lonely planet

Italy

Trentino & South Tyrol
p320

Friuli Venezia Giulia
p428

Turin, Piedmont & Cinque Terre
p176

Milan & the Lakes
p256

Venice & the Veneto
p354

WITHDRAWN

Emilia-Romagna & San Marino
p462

Florence & Tuscany
p506

Umbria & Le Marche
p616

Abruzzo & Molise
p674

Rome & Lazio
p74

Sardinia
p892

Naples & Campania
p692

Puglia, Basilicata & Calabria
p766

Sicily
p826

Brett Atkinson, Alexis Averbuck, Cristian Bonetto, Gregor Clark,
Peter Dragicevich, Duncan Garwood, Paula Hardy, Virginia
Maxwell, Stephanie Ong, Kevin Raub, Brendan Sainsbury,
Regis St Louis, Nicola Williams

Contents

VATICAN CITY P109

Contents

ON THE ROAD

PROCIDA P747

LEONS/SHUTTERSTOCK ©

Contents

COVID-19

We have re-checked every business in this book
before publication to ensure that it is still open after
the COVID-19 outbreak. However, the economic and
social impacts of COVID-19 will continue to be felt
long after the outbreak has been contained, and
many businesses, services and events referenced
in this guide may experience ongoing restrictions.
Some businesses may be temporarily closed, have
changed their opening hours and services, or require
bookings; some unfortunately could have closed permanently. We suggest you check with venues before
visiting for the latest information.

Right: Alfresco
dining in
Trastavere
(p144), Rome

WELCOME TO
Italy

'You can have the Universe, if I can have Italy,' said Italian composer Giuseppe Verdi, and I couldn't agree more. Because after two decades of travel, I see no end to the peninsula's pleasures and surprises. Of course, there is the outstanding artistic heritage, the gorgeous landscapes and the food – my God, the food! – but more than that it is Italy's warm humanity that I admire most. It imbues life's most simple pleasures – a street-corner chat, fresh seasonal produce, a perfect negroni – with reverence and joy. It's a philosophy that soothes the soul.

By Paula Hardy, Writer
🐦 @paula6hardy 📷 paulahardy
For more about our writers, see p1024

ALEXANDER MAZURKEVICH/SHUTTERSTOCK ©

Italy

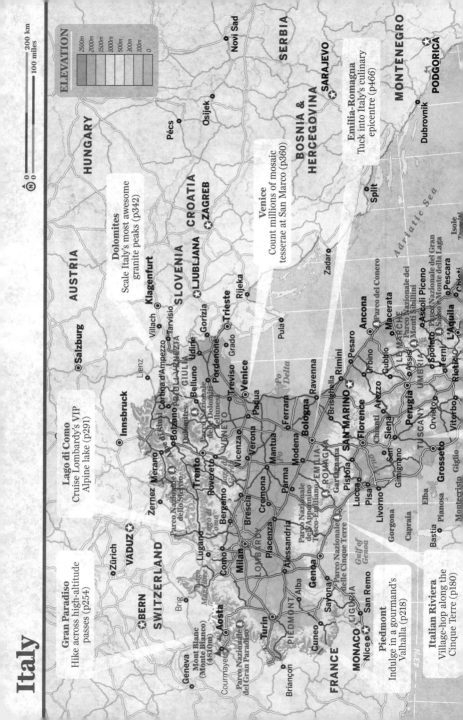

ELEVATION

2500m	
2000m	
1500m	
1000m	
500m	
300m	
100m	
0	

200 km
100 miles

Gran Paradiso
Hike across high-altitude passes (p254)

Lago di Como
Cruise Lombardy's VIP Alpine lake (p291)

Dolomites
Scale Italy's most awesome granite peaks (p342)

Venice
Count millions of mosaic tesserae at San Marco (p360)

Emilia-Romagna
Tuck into Italy's culinary epicentre (p466)

Piedmont
Indulge in a gourmand's Valhalla (p218)

Italian Riviera
Village-hop along the Cinque Terre (p180)

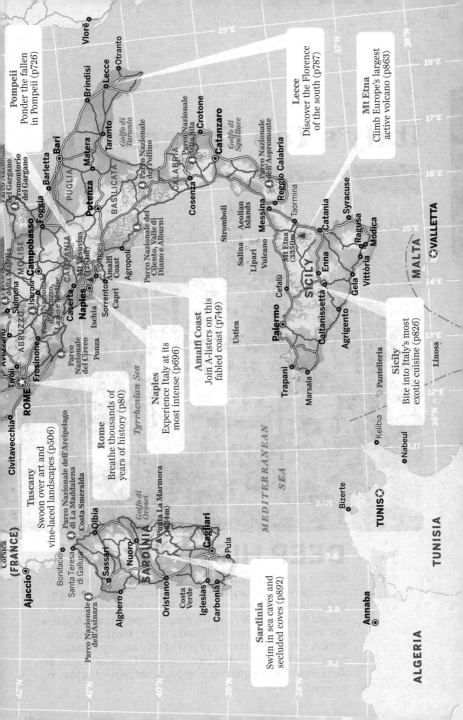

Pompeii
Ponder the fallen in Pompeii (p726)

Lecce
Discover the Florence of the south (p787)

Mt Etna
Climb Europe's largest active volcano (p863)

Sicily
Bite into Italy's most exotic cuisine (p826)

Amalfi Coast
Join A-listers on this fabled coast (p749)

Naples
Experience Italy at its most intense (p696)

Rome
Breathe thousands of years of history (p80)

Tuscany
Swoon over art and vine-laced landscapes (p506)

Sardinia
Swim in sea caves and secluded coves (p892)

19°E
18°E
17°E
16°E
15°E
14°E
13°E
12°E

37°N
36°N
36°N
42°N
41°N
40°N
39°N
38°N

Vlorë
Otranto
Lecce
Brindisi
Bari
Barletta
Promontorio del Gargano
Parco Nazionale del Gargano
Foggia
Campobasso
Isernia
Matera
Taranto
Golfo di Taranto
Crotone
Potenza
PUGLIA
BASILICATA
Parco Nazionale del Pollino
CALABRIA
Catanzaro
Golfo di Squillace
Parco Nazionale dell'Aspromonte
Reggio Calabria
Cosenza
Stromboli
Messina
Taormina
Aeolian Islands
Salina
Lipari
Vulcano
Mt Etna (3350m)
Catania
Syracuse
Ragusa
Modica
SICILY
Enna
Caltanissetta
Gela
Vittoria
Cefalù
Palermo
Agrigento
Trapani
Marsala
Ustica
Pantelleria
Linosa
MALTA
VALLETTA
Sulmona
ABRUZZO
Avezzano
MOLISE
Frosinone
CAMPANIA
Caserta
Mt Vesuvius (1281m)
Pompeii
Naples
Sorrento
Capri
Amalfi Coast
Agropoli
Parco Nazionale del Cilento, Valle di Diano e Alburni
Ischia
Ponza
Parco Nazionale del Circeo
Lazio e Molise
Tivoli
ROME
Civitavecchia
Tyrrhenian Sea
Corsica (FRANCE)
Ajaccio
Bonifacio
Santa Teresa di Gallura
Parco Nazionale dell'Arcipelago di La Maddalena
Costa Smeralda
Olbia
Golfo di Orosei
Punta La Marmora (1834m)
Nuoro
Sassari
SARDINIA
Alghero
Parco Nazionale dell'Asinara
Oristano
Costa Verde
Iglesias
Carbonia
Cagliari
Pula
MEDITERRANEAN SEA
Kelibia
Nabeul
Bizerte
TUNIS
TUNISIA
Annaba
ALGERIA

Italy's Top Experiences

 # DEEP HISTORY

Almost everyone knows what happened in Pompeii and even now Rome's ruined Colosseum telegraphs the might of Europe's first superpower. But Roman brilliance dazzles across the peninsula from the gorgeous mosaics in Aquileia to Carrara's marble quarries and the port town of Ostia Antica. Excavate further and you'll find deeper treasures: fine Greek temples in Agrigento, painted Etruscan tombs in Tarquinia and an ingenious troglodyte settlement in Matera.

Above: Matera (p800)

MARCO RUBINO/SHUTTERSTOCK ©

Visit Hadrian's Playboy Mansion

A showy display of power and wealth, Emperor Hadrian's Villa Adriana is a flashy five-star pad and one of the largest private homes in the ancient world. p162

Right: Villa Adriana

KONTROLAB/GETTY IMAGES ©

POPPY HOLLIS/GETTY IMAGES ©

Explore new finds at Pompeii

The world's most engaging archaeological site, Pompeii keeps on giving with months of lockdown excavation opening up new areas of the site and revealing frescoed treasures. A revamped Antiquarium has also been unveiled. p726

Right: Terracotta frieze, Pompeii

Sleep in a prehistoric cave

The oldest troglodyte town in Italy, and one of the oldest in the world after Aleppo and Jericho, Matera was once the shame of Italy but is now a Unesco heritage site. p800

Right: Cave hotel (p804), Matera

2 MIGHTY MASTERPIECES

Most seminal movements in Western art – from classical, Renaissance and mannerist to baroque, futurist and metaphysical – were forged in Italy by a red-carpet roll call of artists including Giotto, da Vinci, Michelangelo, Botticelli, Caravaggio, Carracci, Boccioni, Balla and de Chirico. This is the reason why touring Italian art cities such as Milan, Venice, Florence, Rome and Naples was considered an essential scholarly pilgrimage in the days of the Grand Tour.

Galleria degli Uffizi

Dazzling, overwhelming, mind-expanding, exhilarating – how to describe a tour of this historic, 101-room palace-museum? It is home to 1500-odd of the world's most dazzling masterpieces and the only place you will see them is here. p512

Below: Galleria degli Uffizi

GIORDANO CANTONE/SHUTTERSTOCK ©

Museo e Galleria Borghese

An epic suburban pleasure villa housing the 'queen of all private art collections' in its gilded salons set in 80 hectares of luxurious parkland. p127

Above: Villa Borghese (p128)

Palazzo Grassi

French billionaire François Pinault's world-class contemporary art collection is showcased against Tadao Ando interior sets in Venice. p372

Right: Palazzo Grassi

3 FEASTING & FORAGING

RADIOKAFKA/SHUTTERSTOCK ©

Italy is a gastronomic powerhouse, a mouth-watering, knee-weakening Promised Land of culinary decadence. To say Italian cuisine is regional is an enormous understatement when striking differences can often be found valley to valley, village to village. Wherever you eat, your tastebuds will be delighted by the sheer diversity of the Italian pantry from Sicily's Middle-Eastern-influenced palette, to the New World–inspired tomato dishes of Naples, Piedmont's truffle-loaded plates and the Swiss-style fonduta of the Valle d'Aosta.

Once-in-a-lifetime dining

Massimo Bottura's Osteria Francescana is regularly voted the best restaurant in the world for its inventive modern take on Italian food. p481

Go truffling

Piedmont is heaven on earth for foodies and there's no better time to visit than autumn when the woods around Alba are filled with truffle hunters and every plate is heaped with them. p235

Street feasting

Palermo's medieval food markets pack a punch when it comes to tasty snacks. From morning to night, you can graze here on fritters, kebabs, riceballs and gelato. p838

Above: Food market, Palermo

4 LA DOLCE VITA

Made famous by Federico Fellini's 1960 film of the same name, 'the sweet life' has come to encapsulate Italy's seemingly effortless ability to deliver on a life full of pleasure and indulgence. Style and flair furnish every aspect of life, from those immaculately knotted ties and seamless espressos to the flirtatious smiles of striking strangers. At the root of it is a dedication to living life well, slowly and beautifully.

Lago di Como

Nestled in the shadow of the Rhaetian Alps, dazzling Lake Como is Lombardy's most spectacular glacial lake surrounded by ravishing formal gardens. p291

Top left: Bellagio (p295), Lake Como

Amalfi Coast

No matter the buzzing summer crowds that fill its cascading towns, the Amalfi Coast will steal your heart with its sapphire blue seas and maquis-laden cliffs. p749

Bottom left: Atrani (p755)

Puglia

A still-hidden corner of Italy where the gently rolling hills of the Valle d'Itria meet the dry sierras of the Salento. Life is slow and Lecce is the 'Florence of the South'. p770

Above: Ostuni (p785)

5 WINE ROUTES

LUCIANO MORTULA · LGM/SHUTTERSTOCK ©

SAMOT/SHUTTERSTOCK ©

The Wine of Kings

Arguably Italy's most famous wine, Barolo is produced in the 11 tiny comunes, southwest of Alba. Explore the wine's history through art and film at Barolo's wine museum. p237

Tuscan Wine Tour

Discover why Chianti isn't just a cheap table wine left over from the 1970s on a leisurely tour of its vineyards, estates and restaurant cellars. p565

Bottom left: Tuscan vineyards

Il Collio's 'super whites'

Equidistant from the Austrian Alps and the Adriatic Sea, the hilly landscape of the Collio has a sunny, breezy microclimate that conspires to produce grapes of astonishing fragrance, yielding Italy's 'super whites'. p450

Top left: Il Collio

In Italy, wine isn't just a drink: it represents history, culture, geography and identity. Each great bottle of wine is a capsule of time, terroir and vintage to be savoured and contemplated. Wine has been cultivated here for 4000 years and while some will be as familiar to you as old flames, including pizza-and-a-movie Chianti or reliable summertime fling pinto grigio, there are dozens of varietals that you'll only find in local cellars.

6 UNSPOILT WILDERNESS

Italy's spectacular wildernesses are often overshadowed by the country's art treasures, which is a shame, because the peninsula is a natural masterpiece. From the icy Alps of the north to the south's fiery craters and turquoise grottoes, this is a place for doing as well as seeing. One day you're tearing down Courmayeur's powdery slopes, the next you could be galloping across the marshes of the Maremma, or diving in coral-studded Campanian waters.

Parco Nazionale del Gran Paradiso

Spectacular hiking trails, Alpine ibex and a refreshing lack of ski resorts at the Valle d'Aosta's mountainous wonderland. p254

Top left: Hikers, Parco Nazionale del Gran Paradiso

Selvaggio Blu

Sardinia's toughest trek doesn't short change on rugged beauty – from cliffs and caves to hypnotic coastal scenery. p933

Above right: The Selvaggio Blu trail

Parco Nazionale dei Monti Sibillini

The border between Umbria and Le Marche has unspoilt ancient woodlands and subalpine meadows home to peregrine falcons, wolves and wildcats. p672

Bottom left: Piano Grande (p648)

7 RETAIL THERAPY

ALEMASCHE7Z/SHUTTERSTOCK ©

MICHELE DEFILIPPIS/SHUTTERSTOCK ©

Quadrilatero d'Oro

Milan's 'Golden Quad' is undoubtedly the world's most fabled shopping district. Even if you don't have the slightest urge to sling a swag of glossy bags over your arm, the people watching is priceless. p267

Top left: Shops, Milan (p279)

Venetian Artistry

All those souvenir tees and kitschy masks are nothing more than decoys for amateurs. Explore Venice's labyrinthine back streets and you'll find one-of-a-kind artisan-made finds. p393

Bottom left: Venetian artisan

Omega

A cult family-run glove factory that supplies the likes of Dior and Hermes. Pick up your own slice of luxury for a fraction of the price at the workshop. p717

Italy's artisans have preserved their heritage crafts in dozens of small family-run businesses. Even now, the country punches above its weight in producing some of the world's most fashionable clothes, shoes and bags. Milan, Rome and Florence remain important fashion centres, but centuries-old artisanal skills can be found everywhere from Venetian glass and Carrara marble to Cremona's violins and Naples' old-school tailoring tradition.

8 LIDO LOVE

The Italian *lido*, or *bagno* (private beach club), is a much-loved 19th-century tradition that is preserved from Venice to Amalfi and beyond. Across Italy's 7600-km coastline some 30,000 private clubs cordon off prime sections of sand, supplying paying punters with loungers and pretty striped beach umbrellas. You'll even find them in the midst of seaside cities such as Trieste or on floating platforms around the Italian lakes. Just don't forget to pack your swimming togs in this season's colours.

Monterosso al Mare

Monterosso is the last of the five small towns that comprise the Cinque Terre. It's best known for its large beach lined with *lidi*. p201

Below: Monterosso al Mare

ELZAUER/SHUTTERSTOCK ©

Spiaggia dei Maronti

If you want to reenact the glamorous life of Dickie and Marge in *The Talented Mr. Ripley,* head to the *lidi* on this sandy strip on the island of Ischia. p744

Above: Spiaggia dei Maronti

I Bagni Misteriosi

Luigi Secchi's gorgeous modernist *lido* in the heart of Milan is an architectural treasure as well as a thriving community hub. p269

Bottom right: I Bagni Misteriosi

9 STREET LIFE

Nowhere else in Italy are people as conscious of their role in the theatre of everyday life as in Naples. And in no other city does daily life radiate such drama and intensity. Naples' ancient streets are a stage, cast with boisterous matriarchs, bellowing baristas and tongue-tied lovers. To savour the flavour, dive into the city's rough-and-tumble La Pignasecca market, book an evening at the opera or just spend the morning propping up the bar at your local café.

La Pignasecca

This buzzing market in Montesanto is the oldest in Naples and a gem in the Neapolitan foodscape. It's buzzing on Sunday before the sacred midday *pranzo* (lunch). p707

Festa di San Gennaro

A tri-annual festival when nearly the whole city flocks to the Duomo to witness the liquefaction of San Gennaro's blood. p713

Above: Festa di San Gennaro

Teatro San Carlo

The symbol of the city and the oldest opera house in Europe, the San Carlo opera and ballet season is well attended by a discerning local crowd. p717

10 HISTORIC GARDENS

First they fixed the drawing room and then they started on the garden: Italy's penchant for the 'outdoor room' has been going strong since wealthy Romans realised the benefits of regular rest and relaxation in natural settings, and designed their holiday villas with extravagant gardens. Medieval humanists revived their interest in botany and Renaissance princes used new engineering techniques to mould Italian landscapes into dynamic symbols of wealth and power.

La Mortella

A unique tropical garden warmed by thermal springs and filled with 800 rare plants native to four continents. But more than a botanic garden, la Mortella is a setting dedicated to the arts and music. p744

Below: La Mortella

Ravello

Possibly Italy's most romantic garden are the tumbling terraces of Villa Rufolo. Visit in the summer to applaud classical music concerts amid the blossom. p758

Above: Villa Rufolo

Villa d'Este

This High Renaissance garden is the model for formal garden design across the continent. It is laid out in a set of rooms aimed to highlight picturesque views and sculpture. p163

Right: Villa d'Este

EZYPIX/GETTY IMAGES ©

11 HITTING THE PEAKS

BOERESCU/SHUTTERSTOCK ©

From the western Maritime Alps to the eastern Dolomites, northern Italy is encircled by an icy ring of Alpine peaks that provide a vast high-altitude playground for all manner of skiers, hikers, climbers and thrill-seekers. They are criss-crossed with thousands of kilometres of *sentieri* (walking trails), cable-bolted vie ferrate and steep cycle routes where Giro d'Italia riders come to train. In addition, the myriad mountain valleys sequester unique cultures and cuisines worth exploring in your down time.

Cortina d'Ampezzo

Italy's most glamorous ski resort offers downhill skiing alongside designer shopping. Expect lots more to come as the resort gears up for the 2026 Winter Olympics. p425

Above: Cortina d'Ampezzo

Alpe di Siusi

Europe's largest alpine plateau situated in the shadow of the pink-hued Rosengarten range offers stunning hiking and skiing. The valleys villages are also a big draw. p345

Valle d'Aosta

French-influenced Valle d'Aosta comprises a single valley and offers some of Italy's best snow facilities. Hike Alta Vie 1, the Giant's Trail, to the highest peaks in Europe. p247

12 MEDIEVAL HILL TOWNS

Italy's most romanticised region, Tuscany and Umbria is tailor-made for fastidious aesthetes. Beyond its elegant Renaissance towns – Florence, Pisa, Siena, Perugia and Assisi – sprawls a timeless landscape of olive groves, vineyards and rolling hills laced with sinuous roads lined with cypress trees. Atop many of them are the regions signature medieval hill towns, stuffed with frescoed churches, ancient brick architecture and down-to-earth trattorias.

Val d'Orcia

The most picturesque of Tuscany's gentle valleys is this Unesco-recognised landscape characterised by conical hills topped by ancient medieval settlements. p577

Left: Montalcino (p577)

Pitigliano

One of Tuscany's most dramatic hilltop treasures perched at the edge of a gorge and composed of Escher-like streets haunted by Jewish influences. p586

Above left: Pitigliano

Spoleto Festival

While Spoleto is visually stunning all-year round, framed as it is by the Apennines, this medieval town kicks into life in summer for its epic arts festival. p645

Above right: Spoleto (p643)

13 PALAZZO STYLE

Murderous intrigues, magnificent balls, secret prisons and fateful love affairs, Italy's royal palaces have seen them all. From the pope's palace in the Vatican and Reggia di Caserta, the largest royal palace in the world, situated just outside Naples, to the Savoy palaces in Turin where the modern Italian state was born, Italy's palazzi chart the country's history and the changing trends in fashions, art and architecture over the centuries.

Reggia di Caserta

As seen in *Star Wars*, this 1200-room palace is the largest royal palace in the world and is the Italian baroque's most spectacular epilogue. p720

Top left: Reggia di Caserta

Palazzo Ducale, Venice

The residence of 120 Venetian Doges spanning nearly 1000 years, this pretty Gothic structure embodies the story of the Venetian Republic. p364

Bottom left: Venice's Palazzo Ducale

Palazzo Ducale, Mantua

The opulence of the Gonzaga residence in Mantua is hard to describe with its maze of internal piazzas and luxuriously frescoed rooms. p314

Above: Mantua's Palazzo Ducale

14 ISLAND HOPPING

Venice

The Venetian archipelago is made up of 118 islands scattered the shallow bowl of a teal-coloured lagoon that supports unique flora and fauna. p360

Isola d'Elba

Napoleon's island of exile, Elba sits just off the coast of northern Tuscany and its quiet coves and bays sit within Europe's largest marine park. p594

Left: Snorkeling off Elba's coast (p597)

Aeolian Islands

Sicily's seven Unesco-protected islands boast silver-grey pumice beaches, lush green vineyards and Stromboli's bubbling volcano. p844

Top: Panarea (p852)

The Italian peninsula is ringed by more than 400 islands, and while showstopper such as Capri, Sicily and Sardinia are world-famous, there are so many more to explore. From charming Ponza, the Roman holiday resort of choice, to jet-set Pantelleria – where the likes of Truman Capote, Giorgio Armani and Sting have holidayed – there's an island for every taste and budget. And, in 2022, tiny Procida will assume the crown of Italian Capital of Culture.

Need to Know

For more information, see Survival Guide (p985)

Currency
Euro (€)

Language
Italian

Visas
Generally not required for stays of up to 90 days (or at all by EU nationals). Some nationalities will need a Schengen visa.

Money
ATMs are widespread in Italy. Major credit cards are widely accepted, but some smaller shops, trattorias and hotels might not take them.

Mobile Phones
Local SIM cards can be used in European, Australian and some unlocked US phones. Other phones must be set to roaming.

Time
Central European Time (GMT/UTC plus one hour)

When to Go

Dry climate
Warm to hot summer, mild winter
Warm to hot summer, cold winter
Mild summer, cold winter
Cold climate

Milan
GO Dec–Mar (skiing), Jan & Sep

Venice
GO Feb–Mar & Sep–Nov

Rome
GO Apr–May, Jul & Nov–Dec

Naples
GO May–Jun & Sep–Oct

Palermo
GO Sep–Oct

High Season (Jul & Aug)
➡ Queues at big sights and on the road, especially in August.

➡ Prices also rocket for Christmas, New Year and Easter.

➡ Late December to March is high season in the Alps and Dolomites.

Shoulder (Apr–Jun & Sep–Oct)
➡ Good deals on accommodation, especially in the south.

➡ Spring is best for festivals, flowers and local produce.

➡ Autumn provides warm weather and the grape harvest.

Low Season (Nov–Mar)
➡ Prices up to 30% lower than in high season.

➡ Many sights and hotels closed in coastal and mountainous areas.

➡ A good period for cultural events in large cities.

Useful Websites

Lonely Planet (www.lonely planet.com/italy) Destination information, hotel bookings, traveller forum and more.

Trenitalia (www.trenitalia.com) Italian railways website.

Agriturismi (www.agri turismi.it) Guide to farm accommodation.

Italia (www.italia.it) Official Italian-government tourism website.

The Local (www.thelocal.it) English-language news from Italy, including travel-related stories.

Italy Magazine (www.italy magazine.com) Travel, culture, accommodation, dining and more.

Important Numbers

From outside Italy, dial your international access code, Italy's country code (39) then the number (including the first '0').

Country code	☑39
International access code	☑00
Ambulance	☑118
Police	☑112, 113
Fire	☑115

Exchange Rates

Australia	A$1	€0.65
Canada	C$1	€0.67
Japan	¥100	€0.77
New Zealand	NZ$1	€0.59
Switzerland	Sfr1	€0.90
UK	UK£1	€1.17
US	US$1	€0.85

For current exchange rates, see www.xe.com.

Daily Costs

Budget: Less than €100

➡ Dorm bed: €20–35

➡ Double room in a budget hotel: €60–110

➡ Pizza or pasta: €6–15

Midrange: €100–250

➡ Double room in a hotel: €110–200

➡ Local restaurant dinner: €25–45

➡ Museum admission: €4–18

Top end: More than €250

➡ Double room in a four- or five-star hotel: €200 plus

➡ Top restaurant dinner: €45–150

➡ Opera ticket: €40–210

Opening Hours

Opening hours vary throughout the year. We've provided high-season hours, which are generally in use over summer. Summer refers to the period between April and September (or October); winter is October (or November) to March.

Banks 8.30am–1.30pm and 2.45pm–4.30pm Monday to Friday

Bars & cafes 7.30am–8pm, sometimes until 1am or 2am

Clubs 10pm–4am or 5am

Restaurants noon–3pm and 7.30pm–11pm (later in summer)

Shops 9am–1pm and 3.30pm–7.30pm (or 4pm to 8pm) Monday to Saturday. In main cities some shops stay open at lunchtime and on Sunday mornings. Some shops close Monday mornings.

Arriving in Italy

Rome: Fiumicino (Leonardo da Vinci) Airport Express trains (€14) take 30 minutes and run from 6.08am to 11.23pm. Buses (€6 to €6.90) take an hour and operate between 6.05am and 12.40am. Taxis (set fare €48) take 45 to 60 minutes.

Milan: Malpensa Airport Trains (€13) take 50 minutes and run every half hour from 5.37am to 12.20am. Buses (€10) run half-hourly between 3.45am and 12.15am. Taxis (€95 set fare) take 50 minutes.

Venice: Marco Polo Airport Water shuttles (€15) take 45 to 90 minutes from the airport ferry dock. Buses to Piazzale Roma (€8) take 25 minutes and run between 5.20am and 12.50am.

Naples International (Capodichino) Airport Shuttle buses (€5) take 15 to 35 minutes and run between 6am and 11.20pm. Taxis (set fares €18 to €27) take 20 to 35 minutes.

Getting Around

Transport in Italy is affordable and reasonably quick and efficient.

Train Moderately priced, with extensive coverage and frequent departures. High-speed trains connect major cities.

Car Handy for travelling at your own pace and visiting regions with minimal public transport. Not a good idea for travelling in major urban areas.

Bus Cheaper and slower than trains. Useful for mountainous areas and remote towns and villages not served by trains.

PLAN YOUR TRIP NEED TO KNOW

For much more on **getting around**, see p998

First Time Italy

For more information, see Survival Guide (p985)

Checklist

➡ Ensure your passport is valid for at least six months past your arrival date

➡ Check airline baggage restrictions

➡ Organise travel insurance

➡ Make bookings (for popular museums, entertainment and accommodation)

➡ Inform your credit- or debit-card company of your travels

➡ Check you can use your mobile (cell) phone

➡ Check requirements for hiring a car

What to Pack

➡ Good walking shoes for those cobblestones

➡ Hat, sunglasses, sunscreen

➡ Electrical adapter and phone charger

➡ A detailed driving map for Italy's rural back roads

➡ A smart outfit and shoes

➡ Patience: for coping with inefficiency

➡ Phrasebook: for ordering and charming

Top Tips for Your Trip

➡ Visit in spring and autumn – good weather and thinner crowds.

➡ Always carry some cash. Some restaurants and hotels only accept cash, while unattended petrol (gas) stations don't always accept foreign credit cards.

➡ If you're driving, head off the main roads: some of Italy's most stunning scenery is best on secondary or tertiary roads.

➡ Don't rely solely on a GPS, which can occasionally lead you too far off the beaten track; cross-check your route on a printed road map.

➡ Avoid restaurants with touts and the mediocre *menu turistico* (tourist menu).

What to Wear

Appearances matter in Italy. Milan, Italy's fashion capital, is rigidly chic. Rome and Florence are marginally less formal, but with big fashion houses in town, sloppy attire just won't do. In the cities, suitable wear for men is generally trousers (including stylish jeans) and shirts or polo shirts, and for women skirts, trousers or dresses. Shorts, T-shirts and sandals are fine in summer and at the beach, but long sleeves are required for dining out. For evening wear, smart casual is the norm. A light sweater or waterproof jacket is useful in spring and autumn, and sturdy, comfortable shoes are good when visiting archaeological sites.

Sleeping

Hotels All prices and levels of quality, from cheap-and-charmless to sleek-and-exclusive boutique.

Farm stays Perfect for families and for relaxation, *agriturismi* range from rustic farmhouses to luxe country estates.

B&Bs Often great value, can range from rooms in family houses to self-catering studio apartments.

Pensions Similar to hotels, though *pensioni* are generally of one- to three-star quality and family-run.

Money

Credit and debit cards can be used almost everywhere with the exception of some rural towns and villages.

Visa and MasterCard are widely recognised. American Express is only accepted by some major chains and big hotels; few places take Diners Club.

ATMs are everywhere but be aware of transaction fees. Some ATMs in Italy reject foreign cards. Try a few before assuming your card is the problem.

Bargaining

Gentle haggling is common in street/flea markets (though not in food markets).

Haggling in stores is generally unacceptable, though good-humoured bargaining at smaller artisan or craft shops in southern Italy is not unusual if making multiple purchases.

Tipping

Italians are not big tippers. The following is a rough guide.

Taxis Optional, but most round up to the nearest euro.

Hotels Tip porters about €5 at high-end hotels.

Restaurants Service (servizio) is generally included – otherwise, a euro or two is fine in pizzerias and trattorias, and 5% to 10% in smart restaurants.

Bars Not necessary, although many leave small change if drinking coffee at the bar, usually €0.10 or €0.20.

Language

Unlike in many other European countries, English is not widely spoken in Italy. Of course, in the main tourist centres you can get by, but in the countryside and off-the-tourist track you'll need to master a few basic phrases. This will improve your experience no end, especially when ordering in restaurants, some of which have no written menu. See the Language chapter (p1003) of this book for all the phrases you need to get by.

 What's the local speciality?
Qual'è la specialità di questa regione?
kwa·le la spe·cha·lee·ta dee kwes·ta re·jo·ne

A bit like the rivalry between medieval Italian city-states, these days the country's regions compete in speciality foods and wines.

 Which combined tickets do you have?
Quali biglietti cumulativi avete?
kwa·lee bee·lye·tee koo·moo·la·tee·vee a·ve·te

Make the most of your euro by getting combined tickets to various sights; they are available in all major Italian cities.

 Where can I buy discount designer items?
C'è un outlet in zona? che oon owt·let in zo·na

Discount fashion outlets are big business in major cities – get bargain-priced seconds, samples and cast-offs for la bella figura.

 I'm here with my husband/boyfriend.
Sono qui con il mio marito/ragazzo.
so·no kwee kon eel mee·o ma·ree·to/ra·ga·tso

Solo women travellers may receive unwanted attention in some parts of Italy; if ignoring fails have a polite rejection ready.

 Let's meet at 6pm for pre-dinner drinks.
Ci vediamo alle sei per un aperitivo.
chee ve·dya·mo a·le say per oon a·pe·ree·tee·vo

At dusk, watch the main piazza get crowded with people sipping colourful cocktails and snacking the evening away: join your new friends for this authentic Italian ritual!

Etiquette

Italy is a surprisingly formal society; the following tips will help avoid awkward moments.

Greetings Greet people in shops, restaurants and bars with a 'buongiorno' (good morning) or 'buonasera' (good evening); kiss both cheeks and say 'come stai' (how are you) to friends.

Asking for help Say 'mi scusi' (excuse me) to attract attention; use 'permesso' (permission) to pass someone in a crowded space.

Dress Cover shoulders, torso and thighs when visiting churches and dress smartly when eating out.

At the table Eat pasta with a fork, not a spoon; it's OK to eat pizza with your hands.

Queues Queue-jumping is common in Italy: be polite but assertive.

What's New

While Italy's politicians and economists are clearly in for a rocky ride returning the country to health after the pandemic, the country's world-class cultural heritage continues to deliver with some exciting new museums, continuing modernisation at some of its top sights and an increasingly determined drive towards a better, more sustainable model of tourism.

Capital of Culture

In 2022, the tiny Italian island of Procida (p747) with its pastel-painted houses and idyllic bays is set to become Italy's Capital of Culture - the first island to ever win the award. Key to the winning bid was the island's emphasis on 'low tourism' and its rich artisanal heritage. Cultural events will span the year with plans for 44 cultural projects involving 240 artists and eight regenerated cultural spaces.

Dante's Way, Ravenna

As the resting place of Italian literary lion Dante Alighieri, Ravenna (p494) commemorates the 700th anniversary of the poet's death in 2021 with a year of exhibi-

tions, concerts and readings. Several new walking routes, the Cammino di Dante and Le Vie di Dante, explore the places that inspired the poet's writings.

Roman SUPER Ticket

The snappily titled SUPER Ticket is a pass covering the Colosseum (p86), Palatino and Roman Forum. Costing €6 more than the regular entrance ticket, it's valid for two days and gives access to extra 'internal' sights, off-limits to regular ticket-holders.

E-Biking

Enterprising bike shop Urban Bikery (p582), in Montepulciano in Tuscany, is

---

LOCAL KNOWLEDGE

WHAT'S HAPPENING IN ITALY

Paula Hardy, Lonely Planet writer

Italy has had a torrid time of it over the past few years and that's not just because of the devastating death toll from COVID-19. Since the populists came to power in 2018, Italy's government has collapsed twice. There has been deadly flash-flooding in Sardinia, Central Italy and the northeast, while in November 2019 nearly 80% of Venice was inundated by high tides. At sea, in 2020, there were stand-offs with refugee rescue boats carrying three times the number of asylum seekers as 2019; and, in the Alps, glaciers threatened to collapse or turned pink with algae – a sign of the warming times. The tide that did recede, however, was tourism, as Italy implemented Europe's first national lockdown in 2020 and Rome recorded a 44% drop in visitors while GDP dropped 9.1% in 2020. But while the pandemic has laid bare urgent climate issues (Covid was more virulent in areas of high pollution), dramatic social inequalities between north and south, the weakness of populist politicians, and the fragility of whole cities entirely reliant on tourism, it has presented a unique opportunity to finally address them. Italy will receive €209 billion from the European Recovery Fund and Mario Draghi, the country's new unelected prime minister, has promised to spend it wisely on the most ambitious reform plans in a generation.

one of many in Italy to pioneer e-bike tourism. Customised off-road e-bikes come equipped with GPS devices programmed with routes of varying difficulty, making light work of two-wheeling Tuscany independently.

Uffizi Ticketing

Visiting the Uffizi (p512) in Florence is finally easier: expect seasonal prices (dramatically lower in winter); a combination ticket covering the Uffizi, Palazzo Pitti and Boboli Gardens; a new 'quick' exit; and, time-slot coupons to reduce ticket queues.

Urban Hostel Boom

The Italian capital is enjoying a hostel boom with the opening of two new-generation hostels: RomeHello (p136), a street-art-adorned hostel whose profits go to worthy local causes; and family-friendly Meininger Roma Hostel (p137) in the Castro Pretorio district north of Termini.

When a hybrid hostel-hotel marks its opening with 'bed talks', live-streaming artistic performances, cultural chats and events à la John Lennon from bed, you know it's on-trend. Rooftop pool, co-working areas and play zones are highlights of Student Hotel (p538), a new-gen hostel-hotel in Florence, Tuscany. A second, with running track and pool on the roof of a former Fiat factory, is scheduled to open in September 2022.

Ocean Space, Venice

Derelict for nearly a century, the Benedictine church of San Lorenzo has been restored to house the ground-breaking Ocean Space (p381) gallery dedicated to exploring climate change through art.

Zipline Majella, Abruzzo

Central Italy panders to cultured thrill-seekers with its first zip line (p684), soaring above the medieval towers, piazzas and red roof-tops of Pacentro, next to Abruzzo's Parco Nazionale della Majella.

LUMEN Museum of Mountain Photography, South Tyrol

Mountain enthusiasts will adore this high-altitude museum (p349), an architecturally

PLAN YOUR TRIP WHAT'S NEW

bold re-rendering of a funicular station at 2275m in Kronplatz. Mountain imagery by international photographers and 360-degree Alpine views are equally dizzying.

Museo Ebraico, Puglia

The Jewish history of medieval Lecce and the greater Salento region in southern Italy comes alive in this 16th-century *palazzo* (mansion) museum (p788). Watch for poignant spoken-word performances some evenings.

Chiesa e Monastero di Santa Caterina d'Alessandria, Palermo

A historic convent (p831) in Palermo has reopened, allowing access to one of the city's grandest baroque churches, a cloister, rooftop views of the city, and a bakery cooking up secret recipes of Sicilian nuns.

Venezia Autentica

Want to connect with locals and support local businesses? Then explore this ethical website (https://veneziaautentica.com), which features Venetian-run restaurants, shops and tours and offers a useful discount pass to signed-up 'Friends'.

Plan Your Trip

Accommodation

Accommodation in Italy is incredibly varied, with everything from family-run *pensioni* and *agriturismi* (farm stays) to idiosyncratic B&Bs, designer hotels, serviced apartments and even *rifugi* (mountain huts) for weary mountain trekkers. Capturing the imagination even more are options spanning luxurious country villas and castles to tranquil convents and monasteries. Book ahead for the high season, especially in popular tourist areas or if visiting cities during major events.

Booking Services

Lonely Planet (lonelyplanet.com/italy/hotels) Find independent reviews, as well as recommendations on the best places to stay – and then book them online.

Agriturismo.it (www.agriturismo.it) Authentic *agriturismi* (farmstays) all over Italy.

BBItalia.it (www.bbitalia.it) Bed-and-breakfasts countrywide.

Camping.it (www.camping.it) Directory of campgrounds in Italy.

In Italia (www.initalia.it) Italy's hotel booking specialists.

Monastery Stays (www.monasterystays.com) Just that.

Accommodation Types

B&Bs

B&Bs are a burgeoning sector of the Italian accommodation market and can be found throughout the country in both urban and rural settings. Options include everything from restored farmhouses, city *palazzi* (mansions) and seaside bungalows to rooms in family houses. In some cases, a B&B can also refer to a self-contained apartment with basic breakfast provisions provided. Tariffs for a double room cover a wide range, from around €60 to €140.

Camping

Most campgrounds in Italy are major complexes with swimming pools, restaurants and supermarkets. They are graded according to a star system. Charges usually vary according to the season, peaking in July and August. Note that some places offer an all-inclusive price, while others charge separately for each person, tent, vehicle and/or campsite. Typical high-season prices range from around €10 to €20 per adult, up to €12 for children under 12, and from €5 to €25 for a site.

Italian campgrounds are generally set up for people travelling with their own vehicle, although some are accessible by public transport. In the major cities, grounds are often a long way from the historic centres. Most but not all have space for RVs. Tent campers are expected to bring their own equipment, although a few grounds offer tents for hire. Many also offer the alternative of bungalows or even simple, self-contained (self-catering) flats. In high season, some only offer deals for a week at a time.

Convents & Monasteries

Some Italian convents and monasteries let out cells or rooms as a modest revenue-making exercise and happily take in tourists, while others only take in pilgrims or people who are on a spiritual retreat. Many impose a fairly early curfew, but prices tend to be quite reasonable.

Two useful publications are Eileen Barish's *The Guide to Lodging in Italy's Monasteries* (2006) and Charles M Shelton's *Beds and Blessings in Italy: A Guide to Religious Hospitality* (2010). Online, St Patrick's American Community in Rome (www.stpatricksamericanrome.org) lists convent and monastery accommodation in Rome, Assisi and Venice. Some of these are simply residential accommodation run by religious orders and not necessarily big on monastic atmosphere. The website doesn't handle bookings; to request a spot, you'll need to contact each individual institution directly. Other websites with useful information on monastery stays are Monastery Stays (www.monasterystays.com) and In Italy Online (www.initaly.com/agri/convents.htm).

Farmhouse Holidays

Live out your bucolic fantasies at one of Italy's growing number of *agriturismi* (farm stays). A long-booming industry in Tuscany and Umbria, farm stays are spreading across the country like freshly churned butter. While all *agriturismi* are required to grow at least one of their own products, the farm stays themselves range from rustic country houses with a handful of olive trees to elegant country estates with sparkling pools or fully functioning farms where guests can pitch in.

Hostels

Ostelli per la gioventù (youth hostels) are run by the **Associazione Italiana Alberghi per la Gioventù** (AIG; ☑06 9826 1462; www.

aighostels.it; Viale Mazzini 88, Rome; ⊘8am-6pm Mon-Fri; 🚇Piazza Giuseppe Mazzini), affiliated with Hostelling International (www.hihostels.com). A valid HI card is required in all associated youth hostels in Italy. You can get this in your home country or directly at many hostels.

A full list of Italian hostels, with details of prices and locations, is available online or from hostels throughout the country. Nightly rates in basic dorms vary from around €15 to €50, which usually includes a buffet breakfast. You can often get lunch or dinner for roughly an extra €10 to €15.

Many hostels also offer singles and doubles, with prices ranging from around €30/50 in cheaper parts of the country to as high as €80/100 in major tourist centres like Rome. Some also offer family rooms. Be aware that some hostels have a curfew of 11pm or midnight.

A growing contingent of independent hostels offers alternatives to HI hostels. Many are barely distinguishable from budget hotels.

Hotels & Pensioni

While the difference between an *albergo* (hotel) and a *pensione* is often minimal, a *pensione* will generally be of one- to three-star quality while an *albergo* can be awarded up to five stars. *Locande* (inns) long fell into much the same category as *pensioni,* but the term has become a trendy one in some parts and reveals little about the quality of a place. *Affittacamere* are rooms for rent in private houses. They are generally simple affairs.

Quality can vary enormously and the official star system gives limited clues. One-star hotels and *pensioni* tend to be basic and usually do not offer private bathrooms. Two-star places are similar, but rooms will generally have a private bathroom. Three-star options usually offer reasonable standards. Four- and five-star hotels offer facilities such as room service, laundry and dry-cleaning.

Prices are highest in major tourist destinations. They also tend to be higher in northern Italy. A *camera singola* (single room) costs from around €40, and from around €60 in more expensive cities like Milan. A *camera doppia* (twin beds) or *camera matrimoniale* (double room with a double bed) will cost from around €60 or €70, even more in places like Milan.

Tourist offices usually have booklets with local accommodation listings. Many hotels are also signing up with (steadily proliferating) online accommodation-booking services.

Mountain Huts

The network of *rifugi* in the Alps, Apennines and other mountains is usually only open from June to late September. While some are little more than rudimentary shelters, many *rifugi* are more like Alpine hostels. Accommodation is generally in dormitories, but some of the larger *rifugi* have doubles. Many *rifugi* also offer guests hot meals and/or communal cooking facilities. Though mattresses, blankets and duvets are usually provided, most *rifugi* will require you to bring your own sleeping bag or travel sheet. Some places offer travel sheets for hire or purchase.

The price per person (which typically includes breakfast) ranges from €20 to €30 depending on the quality of the *rifugio* (it's more for a double room). A hearty post-walk single-dish dinner will set you back another €10 to €15.

Rifugi are marked on good walking maps. Those close to chair lifts and cable-car stations are usually expensive and crowded. Others are at high altitude and involve hours of hard walking. It is important to book in advance. Additional information can be obtained from the local tourist offices.

The Club Alpino Italiano (www.cai.it) owns and runs many of the mountain huts. Members of organisations such as the New Zealand Alpine Club, Fédération Française des Clubs Alpins et de Montagne and Deutscher Alpenverein can enjoy discounted rates for accommodation and meals. See the International Mountaineering and Climbing Federation website (www.theuiaa.org) for details.

Rental Accommodation

Finding rental accommodation in the major cities can be difficult and time-consuming; rental agencies (local and foreign) can assist, for a fee. Rental rates are higher for short-term leases. A studio or one-bedroom apartment anywhere near the centre of Rome will cost around €900 per month and it is usually necessary to pay a deposit (generally one month in advance). Expect to spend similar amounts in cities such as Florence, Milan, Naples and Venice.

OFFBEAT ACCOMMODATION

Looking for something out of the ordinary? Italy offers a plethora of sleeping options that you won't find anywhere else in the world.

➡ Down near Italy's heel, rent a *trullo*, one of the characteristic whitewashed conical houses of southern Puglia.

➡ Ancient *sassi* (cave dwellings) have found new life as boutique hotels in otherworldly Matera, a Unesco World Heritage–listed town in the southern region of Basilicata.

➡ Cruise northern Italy on the Avemaria (p314), a river barge that sails from Mantua to Venice over seven leisurely days, with cultural and foodie pit stops, and the chance to cycle between locations.

➡ In Friuli Venezia Giulia, experience village life in an *albergo diffuso*, an award-winning concept in which self-contained (self-catering) apartments in neighbouring houses are rented to guests through a centralised hotel-style reception.

➡ In Naples, spend a night or two slumbering in the aristocratic *palazzo* (mansion) of a Bourbon bishop. Now the Decumani Hotel de Charme (p714), the property comes complete with a sumptuous baroque salon.

THE SLUMBER TAX

Italy's *tassa di soggiorno* (accommodation tax) sees visitors charged an extra €1 to €7 per night. Exactly how much you're charged may depend on several factors, including the type of accommodation (campground, guesthouse, hotel), a hotel's star rating and the number of people under your booking. Depending on their age and on the location of the accommodation, children may pay a discounted rate or be completely exempt from the tax. In Florence and Siena, for instance, children under 12 are exempt from paying, while in Venice, children aged 10 to 16 pay half-price. It's also worth noting that the maximum number of nights that the tax is charged can vary between cities and regions.

It's always a good idea to confirm whether taxes are included when booking.

Search online for apartments and villas for rent. Another option is to share an apartment; check out university notice-boards for student flats with vacant rooms. Tourist offices in resort areas (coastal towns in summer, ski towns in winter) also maintain lists of apartments and villas for rent.

Best Places to Stay

Best on a Budget

RomeHello (p136) New-gen hostel in the Italian capital plastered in fantastic street art.

Magma Home (p713) B&B mixing Italian design with rooftop terraces, and views of Naples and Mt Vesuvius.

Hotel Scoti (p538) Palazzo living at bargain rates in Italy's favourite Renaissance city, Florence.

Ca' Barba (p388) Exceptionally good-value B&B in Venice by Rialto Market.

Via Stampatori (p227) Budget but insanely stylish B&B in a frescoed Renaissance building in Turin.

Best for Families

Meininger Roma Hostel (p137) The four-bed 'dorms' with bathroom at Rome's hostel newcomer are tip-top for families.

Palm Gallery Hotel (p138) The pool alone at this excellent midrange choice in Rome, in a Liberty-style villa, keeps kids happy post-sightseeing.

Villa Lina (p389) Kid-friendly Venice B&B with canal-side garden, in a 16th-century villa in the grounds of a Murano glassworks.

Eco Park Hotel Azalea (p343) Organic feasting, stupendous mountain views and a warm welcome for families in the action-packed Dolomites.

Agriturismo Guthiddai (p931) Bucolic whitewashed farm amid fig, olive and fruit trees on the island of Sardinia.

ProKite Alby Rondina (p887) Modern cottage accommodation adjoining a top kite-surfing school in western Sicily; a real teen favourite.

Best Unusual Settings

Prendiparte B&B (p472) Snooze, chill and cook up a feast in a 900-year-old tower in Bologna.

Avemaria Boat (p314) Mantua barge hotel offering cultural itineraries on the Po Delta.

Truddhi (p783) Bucolic, self-catering accommodation in *trulli* (traditional conical-roofed houses) in Locorotondo.

Hotel Il Belvedere (p805) What was once a cave is now a boutique hotel in Basilicata's World Heritage–listed Matera.

Month by Month

January

Following hot on the heels of New Year is Epiphany. In the Alps and Dolomites it's ski season, while in the Mediterranean south winters are mild and crowd-free, although many resort towns are firmly shut.

⭐ Regata della Befana

Venice celebrates Epiphany on 6 January with the Regatta of the Witches, complete with a fleet of brawny men dressed in their finest *befana* (witch) drag.

February

'Short' and 'accursed' is how Italians describe February. In the mountains the ski season hits its peak in line with school holidays. Further south it's chilly, but almond trees blossom and herald the carnival season.

⭐ Carnevale

In the period leading up to Ash Wednesday, many Italian towns stage pre-Lenten carnivals. Venice's Carnevale (www.carnevale.venezia.it) is the most famous, while Viareggio's version (htpp://viareggio.ilcarnevale.com) is well known for its giant papier-mâché floats.

🍴 Nero Norcia

An early-spring taste of truffles in the Umbrian town of Norcia, this fair usually runs over two to three weekends in late February and early March. Vsitors sift through booths focusing on all things fungi, alongside other speciality produce. (p648)

March

The weather in March is capricious: sunny, rainy and windy all at once. The official start of spring is 21 March, but the holiday season starts at Easter.

🍴 Taste

Gourmands flock to Florence for Taste (www.pittimmagine.com), a bustling food fair held inside industrial-sleek Stazione Leopolda. Culinary talks, cooking demonstrations and samples of food, coffee and liquor from more than 300 Italian artisan producers.

⭐ Settimana Santa

The Pope leads a candlelit procession to the Colosseum on Good Friday and gives the Easter message and blessing from St Peter's Square on Easter Sunday. Fireworks explode in Florence's Piazza del Duomo, with notable processions in Procida and Sorrento (Campania), Taranto (Puglia), Trapani (Sicily) and Iglesias (Sardinia).

April

April sees the Italian peninsula bloom. The gardens of northern Italy show off tulips and early camellias, and the mountains of Sicily and Calabria fill with wildflowers.

👁 Salone Internazionale del Mobile

Held annually in Milan, the world's most prestigious furniture fair is held at Fiera Milano, with satellite exhibitions in Zona Tortona. Running alongside it is the Fuorisalone (www.fuorisalone.it), with design-related exhibits and events across the city. (p272)

👁 Settimana del Tulipano

Tulips bloom during the Week of the Tulip, held at Lago Maggiore's Villa Taranto in Verbania; the dahlia and dogwood are also in bloom in one of Europe's finest botanical gardens. (p288)

☆ Maggio Musicale Fiorentino

Established in 1933, Italy's oldest art festival brings world-class performances of theatre, classical music, jazz, opera and dance to Florence's opera house and other venues. (p538)

🏃 Sciacchetrail

Runners flock to Cinque Terre for this challenging 47km race along a cliff-edge trail past vineyards and villages. Wine tastings and other events inspired by the area's Sciacchetrà wine are part of the weekend. (www.sciacchetrail.com)

May

The month of roses and cultural festivals is a perfect time to travel. The weather is warm but not too hot, and prices are good value. Especially good for walkers.

☆ Maggio dei Monumenti

As the weather warms up, Naples rolls out a mammoth, month-long program of art exhibitions, concerts, performances and tours. Historical and architectural

treasures usually off-limits are open and free to visit.

🍷 Wine & The City

A 10-day celebration of regional *vino* in Naples, with free wine degustations, *aperitivo* sessions and cultural events in museums and castles, art galleries, boutiques and restaurants. (p712)

☆ La Biennale di Venezia

Europe's premier arts showcase is actually held annually, though the spotlight alternates between art (odd-numbered years) and architecture (even-numbered years). Alongside the main events are showcases of dance, theatre, cinema and music. (p387)

☆ Piano City

Milan dedicates a long weekend to piano concerts held in museums, courtyards, stations, parks and markets. Ears are treated to classical, jazz, rock and world music tunes. Book tickets early. (www.pianocitymilano.it)

June

The summer season kicks off in June. The temperature cranks up quickly, beaches start to open in earnest and some of the big summer festivals commence. Republic Day, on 2 June, is a national holiday.

☆ Napoli Teatro Festival Italia

Naples celebrates a month of theatre, dance and literary events. Held in both conventional and uncon-

ventional venues, the program ranges from classic works to specially commissioned pieces. (p712)

☆ Spoleto Festival

Held in the Umbrian hill town of Spoleto, this is a world-renowned arts event, serving up 17 days of international theatre, opera, dance, music and art. (p645)

☆ Giostra del Saracino

A grandiose affair deep-rooted in neighbourhood rivalry, this medieval jousting tournament sees each *quartiere* (quarter) of Arezzo put forward a team of knights to battle on Piazza Grande; third Saturday in June and first Sunday in September. (www.giostradelsaracinoarezzo.it)

July

School is out and Italians head away from the cities and to mountains or beaches for summer holidays. Prices and temperatures rise. Many cities host summer art festivals.

☆ Il Palio di Siena

Daredevils in tights thrill the crowds with this chaotic bareback horse race around Siena's world-famous medieval piazza. Preceding the race is a dashing medieval-costume parade.

☆ Sagra della Madonna della Bruna

A week-long celebration (www.festadellabruna.it) of Matera's patron saint that culminates on

2 July with a colourful procession that sees the Madonna della Bruna escorted around town in a papier-mâché-adorned chariot. (p804)

✯ Festa di Sant'Anna

The Campanian island of Ischia celebrates the feast day of Sant'Anna: local municipalities build competing floats to sail in a flotilla, with spectacular fireworks and a symbolic 'burning' of the medieval Castello Aragonese. (www.infoischiaprocida.it)

✯ Ravello Festival

High above the Amalfi Coast, Ravello draws world-renowned artists for everything from music and dance to film and art exhibitions. Several events take place in the beautiful gardens of Villa Rufolo. (p758)

☆ Estate Romana

Rome puts on a summer calendar of events that turn the city into an outdoor stage. The program encompasses music, dance, literature and film, with events staged in some of Rome's most evocative venues. (p133)

☆ Ortigia Sound System

One of Sicily's top music festivals, held in Syracuse, ushers in five days of electronica by top-tier artists at venues island-wide. (p869)

August

August is hot, expensive and crowded. Everyone is on holiday; while not everything is shut, many

Top: Settimana Santa celebrations, Taranto (p798)

Bottom: Flags on display at Il Palio di Siena (p37)

businesses close for part of the month.

★ Ferragosto

After Christmas and Easter, Ferragosto, on 15 August, is Italy's biggest holiday. It marks the Feast of the Assumption, but even before Christianity the Romans honoured their gods on Feriae Augusti.

☆ Venice International Film Festival

One of the world's most prestigious silver-screen events. Held at the Lido from late August to early September, it draws the international film glitterati with its red-carpet premieres and paparazzi glamour. (www.labiennale.org/en/cinema)

September

This is a glorious month to travel in Italy. Summer warmth lingers in much of the country and the start of the harvest season sees lots of local *sagre* (food festivals) spring up. September is also the start of the grape harvest.

🏃 Corsa degli Zingari

Each year the first weekend in September sees hundreds of hardy (crazy?) barefoot runners race along sharp, stony mountain paths around the Abruzzo village of Pacentro – as has been the case for the last 550-odd years. (p684)

★ Regata Storica

In early September, gondoliers in period dress work those biceps in Venice's Historic Regatta. Period boats are followed by gondola and other boat races along the Grand Canal. (p387)

🍷 Expo del Chianti Classico

There is no finer opportunity to taste Tuscany's Chianti Classico than at this expo, in Greve in Chianti on the second weekend in September. All of the major producers are represented, with supporting events including musical performances. (p562)

◉ Venice Glass Week

This Venetian festival showcases the work of Murano's finest glass-blowers. The week-long event also offers visitors a peek into what were previously off-limits furnaces. (www.theveniceglassweek.com)

October

October is a fabulous time to visit the south, when the days still radiate with late-summer warmth and the beaches are emptying. Further north temperatures start to drop.

☆ Romaeuropa

Top international artists take to the stage for Rome's premier festival of theatre, opera and dance. Performances at numerous venues across the city. (p133)

🍴 Salone del Gusto & Terre Madre

Hosted by the home-grown Slow Food Movement, this biennial food expo takes place in Turin in even-numbered years. Events include workshops, presentations and tastings of food, wine and beer from Italy and beyond. (p227)

November

Winter creeps down the peninsula in November, but there's still plenty going on. This is truffle season. It's also the time for the chestnut harvest and mushroom picking.

★ Ognissanti

Celebrated all over Italy as a national holiday, All Saints' Day on 1 November commemorates all the saints, while All Souls' Day, on 2 November, honours the deceased.

☆ Opera Season

Italy is home to four of the world's great opera houses: La Scala (Milan), La Fenice (Venice), Teatro San Carlo (Naples) and Teatro Massimo (Palermo). The season traditionally runs from mid-October to March, although La Scala opens on St Ambrose Day (7 December).

December

December is cold and Alpine resorts start to open for the early ski season, although looming Christmas festivities keep life warm and bright.

◉ Natale

The weeks preceding Christmas are studded with religious events. Many churches set up nativity scenes known as *presepi*. On Christmas Eve the Pope serves midnight mass in St Peter's Square.

Itineraries

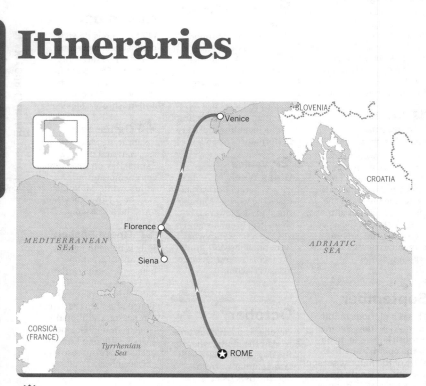

 Italian Highlights

A perfect introduction to Italy, this easy tour ticks off some of the country's most seductive sights, including Roman ruins, Renaissance masterpieces and the world's most beautiful lagoon city.

Start with three days in mighty **Rome**, punctuating blockbuster sights like the Colosseum, Palatino (Palatine Hill) and Sistine Chapel with market grazing in the Campo de' Fiori, boutique-hopping in Monti and late-night revelry in Trastevere.

On day four, head to Renaissance **Florence**. Drop in on Michelangelo's *David* at the Galleria dell'Accademia and pick your favourite Botticelli at the Galleria degli Uffizi. For a change of pace, escape to the Tuscan countryside on day six for a day trip to Gothic **Siena**, home of the biannual Palio horse race.

The following day, continue north for three unforgettable days in **Venice**. Check off musts like the mosaic-encrusted Basilica di San Marco, art-slung Gallerie dell'Accademia and secret passageways of the Palazzo Ducale, then live like a true Venetian, scouring seafood-laden stalls at the Rialto Market, noshing on the city's famous *cicheti* (Venetian tapas) and toasting with a Veneto prosecco.

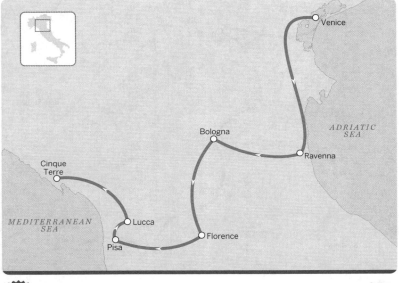

 **Northern Jewels**

This two-week route takes in some of northern Italy's most extraordinary assets, from cultural-powerhouse cities to one of Italy's most arresting stretches of coastline.

Begin with a trio of days in **Venice**, its trading-port pedigree echoed in the Near East accents of its architecture and the synagogues of its 500-year-old Ghetto. Don't miss big-hitters like the Basilica di San Marco and the Gallerie dell'Accademia, but leave time for less well trodden treasures, among them the Chiesa della Madonna dell'Orto. Day four, continue to **Ravenna**, former capital of the Western Roman Empire and home to eight Unesco World Heritage–listed sites, including the basilicas of San Vitale and Sant'Apollinare Nuovo adorned with extraordinary Byzantine mosaics.

Spend days six and seven in erudite **Bologna**, home to the world's fifth-largest church and its oldest university. The university district is the location of the Pinacoteca Nazionale, its powerhouse art collection including works by regional master Parmigianino. Delve into Bologna gastronomy in the Quadrilatero, a district bursting with produce stalls, fragrant delis, restaurants and an appetite-piquing food hall.

Burn off those excess calories with three days exploring **Florence** on foot. Find some of Western art's most revered works, including Michelangelo's chiselled *David* and Botticelli's ethereal paintings *Primavera* and *La nascita di Venere*. The city's Renaissance credentials extend to its architecture, which includes Filippo Brunelleschi's show-stopping Duomo. Even the city's gardens are manicured masterpieces, exemplified by the supremely elegant Giardino di Boboli.

On day 11, pit-stop in **Pisa** to eye-up the architectural ensemble that makes up the Piazza dei Miracoli, then continue to **Lucca**. Pedal 'n picnic atop its centuries-old city walls and meditate on Tintoretto's soul-stirring *Last Supper* in Cattedrale di San Martino. Human ingenuity and natural beauty merge on Liguria's World Heritage–listed **Cinque Terre** – the five colourful villages seemingly defy their precarious natural setting. Enjoy two days exploring medieval village streets, remarkable terraced gardens, *muretti* (dry stone walls) and breathtaking coastal walks.

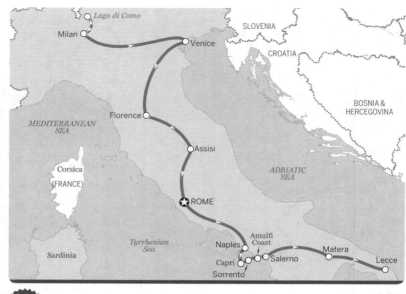

4 WEEKS The Grand Tour

From elegant northern cities and lakes to ancient southern coasts and dwellings, this grand tour encapsulates Italy's inimitable natural and cultural diversity.

Start in style with two days in **Milan**. Shop among coveted boutiques, dine at hotspot restaurants and demand an encore at the gilded La Scala. Come day three, continue to **Lago di Como** (Lake Como), basing yourself in Como or Bellagio and spending two romantic days among its sublime waterside villas and villages. If you haven't been wooed by Hollywood royalty, continue to **Venice** on day five, where the following trio of days burst with Titians and Tintorettos, artisan studios and convivial *bacari* (bars). On day eight, shoot southwest to **Florence**, allowing three days to tackle its heavyweight art collections and sink your teeth into its *bistecca alla fiorentina* (T-bone steak). Gluttonous acts are forgiven on day 11 as you travel to the pilgrimage city of **Assisi**, its Gothic basilica lavished with Giotto frescoes. Head southwest to **Rome** on day 13 and spend three full days exploring its two-millennia-worth of temples, churches, piazzas and artistic marvels.

On day 17, slip south to **Naples** and its explosion of baroque architecture and subterranean ruins. Day-trip to the ruins of Pompeii on day 19, then sail to **Capri** on day 20 for three seductive days of boating, hikes and piazza-side posing. If it's high season, catch a ferry directly to laid-back **Sorrento** on day 23, spending a night in town before hitting the hairpin turns of the glorious Amalfi Coast. Allow two days in chi-chi **Positano**, where you can hike the heavenly Sentiero degli Dei (Walk of the Gods). Spend day 26 in historic **Amalfi** before continuing to sky-high **Ravello**, long-time haunt of composers and Hollywood stars. Stay the night to soak up its understated elegance, and spend the following morning soaking up its uber-romantic gardens. After an evening of barhopping in upbeat **Salerno**, shoot inland to **Matera** on day 28 to experience its World Heritage–listed *sassi* (former cave dwellings) and dramatic Matera Gravina gorge. Come day 30, continue through to architecturally astounding **Lecce**, the 'Florence of the South' and your final cross-country stop.

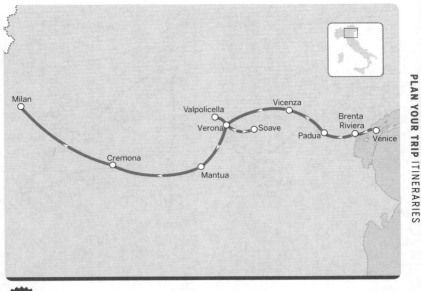

Venice to Milan

Aristocratic villas, renegade frescoes, star-struck lovers and cult-status wines; this easy two-week journey serves up a feast of northern assets. Begin with a couple of days in **Venice**, sampling the city's enviable art, architecture and seafood. In the 16th century the Venetian summer began early in June, when every household loaded onto barges for a summer sojourn along the nearby **Brenta Riviera**. You too can make like a Venetian on a boat trip along the Riviera, marvelling at the Tiepolo frescoes of Villa Pisani Nazionale and snooping around Palladio's Villa Foscari.

Boat trips along the Brenta Riviera end in **Padua** where you can overnight overlooking the Basilica di Sant'Antonio. Book ahead to see Padua's crowning glory, Giotto's frescoed Cappella degli Scrovegni.

Day six train it to **Vicenza**. Spend the afternoon watching sunlight ripple across the soaring facades of Palladio's *palazzi* (mansions) and illuminate the Villa Valmarana 'ai Nani', with frescoes by father and son Giambattista and Giandomenico Tiepolo, then head to **Verona** for three or four days. Here you can view Mantegnas at Basilica di San Zeno Maggiore, ponder modern art at the Galleria d'Arte Moderna Achille Forti, and find tranquillity in the 16th-century oasis of Giardino Giusti. Listen to opera in the Roman Arena and wander balconied backstreets where Romeo wooed Juliet. From Verona, consider also a day trip northwest to **Valpolicella** to sip prized Amarone (red wine), or back east to **Soave** for a sampling of its namesake DOC white wine.

Day 11 dip southwest to **Mantua** for an impressive display of dynastic power and patronage at the Gonzagas' fortified family pad, Palazzo Ducale. Finish with a two-day stop in **Cremona**, where you can chat with artisans in one of the 100 violin-making shops around Piazza del Comune before hearing the instruments in action at the Teatro Amilcare Ponchielli. Wrap up your tour in Italy's financial and fashion epicentre, **Milan**. On-trend shopping and dining aside, the city is home to a string of artistic treasures, among them Leonardo da Vinci's iconic *The Last Supper*.

10 DAYS Central Italian Escape

Revered vineyards, medieval hilltop towns and Unesco-lauded artwork: this trip takes in evocative landscapes, from well-trodden Tuscany to lesser-known Umbria and Le Marche.

Begin with two cultured days in **Florence**, then enjoy a pair of decadent days in **Chianti**, toasting to the area's vino and indulging in lazy lunches and countryside cycling. On day five, head east, pit-stopping in tiny **Sansepolcro** to meditate on Pietro della Francesca's trio of masterpieces and calling it a night in the Umbrian hilltop town of **Gubbio**. Spend the following day exploring the town's Gothic streets, then drive into Le Marche on day seven for a guided tour of the incredible **Grotte di Frasassi** cave system. The same day, head back into Umbria to **Assisi**, one of Italy's most beautiful medieval towns. Stay two nights, taking in the frescoes of the Basilica di San Francesco and finding peace on the hiking trails flanking Monte Subasio. Come day nine, make your way to the lively university city of **Perugia**, where your adventure ends with brooding Gothic architecture and world-famous Baci Perugina chocolates.

2 WEEKS Northeastern Interlude

Laced with cross-cultural influences, hot-list wines, world-famous charcuterie and stunning Alpine landscapes, this lesser-known corner of the country is ripe for discovery. After three days in **Venice**, head east to Trieste via the Roman ruins of **Aquileia** and the medieval heart of **Grado**. Take two days in **Trieste** for its gilded cafes, literary heritage and central European air, then catch a ferry to **Muggia**, the only Italian settlement on the Istrian peninsula. Day seven, head inland for celebrated whites in the **Collio** wine region. Spend two days in **Udine**, dropping in on the Museum of Modern and Contemporary Art and sidestepping to **Cividale dei Friuli**, home to Europe's only surviving example of Lombard architecture and artwork. On day 10, pit-stop in **San Daniele del Friuli** for Italy's best prosciutto before hitting breathtaking mountain scenery on your way to ski town **Cortina d'Ampezzo**. Allow two days to hit the slopes, on winter skis or in summer hiking boots. Head south on day 14 for afternoon bubbles in the prosecco heartland of **Conegliano** before wrapping things up in Venice.

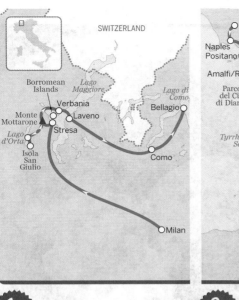

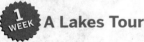 **A Lakes Tour**

Tickling the snowcapped Alps, Italy's glacial lakes have lured romantics for centuries, from European royalty to American silver-screen pin-ups.

A short drive northwest of Malpensa airport, **Milan**, brings you to the edge of serene Lago Maggiore. Start with three nights in belle époque **Stresa** and visit the lavish **Borromean Islands**: Isola Madre for its romantic gardens and wisteria-clad Staircase of the Dead; and Isola Bella for its art collection, ballrooms and shell-encrusted grotto. Take the funicular up to **Monte Mottarone** and day-trip to **Lago d'Orta** and **Isola San Giulio**. Day four, head north from Stresa to **Verbania**, picnicking amid the tulips of Villa Taranto before gliding east across the lake to **Laveno** and onto celebrity haunt **Como**. Amble the flower-laden lakeside to view art exhibits at Villa Olmo, hire a boat and/or hike the mountainous Triangolo Lariano. If you're ambitious you can walk to chic **Bellagio**. Otherwise, take the high and exhilarating 32km lakeside road from Como to Bellagio, lunching with magnificent views before one last romantic night lakeside.

2 WEEKS Southern Coastal Route

Graeco-Roman ruins, a Bourbon palace and beautiful coastline: crank up the romance on this two-week journey through the sun-baked south.

Enjoy three days in exhilarating **Naples**, day-tripping it to **Caserta** to explore Italy's largest royal palace. On day four, head south to the Amalfi Coast for two nights in **Positano** and a day in **Amalfi**. Overnight in **Ravello** en route to to **Salerno**. Week two, continue to the World Heritage–listed temples of **Paestum**, then through the **Parco Nazionale del Cilento, Vallo di Diano e Alburni** to cognoscenti coastal jewel **Maratea**. Spend two nights in town, followed by lunch in **Tropea** (one of Calabria's most beautiful coast towns) on your way to **Villa San Giovanni**. Sail to Sicily and treat yourself to a couple of nights in fashionable **Taormina**, Sicily's former Byzantine capital and home to the world's most spectacularly located Greek amphitheatre. Sun-kissed and relaxed, continue to **Catania** on day 13, taking two days to soak up the city's ancient sites, baroque architecture, vibrant market life and charismatic bar scene.

Arancin

Eat & Drink Like a Local

Gastronomy is one of Italy's raisons d'être. In fact, the country feels like one gargantuan kitchen, jam-packed with superlative produce, irresistible bites and finely tuned culinary know-how. Locals are fiercely proud of their regional specialities, and devouring them is an essential part of any Italian sojourn.

The Year in Food

While *sagre* (local food festivals) go into overdrive in autumn, there's never a bad time to raise your fork in Italy.

Spring (March–May)
Asparagus, artichokes and Easter specialities, plus a handful of festivals like Turin's Cioccolatò and Ascoli Piceno's Fritto Misto all'Italiana.

Summer (June–August)
Eggplants, peppers and berries. Tuck into tuna at Carloforte's Girotonno tuna catch in June and beat the heat with gelato and Sicilian *granita*.

Autumn (September–November)
Food festivals, chestnuts, mushrooms and game. Truffle hunters head to Piedmont, Tuscany and Umbria, while wine connoisseurs hit Elba's wine harvest and Merano's wine festival.

Winter (December–February)
Christmas and Carnevale treats. Fishers serve up sea urchins and mussels on Sardinia's Poetto beach, while Umbria celebrates black truffles with the Mostra Mercato del Tartufo Nero.

Food Experiences

So much produce, so many specialities, so little time! Fine-tune your culinary radar with the following edible musts.

Meals of a Lifetime

Osteria Francescana, Modena Emilia-Romagna's produce gets seriously experimental at this restaurant, named the world's best in 2018 (www.theworlds50best.com). (p481)

President, Pompeii One of Italy's best-priced Michelin-starred restaurants, serving whimsical re-interpretations of Campanian cuisine. (p732)

Piazza Duomo, Alba Langhe produce and Japanese technique fuse to spectacular effect at Enrico Crippa's Michelin-starred blockbuster, rated number 29 in the world in 2019 (www.theworlds50best.com). (p236)

Enoteca Pinchiorri, Florence Tuscany's only Michelin-three-star address, stratospheric and smug in a 16th-century Florentine *palazzo* (mansion). (p543)

Peperino, San Miniato Dinner for two at the world's smallest, and possibly most romantic, restaurant. (p603)

Dal Pescatore, Mantua The first female Italian chef to hold three Michelin stars, Nadia Santini is a self-taught culinary virtuoso. (p315)

Il Frantoio, Puglia Long, legendary Sunday lunches at an olive-grove-fringed *masseria* (working farm) in Italy's deep south. (p786)

Cheap Treats

Pizza al taglio 'Pizza by the slice' is the perfect piazza-side nibble.

Arancini Deep-fried rice balls stuffed with *ragù* (meat sauce), tomato and vegetables.

Porchetta rolls Warm sliced pork (roasted whole with fennel, garlic and pepper) in a crispy roll.

Pane e panelle Palermo chickpea fritters on a sesame roll.

Gelato The best Italian gelato uses seasonal ingredients and natural colours.

Dare to Try

Missoltini Como's sun-dried fish cured in salt and bay leaves.

Lampredotto Cow's stomach boiled, sliced, seasoned and bunged between bread in Florence.

Pani ca meusa A Palermo sandwich of beef spleen and lungs dipped in boiling lard.

Zurrette Sardinian black pudding made of sheep's blood, cooked in a sheep's stomach with herbs and fennel.

Local Specialities

The Italian term for 'pride of place' is *campanilismo,* but a more accurate word would be *formaggismo:* loyalty to the local cheese. Clashes among medieval city-states involving castle sieges and boiling oil have been replaced by competition in producing speciality foods and wines.

Emilia-Romagna

Emilia-Romagna claims some of Italy's most famous exports. Bologna piques appetites with *mortadella* (pork cold cut), *stinco di maiale al forno con porcini* (roasted pork shanks with porcini mushrooms) and *tagliatelle al ragù* (pasta with white wine, tomato, oregano, beef and pork belly). It's also famous for soothing *tortellini in brodo* (pasta stuffed with ground meats in a thin meat broth). While Parma is world-famous for *parmigiano reggiano* cheese (Parmesan) and *prosciutto di Parma* (cured ham), lesser-known claims include *pesto di cavallo* (raw minced horse meat with herbs and Parmesan).

Lombardy

Lombardy is all about *burro* (butter), risotto and gorgonzola cheese. Milan serves up *risotto alla milanese* (saffron and bone-marrow risotto), *panettone* (a yeast-risen sweet bread), uberfashionable restaurants and food emporium Peck. Renaissance Mantua remains addicted to *tortellini di zucca* (pumpkin-stuffed pasta), wild fowl and its *mostarda mantovana* (apple relish). The Valtenesi area is home to some of Italy's finest emerging olive oils, including Comincioli's award-winning Numero Uno.

Naples & Campania

Procida lemons get cheeky in *limoncello* (lemon liqueur), while the region's vines create intense red Taurasi and the dry white Fiano di Avellino. Naples is home to superlative street food, including *pizza fritta* (fried pizza dough stuffed with salami, dried lard cubes, smoked *provola* cheese, ricotta and tomato). The town of Gragnano produces prized pasta, perfect for *spaghetti alle vongole* (spaghetti with clam sauce). Leave room for a *sfogliatella* (sweetened ricotta pastry) and *babà* (rum-soaked sponge cake). Both Caserta and the Cilento produce prime *mozzarella di bufala* (buffalo mozzarella).

Piedmont

Birthplace of the Slow Food Movement. Guzzle Lavazza and Caffè Vergnano coffee in Turin, a city also famed for vermouth,

Limoncello

nougat and its buzzing *aperitivo* scene (pre-dinner drinks). Leave room for *gianduja* (a chocolate hazelnut spread) and a *bicerin* (a chocolate, coffee and cream libation). Alba treats taste buds to white truffles, hazelnuts, and pedigreed Barolo and Barbaresco reds, while Cherasco is celebrated for its *lumache* (snails).

Puglia

Head southeast for peppery olive oil and honest *cucina povera* (peasant cooking). Breadcrumbs lace everything from *strascinati con la mollica* (pasta with breadcrumbs and anchovies) to *tiella di verdure* (baked vegetable casserole), while snacks include *puccia* (bread with olives) and ring-shaped *taralli* (pretzel-like biscuits). In Salento, linger over lunch at a *masseria* and propose a toast with hearty reds like Salice Salentino and Primitivo di Manduria.

Rome & Lazio

Carb-up with *spaghetti alla carbonara* (no cream involved), *bucatini all'amatriciana* (with bacon, tomato, chilli and *pecorino*

Pasta alla Norma

cheese) and *spaghetti cacio e pepe* (with *pecorino* cheese and black pepper). Head to Rome's Testaccio neighbourhood for nose-to-tail staples like *trippa alla romana* (tripe cooked with potatoes, tomato, mint and *pecorino* cheese), and to the Ghetto for kosher deep-fried *carciofi* (artichokes). Southeast of the city in Frascati, tour the vineyards and swill the area's eponymous, delicate white vino.

Sardinia

Sardinia's waters provide *ricci di mare* (sea urchins) and *bottarga* (salted, pressed and dried mullet roe), while its interior delivers *porchetta* (roast suckling pig, often served on a bed of myrtle leaves). Pasta classics include *culurgiones* (pasta pockets stuffed with potato and *casu de fitta* cheese), *fregola* (granular pasta similar to couscous) and *malloreddus* (a gnocchi-pasta hybrid), while its cheeses include top-notch *pecorino*. A lesser-known *formaggio* (cheese) is *casu marzu* (rotten maggoty cheese), though this can be hard to find unless you know a farmer with a stash in the Nuoro region.

Sicily

Channel ancient Arab influences with fish couscous and spectacular sweets like *cannoli* (crisp pastry shells filled with sweet ricotta). In Palermo, snack on *sfincione* (spongy, oily pizza topped with onions and *caciocavallo* cheese), and feast on *pasta con le sarde* (pasta with sardines, pine nuts, raisins and wild fennel) and *involtini di pesce spada* (thinly sliced swordfish fillets rolled up and filled with breadcrumbs, capers, tomatoes and olives). In Catania, tackle *pasta alla Norma* (pasta with basil, eggplant, ricotta and tomato). Further south, taste-test Modica's spiced chocolate.

Tuscany

In Florence, drool over *bistecca alla fiorentina* (T-bone steak), made with Chianina beef from the Val di Chiana. The valley is also famous for *ravaggiolo* (sheep's-milk cheese wrapped in fern fronds). Head to Castelnuovo di Garfagnana for autumnal porcini and chestnuts, and to San Miniato for white truffles (October to December). These prized fungi are celebrated at

TABLE MANNERS

While Italian diners will usually forgive any foreign faux pas, the following few tips should impress any gastro-snob.

➡ Make eye contact when toasting.

➡ Eat spaghetti with a fork, not a spoon.

➡ Don't eat bread with your pasta; using it to wipe any remaining sauce from your plate (called *fare la scarpetta*) is fine.

➡ Never order a coffee *with* your lunch or dinner – and never order a cappuccino at the end of your meal (it's espresso or nothing).

➡ Whoever invites usually pays. Splitting *il conto* (the bill) is common enough; itemising it is not.

San Miniato's white-truffle fair (Mostra Mercato Nazionale del Tartufo Bianco di San Miniato), held in November. Savour *cinta senese* (indigenous Tuscan pig), *pecorino* (sheep's-milk cheese) and prized extra-virgin olive oils in Montalcino, a place also known for its Brunello and Rosso di Montalcino reds. Montepulciano is the home of Vino Nobile red, its equally quaffable second-string Rosso di Montepulciano, and Terre di Siena extra-virgin olive oil. Just leave time for Chianti's world-famous vineyards.

Umbria

Uncork a bottle of Sagrantino di Montefalco red and grate a black truffle from Norcia over fresh *tagliatelle* (ribbon pasta) or *strozzapreti* (an elongated pasta literally meaning 'priest-strangler'). Black truffles aside, Norcia is Italy's capital of pork. Another popular meat is wild boar. In Lago Trasimeno, freshwater fish flavour dishes like *regina alla porchetta* (roasted carp stuffed with garlic, fennel and herbs) and *tegemacchio* (fish stew made with garlic, onions, tomatoes and a medley of underwater critters). Meanwhile, on the Strada dei Vini del Cantico wine trail, the town of Torgiano celebrates wine and olives with two dedicated museums.

Venice & the Veneto

Not all bubbly prosecco and fiery grappa, Italy's northeast peddles *risotto alle seppie* (cuttlefish-ink risotto) and *polenta con le quaglie* (polenta with quails), as well as the odd foreign spice – think *sarde in saor* (grilled sardines in a sweet-and-sour sauce). Sail into Venice for *cicheti* (Venetian bar snacks) at local *bacari* (bars) and to scour Rialto Market produce such as lagoon seafood (look for tags reading *nostrano,* meaning 'ours'). The prime wine region of Valpolicella is celebrated for Amarone, Valpolicella Superiore, Ripasso, Recioto, and inspired renegade *Indicazione geografica tipica* (IGT) red blends from winemakers like Giuseppe Quintarelli and Zýmē.

How to Eat & Drink

Now that your appetite is piqued, it's time for the technicalities of eating *all'italiana*.

When to Eat

Colazione (Breakfast) Often little more than an espresso and a *cornetto* (Italian croissant) or brioche.

Pranzo (Lunch) Traditionally the main meal of the day. Standard restaurant times are noon to 3pm, though most locals don't lunch before 1pm.

Aperitivo Post-work drinks usually take place between 5pm and 8pm, when the price of your drink includes a buffet of tasty morsels.

Cena (Dinner) Traditionally lighter than lunch, though still a main meal. Standard restaurant times are 7.30pm to around 11pm, with southern Italians generally eating later than their northern cousins.

Where to Eat

Ristorante (restaurant) Formal service and refined dishes.

Trattoria Cheaper than a restaurant, with more-relaxed service and regional classics.

Osteria Historically a tavern focused on wine; the modern version is often an intimate trattoria or wine bar offering a handful of dishes.

Enoteca A wine bar often serving snacks to accompany your tipple.

Top: Rialto Market (p375), Venice

Bottom: *Tagliatelle* with truffles

THE *CAFFÈ* LOW-DOWN

➡ Caffè latte and cappuccino are considered morning drinks, with espresso and macchiato the pre-ferred post-lunch options.

➡ Baristas may offer a glass of water, either *liscia* (still) or *frizzante* (sparkling), with your espresso. Many (especially southern Italians) drink it before their coffee to cleanse the palate.

➡ Take the edge off the day with a *caffè corretto*, a shot of espresso spiked with liqueur (usually grappa).

➡ Coffee with dessert is fine, but ordering one with your main meal is a travesty.

Agriturismo A working farmhouse offering food made with farm-grown produce.

Pizzeria Cheap grub, cold beer and a convivial vibe. The best pizzerias are often crowded: be patient.

Tavola calda Cafeteria-style spots serving cheap pre-made food such as pasta and roast meats.

Friggitoria A simple joint selling freshly fried local street food and snacks to go.

Menu Decoder

Antipasto A hot or cold appetiser; for a tasting plate of different appetisers, request an *antipasto misto* (mixed antipasto).

Contorno Side dish; usually *verdura* (vegetable).

Dolce Dessert; including *torta* (cake).

Frutta Fruit; usually the epilogue to a meal.

Menù alla carta Choose whatever you like from the menu.

Menù di degustazione Degustation menu; usually consisting of six to eight 'tasting size' courses.

Menù turistico The 'tourist menu' usually signals mediocre fare – steer clear!

Nostra produzione Made in-house.

Piatto del giorno Dish of the day.

Primo First course; usually a substantial pasta, rice or *zuppa* (soup) dish.

Secondo Second course; often *carne* (meat) or *pesce* (fish).

Surgelato Frozen; usually used to denote fish or seafood not freshly caught.

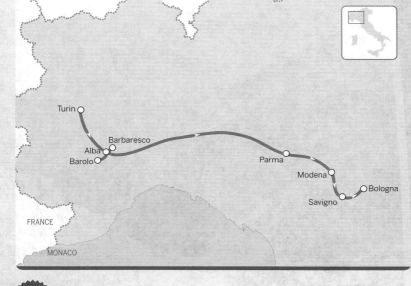

Food Odyssey of the North

2 WEEKS

Begin with two days in **Turin** (p218), foodie Piedmont's regional capital that gave the world its first saleable chocolate bar; it hosts the fun chocolate festival Cioccolatò (www.cioccolato.it) in November. Begin with a sweet mid-morning *bicerin* (a caffeine-charged hot drink of chocolate, coffee and cream) at historic cafe Al Bicerin; a gourmet shopping spree at Eataly Torino Lingotto; chocolate tastings at modern chocolatier Guido Gobino; and, come dusk, a high-end *aperitvo* at Bar Cavour. Buy a bag of *gianduiotto* (triangular chocolates made from hazelnut paste) to take home.

Move southeast next to **Alba** (p235) in the vine-striped Langhe hills for the remainder of week one. Famed for its creamy hazelnuts and white truffles, the town hosts weekend truffle fairs in October and November and an exuberant *vendemia* (grape harvest). Sign up for a guided walk or bike ride through vineyards and chestnut groves at the tourist office, and take day trips to the wine-growing towns of **Barolo** (p237) and **Barbaresco** (p238), famed for exceptional reds.

Week two, motor east to **Parma** (p483), celebrity home to *prosciutto di Parma* and *parmigiano reggiano*. Sample both at their finest at Ristorante Cocchi. Next day drive east to **Modena** (p477). Shop for balsamic vinegar at La Consorteria 1966 and local produce at the region's finest food market, Mercato Albinelli. Depending on your budget, dine at Osteria Francescana (book months ahead) or Trattoria Ermes, an Emilian kitchen going strong since 1963. Next day, another sensational dining experience awaits at Trattoria da Amerigo in the village of **Savigno** (p474), an hour's drive from Modena in truffle country. Overnight above the restaurant.

Bologna (p466) demands at least two days to sample its culinary riches. Spend half a day exploring FICO Eataly World, a one-stop Holy Grail for the culinarily curious with plenty of tasty lunch options. Back in town, deli-hop in the Quadrilatero district and learn how to make pasta during a cookery class at the Culinary Institute of Bologna. Enjoy dinner with food-obsessed locals at Trattoria Bertozzi.

Gran Sasso (678)

Plan Your Trip
Activities

Blessed with mountains, lakes and 7600km of coastline, Italy is like one giant, pulse-racing playground. Whether you're after adrenalin-charged skiing in the Alps, hardcore hiking in the Dolomites, coastal climbs in Sardinia, white-water rafting in Calabria or low-key cycling through Piedmont – Madre Natura (Mother Nature) has you covered.

FAB3B/SHUTTERSTOCK ©

Best Activities

Best Outdoor Experiences

Hiking The Dolomites, Piedmont's Gran Paradiso, Trentino's Stelvio and Calabria's Pollino parks, Umbria's Piano Grande and the coastal tracks of the Cinque Terre, the Amalfi Coast, Sicily and Sardinia.

Cycling The Po Delta and Bolzano offer good networks, as do the wine regions of Franciacorta, Barolo, Barbaresco and Chianti. Urban options include Rome's Via Appia Antica, Ferrara, Lucca, Bologna and Lecce.

Skiing Cross-border into Slovenia at Sella Nevea; skiing and snowboarding in Courmayeur; downhill and cross-country in Cortina d'Ampezzo, the Valle d'Aosta and Sella Ronda.

Diving Marine parks abound. The best are off the Cinque Terre, the Gargano Promontory, Elba, the Sorrento Peninsula, the Aeolian Islands, Ustica and Sardinia.

Best Times to Go

April to June Walk among wildflowers.

July & September Water sports and warm-water diving without the August crowds.

December, February & March The best ski months for atmosphere, snow and value respectively.

Hiking & Walking

Italy is laced with thousands of kilometres of *sentieri* (marked trails). Most local and regional tourist office websites have information about walking in their area. Italian Parks (www.parks.it) lists walking trails through each of the country's 25 national parks, and provides updates on Italy's marine parks and other protected areas. Another useful website is that of Italy's major walking club, the Club Alpino Italiano (www.cai.it) – follow the *rifugi* (mountain huts) link for information about trail routes and accommodation (members of organisations such as the New Zealand Alpine Club, Fédération Française des Clubs Alpins et de Montagne and Deutscher Alpenverein can enjoy discounted rates for accommodation and meals).

Bear in mind that most Italians take their summer holidays in August, so this is when the trails are at their most crowded and the *rifugi* are often jam-packed – you'll need to book weeks, if not months, in advance. On lower terrain, August's intense heat can be oppressive. Sidestep this month if you can. Also note that backcountry or wild camping is not permitted in Italy; if you want to pitch a tent, you'll have to do so at a private campsite.

For detailed information on hiking routes in specific regions, check out the reliable Cicerone (www.cicerone.co.uk) series of walking guides.

The Alps & Dolomites

Italy's wild, lushly wooded Alps stretch from France in the west, via the southern borders of Austria and Switzerland, to Slovenia in the east. For hikers, they offer heady mountain vistas, swooping forested valleys and views over large glacial lakes such as Garda, Como and Maggiore.

In the far west, dropping into Piedmont and Liguria, are the Graian, Maritime and Ligurian Alps, which take in the full sweep of the Valle d'Aosta (p247), the vast Parco Nazionale del Gran Paradiso (p254) and the lesser-known Parco Naturale delle Alpi Marittime, before making a sharp and dramatic descent to the Cinque Terre (p200) and Portofino park on the Ligurian coastline.

To the east in Friuli Venezia Giulia, you'll find the Giulie and Carnic Alps, where you can hike in pursuit of lynx, marmots and eagles amid supercute Tyrolean villages. Heading west, the white ridges pass through Trentino's Parco Nazionale dello Stelvio (p341), northern Italy's (and the Alps') largest national park, and spill into Lombardy. Lombardy's great lakes – encompassing Garda, Como, Iseo, Maggiore and Orta – are prime hiking territory, mixing mountain and lake vistas. Particularly scenic is the crumpled ridge of mountains in Como's Triangolo Lariano and Garda's Monte Baldo.

Soaring across the borders of the Veneto, Trentino and Alto Adige, the enormous limestone fangs of the Dolomites (p342) have the edge when it comes to wild beauty. The Unesco World Heritage–listed mountain range offers some of Italy's most dramatic and vertiginous hiking trails. The multi-day, hut-to-hut alte vie (high routes) that slice through the heart of the range are among the most stunning in Europe. To up the ante somewhat, the region is laced with *vie ferrate,* fixed routes that snake and ladder up the peaks and allow would-be mountaineers to flirt with rock climbing with the security of a cable to hook onto.

Accommodation in the mountains is in *rifugi* (huts) or chalets, which should be booked ahead in high season. For serious hiking you'll need to bring appropriate equipment and get detailed trail maps. Tourist offices and visitor centres provide some information, resources and basic maps for easier tourist routes.

Central Italy

Abruzzo's national parks are among Italy's least explored. Here, you can climb Corno Grande, the Apennines' highest peak at 2912m, and explore vast, silent valleys. A top hike here is the three- to four-day trek through the Majella mountains (p683), which follows an old POW escape route from Sulmona to Casoli.

In neighbouring Umbria, the glacier-carved valleys, beech forests and rugged mountains of Monti Sibillini (p672) and the Piano Grande, a 1270m-high plain flanked by the peaks of the Apennines, are well off the trodden path and beg to be discovered on foot. Both are spattered with a painter's palette of vibrant wildflowers in spring and early summer.

Tuscany's only significant park with good walking trails is in the southern Maremma (p589), where you can sign up for walks of medium difficulty. The tower-topped medieval town of San Gimignano is also a fine base for guided nature walks into the hills. The Apuane Alps and the stunning Garfagnana valleys are for serious hikers, with hundreds of trails encompassing everything from half-day hikes to long-distance treks. For most people, though, an easy amble through the picturesque vineyards of Chianti (p562) suits just fine – with a little wine tasting thrown in for good measure, naturally. Autumn, when the wine and olive harvests start, has a particularly mellow appeal.

Edging northwest, Cinque Terre (p200) is postcard stuff, with its collection of five rainbow-bright villages pasted precariously to the clifftops, looking as though

---

TOP TRAILS

Alpe di Siusi, Alto Adige (p345) Europe's largest plateau ends dramatically at the base of the Sciliar Mountains. Average stamina will get you to Rifugio Bolzano, one of the Alps' oldest mountain huts. The more challenging peaks of the Catinaccio group and the Sassolungo are nearby.

Val Pusteria, Alto Adige (p350) This narrow Tyrolean valley runs from Bressanone to San Candido. At the far end of the valley are the Sesto Dolomites, criss-crossed with spectacular walking trails, including moderate trails around the iconic Tre Cime di Lavaredo (Three Peaks).

Val Gardena, Alto Adige (p344) One of only five valleys where the Ladin heritage is still preserved. Located amid the peaks of the Gruppo del Sella and Sassolungo, there are challenging *alte vie* (high-altitude) trails and easier nature walks such as the Naturonda at Passo di Sella (2244m).

Brenta Dolomites, Trentino (p329) The Brenta group is famed for its sheer cliffs and tricky ascents, which are home to some of Italy's most famous *vie ferrate* (trails with permanent steel cables and ladders), including the Via Ferrata delle Bocchette.

Parco Nazionale delle Dolomiti Bellunesi, Veneto (p424) A Unesco Heritage park offering trails amid wildflowers. This park also harbours the high-altitude Alte Vie delle Dolomiti trails, accessible between June and September.

the slightest puff of wind would make them topple into the Ligurian Sea any second. The area is honeycombed with terrific trails that teeter through the vines and along the precipitous coastline. The star attraction is undoubtedly the serpentine Sentiero Azzuro (p200) linking all five villages, while the Sentiero Rosso presents a highly scenic alternative.

The South

For spectacular sea views hit the Amalfi Coast (p749) and Sorrento Peninsula, where age-old paths such as the Sentiero degli Dei (Path of the Gods) disappear into wooded mountains and ancient lemon groves. Across the water, Capri (p737) subverts its playboy image with a series of bucolic walking trails far from the crowds.

Crossing the border between Calabria and Basilicata is the Parco Nazionale del Pollino (p812), Italy's largest national park. Claiming the richest repository of flora and fauna in the south, its varied landscapes range from deep river canyons to alpine meadows. Calabria's other national parks – the Sila (p815) and Aspromonte (p818) – offer similarly dramatic hiking, particularly the area around Sersale in the Sila, studded with waterfalls and the possibility of trekking through the Valli Cupe canyon.

Close to the heel of the stiletto in the sun-baked region of Puglia, the Parco della Murgia Materana, part of the Matera (p800) Unesco World Heritage Site, is full of fascinating cave churches and is great for birdwatching.

Sicily & Sardinia

With their unique topographies, Sicily and Sardinia provide unforgettable walking opportunities. Take your pick of volcano hikes in Sicily: the mother of them all is Mount Etna (p863), but there's a whole host of lesser volcanoes on the Aeolian Islands, from the slumbering Vulcano (p847), where you can descend to the crater floor, to a three-hour climb to the summit of Stromboli (p850) to see it exploding against the night sky. On Salina, you can clamber up extinct volcano Monte Fossa delle Felci (p849) for staggering views of symmetrically aligned volcanic peaks. From Etna you can also trek across into the Madonie park (p843), or

Hiker, Apuane Alps, Tuscany

on Sicily's northwest coast, you can track the shoreline in the Riserva Naturale dello Zingaro (p889).

Hiking Sardinia's granite peaks is more challenging. The Golfo di Orosei e del Gennargentu (p934) park offers a network of old shepherds' tracks on the Supramonte plateau and incorporates the prehistoric site of Tiscali (p932) and the Gola Su Gorropu (p931) canyon, which requires a guide and a little rock climbing. Arguably the toughest trek in Italy, the island's seven-day Selvaggio Blu (p933) is not for the faint-hearted. Stretching 45km along the Golfo di Orosei, the trek traverses wooded ravines, gorges and cliffs and a string of stunning coves. It's not well signposted (a deliberate decision to keep it natural), there's no water en route and some climbing and abseiling is involved.

Cycling

Whether you're after a gentle ride between trattorias, a 100km road race or a teeth-rattling mountain descent, you'll find a route to suit. Tourist offices can usually

Top: Cycling, Tuscany

Bottom: Horse riding, Sardinia

BIKE TOURS

We Bike Tuscany (p63) Year-round one-day bike tours for riders of every skill level. Transport to Chianti and a support vehicle are provided. It also offers electric-bike tours.

Iseobike (p300) Tours around the Franciacorta wine region, with wine tastings.

Colpo di Pedale (☑333 810 46 88; www.colpodipedale.it; ⊙Apr-Oct) Trips for all levels on racers, mountain bikes and city bikes around Piedmont's Langhe wine region.

Ciclovagando (p785) Half- and full-day tours in Puglia, departing from various Puglian towns including Lecce, Matera and Trani.

Xtreme Malcesine (p307) On Lago di Garda's east bank, mountain-bike tours into the hills departing from the base of the Monte Baldo cable car.

Soul Cycles (p215) Hooks up mountain-bike enthusiasts with qualified guides and some outstanding mountain-biking tracks along Liguria's Riviera di Ponente.

provide details on trails and guided rides, and bike hire is available in most cities and key activity spots.

Tuscany's rolling countryside has enduring appeal for cyclists, with gentle rides between achingly pretty villages, vines and olive groves. The wine-producing Chianti (p562) area south of Florence is a particular favourite. In Umbria, the Valnerina (p647) and Piano Grande at Monte Vettore have beautiful trails and quiet country roads to explore. Further north, the flatlands of Emilia-Romagna (p462) and the terraced vineyards of Barolo (p237), Barbaresco (p238) and Franciacorta are also ideally suited to bike touring, as are the trails rimming Lago di Como (p291) and Lago Maggiore (p285). Cycling meets architecture on the Veneto's Brenta Riviera, which offers 150km of bike routes past glorious Venetian villas. In the south, Puglia's flat countryside and coastal paths are also satisfying.

In summer, many Alpine ski resorts offer wonderful cycling. Mountain bikers are in their element whizzing among the peaks around Lago di Garda (p301), Lago Maggiore and the Dolomites (p342) in Trentino-Alto Adige. Another challenging area is the granite landscape of the Supramonte (p930) in eastern Sardinia.

Friuli Venezia Giulia is another scenic cycling destination, with routes wending their way through the Dolomites, the rolling hills and vineyards of Collio wine country and along the coast. The transnational Ciclovia Alpe Adria Radweg (p431) bike route passes through Friuli and across to the island of Grado off Friuli's

coast en route to Salzburg in Austria. Seasonal summer trains and buses allow cyclists to hop on and off the trail.

A useful first port of call for two-wheel adventures is Italy Cycling Guide (www.italy-cycling-guide.info), which gives the lowdown on major national and international routes in Italy, as well as route options (including maps and GPS files) for a number of regions.

Horse Riding

Almost every region can be explored on horseback. Riding is particularly accessible in southern Tuscany where iconic *butteri* (Maremmese cowboys) herd cows in the Parco Regionale della Maremma. Guided treks can be arranged through the park's main visitor centre in Alberese or contact **Montebelli Agriturismo & Country Hotel** (☑334 2206929; www.montebelli.com; Località Molinetto, Caldana; agriturismo d €132-170, country hotel d €210, ste €240, f €300; ⊙closed Nov-Mar; P❄🅿🛜🏊), one of a handful of hotels in the region to offer horse riding.

Different regions offer different types of treks: In the Valle d'Asota in northern Italy, horseback enthusiasts can explore the protected Parc Nazionale del Gran Paradiso on horseback with Le Traîneau Equestrian Tourism Centre (p254). Not far from Lago di Garda at **Ranch Barlot** (☑348 7234082; www.ranchbarlot.com; Località Porcini, Caprino Veronese; treks per person per day €110-150), you can saddle up an

Skiing, Madonna di Campiglio (p330)

Appaloosa or Argentinian pony and trek for two to eight days Western-style up Monte Baldo or through the lushly forested Adige valley. In southern Italy Horse Riding Tour Naples (p723) visits Parco Nazionale del Vesuvio (weather permitting) and casts an alternative spin on visiting Pompeii.

Sardinia's **Horse Country Resort** (☑0783 8 05 00; www.horsecountry.it; Strada a Mare 24; riding lessons per person from €20) is among Italy's most important equestrian centres, with a stable of Arabian, Andalusian and Sardinian horses. In addition to lessons and various packages, it also offers accommodation.

Favourite *agriturismi* (farm stays) with ample opportunity to hack through the surrounding countryside on horseback include Podere San Lorenzo (p575) near Volterra in central Tuscany, Le Case Rosse di Montebuono (p630) on Lage Trasimeno in Umbria, and the aptly named Eldorado Ranch (p804) in Matera, southern Italy. Riding packages at the Gstatschhof Ponyhof (p348) in the Dolomites include snow treks (January to March).

Rock Climbing

The huge rock walls of the Dolomites set testing challenges for rock climbers of all levels, with everything from simple, single-pitch routes to long, multi-pitch ascents, many of which are easily accessible by road. To combine rock climbing with high-level hiking, clip into the *vie ferrate* (trails with permanent cables and ladders) in the Brenta Dolomites (p329).

Climbs of all grades are found in the Trentino town of Arco, home to the world-famous Rock Master Festival, from short, single-pitch sport routes to lengthier, Dolomite-style climbs.

For hardcore mountaineering, alpinists can pit themselves against Western Europe's highest peaks in the Valle d'Aosta (p247). Courmayeur and Cogne, a renowned ice-climbing centre, make good bases.

To the south, the Gran Sasso (p678) massif is a favourite. Of its three peaks, Corno Grande (2912m) is the highest and Corno Piccolo (2655m) the easiest to get to.

Other hot spots include Monte Pellegrino outside Palermo in Sicily, and Domusnovas, Ogliastra and the Supramonte (p930) in Sardinia.

The best source of climbing information is the Club Alpino Italiano (www.cai.it). Another good information source is the website Climb Europe (www.climb-europe.com), which also sells rock-climbing guidebooks covering Italy.

Italy's largest indoor-climbing centre is Salewa Cube (p334) in Bolzano, South Tyrol.

Skiing & Snowboarding

Most of Italy's top ski resorts are in the northern Alps, where names like Sestriere (p243), Cortina d'Ampezzo (p425), Madonna di Campiglio (p330) and Courmayeur (p251) are well known to serious skiers. Travel down the peninsula and you'll find smaller resorts dotted throughout the Apennines, in Lazio, Le Marche and Abruzzo. The Apennines often receive mega snowfalls and fewer crowds (so shorter lift queues), and historic villages such as Scanno (p685) and Pescocostanzo (p682) are far more charming than some

TOP SKI RESORTS

Spread across the north of the country in the Alps and Dolomites, Italy has a bumper crop of ski resorts, which range from the fast and fashion-conscious to the low-key and affordable. Here's our pick of them at a glance.

Courmayeur

Dominated by spectacular Mont Blanc, Courmayeur (p251) has access to legendary runs like the Vallée Blanche. Besides 100km of downhill skiing geared towards confident intermediates, there's good off-piste, heli-skiing and a pumping après-ski scene.

Cortina d'Ampezzo

In the Veneto Dolomites, Cortina d'Ampezzo (p425) has some serious downhill and cross-country skiing on Italy's most glamorous slopes, including the legendary Staunies black mogul run, and uplifting views of the Dolomites all around.

Breuil-Cervinia

In Matterhorn's shadow and within skiing distance of Zermatt over the mountain in Switzerland, Breuil-Cervinia (p255) in Aosta is a fine choice for late-season snow, intermediate runs and family facilities.

Monte Rosa

Straddling three valleys, the Monte Rosa (p247) ski area has a nicely chilled atmosphere, pretty Walser villages and white-knuckle off-piste skiing and heli-skiing, which figures among Europe's best.

Via Lattea

Italy's Via Lattea (p243), or 'Milky Way', covers a staggering 400km of pistes and links five ski resorts, including one of Europe's most glamorous, Sestriere, which is snow-sure thanks to its 2035m elevation.

Madonna di Campiglio

The Dolomites form a spectacular backdrop to the ultra-fashionable Madonna di Campiglio (p330), which attracts the Italian A-list to its swanky slopes. There's 150km of manicured runs and a snowboarding park to play on.

of the bigger resorts found elsewhere. Even Sicily's Mount Etna (p863) is skiable in winter.

Two snowboarding hot spots are Trentino's Madonna di Campiglio and Valle d'Aosta's Breuil-Cervinia (p255). Madonna's facilities are among the best in the country and include a snowboard park with descents for all levels and a dedicated boarder-cross zone. Breuil-Cervinia, situated at 2050m in the shadow of the Matterhorn, is better suited to intermediate and advanced levels.

Facilities at the bigger centres are generally world-class, with pistes ranging from nursery slopes to tough black runs. As well as *sci alpino* (downhill skiing), resorts might offer *sci di fondo* (cross-country skiing) and *sci alpinismo* (ski mountaineering).

The ski season runs from December to late March, although there is year-round skiing in Trentino-Alto Adige and on Mont Blanc (Monte Bianco) and the Matterhorn in the Valle d'Aosta. Generally, January and February are the best, busiest and priciest months. For better value, consider Friuli's expanding Sella Nevea (p461) runs or Tarvisio (p461), one of the coldest spots in the Alps, where the season is often extended into April.

The best bargain of the ski year is the *settimana bianca* (literally 'white week'), a term used by resorts that generally refers to an all-inclusive ski package that covers accommodation, food and ski passes.

PLAN YOUR TRIP ACTIVITIES

Sailing

Italy has a proud maritime tradition and you can hire a paddle boat or sleek sailing yacht almost anywhere in the country. Sailors of all levels are catered for: experienced skippers can island-hop around Sicily and Sardinia, or along the Amalfi, Tuscan, Ligurian or Triestino coasts on chartered yachts; weekend boaters can explore hidden coves in rented dinghies around Puglia, in the Tuscan archipelago and around the Sorrento Peninsula (p733); and speed freaks can take to the Lombard lakes in sexy speedboats.

Down south, on the Amalfi Coast (p749), prime swimming spots are often only accessible by boat. It's a similar story on the islands of Capri, Ischia, Procida and Elba.

In Sicily, the waters of the Aeolian Islands (p844) are perfect for idle island-hopping. Across in Sardinia, the Golfo di Orosei (p935), Santa Teresa di Gallura (p925) and the Arcipelago di La Maddalena (p926) are all top sailing spots. Sardinia's main sailing portal is www.sailingsardinia.it.

Italy's most prestigious sailing regattas are Lago di Garda's September **Cento-miglia** (www.centomiglia.it), which sails just south of Gargnano, and the Barcolana (p435) held in Trieste in October. The latter is the Med's largest regatta.

Reputable yacht charter companies include Bareboat Sailing Holidays (www.bareboatsailingholidays.com).

Diving

For divers ready to take the plunge, Italy delivers on all fronts, with everything from sea caves, the remnants of old volcanoes and abundant marine life underwater. The best diving is generally found on the clear waters surrounding the country's islands and islets.

Sicily makes an exceptional base, especially the cobalt waters of the Unesco-protected Aeolian Islands (p844), where you can dive in sea grottoes around the remains of old volcanoes. The volcanic island of Ustica (p836), Italy's first marine reserve, is also rich with underwater flora and fauna.

Over on Sardinia, the diving is equally outstanding. Dangling off the northwest coast, Capo Caccia (p916) is the dive site for Sardinia's coral divers and features the largest underwater grotto in the Mediterranean. In the north, the Maddalena marine park boasts translucent waters and diving around 60 islets.

On the craggy shores of the Italian Riviera in Liguria, Cinque Terre Marine Reserve is a good base for diving in the north of the country.

Heading further south, Capri (p737), Ischia (p743) and Procida (p747) in Campania are three islands in the Bay of Naples with exceptional diving amid sun-struck sea caves. In the southeast, the Isole Tremiti (p781) are wind-eroded islands off Puglia's Gargano Promontory, pock-marked with huge sea caves.

Hundreds of diving schools offer courses, dives for all levels and equipment hire. Most open June to October.

ZIP LINE FLIGHTS

How do angels fly? At the speed of light, apparently. Il Volo dell'Angelo (p807; Flight of the Angel) in Basilicata is one of the world's longest (1452m) and fastest (120km/h) zip lines, racing you between two villages: Castelmezzano and Pietrapertosa! If you want to amp up the adventure, this is the ultimate high-wire thrill.

Those who prefer to zip on an aerial wire over medieval towers, piazzas and burnt-red rooftops should try the new Zipline Majella (p684) in Pacentro, by the Parco Nazionale della Majella in Abruzzo. In northern Italy **Lago Maggiore Zipline** (📞333 9467147; www.lagomaggiorezipline.it; Via Giulio Pastore, Alpe Segletta; one ride €39, two-person ride €70; ⊙10am-9pm May-Aug, to 6pm Sep & Oct, 11am-4pm Sat & Sun Nov-Mar, 11am-6pm Apr) offers high-speed flights at 120km/h across one of Europe's prettiest lakes.

Rafting, Kayaking & SUP

A mecca for water rats, the Sesia river in northern Piedmont is Italy's top white-water destination. At its best between April and September, it runs from the slopes of Monte Rosa down through the spectacular

Sailing boat off the Amalfi Coast (p749)

scenery of the Valsesia. Operators in Varallo (p248) offer various solutions to the rapids: there's canoeing, kayaking, white-water rafting, canyoning, hydrospeed and tubing.

In Alto Adige, the Val di Sole (p331) is another white-water destination, as is Lago Ledro in Trentino, where you can canyon beneath invigorating waterfalls. Further south, Monti Sibillini (p672) in Umbria is another good choice for white-water adventures.

On the southwest coast, **Kayak Napoli** (☏338 2109978, 331 9874271; www.kayaknapoli. com; Bagno Sirena, Via Posillipo 357; tours €25-30; ☐140 to Via Posillipo) ✎ offers great tours of the Neapolitan coastline for all levels, ticking off often-inaccessible ruins, neo-classical villas, gardens and grottoes from the water. Liguria's mythical Cinque Terre shoreline can be tranquilly explored with Manarol-based Arbaspàa (p208).

At the southern end of the peninsula, the Lao river rapids in Calabria's Parco Nazion-ale del Pollino (p812) provide exhilarating rafting, as well as canoeing and canyoning. Trips can be arranged in Scalea.

The compelling red granite coastline of Ogliastra in Sardinia is best seen on a relaxed paddle with **Cardedu Kayak** (☏0782 7 51 85, 348 9369401; www.cardedu -kayak.com; Località Perda Rubia, SS125, Km 121.6, Cardedu). On the Friulian Coast ASD Fairplay (p443) organises seasonal kayak and stand-up paddleboard (SUP) courses and tours. In Sicily, Sicily in Kayak (p848) offers kayaking, sailing and SUP tours around Vulcano and the other Aeolians, ranging from half a day to an entire week.

Romantics won't do better than a mel-low SUP foray on Lago Maggiore with Tomaso Surf & Sail (p289), along the canals of Venice with SUP in Venice (p384) or along the river Arno in Renaissance Florence with Firenze Rafting (p537).

Windsurfing & Kitesurfing

Considered one of Europe's prime wind-surfing spots, Lago di Garda (p301) enjoys excellent wind conditions: the northerly *peler* blows in early on sunny mornings, while the southerly *ora* sweeps down in the early afternoon as regular as clockwork.

ALTERNATIVE ACTIVITIES

For a fresh perspective on Italian life, look beyond the obvious big-hitter sights and activities to uncover a ming-boggling host of lesser known, alternative things to do. A few favourites:

Mosaic Art

Mosaic art is alive and well at the Scuola Mosaicisti del Friuli (p457) in Spilimbergo where budding artists can try their hand at the centuries-old art.

Motor Racing

Never say never. Aspiring speedsters can race their own car around Monza's world-famous motor-racing track at the Autodromo Nazionale Monza (p285) in northern Italy.

Photography

Photography tours are just one of the many fun and creative activities cooked up at **Be Tuscan for a Day** (www.betuscanforaday.com), a grass-roots initiative designed to promote sustainable travel in Tuscany. In the impossibly photogenic Cinque Terre on the Ligurian coast, get in touch with Arbaspàa (p208).

Spas & Wellness

Italy is rich in mineral-packed thermal waters and spas countrywide offer relaxing thalassotherapy, hydrotherapy and psammotherapy (hot sand) treatments. Options range from stylish indoor spas such as Terme Meran (p338) in South Tyrol, to rustic woodland pools such as **Bagni San Filippo** (◷24hr) FREE in Tuscany's Val d'Orcia, to island retreats bursting with exotic foliage such as Negombo (p744) on Ischia in the Bay of Naples.

Venetian Rowing

For a very different view of Venice's celebrated canals, learn the traditional art of *voga alla veneta* (rowing standing up like a Venetian gondolier) with non-profit Row Venice (p387).

Vespa & Vintage Motoring

Don your Audrey Hepburn hat and hit the road on the back of an iconic Vespa, in a classic Fiat 500 or a three-wheeled Ape Calessino in Rome with A Friend in Rome (p132). Find similar tours in Florence and other big cities.

Whale Watching

Liguria is the hot spot. **Boats** (✆010 26 57 12; www.whalewatchliguria.it; Ponte Spinola; adult/child €35/20; ◷1pm Tue & 2pm Sat May-early Oct) depart from Genoa and Savona.

The two main centres are Torbole, home of the World Windsurf Championship, and Malcesine (p306), 15km south. **OKSurf** (www.oksurf.it; Parco La Fontanella, Via Rimembranza) is one of many lake schools offering lessons.

For windsurfing on the sea, head to Sardinia. In the north, Porto Pollo, also known as Portu Puddu, is good for beginners and experts – the bay provides protected waters for learners, while experts can enjoy the high winds as they funnel through the channel between Sardinia

and Corsica. To the northeast, there's good windsurfing on the island of Elba (p594), off the Tuscan coast. Competitions such as the Chia Classic are held off the southwest coast in June.

Kitesurfing enthusiasts flock to western Sicily. The shallow waters and gentler winds of the Laguna dello Stagnone, a lagoon between Trapani and Marsala, are ideal for beginners and intermediates. The accommodation, gear rental and lesson packages offered by Prokite Alby Rondina (p887) are good value.

Plan Your Trip
Family Travel

With everything from ancient treasures to dreamy beaches, snowy mountains and the world's best gelato, Italy is made for family travel. Whether you're into history, outdoor activities or seaside fun, there are plenty of adventures to be had in the bel paese (beautiful country). To make the most of your time, plan ahead.

Children Will Love...

History Trips

Colosseum, Rome (p86) Conjure up the drama of ancient Rome at the city's iconic arena.

Pompeii (p726) **& Herculaneum** (p721), **Campania** Evocative ruins with ancient shops, chariot-grooved streets and amphitheatres.

Palazzo Comunale, San Gimignano (p572) Slip on augmented-reality glasses to learn about frescoes and its medieval past.

Matera, Basilicata (p800) One of the world's oldest towns set around two rocky gorges riddled with *sassi* (habitable cave dwellings).

Museo del Monte San Michele, Friuli (p449) The Italian front in WWI is brought to life through an excellent, immersive Virtual Reality experience.

Outdoor Fun

Alpe di Siusi (p345) **& Kronplatz** (www.kronplatz .com) Tip-top downhill skiing in the Dolomites.

Labirinto della Masone (p486) Get lost in the world's largest labyrinth near Parma.

Venice (p360) Learn how to row standing up like a bona fide gondolier.

Lago Maggiore (p285) **& Lago di Garda** (p301) Lakeside beaches, water sports, climbing, mountain biking, canyoning, swimming, horse riding, biking etc.

Zipline Majella (p684) Fly through the air on a zip line in Abruzzos' Parco Nazionale della Majella.

Keeping Costs Down

Sleeping

Book family and four-person hotel rooms well in advance. Some boutique hotels offer family-friendly self-catering apartments.

Eating Out

Many restaurants serve a *menu bambino* (child's menu); if not order a *mezzo porzione* (half-portion) or a simple plate of pasta with butter and Parmesan.

Sightseeing

Kids with EU passports aged under 18 receive free entry into state-run museums; otherwise, under 18s pay half price and under fives are often free.

Transport

A seat on a bus costs the same for everyone (toddlers and babies on laps are free). Children under 12 pay half-fare on trains.

Grado (p443) A kid-friendly island on the Friulian coast with safe, sandy beaches, a water park, tons of water sports and cycling.

Cool Climbs

St Peter's Basilica, Rome (p110) Climbing the dome of the Vatican's most spectacular church is unforgettable.

Duomo, Florence (p518) Summit Brunelleschi's legendary red cupola.

Leaning Tower, Pisa (p598) Snap your kids propping up the tower and climb inside.

Torre dell'Orologio, Venice (☑041 4273 0892; www.museicivicivenezani.it; Piazza San Marco; adult/reduced €12/7; ⊙tours in English 11am & noon Mon-Wed, 2pm & 3pm Thu-Sun) Scale Venice's celebrated clock tower to examine its Renaissance mechanisms and bronze Moors hammering out the hour.

Stromboli, Aeolian Islands (p850) A guided trek to the firework-spitting crater of this volcano is a total thrill for active teenagers.

Rainy Days

Museo Nazionale Scienza e Tecnologia, Milan (p269) Italy's best science-technology museum.

Museo Nazionale del Cinema, Turin (p224) Multimedia displays and movie memorabilia.

Museo Archeologico dell'Alto Adige, Bolzano (p333) Drop in on Iceman Ötzi, Europe's oldest natural human mummy.

Teatro dei Pupi di Mimmo Cuticchio, Palermo (p840) Sicilian puppetry.

Palazzo Vecchio, Florence (p522) Theatrical tours for children and families.

Culinary Experiences

Pasta Challenge your child to taste different shapes and colours of pasta: *strozzapreti* ('priest strangler' pasta) is an Umbrian highlight, while in southern Italy Puglia's *orecchiette con cima di rape* (small ear-shaped pasta with turnip greens) is the perfect way of ensuring your kids eat some vegetables.

Pizza in Naples Hands down the best in Italy. Favourite addresses include Pizzeria Starita (p715), Pizzeria Gino Sorbillo (p715) and Concettina Ai Tre Santi (p714).

Gelato Museum Carpigiani, Anzola (p472) Gelato-themed tours with lots of tasting, or make your own with masters from neighbouring Gelato University; 30 minutes from Bologna in Anzola.

Cook in Venice (www.cookinvenice.com; tours €40-60, courses €150-350) Kid-friendly food tours and cooking classes by Venetian *mamma* of two Monica Cesarato.

Casa del Cioccolato Perugina, Perugia (p625) Perugia's 'House of Perugina Chocolate' offers Wonka-esque guided tours.

GOOD TO KNOW

Look out for the ☑ icon for family-friendly suggestions throughout this guide.

Farmstays Rural Italy's bounty of accommodation on farms, wineries and agricultural estates is family gold: pick olives, feed the pigs, bake bread etc.

Sightseeing Few sights organise specific tours and workshops for children (exceptions are Florence and Venice), but many cater to young minds with multimedia displays, touchscreen gadgets and audio guides (€5); some even have augmented-reality headsets.

Family tickets Save a few euros with family tickets on offer at some larger museums; usually valid for two adults and two children.

Stuff for babies Pharmacies and supermarkets (closed Sundays) sell baby formula, nappies (diapers), ready-made baby food and sterilising solutions. Fresh cow's milk is sold in cartons in supermarkets.

Prams & strollers Cobbled streets and narrow pavements make historic cities like Florence and Siena hard to navigate; bring a back carrier.

Dining out Italian families eat late; few restaurants open before 8pm. Children are warmly welcomed. High chairs *(seggioloni)* are only occasionally available.

Car travel Children under 150cm or 36kg must be buckled into an appropriate child seat for their weight and are not allowed in the front passenger seat.

Eataly Torino Lingotto, Turin (p233) Food counters at this temple to Slow Food allow every member of the family to dine on a different cuisine.

Florence Town, Florence (☑055 28 11 03; www.florencetown.com; Piazza della Repubblica 1; ☉7.30am-8pm summer, 8.30am-6.30pm winter) Gelato classes or pizza-making with a professional *pizzaiolo* for all the family.

Region by Region
Rome & Lazio

Ancient Roman ruins (p90), the spine-tingling Colosseum (p86), creepy catacombs and sensational sliced pizza make Rome an exciting prospect for older kids.

Turin, Piedmont & the Italian Riviera

Egyptian history at Turin's Museo Egizio (p223), chocolate, a state-of-the-art cable car (p251) in the mountainous Valle d'Aosta, backcountry skiing on Monte Rosa and coastal hiking: the variety of activities here is immense.

Milan & the Lakes

Home to Italy's biggest and best science museum (p269), a castle (p261) and grand park (p266), turn-of-the-century trams and canal cruises, Milan is more child-friendly than most imagine. Around the lakes (water-sports alert!), life's a beach. Lago di Garda sports some theme parks.

Trentino & South Tyrol

Ski or snowboard at some of Italy's best family-friendly ski resorts. Summer ushers in mountain hiking and biking for all ages.

Venice & the Veneto

Lido beaches and lagoon picnics, canal trips in Venetian gondolas, carnival mask makers and Murano glass blowers, children's art workshops at the Peggy Guggenheim Collection (p373): this region rocks for kids.

Fruili Venezia Giulia

This little-visited region squirrels away Trieste's spectacular 1930s lighthouse, Europe's only museum (p448) dedicated

Colosseum (p86), Rome

to comic books and illustration, and the Carnic Alps' crowd-free ski slopes.

Emilia-Romagna & San Marino

Teens love seaside Rimini's Roman treasures (p500), pedalling around the world's largest food park (p470) in Bologna, outdoor adventure in Parco Nazionale dell'Appennino Tosco-Emiliano (p482) and the region's clutch of car museums. All ages adore the world's largest labyrinth (p486).

Florence & Tuscany

This cultured region cooks up some fun experiences, including Florence's duomo (p518), Pisa's Leaning Tower (p598) and the pristine island beaches of Elba.

Umbria & Le Marche

Families seeking a natural green detox of wild and mysterious landscapes around Monti Sibillini (p672), white limestone cliffs and picture-postcard beaches in the Parco del Conero (p661), look no further.

Abruzzo & Molise

Roman vestiges in Molise (p689), bucket-and-spade beach fun in Pescara (p686) on the Adriatic coast, mountain hikes in Abruzzo's wild and remote Parco Nazionale della Majella (p682): this region is for outdoorsy families.

Naples & Campania

Gold for every age: subterranean ruins and catacombs (p710) in Naples, gladiator battlefields in Pompeii and natural high drama – think volcanoes, thermal pools and coastal caves.

Puglia, Basilicata & Calabria

Blissful beaches, whitewashed towns, islands loaded with swashbuckling adventure and glorious food add up to summer fun for all the family.

Sicily

Summit volcanoes with sporty teens, laze on the beach with sand-loving tots, explore ancient ruins or eerie **catacombs** (www.catacombepalermo.it; Piazza Cappuccini; adult/child under 8yr €3/free; ⊗9am-1pm & 3-6pm, closed Sun afternoon Nov-Mar), enjoy traditional puppet theatre – Sicily has inspiration and entertainment for one and all.

Sardinia

A natural paradise overflowing with some of Italy's top beaches and water-sports action, horse riding, rock climbing, caving and hikes suitable for all ages and abilities.

Useful Resources

Lonely Planet Kids (www.lonelyplanetkids.com) Loads of activities and great family travel blog content.

Book: City Trails Rome (shop.lonelyplanet.com) Discover Rome's best-kept secrets, amazing stories and loads of other cool stuff.

Italia Kids (www.italiakids.com) Family travel and lifestyle guide to Italy.

Context Travel (www.contexttravel.com) Family guided walks in Italian cities.

Kids' Corner

Say What?

Hello.	Buongiorno. bwon·*jor*·no
Goodbye.	Arrivederci. a·ree·ve·*der*·chee
Thank you.	Grazie. *gra*·tsye
Yes./No.	Sì./No. see/no
My name is ...	Mi chiamo ... mee *kya*·mo ...

Did You Know? ⓘ

• Italy is home to Europe's only three active volcanoes: Etna, Vesuvius and Stromboli.

• The Romans invented toilets.

Have You Tried?

Lampredotto
Tripe burger made from a cow's fourth stomach

Regions at a Glance

Rome & Lazio

History
Art
Scenery

History

Rome's ancient centre is history in 3D. Romulus killed Remus on the Palatino (Palatine Hill), Christians were fed to lions in the Colosseum and rulers soaked at the Terme di Caracalla. Ponder the remains of the great and the good in the catacombs along Via Appia Antica.

Art

The breadth of cultural treasures housed in Rome's museums and galleries is, quite frankly, embarrassing. If you plan on hitting several of them, consider the Roma Pass discount card.

Scenery

Often upstaged by Rome's urban must-sees, the Lazio region harbours lesser-known delights, from the classic Mediterranean beauty of the Isole Pontine to the extraordinary stone village of Civita di Bagnoregio.

p74

Turin, Piedmont & Cinque Terre

Activities
Villages
Food & Drink

Activities

From the slopes of Piedmont's Via Lattea and the Valle d'Aosta to wild coastal hikes along the Cinque Terre, this northwest corner of the country is a pulse-raising paradise.

Villages

With chic medieval fishing villages along the Cinque Terre, quaint wine-growing villages on Langhe hilltops and secret villages in the Valle d'Aosta, it's not hard to find your ideal storybook refuge.

Food & Drink

Birthplace of the Slow Food movement, Piedmont has an cornucopia of culinary riches, from the truffles of Alba to the wines of the Langhe region.

p176

Milan & the Lakes

Shopping
Gardens
Food & Drink

Shopping

Every style maven knows that Milan takes fashion and design as seriously as others take biotech or engineering. Best of all, top-notch discount outlets mean that even mere mortals can make a *bella figura* (good impression) here.

Gardens

Framed by gazebos, blushing bushes of camellias, artfully tumbling terraces and world-class statuary, Lombardy's lakeside villas knock the socks off the 'luxury getaway' concept.

Food & Drink

Bergamo, Brescia, Cremona and Mantua, the cultured cities of the Po Plain, combine a slew of sophisticated, regional restaurants with a growing interest in craft beer and micro-roasted coffee.

p256

Trentino & South Tyrol

Activities
Wellness
Food & Wine

Activities

Ski, hike, ice-climb, sledge-ride or Nordic walk in the Sella Ronda and the remote Parco Nazionale dello Stelvio. Real adrenalin junkies will want to scale the WWI-era *vie ferrate* (trails with permanent cables and ladders).

Wellness

Attend to your wellness in the thermal baths at Terme Merano, then stock up on tisane and cosmetics infused with Alpine herbs, grapes, apples and mountain pine.

Food & Wine

Bolzano beer halls, strudels, Sachertorte, sourdough breads and buckwheat cakes are just some of the region's Austro-Italian specialities. Combine with regional wines such as Gewürztraminer and riesling.

p320

Venice & the Veneto

Art
Architecture
Wine

Art

Action-packed canvases by Titian and Veronese, stirring frescoes by Tintoretto and Tiepolo, all illuminating the path to the modern creativity showcased at Punta della Dogana, Peggy Guggenheim Collection and La Biennale di Venezia.

Architecture

Formidable castles, gracious country villas and an entire city of palaces on the water, many of the Veneto's architectural landmarks admire their own reflections in glassy, historic waterways.

Wine

One of Italy's wine-growing heavyweights, this region is home to Valpolicella's cult-status Amarone, Soave's mineral whites and Conegliano's prosecco, not to mention dozens of innovative blends.

p354

Friuli Venezia Giulia

Culture
Wine
Activities

Culture

The geographic proximity of Mitteleuropa (Central Europe) is echoed in the region's earthy Slavic flavours, Austrian cakes and minority languages, not to mention the cosmopolitan other-worldliness of oft-overlooked Trieste.

Wine

Italy's northeast corner is home to an ever-growing number of small, innovative and often natural wine producers; their products are swilled by locals well-known for their love of fine libations.

Activities

Dramatic, unspoilt Alpine wilderness sets an enticing scene for laid-back winter skiing, sublime summertime hikes and no shortage of wildlife sightings, from foxes and deer to chamois and lynx.

p428

Emilia-Romagna & San Marino

Food
Architecture
Activities

Food

Indulge in Modena's aged balsamic vinegar, Parma's coveted prosciutto and cheese, Ferrara's *cappellacci di zucca* (pumpkin pasta dumplings) and Bologna's rich, comforting *ragù* (meat and tomato sauce).

Architecture

Tour the churches for a quick art-history lesson, from Ravenna's dazzling Byzantine mosaics and Modena's Romanesque cathedral to Bologna's Gothic-Renaissance blockbuster Basilica di San Petronio.

Activities

It's time to hit the pedal. Bologna's cobbled streets recall a continental Oxford, while smaller Modena and Ferrara, the latter with 9km of old city walls, are two of Italy's most bicycle-friendly locales.

p462

Florence & Tuscany

Art
Food & Wine
Scenery

Art

Read the story of the evolving Renaissance within the vibrant frescoes and paintings adorning Florence, Siena, Arezzo and San Gimignano. Genius innovators include Giotto, Masaccio, Ghirlandaio, Lippi and Botticelli.

Food & Wine

Intoxicating white truffles and juicy Chianina *bistecche* (steaks) – few regions whet the appetite so lasciviously. Add a glass of Montepulciano's Vino Nobile or Montalcino's world-famous Brunello, and rediscover bliss.

Scenery

Cypress-lined gardens in Florence, terraced hills in Chianti, the Unesco-lauded beauty of the Val d'Orcia: Tuscany's landscapes seem sketched by its artistic greats.

p506

Umbria & Le Marche

Villages
Scenery
Food & Wine

Villages

Perched snugly on their peaks like so many storks on chimneys, Umbria's hill towns – Perugia, Assisi, Gubbio, Urbino, Spoleto, Todi – are the postcard-pretty protectors of local traditions.

Scenery

Mountainous and wild, views come at you from all angles. Shoot up the *funivia* (cable car) in Gubbio or strike out into the snowcapped ranges of Monti Sibillini and the wildflower-flecked Piano Grande.

Food & Wine

Richly forested and rural, Umbria's larder is stocked with some lovely wines and robust flavours, from wild boar and pigeon to Norcia's *cinta senese* (Tuscan pig) salami and black truffles.

p616

Abruzzo & Molise

Scenery
Activities
Wilderness

Scenery

Vintage Italy lives on in the isolated mountain villages of Pescocostanzo, Scanno and Sulmona. En route from Sulmona to Scanno, the untamed scenery of the Gole di Sagittario gorge will bewitch you.

Activities

From Corno Grande (2912m) to Monte Amaro (2793m), Abruzzo's parks offer hiking and skiing without the northern hordes. The best-loved route: the ascent of Corno Grande.

Wilderness

These regions excel in outstanding natural beauty. Traced with walking trails, the ancient forests of three national parks still rustle with bears, chamois and wolves.

p674

Naples & Campania

Scenery
History
Food & Drink

Scenery

From Ischia's Med-tropical gardens and Capri's vertiginous cliffs, to the citrus-scented panoramas of the Amalfi Coast, the views from this sun-drenched coastline are as famous as the stars who holiday here.

History

Sitting beneath Mt Vesuvius, the Neapolitans abide by the motto *carpe diem*. And why not? All around them – at Pompeii, Herculaneum, Cuma and the Phlegraean Fields – are vivid reminders that life is short.

Food & Drink

Campania produces powerhouse coffee, pizzas, tomato pasta, *sfogliatelle* (sweetened ricotta pastries) and an incredible panoply of seafood, eaten every which way you can.

p692

Puglia, Basilicata & Calabria

Beaches
Wilderness
Food & Wine

Beaches

Lounge beneath white cliffs in the Gargano, gaze on violet sunsets in Tropea and soak up summer on the golden beaches of Otranto and Gallipoli.

Wilderness

A crush of spiky mountains, Basilicata and Calabria are where the wild things are. Burst through the clouds in mountain-top Pietrapertosa, pick bergamot in the Aspromonte and swap pleasantries with quietly curious locals.

Food & Wine

Puglia has turned its poverty into a culinary art: sample vibrant, vegetable-based pasta dishes like *orecchiette con cima di rape* (pasta with broccoli rabe) and wash it down with a Salento red from Italy's heel.

p766

Sicily

Food & Wine
History
Activities

Food & Wine

Sicilian cuisine seduces. Tuna, sardines, swordfish and shellfish come grilled, fried or seasoned with mint or wild fennel – and paired with a crisp white Novello wine perhaps. Desserts – rich in citrus, ricotta, almonds and pistachios – come with a sweet glass of Marsala.

History

A Mediterranean crossroads for centuries, Sicily keeps history buffs busy with Greek temples, Roman and Byzantine mosaics, Phoenician statues, Norman-Romanesque castles and art-nouveau villas.

Activities

Outdoor enthusiasts can swim and dive in Ustica's pristine waters, hike the Aeolian Islands' dramatic coastlines or watch the volcanic fireworks of Stromboli and Etna.

p826

Sardinia

Beaches
Activities
History

Beaches

Famous for its fjord-like coves, crystalline waters and windswept sand dunes, surfers, kite-surfers, sailors and divers from Italy and beyond flock to the Costa Smeralda, Porto Pollo, the Golfo di Orosei and the Archipelago di La Maddalena.

Activities

Sardinia's rugged, awe-inspiring mountains leave hikers and free climbers breathless. Climbs deliver stunning views of the sea, while Supramonte hikes traverse old, atmospheric shepherd routes.

History

The island's grey-granite landscape is littered with strange prehistoric dolmens, menhirs, wells and *nuraghi* (mysterious stone towers built by the island's earliest inhabitants).

p892

On the Road

AT A GLANCE

POPULATION
5.8 million

CHURCHES
900

BEST STREET ART
Street Art in the
Suburbs (p123)

**BEST UNDER-
GROUND CLUB**
Circolo Illuminati
(p151)

**BEST WILD
SWIMMING**
Lazio's Northern
Lakes (p165)

WHEN TO GO
Apr–Jun The best
time for visiting
Rome is spring.
Easter is busy,
though, and peak
rates apply.

Jun & Sep Avoid the
peak summer crowds
on Lazio's beaches
and lakes.

Sep & Oct Festivals
and warm weather
make autumn a good
time for visiting
regional sites.

Rome & Lazio

W ith ancient treasures, medieval towns, remote hilltop monasteries and volcanic lakes, Lazio is one of Italy's great surprise packages.

Its epic capital needs no introduction. Rome has been mesmerising travellers for millennia and still today it casts a powerful spell. It's home to some of the world's most celebrated masterpieces and its romantic cityscape, piled high with haunting ruins and iconic monuments, is achingly beautiful.

Beyond the city, Lazio more than holds its own. Cerveteri and Tarquinia's Etruscan tombs, Hadrian's vast Tivoli estate, Subiaco's monasteries and Ostia Antica's remarkable ruins – these are sights to rival anything in the country.

Add pockets of great natural beauty, fabulous food and wine and you have the perfect recipe for a trip to remember.

INCLUDES

Rome & Lazio Highlights

1 Colosseum
(p86) Getting your first spine-tingling glimpse of Rome's great gladiatorial arena.

2 Sistine Chapel
(p114) Marvelling at Michelangelo's legendary frescoes in the heart of the Vatican Museums.

3 Pantheon (p98)
Gazing heavenwards in this extraordinary Roman temple.

4 St Peter's Basilica (p110) Being blown away by the super-sized opulence of the Vatican's showpiece church.

5 Museo e Galleria Borghese
(p127) Going face to face with sensational baroque sculpture.

6 Area Archeologica di

Map labels

1 km
0.5 miles

Cimitero di Campo Verano

7 Tivoli (30km)
9 Subiaco (70km)

Viale XXI Aprile

NOMENTANO
Bologna Ⓜ
Villa Torlonia

Nomentana
Libia Ⓜ

Sant'Agnese/ Annibaliano Ⓜ

Via Nomentana

TRIESTE

Via Salaria

SALARIO

Viale Regina Margherita

Policlinico Ⓜ

Castro Pretorio Ⓜ

TIBURTINO

Via Tiburtina

SAN LORENZO

Stazione Ⓜ Termini

CASTRO PRETORIO

Via del Foro Italico

Monte Antenna

Campi Sportivi

Villa Ada

Acqua Acetosa

PARIOLI

Viale Liegi

Viale dei Parioli

Euclide

PINCIANO

Viale Bruno Buozzi

See Villa Borghese Map (p130)

Museo e Galleria Borghese 5

Corso d'Italia

Repubblica Ⓜ

Termini Ⓜ

Barberini Ⓜ

Vittorio Ⓜ
Emanuele II

MONTI

Viale Tiziano

FLAMINIO

Flaminio Ⓜ

Villa Borghese

Spagna Ⓜ

See Tridente & Trevi Map (p106)

TRIDENTE

CAMPO MARZIO

COLONNA

Via del Corso

Quirinale

TREVI

Auditorium Parco della Musica

Stadio Flaminio

Via Flaminia

Viale Giuseppe Mazzini

Museo Nazionale delle Arti del XXI Secolo (MAXXI)

Tevere

Cerveteri (35km); Civitavecchia (80km); Tarquinia (90km)

Stadio Olimpico

FORO ITALICO

Parco della Vittoria

TRIONFALE

Viale Angelico

PRATI

Lepanto Ⓜ

Via Cola di Rienzo

Via Crescenzio

Ottaviano- San Pietro Ⓜ

Cipro-Musei Vaticani Ⓜ

See Vatican City, Borgo & Prati Map (p116)

VATICAN CITY

St Peter's Basilica 4

Sistine Chapel 2

BORGO

PONTE

Corso Vittorio Emanuele II

See Centro Storico Map (p100)

Pantheon 3

PIGNA

Stazione San Pietro

8 Tarquinia

9 Subiaco (70km)

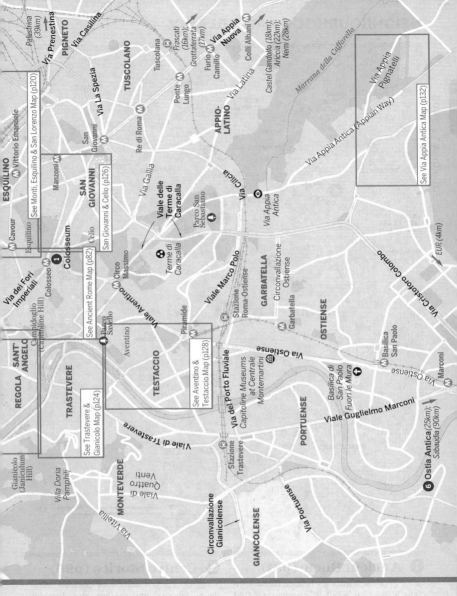

Ostia Antica (p160)
Strolling the fossilised streets of ancient Rome's main seaport.

7 Villa Adriana (p162) Poking around the monumental ruins of Hadrian's vast Tivoli estate.

8 Necropoli di Tarquinia (p164) Delving into frescoed Etruscan tombs in Tarquinia.

9 Monastero di San Benedetto (p171) Exploring this spectacular Subiaco monastery where St Benedict holed up for three years.

10 Palazzo Farnese (p168) Taking in the fabulous interior design of this majestic Renaissance palace near Viterbo.

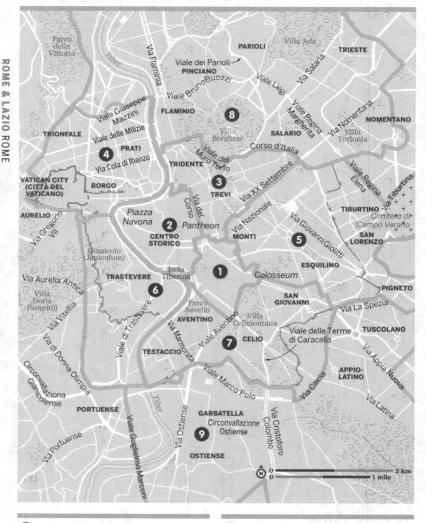

❶ Ancient Rome (p81)

In a city of extraordinary beauty, Rome's ancient heart stands out. It's here you'll find the great icons of the city's past: the Colosseum, the Palatino, the forums and the Campidoglio (Capitoline Hill), the historic home of the Capitoline Museums. Touristy by day, it's quiet at night with few after-hours attractions.

❷ Centro Storico (p96)

A tightly packed tangle of cobbled alleyways, Renaissance palaces and baroque piazzas, the historic centre is the Rome many come to see. Its theatrical streets teem with boutiques, cafes, trattorias and stylish bars, while market traders and street artists work its vibrant squares. The Pantheon and Piazza Navona are the star turns, but you'll also find a host of monuments, museums and churches, many with works by the likes of Michelangelo, Caravaggio, Bernini et al..

❸ Tridente, Trevi & the Quirinale (p103)

Counting the Trevi Fountain and Spanish Steps among its A-list sights, this central part of Rome is debonair and touristy. Designer boutiques, swish hotels and historic cafes and restaurants crowd the streets between Piazza di Spagna and Piazza del Popolo in Tridente, while the streets around Piazza Barberini and the Trevi Fountain, within shouting distance of the president's palace on the Quirinale Hill, are home to multiple art galleries and eateries.

❹ Vatican City, Borgo & Prati (p109)

The Vatican, the world's smallest sovereign state, sits over the river from Rome's historic centre. Radiating out from the domed grandeur of St Peter's Basilica, it boasts some of Italy's most revered artworks, many housed in the vast Vatican Museums (home of the Sistine Chapel), as well as batteries of overpriced restaurants and souvenir shops. Nearby, the landmark Castel Sant'Angelo looms over the Borgo district and upmarket Prati offers excellent accommodation, eating and shopping.

❺ Monti, Esquilino & San Lorenzo (p118)

Centred on transport hub Stazione Termini, this is a large and cosmopolitan area that, upon first glance, can seem busy and overwhelming. But hidden among its traffic-noisy streets are some beautiful churches, Rome's best unsung art museum at Palazzo Massimo alle Terme, and any number of trendy bars and restaurants in the fashionable Monti, student-loved San Lorenzo and bohemian Pigneto districts.

❻ Trastevere & Gianicolo (p122)

With its old-world cobbled lanes, ochre *palazzi,* ivy-clad facades and boho vibe, ever-trendy Trastevere is one of Rome's most vivacious and Roman neighbourhoods. Endlessly photogenic and largely car-free, its labyrinth of backstreet lanes heaves after dark as crowds swarm to its fashionable restaurants, cafes and bars. Rising up behind all this, Gianicolo Hill offers a breath of fresh air and superb views of Rome, which is laid out at your feet.

❼ San Giovanni & Testaccio (p125)

Encompassing two of Rome's seven hills, this sweeping, multifaceted area offers everything from dramatic basilicas and ancient ruins to colourful markets and popular trattorias. Its best-known draws are the Basilica di San Giovanni in Laterano and Terme di Caracalla, but there are heavenly views to be had on the Aventino. Down by the river, Testaccio is a trendy district known for its nose-to-tail Roman cuisine and weekend clubbing.

❽ Villa Borghese & Northern Rome (p127)

This moneyed area encompasses Rome's most famous park (Villa Borghese) and its most expensive residential district (Parioli). Concert-goers head to the Auditorium Parco della Musica, while art-lovers can choose between contemporary installations at MAXXI, Etruscan artefacts at the Museo Nazionale Etrusco di Villa Giulia or baroque treasures at the Museo e Galleria Borghese.

❾ Southern Rome (p129)

Boasting a wealth of diversions, this huge area extends to Rome's southern limits. Glorious ancient ruins and subterranean catacombs await on Via Appia Antica, one of the world's oldest roads, while post-industrial Ostiense offers edgy street art, superb dining and heaving nightlife. Then there's EUR, an Orwellian quarter of wide boulevards and linear buildings.

ROME

POP 2.87 MILLION

History

According to legend Rome was founded by Romulus and Remus in 753 BC. In fact, the city started life as an amalgamation of Etruscan, Latin and Sabine settlements on the Palatino, Esquilino and Quirinale hills. It was initially ruled by Sabine and Etruscan kings, but the death of Tarquinius the Proud paved the way for the birth of the Roman Republic in 509 BC.

Ancient Rome

Over the next five centuries the Republic flourished, growing to become the dominant force in the Western world. Its armies conquered the Etruscans to the north and the Greeks and Carthaginians in the south. At home, it adopted a quasi-democratic system of government, based on a Senate and People's Assemblies – hence SPQR (*Senatus Populusque Romanus,* or the Senate and People of Rome).

The end of the Republic came in the 1st century BC when internal rivalries led to the murder of Julius Caesar in 44 BC and the outbreak of civil war between Octavian and Mark Antony. Octavian emerged victorious and was made Rome's first emperor with the title Augustus.

Augustus ruled well and the city enjoyed a golden age of period of peace and artistic development. A huge fire reduced Rome to tatters in AD 64, but the city bounced back, and by AD 100 it had a population of 1.5 million and was the undisputed *caput mundi* (capital of the world).

ⓘ ROMA PASS

Covering sights admission and public transport, the useful Roma Pass (www. romapass.it) is available online, from tourist information points or participating museums. It comes in two forms:

72 hours (€38.50) Provides free admission to two museums or sites, as well as reduced entry to extra sites, unlimited city transport and discounted entry to other exhibitions and events.

48 hours (€28) Gives free admission to one museum or site, then as per the 72-hour pass.

It couldn't last, though, and when Constantine moved his power base to Byzantium in 330, Rome's glory days were numbered. In 476 Romulus Augustulus, the last emperor of the Western Roman Empire, was deposed.

Christian Roots

By the 6th century, Rome was in a bad way and in desperate need of a leader. Into the breach stepped the Catholic Church. Christianity had been spreading since the 1st century AD thanks to the underground efforts of apostles Peter and Paul, and under Constantine it had received official recognition. In the late 6th century Pope Gregory I did much to strengthen the Church's grip over the city, laying the foundations for its later role as capital of the Catholic world.

Historic Makeovers

During the Middle Ages, Rome was reduced to a semi-deserted battlefield as powerful families battled for supremacy and the bedraggled population trembled in the face of plague, famine and flooding (the Tiber regularly broke its banks).

But out of these dark times grew Renaissance Rome. At the behest of the city's great papal dynasties – the Barberini, Farnese and Pamphilj – the leading artists of the 15th and 16th centuries were summoned to work on projects such as the Sistine Chapel and St Peter's Basilica. But trouble was never far away, and in 1527 the Spanish forces of Holy Roman Emperor Charles V ransacked Rome.

The late 16th and 17th centuries saw a second wave of artistic and architectural activity as the Church sought to restore its authority in the wake of the Protestant Reformation. Exuberant churches, fountains and *palazzi* (palaces) sprouted all over the city as Bernini and Borromini, the two giants of the Roman baroque, competed to produce ever-more spectacular masterpieces.

The next major makeover followed Italian unification and the declaration of Rome as Italy's capital. Mussolini later left an indelible mark, bulldozing new roads and commissioning ambitious building projects such as the monumental suburb of EUR.

More recently, a number of leading contemporary architects have completed projects in the city, adding a hint of modernity to Rome's historic cityscape.

BEST LESSER-KNOWN SIGHTS
•••••••••••••••••••••

Away from Rome's headline sights, there are many lesser-known hits to savour:

Basilica di Santa Prassede (Map p120; Via Santa Prassede 9a; ⏰ 7am-noon & 4-6.30pm; Ⓜ Cavour) This easy-to-miss 9th-century church boasts some of Rome's most brilliant Byzantine mosaics.

Palazzo Spada (Palazzo Capodiferro; Map p100; ☑ 06 683 24 09; www.galleriaspada.benicul turali.it; Piazza Capo Di Ferro 13; adult/reduced €5/2.50; ⏰ 8.30am-7.30pm Wed-Mon; 🚌 Corso Vittorio Emanuele II) A 16th-century palace home to a celebrated optical illusion by baroque architect Borromini, the so-called *Prospettiva* (Perspective).

Cimitero Acattolico per gli Stranieri (Map p128; ☑ 06 574 19 00; www.cemeteryrome.it; Via Caio Cestio 6; voluntary donation €3; ⏰ 9am-5pm Mon-Sat, to 1pm Sun; Ⓜ Piramide) An air of Grand Tour romance hangs over the final resting place of poets Keats and Shelley.

Quartiere Coppedè (🚌 Viale Regina Margherita) A charmingly off-beat neighbourhood full of Tuscan turrets, Liberty sculptures, arches, gargoyles, frescoed facades and palm-fringed gardens.

Chiesa di Santo Stefano Rotondo (Map p126; Via di Santo Stefano Rotondo 7, Celio; ⏰ 10am-1pm & 2-5pm Tue-Sun winter, 10am-1pm & 3.30-6.30pm Tue-Sun summer; 🚌 Via Claudia) One of Rome's oldest churches features a cycle of blood-curdling 16th-century frescoes.

👁 Sights

👁 Ancient Rome

Bocca della Verità MONUMENT
(Mouth of Truth; Map p82; Piazza Bocca della Verità 18; voluntary donation; ⏰ 9.30am-5.50pm summer, to 4.50pm winter; 🚌 Piazza Bocca della Verità) A bearded face carved into a giant marble disc, the *Bocca della Verità* is one of Rome's most popular curiosities. Legend has it that if you put your hand in the mouth and tell a lie, the *bocca* (mouth) will slam shut and bite it off. The mouth, which was originally part of a fountain, or possibly an ancient manhole cover, now lives in the portico of the **Chiesa di Santa Maria in Cosmedin**, a handsome medieval church.

Piazza del Campidoglio PIAZZA
(Map p82; 🚌 Piazza Venezia) This hilltop piazza, designed by Michelangelo in 1538, is one of Rome's most beautiful squares. There are several approaches but the most dramatic is the graceful **Cordonata** staircase, which leads up from Piazza d'Aracoeli.

The piazza is flanked by **Palazzo Nuovo** and **Palazzo dei Conservatori**, together home to the Capitoline Museums (p94), and **Palazzo Senatorio** (⏰ closed to the public), Rome's historic city hall. In the centre is a copy of an equestrian **statue of Marcus Aurelius**. The original dates from the 2nd century AD and is in the Capitoline Museums.

Chiesa di Santa Maria in Aracoeli CHURCH
(Map p82; ☑ 06 6976 3837; Scala dell'Arce Capitolina; ⏰ 9am-6.30pm summer, 9.30am-5.30pm winter; 🚌 Piazza Venezia) Atop the steep 124-step Aracoeli staircase, this 6th-century Romanesque church sits on the highest point of the Campidoglio. Its richly decorated interior boasts several treasures including a wooden gilt ceiling, an impressive Cosmatesque floor, and a series of 15th-century Pinturicchio frescoes illustrating the life of St Bernardino of Siena. Its chief claim to fame, though, is a wooden baby Jesus that's thought to have healing powers.

Vittoriano MONUMENT
(Victor Emanuel Monument; Map p82; https://vitto riano.beniculturali.it/it; Piazza Venezia; ⏰ 9.30am-7.30pm summer, final entry 6.45pm; 🚌 Piazza Venezia) **FREE** Love it or loathe it (as many Romans do), you can't ignore the Vittoriano (aka the Altare della Patria, or Altar of the Fatherland), the colossal mountain of white marble that towers over Piazza Venezia. It was built at the turn of the 20th century to honour Italy's first king, Vittorio Emanuele II – who's immortalised in its vast equestrian statue.

The building provides the dramatic setting for the **Tomb of the Unknown Soldier**. Also inside is the **Complesso del Vittoriano** (☑ 06 871 51 11; www.ilvittoriano.com; Via di San Pietro in Carcere; admission variable; ⏰ 9.30am-7.30pm Mon-Thu, to 10pm Fri & Sat, to 8.30pm Sun; 🚌 Via dei Fori Imperiali), a gallery that regularly

Ancient Rome

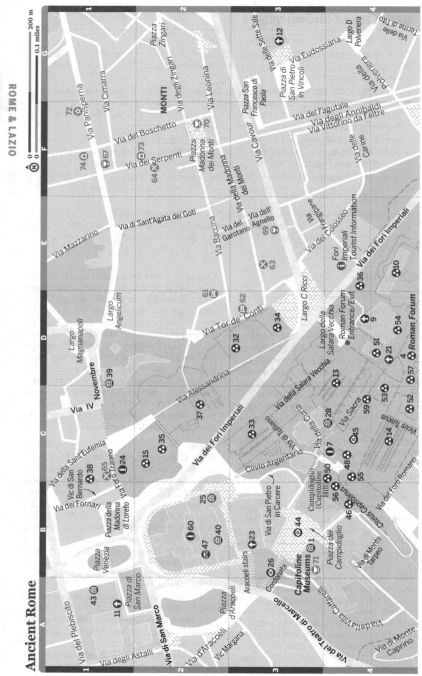

200 m
0.1 miles

N

Via del Plebiscito

Piazza Venezia

Piazza di San Marco

Via di San Marco

Via degli Astalli

Piazza d'Aracoeli

Via del Teatro di Marcello

Vic Margana

Via d'Aracoeli

Aracoeli stairs

Cordonata

Capitoline Museums

Piazza del Campidoglio

Via della Villa Caffarelli

Via di Monte Tarpeo

Via di Monte Caprino

Campidoglio (Capitoline Hill)

Clivius Capitolinus

Via del Foro Romano

Via di San Pietro in Carcere

Clivio Argentario

Via di Tulliano

Via della Curia

Via della Salara Vecchia

Vicus Tuscus

Via Sacra

Roman Forum Entrance/Exit

Largo della Salara Vecchia

Via del Colosseo

Via dei Fori Imperiali

Via Alessandrina

Via IV Novembre

Largo Magnanapoli

Largo Angelicum

Via Mazzarino

Via di Sant'Agata dei Goti

Via Tor de' Conti

Largo C Ricci

Via della Madonna dei Monti

Via Baccina

Via del Garofano

Via dell' Agnello

Via della Madonna dei Monti

Via Cavour

Piazza Madonna dei Monti

MONTI

Via dei Serpenti

Via del Boschetto

Piazza Zingari

Via degli Zingari

Via Leonina

Via Cimarra

Via Panisperna

Via Frangipane

Via delle Carine

Via Vittorino da Feltre

Via degli Annibaldi

Via del Fagutale

Piazza San Francesco di Paola

Piazza San Pietro in Vincoli

Via Eudossiana

Via della Polveriera

Largo D Polveriera

Via delle Terme di Tito

Via di San Bernardo

Vic di San Bernardo

Via dei Fornari

Via della Sant'Eufemia

Piazza della Madonna di Loreto

Via Foro Traiano

Fori Imperiali Tourist Information

Roman Forum

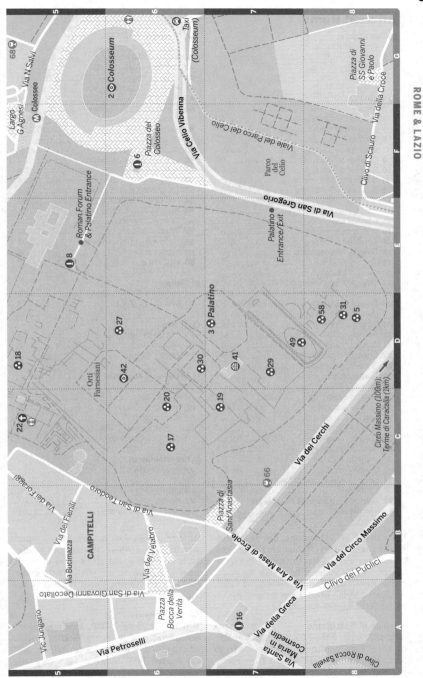

Ancient Rome

hosts major art exhibitions. But as impressive as any of the art on show are the glorious 360-degree views from the top of the monument. See for yourself by taking the panoramic **Roma dal Cielo** (adult/reduced €10/5; ⊙9.30am-7.30pm, last admission 6.45pm) lift up to the Terrazza delle Quadrighe.

Basilica di San Marco   BASILICA
(Map p82; ✆06 679 52 05; Piazza di San Marco 48; ⊙10am-1pm Tue-Sun & 4-6pm Tue-Fri, to 8pm Sat & Sun; ☐Piazza Venezia) Now incorporated into Palazzo Venezia, the early-

4th-century Basilica di San Marco stands over the house where St Mark the Evangelist is said to have stayed while in Rome. Its main attraction is the golden 9th-century apse mosaic showing Christ flanked by several saints and Pope Gregory IV.

Palazzo Venezia   MUSEUM
(Map p82; ✆06 6999 4388; www.museopalazzo venezia.beniculturali.it; Piazza Venezia 3; adult/reduced €10/5; ⊙8.30am-7.30pm Tue-Sun; ☐Piazza Venezia) Built between 1455 and 1464, Palazzo Venezia was the first of Rome's great

Renaissance palaces. For centuries it was the embassy of the Venetian Republic – hence its name – but it's most readily associated with Mussolini, who had his office here and famously made speeches from the balcony of the Sala del Mappamondo (Globe Room). Nowadays, it's home to the **Museo Nazionale del Palazzo Venezia** and its eclectic collection of Byzantine and early Renaissance paintings, ceramics, bronze figures, weaponry and armour.

Mercati di Traiano Museo dei Fori Imperiali
MUSEUM

(Map p82; ☑06 06 08; www.mercatiditraiano.it; Via IV Novembre 94; adult/reduced incl exhibition €11.50/9.50; ⊙9.30am-7.30pm; 🚌Via IV Novembre) This striking museum showcases the **Mercati di Traiano** (Trajan's Markets), the emperor Trajan's towering 2nd-century complex, while also providing a fascinating introduction to the Imperial Forums with multimedia displays, explanatory panels and a smattering of archaeological artefacts.

Sculptures, friezes and the occasional bust are set out in rooms opening onto what was once the Great Hall. But more than the exhibits, the real highlight here is the chance to explore the vast structure, which historians believe housed the forums' administrative offices.

Imperial Forums
ARCHAEOLOGICAL SITE

(Fori Imperiali; Map p82; ☑06 06 08; Piazza Santa Maria di Loreto; adult/reduced €4/3, free 1st Sun of month Oct-Mar; ⊙by reservation; 🚌Via dei Fori Imperiali) The forums of Trajan, Augustus, Nerva and Caesar are known collectively as the Imperial Forums. They were largely buried when Mussolini bulldozed Via dei Fori Imperiali through the area in 1933, but excavations have since unearthed much of

them. The standout sights are the Mercati di Traiano and the landmark **Colonna Traiana** (Trajan's Column).

Little recognisable remains of the **Foro di Traiano** (Trajan's Forum), except for some pillars from the **Basilica Ulpia** and the Colonna Traiana, whose minutely detailed reliefs celebrate Trajan's military victories over the Dacians (from modern-day Romania).

To the southeast, three temple columns arise from the ruins of the **Foro di Augusto** (Augustus' Forum), now mostly under Via dei Fori Imperiali. The 30m-high wall behind the forum was built to protect it from the fires that frequently swept down from the nearby Suburra slums.

The **Foro di Nerva** (Nerva's Forum) was also buried by Mussolini's road-building, although part of a temple dedicated to Minerva still stands. Originally, it would have connected the Foro di Augusto to the 1st-century **Foro di Vespasiano** (Vespasian's Forum), also known as the Foro della Pace or Tempio della Pace. On the other side of the road, three columns on a raised platform are the most visible remains of the **Foro di Cesare** (Caesar's Forum).

Basilica dei SS Cosma e Damiano
BASILICA

(Map p82; ☑06 699 08 08; www.cosmadamiano.com; Via dei Fori Imperiali 1; presepe €1; ⊙10am-1pm & 3-6pm; 🚌Via dei Fori Imperiali) Backing onto the Roman Forum, this 6th-century basilica incorporates parts of the Foro di Vespasiano and Tempio di Romolo (p91), visible at the end of the nave. However, the main reason to visit is to admire its fabulous 6th-century apse mosaic depicting Peter and Paul presenting saints Cosma, Damiano, Theodorus and Pope Felix IV to Christ.

Continued on p96

ROME'S RULES OF CONDUCT

Sitting on the Spanish Steps (p104) is now officially forbidden. The ban, introduced in 2019, came as part of a package of regulations designed to crack down on antisocial behaviour. Other rules include the following:

➡ No wading in the city's fountains.

➡ No 'messy' outdoor eating near historic monuments.

➡ No walking around bare-chested.

➡ No dragging strollers or wheelie suitcases up or down historic staircases.

➡ When drinking from the public drinking fountains known as *nasoni,* don't place your lips on the spout, rather drink from your cupped hands.

People caught breaking these rules risk fines of up to €400 or a temporary ban on entering the area in which they caused the offence.

 TOP SIGHT
COLOSSEUM

An awesome, spine-tingling sight, the Colosseum is the most thrilling of Rome's ancient monuments. It was here that gladiators met in fierce combat and condemned prisoners fought off wild beasts in front of baying, bloodthirsty crowds. Two thousand years on and it's Italy's top tourist attraction, drawing more than seven million visitors a year.

History

The emperor Vespasian (r AD 69–79) originally commissioned the amphitheatre in AD 72 in the grounds of Nero's vast Domus Aurea complex. He never lived to see it finished, though, and it was completed by his son and successor Titus (r 79–81) in AD 80. To mark its inauguration, Titus held games that lasted 100 days and nights, during which some 5000 animals were slaughtered. Trajan (r 98–117) later topped this, holding a marathon 117-day killing spree involving 9000 gladiators and 10,000 animals.

The 50,000-seat arena was Rome's first, and greatest, permanent amphitheatre. For some five centuries it was used to stage lavish spectacles to mark important anniversaries or military victories. Gladiatorial combat was eventually outlawed in the 5th century, but animal shows continued until the mid-6th century.

Following the fall of the Roman Empire, the Colosseum was largely abandoned. It was used as a fortress by the powerful Frangipani family in the 12th century and later plundered of its precious building materials. Travertine and marble stripped from the Colosseum were used to decorate

TOP TIPS

➡ If queues are long, get your ticket at the Palatino at Via di San Gregorio 30.

➡ Alternatively book tickets at www. coopculture.it (€2 booking fee); get the Roma Pass or SUPER ticket; join a tour.

PRACTICALITIES

➡ Colosseo

➡ Map p82

➡ ☎ 06 3996 7700

➡ www.parcocolosseo.it

➡ Piazza del Colosseo

➡ adult/reduced incl Roman Forum & Palatino €16/2, with arena & SUPER sites €22/2

➡ ⊙ 8.30am-1hr before sunset, last entry 1hr before closing

➡ Ⓜ Colosseo

a number of notable buildings, including Palazzo Venezia, Palazzo Barberini and Palazzo Cancelleria.

More recently, pollution and vibrations caused by traffic and the metro have taken a toll. To help counter this, it was given a major clean-up between 2014 and 2016, the first in its 2000-year history, as part of an ongoing €25 million restoration project sponsored by the luxury shoemaker Tod's.

The Exterior

The outer walls have three levels of arches, framed by decorative columns topped by capitals of the Ionic (at the bottom), Doric and Corinthian (at the top) orders. They were originally covered in travertine, and marble statues filled the niches on the 2nd and 3rd storeys. The upper level, punctuated with windows and slender Corinthian pilasters, had supports for 240 masts that held the awning over the arena, shielding the spectators from sun and rain. The 80 entrance arches, known as *vomitoria*, allowed the spectators to enter and be seated in a matter of minutes.

The Seating

The *cavea*, or spectator seating, was divided into three tiers: magistrates and senior officials sat in the lowest tier, wealthy citizens in the middle and the plebs in the highest tier. Women (except for Vestal Virgins) were relegated to the cheapest sections at the top. Tickets were numbered and spectators were assigned a precise seat in a specific sector – in 2015, restorers uncovered traces of red numerals indicating how the sectors were numbered. The podium, a broad terrace in front of the tiers, was reserved for the emperor, senators and VIPs.

The Arena

The stadium had a wooden floor covered in sand – *harena* in Latin, hence the word 'arena' – to prevent combatants from slipping and to soak up spilt blood. Trapdoors led down to the hypogeum, a subterranean complex of corridors, cages and lifts beneath the floor.

Hypogeum

The hypogeum served as the stadium's backstage area where stage sets were prepared and combatants gathered before showtime. Gladiators entered from the nearby Ludus Magnus (gladiator school) via an underground corridor, while a second tunnel, the Passaggio di Commodo, allowed the emperor to arrive without having to pass through the crowds. To hoist people, animals and scenery up to the arena, the hypogeum was equipped with 80 winch-operated lifts, all controlled by a single pulley system.

THE NAME

The arena was originally known as the Flavian Amphitheatre (Anfiteatro di Flavio) after Vespasian's family name. And while it was Rome's most famous arena, it wasn't the biggest – the Circo Massimo could hold up to 250,000 people. The name Colosseum, when introduced in the Middle Ages, wasn't a reference to its size but to the Colosso di Nerone, a giant statue of Nero that stood nearby.

Games staged at the Colosseum usually involved gladiators fighting wild animals or each other. Bouts rarely ended in death as the games' sponsor was required to pay compensation to a gladiator's owner if the gladiator died in action.

TICKETS & TOURS

When you buy a ticket online at www.coop culture.it, bear in mind you'll have to commit to a specific entry time. Note also you'll need to book a guided tour if you want to visit the underground area (hypogeum) and/or upper floors (Belvedere). These cost €9 (or €15 for both) plus the normal Colosseum ticket.

HERCULES MILAS/ALAMY STOCK PHOTO ©

TOP SIGHT
PALATINO

Sandwiched between the Roman Forum and the Circo Massimo, the Palatino (Palatine Hill) is an atmospheric area of towering pine trees, majestic ruins and memorable views. This is where Romulus supposedly founded the city in 753 BC and Rome's emperors lived in palatial luxury.

Historical Development

Roman myth holds that Romulus founded Rome on the Palatino after he'd killed his twin Remus in a fit of anger. Archaeological evidence, however, puts the establishment of a village here to the early Iron Age (around 830 BC).

As the most central of Rome's seven hills, and because it was close to the Roman Forum, the Palatino was ancient Rome's most exclusive neighbourhood. The emperor Augustus lived here all his life and successive emperors built increasingly opulent palaces. But after Rome's fall it fell into disrepair, and in the Middle Ages churches and castles were built over the ruins. Later, wealthy Renaissance families established gardens on the hill.

Most of the Palatino as it appears today is covered by the ruins of Emperor Domitian's vast complex, which served as the main imperial palace for 300 years. Divided into the Domus Flavia, Domus Augustana and a *stadio* (stadium), it was built in the 1st century AD.

Southern Path

On entering the Palatino from Via di San Gregorio, continue left until you come to a gate giving onto a path (open 9am to 3pm). This skirts the hill's southern flank, offering good views up to the ruins and providing a clear chronology of the area's

DON'T MISS

➡ Stadio

➡ Domus Augustana

➡ Casa di Livia and Casa di Augusto

➡ Orti Farnesiani

PRACTICALITIES

➡ Palatine Hill

➡ Map p82

➡ ☏ 06 3996 7700

➡ www.parcocolosseo.it

➡ Via di San Gregorio 30, Piazza di Santa Maria Nova

➡ adult/reduced incl Roman Forum & SUPER sites €16/2, incl Colosseum & Roman Forum €16/2, incl Colosseum, Roman Forum & SUPER sites €22/2

➡ ⊘ 8.30am-1hr before sunset; some SUPER ticket sites Mon, Wed, Fri & morning Sun only

➡ Ⓜ Colosseo

development – as you walk, you're essentially going back in time as the ruins become increasingly older.

Stadio

Back on the main site, the first recognisable construction you'll come across is the stadio. This sunken area, which was part of the imperial palace, was probably used by the emperors for private games. A path to the side of it leads to the towering remains of a complex built by Septimius Severus, comprising baths (**Terme di Settimio Severo**) and a palace (**Domus Severiana**). Here you can enjoy views over the Circo Massimo and, if they're open, visit the **Arcate Severiane** (Severian Arches; admission incl in Palatino ticket; ⊙8.30am-6.45pm Tue & Fri summer, shorter hours Tue & Fri winter; Ⓜ Colosseo), a series of arches built to facilitate further development.

Domus Augustana & Domus Flavia

Next to the *stadio* are the ruins of the Domus Augustana (pictured), the emperor's private quarters in the imperial palace. Also here is the **Aula Isiaca** (⊙9am-6.30pm Mon, Wed & Fri, to 2pm Sun summer, 9am-3.30pm Mon, Wed & Fri, to 1pm Sun winter), a frescoed room from a luxurious Republican-era house, and the **Loggia Mattei**, a Renaissance loggia. To the north is the Domus Flavia, the public part of the palace. This was centred on a grand columned peristyle – the grassy area with the base of an octagonal fountain.

Museo Palatino

The white building next to the Domus Augustana is the **Museo Palatino** (⊙8.30am-1½hr before sunset; Ⓜ Colosseo), a small museum that charts the development of the Palatino through video presentations, models and archaeological finds.

Casa di Livia & Casa di Augusto

Near the Domus Flavia, the **Casa di Livia** (⊙9am-6.30pm Mon, Wed & Fri, to 2pm Sun summer, 9am-3.30pm Mon, Wed & Fri, to 1pm Sun winter; Ⓜ Colosseo) is one of the Palatino's best-preserved buildings. Home to Augustus' wife Livia, it was built around an atrium leading onto frescoed reception rooms. Nearby, the **Casa di Augusto** (⊙9am-6.30pm Mon, Wed & Fri, to 2pm Sun summer, 9am-3.30pm Mon, Wed & Fri, to 1pm Sun winter; Ⓜ Colosseo), Augustus' private residence, features some superb frescoes in vivid reds, yellows and blues.

Orti Farnesiani

Standing on the site of Tiberius' palace, the **Domus Tiberiana**, in the Palatino's northwest, the 16th-century Orti Farnesiani is one of Europe's earliest botanical gardens. A balcony at its northern end commands breathtaking views over the Roman Forum.

SUPER TICKET

To visit the Palatino and Roman Forum's internal sites you'll need to buy a SUPER ticket and plan carefully. The ticket, valid for two consecutive days, covers the Colosseum, Roman Forum and Palatino. On the Palatino, the Casa di Augusto, Casa di Livia, Aula Isiaca and Loggia Mattei are open on Mondays, Wednesdays, Fridays and Sunday mornings; the Museo Palatino and Criptoportico Neroniano open daily. The Roman Forum sites (Tempio di Romolo, Chiesa di Santa Maria in Antiqua, Rampa di Domiziano) are open on Tuesdays, Thursdays, Saturdays and Sunday afternoons.

The Palatino's imperial connection has worked its way into the English language. The word 'palace' is a derivation of the hill's Latin name, *Palatium*.

ROMULUS & REMUS

Rome's mythical founders were supposedly brought up on the Palatino by a shepherd, Faustulus, after a wolf saved them from death. Their shelter, the 8th-century-BC **Capanne Romulee** (Romulean Huts), is situated near the Casa di Augusto.

TOP SIGHT
ROMAN FORUM

The Roman Forum (Foro Romano) was ancient Rome's showpiece centre, a grandiose district of temples, basilicas and vibrant public spaces. Nowadays it's a collection of impressive, if sketchily labelled, ruins that can leave you drained and confused. But if you can get your imagination going, there's something wonderfully compelling about walking in the footsteps of Julius Caesar and other legendary figures of Roman history.

Via Sacra Towards Campidoglio

Entering from Largo della Salara Vecchia (you can also enter directly from the Palatino or via an entrance near the Arco di Tito) you'll see the **Tempio di Antonino e Faustina** ahead to your left. Erected in AD 141, this was transformed into the **Chiesa di San Lorenzo in Miranda** in the 8th century. To your right, the 179 BC **Basilica Fulvia Aemilia** was a 100m-long public hall with a two-storey porticoed facade.

At the end of the path, you'll come to **Via Sacra**, the Forum's main thoroughfare, and the **Tempio di Giulio Cesare** (also known as the Tempio del Divo Giulio). Built by Augustus in 29 BC, this marks the spot where Julius Caesar was cremated after his assassination in 44 BC.

Heading right up Via Sacra brings you to the **Curia**, the original seat of the Roman Senate. This barn-like construction was rebuilt on various occasions and what you see today is a 1937 reconstruction of how it looked in the reign of Diocletian (r 284–305).

In front of the Curia, and hidden by scaffolding, is the **Lapis Niger**, a large slab of black marble that's said to cover the tomb of Romulus.

DON'T MISS

→ Arco di Settimio Severo

→ Tempio di Saturno

→ Chiesa di Santa Maria Antiqua

→ Casa delle Vestali

PRACTICALITIES

→ Map p82

→ ☎ 06 3996 7700

→ www.parcocolosseo.it

→ Largo della Salara Vecchia, Piazza di Santa Maria Nova

→ adult/reduced incl Palatino & SUPER sites €16/2, incl Colosseum & Palatino €16/2, incl Colosseum, Palatino & SUPER sites €22/2

→ ⊙ 8.30am-1hr before sunset; SUPER ticket sites Tue, Thu, Sat & afternoon Sun only, last entry 1hr before closing

→ 🚍 Via dei Fori Imperiali

At the end of Via Sacra, the 23m-high Arco di Settimio Severo was built in AD 203 to commemorate the Roman victory over the Parthians. Close by are the remains of the Rostri, an elaborate podium where Shakespeare had Mark Antony make his famous 'Friends, Romans, countrymen...' speech. Facing this, the Colonna di Foca rises above what was once the Forum's main square, Piazza del Foro.

The eight granite columns behind the Colonna are all that survive of the Tempio di Saturno, an important temple that doubled as the state treasury. Behind it are (from north to south): the ruins of the Tempio della Concordia, the Tempio di Vespasiano and the Portico degli Dei Consenti.

Basilica Giulia & Tempio di Castore e Polluce

On the southern side of Piazza del Foro, you'll see the stubby ruins of the Basilica Giulia, which was begun by Caesar and finished by Augustus. At the end of the basilica, three columns remain from the 5th-century-BC Tempio di Castore e Polluce.

Chiesa di Santa Maria Antiqua

Nearby, the 6th-century Chiesa di Santa Maria Antiqua (⊙9am-6.30pm Tue, Thu & Sat, from 2pm Sun summer, 9am-3.30pm Tue, Thu & Sat, from 2pm Sun winter; ⊟ Via dei Fori Imperiali) is the oldest and most important Christian site on the Forum. Its cavernous interior is a treasure trove of early Christian art containing exquisite 6th- to 9th-century frescoes and a hanging depiction of the Virgin Mary with child, one of the oldest icons in existence.

From the church you can access the Rampa di Domiziano, an underground passageway that allowed the emperors to enter the Forum from their Palatine palaces without being seen.

Via Sacra Towards the Colosseum

Back towards Via Sacra is the Casa delle Vestali, home of the virgins who tended the flame in the adjoining Tempio di Vesta.

Further on, past the circular Tempio di Romolo (Temple of Romulus; ⊙9am-6.30pm Tue, Thu & Sat, from 2pm Sun summer, 9am-3.30pm Tue, Thu & Sat, from 2pm Sun winter; ⊟ Via dei Fori Imperiali), is the Basilica di Massenzio, the largest building on the Forum. Started by the Emperor Maxentius and finished by Constantine in 315, it originally measured approximately 100m by 65m, roughly three times what it now covers.

Beyond the basilica, the Arco di Tito was built in AD 81 to celebrate Vespasian and Titus' victories against rebels in Jerusalem.

THE VESTAL VIRGINS

Despite privilege and public acclaim, life as a Vestal Virgin was no bed of roses. Every year, six physically perfect patrician girls aged between six and 10 were chosen by lottery to serve Vesta, goddess of hearth and household. Once selected, they faced a 30-year period of chaste servitude at the Tempio di Vesta. Their main duty was to ensure the temple's sacred fire never went out. If it did, the priestess responsible would be flogged. If a priestess were to lose her virginity, she risked being buried alive and her partner in crime being flogged to death.

Visit first thing in the morning or late afternoon; crowds are worst between 11am and 2pm.

ROMAN TRIUMPH

Via Sacra was the principal route of the Roman Triumph. This official victory parade, originally awarded by the Senate to victorious generals but later reserved for emperors, was a huge spectacle involving a procession from the *Porta Triumphalis* (Triumphal Gate) through the Forum to the Temple of Jupiter Capitolinus on the Capitoline Hill.

Roman Forum

A HISTORICAL TOUR

In ancient times, a forum was a market place, civic centre and religious complex all rolled into one, and the greatest of all was the Roman Forum (Foro Romano). Situated between the Palatino (Palatine Hill), ancient Rome's most exclusive neighbourhood, and the Campidoglio (Capitoline Hill), it was the city's busy, bustling centre. On any given day it teemed with activity. Senators debated affairs of state in the ① **Curia**, shoppers thronged the squares and traffic-free streets and crowds gathered under the ② **Colonna di Foca** to listen to politicians holding forth from the ② **Rostri**. Elsewhere, lawyers worked the courts in basilicas including the ③ **Basilica di Massenzio**, while the Vestal Virgins quietly went about their business in the ④ **Casa delle Vestali**.

Special occasions were also celebrated in the Forum: religious holidays were marked with ceremonies at temples such as ⑤ **Tempio di Saturno** and ⑥ **Tempio di Castore e Polluce**, and military victories were honoured with dramatic processions up Via Sacra and the building of monumental arches like ⑦ **Arco di Settimio Severo** and ⑧ **Arco di Tito**.

The ruins you see today are impressive but they can be confusing without a clear picture of what the Forum once looked like. This spread shows the Forum in its heyday, complete with temples, civic buildings and towering monuments to heroes of the Roman Empire.

TOP TIPS

➡ Get grandstand views of the Forum from the Palatino and Campidoglio.

➡ Visit first thing in the morning or late afternoon; crowds are worst between 11am and 2pm.

➡ In summer it gets hot in the Forum and there's little shade, so take a hat and plenty of water.

Colonna di Foca & Rostri

The free-standing, 13.5m-high Column of Phocus is the Forum's youngest monument, dating to AD 608. Behind it, the Rostri provided a suitably grandiose platform for pontificating public speakers.

Campidoglio (Capitoline Hill)

ADMISSION

Although valid for two days, admission tickets only allow for one entry into the Forum, Colosseum and Palatino.

Tempio di Saturno

Ancient Rome's Fort Knox, the Temple of Saturn was the city treasury. In Caesar's day it housed 13 tonnes of gold, 114 tonnes of silver and 30 million sestertii worth of silver coins.

IASCIC/SHUTTERSTOCK ©

VIACHESLAV LOPATIN/SHUTTERSTOCK ©

Tempio di Castore e Polluce

Only three columns of the Temple of Castor and Pollux remain. The temple was dedicated to the Heavenly Twins after they supposedly led the Romans to victory over the Latin League in 496 BC.

Arco di Settimio Severo

One of the Forum's signature monuments, this imposing triumphal arch commemorates the military victories of Septimius Severus. Relief panels depict his campaigns against the Parthians.

Curia

This big barn-like building was the official seat of the Roman Senate. Most of what you see is a reconstruction, but the interior marble floor dates to the 3rd-century reign of Diocletian.

Basilica di Massenzio

Marvel at the scale of this vast 4th-century basilica. In its original form the central hall was divided into enormous naves; now only part of the northern nave survives.

Via Sacra

Tempio di Giulio Cesare

JULIUS CAESAR

Julius Caesar was cremated on the site where the Tempio di Giulio Cesare now stands.

Arco di Tito

Said to be the inspiration for the Arc de Triomphe in Paris, the well-preserved Arch of Titus was built by the emperor Domitian to honour his elder brother Titus.

Casa delle Vestali

White statues line the grassy atrium of what was once the luxurious 50-room home of the Vestal Virgins. The virgins played an important role in Roman religion, serving the goddess Vesta.

JUSTIN FOULKES/LONELY PLANET ©

TOP SIGHT
CAPITOLINE MUSEUMS

Housed in two stately *palazzi* on Piazza del Campidoglio, the Capitoline Museums are the world's oldest public museums. Their origins date from 1471, when Pope Sixtus IV donated a number of bronze statues to the city, forming the nucleus of what is now one of Italy's finest collections of classical sculpture. There's also a formidable picture gallery with works by many big-name Italian artists.

Entrance & Courtyard

The entrance to the museums is in Palazzo dei Conservatori, where you'll find the original core of the sculptural collection on the 1st floor, and the Pinacoteca (picture gallery) on the 2nd floor.

Before you head up to start on the sculpture collection proper, take a moment to admire the ancient masonry littered around the ground-floor courtyard, notably a mammoth head, hand and foot. These all come from a 12m-high statue of Constantine that originally stood in the Basilica di Massenzio in the Roman Forum.

Palazzo dei Conservatori

Of the sculpture on the 1st floor, the Etruscan *Lupa Capitolina* (Capitoline Wolf) is the most famous piece. Standing in the Sala della Lupa, the bronze wolf towers over her suckling wards, Romulus and Remus, who were added in 1471. Until recently, the she-wolf was thought to be a 5th-century BC Etruscan work, but carbon-dating has shown it probably dates from the 1200s.

TOP TIPS

➜ Note that ticket prices increase, typically to around €15/13 (adult/reduced), when there's an exhibition on.

➜ Don't miss the views over the Roman Forum from the Tabularium.

➜ The ground-floor bookshop has a €15 museums guide.

PRACTICALITIES

➜ Musei Capitolini

➜ Map p82

➜ 🎟 06 06 08

➜ www.museicapitolini.org

➜ Piazza del Campidoglio 1

➜ adult/reduced €11.50/9.50

➜ ⏱ 9.30am-7.30pm, last entry 6.30pm

➜ 🚌 Piazza Venezia

Other highlights include the *Spinario*, a delicate 1st-century-BC bronze of a boy removing a thorn from his foot in the Sala dei Trionfi, and two works by Gian Lorenzo Bernini: *Medusa* in the Sala delle Oche and a statue of Pope Urban VIII in the frescoed Sala degli Orazi e Curiazi.

Also on this floor, in the modern Esedra di Marco Aurelio, is the original of the equestrian statue of Marcus Aurelius that stands outside in Piazza del Campidoglio. Here you can also see foundations of the Temple of Jupiter, one of the ancient city's most important temples.

Pinacoteca

The 2nd floor of Palazzo dei Conservatori is given over to the Pinacoteca, the museum's picture gallery.

Each room harbours masterpieces, but two stand out: the Sala Pietro da Cortona, which features Pietro da Cortona's famous depiction of the *Ratto delle Sabine* (Rape of the Sabine Women; 1630), and the Sala di Santa Petronilla, named after Guercino's huge canvas *Seppellimento di Santa Petronilla* (The Burial of St Petronilla; 1621–23). This airy hall also boasts two important works by Caravaggio: *La Buona Ventura* (The Fortune Teller; 1595), which shows a gypsy pretending to read a young man's hand but actually stealing his ring, and *San Giovanni Battista* (John the Baptist; 1602), an unusual nude depiction of the youthful saint with a ram.

Tabularium

A tunnel links Palazzo dei Conservatori to Palazzo Nuovo via the Tabularium, ancient Rome's central archive, beneath Palazzo Senatorio. Make sure you check out the views over the Roman Forum.

Palazzo Nuovo

Palazzo Nuovo is crammed to its elegant 17th-century rafters with classical Roman sculpture.

From the lobby, where the curly-bearded Mars glares ferociously at everyone who passes by, stairs lead up to the main galleries where you'll find some real showstoppers. Chief among them is the *Galata morente* (Dying Gaul) in the Sala del Gladiatore. One of the museum's greatest works, this sublime piece, actually a Roman copy of a 3rd-century-BC Greek original, movingly captures the quiet, resigned anguish of a dying Gaul warrior.

Next door, the Sala del Fauno takes its name from the red marble statue of a faun.

Another superb figurative piece is the sensual yet demure portrayal of the *Venere Capitolina* (Capitoline Venus) in the Gabinetto della Venere.

TREATY OF ROME

With frescoes depicting episodes from ancient Roman history and two papal statues – one of Urban VIII by Bernini and one of Innocent X by Algardi – the Sala degli Orazi e Curiazi provided the grand setting for one of modern Europe's key events. On 25 March 1957 the leaders of Italy, France, West Germany, Belgium, Holland and Luxembourg gathered here to sign the Treaty of Rome and establish the European Economic Community, the precursor of the European Union.

Stop by the Terrazza Caffarelli (p147) on the 2nd floor of Palazzo dei Conservatori for coffee and memorable views.

THE CONSERVATORI

Palazzo dei Conservatori takes its name from the *Conservatori* (elected magistrates) who used to hold their public hearings in the *palazzo* in the mid-15th century.

Continued from p85

Also worth a look is the 18th-century Neapolitan **presepe** (nativity scene) in a room off the salmon-orange 17th-century cloister.

Arco di Costantino   MONUMENT

(Map p82; Via di San Gregorio; Ⓜ Colosseo) On the western side of the Colosseum, this monumental triple arch was built in AD 315 to celebrate the emperor Constantine's victory over his rival Maxentius at the Battle of the Milvian Bridge (AD 312). Rising to a height of 25m, it's the largest of Rome's surviving triumphal arches.

◉ Centro Storico

★ Piazza Navona   PIAZZA

(Map p100; 🚇 Corso del Rinascimento) With its showy fountains, baroque *palazzi* and colourful street artists, hawkers and tourists, Piazza Navona is central Rome's elegant showcase square. Built over the 1st-century **Stadio di Domiziano** (Domitian's Stadium; ☑ 06 6880 5311; www.stadiodomiziano.com; Via di Tor Sanguigna 3; adult/reduced €8.50/6.50; ◷ 10am-6.30pm Sun-Fri, to 7.30pm Sat), it was paved over in the 15th century and for almost 300 years hosted the city's main market. Its grand centrepiece is Bernini's **Fontana dei Quattro Fiumi** (Fountain of the Four Rivers), a flamboyant fountain featuring an Egyptian obelisk and muscular personifications of the rivers Nile, Ganges, Danube and Plate.

Legend has it that the Nile figure is shielding his eyes to avoid looking at the nearby **Chiesa di Sant'Agnese in Agone** (☑ 320 0217152; www.santagneseinagone.org; Piazza Navona; ◷ 9am-1pm & 3-7pm Tue-Fri, 9am-1pm & 3-8pm Sat & Sun) designed by Bernini's hated rival Borromini. In truth, Bernini had completed his fountain two years before Borromini started work on the church's facade and the gesture simply indicated that the source of the Nile was unknown at the time.

The **Fontana del Moro** at the southern end of the square was designed by Giacomo della Porta in 1576. Bernini added the Moor holding a dolphin in the mid-17th century, but the surrounding Tritons are 19th-century copies. At the northern end of the piazza, the 19th-century **Fontana del Nettuno** depicts Neptune fighting with a sea monster, surrounded by sea nymphs.

The piazza's largest building is **Palazzo Pamphilj** (www.roma.itamaraty.gov.br/it; ◷ by reservation only), built for Pope Innocent X between 1644 and 1650, and now home to the Brazilian embassy.

Museo Nazionale Romano: Palazzo Altemps   MUSEUM

(Map p100; ☑ 06 68 48 51; www.museonazionaleromano.beniculturali.it; Piazza Sant'Apollinare 46; adult/reduced €10/2; ◷ 9am-7.45pm Tue-Sun; 🚇 Corso del Rinascimento) Just north of Piazza Navona, Palazzo Altemps is a beautiful late-15th-century *palazzo* housing the best of the Museo Nazionale Romano's formidable collection of classical sculpture. Many pieces come from the celebrated Ludovisi collection, amassed by Cardinal Ludovico Ludovisi in the 17th century. Note that the ticket office closes at 7pm.

Prize exhibits include the beautiful 5th-century *Trono Ludovisi* (Ludovisi Throne), a carved marble block whose central relief depicts a naked Venus (Aphrodite) being modestly plucked from the sea. In the neighbouring room, the *Ares Ludovisi*, a 2nd-century-BC representation of a young, clean-shaven Mars, owes its right foot to a Gian Lorenzo Bernini restoration in 1622.

The building itself provides an elegant backdrop, with a grand central courtyard, a finely painted loggia and frescoed rooms. These include the **Sala delle Prospettive Dipinte**, which was adorned with landscapes and hunting scenes for Cardinal Altemps, the rich nephew of Pope Pius IV (r 1560–65) who bought the *palazzo* in the late 16th century.

Also here are pieces from the Museo Nazionale Romano's Egyptian collection.

Note that the museum is one of four that collectively make up the Museo Nazionale Romano. A combined ticket (€15/8), which is valid for three days, includes admission to the other three sites: the Museo Nazionale Romano: Palazzo Massimo alle Terme, the Terme di Diocleziano and the Crypta Balbi. Ticket prices increase when temporary exhibitions are staged here.

★ Chiesa di San Luigi dei Francesi   CHURCH

(Map p100; ☑ 06 68 82 71; http://saintlouis-rome.net; Piazza di San Luigi dei Francesi 5; ◷ 9.30am-12.45pm & 2.30-6.30pm Mon-Fri, 9.30am-12.15pm & 2.30-6.45pm Sat, 11.30am-12.45pm & 2.30-6.45pm Sun; 🚇 Corso del Rinascimento) Church to Rome's French community since 1589, this opulent baroque *chiesa* is home to a celebrated trio of Caravaggio paintings: the *Vocazione di San Matteo* (The Calling of Saint Matthew), the *Martirio di San Matteo* (The Martyrdom of Saint Matthew) and *San Matteo e l'angelo* (Saint Matthew and the Angel), known collectively as the St Matthew cycle. Find them in the Cappella Contarelli to the left of the main altar.

ITALY'S POLITICAL CENTRE

Italy's political nerve centre is formed by a trio of *palazzi* in the historic centre. Overlooking the **Colonna di Marco Aurelio** on Piazza Colonna is **Palazzo Chigi** (Map p100; www.governo.it/visitare-i-palazzi-istituzionali/visitare-palazzo-chigi/palazzo-chigi-prenotazioni -e-calendario; Piazza Colonna 370; ⊘ guided visits 9am-noon Sat, twice monthly Sep-Jul, bookings required; 🚇 Via del Corso) FREE, the official residence of Italy's prime minister. Next door on Piazza di Montecitorio, the Bernini-designed **Palazzo di Montecitorio** (Map p100; 🖉 800 012955; www.camera.it/leg18/1253?conoscere_montecitorio=4; Piazza di Montecitorio; ⊘ guided visits 10.30am-3.30pm 1st Sun of the month; 🚇 Via del Corso) FREE is home to Italy's Chamber of Deputies. A short walk away, **Palazzo Madama** (Map p100; 🖉 06 6706 2177; www.senato.it; Piazza Madama 11; ⊘ guided tours 10am-6pm 1st Sat of the month Sep-Jul; 🚇 Corso del Rinascimento) FREE has been seat of the Italian Senate since 1871.

These three canvases are among the earliest of Caravaggio's religious works, painted between 1600 and 1602, but they are inescapably his, featuring a down-to-earth realism and the stunning use of *chiaroscuro* (the bold contrast of light and dark).

Before you leave, take a moment to enjoy Domenichino's faded 17th-century frescoes of St Cecilia in the second chapel on the right. St Cecilia is also depicted in the altarpiece by Guido Reni, a copy of a work by Raphael.

Basilica di Santa
Maria Sopra Minerva   BASILICA
(Map p100; www.santamariasopraminerva.it; Piazza della Minerva 42; ⊘ 6.50am-7pm Mon-Fri, 10am-12.30pm & 3.30-7pm Sat, 8am-12.30pm & 3.30-7pm Sun; 🚇 Largo di Torre Argentina) Built on the site of three pagan temples, including one dedicated to the goddess Minerva, the Dominican Basilica di Santa Maria Sopra Minerva is Rome's only Gothic church. However, little remains of the original 13th-century structure and these days the main draw is a minor Michelangelo sculpture and the magisterial, art-rich interior.

Inside, to the right of the altar in the **Cappella Carafa** (Cappella della Annunciazione), you'll find some superb 15th-century frescoes by Filipino Lippi and the majestic tomb of Pope Paul IV. Left of the high altar is one of Michelangelo's lesser-known sculptures, *Cristo Risorto* (Christ Bearing the Cross; 1520), depicting Jesus carrying a cross while wearing some jarring bronze drapery. The latter wasn't part of the original composition and was added after the Council of Trent (1545-63) to preserve Christ's modesty.

Chiesa di Sant'Ignazio di Loyola   CHURCH
(Map p100; 🖉 06 679 44 06; https://santignazio. gesuiti.it; Piazza di Sant'Ignazio; ⊘ 7.30am-7pm Mon-Sat, from 9am Sun; 🚇 Via del Corso) Flanking a delightful rococo piazza, this important Jesuit church boasts a Carlo Maderno facade and two celebrated *trompe l'œil* frescoes by Andrea Pozzo (1642-1709). One cleverly depicts a fake dome, while the other, on the nave ceiling, shows St Ignatius Loyola being welcomed into paradise by Christ and the Madonna.

★ Galleria Doria Pamphilj   GALLERY
(Map p100; 🖉 06 679 73 23; www.doriapamphilj.it; Via del Corso 305; adult/reduced €12/8, inc private apartments €14/8; ⊘9am-7pm, last admission 6pm; 🚇Via del Corso) Hidden behind the grimy grey exterior of Palazzo Doria Pamphilj, this wonderful gallery boasts one of Rome's richest private art collections, with works by Raphael, Tintoretto, Titian, Caravaggio, Bernini and Velázquez, as well as several Flemish masters. Masterpieces abound, but the undisputed star is Velázquez' portrait of an implacable Pope Innocent X, who grumbled that the depiction was 'too real'. For a comparison, check out Gian Lorenzo Bernini's sculptural interpretation of the same subject.

The opulent picture galleries are hung with floor-to-ceiling paintings, all ordered chronologically. In the Sala Aldobrandini look out for Titian's *Salomè con la testa del Battista* (Salome with the Head of John the Baptist) – the severed head is possibly Titian's self-portrait and Salome a lover who spurned the artist – and two early Caravaggios: *Riposo durante la fuga in Egitto* (Rest During the Flight into Egypt) and *Maddalene penitente* (Penitent Magdalen). Further highlights include Alessandro Algardi's bust of Donna Olimpia, the formidable woman who supposedly called the shots during Innocent X's papacy, and the *Battaglia nel porto di Napoli* (Battle in the Bay of Naples), one of the few paintings in Rome by Pieter Bruegel the Elder.

Continued on p102

 TOP SIGHT
PANTHEON

A striking 2000-year-old temple, now a church, the Pantheon is Rome's best-preserved ancient monument and one of the most influential buildings in the Western world. Its greying, pockmarked exterior might look its age, but inside it's a different story, and it's a unique and exhilarating experience to pass through its vast bronze doors and gaze up at the largest unreinforced concrete dome ever built.

History

In its current form the Pantheon dates from around AD 125. The original temple, built by Marcus Agrippa in 27 BC, burnt down in AD 80, and although it was rebuilt by Domitian, it was struck by lightning and destroyed for a second time in AD 110. The emperor Hadrian had it reconstructed between AD 118 and 125, and this is the version you see today.

Hadrian's temple was dedicated to the classical gods – hence the name Pantheon, a derivation of the Greek words *pan* (all) and *theos* (god) – but in 608 it was consecrated as a Christian church and it's now officially known as the Basilica di Santa Maria ad Martyres.

Thanks to this consecration, it was spared the worst of the medieval plundering that reduced many of Rome's ancient buildings to near dereliction. But it didn't escape entirely unscathed – its gilded-bronze roof tiles were removed and bronze from the portico was used by Bernini for his baldachin at St Peter's Basilica.

During the Renaissance, the building was much admired – Brunelleschi used it as inspiration for his cupola in Florence and Michelangelo studied it before designing the dome

TOP TIPS

➜ The Pantheon is a working church and Mass is celebrated at 5pm on Saturdays and 10.30am on Sundays.

➜ Visit around midday to see a beam of sunlight stream in through the oculus.

➜ Look down as well as up – the sloping marble floor has 22 almost-invisible holes to drain away the rain that gets in through the oculus.

PRACTICALITIES

➜ Map p100

➜ www.pantheonroma.com

➜ Piazza della Rotonda

➜ ⊙ 8.30am-7.30pm Mon-Sat, 9am-6pm Sun

➜ 🚊 Largo di Torre Argentina

at St Peter's Basilica – and it became an important burial chamber. Today you'll find the tomb of the artist Raphael here alongside those of kings Vittorio Emanuele II and Umberto I.

Exterior

Originally, the Pantheon was on a raised podium, its entrance facing onto a rectangular porticoed piazza. Nowadays its pitted exterior faces onto busy, cafe-lined Piazza della Rotonda. And while its facade is somewhat the worse for wear, it's still an imposing sight. The monumental entrance portico consists of 16 columns, each 11.8m high and each made from a single block of Egyptian granite, supporting a triangular pediment. Behind the columns, two 20-tonne bronze doors – 16th-century restorations of the originals – give onto the central rotunda.

Little remains of the ancient decor, although rivets and holes in the brickwork indicate where marble-veneer panels were once placed.

Interior

Although impressive from outside, it's only when you get inside that you can really appreciate the Pantheon's full size. With light streaming in through the oculus (the 8.7m-diameter hole in the centre of the dome), the cylindrical marble-clad interior seems vast, an effect that was deliberately designed to cut worshippers down to size before the gods.

Opposite the entrance is the church's main altar, over which hangs a 7th-century icon of the *Madonna col Bambino* (Madonna and Child). To the left (as you look in from the entrance) is the tomb of Raphael, marked by Lorenzetto's 1520 sculpture of the *Madonna del Sasso* (Madonna of the Rock). Neighbouring it are the tombs of King Umberto I and Margherita of Savoy. Over on the opposite side of the rotunda is the tomb of King Vittorio Emanuele II.

The Dome

The Pantheon's dome, considered the Romans' greatest architectural achievement, was the largest dome in the world until the 15th century when Brunelleschi beat it with his Florentine cupola. Its harmonious appearance is due to a precisely calibrated symmetry – its diameter is equal to the building's interior height of 43.4m. At its centre, the oculus, which symbolically connected the temple with the gods, plays a vital structural role by absorbing and redistributing the dome's huge tensile forces.

Radiating out from the oculus are five rows of 28 coffers (indented panels). These were originally ornamented, but more importantly served to reduce the cupola's immense weight.

ROME & LAZIO PANTHEON

THE INSCRIPTION

For centuries the Latin inscription over the entrance led historians to believe that the current temple was Marcus Agrippa's original. Certainly, the wording suggests this, reading: 'M.AGRIPPA.L.F.COS. TERTIUM.FECIT' or 'Marcus Agrippa, son of Lucius, in his third consulate built this'. However, excavations in the 19th century revealed traces of an earlier temple and scholars realised that Hadrian had simply kept Agrippa's original inscription over his new temple.

The stripping of the Pantheon's bronze by the Barberini pope Urban VIII gave rise to the saying, still in use today: 'What the barbarians didn't do, the Barberini did.'

PENTECOST AT THE PANTHEON

Each Pentecost, tens of thousands of red petals are rained down on the Pantheon through the oculus. This centuries-old tradition represents the Holy Spirit descending to earth.

Centro Storico

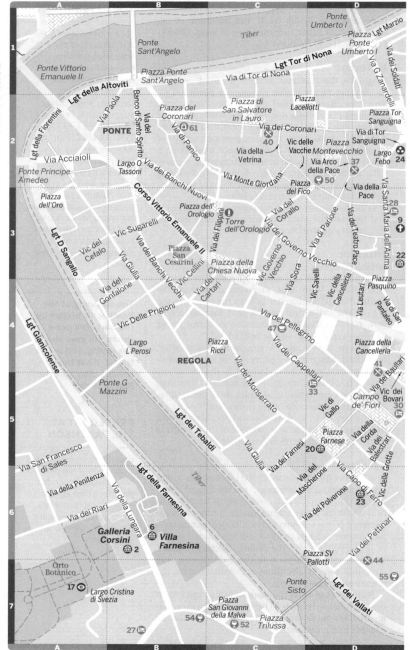

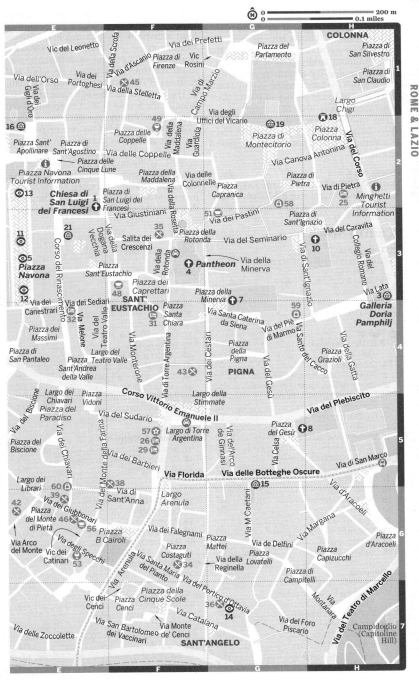

Continued from p97

Palazzo Doria Pamphilj dates from the mid-15th century, but its current look was largely the work of the current owners, the Doria Pamphilj family, who acquired it in the 18th century. The Pamphilj's golden age, during which the family collection was started, came during the papacy of one of their own, Innocent X (r 1644–55).

The excellent free audio guide, narrated by Jonathan Pamphilj, brings the place alive with family anecdotes and background information.

Chiesa del Gesù CHURCH
(Map p100; ☑ 06 69 70 01; www.chiesadelgesu.org; Piazza del Gesù; ⊙ 7am-noon & 4-7.30pm, St Ignatius rooms 4-6pm Mon-Sat, 10am-noon Sun; ☐ Lar-go di Torre Argentina) An imposing example of Counter-Reformation architecture, Rome's most important Jesuit church is a fabulous treasure trove of baroque art. Headline works include a swirling vault fresco by Giovanni Battista Gaulli (aka Il Baciccia) and Andrea del Pozzo's opulent tomb for Ignatius Loyola, the Spanish soldier and saint who founded the Jesuits in 1540. St Ignatius lived in the church from 1544 until his death in 1556 and you can visit his private rooms to the right of the man church.

The church, which was consecrated in 1584, is fronted by an impressive and much-copied facade by Giacomo della Porta. But more than the masonry, the real draw here is the church's lavish interior. The cupola frescoes and stucco decoration were designed

Centro Storico

by Il Baciccia, who also painted the hypnotic ceiling fresco, the *Trionfo del Nome di Gesù* (Triumph of the Name of Jesus).

In the northern transept, the **Cappella di Sant'Ignazio** houses the tomb of Ignatius Loyola. The altar-tomb, designed by baroque maestro Andrea Pozzo, is a sumptuous marble-and-bronze affair with lapis-lazuli-encrusted columns, and, on top, a lapis-lazuli globe representing the Trinity. On either side are sculptures whose titles neatly encapsulate the Jesuit ethos: to the left, *Fede che vince l'Idolatria* (Faith Defeats Idolatry); and on the right, *Religione che flagella l'Eresia* (Religion Lashing Heresy).

Jewish Ghetto   AREA
(Map p100; ☐ Lungotevere de' Cenci) The Jewish Ghetto, centred on lively Via del Portico d'Ottavia, is an atmospheric area studded with artisan's studios, small shops, kosher bakeries and popular trattorias. Crowning everything is the distinctive square dome of Rome's main synagogue.

As you stroll around look out for a series of brass cobblestones. These are memorial plaques commemorating the city's Holocaust victims: each one names a person and gives the date and destination of their deportation and death. They are placed outside the victims' homes.

Rome's Jewish community dates back to the 2nd century BC, making it one of the oldest in Europe. The first Jews came as business envoys, but many more arrived as slaves following the Roman wars in Judaea and Titus' defeat of Jerusalem in AD 70. Confinement to the Ghetto came in 1555 when Pope Paul IV ushered in a period of official intolerance that lasted, on and off, until the 20th century. Ironically, though, confinement meant that the Jewish cultural and religious identity survived intact.

Palazzo Farnese   HISTORIC BUILDING
(Map p100; www.inventerrome.com; Piazza Farnese; tours €9; ⊘ guided tours 3pm, 4pm & 5pm Mon, Wed & Fri; ☐ Corso Vittorio Emanuele II) Home to the French embassy, this towering Renaissance *palazzo*, one of Rome's finest, was started in 1514 by Antonio da Sangallo the Younger, continued by Michelangelo and finished by Giacomo della Porta. Inside, it boasts frescoes by Annibale and Agostino Carracci that are said by some to rival Michelangelo's in the Sistine Chapel. The highlight, painted between 1597 and 1608, is the monumental ceiling fresco *Amori degli Dei* (The Loves of the Gods) in the Galleria dei Carracci.

DON'T MISS

THE ECSTASY OF ST TERESA
....

Designed by Carlo Maderno, the modest **Chiesa di Santa Maria della Vittoria** (☑ 06 4274 0571; www.chiesasantamariavittoriaroma.it; Via XX Settembre 17; ⊘ 8.30am-noon & 3.30-6pm Mon-Sat, 3.30-6pm Sun; Ⓜ Repubblica) is an unlikely setting for an extraordinary work of art – Bernini's extravagant and sexually charged *Santa Teresa trafitta dall'amore di Dio* (Ecstasy of St Teresa). This daring sculpture depicts Teresa, engulfed in the folds of a flowing cloak, floating in ecstasy on a cloud while a teasing angel pierces her repeatedly with a golden arrow. It's in the fourth chapel on the north side.

Watching the whole scene from two side balconies are a number of sculpted figures, including one depicting Cardinal Federico Cornaro, for whom the chapel was built. It's a stunning and major work, bathed in soft natural light filtering through a concealed window. Go in the afternoon for the best effect.

Visits to the *palazzo* are by 45-minute guided tour (in English, French and Italian), for which you'll need to book at least a week in advance – see the website for details.

◉ Tridente, Trevi & the Quirinale

★ **Palazzo Barberini**   GALLERY
(Galleria Nazionale d'Arte Antica – Palazzo Barberini; Map p106; ☑ 06 481 45 91; www.barberinicorsini.org; Via delle Quattro Fontane 13, Trevi; adult/reduced incl Galleria Corsini €12/2, free 1st Sun of the month Oct-Mar; ⊘ 8.30am-7pm Tue-Sun; Ⓜ Barberini) Commissioned to celebrate the Barberini family's rise to papal power, this sumptuous baroque palace impresses even before you view its breathtaking art collection. Many high-profile architects worked on it, including rivals Bernini and Borromini; the former contributed a square staircase, the latter a helicoidal one. Amid the masterpieces on display, don't miss Filippo Lippi's *Annunciazione e due donatori* (Annunciation with Two Donors; 1440-45) and Pietro da Cortona's ceiling fresco *Il Trionfo della Divina Provvidenza* (The Triumph of Divine Providence; 1632-39).

Continued on p107

TOP SIGHT
PIAZZA DI SPAGNA & THE SPANISH STEPS

Forming a picture-perfect backdrop to Piazza di Spagna, this statement sweep of stairs is one of the city's major icons and public meeting points. Though officially named the _Scalinata della Trinità dei Monti_, the stairs are popularly called the Spanish Steps.

Spanish Steps

Piazza di Spagna was named after the Spanish Embassy to the Holy See, but the staircase – 135 gleaming steps designed by the Italian Francesco de Sanctis – was built in 1725 with a legacy from the French. The dazzling stairs reopened in September 2016 after a €1.5 million clean-up job funded by luxury Italian jewellery house Bulgari.

Chiesa della Trinità dei Monti

This landmark **church** (☎06 679 41 79; http://trinitadeimonti. net/it/chiesa/; Piazza Trinità dei Monti 3; ⏰10.15am-8pm Mon, Wed & Thu, to 7pm Tue, noon-9pm Fri, 9.15am-9pm Sat, 9am-8pm Sun) was commissioned by King Louis XII of France and consecrated in 1585. Apart from the great city views offered from its front steps, it is notable for its wonderful frescoes by Daniele da Volterra. His _Deposizione_ (Deposition), in the second chapel on the left, is regarded as a masterpiece of mannerist painting.

Fontana della Barcaccia

At the foot of the steps, the fountain of a sinking boat, the **Barcaccia** (1627), is believed to be by Pietro Bernini, father of the more famous Gian Lorenzo Bernini. It's fed from an aqueduct, the ancient Roman Aqua Virgo (also known as the Acqua Vergine), as are the fountains in Piazza del Popolo and the Trevi Fountain. Here there's not much pressure, so it's sunken as a clever piece of engineering. Bees and suns decorate the structure, symbols of the commissioning Barberini family.

TOP TIPS

➡ No sitting on the steps, please! It is also forbidden to eat and drink or 'shout, squall and sing' on the restored staircase. Doing so risks a fine of up to €400.

➡ To skip the 135-step hike up, take the lift inside the Spagna metro station to the top.

PRACTICALITIES

➡ Map p106

➡ Ⓜ Spagna

TOP SIGHT
TREVI FOUNTAIN

Rome's most famous fountain, the iconic Fontana di Trevi, is a baroque extravaganza – a foaming white-marble and emerald-water masterpiece filling an entire piazza. The flamboyant ensemble, 20m wide and 26m high, was designed by Nicola Salvi in 1732 and depicts the chariot of the sea-god Oceanus being led by Tritons accompanied by seahorses that represent the moods of the sea.

Aqua Virgo

The fountain's water comes from the Aqua Virgo, an underground aqueduct that is over 2000 years old. It was built by General Agrippa under Augustus and brings water from the Salone springs around 19km away. The *tre vie* (three roads) that converge at the fountain give it its name.

Coin-Tossing

The famous tradition (inaugurated in the 1954 film *Three Coins in the Fountain*) is to toss a coin into the fountain, thus ensuring your return to Rome. An estimated €3000 is thrown into the Trevi each day. This money is collected daily and goes to the Catholic charity Caritas, with its yield increasing significantly since the crackdown on people extracting the money for themselves.

Trevi on Camera

Most famously, Trevi Fountain is where movie star Anita Ekberg cavorted in a ballgown in director Federico Fellini's classic *La Dolce Vita* (1960); apparently she wore waders under her iconic black dress but still shivered during the winter shoot.

TOP TIPS

➜ Coin-tossing etiquette: throw with your right hand, over your left shoulder with your back facing the fountain.

➜ Paddling or bathing in the fountain is strictly forbidden, as is eating and drinking on the steps leading down to the water. Both crimes risk an on-the-spot fine of up to €500.

PRACTICALITIES

➜ Fontana di Trevi

➜ Map p106

➜ Piazza di Trevi, Trevi

➜ Ⓜ Barberini

Tridente & Trevi

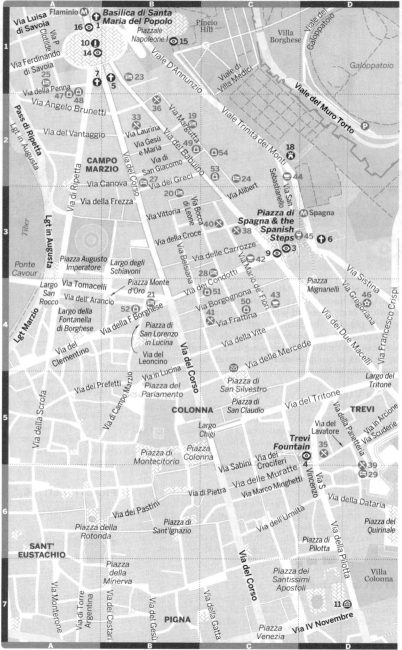

The map shows the following labelled locations and features:

Streets and places:
Via Luisa di Savoia, Via P Clotilde, Via Ferdinando di Savoia, Via della Penna, Via Angelo Brunetti, Pass di Ripetta, Lgt in Augusta, Lgt di Ripetta, Via del Vantaggio, CAMPO MARZIO, Via del Corso, Via Canova, Via della Frezza, Via Laurina, Via del Babuino, Via Gesù e Maria, Via di San Giacomo, Via dei Greci, Via Vittoria, Via della Croce, Via Bocca di Leone, Via Belsiana, Via Margutta, Viale D'Annunzio, Viale di Villa Medici, Viale Trinità dei Monti, Viale del Galoppatoio, Viale del Muro Torto, Galoppatoio, Villa Borghese, Pincio Hill, Piazzale Napoleone I

Basilica di Santa Maria del Popolo

Flaminio M

Tiber, Ponte Cavour, Lgt Marzio, Largo San Rocco, Piazza Augusto Imperatore, Largo degli Schiavoni, Via Tomacelli, Via dell'Arancio, Largo della Fontanella di Borghese, Via della F Borghese, Piazza Monte d'Oro, Piazza di San Lorenzo in Lucina, Via del Clementino, Via del Leoncino, Via dei Prefetti, Via di Campo Marzio, Via in Lucina, Piazza del Parlamento, COLONNA, Via della Scrofa, Via del Corso, Piazza di San Silvestro, Piazza di San Claudio, Largo Chigi, Piazza di Montecitorio, Piazza Colonna, Via del Tritone, TREVI, Via del Lavatore, Via in Arcione, Via delle Scuderie, Via della Panetteria, Largo del Tritone, Via Francesco Crispi, Via dei Due Macelli, Via Sistina, Via Gregoriana, Piazza Mignanelli, Piazza di Spagna & the Spanish Steps, Spagna M, Via San Sebastianello, Via delle Carrozze, Via dei Condotti, Via Mario de' Fiori, Via Borgognona, Via delle Mercede, Via della Vite, Via Frattina, Piazza della Rotonda, SANT' EUSTACHIO, Via Monterone, Via di Torre Argentina, Via dei Cestari, Via del Gesù, Piazza della Minerva, PIGNA, Via della Gatta, Via del Corso, Piazza di Sant'Ignazio, Via dei Pastini, Via di Pietra, Via delle Muratte, Via Marco Minghetti, Via Sabini, Via dei Crociferi, Trevi Fountain, Via S Vincenzo, Via della Dataria, Via dell'Umiltà, Piazza di Pilotta, Piazza del Quirinale, Piazza dei Santissimi Apostoli, Villa Colonna, Via della Pilotta, Piazza Venezia, Via IV Novembre

Numbered markers: 1, 5, 6, 7, 9, 10, 11, 14, 15, 16, 18, 19, 20, 21, 23, 24, 25, 27, 28, 33, 35, 36, 38, 39, 40, 41, 42, 43, 44, 45, 46, 47, 48, 49, 50, 51, 52, 53, 54, 3, 4, 29

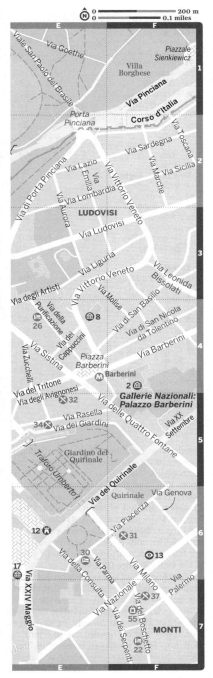

Continued from p103

Other must-sees include Hans Holbein's famous portrait of a pugnacious Henry VIII (c 1540) and Raphael's *La Fornarina* (The Baker's Girl; c 1520), thought to be a portrait of his mistress, who worked in a bakery in Trastevere. Works by Caravaggio include *San Francesco d'Assisi in meditazione* (St Francis in Meditation; 1606), *Narciso* (Narcissus; 1597–98) and the mesmerisingly horrific *Giuditta e Oloferne* (Judith Beheading Holophernes; c 1598–99). Other artistic giants represented include El Greco, Giovanni Bellini, Beccafumi and Perugino. Last entry is one hour before final exit time. The entrance ticket also includes entrance to the Galleria Corsini (p122) in Trastevere.

Convento dei Cappuccini   MUSEUM
(Map p106; ☎06 8880 3695; www.cappuccini viaveneto.it; Via Vittorio Veneto 27, Trevi; adult/reduced €8.50/5; ⊗9am-6.30pm; M Barberini) This church and convent complex safeguards what is possibly Rome's strangest sight: crypt chapels where everything from the picture frames to the light fittings is made of human bones. Between 1732 and 1775 resident Capuchin monks used the bones of 3700 of their departed brothers to create this macabre *memento mori* (reminder of death) – a 30m-long passageway ensnaring six crypts, each named after the type of bone used to decorate (skulls, shin bones, pelvises etc).

Villa Medici   PALACE
(Map p106; ☎06 676 13 11; www.villamedici.it; Viale Trinità dei Monti 1; guided tour adult/reduced €12/6; ⊗10am-7pm Tue-Sun; M Spagna) Built for Cardinal Ricci da Montepulciano in 1540, this sumptuous Renaissance palace was purchased by Ferdinando de' Medici in 1576 and remained in Medici hands until 1801, when Napoleon acquired it for the French Academy. Guided tours (1½ hours) in multiple languages take in the sculpture-filled gardens and orchard, a garden studio exquisitely frescoed by Jacopo Zucchi in 1577 and the cardinal's private apartments. Note the pieces of ancient Roman sculpture from the Ara Pacis embedded in the villa's walls.

Piazza del Popolo   PIAZZA
(Map p106; M Flaminio) This massive piazza was laid out in 1538 to provide a grandiose entrance to what was then Rome's main northern gateway. It has been remodelled several times, most recently by Giuseppe Valadier in 1823. At its southern approach are Carlo Rainaldi's twin 17th-century churches, **Chiesa di Santa Maria dei Miracoli**

ROME & LAZIO SIGHTS

Tridente & Trevi

(☎06 361 02 50; Via del Corso 528; ⊙7.30am-
12.30pm & 4.30-7.30pm) and **Basilica di
Santa Maria in Montesanto** (Chiesa degli Artisti; www.chiesadegliartisti.it; Via del Babuino 198;
⊙10am-noon & 5-8pm Mon-Fri, 10am-noon Sat,
11am-1.30pm Sun) In the centre, the 36m-high
obelisk was brought by Augustus from ancient Egypt; it originally stood in the Circo
Massimo. On the northern flank, the **Porta
del Popolo** was created by Bernini in 1655 to
celebrate Queen Christina of Sweden's defec-
tion to Catholicism, while rising to the east
is the viewpoint of the **Pincio Hill Gardens**.

★**Basilica di Santa
Maria del Popolo**   BASILICA
(Map p106; ☎392 3612243; www.smariadel
popolo.com; Piazza del Popolo 12; ⊙7am-noon &
4-7pm Mon-Sat, 8am-1.30pm & 4.30-7.30pm Sun;
Ⓜ Flaminio) This is one of Rome's richest

Renaissance churches, with a particularly
impressive collection of art, including two
Caravaggios: the *Conversion of St Paul*
(1600–1601) and the *Crucifixion of St Peter*
(1601). These are in the 16th-century **Cerasi
Chapel** to the left of the main altar. Other
fine works include Caracci's *Assumption of
the Virgin* (c 1660) in the same chapel and
multiple frescoes by Pinturicchio (look for
his 1484–90 *Adoration of the Christ Child*
in the **Della Rovere Chapel**).

The church has a central nave and four
chapels on each of its sides. The first chapel
was built here in 1099 to exorcise the ghost
of Nero, who was secretly buried on this spot
and whose ghost was thought to haunt the
area. It was later overhauled, but the church's
most important makeover came when Bramante renovated the presbytery and choir
and Pinturicchio added his series of frescoes

at the end of the 5th century. Bernini further reworked the church in the 17th century.

Look out for the **Cappella Chigi**, designed by Raphael for wealthy banker Agostino Chigi in 1514 but not completed until 100 years later, under Bernini's supervision.

Palazzo del Quirinale   PALACE
(Map p106; ☎ 06 3996 7557; www.quirinale.it; Piazza del Quirinale; tours from €1.50; ☺ 9.30am-4pm Tue, Wed & Fri-Sun, closed Aug; ☐ Via Nazionale, Ⓜ Repubblica) Perched atop the Quirinale Hill, one of Rome's seven hills, this former papal summer residence has been home to the Italian head of state since 1948. Originally commissioned by Pope Gregory XIII (r 1572–85) it was built and added to over 150 years by architects including Ottaviano Mascherino, Domenico Fontana, Francesco Borromini, Gian Lorenzo Bernini and Carlo Maderno. Guided tours of its grand reception rooms should be booked at least five days ahead by telephone, or online at www. coopculture.it. On the other side of the piazza, the palace's former stable building, the **Scuderie al Quirinale** (☎ 06 8110 0256; www. scuderiequirinale.it; Via XXIV Maggio 16; adult/reduced €15/13; ☺ 10am-8pm Sun-Thu, to 9.30pm Fri & Sat), hosts excellent art exhibitions.

Palazzo Colonna   GALLERY
(Map p106; ☎ 06 678 43 50; www.galleriacolonna.it; Via della Pilotta 17; adult/reduced €12/10; ☺ 9am-1.15pm Sat, closed Aug; Ⓜ Colosseo) The guided tours of this opulent palace are among the city's best, introducing visitors to the residence and art collection of the patrician Colonna family. The largest private palace in Rome, it has a formal garden, multiple reception rooms and a grandiose baroque Great Hall built to honour Marcantonio II Colonna, a hero of the 1571 Battle of Lepanto. Guides recount plenty of anecdotes about family members including fascinating Maria Mancini Mazzarino, a feisty favourite of Louis XIV of France.

Le Domus Romane di Palazzo Valentini   ARCHAEOLOGICAL SITE
(Map p82; ☎ 06 2276 1280; www.palazzovalentini.it; Via Foro Traiano 85; adult/reduced €12/8; ☺ 9.30am-6.30pm Wed-Mon; ♿; Ⓜ Barberini) Underneath a grand mansion that's been the seat of the Province of Rome since 1873 lie the archaeological remains of several lavish ancient Roman houses; the excavated fragments have been turned into a fascinating multimedia 'experience'. Tours are held every 30 minutes, but rotate between Italian, English, French, German and Spanish. Book

ahead online or by phone (advance booking fee €1.50), especially during holiday periods.

⊙ Vatican City, Borgo & Prati

★ Castel Sant'Angelo   MUSEUM, CASTLE
(Map p116; ☎ 06 32810; www.castelsantangelo. beniculturali.it; Lungotevere Castello 50; adult/reduced €15/2, free 1st Sunday of the month Oct-Mar; ☺ 9am-7.30pm, last admission 6.30pm; ☐ Piazza Pia) With its chunky round keep, this castle is an instantly recognisable landmark. Built as a mausoleum for the emperor Hadrian, it was converted into a papal fortress in the 6th century and named after an angelic vision that Pope Gregory the Great had in 590. Nowadays, it is a moody and dramatic keep that houses the **Museo Nazionale di Castel Sant'Angelo** and its grand collection of paintings, sculpture, military memorabilia and medieval firearms. Many of these weapons were used by soldiers fighting to protect the castle, which, thanks to a 13th-century **secret passageway to the Vatican** *(Passetto di Borgo)*, provided sanctuary to many popes in times of danger. Most famously, Pope Clemente VI holed up here during the 1527 sack of Rome.

The castle's upper floors are filled with elegant Renaissance interiors, including the lavish **Sala Paolina** with frescoes depicting episodes from the life of Alexander the Great. Two storeys up, the **terrace**, immortalised by Puccini in his opera *Tosca*, offers unforgettable views over Rome and has a busy little cafe (snacks €2.50 to €5).

Fascinating guided Secret Castle (Il Castello Segreto) tours (twice daily in English) take in the hidden *Passetto di Borgo*, the prisons and the steam-heated papal baths of Leo X and Clemente VII.

Ticket prices may increase during temporary exhibitions.

St Peter's Square   PIAZZA
(Piazza San Pietro; Map p116; ☐ Piazza del Risorgimento, Ⓜ Ottaviano-San Pietro) Overlooked by St Peter's Basilica (p110), the Vatican's central square was laid out between 1656 and 1667 to a design by Gian Lorenzo Bernini. Seen from above, it resembles a giant keyhole with two semicircular colonnades, each consisting of four rows of Doric columns, encircling a giant ellipse that straightens out to funnel believers into the basilica. The effect was deliberate – Bernini described the colonnades as representing 'the motherly arms of the church'.

Continued on p118

 TOP SIGHT
ST PETER'S BASILICA

In a city of outstanding churches, none can hold a candle to St Peter's, Italy's largest, richest and most spectacular basilica. A monument to centuries of artistic genius, it boasts many spectacular works of art, including three of Italy's most celebrated masterpieces: Michelangelo's *Pietà*, his soaring dome, and Bernini's 29m-high bronze baldachin (canopy) over the papal altar.

The Facade

Built between 1608 and 1612, Carlo Maderno's immense facade is 48m high and 115m wide. Eight 27m-high columns support the upper attic on which 13 statues stand representing Christ the Redeemer, St John the Baptist and the 11 apostles. The central balcony, the **Loggia della Benedizione**, is where the pope stands to deliver his *Urbi et Orbi* blessing at Christmas and Easter.

Interior – The Nave

Dominating the centre of the basilica is Bernini's 29m-high **baldachin**. Supported by four spiral columns and made with bronze taken from the Pantheon, it stands over the **papal altar**. In front, Maderno's **Confessione** stands over the site where St Peter was originally buried.

Above the baldachin, Michelangelo's **dome** soars to a height of 119m. It's supported by four massive stone **piers**, each named after the saint whose statue adorns its Bernini-designed niche: **St Longinus**, **St Veronica**, **St Helena** and **St Andrew**. At the base of the **Pier of St Longi-**

TOP TIPS

➡ Dress appropriately if you want to get in – no shorts, miniskirts or bare shoulders.

➡ Queues are inevitable at the security checks, but they move quickly.

➡ Lines are generally shorter during lunch hours and late afternoon.

PRACTICALITIES

➡ Basilica di San Pietro

➡ Map p116

➡ ☏ 06 6988 3731

➡ www.vatican.va

➡ St Peter's Sq

➡ ⏱7am-7pm Apr-Sep, to 6.30pm Oct-Mar

➡ 🚇 Piazza del Risorgimento, Ⓜ Ottaviano-San Pietro

nus is Arnolfo di Cambio's much-loved 13th-century bronze statue of St Peter, whose right foot has been worn down by centuries of caresses.

Behind the altar, the tribune houses Bernini's extraordinary Cattedra di San Pietro. A vast gilded bronze throne held aloft by four 5m-high saints, it's centred on a wooden seat that was once thought to have been St Peter's, but in fact dates from the 9th century.

Interior – Left Aisle

In the roped-off left transept, the Cappella della Madonna della Colonna features a marble altar by Giacomo della Porta. To its right, above the tomb of St Leo the Great, is a fine relief by Alessandro Algardi. Under the next arch is Bernini's last work in the basilica, the monument to Alexander VII.

Halfway down the aisle, the Cappella Clementina is named after Clement VIII, who had Giacomo della Porta decorate it for the Jubilee of 1600. Beneath the altar is the tomb of St Gregory the Great and, to the left, a monument to Pope Pius VII.

The next arch shelters Alessandro Algardi's monument to Leo XI. Beyond it is the richly decorated Cappella del Coro. The monument to Innocent VIII in the next aisle arch is a recreation of a monument from the old basilica.

Continuing, the Cappella della Presentazione contains a monument to John XXIII and Benedict XV. Under the next arch are the so-called Stuart monuments.

Interior – Right Aisle

At the head of the right aisle is Michelangelo's hauntingly beautiful Pietà. Sculpted when he was only 25 (in 1499), it's the only work the artist ever signed – his signature is etched into the sash across the Madonna's breast.

Nearby, a red floor disc marks the spot where Charlemagne and later Holy Roman emperors were crowned by the pope.

On a pillar just beyond the Pietà, Carlo Fontana's gilt and bronze monument to Queen Christina of Sweden commemorates the far-from-holy Swedish monarch who converted to Catholicism in 1655.

Moving on, you'll come to the Cappella di San Sebastiano, home of Pope John Paul II's tomb, and the Cappella del Santissimo Sacramento with works by Borromini, Bernini and Pietro da Cortona.

Beyond the chapel, the grandiose monument to Gregory XIII sits near the roped-off Cappella Gregoriana. Much of the right transept is closed off, but you can still make out Canova's monument to Clement XIII.

THE DOME

From the dome (with/without lift €10/8; ⊘8am-6pm Apr-Sep, to 5pm Oct-Mar) entrance on the right of the basilica's main portico, you can walk the 551 steps to the top or take a small lift halfway and then follow on foot for the last 320 steps. Either way, it's a long, steep climb. But make it to the top, and you're rewarded with stunning views from a perch 120m above St Peter's Square.

Contrary to popular belief, St Peter's Basilica is not the world's largest church – the Basilica of Our Lady of Peace in Yamoussoukro on the Ivory Coast is bigger. Still, its measurements are pretty staggering – it's 187m long and covers more than 15,000 sq metres. Bronze floor plates in the nave indicate the respective sizes of the 14 next-largest churches.

TOURS

From February to May, free, two-hour English-language tours of the basilica depart from the Ufficio Pellegrini e Turisti (p157) at 2.15pm weekdays. No tickets are necessary, but check www.pnac.org for details.

TOP SIGHT
VATICAN MUSEUMS

Visiting the Vatican Museums (Musei Vaticani) is a thrilling and unforgettable experience. With some 7km of exhibitions and more masterpieces than many small countries can call their own, this vast museum complex boasts one of the world's greatest art collections. Highlights include a spectacular collection of classical statuary in the Museo Pio-Clementino, a suite of rooms frescoed by Raphael, and the Michelangelo-decorated Sistine Chapel.

Pinacoteca

Often overlooked by visitors, the papal picture gallery displays paintings dating from the 11th to 19th centuries, with works by Giotto, Fra' Angelico, Filippo Lippi, Perugino, Titian, Guido Reni, Guercino, Pietro da Cortona, Caravaggio and Leonardo da Vinci.

Look out for a trio of paintings by Raphael in Room VIII – the *Madonna di Foligno* (Madonna of Folignano), the *Incoronazione della Vergine* (Crowning of the Virgin) and *La Trasfigurazione* (Transfiguration), which was completed by his students after his death in 1520. Other highlights include Filippo Lippi's *L'Incoronazione della Vergine con Angeli, Santo e donatore* (Coronation of the Virgin with Angels, Saints and Donors); Leonardo da Vinci's haunting and unfinished *San Gerolamo* (St Jerome); and Caravaggio's *Deposizione* (Deposition from the Cross).

TOP TIPS

➜ Last Sunday of the month the museums are free (and busy).

➜ Exhibits are simply labelled – consider an audio guide (€8) or Guide to the Vatican Museums and City (€13).

➜ Check website for excellent tours.

PRACTICALITIES

➜ Map p116

➜ ☎ 06 6988 4676

➜ www.museivaticani.va

➜ Viale Vaticano

➜ adult/reduced €17/8, free last Sun of the month

➜ ⊙ 9am-6pm Mon-Sat, to 2pm last Sun of month, last admission 2hr before close

➜ 🚇 Piazza del Risorgimento, Ⓜ Ottaviano-San Pietro

Museo Chiaramonti & Braccio Nuovo

This museum is effectively the long corridor that runs down the lower east side of the Palazzetto di Belvedere. Its walls are lined with thousands of statues and busts representing everything from immortal gods to playful cherubs and ugly Roman patricians.

Near the end of the hall, off to the right, is the Braccio Nuovo (New Wing), which contains a celebrated statue of the Nile as a reclining god covered by 16 babies.

Museo Pio-Clementino

This stunning museum contains some of the Vatican's finest classical statuary, including the peerless *Apollo Belvedere* and the 1st-century BC *Laocoön,* both in the Cortile Ottagono (Octagonal Courtyard).

Before you go into the courtyard, take a moment to admire the 1st-century *Apoxyomenos,* one of the earliest known sculptures to depict a figure with a raised arm.

To the left as you enter the courtyard, the *Apollo Belvedere* is a 2nd-century Roman copy of a 4th-century-BC Greek bronze. A beautifully proportioned representation of the sun god Apollo, it's considered one of the great masterpieces of classical sculpture. Nearby, the *Laocoön* depicts the mythical death of the Trojan priest who warned his fellow citizens not to take the wooden horse left by the Greeks.

Back inside, the Sala degli Animali is filled with sculpted creatures and magnificent 4th-century mosaics. Continuing on, you come to the Sala delle Muse (Room of the Muses), centred on the *Torso Belvedere,* another of the museum's must-sees. A fragment of a muscular 1st-century-BC Greek sculpture, this was found in Campo de' Fiori and used by Michelangelo as a model for his *ignudi* (male nudes) in the Sistine Chapel.

The next room, the Sala Rotonda (Round Room), contains a number of colossal statues, including a gilded-bronze *Ercole* (Hercules) and an exquisite floor mosaic. The enormous basin in the centre of the room was found at Nero's Domus Aurea and is made out of a single piece of red porphyry stone.

Museo Gregoriano Egizio

Founded by Pope Gregory XVI in 1839, this Egyptian museum displays pieces taken from Egypt in ancient Roman times. There are fascinating exhibits, including a fragmented statue of the pharaoh Ramses II on his throne, vividly painted sarcophagi dating from around 1000 BC, and a macabre mummy.

SKIP THE LINE

To avoid horrendous queues, book tickets (€4 fee) online (http://biglietteriamusei.vatican.va/musei/tickets/do; print voucher and swap it for a ticket at the appointed time at the entrance) or at Ufficio Pellegrini e Turisti. Alternatively, sign up for a tour. Also, time your visit: Tuesdays and Thursdays are quietest; Wednesday mornings are good too; afternoons are better than mornings; avoid Mondays when other museums close, and rainy days.

From mid-April to October, the museums open late every Friday evening (7pm to 11pm). To visit at this special time you'll need to book online.

MICHELANGELO'S SELF-PORTRAITS

Hidden amid the mass of bodies in the Sistine Chapel frescoes are two Michelangelo self-portraits. On the *Giudizio Universale* look for the figure of St Bartholomew, holding his own flayed skin beneath Christ. The face in the skin is said to be Michelangelo's, its anguished look reflecting the artist's tormented faith. His stricken face is also said to be that of the prophet Jeremiah on the ceiling.

Museo Gregoriano Etrusco

At the top of the 18th-century Simonetti staircase, this fascinating museum contains artefacts unearthed in the Etruscan tombs of northern Lazio, as well as a superb collection of vases and Roman antiquities. Of particular interest is the *Marte di Todi* (Mars of Todi), a black bronze of a warrior dating from the late 5th century BC, located in Room III.

Galleria delle Carte Geografiche & Sala Sobieski

One of the unsung heroes of the Vatican Museums, the 120m-long Map Gallery is hung with 40 huge topographical maps. These were created between 1580 and 1583 for Pope Gregory XIII based on drafts by Ignazio Danti, one of the leading cartographers of his day. Beyond the gallery, the Sala Sobieski is named after an enormous 19th-century painting depicting the victory of the Polish King John III Sobieski over the Turks in 1683.

Stanze di Raffaello

These four frescoed chambers, currently undergoing partial restoration, were part of Pope Julius II's private apartments. Raphael himself painted the Stanza della Segnatura (1508–11) and the Stanza d'Eliodoro (1512–14), while the Stanza dell'Incendio di Borgo (1514–17) and Sala di Costantino (1517–24) were decorated by students following his designs.

The first room you come to is the Sala di Costantino, originally a ceremonial reception room, which is dominated by the *Battaglia di Costantino contro Maxentius* (Battle of the Milvian Bridge) showing the victory of Constantine, Rome's first Christian emperor, over his rival Maxentius.

The Stanza d'Eliodoro, which was used for the pope's private audiences, takes its name from the *Cacciata d'Eliodoro* (Expulsion of Heliodorus from the Temple), an allegorical work reflecting Pope Julius II's policy of forcing foreign powers off Church lands. To its right, the *Messa di Bolsena* (Mass of Bolsena) shows Julius paying homage to the relic of a 13th-century miracle at the lakeside town of Bolsena. Next is the *Incontro di Leone Magno con Attila* (Encounter of Leo the Great with Attila), and, on the fourth wall, the *Liberazione di San Pietro* (Liberation of St Peter), a brilliant work illustrating Raphael's masterful ability to depict light.

The Stanza della Segnatura, Julius' study and library, was the first room that Raphael painted, and it's here that you'll find his great masterpiece, *La Scuola di Atene* (The School of Athens), featuring philosophers and scholars gathered around Plato and Aristotle. The seated figure in front of the steps is believed to be Michelangelo, while the figure of Plato is said to be a portrait of Leonardo da Vinci, and Euclide (the bald man bending over) is Bramante. Raphael also included a self-portrait in the lower right corner – he's the second figure from the right in the black hat. Opposite is *La Disputa del Sacramento* (Disputation on the Sacrament), also by Raphael.

The most famous work in the Stanza dell'Incendio di Borgo, the former seat of the Holy See's highest court and later a dining room, is the *Incendio di Borgo* (Fire in the Borgo). This depicts Leo IV extinguishing a fire by making the sign of the cross. The ceiling was painted by Raphael's master, Perugino.

From the Raphael Rooms, stairs lead to the Appartamento Borgia and the Vatican's collection of modern religious art.

Sistine Chapel

The jewel in the Vatican crown, the Cappella Sistina (www.museivaticani.va; Viale Vaticano; adult/reduced €17/8, last Sun of the month free; 9am-6pm Mon-Sat, to 2pm last Sun of the month, last entry 2hr before close) is home to two of the world's most famous works of art – Michelangelo's ceiling frescoes and his *Giudizio Universale* (Last Judgment).

SISTINE CHAPEL CEILING

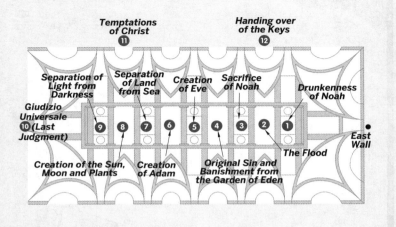

Temptations of Christ ⓫

Handing over of the Keys ⓬

Separation of Light from Darkness

Separation of Land from Sea

Creation of Eve

Sacrifice of Noah

Drunkenness of Noah

Giudizio Universale ⓾ (Last Judgment)

⑨ ⑧ ⑦ ⑥ ⑤ ④ ③ ② ①

East Wall

The Flood

Creation of the Sun, Moon and Plants

Creation of Adam

Original Sin and Banishment from the Garden of Eden

🏃 Sight Tour
Sistine Chapel

LENGTH 30 MINUTES

On entering the chapel via the stairway in the northwest corner, head over to the main entrance in the far (east) wall for the best views of the ceiling.

Michelangelo's design, which took him four years to complete, covers the entire 800-sq-metre surface. With painted architectural features and a colourful cast of biblical figures, it centres on nine panels depicting stories from the Book of Genesis.

As you look up from the east wall, the first panel is the ❶ **Drunkenness of Noah**, followed by ❷ **The Flood**, and the ❸ **Sacrifice of Noah**. Next, ❹ **Original Sin and Banishment from the Garden of Eden** famously depicts Adam and Eve being sent packing after accepting the forbidden fruit from Satan, represented by a snake with the body of a woman coiled around a tree. The ❺ **Creation of Eve** is then followed by the ❻ **Creation of Adam**. This, one of the most famous images in Western art, shows

a bearded God pointing his finger at Adam, thus bringing him to life. Completing the sequence are the ❼ **Separation of Land from Sea**; the ❽ **Creation of the Sun, Moon and Plants**; and the ❾ **Separation of Light from Darkness**, featuring a fearsome God reaching out to touch the sun. Set around the central panels are 20 athletic male nudes, the so-called *ignudi*.

Straight ahead of you on the west wall is Michelangelo's mesmeric ❿ **Giudizio Universale** (Last Judgment), showing Christ – in the centre near the top – passing sentence over the souls of the dead as they are torn from their graves to face him. The saved get to stay in heaven (in the upper right) while the damned are sent down to face the demons in hell (in the bottom right).

The chapel's side walls also feature stunning Renaissance frescoes, representing the lives of Moses (to the left) and Christ (to the right). Look out for Botticelli's ⓫ **Temptations of Christ** and Perugino's great masterpiece, the ⓬ **Handing over of the Keys**.

Vatican City, Borgo & Prati

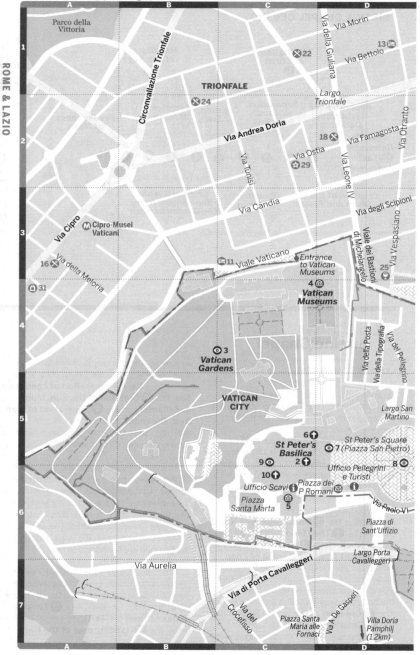

Parco della Vittoria

Via Morin

Via della Giuliana

Via Bettolo

13

TRIONFALE

24

Largo Trionfale

Circonvallazione Trionfale

Via Andrea Doria

18

Via Famagosta

Via Otranto

Via Tunisi

Via Ostia

29

Via Leone IV

Via Candia

Via degli Scipioni

Via Vespasiano

Via Cipro

M Cipro-Musei Vaticani

Viale dei Bastioni di Michelangelo

11 Viale Vaticano

Entrance to Vatican Museums

16 Via della Meloria

4 Vatican Museums

25

Via della Posta

Via della Tipografia

Via del Pellegrino

31

3 Vatican Gardens

VATICAN CITY

Largo San Martino

6

St Peter's Square (Piazza San Pietro)

7

St Peter's Basilica

2

9

8

10

Ufficio Pellegrini e Turisti

Ufficio Scavi

Piazza del P Romani

Piazza Santa Marta

5

Via Paolo VI

Piazza di Sant'Uffizio

Via Aurelia

Largo Porta Cavalleggeri

Via di Porta Cavalleggeri

Via del Crocefisso

Piazza Santa Maria alle Fornaci

Via A De Gasperi

Villa Doria Pamphilj (1.2km)

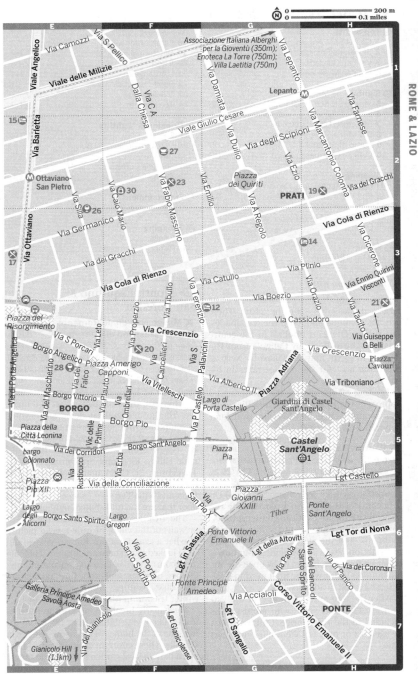

ROME & LAZIO

N 0 ———————————— 200 m
0 ———————————— 0.1 miles

E

Via Camozzi
Viale Angelico
Via S Pellico
Viale delle Milizie
Via C A Dalla Chiesa
Via Barletta
15
Ottaviano-San Pietro
Via Sila
Via Caio Mario
26
30
Via Germanico
Via Ottaviano
Via dei Gracchi
17
Via Cola di Rienzo
Piazza del Risorgimento
Via S Porcari
Via Leto
Borgo Angelico
Via del Falco
28
Piazza Amerigo Capponi
Via del Mascherino
Via di Porta Angelica
Borgo Vittorio
BORGO
Vic delle Palline
Piazza della Città Leonina
Largo Colonnato
Via dei Corridori
Via Rusticucci
Piazza Pio XII
Via della Conciliazione
Largo degli Alicorni
Borgo Santo Spirito
Largo Gregori
Via di Porta Santo Spirito
Galleria Principe Amedeo Savoia Aosta
Via del Gianicolo
Gianicolo Hill (1.1km)
Lgt Gianicolense

F

Via S Pellico
Associazione Italiana Alberghi per la Gioventù (350m); Enoteca La Torre (750m); Villa Laetitia (750m)
Via Damiata
Viale Giulio Cesare
27
23
Via Fabio Massimo
Via Emilio
Via dei Gracchi
Via Catullo
Via Cola di Rienzo
Via Tibullo
Via Properzio
Via Crescenzio
12
Via Terenzio
20
Via Cancellieri
Via S Pallavicini
Via Plauto
Via Vitelleschi
Via Ombrellari
Via P Castello
Borgo Pio
Largo di Porta Castello
Borgo Sant'Angelo
Piazza Pia
Via in Sassia
Via San Pio X
Piazza Giovanni XXIII
Ponte Vittorio Emanuele II
Ponte Principe Amedeo
Via Acciaioli
Lgt D Sangallo

G

Via Lepanto
Lepanto
Via Duilio
Via degli Scipioni
Via Ezio
Piazza dei Quiriti
Via A Regolo
PRATI
19
Via Cola di Rienzo
14
Via Plinio
Via Boezio
Via Orazio
Via Cassiodoro
Piazza Adriana
Via Alberico II
Giardini di Castel Sant'Angelo
Castel Sant'Angelo
1
Tiber
Ponte Sant'Angelo
Lgt Castello
Lgt della Altoviti
Via Paola
Via del Banco di Santo Spirito
Corso Vittorio Emanuele II

H

Via Marcantonio Colonna
Via Farnese
Via dei Gracchi
Via Cicerone
Via Ennio Quirini Visconti
Via Tacito
21
Via Guiseppe G Belli
Via Crescenzio
Piazza Cavour
Via Triboniano
Lgt Tor di Nona
Via di Panico
Via dei Coronari
PONTE

Vatican City, Borgo & Prati

Continued from p109

The scale of the piazza is dazzling: at its largest it measures 320m by 240m. There are 284 columns and, atop the colonnades, 140 saints. The 25m **obelisk** in the centre was brought to Rome by Caligula from Heliopolis in Egypt and later used by Nero as a turning post for the chariot races in his circus.

Leading off the piazza, the monumental approach road, **Via della Conciliazione**, was commissioned by Mussolini and built between 1936 and 1950.

★ **Vatican Gardens**   GARDENS
(Map p116; ☏ 06 6988 3145; www.museivaticani. va; adult/reduced incl Vatican Museums €34/25, by open-air bus €37/23; ☉ by reservation only; ☐ Piazza del Risorgimento, Ⓜ Ottaviano-San Pietro) Up to a third of the Vatican is covered by the perfectly manicured Vatican Gardens, which contain fortifications, grottoes, monuments, fountains, and the state's tiny heliport and train station. Visits are by guided tour only – either on foot (two hours) or by open-air bus (45 minutes) – for which you'll need to book at least a week in advance.

After the tour you're free to visit the Vatican Museums on your own; admission is included in the ticket price. Children must be aged six or over to take the open-air bus tour.

◉ Monti, Esquilino & San Lorenzo

★ **Museo Nazionale Romano: Palazzo Massimo alle Terme**   MUSEUM
(Map p120; ☏ 06 3996 7700; www.museonazi onaleromano.beniculturali.it; Largo di Villa Peretti 1; adult/reduced €10/2, free 1st Sun of month Oct-Mar; ☉ 9am-7.45pm Tue-Sun, last admission 7pm; Ⓜ Termini) One of Rome's pre-eminent museums, this treasure trove of classical art is a must-see. The ground and 1st floors are devoted to sculpture, with some breathtaking pieces – don't miss *The Boxer*, a 2nd-to-1st-century-BC Greek bronze excavated on the Quirinale Hill in 1885, and the *Dying Niobid*, a 4th-century-BC Greek marble statue. But it's the magnificent and vibrantly coloured Villa Livia and Villa Farnesia frescoes on the 2nd floor that are the undisputed highlight.

The frescoes, which adorned the interior walls of the villas, provide a vivid picture of what a grand ancient Roman villa would have looked like. There are intimate cubicula (bedroom) frescoes focusing on nature, mythology, domestic and erotic life, and delicate landscape paintings from a dark-painted winter triclinium (living and dining area).

Particularly breathtaking are the frescoes from Villa Livia (dating from 30 BC to 20 BC), one of the homes of Augustus' wife Livia Drusilla. These cover an entire room and depict a paradisiacal garden full of a wild tangle of roses, pomegranates, irises and camomile under a deep-blue sky. They once decorated a summer triclinium built half underground to provide protection from the heat.

The 2nd floor also features some exquisitely fine floor mosaics and rare inlay work. That these mosaics carpeted the floors of plush villas of aristocratic Romans in the 13th and 14th centuries is quite extraordinary.

On the 1st floor, there's a fascinating display of bronze fittings from two ships recovered at the bottom of Lake Nemi in Lazio in the 1930s. They had been built by order of Caligula and were used by as floating palaces.

In the basement, the unexciting-sounding coin collection is far more absorbing than you might expect, tracing the Roman Empire's propaganda offensive through its coins. There's also jewellery dating back several millennia, and the disturbing remains of a mummified eight-year-old girl, the only known example of mummification dating from the Roman Empire.

The museum is one of four that collectively make up the Museo Nazionale Romano. A combined ticket (€15/8), which is valid for three days, includes admission to the other three sites: the Terme di Diocleziano, Palazzo Altemps (p96) and the **Crypta Balbi** (Map p100; ☑06 678 01 67; www.museonazionaleromano.beniculturali.it; Via delle Botteghe Oscure 31; adult/reduced €10/5, incl Palazzo Altemps, Terme di Diocleziano & Palazzo Massimo alle Terme €12/6; ⊙9am-7.45pm Tue-Sun; 🚇Via delle Botteghe Oscure). An audio guide costs €5.

Museo Nazionale Romano: Terme di Diocleziano   MUSEUM
(Map p120; ☑06 3996 7700; www.museonazionaleromano.beniculturali.it; Viale Enrico de Nicola 78; adult/reduced €10/5, free 1st Sun of month Oct-Mar; ⊙9am-6.30pm Tue-Sun; 🇲Termini) Able to accommodate some 3000 people, the Terme di Diocleziano was ancient Rome's largest bath complex. Now an epigraphic museum, its exhibits provide a fascinating insight into ancient Roman life, with the highlight being the upstairs exhibition relating to cults. There's also a temporary exhibition area in the massive baths hall and a 16th-century cloister that was built as part of the charterhouse of **Santa Maria degli Angeli e dei Martiri** (☑06 488 08 12; www.santamariadegliangeliroma.it; Piazza della Repubblica; ⊙7.30am-6.30pm Mon-Sat, to 8pm Sun; 🇲Repubblica). The cloister's design was based on drawings by Michelangelo.

Palazzo delle Esposizioni   CULTURAL CENTRE
(Map p106; ☑06 3996 7500; www.palazzoesposizioni.it; Via Nazionale 194; ⊙10am-8pm Tue-Thu

& Sun, to 10.30pm Fri & Sat; 🚇Via Nazionale) This huge neoclassical palace was built in 1882 as an exhibition centre, though it has since served as headquarters for the Italian Communist Party, a mess hall for Allied servicemen, a polling station and even a public loo. Nowadays it's a splendid cultural hub, with cathedral-scale exhibition spaces hosting blockbuster art exhibitions and sleekly designed art labs, as well as an upmarket restaurant (p144) serving dinner and a bargain-priced weekday lunch or weekend brunch buffet beneath a dazzling glass roof.

★**Basilica di Santa Maria Maggiore**   BASILICA
(Map p120; ☑06 6988 6800; Piazza Santa Maria Maggiore; ⊙7am-6.45pm, loggia guided tours 9.30am-5.45pm; 🇲Termini or Cavour) **FREE** One of Rome's four patriarchal basilicas, this 5th-century church stands on Esquiline Hill's summit, on the spot where snow is said to have miraculously fallen in the summer of AD 358. Every year on 5 August the event is recreated during a light show in Piazza Santa Maria Maggiore. Much altered over the centuries, the basilica is an architectural hybrid with 14th-century Romanesque campanile, Renaissance coffered ceiling, 18th-century baroque facade, largely baroque interior and a series of glorious 5th-century mosaics. The exterior fronting Piazza Santa Maria Maggiore is decorated with glimmering 13th-century mosaics that are screened by Ferdinand Fuga's baroque loggia (1741). Rising behind, the campanile – Rome's tallest – tops out at 75m.

The vast interior retains its original structure, despite the basilica's many overhauls. Particularly spectacular are the 5th-century mosaics in the triumphal arch and nave, depicting Old Testament scenes. The central image in the apse, signed by Jacopo Torriti, dates from the 13th century and represents the coronation of the Virgin Mary. Beneath your feet, the nave floor is a fine example of 12th-century Cosmati paving.

The 18th-century baldachin over the high altar is heavy with gilt cherubs; the altar is a porphyry sarcophagus, which is said to contain the relics of St Matthew and other martyrs. A plaque on the floor to the right of the altar marks the spot where Gian Lorenzo Bernini and his father Pietro are buried. Steps lead down to the *confessio* (a crypt in which relics are placed), where a statue of Pope Pius IX kneels before a reliquary that is claimed to contain a fragment of Jesus' manger.

Monti, Esquilino & San Lorenzo

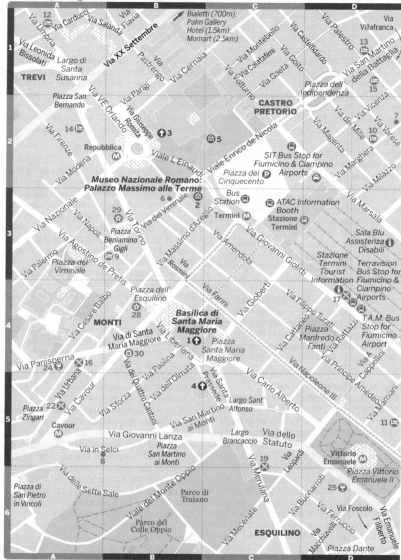

The sumptuously decorated **Cappella Sistina**, last on the right, was built by Domenico Fontana in the 16th century and contains the tombs of Popes Sixtus V and Pius V. Not as sumptuous but far more beautiful is the **Cappella Sforza** on the left, which was designed by Michelangelo.

Guided tours of the **Loggia delle Benedizioni** (upper loggia) were suspended at the time of research. If reinstated, they allow participants a close look at the 13th-century mosaics on the facade, which were created by Filippo Rusuti.

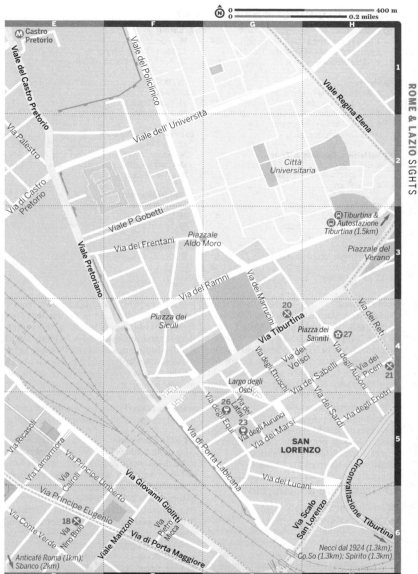

Basilica di San Pietro in Vincoli BASILICA
(Map p82; ☎ 06 9784 4950; Piazza di San Pietro in Vincoli 4a; ⊙ 8am-12.20pm & 3-6.50pm summer, to 5.50pm winter; Ⓜ Cavour) Pilgrims and art lovers flock to this 5th-century basilica for two reasons: to marvel at Michelangelo's colossal *Moses* sculpture (1505) and to see the chains that are said to have bound St Peter when he was imprisoned in the Carcere Mamertino ('in Vincoli' means 'in Chains'). Also of note is a lovely 7th-century mosaic icon of St Sebastian. Access to the church is via a steep flight of steps leading up from Via Cavour and passing under a low arch.

Monti, Esquilino & San Lorenzo

Domus Aurea ARCHAEOLOGICAL SITE
(Golden House; Map p126; ☑06 3996 7700; www.
coopculture.it; Viale della Domus Aurea 1, Parco
del Colle Oppio; adult/reduced €14/10; ☺9.15am-
4.15pm Sat & Sun; Ⓜ Colosseo) Nero had his Domus Aurea constructed after the fire of AD
64 (which he is rumoured to have started to
clear the area). Named after the gold that
lined its facade and interiors, it was a huge
complex covering almost one third of the city.
Making some use of video and virtual reality,
multi-language guided tours of its ruins shed
light on how it would have appeared in its
prime. Advance online reservations (€2) are
obligatory. Enter from Via Labicana.

⊙ Trastevere & Gianicolo

★ **Basilica di Santa
Maria in Trastevere** BASILICA
(Map p124; ☑06 581 48 02; Piazza Santa Maria in
Trastevere, Trastevere; ☺7.30am-9pm Sat-Thu, 9am-
9pm Fri Sep-Jul, 8am-noon & 4-9pm Aug; 🚍Viale di
Trastevere, 🚋Belli) Nestled in a quiet corner of
Trastevere's focal square, this is said to be
the oldest church dedicated to the Virgin
Mary in Rome. In its original form, it dates
from the early 3rd century, but a major 12th-
century makeover saw the addition of a
Romanesque bell tower and a glittering facade. The portico came later, added by Carlo Fontana in 1702. Inside, the 12th-century
mosaics are the headline feature. In the apse,

look out for Christ and his mother flanked
by various saints and, on the far left, Pope
Innocent II holding a model of the church.
Beneath this are six mosaics by Pietro Cavallini illustrating the life of the Virgin (c 1291).

According to legend, the church stands
on the spot where a fountain of oil miraculously sprang from the ground in 32 BC.
It incorporates 24 ancient Roman columns,
some plundered from the Terme di Caracalla, and boasts a 17th-century wooden ceiling.

★ **Villa Farnesina** HISTORIC BUILDING
(Map p100; ☑06 6802 7268; www.villafarnesina.
it; Via della Lungara 230, Trastevere; adult/reduced
€10/9, more when special exhibitions staged;
☺9am-2pm Mon-Sat, to 5pm 2nd Sun of the month;
🚍Lungotevere della Farnesina) The interior of
this gorgeous 16th-century villa is fantastically frescoed from top to bottom. Several
paintings in the **Loggia of Cupid and Psyche** and the **Loggia of Galatea**, both on the
ground floor, are attributed to Raphael. On
the 1st floor, Peruzzi's dazzling frescoes in
the **Salone delle Prospettive** are a superb
illusionary perspective of a colonnade and
panorama of 16th-century Rome.

★ **Galleria Corsini** GALLERY
(Palazzo Corsini; Map p100; ☑ 06 6880 2323; www.
barberinicorsini.org; Via della Lungara 10; adult/
reduced incl Palazzo Barberini €12/6; ☺8.30am-
7pm Wed-Mon; 🚍Lungotevere della Farnesina)

Once home to Queen Christina of Sweden, whose bedroom reputedly witnessed a steady stream of male and female lovers, the 16th-century Palazzo Corsini was designed by Ferdinando Fuga in grand Versailles style, and houses part of Italy's national art collection. Highlights include Caravaggio's *San Giovanni Battista* (St John the Baptist), Guido Reni's *Salome con la Testa di San Giovanni Battista* (Salome with the Head of John the Baptist), and Fra' Angelico's Corsini Triptych, plus works by Rubens, Poussin and Van Dyck.

Orto Botanico   GARDENS
(Botanical Garden; Map p100; ☑06 4991 7107; Largo Cristina di Svezia 24; adult/reduced €8/4; ⊙9am-6.30pm Mon-Sat summer, to 5.30pm winter; ☐Lungotevere della Farnesina, Piazza Trilussa) Formerly the private grounds of Palazzo Corsini, Rome's 12-hectare botanical gardens are a little-known, slightly neglected gem and a great place to unwind in a tree-shaded expanse covering the steep slopes of the Gianicolo. Plants have been cultivated here since the 13th century and the current gardens were established in 1883, when the grounds of Palazzo Corsini were given to the University of Rome. They now contain up to 8000 species, including some of Europe's rarest plants.

Tempietto di Bramante &
Chiesa di San Pietro in Montorio   CHURCH
(Map p124; ☑06 581 3940; www.sanpietro inmontorio.it; Piazza San Pietro in Montorio 2; ⊙chiesa 8.30am-noon & 3-4pm Mon-Fri, tempietto 10am-6pm Tue-Sun; ☐Via Garibaldi) Considered the first great building of the High Renaissance, Bramante's sublime *tempietto* (Little Temple; 1508) is a perfect surprise, squeezed into the courtyard of the Chiesa di San Pietro in Montorio, on the spot where St Peter is said to have been crucified. It's small but perfectly formed; its classically inspired design and ideal proportions epitomise the Renaissance zeitgeist.

Gianicolo   HILL
(Janiculum; ☐115, 870) The verdant hill of Gianicolo (or Janiculum) is dotted by monuments to Garibaldi and his makeshift army, who fought pope-backing French troops in one of the fiercest battles in the struggle for Italian unification on this spot in 1849. The Italian hero is commemorated with a massive monument in Piazzale Giuseppe Garibaldi, while his Brazilian-born wife, Anita, has her own monument about 200m away in Piazzale Anita Garibaldi; she died from malaria, together with their unborn child, shortly after the siege.

★**Basilica di Santa**
Cecilia in Trastevere   BASILICA
(Map p124; ☑06 4549 2739; www.benedettine santacecilia.it; Piazza di Santa Cecilia 22, Trastevere; fresco & crypt each €2.50; ⊙basilica & crypt 10am-12.30pm & 4-6pm Mon-Sat, 11.30am-12.30pm & 4.30-6pm Sun, fresco 10am-12.30pm Mon-Sat, 11.30am-12.30pm Sun; ☐Viale de Trastevere, ☐Belli) The last resting place of

---

STREET ART IN THE SUBURBS

Street art in Rome is edgy, exciting and a fabulous excuse to delve into the city's gritty southern suburbs. Tourist kiosks have maps marked up with key works, and 15 street-art itineraries can be found under 'Itineraries' at www.turismoroma.it.

With over 30 works, ex-industrial Ostiense is one of the best places to enjoy the outdoor gallery of colourful wall murals. Note, however, that these works are ephemeral and many past masterpieces have faded away or been destroyed by development.

Highlights include the fading murals at **Caserma dell'Aeronautica** (Via del Porto Fluviale; Ⓜ Piramide), a former military warehouse where Bolognese artist Blu painted a rainbow of sinister faces in 2014.

The signature stencil art of Italian street artists Sten & Lex is well represented in Ostiense with a B&W mural of an anonymous student at Via delle Conce 14 and the giant *Peassagio Urbano XVIII* (2016) emblazoning the pedestrian entrance to Stazione Roma-Ostiense. Nearby, on Via dei Magazzini Generali, a line-up of larger-than-life portraits by Sten & Lex provide an admiring audience for the iconic *Wall of Fame* by Rome's JBRock.

In 2017, a 19th-century soap factory opened its doors as a gallery, the **Ex Mira Lanza Museum** (☑351 0317563; www.999contemporary.com/exmiralanza; Via Amedeo Avogadro; ⊙24hr; Ⓜ Stazione Trastevere) FREE. This public-art project invited French globe-painter Seth to spruce up the site with a series of large-scale installations and murals. See the website for further information.

Trastevere & Gianicolo

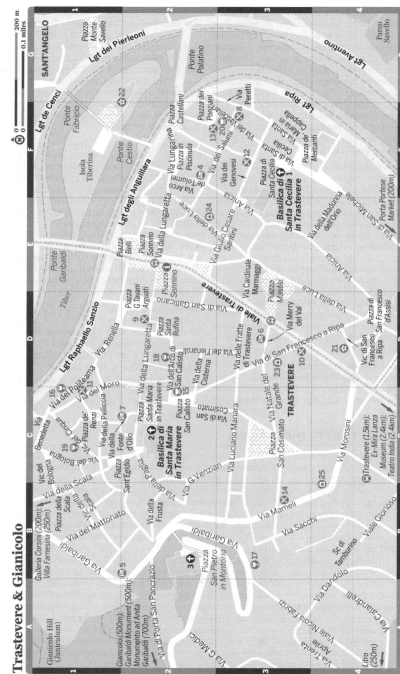

Trastevere & Gianicolo

ROME & LAZIO SIGHTS

the patron saint of music features Pietro Cavallini's exquisite 13th-century fresco in the nuns' choir of the hushed convent adjoining the church. Inside the church itself, Stefano Maderno's mysterious sculpture depicts St Cecilia's miraculously preserved body, unearthed in the Catacombs of San Callisto in 1599. You can also visit the excavations of Roman houses, one of which was possibly Cecilia's. The church is fronted by a gentle fountain surrounded by roses.

⊙ San Giovanni & Testaccio

★**Basilica di San
Giovanni in Laterano** BASILICA
(Map p126; ☑ 06 6988 6493; Piazza di San Giovanni in Laterano 4; basilica free, cloister €5 incl Museo del Tesoro; ⊙ 7am-6.30pm, cloister 9am-6pm; Ⓜ San Giovanni) For a thousand years this monumental cathedral was the most important church in Christendom. Commissioned by the emperor Constantine and consecrated in AD 324, it was the first Christian basilica built in Rome and, until the late 14th century, was the pope's main place of worship. It's still Rome's official cathedral and the pope's seat as the bishop of Rome.

The basilica has been revamped several times, most notably by Borromini in the 17th century, and by Alessandro Galilei, who added the immense white facade in 1735.

This towering structure, surmounted by 15 7m-high statues – Christ, St John the Baptist, John the Evangelist and the 12 Apostles – is an imposing example of late-baroque classicism. The central bronze doors in the porch

were moved here from the Curia in the Roman Forum, while, on the far right, the Holy Door is only opened in Jubilee years.

The cavernous interior owes much of its present look to Francesco Borromini, who refurbished it for the 1650 Jubilee. It's a breathtaking sight with a golden gilt ceiling, a 15th-century mosaic floor, and a wide central nave lined with muscular 4.6m-high sculptures of the apostles.

At the head of the nave, the Gothic baldachin over the papal altar is said to contain the relics of the heads of saints Peter and Paul. In front, a double staircase leads down to the confessio where you'll see a wooden statue of St John the Baptist and the Renaissance tomb of Pope Martin V.

Behind the altar, the massive apse is decorated with sparkling mosaics. Parts of these date from the 4th century, but most were added in the 1800s. To the right of the apse, through a small gift shop, the Museo del Tesoro contains a small collection of religious artefacts and vestments.

At the other end of the basilica, on the first pillar in the right-hand aisle, is an incomplete Giotto fresco. While admiring this, cock your ear towards the next column, where a monument to Pope Sylvester II (r 999–1003) is said to sweat and creak when the death of a pope is imminent.

Outside the church, the beautiful 13th-century cloister, accessible to the left of the altar, is a lovely, peaceful place with graceful twisted columns set around a central garden.

San Giovanni & Celio

San Giovanni & Celio

★ **Basilica di San Clemente**   BASILICA
(Map p126; ☎06 774 00 21; www.basilicasan
clemente.com; Piazza di San Clemente; basilica free,
excavations adult/reduced €10/5; ⊙9am-12.30pm
& 3-6pm Mon-Sat, 12.15-6pm Sun, last entries 30
minutes before closing; 🚇Via Labicana) Nowhere
better illustrates the stages of Rome's turbulent past than this multilayered church. The
ground-level 12th-century basilica sits over
a 4th-century church, which stands over a
2nd-century pagan temple and a 1st-century
Roman house. Beneath everything are foundations dating from the Roman Republic.

The street-level *basilica superiore* features a marvellous 12th-century apse mosaic
depicting the *Trionfo della Croce* (Triumph
of the Cross) and wonderful 15th-century
frescoes by Masolino in the **Cappella di
Santa Caterina** showing a crucifixion scene
and episodes from the life of St Catherine.

Steps lead down to the 4th-century *basilica inferiore,* mostly destroyed by Norman invaders in 1084, but with some faded
11th-century frescoes illustrating the life of St
Clement, a 1st-century bishop who became
the fourth pope in AD 88. Follow the steps
down another level and you'll come to a
1st-century Roman house and a 2nd-century
temple to Mithras, with an altar showing the
god slaying a bull. Beneath it all, you can hear
the eerie sound of a subterranean river flowing through a Republic-era drain.

★ **Terme di Caracalla**   RUINS
(☎06 3996 7700; www.coopculture.it; Viale delle
Terme di Caracalla 52; adult/reduced €8/4, free 1st
Sun of month Oct-Mar; ⊙9am-1hr before sunset
Tue-Sun, 9am-2pm Mon; 🚇Viale delle Terme di Caracalla) The remains of the emperor Caracalla's
vast baths complex are among Rome's most
awe-inspiring ruins. Inaugurated in AD 212,
the original 10-hectare site, which comprised
baths, gyms, libraries, shops and gardens,
was used by up to 8000 people daily. To evoke
what the site would have looked like in its

heyday, hire a virtual reality headset (€7) from the ticket office. The focal point is the central bathhouse, a huge rectangular edifice bookended by two palestre (gyms).

The bathouse was centred on a frigidarium (cold room), where bathers would stop after the warmer tepidarium and dome-capped caldarium (hot room). While the customers enjoyed the luxurious facilities, below ground hundreds of slaves sweated in a 9.5km tunnel network, tending to the complex plumbing systems.The baths remained in continuous use until AD 537, when the Visigoths cut off Rome's water supply. Excavations in the 16th and 17th centuries unearthed important sculptures, many of which found their way into the Farnese family's art collection.

In summer, the ruins are used to stage spectacular music and ballet performances.

Note that the ticket office closes one hour before the site closes.

Basilica di Santa Sabina   BASILICA
(Map p128; ☑ 06 57 94 01; Piazza Pietro d'Illiria 1; ⏰ 7.15am-12.45pm & 3-8pm; ☐ Lungotevere Aventino) This solemn basilica, one of Rome's most beautiful early Christian churches, was founded by Peter of Illyria around AD 422. It was enlarged in the 9th century and again in 1216, just before it was given to the newly founded Dominican order – note the tombstone of Muñoz de Zamora, one of the order's founding fathers, in the nave floor. The interior was further modified by Domenico Fontana in 1587. A 20th-century restoration subsequently returned it to its original look.

Villa del Priorato di Malta   HISTORIC BUILDING
(Villa Magistrale; Map p128; Piazza dei Cavalieri di Malta; ☐ Lungotevere Aventino) Fronting a cypress-shaded piazza, the Roman headquarters of the Sovereign Order of Malta, aka the *Cavalieri di Malta* (Knights of Malta), boasts one of Rome's most celebrated views. It's not immediately apparent, but look through the keyhole in the green door and you'll see the dome of St Peter's Basilica perfectly aligned at the end of a hedge-lined avenue.

👁 Villa Borghese & Northern Rome

★ **Museo e Galleria Borghese**   MUSEUM
(Map p130; ☑ 06 3 28 10; http://galleriaborghese. beniculturali.it; Piazzale del Museo Borghese 5; adult/reduced €13/2 plus €2 booking fee, free some Sundays & every 2nd Wednesday of the month; ⏰ 9am-7pm Tue-Sun; ☐ Via Pinciana) Housing what's often referred to as the 'queen of all private art collections', this gallery has works commissioned and acquired by Cardinal Scipione Borghese (1577–1633). It boasts paintings by Caravaggio, Raphael and Titian, as well as magnificent sculptures by Bernini. Highlights abound, but look for Bernini's *Ratto di Proserpina* (Rape of Proserpina, 1621–22) and Canova's *Venere vincitrice* (Venus Victrix).

Daily admissions are limited, with visitors being admitted at two-hourly intervals – pre-book your tickets well in advance.

Cardinal Borghese was the most knowledgeable and ruthless art collector of his day. He originally housed his collection in the cardinal's residence near St Peter's, but in the 1620s he had it transferred to his new villa just outside Porta Pinciana. And it's here, in the villa's central building, the Casino Borghese, that you'll see it today. Over the centuries, the villa has undergone several overhauls, most notably in the late 1700s when Prince Marcantonio Borghese added much of the lavish neoclassical decor.

The museum is divided into two parts: the ground-floor gallery, with its superb sculptures, intricate Roman floor mosaics and over-the-top frescoes, and the upstairs picture gallery.

Stairs lead up to a portico flanking the grand entrance hall, decorated with 4th-century floor mosaics of fighting gladiators and a 2nd-century *Satiro Combattente* (Fighting Satyr). High on the wall is a bas-relief of a horse and rider falling into the void *(Marco Curzio a Cavallo)* by Pietro Bernini (Gian Lorenzo's father).

The statuesque scene-stealer of Sala I is Antonio Canova's daring depiction of Napoleon's sister, Paolina Bonaparte Borghese, reclining topless as *Venere vincitrice* (1805–08). Further on, in Sala III, Gian Lorenzo Bernini's *Apollo e Dafne* (1622–25), one of a series depicting pagan myths, captures the exact moment Daphne's hands start morphing into leaves. Sala IV is home to Bernini's masterpiece *Ratto di Proserpina*. This flamboyant sculpture brilliantly reveals the artist's virtuosity – just look at Pluto's hand pressing into the seemingly soft flesh of Persephone's thigh.

Caravaggio dominates Sala VIII. Look for his dissipated-looking self-portrait, *Bacchino malato* (Young Sick Bacchus; 1592–95), the strangely beautiful *La Madonna dei Palafrenieri* (Madonna with Serpent; 1605–06) and the much-loved *Giovane col Canestro di Frutta* (Boy with a Basket of Fruit; 1593–95).

Aventino & Testaccio

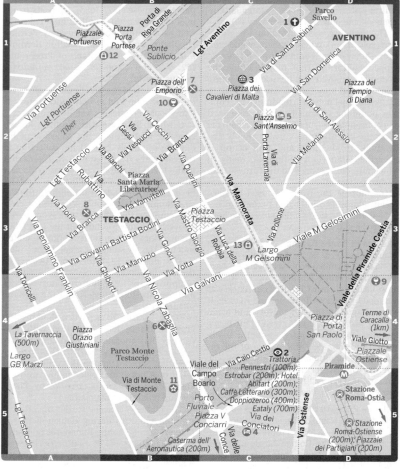

Upstairs, the **pinacoteca** offers a wonderful snapshot of Renaissance art. Don't miss Raphael's extraordinary *La Deposizione di Cristo* (The Deposition; 1507) and his *Dama con liocorno* (Lady with a Unicorn; c1506) in **Sala IX**. In the same room is Fra Bartolomeo's superb *Adorazione del Bambino* (Adoration of the Christ Child; 1495) and Botticelli's *Madonna col Bambino, San Giovannino e angeli* (Virgin and Child with the Infant St John and Angels; c1488).

Other highlights include Lucas Cranach the Elder's *Venere e Amore che reca il favo di miele* (Venus and Cupid Carrying the Honeycomb; 1531) in **Sala X**; Bernini's

self-portraits in **Sala XIV**; and Titian's great masterpiece, *Amor Sacro e Amor Profano* (Sacred and Profane Love; 1514) in **Sala XX**.

Audio guides cost €5 and can be picked up in the basement ticket area, where there is also a coat check and a small cafe.

Villa Borghese PARK
(Map p130; entrances at Piazzale San Paolo del Brasile, Piazzale Flaminio, Via Pinciana, Via Raimondo, Largo Pablo Picasso; ☉ sunrise-sunset; 🚇 Via Pinciana) Locals, lovers, tourists, joggers – no one can resist the lure of Rome's most celebrated park. Originally the 17th-century estate of Cardinal Scipione Borghese, it covers about 80 hectares of wooded glades, gardens

Aventino & Testaccio

and grassy banks. Among its attractions are the landscaped **Giardino del Lago**, **Piazza di Siena**, a dusty arena used for Rome's top equestrian event in May, and a panoramic terrace on the Pincio Hill (p108).

⭐**Museo Nazionale
Etrusco di Villa Giulia** MUSEUM
(Map p130; ☎06 322 65 71; www.villagiulia. beniculturali.it; Piazzale di Villa Giulia 9; adult/ reduced €10/2, free 1st Sun of month Oct-Mar; ◎9am-7.30pm Tue-Sun; 🚊Via delle Belle Arti) Pope Julius III's 16th-century villa provides the often-overlooked but charming setting for Italy's finest collection of Etruscan and pre-Roman treasures. Exhibits, many of which came from tombs in the surrounding Lazio region, range from bronze figurines and black *bucchero* tableware to temple decorations, terracotta vases and a dazzling display of sophisticated jewellery.

⭐**La Galleria Nazionale** GALLERY
(Galleria Nazionale d'Arte Moderna e Contemporanea; Map p130; ☎06 3229 8221; http://lagalle rianazionale.com; Viale delle Belle Arti 131; adult/ reduced €10/5, free 1st Sun of month Oct-Mar; ◎8.30am-7.30pm Tue-Sun; 🚊Piazza Thorvaldsen) 🖉 Housed in a vast belle époque palace, this oft-overlooked modern-art gallery, known locally as GNAM, is an unsung gem. Its superlative collection runs the gamut from neoclassical sculpture to abstract expressionism, with works by many of the most important exponents of 19th- and 20th-century art. There are canvases by the *macchiaioli* (Italian Impressionists) and futurists Boccioni and Balla, as well as sculptures by Canova and major works by Modigliani, de Chirico and Guttuso. International artists represented include Van Gogh, Cézanne, Monet, Klimt, Kandinsky, Mondrian and Man Ray.

An accessible entrance is at Via Antonio Gramsci 71.

MAXXI GALLERY
(Museo Nazionale delle Arti del XXI Secolo; ☎06 320 19 54; www.maxxi.art; Via Guido Reni 4a, Flaminio; adult/reduced €12/9; ◎11am-8pm Tue, Fri & Sat, to 7pm Wed, Thu & Sun; 🚊Viale Tiziano) The Zaha Hadid–designed building that Rome's leading contemporary-art gallery occupies is certainly striking. Formerly a barracks, the curved concrete structure has a multi-layered geometric facade and a cavernous interior full of snaking walkways and suspended staircases. A changing selection of works from the gallery's impressive collection are on display in Gallery 1, but the main drawcards here are the temporary exhibitions, which feature big-name and up-and-coming artists from Italy and around the world. Great cafe and gift shop, too.

👁 Southern Rome

⭐**Via Appia Antica** HISTORIC SITE
(Appian Way; ☎06 513 53 16; www.parcoappiaan tica.it; ◎main site 24hr, individual sites hours vary; 🚌Via Appia Antica) Named after consul Appius Claudius Caecus, who laid the first 90km section in 312 BC, ancient Rome's *regina viarum* (queen of roads) was extended in 190 BC to reach Brindisi. Via Appia Antica has long been one of Rome's most exclusive addresses, a beautiful cobbled thoroughfare flanked by grassy fields, Roman structures and towering pine trees. Most splendid of the ancient houses was Villa dei Quintili (p131), which was so desirable that Emperor Commodus murdered its owner and took it for himself.

The Appian Way has a dark history – it was here that Spartacus and 6000 of his slave rebels were crucified in 71 BC, and the early Christians buried their dead here in 300km of **underground catacombs**. You can't visit all 300km, but three major catacombs – San Callisto (p131), San Sebastiano (p130) and

Villa Borghese

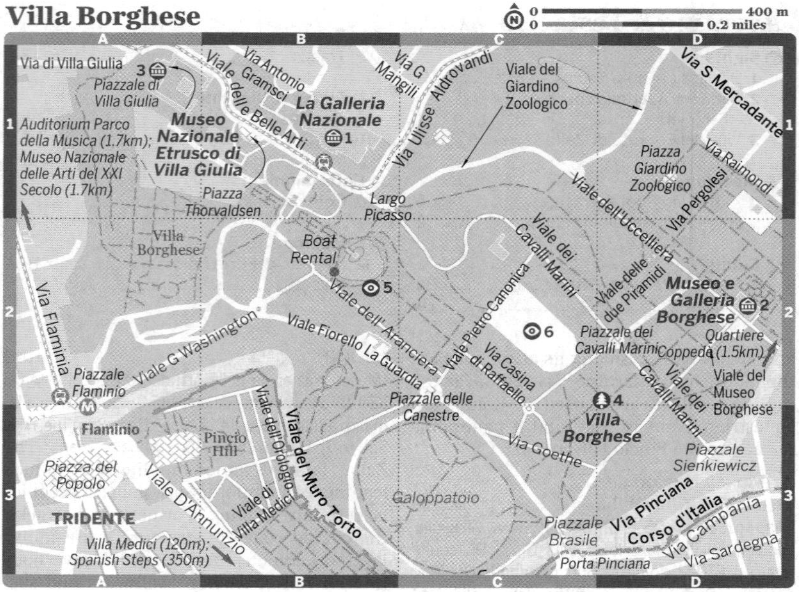

Villa Borghese

Top Sights

Sights

Santa Domitilla (☎06 511 03 42; www.domitilla.info; Via delle Sette Chiese 282; adult/reduced €8/5; ⏰9am-noon & 2-5pm Wed-Mon mid-Jan–mid-Dec) – are open for guided exploration.

The most pleasurable way of exploring the Appian Way is by foot and bicycle. Rent a bike and pick up detailed maps at the **Service Center Appia Antica** (☎06 513 53 16; www.parcoappiaantica.it; Via Appia Antica 58-60; ⏰9.30am-1pm & 2-5pm Mon-Fri, 9.30am-5pm Sat & Sun Nov-Feb, to 6pm Mon-Fri, to 7pm Sat & Sun Mar-Oct; 📶) at the northern end of the road, follow the access road between the centre and the Catacombe di San Callisto and then proceed to the southern stretch of the road with its good longer-distance rides. Alternatively book one of its guided tours by bike, on foot or by electric golf cart.

★**Catacombe di San Sebastiano** CATACOMB

(Map p132; ☎06 785 03 50; www.catacombe.org; Via Appia Antica 136; adult/reduced €8/5; ⏰10am-5pm Mon-Sat, closed late Nov–late Dec; 🚌Via Appia Antica) Extending beneath the **Basilica di San Sebastiano** (www.sansebastianofuorilemura.org; ⏰9am-5.30pm), these underground burial chambers were the first to be called catacombs – derived from the Greek *kata* (near) and *kymbas* (cavity), because they were located near a quarry. Entombments occurred here from the 1st century (including the Apostles Peter and Paul), with mausoleums added in the 2nd century and underground catacombs in the 3rd century. Tours are offered in several languages and last about 45 minutes, with moderate stair climbing.

The 1st level is now almost completely destroyed, but frescoes, stucco work and epigraphs can be seen on the 2nd level. There are three perfectly preserved mausoleums and a plastered wall with hundreds of invocations to Peter and Paul, engraved by worshippers in the 3rd and 4th centuries. There's even a section of pagan Roman tombs.

Above the catacombs, the basilica, a much-altered 4th-century church, preserves one of the arrows allegedly used to kill St Sebastian, and the column to which he was tied. It's also home to the last sculpture created by Gian Lorenzo Bernini, a marble bust of Jesus known as the *Salvator Mundi* (1679).

★**Catacombe di San Callisto** CATACOMB
(Map p132; ☑06 513 01 51; www.catacombe.roma.
it; Via Appia Antica 110-126; adult/reduced €8/5;
☺9am-noon & 2-5pm Thu-Tue, closed late Jan–late
Feb; ☐Via Appia Antica) These are the largest
and busiest of Rome's catacombs. Founded
at the end of the 2nd century and named after Pope Calixtus I, they became the official
cemetery of the newly established Roman
Church. In the 20km of tunnels explored to
date, archaeologists have found the tombs
of 16 popes, 63 martyrs and thousands upon
thousands of Christians. Tours (in English
and many other languages) last about 45
minutes and give a good idea of the seemingly endless corridors stretching underground.

Villa di Massenzio RUINS
(Map p132; ☑06 06 08; www.villadimassenzio.
it; Via Appia Antica 153; ☺10am-4pm Tue-Sun, last
entry 3.30pm; ☐Via Appia Antica) FREE The outstanding feature of Maxentius' enormous
4th-century palace complex is the Circo di
Massenzio, Rome's best-preserved ancient
racetrack. Above the arena are the ruins of
Maxentius' imperial residence. Near the racetrack, the Mausoleo di Romolo was built by
Maxentius for his 17-year-old son Romulus.
Fully seeing the sights will require a pleasant and pastoral stroll through the vast site.
Panels near the entrance have details on the
wildflowers and plants throughout the area.

The villa itself, which is on a hill behind
the Circo, is closed for long-term research;
the rest of the site is open. Entry to this State-
owned site is free – don't feel pressured into
making a donation unless you wish to do so.

★**Villa dei Quintili** RUINS
(☑06 712 91 21; www.coopculture.it; main entrance:
Via Appia Antica 251, east entrance: Via Appia Nuova
1092; adult/reduced incl Mausoleo di Cecilia Metella
valid for 2 days €5/2; ☺9am-1hr before sunset Tue-
Sun; ☐Via Appia Nuova) Towering over green
fields, this 2nd-century villa is one of Rome's
unsung splendours. It was the luxurious
abode of two consuls, the Quintili brothers,
but its splendour was in fact their downfall:
the emperor Commodus had them both
killed, taking over the villa. The ruins are
fabulously impressive. The highlight is the
well-preserved baths complex with a pool,
caldarium (hot bath) and *frigidarium* (cold
bath). The small museum has good exhibits.

Museo Capitoline
Centrale Montemartini MUSEUM
(Museums at Centrale Montemartini; ☑06 06 08;
www.centralemontemartini.org; off Via Ostiense 106;
adult/reduced €7.50/6.50, incl Capitoline Museums

€12.50/10.50, ticket valid 7 days; ☺9am-7pm Tue-
Sun; ☐Via Ostiense) Housed in a former power
station, this bold outpost of the Capitoline
Museums (p94) (Musei Capitolini) juxtaposes classical sculpture with diesel engines and
giant furnaces. The collection's highlights are
in the Sala Caldaia, where ancient statuary
strike poses around the giant furnace. Beautiful pieces include the *Fanciulla Seduta*
(Seated Girl) and *Musa Polimnia* (Muse Pol-
yhymnia), and there are also some exquisite
Roman mosaics, depicting favourite subjects
such as hunting scenes and foodstuffs.

Basilica di San Paolo Fuori le Mura BASILICA
(Basilica of St Paul Outside the Walls; ☑06 6988
0803; www.basilicasanpaolo.org; Piazzale San Paolo
1; cloisters adult/reduced €4/3; ☺7am-6.30pm;
MBasilica San Paolo) The largest church
in Rome after St Peter's (and the world's
third-largest), this vast basilica stands on the
site where St Paul was buried in AD 67. Built
by Constantine in the 4th century, it was
largely destroyed by fire in 1823 and much
of what you see is a 19th-century reconstruction. The echoey results have a modern feel
and draw large groups of pilgrims who are
dwarfed by the huge interior.

Many treasures survived, including the
5th-century triumphal arch, with its heavily
restored mosaics, and the Gothic marble tabernacle over the high altar. This was designed
around 1285 by Arnolfo di Cambio together
with another artist, possibly Pietro Cavallini.
To the right of the altar, the elaborate Romanesque Paschal candlestick was fashioned by
Nicolò di Angelo and Pietro Vassalletto in the
12th century and features a grim cast of an-
imal-headed creatures. The cloisters would
be a wonderful lavender-scented refuge if
they let you sit down (there are no benches
or seats). St Paul's tomb is in the nearby confessio, somewhat lost in the unfortunately
weed-choked grounds.

Looking upwards, doom-mongers should
check out the papal portraits beneath the
nave windows. Every pope since St Peter
is represented here, and legend has it that
when there is no longer room for the next
portrait, the world will fall. Note that there
are only six blank spots left after Francis.

Also well worth a look is the polychromatic 13th-century Cosmati mosaic work
that decorates the columns of the cloisters
of the adjacent Benedictine abbey.

EUR District AREA
(MEUR Palasport) This Orwellian quarter of
wide boulevards and linear buildings was

Via Appia Antica

built for an international exhibition in 1942, and although war intervened and the exhibition never took place, the name stuck – Esposizione Universale di Roma (Roman Universal Exhibition) or EUR. The area's main interest lies in its rationalist architecture, which finds perfect form in the iconic **Palazzo della Civiltà Italiana** (Palace of Italian Civilisation; ☑06 3345 0970; www.fendi.com; Quadrato della Concordia, EUR; ⊙depends on exhibition; ⓂEUR Magliana) FREE, aka the Square Colosseum, where Italian fashion house Fendi has had its global headquarters since 2015.

The sensational modern building is a masterpiece of rationalist architecture with its symmetrical rows of 216 arches and gleaming white travertine marble. For much of its 72-year history – it was completed in 1943 – it remained unoccupied. Fendi regularly has contemporary-art exhibitions in the ground-floor exhibition space of the building; check what's on when you're in town.

Massimiliano and Doriana Fuksas' cutting-edge 2016 **Rome Convention Centre La Nuvola** (☑06 5451 3710; www.romaconventiongroup.it; Viale Asia, entrance cnr Via Cristoforo Colombo,

EUR; ⊙open for exhibitions, fairs & events; ⓂEUR Fermi) – the largest building to open in Rome in half a century – is the most dramatic piece of contemporary architecture. The striking building comprises a transparent, glass-and-steel box (40m high, 70m wide and 175m long) called **Le Theca** ('The Shrine'), inside of which hangs organically shaped **La Nuvola** ('The Cloud') containing an auditorium and conference rooms seating up to 8000 people. A separate black skyscraper called **La Lama** ('The Blade') once contained a hotel that closed shortly after it opened as the entire complex fell into fiscal trouble, but it has now reopened as a Hilton.

While strolling EUR, watch out for artwork honouring the Fascists, which remains decades after their fall.

🍴 Courses

Vino Roma   WINE
(Map p120; ☑328 4874497; www.vinoroma.com; Via in Selci 84g, Esquilino; 2hr tastings per person €50; ⓂCavour) With beautifully appointed century-old cellars and a chic tasting studio, Vino Roma guides both novices and wine enthusiasts in the basics of Italian wine under the knowledgeable stewardship of sommelier Hande Leimer and her expert team.

Divulgazione Lingua Italiana   LANGUAGE
(Map p120; ☑06 446 25 93; www.dilit.it; Via Marghera 22; ⊙8.30am-7pm Mon-Fri) Offers a range of language and cultural courses. Check the website for course dates and prices.

👉 Tours

A Friend in Rome   TOURS
(☑340 5019201; www.afriendinrome.it) Silvia Prosperi and her team offer a range of

private tours, including a popular walking tour around the *centro storico* (historic centre) and tours of the Vatican and Colosseum. Rates start at €165 for a basic three-hour tour (up to eight people); add €55 for every additional hour.

Casa Mia Tours TOURS
(☑346 8001746; www.casamiatours.com; 3hr tour with tastings 1/2/3/4 people €410/450/480/510) Serious food and wine tours, including a Trastevere and Jewish Quarter neighbourhood tour, with tastings and behind-the-scene meetings with shopkeepers, producers, chefs and restaurateurs. Also offers three-hour sommelier-led private **wine tastings** (1/2/3/4 people €440/500/600/680) and five-hour **cooking classes** (2/3/4/5 people €320/450/580/680) suitable for adults and children, beginners and experienced cooks; these include lunch or dinner. Single participants pay for two-person minimum.

GT Food & Travel TOURS
(☑320 7204222; www.gtfoodandtravel.com; tours with tastings per person €130; ◷noon Thu-Tue) Small-group food-lover tours, including a three-hour Food Lover's tour in the *centro storico* and neighbourhood market tours in Testaccio, the Jewish Ghetto and Trionfale near the Vatican. Wine tastings also available.

The Tour Guy TOURS
(☑06 9480 4747; https://thetourguy.com) A professional set-up that organises a wide range of group and private tours. Packages, led by English-speaking experts, include skip-the-line visits to the Vatican Museums and St Peter's Basilica (€60), tours of the Colosseum and Roman Forum (€65), and foodie tours of Trastevere (€90 including dinner). Day trips to Florence and Pompeii also available.

Bici & Baci TOURS
(Map p120; ☑06 482 84 43; www.bicibaci.com; Via del Viminale 5, Esquilino; bike/Vespa tours from €30/120; ◷8am-7pm; Ⓜ Repubblica) Bici & Baci runs a range of daily walking, bike and Segway tours taking in the main historical sites and Via Appia Antica; these are in English or Dutch. Also offers tours on vintage Vespas, classic Fiat 500 cars or funky three-wheeled Ape Calessinos.

☆ Festivals & Events

Easter RELIGIOUS
(◷Mar/Apr) On Good Friday, the pope leads a candlelit procession around the Colosseum. At noon on Easter Sunday he blesses the crowds in St Peter's Square.

Mostra delle Azalee CULTURAL
(Piazza di Spagna; ◷Apr–May; Ⓜ Spagna) Following an 80-year-old tradition, the Spanish Steps are decorated with hundreds of vases of blooming, brightly coloured azaleas from early April to mid-May weather permitting.

Natale di Roma CULTURAL
(www.nataledroma.it; ◷21 Apr) Rome celebrates its birthday with music, processions, historical re-enactments and fireworks. Action is centred on Via dei Fori Imperiali and Circo Massimo.

Primo Maggio MUSIC
(www.primomaggio.net; Piazza di San Giovanni in Laterano; ◷1 May; Ⓜ San Giovanni) Rome's May Day rock concert attracts huge crowds and big-name Italian performers to Piazza di San Giovanni in Laterano.

Estate Romana CULTURAL
(www.estateromana.comune.roma.it; ◷Jun-Sep) Rome's big summer festival involves everything from concerts and dance performances to book fairs, puppet shows and late-night museum openings.

Lungo il Tevere STREET CARNIVAL
(www.lungoiltevereroma.it; ◷mid-Jun–Aug) A summer-long festival, with live music, film screenings, exhibitions, craft stalls and bars, all on the banks of the Tiber between Ponte Sublicio and Ponte Sisto.

Roma Incontra il Mondo MUSIC
(www.villaada.org; Villa Ada; ◷late Jun-Aug; ☑Via Salaria) Villa Ada is transformed into a colourful multi-ethnic village for this popular summer-long event. There's a laid-back party vibe and an excellent program of gigs, ranging from reggae to jazz and world music.

Festa dei Santi Pietro e Paolo RELIGIOUS
(◷29 Jun) Rome celebrates its two patron saints, Peter and Paul, with flower displays on St Peter's Square and festivities near the Basilica di San Paolo Fuori-le-Mura.

Festa de' Noantri CULTURAL
(www.festadenoantri.it; ◷late Jul) Trastevere celebrates its roots with a raucous street party in the last two weeks of July. Events kick off with a religious procession and continue with much eating, drinking, dancing and praying.

Romaeuropa PERFORMING ARTS
(http://romaeuropa.net; ◷mid-Sep–mid-Nov) Top international artists take to stages across town for Rome's autumn festival of theatre, opera and dance.

Festa del Cinema di Roma FILM
(www.romacinemafest.it; Viale Pietro de Coubertin
10, Auditorium Parco della Musica; ☉ late Oct; 🚇 Viale Tiziano) Held at the Auditorium Parco della Musica, Rome's film festival rolls out the
red carpet for big-screen big shots.

🛏 Sleeping

🛏 Ancient Rome

⭐**Residenza Maritti** GUESTHOUSE €€
(Map p82; ☎ 06 678 82 33; www.residenzamaritti.
com; Via Tor Dè Conti 17; s €100, d €130-180, tr €150-
200, q €170-210; ❄🛜; Ⓜ Cavour) With stunning
views over the nearby forums and Vittoriano,
this hidden gem has 13 rooms spread across
three floors. Some are bright and modern
while others are more cosy with antiques,
original tiled floors and family furniture.
There's a fully equipped kitchen and a buffet
breakfast is served in the bistro next door.

⭐**Inn at the
Roman Forum** BOUTIQUE HOTEL €€€
(Map p82; ☎ 06 6919 0970; www.theinnatthero
manforum.com; Via degli Ibernesi 30; d €228-422;
Ⓜ Cavour) Hidden on a quiet backstreet near
the Imperial Forums, this chic boutique
hotel offers five-star service and a refined
contemporary look. Rooms are individually
styled, marrying modern design with timber
beams and Murano chandeliers, while up
top there's a terrace for aperitifs and romantic views. Check out the hotel's own ancient
ruins – a 1st-century BC tunnel complex.

🛏 Centro Storico

⭐**Navona Essence** BOUTIQUE HOTEL €€
(Map p100; ☎ 06 8760 5186; www.navonaessence
hotel.it; Via dei Cappellari 24; d €70-200; ❄🛜;
🚇 Corso Vittorio Emanuele II) Bed down in the
heart of the action at this snug boutique hotel.
Situated on a narrow backstreet near Campo
de' Fiori, it's something of a squeeze but its
location is handy for pretty much everywhere
and its rooms are attractive, sporting a pared-
down modern look and designer bathrooms.

9 Hotel Cesàri HISTORIC HOTEL €€
(Map p100; ☎ 06 674 97 01; www.9-hotel-cesari
-rome.it; Via di Pietra 89a; s €130-170, d €145-280;
❄🛜; 🚇 Via del Corso) This friendly three-star
has been welcoming guests since 1787 and
both Stendhal and Giuseppe Mazzini are
said to have slept here. Modern-day visitors can expect traditionally attired rooms,
a stunning rooftop terrace and a wonderful
central location.

The panoramic terrace bar, which is also
open to nonguests, opens daily in summer
from 6pm to midnight but closes on Sundays and Mondays in winter.

Hotel Navona HOTEL €€
(Map p100; ☎ 06 6821 1392; www.hotelnavona.
com; 2nd fl, Via dei Sediari 8; s €110-170, d €125-
260, q €195-400; ❄🛜; 🚇 Corso del Rinascimento) This well-placed hotel offers a range of
handsome rooms in a 15th-century *palazzo*
near Piazza Navona. The fresh, crisp decor
marries white walls with blond-wood floors,
large padded bedsteads and the occasional ceiling fresco to striking effect. Family
rooms, including a deluxe suite as large as
a mid-size apartment, are also available.
Breakfast costs €10 extra.

Hotel Barrett PENSION €€
(Map p100; ☎ 06 686 8481; www.pensionebarrett.
com; Largo di Torre Argentina 47; s €115-135, d €135-
150, tr €165-175; ❄🛜; 🚇 Largo di Torre Argentina)
This exuberant *pensione* is unique. Boasting
a convenient central location, its decor is fla-
grantly over the top with statues, busts and
vibrant stucco set against a forest of leafy pot
plants. Rooms, which are on the small side,
come with thoughtful extras like foot spas,
coffee machines and fully stocked fridges.

Hotel Mimosa PENSION €€
(Map p100; ☎ 06 6880 1753; www.hotelmimosa.
net; 2nd fl, Via di Santa Chiara 61; s €95-135, d €125-
145, tr €135-175, q €145-185; ❄ @ 🛜; 🚇 Largo di
Torre Argentina) This long-standing *pensione*
makes an excellent central base, offering a
warm welcome and a top location near the
Pantheon. Rooms are spacious and comfortable with jazzy patterned wallpaper, lami-
nated floors and cooling low-key colours.

⭐**Argentina Residenza
Style Hotel** BOUTIQUE HOTEL €€€
(Map p100; ☎ 06 6821 9623; www.argentinaresi
denzastylehotel.com; Via di Torre Argentina 47, 1st
fl; r €180-280; ❄🛜; 🚇 Largo di Torre Argentina)
A prime central location, stellar service
and sleek contemporary design await at
this elegant boutique hotel. Housed in a
former monastery, its 12 individually styled
rooms sport a minimalist white look while
effortlessly incorporating features from the
original building: wood-beamed ceilings,
frescoes and stone door frames. Extras include a popular daily aperitif served in the
timber-beamed breakfast hall.

⭐**Hotel Campo de' Fiori** BOUTIQUE HOTEL €€€
(Map p100; ☎ 06 6880 6865; www.hotelcam
podefiori.com; Via del Biscione 6; r €280-430, apt

€230-350; ❋@🛜; 🚇Corso Vittorio Emanuele II) This rakish four-star has got the lot – enticing boudoir decor, an enviable location off Campo de' Fiori, super-helpful staff and a fabulous panoramic roof terrace. The interior feels delightfully decadent with its boldly coloured walls, low wooden ceilings, gilt mirrors and heavy crimson damask. Also available are 13 apartments, each sleeping two to five people. Rates drop considerably in the low season – check the website for deals.

⭐**Eitch Borromini**   HOTEL €€€
(Map p100; 🌐06 686 14 25; www.eitchborromini. com; Via di Santa Maria dell'Anima 30; r €300-600; ❋🛜; 🚇Corso del Rinascimento) A sense of history pervades this ravishing hotel, housed in a 17th-century *palazzo* designed by Borromini and overlooking Piazza Navona. Rooms are bright and quietly elegant with period furniture, wood-beamed ceilings and even the occasional fresco, and there are dreamy views from two panoramic roof terraces.

🛏 Tridente, Trevi & the Quirinale

La Controra   HOSTEL €
(Map p120; 🌐06 9893 7366; rome@lacontro ra.com; Via Umbria 7; d/tr €110/120; ❋@🛜; Ⓜ Barberini, Ⓜ Repubblica) Quality budget accommodation is thin on the ground in the upmarket area north of Piazza Repubblica, but this great little hostel is a top choice. It has a friendly, laid-back vibe, helpful staff and rooms with private bathrooms; email and ask about the possibility of a dorm bed (€40). Minimum two-night stay.

⭐**Casa Fabbrini: Campo Marzio**   B&B €€
(Map p106; 🌐06 324 37 06; https://campomar zio.casafabbrini.it; Vicolo delle Orsoline 13; r from €155; 🛜; Ⓜ Spagna) There are only four B&B rooms on offer in this 16th-century townhouse secreted in a pedestrianised lane near the Spanish Steps, ensuring an intimate stay. Owner Simone Fabbrini has furnished these with a mix of antiques and contemporary pieces, and the result is quite delightful. Common areas include a mezzanine lounge and a kitchen where breakfast is served.

BDB Luxury Rooms   GUESTHOUSE €€
(Map p106; 🌐06 6821 0020; www.bdbluxury rooms.com; Via Margutta 38; r from €75; ❋🛜; Ⓜ Flaminio) For your own designer pied-à-terre on one of Rome's prettiest and most peaceful pedestrian streets, reserve yourself one of the seven well-equipped rooms on the upper floors (no lift) of this 17th-century *palazzo* on Via Margutta. The ground-floor reception is, in fact, a contemporary art gallery and bold wall art is a prominent feature of the decor. Breakfast costs €10.

Hotel Modigliani   HOTEL €€
(Map p106; 🌐06 4281 5226; www.hotelmodigli ani.com; Via della Purificazione 42; s/d €175/200; ❋🛜; Ⓜ Barberini) Run by Italian writer Marco and musician Giulia, this three-star hotel is all about attention to detail. Twenty-three modern rooms sport a soothing, taupe-and-white palette; all have good bathrooms and some have balconies with superb views. The garden apartments sleep up to six and are great choices for families. Pretty courtyard patio garden too.

Hotel Forte   HISTORIC HOTEL €€
(Map p106; 🌐06 320 76 25; www.hotelforte.com; Via Margutta 61; s & d €200, tr €210; ❋🛜; Ⓜ Spagna) Elegant 18th-century Palazzo Alberto is on one of Rome's prettiest ivy-draped streets, and this three-star hotel within it is a reliable midrange choice for those seeking an old-style Roman ambience (it opened in 1923) and a convenient location. Its 20 rooms are well maintained and comfortable, with satellite TV. Good buffet breakfast.

Hotel Mozart   HOTEL €€
(Map p106; 🌐06 3600 1915; www.hotelmozart.com; Via dei Greci 23b; s €150, d €170-200, tr €200-230; ❋@🛜; Ⓜ Spagna) Ticks all the boxes: its location is central; the classic rooms (some with balcony) are comfortable and well equipped with satellite TV and kettles; the breakfast buffet is generous; and far-better-than-average facilities include a sunny rooftop garden and lounge with fireplace.

⭐**Palazzo Scanderbeg**   BOUTIQUE HOTEL €€€
(Map p106; 🌐06 8952 9001; www.palazzoscan derbeg.com; Piazza Scanderbeg 117; r/ste from €360/1000; ❋🛜; Ⓜ Barberini) Suite hotels are a dime a dozen in central Rome, but few are as attractive and comfortable as this boutique offering in a 15th-century *palazzo* near the Trevi Fountain. All of the guest rooms are spacious and elegantly appointed; suites have kitchens. Enjoy breakfast in the chic breakfast room or have the butler bring it to your room.

Fendi Private Suites   DESIGN HOTEL €€€
(Map p106; 🌐06 9779 8080; www.fendiprivate suites.com; Via della Fontanella di Borghese 48, Palazzo Fendi; ste €950; ❋@🛜; 🚇Via del Corso) Comfortably at home on the 3rd floor of Palazzo Fendi (the Roman fashion house's flagship store is below), this exclusive boutique hotel

ROME & LAZIO SLEEPING

is pure class. Original artworks, photographs of the city snapped by Fendi creative director Karl Lagerfield, Fendi Casa furniture and haute-couture fabrics in soothing greys and blues adorn the seven spacious suites. Dress the part.

Lungarno Collection: Portrait Roma
BOUTIQUE HOTEL €€€

(Map p106; ✆06 6938 0742; www.portraitsuites. com; Via Bocca di Leone 23; ste €670-2800; ❊❋; MFlaminio) As exclusive as Roman accommodation comes, this residence boasts exquisite suites in a townhouse near the Spanish Steps. Interiors evoke the 1950s style and panache of Italian design king Salvatore Ferragamo, and rooms have comforts and gadgets galore; all have a kitchenette and one has its own sauna and mini-gym. The 360-degree city panorama from the roof terrace is exhilarating.

Hotel Locarno
HOTEL €€€

(Map p106; ✆06 361 08 41; www.hotellocarno. com; Via della Penna 22; d €320-440, ste €470-830; ❊❋; MFlaminio) With its stained-glass doors and rattling cage-lift, this 1925 hotel is an art nouveau classic – the kind of place Agatha Christie's famous detective Hercule Poirot might stay if he were in town. Rooms have period furniture, marble bathrooms and vintage charm. The roof garden, wisteria-draped courtyard, restaurant and fin-de-siècle cocktail bar (◷7pm-1am) with wintertime fireplace are major draws.

🛏 Vatican City, Borgo & Prati

Colors Hotel
HOTEL €

(Map p116; ✆06 687 40 30; www.colorshotel.com; Via Boezio 31; s €70-95, d €80-130, q €120-160; ❊@❋; ᄆVia Cola di Rienzo) This welcoming hotel in an elegant four-storey building impresses with its fresh, artful design and clean, colourful rooms. These come in various shapes and sizes, including cheaper ones with shared toilets (sinks and showers in the room). A buffet breakfast is included in some web rates. There's a small rooftop terrace.

Hotel San Pietrino
HOTEL €

(Map p116; ✆06 370 01 32; www.sanpietrino.it; Via Bettolo 43; s €40-70, d €55-80, tr €75-100, q €95-130; ❊❋; MOttaviano-San Pietro) Within easy walking distance of St Peter's Basilica, this family-run *pensione* is an excellent budget choice. Its 11 compact rooms, squeezed into a 3rd-floor apartment (with elevator), are characterful and prettily decorated with terracotta-tiled floors and the occasional statue. It has a good location near cafes.

★Le Stanze di Orazio
BOUTIQUE HOTEL €€

(Map p116; ✆06 3265 2474; www.lestanzedio razio.com; Via Orazio 3; r €80-200; ❊❋; ᄆVia Cola di Rienzo, MLepanto) This five-room boutique hotel makes for an attractive home away from home in the heart of the elegant Prati district, a single metro stop from the Vatican. The rooms have refined decor from a modern colour palette. There are top-end luxuries and well-appointed bathrooms. The breakfast area is small and stylish.

Quod Libet
B&B €€

(Map p116; ✆347 1222642; www.quodlibetro ma.com; 4th fl, Via Barletta 29; r €140-240; ❊❋; MOttaviano-San Pietro) A family-run guesthouse offers four big colourful rooms and a convenient location near Ottaviano-San Pietro metro station. Rooms are spacious with hand-painted bright watercolours and homey furnishings, and it also has a kitchen for guest use plus an elevator. Enjoy breakfast on the large garden terrace. Hosts Gianluca and Connie extend a warm welcome.

★Villa Laetitia
BOUTIQUE HOTEL €€€

(✆06 322 67 76; www.villalaetitia.com; Lungotevere delle Armi 22; r €140-400; ❊❋; ᄆLungotevere delle Armi) Gorgeous Villa Laetitia is in a riverside art nouveau villa. Its 20 rooms and mini apartments, spread over the main building and a separate Garden House, were all individually designed by Anna Venturini Fendi of the famous fashion house. Interiors marry modern design touches with family furniture, vintage pieces and rare finds, such as a framed Picasso scarf in the Garden Room.

🛏 Monti, Esquilino & San Lorenzo

★RomeHello
HOSTEL €

(Map p120; ✆06 9686 0070; https://the romehello.com/; Via Torino 45; dm/r from €15/45; ❊@❋; MRepubblica) ∅ Funnelling all of its profits into worthy social enterprises, this street-art-adorned hostel is the best in the city. It offers 200 beds, a communal kitchen, courtyard, lounge and laundry. Dorms max out at 10 beds (most have four) and have good mattresses and en-suite bathrooms; each bed has a locker, reading light, USB plug and power point.

★Beehive
HOSTEL €

(Map p120; ✆06 4470 4553; www.the-beehive. com; Via Marghera 8; dm from €25, s €70, without bathroom €50, d €100, without bathroom €80; ◷reception 7am-11pm; ❊@❋; MTermini) ∅ More boutique chic than backpacker grungy, this small and stylish hostel has a glorious summer garden and a friendly traveller vibe. Dynamic American owners Linda and Steve exude energy and organise yoga sessions, storytelling evenings and tri-weekly vegetarian and organic dinners around a shared table (€10). Private rooms come with or without bathrooms and air-con; dorms are mixed or female-only.

Meininger Roma Hostel HOSTEL €
(Map p120; ☑06 9480 1352; www.meininger-ho tels.com; Via San Martino della Bataglia 16; dm/s/ tw/tr/f from €17/49/50/63/68; ❋ 🖲; Ⓜ Castro Pretorio) A newcomer to Rome's hostel scene, this family-friendly German-owned place is a different proposition to its party-focused competitors. Rooms have single beds, and dorms – most of which have four beds – have a mix of single beds and bunks; all have excellent bathrooms. Facilities include a communal kitchen, bar, and breakfast room where a generous buffet (€7.90) is served.

Generator Hostel HOSTEL €
(Map p120; ☑06 49 23 30; https://generator hostels.com; Via Principe Amedeo 251; dm/d from €15/40; ❋ @ 🖲; Ⓜ Vittorio Emanuele) Rome is blessed with a number of designer hostels, and this is one of the best. Though small, private rooms are bright and have good bathrooms. Comfortable dorms sleep between three and six. Facilities include a bar and a cafe where breakfast (€5) is served. Sadly, the hostel is located in one of central Rome's least-attractive pockets.

Yellow Hostel HOSTEL €
(Map p120; ☑06 446 35 54; www.the-yellow.com; Via Palestro 51; dm/d €45/130; ❋ @ 🖲; Ⓜ Castro Pretorio) This sharp, 374-bed party hostel offers mixed and female-only dorms (some with en suites), private en-suite rooms, two communal lounges and a clean, well-equipped kitchen. Each dorm bed has a reading light, power point and luggage cage (BYO padlock). The hostel is rapidly colonising the entire street – aka the 'Yellow Square' – with its restaurant, bar, gelateria and bike shop.

★ **66 Imperial Inn** B&B €€
(Map p120; ☑06 4890 7682, 333 3520294; ww w.66imperialinn.com; Via del Viminale 66, 4th fl; d €150, tr & q €210; ❋ 🖲; 🚇 Via Nazionale) A particularly charming B&B, this place on an upstairs floor of an attractive building near Rome's opera house offers five rooms, each named after a colour (or animal in the case of B&W-striped Zebra). All have cable TV, a kettle and a good-sized marble bathroom.

Guests love the complimentary water and bottle of wine. Book ahead.

Hotel Artorius HOTEL €€
(Map p106; ☑06 482 11 96; www.hotelartorius rome.com; Via del Boschetto 13; s/d €140/160; ❋ @ 🖲; Ⓜ Cavour) Let's start with the main draw: location, location, location. But that's not the only reason to stay in this friendly family-run hotel in two buildings on one of Monti's most popular eating, drinking and shopping streets – it also offers neat and comfortable, albeit dated, rooms. Guests enjoy the continental breakfast too.

★ **Villa Spalletti Trivelli** BOUTIQUE HOTEL €€€
(Map p106; ☑06 4890 7934; www.villaspalletti. it; Via Piacenza 4; d/ste from €540/830; ❋ @ 🖲; Ⓜ Repubblica) Furnished with 16th-century tapestries, antique books and original period furnishings, this mansion was built by Gabriella Rasponi, niece of Carolina Bonaparte (Napoleon's sister), and its magnificent salons evoke this illustrious past quite wonderfully. The 14 romantic rooms and suites are elegantly decorated, with excellent bathrooms and amenities. Guests are offered personalised service, a lavish buffet breakfast and complimentary daily *aperitivo*.

🛏 Trastevere & Gianicolo

★ **Relais Le Clarisse** HOTEL €€
(Map p124; ☑06 5833 4437; www.leclarisse trastevere.com; Via Cardinale Merry del Val 20; r €120-200; ❋ 🖲; 🚊 Viale di Trastevere, 🚊 Trastevere/Mastai) Set around a pretty internal courtyard with a gnarled old olive tree, orange trees and a scattering of tables, this is a peaceful 18-room oasis in Trastevere's bustling core. In contrast to the urban mayhem outside, the hotel is all farmhouse charm. Rooms are decorated in rustic style with wrought-iron bedsteads and wood-beamed ceilings. Suites open on to the garden.

★ **Arco del Lauro** GUESTHOUSE €€
(Map p124; ☑06 9784 0350; www.arcodellau ro.it; Via Arco de' Tolomei 27; r €110-145; ❋ @ 🖲; 🚊 Viale di Trastevere, 🚊 Viale di Trastevere) Perfectly placed on a peaceful cobbled lane on the 'quiet side' of Trastevere, this ground-floor guesthouse sports six gleaming white rooms with parquet floors, a modern low-key look and well-equipped bathrooms. Guests share a fridge, a complimentary fruit bowl and cakes. Breakfast (€5) is served in a nearby cafe. Daniele and Lorenzo, who run the place, could not be friendlier or more helpful.

A CONVENT STAY

Many of Rome's religious institutions offer basic, no-frills accommodation. For a bargain Vatican stay, the **Casa di Accoglienza Paolo VI** (Map p116; ☑ 06 390 91 41; www.casapaolosesto.it; Viale Vaticano 92; s/d/tr/q €40/70/90/ 100; ✱ ⬙ ; ▢ Viale Vaticano) is a tranquil, palm-shaded convent near the Vatican Museums. The resident nuns keep everything shipshape and the 30 small, sunny rooms are clean as a pin, if institutional in feel. No breakfast, but there's a fridge and microwave for guests to use plus a small rooftop terrace.

★**Villa Della Fonte**   B&B €€

(Map p124; ☑ 06 580 37 97; www.villafonte.com; Via della Fonte d'Olio 8; s €150-170, d €160-200; ✱ ⬙ ; ▢ Via della Scala) A lovely terracotta-hued, ivy-shrouded gem in a 17th-century town-house, Villa della Fonte is precisely what Rome's *la dolce vita* is about. Five rooms with basic decor, some with original red brick and wood-beam ceilings, are comfortable. The crowning glory is the trio of rooftop gardens, strewn with sun lounges, potted pomegranate trees and fragrant citrus plants.

★**Donna Camilla Savelli Hotel**   HOTEL €€€

(Map p124; ☑ 06 58 88 61; www.hoteldonnacamilla-savelli.com; Via Garibaldi 27; r €200-300; ✱ @ ⬙ ; ▢ Via Garibaldi) It's seldom you can stay in a 16th-century convent designed by baroque genius Borromini. This four-star hotel is exquisitely appointed – muted colours complement the serene concave and convex curves of the architecture – and service is excellent. The best rooms overlook the cloister garden or have views of Rome. Enjoy the roof garden and view with a drink from the bar.

Buonanotte Garibaldi   B&B €€€

(Map p100; ☑ 06 5833 0733; www.buonanotte-garibaldi.com; Via Garibaldi 83; r €210-280; ⊙ reception 9am-7pm; ✱ @ ⬙ ; ▢ Via Garibaldi) With only three rooms in a divinely pretty villa set around a courtyard in Gianicolo, this upmarket B&B is a haven. The rooms – themed Rome (inspired by the magnificent sunsets over Rome as seen from Gianicolo), Chocolate and Tinto – are beautifully decorated. There are works of art and sculpture all over the place; this is artist Luisa Longo's house.

⛺ San Giovanni & Testaccio

★**Althea Inn Roof Terrace**   B&B €

(Map p128; ☑ 339 4353717, 06 9893 2666; www.altheainnroofterrace.com; Via dei Conciatori 9; d €100-120; ✱ ⬙ ; Ⓜ Piramide) In a workaday apartment block near the Aurelian Walls, this friendly B&B offers superb value for money and easy access to Testaccio's bars, clubs and restaurants. Its spacious, light-filled rooms sport a modish look with white walls and tasteful modern furniture, and some also come with their own al fresco terrace.

Hotel Lancelot   HOTEL €€

(Map p126; ☑ 06 7045 0615; www.lancelothotel.com; Via Capo d'Africa 47; s €80-128, d €100-196, f €230-278; ✱ ⬙ ; ▢ Via di San Giovanni in Laterano) A great location near the Colosseum, striking views and super-helpful English-speaking staff – the family-run Lancelot scores across the board. The lobby and communal areas gleam with marble and crystal, while the airy rooms exhibit a more restrained classic style. The best, on the 6th floor, also come with their own terrace. Parking is available on request for €10 per day.

★**Hotel Sant'Anselmo**   BOUTIQUE HOTEL €€€

(Map p128; ☑ 06 57 00 57; www.aventinohotels .com; Piazza Sant'Anselmo 2; s €129-254, d €179-334; ✱ ⬙ ; ▢ Via Marmorata) A ravishing hideaway in the romantic Aventino district. Housed in an elegant villa, its individually decorated rooms are not the biggest but they are stylish, juxtaposing parquet floors, Liberty-style furniture and ornate decorative flourishes with modern touches and contemporary colours. They also come with smartphones that guests are free to use during their stay.

⛺ Villa Borghese & Northern Rome

★**Palm Gallery Hotel**   HOTEL €€

(☑ 06 6478 1859; www.palmgalleryhotel.com; Via delle Alpi 15d; s/d/f from €140/180/250; ✱ ⬙ ; ▢ Via Nomentana, ▢ Viale Regina Margherita) Housed in a 1905 Liberty-style villa, this gorgeous hotel sports an eclectic look that effortlessly blends African and Middle Eastern art with original art deco furniture, exposed brickwork and hand-painted tiles. Rooms are individually decorated, with the best offering views over the wisteria and thick greenery in the surrounding streets. In an adjacent building, a small swimming pool provides a welcome respite from the summer heat.

🛏 Southern Rome

Hotel Abitart
HOTEL €€

(☑06 454 31 91; www.abitarthotel.com; Via Pellegrino Matteucci 10-20; r €120-170; 🖳Via Ostiense, ⓂPiramide) Changing contemporary-art exhibitions by local Roman artists decorate this stylish 66-room hotel in gentrifying Ostiense. Standard rooms are a riot of bright colours, and themed suites evoke different art periods (cubism, 1970s, pop art) and genres (poetry, photography). Pluses include the restaurant-bar Estrobar (☑06 5728 9141; www.estrobar.com; menu €29, meals €35-50; ⊙9am-midnight) with its attractive summertime terrace, and garage parking (€25 per night) next door.

🍴 Eating

This is a city that lives to eat. Food feeds the Roman soul, and a social occasion would be nothing without it. Over recent decades the restaurant scene has become increasingly sophisticated, but traditional no-frills trattorias still provide Rome's most memorable gastronomic experiences. And everywhere, cooking with local, seasonal ingredients remains the norm, as it has been for millennia.

🍴 Ancient Rome

Terre e Domus
LAZIO €€

(Map p82; ☑06 6994 0273; Via Foro Traiano 82-4; meals €30-40; ⊙9.30am-9.30pm Wed-Mon; ✳🖘; 🖳Via dei Fori Imperiali) Staffed by young graduates from a local *scuola alberghiera* (catering college), this slightly scruffy casual eatery is one of the few decent options in the touristy Forum area. With large windows overlooking the Colonna Traiana (p85), it's a relaxed spot to sit down to rustic local staples, all made with locally sourced ingredients, and a glass or two of regional wine.

🍴 Centro Storico

⭐ Forno Roscioli
BAKERY €

(Map p100; ☑06 686 40 45; www.anticoforno roscioli.it; Via dei Chiavari 34; pizza slices from €2, snacks €2.50; ⊙7am-8pm Mon-Sat, 8.30am-6pm Sun; 🖘; 🖳Via Arenula) This is one of Rome's top bakeries, much loved by lunching locals who crowd here for fabulous sliced pizza, delectable pastries and hunger-sating *supplì* (risotto balls). The pizza margherita is superb, if messy to eat, and there's also a counter serving hot pastas and vegetable side dishes. Try to come just before noon to beat the crowds.

I Dolci di Nonna Vincenza
PASTRIES €

(Map p100; ☑06 9259 4322; www.dolcinonna vincenza.it; Via Arco del Monte 98a; pastries from €2.50; ⊙7.30am-8.30pm Mon-Sat, to 8am Sun; 🖳Via Arenula) Bringing the sweet flavours of Sicily to Rome, this pastry shop is a delight. Browse the traditional cakes and tempting *dolci* (sweet pastries) arrayed in the old wooden dressers, before adjourning to the adjacent bar to tear into creamy, flaky, puffy pastries and ricotta-stuffed *cannoli*.

Antico Forno Urbani
BAKERY €

(Map p100; ☑06 689 32 35; Piazza Costaguti 31; pizza slices from €1.50; ⊙7am-2.30pm & 5-7pm Mon-Fri, 7.30am-1.30pm Sat, 9.30am-1pm Sun; 🖳Via Arenula) This Ghetto kosher bakery makes some of the best *pizza al taglio* (sliced pizza) in town. It can get extremely busy, but once you catch a whiff of the yeasty smell it's impossible to resist a quick stop. Everything's good, including its fabulous pizza *con patate* (pizza topped with thin slices of potato).

Gelateria del Teatro
GELATO €

(Map p100; ☑06 4547 4880; www.gelateriadel |teatro.it; Via dei Coronari 65-66; gelato from €3; ⊙10am-11pm; 🖳Via Zanardelli) All the gelato served at this excellent gelateria is prepared on-site – peer through the window and you'll see how. There are numerous flavours, all made from premium seasonal ingredients, ranging from evergreen favourites such as pistachio and hazelnut to inventive creations such as rosemary, honey and lemon.

Caffetteria Chiostro del Bramante
CAFE €

(Map p100; ☑06 6880 9036; www.chiostrodel-bramante.it; Via Arco della Pace 5; meals €15-25; ⊙10am-8pm Mon-Fri, to 9pm Sat & Sun; 🖘; 🖳Corso del Rinascimento) Few cafes are as beautifully located as this one on the 1st floor of Bramante's elegant Renaissance cloisters. With tables above the central courtyard and sofas in a vintage-styled room overlooking Raphael's frescoes in the Chiesa di Santa Maria della Pace, it serves everything from cakes to baguettes, risottos and avocado starters.

⭐ La Ciambella
ITALIAN €€

(Map p100; ☑06 683 29 30; www.la-ciambella. it; Via dell'Arco della Ciambella 20; meals €35-45; ⊙noon-11pm Tue-Sat, to 10pm Sun; 🖳Largo di Torre Argentina) Near the Pantheon but as yet largely undiscovered by the tourist hordes, this friendly restaurant beats much of the local competition. Its light-filled interior is set over the ruins of the Terme di Agrippa, visible through transparent floor panels, an attractive stage for interesting, imaginative food.

★ **Pianostrada** BISTRO €€
(Map p100; 📞06 8957 2296; www.facebook.com/pianostrada; Via delle Zoccolette 22; meals €40-45; ⏱1-4pm & 7pm-midnight Tue-Fri, 10am-midnight Sat & Sun; 🌱; 🚌Via Arenula) This chic contemporary bistro has a dining space adorned with vintage and designer furnishings as well as a lovely rear summer courtyard. Reserve ahead, or settle for a stool at the bar and enjoy views of the talented chefs at work. The cuisine is creative and seasonal, including gourmet open sandwiches, delicate pastas and delectable meat, fish and vegetable mains.

Ba'Ghetto JEWISH €€
(Map p100; 📞06 6889 2868; www.baghetto.com; Via del Portico d'Ottavia 57; meals €30-35; ⏱noon-11pm Mon-Thu & Sun, to 3pm Fri, from 6pm Sat; 🚌Via Arenula) This historic kosher restaurant whips up Roman Jewish fare such as *amatriciana* with beef instead of the classic pork, plus grilled meats and North African offerings including falafel, *burik* (savoury pastries) and couscous. Close by (separated in accordance with Jewish dietary laws), **Ba'Ghetto Milky** specialises in fish- and dairy-based dishes. Both serve the iconic *carciofi alla giudia* (fried whole artichokes).

★ **Emma** PIZZA €€
(Map p100; 📞06 6476 0475; www.emmapizzeria.com; Via del Monte della Farina 28-29; pizzas €8-20, pastas €13-21; ⏱12.30-3pm & 7-11.30pm; 🌱🍴; 🚌Via Arenula) Offering brisk but friendly service, a contemporary vibe and excellent food, Emma is an all-round winner. Sit on the front terrace or in the airy interior to enjoy excellent antipasti, thin-crust pizzas and classic Roman pasta dishes. The quality of ingredients here is top-notch – think buffalo mozzarella from Paestum, organic tomatoes from the slopes of Vesuvius and Cantabrian anchovies. Yum.

Grappolo D'Oro TRATTORIA €€
(Map p100; 📞06 689 70 80; www.hosteriagrappolodoro.it; Piazza della Cancelleria 80; meals €35; ⏱12.30-3pm & 6.30-11pm, closed Wed lunch; 🚌Corso Vittorio Emanuele II) This welcoming modern trattoria stands out among the many lacklustre options around Campo de' Fiori. The emphasis is on updated regional cuisine, so look out for dishes such as pasta with anchovies, *pecorino* and cherry tomatoes, and rich desserts like *zabaglione* spiked with fortified Marsala wine.

Armando al Pantheon TRATTORIA €€
(Map p100; 📞06 6880 3034; www.armandoalpantheon.it; Salita dei Crescenzi 31; meals €35-40;

⏱12.30-3pm Mon-Sat & 7-11pm Mon-Fri; 🚌Largo di Torre Argentina) With its cosy traditional interior and unwavering dedication to old-school Roman cuisine, family-run Armando's is almost as well known as its neighbour, the Pantheon. It's been on the go for nearly 60 years and remains as popular as ever, its cosy interior usually packed with locals and out-of-towners. Reservations essential.

Salumeria Roscioli DELI €€€
(Map p100; 📞06 687 52 87; www.salumeriaroscioli.com; Via dei Giubbonari 21; meals €55-60; ⏱12.30-4pm & 7pm-midnight Mon-Sat, open Sun in Dec; 🚌Via Arenula) The name Roscioli has long been a byword for foodie excellence in Rome, and this deli-restaurant is one of a clutch of venues the family operates near the Campo de' Fiori. The produce here is top-notch and the wine list is marvellous, but the surroundings are cramped and noisy, and the dining experiences is often rushed.

The bar is great for solo diners; couples and larger groups will be happiest sitting in the main hall.

Retrobottega RISTORANTE €€€
(Map p100; 📞06 6813 6310; www.retro-bottega.com; Via della Stelletta 4; à la carte meals €45, 4-/7-course menus €55/75; ⏱6.30-11.30pm Mon, from noon Tue-Sun; 🚌Corso del Rinascimento) Fine dining goes casual at trendy Retrobottega. Here you'll be sitting on a stool at a high communal table or chatting with the chef during plating of dishes at the counter. The food, in keeping with the experimental vibe and contemporary decor, is original and creative Italian.

🍴 Tridente, Trevi & the Quirinale

Fatamorgana Corso GELATO €
(Map p106; 📞06 3265 2238; www.gelateriafatamorgana.com; Via Laurina 10, Tridente; cups & cones €2.50-5; ⏱noon-11pm; Ⓜ Flaminio) Ambrosial flavours abound at this artisanal *gelateria* near the Spanish Steps, all made using the finest seasonal ingredients. There are several other branches around town.

Pompi DESSERTS €
(Map p106; 📞06 2430 4431; www.barpompi.it; Via della Croce 82, Tridente; tiramisu €4; ⏱11am-9.30pm Sun-Thu, to 10.30pm Fri-Sat; Ⓜ Spagna) Now a chain operation, Rome's most famous vendor of tiramisu (which literally means 'pick me up') sells takeaway cartons of the deliciously rich yet light-as-air dessert. As well as the classic version, it serves

CULINARY NEIGHBOURHOODS

Most entrenched in culinary tradition is the Jewish Ghetto (p103), with its hearty Roman-Jewish cuisine. Deep-frying is a staple of *cucina ebraico-romanesca* (Roman-Jewish cooking), which developed between the 16th and 19th centuries when the Jews were confined to the ghetto. To add flavour to their limited ingredients – those spurned by the rich, such as courgette (zucchini) flowers – they began to fry everything from mozzarella to *baccalà* (cod). Particularly addictive are the locally grown artichokes, which are deep-fried to a golden crisp and salted to become *carciofo alla giudia*. By contrast, *carciofo alla romana* (Roman-style artichokes) are stuffed with parsley, mint and garlic, then braised in an aromatic mix of broth and white wine until soft.

For the heart (and liver and brains) of *cucina romana*, head to Testaccio, a traditional working-class district clustered around the city's former slaughterhouse. In the past, butchers who worked in the city abattoir were often paid in cheap cuts of meat as well as money. Neighbourhood staples include *coda alla vaccinara* (braised oxtail), which is cooked for hours to create a rich sauce with tender slivers of meat, and pasta with pajata (veal intestines).

strawberry, pistachio, hazelnut and banana-chocolate. Scoff on the spot (standing) or buy frozen portions to take with you.

Pastificio Guerra   FAST FOOD €
(Map p106; ☑06 679 31 02; Via della Croce 8; pastas €4; ☺1-9.30pm; Ⓜ Spagna) A brilliant budget find, this old-fashioned pasta shop (1918) serves up two choices of pasta from its kitchen hatch. It's fast food, Italian style – freshly cooked (if you time it right) pasta, with a glass of water included. Grab a space to stand and eat between shelves packed with packets of dry pasta or take it away.

★ Piccolo Arancio   TRATTORIA €€
(Map p106; ☑06 678 61 39; www.piccoloarancio.it; Vicolo Scanderbeg 112, Trevi; meals €35-40; ☺noon-3pm & 7pm-midnight Tue-Sun; Ⓜ Barberini) In a 'hood riddled with tourist traps, this backstreet eatery – tucked inside a little house next to grandiose Palazzo Scanderberg – stands out. The kitchen mixes Roman classics with more contemporary options and, unusually, includes a hefty number of seafood choices – the *linguini alla pescatora* (handmade pasta with shellfish and baby tomatoes) and fried fillet of *baccalà* (cod) are sensational.

★ Hostaria Romana   TRATTORIA €€
(Map p106; ☑06 474 52 84; www.hostariaroma na.it; Via del Boccaccio 1, Trevi; meals €40-45; ☺12.30-3pm & 7.15-11pm Mon-Sat; Ⓜ Barberini) Beloved of locals and tourists alike, this bustling place in Trevi is everything an Italian trattoria should be. Order an antipasto or pasta (excellent) and then move onto a main – traditional Roman dishes including *saltimbocca* (pan-fried, prosciutto-wrapped veal escalopes) and *trippa* (tripe) are on offer, as are lots of grilled meats.

★ Colline Emiliane   EMILIAN €€
(Map p106; ☑06 481 75 38; www.collineemiliane. com; Via degli Avignonesi 22, Trevi; meals €45-50; ☺12.45-2.45pm & 7.30-10.45pm Tue-Sat, 12.45-2.45pm Sun; 🛜; Ⓜ Barberini) Serving sensational regional cuisine from Emilia-Romagna, this restaurant has been operated by the Latini family since 1931. Our three recommendations when eating here: start with the *antipasti della casa* (€26 for two persons) and progress to pasta. Seasonal delights include white truffles in winter and fresh porcini mushrooms in spring, but the menu is delectable whatever the season.

★ Il Margutta   VEGETARIAN €€
(Map p106; ☑06 3265 0577; www.ilmargutta.bio; Via Margutta 118, Tridente; lunch buffet weekdays/weekends €15/25, meals €35-40; ☺8.30am-11.30pm; 🖋; Ⓜ Spagna) This chic, art-adorned restaurant is packed at lunchtime with Romans feasting on its good-value buffet deal. Everything on its menu is organic, and vegetables and pulses are combined and presented with care and flair. Among the various tasting menus is a vegan option.

VyTA Enoteca Regionale del Lazio   LAZIO €€
(Map p106; ☑06 8771 6018; www.vytaenote calazio.it/en; Via Frattina 94, Tridente; cicchetti & panini from €3, platters €15, restaurant meals €55-60; ☺9am-midnight Sun-Thu, to 1am Fri & Sat; Ⓜ Spagna) Showcasing food and wine of the Lazio region, this mega-stylish address owes its design to fashionable Roman architect Daniela Colli and its contemporary menu to chef Dino De Bellis. The burnished copper bar is a perfect perch for enjoying *panini* (sandwiches), *cicheti* (snacks) and *taglieri* (cheese and meat plates) – it also

offers a tempting *aperitivo* spread. Up-stairs, a glam restaurant awaits.

Il Chianti TUSCAN €€
(Map p106; 📞06 679 24 70; www.vineriailchianti. com; Via del Lavatore 81-82a, Trevi; pizzas €8-13, taglieri €14, meals €45-50; ⊘noon-3.30pm & 7-11pm; MBarberini) The name says it all: this pretty ivy-clad place specialises in Tuscan-style wine and food. Cosy up inside its bottle-lined interior or grab a table on the lovely street terrace and dig into Tuscan favourites including crostini (toasts with toppings), *taglieri* (platters of cheese and cured meats), hearty soups, handmade pasta and Florence's iconic T-bone steak. Pizzas are available too.

🍴 Vatican City, Borgo & Prati

⭐**Gelateria dei Gracchi** GELATO €
(Map p116; 📞06 321 66 68; www.gelateriadeigracc hi.it; Via dei Gracchi 272, Prati; gelato from €2.50; ⊘noon-midnight; 🚌Piazza Cola Di Rienzo) This is the original location of a small and highly regarded local chain of artisanal *gelaterie*. The proprietors here only use fresh fruit in season, so flavours vary. What stays constant is the quality of their icy delights. Other branches include one at **Via di Ripetta 261** (📞06 322 47 27; Via di Ripetta 261; ⊘11.30-10pm; MFlaminio), near Piazza del Popolo, and at Via di San Pantaleo 61, just off Piazza Navona.

⭐**Panificio Bonci** BAKERY €
(Map p116; 📞06 3973 4457; www.bonci.it; Via Trionfale 36; snacks €2-6; ⊘8.30am-3pm & 5-8.30pm Mon-Thu, 8.30am-8.30pm Fri & Sat; 🍴; 🚌Largo Trionfale) From Gabriele Bonci of the vaunted Bonci Pizzarium, this mellow bakery and deli offers a wide range of splendid takeaway fare, starting with the signature thin and crispy pizza slices. There are sandwiches, wholegrain breads and superb pastries. Seating (there's none) will be your main challenge. Enjoy *panini* stuffed with slow-roasted porchetta (pork) and tangy gorgonzola.

⭐**Fa-Bio** VEGETARIAN €
(Map p116; 📞06 3974 6510; Via Germanico 57-63, Borgo; dishes €5-15; ⊘7am-8pm Mon-Sat, 7.30am-4pm Sun; 🚌Piazza del Risorgimento, MOttaviano-San Pietro) 🌿 Sandwiches, wraps, salads, breakfast bowls, soup and fresh juices are all prepared with speed, skill and fresh locally sourced organic ingredients at this busy place, which is vegan and vegetarian friendly. Locals, Vatican tour guides and in-the-know visitors come here to grab a quick lunchtime bite to eat in or take away.

⭐**Bonci Pizzarium** PIZZA €
(Map p116; 📞06 3974 5416; www.bonci.it; Via della Meloria 43; pizza slices €5; ⊘11am-10pm Mon-Sat; MCipro) Gabriele Bonci's acclaimed *pizzeria a taglio* serves Rome's best pizza by the slice, bar none. Scissor-cut squares of soft, springy base are topped with original combinations of seasonal ingredients and served for immediate consumption. Often jammed, there are only a couple of benches and stools for the tourist hordes; head across to the plaza at the metro station for a seat.

Fatamorgana GELATO €
(Map p116; 📞06 3751 9093; www.gelateriafata morgana.it; Via Leone IV 52; gelato €2.50-5; ⊘noon-11pm summer, to 9pm winter; MOttaviano-San Pietro) The Prati branch of Rome's trendy gelateria chain. As well as all the classic flavours, there are some wonderfully esoteric creations, including a delicious *basilico*, *miele e noci* (basil, honey and hazelnuts), carrot cake, and pineapple and ginger.

Il Sorpasso ITALIAN €€
(Map p116; 📞06 8902 4554; www.sorpasso.info; Via Properzio 31-33; meals €20-35; ⊘7.30am-1am Mon-Fri, 9am-1am Sat; 🛜; 🚌Piazza del Risorgimento) This bar-restaurant hybrid with a vintage cool look – vaulted stone ceilings, exposed brick, rustic wooden tables and summertime outdoor seating – is a Prati hotspot. Open throughout the day, it caters to a fashionable crowd, serving everything from salads and pasta specials to *trapizzini* (pyramids of stuffed pizza), cured meats and cocktails.

Stilelibero ITALIAN €€
(Map p116; 📞06 321 96 57; Via Fabio Massimo 68; meals €30-40; ⊘noon-3pm & 7pm-1am Tue-Sun; 🛜🍴; MLepanto) This eclectic restaurant and bar seamlessly marries fashion, food and cocktails. Italian dishes are playfully revisited, such as *amatriciana*-stuffed *tortello*, while bags and accessories from local designers adorn the walls, doubling as decor. Downstairs, a sleek cocktail bar with a piano serves up drinks and live music till late.

Tordomatto LAZIO €€€
(Map p116; 📞06 6935 2895; www.tordomatto ma.com; Via Pietro Giannone 24; meals €70, tasting menus €70-90; ⊘1-2.30pm Fri-Sun, 7.30-10.45pm Thu-Tue; 🚌Trionfale/Telesio) The dining room is elegant simplicity itself at this Michelin-starred restaurant, which puts the food ahead of fuss. With a corner spot on genteel streets, Tordomatto promises a relaxed evening of fine cuisine. See Michelin-starred chef Adriano Baldassarre and his team in

action by booking the kitchen table well in advance. Look for Roman classics, exquisitely imagined and prepared.

Enoteca La Torre RISTORANTE €€€
(☑06 4566 8304; www.enotecalatorreroma.com; Villa Laetitia, Lungotevere delle Armi 22; fixed-price lunch menu €60, tasting menus €105-130; ⊙12.30-2.30pm Tue-Sat, 7.30-10.30pm Mon-Sat; ☐Lungotevere delle Armi) The romantic art nouveau Villa Laetitia (p136) provides an aristocratic setting for this refined Michelin-starred restaurant. It's a solid member in good standing in Rome's fine-dining scene, and people book weeks in advance. Expect sophisticated contemporary cuisine with seasonal dishes beautifully presented. The wine list is stellar and the service sublime. Many come just to gape at the noted interior dining-room windows.

L'Arcangelo RISTORANTE €€€
(Map p116; ☑06 321 09 92; www.larcangelo.com; Via Giuseppe Gioachino Belli 59, Prati; meals €50, 7-course tasting menu €65; ⊙1-2.30pm Mon-Fri, 8-10.30pm Mon-Sat; ❋🐾; ☐Piazza Cavour) Styled as an informal bistro with wood panelling, leather banquettes and casual table settings, L'Arcangelo enjoys a stellar local reputation. Dishes are modern and creative yet still undeniably Roman in their execution, with an emphasis on seasonal ingredients. A further plus is a well-curated wine list, with better-than-usual choices by the glass. The 3-course lunch menu (€30) is excellent value.

✖ Monti, Esquilino & San Lorenzo

★ Alle Carrette PIZZA €
(Map p82; ☑06 679 27 70; www.facebook.com/allecarrette; Via della Madonna dei Monti 95, Monti; pizza €4.50-8; ⊙11.30am-4pm & 7pm-midnight; ⓜCavour) Authentic pizza, super-thin and swiftly cooked in a wood-fired oven, is what this traditional Roman pizzeria on one of Monti's prettiest streets has done well for decades. Romans pile in here at weekends for good reason – it's cheap, friendly and delicious. All of the classic toppings are available, as well as gourmet choices such as anchovy and zucchini flower.

★ Said DESSERTS €
(Map p120; ☑06 446 92 04; www.said.it; Via Tiburtina 135; praline assortment €8, desserts €8-10; ⊙10am-12.30am Tue-Thu, to 1.30am Fri, noon-1.30am Sat, noon-midnight Sun; 🐾; ☐Reti) Housed in a 1920s chocolate factory, this hybrid cafe-bar, restaurant and boutique

is San Lorenzo's most fashionable address. Its top-quality chocolate can be indulged in here or purchased to take home. Enjoying a coffee, dessert or meal in the urban-chic interior will give you lots of opportunities to people-watch as the place literally heaves at night, particularly on weekends.

★ Panella BAKERY €
(Map p120; ☑06 487 24 35; www.panellaroma.com; Via Merulana 54, Esquilino; hot dish €10-15, foccacia €8-12; ⊙7am-11pm Mon-Thu & Sun, to midnight Fri & Sat; ⓜVittorio Emanuele) Freshly baked pastries, fruit tartlets, *pizza al taglio* (pizza by the slice) and focaccia fill display cases in this famous bakery, and there's also a *tavola calda* ('hot table') where an array of hot dishes is on offer. Order at the counter and eat at bar stools between shelves of gourmet groceries, or sit on the terrace for waiter service.

Zia Rosetta SANDWICHES €
(Map p120; ☑06 3105 2516; www.ziarosetta.com; Via Urbana 54; salads €6-8, panini mini €2-3.50, regular €4.50-7; ⊙11am-4pm Mon-Thu, to 10pm Fri-Sun; ⓜCavour) Grab a pew at a marble-topped table and brace your taste buds for a torturous choice between 25-odd gourmet *panini* and another dozen specials – all creatively stuffed with unexpected combinations, and with catchy names like Amber Queen, Strawberry Hill and Lady Godiva. If you really can't decide, pick a trio of mini *panini*. Freshly squeezed juices (€3.50) too. Glam and gluten-free.

Palazzo del Freddo di Giovanni Fassi GELATO €
(Map p120; ☑06 446 47 40; www.palazzodelfreddo.it; Via Principe Eugenio 65; gelato from €1.60; ⊙noon-10pm Mon-Thu, to midnight Fri & Sat, 10am-11pm Sun; ⓜVittorio Emanuele) Established in 1880, this vast temple to gelato is now operated by the founder's great-grandson, Andrea Fassi. Choose from myriad flavours of gelato, or opt for an iced dessert instead – the *tronchetto* (ice-cream cake), cassata, *Sanpietrino* (a semifreddo of zabaglione, coffee, nuts and chocolate) and *tramezzini* (ice-cream wafer 'sandwiches' filled with *Sanpietro*) deserve special mention.

Aromaticus HEALTH FOOD €
(Map p120; ☑06 488 13 55; www.aromaticus.it; Via Urbana 134; dishes €7-12; ⊙11.30am-9.30pm Tue-Sun; 🐾✏; ⓜCavour) Few addresses exude such a healthy vibe. Set within a shop selling aromatic plants and edible flowers, this inventive little cafe is the perfect place to satisfy cravings for fresh and unadorned food.

Its daily changing menu features creative salads, soups, and dishes suitable for vegans and those who are gluten-free. To drink, order a juice or detox smoothie.

Mercato Centrale   FOOD HALL €

(Map p120; www.mercatocentrale.it/roma; Stazione Termini, Via Giolitti 36; snacks/meals from €3/10; ⊗8am-midnight; 🛜; Ⓜ Termini) A gourmet oasis for hungry travellers at Stazione Termini (p158), this food hall with its vaulted 1930s ceiling hosts stalls selling good-quality fast food and fresh produce. Consider purchasing a *panino* filled with artisanal cheese from **Beppe Giovali**; a slice of focaccia or pizza from **Gabriele Bonci**; or a Chianina burger from **Enrico Lagorio**. Craft beer and wine are also available.

La Barrique   OSTERIA €€

(Map p106; 🖉06 4782 5953; www.facebook.com/la.barrique.94/; Via del Boschetto 41b, Monti; meals €40-45; ⊗1-3pm & 7.30-11pm Mon-Fri, 7.30-11pm Sat; ✳🛜; ⓂCavour) As popular with local residents as it is with tourists, this *osteria* (casual tavern) offers a menu of creative pastas and mains inspired by what's fresh at the local markets; lunch dishes (€10 to €14) offer particularly good value. The interesting wine list is mostly sourced from small producers and includes plenty of natural wines.

Temakinho   SUSHI €€

(Map p82; 🖉06 4201 6656; www.temakinho.com; Via dei Serpenti 16; dishes €8-15; ⊗12.30-3.30pm & 7pm-midnight; 🛜; ⓂCavour) In a city where most food is still resolutely (though deliciously) Italian, this chain of Brazilian-Japanese hybrid restaurants makes for a refreshing change. As well as sushi and ceviche, it serves delicious, strong *caipirinha* cocktails, which combine Brazilian *cachaça*, sugar, lime and fresh fruit; there are also 'sakehinhas' made with sake. It's very popular so book ahead.

Tram Tram   TRATTORIA €€

(Map p120; 🖉06 49 04 16; www.tramtram.it; Via dei Reti 44; meals €35; ⊗noon-3pm & 7-11pm Tue-Sun; 🚉Reti) Taking its name from the trams that rattle by outside, this old-style trattoria is known as a Slow Food hub. A family-run affair, its kitchen mixes classical Roman dishes with seafood from Puglia in Italy's sultry south. Taste sensation *tiella riso, patate e cozze* (baked rice dish with rice, potatoes and mussels) is not to be missed. Book ahead.

Antonello Colonna Open   GASTRONOMY €€€

(Map p106; 🖉06 4782 2641; www.antonellocolonna.it; Via Milano 9a; lunch/brunch €16/30, à la carte meals €80-100; ⊗12.30-3.30pm & 7-11pm

Tue-Sat, 12.30-3.30pm Sun; ✳; Ⓜ Repubblica) Spectacularly set at the back of the Palazzo delle Esposizioni (p119), Antonello Colonna's restaurant lounges dramatically under a dazzling all-glass roof. Cuisine is new Roman – innovative takes on traditional dishes, cooked with wit and flair. On sunny days, dine al fresco on the rooftop terrace. The all-you-can-eat weekday lunch buffet and weekend brunch are cheap but unremarkable.

🗡 Trastevere & Gianicolo

★Fior di Luna   GELATO €

(Map p124; 🖉06 6456 1314; http://fiordiluna.com; Via della Lungaretta 96; gelato from €2.50; ⊗noon-10pm Tue, Thu, Fri & Sun, to 11pm Wed & Sat Sep-May, 1pm-midnight Tue-Sun Jun-Aug; 🚉Belli, 🚉Viale di Trastevere) Many Romans believe that Fior di Luna makes the best handmade gelato and sorbet in the city. Produced in small batches using natural, seasonal ingredients and with the help of a local restaurateur, it serves seasonally driven classics as well as 'gastronomic' inventions such as parmesan and apricot. Also sells *cafe bio* (organic coffee; €1).

Giselda   ITALIAN €

(Map p124; 🖉06 4566 5090; http://giseldaforno roma.com; Viale di Trastevere 52; meals from €9; ⊗7am-11pm; 🛜) The coffee bar at this bright and airy cafe buzzes all day. Grab a table amid the industrial chic and tuck into one of the €6 lunch specials. It's all Italian standards made with care, passion and the best ingredients. The bakery sells pizza slices topped with buttery mortadella that will make you weep. Also good are the pastries and the desserts.

La Renella   BAKERY €

(Map p124; 🖉06 581 72 65; http://larenella.com; Via del Moro 15, Trastevere; pizza slices from €2.50, panini €3-5; ⊗7am-midnight Sun-Thu, to 3am Fri & Sat; 🚉Piazza Trilussa) Watch pizza masters at work at this historic Trastevere bakery. Savour the wood-fired ovens, bar-stool seating and heavenly aromas of pizza, bread (get the *casareccia*, crusty Roman-style bread) and biscuits. Piled-high toppings (and fillings) vary seasonally, to the joy of everyone from punks with big dogs to old ladies with little dogs. It's been in the biz since 1870.

★Trattoria Da Cesare al Casaletto   TRATTORIA €€

(🖉06 53 60 15; www.trattoriadacesare.it; Via del Casaletto 45; meals €30-50; ⊗12.45-3pm & 7.45-11pm Thu-Tue; 🚉Casaletto) Rome's best trattoria? Many think so. This out-of-the-way restaurant is simplicity itself: dozens of tables in a plain interior and a summer-only vine-covered arbour on a vast terrace. The food is rightfully the star – Roman standards prepared with precision, skill and love. To seal the deal, there's a great house wine, and service is efficient and relaxed.

★**La Tavernaccia** TRATTORIA **€€**
(☑06 581 27 92; www.latavernacciaroma.com; Via Giovanni da Castel Bolognese 63; meals €35-40; ☺1-3pm & 7.30-11pm Thu-Tue; ❀; 🚊Stazione Trastevere) This family-run neighbourhood trattoria bustles every minute it's open. The setting is simplicity itself, and the Roman classics that dominate the menu are given stellar treatment (the pastas, eggplant parmigiana and roast suckling pig are all notable). Staff are cheery and helpful.

Da Enzo TRATTORIA **€€**
(Map p124; ☑06 581 22 60; www.daenzoal29.com; Via dei Vascellari 29, Trastevere; meals €30; ☺12.30-3pm & 7.30-11pm Mon-Sat; 🚊Lungotevere Ripa, 🚊Belli) A tiny and staunchly traditional trattoria with a menu featuring all the Roman classics, Da Enzo carefully sources its produce, relying on farms in Lazio. The seasonal, deep-fried Jewish artichokes and the *pasta cacio e pepe* (cheese and black-pepper pasta) are highlights. Expect to wait a while for a table, even if you've booked.

Spirito DiVino ITALIAN **€€**
(Map p124; ☑06 589 66 89; www.ristorantespiritodivino.com; Via dei Genovesi 31; meals €35-45; ☺7pm-midnight Mon-Sat; 🚊Belli) Chef and Slow Food aficionado Eliana Catalani buys ingredients directly from local producers. The restaurant's trademark dish is *maiale alla mazio,* an ancient pork and red-wine stew said to have been a favourite of Caesar. Between courses diners can visit the wine cellar, which dates from 80 BC. Note the ancient columns on the side facade with old Hebrew inscriptions.

Trattoria Da Teo TRATTORIA **€€**
(Map p124; ☑06 581 83 55; www.facebook.com/Trattoria.da.teo; Piazza dei Ponziani 7; meals €35-40; ☺12.30-3pm & 7.30-11.30pm Mon-Sat; 🚊Viale di Trastevere, 🚊Belli) One of Rome's classic trattorias, Da Teo buzzes with locals tucking into steaming platefuls of Roman standards as well as seasonal specials built around products such as artichokes, zucchini flowers, puntarelle (a type of chicory), truffles, porcini mushrooms and *fragoline di bosco* (wild strawberries). More seafood on the menu here than is usual, which is a nice change.

Zia Restaurant FUSION **€€€**
(Map p124; ☑06 2348 8093; www.ziarestaurant.com; Via Goffredo Mameli 45; meals €30-55; ☺7.30-10pm Mon-Wed, 12.30-2pm & 7.30-10pm Thu-Sat; ☎🍴; 🚊Trastevere/Min P Istruzione) After cutting his teeth in the kitchens of a few of the culinary world's most reputable names (think Georges Blanc and Gordon Ramsay), up-and-coming chef Antonio Ziantoni forges out on his own with solo venture Zia. The menu exquisitely mates Italian and French cuisine; pasta stuffed with blue cheese in an onion and clove broth and foie gras macarons shine.

🍴 San Giovanni & Testaccio

★**Sbanco** PIZZA **€**
(☑06 78 93 18; https://sbanco.eatbu.com; Via Siria 1; pizzas €7-13; ☺7.30pm-midnight Tue-Sat, 12.30-11.30pm Sun; 🚊Piazza Zama) With its informal warehouse vibe and buzzing atmosphere, Sbanco is one of the capital's best modern pizzerias. It's made a name for itself with its sumptuous fried starters and inventive, wood-fired pizzas, including a *cacio e pepe* (pecorino cheese and black pepper) pizza baked with ice. To top things off, you can quaff on delicious craft beer.

★**Trapizzino** FAST FOOD **€**
(Map p128; ☑06 4341 9624; www.trapizzino.it; Via Branca 88; trapizzini from €4; ☺noon-1am Tue-Sun; 🚊Via Marmorata) The original of a growing countrywide chain, this is the birthplace of the *trapizzino,* a kind of hybrid sandwich made by stuffing a cone of doughy focaccia with fillers like *polpette al sugo* (meatballs in tomato sauce) or *pollo alla cacciatore* (stewed chicken). They're messy to eat but quite delicious. Eat in or take away; beer and wine available.

There's another branch in the Mercato Centrale, next to Stazione Termini.

Flavio al Velavevodetto TRATTORIA **€€**
(Map p128; ☑06 574 41 94; www.ristorantevelavevodetto.it; Via di Monte Testaccio 97-99; meals €30-35; ☺12.30-3pm & 7.45-11pm; 🚊Via Galvani) This cavernous trattoria is celebrated locally for its earthy, no-nonsense *cucina romana* (Roman cuisine). Antipasti and pastas are very good and the wine list is extremely well priced, but mains and desserts are often disappointing and foreigners are often relegated to the worst tables in the house – if you don't like where you've been seated, ask to move.

✖ Villa Borghese & Northern Rome

★ Neve di Latte   GELATO €

(☑06 320 84 85; www.facebook.com/Nevedilat-teRomaFlaminio; Via Poletti 6, Flaminio; gelato from €2.50; ◔11am-11pm; 🚊 Viale Tiziano) Behind the MAXXI (p129) gallery, opposite the tram terminus, this out-of-the-way *gelateria* may well be the best in Rome. There are few exotic flavours; rather the onus is on the classics, all prepared with high-quality seasonal ingredients. The pistachio, made with nuts from the Sicilian town of Bronte, is particularly delicious. There's another branch on Piazza Cavour in Prati.

★ All'Oro   GASTRONOMY €€€

(☑06 9799 6907; www.ristorantealloro.it; Via Giuseppe Pisanelli 23-25, Flaminio; meals €90, tasting menus €88-150; ◔7-11pm daily, plus 1-2.45pm Sat & Sun; ❄🅿; Ⓜ Flaminio) This Michelin-starred restaurant, in the five-star H'All Tailor Suite hotel, is one of Rome's top fine-dining tickets. At the helm is chef Riccardo Di Giacinto, whose artfully presented food is modern and innovative while still being recognisably Italian. Complementing the cuisine, the decor strikes a contemporary club look with dark-wood ceilings, brass lamps and a fireplace.

★ Metamorfosi   RISTORANTE €€€

(☑06 807 68 39; www.metamorfosiroma.it; Via Giovanni Antonelli 30; tasting menus €100-130; ◔12.30-2.30pm & 8-10.30pm, closed Sat lunch & Sun; 🚊 Via Giovanni Antonelli) This Michelin-starred Parioli restaurant provides one of Rome's best dining experiences, offering international fusion cuisine and a contemporary look that marries linear clean-cut lines with warm earthy tones. Chef Roy Caceres' cooking is eclectic, often featuring playful updates of traditional Roman dishes, such as his signature Uovo 65° carbonara antipasto, a deconstruction of Rome's classic pasta dish.

✖ Southern Rome

★ Doppiozeroo   BISTRO €

(☑06 5730 1961; www.doppiozeroo.com; Via Ostiense 68; cheese & meat platters €10-29, meals €35-40; ◔6pm-2am; 🚊 Via Ostiense, Ⓜ Piramide) This easy-going cafe, restaurant and wine bar hybrid was once a bakery, hence the name ('double zero' is a type of flour). These days it attracts trendy Romans who pile in here to enjoy the famously lavish *aperitivi* buffet (pre-dinner drinks and snacks; 6pm to 9pm), *taglieri* (cheese or meat platters)

at the bar, or dinners in the sleek dining area. Its next-door cafe (7am to 6pm) sells bread, sandwiches and pastries to eat in or take away.

Verde Pistacchio   VEGETARIAN, VEGAN €

(☑06 4547 5965; www.facebook.com/verdepistacchioroma; Via Ostiense 181; meal deals from €5; ◔11am-3pm & 6.30 pm-midnight Mon-Thu, to 1am Thu, 6pm-2am Sat; 🚭🅿; 🚊 Via Ostiense, Ⓜ Garbatella) Camilla, Raffaele and Francesco are the friends behind Green Pistachio, a stylish bistro-cafe with a minimalist, vintage interior and pavement tables. They cook up fantastic vegetarian and vegan cuisine using local produce, and the lunchtime deal is a steal. Lunch here before or after visiting Rome's second-largest church just over the road.

Eataly   FOOD & DRINK

(☑06 9027 9201; www.eataly.net/it_it/negozi/roma; Piazzale XII Ottobre 1492; ◔shops 9am-midnight, restaurants typically noon-3.30pm & 7-11pm; 🚭; Ⓜ Piramide, 🚉 Ostiense) Be prepared for some serious taste-bud titillation in this flash food emporium of gargantuan proportions built in the former terminal for airport buses. Four shop floors showcase every conceivable Italian food product (dried and fresh), while multiple themed food stalls and restaurants offer plenty of opportunity to taste or feast on Italian cuisine.

★ Trattoria Pennestri   LAZIO €€

(☑06 574 24 18; www.facebook.com/Trattoria Pennestri; Via Giovanni da Empoli 5; meals €25-35; ◔7-11pm Tue-Thu, noon-3pm & 7-11pm Fri-Sun; 🅿; Ⓜ Piramide) Headed by a Danish-Italian chef Tommaso Pennestri, this mellow trattoria pays its respects to staunch Roman classics (think carbonara and tripe) but is at its best when dishing out bright, bold comfort food, such as gnocchi tumbled with prawns and *stracciatella* cheese or suckling pig glazed in juniper with apple chutney. Save room for the heavenly chocolate and rosemary mousse.

Qui Nun Se More Mai   LAZIO €€

(☑06 780 39 22; www.facebook.com/qvinunsemoremai; Via Appia Antica 198; meals €35-45; ◔noon-3pm & 7.30-11.45pm Tue-Sat, 12.30-3pm Sun; 🚊 Via Appia Antica) This small, charismatic restaurant in an old stone house has an open fire for grilling, plus a small terrace. The menu offers Roman classics such as pasta *amatriciana* (pig's cheek with onions and tomato), carbonara, *alla gricia* (cured pork and *pecorino* cheese) and *cacio e pepe* (cheese and pepper) – just the thing to set you up for the road ahead.

🍸 Drinking & Nightlife

There's simply no city with better backdrops for a coffee or drink than Rome: you can sip espresso in historic cafes, claim piazza seating for an *aperitivo* (pre-dinner drink and snacks) or wander from wine bar to restaurant to late-night drinking den, getting happily lost down picturesque cobbled streets in the process.

🍷 Ancient Rome

BrewDog Roma CRAFT BEER
(Map p82; ☑ 06 4555 6932; www.brewdog.com/bars/worldwide/roma; ⊗ noon-1am Sun-Thu, to 2am Fri & Sat; Ⓜ Colosseo) Quaff craft beer in the shadow of the Colosseum at this bar by Scottish brewery BrewDog. With its stripped-down grey-and-brick look and up to 20 brews on tap, including IPAs, stouts and pale ales, it's a fine spot to kick back after a day doing the sights.

Terrazza Caffarelli CAFE
(Caffetteria dei Musei Capitolini; Map p82; ☑ 06 6919 0564; Piazzale Caffarelli 4; sandwiches, panini & foccacia from €3; ⊗ 9.30am-7pm; ⬚ Piazza Venezia) On the 2nd floor of the Capitoline Museum (p94) and with a terrace commanding views over the city's domes and rooftops, this cafe has waiter service on the terrace and a cheaper self-service cafeteria inside. You don't need a museum ticket to reach the cafe, which can be accessed from Piazzale Caffarelli as well as from inside the museum itself.

0,75 BAR
(Map p82; ☑ 06 687 57 06; www.075roma.com; Via dei Cerchi 65; ⊗ 11am-2am; 🛜; ⬚ Via dei Cerchi) This welcoming bar overlooking the Circo Massimo is good for a lingering evening drink, an *aperitivo* or casual meal (mains €6 to €17). It's a friendly place with a laid-back vibe, an international crowd, an attractive wood-beamed look and cool tunes.

Cavour 313 WINE BAR
(Map p82; ☑ 06 678 54 96; www.cavour313.it; Via Cavour 313; cheese & meat platters €9-14; ⊗ 12.30-2.45pm daily & 6-11.30pm Mon-Thu, to midnight Fri & Sat, 7-11pm Sun, closed Aug; Ⓜ Cavour) A historic wine bar, Cavour 313 is a snug, wood-panelled retreat frequented by everyone from tourists to actors and politicians. Housed in a *bottega* (artisan's workshop) dating from 1904, it serves a selection of cold cuts and cheeses, as well as daily specials, but the headline act is the wine – there are over 1000 mainly Italian labels to choose from.

🍷 Centro Storico

★ Rimessa Roscioli BISTRO €€€
(Map p100; ☑ 06 6880 3914; www.winetastingrome.com; Via del Conservatorio 58; meals €40-50, tasting menus €42-67; ⊗ 6.30-midnight Mon-Fri, 12.30-3.30pm & 6.30-midnight Sat & Sun; 🛜; ⬚ Lungotevere dei Tebaldi) An offshoot of the Roscioli empire, Rimessa is particularly geared to wine lovers: quality drops from all over Italy and further afield crowd the shelves, and the affable sommeliers really know their craft. The food is equally impressive, *cucina romana* (Roman cuisine) executed with a modern sensibility. Come for a curated wine-and-food tasting or order à la carte.

★ Caffè Sant'Eustachio COFFEE
(Map p100; ☑ 06 6880 2048; www.santeustachioilcaffe.it; Piazza Sant'Eustachio 82; ⊗ 7.30am-1am Sun-Thu, to 1.30am Fri, to 2am Sat; ⬚ Corso del Rinascimento) Always busy, this small and unassuming cafe near the Pantheon serves the best coffee in town. Its secret? Baristas beat the first drops of an espresso with several teaspoons of sugar to create a frothy paste to which they add the rest of the coffee. The result is superbly smooth. Ask for yours '*senza zucchero*' if you don't want sugar.

★ Open Baladin CRAFT BEER
(Map p100; ☑ 06 683 89 89; www.openbaladinroma.it; Via degli Specchi 6; ⊗ noon-2am; 🛜; ⬚ Via Arenula) This modern pub near Campo de' Fiori has long been a leading light in Rome's craft-beer scene, and with 40 beers on tap and up to 100 bottled brews (many from Italian artisanal microbreweries) it's a top place for a pint. As well as great beer, expect burgers (€9 to €18), a laid-back vibe and a young, international crowd.

★ Barnum Cafe BISTRO
(Map p100; ☑ 06 6476 0483; www.barnumcafe.com; Via del Pellegrino 87; breakfast dishes €4-10, meals €30-35; ⊗ 8.30am-4pm & 6pm-1am Mon-Sat; 🛜; ⬚ Corso Vittorio Emanuele II) This on-trend cafe, bistro and cocktail bar hybrid is the sort of place where customers come for a breakfast of muesli and smashed avocado toast accompanied by third-wave coffee and end up returning for pasta lunches, snack-fuelled *aperitivo* hours (6pm to 8pm) and casual dinners. The bartenders and baristas here know their crafts, and the food is all house-made and tasty. Love it.

Club Derrière COCKTAIL BAR
(Map p100; ☑ 329 0452505; www.facebook.com/clubderriereroma; Vicolo delle Coppelle 59;

10pm-4am; 🔊; 🚇 Corso del Rinascimento) Found in the back room of an unassuming trattoria (Osteria delle Coppelle) but accessed through a dedicated entrance, this speakeasy has bartenders who sling sleek cocktails that are often inspired by cultural figures, such as their Edgar Allan Poe: a heady mix of sherry, Knob Creek rye, chocolate and Angostura bitters.

Roscioli Caffè   CAFE
(Map p100; ☑06 8916 5330; www.rosciolicaffe.com; Piazza Benedetto Cairoli 16; ⏱7am-11pm Mon-Sat, 8am-6pm Sun, closed mid-Aug; 🚇Via Arenula) In Rome, the Roscioli name is a guarantee of good things to come: the family runs one of Rome's most celebrated delis (p140) and a hugely popular bakery (p139), and this cafe doesn't disappoint either. The coffee is luxurious and the artfully crafted pastries, petits fours and *panini* taste as good as they look.

La Casa del Caffè Tazza d'Oro   COFFEE
(Map p100; ☑06 678 97 92; www.tazzadorocoffeeshop.com; Via degli Orfani 84-86; ⏱7am-8pm Mon-Sat, 10.30am-7.30pm Sun; 🚇Via del Corso) A busy cafe with 1940s fittings, this is one of Rome's best coffee houses. Its position near the Pantheon makes it touristy but its coffees are brilliant – the espresso hits the mark every time and there's a range of delicious *caffè* concoctions, including *granita di caffè*, a crushed-ice coffee with whipped cream.

Etablì   BAR, CAFE
(Map p100; ☑06 9761 6694; www.etabli.it; Vicolo delle Vacche 9a; ⏱7.30am-1am Sun-Wed, to 2am Thu-Sat; 🔊; 🚇 Corso del Rinascimento) Housed in a 16th-century *palazzo*, Etablì is a rustic-chic lounge bar-restaurant popular for coffee, *aperitivo* or a late-night drink. It's laid-back and good-looking, with Provence-inspired country decor – leather armchairs, rough wooden tables and a fireplace for the winter months. Avoid eating here, though – the quality of the food leaves a lot to be desired.

🍷 Tridente, Trevi & the Quirinale

Zuma Bar   COCKTAIL BAR
(Map p106; ☑06 9926 6622; www.zumarestaurant.com; Via della Fontanella di Borghese 48, Palazzo Fendi; ⏱6pm-1am Sun-Thu, to 2am Fri & Sat; 🔊; 🚇Spagna) Dress up for a drink on the rooftop terrace of Palazzo Fendi of fashion-house fame – few cocktail bars in Rome are as sleek, hip or achingly sophisticated as this. City rooftop views are predictably fabulous;

cocktails mix exciting flavours like shiso with juniper berries, elderflower and prosecco. DJs spin Zuma playlists at weekends.

★ Antico Caffè Greco   CAFE
(Map p106; ☑06 679 17 00; www.facebook.com/AnticoCaffeGreco; Via dei Condotti 86, Tridente; ⏱9am-9pm; 🚇Spagna) Casanova, Goethe, Wagner, Keats, Byron, Shelley and Baudelaire were all regulars at Rome's oldest and most elegant cafe, which opened in 1760. Prices reflect this amazing heritage: pay nearly four times more if you sit at a table rather than stand at the bar. If you opt for the latter, be sure to exit through the elegant interior salons to admire the furnishings.

★ Stravinskij Bar   BAR
(Map p106; ☑06 3288 88 74; www.roccofortehotels.com/hotels-and-resorts/hotel-de-russie; Via del Babuino 9, Hotel de Russie; ⏱9am-1am; 🚇Flaminio) Can't afford to stay at the celeb-magnet Hotel de Russie? Then splash out on a drink at its swish bar. There are sofas inside, but the sunny courtyard is the fashionable choice, with sun-shaded tables overlooked by terraced gardens. In the best *dolce vita* style, it's perfect for a pricey cocktail or beer accompanied by appropriately posh snacks.

Il Palazzetto   COCKTAIL BAR
(Map p106; ☑06 6993 4560; Vicolo del Bottino 8; ⏱noon-8.30pm winter, 4pm-midnight summer, closed in bad weather; 🚇Spagna) Enjoy fine views of the Spanish Steps over an expertly shaken cocktail at this terrace bar. Ride the lift up from the discreet entrance on narrow Vicolo del Bottino or look for stairs leading to the bar from the top of the steps. Given everything is alfresco, the bar is only open in warm, dry weather.

Caffè Ciampini   CAFE
(Map p106; ☑06 678 56 78; www.caffeciampini.com; Viale Trinità dei Monti, Villa Borghese; gelato €7-10; ⏱8am-11pm Mar-Oct; 🚇Spagna) Hidden away a short walk from the top of the Spanish Steps towards the Pincio Hill Gardens (p108), this cafe has a vintage garden-party vibe, with green wooden latticework and orange trees framing its white-clothed tables. There are lovely views over the backstreets behind Spagna, and the gelato – particularly the *tartufo al cioccolato* (chocolate truffle) – is renowned. Serves food too.

Bar Frattina   CAFE
(Map p106; ☑06 679 26 93; www.barfrattina.com; Via Frattina 142; ⏱7am-10pm; 🚇Spagna) Yes, the Spanish Steps offer a primo people-watching opportunity. But so too does the

street-side terrace of this nearby cafe, which has been hugely popular with local workers and residents ever since opening back in the 1950s. Come for coffee or a drink, not to eat.

Vatican City, Borgo & Prati

Sciascia Caffè
CAFE

(Map p116; ☑06 321 15 80; http://sciascia caffe1919.it; Via Fabio Massimo 80/a, Prati; ☺7.30am-8.30pm Mon-Sat, from 8am Sun; Ⓜ Ottaviano-San Pietro) There are several contenders for the best coffee in town, and the *caffè eccellente* served at this polished old-school cafe in Prati, which opened in 1919, is most definitely one of them. The house speciality is velvety smooth espresso served in a delicate cup lined with melted chocolate, but the standard espresso is top-notch, too.

L'Osteria di Birra del Borgo Roma
CRAFT BEER

(Map p116; ☑06 8376 2316; http://osteria.bir radelborgo.it; Via Silla 26, Prati; ☺noon-2am; ☏; Ⓜ Ottaviano-San Pietro) Italy is no longer just about wine: there's a growing demand for locally produced craft beer. Try some of the best at this contemporary brewhouse with its bar area dominated by working vats. There are 24 beers on tap – the popular of which is the house-made Lisa lager – and food choices including pizzas, burgers and ribs (€10 to €18).

Zazie
JUICE BAR

(Map p116; ☑06 6830 0466; www.lazazie.com; Via del Falco 37-38; juice €4-6; ☺9am-7pm Mon-Sat; ☏; Ⓜ Ottaviano-San Pietro) Fresh juices and vegetarian and vegan dishes are the order of the day at this mod juicery – perfect for a post-Vatican pick-me-up. Choose from seasonal fruit and produce, most of it grown in Italy, and staff will create your bespoke juice.

Be.re
CRAFT BEER

(Map p116; ☑06 9442 1854; www.facebook.com/ BeRe-541249312736140/; Piazza del Risorgimento, cnr Via Vespasiano; ☺10am-2am; ⬚Piazza del Risorgimento) With its high vaulted ceilings and narrow pavement tables, this is a good spot for Italian craft beers – there are 23 on tap. And should hunger strike, there's a branch of hit takeaway Trapizzino, right next door, that offers table service at Be.re.

Monti, Esquilino & San Lorenzo

★Blackmarket Hall
COCKTAIL BAR

(Map p120; ☑349 1995295; www.facebook.com/ blackmarkethall/; Via de Ciancaleoni 31; ☺6pm-

ROME AFTER DARK

Night-owl Romans tend to eat late, then drink at bars before heading off to a club at around 1am. Like most cities, Rome is a collection of districts, each with its own character, which is often completely different after dark. The *centro storico* (historic centre) and Trastevere pull in a mix of locals and tourists as night falls. Ostiense and Testaccio are the grittier clubbing districts, with clusters of clubs in a couple of locations – Testaccio has a parade of crowd-pleasing clubs running over the hill of Monte Testaccio. There are also subtle political divisions. San Lorenzo and Pigneto, to the east of central Rome, are popular with a left-leaning, alternative crowd, while areas to the north (such as Ponte Milvio and Parioli) attract a more right-wing, bourgeois milieu.

2am; Ⓜ Cavour) One of Monti's best bars, this multiroomed speakeasy in a former monastery has an eclectic vintage-style decor and plenty of cosy corners where you can enjoy a leisurely, convivial drink. It serves *aperitivo* (€10 to €12 including one drink) between 6pm and 8.30pm and the kitchen stays open until at least midnight. There's also often live jazz – check the Facebook feed for details.

★Ai Tre Scalini
WINE BAR

(Map p82; ☑06 4890 7495; www.facebook.com/ aitrescalini; Via Panisperna 251; ☺noon-2am; Ⓜ Cavour) A firm favourite since 1895, the 'Three Steps' is inevitably packed with young patrons spilling out of its two-room interior and into the street. Its a perfect spot to enjoy an afternoon drink or a simple meal of cheese, salami and home-style mains (including vegan and gluten-free options), washed down with excellent choices of beer or wine by the glass.

★Necci dal 1924
CAFE

(☑06 9760 1552; www.necci1924.com; Via Fanfulla da Lodi 68; ☺8am-1am Sun-Thu, to 2am Fri & Sat; ☏⬚; ⬚Prenestina/Officine Atac) An all-round hybrid in Pigneto, iconic Necci opened as a gelateria in 1924 and later became a favourite drinking destination of film director Pier Paolo Pasolini. These days it caters to a buoyant hipster crowd, offering a laid-back vibe, retro interior and all-day food. Huge kudos for the fabulous summertime terrace, which is very family friendly.

★ La Bottega del Caffè
CAFE

(Map p82; ☑ 06 474 15 78; Piazza Madonna dei Monti 5, Monti; sandwiches & panini €3-6; ☺8am-2am; ☎; Ⓜ Cavour) On one of Rome's prettiest squares in Monti, La Bottega del Caffè – named after a comedy by Carlo Goldoni – is the hotspot in Monti for lingering over excellent coffee, drinks, snacks and lunch or dinner. Heaters in winter ensure balmy alfresco action year-round.

Artisan
CRAFT BEER

(Map p120; ☑ 327 9105709; www.facebook.com/art.isan.90/; Via degli Arunci 9; ☺6pm-1am Sun & Mon, to 2am Tue-Thu, to 3am Fri & Sat; ☒ Reti) A mecca for those who enjoy drinking craft beer, this hipster bar stocks artisanal tipples from around the globe and serves simple but tasty global food too.

Gatsby Café
BAR

(Map p120; ☑ 06 6933 9626; www.facebook.com/gatsbycafe; Piazza Vittorio Emanuele II 106; ☺8am-midnight Sun-Wed, to 1am Thu, to 2am Fri & Sat; Ⓜ Vittorio Emanuele) There's good reason why the friendly bartenders here all wear flat caps, feather-trimmed trilbys and other traditional gents' hats: this fabulous 1950s-styled space with vintage furniture and flashes of geometric wallpaper was originally a milliner's shop called Galleria Venturini. Delicious *spritz*, craft cocktails, gourmet *panini* and *taglieri* (salami and cheese platters) make it a top *aperitivo* spot.

Officina Beat
COCKTAIL BAR

(Map p120; ☑ 06 9521 8779; https://officinebeat.it/; Via degli Equi 29; ☺6pm-1am Sun-Thu, to 2am Fri & Sat; ☎; ☒ Reti) We like Officina's style. A friendly drinking den with tiled floor, vintage furniture and book-lined walls, it focuses on quality craft beers and expertly made cocktails, but also offers good food. Reason alone to head to San Lorenzo.

Co.So
COCKTAIL BAR

(☑ 06 4543 5428; www.facebook.com/COSORO MA; Via Braccio da Montone 80; ☺6.30pm-3am Mon-Sat; ☒ Via Prenestina/Officine Atac) Tiny Co. So (meaning 'Cocktails & Social') was founded by Massimo D'Addezio (a former master mixologist at Hotel de Russie) and is hipster to the hilt. Think Carbonara Sour cocktails (with pork-fat-infused vodka), bubblewrap coasters, and popcorn and M&M bar snacks.

🍷 Trastevere & Gianicolo

★ Terra Satis
CAFE, WINE BAR

(Map p124; ☑ 06 9893 6909; Piazza dei Ponziani 1a, Trastevere; ☺7am-midnight Mon-Fri, from 7.30am Sat; ☎; ☒ Viale di Trastevere, ☒ Belli) This friendly neighbourhood cafe and bar in Trastevere serves great coffee and offers a lavish, predominantly vegetarian *aperitivo* buffet between 6pm and 9pm that costs €10, including a drink, and can easily double as dinner. On warm days the laid-back action spills out from the art-laden interior to a vine-covered terrace on cobbled Piazza di Ponziani. Other snacks include pizzas (€6 to €8) and burgers (€6 to €8), including a vegan version.

★ Bar San Calisto
BAR

(Map p124; Piazza San Calisto 3-5, Trastevere; ☺6am-2am Mon-Sat; ☒ Viale di Trastevere, ☒ Viale di Trastevere) Head to 'Sanca' for its basic, stuck-in-time atmosphere, cheap prices and large terrace. It attracts everyone from intellectuals to people-watching idlers and foreign students. Expect occasional late-night jam sessions. The coffee isn't much good, but the place is famous for its chocolate – come here for hot chocolate with cream in winter, and chocolate gelato in summer.

★ Rivendita Libri, Cioccolata e Vino
COCKTAIL BAR

(Map p124; ☑ 06 5830 1868; www.facebook.com/cioccolateriatrasterevere; Vicolo del Cinque 11a; ☺6.30pm-2am Mon-Fri, 2pm-2am Sat & Sun; ☒ Piazza Trilussa) Think of this as Ground Zero of Rome's recent crackdown on debauched drinking. The drinks of a million hen parties – French Kiss, Orgasm and One Night Stand – highlight the cocktail list. The bar is packed every night from around 10pm with a squealing, drinking-pounding crowd. Some cocktails are served in miniature chocolate cups topped with whipped cream.

Keyhole
COCKTAIL BAR

(Map p124; Via dell'Arco di San Calisto 17; ☺midnight-5am; ☒ Viale di Trastevere, ☒ Belli) This achingly hip, underground speakeasy ticks all the boxes: no identifiable name or signage outside; a black door smothered in keyhole plates; and Prohibition-era decor including chesterfield sofas and dim lighting. Not sure what to order? The mixologists will create your own bespoke cocktail (around €10). No password is required to get into Keyhole, but you need to fill in a form to become a member (€5). No phones.

Pimm's Good
BAR

(Map p100; ☑ 06 9727 7979; www.pimmsgood.it; Via di Santa Dorotea 8; ☺10am-2am; ☎; ☒ Piazza Trilussa) 'Anyone for Pimm's?' is the catchphrase of both the namesake fruity English liqueur and this eternally popular bar. It has a part red-brick ceiling and does indeed serve Pimm's – the classic way or in a variety of cocktails. The lively bartenders are serious mixologists and well-crafted cocktails are their thing. Look for the buzzing street-corner pavement terrace.

Ma Che Siete Venuti a Fà   PUB
(Map p100; ✆06 6456 2046; www.football-pub.com; Via Benedetta 25, Trastevere; ⊙11am-2am; ⬚Piazza Trilussa) Named after a football chant, which translates politely as 'What did you come here for?', this pint-sized Trastevere pub is a beer-buff's paradise, packing in around 15 international craft beers on tap and even more by the bottle.

Il Baretto   BAR
(Map p124; ✆06 589 60 55; Via Garibaldi 27; ⊙7am-2am; ⬚Via Garibaldi) Venture up a steep flight of steps from Trastevere – go on, it's worth it. Because here you'll discover this good-looking cocktail bar where the bass lines are meaty, the bar staff hip, and the interior a mix of vintage and pop art. Better yet, stop here on your way *down* from Gianicolo and have something cold on the tree-shaded terrace.

Freni e Frizioni   BAR
(Map p124; ✆06 4549 7499; www.freniefrizioni.com; Via del Politeama 4, Trastevere; ⊙6.30pm-2am; ⬚Piazza Trilussa) This perennially cool Trastevere bar is housed in an old mechanic's workshop – hence its name ('brakes and clutches') and shabby facade. It draws a young crowd that swells onto the piazza outside to sip well-mixed cocktails and seasonal punches, and fill up on its lavish, complimentary and mainly vegetarian, *aperitivo* buffet (7pm to 10pm). Table reservations essential Friday and Saturday evenings.

🍷 San Giovanni & Testaccio

Wine Concept   WINE BAR
(Map p126; ✆06 7720 6673; www.wineconcept.it; Via Capo d'Africa 21, Celio; ⊙11am-3pm & 6pm-midnight Mon-Fri, 6pm-midnight Sat; 🛜; ⬚Via Labicana) One for wine buffs, this smart *enoteca* (wine bar) is run by expert sommeliers and has an extensive list of Italian regional labels and European vintages, as well as a limited food menu. Wines are available to drink by the glass or to buy by the bottle, and there are also daily tastings (three wines for €15).

Barnaba   WINE BAR
(Map p128; ✆06 2348 4415; www.facebook.com/barnabawinebarecucina; Via della Piramide Cestia 45-51; meal €38; ⊙12.30pm-12.30am; 🛜;

⬚Piramide) Hands-down Testaccio's most sought-out spot after dark, wine bar Barnaba favours natural and independent producers spanning the *bel paese*. It also features an impressive champagne selection and more than 20 wines by the glass. Food depends on how hungry you are: choose upmarket snacks like oysters and crostini with *burrata* cheese and sun-dried tomatoes or filling meat and pasta dishes.

Rec 23   BAR
(Map p128; ✆06 8746 2147; www.rec23.com; Piazza dell'Emporio 2; ⊙6.30pm-2am daily, plus 12.30-3.30pm Sat & Sun; ⬚Via Marmorata) All exposed brick and mismatched furniture, this large, New York–inspired venue caters to all moods, serving *aperitivo* (drink plus buffet €10), restaurant meals and a weekend brunch (€18). Arrive thirsty to take on a 'Testaccio mule', one of its original cocktails, or keep it simple with an Italian prosecco, Scottish whisky or Latin American rum.

🍷 Villa Borghese & Northern Rome

Lanificio 159   CLUB
(✆06 4178 0081; www.lanificio.com; Via Pietralata 159a; ⊙club nights 11pm-4.30am Fri & Sat; ⬚Via Pietralata) Occupying an ex-wool factory in Rome's northeastern suburbs, this cool underground venue hosts live gigs and hot clubbing action, led by top Roman crews and international DJs – check the website for the schedule. The club is part of a larger complex that stages more reserved events such as Sunday markets, exhibitions and *aperitivi*.

🍷 Southern Rome

★ Circolo Illuminati   CLUB
(✆327 7615286; www.circolodegliilluminati.it; Via Giuseppe Libetta 3, Ostiense; ⊙10.30pm-late Wed-Sun; ⬚Garbatella) Tech house, hip-hop, chill music and top DJs rev up clubbers into the night Wednesday to Sunday. Earlier in the evening patrons can enjoy showy cocktails and stylish bites at the onsite **Azienda Cucineria** lounge (kitchen 7pm to midnight Tuesday to Saturday), which has a courtyard garden with potted plants and olive trees.

★ Goa   CLUB
(✆06 574 82 77; www.goaclub.com; Via Giuseppe Libetta 13, Ostiense; ⊙11.30pm-5am Thu-Sat; ⬚Garbatella) At home in a former motorbike-repair shop down a bamboo-lined dead-end alley in post-industrial-style Ostiense, Goa is Rome's

serious super-club with exotic India-inspired decor and international DJs mixing house and techno. Expect a fashion-forward crowd, podium dancers, thumping dance floor, sofas to lounge on and heavies on the door.

Vinile
CLUB

(☑06 5728 8666; www.vinileroma.it; Via Giuseppe Libetta 19; ☻8pm-2am Tue & Wed, to 3am Thu, to 4am Fri & Sat, 12.30-3.30pm & 8pm-2am Sun; ⓜGarbatella) On weekends a mixed bag of Romans hits the dance floor at Vinyl, a buzzing bar and club cooking up food, music and party happenings on the Via Giuseppe Libetta strip. Inside its cavernous interior – with part-vegetal, part-frescoed ceiling – the night starts with an *aperitivo* banquet from 8pm; DJ sets start at 11.30pm. On Sunday students pile in for the unbeatable-value brunch.

☆ Entertainment

Watching the world go by in Rome is often entertainment enough, but there are plenty of organised events to capture your attention too. As well as gigs and concerts in every genre, there are some excellent arts festivals (especially in summer), opera performances with Roman ruins as a backdrop, and football games that bring the city to a standstill.

Classical Music & Opera

★ Auditorium Parco della Musica
CONCERT VENUE

(☑06 8024 1281; www.auditorium.com; Viale Pietro de Coubertin 30; ☻ticket office 11am-6pm Mon-Sat, from 10am Sun Oct-Mar, to 8pm Apr-Sep; ⓠViale Tiziano) The hub of Rome's thriving cultural scene and home to Rome's world-class Orchestra dell'Accademia Nazionale di Santa Cecilia (www.santacecilia.it), the Auditorium Parco della Musica is the capital's premier concert venue. Its three concert halls

offer superb acoustics and, together with a 3000-seat open-air arena, stage everything from classical music concerts to jazz gigs, public lectures and film screenings.

Teatro dell'Opera di Roma
OPERA

(Map p120; ☑06 48 17 55; www.operaroma.it; Piazza Beniamino Gigli 1, Monti; ☻box office 10am-6pm Mon-Sat, 9am-1.30pm Sun; ⓜRepubblica) Rome's premier opera house, aka Teatro Costanzi, boasts a dramatic red-and-gold interior, a Fascist 1920s exterior and an impressive history: it premiered both Puccini's *Tosca* and Mascagni's *Cavalleria rusticana*. Opera and ballet performances are staged between October and June. In July and August, the opera action moves to the Baths of Caracalla.

Terme di Caracalla
OPERA

(www.operaroma.it; Viale delle Terme di Caracalla 52; ☻Jun–early Aug; ⓠViale delle Terme di Caracalla) The hulking ruins of this vast 3rd-century baths complex (p126) set the memorable stage for the Teatro dell'Opera's summer performance season.

Live Music

Caffè Letterario
LIVE MUSIC

(☑06 5730 2842; www.caffeletterarioroma.it; Via Ostiense 95, Ostiense; ☻hours vary; ⓠVia Ostiense, ⓜPiramide) An intellectual hang-out housed in the funky, somewhat underground, post-industrial space of a former garage. It combines designer looks, a bookshop, gallery, co-working space, performance area and lounge bar. There are also occasional live music gigs.

Nuovo Cinema Palazzo
ARTS CENTRE

(Map p120; www.facebook.com/nuovocinemapalazzo; Piazza dei Sanniti 9a, San Lorenzo; ☻hours vary; ⓠVia Tiburtina) Students, artists and activists are breathing new life into San Lorenzo's

---

LGBTQ+ ROME

There is only a smattering of dedicated gay and lesbian clubs and bars in Rome, but the Colosseum end of Via di San Giovanni in Laterano is a favourite hang-out and many clubs host regular gay and lesbian nights. The **Circolo Mario Mieli di Cultura Omosessuale** (☑06 541 39 85, Rainbow Help Line 800 110611; www.mariomieli.org; Via Efeso 2a; ☻11am-6pm Mon-Fri; ⓜBasilica San Paolo) organises social functions. Its website has info and listings of forthcoming events.

Most gay venues (bars, clubs and saunas) require you to have an Arcigay membership card. These cost €10 and are available from the **Arcigay** (☑06 6450 1102, Helpline 800 713713; www.arcigayroma.it; Via Nicola Zabaglia 14; ☻4-8pm Mon-Sat; ⓠVia Marmorata) headquarters in Testaccio or at any venue that requires one.

The biggest LGBTIQ+ event of the year is Gay Village, which runs from June to early September. It attracts crowds of partygoers and an exuberant cast of DJs, musicians and entertainers to Testaccio's bars, cafes and clubs.

former Palace Cinema with a bevy of exciting creative happenings: think film screenings, theatre performances, DJs, concerts, live music, breakdance classes and other arty events. In warm weather, the action spills outside onto the street terrace. Check the Facebook page for event details.

Alexanderplatz
JAZZ

(Map p116; ☑ 06 8377 5604; www.alexander platzjazzclub.com; Via Ostia 9, Trionfale; tickets €15-20 including one drink; ⊙8.30pm-1.30am; ⓂOttaviano-San Pietro) Intimate, underground and hard to find – look for the discreet black door near the corner – Rome's most celebrated jazz club draws top Italian and international performers and a respectful cosmopolitan crowd. Book a table for the best stage views or to dine here, although note that it's the music that's the star act. Performances begin at 9.30pm.

ConteStaccio
LIVE MUSIC

(Map p128; www.facebook.com/contestaccio; Via di Monte Testaccio 65b; ⊙6pm-5am Wed-Sat; ☐Via Galvani) A fixture on Rome's music scene, ConteStaccio is one of the top venues on the Testaccio clubbing strip. It's known for its free gigs, which feature both emerging groups and established performers, spanning a range of styles – indie, pop, rock, acoustic, reggae and new wave. Also serves food.

Gregory's Jazz Club
JAZZ

(Map p106; ☑ 06 679 63 86, WhatsApp messaging 351 645 7888; www.gregorysjazz.com; Via Gregoriana 54, Tridente; obligatory drink €15-20; ⊙7.30pm-2am Tue-Sun; 🛜; ⓂBarberini) If Gregory's were a tone of voice, it'd be husky: unwind over a whisky in the downstairs bar, then unwind some more on squashy sofas upstairs to slinky live jazz and swing, with quality local performers who also like to hang out here.

Big Mama
BLUES

(Map p124; ☑ 06 581 25 51; www.bigmama.it; Vicolo di San Francesco a Ripa 18, Trastevere; ⊙9pm-1.30am, shows 10.30pm, closed summer; ☐Viale di Trastevere, ☐Trastevere/Mastai) Head to this cramped basement for a mellow night of Eternal City blues. A long-standing venue, it also stages jazz, funk, soul and R&B acts, as well as popular cover bands.

Charity Café
LIVE MUSIC

(Map p82; ☑ 06 4782 5881; www.charitycafe.it; Via Panisperna 68, Monti; ⊙6.30pm-2am Tue-Sun; ⓂCavour) Think narrow space, spindly tables, dim lighting and a laid-back vibe: this is a place to snuggle down and listen to some live jazz, soul or blues. It's civilised, relaxed,

---

ⓘ TICKETS

Tickets for concerts, live music and theatrical performances are widely available across the city. Prices range enormously depending on the venue and artist. Hotels can often reserve tickets for guests, or you can contact the venue or organisation directly – check listings publications for booking details. Otherwise you can try the following:

Vivaticket (☑892 234; www.vivaticket.it)

Orbis Servizi (Box Office Lazio; Map p120; ☑06 482 79 15; www.boxofficelazio. it; Piazza dell'Esquilino 37; ⊙10am-7.30pm Mon-Fri, to 1pm Sat; ⓂTermini) Opposite Basilica di Santa Maria del Maggiore.

---

untouristy and very Monti. Gigs usually take place from 9pm or 10pm; on Sundays there's an open buffet and live music from 6.30pm to 9pm. Check the website to see who's performing. It's closed on Sundays in summer.

Cinema

Isola del Cinema
OUTDOOR CINEMA

(Map p124; ☑06 9021 4524; www.isoladelcinema. com; Piazza San Bartolomeo all'Isola, Isola Tiberina; ⊙mid-Jun–Sep) Running from mid-June to September in conjunction with the riverside Lungo il Tevere festival, the Isola Tiberina sets the stage for a season of outdoor cinema, featuring Italian and international films, some shown in their original language. There are also meetings with actors and directors, masterclasses and film-related events.

Theatre

Teatro Argentina
THEATRE

(Map p100; ☑box office 06 68400 0314; www.te atrodiroma.net; Largo di Torre Argentina 52; ⊙box office 10am-7pm Tue-Sun; ☐Largo di Torre Argentina) Founded in 1732, Rome's top theatre is one of three managed by the Teatro di Roma, along with the **Teatro India** (☑06 8775 2210; Lungotevere Vittorio Gassman 1, Portuense; ⊙box office open before performances; ☐Stazione Trastevere) and Teatro di Villa Torlonia. Rossini's *Barber of Seville* premiered here in 1816, and these days it stages a wide-ranging program of classic and contemporary drama (mostly in Italian), plus dance and classical music.

Sport

Stadio Olimpico
STADIUM

(☑06 3685 7563; Viale dei Gladiatori 2, Foro Italico; ☐Lungotevere Maresciallo Cadorna) A trip to Rome's impressive Stadio Olimpico offers an unforgettable insight into Rome's sporting heart. Throughout the football season (late August to May) there's a game on most Thursdays and Sundays featuring one of the city's two Serie A teams (AS Roma or Lazio), and during the Six Nations rugby tournament (February to March) it hosts Italy's home games. Tickets can be bought at Lottomatica (lottery centres), the stadium, ticket agencies, www.listicket.it or one of the many Roma or Lazio stores around the city.

🔒 Shopping

Rome has a huge and diverse array of specialist shops, fashion boutiques and artisans' workshops, with a particularly impressive portfolio of food, clothing and accessory boutiques. Many of these businesses are family owned, having been passed down through the generations. Others have grown from their modest origins into global brands known for their classic designs and quality workmanship.

🔒 Centro Storico

Marta Ray   SHOES
(Map p100; ☑06 6880 2641; www.martaray.it; Via dei Coronari 121; ⊙10am-8pm; 🚇Via Zanardelli) Women's ballet flats and elegant, everyday bags in rainbow colours and super-soft leather are the hallmarks of the Rome-born Marta Ray brand. At this store, one of three in town, you'll find a selection of trademark ballerinas as well as ankle boots and an attractive line in modern, beautifully designed handbags.

★Salumeria Roscioli   FOOD & DRINKS
(Map p100; ☑06 687 52 87; www.salumeriaroscioli.com; Via dei Giubbonari 21; ⊙8.30am-8.30pm Mon-Sat; 🚇Via Arenula) Rome's most celebrated deli showcases a spectacular smörgåsbord of prize products ranging from cured hams and cheeses to conserves, dried pastas, olive oils, aged balsamic vinegars and wines. Alongside celebrated Italian fare you'll also find top international foodstuffs such as French cheese, Iberian ham and Scottish salmon.

★Confetteria Moriondo
& Gariglio   CHOCOLATE
(Map p100; ☑06 699 08 56; Via del Piè di Marmo 21-22; ⊙9am-7.30pm Mon-Sat; 🚇Via del Corso) Roman poet Trilussa was so smitten with this chocolate shop – established by the Torinese confectioners to the royal house of Savoy – that he was moved to mention it in verse. And we agree: it's a gem. Decorated like an elegant tearoom, it specialises in handmade chocolates and confections such as marrons glacés, many prepared according to original 19th-century recipes.

Ibiz – Artigianato
in Cuoio   FASHION & ACCESSORIES
(Map p100; ☑06 6830 7297; www.ibizroma.it; Via dei Chiavari 39; ⊙10am-7.30pm Mon-Sat; 🚇Corso Vittorio Emanuele II) In her diminutive family workshop, Elisa Nepi and her team craft beautiful butter-soft leather wallets, bags, belts, keyrings and sandals in elegant designs and myriad colours. You can pick up a belt for about €39, while for a shoulder bag you should bank on around €165.

Bartolucci   TOYS
(Map p100; ☑06 6919 0894; www.bartolucci.com; Via dei Pastini 96-99; ⊙10am-10pm; 🚇Via del Corso) It's difficult to resist going into this magical toyshop where everything is carved out of wood. By the main entrance, a Pinocchio pedals his bike robotically, perhaps dreaming of the full-size motorbike parked nearby, while inside there is all manner of ticking clocks, rocking horses, planes and more Pinocchios than you're likely to see in your whole life.

🔒 Tridente, Trevi & the Quirinale

Chiara Baschieri   CLOTHING
(Map p106; ☑333 6364851; www.chiarabaschieri.it; Via Margutta, cnr Vicolo Orto di Napoli, Tridente; ⊙3.30-7.30pm Mon, from 11am Tue-Sat; 🚇Spagna) An independent Roman designer, Chiara Baschieri sells age-neutral clothing, featuring quality fabrics, from her small boutique located on one of Rome's most attractive streets.

★Bomba   CLOTHING
(Map p106; ☑06 361 28 81; www.cristinabomba.com; Via dell'Oca 39, Tridente; ⊙11am-7.30pm Tue-Sat, from 3.30pm Mon; 🚇Flaminia) Opened by designer Cristina Bomba over four decades ago, this gorgeous boutique is now operated by her fashion-designing children Caterina (womenswear) and Michele (menswear). Using the highest-quality fabrics, their creations are tailored in the next-door atelier (peek through the front window); woollens are produced at a factory just outside the city. Pricey but oh so worth it.

★Gente   FASHION & ACCESSORIES
(Map p106; ☑06 320 76 71; www.genteroma.com; Via del Babuino 77, Tridente; ⊙10.30am-7.30pm Mon-Thu, to 8pm Fri & Sat, 11.30am-7.30pm Sun; 🚇Spagna) This multilabel boutique was the first in Rome to bring all the big-name luxury

designers – Italian, French and otherwise – under one roof and its vast emporium-styled space remains an essential stop for every serious fashionista. Labels include Dolce & Gabbana, Prada, Alexander McQueen, Sergio Rossi and Missoni.

★ **Fausto Santini** SHOES
(Map p106; ☑ 06 678 41 14; www.faustosantini. com; Via Frattina 120; ☺10am-7.30pm Mon-Sat, 11am-2pm & 3-7pm Sun; Ⓜ Spagna) Rome's best-known shoe designer, Fausto Santini is famous for his beguilingly simple, architectural shoe designs, realised in boots and shoes made with butter-soft leather. Colours are beautiful, and the quality is impeccable. Seek out the end-of-line discount shop (Map p120; ☑ 06 488 09 34; Via Cavour 106; ☺10am-1pm & 3.30-7.30pm Mon-Fri, 10am-1pm & 3.30-7.30pm Sat; Ⓜ Cavour) in Monti to source a bargain – its stock is regularly refreshed.

Federico Buccellati JEWELLERY
(Map p106; ☑ 06 679 03 29; www.facebook.com/ federico-buccellati-orafo-311172238241; Via dei Condotti 31, Tridente; ☺10am-1.30pm & 3-7pm Tue-Fri, 10am-1.30pm & 2-6pm Sat, 3-7pm Mon; Ⓜ Spagna) Run today by the third generation of one of Italy's most prestigious silver- and goldsmiths, this historical shop opened in 1926. Everything is handcrafted and often delicately engraved with decorative flowers, leaves and nature-inspired motifs. Don't miss the Silver Salon on the 1st floor showcasing some original silverware and jewellery pieces by grandfather Mario.

Artisanal Cornucopia CONCEPT STORE
(Map p106; ☑342 8714597; www.artisanalcornu-copia.com; Via dell'Oca 38a; ☺10.30am-1.30pm & 3-7.30pm Mon-Sat; Ⓜ Flaminio) One of several stylish boutiques on Via dell'Oca, Elif Sallorenzo's chic concept store showcases exclusive handmade pieces by Italian designers alongside her own clothing designs and objects from around the globe. There are loads of bags, shoes, candles, jewellery pieces, homewares and other objects to covet.

Fendi FASHION & ACCESSORIES
(Map p106; ☑ 06 3345 0890; www.fendi.com; Largo Carlo Goldoni 420, Palazzo Fendi; ☺10am-7.30pm Mon-Sat, from 10.30am Sun; Ⓜ Spagna) With travertine walls, stunning contemporary art and sweeping red-marble staircase, the flagship store of Rome's iconic fashion house inside 18th-century Palazzo Fendi is dazzling. Born in Rome in 1925 as a leather and fur workshop on Via del Plebiscit, this luxurious temple to Roman fashion is as much concept store as *maison* selling ready-to-wear clothing for men and women.

La Bottega del Marmoraro ART
(Map p106; ☑ 06 320 76 60; Via Margutta 53b; ☺8am-7.30pm Mon-Sat; Ⓜ Flaminio) Watch *marmoraro* (marble artist) Sandro Fiorentini chip away in this atelier filled with his decorative marble plaques engraved with various inscriptions: *la dolce vita, la vita e bella* (life is beautiful) etc. Plaques start at €10 and Sandro will engrave any inscription you like (from €15).

🏛 Vatican City, Borgo & Prati

★ **Paciotti** FOOD & DRINKS
(Map p116; ☑ 06 3973 3646; www.paciotti salumeria.it; Via Marcantonio Bragadin 51-53; ☺7.30am-8.30pm Mon-Wed, Fri & Sat, 12.30-8.30pm Thu; Ⓜ Cipro) This family-run deli is a fantasyland of Italian edibles. Whole prosciutto hams hang in profusion. Cheeses, olive oil, dried pasta, balsamic vinegar, wine and truffle pâtés crowd the shelves, and can be bubbled-wrapped and vacuum-sealed for travel. Patriarch Antonio Paciotti and his three affable sons merrily advise customers in both Italian and English.

Il Sellaio FASHION & ACCESSORIES
(Map p116; ☑06 321 17 19; www.serafinipelletteria.it; Via Caio Mario 14, Borgo; ☺9.30am-7.30pm Mon-Fri, 9.30am-1pm & 3.30-7.30pm Sat; Ⓜ Ottaviano-San Pietro) During the 1960s Ferruccio Serafini was one of Rome's most sought-after artisans, making handmade leather shoes and bags for the likes of Liz Taylor and Marlon Brando. Come here to pick up beautiful hand-stitched bags, belts and accessories. Have designs made to order or get your leather handbags and luggage reconditioned.

🏛 Monti, Esquilino & San Lorenzo

Perlei JEWELLERY
(Map p106; ☑ 06 4891 3862; www.perlei.com; Via del Boschetto 35; ☺11am-7pm Mon-Sat; Ⓜ Cavour) This tiny artisanal jeweller on Monti's best shopping street showcases handmade pieces by Tammar Edelman and Elinor Avni that will appeal to those with a modernist aesthetic – their graceful arcs, sinuous strands and architectural arrangements are elegant and eye-catching.

★ **Tina Sondergaard** FASHION & ACCESSORIES
(Map p82; ☑ 06 8365 5761; www.facebook.com/ tina.sondergaard.rome; Via del Boschetto 1d;

ROME & LAZIO INFORMATION

156

LOCAL KNOWLEDGE

PORTA PORTESE MARKET

Head to the mammoth **Mercato di Porta Portese** (Map p128; Piazza Porta Portese; ⊙ 6am-2pm Sun; ⊒ Viale di Trastevere, ⊒ Trastevere/Min P Istruzione) to see Rome bargain-hunting. Thousands of stalls sell everything from rare books and fell-off-a-lorry bikes to Peruvian shawls and off-brand phones. It's crazily busy and a lot of fun. Keep your valuables safe and wear your haggling hat for the inevitable discovery of a treasure amid the dreck.

⊙ 10.30am-7.30pm Mon-Wed, to 8.30pm Thu & Fri, to 9pm Sat, 11am-1.30pm & 2.30-7pm Sun, closed Aug; Ⓜ Cavour) Sublimely cut and whimsically retro-esque, Tina Sondergaard's handmade creations for women are a hit with the local fashion cognoscenti. Styles change by the week rather than the season, femininity is the leitmotif, and you can have adjustments made (included in the price). Everything is remarkably well priced considering the quality of the fabrics and workmanship.

Pifebo   VINTAGE
(Map p82; ☑ 06 8901 5204; www.pifebo.com; Via dei Serpenti 135, Monti; ⊙ 11am-3pm & 4-8pm Mon-Sat, noon-8pm Sun; 🗺; Ⓜ Cavour) Seek out a secondhand steal at Pifebo, the city's top vintage boutique. Shelves and racks brim with sunglasses, boots, clothing (including lots of denim), bags and an impressive sports jersey collection, all hailing from the '70s, '80s and '90s. The shop also specialises in rehabbing and restoring leather items, handily returning them to their original splendour. There's another store in at Via dei Valeri 10 in San Giovanni.

🏛 Trastevere & Gianicolo

Antica Caciara Trasteverina   FOOD & DRINKS
(Map p124; ☑ 06 581 28 15; www.facebook.com/anticacaciaratrasteverina; Via di San Francesco a Ripa 140; ⊙ 7.30am-8pm Mon-Sat; ⊒ Viale di Trastevere, ⊒ Trastevere/Mastai) The fresh ricotta is a prized possession at this century-old deli, and it's usually gone by lunchtime. If you're too late, take solace in the luscious *ricotta infornata* (oven-baked ricotta), wheels of *pecorino romano,* Sicilian anchovies, gourmet pasta and local wines. The lovely, caring staff answer questions and plastic-wrap cheese and hams for transport home.

★ **Biscottificio Innocenti**   FOOD
(Map p124; ☑ 06 580 39 26; www.facebook.com/biscottificioInnocenti; Via della Luce 21; ⊙ 8am-8pm Mon-Sat, 9.30am-2pm Sun; ⊒ Viale di Trastevere, ⊒ Belli) For homemade biscuits, bite-sized meringues and fruit tarts large and small, there is no finer address in Rome than this vintage *biscottificio* with ceramic-tiled interior, fly-net door curtain and a set of old-fashioned scales on the counter to weigh biscuits (€17 to €25 per kilo). The shop has been run with much love and passion for several decades by the ever-dedicated Stefania.

Les Vignerons   WINE
(Map p124; ☑ 320 8763378; www.lesvignerons.it; Via Mameli 61, Trastevere; ⊙ 11am-9pm Mon-Sat, noon-8pm Sun; ⊒ Viale di Trastevere, ⊒ Trastevere/Min P Istruzione) If you're looking for interesting vintages, search out this lovely wine shop near the Mercato di Piazza San Cosimato. It boasts one of the capital's best collections of natural wines, mainly from small Italian and French producers, as well as a comprehensive selection of spirits and international craft beers. Staff offer great advice.

🏛 San Giovanni & Testaccio

Volpetti   FOOD & DRINKS
(Map p128; ☑ 06 574 23 52; www.volpetti.com; Via Marmorata 47, Testaccio; ⊙ 8.30am-2pm & 4.30-8.15pm Mon-Fri, 8.30am-8.30pm Sat; ⊒ Via Marmorata) This super-stocked deli, one of the best in town, is a treasure trove of gourmet delicacies. Helpful staff will guide you through its extensive selection of Italian cheese, homemade pasta, olive oil, vinegar, cured meat, wine and grappa. It also serves excellent, though pricey, sliced pizza.

ℹ Information

INTERNET ACCESS
➤ Free wi-fi is widely available in hostels, B&Bs and hotels, though signal quality varies. Some places also provide laptops/computers.

➤ Many bars and cafes offer wi-fi.

➤ There are many public wi-fi hotspots across town run by WiFimetropolitano (www.cittametropolitanaroma.gov.it/wifimetropolitano). To use these, you'll need to register online using a credit card or Italian mobile phone.

MEDICAL SERVICES
For emergency treatment, you can go to the *pronto soccorso* (casualty department) of an *ospedale* (public hospital). For less serious ail-

ments call the **Guardia Medica Turistica** (☑ 06 7730 6650; Via Emilio Morosini 30; ☺ 24hr; ☐ Viale di Trastevere, ☐ Viale di Trastevere) or seek advice at a pharmacy.

English-speaking doctors are available for house calls or appointments at the private clinic, **Doctors in Italy** (☑ 370 1359521, 06 679 06 95; www.doctorsinitaly.com; 3rd fl, Via Frattina 48; ☺ 10am-8pm Mon-Fri; Ⓜ Spagna).

If you need an ambulance, call ☑ 118.

Farmacia Gruppo Farmacrimi (☑ 06 474 54 21; https://farmacrimi.it; Via Marsala 29; ☺ 7am-10pm; Ⓜ Termini) Pharmacy located in Stazione Termini, next to Platform 1.

Policlinico Umberto I (☑ 06 4 99 71; www. policlinicoumberto1.it; Viale del Policlinico 155; Ⓜ Policlinico, Castro Pretorio) Rome's largest hospital is located near Stazione Termini.

POST OFFICES

Main Post Office (Map p106; ☑ 06 6973 7205; www.poste.it; Piazza di San Silvestro 19; ☺ 8.20am-7pm Mon-Fri, to 12.35pm Sat; Ⓜ Spagna)

Vatican Post Office (Map p116; ☑ 06 6989 0400; St Peter's Sq; ☺ 8.30am-6.30pm Mon-Sat) Letters can be posted in yellow Vatican postboxes only if they carry Vatican stamps.

MONEY

ATMs are widespread. Major credit cards are widely accepted but some smaller shops, trattorias and hotels might not take them.

TOURIST INFORMATION

There are tourist information points at **Fiumicino** (International Arrivals, Terminal 3; ☺ 8am-8.45pm) and **Ciampino** (Arrivals Hall; ☺ 8.30am-6pm) airports, as well as locations across the city. Each can provide city maps and sell the Roma Pass (p80).

Information points:

Castel Sant'Angelo (www.turismoroma.it; Piazza Pia; ☺ 9.30am-7pm summer, 8.30am-6pm winter; ☐ Piazza Pia)

Imperial Forums (Map p82; Via dei Fori Imperiali; ☺ 9.30am-7pm, to 8pm Jul & Aug; ☐ Via dei Fori Imperiali)

Stazione Termini (Map p120; ☑ 06 06 08; www.turismoroma.it; Via Giovanni Giolitti 34; ☺ 8am-6.45pm; Ⓜ Termini) In the hall adjacent to platform 24.

Trastevere (Map p124; www.turismoroma.it; Piazza Sonnino; ☺ 10.30am-8pm; ☐ Viale di Trastevere, ☐ Belli)

Via Marco Minghetti (Map p100; ☑ 06 06 08; www.turismoroma.it; Via Marco Minghetti; ☺ 9.30am-7pm; ☐ Via del Corso) Between Via del Corso and the Trevi Fountain.

For information about the Vatican, contact the **Ufficio Pellegrini e Turisti** (Map p116;

☑ 06 6988 1662; www.vatican.va; St Peter's Sq; ☺ 8.30am-6.30pm Mon-Sat; ☐ Piazza del Risorgimento, Ⓜ Ottaviano-San Pietro).

Rome's official tourist website, **Turismo Roma** (www.turismoroma.it), has comprehensive information about sights, accommodation and city transport, as well as itineraries and up-to-date listings.

The **Comune di Roma** (☑ 06 06 08; www.060608.it; ☺ 9am-7pm) runs a free multilingual tourist information phone line providing info on culture, shows, hotels, transport etc. Its website is also an excellent resource.

For practical questions such as 'Where's the nearest hospital?' or 'Where can I park?', phone the **ChiamaRoma** (☑ 06 06 06; ☺ 24hr) call centre.

USEFUL WEBSITES

060608 (www.060608.it) Great for practical details on sights, transport, upcoming events and more.

Coopculture (www.coopculture.it) Information and ticket booking for Rome's monuments.

Lonely Planet (www.lonelyplanet.com/rome) Destination information, hotel bookings, traveller forum and more.

Romeing (www.romeing.it) English-language magazine with events listings, thematic sections and features.

Vatican Museums (www.museivaticani.va) Book tickets and guided tours to the museums and other Vatican sites.

ⓘ Getting There & Away

AIR

Rome's main international airport, **Leonardo da Vinci** (☑ 06 6 59 51; www.adr.it/fiumicino), aka Fiumicino, is 30km west of the city. It currently has two operational terminals, T1 and T3, both within walking distance of each other.

Ciampino Airport (☑ 06 6 59 51; www.adr.it/ciampino), 15km southeast of the city centre, is used by Ryanair (www.ryanair.com) for European and Italian destinations. It's not a big airport, but there's a steady flow of traffic, and at peak times it gets extremely busy.

BOAT

The nearest port to Rome is at Civitavecchia, about 80km north of town. Ferries sail here from Barcelona and Tunis, as well as Sicily and Sardinia. Check www.traghettiweb.it for route details, prices and bookings.

Bookings can also be made at the Termini-based **Agenzie 365** (☑ 06 4782 5179; www.agenzie365.it; Stazione Termini, Via Giolitti 34; ☺ 8am-9pm; Ⓜ Termini), at travel agents or directly at the port.

From Civitavecchia there are half-hourly trains to Stazione Termini (€4.60 to €16, 45 minutes to 1½ hours). Civitavecchia's station is about 700m from the entrance to the port.

BUS

Long-distance national and international buses use **Autostazione Tibus** (Autostazione Tiburtina; 📞 06 44 25 95; www.tibusroma.it; Largo Guido Mazzoni; Ⓜ Tiburtina). Get tickets at the bus station or at travel agencies.

From the bus station, cross under the overpass for the Tiburtina train station, where you can pick up metro line B and connect with Termini for onward buses, trains and metro line A.

Bus operators include the following:

FLiXBUS (www.flixbus.it) To/from Siena, Florence and other destinations.

Interbus (📞 091 34 25 25; www.interbus.it) To/from Sicily.

Marozzi (📞 080 579 02 11; www.marozzivt.it) To/from Sorrento, Bari and Puglia.

Sulga (www.sulga.eu) To/from Perugia, Assisi, Ravenna and Naples.

CAR & MOTORCYCLE

Rome is circled by the Grande Raccordo Anulare (GRA) to which all *autostrade* (motorways) connect. The main *autostrade* serving Rome:

A1 The principal north–south artery, which runs from Milan to Naples, via Bologna, Florence and Rome.

A12 Runs to/from Civitavecchia and connects with the A91 Rome–Fiumicino Airport.

Car & Scooter Hire

Car hire is available at both Rome's airports and Stazione Termini. Reckon on from €20 per day for a small car.

Avis (Termini office 06 481 43 73; www.avis autonoleggio.it)

Europcar (Termini office 06 488 28 54; www.europcar.it)

Hertz (Termini office 06 488 39 67; www.hertz.it)

Maggiore National (Termini office 06 488 00 49; www.maggiore.it)

To hire a scooter, prices range from about €30 to €120 depending on the size of the vehicle. Reliable operators include the following:

Eco Move Rent (📞 06 4470 4518; www.ecomoverent.com; Via Varese 48-50; scooter/Vespa per day from €40/45; ⊙ 8.30am-7.30pm; Ⓜ Termini)

On Road (📞 06 481 56 69; www.scooterhire.it; Via Cavour 80a; scooter rental per day from €44; ⊙ 9am-7pm; Ⓜ Termini)

Treno e Scooter (📞 342 7693291; www.trenoescooter.com; Piazza dei Cinquecento; scooter rental per day €28-79; ⊙ 9am-7pm Mon-Sat, 9am-2pm & 4-7pm Sun; Ⓜ Termini)

TRAIN

Rome's main station and principal transport hub is **Stazione Termini** (www.romatermini.com; Piazza dei Cinquecento; Ⓜ Termini). It has regular connections to other European countries, all major Italian cities and many smaller towns.

Train information is available from the Customer Service area on the main concourse to the left of the ticket desks. Alternatively, check www.trenitalia.com or phone 89 20 21.

From Termini, you can connect with the metro or take a bus from Piazza dei Cinquecento out the front. Taxis are outside the main entrance/exit.

Left luggage (Stazione Termini; 1st 5hr €6, 6-12hr per hour €1, 13hr & over per hour €0.50; ⊙ 6am-11pm; Ⓜ Termini) is available by platform 24 on the Via Giolitti side of the station.

🛈 Getting Around

TO/FROM THE AIRPORT
Fiumicino (Leonardo da Vinci)
Leonardo Express (www.trenitalia.com; one-way €14, child 4-12 one child free for each paying adult, child under 4 free) Runs to/from Stazione Termini. Departures from the airport every 30 minutes between 6.08am and 11.23pm, and from Termini between 5.20am and 10.35pm. Journey time is approximately 30 minutes.

FL1 (www.trenitalia.com; one way €8) Connects to Trastevere, Ostiense and Tiburtina stations, but not Termini. Departures from the airport every 15 minutes (half-hourly on Sundays and public holidays) between 5.57am and 10.42pm; from Tiburtina every 15 to 30 minutes between 5.01am and 10.01pm.

SIT Bus (www.sitbusshuttle.com; one way €6) Regular departures to the Via Marsala stop (Map p120; Via Marsala 5) outside Stazione Termini from 7.15am to 12.40am; from Termini between 4.45am and 8.30pm. All buses stop near the Vatican (Via Crescenzio 2) en route. Tickets are available on the bus. Journey time is approximately one hour.

Taxi The set fare to/from the city centre is €48, which is valid for up to four passengers including luggage. Note that taxis registered in Fiumicino charge more, so make sure you catch a Comune di Roma taxi – these are white with a taxi sign on the roof and Roma Capitale written on the door along with the taxi's licence number. Journey time is approximately 45 to 60 minutes depending on traffic.

Ciampino
Schiaffini Rome Airport Bus (📞 06 713 05 31; www.romeairportbus.com; Via Giolitti; one

way/return €5.90/9.90) Regular departures to/from Via Giolitti outside Stazione Termini. From the airport, services are between 4am and 11.45pm; from Via Giolitti, between 4.20am and midnight. Buy tickets on board, online, at the airport or at the bus stop. Journey time is approximately 40 minutes.

SIT Bus (☑06 591 68 26; www.sitbusshuttle. com; one way airport €6, return €11) Regular departures from the airport to Via Marsala outside Stazione Termini between 7.45am and 12.15am; from Termini between 4.30am and 9.30pm. Get tickets online, on the bus or at the desk at Ciampino. Journey time is 45 minutes.

Atral (www.atral-lazio.com) Runs regular buses between the airport and Anagnina metro station (€1.20) and Ciampino train station (€1.20), from which you can get a train to Termini (€1.50).

Taxi The set rate to/from the airport is €30. Journey time is approximately 30 minutes depending on traffic.

CAR & MOTORCYCLE

➡ Driving around Rome is not recommended. Riding a scooter or motorbike is faster and makes parking easier, but Rome is no place for learners, so if you're not an experienced rider, give it a miss. Hiring a car for a day trip out of town is worth considering.

➡ Most of Rome's historic centre is closed to unauthorised traffic from 6.30am to 6pm Monday to Friday, from 2pm to 6pm Saturday, and from 11pm to 3am Friday and Saturday. Restrictions also apply in Tridente, Trastevere and Monti; evening-only Limited Traffic Zones (ZTLs) are operative in San Lorenzo and Testaccio, typically from 9.30pm or 11pm to 3am on Fridays and Saturdays (also Wednesdays and Thursdays in summer).

➡ All streets accessing the ZTL are monitored by electronic-access detection devices. If you're staying in this zone, contact your hotel. For further information, check https://roma mobilita.it.

Parking

➡ Blue lines denote pay-and-display parking – get tickets from meters (coins only) and *tabacchi* (tobacconist's shops).

➡ Expect to pay up to €1.20 per hour between 8am and 8pm (11pm in some places) in central areas. After 8pm (or 11pm) parking is free until 8am the next morning.

➡ Traffic wardens are vigilant and fines are not uncommon. If your car gets towed away, call the **traffic police** (☑06 6 76 91).

➡ There's a comprehensive list of car parks on www.060608.it – click on the transport tab then car parks.

➡ Useful car parks include the following:

Piazzale dei Partigiani (www.atac.roma.it; per hour €1; ⊙8am-7pm Mon-Sat; Ⓜ Piramide)

Stazione Termini (Map p120; ☑800 909636; www.parkinstation.it; Piazza dei Cinquecento; per hr/day €2.50/20; ⊙24hr; 🚉Piazza dei Cinquecento)

Villa Borghese (Map p106; ☑06 322 59 34; www.sabait.it; Viale del Galoppatoio 33; per hour/day €2.30/22; ⊙24hr; 🚉Via Pinciana)

PUBLIC TRANSPORT
Metro

➡ Rome has two main metro lines, A (orange) and B (blue), which cross at Termini. A branch line, 'B1', serves the northern suburbs, while work continues on a third line C, which

---

ⓘ TICKETS & PASSES

Public-transport tickets are valid on all buses, trams and metro lines, except for routes to Fiumicino airport. Children under 10 travel free. Ticket options are as follows:

BIT (a single ticket valid for 100 minutes; in that time it can be used on all forms of transport but only once on the metro) €1.50

Roma 24h (24 hours) €7

Roma 48h (48 hours) €12.50

Roma 72h (72 hours) €18

CIS (weekly ticket) €24

Abbonamento mensile (a monthly pass) For a single user €35

Buy tickets from *tabacchi* (tobacconist's shops), newsstands and vending machines at main bus stops and metro stations. Validate in machines on buses, at metro entrance gates or at train stations. Ticketless riders risk a fine of at least €50.

The Roma Pass (48/72 hours €28/38.50) comes with a travel pass valid within the city boundaries.

currently runs through the southeastern outskirts from San Giovanni. However, you're unlikely to need these two lines.

➡ Trains run between 5.30am and 11.30pm (to 1.30am on Fridays and Saturdays).

➡ All stations on line B have wheelchair access and lifts except Circo Massimo, Colosseo and Cavour. On line A, Cipro and Termini are equipped with lifts.

➡ Take line A for the Trevi Fountain (Barberini), Spanish Steps (Spagna) and St Peter's (Ottaviano-San Pietro).

➡ Take line B for the Colosseum (Colosseo).

Bus

➡ Rome's public bus service is run by **ATAC** (🖉 06 5 70 03; www.atac.roma.it).

➡ The **main bus station** (Map p120; Piazza dei Cinquecento) is in front of Stazione Termini, where there's an **information booth** (☺ 8am-8pm).

➡ Other important hubs are at Largo di Torre Argentina and Piazza Venezia.

➡ Buses generally run from about 5.30am until midnight, with limited services throughout the night.

➡ Rome's night bus service comprises more than 25 lines, many of which pass Termini and/or Piazza Venezia. Buses are marked with an 'n' before the number and bus stops have a blue owl symbol. Departures are usually every 15 to 30 minutes, but can be much slower.

➡ For route planning and real-time information, Roma Bus is a useful phone app.

Tram

Rome has a limited tram network. For route maps see www.atac.roma.it.

TAXI

➡ Official licensed taxis are white with a taxi sign on the roof and Roma Capitale written on the front door along with the taxi's licence number.

➡ Always go with the metered fare, never an arranged price (the set fares to/from the airports are exceptions).

➡ In town (within the ring road) flag fall is €3 between 6am and 10pm on weekdays, €4.50 on Sundays and holidays, and €6.50 between 10pm and 6am. Then it's €1.10 per kilometre. Official rates are posted in taxis and at https://romamobilita.it/it/media/muoversiaroma/muoversi-taxi.

➡ You can hail a taxi, but it's often easier to wait at a rank or phone for one. There are taxi ranks at the airports, Stazione Termini, Piazza della Repubblica, Piazza Barberini, Piazza di Spagna, Piazza Venezia, the Pantheon (Map p100), the Colosseum (Map p82; Piazza del Colosseo, cnr Via Capo d'Africa), Largo di Torre

Argentina (Map p100), Piazza Belli, Piazza Pio XII (Map p116) and Piazza del Risorgimento (Map p116).

➡ To book call the automated **taxi line** (🖉 in Italian 06 06 09), which sends the nearest car available; a taxi company direct; or use the ChiamaTaxi app.

➡ MyTaxi is another good app. It allows you to order a taxi without having to deal with potentially tricky language problems.

➡ Note that when you order a cab, the meter is switched on straight away and you pay for the cost of the journey from wherever the driver receives the call.

Pronto Taxi (🖉 06 66 45; www.6645.it)
Radiotaxi 3570 (🖉 06 35 70; www.3570.it)
Samarcanda (🖉 06 55 51; https://065551.it)
Taxi Tevere (🖉 06 49 94, 06 41 57; www.taxitevere.it)

LAZIO

Ostia Antica

An easy train ride from Rome, Ostia Antica is one of Italy's most thrilling archaeological sites.

Founded in the 4th century BC, Ostia started life as a fortified military camp guarding the mouth of the Tiber – hence the name, a derivation of the Latin word *ostium* (mouth). It quickly grew, and by the 2nd century AD it had become a thriving port with a population of around 50,000.

Decline set in after the fall of the Roman Empire, and by the 9th century it had largely been abandoned, its citizens driven off by barbarian raids and outbreaks of malaria. Over subsequent centuries, it was plundered of marble and building materials and its ruins were gradually buried in river silt, thus ensuring their survival.

◉ Sights

⭐ **Area Archeologica di Ostia Antica** ARCHAEOLOGICAL SITE
(🖉 06 5635 8099; www.ostiaantica.beniculturali.it/; Viale dei Romagnoli 717; adult/reduced/under 18 €12/2/free, free 1st Sunday of the month Oct-Mar; ☺ 8.30am-7.15pm Tue-Sun Apr-Aug, earlier closing winter) One of Lazio's prize sights, the ruins of ancient Rome's seaport are wonderfully complete, like a smaller version of Pompeii. Highlights include the Terme di Nettuno (Baths of Neptune), a steeply stacked am-

Lazio

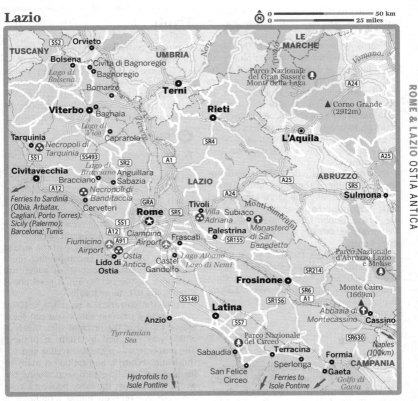

phitheatre, some exquisite mosaics and an ancient cafe, complete with traces of its original menu.

Note that the site is huge and you'll need a few hours to do it justice. Busy at weekends, it is much quieter on weekdays. Last admission can sometimes be as early as 3.30pm.

To help with navigation, it's worth arming yourself with a site map, which you can buy for €2 at the ticket office. Audio guides are also available for €10.

Just beyond the ticket office, Porta Romana gives onto the Decumanus Maximus, the site's central drag, which runs over 1km to Porta Marina, the city's original sea-facing gate. At the time of research, however, it was blocked off about two-thirds of the way down, by the Tempio dei Fabri Navales.

On the Decumanus, the Terme di Nettuno is a must-see. This baths complex, one of

20 that originally stood in town, dates from the 2nd century and boasts some superb mosaics, including one of Neptune riding a seahorse chariot. In the centre of the complex are the remains of an arcaded palestra (gym).

Near the Terme is the Teatro, an amphitheatre originally built at the end of the 1st century BC by Agrippa and later enlarged to hold 4000 people.

The grassy area behind the amphitheatre is the Piazzale delle Corporazioni (Forum of the Corporations), home to the offices of Ostia's merchant guilds. The mosaics that line the perimeter – ships, dolphins, a lighthouse, elephants – are thought to have represented the businesses housed on the square: ships and dolphins indicated shipping agencies, while elephants probably signalled businesses involved in the ivory trade.

Further down the Decumanus, the Forum, Ostia's main square, is overlooked by what remains of the **Capitolium**, a temple built by Hadrian and dedicated to Jupiter, Juno and Minerva.

Nearby is another highlight: the **Thermopolium**, an ancient cafe, complete with bar, fragments of its original frescoed menu, and a small courtyard where customers would have relaxed around a fountain. To the north of this are two of the so-called **case decorate**. These frescoed houses are off limits to unaccompanied visitors but can be entered on a free guided tour at 10.30am each Sunday – email pa-oant.domusostia@ beniculturali.it.

Over on the other side of the Decumanus are the remains of the 2nd-century **Terme del Foro**, originally the city's largest and most important baths complex. Here, in the *forica* (public toilet), you can see 20 well-preserved latrines set sociably in a long stone bench.

For more modern facilities, you'll find a cafeteria, toilets and a gift shop to the north of the Decumanus (head up Via dei Molini). Nearby, a small **museum** (⊗9.30am-3.30pm) displays statues and sarcophagi excavated on the site.

✖ Eating

Ristorante Monumento   ITALIAN **€€**
(☑06 565 00 21; www.ristorantemonumento.it; Piazza Umberto I 8; meals €30-35; ⊗12.30-3.30pm & 8-11pm; ☞) In Ostia's tiny medieval centre, this historic restaurant started life in the 19th century, catering to the labourers working on reclaiming the local marshlands. Nowadays, it does a brisk business feeding sightseers from the nearby ruins. The menu is equally weighted with seafood and meat dishes, acknowledging the restaurant's proximity to the seashore. Bookings are recommended here, particularly at weekends.

❶ Getting There & Away

From Rome, take the Roma–Lido train from Stazione Porta San Paolo (next to Piramide metro station) to Ostia Antica (every 15 minutes). The 25-minute trip is covered by a standard Rome public transport ticket (€1.50).

By car, take Via del Mare, which runs parallel to Via Ostiense, and follow signs for the *scavi* (excavations).

Tivoli
POP 56,500

A summer retreat for ancient Romans and the Renaissance rich, the hilltop town of Tivoli is home to two Unesco World Heritage Sites: Villa Adriana, the sprawling estate of Emperor Hadrian, and the 16th-century Villa d'Este, a Renaissance retreat famous for its landscaped gardens and lavish fountains.

◎ Sights

★ **Villa Adriana**   ARCHAEOLOGICAL SITE
(☑0774 38 27 33; www.villaadriana.beniculturali.it; Largo Marguerite Yourcenar 1; adult/reduced €10/2, free 1st Sun of month Oct-Mar; ⊗8.30am-1hr before sunset) The ruins of Hadrian's vast country estate, 5km outside of Tivoli proper, are quite magnificent, easily on a par with anything you'll see in Rome. Built between AD 118 and 138, the villa was one of the largest in the ancient world, encompassing more than 120 hectares, about 40 of which are now open to the public. You'll need about three hours to explore it fully.

From the entrance, a road leads 400m or so up to a pavilion where you can see a plastic model of the original villa, much of which was designed by Hadrian himself. The emperor was a great traveller and enthusiastic architect, and he based many of his ideas on buildings he'd seen around the world. The **pecile**, the large pool area near the walls, is a reproduction of a building in Athens. Similarly, the **canopo** is a copy of a sanctuary in the Egyptian town of Canopus, with a narrow 120m-long pool flanked by sculptural figures. At its head, the **Serapaeum** is a semi-circular *nymphaeum* (shrine to the water nymph) that was once used to host summer banquets. Flanking the water is the **antiquarium** where temporary exhibitions are sometimes held.

To the northeast of the *pecile*, the **Teatro Marittimo** is one of the site's signature buildings. A circular mini-villa set in an artificial pool, this was Hadrian's personal refuge that could only be accessed by swing bridges.

To the southeast, **Piazza d'Oro** makes for a memorable picture, particularly in spring, when its grassy centre is cloaked in wild yellow flowers.

There are also several bath complexes, temples and barracks.

Parking (€3) is available at the site. Last admissions are 1hr before closing.

Villa d'Este · HISTORIC BUILDING

(📞 0774 33 29 20; www.villadestetivoli.info; Piazza Trento 5; adult/reduced €10/2; ⏰ 8.30am-4.45pm Tue-Sun, from 2pm Mon Dec-Feb, extended hours Mar-Nov) The steeply terraced grounds of this Renaissance villa In the hilltop town of Tivoli are adorned with monumental fountains, tree-lined avenues including the 130m-long Avenue of the Hundred Fountains, and landscaped grottoes. The villa, originally a Benedictine convent, was converted into a luxury retreat by Lucrezia Borgia's son, Cardinal Ippolito d'Este, in the late 16th century and later provided inspiration for composer Franz Liszt, who wrote *The Fountains of the Villa d'Este* after spending time here between 1865 and 1886.

Before heading out to the gardens, take time to admire the villa's rich mannerist frescoes. Outside, the manicured park features water-spouting gargoyles and shady lanes flanked by lofty cypress trees. The garden's most unusual feature is the Bernini-designed Fountain of the Organ, which uses water pressure to play music through a concealed instrument. Hear it play every day at 10.30am, 12.30pm, 2.30pm and 4.30pm.

Last admissions are 1hr before closing.

🛏 Sleeping & Eating

⭐ **Residenze Gregoriane** · BOUTIQUE HOTEL €€€

(📞 0774 43 69 03, 347 7136854; www.residenzegregoriane.it; Via Domenico Giuliani 92; ste €230-250; ❄️ 🛜 ♿) Steeped in history, the Residenze Gregoriane offers a night to remember. Its four suites, all decorated in classic antique style, occupy the 16th-century Palazzo Mancini-Torlonia. Frescoes adorn the historic building, many by the same artists who worked on Villa d'Este, and there's a magnificent internal courtyard adorned with ceramic tiles and seashell mosaics.

Sibilla · RISTORANTE €€€

(📞 0774 33 52 81; www.ristorantesibilla.com; Via della Sibilla 50; meals €40-50; ⏰ 12.30-3pm & 7.30-10pm Tue-Sun, closed Sun evenings in winter; 🛜) With tables set next to the 2nd-century BC Tempio di Vesta and water cascading down the green river gorge below, this elegant restaurant is the most atmospheric eatery in town. Expect classic Italian food prepared with fresh, seasonal ingredients and paired with good local wines. The pastas are particularly good here.

The restaurant is a 10-minute walk downhill from the Villa d'Este.

ℹ️ TIVOLI IN A DAY

Tivoli makes an excellent day trip from Rome, but to cover its two main sights you'll have to start early. The best way to see both is to visit Villa d'Este first, then have lunch up in the centre, before heading down to Villa Adriana. To get to Villa Adriana from the centre, take local CAT bus 4 or 4X (€1.30, 10 minutes, half-hourly) from Piazza Garibaldi. After you've visited Villa Adriana, pick up the Cotral bus back to Rome.

ℹ️ Information

Tourist Information Point (📞 0774 31 35 36; Piazzale delle Nazioni Unite; ⏰ 9.30am-5.30pm) This information kiosk is located near the arrival point for the bus from Rome.

ℹ️ Getting There & Away

Tivoli, 30km east of Rome, is accessible by **Cotral** (📞 800 174471, from a mobile 06 7205 7205; www.cotralspa.it) bus (€1.30, 50 minutes, at least twice hourly) from Rome's Ponte Mammolo metro station.

By car you can either take Via Tiburtina or the quicker Rome–L'Aquila autostrada (A24).

Trains run from Rome's Stazione Tiburtina to Tivoli (€2.60, one to 1¼ hours, at least hourly).

Cerveteri

POP 38,000

A quiet provincial town 35km northwest of Rome, Cerveteri is home to one of Italy's great Etruscan treasures – the Necropoli di Banditaccia. This ancient burial complex, now a Unesco World Heritage Site, is all that remains of the formidable Etruscan city that once stood here.

Founded in the 9th century BC, the city the Etruscans knew as Kysry, and Latin speakers called Caere, was a powerful member of the Etruscan League, and, for a period between the 7th and 5th centuries, it was one of the Mediterranean's most important commercial centres. It eventually came into conflict with Rome and, in 358 BC, was annexed into the Roman Republic.

👁 Sights

⭐ **Necropoli di Banditaccia** · ARCHAEOLOGICAL SITE

(📞 06 994 00 01; www.polomusealelazio.beni culturali.it/index.php?it/145/antichit; Via della

Necropoli 43/45; adult/reduced €6/2, incl museum €10/4; ⊙8.30am-1hr before sunset Tue-Sun) This haunting, 12-hectare Etruscan necropolis is a veritable city of the dead, with streets, squares and terraces of *tumuli* (circular tombs cut into the earth and capped by turf). Some tombs, including the 6th-century-BC Tomba dei Rilievi, retain traces of painted reliefs, many of which illustrate endearingly domestic household items, as well as figures from the underworld.

Another interesting tomb is the 7th-century-BC Tumulo Mengarelli, whose plain interior shows how the tombs were originally structured.

In total, there are reckoned to be around 2000 tombs spread across the site, which is vast and not well signposted, so allow yourselves at least two hours to explore it.

Note also that if you're planning to continue your Etruscan exploration at Tarquinia, you can buy a combined ticket that covers Tarquinia's museum and necropolis as well as Cerveteri's two Etruscan sites. Valid for seven days, it costs €15/8 (adult/reduced).

Museo Nazionale Cerite   MUSEUM
(⊘06 994 13 54; www.polomusealelazio.beni culturali.it/index.php?en/145/antiquity; Piazza Santa Maria 1; adult/reduced €6/2, incl necropolis €10/4; ⊙8.30am-7.30pm Tue-Sun) Housed in a medieval fortress on what was once ancient Caere's acropolis, this interesting little museum houses archaeological artefacts unearthed at the nearby Necropoli di Banditaccia (p163).

Exhibits, which are displayed in two halls, include terracotta vases, black bucchero tableware and jewellery. The highlight is the *Euphronios Krater,* a celebrated 1st-century-BC vase that was returned to Cerveteri in 2015 after an extended period in New York and Rome.

✕ Eating

Da Bibbo   OSTERIA €€
(⊘388 6598858; Via Agillina 41; meals €30-35; ⊙noon-3pm & 7-11pm) A popular choice in Cerveteri's historic centre, this coolly casual *osteria* looks the part with its low brick arches, exposed stone walls and decorative wine cases. Food-wise, it serves an imaginative menu of modern, well-executed *mare* (sea) and *terra* (land) dishes prepared with prime Italian ingredients.

❶ Information

Tourist Information Point (⊘06 9955 2637; Piazza Aldo Moro; ⊙9.30am-12.30pm & 5.30-7.30pm Tue-Sat, 10am-1pm Sun summer, 9.30am-12.30pm Tue-Sat, 10am-1pm Sun winter) A kiosk by the entrance to the historic centre.

❶ Getting There & Around

Cerveteri is easily accessible from Rome by Cotral (⊘800 174471, from a mobile 06 7205 7205; www.cotralspa.it) bus (€2.80, one to 1¼ hours, twice hourly Monday to Saturday, hourly Sunday) from Cornelia metro station (line A).

By car, take either Via Aurelia (SS1) or the Civitavecchia autostrada (A12) and exit at Cerveteri–Ladispoli.

Once in town, buses serve the necropolis from Piazza Aldo Moro near the tourist information point, although services are limited. On Sundays, take bus 41 or 42 (€1.10, five minutes, approximately hourly); from Tuesday to Saturday, take bus 24 and 25, though check with the driver as not all scheduled runs stop at the necropolis.

Tarquinia

POP 16,300

Some 90km northwest of Rome, Tarquinia is the pick of Lazio's Etruscan towns. The star attraction is the magnificent Unesco-listed necropolis and its extraordinary frescoed tombs, but there's also a fantastic Etruscan museum (the best outside of Rome) and an atmospheric medieval centre.

Legend holds that Tarquinia was founded towards the end of the Bronze Age in the 12th century BC. It was later home to the Tarquin kings of Rome, reaching its peak in the 4th century BC, before a century of struggle ended with surrender to Rome in 204 BC.

⊙ Sights

★Necropoli di Tarquinia   ARCHAEOLOGICAL SITE
(Necropoli dei Monterozzi; ⊘0766 85 63 08; www.polomusealelazio.beniculturali.it/index.php?it/145/antichit; Via Ripagretta; adult/reduced €6/2, incl museum €10/4; ⊙8.30am-7.30pm Tue-Sun summer, to 1hr before sunset winter) This remarkable 7th-century-BC necropolis is one of Italy's most important Etruscan sites. At first sight, it doesn't look like much – a green field littered with corrugated huts – but once you start ducking into the tombs and seeing the

vivid frescoes, you'll realise what all the fuss is about.

Some 6000 tombs have been excavated in this area since digs began in 1489, of which 140 are painted and 22 are currently open to the public.

For the best frescoes search out the **Tomba della Leonessa**; the **Tomba della Caccia e della Pesca**, with some wonderful hunting and fishing scenes; the **Tomba dei Leopardi**; and the **Tomba della Fustigazione**, which is named after a scratchy scene of an S&M threesome.

To get to the necropolis, about 1.5km from the centre, take bus D (€1) from near the tourist office. Alternatively, it's about 20 minutes on foot – head up Corso Vittorio Emanuele, turn right into Via Porta Tarquinia and continue along Via Ripagretta.

Note that you can buy a combined ticket that gives admission to the site and the Museo Archeologico Nazionale Tarquiniense as well as Cerveteri's Etruscan museum and necropolis (p163). Valid for seven days, it costs €15/8 (adult/reduced).

Museo Archeologico
Nazionale Tarquiniense   MUSEUM
(📞0766 85 60 36; www.polomusealelazio.beni culturali.it/index.php?it/145/antichit; Via Cavour 1; adult/reduced €6/2, incl necropolis €10/4; ⊙8.30am-7.30pm Tue-Sun) This charming museum, beautifully housed in the 15th-century Palazzo Vitelleschi, is a treasure trove of locally found Etruscan artefacts. Highlights include the *Cavalli Alati*, a magnificent frieze of two winged horses, and, in the next room, the *Mitra Tauroctono*, a striking sculpture of the headless, handless god Mithras killing a bull.

🛏 Sleeping & Eating

Camere Del Re   HOTEL €
(📞327 7639742, 0766 85 58 31; www.cameredelre. com; Via San Pancrazio 41; s €55-70, d €69-89, tr €89-119, q €99-129; ❊ ❋ ➡) This modest hotel is housed in a 19th-century *palazzo* just off the historic centre's main strip. A welcoming spot, it has spacious, if slightly dated, rooms decorated in simple, monastic style with tiled floors and wrought-iron bedsteads. The best also sport original vaulted ceilings and the occasional fresco.

Il Cavatappi   LAZIO €€
(📞0766 84 23 03; www.cavatappirestaurant.it; Via dei Granari 2; meals €25-30; ⊙12.30-2pm Fri-Sun year-round, also 7.30-10pm Wed-Mon summer,

7-10pm Wed-Mon winter) Tarquinia has several decent eateries, including this family-run restaurant in the *centro storico*. Bag a table in the tastefully cluttered interior or out on the summer terrace, and dive into generous helpings of earthy regional food – cured meat and cheese platters, seasonal vegetable soups and flavoursome grilled steaks.

ℹ Information

Tourist Office (📞0766 84 92 82; www. tarquiniaturismo.it; Largo Barriera San Giusto; ⊙9am-1pm & 4-7pm summer, 10am-12.30pm & 3-5pm winter) Helpful office in the town's medieval gate (Barriera San Giusto).

ℹ Getting There & Away

The best way to reach Tarquinia from Rome is by train from Termini (€5.60, 1½ hours, hourly). From Tarquinia station, catch the hourly BC bus to the hilltop historic centre (€1).

By car, take the A12 autostrada for Civitavecchia and then Via Aurelia (SS1).

WORTH A TRIP

LAZIO'S NORTHERN LAKES

North of Rome, Lazio's verdant landscape is pitted with volcanic lakes. The closest to the capital is **Lago di Bracciano**, a beautiful blue expanse surrounded by picturesque medieval towns. There's a popular lakeside beach at **Anguillara Sabazia** and you can visit a 15th-century castle, **Castello Odescalchi** (📞06 9980 4348; www. odescalchi.it; Via del Lago 1; adult/reduced €8.50/6; ⊙10am-6pm Mon-Fri, to 7pm Sat & Sun summer, 10am-5pm Mon-Fri, to 6pm Sat & Sun winter) at **Bracciano**.

Both towns are accessible by half-hourly trains from Roma Ostiense (Anguillara €2.60, 55 minutes; Bracciano €3.60, 70 minutes).

In the north of the region, **Lago di Bolsena** is one of Europe's largest volcanic lakes. Its main town is **Bolsena**, a charming place with a hilltop medieval centre and a famous 13th-century miracle story.

Hourly Cotral buses serve Bolsena from Viterbo (€2.20, 45 minutes).

Viterbo

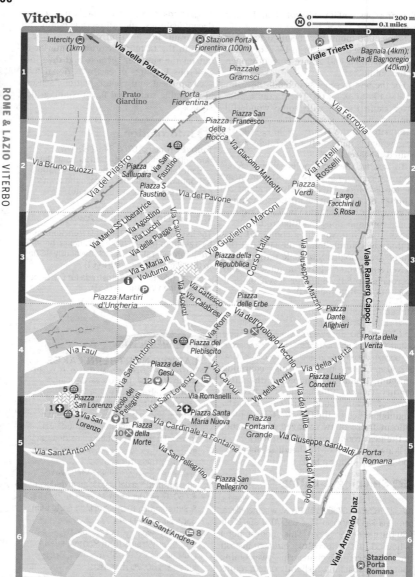

Viterbo

POP 67,800

The largest town in northern Lazio, Viterbo is a much-overlooked gem with a charming medieval *centro storico* and a laid-back, provincial vibe.

Founded by the Etruscans and later taken over by the Romans, it developed into an important medieval centre, and in the 13th century was briefly the seat of the papacy. It was heavily bombed in WWII, but much of its historic core survived and this attractive tangle of grey-stone buildings is today in

Viterbo

remarkably good shape. This, together with its good bus connections, makes it an attractive base for exploring Lazio's far-flung northern reaches.

⊙ Sights

Palazzo dei Papi   HISTORIC BUILDING
(☑320 7911328; www.archeoares.it/palazzo-dei-papi-2; Piazza San Lorenzo; incl Cattedrale & Museo Colle del Duomo adult/reduced €9/7; ⊗10am-7pm summer, 10am-1pm & 3-6pm winter) Flanking Piazza San Lorenzo, this handsome Gothic *palazzo* was built for the popes who lived in Viterbo from 1257 to 1281. Its most obvious feature is the Loggia delle Benedizione, an elegant arched balcony onto which newly elected popes would emerge from the Aula del Conclave, scene of the first and longest-ever papal conclave.

Cattedrale di San Lorenzo   CATHEDRAL
(www.archeoares.it/cattedrale-di-san-lorenzo; Piazza San Lorenzo; ⊗10am-7pm summer, 10am-1pm & 3-6pm winter) With its black-and-white bell tower, Viterbo's 12th-century cathedral looms over Piazza San Lorenzo, the religious nerve centre of the medieval city. Originally built to a simple Romanesque design, it owes its current Gothic look to a 14th-century makeover and a partial post-WWII reconstruction.

Inside, look out for *Redentore e Santi* (1472) by Gerolamo da Cremona and the tomb of Pope Giovanni XXI (r 1276–77). A second pope, Alessandro IV (r 1254–61), is also buried in the cathedral, but the location of his body is a long-standing mystery.

Many of the cathedral's art treasures are today housed in the adjacent Museo Colle del Duomo (☑320 7911328; www.archeoares.it/museo-colle-del-duomo; Piazza San Lorenzo 8; €3, incl Cattedrale & Palazzo dei Papi adult/reduced €9/7; ⊗10am-7pm summer, 10am-1pm & 3-6pm winter).

The cathedral is free to enter but certain areas can only be accessed with a ticket (adult/reduced €9/7); this also covers admission to the Museo Colle and Palazzo dei Papi.

Chiesa di Santa Maria Nuova   CHURCH
(Piazza Santa Maria Nuova; ⊗church 7am-7pm, cloisters 10am-noon & 3-5pm Fri-Sun) This 11th-century Romanesque church, the oldest in Viterbo, was restored to its original form after sustaining bomb damage in WWII. A series of 13th- to 16th-century frescoes line the solemn, grey interior, while outside you can see a stone pulpit where St Thomas Aquinas preached in 1266. Also of note is the church's cloister, the so-called Chiostro Longobardo.

Palazzo dei Priori   HISTORIC BUILDING
(Piazza del Plebiscito 14, Via Ascenzi 1; ⊗9am-1pm & 3-6.30pm Mon-Fri, 9am-noon & 3-7pm Sat, 9am-noon Sun) FREE Viterbo's 15th-century city hall overlooks Piazza del Plebiscito, the elegant Renaissance square that has long been the city's political and social hub. It's not all open to the public, but you can visit a series of impressively decorated halls on the 1st floor whose 16th-century frescoes colourfully depict Viterbo's ancient origins. During the week, the entrance is at Via Ascenzi 1; at weekends it's on Piazza del Plebiscito.

Museo Nazionale Etrusco   MUSEUM
(☑0761 32 59 29; Piazza della Rocca; adult/reduced €6/2; ⊗8.30am-7.30pm Tue-Sun) The Albornaz fortress, built in the 14th century to guard the city and later modified by Renaissance architect Bramante, houses Viterbo's modest Etruscan museum. Reconstructions and locally found artefacts illustrate the Etruscan lifestyle, while a series of life-sized statues harks back to the city's Roman past.

⊨ Sleeping

★B&B Centro Storico   B&B €
(☑389 2386283; Via Romanelli 24; s €68-82, d €59-82, q €84-107; ❋ 🛜) A great little bolthole in the heart of the historic centre. Its three cool, tastefully attired rooms, including a mini-apartment for four, are up a steep set

of stairs (no lift) on the 1st floor of a 14th-century *palazzo*, about 200m from Piazza del Plebiscito. Kettles are provided, along with some lovely homemade biscuits; otherwise breakfast is served in a nearby bar.

It's not the easiest place to find but your host, Daniele, can help you out on that front.

Medieval House   B&B €

(☑ 347 2562690; www.bbmedievalhouse.com; Via Sant'Andrea 78; s €45-55, d €60-70; ⊛🛜) Run by the gregarious Matteo, this welcoming B&B enjoys a tranquil location just inside the town's medieval walls. It's a cosy set-up with seven rooms – some in the main house, others over the road – and a look that combines homey furniture with exposed stone walls and wood-beamed ceilings. Breakfast is another highlight, a feast of *cornetti* (croissants) and cured meats.

✖️ Eating

★ Il Gargolo Ristorantino   ITALIAN €€

(☑ 0761 95 88 30; Piazza della Morte 14; meals €30; ☺ noon-3pm & 7.30-11pm) A casual meal on an atmospheric piazza is one of the joys of eating out in Italy, and that's exactly what you get at Il Gargolo. Its al fresco tables, shaded by leafy trees, are a wonderful place to tuck into scrumptious pastas – try the *tonnarelli* (thick square spaghetti) with *pecorino*, *guanciale* (cured pig's cheek) and black truffle – and rich, creamy desserts.

Al Vecchio Orologio   LAZIO €€

(☑ 335 337754; www.alvecchioorologio.it; Via dell'Orologio Vecchio 25; pizzas €8-10, meals €30; ☺ 7.30-10.30pm Mon & Tue, 12.30-2.30pm & 7.30-10.30pm Wed-Sun) A much-frequented local favourite, Al Vecchio Orologio wins you over with its charming stone-vaulted setting and updated seasonal cuisine. There's a full range of pizzas, but to get the best out of the kitchen opt for the main menu and dishes like *acquacotta viterbese* (a winter vegetable soup with egg) and saffron-flavoured pasta with zucchini and Lake Bolsena perch.

🍷 Drinking & Nightlife

Tredici Gradi Slow Bar   WINE BAR

(☑ 0761 22 03 66; Piazza del Gesù 18; ☺ 7am-11pm) A glass of local Sangiovese accompanied by a side-plate of bruschetta is a fine way to kick start your evening. And with an enviable setting on Piazza del Gesù, a casual vibe and a cosy interior, this inviting wine bar is a cool place to have one.

Magnamagna   BAR

(☑ 329 8054913; Vicolo dei Pellegrini 2; ☺ 12.30-3pm & 6.30pm-1am, closed Mon & Tue lunch) Join the crowds for a glass of wine in the atmospheric setting of Piazza della Morte. The bar, which also serves craft beers and local foodie specialities, is standing room only, but there's seating outside in the piazza and in a vaulted hall known as the Winter Garden,

---

OFF THE BEATEN TRACK

AROUND VITERBO

Largely overlooked by travellers, the lush, emerald-green countryside around Viterbo hides some wonderful treasures. Chief among them is Palazzo Farnese (☑ 0761 64 60 52; Piazza Farnese 1; adult/reduced €5/2; ☺ 8.30am-7.30pm Tue-Sun), 20km southeast of Viterbo in Caprarola. A 16th-century Renaissance *palazzo*, it features a distinct pentagonal design and, inside, an internal circular courtyard and extraordinary columned staircase. Visits take in the richly frescoed rooms and, on weekdays, the beautiful hillside gardens.

For more horticultural splendours, head to Bagnaia and Villa Lante (☑ 0761 28 80 08; www.polomusealelazio.beniculturali.it; Via Barozzi 71; adult/reduced €5/2; ☺ 8.30am-1hr before sunset Tue-Sun), whose 16th-century mannerist gardens feature monumental fountains and an ingenious water cascade.

Some 30km north of Viterbo, Bagnoregio is home to one of Lazio's most dramatic apparitions, the Civita di Bagnoregio (www.civitadibagnoregio.cloud; €5; ☺ ticket office 8am-8pm), aka *il paese che muore* (the dying town). This medieval village, accessible by a scenic footbridge, sits atop a huge stack of slowly crumbling rock in the deep-cut Valle dei Calanchi.

The best way to get around the area is by car, although you can also get to all the places listed here by Cotral (☑ 800 174471, from a mobile 06 7205 7205; www.cotralspa.it) bus from Viterbo.

where you can kick back to cocktails and the occasional DJ set.

ℹ Information

Tourist Office (☑ 0761 32 59 92; www.visit. viterbo.it; Piazza Martiri d'Ungheria; ⊙10am-1pm & 3-7.30pm Tue-Sun) By the Piazza Martiri d'Ungheria car park. You can pick up useful city information and make use of its public toilets (€0.50).

ℹ Getting There & Away

From Rome, **Cotral** (☑ 800 174471, from a mobile 06 7205 7205; www.cotralspa.it) buses serve Viterbo from Saxa Rubra station (€4.50, 1½ hours, half-hourly) – get to Saxa Rubra by Ferrovia Roma-Nord train from Piazzale Flaminio.

In Viterbo, make sure you get off at Porta Romana, not the intercity bus station at Piazza Giordano Bruno, which is a kilometre or so northwest of Porta Fiorentina.

By car, Viterbo is about a 1½-hour drive up Via Cassia (SR2). Once in town, the best bet for parking is Piazza Martiri d'Ungheria (€1 for the first hour, then €0.50 per hour from 7am to 9.30pm; €0.50 for the night from 9.30pm to 7am). Note, however, the car park is closed Saturday from 6am to 3pm.

Trains from Rome's Ostiense station to Viterbo Porta Romana (€5.60, 1¾ hours) depart hourly from Monday to Saturday and every two hours on Sundays.

Castelli Romani

A pretty pocket of verdant hills and volcanic lakes 20km southeast of Rome, the Colli Albani (Alban Hills) and their 13 towns are collectively known as the Castelli Romani. Since ancient times they've provided a green refuge from the city and still today Romans flock to the area on hot summer weekends. Highlights include the famous wine town of Frascati, hilltop Castel Gandolfo and the scenic Lago Albano.

Frascati

POP 22,450

An easy train ride from Rome, the elegant and well-to-do wine town of Frascati makes for a refreshing day trip with its compact historic centre and delicious food and drink.

The town is also famous for its aristocratic villas, built as summer retreats by rich Roman families in the late Renaissance and early baroque period.

◉ Sights

Scuderie Aldobrandini　　　MUSEUM
(☑ 06 941 71 95; www.scuderiealdobrandini.it; Piazza Marconi 6; adult/reduced €3/1.50, plus exhibition €5.50/3; ⊙10am-6pm Tue-Fri, to 7pm Sat & Sun) The former stables of Villa Aldobrandini, restored by architect Massimiliano Fuksas, house Frascati's single museum of note, the **Museo Tuscolano**. Dedicated to local history, its collection includes ancient Roman artefacts and models of the Ville Tuscolane, a series of patrician villas built in the surrounding countryside between the 16th and 17th centuries.

Villa Aldobrandini Gardens　　GARDENS
(☑ 06 942 25 60; Via Cardinal Massai 18; ⊙ 8.30am-5.30pm Mon-Fri) FREE Looming over Frascati's main square, Villa Aldobrandini is a haughty 16th-century villa designed by Giacomo della Porta and built by Carlo Maderno. It's closed to the public, but you can visit its baroque gardens, complete with a celebrated water theatre and panoramic terrace.

✗ Eating

Cantina Simonetti　　　OSTERIA €
(☑ 347 6300269; Piazza San Rocco 4; meals €25; ⊙8pm-midnight Tue-Sun summer, 1-4pm Sat & Sun & 8pm-midnight Wed-Sun winter) For an authentic *vino e cucina* (wine and food) experience, search out this traditional *cantina* and sit down to a mountainous meal of *porchetta,* cold cuts, cheese and Roman pastas, all accompanied by jugs of local white wine. In keeping with the food, the decor is rough-and-ready rustic with strings of hanging garlic and plain wooden tables.

★ **Cacciani**　　　RISTORANTE €€€
(☑ 06 942 03 78; www.cacciani.it; Via Armando Diaz 13; meals €50; ⊙12.30-2.30pm & 8-10.30pm, closed Sun dinner & Mon) One of Frascati's most renowned restaurants, Cacciani offers fine food and twinkling terrace views. The menu lists much-loved regional classics like *tonnarello a cacio e pepe* (egg spaghetti with *pecorino* cheese and black pepper) alongside more modern compositions prepared with seasonal ingredients from small local producers. Aficionados will also appreciate the weighty wine list.

ℹ Information

Frascati Point Tourist Office (☑ 06 9418 4409; Piazza Marconi 5; ⊙10am-7pm) Helpful office that can provide information about the town and tours of local vineyards.

LOCAL KNOWLEDGE

FRASCHETTE IN ARICCIA

The Castelli are famous for their *fraschette*: rustic, no-frills *osterie* serving local food and wine. Ariccia is the area's *fraschette* capital, and on weekends, national holidays and hot summer evenings, the small town heaves with hungry Romans and out-of-towners.

Their menus are all variations on a theme, offering hefty starters of *porchetta* (the herbed, spit-roasted pork for which Ariccia is famous), marinated veggies, cured meats, cheese, mozzarella, olives and crusty local bread. To follow, there will be a limited choice of classic Roman pastas and mains of char-grilled steaks.

Recommended *fraschette* include **Osteria da Angelo** (✆06 933 17 77; www.osteria daangelo.it; Via dell'Uccelliera 24; fixed-price menus €15-20; ⊙noon-4pm & 7pm-midnight Thu-Tue), one of several strung along Via dell'Uccelliera, **La Rupe** (✆06 932 39 61; www.fraschettalarupe.it; Piazzale Menotti Garibaldi 1; meals €25, pizzas €7-10; ⊙11am-4pm & 6pm-midnight), a hospitable family-run outfit near the entrance to town, and **La Selvotta** (✆06 932 45 21; www.laselvottadiariccia.it; Via Selvotta 43; meals €15-20; ⊙noon-4pm & 7.30pm-midnight Apr-Oct), a spartan outdoor set-up in a shady patch of woodland.

Ariccia is on Via Appia (SS7) about 25km south of Rome.

❶ Getting There & Away

The best way to get to Frascati from Rome is by train. Regular services run from Stazione Termini (€2.10, 30 minutes, hourly Monday to Saturday, every two hours Sunday).

By car, it's a straight drive up Via Tuscolana (SS215).

Castel Gandolfo & Lago Albano

POP 8900

One of the Castelli's prettiest towns, Castel Gandolfo is a refined hilltop *borgo* (medieval town). For centuries, the popes spent their summers here, relaxing in the elegant Palazzo Apostolico and enjoying exquisite views down to Lago Albano. The popes no longer holiday here, but the town still draws plenty of visitors who come to admire the papal palace and its extensive gardens. The lake attracts fewer foreign visitors but is much frequented by locals and day-tripping Romans.

◉ Sights

Palazzo Apostolico   PALACE
(✆06 6988 3145; www.museivaticani.va; Piazza della Libertà; adult/reduced €11/5; ⊙8.30am-2pm Mon-Fri, to 5.30pm Sat, 10am-3pm Sun) Dominating Castel Gandolfo's skyline, the 17th-century Palazzo Apostolico was the pope's traditional summer residence. However, since 2016 it has been open to the public and you can now visit the papal apartments and explore the palace's marble halls. Look out for portraits of around 50 popes as well

as costumes, robes and assorted Vatican paraphernalia, including the BMW that Pope John Paul II used when he stayed at the palace.

Giardini di Villa Barberini   GARDENS
(Villa Barberini Gardens; ✆06 6988 3145; www. museivaticani.va; Via Rosselli; tours adult/reduced €20/15, Sat morning walk €12/5; ⊙9.30am-2.30pm) For centuries a closed world, the papal gardens at Castel Gandolfo can now be visited, albeit accompanied and in groups. The regular one-hour tour involves a mini train ride through the extensive gardens, taking in Roman ruins, flower displays, woods, fruit-and-veg patches and the papal helipad.

✗ Eating

**Antico Ristorante
Pagnanelli**   RISTORANTE €€€
(✆06 936 00 04; www.pagnanelli.it; Via Gramsci 4; meals €60; ⊙noon-3.30pm & 6.30-11.45pm) A local landmark for more than a century, this colourful wisteria-clad restaurant oozes romance, particularly on warm summer nights when the views over Lago Albano melt the heart. The seasonally driven Italian food rises to the occasion too, especially when paired with outstanding wine from the terrific list – bottles are racked in an amazing cellar carved into tufa rock.

❶ Getting There & Away

The best way to get to Castel Gandolfo and Lago Albano by public transport is to take the Albano

Laziale train from Stazione Termini (€2.10, 45 minutes, hourly Monday to Saturday, every two hours Sunday). From the train station, it's a 1km walk down to the lake. By car, take Via Appia Nuova (SS7).

Palestrina

POP 21,900

Largely overlooked by foreign visitors, hilltop Palestrina hosts some extraordinary archaeological treasures. In ancient times the town, then known as Praeneste, was home to a spectacular temple, the Santuario della Fortuna Primigenia, which covered much of what is now the *centro storico*. The sanctuary has long since been built over, but you can still explore its few remaining terraces at the Museo Archeologico Nazionale di Palestrina, the town's excellent museum.

Palestrina stands on the slopes of Monte Ginestro about 40km east of Rome.

The delightful Museo Archeologico Nazionale di Palestrina (☑06 953 81 00; Piazza della Cortina; admission incl sanctuary adult/reduced €5/2.50; ☉9am-8pm, sanctuary 9am-1hr before sunset) occupies Palazzo Colonna Barberini, a Renaissance palace built atop the 2nd-century-BC Santuario della Fortuna Primigenia. Its airy halls display an interesting collection of ancient sculpture and funerary artefacts, as well as some huge Roman mosaics. But the crowning glory is the breathtaking *Mosaico Nilotico,* a detailed 2nd-century BC mosaic depicting the flooding of the Nile and everyday life in ancient Egypt.

Hidden down a side alley near the cathedral, Zi' Rico (☑06 8308 2532; www.zirico.it; Via Enrico Toti 2; meals €40; ☉12.30-3pm Tue-Sun & 8-11pm Tue-Sat) is a smart restaurant that impresses with its seasonal menu of updated Italian fare. Dishes such as *pappardelle al ragù bianco di cinghiale* (pasta ribbons with wild boar sauce) stand out alongside excellent wines from the well-stocked wine cellar. Reservations recommended.

❶ Getting There & Away

Cotral (☑800 174471, from a mobile 06 7205 7205; www.cotralspa.it) buses run to Palestrina from Rome's Ponte Mammolo metro station (€2.80, 50 minutes, at least hourly).

By car, follow Via Prenestina (SR155) for approximately 40km.

Subiaco

POP 8920

Set amid the steep wooded hills of the Valle dell'Aniene in Lazio's remote eastern reaches, Subiaco is one of the region's unsung pearls. Nero had a huge villa here – you can still see a few scant ruins just outside town – but it was St Benedict (480–543) who put the town on the map when he spent three years meditating in a local cave. This grotto is now incorporated into the Monastero di San Benedetto, one of the town's two historic Benedictine monasteries.

◎ Sights

★ Monastero di
San Benedetto   MONASTERY
(Santuario del Sacro Speco; ☑0774 8 50 39; www.benedettini-subiaco.org; ☉9am-12.30pm & 3-6pm) This spectacularly sited hilltop monastery is carved into the rock over the cave where St Benedict supposedly spent three years meditating. As well as its setting, described by Petrarch as 'the edge of Paradise', it boasts an interior almost entirely covered in 13th-to 15th-century frescoes. The Chiesa Superiore (Upper Church) features works by the 14th-century Sienese school and later 15th-century works illustrating episodes from the life of Benedict. Downstairs, the Chiesa Inferiore (Lower Church) has works from the 13th-century Roman school.

Accessible from the lower church, the Grotta di San Benedetto is in better shape now than when Benedict, here represented by Antonio Raggi's delicate marble statue, did his time here in around AD 500.

Another highlight is a painting of St Francis in the Capella di San Gregorio. This is reckoned to be one of the earliest known depictions of the saint, who is portrayed standing up and without his stigmata. This, scholars reckon, dates the painting to some time before 1224, the year St Francis supposedly received the stigmata.

Monastero di Santa Scolastica   MONASTERY
(☑0774 8 55 69; www.benedettini-subiaco.org; ☉9am-12.30pm & 3.30-7pm summer, to 6.15pm winter) Subiaco's Monastero di Santa Scolastica is the only one of the 13 monasteries built by St Benedict still standing in the Valley of the Amiene – and still occupied by monks. Visitable by free guided tour, it's a fascinating place centred on three internal cloisters, each dating from a separate period: the first

from the Renaissance, the second from the Gothic 14th century, and the third from the 1200s. Towering over everything is the monastery's landmark bell tower, virtually unchanged since the 12th century.

As well as its fascinating architecture, the monastery also boasts an important place in history as the site of Italy's first ever printing press. This was established by two visiting German monks in 1464.

🛏 Sleeping & Eating

Foresteria MONASTERY €
(📞 0774 8 55 69; www.benedettini-subiaco.org; B&B/half-board per person €37/51) For a contemplative night's stay, the Monastero di Santa Scolastica offers basic, institutional-style accommodation and a tranquil setting just outside town. Simple, homespun meals are also available, served at communal tables in the airy refectory (€20 to €25). Book ahead.

Il Cantuccio TRATTORIA €€
(📞 0774 8 34 14; www.ilcantucciosubiaco.it; Via Filzi 38; meals €25-30; ⊙ noon-2.30pm & 7.30-10pm Wed-Mon) Decamp to this family-run trattoria on a *centro storico* side street for a taste of authentic local cooking. Starters feature cheeses, cured meats and grilled veggies, setting you up nicely for earthy pastas paired with the likes of sausage and porcini mushrooms.

ℹ Information

Tourist Office (📞 0774 8 50 50; www.subiaco turismo.it; Corso Cesare Battisti; ⊙10am-6pm Tue-Sun) At the western end of town.

ℹ Getting There & Around

To get to Subiaco from Rome, take the **Cotral** (📞 800 174471, from a mobile 06 7205 7205; www.cotralspa.it) bus (€4.30, 1¼ hours, twice hourly, less frequently at weekends) from Ponte Mammolo metro station.

By car, take the A24 autostrada, exit at Vicovaro and follow the signs. It's about 60km.

Once in Subiaco, three weekday buses (two at weekends) serve the monasteries (€1.10) from the **Cotral bus stops** (Via Carlo Alberto Dalla Chiesa) near the tourist office.

South Coast

Lazio's southern coast boasts the region's best beaches and tracts of beautiful, unspoiled countryside, particularly around Monte Circeo, a rocky promontory that rises to 541m as it juts into the sea.

The main centres of interest are Anzio, a buzzing port known for its harbour-side fish restaurants; Sabaudia, a popular beach destination; and Sperlonga, an attractive seafront town with a hilltop medieval centre. Off-shore, the Isole Pontine provide plenty of laid-back island charm.

Anzio

POP 54,700

Anzio is a likeable fishing port popular with day-trippers who pile in on summer weekends to eat at its excellent seafood restaurants and hang out on its sandy beaches.

Situated 40km south of Rome, the town was at the centre of ferocious WWII fighting in the wake of a major Allied landing on 22 January 1944.

One of a string of seafood restaurants lined along the harbour front, bustling trattoria **La Nostra Paranza** (📞 338 2303844; Via Porto Innocenziano 23; set menu €20; ⊙ 12.45-2.45pm & 7.45-10.30pm, closed Wed & Sun dinner) is a real find. The menu is fixed, but you won't be short of choice as the multi-dish antipasto gets the four-course feast off to a superlative start. Continue with pasta before digging into freshly fried calamari or baked catch of the day and a cooling sorbet dessert. Booking is essential for weekends.

No summer day out would be complete without a gelato, and **Gelateria Fornai** (Piazza Garibaldi 8; gelato €1-3; ⊙ 2-8.30pm Mon-Thu, to midnight Fri, 11am-12.30am Sat, 11-8.30pm Sun) is one of the best in town. Among the flavours are some unusual and creative choices, including Sri Lankan coconut and *bacio al rhum* (chocolate-hazelnut with rum), as well as staples like intense, dark chocolate and Sorrento lemon.

ℹ Getting There & Away

Trains serve Anzio from Rome's Stazione Termini (€3.60, 70 minutes) every hour (every two hours on Sundays). If driving, take Via Pontina (SS148) and then Via Nettunense (SR207).

Sabaudia

POP 20,500

Set in the heart of the Parco Nazionale del Circeo, Sabaudia can lay claim to one of southern Lazio's finest beaches, a glorious, unspoilt stretch of sand backed by low-lying dunes. The town itself was founded in 1934 by Mussolini and, while not the most attractive of places, does possess some striking works of rationalist architecture.

◎ Sights

Spiaggia di Sabaudia   BEACH
(Strada Lungomare) Sabaudia's fabulous beach stretches for kilometres. A wide expanse of fine, soft sand flanked by billowing dunes capped by Mediterranean scrub, it's largely free of invasive development, with facilities concentrated at the end nearest town. The sea is clean and excellent for swimming, though it can get choppy when the wind whips in.

You'll need your own wheels (a car or bike) to get here, and note that parking can be a headache in peak summer months.

Parco Nazionale del Circeo   NATIONAL PARK
(www.parcocirceo.it) Encompassing around 85 sq km of billowing sand dunes, scratchy scrubland, forests, wetlands and four coastal lakes, the Circeo National Park offers a range of activities including hiking, fishing, birdwatching and cycling. Pick up trail maps and other information at the visitor centre (☑0773 51 22 40; Via Carlo Alberto 188; ☺9am-1pm & 2-4.30pm) in Sabaudia.

🛏 Sleeping & Eating

Agriturismo I Quattro Laghi   AGRITURISMO €
(☑338 2894796, 0773 59 31 35; www.quattrolaghi. it; Strada Sacramento 32; d €65, half-board per person €52-78; 图🛜) This welcoming year-round *agriturismo* sits on a 15-hectare farm about 800m inland from the beach. There's a genuine, workaday feeling to the place with its rustic, high-ceilinged rooms and restaurant specialising in filling farmhouse fare – meals cost €25 to €34. Kids will also enjoy the wide open spaces and occasional sight of animals grazing on the grass. No credit cards.

Pasticceria da Gigi   PASTRIES €
(☑0773 51 51 15; Via Cesare Battisti 2; pastries from €1.20, gelato €2-4; ☺7am-8pm Tue-Sun summer, shorter hours winter) A local institution, this pocket-size *pasticceria* tantalises with an array of artful *dolci* – try the delicious *cannoli* (pastry tubes filled with creamy ricotta) – and tasty gluten-free ice cream. It also does a good *cornetto* (croissant) and cappuccino, ideal for a classic Italian breakfast.

ℹ Information

Tourist Office (☑0773 51 50 46; www. prolocosabaudia.it; Piazza del Comune 18; ☺9.15am-12.30pm daily & 4.30-7.30pm Mon-Fri, 4.15-6.30pm Sat) Pick up the useful *Sabaudia Dove* booklet, which has basic maps and extensive local listings (in Italian and English). You can also buy bus and train tickets here.

ℹ Getting There & Away

From Laurentina metro station in Rome, **Cotral** (☑800 174471, from a mobile 06 7205 7205; www.cotralspa.it) buses cover the 90km to Sabaudia (€5, two hours, nine daily Monday to Friday, seven on Saturday).

On Sundays (and Saturdays in winter) you'll need to get a train from Termini to Priverno-Fossanova (€5.10, one hour, at least hourly) and then a connecting Cotral bus.

By car, Sabaudia is signposted off the main coastal road, Via Pontina (SS148).

ℹ Getting Around

For exploring the area, consider hiring a bike. **Zicchieri** (☑0773 51 01 37; www.zicchieri sabaudia.it; Corso Vittorio Emanuele III 102; ☺8am-1pm & 3-8pm daily summer, 9am-1pm & 3-6.30pm Mon-Sat winter) has a range to choose from, costing from €8 per day; mountain bikes and electric bikes are available for €20. Helmets cost €2 extra.

Sperlonga
POP 3300

The pick of Lazio's southern coastal towns, Sperlonga is a fashionable summer destination, much frequented by weekending Romans and Neapolitans. It has two sandy beaches either side of a rocky promontory and a hilltop medieval centre whose narrow whitewashed lanes are lined with boutiques, cafes and restaurants.

◎ Sights

Museo Archeologico di
Sperlonga e Villa di Tiberio   MUSEUM
(☑0771 54 80 28; Via Flacca, Km 16.3; adult/reduced €5/2; ☺8.30am-7.30pm) Other than the beach – and great views from the historic centre – Sperlonga's main attraction is this seafront archaeological museum. Here you can admire striking ancient sculpture, including a muscular depiction of the cyclops Polyphemus being blinded, and poke around the ruins of Villa Tiberio, the Emperor Tiberius' waterfront villa set around a gaping sea cave.

The museum is south of town, off the main coastal road, Via Flacca (SS123). On foot it's a 1.5km walk from the small marina on the southern side of the *centro storico*.

🛏 Sleeping & Eating

Hotel Mayor   HOTEL €€
(☑ 0771 54 92 45; www.hotelmayor.it; Via 1 Romita 24-36; s €45-110, d €55-200, tr €85-170, q €105-290; ✸ @ 🛜) Within easy walking distance of the beach and historic centre, the three-star Mayor is an old-school, family-run hotel with sunny, crisp-white rooms and its own stretch of private beach (room rates include a complimentary umbrella and sun-lounger). Note that minimum-stays of three to seven nights apply in summer.

★ **Altrò**   SEAFOOD €€
(☑ 320 1619390; http://altrosperlonga.it; Via Colombo 58; meals €40; ☉ 12.30-2.45pm & 7-11.30pm) With a strategic position at the bottom of the historic centre, this modern restaurant is raising the bar for seafood dining in Sperlonga. Tuna tartares and carpaccios paired with strawberries pave the way for delicately fried calamari and decadent fish grills, all plated with panache and served in a modern black-and-white interior.

★ **Gli Archi**   SEAFOOD €€
(☑ 0771 54 83 00; www.gliarchi.com; Via Ottaviano 17; meals €40; ☉ 12.30-3pm & 7.30-10.30pm Thu-Tue) One of the best restaurants in the medieval centre, Gli Archi provides a lovely setting for fresh fish. Sit down in the coolly elegant arched interior or go al fresco on the terrace and dig into seafood salad starters followed by risottos and pastas laced with super-fresh clams, mussels, prawns and scampi.

ℹ Getting There & Away

To get to Sperlonga, take the train from Termini to Fondi-Sperlonga (€7, 1¼ hours, half-hourly) and then a connecting **Piazzoli** (☑ 0771 51 90 67; www.piazzoli.it) bus (€1.50, 10 minutes, up to 12 daily).

By car, Sperlonga is 112km from Rome. Take Via Pontina (SS148) and follow signs to Terracina and then Sperlonga.

Isole Pontine

Off the southern Lazio coast, this group of volcanic islands serves as an Italian Hamptons. Between mid-June and the end of August, **Ponza** and **Ventotene** – the only two inhabited islands – buzz with holidaymakers and weekenders who descend in droves to eat shellfish at terrace restaurants, swim in emerald coves and cruise around the islands' craggy, cave-pitted coastlines. Outside of summer, the islands are very quiet, and, although expensive, a joy to explore.

Action centres on Ponza town, which rises above the harbour in a medley of white blocks and pastel hues, offering the usual array of souvenir shops, cafes and restaurants, as well as a small sandy beach.

◉ Sights

Spiaggia di Frontone   BEACH
A thin strip of pebbly sand fronting pristine waters and framed by pale rock faces, this is Ponza's top beach. It's a beautiful place, but

---

WORTH A TRIP

ABBAZIA DI MONTECASSINO

Dramatically perched on a mountaintop near the regional border with Campania, the **Abbazia di Montecassino** (☑ 0776 31 15 29; www.abbaziamontecassino.org; abbey free, museum adult/reduced €5/3; ☉ 8.45am-7pm daily summer, 9am-4.45pm Mon-Sat & 8.45am-5.15pm Sun winter) 🆓 was one of the most important Christian centres in the medieval world. St Benedict founded it in AD 529, supposedly after three ravens led him to the spot, and lived there until his death in 547.

The abbey's history, which is illustrated in its small museum, has been turbulent and it has been destroyed and rebuilt several times, most recently after WWII.

During the war, it was at the centre of heavy fighting as the Germans sought to stop the Allied push north. After almost six months of bloody deadlock, the Allies bombed it to rubble in May 1944 in a desperate bid to break through German defences.

To reach the abbey from Rome, take one of the half-hourly trains from Stazione Termini to Cassino (€8.40, 1½ to two hours) and then one of the three daily buses that run up from the station.

it gets very busy in summer so try to get a spot early. The best way to reach it is by boat from Ponza harbour – in summer, Cooperativa Barcaioli Ponzesi runs regular ferries (€5 return); the first departs at 9am, the last returns from the beach at 6pm.

☞ Tours

Cooperativa Barcaioli Ponzesi　　　　BOATING

(☎0771 80 99 29; www.barcaioliponza.it; Sotto il Tunnel di S Antonio; ⊙9am-midnight summer, shorter hours winter) Cooperativa Barcaioli is one of several outfits in Ponza offering island cruises – from €12.50 for an hour-long mini-cruise to €27.50 for an all-day excursion including lunch and a swimming stop. It also runs boats to the beach at Frontone.

🛏 Sleeping & Eating

Villa Ersilia　　　　B&B €€

(☎0771 8 00 97, 328 7749461; www.villaersilia.it; Via Scotti 2, Ponza; d €85-160; ⊙May-Sep; ❄🐱) Housed in a panoramic villa a short but calf-busting walk up from the harbour, this homey B&B wins you over with its simple rooms, manicured gardens and tasty breakfast. But what sticks in the memory most is the blissful sea view that unfurls before you from the terrace.

Oresteria by Ponza　　　　SEAFOOD €€

(☎347 3011376; www.oresteria.it; Corso Pisacane 51; meals €35; ⊙noon-2.30pm & 7-11pm) With its turquoise look and driftwood fish designs, Oresteria by Ponza is the very picture of a summery waterfront restaurant. Overlooking the port, it presents immaculate plates of finely cooked seafood, from octopus on a bed of sharply flavoured potato to risotto spiked with juicy mussels, capers and fried breadcrumbs.

ℹ Information

Tourist Office (☎0771 8 00 31; www.proloco diponza.it; Via Molo Musco; ⊙9am-1pm & 4-8pm daily summer, shorter hours winter) Can provide an island guide with a stylised map and lists of local services, as well as accommodation and eating options.

ℹ Getting There & Away

Ponza and Ventotene are accessible from Anzio, Terracina and Formia. Some services run year-round, including daily ferries from Terracina, but most operate from June to September.

The major ferry companies:

Laziomar (☎0771 83 16 40; www.laziomar. it) Services to Ponza from Terracina (ferry one way €10, 2½ hours), Formia (ferry one way €15, 2½ hours; fast ferry one way €22.50, 1½ hours) and Anzio (fast ferry one way €23.40, 1½ hours). Note there's a €2.50 port tax to add to the ticket prices quoted here.

Navigazione Libera del Golfo (NLG; ☎348 3706673; www.navlib.it) Hydrofoils from Terracina to Ponza (return €49.50, 50 minutes) and Ventotene (return €52.50, 1¾ hours).

Vetor (☎06 984 50 83; www.vetor.it) Hydrofoils from Anzio to Ponza (one way €25 to €44, 70 minutes). Extra charges apply for luggage: bags up to 10/20/30kg €5/15/25.

ℹ Getting Around

Autolinee Schiaffini (☎0771 8 03 68; www. schiaffini.com) runs buses from the port to points across the island. Tickets cost €1.50; bags are an extra €0.50. Timetables are posted at the tourist office.

To get your own wheels, **Noleggio Pilato** (☎338 4990565; Via Dante, Ponza; ⊙8am-midnight summer, to 8pm winter) rents out scooters (€30 to €40 per day including helmet and petrol) and cars/mini-mokes (€50 to €60 per day).

POPULATION
5.96 million

**CHOCOLATE
PRODUCTION**
85,000 tons per
annum

**BEST SEASIDE
HAMLET**
Camogli (p194)

BEST FOCACCIA
Antico Forno della
Casana (p191)

BEST BAROLO
More e Macine (p241)

WHEN TO GO
Jan–Mar Most
reliable snow cover
for skiing in the Alps.

Apr Fewer crowds
and fine days on the
Ligurian coast.

Sep & Oct Autumn
food festivals in Turin
and the Langhe.

Manarola (p207)

Turin, Piedmont & Cinque Terre

The beauty of northwestern Italy is its diversity. Piedmont's capital, Turin, is an elegant, easy city of baroque palaces, cutting-edge galleries and fittingly fabulous dining. While the region might have been one of Italy's 20th-century industrial success stories, it has also retained deep, lasting links to the soil, its wines and culinary offerings earning it the name of the 'new Tuscany'.

To the south, Liguria's slim, often vertical, sliver is home to Italy's Riviera, the fabled port city of Genoa and the beguiling villages of Cinque Terre. Expect dramatic coastal topography, beautifully preserved architecture and some of Italy's most memorable cuisine.

Head north and you'll soon hit the Alps and the semi-autonomous region of Aosta, where you can ski or hike beneath Europe's highest mountains.

Turin, Piedmont & Cinque Terre Highlights

❶ Museo Egizio (p223) Exploring the largest collection of Egyptian history outside of Cairo.

❷ Musei di Strada Nuova (p182) Discovering the art and architecture of Genoa's once-great maritime empire.

❸ Barolo (p237) Discussing terroir, tannins and tenacity with some of the world's most revered winemakers.

❹ Cinque Terre (p200) Hiking the fabulous trails along sea cliffs, through vineyards and up to lofty promontories.

❺ Funivie Monte Bianco (p251) Jumping the border aboard the state-of-the-art cable-car in Valle d'Aosta.

❻ Truffle festival (p235) Braving the crowds of truffle-snorting high rollers in Alba in October.

❼ Lerici (p212) Swimming in the Golfo di Poeti and remembering Shelley and Byron.

❽ Finale Ligure (p214) Exploring medieval architecture followed by a refreshing dip off pretty beaches.

❾ Parco Nazionale del Gran Paradiso (p254) Spotting chamois and gazing at waterfalls on magnificent mountain hikes.

THE ITALIAN RIVIERA

Italy's famed crescent of Mediterranean coast, where the Alps and the Apennines cascade into the sea, is defined by its sinuous, giddy landscapes. The Italian Riviera, synonymous with the Ligurian region, is shaped by its extreme topography – its daily life is one of ascents and descents, always in the presence of a watery horizon.

Anchored beside the region's best natural harbour is noble Genoa. Known as La Superba (the Superb One) to biased locals, it's a city that ruled over one of the finest maritime empires in medieval Europe. Fanning out on either side is the Riviera, home to many alluring destinations including the Portofino peninsula, the legendary Cinque Terre and more low-key seaside towns to Genoa's west.

This is both a deeply historic destination and a fabulously in-the-moment pleasure-seeking one, where you can explore lavish *palazzi* (mansions) or humble village churches and then simply swim, eat, walk or stare at the sea.

Genoa

📞 010 / POP 580,000

Italy's largest sea port is indefatigably contradictory, full at once of grandeur, squalor, sparkling light and deep shade. It's a gateway to the Riviera for many travellers today, but a weighty architectural heritage speaks of its former glory – the Most Serene Republic of Genoa ruled over the Mediterranean waves during the 12th to the 13th centuries – and history feels alive in Genoa. No more is this true than in its extensive old city, an often confronting reminder of premodern life with its twisting maze of *caruggi* (narrow streets), largely intact. Emerge blinking from this thrillingly dank heart to Via Garibaldi and the splendid Enlightenment-era gold-leaf halls of the Unesco-listed Palazzi dei Rolli.

Liguria

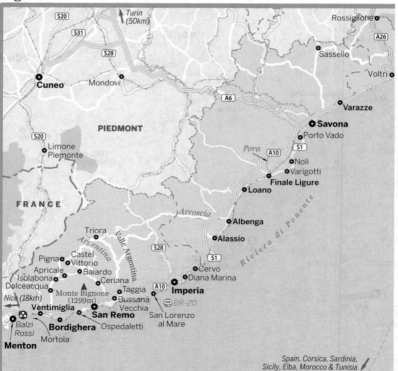

The city's once-tatty port area now hosts museums and a number of eating and drinking options. Its old town, too, has had its own far more organic revitalisation, with a bright new crop of fashionable shops, restaurants and bars lighting the way.

⊙ Sights & Activities

Keen museum-goers should pick up the Card Musei (24/48hr €12/20). The card gives free admission to over 20 of Genoa's museums and discounted access to several more. You can buy it at various museums, information booths and tourist offices.

Old City   AREA
(Centro Storico) The heart of medieval Genoa – bounded by ancient city gates Porta dei Vacca (Via del Campo) and Porta Soprana (Via di Porta Soprana), and the streets of Via Cairoli, Via Garibaldi and Via XXV Aprile – is famed for its *caruggi*. Looking up at the washing pegged on lines everywhere, it becomes obvious that these dark, cave-like laneways and blind alleys are still largely residential, although the number of fashionable bars, shops and cafes continues to grow.

Parts of the *caruggi* can feel somewhat unnerving, especially after dark. Although it's not particularly dangerous, do take care in the zone west of Via San Luca and south to Piazza Banchi, where most street prostitution and accompanying vice concentrates. East of the piazza is Via Orefici, where you'll find market stalls.

Primo Piano   GALLERY
(www.hotelpalazzogrillo.it; Vico alla Chiesa delle Vigne 18r; admission varies; ⊙4-8pm Wed-Sun) FREE A beautiful historical space that runs a program of modern and contemporary shows along interesting curatorial themes. The focus is often on photography. It's part of the Palazzo Grillo (p190) hotel but has a separate backstreet entrance.

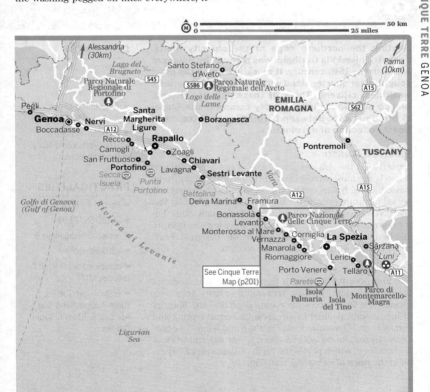

TOP SIGHT
MUSEI DI STRADA NUOVA

Skirting the northern edge of the old city limits, pedestrianised Via Garibaldi was planned by Galeazzo Alessi in the 16th century. It quickly became the most sought-after quarter, lined with the palaces of Genoa's wealthiest citizens. Three of these *palazzi* – Rosso, Bianco and Doria-Tursi – today comprise the Musei di Strada Nuova. Between them, they hold the city's finest collection of old masters.

Palazzo Rosso

Named after the rich red (*rosso*) hue of the facade, Palazzo Rosso is the most atmospheric of the bunch, and not to be missed. Lavishly frescoed rooms set with decorative art and period furniture provide the backdrop to fine works by Van Dyck, Veronese, Dürer and Strozzi, among many other European masters. There is also some surprising architecture and design on display, as well as an artfully designed courtyard and a viewing platform on the rooftop.

Frescoes

The 2nd floor is awash with frescoes painted by some of the Italian Riviera's greatest 17th-century artists. Standouts include the four successive rooms depicting the allegory of the seasons, painted by Gregorio de Ferrari (spring and summer) and Domenico Piola (autumn and winter). *Loggia Delle Rovine (Ruins of the Loggia)* is a wonderful work of *trompe l'oeil*, which places the myth of Diana and Endymion in the ruins of a classical mansion.

DON'T MISS

→ Gregorio de Ferrari's striking frescoes in Palazzo Rosso.

→ The Hall of Tapestries in Palazzo Doria-Tursi.

→ Rubens' *Venere e Marte* (*Venus and Mars*) in Palazzo Bianco.

PRACTICALITIES

→ Palazzi dei Rolli

→ ☏ 010 557 21 93

→ www.museidigenova.it

→ Via Garibaldi

→ combined ticket adult/reduced €9/7

→ ⊙ 9am-7pm Tue-Fri, 10am-7.30pm Sat & Sun Apr-Sep, 9.30am-6.30pm Oct-Mar

Paintings

The wealthy noble Gio Francesco Brignole commissioned Van Dyck – one of the greatest artists of his time – to paint full-length portraits of his family members in 1627. These exquisite works would later hang in the family home of Palazzo Rosso, where they remain today. They are joined by other Van Dyck masterpieces, including *Christ Carrying the Cross* and *Portrait of a Gentleman of the Spinola Family*. Other standouts include Guido Reni's *San Sebastiano* and Guercino's *La morte di Cleopatra (The Death of Cleopatra)*, as well as the lifelike *Pifferaio (Flute Player)* by Bernardo Strozzi and Veronese's macabre *Judith and Holofernes*.

Albini Apartments

The 3rd floor of Palazzo Rosso hides an Italian mid-century gem – an apartment designed by one of Italy's best-loved 20th-century architects, Franco Albini (1905–1977). Its mix of signature Albini furniture, clean modern lines and Genovese excess will delight design fans (the city views aren't bad either).

Palazzo Bianco

Flemish, Spanish and Italian artists feature at Palazzo Bianco, the second of the triumvirate of *palazzi*. Rubens' sensual and lushly painted *Venere e Marte (Venus and Mars)* and Van Dyck's *Vertumno e Pomona* – painted during his Genoese period – dominate room 18. Other splendid works showcase the talents of Hans Memling, Filippino Lippi and Murillo. There's also an assortment of 15th-century religious icons.

Courtyards

The palace has several elegant courtyards spread across two different levels. The first, accessed from the 1st floor of the museum, maintains its 18th-century design, complete with cobblestone mosaic paths, fountains and ornamental gardens. The second courtyard – reached on the pathway to Palazzo Doria-Tursi – contains the remains of a once impressive Gothic church. From here, you'll continue on into the galleries of Palazzo Doria-Tursi (no need to exit back onto the street).

Textile Collections

On the mezzanine floor, Palazzo Bianco's textile collections hold a trove of men's and women's fashion from several centuries. Garments here hail from across the globe, and include elaborate Kashmir shawls, 19th-century dresses of the Ottoman Empire, 18th-century French Argentan laces, and finely embroidered silks and gala costumes of the Napoleonic era.

TOP TIPS

➡ Go right at opening time to beat the crowds. Start with Palazzo Rosso.

➡ You get free admission to the Musei di Strada Nuova at the end of the historic-centre walking tour offered by Genoa's tourist office.

➡ For the full experience rent an audioguide (€5).

After visiting the palazzi, be sure to check out the other grand buildings on this street. Some have courtyards that are open to the public.

TAKE A BREAK

Get your daily gelato infusion a short walk from Via Garibaldi at the excellent **Gelateria Profumo** (www.villa1827.it; Vico Superiore del Ferro 14; cones from €2.50; ⊙ noon-7.30pm Tue-Sat), or pick up a slice of focaccia and other freshly baked goodies at **Pane e Tulipani** (✆ 010 817 88 41; Via dei Macelli di Soziglia 75; snacks from €2; ⊙ 6am-7.30pm Mon-Sat).

TURIN, PIEDMONT & CINQUE TERRE MUSEI DI STRADA NUOVA

Palazzo Doria-Tursi

Boasting a grand facade of marble, sandstone and slate, Palazzo Doria-Tursi was built in the late 16th century for Nicolò Grimaldi, who had deep ties to royalty. It later passed to Giovanni Andrea Doria, prince of Melfi, who enhanced the edifice with hanging gardens and side galleries. He also assembled a collection of tapestries and artworks from England and Flanders. In the 19th century, the palace saw more transformations – including the adding of the clock turret – under the ownership of Vittorio Emanuele I of Savoy. In the second half of the 19th century, the halls were decorated with frescoes.

Sala degli Arazzi

The aptly named *Sala degli Arazzi* (Hall of Tapestries) displays an impressive collection of textile art. It was assembled in part thanks to the close economic ties Genoa had with Flanders dating back to the 14th century. Among the treasures are several fine Flemish tapestries depicting events from the life of Alexander the Great.

Sala Paganini

The final rooms feature a small but absorbing collection of legendary violinist Niccolò Paganini's personal effects. Pride of place goes to the great musician's Cannone violin, made in Cremona in 1743. One lucky musician gets to play the maestro's violin during October's Paganini festival. Other artefacts on show include letters, musical scores and his travelling chess set. Enter the galleries via Palazzo Bianco.

Town Hall

In addition to fine art and priceless musical instruments, the palace also houses Genoa's town hall – a role it's held since 1848. There's no charge to wander around the courtyard and admire the design from the staircases (simply enter via the main palace entrance at number 9).

TOP SIGHT
PALAZZO REALE

If you only get the chance to visit one of the Palazzi dei Rolli (group of palaces belonging to the city's most eminent families), make it this one. A former residence of the Savoy dynasty, it has terraced gardens, exquisite furnishings, a fine collection of 17th-century art and a gilded Hall of Mirrors that is worth the entry fee alone.

History

The palace was built by the wealthy Balbi family in the 1640s but went through various transformations as the Durazzo family bought the building in 1679 and redecorated many of the rooms, redesigned the facade on Via Balbi and rebuilt the Teatro del Falcone. Renovations of the early 18th century added some of the *palazzo's* most dramatic features. Hard times forced the Durazzos to sell the building, which ultimately became a royal palace after it was purchased by Vittorio Emanuele I, King of Sardinia, in 1824. The Emanuele clan renovated various rooms, creating a throne room, audience chamber and ball room among other refitting. It remained a royal residence until 1919, when King Vittorio Emanuele III ceded it to the Italian State.

Second Floor

The grandeur of this noble residence is apparent as you ascend the stairs and wander through a series of elaborately decorated rooms. Through these photogenic chambers you'll find a mix of oversized oil paintings, lavish stucco details, Classical marble sculptures, Flemish tapestries and dazzling ceiling frescoes. Highlights include the Hall of Mirrors, designed by Domenico Parodi in the 1720s and 1730s. Influenced by the Galerie des Glaces in Versailles, the staggering room is lined with exquisitely carved statues of Roman deities, like *Adonis*, a 17th-century work by Filippo Parodi – the greatest Genoese sculptor of his time. Further along, the King's Bedroom features frescoes by Tommaso Aldrovandini and the palace's greatest treasure – the painting *Cristo Spirante* (Christ Crucified) by Van Dyck.

First Floor

The 1st floor of the palace houses the apartments of the hereditary princes, also called Appartamento del Duca degli Abruzzi (the Duke of Abruzzi), after the last member of the House of Savoy who lived there, Luigi Amedeo di Savoia-Aosta. The ten rooms provide a fascinating portrait of life among the 19th-century royals, with intact furnishings, tapestries and artworks.

DON'T MISS

➡ The dazzling Versailles-like Galleria degli Specchi (Hall of Mirrors).

➡ Lifelike sculptures by the great 17th-century artist Filippo Parodi.

➡ The magnificent painting *Cristo Spirante* (Christ Crucified) by Van Dyck.

PRACTICALITIES

➡ ☑ 010 271 02 36

➡ www.palazzoreale genova.beniculturali.it

➡ Via Balbi 10

➡ adult/reduced €6/2

➡ ⊙ 9am-6.30pm Tue-Fri, 1.30-7pm Sat & Sun

TURIN, PIEDMONT & CINQUE TERRE PALAZZO REALE

Genoa

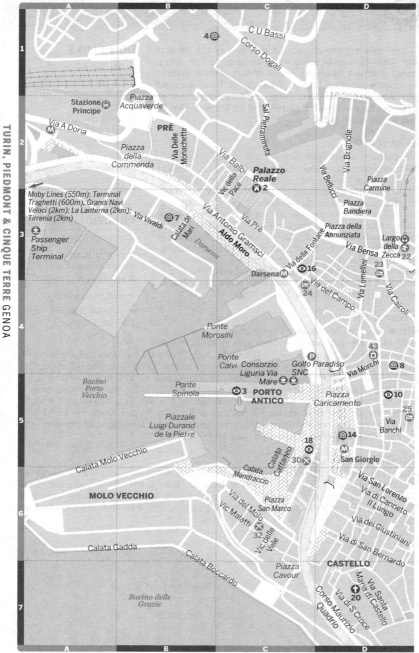

C U Bassi

Corso Dogali

4

Stazione Principe

Piazza Acquaverde

PRÉ

Via A Doria

Piazza della Commenda

Via Delle Monachette

Via Balbi

Sa Pietraminuta

Palazzo Reale
2

Via della Pace

Via Pre

Via Antonio Gramsci

Aldo Moro

Via Birgnole

Via Bellucci

Piazza Carmine

Piazza Bandiera

Piazza della Annunziata

Via Bensa

Largo della Zecca
22

Via Lomellini

23

Via Cairoli

Moby Lines (550m); Terminal Traghetti (600m); Grandi Navi Veloci (2km); La Lanterna (2km); Tirrenia (2km)

Passenger Ship Terminal

Via Vivaldi

Calata de Mari

7

Darsena

Darsena M

Via delle Fontane

16

Via del Campo

24

Bacino Porto Vecchio

Ponte Morosini

Ponte Calvi

Ponte Spinola

Consorzio Liguria Via Mare

Golfo Paradiso SNC

3

PORTO ANTICO

Piazza Caricamento

Via Morchi

43

8

10

Piazza

25

Via Banchi

Piazzale Luigi Durand de la Pierre

Calata Molo Vecchio

Calata Cattaneo

18

30

14

San Giorgio

Via San Lorenzo

Via di Canneto Il Lungo

MOLO VECCHIO

Via del Molo

Vic Malatti

Calata Mandraccio

Piazza San Marco

32

Vic delle Vele

Via dei Giustiniani

Via di San Bernardo

Calata Gadda

Calata Boccardo

Piazza Cavour

CASTELLO

Bacino delle Grazie

Corso Maurizio Quadrio

Via di S Croce

20

Via Santa Maria di Castello

Galleria Nazionale di
Palazzo Spinola   GALLERY

(www.palazzospinola.beniculturali.it; Piazza Superiore di Pellicceria 1; adult/reduced €6/2; ☺8.30am-7.30pm Tue-Sat, 1.30-7.30pm Sun) This gallery's paintings are wonderfully displayed over four floors of the 16th-century Palazzo Spinola, once owned by the Spinola family, one of Genoa's most formidable dynasties. The main focus is Italian and Flemish Renaissance art of the so-called Ligurian School (look out for Van Dyck, Rubens and Strozzi), but it's also worth visiting to gape at the decorative architecture.

Cattedrale di San Lorenzo   CATHEDRAL

(Piazza San Lorenzo; ☺8am-noon & 3-7pm) Genoa's zebra-striped Gothic–Romanesque cathedral owes its continued existence to the poor quality of a British WWII bomb that failed to ignite here in 1941; it still sits on the right side of the nave like an innocuous museum piece.

The cathedral, fronted by three arched portals, twisting columns and crouching lions, was first consecrated in 1118. The two bell towers and cupola were added later in the 16th century.

Inside, above the central doorway, there's a great lunette with a painting of the *Last Judgment,* the work of an anonymous Byzantine painter of the early 14th century. In the sacristy, the Museo del Tesoro (🗷010 209 18 63; Piazza San Lorenzo; adult/child €6/5; ☺9am-noon & 3-6pm Mon-Sat, 3-6pm Sun) preserves various dubious holy relics, including the medieval *Sacro Catino,* a glass vessel once thought to be the Holy Grail. Other artefacts include the polished quartz platter upon which Salome is said to have received John the Baptist's head, and a fragment of the True Cross.

Palazzo Ducale   MUSEUM

(www.palazzoducale.genova.it; Piazza Giacomo Matteotti 9; price varies by exhibition; ☺hours vary) Once the seat of the independent republic, this grand palace was built in the Mannerist style in the 1590s and was largely refurbished after a fire in the 1770s. Today it hosts high-profile temporary art exhibitions, several smaller galleries and occasional markets in its lofty atrium. The *palazzo* also has a bookshop and cafe.

Piazza de Ferrari   PIAZZA

Genoa's fountain-embellished main piazza is ringed by magnificent buildings that include the art nouveau Palazzo della Borsa, which was once the country's stock exchange, and

Genoa

the hybrid neoclassical-modernist Teatro Carlo Felice (☎010 58 93 29; www.carlofelice. it; Passo Eugenio Montale 4), bombed in WWII and not fully rebuilt until 1991.

Chiesa del Gesù
CHURCH

(Piazza Giacomo Matteotti; ⊙3.30-7.30pm Mon, 7am-1pm & 3.30-7.30pm Tue-Sat, 8am-1pm & 4-10pm Sun) Hidden behind Piazza de Ferrari (p187), this former Jesuit church dating from 1597 has an intricate and lavish interior. The wonderfully frescoed walls and ceiling are anchored by two works by the great Dutch artist Rubens. *Circoncisione (Circumcision)* hangs over the main altar, and *Miracolo di San Ignazio* is displayed in a side chapel.

Santa Maria di Castello
ABBEY

(☎010 860 36 90, 347 9956740; www.santamariadicastello.it; Salita di Santa Maria di Castello 15; ⊙10-1pm & 3-6pm) Built on the site of the original settlement, and sheltering under the 11th-century Embriaci Tower, this Romanesque church and convent, itself built before AD 900, is an extraordinary, little-visited historic site. Its walls are covered

with treasures that were commissioned by the noble families of Genoa from the earliest times, though some of the notable frescoes also date to the 16th and 17th century. Private tours, by coin donation, are possible.

Porto Antico
AREA

(www.portoantico.it; 🚻) The port that once controlled a small empire is now one of the most popular places to enjoy a *passeggiata* (evening stroll). Superyacht lovers are particularly well catered for and those with kids will love the aquarium, the futuristic Bigo (lookout), the small public swimming pool and the pirate ship.

Palazzo San Giorgio
HISTORIC BUILDING

(Palazzo San Giorgio 2) One of the most famous monuments on Genoa's waterfront is this mural-covered building constructed in 1260. St George is one of Genoa's patron saints, and the dragon slayer is featured prominently underneath the clock. The six men depicted below St George represent some of Genoa's most famous native sons, including Christopher Columbus, second from left.

The *palazzo* has fulfilled many roles over the years as the seat of civic power during the Middle Ages, as a customs office for maritime trade, and later in the 15th century as the headquarters for the Casa delle Compere e dei Banchi di San Giorgio, which became one of the world's first banks. The building was also used as a prison, and allegedly held Marco Polo here in 1298.

Acquario
AQUARIUM

(☑ 010 2 34 51; www.acquariodigenova.it; Ponte Spinola; adult/reduced €32/21; ⊙ 9am-8pm Mar-Jun & Sep & Oct, 8.30am-9pm Jul & Aug, 9.30am-8pm Nov-Feb) Genoa's much-vaunted aquarium is one of the largest in Europe, with more than 600 species of sea creatures, including sharks. Moored at the end of a walkway is the ship *Grande Nave Blu*, a unique floating display with exhibits of coral reefs. The aquarium's 'cetaceans pavilion' may concern some visitors: while the dolphins do not perform tricks and the aquarium fulfils its international legal requirements, including rehousing abused dolphins, animal welfare groups claim keeping dolphins in enclosed tanks is harmful.

Buy tickets online to save a few euros and to avoid long, hot queues (and harassment from street traders) in summer; a combination ticket (adult/reduced €57/40) gives you access to other port attractions, the Galata Museo del Mare, the Biosphere and the panoramic lift. Note that the last entrance is two hours before closing.

Galata Museo del Mare
MUSEUM

(www.galatamuseodelmare.it; Calata de Mari 1; adult/child €13/8; ⊙ 10am-7.30pm daily Mar-Oct, 10am-6pm Tue-Fri, to 7.30pm Sat & Sun Nov-Feb) Genoa was rivalled only by Barcelona and Venice as

a medieval and Renaissance maritime power, so its 'museum of the sea' is, not surprisingly, one of its most relevant and interesting. High-tech exhibits trace the history of seafaring, from Genoa's reign as Europe's greatest dockyard to the ages of sail and steam.

Boccadasse
VILLAGE

(near Via Boccadasse) When the sun is shining, do as the Genovese do and decamp for a *passeggiata* (late afternoon stroll) along the oceanside promenade, Corso Italia, which begins around 3km east of the city centre. This broad 2.5km-long pavement lined with Liberty villas leads to Boccadasse, a once separate fishing village that appears like a sawn-off chunk of Cinque Terre. Its pebble beach is a perfect gelato-licking location by day and its gaggle of small bars serve up *spritz* (cocktail made with Prosecco) to happy crowds on summer evenings.

Bus No 42 goes to Boccadasse from Via Dante near the De Ferrari metro station. Bus 31 also goes there from Brignole Station.

⭐ Festivals & Events

Parole Spalancate
PERFORMING ARTS

(Festival Internazionale di Poesia di Genova; www.parolespalancate.it; ⊙ Jun) Held over 11 days in June, this international poetry festival features much more than just artful wordplay. Concerts, special art exhibitions, video installations, dance performances and guided tours are all part of the draw – along with notable authors from 30 different countries (including the occasional Nobel Prize winner).

Slow Fish
FOOD & DRINK

(http://slowfish.slowfood.it; ⊙ May) 🌱 FREE Every odd-numbered year in early May, this

---

BEST CITY PANORAMAS

Spianata Castelletto Admire the beauty of Genoa from this leafy lookout in the hills, packed with gelato-licking locals at weekends. Get there via the Art Nouveau lift on Piazza del Portello, or take the steep lane/staircase of Salita San Gerolamu.

Castello d'Albertis (Museum of World Cultures; ☑ 010 272 38 20; www.museidigenova.it; Corso Dogali 18; adult/child €6/4.50; ⊙ 10am-6pm Tue, Wed & Fri, 1-10pm Thu, 10am-7pm Sat & Sun Apr-Sep, 10am-5pm Tue-Fri, to 6pm Sat & Sun Oct-Mar) The leafy grounds of this late 19th-century, neo-Gothic castle offer fine city views. Inside, admire ethnographic artefacts from around the globe, assembled by Italian navigator and philanthropist Enrico d'Albertis during his travels. The castle is a steep 700m climb from Genoa's Piazza Principe train station, or save your legs by taking the Ascensore Montegalletto on Via Balbi.

La Lanterna (www.lanternadigenova.it; Via alla Lanterna; adult/reduced €6/5; ⊙ 2-6.30pm Sat & Sun) Genoa's lighthouse (1543) is one of the world's oldest and tallest – and it still works, beaming its light over 50km to warn ships and tankers. Stagger up 172 steps to ponder big sea views and exhibits, in an adjacent museum, of lamps, lenses and related history.

festival celebrates seafood with a fish market and tastings. Affiliated with the Slow Food movement, it also runs free workshops focusing on water pollution, good fishing practices and aquaculture.

🛏 Sleeping

Manêna HOSTEL €
(🖉 346 3521928; www.manenahostel.com; Vico alla Chiesa della Maddalena 9/1; dm €23-28; 🏵 🛜) In a quiet lane near the Maddalena church, the easy-going Manêna was Genoa's first hostel to open in the historic centre back in 2012, and it's still one of the best. Dorms have five to 12 beds, with tall ceilings, decent natural light, and privacy curtains (and reading lights) in the bunks. There's also a kitchen.

La Superba B&B €
(🖉 010 869 85 89; www.la-superba.com; Via del Campo 12; s/d €85/95; 🏵 🛜) This lovingly cared-for, well-equipped place at a bargain price has rooms spread over the two top floors of an old *palazzo*. Top-floor rooms have pretty mansard ceilings and one a tiny terrace with spectacular port and city views (along with the Genovese soundtrack of crosstown traffic). There are also generous lounge and breakfast areas.

Hotel Cairoli HOTEL €
(🖉 010 246 14 54; www.hotelcairoligenova.com; Via Cairoli 14/4; d €70-160, tr €100-180, q €115-200; 🏵 🛜) For five-star service at three-star prices, book at this artful hideaway. Rooms, on the 3rd floor of a towering *palazzo,* are themed on modern artists and feature works inspired by the likes of Mondrian, Dorazio

and Alexander Calder. Add in a reading room, chill-out area, small gym and terrace, and you have the ideal bolthole.

Cheaper rates are available without breakfast. The hotel also has several apartments, sleeping up to eight people

Hotel Suisse HOTEL €
(🖉389 6669171; www.hotelsuissegenova.it; 3rd fl, Via XX Settembre 21; s/d/tr/q from €65/70/85/95; 🛜) Clean, uncluttered rooms, service with a smile and excellent prices all inside an art-nouveau beauty. What more could you want? Climb the stairs to the 3rd floor of this strapping Genoa building near Stazione Brignole for a bit of faded fin-de-siècle magic.

★ Palazzo Grillo DESIGN HOTEL €€
(🖉 010 247 73 56; www.hotelpalazzogrillo.it; Piazza delle Vigne 4; d €130-300; 🏵 🛜) In a once derelict *palazzo*, Genovese locals Matteo and Laura have created the extraordinary place to stay that Genoa has been crying out for. Stunning public spaces are dotted with spot-on contemporary design pieces, character-filled vintage finds and – look in any direction – original 15th-century frescoes. Rooms are simple but superstylish with Vitra TVs and high ceilings.

Genova 46 GUESTHOUSE €€
(🖉 010 859 58 01; www.genova46.it; Via Assarotti 46/11; d €110-200; 🏵 🛜) On the top floor of an elegant 1891 mansion, Genova 46 has five spacious rooms and suites, all set with original details (like stucco ceilings) and vibrant contemporary artwork on the walls (borrowed from the Galleria Rotta Farinelli). The warm welcome adds to the appeal.

LOCAL KNOWLEDGE

MOUNTAIN ESCAPE

On sunny weekend days, the Genovese escape the busy lanes of the city centre and head for the hills for walks, picnics and long, leisurely meals at rustic country restaurants. The **Funicolare Zecca-Righi** (Largo della Zecca) travels high above Genoa, stopping at several stations before reaching a terminus at Zecca-Righi. From there, you can make the 3km walk through woodlands of the Area Naturale della Mura and up to Forte Sperone, an abandoned fortification that was once an essential part of the city's 19th-century defences. From there, you can keep walking, all the way up past a series of other towers and forts, eventually leading to Forte Diamante. Perched on a ridge at 667m above sea level, this iconic 17th-century fortress offers sweeping 360-degree views over Genoa and the rolling, craggy hillsides surrounding the city.

Another option for a relaxing getaway is to take the narrow-gauge **Ferrovia Genova Casella** (www.ferroviagenovacasella.it; one way €4.50, family one way/return €20), which snakes 25km north from the cute Stazione di Genova Piazza Manin to the village of Casella in the Valle Scrivia. Memorable walks intersect at various stations along the way, including at Trensacaso, where you can pick up the trail heading west to Forte Diamante.

It's a 15-minute stroll into the old town, but a steep (uphill) walk back from there.

Le Nuvole
BOUTIQUE HOTEL €€

(📋 010 251 00 18; www.hotellenuvole.it; Piazza delle Vigne 6; d €130-160, ste €140-180; ✴ 🛜) A lovely small hotel where smart modern furniture and slick bathrooms make the most of an ancient *palazzo*'s original architecture and its knockout lofty ceilings, lovingly restored plaster mouldings and beautiful tilework. Owners are hands-on and helpful; breakfast is taken in the beautiful rooftop space at neighbouring Palazzo Grillo.

🍴 Eating

Genoa is a delight to the culinary inclined. Ubiquitous local specialities beyond pesto include focaccia and *farinata* (chickpea flour flat bread), *torta pasqualina* (spinach, artichoke, ricotta and egg tart), *polpettone* (a gratined potato and egg slice, rather than meatballs), *pansotti* (a filled pasta of wild, wilted greens with a creamy walnut sauce) and Russian salad. The freshly caught seafood is also unmissable.

Mercato Orientale Genova
ITALIAN €

(MOG; 📋 010 897 30 00; www.moggenova.it; Via XX Settembre 75; mains from €8; ⏰10am-11.45pm; 📋) This gourmet food hall in Genoa's oldest market offers nearly a dozen different stands. You can dine on wood-oven-fired pizzas, pastas, burgers, focaccia, *panini* (sandwiches), tacos and fresh seafood. A square bar stands at the centre of the vast 19th-century hall, and there's also a wine bar and a high-end restaurant helmed by the celebrated young chef Daniele Rebosio.

Antico Forno della Casana
BAKERY €

(Vico della Casana 17; focaccia from €1.50; ⏰7am-8pm Mon-Sat) A much-loved local institution, this back-lane bakery fires up some of Genoa's best focaccia, which are available in countless varieties. The Antico Forno della Casana also whips up delicious *torta di verdura* (a quiche-like vegetable tort) and satisfying slices of *farinata*.

Rooster
FAST FOOD €

(📋 010 899 69 14; www.roosterrotisserie.com; Piazza Giacomo Matteotti 41; sandwiches around €6; ⏰10.30am-10pm Mon-Sat, to 3pm Sun) A cute little hole in the wall that breathes new life into the traditional rotisserie chicken. Birds are all free range and local; buy them whole (from €9) for a picnic or eat in for one of their special *panini*, which may come with the likes of eggplant and mozzarella, or with pesto and cheese curd.

La Botega Del Gusto
LIGURIAN €

(Vico Superiore del Ferro 3; dishes €7-10; ⏰11.30am-5pm Mon-Thu, to 10pm Fri & Sat) Genovese fast food done in the most authentic and enticing of ways can be had at this backstreet hole in the wall. Come for a quick and easy plate of *pansotti* (filled pasta with wild greens), quiche-like spinach-and-artichoke *torta pasqualina*, baked rabbit or steamed salt cod.

Trattoria Da Maria
TRATTORIA €

(📋 010 58 10 80; Vico Testadoro 14r; meals €10-20; ⏰11.45am-2.45pm Mon-Sat, 6.15-10pm Thu & Fri) Brace yourself for lunchtime mayhem. This is a totally authentic, if well touristed, workers' trattoria and there's much squeezing into tiny tables, shouted orders and a fast and furious succession of plates plonked on tables. A daily hand-scrawled menu is a roll call of elemental favourites that keep all comers full and happy, along with the jugs of ridiculously cheap wine.

⭐ Trattoria Rosmarino
TRATTORIA €€

(📋 010 251 04 75; www.trattoriarosmarino.it; Salita del Fondaco 30; meals €28-34; ⏰12.30-2.30pm & 7.30-10.30pm Mon-Sat) Rosmarino cooks up the standard local specialities, yes, but the straightforwardly priced menu has an elegance and vibrancy that sets it apart. With two nightly sittings, there's always a nice buzz (though there are also enough nooks and crannies that a romantic night for two isn't out of the question). Call ahead for an evening table.

Osteria di Vico Palla
LIGURIAN €€

(📋 010 246 65 75; www.osteriadivicopalla.com; Vico Palla 15; meals €26-36; ⏰12.30-3pm & 7.30-11pm Tue-Sun) This old-fashioned tavern near the waterfront has been around in one form or another since the 1600s. Wooden tables, low-arched brick ceilings and a few nautical knick-knacks set the scene for seafood feasting with a minimum of fuss. The changing chalkboard menu (brought to your table) is replete with Genovese delicacies.

Bella Bu
LIGURIAN €€

(📋 010 247 42 09; http://bellabubistrot.com; Vico Inferiore del Ferro 9; meals €25-40; ⏰6.30pm-1am Mon-Thu, to 2am Fri & Sat) An atmospherically lit spot for tapas and cocktails early in the evening, or a proper dinner later in the night. The youthful owners showcase quality seasonal and market-fresh ingredients in

ℹ️ MENU DECODER: LIGURIAN DISHES

Pesto genovese: It would be criminal to come to Genoa and not try *pesto genovese*. The city's famous pasta sauce – a pounded mix of basil, pine nuts, olive oil and sometimes garlic – really does taste, and look, better here than anywhere else. This is a result of the basil that's used (the leaves of very young plants are plucked daily from hothouses on city hillsides), as well as techniques honed through generations.

Farinata: a chickpea flour flat bread, like the Niçoise *panisse* and *socca*; usually made in dedicated shops where you can buy by the slice, though often found on restaurant menus, too.

Polpettone: bubble-and-squeak-like slice of potato, green beans or other seasonal vegetables and eggs, scented with marjoram, baked and topped with breadcrumbs and cheese.

Corzetti: handmade disc-shaped pasta, often embossed with a stamp and traditionally 'flavoured' with a few drops of the local white wine, Pigato.

Salsa di noce: a pesto-like pasta sauce made from ground walnuts, olive oil, garlic and soaked bread as a thickener; usually served either with *corzetti* or with ravioli filled with bitter wild greens.

Torta pasqualina: an Easter-time special that's also served year-round, a quiche-like mix of eggs, cheese and sautéed spring artichokes baked in a short pastry crust.

Cappon magro: a celebratory layered salad of eggs, green beans, celery and other vegetables on top of dry olive-oil biscuits and topped with lobster, prawns and other seafood, as well as green olives and artichokes.

creative plates that pull from both Ligurian and Spanish recipes, all of which pair nicely with the natural wines on offer.

⭐ **Il Marin**   SEAFOOD €€€

(Eataly Genova; ☑ 010 869 87 22; www.eataly.net; Porto Antico; meals €50-60, 8-course menu €75; ⊙12.30-3pm & 7.30-10.30pm Wed-Mon) Eating by the water often means a compromise in quality, but Eataly's 3rd-floor fine-dining space delivers both panoramic port views and Genoa's most innovative seafood menu. Rustic wooden tables, Renzo Piano–blessed furniture and an open kitchen make for an easy, relaxed glamour, while dishes use unusual Mediterranean-sourced produce and look gorgeous on the plate. Book ahead.

To save some cash, come midday for the chef's three-course lunch menu (€25 to €35).

🍷 Drinking & Nightlife

Aperitivo spritzes can be had anywhere, but never underestimate the lure of the *caruggi* later on. You'll find a number of new drinking spots intermingled with old-time favourites throughout the city, particularly in the streets just northwest of Piazza de Ferrari. Piazza delle Erbe pulls the city's young for cheap and cheerful *aperitivi* (predinner drinks) and occasionally gets rowdy well into the night.

⭐ **Cantine Matteotti**   WINE BAR

(☑ 010 868 70 00; Archivolto Baliano 4-6/r; ⊙6pm-1am Sun-Thu, to 2am Fri & Sat) The Puccini wafting up the laneway gives you some clue that this is a special little place. The owners here have a passion for good music and brilliant wine, and will pour you some amazing local drops and stave off your hunger with creatively topped crostini, pesto lasagna or generous cheese platters.

⭐ **Les Rouges**   COCKTAIL BAR

(☑ 329 3490644; www.lesrouges.it; 1st fl, Piazza Campetto 8a; ⊙6-11.45pm Sun-Thu, to 12.45am Fri & Sat) One of Genoa's surfeit of crumbling *palazzi* is being put to excellent use in this atmospheric cocktail bar. Three bearded, vest-wearing, red-headed brothers – the 'rouges' of the name – man the floor and shake up some of the city's best cocktails, using top-shelf ingredients and herbal or floral flavours such as chamomile and kaffir lime.

Malkovich   COCKTAIL BAR

(www.facebook.com/MalkovichGenova; Via ai Quattro Canti di San Francesco 32r; ⊙9pm-1am Sun-Thu, to 3am Fri & Sat) Tucked under the bar Groove, Malkovich is one of Genoa's most atmospheric and secretive drinking dens. To get in, you'll have to provide the password (check the Facebook page for the question, which you'll have to answer!). Once inside, flickering candles, upbeat jazz and vintage furnishings scattered about the various rooms evoke Prohibition-era glam. There's even an artfully placed bathtub.

Scurreria Beer & Bagel BEER HALL
(Via di Scurreria 22r; ⊘6pm-1am Mon-Fri, from noon Sat & Sun; ☎) A little bit of Brooklyn or Melbourne in the *caruggi*, this brewpub packs out with Genoa's black-clad young. There are over a dozen taps of local and imported beers and a staggering by-the-bottle list. And, yes, they do bagels, stuffed in a way that only an Italian can do, along with other belly-liners.

🛍 Shopping

Heading southwest, elegant Via Roma, adjacent to the glass-covered Galleria Giuseppe Mazzini (Off Via XXV Aprile; ⊘8am-10pm), is Genoa's designer shopping street. It links Piazza Corvetto with Piazza de Ferrari. The old city's lanes are full of all kinds of traditional shops as well as many new independent fashion, vintage and homewares boutiques.

★ Via Garibaldi 12 HOMEWARES
(☏010 253 03 65; www.viagaribaldi12.com; Via Garibaldi 12; ⊘10am-2pm & 3.30-7pm Tue-Sat) Even if you're not in the market for designer homewares, it's worth trotting up the noble stairs just to be reminded how splendid a city Genoa can be. There's an incredibly canny collection of contemporary furniture and objects, as well as 'interventions' by contemporary artists such as Damian Hirst and Sterling Ruby, with works occasionally loaned from New York's Gagosian gallery.

Temide DESIGN
(www.temidestore.it; Vico del Fieno 40; ⊘3.30-7.30pm Mon, 10.30am-2pm & 3.30-7.30pm Tue-Sat) A showcase of Ligurian creativity, Temide sells works by local artists and artisans, including delicate ceramics, eye-catching jewellery, colourfully embroidered bags, hand-painted silk scarves, homewares made from recycled materials, and art-naïf sculptures and paintings. In short, you'll find plenty of original gift ideas. Temide also has a store in Savona.

La Medina Genova FOOD
(Via San Luca 82; ⊘8am-1pm & 3.30-7.30pm Mon-Sat) Evoking all the exoticism of far-flung travels to North Africa and beyond, this tiny shop has shelves packed with jars of fragrant spices, nuts, colourful dried fruits, roasted coffee beans and smokey loose-leaf teas. You can also pick up woven shopping bags or Moroccan ceramics here.

Pietro Romanengo fu Stefano CHOCOLATE
(www.romanengo.com; Via Soziglia 74r; ⊘3.15-7.15pm Mon, 9am-1pm & 3.15-7.15pm Tue-Sat) An intriguing historic chocolate shop (established 1780) that specialises in candied flowers and floral waters: it really does feel as if nothing has changed since *long* before the Risorgimento.

ℹ Information

Tourist Office (☏010 557 29 03; www.visitgenoa.it; Via Garibaldi 12r; ⊘9am-6.20pm) Helpful office in the historic centre.

Tourist Office (☏010 557 29 03; Arrivals Hall, Cristoforo Colombo Airport; ⊘10am-8pm)

ℹ Getting There & Around

AIR
Regular domestic and international services, including Ryanair flights to London Stansted, use **Cristoforo Colombo Airport** (☏010 6 01 51; www.airport.genova.it), 6km west of the city in Sestri Ponente.

The AMT **Volabus** (☏848 000030; www.amt.genova.it; one way €6) runs to/from Genoa's two main train stations (Piazza Principe and Brignole). Services are at least hourly between 5am and 11.45pm to the airport, 5.50am to 12.20am from the airport. Buy tickets for the 30-minute journey on board.

A taxi to or from the airport will cost around €20 to €30.

BOAT
Information and tickets for boat trips around the port and destinations further afield are available from the **ticket booths** (Ponte Spinola; ⊘9.30am-6.30pm Sep-Jun, 9am-8pm Jul & Aug) beside the aquarium at Porto Antico.

From June to September, **Golfo Paradiso SNC** (☏392 1375558; www.golfoparadiso.it) operates boats from Porto Antico to Camogli (one way/return €10/17), Portofino (€15/24) and Cinque Terre (€21/38).

Consorzio Liguria Via Mare (www.liguriaviamare.it) runs a range of seasonal trips to Camogli, San Fruttuoso and Portofino; Monterosso in Cinque Terre; and Porto Venere.

Only cruise ships use the 1930s Ponte dei Mille terminal while ferries sailing to Spain, Sicily, Sardinia, Corsica, Morocco and Tunisia use the neighbouring international passenger terminals or the **Terminal Traghetti** (Ferry Terminal; Via Milano 51).

Fares listed here are for one-way, high-season deck-class tickets. Ferry operators include the following:

Grandi Navi Veloci (GNV; ☏010 209 45 91; www.gnv.it) Ferries to Sardinia (Porto Torres from €51) and Sicily (Palermo from €81). Also to Barcelona (Spain, from €68) and Tunis (Tunisia, from €88).

Moby Lines (☑ 800 804020; www.mobylines.com) Ferries year-round to the Sardinian ports of Olbia (from €69 return) and Porto Torres (from €65 return).

Tirrenia (☑ 89 21 23; www.tirrenia.it) To/from Sardinia (Porto Torres from €72 return; Olbia from €75 return).

TRAIN

Genoa's Stazione Principe and Stazione Brignole are linked by very frequent trains to Milan (€13.50 to €22, 1½ to two hours), Pisa (€27, two hours), Rome (€64, five hours) and Turin (€12.40, two hours).

Stazione Principe tends to have more trains, particularly going west to San Remo (€12 to €18, two hours, eight daily) and Ventimiglia (€14 to €21, 2½ hours, 10 daily).

Tigullio & Baia del Levante

Beyond Genoa's claustrophobic eastern sprawl, this narrow strip of coast between the deep blue waters of the Mediterranean and the ruggedly mountainous Ligurian hinterland is home to some of Italy's most elite resorts, including jet-set favourite Portofino and the gently faded Santa Margherita Ligure. Anything but off the beaten track, this glittering stretch of coast is hugely popular, but retains pockets of extreme natural beauty and profound authenticity.

Nervi

☑ 010 / POP 10,700

A former fishing village engulfed by Genoa's urban sprawl, modern Nervi serves as Genoa's summer playground with a string of resort-style beach clubs and seasonal bars along the waterfront. Its bounty of museums and galleries, and the 2km cliff-side promenade, the Passeggiata Anita Garibaldi, make for a pleasant, evocative day trip, whatever the season.

All three of Nervi's museums and galleries can be accessed in a combined ticket (€10) or they're included on the Genoa Museum Card.

Some 18,000 items from the period 1880–1945 are displayed in the Wolfsoniana (www.wolfsoniana.it; Via Serra Gropallo 4; adult/reduced €5/4; ⊙ 11am-6pm Tue-Fri, noon-7pm Sat & Sun summer, 11am-5pm Tue-Sun winter), including paintings, sculptures, furniture, decorative arts, propaganda, everyday objects and industrial design. Absolute eye-candy for 20th-century design and interiors fans, they also form an incredibly rich, and sometimes troubling, document of post-Risorgimento Italy's cultural complexity.

The Galleria d'Arte Moderna (www.museidigenova.it; Via Capolungo 3; adult/reduced €6/5; ⊙ 11am-6pm Tue-Fri, noon-7pm Sat & Sun Apr-Oct, 11am-5pm Tue-Sun Nov-Mar), set in the 16th-century Villa Saluzzo, displays the former Prince Odone di Savoia's collection, mostly works by 19th- and early-20th-century artists such as futurist Fortunato Depero, semiofficial fascist sculptor Arturo Martini and the lyrical eccentric Filippo De Pisis.

❶ Getting There & Away

Nervi is 7km east of Genoa and is best reached by frequent trains from Stazione Brignole and Stazione Principe (€1.30, 15 to 25 minutes).

Camogli

☑ 0185 / POP 5300

Camogli, 25km east of Genoa, is most famous for its sheer number of *trompe l'œil* villas, its photogenic terraced streets winding down to a perfect cove of pebble beach amid a backdrop of umbrella pines and olive groves. While tourists flock to Portofino, this is where many of northern Italy's intellectuals and creatives have their summer apartments. Still, as pretty as the town is, it remains a working fishing hub – the town's name means 'house of wives', hailing from the days when the womenfolk ran the show while the husbands were away at sea. Come the second weekend in May, the town celebrates its maritime heritage with the Sagra del Pesce (Fish Festival; Piazza Cristoforo Colombo; ⊙ May) and a huge fish fry – hundreds are cooked in 3m-wide pans along the waterfront.

◎ Sights & Activities

Centro Visito Batterie Silvio Sommazzi   HISTORIC SITE
(☑ 348 0182556; www.parcoportofino.com; Chiappa; guided tour adult/child €5/3; ⊙ 10am-5pm Sat & Sun Mar–mid-Jun & Sep) This free visitor centre provides insight into the military installations scattered in the surrounding hillside. The 202nd Batteria Chiappa guarded the coast during the Second World War, and you can still poke around the various bunkers, sentinel posts, barracks and armoury (pick up a map to see the layout). The visitor centre runs one-hour guided tours of the military post.

It also offers longer tours of other parts of the island, which you'll need to book in advance (these depart from San Rocco, and cost €100 per group for a half day).

You can get there on foot along the scenic trail from Camogli (about a 90-minute walk via San Rocco) or take a ferry to Punta Chiappa and hike up from there – it's a short but steep climb that ascends 250m (around 30 minutes).

Punta Chiappa   SWIMMING
(www.golfoparadiso.it; ☺ boats hourly in summer, 3-5 times per day rest of year) From the main esplanade, Via Garibaldi, boats sail to the Punta Chiappa (one way/return €6/11), a rocky outcrop on the Portofino promontory where you can swim and sunbathe like an Italian. By sea it's a 5-minute trip; otherwise it's an easy 3km walk along the trail that begins at the end of Via San Bartolomeo.

🛏 Sleeping & Eating

★**Villa Rosmarino**   B&B €€€
(📞 0185 77 15 80; www.villarosmarino.com; Via Figari 38; d €240-290; ☺ Mar-Oct; P ❄ 🛜 🏊) Villa Rosmarino's motto is 'you don't stay, you live' and it's apt. Simply taking in the views here is life affirming. This elegant pink 1907 villa is a typical Ligurian beauty on the outside, a calming oasis of modernity on the inside.

Mario and Fulvio's collection of 20th-century furniture and contemporary artworks is scattered throughout the lounge, library and light-filled rooms. Despite the haute design credentials, there's a sensual warmth to it all. Even breakfasts – taken around the dining table – pop with colour and texture. The setting is sublimely tranquil but Camogli's bustle, and the beach, is just a 15-minute walk down a picturesque lane. Note prices in March and October drop substantially.

★**La Cucina di Nonna Nina**   TRATTORIA €€
(📞 0185 77 38 35; www.nonnanina.it; Via F Molfino 126, San Rocco di Camogli; meals €35-50; ☺ 12.30-3pm & 7.30-10.30pm Thu-Tue) 🌿 In the leafy heights of San Rocco di Camogli you'll find the only Slow Food–recommended restaurant along the coast, named for grandmother Nina, whose heirloom recipes have been adapted with love by Paolo Delphin. Your culinary odyssey will include traditional dishes such as air-dried cod stewed with pine nuts, potatoes and local Taggiasca olives, and *rossetti* (minnow) and artichoke soup.

ℹ Information

Tourist Office (📞 0185 77 10 66; www.camogliturismo.it; Via XX Settembre 33; ☺ 9.15am-12.15pm & 3.30-6.30pm Tue-Sat, from 10am Mon, 9.15am-12.15pm Sun) Has a list of diving schools and boat-rental operators.

ℹ Getting There & Away

Camogli is on the Genoa–La Spezia train line, with regular connections to Santa Margherita Ligure (€2.20, five minutes), Rapallo (€2.20, 10 minutes) and Genoa (€3.60, 46 minutes).

The **Golfo Paradiso SNC** (📞 0185 77 20 91; www.golfoparadiso.it; Via Piero Schiaffino 14) runs boats year-round to Punta Chiappa (one

---

DON'T MISS

BREAKING FOCACCIA WITH THE LOCALS

Spend a week frequenting the bars and bakeries of the Italian Riviera and you'll quickly ascertain that no two focaccias are alike. The classic focaccia, called *'alla genovese'*, is a simple oven-baked flat bread made with flour, yeast, water, salt and olive oil, and topped with salt, oil and sometimes rosemary. But various regional variations crop up only a short train ride away. To the east, the *galletta di Camogli* is a crisp focaccia more akin to a biscuit that was supposedly invented for the town's sailors to take on long voyages. In nearby Recco, the delicious *focaccia col formaggio* spreads mild creamy cheese (usually *crescenza*) between two thin slices of bread made without yeast. It traces its roots back to the Saracen invasions of the Early Middle Ages. San Remo, on the Riviera di Ponente, has concocted *sardenara*, a pizza-like focaccia topped with tomatoes, onions, capers and – as the name implies – sardines. And, yes, you've seen right: Ligurians think nothing of dipping a slice of *alla genovese* into their morning coffee.

In Camogli, assuming you're not on a mission to taste-test every town's *focacceria*, Revello (📞 0185 77 07 77; www.revellocamogli.com; Via Garibaldi 183; focaccia from €2; ☺ 8am-7.30pm) is a respectable choice for slices of focaccia di Recco – a slightly flaky variety stuffed with stracchino cheese – or others topped with anchovies, fresh tomatoes and Ligurian olives.

way/return €6/11) and San Fruttuoso (€9/14). Between April and September there are services to Genoa's Porto Antico (€10/17), Portofino (€11/19) and Cinque Terre (€20/33).

Portofino

📞 0185 / POP 420

Even the trees are handsome in Portofino, a small but perfectly coiffured coastal village that sits on its own peninsula, seemingly upping the exclusivity factor by mere geography. Hotels here are hushed and headily priced, but a drink by Portofino's yacht-filled harbour or a stroll around its designer shops can be easily enjoyed on a day trip from Genoa.

◎ Sights & Activities

Various boat-taxi operators around the harbour host snorkelling and sightseeing trips (from €30).

Castello Brown CASTLE
(www.castellobrown.com; Via alla Penisola 13a; admission €5; ☺ 10am-7pm daily summer, to 5pm Sat & Sun winter) A flight of stairs signposted 'Salita San Giorgio' leads from the harbour and past the Chiesa di San Giorgio to Portofino's unusual castle, a 10-minute walk altogether (do confirm it's open with the tourist office before setting out, as the castle often closes for private events). The Genoese-built bulwark saw action against the Venetians, Savoyards, Sardinians and Austrians, and later fell to Napoleon.

In 1867 it was transformed by the British diplomat Montague Yeats Brown into a private mansion. The fabulous tiled staircase is one of the showpieces of the neo-Gothic interior, while there are great views from the garden. For a better outlook, continue

WORTH THE WALK

Situated at the base of Portofino's lighthouse, terrace bar Al Faro di Portofino (📞 320 308 70 36; Via alla Penisola 18) has mesmerising views over the sea from its clifftop perch. Keep your eyes peeled for dolphins leaping through the waves while you sip a first-rate *spritz* from a deck chair. It's a 20-minute walk from Portofino's main square.

To get there, follow signs to San Giorgio church, then on to Castello Brown and continue along the same road, which ends at the lighthouse.

for another 400m or so along the same track to the lighthouse (Faro di Portofino).

Parco Naturale Regionale di Portofino HIKING
(www.parks.it/parco.portofino) The Portofino peninsula's 60km of narrow trails are a world away from the sinuous sports-car-lined road from Santa Margherita. Many of them are absolutely remote and all of them are free of charge. The tourist office has maps.

A good but tough day hike (there are very exposed sections) is the 18km coastal route from Camogli to Santa Margherita Ligure via San Fruttuoso and Portofino. There are handy train connections at both ends.

🛌 Sleeping & Eating

Eight Hotels Paraggi HOTEL €€€
(📞 0185 28 99 61; www.paraggi.eighthotels.it; Via Paraggi a Mare 8; d €550-960; ❄ ❸) This low-key hotel has simple, luxurious rooms, but its real appeal is the location. Right on the perfect crescent of Paraggi beach, there's a sense of calm here that can be elusive around the cove in Portofino proper. Such beauty doesn't come cheap, however: rooms with balconies start at €750 per night.

Ristorante Puny LIGURIAN €€
(📞 0185 26 90 37; Piazza Martiri dell'Olivetta; meals €40-50; ☺ noon-3pm & 7-11pm Fri-Wed) Puny's harbourside location is the one you've come to Portofino for and the owners treat *everyone* like they're a visiting celeb. The food sticks loyally to Ligurian specialities, especially seafood.

Caffè Excelsior LIGURIAN €€
(📞 0185 26 91 23; www.excelsiorportofino.it; Piazza Martiri dell'Olivetta 54; meals €35-45; ☺ 10am-11pm May-Oct) A fashionable restaurant overlooking the port, Caffè Excelsior is a good perch with romantic outdoor booths – where Greta Garbo used to hide behind dark glasses – serving up octopuses and prawns.

❶ Information

Tourist Office (Via Roma 35; ☺ 10am-6pm summer, 10am-3pm Thu-Sun winter) Has free trail maps for the Parco Naturale Regionale di Portofino and information on mountain-bike rental, as well as seasonal sailboat and motorboat rental.

❶ Getting There & Away

ATP (www.atp-spa.it) bus 82 runs to Portofino from outside the tourist office in Santa Margherita Ligure (€1.80, every 15 to 30 minutes), but

---

WORTH A TRIP

SAN FRUTTUOSO
....

San Fruttuoso is a slice of ancient tranquillity preserved amid some of Italy's busiest coastal resorts. There are no roads here – come here with the Ligurians to swim, stroll, sunbake and feast on seafood on the shaded terrace of **Da Laura** (☑ 339 5208537; meals €36-46; ⏰ 12.30-2pm) (reserve in advance).

The hamlet's sensitively restored Benedictine abbey exudes a calm simplicity and its charming everyday collection of ancient monkish things feels touchingly close and human. **Abbazia di San Fruttuoso** (www.visitfai.it/sanfruttuoso; adult/reduced €7.50/4; ⏰ 10am-5.45pm summer, to 3.45pm winter) was built as a final resting place for Bishop St Fructuosus of Tarragona, martyred in Spain in AD 259, and was rebuilt in the mid-13th century with the assistance of the Doria family.

San Fruttuoso's blissful isolation means you have only two transport options: foot or sea. Walk in from Camogli or Portofino, a steep but easier 5km cliff-side walk. Both hikes take about 2½ hours one way. Alternatively, you can catch a boat from Camogli (one way/return €9/14), Portofino (€9/13), Santa Margherita Ligure (€11/17) and, in summer, Genoa (€15/24).

---

by far the best way is to walk. A designated path tracks the gorgeous coastline for 3km.

From April to October, Servizio Marittimo del Tigullio (www.traghettiportofino.it) runs daily ferries from Portofino to/from San Fruttuoso (one way/return €9/13), Rapallo (€9/15) and Santa Margherita Ligure (€7/12). Golfo Paradiso (www.golfoparadiso.it) also has a regular service from Camogli (€11/19). From June to September, Golfo Paradiso SNC (p193) operates boats from Genoa to Portofino (€15/24).

Motorists can only park in the car park at the village entrance, with fees starting from €8 per hour (cash only).

Santa Margherita Ligure
☑ 0185 / POP 9100

Santa Margherita Ligure materialises like a calm Impressionist painting. You wouldn't want to change a single detail of the picture-perfect seaside promenade in this fishing village turned retirement spot, where elegant hotels with Liberty facades overlook yachts. It's decidedly less bling than Portofino, with some affordable hotel options and a surprisingly workaday town behind the waterfront.

◉ Sights & Activities

An idyllic position on a sheltered bay on the turquoise Golfo di Tigullio makes the town a good base for sailing, water skiing and scuba diving. Those feeling less active can simply stretch out on its popular beach.

Villa Durazzo   GARDENS
(www.villadurazzo.it; Piazzale San Giacomo 3; gardens free, villa adult/child €5.50/3; ⏰ gardens

9am-7pm, villa 9am-1pm & 2-6pm) **FREE** This exquisitely turned-out mansion and gardens, part of a 16th-century castle complex, overlooks the sea. In the lavish Italian gardens, you can take an aromatic stroll among lemon trees, hydrangea and camellia hedges, and other flora typical of the town's mild climate, or wander among its recently restored collection of 17th-century paintings.

Santuario di Nostra Signora della Rosa   CHURCH
(Piazza Caprera) You'll gasp audibly when entering Santa Margherita Ligure's small yet lavish baroque church, not just at the truly dazzling array of gold leaf, frescoes, chandeliers and stained glass, but also at the sheer serendipity of it being here at all.

⎘ Sleeping & Eating

★ Blu di Te House   BOUTIQUE HOTEL €€€
(☑ 0185 28 71 87; www.bludite.com; Via Favale 30; s/d €280/380; ⓟ ❈ ☎) Once a rambling old Ligurian villa, the Blu di Te now has 20 clean-lined rooms. Colours echo the Ligurian landscape and there is a combination of midcentury classics and more traditional pieces scattered across the hotel. A rooftop terrace overlooks a baroque church and treetops to the blue of the gulf.

L'Altro Eden   SEAFOOD €€
(☑ 0185 29 30 56; www.laltro.ristoranteeden. com; Calata del Porto 11; meals €40-60; ⏰ noon-11.30pm Mon-Fri, noon-2.30pm & 7-11.30pm Sat & Sun) A seafood place right on the docks, yes, but this grey-and-white streamlined vaulted space is a maritime kitsch-free zone.

LOCAL KNOWLEDGE

LUNCH INLAND

About 5km inland in the hamlet of San Massimo di Rapallo, **uGiancu** is a cult restaurant run by comic-book collector Fausto Oneto. Half of his collection decorates the walls and, being away from the coast, the kitchen focuses on meat and vegetables, including an incredibly succulent herb-battered suckling lamb with field greens from the kitchen gardens.

Romantic and cosy on colder evenings, outside tables are right by the boats in summer. Fish is done by weight and to order, but they are best known for *crudo* (raw fish) and risotto with fresh prawns or, in season, squid ink.

Drinking & Nightlife

Sabot Italia BAR
(www.facebook.com/sabotitalia; Piazza Martiri della Libertà 32; ⊙5pm-3am Mon-Fri, from 10am Sat & Sun; ⊗) Just around the corner from the historic centre, Sabot serves some of Santa Margherita Ligure's best *aperitivi*, where a generous platter of snacks accompanies the drink orders from 5pm to 9pm. Sink into one of the sofas, or grab a street-side table and enjoy the well-made cocktails, upbeat jazzy grooves, and friendly banter with the staff.

ⓘ Information

Tourist Office (www.lamialiguria.it; Piazza Vittorio Veneto; ⊙9.30am-noon & 2.30-5.30pm Mon-Sat)

ⓘ Getting There & Away

ATP Tigullio Trasporti (www.atpesercizio.it) runs buses to/from Portofino (every 20 minutes) and Camogli (every 30 minutes), both with the Portofino Pass one way/return €4/6.

By train, there are fast hourly services to/from Genoa (€8.50, 30 minutes) and La Spezia (€10, one hour).

Servizio Marittimo del Tigullio (www.traghettiportofino.it) runs seasonal ferries to/from Cinque Terre (one way/return €25/40), Porto Venere (€25/40), San Fruttuoso (€11/17), Portofino (€7/12) and Rapallo (€4.50/6).

Rapallo

📱 0185 / POP 29,700
WB Yeats, Max Beerbohm and Ezra Pound all garnered inspiration in Rapallo and it's not difficult to see why. With its bright-blue changing cabins, palm-fringed beach and diminutive 16th-century castle perched above the sea, the town has a poetic and nostalgic air. It's at its busiest on Thursdays, when market stalls spread along the waterfront.

⊙ Sights & Activities

Lungomare Vittorio Veneto AREA
Rapallo's scenic seafront promenade hosts a daily parade of locals and visitors. This is also the setting for the Mercato del Giovedì (Thursday market).

La Funivia Rapallo-Montallegro CABLE CAR
(Piazzale Solari 2; one way/return €5.50/8; ⊙9am-12.30pm & 2-6pm) When you've had your fill of the promenade poseurs, rise above them in a 1934-vintage cable car up to **Santuario Basilica di Montallegro** (612m), built on the spot where, in 1557, the Virgin Mary was reportedly sighted. Walkers and mountain bikers can follow an old mule track (5km, 1½ hours) to the hilltop site.

🛏 Sleeping & Eating

Europa Hotel Design Spa 1877 HOTEL €€
(📱0185 66 95 21; www.hoteleuropa-rapallo.com; Via Milite Ignoto 2; s €125-190, d €170-255; 🅿❄🛜) Close to the beach and with its own spa facilities – a thermal bath and steam room – this beautifully refurbished place is super relaxing. The modern rooms here have subtle design touches and are well appointed with marble bathrooms, double-insulated windows and high-quality bedding.

Ö Bansin TRATTORIA €
(📱0185 23 11 19; www.trattoriabansin.it; Via Venezia 105; meals €18-27; ⊙noon-2pm Mon, noon-2pm & & 7-9.30pm Tue-Sun) Ligurian comfort food – salt cod fritters, chickpea soup, spinach-stuffed pasta with walnut sauce, mussels gratin – gets served up here with a minimum of fuss and not just a little bit of love. Lunch menus, with two courses and house wine or water, are €10 (or €5 with just a first course and side), and there's a garden courtyard in summer.

ⓘ Information

Tourist Office (📱0185 23 03 46; www.lamialiguria.it; Lungomare Vittorio Veneto 38; ⊙9am-1pm & 3-5pm mid-Apr–Sep 10am-noon & 2-4pm Oct-Mar) Details of walks in the area, plus maps.

ℹ Getting There & Away

Fast intercity trains run along the coast to Genoa (€8.50, 35 minutes) and La Spezia (€10, one hour).

Servizio Marittimo del Tigullio (www.traghetti portofino.it) runs boats to/from Santa Margherita Ligure (one way/return €4.50/6), Portofino (€9/15), San Fruttuoso (€12/18), the Cinque Terre (€25/40) and Porto Venere (€25/40). Not all operate daily, and many are seasonal – the website posts updated schedules.

Levanto

📞 0187 / POP 5400

Just north of Monterosso, the slumbering seaside town of Levanto (LAY-vahn-toh) makes a fine base for exploring the Cinque Terre with somewhat smaller crowds. A settlement has existed here since the Roman times (when it was known as Ceula), with fragments of its storied past still sprinkled around town. Among other things, Levanto is home to a Unesco-listed 13th-century *loggia*, a rare example of late medieval architecture that survives intact up to the present.

Most visitors, however, come for the wide pebble-and-sand beach, with a scenic promenade elevated above the shoreline. Levanto is also the start and end point for a gorgeous walk to Monterosso over the Punta Mesco. You can also hire a bike for a spin to the nearby villages of Bonassola and Framura beyond.

◉ Sights & Activities

Spiaggia di Levanto   BEACH

(Off Lungomare Amerigo Vespucci) One of the best beaches within easy reach of Cinque Terre, Levanto's seaside is long and wide, and flanked by green hills sloping down to the wave-kissed shoreline. Like most other beaches in the Italian Riviera, the surface is pebbly rather than sandy, but the water is inviting, and it's a scenic spot for a walk or a swim. It has free sections sprinkled among the private access areas.

The beach is just steps from Levanto's train station.

Via Guani   STREET

This atmospheric lane, located a few blocks from the beach, winds its way past some of Levanto's oldest buildings. Don't miss stately former noble residences like number 37, known as Palazzo delle Sirene, dating back to the 16th century. The street intersects with the picturesque Piazza del Popolo, where you'll find the *loggia medievale,* its columns hiding a small enclosure with the remains of a 13th-century fresco.

🍴 Eating

Ristorante Moresco   LIGURIAN €€

(📞 0187 80 72 53; Via Jacopo da Levanto 24; meals €30-40; ⊗noon-2pm & 7-10pm) In a vaulted-ceiling dining room a few blocks from the beach, Moresco is a chef-driven restaurant that has a loyal local following for its superb seafood and pasta dishes served at reasonable prices. Stuffed mussels, *spaghetti alle vongole* (spaghetti with clams), sea bass ravioli and *pansotti alla genovese* (stuffed pasta with walnut sauce) are among the many standouts. Reserve ahead.

ℹ Getting There & Away

Frequent regional trains run along the coast to Genoa (€6, 51 minutes) and La Spezia (€4, 30 minutes).

TURIN, PIEDMONT & CINQUE TERRE TIGULLIO & BAIA DEL LEVANTE

OFF THE BEATEN TRACK

BIKING TO BONASSOLA

Hire a bike in Levanto from **Sensafreni Bike Shop** (📞0187 80 71 28; Piazza del Popolo 1; bike hire per hr/half day/full day from €3/5/15; ⊗9am-1pm & 4-8pm Mon-Sat) for a short but pleasant ride to several other villages along a smooth, flat promenade. The tranquil settlement of Bonassola lies just 2.5km north of Levanto, and it has flower-lined streets, a few seafood restaurants and a stretch of grey sand beach framed by forested hills. The ride here follows an abandoned railway line that's been converted into a biking and pedestrian thoroughfare, which encompasses a series of well-lit train tunnels that open up every few hundred meters to striking views of wave-dashed cliffs and rocky shoreline.

Once in Bonassola, you can stop for refreshment at one of the outdoor cafes just one block back from the waterfront, or time your visit to coincide with a meal at **Osteria Antica Guetta** (📞0187 81 37 97; Via Marconi 1; meals €30-40; ⊗noon-3pm & 7-11pm Thu-Tue) overlooking the shoreline. Afterwards, you can continue another 3km to the village of Framura. This stretch is mostly through dark, dripping tunnels so it's a rather dreary walk, but an intriguing (and fast) bike ride.

From late March to October, **Consorzio Maritimo Turistico Cinque Terre Golfo dei Poeti** (📞 0187 73 29 87; www.navigazionegolfodei poeti.it) sails from Levanto to/from Cinque Terre villages (all day, all stops €35, one way €27), Porto Venere (one way €21) and Lerici (one way €26). Note that boats typically have only two morning departures from Levanto and two late afternoon arrivals back to Levanto.

Cinque Terre

📞 0187

Set amid some of the most dramatic coastal scenery on the planet, these five ingeniously constructed fishing villages can bolster the most jaded of spirits. A Unesco World Heritage Site since 1997, Cinque Terre isn't the undiscovered Eden it once was but, frankly, who cares? Sinuous paths traverse seemingly impregnable cliff sides, while a 19th-century railway line cut through a series of coastal tunnels ferries the footsore from village to village. Thankfully cars were banned over a decade ago.

Rooted in antiquity, Cinque Terre's five villages date from the early medieval period. While much of this fetching vernacular architecture remains, Cinque Terre's unique historical draw is the steeply terraced cliffs bisected by a complicated system of fields and gardens that have been hacked, chiselled, shaped and layered over the course of nearly two millennia. The extensive *muretti* (low stone walls) can be compared to the Great Wall of China in their grandeur and scope.

🏃 Activities

⭐ Alta Via delle Cinque Terre   HIKING
Just a few kilometres shy of a full-blown marathon, the 38km Alta Via Delle Cinque Terre (marked AV5T on maps) – which runs from Porto Venere to Levanto – dangles a tempting challenge to experienced walkers who aim to complete it in one (very long) or two days.

⭐ Sentiero Azzurro   HIKING
(Blue Trail; admission with Cinque Terre card) The Sentiero Azzurro (Blue Trail; marked SVA on maps), a 12km old mule path that once linked all five oceanside villages by foot, is Cinque Terre's showcase hike, narrow and precipitous. Owing to bad storms and landslides in years past, only two sections of the trail remain open: from Monterosso to Vernazza and Vernazza to Corniglia.

Crazy Boat Cinque Terre   BOATING
(📞 328 9365595; www.crazyboatcinqueterre.com; boat hire per hr €100) Escape the crowds on a small-boat tour run by this reputable outfit based in Manarola and La Spezia. You can create a customised tour, stopping for a swim off Guvano Beach, checking out the waterfall (acqua pendente) near Monterosso or having a look at unusual cave formations along the coast. Crazy Boat also runs three-hour sunset tours for €60 per person (five person minimum).

ℹ️ Information
Online information is available at www.cinque terre.it and www.cinqueterre.com.

WORTH A TRIP

SESTRI LEVANTE
....

Located roughly halfway between Genoa and Cinque Terre, the pretty seaside town of Sestri Levante has enchanted countless generations of visitors. Hans Christian Andersen fell for the setting while renting a room here in 1833 and Baia delle Favole (Bay of Fables) – the long palm-fringed shoreline – was later named in his honour. Beachfront aside, Sestri Levante also has a small historic quarter, sprinkled with Liberty-style buildings, easy-going shops, cafes and al fresco restaurants. The cellar-like, two-room Osteria Mattana (📞0185 45 76 33; www.osteriamattana.com; Via XXV Aprile 34; meals €20-30; ⏰7-10.30pm daily May-Sep, closed Mon & also open noon-2.30pm Sat & Sun Oct-Apr) is a locally loved lunchtime spot for hearty home-cooked dishes at outstanding prices: cuttlefish stew with potatoes and artichokes perhaps, spaghetti with mussels and clams, or braised rabbit. Start off with *farinata* fired up from the wood-burning oven in front. Cash only.

Just south of the cobblestones is the scenic Baia del Silenzio (Bay of Silence), with a small pretty beach backed by scenic villas. Some fine walks also lead south of town, proffering dramatic views overlooking a town sometimes described as having '*due mari*' (two seas).

Cinque Terre

Parco Nazionale (www.parconazionale5terre.
it; ⊙8am-8pm summer, 8.30am-12.30pm &
1-5.30pm winter) Offices in the train stations
of all five villages and La Spezia station; has
comprehensive information about hiking trail
closures.

❶ Getting There & Away

BOAT

In summer the **Golfo Paradiso SNC** (☎0185
77 20 91; www.golfoparadiso.it) runs boats
to Cinque Terre from Genoa (one way/return
€21/38). Seasonal boat services to/from
Santa Margherita (€25/40) are handled by the
Servizio Marittimo del Tigullio (www.traghetti-
portofino.it).

CAR & MOTORCYCLE

Private vehicles are not allowed beyond village
entrances and during high-volume days roads
between villages can be closed. If you're arriving
by car or motorcycle, you'll need to pay to park
in designated car parks (€12 to €25 per day)
though these are often full. In some villages,
minibus shuttles depart from the car parks (one
way/return €1.50/2.50) – park offices have
seasonal schedules.

TRAIN

Between 6.30am and 10pm, one to three trains
an hour trundle along the coast between Genoa
and La Spezia, stopping at each of Cinque
Terre's villages (Trenitalia has renamed its usual

service the Cinque Terre Express in summer).
Unlimited 2nd-class rail travel between Levanto
and La Spezia is covered by the Cinque Terre
Train card (one/two day €16/29), or you can buy
a €4 ticket for travel between any two villages.

Monterosso

☑ 0187 / POP 1420

The most accessible village by car and the
only Cinque Terre settlement to sport a
proper stretch of beach, the westernmost
Monterosso is the least quintessential of the
quintet. The village, known for its lemon
trees and anchovies, is delightful. Split in
two, its new and old halves are linked by an
underground tunnel burrowed beneath the
blustery San Cristoforo promontory.

◉ Sights & Activities

Convento dei Cappuccini   CHURCH
(Salita San Cristoforo) Monterosso's most interesting church and convent complex is set on
the hill that divides the old town from the
newer Fegina quarter. The striped church,
the Chiesa di San Francesco, dates from
1623 and has a painting attributed to Van
Dyck (Crocifissione) to the left of the altar.
The convent welcomes casual visitors but
also has a program of spiritual retreats and
workshops.

Cinque Terre

Climb above the crowds on Cinque Terre's terraced cliffs and you might have to pinch yourself to check that you're still in the 21st century. Rooted in antiquity and bereft of modern interferences, these five historic fishing villages have embellished the Ligurian coastline with subtle human beauty and a fascinating medieval heritage.

Manarola

Grapes grow abundantly on Cinque Terre's terraced plots, especially around the village of Manarola (p207). The area's signature wine is the sweet white Sciacchetrà, a blend of Bosco, Albarola and Vermentino grapes best sampled with cheese or sweet desserts.

1. Manarola (p207) **2.** Riomaggiore (p208) **3.** Vernazza (p205)

Riomaggiore

The pleasantly peeling medieval houses of the unofficial capital (p208) are tucked into a steep ravine. Jump on a boat to best experience one of the Cinque Terre's most iconic views: the warm pastel glow of Riomaggiore's pastel facades as the sun sets.

Vernazza

Sporting the best natural harbour of the five towns, Vernazza (p205) rises tightly from its central square. Its closely clustered streets and lanes are a labyrinth of steep, switchback stairs rewarding the strong of thigh with stunning sea views from a cluster of handkerchief-sized terraces.

Terraced Fields

Cinque Terre's cleverly cultivated cliff terraces are so old no one truly knows who built them. Held in place by hundreds of kilometres of dry stone walls, they add a strange human beauty to a stunning natural landscape.

ⓘ CINQUE TERRE CARD

If you plan to hike between villages, the best way to get around Cinque Terre is with a Cinque Terre card. Two versions are available: with or without train travel. Both include unlimited use of walking paths and electric village buses, as well as cultural exhibitions. The basic one-/two-day card for those aged over four years costs €7.50/14.50. With unlimited train trips between the towns, the card costs €16/29. A one-day family card for two adults and two children (under 12) costs €42/20 with/without train travel.

Both versions of the card are sold at all Cinque Terre park information offices and each of Cinque Terre's train stations. You can also purchase trail admission at each of the trailheads (cash only).

Monterosso to Santuario della Madonna di Soviore   WALKING

From Via Roma in the village, follow trail 509 up through forest and past the ruins of an old hexagonal chapel to an ancient paved mule path that leads to Soviore, the Italian Riviera's oldest sanctuary dating from the 11th century. Here you'll find a bar, restaurant and views as far as Corsica on a clear day. It's a two-hour walk to get there.

Buranco   WINE

(☑0187 817 677; www.burancocinqueterre.it; Via Buranco 72; ☺noon-6pm by advanced booking) A short stroll from Monterosso, Buranco is a verdant oasis that produces some fine DOC Cinque Terre white wines as well as grappa, *limoncino* (the Italian Riviera's answer to the Amalfi Coast's lemon-flavored *limoncello*) and one dessert wine that's even harder to produce than it is to pronounce: Sciacchetrà (shah-keh-TRAH). Before or after a tasting on the verandah, you can wander the vineyards to get a sense of the challenges of working the steeply terraced hillsides. Buranco also rents out three fully equipped apartments on the property (around €270 per night), all with terraces (two overlooking the vineyards).

🛏 Sleeping

Unlike the other four towns, Monterosso has quite a lot of hotels to choose from.

Hotel La Spiaggia   HOTEL €€

(☑0187 81 75 67; www.laspiaggiahotel.com; Via Lungomare 98; d €195; ❄🛜) This aptly named hotel is right on Monterosso's *spiaggia* (beach) and its 20 largish rooms are popular – book early (up to six months in advance). If you don't get lucky with the fabulous views from the sea-facing rooms, console yourself with a back one with terrace instead.

★ La Sosta di Ottone III   BOUTIQUE HOTEL €€€

(☑0187 81 45 02; www.lasosta.com; Località Chiesanuova 39; d €270; ☺Apr-Oct; 🅿🛜) Up in the hills between the beautiful, almost Cinque Terre, beach town of Levanto and Monterosso, La Sosta di Ottone III is a lovely hideaway that's also in prime position for striking out to Cinque Terre by foot or car. The owners have revitalised a village house with extreme attention to detail that also feels effortless.

🍴 Eating

Il Massimo della Focaccia   STREET FOOD €

(Via Fegina 50; focaccia €2-5; ☺9am-6pm Thu-Tue) Just below the train station, this photogenic takeaway fires up the best focaccia in all of Cinque Terre. You can order that perfectly crisped bread topped with pesto, tomatoes and olives, sweet onions, with cheese or in various other fashions. There's also quiche-like *torta* (savoury pie) and a few sweet dessert items.

Da Eraldo   LIGURIAN €

(☑366 3388440; Piazza Giacomo Matteotti 6; meals €22-34; ☺noon-2.30pm & 6.30-9.30pm Fri-Wed) One of the liveliest restaurants in town, Eraldo's is a family-style spot where you dine amid arched brick ceilings and red-and-white tablecloths, with the songs of Andrea Bocelli wafting overhead. Sure, it's a bit of a cliché, but the unfussy home-style cooking is quite good (Eraldo honed his cooking skills from the village grandmothers), and the prices and portion sizes are excellent.

San Martino Gastronomia   LIGURIAN €

(☑346 1860764; Via San Martino 3; mains €9-13; ☺noon-3pm & 6-8.30pm Tue-Sun) The go-to place for delicious market-fresh fair at reasonable prices, San Martino has a changing chalkboard menu posted out front and just a couple of tables for the lucky few; most locals order to take away. Linguine with seafood, grilled swordfish and *pansotti* (a stuffed pasta) with walnuts are among the many hits.

Trattoria da Oscar   SEAFOOD €€

(☑345 8714789; Via V Emanuele 67; meals €32-42; ☺noon-2.30pm & 7-9.30pm Fri-Wed) Behind Piazza Matteoti, in the heart of the old town, this tiny vaulted dining room is run by a young, friendly team and attracts a loyal local crowd. The town's famed anchovies dominate the small menu; there's also excellent gnocchi with pesto, seafood spaghetti and grilled swordfish. There are some lovely laneway tables. Reserve ahead. Cash only.

Torre Aurora LIGURIAN €€€
(☑366 1453702; www.torreauroracinqueterre.com; Via Bastione 5; meals €50-60; ⊙noon-10.30pm Apr-Oct) Monterosso's most memorable setting for a meal is undoubtedly this 13th-century tower with a terrace overlooking the sea. Painstakingly prepared seafood (squid-ink pasta with anchovies), mouth-watering grass-fed Fassona beef and excellent wines go nicely with the sweeping views. You can also stop by for an afternoon *aperitivo*, or a postdinner nightcap (during the summer the bar stays open until midnight).

Vernazza

☑0187 / POP 870

Vernazza's small harbour – the only secure landing point on the Cinque Terre coast – guards what is perhaps the quaintest, and steepest, of the five villages. Lined with little cafes, a main cobbled street (Via Roma) links seaside Piazza Marconi with the train station. Side streets lead to the village's trademark Genoa-style *caruggi*, where sea views pop at every turn.

◎ Sights & Activities

Castello Doria CASTLE
(Off Via Guidoni; admission €1.50; ⊙10am-9pm May-Aug, to 7pm Sep-Apr) This castle, the oldest surviving fortification in the Cinque Terre, commands superb views. Dating to around 1000, it's now largely a ruin except for the circular tower in the centre of the esplanade. To get there, head up the steep, narrow staircase by the harbour.

Chiesa di Santa Margherita d'Antiochia CHURCH
(Piazza Matteotti) The waterfront is framed by this small Ligurian-Gothic church, built on a small seafront promontory in 1318 on the site of an 11th-century Romanesque building. According to legend, the church was constructed here after a box containing the bones of St Margaret washed up on a nearby beach. It is notable for its unusual 40m-tall octagonal tower topped with a dome.

Vernazza to Santuario della Madonna di Reggio WALKING
From underneath Vernazza's railway bridge, follow trail 508 up numerous flights of steps

and past 14 sculpted Stations of the Cross to an 11th-century chapel with a Romanesque facade. It's approximately a 45-minute walk.

Sleeping

★La Mala BOUTIQUE HOTEL €€
(☑334 2875718; www.lamala.it; Via San Giovanni Battista 29; d €160-250; ❋❄🛜) These four rooms are some of Cinque Terre's nicest. Up in the cliff-side heights of the village, they are in a typical Ligurian house that's run by the grandson of the original owner. The fit-out is a clean-lined contemporary one, providing both comfort and a place to soak in some fabulous sea views, either from bed or a sunny terrace.

Gianni Franzi Rooms B&B €€
(☑0187 81 22 28; www.giannifranzi.it; Via San Giovanni Battista 41; d €120-160; 🛜) Spread over two locations, one above the attached restaurant (☑0187 81 22 28; www.giannifranzi.it; Piazza Matteotti 5; meals €30-45; ⊙8am-11pm Thu-Tue mid-Mar–early Jan), the other up the hill, rooms here are an atmospheric mix of antique furniture and simple traditional architecture, all kept with care. Breakfast on their deck delivers not just *cornetti* (croissants) and cappuccino, but sublime sea-drenched views; there's a small garden under the Doria castle for guest use.

✗ Eating

Il Porticciolo GELATO €
(www.facebook.com/gelateriailporticciolo; Piazza Marconi 12; gelato from €2.50; ⊙11.30am-11pm) In a perfect location on the waterfront, Il Porticciolo whips up heavenly perfection in its all-natural gelato. Indulge in fruit flavors like strawberry, lemon (locally sourced) or green apple, or opt for Greek yoghurt with local honey, hazelnut or *ambrogio* (a combination of nuts, cream and chocolate).

Gambero Rosso SEAFOOD €€
(☑0187 81 22 65; www.ristorantegamberorosso.net; Piazza Marconi 7; meals €35-45; ⊙noon-3pm & 7-10pm Fri-Wed) If you've been subsisting on focaccia, Gambero's house specials – *tegame di Vernazza* (anchovies with baked potatoes and tomatoes), grilled rock octopus or stuffed mussels – will really hit the spot; and the fresh fish baked in sea salt is outstanding. It tastes all the better in the excellent waterfront location. Bookings recommended.

Belforte SEAFOOD €€€
(☑0187 81 22 22; www.ristorantebelforte.it; Via Guidoni 42; meals €35-55; ⊙noon-3pm & 7-10pm

Wed-Mon) A Vernazza classic for more than 50 years, Belforte serves beautifully prepared seafood dishes in an 11th-century castle. You can dine in the atmospheric stone-walled interior or enjoy the breezy views from one of the terraces. The prices are steep, but most diners rate the experience highly. Reserve ahead.

🛍 Shopping

Gocce di Byron   PERFUME
(www.goccedibyron.it; Via Roma 35; ⊙10.30am-7pm daily Apr-Oct, to 9pm Jun-Aug) Cinque Terre's lemon trees, vineyards and seashore are among the inspirations for the alluring fragrances created by the locally based perfume maker. At this sunny little shop, you can browse the five signature scents, each named after Cinque Terre places (like Guvano, made of white musk and sandalwood). It also sells skincare products, scented candles and diffusers. Each fragrance also features a line from a Lord Byron poem ('pleasure's a sin, and sometimes sin's a pleasure'). Byron fell in love with the region, particularly Porto Venere. There, you'll find a second **Gocce di Byron** (www.goccedibyron.it; Via Capellini 127; ⊙10am-1pm & 3-7pm) store.

Corniglia

📍 0187 / POP 190

Corniglia is the 'quiet' middle village that sits atop a 100m-high rocky promontory surrounded by vineyards. It is the only Cinque Terre settlement with no direct sea access, although steep steps lead down to a rocky cove. Narrow alleys and colourfully painted four-storey houses characterise the ancient core, a timeless streetscape that was name-checked in Boccaccio's *Decameron*. To reach the village proper from the railway station you must first tackle the **Lardarina**, a 377-step brick stairway, or jump on a shuttle bus.

👁 Sights & Activities

Corniglia, by virtue of its elevation and central position, is the only place you can see all five settlements in the same panorama.

Belvedere di Santa Maria   VIEWPOINT
Enjoy dazzling 180-degree sea views at this heart-stopping lookout in hilltop Corniglia. To find it, follow Via Fieschi through the village until you reach the clifftop balcony.

Guvano Beach   BEACH
This lovely, hard-to-reach beach was once a famous nudist spot from the 1960s to the 1990s, when it was accessed by walking through an abandoned railway tunnel. Unfortunately, landslides have led to the tunnel's closure, and the only way to reach Guvano today involves hiring a kayak or arranging a visit on a private boat tour.

**Santuario della
Madonna delle Grazie**   WALKING
This sanctuary can be approached from either Corniglia (on trail 587) or Vernazza (trail 507); both take around an hour. The latter is considered more scenic. Branch off the Sentiero Azzurro and ascend the spectacular Sella Comeneco to the village of San Bernardino, where you'll find the church with its adored image of Madonna and Child above the altar.

🛏 Sleeping

⭐**Il Magan**   B&B €
(📞342 3505356; www.vernazzani5terre.it; Via Fieschi 204; r €100-120; 🛜) Four appealingly simple, rustic rooms all have spectacular views, including the single room; two have terraces. Private bathrooms are new, if basic, and breakfast is taken in the town's best bar, La Scuna. Il Magan also rents out an attractive modern apartment. A rare find.

Ostello di Corniglia   HOSTEL €
(📞0187 81 25 59; www.ostellocorniglia.com; Via alla Stazione 3; dm/d €28/75; 🛜) One of only two hostels in Cinque Terre, Ostello di Corniglia is perched at the top of the village and has two eight-bed dorms and four doubles (with private bathroom). Prices are negotiable. There's a lockout from 1pm to 3pm. No breakfast.

Heart of Cinque Terre   GUESTHOUSE €€
(📞348 0459085; www.theheartofcinqueterre.com; Prevo; r €75-140, ste €300, villa €600; 🅿❄🛜) Located at the midpoint of the Sentiero Azzurro hiking trail between Corniglia and Vernazza, this friendly place has spectacular views overlooking the coastline. There's accommodation here for all budgets, with two small, simply furnished rooms (with air-con or wi-fi), a roomier, better equipped Panoramic Room, and a spacious 3-bedroom suite (that sleeps up to 10).

🍴 Eating & Drinking

Corniglia has the most local and surprisingly lively nightlife options. That said, don't expect a very late night.

Alberto Gelateria GELATO €

(Via Fieschi 74; gelato from €2; ⊙11am-11pm)
A Corniglia mainstay since 1999, Alberto
Melandri serves some of the best gelato for
miles around. Try the *basilico*, made from
basil grown in his garden or *miele de Corniglia* (made of Corniglia honey), *limone*
(lemon) or the perfection of simplicity in
cannella (cinnamon). You can also opt for
a *granita* (crushed ice) made from locally
grown lemons.

Il Gabbiano CAFE €

(Prevo; snacks from €4; ⊙9am-6pm) One of the
only places where you'll find refreshment
on the Sentiero Azzurro, this cafe sits alongside the trail (on the Mediterranean side)
in Prevo. Il Gabbiano serves up cold drinks
(smoothies, iced coffee, *granite*) as well as
panini and other snacks. Perched right over
the cliff, the shaded outdoor tables have
magnificent views.

★ **La Scuna** BAR

(☑349 635 5081; Via Fieschi 185; ⊙8.30am-
11.30pm) Craft beer on draft, first-rate
cocktails and creative appetisers make a
great combo at this surprisingly hip little
spot in this most traditional of regions. The
best feature, however, is the jaw-dropping
terrace, with its mesmerising views over a
hill-studded stretch of coastline.

❶ Getting There & Away

The village is on the main train line for the Trenitalia Cinque Terre Express trains, accessible
from there via a 377-step brick stairway; a shuttle bus (€2.50) meets the train.

Manarola

🏠 0187 / POP 360

With more grapevines than any other Cinque
Terre village, Manarola is famous for its
sweet Sciacchetrà wine. It's also awash with
priceless medieval relics, supporting claims
that it is the oldest of the five. The spirited
locals here speak an esoteric local dialect
known as Manarolese. Due to its proximity
to Riomaggiore (852m away), the village is
heavily trafficked, especially by Italian school
parties along with the regular tourists.

◉ Sights & Activities

Punta Bonfiglio VIEWPOINT

Manarola's prized viewpoint is on a rocky
promontory just above the village. A rest
area, including a kids' playground, has been
constructed here and there's also a bar just
below. Nearby are the ruins of an old chapel
once used as a shelter by local farmers.

**Santuario della
Madonna delle Salute** WALKING

The pick of all the sanctuary walks is this
breathtaking traverse (trail 506) through
Cinque Terre's finest vineyards to a diminutive Romanesque-meets-Gothic chapel in
the tiny village of Volastra. It takes around
30 minutes. You can also keep going all the
way to Corniglia.

Via dell'Amore WALKING

This beautiful coastal path that links Riomaggiore to Manarola in a leisurely 20-
minute stroll was, until rockslides caused its
closure in 2012, Cinque Terre's most popular.

DON'T MISS

CINQUE TERRE WINE FLIGHTS

One of the best places in Cinque Terre to discover the wines of the region is the **Enoteca Internazionale** (☑0187 81 72 78; www.enotecainternazionale.com; Via Roma 62;
⊙noon-midnight early Apr-Oct) in Monterrosso. The family-run wine shop offers various
tastings, including flights, from its selection of over 500 different wines. Enjoy by the
glass (€4.50 to €6) on the small terrace in front. Food pairings too.

In Corniglia, savour local wines by the glass (€5–8) or flights with food pairings (from
€15) and pretty views of vineyards tumbling down to the water from the vine-covered
terrace of **Terra Rossa** (Via Fieschi 58; ⊙11am-10pm) wine bar.

Manarola's go-to wine-tasting address is **A Piè de Campu** (☑338 2220088; apiede
campu@gmail.com; Via Discovolo; wine tasting €30-50, vineyard tour from €50). Reserve in
advance for guided wine tastings led by a sommelier with deep knowledge of the wines
of Cinque Terre and beyond; there are pesto-making and pasta-making courses, and
vineyard (and tasting) tours too. Or head to **Cantina Nessun Dorma** (www.nessundor
macinqueterre.com; Piazza Papa Innocenzo IV; ⊙2-8pm Wed-Mon, to 10pm Jul & Aug, closed
Nov-Feb), a tiny shop selling Cinque Terre wines by the bottle and glass, with tastings.

LOCAL KNOWLEDGE

OUTDOOR ACTION KNOW-HOW

The best locally based tour operator in Cinque Terre, Arbaspàa (📞0187 76 00 83; www.arbaspaa.com; Via Discovolo 252; ⬛) offers a vast range of activities, including wine-tasting at a local vineyard, boat trips, kayaking excursions, photography tours, hiking trips and more. Arbaspàa also hires out apartments (📞0187 198 77 30; www.arbaspaa.com; Via Discovolo 252) in all of the Cinque Terre villages as well as in La Spezia.

The name is a nod to the number of marriages the opening of the path engendered between villagers of the once geographically divided hamlets.

🛏 Sleeping

Hotel Marina Piccola   BOUTIQUE HOTEL €€
(📞0187 92 07 70; www.hotelmarinapiccola.com; Via Birolli 120; s/d/tr €130/150/195, ste €165-250; ❄🏶) This choice Manarola hotel has 12 big, comfortable, contemporary rooms, with a few looking over the sea. The lovely lobby and lounge area, which sports a surprisingly on-trend interior, is a welcome respite from the busy day-time streets. A real find at this price, although there is a minimum two-day stay in summer.

Hotel Ca' d'Andrean   HOTEL €€
(📞0187 92 00 40; www.cadandrean.it; Via Doscovolo 101; s €110, d €150-170; ⊙Mar–mid-Nov; ❄🏶) An excellent family-run hotel in the upper part of Manarola. Rooms are large with soothing, stylish white-grey tones and slick bathrooms; some have private terraces. Breakfast (€7) is optional.

★ La Torretta Lodge   BOUTIQUE HOTEL €€€
(📞0187 92 03 27; www.torrettas.com; Vico Volto 20; d/ste €350/550; ❄🏶) Sitting high up above the village, a collection of both private and public terraces command spectacular views while decor differs in each of the rooms, with a seductive Italian maximalist mash of contemporary pieces, mosaic tiles, antiques and murals.

🍴 Eating & Drinking

Manarola's restaurants cluster around the port; don't miss the gelato here.

Cappun Magru   LIGURIAN €
(Via Discovolo; mains €8-12; ⊙8.15am-6.30pm Tue-Sun) Near the Chiesa di San Lorenzo (Piazzale Papa Innocenzo IV), Cappun Magru is a favourite among locals for its home-style cooking, its delicious cakes and Manarola's best espressos. The seafood sandwiches made with anchovies, shrimp, salted cod and octopus are excellent, and pair well with the good DOC Cinque Terre wines.

★ Trattoria dal Billy   SEAFOOD €€
(📞0187 92 06 28; www.trattoriabilly.com; Via Rollandi 122; meals €30-40) Hidden off a narrow lane in the upper reaches of town, the Trattoria dal Billy fires up some of the best seafood dishes anywhere in Cinque Terre. Start off with a mixed appetiser platter – featuring 12 different hot and cold dishes (octopus salad, lemon-drizzled anchovies, tuna with sweet onion) – then tuck into lobster pasta or swordfish with black truffle.

On clear days, book a table on the terrace for superb views. Reservations essential.

★ Nessun Dorma   BAR
(📞340 8884133; www.nessundormacinqueterre. com; Punta Bonfiglio; ⊙noon-9.30pm) On a wave-kissed promontory overlooking the pastel-coloured houses of Manarola, this leafy terrace bar makes a magical setting for a sundowner. Great wine selection and plenty of creative cocktails (try a *limoncino spritz*) pair with sandwiches, salads, bruschetta and cheese platters.

This all-outdoor spot closes on rainy days.

Riomaggiore
📞0187 / POP 1490

Cinque Terre's easternmost village, Riomaggiore is the largest of the five and acts as its unofficial HQ (the main park office is based here). Its peeling pastel buildings march down a steep ravine to a tiny harbour – the region's favourite postcard view – and glow romantically at sunset. If you are driving, the hills between here and La Spezia are spectacular to explore.

⊙ Sights & Activities

Fossola Beach   BEACH
This small pebbly beach is immediately southeast of Riomaggiore marina. Take the short trail that leads just past the harbour to get here. The shore is rugged and delightfully secluded from the village (though it gets packed in the summer); it's also remarkably photogenic with the waters framed by the

steep hillsides. Swimmers should be wary of currents here.

Riomaggiore to Santuario della Madonna di Montenero   WALKING
Trail 593V ascends for around an hour from Riomaggiore, up steps and past walled gardens to a restored 18th-century chapel with a frescoed ceiling, which sits atop an astounding lookout high above the coastline.

Find the trailhead down by the waterfront. An alternative route up to the sanctuary, SVA (formerly number 3) starts at the top of Riomaggiore; take Via Colombo uphill and look for the signs.

🛏 Sleeping

If you're looking for help with reservations, **Riomaggiore Reservations** (☑ 0187 76 05 75; www.riomaggiorereservations.com; Via Colombo 181), run by a local and his American wife, has a large number of simple, but well-vetted properties. The operators are super helpful and efficient to deal with.

🍴 Eating & Drinking

Il Pescato Cucinato   SEAFOOD €
(Via Colombo 199; snacks around €6; ⊙ 11.30am-11pm) Riomaggiore's standout street food is a mound of fresh fried seafood – calamari, anchovies, shrimp, cod – stuffed into a paper cone and served on the go. Vegetarians can opt for chips (fries) or fried veggies. Take your seafood treat down to the waterfront for munching on million-dollar views.

Colle del Telegrafo   LIGURIAN €€
(☑ 0187 76 05 61; Località Colle del Telegrafo; meals €25-35; ⊙ 9am-8pm Tue-Sun) Perched on a ridge south of Riomaggiore, where the old telegraph line used to be strung, the views from the Colle del Telegrafo are spectacular. But they don't overshadow the carefully prepared dishes of pasta with Cinque Terre cooperative pesto, white bean soup and superfresh whitebait. During the day, join hikers for bolstering rounds of cake and espresso.

La Cantina del Macellaio   STEAK €€
(☑ 0187 92 07 88; www.facebook.com/lacantinadelmacellaio.rio; Via Colombo 103; meals €35-45; ⊙ noon-3pm & 7-11pm) A surprising find in seafood-centric Cinque Terre, La Cantina del Macellaio fires up melt-in-your-mouth braised beef, pasta with wild boar and a few other simple but beautifully executed dishes. The incredibly accommodating staff and good wines on hand make for a memorable night out.

A Pié de Mà   BAR
(☑ 0187 92 10 37; www.facebook.com/apiedemariomaggiore; Via dell'Amore 55; ⊙ 11am-6.30pm Wed-Mon Oct-May, to 11pm Jun-Sep) A delightful spot for an afternoon pick-me-up, this open-air gem has a terrace perched right over Riomaggiore's wave-kissed shoreline. You'll find local craft beers (including La Spezia's Birrificio del Golfo on draft) as well as coffees, a few desserts and a fine selection of both red and white wines from Cinque Terre.

Golfo dei Poeti
☑ 0187
Back when Cinque Terre was but a collection of remote hardscrabble fishing villages, the Golfo dei Poeti (Gulf of Poets) was already drawing an it-crowd. Renamed for the English poets Lord Byron and Percy Bysshe Shelley, who escaped here in the 1820s, its natural beauty had inspired writers and artists as far back as Petrarch and Dante.

The port of La Spezia, Italy's largest naval base, is the main town and makes for a nicely urban, if supremely easygoing, base. Around each side of the bay, mountains loom on the horizon and cliffs plummet into the sea, and there's a deliciously remote feeling to the many forest-fringed sandy coves. Bumping up against Tuscany, there are the ridiculously beautiful, discrete resort towns of Lerici, San Terenzo and Tellaro, while at the other end sits the historic sentinel village of Porto Venere. Each has its own charm, but all share the evocative vertiginous tumble of pastel houses.

La Spezia
☑ 0187 / POP 93,500
It's an understandable oversight. Situated minutes to the east of Cinque Terre by train, and sidling up to the exquisite Lerici and Tellaro, this hard-working port town and home to Italy's largest naval base is routinely overlooked. But it's not only an affordable place to overnight if you're heading to the Cinque Terre, it's really worthy of exploring – the winding streets of the old town are hugely atmospheric and there are plenty of cosy trattorias showcasing the Ligurian kitchen's finest.

La Spezia's bustle peaks on 19 March, the feast day of the city's patron saint, San Giuseppe (St Joseph). Celebrations see a giant market fill the port and surrounding streets, and the naval base (off-limits the rest of the year) opens to the public.

OFF THE BEATEN TRACK

ESCAPE TO THE HILLS

The beaches of Lerici and San Terenzo are quite inviting, but the sands can get incredibly packed during the summer months. When you need a break from the crowds, look to the hills. A network of trails run inland, providing fabulous views over the coastline, and an intriguing way of connecting towns like Lerici with Tellaro without having to step into a vehicle. And unlike the trails in Cinque Terre, you won't encounter heavy crowds while out enjoying nature.

One beautiful walk begins near Lerici's Piazza Garibaldi and travels along a narrow lane (the Via Andrea Doria) up to the hillside village of **La Serra**. From there you can stop to admire the views before taking trail 464 through dense Mediterranean scrub to **Barbazzano**. The ruins of this ancient village, abandoned in the 16th century, have been almost entirely reclaimed by the forest. From there, trail 433 follows a hillside route to **Portesone** – yet another abandoned village (this one deserted owing to a medieval plague epidemic). It's an easy descent down to the enchanting village of Tellaro from there.

The whole trip, around 6km, takes about 1½ to two hours. Be sure to pick up a map at a tourist office before heading out, or have a look at the trail network on www.lericicoast.it.

◉ Sights

Museo Amedeo Lia   MUSEUM
(http://museolia.spezianet.it; Via del Prione 234; adult/reduced €10/7; ⊙10am-6pm Tue-Sun) This fine-arts museum in a restored 17th-century friary is La Spezia's star cultural attraction. The collection spans from the 13th to 18th centuries and includes paintings by masters such as Tintoretto, Montagna, Titian and Pietro Lorenzetti. Also on show are Roman bronzes and ecclesiastical treasures, such as Limoges crucifixes and illuminated musical manuscripts.

Museo Tecnico Navale della Spezia MUSEUM
(🗷0187 78 47 63; Viale Amendola 1; admission €1.55; ⊙8.30am-7.30pm) Maritime lovers shouldn't miss the world's oldest naval museum, which is reached via a narrow bridge a few blocks southwest of Parco Salvador Allende. The halls contain all manner of naval curiosities, including small models of sailing vessels from around the globe, otherworldly diving suits and a special area dedicated to Marconi's wireless invention. Upstairs, the Sala delle Polene is a hauntingly beautiful room with 28 figureheads that once adorned large sailing ships. The oldest, a sword- and shield-wielding Minerva, dates from 1738.

⛏ Sleeping & Eating

Alta Marea   B&B €
(🗷377 5448365; www.affittacamerealtamarea.it; Via Torino 70; d €100-120; ▣🛜) Friendly Andrea will be there to greet you at this small B&B and can be counted on for his local knowledge and restaurant tips. Rooms are spotless, airy and bright, with wooden floors

and signature graphic design, and the location is handy for making an early morning train to Cinque Terre.

La Pia Centenaria   LIGURIAN €
(www.lapia.it; Via Magenta 12; farinata/pizza from €2/4; ⊙10am-10pm) Founded in 1887, La Pia is a much-loved icon in La Spezia. Piping hot slices of *farinata* is the big draw, though there's also perfectly cooked slabs of pizzas, satisfying focaccia (including the cheese-packed *focaccia di Recco*) and quiche-like vegetable tort. The dining room is a casual affair, though there's also a takeaway window next door.

Dai Pescatori   SEAFOOD €
(Viale Italia; meals €15-20; ⊙noon-3pm & 7-9pm Tue-Sun) On the waterfront, this casual spot is a local institution for delicious plates of octopus salad, steamed mussels and fried fish plates. It's quite popular but not fancy in the least – think cafeteria-style self-service. Go right at opening time to beat the long lines.

★ Il Papeoto   VEGETARIAN €€
(🗷0187 150 95 68; www.facebook.com/ristorante vegetariano; Via Urbano Rattazzi 25; meals €26-32; ⊙7.30-10.30pm Mon-Sat; 🗷) This friendly *osteria* (casual tavern) turns out Insta-worthy plates of creative, cruelty-free delicacies. Rich, complex flavours feature prominently in dishes like gnocchi with salty ricotta cheese and almonds or crispy egg asparagus with saffron sauce; don't overlook the imaginative desserts. The setting inspires zen-like calm, with vintage botanical prints on the walls, chic industrial fixtures, and touches of greenery. Reservations recommended.

🍷 Drinking & Nightlife

Resilience Cafe BAR
(www.facebook.com/resiliencecafe; Via Vanicella 8; ⊙ 6pm-midnight Mon-Thu, to 1am Fri & Sat) An atmospheric spot for a pre- or post-dinner drink, the Resilience Cafe exudes effortless style, with its wine red walls, shelves of books, twinkling chandeliers and vintage furniture. The well-made cocktails are served in fine glassware and you can design your own bruschetta, and cheese and meat boards. Outdoor seating on the lane in front.

ⓘ Information

Tourist Office (www.myspezia.it; Via del Prione; ⊙ 10am-1pm & 2-5pm)

There's also a **Cinque Terre Park Office** (⌨ 0187 74 35 00; www.parconazionale5terre.it; ⊙ 7am-8pm) inside La Spezia's train station.

ⓘ Getting There & Away

Buses, marked 11 or P, run to Porto Venere (€2.50); these depart hourly from Via Fiume, the busy street just below the train station, and every 15 minutes from Via Chiodo just opposite the Giardini Publici. Buses to Lerici, marked L or S (€2.50, approximately every 15 minutes) go from Via Fiume, below the train station. Check Azienda Trasporti Consortile (www.atcesercizio.it) for schedules.

La Spezia is on the Genoa–Rome railway line and is also connected to Milan (€29, 3½ hours, every two hours), Turin (€40 to €42, 3½ hours, several daily) and Pisa (€8 to €16, 50 to 80 minutes, almost hourly). The Cinque Terre and other coastal towns are easily accessible by train and boat.

Porto Venere

⌨ 0187 / POP 3600

Perched on the dreamy Golfo dei Poeti's western promontory, the historic fishing port's sinuous seven- and eight-storey harbourfront houses form an almost impregnable citadel around the muscular Castello Doria.

The Romans built Portus Veneris as a base en route from Gaul to Spain, and in later years the Byzantines, Lombards, Genovese and Napoleon all passed through here and made the most of its spectacular natural defences. Its appeal, however, is not just strategic: its beauty drew the poet Byron, who famously swam from the now collapsed Grotta Arpaia's rocky cove to San Terenzo to visit fellow poet Percy Shelley (it was to be renamed Grotta di Byron for him). The town remains a romantic, scenic place for a day trip, or a relaxing base for exploring the coast. Serene by comparison to its Cinque Terre neighbours, weekends and summer evenings do bring Ligurians from far and wide for the *passeggiata*.

⊙ Sights

★ Grotta di Byron VIEWPOINT
(Grotta Arpaia) At the end of the quay, a Cinque Terre panorama unfolds from the rocky terraces of a cave formerly known as Grotta Arpaia. Despite the cave's collapse, the rocky terraces remain quite beautiful and suitably dishevelled and affecting.

To add to the frisson, know that traces of a pagan temple dedicated to Venus (hence a suggestion to the name 'Venere') have been uncovered here, as well as inside the black-and-white-marble Chiesa di San Pietro. Just off the promontory, you can see the tiny islands of **Palmaria**, **Tino** and **Tinetto**.

Chiesa di San Pietro CHURCH
(www.parrocchiaportovenere.it; ⊙ 8.30am-7pm Jun-Sep, to 5.30pm Oct-May) This stunning wind- and wave-lashed church, built in 1198 in Gothic style, stands on the ruins of a 5th-century palaeo-Christian church, with its extant floor still partially visible. Before its Christianisation, it was a Roman temple dedicated to the goddess Venus, born from the foam of the sea, from whom Porto Venere takes its name.

After visiting the church, be sure to climb the stairs just out front to a terrace with staggering views over the cliffs.

Palmaria ISLAND
The largest island of the Italian Riviera is largely undeveloped (it's home to around 50 residents) and lies just a short ferry ride from Porto Venere. Set with towering cliffs, picturesque coves and rocky beaches, the 1.9 sq km Palmaria makes a fascinating destination for a day trip. There are several well-maintained hiking trails on the island including the 510, which circles the island and takes you up high slopes, through Mediterranean forest and past pristine shorelines on a moderately difficult three-hour walk.

If you prefer to lounge on the beach, you can join sunseekers on the shore near Punta Secca, opposite Porto Venere. The best beach though is at Pozzale on the southeast side of the island. Ferries run every 30 minutes during summer (and every couple of hours off season) from Porto Venere to Punta Secca (€5, five minutes).

ℹ Information

Tourist Office (www.prolocoportovenere.it; Piazza Bastreri 7; ⊘10am-noon & 3-7pm Jun-Aug, to 6pm Thu-Tue Sep-May)

ℹ Getting There & Away

Porto Venere is served by daily buses from La Spezia. Note that you can't park in the town during summer; a parking area is located just outside the town and a shuttle service (€1 per person) operates all day.

From late March to October, **Consorzio Marittimo Turistico Cinque Terre Golfo dei Poeti** (☑0187 73 29 87; www.navigazionegolfodei poeti.it) sails from Porto Venere to/from Cinque Terre villages (all day, all stops €35, one way €27, afternoon-only ticket €27) and runs one-hour excursions to the islands of Palmaria, Tino and Tinetto (€13).

Lerici, San Terenzo & Tellaro

Magnolia, yew and cedar trees grow in the 1930s public gardens at Lerici, an exclusive retreat of terraced villas clinging to the cliffs along its beach, and in another age Byron and Shelley sought inspiration here.

From Lerici, a scenic 3km coastal stroll leads northwest to San Terenzo, a seaside village with a sandy beach and Genoese castle. The Shelleys lived in the waterfront Villa Magni (sadly closed to visitors) in the early 1820s and Percy drowned here when his boat sank off the coast in 1822, on an ill-fated return trip from Livorno.

Another coastal stroll or drive, 4km southeast, takes you past magnificent little bays to Tellaro, a fishing hamlet with ink-and-orange houses cluttering narrow lanes and tiny hidden squares. Sit on the square near the village church and imagine an octopus ringing the church bells – which, according to legend, it did to warn the villagers of a Saracen attack. Nearby Fiascherino (a little over 1km north) has splendid sandy beaches, set on two sheltered bays that are ideal for swimming. It's hard not to fall for this area, as English writer DH Lawrence did while living here in 1913.

◉ Sights

Castello di Lerici   CASTLE
(Piazzetta San Giorgio, Lerici; ⊘10am-noon & 3-6pm Tue-Sun May, Jun & mid-Sep–Oct, 10am-noon & 6-11pm daily Jul–mid-Sep) **FREE** On a promontory high above the shoreline, Lerici's castle has played a pivotal role protecting the city since the Middle Ages. Rebuilt var-

ious times over the years, the citadel today hosts changing exhibitions spread among various stone-walled chambers. There are also fabulous views from its lofty terraces.

The easiest way to reach the castle is by taking the lift, which is hidden inside a tunnel leading off the waterfront (Via Giuseppe Mazzini). You can also follow the stairs heading up from near Piazza Garibaldi.

Spiagge di San Giorgio   BEACH
(Lerici) Hidden behind the Castello di Lerici are a series of wild cliff-backed beaches extending along the southern shoreline. Reach the first by heading through the tunnel (under the castle) that leads off Via Giuseppe Mazzini and taking the stairs down to the water. To reach the other beaches, you'll have to clamber over the rocks (wear good shoes) – not advised if you have children in tow.

🛏 Sleeping & Eating

There is little in the way of budget hotels in this upmarket enclave, although midrange (often delightfully old-fashioned) places can be good value in shoulder season. Apartment and villa rentals are also a good option.

Eco Del Mare   RESORT €€€
(☑0187 96 86 09; www.ecodelmare.it; Via Fiascherino 4, Tellaro; d €390-690; ⊘May-Sep; P☎) One of the Riviera's loveliest beaches is home to this exclusive, remote-seeming hotel and beach club. An insouciant boho glamour pervades here; rooms are deeply romantic, filled with an idiosyncratic mix of decor, muted crumpled linen and classical chairs, while the restaurant, despite the prices, gives off beach-shack vibes.

Dal Pudu   LIGURIAN €
(Piazza Garibaldi 10, Lerici; mains €10-18; ⊘noon-3pm & 7-10pm) Just across from Piazza Garibaldi, Dal Pudu is a tiny storefront serving up some of the best seafood in town. A chalkboard menu lists the day's specials, which might include *stoccafisso* (a delectable fish stew), spaghetti with anchovies, lobster salad or lightly battered fried squid. Go early to score a seat at one of the three tables out front. You can also order takeaway and have your feast down by the water.

ℹ Information

There are several tourist information kiosks in the area including on the Lerici waterfront (near Piazza Garibaldi) and on Piazza Rainuso in Tellaro.

❶ Getting There & Away

ATC Esercizio (www.atceserzicio.it) buses run to Lerici and San Terenzo from La Spezia's train station, a 35-minute trip. Tickets can be bought on board, though they are cheaper from a *tabaccheria* (€2.50). If heading to Tellaro, you'll have to change in Lerici.

Riviera di Ponente

✒ 0184

Curving west from Genoa to the French border, the Ponente stretch of the Italian Riviera coast is more down-to-earth than the flashy Riviera east of Genoa. As a result, it shelters some relatively well-priced escape hatches, particularly along the stretch of coast from Noli to Finale Ligure.

Savona

✒ 019 / POP 60.400

Behind Savona's sprawling port facilities, the city's unexpectedly graceful medieval centre is well worth a stop. Among the old-town treasures to survive destruction by Genoese forces in the 16th century are the baroque Cattedrale di Nostra Signora Assunta and the lumbering Fortezza del Priamàr. There's also a nice urban buzz, with lots of new shops, bars and restaurants regenerating the old centre.

◉ Sights & Activities

Museo d'Arte di Palazzo Gavotti GALLERY
(http://musa.savona.it; Piazza Chabrol 1/2; adult/reduced €8/5; ⊙10am-1.30pm Wed & Sun, 10am-1.30pm & 3.30-6.30pm Thu-Sat) Set amid two adjoining *palazzi*, Savona's premier art collection features an impressive collection of paintings dating all the way back to the 14th century, including *Madonna and Child* by Taddeo di Bartolo, *The Crucifixion* by Donato de' Bardi and Giovanni Battista Carlone's emotionally charged painting of *Venus and Mars*. Another area of the museum showcases 20th-century art, with pieces by Magritte, de Chirico, Man Ray and Picasso. The museum also houses the Italian Riviera's best collection of ceramics, with pieces spanning some six centuries.

Cappella Sistina CHAPEL
(www.cattedralesavona.it; Piazza del Duomo; admission €2; ⊙10am-12.30pm Sun) Dating from the 1480s, Savona's Sistine Chapel (like the one in Rome) was created by Pope Sixtus IV. Though far less famous than its Roman counterpoint, this site – a funerary chapel for Sixtus' deceased parents – is a striking work of art. It's well worth seeing if you happen to be around the one day a week it's open.

Fortezza del Priamàr FORTRESS
(www.museoarcheosavona.it; Corso Mazzini 1; ⊙9am-6.30pm mid-Sep–mid-Jun, to midnight mid-Jun–mid-Sep) FREE Among Savona's treasures to survive destruction by Genoese forces in the 16th century is the lumbering Fortezza del Priamàr. This imposing fortress, which has suffered some years of neglect, guards several small museums including the **Civico Museo Storico Archeologico** (www.museo archeosavona.it; adult/reduced €5/3; ⊙10am-1pm Thu, 10am-2pm & 5-7pm Sat & Sun, reduced hours winter). The citadel also has various terraces overlooking the seaside, an overgrown playground and a small cafe.

Whale Watch Liguria WHALE WATCHING
(www.whalewatchliguria.it; Marinai d'Italia; tickets €40) Seven- to eight-hour whale-watching trips depart Savona at 9.15am on Thursdays from late July to mid-September. A marine biologist on board provides info on the eight different cetacean species that inhabit the area. Reservations are essential. The boat departs from the pier near the medieval tower overlooking the waterfront.

🛏 Sleeping & Eating

Mare Hotel HOTEL €€
(✒019 26 40 65; www.marehotel.it; Via Nizza 41; d €180-260; ❄@🛜🏊) The four-star seafront Mare with its infinity pool, private beach and candlelit open-air restaurant is Italian beach bling in action. New rooms adopt a Milanese nightclub aesthetic, while older rooms are comfortable, if a little frumpy. It's 2km west along the beach from the station – regular buses run there.

Vino e Farinata ITALIAN €
(www.vinoefarinata.it; Via Pia 15; meals €18-28; ⊙noon-2pm & 6.30-9.30pm Tue-Sat) In the cobbled centre, this much-loved local spot serves up outstanding *farinata*, as well as delectable, simply prepared seafood. All goes down nicely with the local wines.

Green LIGURIAN €
(✒019 80 30 29; www.greenristorantesavona.it; Via Domenico Cimarosa 4; meals €22-32; ⊙7-11pm Mon-Sat, 12.30-2.30pm & 7-11pm Sun) A popular gathering spot for all – families, young couples, visitors, old timers with small dogs – Green is easy-going with a spacious covered terrace overlooking the sea. The menu encompasses abundant seafood and good pizzas.

ℹ️ Information

Tourist Office (Via dei Maestri d'Ascia 7; ⊙ 8.30am-4pm Sat & Sun) Near the cruise-ship terminal.

ℹ️ Getting There & Away

ACTS buses (www.tpllinea.it), departing from the train station, are the best option for reaching points inland.

Trains run along the coast to Genoa's Stazione Piazza Principe (€5, one hour, every 30 minutes) and San Remo (€8.40, 1½ hours, every 30 to 60 minutes).

Corsica Ferries (www.corsica-ferries.fr) runs up to three boats daily between Savona's Porto Vado and Corsica.

Finale Ligure

📞 019 / POP 11,800

The scenic area of Finale Ligure is an ideal setting for outdoor adventures, with excellent hiking and mountain biking in the hills above the village. There's also plenty of seaside fun coupled with historic cobblestone districts ripe for exploring.

Set amid lush Mediterranean vegetation, this township comprises several districts. **Finale Ligure** has a wide, fine-sand beach. The walled medieval centre, known as **Finalborgo**, is a knot of twisting alleys set 1km back from the coast on the Pora river. **Finale Marina** sits on the waterfront, the more residential **Finale Pia** runs along the Sciusa river and the **Finalese** rises up into the hinterland.

🏃 Activities

Finalborgo is a prime destination for outdoor activities. Aside from some fine walks in the region, there's excellent mountain biking here. Many outfitters hire out bikes and gear, and run shuttles to some excellent tracks out of town.

🛏️ Sleeping

⭐ **Valleponci** AGRITURISMO €

(📞 329 3154169; www.valleponci.it; Val Ponci 22, Localita Verzi; d €80-100, apt €165) Only 4km from the beach, Val Ponce feels deliciously wild, tucked away in a rugged Ligurian valley. Horses graze, grapevines bud and the restaurant turns out fresh Ligurian dishes, with vegetables and herbs from a kitchen garden. On weekend evenings and Sunday lunch, there's live music or classic vinyl. Rooms are simple but show the keen eye of the Milanese escapee owners.

There are some wonderful hiking and mountain-biking paths around here: ask the knowledgeable Giorgio for a map and tips on the historical and archaeological sites to look out for. Vallepanci is around 6km northeast of Finale Ligure.

Paradiso di Manù HOTEL €€

(📞 019 749 01 10; www.paradisodimanu.it; Via Chiariventi 35, Noli; d €185-250; 🅿 @ 🏊) Overlooking the Gulf of Spotorno, this 'diffusion' hotel is a revitalised hamlet with six elegant Provençal-style rooms located in a variety of stone buildings overlooking florid terraces, two with outdoor jacuzzis. Paradiso di Manù lies near the village of Noli, roughly midway between Savona and Finale Ligure.

🍴 Eating

In Finale Ligure, the promenade along Via San Pietro and Via Concezione is crammed with restaurants. Finalborgo's atmospheric cobblestone streets are dotted with charming places to eat, many with outdoor tables.

Salumeria Chiesa DELI €

(📞 019 69 25 16; Via Pertica 15; small plates from €6; ⊙ 11am-2.30pm & 6-8.30pm May-Oct, closed Sun Nov-Apr) Presided over by Laura Chiesa, this delicatessen offers a huge array of seafood salads, salamis, cheeses and gnocchi with pesto, of course. Order what you like in the shop and eat it at the *tavola calda* ('warm table', a casual eatery) round the corner on Vico Gandolino.

Osteria ai Cuattru Canti OSTERIA €€

(📞 019 68 05 40; Via Torcelli 22; meals €25-35; ⊙ noon-2pm & 7.30-10pm Tue-Sun) Simple, good Ligurian specialities are cooked up at this rustic place in Finalborgo's historic centre.

ℹ️ Information

Finalborgo Tourist Office (Piazza Santa Caterina; ⊙ 9.30am-12.30pm & 3.30-7.30pm Wed-Sun) Pick up info on walking, biking and other outdoor activities from this helpful office in the historic centre.

Finalmarina Tourist Office (Via San Pietro 14, Finalmarina; ⊙ 9am-12.30pm & 2.30-5.30pm Tue-Sat, 9am-12.30pm Sun) From the train station on Piazza Vittorio Veneto, at Finale Marina's western end, walk down Via Saccone to the sea and this office.

ℹ️ Getting There & Around

TPL (📞 019 220 12 31; www.tpllinea.it) buses yo-yo every 30 minutes to/from Finale Ligure and Savona (€2.50, 50 minutes), stopping en route in Finalborgo (€1.30, five minutes) and Noli (€1.80, 20 minutes). Catch bus 40/ from Savona's train station. Note the '/' on the sign indicates the bus travels to Finalborgo; bus 40 (without '/') goes only to Finale Ligure.

Rent mountain bikes and e-bikes at **Soul Cycles** (☑ 019 528 39 73; www.soulcycles finaleligure.com; Viale Dante Alighieri 88, Finalborgo; mountain bike/e-bike per day €50/60; ☺ 8.30am-12.30pm & 3.30-7.30pm), just outside the walls of the old town (on the road leading down to Finale Ligure).

San Remo

☑ 0184 / POP 55,000

Fifty kilometres east of Europe's premier gambling capital lies San Remo, Italy's own Monte Carlo, a sun-dappled Mediterranean resort with a casino, a clutch of ostentatious villas and lashings of Riviera-style grandeur. Beaches aside, San Remo (spelled Sanremo in Italian) hides the atmospheric lanes of a medieval district called La Pigna.

Known colloquially as the City of Flowers for its colourful summer blooms, San Remo also stages an annual music festival (the supposed inspiration for the Eurovision Song Contest) and the world's longest professional one-day cycling race, the 298km Milan–San Remo classic.

During the mid-19th century the city became a magnet for regal European exiles, such as Empress Elisabeth of Austria and Tsarina Maria Aleksandrovna, who favoured the town's balmy winters. Swedish inventor Alfred Nobel maintained a villa here, and an onion-domed Russian Orthodox church

reminiscent of Moscow's St Basil's Cathedral still turns heads down by the seafront.

◉ Sights & Activities

Curling around the base of San Remo is a 24km **bike and walking path** (www.pistacicla bile.com) that tracks the coast as far as San Lorenzo.

La Pigna HISTORIC SITE
(Off Via Santo Stefano; 🚶) San Remo's little-visited old town is a labyrinth of quiet, twisting lanes set on a hilltop above the bustling centre. Get there by taking Via Santo Stefano uphill and losing yourself among the cobblestone paths. If you keep ascending, you'll eventually reach the Giardina Regina Elena, a pine-shaded terrace (with a playground) that has fine views over town.

Il Casinò Municipale CASINO
(www.casinosanremo.it; Corso degli Inglesi 18; ☺ 10am-2.30am Sun-Thu, to 3.30am Fri & Sat) San Remo's belle époque casino, one of only four in Italy, was dealing cards when Vegas was still a waterhole in the desert. The building dates from 1905 and was designed by Parisian architect Eugenio Ferret. Slot machines (more than 400 of them) open at 10am; other games (roulette, blackjack, poker etc) kick off at 2.30pm. Dress smart-casual and bring ID (the minimum age for entry is 18).

Chiesa Russa Ortodossa CHURCH
(Via Nuvoloni 2; admission €1; ☺ 9.30am-12.30pm & 3-6.30pm) Built for the Russian community that followed Tsarina Maria Aleksandrovna (wife of Tsar Alexander II) to San Remo in

TURIN, PIEDMONT & CINQUE TERRE RIVIERA DI PONENTE

OFF THE BEATEN TRACK

VILLAGE ESCAPES INLAND

Seven kilometres northeast of San Remo lies the intriguing artists' colony of **Bussana Vecchia** (www.bussanavecchia.it). On Ash Wednesday 1887, an earthquake destroyed the village and it remained a ghost town until the 1960s when artists and counterculture devotees moved in and began rebuilding the ruins, using the original stones from the rubble. A thriving community of international artists remains in residence today. Take a bus to Bussana, 5km east of San Remo, then walk the 2km up.

Alternatively escape the coastal crowds with a flit up a narrow, dead-end valley to **Dolceaqua**, a serene medieval town 23km from San Remo whose beauty once inspired Monet. Its original, steeply sited heart is watched over by a recently restored castle, while its new town, a typical 19th-century affair, sits across a fast-flowing river, joined by an ancient humpback stone bridge. A number of small, unpretentious places serving very good Ligurian dishes hide in the tangle of the old town's core. Or join the fashionably dressed French-border hoppers at **Casa e Bottega** (☑ 340 5665339; www.ristocasaebot tega.it; Piazza Garibaldi 2; meals €30-40; ☺ noon-2.30pm daily & 7.30-10pm Fri-Sun), a stylishly bucolic restaurant, cafe, homewares shop and general village epicentre.

San Remo

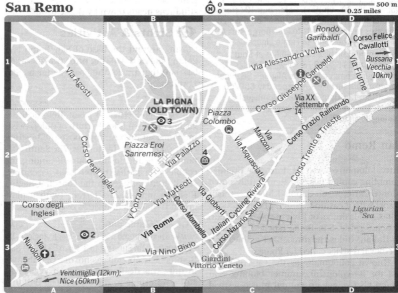

San Remo

◎ Sights

◎ Sleeping

◎ Eating

1906, the Russian Orthodox church of Cristo Salvatore – with its onion domes and heavenly pale-blue interior – was designed by Alexei Shchusev, who later planned Lenin's mausoleum in Moscow. Icons and murals of Christian saints line the interior, and liturgical services are still held on Saturday evenings and Sunday mornings for the Russian expat community.

Museo Civico MUSEUM
(Palazzo Borea d'Olmo; Corso Matteotti 143; adult/reduced €5/3; ⊙ 8.30am-noon & 2-6.30pm Tue-Sat) Housed in a 15th-century *palazzo*, several rooms in this museum, some with fine frescoed ceilings, display local prehistoric and Roman archaeological finds, paintings and temporary exhibitions. Highlights include Maurizio Carrega's 1808 homage, *Gloria di San Napoleone*, and bronze statues by Franco Bargiggia.

🛏 Sleeping & Eating

Lolli Palace Hotel HOTEL €€
(📞 0184 53 14 96; www.lollihotel.it; Corso Imperatrice 70; €125-175; ❄ 🕾) Set in a lovely art-nouveau building near the waterfront, this well-equipped three-star makes a fine base for exploring the town. It has pleasantly furnished modern rooms with good mattresses, and some have sea views. The rooftop terrace is a nice bonus.

★ A Cuvèa ITALIAN €
(Corso Giuseppe Garibaldi 110; meals €15-30; ⊙ noon-2.45pm & 7.15-9.45pm) This cosy, warmly lit place lined with wine bottles overflows with locals tucking into homemade traditional dishes such as *tagliolini* with seafood or *zimino di seppie* (cuttlefish stew); it also has the most genial host in town. The set menus (three courses with water, wine and coffee for €28) are a fabulous deal, available at lunch and dinner.

Urbicia Vivas LIGURIAN €€

(☑ 0184 84 44 60; Piazza Dolori 5; meals €30-40; ⊙ noon-2.30pm & 7pm-midnight Tue-Sun) Basking in a quiet medieval square in San Remo's remarkable old town, Urbicia is slavishly faithful to old Ligurian recipes, with a strong bias towards seafood. Highlights include ravioli of borage (a Mediterranean herb with a faint cucumber taste), grilled squid with lime and pepper sauce, and spaghetti with clams.

ⓘ Information

Tourist office (☑ 0184 58 05 00; Corso Giuseppe Garibaldi; ⊙ 9.30am-1pm daily, plus 3-6.30pm Tue & Thu-Sat)

ⓘ Getting There & Away

Riviera Trasporti buses leave regularly from the **bus station** (Piazza Colombo 42) for the French border, and destinations east along the coast and inland.

From San Remo's underground train station there are trains to/from Genoa (€12, two hours, every one to two hours), Ventimiglia (€2.80, 15 minutes, hourly) and stations in between.

Ventimiglia

☑ 0184 / POP 24,200

Bordertown Ventimiglia once harboured a stoic Roman town known as Albintimulium, which survived until the 5th century AD, when it was besieged by the Goths. These days it's besieged by a weekly horde of French bargain hunters who cross the border each market day.

The rocky beach makes for a pleasant dip, though the the real draw to Ventimiglia is exploring its medieval district – set on a hill across the river from the modern part of town.

⊙ Sights

Centro Storico AREA

(Off Via Garibaldi) The small village on the hill is upper Ventimiglia, home to one of the largest historic centres in the Italian Riviera. Medieval walls surround the lofty district, which is sprinkled with photogenic churches, architecturally striking buildings and hidden plazas bristling with olive trees. Shadowy cobblestone *caruggi* meander through this surprisingly residential neighbourhood, with locals exchanging gossip at cafes along Via Garibaldi.

Cattedrale di Santa Maria Assunta CATHEDRAL

(Via del Capo; ⊙ 8am-6.30pm) A must-see when exploring the historic centre, this cathedral has original 13th-century elements, including a portal with an acute arch, Romanesque columns and a baptistery set inside an atmospheric lower chamber.

Mercato del Venerdì MARKET

(Lungo Roja Rossi; ⊙ 6am-6pm Fri May-Oct, to 5pm Fri Nov-Apr) Ventimiglia is best known for its huge Friday market when hundreds of stalls sell food, clothes, leather goods, homewares, baskets and everything else under the sun. The market is concentrated along the riverside from the bridge across the Roya south to Via Chiappori.

Giardini Botanici Hanbury GARDENS

(www.giardinihanbury.com; Corso Montecarlo 43, La Mortola; adult/reduced €9/7.50; ⊙ 9.30am-6pm Mar–mid-June, to 7pm mid-Jun–mid-Oct, to 5pm mid-Oct–Feb, closed Mon Nov-Feb) Established in 1867 by English businessman Sir Thomas Hanbury, the 18-hectare Villa Hanbury estate is planted with 5800 botanical species from five continents, including cacti, palm groves and citrus orchards. Today it's a protected area, under the care of the University of Genoa.

Take bus 1 from Via Cavour in Ventimiglia (there's a stop two blocks from the train station beside a Calzedonia shop) to 'La Mortola' stop. The bus continues on to the Ponte San Lodovico frontier post, from where you can walk down to the Balzi Rossi caves and beach on the French border.

✖ Eating

Cheap, cheerful places to eat congregate around Via Cavour. You'll be competing with the French who come over the border for lunch or dinner, so nab a table early.

Pasta & Basta LIGURIAN €€

(☑ 0184 23 08 78; www.pastaebastaventimiglia.com; Via Marconi 20a; meals €25-40; ⊙ noon-3pm & 7.30-10pm Tue-Sun) Near the seafront on the border side of town (overlooking the new marina) you'll find elegant Pasta & Basta. Various house-made fresh pasta can be mixed and matched with a large menu of sauces, including a good pesto or *salsa di noci* (walnut purée), and washed down with a carafe of pale and refreshing Pigato, a local white.

ℹ Information

Tourist Office (📱 0184 192 83 09; Lungo Roja Rossi; ⊙ 9.30am-12.30pm Tue-Thu & Sat, 9.30am-12.30pm & 3.30-6.30pm Fri) Near the riverside, just south of the vehicle bridge, this office provides basic info and also rents out free e-bikes. Be sure to bring ID.

ℹ Getting There & Away

From the **train station** (Via della Stazione), Via della Repubblica leads to the beach. Trains connect Ventimiglia with Genoa (€14, 2½ hours, hourly), Nice (€8, 1 hour, hourly) and other destinations in France.

PIEDMONT

POP 4.36 MILLION

Italy's second-largest region is arguably its most elegant: a purveyor of Slow Food and fine wine, regal *palazzi* and an atmosphere that is superficially more *français* than *italiano*. But dig deeper and you'll discover that Piedmont has 'Made in Italy' stamped all over it. Emerging from the chaos of the Austrian wars, the unification movement first exploded here in the 1850s, when the noble House of Savoy provided the nascent nation with its first prime minister and its dynastic royal family.

Most Piedmont journeys start in stately Turin, famous for football and Fiats. Beyond the car factories, Piedmont is notable for its food – everything from rice to white truffles – and pretty pastoral landscapes not unlike nearby Tuscany.

The region's smaller towns were once feuding fiefdoms that bickered over trade and religion. Today the biggest skirmishes are more likely to be over recipes and vintages as they vie for the gourmet traveller euro.

ℹ CENT SAVER

Along with the Torino + Piemonte Card (one/two/three/five days €27/36/43/51), which covers admission to 190 of the region's monuments and museums, Turin has the Torino Contemporary Card (adult and one child €29), which gives free admission to the Castello di Rivoli, GAM, various Fondazione and both Ettore Fico and the Agnelli museums, along with a taxi discount. It's valid for seven days.

Turin

📱 011 / POP 878,000 / ELEV 240M

There's a whiff of Paris in Turin's elegant tree-lined boulevards and echoes of Vienna in its stately art-nouveau cafes, but make no mistake – this elegant, Alp-fringed city is utterly self-possessed. The industrious Torinese gave the world its first saleable hard chocolate and Italy's most iconic car, the Fiat.

Its booming contemporary art, architecture and live-music scene and innovative food and wine culture are definitely aspects you'll want to discover.

History

The ancient Celtic-Ligurian city of Taurisia was destroyed by Hannibal in 218 BC and the Roman colony of Augusta Taurinorum, established here almost two centuries later, saw succeeding invasions of Goths, Lombards and Franks. In 1563 the Savoys abandoned their old capital of Chambéry (now in France) to set up court in Turin, which shared the dynasty's fortunes thereafter. The Savoys annexed Sardinia in 1720, but Napoleon put an end to their power when he occupied Turin in 1798. Turin was then controlled by Austria and Russia before Vittorio Emanuele I restored the House of Savoy and re-entered Turin in 1814. Nevertheless, Austria remained the true power throughout northern Italy until the Risorgimento in 1861, when Turin became the nation's inaugural capital. Piedmont, with its wily president, the Count of Cavour, was the engine room of the Risorgimento (literally 'the Resurgence', or Italian unification). Its capital status lasted only until 1864, and the parliament had already moved to Florence by the time full-sized chambers were completed.

Turin adapted quickly to its loss of political significance, becoming a centre for industrial production during the early 20th century. Giants such as Fiat lured hundreds of thousands of impoverished southern Italians to Turin and housed them in vast company-built and -owned suburbs. Fiat's owners, the Agnelli family (who also happen to own the Juventus football club, Turin's local newspaper and a large chunk of the national daily *Corriere della Sera*), remain one of Italy's most powerful establishment forces. Fiat's fortunes declined later in the 20th century, however, and only revived around a decade ago.

The highly successful 2006 Winter Olympics were a turning point for the city. The Olympics not only ushered in a building boom, including a brand-new metro system, but also transformed Turin from a staid industrial centre into a vibrant metropolis. Turin was European Capital of Design in 2008, hosting conferences and exhibitions, and the national focus of celebrations of the 150th anniversary of the Risorgimento in 2011.

⊙ Sights

Got a week? You might need it to see all the sights Turin has to offer. The time-poor can concentrate on a trio of highlights: the Museo Egizio, the Mole Antonelliana and the Museo Nazionale dell'Automobile.

⊙ Central Turin

Piazza Castello   PIAZZA
(Via Roma) Turin's central square is lined with museums, theatres and cafes. The city's Savoy heart, although laid out from the mid-1300s, was mostly constructed from the 16th to 18th centuries. Dominating it is the part-medieval, part-baroque Palazzo Madama, the original seat of the Italian parliament. To the north is the exquisite facade of Palazzo Reale, the royal palace built for Carlo Emanuele II in the mid-1600s.

★ Palazzo Reale   MUSEUM
(www.museireali.beniculturali.it; Piazza Castello; adult/reduced €15/2, 1st Sun of month free; ⊙10am-7pm Tue-Sun) Statues of the mythical twins Castor and Pollux guard the entrance to this eye-catching palace and, according to local hearsay, also watch over the magical border between the sacred and diabolical halves of the city. Built for Carlo Emanuele II around 1646, its lavishly decorated rooms complete with jaw-dropping coffered ceilings house an assortment of furnishings, porcelain, and other finery. The Giardino Reale (Royal Garden; ⊙8.30am-7.30pm Tue-Sun) FREE, north and east of the palace, was designed in 1697 by André Le Nôtre, who also created the gardens at Versailles.

The Palazzo Reale ticket includes admission to a sprawling collection, including Greek and Roman archaeological treasures in the Museo di Antichità, a dazzling armoury hall and temporary shows in the Sala Chiablese. Also within the palace confines is the stunning Cappella della Sacra Sindone (Chapel of the Holy Shroud), a 17th-century architectural masterpiece that reopened in 2018 after being closed for some 30 years following a devastating fire. The religious relic (saved by firefighters from the flames) is today kept out of sight in the nearby Cattedrale di San Giovanni Battista.

If time is limited, focus on the Galleria Sabauda, the personal art collection of the Savoy monarchy. Amassed over 400 years, the trove includes works by Van Dyck, Rubens, Veronese and Rembrandt. On Thursdays from June to mid-October, admission is free from 5pm to 7pm.

Cattedrale di San
Giovanni Battista   CATHEDRAL
(☑011 436 15 40; www.duomoditorino.it; Via XX Settembre 87; ⊙7am-12.30pm & 3-7pm, Mon-Sat, from 8am Sun) Turin's cathedral was built between 1491 and 1498 on the site of three 14th-century basilicas and, before that, a Roman theatre. Plain interior aside, as home to the Shroud of Turin (traditionally believed to be the burial cloth in which Jesus' body was wrapped), this is a highly trafficked church. The famous cloth is not on display, but you can see where it is kept and watch explanatory video presentations.

The separate Romanesque-style bell tower looks older than it really is; it was designed by Juvarra and built in 1723. Just to the north lie the remains of a 1st-century Roman amphitheatre (Teatro Romano; Via XX Settembre 88), while a little further to the northwest lies Porta Palatina (Piazza Cesare Augusto), the red-brick remains of a Roman-era gate.

Palazzo Madama   PALACE
(☑011 443 35 01; www.palazzomadamatorino.it; Piazza Castello; adult/reduced €10/8; ⊙10am-6pm Wed-Mon) A part-medieval, part-baroque castle built in the 13th century on the site of the old Roman gate, this *palazzo* is named after Madama Reale Maria Cristina, the widow of Vittorio Amedeo I (Duke of Savoy, 1630–37). Today, much of the building houses the expansive Museo Civico d'Arte Antica, which contains four floors of mostly decorative arts from medieval to the post-unification period, along with temporary exhibitions of contemporary art.

Museo della Sindone   MUSEUM
(www.sindone.it; Via San Domenico 28; adult/reduced €8/6; ⊙9am-noon & 3-7pm) Encased in the crypt of Santo Sudario church, this fascinating museum documents one of the most studied objects in human history: the

Piedmont

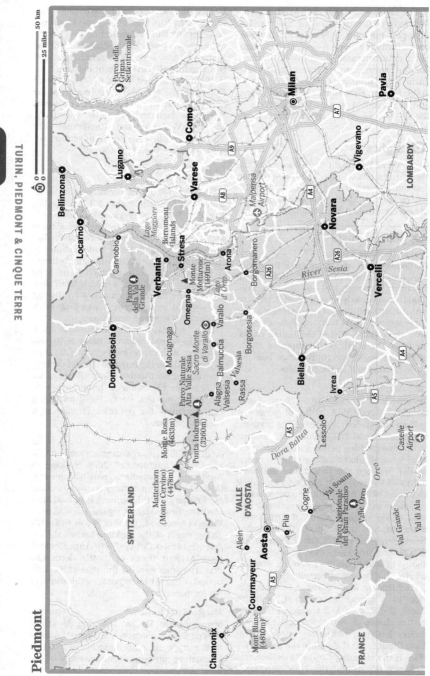

0 N

0 50 km
0 25 miles

SWITZERLAND

Mont Blanc (4810m)
Chamonix
Courmayeur
A5
Allein
Aosta
Pila
VALLE D'AOSTA
Cogne
Val Soana
Parco Nazionale del Gran Paradiso
Valle Orco
Val Grande
Val di Ala
Orco
Caselle Airport
Lessolo
Dora Baltea
Ivrea
Biella
A5
A4

Matterhorn (Monte Cervino) (4478m)
Monte Rosa (4633m)
Punta Indren (3260m)
Macugnaga
Alagna Valsesia
Rassa
Balmuccia
Valsesia
Borgosesia
Parco Naturale Alta Valle Sesia
Sacro Monte di Varallo
Varallo
Borgomanero
A26

Domodossola
Parco della Val Grande
Monte Mottarone (1491m)
Omegna
Verbania
Stresa
Arona
Lago d'Orta
River Sesia
Vercelli
A4
A26
Novara

Cannobio
Locarno
Bellinzona
Lugano
Borromean Islands
Lago Maggiore
Varese
A8
Malpensa Airport
A9
A4

Parco della Grigna Settentrionale
Como
Milan
A7
Vigevano
Pavia
LOMBARDY

FRANCE

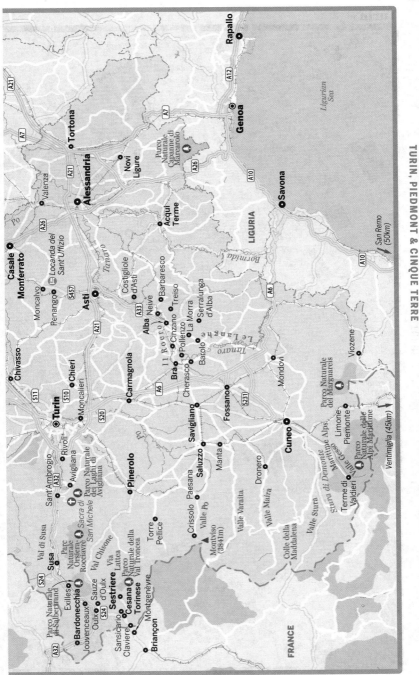

Turin

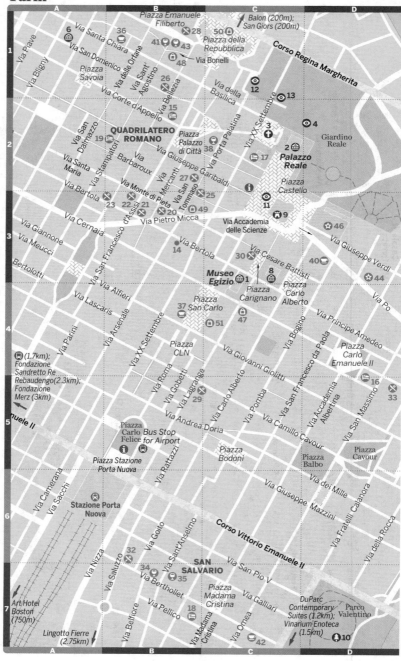

Piazza Emanuele Filiberto

Balon (200m); San Giors (200m)

Corso Regina Margherita

Via Plave

Via Bligny

Via Santa Chiara

Via San Domenico

Piazza Savoia

Via Corte d'Appello

Via delle Orfane

Via Sant' Agostino

Via Bellezia

Piazza della Repubblica

Via Bonelli

Via della Basilica

QUADRILATERO ROMANO

Via San Dalmazzo

Via Santa Maria

Via Bertola

Via Stampatori

Via Barbaroux

Piazza Palazzo di Città

Via Giuseppe Garibaldi

Via Porta Palatina

Via XX Settembre

Palazzo Reale

Giardino Reale

Piazza Castello

Via Monte di Pietà

Via Mercanti

Via San Tommaso

Via Cernaia

Via Giannone

Via Meucci

Via San Francesco d'Assisi

Via Pietro Micca

Via Accademia delle Scienze

Via Giuseppe Verdi

Bertolotti

Via Bertola

Via Cesare Battisti

Via Po

Via Alfieri

Museo Egizio

Piazza Carignano

Piazza Carlo Alberto

Via Lascaris

Via Arsenale

Via XX Settembre

Piazza San Carlo

Via Principe Amedeo

(1.7km); Fondazione Sandretto Re Rebaudengo(2.3km); Fondazione Merz (3km)

Piazza CLN

Via Roma

Via Gobetti

Via Lagrange

Via Carlo Alberto

Via Giovanni Giolitti

Via Bogino

Piazza Carlo Emanuele II

Via Parini

Via Andrea Doria

Via Francesco da Paola

Via Accademia Albertina

Via San Massimo

nuele II

Piazza Carlo Felice

Bus Stop for Airport

Piazza Stazione Porta Nuova

Via Camerana

Via Sacchi

Via Rattazzi

Via Pomba

Via Camillo Cavour

Piazza Bodoni

Piazza Balbo

Piazza Cavour

Stazione Porta Nuova

Via Nizza

Via Salluzzo

Via Goito

Via Sant'Anselmo

Corso Vittorio Emanuele II

Via San Pio V

Via Giuseppe Mazzini

Via dei Mille

Via Fratelli Calandra

Via della Rocca

Art Hotel Boston (750m)

Lingotto Fierre (2.75km)

Via Belfiore

Via Berthollet

Via Pellico

SAN SALVARIO

Piazza Madama Cristina

Via Madama Cristina

Via Galliari

Via Ornea

DuParc Contemporary Suites (1.2km); Vinarium Enoteca (1.5km)

Parco Valentino

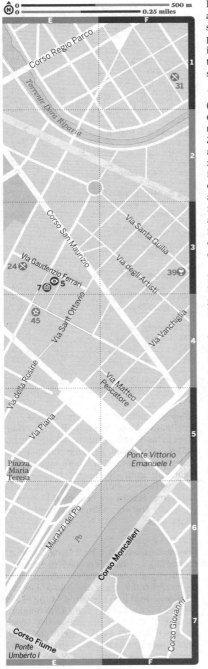

Holy Shroud. Despite the shroud's debated authenticity, its story unfolds like a gripping suspense mystery, with countless plots, subplots and revelations. Note the shroud itself is not on display here; it's kept in the Cattedrale di San Giovanni Battista (p219) and shown occasionally by decree of the Pope.

★**Museo Egizio** MUSEUM
(Egyptian Museum; ☎011 440 69 03; www.museoegizio.it; Via Accademia delle Scienze 6; adult/reduced €15/11; ⊙9am-6.30pm Tue-Sun, 9am-2pm Mon) Opened in 1824 and housed in the austere Palazzo dell'Accademia delle Scienze, this Turin institution houses the most important collection of Egyptian treasures outside Cairo. Among its many highlights are a statue of Ramses II (one of the world's most important pieces of Egyptian art) and a vast papyrus collection. There are also 500 funerary and domestic items from the tomb of royal architect Kha and his wife Merit, dating to 1400 BC and found in 1906.

Both anthropomorphic coffins are incredibly moving, but Merit's image, rendered in *cartonnage* (layers of plaster and linen), gold leaf and glass inlays, is one of the most hauntingly beautiful ever displayed.

A major renovation was completed in recent years and, although the old museum's rambling rooms had their dusty charm, the new minimalist spaces almost double the amount of the collection available for public display. Modern museological techniques – splicing in documentary photographs and films about the early 20th-century digs, dramatic lighting and a well-articulated chronological narrative – make for an absorbing experience. Allow ample time: you can easily spend half a day here.

Museo Nazionale del Risorgimento Italiano MUSEUM
(☎011 562 11 47; www.museorisorgimentotorino.it; Via Accademia delle Scienze 5; adult/reduced €10/8; ⊙10am-6pm Tue-Sun) After extensive renovations, this significant museum reopened in 2011 to coincide with the centenary of the Risorgimento (reunification period). An astounding 30-room trajectory illustrates the creation of the modern Italian state in the very building (the baroque Palazzo Carignano) where many of the key events happened. Not only was this the birthplace of Carlo Alberto and Vittorio Emanuele II, but it was also the seat of united Italy's first parliament from 1861 to 1864.

Turin

Mole Antonelliana LANDMARK
(www.gtt.to.it/cms/turismo/ascensore-mole; Via Montebello 20; lift adult/reduced €8/6, incl Museo €15/12; ☉lift 9am-8pm Sun, Mon & Wed-Fri, to 11pm Sat) The symbol of Turin, this 167m tower with its distinctive aluminium spire appears on the Italian two-cent coin. It was originally intended as a synagogue when construction began in 1862, but was never used as a place of worship, and nowadays houses the **Museo Nazionale del Cinema** (☎011 813 85 63; www.museocinema.it; adult/reduced €11/9, incl lift €15/12; ☉9am-8pm Sun, Mon & Wed-Fri, to 11pm Sat). For dazzling 360-degree views, take the **Panoramic Lift** up to the 85m-high outdoor viewing deck.

★**Museo Casa Mollino** ARCHITECTURE
(☎011 812 98 68; cm@carlomollino.org; Via Napione 2; 1-2hr tour €30; ☉by appointment) Architect-designer-artist Carlo Mollino is perhaps Turin's most intriguing son and a quintessentially 20th-century Torinese. The little-known Museo Casa Mollino is a testament to his deliriously lush aesthetic and his skill as a craftsman, as well as his manifold obsessions. It was also where many of his theatrical, erotically charged Polaroid portraits were shot. Father and son Fulvio and Napoleone Ferrari are dedicated keepers of his legacy and compelling interpreters and storytellers.

Museo Lavazza MUSEUM
(www.museo.lavazza.com; Via Bologna 32a; adult/reduced €10/8; ☉10am-6pm Wed-Sun) Set in the architecturally striking new headquarters of the famed coffee chain, the Museo Lavazza takes you deep into the world of the heady caffeine-filled brew. The hypermodern three-floor museum has interactive touch screens that show every stage of the cycle, from shade grown plants to roasteries and then on to cafes around the globe. You'll also

learn about the Lavazza family, and its role in shaping Italy's love for espresso from a tiny grocery in the 19th century.

Galleria Civica d'Arte
Moderna e Contemporanea
GALLERY

(GAM; ☑ 011 442 95 18; www.gamtorino.it; Via Magenta 31; adult/reduced €10/8; ⊙ 10am-6pm Tue-Sun) GAM was one of Italy's first modern-art museums and has an astounding 45,000 works in its vaults dedicated to 19th- and 20th-century European artists, including de Chirico, Otto Dix and Klee. It's a great place to expand your knowledge of Italy's post-war period: Paolini, Boetti, Anselmo, Penone and Pistoletto are all well represented.

Fondazione Sandretto
re Rebaudengo
GALLERY

(FSRR; ☑ 011 379 76 00; www.fsrr.org; Via Modane 16; adult/reduced €7/5, Thu free; ⊙ 8-11pm Thu, noon-7pm Fri-Sun) This classic white-cube contemporary gallery space was created with Italian super curator Francesco Bonami and runs a great exhibition program showcasing outstandingly talented artists. Provocative thematic shows grapple with themes like globalisation, refugees, labour rights and other contemporary topics in surprising ways.

Fondazione Merz
GALLERY

(☑ 011 1971 9437; http://fondazionemerz.org; Via Limone 24; adult/reduced €6/3.50; ⊙ 11am-7pm Tue-Sun) The Arte Povera powerhouse, Mario Merz, was born in Milan but spent most of his creative life in Turin. This foundation space, an evocative reworking of the former Lancia heating plant, holds regular exhibitions of his work and an astute program of Italian contemporary art. It also hosts concerts, poetry slams, author readings and other cultural fare (the majority of which are admission-free).

Parco Valentino
PARK

(www.parcovalentino.com) Opened in 1856, this 550,000-sq-metre French-style park kisses the banks of the Po and is filled with joggers, promenaders and lovers night and day. Walking southwest along the river brings you to Castello del Valentino (open for events only), a gorgeous mock château built in the 17th century. The park is also home to the Borgo Medievale.

Borgo Medievale
OLD TOWN

(www.borgomedievaletorino.it; Viale Virgilio 107; €5; ⊙ 9am-7pm Tue-Sun Nov-Mar, to 8pm Tue-Sun Apr-Oct; ⊕) Perched over a scenic stretch of the Po River, the Borgo Medievale is a small re-created 15th-century village that was actually built for the 1884 Turin Expo. Enter via the drawbridge, then wander amid gardens, arcades, artisan shops and trickling fountains beneath imposing crenellated castle walls. It's a hit with families.

⊙ Lingotto

Lingotto
LANDMARK

(Via Nizza 294; Ⓜ Lingotto) Turin's former Fiat factory, one of Italy's most praised examples of early-20th-century industrial architecture, is 5km south of the city centre. It was redesigned by architect Renzo Piano in the 1980s to house an exhibition centre, a university campus and hotels. The starkly beautiful space today houses the 8 Gallery shopping mall, the Pinacoteca Giovanni e Marella Agnelli and a former rooftop car test track.

Pinacoteca Giovanni
e Marella Agnelli
GALLERY

(Lingotto; www.pinacoteca-agnelli.it; Via Nizza 230; adult/reduced €10/8; ⊙ 10am-7pm Tue-Sun; Ⓜ Lingotto) On the rooftop of the Lingotto building, 3km south of the centre, this intimate gallery houses the personal collection of late Fiat head Gianni Agnelli, with masterpieces by Renoir, Manet, Modigliani, Matisse and Picasso, among others. Apart from the paintings, your ticket grants you access to the Lingotto's famous rooftop test track.

It also has an attached bookshop, full of wonderful art and design titles. When there's no temporary exhibition showing, the gallery admission is €8.

⊙ Out of Town

Museo Ettore Fico
GALLERY

(MEF; ☑ 011 85 30 65; www.museofico.it; Via Francesco Cigna 114; adult/reduced €10/5; ⊙ 11am-7pm Wed-Sun) This sleek, contemporary gallery joins Turin's already stellar collection of pivotal art foundations. Set in an old factory in a hipster, postindustrial neighbourhood north of the Dora River, MEF has three major shows per year, with high-profile monographic exhibitions as well as installation work by contemporary artists, along with design, fashion or film-based shows. Work by Ettore Fico, the late Torinese painter to whom the museum is dedicated, also features.

WORTH A TRIP

GET UP HIGH: BASILICA DI SUPERGA

Vittorio Amedeo II's 1706 promise, to build a basilica to honour the Virgin Mary if Turin was saved from besieging French and Spanish armies, resulted in this wedding-cake edifice (www.basilicadisuperga.com; Strada della Basilica di Superga 75; adult/reduced €5/4; ⊙10am-1.30pm & 2.30-7pm Mar-Oct, to 6pm Nov-Feb, closed Wed year-round), built on a hill across the Po river. Architect Filippo Juvarra's Basilica di Superga became the final resting place of the Savoy family, whose lavish tombs make for interesting viewing, as does the dome. In 1949 the basilica gained less welcome renown when a plane carrying the entire Turin football team crashed into the church in thick fog, killing all on board. Their tomb rests at the rear of the church.

Take tram 15 from Piazza Vittorio Veneto to the Sassi–Superga stop on Corso Casale, then walk 20m to Stazione Sassi, from where an original 1934 tram rattles the 3.1km up the hillside in 18 minutes, every day except Wednesday.

Catch bus 46 from Piazza XVIII Dicembre. A taxi from the centre will cost you around €8.

★ **Reggia di Venaria Reale**　　PALACE
(☑ 011 499 23 33; www.lavenaria.it; Piazza della Repubblica; admission incl exhibitions €25, Reggia & gardens €16, gardens only €5; ⊙9am-5pm Tue-Fri, to 6.30pm Sat & Sun) OK, it may not enjoy the weighty publicity of its French counterpart, but this is one of the largest royal residences in the world, rescued from ruin by a €235 million 10-year-long restoration project. Humongous, ostentatious, regal, yet strangely underpublicised, this Unesco-listed baroque palace some 14km northwest of Turin was built as a glorified hunting lodge in 1675 by the frivolous Duke of Savoy, Carlo Emanuele II.

Among the jewels bequeathed by its erstwhile royal rulers are a vast garden complex, a glittering stag fountain (with water shows), a conspicuous consumption style Grand Gallery, plus the attached Capella di Sant'Uberto and Juvarra stables. The last three were all designed by the great Sicilian architect Filippo Juvarra in the 1720s.

To enjoy the permanent exhibition alone, you'll need to walk 2km through the aptly named Theatre of History and Magnificence, a museum journey that relates the 1000-year history of the Savoy clan set in their former royal residential quarters, with a Brian Eno soundtrack and film installations care of Peter Greenaway.

On top of this are numerous temporary exhibitions, regular live concerts, an on-site cafe and restaurant, and an adjacent *borgo* (medieval town), now engulfed by Turin's suburbs, that's full of cosy places to eat and

drink. Take note of the scale and leave the best part of a day to visit. You can reach the palace complex via the Venaria Express shuttle, one of the tourist office's summer sightseeing buses or bus 11 or 72 from Porta Nuova station.

★ **Castello di Rivoli**　　GALLERY
(Museo d'Arte Contemporanea; ☑ 011 956 52 22; www.castellodirivoli.org; Piazza Mafalda di Savoia; adult/reduced €8.50/6.50, Villa Cerruti incl shuttle & tour adult/reduced €26.50/19.50; ⊙10am-5pm Tue-Fri, to 7pm Sat & Sun) Some 21km west of Turin, the Castello di Rivoli Museum of Contemporary Art is a giant of modern art in Piedmont. Its ambition and reach, not to mention healthy regional funding, has been the envy of Milan, Venice and Rome's art worlds. The permanent collection has a sizeable number of Arte Povera works, which are beautifully displayed in the historical setting, along with pieces from the Transavanguardia, Minimal, Body and Land Art movements.

Juventus Museum　　MUSEUM
(www.juventus.com; Strada Comunale di Altessano 131; museum €15, incl stadium visit €22; ⊙10.30am-7pm Mon & Wed-Fri, to 7.30pm Sat & Sun) The state-of-the-art Juventus Stadium has a museum that will blind you with its silverware (32 Serie A titles – and the rest!) and proudly recounts how it was all amassed. On match days your museum visit can include viewing the team's match prep behind the scenes (€30).

The museum lies about 8km northwest of the centre. Get there via bus No 72, which stops near the corner of Via XX Settembre and Via Bertola.

✦ Festivals & Events

Salone del Gusto & Terre Madre
FOOD & DRINK

(www.salonedelgusto.com; ⊙ late Sep) Held each even-numbered year in venues across Turin, Slow Food's global symposium features producers, chefs, activists, restaurateurs, farmers, scholars, environmentalists, epicureans and food lovers from around the world... not to mention the world's best finger food. Avoid queues by purchasing day passes online for around €11, or get a five-day pass for €35.

Torino Film Festival
FILM

(www.torinofilmfest.org; ⊙ Nov) Well-respected international festival with screenings held at several cinemas during the last weeks of November. One of the main venues is the **Cinema Massimo** (☑011 813 85 74; www.cinemamassimotorino.it; Via Verdi 18) around the corner from the Mole Antonelliana.

Cioccolatò
FOOD & DRINK

(www.cioccola-to.eu; ⊙ Nov) Turin celebrates chocolate and its status as a world chocolate capital for 10 days in November. Scores of artisan producers showcase their delicacies along Via Roma and on Piazza San Carlo. The event also features tastings, discussions, cooking demonstrations and hands-on activities for kids.

🛏 Sleeping

★ Tomato Backpackers Hotel
HOSTEL €

(☑011 020 94 00; www.tomato.to.it; Via Pellico 11; dm/s/d/tr €24/43/72/84; 🛜) 🗗 This eco-friendly hostel in the nightlife-loving San Salvario area is one of the few central places that caters to budget travellers. And it does so with style and soul, offering pristine dorms, smart private rooms, a kitchen, bar area, and a vine-trimmed terrace. There's a relaxed, inclusive vibe and a long list of extras including bike hire, laundry facilities and luggage storage.

★ Via Stampatori
B&B €

(☑339 2581330; www.viastampatori.com; Via Stampatori 4; d €110; ❋🛜) This utterly lovely B&B occupies the top floor of a frescoed Renaissance building, one of Turin's oldest. Its bright, stylish and uniquely furnished rooms overlook either a sunny terrace or a leafy inner courtyard. The owner's personal collection of 20th-century design is used throughout, including in the two serene common areas. It's central but blissfully quiet.

Hotel Dogana Vecchia
HOTEL €

(☑011 436 67 52; www.hoteldoganavecchia.com; Via Corte d'Appello 4; s/d/tr €80/95/125; 🅿❋🛜) Mozart, Verdi and Napoleon are among those who have stayed at this historic three-star inn. Renovations have fortunately preserved much of its old-world charm, and while it's unrepentantly dowdy, its location in the Quadrilatero Romano is hard to beat.

San Giors
BOUTIQUE HOTEL €

(☑011 521 63 57; www.sangiors.it; Via Borgo Dora 3; s €75-130, d €86-150; ❋🛜) If you're not perturbed by a still-gentrifying neighbourhood, this welcoming family-run place offers individual artist-decorated rooms that are basic, but often include beautiful vintage design pieces and a witty, bohemian eye. The restaurant comes highly recommended, and come Saturday, you're in the thick of the Balon (p234), one of Italy's best flea markets.

★ DuParc Contemporary Suites
DESIGN HOTEL €€

(☑011 012 00 00; www.duparcsuites.com; Corso Massimo d'Azeglio 21; r €95-175; 🅿❋🛜) A business-friendly location doesn't mean this isn't a great choice for all travellers. Staff are young, clued-up and friendly, and the building's iconic modern lines are matched with a fantastic contemporary art collection and comfortable furnishings along with stunning Italian lighting. Best of all, even the cheapest rooms here are sumptuously large (50 sq m), with king beds, huge baths, and floor-to-ceiling windows.

There's a gym and basement spa area with saunas and a large whirlpool. Note that the location puts you in walking distance of the bars and restaurants of San Salvario and the elegant green paths of the riverside Parco Valentino (p225).

Art Hotel Boston
BOUTIQUE HOTEL €€

(☑011 036 14 00; www.hotelbostontorino.it; Via Massena 70; s €90-120, d €120-160, ste €180-250; ❋🛜) The Boston's austere classical facade gives no inkling of the interiors that await inside. Common areas are filled with original works by Warhol, Lichtenstein and Aldo Mondino, while individually styled suites and deluxe rooms are themed on subjects as diverse as Lavazza coffee, Ayrton Senna and Pablo Picasso.

Palazzo Chiablese
B&B €€

(☑333 886 26 70; www.bbpalazzochiablese.com; Vicolo San Lorenzo 1; s/d €130/140; 🅿🛜) Marta and Riccardo's three B&B rooms are the

Around Turin

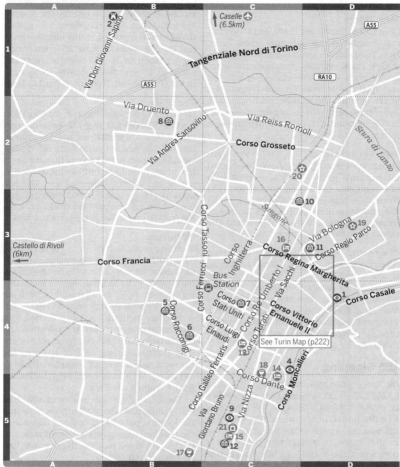

epitome of pared back Torinese elegance, and mix warm midcentury Italian design with contemporary paintings, beautiful linen, design-centric bathrooms and large white-draped windows. Breakfast is taken in the apartment's stylish kitchen, adding to the feeling you're staying with friends, rather than at a hotel.

NH Lingotto Congress BUSINESS HOTEL €€
(☑ 011 664 20 00; www.nh-hotels.com; Via Nizza 262; d €90-200; P ✳ @ 🛜) The 20th-century industrial bones mean rooms are huge and bright, while the fit-out is high-2000s designer slick with an industrial edge. This corporate favourite has comprehensive facilities and free access to a quality gym next door. The culinary wonder of Eataly is also nearby.

**NH Collection Torino
Piazza Carlina** DESIGN HOTEL €€€
(☑ 011 860 16 11; www.nh-hotels.com; Piazza Carlo Emanuele II; d €180-250; P ✳ 🛜) Overlooking one of Turin's most beautiful squares, this sprawling property occupies a 17th-century building, once the Albergo di Virtù, a Savoy charitable institution (and home to the famous political theorist Antonio Gramsci). The decor is cutting edge, highly atmos-

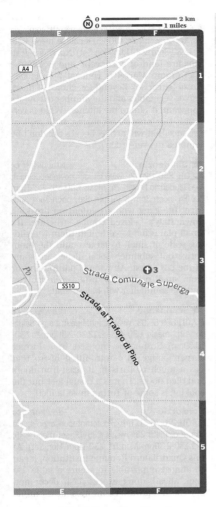

TURIN, PIEDMONT & CINQUE TERRE TURIN

za, tapas or cheap eats, head to San Salvario in the city's south.

Sciamadda　　　　　　　　LIGURIAN €
(📞011 020 51 84; Via Maria Vittoria 32; snacks €5-7; ⊙11.30am-3pm & 6.30-11pm Tue-Sun) This much-loved local snack spot serves up Ligurian delicacies, including fried anchovies and calamari, *pasqualina* (an artichoke tort), *trofie al pesto* (a type of pesto pasta) and fresh-from-the-oven focaccia. It's a tiny space, so order your mini feast *da portare via* (takeaway) or hunker down at one of the stools where you can watch the cooks in action.

Gofri Piemontéisa　　　　　FAST FOOD €
(www.gofriemiassepiemontesi.it; Via San Tommaso 7; gofri around €5; ⊙11.30am-7.30pm Tue-Sat, to 4pm Sun) *Gofri*, thin waffles snap cooked

pheric and deeply luxurious. There's a great downstairs bar and guests have access to rooftop terraces and a gym.

Breakfast is served in a stately courtyard among the hotel's own lemon trees.

✖ Eating

Turin is blessed with a hinterland fabulously rich in produce and tradition. Both can be found in its deliciously ancient grand cafes and dining rooms, as well as in its booming new bar and restaurant scene.

The Quadrilatero Romano has a concentrated clutch of small casual places; for piz-in hot irons, are a traditional dish from the mountainous regions of northern Piedmont and have been reinvented here by a local chef as tasty fast food. Try the house *gofre* with ham, *toma* (alpine cheese) and artichokes or one of the equally delicious *mi-asse*, a corn-based variation, also adapted from ancient recipes.

Perino Vesco
BAKERY €

(☑ 011 068 60 56; www.perinovesco.it; Via Cavour 10; snacks from €5; ☺ 7.30am-7.30pm Mon-Sat) 🏃 Cult Slow Food baker Andrea Perino turns out dense, fragrant *torta langarola* (hazelnut cake), naturally yeasted *panettone* (sweet bread) and focaccia that draws sighs from homesick Ligurians. Join the queues for takeaway pizza and focaccia slices (grab a ticket upon entering) or head out the back and nab a seat for sandwiches, pizza slices, savoury tarts and coffee.

Margutte Polenta da Strada
STREET FOOD €

(☑ 393 886 21 48; Via San Tommaso 6; polenta €5-7; ☺ noon-3pm & 5.30-8.30pm Mon-Sat, noon-8.30pm Sun) For a satisfying midday snack, make your way to this tiny shop with just a handful of seats a few blocks from Piazza Castelo. Creamy rich polenta is topped by various cheeses (gorgonzola, parmigiano, taleggio), mushrooms, pesto and other delicacies. There are also dessert options (like pear and ginger) and excellent-value wines by the glass.

Ruràl Pizza
PIZZA €

(☑ 011 235 91 79; www.ruralpizza.it; Via Mantova 27; pizza €18-24; ☺ 7.30-11.30pm) This happy, pretty pizzeria set in an old glassworks does Sicilian-style pizza using good-quality ingredients, along with rather fancy desserts.

È Cucina
MODERN ITALIAN €

(☑ 011 562 90 38; www.cesaremarretti.com; Via Bertola 27a; meals €10-25, 4-course menu €30; ☺ 12.30-3pm & 8-11pm Mon-Sat) Northern Italians are fond of a 'concept' and Bolognese chef Cesare Marretti's concept here is *sorpresa* (surprise). Beyond the choice of meat, fish or vegetables and the number of courses you want, it's up to the kitchen. What *is* certain is the innovative cooking and excellent produce that will arrive. Local's tip: don't be tempted to over-order.

★ Gaudenzio
PIEDMONTESE €€

(☑ 011 860 02 42; www.gaudenziovinoecucina.it; Via Gaudenzio Ferrari 2h; meals €30-55; ☺ 7-11pm Tue-Fri, noon-3pm & 7-11pm Sat, noon-3pm Sun) Meet the gang who are intent on breaking down Italy's beloved course structure. It's small plates here – although there is a sliding scale of small to large – and the innovative but sublimely local dishes are some of the city's best. All wine is natural and/or from small producers; in lieu of a list, you and the sommelier will have a chat.

★ Scannabue
PIEDMONTESE €€

(☑ 011 669 66 93; www.scannabue.it; Largo Saluzzo 25h; meals €30-42; ☺ 12.30-2.30pm & 7.30-10.30pm) Scannabue, housed in a former corner garage, is a retro-fitted bistro that has a touch of Paris in its cast-iron doors and tiled floors. There's a casual feel, but the cooking is some of Turin's most lauded.

Consorzio
PIEDMONTESE €€

(☑ 011 276 76 61; http://ristoranteconsorzio.it; Via Monte di Pietà 23; meals €35-42, set menu €35; ☺ 12.30-2.30pm Mon-Fri, 7.30-11pm Mon-Sat) At this Quadrilatero Romano institution, it can be almost impossible to secure a table. Do book ahead, don't expect flash decor and pay the not-always-chummy staff no mind.

DON'T MISS

APERICENA

Who needs *cena* (dinner) when you've got bar snacks the size of...well...dinners? Turin's answer to the aperitif is the *apericena*, where bar-side buffets resemble full-blown meals. You'll find fabulous buffet spreads all across town, particularly in student-loving San Salvario, with its array of bohemian bars with ample food on the side. One of the best is **Beerba** (Via Sant'Anselmo 13b; ☺ 7pm-1am), which spreads creative salads, cheese-topped grilled veggies, pastas, focaccia, artichoke pies and risotto. The Quadrilatero quarter is another buffet wonderland – Pastis (p232) on Piazza Filiberto do a full carb-heavy spread, or keep it classy with just cheese at **I Tre Galli** (☑ 011 521 60 27; www.3galli.com; Via Sant'Agostino 25; ☺ 12.30pm-2.30pm & 6.30pm-midnight Mon-Wed, to 2am Thu-Sat). Expect to pay between €7 and €14 for an *apericena*-hour drink.

Everyone is here for the pristinely sourced, spot-on Piedmontese cooking that's so traditional it's innovative.

Banco vini e alimenti
PIEDMONTESE €€

(☑011 764 02 39; www.bancovinialimenti.it; Via dei Mercanti 13f; meals €30-40; ☺12.30pm-12.30am Tue-Sat, from 6pm Mon) A hybrid restaurant-bar-deli, this smartly designed, low-key place does clever small-dish dining for lunch and dinner. While it might vibe casual wine bar, with young staff in T-shirts, don't underestimate the food: this is serious Piedmontese cooking. Open all day, you can also grab a single-origin pour-over here after lunch, or a herbal house *spritz* late afternoon.

EDIT
ITALIAN €€

(☑011 1932 9700; www.edit-to.com; Piazza Teresa Noce 15; meals €25-50; ☺bakery 8.30am-midnight, pub noon-midnight, restaurant 7.30-10.30pm Tue-Sat; 🐾🍷) Breathing new life into a former industrial district, EDIT (which stands for Eat Drink Innovate Together) is set in a capacious two-storey building that houses a bakery, pub, cocktail bar and high-end restaurant. The artfully configured space (once an electric cable factory) aims to showcase both classic comfort food and culinary pyrotechnics, with open kitchens, decent in-house microbrews and excellent regional products.

Reserve ahead for the restaurant. The number 4 trolley, which runs up Via Milano, stops a few blocks away on Corso Novara.

L'Acino
PIEDMONTESE €€

(☑011 521 70 77; Via San Domenico 2a; meals €28-35; ☺7.30-11pm Mon-Sat) Half a dozen tables and a legion of enamoured followers mean this inviting restaurant is hard to get into. Book ahead or arrive at the stroke of 7.30pm for anchovies, baked peppers with *bagna caòda* sauce and stewed beef cooked in Roero wine, or classic Piedmontese pasta staples such as *plin* (ravioli).

Their *bonèt* (chocolate pudding with Amaretti and rum) is considered one of the city's best.

Ristorante Del Cambio
GASTRONOMY €€€

(☑011 54 66 90; www.delcambio.it; Piazza Carignano 2; set menus €110-135, lunch 2-/3-course €45/65; ☺7.30-10.30pm Tue, 12.30-2.30pm & 7.30-10.30pm Wed-Sat, 12.30-2.30pm Sun) Crimson velvet, glittering chandeliers, baroque mirrors and a timeless air greet you at this grande dame of the Turin dining scene, reg-

ularly patronised by Count Cavour in his day. It first opened its doors in 1757, and classic Piedmont cuisine still dominates the menu, although you'll eat in the company of some great contemporary art now, too. Bookings and smart dress are advised.

🍷 Drinking & Nightlife

Nightlife – including the nightly *aperitivo* crawl – concentrates in the riverside area around Piazza Vittoria Veneto, the Quadrilatero Romano district and, with a younger crowd, the southern neighbourhood of San Salvarino. The Po-side enclaves of Vanchiglia and Dora are the city's new cool zones – both have some excellent wine bars and great live venues and club nights.

Orso - Laboratorio Caffè
CAFE

(Via Berthollet 30; ☺8am-6pm) Pouring some of the best espresso in town, Orso is a cosy coffee-lover's den with reclaimed wood furnishings, coffee gadgetry galore (Chemex, Syphon, cold brew, Napoletana) and a big picture window for watching the tousle-haired residents of San Salvario stroll by. The high-quality roasts made of single-origin beans from Tanzania, Rwanda, Guatemala and India make for excellent pour-overs.

Vinarium Enoteca
WINE BAR

(☑011 650 52 08; www.facebook.com/Vinarium Enoteca; Via Madama Cristina 119; ☺3-10.30pm Mon, from 10am Tue-Sat) Hidden in the southern

LOCAL KNOWLEDGE

GRAND CAFES

While Turin's contemporary food and wine scene continues to boom, its classic cafes – around for ions – scarcely change. Our favourite trio:

Caffè Al Bicerin (www.bicerin.it; Piazza della Consolata 5; ☺8.30am-7.30pm Thu-Tue, closed Aug) Founded in 1763, with an exquisitely simple boiserie interior dating to the early 1800s, this one-room cafe takes its name from its signature drink, a potent combination of chocolate, coffee and cream. Fuelling the likes of Dumas, Puccini, Nietzsche and Calvino, along with Savoy royalty and Turin's workers, the price didn't rise for a century to ensure no one missed out.

Caffè Torino (www.caffe-torino.it; Piazza San Carlo 204; ☺8am-midnight) This chandelier-lit showpiece opened in 1903. A brass plaque of the city's emblem, a bull (Torino in Italian means 'little bull'), is embedded in the pavement out front; rub your shoe across it for good luck (you won't have to queue like in Milan).

Fiorio (www.caffefiorio.it; Via Po 8; ☺8am-midnight Mon-Thu, to 1am Fri & Sat, 8am-9pm Sun) Garner literary inspiration in Mark Twain's old window seat as you contemplate the gilded interior of a cafe where 19th-century students once plotted revolutions and the Count of Cavour deftly played whist. The bittersweet hot chocolate remains inspirational.

reaches of San Salvario, Vinarium has a laid-back, free-spirited ethos, with beautifully balanced wines by the glass (from €2.50 to €7) to be enjoyed at long communal tables among the bottle-lined shelves that stretch high to the ceiling. Staff have excellent suggestions if you're looking for a unique bottle from the 1300 labels (priced from €7 to upwards of €500).

Farmacia Del Cambio   BAR
(☏011 1921 1250; www.delcambio.it/farmacia; Piazza Carignano 2; ☺9am-9.30pm) Cambio Corner – home to one of Turin's best restaurants, not to mention bars – also has this 'informal' but glamorous all-day space, set within an old pharmacy dating to 1833. Pop in for morning coffee or to pick up deli goods, but do come back for *aperitivo*, either beneath the dark shelves, by the theatrically open kitchen or out on the piazza.

Bar Cavour   COCKTAIL BAR
(☏011 1921 1270; http://delcambio.it; Piazza Carignano 2; ☺7pm-1.30am Tue-Sat, to midnight Sun) Named for its most famous barfly, the ubiquitous Count Cavour, this beautiful historical room combines a magical, mirrored setting with a great collection of contemporary art and design savvy. Upstairs from Del Cambio (p231), a Michelin-starred restaurant, the *aperitivo* here doesn't come cheap (around €15) but features artfully prepared cocktails served with quality snacks (including a mini tin of polenta). Reserve ahead.

Enoteca Botz   WINE BAR
(☏340 215 04 97; www.facebook.com/enoteca botz; Via Santa Giulia 48; ☺6pm-midnight Sun-Thu, to 3am Fri & Sat) Come to this Vanchiglia triangle stalwart for good wine served by serious wine pros at reasonable prices. Plus you get to hang out with some of the neighbourhood's cool kids at the same time. A good choice when you're too old (or tired) for clubs, but too young (or excited) to go home.

Caffè-Vini Emilio Ranzini   WINE BAR
(☏011 765 04 77; Via Porta Palatina 9g; ☺9:30am-3pm & 5.40-8.30pm Mon-Fri, 10:30am-3pm Sat) Location scouts looking for a neighbourhood bar from Turin's midcentury glory days would jump on this little place. A crew of local shopkeepers, creatives and students frequently prop up its dark wooden bar and loll about the summer courtyard with wines by the glass, delicious sandwiches and small plates.

Pastis   WINE BAR
(Piazza Emanuele Filiberto 9; ☺9am-3pm Mon, 9am-3pm & 6pm-2am Tue-Sun) A cute take on Paris in the '60s, this day-night bar has a loyal local following. Young Torinese come for big weekend brunches, a nightly *aperitivo* spread or a late-night *amaro* or three.

Hiroshima Mon Amour   CLUB
(www.hiroshimamonamour.org; Via Bossoli 83; admission free-€20; ☺hours vary) This legendary dance club features everything from folk

and punk to tango and techno. Check the website for specific opening hours and details on the weekend night bus.

Astoria   CLUB
(☎ 345 448 31 56; www.astoria-studios.com; Via Berthollet 13; ⊙ 6pm-2am Thu-Sat) A street-side cocktail bar hides a basement venue that showcases some excellent international and local indie talent as well as club nights. Thursday night Xänäx Party draws out the beauty crowd, who come for electropop grooves on the compact but heavily fired-up dance floor.

☆ Entertainment

Most live-music venues are out of the centre either south in Lingotto and San Salvarino or to the north in Vanchiglia and Dora.

Teatro Regio Torino   THEATRE
(☎ 011 881 52 41; www.teatroregio.torino.it; Piazza Castello 215; ⊙ ticket office 10.30am-6pm Tue-Fri, to 4pm Sat & 1hr before performances) Sold-out performances can sometimes be watched free on live TV in the adjoining Teatro Piccolo Regio, where Puccini premiered *La Bohème* in 1896, and it's always worth popping into the box office to see what might not be sold out. Sadly, some of Carlo Mollino's visionary midcentury fit-out did not survive subsequent renovations, but the seductive red, rhythmic foyer is still a treat.

Bunker   LIVE MUSIC
(www.variantebunker.com; Via Niccolò Paganini 0/200; ⊙ hours vary) This multidisciplinary collective organises one of winter's best electronic and techno club nights, as well as live concerts. Also worth checking out for their street-art exhibitions and various other hard-hitting cultural activities. Check the website for upcoming events.

Blah Blah   LIVE MUSIC
(☎ 392 7045240; www.blahblahtorino.com; Via Po 21; ⊙ 11am-2am Mon-Thu, to 3am Fri & Sat, 9am-2am Sun) An intriguing, and very Torinese, venue that will feed you breakfast or lunch, surprise you with an alternative cinema screening pre-*aperitivo*, have an electro punk or metal band serenade you after dinner and then keep you dancing till the early hours.

Spazio 211   LIVE MUSIC
(☎ 011 1970 5919; www.spazio211.com; Via Cigna 21) This long-established live-music venue, a 10-minute taxi ride north of the city centre,

is the city's main venue for international indie acts, interesting theme nights, as well as big Italian names like Guida. Book tickets on the website.

🛍 Shopping

★ **Eataly Torino Lingotto**   FOOD & DRINKS
(www.facebook.com/eatalytorino; Via Nizza 230; ⊙ 10am-10.30pm) 🥢 The global Slow Food phenomenon began here in Lingotto. Set in a vast converted factory, the Eataly mothership houses a staggering array of sustainable food and drink, along with beautiful affordable kitchenware and cookbooks. Specialist counters that correspond to their produce area – bread and pizza, cheese, pasta, seafood, Piedmontese beef – serve lunch from 12.30pm to 2.30pm. Food lovers' heaven!

Events range from vermouth-tasting parties with DJs to multicourse dinners built around a show-stopping ingredient, such as Parmigiano Reggiano. Check the Facebook page to see what's on. **Somewhere** (☎ 011 668 05 80; www.somewhere.it; Via Botero 15) operates foodie tours here.

★ **Laboratorio Zanzara**   ARTS & CRAFTS
(☎ 011 026 88 53; www.laboratoriozanzara.it; Via Bonelli 3a; ⊙ 9.30am-12.30pm & 2-4pm Mon-Fri, 10.30am-12.30pm & 3.30-7.30pm Sat) A delightfully eccentric collection of handmade objects, light fittings, posters, textiles, cards and calendars fills this bright shop, which is run as a nonprofit cooperative, employing people with intellectual disabilities. It's a noble enterprise, yes, but its wares are the model of Torinese cool. The co-op's director, Gianluca Cannizzo, is also one of the city's most celebrated creatives.

Latteria Bera   FOOD & DRINKS
(☎ 328 016 68 54; www.latteriabera.com; Via San Tommaso 13; ⊙ 9.30am-1.30pm & 3-7.30pm Mon & Tue, 9.30-1.30pm Wed, 9.30am-2pm & 3-7.30pm Thu-Sat) A neighbourhood icon since 1958, this tiny family-run shop and deli draws gourmands from near and far, who fawn over the delectable cheese counter (over 50 varieties!) plus antipasti, biscotti, olive oils, jams, candies and chocolates. The old-fashioned storefront (with artfully arranged displays) adds to the allure.

Guido Gobino   CHOCOLATE
(☎ 011 566 07 07; www.guidogobino.it; Via Lagrange 1; ⊙ 3-8pm Mon, 10am-8pm Tue-Sun) Guido Gobino's extreme attention to detail, flair and innovation have made him Turin's

DON'T MISS

MARKET DATES

Porta Palazzo (http://scopriporta palazzo.com; Piazza della Repubblica; ⊙ 7am-1pm Mon-Fri, to 7pm Sat) Europe's largest food market: frantic, fun and fabulously multicultural.

Balon (www.balon.it; Via Borgo Dora; ⊙ 7am-7pm Sat) Sprawling flea market around since 1857; watch for the **Grand Balon**, with more specialised antique and vintage dealers, on the second Sunday of the month, from 8am.

favourite modern chocolatier. Have a box of his tiny tile-like ganache chocolates made to order: highly evocative flavours include vermouth, Barolo, and lemon and clove. Or grab a bag of his classic *gianduiotto* (triangular chocolates made from *gianduja* – Turin's hazelnut paste).

Via Stampatori Perfumeria PERFUME
(☑ 339 258 13 30; www.viastampatoriparfum.com; Via Stampatori 4; ⊙ 3.30-7pm Tue & Wed, 10am-7.30pm Thu-Sat) Elena Boggio, who owns the Via Stampatori B&B (p227) upstairs, has a passion for natural perfumes. She grows many of the botanical elements that go into her range of scents (which can be both worn on the skin or used as room sprays) herself.

San Carlo dal 1973 FASHION & ACCESSORIES
(San Carlo 1; ☑ 011 511 41 11; www.sancarlodal1973.com; Piazza San Carlo 201; ⊙ 3-7pm Mon, 10.30am-7pm Tue-Sat) This Torinese fashion institution – the city's first 'concept store' – stocks a tightly curated selection of Italian and European high fashion, along with a selection of perfumes and candles. It's Turin at its most edgily elegant.

ℹ Information

Piazza Carlo Felice Tourist Office (☑ 011 53 51 81; www.turismotorino.org; Piazza Carlo Felice; ⊙ 10am-4pm) On the piazza in front of Stazione Porta Nuova.

Piazza Castello Tourist Office (☑ 011 53 51 81; www.turismotorino.org; Piazza Castello; ⊙ 9am-1pm & 2-6pm Mon-Sat, 10am-4pm Sun) Central and multilingual.

ℹ Getting There & Away

AIR

Turin's **Caselle** (☑ 011 567 63 61; www.aero portoditorino.it; Strada Aeroporto 12) airport,

16km northwest of the city centre in Caselle, has connections to European and national destinations. Budget airline Ryanair operates flights to London Stansted, as well as several other European and southern Italian destinations.

BUS

Most international, national and regional buses terminate at the **bus station** (www.autostaz ionetorino.it), 2km northwest from Stazione Porta Nuova along Corso Vittorio Emanuele II, including services to Milan's Malpensa airport.

TRAIN

Regular daily trains connect Turin's **Stazione Porta Nuova** (Piazza Carlo Felice) to the following destinations.

Destination	Fare (€)	Duration (hr)	Frequency
Milan	12.45	2	28
Aosta	9.45	2½	21
Venice	72	4½	17
Genoa	12.40	2	16
Rome	98	4½	11

Some trains also depart from **Stazione Porta Susa** (Corso Inghilterra) terminal and **Stazione di Torino Lingotto**.

ℹ Getting Around

TO/FROM THE AIRPORT

Sadem (☑ 800 801600; www.sadem.it; one way €7.50) runs buses to the airport from a **bus stop** (Piazza Carlo Felice 39) near Stazione Porta Nuova opposite Piazza Carlo Felice (one-way/return €7.50/12, 50 minutes), also stopping at Stazione Porta Susa (42 minutes). Buses depart every 30 minutes between 5.15am and 11.30pm during the week and 5.30am to 10.30pm on weekends. They run from 6.10am to 12.30am from the airport during the week and 6.10am and 11.45pm on weekends.

A taxi between the airport and the city centre will cost around €35 to €40.

BICYCLE

Turin's ever-expanding bike-sharing scheme, **[To]Bike** (www.tobike.it; 1-/2-day pass €8/13), is one of the largest in Italy. Passes for use of the bright-yellow *biciclette* can be bought at the Piazza Castello tourist office. For longer subscriptions, see the website.

With a smartphone, you can also access the free-floating **Mobike** network, which has hundreds of bikes across the city (€1.50 per 20 minutes).

PUBLIC TRANSPORT

The city boasts a dense network of buses, trams, a metro system and a cable car, all run by the **Gruppo Torinese Trasporti** (www.gtt. to.it/en). They have an **information office** (GTT; 📞 011 562 89 85; www.gtt.to.it; Porta Nuova, via Sacchi; ⏱ 7.15am-7pm Mon-Fri, 9am-5pm Sat & Sun) at Stazione Porta Nuova, if you're happy to take a ticket and wait in line for minimal information. Buses and trams run from 6am to midnight and tickets cost €1.70 (100 minutes) or €4 (one-day pass). Purchase tickets from metro stations or any *tabaccheria*. You can also download the free smartphone app **GTT Mobile**, where you can purchase credits (same price as paper tickets, though daily passes cost €3 rather than €4).

The Langhe & Monferrato

📞 0173

Gourmets get ready to indulge: the rolling hills, valleys and townships of southern Piedmont are northern Italy's most redolent pantry, weighed down with sweet hazelnuts, rare white truffles, arborio rice, delicate veal, precious cheeses and Nebbiolo grapes that metamorphose into the magical Barolo and Barbaresco wines.

Alba

📞 0173 / POP 31,500 / ELEV 172M

A once-powerful city-state whose centre sported more than 100 towers, Alba is considered the capital of the Langhe, and has big-city confidence and energy while retaining all the grace and warmth of a small rural town. Alba's considerable gastronomic reputation comes courtesy of its white truffles, dark chocolate and wine. Its annual autumn truffle fair draws huge crowds and the odd truffle-mad celebrity. The *vendemmia* (grape harvest) remains refreshingly local and low key, if ecstatic in its own way.

The vine-striped Langhe Hills radiate out from the town like a giant undulating vegetable garden, replete with grapes, hazelnut groves and wineries. Exploring Alba's fertile larder on foot or with two wheels is a delicious pleasure.

👁 Sights & Activities

Centro Culturale
San Giuseppe   CULTURAL CENTRE
(📞 0173 29 31 63; www.centroculturalesangiuseppe.it; Via Vernazza 6; ⏱ church 2.30-6.30pm Tue-Sun, exhibitions vary) A converted church

turned cultural centre, this is a lovely place to catch a choral or chamber music performance, or undertake a bracing hike up 134 steps to the 36m belltower (€1). In the basement, 2nd-century archaeological remains from the vanquished Roman Empire have been uncovered, and they also host temporary art exhibitions here.

Consorzio Turistico
Langhe Monferrato Roero   FOOD & DRINK
(📞 0173 36 25 62; www.booking-experience.tartufoevino.it; Piazza Risorgimento 2) This Alba-based consortium organises a wide variety of tours and courses unique to the Alba region. Truffle hunting can be arranged seasonally for white (September to December) or black (May to September) truffles for €70 per person. Year-round, you can tour a hazelnut farm for €30 or take part in a three-hour cooking course for €95.

There are various wine-themed excursions, including a guided tour and tasting in a Barolo winery (€15), as well as the ostensibly nonfoodie horse riding and donkey trekking. All tours can be booked up to a day in advance at Alba's tourist office (p237).

✨🍴 Festivals & Events

Fiera del Tartufo   FOOD & DRINK
(Truffle Festival; www.fieradeltartufo.org; ⏱ Oct-Nov) October's precious white-truffle crop is bought, sold and celebrated at this annual festival, held every weekend from mid-October to mid-November. Come and watch princely sums exchanged and sample autumn's bounty. Book accommodation, and restaurants, well ahead.

🛏 Sleeping

Le Camere di Gio   GUESTHOUSE €
(📞 0173 06 20 86; www.facebook.com/le.camere.di.Gio; Via Gioberti 2; s/d from €65/80; ❄ 📶) In the heart of the old quarter, you'll find these spacious, comfortably equipped rooms, each set with a king-sized bed, minifridge and a Lavazza espresso pod machine. Quilted bedspreads and the odd framed print add a homey touch. The best room has a balcony facing the photogenic Chiesa di Santa Maria Maddalena, but beware the 7am bells.

Hotel Langhe   HOTEL €
(📞 0173 36 69 33; www.hotellanghe.it; Strada Profonda 21; d €98-160; 🅿 ❄ ♨) Two kilometres from the city centre, Hotel Langhe sits on the edge of vineyards that push up against Alba's not entirely unpleasant suburban

sprawl. Staff are friendly and the pace relaxed, with a wine conservatory, a bright breakfast area, an inviting pool, and downstairs rooms with French windows that open onto a sunny forecourt.

Casa Dellatorre B&B €€

(☑ 0173 44 12 04; Via Elvio Pertinace 20; d €130-170; ❋ ⓐ) Three sisters run this central, upmarket B&B – which was once their family home – with love. Three classically decorated, antique-filled rooms share a flowery internal courtyard. Breakfast is served in the courtyard in summer, and in the sisters' pretty cafe in winter.

✗ Eating

Alba's fantastic cuisine comes in the Michelin-starred variety, but also represents the most sublime of quotidian pleasures in its word-of-mouth, no-menu *osteria*.

Osteria dei Sognatori OSTERIA €

(Via Macrino 8b; meals €20-30; ⓐ noon-2.30pm & 7.30-10pm Wed-Mon) Menu? What menu? You get whatever's in the pot at this dimly lit place. Munch on the theatrically large breadsticks while you wait for an array of antipasti to arrive, then try to keep up as the dishes mount up. Walls are bedecked with football memorabilia and B&W snaps of bearded wartime partisans look over rowdy tables of locals.

Beat the queues by going right at opening time to score a table. Reservations not accepted.

★ La Piola PIEDMONTESE €€

(☑ 0173 44 28 00; www.lapiola-alba.it; Piazza Risorgimento 4; meals €30-45; ⓐ 12.15-2.30pm & 7.15-10pm Mon-Sat, closed Mon in summer) Part of the Ceretto family's small empire, La Piola offers a faithful menu of traditional Piedmontese dishes, but at the same time manages to be stylish, modern and relaxed (let's put it down to *sprezzatura* – the Italian art of studied nonchalance).The kitchen is overseen by one of Italy's most respected chefs, Enrico Crippa, from gastronomic Piazza Duomo upstairs.

Expect wonderful produce – the vegetables and herbs all come from the Cerettos' own garden – and technique, along with a sense-grabbing flair. Engaged young staff and great contemporary artwork (including specially commissioned 'show' plates) make the experience a special one. Don't miss their version of *vitello tonnato* (sliced cold

veal and tuna sauce) and *bonet* (chocolate pudding): both the apotheosis of their respective genres.

Soda VEGAN €€

(☑ 346 593 88 38; www.facebook.com/sodavegan food; Corso Italia 6; meals €20-30; ⓐ 6.30pm-1am; ☑) ⌀ A stylish, minimalist space near the south side of the old town that serves outstanding vegan cuisine. Here you'll find beautifully prepared pad thai, flavour-packed black-bean burgers and imaginative combinations like chickpea meringue. Even if you're not hungry, it's worth stopping by for a creative cocktail. Soda serves some of the best drinks in town.

Piazza Duomo GASTRONOMY €€€

(☑ 0173 44 28 00; www.piazzaduomoalba.it; Piazza Risorgimento 4; meals around €200, degustation €260-290; ⓐ 12.30-2pm & 7.30-10pm Tue-Sat, closed 3 weeks Aug) Enrico Crippa's Michelin-starred restaurant is now in its second decade and is considered one of Italy's best. Dreamlike frescoes by Francesco Clemente fill the fleshy pink dining room, which is otherwise a bastion of elegant restraint. On the plate, expect the high concept play beloved of Italian fine-dining chefs, along with spectacular local – and some homegrown – produce (this *is* white truffle country).

Four elegant rooms (from €240 a night) are available for restaurant guests who just want to fall in a heap after a long night of degustation dining.

🍸 Drinking & Nightlife

Monviso Coffee Factory COFFEE

(Vicolo dell'Arco 1; ⓐ 7.30am-7.30pm Tue-Sat, from 9.30am Sun) Hidden on a tiny lane just south of Piazza del Risorgimento, Monviso pours the best coffee in town. Amid low-playing indie rock, recycled furnishings and a menu of fanciful preparations (flat white, V60, chai latte), the friendly barista-owner happily provides suggestions if you're seeking something new.

Voglia di Vino WINE BAR

(☑ 0173 20 93 12; www.lavogliadivino.com; Via Pertinace 7; ⓐ 6pm-11pm Tue, noon-3pm & 6-11pm Wed-Sun) What started as a wine shop in 2014 has quickly morphed into an elegant wine bar and restaurant. The variety is astonishing, with more than 400 types of wine from some 160 producers, and there are dozens of wines by the glass.

Boia Fauss Pensavo Peggio   BREWERY
(Corso Langhe 59; ☺8am-10.30pm Tue-Sat) A
15-minute walk from the old town, this
microbirrificio e ristoro (brewery and
restaurant) is also one of the city's liveliest
places for a drink. Join Alba's younger set
over excellent microbrews and interesting
wines, including Nascetta, a little-known
white from the Langhe. Come early at *aperitivo* time (6pm to 10pm) for the extensive
(and extremely popular) buffet, which costs
just €2.

ℹ Information

Tourist Office (☑0173 3 58 33; www.langhe
roero.it; Piazza Risorgimento 2; ☺9am-6pm
Mon-Fri, from 10am Sat & Sun)

ℹ Getting There & Away

From the **bus station** (Corso Matteotti 10) there
are frequent buses to/from Turin (two hours,
€5.70, up to 10 daily) and infrequent buses to/
from Barolo (25 minutes, €2.30, one to two daily
when school is in session; none on Sunday) and
other surrounding villages.

From Alba's **train station** (Piazza Trento e
Trieste) regular trains run to/from Turin via Bra/
Asti (1¼ hours, €5.75, every two hours).

The irregularity of buses makes touring the
Langhe by car or bike the better option. For bike
hire (from €20 a day) book through the tourist
office. Car hire goes from about €35 per day or
the tourist office can hook you up with a driver
(prices vary).

Barolo

☑ 0173 / POP 700

The tiny, 1800-hectare parcel of undulating
land immediately around this hilltop village
knocks out what is arguably the finest *vino*
in Italy and currently the next big thing
with anglophone collectors. No flash in the
pan, Barolo has been a viticultural hub for
at least four centuries and is far too deeply
rooted in the soil and the seasons to have
wine-snob attitude. The ancient streets are
delightful enough themselves to warrant a
stroll even if wine is not your thing, but being able to taste its precious, aromatic wines
in a relaxed and welcoming tasting room
makes visiting a sublime experience indeed.

◉ Sights & Activities

Museo del Vino a Barolo   MUSEUM
(www.wimubarolo.it; Castello Comunale Falletti
di Barolo; adult/reduced €8/6; ☺10.30am-7pm,
closed Jan & Feb) A capricious jaunt through

the history of viticulture via light, film and
installations, care of the imagination of
Swiss designer François Confino (who also
designed Turin's cinema museum; p224). It's
set over three floors of the village's stunning
medieval castle and is best braved *after* a
tasting session, when it all will seem to make
sense.

★ Agrilab Wine Tasting Tour   WINE
(www.barolowinetastingtour.com; Piazza Falletti
2; tasting €1-4; ☺10am-6pm Tue-Fri, to 7pm Sat
& Sun) Tucked behind the castle, this lively,
modern tasting room brings a dash of verve
to Barolo. Here you can try some 36 different wines, including Barolo, Barbaresco and
Barbera, as well as more obscure varietals
like Nascetta, Ruche and Pelaverga.

It's a clever and simple system: pick up a
card and use it to select the wine you like,
noting how much of each you want (from
small sips to half pours). While drinking,
you can listen to audio content (in English
or Italian) that describes interesting features, historical tidbits and legends about
the wines. At the end, you'll pay for whatever you've consumed on the card.

Marchesi di Barolo   WINE
(☑0173 56 44 91; www.marchesibarolo.com; Via
Roma 1; ☺10.30am-5.30pm) A venerable winery that was first established by the fascinating Juliette Colbert de Maulévrier, a French
noblewoman and social reformer, in the early years of the 19th century. You can pop in
to buy a bottle, but better to book for a tour
and guided tasting. If you're lucky, you'll be
taken around the sprawling, historic cellars
by 6th-generation Barolo makers Valentina
or Davide Abbona.

Marchesi's reputation is for its single-
vineyard Barolo, but it also produces good
Barbera and local whites, Arneis and
Cortese.

🛏 Sleeping

Casa Svizzera   AGRITURISMO €
(☑0173 56 64 08; www.casasvizzera.com; Via Roma
65; d €110-140; 🅿 🛜) Five minutes from the
Germano family's vines, these three pretty,
balconied rooms sit above their central *enoteca* (wine bar) and former bottling plant.
It's quiet and ridiculously atmospheric, but
also puts you within toddling distance of all
the village's tasting rooms and restaurants.
Kind staff will happily make local recommendations and reservations for you.

Hotel Barolo
HOTEL €

(☑ 0173 5 63 54; www.hotelbarolo.it; Via Lomondo 2; s €80-100, d €120-200; P @ ≋) Overlooked by the famous *enoteca*-castle, Hotel Barolo is an old-school place; sit back on the terrace with a glass of you-know-what, contemplating the 18th-century Piedmontese architecture that guards its shimmering swimming pool. Follow up with a meal at the in-house Brezza restaurant (it's been serving up truffles and the like for three generations, and making wine since 1885).

★ Palas Cerequio
BOUTIQUE HOTEL €€€

(☑ 0173 5 06 57; www.palascerequio.com; Borgata Cerequio; d €190-350; P ✳ 🛜 ≋) Located halfway between Barolo and La Morra, this vineyard-surrounded hotel puts you right in the heart of Italy's fabled wine country. It has nine luxuriously appointed suites, set in either a vintage or a contemporary style. There are lovely views over the vine-covered hills from the terrace and small pool.

Palas Cerequio has an outstanding restaurant (meals €40 to €45) and a beautiful wine cellar, stocked with legendary Barolo vintages, with wine tasting available. Foodies can sign up for a cooking class with head chef Vincenzo La Corte.

✖ Eating

Neighbouring towns may offer more variety and less hectic lunch services, but there's still some lovely places to eat in the village. Most cellars have dining rooms, too.

La Cantinetta
PIEDMONTESE €€

(☑ 0173 5 61 98; Via Roma 33; meals €32-36; ⊘ 12.30-3pm & 7-10pm Fri-Wed) A sunny outside terrace is the big draw here, although you'll be far from unhappy with the menu of local dishes: Ligurian rolled rabbit, risotto with radicchio, wild boar with Barbera wine sauce. Don't miss the antipasto dish of egg in pasta (€7), one of those better-than-the-sum-of-its-parts culinary experiences.

Barolo Friends
PIEDMONTESE €€

(☑ 0173 56 05 42; www.barolofriends.it; Piazza Castello 3; meals €30-40; ⊘ 11am-10pm Thu-Tue) An easy, contemporary place that does Piedmontese staples but, helpfully, doesn't keep to rigid service hours or menu formats. Need a quick *vitello tonnato* (cold sliced veal with tuna sauce) or ravioli with sage and butter? Fancy a late afternoon glass of something special as the sun dips over the vines? This is your place.

🍷 Drinking & Nightlife

You're probably here to taste one of the world's best reds and that will be taken care of nicely. There are a few wine bars that do stay open a little later to cater to the pickers and other young wine professionals, but head to Alba for proper nightlife.

★ La Vite Turchese
WINE BAR

(☑ 366 455 67 44; www.laviteturchese.com; Via Alba 5; ⊘ 2-8pm Mon & Wed, 10am-8pm Thu-Sun) This friendly *enoteca* is run by passionate young staff who will talk you through their good stock of local wines – from a cheap and cheerful Nebbiolo or Arneis to a 2003 Casa Nere Barolo at €55 a glass – and they also branch out to some other Italian regions. Daily cheese and *salumi* (cured meats/charcuterie) choices are sourced with love and it's a local favourite for *aperitivo*.

Wine flights are an excellent way to learn about the great wines produced around the region, and range from €15 to sample four Barberas, to €25 for four remarkable DOCG Barolos. For something lighter, you can also discover some great white wines (from €9 for three tastings).

ℹ Getting There & Away

Infrequent buses run from Alba (25 minutes, €2.30, one to two daily Monday to Saturday), the nearest train station. It's also possible to get a taxi from there.

Barbaresco

☑ 0173 / POP 650

Delightful Barbaresco is surrounded by vineyards and characterised by its 30m-high, 11th-century tower, visible from miles around. There are more than 40 wineries and two *enoteche* in the area. Only a few kilometres separate Barolo from Barbaresco; a rainier microclimate, nutrient-rich soil and fewer ageing requirements have made the latter's wine into a softer, more ethereal red that plays 'queen' to Barolo's 'king'. The village itself is similarly a little softer, less in your face than Barolo. The hilltop hamlet of Treiso, 15 minutes' drive away, also produces Barbaresco.

👁 Sights & Activities

Torre di Barbaresco
VIEWPOINT

(www.facebook.com/torredibarbaresco; Via Torino; adult/child €5/free; ⊘ 10am-7pm) Take the lift to the rooftop of this restored medieval tower for a sublime view over wine country.

You'll see the meandering Tanaro River, various other settlements (Alba, Neive, Treiso, Asti) and the vineyard-covered rolling hills of Langhe and Roero stretching off to the horizon.

★ **Le Rocche dei Barbari**   WINE
(☑0173 63 51 38; www.rocchedeibarbari.it; Via Torino 62; ◎10am-5.30pm) This historic winery has a moody tasting room and cellar, with wines that are not retailed elsewhere. Generous complimentary tastings are conducted by the owner, cheese and hazelnuts are offered on pewter platters and the stories of each vintage are enchanting. A quiet Langhe highlight.

Enoteca Regionale del Barbaresco   WINE
(☑0173 63 52 51; www.enotecadelbarbaresco.it; Piazza del Municipio 7; ◎10am-7pm) Fittingly for a wine that conjures such reverence, this intimate *enoteca* is housed inside a deconsecrated church, with wines lined up where the altar once stood. It costs €3 per tasting glass; four Barbaresco wines are available to try each day.

🛌 **Sleeping & Eating**

Casa Boffa   PENSION €
(☑0173 63 51 74; www.boffacarlo.it; Via Torino 9a; d/ste €97/125; P🅿❄🐾) In a lovely house in the centre of the village, Boffa offers four modern rooms and one suite above a stunning terrace with limitless Langhe valley views. Boffa's cellars are open for tasting daily (from 11am to 6pm).

Ristorante Rabayà   ITALIAN €€
(☑0173 63 52 23; www.rabayaristorante.it; Via Rabayà 9; meals €35-45, set menu €38; ◎noon-2pm Tue-Sun, 7.30-9pm Tue-Sat) Rabayà, on the southern fringe of the village, has the ambience of dining at a private home. The signature veal shoulder in Barbaresco works better in its antique-furnished dining room in front of a roaring fire, but its terrace set high above the vineyards is perfect for a summer evening, even if it's just for a plate of cheese.

A truffle menu also makes an appearance in autumn. Rabayà is located about 750m south of Barbaresco's main street (Via Torino).

ⓘ **Getting There & Away**

Buses run from Alba (25 minutes, €3.10, twice daily), the nearest train station. It's also possible to get a taxi from there.

Bra & Pollenzo
📞0172 / POP 29,630
Bra seems like a small, unassuming Piedmontese town, but as the place where the Slow Food movement first took root in 1986, it's also something of a gastronomic pilgrimage site. There are defiantly no supermarkets in the historic centre, where small, family-run shops are replete with organic sausages, handcrafted chocolates and fresh local farm produce. Naturally, shops shut religiously for a 'slowdown' twice a week. Just down the hill sits Pollenzo, a slightly less picturesque but still pretty town, with the Slow Food movement's very own University of Gastronomic Sciences at its heart.

🏃 **Activities**

Banca del Vino   WINE
(☑0172 45 84 18; www.bancadelvino.it; Piazza Vittorio Emanuele II 13, Pollenzo; ◎10am-7pm Tue-Sat, to 1pm Sun) Slow Food's Università di Scienze Gastronomiche oversees this extensive wine cellar 'library' of Italian wines. Free guided tastings are available by reservation. Or you can stop in and sample your way through some exquisite vintages, ranging from €2 to €6 per glass.

Università di Scienze Gastronomiche   WINE
(University of Gastronomic Sciences; www.unisg.it; Piazza Vittorio Emanuele 9, Pollenzo) 🚶 Another creation of Carlo Petrini, founder of the Slow Food movement, this university, established in the village of Pollenzo (4km southeast of Bra) in 2004, occupies a former royal palace and offers three-year courses in gastronomy and food management. The Banca del Vino is here.

🎉 **Festivals & Events**

Cheese   FOOD & DRINK
(www.cheese.slowfood.it; Bra; ◎mid-Sep) `FREE`
Held on odd-numbered years in September, this Slow Food festival celebrates cheese with tastings, workshops and special dinners. The event happens all over Bra's streets and squares.

🛌 **Sleeping & Eating**

Albergo Dell'Agenzia   HOTEL €€
(☑0172 45 86 00; www.albergoagenzia.it; Via Fossano 21, Pollenzo; s/d €165/190; P🅿❄🐾🏊) Part of the same sprawling complex that houses Pollenzo's Università di Scienze Gastronomiche , the rooms are spacious and elegantly

furnished, with huge beds, walk-in wardrobes, marble bathrooms and the occasional roof terrace that looks over village rooftops. With a restaurant run by people who really know their business, a well-stocked wine cellar and a park, its ever-so-slight corporate edge soon melts away.

Albergo Cantine Ascheri DESIGN HOTEL €€
(☑ 0172 43 03 12; www.ascherihotel.it; Via Piumati 25, Bra; s/d/ste €110/130/170; P ☀ ⛵) Built around the Ascheri family's 1880-established winery, incorporating wood, steel mesh and glass, this ultracontemporary hotel includes a mezzanine library, 27 sun-drenched rooms and a vine-lined terrace overlooking the rooftops. From the lobby you can see straight down to the vats in the cellar (guests get a free tour). It's just one block south of Bra's train station.

Osteria del Boccondivino OSTERIA €€
(☑ 0172 42 56 74; www.boccondivinoslow.it; Via Mendicità Istruita 14, Bra; meals €28-38, set menus €20-24; ☺ noon-2.30pm & 7-10pm Tue-Sat) ☀ On the 1st floor of the Slow Food movement's backstreet headquarters, this bottle-lined dining room was the first to be opened by the emerging organisation back in the 1980s. The menu, which changes daily, is, as you'd expect, a picture of precise providence and seasonality, with dishes that are beautifully prepared. You can dine in the courtyard on warm days.

❶ Information

Tourist office (☑ 0172 43 01 85; www.langheroero.it; Piazza Caduti della Liberta 20, Bra; ☺ 9am-1pm & 2.30-6pm Mon-Fri, 9am-12.30pm Sat & Sun)

❶ Getting There & Away

From the train station on Piazza Roma, trains link Bra with Turin (45 minutes, €4.60), via Carmagnola, while buses connect Bra (train station) with Pollenzo (20 minutes, €2).

La Morra

☑ 0173 / POP 2760

Atop a hill surrounded by vines with the Alps as a backdrop, La Morra is bigger and quieter than Barolo, though no less beguiling. The village's *cantina comunale* (communal wine seller) provides lists of places to do tastings.

◉ Sights & Activities

Torre Campanaria VIEWPOINT
(Piazza Castello; ☺ 10am-5pm Fri-Sun Mar-Nov) FREE Dating back to the early 1700s, La Morra's stolid bell tower soars 31m above Piazza Castello. Make your way up the narrow staircases for fine 360-degree views over the terracotta roofs of town and the patchwork fields of vineyards stretching off into the distance.

★**Cappella del Barolo** PUBLIC ART
(www.ceretto.com/en/experience/art-design/the-chapel-of-barolo; Borgata Cerequio) Alba's winemaking and restaurateuring Ceretti family has commissioned a number of site-specific artworks in the region, and this never-consecrated chapel is one of the most wonderful. Its Sol LeWitt exterior and David Tremlett interiors were added in 1999. Lewitt's playful intervention is visible from across the vines, but don't miss Tremlett's work inside, which is both serene and enlivening. It's always open, just push the door.

It's located around 2km southeast of (and downhill from) La Morra and is set among rolling vineyards.

Cantina Comunale di La Morra WINE
(☑ 0173 50 92 04; Via Carlo Alberto 2; wine tasting €15; ☺ 10am-12.30pm & 2.30-6.30pm Wed-Mon) One of the best places in town to learn about the range of wines produced in the region, this cellar organises walk-in tastings that feature a changing line-up of quality wines. When last we passed through, visitors could taste one Dolcetto, two Barberas, one Nebbiolo and four Barolos – an excellent value at €15.

🛏 Sleeping

★**Brandini** AGRITURISMO €€
(www.agriturismolamorra.com; Borgo Brandini 16; s €100, d €140-210; P ☀ ⛵ 🐾) ☀ A five-minute drive below La Morra, this vineyard restaurant and cellar has five cosy, modern rooms. Each is named for a writer and graced with appropriate quotes and reading material, along with equally inspiring views of the Alps. All fittings, from paint to wood to bedding, are made from sustainable, nontoxic materials in line with their organic agricultural practices.

Cooking classes that explore the specialities of the Langhe can be organised for groups or individuals in English or Italian.

Arborina Relais   BOUTIQUE HOTEL **€€€**
(📞 0173 50 03 51; www.arborinarelais.it; Frazione Annunziata 27; d €260-370; [P][❄][🛜][🏊]) A gorgeous contemporary design is a departure from the usual stately traditional upmarket hotels of this region. The look throughout is dark glamour, with extensive use of grey and dark wood. Beds are large and luxuriously made-up, there's a variety of terraces and vineyard-side gardens to loll about in and both an on-site restaurant and a wine/produce shop at reception.

✖️ Eating

★ **More e Macine**   PIEDMONTESE **€**
(📞 0173 50 03 95; Via XX Settembre 18; meals €25-30; ⏱ noon-2.30pm & 7-11pm) A rambunctious, casual and seemingly chaotic place that turns out some of the town's best food. This is the Piedmontese kitchen at its most essential: come for a mountainous swirl of the signature fine *tajarin* pasta with *ragú*, risotto with whatever vegetable's in season, spicy sauced tongue or sliced octopus. But the star of the menu here is the Barolo by-the-glass list.

Brandini   PIEDMONTESE **€€**
(📞 0173 5 02 66; www.agriturismolamorra.com; Borgo Brandini 16; meals €30-40; ⏱ 12.30-2.30pm Thu-Tue & 7-10pm Fri & Sat) There's a stunning view across vineyards to a wall of snow-capped mountains from the rustic farmhouse tables that grace the light open space at Brandini, while the food is similarly a coming together of tradition and fresh ideas using local produce and organic vegetables from Brandini's own gardens. Ask about the cooking classes if you're keen to reproduce the Piedmontese kitchen at home.

Osteria Arborina   GASTRONOMY **€€€**
(📞 0173 50 03 40; www.osteriarborina.it; Frazione Annunziata 27; meals around €50, menu €75-100; ⏱ dining room 12.30-2pm & 7.30-10pm Tue-Sat, 12.30-2pm Sun, terrace 11.30am-11pm Thu-Tue) Part of the Arborina Relais hotel, this very smart dining room offers gastronomic menus that either rework Piedmontese standards in surprising ways or go for complete culinary poetry and use the global influences that the widely travelled chef has gathered. The sommelier is one of the region's most revered and overall service is extremely attentive and personal.

In summer, head to the rooftop terrace if you'd prefer a casual grill or plate of *crudo* (they do both raw fish and beef), or simply to linger over a phenomenal glass of wine outside of meal times.

❶ Getting There & Away

Buses run from Alba (30 minutes, €3.10, three daily Monday to Saturday), the nearest train station. It's also possible to get a taxi from there.

Neive
📞 0173 / POP 3050

Ping-ponged between Alba and Asti during the Middle Ages, Neive is a quieter proposition these days, its hilltop medieval layout earning it a rating as one of Italy's *borghi più belli* (most beautiful towns). Come here to taste the village's four legendary wines – Dolcetto d'Alba, Barbaresco, Moscato and Barbera d'Alba – among sun-dappled squares and purple wisteria.

⚡ Activities

La Casetta del Castello   WINE
(📞 329 212 51 71; www.castellodineive.it/en/caseta; Via Castelborgo 1; tour €10; ⏱ 10.30am-6pm Wed-Mon, tours 11am, 2.30pm & 4.30pm) Set inside a medieval castle, this winery offers guided tours of its historic cellars three times daily; the one-hour tour ends with a tasting of your choice among three different wines (Arneis, Dolcetto or Moscato). You can also stop in the tasting room, for more extensive samplings, with more than 18 different wines on offer (priced at €4 to €9 per glass).

Cantina del Glicine   WINE
(📞 0173 6 72 15; www.cantinadelglicine.com; Via Giulio Cesare 1; tasting €10; ⏱ 10am-noon & 3-6pm Thu-Mon) Breathe in Neive's tannic history while sipping a Barbaresco inside the 16th-century brick cellars of this small family-run winery. Cheese and hazelnuts accompany the tasting of several different wines. It's located toward the north end of the village.

🛏 Sleeping

Al Palazzo Rosso   B&B **€**
(📞 333 117 91 27; http://al-palazzo-rosso.it; Piazza Italia 6; s/d/ste €90/110/140; [❄][🛜]) Looking out to Piazza Italia, this cute, rather modern place has four stylish rooms. Some are decked out in grey, white and black tones, while others come with wood and earthy-toned accents. The suite has huge windows, some have fireplaces and all have wooden floorboards.

Borgo Vecchio
APARTMENT €€

(☑ 335 800 82 82; Via Rocca 13; ste €160-260; ❄ 🛜) These large, luxuriously furnished and very pretty apartment-style suites can sleep two to four; they have small terraces and, in the largest, a Jacuzzi. The excellent breakfast is served in the fine restaurant (with terrace) downstairs. There are amazing views and a garden, too.

🍴 Eating

Osteria del Borgo Vecchio
PIEDMONTESE €

(☑ 377 491 17 05; Via Borgese 10; meals €22-28, set menus €20-33; 🍴) A sweet surprise in meat-centric Piedmont, Osteria del Borgo Vecchio does parallel vegetarian and meat menus, with all organic ingredients and all pasta made in-house. Despite these 21st-century conceits, you could still be in your Piedmontese nonna's dining room with delightful tiled floors, farmhouse chairs and a deep red, green and brown palette.

Rather ironically, the steak here is sensational, but so too are the meat-less meatballs.

Donna Selvatica
PIEDMONTESE €€

(☑ 335 800 82 82; Via Rocca 13; meals €40-50, set menu €48; ⊘ 12-3pm & 7-10pm) On the Barbaresco hills overlooking the village, the name Donna Selvatica honours the local grappa producer Romano Levi for whom the 'wild woman' was a symbol. This is an upmarket but still pleasantly rustic dining room with a lovely terrace from which to enjoy the view in summer. Dishes are carefully prepared using top-quality ingredients like Fassone beef, 36-month-aged Parmigiano Reggiano and truffles.

Al Nido Della Cinciallegra
WINE BAR

(☑ 0173 6 73 67; www.alnidodellacinciallegra.com; Piazza Cocito 8; ⊘ 8am-7.30pm) Join Neive's winemakers and restaurateurs here for a wine and a generous *aperitivo* plate; if the weather's warm, you'll all boisterously spill out onto the pretty square. This is the Langhe at its unpretentious best: on one side of the shop buy a brilliant Barolo; on the other, batteries or a ballpoint pen (it's both *enoteca* and village corner shop).

ℹ Information

Tourist Office (www.langheroero.it; Via Borgese 1; ⊘ 10.30am-1.30pm & 3-8pm Fri-Tue Mar-Dec)

ℹ Getting There & Away

Bus 45FS from Alba's Stazione Ferroviaria (train station) runs to Neive (15 minutes, €3.10) half-hourly from Monday to Saturday and only every few hours on Sundays.

Asti

☑ 0141 / POP 76,100 / ELEV 123M

Just 30km apart, Asti and Alba were fierce rivals in medieval times, when they faced off against each other as feisty, independent strongholds ruled over by feuding royal families. These days the two towns maintain a friendly rivalry – stately but workaday Asti sniffs at Alba's burgeoning glamour – but are united by viticulture. Asti is famed for sparkling white Asti Spumante wine made from white muscat grapes, though it is actually made in Canelli and other nearby areas.

⊙ Sights

Palazzo Mazzetti
MUSEUM

(www.palazzomazzetti.it; Corso Alfieri 357; incl in Smarticket €10; ⊘ 10am-7pm Tue-Sun) FREE This 18th-century residence of the Mazzetti family houses the civic museum and an information office. Downstairs you'll find Roman artefacts and a scale model of the city. Upstairs there are Italian paintings from the 17th to 19th centuries.

Torre Troyana o Dell'Orologio
LANDMARK

(☑ 0141 39 94 89; www.comune.asti.it; Piazza Medici; incl in Smarticket €10; ⊘ 10am-1pm & 4-7pm Tue-Sun Apr-Sep) FREE During the late 13th century the region became one of Italy's wealthiest, with 150-odd towers springing up in Asti alone. Of the 12 that remain, only this one can be climbed. Troyana is a 38m-tall tower that dates from the 12th century. The clock was added in 1420.

★ Cantine Bosca
WINERY

(☑ 335 799 68 11; www.bosca.it; Via Giuliani 23, Canelli; ⊘ visits by appointment) Some 28km south of Asti, the Cantine Bosca is one of several historic wineries that produce the famed sparkling wine of the area (the DOCG Asti Spumante, made from Moscato grapes). Bosca is also known for its 'underground cathedrals', an impressive series of brick-walled halls and tunnels built below the hamlet of Canelli. You can book free visits online or over the phone, but advanced reservations are essential.

✨ Festivals & Events

Palio d'Asti   SPORTS
(www.astiturismo.it/en/content/palio-asti; Piazza
Alfieri; ⊘ Sep) Held on the first Sunday of September, this bareback horse race commemorates a victorious battle against Alba during
the Middle Ages and draws over a quarter
of a million spectators from surrounding villages. Cheeky Alba answers with a donkey
race on the first Sunday in October.

🛏 Sleeping

Relais Cattedrale   B&B €€
(📞 0141 09 20 99; www.relaiscattedrale.it; Via
Cattedrale 7; s/d €175/250; 🛜) Set in an 18th-
century palazzo in the old quarter, this
friendly six-room guesthouse has atmospheric rooms set with a mix of period furnishings and artful modern flourishes.
Guests can enjoy the terrace or linger in the
inviting lounge with stylish furnishings and
a record player.

Hotel Palio   HOTEL €€
(📞 0141 3 43 71; www.hotelpalio.com; Via Cavour
106; s/d €120/175; 🅿 ❄ 🛜) Wedged between
the train station and the old town, the Palio's
utilitarian exterior belies comfortable facilities inside and its rather charming rooms.

🍴 Eating

Pompa Magna   PIEDMONTESE €
(Via Aliberti 65; meals €20-30; ⊘ noon-2.30pm
Tue-Sun, 6-10.30pm Thu-Sat) This enticing
brasserie with vaulted brick ceilings and
a knowledgeable garrulous host is a great
spot for thoughtfully prepared Piemontese
dishes. You can't go wrong with anything on
the small menu, whether opting for gnocchi
with Castelmagno cheese, pork loin with hazelnuts and Moscato, or warm octopus and
potato salad. All go well with the great (and
reasonably priced) wines on hand.

Osteria del Diavolo   PIEDMONTESE €€
(📞 0141 3 02 21; www.osteriadeldiavolo.it; Piazza
San Martino 6; meals around €30; ⊘ 7.30-10pm
Mon-Fri, noon-2.30pm & 7.30-10pm Sat) For one
of Asti's best dining experiences, book a table at this award-winning *osteria* that offers
beautiful Piedmont and Ligurian dishes.
Cappon magro (a stacked seafood and vegetable appetiser), braised beef cheek with
Barbera wine and hearty seafood soup are
among the standouts. You can dine outside
on the small piazza on warm evenings.

ℹ MUSEUM TICKETING

Asti's cumulative **Smarticket** (www.
fondazioneastimusei.it; adult/reduced
€10/8) offers admission to the major sites in town, including Palazzo
Mazzetti, Torre Troyana and five other
historical sites. As such, there is no
longer a single admission cost for these
individual sites; in fact, several sites do
not have staff on hand as admission is
by automated entry with the Smarticket. Purchase the ticket at Palazzo
Mazzetti .

ℹ Information

Tourist Office (www.astiturismo.it; Piazza
Alfieri 34; ⊘ 9am-1pm & 2-6pm Mon-Sat, to
5.30pm Sun) Has details of September's flurry
of wine festivals and lists of wine cellars open
to visitors.

ℹ Getting There & Away

Asti is on the Turin–Genoa railway line and
is served by hourly trains in both directions.
Journey time is 36 to 54 minutes to/from Turin
(€5.25) and 1½ hours to/from Genoa (€9.45). To
get to Alba, you must take a bus.

Via Lattea

Piedmont's Via Lattea (Milky Way) consists
of two parallel valleys just west of Turin that
offer top-notch skiing facilities. The more
northern of the two, **Val di Susa**, meanders
past a moody abbey, the old Celtic town
of Susa and pretty mountain villages. Its
southern counterpart, the **Val Chisone**, is
pure and simple ski-resort territory. The valleys hosted many events at the 2006 Winter
Olympics, and the facilities and infrastructure remain state of the art.

Built in the 1930s by the Agnelli clan of
Fiat fame, **Sestriere** (pop 950) ranks among
Europe's most glamorous ski resorts due to
its enviable location in the snowy eastern
realms of the vast Via Lattea ski area. You'll
either love or hate the architecture.

◉ Sights & Activities

★**Sacra di San Michele**   ABBEY
(www.sacradisanmichele.com; Via alla Sacra 14, Avigliana; adult/reduced €8/6; ⊘ 9.30am-12.30pm &
2.30-6pm, to 5pm mid-Oct–mid Mar) This Gothic-
Romanesque abbey, brooding above the

OFF THE BEATEN TRACK

RURAL BOLTHOLES

A great find in not-always-budget-friendly Piedmont, **Cascina Rosa** (☑ 0141 92 52 35; www.cascinarosa33.it; Viale Pininfarina 33, Grazzano Badoglio; s/d €65/95; P ※ ♠ ☎) is a farmhouse B&B atop a hilltop with a 360-degree panorama of the lush Monferrato countryside. Switched-on owners really want you to unwind and enjoy the region, and besides providing simple, stylish and suitably rustic rooms, offer up a host of ideas for rides, walks and other leisurely pursuits. Count a 30-minute drive north from Asti.

Around a 15-minute drive south of Asti, surrounded by vineyards and rolling hills, **Villa Pattono** (☑ 0141 96 20 21; www.villapattono.com; Strada Drotte, Costiglione d'Asti; d €190-250, ste €290-390; ☺ late-Mar–Dec; P ※ ♠ ☎) is a painstakingly restored 18th-century country mansion with frescoed ceilings, dark wood floors and marble bathrooms. Part of the Renatto Ratto winery, it can arrange guided tastings and cellar visits.

road 14km from Turin, has kept sentry atop Monte Pirchiriano (962m) since the 10th century. It housed a powerful, bustling community of Benedictine monks for over 600 years and was a staging point for high-social-level pilgrims. Look out for the whimsical 'Zodiac Door', a 12th-century doorway sculpted with *putti* (cherubs) pulling each other's hair. The monastery was the likely inspiration for Umberto Eco's masterpiece *The Name of the Rose*.

To get to the abbey by public transport, there's a steep 90-minute hike from Sant'Ambrogio station. Alternatively, there's a special bus from Avigliana train station six times a day from May to September. If coming by private vehicle, there are various car parks on the road to the abbey, including a pay lot just outside the entrance (€1.50 per hour).

Via Lattea   SKIING
(www.vialattea.it) The Via Lattea ski domain embraces 400km of pistes and seven interlinked ski resorts: Sestriere (2035m), Sauze d'Oulx (1509m), Sansicario (1700m), Cesana Torinese (1350m), Pragelato (1524m) and Claviere (1760m) in Italy; and Montgenèvre (1850m) in neighbouring France. A single daily ski pass costing €40 covers the Italian Via Lattea, or €50 including the French slopes.

ℹ Information

There are numerous tourist offices in the valleys.
Cesana Torinese Tourist Office (☑ 0122 8 92 02; Piazza Vittorio Amedeo 3, Cesana Torinese; ☺ 9am-1pm & 2-6pm)

Sauze d'Oulx Tourist Office (☑ 0122 85 80 09; www.consorziofortur.it; Viale Genevris 7, Sauze d'Oulx; ☺ 9am-12.30pm & 2.30-6.30pm)

Sestriere Tourist Office (☑ 0122 75 54 44; www.turismotorino.org; Via Pinerolo/SS23; ☺ 9am-1pm & 2-6pm)

ℹ Getting There & Away

Turin-based Sadem buses link Susa with Avigliana (€4.40, 35 minutes), Oulx (€5.25, 45 minutes), Turin (€6.35, 1¼ hours) and the Via Lattea resorts. It's a 45-minute drive or 1¼ hour train journey from Turin (€5.25).

To/from Sestriere, there are bus links to Cesana Torinese (€2.70, 25 minutes), Oulx (€3.05, 45 minutes) and Turin (€7.80, two to three hours, up to five times daily).

Cuneo

☑ 0171 / POP 56,300 / ELEV 543M

There are a raft of reasons why you should drop by stately Cuneo, not least being the food, the bike friendliness, the hiking possibilities nearby and, last but certainly not least, the city's signature rum-filled chocolates.

Sitting on a promontory of land between two rivers, Cuneo also provides excellent Alpine views framed by the high pyramid-shaped peak of Monte Viso (3841m) in the Cottian Alps.

⊙ Sights

Piazza Galimberti   PIAZZA
Arriving in Cuneo's gargantuan main piazza, you'd think you'd just touched down in a capital city. Finished in 1884, it sits aside an older portico-embellished town founded in 1198.

Museo Civico di Cuneo   MUSEUM
(Via Santa María 10; adult/reduced €3/2; ☺ 3.30-6.30pm Tue-Sun) Cuneo has some wonderfully dark and mysterious churches. The oldest

is the deconsecrated San Francisco convent and church, which today hosts this museum tracking the history of the town and province.

🛏 Sleeping

Hotel Ligure
HOTEL €

(☑ 0171 63 45 45; www.ligurehotel.com; Via Savigliano 11; s/d/tr/q €65/80/110/130; P ❄ 🛜) In the heart of the old town, this two-star hotel is run by a charming, elegant family and has simple but spotless rooms and self-catering apartments for longer stays.

Hotel Palazzo Lovera
HOTEL €€

(☑ 0171 69 04 20; www.palazzolovera.com; Via Roma 37; d €110-130, ste €150-170; P ❄ 🛜) A French king and an Italian pope have stayed at this hotel in the heart of the old quarter, which hints at the Lovera's stately past. Rooms are comfortable and the hotel offers rare small-town Italian extras, such as a gym, sauna and good on-site restaurant.

🍴 Eating

Cuneo is an under-the-radar culinary powerhouse and has some standout places to wine and dine.

Arione
SWEETS €

(www.arionecuneo.it; Piazza Galimberti 14; cake €2-5; ⏰ 8am-8pm Tue-Sat, 8am-1pm & 3.30-8pm Sun) This 1920s vintage chocolatier and cafe invented the *Cuneesi al Rhum*, a large, rum-laced praline wrapped in cellophane. The chocolates came to the attention of Hemingway, who made a detour from Milan en route to Nice in 1954 to try them; there's a photograph of his visit in the window. We're with Hemingway: buy a bag. Actually, buy two.

Bove's
STEAK, PIEDMONTESE €

(☑ 0171 69 26 24; www.boves1929.it; Via Dronero 2; meals €20-30; ⏰ 12.15-2.30pm & 7.15-10.30pm Thu-Tue) This dark corner bar may seem like a Brooklyn transplant with its tiles and high stools, but it's the real deal, serving up high quality Piedmontese *cruda* (raw minced beef) and steaks since 1929. These days they've added an ever-so-slightly-international burger menu: there's even a good veggie burger (made from lentils and leeks, and topped with mozzarella).

★ 4 Ciance
PIEDMONTESE €€

(☑ 0171 48 90 27; www.4cianceristorante.it; Via Dronero 8c; meals €32-42, tasting menu €40; ⏰ 12.30-2.30pm & 7.45-10pm Tue-Thu & Sat, 7.30-10.30pm Fri, 12.30-2.30pm Sun) A warm, unpretentious place where everything is made from scratch, including the bread. The chef's specialities showcase the Piedmont's quality produce in simple but elegant dishes like ravioli stuffed with borage and herbs with hazelnut butter, or lamb with broad beans and potatoes.

Osteria della Chiocciola
GASTRONOMY €€

(☑ 0171 6 62 77; www.osteriadellachiocciola.it; Via Fossano 1; meals €30-35, degustation €38; ⏰ restaurant 12.30-2pm & 7.30-10pm Mon-Sat, enoteca 10am-3.30pm Mon-Sat) 🍃 Slow Food–affiliated Chiocciola's upstairs dining room is the colour of buttercups and makes for a soothing setting to linger over expertly crafted local, seasonal dishes. Its weekday lunch menu (meals €15 to €25) is a fabulous deal, or if on the fly, you can stop by for a glass of wine with cheese in the ground-floor *enoteca*.

WORTH A TRIP

ROMAN SUSA

Susa has a palpable sense of confidence that dates back millennia. It was an important Gaulish city that agreed to be Romanised in the 1st-century BC, then continued as a cosmopolitan trading post during the Medieval and Renaissance periods. Its Roman ruins make for an interesting stop on the way to the western ski resorts and it can make a very pleasant base for exploration and hiking, or a cheaper alternative to the resorts in winter.

The pristine and impressive triumphal **Arco d'Augusto** (Arch of Augustus), dating to 9BC, sits just outside the centre of town on Via Impero Romano. It marks the transition of power between the Celtic-Ligurian Marcus Julius Cottius and Roman Emperor Augustus, who in fact inaugurated it on his way home from Gaul. Its beautifully peaceful position makes it all the more enthralling, plus you'll often get it all to yourself.

ℹ Information

Tourist Office (☑ 0171 69 02 17; www.comune.cuneo.it; Via Roma 28; ⊘8.30am-1pm & 2.30-6pm Mon-Fri, 10am-4pm Sat & Sun)

ℹ Getting There & Away

Regular trains run from Cuneo's central train station, at Piazzale Libertà, to Turin (€7, 1¼ hours, up to eight daily) and Ventimiglia (€8.30, 2¾ hours, one daily), from where you can continue over the border to Nice.

Limone Piemonte & the Maritime Alps

☑ 0171 / ELEV 1525M

Shoehorned between the rice-growing plains of Piedmont and the sparkling coastline of Liguria lie the brooding Maritime Alps – a small pocket of dramatically sculpted mountains that rise like stony-faced border guards along the frontier of Italy and France. Smaller yet no less majestic than their Alpine cousins to the north, the Maritimes are speckled with mirror-like lakes, foraging ibexes and a hybrid cultural heritage that is as much southern French as northern Italian.

There's a palpable wilderness feel to be found among these glowering peaks. Get out of the populated valleys and onto the imposing central massif and you'll quickly be projected into a high-altitude Shangri-La. Whistling marmots scurry under rocky crags doused in mist above a well-marked network of mountain trails where the sight of another hiker – even in peak season – is about as rare as an empty piazza in Rome. This is Italy at its most serene and serendipitous.

🏃 Activities

The main hiking trailheads lie to the south of the city of Cuneo in a couple of ruggedly attractive regional parks: the **Parco Naturale Alpi Marittime** (www.parcoalpimarittime.it) and the **Parco Naturale del Marguareis** (www.parcomarguareis.it).

Maritime Alps Circuits   HIKING
(www.limoneturismo.it) The Lago di Valscura Circuit (21km) starts in the airy spa of Terme di Valdieri and follows an old military road via the Piano del Valasco to an icy lake near the French border. It loops back past the Rifugio Questa before descending via the same route.

For a two-day hike try the Marguareis Circuit (35km), which begins in the small ski centre of Limone Piemonte and tracks up across passes and ridges to the Rifugio Garelli. Day two involves looping back through a small segment of France to your starting point in Limone.

Limone Piemonte   SKIING
(www.riservabianca.it) Limone Piemonte, 20km south of Cuneo, has been a ski station since 1907 and maintains 15 lifts and 80km of runs, including some put aside for Nordic skiing. The town (population 1600) has numerous hotels and ski-hire shops.

🛏 Sleeping

Borgo Fantino   APARTMENT €
(☑ 0171 92 66 69; www.borgofantino.it; Corso Nizza 54; 4-person apt €130-180; 🅿 🐾) These modern apartments in a low-slung structure of wood and stone are both stylish and comfortingly rustic. There's a communal games room, a spa and a shuttle service to town and the lifts. Apartments sleep up to four people.

Rifugio Garelli   CHALET €
(☑ 0171 73 80 78; www.rifugiogarelli.com; Al Pian del Lupo; dm €26, with half-board €49; ⊘mid-Jun–mid-Sep) Mountain hut in the Maritime Alps at 1970m. The restaurant meals are good; note you'll have to pay a few extra euros for showers and sheets.

ℹ Getting There & Away

Limone is on the main train line from Turin (two hours, €8.70) which continues to the French border at Ventimiglia (two hours, €6.55), though you may have to change at Cuneo. There are winter and summer shuttle buses to the lifts and hotels can arrange train station pick-ups.

Varallo & the Valsesia

☑ 0163

Situated 66km northwest of Vercelli in northern Piedmont, this wild, remote region is a place for either contemplation or for adventure along the lines of black skiing, rafting, canyoning or fishing. Varallo is home to the occasionally macabre pilgrimage site of the Sacro Monte di Varallo, while beyond here, the Sesia river heads spectacularly north to the foot of the Monte Rosa massif. Alpine slopes climb sharply, offering numerous walking, cycling and white-water rafting possibilities. The valley's last village,

Alagna Valsesia, is an ancient Swiss-Walser settlement turned ski resort, which is part of the Monte Rosa Ski Area. It is well known for its off-piste runs.

◉ Sights & Activities

Sacro Monte di Varallo   MOUNTAIN
(☑0163 5 11 31; www.sacromontedivarallo.it; ⊕8.30am-12.20pm & 2.15pm-6.30pm) FREE Situated 66km northwest of Vercelli in northern Piedmont, Varallo guards the Sacro Monte di Varallo, the oldest of Italy's nine Sacri Monti (Sacred Mountains), all a Unesco World Heritage site from 2003. The complex consists of an astounding 45 chapels, with 800 statues depicting the Passion of Christ set on a rocky buttress on the slopes of Monte Tre Croci.

A Franciscan friar created the site in 1491, hoping to reproduce an alpine simulacrum of Jerusalem for locals who could not make the pilgrimage to the real deal. The complex is anchored by a basilica dating from 1614, and the subsequent chapels follow the course of Christ's life told through frescoes and life-size terracotta statues. The scenes are sometimes macabre. The Monte is accessed via a winding walking path from Piazza Ferrari in town.

Monte Rosa Ski Area   SKIING
(www.visitmonterosa.com) The Monte Rosa ski area consists of three valleys. Champoluc anchors the Valle d'Ayas, Gressoney lights up the Val de Gressoney and Alagna Valsesia is the focal point in the Valsesia. These valleys have a less manic resort scene and harbour some quiet Walser villages. The skiing, however, is white-knuckle, with some of Europe's best off-piste and heli-skiing possibilities, particularly in the Valsesia.

Corpo Guide Alagna   OUTDOORS
(☑340 583 57 38; www.guidealagna.com; Piazza Grober 1, Alagna) From Alagna, the Corpo Guide Alagna organises a smorgasbord of winter and summer activities. A highlight is its summer two-day trip up to the highest *rifugio* in Europe, the **Capanna Regina Margherita** (www.rifugimonterosa. it; dm with breakfast/half board €70/100; ⊕late Jun-early Sep) perched atop Punta Gnifetti on the Swiss–Italian border at an astounding 4554m. Guided ascents cost €300 to €450 per person depending on group size.

⬛ Sleeping

There are some really lovely small hotels and B&Bs in Alagna and some spectacular mountain huts.

Rifugio Camparient   CHALET €
(☑0163 7 80 02; www.rifugiocamparient.com; Via alla Chiesa 4, Alpe di Mera; d with half board €85-110; P❧) A beautifully sited family-run place that's a great base for exploring the region, both in winter and summer.

❶ Getting There & Away

This region is in fact closer to Milan than to Turin, although it's an easy two or so hours' drive from the Piedmontese capital. The closest train station is Vercelli, from there it's a two- to three-hour bus ride to Alagna Valsesia (€9.80, three daily).

VALLE D'AOSTA
☑0165 / POP 125,800

While its Dolomite cousins tend to the Tyrolean, Aosta's nuances are French. The result is a hybrid culture known as Valdostan, a long-ago mingling of the French Provençal and northern Italian that is notable in the local architecture, the dining table and in the survival of an esoteric local language, Franco-Provençal or Valdôtain.

Comprising one large glacial valley running east–west, bisected by several smaller valleys, the semi-autonomous Valle d'Aosta is overlooked by some of Europe's highest peaks, including Mont Blanc (4810m), the

---

WORTH A TRIP

LOCAL VIN

The Valle d'Aosta is home to vineyards producing sought-after wines that are rarely available outside the region. Cooperative **Cave Mont Blanc de Morgex et La Salle** (☑0165 80 19 49; www.cavemontblanc.com; Strada des Iles 31, La Ruine-Morgex; ⊕10am-noon & 3.30-6.30pm Mon, Tue & Thu-Sat, 10am-noon Wed), 25km west of Aosta, processes the grapes from the 90 or so local smallholdings within Europe's highest vineyard, named for the two villages that are strung together by its vines.

Valle d'Aosta

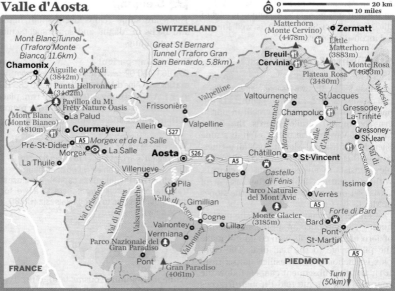

Matterhorn (Monte Cervino; 4478m), Monte Rosa (4633m) and Gran Paradiso (4061m). Not surprisingly, the region offers some of the best snow facilities on the continent: descend hair-raisingly into France and Switzerland over glaciers or via cable cars.

The hiking is just as extraordinary, with access to the 165km Tour du Mont Blanc, Parco Nazionale del Gran Paradiso, and Aosta's two blue-riband, high-altitude trails: the Alte Vie 1 and 2.

Aosta

📞 0165 / POP 33,900 / ELEV 565M

Jagged Alpine peaks rise like marble cathedrals above the regional capital Aosta, a once-important Roman settlement that retains a charming historic centre, while also sprawling rather untidily across the valley floor. Bounced around between Burgundy (France) and Savoy (Italy) in the Middle Ages, the modern town remains bilingual, with a Valdostan culture that can be heard in its musical local dialect and simple but hearty cuisine.

👁 Sights & Activities

Aosta's 2000-year-old centre is awash with Roman ruins. The grand triumphal arch,

Arco di Augusto (Piazza Arco di Augusto), has been strung with a crucifix in its centre since medieval times. From the arch, head east across the Buthier river bridge to view the cobbled **Roman bridge** – in use since the 1st century AD.

Backtracking west 300m along Via Sant'Anselmo brings you to **Porta Praetoria**, the main gate to the Roman city. Heading north along Via di Bailliage and down a dust track brings you to Aosta's **Teatro Romano** (Via Porta Praetoria; incl admission to 3 other sites €7; ⊙ 9am-7pm Sep-Jun, to 8pm Jul & Aug). Part of its 22m-high facade is still intact. Further north, the forbidding 12th-century **Torre dei Balivi** (Via Guido Rey), a former prison, marks one corner of the Roman wall and peers down on the smaller **Torre dei Fromage** (Via Baillage) – named after a family rather than a cheese. The city's Roman forum, the **Criptoportico Forense** (Piazza Giovanni XXIII; incl admission to 3 other sites €7; ⊙ 9am-7pm Apr-Sep, 10am-1pm & 2-6pm Oct-Mar), was another couple of blocks west, beneath what's now Piazza Giovanni XXIII.

Museo Archeologico Regionale MUSEUM
(Piazza Roncas 12; incl admission to 3 other sites €7; ⊙ 9am-7pm Apr-Sep, 10am-1pm & 2-6pm Oct-Mar) **FREE** Aosta's little city museum does an excellent job of detailing the city's Roman

history with a scale model of Aosta's Roman layout plus various antediluvian remains and some fascinating finds from a necropolis discovered at the gates of the Roman city.

Cattedrale Santa Maria Assunta   CATHEDRAL
(Piazza Giovanni XXIII; ⊘7am-noon & 3-7pm) The neoclassical facade of Aosta's cathedral belies the impressive Gothic interior. Inside, the carved 15th-century walnut-wood choir stalls are particularly beautiful. Two mosaics on the floor, dating from the 12th to the 13th centuries, are also notable, as are the treasures displayed in the lovingly attended **Museo del Tesoro** (€4).

Pila   SKIING
(www.pila.it; half-/full-day pass €32/41; ⊘mid-Dec–mid-Apr) The 1800m-high resort of Pila is accessible by the Aosta–Pila cable car or a zigzagging 18km drive south of Aosta. Its 70km of runs, served by 13 lifts, form one of the valley's largest ski areas. Its highest slope, in the shadow of Gran Paradiso, reaches 2700m and sports an ace snow park with a half-pipe, jump and slide, as well as freestyle area for boarders and freestyle skiers.

🛏 Sleeping

Maison Colombot   GUESTHOUSE €
(☏0165 23 57 23; www.aostacamere.com; Via Torre del Lebbroso 3; s/d €65/92; 🛜) This sweetly old-fashioned place has six rooms with rustic furniture, wood floors and ceilings, and vintage prints on the walls (plus electric kettles with tea). It has a great location a few steps from shop- and restaurant-lined Via Edouard Aubert.

★ Le Rêve Charmant   GUESTHOUSE €€
(☏0165 23 88 55; www.lerevecharmant.com; Via Marché Vaudan 6; d €130-180; 🅿❄🛜) Tucked away in a quiet historic alley, this six-room hotel is full of traditional Aostan furniture and decoration but keeps it simple and rather stylish. A warm, welcoming lounge leads to surprisingly spacious rooms that have beautiful modern bathrooms and high ceilings. The young owners are charming and service is top rate.

Hotel Milleluci   HOTEL €€€
(☏0165 23 52 78; www.hotelmilleluci.com; Loc Porossan 15; d €215-330; 🅿🛜🏊) Old wooden skis, traditionally carved wooden shoes, claw-foot baths, indoor and outdoor pools,

a Jacuzzi, sauna and gym, and sumptuous skiers' breakfasts make this large, family-run converted farmhouse seem more like a luxury resort. Set on a hillside above town, its balconied rooms look out to the eponymous 'thousand lights' twinkling from Aosta below.

🍴 Eating

Bataclan   PIZZA €
(☏393 3026153; www.facebook.com/ristorante bataclan; Piazza Arco D'Augusto 15; pizza €8-14, meals €18-30; ⊘noon-2.30pm & 7pm-midnight) You might be lured here by the pizza (which is good), but you'll stay on for the atmosphere, with convivial staff, happy locals and a wonderful position by the Roman ruins.

Croix de Ville   ITALIAN €
(☏0165 23 07 38; Via Croix de Ville 25; dishes €15-18; ⊘noon-2.30pm & 7-11pm Mon-Wed, Fri & Sat, 10am-10pm Sun; 🛜) Croix de Ville's smart, bustling dining room serves up contemporary Italian favourites such as beef *tagliata* (rare slices) with rocket and Parmesan, and Mediterranean-tinged pastas, dispensing with the strict first- and second-course format. Similarly, the wine list takes it pan-Italian and international, though there's no reason to stray from the beautiful Aostan drops on offer.

Trattoria degli Artisti   TRATTORIA €€
(☏0165 4 09 60; www.trattoriadegliartisti.it; Via Maillet 5-7; meals €25-33; ⊘12.30-2pm & 7.30-10pm Tue-Sat; 🛜) Fabulous Valdostan cuisine is dished up at this dark and cosy trattoria, tucked down an alleyway off Via E Aubert. Antipasti such as puff pastry filled with Valdostan fondue, cured ham and regional salami are followed by dishes such as roe venison with polenta, and beef braised in Morgex et de La Salle white wine.

> ### ℹ ARCHAEOLOGICAL TICKET
> A joint ticket (*biglietto cumulativo*) provides admission to four of Aosta's most important historical sites (adult/child €7/2):
> ➡ Teatro Romano
> ➡ Criptoportico Forense
> ➡ Museo Archeologico Regionale
> ➡ Basilica paleocristiana di San Lorenzo

Aosta

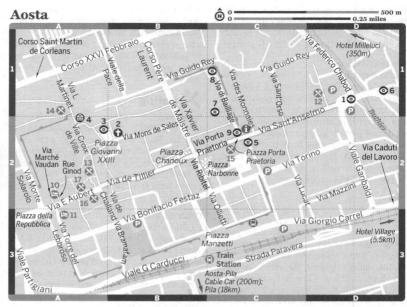

0 _____ 500 m
0 _____ 0.25 miles

Aosta

⊙ Sights
1	Arco di Augusto	D1
2	Cattedrale Santa Maria Assunta	B2
3	Criptoportico Forense	A2
4	Museo Archeologico Regionale	A2
5	Porta Praetoria	C2
6	Roman Bridge	D1
7	Teatro Romano	C1
8	Torre dei Balivi	C1
9	Torre dei Fromage	C2

🛏 Sleeping
10	Le Rêve Charmant	A2
11	Maison Colombot	A3

🍴 Eating
12	Bataclan	D1
13	Croix de Ville	A2
14	Il Vecchio Ristoro	A1
15	L'Osteria 1880	C2
16	Osteria dell'Oca	A2
17	Trattoria degli Artisti	A2

L'Osteria 1880   ALPINE €€
(☑0165 4 01 11; www.facebook.com/losteria1880; Via Porta Pretoria 13; meals €25-35, menu €22; ⊙noon-3pm & 7.30-11pm Tue-Sat, noon-3pm Sun) A hip but friendly spot on the main drag, L'Osteria serves heart-warming Aostian comfort fare: wild boar in pinot noir with rosemary over polenta, creamy rich fondue, and Valpellinentze (a meaty soup with cabbage, pancetta, rye bread and *fontina* cheese). Dine in the easy-going back room, amid globe lights and curious wood carvings.

Osteria dell'Oca   ALPINE €€
(☑0165 23 14 19; www.ristoranteosteriadelloca. com; Via E Aubert 15; meals €25-35, pizza €7-10; ⊙12.30-2.30pm & 7.30-10.30pm Tue-Sun) *Oca*

means 'goose' and there are plenty, both on the menu and reproduced in hilariously kitsch china forms around the room. This quaint perch under an archway off Via E Aubert is Valdostan food heaven: dig into one-plate wonders like veal stew spooned over polenta or sausages covered in *fontina*.

Il Vecchio Ristoro   GASTRONOMY €€€
(☑0165 3 32 38; www.ristorantevecchioristoro.it; Via Tourneuve 4; meals €50, menu degustazione €80; ⊙12.30-2.30pm & 7.30-10.30pm Tue-Sat) Originating from the Valtellina, Alfio Fascendini knows a thing or two about good food and wine. Sample creamy polenta with gorgonzola and egg, boneless rabbit stuffed with chestnuts, or branzino with beets and curry.

ℹ️ Information

Aosta Tourist Office (www.lovevda.it; Piazza Porta Praetoria 3; ⊙9am-7pm; 📞)

ℹ️ Getting There & Away

Buses operated by Savda (www.savda.it) run to Milan's Lampugnano station (€17, 2½ hours, two to four daily), Turin (€12, two hours, three daily) and Courmayeur (€2.90, 50 minutes, up to six daily), as well as to French destinations, including Chamonix. Services leave from Aosta's **bus station** (Via Giorgio Carrel), almost opposite the train station. To get to Breuil-Cervinia, take a Turin-bound bus to Châtillon (€2.50, 35 minutes, eight daily), then a connecting bus (€3.50, one hour, seven daily) to the resort.

Aosta's train station, on Piazza Manzetti, is served by trains from most parts of Italy. All trains to Turin (€9.45, two to 2½ hours, hourly) change at Ivrea.

Aosta is on the A5, which connects Turin with the Mont Blanc tunnel and France. Another exit road north of the city leads to the Great St Bernard tunnel and on to Switzerland.

Courmayeur

📱 0165 / POP 2780 / ELEV 1224M

Flush up against France and linked by a dramatic cable-car ride to its cross-border cousin in Chamonix, Courmayeur is an activity-oriented Aosta village that has grafted upmarket ski facilities onto an ancient Roman bulwark. Its pièce de résistance is lofty Mont Blanc, Western Europe's highest mountain – 4810m of solid rock and ice that rises like an impregnable wall above the narrow valleys of northwestern Italy, igniting awe in all who pass.

In winter Courmayeur is a fashion parade of skiers bound for the high slopes above town that glisten with plenty of late-season snow. In summer it wears a distinctly different hat: the Società delle Guide Alpine di Courmayeur is bivouacked here and the town is an important staging post on three iconic long-distance hiking trails: the Tour du Mont Blanc (TMB), Alta Via 1 and Alta Via 2.

👁️ Sights

Pavillon du Mt Fréty
Nature Oasis   NATURE RESERVE
A protected zone of 1200 hectares tucked between glaciers, this nature oasis is accessible from the Pavillon du Mt Fréty. Enjoy numerous trails, including the Sentiero Francesco e Giuditta Gatti.

Giardino Botanico
Alpino Saussurea   GARDENS
(www.saussurea.it; admission €3, with cable-car ticket in high summer free; ⊙9am-5pm late Jun-late Sep) Walk through this flower-filled Alpine garden in summer (it's blanketed by snow in winter) and enjoy numerous other trails, including the Sentiero Francesco e Giuditta Gatti, where you have a good chance of spotting ibexes, marmots and deer.

🏃 Activities

Courmayeur is heaven for outdoorsy types, with both summer and winter activities at your doorstep.

⭐ **Funivie Monte Bianco**   CABLE CAR
(Skyway; www.montebianco.com; Strada Statale 26; return €52, Pavillon du Mt Fréty return €28;

(side margin) TURIN, PIEDMONT & CINQUE TERRE COURMAYEUR

WORTH A TRIP

FORTE DI BARD

When a diversion from skiing or hiking beckons, plan a great day out at Forte di Bard (www.fortedibard.it; Bard; fort entrance free, museums €5-10, cumulative ticket €15; ⊙10am-6pm Tue-Fri, to 7pm Sat & Sun), around 70 minutes from Aosta by bus.

A fort has existed here for millennia and the current 1830s Savoy edifice is an imposing one, set high up upon a rocky escarpment at the jaws of the Valle d'Aosta. Ride up a series of supermodern panoramic lifts, where you can admire the inspiring Alpine views and visit the Vallée Culture rooms, which offer interesting nuggets of information on Aosta's history and traditions.

The Museo delle Alpi, a clever, interactive museum, takes you on a journey across the entire Alps – children love the Flight of the Eagle, a cinematic simulation of a bird's flight over valleys, villages, lakes and snow-capped peaks. The Museo Ferdinando details the region's military history. The fort's prisons, which were still in use right up until the end of WWII, can also be visited (adult/reduced €5/4), and there's an excellent program of big-ticket 20th-century art and photography shows in another space.

8.30am-4pm) The Mont Blanc cable car might not be the world's highest, but it's surely the most spectacular. This astounding piece of engineering reaches three-quarters of the way up Western Europe's highest mountain before heading across multiple glaciers into France. New stations, with glass surfaces and futuristic cantilevers, opened in summer 2015, along with state-of-the-art 360-degree rotating cabins. It departs every 20 minutes from the village of La Palud, 15 minutes from Courmayeur's main square by a free bus.

First stop is the 2173m-high midstation Pavillon du Mt Fréty, while at the top of the ridge is Punta Helbronner (3462m). All three stations have restaurants and other facilities; there's a sparkling wine cellar and, in summer, the Giardino Botanico Alpino Saussurea (p251) and a crystal display at Helbronner. Take ample warm clothes and sunglasses for the blinding snow, and head up early in the morning to avoid the heavy weather that often descends in the early afternoon.

From Punta Helbronner another cable car (from late May to late September, depending on weather conditions, €35) takes you on a breathtaking 5km transglacial ride across the Italian border into France to the Aiguille du Midi (3842m), from where the world's highest cable car transports you down to Chamonix (€80). The return trip from Chamonix to Courmayeur by bus is €15 (45 minutes). Not a cheap day out, but a spectacular one.

Società delle Guide Alpine di Courmayeur   OUTDOORS

(📞 0165 84 20 64; www.guidecourmayeur.com; Strada del Villair 2; ⊙ 8.30am-1pm & 4-7pm Tue-Sun, 4-7pm Mon) Founded in 1859, this is Italy's oldest guiding association. In winter, guides lead adventure seekers off-piste, up frozen waterfalls and on heli-skiing expeditions. In summer, rock climbing, canyoning, canoeing, kayaking and hiking are among its many outdoor activities.

Skiing

Courmayeur offers some extraordinary skiing in the spectacular shadow of Mont Blanc. The two main ski areas – the Plan Chécrouit and Pré de Pascal – are interlinked by various runs (100km worth) and a network of chairlifts. Three lifts leave from the valley floor: one from Courmayeur itself, one from the village of Dolonne and one from nearby

Val Veny. They are run by Funivie Courmayeur Mont Blanc (www.courmayeur-montblanc. com; Strada Regionale 47). Daily ski passes (€59) give you access to Courmayeur and Mont Blanc, three-day passes and above include all of Aosta's resorts (three-/seven-day pass €137/282). Queues are rarely an issue.

Vallée Blanche   SKIING

This is an exhilarating off-piste descent from Punta Helbronner across the Mer de Glace glacier into Chamonix, France. The route itself is not difficult – anyone of intermediate ability can do it – but an experienced guide is essential to steer you safely round the hidden crevasses. The Società delle Guide Alpine di Courmayeur has top-notch guides.

All up, the 24km Vallée Blanche takes around four to five hours, allowing time to stop and take in the view.

Toula Glacier   SKIING

Only highly experienced, hard-core skiers need apply for this terrifying descent, which also takes off from Punta Helbronner and drops for six sheer kilometres to La Palud. A guide is essential; it's usually easy to join a group.

Walking

Tour du Mont Blanc   WALKING

For many walkers (some 30,000 each summer), Courmayeur's trophy hike is the Tour du Mont Blanc (TMB). This 169km trek cuts across Italy, France and Switzerland, stopping at nine villages en route. Snow makes it impassable for much of the year. The average duration is anything from one week to 12 days; smaller sections are also possible.

You can undertake the hike solo, but if you're unfamiliar with the area, hooking up with a local guide is a good idea as the route traverses glacial landscapes. The Società delle Guide Alpine di Courmayeur is a great place to arrange a trek. Easy day hikes will take you along the TMB as far as the Rifugio Maison Vieille (6.6km, one hour and 50 minutes) and Rifugio Bertone (4.5km, two hours). Follow the yellow signposts from Piazzale Monte Bianco in the centre of Courmayeur.

Swimming

Plan Chécrouit Swimming Pool   SWIMMING

(half-day/day lift & pool €18/25; ⊙ 10.30am-5pm mid-Jul–Aug) Yes, there is a highest heated swimming pool in Europe and, at 1700m, this is it. Take the Dolonne cable car for a dip with a view and a laze among lush green surrounds, or hike up from Courmayeur in around an hour.

🛏 Sleeping

There are plenty of hotels in the village but they book out quickly. Ask the tourist office for a list of *rifugi* (mountain huts), usually open from late June to mid-September.

Auberge de la Maison   CHALET €€
(📞 0165 86 98 11; www.aubergemaison.it; Via Passerin d'Entrèves 16, Entrèves; d €180-360; P 🛜) Overlooking the Courmayeur valley, this *auberge* (inn) is located in the village of Entrèves. Crackling fires welcome you into warmly traditional Alpine rooms, where majolica stoves and wooden beds await.

Hotel Bouton d'Or   HOTEL €€
(📞 0165 84 67 29; www.hotelboutondor.com; Strada Statale 26/10; s/d €110/180; P ✳ @ 🛜) Charmingly folksy Bouton d'Or is in the centre of Courmayeur and not only has incredible views of the imposing hulk of Mont Blanc, but also a sauna, a lounge full of interesting Alpine paraphernalia and, in summer, a peaceful garden.

★ Grand Hotel Courmayeur Mont Blanc   SPA HOTEL €€€
(📞 0165 84 45 42; www.grandhotelcourmayeur montblanc.it; Strada Grand Ru 1; d €220-370, ste €460-820; P ✳ 🛜 ≋) This 72-bed luxury place hits all the right notes, with exquisitely comforting yet Alpine-sleek rooms with soft wool blankets, light wood and dark furniture. There's everything you need here, from a spa and pool, to restaurants and après-ski, and of course Alpine views. But you're also close to the lifts and the town's happy bustle.

🍴 Eating & Drinking

Bars, cafes and restaurants line Via Roma.

La Terraza   INTERNATIONAL €€
(📞 0165 84 33 30; www.ristorantelaterrazza.com; Via Circonvallazione 73; meals €40-50; ⊙ noon-2.30pm & 7-10.30pm) This attractive, lively, central bar-restaurant-pizzeria has an array of Valdostan dishes and local specialities – including polenta with *fontina* and hazelnut butter, trout with Aostan-white-wine sauce, and onion soup baked in a crispy bread crust – plus daily chalkboard specials. The free shot of limoncello makes a nice finish.

La Chaumière   ITALIAN €€
(📞 392 9585987; www.lachaumiere.it; Località Planchecrouit 15; meals €30-45; ⊙ 9am-5pm)

THERMAL SPA TIME

Bubbling up a natural 37°C from the mountains' depths, the thermal water at Pré-Saint-Didier, a 10-minute drive south of Courmayeur, has been a source of therapeutic treatments since the bath-loving Romans marched into the valley. A spa opened here in 1838, with the newest addition, **Terme di Pré-Saint-Didier** (📞 0165 86 72 72; www.qcterme.com; Allée des Thermes; admission €44-54; ⊙ 9.30am-9pm Mon-Thu, 8.30am-11pm Fri & Sat, 8am-9pm Sun), dating to the 1920s. Go online to reserve a time and date in advance.

Set on the slopes above Courmayeur, within walking distance of the cable car, is the fabulous sun-kissed terrace of La Chaumière. Views straight down the Aosta valley are accompanied by superlative polenta and 38 carefully sourced wines.

La Bouche   BAR
(www.facebook.com/LaBouchedeCourmayeur; Via Regionale 12; ⊙ 5pm-2am Tue-Sun) A short walk south of Via Roma, La Bouche creates Courmayeur's most imaginative cocktails. Nattily attired bartenders in leather aprons are more like alchemists, using tiny blow torches to fire up smoked negronis and other elixirs. It's a small but festive space, with outdoor sipping on warm nights, and the odd rockabilly band playing on weekends.

ℹ Information

Tourist Office (📞 0165 84 20 60; www. lovevda.it; Piazzale Monte Bianco 15; ⊙ 9am-1pm & 2.30-6.30pm)

ℹ Getting There & Away

Three trains a day from Aosta terminate at Pré-Saint-Didier, with bus connections (20 to 30 minutes, eight to 10 daily) to **Courmayeur bus station** (Piazzale Monte Bianco), outside the tourist office. There are up to eight direct Aosta–Courmayeur buses daily (€2.90, 50 minutes), and long-haul buses serve Milan (€19.50, four hours, three to five daily) and Turin (€15.50, 3½ hours, two to four daily).

Immediately north of Courmayeur, the 11.6km Mont Blanc Tunnel leads to Chamonix in France (one way/return €46.40/57.90). At the Italian entrance, a plaque commemorates Pierlucio Tinazzi, a security employee who died while saving at least a dozen lives during the 1999 disaster when a freight truck caught fire in the tunnel.

Parco Nazionale del Gran Paradiso

☎0165

Italy's oldest national park, the Gran Paradiso, was created in 1922 after Vittorio Emanuele II gave his hunting reserve to the state, ostensibly to protect the endangered ibex. The park preceded the rise of the modern ski resort and has so far resisted the lucrative mass tourist trade. Its tangible wilderness feel is rare in Italy.

Gran Paradiso incorporates the valleys around the eponymous 4061m peak (Italy's seventh highest), three of which are in the Valle d'Aosta: the Valsavarenche, Val di Rhêmes and the beautiful Valle di Cogne. On the Piedmont side of the mountain, the park includes the valleys of Soana and Orco.

The main stepping stone into the park is tranquil **Cogne** (population 1500, elevation 1534m), a refreshing antidote to overdeveloped Breuil-Cervinia on the opposite side of the Valle d'Aosta. Aside from its plethora of outdoor opportunities, Cogne is known for its lace-making, and you can buy local products at several craft and antique shops.

Sights & Activities

Gran Paradiso is one of Italy's best walking areas, with over 700km of trails linked by a recuperative network of *rifugi* (mountain huts). The tourist office has free winter and summer trail maps for walkers and skiers.

Giardino Alpino Paradisia GARDENS
(☎0165 7 53 01; www.pngp.it; Frazione Valnontey 44, Cogne; adult/reduced €3/1.50; ⏲10am-5.30pm Jun & early Sep, to 6.30pm Jul & Aug) The park's amazing biodiversity, including butterflies and Alpine flora, can be seen in summer at this fascinating Alpine botanical garden in the tiny hamlet of Valnontey (1700m), 3km south of Cogne. Guided nature walks are available from July to September.

Associazione Guide della Natura WALKING
(☎0165 7 48 35; www.cogneturismo.it; Rue Bourgeois 33, Cogne; ⏲9am-noon Mon, Wed & Sat) Guided nature walks from July to September are organised by the Associazione Guide della Natura.

Le Traîneau Equestrian Tourism Centre HORSE RIDING
(☎333 3147248; Frazione Valnontey; ⏲10am-12.30pm & 2-7pm) This group in Valnontey organises horse riding and 45-minute horse-and-carriage rides through the mountain meadows.

Sleeping & Eating

There are a number of good hotels in Cogne. Wilderness camping is forbidden in the park, but there are 11 *rifugi* (mountain huts) and a decent campground. The tourist office has a list.

Hotel Ristorante Petit Dahu GUESTHOUSE €
(☎393 8285300; www.hotelpetitdahu.com; Frazone Valnontey 27; d from €110; P 📶) Straddling two traditional stone-and-wood buildings, this friendly, family-run spot has cosy, all-wood rooms in a peaceful location a short stroll from the Cogne village centre. There's a wonderful restaurant (open only to guests) that features rustic mountain cooking using wild Alpine herbs.

Locanda Grauson HOTEL €
(☎0165 7 40 01; www.hotelgrauson.it; Frazione Gimillan 126; s/d from €54/90; 📶) Set in the village of Gimillan, overlooking Cogne and the towering peaks beyond, the friendly Locanda Grauson has a range of pine-panelled rooms with simple furnishings and floral accents. The best have balconies with staggering views.

★ **Hotel Bellevue** HERITAGE HOTEL €€€
(☎0165 7 48 25; www.hotelbellevue.it; Rue Grand Paradis 22; d €240-330, 2-person chalet €360; ⏲mid-Dec–mid-Oct; P 🏊) Overlooking meadows, this green-shuttered mountain hideaway evokes its 1920s origins with romantic canopied timber 'cabin beds', weighty cowbells strung from old beams, claw-foot baths and the occasional open fire (it's definitely not for minimalists). Afternoon tea is included in the price, as is use of the health spa, and you can also rent mountain bikes and snowshoes.

Its four restaurants include a Michelin-starred gourmet affair, a wonderful cheese restaurant (goat raclette!) with produce from the family's own cellar, a lunchtime terrace restaurant and a dark, historic brasserie on the village's main square, a few moments' stroll away.

★ **La Brasserie de Bon Bec** ALPINE €€

(☑ 0165 74 92 88; Rue Bourgeois 72, Cogne; meals €28-38; ☺ noon-2.30pm & 7-10pm Tue-Sun) In a warmly lit dining room adorned with old farm tools and glossy oil paintings, Bon Bec serves up outstanding mountain cuisine. Start off with house-smoked trout (sourced from nearby Lillaz) or classic Valdostan polenta, before moving on to grilled Angus beef or rich *tartiflette* (a dish from the Savoy made with potatoes, reblochon cheese, onions and lardons).

ℹ Information

Tourist Office (☑ 0165 7 40 40; www.cogne turismo.it; Rue Bourgeois 34, Cogne; ☺ 9am-1pm & 3-6pm Sep-Jun, 9am-1pm & 3-7pm Jul & Aug)

ℹ Getting There & Around

Up to 10 buses run daily between Cogne and Aosta (€2.90, 50 minutes). Cogne can also be reached by cable car from Pila.

Free valley buses run up to 10 times daily, and link Cogne with Valnontey (five minutes), Lillaz (five minutes) and Gimilllan (10 minutes). Pick up a schedule at the tourist office.

Valtournenche

☑ 0166

One of Europe's most dramatic – and deadly – mountains, the Matterhorn (4478m) frames the head of Valtournenche. Byron once stood here and marvelled at 'Europe's noble rock'. Today he'd also get an eyeful of one of the Alps' most architecturally incongruous ski resorts, Breuil-Cervinia (www.cervinia.it). Ugly or not, Cervinia's ski facilities are second to none; you can hit the snow year-round up here and even swish across to Zermatt in Switzerland.

Plateau Rosa (3480m) and the Little Matterhorn (3883m) in the Breuil-Cervinia ski area offer some of Europe's highest skiing, while the Campetto area has introduced the Valle d'Aosta to night skiing. A couple of dozen cable cars, four of which originate in Breuil-Cervinia, serve 200km of downhill pistes. Ski passes covering Breuil-Cervinia and Valtournenche cost €46/129/265 for one/three/seven days.

Contact Breuil-Cervinia's Scuola di Sci del Breuil Cervinia (www.scuolascibreuil. com) or Scuola Sci del Cervino (www.scuola cervino.com) for skiing and snowboarding lessons, and its mountain-guide association Società Guide del Cervino (www.guide delcervino.com; Via J Antoine Carrel 20) to make the most of the Matterhorn's wild off-piste opportunities.

Between July and September several cable cars and lifts to Plateau Rosa continue to operate, allowing year-round skiing on the Swiss side of the mountain. A one-day international ski pass costs €59.

ℹ Getting There & Away

Savda (www.savda.it) operates buses from Breuil-Cervinia to Châtillon (€3.50, one hour, seven daily), from where there are connecting buses to/from Aosta.

TURIN, PIEDMONT & CINQUE TERRE VALTOURNENCHE

AT A GLANCE

POPULATION
10.03 million

GDP PER CAPITA
€38,860

BEST PASTRIES
Pasticceria
Marchesi (p273)

**BEST INTERIOR
DESIGN**
Villa Necchi
Campiglio (p266)

BEST GARDEN
Villa Balbianello
(p297)

WHEN TO GO
Apr–Jun The Salone
furniture fair and
fashion weeks make
Milan busy. Full boat
services start on the
lakes.

Jul–Aug Cities are
hot and humid, so
everyone heads to
the lakes and
mountains for hiking
and boating.

Dec Opera season
starts in Milan,
followed by
Christmas fairs.

Galleria Vittorio Emanuele II (p261), Milan
©LAVSH12/SHUTTERSTOCK

Milan &
the Lakes

Wedged between the Alps and the Po valley, the glacial lakes of Lombardy (Lombardia) have been a popular holiday spot since Roman times. At its heart is Milan, Italy's second-largest metropolis. Home to the nation's stock exchange, one of Europe's biggest trade-fair grounds and an international fashion hub, it's also Italy's economic powerhouse.

Beyond Milan pretty countryside unfolds, dotted with patrician towns including Pavia, Monza, Bergamo, Cremona and Mantua; all are steeped in history, hiding fabulous monuments and world-class museums. To the north a burst of Mediterranean colour awaits around lakes Orta, Maggiore, Como, Garda and Iseo. Ringed by hot-pink oleanders in luxurious tiered gardens, the lakes are powerfully seductive. No wonder European aristocrats, Arab princes and Hollywood celebrities choose to call this home.

Milan & the Lakes Highlights

1 **The Last Supper** (p268) Pondering the power of Leonardo da Vinci's ageless painting.

2 **Il Duomo** (p262) Climbing Milan's marble cathedral for views of spires and flying buttresses.

3 **Museo del Novecento** (p260) Discovering the modernists who shaped Milan.

4 **Museo Nazionale Scienza e Tecnologia Leonardo da Vinci** (p269) Exploring past and present inventions in Italy's best Science Museum.

5 **Accademia Carrara** (p309) Coming face to face with hundreds of Old Masters in Bergamo's academy.

6 **Isola Bella** (p853) Strolling in Lago Maggiore's most spectacular island garden.

7 **Lago di Como** (p291) Touring this famous lake James Bond–style, in your own cigarette boat.

8 **Riva del Garda** (p305) Sailing, surfing and kayaking beneath the snow-capped peaks.

9 **Palazzo Ducale** (p314) Marvelling at Mantua's marvellous Renaissance frescoes.

10 **Orta San Giulio** (p290) Discovering lake-side bliss in this enchanting lakeside town.

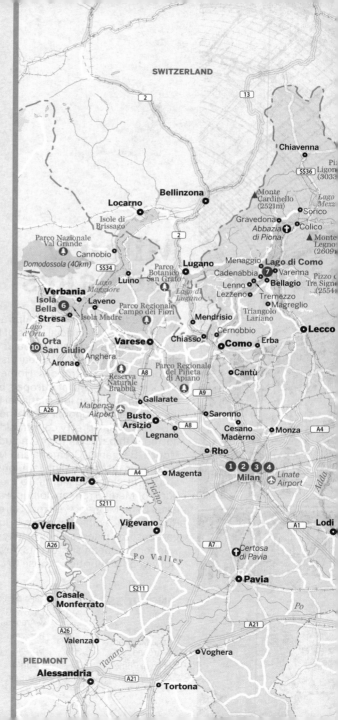

MILAN

Milan is Italy's city of the future, a fast-paced metropolis with New World qualities: ambition, aspiration and a highly individualistic streak. In Milan appearances really do matter and materialism requires no apology. The Milanese love beautiful things, luxurious things, and it is for that reason perhaps that Italian fashion and design maintain their esteemed global position.

But like the models that work the catwalks, Milan is considered by many to be vain, distant and dull. However, this superficial lack of charm disguises a city of ancient roots and many treasures, which, unlike in the rest of Italy, you'll often get to experience without the queues. So while the Milanese may not always play nice, jump in and join them regardless in their intoxicating round of pursuits, whether that means precision-shopping, browsing edgy contemporary galleries or loading up a plate with local delicacies while downing an expertly mixed negroni.

History

From its founding as a Celtic settlement, Milan (or Mediolanum – 'middle of the plain') was always an important crossroads. It was here that Christianity was declared the official religion of the Roman Empire in AD 313. As a powerful medieval city-state, Milan expanded its influence by conquest under a series of colourful (and often bloody) dynasties – the Torrianis, the Viscontis and finally the Sforzas. However, under Spanish rule from 1525 and then the Austrians from 1713, Milan lost some of its brio. In 1860, it joined the nascent united Kingdom of Italy.

Benito Mussolini founded the Fascist Party in Milan in 1919 and his lifeless body was strung up in the same city, in Piazzale Loreto, by the partisans who had summarily executed him towards the end of WWII in 1945. Allied bombings during WWII destroyed much of central Milan. Treasures that survived include the Duomo, Leonardo da Vinci's *Last Supper* (just), the Castello Sforzesco and the Teatro alla Scala opera house. Milan was quick to get back on its feet after the war and what still sets it apart today is its creative streak and can-do attitude.

At the vanguard of two 20th-century economic booms, Milan cemented its role as Italy's financial and industrial capital. Immigrants poured in from the country's south and were later joined by others from China, Africa, Latin America, India and Eastern Europe, making for one of the least homogeneous cities in Italy. Culturally, the city was the centre of early Italian film production, and in the 1980s and '90s it ruled the world as the capital of design innovation and production. Milan's self-made big shot and media mogul Silvio Berlusconi made the move into politics in the 1990s and was then elected prime minister three times – scandal and financial Armageddon finally forced him from office in 2011.

Since that nadir, leading up to the Expo2015 World Fair and beyond, Milan has undergone a series of sweeping redevelopments. New districts such as Porta Nuova and CityLife have been constructed, breathing life into unused areas; the enormous exhibition centre now has an even bigger new home at Rho; museums have been modernised; the city's infrastructure has been improved; and the old dock area has been rehabilitated. The mood in the city is buoyant, and for now, the Milanese are quietly pleased with the forward-looking, confident, modern city that is emerging.

◉ Sights

◉ Duomo & San Babila

★ **Museo del Novecento**   GALLERY
(Map p270; ☑02 8844 4061; www.museodelnovecento.org; Piazza del Duomo 8; adult/reduced €5/3; ⊙2.30-7.30pm Mon, from 9.30am Tue, Wed, Fri & Sun, to 10.30pm Thu & Sat; Ⓜ Duomo) Overlooking Piazza del Duomo, with fabulous views of the cathedral (p262), is Mussolini's Arengario, from where he would harangue huge crowds in his heyday. Now it houses Milan's museum of 20th-century art. Built around a futuristic spiral ramp (an ode to the Guggenheim), the collection includes the likes of Boccioni, Campigli, Giorgio de Chirico and Marinetti.

Ascend the spiral ramp and begin your exploration of chronologically arranged rooms, which take you from Volpedo's powerful neo-impressionist painting of striking workers, *Il quarto stato,* through to the dynamic work of futurist greats such as Umberto Boccioni, Carlo Carra, Gino Severini and Giacomo Balla. The collection then continues on to the Italian Novecento, abstractionism and Arte Povera, before finishing up with kinetic art, pop art and large-scale installations. Aside from the general coherence of the collection, it provides a fascinating social commentary on Italy's trajectory through fascism, two world wars and into the new dawn of the technological era.

Other than the exceptional collection, the museum also houses Giacomo Arengario (☑02 7209 3814; www.giacomoarengario.com; Via Guglielmo Marconi 1; meals €60-75; ☺noon-midnight; ❖), a top-notch bistro located on the 3rd floor, from where you can enjoy excellent views of the Duomo.

Gallerie d'Italia   MUSEUM
(Map p270; www.gallerieditalia.com; Piazza della Scala 6; adult/reduced €10/7; ☺9.30am-7.30pm Tue-Wed & Fri-Sun, to 10.30pm Thu; M Duomo) This fabulously decorated *palazzo* (mansion) is home to part of the enormous collection of Fondazione Cariplo and Intesa Sanpaolo bank, which pays homage to 18th- and 19th-century Lombard painting. From a magnificent sequence of bas-reliefs by Antonio Canova to luminous Romantic masterpieces by Francesco Hayez, the works span 23 rooms and document Milan's significant contribution to the rebirth of Italian sculpture, the patriotic romanticism of the Risorgimento (reunification period) and the birth of futurism at the dawn of the 20th century.

Biblioteca e Pinacoteca Ambrosiana   GALLERY
(Map p270; ☑02 80 69 21; www.ambrosiana.it; Piazza Pio XI 2; adult/reduced €15/10; ☺10am-6pm Tue-Sun; M Duomo) One of Europe's earliest public libraries (built 1609), the Biblioteca Ambrosiana was more a symbol of intellectual ferment than of quiet scholarship. It houses more than a million volumes and nearly 40,000 manuscripts, including Leonardo da Vinci's priceless collection of drawings, the *Codex Atlanticus*. An art gallery – the Pinacoteca – was added later. It exhibits Italian paintings from the 14th to the 20th century and famously features Caravaggio's *Canestra di frutta* (Basket of Fruit), which launched both his career and Italy's ultrarealist traditions.

Galleria Vittorio Emanuele II   HISTORIC BUILDING
(Map p270; Piazza del Duomo; M Duomo) So much more than a shopping arcade, the neoclassical Galleria Vittorio Emanuele II is a soaring structure of iron and glass. Nicknamed *'il salotto di Milano'*, the city's drawing room, it's been at the centre of city life since 1877. Its known for its high-end boutiques (the original Prada store is located here) and equally lofty dining. While it's packed by day, a stroll during the late evening gives you a chance to experience its beauty without distraction.

Palazzo Reale   MUSEUM
(Map p270; ☑02 8844 5181; www.palazzoreale milano.it; Piazza del Duomo 12; admission varies; ☺2.30-7.30pm Mon, from 9.30am Tue, Wed, Fri & Sun, to 10.30pm Thu & Sat; M Duomo) Empress Maria Theresa's favourite architect, Giuseppe Piermarini, gave this town hall and Visconti palace a neoclassical overhaul in the late 18th century. The supremely elegant interiors were all but destroyed by WWII bombs; the Sala delle Cariatidi remains unrenovated as a reminder of war's indiscriminate destruction. Now the once opulent palace hosts blockbuster art exhibits, attracting serious crowds to shows featuring artists as diverse as Escher, Caravaggio and Arnaldo Pomodoro.

⊙ Brera & Parco Sempione

★ **Pinacoteca di Brera**   GALLERY
(Map p270; ☑02 7226 3264; www.pinacoteca brera.org; Via Brera 28; adult/reduced €12/8; ☺8.30am-7.15pm Tue-Sun; M Lanza, Montenapoleone) Located upstairs from one of Italy's most prestigious art schools, this gallery houses Milan's collection of Old Masters, much of it 'lifted' from Venice by Napoleon. Rubens, Goya and Van Dyck all have a place, but you're here for the Italians: Titian, Tintoretto, Veronese and the Bellini brothers. Much of the work has tremendous emotional clout, most notably Mantegna's brutal *Lamentation over the Dead Christ*.

Audio guides are available in Italian, French, English, Spanish, German and Russian (€5). Highlights include the glass-walled restoration laboratory, where you can see conservators at work. Additionally, every third Thursday atmospheric musical concerts are held amid the artworks, and entrance to the museum is just €3. There's also an elegant bar/cafe for light snacks or cocktails.

Much anticipated is the opening of the beautifully restored 18th-century Palazzo Citterio, now scheduled for 2022 after suffering structural and bureaucratic setbacks. It will provide a new 6500-sq-metre home to Brera's modernist collection, as well as showcasing exciting temporary exhibitions in James Stirling's austere concrete bunker beneath the palace's frescoed halls.

★ **Castello Sforzesco**   CASTLE
(Map p270; ☑02 8846 3703; www.milano castello.it; Piazza Castello; adult/reduced €5/3; ☺9am-5.30pm Tue-Sun; M Cairoli) Originally a Visconti fortress, this iconic red-brick castle

Continued on p266

MILAN & THE LAKES MILAN

TOP SIGHT
DUOMO

A vision in pink Candoglia marble, this cathedral embodies Milan's verve and ambition. Begun by Giangaleazzo Visconti in 1387, its design was originally considered unfeasible. Canals were dug to transport the vast quantities of marble to the city centre, and new technologies were invented to cater for the never-before-attempted scale. Now its pearly white facade and extravagant details are the city's crown attraction.

The Exterior & Roof Terraces

During his stint as king of Italy, Napoleon offered to fund the Duomo's completion in 1805, in time for his coronation. The architect piled on the neo-Gothic details, a homage to the original design that displayed a prescient use of fashion logic – ie everything old is new again. The petrified pinnacles, cusps, buttresses, arches and more than 3000 statues are almost all products of the 19th century. Climb to the roof terraces where you'll be within touching distance of the elaborate 135 spires and their forest of flying buttresses. In the centre rises the 15th-century spire, on top of which is the golden Madonnina (erected in 1774). She was the highest point in the city (108.5m) until the Pirelli skyscraper outdid her in 1958.

The Interior

Initially designed to accommodate Milan's then population of around 40,000, the cathedral's sublimely spiritual architecture can transport 21st-century types back to a medieval mindset. Once your eyes have adjusted to the surreal proportions inside (there are five grandiose naves supported by 52 columns), stare up to the enormous stained-glass windows, with 144 panes illuminating stories from the Bible.

TOP TIPS

➡ Hours for the crypt, baptistry and roof vary, so check the website for details.

➡ Ascend to the roof via the 251 steps rather than the elevator, which attracts a long queue.

PRACTICALITIES

➡ Map p270

➡ ☎ 02 7202 3375

➡ www.duomomilano.it

➡ Piazza del Duomo

➡ adult/reduced Duomo €3/2, roof terraces via stairs €10/5, lift €14/7, archaeological area €7/3 (incl Duomo)

➡ ⏲ Duomo 8am-7pm, roof terraces 9am-7pm, archaeological area 9am-7pm

➡ Ⓜ Duomo

Then look down and marvel at the polychrome marble floor that sweeps across 12,000 sq metres. The design was conceived by Pellegrino Tibaldi and took 400 years to complete. The pink and white blocks of Candoglia marble came from the cathedral's own quarries at Mergozzo, and are inlaid with black marble from Varenna and red marble from Arzo.

Artworks

Bisecting the nave, the transept is especially rich in works of art. At either end there are marble altars, the most elaborate being the *Altar to the Virgin of the Tree* on the north side. Although this area is now restricted to mass-goers, you can still admire from a distance the 5m-high Trivulzio candelabrum. A masterpiece of medieval bronze work. Also located here is the cathedral's most unusual statue, the 1562 figure of St Bartholomew by Marco d'Agrate, a student of Leonardo da Vinci. It depicts St Bartholomew post-torture with his skin flayed from his flesh and cast about his neck like a cape. This Christian martyr was a favourite subject for 16th-century sculptors, enabling them to show off their anatomical knowledge as well as their technique.

The Crypt

From the ambulatory that encircles the choir are the stairs down to the crypt or Winter Choir. Designed by Tibaldi, this jewel-like chapel with its red porphyry pillars, polychrome marble floor and stucco ceiling contains a casket holding the relics of various saints and martyrs. A wooden choir stall encircles the room. On the opposite side of the crypt is the memorial chapel housing the remains of saintly Carlo Borromeo (cardinal archbishop of Milan; 1564–84), contained in a rock-crystal casket atop a silver altar.

Sundial

On the floor by the main entrance you may notice a brass strip lined with signs of the zodiac. This is, in fact, an 18th-century sundial, installed by astronomers from the Accademia di Brera in 1783. A hole in the vault of the south aisle casts a ray of sunlight at various points along its length (depending on the season) at astronomical noon. All the city's clocks were set by it up until the 19th century.

Il Grande Museo del Duomo

In the Duomo's museum (Piazza del Duomo 12; adult/reduced €3/1; ☉10am-6pm Thu-Tue) gargoyles leer down through the shadows; shafts of light strike the wings of heraldic angels; and a monstrous godhead, once intended for the high altar, glitters awesomely in copper. Arranged through 26 rooms, it tells the 600-year story of the cathedral's construction through sculptures, paintings, stained glass, tapestries and bejewelled treasures.

VENERANDA FABBRICA DEL DUOMO

The epic building of Milan's cathedral necessitated the creation of a 'factory' for all operational activities and maintenance. The Fabbrica del Duomo oversaw construction from 1387 until the last gate was inaugurated in 1965. Today it continues the work of restoring and maintaining the cathedral. It's possible to visit the Fabbrica's marble quarries near Lago di Mergozzo.

MILAN & THE LAKES DUOMO

The Fast Track ticket lets you join shorter queues with priority entrance to the cathedral and roof.

The Duomo **ticket office** (☑02 7202 3375; www.duomomilano.it; Piazza del Duomo 14a; ☉9am-6pm May-Oct, 9.30am-4.30pm Mon-Fri, 9am-5pm Sat & Sun Nov-Apr; Ⓜ Duomo) opens at 9.30am. While queues are unavoidable unless you come early, they move fairly fast if you opt for the self-service machines. We recommend purchasing the combined Duomo ticket, which gives you access to the whole complex, allowing you to visit over three days.

Milan

MILAN & THE LAKES MILAN

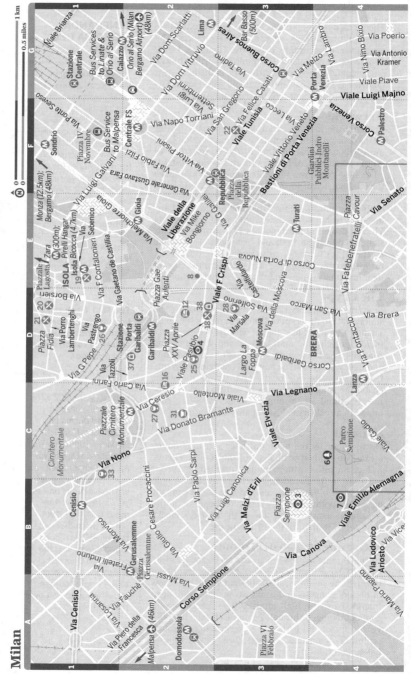

0 — 1 km
0 — 0.5 miles

Via Cenisio

Via Piero della Francesca

Via Losanna

Domodossola

Via Fauché

Malpensa (46km)

Piazza VI Febbraio

Corso Sempione

Via Mussi

Via Giulio Cesare Procaccini

Via Paolo Sarpi

Via Luigi Canonica

Piazza Sempione

Via Canova

Via Melzi d'Eril

Via Mario Pagano

Via Lodovico Ariosto

Via Vice

Viale Emilio Alemagna

Parco Sempione

Viale Gadio

Via Pontaccio

Via Brera

Via Fatebenefratelli

Piazza Fratelli Cavour

Via Senato

Via G Pepe

Via Carlo Farini

Piazzale Cimitero Monumentale

Cimitero Monumentale

Cenisio

Via Nono

Via Donato Bramante

Viale Elvezia

Via Legnano

Viale Montello

Corso Garibaldi

BRERA

Lanza

Via della Moscova

Via San Marco

Corso di Porta Nuova

Via Castelfidardo

Via Moscova

Largo La Foppa

Via Marsala

Via Solferino

Piazza Gae Aulenti

Viale Pasubio

Piazza XXV Aprile

Stazione Porta Garibaldi

Via Pastengo

Via Lambertenghi

Via Porro

Piazza Fidia

Via Borsieri

Via F Confalonieri

ISOLA

Piazzale Lagosta

Via Zara

Via Sebenico

Via Gaetano de Castillia

Piazzale Lagosta

Via Melchiorre Gioia

Via Gioia

Viale della Liberazione

Via Mike Bongiorno

Piazza della Repubblica

Repubblica

Bastioni di Porta Venezia

Giardini Pubblici Indro Montanelli

Corso Venezia

Porta Venezia

Viale Luigi Majno

Viale Vittorio Veneto

Viale Tunisia

Via Tadino

Corso Buenos Aires

Bar Basso (500m)

Via Melzo

Via Lambro

Via Poerio

Via Antonio Kramer

Viale Piave

Palestro

Via Nino Bixio

Via Lecco

Via Felice Casati

Via San Gregorio

Via Napo Torriani

Via Luigi Settembrini

Via Vittor Pisani

Via Fabio Filzi

Via Generale Gustavo Fara

Via Fabio Filzi

Piazza IV Novembre

Via Galilei

Viale F Crispi

Viale della Liberazione

Stazione Centrale

Bus Services to Linate & Orio al Serio

Orio al Serio (Milan) Bergamo Airport (48km)

Calazzo

Centrale FS

Bus Service to Malpensa

Sondrio

Via Ponte Seveso

Via Brianza

Viale Brianza

Via Dom Scarlatti

Via Dom Vitruvio

Lima

Via G Galilei

Turati

Monza (12.5km); Bergamo (48km)

Pirelli Hangar Bicocca (4.7km)

Pirelli (300m)

22

8

12

38

28

18

4

25

16

37

26

21

20

27

31

33

7

6

3

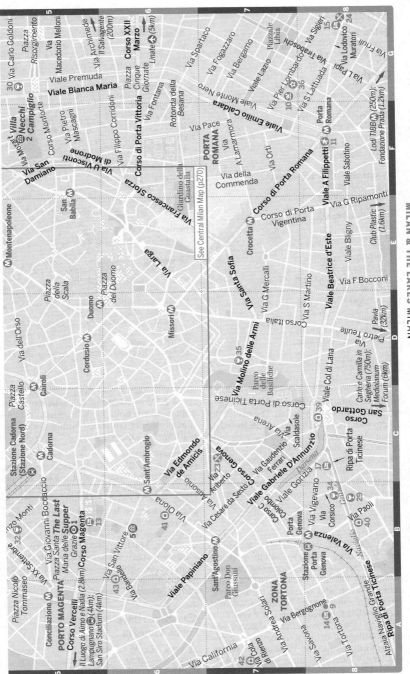

MILAN & THE LAKES MILAN

Milan

Continued from p261

was later home to the mighty Sforza dynasty, who ruled Renaissance Milan. The castle's defences were designed by the multitalented da Vinci; Napoleon later drained the moat and removed the drawbridges. Today, it houses seven specialised museums, which gather together intriguing fragments of Milan's cultural and civic history, including Michelangelo's final work, the *Rondanini Pietà,* now housed in the frescoed hall of the castle's Ospedale Spagnolo (Spanish Hospital).

Parco Sempione PARK
(Map p264; ⊙6.30am-nightfall; ﹢; ⧄Cadorna, Lanza) Situated behind Castello Sforzesco, Parco Sempione was once the preserve of hunting Sforza dukes. Then Napoleon came to town and set about landscaping. First the French carved out orchards; next they mooted the idea in 1891 of a vast public park. It was a resounding success, and today Milanese of all ages come to enjoy its winding paths and ornamental ponds. Giò Ponti's 1933 steel tower (☎02 331 41 20; €5; ⊙3-7pm & 8.30pm-midnight Tue, Thu & Fri,

10.30am-12.30pm & 3pm-midnight Wed, 10.30am-2pm & 2.30pm-midnight Sat & Sun summer, closes 6.30pm winter), built for a Triennale exhibition, provides a fantastic 108m-high viewing platform over the park.

Triennale di Milano MUSEUM
(Map p270; ☎02 72 43 41; www.triennale.org; Viale Emilio Alemagna 6; adult/reduced €18/14; ⊙10.30am-8.30pm Tue-Sun; ℗; ⧄Cadorna) Italy's first Triennale took place in 1923 in Monza. It aimed to promote Italian design and applied arts, and its success led to the construction of Giovanni Muzio's **Palazzo d'Arte** in Milan in 1933. Since then, this exhibition space has championed design in all its forms, although the triennale formula has been replaced by long annual exhibits and international shows.

◉ Quadrilatero d'Oro & Porta Venezia

★**Villa Necchi Campiglio** MUSEUM
(Map p264; ☎02 7634 0121; www.visitfai.it/vil lanecchi; Via Mozart 14; adult/reduced €12/7;

⊙10am-6pm Wed-Sun; Ⓜ San Babila) Designed by homegrown talent Piero Portaluppi, this exquisitely restored 1930s villa was commissioned by Pavian heiresses Nedda and Gigina Necchi (of the Necchi sewing-machine empire), and Gigina's husband Angelo Campiglio. When it was completed the trio were proud owners of a home that embodied 'new' luxury, complete with a swimming pool, central heating and electronic shuttering. Portaluppi's commingling of art deco and rationalist styles powerfully evokes Milan's modernist imaginings. However, purists will lament later classical renovations by Tomaso Buzzi, favoured architect of the bourgeoisie.

Museo Poldi Pezzoli   MUSEUM
(Map p270; ☑02 79 48 89; www.museopoldi pezzoli.it; Via Manzoni 12; adult/reduced €10/7; ⊙10am-6pm Wed-Mon; Ⓜ Montenapoleone) At the age of 24 Gian Giacomo Poldi Pezzoli had inherited not only his family fortune, but also his mother's love of art. After extensive travels in which he took inspiration from European art trends, he transformed his apartments into a series of themed rooms based on the great art periods (the Middle Ages, early Renaissance, baroque etc). Crammed with big-ticket Renaissance artworks, these Sala d'Artista are exquisite works of art in their own right.

Museo Bagatti Valsecchi   MUSEUM
(Map p270; ☑02 7600 6132; www.museobagatt ivalsecchi.org; Via Gesù 5; adult/reduced €10/7; ⊙1-5.45pm Tue-Sun; Ⓜ Montenapoleone) Though born a few centuries too late, the Bagatti Valsecchi brothers, Fausto and Giuseppe, were determined to be Renaissance men, and from 1878 to 1887 they built their home as a living museum of the Quattrocento up to the 16th century. Decorated in the style of the ducal palaces in Mantua, the apartments are full of Renaissance furnishings, ceiling friezes, tapestries and paintings. They even had a period stone bath, although it was discreetly retrofitted for running water.

⊙ Corso Magenta & Sant'Ambrogio

Basilica di Santa Maria delle Grazie   BASILICA
(Map p264; ☑02 467 61 11; www.legraziemilano.it; Piazza Santa Maria delle Grazie; ⊙7am-12.55pm & 3-7.30pm Mon-Fri, 7.30am-12.30pm & 3.30-9pm Sat-Sun; Ⓜ Cadorna) Begun by Guiniforte Solari in 1463, with later additions by Bramante, this handsome Lombard church encapsulates the magnificence of the Milanese court of Ludovico Sforza and Beatrice d'Este, as well as famously containing *The Last Supper* (p268). Articulated in fine brickwork and terracotta, the building is robust but fanciful; its apse is topped by a masterful, drum-shaped dome attributed to Bramante, and its interior is lined with frescoed chapels decorated by the likes of Bernardo Zenale, Antonello da Messina, Bramantino and Paris Bordone, a student of Titian.

Basilica di Sant'Ambrogio   BASILICA
(Map p270; ☑02 8645 0895; www.basilicasant ambrogio.it; Piazza Sant'Ambrogio 15; ⊙10am-noon & 2.30-6pm Mon-Sat, 3-5pm Sun; Ⓜ Sant'Ambrogio) FREE St Ambrose, Milan's patron saint and one-time superstar bishop, is buried in the crypt of this red-brick cathedral, which he founded in AD 379. It's a fitting legacy, built and rebuilt with a purposeful simplicity that is truly uplifting: the seminal Lombard Romanesque basilica. Shimmering altar mosaics and a biographical golden altarpiece (835), which once served as the cladding for the saint's sarcophagus, light up the shadowy vaulted interior.

Chiesa di San Maurizio   CHURCH
(Map p270; ☑02 2040 4175; Corso Magenta 15; ⊙9.30am-7.30pm Tue-Sun; Ⓜ Cadorna) FREE This 16th-century royal chapel and one-time Benedictine convent is Milan's hidden crown jewel. Its somewhat sombre facade belies a gorgeous interior, every inch covered in breathtaking frescoes, most of them executed by Bernardino Luini, who worked with Leonardo da Vinci. Many of the frescoes immortalise Ippolita Sforza, Milanese literary maven, and other members of the powerful Sforza and Bentivoglio clans who paid for the chapel's decoration.

DON'T MISS

THE GOLDEN QUAD

A stroll around the Quadrilatero d'Oro, the world's most famous shopping district, is a must even for those not sartorially inclined. The quaintly cobbled quadrangle of streets – loosely bound by Via Monte Napoleone, Via Sant'Andrea, Via Senato and Via Manzoni – have long been synonymous with elegance and money, and even if you don't have the slightest urge to sling a swag of glossy shopping bags, the window displays and people-watching are priceless.

MILAN & THE LAKES MILAN

 TOP SIGHT
THE LAST SUPPER

Milan's most famous painting, Leonardo da Vinci's *The Last Supper*, is hidden away on a wall of the refectory adjoining the Basilica di Santa Maria delle Grazie (p267). Depicting Christ and his disciples at the dramatic moment when Christ reveals he is aware of the betrayal afoot, it is a masterful psychological study and one of the world's most iconic images.

The Painting

The Last Supper is a landmark painting. Art historians identify it as the beginning of the High Renaissance. But it isn't just technique that sets the 40-sq-metre mural apart from everything that came before; even today it possesses a subtlety of tone and vivid narrative power that few images possess, and the baggage of a million dodgy reproductions are quickly shed once you are face to face with the luminous original.

Twenty-two years of delicate restoration were required to stabilise the fragile image. Da Vinci himself is partly to blame: his experimental mix of oil and tempera was applied between 1495 and 1498, rather than within a week as is typical of fresco techniques. The Dominicans didn't help matters when in 1652 they raised the refectory floor, hacking off Jesus' feet. The most damage, however, was caused by restorers in the 19th century, whose use of alcohol and cotton wool removed an entire layer. But the work's condition does little to lessen its astonishing beauty and enthralling psychological power.

TOP TIPS

➡ Reservations must be made weeks in advance.

➡ At shorter notice (a few days) you can take a €75 city tour with Autostradale Viaggi (p271) that guarantees a visit to the mural.

➡ Visiting time is in allocated 15-minute slots.

PRACTICALITIES

➡ Il Cenacolo

➡ Map p264

➡ ☎ 02 9280 0360

➡ www.cenacolovinciano.net

➡ Piazza Santa Maria delle Grazie 2

➡ adult/reduced €15/2, plus booking fee €2

➡ ⏱ 8.15am-7pm Tue-Sun

➡ Ⓜ Cadorna

**Museo Nazionale Scienza
e Tecnologia Leonardo da Vinci** MUSEUM
(Map p264; ☏ 02 48 55 51; www.museoscienza.org;
Via San Vittore 21; adult/child €10/7.50, submarine
tours €8; ⊕9.30am-5pm Tue-Fri, to 6.30pm Sat
& Sun; ☂; Ⓜ Sant'Ambrogio) Kids and would-
be inventors will go goggle-eyed at Milan's
science museum, the largest of its kind in
Italy. It is a fitting tribute in a city where
arch-inventor Leonardo da Vinci did much
of his finest work. The 16th-century monastery where it's housed features a collection
of more than 15,000 items, including models
based on da Vinci's sketches, with outdoor
hangars housing steam trains, planes and
Italy's first submarine, *Enrico Toti* (tours
available in English and Italian).

The museum's MUST Shop (☏ 02 4855
5340; www.mustshop.it; Via Olona 6; ⊕10am-
7pm Tue-Sun; ☎☂) is the place for all manner of science-inspired books, design items,
gadgets and games. Access it through the
museum or from Via Olona.

◉ Porta Romana &
Porta Vittoria

★**Fondazione Prada** GALLERY
(☏ 02 5666 2611; www.fondazioneprada.org; Largo Isarco 2; adult/reduced €10/8; ⊕10am-7pm
Mon, Wed & Thu, to 8pm Fri-Sun; Ⓜ Lodi TIBB)
Conceived by designer Miuccia Prada and
architect Rem Koolhaas, this museum is as
innovative and creative as the minds that
gave it shape. Seven renovated buildings
and three new structures have transformed
a century-old gin distillery into 19,000 sq
metres of exciting, multilevel exhibition
space. The buildings, including the shimmering Haunted House clad in gold leaf and
a bold 60m-high white concrete tower, work
seamlessly together, presenting some stunning visual perspectives.

Inside, temporary and permanent exhibits fill the diverse spaces that finally allow
for the display of the foundation's extensive
contemporary collection, which includes
pieces by Anish Kapoor, Louise Bourgeois,
Francesco Vezzoli and Nathalie Djurberg.
Film screenings, performances and events
are also part of the cultural program.

Almost as popular as the exhibits is the
Wes Anderson–designed cafe, Bar Luce,
with its wallpapered 1950s-inspired interior,
complete with jukebox, themed pinball machines and rows of candy jars. The 6th-floor
Torre restaurant is also worth a stop, especially for its skyline views.

I BAGNI MISTERIOSI

Conceived as a community hub by
architect Luigi Secchi in 1939, I Bagni
Misteriosi (Map p264; ☏ 02 8973 1800;
www.bagnimisteriosi.com; Via Carlo Botta
18; adult €7-15, reduced €5-12, depending
on time of day; ⊕10am-6pm Sun-Mon &
Wed, 10am-midnight Thu, 10am-10pm Fri
& Sat; ☂; Ⓜ Porta Romana) is a spectacular modernist *lido* (beach). Recently
restored, its enormous heated pools,
shaded porticos and bar are once again
a favourite summer retreat.

One of the pools, featuring a fountain
with flamingos, is dedicated to children,
while the other, Olympic-sized pool
is adults only. In addition, there's tai
chi, art classes, and dance and music
concerts hosted by the adjoining Teatro
Franco Parenti (p279).

In winter, the complex is made over
into an ice-skating rink. The best time
to visit is between 6.30pm and 9pm for
an unforgettable *aperitivo* (pre-dinner
drink) around the pools. Both the bar
and bistro are accessible from Via Sabina without having to pay the entry fee.

◉ Porta Garibaldi & Isola

★**Cimitero Monumentale** CEMETERY
(☏ 02 8844 1274; Piazzale Cimitero Monumentale;
⊕8am-6pm Tue-Sun; Ⓜ Monumentale) FREE Behind striking Renaissance-revival black-and-
white walls, Milan's wealthy have kept their
dynastic ambitions alive long after death
with grand sculptural gestures since 1866.
Nineteenth-century death-and-the-maiden
eroticism gives way to some fabulous abstract
forms from mid-century masters. Studio BB-
PR's geometric steel-and-marble memorial to
Milan's WWII concentration-camp dead sits
in the centre, stark and moving. The tombs
are divided into three zones: Catholics lie
centre stage, while people of Jewish descent
rest on the right and non-Catholics on the
left. Grab a map inside the forecourt.

Fondazione Feltrinelli ARCHITECTURE
(Map p264; ☏ 02 495 83 41; www.fondazionefeltr
inelli.it; Viale Pasubio 5; ⊕9.30am-5.30pm Mon-Fri;
Ⓜ Monumentale) Herzog & de Meuron's first
public buildings in Italy, these two elongated,
slanted structures look reminiscent of greenhouses. The Feltrinelli Foundation, which occupies one of the buildings, is home to one of

Central Milan

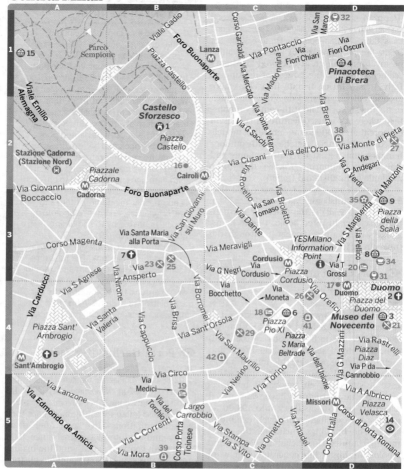

its namesake **bookshops** (open 8am to 11pm Monday to Friday, 9.30am to 11pm Saturday and Sunday), an extremely good **cafe** (☎02 6379 3977; www.facebook.com/BabitongaFeltrinelli; Viale Pasubio 11/13; ☺8am-11pm Mon-Fri, from 10am Sat, 10am-9pm Sun; ☎), a reading room and a conference/events space. The other building is home to Microsoft's Italian hub.

🏃 Activities

QC Terme Milano   SPA
(Map p264; ☎02 5519 9367; www.termemilano. com; Piazzale Medaglie d'Oro 2; day ticket weekdays/ weekend €48/54; ☺9.30am-midnight Mon-Fri, from 8.30am Sat & Sun; ⓂPorta Romana) Pad down

the hallways of Milan's former tram depot and make yourself comfortable in a historic pine-clad tram for a bio sauna session. Such is the ingenuity of this remodelled spa, which has turned the art nouveau building into a luxurious wellness centre. Outside, the garden is dotted with Jacuzzi pools around which fatigued high-flyers snooze.

👣 Tours

Ad Artem   CULTURAL
(Map p264; ☎02 659 77 28; www.adartem.it; Via Melchiorre Gioia 1; adult €8-25, child €8-15; ☺9am-1pm & 2-6pm Mon-Fri; ♿; ⓂGaribaldi, Gioia) Unusual cultural tours of Milan's museums

Central Milan

and monuments with qualified art histori- ans and costumed actors. Highlight tours include a walk around the Castello Sforzes- co battlements; explorations of the cas- tle's subterranean Ghirlanda passageway; and family-friendly tours of the Museo del Novecento, where kids are invited to make their own artwork. Tours can be tailored specifically for your group.

Autostradale Viaggi TOURS
(Map p270; ☎02 3008 9900; www.autostradale viaggi.com; Piazza Castello 1; tours €55-125; ☺9am-6pm Mon-Fri, to 4pm Sat; ⓜCairoli) Au- tostradale's 3½-hour 'Leonardo' bus tour (adult/child €75/45) includes admission to

The Last Supper (Il Cenacolo), the Duomo and the Teatro alla Scala (La Scala) muse- um. Tours run Wednesday and Sunday and depart either from Stazione Centrale (p281) at 9am or near the taxi rank on the western side of Piazza del Duomo at 9.30am.

✯ Festivals & Events

Carnevale Ambrosiano RELIGIOUS
(☉Feb; 👣) Lent comes late to Milan, with Carnevale held on the Saturday that falls after everyone else's frantic Fat Tuesday. Dedicated to the city's patron saint, St Ambrose, it's said his delayed arrival led to the festival's postponement. Now it's an excuse for festivities and stuffing yourself with fried doughy sweets, such as crunchy *chiacchiere* or custard-filled *tortelli*.

Salone Internazionale del Mobile FAIR
(International Furniture Fair; www.salonemilano.it; Fiera Milano; tickets €26; ☉Apr; Ⓜ Rho-Fiera) The world's most prestigious annual furniture fair brings in crowds of more than 370,000 from all over the world. A mostly trade event, the fair runs alongside its ever-popular sidekick **Fuorisalone** (http://fuorisalone.it; ☉Apr), which as the name suggests, covers all design events 'outside' of the Salone.

**Festa di Sant'Ambrogio &
Fiera degli Obej Obej** RELIGIOUS
(☉Dec; 👣) The feast day of Milan's patron saint, St Ambrose, is celebrated on 7 December with a special mass at the Basilica di Sant'Ambrogio and the large Christmas Fair Obej! Obej! (pronounced o-bay, o-bay). The market sets up both in and around Castello Sforzesco (p261), with stalls selling regional foods, sweets and seasonal handicrafts.

🛏 Sleeping

★ Ostello Bello HOSTEL €
(Map p270; ☎ 02 3658 2720; www.ostellobello.com; Via Medici 4; dm €45-50, d €145-175; ⊕ 🛜; 🚇 2, 3, 14) A breath of fresh air in Milan's stiffly suited centre, this is the best hostel in town (and hands down the most social). Entrance is through its lively bar-cafe, where you're welcomed with a complimentary drink. Beds are in bright mixed dorms or private rooms. It also has a kitchen, a sunny terrace, and a basement lounge with board games and table football.

Casa Base DESIGN HOTEL €
(Map p264; https://base.milano.it/casabase; Via Bergognone 34; dm with/without bathroom €45/40, d €110/70; ⊕ 🛜; Ⓜ Porta Genova) Hot on the heels of the co-working trend is this co-living artists' residence and guesthouse styled by Stella Orsini, who's imbued its 10 rooms with a rustic '50s vintage vibe. Part of

the massive renovated Ansaldo steelworks, it also includes access to the co-working space and bar, and has cool events on constant rotation. Check-in is between 2pm and 6pm only; otherwise pay a €25 surcharge.

Foresteria Un Posto a Milano GUESTHOUSE €
(Map p264; ☎ 373 8955768; www.unpostoamilano.it; Via Cuccagna 2; s €70-115, d €90-144, q €235; 🛜; Ⓜ Porta Romana, Lodi) Check in to this rustic 'farmhouse' in downtown Milan. Four comfortable rooms offer simply styled accommodation with distressed walls and functional furniture. Beds are from Pino Pedano, who has dedicated 25 years to creating the optimum sleeping system. Perks include a 10% discount at adjoining restaurant Un Posto a Milano (p276) and a country-style garden perfect for lounging.

★ Atellani Apartments APARTMENT €€
(Map p264; ☎ 375 5289922; www.atellaniapartments.com; Corso Magenta 65; 1-bed apt €170-230, 2-bed apt €260-300; 🅿 ❄ 🛜; Ⓜ Conciliazione, 🚋 16) Now you can bed down in the 15th-century *palazzo* where Leonardo himself lodged while painting *The Last Supper*. Six boutique apartments run by Portaluppi's grandchildren feature the architect's inspired modernist design, along with parquet floors, contemporary decor by local artisans and views over the Santa Maria delle Grazie. Guests can also access the house museum and resplendent garden with Leonardo's own vineyard.

LaFavia B&B €€
(Map p264; ☎ 347 7842212; www.lafaviamilano.com; Via Farini 4; s €90-105, d €100-125; ❄ 🛜; Ⓜ Garibaldi) Marco and Fabio's four-room B&B in the former Rabarbaro Zucca factory is a multicultural treat with rooms inspired by their travels through India, Mexico and Europe. Graphic wallpapers by Manuel Canovas in zippy greens and oranges are complemented by lush window views onto plant-filled verandas. Best of all is the rooftop garden, where an organic breakfast is served in summer.

Hotel Gran Duca di York HOTEL €€
(Map p270; ☎ 02 87 48 63; www.ducadiyork.com; Via Moneta 1; s €100-200, d €180-300; ❄ @ 🛜; Ⓜ Duomo) This golden-yellow *palazzo*, literally a stone's throw from the Duomo, was once a residence for scholars working in the nearby Ambrosiana library. While its looking a touch dated, it still offers solid service and 33 spotless rooms (some with private balconies), fitted out with wood floors, candy-striped walls, Kartell chairs and flat-screen TVs.

★ **Maison Borella** BOUTIQUE HOTEL €€€
(Map p264; ✆02 5810 9114; www.hotelmaisonbo
rella.com; Alzaia Naviglio Grande 8; d €195-260, ste
€350-600; P❉🛜; Ⓜ Porta Genova) With balconies overhanging the Naviglio Grande and
vintage furniture selected by collector Raimondo Garau, this canalside hotel offers a
touch of class in a bohemian neighbourhood.
Converted from an old *casa di ringhiera*
(railing house), its main rooms are arranged
around an inner courtyard draped in ivy
and offer charming features such as parquet
floors and elegant sculpted panelling.

★ **3Rooms** B&B €€€
(Map p264; ✆02 62 61 63; www.3rooms-10corso
como.com; Corso Como 10; d €340; P❉@🛜;
Ⓜ Garibaldi) Can't drag yourself away from
concept shop Corso Como? You don't have
to – the *palazzo's* three guest rooms (mini-
apartments with bedroom, bathroom and
living room) let you sleep between Eames
bedspreads, lounge on Arne Jacobsen chairs
and sip tea off Verner Panton tables. Vintage
items and eye-catching artworks by Kris Ruhs
are thrown in, just to keep you on your toes.

Room Mate Giulia DESIGN HOTEL €€€
(Map p270; ✆02 8088 8900; www.room-mate
hotels.com; Via Pellico 4; d €265-350, tr €335-430;
🛜; Ⓜ Duomo) Chic design accommodation,
a stone's throw away from the Duomo,
showcases the unique aesthetic of celebrated Spanish designer and architect Patricia
Urquiola. Pastel colours, geometric designs
and a homely vintage feel are all part of the
look, which references Milan in the 1950s.
The private spa and sauna, plus buffet
breakfast till noon (extra €16.95), are nice
additional touches.

✖ Eating

★ **Pasticceria Marchesi** PASTRIES €
(Map p270; ✆02 86 27 70; www.pasticceria
marchesi.it; Via Santa Maria alla Porta 11a; ⊙7.30am-
8pm Tue-Sat, 8.30am-1pm Sun; Ⓜ Cairoli, Cordusio)
Since 1824 the original Marchesi *pasticceria*
(pastry shop) has been charming customers
with its refined features and picture-perfect
petit fours. Indulge your sweet tooth with
any number of *bignes* (cream puffs), pralines,
sugared almonds and fruit gels, and sample
some of the best *panettone* (yeast-risen sweet
bread) in Milan. The dining area out back
also makes for an elegant pit stop.

★ **Pavé** PASTRIES €
(Map p264; ✆02 9439 2259; www.pavemilano.
com; Via Felice Casati 27; pastries €1.50-6, panini
€6-10; ⊙8am-9pm Tue-Fri, 8.30am-7pm Sat & Sun;

🛜 🍴; Ⓜ Porta Venezia) Try not to argue over
the *frolla con ganache*, an insanely good
tart filled with dark chocolate ganache and
topped with crunchy cacao nuggets. After
all, it's just one of the temptations dreamed
up by pastry maestros Diego, Luca and Giovanni. There are also custard-filled croissants, mille-feuille and a lunch menu for
those who can't tear themselves away.

Casa Ramen RAMEN €
(Map p264; ✆02 3944 4560; www.casa-ramen.it;
Via Porro Lambertenghi 25; meals €15-25; ⊙12.30-
3pm & 7.30-11.30pm Tue-Sat; Ⓜ Isola) Join the
back of the queue at Luca Catalfamo's roar-
ingly successful original ramen bar and just
pray for a seat. If you're lucky, you'll get to
savour his durum wheat noodles simmered
in a rich broth filled with tender braised
pork and a soupy egg. His uncompromising
approach earned him an invitation to open
a space in Tokyo's Shin-Yokohama Raumen
Museum. If you're not in the mood to queue,
book a spot at sibling **Casa Ramen Super**
(Map p264; ✆02 8352 9210; www.casaramensuper.
com; Via Ugo Bassi 26; meals €15-35; ⊙12.30-3pm
& 7.30-11.30pm Tue-Sat; ❉ 🍴; Ⓜ Isola), which offers the same crowd-pleasing ramen, along
with other tempting Asian dishes.

Macelleria Popolare STREET FOOD €
(Map p264; ✆02 3946 8368; www.mangiaridist
rada.com; Piazza XXIV Maggio; panini €5-8, small
dishes €2.50-14; ⊙11am-11pm Tue-Fri, to midnight
Sat; 🚇9) Inside the **Mercato Comunale**
(⊙8.30am-1pm & 4-7.30pm Tue-Sat, 8.30am-1pm
Mon) you'll find the aptly named 'Popular
Butcher' selling high-quality cuts from animals grazed in pasture. But that's not the
only reason to drop by: people queue for the
quality street food on offer, which emphasis-
es Italian specialities such as *lampredotto*
(cow stomach) and *mondeghili* (Milanese
meatballs). Also serves wine by the glass.

Berberè PIZZA €
(Map p264; ✆02 3670 7820; www.berberepizza.
it; Via Sebenico 21; pizza €5.90-12.80; ⊙7-11.30pm
Mon-Fri, 12.30-3pm & 7-11.30pm Sat & Sun; Ⓜ Isola)
Fantastically light pizzas and craft beer are
what Calabrian brothers Matteo and Salvatore promise you, at this pizzeria housed
in an atmospheric 1950s cooperative.
Everything from the bio flour (using variations of spelt, enkir and the superior Sen-
atore Cappelli durum wheat) to the Torre
Guaceto tomatoes and buffalo mozzarella
from Caserta is sourced obsessively for the
optimum flavour punch. Book ahead.

(sidebar) MILAN & THE LAKES MILAN

Milan Design

Better living by design: what could be more Italian? From the cup that holds your morning espresso to your bedside light, there's a designer responsible and almost everyone in Milan will know their name. Design here is a way of life.

Modern Italian Design

The roots of Italian design stretch back to early-20th-century Milan, with the development of the Fiera trade fair, the rebuild of the Rinascente department store (Giorgio Armani started there as window dresser), the founding of architectural and design magazines *Domus* and *Casabella* and the opening of the Triennale in 1947. Where elaborate French rococo and ornate Austrian art nouveau had captured the imagination of a genteel prewar Europe, the dynamic deco style of Italian futurism was a perfect partner for the industrial revolution and Fascist philosophies.

Fascist propaganda co-opted the radical, neoclassical streamlining that futurism inspired and Italy implemented these ideas into architecture and design. Modern factories had to aid the war effort and Fascist tendencies towards centralised control boosted Italian manufacturing. Through an inherent eye for purity of line, modern Italian design found beauty in balance and symmetry. This refreshing lack of detail appealed to a fiercely democratising war-torn Europe where minimalism and utility came to represent the very essence of modernity.

'From the Spoon to the City'

Milan's philosopher-architects and designers – Giò Ponti, Vico Magistretti,

1. Vespa 2. Alessi moka pots 3. Alfa Romeo

Gae Aulenti, Achille Castiglioni, Ettore Sottsass and Piero Fornasetti – saw their postwar mission as not only rebuilding the bombed city but redesigning the urban environment. A defining statement came from Milanese architect Ernesto Rogers, who said he wished to design 'everything, from the spoon to the city'.

Far from being mere intellectual theorists, this cadre of architect-designers benefited from a unique proximity to artisanal businesses located in Brianza province, north of Milan. This industrial district grew from rural society and thus retained many specialist peasant craft skills. While these production houses remained true to the craft aspect of their work, they were able to use modern sales and production techniques via the central marketplace of the Triennale. This direct connection between craftsperson, producer and marketplace allowed for a happy symbiosis between creativity and commercialism, ultimately fine-tuning Italian design to achieve the modernist ideal of creating beautiful, useful objects.

DESIGN CLASSICS

Alessi Crafted kitchen utensils designed by big-name architect-designers.

Vespa 1946 Piaggio mini-motor scooter that transformed the lives of urbanites.

Cassina 'Masters' collection furniture by Le Corbusier, Frank Lloyd Wright and Giò Ponti.

Alfa Romeo This legendary roadster, launched in 1910, is the most famous product from Milanese petrolheads.

Trattoria da Pino
MILANESE €

(Map p270; ☑ 02 7600 0532; Via Cerva 14; meals €20-25; ☻noon-3pm Mon-Sat; Ⓜ San Babila) In a city full of fashion models in Michelin-starred restaurants, working-class da Pino offers the perfect antidote. Sit elbow to elbow at packed wooden tables and enjoy hearty plates of *bollito misto* (mixed boiled meats), sausages and potatoes, and comforting classic pastas. Arrive early or prepare to queue.

Luini
FAST FOOD €

(Map p270; ☑ 02 8646 1917; www.luini.it; Via Santa Radegonda 16; panzerotti €2.80; ☻10am-3pm Mon, to 8pm Tue-Sat; ☝; Ⓜ Duomo) This historic joint is the go-to place for *panzerotti,* delicious pizza-dough parcels stuffed with a combination of mozzarella, spinach, tomato, ham or spicy salami, and then fried up or oven baked (although the favourite by far is the fried version). Queues may be long, but they move fast.

Un Posto a Milano
ITALIAN €€

(Map p264; ☑ 02 545 77 85; www.unpostoamilano.it; Via Cuccagna 2; meals €15-35; ☻10am-midnight, to 1am Fri & Sat; ☝☝; Ⓜ Porta Romana, Lodi) This country *cascina* (farmstead) was a derelict ruin until a collection of cooperatives and cultural associations returned it to multifunctional use as a restaurant, bar, social hub and guesthouse (p272). Delicious salads, homemade focaccia, soups and snacks are on offer throughout the day at the bar, while the restaurant serves up modern Italian food, with an emphasis on vegetarian dishes, using locally sourced ingredients.

Trattoria Milanese
MILANESE €€

(Map p270; ☑ 02 8645 1991; Via Santa Marta 11; meals €30-45; ☻noon-3pm & 7-11.30pm Mon-Fri; ☐2, 3, 14) Like an old friend you haven't seen in years, this trattoria welcomes you with generous goblets of wine, hearty servings of traditional Milanese fare and convivial banter. Regulars slide into their seats, barely needing to order as waiters bring them their usual: meatballs wrapped in cabbage, minestrone or a soul-warming *risotto al salto* (pan-fried risotto).

★ Seta
GASTRONOMY €€€

(Mandarin Oriental; Map p270; ☑ 02 8731 8897; www.mandarinoriental.com; Via Andegari 9; meals €110; ☻12.30-2.30pm & 7.30-10.30pm Mon-Sat; Ⓟ☀☎; Ⓜ Montenapoleone) Smooth as the silk after which it's named, Seta is Michelin-starred dining at its best: beautiful, inventive and full of flavour surprises. Diners sit on their teal-coloured velvet chairs in keen anticipation of Antonio Guida's inspired dishes, such as blue lobster with *zabaglione* (egg and Marsala custard) and white miso. If weather permits, dine in the outdoor courtyard where you can glimpse the kitchen in action.

★ Alice Ristorante
ITALIAN €€€

(Map p264; ☑ 02 4949 7340; www.aliceristorante.it; Piazza XXV Aprile, Eataly; meals €70-110, lunch menu €55; ☻12.30-2.30pm & 7.30-10pm Mon-Sat; ☀☝; Ⓜ Moscova, Garibaldi) The one-Michelin-starred restaurant of talented chef Viviana Varese and sommelier and fish expert Sandra Ciciriello is the pride of Eataly's foodstore. The artful furnishings and views over Piazza XXV Aprile are a match for the superlative food and playful menu, with dishes such as Polp Fiction (roasted octopus with string beans) and Mr Crab (unshelled crab in broth).

★ Tokuyoshi
FUSION €€€

(Map p264; ☑ 02 8425 4626; www.ristorantetokuyoshi.com; Via San Calocero 3; meals €50-75; tasting menu €135; ☻7-10.30pm Tue-Sat, 12.30-2.30pm & 7-10.30pm Sun; ☐2, 14) Take a creative culinary voyage from Japan to Italy with Yoji Tokuyoshi at the helm. One-time sous-chef of world-renowned Osteria Francescana, this talented chef has already received a Michelin star for his efforts. Expect the unexpected, such as Parmesan tiramisu or cod-filled Sicilian *cannoli* (pastry shells).

La Brisa
ITALIAN €€€

(Map p270; ☑ 02 8645 0521; www.ristorantelabrisa.it; Via Brisa 15; meals €50-70; ☻12.45-2.30pm & 7.45-10.30pm Mon-Fri, 7.45-10.30pm Sun; ☀; Ⓜ Cairoli, Cordusio) Discreet, elegant and exquisitely romantic. Push past the velvet curtain and the maître d' will guide you to a table beneath centuries-old linden trees in a secluded ivy-covered courtyard. Chef Antonio Facciolo's seasonal menus are similarly refined, featuring a mix of artfully arranged Italian and modern dishes, such as Iberian suckling pig with rocket salad and a broad bean puree.

Il Baretto al Baglioni
MILANESE €€€

(Map p270; ☑ 02 78 12 55; www.ilbarettoalbaglioni.it; Via Senato 7; meals €60-75; ☻12.30-3pm & 7.30-11pm; ☀☎; Ⓜ San Babila) Il Baretto's cosy, clubby atmosphere and top-notch, no-nonsense Milanese menu keep its wood-panelled dining rooms packed with silver-haired foxes and their bejewelled partners. The typical Milanese repertoire here includes not only *cotoletta* (breaded veal) and osso buco, but also a wonderfully fresh *astice alla catalana* (Catalonian-style lobster). A not-so-secret back entrance means you can also enter from Via della Spiga 6.

🍺 Drinking & Nightlife

★ Bamboo Bar
BAR

(Armani Hotel; Map p270; 📞 02 8883 8888; www.armanihotelmilano.com; Via Manzoni 31; ⊗ 11am-1am; 📶; Ⓜ Montenapoleone) In a city full of designer drinking dens, the Bamboo Bar literally raises the bar with its double-height windows offering up incredible city views. Expert cocktails such as the signature Mary Caprese are also bound to impress, while the black onyx floor and white leather sofas exude cold elegance – Patrick Bateman would surely approve.

★ Pasticceria Cova
CAFE

(Map p270; 📞 02 7600 5599; www.pasticceriacova.com; Via Monte Napoleone 8; ⊗ 7.45am-8.30pm Mon-Sat, 9.30am-7.30pm Sun; Ⓜ Montenapoleone) In operation for 200 years, the Quadrilatero's most historic bar was bought by LVMH and got a subsequent subtle nip-and-tuck eschewing any showy modernisations. Instead, cushioned banquettes gleam in midnight-blue velvet, offsetting dazzling chandeliers and gilt-framed mirrors. It's the perfect spot for tea or a smoked salmon *panino* (sandwiches), followed by a slice of devilishly good Sachertorte.

★ Nottingham Forest
COCKTAIL BAR

(Map p264; 📞 02 79 83 11; www.nottingham-forest.com; Viale Piave 1; ⊗ 6.30pm-2am Tue-Sat, 6pm-1am Sun; 🚌 9, 23) If Michelin awarded stars for bars, Nottingham Forest would have one. This eclectically decorated Asian/African tiki bar is the outpost of molecular mixologist Dario Comino, who conjures smoking cocktails packed with dry ice and ingenuity. Unique cocktails include the Elite, a mix of vodka, ground pearls and sake – supposedly an aphrodisiac. Only downside? It doesn't take bookings, so prepare to queue.

★ oTTo
CAFE

(Map p264; www.sarpiotto.com; Via Paolo Sarpi 8; ⊗ 7pm-2am Mon, 10am-2am Tue-Sun; 📶; Ⓜ Garibaldi FS) How to define oTTo? It's where you go to feel at home when you don't want to be at home (or in your hotel). Come here for breakfast; hang out with the global nomads mid-morning; break for sociable lunches, cake-filled tea times and Aperol-fuelled *aperitivi*. The Danish-inspired *smørrebrøds* (open sandwiches) are delicious and healthy. It also hosts film nights and events.

Ceresio 7
BAR

(Map p264; 📞 02 3103 9221; www.ceresio7.com; Via Ceresio 7; ⊗ 12.30pm-1am; 📶; 🚌 2, 4) Heady views match the heady price of *aperitivi* (pre-dinner drinks) at Milan's swanky rooftop bar, sitting atop the former 1930s Enel (electricity company) HQ. Two pools, a bar headed by master mixologist Guglielmo Miriello, and a restaurant by former Bulgari head chef Elio Sironi make this a hit with Milan's beautiful people. In summer you can book a whole day by the pool (from €110, including food and drinks).

Mag Cafè
BAR

(Map p264; 📞 02 3956 2875; Ripa di Porta Ticinese 43; ⊗ 7.30am-2am Mon-Fri, 9am-2am Sat & Sun; 🚌 9) Don't get distracted by the cosy eclectic decor, complete with wingback armchairs, marble-topped tables, a patchwork of Persian rugs and huge lampshades that look like birds' nests. The focus is the cocktails, which are creatively crafted, utilising curious herbs and syrups, and served up in shiny vintage glassware. Opt for the cocktail of the month if you're feeling adventurous.

Pasticceria Marchesi
CAFE

(Map p270; 📞 02 9418 1710; www.pasticceriamarchesi.it; Galleria Vittorio Emanuele II; ⊗ 7.30am-9pm; Ⓜ Duomo) After acquiring an 80% stake in the historic Marchesi pastry shop, Prada opened a more modern cafe version of it in the Galleria. Decked out in green floral jacquard wallpaper and velvet chairs, it's the place for high tea and delicate pastries. Set above the Prada men's store (the entrance is easy to miss), it overlooks the mosaics down below.

Club Plastic
CLUB

(www.facebook.com/clubplasticmilano; Via Gargano 15; ⊗ 11pm-5am Thu-Sat; 🚌 24, Ⓜ Brenta) This is Milan's most historic club – its original location was frequented by the likes of Andy Warhol and Keith Haring (you can still see the door Haring painted). Little has changed since its '80s golden era, not the heaving gay-friendly crowd, the mildly claustrophobic atmosphere nor the strict door policy. Even DJ Nicola Guiducci has been manning the console for 30 years.

Camparino in Galleria
BAR

(Map p270; 📞 02 8646 4435; www.camparino.it; Piazza del Duomo 21; ⊗ 8am-9pm Mon, to 10pm Tue-Fri, 8.30am-10pm Sat & Sun; Ⓜ Duomo) With a history dating back to the inauguration of the Galleria Vittorio Emanuele II arcade in 1867, this art nouveau bar has served drinks to the likes of Verdi, Toscanini and Dudovich. Cast-iron chandeliers and mirrored walls trimmed with mosaics of birds and flowers set the tone for a classy Campari-based cocktail.

Ricerca Vini   WINE BAR
(Map p264; ☑02 46 04 71; www.ricercavini.it; Via Vicenzo Monti 33; ☺10am-1pm & 3.30-10pm Tue-Sat, 4-10pm Mon; ⓂCadorna) Sure, it's a wine shop, but it's a bar and a rather good restaurant, too. What better place to sample your options before committing to carry home one of the 2500 wines on offer here. It's one of the largest selections in the city, and the *aperitivo* platters of prosciutto and cheese are excellent. Some evenings it hosts tastings.

Dry   COCKTAIL BAR
(Map p264; ☑02 6379 3414; www.drymilano.it; Via Solferino 33; ☺7pm-2am Tue-Sun; ☏; ⓂMoscova) The brainchild of Michelin-starred chef Andrea Berton, Dry brings together everyone's favourites: cocktails and gourmet pizza. The inventive cocktail list includes its signature drinks (simply numbered 001 to 008), twists on classics like dry martini, and a weekly pairing with pizza and dessert. Dine to a soundtrack of blaring techno and get your night started early.

N'Ombra de Vin   WINE BAR
(Map p270; ☑02 659 96 50; www.nombradevin. it; Via San Marco 2; ☺10am-2am Mon-Wed, to 3am Thu-Sat, 11am-2am Sun; ☏; ⓂLanza, Moscova) Set in the atmospheric surrounds of a one-time Augustine refectory, this *enoteca* (wine bar) gets packed with an older upmarket kind of crowd, especially on weekends. Choose from an enormous selection of Italian and French wines, along with coveted Krug champagnes. They go nicely with cold cuts from the in-house *salumeria* (delicatessen) and tapas-style dishes such as caviar and tartare.

Botanical Club   BAR
(Map p264; ☑02 3652 3846; www.thebotanical club.com; Via Pastrengo 11; ☺12.30-2.30pm & 6.30-10.30pm Mon-Fri, 6.30-10.30pm Sat; ☏; ⓂIsola) This bar-bistro is Italy's first foray into microdistillery and a favoured haunt for gin-and-tonic lovers. The inventive cocktails include unusual botanicals such as Serbian juniper, and you can also choose from over 150 gins, including the house brand, Spleen et Idéal. Additionally, it has a top-notch selection of Asian-inspired and modern Italian dishes.

Bar Basso   BAR
(☑02 2940 0580; www.barbasso.com; Via Plinio 39; ☺9am-1.15am Wed-Mon; ⓂLima) This iconic Milanese bar is not only said to have invented the *aperitivo* concept, but also the ever-popular *negroni sbagliato* (made with prosecco not gin). A supersized goblet of the stuff is practically mandatory, served up by black-tied waiters in an elegant setting that hasn't changed since the '50s. It's the creatives' bar of choice come Design Week.

VOLT   CLUB
(Map p264; ☑table booking & guest list 342 7976858; www.voltclub.it; Via Molino delle Armi 16; €15-20; ☺11.30pm-5am Thu-Sat; ☐94, ☐3) Owned by fashion guru Claudio Antonioli, this is possibly Milan's most beautiful club. Set against a sleek all-black interior, it attracts an affluent crowd of wanna-be-seeners. Thursday's Uptown party focuses on hip-hop and R&B, while Friday and Saturday nights draw in big-name DJs playing house, techno and electronica. The door policy is fierce, so follow their advice and 'make it look good'.

Ugo   COCKTAIL BAR
(Map p264; ☑02 3981 1557; www.ugobar.it; Via Corsico 12; ☺6pm-2am Tue-Sun; ⓂPorta Genova) Hipster home Ugo has a retro vibe that will appeal to those who find themselves in need of a rum or whisky-based cocktail such as Whip & Stool (whisky, ginger, pimento, herbal liquor, pear and lemon). Accompany it with a classic burger, tartare of superior Fassona beef or any number of tasty plates.

Tempio del Futuro Perduto   CLUB
(Map p264; www.facebook.com/tempiodelfuturo perduto; Via Nono 9; €10; ☺varies; ⓂCenisio) With its ominous-sounding name (literally 'Temple of the Lost Future') and abandoned industrial locale, you can't help but imagine this will be the place to party when the world ends. Started by a cultural group of young under-35s, it's *the* venue for electronic-music club nights. Entry is half-price if you bring a secondhand T-shirt or book.

☆ Entertainment

Teatro alla Scala   OPERA
(La Scala; Map p270; ☑02 7200 3744; www. teatroallascala.org; Piazza della Scala; tickets €30-300; ⓂDuomo) One of the most famous opera stages in the world, La Scala's season runs from early December to July. You can also see theatre, ballet and classical-music concerts here year-round (except August). Buy tickets online, by phone or from the box office (☑02 7200 3744; Largo Ghiringhelli; ☺10.30am-6pm Mon-Sat, noon-6pm Sun; ⓂDuomo) up to two months before the performance. Heavily discounted same-day tickets are also available from the box office.

Mediolanum Forum STADIUM
(📞02 48 85 71; www.mediolanumforum.it; Via Giuseppe di Vittorio 6; Ⓜ Assago Milanofiori Forum)
Most big-name music artists that play Milan do so at major venues outside the city centre. Mediolanum Forum is one of the largest venues and has hosted the likes of Rihanna and U2, along with festivals and minor sporting events.

★**Teatro Franco Parenti** THEATRE
(Map p264; 📞02 5999 5206; www.teatrofranco parenti.it; Via Pier Lombardo 14; Ⓜ Porta Romana) Having made a name for itself with a program boasting some of the finest names in Italian cinema and theatre, Franco Parenti cemented its role as a community hub with the opening of I Bagni Misteriosi (p269). Aside from theatre, there are concerts, film screenings, book readings and a variety of outdoor events.

🏠 **Shopping**

★**Peck** FOOD & DRINKS
(Map p270; 📞02 802 31 61; www.peck.it; Via Spadari 9; ⊙3-8pm Mon, from 9am Tue-Sat; 📶; Ⓜ Duomo) Milan's historic deli is a bastion of the city's culinary heritage, with the huge ground floor turning out a colourful cornucopia of fabulous foods. It showcases a mind-boggling selection of cheeses, chocolates, pralines, pastries, freshly made gelato, pasta, seafood, meat, caviar, pâté, olive oils and balsamic vinegars; it also has a downstairs wine cellar.

The in-house cafe is worth a lunch or tea stop to sample some of the stunning array, from canapés and cold cuts to freshly made pastries. Peck also runs an all-day restaurant, Peck Italian Bar (Map p270; 📞02 869 30 17; Via Cantù 3; meals €40-55; ⊙8am-3.30pm & 6-10pm Mon-Fri, from 10am Sat; ❄📶; Ⓜ Duomo).

Aspesi FASHION & ACCESSORIES
(Map p270; 📞02 7602 2478; www.aspesi.com; Via San Pietro all'Orto 24; ⊙10am-7pm Mon-Sun; Ⓜ San Babila, Montenapoleone) The sheer size of this shop is a clue to just how much Italians love this label – Aspesi outerwear is *de rigueur* for mountain and lake weekends, while its smart casual wear helps you segue back to city living in comfort. The bold industrial sprawl also showcases artwork and installations, which go hand-in-hand with the brand's unconventional spirit.

★**10 Corso Como** FASHION & ACCESSORIES
(Map p264; 📞02 2900 2674; www.10corsocomo. com; Corso Como 10; ⊙10.30am-7.30pm Fri-Tue, to

OFF THE BEATEN TRACK

BEHIND THE SCENES AT LA SCALA

To glimpse the inner workings of La Scala, visit the enormous **Ansaldo Workshops** (Map p264; 📞02 4335 3521; www.teatroallascala.org; Via Bergognone 34; per person €25; ⊙9am-noon & 2-4pm Tue & Thu; Ⓜ Porta Genova) where the stage sets are crafted and painted, and around 1000 new costumes are handmade each season. Tours take place two or three times a month (book online in advance) and are guided in conjunction with the heads of each department.

9pm Wed & Thu; Ⓜ Garibaldi) This might be the world's most hyped 'concept shop', but Carla Sozzani's selection of desirable things (Maison Margiela jewellery, Gucci bathers, Yayoi Kusama mugs) makes 10 Corso Como a fun window-shopping experience. It also has a bookshop upstairs with art and design titles, a photo gallery plus rooftop terrace, and a hyper-stylish bar and restaurant with an ivy-draped courtyard.

Bargain hunters take note: the **outlet store** (Map p264; 📞02 2901 5130; Via Tazzoli 3; ⊙11am-7pm; Ⓜ Garibaldi) nearby sells last season's stock at a discount.

★**Eataly** FOOD
(Map p264; 📞02 4949 7301; www.eataly.net/ it_it/negozi/milano-smeraldo; Piazza XXV Aprile 10; ⊙8.30am-midnight; 📶❄; Ⓜ Moscova, Garibaldi) A cult destination dedicated to Italian gastronomy, this three-level mega-emporium showcases the best locally sourced products, including artisanal gelato from Làit and mozzarella made fresh daily from Miracolo a Milano. In addition, there are 12 different eateries, rooms for food workshops and the Michelin-starred restaurant Alice.

Alessi HOMEWARES
(Map p270; 📞02 79 57 26; www.alessi.com; Via Manzoni 14-16; ⊙10am-7pm; Ⓜ Montenapoleone) Established in Omegna in 1921, Italy's most famous design factory has gone on to transform our homes with more than 22,000 crafted utensils, many of which have been designed by the world's leading architect-designers. Some of them now reside in the V&A in London and New York's MoMA, but you can find all the best signature pieces at this flagship store.

Mercatone dell'Antiquariato   MARKET
(Map p264; www.navigliogrande.mi.it; Naviglio
Grande; ☉last Sun of month; Ⓜ Porta Genova,
🚋9) This antiques market is the city's most
scenic market. Set along a 400m stretch
of the pretty Naviglio Grande, it has stalls
from over 380 well-vetted antique and secondhand traders. Hours of treasure-hunting
pleasure can be had immersed in the vintage
furniture, clothing, pre-loved books and
eye-catching jewellery.

Wait and See   FASHION & ACCESSORIES
(Map p270; ☑02 7208 0195; www.waitandsee.
it; Via Santa Marta 14; ☉3.30-7.30pm Mon, from
10.30am Tue-Sat; Ⓜ Duomo, Missori) With collaborations with international brands and
designers such as Missoni, Etro and Anna
Molinari under her belt, Uberta Zambeletti
launched her own collection in 2010. Quirky
Wait and See indulges her eclectic tastes and
playful sense of women's fashion, featuring
unfamiliar niche brands alongside more established names

Cavalli e Nastri   FASHION & ACCESSORIES
(Map p270; ☑02 7200 0449; www.cavallienastri.
com; Via Brera 2; ☉10.30am-7.30pm Mon-Sat, from
noon Sun; Ⓜ Montenapoleone) This gorgeously
colourful shop is known for its high-end
vintage clothes and accessories (which are
priced accordingly). It specialises in lovingly curated frocks, bags, jewellery and even
shoes, from fashion giants such as Gucci,
Hermès and Sonia Rykiel. You'll find its
menswear store (Map p270; ☑02 4945 1174;
☉10.30am-7.30pm Mon-Sat, noon-7.30pm Sun;
🚋2, 14) at Via Mora 3.

★**Spazio Rossana Orlandi**   DESIGN
(Map p264; ☑02 467 44 71; www.rossanaorlan
di.com; Via Bandello 14; ☉10am-7pm Mon-Sat;
Ⓜ Sant'Ambrogio) Installed in a former tie factory not far from Corso Magenta, this iconic interior-design studio is a challenge to
find. Once inside, though, it's hard to leave
the dream-like treasure trove stacked with
vintage and contemporary limited-edition
furniture, light fixtures, rugs, art and highly
desirable homeware accessories from young
and upcoming artists.

★**NonostanteMarras**   FASHION & ACCESSORIES
(Map p264; ☑393 8934340; Via Cola di Rienzo
8; ☉10am-7pm Mon-Sat, noon-7pm Sun; 🚋14)
Brainchild of Sardinian fashion designer
Antonio Marras, this eccentric concept store
has an almost cinematic feel. Hidden in an
ivy-draped courtyard, the industrial-style
loft is artfully arranged, featuring racks of
dreamy womenswear together with seemingly random objects, like a silken settee,
framed landscape paintings or a wall of oddly shaped mirrors.

La Rinascente   DEPARTMENT STORE
(Map p270; ☑02 8 85 21; www.rinascente.it; Piazza
del Duomo; ☉9.30am-9pm Mon-Thu, to 10pm Sat,
10am-9pm Sun; Ⓜ Duomo) Italy's most prestigious department store doesn't let the fashion capital down – come for Italian diffusion
lines, French lovelies and LA upstarts. The
basement also hides a design supermarket
with emphasis on 'Made in Italy', while chic
hairdresser Aldo Coppola is on the top floor.
Purchase edible souvenirs from the 7th-floor
food market and dine on Obikà's terrace
with views of the Duomo.

ⓘ Information

DANGERS & ANNOYANCES
Milan is a safe and affluent destination; however,
as with any major city there are a few things of
which to be wary.
➔ Pickpocketing can be an issue at busy train
stations (especially around Cadorna and
Centrale).
➔ Certain areas such as Via Gola and around
Rogoredo Station have a reputation for drugs
and are best avoided.
➔ Buses 90, 91, 92 and 93 are considered some
of the worst in the city. It's not advised to take
them alone late at night.

MEDICAL SERVICES
American International Medical Centre
(AIMC; ☑02 5831 9808; www.aimclinic.it; Via
Mercalli 11; ☉9am-1pm Mon-Fri; Ⓜ Missori)
Private, international health clinic with
English-speaking staff.
Ospedale Maggiore Policlinico (☑24hr 02
5 50 31; www.policlinico.mi.it; Via Francesco
Sforza 35; Ⓜ Crocetta) Milan's main hospital;
offers an outpatient service.

POLICE
Police Station (Questura; ☑02 6 22 61;
http://questure.poliziadistato.it/milano; Via
Fatebenefratelli 11; ☉8am-2pm & 3-6pm Mon-
Fri; Ⓜ Turati) Milan's main police station.

TOURIST INFORMATION
Milan Tourist Office (Map p270; ☑02 8845
5555; www.yesmilano.it; Piazza Duomo 14;
☉9am-7pm Mon-Fri, 10am-1pm Sat & Sun;
Ⓜ Duomo) Has helpful English-speaking staff
and information on new exhibitions and events.
YESMilano Information Point (Map p270;
☑02 8515 5931; www.yesmilano.it; Palazzo Gi-
ureconsulti, Via dei Mercanti 8; ☉9am-6.30pm
Mon-Fri, 1.30-5.30pm Sat & Sun; Ⓜ Cordusio)

Interactive information point open at the weekends, when the tourist office is closed.

❶ Getting There & Away

AIR

In addition to its own airports, Milan has direct links to Bergamo's Orio al Serio airport (p312).

Aeroporto Malpensa (MXP; ☑ 02 23 23 23; www.milanomalpensa-airport.com; 🚆 Malpensa Express) Northern Italy's main international airport is located 50km northwest of Milan. Services include car rental, banks and a VAT refund office.

Aeroporto Linate (LIN; ☑ 02 23 23 23; www.milanolinate-airport.com; Viale Forlanini) Handles the majority of domestic and a handful of European flights. It is located 7km east of the city centre.

BUS

Buses converge on Milan from most major European cities. Most services depart from and terminate in **Lampugnano Bus Terminal** (Via Natta; Ⓜ Lampugnano).

CAR

The A1, A4, A7 and A8 motorways converge on Milan from all directions.

TRAIN

Milan is a major European rail hub. High-speed services arrive from across Italy, and from France, Switzerland, Austria and Germany at the **Stazione Centrale** (www.milanocentrale.it; Piazza Duca d'Aosta; ☺4am-1am; ⓂCentrale). For train timetables and fares, check out **Trenitalia** (☑89 20 21; www.trenitalia.it), www.sncf.com, www.sbb.ch and www.bahn.de.

❶ Getting Around

TO/FROM THE AIRPORTS
Aeroporto Malpensa

Malpensa Express (☑02 7249 4949; www.malpensaexpress.it; one-way €13) trains run from both airport terminals to the city centre (approximately 50 minutes) every 30 minutes from 5.37am to 12.20am. The **Malpensa Shuttle** (Map p264; ☑02 5858 3185; www.malpensashuttle.it; one-way/return €10/16; Ⓜ Centrale) bus runs roughly half-hourly between 3.45am and 12.15am. Taxis into central Milan are €95 set fare (50 minutes).

Aeroporto Linate

Airport Bus Express (Map p264; ☑02 3008 9000; www.airportbusexpress.it; one-way/return €5/9; ⓂCentrale) coaches run from Stazione Centrale (25 minutes) every 30 minutes between 5.30am and 10pm; **Air Bus** (www.atm-mi.it; Piazza Luigi Savoia; one-way/return €5/9; ⓂCentrale) offers a similar service. ATM

city bus 73 departs to Via Gonzaga (€1.50, 25 minutes) every 15 to 30 minutes between 5.35am and 1.06am. Taxis cost €20 to €30.

Aeroporto Orio al Serio

The **Orio Shuttle** (☑ 035 31 93 66; www.orioshuttle.com; adult/reduced €7/5; Ⓜ Centrale) runs to Stazione Centrale every 30 minutes from 4.25am to 11.40pm. **Autostradale** (Map p270; ☑ 02 3008 9000; www.autostradale.it) runs a similar service.

BICYCLE

Mobike (https://mobike.com) offers dockless bike sharing through its app. Alternatively, **BikeMi** (☑ 02 4860 7607; www.bikemi.it) is a public bicycle system with stops all over town. Subscribe and register for all services online or through its apps. For BikeMi you can also register at the ATM Info Point at the Duomo, Cadorna or Centrale metro stops.

If you fancy your 'own' bike, consider renting one from **Rossignoli** (☑ 02 80 49 60; http://rossignoli.it; Corso Garibaldi 71; bike rental 1 day/week €12/65; ☺ 2.30-7.30pm Mon, 9am-1pm & 2.30-7.30pm Tue-Sat; Ⓜ Moscova), Milan's oldest bike outfit, or **AWS Bici** (☑ 02 6707 2145; https://awsbici.com; Via Ponte Seveso 33; bike rental per day from €13; ☺ 9am-1pm & 3-7pm Tue-Sat; Ⓜ Sondrio, Stazione Centrale), a stone's throw from Stazione Centrale.

CAR & MOTORCYCLE

It simply isn't worth having a car in Milan. Many streets have restricted access and parking is a nightmare. A congestion zone, Area C, is enforced between 7.30am and 7.30pm Monday to Friday. To enter buy a daily pass (€5) at www.muoversi.milano.it. Electric cars and most motorcycles and scooters enter freely.

Street parking is colour coded: yellow for residents, white is free and blue requires payment, usually of between €1.20 and €4.50 per hour. Payment can be made via parking meters, SMS (48444) or by downloading the free apps MiCero, Easypark or TelePass Pay.

Underground car parks charge between €25 and €40 for 24 hours.

PUBLIC TRANSPORT

ATM (Azienda Trasporti Milano; ☑ 02 4860 7607; www.atm.it) runs Milan's public-transport network, including buses, trams and the metro.

The metro is the most convenient way to get around and consists of five major lines. Services operate between 5.30am and 12.30am (from 6am on Sunday).

A ticket for the metro or tram costs €2 and is valid for 90 minutes; it can only be used for one metro ride. Tickets are sold at electronic ticket machines in the station, or at tobacconists and newsstands.

MILAN & THE LAKES MILAN

Milan Fashion

Northern Italian artisans and designers have been dressing and adorning Europe's affluent classes since the early Middle Ages. At that time Venetian merchants imported dyes from the East and Leonardo da Vinci helped design Milan's canal system, connecting the wool merchants and silk weavers of the lakes to the city's market places. Further south, Florence's wool guild grew so rich it was able to fund a Renaissance.

Global Powerhouses

In the 1950s Florence's fashion houses, which once produced only made-to-measure designs, began to present seasonal collections to a select public. But Milan literally stole the show in 1958, hosting Italy's first Fashion Week. With its ready factories, cosmopolitan workforce and long-established media presence, Milan created ready-to-wear fashion for global markets.

Recognising the enormous potential of mass markets, designers such as Armani, Missoni and Versace began creating and following trends, selling their 'image' through advertising and promotion. In the 1980s Armani's power suits gave rise to new unisex fashions, became a byword for Italian sex appeal and Miuccia Prada transformed her father's ailing luxury luggage business by introducing democratic, durable totes and backpacks made out of radical new fabrics (like waterproof Pocono, silk faille and parachute nylon).

Fashion Mecca Milan

Milan's rise to global fashion prominence was far from random. No other Italian

CATWALKPHOTOS/SHUTTERSTOCK ©

PORLICIATTI/SHUTTERSTOCK ©

1. Models at a fashion show **2.** Versace store, Milan **3.** Bag at Milan Men's Fashion Week

ANDERSPHOTO/SHUTTERSTOCK ©

city, not even Rome, was so well suited to take on this mantle. First, thanks to its geographic position, the city had historically strong links with European markets. It was also Italy's capital of finance, advertising, television and publishing, with both *Vogue* and *Amica* magazines based there. What's more, Milan always had a fashion industry based around the historic textile and silk production of upper Lombardy. And, with the city's postwar focus on trade fairs and special events, it provided a natural marketplace for the exchange of goods and ideas.

As a result, by 2011 Milan emerged as Italy's top (and the world's fourth-biggest) fashion exporter. The Quadrilatero d'Oro is now dominated by more than 500 fashion outlets in an area barely 6000 sq metres. Such is the level of display, tourists now travel to Milan to 'see' the fashion. Helping them do just that, in 2015 King Giorgio opened Armani Silos, a museum showcasing 600 couture outfits and 200 accessories.

FASHION WEEK

The winter shows are held in January (men) and February (women) and the spring/summer events are in June (men) and September (women). You'll enjoy the full carnival effect as more than 100,000 models, critics, buyers and producers descend on the city to see 350-plus shows.

For a full timetable check out www.cameramoda.it or http://milanfashionweeklive.com.

Tram 1, which cuts through the historic centre, is a retro yellow beauty with wooden benches and original fittings. Trams 2 and 3 are good for sightseeing, while trams 9 and 10 together loop around the centre via Porta Venezia, Porta Genova and Porta Garibaldi.

Bus-based night services run every half-hour between 12.30am and 5.10am, after the metro has closed.

Download the free ATM app for network maps and timetables.

TAXI

Pick up taxis at designated ranks, usually outside train stations, large hotels and in major piazzas. Otherwise, you can book on 02 40 40, 02 69 69 or 02 85 85, or through the app mytaxi. Be aware that the meter runs from receipt of the call, not pick-up. Uber is also an option although prices are not that competitive.

The average short city ride costs €10.

AROUND MILAN

Monza

📞 039 / POP 122,700

Monza is best known for its racing track, the spiritual home of thousands of fanatical *tifosi* (fans) who decamp here annually to worship their idols at the Italian Grand Prix. But motor racing is less than half the story. Monza protects Europe's largest walled park, one of Italy's grandest palaces and a spectacular cathedral containing the priceless crown that was once worn by the epoch-defining Frankish-Lombard king, Charlemagne.

⊙ Sights

★ Villa Reale   PALACE
(📞 039 578 34 27; www.villarealedimonza.it; Viale Brianza 1; adult/reduced royal apartments €10/8,

royal apartments & exhibitions €19/16; ⊙ 10am-7pm Tue-Sun) In Monza's colossal park stands this equally colossal palace. Built between 1777 and 1780 as a viceregal residence for Archduke Ferdinand of Austria, Giuseppe Piermarini's vast Villa Reale was modelled on Vienna's Schönbrunn Palace. It served as the summer home for Italian royalty, but was abandoned following the assassination of Umberto I in 1900. Years of restoration have revived its glorious 3500-sq-metre frescoed, stuccoed and gilded interior containing royal apartments, a theatre, an orangery and a chapel.

★ Museo e Tesoro del Duomo   MUSEUM
(📞 039 32 63 83; www.museoduomomonza.it; Piazza del Duomo; adult/reduced €8/6, incl Duomo €14/12; ⊙ 9am-6pm Tue-Sun) Religious art museums are often dull, full of faded priestly vestments and tarnished silver that hasn't been polished since the Risorgimento. But this museum is in a different class and arguably worth a Monza visit in its own right. Rare treasures include artefacts from the often glossed over Carolingian period of European history (8th and 9th centuries) as well as the priceless *Croce di Agilulfo,* an embroidered cross dating from the early 7th century.

Duomo   CATHEDRAL
(📞 039 38 94 20; www.duomomonza.it; Piazza del Duomo; Corona Ferrea adult/reduced €4/3; ⊙ 9am-6pm) The Gothic Duomo, with its white-and-green-banded facade, contains a key early-medieval treasure, the Corona Ferrea (Iron Crown), fashioned according to legend with one of the nails from the Crucifixion. Charlemagne, King of the Franks and the first Holy Roman Emperor, saw it as a symbol of empire, and he was not alone. Various other Holy Roman emperors, including Frederick I (Barbarossa) and Napoleon, had

---

WORTH A TRIP

CERTOSA DI PAVIA

One of the Italian Renaissance's most notable buildings is the splendid Certosa di Pavia (📞 0382 92 56 13; www.certosadipavia.com; Viale Monumento; entry by donation; ⊙ 9-11.30am & 2.30-6pm Tue-Sun summer, to 4.30pm winter). Giangaleazzo Visconti of Milan founded the monastery, 10km north of Pavia, in 1396 as a private chapel and mausoleum for the Visconti family. Originally intended as an architectural companion piece to Milan's Duomo, the same architects worked on its design; the final result, however, completed more than a century later, is a unique hybrid between late-Gothic and Renaissance styles.

Pavia is connected to Milan via the S13 suburban railway service, which stops at Porta Venezia and Stazione Centrale (€4 to €9, 25 to 40 minutes). Buses link Pavia bus station and Certosa di Pavia (€1.80, 15 minutes, every 30 minutes).

themselves crowned with it. It's on show in the chapel (from Tuesday to Sunday) dedicated to the Lombard queen Theodolinda.

🏃 Activities

Autodromo Nazionale Monza   CAR RACING
(📞039 2 48 21; www.monzanet.it; Via Vedano 5, Parco di Monza; ⏰7am-7pm) Monza's racetrack with its long straights, tricky chicane and sweeping Curva Parabolica is one of the most famous racetracks in the world – and one of the oldest. In addition to glitzy Formula One race days, the track hosts year-round events including cycle races, bike fests and even marathons.

In winter you can roll up in your own vehicle and tool around the infamous chicane; or go all out and take a spin in a Ferrari (from €299; www.puresport.it).

ℹ Getting There & Away

Frequent trains connect from Milan's Stazione Centrale (€2.20, 10 to 20 minutes).

THE LAKES

Writers from Goethe and Stendhal to DH Lawrence and Hemingway have lavished praise on the Italian Lakes, a dramatic region of vivid-blue waters ringed by snow-powdered peaks. Curling Lago Maggiore is home to the bewitching Borromean Islands and offers a blast of the belle époque. Mountain-fringed Lago di Como delivers extravagant villas and film-star glamour. Families find fun in the southern amusement parks of Lago di Garda while adrenaline junkies are drawn to the spectacular mountains in the north. Little Lago d'Iseo serves up soaring slopes while the villages and islands of diminutive, often bypassed Lago d'Orta are laced with laid-back charm.

Lago Maggiore & Around

Italy's second-largest lake, Maggiore is one of Europe's more graceful corners. Arrayed around the lakeshore are a series of pretty towns (Stresa, Verbania, Cannobio and, on the Swiss side of the border, Locarno) which serve as gateways to the gorgeous Maggiore islands. Behind the towns, wooded hillsides are dotted with decadent villas, lush botanical gardens and even the occasional castle. Further still, the snow-capped peaks of Switzerland provide the perfect backdrop.

ℹ LAGO MAGGIORE EXPRESS

The Lago Maggiore Express (📞091 756 04 00; www.lagomaggioreexpress.com; adult/child 1-day tour €34/17, 2-day tour €44/22) is a picturesque day trip you can do under your own steam. It includes train travel from Arona or Stresa to Domodossola, from where you get the charming Centovalli (Hundred Valleys) train to Locarno in Switzerland, before hopping on a ferry back to Stresa. Tickets are available from Navigazione Lago Maggiore ticket booths at each port.

ℹ Getting There & Around

BOAT

Navigazione Lago Maggiore (📞800 551801; www.navigazionelaghi.it) Operates car and passenger ferries and hydrofoils around the lake; ticket booths are next to embarkation quays. Services include those connecting Stresa with Arona (€6.20, 50 to 70 minutes), Angera (€6.20, 40 to 60 minutes) and Verbania Pallanza (often just called Pallanza; €5, 40 minutes). Day passes include a ticket linking Stresa with Isola Superiore, Isola Bella and Isola Madre (adult/child €16.90/8.50). Services are drastically reduced in autumn and winter.

BUS

SAF (📞0323 55 21 72; www.safduemila.com) The daily Verbania Intra–Milan service links Stresa with Arona (€2.70, 20 minutes), Verbania Pallanza (€2.70, 20 minutes), Verbania Intra (€2.70, 25 minutes) and Milan (€9.20, 1¾ hours). SAF also runs the Alibus, a pre-booked shuttle bus linking the same towns with Malpensa airport (€15).

TRAIN

Lake Maggiore is well served by rail, with trains running the length of the east bank and up the west bank to Stresa before continuing on to Domodossola.

Stresa

📞0323 / POP 5000
Perhaps more than any other Lake Maggiore town, Stresa, with a ringside view of sunrise over the lake, captures the lake's prevailing air of elegance and bygone decadence. This is most evident in the string of belle-époque villas along the waterfront, a legacy of the town's easy access from Milan, which has made it a favourite for artists and writers since the late 19th century.

WORTH A TRIP

SACRO MONTE DI SAN CARLO

Just south of Stresa is the lakeside town of Arona, the birthplace of San Carlo Borromeo (1538–84), the son of the Count of Arona and Margherita de' Medici. He went on to be canonised in 1610, and his cousin Federico ordered the creation of a 'sacred mountain' in his memory.

A church and three chapels were built, along with a gigantic, hollow 35m bronze-and-copper statue of the saint completed in 1698. Commonly known as the Sancarlone (Big St Charles; ☑ 0322 24 96 69; www.statuasancarlo.it; Piazza San Carlo; €6, exterior only €3.50; ⊙ 9am-12.30pm & 2-6pm mid-Mar–mid-Oct, to 4.30pm Sun Nov, Dec & 1-15 Mar, closed Jan & Feb), you can climb inside to discover heavenly views through the saint's eyes (and even nostrils).

⊙ Sights & Activities

Lungolago di Stresa   WATERFRONT
For the best *passeggiata* (afternoon stroll) on Lake Maggiore head for Stresa, where a 2km-long lakeside promenade meanders through florid gardens and past grand Liberty-style hotels, with the attractive hump of Isola Bella omnipresent across the water. The journey northwest from the Stresa ferry dock takes you past a couple of cafes, several prestigious hotels and a variety of statues, fountains and sculptures, many of them dedicated to events and personalities from WWII.

Funivia Stresa–Mottarone   CABLE CAR
(☑ 0323 3 02 95; www.stresa-mottarone.it; Piazzale della Funivia; adult/reduced return €19/12, to Alpino station €13.50/8.50; ⊙ 9.30am-5.40pm Apr-Oct, 8.10am-5.20pm Nov-Mar) Captivating lake views unfold during a 20-minute cable-car journey to the top of the 1491m-high Monte Mottarone. On a clear day you can see Lago Maggiore, Lago d'Orta and Monte Rosa on the Swiss border. At the Alpino midstation (where you change cars) a profusion of alpine plants flourish in the Giardino Botanico Alpinia (☑ 0323 92 71 73; Viale Mottino 26; adult/reduced €4/3.50; ⊙ 9.30am-6pm mid-Apr–early Oct). The mountain itself offers good hiking and biking trails, and there's a small winter ski station at the top. The ticket includes a short chairlift ride that transports you from the top of the Funivia to the mountain's summit. Rates are cheaper from November to March (adult/reduced €13.50/8.50, to Alpino station €8/5.50).

🛌 Sleeping

Hotel Saini Meublè   HOTEL €
(☑ 0323 93 45 19; www.hotelsaini.it; Via Garibaldi 10; s/d €75/102; 🛜) A classic small-town Italian hotel where you'll be greeted like a prodigal family member, given the best local tips and made to feel like it's your own *casa*. Rooms fall into the simple-but-cosy category with comfortable old-style TVs, bidets and those oddly nonabsorbent 'tablecloth' towels.

Hotel Elena   HOTEL €
(☑ 0323 3 10 43; www.hotelelena.com; Piazza Cadorna 15; s/d €65/90; 🛜) Adjoining a cafe, the old-fashioned Elena is a no-frills family-run classic that you can rely on for the basics: comfortable rooms, simple furnishings and balconies, many of which overlook the piazza. There's a lift, and wheelchair access is possible. Check-in is in the timeless downstairs restaurant.

🍴 Eating

Bar Pasticceria Jolly   CAFE €
(☑ 0323 3 11 74; Via Tomasso 17; cakes €2-6; ⊙ 8am-12.30pm & 4-8pm) Living up to its name, Jolly offers service at a jaunty allegro pace and is one of the best places in town to bag your early-morning Italian breakfast (ie a brioche and cappuccino). It's also a proud purveyor of Stresa's culinary gift to the world – the sweet *margheritine* biscuit.

★ Ristorante Il Vicoletto   RISTORANTE €€
(☑ 0323 93 21 02; www.ristorantevicoletto.com; Vicolo del Pocivo 3; meals €32-38; ⊙ noon-2pm & 7-10pm Fri-Wed) One of Stresa's most gourmet restaurants doesn't advertise itself from its modest perch up a narrow side street. It doesn't need to. Local word of mouth means the small interior is often full, with diners spilling out onto a heated front patio. Walk by and you'll see them demolishing cod carpaccio, saffron, asparagus and anchovy risotto, and lamb stewed in Nebbiolo wine.

Lo Stornella   TRATTORIA €€
(☑ 0323 3 04 44; www.ristorantelostornello-stresa.it; Via Cavour 35; meals €32-35; ⊙ 11.30am-2.30pm & 7-11.30pm; 🌱) The street profile isn't a knock-out and the interior isn't particularly exciting either, but a quick opinion poll of local tastes will reveal that Stornella is the dark horse of Stresa restaurants. Traditional Italian food is given a creative spin here with red potato gnocchi in Gorgonzola sauce, *orecchiette* ('little ears'; pasta) with rabbit *ragù* and a proper 'vegetarian corner' featuring quinoa and other such noncarnivorous delicacies.

Piemontese   PIEDMONTESE €€€

(☑0323 3 02 35; www.ristorantepiemontese.
com; Via Mazzini 25; meals €39-55; ☺noon-3pm
& 7-11pm Tue-Sun) Reminding you that Lake
Maggiore's west shore is in Piedmont, this
refined dining room peddles such regional
delicacies as gnocchi with Gorgonzola and
hazelnuts, and baked perch with black venere rice. The Lake Menu (€39) features
carp, trout, perch and pike, while the *menù
degustazione* (€55) takes things up a notch
with a decadent spread of *lumache* (snails),
capesante (scallops) and foie gras.

Drinking & Nightlife

**Grand Hotel des
Iles Borromées**   COCKTAIL BAR

(☑0323 93 89 38; www.borromees.it; Corso Umberto I 67; ☺6pm-late) You might baulk at
room prices (guests have included Princess
Margaret and the Vanderbilts) but you can
still slug back a Manhattan on the terrace
with cinematic views. And if the cocktails
are too expensive, just nose around the corridors and common areas to see how the top
0.1% live.

Information

Tourist Office (☑0323 3 13 08; www.stresa
turismo.it; Piazza Marconi 16; ☺10am-12.30pm
& 3-6.30pm summer, closed Sat afternoon &
Sun winter) Located at the ferry dock.

Borromean Islands

Forming Lake Maggiore's most beautiful
corner, the Borromean Islands (Isole Bor-
romee) can be reached from various points
around the lake, but Stresa and Verbania offer the best access. Three of the four islands
– Bella, Madre and Superiore (aka Isola dei
Pescatori) – can all be visited, but tiny San
Giovanni is off limits. The Borromeo family,
a noble family from Milan, has owned these
islands (they own six of the lake's nine islands) since the 17th century.

The grandest and busiest of Maggiore's
three main islands, Isola Bella is the centrepiece of the Borromean archipelago. The
island took the name of Carlo III's wife, the
bella Isabella, in the 17th century, when
Palazzo Borromeo was built for the Borromeo family. By contrast, tiny Isola dei Pescatori, 'Fishermen's Island', retains much of
its original fishing-village atmosphere. Many
visitors make it their port of call for lunch,
or stay overnight.

Sights

Palazzo Borromeo   PALACE

(☑0323 93 34 78; www.isoleborromee.it; Isola Bella; adult/child €17/9, incl Palazzo Madre €24/10.50;
☺9am-5.30pm Apr-Sep, shorter hours rest of year,
closed 2 Nov-19 Mar) Presiding over 10 tiers of
spectacular terraced gardens roamed by peacocks, this baroque palace is arguably Lake
Maggiore's finest building. Wandering the
grounds and 1st floor reveals guest rooms,
studies and reception halls. Particularly striking rooms include the Sala di Napoleone,
where Napoleon stayed with his wife in 1797;
the grand Sala da Ballo (Ballroom); the stucco-laced Sala del Trono (Throne Room); and
the Sala delle Regine (Queens' Room). Paintings from the 130-strong Borromeo collection
hang all around.

Isola Madre   ISLAND

(☑0323 93 34 78; www.isoleborromee.it; adult/
child €13.50/7, incl Palazzo Borromeo €24/10.50;
☺9am-5.30pm Apr-Sep, shorter hours rest of year,
closed 2 Nov-19 Mar) The closest of the three
islands to Verbania, Isola Madre is entirely taken up by the Palazzo Madre and the
lovely gardens that surround it. The 16th- to
18th-century Palazzo Madre is a wonderfully
decadent structure crammed full of all manner of antique furnishings and adornments.
Highlights include Countess Borromeo's doll
collection, a neoclassical puppet theatre designed by a scenographer from Milan's La
Scala, and a 'horror' theatre with a cast of
devilish marionettes.

Sleeping & Eating

Albergo Verbano   HOTEL €€

(☑0323 3 04 08; www.hotelverbano.it; Via Ugo
Ara 2; d €140-210; ☺Mar-Dec; ☎) If you want
to join a guestbook that includes Hemingway, GB Shaw, D'Annunzio and British royalty, head for this rust-red hotel set at the
southern tip of enchanting Isola Superiore.
Albergo Verbano has been putting up guests
in its 12 sunny rooms (all of them named after flowers) since 1895. It's equally acclaimed
for its fish-focused Piedmontese restaurant.

Faculties include a private boat-dock,
communal lounge and relaxing terrace.
There are no TVs, but plenty of romance.

The hotel will send out its own boat free
for guests once the ferries have stopped
running.

Elvezia   ITALIAN €€

(☑0323 3 00 43; Via de Martini 35; meals €32-42;
☺9am-6pm Tue-Sun Mar-Oct, Fri-Sun only Nov-
Feb) With its rambling rooms, fish-themed

portico and upstairs pergola-and-balcony dining area, this is the best of the few spots on Isola Bella for home cooking. Dishes include ricotta-stuffed ravioli, various risottos and lake fish such as *coregone alle mandorle* (lake whitefish in almonds). There's also a little snack bar out front if you've got a boat to catch. For those who want to experience the magic of the island after dark when all the day trippers have gone home, there are seven elegant bedrooms above the restaurant (doubles €134 to €170).

★Casabella RISTORANTE €€€
(🖉0323 3 34 71; Via del Marinaio 1; meals €30-50, 5-course tasting menu €55; ⊙noon-2pm & 6-8.30pm Feb-Nov) A small restaurant on a small island with a big reputation. This bewitching place has an admirably short menu, which might feature octopus confit, black ravioli in a saffron sauce or perfectly cooked lake fish. Leave room for dessert; the pear cake with chocolate fondant is faultless.

Verbania
🖉0323 / POP 30,800

Verbania, the biggest town on Lake Maggiore, makes a good base for exploring the west bank. The town is strung out along the lakeshore and consists of three districts. Verbania Pallanza, the middle chunk, is the most interesting, with a pretty waterfront and a ferry stop. Running north from Pallanza the waterfront road has a jogging and cycling path that follows the lakefront. It connects Pallanza with Villa Taranto and Verbania Intra.

◉ Sights

Villa Taranto GARDENS
(🖉0323 55 66 67; www.villataranto.it; Via Vittorio Veneto 111, Verbania Pallanza; adult/child €11/5.50; ⊙8.30am-6.30pm Apr-Sep, shorter hours rest of year, closed Nov-Feb; 🅿) At Villa Taranto it's all about the gardens (the house is not open to the public). The grounds of this late-19th-century villa are one of Lake Maggiore's highlights. A Scottish captain, Neil McEacharn, bought the Normandy-style villa from the Savoy family in 1931 after spotting an ad in the *Times*. He planted some 20,000 plant species over 30 years, and today it's considered one of Europe's finest botanic gardens. Even the main entrance path is a grand affair, bordered by lawns and colourful flowers.

Museo del Paesaggio MUSEUM
(🖉0323 55 66 21; www.museodelpaesaggio.it; Via Ruga 44, Verbania Pallanza; adult/reduced €5/3;

⊙10am-6pm Tue, Thu & Fri, to 10pm Thu, to 7pm Sat & Sun) Set in a stately 17th-century *palazzo* tucked down one of Pallanza's back lanes, this museum houses an exquisite collection of works by sculptor Paolo Troubetzkoy. Though not well known today, Troubetzkoy, who was born nearby in 1866, was celebrated as one of the great artists of the 20th century, and he created vivid busts of luminaries such as Toscanini, Tolstoy and George Bernard Shaw among others.

🛌 Sleeping & Eating

Aquadolce HOTEL €
(🖉0323 50 54 18; www.hotelaquadolce.it; Via Cietti 1, Verbania Pallanza; d €90-105, tr €120; 🕸🌐) Ask for a room at the front of this bijou waterfront address and your window will be filled with a glittering lake backed by the mountains rearing up behind. Inside it's a beautifully lit, genteel affair, with all the quiet assurance of a well-run hotel.

Hotel Belvedere HOTEL €€
(🖉0323 50 32 02; www.pallanzahotels.com; Viale Magnolie 6, Verbania Pallanza; d €120-180; 🕸🌐) One of three hotels in the same group, all encased in Liberty-style buildings on Pallanza's waterfront, the Belvedere is all heavy drapes, creamy colours and hearty buffet breakfasts. The service is at once friendly and professional, while the refined rooms are well sized – it's worth paying extra for one with a *belvedere* (good view).

Osteria Castello OSTERIA €€
(🖉0323 51 65 79; www.osteriacastello.com; Piazza Castello 9, Verbania Intra; meals €25-35; ⊙11am-2.30pm & 6pm-midnight Mon-Sat) Its 100-plus years of history run like a rich seam through this enchanting *osteria* (casual tavern), where archive photos and bottles line the walls in a display of beautiful clutter. Order a glass of wine from the vast selection; sample some rustic ham; or tuck into the pasta or lake fish of the day.

★Ristorante Milano MODERN ITALIAN €€€
(🖉0323 55 68 16; www.ristorantemilanolagomaggiore.it; Corso Zanitello 2, Verbania Pallanza; meals €68-80; ⊙noon-2pm & 7-9pm Wed-Mon; 🕸) The setting really is hard to beat: Milano directly overlooks Pallanza's minuscule horseshoe-shaped harbour (200m south of the ferry jetty), with a scattering of tables sitting on lakeside lawns amid the trees. It's an idyllic if pricey spot to enjoy lake fish, local lamb and some innovative Italian cuisine, such as pigeon with pâté and red-currant reduction.

❶ Information

Verbania Tourist Office (☑ 0323 50 32 49; www.verbania-turismo.it; Via Ruga 44, Verbania Pallanza; ◷ 9.30am-12.30pm & 3-5pm Mon-Sat) Located in the same complex as the Museo del Paesaggio.

Cannobio

☑ 0323 / POP 5200

Almost kissing the border with Switzerland, Cannobio has delightfully quaint toy-town cobblestone streets. Nicely set apart from the busier towns to the north and south, it's a dreamy place that makes for a charming lake base. There's a public beach at the north end of town, which is also the departure point for a whole network of trails along the Cannobino River and in the wider valley.

✖ Activities

Tomaso Surf & Sail   WATER SPORTS
(☑ 333 7000291; www.tomaso.com; Via Nazionale 7; ◷ 9.30am-7pm Jun-Sep, 11am-5.30pm Oct-May) For a day out on the water, hit German-run Tomaso's at the town *lido*. You can hire SUP boards (one/two hours €20/35), windsurfing gear (one/five hours from €25/105), canoes (two/four hours €20/45) and motorboats. If you lack the know-how, Tomaso also offers lessons in windsurfing (per hour €95), sailing (per hour from €110) and waterskiing (per half-hour €90).

🛏 Sleeping & Eating

★Hotel Pironi   HOTEL €€
(☑ 0323 7 06 24; www.pironihotel.it; Via Marconi 35; s €120, d €160-195; ℗🛇) Set in a 15th-

century mini-monastery (later home of the noble Pironi family) high in Cannobio's cobbled maze, Hotel Pironi is, in a word, beautiful. Thick-set stone walls shelter interiors evocative of another era; it's full of antiques, frescoed vaults, exposed timber beams and stairs climbing off in odd directions.

Oggi Pasta   ITALIAN €€
(☑ 0323 73 96 62; www.oggipasta.net/?/oggi-pas ta; Via Umberto 25; meals €25-30; ◷ 11am-9pm) For a quick Cannobio lunch (and flashbacks to your school days), sit down at a requisitioned lift-up school desk and order something from the blackboard of daily specials. If you're lucky, the sausage risotto cooked in Barbera wine will be making an appearance. It arrives quickly, accompanied by a generous basket of homemade bread, but doesn't scrimp on deep rice-absorbed flavours.

★Lo Scalo   MODERN ITALIAN €€€
(☑ 0323 7 14 80; www.loscalo.com; Piazza Vittorio Emanuele III 32; meals €45-55; ◷ noon-2.30pm & 7-11pm Wed-Sun, 7-11pm Tue) Cannobio's best restaurant, Lo Scalo serves cuisine that is sophisticated and precise, featuring dishes such as a suckling pig with spring onions and black garlic, and ricotta and tomato gnocchi with clams. The two-course lunch (€25) and five-course *menù degustazione* (€55) are both great-value treats, best enjoyed at a table on the waterfront promenade.

❶ Information

Tourist Office (☑ 0323 7 12 12; www.procan nobio.it; Via Giovanola 25; ◷ 9am-noon & 4-7pm Mon-Sat, 9am-noon Sun) Located next to the Romanesque bell tower.

OFF THE BEATEN TRACK

WALKING TO ORRIDO DI SANT'ANNA

The 3km walk to Orrido di Sant'Anna is a splendid way to see some of Cannobio's natural beauty. From the beach just north of the centre, follow the Cannobino River inland, crossing the second bridge, and take the well-marked trail along the northern bank. This passes besides woods to tranquil shallows at the base of a cliff topped by a small church (the 17th-century Chiesa di Sant'Anna). The rocky beach here makes a fine spot for a dip. Just past the church is the Orrido di Sant'Anna, a tight ravine where the rushing water has carved a path through the mountains on its descent to the lake. From here, you can retrace your steps back to town, or loop back to Cannobio by taking the road from here. Take the trail leading uphill off to the right near the Camping Valle Romantica, which offers pretty views on the return to Cannobio.

Allow two hours for the walk – though it's worth timing your arrival at Orrido di Sant'Anna to allow a lunchtime stop at the Grotto Sant'Anna (☑ 0323 7 06 82; Via Sant'Anna 30, Orrido Sant'Anna; meals €35-45; ◷ noon-1.30pm & 7-9.30pm Tue-Sat, noon-1.45pm Sun Apr-Oct), next to the ravine (reserve ahead). Pick up a map and get other walking suggestions at the tourist office.

Lago d'Orta

Enveloped by thick, dark-green woodlands, tranquil Lake Orta (aka Lake Cusio) could make a perfect elopers' getaway, particularly if you come during the week when you'll have the place largely to yourself. The focal point of the lake is the captivating medieval village of Orta San Giulio, often referred to simply as Orta. The village and the surrounding hill topped by the Sacro Monte di San Francesco can be circumnavigated on a series of walking paths measuring around 3km in length.

◉ Sights

Orta San Giulio   VILLAGE
Overlooking the forest-lined banks of the shimmering Lake Orta, this shore-hugging village has abundant allure. It occupies a kidney-shaped peninsula with most of the narrow lanes running parallel to the water where they converge on **Piazza Mario Motta** and its small port.

Isola San Giulio   ISLAND
Anchored barely 500m in front of Piazza Mario Motta is Isola San Giulio. The island is dominated by the 12th-century **Basilica di San Giulio** (Isola San Giulio; ⊘ 9.30am-6pm Tue-Sun, 2-5pm Mon Apr-Sep, 9.30am-noon & 2-5pm Tue-Sun, 2-5pm Mon Oct-Mar), full of vibrant frescoes that alone make a trip to the island worthwhile. The frescoes mostly depict saints (and sometimes their moment of martyrdom – St Laurence seems supremely indifferent to his roasting on a grate). Step inside after mass, when the air is thick with incense and the frescoes seem to take on a whole new power.

Sacro Monte di San Francesco   CHAPEL, PARK
Beyond the lush gardens and residences that mark the hill rising behind Orta is a kind of parallel 'town' – the *sacro monte*, where 20 small chapels dedicated to St Francis of Assisi dot the hillside. The views down to the lake are captivating, and meandering from chapel to chapel is a wonderfully tranquil way to pass a few hours.

🛏 Sleeping

Locanda di Orta   BOUTIQUE HOTEL €
(☑0322 90 51 88; www.locandaorta.com; Via Olina 18; s €70, d €85-90, ste €160; 🐾) When old and new combine it can be a beautiful amalgamation. White leather and bold pink are juxtaposed with medieval grey stone walls in this tasteful boutique hotel. Because of the age and size of the building, the cheaper rooms are tiny, but still delightful. Suites are roomier; each features a Jacuzzi and a pocket-sized balcony overlooking the cobbled lane.

Hotel Leon d'Oro   HOTEL €€
(☑0322 91 19 91; www.albergoleondoro.it; Piazza Mario Motta 42; r €150-185; ⊘Feb-Dec; 🏳🐾) A red carpet leads you through the front door and regal furniture greets you in the lobby at this 200-year-old lakefront beauty. Sunny yellows and deep blues dominate the decor, with heavy window curtains, timber furniture and tiled floors; though you should avoid the cramped standard rooms. It also has some smallish suites with attractive spiral staircases. The waterfront terrace is *the* place for gorgeous Isola San Giulio views. You can take a dip in the lake from here.

🍴 Eating

Enoteca Al Boeuc   PIEDMONTESE €
(☑339 5840039; www.alboeuc.beepworld.it; Via Bersani 28; plates €10-18; ⊘11.30am-3pm & 6pm-midnight Wed-Mon) Cross the threshold from the sunny street to the dark stone and wood interior of this suitably lived-in old cantina where a bar the size of a residential garage provides a haven for lovers of wine and aged cheese. It's a tight but smooth operation where small plates of bruschetta (try the truffle, mushroom and cream of radicchio) make a perfect accompaniment to the kings and queens of Italian wine (take a bow Barolo and Barbaresco).

★**Cucchiaio di Legno**   AGRITURISMO €€
(☑339 5775385; www.ilcucchiaiodilegno.com; Via Prisciola 10, Legro; set menu €32; ⊘6-9pm Thu-Sun, noon-2.30pm Sat & Sun; 🅿🏳🐾) Delicious home cooking emerges from the kitchen of this

honest-to-goodness *agriturismo* (the name translates as 'wooden spoon'); expect fish fresh from the lake, and salami and cheese from the surrounding valleys. When eating al fresco on the vine-draped patio it feels rather like you're dining at the house of a friend. Limited opening; bookings essential.

★**Locanda di Orta**   MODERN ITALIAN €€€
(☑ 0322 90 51 88; www.locandaorta.com; Via Olina 18; meals €55-80, menus €75-90; ⊙ noon-2.30pm & 7.30-9pm Wed-Mon) This is as good as it gets food-wise in a town where the bar is already set high. The wisteria-draped Locanda di Orta, squeezed into the heart of the old town, runs a stylish, intimate restaurant (it only seats around 17 people) alongside its boutique hotel. Come and see culinary alchemy convert traditional Lake Orta ingredients into food art.

❶ Information

Tourist Office (☑ 0322 91 19 72; www.distrettolaghi.it; Via Panoramica; ⊙ 10am-1pm & 2-6pm Wed-Mon) Located on the road into Orta San Giulio this office provides information on the whole of Lake Orta.

Pro Loco (☑ 339 5267436; Via Bossi 11; ⊙ 11am-1pm & 2-4pm Mon, Tue & Thu, 10am-1pm & 2-4pm Fri-Sun) A more convenient information office inside the town hall.

❶ Getting There & Around

Navigazione Lago d'Orta (☑ 345 5170005; www.navigazionelagodorta.it) Operates ferries from Piazza Motta to places including Isola San Giulio (return €3.15), Omegna, Pella and Ronco. A day ticket for unlimited travel anywhere on the lake costs €8.90.

Orta-Miasino Station (Via Stazione) Located a 2km walk from the centre of Orta.

Lago di Como & Around

Set in the shadow of the snow-covered Rhaetian Alps and hemmed in on both sides by steep, verdant hillsides, Lake Como (aka Lake Lario) is the most spectacular of the three major lakes. Shaped like an upside-down Y, it is surrounded by villages, including exquisite Bellagio and Varenna. Where the southern and western shores converge is the lake's main town, Como, an elegant, prosperous Italian city.

❶ Getting There & Away

Rail services connect Lake Como to Milan – both from Como (€4.80, one hour, hourly) on the

southwest corner and Lecco (€4.80, 40 minutes, every 45 minutes) on the southeast corner.

ASF Autolinee (SPT; ☑ 031 24 72 49; www.asfautolinee.it) bus service connects Como with Bergamo (€6.20, 2¼ hours, up to six daily).

By car, take the A8 and A9 from Milan to Como (one hour, 52km). For east-side destinations, take the SS36 from Milan to Lecco (one hour, 56km).

❶ Getting Around

Navigazione Lago del Como (☑ 800 551801; www.navigazionelaghi.it; Lungo Lario Trento) ferries and hydrofoils depart year-round from Como's jetty at the north end of Piazza Cavour. Single fares range from €2.50 (Como–Cernobbio) to €12.60 (Como–Lecco or Como–Gravedona). Return fares are double. Hydrofoil services entail a supplement of €1.40 to €4.90. Car ferries connect Bellagio with Varenna and Cadenabbia.

ASF Autolinee (☑ 031 24 72 47; www.asfautolinee.it) operates buses around the lake, which in Como depart from the **bus station** (⊙ ticket office 6.30am-8pm Mon-Sat, 8am-noon & 2-7pm Sun & holidays) on Piazza Matteotti. Key routes include Como to Colico (€6.20, two hours, three to five daily), via the villages on the western shore, and Como to Bellagio (€3.40, 70 minutes, hourly).

Como

☑ 031 / POP 84,700

Sitting in a lush basin at the southern tip of its namesake lake, Como is a self-confident and historic town, established by Julius Caesar as an Alpine garrison and Roman holiday resort in the 1st century BC. The town's medieval watchtowers were built by Frederick Barbarossa and its three impressive Romanesque basilicas rise from the remains of once-rich convents. Eighteenth-century Austrian rule subsequently gave the town its Central European air and vibrant cafe culture; while the wealth of the silk industry paid for dozens of *Stile Liberty* (Italian art nouveau) villas. Nowadays, Como is reimagining itself as the lake's coolest hub, full of hip hotels, creative restaurants and youthful bar-lined piazzas.

Como

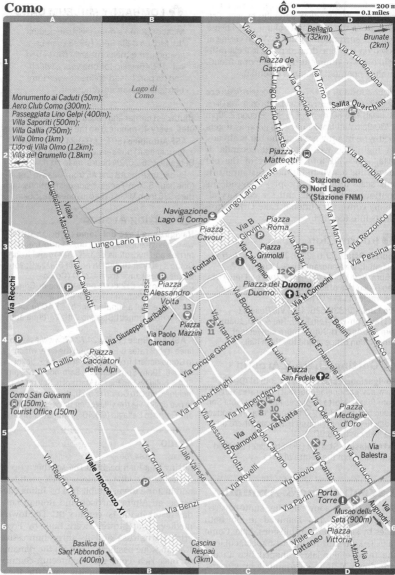

Map labels:

Lago di Como

Bellagio (32km)

Brunate (2km)

Viale Geno

Piazza de Gasperi

Via Prudenziana

Via Torno

Via Coloniola

Salita Quarchino

6

Via Brambilla

Monumento ai Caduti (50m);
Aero Club Como (300m);
Passeggiata Lino Gelpi (400m);
Villa Saporiti (500m);
Villa Gallia (750m);
Villa Olmo (1km);
Lido di Villa Olmo (1.2km);
Villa del Grumello (1.8km)

Lungo Lario Trieste

Piazza Matteotti

Stazione Como Nord Lago (Stazione FNM)

Via A Marzoni

Via Rezzonico

Via Pessina

Navigazione Lago di Como

Lungo Lario Trieste

Piazza Cavour

Piazza Roma

Via B Giovini

Piazza Grimoldi

Via Rodari

5

Lungo Lario Trento

Viale Guglielmo Marconi

Viale Cavallotti

Via Recchi

Viale Grassi

Via Fontana

Via Calo Plinio

12

Piazza del Duomo

Duomo

1

Via M Comacini

Via Bellini

Viale Lecco

Piazza Alessandro Volta

13

Via Giuseppe Garibaldi

Piazza Mazzini

11

Via Vitani

Via Boldoni

Via Luini

Via Vittorio Emanuele II

Via T Gallio

Piazza Cacciatori delle Alpi

Via Paolo Carcano

Via Cinque Giornate

Piazza San Fedele

2

Piazza Medaglie d'Oro

Via Odescalchi

Via Balestra

Como San Giovanni (150m); Tourist Office (150m)

Via Lambertenghi

Via Alessandro Volta

Via Indipendenza

4

8 10

Via Paolo Carcano

Via Natta

Via Raimondi

7

Via Cantù

Via Giovio

Via Carducci

Viale Innocenzo XI

Via Torriani

Viale Varese

Via Rovelli

Porta Torre

9

Museo della Seta (900m)

Via Auguadri

Via Milano

Via Regina Theodolinda

Via Parini

Viale C Cattaneo

Piazza Vittoria

Via Benzi

Basilica di Sant'Abbondio (400m)

Cascina Respaù (3km)

◉ Sights

★ Duomo

CATHEDRAL

(Cattedrale di Como; ☎031 331 22 75; Piazza del Duomo; ⊗10.30am-5.30pm Mon-Fri, 10.45am-4.30pm Sat, 1-4.30pm Sun) FREE Como's awesome marble-clad cathedral is one of the most important buildings on the lake, incorporating a variety of styles – Romanesque, Renaissance and Gothic topped by a rococo cupola – over its centuries-long construction between 1396 and 1770. Inside, Renaissance chapels flank a wide cross-vaulted nave, which is hung with huge tapestries woven in gold thread in Ferrara, Florence and Ant-

Como

⊙ Top Sights
1 Duomo C3

⊙ Sights
2 Basilica di San Fedele..........................D4

⊕ Activities, Courses & Tours
3 Funicolare Como–Brunate...................C1

⊜ Sleeping
4 Avenue Hotel C5
5 Le Stanze del Lago...............................D3

6 Quarcino D2

⊗ Eating
7 Castiglioni...D5
8 Il Comacino...C5
9 Mercato Mercerie di Como..................D6
10 Natta Café...C5
11 Osteria del Gallo..................................C4
12 Sartoria Ciclistica C3

⊙ Drinking & Nightlife
13 Vintage Jazz Food & Wine...................B4

werp. Statues of Pliny the Elder and Pliny the Younger adorn the facade, an unusual honour for two humanist philosophers.

Passeggiata Lino Gelpi　　WATERFRONT
One of Como's most charming walks is the lakeside stroll west from Piazza Cavour. Passeggiata Lino Gelpi leads past the **Monumento ai Caduti** (Viale Puecher 9; ⊙3-6pm Sun summer), a 1931 memorial to Italy's WWI dead. Next you'll pass a series of mansions and villas, including **Villa Saporiti** (Via Borgo Vico 148) and **Villa Gallia** (Via Borgo Vico 154), both now owned by the provincial government and closed to the public, before arriving at the garden-ringed Villa Olmo (p294).

Basilica di Sant'Abbondio　　BASILICA
(Via Regina; ⊙8am-6pm summer, to 4.30pm winter) About 500m south of Como's city walls is this austere 11th-century Romanesque church, once the seat of a bishopric built on the orders of St Amantius of Como in order to house precious relics of no less than Sts Peter and Paul. The highlights are the soaring frescoes inside the apse that depict scenes from the life of Christ, from the Annunciation to his burial. The adjoining cloister is now home to a law faculty.

Museo della Seta　　MUSEUM
(Silk Museum; ☑031 30 31 80; www.museosetaco mo.com; Via Castelnuovo 9; adult/reduced €10/7; ⊙10am-6pm Tue-Sun) Far from being a flashy collection of silk scarves, this highly educational study of Como's long-standing textile industry explains the full silk-making process from mulberry leaf–eating silkworm to debonair tie. An accompanying booklet and various museum panels fascinatingly relate how this most expensive and sought-after of fabrics is essentially the work of an ugly worm-turned-moth. There are plenty of looms, dyeing machines and old photos to look at, plus a small collection of scarves and dresses to admire at the end.

Basilica di San Fedele　　BASILICA
(Piazza San Fedele; ⊙8am-noon & 3.30-7pm) Hemmed in by houses and enclosing one side of what was once a medieval grain market, this Lombard Romanesque basilica dates back to the 7th century, although what you see now was built in 1120 after the relics of Roman martyr San Fedele were entombed in the altar. Inside, its three naves and apses are covered in 16th- and 17th-century frescoes; a handful of older ones also survive, including the *Beheading of San Fedele*.

🏃 Activities

★ Funicolare Como–Brunate　　CABLE CAR
(☑031 30 36 08; www.funicolarecomo.it; Piazza de Gasperi 4; one way/return adult €3.10/5.70, reduced €2.10/3.30; ⊙half-hourly departures 6am-midnight summer, to 10.30pm winter) Prepare for some spectacular views. The Como–Brunate cable car (built in 1894) takes seven minutes to trundle up to the quiet hilltop village of **Brunate** (720m), revealing a memorable panorama of mountains and lakes. From there a steep 30-minute walk along a stony track leads to **San Maurizio** (907m), where 143 steps climb to the top of a lighthouse built in 1927 to mark the centenary of Alessandro Volta's death. The Como tourist office (p295) can provide a map with a range of suggested walks around Brunate. It's best to book a return ticket: the meandering path between Como and Brunate is narrow, steep and poorly signed.

Aero Club Como　　SCENIC FLIGHTS
(☑031 57 44 95; www.aeroclubcomo.com; Viale Masia 44; 30min flight per person €120) For a true touch of glamour, take one of these seaplane tours and buzz about the skies high above Como. The often bumpy take-off and landing on the lake itself is thrilling, as are the views down onto the villas and villages dotted far below. Flights are popular; book

THE KILOMETRE OF KNOWLEDGE (& BEAUTY)

On Sundays, the interconnected grounds of three Como villas open to the public (from about 10am to 6pm). Dotting the shore just northwest of the centre, a 1km promenade connects the **Villa Olmo** (☑ 031 25 23 52; www.villa olmocomo.it; Via Cantoni 1; gardens free, villa entry varies by exhibition; ☺ villa 10am-6pm Tue-Sun during exhibitions, gardens 7am-11pm Apr-Sep, to 8pm Oct-Mar), the **Villa del Grumello** (www.villadelgrumel lo.it; Via per Cernobbio 11; ☺ grounds 10am-7pm Sun year-round, daily in Aug) and the **Villa Sucota** (☑ 031 338 49 76; www. fondazioneratti.org; Via per Cernobbio 19; ☺ gardens 10am-6pm Sun year-round, daily in Aug, museum hours vary). Sometimes referred to as the Chilometro della Conoscenza (Kilometre of Knowledge), this stroll takes in fragrant gardens and hilltop views of lovely Lake Como.

three or four days ahead in summer. Maximum group size four.

🛌 Sleeping

Quarcino HOTEL €
(☑ 031 30 39 34; www.hotelquarcino.it; Salita Quarchino 4; s €55-70, d €70-130, apt €150-170; P❀🛜) The Quarcino is one of those modern Italian hotels where a relatively run-of-the-mill building gets a lesson in clever design aesthetics. What doesn't look particularly interesting from the outside is far more enticing within, starting with the garden-facing breakfast area and continuing upstairs with small but high-tech rooms that make excellent use of the limited space.

⭐ **Avenue Hotel** BOUTIQUE HOTEL €€
(☑ 031 27 21 86; www.avenuehotel.it; Piazzolo Terragni 6; d €165-210, ste €250-290; P❀🛜) An assured sense of style at this à la mode boutique hotel sees modern, minimalist rooms team crisp white walls with shots of purple or fuchsia pink. Unusual art (two giant zebras in the breakfast room) melds with unusual design (square toilets) to leave a memorable impression, lent weight by warm but discreet service and fun extras (you can borrow bikes gratis).

Le Stanze del Lago APARTMENT €€
(☑ 031 30 11 82; www.lestanzedellago.com; Via Rodari 6; apt €135-180; ❀🛜) For a touch of loft

living Como-style, check into one of these five serviced apartments, where sloping wooden ceilings and rough stone walls are given bright furnishings. The ample space (including a kitchenette and a dining area) and the location in the heart of Como make them a great deal.

🍴 Eating

Como's **food market** (Viale C Battisti; ☺ 8.30am-1pm Tue & Thu, to 6.30pm Sat) is held outside Porta Torre.

⭐ **Cascina Respaù** ITALIAN €
(☑ 031 52 36 62; www.cascinarespau.it; Via Santa Brigide e Respaù; meals €15-25; ☺ noon-3pm & 7-10pm Sat & Sun) ✍ Amid the lush greenery high above Como, this small rustic restaurant feels like an idyllic escape from the sometimes maddening crowds along the lake. Charming hosts, delicious homemade dishes and a cosy setting (with outdoor seating on warm days) add to the appeal – as does the attention to locally sourced ingredients, like fall-off-the-bone pork and organic wines from small producers. Call ahead to let them know you're coming. There's also a delightful hostel (dorms from €21) here.

Sartoria Ciclistica CAFE €
(www.sartoriaciclistica.cc; Via Pretorio 7; snacks €4-10; ☺ 7.30am-5pm Mon & Tue, to 9pm Thu-Sat, to 8.30pm Sun; 🛜✍) Sartoria is part cafe plying its own coffee beans (backed up by muffins and toasted *panini*), and part bike store selling cycling paraphernalia – we're talking old-fashioned pink Giro jerseys, soft peaked caps, and books about erstwhile 'kings of the mountains' rather than the bikes themselves.

⭐ **Natta Café** CAFE €€
(☑ 031 26 91 23; www.facebook.com/nattacafe como; Via Natta 16; meals €20-35; ☺ 12.30-3pm & 7.30-11pm Tue-Sun; 🛜✍) ✍ Atmosphere counts for a lot in this old stone-arched cafe-cum-bistro-cum–wine bar. Add mood lighting, mezzanine tables, and a trance-y music soundtrack to the fast-appearing, simple-but-effective food and you've got a recipe for plenty of repeat visits. The blackboard menu chalks up mint ravioli, fish *ragù* and a litany of light lunch wraps (€8). There are good veggie options too.

⭐ **Osteria del Gallo** ITALIAN €€
(☑ 031 27 25 91; www.osteriadelgallo-como.it; Via Vitani 16; meals €26-32; ☺ 12.30-3pm Mon-Sat, 7-9pm Tue-Sat) An ageless *osteria* that looks exactly the part. In the wood-lined checker-

clothed dining room, wine bottles and other goodies fill the shelves, and diners sit at small timber tables to tuck into traditional local food. The menu is chalked up daily and might include a first course of *zuppa di ceci* (chickpea soup), followed by lightly fried lake fish.

Crotto del Sergente   TRATTORIA €€
(📋 031 28 39 11; www.crottodelsergente.it; Via Crotto del Sergente 13; meals €35-45; ⏱ noon-2pm & 7-10pm Sun-Tue, Thu & Fri, 7-10pm Sat) Although it's a bit of a trek (4km southeast of Como's centre), the delectable Slow Food cooking at this characterful *crotto* ('grotto') makes it well worth the effort. Set in a barrel-vaulted brick dining room, Crotto del Sergente serves excellent grilled meats and seafood (including a flavoursome bouillabaisse), best matched with a fine glass of Nebbiolo. Reserve ahead.

Castiglioni   TRATTORIA €€
(📋 031 26 33 88; www.castiglionistore.com; Via Cantù 9; meals €20-25; ⏱ deli 8am-2pm & 4-7pm Mon-Fri, 8am-7.30pm Sat, restaurant noon-2.30pm Mon-Sat; 📋) Going strong since 1958, Castiglioni's wonderful deli has evolved to include an *enoteca* (situated 50m around the corner) and a lunch-only restaurant. Sample dozens of local vintages with plates of sweet prosciutto, or take lunch on the pleasant outdoor patio. The menu, which includes all manner of charcuterie plates, lake fish and mountain meat dishes, is surprisingly refined and superb value.

★ **Il Comacino**   ITALIAN €€€
(📋 031 27 21 86; www.comacino.it; Piazzolo Terragni 7; meals €50; ⏱ 5.30-11.30pm Tue-Thu, to midnight Fri, to 1am Sat, 3-11pm Sun) A new venture affiliated with the plush Avenue Hotel, Comacino offers food as theatre, especially if you sit at the chef's table (technically a couple of bar stools), which brings your eyeball to eyeball with the guy cooking your dinner. Watch carefully as he calmly squeezes ricotta into your zucchini flowers or rolls out the dough for your breadsticks.

🍷 **Drinking & Nightlife**

Vintage Jazz Food & Wine   BAR
(📋 031 414 13 46; www.vintagejazzcomo.com; Via Olginati 14; ⏱ 9.30am-midnight Tue-Thu, to 1.30am Fri & Sat, from 5pm Sun) Flickering candles, walls covered with bric-a-brac, and a jazzy (often live) soundtrack make a fine setting for an evening drink and/or snack (burgers are best). Anyone vaguely hip in Como has passed through here at some point to imbibe their cocktails from a jam jar and eat French fries out of a frying pan.

ℹ️ **Information**

Tourist Office (📋 031 26 42 15; Via Albertoli 7; ⏱ 9am-6pm) Well supplied with hiking maps and multilingual information on events in Como and around the lake. There's another information point inside San Giovanni **train station** (📋 342 0076403; Como San Giovanni, Piazzale San Gottardo; ⏱ 9am-5pm summer, 10am-4pm Wed-Mon winter).

Bellagio
📋 031 / POP 3700
Bellagio's waterfront of bobbing boats, its maze of steep stone staircases, and its dark cypress groves and rhododendron-filled gardens are a true joy. Sitting at the crux of the inverted Y that is Lake Como, the village's beauty is reflected in the lake at every turn. Inevitably this charm draws the summer crowds – stay overnight for a more authentic feel and the full magical effect.

◎ **Sights**

Before setting out to explore Bellagio, pick up the three self-guided walking tour brochures from the tourist office. They range from one hour (*Historical Tour & Itinerary of the Central Part of Town*) to a three-hour walk that takes in neighbouring villages, including Pescallo, a small one-time fishing port about 1km from the centre, and Loppia, with the 11th-century Chiesa di Santa Maria, which is only visitable from the outside.

Villa Melzi d'Eril   GARDENS
(📋 333 4877427; www.giardinidivillamelzi.it; Lungo Lario Manzoni; adult/reduced €6.50/4; ⏱ 9.30am-6.30pm Mar-Oct) The grounds of neoclassical Villa Melzi d'Eril are a highlight among Lake Como's (many) delightful places. The villa was built in 1808 for one of Napoleon's associates and is coloured by flowering azaleas and rhododendrons in spring. The statue-studded garden was the first English-style park on the lake. Within its walls you'll stumble upon a Japanese garden, a grotto and an Orangerie museum displaying a succinct collection of Roman busts and Etruscan tombs.

Villa Serbelloni   GARDENS
(📋 031 95 15 55; Piazza della Chiesa 14; adult/child €9/5; ⏱ tours 11am & 3.30pm Tue-Sun mid-Mar–early Nov) The lavish gardens of Villa Serbelloni cover much of the promontory on which Bellagio sits. The villa has been a magnet for Europe's great and good, including Austria's

---

LOCAL KNOWLEDGE

LAKESIDE LIDO

With its smart, sand-covered decking, diving platforms and gazebos, Bellagio's lido (☑ 031 95 11 95; www.lidodibellagio. com; Via Carcano 1; per half-/full day €6/10; ⊘10am-6.30pm Tue-Sun May, Jun & Sep, daily Jul & Aug) is a prime place to laze on a sun lounger or plunge into the lake.

---

emperor Maximilian I, Ludovico il Moro and Queen Victoria. The interior is closed to the public, but you can explore the terraced park and gardens, by guided tour only. Numbers are limited to between six and 30 people per group; tickets are sold at the PromoBellagio information office near the church.

🛶 Courses

Bellagio Cooking Classes   COOKING
(☑ 333 7860090; www.gustoitalianobellagio.com; Salita Plinio 5; per person €90) A wonderful way to really get to know Bellagio, these cooking classes have a personal touch – they take you to the village shops to buy the food and then local home-cooks lead the sessions. Classes are small (a minimum of three, maximum of seven). Payment in cash only.

☞ Tours

Bellagio Water Sports   KAYAKING
(☑ 340 3949375; www.bellagiowatersports.com; Pescallo Harbour; tours from €35; ⊘8.30am-4.30pm Mon-Sat, to 2.30pm Sun) Experienced outfitter based in Pescallo, on the east side of the Bellagio headland. Offers five different kayaking tours, from a 1½-hour trip taking in nearby historical villas to a three-hour dig-deep paddle to Varenna. All tours can also be done with stand-up paddle-boards. Reserve at least a day in advance.

Barindelli's   BOATING
(☑ 338 2110337; www.barindellitaxiboats.it; Piazza Mazzini; tours per hour €220) For a touch of film-star glamour, take a tour in one of Barindelli's chic mahogany cigarette boats. The group offers hour-long sunset tours around the Bellagio headland and can also tailor-make outings around the lake.

🛏 Sleeping & Eating

Locanda Barchetta   B&B €
(☑ 031 95 10 30; www.ristorantebarchetta.com; Via Centrale 13; d €100; ⊘Apr-Oct; 🛜) Tradition rules at Barchetta amid the swanky hordes

that often populate Bellagio. Suspended above one of those old family-run restaurants decorated with sepia-toned photos from another era, lie four small, unfussy but spruce rooms that might have sprung from a Neapolitan back alley. Breakfast in the co-owned restaurant costs extra.

Hotel Silvio   HOTEL €€
(☑ 031 95 03 22; www.bellagiosilvio.com; Via Carcano 10; d €75-115, apt from €110; 🅿 ❋ 🛜 ⊠) Located above the fishing hamlet of Loppia a short walk from the village, this family-run hotel is one of Bellagio's most relaxing spots. Here you can wake up in a contemporary Zen-like room and gaze out over the gardens of some of Lago di Como's most prestigious villas, then spend the morning at Bellagio's *lido* (free for hotel guests). The hotel also has a well-regarded restaurant, complete with terrace for sunset dining.

Residence Il Borgo   APARTMENT €€
(☑ 031 95 24 97; www.borgoresidence.it; Salita Plinio 4; apt €75-135; ❋ 🛜) With their blond-wood beams and sleek lines, these stylish apartments make it easy to imagine living in Bellagio full time. Especially as you're just a minute's walk down an atmospheric lane to the lake and are surrounded by countless eateries and bars. Count on spacious kitchens, mezzanines and bedrooms.

★ Ittiturismo da Abate   SEAFOOD €€
(☑ 031 91 49 86; www.ittiturismodabate.it; Frazione Villa 4, Lezzeno; meals €28-38; ⊘7-10.30pm Tue-Sun, noon-2.30pm Sun; 🅿 🚻) Most dishes at Slow Food–focused Da Abate feature fish that's been caught that day in the lake (the restaurant will only open if they've caught enough), so you can sample *lavarello* (white fish) in balsamic vinegar, linguine with perch and black olives, and the robust *missoltino* (fish dried in salt and bay leaves).

Da Abate is 8km south of Bellagio. Booking advised.

🍷 Drinking & Nightlife

★ Enoteca Cava Turacciolo   WINE BAR
(☑ 031 95 09 75; www.cavaturacciolo.it; Salita Genazzini 3; ⊘10.30am-1am Thu-Tue Apr-Oct, shorter hours Nov, Dec & Mar, closed Jan & Feb) A contender for Bellagio's most charming address, this cosy wine bar occupies a candlelit, stonewalled space tucked down a lane near the waterfront. The encyclopedic wine list covers every region in Italy, and there's excellent charcuterie and cheese boards on offer – as well as a few pasta and fish plates.

🛍 Shopping

Alimentaria Gastronomia   FOOD
(Via Bellosio 1; ⊙ 7.30am-9pm) A deli-cum-grocery shop piled high with Larian goodies, among them dried porcini mushrooms, DOP Laghi Lombardi-Lario olive oil, *missoltini* (dried fish) and some rather irreverently shaped bottles of *limoncello* (lemon liqueur). There's an excellent cheese and meat counter, and staff can happily assemble sandwiches with your ingredients of choice.

ⓘ Information

Tourist Office (☑ 031 95 02 04; www.bellagio lakecomo.com; Piazza Mazzini; ⊙ 9.30am-12.30pm & 1-5.30pm, shorter hours winter) Next to the boat landing stage.

PromoBellagio (☑ 031 95 15 55; www.bellagio lakecomo.com; Piazza della Chiesa 14; ⊙ 9.30am-1pm Mon, 9-11am & 2.30-3.30pm Tue-Sun Apr-Oct) A consortium of local businesses that provides useful information. Book guided tours of Villa Serbelloni (p295) here.

Cernobbio to Lenno

The sunny, western lakefront stretch from Cernobbio to Lenno is one of Lago di Como's most glamorous. The big draws here are the blockbuster villas; some are open to the public (such as the bewitching Villa Balbianello); some are most definitely closed (including George Clooney's place, Villa Oleandra, in Laglio).

◉ Sights & Activities

★ **Villa Balbianello**   VILLA
(☑ 0344 5 61 10; www.fondoambiente.it; Via Comoedia 5, Località Balbianello; adult/reduced villa & gardens €20/10, gardens only €10/5; ⊙ gardens 10am-6pm, villa 10am-4.30pm Tue & Thu-Sun mid-Mar–mid-Nov) A 1km walk along the (partially wooded) lake shore from Lenno's main square, Villa Balbianello has cinematic pedigree: this was where scenes from *Star Wars Episode II* and the 2006 James Bond remake of *Casino Royale* were shot. The reason? It is one of the most dramatic locations anywhere on Lake Como, providing a genuinely stunning marriage of architecture and lake views.

Greenway del Lago di Como   HIKING
(www.greenwaydellago.it) Following the erstwhile Strada Regina, an old Roman road that linked Milan and Switzerland, this refreshingly well-signposted path winds its way along Lake Como's western shore between Colonno and Cadenabbia, avoiding the traffic-choked highway and dipping into plenty of *bella* villages along its course.

🛏 Sleeping & Eating

Villa Regina Teodolinda   LUXURY HOTEL €€€
(☑ 031 40 00 31; www.villareginateodolinda.com; Via Vecchia Regina 58, Laglio; r €190-450; ⊙ Mar-Oct; P ✳ @ 🛜 🏊) For a taste of the A-lister lifestyle, head for this sumptuous villa, slightly north of the village of Laglio, allegedly once targeted by George Clooney (who ultimately bought Villa Oleandra, 1km to the south). Elegant and deliciously tasteful rooms, many with lake views, emit refined sophistication; the welcome is discretion itself. Approach by the lake road or by boat via the private landing stage. It's a popular place with newlyweds.

★ **Antica Trattoria del Risorgimento**   ITALIAN €€
(☑ 0344 4 17 89; Via San Abbondio 8, Mezzegra; meals €30-38; ⊙ 7-10.30pm Tue-Sun, noon-2.30pm Sat & Sun; 🛜 🍴) Tucked down a narrow lane in the tiny village of Mezzegra, this wonderful old stone building with its dark wood furnishings (including antique fireplace) cooks up beautifully prepared regional dishes. It's family-run with a small revolving menu featuring three choices of starter, first course and second course. Delicacies might include lake trout cooked on a stone, risotto with wild nettles, and suckling pig.

Reserve ahead. Mezzegra is about 1.5km north of Lenno (and 2km south of Tremezzo).

★ **Materia**   ITALIAN €€€
(☑ 031 207 55 48; www.ristorantemateria.it; Via Cinque Giornate 32; meals €45-55, menus €52-90; ⊙ noon-2.30pm Wed-Sun, 7-10.30pm Tue-Sun) The talk of the town is this enticing Zen-like space, a 10-minute walk from the waterfront. Materia sources many herbs (including unusual varieties) and vegetables from its own greenhouse, and its daring menu pushes flavour notes you won't find elsewhere. Think pigeon with rose-hip and cherries, risotto with woodruff and herring caviar and an intriguing dessert simply named 'Banksy'.

Tremezzo

☑ 0344 / POP 1260

Tremezzo is high on everyone's list for a visit to one of Como's loveliest villas, whose art-packed interior is slightly overshadowed by the stunning gardens surrounding it.

◉ Sights

★ Villa Carlotta — HISTORIC BUILDING
(☑0344 4 04 05; www.villacarlotta.it; Via Regina 2; adult/reduced €12/6; ☺9am-6.30pm Mar-Sep, shorter hours rest of year) The star of the show on a lake shore not bereft of elegant touches, the Villa Carlotta is a fabulous fusion of neoclassical architecture and harmonious garden design. The botanic gardens are filled with colour from orange trees interlaced with pergolas, while some of Europe's finest rhododendrons, azaleas and camellias bloom. The 8-hectare gardens also contain a lush fern valley, a bamboo grove, a Zen-style rock garden, towering cedars and a high-up lookout fringed by olive trees.

⌕ Sleeping & Eating

★ Hotel La Perla — HOTEL €€
(☑0344 4 17 07; www.laperlatremezzo.com; Via Romolo Quaglino 7; d €125-160, with lake views €165-180, family ste €250; P❋≋) Suspended high above the lake in an artfully converted 1960s villa, La Perla is an impeccably run bustle-free tranquillity zone save for the pealing of nearby church bells. Creamy rooms are immaculate; service is warm and friendly; and the vantage point from the hillside with terraces and shapely pool is rockstar lavish. It's worth paying extra for a room with a view.

Al Veluu — RISTORANTE €€€
(☑0344 4 05 10; www.alveluu.com; Via Rogaro 11; meals €45-75; ☺noon-2.30pm & 7-10pm Wed-Mon; ☝) Situated on a steep hillside with panoramic lake views from its terrace, this excellent restaurant serves up home-cooked dishes that are prepared with great pride. They also reflect Lake Como's seasonal produce, so expect butter-soft, milk-fed kid with rosemary at Easter or wild asparagus and polenta in spring.

❶ Information

Tremezzo Tourist Office (☑0344 4 04 93; Via Statale Regina; ☺9am-noon & 3.30-6.30pm Wed-Mon Apr-Oct) is by the boat jetty.

Varenna
☑0341 / POP 750

Varenna, a beguiling village bursting with florid plantlife, is a short ferry ride away from its rival in Como-esque beauty, Bellagio. In many ways the villages are similar: pastel-coloured houses stacked up on mountain slopes defying the standard laws of physics and narrow lanes which are often little more than long staircases. Walk up to Castello di Vezio for panoramic views over the lake or drive the SP65, village-hopping down the Val d'Esino.

◉ Sights

Castello di Vezio — CASTLE
(☑333 4485975; www.castellodivezio.it; Vezio, near Varenna; adult/reduced €4/3; ☺10am-7pm Mon-Fri, to 8pm Sat & Sun Jun-Aug, to 6pm Mar-May, Sep & Oct) High above the terracotta rooftops of Varenna, the imposing Castello di Vezio offers magnificent views over Lake Como. The 13th-century building was once part of a chain of early-warning medieval watchtowers. Get there by taking a steep cobblestone path (about a half-hour hike) from Olivedo (the northern end of Varenna) to Vezio. You can also take a path (around 40 minutes' walk) along the Sentiero Scabium, reached by taking the uphill ramp just opposite the Villa Monastero.

Villa Monastero — HISTORIC BUILDING
(☑0341 29 54 50; www.villamonastero.eu; Via IV Novembre; villa & gardens €9, gardens only €6; ☺9.30am-7pm May-Aug, 10am-6pm Apr & Sep, to 5pm Mar & Oct, 11am-5pm Sun only Jan & Feb) At Villa Monastero elegant balustrades and statues sit amid exotic shrubs; spiky yucca trees frame lake and mountain views. The villa itself is a former convent that was turned into a private residence in the 18th century – which explains the giddy opulence of some of the 11 rooms.

⌕ Sleeping

Albergo Milano — HOTEL €€
(☑0341 83 02 98; www.varenna.net; Via XX Settembre 35; s €140, d €195-230; ☺Mar-Oct; ❋@☎) In the middle of Varenna on the pedestrian main street (well, lane), hillside Albergo Milano opens onto a terrace with magnificent lake vistas. Most of the 12 rooms have some kind of lake view and balcony – they're also tastefully appointed, with gaily painted iron bedsteads, original floor tiles and super-modern bathrooms. You can dine on the **terrace** (☑0341 83 02 98; meals €42-50; ☺7-10pm Wed-Fri & Mon, 12.30-2.30pm & 7-10pm Sat & Sun Apr-Oct) or just sip a cocktail.

Varenna Caffè Bistrot — CAFE €
(☑0341 83 04 59; Contrada Scoscesa 13; snacks €4-10; ☺8.30am-midnight) Should you need 'una pausa' while you're waiting for your Varenna ferry, enter this nouveau-rustic bistro-cafe and peruse the cake case (the

chocolate and pear ought to do nicely), then choose your caffeine from a list of two dozen infusions, and finally grab a pew outside by the water where the wake of a passing boat might splash your shoes.

Il Cavatappi   ITALIAN €€
(☑0341 81 53 49; www.cavatappivarenna.it; Via XX Settembre 10; meals €30-40; ☺noon-2pm & 6.30-9pm Thu-Tue, closed Jan & Feb; ☑) Set along a narrow pedestrian lane in the upper part of Varenna, Il Cavatappi is an intimate spot with just seven tables set amid arched ceilings and stone walls, as opera plays quietly in the background. The cooking is outstanding, with creative twists on regional recipes.

Osteria Quatro Pass   ITALIAN €€
(☑0341 81 50 91; www.quattropass.com; Via XX Settembre 20; meals €35-42; ☺noon-2pm & 7-10pm, closed Mon-Wed winter) Places that don't have a lake view in Varenna are at a distinct disadvantage, which is why this place works just that extra bit harder with the food and service. The menu is fish-forward led by dried salted lake herring served with polenta. Also in the pescatarian line are lake char, perch, snapper, squid and scallops.

🍷 Drinking & Nightlife

Il Molo   BAR
(☑0341 83 00 70; www.barilmolo.it; Via Riva Garibaldi 14; ☺9am-1.30am Apr-Oct) The tiny terrace of Bar Il Molo is Varenna's most sought-after *aperitivi* spot, although the cocktails sometimes morph into huge pitchers of beer. It's raised above the water with cracking views north right up the lake and there's live music in the summer. Molo is also a fine spot for lunch – try the warm ciabatta *panini* served on small bread boards.

ℹ️ Information

Tourist Office (☑0341 83 03 67; www.varennaitaly.com; Via 4 Novembre 3; ☺10am-3pm Mon, 10am-1pm & 2-6pm Tue-Sun Jul, shorter hours rest of year) Located just west of Villa Monastero this office provides information on the lake's entire eastern shore.

ℹ️ Getting There & Away

If driving to Varenna, take the slip road just before the tunnel (coming from either north or south). There's an underground car park (€2 per hour) opposite the entrance to Villa Monastero.

Regular ferries connect Varenna with Como (€11.60, 2¼ hours) and Bellagio (€4.60, 15 to 20 minutes). A car ferry runs to Bellagio (€8.60).

Lago d'Iseo

Cradled in a deep glacial valley and shut in by soaring mountains, little-known Lake Iseo (aka Sebino) is a magnificent sight. The main town, picturesque Iseo (population 9200), is tucked into the southwest shore. To the west, the lovely old town of Sarnico (population 6640) features Liberty villas, while in the north Lovere (population 6630) is a working harbour with a higgledy-piggledy old centre and a wealth of walking trails.

👁 Sights & Activities

Monte Isola   ISLAND
Monte Isola towers from the south end of Lake Iseo, making it easily the lake's most intriguing feature. It's Europe's largest lake island, at 4.28 sq km, and today remains dotted with fishing villages. From Carzano in the northeast – where many ferries land – or Peschiera Maraglio in the southeast you can climb rough stairs to the scattered rural

---

OFF THE BEATEN TRACK

HIKING MONTE ISOLA

Hiking (or biking) is practically obligatory on Monte Isola where cars are mercifully banned, so you might as well go the whole hog and aim to conquer the island's highest point, crowned by the beautifully weathered Santuario Madonna della Ceriola. A path leads steeply out of Peschiera Maraglio and winds up through woodland to the hamlet of Curia high on the hillside, from where it's a short punt to the summit (via two different routes). Both are well-signposted and neither is particularly steep. At the top, you can admire the heady lake views.

To make the walk into a circuit, descend to the island's northwest shore via the hamlets of Masse and Olzano before finally dropping into the tiny port of Carzano where you can have lunch at Locanda al Lago (p300). From Carzano it's a sedate 2.7km stroll along a car-free lakeside esplanade back to Peschiera Maraglio.

The whole walk should take around three hours – more with stops. The information office in Iseo can provide an island map.

MILAN & THE LAKES LAGO D'ISEO

WINE TOURING IN FRANCIACORTA

You could spend days exploring the vineyards of the Franciacorta region (www.stradadelfranciacorta.it), which sits to the south of Lake Iseo. Most tourist offices in the region have a copy of the *Franciacorta Wine Route* brochure, which details hiking and cycling itineraries (some of which are possible by car), and includes a list of over 100 local wineries.

settlements and follow a path to the top of the island (599m).

Accademia Tadini   GALLERY
(📞035 96 27 80; www.accademiatadini.it; Via Tadini 40, Lovere; adult/reduced €7/5; ⏱3-7pm Tue-Sat, 10am-noon & 3-7pm Sun May-Sep, weekends only Apr & Oct) A gallery concentrating on Venetian and Lombard art that's been around for nearly 200 years. Look out for works by Jacopo Bellini, Giambattista Tiepolo and Antonio Canova. The museum is set in an imposing neoclassical palace on the lakefront in Lovere.

Iseobike   CYCLING
(📞340 3962095; www.iseobike.com; Via per Rovato 26, Iseo; bike rental 1/5hr €4/16; ⏱9.30am-12.15pm & 2.30-7pm Apr-Sep) Iseobike hires out bikes and can put together tailor-made cycling tours around the lake into the Franciacorta wine region. Electric bikes are also available from €15 per hour.

🛏 Sleeping & Eating

Hotel Milano   HOTEL €
(📞030 98 04 49; www.hotelmilano.info; Lungolargo Marconi 4, Iseo; s/d from €60/95; ❄@🛜) One of several hotels in the centre of Iseo, the two-star, lakefront Milano is an excellent deal. The lake views are better than the slightly dated rooms, though you'll quickly forget about the furnishing details when you take a seat on the balcony to watch the sunset behind the mountains. There's a one-week minimum stay from mid-July to mid-August.

⭐ Locanda al Lago   ITALIAN €€
(📞030 988 64 72; www.locandaallago.it; Località Carzano 38, Monte Isola; meals €27-37; ⏱noon-2.30pm & 7-9pm Wed-Sun) The Soardi family

has been serving up local dishes since 1948, perfecting deceptively simple treatments of lake fish. It means you can sit on their waterside terrace and feast on fish lasagna or the day's catch combined with *trenette* (a flat pasta) and lashings of extra virgin Monte Isola olive oil.

La Tana dell'Orso   RISTORANTE €€
(📞030 982 16 16; Vicolo Borni 19, Iseo; meals €32-42; ⏱7-9.30pm Mon, Tue & Thu, noon-2pm & 7-9.30pm Fri-Sun) For an intimate ambience and fine local fare head to this excellent eatery where a barrel ceiling sits above rough stone walls. 'The Bear's Den' is hidden away down a cobbled *vicolo* off Piazza Garibaldi. The gnocchi with mussels and clams, beef with polenta, and *casoncelli* (stuffed pasta) are all crowd-pleasers.

L'Isola dei Sapori   MEDITERRANEAN €
(📞366 8237100; www.prodottitipicimonteisola.it; Via Peschiera Maraglio 149; plates from €10; ⏱10am-7.30pm Mon-Thu, to 10pm Fri-Sun) Only those of strong resolve will manage to walk past the al fresco bar at this deli-restaurant on Peschiera Maraglio's harbourfront without stopping. From a line of frosty taps, a quartet of hoppy craft brews are dispensed. Most customers stroll off sipping the suds from plastic cups, but you can also grab a table outside and pair the beer with a plate of fresh-from-the-lake sardines.

ℹ Information

Iseo Tourist Office (📞030 374 87 33; www.iseolake.info; Lungolago Marconi 2, Iseo; ⏱10am-12.30pm & 3.30-6.30pm May-Sep, shorter hours winter) Provides information on the region, including wine-tasting days in Franciacorta.

ℹ Getting There & Around

Iseo Train Station (Via XX Settembre) Links Iseo with Brescia (€3.30, 30 minutes, one to two hourly), where you can connect to Bergamo (from €6.70, 90 minutes).

Navigazione sul Lago d'Iseo (📞035 97 14 83; www.navigazionelagoiseo.it) Operates ferries on the lake. There are regular runs between Lovere and Pisogne. M boats link Iseo with Peschiera Maraglio on Monte Isola (one way/return €4/7, 30 minutes, half-hourly).

SAB (📞035 28 90 11; www.arriva.it) Runs regular buses between Sarnico and Bergamo (€4, 50 minutes).

Lago di Garda & Around

Covering 370 sq km, Lake Garda is the largest of the Italian lakes, straddling the border between three regions: the Lombard plains to the west, Alpine Trentino Alto-Adige to the north and the rolling hills of the Veneto to the east. Look around and you'll be surprised to see a Mediterranean landscape of vineyards, olive groves and citrus orchards that is thanks to the lake's uniquely mild microclimate.

ℹ Getting There & Around

BOAT

Navigazione Lago di Garda (☑ 800 551801; www.navigazionelaghi.it) Operates an extensive ferry network. One-day, unlimited-travel foot-passenger tickets include lake-wide (adult/reduced €34.30/17.60); lower lake (€23.40/12.40); and upper lake (€20.50/11). Single passenger fares include Sirmione to Salò (adult/reduced €9.80/5.90) and Riva del Garda to Sirmione (adult/reduced €13.70/7.80). Car ferries link Toscolano-Maderno with Torri del Benaco and (seasonally) Limone with Malcesine.

BUS

ATV (☑ 045 805 79 22; www.atv.verona.it) Runs buses up the east and west shore, including regular connections between Desenzano del Garda train station and Riva del Garda, via Salò and Gardone, and between Riva del Garda and Verona, via Garda.

SIA (☑ 840 620001; www.arriva.it) Operates buses from Brescia up the western side of the lake to Riva del Garda (€9, three hours, two-hourly). Hourly buses also link Brescia with Desenzano, Sirmione and Verona.

Trentino Trasporti (☑ 0461 82 10 00; www.ttesercizio.it) Connects Riva del Garda with Trento (€4, 1¼ hours, every two hours).

CAR

Car is the fastest way to get to Lake Garda: the A4 motorway skirts the southern shores on its way between Verona and Brescia.

TRAIN

There are two railway stations on the southern shores of Lake Garda – one in Desenzano, the other in Peschiera. Both are served by direct trains from Verona and Brescia.

Sirmione

☑ 030 / POP 8200

Built on the end of an impossibly thin peninsula sticking out from the southern shore of Lake Garda, Sirmione has drawn the likes of Catullus and Maria Callas over the centuries. Today millions of visitors follow in their footsteps for a glimpse of Lake Garda's prettiest village and a dip in its only hot spring.

◉ Sights & Activities

★**Grotte di Catullo**   ARCHAEOLOGICAL SITE
(☑ 030 91 61 57; www.polomuseale.lombardia.beni culturali.it/index.php/grotte-di-catullo; Piazzale Orti Manara 4; adult/reduced €8/4, with Rocca Scaligera €12/6; ⊙ 8.30am-7.30pm Mon & Wed-Sat, 9.30am-7pm Sun late Mar-late Oct, 8.30am-5pm Mon & Wed-Sat, to 2pm Sun late Oct-late Mar) Occupying 2 hectares at Sirmione's northern tip, this ruined 1st-century-AD Roman villa is a picturesque complex of teetering stone arches and tumbledown walls, some three storeys high. It's the largest domestic Roman villa in northern Italy and wandering its terraced hillsides offers fantastic views.

★**Aquaria**   SPA
(☑ 030 91 60 44; www.termedisirmione.com; Piazza Piatti; pools per 90min/day €19/53, treatments from €40; ⊙ pools 9am-10pm Sun-Wed, to midnight Thu-Sat Mar-Jun & Sep-Dec, 9am-midnight daily Jul & Aug, hours vary Jan & Feb) Sirmione is blessed with a series of offshore thermal springs that pump out water at a natural 37°C. They were discovered in the late 1800s and the town's been tapping into their healing properties ever since. At the Aquaria spa you can enjoy a soothing wallow in two thermal pools – the outdoor one is set right beside the lake.

Rocca Scaligera   CASTLE
(Castello Scaligero; ☑ 030 91 64 68; adult/reduced €6/2, with Grotte di Catullo €12/6; ⊙ 8.30am-7.30pm) Expanding their influence northwards, the Scaligeri of Verona built this enormous square-cut castle right at the entrance to old Sirmione. Rising out of the still waters of the lake it guards the only bridge into town, looming over the scene with impressive crenellated turrets and towers. There's not a lot in the way of exhibits inside, but the climb up 146 steps to the top of the tower affords beautiful views over Sirmione's rooftops and the enclosed harbour.

🛏 Sleeping

★**Meublé Grifone**   HOTEL €
(☑ 030 91 60 14; www.gardalakegrifonehotel.eu; Via Gaetano Bocchio 4; s €70-85, d €95-115; ❄ 🌐) The location is superb: set right beside the shore, Grifone's many bedrooms directly overlook the lake and Sirmione's castle,

meaning you get five-star views for two-star prices. Inside it's all old-school simplicity, but with large beds, air-con units and fans. It's family-run and super-accommodating. Breakfast and a balcony cost €10 extra each.

Hotel Marconi HOTEL €€
(☑ 030 91 60 07; www.hotelmarconi.net; Via Vittorio Emanuele II 51; s €45-75, d €80-150; P ☀ ⬚) Blue-and-white-striped umbrellas line the lakeside deck at this stylish, family-run hotel. The quietly elegant, light-filled rooms, some with balconies and lake views, sport subtle shades and crisp fabrics, while the breakfasts involving freshly baked bread and cakes in an elegant dining room are a treat.

✖ Eating

Al Boccondivino LOMBARD €€
(Piazzetta Mosaici; meals €25-30; ⊙ 11am-2am) A small restaurant close to Sirmione's castle with tables pushed close together and every inch of wall covered by a mix of old movie stills and wispy watercolours (they've even managed to paint stars on the ceiling). Wait staff weave like dancers around the tables delivering recipes such as duck sautéed in Valpolicella wine, lake trout with polenta and stewed beef with roast potatoes. Arrive early to bag a table.

La Fiasca TRATTORIA €€
(☑ 030 990 61 11; www.trattorialafiasca.it; Via Santa Maria Maggiore 11; meals €25-40; ⊙ noon-2.30pm & 6.45-10.15pm Thu-Tue) In this small authentic trattoria, tucked away in a backstreet just off the main square, the atmosphere is warm and bustling, and the dishes are packed with traditional Lake Garda produce. Prepare for some gutsy flavours: *bigoli* (thick spaghetti) with sardines, fillets of perch with aspara-

gus, and duck with honey and orange. Reservations recommended.

★ Ristorante Il Girasole ITALIAN €€€
(☑ 030 91 91 82; Via Vittorio Emanuele 72; meals €40-55; ⊙ noon-2.30pm & 7-10.30pm) Sirmione's best dining experience excels in congenial, well-organised service and traditional food skilfully executed. The three-ingredient *cacio e pepe* (pasta with cheese and pepper) topped with black truffles might be the simplest thing on the menu but it's also the most sublime, while the extra-crunchy breadsticks could be the best of the 100 or so you bite into in Italy.

❶ Information

Tourist Office (☑ 030 374 87 21; iat.sirmione@provincia.brescia.it; Viale Marconi 8; ⊙ 10am-12.30pm & 3-6pm Mon-Fri, 9.30am-12.30pm Sat) Efficient if visitor-weary office on the main road into Sirmione.

Valtenesi

The Valtenesi stretches languidly between Desenzano and Salò, its rolling hills etched with vine trellises and flecked with olive groves. The main lake road heads inland, allowing for gentle explorations of small towns, including Padenghe sul Garda, Moniga del Garda, Manerba del Garda and San Felice del Benaco. The tourist office in Desenzano stocks information on the region.

◉ Sights

★ Parco Archeologico Rocca di Manerba NATURE RESERVE
(☑ 0365 55 25 33; www.riservaroccamanerba.com; Via Rocca 20, Manerba del Garda; ⊙ 10am-6pm Wed-Mon Apr-Sep, 9am-1pm Wed-Fri, 10am-5pm

---

LAKE GARDA FOR KIDS

Gardaland (☑ 045 644 97 77; www.gardaland.it; Via Dema 4, Castelnuovo del Garda; adult/reduced €41/36; ⊙ 10am-11pm mid-Jun–mid-Sep, to 5pm Apr–mid-Jun; ⊕) is essentially Italy's Disneyland and is considered to be one of the top 10 theme parks in Europe. Expect larger-than-life dinosaurs, pirate ships and roller coasters, and an aquarium with a glass tunnel where sharks swim overhead.

CanevaWorld (☑ 045 696 99 00; www.canevaworld.it; Località Fossalta 58) contains two theme parks. **Aquapark** (www.canevapark.it; adult/child €26/20; ⊙ 10am-7pm Jul & Aug, to 6pm mid-May–Jun & Sep) features plenty of exhilarating waterslides, while **Movieland Studios** (www.movieland.it; adult/reduced €26/20; ⊙ 10am-6pm Apr, May & Sep, to 7pm Jun & Jul, to 11pm Aug) has stunt-packed action shows. You can even take part yourself at the house of horrors, on a simulated submarine experience or a roller coaster that plunges both forwards and backwards. Opening hours vary, so check the website.

Sat & Sun Oct-Mar) FREE Protected by Unesco, the gorgeous 'rock of Minerva' juts out scenically into the lake just north of Moniga del Garda. The park contains the remaining low rubble walls of a medieval castle, a restful nature reserve of evergreen woods, orchid meadows and walking trails, and some of the best beaches on the lake. There's also a small archaeological museum close to where you can park just outside the village of Montinelle.

Santuario della
Madonna del Carmine   MONASTERY
(☑0365 6 20 32; www.santuariodelcarmine-san felice.it; Via Fontanamonte 1, San Felice del Benaco; ⊙7am-noon & 3-6pm; P) The sanctuary of the Madonna del Carmine dates from 1452. Its simple Gothic-Romanesque exterior does little to prepare you for the technicolour frescoes inside, depicting images of Christ and the Virgin and scenes resonant with the Carmelite Order.

🏃 Activities

Cicli Mata   CYCLING
(☑0365 55 43 01; www.matabikeshop.com; Via Nazionale 63, Raffa di Puegnago; half-/full day €20/27; ⊙9am-1pm & 2.30-7.30pm Tue-Sat, 2.30-7.30pm Sun & Mon) The Valtenesi is perfect cycling country, so pick up a bike from Cicli Mata in Raffa di Puegnago.

Comincioli   FOOD
(☑0365 65 11 41; www.comincioli.it; Via Roma 10, Puegnago del Garda; ⊙by reservation 9.30am-noon & 2.30-7pm Mon-Sat) 🍷 FREE Comincioli produces some of Italy's best olive oils – its Numero Uno is legendary. The family has been harvesting olives for nearly 500 years. Get an insight into that complex process and indulge in a tutored tasting at their farm-vineyard deep in the Valtenesi hills. You can also taste some of the wine that is made here.

La Basia   HORSE RIDING
(☑0365 55 59 58; www.labasia.it; Via Predefitte 31, Puegnago del Garda; per hour €25) At this rambling vineyard and riding school you can have a formal riding lesson or head out for a trot among the vines, before sampling wines and wild honey on the terrace. Between March and September you can also bed down in one of the family-sized *agriturismo* apartments (from €345 to €550 per week).

🍴 Sleeping & Eating

Campeggio Fornella   CAMPGROUND €
(☑0365 6 22 94; www.fornella.it; Via Fornella 1, San Felice del Benaco; campsite per person/car & tent €14/23.50; P ❋ ≋) This luxury, four-star campground has a private beach, lagoon pool, Jacuzzi, children's club, boat centre, tennis courts, restaurant, bar and pizzeria. You pay considerably more for a lakeside pitch.

★Agriturismo i Vegher   AGRITURISMO €€
(☑0365 65 44 79; www.agriturismovegher.it; Via Mascontina 6, Puegnago del Garda; meals €25-35; ⊙7-10pm Wed-Sat & Mon, noon-2.30pm Sun; P 🐾) Well worth the journey along unsurfaced roads and the long booking lead times (book at least a month in advance for holiday weekends, otherwise about two weeks), I Vegher is a place you'll want to arrive at hungry. Awaiting you are numerous delicious antipasti courses, homemade pasta and the unrivalled meat *secondi* (second courses). It's encircled by rows of silver-green olive trees.

Salò
☑0365 / POP 10,600
Wedged between the lake and the foothills of Monte San Bartolomeo, Salò exudes an air of courtly grandeur, a legacy of its days as Garda's capital when the Venetian Republic held sway over the lake. Devoid of sights, Salò's historic centre is lined with fine *Stile Liberty* buildings, small, ordinary shops and restaurants. In 1901 an earthquake levelled many of its older *palazzi,* although a few fine examples remain, including the Torre dell'Orologio (the ancient city gate) and the late-Gothic *duomo* (cathedral).

◉ Sights

★Museo di Salò   MUSEUM
(Musa; www.museodisalo.it; Via Brunati 9; adult/reduced €14/11; ⊙10am-7pm, to 8pm Jun-Sep) Opened in the mid-2010s and housed in an old monastery a block back from Salò's ferry dock, Musa's exhibits are split between a permanent collection that tells the town's history through art and sculpture, and a temporary gallery that has – so far – pulled in several artistic heavy-punchers (exhibitions on Mussolini's personality cult and 'madness in art' have recently featured).

Republic of Salò
AREA

In 1943 Salò was named the capital of the Social Republic of Italy as part of Mussolini and Hitler's last efforts to organise Italian Fascism in the face of advancing American forces. This episode, known as the Republic of Salò, saw more than 16 public and private buildings in the town commandeered and turned into Mussolini's ministries and offices. Strolling between the sites is a surreal tour of the dictator's doomed mini-state. Look out for the multilingual plaques scattered around town.

🛏 Sleeping

Hotel Laurin HISTORIC HOTEL €€
(☑ 0365 2 20 22; www.hotellaurinsalo.it; Viale Landi 9; d €155-300; P ❄ 🛜 🏊) An art nouveau treat with some real history behind it, the Hotel Laurin (formerly the Villa Simonini) was the Foreign Ministry during Mussolini's short-lived Republic. Downstairs salons retain wonderful details: frescoes by Bertolotti, intricate parquet floors, and wood inlay and wrought-iron volutes. Rooms mix tradition with modernity; some have terraces and king-size beds.

★**Villa Arcadio** VILLA €€€
(☑ 0365 4 22 81; www.hotelvillaarcadio.it; Via Navelli 2; d €150-270, ste €300-450; P ❄ @ 🛜 🏊) Perched above Salò and surrounded by olive groves, this converted convent lays on restrained luxury in a semi-rural setting. Enjoy the vista of glassy lake and misty mountains from the cheese-wedge-shaped pool or retreat inside to frescoed rooms and ancient wood-beamed halls.

🍴 Eating

★**Al Cantinone** TRATTORIA €€
(☑ 0365 2 02 34; Piazza Sant'Antonio 19; meals €25-30; ⏰ noon-2.30pm & 7-10pm Fri-Wed) It's well worth heading just a few streets back from the waterfront to track down this friendly neighbourhood trattoria, home to gingham tablecloths, fabulous cooking smells and a clutch of regulars playing cards in the corner. Good-value dishes draw on Salò's lake-meets-mountains setting.

Osteria di Mezzo OSTERIA €€€
(☑ 0365 29 09 66; www.osteriadimezzo.it; Via di Mezzo 10; meals €42-55; ⏰ noon-11pm Wed-Mon) At this intimate *osteria* guarded by hydrangeas a constant stream of hearty meals heads into a dining room lined with antique mirrors and weathered stone. King salmon carpaccio with caviar and shredded beef with truffles are just some of the delights to choose from.

Gardone Riviera
☑ 0365 / POP 2500

Once Lake Garda's most prestigious corner, Gardone is flush with belle-époque hotels and extravagant gardens. They tumble down the hillside from the historic centre, Gardone Sopra, to the cobbled *lungolago* (lakefront) of Gardone Sotto, which is lined with cafes. Although the glamour of Gardone's 19th-century heyday is long gone it is a pleasant place for a stroll and drink, although you'll probably want to base yourself elsewhere.

An hour uphill is the pretty mountain village of San Michele, from where you can pick up a number of walking trails. Ask at the tourist office in Gardone Sotto for details.

◉ Sights

★**Il Vittoriale degli Italiani** MUSEUM
(☑ 0365 29 65 11; www.vittoriale.it; Piazza Vittoriale; gardens & museums adult/reduced €16/13; ⏰ 9am-8pm Apr-Oct, to 5pm Tue-Sun Nov-Mar; P) Poet, soldier, hypochondriac and proto-Fascist, Gabriele d'Annunzio (1863–1938) defies easy definition, and so does his estate. Bombastic, extravagant and unsettling, it's home to every architectural and decorative excess imaginable and is full of quirks that help shed light on the man. Visit and you'll take in a dimly lit, highly idiosyncratic villa (for which the tour is guided), three distinct museums and tiered gardens complete with full-sized battleship.

Giardino Botanico
Fondazione André Heller GARDENS
(☑ 336 410877; www.hellergarden.com; Via Roma 2; adult/reduced €12/6; ⏰ 9am-7pm Mar-Nov) Gardone's heyday was due in large part to its mild climate, something which benefits the thousands of exotic blooms that fill artist André Heller's sculpture garden. Laid out in 1912 by Arturo Hruska, the garden is divided into pocket-sized climate zones, with tiny paths winding from central American plains to African savannah, via swaths of tulips and bamboo.

🛏 Sleeping

⭐ Locanda Agli Angeli   B&B €€
(☑ 0365 2 09 91; www.agliangeli.biz; Via Dosso 7; d from €105; [P][❄][❅]) It's a perfect hillside Lago di Garda bolthole: a beautifully restored, rustic-chic *locanda* (inn) with a kidney-shaped pool, a terrace dotted with armchairs and Italian-meets-Balinese decor. Ask for room 29 for a balcony with grandstand lake and hill views, but even the smaller bedrooms are full of charm.

ℹ Information

Tourist Office (☑ 0365 374 87 36; Corso della Repubblica 8; ⊙ 9am-12.30pm & 2.15-6pm Mon-Sat) Stocks information on activities and nearby hikes.

Riva del Garda & Around

POP 17,400 / ELEV 73M

Get off the boat in Riva at Garda's northern tip and you'll quickly notice a whiff of the Tirol in the air. For centuries Riva was a key access point for northern armies into Italy. In the Middle Ages the town was a port for the Prince-Bishops of Trento, and throughout its history Riva was much fought over. In 1815 it became part of the Austrian Empire and soon became a popular holiday resort for the Archduke and northern European intelligentsia. Stendhal, Thomas Mann and Kafka all summered here. These days it's a nexus for serious rock-climbers.

👁 Sights & Activities

East of the town centre at Punta Lido, Riva's waterfront is given over to pebble beaches, parkland and picnic spots. Most of the water-sports agencies are based here and it provides the launchpad for all manner of sailing, windsurfing and kitesurfing activities. It's particularly popular on Sunday mornings when all Riva seems to take a well-dressed amble here.

⭐ Cascata del Varone   WATERFALL
(☑ 0464 52 14 21; www.cascata-varone.com; Via Cascata 12; €6; ⊙ 9am-7pm May-Aug, to 6pm Apr & Sep, to 5pm Mar & Oct, 10am-5pm Nov-Feb) An unusual 100m waterfall that thunders through a vertical limestone tunnel rather than off an open cleft. With the help of metal walkways, you can enter the gorge to see the torrent – and get a soaking in the process. A botanical garden has taken root on the terraced hillside, making use of the perpetual

downpour. The waterfall is just outside the village of Varone and 3km northwest of Riva's centre. Bus number 1 will get you there, or you can walk up on bike paths.

⭐ La Strada del Ponale   HIKING
(www.ponale.eu) Once the main (and only) road linking Riva with Limone, the Ponale has been reborn as a dedicated cycling and walking path that cuts into the cliff face like a horizontal crevasse close to Lake Garda's northern tip. From a distance it looks like a *via ferrata* (trail with permanent cables and ladders), but up close it's wide enough for mountain bikers and hikers to share the road.

Arco Mountain Guide   CLIMBING
(☑ 330 567285; www.arcomountainguide.com) For information on some of the best climbing in Italy (courses and routes), as well as winter skiing and snowboarding, contact Arco Mountain Guide. Guided climbs start at €55, and they also do *via ferrate*.

The main meeting point is the Caneve car park in the village of Arco.

Canyon Adventures   OUTDOORS
(☑ 334 8698666; www.canyonadv.com; Via Matteotti 12; ⊙ May-Oct) Arranges trips to the Palvico and Rio Nero gorges in the Val di Ledro and the Vione canyon in Tignale as well as kayaking, *via ferrata* trips, caving and climbing. Four-hour canyoning trips start at around €75.

Surfsegnana   WATER SPORTS
(☑ 0464 50 59 63; www.surfsegnana.it; Foci del Sarca, Torbole) Operates from Lido di Torbole. Runs lessons in windsurfing (€59), kitesurfing (€119) and sailing (€75), and hires out windsurfing kits (per half-day €45), sail boats (per two hours €45 to €75) and SUPs (per two hours €25). It's also at Porfina Beach in Riva.

🎪 Festivals & Events

Rockmaster Festival   SPORTS
(☑ 0464 47 25 67; www.rockmasterfestival.com; ⊙ late Aug) Arco is one of Europe's most popular climbing destinations and is the location of the Rockmaster festival and climbing competition in late summer.

🛏 Sleeping

Hotel Garni Villa Maria   HOTEL €
(☑ 0464 55 22 88; www.garnimaria.com; Viale dei Tigli; d €95, ste €120-160; [P][❄][❅]) Beautifully designed, uber-modern rooms make this

small family-run hotel a superb deal. Pristine bedrooms have a Scandinavian vibe, with all-white linens, sleek modern bathrooms and accents of orange and lime green. There's a tiny roof garden, and bedrooms with balconies offer impressive mountain views.

Villa Angelica
VILLA €€

(☑ 0464 55 67 91; www.villaangelicariva.com; Via San Giacomo 48; d €150-270, q €130-450; P 🛜) Located 1.6km outside Riva, the Angelica is classified as one of Lake Garda's historic villas with antecedents in the 14th century. Inside, the handsome apartments sleeping up to four seem almost too good to be true. Unlike other villas, the place is family-run and the owners are happy to share the house's history.

★ Lido Palace
HISTORIC HOTEL €€€

(☑ 0464 02 18 99; www.lido-palace.it; Viale Carducci 10; d/ste from €300/450; P 🌡 @ 🛜 🌊) If you're flush with euros, Riva's captivating Lido Palace is the place to offload them. The exquisite building dates back to 1899 when it opened as a resort for holidaying Austrian royalty. A recent renovation means super-modern bedrooms with muted colour schemes now embellish the grand Liberty-style villa, offering peerless views over lawns and lake.

🍴 Eating

Cristallo Caffè
CAFE €

(☑ 0464 55 38 44; www.cristallogelateria.com; Piazza Catena 17; cones €2.50; ⊙ 7am-midnight, closed Nov-Mar) There's a clockwork efficiency about Cristallo that isn't always present in tourist-heavy lakeside cafes in Italy. Plying ice cream since 1892, the 60 flavours of artisanal gelato are what the cafe is most famous for. But it's also a fine place to digest well-crafted economical pastas, pizzas and *piadine* (Italian flat-bread sandwiches) with prices that rarely sail north of €10.

★ Osteria Le Servite
OSTERIA €€

(☑ 0464 55 74 11; www.leservite.com; Via Passirone 68, Arco; meals €30-45; ⊙ 7-10.30pm Tue-Sun Apr-Sep, 7-10.30pm Wed-Sat Oct-Mar; P 🍴) Tucked away in Arco's wine-growing region, this elegant little *osteria* serves dishes that are so seasonal the menu changes weekly. You might be eating mimosa gnocchi, tender *salmerino* (Arctic char) or organic ravioli with *stracchino* cheese.

★ Restel de Fer
ITALIAN €€

(☑ 0464 55 34 81; www.resteldefer.com; Via Restel de Fer 10; meals €36-60; ⊙ noon-2.30pm & 7-11pm daily Jul & Aug, Thu-Tue Sep, Oct & Dec-Jun; P 🛜) Set in a quiet residential quarter, this family-run *locanda* feels like dropping by a friend's rustic-chic house: expect worn leather armchairs, copper cooking pots and a suit of armour greeting you at the door. The menu focuses on seasonal, local delicacies such as pork wrapped in smoked mountain ham, pressure-cooked Garda trout, and veal with Monte Baldo truffles.

Osteriva
OSTERIA €€

(☑ 0464 55 26 53; Via Fiume 15; meals €25-30; ⊙ 6-11.30pm Mon-Wed, 11am-2.30pm & 6-11.30pm Fri-Sun) If you're just off the Lake Garda ferry from 'down south' (ie Lombardy), welcome to Trentino where Teutonic influences prevail and sausages are king. If you're heading deeper into the Dolomites, treat the speck (smoked cured ham), apple strudel and unfortunately named *stinco* (pork shank) as a shape of things to come.

ℹ Information

Tourist Office (☑ 0464 55 44 44; www. gardatrentino.it; Largo Medaglie d'Oro; ⊙ 9am-7pm daily May-Sep, to 6pm Mon-Fri Oct-Apr) By the main bus stop. Can advise on everything from climbing and paragliding to wine tasting and markets.

Malcesine

☑ 045 / POP 3700

With the lake lapping right up to the tables of its harbourside restaurants and the chunky, snow-capped ridge of Monte Baldo looming behind, Malcesine is quintessential Lake Garda. Alas, its privileged setting and mountain-ascending cable car attract hundreds of day trippers, who flood the town's tiny streets.

🏃 Activities

Funivia Malcesine–Monte Baldo
CABLE CAR

(☑ 045 7440 02 06; www.funiviedelbaldo.it; Via Navene Vecchia 12; adult/reduced return €22/15; ⊙ 8am-7pm Apr-Sep, to 5pm Oct-Mar) Jump aboard this cable car and glide 1760m above sea level for spectacular views – circular rotating cabins reveal the entire lake and surrounding terrain. For the first 400m the slopes are covered in oleanders and olive and citrus trees – after that, oak and chestnut take over. Mountain-bike trails wind down from the summit.

Getting off the cable car at the intermediate station of San Michele (from Malcesine one way/return €6/10) opens up some excellent hikes; pick up a map from the tourist office before you set out. The hour-long walk back to Malcesine reveals a rural world of hillside houses and working farms.

Xtreme Malcesine   CYCLING
(☑ 045 740 01 05; www.xtrememalcesine.it; Via Navene Vecchia 10; road/mountain bike per day €15/25; ☺ 8am-7pm) Rents bikes from its shop at the base of the Monte Baldo cable car. There's also a bike cafe, and the owners run mountain-bike tours into the hills.

🍴 Eating

★ Speck Stube   BARBECUE €
(☑ 045 740 11 77; www.speckstube.com; Via Navene Vecchia 139; meals €15-25; ☺ noon-11pm Mar-Oct; 🅿 🖼) You could be forgiven for thinking you'd just arrived in rural Bavaria at this popular Lake Garda haunt. On sunny days, multitudes of bikers and motorists pull over to tuck into sizzling meat straight off the grill washed down with German-sized pitchers of cold beer. Forsake the scent of alpine flowers for the afternoon and enjoy the aroma of sausages, pork on the bone and barbecued chicken.

Vecchia Malcesine   GASTRONOMY €€€
(☑ 045 740 04 69; www.vecchiamalcesine.com; Via Pisort 6; menus €95; ☺ noon-2pm & 7-10pm Thu-Tue) Hillside Vecchia Malcesine is at once creative, fun and very, very tasty. The Michelin-starred menu (propped up by superb lake views) is exquisitely presented using the likes of trout with horseradish, smoked caviar and white chocolate, or fake tomato (we won't ruin the surprise).

The restaurant is well signposted, but hard to find. Don't try to drive to the gates as you'll get stuck in the narrow lanes.

🛍 Shopping

Consorzio Olivicoltori di Malcesine   FOOD
(☑ 045 740 12 86; www.oliomalcesine.it; Via Navene 21; ☺ 9am-12.30pm & 3.30-6.30pm Mon-Sat, 9am-1pm Sun, shorter hours winter) Olives harvested around Malcesine are milled into first-rate extra virgin olive oil by this local consortium. You can sample the product here. Known as 'El nos Oio' (Our Oil), it's a gold-green liquid that's low in acidity and

has a light, fruity, slightly sweet taste. Prices of the cold-pressed extra virgin DOP oil start at €8.50 for 0.25L.

ℹ Information

Tourist office (☑ 045 740 00 44; www.tourism.verona.it; Via Gardesana 238; ☺ 9.30am-12.30pm & 3-6pm Mon-Sat, 9.30am-12.30pm Sun) Set back from the lake beside the bus station.

Garda & Punta San Vigilio
POP 4000

Situated in the shade of the Rocca del Garda is the 10th-century fishing village that gave the lake its name. Sadly, the picturesque town is now cut through by the main perimeter road around the lake making summer traffic overwhelming. Out of season, Garda's perfectly curved bay and fine shingle beaches make it a great lunch spot.

The leafy headland of Punta San Vigilio (adult/reduced incl Parco Baia delle Sirene €13/6; 🅿) curls out into the lake 3km north of Garda. An avenue of cypress trees leads from the car park towards a gorgeous crescent of bay backed by olive groves. There the Parco Baia delle Sirene (☑ 045 725 58 84; www.parcobaiadellesirene.it; adult/reduced incl Punta San Vigilio €13/6, cheaper after 2.30pm; ☺ 10am-7pm Apr & May, 9.30am-8pm Jun-Aug; 🅿) offers sun loungers beneath the trees; there's also a children's play area.

Locanda San Vigilio (☑ 045 725 66 88; www.punta-sanvigilio.it; Punta San Vigilio; d €270-375, ste €440-900; 🅿 ❄ @ 🏊) is not the sort of place you want to rock up to with a backpack and no reservation. This enchanting 16th-century *locanda* feels just like a luxurious English manor house. Worthy of Napoleon, Churchill and Prince Charles (yep, they've all stayed here), the elegant dark wood, stone floors and plush furnishings ensure an old-world-meets-new-luxury feel.

Bardolino
☑ 045 / POP 7000

On the eastern Veneto shore of Lake Garda, prosperous Bardolino is a town in love with the grape. More than 70 vineyards and wine cellars grace the gentle hills that roll east from Bardolino's shores. The best time to visit is in early October during the Festa dell'Uva e del Vino, when the town's waterfront fills with food stands, as well as

LOCAL KNOWLEDGE

COUNTRYSIDE SPA DAY

The **Parco Thermale del Garda** (☑ 045 759 09 88; www.villadeicedri. it; Piazza di Sopra 4, Colà; adult/reduced €26/17; ⏰ 9.30am-11pm Sun-Fri, to 1am Sat) is an enormous, 5-hectare natural spa complete with thermal lakes, pools and Jacuzzis set in a beautiful park replete with rare trees and plants. The lakes average 33–34°C and are equipped with jets, fountains, cascades and geysers. They are lit in the evening so night-time bathing is possible, and the park is attached to the Villa dei Cedri where a gym and massage treatments are available. The main lake is set infront of the Wintergarten Pavilion, a glass-and-steel summerhouse now housing the changing rooms and a restaurant. The park is 7km southeast of Lazise.

musicians and dancers. The tourist office stocks a map of local producers on the Bardolino Strada del Vino (www.stradadelbardolino.com).

◎ Sights & Activities

Pieve di San Zeno CHURCH
(Corte San Zeno) There's old and there's...*old.* Hemmed in by houses and guarded by an agreeably shabby courtyard north of the main road, this tiny church, dating from the 9th century, is one of the finest pieces of Carolingian architecture to have survived in northern Italy. Its almost windowless form and moody interior give visitors a good impression of how early-Christian worship must have felt.

Museo del Vino MUSEUM
(☑ 045 622 83 31; www.museodelvino.it; Via Costabella 9; ⏰ 9am-12.30pm & 2.30-7pm mid-Mar–Sep, hours vary Oct–mid-Mar) FREE Just off the main lake road and walkable from town, the Museo del Vino is set within the Zeni Winery, and rarely has a museum smelt this good. Rich scents waft around displays of wicker grape baskets, coopers' tools, drying racks and gigantic timber grape presses. Tastings of Zeni's red, white and rosé wines are free, or pay to sample pricier vintages, including barrel-aged Amarone.

Zeni Winery WINE
(☑ 045 721 00 22; www.zeni.it; Via Costabella 9; ⏰ 9am-12.30pm & 2.30-7pm) Zeni has been crafting quality wines from Bardolino's morainic hills since 1870. Get an insight into that process with an hour-long winery tour that ends with a mini-tasting in the *cantina.* Reservations aren't necessary. English tours kick off at 10.30am on Wednesday (€5). There's a free-entry wine museum on-site and free tastings for the 13 varieties of cheaper wines on offer.

🛏 Sleeping & Eating

Corte San Luca APARTMENT €
(☑ 345 8212906; www.cortesanluca.com; Piazza Porta San Giovanni 15; d €100, 4-person apt from €250; 🅿✳🛜) Someone with a flair for design has created 11 smart central apartments – expect suspended furniture, moulded chairs and glass-topped tables. With their fully kitted-out kitchens, laundries and 32in TVs, the apartments are a particularly smart home away from home. There's a minimum stay of a week in July and August.

Il Giardino delle Esperidi OSTERIA €€
(☑ 045 621 04 77; Via Goffredo Mameli 1; meals €40-50; ⏰ 7-10pm Mon & Wed-Fri, noon-2.30pm & 7-10pm Sat & Sun) Holidaying gourmets should head for this intimate little *osteria,* where sourcing local delicacies is a labour of love for its sommelier-owner. The intensely flavoured baked truffles with *parmigiano reggiano* (Parmesan) are legendary, and the highly seasonal menu may feature rarities such as nettle gnocchi or lamb fillet in Marsala reduction.

🍷 Drinking & Nightlife

★**La Bottega del Vino** WINE BAR
(☑ 348 6041800; Piazza Matteotti 46; ⏰ 9.30am-2am) Welcome to wine country. You can get straight off the boat and into vino-tasting mode at this no-nonsense bar in the centre of town that looks and feels more like a pub. Inside, a stream of lively banter passes between staff and locals sinking €6.50 glasses of Amorone paired with crunchy cheese and ham sandwiches.

❶ Information

Tourist Office (☑ 045 721 00 78; www. tourism.verona.it; Piazzale Aldo Moro 5; ⏰ 9am-noon & 3-6pm Mon-Sat, 10am-2pm Sun) Operates a hotel booking service and can advise on the surrounding wine region.

THE PO PLAIN

Stretching from the foot of the pre-Alps to low-lying, lake-fringed plains, this is a region that's often, but unjustifiably, overlooked. In the north, framed by mountains and encircled by defensive walls, you'll find Bergamo, an ancient hill town rich in architecture and art. Nearby, Brescia showcases gutsy cuisine and impressive fragments of its Roman past. In Cremona, once home to Antonio Stradivari, discover a vibrant musical heritage and old-town vibe. And in the east is captivating Mantua, surrounded by lakes, and packed with fresco-filled palaces.

Bergamo

☑ 035 / POP 120,000

Of Lombardy's four great historic cities, Bergamo might just be the finest, courtesy of its handsomely walled old town, antique but atmospheric main piazza and – lest we forget – overachieving Serie A football team (Atalanta). Split into two sections: *alto* (the old town atop a hill) and *basso* (the newer town inhabiting the plains below), Bergamo juxtaposes medieval monuments with the footprints of 21st-century hipsters.

◉ Sights

The best way to explore Bergamo's old town is to simply wander without haste. Via Bartolomeo Colleoni and Via Gombito are lined with all sorts of curious shops and eateries. For rewarding panoramas circumnavigate the city's 5.3km-long, Venetian-era defensive walls, which were recognised by Unesco as a World Heritage Site in 2017.

★ **Accademia Carrara**   GALLERY
(☑ 035 23 43 96; www.lacarrara.it; Piazza Carrara 82; adult/reduced €10/8; ⊙ 9.30am-5.30pm Wed-Mon) Just east of the old city walls is one of Italy's great art repositories. Founded in 1780, it contains an exceptional range of Italian masters. Raphael's *San Sebastiano* is a highlight, and other artists represented include Botticelli, Canaletto, Mantegna and Titian.

The collection was started by local scholar Count Giacomo Carrara (1714–96) and has now swelled to 1800 paintings dating from the 15th to 19th centuries. Reopened after a seven-year renovation, the gallery's displays revolve around 28 rooms. Highlights include the sections on Giovanni Bellini, Florence

and the major local artists Lorenzo Lotto and Giovanni Battista Moroni.

★ **Torre del Campanone**   TOWER
(☑ 035 24 71 16; Piazza Vecchia; adult/reduced incl Podestà €5/3; ⊙ 10am-6pm Tue-Fri, to 8pm Sat & Sun Apr-Oct, reduced hours winter) Bergamo's colossal, square-based Torre del Campanone soars 52m above the city. It still tolls a bell at 10pm, the legacy of an old curfew. Taking the lift to the top of the tower reveals sweeping views down onto the town, up to the pre-Alps and across to the Lombard plains.

There's a 230-step staircase if you're feeling energetic.

Entry also includes the **Palazzo del Podestà** (Museo Storico dell'Età Veneta; ☑ 035 24 71 16; www.palazzodelpodesta.it; Piazza Vecchia; adult/reduced incl Torre del Campanone €5/3; ⊙ 10am-1pm & 2.30-6pm Tue-Fri, 10am-7pm Sat & Sun).

Basilica di Santa Maria Maggiore BASILICA
(www.www.fondazionemia.it; Piazza del Duomo; ⊙ 9am-12.30pm & 2.30-6pm Mon-Fri, 9am-6pm Sat & Sun Apr-Oct, shorter hours Nov-Mar) Bergamo's most striking church, begun in 1137, is quite a mishmash of styles. To its whirl of Romanesque apses (on which some external frescoes remain visible), Gothic additions were added. Influences seem to come from afar, with dual-colour banding (black and white, and rose and white) typical of Tuscany and an interesting *trompe l'œil* pattern on part of the facade. Highlights include wooden marquetry designed by Lorenzo Lotto and the funerary tomb of the great Bergamo-born composer Gaetano Donizetti.

Cappella Colleoni   CHAPEL
(Piazza del Duomo; ⊙ 9am-12.30pm & 2-6.30pm Mar-Oct, to 4.30pm Tue-Sun Nov-Feb) The Cappella Colleoni, attached to the north side of the Basilica di Santa Maria Maggiore, was built between 1472 and 1476 as a magnificent mausoleum-cum-chapel for the Bergamese mercenary commander Bartolomeo Colleoni (c 1400–75), who led Venice's armies in campaigns across northern Italy. He lies buried inside in a magnificent tomb.

**Galleria d'Arte Moderna
e Contemporanea**   GALLERY
(GAMeC; ☑ 035 27 02 72; www.gamec.it; Via San Tomaso 53; adult/reduced €6/4; ⊙ 10am-6pm Wed-Mon) GAMeC, as the gallery is known, sits opposite the more prestigious Accademia Carrara and displays modern works by Italian artists like Giacomo Balla, Giorgio

MILAN & THE LAKES BERGAMO

Bergamo

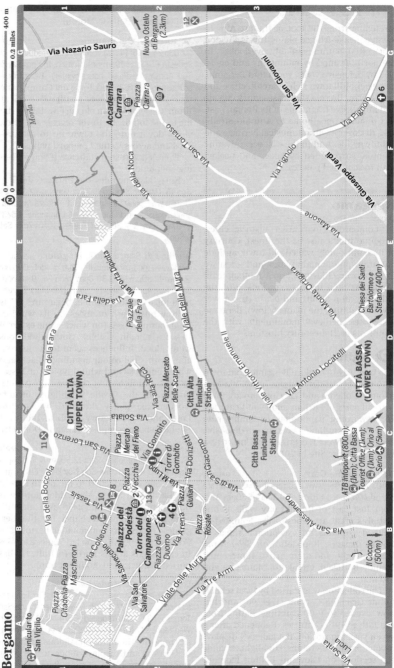

400 m
0.2 miles

Via Nazario Sauro

Nuovo Ostello di Bergamo (2.3km)

Via San Giovanni

Accademia Carrara 1
Piazza Carrara

7

6

Via della Noca

Via San Tomaso

Via Pignolo

Via Giuseppe Verdi

Morla

Via Masone

Via della Fara

Piazzale della Fara

Via della Fara

Via Porta Dipinta

Viale delle Mura

Chiesa dei Santi Bartolomeo e Stefano (400m)

CITTÀ BASSA (LOWER TOWN)

Via Monte Ortigara

Viale Vittorio Emanuele II

Via Antonio Locatelli

CITTÀ ALTA (UPPER TOWN)

Via alla Rocca

Via Solata

Piazza Mercato delle Scarpe

Città Alta Funicular Station

Città Bassa Funicular Station

ATB Infopoint (800m); (3km); Città Bassa Tourist Office (1km); Orio al Serio (5km)

11

Via San Lorenzo

Piazza Mercato del Fieno

Via al Gombito

Torre di Gombito

Via Donizetti

Via di San Giacomo

Via della Boccola

Piazza Vecchia

8

10

Via Tassis

9

Via Colleoni

Via San Salvatore

Piazza del Duomo

Torre del Campanone

Palazzo del Podestà 2

13

5

4

Piazza Giuliani

Piazza Rosate

Via San Alessandro

Il Coccio (500m)

Piazza Cittadella Piazza Mascheroni

Via Arena

Viale delle Mura

Via Tre Armi

Via Santa Lucia

Funicular to San Vigilio

Bergamo

Morandi, Giorgio de Chirico and Filippo de Pisis. A contribution from Vassily Kandinsky lends an international touch.

Chiesa del Santo Spirito　　CHURCH
(Church of the Holy Spirit; Via Tasso 100; ⊙8-11am & 3-6pm Thu-Tue) Look for the Venetian-inspired countryside and colour palette that defines Lorenzo Lotto's *Pala di Santo Spirito* (1521), where the Madonna sits beneath a garland of energetic winged *putti* (cherubs). It's on the right-hand side as you face the altar.

🛏 Sleeping

Albergo Il Sole　　HOTEL €
(☎035 21 82 38; www.ilsolebergamo.com; Via Colleoni 1; s/d/tr €65/85/110; 🅿🤝) It may be metres from Bergamo's main square, but Il Sole has the unhurried feel of a family-run B&B in a quiet Italian village. Enter via the eponymous restaurant and find your room amid a dense warren of corridors and stairs.

Hotel Piazza Vecchia　　HOTEL €€
(☎035 25 31 79; www.hotelpiazzavecchia.it; Via Colleoni 3; r €140-240; 🌀@🤝) An air of elegance pervades this 14th-century townhouse in the Città Alta which cleverly fuses *vecchia* (old) with new with its honey-coloured beams, striped wallpaper and Van Gogh and Gauguin reproductions on the walls. Rooms have parquet floors and bathrooms that

gleam with chrome; the deluxe ones have a lounge and a balcony with mountain views.

★ Da Vittorio　　BOUTIQUE HOTEL €€€
(☎035 68 10 24; www.davittorio.com; Via Cantalupa 17, Brusaporto; s €300-350, d €400-450; 🅿🌀🤝) Da Vittorio is not only a noteworthy gourmet hideout (p312) 9km east of town, but also offers 10 quality suites in its low-slung country estate. Each of the generous rooms enjoys its own sumptuous decor, with beautifully woven fabrics and marble bathroom. Indulge in a tasting menu breakfast, with a series of miniportions of various sweet and savoury options.

🍴 Eating

Il Coccio　　ITALIAN €
(☎035 093 23 38; www.trattoriailcoccio.it; Via Sant'Alessandro 54; meals €12-20; ⊙11am-3pm Tue-Sun; 🍴) If you're staying in the Città Alta, it's worth letting gravity carry you downhill to seek out this lunch-only, four-table cafe with an out-of-the-ordinary Italian menu catering for all kinds of lactose, gluten and vegetarian requirements. Everything on the ever-changing menu-board is homemade. There are usually a couple of lasagne and cannelloni options plus plenty of vegetable *contorni* (side dishes).

Il Fornaio　　PIZZA, BAKERY €
(Via Colleoni 1; pizza slices around €3-4; ⊙8am-8pm) With its wedges of focaccia-style pizza displayed like colourful art in the front window, it's no wonder this bakery-cafe is perennially crowded. This is the kind of food that makes you hungry just looking at it, big square slabs of pizza generously topped with everything from folded cured meats to gleaming white cheese.

★ Noi　　ITALIAN €€
(☎035 23 77 50; www.noi-restaurant.it; Via Alberto Pitentino 6; meals €35-45; ⊙7.30pm-midnight Mon, 12.30-2.30pm & 7.30pm-midnight Tue-Sat; 🤝) More esoteric than your average trattoria, Noi is a chameleonic restaurant that changes it spots between lunch and dinner (they even change the restaurant sign). Lunch (under the moniker 'Rame-noi') has an Asian-fusion theme with ramen noodles heading the bill, while at dinner, it returns to its Italian roots with five-course tasting menus endowing local food with fusion influences and presenting it like food art.

La Tana ITALIAN €€
(☑ 035 21 31 37; www.tanaristorante.it; Via San Lorenzo 25; meals €32-42; ☺ noon-2.30pm & 7-10pm Wed-Sun, 7-10pm Tue) In the upper town, tucked close to the Venetian walls, La Tana remains exceptionally popular for painstakingly prepared Bergamesque dishes served in a sun-drenched interior of exposed brick and colourful artwork, or out on the small front terrace.

★ **Da Vittorio** GASTRONOMY €€€
(☑ 035 68 10 24; www.davittorio.com; Via Cantalupa 17, Brusaporto; set menu lunch €80, dinner €190-280; ☺ 12.30-2.30pm & 7-10pm Thu-Tue Sep-Jul) Bergamo's Vittorio is set in a country house 9km east of town and, with over 50 years and three Michelin stars under its belt, is up there with the best restaurants in Italy, thanks to the celebrated talents of Bergamo-born chef Enrico Cerea. Many of its creative dishes such as *orrecchia di elefante* and *egg 'à la egg'* have become legendary.

🍷 Drinking & Nightlife

Bugan Coffee Lab COFFEE
(☑ 035 31 71 47; www.bugancoffeelab.com; Via Quarenghi 32; ☺ 8.30am-6.30pm Mon-Fri, to 7.30pm Sat & Sun) Challenging the hegemony of Lavazza and Illy, Bugan was Italy's first coffee 'laboratory' when it opened in 2014. Headquartered in this Città Bassa roastery, tasting room, shop and training school for baristas it offers coffee samples any time of day. Try an espresso made from whatever beans are on offer (a fruity Rwandan concoction was circulating at last visit). There's a second tasting room in the Città Alta, handily located just off the main piazza.

Caffè del Tasso CAFE
(☑ 035 23 79 66; Piazza Vecchia 3; ☺ 8.30am-12.30am) They could serve mud-water in this cafe on Bergamo's main square, so delightful is the setting. Notwithstanding, the drinks still taste just as good as they did in 1476 when this venerable establishment first opened its doors. Inside the ambience is classic old-school Italy with marble tables guarded by gossiping *nonnas* just back from a dye and set at the hairdressers.

❶ Information

Airport Tourist Office (☑ 035 32 04 02; www.visitbergamo.net; arrivals hall; ☺ 8am-8pm Mon-Sat, 10am-6pm Sun) In the arrivals hall.

Città Alta Tourist Office (☑ 035 24 22 26; www.visitbergamo.net; Via Gombito 13; ☺ 9am-5.30pm) Helpful multilingual office in the heart of the Upper Town.

Città Bassa Tourist Office (☑ 035 21 02 04; www.visitbergamo.net; Viale Papa Giovanni XXIII 57; ☺ 9am-12.30pm & 2-5.30pm) New office near the train and bus stations, in the Lower Town.

❶ Getting There & Away

AIR

Orio al Serio (☑ 035 32 63 23; www.sacbo.it) Has regular flights to/from the UK and other European destinations, the bulk of them with **Ryanair** (www.ryanair.com).

BUS

Bus station (☑ 800 139392; www.bergamo trasporti.it) Located across from the train station on Piazzale Marconi. **SAB** (☑ 035 28 90 11; www.arriva.it) operates services to Brescia, Mantua and the lakes.

CAR

From Milan or Brescia, take the A4 motorway and follow the Bergamo exits.

Traffic is restricted in the Città Alta. Instead, use metered parking or car parks in the Lower Town.

TRAIN

Train station (☑ 035 24 79 50; Piazza Marconi) One or two trains run every hour to Milan (€5.50, 50 to 65 minutes) and Brescia (€4.80, one to 1½ hours), where you can change for Cremona or Mantua.

❶ Getting Around

TO/FROM THE AIRPORT

ATB (☑ 035 23 60 26; www.atb.bergamo.it) bus 1 runs between the airport and Bergamo bus and train stations (€2.30, 15 minutes, every 20 minutes). Direct buses also connect with Milan and Brescia.

PUBLIC TRANSPORT

ATB bus 1 connects the train station with the **funicular** (☑ 035 23 60 26; www.atb.bergamo. it; ☺ 7.30am-11.45pm) to the Upper Town and Colle Aperto (going the other way not all buses stop right at the station but at the Porta Nuova stop). From Colle Aperto, either bus 21 or a funicular continues uphill to San Vigilio. Buy tickets, valid for 75 minutes, for €1.30 from machines at the train and funicular stations or at newspaper stands.

There's a taxi rank at the train station.

Brescia

📍 030 / POP 196.000

The largest of the four great Eastern Lombard towns, Brescia is also the most Roman of the quartet. Indeed, the settlement known in antiquity as Brixia guards the most important Roman ruins in northern Italy. Backing them up is a huge monastic complex founded in the 8th century, a museum dedicated to a marathon car race and not one but *two* cathedrals residing side-by-side in the main square.

◉ Sights

★ **Santa Giulia**   MUSEUM, MONASTERY
(Museo della Città; 📞 030 297 78 33; www.brescia musei.com; Via dei Musei 81; adult/reduced €10/7.50, combined ticket incl Tempio Capitolino €15/10; ⏱ 9am-5pm Tue-Fri, 10am-9pm Sat, 10am-6pm Sun) You could spend a whole day in this monster of a museum housed in an ex-monastery and still have plenty left for another visit. Those with limited time should skip to the best bits headlined by Brescia's extraordinary Roman remains and an original church dating from the 8th century AD. Other exhibits include the history of the building itself, medieval jewels (including the early-Christian *Croce di Desiderius*) and remnants from Brescia's Venetian era.

The building of the monastery, which started as early as the 8th century, absorbed two *domus* (Roman houses), which were left standing in what would become the monk's garden (Ortaglia) near the north cloister. The remains have become known as the **Domus dell'Ortaglia**. Raised walkways allow you to wander round the **Domus di Dioniso** (so called because of a mosaic of Dionysius, god of wine) and the **Domus delle Fontane** (named after two marble fountains). The beautiful floor mosaics and colourful frescoes in these two *domus* rank among the highlights of the monastery-museum.

Other highlights of the monastery range from 1st-century-AD bronzes (including a beautifully rendered *Winged Victory*) to the Coro delle Monache (Nun's Choir), a marvellous two-storey chamber completed in the 16th century that is decorated with lavish frescoes.

Brixia Parco Archeologico   RUINS
(Via dei Musei; adult/reduced €8/6; ⏱ 9am-5pm Tue-Fri, 10am-6pm Sat & Sun) Brescia's impressive archaeological complex cleverly reconstructs the city's Roman past from fragments first discovered in the 1820s. It consists of three parts. Above ground, a (very) ruined **Roman theatre** stands next to an erstwhile Roman temple known as the **Tempio Capitolino** that was commissioned by Emperor Vespasian in AD 73. The temple was partly reconstructed in the 1850s with six Corinthian columns and a series of cells.

Duomo Vecchio   CHURCH
(Old Cathedral; Piazza Paolo VI; ⏱ 9am-noon & 3-6pm Tue-Sat, 9-10.45am & 3-7pm Sun) The most compelling of all Brescia's religious monuments is the 11th-century Duomo Vecchio, a rare example of a circular-plan Romanesque basilica, built over a 6th-century church. The inside is surmounted by a dome borne by eight sturdy vaults resting on thick pillars.

Museo Mille Miglia   MUSEUM
(📞 030 336 56 31; www.museomillemiglia.it; Viale della Rimembranza 3; adult/reduced €8/6; ⏱ 10am-6pm) The original Mille Miglia (Thousand Miles) ran between 1927 and 1957 and was one of Italy's most legendary endurance car races – it started in Brescia and took some 16 hours to complete. The race's colourful museum is loaded with some of the greatest cars to cross the finish line, as well as old-style petrol pumps and archived race footage.

🍴 Sleeping & Eating

★ **Albergo Orologio**   HOTEL €
(📞 030 375 54 11; www.albergoorologio.it; Via Beccaria 17; s/d €64/84; ❋ @ 🛜) A budget city centre hotel with splashes of elegance in its recently renovated rooms. Bank on bathroom slippers, browsable art books, and a 'welcome home' sign pinned to your door, as well as well-positioned reading lamps, refined writing desks and stylish drapes.

La Vineria   ITALIAN €€
(📞 030 28 05 43; www.lavineriabrescia.it; Via X Giornate 4; meals €28-36; ⏱ noon-3pm & 7-11pm Tue-Sat, noon-3pm Sun) Near the Piazza della Loggia, La Vineria serves up delectable regional cuisine at al fresco tables under a portico or in a classy dining room with vaulted ceilings. Try dishes like linguine with dried sardines and almond butter, or *bigoli* (thick spaghetti) with duck *ragù*. Not surprisingly, 'the winery' has good wine selections.

Osteria al Bianchi   OSTERIA €€
(📞 030 29 23 28; www.osteriaalbianchi.it; Via Gasparo da Salò 32; meals €24-30; ⏱ 10am-2pm & 6pm-midnight Mon-Fri, 9am-2pm & 6pm-midnight

HOLIDAY AFLOAT

Peek out of your porthole at banks of wildflowers and cormorants sunning themselves on branches as you glide (sustainably) down the Mincio and Po rivers all the way to Venice. **Avemaria Boat** (📞 0444 127 84 30; www.avemaria boat.com; Via Conforto da Costozza 7, Vicenza; 7 days per person €990; 🖥️) 🖊️ hotel offers week-long bike-and-barge trips exploring the peaceful nooks and crannies of the delta.

Sat & Sun) Al Bianchi is your classic Italian bar with restaurant out back, in business since the callow years of the Risorgimento and probably serving the same reliable (and economical) dishes such as *pappardelle al taleggio e zucca* (broad ribbon pasta with Taleggio cheese and pumpkin) and *brasato d'asino* (ahem – braised donkey). Don't forgo the €4 desserts.

ℹ️ Information

Main Tourist Office (📞 030 240 03 57; www.turismobrescia.it; Via Trieste 1; ⏰ 9am-7pm Mon-Sat, 10am-6pm Sun) On the edge of Piazza Paolo VI.

Tourist Office (📞 030 306 12 40; www.turis-mobrescia.it; Piazzale Stazione; ⏰ 9am-7pm Mon-Sat, 10am-6pm Sun) At the train station.

ℹ️ Getting There & Around

Bus Station (📞 030 288 99 11; Via Solferino) Buses operated by **SIA** (📞 030 288 99 11; www.arriva.it) serve destinations all over Brescia province. Some leave from another station off Viale della Stazione.

Train Station (📞 030 4 41 08; Viale della Stazione 7) Brescia is on the Milan–Venice line, with regular services to Milan (€7.30 to €20, 45 minutes to 1¼ hours) and Verona (€7.05, 40 minutes). There are also secondary lines to Cremona (€5.50, one hour), Bergamo (€4.80, one hour) and Parma (€7.95, two hours). A metro links the train station with Piazza della Vittoria (single €1.40) in the heart of the old town, or San Faustino for the castle.

Bike Station (Il Parcheggio Biciclette; 📞 030 306 11 00; Piazzale Stazione; ⏰ 7am-7.30pm Mon-Fri, 7.30am-1.40pm Sat) You can hire a bike (€1/4 per two hours/day) from in front of the train station.

Mantua

📞 0376 / POP 49,000

Sharing more in common with Ferrara in Romagna than its Lombard cohorts, Mantua (Mantova) is a city protected by lakes, anchored by Unesco-listed Renaissance architecture and coloured by a history that resounds to the daring, sometimes despotic deeds of one family: the House of Gonzaga. Reigning for 400 years from the early 14th to 18th centuries, the Gonzaga made Mantua a centre of the Renaissance, commissioned several massive palaces, and cemented power by intermarrying with the powerful d'Este clan of Ferrara. Much of the city today was built in their image.

◉ Sights

★ **Palazzo Ducale**   PALACE
(📞 041 241 18 97; www.ducalemantova.org; Piazza Sordello 40; adult/reduced €13/6.50; ⏰ 9.15am-7.15pm Tue-Sat, 8.30am-1.30pm Sun) For more than 300 years the enormous Palazzo Ducale was the seat of the Gonzaga – a family of wealthy horse breeders who rose to power in the 14th century to become one of Italy's leading Renaissance families. Their 500-room, 35,000-sq-metre palace is vast; a visit today winds through 40 of the finest chambers split into three historical parts: the **Corte Vecchia**, the **Corte Nuova** and the **Castello di San Giorgio**. Outside is a courtyard garden known as the **Giardino dei Semplici**.

Along with works by Morone and Rubens, the highlight of the palace is the witty mid-15th-century fresco by Mantegna in the **Camera degli Sposi** (Bridal Chamber). Executed between 1465 and 1474, the room, which is entirely painted, shows the marquis, Lodovico, going about his courtly business with family and courtiers in tow in impressive 3D. Painted naturalistically and with great attention to perspective, the arched walls appear like windows on the courtly world – looking up at the duke's wife, Barbara, you can even see the underside of her dress as if she's seated above you. Most playful of all though is the *trompe l'œil* oculus featuring bare-bottomed *putti* – the point of view is quite distastefully realistic in places – balancing precariously on a painted balcony, while smirking courtly pranksters appear ready to drop a large potted plant on gawping tourists below.

Other palace highlights are the Sala di Troia, Frederico II's council chamber entirely done out in Trojan War scenes and Rubens' *Adoration of the Holy Trinity* in the Sala degli Arcieri (Room of Archers), which Napoleonic troops brutally dismembered in 1797. In room 8, the Sala del Pisanello, fragments and preliminary sketches of Pisanello's frescoes of Arthurian knights remain, while room 24, the Sala dello Zodiaco, sports a ceiling representing the heavens studded with starry constellations.

★ **Palazzo Te**   PALACE
(🖉 0376 36 58 86; www.palazzote.it; Viale Te 13; adult/reduced €12/8; ◎ 1-7.30pm Mon, 9am-7.30pm Tue-Sun) Palazzo Te was where Frederico II Gonzaga escaped for love trysts with his mistress Isabella Boschetti, and it's decorated in playboy style with stunning frescoes, playful motifs and encoded symbols. A Renaissance pleasure-dome, it is the finest work of star architect Giulio Romano, whose sumptuous mannerist scheme fills the palace with fanciful flights of imagination.

Basilica di Sant'Andrea   BASILICA
(Piazza Mantegna; ◎ 8am-noon & 3-7pm) Easily usurping Mantua's cathedral, this towering basilica safeguards the golden vessels said to hold earth soaked by the blood of Christ. Longinus, the Roman soldier who speared Christ on the cross, is said to have scooped up the earth and buried it in Mantua after leaving Palestine. Today, these containers rest beneath a marble octagon in front of the altar and are paraded around Mantua in a grand procession on Good Friday.

The first chapel on the left contains the tomb of Andrea Mantegna, the man responsible for the splendours of Mantua's most famous paintings – those in the Camera degli Sposi in the Palazzo Ducale. The chapel is beautifully lit and also contains a painting of the Holy Family and John the Baptist, attributed to Mantegna and his school.

Teatro Bibiena   THEATRE
(Teatro Scientifico; 🖉 0376 28 82 08; Via dell'Accademia 47; adult/reduced €2/1.20; ◎ 10am-1pm & 3-6pm Tue-Fri, 10am-6pm Sat & Sun) If ever a theatre were set to upstage the actors, it's the 18th-century Teatro Bibiena. Dimly lit and festooned with plush velvet, its highly unusual, intimate bell-shaped design sees four storeys of ornate, stucco balconies arranged around curving walls. It was specifically intended to allow its patrons to be seen – balconies even fill the wall behind the stage. You can wander round at will during the day or come to an evening performance to see the building come alive.

🏃 **Activities**

La Rigola   CYCLING
(🖉 0335 605 49 58; Via Trieste 5; per hour/day €5/15; ◎ 9.30am-12.30pm & 2.30-7.30pm) Rent bikes by the day to explore the surrounding lakes, the Po river and the Parco del Mincio (www.parcodelmincio.it). The shortest route (a couple of hours) takes cyclists around Lago Superiore to the Santuario di Santa Maria delle Grazie, while longer routes meander south to the abbey of San Benedetto Po and the Gonzaga town of Sabbioneta.

MILAN & THE LAKES MANTUA

WORTH A TRIP

DAL PESCATORE RESTAURANT

Petals of egg pasta frame slices of guinea fowl caramelised in honey saffron; silky tortellini are stuffed to bursting with pumpkin, nutmeg, cinnamon and candied *mostarda* (fruit in a sweet-mustard sauce). You practically eat the Mantuan countryside in Nadia Santini's internationally acclaimed restaurant Dal Pescatore (🖉 0376 72 30 01; www.dalpescatore.com; Località Runate, Canneto sull'Oglio; meals €150-250; ◎ noon-4pm & 7.30pm-late Thu-Sun, 7.30pm-late Wed; P 🅰).

What's even more surprising is that the triple-Michelin-starred chef is entirely self-taught and has only ever cooked here, in what was originally the modest trattoria of her husband's family. Beneath the tutelage of her mother-in-law, who still cooks in the kitchen, Nadia learnt to create Mantuan cuisine deftly and creatively. Despite a background in food science, her food isn't remotely high-tech, but rather quietly brilliant, focusing on the essentials and balancing simplicity with the very finest natural produce.

The restaurant is located 40km west of Mantua in a green glade beside the Oglio river. Nearby, 9 Muse B&B (🖉 335 8007601; www.9muse.it; Via Giordano Bruno 42a, Canneto sull'Oglio; s/d €55/85; P 🅰 @) provides elegant and charming accommodation.

Mantua

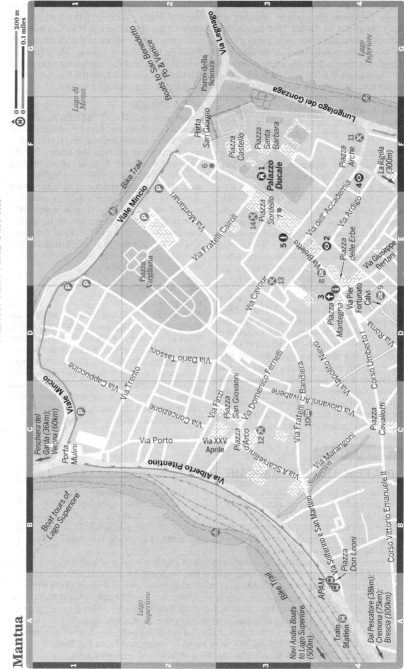

Lago di Mezzo

Lago Inferiore

Parco della Scienza

Boats to San Benedetto Po & Venice

Via Legnago

Lungolago del Gonzaga

Porta San Giorgio

Piazza Castello

Piazza Santa Barbara

1 Palazzo Ducale

Piazza Arche

11

La Rigola (300m)

4

Viale Mincio

Via Montanari

Via dell' Accademia

Via Ardigo

Piazza Sordello

14

5

Via Fratelli Cairoli

Via Boletto

Piazza delle Erbe

2

Via Giuseppe Bertani

Piazza Virgiliana

Via Cavour

13

8

Via Pier Fortunato Calvi

9

Via Trento

Via Dario Tassoni

3

Piazza Mantegna

Via Roma

Via Cappuccine

Viale Mincio

Porta Mulini

Peschiera del Garda (36km); Verona (60km)

Via Alberto Pitentino

Via Concezione

Via Finzi

Piazza San Giovanni

Via Domenico Fernelli

Via Ippolito Nievo

Via Giovanni Arrivabene

Via Fratelli Bandiera

Corso Umberto I

Piazza Cavallotti

Via Porto

Via XXV Aprile

Via d'Arco

Piazza d'Arco

12

Via A Scarsellino

10

Via Marangoni

Sottoriva

Bike Trail

Lago Superiore

Boat tours of Lago Superiore

Navi Andes Boats to Lago Superiore (500m)

Train Station

APAM

Via Solferino e San Martino

Piazza Don Leoni

Dal Pescatore (38km); Cremona (75km); Brescia (100km)

Corso Vittorio Emanuele II

200 m
0.1 miles

6

Mantua

☞ Tours

★**Visit Mantua**   WALKING

(☎347 4022020; www.visitmantua.it; tours per 2 people 90min/5hr €100/300) Get the insider view of Renaissance dukes and duchesses – what they ate for breakfast, how they conspired at court and the wardrobe crises of the day – with art historian Lorenzo Bonoldi's fascinating conversational tours of Mantua's highlight palaces. Tours leave from Piazza Sordello 40.

Motonavi Andes   BOATING

(☎0376 32 28 75; www.motonaviandes.it; Via San Giorgio 2) Motonavi Andes organises frequent boat tours of Mantua's lakes (starting from €9 for 1½ hours) as well as other occasional cruises along the Po and to the Parco del Mincio.

🛏 Sleeping

La Zucca Guesthouse   B&B €

(☎392 3827503; www.lazucca.mn.it; Via Spagnoli 10; s/d without bathroom from €70/90; @ 🖤) The top deal in the city centre, this three-room B&B up an ancient staircase off Via Spagnoli is pure delight. Rooms flutter in bright fabrics, beds are comfortable and pleasant aromas fill the air throughout. Breakfast is self-service and laid out all day, and the wi-fi is speedy. The only downside is the shared bathroom. Prior booking essential.

★**Ca' delle Erbe**   B&B €€

(☎0376 22 61 61; www.cadelleerbe.it; Via Broletto 24; d €130-165; ❄🖤) In this gorgeous 16th-century townhouse historic features have undergone a minimalist remodelling: exposed creamy stone walls surround pared-down furniture; whitewashed beams cohabit with lavish bathrooms and modern art. The pick of the bedrooms must be the one with the balcony overlooking the iconic Piazza delle Erbe, a candidate for the town's best room.

Palazzo Arrivabene   B&B €€

(☎0376 32 86 85; www.palazzoarrivabene.net; Via Bandiera 20; s €100-120, d €120-140; ❄🖤) You may well feel like a duke or duchess, lounging around this 15th-century *palazzo*, delighting in the frescoed ceilings, vast marble fireplaces and cherub-framed doors. The grand style continues into the bedrooms, one of which is cheekily called the *camera degli sposi* (bridal chamber) after the iconic room in Mantua's Palazzo Ducale. It's way, way grander than your traditional B&B.

✖ Eating

★**Osteria delle Quattro Tette**   OSTERIA €

(☎0376 32 94 78; Vicolo Nazione 4; meals €10-15; ⊙12.30-2.30pm Mon-Sat) At the wonderfully esoteric *osteria* of the 'four breasts', you can pull up a pew (literally, an old church pew) and enjoy yet-to-be-exported Italian gems such as tripe and beans, horsemeat steak and sweet desserts smeared with alcoholic custard. This is a slice of gritty unwrapped Italy where service is fast, prices cheap and rough-hewn tables are spaced only centimetres apart.

Ristorante Affresco   ITALIAN €€

(☎0376 196 16 12; www.ristoranteaffrescomantova. com; Piazza Sordello 14; meals €25; ⊙noon-3pm & 7-10:30pm) After several hours wandering around the gargantuan Palazzo Ducale, getting neck-ache looking at frescoes, you'll probably appreciate a quick light lunch at this new restaurant located just across the square and encased in a pretty townhouse with – erm – more ceiling frescoes. The menu is a simple precis of Mantovese food.

Generous portions of *risotto alla pilota* (rice with crumbled sausage) or *tortelli di zucca artiginale* (pumpkin ravioli with melted butter and sage) ought to keep the hunger pangs at bay until dinnertime.

Fragoletta   LOMBARD €€
(☑ 0376 32 33 00; www.fragoletta.it; Piazza Arche
5; meals €25-35; ☺ noon-3pm & 8pm-midnight
Tue-Sun) Wooden chairs scrape against the
tiled floor as diners eagerly tuck into Slow
Food–accredited *culatello di Zibello* (lard)
at this 250-year-old trattoria. Other Mantuan specialities feature, such as *risotto alla
pilota* and local classic *tortelli di zucca*.

Il Cigno dei Martini   MODERN ITALIAN €€€
(☑ 0376 32 71 01; www.ristoranteilcignomantova.it;
Piazza d'Arco 1; meals €60; ☺ 12.30-1.45pm & 7.30-
9.45pm Wed-Sun) The building is as beautiful
as the food: a lemon-yellow facade dotted
with faded olive-green shutters. Inside, Mantua's gourmands graze on delicately steamed
risotto with spring greens, veal sautéed in
white wine with polenta or gamey guinea
fowl with spicy Mantuan *mostarda*.

❶ Information

Tourist Office (☑ 0376 43 24 32; www.turis
mo.mantova.it; Piazza Mantegna 6; ☺ 9am-7pm
Sun-Thu, to 6pm Fri & Sat) Enquire about the
Mantova Card here to secure discounts on all
the main sights.

❶ Getting There & Away

Bus Station (Piazza Don Leoni) City and
regional buses are operated by **APAM** (☑ 0376
23 03 39; www.apam.it). They head to Sabbioneta, San Benedetto Po and Brescia. Some leave
from Viale Risorgimento.

Car Mantua is just west of the A22 Modena–
Verona–Trento autostrada. Much of the historic
centre is a traffic-restricted zone.

Train Station (Piazza Don Leoni) Direct trains
link Mantua with Verona (€4.20, 50 minutes,
hourly) and Milan (€11.50, two hours, every two
hours). The trip to Peschiera del Garda train
station (€6.25, 70 minutes, hourly) involves a
change in Verona.

Cremona
☑ 0372 / POP 72,000

Just as Bergamo has its Venetian walls and
Brescia has its Roman ruins, Cremona has
its own defining feature – violins. Its love
affair with the fiddle dates back to the early
18th century and the travails of the legendary Antonio Stradivari, who crafted over
1000 stringed instruments in an 80-year
career. But once you've rosined your bow
in the Museo del Violino and nosed in the
windows of the specialist luthiers' work-

shops that still crowd Cremona's old quarter,
there's plenty more to see.

◉ Sights

★ **Museo del Violino**   MUSEUM
(☑ 0372 08 08 09; www.museodelviolino.org; Piazza Marconi 5; adult/reduced €10/7; ☺ 10am-6pm
Tue-Sun) Cremona's history echoes to sound
of violins and violin-making, meaning a
visit to this relatively new, state-of-the-art
museum is practically obligatory should
you desire to understand the city properly.
Essential pit stops include a small workshop
where you can see a luthier (violin-maker)
in action, a dramatically lit corridor full
of gorgeous Cremona-made violins dating
back to the 17th century, and a special room
containing the drawings, moulds and tools
legendary craftsman Stradivari used in his
workshop.

Cattedrale di Cremona   CATHEDRAL
(Duomo; www.cattedraledicremona.it; Piazza del
Comune; ☺ 10.30am-noon & 3.30-5pm Mon-Sat,
noon-12.30pm & 3-5pm Sun) Welcome to an ecclesial colossus. Cremona's cathedral started
out as a Romanesque basilica, but the simplicity of that style later gave way to an extravagance of designs. The interior frescoes
are utterly overwhelming, with the *Storie di
Cristo* (Stories of Christ) by Pordenone perhaps the highlights. One of the chapels contains what is said to be a thorn from Jesus'
crown of thorns.

Torrazzo   TOWER
(Piazza del Comune; adult/reduced €5/4, incl Baptistry €6/5; ☺ 10am-1pm & 2.30-6pm, closed Mon
winter) Cremona's 111m-tall *torrazzo* (bell
tower, although '*torrazzo*' translates literally as 'great, fat tower') is the third tallest
brick bell tower in the world. A total of 502
steps wind up to the top (there's no lift). The
effort is more than repaid with marvellous
views across the city. A 'vertical museum' inside the tower's lean frame is dedicated to
astronomy, time measurement and clocks,
including a Foucault's pendulum exhibit.

✯ Festivals & Events

Stradivari Festival   MUSIC
(www.stradivarifestival.it; ☺ mid-Sep–mid-Oct)
Focusing on music for string instruments.
Held between mid-September and mid-
October, it's organised by the Museo del
Violino.

Festa del Torrone FOOD & DRINK

(www.festadeltorronecremona.it; ⊘Nov) A weekend full of exhibitions, performances and tastings dedicated to that toffee-tough Cremona-made Christmas sweet: *torrone* (nougat).

🛏 Sleeping

L'Archetto HOSTEL €

(☑0372 80 77 55; www.ostellocremona.com; Via Brescia 9; dm/s/d €30/45/60; ✳@ 🛜) Cost-conscious musicians love this central, fairly luxurious hostel where cheerful, modern bedrooms and four-bed dorms are pristine and thoughtfully furnished. Sadly, the limited reception hours (8am to 10am and 5pm to 9pm) – and no option to leave luggage – might be inconvenient.

Hotel Continental HOTEL €

(☑0372 43 41 41; www.hotelcontinentalcremona.it; Piazza della Libertà 26; s/d from €70/97; 🅿✳🛜) A short stroll outside the historic centre, the Hotel Continental is a self-proclaimed 'lifestyle' hotel that pricks your interest with a dynamically designed lobby replete with retro loungers, book shelves, an honesty bar and a Nespresso machine. Take this as a gateway to more fun including a rooftop cocktail bar (negronis €6), a pizza restaurant (margheritas €4.50) and a modern gym.

★ **Dellearti Design Hotel** DESIGN HOTEL €€

(☑0372 2 31 31; www.dellearti.com; Via Bonomelli 8; d €120, ste €199; ✳🛜) It's what Italians do best. Cremona's hippest hotel is a high-tech blend of glass, concrete and steel. Stylish bedrooms feature clean lines, bold colours and artful lighting. There are also some whimsical flourishes: undulating gold, corrugated corridors with walls that curve like Cremonan violins, and a bowl of liquorice allsorts on the front desk.

🍴 Eating

Tramezzo 1925 SANDWICHES €

(☑320 703 03 82; Piazza Stradivari 2; panini €4-8; ⊘10am-4pm & 6-10pm) If you're darting between sights in Cremona, dip into this small cafe where they'll make up a toasted *panino* as you wait from a menu with 123 different combos. The light warm bread is delightfully crumbly – so crumbly you'll quickly have pigeons amassing around you if you eat it out in the square.

CREMONA'S VIOLINS

Some 100 violin-making workshops occupy the streets around Piazza del Comune. To visit a workshop, you generally need to be looking to buy a violin, but the **Consorzio Liutai Antonio Stradivari** (☑0372 46 35 03; www.cremonaliuteria.it; Piazza Stradivari 1; ⊘9.30am-1pm Mon & Sat, 9.30am-1pm & 3-6.30pm Tue-Fri), which represents the workshops, can make appointments for visits. Count on €60 to €80 per group for a one-hour visit.

To hear Cremona's violins in action, attend one of the concerts held at the 19th-century **Teatro Amilcare Ponchielli** (☑0372 02 20 01; www.teatroponchielli.it; Corso Vittorio Emanuele II 52; ⊘box office 10.30am-1.30pm & 4.30-7.30pm Mon-Sat) between October to June.

Hosteria 700 LOMBARD €€

(☑0372 3 61 75; www.hosteria700.com; Piazza Gallina 1; meals €33-40; ⊘noon-2.45pm Wed-Mon, 7-11pm Wed-Sun) Behind the dilapidated facade lurks a diamond in the rough. Some of the vaulted rooms come with ceiling frescoes, dark timber tables come with ancient wooden chairs, and the hearty Lombard cuisine comes at a refreshingly competitive cost.

Il Violino ITALIAN €€€

(☑0372 46 10 10; Via Vescovo Sicardo 3; meals €45-60; ⊘12.30-2pm daily, 7.30-10pm Mon-Sat) Il Violino is Cremona's timeless classy option. Smooth service is key to this elegant spot, where you can peruse a menu filled with intriguing names such as '*un* must have' (pumpkin and mustard risotto), '*E tu hai fagato?*' (veal pâté with caramelised red onion) and 'Black is back' (inky squid and rice).

ℹ Information

Tourist Office (☑0372 40 70 81; www.turismocremona.it; Piazza del Comune 5; ⊘10am-6pm) Helpful staff in an office across from the cathedral.

ℹ Getting There & Away

Train station (Via Dante) The most convenient way to reach Cremona. Served by trains from Milan (from €7.30, one to two hours, several daily) and Brescia (€5.50, one hour, hourly).

MILAN & THE LAKES CREMONA

Val di Fassa (p343)
DMITRY NAUMOV/SHUTTERSTOCK ©

Trentino & South Tyrol

Home to the spectacular sawtoothed Dolomites, the semi-autonomous provinces of Trentino and South Tyrol are packed with stunning landscapes. The region has long enticed hikers, climbers, poets and fresh-air fanciers, with the scenic Sella Ronda remaining one of the world's most iconic skiing and cycling circuits.

Alpine influences abound here. Many residents speak German or the ancient Ladin language, trains run with Swiss precision, and pristine recreation paths wind through vine- and orchard-covered hillsides. The region's cities – Trento, Bolzano and Merano – are alluringly cultured and dynamic, while accommodation – be it a humble mountain hut or a five-star spa – is unfailingly welcoming and well run.

Trentino & South Tyrol Highlights

1 Sella Ronda (p343) Working up a high-altitude appetite on the slopes, then hitting the fine-dining hot spots of Alta Badia.

2 Alpe di Siusi (p345) Riding across the enchanting high pastures on a pretty horse.

3 Brenta Dolomites (p329) Testing your mettle on a vertiginous *via ferrata* climb.

4 Terme Merano (p338) Floating away at this spa beneath palm trees and snowy peaks.

5 Südtiroler Weinstrasse (p337) Tasting Italy's most elegant white wines along this gourmet route.

6 Museo Archeologico dell'Alto Adige (p333) Meeting Ötzi the iceman and uncovering his Copper Age lifestyle.

7 MART (p328) Uncovering the excellent modern and contemporary art collections in Rovereto.

8 Val Pusteria (p350) Feasting on schnitzel and strudel in this traditional valley.

9 Ferrari (p326) Discovering Trento DOC sparkling wine at this Trentino legend.

10 Val di Sole (p331) Mountain biking through orchard-clad hills.

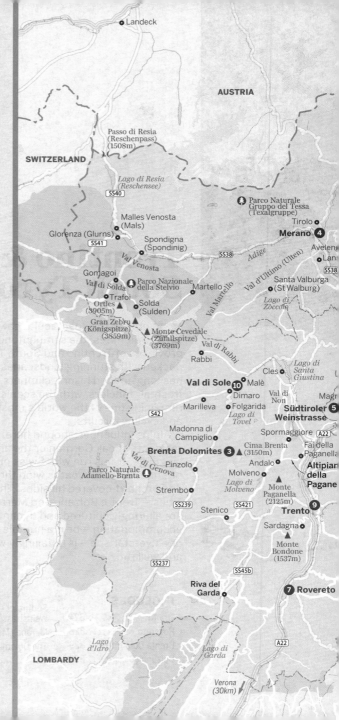

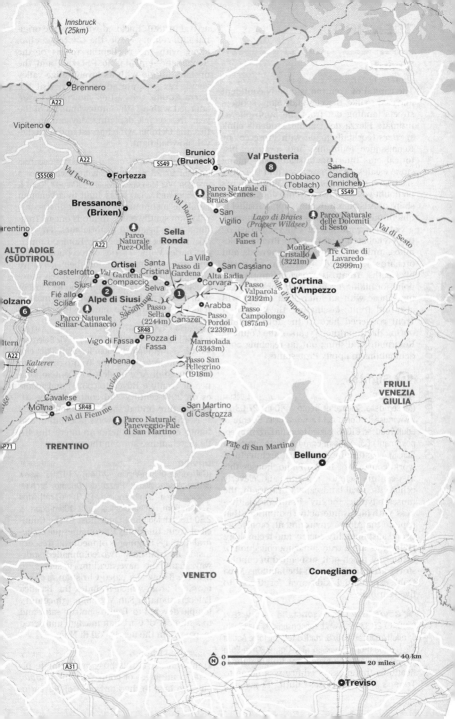

TRENTINO

Trento

📞 0461 / POP 117,400 / ELEV 194M

The capital of Trentino is quietly confident and easy to like. Bicycles glide along spotless streets fanning out from the atmospheric, intimate Piazza del Duomo, students clink *spritzes* (cocktails made with Prosecco) by Renaissance fountains, and a dozen historical eras intermingle seamlessly among stone castles, shady porticoes and the city's signature medieval frescoes. While there's no doubt you're in Italy, Trento does have its share of Austrian influence: apple strudel is ubiquitous and beer halls not uncommon.

Set in a wide glacial valley guarded by the crenellated peaks of the Brenta Dolomites, amid a patchwork of vineyards and orchards transected by 400km of paved bike paths, Trento is a perfect jumping-off point for hiking, cycling, skiing or wine tasting. Those with an interest in history will also find Trento fascinating: the Council of Trent convened here in the 16th century, during the tumultuous years of the Counter-Reformation, dishing out far-reaching condemnations to uppity Protestants.

⊙ Sights

★ MUSE   MUSEUM
(Museo delle Scienze di Trento; 📞 0461 27 03 11; www.muse.it; Corso del Lavoro e della Scienza 3; adult/reduced €10/8, guided tours (in English by appointment) €3; ⊙ 10am-6pm Tue-Fri, to 7pm Sat & Sun; 🚻) A stunning modernist architectural work, courtesy of Renzo Piano, houses this 21st-century science museum and cleverly echoes the local landscape. Curatorially, the museum typifies the city's brainy inquisitiveness, with highly interactive exhibitions that explore the Alpine environment, biodiversity and sustainability, society and technology. Highlights are a truly amazing collection of taxidermy, much of it suspended in a multi-storey atrium, along with the fabulous Maxi Ooh! experiential kids area for three- to five-year-olds.

★ Castello del Buonconsiglio   MUSEUM
(📞 0461 23 37 70; www.buonconsiglio.it; Via Clesio 5; adult/reduced €10/8, guided tour of Torre Aquila €2; ⊙ 10am-6pm Tue-Sun May-Oct, 9.30am-5pm Tue-Sun Nov-Apr) Guarded by hulking fortifications, this massive edifice was home to Trento's bishop-princes until Napoleon's arrival in 1801. Enclosed within is the original 13th-century castle, the Castelvecchio, along with the residential rooms of the Renaissance-era Magno Palazzo, and the upstairs loggia with its lovely Adige valley views. Pay separate admission to visit the Torre Aquila, the castle's showpiece tower, adorned with a 14th-century 'months of the year' fresco cycle depicting May garden parties, the October wine harvest and a medieval snowball fight.

Villa Margon   HISTORIC BUILDING
(📞 0461 97 23 61; www.ferraritrento.com/en/villa-margon; Via Margone, Ravina; ⊙ 10am-12.30pm & 2.30-5pm Wed & Sat) FREE Built by a Venetian family as a summer house in the 1540s, this villa 7km southwest of Trento is one of Trentino's most beautiful historic sites. Frescoes documenting the life of Holy Roman Emperor Charles V line a series of reception rooms and are startling both for their narrative content and for their vivid, and entirely untouched, colour. The setting is no less lovely, with a forest and mountain backdrop making it feel far more remote than it actually is.

Galleria Civica di Trento   GALLERY
(📞 0461 98 55 11; www.mart.trento.it; Via Belenzani 44; €2; ⊙ 10am-1pm & 2-6pm Tue-Sun) This city gallery/project space is the Trento campus of the Museo di Arte Moderna e Contemporanea di Trento e Rovereto (p328) and focuses on 20th-century and contemporary art, architecture and design. The small space's seasonal program is always fascinating and tightly curated and there's an interesting little merchandise shop in the entrance.

Duomo   CATHEDRAL
(Cattedrale di San Vigilio; 📞 0461 23 12 93; www.cattedralesanvigilio.it; Piazza del Duomo; archaeological area adult/reduced €2/1; ⊙ cathedral 6.30am-6pm, archaeological area 10am-noon & 2.30-5.30pm Mon-Sat) Once host to the Council of Trent, this dimly lit Romanesque cathedral displays fragments of medieval frescoes inside its transepts. Two colonnaded stairways flank the nave, leading, it seems, to heaven. Below is a paleo-Christian archaeological area, which includes the Basilica Paleocristiana di San Vigilio, a 4th-century temple devoted to Trento's patron saint and to a number of Christian martyrs murdered by pagans in the nearby Val di Non.

Piazza del Duomo   PIAZZA
Trento's heart is this busy yet intimate piazza, dominated, of course, by the *duomo*, but also host to the Fontana del Nettuno,

Trentino

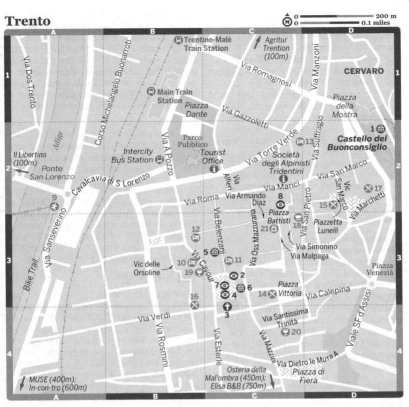

Trento

a flashy late-baroque fountain rather whimsically dedicated to Neptune. Intricate, allegorical frescoes decorate the 16th-century facades of the Case Cazuffi-Rella, two private Renaissance houses on the piazza's northern side.

Museo Diocesano Tridentino MUSEUM

(Palazzo Pretorio; ☑0461 23 44 19; www.museo diocesanotridentino.it; Piazza del Duomo 18; adult/reduced incl archaeological area €7/2; ⊙10am-1pm & 2-6pm Wed-Mon Jun-Sep, 9.30am-12.30pm & 2-5.30pm Mon & Wed-Sat, 10am-1pm & 2-6pm Sun Oct-May) Sitting alongside the *duomo,* this former bishop's residence dates from the 11th century. It now houses one of Italy's most important ecclesiastical collections, with enormous documentary paintings of the Council of Trent, along with Flemish tapestries, illustrated manuscripts, vestments, and some particularly opulent reliquaries. Admission price includes entry to the paleo-Christian archaeological area beneath the duomo (p325). A ground-floor gallery also hosts temporary contemporary art exhibitions.

Giardino Botanico Alpino GARDENS

(Botanical Alpine Gardens; ☑0461 94 80 50; www2. muse.it/giardinobotanico; Viote de Monte Bondone; adult/reduced €3.50/2.50; ⊙9am-5pm Jun & Sep, to 6pm Jul & Aug) This is one of the oldest and largest gardens in the Alps; more than 2000 species of rare high-altitude plants are nurtured in this beautiful, fragile environment. Now overseen by MUSE (p324), there is a program of talks and walks, as well as a forest playground constructed from natural elements.

Tridentum Spazio Archeologico Sotterraneo del SAS ROMAN SITE

(SASS; ☑0461 23 01 71; Piazza Battisti; adult/reduced €2.50/1.50; ⊙9.30am-1pm & 2-6pm Tue-Sun Jun-Sep, 9am-1pm & 2-5.30pm Tue-Sun Oct-May) Explore Roman Tridentum's city walls, paved streets, tower, domestic mosaics and workshop. The site was, rather incredibly, only discovered less than two decades ago, during restoration works on the nearby theatre.

🏃 Activities

Ferrari WINE

(☑0461 97 23 61; www.ferraritrento.it; Via Ponte di Ravina 15, Ravina; tours €15-48; ⊙9am-1pm & 2-6pm Mon-Fri, 10am-5pm Sat) Ferrari is a richly storied and hugely respected producer of Italy's 'other' sparkling wine, Trento DOC. Tours here must be prebooked and you can choose from six different levels of tasting – from the starter package (€15 per person) to the 'Grandi Riserve' tour, which includes a number of the marque's reserve-label drops (€48 per person).

Funivia Trento–Sardagna CABLE CAR

(☑0461 23 21 54; www.ttesercizio.it/Funivia; Via Monte Grappa 1; one-way/return €3/5; ⊙7am-10pm) A brief but spectacular cable-car ride from Trento's valley floor delivers you to the pretty village of Sardagna – admire the vista over a grappa or two. You can take bicycles on board, too. There are departures every 15 to 30 minutes – see the timetable online.

Monte Bondone SKIING

(www.montebondone.it; ski pass 1/3/7 days €34/87/157) A short drive southwest of Trento, the small, down-to-earth ski station of Vaneze (1300m) and its higher counterpart Vason (1654m) offer access to the gentle slopes of Monte Bondone (2180m), criss-crossed by 37km of cross-country ski trails and 16 downhill runs. From January through March, Skibus Monte Bondone, run by Trentino Trasporti (p328), wends its way from Trento to Vaneze and Vason (free with Trentino Guest Card, one way €2.90, 45 minutes).

🛏 Sleeping

Al Palazzo Malfatti B&B €

(☑0461 92 21 33; www.bbpalazzomalfatti.it; Via Belenzani 47; s €65-70, d €90-110; ❇🛜) Perched on a rooftop, this beautifully designed B&B offers a calm, airy retreat right in Trento's centre. Upstairs rooms are super private, but the property retains the feeling of a welcoming home with a shared terrace and an elegant living area (complete with grand piano) to relax in. The charming hosts dispense organic breakfasts, along with invaluable local tips.

Elisa B&B B&B €

(☑0461 92 21 33; www.bbelisa.com; Viale Rovereto 17; s/d from €65/90; ❇🛜) This is a true B&B in an architect's beautiful family home, with two private, stylish rooms and breakfasts that are a feast of home-baked cakes, freshly squeezed juice and artisanal cheese. It's located in a smart residential neighbourhood, a pleasant 15-minute stroll from Trento's city centre, with lots of eating, shopping and drinking options along the way.

Hotel America HOTEL €€

(☑0461 98 30 10; www.hotelamerica.it; Via Torre Verde 50; d €99-145; ❇🛜) Hotel America's extremely central location, within five minutes' walk of the train station, the *duomo* and the *castello,* makes it an excellent option for anyone who prefers the hotel lifestyle over a B&B. Some of the upstairs rooms have fabulous city views and there are solid three-star amenities throughout, including air-con, an elevator and an onsite restaurant.

Al Cavour 34   B&B €€
(☑ 349 4155814; www.alcavour34.it; Via Cavour
34; s €65-90, d €90-130, tr €120-150, q €140-180;
❄ 🛜) A stone's throw from the *duomo,* this
four-room B&B is run by five-star hospitality veterans Elisa and Carlo, who infuse all
with a wonderful mix of genuine warmth
and absolute professionalism. Rooms are
large and decorated in contemporary style;
breakfast is taken around a large table with
daily homemade treats and surprises from
the local artisan baker.

Albergo Accademia   HOTEL €€
(☑ 0461 23 36 00; www.accademiahotel.it; Vicolo
Colico 4/6; s €79-113, d €113-154; P ❄ @) This
elegant small hotel in a historic medieval
house features rooms that are modern and
airy (if a little on the staid side). Its central
location, midway between the train station
and the *duomo,* is its big selling point.

🍴 Eating

Gusto Giusto   BURGERS €
(☑ 0461 159 23 49; www.gustogiusto-trento.it;
Piazza Vittoria 1; burgers €5.50-10.50; ⏱ 11.30am-
2.30pm Mon-Sat) This ever-popular shack
serves up a variety of burgers, including
unconventional offerings that pair a beef
patty with melted brie, caramelised shallots,
walnuts and rocket (arugula), or cream of
zucchini, bacon and Gorgonzola – all accompanied by artisan beers. In the evenings, it
offers home delivery.

★**Il Libertino**   ALPINE €€
(☑ 0461 26 00 85; Piazza Piedicastello 4-6; meals
€35-43; ⏱ noon-2.30pm & 7-10.30pm Wed-Mon)
Stroll the bridge over the fast-flowing Adige
to this charming wood-panelled restaurant
for carefully prepared traditional dishes.
Think venison, chestnuts, radicchio, boar
sausage and river trout, along with an encyclopedic wine list of Trentino DOCs and
a memorable *tavolozza di dolci* (sampler of
four scrumptious desserts). Best of all, it's
open for Sunday lunch.

★**Il Cappello**   TRENTINO €€
(☑ 0461 23 58 50; www.osteriailcappello.it; Piazzetta Lunelli 5; meals €36-41; ⏱ noon-2pm &
7.30-10pm Tue-Sat, noon-2pm Sun) Decked out
with linen tablecloths, wooden beams and a
quiet courtyard terrace, this intimate dining
room hidden away between Trento's *duomo*
and castle woos guests with a mix of rustic-
ity and elegance. The menu is Trentino to
the core, and simple presentation makes the
most of beautiful artisan produce. Wines,
too, are local and rather special.

Terramia   SEAFOOD €€
(☑ 0461 26 26 66; www.ristoranteterramia.eu;
Parco San Marco, Via San Marco 64; meals €33-43;
⏱ noon-2.30pm & 6-10.30pm Tue-Sun) A little
escape to the Med in the mountains, this
Sicilian-run restaurant enjoys a dreamy setting within a walled public garden near the
Castello del Buonconsiglio. There's a trolley of
freshly transported fish that you can choose
to have grilled or fried, or make a meal from
the interesting menu of antipasti – say fish-
stuffed eggplant – and seafood pastas.

★**Osteria a le Due Spade**   GASTRONOMY €€€
(☑ 0461 23 43 43; www.leduespade.com; Via Don
Arcangelo Rizzi 11; meals €45-55, tasting menus €65-
75, 2-course lunch menu €30; ⏱ noon-2pm Tue-Sat
& 7.30-10pm Mon-Sat) You usually have to book
ahead to secure a table at this tiny, vaulted place, but it's always worth braving the
heavy door and drapes to see if they have a
spare spot. The kitchen here really celebrates
the local. Let out all the stops with their
seven-course fish or meat tasting menus, or
come midday for the great value two-course
lunch deal.

★**Locanda Margon**   GASTRONOMY €€€
(☑ 0461 34 94 01; www.locandamargon.it; Via Margone 15, Ravina; meals €40-70, 4-course degustation
€90, 5-course degustation incl wine €180) Proud
owners of Trentino's only twinset of Michelin stars, the Lunelli family who make Trento's Ferrari sparkling wines preside over this
gourmet aerie among the vines in the Brenta
Dolomites foothills. It's a thrilling drive up
and a heady experience once you're there.
Choose between the tiny, darkly glamorous
gastronomic salon or the informal 'veranda'.

🍷 Drinking & Nightlife

Palazzo Roccabruna   WINE BAR
(Enoteca Provinciale del Trentino; ☑ 0461 88 71 01;
www.palazzoroccabruna.it; Via Santissima Trinità 24;
⏱ 5-10pm Thu-Sat) For an excellent introduction to Trentino region wines, stop in at this
provincial government-sponsored *enoteca*
(wine bar) in a historic *palazzo* (mansion),
where you're invited to sample sparkling,
white and red vintages (three small glasses from €5), accompanied by local cheeses
and smoked meats. Buy bottles to go at the
attached shop.

Locanda Gatto Gordo   BAR
(☑ 0461 148 41 66; www.facebook.com/locandadel
gattogordo; Via Cavour 40; ⏱ 5.30pm-12.30am
Tue, 11.30am-12.30am Wed, Thu & Sun, 11.30am-
2am Fri & Sat) A central but very neighbourly
bar that attracts a young, relaxed but not so

studenty crowd. *Spritzes* and wines by the glass are well priced and there is a wide selection of 0km artisan beers.

Casa del Caffe COFFEE
(☑0461 98 51 04; www.casadelcaffetn.it; Via San Pietro 38; ⊗8am-12.30pm & 3-7pm Mon-Sat) Follow your nose to this coffee bar and chocolate shop for Trento's best espresso. Beans are roasted on the premises and the crowded shelves feature some of the country's best boutique chocolates, sweets and biscotti.

🛍 Shopping

In-con-tro FASHION & ACCESSORIES
(☑0461 23 01 30; www.in-con-tro.com; Viale della Costituzione 40; ⊗3.30-7pm Mon, 9.30am-12.30pm & 3.30-7pm Tue-Sat) The Trentini have a particular pared-back, intellectual elegance and this shop – the latest in three branches – encapsulates that style. It stocks global conceptual fashion from Martin Margiela, Comme des Garçons et al, but come for the more interesting independent Italian labels or a peek at the whimsical displays, and enjoy a slice of *torta* and an espresso in the in-store cafe.

Raccolta Differenziata FASHION & ACCESSORIES
(☑0461 26 12 92; www.facebook.com/raccolta differenziatatrento; Via Malpaga 16; ⊗10am-7pm Tue-Sat) Luigi Andreis has long been Trento's superstylist and it's worth seeking out his shop, tucked away in a quiet courtyard of an ancient *palazzo* from the 1400s, to experience his fascinating eye and treat yourself to one of the beautiful pieces from mostly Italian designers.

ℹ Information

Tourist Office (☑0461 21 60 00; www.discov ertrento.it; Piazza Dante 24; ⊗9am-7pm)
Hospital (Ospedale Santa Chiara; ☑0461 90 31 11; Largo Medaglie d'Oro 9; ⊗24hr)

ℹ Getting There & Away

Trento is situated on the A22 that runs north from Verona to the Austrian border at the Brenner Pass. Regular trains leave from the main train station (Piazza Dante) for the following destinations:
Bologna (€15.55, 2¾ hours, every two hours)
Bolzano (€7.30, 35 to 55 minutes, at least hourly)
Venice (€11.20, 2½ to 3½ hours, hourly)
Verona (€7.85, 1¼ hours, half hourly)

Next door to the main station, the regional train line **Ferrovia Trento–Malè–Mezzana** (☑0461 23 83 50; www.trentinotrasporti.it/en/travel-with-us/train) connects Trento with several towns in the Val di Non and Val di Sole.

From the **InterCity bus station** (Autostazione di Trento; Via Andrea Pozzo), local bus company **Trentino Trasporti** (☑0461 82 10 00; www.trentinotrasporti.it) runs buses to and from Madonna di Campiglio, Canazei, Rovereto and several other destinations.

Rovereto

☑0464 / POP 39,490

In the winter of 1769, Leopold Mozart and his soon-to-be-famous musical son visited Rovereto and found it to be 'rich in diligent people engaged in viticulture and the weaving of silk'. The area is no longer known for silk, but still produces some outstanding wines, including the inky, cherry-scented Marzemino (the wine's scene-stealing appearance in *Don Giovanni* suggests it may have been a Mozart family favourite). Those on a musical pilgrimage come for the annual **Festival Settenovecento** (www.settenovecento.it; ⊗mid-Apr–mid-May), and the town that Mozart knew still has its haunting, tightly coiled historic-centre streets. But it's the shock of the new that now lures most: Rovereto is home to one of Italy's finest contemporary art museums.

◉ Sights

★**Museo di Arte Moderna e Contemporanea Rovereto** GALLERY
(MART; ☑0464 43 88 87; www.mart.trento.it; Corso Bettini 43; adult/reduced €11/7, incl Casa d'Arte Futurista Depero & Galleria Civica di Trento €14/10; ⊗10am-6pm Tue-Thu, Sat & Sun, to 9pm Fri) This four-storey, 12,000-sq-metre steel, glass and marble behemoth, designed by Ticinese architect Mario Botta, is both imposing and human in scale, with mountain light gently filling a central atrium from a soaring cupola. On either side are the museum's monumental galleries of modern and contemporary art. Among the collections (though not always on display) are some huge 20th-century works, including Warhol's *Four Marilyns,* several Picassos, and a clutch of others, including Bill Viola, Kara Walker, Arnulf Rainer and Anselm Kiefer.

Casa d'Arte Futurista Depero MUSEUM
(☑0464 43 18 13; www.mart.trento.it/casadepe ro; Via Portici 38; adult/reduced €7/4, incl MART & Galleria Civica di Trento €14/10; ⊗10am-6pm Tue-Sun) Those Futurists were never afraid of a spot of self-aggrandisement and local lad Fortunato Depero was no exception. This Depero-designed museum was first launched shortly before his death in 1960, and was then restored and reopened by MART in recent

years. The obsessions of early 20th-century Italy mix nostalgically, somewhat unnervingly, with a historic past – bold tapestries and machine-age-meets-troubadour-era furniture decorate a made-over medieval townhouse.

✖ Eating

Maso Palù   TRENTINO €€
(☑0464 39 50 14; www.masopalu.com; Via Graziani 56, Brentonico; meals €35-40; ☺12.30-2.30pm & 7.30-9.15pm Wed-Mon) For a real treat, head 17km into the countryside southwest of Rovereto to this converted farmstead specialising in seasonal Trentino cuisine. The monthly changing *menu degustazione* takes diners through a multicourse feast of traditional dishes, served in smaller portions so you can sample them all. In summer, the kids' play area out back leaves grown-ups free to linger.

Trattoria Bella Vista   TRENTINO €€
(☑0464 43 99 51; Via Paganini 17; meals €25-35; ☺9am-6pm Mon-Thu, 11.30am-6pm Fri, 11.30am-3.30pm Sun) A cute-as-a-button historic trattoria that's worth it for the decor alone, but also serves up hearty pastas, occasionally inventive mains (say trout strudel) and trad desserts all made from almost all organic ingredients. At lunch they also do a €10 vegetarian or meat special.

❶ Information

Tourist Office (☑0464 43 03 63; www.visitrovereto.it; Corso Rosmini 21; ☺10am-1pm Mon & Sun, 9am-1pm & 2-6pm Tue-Sat) The tourist office has lots of information on Rovereto, town maps and details of cycling trails.

❶ Getting There & Away

Rovereto is on the A22 that runs north from Verona, and continues up to the Austrian border via Trento and Bolzano. It's around 15 minutes by train from Trento on the Bologna–Brennero line (€6.80, half hourly).

Brenta Dolomites

The Brenta group lies like a rocky island to the west of the main Dolomite range. Protected by the **Parco Naturale Adamello Brenta** (☑0463 45 10 33; www.pnab.it; Casa del Parco Lago Rosso, Tovel; ☺visitors centre 10am-1pm & 2-6pm Jun-Oct), these sharp, majestic peaks are well known among mountaineers for their sheer cliffs and tricky ascents. They are home to some of the world's most famous *vie ferrate* (trails with permanent cables and ladders), including the Via Ferrata delle Bocchette, pio-

neered by trailblazing British climber Francis Fox Tuckett in the 1860s.

On the densely forested western side of the Brenta group is the popular resort of Madonna di Campiglio, while on the eastern side is the Altopiano della Paganella, a high plateau offering some skiing and a huge range of outdoor adventures. The wiggly S421, S237 and S239 linking the two make for some scenic driving.

❶ Getting There & Away

From Trento, the Brenta Dolomites are accessed either via the northern SS421 or the southern SS237.

Trentino Trasporti (☑0461 82 10 00; www.trentinotrasporti.it) Offers bus connections between Trento and towns throughout the region during the summer and winter high seasons.

Ferrovia Trento–Malè (☑0461 23 83 50; www.trentinotrasporti.it/en/travel-with-us/train) Has frequent services from Trento to towns in the Val di Non and Val di Sole, including Cles, Malè, Dimaro and Mezzana.

Altipiano della Paganella

ELEV 2098M

Less than an hour's drive northwest of Trento, this dress-circle plateau looks out onto the towering Brenta Dolomites. The Altipiano incorporates five villages: ski resorts **Fai della Paganella** and **Andalo**, lakeside **Molveno** and little **Cavedago** and **Spormaggiore**. Molveno, with its wide selection of hotels and good swimming opportunities, is especially popular with families, while Andalo offers central location and ready access to the ski slopes, and Fai della Paganella enjoys some of the region's most beautiful mountain vistas.

◉ Sights & Activities

Casa Museo del Parco Orso   ANIMAL SANCTUARY
(☑0461 65 36 22; www.parcofaunistico.tn.it/sito/museo-parco-orso; Spormaggiore; adult/reduced €3/2; ☺10am-12.30pm & 2.30-6.30pm Tue-Sun Jul & Aug) Part of the larger **Parco Faunistico**, and with cute displays for kids, this is *the* place to see the 20-odd population of brown bears of the Parco Naturale Adamello Brenta. Outside the peak July and August season, hours are variable; call or check the website for details. With advance notice, you can book to see the bears in winter dormancy via infrared camera. It's 15km northeast of Molveno.

Paganella Ski Area   SKIING
(www.paganella.net; Cima Paganella) This ski area is accessible from Andalo by cable car and

WORTH A TRIP

VAL DI GENOVA

Northwest of Pinzolo is the entrance to the Val di Genova, renowned as one of the Alps' most beautiful valleys. It's great walking country, lined with a series of spectacular waterfalls along the 16km **Sentiero delle Cascate** (Waterfalls Trail). Four mountain huts strung out along the valley floor – from east to west, Chalet da Gino (www.chaletdagino.com), Rifugio Fontana Bona (www.rifugiofontanabona.it), Rifugio Stella Alpina (www.facebook.com/StellaAlpinaValGenova) and Rifugio Bedole (www.sites.google.com/site/rifugiobedole) – offer food and accommodation en route; Pinzolo's **tourist office** (📞0465 50 10 07; www.campigliodolomiti.it; Piazza S Giacomo; ⏰9am-12.30pm & 2.30-6.30pm Dec-Apr & mid-Jun–mid-Sep; reduced hours rest of year) has details. From early July through early September, private vehicles are prohibited and a free shuttle bus runs the length of the valley.

Fai della Paganella by chairlift. It has cross-country skiing trails and 50km of downhill ski slopes, ranging from beginner-friendly green runs to the heart-pounding black.

🍴 Sleeping & Eating

⭐ **Agriturismo Florandonole**   FARMSTAY €€
(📞0461 58 10 39; www.florandonole.it; Via ai Dossi 22, Fai della Paganella; d €90-130; 🅿🛜) 🍃 This modern farmhouse may look like every other from the outside, but inside the smart local-wood furniture and crisp goose-down duvets give it a luxury feel. Pretty views over the fields towards the Brenta Dolomites or Paganella will tempt you to grab a complimentary mountain bike. This is also a working **honey farm**, with hives, production facilities and a shop to explore.

Al Penny   TRENTINO €€
(📞0461 58 52 51; Viale Trento 23, Andalo; pizzas €8-12, meals €30-35; ⏰11am-2.30pm & 5pm-midnight) First impressions may clock the decor as a little too Alpine-for-dummies, but this is a genuinely cosy spot. A glass of warming Marzemino sets the scene, then out come authentic and tasty Trentino specialities – *taiadèle smalzàde* (pan-fried noodles with venison and pine-nut *ragù*) or beef fillet with porcini mushrooms and polenta, all served with homemade bread. The pizza also rates.

ℹ Information

Fai della Paganella Tourist Office (📞0461 58 31 30; www.visitdolomitipaganella.it; Piazza Italia Unita 6, Fai della Paganella; ⏰9am-12.30pm Mon, 9am-12.30pm & 3-6.30pm Tue-Sat, 9.30am-12.30pm Sun)

ℹ Getting There & Away

Altipiano della Paganella is best accessed from Trento, along the A22 then onto the SS421.
   Trentino Trasporti (📞0461 82 10 00; www.trentinotrasporti.it) serves all five villages with

bus service to Trento, Madonna di Campiglio and Riva del Garda; tourist offices have timetables. Free ski buses serve the area in winter.

Madonna di Campiglio & Pinzolo

Welcome to the Dolomites' bling belt, Madonna di Campiglio (population 1000, elevation 1522m), where ankle-length furs are standard après-ski wear and the formidable downhill runs are often a secondary concern to the social whirl and Michelin-starred dining. Austrian royalty set the tone in the 19th century, in particular Franz Joseph and wife Elisabeth (Sissi). This early celeb patronage is commemorated in late February or early March, when fireworks blaze and costumed pageants waltz through town for the annual **Habsburg Carnival**. Despite the traffic jams and hotel complexes, the town has a certain charm, overlooked by a pretty stone church and the jutting battlements of the Brenta Dolomites beyond. In summer this is an ideal base for hikers and *via ferrata* enthusiasts.
   Pinzolo (population 2000, elevation 800m), in a lovely valley 16km south, misses out on the most spectacular views but has a lively historic centre and more down-to-earth prices.

🏃 Activities

Funivie Madonna di Campiglio   CABLE CAR
(📞0465 44 77 44; www.funiviecampiglio.it; round-trip summer €12.70-19.40, various single-run and pass prices winter) A network of cable cars takes skiers and boarders from Madonna to its numerous ski runs and a snowboarding park in winter and to walking and mountain-biking trails in summer. In Campo Carlo Magno, 2km north of Madonna, the Cabinovia Grostè takes walkers to the Passo Grostè (2440m), and Brenta's most famous *via ferrata,* the **Via delle Bocchette** (trail No 305), leaves from its upper station.

Dolomiti di Brenta Bike CYCLING
(📞0463 42 30 02; www.dolomitibrentabike.it)
This agency organises mountain-bike tours
around the Brenta Dolomites, providing
luggage transfers and arranging accommodation in cyclist-friendly hotels, *rifugi* and
agriturismi. For further info, see the website
or inquire at the Madonna tourist office.

🛏 Sleeping & Eating

Camping Parco Adamello CAMPGROUND €
(📞338 1919608, 0465 50 17 93; www.campingpar
coadamello.it; Località Magnabò, Carisolo; camping
2 people, car & tent €32-40, s/d/q apt per week from
€400/500/700; 🅿) Beautifully situated within the national park 1km north of Pinzolo,
this campground is a natural starting point
for outdoor adventures such as skiing, snowshoeing, walking and biking. Weekly rates
are cheaper and five-day stays obligatory in
July and August.

★Chalet Fogajard AGRITURISMO €€
(📞0465 44 26 19; www.chaletfogajard.it; Località
Fogajard 36, Madonna di Campiglio; d €110-150,
with half-board €170-230; 🛜) 🍴 If you're looking for a mountain retreat, this six-room
Alpine idyll will fit the bill. Its remote location, down a steep dirt track way south of
Madonna's resort row, is stupefyingly beautiful and blissfully silent. Rooms have a craft
ethos that seems from another era, and an
atmospheric dining room delivers hearty,
wholesome, locally sourced meals.

DV Chalet DESIGN HOTEL €€€
(📞0465 44 31 91; www.dvchalet.it; Via Castelletto
Inferiore 10, Madonna di Campiglio; d from €260;
🅿❄🛜🏊) The most fashionable of Madonna's
ultraluxe hotels, DV is a relaxed place with
friendly staff and a quiet, wooded setting.
The bar keeps the Milanese fashion set happy
come *aperitivo* hour, there's a worthy Michelin-starred restaurant, **Dolomieu** (8-course
tasting menu €95), and once upstairs, guests are
cocooned in beautiful, earthy rooms.

Il Convivio GASTRONOMY €€€
(📞0465 44 01 00; www.alpensuitehotel.it; Viale
Dolomiti di Brenta 84, Madonna di Campiglio; meals
€48-60; ⊙7.30-9.30pm) Places like Conviv-
io are what Madonna is all about – return
guests and long-held traditions. While it
won't win any prizes for decor, the carefully
prepared food is a showcase of local produce. Risotto comes scented with pine, rack
of lamb is cooked in a bed of mountain hay,
and the organic beef carpaccio comes from
the rare local Rendena breed.

ℹ Information

Madonna Tourist Office (📞0465 44 75 01;
www.campigliodolomiti.it; Via Pradalago 4;
⊙9am-12.30pm & 2.30-6.30pm Dec-Apr &
mid-Jun–mid-Sep; reduced hours rest of year)
Madonna's tourist office teams up with the
Parco Naturale Adamello-Brenta in high summer to run guided thematic walks.

ℹ Getting There & Away

These two towns are accessed either via the
northern SS421 (from Trento or Bolzano) or the
southern SS237 (from Venice or Verona and also
from Trento).

Trentino Trasporti (📞0461 82 10 00; www.
trentinotrasporti.it) buses from Trento (€6.20,
1½ hours, five daily) serve both Madonna di
Campiglio and Pinzolo. On Saturdays and Sundays from early December to early April, the
Flyski (📞0461 39 11 11; www.flyskishuttle.com;
transfers from €35) shuttle runs services to
Madonna and Pinzolo from Milan, Verona, Bergamo, Treviso and Venice airports, as well as from
Trento's train station.

Val di Sole, Val di Rabbi & Val di Pejo

Centred on the main town of **Malé**, the aptly
named Val di Sole (Valley of the Sun) traces
the course of the foaming river Noce. Popular with young Trentini, it's a renowned hub
for outdoor pursuits, including rafting, fishing and cycling.

Two spectacular Alpine side valleys
branch off to the west, offering access to the
Trentino section of Parco Nazionale dello
Stelvio (p341). Narrow, deep-green Val di
Rabbi, among the few local valleys not developed for skiing, is refreshingly tranquil
and picturesquely rustic. Visitors come for
the Terme di Rabbi's spa treatments, or to
explore the network of paths just upstream,
which fan out into the national park's forests, meadows and waterfalls, some connecting to Val Martello in Alto Adige.

About 15km further southwest, Val di Pejo
is home to the Pejo 3000 ski area, a national park visitor centre and a nature centre
where you can meet some of the local mountain wildlife.

◉ Sights

Segheria Veneziana dei Bègoi HISTORIC SITE
(⊙variable hours Mon & Thu mid-Jun–early Sep)
This working 18th-century 'Venetian saw-
mill', powered by the rushing waters of the
Torrente Rabbiés and built according to a
design reputedly conceived by Leonardo da

Vinci, is one of the valley's most prized historical features. In summer, free guided tours allow visitors to watch its ingenious hydraulic mechanisms sawing wood in rapid-fire motion; consult the park office for exact hours.

Area Faunistica Pejo WILDLIFE RESERVE
(☑ 0463 98 90 75; Località Runcal, Pejo Fonti, Val di Pejo; ⊙ 10am-noon & 2-5pm Mon-Fri early May–mid-Jun, 9am-1pm & 3-7pm daily mid-Jun–Sep; ⊞) For an up-close look at the red and roe deer indigenous to Parco Nazionale dello Stelvio, visit this small hillside wildlife centre, dedicated to caring for and rehabilitating injured animals.

🏃 Activities

Terme di Rabbi THERMAL BATHS
(☑ 0463 98 30 00; www.termedirabbi.it; Località Fonti di Rabbi 162, Val di Rabbi; baths from €20; ⊙ 8.30am-noon & 4-8pm Mon-Sat late May-late Sep, plus 5-8pm Sun Jul & Aug) Europeans come to this remote spa to take the supposedly curative Antica Fonte spring waters; a wide range of traditional spa treatments is also available.

Centro Rafting Val di Sole RAFTING
(☑ 340 2175873, 0463 97 32 78; www.raftingcenter.it; Via Gole 105, Dimaro, Val di Sole; ⊙ by appointment May-Sep, phone hrs 9am-9pm) Runs rafting trips (from €39) on the Fiume Noce – touted as Italy's best water-sports river, along with kayaking, canyoning, hydrospeeding (riding the current downstream on a riverboard), mountain biking, Nordic walking, zip lining, paintball and other adventures.

🛏 Sleeping & Eating

Maso Fior di Bosco FARMSTAY €
(☑ 0463 98 55 43; www.masofiordibosco.it; Località Pralongo, Val di Rabbi; d from €90, with half-board from €110; 🛜) Lovingly overseen by two generations of the Casna family, this beautifully restored *maso* (traditional farmstead) on a bucolic hillside makes a perfect base for excursions into the Val di Rabbi. Taking half board here is a no-brainer: delicious home-cooked dinners of hearty Alpine fare are available for just a tiny surcharge over the cost of bed and breakfast.

Agritur il Tempo delle Mele B&B €
(☑ 347 9558401, 0463 90 13 89; www.agriturdellemele.it; Via Strada Provinciale 65, Caldes, Val di Sole; d €90-120; 🅿🛜) 🖉 Adventurous-spirited, well-travelled owner Fabiana and her husband Michele run this lovely B&B overlooking the Val di Sole's orchards. Modern,

spacious and comfortable wood-clad rooms offer easy access to the Pejo 3000 and Folgarida-Marilleva slopes, from where you can ski over to Madonna di Campiglio. Breakfasts feature strudel and juice from home-grown apples. Prices rise in February, August and around Christmastime.

★ Baita Tre Larici ALPINE €€
(☑ 349 7157786; www.vacanzadelgusto.it; Località Mezoli, Val di Pejo; meals €25-35; ⊙ 9am-6pm) This convivial place straddling the Val di Pejo's ski slopes serves delicious meals featuring steaks and raw-milk gelato from their home-raised Highlander cattle, along with Birra Pejo craft brews and carafes of Teroldego red wine from the Adige valley. In warm weather, enjoy fine mountain views from picnic tables on the wooden deck out front.

ℹ Information

Val di Sole Tourist Office (☑ 0463 90 12 80; www.valdisole.net; Via Marconi 7, Malé; ⊙ 8.30am-noon & 2-6pm Mon-Sat) Has good information on the entire Val di Sole and can advise you on ski facilities and walking trails in nearby Stelvio (p341).

ℹ Getting There & Away

The Val di Sole can be reached directly from Bolzano Sud on the SS42. To reach the Val di Rabbi, turn west onto the SP86 between Terzolas and Malé; for Val di Pejo, head west onto the SP87 at Ossana.

Ferrovia Trento–Malè (☑ 0461 23 83 50; www.trentinotrasporti.it/en/travel-with-us/train) has frequent services from Trento to Malè and on to Dimaro and Mezzana. Travel in the Val di Pejo and Val di Rabbi is much easier with your own wheels.

SOUTH TYROL (SÜDTIROL)

Bolzano (Bozen)
☑ 0471 / POP 106,950 / ELEV 262M

Bolzano, the provincial capital of South Tyrol, is anything but provincial. Once a stop on the coach route between Italy and the flourishing Austro-Hungarian Empire, this small city is worldly and engaged, a long-time conduit between cultures that has more recently become home to Europe's first trilingual university. Its quality of life – one of Italy's highest – is reflected in its openness, youthful energy and an all-pervading greenness. A stage-set-pretty backdrop of grassy, rotund hills sets off rows of pastel-painted townhouses, while bicycles ply riverside paths and wooden market stalls are laid out with Alpine cheese, speck (cured ham) and dark, seeded loaves. German may be the first language of 95% of the region, but Bolzano is an anomaly. Today its Italian-speaking majority – a legacy of Mussolini's brutal Italianisation program of the 1920s and the more recent siren call of education and employment opportunities – looks both north and south for inspiration.

◎ Sights

★ Museo Archeologico dell'Alto Adige
MUSEUM

(☑0471 32 01 00; www.iceman.it; Via Museo 43; adult/reduced €9/7; ☉10am-6pm Tue-Sun) The star here is Ötzi, the Iceman, with almost the entire museum given over to the Copper Age mummy. Kept in a temperature-controlled 'igloo' room, he can be viewed through a small window (peer closely enough and you can make out faint tattoos on his legs). Ötzi's clothing – a wonderful get-up of patchwork leggings, rush-matting cloak and fur cap – and other belongings are also displayed.

Museion
GALLERY

(☑0471 22 34 13; www.museion.it; Piazza Piero Siena 1; adult/reduced €7/3.50, from 6pm Thu free; ☉10am-6pm Tue, Wed & Fri-Sun, to 10pm Thu) Bolzano's four-storey contemporary art space is housed in a huge multifaceted glass cube, a brave architectural surprise that beautifully vignettes the old-town rooftops and surrounding mountains from within. There's an impressive permanent collection of Italian and international artwork; temporary shows are a testament to the local art scene's vibrancy, or often highlight an ongoing dialogue with artists and institutions from around the world. The river-facing cafe has a terrace perfect for a post-viewing *spritz*.

BZ '18-'45
MUSEUM

(☑0471 99 75 88; www.monumenttovictory.com; Piazza Vittoria; ☉11am-1pm & 2pm-5pm Tue, Wed & Fri-Sun, 3-9pm Thu Apr-Sep, reduced hours Oct-Mar) FREE This dense but visually seductive museum explores Bolzano's turbulent interwar years via the history of the fascist Monument to Victory, where it is sited. It's a thoughtful and overdue examination of a highly complex time in the South Tyrol's past and covers Bolzano's post-WWI handover to Italy and the later Nazi occupation. The displays on the radical urban transformation of the 1920s – the enduring face of Mussolini's 'Italianisation' project – are particularly fascinating.

Messner Mountain Museum Firmiano
MUSEUM

(MMM Firmian; ☑0471 63 12 64; www.mess ner-mountain-museum.it; adult/reduced €12/10; ☉10am-6pm Fri-Wed late Mar–mid-Nov) The imposing Castel Firmiano, dating back to AD 945, is the centrepiece of mountaineer Reinhold Messner's six museums. Based around humankind's relationship with the mountains across all cultures, the architecture itself suggests the experience of shifting altitudes, and requires visitors to traverse hundreds of stairs and mesh walkways. The collection is idiosyncratic, but when it works, it's heady stuff. Messner's other museums are scattered across the region, including his newest, at Kronplatz (MMM Corones; ☑0474 50 13 50; www.messner-mountain-mu seum.it; Kronplatz ski area; adult/reduced €10/8.50; ☉10am-4pm Jun–mid-Oct & Dec–mid-Apr), and his most remote, at Ortles (p342).

There's a shuttle from Piazza Walther in summer, or you can catch a taxi or take the suburban train to Ponte Adige/Sigmundskron (beware there is then a long walk up a truck-laden road). By bike it's a 25-minute ride along a riverside path.

Castel Roncolo
CASTLE

(Schloss Runkelstein; ☑0471 32 98 08; www.run kelstein.info; Via San Antonio 15; adult/reduced €8/5.50; ☉10am-6pm Tue-Sun mid-Mar–, to 5pm Nov–mid-Mar) This stunningly located castle was built in 1237 but is renowned for its vivid 14th-century frescoes. These are particularly rare, with themes that are drawn from secular literature, including the tale of Tristan and Isolde, as well as depictions of day-to-day courtly life. From April through October, a free shuttle runs from Piazza Walther; alternatively, catch suburban bus 12 or 14.

🏃 Activities

Bolzano's trio of *funivie* (cable cars) whisk you up into the hills, affording spectacular views over the city and valley floor, then of terraced vineyards, tiny farms, ancient mountain chapels and towering peaks beyond. The respective villages might be delightful destinations in themselves but they are also a great jumping-off point for rambles or serious hikes. Walks can also be done from the city centre – ask at the tourist office (p337) for a comprehensive map marked with all the easily accessible routes.

★ **Salewa Cube**   CLIMBING

(📞 0471 188 68 67; www.salewa-cube.com; Via Waltraud-Gebert-Deeg 4, Bolzano Sud; adult/reduced €13/10; ⏱ 9am-11pm) Part of the outdoor-clothing empire's HQ, this is Italy's largest indoor-climbing centre. There are over 2000 sq metres of climbing surface and 180 different routes. In good weather the enormous entrance is open, so climbing has an outdoor feel. Take bus 18 from the centre.

Funivia del Renon   CABLE CAR

(Rittner Seilbahn; 📞 0471 35 61 00; www.ritten.com; Via Renon; one-way/return €6/10; ⏱ 6.30am-10.45pm Mon-Sat, 7.10am-10.45pm Sun) The 12-minute journey over the Renon (Ritten) plateau to Soprabolzano (Oberbozen) runs along the world's longest single-track aerial tramway, stretching for 4.56km, passing over eerie red-earth pyramids and farm-, vine- and spire-dotted valleys. Departures are every four minutes.

Funivia San Genesio   CABLE CAR

(Seilbahn Jenesien; 📞 0471 35 41 96; www.sii.bz.it; Via Rafenstein 15; one-way/return €3/5; ⏱ 8.30am-noon & 3-6.30pm) An ultra-steep eight-minute ascent whisks you 740 vertical metres up to the beautiful terraced village of San Genesio (Jenesien), where there are roof-of-the-world views and forest trails to follow. Take bus 12 or 150 from the centre to the cable car's base station.

Bike Rental   CYCLING

(Noleggio Bici, Fahrradverleih; 📞 0471 99 75 78; Via della Stazione 2; rental 6hr/full day €2/5; ⏱ 7.30am-8pm Mon-Sat late Apr–mid-Oct) Bicycles can be rented at Bolzano's municipal open-air bike-rental stall near the train station. You'll need cash for a deposit plus ID.

Funivia del Colle   CABLE CAR

(Kohlerer Seilbahn; 📞 0471 97 85 45; Via Campegno 4; one-way/return €4/8; ⏱ 7am-7pm Mon-Sat, 8am-noon & 1-7pm Sun Mar-Oct, shorter hours Nov-Feb) This is the world's oldest cable car, dreamt up by a canny innkeeper in 1908. Up top you'll find a pristine village, a tall wooden tower offering panoramic views of the Dolomites, and a network of hiking trails.

Club Alpino Italiano   WALKING

(📞 0471 97 81 72; www.caibolzano.it; Piazza delle Erbe 46; ⏱ 10am-noon & 2.30-6.30pm Mon-Fri) A serious alpinist's organisation that can provide details of mountain trails and huts as well as club activities, either in person or online.

🛏 Sleeping

Villa Anita   GUESTHOUSE €

(📞 348 9351120; www.villaanitabolzano.it; Via Castel Roncolo 16; s/d/f without bathroom from €61/70/84; 🅿🛜) Although it's just a short walk from the historic centre, the surrounding gardens make this beautiful 1905 villa seem like you're already out in the countryside. Rooms are spacious and light, the shared bathrooms are modern and spotlessly maintained and the owner is gracious and kind. You can pay a little extra for a room with a balcony or for the spacious self-catering apartment.

Goethe Guesthouse   GUESTHOUSE €

(📞 335 8258599, 070 58 38 346; www.bookingbolzano.com; Via Goethe 28; d without breakfast €92-116; ❄🛜) If you don't mind hopping down the stairs to a *pasticceria* or the market for breakfast and don't need front desk or other hotel facilities, these historic townhouse rooms are superstylish. Contemporary furnishings are minimal but comfortable, while floorboards, subtle lighting and dramatic exposed stone add atmosphere. Check-in is DIY or at the central **Booking Bolzano office** (📞 327 1135751, 0471 98 00 23; www.bookingbolzano.com; Via Piave 7b).

Youth Hostel Bolzano   HOSTEL €

(Jugendherberge Bozen; 📞 0471 30 08 65; www.bozen.jugendherberge.it; Via Renon 23; dm/s €24/33; 🛜) The three- and four-bed dorms in this airy and friendly hostel are well designed and configured for privacy. Single rooms can squeeze in a fold-out if needed. Rooms at the back have balconies, but sadly no view.

★ **Parkhotel Laurin**   HOTEL €€

(📞 0471 31 10 00; www.laurin.it; Via Laurin 4; s €88-134, d €129-347; 🅿🛜🏊) Set in its own lush gardens in the centre of town, this five-star hotel has large rooms overlooking the Dolomites or the Duomo, all endowed with a weighty, old-fashioned opulence, and staff that mesh haute-professionalism with relaxed Alpine charm. There's a distinctly individual style throughout, from the beloved vintage elevator to the idiosyncratic mix of contemporary artwork and Tyrolean antiques.

★ **Hotel Greif**   DESIGN HOTEL €€

(📞 0471 31 80 00; www.greif.it; Piazza Walther; s/d €100-125, d €154-320; ❄🛜) The Greif's pedigree dates back to its founding in 1816 as one of Bolzano's original hotels; Ezra Pound even immortalised it in poetry (his quote adorns the entrance staircase). Largely destroyed in WWII, it has fully embraced its design-hotel reincarnation. Each of the 33 spacious, light-

Bolzano

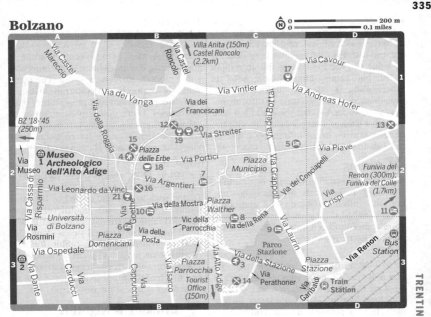

filled rooms is unique but all are beautifully decorated with art and antiques from the owner's wide-ranging collection.

Residence Fink APARTMENT €€
(☑0471 09 50 91; www.residence-fink.it; Via della Mostra 9; apt 2/4 people from €112/118; 🛜) If you don't need hotel facilities or service, these stylish, atmospheric apartments can't be beaten for their living-like-a-local position and facilities. They range in size from studios to two bedrooms with enough room for eight people. Rates are cheaper for singles.

Hotel Figl HOTEL €€
(☑0471 97 84 12; www.figl.net; Piazza del Grano 9; s/d/apt without breakfast €100/147/172; ❄@) Affable staff and a busy downstairs bar lend this place a home-away-from-home feel. Mod-Euro rooms are sleek but also fabulously cosy and look out over a pretty square or town rooftops. Business travellers and long-stay guests can negotiate discounts. Breakfast is extra: €4 for the Italian option, €8 for continental or €16 for the big buffet.

Hotel Belvedere
HOTEL €€€

(📞0471 35 41 27; www.belvedere-hotel.it; Via Pichl 15, San Genesio; d with half-board from €332; ⊙late Mar–mid-Dec; 🏡🐾) Ten minutes from Bolzano by cable car, the location of this incredibly stylish but unpretentious 'hiking hotel' is otherworldly. It offers a number of wellness-themed programs (stays of three nights plus are cheaper, too) but you could just hole up with a book and eat yourself silly, with the occasional swim in the infinity pool, hike or massage to break up the exquisite monotony.

✗ Eating

Redolent of rural mountain life one minute, Habsburg splendour the next, Bolzano's restaurants – often in the guise of a traditional wood-panelled dining room called a *stube* – are a profound reminder of just how far north of Rome you've come.

Stars
BURGERS €

(📞0471 32 45 07; www.stars-burgers.com; Piazza delle Erbe 39; burgers €8; ⊙noon-2.30pm & 6-10pm Tue-Thu, noon-11pm Fri & Sat) 🌿 This may look like just another hipster burger place, but the people behind it (and its Merano sibling) have serious culinary credentials, including local Michelin-starred chef Theodor Falser. Burgers are made with beef from a local farmer-butcher, vegetables are all 0km, sauces are house-made, the bread is long-risen, and all soft drinks and beers are from artisan producers.

Pur Südtirol
CAFE €

(📞0471 09 56 51; www.pursuedtirol.com; Via Perathoner 9; snacks & light meals €5-13; ⊙7.30am-7.30pm Mon-Fri, 8.30am-5pm Sat) Merano's Slow Food–driven produce shop, cafe and wine bar concept has been rolled out to big-city Bolzano. Window seats are a great place for morning pastries and coffee or afternoon *aperitivi* accompanied by plates of cheeses and cured meats. You can also pick up some beautiful deli goods for picnics.

Franziskaner Stuben
OSTERIA €€

(📞0471 97 61 83; www.franziskanerstuben.com; Via dei Francescani 7; meals €32-45; ⊙11.45am-2.30pm & 6-10pm Mon-Sat) Going strong for nearly a century, this wood-panelled *osteria* (tavern) next door to the Chiesa dei Francescani is a welcoming venue for Tyrolean specialities. Waiters clad in red-and-black vests parade through the elegant dining room bearing baskets of seeded bread and plates piled high with homemade dumplings, saffron-vegetable risotto, Wienerschnitzel, beef goulash, chestnut mousse and apple strudel.

Löwengrube
ALPINE €€

(📞0471 97 00 32; www.loewengrube.it; Piazza Dogana 3; meals €38-45; ⊙11am-3pm & 6pm-midnight Mon-Sat) A glorious 16th-century *stube* is the surprise design element in an otherwise super-modern, glamorous fit-out. The menu ranges across local and Mediterranean dishes, and its combinations and presentation push boundaries. Don't miss a peek at the wine cellar (dating back to 1280). It holds a vast collection that honours international-name vineyards as well as local microproducers.

Vögele
ALPINE €€

(📞0471 97 39 38; www.voegele.it; Via Goethe 3; meals €28-44; ⊙11am-4pm & 6-11pm Mon-Sat) Dating back to 1277 and owned by the same family since 1840, this multilevel, wood-panelled, antique-stuffed restaurant is well loved for its schnitzels and steaks along with local favourites risotto with rabbit *ragù* and rosemary, or jugged venison with polenta. There are some good vegetarian options and much of the produce is organic. The attached bar is pleasantly rowdy, too.

🍷 Drinking & Nightlife

Bolzano after dark makes for a delightful wander. Follow the locals heading for Piazza delle Erbe's bar strip or the beer halls and wine bars along Via Argentieri, Via Leonardo da Vinci, Via Streiter and Via Goethe. A younger local crowd frequents the bars across the river in the 'Italian town'.

★ Franzbar
WINE BAR

(📞0471 30 02 52; Via Leonardo da Vinci 1; ⊙8am-1am Mon-Sat) A perennial local favourite, Franzbar straddles the wine-bar/beer-hall and student/grown-up divides. Join the crowds for scrumptious *tartine* (miniature open-faced sandwiches) at *aperitivo* hour, stop in for a meal at lunchtime or pop in after dark for a rowdier nighttime scene.

★ Café Bistro Thaler Arôme
CAFE

(📞0471 31 30 30; www.thaler.bz.it; 5th fl, Via Portici 69; ⊙9am-11pm Mon-Sat) On the top floor of Bolzano's luxe perfumerie and skincare department store, this glamorous bar is a great place to celebrate any time of day, with espresso drinks, wines by the glass and sweeping vistas from the rooftop terrace. Lunch (noon to 2.30pm) and dinner (7pm to 10pm) are also served. Its sister champagne bar on the 2nd floor is equally chic.

Aperitif Bar Thaler Perlage
WINE BAR

(📞0471 31 30 14; www.thaler.bz.it; 2nd fl, Via Portici 69; ⊙10am-8pm Mon-Fri, to 7pm Sat) Fuchsiahued velvet couches and bookshelf-lined walls set the tone at this champagne bar on the 2nd floor of the Thaler department store. The sparkling wine list includes over 250 international labels, from French classics to local producers in Trentino and Franciacorta.

Batzen-bräu PUB
(📞 0471 05 09 50; www.batzen.it; Via Andreas Hofer 30; ⏱11am-1am) Dating back to 1404, with a cosy interior with leaded glass windows and a sunny beer garden, this centrally located brewery cranks out an appealing mix of ales; try a six-beer sampler for €6.50, snack on burgers, sausages or dumplings (€5 to €9) or linger over the €10.50 daily lunch special. A basement theatre space turns into a night-club on weekends.

Fischbänke WINE BAR
(📞 340 5707468; Via Streiter 26; ⏱noon-sunset Mon-Fri) Pull up a stool at one of the original marble-slab counters decorated with bas-reliefs of fish at this lively streetside bar on the site of a fish market dating back to 1327. It's a lively spot for late afternoon glasses of local wines accompanied by bruschetta, all care of bon vivant Cobo.

Enovit WINE BAR
(📞0471 97 04 60; Via Streiter 30; ⏱10am-2pm & 3.30-8pm Mon-Fri, 10am-2pm Sat) An older, well-dressed lot frequents this warm, woody corner bar and shop for expertly recommended, generously poured local wine by the glass. There's a crowd – and on Fridays there *always* is – it kicks on past demarcated closing.

ℹ Information

Tourist Office (📞 0471 30 70 00; www.bolzano-bozen.it; Via Alto Adige 60; ⏱9am-7pm Mon-Fri, 9.30am-6pm Sat year-round, 10am-3pm Sun May-Oct)

ℹ Getting There & Away

The city is on the A22 which runs from Verona to Austria.

Local **SAD** (📞 840 000471, 0471 45 01 11; www.sad.it; ⏱6am-8pm Mon-Sat, 7.30am-8pm Sun) buses leave from Bolzano's brand-new **bus station** (Via Renon) for destinations throughout the province, including hourly routes to Val Gardena, Brunico and Merano. SAD buses also head for resorts outside the province, including Cortina d'Ampezzo.

Bolzano's train station is connected by hourly or half-hourly trains with Merano (€6, 40 minutes), Trento (€7.30, 35 to 55 minutes) and Verona (€14.55, 1¾ to 2¼ hours), with slightly less frequent connections to Bressanone (€7,

30 minutes). All regional trains within South Tyrol and right down to Trento are covered by the Museumobil card. Deutsche Bahn trains run south to Venice and north to Innsbruck and Munich via Brennero.

At the time of research all commercial flights at Bolzano's small **airport** (Aeroporto di Bolzano; 📞 0471 25 52 55; www.abd-airport.it; Via Baracca 1) had been suspended.

Südtiroler Weinstrasse
📞 0471

You might only be an hour or so south of the Brenner pass, but there's no mistaking the Mediterranean vibe along South Tyrol's Weinstrasse, or the Strada del Vino. It begins northwest of Bolzano in **Nals**, meanders past **Terlano** (Terlan) through **Upper Adige** (Überetsch) and **Lower Adige** (Unterland), until it reaches **Salorno** (Salurn). Grapevines cover gentle rolling hills, fringed with palm trees and apple orchards. It's a gentle, relaxed place where you can taste the region's world-famous wines made from native grape varieties (Lagrein, Vernatsch and Gewürztraminer) along with well-adapted imports pinot blanc, sauvignon, merlot and cabernet, or you can swim, windsurf or sun-worship at its central lake the Kalterer See, the warmest body of water in the region. Of course, glimpses of the mighty Dolomites at every turn will remind you that you're still in the Alps.

🛏 Sleeping

⭐ **Das Wanda** BOUTIQUE HOTEL €€€
(📞 0471 66 90 11; www.das-wanda.com; Garnellenweg 18, Caldaro (Kaltern); d €216-360, adults only; ⏱Apr–mid-Nov; P❄🐶🏊) Verena Huf is a third-gen hotelier and her gorgeous 12-suite place combines that rich lineage with youthful enthusiasm and a relaxed style. Rooms are spacious and clean-lined but deliciously cosy, and all have huge bathrooms, balconies (some two) overlooking the vines, palm-clad gardens and Dolomite peaks beyond. Swim laps or sauna with vine views in the dramatically low-lit spa area, or laze by the outdoor pool in summer.

Seehotel Ambach DESIGN HOTEL €€€
(📞0471 96 00 98; www.seehotel-ambach.com; Klughammer 3, Caldaro (Kaltern); s €181-199, d €258-394, all with half-board; ⏱mid-Apr–early Nov; P❄🐶🏊) This Othmar Barth–designed hotel dates to 1973 and is remarkably intact. Gentle revamping has not altered its fabulous 20th-century charm. All rooms from single to suite offer a view of the lake and

feature design classics from 1920s Eileen Gray lamps to 1960s Magistretti chairs to contemporary Italian and Scando pieces.

Drinking & Nightlife

★ **Alois Lageder Paradeis**   WINE BAR
(📞0471 80 95 80; www.aloislageder.eu/alois-laged er-paradeis/vineria-restaurant; Casòn Hirschprunn Strasse 1, Magrè (Margreid); meals €34-41; ⊙10am-6pm Mon-Sat Mar-Oct, to 5pm Nov & Dec; 11am-3pm Mon-Sat Jan & Feb) 🍴 Take a seat at the long communal table, crafted from the wood of a 250-year-old oak tree, at fourth-generation winemaker Alois Lageder's biodynamic *vineria* (winery), and start tasting. Book for lunch in the stunning dining room where simple, 'meat-light' dishes are prepared with biodynamic produce, or linger over a bottle and plate of cheese in the pretty courtyard.

Getting There & Away

To reach the Weinstrasse, take the SS42 southwest from Bolzano Sud, then continue south onto the SP14 for Kaltern, following the Weinstrasse signage.

The main villages of the Weinstrasse are well connected by regular train services to Bolzano in the north, Trento, and on to Verona to the south. There is also a good network of local buses from Bolzano operated by SAD (www.sad.it). Hotels can arrange a taxi to take you between villages if you're tasting or out to eat.

Merano (Meran)
📞0473 / POP 40,050 / ELEV 325M

With its leafy boulevards, birdsong, oleanders and cacti, Merano feels like a northern Italian Shangri-La. Lauded for its sunny microclimate, this poignantly pretty town (and one-time Tyrolean capital) was a Habsburg-era spa and the hot destination of its day, favoured by the Austrian royals plus Freud, Kafka and Pound. The Jugendstil (art nouveau) villas, recuperative walks and grand riverside Kurhaus fan out from its intact medieval core. The city's therapeutic traditions have served it well in the new millennium, with spa hotels drawing a new generation of health-conscious visitors and bolstering the region's booming organics movement. German is spoken more widely than Italian here, sausage and beer stalls dot the streets and an annual open-air play celebrates Napoleonic-era Tyrolean freedom fighter Andreas Hofer. Despite the palm trees, you're closer to Vienna than Rome. Merano also makes an attractive urban base for skiing, cycling or hiking.

◎ Sights

★ **Schloss Trauttmansdorff Gardens**   GARDENS
(📞0473 25 56 00; www.trauttmansdorff.it; St-Valentin-Strasse 51a; garden & museum adult/reduced €14/11; ⊙9am-7pm Apr–mid-Oct, to 5pm mid-Oct–mid-Nov, plus to 11pm Fri Jun-Aug) You could give an entire day to these beautiful botanical gardens a little outside Merano (and they do suggest it). Exotic cacti and palms, fruit trees and vines, beds of lilies, irises and tulips all cascade down the hillside surrounding a mid-19th-century castle where Sissi – Empress Elisabeth – spent the odd summer. Inside, **Touriseum** charts two centuries of travel in the region. There's also a restaurant and a cafe by the lily pond.

Schloss Tirol   MUSEUM
(Castel Tirolo; 📞0473 22 02 21; www.schlosstirol. it; Schlossweg 24, Tirol; adult/reduced €7/3.50; ⊙10am-5pm Tue-Sun mid-Mar–early Dec) Clinging to a steep crag high above the Adige valley, the ancestral seat of the counts of Tyrol houses a dynamically curated museum of Tyrolean history, including a series of exhibits on the turbulent years of the 20th century. To get here, take the chairlift or drive from Merano to the higher village of Tirolo (Dorf Tirol). From here, a pretty 1km walk snakes up through terraced vineyards to the castle. Book ahead for English-language tours.

🏊 Activities

★ **Therme Meran**   THERMAL BATHS
(Terme Merano; 📞0473 25 20 00; www.termemerano.it; Thermenplatz 9; bathing pass 2hr/all-day from €13/19, with sauna from $18/25; ⊙9am-10pm) Bolzano-born Matteo Thun's striking redevelopment of Merano's historic thermal baths features 13 indoor pools sitting within a massive glass cube; there are also 12 outdoor pools in summer. Swim through the sluice and be met by a vision of palm-studded gardens and snow-topped mountains beyond.

Merano 2000   SKIING
(www.hafling-meran2000.eu; Avelengo (Hafling)) Some 6km east of town, a cable car carries winter-sports enthusiasts up to Merano 2000, which has 30km of mostly beginner, but very pleasant, slopes. This is a great choice for families, with ski kindergartens, designated children's ski areas and nature-based playgrounds. Local bus 1 and SAD (www.sad.it) bus 225 (Meran-Hafling-Falzeben) link Merano with the Naif valley station (20 minutes).

MERANO'S GARDEN WALKS

The promenade or *passeggiata* (evening stroll) has long been a Merano institution. Fin-de-siècle-era walks trace the river, traverse pretty parks, weave past elegant mansions and skirt Monte Benedetto (514m). The tourist office can give you a detailed map; all routes have helpful signage.

Winterpromenade & Sommerpromenade Merano's most centrally located walking paths follow opposing sides of the river, the shady Sommerpromenade tracing the south bank and the sunny Winterpromenade running along the north. Watch for the **Wandelhalle** on the Winterpromenade, a narrow, late-19th-century pavilion where thermal cure seekers would gather in the sun while bands played. Now lined with 1930s Alpine landscape painting, it still attracts evening *aperitivo*-takers.

Gilfpromenade (Passeggiata Gilf) Winding through a narrow river gorge and lush subtropical gardens east of the centre, the short but sweet Gilfpromenade features some whimsical topiary creations and poems carved on wooden benches (also handy for a breather).

Sissiweg (Sentiero di Sissi, Sissi's Path) Tracing the route that Empress Elisabeth of Austria herself once trod from downtown Merano to her summer home at Trauttmansdorff Castle, this easy 3km, 45-minute walking route offers a glimpse of some of Merano's most refined neighbourhoods, passing a series of villas, manors, parks and gardens on its way up the hill.

Tappeinerweg (Passeggiata Tappeiner) Meandering above town for 4km, this lovely garden-fringed promenade with splendid views over the city and surrounding mountains is Merano's most evocative walk. The easiest two ways to pick it up are by following signs uphill from Gilfpromenade or taking the zigzag path uphill from the Dorf Tirol chairlift.

🛏 Sleeping

Youth Hostel Merano HOSTEL €
(☑ 0473 20 14 75; www.meran.jugendherberge.it; Carduccistrasse 77; dm/s €25/28.50; 🅿 @ 🛜) A five-minute stroll from both Merano's train station and the riverside promenade, this hostel is bright and modern, with a sunny terrace and other downtime extras. It has 59 beds, either singles or en-suite dorms.

Garni Domus Mea B&B €€
(☑ 0473 23 67 77; www.domusmea.com; Piavestrasse 8; s €48-61, d €92-118; 🛜) Owner Massimo's warm-hearted welcome makes all the difference at this old family flat converted into a low-key B&B. The Terme Merano are a stone's throw away, the city centre is just across the bridge, and there's limited free parking out back.

Hotel Aurora HOTEL €€
(☑ 0473 21 18 00; www.hotel-aurora-meran.com; Passerpromenade 38; d €129-189; 🅿 ❄ 🛜) This traditional family hotel, just across the river from the Terme, works some fresh ideas. 'New' rooms are Italian designed, bright and slick, but the parquetry-floored '60s to '80s originals have their own vintage charm, along with some river-facing balconies. The corridors, too, are littered with original but pristine midcentury pieces. Service is attentive and kind.

★ Miramonti BOUTIQUE HOTEL €€€
(☑ 0473 27 93 35; www.hotel-miramonti.com; St Kathreinstrasse 14, Avelengo (Hafling); d from €318; 🅿 ❄ 🛜) 🍴 This extraordinary small hotel, a 15-minute drive from Merano, nestles high on a secluded mountainside at 1230m. Run by an incredibly vibrant young couple, the whole place exemplifies Südtirolean hospitality, relaxed but attentive to every detail. Deeply comfortable original rooms have been joined by a new batch of clean-lined design suites, including some very glamorous lofts.

★ Ottmanngut BOUTIQUE HOTEL €€€
(☑ 0473 44 96 56; www.ottmanngut.it; Verdistrasse 18; s €132, d €264-314; 🛜) 🍴 This boutique hotel encapsulates Merano's beguiling mix of stately sophistication, natural beauty and gently bohemian backstory. The remodelled townhouse has nine rooms scattered over three floors, and is set among terraced vineyards a scant five-minute walk from the arcades of the centre. Individually furnished, antique-strewn rooms evoke different moods, each highlighting the different landscape glimpsed from the window.

✗ Eating

★ Pur Südtirol   DELI €

(📞 0473 01 21 40; www.pursuedtirol.com; Freiheitsstrasse 35; snacks & light meals €5-13; ☺ 9am-7.30pm Mon-Fri, to 2pm Sat; 🚲) 🍴 This stylish regional showcase – now a chain with branches in Bolzano and Brunico – has an amazing selection of farm produce: wine, cider, some 80 varieties of cheese, speck and sausage, pastries and breads, tisanes and body care. Everything is local (take Anton Oberhöller's chocolate, flavoured with apple, lemon balm or dark bread crisps).

Trattoria Mainardo   TRATTORIA €€

(📞 345 1575412; Meinhardstrasse 19; meals €30-40; ☺ noon-2pm & 7-10pm Mon-Sat) Marco and Sabina's cute and humble trattoria serves a tempting mix of Italian- and Alpine-style home cooking – from tagliatelle with zucchini, cherry tomatoes and squash blossoms, to roast pork with potatoes, to fantastic *canederli* (dumplings) with *parmigiano reggiano* (Parmesan) and *burro fuso* (melted butter). It's a popular gathering spot for Merano's native Italian speakers.

Trattoria Al Boia   SICILIAN €€

(Henker Haus; 📞 329 8782673; www.henkerhaus.it; Ortensteingasse 9; meals €30-40; ☺ noon-2pm & 6pm-midnight Tue-Sat, noon-2pm Sun) Agrigento transplant Marco has created this sweet Sicilian trattoria, sporting a welcoming front courtyard, a warm stone-walled interior and a cool jazz and blues soundtrack. Authentic, perfectly prepared Sicilian classics like *caponata* (a sweet-and-sour mix of vegetables, capers and olives) and *pasta alla norma* (pasta with aubergines, tomatoes and ricotta) offer a welcome alternative to Merano's ubiquitous South Tyrolean cuisine.

Sigmund   ALPINE €€

(📞 0473 23 77 49; www.restaurantsigmund.com; Freiheitsstrasse 2; meals €35-45; ☺ noon-2.15pm & 6-9.30pm Thu-Tue) This intimate place is what Merano is all about: gentility and tradition. A few Italian dishes (steak *tagliata, tagliatelle alla bolognese*) sit side-by-side with Tyrolean classics (schnitzel, boiled calf's head with onion) and more innovative dishes such as pork in a black-bread crust with local asparagus or risotto with wild-garlic pesto. The terrace is lovely in summer, too.

Sissi   GASTRONOMY €€€

(📞 0473 23 10 62; www.sissi.andreafenoglio.com; Galileo Galilei-Strasse 44; meals €60, 4-/5-/7-course menu €80/85/95; ☺ 12.15-2.30pm Wed-Sun & 7-10pm Tue-Sun) Andrea Fenoglio is one of the region's best-loved chefs and his big personality fills this small early 20th-century room. The food here is inventive, for sure, but the experience is warm and refreshingly relaxed. Even the most experimental dish retains a connection to the traditional, or what Fenoglio calls 'memory food'.

🍸 Drinking & Nightlife

Why Not?   COCKTAIL BAR

(📞 338 8015278; www.facebook.com/whynot lab; Freiheitsstrasse 15; ☺ 8.30am-1am Tue-Sat, 9.30am-1am Sun) At this loud, shiny and fun spot in Merano's pedestrian zone, the owner-bartender Stefano Urru loves what he does, and most of the cocktail ingredients are homemade. If you're more interested in an *aperitivo*, there's an interesting *spritz* menu to choose from.

Bistro Sieben   BAR

(📞 0473 21 06 36; www.bistrosieben.it; Laubengasse 232; ☺ 8.30am-midnight Mon-Sat, 9.30am-4pm Sun) You'll probably end up staying for a bite at this beautifully sited casual restaurant under stunning vaulted ceilings, but it's a great spot for an afternoon Hugo (elderflower-and-prosecco *spritz*) or kicking on after you've been elsewhere.

🛍 Shopping

Meraner Markt   MARKET

(Mercato Meranese; Freiheitsstrasse; ☺ 9am-1pm Sat Apr-Oct) Meranese designer Martino Gamper is behind this weekly artisan and produce market that showcases South Tyrolean traditions and includes seasonal farm products, speck, wild berries, wine, spirits and bread, as well as crafts using wool, felt and lace, jewellery, glass, and local skincare. There is often also music and other performances.

ℹ️ Information

Tourist Office (📞 0473 27 20 00; www.mer ano.eu; Freiheitsstrasse 45; ☺ 9am-6pm Mon-Fri, to 4pm Sat, 10am-12.30pm Sun Apr-Dec, 9am-1pm & 2.30-5pm Mon-Fri, 10am-12.30pm Sat Jan-Mar)

ℹ️ Getting There & Away

Merano is on the SS38, which runs north-west just south of Bolzano. **SAD** (📞 840 000471, 0471 45 01 11; www.sad.it) buses leave Merano **bus station** (Bahnhofsplatz) for villages in the Gruppo del Tessa, Silandro, and the valleys leading into the Parco Nazionale dello Stelvio and Ortles (Ortler) range.

By train, Bolzano (€6, almost hourly) is an easy 40-minute trip from Merano train station (Piazza Stazione), while the Venosta/Vinschgau line heads west to Malles, from where you can catch buses to Switzerland or Austria.

Parco Nazionale Dello Stelvio

It's not quite Yellowstone, but 1346-sq-km Parco Nazionale dello Stelvio (☑0473 83 04 30; www.parks.it/parco.nazionale.stelvio) is the Alps' largest national park, spilling into the next-door region of Lombardy and bordering Switzerland's Parco Nazionale Svizzero. The sprawling park is divided into three distinct regional sectors, each administered separately: the South Tyrol sector to the north (www.stelviopark.bz.it), Trentino to the south (www.parcostelviotrentino.it) and Lombardy to the west (http://lombardia.stelviopark.it).

The park is primarily the preserve of walkers who come for the extensive network of well-organised mountain huts and marked trails that, while often challenging, don't require the mountaineering skills necessary elsewhere in the Dolomites. Stelvio's central massif is guarded over by Monte Cevedale (Zufallspitze; 3769m) and Ortles (Ortler; 3905m), protecting glaciers, forests and numerous wildlife species, not to mention many mountain traditions and histories.

❶ Getting There & Away

The South Tyrol sector of the park is reached via the SS38 from Merano. From June to September, subject to late or early snowfall, you can travel to and from Bormio in Lombardy via the Passo di Stelvio (2757m), the second-highest pass in the Alps and one of Europe's most spectacular roads. The excellent Vinschgau rail service between Merano and Mals – 100% owned and operated by South Tyrol – makes much of this region easily accessible, as do numerous bike trails.

Val Venosta (Vinschgau)

The northwestern valley of Val Venosta (Vinschgau) is prettily pastoral, dotted with orchards, farms and small-scale, often creative, industries including marble quarries and workshops. It may feel remote, nestled as it is within the embrace of towering, snowy peaks along the Swiss and Austrian borders, but for much of its history it was a vibrant border zone, long on the road to somewhere. Come and enjoy its gentle way of life, the excellent bike trails – including an easy 80km route that traces the ancient Via Claudia Augusta between Merano and Malles – and easy access to some interesting local ski areas.

◎ Sights & Activities

Reschensee   LAKE
(Lago di Resia) Just south of Reschenpass (Passo di Resia) and the Austrian border is the deep blue Reschensee, a result of 1950s dam projects. The drowned Romanesque church tower here, just offshore from the village of Graun im Vinschgau (Curon Venosta), is an odd and deeply affecting sight, and the region's obligatory roadside photo op. The lake is also popular for sailing and kiteboarding in summer and ice-fishing and snowkiting in winter, and a gateway to the Skiparadies Reschenpass ski area.

Glorenza   VILLAGE
A walled medieval town, Glorenza (Glurns) was once a kingpin in the region's salt trade. Its pristine burgher houses, colonnaded shops, town gates, fortifications and ramparts were faithfully restored in the 1970s, and while it's certainly picturesque, it retains a comforting normalcy, with the road to Switzerland passing through its very centre.

★ Vinschger Radweg   CYCLING
(Pista Ciclabile della Val Venosta; www.suedtirol-it.com/valvenosta/ciclabile-val-venosta.html) This dreamy bike route follows the Adige River downstream for 86.3km from Resia (Reschen) near the Austrian border to Merano, tracing the ancient Roman Via Claudia Augusta that once connected Italy's Po Valley with modern-day Bavaria. For an exhilarating day ride, catch the weekly Taxi Iris (☑333 5657464; www.taxi-iris.com; per person incl bike €20; ☉ Wed May-Oct) bike shuttle from Merano to the border, then cycle downhill back to Merano.

🛏 Sleeping

Josephus   LODGE €€
(☑338 4241710; www.josephus.it; Unser Frau 42, Senales (Schnals); 2-/4-person apt €130/220; ℗🛜) Incorporating historical furniture from the original farmhouse along with beautiful contemporary design and the wool and wood of the region, these thoroughly South Tyrolean apartments in the gorgeous

Val Senales (Schnalstal) – a side valley branching north from Val Venosta – are incredibly evocative. Set high on a pretty green hillside, they offer magnificent views and come equipped with full cooking facilities.

❶ Getting There & Away

Val Venosta is on the SS40, which runs from Merano to the Austrian and Swiss borders. It's also serviced by the Vinschgerbahn (Ferrovia della Val Venosta) train line that runs west from Merano to Malles; from Malles, Swiss Post buses run to Zernez across the Swiss border (€12, 1½ hours) and SAD (www.sad.it) bus 273 runs to Nauders in Austria (€4.50, 35 minutes). From early April to late October, SüdtirolExpress (www.suedtirolexpress.ch) runs coaches (one-way/return CHF120/180) from various points in Val Venosta to Zurich and St Gallen, Switzerland.

Val di Solda (Suldental) & Val di Trafoi (Trafoital)

The neighbouring Val di Solda and Val di Trafoi are two of Parco Nazionale dello Stelvio's most dramatic valleys, branching off from one another in the hamlet of Gomagoi.

You can reach the village of **Solda** (Sulden; 1906m) by winding your way up the deep, dark valley of the same name. It is surrounded by 14 peaks over 3000m high, including the legendary **Ortles** (Ortler; 3905m). First climbed in 1804, this is South Tyrol's loftiest summit and was long revered as the highest peak in the Austro-Hungarian empire. This low-key ski resort becomes a busy base for walkers and climbers in summer.

Just to the west, the adjoining Val di Trafoi is the gateway to the imposing Passo dello Stelvio (2757m), the Alps' second-highest pass. From the village of **Trafoi** (1543m), one of Europe's most spectacular roads climbs to the summit via a series of 48 tight switchbacks covering 15km, with some very steep gradients.

◉ Sights

Messner Mountain Museum MUSEUM
(MMM Ortles; ☎0473 61 35 77; www.messner-mountain-museum.it; Forststrasse 55, Solda (Sulden); adult/reduced €8/6.50; ☺1-6pm Wed-Mon Jul & Aug, 2-6pm Wed-Mon Jun, Sep–mid-Oct & mid-Dec–Apr) Located – quite literally – inside a hill, the unique Messner Mountain Museum Ortles articulates the theme of 'ice' with artistically presented exhibits on glaciers, ice-climbing and pole expeditions, all at 1900m. Especially evocative is the museum's collection of out-

door gear, from climbing axes to sleds used on polar expeditions. Downstairs you'll find a minicinema showing snow- and ice-related films including one about Messner's voyage across Antarctica.

✖ Eating

Yak & Yeti ALPINE €€
(☎380 6574967; www.yakundyeti.it; Forststrasse 55, Solda (Sulden); meals €25-30; ☺noon-2pm & 6.30-9pm Wed-Mon) The Yak & Yeti is a 17th-century farmhouse that Messner has transformed into a restaurant, 'bio-homestead' and yak farm; the menu features typical food of the Solda valley – slow-cooked meats, dumplings, pasta – with a few yak-based specials, from yak carpaccio to Tibetan momos, thrown in for a Himalayan touch.

❶ Getting There & Away

Both valleys are accessed via the SS38 west of Merano. In Gomagoi, about 9km south of Spondigna (Spondinig), the SS622 branches southeast to Solda while the SS38 continues southwest through the village of Trafoi to Passo dello Stelvio.

SAD (www.sad.it) buses connect Merano with Solda (via Silandro and Spondigna, two hours, €11) and Trafoi (via Silandro, Spondigna and Gomagoi, three hours, €11.50).

THE DOLOMITES

The jagged peaks of the Dolomites span the provinces of Trentino and Alto Adige, jutting into neighbouring Veneto. Europeans flock here in winter for highly hospitable resorts, sublime natural settings and extensive, well-coordinated ski networks. Come for downhill or cross-country skiing and snowboarding or get ready for *sci alpinismo* (an adrenaline-spiking mix of skiing and mountaineering), freeride, and a range of other winter adventure sports including those on legendary circuit Sella Ronda. This is also a beautiful summer destination, offering excellent hiking, sublime views and lots of fresh, fragrant air.

❶ DOLOMITI SUPERSKI

Dolomiti Superski (www.dolomitisuperski.com; ☺1-/3-/7-day pass €55/155/290) gives you access to 450 lifts and some 1200km of ski runs, spread over 12 resorts in the Dolomites.

Val di Fiemme

In a region where few valleys speak the same dialect, let alone agree on the same cheese recipe, the Val di Fiemme's proud individualism is above and beyond. In the 12th century, independently minded local nobles even set up their own quasi-republic here, the Magnificent Community of Fiemme, and the ethos and spirit of the founders lives on.

Come here for relaxed skiing at Cermis, access to other Dolomiti Superski resorts, or for adventurous, high-altitude ski excursions and summertime ascents on the gnarly Pale di San Martino and other extraordinary peaks.

◉ Sights & Activities

**Palazzo Magnifica
Comunità di Fiemme** PALACE
(www.palazzomagnifica.eu; Piazza Battisti 2; adult/
reduced €5/2; ⊙10am-noon & 3-6.30pm Fri-Sun
Dec-Apr, Jul & Aug) The modern-day Magnificent Community of Fiemme is headquartered in the wonderfully frescoed Palazzo Vescovile in Val di Fiemme's main town of Cavalese. Visitors can tour a dozen of its rooms, including the grand 16th-century Audience Room, adorned with beamed ceilings, portraits of prince-bishops and other dignitaries, and friezes of cherubs and vines. Even when the building is closed, it's still worthy of an admiring look at its facade.

Cermis Ski Area SKIING
(www.alpecermis.it; Masi di Cavalese; ⊙ski lifts
8.15am-4.30pm) This ski resort just outside
Val di Fiemme's main town of Cavalese has
26 downhill runs for all skill levels.

🍽 Sleeping & Eating

⭐**Eco Park Hotel Azalea** SPA HOTEL €€
(☎0462 34 01 09; www.ecoparkhotelazalea.it; Via
delle Cesure 1, Cavalese; d incl half board €125-192;
P🗗) 🏵 This hotel combines impeccable
eco-credentials, super-stylish interiors and
a warm, welcoming vibe. Rooms are individually decorated and make use of soothing, relaxing colours; some have mountain views, others look across the village's pretty vegetable gardens.

⭐**El Molin** GASTRONOMY €€€
(☎0462 34 00 74; www.elmolin.info; Piazza Battisti 11, Cavalese; meals €55-60, degustation menus
€90-130; ⊙7.30-10pm Wed-Mon) A legend in the
valley, this Michelin-starred restaurant in an

SELLA RONDA
....

One of the Alps' most iconic ski routes, Sella Ronda (http://sellaronda.info) is a 40km circumnavigation of the Gruppo del Sella range (3151m, at Piz Boé). It is linked by various cable cars and chairlifts, and takes in four passes and their surrounding valleys: Alto Adige's **Val Gardena** and **Val Badia**, the Veneto's **Arabba**, and Trentino's **Val di Fassa**. Experienced skiers can complete the clockwise (orange) or anticlockwise (green) route in a day.

old mill sits at the historic heart of Cavalese. Downstairs, next to the waterwheels, you'll find playful gastronomic dishes featuring ultralocal, seasonal ingredients. Streetside, the wine bar does baked-to-order eggs with Trentingrana or truffles, burgers, hearty mains and creative desserts, while around the corner the sister restaurant Excelsior specialises in pizzas and salads.

❶ Information

Val di Fiemme Tourist Office (☎0462 24 11
11; www.visitfiemme.it; Via Bronzetti 60, Cavalese; ⊙9am-noon & 3.30-7pm Mon-Sat)

❶ Getting There & Away

The valley is on the SS48, off the A22. Public transport is limited, so you're better off with your own wheels.

Val di Fassa

Val di Fassa is Trentino's only Ladin-speaking valley, framed by the stirring peaks of the **Gruppo del Sella** to the north, the **Catinaccio** to the west and the **Marmolada** (3342m) to the southeast. The valley has two hubs: **Canazei** (population 1866, elevation 1465m), beautifully sited but verging on overdeveloped, and the pretty riverside village of **Moena** (population 2690, elevation 1114m), more down to earth and increasingly environmentally conscious.

Fassa is the nexus of Italy's cross-country skiing scene. Italian cross-country champ Cristian Zorzi hails from Moena and the town also plays host to the sport's most illustrious mass-participation race, the annual Marcialonga.

◉ Sights

Museo Ladin de Fascia   MUSEUM
(☑ 0462 76 01 82; www.istladin.net/en/muse um-ladin-de-fascia; Strada de Sèn Jan 5, Vigo di Fas-sa; adult/reduced €5/3; ⊙ 10am-12.30pm & 3-7pm mid-Jun–mid-Sep, closed May & Nov, 3-7pm Tue-Sat rest of year) One of the Ladin valleys' fasci-nating cultural museums, this three-storey structure in the village of Vigo di Fassa is packed with beautiful wood carvings and quotidian objects, along with informational displays about everything from music, farm-ing and family life to furniture-, bread- and cheese-making.

🛏 Sleeping

Garnì Ladin   B&B €
(☑ 0462 76 44 93; www.ladin.it; Strada de la Pi-azedela 9, Vigo di Fassa; s €59-65, d €90-100; P 🛜) Right in the middle of Vigo di Fassa village, midway between Moena and Canazei, the five individually themed and decorated rooms here sport a mix of sweetly kitsch Ladin-alia and ultramodern bathrooms.

Agritur Weiss   AGRITURISMO €€
(☑ 0462 76 91 15; www.agriturweiss.com; Strada de San Pozat 11, Località Tamion, Vigo di Fassa; d €100-140, incl half board €140-180; P 🛜) Fans of the authentic *agriturismo* (farm-stay accom-modation) experience need look no further than Monica and Luigi Weiss's family-run working dairy farm on a mountainside with 360-degree views, high above Vigo di Fassa. The eight spacious wood-clad rooms, decked out with rustic details such as handmade lace curtains and recycled barn-door coun-tertops, all enjoy wonderful views over the surrounding farmland and mountains.

🍴 Eating

Wurstelstand Pippotto   FAST FOOD €
(Piazza Marconi, Canazei; sausages €4; ⊙ 11am-6.30pm Sep-Jun, 10am-10pm Jul & Aug) The fork-wielding Ladin sausage cooks are a Canazei institution at this roadside stall just by the bus stop. It draws queues of ravenous skiers all winter long and keeps hikers hap-py into the night in summer.

El Paèl   ALPINE €€
(☑ 0462 60 14 33; www.elpael.com; Streda Roma 58, Canazei; meals €35-45, pizzas €6-13; ⊙ noon-2pm & 6.30-10pm) This *osteria tipica trenti-na* (traditional, casual Trentino tavern) was originally known for its traditional Ladin specialities, but now mixes things up with a contemporary Italian slickness. For samples of several house specialities – including ven-ison, sausage, polenta, mushrooms, *spätzle* and *canederli* – order the *piattone gastro-nomico*. There's also good pizza for those on a tighter budget.

Malga Panna   GASTRONOMY €€€
(☑ 0462 57 34 89; www.malgapanna.it; Strada de Sort 64, Moena; meals €50-60, tasting menus €70-80; ⊙ 12.30-2pm & 7.30-10pm Tue-Sun) Fine-dining interpretations of mountain food stay true to their culinary roots and are served in an evocatively simple setting high on a hill-side above Moena. Expect to encounter the flavours of Alpine herbs and flowers and lots of game.

ℹ Information

Canazei Tourist Office (☑ 0462 60 96 00; www.fassa.com; Piazza Marconi 5; ⊙ 8.30-12.30pm & 3-7pm daily Jul-Mar, reduced hours Apr-Jun)

ℹ Getting There & Away

The Val di Fassa is on the SS241, which runs off the A22.

SAD (☑ 840 000471, 0471 45 01 11; www.sad. it) buses serve Canazei from Bolzano (transfer at Selva di Val Gardena). **Trentino Trasporti** (☑ 0461 82 10 00; www.trentinotrasporti.it) runs buses to the Val di Fassa from Trento year-round. Free ski buses also serve the region in winter.

Val Gardena

Despite its proximity to Bolzano, Val Garde-na's historical isolation among the turrets of Gruppo del Sella and Sassolungo has ensured the survival of many pre-mass-tourism traditions. Ladin is a majority tongue and this linguistic heritage is care-fully maintained. The pretty and bustling villages are full of reminders of this distinct culture, too, with folksy vernacular architec-ture and a profusion of woodcarving shops.

In recent times the valley, part of Dolo-miti Superski (p342), has become an 'every-man' ski area, with the emphasis firmly on classic runs and fine powder. The valley's main trilingual towns, **Ortisei** (St Ulrich; population 6000, elevation 1236m), **Santa Cristina** (population 1900, elevation 1428m) and **Selva** (Wolkenstein; population 2580, elevation 1563m) all have good facilities.

Sights & Activities

Museum de Gherdëina   MUSEUM
(☑ 0471 79 75 54; www.museumgherdeina.it; Via
Rezia 83, Ortisei; adult/reduced €8/2.50; ⊙ 10am-
12.30pm & 2-6pm Mon-Fri mid-May–Jun & Sep–
mid-Oct, 10am-1pm & 2-6pm Mon-Sat Jul & Aug,
2-6pm Tue-Fri mid-Dec–Mar, closed rest of year)
Ortisei's folky Museum de Gherdëina has a
particularly exquisite collection of wooden
toys and sculptures, along with other artefacts and exhibits related to Ladin history
and culture.

Scuola di Alpinismo Catores   OUTDOORS
(☑ 0471 79 82 23; www.catores.com; Streda Rezia
5, Ortisei; ⊙ 8.30-11.30am & 4-6.30pm) All-round
Alpine adventure specialist offering courses, equipment rental and lots more – from
snowshoeing to ice climbing, and botanical
walks to glacier excursions.

Sleeping & Eating

Hotel Am Stetteneck   HOTEL €€
(☑ 0471 79 65 63; www.stetteneck.com; Via Rezia 14, Ortisei; d €106-214, half board €154-262,;
P☂@☀) This elegant hotel in the heart of
Ortisei dates from 1913 (during WWI Italian troops were bivouacked here). Come
for graceful service, and lovely village and
mountain views from big bay windows.
Weekly stays during ski season (January to
March) are good value. Seven-night minimum from Christmas to Easter.

★ **Chalet Gerard**   HOTEL €€€
(☑ 0471 79 52 74; www.chalet-gerard.com; Plan de
Gralba 37, Selva; d with half board €220-380; ☎)
This modern family-run chalet, launched
in the 1970s by award-winning skier Gerard
Mussner and now lovingly managed by
his two well-travelled daughters, enjoys
stunning panoramic views from its perch
10 minutes' drive above Selva on the road
to Passo Gardena. Supercute rooms are
complemented by spots for cosy lolling by
the (architect-designed) fire, a sauna and a
mountain-facing outdoor hot tub.

Costamula   ALPINE €€
(☑ 339 1467266; www.costamula.com; meals from
€40; ⊙ noon-3pm daily, 7pm-midnight Tue-Sat)
Slip off the Lalongia slopes into the warren of cosy wood-panelled rooms at this
painstakingly restored 17th-century *baita*
(mountain cabin), and settle in for some
of Val Gardena's finest Alpine fare, from
spectacular *crafuncins* (rye pasta pockets
stuffed with spinach and ricotta) to deli-

cious apple strudel. Prices are high-end for
a slope-side hut, but quality and views are
both exceptional.

Information

Ortisei Tourist Office (☑ 0471 77 76 00;
www.valgardena.it; Streda Rezia 1, Ortisei;
⊙ 8.30am-12.30pm & 2.30-6pm Mon-Sat,
9.30am-noon & 4.30-6pm Sun, reduced hours
Apr, May, Oct & Nov)

Getting There & Away

Year-round access is via the SS242 from the
A22. The Gardena Pass links Selva to Corvara in
Alta Badia and is open year-round but subject to
avalanche risk closures.

The Val Gardena is accessible from Bolzano
and Bressonone by **SAD** (☑ 840 000471, 0471
45 01 11; www.sad.it) buses year-round, and the
neighbouring valleys in summer.

Alpe di Siusi & Parco Naturale Sciliar-Catinaccio

There are few more jarring or beautiful juxtapositions than the undulating green pastures of the Alpe di Siusi – Europe's largest
plateau – ending dramatically at the base of
Sassolungo and the towering Sciliar massif.
To the southeast lies the jagged Catinaccio
range, its German name of Rosengarten an
apt description of the eerie pink hue given
off by the mountains' dolomite rock at sunset. Both areas fall within the Parco Naturale
Sciliar-Catinaccio. While great skiing and
hiking are a huge draw, the villages that dot
the valleys – including Castelrotto (Kastel-
ruth), Fiè allo Sciliar (Völs am Schlern) and
Siusi – signposted by their onion-domed
churches, are lovingly maintained, unexpectedly sophisticated and far from mere
resorts. Horses are a big part of local life and
culture and there's nothing more picturesque than a local chestnut Haflinger pony
galloping across endless pastureland.

Sights & Activities

Parco Naturale Sciliar-Catinaccio   PARK
(http://nature-parks.provinz.bz.it/schlern-rosen
garten-sciliar-catinaccio-nature-park.asp)   This
7291-hectare park takes in some of the Dolomites' most spectacular landscapes, including the Sciliar and Catinaccio massifs as well
as pine forests, pastureland and lakes.

TRENTINO & SOUTH TYROL ALPE DI SIUSI & PN SCILIAR-CATINACCIO

LUBOS CHLUBNY/SHUTTERSTOCK ©

LUC KOHNEN/SHUTTERSTOCK ©

1. Bolzano (p332)
Bolzano's Museo Archeologico dell'Alto Adige is home to Ötzi, the Iceman, a reproduction of whom is pictured here.

2. Brenta Dolomites (p329)
These sharp, majestic peaks are well known among mountaineers for their sheer cliffs and tricky ascents, and are home to some of the world's most famous *vie ferrate* (trails with permanent cables and ladders).

3. Alpe di Siusi (p345)
There are few more jarring or beautiful juxtapositions than the mountains and undulating green pastures of the Alpe di Siusi.

4. Rovereto (p328)
The Museo di Arte Moderna e Contemporanea Rovereto, designed by Ticinese architect Mario Botta, is both imposing and human in scale, with mountain light gently filling a central atrium from a soaring cupola.

Alpe di Siusi Cableway   CABLE CAR

(Seiser Alm; ✆ 0471 70 42 70; www.seiseralm bahn.it; Via Sciliar 39; one-way/return €11.50/18; ⊙ 8am-6pm mid-Dec–Mar & mid-May–Oct, to 7pm summer) This is a dizzying 15-minute, 4300m trip (800m ascent) from Siusi to Compaccio. The road linking the two is closed to normal traffic when the cableway is open.

Panorama Chairlift   CABLE CAR

(✆ 0471 72 78 16; www.panoramaseiseralm.info; Via Saltria 1, Compaccio; one-way/return €6/8.50; ⊙ 8.30am-5pm Dec-early Apr & late May–mid-Oct) This scenic chairlift runs from Compaccio at the lower end of Alpe di Siusi up to the Alpenhotel Panorama, which is a good base for walkers.

For one of the region's best hikes, take the chairlift from Compaccio to the Alpenhotel, followed by paths S, No 5 and No 1 to the Rifugio Bolzano, which rests at 2457m, just under Monte Pez (2564m), the Sciliar's summit.

Gstatschhof Ponyhof   HORSE RIDING

(✆ 0471 72 78 14; www.gstatschhof.com; Via Alpe di Siusi 39, Castelrotto) This farm stay offers horse-riding programs, including half-day snow rides (€70) from January to March, and accommodation in one- and two-bedroom apartments (€70 to €135).

🛏 Sleeping & Eating

Stiner Hof   APARTMENT €

(✆ 339 3555534; www.stinerhof.it; Via Peterbuehel 16, Fié allo Sciliar; 2-person apt €55-70, 4-person apt €75-95; 🛜) Just outside the pretty village of Fié allo Sciliar, this pair of well-equipped apartments on a working farm enjoys gorgeous views down into the Isarco gorge on one side and up to Sciliar on the other. South-facing windows let in lots of natural light, and breakfasts feature farm-fresh eggs, butter, cheese and speck, along with homemade marmalade, yoghurt and bread.

★ Hotel Heubad   SPA HOTEL €€

(✆ 0471 72 50 20; www.hotelheubad.com; Via Sciliar 13, Fiè allo Sciliar; d incl half board €166-276; P ✳ @ ⊠) As if the views, pretty garden and lounge areas here weren't relaxing enough, the spa is known for its typically Tyrolean hay baths, which have been on offer since 1903 and give the hotel its name. Delightful service is courtesy of the founder's great- and great-great-grandchildren, while rooms are modern, light and spacious.

Alpina Dolomites   HOTEL €€€

(✆ 0471 79 60 04; www.alpinadolomites.it; Compatsch; d incl half board €428-708; P ✳ 🛜 ⊠) A suitably high-style super-luxe lodge for one of the world's most beautiful high-altitude plateaus. A stunning contemporary building of wood, stone and glass houses calming, cosy rooms and suites, indoor and outdoor pools, a wellness centre, and restaurant, bar and lounging areas. Views are spectacular.

★ Gostner Schwaige   ALPINE €€

(✆ 347 8368154; www.gostnerschwaige.com; Via Saltria 13, footpath No 3 from Compaccio; meals €35-45; ⊙ 8.30am-6pm late May–mid-Oct & mid-Dec–mid-Apr, dinner by reservation only from 7pm) Chef Franz Mulser gives new meaning to the tag 'locally sourced' at his mountain refuge (elevation 1930m) on the beautiful Alpe di Siusi. The butter and cheese come from the barn next door, while salads are decorated with flowers from the adjacent garden and pastures. Other innovative specialities include hay soup, home-cured meats and refreshing herb-infused soft drinks bottled on-site.

ℹ Information

Castelrotto Tourist Office (✆ 0471 70 63 33; www.seiseralm.it; Piazza Kraus 1; ⊙ 8.30am-noon & 3-6pm Mon-Sat)

ℹ Getting There & Away

This region is accessed from the A22. **SAD** (✆ 840 000471, 0471 45 01 11; www.sad.it) runs buses to the Alpe di Siusi from Bolzano, the Val Gardena and Bressanone.

Note that if you're headed all the way up to Alpe di Siusi, the final climb between the villages of Siusi and Compaccio is off limits to motorists for much of the year; whenever the Alpe di Siusi Cableway is running, you'll need to park your car at the base station and take the cable car the rest of the way.

Val Badia & Alpe di Fanes

For centuries potent Ladin legends have resonated across this mystical landscape, which inspired the fantasies of JRR Tolkien. Not surprisingly, the Badia valley and the adjoining high plains of Fanes are often touted as one of the most evocative places in the Dolomites. Since 1980 they have been protected as part of the Parco Naturale di Fanes-Sennes-Braies. Colfosco (1645m), Pedraces (1324m), La Villa (1433m), San

Cassiano (St Kassian; 1537m) and Corvara (1568m) form the Alta Badia ski area. While undoubtedly upmarket, they remain relatively low key and retain something of their original, and highly individual, village character.

◉ Sights

★ Museo Ladin   MUSEUM
(☑ 0474 52 40 20; www.museumladin.it; Strada Tor 65, San Martin de Tor; adult/reduced €8/6.50; ⊙ 10am-5pm Tue-Sat, 2-6pm Sun May-Oct, 3-7pm Thu-Sat Jan-Mar, closed Apr, Nov & Dec) Atmospherically set in a castle 15km south of Brunico and full of folk treasures, this is the best of three museums in this region devoted to Ladin history and culture. The wide-ranging exhibits cover everything from Ladin language, geology and winter sports to rituals of everyday life, with reconstructed rooms from traditional homes and a treasure trove of touch-screen displays through which you can glean background information on a variety of topics.

☞ Tours

Alta Badia Guides   OUTDOORS
(☑ 0471 83 68 98; www.altabadiaguides.com; Strada Col Alt 94, Corvara; ⊙ office 5-7pm) This group runs freeride, ski circuits, and ice-climbing courses and tours, as well as snowshoe walks in winter. In summer it organises climbs, including *vie ferrate* (trails with permanent cables and ladders), trekking and excursions to the natural parks and WWI sites.

🛌 Sleeping

Camping Sass Dlacia   CAMPGROUND €
(☑ 0471 84 95 27; www.campingsassdlacia.it; Strada Sciarè 11, Sciarè; camping 2 people, car & tent €21-38) Backed by a spectacular mountain ridge at 1680m, this campground just southeast of San Cassiano proudly advertises itself as the Dolomites' highest. Evergreen-shaded sites are nicely complemented by a restaurant-pizzeria, a sauna and a small store.

★ Berghotel Ladinia   BOUTIQUE HOTEL €€
(☑ 0471 83 60 10; www.berghotelladinia.it; Pedecorvara 10, Corvara; s/d incl half board from €112/164; [P][❄][🌐]) The family owners of Hotel La Perla have taken over this traditional small hotel just up the hill from their luxurious place. Rooms are exquisitely simple and rustic, and the location is sublime. Four-course dinners at the hotel's own restaurant are included, or a food credit (€40

LUMEN MUSEUM

Anyone passionate about the mountains should make a beeline for the captivating LUMEN Museum of Mountain Photography (☑ 0474 43 10 90; www.lumenmuseum.it; Kronplatz summit; adult/reduced €17/12; ⊙ 10am-4pm), located at the summit of Kronplatz ski resort. The architecturally bold re-rendering of a former funicular station houses four floors of stunning mountain imagery from a rotating cast of international photographers. The setting alone is worth the trip, with swoon-inducing perspectives on the surrounding mountains.

per person per day) can be used at any of La Perla's restaurants instead.

Lagacio Mountain
Residence   APARTMENT €€€
(☑ 0471 84 95 03; www.lagacio.com; Strada Micurá de Rü 48, San Cassiano; 2-person apt €250-470, 4-person apt €470-990; [P][❄][🌐]) 🅿 A stylish residence-hotel with young, happy staff and a casual vibe. Suites are decorated with wood, wool and leather; all have heated floors, big baths and balconies. Attention to detail is keen: kitchens come with top-of-the-line equipment, Nespresso machines and filtered mountain water. There is a guest-only bar and lavish all-organic breakfast served in a traditional *Stube* (living room).

✕ Eating

Restaurant Ladinia   ALPINE €€
(☑ 0471 83 60 10; www.berghotelladinia.it; Pedecorvara 10, Corvara; meals €38-45; ⊙ noon-2pm & 7-9pm, closed Apr & Nov) The dining room of Berghotel Ladinia is appealingly cosy, or you can soak up the sun on the protected terrace on warmer days. Mountain-style food is done in a fresh but unpretentious way: dishes such as salmon with mashed purple carrots and artichokes or roe deer medallions with caramelised walnuts, radicchio and apple sauce will reinvigorate even the most stew-and-dumpling-dulled palate.

★ Prè de Costa   ALPINE €€€
(☑ 0471 84 94 43; www.predecosta.it; Strada Pre de Costa 20, Armentarola; meals €40-50; ⊙ noon-3pm Mon, noon-3pm & 7-9pm Wed-Sun) Housed in an old barn with a stunning mountain

backdrop, the Crazzolara family's farm-to-table gem is a long-standing local favourite. Chef Norbert creates spectacular heritage Ladin dishes, from hearty bowls of goulash, barley soup and *pasta e fagioli* (pasta and bean soup), to ravioli stuffed with beets or pumpkin and smoked ricotta, and mains featuring wild boar, roe deer and other local game.

La Siriola   GASTRONOMY €€€
(Hotel Ciasa Salares; ☑ 0471 84 94 45; www.ciasasalares.it; Pré de Ví 31, Armentarola; menus €138-198, incl wine pairings €191-275; ☉ 7.15-9.30pm Tue-Sun) Honoured in 2017 as the youngest Italian chef to earn two Michelin stars, Matteo Metullio runs this gastronomic spot nestled just outside San Cassiano, and offers a menu that ranges from crowd-pleasers to the more creative. The wine-by-the-glass selection is broader than most fine-dining places, and sweet tooths will appreciate the unlimited tastings of chocolate in the dedicated 'chocolate room'.

St Hubertus   GASTRONOMY €€€
(Hotel Rosa Alpina; ☑ 0471 84 95 00; www.rosalpina.it/italy-michelin-star-restaurants.htm; Strada Micurá de Rü 20, San Cassiano; degustation menus €200-280, wine pairing €110-150; ☉ 7-10pm Wed-Mon) Part of the luxurious Rosa Alpina Hotel & Spa, this quietly elegant foodie destination earned its third Michelin star in 2018. The mountain beef cooked in salt and hay is a menu stalwart, as is the crispy suckling pig. Many of Norbert Niederkofler's dishes take a whimsical turn, while desserts such as the exquisite tarte Tatin are pared back to essentials.

ℹ Information

Corvara Tourist Office (☑ 0471 83 61 76; www.altabadia.org; Strada Col Alt 36, Corvara; ☉ 9am-noon & 3-7pm Mon-Sat, 10-noon & 4-6pm Sun Dec-Mar, Jul & Aug, reduced hours Apr-Jun & Sep-Nov)

ℹ Getting There & Away

This region can be reached from Bolzano via the A22, then the SS242 and, subject to high-altitude pass closures, from Cortina d'Ampezzo via the SS48 and SS24.

SAD (☑ 840 000471, 0471 45 01 11; www.sad.it) buses link the Alta Badia villages with Bolzano (2½ hours) and Brunico (1¼ hours) roughly hourly. Summer services link Corvara with the Val Gardena, Passo di Sella and Passo di Pordoi, Canazei and the Passo Falzarego.

Val Pusteria (Pustertal)

Running from the junction of the Valle Isarco at Bressanone (Brixen) to San Candido (Innichen) in the far east, the narrow, verdant Val Pusteria is profoundly Tyrolean and almost entirely German speaking. It's a gentle, traditional alternative to the more glamorous Dolomites resorts during the ski season, and offers plenty to do in summer, too.

Dobbiaco (Toblach), where Gustav Mahler once holed up and wrote his troubled but ultimately life-affirming *Ninth Symphony,* is the gateway to the ethereal **Parco Naturale delle Dolomiti di Sesto**, home of the much-photographed **Tre Cime di Lavaredo** ('Three Peaks' or, in German, Drei Zinnen). Down yet another deeply forested valley twist are the jewel-like **Lago di Braies** (Pragser Wildsee) and its serious Alta Via No 1 walking route.

Bumping the Austrian and Veneto borders in the far northeast is a vast, wild territory, the **Sesto Dolomiti**, which is criss-crossed with spectacular walking and cross-country ski trails.

ℹ Getting There & Away

Half-hourly trains run the length of the valley from Fortezza in the west to San Candido in the east, passing through the main towns of Brunico and Dobbiaco, and continuing east to Lienz (Austria). At Fortezza there are frequent, well-timed connections to mainline trains running south to Bolzano and Trento and north to Innsbruck.

SAD (☑ 840 000471, 0471 45 01 11; www.sad.it) buses connect Brunico and Cortina to San Candido. Buses also connect Brunico with Bolzano, via Bressanone.

Brunico (Bruneck)

☑ 0474 / POP 16,400 / ELEV 835M

As Val Pusteria's big smoke, Brunico is often relegated to a quick stop on the way to the slopes. Its quintessentially Tyrolean historic centre offers a delightful detour, however, and its great local eating and drinking scene, not to mention easy access to good skiing and hiking, makes longer stays a very attractive option.

◉ Sights

Messner Mountain Museum Ripa   MUSEUM
(☑ 0474 41 02 20; www.messner-mountain-museum.it; Schlossweg 2; adult/reduced €11/9; ☉ 10am-

VAL DI FUNES

If there's a single image that sums up the Dolomites' compelling mix of raw natural beauty and loving human stewardship, it would be the Chiesetta di San Giovanni in Ranui (p352), just east of the village of Santa Maddalena di Funes (21km southeast of Bressanone). Sitting alone in a meadow below the gargantuan spiky peaks of the Odle group, this teensy onion-steepled baroque church (built in 1744) is one of South Tyrol's most iconic photo-ops.

The surrounding **Val di Funes** is a land of small villages and working farmsteads that cling photogenically to emerald green slopes against a stunning mountain backdrop. The valley's two main settlements are **Santa Maddalena (St Magdalena)** and the slightly larger **San Pietro (St Peter)** 3km to the west; both offer accommodation and food. For a picturesque setting, it's hard to beat **Hotel Ranuimüllerhof** (☑ 0472 84 01 82; www.ranuimuellerhof.com; St Johann 1, Santa Maddalena di Funes; ☺ d incl half board €158-202; 🛜), a stone's throw from the church at the eastern edge of Santa Maddalena. Back down in San Pietro, Viel Nois (p353) is a great spot for lunch or dinner, serving up a tempting mix of Italian and South Tyrolean treats, from pizza and gelato to dumplings and *Wienerschnitzel*.

For bird's-eye perspectives on the valley, snake your way uphill from San Pietro to the **Passo delle Erbe (Würzjoch)**. The road up to the 2006m pass is intensely narrow (allow half an hour for the 17km drive) but amazingly scenic, and you'll find one of the Dolomites' best loop hikes at the top. Park your car at the pass and take the signposted **Rode de Pütia** trail (trails 8A and 8B) towards **Sass de Pütia (Peitlerkofel)**, the hulking 2875m mountain to your south. The 13km loop hike takes about four hours to complete, and there are several mountain huts along the way where you can refuel with food and drink.

6pm Wed-Mon mid-May–Oct, noon-6pm Wed-Mon late Dec-late Apr) Brunico's 13th-century hilltop castle is the evocative setting for mountaineer Reinhold Messner's fifth 'Mountain Museum'. Opened in 2011, it documents the cultures of mountain peoples on four continents (Asia, Africa, South America and Europe). Displays range from photographs, textiles and furniture to a traditional tent used by yak-herding Tibetan nomads and a reconstructed Tyrolean farm kitchen.

Kriegerfriedhof CEMETERY
(Cimitero di Guerra; Reischacher Strasse) This pristinely maintained cemetery set in a forest on Kühbergl just behind the town has graves of soldiers from the nearby WWI front as well as a section of WWII dead. Most of the WWI soldiers buried here are from the Slavic regions of the old Austro-Hungarian empire, and there are Christian, Muslim and Jewish graves. It's a peaceful and solemn place.

🛏 Sleeping

⭐**Niedermairhof** B&B €€
(☑ 348 2476761; www.nmhof.it; Herzog-Diet-Strasse 1; ste €176-244; 🅿 ❄ 🛜) Niedermairhof is a delightful meeting of family B&B and stylish boutique hotel, set in a rambling old 13th-century farmhouse on Kathrin Mair and Helmuth Mayr's working vegetable farm. There are eight spacious, beautifully designed rooms here, all different and all utterly charming. They variously feature balconies, big baths or mountain views and there's an airy guest loft for relaxing or kids' play.

Berggasthof Haüsler B&B €€
(☑ 0474 40 32 28; www.berggasthof-haeusler.com; Elle 12, San Lorenzo di Sebato; s €69-104, d €118-148, all incl half board) Carsickness-prone passengers may not appreciate the long, tortuous ride up the mountainside to this family-run guesthouse, 13km southwest of Brunico – but the views up top are truly staggering. Meanwhile, the warm welcome from the Oberhammer family, the tastebud-pleasing half board and the delightful high-country trails on your doorstep will surely tempt you to linger.

🍽 Eating

Acherer Patisserie & Blumen PASTRIES €
(☑ 0474 41 00 30; www.acherer.com; Stadtgasse 8; items from €2; ☺ 9am-12.30pm & 2.30-7pm Mon-Fri, 8am-1pm & 2-6pm Sat) Right by the

town gate, Acherer Patisserie & Blumen sells strudel and Sachertorte that may just be the region's best; the young owner reopened his grandfather's former bakery after apprenticing in Vienna. His inventive, rather fancy cakes, chocolates and seasonal preserves now grace many of the region's five-starred pillows and breakfast buffets. Gluten-free options are also available.

Pur Südtirol CAFE €
(☑ 0474 05 05 00; www.pursuedtirol.com; Herzog-Sigmund-Strasse 4a; snacks & light meals €5-13; ⊙ 7.30am-7.15pm Mon-Fri, to 5pm Sat) Sit-down lunches are a great option at the bustling Brunico branch of Merano's famous gourmet shop – especially if you're needing a break from goulash or schnitzel. There are plenty of sandwiches and burgers, but follow the locals' lead and order one of the smoked fish or vegetarian salads, washed down with a glass of small-producer white wine or local apple juice.

Rienzbräu Bruneck ALPINE €€
(☑ 0474 53 13 07; www.rienzbraeu.bz.it; Stegenerstrasse 8; meals €33-45; ⊙ restaurant 11.30am-2.30pm & 6-11pm, bar 10am-midnight) It would be sad to stop at this backstreet brewery for just a beer. Join big tables of locals by the vats for a sample of no-frills dishes ranging from bar snacks such as smoked beef and cheese plates, to barley minestrone, simple pastas, schnitzels and steaks. There's also rather good pizza.

🍴 Drinking & Nightlife

Brunegg'n BAR
(www.facebook.com/bruneggn; Kapuzinerplatz 1; ⊙ 2pm-1am Wed & Thu, to 3am Fri & Sat, 3-11pm Sun) Fire pits and art-school-style video projections give this bar a big-town feel but it's beloved by locals and the staff is fabulously welcoming. The *aperitivo* (predinner drinks) scene is also the town's best and it kicks on nicely, plus there's a weekly *aperitivo lungo* – a big buffet – on Thursday evenings. Weekends are all about cocktails; Saturday nights bring DJs or live acts.

ℹ️ Information

Brunico Tourist Office (☑ 0474 55 57 22; www.bruneck.com; Rathausplatz 7; ⊙ 9am-12.30pm & 3-6pm Mon-Fri, 9.30am-12.30pm Sat)

ℹ️ Getting There & Away

Brunico is on the E66, which leaves the A22 a little north of Bolzano. The SS49 continues to the Austrian border and then to Lienz.

SAD (☑ 840 000471, 0471 45 01 11; www.sad.it) buses connect Brunico (45 minutes, hourly) and Cortina (one hour, four daily) to San Candido. Buses run directly between Brunico and Bressanone (€5.50, one hour, half-hourly).

Brunico is easily accessible by train from both Bolzano (€7, 1½ hours, hourly via Fortezza) and from Lienz (Austria). All regional trains are covered by the **HolidayPass** that most hotels offer to guests or can be purchased from tourist offices.

Bressanone (Brixen)

☑ 0472 / POP 21,700 / ELEV 560M

Alto Adige's oldest city, dating to 901, might be the picture of small-town calm, but it has a grand ecclesiastical past and a lively, cultured side. Stunning baroque architecture is set against a beguiling Alpine backdrop; a stately piazza leads into a tight medieval core; and pretty paths trace the fast-moving Isarco river. Come for excellent hiking in summer, or the spectacular views and beautiful 11km ski run at town mountain Plose in winter or, by all means, just stay, eat, drink and shop any time.

👁️ Sights

Chiesetta di San Giovanni in Ranui CHURCH
(Santa Maddalena di Funes) Sitting alone in a meadow below the gargantuan spiky peaks of the Odle mountain group, this tiny and almost impossibly picturesque onion-steepled church (built in 1744) is one of the Dolomites' most iconic photo-ops. Look for it about 1km east (and uphill) from the village of Santa Maddalena di Funes.

Dom CATHEDRAL
(Duomo; Domplatz; ⊙ 6am-6pm Apr-Oct & Dec, 6am-noon & 3-6pm Nov & Jan-Mar) The lofty two-spired baroque cathedral you see today was built on top of the AD 980 Gothic-Romanesque original in 1745. While the bishop decamped to Bolzano some years back, this remains South Tyrol's most important church. Interiors feature Michelangelo Unterberger's altar work depicting the death of Mary, and ceilings by Paul Troger.

🛏 Sleeping

★ **Hotel Elephant** HISTORIC HOTEL €€
(📞 0472 83 27 50; www.hotelelephant.com; Weiss-lahnstrasse 4; s €112-141, d €192-284; 🅿 ❈ 🛜 🏊) This 15th-century inn marks the entrance to old Bressanone and, as the name suggests, once gave shelter to an Indian elephant, a gift on its way to Archduke Maximilian of Austria. The quince-toned exterior hints at what's inside: extremely comfortable rooms and serenely professional service, exquisite historic *stufas* (tiled stoves) in the dining room and museum-worthy paintings lining the stairs.

Hotel Pupp DESIGN HOTEL €€€
(📞 0472 26 83 55; www.small-luxury.it; Alten-marktgasse 36; d €170-260; 🅿 ❈ 🛜) Things take a totally contemporary turn at this small and fun hotel, even if its hospitality lineage reaches way back (the owners have branched out from the venerable bakery opposite). Fabulously designed rooms are suite-sized and come with Nespresso machines and wine-stocked fridges; several have terraces, including three with private hot tubs. Adults only.

🍴 Eating

Viel Nois ALPINE €€
(📞 0472 84 05 26; www.vielnois.com; Peterweg 8, San Pietro di Funes; pizza €6.50-11, meals €30-38; ⏱ 11.30am-2pm & 5.30-11pm Tue-Sun) Warm and welcoming, this bustling restaurant in the heart of San Pietro di Funes does everything from homemade pastries and gelato to pizza and *Wienerschnitzel* (breaded pork cutlets) with lingonberries. Alpine comfort-food junkies need look no further than the Tiroler Tris: *Schlutzkrapfen* (spinach-ricotta ravioli) accompanied by a pair of hearty Austrian-style dumplings.

Finsterwirt ALPINE €€€
(Oste Scuro; 📞 0472 83 53 43; www.finsterwirt.com; Domgasse 3; meals €45-55; ⏱ 11.30am-2.15pm & 6.30-9.15pm Tue-Sat, 11.30am-2.15pm Sun) This place would be worth a visit for the decor alone; it's a wonderful series of dark-wooded rooms strewn with moody mountain paintings and Alpine curios. The food here is excellent, if seriously rich – cheese and truffle millefeuille, polenta dumplings with venison *ragù*, rhododendron honey-glazed duck in citrus sauce, and a homemade apple strudel with Bourbon vanilla gelato.

DON'T MISS

DURNWALD

Hidden away in the pastoral Val di Casies (Gsiesertal), **Durnwald** (📞 0474 74 68 86; http://restaurantdurnwald.it; Nikolaus-Amhof-Strasse 6, Pichl, Gsies; meals €30-42; ⏱ noon-2pm & 7-9pm Tue-Sun) is a gem of a family-run restaurant, specialising in ultra-fresh, locally sourced seasonal South Tyrolean cuisine. Plates of venison goulash with polenta, pork medallions with chanterelles and porcini, spinach dumplings, house-cured meats and smoked trout mousse are all served with a smile and best finished off with scrumptious desserts such as homemade apple fritters.

🍷 Drinking & Nightlife

Pupp Konditorei Cafe CAFE
(www.pupp.it; Altenmarktgasse 37; items from €2; ⏱ 7am-7pm Tue-Sat) This Bressanone favourite has been in the Pupp family for almost a hundred years. The cosy velvet booths of this oh-so-'80s cafe are perpetually filled with locals scoffing great coffee and cake. The poppy seed or walnut *potize* (stuffed brioche) is known throughout the valley.

Vinus WINE BAR
(Peter's Weinbistro; 📞 0472 83 15 83; www.vinothekvinus.it; Altenmarktgasse 6; ⏱ 10am-1pm & 4-9pm Mon, Tue & Thu, to midnight Wed & Fri, 10am-6pm Sat) A classy dark, low-ceilinged space with an extensive wine-by-the-glass list. Peter offers a nightly *tavola calda* (a limited hot menu; mains €22) on Wednesdays and Fridays and at Saturday lunch, and sometimes keeps pouring local drops until midnight.

ℹ Information

Tourist Office (📞 0472 27 52 52; www.brixen.org; Regensburger Allee 9; ⏱ 8.30am-12.30pm & 2-6pm Mon-Fri, 9am-1pm Sat)

ℹ Getting There & Away

Bressanone is on the A22/SS12 halfway between Bolzano and the Brenner Pass border with Austria. It's also on the main Bolzano–Innsbruck train line, with frequent services to Bolzano (30 minutes, €9.40). For travel to Val Pusteria destinations such as Brunico, change trains just north of town at Fortezza (Franzensfeste).

AT A GLANCE

POPULATION
4.88 million

BIRTH RATE
1.36

BEST VIEW
Row Venice (p387)

**BEST LOCAL
MARKET**
Padua Market (p401)

BEST SKIING
Cinque Torri (p427)

WHEN TO GO
Dec–Feb Snow-
covered gondolas,
skiers in the
Dolomites and
Carnevale parties.

Apr–Jun Warming
weather, canalside
dining and Biennale
openings.

Sep–Nov Venice
International Film
Festival, wild duck
pasta and palatial
accommodation for
less.

Murano p384
YASONYA/SHUTTERSTOCK ©

Venice & the Veneto

Venice really needs no introduction. This incomparable union of art, architecture and lagoon-based living has been a fabled destination for centuries. No matter how many photographs, films or paintings you've seen, the reality is more surprising than you could ever imagine.

Most visitors to the Veneto devote all their time to Venice, which is understandable – until you discover the rich variety of experiences that await nearby. Firstly, there are the city-states Venice annexed in the 15th century: Padua, with its pre-Renaissance frescoes; Vicenza, with Palladio's peerless architecture; and Verona, with its sophisticated bustle atop Roman foundations. Then there are the wines, in particular Soave, prosecco and Valpolicella's bold Amarone.

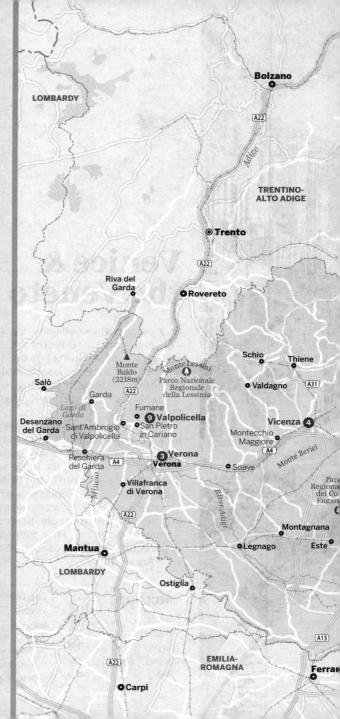

Venice & the Veneto Highlights

1 Venice (p360)
Realising what all the fuss is about in this extraordinary city of canals, churches and palaces.

2 Padua (p401)
Gazing in awe at the Cappella degli Scrovegni, Padua's answer to the Sistine Chapel.

3 Verona (p408)
Enjoying the world's finest open-air opera festival in a Roman amphitheatre.

4 Vicenza (p415)
Admiring the perfect proportions of Palladio's home town.

5 Cinque Torri (p427) Hiking the ruins of WWII trenches beneath these rocky peaks.

6 Treviso (p398)
Discovering the Veneto's underappreciated modern art in the Museo Luigi Bailo.

7 Asolo (p422)
Lingering over unusual regional dishes and hilltop views at Due Mori.

8 La Strada del Prosecco (p422)
Taking a wine-fuelled tour of the prosecco vineyards.

9 Valpolicella (p413) Sampling modern takes on classic wines.

10 Sacrario Militare del Monte Grappa (p419) Paying tribute to past heroism at Monte Grappa's epic mausoleum.

NEIGHBOURHOODS AT A GLANCE

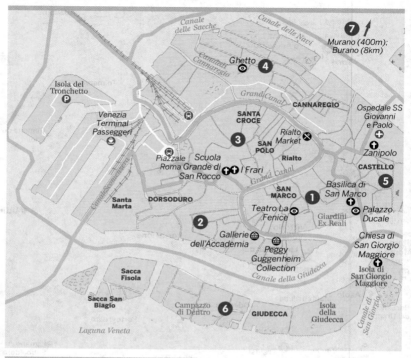

VENICE & THE VENETO VENICE

❶ San Marco (p361)

San Marco is packed with so many world-class attractions that some visitors never leave – and others are loath to visit, fearing the crowds. But why deny yourself the pleasures of two of the most famous buildings in the world, Basilica di San Marco and Palazzo Ducale, not to mention the wonderful Museo Correr and Venice's famous jewel-box opera house La Fenice? Judge for yourself whether they earn their reputations – and don't stop there: San Marco's backstreets are packed with galleries, boutiques and *bacari* (wine bars).

❷ Dorsoduro (p372)

Dorsoduro covers prime Grand Canal waterfront with Ca' Rezzonico's golden-age splendour, the Peggy Guggenheim Collection's modern edge, Gallerie dell'Accademia's Renaissance beauties and Punta della Dogana's ambitious installation art. The neighbourhood lazes days away on the sun-drenched Zattere, and convenes in Campo Santa Margherita for *spritz* and flirtation. While the eastern tip is heavily tourist focused, it develops a more local feel the further west you go.

❸ San Polo & Santa Croce (p374)

Heavenly devotion and earthly delights co-exist in San Polo and Santa Croce, where divine art rubs up against the ancient red-light district, now home to artisan workshops and *osterie* (taverns). Don't miss fraternal-twin masterpieces: Titian's glowing *Madonna* at I Frari and turbulent Tintorettos at Scuola Grande di San Rocco. Quirky museums fill Grand Canal *palazzi* (mansions) with fashion and natural history oddities, while island-grown produce crams the stalls of the Rialto Market.

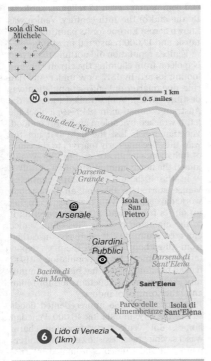

(1km)

➎ Castello (p379)

The crenellated walls of the Arsenale still dominate Venice's largest *sestiere* (district), but where it was once the secret preserve of highly skilled artisans serving Venice's naval war machine, it is now thrown open annually to alternating throngs of art and architecture lovers during the annual Biennale. The Riva degli Schiavoni is Venice's prime waterfront promenade, but step back into the maze of lanes and you'll still find washing lines strung between buildings and little neighbourhood cafes on sunny squares.

➏ Giudecca, Lido & the Southern Islands (p381)

The most evocative of Venice's southern islands are tiny specks capped with monasteries such as San Servolo, San Lazzaro degli Armeni and (especially) San Giorgio Maggiore, its gracious Palladio church forming the essential backdrop for dreamy lagoon views. The much larger crescent of Giudecca has its own Palladian masterpieces and is a fascinating mash-up of luxury hotels, workaday apartments, the remnants of industry and a still-functioning women's prison. Lido is Venice's 12km beach escape, its A-list film festival a hangover from its days as one of Europe's most glamorous resorts.

➍ Cannaregio (p376)

Anyone could adore Venice on looks alone, but in Cannaregio you'll fall for its personality. A few streets over from bustling Strada Nova, footsteps echo along moody Fondamenta de la Misericordia, and there's not a T-shirt kiosk in sight. Between the art-filled Chiesa della Madonna dell'Orto, the Renaissance miracle of Chiesa di Santa Maria dei Miracoli and the tiny island Ghetto, a living monument to the outsized contributions of Venice's Jewish community, are some of Venice's top casual eateries and *cicheti* (Venetian tapas) bars.

➐ Murano, Burano & the Northern Islands (p384)

Venetian life had its origins in the northern reaches of the lagoon, and when things get too frantic in the city proper, these ancient island settlements remain the best escape. Serious shoppers head to Murano for one-of-a-kind glass art. Others prefer to head to the islands of Burano and Mazzorbo for extended seafood feasts, or to Torcello for glimpses of heaven in the golden mosaics.

VENICE

POP 53,835

Imagine the audacity of deciding to build a city of marble palaces on a lagoon. Instead of surrendering to the *acque alte* (high tides) like reasonable folk might do, Venetians flooded the world with vivid paintings, baroque music, spice-route cuisine and a canal's worth of *spritz*, the city's signature prosecco-based cocktail.

Never was a thoroughfare so aptly named as the Grand Canal, reflecting the architectural glories lining its banks. The city that made walking on water seem easy remains as unique and remarkable as it ever was. Today, cutting-edge architects and billionaire benefactors are spicing up the art scene, and culinary traditions are being kept alive and continually tweaked in restaurants scattered along quiet canals and far-flung islands.

History

When barbarian hordes sacked the Roman towns along the Veneto's Adriatic coast in the 5th and 6th centuries, refugees fled to safety on the murky wetlands of the lagoon. They settled first on the island of Torcello before spreading out to the surrounding islands and finally the Rivoalto (meaning 'high bank', shortened to Rialto).

In 726 the people of Venice elected Orso Ipato as their doge (duke), the first of 118 elected Venetian dogi that would lead the city for more than 1000 years.

Next Venice shored up its business interests, positioning itself as a neutral party between the western Holy Roman Empire and the eastern Byzantine Empire. Even at the outset of the Crusades, Venice maintained strategic neutrality, continuing to trade with Muslim leaders from Syria to Spain while its port served as the launching pad for crusaders bent on wresting the Holy Land from Muslim control. Always with an eye for a business opportunity, in 1203 Venice persuaded the Fourth Crusade to stop off and sack Christian Constantinople on the way, claiming a hefty share of the spoils and control over the Dalmatian coast. This backfired for Venice when a much-weakened Constantinople fell to the Ottoman Turks in 1453, followed by the Venetian territory of Morea (in Greece) in 1499. At the same time as they lost control over the Mediterranean trade routes, the Age of Exploration opened up routes across the Atlantic that Venice had no access to.

Once it could no longer rule the seas, Venice changed tack and began conquering Europe by charm. Venetian art was incredibly daring, bringing sensuous colour and sly social commentary even to religious subjects. By the end of the 16th century, Venice was known across Europe for its painting, catchy music and 12,000 registered prostitutes.

Venice's reputation did nothing to prevent Napoleon from claiming the city in 1797 and looting its art. By 1817, now under Austrian rule, one-quarter of Venice's population was destitute. When Venice rallied to resist the Austrian occupation in 1848–49, a blockade left it wracked by cholera and short on food. Venetian rebels lost the fight but not the war: they became early martyrs to the cause of Italian independence, and in 1866 Venice joined the newly minted Kingdom of Italy.

In the 19th and early 20th centuries, Venice started to take on an industrious workaday aspect, with factories springing up on its fringes and a road connecting it to the mainland built by Mussolini. Venice emerged from WWII relatively unscathed from Allied bombing – but the mass deportation of Venice's Jewish population in 1943 had all but annihilated that historic community. Postwar, many Venetians left for Milan and other centres of industry.

In November 1966 unprecedented floods struck the city, inundating 16,000 Venetian homes. But Venice's cosmopolitan charm was a saving grace: assistance from admirers poured in and Unesco coordinated international charities to redress the ravages of the flood. It was decided to commission a system of barriers at the three mouths of the lagoon, which could be raised to prevent flooding during high tides. Initial costs were estimated at €1.5 billion with a completion date set for 1995. After a high-profile corruption scandal that claimed the scalp of the mayor, MoSE is not expected to be fully completed until 2022 and the price tag has risen to €5.5 billion.

Just as public opinion questions the efficacy of MoSE as a solution to rising sea levels and a sinking city, Venice faces another rising tide – the boom in tourism – which threatens to overwhelm the city. Grassroots activists are demanding immediate measures to tackle the lack of affordable housing, a complete ban on cruise ships entering the lagoon and the creation of a sustainable, long-term tourism strategy.

⊙ Sights

As Venetian author Tiziano Scarpa observed, the Rialto islands really do look like a fish, made up of the six *sestieri* (neighbourhoods):

San Marco, San Polo, Santa Croce, Dorsoduro, Cannaregio and Castello, with the island of Giudecca underscoring it like a wavy tilde. So many world-class attractions are concentrated here that some visitors never leave. But Venice's origins lie northeast on the glass-manufacturing island of Murano, the fisherfolk island of Burano and historic Torcello. East are the city's parks, farms and gardens on the islands of La Certosa, Le Vignole and Sant'Erasmo; south, a smattering of small islands between the city and the sea once used for quarantine and asylum centres. The barrier islands of Lido and Pellestrina enclose the lagoon and are the site of Venice's few beaches on their seaward-facing side.

◉ San Marco

★ Campanile　　　　　　　　　　TOWER
(Map p374; www.basilicasanmarco.it; Piazza San Marco; adult/reduced €8/4; ⊗8.30am-9pm mid-Apr-Sep, 9.30am-5.30pm Oct-Mar, shorter hours rest of year; ⛴San Marco) Basilica di San Marco's 99m-tall bell tower has been rebuilt twice since its initial construction in AD 888. Galileo Galilei tested his telescope here in 1609 but modern-day visitors head to the top for 360-degree lagoon views and close encounters with the **Marangona**, the booming bronze bell that originally signalled the start and end of the working day for the *marangoni* (artisans) at the Arsenale shipyards. Today it rings twice a day, at noon and midnight.

★ Museo Correr　　　　　　　　MUSEUM
(Map p374; ☑041 240 52 11; www.correr.visitmuve.it; Piazza San Marco 52; adult/reduced incl Palazzo Ducale €20/13, with Museum Pass free; ⊗10am-7pm Apr-Oct, to 5pm Nov-Mar; ⛴San Marco) Napoleon pulled down an ancient church to build his royal digs over Piazza San Marco, and then filled them with the riches of the doges while taking some of Venice's finest heirlooms to France as trophies. When he lost Venice to the Austrians, Empress Sissi remodelled the palace, adding ceiling frescoes, silk cladding and brocade curtains. It's now open to the public and full of many of Venice's reclaimed treasures, including ancient maps, statues, cameos and four centuries of artistic masterpieces.

★ La Fenice　　　　　　　　　　THEATRE
(Map p374; ☑041 78 66 75; www.teatrolafenice.it; Campo San Fantin 1977; ⊗9.30am-6pm; ⛴Giglio) Once its dominion over the high seas ended, Venice discovered the power of the high Cs, opening La Fenice in 1792. Rossini, Donizetti and Bellini staged operas here; Verdi premiered *Rigoletto* and *La Traviata;* and international greats Stravinsky, Prokofiev and Britten composed for the house, making La Fenice the envy of Europe. From January to July and September to October, opera season is in full swing. If you can't attend a **performance** (☑041 78 66 54; tickets €15-380), it's possible to explore the theatre with an audio guide (adult/reduced €11/7).

Chiesa di Santo Stefano　　　　CHURCH
(Map p374; ☑041 522 50 61; www.chorusvenezia.org; Campo Santo Stefano; museum €3, with Chorus Pass free; ⊗10.30am-4.30pm Mon-Sat, to 7pm Sun; ⛴Sant'Angelo) **FREE** The free-standing bell tower, visible from the square behind, leans disconcertingly, but this brick Gothic church has stood tall since the 13th century. Credit for shipshape splendour goes to Bartolomeo Bon for the marble entry portal and to Venetian shipbuilders, who constructed the vast wooden *carena di nave* (ship's keel) ceiling that resembles an upturned Noah's ark.

ⓘ BYLAWS & TOURIST TAXES

Tourism numbers have seen the attitudes of long-suffering Venetian locals harden towards behaviours they find disrespectful or inconvenient, which in turn has led to the city banning various activities. Some are obvious, such as littering, graffiti and posting bills, but it's also forbidden to sit and picnic in any of the squares or on the streets. Swimming in the canals is strictly forbidden, as is riding bikes, or walking around shirtless or in swimwear in the centre of town. Photo snappers can no longer clog city bridges, and stag and hen parties need to restrict their outdoor carousing to daytime and on the weekends. Store-bought alcohol can't be consumed on the streets between 8pm and 8am.

The authorities aren't joking about enforcement either. In 2019, two German backpackers found this out the hard way when they were fined €950 and expelled from the city after lighting up a portable stove and making coffee just metres from the busy Rialto Bridge. A tourist tax has also come into force, targeting day-trippers (overnight stays already have a tax attached). Rates vary throughout the year but rise to €10 at the absolute peak times.

TOP SIGHT
BASILICA DI SAN MARCO

In a city packed with architectural wonders, nothing beats Basilica di San Marco for sheer spectacle and bombastic exuberance. In AD 828, wily Venetian merchants allegedly smuggled St Mark's corpse out of Egypt in a barrel of pork fat to avoid inspection by Muslim authorities. Venice built a basilica around its stolen saint in keeping with the city's own sense of supreme self-importance.

Construction

Church authorities in Rome took a dim view of Venice's tendency to glorify itself and God in the same breath, but the city defiantly created a private chapel for their doge that outshone Venice's official cathedral (the Basilica di San Pietro in Castello) in every conceivable way. After the original St Mark's was burned down during an uprising, Venice rebuilt the basilica twice (mislaying and rediscovering the saint's body along the way). The current incarnation was completed in 1094, reflecting the city's cosmopolitan image, with Byzantine domes, a Greek cross layout and walls clad in marbles looted from Syria, Egypt and Palestine. Unbelievably, Basilica di San Marco only replaced San Pietro as Venice's cathedral in 1807, after the fall of the Republic.

Facade

The front of the basilica ripples and crests like a wave, its five niched portals capped with shimmering mosaics and frothy stonework arches. It's especially resplendent just before sunset, when the sun's dying rays set the golden mosaics ablaze. Grand entrances are made through the central portal, under an ornate triple arch featuring Egyptian purple porphyry columns and intricate 13th- to 14th-century stone re-

DON'T MISS

➡ Pala d'Oro

➡ Dome of Genesis

➡ Loggia dei Cavalli

➡ Ascension Cupola

➡ St Mark's sarcophagus

PRACTICALITIES

➡ St Mark's Basilica

➡ Map p374

➡ ☎ 041 270 83 11

➡ www.basilicasanmarco.it

➡ Piazza San Marco

➡ ⊙ 9.30am-5pm Mon-Sat, 2-5pm Sun mid-Apr–Oct, to 4.30pm Sun Nov–mid-Apr

➡ ⬇ San Marco

liefs. The oldest mosaic on the facade, dating from 1270, is in the lunette above the far-left portal, depicting St Mark's stolen body arriving at the basilica. The theme is echoed in three of the other lunettes, including the 1660 mosaics above the second portal from the right, showing turbaned officials recoiling from the hamper of pork fat containing the sainted corpse.

Ceiling Mosaics

Blinking is natural upon your first glimpse of the basilica's 8500 sq metres of glittering mosaics, many made with 24-carat gold leaf fused onto the back of the glass. Just inside the narthex (vestibule) glitter the basilica's oldest mosaics, Apostles with the Madonna, standing sentry by the main door for more than 950 years. The atrium's medieval Dome of Genesis depicts the separation of sky and water with surprisingly abstract motifs.

Inside the church proper, three golden domes vie for your attention. The images are intended to be read from the altar end to the entry, so the Cupola of the Prophets shimmers above the main altar, while the Last Judgment is depicted in the vault above the entrance (and best seen from the museum). The dome nearest the door is the Pentecost Cupola, showing the Holy Spirit represented by a dove shooting tongues of flame onto the heads of the surrounding saints. In the central 13th-century Ascension Cupola, angels swirl around the central figure of Christ hovering among the stars. Scenes from St Mark's life unfold around the main altar, which houses the saint's simple stone sarcophagus.

Treasury

Holy bones and booty from the Crusades fill the Tesoro (admission €3). Don't miss the bejewelled 12th-century Archangel Michael icon, featuring tiny, feisty enamelled saints. In a separate room, velvet-padded boxes preserve the remains of sainted doges alongside the usual assortment of credulity-challenging relics.

Pala d'Oro

Tucked behind the main altar (admission €2), this stupendous golden screen is studded with 2000 gemstones. But the most priceless treasures here are biblical figures in vibrant cloisonné, begun in Constantinople in AD 976 and elaborated by Venetian goldsmiths in 1209. The enamelled saints have unkempt beards and wide eyes fixed on Jesus, who glances sideways at a studious Mark as Mary throws up her hands in wonder – an understandable reaction to such a captivating scene.

SERVICES

Those simply wishing to pray or attend Mass can enter from the Porta dei Fiori, on the north side of the church. Attending evening vespers, a sung service held before the main evening Mass, allows you to enter the basilica after hours, when the tour groups are long gone. Everyone is welcome, as long as you sit quietly and behave respectfully.

TOP TIPS

➡ There's no charge to enter the church and wander around the roped-off central circuit.

➡ Dress modestly (ie knees and shoulders covered) and leave large bags at the Ateneo San Basso Left Luggage Office (Piazza San Marco; max 1hr free; ⊗ 9.30am-5pm; ☒ San Marco).

➡ Between April and October, reserve 'Skip the Line' access through the website (€3 per person; children under five free) and head directly into the central portal. Present your voucher at the entrance.

➡ The best chance of beating the crowds is to get here early and wait for the doors to open.

VENICE & THE VENETO BASILICA DI SAN MARCO

TOP SIGHT
PALAZZO DUCALE

Don't be fooled by its genteel Gothic elegance: behind that lacy pink-and-white patterned facade, the doge's palace shows serious muscle and a steely will to survive. The seat of Venice's government for more than seven centuries, this powerhouse stood the test of storms, crashes and conspiracies – only to be outwitted by Casanova, the notorious seducer who escaped from the attic prison.

Exterior

The doge's official residence probably moved to this site in the 10th century, although the current complex only began to take shape around 1340. In 1424 the wing facing Piazzetta San Marco was added and the palace assumed its final form, give or take a few major fires and refurbishments. The 1st-floor loggia fronting the square may seem like a fanciful flourish, but it served a solemn purpose: death sentences were read between the darker coloured ninth and 10th columns from the left. Abutting Basilica di San Marco, Zane and Bartolomeo Bon's 1443 Porta della Carta (Paper Door) was an elegant point of entry for dignitaries, and served as a public bulletin board for government decrees.

Courtyard

Entering through the colonnaded courtyard you'll spot Sansovino's brawny statues of *Apollo* and *Neptune* flanking Antonio Rizzo's Scala dei Giganti (Giants' Staircase). Recent restorations have preserved charming cherubim propping up the pillars, though slippery incised-marble steps remain off-limits. Just off the courtyard in the wing facing

DON'T MISS

➡ Sala del Maggior Consiglio (Grand Council Chamber)

➡ Sala dello Scudo (Shield Room)

➡ Scala d'Oro (Golden Staircase)

➡ Anticollegio (Council Antechamber)

PRACTICALITIES

➡ Map p374

➡ ☑ 041 271 59 11

➡ www.palazzoducale. visitmuve.it

➡ Piazzetta San Marco 1

➡ adult/reduced incl Museo Correr €25/13, with Museum Pass free

➡ ⊙ 8.30am-9pm Mon-Thu, to 11pm Fri & Sat Apr-Oct, 8.30am-7pm Nov-Mar

➡ ⛴ San Zaccaria

the square is the Museo dell'Opera, displaying a collection of stone columns and capitals from previous incarnations of the building.

The Main Circuit
A standard entry ticket takes you on a circuit through main state and institutional rooms of the palace as well as the armoury and prisons.

Level 2
From the loggia level, head to the top of Sansovino's 24-carat gilt stucco-work Scala d'Oro (Golden Staircase) and emerge into rooms covered with gorgeous propaganda. In Palladio-designed Sala delle Quattro Porte (Hall of the Four Doors), ambassadors awaited ducal audiences under a lavish display of Venice's virtues by Giovanni Cambi, whose over-the-top stucco work earned him the nickname Bombarda. Other convincing shows of Venetian superiority include Titian's 1576 *Doge Antonio Grimani Kneeling Before Faith,* amid approving cherubim, and Tiepolo's 1740s *Venice Receiving Gifts of the Sea from Neptune,* where Venice is a gorgeous blonde figure casually leaning on a lion.

Delegations waited in the Anticollegio (Council Antechamber), where Tintoretto drew parallels between Roman gods and Venetian government: *Mercury and the Three Graces* rewards Venice's industriousness with beauty, and *Minerva Dismissing Mars* is a Venetian triumph of savvy over brute force. The recently restored ceiling is Veronese's 1577 *Venice Distributing Honours,* while on the walls is a vivid reminder of diplomatic behaviour to avoid: Veronese's *Rape of Europe.*

Few were granted an audience in the Palladio-designed Collegio (Council Chamber), where Veronese's 1575–78 *Virtues of the Republic* ceiling shows Venice again as a blonde figure waving her sceptre like a wand over Justice and Peace. Father-son team Jacopo and Domenico Tintoretto attempt similar flattery, showing Venice keeping company with Apollo, Mars and Mercury in their *Triumph of Venice* ceiling for the Sala del Senato (Senate Chamber), but frolicking lagoon sea monsters steal the scene.

Government cover-ups were never so appealing as in the Sala Consiglio dei Dieci (Chamber of the Council of Ten), where Venice's star chamber plotted under Veronese's *Juno Bestowing her Gifts on Venice,* depicting a glowing goddess strewing gold ducats. Above the slot where anonymous treason accusations were slipped into the Sala della Bussola (Compass Room) is Veronese's *St Mark in Glory* ceiling. The route then finishes in the weapon-laden Armoury.

DEATH OF A DOGE

On the death of the doge, the Council announced: 'With much displeasure we have heard of the death of the most serene prince, a man of such goodness and piety; however, we shall make another.' The signet ring, symbol of his power, was then slipped from his finger and broken in half. The doge's family had three days to vacate the palace and remove all their furniture. Three Inquisitors were also appointed to scrutinise the doge's past office and, if necessary, punish his heirs for any fraud or wrongdoing.

TOP TIPS

➡ Book tickets online in advance to avoid queues.

➡ Tickets (valid for three months) include Museo Correr (p361) but it's worth paying an extra €5 for a Museum Pass, which gives access to several other high-profile civic museums.

➡ Last admission is one hour prior to closing.

➡ Don't leave your run until too late in the day, as some parts of the palace, such as the prisons, may close early.

➡ Get here when the doors open to avoid groups, which start arriving at around 9.30am to 10am.

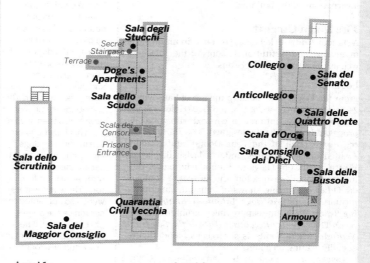

PALAZZO DUCALE

Sala degli Stucchi
Secret Staircase
Terrace
Doge's Apartments
Sala dello Scudo
Scala dei Censori
Prisons Entrance
Sala dello Scrutinio
Quarantia Civil Vecchia
Sala del Maggior Consiglio

Collegio
Anticollegio
Sala del Senato
Sala delle Quattro Porte
Scala d'Oro
Sala Consiglio dei Dieci
Sala della Bussola
Armoury

Level 1   **Level 2**

Level 1

After exiting the Armoury, stairs lead down to the chambers of the Quarantia Civil Vecchia (Council of Forty), a kind of court, split into sections dealing with criminal matters, civil disputes concerning Venetians and civil disputes pertaining to Venice's other territories. This last room is now used by restorers; peer through the windows to see them at work.

Beyond is the cavernous 1419 Sala del Maggior Consiglio (Grand Council Chamber), where the doge's throne once stood in front of the staggering 22m-by-7m *Paradise* backdrop (by Tintoretto's son, Domenico) that's more politically correct than pretty: heaven is crammed with 500 prominent Venetians, including several Tintoretto patrons. Veronese's political posturing is more elegant in his oval *Apotheosis of Venice* ceiling, where gods marvel at Venice's coronation by angels, with foreign dignitaries and blonde Venetians rubbernecking on the balcony below. A frieze along the top of the room depicts the first 76 doges of Venice, but note the black space: Doge Marin Falier would have appeared here had he not lost his head for treason in 1355.

This room opens out onto the only slightly less vast Sala dello Scrutinio (Ballot Room), a former library that was subsequently used for elections of the doge and the various councils of state. From here the route backtracks and passes through more rooms relating to the Quarantia Civil Vecchia, before entering the prisons.

Prisons & Loggia Level

Follow the path of condemned prisoners across the Ponte dei Sospiri (Bridge of Sighs; Map p386; 🚊 San Zaccaria) to Venice's 16th-century Priggione Nove (New Prisons). Dank cells covered with graffitied protestations of innocence are spread over three floors, with a central courtyard. One room has a small display of archaeological finds. After crossing back over the bridge, the route descends to the loggia level and through the rooms of the censors, state advocates and naval captains.

Doge's Apartments

The doge's suite of private rooms takes up a large chunk of the 1st floor above the loggia. The 18 roaring lions decorating the Sala degli Stucchi are a reminder that Venice's most powerful figurehead lived like a caged lion in his gilded suite, which he could not leave without permission. Still, consider the real estate: a terrace garden with private entry to Basilica di San Marco, and a dozen salons with splendidly restored marble fireplaces carved by Tullio and Antonio Lombardo.

The most intriguing room is the Sala dello Scudo (Shield Room), which is covered with world maps that reveal the extent of Venetian power (and the limits of its cartographers) c 1483 and 1762. The New World map places California near *Terra Incognita d'Antropofagi* (Unknown Land of the Maneaters), aka Canada, where Cuzco is apparently located.

This space is now used for high-profile temporary art exhibitions, which are ticketed separately (around €10 extra). These include diverse shows such as 'Venice, the Jews & Europe', 'Treasures of the Mughals & the Maharajas' and, most recently, 'Canaletto & Venice'.

Secret Itineraries Tour

Further rooms, too small for the masses, can be visited on a fascinating 75-minute guided tour (☏041 4273 0892; adult/reduced €20/14; ☉ tours in English 9.55am, 10.45am & 11.35am). It takes in the damp ground-floor cells known as Pozzi (wells) and then heads up through a hidden passageway into the cramped, unadorned Council of Ten Secret Headquarters. Beyond this ominous office suite, the vast Chancellery is lined with drawers of top-secret files, including reports by Venice's far-reaching spy network, accusations by Venetians against their neighbours, and judgements copied in triplicate by clerks. The accused might be led to the windowless Torture Chamber, where until 1660 confessions were sometimes extracted from prisoners dangling from a rope. Upstairs lie the Piombi (Leads), the attic prison cells where Casanova was condemned to five years' confinement in 1756 for corrupting nuns and the more serious charge of spreading Freemasonry. As described in his memoirs, Casanova made an ingenious escape through the roof, then convinced a guard he was an official locked into the palace overnight. He would later return to Venice, enlisted as a spy for the Consiglio dei Dieci (Council of Ten).

THE LION'S MOUTH

On the terrace of the loggia level look for the face of a grimacing man with his mouth agape. This *bocca di leoni* (lion's mouth) was a postbox for secret accusations. These slanders reported any number of unholy acts, from cursing and tax avoidance (forgivable) to Freemasonry (punishable by death). The notes, which had to be signed by two accusers, were then investigated by Venice's dreaded security service, led by the Council of Ten.

BRIDGE OF SIGHS

Easily the most overrated architectural feature in Venice, the Ponte dei Sospiri, which links the palace with the prisons, was popularised by the famous British libertine Lord Byron (1788–1824), who mentioned it in one of his poems. Condemned prisoners were said to sigh as they passed through the enclosed bridge and caught their last glimpse of the beauty of the lagoon. Now the sighs are mainly from people trying to dodge the photo-snapping masses as they attempt to cross the neighbouring bridges.

VENICE & THE VENETO PALAZZO DUCALE

TOP SIGHT
GALLERIE DELL'ACCADEMIA

Hardly academic, these galleries contain more murderous intrigue, forbidden romance and shameless politicking than the most outrageous Venetian parties. The former Scuola della Carità complex maintained its serene composure for centuries, but ever since Napoleon installed his haul of Venetian art trophies here in 1807 – mainly looted from various religious institutions – there's been nonstop visual drama inside these walls.

Layout & Gallery Restoration

The bulk of the collection's treasures are on the 1st floor, and this is the best place to start your visit. Ordinarily you can trace a circular route through the numbered rooms (each floor is numbered separately). However, at the time of writing, the gallery was in the midst of a lengthy restoration and several rooms were closed. An attempt has been made to move some of the most famous works into spaces usually used for temporary exhibitions, but don't be surprised if some of the masterpieces that we've described are not on view or are not where we've said they'll be.

The ground floor houses major exhibitions, sculpture and a less showstopping collection of paintings from 1600 to 1880. These rooms may also be affected by the restoration. At the time of writing, the ground floor's Rooms 1 to 3 could be accessed from behind the ticket desk, while Rooms 7 to 13 could only be approached from the central staircase on the 1st floor.

DON'T MISS

→ Bellini's *Miracle of the Reliquary of the Cross at San Lorenzo Bridge*

→ Titian's *Presentation of the Virgin*

→ Tintoretto's *Creation of the Animals*

→ Giorgione's *The Storm*

PRACTICALITIES

→ Map p374

→ ☎ 041 522 22 47

→ www.gallerieaccademia.it

→ Campo de la Carità 1050

→ adult/reduced €12/2

→ ⊙ 8.15am-2pm Mon, to 7.15pm Tue-Sun

→ 🚤 Accademia

First Floor

Take the stairs up from the grand entry hall and prepare to be overwhelmed by the sensory overload of Room 1, where a swarm of angels flutter their golden wings from the carved ceiling, gazing down upon a swirling polychrome marble floor. Competing valiantly for your attention are a collection of vivid 14th- and 15th-century religious works that show Venice's precocious flair for colour and drama.

UFO arrivals seem imminent in the eerie, glowing skies of Carpaccio's lively *Crucifixion and Glorification of the Ten Thousand Martyrs of Mount Ararat* (Room 2). Lock eyes with fascinating strangers across Room 4. Hans Memling captures youthful stubble and angst with exacting detail in *Portrait of a Young Man*. Venice's Renaissance awaits in Room 6, where you'll find Titian and Tintoretto.

Room 20 is full of large canvases taken from the Scuola Grande di San Giovanni Evangelista. Among them is Gentile Bellini's *Miracle of the Reliquary of the Cross at San Lorenzo Bridge*, thronged with cosmopolitan crowds. The artist's *Procession in Piazza San Marco* offers an intriguing view of Venice's most famous square before its 16th-century makeover. The former church (Room 23) is a serene showstopper fronted by a Bellini altarpiece. Sharing the space is Giorgione's highly charged *The Storm*. The rear of the church displays massive canvases looted from the Scuola Grande di San Marco.

The final room (Room 24) has been left untouched from when it was the Scuola della Carità's boardroom. Board meetings would not have been boring here, under a lavishly carved ceiling and facing Antonio Vivarini's *Madonna Enthroned with Child in the Heavenly Garden*. Titian closes the 1st-floor circuit with his touching *Presentation of the Virgin*. Here, a young, tiny Madonna trudges up an intimidating staircase while a distinctly Venetian crowd of onlookers point at her.

Ground Floor

The highlight of the ground-floor collection is Room 2, which is devoted to 18th-century Venice's go-to ceiling guy Giambattista Tiepolo. The focal point is a large fresco which originally adorned the ceiling of a church in Castello.

Rooms 7, 10 and 13 feature the work of the city's most famous sculptor, Antonio Canova, including funeral steles, classical figures and sycophantic effigies of Venice's new French overlords, the Bonapartes. There's a Canaletto tucked away in Room 9 – one of only a couple of works by the artist on public display in his home town.

ACCADEMIA ARCHITECTURE

The Accademia inhabits three conjoined buildings. The Scuola della Carità (founded 1260) was the oldest of Venice's six *scuole grandi* (religious confraternities); the current building dates to 1343. Bartolomeo Bon completed the spare, Gothic-edged facade of the Chiesa di Santa Maria della Carità (Church of Our Lady of Charity) in 1448. A century later, Palladio took a classical approach to the Convento dei Canonici Lateranensi. From 1949 to 1954, Carlo Scarpa chose a minimalist approach to restorations; his restrained style is most apparent in the central staircase.

TOP TIPS

➤ There's free admission to the gallery on the first Sunday of each month.

➤ To avoid high-season queues, arrive at opening time or towards the end of the day. Last entry is 45 minutes before closing, but a proper visit takes at least 1½ hours.

➤ To skip ahead of the queues, book timed tickets in advance online (booking fee €1.50).

➤ The audio guide (€6) is largely unnecessary.

Venice

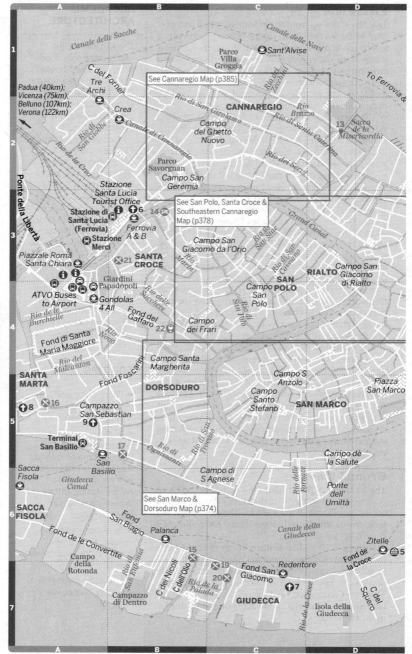

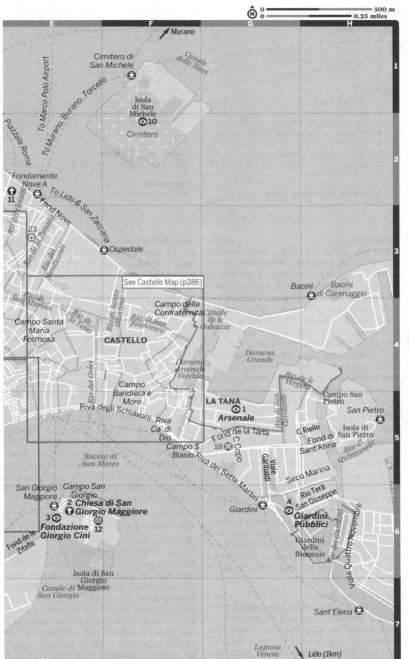

0 ——— 500 m
0 ——— 0.25 miles

To Murano

Cimitero di
San Michele

Isola
di San
Michele
◎10

Cimitero

Canale
delle Navi

To Marco Polo Airport

To Murano, Burano, Torcello

Piazzale Roma

Fondamente
Nove A
⊗ To Lido & San Zaccaria
11
Fond Nove

Rio di la Panada

23

Rio dei Mendicanti

⊗ Ospedale

Rio di
San Marina

Campo Santa
Maria
Formosa

Rio di la Tetta

Rio di Santa
Giustina

CASTELLO

Campo della
Confraternita

Rio di San
Francesco

Canale
de le
Galeazze

Bacini
⊕ di Carenaggio

Bacini

Rio dei Greci

Campo
Bandiera e
Moro

Riva degli Schiavoni

Darsena
Arsenale
Vecchia

Darsena
Grande

Rio de le
Vergini

Riva
Ca' di
Dio

Fond de la Tana

LA TANA
◎1
Arsenale

Rio di San
Gerolamo

Campo San
Pietro

San Pietro
⊕

Isola di
San Pietro
⊕

Rio di
Quintavalle

Campo S
Biasio

18 ⊗ C Copo

Riva dei Sette Martiri

C Riello

Fond di
Sant'Anna

Viale
Garibaldi

Seco Marina

*Bacino di
San Marco*

San Giorgio
Maggiore

Campo San
Giorgio

⊕
2 **Chiesa di San
Giorgio Maggiore** ⊕

3 ◎

**Fondazione
Giorgio Cini**

Fond de le
Zitelle

🏛12

Giardini ⊕

Rio Tera
San Giuseppe

4
**Giardini
Pubblici**

Rio del Giardini

Giardini
della
Biennale

Viale Quattro Novembre

Isola di San
Giorgio
Maggiore

*Canale di
San Giorgio*

Sant'Elena ⊕

*Laguna
Veneta*

↘ Lido (1km)

See Castello Map (p386)

Venice

Museo Fortuny   MUSEUM
(Map p374; ☑041 520 09 95; www.fortuny.visit
muve.it; Campo San Beneto 3958; adult/reduced
€10/8; ☺10am-6pm Wed-Mon; ☒Sant'Angelo)
Find design inspiration at the palatial home
studio of art nouveau designer Mariano Fortuny y Madrazo (1871–1949), whose uncor-
seted Delphi-goddess frocks set the standard
for bohemian chic. The 1st-floor salon walls
are eclectic mood boards: Fortuny fashions
and Isfahan tapestries, family portraits and
artfully peeling plaster. Interesting temporary exhibitions spread from the basement
to the attic, the best of which use the general
ambience of grand decay to great effect.

Scala Contarini del Bovolo   NOTABLE BUILDING
(Map p374; ☑041 309 66 05; www.gioiellinas
costidivenezia.com; Calle Contarini del Bovolo 4299;
adult/reduced €7/6; ☺10am-6pm; ☒Sant'Angelo)
Under the Republic, only the Church and
state were permitted to erect towers, as the
structures could conceivably be used for military purposes. In around 1400 the Contarini
family, eager to show off their wealth and
power, cheekily built this non-tower instead.
Combining Venetian Gothic, Byzantine and
Renaissance elements, this romantic 'staircase' looks even higher than its 26m due to
the simple trick of decreasing the height of
the arches as it rises.

Museo di San Marco   MUSEUM
(Map p374; ☑041 2730 8311; www.basilicasanmar
co.it; Basilica di San Marco; adult/reduced €5/2.50;
☺9.45am-4.45pm; ☒San Marco) Accessed by a
narrow staircase leading up from the atrium of the Basilica di San Marco (p362), this
museum transports visitors to the level of

the church's rear mosaics and onto the Loggia dei Cavalli, the terrace above the main
facade. The four magnificent bronze horses
positioned here are actually reproductions
of the 2nd-century originals, plundered
from Constantinople's hippodrome, displayed inside.

Palazzo Grassi   GALLERY
(Map p374; ☑041 200 10 57; www.palazzograssi.
it; Campo San Samuele 3231; adult/reduced incl
Punta della Dogana €18/15; ☺10am-7pm Wed-Mon
mid-Mar–Nov; ☒San Samuele) Grand Canal gondola riders gasp at their first glimpse of the
massive sculptures by contemporary artists
docked in front of Giorgio Masari's neoclassical palace (built 1748–72). The provocative
collection of French billionaire François
Pinault overflows Palazzo Grassi, while clever curation and shameless art-star name-
dropping are the hallmarks of rotating temporary exhibits. Despite the artistic glamour,
it's Tadao Ando's creatively repurposed interi-
or architecture that steals the show.

◎ Dorsoduro

★ **Ca' Rezzonico**   MUSEUM
(Museum of 18th-Century Venice; Map p374; ☑041
241 01 00; www.visitmuve.it; Fondamenta Rezzonico
3136; adult/reduced €10/7.50, or with Museum Pass;
☺10am-5pm Wed-Mon; ☒Ca' Rezzonico) Baroque
dreams come true at this Baldassare Longhena–designed Grand Canal *palazzo* (mansion), where a marble staircase leads to a
vast gilded ballroom and sumptuous salons
filled with period furniture, paintings, porcelain and mesmerising ceiling frescoes, four of
which were painted by Giambattista Tiepolo.

The building was largely stripped of its finery when the Rezzonico family departed in 1810, but this was put right after the city acquired it in 1935, and refurnished it with pieces salvaged from other decaying palaces.

★ **Peggy Guggenheim Collection** MUSEUM
(Map p374; ☑041 240 54 11; www.guggen heim-venice.it; Calle San Cristoforo 701; adult/ reduced €15/9; ⊙10am-6pm Wed-Mon; 🚊Accademia) After losing her father on the *Titanic,* heiress Peggy Guggenheim became one of the great collectors of the 20th century. Her palatial canalside home, Palazzo Venier dei Leoni, showcases her stockpile of surrealist, futurist and abstract expressionist art, with works by up to 200 artists, including her ex-husband Max Ernst, Jackson Pollock (among her many rumoured lovers), Pablo Picasso and Salvador Dalí.

★ **Basilica di Santa**
Maria della Salute BASILICA
(Our Lady of Health Basilica; Map p374; www.ba silicasalutevenezia.it; Campo de la Salute 1; sacristy adult/reduced €4/2; ⊙9.30am-noon & 3-5.30pm; 🚊Salute) FREE Baldassare Longhena's magnificent basilica is prominently positioned near the entrance to the Grand Canal, its white stones, exuberant statuary and high domes gleaming spectacularly under the sun. The church makes good on an official appeal by the Venetian Senate directly to the Madonna in 1630, after 80,000 Venetians had been killed by plague. The Senate promised the Madonna a church in exchange for her intervention on behalf of Venice – no expense or effort spared.

★ **Punta della Dogana** GALLERY
(Map p374; ☑041 200 10 57; www.palazzograssi.it; Fondamenta Salute 2; adult/reduced €15/10, incl Palazzo Grassi €18/15; ⊙10am-7pm Wed-Mon Apr-Nov; 🚊Salute) Fortuna, the weathervane atop Punta della Dogana, swung Venice's way in 2005, when bureaucratic hassles in Paris convinced art collector François Pinault to showcase his works in Venice's long-abandoned customs warehouses. Built by Giuseppe Benoni in 1677 to ensure no ship entered the Grand Canal without paying duties, the warehouses reopened in 2009 after a striking reinvention by Japanese architect Tadao Ando. The space now hosts exhibitions of ambitious, large-scale artworks from some of the world's most provocative creative minds.

Chiesa di San Pantalon CHURCH
(St Pantaleon's Church; Map p374; Campo San Pantalon 3703; ⊙10am-noon & 3.30-6pm; 🚊San Tomà) FREE It's not the prettiest from the outside, but the bald brick facade of this 17th-century church (rent by a concerning crack), doesn't give any indication of the drama contained within. The entire ceiling is engulfed in a vast, overwhelming *trompe l'oeil* fresco by Gianantonio Fumiani, featuring a dark cacophony of saints and angels seemingly bursting through the roof. This extraordinary 1704 fresco may have been the artist's last: he's said to have fallen to his death while working on it.

Chiesa di San Sebastiano CHURCH
(St Sebastian's Church; Map p370; www.chorusven ezia.org; Campo San Sebastian 1687; adult/reduced €3/1.50, free with Chorus Pass; ⊙10.30am-4.30pm Mon-Sat; 🚊San Basilio) Antonio Scarpignano's relatively austere 1508–48 facade creates a sense of false modesty at this neighbourhood church. The interior is adorned with floor-to-ceiling masterpieces by Paolo Veronese, executed over three decades. According to popular local legend, Veronese found sanctuary at San Sebastiano in 1555 after fleeing murder charges in Verona, and his works in this church deliver lavish thanks to the parish and an especially brilliant poke in the eye to his accusers.

Chiesa di San Nicolò dei Mendicoli CHURCH
(St Nicholas of the Beggars Church; Map p370; ☑041 528 45 65; Campo San Nicolò dei Mendicoli 1907; ⊙10am-noon & 3-5.30pm Mon-Sat, 9am-noon Sun; 🚊Santa Marta) FREE Other churches might be grander, but none is more quintessentially Venetian than this 12th-century church with a history of service to the poor. Its cloisters once functioned as a women's refuge and its portico sheltered the *mendicoli* (beggars) to whom it owes its name. The tiny, picturesque *campo* (square) out front is Venice in miniature, surrounded on three sides by canals and featuring a pillar bearing the lion of St Mark.

---

❶ THE BUDGET GONDOLA

A *traghetto* is the gondola service locals use to cross the Grand Canal between its widely spaced bridges. *Traghetti* rides cost just €2 for nonresidents and typically operate from 9am to 6pm, although some routes finish by noon. You'll find *traghetto* crossings at Campo San Marcuola, the Rialto Market, Riva del Vin, San Tomà, Ca' Rezzonico and beside the Gritti Palace, though note that service can be spotty at times at all crossings.

VENICE & THE VENETO VENICE

San Marco & Dorsoduro

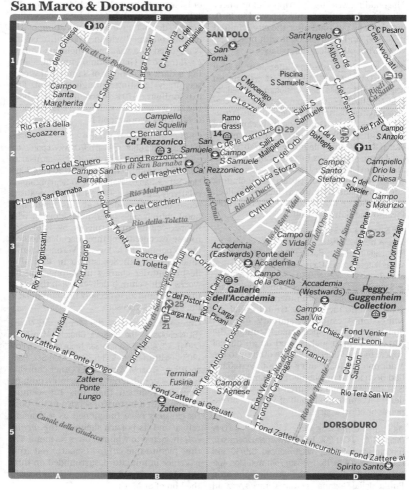

San Polo & Santa Croce

★ I Frari
BASILICA
(Basilica di Santa Maria Gloriosa dei Frari; Map p378; ☑041 272 86 18; www.basilicadeifrari.it; Campo dei Frari 3072, San Polo; adult/reduced €3/1.50, with Chorus Pass free; ⏰9am-6pm Mon-Sat, 1-6pm Sun; ⛴San Tomà) A soaring Gothic church, the Friary's assets include marquetry choir stalls, Canova's pyramid mausoleum, Bellini's achingly sweet *Madonna with Child* triptych in the sacristy, and Longhena's creepy Doge Pesaro funereal monument. Upstaging them all, however, is Titian's 1518 *Assunta* (Assumption) altarpiece, in which a radiant red-cloaked Madonna reaches heavenward, steps onto a cloud and escapes this mortal coil. Titian himself – lost to the plague in 1576 at the age 94 – has his memorial here.

★ Scuola Grande di San Rocco
HISTORIC BUILDING
(Map p378; ☑041 523 48 64; www.scuolagrandesanrocco.org; Campo San Rocco 3052; adult/reduced €10/8; ⏰9.30am-5.30pm; ⛴San Tomà) Everyone wanted the commission to paint this building dedicated to St Roch, patron saint of the plague-stricken, so Tintoretto cheated: instead of producing sketches like rival Veronese, he gifted a splendid ceiling panel of the saint, knowing it couldn't be refused, or

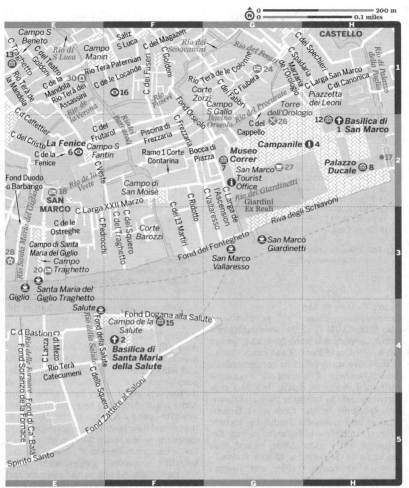

matched by other artists. This painting still crowns the Sala dell'Albergo, upstairs, and Tintoretto's work completely covers the walls and ceilings of all the main halls.

⭐ **Rialto Market**   MARKET

(Rialto Mercato; Map p378; 📞 041 296 06 58; Campo de la Pescaria; ⏰ 7am-2pm; 🚤 Rialto Mercato) Venice's main market has been whetting appetites for seven centuries, with fruit and vegetable stands abutting the rather more pungent **Pescaria** (Fish Market; Campo de la Pescaria; ⏰ 7am-2pm Tue-Sun). To see it at its best, arrive in the morning along with the trolley-pushing shoppers and you'll be rewarded with pyramids of colourful seasonal produce like Sant'Erasmo *castraure* (baby artichokes), *radicchio trevisano* (bitter red chicory) and thick, succulent white asparagus. If you're in the market for picnic provisions, vendors may offer you samples.

Ponte di Rialto   BRIDGE

(Map p378; 🚤 Rialto) A superb feat of engineering, Antonio da Ponte's 1592 Istrian stone span took three years and 250,000 gold ducats to construct. Adorned with stone reliefs depicting St Mark and St Theodore on the north side and the Annunciation on the other, the bridge crosses the Grand Canal at its narrowest point, connecting the neighbourhoods of San Polo and San Marco.

San Marco & Dorsoduro

Scuola Grande di San Giovanni Evangelista HISTORIC BUILDING
(Map p378; ☑041 71 82 34; www.scuolasangio vanni.it; Campiello de la Scuola 2454; adult/reduced €10/8; ⊙9.30am-5.15pm; ☷San Tomà) One of Venice's five main religious confraternities, the lay brothers of St John the Evangelist performed works of charity but also supported the arts by lavishing their clubrooms with treasures by the city's most famous painters and architects. Highlights include Pietro Lombardo's elaborately carved Renaissance entry gate (1481), topped with the eagle of St John; a Mauro Codussi–designed staircase (1498); and Giorgio Massari's spectacularly ostentatious St John's Hall (1727–62).

Ca' Pesaro MUSEUM
(Map p378; ☑041 72 11 27; www.capesaro.visit muve.it; Fondamenta Ca' Pesaro 2076; adult/reduced €10/7.50, with Museum Pass free; ⊙10am-5pm Tue-Sun; ☷San Stae) The stately exterior of this Baldassare Longhena–designed 1710 *palazzo* hides two intriguing art museums that could hardly be more different: the Galleria Internazionale d'Arte Moderna and the Museo d'Arte Orientale. While the former includes art showcased at La Biennale di Venezia, the latter holds treasures from Prince Enrico di Borbone's epic 1887–89 souvenir-shopping spree across Asia. Competing with the artworks are Ca' Pesaro's

fabulous painted ceilings, which hint at the power and prestige of the Pesaro clan.

Palazzo Mocenigo MUSEUM
(Map p378; ☑041 72 17 98; www.mocenigo.visit muve.it; Salizada San Stae 1992; adult/reduced €8/5.50, with Museum Pass free; ⊙10am-4pm; ☷San Stae) Venice received a dazzling addition to its property portfolio in 1945 when Count Alvise Nicolò Mocenigo bequeathed his family's 17th-century *palazzo* to the city. While the ground floor hosts temporary exhibitions, the *piano nobile* (main floor) is where you'll find a dashing collection of historic fashion, including exquisitely embroidered men's silk waistcoats. Adding to the glamour and intrigue is an exhibition dedicated to the art of fragrance – an ode to Venice's 16th-century status as Europe's capital of perfume.

◎ Cannaregio

★ **The Ghetto** JEWISH SITE
(Map p385; ☷Guglie) In medieval times this part of Cannaregio housed a *getto* (foundry), but it was as the designated Jewish quarter from the 16th to 19th centuries that the word acquired a whole new meaning. In accordance with the Venetian Republic's 1516 decree, by day Jewish lenders, doctors and clothing merchants were permitted to attend to Venice's commercial interests, but at night and on Christian holidays they were

locked within the gated island of the Ghetto Nuovo (New Foundry).

When Jewish merchants fled the Spanish Inquisition for Venice in 1541, there was no place left in the Ghetto to go but up: in buildings around the Campo del Ghetto Nuovo, upper storeys housed new arrivals, synagogues and publishing houses. A plain wooden cupola in the corner of the *campo* (square) marks the location of the Schola Canton (Corner Synagogue). Next door is the Schola Tedesca (German Synagogue), while the rooftop Schola Italiana (Italian Synagogue) is a simple synagogue built by newly arrived and largely destitute Italian Jews, who had fled from Spanish-controlled southern Italy.

As numbers grew, the Ghetto was extended into the neighbouring Ghetto Vecchio (Old Foundry), creating the confusing situation where the older Jewish area is called the New Ghetto and the newer is the Old Ghetto. Sephardic Jewish refugees raised two synagogues in Campo del Ghetto Vecchio that are considered among the most beautiful in northern Italy, lavishly rebuilt in the 17th century. The Schola Levantina (Levantine Synagogue), founded in 1541, has a magnificent 17th-century woodworked pulpit, while the Schola Spagnola (Spanish Synagogue), founded around 1580, shows just how Venetian the community had become through a demonstrated flair for Venetian architectural flourishes: repeating geometric details, high-arched windows, and exuberant marble and carved-wood baroque interiors.

After Venice fell to Napoleon in 1787 the city's Jews experienced six months of freedom before the Austrian administration restricted them to the Ghetto once again. It wasn't until Venice joined with Italy in 1866 that full emancipation was gained, but even that was short-lived. Many of Venice's Jews fled before the Nazi occupation, but 246 were arrested and sent to concentration camps between 1943 and 1944; only eight survived. A memorial consisting of harrowing bas-reliefs and the names and ages of those killed now lines two walls facing Campo del Ghetto Nuovo.

You can stroll around this peaceful precinct by day and night, but the best way to experience the Ghetto is on a guided tour of three of the synagogues offered by the Museo Ebraico (Jewish Museum; Map p385; ☑041 71 53 59; www.museoebraico.it; Campo del Ghetto Nuovo 2902b; adult/reduced €8/6, incl tour €12/10; ⊙10am-7pm Sun-Fri Jun-Sep, to 5.30pm Sun-Fri Oct-May), departing hourly from 10.30am.

★ Chiesa della Madonna dell'Orto   CHURCH
(Map p385; www.madonnadellorto.org; Campo de la Madonna dell'Orto 3520; adult/reduced €3/2; ⊙10am-5pm Mon-Sat; ⊠Orto) This elegantly spare 1365 brick Gothic church remains one of Venice's best-kept secrets. It was the parish church of Venetian Renaissance painter Tintoretto (1518–94), who is buried in the chapel to the right of the altar. Inside, you'll find two of Tintoretto's finest works: *Presentation of the Virgin in the Temple* and *Last Judgment*, where lost souls attempt to hold back a teal tidal wave while an angel rescues one last person from the ultimate *acqua alta* (high tide).

★ Chiesa di Santa
Maria dei Miracoli   CHURCH
(Map p378; Campo dei Miracoli 6074; adult/reduced €3/1.50, with Chorus Pass free; ⊙10.30am-4.30pm Mon-Sat; ⊠Fondamente Nove) This magnificent church was built between 1481 and 1489 to house Nicolò di Pietro's Madonna icon after the painting began to miraculously weep in its outdoor shrine. Aided by public fundraising, Pietro and Tullio Lombardo's design used marble scavenged from slag heaps in San Marco and favoured the human-scale of radically new Renaissance architecture in place of the grandiose Gothic status quo.

★ Galleria Giorgio
Franchetti alla Ca' d'Oro   MUSEUM
(Map p378; ☑041 522 23 49; www.cadoro.org; Calle di Ca' d'Oro 3932; adult/reduced €8.50/2; ⊙8.15am-2pm Mon, to 7.15pm Tue-Sun, 2nd fl 10am-6pm Tue-Sun; ⊠Ca' d'Oro) One of the most beautiful buildings on the Grand Canal, with a lacy Gothic facade, 15th-century Ca' d'Oro is resplendent even without the original gold-leaf details that gave the palace its name (Golden House). Baron Franchetti (1865–1922) bequeathed this treasure-box palace to Venice, packed with his collection of masterpieces, many of which were originally plundered from Veneto churches during Napoleon's conquest of Italy. The baron's ashes are interred beneath an ancient purple porphyry column in the magnificent open-sided, mosaic-floored court downstairs.

I Gesuiti   CHURCH
(Santa Maria Assunta; Map p370; ☑041 528 65 79; Salizada dei Specchieri 4882; €1; ⊙10.30am-1pm & 3.30-5pm; ⊠Fondamente Nove) Giddily over the top even by rococo standards, this glitzy 18th-century Jesuit church is difficult to take in all at once, with staggering white-and-green intarsia (inlaid marble) walls that look like a version of Venetian flocked

San Polo, Santa Croce & Southeastern Cannaregio

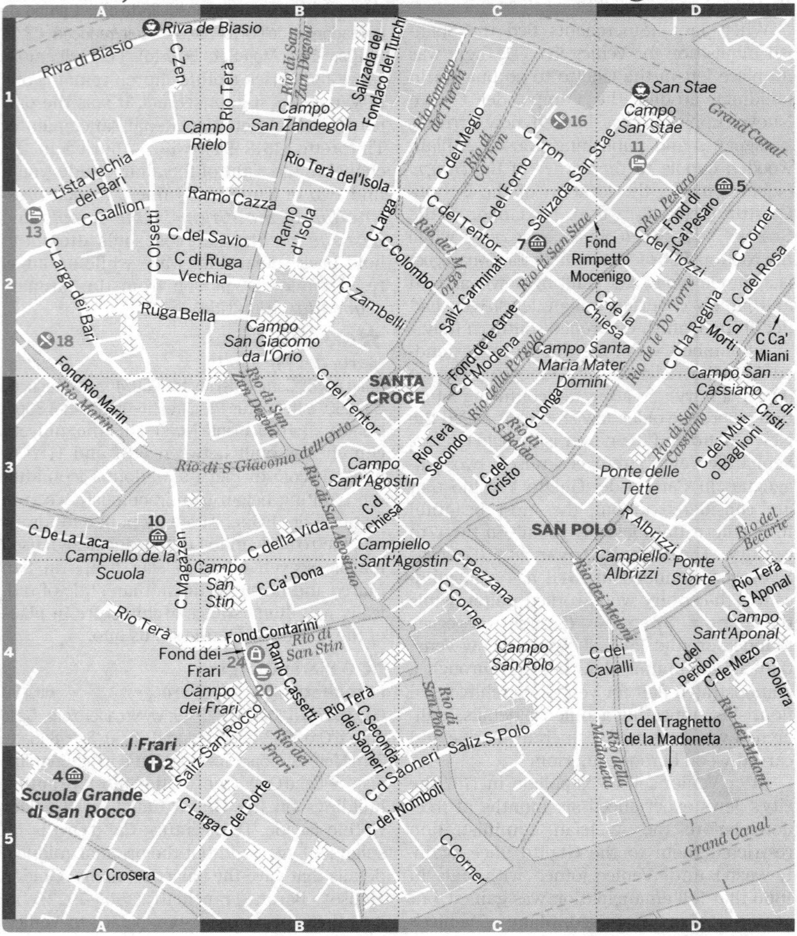

wallpaper, marble curtains draped over the pulpit and a marble carpet spilling down the altar stairs. While the ceiling is a riot of gold-and-white stuccowork, gravity is provided by Titian's uncharacteristically gloomy *Martyrdom of St Lawrence,* on the left as you enter the church.

Chiesa dei Scalzi CHURCH
(Chiesa di Santa Maria di Nazareth; Map p370; ☎041 71 51 15; www.carmeloveneto.it; Fondamenta dei Scalzi 55-57; suggested donation €1; ⏲7.30-11.50am & 4-6.50pm; ⛴Ferrovia) An unexpected outburst of baroque extravagance, this Longhena-designed church (built 1654–80) has a facade by Giuseppe Sardi that ripples with columns and statues in niches. This is an unusual departure for Venice, where baroque ebullience was usually reserved for interiors of Renaissance-leaning buildings – in fact it was a deliberate echo of a style often employed in Rome, intended to help make the Discalced (meaning 'barefoot'; *scalzi* in Italian) Carmelites posted here from Rome feel more at home.

Chiesa di Sant'Alvise CHURCH
(Map p385; Campo Sant'Alvise 3025; adult/reduced €3/1.50, with Chorus Pass free; ⏲10.30am-4.30pm Mon-Sat; ⛴Sant'Alvise) Don't be fooled by the bare brick exterior of this 1388 church, attached to an Augustinian convent. Inside it's

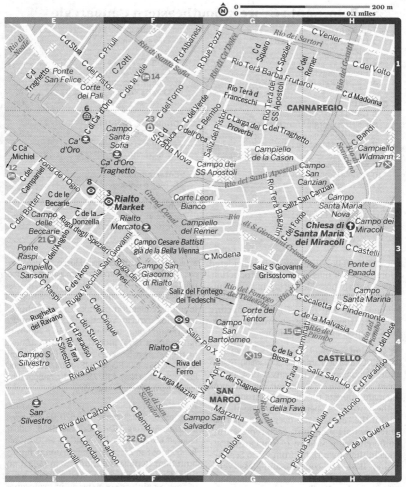

a riot of colour, with extraordinary *trompe l'œil* ceiling frescoes and massive canvases all around. Look out for Tiepolo's *La salita al Calvario* (The Road to Calvary), a distressingly human depiction of one of Christ's falls under the weight of the cross.

👁 Castello

⭐ Zanipolo

BASILICA

(Basilica di San Giovanni e Paolo; Map p386; ☑ 041 523 59 13; www.basilicasantigiovanniepaolo. it; Campo Zanipolo; adult/reduced €3.50/1.50; ⏱ 9am-6pm Mon-Sat, noon-6pm Sun; 🚤 Ospedale) Commenced in 1333 but not finished until the 1430s, this vast church is similar in style and scope to the Franciscan Frari in San Polo, which was being raised at the same time. Both oversized structures feature red-brick facades with high-contrast detailing in white stone. After its completion, Zanipolo quickly became the go-to church for ducal funerals and inside you'll find 25 of their lavish tombs, plus works by Bellini, Lorenzetti and Veronese.

⭐ Arsenale

HISTORIC SITE

(Map p370; Campo de l'Arsenale; 🚤 Arsenale) Founded in 1104, the Arsenale soon became the greatest medieval shipyard in Europe, home to 300 shipping companies employing up to 16,000 people. Capable of turning

San Polo, Santa Croce & Southeastern Cannaregio

out a new galley in a day, it is considered a forerunner of mass industrial production. Access is only possible during major events and exhibitions such as Carnival, the Arte Laguna Prize and the art and architecture Biennale, when it forms an awesome backdrop to international exhibitions.

★**Giardini Pubblici**   GARDENS
(Map p370; Riva dei Partigiani; 🚤 Giardini) Begun under Napoleon as the city's first public green space, these leafy gardens are now the main home of the Biennale. Around half of the gardens is open to the public all year round; the rest given over to the permanent Biennale pavilions, each representing a different country. Many of them are attractions in their own right, from Carlo Scarpa's daring 1954 raw-concrete-and-glass Venezuelan Pavilion to Denton Corker Marshall's 2015 Australian Pavilion in black granite.

★**Scuola Dalmata di
San Giorgio degli Schiavoni**   CHURCH
(Map p386; 🕿 041 522 88 28; Calle dei Furlani 3259a; adult/reduced €5/3; ⏰ 1.30-5.30pm Mon, 9.30am-5.30pm Tue-Sat, 9.30am-1.30pm Sun; 🚤 San Zaccaria) This 15th-century Dalmatian religious-confraternity house is dedicated to favourite Slavic saints George, Tryphon and Jerome, whose lives are captured with precision and glowing early-Renaissance grace by 15th-century master Vittore Carpaccio.

Padiglione delle Navi   MUSEUM
(Ships Pavilion; Map p386; 🕿 041 24 24; www. visitmuve.it; Fondamenta de la Madonna 2162c; adult/reduced €10/7.50, incl Museo Storico Navale; ⏰ 11am-6pm summer, to 5pm winter; 🚤 Arsenale) The Padiglione delle Navi is a vast 2000-sq-metre warehouse containing a fabulous collection of model historic boats, including typical Venetian luggers, gondolas, racing boats, military vessels, a funerary barge and a royal motorboat. It's an annexe of the Museo Storico Navale (Naval History Museum; Riva San Biagio 2148; adult/reduced incl Padiglione delle Nave €10/7.50; ⏰ 10am-6pm summer, to 5pm winter; 🚤 Arsenale).

Palazzo Grimani   MUSEUM
(Map p386; 🕿 call centre 041 520 03 45; www. palazzogrimani.org; Ramo Grimani 4858; adult/ reduced €5/2, incl Ca' D'Oro €10/4; ⏰ 10am-7pm Tue-Sun; 🚤 San Zaccaria) The Grimani family built their Renaissance *palazzo* in 1568. Cardinal Giovanni Grimani hired a dream team of fresco painters specialising in grotesques and Pompeii-style mythological scenes. The Sala ai Fogliami (Foliage Room) is the most memorable room. Painted by Mantovano, its ceiling and walls are awash with realistic plant- and birdlife. They even include New World species only recently been discovered by Europeans, including two that would come to be staples of Venetian life: tobacco and corn.

Fondazione Querini Stampalia   MUSEUM
(Map p386; 🕿 041 271 14 11; www.querinistampalia. it; Campiello Querini Stampalia 5252; adult/reduced €14/10; ⏰ 10am-6pm Tue-Sun; 🚤 San Zaccaria) In 1869 Conte Giovanni Querini Stampalia made a gift of his ancestral 16th-century

palazzo to the city on the forward-thinking condition that its 700-year-old library operate late-night openings. Downstairs, savvy drinkers take their *aperitivi* (pre-dinner drinks) in Carlo Scarpa's modernist garden, while the museum's temporary exhibitions, art-filled salons and rare numismatic collection from the Venetian mint offer an interesting insight into how the Venetian aristocracy lived with and collected art.

Ocean Space GALLERY
(Chiesa di San Lorenzo; Map p386; www.tba21. org; Campo San Lorenzo 5069; ⊙11am-7pm Tue-Sun; ⛴San Zaccaria) FREE Austrian powerhouse Francesca von Habsburg has restored the epic San Lorenzo church – derelict for nearly a century after suffering damage in WWI – to house the Ocean Space Centre. This cross-disciplinary centre showcases the work of the TBA21 Academy and offers a platform to artists, scientists and policymakers tackling the challenge of climate change. Via a programme of lectures, workshops and events, the academy hopes to transform Venice itself into a lab for the future rather than a relic of the past.

⊙ **Giudecca**

Chiesa del Santissimo Redentore CHURCH
(Church of the Most Holy Redeemer; Map p370; www.chorusvenezia.org; Campo del SS Redentore 194; adult/reduced €3/1.50, with Chorus Pass free; ⊙10.30am-4.30pm Mon-Sat; ⛴Redentore) Built to celebrate the city's deliverance from the Black Death, Palladio's Il Redentore was completed under Antonio da Ponte (of Rialto Bridge fame) in 1592. The theme is taken up in Paolo Piazza's monochrome *Venice's Offering for Liberation from the Plague of 1575–77* (1619), high above the entry door. Look for Tintoretto's *The Flagellation of Christ* (1588) on the third altar to the right.

Casa dei Tre Oci GALLERY
(Map p370; ☎041 241 23 32; www.treoci.org; Fondamenta de le Zitelle 43; adult/reduced €12/10; ⊙10am-7pm Wed-Mon; ⛴Zitelle) FREE Acquired by the Fondazione di Venezia in 2000, the fanciful neo-Gothic 'House of Three Eyes' was built in 1913 by artist and photographer Mario de Maria, who conceived its distinctive brick facade with its three unusually shaped arched windows. It now houses his photographic archive and interesting exhibitions of contemporary art, especially photography. The gift shop is worth a browse.

◉ **Isola di San Giorgio Maggiore**

★**Chiesa di San Giorgio Maggiore** CHURCH
(St George's Church; Map p370; ☎041 522 78 27; www.abbaziasangiorgio.it; Isola di San Giorgio Maggiore; bell tower adult/reduced €6/4; ⊙9am-6pm; ⛴San Giorgio Maggiore) FREE Begun in 1565 and completed in 1610, this dazzling Benedictine abbey church owes more to ancient Roman temples than the bombastic baroque of Palladio's day. Inside is a generously proportioned nave, with high windows distributing filtered sunshine. Two of Tintoretto's masterworks flank the altar, and a lift whisks visitors up the 60m-high bell tower for stirring panoramas – a great alternative to queuing at San Marco's *campanile*.

★**Fondazione Giorgio Cini** CULTURAL CENTRE
(Map p370; ☎041 271 02 37; www.cini.it; Isola di San Giorgio Maggiore; adult/reduced €13/10; ⊙tours 10am-6pm daily Apr-Nov, to 4pm Wed-Mon Dec-Mar; ⛴San Giorgio Maggiore) In 1951, industrialist and art patron Vittorio Cini – a survivor of Dachau – acquired the monastery of San Giorgio and restored it in memory of his son, Giorgio Cini. The rehabilitated complex is an architectural treasure incorporating designs by Andrea Palladio and Baldassare Longhena. Tours allow you to stroll through the cloisters, visit the refectory and libraries, and gaze down on the Borges Labyrinth – an intricate garden maze built to honour Argentinian writer Jorge Luis Borges.

Le Stanze del Vetro GALLERY
(Map p370; ☎041 522 91 38; www.lestanzedel vetro.org; Isola di San Giorgio Maggiore 8; ⊙10am-4.30pm Thu-Tue, extended hours summer; ⛴San Giorgio) FREE Once part of a boarding school, 'The Glass Rooms' are now home to a constant flow of temporary exhibitions, all of them based on glass. Often the displays continue outside, with glass installations in the garden. There is a well-stocked gift shop and a fantastic collection of books about glass art.

WORTH A TRIP

ISOLA DI SAN MICHELE
This picturesque walled islet, positioned between Murano and the city, is Venice's main cemetery (Map p370; ⊙7.30am-6pm Apr-Sep, to 4.30pm Oct-Mar; ⛴Cimitero) FREE. *Vaporetti* 4.1 and 4.2 stop here, en route between Fondamente Nove and Murano.

Grand Canal

A WATER TOUR

The 3.5km route of vaporetto (passenger ferry) No 1, which passes some 50 palazzi (mansions), six churches and scene-stealing backdrops featured in four James Bond films, is public transport at its most glamorous.

The Grand Canal starts with controversy: **① Ponte di Calatrava** a luminous glass-and-steel bridge that cost triple the original €4 million estimate. Ahead are castle-like **② Fondaco dei Turchi**, the historic Turkish trading-house; Renaissance **③ Palazzo Vendramin**, housing the city's casino; and double-arcaded **④ Ca' Pesaro**. Don't miss **⑤ Ca' d'Oro**, a 1430 filigree Gothic marvel.

Points of Venetian pride include the **⑥ Pescaria**, built in 1907 on the site where fishmongers have been slinging lagoon crab for 600 years, and neighbouring **⑦ Rialto Market** stalls, overflowing with island-grown produce. Cost overruns for 1592 **⑧ Ponte di Rialto** rival Calatrava's, but its marble splendour stands the test of time.

The next two canal bends could cause architectural whiplash, with Sanmicheli-designed Renaissance **⑨ Palazzo Grimani** and Mauro Codussi's **⑩ Palazzo Corner-Spinelli** followed by Giorgio Masari-designed **⑪ Palazzo Grassi** and Baldassare Longhena's baroque jewel box, **⑫ Ca' Rezzonico**.

Wooden **⑬ Ponte dell'Accademia** was built in 1930 as a temporary bridge, but the beloved landmark remains. Stone lions flank the **⑭ Peggy Guggenheim Collection**, where the American heiress collected ideas, lovers and art. You can't miss the dramatic dome of Longhena's **⑮ Chiesa di Santa Maria della Salute** or **⑯ Punta della Dogana**, Venice's triangular customs warehouse reinvented as a contemporary art showcase. The Grand Canal's grand finale is pink Gothic **⑰ Palazzo Ducale** and its adjoining **⑱ Ponte dei Sospiri**.

Palazzo Grassi
French magnate François Pinault scandalised Paris when he relocated his contemporary art collection here, to be displayed in galleries designed by Gae Aulenti and Tadao Ando.

Ca' Rezzonico
See how Venice lived in baroque splendour at this 18th-century art museum with Tiepolo ceilings, silk-swagged boudoirs and even an in-house pharmacy.

⑬ Ponte dell'Accademia

Peggy Guggenheim Collection

Chiesa di Santa Maria delle Salute

Punta della Dogana
Minimalist architect Tadao Ando creatively repurposed abandoned warehouses as galleries, which now host contemporary art installations from François Pinault's collection.

Ponte di Calatrava
With its starkly streamlined fish-fin shape, the 2008 bridge was the first to be built over the Grand Canal in 75 years.

Fondaco dei Turchi
Recognisable by its double colonnade, watchtowers, and dugout canoe parked at the Museo di Storia Naturale's ground-floor loggia.

Ca' d'Oro
Behind the triple Gothic arcades are priceless masterpieces: Titians looted by Napoleon, a rare Mantegna and semiprecious stone mosaic floors.

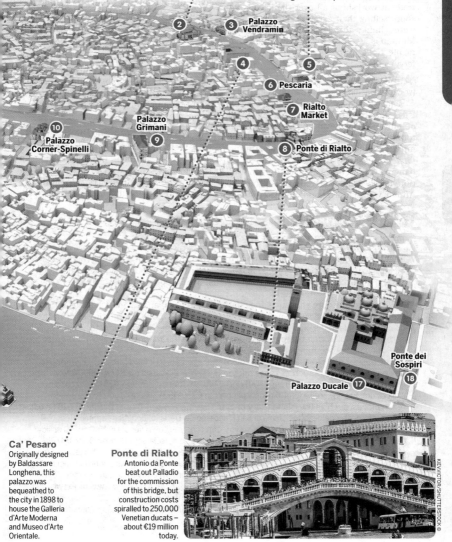

Ca' Pesaro
Originally designed by Baldassare Longhena, this palazzo was bequeathed to the city in 1898 to house the Galleria d'Arte Moderna and Museo d'Arte Orientale.

Ponte di Rialto
Antonio da Ponte beat out Palladio for the commission of this bridge, but construction costs spiralled to 250,000 Venetian ducats – about €19 million today.

👁 Murano

Venetians have been working in glass since the 10th century, but due to the fire hazards of glass-blowing, the industry was moved to the island of Murano in the 13th century. This history is showcased in the Museo del Vetro (Glass Museum; ☎041 243 49 14; www.museovetro. visitmuve.it; Fondamenta Giustinian 8; adult/reduced €14/11.50, free with Museum Pass; ⏱10am-5pm; ⛴Museo) in the 17th-century Palazzo Giustinian. Today, glass artisans continue to ply their trade at workshops all over the island, with shops selling their extraordinarily expensive wares lining the Fondamenta dei Vetrai. Murano is less than 10 minutes from Fondamente Nove by *vaporetto* (small passenger ferry) and services are frequent.

⭐ Basilica dei SS Maria e Donato   CHURCH
(www.sandonatomurano.it; Campo San Donato; ⏱9am-6pm Mon-Sat, 12.30-6pm Sun; ⛴Museo) FREE Fire-breathing is the unifying theme of Murano's medieval church, with its astounding 12th-century gilded-glass apse mosaic of the Madonna made in Murano's *fornaci* (furnaces) and the bones of a dragon hanging behind the altar. According to tradition, this beast was slayed by St Donatus of Arezzo, whose mortal remains also rest here.

The other masterpiece here is underfoot: a Byzantine-style 12th-century mosaic pavement of waving geometric patterns, griffons, eagles and peacocks rendered in porphyry, serpentine and other precious stones.

Santa Chiara –
The Glass Cathedral   WORKSHOP
(☎041 73 69 98; www.santachiaramurano.com; Fondamenta Manin 1; summer/winter €7/5; ⛴Colonna) There are authentic glass factories on Murano offering cheaper demonstrations and turning out far finer work, but this furnace – housed within a deconsecrated 16th-century church (founded 1231) – delivers an entertaining and highly informative experience tailored unapologetically to tourists. It has bleacher seating, musical accompaniment, a mirror ball and plenty of opportunities for photos of the handsome artisans at work. You might want to save your purchases for another shop, though.

👁 Burano & Mazzorbo

Once Venice's lofty architecture leaves you feeling overwhelmed, Burano brings you back to your senses with a reviving shock of colour. The 50-minute ferry ride on line 12 from the Fondamente Nove is packed with

---

OFF THE BEATEN TRACK

EXPLORING THE LAGOON

Seeing and understanding something of the lagoon's patchwork of shifting mudflats is integral to understanding Venice. Unesco recognised this by specifically including the 550-sq-km expanse – the largest coastal wetland in Europe – in its designation of Venice as a World Heritage Site in 1987.

Rich in unique flora and fauna, the tidal *barene* (shoals) and salt marshes are part of the city's psyche. Between September and January over 130,000 migrating birds nest, dive and dabble in the shallows, while year-round fishermen tend their nets and traps, and city-council workers dredge canals and reinforce the shifting islands of cord-grass and saltwort so essential to the lagoon's survival.

The easiest and cheapest way to explore the lagoon is to island hop with a *vaporetto* day pass. A boat tour, such as those offered by Terra e Acqua (☎347 4205004; www. veneziainbarca.it; ⏱day trips from €400) and Eolo Cruises (☎349 7431551; www.cruising venice.com; full-day cruise for 4-6 people per person €350-450), will take you to harder-to-reach places, such as the island friary of San Francesco del Deserto (☎041 528 68 63; www.sanfrancescodeldeserto.it; Isola di San Francesco del Deserto; donations appreciated; ⏱9-11am & 3-5pm Tue-Sun) FREE. Otherwise you can rent your own vessel with CBV (Classic Boats Venice; ☎041 523 67 20; www.classicboatsvenice.com; Isola della Certosa; 1/2/3/4/8hr rental €80/130/180/225/295; ⏱9am-7pm Apr-Feb; ⛴Certosa) 🚣 or Brussa Is Boat (Map p385; ☎041 71 57 87; www.brussaisboat.it; Fondamenta Labia 331; 7m boat per hr/day incl fuel €43/196; ⏱7.30am-5.30pm Mon-Fri, to 12.30pm Sat & Sun; ⛴Ferrovia) and go it alone. If you don't mind working up a sweat, both Venice Kayak (☎346 4771327; www.venicekayak. com; Vento di Venezia, Isola della Certosa; half-/full-day tours €95/125) and SUP in Venice (Map p385; ☎389 9851866; www.supinvenice.com; Fondamenta Contarini 3535; tours from €70; ⏱Apr-Oct; ⛴Orto) also offer lagoon excursions.

Cannaregio

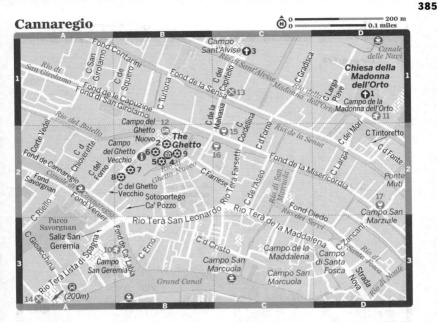

amateur photographers preparing to bound into Burano's backstreets, snapping away at pea-green stockings hung to dry between hot-pink and royal-blue houses.

Burano is famed for its handmade lace, which once graced the décolletage and ruffs of European aristocracy. Unfortunately, the ornate styles and expensive tablewear fell out of vogue in lean post-WWII times and the industry has since suffered a decline. Some women still maintain the traditions, but few production houses remain; with a couple of notable exceptions, most of the lace for sale in local shops is of the imported, machine-made variety.

If you fancy a stroll, hop across the 60m bridge to Burano's even quieter sister island, Mazzorbo. Little more than a broad grassy knoll, Mazzorbo is a great place for a picnic or a long, lazy lunch. Line 12 also stops at Mazzorbo, and line 9 runs a shuttle between Burano and Torcello.

◉ Torcello

On the pastoral island of Torcello, sheep vastly outnumber the 14 or so human residents. This bucolic backwater was once a Byzantine metropolis of 20,000, but rivalry with its offshoot Venice and a succession of malaria epidemics systematically reduced its population. Of its original nine churches and two abbeys,

all that remain are the Basilica di Santa Maria Assunta and the 11th-century Chiesa di Santa Fosca (Piazza Torcello; ⊙10am-4.30pm;

Castello

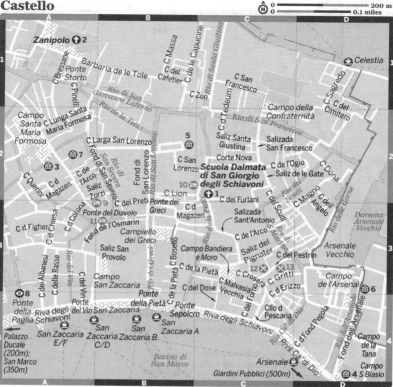

Castello

⬛Torcello) **FREE**. Not all line 12 *vaporetto* services stop at Torcello, but those that do provide a direct link to Burano, Mazzorbo, Murano and Fondamente Nove. The more frequent line 9 shuttles to and from Burano.

★ **Basilica di Santa Maria Assunta** CHURCH
(📞041 73 01 19; Piazza Torcello; adult/reduced €5/4, incl museum & campanile €12/10; ⏰10.30am-5.30pm; ⬛Torcello) Life choices are presented in no uncertain terms in the dazzling mosaics of the Assumption Basilica. Look ahead to a golden afterlife amid saints and a beatific Madonna and Child, or turn your back on them and face the wrath of the devil gloating over lost souls in an extraordinary *Last Judgment* scene. In existence since the 7th century, this former cathedral is the lagoon's oldest Byzantine-Romanesque structure.

Museo di Torcello MUSEUM
(📞041 73 07 61; www.museoditorcello.provincia.venezia.it; Piazza Torcello; adult/reduced €3/1.50, incl basilica €8/6; ⏰10.30am-5.30pm Tue-Sun;

⊡ Torcello) Occupying two buildings across the square from the Basilica di Santa Maria Assunta, this museum is dedicated to Torcello's venerable history. The main building, the 13th-century Palazzo del Consiglio, displays mainly religious art recovered from the island's many long-lost churches. The annexe focuses on ancient archaeological treasures, many of which were discovered in the abandoned Roman city of Altinum (Altino) on the mainland. The collection includes tiny Egyptian figurines, Etruscan bronzes, Greek pottery and some lovely Roman cameos.

☞ Tours

★ Best Venice Guides
TOURS

(http://bestveniceguides.it; per hr €65-85) Visiting Venice with a guide opens your eyes to the city's personal stories and secrets, as well as its extraordinary art, architecture and environment. Whatever your interests, find your ideal guide or tour at this one-stop shop, which features the city's most highly qualified guides. If you have special needs, you can contact them and they'll advise you on suitable itineraries.

★ Row Venice
BOATING

(Map p370; ☏347 7250637; www.rowvenice.org; Fondamenta Contarini; 90min lessons per 1-2 people €85, 3/4 people 120/140; ⊡Orto) The next best thing to walking on water is rowing a traditional *batellina coda di gambero* (shrimp-tailed boat) standing up as gondoliers do. Tours must be pre-booked, and commence at the Sacca Misericordia boat marina. After you've found your sea legs, try out the bar-hopping Cichetto Row (two/four people €240/280) or the fantastically atmospheric evening row on the Grand Canal (€180).

🎊 Festivals & Events

★ La Biennale di Venezia
ART

(www.labiennale.org; Giardini della Biennale; ⊘mid-May–Nov; ⊡Giardini Biennale) Europe's premier arts showcase since 1907 is something of a misnomer: the Biennale is now actually held every year, but the spotlight alternates between art (odd-numbered years) and architecture (even-numbered years). Running alongside the main events are annual showcases of dance, theatre, cinema and music.

Regata Storica
CULTURAL

(www.regatastoricavenezia.it; ⊘Sep) Sixteenth-century costumes, eight-oared gondolas and ceremonial barques feature in this historical procession (usually held in early September) along the Grand Canal, which re-enacts the arrival of the Queen of Cyprus and precedes gondola races.

🛏 Sleeping

Although Venice is a small city, getting around it amid tourist crowds and on slow *vaporetti* (small passenger ferries) can take time, so plan where you stay carefully. Easy access to the Grand Canal or a convenient *vaporetto* stop is key, although San Marco has all the best sights, and *sestieri* such as Dorsoduro, Cannaregio and Castello have all the best restaurants and bars. For those on a budget, Giudecca, Murano and the Lido are all within 15 to 30 minutes of the Rialto and are cheaper, quieter and more authentically Venetian.

🛏 San Marco

★ Locanda Fiorita
BOUTIQUE HOTEL €€

(Map p374; ☏041 523 47 54; www.locandafiorita.com; Campiello Novo 3457a; d €80-180; ❄🛜; ⊡ San Samuele) Few budget digs can match this smart 10-room hotel with flower-draped terraces and dreamy views of Chiesa di Santo Stefano from its rooms. Petite bedrooms offer a chic, updated take on Venetian style, with Rubelli-style fabrics and period furnishings. Room 10 has a private terrace. Head out for *aperitivo* on the roof terrace of adjoining B&B Bloom (same management) and breakfast in Campiello Novo.

B&B Al Teatro
B&B €€

(Map p374; ☏333 9182494; www.bedandbreakfastalteatro.com; Fondamenta de la Fenice 2554; d from €170; 🛜; ⊡Giglio) With La Fenice opera house for your neighbour and a chorus of singing *gondolieri* passing beneath your windows, you'll need to book early to nab one of the three rooms in Eleonora's 15th-century family home. Inside, old-world elegance meets a minimalist style with white linen and Murano chandeliers. Eleonora hosts breakfast every morning, sharing recommendations over freshly brewed coffee.

★ Gritti Palace
HOTEL €€€

(Map p374; ☏041 79 46 11; www.thegrittipalace.com; Campo di Santa Maria del Giglio 2467; r from €874; ❄🛜; ⊡Giglio) Guests at the Gritti Palace on the Grand Canal don't need to leave their balconies to sightsee. This landmark 1525 doge's palace features Grand Canal rooms with Rubelli silk damask lining, antique fainting couches, stucco ceilings, hand-painted vanities and bathrooms sheathed in rare marble.

★ **Rosa Salva Hotel** BOUTIQUE HOTEL €€€
(Map p374; 📞 041 241 33 23; www.rosasalvaho
tel.it; Calle Fiubera 951; d from €205; 🕸🛜; 🚇San
Marco) Run by the same family as the well-
regarded Rosa Salva pastry shop next door,
this high-standard hotel features contemporary rooms the colour of a good cappuccino,
finished with beautiful parquet floors, large
beds with coil-spring mattresses, luxe drapes
and large wardrobes. Service is highly personal, and breakfast includes a selection of
divine pastries from its cafe next door.

★ **Corte di Gabriela** HOTEL €€€
(Map p374; 📞 041 523 50 77; www.cortedigabriela
.com; Calle dei Avvocati 3836; r from €300; 🕸🛜;
🚇Sant'Angelo) This is a 19th-century *palazzo*,
but there's nothing traditional about its 11
rooms, which inventively play with the palace's historic features. Frescoed ceilings and
terrazzo floors meet with contemporary design pieces, high-spec gadgets and a modern
colour palette. The central wisteria-draped
courtyard is super romantic and the lavish
breakfast is one of the best in Venice.

★ **Novecento** BOUTIQUE HOTEL €€€
(Map p374; 📞 041 241 37 65; www.novecento.
biz; Calle del Dose 2683/84; d from €190; 🕸🛜;
🚇Giglio) Run by the Romanelli family for
more than 50 years, this hotel is a home
away from home. Nine individually designed rooms are inspired by designer Mario
Fortuny and come finished with Turkish kil-
im pillows, velvet draperies and carved bedsteads. You can mingle with creative fellow
travellers around the honesty bar, while the
garden is a lovely spot in which to linger
over breakfast.

ℹ BOOKING SERVICES

Luxrest Venice (Map p378; 📞 041 296
05 61; www.luxrest-venice.com; Ponte del
Pistor 5990, Castello) Carefully curated,
hand-picked selection of apartments.

Venice Prestige (www.veniceprestige.
com) Venetian apartments to rent in
aristocratic palaces in the best locations
in town.

Views on Venice (📞 041 241 11 49; www.
viewsonvenice.com) Apartments picked
for their personality, character and view,
of course.

Fairbnb Venice (https://fairbnb.
coop/venice) A community-powered
home-sharing platform where 50% of
booking fees support local projects.

🛏 Dorsoduro

★ **Hotel Nani
Mocenigo Palace** HERITAGE HOTEL €€€
(Map p374; 📞041 520 01 45; www.hotelnani
mocenigo.com; Fondamenta Nani 960; s/d from
€163/200; 🕸🛜; 🚇Accademia) Live like a
doge in a 15th-century Venetian-Gothic palace that once belonged to one of the most
famous of them: Agostino Barbarigo, who
was responsible for commissioning some of
the most significant buildings on Piazza San
Marco. This gorgeous hotel, just steps from
the Accademia, offers a variety of tastefully
furnished rooms and charming communal
spaces, including a hidden garden.

🛏 San Polo & Santa Croce

★ **Ca' Barba** B&B €
(Map p378; 📞328 2144979; www.cabarba.com;
Calle Ca' Michiel 1825; r/ste/apt from €106/123/166;
🕸🛜; 🚇Rialto Mercato) Hidden down a quiet
lane just around the corner from Rialto Market, this B&B offers exceptionally good value
with four spacious rooms with wooden ceiling beams, black-and-white Venice photographs, modern bathrooms, coffee machines
and huge smart TVs. A breakfast basket is
delivered to the room every day. Host Alessandro is a good source of advice, even loan-
ing out Venice-themed books.

★ **Al Ponte Mocenigo** HERITAGE HOTEL €€
(Map p378; 📞041 524 47 97; www.alpontemoc
enigo.com; Fondamenta Rimpetto Mocenigo 2063;
r €144-191; 🕸🛜; 🚇San Stae) A doge of a deal
near the Grand Canal, this historic *palazzo*
is just steps from the San Stae *vaporetto*
stop. Reached via a petite bridge, this little oasis offers elegant guest rooms, some
with Murano chandeliers illuminating high
wood-beamed ceilings, four-poster beds,
gilt-edged armoires and salon seating. Ask
for a room overlooking either Rio San Stae
or the courtyard.

★ **Il Giardino di Giulia** B&B €€
(Map p378; 📞041 200 77 86; www.ilgiardinodi
giulia.com; Salizada de la Chiesa 965; s/d €70/120;
🕸🛜; 🚇Riva de Biasio) The three atmospheric
guest rooms at the bottom of this tower-like
house have wooden beams and antique furniture, and each has its own theme: maritime, rock music or Italian actor Marcello
Mastroianni. It's a reflection of the personality of charming, chatty owner Marco Bu-
setto, who also happens to serve some of the
best B&B breakfasts in Venice.

⭐ Hotel Canal Grande   HERITAGE HOTEL €€€

(Map p370; ☑ 041 244 01 48; www.hotelcanal grande.it; Campo San Simeon Grande 932; s/d/ ste from €208/215/288; ❄ 🛜; 🚤 Riva de Biasio) The 24 sumptuous rooms are split between a Grand Canal *palazzo* and a humbler building a few doors down, but both swirl with old Venetian glamour. There are canopy beds, damask wall claddings, Murano sconces, and even the TVs are cunningly hidden within gilded Venetian mirrors. Breakfasts are served on a deck jutting romantically over the canal.

🛏 Cannaregio

⭐ Locanda Ca' Le Vele   B&B €€

(Map p378; ☑ 041 241 39 60; www.locandalevele. com; Calle de le Vele 3969; d €122-148, ste €165-183; ❄🛜; 🚤 Ca' d'Oro) The lane may be quiet and the house may look demure but inside it's Venetian glam all the way. The six guest rooms are a surprisingly stylish riot of terrazzo floors, damask furnishings, Murano glass sconces and ornate gilded beds with busy covers. Pay a little extra for a canal view.

⭐ Giardino dei Melograni   HOTEL €€

(Map p385; ☑ 041 822 61 31; www.pardesrimonim. net; Campo del Ghetto Nuovo 2874; d €160-200, tr €230-260; ⏱Feb-Dec; ❄🛜; 🚤 Guglie) Run by Venice's Jewish community, to which all proceeds go, the 'Garden of Pomegranates' is a sparkling kosher residence. You don't have to be Jewish to enjoy the 20 modern rooms, with artwork themed around local plants. Some have canal views while others face the *campo* (square). Families may prefer the brand-new one- and three-bedroom apartments, also located in the Ghetto.

🛏 Castello

⭐ Ai Tagliapietra   B&B €

(Map p386; www.aitagliapietra.com; Salita Zorzi 4943; s €70, d €75-110; 🛜; 🚤 San Zaccaria) Ai Tagliapietra is exactly what a B&B should be: well located, welcoming, unpretentious, comfortable and very reasonably priced. This is all down to excellent host Lorenzo, who knows what travellers need and is on hand to supply good coffee, fresh breakfasts and excellent recommendations. There are only three simple, but smart, rooms so book early to avoid disappointment.

B&B San Marco   B&B €

(Map p386; ☑ 041 522 75 89; www.realvenice. it; Fondamente San Giorgio dei Schiavoni 3385I; r €135, without bathroom €105-135; ❄; 🚤 San Zac-

caria) Alice and Marco welcome you warmly to their home overlooking Carpaccio's frescoed Scuola Dalmata. The 3rd-floor apartment (no lift), with its parquet floors and large windows, is furnished with family antiques and offers photogenic views over the terracotta rooftops and canals. The hosts live upstairs, so they're always on hand with great recommendations.

⭐ Residenza de L'Osmarin   B&B €€

(Map p386; ☑ 347 4501440; www.residenza delosmarin.com; Calle Rota 4960; d €170-250; ❄🛜; 🚤 San Zaccaria) This B&B is good value, especially considering it is barely 300m from Piazza San Marco. Rooms – one with a roof terrace and another with a courtyard-facing terrace – are quaintly decorated with quilted bedspreads, painted wardrobes and period furnishings. The hosts make guests feel welcome with slap-up breakfasts of homemade cakes, brioche and platters of ham and cheese.

🛏 Murano

⭐ Villa Lina   B&B €€

(☑041 73 90 36; www.villalinavenezia.com; Calle Dietro gli Orti 12, Murano; r from €160; ❄🛜; 🚤Colonna) Finding 16th-century Villa Lina in the grounds of the Nason Moretti glassworks is like chancing upon a wonderful secret. The home of Carlo Nason and his wife Evi has a mod 1950s vibe and is scattered with Carlo's glass designs. Bedrooms are large, comfortable and contemporary, and the flower-filled garden backs on to the Serenella Canal.

⭐ Murano Palace   HOTEL €€

(☑ 041 73 96 55; www.muranopalace.com; Ramo dei Vetrai 77, Murano; r €110-195; ❄🛜; 🚤Faro) Come here for designer fabulousness at an outlet price. Jewel-toned colour schemes and (naturally) Murano glass chandeliers illuminate high-ceilinged, wooden-floored rooms, and there are free drinks and snacks in the minibar. Expect canal views and unparalleled art-glass shopping in the vicinity, but an eerie calm descends once the shops close around 6pm.

🍴 Eating

🍴 San Marco

⭐ Suso   GELATO €

(Map p378; ☑ 348 5646545; www.gelatoven ezia.it; Calle de la Bissa 5453; scoops €1.60; ⏱10am-midnight; 🚤Rialto) 🌿 Suso's gelati are locally made and free of artificial colours.

Indulge in rich, original seasonal flavours such as marscapone cream with fig sauce and walnuts. Gluten-free cones are available.

★**Ristorante Quadri** ITALIAN €€€
(Map p374; ☑ 041 522 21 05; www.alajmo.it; Piazza San Marco 121; meals €140-225; ⊙12.30-2.30pm & 7.30-10.30pm Tue-Sun; ⚓San Marco) When it comes to Venetian glamour, nothing beats this historic Michelin-starred restaurant overlooking Piazza San Marco. A small swarm of servers greets you as you're shown to your table in a room decked out with silk damask, gilt, painted beams and Murano chandeliers. Dishes are precise and delicious, deftly incorporating Venetian touches into an inventive modern Italian menu.

✕ Dorsoduro

★**Cantine del Vino già Schiavi** VENETIAN €
(Map p374; ☑ 041 523 00 34; www.cantinaschiavi .com; Fondamenta Priuli 992; cicheti €1.50; ⊙8.30am-8.30pm Mon-Sat; ⚓Zattere) It may look like a wine shop and function as a bar, but this legendary canalside spot also serves the best *cicheti* (Venetian tapas) on this side of the Grand Canal. Choose from the impressive counter selection or ask for a filled-to-order roll. Chaos cheerfully prevails, with an eclectic cast of locals propping up the bar.

★**Osteria Bakán** ITALIAN €€
(Map p370; ☑ 041 564 76 58; Corte Maggiore 2314a; meals €36-44; ⊙8am-3pm & 6-10pm Wed-Mon; ⚓Santa Marta) A strange mix of local drinking den and surprisingly adventurous restaurant, Bakán has bucketloads of atmosphere – with old beams and soft jazz inside, and tables on a tucked-away courtyard. The homemade pasta is excellent, or you could opt for the likes of *guance di vitello* (veal cheeks) or ginger prawns with pilaf rice.

★**Riviera** ITALIAN €€€
(Map p370; ☑ 041 522 76 21; www.ristoranteriviera. it; Fondamenta Zattere al Ponte Lungo 1473; meals €67-157; ⊙12.30-3pm & 7-10.30pm Fri-Tue; ⚓Zattere) A former rock musician, GP Cremonini now focuses his considerable talents on ensuring his top-end restaurant – Dorsoduro's finest – delivers exemplary service and perfectly cooked seafood: think homemade pasta with scallops or sea-bass poached with prawns. The setting, overlooking the Giudecca Canal, is similarly spectacular. For serious gourmands, the 11-course tasting menu (€150) with wine pairings (€55) is an unmissable experience.

✕ San Polo & Santa Croce

★**Osteria Trefanti** VENETIAN €€
(Map p378; ☑ 041 520 17 89; www.osteriatre fanti.it; Fondamenta del Rio Marin o dei Garzoti 888; meals €40-45; ⊙noon-2.30pm & 7-10.30pm Tue-Sun; 📷; ⚓Riva de Biasio) La Serenissima's spice trade lives on at simple, elegant Trefanti, where gnocchi might get an intriguing kick from cinnamon, and turbot is flavoured with almond and coconut. Seafood is the focus; try the 'doge's fettucine', with mussels, scampi and clams. Furnished with recycled copper lamps, the space is small and deservedly popular – so book ahead.

★**Zanze XVI** VENETIAN €€€
(Trattoria dalla Zanze; Map p370; ☑ 041 71 53 94; www.zanze.it; Fondamenta dei Tolentini 231; lunch set menu €25, meals €46-51; ⊙12.30-2.30pm & 7.30-10.30pm Sun & Tue-Fri, 7.30-10.30pm Sat; 🌸; ⚓Piazzale Roma) These sophisticated culinary adventurers offer a contemporary spin on Venetian traditions. Opt for a 'surprise' five-course *mare* (seafood; €70) or *terra* (meat and local produce; €50) menu, or leap straight into the eight-course 'soul' menu (€80). If you've got trust issues or a fussy dining partner, there are à la carte options too. The two-course set lunches include coffee.

★**Glam** VENETIAN €€€
(Map p378; ☑ 041 523 56 76; www.enricobarto lini.net; Calle Tron 1961; meals €108-168; ⊙12.30-2.30pm & 7.30-10.30pm; ⚓San Stae) Step out of your water taxi into the canalside garden of this inventive Michelin-starred restaurant in the Hotel Palazzo Venart. The contemporary menu focuses on local ingredients, pepping up Veneto favourites with unusual spices that would once have graced the tables of this trade-route city. The service and the wine list are equally impressive.

✕ Cannaregio

★**Pasticceria Dal Mas** BAKERY €
(Map p385; ☑ 041 71 51 01; www.dalmaspasticce ria.it; Rio Terà Lista di Spagna 150; pastries €1.30-6.50; ⊙7am-9pm; 📷; ⚓Ferrovia) This historic Venetian bakery-cafe sparkles with mirrors, marble and metal trim, fitting for the pastries displayed within. Despite the perpetual morning crush, the efficient team dispenses top-notch coffee and *cornetti* (Italian-style croissants) with admirable equanimity. Come mid-morning for mouthwatering, still-warm quiches. The hot chocolate is also exceptional – hardly surprising given the sibling chocolate shop next door.

★ Anice Stellato
VENETIAN €€

(Map p385; ☑ 041 72 07 44; www.osterianice stellato.com; Fondamenta de la Sensa 3272; meals €40-50; ☉ 12.15-2pm & 7.15-10pm Tue-Sat; ⬛ Sant'Alvise) Tin lamps, unadorned rustic tables and a small wooden bar set the scene for quality seafood and other Venetian specialities at this excellent canalside *bacaro* (bar). You can munch on *cicheti* or go for the full menu and swoon over mantis shrimps with pomegranate puree; market-fresh fish; or guinea fowl, radicchio and a decadent port sauce. Reservations recommended.

★ Osteria Boccadoro
VENETIAN €€€

(Map p378; ☑ 041 521 10 21; www.boccadoroven ezia.it; Campiello Widmann 5405a; meals €40-55; ☉ noon-3pm & 7-11pm Tue-Sun; ⬛ Fondamente Nove) The sweetly singing birds in this *campo* (square) are probably angling for your leftovers, but they don't stand a chance. Chef-owner Luciano and son Simone's creative *crudi* (raw seafood) are two-bite delights, and cloud-like gnocchi and homemade pasta are gone too soon. Fish is sourced from the lagoon or the Adriatic, and vegetables come from the restaurant's kitchen garden.

✖ Castello

★ Salvmeria
VENETIAN €

(Map p370; ☑ 041 523 39 71; www.salvmeria.com; Via Garibaldi 1769; meals €15-25; ☉ 10am-11pm Tue-Sun; ⬛ Arsenale) Fashioned from an old deli, Marco Ginepri's cool *cichetteria* serves accomplished food and excellent Veneto wines by the glass. Gourmet *cicheti* include fluffy *baccalá* (cod) on polenta, marinated shrimps and Fassone beef with peppers, while main plates include succulent tuna in a sesame crust, warm potato salad with radicchio and belly-warming fish lasagne. Trust them to recommend interesting wine pairings.

★ CoVino
VENETIAN €€

(Map p386; ☑ 041 241 27 05; www.covinovenezia. com; Calle del Pestrin 3829; fixed-price menu lunch €27-38, dinner €40; ☉ 12.45-2.30pm & 7pm-midnight Thu-Mon; ☎; ⬛ Arsenale) Tiny CoVino has only 14 seats but demonstrates bags of ambition with its inventive, seasonal menu inspired by the Venetian terroir. Speciality products are selected from Slow Food Foundation producers, and the charming waiters make enthusiastic recommendations from the wine list. Only a three-course set menu is available at dinner; however, you can choose from two fixed-price options at lunch.

★ Trattoria Corte Sconta
VENETIAN €€€

(Map p386; ☑ 041 522 70 24; www.cortesconta venezia.it; Calle del Pestrin 3886; meals €45-55; ☉ 12.30-2pm & 7-9.30pm Tue-Sat, closed Jan & Aug; ✳ ✍; ⬛ Arsenale) Well-informed visitors and celebrating locals seek out this vine-covered *corte sconta* (hidden courtyard) for its trademark seafood antipasti and imaginative house-made pasta. Inventive flavour pairings transform the classics: clams zing with ginger; prawn and courgette linguine is recast with an earthy dash of saffron; and the roast eel loops like the Brenta river in a drizzle of balsamic reduction.

✖ Giudecca

★ La Palanca
VENETIAN €€

(Map p370; ☑ 041 528 77 19; www.facebook.com/ LaPalancaGiudecca; Fondamenta Sant'Eufemia 448, Giudecca; meals €24-40; ☉ 7am-8.30pm Mon-Sat; ☎ ✍; ⬛ Palanca) Locals of all ages pour into this humble bar for *cicheti,* coffee and a *spritz.* However, it's at lunchtime that it really comes into its own, serving surprisingly sophisticated fare like swordfish carpaccio with orange zest alongside more rustic dishes, such as a delicious *pasta e fagioli* (pasta and bean soup). In summer, competition for waterside tables is stiff.

★ Trattoria ai Cacciatori
VENETIAN €€

(Map p370; ☑ 328 7363346; www.aicacciatori. it; Fondamenta del Ponte Piccolo 320, Giudecca; meals €34-47; ☉ noon-3pm & 6.30-10pm Tue-Sun; ☎; ⬛ Palanca) If you hadn't guessed from the oversized gun hanging from the ceiling beams, the restaurant is named for the hunters who once bagged lagoon waterfowl. Dishes are hearty but sophisticated, including both game and local seafood.

★ Trattoria Altanella
VENETIAN €€

(Map p370; ☑ 041 522 77 80; Calle de le Erbe 268, Giudecca; meals €41-46; ☉ 12.30-2pm & 7.30-9pm Wed-Sun; ✳; ⬛ Redentore) Founded by fisherfolk in 1920 and still run by the same family, this cosy restaurant serves classic Venetian fare such as potato gnocchi with cuttlefish, stuffed squid and perfectly grilled fish. The vintage interior is hung with paintings, reflecting the restaurant's popularity with local artists, and there are also tables on a flower-fringed balcony jutting out over the canal.

✖ Burano & Mazzorbo

★ Trattoria Maddalena
VENETIAN €€

(☑ 041 73 01 51; www.trattoriamaddalena.com; Fondamenta di Santa Caterina 7b, Mazzorbo; meals

€26-46; ⊘noon-3pm & 7-9pm Fri-Wed; ⊛Mazzorbo) Just a footbridge away from Burano's photo-snapping crowds, this pretty Mazzorbo restaurant is a great place for a lazy seafood lunch. Relax by the canal or in the garden out the back, sampling fresh fish dishes and, during autumn hunting season, the signature pasta with wild-duck *ragù* (meat and tomato sauce). It pays to call ahead, as the hours are sporadic in the low season.

★ **Trattoria al Gatto Nero**　　VENETIAN €€€
(☑041 73 01 20; www.gattonero.com; Fondamenta della Giudecca 88, Burano; meals €42-70; ⊘12.30-3pm & 7.30-9pm Tue-Sun; ⊛Burano) Don't expect fancy tricks from this 'Black Cat' – just excellent, traditional fare. Once you've tried the homemade *tagliolini* (ribbon pasta) with spider crab, whole grilled fish and perfect house-baked biscuits, the ferry ride to Burano seems a minor inconvenience – a swim back here from Venice would be worth it for the mixed seafood grill alone. Call ahead and plead for canalside seating.

🍷 Drinking & Nightlife

★ **Vino Vero**　　WINE BAR
(Map p385; ☑041 275 00 44; www.facebook.com/vinoverovenezia; Fondamenta de la Misericordia 2497; ⊘noon-midnight Tue-Sun, from 5pm Mon; ⊛San Marcuola) Lining the exposed-brick walls of this canalside bar are small-production wines, including a great selection of natural and biodynamic labels. The *cicheti* here lift this place above the ordinary, with arguably the best selection of *crostini* (open-face sandwiches) in the city, including wild-boar sausage with aubergine and baba ganoush topped with prosciutto.

★ **Bar Longhi**　　COCKTAIL BAR
(Map p374; ☑041 79 47 81; www.hotelgrittipalacevenice.com; Campo di Santa Maria del Giglio 2467; ⊘11am-1am; ⊛Giglio) Gritti Palace's beautiful Bar Longhi may be pricey, but if you consider your surrounds – Fortuny fabrics, an intarsia marble bar, 18th-century mirrors and million-dollar Piero Longhi paintings – the price of a signature orange martini starts to seem reasonable. In summer you'll have to choose between the twinkling interior and a spectacular Grand Canal terrace.

★ **Malvasia all'Adriatico Mar**　　WINE BAR
(Map p370; ☑041 476 43 22; www.facebook.com/MalvasiaAdriaticoMar; Calle Crosera 3771; ⊘5-10pm Mon, 10am-10pm Tue-Sun; ⊛San Tomà) Wine lovers should stake out a place in this small, upmarket and extremely welcoming bar and let owner Francesco guide them through the range of naturally produced regional wines. Bar snacks include delicious cheeses and meats on tasty bread. Squeeze onto the tiny deck in the warmer months and watch the gondolas go by.

★ **Marciano Pub**　　PUB
(Map p385; ☑041 47 62 55; www.facebook.com/marcianopubvenezia; Calle Gheltof o Loredan 1863c; ⊘5pm-1am Fri-Wed; ⊛San Marcuola) With its wooden bar and gleaming brass beer taps, this Anglo-Venetian hostelry certainly looks authentic. Marciano takes booze seriously, stocking craft beers from around the globe, including its own brew. The same goes for the food menu of sustainably sourced burgers (€12 to €16) and steaks, including kangaroo and ostrich. There's also an oyster bar and dedicated cocktail area.

★ **Al Timon**　　WINE BAR
(Map p385; ☑041 524 60 66; www.altimon.it; Fondamenta dei Ormesini 2754; ⊘5pm-1am; ⊛San Marcuola) Find a spot in the wood-lined interior or, in summer, on the boat moored out the front along the canal, and watch the motley parade of drinkers and dreamers arrive for steak platters and quality wines by the *ombra* (half-glass) or carafe. Musicians play sets canalside when the weather obliges.

★ **Caffè Florian**　　CAFE
(Map p374; ☑041 520 56 41; www.caffeflorian.com; Piazza San Marco 57; ⊘9am-midnight Apr-Oct, shorter hours in winter; ⊛San Marco) The oldest still-operating cafe in Europe and one of the first to welcome women, Florian maintains rituals (if not prices) established in 1720: besuited waiters serve cappuccino on silver trays; lovers get cosy on plush banquettes; and the orchestra strikes up as the sunset illuminates San Marco's mosaics. Piazza seating during concerts costs €6 extra, but dreamy-eyed romantics will hardly notice.

★ **Grancaffè Quadri**　　CAFE
(Map p374; ☑041 522 21 05; www.alajmo.it; Piazza San Marco 121; ⊘9am-midnight; ⊛San Marco) Powdered wigs seem appropriate inside this baroque bar-cafe that's been serving happy hours since 1638. During Carnevale, costumed Quadri revellers party like it's 1699 – despite prices shooting up to €15 for a *spritz*. Grab a seat on the piazza to watch the best show in town: the basilica's golden mosaics ablaze in the sunset.

★ **Il Mercante**　　COCKTAIL BAR
(Map p378; ☑041 476 73 05; www.ilmercantevenezia.com; Campo dei Frari 2564; ⊘6pm-1am; ⊛San Tomà) An hour's changeover is all it takes for

historic **Caffè dei Frari** (⊙9am-5pm) to transform itself into its night-time guise as Venice's best cocktail bar. If you can't find anything that takes your fancy on the adventurous themed cocktail list, the expert bar team will create something to suit your mood. In winter, snuggle on a velvet sofa upstairs.

⭐ **Cantina Do Spade**   WINE BAR
(Map p378; ☑041 521 05 83; www.cantinado spade.com; Sotoportego de le Do Spade 860; ⊙10am-3pm & 6-10pm Wed-Mon, 6-10pm Tue; 🛜; 🚤Rialto Mercato) Famously mentioned in Casanova's memoirs, cosy 'Two Spades' was founded in 1488 and continues to keep Venice in good spirits with its bargain Tri-Veneto and Istrian wines and young, laid-back management. Come early for the market-fresh *fritture* (fried battered seafood) and grilled squid, or linger longer with satisfying, sit-down dishes such as *bigoli in salsa* (pasta in anchovy and onion sauce).

⭐ Entertainment

Teatro Goldoni   THEATRE
(Map p378; ☑041 240 20 14; www.teatrostabile veneto.it; Calle del Teatro 4650b; 🚤Rialto) Named after the city's great playwright, Carlo Goldoni, Venice's main theatre has an impressive dramatic range that runs from Goldoni's comedy to Shakespearean tragedy (mostly in Italian), plus ballets and concerts. Don't be fooled by the huge 20th-century bronze doors: this venerable theatre dates from 1622, and the jewel-box interior seats just 800.

Musica a Palazzo   OPERA
(Map p374; ☑340 9717272; www.musicapalazzo. com; Palazzo Barbarigo Minotto, Fondamenta Duodo o Barbarigo 2504; tickets incl beverage €85; ⊙from 8pm; 🚤Giglio) Hang onto your prosecco and brace for impact: in historic salons the soprano's high notes imperil glassware, and thundering baritones reverberate through inlaid floors. During performances of opera from Verdi or Rossini, the drama progresses from receiving-room overtures to parlour duets overlooking the Grand Canal, followed by second acts in the Tiepolo-ceilinged dining room and bedroom grand finales.

🛍 Shopping

⭐ **ElleElle**   GLASS
(☑041 527 48 66; www.elleellemurano.com; Fondamenta Manin 52, Murano; ⊙10.30am-6pm; 🚤Faro) Nason Moretti has been making modernist magic happen in glass since the 1950s, and the third-generation glass designers are in fine form in this showroom. Everything is

signed, including an exquisite (and expensive) range of hand-blown drinking glasses, jugs, bowls, vases, tealight holders, decanters and lamps.

⭐ **Cesare Toffolo**   GLASS
(☑041 73 64 60; www.toffolo.com; Fondamenta dei Vetrai 37, Murano; ⊙10am-6pm; 🚤Colonna) Mind-boggling miniatures are the trademarks of this Murano glass-blower, but you'll also find some dramatic departures: chiselled cobalt-blue vases, glossy black candlesticks that look like minarets, and drinking glasses so fine that they seem to be made out of air.

⭐ **Vittorio Costantini**   GLASS
(Map p370; ☑041 522 22 65; www.vittoriocostan tini.com; Calle del Fumo 5311; ⊙9.30am-1pm & 2.15-5.30pm Mon-Fri; 🚤Fondamente Nove) Kids and adults alike are thrilled at the magical, miniature insects, butterflies, shells and birds that Vittorio Costantini fashions out of glass using a lampwork technique. Some of the iridescent beetles have bodies made of 21 segments that need to be fused together with dazzling dexterity and speed.

⭐ **Chiarastella Cattana**   HOMEWARES
(Map p374; ☑041 522 43 69; www.chiarastella cattana.com; Salizada San Samuele 3216; ⊙11am-1pm & 3-7pm Mon-Sat; 🚤San Samuele) Transform any home with these locally woven, strikingly original Venetian linens. Whimsical cushions feature chubby purple rhinoceroses and grumpy scarlet elephants straight out of Pietro Longhi paintings, and hand-tasselled jacquard hand towels will dry your guests in style. Decorators and design aficionados should save an afternoon to consider dizzying woven-to-order napkin and curtain options.

⭐ **Feelin' Venice**   DESIGN
(Map p378; ☑041 887 86 39; www.feelinvenice. com; Strada Nova 4194; ⊙9.30am-8pm; 🚤Ca' d'Oro) Tired of bemoaning the increasing number of tatty souvenir shops, Venetians Mattia and Filippo decided to open a design-led alternative featuring the work of local graphic artists. Their cool, contemporary designs adorn high-quality fabric totes, 100% organic cotton T-shirts, posters, notebooks and graphite pens. If you're looking for a memorable souvenir, this is the place.

⭐ **Process Collettivo**   GIFTS & SOUVENIRS
(Map p378; ☑041 524 31 25; www.rioteradeipen sieri.org; Fondamenta dei Frari 2559a; ⊙10am-8pm; 🚤San Tomà) 🖉 A nonprofit cooperative runs this little shop, selling goods made by inmates of Venice's prisons as part of a social

reintegration program. The toiletries are made from plants grown in the garden of the women's prison on Giudecca, while the very hip satchels and shoulder bags constructed from recycled advertising hoardings are made at the men's prison in Santa Croce.

★ **Libreria Linea d'Acqua** BOOKS (Map p374; ☑041 522 40 30; https://lineadacqua. it; Calle de la Mandola 3717d; ⊗9am-1pm & 3-7pm Mon-Fri, 10am-1pm Sat; ⬚Rialto) This beautiful store selling antiquarian books, first editions, maps, sculptures and engravings is much more than a shop: it's a guardian of Venice's soul. Owner Luca Zentilini is a scholar and artist, preserving books and publishing a line of beautifully illustrated and affordable titles on Venetian history, culture, art and food. Check out its online magazine, In Time (https://intimemagazine.com).

🛈 Information

MEDICAL SERVICES

First Aid Point Piazza San Marco (Procuratie Nuove 63/65, Piazza San Marco; ⊗8am-8pm) Dedicated to tourists, this well-equipped first-aid point performs diagnostics and minor surgery, and issues drug prescriptions and referrals for further hospital treatment.

First Aid Point Piazzale Roma (Piazzale Roma 496; ⊗8am-8pm; ⬚Piazzale Roma) Offers similar services to the San Marco first-aid point, including minor surgeries and drug prescriptions.

Guardia Medica (☑041 238 56 00) This service of night-time call-out doctors in Venice operates from 8pm to 8am on weekdays and from 10am the day before a holiday (including Sunday) until 8am the day after.

Ospedale dell'Angelo (☑041 965 71 11; www. ulss12.ve.it; Via Paccagnella 11, Mestre) Vast modern hospital on the mainland.

Ospedale SS Giovanni e Paolo (☑041 529 43 11; www.aulss3.veneto.it; Campo Zanipolo 6777; ⬚Ospedale) Venice's main hospital; provides emergency care and dental treatment. The entrance is on the water near the Ospedale *vaporetto* stop.

TOURIST INFORMATION

Vènezia Unica (☑041 24 24; www.venezia unica.it) runs tourist information services in Venice. It provides information on sights, itineraries, transport, special events and exhibitions. Discount passes can be prebooked online.

Piazzale Roma Garage ASM Tourist Office (Map p370; ☑041 24 24; Garage ASM, L1, Piazzale Roma 496u; ⊗7am-8pm; ⬚Piazzale Roma)

Piazzale Roma Tourist Office (Map p370; ☑041 24 24; ACTV office, Piazzale Roma;

⊗7am-8pm; ⬚Piazzale Roma Santa Chiara)

San Marco Tourist Office (Map p374; ☑041 24 24; Piazza San Marco 71f; ⊗9am-7pm; ⬚San Marco)

Stazione Santa Lucia Tourist Office (Map p370; ☑041 24 24; ⊗7am-9pm; ⬚Ferrovia)

🛈 Getting There & Away

AIR

Venice's main international airport, **Marco Polo Airport** (☑flight info 041 260 92 60; www.venice airport.it; Via Galileo Gallilei 30/1, Tessera), is located in Tessera, 12km east of Mestre.

Inside the terminal you'll find ticket offices for water taxis and Alilaguna water bus transfers, an ATM, currency exchange offices, a **left-luggage office** (first 6hr per item €6, thereafter per hr €0.30, bikes per 24hr €14; ⊗5am-9pm) and a **Vènezia Unica tourist office** (☑041 24 24; www. veneziaunica.it; ⊗8.30am-7pm), where you can pick up pre-ordered travel cards and a map.

BUS

Urban, regional and long-distance buses arrive at the **bus station** (Map p370) in Piazzale Roma, from where *vaporetti* connect with the rest of the city. You can search routes and buy tickets through the **daAaB app** (www.daaab.it). Services include:

ACTV (Azienda del Consorzio Trasporti Veneziano; ☑041 272 2111; http://actv.avmspa.it/ en) Venice's public-transport company. Runs buses to Mestre and surrounding areas. The main **ticket office** (www.actv.it; ⊗6.30am-8pm) is in Piazzale Roma.

ATVO (Map p370; ☑0421 59 46 71; www.atvo. it; Piazzale Roma 497g; ⊗6.40am-7.30pm; ⬚Piazzale Roma) Operates buses from Piazzale Roma to destinations all over the eastern Veneto, including airport connections.

Flixbus (www.flixbus.it; 📱) Operates a wide range of national and international routes in fuel-efficient buses. Book online and store tickets in the downloaded app.

CAR & MOTORCYCLE

To get to Venice by car or motorcycle, take the often-congested Trieste–Turin A4, which passes through Mestre. From Mestre, take the 'Venezia' exit. Once over Ponte della Libertà from Mestre, cars must be left at a car park in Piazzale Roma or on the Isola del Tronchetto. Be warned: you'll pay a hefty price in parking fees, and traffic backs up at weekends.

TRAIN

Direct intercity services operate out of Venice to most major Italian cities, as well as points in France, Germany, Austria, Switzerland, Slovenia and Croatia.

ⓘ Getting Around

TO/FROM THE AIRPORT
Bus

ACTV (☑ 041 272 2111; http://actv.avmspa. it/en) Runs bus 5 between Marco Polo Airport and Piazzale Roma (€8, 30 minutes, four per hour) with a limited number of stops en route. Alternatively, a bus+*vaporetto* ticket covering the bus journey and a one-way *vaporetto* trip within a total of 90 minutes costs €14.

ATVO (☑ 0421 59 46 71; www.atvo.it) Runs a direct bus service between the airport and **Piazzale Roma** (Map p370) (€8, 25 minutes, every 30 minutes from 8am to midnight). At Piazzale Roma you can pick up the ACTV *vaporetti* to reach locations around Venice.

Ferry

Alilaguna (☑ 041 240 17 01; www.alilaguna.it; airport transfer one-way €15) operates three water shuttles that link the airport with various parts of Venice at a cost of €8 to Murano and €15 to all other landing stages. Passengers are permitted one suitcase and one piece of hand luggage. All further bags are charged at €3 per piece. Expect it to take 45 to 90 minutes to reach most destinations; it takes approximately 1¼ hours to reach Piazza San Marco. Lines include the following:

Linea Blu (Blue Line) Stops at Murano, Fondamente Nove, the Lido, San Marco, the Stazione Marittima and points in-between.

Linea Rossa (Red Line) Stops at Murano, the Lido, San Marco, Giudecca and the Stazione Marittima.

Linea Arancia (Orange Line) Stops at Fondamente Nove and Guglie in Cannaregio, Rialto and San Marco via the Grand Canal.

Taxi

A taxi from the aiport to Piazzale Roma costs €40; the taxi rank (Map p370) is located by the bus station. From there you can either hop on a *vaporetto* or pick up a water taxi at the nearby Fondamente Cossetti.

Water Taxi

The dock for water transfers to the historic centre is a 10- to 15-minute walk from the arrivals hall, via a raised, indoor walkway accessed on the 1st floor of the terminal building. Luggage trolleys (requiring a €1 deposit) can be taken to the dock.

Private water taxis can be booked at the **Consorzio Motoscafi Venezia** (☑ 041 240 67 12; www.motoscafivenezia.it; ⊗ 9am-6pm Mon-Fri) or **Venezia Taxi** (☑ info 328 2389661; www.veneziataxi.it) desks in the arrivals hall, or directly at the dock. Private taxis cost from €110 for up to four passengers and all their luggage. Extra passengers (up to a limit of 12 or 16) carry a small surcharge.

ⓘ VAPORETTO PASSES

The ACTV Tourist Travel Cards allow for unlimited travel on *vaporetti* (small passenger ferries) and Lido buses within the following time blocks:

24 hours €20

48 hours €30

72 hours €40

One week €60

If you don't have a large group, there is also the option of a **Venice Shuttle**. This is a shared water taxi and costs from €25 per person with a €6 surcharge for night-time arrivals. Seats should be booked online at www.venicelink. com. Boats seat a maximum of eight people and accommodate up to 10 bags. Those opting for a shared taxi should be aware that the service can wait for some time to fill up and has set drop-off points in Venice; only private transfers will take you directly to your hotel.

GONDOLA

A gondola ride offers a view of Venice that is anything but pedestrian. Official daytime rates are €80 for 40 minutes (€100 for 40 minutes from 7pm to 8am), not including songs or tips. Additional time is charged in 20-minute increments (day/night €40/50). You may negotiate a price break in overcast weather or around noon. Agree on a price, time limit and singing in advance to avoid unexpected surcharges.

Gondolas cluster at *stazi* (stops) along the Grand Canal and near major monuments and tourist hotspots, but you can also book a pick-up by calling **Ente Gondola** (☑ 041 528 50 75; www.gondolavenezia.it).

Gondolas 4 All (Map p370; ☑ 328 2431382; www.gondolas4all.com; Fondamente Cossetti; per 30min €80; 🚹 Piazzale Roma), supported by the Gondoliers Association, offers gondola rides to wheelchair users in a specially adapted gondola. Embarkation is from a wheelchair-accessible pier at Piazzale Roma.

PUBLIC TRANSPORT

ACTV (☑ 041 272 2111; http://actv.avmspa.it/ en) runs all public transport in Venice, including the *vaporetto* (small passenger ferry) service. Although the service is efficient and punctual, boats on main lines fill up and are prone to overcrowding in peak season. One-way tickets cost €7.50.

To plan itineraries, check schedules and buy tickets download the useful *vaporetto* app **daAaB** (www.daaab.it). If you purchase tickets through the app, you can then scan your phone at the barriers in place of a ticket.

AROUND VENICE

Mestre

POP 183,000

Set on the mainland at the other end of the causeway from Venice, Mestre could hardly offer more of a contrast. Where Venice dazzles with history and extraordinary beauty, Mestre is modern and ordinary. Although there has been a town here since the Middle Ages, Mestre only really began to develop in the 1920s, when migrant workers flocked here to work in the nearby industrial complex of Porto Marghera. Then in the 1960s, as tourism took off in Venice, Venetians too crossed over to the mainland, abandoning their historic home for Mestre's modern amenities and car-filled streets.

Today Mestre still acts largely as a dormitory for workers in Venice, although increasingly tourists in search of cheap accommodation also bed down here. A modern museum and a slew of new designer hostels and hotels hope to improve the city's image, although it's unlikely such an unlovely suburb will ever compete with Venice.

◉ Sights

M9   MUSEUM
(Il Museo del Novecento; ☑ 041 238 72 30; www.m9digital.it; Via Pascoli 11; adult/reduced €14/10, incl temporary exhibit €16/13; ☉ 10am-7pm Wed-Fri & Mon, 11am-10pm Sat & Sun in summer, 9am-6pm Wed-Fri & Mon, 10am-7pm Sat & Sun in winter; ◻ 4/Mestre Centro) Aiming to put Mestre on the map, this multimedia museum tells the story of Italy in the 20th century through imaginative interactive exhibits involving film, photography, audio and virtual reality. Spreading across two floors, the exhibit moves mesmerised visitors through distinct spaces dealing with demographics, food, war, politics, crime, popular culture and much more. Although there are no physical artefacts, the displays are cleverly designed and absorbing.

🛏 Sleeping

Anda Hostel   HOSTEL €
(☑ 041 862 22 91; www.andavenice.com; Via Ortigara 10; dm beds €19-25, d €80-90; ❄ 🛜; ◻ 4/Mestre Stazione) A 2019 Hoscar's winner, this eight-storey, 769-bed buzzing design hostel is one of a new breed of mega-hostels offering slick contemporary accommodation to so-called global nomads. Choose between spartan Scandi-style six- to nine-bed male and female dorms or en suite private rooms. Communal areas include a fully equipped kitchen, breakfast area and a cocktail bar that hosts occasional DJ sets.

Hotel Al Vivit   HOTEL €€
(☑ 041 95 13 85; www.hotelvivit.com; Piazza Ferretto 73; d €80-140; 🅿 ❄ 🛜; ◻ 4/Mestre Centro) Facing on to buzzing Piazza Ferretto is this characterful three-star hotel, which has large, smart rooms decked out in extravagant faux-Venetian decor. Aside from its unbeatable location, it offers lots of great extras: private parking, free bicycles, public-transport ticket sales and baggage storage, while the very helpful staff happily hand out brochures and maps and help with restaurant and event bookings.

🍴 Eating & Drinking

Aki   JAPANESE €€
(☑ 041 531 60 71; www.akirestaurant.it; Via Torino 6; meals €35-40; ☉ 7-11pm Tue-Sun; ❄; ◻ 4/Mestre Centro) For something different, head to Japanese restaurant Aki on the 17th floor of a concrete tower block with 360-degree views over the shipyards. Chef Nakasuga was born in Brazil, hence the fusion menu, which features classic sushi alongside creative dishes such as tuna with *leche de tigre* (citrus-based marinade) spiced with aji Amarillo. Opt for the tasting plate for the full experience.

Casa Fortuna   VENETIAN €€€
(☑ 041 94 32 44; www.casafortunamestre.it; Corte Bettini 14; meals €50; ☉ 10.30am-3pm & 5.30-11pm Wed-Sun; ◻ 4/Mestre Centro) This picturesque villa in Mestre is home to one of the town's best fish restaurants. Downstairs, the focus is more on the wine and *cicheti*, and is particularly busy for pre-dinner drinks. Upstairs, the dining room has a more rustic vibe. Dishes include homemade gnocchi with spider crab and asparagus, and spaghetti with clams, broccoli and anchovies.

Oltre il Giardino   WINE BAR
(☑ 041 802 12 53; www.oltreilgiardinobistrot.it; Via Torre Belfredo 24; ☉ 6.30-11pm Tue-Sat; ◻ 4/Mestre Centro) A smart contemporary bistro and wine bar in a historic part of Mestre serving an interesting selection of natural and biodynamic wines and beer. Take a pew in the cosy interior, which is lined with blonde wood and artfully decorated. Freshly made *crostini* and focaccia accompany aperitifs between 6.30pm and 8.30pm. Those wanting to dine need to book.

LIDO DI JESOLO

This 13km strand of golden sand on the mainland east of Venice is far and away Venetians' preferred beach and is a magnet for regional and international holidaymakers. Billed by holiday operators as the Venetian Riviera, its sandy beaches are lined with sun-loungers (beds and umbrellas per day €14 to €20) and backed by hotels, apartments, a water park, a large aquarium complex, and a stretch of family-friendly restaurants and bars. The resort is organised and well managed with on-duty lifeguards and convenient first-aid points.

Amid the pizzerias and ice-cream parlours are a handful of very good fish restaurants, the best of which are **Ristorante da Omar** (☑ 0421 9 36 85; www.ristorantedaomar.it; Via Dante Alighieri 21, Lido di Jesolo; meals €40-65; ⊗ noon-3.30pm & 7.30pm-midnight Thu-Tue) and **Ristorante da Guido** (☑ 0421 35 03 80; www.ristorantedaguido.com; Via Roma Sinistra 25, Jesolo; meals €50-75; ⊗ noon-3pm & 7.30-11pm Wed-Sun, 7.30-11pm Tue; ✦), while **Bariolè** (☑ 0421 97 25 45; Via Bafile 444, Lido di Jesolo; ⊗ 6pm-2am Wed-Mon) serves up quality burgers and excellent cocktails. Aside from the beach, the other attraction of Lido di Jesolo is its summertime nightclubs. Keep an eye out for flyers around Venice advertising club nights and beach concerts. Note that the main clubs are set back from the beach, about 2km west of the bus station. For more information on things to do and see in Jesolo, call into the **Casa del Turismo** (☑ 041 37 06 01; www.jesolo.it; Piazza Brescia 13, Jesolo; ⊗ 8.30am-6.30pm Mon-Fri, 9am-6pm Sat & Sun; ⊒ 23a).

Getting to Lido di Jesolo from Venice takes about an hour by car. If you plan to come by public transport, ATVO has buses departing from Piazzale Roma roughly hourly from 6am until about 11pm (€5, 70 minutes). Another option is to catch a *vaporetto* to Punta Sabbioni on the tip of the peninsula (lines 14, 15, 17 and 22) and then catch bus 23A (€3, 38 minutes). If you're planning a club night, the problem is getting back. Taxis cost upwards of €95, so you might want to wait for the first buses. The 23A to Punta Sabbioni stops near the main clubs from around 5.20am.

ⓘ Getting There & Away

BUS

Urban, regional and long-distance buses arrive at Mestre's bus station on Viale Stazione beside the train station. You can search for routes and buy tickets through the **daAaB app** (www.daaab.it).

TRAIN

Stazione Venezia Mestre (www.venezia mestre.it; Piazzale Pietro Favretti) is located directly across the causeway from Venice. Services from the station include high-speed Le Frecce and Italo trains connecting Mestre with Rome, Milan and Florence, as well as Eurocity trains to Munich.

Frequent trains connect Mestre with Stazione Venice Santa Lucia in Venice (10 minutes, every 15 minutes). Inside the station, you'll find a tourist information office, currency exchange and a **left-luggage depot** (per piece 1st 5hr €6, next 6hr €0.90, thereafter per hr €0.40; ⊗ 8am-8pm).

TRAM

The T1 tram line runs from Piazzale Cialdini in Mestre to Piazzale Roma in Venice. It stops at all the essential locations in Mestre and is wheelchair accessible. Tickets cost just €1.50 per ride.

Treviso

POP 83,950

Treviso has everything you could want from a mid-sized Veneto city: medieval city walls, lots of pretty canals, narrow cobbled streets and frescoed churches. Despite this, it receives few visitors, eclipsed by its more impressive neighbours. If you want to experience authentic Veneto life away from the tourist crowds, this is a great place to come.

Die-hard sports fans may also find their way here thanks to the city's rugby links. Benetton Rugby Treviso plays in the highest European competitions, and international matches are held at its stadium.

◎ Sights

★ **Museo Collezione Salce**　　　MUSEUM
(☑ 0422 59 19 36; www.collezionesalce.beniculturali. it; Via Carlo Alberto 31; adult/reduced €8/4; ⊗ 10am-6pm Wed-Sun) When Treviso-born Nando Salce donated his collection of Italian advertising posters to the Italian state in 1962, he established a unique Italian graphic-art archive with global significance. The collection spans the years between 1844 and 1962 and

numbers some 25,000 posters, including in its ranks all the great Italian graphic artists like Leonetto Cappiello and Bruno Munari. A limited rotating exhibit, curated according to themes and monographs, is currently housed in the San Gaetano complex.

★ **Museo Luigi Bailo** MUSEUM
(☑0422 65 89 51; www.museicivicitreviso.it; Borgo Cavour 24; adult/reduced €6/4; ☺10am-6pm Tue-Sun) The contemporary white marmorino entrance to Treviso's modern-art museum is a sign of good things to come. Namely, a stunningly good 20th-century art collection, featuring portraits by Luigi Serena, Lino Selvatico and Bepi Fabiano, sculpture by underappreciated talents like Ottone Zorlini, and the largest collection of works by Arturo Martini. The latter is wide-ranging and shows Martini's incredible talent in graphic art, monumental sculpture, terracotta modelling and bronze casting.

Gallerie delle Prigione CULTURAL CENTRE
(Piazza del Duomo 20; ☺3-7pm Tue-Fri, 10am-1pm & 3-7pm Sat & Sun) **FREE** Treviso's old Habsburg prison has been reborn thanks to Fondazione Benetton and visionary architect Tobia Scarpa (son of Carlo Scarpa). Now its stark whitewashed corridors, tiny cells, refectory and infirmary display contemporary artworks by young, unknown and up-and-coming artists. Luciano Benetton's Imago Mundi collection, which includes works from around the world, is housed here and augmented by interesting temporary exhibitions and cultural events.

Fontana delle Tette STATUE
(Calle del Podestà 9) Treviso's best-known piece of statuary is the 16th-century naked female torso called the *Fontana delle Tette*, a snigger-worthy translation coming in as 'Tits Fountain'. Essentially created as a free wine dispenser (white wine flowed from one breast, red from the other) for the celebrating masses during autumn wine festivals, it now stands in a courtyard off Calle del Podestà – the wine has, sadly, long since been replaced with water.

Chiesa di Santa Lucia CHURCH
(www.santaluciatreviso.it; Piazza San Vito; ☺8am-noon Mon-Fri, to noon & 4-6.30pm Sat, 9am-12.30pm & 4-6.30pm Sun) **FREE** The small Chiesa di Santa Lucia adjoins the larger Chiesa di San Vito and is an absolute beauty. Its vaulted ceiling and walls are covered with colourful 14th- and 15th-century frescoes, including the *Madonna del Pavejo* (c 1450) by Tommaso da Modena.

Il Complesso di Santa Caterina MUSEUM
(☑0422 65 84 42; www.museicivicitreviso.it; Piazzetta Mario Botter 1; adult/reduced €6/4, combined ticket with Museo Luigi Bailo €10/6; ☺9am-12.30pm & 2.30-6pm Tue-Sun) Housed in the 14th-century convent complex of St Catherine, Treviso's civic museum presents the history of the city from the Palaeolithic era to Roman times. The material is fairly dry, but a visit is worth it for the wonderful fresco cycle rescued from the bomb-damaged church of Santa Margherita. Depicting the troubled life of St Orsola, they were painted by Tommaso da Modena in 1358 and represent one of the most important fresco cycles of the period.

🛏 Sleeping

★ **Ai Bastioni** BOUTIQUE HOTEL €€
(☑0422 59 07 55; Viale Fratelli Bandiera 18; s €110-130, d €140-180; ⓟ❊🛜) This hybrid hair salon, beauty spa and contemporary hotel is delightfully unconventional and super-smart. Rooms have every imaginable mod con: Netflix movies, sleek bathrooms with underfloor heating, giant king-sized beds and stylish decor mixing choice vintage pieces with artful bespoke furniture. Your hosts dish out excellent advice, and the hair salon offers an interesting insight into local life.

Maison Matilda B&B €€€
(☑0422 58 22 12; www.maisonmatilda.com; Via Riccati 44; d €160-225, ste €280; ⓟ🛜) This darkly beautiful townhouse is the perfect display of contemporary Italian design, from its Carrara marble bathrooms and art deco bedrooms to its sleek modernist furniture. There are only six rooms, so book ahead.

🍴 Eating & Drinking

★ **Osteria Dalla Gigia** OSTERIA €
(Via Barberia 20; snacks €1.30-3; ☺9.30am-2pm & 4-8.30pm Mon-Sat) This friendly and authentic snack bar is a great place to rub shoulders with locals. Everyone crams in to enjoy the legendary *mozzarella alla Gigia*, a tiny deep-fried sandwich filled with molten mozzarella and either prosciutto or sardines, washed down with an equally tiny beer.

Gelateria Dassie GELATO €
(www.stefanodassie.it; Via Sant'Agostino 42; servings from €1.50; ☺10.30am-midnight Tue-Sun summer, to 10pm winter) No one should leave Treviso without savouring an award-winning gelato by Stefano Dassie, one of Italy's top *gelatisti*. The Dassie family has a 45-year tradition of gelato production, but Stefano has taken things to new levels,

grabbing prize after international prize at ice-cream competitions. Ingredients are meticulously sourced from around the world.

★ **Toni del Spin**   TRATTORIA €€
(☑0422 54 38 29; www.ristorantetonidelspin.com; Via Inferiore 7; meals €35-50; ⊙noon-2.30pm & 7.15-10.30pm Tue-Sun, 7.15-10.30pm Mon) This trattoria has been a reference point since 1880, and the original wood-panelled dining room is reassuringly full of diners hunched over silky plates of risotto full of white asparagus and bowls of tagliatelle with duck *ragù*. In the evening, turn the corner into a second contemporary dining room where you'll find a slick bar serving the best of the region's labels from its 3000-bottle cellar.

Osteria Muscoli   VENETO €€
(☑0422 58 33 90; Via Pescheria 23; meals €30; ⊙9am-2pm & 5pm-1am Mon-Tue & Thu, to 2am Fri & Sat, 8am-2pm & 4-8pm Sun) This Venetian-style *cichetteria* is located opposite the fish market, which makes for perfect people-watching and even better *cicheti*, bowls of pasta with baby octopus and eel, and plates of radicchio and beans. Pair with a glass of prosecco.

★ **Cloakroom Cocktail Lab**   COCKTAIL BAR
(☑0422 57 99 72; www.cocktaillab.it; Piazza Monte di Pietà 4; ⊙6pm-2am) This dark speakeasy with a glittering bar stacked with top-quality spirits, unusual bitters and distillates is one of the top 10 bars in Italy. It stocks over 150 gins and makes all its own syrups. The bartender can make a bespoke cocktail just for you.

🛍 Shopping

Pinarello   SPORTS & OUTDOORS
(☑0422 54 38 21; www.pinarello.com; Borgo Mazzini 9; ⊙9am-12.30pm & 3.30-7.30pm Tue-Sat, 3.30-7.30pm Mon) Yes, this is the shop of the legendary Pinarello cycling brand, manufacturers of some of the best handmade road, track and cyclocross bikes, including 13 winners of the Tour de France. Even if you can't afford the bikes, it's nice to admire them and the shop is full of top-quality cycling accessories.

ⓘ Information

Centro Guide e Servizi Turistici (☑0422 5 64 70; www.guideveneto.it; Vicolo del Cristo 4; half-/full-day €110/250) Authorised guides offering walking tours of Treviso, as well as bike rides along the canals, visits to Venetian country villas and food and prosecco tours.

Tourist Office (☑0422 54 76 32; www.marcatreviso.it; Via Fiumicelli 30; ⊙10am-1pm Mon, to 5pm Tue-Sat, to 4pm Sun) Very helpful office, well signposted from the train station.

ⓘ Getting There & Away

AIR

Treviso's **airport** (☑0422 31 51 11; www.trevisoairport.it; Via Noalese 63) serves Ryanair flights from across Europe and some Wizz Air services. It is located around 5km west of Treviso. ACTT **buses** (line 6; ☑ call centre 840 011222; www.mobilitadimarca.it) run from the airport to the train station in Treviso (€3.50, 15 minutes, at least two per hour, 6am to 11pm). **Barzi Bus Service** (☑0422 68 60 83; www.barziservice.com) runs services from the airport to Venice Mestre and Tronchetto, as well as to towns around Treviso.

TRAIN

Treviso Centrale station, located just south of the city centre, has at least hourly connections with Venice (€3.55, 30 minutes) and Vicenza (€7, one hour).

Brenta Riviera

Every 13 June for 300 years, summer officially kicked off with a traffic jam along the Grand Canal, as a flotilla of fashionable Venetians headed to their villas along the banks of the Brenta. Every last ball gown and poker chair was loaded onto barges for dalliances that stretched until November. The party ended when Napoleon arrived in 1797, but 80 villas still strike elegant poses along the Brenta, six of them now open to the public at various times of the year.

◎ Sights & Activities

Villa Foscari   HISTORIC BUILDING
(☑041 5203 9662; www.lamalcontenta.com; Via dei Turisti 9, Malcontenta; adult/reduced €10/8; ⊙9am-noon Tue, Wed & Fri-Sun Apr-Oct) The most romantic Brenta villa, the Palladio-designed, Unesco-listed Villa Foscari (built 1555–60) got its nickname La Malcontenta from a grande dame of the Foscari clan who was reputedly exiled here for cheating on her husband – though these bright, sociable salons hardly constitute a punishment. Giovanni Zelotti's frescoes have been restored to splendour.

Villa Widmann Rezzonico Foscari   HISTORIC BUILDING
(☑041 42 49 73; https://villawidmann.servizimetropolitani.ve.it; Via Nazionale 420, Mira; adult/reduced €5.50/4.50; ⊙10am-1pm & 1.30-4.30pm Tue-Sun May-Oct) To appreciate both gardening and Venetian-style social engineering, stop just west of Oriago at Villa Widmann Rezzonico Foscari. Originally owned by Persian-Venetian nobility, the 18th-century

villa captures the Brenta's last days of rococo decadence, with Murano sea-monster chandeliers and a frescoed grand ballroom with upper viewing gallery. Head to the gallery to reach the upstairs ladies' gambling parlour where, according to local lore, villas were once gambled away in high-stakes games.

Villa Barchessa Valmarana   HISTORIC BUILDING
([✉] 041 426 63 87; www.villavalmarana.net; Via Valmarana 11, Mira; adult/reduced €6/5; ⊙10am-6pm Tue-Sun Mar-Oct, to 4.30pm Sat & Sun Nov-Feb, or by appointment during the week) Debuting on the riviera in the 17th century, Villa Barchessa Valmarana was commissioned by Vicenza's aristocratic Valmarana family. You'll find them enjoying *la dolce vita* (the sweet life) in the villa's fanciful frescoes, painstakingly restored in 1964. These days, the elegant building is mainly used as a function centre, but is still fully accessible to the public.

Villa Pisani Nazionale   HISTORIC BUILDING
([✉]049 50 20 74; www.villapisani.beniculturali.it; Via Doge Pisani 7, Stra; adult/reduced €10/5, park only €7.50/4.50; ⊙9am-8pm Tue-Sun Apr-Sep, to 6pm Oct, to 5pm Nov-Mar) To keep hard-partying Venetian nobles in line, Doge Alvise Pisani provided a Versailles-like reminder of who was in charge. The 1774, 114-room Villa Pisani Nazionale is surrounded by huge gardens, a labyrinthine hedge maze, and pools to reflect the doge's glory. Here you'll find the

bathroom with a tiny wooden throne used by Napoleon; the sagging bed where new king Vittorio Emanuele II slept; and, ironically, the reception hall where Mussolini and Hitler met in 1934 under Tiepolo's ceiling depicting the *Geniuses of Peace*.

Villa Foscarini Rossi   HISTORIC BUILDING
([✉]049 980 10 91; www.museodellacalzatura.it; Via Doge Pisani 1/2, Stra; adult/reduced €7/5; ⊙9am-1pm & 2-6pm Mon-Fri, 2.30-6pm Sat & Sun Apr-Oct, 9am-1pm & 2-6pm Mon-Fri Nov-Mar) Well-heeled Venetians wouldn't have dreamed of decamping to the Brenta without their favourite cobblers, sparking a local tradition of shoemaking. Today, 538 companies produce around 19 million pairs of shoes annually. Their contribution is celebrated with a **Shoemakers' Museum** at this 18th-century villa, its collection including 18th-century slippers and kicks created for Marlene Dietrich. Admission includes access to the villa's 17th-century *foresteria* (guesthouse), which wows with allegorical frescoes by Pietro Liberi and *trompe l'œil* effects by Domenico de Bruni.

Veloce   CYCLING
([✉]0586 40 42 04; www.rentalbikeitaly.com; touring/mountain/racing bicycle per day €20/25/35; ⊙8am-8pm) The scenic Brenta Riviera plains make an easy, enjoyable bicycle ride, and you can speed past those tour boats along 150km of cycling routes. Veloce is a friendly bike-rental outlet with branches in many Veneto towns offering mountain and city bikes, plus pre-loaded GPS units (€10), guided tours (€80 per person), roadside assistance and advice in English on itineraries and local restaurants. Bikes need to be pre-booked.

❶ Getting There & Away

ACTV's Venezia–Padova Extraurbane bus 53 leaves from Venice's Piazzale Roma about every half-hour, stopping at key Brenta villages en route to Padua.

Venice–Padua train services stop at Dolo (€3.55, 25 minutes, one to three per hour).

By car, take SS11 from Mestre-Venezia towards Padua and take the A4 autostrada towards Dolo/Padua.

RIVER CRUISES

Watch 50 villas drift by on the **Il Burchiello** ([✉] 049 876 02 33; www.ilburchiello.it; half-day cruise adult/child €70/55; ⊙ Tue-Sun Apr-Nov) barge, a modern version of the pleasure boats that ferried aristocrats to and from their country villas. Full-day cruises run between Venice and Padua, stopping at Malcontenta, Widmann (or Barchessa Valmarana) and Pisani villas.

From Venice, cruises depart from Pontile della Pietà pier on Riva degli Schiavoni (Tuesday, Thursday and Saturday). From Padua, cruises depart from Pontile del Portello pier (Wednesday, Friday and Sunday). There are also half-day tours stopping at one or two villas, running to Oriago from Venice (Tuesday, Thursday and Saturday) and Padua (Wednesday, Friday and Sunday), and from Oriago to Venice (Wednesday, Friday and Sunday) and Padua (Tuesday, Thursday and Saturday). Book online.

PADUA
POP 209,800

Though less than an hour from Venice, Padua (Padova in Italian) seems a world away with its medieval marketplaces, Fascist-era facades and hip student population. As a medieval city-state and home to Italy's second-oldest university, Padua challenged both Venice and Verona for regional hegemony. A series of extraordinary fresco cycles recalls this golden age – including in Giotto's blockbuster Cappella degli Scrovegni, Menabuoi's heavenly gathering in the baptistry and Titian's *St Anthony* in the Scoletta del Santo. For centuries, Padua and Verona fought for dominance over the Veneto plains. But Venice finally occupied Padua permanently in 1405.

As a strategic military-industrial centre, Padua became a parade ground for Mussolini speeches, an Allied bombing target and a secret Italian Resistance hub (at its university). Even today, Padua remains an important industrial city – its industrial zone employs some 50,000 people – a dynamic university town and an important pilgrimage centre.

⊙ Sights

★ **Cappella degli Scrovegni**   CHAPEL
(Scrovegni Chapel; ☑049 201 00 20; www.capp elladegliscrovegni.it; Piazza Eremitani 8; adult/reduced €14/10, night ticket €8/6; ⊘9am-7pm, night ticket 7-9.20pm) Padua's version of the Sistine Chapel, the Cappella degli Scrovegni houses one of Italy's great Renaissance masterpieces – a striking cycle of Giotto frescoes. Dante, da Vinci and Vasari all honour Giotto as the artist who ended the Dark Ages with these 1303–05 paintings, whose humanistic depiction of biblical figures was especially well suited to the chapel Enrico Scrovegni commissioned in memory of his father (who as a moneylender was denied a Christian burial).

It's a simple brick building, with little indication from the outside of what lies within. It took Giotto two years to finish the frescoes, which tell the story of Christ from Annunciation to Ascension. Scrovegni's chapel once adjoined the family mansion (demolished in 1824) – the city of Padua acquired the chapel in 1881.

Giotto's moving, modern approach helped change how people saw themselves: no longer as lowly vassals, but as vessels for the divine, however flawed. Where medieval churchgoers had been accustomed to blank stares from saints on high thrones, Giotto introduced biblical figures as characters in recognisable settings. Onlookers gossip as middle-aged Anne tenderly kisses Joachim, and Jesus stares down Judas as the traitor puckers up for the fateful kiss. Giotto also used unusual techniques such as impasto, building paint up into 3D forms. A 10-minute

PADUA MARKETS

One of the most enjoyable activities in Padua (Padova) is browsing the markets in **Piazza delle Erbe** and **Piazza della Frutta**, which operate very much as they've done since the Middle Ages. Dividing them is Europe's oldest covered market, housed in the Gothic **Palazzo della Ragione** (☑049 820 50 06; Piazza delle Erbe; adult/reduced €6/4; ⊘9am-7pm Tue-Sun Feb-Oct, to 6pm Nov-Jan). The *palazzo* (mansion) arcades – known locally as **Sotto il Salone** – rumble with specialist butchers, cheesemakers, fishmongers, *salumerie* (delicatessens or sausage shops) and fresh-pasta producers. The markets are open all day, every day, except Sunday, although the best time to visit is before midday.

introductory video provides some helpful insights before you enter the church itself.

Visits must be pre-booked. Tickets are available at the Musei Civici agli Eremitani (p403), where you access the chapel, or at the tourist office. Chapel visits last 15 to 20 minutes (depending on the time of year), plus another 10 minutes for the video. Arrive at least 15 to 30 minutes before your tour starts, or an hour before if you want to get around the Musei Civici agli Eremitani beforehand.

★ **Palazzo Bo**   HISTORIC BUILDING
(☑049 827 39 39; www.unipd.it/en/guidedtours; Via VIII Febbraio 2; adult/reduced €7/3; ⊘ see website for tour times) This Renaissance *palazzo* is the seat of Padua's history-making university. Founded by renegade scholars from Bologna seeking greater intellectual freedom, the university has employed some of Italy's greatest and most controversial thinkers, including Copernicus, Galileo, Casanova and the world's first female doctor of philosophy, Eleonora Lucrezia Cornaro Piscopia (her statue graces the stairs). Admission is on a 45-minute guided tour only, which includes a visit to the world's first **anatomy theatre** and the Aula Magna (Great Hall) where Galileo lectured.

★ **Musme**   MUSEUM
(www.musme.it; Via San Francesco 94; adult/reduced/child €10/8/6; ⊘2.30-7pm Tue-Fri, 9.30am-7pm Sat & Sun) Padua's Museum of Medical History is a fascinating mash-up of historical artefacts and high-tech exhibits that detail

Padua

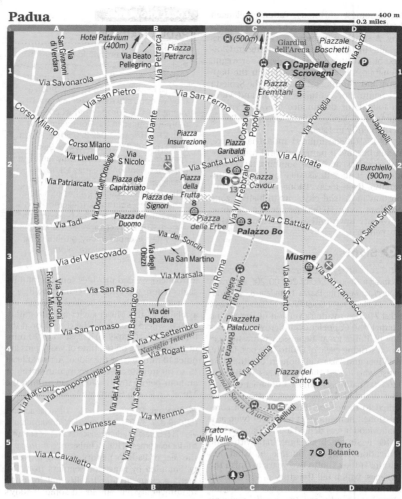

0 | 400 m
0 | 0.2 miles

Via San Givanni di Verdara
Hotel Patavium (400m)
Via Beato Pellegrino
Via Petrarca
Piazza Petrarca
(500m)
Giardini dell'Arena
Piazzale Boschetti
Via Gozzi

Via Savonarola
1 Cappella degli Scrovegni

Corso Milano
Via San Pietro
Via San Fermo
Piazza Eremitani
5
Via Porciglia
Via Jappelli

Corso Milano
Via Dante
Piazza Insurrezione
Piazza Garibaldi
Corso del Popolo
Via Altinate
Il Burchiello (900m)

Via Livello
Via S Nicolo
Via Santa Lucia
6
13
Piazza Cavour

Via Patriarcato
Via Dondi dell'Orologio
Piazza del Capitaniato
Piazza della Frutta
Via VIII Febbraio
Via Santa Sofia

Tronco Maestra
Piazza dei Signori
8
Piazza delle Erbe
3
Via C Battisti

Via Tadi
Piazza del Duomo
Via dei Soncin
Palazzo Bo

Via del Vescovado
Via degli Obizzi
Via San Martino
Musme
12
2
Via San Francesco

Via San Rosa
Via Marsala
Via Roma
Riviera Tito Livio
Via del Santo

Via Speroni
Riviera Mussato
Via Barbarigo
Via dei Papafava
Piazzetta Palatucci

Via San Tomaso
Via XX Settembre
Naviglio Interno
Via Rogati
Riviera Ruzante
Piazza del Santo
4

Via Marconi
Via Camposampiero
Via dei A Abardi
Via Seminario
Via Umberto I
Canale Santa Chiara
Via Rudena

Via Memmo
10
Via Luca Belludi

Via Dimesse
Via Marin
Prato della Valle
7 Orto Botanico
5

Via A Cavalletto
9

the city's outsized contribution to world medicine between the 16th and 18th centuries. Virtual guides representing Padua's most famous physicians narrate the university's greatest discoveries in thematic displays covering how the human body functions, fails and is treated. The journey ends in an Anatomical Theatre, mimicking the original theatre in Palazzo Bo (p401), where a giant mannequin lies on a dissection table ready for an augmented-reality investigation.

Basilica di Sant'Antonio
CHURCH

(Il Santo; ☑049 822 56 52; www.basilicadelsanto.org; Piazza del Santo; ⊙6.20am-7.45pm) FREE A

pilgrimage site and the burial place of St Anthony of Padua (1193–1231), this huge church was begun in 1232, its polyglot style incorporating rising eastern domes atop a Gothic brick structure crammed with Renaissance treasures. Behind the high altar, nine radiating chapels punctuate a broad ambulatory homing in on the **Cappella delle Reliquie** (Relics Chapel), with relics of St Anthony.

Orto Botanico
GARDENS

(☑049 827 39 39; www.ortobotanicopd.it; Via dell'Orto Botanico 15; adult/reduced €10/8, with PadovaCard €5; ⊙9am-7pm Tue-Sun Apr-Sep, to 6pm Oct, to 5pm Nov-Mar) Planted in 1545 by Pad-

Padua

ua University's medical faculty to study the medicinal properties of rare plants, Padua's World Heritage–listed Orto Botanico is the world's original botanical garden. The oldest tree is nicknamed 'Goethe's palm'; planted in 1585, it was mentioned by the German writer in *Italienische Reise* (Italian Journey). The garden is still used as a learning and research environment; studies now focus on the preservation of rare indigenous plants and the maintenance of biodiversity.

**Museo del Risorgimento
e dell'Età Contemporanea**   MUSEUM
(☎049 878 12 31; Galleria Pedrocchi 11; adult/reduced €4/2; ⊙9.30am-12.30pm & 3.30-6pm Tue-Sun) Since 1831, this neoclassical landmark has been a favourite of Stendhal and other pillars of Padua's cafe society for the heart-poundingly powerful coffee and *caffè correto* (coffee-based cocktails) served at the ground-floor **Caffè Pedrocchi** (www.caffe pedrocchi.it; ⊙8am-midnight Sun-Thu, to 1am Fri & Sat). The grand 1st floor – decorated in styles ranging from ancient Egyptian to imperial – houses the museum, recounting local and national history from the fall of Venice in 1797 until the republican constitution of 1848 in original documents, images and mementos.

Musei Civici agli Eremitani   MUSEUM
(☎049 820 45 51; Piazza Eremitani 8; adult/reduced €10/8; ⊙9am-7pm Tue-Sun) The ground floor of this monastery houses artefacts dat-

ing from Padua's Roman and pre-Roman past, including some delicate glass, serviceable Roman surgical instruments and Etruscan bronze figures. Upstairs, a rambling but interesting collection boasts a few notable 14th- to 18th-century works by Bellini, Giorgione, Tintoretto and Veronese. Among the showstoppers are a monster Brussels tapestry and an 18th-century painting by Georgio Fossati that shows the Prato della Valle when it was still a sports ground.

🍴 Sleeping & Eating

Belludi37   BOUTIQUE HOTEL €€
(☎049 66 56 33; www.collezionebelludi.it; Via Luca Belludi 37; s €80, d €110-180; ❄️🖥📶) Graced with smart contemporary furniture and Flos bedside lamps, the neutrally toned rooms at Belludi37 feature high ceilings, queen-sized beds and a free minibar. Extra perks include a central location and helpful staff always on hand with suggestions for biking itineraries and walking tours.

★**Da Nane della Giulia**   OSTERIA €€
(☎049 66 07 42; Via Santa Sofia 1; meals €25-30; ⊙12.30-2pm & 7pm-midnight Wed-Sun; 🍴) Enter the blood-red, candlelit dining room of Padua's oldest tavern and you'll immediately be transported back to another era. Diners settle in at dark wooden tables beneath vaulted ceilings and peruse the seasonal, local menu. It includes traditional dishes such as chicken in red grappa with pancetta and polenta and vegetarian-friendly plates of white asparagus, courgettes and local cheese.

★**Belle Parti**   ITALIAN €€€
(☎049 875 18 22; www.ristorantebelleparti.it; Via Belle Parti 11; meals €50; ⊙12.30-2.30pm & 7.30-10.30pm Mon-Sat) Prime seasonal produce, impeccable wines and near-faultless service meld into one unforgettable whole at this stellar fine-dining restaurant, resplendent with 18th-century antiques and 19th-century oil paintings. Seafood is the forte, with standout dishes including an arresting *gran piatto di crudità di mare* (raw seafood platter). Dress to impress and book ahead.

ℹ Information

Hospital (☎049 821 11 11; Via Giustiniani 1)
Tourist Office (☎049 520 74 15; www. turismopadova.it; Vicolo Pedrocchi; ⊙9am-7pm Mon-Sat, 10am-4pm Sun) Ask about the PadovaCard here. There is a second **tourist office** (☎049 201 00 80; Piazza di Stazione; ⊙9am-7pm Mon-Sat, 10am-4pm Sun) at the train station.

VENICE & THE VENETO PADUA

❶ PADOVACARD

A PadovaCard (€16/21 per 48/72 hours) gives one adult and one child under 14 free use of city public transport and access to almost all of Padua's major attractions, including the Cappella degli Scrovegni (plus €1 booking fee; reservations essential). PadovaCards are available at Padua tourist offices, Musei Civici agli Eremitani and the hotels listed on the PadovaCard section of the tourist-office website (www.turismopadova.it).

❶ Getting There & Away

CAR & MOTORCYCLE

Padua can be reached via the congested Turin–Trieste A4 or the Padova–Bologna A13. There is a restricted access ZTL zone covering the centre of the city, but cars are allowed entry to drop luggage at hotels. Check www.parcheggipadova. it for information on secure parking lots.

TRAIN

Train is by far the easiest way to reach Padua from virtually anywhere. The station is about 500m north of Cappella degli Scrovegni and linked to the centre by a monorail tram-bus. Connections include the followin Venice (€4.35 to €19, 25 to 50 minutes, one to nine per hour), Verona (€7.50 to €23, 40 to 80 minutes, one to four per hou) and Vicenza (€4.35 to €17, 15 to 25 minutes, one to five per hour).

❶ Getting Around

BICYCLE

Bikes are the preferred mode of transport in Padua and the **GoodBike Padova** (☑800 204303; www.goodbikepadova.it) bike-sharing scheme has a network of 25 stations dotted around the city. To use it, subscribe online, where you can sign up for a weekly membership (€5), or pay a flat fee of €8/13 for 24/48 hours, which allows for four or eight hours' use of the bikes.

TRAM

It is easy to get to all the sights by foot from the train and bus stations, but the city's unusual single-branch monorail tram-bus running from the train station passes within 100m of all the main sights. Tickets (€1.30) are available at tobacconists and newsstands.

Colli Euganei

Southwest of Padua, the Euganean Hills, with their walled hilltop towns, misty vineyards and bubbling hot springs, feel a world away from the Veneto's cities. The natural-

hot-spring resorts of Abano Terme and Montegrotto Terme (www.visitabanomontegrotto. com) have been active since Roman times when the Patavini built their villas on Mt Montirone. The towns are uninspired, but some of the spas, such as Mioni Pezzato (☑049 866 83 77; www.hotelmionipezzato.it; Via Marzia 34, Abano Terme; day pass €60-94, treatments €117-348), are fabulous.

In Arquà Petrarca (www.arquapetrarca. com), look for the house (☑0429 71 82 94; www.arquapetrarca.com; adult/reduced €4/2; ⏱10am-12.30pm & 3.30-7pm Tue-Sun Mar-Oct, 9am-12.30pm & 2.30-5.30pm Tue-Sun Nov-Feb) where the great Italian poet Petrarch spent his final years in the 1370s. At the southern reaches of the Euganei, you'll find Monselice, with its remarkable medieval castle (☑0429 7 29 31; www.castellodimonselice.it; Via del Santuario 11; adult/reduced €8/6; ⏱1hr guided tours 9am, 10am, 11am, 3pm, 4pm & 5pm Mar-Oct, 10am, 11am, 3pm & 5pm Nov-Feb); Montagnana, with its magnificent 2km medieval defensive walls; and Este, with its rich architectural heritage and important archaeological museum (☑0429 20 85; www.atestino.beniculturali.it; Via Guido Negri 9c; adult/reduced €5/2; ⏱8.30am-7.30pm).

◉ Sights & Activities

Parco Regionale dei Colli Euganei   PARK
(www.parcocollieuganei.com) The Ancient Veneto survives in this 18,694-hectare park in which about a sixth of Italy's botanical species thrive thanks to its unique location and volcanic origin. The park is criss-crossed by a network of trails; see the website for a full list of itineraries and events.

**Villa Barbarigo
Pizzoni Ardemani**   HISTORIC SITE
(☑049 913 10 65; www.valsanzibiogiardino.it; Via Diana 2, Valsanzibio di Galzignano Terme; adult/reduced €11/6.50; ⏱10am-1pm & 2pm-sunset summer) Located in the town of Galzignano Terme, Villa Barbarigo Pizzoni Ardemani is home to one of the finest historical gardens in Europe, shot through with streams, fish ponds and Bernini fountains. It's near Padova Golf Club, southwest of the city.

🛏 Sleeping & Eating

★**Agriturismo Barchessa**   AGRITURISMO €
(☑0429 603 46 10; www.agriturismobarchessa. com; Via Cappuccini 9, Este; 2-person apt €80-90; 🅿❄🛜) This elegant neoclassical villa, renovated by architect-owner Graziano, sits in the shadow of the grand Villa Contarini degli Scrigni, to which it was once attached. It shares the same sober elegance and now

houses four delightful apartments each with a kitchen/living room. They are beautifully finished and furnished sparely with quality antiques. Beds can be provided for children.

Hostaria San Benedetto ITALIAN €€
(✎ 0429 80 09 99; http://hostariasanbenedetto.it; Via Andronalecca 13, Montagnana; meals €35-40; ⊙ noon-2pm & 8-10pm Thu-Tue) For a deep dive into the cuisine of the Colli Euganei, book a table on the terrace of this renowned local restaurant. A single-page menu showcases Montagnana's DOP prosciutto, sweet Venetian gnocchi with raisins, sugar and cinnamon, and saddle of veal with aged Asiago cheese and seared *carletti* (wild buds). Wine pairings are equally good, and the €32 tasting menu is great value.

ℹ Information

Visit www.parcocollieuganei.com or grab information at the Padua tourist offices.

ℹ Getting There & Away

Buses run from Padua to the Colli Euganei area, and trains serve all towns except Arquà Petrarca, but to really enjoy things here you'll need a hire car.

VERONA

POP 257,350

Best known for its Shakespeare associations, Verona attracts a multinational gaggle of tourists to its pretty piazzas and knot of lanes, most in search of Romeo, Juliet and all that. But beyond the heart-shaped kitsch and Renaissance romance, Verona is a bustling centre, its heart dominated by a mammoth, remarkably well-preserved 1st-century amphitheatre, the venue for the city's annual summer opera festival. Add to that countless churches, a couple of architecturally fascinating bridges over the Adige, regional wine and food from the Veneto hinterland and some impressive art, and Verona shapes up as one of northern Italy's most attractive cities. And all this just a short hop from the shores of stunning Lake Garda.

History

Shakespeare placed star-crossed lovers Romeo Montague and Juliet Capulet in Verona for good reason: romance, drama and fatal feuding have been the city's hallmark for centuries. From the 3rd century BC, Verona was a Roman trade centre with ancient gates, a forum (now Piazza delle Erbe) and a grand Roman arena, which still serves as one of the world's great opera venues. In the Middle Ages the city flourished under the della Scala clan, who were as much energetic patrons of the arts as they were murderous tyrants. Their elaborate Gothic tombs, the Arche Scaligere, are just off Piazza dei Signori.

Under Cangrande I (1308–28) Verona conquered Padua and Vicenza, with Dante, Petrarch and Giotto benefiting from the city's patronage. But the fratricidal rage of Cangrande II (1351–59) complicated matters, and the della Scala family was run out of town in 1387. Venice took definitive control in 1404, ruling until Napoleon's arrival in 1797.

The city became a Fascist control centre from 1938 to 1945, a key location for Resistance interrogation and a transit point for Italian Jews sent to Nazi concentration camps. Today, the city is a Unesco World Heritage Site and a cosmopolitan crossroads, especially in summer when the 2000-year-old arena hosts opera's biggest names.

◎ Sights

★ **Roman Arena** RUINS
(✎ 045 800 51 51; www.arena.it; Piazza Brà 1; adult/reduced €10/7.50; ⊙ 8.30am-7.30pm Tue-Sun, 1.30-7.30pm Mon) Built of pink-tinged marble in the 1st century AD, Verona's Roman amphitheatre survived a 12th-century earthquake to become the city's legendary open-air opera

VENICE & THE VENETO VERONA

ROMEO & JULIET IN VERONA

Shakespeare had no idea what he'd start when he set his tale of star-crossed lovers in Verona, but the city has seized the commercial possibilities with both hands – everything from *osterie* and hotels to embroidered kitchen aprons get the R&J branding. While the play's depiction of feuding families has genuine provenance, the lead characters themselves are fictional.

Undaunted, in the 1930s the authorities settled on a house in Via Cappello (think Capulet) as Juliet's and added a 14th-century-style balcony and a bronze statue of our heroine. You can squeeze onto the balcony itself at the altogether underwhelming Casa di Giulietta (Juliet's House; ✎ 045 803 43 03; Via Cappello 23; adult/reduced €6/4.50, free with VeronaCard; ⊙ 1.30-7.30pm Mon, 8.30am-7.30pm Tue-Sun), or – more sensibly – see the circus from the square below, a spot framed by a slew of lovesick sticky notes.

Verona

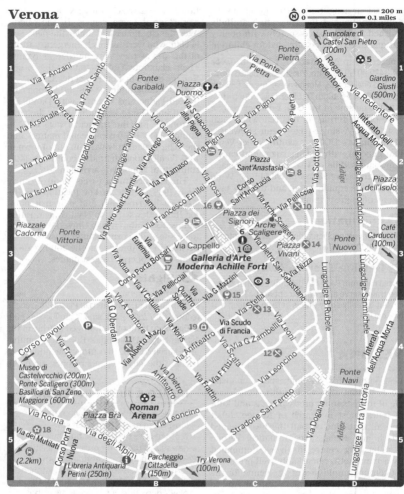

house, with seating for 30,000 people. You can visit the arena year-round, though it's at its best during the summer opera festival (p408). In winter months, concerts are held at the **Teatro Filarmonico** (📞045 800 28 80; www.arena.it; Via dei Mutilati 4; tickets from €25). From October to May, admission is €1 on the first Sunday of the month.

★ Galleria d'Arte
Moderna Achille Forti　　　　　　GALLERY
(Palazzo della Ragione; 📞045 800 19 03; https:// gam.comune.verona.it; Cortile Mercato Vecchio; adult/reduced €4/2.50, incl Torre dei Lamberti €8/5; ⏰10am-6pm Tue-Fri, 11am-7pm Sat & Sun)

In the shadow of the Torre dei Lamberti, the Romanesque Palazzo della Ragione is home to Verona's jewel-box Gallery of Modern Art. Reached via the Gothic **Scala della Ragione** (Stairs of Reason), the collection of paintings and sculpture spans the period from 1840 to 1940 and includes influential Italian artists such as Giorgio Morandi and Umberto Boccioni. Among the numerous highlights are Francesco Hayez' arresting portrait *Meditazione* (Meditation), Angelo Dall'Oca's haunting *Foglie cadenti* (Falling Leaves) and Ettore Berladini's darkly humorous *I vecchi* (Old Men).

Verona

★ **Giardino Giusti**   GARDENS

(☑045 803 40 29; http://giardinogiusti.com; Via Giardino Giusti 2; adult/reduced €8.50/5; ☺9am-7pm) Across the river from the historic centre, these sculpted gardens are considered a masterpiece of Renaissance landscaping, and are named after the noble family that has tended them since opening the gardens to the public in 1591. The vegetation is an Italianate mix of the manicured and natural, graced by soaring cypresses, one of which the German poet Goethe immortalised in his travel writings.

★ **Museo di Castelvecchio**   MUSEUM

(☑045 806 26 11; https://museodicastelvecchio.comune.verona.it; Corso Castelvecchio 2; adult/reduced €6/4.50, free with VeronaCard; ☺1.30-7.30pm Mon, 8.30am-7.30pm Tue-Sun) Bristling with fish-tail battlements along the Adige, Castelvecchio was built in the 1350s by Cangrande II. Severely damaged by Napoleon and WWII bombings, the fortress was reinvented by architect Carlo Scarpa, who constructed bridges over exposed foundations, filled gaping holes with glass panels, and balanced a statue of Cangrande I above the courtyard on a concrete gangplank. The complex is now home to a diverse collection of statuary, frescoes, jewellery, medieval artefacts and paintings.

Torre dei Lamberti   TOWER

(☑045 927 30 27; Via della Costa 1; adult/reduced incl Galleria d'Arte Moderna Achille Forti €8/5, with VeronaCard €1; ☺10am-6pm Mon-Fri, 11am-7pm Sat & Sun) One of Verona's most popular attractions, this 84m-high watchtower provides panoramic views of Verona and nearby mountains. Begun in the 12th century and finished in 1463 – too late to notice invading Venetians – it sports an octagonal bell tower

whose two bells retain their ancient names: Rengo once called meetings of the city council, while Marangona warned citizens of fire. A lift whisks you up two-thirds of the way, but you have to walk the last few storeys.

Duomo   CATHEDRAL

(Cattedrale Santa Maria Matricolare; ☑045 59 28 13; Piazza Duomo; €3, free with VeronaCard; ☺10am-5.30pm Mon-Sat, 1.30-5.30pm Sun Mar-Oct, to 5pm Nov-Feb) Verona's 12th-century *duomo* is a striking Romanesque creation, with bug-eyed statues of Charlemagne's paladins Roland and Oliver, crafted by medieval master Nicolò, on the west porch. Nothing about this sober facade hints at the extravagant 16th- to 17th-century frescoed interior with angels aloft amid *trompe l'œil* architecture. At the left end of the nave is the **Cartolari-Nichesola Chapel**, designed by Renaissance master Jacopo Sansovino and featuring a vibrant Titian *Assumption*.

Teatro Romano e
Museo Archeologico   ARCHAEOLOGICAL SITE

(☑045 800 03 60; Regaste Redentore 2; adult/reduced €4.50/3, with VeronaCard free; ☺8.30am-7.30pm Tue-Sun, 1.30-7.30pm Mon) Just north of the historic centre you'll find a Roman theatre. Built in the 1st century BC, it is cunningly carved into the hillside at a strategic spot overlooking a bend in the river. Take the lift at the back of the theatre to the former convent above, which houses an interesting collection of Greek and Roman pieces.

🏃 Activities

★ **Adige Rafting**   RAFTING

(☑347 8892498; www.adigerafting.it; Via del Perloso 14a; adult/reduced €25/18) The Adige river is

---

ⓘ VERONA DISCOUNT CARDS

VeronaCard (per 24/48 hours €20/25; www.veronatouristoffice.it) is available at tourist sights, tobacconists and numerous hotels, and offers access to most major monuments and churches, unlimited use of town buses, and discounted tickets to selected concerts and opera and theatre productions.

If you're planning on seeing Verona's four main churches – the Duomo, San Zeno, Sant'Anastasia and San Fermo – invest in a cumulative ticket (adult/reduced €6/5, valid until end Dec). Included is an audio guide in six languages.

---

the second-longest river in Italy after the Po, running from the Reschen Pass in Austria to the Adriatic Sea. It is a defining feature of Verona, and rafting along it offers a surprising, new perspective as you pass beneath a dozen bridges past the Castelvecchio to finish at the ruins of the Venetian customs house.

Funicolare di Castel San Pietro CABLE CAR (☑342 8966695; www.funicolarediverona.it; Via Fontanelle Santo Stefano 6; one-way/return €1/2; ⊙10am-9pm Apr-Oct, to 5pm Nov-Mar) For the best view of Verona, take a ride up the cable railway to the cypress-ringed Castel San Pietro (closed for restoration). Its ramparts are the domain of kissing couples enjoying the view of the medieval city embraced within the swooping bends of the Adige river. To descend, take the zigzagging staircase that leads back to the Ponte Pietra.

🎭 Festivals & Events

Verona's Opera Festival PERFORMING ARTS (☑045 800 51 51; www.arena.it; Via Dietro Anfiteatro 6; ⊙late Jun-late Aug) Around 14,000 music lovers pack the Roman Arena on summer nights during the world's biggest open-air lyrical music event, which draws international stars. Performances usually start at 8.45pm or 9pm. Tucking into a pre-show picnic on the unreserved stone steps is fine, so decant that wine into a plastic bottle (glass and knives aren't allowed), arrive early, rent a cushion and prepare for an unforgettable evening.

🛏 Sleeping

★**Agriturismo San Mattia** AGRITURISMO €€ (☑045 91 37 97; www.agriturismosanmattia.it; Via Santa Giuliana 2a; s €70-110, d €90-140, apt from €160; 🅿❄🛜) Make friends with the chickens, ducks and horses as you wander through San

Mattia's olive groves, orchards and vineyards, then sit back on the patio and soak up the stunning views of Verona. Host Giovanni Ederle is the tour de force behind this 14-room farm, its popular Slow Food–focused restaurant and Valpolicella vintages. Located around 2km north of the city centre.

Corte delle Pigne B&B €€ (☑333 7584141; www.cortedellepigne.it; Via Pigna 6a; s €60-110, d €90-150, tr €110-170; 🅿❄🛜) In the heart of the historic centre, this tiny three-room B&B is set around a quiet internal courtyard. It offers tasteful rooms and plenty of personal touches: sweets jars, luxury toiletries and even a Jacuzzi for one lucky couple.

★**Hotel Gabbia d'Oro** HOTEL €€€ (☑045 800 30 60; www.hotelgabbiadoro.it; Corso Porta Borsari 4a; d from €290; ❄🛜) One of the city's top addresses and also one of its most romantic, the Gabbia d'Oro features luxe rooms inside an 18th-century *palazzo* that manage to be both elegant and cosy. The rooftop terrace and central location are the icing on the proverbial cake.

★**Due Torri Hotel** HOTEL €€€ (☑045 59 50 44; http://hotelduetorri.duetorriho tels.com/en; Piazza Sant'Anastasia 4; d €298-512; 🅿❄@🛜) This former Della Scala palace exudes luxury from the velvet-clad sofas in the cavernous lobby to walls clad in tapestries. Suites for the deep of pocket feature burnished antiques, embossed leather books and monogrammed towels. Significant discounts (up to 70%) apply if you book online, in advance.

🍴 Eating

★**Pasticceria Flego** CAFE € (☑045 803 24 71; www.pasticceriaflego.com; Via Stella 13; pastries €1.30-1.60; ⊙7.30am-7.30pm Tue-Sun) The gold standard for pastry in Verona is Flego, where you'll find at least 10 different croissant options every morning, including the divine myrtle-berry croissant, alongside the classic Risino, a typical Veronese cake made with rice. It also specialises in coffee and macarons and, come lunchtime, offers a range of savoury puff-pastry snacks, salads and sandwiches.

Hostaria La Vecchia Fontanina TRATTORIA € (☑045 59 11 59; www.ristorantevecchiafontani na.com; Piazzetta Chiavica 5; meals €20-25; ⊙10.30am-3.30pm & 6.30-11pm) With tables on a pint-sized piazza, cosy indoor rooms and excellent food, this historic, knick-knack-filled eatery stands out from the crowd. The menu features typical Veronese dishes alongside a number of more unusual creations such as *bigoli con ortica e ricotta affumicata* (thick spaghetti with nettles and smoked ricotta) and several heavenly desserts. Queuing to get in is normal.

★**Café Carducci** BISTRO €€
(📞 045 803 06 04; www.cafecarducci.it; Via Carducci 12; meals €25-45; ⊗8am-3pm & 6-10pm Mon-Sat; ✿) A charming 1920s-style bistro where stylish diners relax in the mirror-lined interior at linen-topped tables set with candles and plates of exquisitely sweet salami and local cheeses. The menu is as classic as the surroundings, offering risotto in an Amarone reduction and black rice with scallops. In cherry season, don't miss the cream gelato with Bigarreau cherries doused in grappa.

★**Locanda 4 Cuochi** ITALIAN €€
(📞 045 803 03 11; www.locanda4cuochi.it; Via Alberto Mario 12; meals €40, 5-course set menu €43; ⊗12.30-2.30pm & 7.30-10.30pm, closed lunch Mon & Tue; 📞) With its open kitchen, urbane vibe and hotshot chefs, you're right to expect great things from Locanda. Culinary acrobatics play second fiddle to prime produce cooked with skill and subtle twists. Whether it's perfectly crisp suckling pig lacquered with liquorice, or an epilogue of *gianduja* ganache with sesame crumble and banana, you will be gastronomically impressed.

Osteria da Ugo VENETIAN €€
(📞 045 59 44 00; www.osteriadaugo.com; Vicolo Dietro Sant'Andrea 1b; meals €30-35; ⊗noon-3.30pm & 7.30pm-midnight Mon-Sat, to 4pm Sun) Tucked away in a backstreet, this *osteria* (casual tavern) is a popular treat typically frequented at mealtimes by whole families. The vintage Liberty-style interiors and smartly dressed tables create an old-fashioned refined atmosphere, while the menu showcases Veronese specialities such as Lessinia prosciutto, *maccheroncini* (macarone) with Amarone-enriched *ragù*, and an old-school dessert trolley stacked with crème caramel and fruit tarts.

★**Pescheria I Masenini** SEAFOOD €€€
(📞 045 929 80 15; www.imasenini.com; Piazzetta Pescheria 9; meals €40-50; ⊗12.40-2pm & 7.40-10pm, closed Sun evening & Mon) Located on the piazza where Verona's Roman fish market once held sway, softly lit Masenini quietly serves up Verona's most imaginative, modern fish dishes. Inspired flavour combinations might see fresh sea-bass carpaccio paired with zesty green apple and pink pepper, black-ink gnocchi schmoozing with lobster *ragù,* or sliced amberjack delightfully matched with crumbed almonds, honey, spinach and raspberries.

🍷 Drinking & Nightlife

★**Antica Bottega del Vino** WINE BAR
(📞045 800 45 35; www.bottegavini.it; Vicolo Scudo di Francia 3; ⊗noon-2.40pm & 7-11pm) While *vino* is the primary consideration at this historic, baronial-style wine bar (the cellar holds around 18,000 bottles), the linen-lined tables promise a satisfying feed. Ask the sommelier to recommend a worthy vintage to go with your braised donkey, Vicenza-style codfish or Venetian liver – some of the best wines here are bottled specifically for the *bottega*.

Cafe Borsari COFFEE
(📞045 803 13 13; Corso Porta Borsari 15d; ⊗7.30am-8.15pm) It might look like a ceramics shop from the outside, but open the door and you'll discover a magically minuscule coffee house that's been roasting its own coffee and supplying hot chocolate to tables since 1969. It also sells quirky Christmas gifts year-round.

Archivio COCKTAIL BAR
(📞 345 8169663; Via Rosa 3; ⊗8am-midnight Mon-Thu, to 1am Fri & Sat, 11am-midnight Sun) Fragrant with aromatic cocktail ingredients, this side-street micro-bar is one of the best places for a night-launching drink. Imaginative mixology combines with craft beers to give a lot of choice to drinkers.

🛍 Shopping

★**Libreria Antiquaria Perini** ANTIQUES
(📞045 803 00 73; www.libreriaperini.com; Via Sciesa 11; ⊗9.30am-12.30pm & 3.30-7.30pm Tue-Sat, 3.30-7.30pm Mon) Don't be fooled by the name – this is no ordinary dusty antique shop. Rather, it is a treasure trove of vintage posters, maps, prints, engravings and books. Service is friendly, so ask away – there are wonderful things buried in the store room.

Cordovano FASHION & ACCESSORIES
(📞045 252 47 87; www.cordovano.it; Piazzetta Scala 2; ⊗9.30am-7pm Mon-Sat) Despite its modern demeanour, this leather showroom is the artisan studio of Mario Gastaldi, who handmakes all the leather products downstairs. His naturally tanned leather is beautifully soft and supple, and you can get all his bags, belts, wallets, purses and sandals in a wide selection of colours.

VENICE & THE VENETO VERONA

Shakespeare's Veneto

There is much debate about whether Shakespeare ever visited Italy, but his Italian plays are full of local knowledge. Venetian writer, architect and presenter Francesco da Mosto spoke to *Lonely Planet Traveller* magazine about the playwright's favourite Italian cities.

Verona

Verona was not thought of as a city of romance before *Romeo and Juliet* – in fact, not many people would have heard of it as it was very much in the shadow of Venice at that time. We don't know whether Romeo and Juliet existed, although Italian poet Dante did mention two feuding families, called the Montecchi and the Cappelletti. The famous balcony where Romeo is said to have declared his love to Juliet is close to Verona's main promenade – although, since the balcony was apparently added to a suitably old house in 1936, it's doubtful it is the original! My favourite site in Verona is Juliet's tomb. People go there to pay tribute to Juliet and Shakespeare – even Dickens visited.

Padua

The University of Padua was one of the first in the world, and in Shakespeare's time, the city was very well known throughout Europe as a centre of learning – Galileo (of telescope fame) and Casanova (of sexual-conquest fame) are both alumni. Shakespeare used its reputation, rather than actual locations, as a backdrop for *The Taming of the Shrew* – apart from the university,

1. Piazza San Marco
(p361), Venice 2. Casa
di Giulietta (p405),
Verona 3. Padua (p400)

he rarely mentions specific sites. The best way to experience Shakespeare's Padua is by having a stroll around the university. It feels like a little world unto itself, detached from the rest of the city. There is a marvellous wooden anatomical amphitheatre in the Medical School that was built in the 16th century, where they dissected humans and animals for the students. The life of the university runs through the city. It's lovely to walk through the portico walkways that run under the houses, and into the Prato della Valle, one of the main city squares.

Venice

Shakespeare set *Othello* in Venice, and *The Merchant of Venice* mentions the Rialto Market area several times.

He even talked about gondolas and 'the tranect', which could refer to the *traghetto* ferry, which transported people from Venice to the mainland. If he did visit, Shakespeare would have spent his time wandering the streets, eavesdropping on people's conversations and observing the goings-on in shops and at the market. A walk to the Rialto is certainly evocative of that time. The Palazzo Ducale, with its magnificent Gothic facades and huge council hall, is probably what Shakespeare had in mind as the setting for the final courtroom scene in *The Merchant of Venice,* while the two bronze figures on top of the Torre dell'Orologio clock tower in Piazza San Marco are known as 'i Mori', or 'the Moors', which is a key reference in *Othello.*

Sunday Flea Market MARKET
(Piazza San Zeno; ☺8am-5pm Sun) The flea market fills Piazza San Zeno and the surrounding streets, and is a feast of art nouveau light fittings, gramophone players, Fascist-era bike parts and lots of alarm clocks – a real mix of antiques and junk that you could spend all day browsing.

ℹ Information

Farmacie Internazionale (☏ 045 59 61 39; www.farmacia-internazionale.it; Piazza Brà 28; ☺9am-12.45pm & 3.30-7.45pm Mon-Fri, to 12.45pm Sat) A large, well-stocked pharmacy offering excellent multilingual advice on the main square.

Guardia Medica (☏ 045 761 45 65; ☺8pm-8am Mon-Sat, 8am-8pm Sun) A locum doctor service – doctors usually come to you.

Ospedaliera Universitaria Integrata di V erona (Borgo Trento; ☏ 045 812 11 11; www.aovr.veneto.it; Piazzale Aristide Stefani 1; ☺24hr) Verona's hospital operates out of two sites, Borgo Trento and Borgo Roma.

Tourist Office (☏ 045 806 86 80; www.verona touristoffice.it; Via degli Alpini 9; ☺8am-7pm Mon-Sat, 10am-6pm Sun)

ℹ Getting There & Away

AIR

Verona-Villafranca Airport (☏045 809 56 66; www.aeroportoverona.it) is 12km outside town and accessible by ATV Aerobus to/from the train station (€6, 15 minutes, every 20 minutes, 6.30am to 11.30pm). A taxi costs between €25 and €30. Flights arrive from all over Italy and some European cities.

BUS

The main intercity bus station is in front of the train station in the Porta Nuova area. Buses run to Padua, Vicenza and Venice.

ATV (Azienda Trasporti Verona; www.atv.verona. it; Stazione FS Porta Nuova; ☺6.30am-7pm Mon-Sat) city buses 11, 12 and 13 (bus 92 or 93 on Sundays and holidays) connect the train station with Piazza Brà. Buy tickets from newsagents, tobacconists, ticket machines or the ATV office within the train station before you board the bus (tickets valid for 90 minutes, €1.30).

CAR & MOTORCYCLE

Verona sits at the intersection of two motorways, the north–south A22, which connects Modena with Innsbruck in Austria, and the busy east–west A4, connecting Milan with Venice.

Traffic is restricted in the historic centre, although guests of hotels are allowed entry to drop off bags.

There's pay-and-display parking all around the ZTL zone (€1 to €2 per hour). Otherwise, park in one of the 24-hour parking lots just outside the centre. **Parcheggio Cittadella** (☏ 045 59 65 00; www.apcoa.it; Piazza Cittadella; ☺24hr) is convenient for Piazza Bra.

TRAIN

Verona Porta Nuova station is a major stop on the Italian rail network with direct services to numerous northern Italian towns and cities, including Milan (€13 to €20, 1¼ to two hours, one to three hourly), Padua (€7.50 to €20, 40 to 80 minutes, one to four hourly), Venice (€9.50 to €25, 70 minutes to 2¼ hours, one to four hourly) and Vicenza (€6 to €17, 25 to 55 minutes, one to four hourly). There are also direct international services to Austria, Germany and France.

VERONA'S WINE COUNTRY

A drive through Verona's hinterland is a lesson in fine wine. To the north and northwest are Valpolicella vineyards, which predate the arrival of the Romans, and east on the road to Vicenza lie the white-wine makers of Soave. If you don't have your own wheels, **Pagus Wine Tours** (☏327 7965380; www.pagusvalpo licella.net; Via San Giuseppe 18; group tour half day €75-95, full day €120-140; ☺10am-1pm & 2-6pm Mon-Fri, to 1pm Sat) and **Try Verona** (www.try verona.com; Via Pallone 16; half-day tours per person €60-120) run group tours from Verona.

Valpolicella

The 'valley of many cellars', from which Valpolicella gets its name, has been in the business of wine production since the ancient Greeks introduced their *passito* technique (the use of partially dried grapes) to create the blockbuster flavours we still enjoy in the region's Amarone and Recioto wines.

Situated in the foothills of Monte Lessini, the valleys benefit from a happy microclimate created by the enormous body of Lake Garda to the west and cooling breezes from the Alps to the north. No wonder Veronese nobility got busy building weekend retreats here. Many of them, like the extraordinary Villa della Torre, still house noble wineries, while others have been transformed into idyllic places to stay and eat.

◉ Sights

★**Villa della Torre** HISTORIC BUILDING
(☏ 045 683 20 70; www.villadellatorre.it; Via della Torre 25, Fumane; villa guided tours €10, with wine tasting & snack €30-40; ☺villa tours 11am & 4pm

Mon-Sat by appointment; [P]) The jewel in the Allegrini crown, this historic villa dates to the mid-16th century and was built by intellectual and humanist Giulio della Torre. Numerous starchitects contributed to its construction: the classically inspired peristyle and fish pond are attributed to Giulio Romana (of Palazzo Te fame), the chapel to Michele Sanmicheli, and the monstrous, gaping-mouthed fireplaces to Bartolomeo Ridolfi and Giovanni Battista Scultori.

Villa Serego Alighieri   WINERY
([✆]045 770 36 22; www.seregoalighieri.it; Via Giare 277, Località Gargagnago; tours & tastings €18; ⊙by appointment) Fleeing false charges of corruption in Florence, Italy's great medieval poet Dante Alighieri escaped to Verona and the protection of the Scala family. With the family settled in the Veneto, his son Pietro acquired a grand villa in 1353, the Casal dei Ronchi, which remains in the family today and forms the Villa Serego winery. Tours of the property and winery can be booked and are well worth it just to hear the fascinating story.

Pieve di San Floriano   CHURCH
(Via della Pieve 49, Località San Floriano; ⊙ 7.30am-7.30pm) **FREE** Considered one of the most attractive Romanesque churches in the region, this austere place of worship dates back to between the 10th and 13th centuries. Particularly impressive are the cloisters, a peaceful stone oasis with a truly ancient feel.

Pieve di San Giorgio   CHURCH
(www.infovalpolicella.it; Piazza della Pieve 22, San Giorgio di Valpolicella; ⊙ 7am-8pm summer, 8am-5pm winter) **FREE** In the tiny hilltop village of San Giorgio, around 6km northwest of San Pietro in Cariano, you'll find this fresco-filled, cloistered 8th-century Romanesque church. Not old enough for you? In the little garden to its left you can also see a few fragments of an ancient Roman temple.

☞ Tours

Details of wineries, restaurants and themed itineraries can be found at www.stradadel vinovalpolicella.it.

★ Damoli   WINE
([✆]340 8762680; www.damolivini.com; Via Jago di Mezzo 5, Negrar; tastings per person €30; ⊙by appointment) The Damoli family have been cultivating wines in Negrar since 1623, first as tenant farmers and then as owners of their own small vineyard. Their passion and dedication show in their classic Amarones and the three-hour-long tastings where Lara Da-

moli explains the attention to detail in their production process. The award-winning Checo wine is also extremely well priced at €30.

★ Giuseppe Quintarelli   WINE
([✆]045 750 00 16; giuseppe.quintarelli@tin.it; Via Cerè 1, Negrar; wine tastings per person €30; ⊙by appointment) The late Giuseppe Quintarelli put the Valpolicella region on the world wine map, and his benchmark estate is now run by daughter Fiorenza and her family. Quintarelli's extraordinary, limited-production Amarone – made using Corvina, Corvinone, Rondinella, cabernet, Nebbiolo, Croatina and Sangiovese grapes – is a Holy Grail for serious oenophiles. Given how expensive and hard to find the estate's wines are, the €30 tasting is fantastic value for money.

Allegrini   WINE
([✆]045 683 20 11; www.allegrini.it; Via Giare 9/11, Fumane; vineyard tour per person €60; ⊙by appointment) The Allegrini family has been tending vines in Fumane, Sant'Ambrogio and San Pietro since the 16th century. Pride of place goes to the *cru* wines produced from Corvinia and Rondinella grapes grown on the La Grola hillside (La Poja, La Grola and Palazzo della Torre). Tours of Allegrini's six different vineyards are possible for wine enthusiasts and explore the details of terroir and cultivation; otherwise, wine tastings are held in the historic 16th-century Villa della Torre.

Villa Mosconi Bertani   WINE
([✆]045 602 07 44; www.mosconibertani.it; Via Novare, Arbizzano; tours €9, tastings €22-35; ⊙wine tastings & tours 2pm & 4pm Sun-Fri, & 10am Tue-Sun) This lovely winery housed in a small manor offers both wine tastings and tours of the neoclassical building, a historic landmark with a richly frescoed chamber designed for operatic performances. There is a choice of four tasting sessions, most of them involving superior Valpolicello wines such as Lepia Soave DOC, Amarone Classico DOCG and Torre Pieve chardonnay. Pre-booking advised.

Fratelli Vogadori   WINE
([✆]328 9417228; www.amaronevalpolicella.org; Via Vigolo 16, Negrar; tastings per person €25; ⊙8am-noon & 1-6pm Mon-Sat, 8am-noon Sun) ⚓ The eponymous brothers (*fratelli*) of Vogadori produce organic wines using unusual native varieties such as Oseleta and Negrara. The result: the wonderfully full-bodied Amarone Riserva Forlago (2004) and the deservedly famous 2007 Recioto della Valpolicella, which pairs wickedly with dark chocolate cake. Cellar-door wine-tasting sessions take

place throughout the day; book ahead. Rooms are also available (doubles €70).

🛏 Sleeping

La Meridiana   B&B €

(☑045 683 91 46; www.lameridiana-valpolicella. it; Via Osan 16c, Fumane; s/d €60/90; [P][🛜]) This delightful B&B is set in a 1600s stable, with five beautifully renovated guest rooms with a rustic feel – ask for the garden room with the barrel-vaulted stone ceiling – and bountiful breakfasts at the Enoteca della Valpolicella, run by the same owners as the B&B. It's also possible to swim at a pool 1km away.

La Caminella   B&B €€

(☑045 680 05 63; www.lacaminella.it; Via Don Gaspare Bertoni 24, San Pietro in Cariano; d/q €115/175; [P][❄][🛜][🏊]) This pretty B&B is housed in an old stone structure once used for drying tobacco leaves. It's been transformed to provide chic accommodation in atmospheric rooms characterised by bare stone walls, terracotta-tiled floors and chic country-house furnishings. It's part of the Carilius winery, so there's wine tasting on the doorstep, as well as a pool.

🍴 Eating

⭐**Enoteca della Valpolicella**   VENETIAN €€

(☑045 683 91 46; www.enotecadellavalpolicella. it; Via Osan 47, Fumane; meals €25-35; ☺noon-2.30pm & 7pm-midnight Tue-Sat, to 3pm Sun) Gastronomes flock to the town of Fumane, just a few kilometres north of San Pietro in Cariano, where an ancient farmhouse has found renewed vigour as a rustically elegant restaurant. Put your trust in gracious owners Ada and Carlotta, who will eagerly guide you through the day's menu, a showcase for fresh, local produce.

⭐**Osteria Numero Uno**   OSTERIA €€

(☑045 770 13 75; www.osterianumero1.com; Via Flaminio Pellegrini 2, Fumane; meals €20-30; ☺noon-2.30pm & 7-10.30pm Thu-Mon) The archetypal *osteria* with a wooden bar packed with overall-clad vintners and delicious aromas wafting out of the kitchen. Glasses of Valpolicella (around 120 types) range from just €2 to €5 for a good Amarone. Pair them with salty speck and belly-filling duck with wild garlic and gnocchi.

ℹ️ Information

Valpolicella Tourist Office (☑045 770 19 20; www.valpolicellaweb.it; Via Ingelheim 7, San Pietro in Cariano; ☺9am-1pm Mon-Fri)

ℹ️ Getting There & Away

To get the most out of the Valpolicella area, you need a car. From Verona, take the SP1 northwest out of the city. This changes into the SP12; all villages in the wine region can be found off this road.

Soave

POP 7145

East of Verona and an easy day trip, Soave serves its namesake DOC (Denominazione di Origine Controllate) white wine in a storybook setting. The town is entirely encircled by medieval fortifications, including 24 bristling watchtowers guarding a medieval castle. Wine is the main reason to come here, with tastings available throughout the year.

👁 Sights & Activities

Castello di Soave   CASTLE

(☑045 768 00 36; www.castellodisoave.it; adult/reduced €7/4; ☺9am-noon & 3-6.30pm Apr-Oct, to noon & 2-4pm Nov-Mar) Built on a medieval base by Verona's fratricidal Scaligeri family, the Castello complex encompasses an early-Renaissance villa, grassy courtyards, the remnants of a Romanesque church and the Mastio (the defensive tower, apparently used as a dungeon – during restoration, a mound of human bones was unearthed here). The highlight for most, however, will be the panoramas of the surrounding countryside from the many rampart viewing points.

⭐**1898 Cantina di Soave**   WINE

(☑045 613 98 45; www.cantinasoave.it; Via Covergnino 7; ☺9am-7pm Mon-Sat May-Sep, 8.30am-12.30pm & 2.30-7pm Mon-Sat Oct-Apr) Going strong for over a century and once an official supplier to Italian royalty, this cooperative of 2000 Soave producers is a must-visit. It is housed in a small hamlet, Borgo Rocca Sveva, set against the castle wall, where you can visit the cellars, wine shop and botanical garden. Book tours.

⭐**Suavia**   WINE

(☑045 767 50 89; www.suavia.it; Via Centro 14, Fittà; ☺9am-1pm & 2.30-6.30pm Mon-Fri, to 1pm Sat & by appointment) Soave is not known as a complex white, but this trailblazing winery, located 8km outside Soave via the SP58, has been changing the viticultural landscape in recent years. Don't miss the award-winning DOC Monte Carbonare Soave Classico, with its mineral, ocean-breeze finish. Book tours.

Azienda Agricola Coffele   WINE

(☑045 768 00 07; www.coffele.it; Via Roma 5; wine tasting €12-25; ☺9.30am-7.30pm Mon-Sat,

10am-1pm & 2-7pm Sun) Across from the old-town church, this family-run winery offers tastings of lemon-zesty DOC Soave Classico and an elegant, creamy DOC Coffele Ca' Visco Classico. The family also rents out rooms among vineyards a few kilometres from town. Book wine tastings in advance; at least a day ahead in winter and about a week ahead in summer.

✕ Eating

Trattoria alla Rocca   TRATTORIA €

(☑ 045 768 02 35; Corso Vittorio Emanuele II 155, Soave; meals €15-20; ⊙noon-2pm & 7-10.15pm Tue-Sat, 7-10.15pm Sun) Cheap and cheerful Alla Rocca is known as La Bigoleria because it focuses on the region's signature pasta *(bigoli)* served with dozens of different sauces. The slow-cooked wild-boar sauce is particularly good and plentiful.

Locanda Lo Scudo   ITALIAN €€

(☑045 768 07 66; www.loscudo.vr.it; Via Covergnino 9; meals €35; ⊙noon-2.30pm & 7.30-10.30pm Tue-Sat, to 2.30pm Sun; 🖘) Just outside the medieval walls of Soave, Lo Scudo is half country inn and half high-powered gastronomy. Cult classics include a risotto of scallops and porcini mushrooms, though – if it's on the menu – only a fool would resist the extraordinary dish of tortelloni stuffed with local pumpkin, Grana Padano, cinnamon, mustard and Amaretto, and topped with crispy fried sage.

❶ Information

Soave's **tourist office** (☑045 619 07 73; www.soaveturismo.it; Piazza Foro Boario I; ⊙10am-4pm Tue-Fri, to 2pm Sat & Sun) is just outside the medieval wall, in front of the central bus stop.

❶ Getting There & Away

Soave is 23km east of Verona. To reach Soave by bus from Verona, take ATV bus 130 (€3.40, around one hour) from Corso Porta Nuova. Buy tickets from the machines on the platforms. If driving, exit the A4 autostrada at San Bonifacio and follow the Viale della Vittoria 2km north into town. A taxi will cost €45 to €60.

VICENZA
POP 111.620

When Palladio escaped an oppressive employer in his native Padua, few would have guessed the humble stonecutter would, within a few decades, transform not only his adoptive city but also the history of European architecture. By luck, a local count recognised his talents in the 1520s and sent him to study the ruins in Rome. When he returned to Vicenza, the autodidact began producing his extraordinary buildings, structures that marry sophistication and rustic simplicity, reverent classicism and bold innovation. His genius would turn Vicenza and its surrounding villas into one grand Unesco World Heritage Site. And yet, the Veneto's fourth-largest city is more than just elegant porticoes and balustrades – its dynamic exhibitions, bars and restaurants provide a satisfying dose of modern vibrancy.

◉ Sights

★ La Rotonda   HISTORIC BUILDING

(☑049 879 13 80; www.villalarotonda.it; Via della Rotonda 45; adult/child villa & gardens €10/5, gardens €5/free; ⊙villa 10am-noon & 3-6pm Wed & Sat mid-Mar–mid-Nov, gardens 10am-noon & 3-6pm Tue-Sun year-round) No matter how you look at it, this villa is a showstopper: the namesake dome caps a square base, with identical colonnaded facades on all four sides. This is one of Palladio's most admired creations, inspiring variations across Europe and the USA, including Thomas Jefferson's Monticello. Inside, the circular central hall is covered from the walls to the soaring cupola with *trompe l'œil* frescoes. Catch bus 8 (€1.30, €2 on board) from in front of Vicenza's train station, or simply walk (about 25 minutes).

★ Teatro Olimpico   THEATRE

(☑0444 96 43 80; www.teatrolimpicovicenza.it; Piazza Matteotti 11; adult/reduced €11/8, or free with MuseumCard; ⊙9am-5pm Tue-Sun Sep-Jun, 10am-6pm Jul & Aug) Behind a walled garden lies a Renaissance marvel: the Teatro Olimpico, which Palladio began in 1580 with inspiration from Roman amphitheatres. Vincenzo Scamozzi finished the elliptical theatre after Palladio's death, adding a stage set modelled on the ancient Greek city of Thebes, with streets built in steep perspective to give the illusion of a city sprawling towards a distant horizon. Today, Italian performers vie to make an entrance on this extraordinary stage; check the website for opera, classical and jazz performances.

★ Palazzo Leoni Montanari   MUSEUM

(☑800 578875; www.gallerieditalia.com; Contrà di Santa Corona 25; adult/reduced €5/3, or free with MuseumCard; ⊙10am-6pm Tue-Sun) An extraordinary collection of treasures awaits inside Palazzo Leoni Montanari,including ancient pottery from Magna Graecia and grand salons filled with Canaletto's misty lagoon landscapes and Pietro Longhi's 18th-century

Vicenza

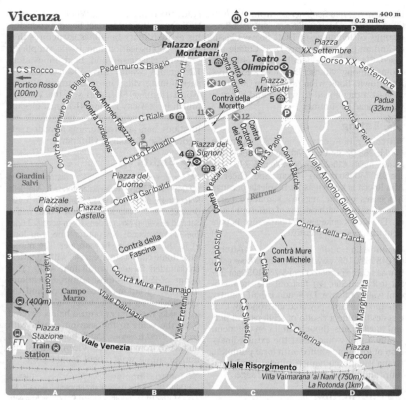

Vicenza

satires. A recent addition is Agostino Fasolato's astounding *The Fall of the Rebel Angels,* carved from a single block of Carrara marble and featuring no less than 60 angels and demons in nail-biting battle. Topping it all off is a superb collection of 400 Russian icons.

Palazzo Chiericati   MUSEUM
(📞 0444 22 28 11; www.museicivicivicenza.it; Piazza Matteotti 37/39; adult/reduced €7/5; ⊙ 9am-5pm Tue-Sun Sep-Jun, 10am-6pm Tue-Sun Jul & Aug) Vicenza's civic art museum occupies one of Palladio's finest buildings, designed in 1550. The ground floor, used for temporary exhibitions, is where you'll find the *Sala dal Firmamento* (Salon of the Skies) and its blush-inducing ceiling fresco of Diana and an up-skirted Helios by Domenico Brusasorci. Highlights in the upstairs galleries include Anthony Van Dyck's allegorical *The Four Ages of Man* and Alessandro Maganza's remarkably contemporary *Portrait of Maddalena Campiglia.*

Palladio Museum MUSEUM
(Palazzo Barbarano; ☑ 0444 32 30 14; www.palladiomuseum.org; Contrà Porti 11; adult/reduced €8/6, or free with MuseumCard; ◷ 10am-6pm Tue-Sun) To better understand architect Andrea Palladio and his legacy, explore the frescoed halls of this modern museum. Artefacts include historical copies of Palladio's celebrated *Quattro libri dell'architettura* (Four Books of Architecture; 1570) and intriguing architectural models of his lauded *palazzi* and villas, as well as video footage of experts discussing various aspects of the maverick's craft and genius.

Piazza dei Signori SQUARE
The heart of historic Vicenza is Piazza dei Signori, where Palladio lightens the mood of government buildings with his trademark play of light and shadow. Dazzling white Piovene stone (a local limestone) arches frame shady double arcades at the Basilica Palladiana while, across the piazza, white stone and stucco grace the exposed red-brick colonnade of the 1571-designed **Loggia del Capitaniato**.

Basilica Palladiana GALLERY
(☑ 0444 22 21 22; ww.museicivicivicenza.it; Piazza dei Signori; basilica adult/reduced €4/2, exhibitions €10-13; ◷ 10am-4pm Tue-Sun) Now a venue for world-class exhibitions, the Palladian Basilica is capped with an enormous copper dome reminiscent of the hull of a ship. The building, modelled on a Roman basilica, once housed the law courts and Council of Four Hundred. Palladio was lucky to secure the commission in 1549 (it took his patron 50 years of lobbying the council), which involved restructuring the original, 15th-century *palazzo* and adding a double order of loggias, supported by Tuscan and Ionic columns topped by soaring statuary.

The building is also home to the elegant **Museo del Gioiello** (☑ 0444 32 07 99; www.museodelgioiello.it; adult/reduced €8/6; ◷ 3-7pm Mon-Fri, 11am-7pm Sat & Sun) and its dazzling collection of historic and contemporary jewellery.

🛏 Sleeping

★ Portico Rosso B&B €
(☑ 348 0847714; www.porticorosso.it; Contrà San Rocco 28; d €80-120; ☎) Set your bags down in this friendly Vicentine house, whose owner has decorated it with colour and flair. The 600-year-old house was once owned by a count who fitted it with roaring fireplaces and balconied bedrooms. Sleep in the countess's carved bed and breakfast on warm *panettone* (sweet bread) and local ham and cheese in the beautiful garden come morning.

Palazzo Valmarana
Braga Rosa APARTMENT €€
(www.palazzovalmaranabraga.it; Corso Antonio Fogazzaro 16; studio/apt €70/150) Designed by Palladio in the 1560s, this elegant palace was raised for noblewoman Isabella Nogarola Valmarana in memory of her husband Giovanni Alvise. More recently the palace has been divided into seven magnificent apartments enjoying antique furnishings, family paintings and the original dreamy frescoes.

Hotel Palladio HOTEL €€
(☑ 0444 32 53 47; www.hotel-palladio.it; Contrà Oratorio dei Servi 25; s/d €110/170; P ✺ ☎) The top choice in central Vicenza, this renovated Renaissance *palazzo* delivers crisp, contemporary rooms with beamed ceilings, polished wooden floors and super-swish, glassed-in bathrooms with large power-showers. Staff are friendly, and breakfast is a generous buffet of cereal, pastries and cooked-to-order eggs and bacon.

🍴 Eating

★ Sòtobotega VENETIAN €
(☑ 0444 54 44 14; www.gastronomiailceppo.com; Corso Palladio 196; meals €25, set tasting menus €26; ◷ 11.30am-3.30pm) Drop into cult-status deli **Gastronomia Il Ceppo** (prepared dishes per 100g from around €2.50; ◷ 8am-7.45pm Tue-Sat, 9am-4pm Sun) for picnic provisions, or head down into its cellar for sensational sit-down dishes like expertly crafted *bigoli* (a type of pasta) with the sauce of the day, or the star of the show, *bacalà alla vicentina*, Vicenza's signature codfish dish. Some 500 mostly Italian wines line the walls, and transparent floor panels reveal an ancient Roman footpath and the foundations of an 11th-century dwelling.

★ Fuorimodena EMILIAN €€
(☑ 0444 33 09 94; www.fuorimodena.it; Contrà San Gaetano da Thiene 8; meals €40-45; ◷ 7.30-11.30pm Tue-Sun; ✺) Two hundred kilometres separate Vicenza and Modena, but enter this restaurant and you'll enjoy the finest Emilian cooking courtesy of Lorenzo Roncaccioli, whose grandparents emigrated here in 1949. Exquisite plates of the Culatello di Zibello DOP (aged for 32 months) are followed by *passatelli* pasta with Zocca chestnuts and saffron, and then delicate guinea fowl with creamy polenta and chargrilled fennel.

VENICE & THE VENETO VICENZA

★ **Al Pestello** VENETIAN €€
(☑ 0444 32 37 21; Contrà San Stefano 3; meals €35; ⊙ 7.30-11.45pm Mon & Wed-Fri, 12.30-2pm & 7.30-11.45pm Sat & Sun; 🛜) Homely Al Pestello dishes out intriguing, lesser-known *cucina vicentina* such as *la panà* (bread soup), red-wine-braised donkey and *bresaola* 'lollies' filled with grappa-flavoured Grana Padano and mascarpone. The kitchen is obsessed with local ingredients, right down to the Colli Berici truffles, while the collection of harder-to-find *digestivi* makes for an enlightening epilogue. Book ahead.

❶ Information

Tourist Office (☑ 0444 32 08 54; www.vicenzae.org; Piazza Matteotti 12; ⊙ 9am-5.30pm) Ask the helpful staff about the excellent-value MuseumCard (adult/reduced €15/12), which offers admission to eight city museums, including the Teatro Olimpico. They also have information on city events and transport to sites in the surrounding area.

❶ Getting There & Away

BUS

FTV (☑ 0444 22 31 11; www.ftv.vi.it) buses leave for outlying areas from the bus station, located next to the train station.

TRAIN

Vicenza has train connections to Padua (€4.35 to €17, 15 to 25 minutes, up to five hourly), Ven-

---

THE PROSECCO LOWDOWN

Prosecco can be traced back to the Romans. It was then known as 'Pucino' and was shipped directly to the court of Empress Livia from Aquileia, where it was produced with grapes from the Carso. In the 16th century, during the time of the Venetian Republic, the vines were transferred to the sunny hillsides just north of the Piave river between the towns of Valdobbiadene, Conegliano and Vittorio Veneto.

You can spot a good prosecco by its straw-like yellow colouring, which is touched with a tinge of green. Its bubbles should be tiny, numerous and long-lasting in your glass. On the nose it is fragrant with the scent of white fruits and freshly mown grass, while in the mouth it is crisp and aromatic. These characteristics are not long lasting, so drink it young when it is full of fizz.

---

ice (€6.50 to €18, 45 to 80 minutes, up to five hourly) and Verona (€6 to €18, 25 to 55 minutes, up to four hourly).

PROSECCO COUNTRY

In the foothills of the Alps, the area between Conegliano and Valdobbiadene is the toast of the Veneto. The vine-draped hillsides hereabouts produce prosecco, a dry, crisp white wine made in *spumante* (bubbly), *frizzante* (sparkling) and still varieties. In 2009, Conegliano's prosecco was promoted to DOCG (guaranteed-quality) status, Italy's highest oenological distinction.

Plot a tasting tour along La Strada del Prosecco from Conegliano to Valdobbiadene to see what all the fuss is about. It is Italy's oldest wine route and covers 120 wine producers in 60km.

Bassano del Grappa

POP 43,400

Bassano del Grappa sits charmingly on the banks of the river Brenta as it winds its way free from Alpine foothills through the Veneto plains to the Venetian lagoon. The town is famous for its namesake spirit, grappa – a distillation made from the discarded skins, pulp, seeds and stems of winemaking – although there is plenty to enjoy in this lovely Veneto town with its Palladian architecture and ancient historic core.

Subject to Venetian rule between 1404 and 1815, Bassano has long been a flourishing manufacturing town, while in the 18th century the local Remondini printing house grew to become the largest in Europe. But the strategic location that gave Bassano its commercial edge also put it on the front line in both world wars. In 1928, the town's name was changed to Bassano del Grappa in honour of the thousands of soldiers who died in the battle of Monte Grappa.

◉ Sights

★ **Palazzo Sturm** MUSEUM
(☑ 0424 51 99 40; www.museibassano.it; Via Schiavonetti 40; adult/reduced €5/3.50; ⊙ 9am-1pm & 3-6pm Mon-Sat, 10am-7pm Sun) Pretty Palazzo Sturm sits overlooking the Brenta river. It was built in the mid-18th century by wealthy industrialist and silk merchant Vincenzo Ferrari, who decorated it with bourgeoisie baroque frescoes by Veronese painter Giorgio Anselmi. Set against this florid pastel backdrop is a permanent collection of

extravagant (and outlandish) historic ceramics and a fascinating exhibit celebrating Bassano's world-famous printers, the Remondinis. Aside from the detailed description of the printing process, there are stunning etchings and woodcuts by Dürer, Mantegna and Tiepolo.

Ponte degli Alpini BRIDGE
Spanning the river is Palladio's photogenic 1569 wooden bridge. Fragile as it seems, it is cleverly engineered to withstand the rush of spring meltwaters from Monte Grappa. It's always been critical in times of war: Napoleon bivouacked here and during WWII the bridge was destroyed by the Germans, only to be reconstructed by the Italian Alpine brigade, who adopted it as their emblem.

Poli Museo della Grappa MUSEUM
(☑0424 52 44 26; www.poligrappa.com; Via Gamba 6; ⊙museum 9am-7.30pm, distillery guided tours 9am-1pm & 2-6pm Mon-Fri) FREE Explore four centuries of Bassano's high-octane libation at this interactive museum, which includes tastings and the chance to tour the distillery of esteemed producer Poli (book tours online; €3 per person). Although grappa is made all over Italy, and indeed inferior versions are distilled well beyond the peninsula, the people of the Veneto have been doing it since at least the 16th century. In fact, an institute of grappa distillers was created in Venice in 1601.

Museo Civico MUSEUM
(☑0424 51 99 01; www.museibassano.it; Piazza Garibaldi 34; adult/reduced €7/5; ⊙10am-7pm Wed-Mon) Bassano del Grappa's Museo Civico is beautifully housed around the cloisters of the Convento di San Francesco. Endowed in 1828 by the naturalist Giambattista Brocchi, the museum features an extensive archaeological collection alongside 500 paintings, including masterpieces such as the 1545 *Flight into Egypt* by local son Jacopo Bassano.

🏃 Activities

★**Valsugana Bike Path** CYCLING
(www.visitvalsugana.it) The mighty Brenta, on whose banks Bassano del Grappa sits, flows down from the Alps through the Valsugana Valley connecting Bassano del Grappa with Trento. It has been an important communication route for centuries, and now an 80km cycle path (mostly flat) runs along its length to Lake Caldonazzo. Valsugana Rent Bike (www.valsuganarentbike.it) and In Bike Valsugana

(www.inbikevalsugana.it) both rent bikes and offer pick-up and drop-off points along the route, as well as service stations.

★**Vignaioli Contra Soarda** WINE
(☑0424 50 55 62; www.contrasoarda.it; Strada Soarda 26, San Michele di Bassano del Grappa; tastings per person €25; ⊙6.30-11pm Mon-Thu, 5.30pm-midnight Fri & Sat) Grappa isn't the only reason to visit Bassano: there are also some exceptional vineyards such as Contra Soarda. Located in a volcanic zone at the start of the Valsugana Valley, the vineyard's autochthonous Garganega, Marzemino and Grupello wines are award-winning, as is the ecofriendly cellar, which is tucked into the hillside.

🛏 Sleeping

★**Le 33** B&B €
(☑347 2161224; www.le33bnb.com; Via Ferracina 33; d €80-90; P☀🐕) This home-away-from-home offers three rooms with river views in a historic *palazzo*. Rooms are furnished with great care: vintage finds, mid-century modern furnishings, photos and books. Host, Julie, a French chef, rustles up a memorable breakfast and runs great cookery classes. Cyclists, too, are welcome, and Julie can help with bike rental and itineraries and even find you a cycle buddy.

Hotel Al Castello BOUTIQUE HOTEL €€
(☑0424 22 86 65; www.hotelalcastello.it; Via Lazzaro Bonamigo 19; d €77-115; P☀🐕) One of the only hotels in the pedestrianised centre of Bassano is this charming, family-owned pink *palazzo*. The cosy rooms come in duck-egg blue and the softest pink with beamed ceilings and glossy wooden floors. Service is

kind and generous, and the vintage hotel bar with its pink-velour banquettes and terrazzo floor is a buzzing local hub.

✕ Eating & Drinking

TIPIC ficusbar
ITALIAN €€

(☑ 334 8715566; Via Lazzaro Bonamigo 39; meals €20-35; ⏱ 5.30pm-midnight Tue-Wed & Fri, 10am-midnight Thu, Sat & Sun) This hipster bar gets everything right, from the cool industrial decor to the organic *cicheti* and the 30 top-quality wines by the glass, which are offered up daily. It also rustles up some interesting cocktails based on an organic vodka produced in Tuscany, and at the weekend, everyone piles in for the excellent bagel-fuelled brunches (11.30am to 2pm).

★ Palazzo delle Misture
COCKTAIL BAR

(☑ 0424 28 04 65; www.palazzodellemisture.it; Piazzotto Montevecchio 23; ⏱ 6pm-2am Mon-Sat, 3pm-2am Sun) A cocktail bar in a palace, what's not to like? Other than the glamorous environment and towering bar, there's live jazz and cabaret. Most of the classic cocktails are on offer alongside revived drinks such as the Pegu Club, while the house signatures are absinthe-based drinks from the late 19th century, to which a whole room is dedicated.

🛍 Shopping

★ Libreria Palazzo Roberti
BOOKS

(☑ 0424 52 25 37; www.palazzoroberti.it; Via Jacopo da Ponte 34; ⏱ 9am-12.30pm & 3.30-7.30pm Tue-Sat, from 10.30am Sun; 🛜) This gorgeous bookshop, housed in an 18th-century noble palace, is one of the most beautiful in Italy, if not the world. Owned by the three Manfrotto sisters, its beautiful walnut shelves are crammed with well-curated titles spanning all genres, while the frescoed hall on the top floor is given over to music concerts, photography exhibitions and author readings.

Carteria Tassotti
ARTS & CRAFTS

(☑ 0424 52 30 13; www.tassotti.it; Via Ferracina 16/18; ⏱ 10am-12.30pm & 3.30-7pm) Freelance journalist Giorgio Tassotti started his printing works in 1958 after seeing an exhibition about Bassano's world-famous Remondini printers. With the aim of reviving the Remondinis' high-quality paper products, he set about crafting coloured handprints, decorative papers, origami sets and stationery, which you can now buy from the historic printing house overlooking the Ponte Vecchio.

ℹ Getting There & Away

BUS

Ferrovie Tramvie Vicentine (www.ftv.vi.it) buses are the quickest way to reach Bassano del Grappa from Vicenza (€4.30, one hour, every 30 minutes).

TRAIN

Train is the easiest way to reach Bassano del Grappa. The train station is 150m east of the centre. The town has the following connections:
Padova €5.10, one hour, hourly.
Trento €7.05, two hours, hourly.
Venice €6.40, 90 minutes, twice hourly.

Asolo
POP 9100

Known as the 'town of 100 vistas' for its panoramic hillside location, the medieval walled town of Asolo has long been a favourite of literary types. Robert Browning bought a house here, but the ultimate local celebrity is Caterina Corner, the 15th-century queen of Cyprus, who was given the town, its castle (now used as a theatre) and the surrounding county in exchange for her abdication. She promptly became queen of the literary set, holding salons that featured writer and later cardinal Pietro Bembo.

⊙ Sights

Villa Freya
GARDENS

(☑ 0423 56 54 78; www.bellasolo.it; Via Forestuzzo; adult/reduced €3/2; ⏱ 1st 3 Sat each month, closed Aug & Dec) When she wasn't exploring the furthest reaches of the Empty Quarter or negotiating with future Arab heads of state, legendary explorer and travel writer Freya Stark retired to Asolo to tend her flower-filled gardens. Inevitably she brought back exotic botanical specimens, which still thrive on the sunny slopes that originally formed part of a Roman theatre complex. The ticket price includes a guided tour by **BellAsolo** (☑ 0423 56 54 78; www.bell asolo.it; Via Schiavonesca Marosticana 15; English-speaking guide half-/full-day €130/230) at 10am and 11am.

Museo Civico di Asolo
MUSEUM

(☑ 0423 95 23 13; www.asolo.it; Via Regina Cornaro 74; adult/reduced €5/4; ⏱ 9.30am-12.30pm & 3-6pm Sat & Sun) Explore Asolo's Roman past and wander through a small collection of paintings, including a pair of Tintoretto portraits. The museum also includes rooms devoted to actress Eleonora Duse (1858–1924) and Freya Stark (1893–1993).

Rocca   RUINS
(☏ 329 8508512; €2; ⊙ 10am-7pm Sat & Sun Apr-Jun, Sep & Oct, 10am-noon & 3-7pm Sat & Sun Jul & Aug, 10am-5pm Sat & Sun Nov-Mar) Perched on the summit of Monte Ricco and looking down on central Asolo are the hulking ru-ins of a fortress dating back to the 12th to early 13th centuries. The still-visible cistern well was constructed between the 13th and 14th centuries, while the heavily restored buttresses offer a breathtaking panorama that takes in soft green hills, snow-capped mountains and the industrious Po Valley. At the time of writing, the fortress was closed for maintenance work.

TUCKED-AWAY TREASURES IN PROSECCO COUNTRY

Tucked in a broad curve of the Piave river between the towns of Conegliano, Vittorio Veneto and Valdobbiadene, prosecco country is deeply rural. Narrow country roads me-ander through a patchwork of vineyards, the majority of which are small, family-run af-fairs. Tastings, which can be arranged between Monday and Saturday, should be booked in advance and you'll need your own set of wheels to get between vineyards. Alternative-ly, tour operators in Venice, Padua and Asolo can help organise visits.

Gypsotheca e Museo Antonio Canova (☏ 0423 54 43 23; www.museocanova.it; Via Canova 74, Possagno; adult/reduced €10/6; ⊙ 9.30am-6pm Tue-Sat, to 7pm Sun) Antonio Canova was Italy's master of neoclassical sculpture. He made marble come alive, and you can see his fascinating modelling technique at the beautiful Gypsotheca, fashioned by modernist master Carlo Scarpa in 1957. Inside, plaster casts reveal the laborious process through which Canova arrived at his glossy, seemingly effortless marbles. Rough clay models give way to plaster figures cast in gesso, which were then used to map out the final marble in minute detail with small nails.

Villa di Maser (Villa Barbaro; ☏ 0423 92 30 04; www.villadimaser.it; Via Cornuda 7, Maser; adult/reduced €9/7; ⊙ 10am-6pm Tue-Sat, from 11am Sun Apr-Oct, 11am-5pm Sat & Sun Nov-Mar; P) A World Heritage Site, the 16th-century Villa di Maser is a spectacular monument to the Venetian *bea vita* (good life). Designed by the inimitable Andrea Palladio, its sublimely ele-gant exterior is matched by Paolo Veronese's wildly imaginative *trompe l'œil* architecture inside. Vines crawl up the Stanza di Baccho; a watchdog keeps an eye on the painted door of the Stanza di Canuccio (Little Dog Room); and in a corner of the frescoed grand salon, the painter has apparently forgotten his spattered shoes and broom.

Cantina Bisol (☏ 0423 90 47 37; www.bisol.it; Via Follo 33, Santo Stefano di Valdobbiadene; ⊙ 10am-1pm & 3-6pm Mon-Sat, 10am-1pm Sun) Twenty-one generations of the Bisol family have been striving to produce the best prosecco in the world since 1542. Their vineyard, the most important in the area, occupies steep hillsides angled towards the sun, making them perfect for Glera-grape growing. Tastings take place in the atmospheric under-ground cellars. Their signature labels are the award-winning Cartizze Dry and Jeio Brut.

Azienda Agricola Barichel (☏ 0423 97 57 43; www.barichel.it; Via Roccat e Ferrari 12, Valdobbiadene) Like the prodigal son, ultra-marathon runner and vintner Ivan Geronazzo returned to his grandfather's vineyard in Valdobbiadene after years of working at larger, high-capacity wineries. Here he tends his 7 hectares by hand, producing up to 60,000 bottles of natural, *frizzante,* extra dry and brut prosecco with a pale, straw-yellow colour and apple-and-pear fragrances. Prices range from €5 to €8 per bottle.

Azienda Agricola Campion (☏ 0423 98 04 32; www.campionspumanti.it; Via Campion 2, San Giovanni di Valdobbiadene; s/d €85/110; ⊙ tasting room 9am-noon & 2-6pm; P ✿ ☎ ≋) Why not quit worrying about the challenges of prosecco tasting and driving, and instead bed down at this farmstay amid 14 hectares of vines in the heart of Valdobbiadene? The four rooms occupy converted farm buildings, with warm, rustic styling and the added perk of a kitchenette in each.

Agriturismo Da Ottavio (☏ 0423 98 11 13; Via Campion 2, San Giovanni di Valdobbiadene; meals €15-20; ⊙ noon-3pm Sat, Sun & holidays, closed Sep; P) Prosecco is typically drunk with *sopressa,* a fresh local salami, as the sparkling *spumante* cleans the palate and refreshes the mouth. There's no better way to test this than at Da Ottavio, where everything on the table, *sopressa* and prosecco included, is homemade by the Spada family.

🛏 Sleeping & Eating

⭐ **Albergo del Sole**   BOUTIQUE HOTEL €€€
(☑ 0423 95 13 32; www.albergoalsoleasolo.com;
Via Collegio 33; s €110-180, d €200-450; P ❋ 🛜)
Even for ridiculously charming Asolo, the
Albergo del Sole is super-romantic. Overlooking the main square the 16th-century
pink villa houses 23 beautifully decorated
rooms finished with polished wooden floors
and brass beds, some of which are tucked
beneath the roof beams. All of them, along
with the pretty dining terrace, have stunning views of the dreamy landscape.

⭐ **Due Mori**   ITALIAN €€€
(☑ 0423 95 09 53; www.2mori.it; Piazza Gabriele
D'Annunzio 5; meals €40-50; ⊙ 12.30-2.30pm
& 7.30-9.30pm Tue-Sun) If ever there was a
table with a view, the dining room of Due
Mori provides it, with floor-to-ceiling windows overlooking Asolo and the layered
Veneto hillsides. Nor does the food disappoint. Refined rustic dishes are cooked on
a wood-burning stove that yields a delicious depth of flavour. Try the ravioli with
poison-oak leaves and ricotta, or the rich
guinea fowl *ragù*.

🛍 Shopping

⭐ **Mercatino dell'Antiquariato**   ANTIQUES
(Antiques Market; ☑ 0423 52 46 75; www.asolo.
it; Piazza Garibaldi; ⊙ 2nd Sun of month) Taking
over the town's main piazza and surrounding streets, Asolo's monthly antiques market is one of the region's finest, peddling
anything and everything from 18th-century
clocks and furniture, to vintage lithographs,
ceramics, cufflinks and books.

ℹ Getting There & Away

The best way to reach Asolo if you don't have
your own car is to take the train to Treviso where
you change onto local bus 112 (€3.60, one hour,
hourly).

Conegliano

POP 35,100

If you've ever admired the paintings of
sweet Madonnas and saints by local boy
Giovanni Battista Cima (aka Cima da Conegliano), you'll most likely feel a sense of
déjà vu when you arrive in the town of
Conegliano. Draped attractively over a
prominent hill in the foothills of the Alps,
the town and the surrounding countryside
were Giovanni's go-to backdrops, and it's no

wonder given their sense of timeless pastoral beauty. These days Conegliano remains
a sleepy rural town and is the starting point
for Italy's oldest wine route, **La Strada del
Prosecco** (The Prosecco Road; www.conegliano
valdobbiadene.it).

◉ Sights

The principal street of the historic centre,
Via XX Settembre, historically known as
Contrada Grande, leads off in either direction from impressive Piazza Cima, and offers
a lovely procession of palaces and arcades.

Castello di Conegliano   CASTLE
(Piazzale San Leonardo; ⊙ 24hr) FREE Head up
steep Calle Madonna della Neve, following
an intact section of 13th-century defensive
walls all the way to a summit, where the
last remaining tower of Conegliano's 10th-
century castle dominates an attractive set of
gardens. The tower is home to a small museum (adult/reduced €2.50/1.50), but the real
joy here is the views across the surrounding
hills. It's also a superb place to unfurl the
picnic blanket, or to spend a sleepy afternoon in the company of a good book.

🛏 Sleeping & Eating

Hotel Canon d'Oro   HISTORIC HOTEL €€
(☑ 0438 3 42 46; www.hotelcanondoro.it; Via XX
Settembre 131; s €76-90, d €90-120; P 🛜) If you
decide to spend the night in town, Hotel
Canon d'Oro provides classic elegance and
modern comforts in a 15th-century *palazzo*.
Rooms are plush, and the breakfast is good.
Staff are very friendly here and can help
plan wine-tasting and cycling itineraries.

Al Castello   CAFE €€
(☑ 0438 2 23 79; www.ristorantealcastello.it;
Piazzale San Leonardo 7, Conegliano; meals €30-
40; ⊙ 12.15-2.15pm & 7.30-10pm Wed-Sun, 12.15-
2.15pm Mon) In the grounds of the *castello*,
the combination of good Italian food and
the incredible views across the surrounding hills make this place well worth the
hike uphill from the centre. Go for the full
experience, involving duck *tagliata* (sliced
grilled meat) with orange sauce or codfish
Vicentina.

ℹ Information

APT Tourist Office (☑ 0438 2 12 30; Via XX
Settembre 132; ⊙ 9am-1pm Tue & Wed, to 1pm
& 2-6pm Thu-Sun) This has limited opening
hours, so it's best to arrive in the morning, pick
up a map (not really necessary) and confirm

opening hours, so you're not caught out by three-hour lunchtime closures.

ℹ Getting There & Away

The easiest way to reach Conegliano is by train. The town has the following connections:

Belluno €5.10, one hour, hourly.

Treviso €3.55, 20 minutes, at least twice hourly.

Venice €5.80, one hour, at least twice hourly.

VENETO DOLOMITES

The spiked peaks and emerald-green valleys of the Venetian Dolomites are encompassed within the 315-sq-km Parco Nazionale delle Dolomiti Bellunesi, just north of the Piave river and the historic town of Belluno. Further north, fashionably turned-out Italian snow bunnies flock to Cortina d'Ampezzo for excellent skiing in the Cinque Torri and the Parco Naturale di Fanes-Sennes-Braies (the latter sits in the neighbouring region of Trentino-Alto Adige). In summer, there's excellent hiking and climbing here too.

Feltre

The 'painted city' of Feltre sits in a gorgeous natural setting at the foot of the Dolomites on the banks of the Piave river in Valbelluna. Since 1404, the city has been fiercely linked to Venice, demonstrating unflinching loyalty in the face of the Holy Roman army, which ransacked the city and massacred the inhabitants in 1510 during the League of Cambrai's war with the Venetian Republic.

In reward for its faithfulness the republic refinanced the city's reconstruction, paying for its frescoed and porticoed *palazzi* and elegant squares. Wander up Via Mezzaterra and Via Lorenzo Luzzo to admire the frescoed facades until you reach Piazza Maggiore, which is overlooked by the Alboino Castle. In August, one of the most famous historical re-enactments takes place here, with hundreds of citizens dressed in Renaissance garb.

◎ Sights

★ Santuario dei Santi
Vittore e Corona   CHRISTIAN SITE
(✏ 0439 21 15; www.santivittoreecorona.it; Località Anzù; ⊙ 9am-noon & 3-7pm summer, to 6pm winter) FREE This 12th- to 15th-century

Byzantine-Romanesque church, perched on Monte Miesna, is one of the most beautiful monuments in the Dolomites. Its interior is richly decorated with Giotto-style frescoes, which have been painted over one another with such exuberance as to pose a problem for restoration. Easily visible are depictions of the *Adoration of Magi* and the *Assumption,* with older frescoes, such as a 14th-century *Last Supper,* layered underneath. The oldest paintings are the *Universal Judgement* and the *Baptism of Jesus* on the counter facade, which date to the 10th to 11th centuries.

★ Galleria d'Arte
Moderna Carlo Rizzarda   MUSEUM
(✏ 0439 88 52 34; http://musei.comune.feltre.bl.it; Via Paradiso 8; adult/reduced €4/1.50; ⊙ 10.30am-12.30pm & 3-6pm Tue-Sun) Feltre-born Carlo Rizzarda was a world-class blacksmith, who trained at Milan's Fine Art Academy and under the guidance of legendary craftsman Alessandro Mazzucotelli. He bought Palazzo Villabruna in 1926 to house his growing collection of modern artworks, including pieces by Egon Schiele, Felice Casorati and Adolfo Wildt. On his premature death in 1931, his palace and collection were left to the city, creating this wonderful museum, which also houses some amazing examples of his ironwork.

Museo Civico   MUSEUM
(✏ 0439 88 52 41; http://musei.comune.feltre.bl.it/MuseoCivico; Via Luzzo 23; adult/reduced €4/1.50; ⊙ 9.30am-6pm Tue-Sun mid-Jun–mid-Sep, 10.30am-12.30pm & 3-6pm Tue-Sun mid-Sep–mid-Jun) Feltre's civic museum thoughtfully tells the rich history of this charming town. The display starts with the coats of arms of Feltre's most noble families in the entrance, then revisits the town's deep Roman history on the ground floor before travelling through a series of reconstructed traditional rooms showing how wealthy Feltrini lived, and finishing with a good collection of Renaissance paintings on the 2nd floor.

☆ Festivals & Events

Palio di Feltre   CULTURAL
(www.paliodifeltre.it; ⊙ 1st weekend Aug) One of the most important re-enactment festivals in Italy is Feltre's lively Palio. It includes processions, markets, concerts and horse races. And the whole town dresses up in Renaissance gear.

📖 Sleeping & Eating

Bus de l'Och   B&B €
(📞 0439 8 13 22; www.busdeloch.it; Salita Giovanni
da Vidor 11; s €45-55, d €65-100; 🅿️) It may require sturdy legs to get there, but this sweet
B&B, located at the top of the Colle delle Ca-
pre hill in the historic centre, rewards those
who persevere with wonderful views and
warm hospitality. There are two lovely bedrooms with pine beds, wooden floors and
beamed ceilings, as well as a small kitchen
area where breakfast is served.

Osteria Crash   OSTERIA €
(📞 0439 8 11 69; Via Paradiso 46; meals €16-24;
🕐 8.30am-3pm & 5pm-midnight Tue-Sat, 10am-
3pm Sun; 🍴) Just inside the Imperial Gate
you'll find this buzzing local *osteria* with
low, beamed ceilings and the day's specials
chalked up on the blackboard. There's often
bigoli with tomatoey seafood, risotto and
even vegetarian lasagne. Desserts are homemade and worth saving room for.

ℹ️ Getting There & Away

Feltre is served by Dolomiti Bus (www.dolomiti
bus.it) service, which connects the town with
Belluno (55 minutes).

Otherwise, the easiest way to reach Feltre is
by train from Belluno (€4.35, 40 minutes, hourly), Treviso (€6, 70 minutes, hourly) or Venice
(€7.50 to €8, two hours, hourly).

WORTH A TRIP

PARCO NAZIONALE DELLE DOLOMITI BELLUNESI

Just over 17km northwest of Belluno,
**Parco Nazionale delle Dolomiti
Bellunesi** (www.dolomitipark.it) offers
trails for hikers of every level, wildflowers in spring and summer, and
restorative gulps of crisp mountain air
year-round. Between late June and early
September, several spectacular Alte Vie
delle Dolomiti (high-altitude Dolomites
walking trails) traverse the park connected by *rifugi* (mountain huts). The
excellent tourist office in Belluno and
the main **headquarters** (📞 0439 33
28; www.infodolomiti.it; Piazzale Zancanaro
1; 🕐 9am-noon & 3-5pm Mon, Wed & Thu,
to noon Tue & Fri) in Feltre can help with
maps and routes.

Belluno

POP 35,875 / ELEV 390M

Perched on high bluffs above the Piave
river and backed majestically by the snow-
capped Dolomites, Belluno makes a scenic
and strategic base to explore the surrounding mountains. The historical old town is
its own attraction, mixing stunning views
with Renaissance-era buildings. And you'll
be happy to fuel up for hikes in the nearby mountains on the city's hearty cuisine,
including Italy's most remarkable cheeses:
Schiz (semi-soft cow's-milk cheese, usually
fried in butter) and the flaky, butter-yellow
Malga Bellunese.

◉ Sights

Museo Civico di Palazzo Fulcis   MUSEUM
(📞 0437 95 63 05; https://mubel.comune.belluno.
it; Via Roma 28; adult/reduced €8/5; 🕐 9.30am-
12.30pm & 3.30-6.30pm Tue-Wed & Fri, to 12.30pm
Thu, 10am-6.30pm Sat & Sun) Although Belluno's Civic Museum has some 600 notable regional works of art, including some stunning
canvases by local talent Sebastiano Ricci, the
real star of the show is the beautiful Palazzo
Fulcis that houses the collection. One of the
best-preserved 18th-century palaces in the
Veneto, its interior is extravagantly embellished with frescoes and stuccowork, while
underfoot terrazzo floors swirl with florid
rococo motifs.

Piazza dei Martiri   SQUARE
Belluno's main pedestrian square is the Piazza dei Martiri (Martyrs' Sq), named after
the four partisans hanged here in WWII. On
the north side various bars, restaurants and
shops seek shade under arcading; the rest of
the square is pleasant parkland.

📖 Sleeping & Eating

Parco Dolomiti Fisterre B&B   B&B €
(📞 0437 93 20 16; Via Michele Cappellari 55; s/d
€39/76; 🅿️🛜) This three-room B&B offers
one of the warmest welcomes in the Dolomites, with extremely friendly and helpful
owners, tasty breakfasts and a tranquil location just next to the Ardo river, 10 minutes
on foot from the train station. Bathrooms
are shared and the check-in time is a little
late (5pm), but these are small irritations.

★ Ristorante Taverna   VENETO €€
(📞 0437 2 51 92; www.ristorantetaverna.it; Via Cipro 7; set menu €45; 🕐 noon-2.30pm & 7.30-10pm

Mon-Sat) Tucked away on Via Cipro, where Cypriot wine was once sold, this traditional tavern offers a warm welcome in its cosy, wood-panelled interior. While service can be slow – relax! – the food is worth the wait: plates come laden with polenta and Schiz cheese, delicate trout scooped out of mountain rivers and blueberry pappardelle with wild-boar *ragù*.

Al Borgo ITALIAN €€
(✆0437 92 67 55; www.alborgo.to; Via Anconetta 8; meals €30-40; ◷noon-2.30pm Mon, to 2.30pm & 7.30-10.30pm Wed-Fri, 7.30-10.30pm Sat) If you have a car or strong legs, seek out this delightful restaurant in an 18th-century villa in the hills about 3km south of Belluno. Considered the area's best, the kitchen produces everything from homemade salami and roast lamb to artisanal gelato. Wines are also skilfully chosen, and the grappa is locally sourced.

ⓘ Information

Tourist Office (✆334 2813222; Piazza del Duomo 2; ◷9.30am-12.30pm & 2.30-6.30pm Mon-Sat, 10am-noon Sun) Has lots of useful information on Belluno, Nevegal and the Parco Nazionale delle Dolomiti Bellunesi, as well as public transport.

ⓘ Getting There & Away

The train station is around 700m northwest of the central Piazza dei Martiri. Belluno has the following connections:
Conegliano €5.10, one hour, hourly.
Treviso €7.50, one hour 50 minutes, hourly.
Venice €8.50, two hours 20 minutes, hourly (change in Conegliano).

Cortina d'Ampezzo

POP 5850 / ELEV 1224M
The Italian supermodel of ski resorts, Cortina d'Ampezzo is icy, pricey and undeniably beautiful. The town's stone church spires and pleasant cascading piazzas are framed by magnificent mountains. It doubles as a slightly less glamorous but still stunning summertime base for hiking, biking and rock climbing.

🏃 Activities

Winter crowds arrive in December for top-notch downhill and cross-country skiing

and stay until late March or April, while from June until October summertime adventurers hit Cortina for climbing and hiking. Two cable cars whisk skiers and walkers from Cortina's town centre to a central departure point for chairlifts, cable cars and trails. Lifts usually run from 9am to 5pm daily mid-December to April and resume June to October.

Ski Pass Cortina SKIING
(✆0436 86 21 71; www.skipasscortina.com; Via Marconi 15; Valley Pass 1/3/7 days €50/144/269; ◷8.30am-12.30pm & 3-6.30pm Mon-Fri) Ski and snowboard runs range from bunny slopes to the legendary Staunies black mogul run, which starts at 3000m. The Dolomiti Superski pass provides access to 12 runs in the area, or you can opt for a Valley Pass that includes San Vito di Cadore and Auronzo/Misurina; both are sold at the Ski Pass Cortina office.

Dolomiti SkiRock CLIMBING
(✆324 7473939; www.dolomitiskirock.com; Corso Italia 14; ◷5-7.15pm) National instructor Mario Dibona Moro's mountaineering outfit synthesises his two main passions of skiing and rock climbing, answering to the increasing interest in climbing in the Dolomites. It offers lessons for all abilities in skiing, climbing, ice climbing and mountaineering, and creates environmentally aware treks, ascents, climbs, and bike and ski itineraries.

Guide Alpine Cortina d'Ampezzo HIKING, CLIMBING
(✆0436 86 85 05; www.guidecortina.com; Corso Italia 69a; ◷8.30-10.30am & 5-7pm Mon-Sat, 5-7pm Sun) In milder weather, guides from this reputable outfit run rock-climbing courses, mountain-climbing excursions and

MESSNER MOUNTAIN MUSEUM

Part of Reinhold Messner's five-museum ode to the Dolomites, Messner Mountain Museum (Fort Monte Rite; ☑ 388 1568007; www.messner-mountain-museum.it; Località Monte Rite, Cibiana di Cadore; adult/reduced €8/6.50; ☺ 10am-5pm Jun & Sep, to 6pm Jul & Aug) on Monte Rite (2181m) offers a complete 360-degree panorama of the Dolomites from its crystal-shaped glass lantern. It is housed in the defensive fort of Monte Rite, which played a critical role in the Italian line of defence against the Austro-Hungarian advance in WWI, and later offered shelter to partisans during WWII.

Inside the fort, the museum explores the geology of the Dolomites through the artefacts, journals and paintings of the first mountaineers and natural scientists, who wrote the story of these mountains as they explored its hidden reaches and pioneered new ascents. You'll need to park your car at Passo Cibiana and take the shuttle bus, or follow the walking path (6.5km).

guided nature hikes (prices vary). In winter it also offers ad hoc courses in off-trail skiing, snowshoeing and challenging *via ferrata* (a trail with permanent cables and ladders) climbs.

Olympic Ice Stadium
SKATING
(☑ 0436 88 18 11; Via Bonacossa 1; adult/reduced incl skate rental €10/9; ☺ 10.30am-12.30pm & 4-5.30pm Dec-Apr) During whiteouts, take a spin around this beautiful ice-skating rink built for the 1956 Winter Olympics. The venue also hosts ice-hockey matches, curling and figure-skating competitions.

🛏 Sleeping

Hotel Montana
HOTEL €
(☑ 0436 86 21 26; www.cortina-hotel.com; Corso Italia 94; s €52-87, d €82-168; 🤶) Right in the heart of Cortina, this friendly, vintage 1920s Alpine hotel offers simple but well-maintained rooms. Facilities include a ski room with a waxing table and rather nice boot warmer. In winter, there's a seven-night minimum (€310 to €570 per person), but call for last-minute cancellations. Reception areas double as gallery space for local artists. Pets are welcome.

★ Rifugio Ospitale
CHALET €€
(☑ 0436 45 85; www.ristoranteospitale.com; Località Ospitale 1; d €120-182; ☺ closed Jun; 🅿🤶) A 10km, forest-shaded drive from Cortina, this stylish place is astounding value, with spectacular mountain views from its large rooms. The well-regarded restaurant (open 9am to 11pm, Tuesday to Sunday) has an unexpected elegance: choose from a modern communal dining table or cosy *stuben* (traditional dining room). Make sure to ask

for the key to the fresco-filled 13th-century church that nestles below the hotel.

🍴 Eating

★ Agriturismo El Brite de Larieto
VENETO €€
(☑ 368 7008083; www.elbritedelarieto.it; Passo Tre Croci, Località Larieto; meals €25-35; ☺ noon-3pm & 7-10pm, closed Thu out of season; 🅿) 🌿 This idyllic farm enjoys a sunny situation amid thick larch forest with fabulous views from its terrace and a quaint Alpine interior. It produces its own dairy products and vegetables and much of the meat on the menu. Cured charcuterie and *canederli* (dumplings) are a highlight. It's located 5km northwest of Cortina off the SR48 towards Passo Tre Croci.

★ SanBrite
VENETO €€€
(☑ 0436 86 38 82; www.sanbrite.it; Località Alverà; meals €50-80; ☺ noon-2.30pm & 7.45-9.45pm Thu-Tue; 🅿) Attached to a renowned dairy with a vegetable garden out front, the ambition of this beautiful restaurant is to reinterpret traditional mountain cuisine in a contemporary way. Riccardo's dishes range from speck tartare to corn pasta with venison *ragù* or mugo pine and wild herbs. They are as beautiful as they are tasty, and are accompanied by a list of biodynamic wines.

ℹ Information

Tourist Office (☑ 0436 86 90 86; www.dolomiti.org; Corso Italia 81; ☺ 9am-7.30pm Mon-Sat, 10am-7pm Sun)

ℹ Getting There & Away

The nearest train stations are Calalzo di Cadore, 35km south of Cortina, and Dobbiaco/Toblach,

30km north of Cortina. Convenient bus services depart from outside these train stations, taking you to the centre of Cortina. Trains from Calalzo di Cadore head to Belluno (€5, 45 minutes), while trains from Dobbiaco/Toblach head to Innsbruck.

The following companies also operate out of Cortina's **bus station** (Via G Marconi):

Cortina Express (☑ 0437 86 73 50; www.cortinaexpress.it) Daily direct services to Mestre train station (€27, 2¼ hours), Venice airport (€18, two hours) and Dobbiaco (€5, 40 minutes, July and August).

Dolomiti Bus (☑ 0437 21 71 11; www.dolomitibus.it) For Calalzo di Cadore (€3.80, one hour) and smaller mountain towns.

SAD Buses (☑ 0471 45 01 11; www.sad.it) Services to Bolzano, Dobbiaco (€5, 40 minutes) and other destinations in Alto Adige (Südtirol).

Cinque Torri

At the heart of the Dolomites, just 16km west of Cortina at the confluence of the Ampezzo, Badia and Cordevole Valleys, is the gorgeous area of Cinque Torri. Hard though it is to believe, some of the fiercest fighting of WWI took place in these idyllic mountains between Italian and Austro-Hungarian troops. Now you can wander over 5km of restored trenches in an enormous open-air museum between Lagazuoi and the Tre Sassi fort. Guided tours are offered by the Gruppo Guide Alpine, and in winter you can ski the 80km Great War Ski Tour with the Dolomiti Superski ski pass. En route, mountain refuges provide standout meals and beds with spectacular views. The Cinque Torri (www.5torri.it) website has useful information.

🛏 Sleeping & Eating

⭐ **Rifugio Ristorante Peziè de Parù** HUT €

(☑ 0436 86 20 68; www.peziedeparu.it; Località Peziè de Parù, 1535m; d/q €95/120; ⊘ Dec-Mar & Jul-Sep; 🅿 🛜) This idyllic Alpine hut sits in a meadow encircled by a crown of high peaks. In summer, guests lounge on the lawn with the cow, then retire to the terrace for bowls of *canederli* and glasses of bilberry-flavoured grappa. Three rustic-chic bed-

rooms with smart modern bathrooms and stunning views are also available for the lucky few who book ahead.

Rifugio Scoiattoli HUT €€

(☑ 333 8146960; www.rifugioscoiattoli.it; Località Potor, 2255m; dm/d €65/140; ⊘ mid-Jun–Oct & Dec-Easter; 🛜) In 1969 Alpine guide Lorenzo Lorenzi built this *rifugio*, and it is still managed by his family today. Accessible by foot from the Cinque Torri chairlift, the terrace offers gorgeous panoramic views to accompany typical Ampezzo dishes, such as pasta with wild blueberries. From here you can also see climbers in action on the 5 Torri. The outdoor hot tub is a bonus.

Rifugio Averau HUT €€

(☑ 0436 46 60; www.rifugioaverau.org; Forcella Averau, 2416m; half-board dm/s/d €75/120/240, meals €35-50; ⊘ 9am-10pm) The Rifugio Averau, a rough-hewn cabin tucked dramatically under the rocky spears of the Averau peak, has a hostel-style dormitory where guests can spend the night and an excellent restaurant. With views of the pink-tinged peaks, settle down by the wood-burning stove for a dinner of house-made pasta, succulent lamb chops, speck-fried potatoes and deeply perfumed mountain bread.

Ristorante Da'Aurelio GASTRONOMY €€€

(☑ 0437 72 01 18; www.da-aurelio.it; Passo Giau 5, Colle Santa Lucia; meals €45-55; ⊘ noon-2pm & 6.30-10pm; 🅿) Located at an altitude of 2175m, on the road between Cortina and Selva (SP638), Da'Aurelio serves Michelin-starred mountain cuisine in a classic chalet-style restaurant. Luigi 'Gigi' Dariz produces startling flavours from mountain ingredients, such as his rich, yellow egg with fragrant *finferlo* mushrooms and a rack of lamb crusted with mountain herbs. The restaurant also offers two comfortable rooms.

ℹ Getting There & Away

The area is accessible from Cortina by buses – **Cortina Express** (☑ 0437 86 73 50; www.cortinaexpress.it) ski shuttles in winter (free to ski-pass holders) and a Dolomiti Bus (www.dolomitibus.it) service in summer – which connect with the lifts at Passo Falzarego.

VENICE & THE VENETO CINQUE TORRI

AT A GLANCE

POPULATION
1.21 million

CAPITAL
Trieste

BEST SEASIDE WALK
Rilke Trail (p440)

BEST COUNTRY INN
La Subida (p451)

BEST CARNIVAL
Plodar Vosenocht (p460)

WHEN TO GO
Feb Ski the uncrowded slopes of the Carnic and Giulie Alps, and join in Sappada's ancient Carnival.

May–Jun Prime cycling time co-incides with San Daniele's annual prosciutto festival.

Sep–Oct Watch sails fill the horizon at Trieste's Barcolana Regatta and enjoy uncrowded beaches.

Castello di Miramare (p440)
BUTTERFLY MEDIA/SHUTTERSTOCK ©

Friuli Venezia Giulia

With its triple-barrelled moniker, Friuli Venezia Giulia's multifaceted nature should come as no surprise. Cultural complexity is cherished in this little-visited region on Italy's northeastern borders with Austria and Slovenia. Its landscapes offer profound contrasts too, with the snowy Giulie and Carnic Alps in the north, idyllic grapevine-clad hills in the centre, sandy beaches and lagoons along the shore, and karst cliffs encircling the regional capital, Trieste.

While there's an amazing reserve of historical sights, from Roman ruins to Austro-Hungarian palaces to world war museums, this is also a destination for simply kicking back with the locals, tasting the region's renowned wines and discovering a culinary heritage that will broaden notions of the Italian table.

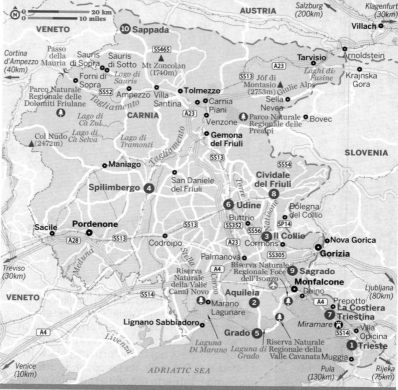

Friuli Venezia Giulia Highlights

1 Trieste (p431)
Communing with the literary ghosts in Italy's most multicultural city.

2 Basilica di Santa Maria Assunta (p444) Being enthralled by the 4th-century mosaic floors of this Aquileia church.

3 Il Collio (p450)
Discovering some of Italy's most outstanding white wines.

4 Scuola Mosaicisti del Friuli (p457) Wandering,

mouth agape, through Europe's only professional mosaic school.

5 Mirko Boat (p443)
Exploring the islands, birdlife and traditional reed huts of Grado's pristine lagoon.

6 Vitello d'Oro (p454)
Dining in exquisite contemporary style in Udine's oldest restaurant.

7 La Costiera Triestina (p440) Hiking, diving and castle-hopping along this pretty, pine-clad coastline.

8 Tempietto Longobardo (p455) Marvelling at the 8th-century Lombard chapel in Cividale del Friuli.

9 Museo del Monte San Michele (p449) Coming face to face with the horrors of WWI in this creative digital museum.

10 Sappada (p460)
Discovering the skiing, hiking and fine dining in this picture-postcard mountain village.

History

The semi-autonomous region of Friuli Venezia Giulia came into being as recently as 1954; its new capital, Trieste, had already traded national allegiances five times since the be-

ginning of the century. Such is the region's history, a rollicking, often blood-stained one of boom, bust and conquest that began with the Romans in Aquileia, saw Cividale rise to prominence under the Lombards, and witnessed the Venetians do their thing in Pordenone and Udine. It was Austria, however, that established the most lasting foothold, with Trieste as its main, and free, seaport. While the region today is a picture of quiet prosperity, much of the 20th century was another story. War, poverty, political uncertainty and a devastating earthquake saw Friulians become the north's largest migrant population, most bound for Australia and Argentina.

ⓘ Getting There & Away

Most travellers arrive in Friuli Venezia Giulia via Venice's Marco Polo airport, Trieste Airport or overland by train.

AIR

Friuli Venezia Giulia Airport (TRS; ☑ flight information 0481 77 32 24; www.triesteairport. it; Via Aquileia 46, Ronchi dei Legionari), aka Trieste Airport, sits just off the A4, 33km northwest of Trieste and 40km southeast of Udine, near Ronchi dei Legionari. Direct flights from Rome, Munich, Barcelona, Valencia and London Stansted arrive here.

The airport is served by Micotra trains to/from Austria via Udine, and Trenitalia services to Ljubljana in Slovenia. In addition, the airport is connected to the Italian national rail network and cities throughout Italy.

Buses depart the airport to Trieste, Udine and Gorizia as well as Venice, Croatia and Slovenia. A taxi to Trieste costs around €65.

BICYCLE

With some of the lowest border crossings in the Alps and excellent bike-carrying trains (look for the bike symbol on the timetable), cycling to Friuli Venezia Giulia is a great way to arrive. The following are the main routes:

➡ FVG1 forms part of the Ciclovia Alpe Adria Radweg (www.alpe-adria-radweg.com) that starts in Salzburg and heads to Grado on the Adriatic coast.

➡ FVG2 is part of the EuroVelo 8 route that crosses Italy with France at one end and Croatia at the other.

➡ FVG3 is part of the Ciclovia Pedemontana cycle route that follows the arc of the Alps across northern Italy.

➡ FVG4 starts on the border with Slovenia and heads west via Cividale del Friuli, Udine and Pordenone to the Veneto.

Trieste

☑ 040 / POP 204,200

Tumbling down to the Adriatic from a wild, karstic plateau and almost entirely surrounded by Slovenia, Trieste is physically and psychologically isolated from the rest of the

Italian peninsula. As such, it preserves its own unique border-town culture and retains a fascinating air of fluidity encapsulated in the Triestini dialect, a strange melange of Italian, Austrian-German, Croatian and Greek.

Once the great seaport of the Habsburg Empire, its fabulous waterfront is lined with portentous neoclassical architecture on a par with London's, although its view across the blazing blue bay is considerably finer. It is this view, plus the marina chock-full of sleek white yachts, the city *lidi*, the long, sandy beaches and the vineyard-draped hinterland of the karst that hold the real magic of Trieste. Without much effort, life is slow and sweet. Like those before you, you might find yourself staying on longer than you'd planned.

◉ Sights

★ **Museo Revoltella**   MUSEUM
(☑ 040 675 43 50; www.museorevoltella.it; Via Diaz 27; adult/reduced €7/5; ⓧ 10am-7pm Wed-Mon) This extraordinary house-museum was the home of wealthy Triestini merchant Pasquale Revoltella, who made his fortune in the timber industry and had a hand in the Suez Canal. Aside from his lavish accommodation, he spent much of his money supporting contemporary Triestini artists, patronage that the city continues as part of his bequest. The result is an enormous collection of late 19th- and 20th-century art that now covers several floors in the adjoining Palazzo Brunner.

You'll need several hours to browse the curious collection, which eschews the typical roll call of Italian artists for lesser-known Friuliano and Central European names. Look out for the impressively fleshy sculptures by Rovan Ruggero and standout portraits by Carlo Wostry, Isidoro Grunhut and Gino Parin. There's also a pretty rooftop cafe and a good bookshop.

ⓘ REGIONAL DISCOUNT CARD

FVG Card (48 hours/72 hours/seven days €25/29/39) provides free admission to all civic museums; free transport in Udine, Lignano and on the Udine–Cividale del Friuli train; and free audio tours plus numerous discounts in the region's shops, spas, beaches and parks. The cards are available from all FVG tourist offices, some hotels and online (www.turismofvg.it).

Trieste

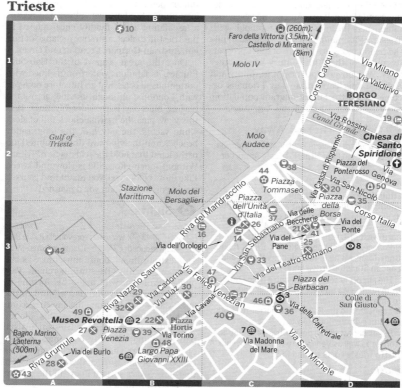

★ **Chiesa di Santo Spiridione**   CHURCH
(☑ 040 63 13 28; www.comunitaserba.org; Via Filzi; ⊙ 8.30am-12.30pm & 5-8pm Mon-Sat, 8.30am-12.30pm Sun) Constructed from pearly white Istrian stone in 1868, the Serbian Orthodox church has a typical Byzantine style, its large central dome flanked by four hemispherical cupolas. Built by wealthy Serb ship owners, it has an unmistakably Eastern look and is an important repository of Serbian culture. Inside, it is richly decorated with glittering mosaics and 19th-century gold and silver icons from Russia.

★ **Faro della Vittoria**   LIGHTHOUSE
(☑ 0432 82 12 10; www.farodellavittoria.it; Strada del Friuli 141; ⊙ 10am-1pm & 4-7pm Wed-Sun Jul & Aug, 3-7pm Fri, 10am-1pm & 3-7pm Sat & Sun Apr-Jun & Sep-Oct) FREE Trieste's elegant lighthouse, with its 68m-high, fluted tower and copper dome sporting a soaring Winged Victory, is perched on the Gretta Hill and worth a visit for the spectacular views it af-fords of the Gulf of Trieste. Built both as a lighthouse and a memorial to soldiers who died in WWI, it bears an inscription at the base that reads: 'Shine in memory of those who died at sea'.

During the Barcolana, the lighthouse is open every day from 9am to 5.30pm. Take bus 42 or 44 from Piazza Oberdan.

Risiera di San Sabba   MEMORIAL
(☑ 040 82 62 02; www.risierasansabba.it; Via Palatucci 5; tours €3; ⊙ 9am-7pm) FREE This former rice-husking plant became a concentration camp in 1943 and has been a national monument and museum since the 1960s. The site commemorates the 5000 people who perished here and the many thousands more who passed through on the way to Nazi forced labour and death camps. These included a great many of the city's Jewish population along with Triestine and Slovenian resistance fighters.

during WWII, it has been meticulously restored and remains one of the most important, and profoundly beautiful, synagogues in Italy. It's not necessary to book the tours; just arrive five minutes before they start.

Museo Joyce & Svevo
MUSEUM

(☑040 675 81 70; www.museojoycetrieste.it; 2nd fl, Via Madonna del Mare 13; tours €4; ⊙9am-1pm Mon-Sat & 3-7pm Wed-Fri) **FREE** James Joyce would enjoy the irony: his museum really belongs to friend and fellow literary great, Italo Svevo, housing a significant collection of the Triestini's first editions, photos and other memorabilia. Joyce, who lived in Trieste from 1904 to 1920, is dealt with ephemerally, with a wall map of his haunts and homes and a Bloomsday bash in June (Svevo's birthday is also celebrated, on 19 December). There's an interesting English video of Joyce's time in Trieste (ask the staff to play it). Staff can also give you suggestions for a DIY walking tour of Joyce sites.

Arco di Riccardo
ROMAN SITE

(Via del Trionfo) The Arco di Riccardo is one of the Roman town gateways, dating from 33 BC, and overlooks a pretty residential square. The gate is named for the English King Richard, who was supposed to have passed through en route from the Crusades.

Castello di San Giusto
MUSEUM

(☑040 30 93 62; www.castellodisangiustotrieste. it; Piazza della Cattedrale 3; adult/reduced €3/2; ⊙10am-7pm daily summer, 10am-7pm Tue-Sun winter) Once a Roman fort, this sturdy 15th-century castle was begun by Frederick of Habsburg and finished off by blow-in Venetians. The city museum is housed here, with temporary exhibitions and a well-stocked armoury. Wander around the walls for magnificent views. To reach it, take the lift at the back of the underground car park to the right of the Roman Theatre which exits at the castle, or bus 24.

Roman Theatre
ROMAN SITE

(Via del Teatro Romano) Behind Piazza dell'Unità d'Italia rise remains of the Roman theatre, which was built between the 1st and 2nd centuries AD. Concerts are held here occasionally during summer.

Chiesa di Sant'Antonio Taumaturgo
CHURCH

(www.diocesi.trieste.it; Via Della Zonta) Sitting at the end of the so-called 'Grand Canal', the Church of Sant'Antonio is Trieste's most instagrammable monument. Built between 1825 and 1849, its harmonious neoclassical structure fronts the waterway with a majestic

Civico Museo Sartorio
MUSEUM

(☑040 30 14 79; www.museosartoriotrieste.it; Largo Papa Giovanni XXIII 1; ⊙10am-5pm Thu-Sun) **FREE** This elegant urban villa set in a large garden belonged to the haute bourgeoisie Sartorio family, who amassed a huge collection of art, ceramics and jewellery in once-trendy Empire, Biedermeier and neo-Gothic styles. The house itself is similarly opulent with a genuine Roman mosaic in the basement and a glyptotheque for the sculpture collection. Don't miss the room of superb **Tiepolo drawings** or the **Triptych of Santa Chiara**, an exquisitely detailed wooden altarpiece from the 14th century.

Synagogue
SYNAGOGUE

(☑040 37 14 66; www.triestebraica.it; Via San Francesco d'Assisi 19; adult/reduced €3.50/2.50; ⊙guided tours 4pm & 5.30pm Mon & Wed, 10am & 11.30am Tue, 10am, 11am & noon Sun) This imposing and richly decorated neoclassical synagogue, built in 1912, is testament to Trieste's once significant Jewish community. Heavily damaged

Trieste

porch supported by six Ionic columns topped by the patron saints of the city: Justus, Sergius, Servulus, Maurus, Euphemia and Thecla. Inside, the austere, soaring interior is crowned by a Pantheon-like dome. At the time of research it was undergoing restoration and was closed to the public.

🏃 Activities & Tours

La Diga BEACH
(☎0345 908 98 90; www.ladigaditrieste.it; ⊙9am-7pm, bar to 11pm Jun-Sep) La Diga – 'the dam' – is not exactly a swimming beach but it's Trieste's idea of a perfect beach club, moored just off the waterfront, opposite Mole Audace. Pre-book a chair and umbrella (€6 to €18) or just sail over for some briny air, a gelato or a yoga-flow class. In the evenings it becomes more club than beach. A free shuttle leaves Mole Audace half-hourly.

Bagno Marino Lanterna SWIMMING
(El Pedocin; ☎040 30 59 22; Molo Fratelli Bandiera 3; adult €1; ⊙7.30am-7.30pm Jun-Sep, open year-

round for sunbathing) For sun-worshipping and a dip in town, head to Bagno Marino Lanterna, tucked away behind the city's disused 19th-century lighthouse (it's often referred to as 'el pedocìn' by locals). A living piece of Austro-Hungarian history, this pebbly beach is still genteelly gender-segregated.

No 2 Tram TOURS
(www.triestetrasporti.it; Piazza Oberdan; hourly/daily €1.60/4.50; ⊙departures every 20min 7am-8pm) A vintage tram to Villa Opicina, with wonderful views. For most of the 5km journey from Piazza Oberdan it's a regular tram, but a funicular section tackles the steep gradient as it heads up into the Carso. An accident in 2016 forced the tram to close for urgent maintenance; it is expected to reopen in late 2021.

Walking Tours WALKING
(www.discover-trieste.it; €10, free with FVG card) Themed tours of the city centre in English. Book through the tourist office (p439), where you can also pick up self-guided audio

tours (per person €5) covering 22 points of interest.

✈ Festivals & Events

★ Barcolana Regatta   SPORTS
(Coppa Autunno; www.barcolana.it; ⊙2nd Sun in Oct) Trieste's 'Autumn Cup' is the largest regatta in the world. Over 2500 boats fill the bay in front of the city while the seafront promenade is filled with food stalls, bars and entertainment. The race runs from the Barcola Marina to the Miramare Castle and back, finishing in front of Piazza dell'Unità d'Italia. For Triestinis, it is the city's signature event. Although the race takes place on the second Sunday of October, the festival is preceded by 10 days of minor regattas, exhibitions and events.

🛌 Sleeping

★ B&B Lidia Polla Trieste   B&B €
(☑0334 7150231; www.atelierlidiapolla.com; Via del Coroneo 1; s €70, d €90-100) A very special B&B where you'll find exquisite parquetry floors, antique furniture and objects set against contemporary textiles and a simple sensibility. The quality of the linens, duvets, towels and bathrobes is a rare find at this price. Bathrooms *are* in the hall, but are exclusive to each room, plus one has a clawfoot bath and all are beautiful.

Residenzale 6a   BOUTIQUE HOTEL €
(☑040 672 67 15; www.residenzale6a.it; Via Santa Caterina 7; s/d €75/110; ❉🛰) Upstairs in an imposing Borgo Teresiano building, this small, cosy hotel mixes traditional furnishings with bright, modern bathrooms, a large lounge and an internal courtyard. Poetically, each of the elegant rooms is named and decorated for one of Italo Svevo's female characters.

★ Seven Historical Suites BOUTIQUE HOTEL €€
(☑040 760 08 17; www.seventrieste.com; Via Filzi 4; apt s/d €160/180; ℗❉🛰) Yes, there are seven suites and they are, indeed, historical, nestled on the beamed attic floor of a grand 1884 commercial building. Still, their lavish size, a slick contemporary way with glass, marble, stone and iron, and their incredible collections of Sicilian objects and antique furniture, are a surprise departure from Trieste's usual haute Habsburg style. Parking costs €23 per night.

Hotel All'Arco   HOTEL €€
(☑040 260 73 89; http://hotelallarco.com; Piazzetta S Silvestro 4; s €50-80, d €70-150; ❉🛰) Located in a quiet winding street that leads

to trendy Piazza Barbacan, All'Arco offers 12 pared-back, wood-beamed rooms with soothing contemporary furnishing. The management are helpful and friendly and offer great suggestions for nearby bars and restaurants.

Forvm Boutique Hotel   BOUTIQUE HOTEL €€
(☑040 372 08 93; www.forvmboutiquehotel.it; Via Valdirivo 30; s €90, d €115-140; ❉🛰) On an upper floor of a nondescript 19th-century office building, the hushed, dramatically lit lounge of this small hotel immediately soothes the weary traveller. Well that, and the complimentary welcome *aperitivo*. Rooms aren't large but they are comfortable, plush and rather sexy; elegant staff are ever on hand when you need city tips or an espresso or herbal tea. Breakfast costs €10 extra.

L'Albero Nascosto   BOUTIQUE HOTEL €€
(☑040 30 01 88; www.alberonascosto.it; Via Venezian 18; s €90, d €140-180; ❉🛰) A delightful little hotel in the middle of the old town, Nascosto is a model of discreet style. Rooms are spacious and tastefully decked out with parquet floors, original artworks, books and a vintage piece or two; most also have a small kitchen corner. Breakfasts are simple but thoughtful, with local cheeses, top-quality preserves and Illy coffee.

★ Hotel Savoia Excelsior Palace HOTEL €€€
(☑040 7 79 41; http://savoiaexcelsiorpalace.starhotels.com; Riva del Mandracchio 4; d €190-280;

WORTH A TRIP

MUGGIA

The village of Muggia, 5km south of Trieste, is the only Italian settlement on the historic Istrian peninsula, which Italy was forced to cede to the former Yugoslavia following the 1947 war settlement. Nowadays, it is a sleepy fishing village with a picturesque old-town square dominated by a Venetian-Gothic church. The Venetian influence extends to the winding *calli* (alleys) of **Muggia Vecchia**, which snake up the hillside to the castle, now the private home of sculptor Villi Bossi.

Carry on up and you'll reach the top of Monte Castellier (170m), from where there is a fantastic view. Boats depart from the Stazione Marittima to Muggia year-round (one way/return €4.35/8.15, 30 minutes, six to 10 times daily).

P ✳ 🛜) The Habsburg-era, seafront Grand Hotel is Trieste's other luxury hotel, offering sumptuous contemporary glamour in place of the Duchi's tradition and history. It offers the most sumptuous public spaces and plush sea-view rooms in the city. The bar, with its crushed-velvet sofas, handmade silk lampshades and shining marble floor is the place to be seen at *aperitivo* time.

Grand Hotel Duchi d'Aosta LUXURY HOTEL €€€
(📞 040 760 00 11; www.grandhotelduchidaosta .com; Piazza dell'Unità d'Italia 2; d €170-275; ✳ 🛜 ≋) There's been a hotel of sorts on this prime site since Roman times, and the Duchi remains Trieste's grand dame. Public spaces are hushed and intimate, and the rooms are opulently traditional – the way repeat visitors like them. The bathrooms might be a tad frumpy for some five-star tastes, but the moody basement pool is a good trade-off.

Next door, the Duchi has a modern offshoot, **Hotel Vis a Vis** (www.hotelvisavis.net; Piazza dello Squero Vecchio 1; s €125, d €145-190; ✳ 🛜), with small-ish but luxurious, all-modcon rooms. A great choice if your tastes tend towards the contemporary, but you'd like in on the Duchi facilities.

🍴 Eating

⭐**Gelato Marco** ICE CREAM
(📞 392 0788230; Via Malcanton 16a; 1 scoop €1.30; ⏰10am-11pm Tue-Sun) The crush spilling out the door and down the street says it all: San Marco is Trieste's best gelateria. Gelato and sorbet (many of them dairy and gluten-free) are prepared daily with seasonal fruit and highest-quality ingredients. The pineapple and rosemary gelato is sensational, as is the mojito granita.

⭐**L'Osteria Salvagente** SEAFOOD €
(📞040 260 66 99; Via dei Burlo 1; mains €22; ⏰noon-3pm & 7-10pm Wed-Sun) After meeting Marco and Valentina, the 80-year-old couple who owned this old seafood place finally felt comfortable passing on their life's work. It's indeed in good hands. The young team have changed little of the original maritime-themed decor but have instead relaxed the menu to include a huge array of Venetian-style mix-and-match *cicheti* (bar snacks).

⭐**Rustiko** SERBIAN €
(📞040 064 50 20; www.rustiko-trieste.com; Via Madonnina 19a; sandwiches €5.50-10, mains €8-15; ⏰noon-3pm & 7-11.30pm Mon-Sat, 7pm-midnight Sun) This colourful and chaotic fast-food joint may be the size of a train carriage, but it has a big Serbian personality. Come early to grab one of the four or five tables and wrack your brains to choose from the bountiful menu, which features spicy Serbian sandwiches, soups, moussaka and a hefty mixed grill. Pair with black beer.

Mimì e Cocotte INTERNATIONAL
(📞348 8369072; Via Cadorna 19; ⏰8am-3pm & 6.30-11pm Tue-Sat, 8am-3pm Sun; 🍽) Shared tables, upcycled furniture and a relaxed and welcoming vibe are the hallmarks of this all-day eatery, which serves simple, organic dishes packed with flavour. Snacks include delicious crostini with creamed mackerel and horseradish, salads and Buddha bowls, or drop by for the traditional Irish breakfast on Saturday and Sunday.

Gelateria Soban GELATO €
(📞391 4617405; www.gelateriasoban.com; Via Cicerone 10; gelato €3-4.50; ⏰11am-11pm) Chiara Soban is from a family of artisan gelato makers originally from the idyllic Val di Zoldo in the Dolomites. Now a Gambero Rosso award-winning operation, you can expect only the best natural gelato, using minimal and ultra-seasonal ingredients, local milk and eggs, and slow, flavour-enhancing techniques.

⭐**De Scarpon** FRIULIAN €€
(📞040 36 76 74; www.facebook.com/descarpon; Via della Ginnastica 20; meals €25-30; ⏰noon-2.15pm & 7-10pm Tue-Sun) No fuss, no frills, just a large, vintage dining room with tiled floors and walls huge with theatre posters, and an utterly authentic Giulian menu. Fish is the focus here, from the classic stockfish to the bountiful seafood pasta, which comes served in the pan. Other dishes worth trying are the Barcola sardines and anything with mussels from Duino.

Trattoria Nerodiseppia SEAFOOD €€
(📞040 30 13 77; www.trattorianerodiseppia.com; Via Cadorna 23; meals €28-32; ⏰noon-2.30pm & 7-11pm Tue-Sat) A simple place that's full of youthful enthusiasm. The menu keeps it simple – fish *ragù*, fish tartares, risotto with local clams, *fritto misto* (fried seafood) of both fish and vegetables – but is not afraid to roam further into the Italian kitchen than is usual in these parts. Pesto, aubergine, mozzarella and capers pop up all over the place, adding welcome colour and punch.

> ### DON'T MISS
>
> ## BUFFET, TRIESTE-STYLE
>
> You'll be sure to eat well, in fact extremely well, at a Triestine buffet. These rowdy bar-restaurants are yet another legacy of the city's Austro-Hungarian past. Usually all-day, and night, affairs, small snacks are available from early morning to *aperitivo* time. Beef brisket may be a stalwart, but pork – baked, boiled, cured, stuffed into a sausage or fried – is the star attraction. Fresh grated *kren* (horseradish), *capuzi* (sauerkraut) and *patate in tecia* (mashed potatoes) are traditional accompaniments. City favourites include:
>
> **Da Siora Rosa** (☑040 30 14 60; Piazza Hortis 3; meals €25; ⊙8am-3.30pm & 5-10pm Tue-Sat) Opened before WWII, a well-loved, family-run buffet with a retro interior.
>
> **Buffet da Pepi** (www.buffetdapepi.it; Via Cassa di Risparmio 3; meals €20-25; ⊙8.30am-10pm Mon-Sat, 10am-4pm Sun) Pepi's counter is a site of porcine carnage and there's take-away brisket at lunchtime.
>
> **Buffet Rudy** (Via Valdirivo 32; meals €20; ⊙10am-1am Mon-Sat) Concocting traditional boiled meats, cold cuts and beer since, oh, 1897. This is the beer-iest of all the buffets.

Ristorante Ai Fiori
SEAFOOD €€

(☑040 30 06 33; www.aifiori.com; Piazza Hortis 7; meals €40-45; ⊙12.30-2.30pm & 7.30-11pm Tue-Sat, 7.30-11pm Mon) As the pretty name suggests (*fiori* means 'flowers'), there's a dedication to the seasons at this discreet little restaurant and an emphasis on freshness. In summer that might be a surprise cold spaghetti with spanner crab or one of the darker, tastier fish dishes with horseradish, apple and potatoes in winter. The wine list includes a few rarities and celebration-priced French drops.

Chimera di Bacco
FRIULIAN €€

(☑040 36 40 23; Via del Pane 2; meals €35-50; ⊙noon-2.30pm & 7.30-11pm Mon-Sat) Much more than the *'picolo enotect'* that it describes itself as, La Chimerina does an interesting regional menu of both local seafood and meat. Don't miss the Istrian-style *fusi* pasta (hand-cut and rolled diamonds served with a meat *ragú*) if it's on the menu, or do the literary tasting menu composed of small dishes from the book *Italo Svevo's Table.*

Joia
SEAFOOD €€

(☑040 265 41 54; www.ristorantejoiatrieste.it; Riva Gulli 4a; meals €30-40; ⊙noon-3pm & 7-11pm) A smart, calm place presided over by Neapolitan chef Pasquale Sorrentino who specialises in local fish and seafood dishes as well as serving top-quality meat. The occasionally over-ambitious menu plays with Italian traditions and highlights the best of Adriatic flavours. There's also a fun aperi-fish, a sort of fish happy hour with small plates of fish balls, tartare and fried fish.

★Harry's Piccolo
ITALIAN €€€

(Hotel Duca d'Aosta; ☑040 66 06 06; www.harrystrieste.it; Piazza dell'Unità d'Italia 2; meals €90-145; ⊙7.30-10pm Tue-Sat; ❉🅿) Trieste's only Michelin-starred restaurant has an enviable setting on lovely Piazza dell'Unità. The menu is modern, executing classic ideas in innovative ways. Try the deceptively simple ricotta gnocchi, which has a cloud-like texture and a three-tomato sauce that makes your taste buds pop. Other crowd pleasers include pigeon foie gras and grilled octopus with lemon potatoes. Advice on wine pairings is excellent. The fine dining restaurant seats just 12, but there's a larger, more informal bistro (open 12.30pm to 2pm and 7.30pm to 10pm daily, meals €65 to €90) next door.

🍸 Drinking & Nightlife

★The Roof, Pier
ROOFTOP BAR

(☑040 322 92 96; www.piert.it; Molo Venezia 1; ⊙9am-1am Sun-Thu, to 2am Fri & Sat) Simply the best place in Trieste for sundowners is this bar perched atop the Marina San Giusto yacht club. Dressed with artificial grass and potted plants this airy 'garden' with killer marina views is decked out with two bars, deckchairs, poufs and common tables where Triestini flock for quality cocktails, live music and tasty fried-fish snacks (€4 to €10).

Downstairs there's also a rather fine fish restaurant (meals €35 to €45) with a deck over the water.

★BarBacan
BAR

(Via S Michele 2a; ⊙7.30am-2pm Mon-Sat plus 4-10pm Tue-Sat) Sandwiched between the Rotonda Pancera and the Roman Arco di

Riccardo in pretty Piazza Barbacan is this popular local wine bar with piazza seating. It's a favourite with local creatives, who converge here for great coffee and savoury, stuffed brioche and pizzette throughout the day and a list of well-curated local wine and craft beer come *aperitivo* time.

Knulp
BAR

(☎040 30 00 21; www.knulp.org; Via Madonna del Mare 7a; ⊙10am-midnight Mon-Sat; 🐾) Named after Hermann Hesse's amiable vagabond, this alternative bar-library-shop-bicycle rental is a bohemian place where alternative Triestini come to hang out, talk books and listen to live music. Channel Knulp's charm, dive in and make new friends.

Al Ciketo
BAR

(☎348 6444034; www.facebook.com/alciketo; Via San Sebastiano 6a; ⊙10am-11pm Mon-Thu, to 1am Fri & Sat) Trieste does do glamour and this bar, which convivially spills out into the alley beside it, attracts a slightly older, very well-put-together crowd come Friday and Saturday evening. There are lots of bottles of sparkling doing the rounds, and this being Trieste, the big wooden platters of *stuzzichini* – bread topped with all kinds of pork – are not far behind them.

Cantina del Vescovo
WINE BAR

(☎329 3241750; Via Torino 32; ⊙4.45pm-midnight Mon & Tue, 6pm-midnight Wed-Fri, to 3am Sat) Trieste's cosmopolitan gaze usually faces east, but here we have a bar that feels like you've been transported to an ultra-hip neighbourhood of Madrid. The city's most fashionable pack out this moody industrial space for bold Spanish wines, *pintxos* (tapas plates) of piquillo peppers, *jamón* (ham) or *patatas bravas* and late-night burgers.

Osteria da Marino
WINE BAR

(☎040 36 65 96; www.osteriadamarino.com; Via del Ponte 5; ⊙5pm-2am Sun, Mon, Tue, to 3am Fri & Sat) If you can't make it to the Carso wine region, get the owner here to ply you with indigenous grape varieties (the Vitovska selection is encyclopedic). Or just settle in with a Franciacorte sparkling or a Tuscan red and wait for the little meatballs to appear. It also has a menu of good local dishes that can be eaten out the back or at the bar.

☆ Entertainment

★ Stazione Rogers
LIVE MUSIC

(☎040 322 94 16; www.stazionerogers.org; Riva Grumula 14; ⊙6pm-midnight Tue-Sat, 10.30am-1.30pm Sun) This quirky 1953 petrol station, designed by Ernesto Rogers (Richard Rogers' cousin) and the BBPR firm, was saved from dereliction in 2008 and turned into a vibrant cultural hub. Now, it serves up cocktails and wine instead of fuel in the forecourt and hosts a hip program of performances, concerts and DJs.

Teatro Verdi
OPERA

(☎040 672 21 11; www.teatroverdi-trieste.com; Riva III Novembre 1) Trieste's opera house is a little

CAFE CULTURE

Trieste is Italy's coffee capital and the city has its own confounding coffee terminology. For an espresso ask for *un nero*, for a cappuccino, order a *caffe latte*, for a macchiato order a *capo* – a cappuccino – and, for either in a glass, specify *'un b'* – the 'b' short for *bicchiere*, a glass. For the full experience take a seat in one of the following historic cafes:

Antico Caffè San Marco (☎040 064 17 24; www.caffesanmarcotrieste.eu; Via Battisti 18; ⊙8.30am-11pm Mon-Sat, 9am-9pm Sun) Opening just before WWI, and a favourite of writers Svevo, Saba and Joyce, this Viennese Secession giant is spectacular.

Caffè degli Specchi (☎040 66 19 73; www.caffespecchi.it; Piazza Unità d'Italia 7; ⊙8am-9pm) This veritable hall of mirrors (*specchi*) first opened in 1839 and is the ultimate Piazza dell'Unità d'Italia perch.

Antico Caffè Torinese (☎040 260 01 53; www.anticocaffetorinese.ts.it; Corso Italia 2; ⊙7.30am-midnight Mon-Sat) The smallest of the historic cafes with an exquisite room that's just perfect for a *capo un'b* (macchiato in a glass).

Caffè Tommaseo (☎040 36 26 66; www.caffetommaseo.it; Riva III Novembre; ⊙10am-10pm) With its ceiling frescoes and primrose-yellow walls, the Tommaseo is unchanged since its 1830 opening.

bit Scala and a little bit Fenice (thanks to a pair of duelling architects), but wears the mix well. Don't miss a chance to see a performance here; the Triestini are passionate opera lovers and make a great audience.

🛍 Shopping

★ Pirona   FOOD
(📞 040 233 54 76; www.pirona1900.com; Largo della Barriera Vecchia 12; ⊙ 7.30am-8pm Tue-Sat, 9am-2pm Sun) This jewel-box pastry shop and cafe was one of Joyce's favourites. Its nutty, spicy, boozy Triestine speciality cakes – *putizza*, *presnitz* and *pinza* – are particularly good. It also does an artful line of house-made chocolates.

Pasticceria La Bomboniera   FOOD
(📞 040 63 27 52; www.pasticcerialabomboniera. com; Via XXX Ottobre 3; ⊙ 8.30am-3pm Tue-Sat, 9am-1pm Sun) This very lovely sugary boutique sells every imaginable sweet treat from its period vitrines. Engage in the impossible task of choosing between fruit tarts topped with wild strawberries or Triestini treats such as myrtle berry *Linzertorte* and *Lettere d'Amore* (Love Letters), hand-rolled puff pastries filled with rum cream.

Delikatessen   VINTAGE
(📞 040 30 58 59; Via Venezian 10c; ⊙ 9.30am-12.30pm Mon-Sat plus 4.30-7.30pm Tue-Sat) Windows full of vintage treasures lure curious passersby into this Aladdin's cave where you can find 1950s signage, good-as-new Artemide lamps, pinball machines and quality mid-century modern furniture. The period postcards, posters and glassware make great souvenirs.

Enoteca Bischoff   WINE
(📞 040 63 14 22; www.bischoff.it; Via Mazzini 21; ⊙ 9.30am-1pm & 4-7.30pm Mon-Sat) Founded in 1777 by a Swiss immigrant who was on to the potential of Trieste's free-port status, Bischoff is one of Trieste's – and the world's – longest-running shops. It can sell you a bottle of one of its 2500 Italian labels or you can do tastings and get advice on wine pairings, serving and storage.

Dezen Dezen   CLOTHING
(📞 040 265 14 57; www.dezendezen.com; Via Duca d'Aosta 6b; ⊙ 11am-7.30pm Tue-Fri) Marco and Michele's handprinted textiles are inspired by traditional Balkan scarves. In fact, their workshop has revived a family business that once supplied the Balkan states, but now turns out scarves, bags, T-shirts and shawls

fit for urban fashionistas. The production is sustainable and they only use natural fibres in their limited-edition prints, including silk from Como.

Eataly   FOOD & DRINKS
(📞 040 246 57 01; www.eataly.net; Riva Tommaso Gulli 1; ⊙ 9am-10.30pm Sun-Thu, to midnight Fri & Sat) Possibly the most beautiful of the Eataly family of food and wine superstores, set in an old dockside warehouse, with two floors of windows overlooking the marina and lighthouse. The usual great line-up of pan-Italian produce is here, along with some excellent Friulian specialities and wine.

Ballarin Pelleterie   SHOES
(📞 040 63 87 65; www.ballarinpelletterie.it; Via Dante Alighieri 2; ⊙ 3.30-7.30pm Mon, 9am-1pm & 3.30-7.30pm Tue-Fri, 9am-1pm Sat) Beautiful supple moccasin shoes in rainbow colours, soft leather sandals and slouchy bags and made-to-last (and love) briefcases fill the windows of Ballarin along smart Via Dante. Prices are surprisingly affordable for such stylish design and Made in Italy quality.

Combiné   ARTS & CRAFTS
(www.combinetrieste.com; Piazza del Barbacan 4; ⊙ 11am-7.30pm Tue-Sat) Ludovika, a jewellery designer, and Nika, a photographer, showcase the work of Trieste's young creatives in this beautifully bohemian shop front. Their prints and wearable pieces are very affordable.

ℹ Information

Tourist Office (📞 040 347 83 12; www.turismofvg.it; Via dell'Orologio 1; ⊙ 9am-7pm) Dispenses information on the city, excursions to the surrounding area and transport. It also sells the FVG Card (p431) and can book guided tours.

ℹ Getting There & Away

Trieste is accessible along the main A4/E70 autostrada (tolls apply) from Venice. It heads east into Slovenia in the form of the E61, and south into Croatia in the form of the E751.

BOAT

From June to September **APT** (www.aptgorizia. it) Linea Marittima ferry services run to and from Grado (single/return €7.20/10.95).

Shuttle boats operated by **Trieste Trasporti** (📞 800 016675; www.triestetrasporti.it) depart from the Stazione Marittima to Muggia year-round (one way/return €4.35/8.15, 30 minutes, six to 10 times daily). From June to August four ferries run daily from Molo Bersaglieri in Trieste to Grignano (€4.40, 40 minutes) and Sistiana (€7, 1¼ hours). Purchase tickets onboard. In summer, the boats carry bikes as well.

BUS

National and international services operate from the **bus station** (☑ 040 41 44 82; www.auto stazionetrieste.it; Via Severo 24).

APT (☑ 800 955957; www.aptgorizia.it) Buses run to Udine (€7, 1¼ hours, hourly), Aquileia (€5.90, one to 1¼ hours, up to eight daily), Grado (€5.90, 1¼ hours, 12 daily) and Gorizia (€5.90, one hour).

Flixbus (www.flixbus.it; ☎) Operates a wide range of national and international routes in fuel-efficient buses to and from Trieste and Trieste Airport. Book online and store tickets in the app.

Florentia Bus (www.florentiabus.it) Services international destinations such as Ljubljana (€17, 2¾ hours, daily Monday to Saturday), Zagreb (€30, five hours, daily Monday to Saturday), Belgrade (€55, 10 hours, two days a week) and Sofia (€65, 16½ hours, daily).

TRAIN

The **train station** (Piazza della Libertà 8) serves Gorizia (€4.90, 50 minutes, hourly), Udine (€9, one hour, at least hourly), Venice (€19.30, two hours, at least hourly) and Rome (€60 to €98, 6½ to 7½ hours; most require a change at Mestre).

❶ Getting Around

Trieste Trasporti (☑ 800 016675; www.trieste trasporti.it) bus 30 connects the train station with Via Roma and the waterfront; bus 24 runs from the station to Castello di San Giusto; bus 36 links Trieste bus station with Miramare; and buses 42, 43, 44 and 46 to the Carso. One-hour tickets cost €1.30; all-day €4.50.

Radio Taxi Trieste (☑ 040 30 77 30; https:// radiotaxitrieste.it) operates 24 hours; from the train station to the centre will cost around €10, and there's a flat fee of €58 to the airport.

La Costiera Triestina

Northwest of Trieste, the 20km Strada Costiera (coastal road) is bookended by two Habsburg castles: the fanciful Gothic-Revival Miramare Castle at the southeastern end and the 14th-century Duino Castle, situated on a rocky karst outcrop at the northwestern extremity. Triestini treat it as an extension of the city, decamping en masse during summer evenings and at the weekends to the beaches, bars and restaurants of Grignano, Sistiana and Duino.

◉ Sights

★ Castello di Miramare CASTLE

(☑ 040 22 41 43; www.castello-miramare.it; Viale Miramare; adult/reduced €8/2; ◷ 9am-7pm) Sitting on a rocky outcrop 7km from Trieste, Castello di Miramare is the city's elegiac bookend, the fanciful neo-Gothic home of the hapless Archduke Maximilian of Austria. The castle's decor reflects Maximilian's wanderlust and various obsessions of the imperial age: a bedroom modelled like a frigate's cabin, ornate orientalist salons and a red silk-lined throne room. Upstairs, a suite of rooms used by military hero Duke Amadeo of Aosta in the 1930s is also intact, furnished in the Italian Rationalist style.

Portopiccolo AREA

(☑ 040 29 12 91; www.portopiccolosistiana.it; Sistiana; Ⓟ▥) ✦ After 40 years of wrangling and €400 million, this immaculate, white-washed resort has finally emerged from what was an abandoned quarry. Come for a day of first-class posing on the white shingle beach at **Maxi's beach club** (two sunbeds and umbrella €32 to €48) or check into the stunning **Bakel Spa** for head-to-toe pampering (10am to 8pm, half day €24 to €34, full day €44 to €54).

Castello di Duino CASTLE

(☑ 040 20 81 20; www.castellodiduino.it; Frazione di Duino 32, Duino; adult/reduced €8/6; ◷ 9.30am-5.30pm Wed-Mon Apr-Sep, 9.30am-4pm Sat & Sun Nov–mid-Mar) Fourteen kilometres northwest along the coast from Miramare, this 14th- and 15th-century bastion picturesquely marches down the cliff, surrounded by a verdant garden and mind-blowing views. Poet Rainer Maria Rilke was a guest here during the winter of 1911–12, a melancholy and windswept stay which produced the *Duino Elegies*. The castle is still in private hands and the collection is idiosyncratic to say the least, but delightfully so. To get here, take bus 41 from Trieste's Piazza Oberdan.

☈ Activities

★ Rilke Trail WALKING

(Sentiero Rilke; www.turismofvg.it/code/68293/ Rilke-Trail; Frazione di Duino, Duino) FREE The path that inspired poet Rainer Maria Rilke during his stay in Duino is now an easy, even 1.7km walk from the Castello di Duino to the town of Sistiana. The extreme beauty of fragrant holyoak- and hornbeam-dotted limestone cliffs tumbling towards the sea can, like Rilke's master work, feel poetic, mystical and, when the Bora blows, profoundly existential.

Miramare Marine Reserve   DIVE SITE
(☑040 22 41 47; www.riservamarinamiramare. it; Viale Miramare 345; snorkelling per person €25, 8-person group dive €240; ☺Jun-Sep) Surrounding the Miramare Castle is a 30-hectare natural reserve, incorporating a walk section of the Carso plateau and a marine reserve where the WWF conducts research of the marine environment of the Upper Adriatic. Join them for some fantastic hiking, snorkelling, diving and boat tours with knowledgeable science guides. Sign up at the visitor centre, which is located in the old stables of the Miramare Castle, where you'll also find a small museum, **BioMa** (BIOdiversitario MArino; ☑040 22 43 46; www.riservamarinamiramare.it/ informazioni/il-centro-visite; adult/reduced €6/4; ☺10am-6pm Tue-Sun summer, 2-6pm Fri, 10am-6pm Sat & Sun winter), showcasing the biodiversity of the gulf.

🛏 Sleeping

★**Ostello Tergeste**   HOSTEL €
(☑040 22 41 02; http://ostellotergeste.com; Viale Miramare 331; dm €22-25, d €70-90; P🛜) This lemon-yellow 1920s villa offers dorms and doubles with dreamy sea views and even balconies. Neat, if spartan, rooms come with private bathrooms and are filled with sunshine, and there's a lovely wisteria-shaded terrace, to boot. It's within walking distance to the Castello di Miramare, the beach and the nightlife in Barcola. Bike rental is available.

Villa Gruber   BOUTIQUE HOTEL €€
(☑040 20 81 15; https://villagruber.com; Frazione di Duino 61; s/d €90/130; P🛜) This period seaside villa was the summer home of a family of Triestini writers and intellectuals who retreated here right up until the year 2000 to enjoy Duino's lovely laid-back vibe. There are eight rooms with balconies overlooking the sea, still filled with the family's furniture and *objets d'art*. There's also a well-tended garden with loungers and a terrace where breakfast is served in style.

Hotel Miramare   HOTEL €€
(☑040 224 70 85; www.hotelmiramaretrieste.it; Viale Miramare 325; s €99, d €130-200; P❄🛜) There are beautiful sea views from all the rooms, a simple beachy design and a well-priced but stylish – love those Cassina leather chairs – restaurant and summery bar.

★**Hotel Riviera &**
Maximilian's   HISTORIC HOTEL €€€
(☑040 22 45 51; www.rivieramax.eu; Strada Costiera 22; d €225-350; P❄🛜🏊) Along the coast from the city, just north of Castello di Miramare, this hotel has the feel of a gracious Habsburg summer resort but with light, if classically decorated, rooms and modern spa facilities. Its absolute waterfront position is rare and views are accordingly a knockout.

❶ Getting There & Away

The Strada Costiera (SS14) runs from Trieste to Duino via the Miramare Castle and Sistiana. Trains and buses serve Grignano (where Castello di Miramare is located) and Duino from Trieste.

Trieste Trasporti (☑800 016675; www. triestetrasporti.it) operates four ferries daily between June and August from Molo Bersaglieri in Trieste to Grignano (€4.40, 40 minutes) and Sistiana (€7, 1¼ hours). Purchase tickets onboard. In summer, boats carry bikes.

Il Carso

Dramatically shoehorned between Slovenia and the Adriatic, the Carso (*Karst* in German, *kras* in Slovenian) is a windswept calcareous tableland riddled with caves and sinkholes. This wild landscape has long inspired myths and legend. It's a compelling place to visit in any season but is particularly pretty in spring, when the hills are speckled with blossom, or in autumn, when the vines and *ruje* (smoke trees) turn crimson.

The Carso's big-ticket attraction is **Grotta Gigante** (☑040 32 73 12; www.grottagigante.it; Località Borgo Grotta Gigante 42, Sgonico; adult/ reduced €12/9; ☺50min guided tours hourly 9am-6pm daily summer, 10am-4pm Tue-Sat winter), an enormous underground cavern near the town of Opicina. At 120m high, 280m long and 65m wide, it's one of the largest caves in the world, filled with stalactites and stalagmites. Knowledgeable guides point out the cave's features, which include two huge pendulums that monitor the movement of the earth's crust. Upstairs there's a small Speleological Museum, which includes fossils and objects found in the cave, including the skeleton of a now-extinct karst bear. To reach the cave from Trieste take bus 42, or tram 2 and bus 42 in the other direction.

Southeast of Trieste is **Val Rosandra** (☑040 832 64 35; www.riservavalrosandra-glinsci ca.it), a natural wilderness shaped by the passage of the Rosandra stream, which starts in

FRIULI VENEZIA GIULIA THE FRIULIAN COAST

OSMIZE: THE CARSO'S POP-UP WINE CELLARS

Osmize (or *osmice*) originated with an 18th-century Austrian law that gave Carso farmers the right to sell surplus from their barns or cellars once a year (the term *osmiza* comes from the Slovenian word for 'eight', the number of days of the original licence). It's mainly vineyards that hold *osmize* today, and farm cheeses and cured meats are always on offer too. Finding an *osmiza* is part of the fun. Look along Carso roads for the red arrows. Then look up, to signposts, gates or lintels bearing a *frasca* – a leafy branch hung upside down announcing that an *osmiza* is open for business.

On arrival, sample the Carso's native wines: the complex, often cloudy, white Vitovska; or Terrano, aka Teran, a berry-scented red. Internationally known winemakers Zidarich (☑ 040 20 12 23; www.zidarich.it; Prepotto 23, Prepotto) and Skerk (☑ 040 20 01 56; www. skerk.com; Prepotto 20, Prepotto) announce *osmiza* dates on their websites, as do smaller producers David Sardo (☑ 040 22 92 70; www.osmize.com/samatorza/sardo-david; Samatorza 5, Samatorza) and Le Torri di Slivia (☑ 338 3515876; www.letorridislivia.net; Aurisina Cave 62, Duino). And, OK, there is now an online calendar: www.osmize.com.

Slovenia, tumbles off the Karst plateau and empties into the Bay of Muggia. The reserve is popular with climbers, hikers and botany enthusiasts who are attracted by its unique flora. One of the best hiking and cycling routes is the 16km Pista Cottur (www.turismofvg.it), which traces the old railway line from Trieste to Draga Sant'Elia in Slovenia. Ask the Trieste tourist office for details.

🛈 Getting There & Away

Trieste Trasporti (☑ 800 016675; www. triestetrasporti.it) runs buses 42, 43, 44 and 46 from Trieste, but you'll need a car to explore properly.

The Friulian Coast

Friuli's marshy, lagoon-filled Adriatic coast combines seaside charm and some of the least-visited Roman sites in the country. Sandwiched between the family-friendly beach resort of Grado and the party town of Lignano Sabbiadoro, the wild Laguna di Marano is an important European wetland with a wonderful lost-in-time quality.

Grado

☑ 0431 / POP 8220

The vintage beach resort of Grado, 14km south of Aquileia, spreads along a narrow island backed by lagoons and is linked to the mainland by a causeway. Behind the family-friendly beaches you'll find a maze-like medieval centre, criss-crossed by narrow *calli* (lanes). Belle époque mansions, beach huts and thermal baths line the cheerful seafront – the greyish local sand is considered

curative and is used in treatments. Grado comes alive from May to September, but is also prime *passeggiata* (evening stroll) territory on any sunny Sunday.

◉ Sights

★ **Santuario di Barbana**   CHURCH
(☑ 0431 8 04 53; www.santuariodibarbana.it) Situated on an island in the lagoon, the Barbana sanctuary is an ancient shrine, the origins of which date back to 582. The current church dates to the 1930s and has a strikingly original interior decorated in art deco frescoes and luminous stained-glass windows. Also of interest are the hand-drawn pictures that cover the back wall: they depict accidents which local congregants have survived and offer a fascinating historical snapshot of local dangers dating back to the late 19th century.

There's a cafe on the island serving a simple fixed menu. Motoscafisti Gradesi (☑ 0431 8 01 15; www.motoscafistigradesi.it; Riva Scaramuzza; adult/child €6/3; ☉ daily summer, Sun only winter) runs services to the sanctuary from Grado.

Basilica di Sant'Eufemia   BASILICA
(Campo dei Parriarchi; ☉ 8am-6pm) Grado's historic core is dominated by this Romanesque basilica, dating to AD 579. Its rich interior decoration indicates its early importance when the church became the seat of the Patriarch after Attila's hordes drove the citizens of Aquileia onto the island. Roman marble columns line the nave and frame the frescoed apse, while the floor is decorated with a 6th-century, Byzantine-style mosaic.

Riserva Naturale Regionale
Foce dell'Isonzo   NATURE RESERVE
(www.parks.it/riserva.foce.isonzo; Isola della Cona; adult/reduced €5/3.50; ⊙9am-sunset) The final stretch of the Isonzo river's journey into the Adriatic flows through this 23.5-sq-km nature reserve where visitors can birdwatch, horse ride or walk around salt marshes and mudflats. There's also a cycle path that runs along the shoreline all the way back to Grado, via the Valle Cavanata (☑340 4005752; www.vallecavanata.it; ⊙10am-6pm Fri-Wed summer, 10.30am-3.30pm Sat-Mon winter) `FREE`. There's a small cafe at the visitor centre.

🏃 Activities & Tours

Spiaggia e Terme Marine   THERMAL BATHS
(☑0431 89 93 09; www.gradoit.it; Viale Dante Alighieri 72; ⊙thermal baths 8.30am-3pm Apr-Jun & Sep-Oct, 8am-1.30pm Jul & Aug, wellness centre 10am-8pm) This swish contemporary spa offers thalassotherapy, hydrotherapy and psammotherapy (sand) treatments. Included in the complex are two 32°C seawater pools, a Turkish bath, a full-service spa and a water park (☑0431 89 92 20; www.gradoit.it; adult/child €12/8; ⊙10am-6pm May-Aug; 🚻) set beside the main beach. The south-facing, 3km beach has shallow waters presided over by lifeguards. There are loungers and umbrellas, a bar, a children's playground and hot showers. The FVG card (p431) entitles you to a 25% discount.

ASD Fairplay   WATER SPORTS
(☑346 3667866; www.asdfairplay.it; Spiaggia Costa Azzurra; ⊙Jun-Aug) One-stop shop for canoe, windsurf and SUP hire. It also offers swimming, skateboarding and SUP lessons. Find it inside the Stabilimento Tivoli on the Costa Azzurra beach.

Mirko Boat   BOATING
(☑345 4686207; www.mirkotaxiboat-grado.com) To explore the lagoon in style step aboard Mirko's beautiful mahogany cigarette boat and head out to the Barbana sanctuary, the fish farms and *casoni* (traditional reed huts), or Anfora Island for a fish feast at Trattoria Ai Ciodi. Tours cost €10 to €20 per person for a group of six, or you can hire the boat exclusively.

🎉 Festivals & Events

★ Perdòn de Barbana   RELIGIOUS
(⊙Jul) On the first Sunday in July, a joyful and colourful votive procession transports the statue of the Virgin from the Basilica di Sant'Eufemia to the Santuario di Barbana. Fishermen have done this since 1237 when the Madonna of Barbana was claimed to have miraculously saved the town from the plague. The procession is preceded by the Sabo Grande (Grand Saturday), a day of celebration and feasting, when the historic centre is filled with food stalls, music and dancing.

🛏 Sleeping

Belvedere Pineta
Camping Village   CAMPGROUND
(☑0431 9 10 07; www.belvederepineta.com; Località Belvedere; adult/child/tent €10/7/26, 4-person bungalow €104-160; ⊙May-Sep) This huge campsite is located on the mainland just over the causeway from Grado. Set in a fragrant pine forest it offers shady pitches for tents; fully equipped shower, toilet and washing facilities; plus some rather plush three-room bungalows overlooking the lagoon. The site also has two tennis courts, a mini-golf course and a beach.

Albergo Alla Spiaggia   HOTEL €€
(☑0431 8 48 41; www.albergoallaspiaggia.it; Via Mazzini 2; s €110-130, d €140-178; ⊙Apr-Oct; P🚫@) The Spiaggia is set in a lovely prewar modernist building, with a fresh maritime-toned fit-out. It's in a great position, wedged between pedestrian zone, historic centre and beach. Rates outside summer are great value and the downstairs bar makes the best cocktails in Grado.

🍴 Eating

★ Tavernetta all'Androna   SEAFOOD €€
(☑0431 8 09 50; www.androna.it; Calle Porta Piccola 4; meals €40-45; ⊙6-11pm Mon-Fri, noon-3pm & 6-11pm Sat & Sun) Hidden down a narrow alley

---

BEACH LOWDOWN

Grado's well-organised beachfront caters to pretty much every holiday need.

Spiaggia Principale (umbrella & 2 loungers €16.50-30.50; ⊙9am-7pm) Grado's south-facing, 3km-long main beach is perfect for families.

Costa Azzurra Grado's westernmost beach is free and full of activity providers.

Lido di Fido (Entrance 8, Viale del Sole) A specially designated dog-friendly beach complete with doggie 'cots'.

behind the basilica, this elegant family restaurant enjoys a tiny piazza all to itself. Take a seat and let your host guide you through the thoughtful menu, which creatively showcases traditional seafood. The sweet mantis shrimp paired with apple and walnut is a triumph, as is the contemporary take on Russian salad with succulent lobster.

Zero Miglia Osteria di Mare   SEAFOOD €€
(☑ 0431 8 02 87; www.zeromiglia.it; meals €30-40; ☺ noon-2pm & 6-10pm Fri & Sat, noon-2pm Sun) Grado's Fishing Cooperative isn't joking when they tell you the food here has travelled 0km. Cuttlefish, mullet, sea bass, mussels et al are fished during the night by the flotilla of boats docked beside the restaurant, and land on your plate a few hours later in dishes that would make a Gradesi grandmother proud.

🍷 Drinking & Nightlife

Campiello della Torre   WINE BAR
(☑ 0431 8 38 69; Campiello della Torre 7; ☺ 10am-2pm & 5-10pm) Drop into this friendly, local wine bar for a coffee, a craft beer or a glass of regional wine chalked up on the board. Locals linger over boards of sliced prosciutto from Sauris and San Daniele or delicious plates of cheese from Fagagna.

Osteria da Sandra   WINE BAR
(☑ 0431 87 60 14; Campo San Niceta 16; ☺ 10am-11pm Tue-Sun) Cute hole-in-the-wall bar on an old-town corner that attracts a local crew for an early-evening *spritz* (cocktail made with Prosecco) or three. Has an excellent chilled white selection available for purchase if you're considering a picnic.

ⓘ Information

Tourist Office (☑ 0431 87 71 11; Viale Dante Alighieri 66; ☺ 9am-6pm Mon-Sat, 9am-1pm Sun summer, 9am-1pm & 2-6pm winter)

ⓘ Getting There & Away

Regular **APT** (☑ 800 955957; www.aptgorizia.it) buses link Grado with Trieste (€5.90, 1½ hours), Aquileia (€2.20, 10 minutes) and Palmanova (€3.40, 45 minutes, up to eight daily). Trains to Venice and Trieste run to the Cervignano-Aquileia-Grado station, in Cervignano, around 15km away.

Between June and August, APT's Linea Marittima boat shuttle also runs to Grado from Trieste (single/return/bike €7.20/10.95/0.85, 1¼ hours, three daily).

ⓘ Getting Around

There are plenty of cycle paths in the area; **Mauro Bike** (☑ 324 6009263; www.maurobike.com; Riva Scaramuzza 8a; 1hr/day €3/10; ☺ 8am-12.30pm & 2.30-7pm Mon-Sat, 8am-12.30pm Sun) can get you on your way.

Aquileia

☑ 0431 / POP 3320

Conferred with a Unesco World Heritage listing in 1998, this charming rural town and living museum rather thrillingly lies above one of the most complete, unexcavated Roman sites in Europe. And there's plenty to see above ground too, including a medieval basilica with a spectacular Roman-era mosaic floor and frescoed crypt, a nationally important archaeological museum and the scattered remains of the Roman port.

Colonised in 181 BC, Aquileia was once one of the largest and richest cities of the Roman Empire – at times second only to Rome – with a population of at least 100,000 at its peak. After the city was levelled by Attila's Huns in AD 452, its inhabitants fled south and west, founding Grado and then Venice.

◉ Sights

★ **Basilica di Santa Maria Assunta**   CHURCH
(www.basilicadiaquileia.it; Piazza Capitolo; basilica complex adult/reduced €10/7.50; ☺ 9am-7pm Apr-Sep, to 6pm Mar & Oct, to 5pm Nov-Feb, bell tower Apr-Oct only) The entire floor of the Latin cross-shaped basilica, rebuilt after an earthquake in 1348, is covered with one of the largest and most spectacular Roman-era mosaics in the world. The 760-sq-metre floor of the basilica's 4th-century predecessor is protected by glass walkways, allowing visitors to wander above the long-hidden tile work.

Images in the msaic include astonishingly vivid episodes from the story of Jonah and the whale, the Good Shepherd, exacting depictions of various lagoon wildlife, and portraits of wealthy Roman patrons and their quotidian business interests.

Treasures also fill the basilica's two crypts. The 9th-century **Cripta degli Affreschi** (Crypt of Frescoes) is adorned with faded 12th-century frescoes depicting the trials and tribulations of saints, while the **Cripta degli Scavi** (Excavations Crypt) reveals more mosaic floors in varying states of

WORTH A TRIP

PALMANOVA

Palmanova is the literal 'star' of a transnational Unesco site incorporating six fortress cities: also Bergamo; Peschiera del Garda; Zadar and Šibenik, Croatia; and Kotor, Montenegro. Spread over 1000km, they were built by Venice in the 16th and 17th centuries to defend the Republic's valuable trade routes from northern European and Ottoman aggression. Shaped like a nine-pointed star, Palmanova (built 1593) represents the ideal fortified city. So impregnable were its defences that Napoleon used and extended them in the late 1700s, as did the Austrians during WWI. To this day the Italian army maintains a garrison here.

While the town's unique character is reason enough to visit, don't miss dining at **Caffetteria Torinese** (☑ 0432 92 07 32; www.caffetteriatorinese.com; Piazza Grande 9; sandwiches €6-15, meals €40-45; ⊙ 7.30am-midnight Mon, Tue & Thu-Sat, 8am-11pm Sun), set at the edge of Piazza Grande and twice voted the best bar in Italy.

preservation. Some images were destroyed or badly damaged by the erection of the basilica's 73m-high bell tower, built in 1030 with stones from the Roman amphitheatre. The FVG Card (p431) offers free admission.

Museo Archeologico Nazionale MUSEUM
(☑ 0431 9 10 35; www.museoarcheologicoaquileia. beniculturali.it; Via Roma 1; adult/reduced €10/2; ⊙ 10am-7pm Tue-Sun) Opened in 1882, Aquileia's archaeological museum is one of the oldest in Italy. Recently renovated, its rich and varied collection has been superbly rearranged across three floors, moving from monumental sculptures and artefacts that played a role in civic and religious life to intimate, upstairs rooms filled with intriguing personal belongings. Standouts include a bronze relief of Boreas, the God of Wind, his hair licked by the breeze; exquisite mosaic panels; and an extraordinary glass display organised in colour blocks.

Porto Fluviale ROMAN SITE
(River Port; Via Sacra; ⊙ 8.30am-1hr before sunset) FREE Scattered remnants of the Roman town include extensive ruins of the Porto Fluviale, the old port, which once linked the settlement to the sea. Also free to visit are the partially restored remains of houses, roads and the standing columns of the ancient Forum on Via Giulia Augusta.

🏃 Activities

Lagoon Boat Excursions BOATING
(☑ 333 2571259; www.lagoonboatexcursions aquileia.it) Lagoon lover Marco offers all manner of excursions in the Marano Lagoon, from full-day explorations (€300 for boat and guide) of the waterways and *casoni* (traditional reed huts) to boat+bike trips

to Grado, where travellers head out by boat and return to Aquileia via the Alpe-Adria cycle route (per person €15 to €25). The boat is also certified to carry passengers with disabilities.

🛏 Sleeping

Camping Aquileia CAMPGROUND €
(☑ 0431 9 10 42; www.campingaquileia.it; Via Gemina 10; camping €24, d cabin €49, 4-bed bungalow €87; P 🛜 🏊) This well-maintained campground is set beside pretty fields; its comfortable bungalows look towards the basilica and old Roman port.

Ostello Domus Augusta HOSTEL €
(☑ 0431 9 10 24; www.ostelloaquileia.it; Via Roma 25; s/d €39/50; P 🛜) A spotless if rather institutional hostel with two- to six-bed rooms and private bathrooms down the hall. Friendly, relaxed staff are helpful and happy to dole out maps and timetables.

ℹ Information

Tourist Office (☑ 0431 91 94 91; Via Giulia Augusta; ⊙ 9am-7pm Mon-Sat, 9am-1pm Sun summer, to 5.30pm Mon-Sat, 9am-1pm Sun winter) Offers audio guides for the basilica and can book guided tours.

ℹ Getting There & Away

Regular **APT** (☑ 800 955957; www.aptgorizia. it) buses link Aquileia with Grado (€2.20, 10 minutes), Trieste (€5.90, 1¼ hours, 12 daily) and Udine (€4.90, one hour, 12 daily). The nearest train station is at Cervignano. You can also reach Grado by boat with Lagoon Boat Excursions.

By car from Trieste take the E70 autostrada and exit at Ronchi dei Legionari onto the SS14. From Grado, it's a 10km drive on the SR352.

Coffee Culture

From Trapani to Tarvisio, every day begins with coffee. A quick cup from a stovetop moka pot might be the first, but the second (third, fourth and fifth) will inevitably be from a neighbourhood bar. Italians consider these visits a moment to pause, but rarely linger. It's a stand-up sniff, swirl and gulp, a *buon proseguimento* to the barista, and on your way.

Origins

Coffee first turned up in mid-16th-century Venice, then a few years later in Trieste, care of the Viennese. While basic espresso technology made an appearance in the early 19th century, it wasn't until 1948 that Gaggia launched the first commercial machines. These reliably delivered full-bodied espresso shots with the characteristic aromatic *crema*: Italy was hooked. The machines, in fact the whole espresso ritual, spoke of a hopeful modernity as Italy reimagined itself as an urban, industrial postwar nation.

Today's Cup

Italy's superior coffee-making technology took seed around the world, carried by postwar immigrants. Global coffee culture today may embrace latte art and new brewing technologies, but in Italy tradition holds sway. Italians still overwhelmingly favour Arabica and Robusta blends with a dense *crema*, high caffeine jolt and, crucially, a price point everyone can afford. Roasts remain dark and often bitter – Italians routinely sweeten coffee – but Italian baristas use far less coffee per shot and ultra-smooth blends. Espresso is the overwhelming order of choice and

1. Coffee being prepared, Florence
2. Caffè Gambrinus (p716), Naples
3. Espresso

takeaway cups uncommon. Why? Clutching a coffee on the move misses coffee's dual purpose for Italians: contemplation and social belonging.

Bean Hunting

Finding your ultimate Italian espresso is trial and error, albeit enjoyable and inexpensive. Best-of lists will only get you so far: Rome's famed Caffè Sant'Eustachio, Florence's Gilli and Naples' Caffè Gambrinus will almost certainly get it right, but so too will many small town bars. Take note of *torrefazionie* (bean roasters): global giants like Trieste's Illy and Turin's Lavazza are reliable, but do seek out regional favourites, such as Verona's Giamaica, Parma's Lady, Piedmont's Caffè Vergnano and Pascucci from Le Marche.

BARISTA BASICS

Caffè, espresso Short shot of black coffee

Ristretto Short espresso

Lungo Long espresso

Americano Espresso with added hot water

Macchiato Espresso 'stained' with a little milk

Cappuccino Espresso with steamed milk

Cappuccino scuro Strong (dark) cappuccino

Marochino Small cappuccino with cocoa

Latte macchiato Dash of coffee in steamed milk

Deca Decaf

Corretto Spiked espresso, usually with grappa

Pordenone

POP 51,100

Pordenone is the kind of place you wouldn't mind calling home. The fading, frescoed *palazzi* (mansions) that line the elegant curve of Corso Vittorio Emanuele II from Piazza Cavour to the cathedral attest to its past importance and provide a charming contemporary outdoor museum. Lined by an almost unbroken chain of covered *portici* (porches), the historic streetscape buzzes with smart shops and busy cafes reminding one this is a young and social town.

◎ Sights

★ PAFF!   GALLERY

(Palazzo Arti Fumetto Friuli; ☑ 0434 39 29 41; www. paff.it; Viale Dante 33; adult/reduced €8/5; ⊗4-8pm Tue-Fri, 10am-8pm Sat & Sun) This unique museum dedicated to the art of comic books and illustration is the only one of its kind in Europe and is the brainchild of Pordenone's dynamic community of graphic artists. They have housed it in the lovely villa in the Galvani Park and plan to make it a reference point for all forms of graphic art. If the inaugural show 'From Leonardo to Picasso: A Comics' Journey into the History of Art' is anything to go by, they're on the right track.

Galleria Harry Bertoia   GALLERY

(☑ 0434 39 29 16; Corso Vittorio Emanuele II 60; adult/reduced €3/1; ⊗ 3-7pm Wed-Fri, 10am-1pm & 3-7pm Sat & Sun) Named for designer Arieto Bertoia, author of the famous 1951 'Diamond Chair' (a web-like chrome chair in the shape of a diamond), this smart little museum hosts some excellent exhibitions. Thoughtfully curated, they cover themes of design, crafts and even photography. Recent shows include an excellent Steve McCurry exhibition and a show devoted to the depiction of women in art noveau *objets d'art*.

Duomo di San Marco   CATHEDRAL

(Piazza San Marco; ⊗7am-noon & 3-7pm) The Romanesque-Gothic facade of the cathedral betrays frequent alteration down the centuries. Inside, among the frescoes and other artworks, is the *Madonna della Misericordia*, by the town's Renaissance master Il Pordenone (1484–1539), aka Giovanni Antonio de Sacchis.

Museo Civico d'Arte   MUSEUM

(Palazzo Ricchieri; ☑0434 39 23 11; Corso Vittorio Emanuele II 51; adult/reduced €3/1; ⊗3.30-7.30pm Tue-Sat, 10am-1pm & 3.30-7.30pm Sun) The medieval Palazzo Ricchieri houses the civic art museum in its richly decorated upper rooms. It is composed of a collection of rare wooden statues, and Friulian and Veneto paintings from the 15th to the 18th centuries. The building is also a treasure, with painted timber ceilings and the remains of 14th-century frescoes suddenly appearing throughout.

🛏 Sleeping & Eating

Best Western Plus Park Hotel   HOTEL €€

(☑ 0434 2 79 02; www.parkhotelpordenone.it; Via Mazzini 43; s €70-80, d €109-121; P ❋ 🛜) This is a super little hotel, with smart, designer-y rooms, a small bar and a friendly, young team who dish out good recommendations. It is well positioned in the historic centre near all the sights and has the added bonus of a parking lot. Breakfast is also good: a large buffet stacked with homemade cakes, pastries and fruit.

Vecia Osteria del Moro   OSTERIA €

(☑ 0434 2 86 58; www.laveciaosteriadelmoro.it; Via Castello 2; meals €25; ⊗ noon-2.30pm & 7.15-10.30pm Mon-Sat) Just off the Corso, a vaulted den offering snacks, grills and Venetian-style *baccalà* (cod).

★ Al Gallo   SEAFOOD €€€

(☑ 0434 52 16 10; www.ristorantealgallo.com; Via San Marco 10; meals €45-50; ⊗ noon-2.30pm & 7-10.30pm Tue-Sat, noon-2.30pm Sun) Bright, forward-looking Al Gallo is all crisp white walls and vibrant blue, sea-inspired paintings by Grado artist Gianni Maran. It sets the scene perfectly for the elegant fish dishes that soon arrive: Catalan crustaceans in a bell jar, octopus with *friggitelli* (sweet Italian chillis) and burrata and tuna in a crust of white and black sesame seeds.

❶ Getting There & Away

Frequent trains run from Udine (€4.90, 30 to 40 minutes). From Venice (Mestre) trains run half-hourly (€7.15, 1¼ to 1½ hours). **ATAP** (☑ 0434 22 44 11; www.atap.pn.it; Piazzale Nassiriya; ⊗ ticket office 6.45am-7.15pm Mon-Sat) runs buses to the surrounding towns. Take the A28 to reach Pordenone by car.

Gorizia

☑ 0481 / POP 34,800 / ELEV 84M

Gorizia's appeal lies in the aristocratic ambience of its centre, its unique Friulian-Slovenian cooking and its easy access to the

WORTH A TRIP

MUSEO DEL MONTE SAN MICHELE

This excellent interactive **museum** (☏0481 9 20 02; www.museodelmontesanmichele.it; Via Zona Sacra, Cima del Monte San Michele; adult/reduced €6/4; ☺10am-4pm Tue-Sun) deploys digital displays and a virtual-reality experience to explore the horrors of the Italian front in WWI. Knowledgeable guides take you through archival material. Alongside them, well-chosen artefacts resonate powerfully: a rudimentary gas mask that failed miserably in a chemical attack in June 1916, a small hand-held pick to hack through the mountains, and a short club meant to finish off victims choking on gas.

The VR experience is also moving, immersing you in the trenches and sending you soaring over the Tagliamento River in a biplane. Afterwards, visit the gunners' gallery and spend some time on the viewing platform reflecting on the beautiful view over what was once a horrifying battleground. The museum can be visited as part of an itinerary linking various WWI sites, including the epic **Redipuglia war memorial** (Via III Armata, Redipuglia).

surrounding countryside, famed for its wine and rustic restaurants. Considering this serene modern incarnation, you'd never guess the turmoil of Gorizia's past. An oft-shifting border zone throughout much of its history and the scene of some of the most bitter fighting of WWI's eastern front, it was most recently an Iron Curtain checkpoint.

◉ Sights

Castello di Gorizia   CASTLE
(☏0481 53 51 46; Borgo Castello 36; adult/reduced €3/1.50; ☺9.30-11.30am Mon, 10am-7pm Tue-Sun) Gorizia's main sight is its castle; perched atop a knoll-like hill it has served as a fortress, barracks and prison. It has some convincing recreations and a fine wood-panelled great hall, and the panoramic views from the windows are impressive, taking in the gentle slopes of the Collio and the winding Isonzo river. The castle is a popular venue for cultural initiatives and often hosts exhibitions and re-enactments.

Palazzo Coronini Cronberg   PALACE
(☏0481 53 34 85; www.coronini.it; Viale XX Settembre 14; adult/reduced €5/3; ☺10am-1pm & 3-6pm Wed-Sun) This 16th-century residence is jammed with antiquities and artworks, and is surrounded by lush gardens, which are free to visit on their own and open until 9pm in summer.

Musei Provinciali di Borgo Castello   MUSEUM
(☏0481 53 39 26; https://musei.regione.fvg.it; Borgo Castello 13-15; adult/reduced €6/3; ☺9am-7pm Tue-Sun) Below the castle in three adjacent building (Casa Domberg, Tasso and Formentini) are the provincial museums of

Gorizia. The most interesting is the **Museo della Grande Guerra**, in which the tragic history of the WWI Italian-Austrian front is explored, including a to-scale recreation of a trench, along with a room dedicated to the much-loved general, Armando Diaz. Next door, the **Museo della Moda e delle Arti Applicate** displays 19th- and early-20th-century textiles, including some fine examples of Gorizian lace.

🛏 Sleeping & Eating

★**Palazzo Lantieri**   B&B €€
(☏0481 53 32 84; www.palazzo-lantieri.com; Piazza Sant'Antonio 6; s/d €100/140; P🅿🛜) This *palazzo*-stay offers light, spacious rooms in the main house or self-catering apartments in former farm buildings, all overlooking a glorious Persian-styled garden. Goethe, Kant and Empress Maria Theresa were repeat guests back in the day. Antiques fill both public and private spaces, but the charming Lantieri family are far from stuck in the past.

Trattoria Ai Tre Amici   GORIZIAN €
(☏340 6323992; Via Oberdan 11; meals €25; ☺6.30-11.30pm Thu-Tue, plus 11.30am-3.30pm Sun) Simple decor and a short menu featuring Mitteleuropean dishes are the hallmarks of this trattoria where the pasta is homemade and the bread is baked in a wood-fired oven. Order the *ljubljanska* (a super-charged wiener schnitzel made of two slices of veal or pork stuffed with ham and cheese, breaded and fried), or the goulash and polenta.

Majda   GORIZIAN €
(☏0481 3 08 71; Via Duca d'Aosta 71; meals €25; ☺7.30-10.30pm Tue, noon-11.30pm Wed-Sat) With

a courtyard bar, friendly staff and enthusiastic decor, Majda is a happy place to sample local specialities such as ravioli filled with potato (Slovenian-style) or beetroot and local herbs, wild boar on polenta and interesting sides like steamed wild dandelion.

Rosenbar
GORIZIAN €€

(☑ 0481 52 27 00; www.rosenbar.it; Via Duca d'Aosta 96; meals €30; ⊙ noon-3pm & 7.30-10pm Tue-Sat) Rosenbar is a traditional dining room set in an airy shop front. It's known for attention to detail, in both preparation and in the always-local and mostly organic produce it uses. Along with dishes capturing Gorizia's cross-border culinary spirit, there are also a few Adriatic fish and seafood options on the menu.

🍷 Drinking & Nightlife

Caffè Garibaldi
CAFE

(☑ 0481 53 01 31; Corso Italia 49; ⊙ 7.30am-10.30pm Mon-Thu, 7.30am-12.30am Fri & Sat, 8am-9pm Sun) This historic bar has a prime location and outdoor seating where you can linger in the sun over strong coffee and *Krapfen* or enjoy a well-made *spritz* come *aperitivo* time. The list of local wines is also good.

Bierkeller
BEER HALL

(☑ 0481 53 78 91; Via Lantieri 4; ⊙ 5pm-midnight Mon-Fri, 11am-1am Sat & Sun) Venture down into this ancient vaulted cellar for a little piece of Bavaria, with pretzels, football on the big screen or DJs on weekends. Staff are delightful and in summer there's a pretty walled beer garden.

ℹ Information

Tourist Office (☑ 0481 53 57 64; Corso Italia 9; ⊙ 9am-1pm & 2-6pm Mon-Sat, 9am-1pm Sun)

ℹ Getting There & Away

The **train station** (Piazzale Martiri Libertà d'Italia), 2km southwest of the centre, has regular trains to Udine (€3.30, 30 minutes, at least hourly) and Trieste (€3.90, 50 minutes, hourly). Trains to Slovenia depart from **Stazione Nova Gorica** (Kolodvorska pot 6, Slovenia) in the centre of town.

APT (☑ 800 955957; www.aptgorizia.it) runs buses from the central train station to Trieste (€5.90, one hour) and across the border to Nova Gorica bus station (€1.30, 25 minutes). Gorizia sits just off the A34.

Il Collio

Equidistant from the Austrian Alps and the Adriatic Sea, Il Collio has a sunny, breezy microclimate that conspires with the marlstone soil to produce grapes of astonishing fragrance and minerality, which yield some of the finest white wines in Italy recognised by a DOC accreditation.

Set on the western edge of the Isonzo river, 12km west of Gorizia, the region straddles the border with Slovenia, although the Italian part focuses on the charming hamlets of San Floriano del Collio, Cormòns and Dolegna del Collio.

In Dolegna del Collio you can find the family-run cellar **Venica & Venica** (☑ 0481 6 12 64; www.venica.it; Località Cerò 8; tastings per person €25-40; ⊙ 10am-5pm Mon-Sat); the Venica brothers are the grandsons of the original winemaker. Book ahead for a two-hour tour and extensive tasting. The Ronco delle Mele Sauvignon Blanc is one of Italy's most acclaimed sauvignons with a gorgeous *sambuca* (aniseed-flavoured liqueur) aroma. Above the cellars there are six smart rooms (single €110 to €120, double €140 to €160 March to November).

This hamlet is also home to **L'Argine a Vencò** (☑ 0481 199 98 82; www.largineavenco.it; Località Vencò; tasting menus €70-110; ⊙ 7.45pm-midnight Wed-Mon, plus 12.45-4pm Fri-Sun; 🅿). After several years running the acclaimed restaurant Venissa in Venice, Antonia Klugmann decided to pursue her own culinary vision at this off-the-beaten-track mill deep in the Friuli countryside. Three tasting menus showcase her elegant, creative cooking which reflects the season and produce of the moment in dishes such as chicory ravioli with fig, lemon and greens, accompanied by top-class regional wines.

In Corno di Rosazzo is the historic **Perusini** (☑ 0432 67 50 18; www.perusini.com; Via del Torrione 13, Località Gramogliano; 1-bedroom apt €75-95, 2-bedroom apt €140-160; 🅿 ❄). Calling it a 'farm stay' is something of an understatement; established by Giacomo Perusini in the 18th century, the estate is classified a historic winery and has been instrumental in preserving several Friulian varietals on the hills overlooking the Judrio river. A number of farm buildings now provide chic, rustic, self-catering accommodation on the doorstep of the vineyards.

Cormòns

☑ 0481 / POP 7380

This mini Habsburg town, which was part of the Austro-Hungarian Empire up until WWI, is the beating heart of the Collio wine region. It sits at the foot of Mt Quarin, which is topped with the ruins of a Roman settlement and back to prehistoric times. In Piazza XXIV Maggio, locals and visitors sit at shaded tables enjoying some of the best white wine in Italy.

🛏 Sleeping & Eating

Picech AGRITURISMO
(☑ 0481 6 03 47; www.picech.com; Località Pradis 11; d €110-125; 🅿 ❄ 🛜) A historic winery turned welcoming *agriturismo* with three cosy doubles, a small apartment and a room with a view in the tower. The highlight is the sumptuous breakfast which features hand-cut prosciutto, cheeses and homemade cakes. Indulge in a wine tasting while you're here and go exploring on the farm's Vespa.

★ La Subida FRIULIAN €€€
(☑ 0481 6 05 31; www.lasubida.it; Via Subida; meals €55-65; ⊙ 7-10pm Thu-Mon, plus noon-2.30pm Sat & Sun) A famous family-run inn, with border-crossing dishes and ingredients – rabbit, boar, flowers and berries – that bring the landscape to the plate in a very modern way. Stay over in one of the stunning forest houses (doubles from €170) and wake to birdsong and rustling leaves. Across the way there is an *osteria* (tavern) with a terrace (meals €15 to €25) and great natural orange wines (skin-contact whites) from Paraschos.

Terra e Vini FRIULIAN €€€
(☑ 0481 6 00 28; www.facebook.com/terraevini; Via XXIV Maggio, Brazzano di Cormòns; meals €52; ⊙ noon-2.30pm Tue-Sun, 7-10pm Tue-Sat) The Felluga family are Friulian wine royalty and their cosy 19th-century *osteria* looks out over the plantings. Feast on tripe on Thursdays, salt cod on Fridays and goose stew or herbed frittata any day of the week. Book ahead for Sunday lunch.

🍷 Drinking & Nightlife

Enoteca di Cormòns WINE BAR
(☑ 0481 63 03 71; www.enoteca-cormons.it; Piazza XXIV Maggio 21; ⊙ 11am-10pm Wed-Mon) A local wine collective wine shop where you can do tastings, chat to winemakers and nibble on a plate of Montasio cheese. They're also happy to provide information on local wineries.

ℹ Getting There & Away

Trains arrive from Trieste (€5.60, one hour, hourly), Udine (€2.70, 20 minutes, hourly) and Gorizia (€1.75, 10 minutes, hourly).

APT (☑ 800 955957; www.aptgorizia.it) buses from Gorizia (€2.15, 30 minutes) and SAF (☑ 0432 60 81 11; www.saf.ud.it) buses from Udine (€3.30, 45 minutes) also stop in Cormòns. However, to really explore the wineries you'll need your own car.

Udine

☑ 0432 / POP 99,300 / ELEV 113M

While reluctantly ceding its premier status to Trieste in the 1950s, this confident, wealthy provincial city remains the spiritual and gastronomic capital of Friuli. Udine gives little away in its sprawling semi-rural suburbs, but encased inside the peripheral ring road lies an infinitely grander medieval centre: a dramatic melange of Venetian arches, Grecian statues and Roman columns. The old town is pristine, but also very lively. Bars here are not just for posing; for the Udinese, kicking on is the norm.

◉ Sights

★ Museum of Modern and Contemporary Art GALLERY
(Casa Cavazzini; ☑ 0432 127 37 72; www.civici museiudine.it; Via Cavour 14; adult/reduced €5/2.50; ⊙ 10am-6pm Tue-Sun) Udine's modern and contemporary hub brings together a number of bequests, creating a substantial collection of 20th-century Italian artists, including De Chirico, Morandi, Campigli and Mušič. There's also a surprise stash of notable 20th-century American work, including by Donald Judd, Sol LeWitt and Carl Andre, which were donated by the artists after the 1976 Friulian earthquake. The gallery itself is a beautiful cultural asset, its bold reconstruction designed by the late Gae Aulenti.

★ Oratorio della Purità CHURCH
(Piazza del Duomo; ⊙ 10am-noon, ask for key at cathedral if closed) FREE This intimate oratory has a dramatic ceiling painting of the Assumption by Giambattista Tiepolo, with a glowing Madonna framed by tumbling, rather mischievous looking cherubs. It's a wondrous work. Eight biblical scenes in

Udine

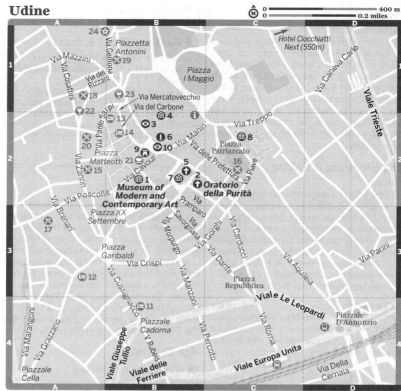

far more sombre chiaroscuro on the walls are by his son, Giandomenico. The building opened as a theatre in 1680 but the patriarch of Aquileia ordered its transformation 80 years later, repulsed that such a devilish institution existed so close to a cathedral.

Piazza della Libertà
PIAZZA

A shimmering Renaissance epiphany materialising from the surrounding maze of medieval streets, Piazza della Libertà is dubbed the most beautiful Venetian square on the mainland. The arched **Palazzo del Comune** (Town Hall) is a clear Venetian keepsake, as is the **Loggia di San Giovanni** opposite, its clock tower modelled on the one gracing Venice's Piazza San Marco. The **Arco Bollani** (Bollani Arch), next to the Loggia, is an Andrea Palladio work from 1556; it leads up to the castle once used by Venetian governors.

Museo Diocesano & Tiepolo Galleries
GALLERY

(☎0432 2 50 03; www.musdioc-tiepolo.it; Piazza Patriarcato 1; adult/reduced €7/5; ⊙10am-1pm & 3-6pm Wed-Mon) The drawcards here are the two rooms featuring early frescoes by Giambattista Tiepolo, including the wonderfully over-the-top *Expulsion of the Rebellious Angels* (1726) at the apex of a grand staircase.

Castello
MUSEUM

(☎0432 127 25 91; www.civicimuseiudine.it; adult/reduced €5/2.50; ⊙10am-6pm Tue-Sun) Rebuilt in the mid-16th century after an earthquake in 1511, Udine's castle affords rare views of the city and snowy peaks beyond. It houses a number of different collections, all fascinating. The **Museo del Risorgimento** is both compellingly designed and set in a series of beautiful rooms, while the **Museo Archeologico** highlights both locally found objects

Udine

FRIULI VENEZIA GIULIA UDINE

as well as the region's archaeological heyday of the late 19th century.

The sprawling upper floors are given to the **Galleria d'Arte Antica** (adult/reduced €5/2.50 incl Castello; ☉10am-6pm Tue-Sun), which has a reproduction of Caravaggio's *St Francis* in room 7 and several stunning Tiepolos in room 10, along with lesser-known Friulian painters and religious sculpture.

Cathedral   CATHEDRAL
(www.cattedraleudine.it; Piazza del Duomo; ☉8am-noon & 4-6pm) The chapels of Udine's 13th-century Romanesque-Gothic cathedral house the **Museo del Duomo** (☑0432 50 68 30; ☉10am-noon & 4-6pm Tue-Sat, 4-6pm Sun) **FREE**, with 13th- to 17th-century frescoes in the Cappella di San Nicolò.

🎇 Festivals & Events

More Than Jazz   MUSIC
(☉Jun) Udine's jazz festival attracts topnotch regional artists and showcases the talents of graduates from the city's conservatories. There are jam sessions, concerts and marching bands that move through the city in tribute to Louis Armstrong.

🛏 Sleeping

⭐ **Dimora Montegnacco**   B&B €
(☑333 3357540; www.dimoramontegnacco.it; Via Cussignacco 48/3; d €65-85; P❄🛜) This charming B&B is housed in a lovely art nouveau building in the city centre. Renovated by the two architect-owners, the three double bedrooms are artfully furnished

and comfortable. All of them overlook a delightful garden where breakfast is served in summer beneath a bower of wisteria. The owners are full of excellent information, and there's private parking (€5 per day).

Hotel Allegria   BOUTIQUE HOTEL €
(☑0432 20 11 16; www.hotelallegria.it; Via Grazzano 18; s €75, d €85-105; P❄@) 🍃 This hotel occupies a historic townhouse opposite one of Udine's loveliest little churches. The rooms are large and what might be described as Udinese-organic in style, with lightwood beams, parquetry floors and shuttered windows. Quirk factor points: the hotel has a *bocciofila* (bowling area) on-site.

Mercatovecchio Luxury Suites   BOUTIQUE HOTEL €€
(☑0432 50 00 27; www.mercatovecchio.it; Via del Carbone 1; s €120, d €140-160) Artist Antonella Arlotti has created Udine's ultimate place to stay. Six elegantly designed suites are packed with various extras, from full kitchens in some to coffee machines and luxe linen throughout. A stylish, simple breakfast spread of sweet and savoury pastries, juice and DIY coffee can be taken at a big table in reception or whisked back to your room.

🍴 Eating

⭐ **L'Alimentare**   ITALIAN, DELI €
(☑0432 150 37 27; www.lalimentare.it; Via D'Aronco 39; meals €22; ☉10.30am-2.30pm Mon, 10.30am-2.30pm & 6-10.30pm Tue-Sat) A bright, young, cool, casual and friendly addition to Udine's dining scene, L'Alimentare serves

up eat-in or takeaway meals that strike out beyond the borders. Vegetable curries sit beside Piedmontese meatballs and there's a number of healthy vegetable sides. Friuli's not forgotten though, with excellent local *salumi* (cured meats) and cheese and great Collio wines like Bastianich's Vespa Bianco on offer.

Oggi
GELATO €

(www.oggigelato.it; Via Paolo Sarpi 3a; cones & cups €2.50-3.50; ☺3-8.30pm Mon, 11am-8.30pm Tue-Sun) If you're lucky, one of the owners of this fabulous Friulian startup, Andrea, will be on hand to take you through Oggi's 0km ethos. Gelato here is made entirely from Friulian milk and local eggs and while there are concessions to favourite flavours and ingredients from across Italy, there's always a local special: try the *biscotto di mais* (cornmeal biscuit) and chocolate.

Alla Ghiacciaia
FRIULIAN €

(☑0432 50 24 71; Via Zanon 13; meals €20-25; ☺11am-3pm & 6pm-midnight Tue-Sun) In the summer, it's hard to beat the wisteria-shaded terrace of this trattoria which hangs over a canal framed by weeping willows. The menu is simple and local, offering large platters of San Daniele ham and local cheese and *cjarsons*, a type of Friulano ravioli stuffed with potato, smoked ricotta, herbs, raisins and cinnamon.

★ La Frasca
FRIULIAN €€

(☑0432 67 51 50; www.lafrasca.com; Viale Grado 10, Pavia di Udine; meals €35; ☺noon-3pm & 7-10pm Thu-Tue) A *frasca* is similar to an *osmize*, a rustic place serving *salumi* and wine, and takes its name from the same practice of hanging a branch out as a shingle. Walter Scarbolo's relaxed roadside dining room has retained the *frasca* experience, and his fans gather for his artisan cured meats, menus that highlight a single seasonal crop, and, naturally, the wonderful Scarbolo wines.

Fred
FRIULIAN €€

(☑0432 50 50 59; www.enotecafredudine.com; Via del Freddo 6; meals €25-28; ☺11am-3pm & 6-11.30pm Mon-Sat; 🖭) Fred's dark wood and produce-lined shelves are of the stylish variety but there's a very traditional attention to detail here at what is at heart a serious wine purveyor. Meals will be seasonal and often light and fresh: think a salad of shaved raw asparagus or a simple baked chicken breast.

Caffè Tomaso
FRIULIAN €€

(☑0432 50 43 87; www.fvgusto.it; Via della Prefettura 16; meals €25-32; ☺11am-2.30pm & 6-10.30pm Mon-Sat) Local produce and fresh takes on Friulian standards are served in this dark and highly atmospheric dining room filled with bright wooden furniture under a canopy of vintage lamps. Smart young Friulians come here for dishes that are highly in sync with the seasons, with lots of vegetable options for pork-overloaded palates. In summer there are tables overlooking a beautiful garden.

Trattoria ai Frati
FRIULIAN €€

(☑0432 50 69 26; www.trattoriaaifrati.it; Piazzetta Antonini 5; meals €25-30; ☺noon-3pm & 7-10.30pm Mon-Sat) A popular old-style eatery on a cobbled cul-de-sac where you can expect local specialities such as *frico* (fried cheese), pumpkin gnocchi with smoked ricotta or, in season, white asparagus and fish stew. It's loved by locals, including the university set, for its whopper steaks and its raucous front bar.

★ Vitello d'Oro
SEAFOOD €€€

(☑0432 50 89 82; www.vitellodoro.com; Via Valvason 4; meals €45-55; ☺noon-2.30pm Tue-Sat, 7-10.30pm Mon-Sat; 🖭) Udine's oldest restaurant, dating to 1849, now has a new lease of life courtesy of its fabulous new interior, which reveals the beauty of the restaurant's history – the city wall it leans against, the ancient wooden beams and terrazzo floors – while giving it an utterly contemporary look. It successfully complements the restaurant's refined seafood cuisine.

🍷 Drinking & Nightlife

Caffè Contarena
CAFE

(www.contarena.it; Via Cavour 11; ☺8am-1am Sun-Thu, to 2am Fri & Sat) Beneath the arcades of Palazzo D'Aronco, Contarena's soaring domed ceilings glitter with gold leaf and other Liberty fancy. Designed by Raimondo d'Aronco, a master of the genre and one-time local, it's a glamorous espresso stop or late-night cocktail venue, and beloved by everyone from senior citizens to students.

Osteria Al Cappello
WINE BAR

(☑0432 29 93 27; www.osteriaalcappello.it; Via Paolo Sarpi 5; ☺10.30am-3pm & 5.30-11pm Tue-Fri, to midnight Sat summer, also 10am-3pm & 5.30-9pm Sun winter) Follow the locals' lead and order what may be northern Italy's most reasonably priced *spritz* (€1 to €2.50) through the window. *Stuzzichini* here are generous enough to constitute dinner, or you can eat well at one of the tables. Upstairs, Locanda Al Cappello (s/d €70/110; ❄🛜) has six cosy bedrooms decorated with rich colours and antiques.

Leon d'Oro   BAR
(📞0432 50 87 78; www.leondoroudine.it; 2 Via dei Rizzani; ⏱10am-3pm & 5-11pm Mon-Sat) A particularly good choice if the weather is balmy (or in any way warm) and the young, good-looking crowd spills out onto the corner terrace, giving it a street-party vibe. Look out for the complimentary plates of fried potatoes doing the rounds: perfect for sopping up the extra *spritz* you're bound to have here.

Osteria Pieri Mortadele   WINE BAR
(📞 0432 50 92 34; www.pierimortadele.com; Riva Bartolini 8; ⏱10am-10pm Mon-Sat) Yes, there's a popular restaurant out back, but it's the spill-onto-the-road front bar that will hold your interest. A rock-and-roll soundtrack, excellent wine by the glass, bountiful *stuzzichini* and great company make this a one-drink-or-many destination.

☆ Entertainment

Caffè Caucigh   LIVE MUSIC
(www.caucigh.com; Via Gemona 36; ⏱7am-11pm Tue-Sun, to 1am Fri) This ornate, dark-wooded bar is a perfect Udinese compass point – it feels far more like Prague than points south. Regulars take glasses of red to the pavement for a chat with passing strangers. A calendar of jazz acts – Friuli's finest and some international surprises – play from 10pm on Friday nights.

❶ Information

Tourist Office (📞 0432 29 59 72; www.turismofvg.it; Piazza I Maggio 7; ⏱9am-6pm Mon-Sat, 9am-1pm Sun) Can book local wine tours.

❶ Getting There & Away

From the **bus station** (📞 0432 50 69 41; Viale Europa Unita 31), services operated by APT (📞 800 955957; www.aptgorizia.it) go to and from Trieste (€7, 1¼ hours, hourly), Aquileia (€3.40, one to 1¼ hours, up to eight daily) and Grado (€4.90, 1¼ hours, 12 daily). Buses also link Udine and Friuli Venezia Giulia airport (p431) (€4.90, one hour, hourly).

From Udine's **train station** (Viale Europa Unita) services run to Trieste (€9, one to 1½ hours), Venice Mestre (€12.35, 1¾ to 2½ hours, several

daily), Gorizia (€4.15, 25 to 40 minutes, hourly) and Salzburg (€29, four hours).

The north–south A23/E55 autostrada connects Udine with Trieste, the coast and the Alps. For Pordenone and the Veneto take the SS13.

Cividale del Friuli

📞 0432 / POP 11,200 / ELEV 138M

Cividale del Friuli, 15km east of Udine, is hauntingly picturesque. Rambling around its dark stone streets makes for a rewarding morning or, better still, stay to enjoy its hearty table and cracking bars. It may be a small country town these days, but in terms of Friulian history it remains hugely significant. Founded by Julius Caesar in 50 BC as Forum de Lulii (ultimately condensed into 'Friuli'), the settlement reached its apex under the Lombards, who arrived in AD 568. The well-preserved Lombard church here is unique in Europe.

👁 Sights

Tempietto Longobardo   CHAPEL
(Oratorio di Santa Maria in Valle; 📞0432 70 08 67; www.tempiettolongobardo.it; Via Monastero Maggiore 34; adult/reduced €4/3; ⏱10am-1pm & 3-6pm Mon-Fri, 10am-6pm Sat & Sun summer, 10am-1pm & 2-5pm Mon-Fri, 10am-5pm Sat & Sun winter) Cividale's most important sight is this stunning complex that houses the only surviving example of Lombard architecture and artwork in Europe. Built in the 8th century, it was originally the chapel of a palace accommodating the representative of the Lombard king before being donated to a Benedictine monastery. The expressive 8th-century frescoes are extremely rare and moving examples of Greek-Byzantine art, while the later stucco work is unusually naturalistic, its luminous whiteness accented by the dark wood choir stalls.

Ponte del Diavolo   BRIDGE
(Corso d'Aquileia) Splitting the town in two is the symbolic Devil's Bridge that crosses the emerald green Natisone river. The 22m-high bridge was first constructed in the 15th century with its central arch supported by a huge rock said to have been thrown into the river by the devil. It was rebuilt post-WWI, after it was blown up by retreating Italian troops.

Duomo & Museo Cristiano   CATHEDRAL
(Piazza del Duomo; museo adult/reduced €4/3; ⏱ museo 10am-1pm & 3-6pm Wed-Sun) Cividale's 16th-century, Venetian-Gothic cathedral

sits on an ancient 8th-century church and is filled with unusual treasures. Among them is the lacquered wooden statue of Cividale hero Marcantonio da Manzano, a 13th-century wooden crucifix and a bejewelled altarpiece – a medieval masterpiece. Commissioned by Patriarch Pellegrino II, it consists of 123 embossed and gilded silver plates depicting the Madonna and Child surrounded by 25 saints. The adjacent Museo Cristiano houses the 8th-century stone Altar of Ratchis, a stunning Lombard relic.

🏃 Activities

Bastianich   WINE

(📞0432 70 09 43; www.bastianich.com; Via Darnazzacco 44/2, Gagliano) Joe Bastianich is a certified celebrity in the US, but his Italian vineyards, a few minutes' drive from Cividale, remain all about the wine and gracious Friulian hospitality. Pull up a stool at the new tasting room and sniff and swirl your way through drops made from the surrounding plantings and the Bastianich holdings in nearby Buttrio.

🎊 Festivals & Events

Palio di San Donato   RELIGIOUS

(www.paliodicividale.it; ⊙end Aug) Taking place on the weekend closest to the Feast of San Donato (21 August), this festival has been taking place annually in Cividale since 1368. Members of the city's five districts compete in races and archery competitions in order to win the gonfalcon (heraldic flag) of San Donato, which is then displayed in the winning quarter's parish church for the rest of the year.

🛏️ Sleeping & Eating

La Casa di Matilde   B&B €

(📞346 5170478; casadimatilde@gmail.com; Via Borgo Brossana 62; s €60, d €70-100; 🅿) Perched beside the Natisone river in the historic centre, this 14th-century townhouse has smartly refurbished bedrooms full of characterful antiques. Most rooms have river views and breakfast in the garden is delightful. It's steps away from the Tempietto and there's access to a nice walking path along the river.

Antico Leon d'Oro   FRIULIAN €

(📞0432 73 11 00; www.anticoleondoro.it; Via Borgo di Ponte 24; meals €20-25; ⊙noon-2.30pm & 7-10.30pm Thu-Tue) Eat in the courtyard of this friendly, festive place, just over the Ponte del Diavolo, and, if you're in luck, watch a polen-

ta cook stir the pot. Dishes here couldn't be more regional: sublime d'Osvaldo *prosciutto crudo* (cured ham); seasonal pasta enlivened with asparagus and *sclupit* (a mountain herb); a Friulian tasting plate of *frico*, salami and herbed frittata; and roast venison.

Trattoria alla Frasca   TRATTORIA €€

(📞0432 73 12 70; www.allafrasca.it; Stretta Rubeis 10a; meals €35-40; ⊙11am-2pm & 7-10.30pm Tue-Sun) This family-run trattoria in the historic centre focuses its energy on showcasing the region's wild mushrooms. They come with pappardelle pasta and bacon, in puff pastry baskets and with smoked cheese, and there's even a mushroom tasting menu. Alternatively, choose from other forest delicacies, such as wild boar or snail bourguignon.

🍷 Drinking & Nightlife

★ Enoteca de Feo   WINE BAR

(📞0432 70 14 25; Via Ristori 29; ⊙11am-3pm & 6-11pm) This elegant *osteria* both sells and serves some of the best Friulano and Collio wines alongside a short, seasonal menu featuring asparagus soufflé with Frant cheese, pumpkin torta and risotto with Mangalica pork cheek. It also does a delicious variation on *frico* with artichokes, when they're in season. Occasionally there's live music here too.

ℹ️ Information

Tourist Office (📞0432 71 04 60; Piazza Diacono 10; ⊙10am-1pm & 3-5pm summer, 10am-noon & 2.30-4.30pm winter) Has information on walks in the town.

ℹ️ Getting There & Away

Private trains run by **Ferrovie Udine Cividale** (📞0432 58 18 44; www.ferrovieudinecividale.it) connect Cividale with Udine (€2.85, 20 minutes, hourly). **SAF** (📞0432 60 81 11; www.saf.ud.it) buses also serve Udine (€2.95, 40 minutes) and Gorizia, by way of Cormòns. By car, Cividale is 20km east of Udine on the SS54.

San Daniele del Friuli

📞0432 / POP 8010

Hilltop San Daniele sits above an undulating landscape that comes as a relief after the Venetian plains, with the Carnic Alps jutting up suddenly on the horizon. While ham is undoubtedly the town's *raison d'être*, there's a broad gastronomic bent in play, with a ridiculous number of good *alimentari* (grocery stores), as well as a number of new culinary industries springing up, such as sustainably farmed local trout.

Sights

FRIULI VENEZIA GIULIA SAN DANIELE DEL FRIULI

Biblioteca Guarneriana   LIBRARY
(☑0432 95 79 30; www.guarneriana.it; Via Roma 1; guided tours €10; ⊙9am-noon & 3-6pm Wed, 3-6pm Sat Sep-Jul) The historic, wood-panelled library is one of Italy's oldest and most venerated libraries, founded in 1466 by humanist Guarniero d'Artegna and later enriched with the collection of Archbishop Fontanini. It contains 12,000 well-preserved antique books, on vellum and parchment, including a priceless 12th-century Byzantine bible, an original manuscript of Dante's *Inferno* and a 1524 illustrated account of Cortez' conquest of Mexico.

To see these fabulous treasures, join one of the Saturday morning tours (in Italian and English) at 10.45am or make an appointment. Much of the collection has now been digitised and can also be viewed online.

Chiesa di San Antonio Abate   CHURCH
(Via Garibaldi; ⊙7.30am-6.30pm) More beautiful than the cathedral is the deconsecrated church of San Antonio Abate (the patron saint of butchers), which is covered in vibrant frescoes by Pellegrino da San Daniele, aka Martino da Urbino (1467–1547). The cycle is considered the best in Friuli, lending the church the nickname the 'little Sistine Chapel of Friuli'.

Tours

★La Casa del Prosciutto   FOOD & DRINK
(☑0432 95 74 22; www.lacasadelprosciutto.com; Via Ciconi 24; tours per person €40; ⊙noon-3pm & 7-10pm Sat, 11am-5pm Sun) With a heritage that dates back to the 1700s, this artisanal

prosciuttificio is the only ham business to remain in the historic centre. Run by the Alberti family for five generations, guided tours take you underground into the state-of-the-art production facility where hams are salted, massaged and smothered in fat before being hung to dry. Stringent quality checks involving 40 test parameters take place before any ham is fit to hit the tasting plates which round out the tour.

Festivals & Events

Aria di San Daniele   FOOD & DRINK
(Le Festa; www.ariadisandaniele.it; ⊙late Jun) San Daniele holds the Aria di Festa, a four-day feeding frenzy of a festival each summer. *Prosciuttifici* do mass open-house tours and tastings, musicians entertain and everyone tucks in.

Sleeping & Eating

Casa Rossa Ai Colli   AGRITURISMO €
(☑0432 03 01 15; www.casarossaaicolli.it; Via Ai Colli 2, Ragogna; s/d €55/80; P🐾) Situated in a verdant setting, 6km northwest of San Daniele, Casa Rossa is a period farmhouse offering chic rustic accommodation. The charming beamed rooms are furnished simply with painted dressers, oak beds and wrought-iron beds and desks looking out at views over the broad Tagliamento river. The restaurant, too, is highly regarded and sources all its ingredients from local farms.

★Ai Bintars   ITALIAN €€
(☑0432 95 73 22; www.aibintars.com; Via Trento Trieste 67; meals €20-30; ⊙12.30-2.30pm & 7.30-9.30pm Fri-Tue, 12.30-2.30pm Wed; P) No menu, no fuss, no kerbside appeal; simply serves the best prosciutto and salami alongside small plates of marinated vegetables, local

WORTH A TRIP

SPILIMBERGO

Scuola Mosaicisti del Friuli (☑0427 22 74; https://scuolamosaicistifriuli.it; Via Corridoni 6) in Spilimbergo is one of Friuli's most fascinating places. Although established in 1922 in a postwar effort to provide vocational skills for the poverty-stricken area, the mosaic tradition here is centuries old. Artisans from this mosaic school decorated much of Renaissance Venice, the Foro Italico in Rome, the Church of the Holy Sepulchre in Jerusalem and the subway station at Ground Zero in New York.

Tours run on Saturday at 3pm (book via the tourist office or the school) and take you through classrooms, often with students still at work, explaining the different styles of mosaic taught: Roman, Byzantine and some stunning free-form modern mosaics. The school itself is a canvas with every surface covered in different styles of mosaic. Summer classes and short courses (€220 to €460) are available for those inspired by what they see.

cheeses and generous hunks of bread. You won't find anything else on the menu.

Drinking & Nightlife

Enoteca la Trappola   WINE BAR
(☑0432 94 20 90; www.enotecalatrappola.it; Via Cairoli 2; ☺9am-10pm Tue-Sun) Head to dark and moody Trappola for crowd-pleasing platters of prosciutto (from €6), cheese (€6 to €8) or smoked trout (€8) and well-priced wine and craft beers with a very local, very vocal crowd.

Shopping

Bottega del Prosciutto   FOOD & DRINKS
(☑0432 95 70 43; www.bottegadelprosciutto.com; Via Umberto I 2; ☺9am-1pm Mon-Sat, 3.30-7pm Tue & Thu-Sat) Levi Gregoris' prosciutto is known for its sweetness and perfume and you can buy as much as your heart and stomach desire at his Bottega del Prosciutto, as well as browsing the regional cheeses and wines and an excellent selection of pan-Italian produce.

Information

Tourist Office (☑0432 94 07 65; Via Roma 3; ☺9am-1pm & 2.30-6.30pm Mon-Fri, 10.30am-12.30pm & 3.30-6.30pm Sat & Sun) Books tours of the library and visits to prosciutto factories.

Getting There & Away

Regular buses run to San Daniele from Udine (€4.90, 45 minutes), 25km to the southeast.

By car from Udine take the SR464 to Ciconic-co, then the SP10 and SP116 north.

The Carnic Alps

Stretching as far west as the Veneto Dolomites and as far north as the border with Austria, Carnia is intrinsically Friulian – the language is widely spoken here in lieu of Italian – and named after its original Celtic inhabitants, the Carnics. Geographically, it contains the western and central parts of the Carnic Alps and presents both down-to-earth ski areas, wild and beautiful walking country, and curious, pristinely rustic villages.

Tolmezzo

☑0433 / POP 10,300 / ELEV 323M

Stunningly sited Tolmezzo is the Carnic region's capital and gateway, a historic (and current) crossroads between Italy and Austria. **Borgàt**, the historic centre, is a charming nucleus set along two parallel streets, Via Roma and Via Linussio, lined with arcaded *palazzi*. An interesting detour 6km northeast of the town is **Illegio**, a 4th-century hill village with a still-operating 16th-century mill and dairy.

Sights

Museo Carnico delle Arti e Tradizioni Popolari   MUSEUM
(☑0433 4 32 33; www.carniamusei.org; Via della Vittoria 2; adult/reduced €5/3; ☺9am-1pm & 3-6pm Tue-Sun summer, 9am-1pm & 3-6pm Tue & Thu-Sun, 9am-1pm Wed winter) This four-storey museum has a rich display of artisanal furniture and folkloric objects dating from the 14th to the early 19th century. They're atmospherically displayed in 30 rooms in 17th-century Palazzo Campeis, making it one of the most significant ethnographic museums on mountain life in Europe. The carved cabinetry, wrought iron and weird and wonderful mask collection are quite outstanding.

Sleeping & Eating

Albergo Roma   HOTEL €
(☑0433 46 80 31; www.albergoromatolmezzo.it; Piazza XX Settembre 14; s €50-62, d €90; P ❄ 🗢) This vintage hotel has been serving travellers since 1889 and enjoys a prime position on the main piazza. Rooms are large and pleasant with flowery bed spreads and mountain views. The downstairs bar with its traditional fireplace is a popular local hangout and serves good mountain food.

Antica Osteria Al Borgat   FRIULIAN €
(☑0433 4 03 72; Piazza Mazzini 7b; meals €20-25; ☺10am-3pm & 5-10pm Mon & Wed-Sat, 10am-3pm Sun) This historic Tolmezzo tavern is the perfect place for cold winter nights. Strung with bottles, its low-beamed ceilings and stone walls make for an atmospheric dining room where you can enjoy heavy cheese *frico* with polenta and a glass of Friulian beer.

★ **La Buteghe di Pierute**   FRIULIAN €€
(☑0433 4 11 40; Via Damarie 2, Illegio; meals €25-40; ☺10am-6pm Fri-Sun) A warm and welcoming mountain restaurant in Illegio, with heavy wood-beamed ceilings and a beautiful hand-carved bar. The plate of cold cuts and cheese is excellent, as are the mountain mushrooms and polenta, the slow-cooked pork cheek and the fragrant apple strudel. It's hidden down a small alley off Via Lovea.

Terazzo Tamai ALPINE €€
(www.laugiane.it; Monte Zoncalan; meals €28-38; ⊙Dec-late Mar, Jun-Sep) A short drive from Tolmezzo and a cable car or snowmobile ride up into the Carnic Alps and you'll find this lively spot. There's an all-day sausage stand and bar as well as a restaurant serving up lunches of game, seafood, Friulian-style pastas and the occasional international dish such as paella or tataki of tuna.

❶ Information

Tourist Office (☑0433 4 48 98; Via della Vittoria 4; ⊙9am-1pm daily plus 2-6pm Mon-Sat) Provides information on hiking routes and the whole Carnia region.

❶ Getting There & Away

SAF (☑0432 60 81 11; www.saf.ud.it) buses run to Udine hourly (€5.90, 1¼ hours) from Via Carnia Libera and head north to Sappada (€5.90, 1¼ hours).

Sauris
POP 410 / ELEV 1212M
Up towards Friuli's far northwest border, an insanely twisted road takes you past the plunging Lumiei Gorge to emerge at the intensely blue Lago di Sauris. Another 4km west is the village of Sauris di Sotto and another 4km on, eight switchbacks and a few dripping rock tunnels included, is the breathtakingly pretty Sauris di Sopra. These twin hamlets (in German, Zahre) are an island of unique dark timber houses and German-speakers, and are known for their fine hams, sausages and locally brewed beer.

🛏 Sleeping

Albergo Diffuso Sauris APARTMENT €
(www.albergodiffusosauris.com; 2-6 bed apt €110-180) Part of the larger alberghi diffusi (diffuse hotels) movement in the Carnic region, the Sauris network offers various apartments in a collection of refurbished village houses, all constructed in the unusual local vernacular style, with deep verandahs screened with horizontal slats. Breakfast arrives in a hamper and is composed of warm croissants, mountain honey, homemade yoghurt and, in summer, apricots.

Borgo Eibn LODGE €€€
(☑0433 32 01 94; www.borgoeibn.it; Stavoli Eibn 80, Sauris di Sotto; ste €290-400) In a secluded location, up a steep winding road, Borgo Eibn has created a folk-luxe playground.

Three large chalets of reclaimed timber and local stone house 15 apartments and suites which have traditional stufa (stove) fireplaces, lots of pretty wooden furniture and cosy contemporary textiles. Breakfasts are served to your room.

🍴 Eating

★**Hotel Neider Restaurant** FRIULIAN €€
(☑0433 32 02 14; www.neider.it; Sauris di Sopra 38; meals €25-35; ⊙restaurant 8am-11pm Fri-Wed) This friendly small hotel has a super restaurant, where owner Danila fusses over her guests as if they were her own children; let her guide your choices. The local Wolf prosciutto is always a great start, followed by gnocchi with Moseanda cheese and then a hefty pork chop or plate of roasted veal with roasted potatoes.

Maanja Restaurant FRIULIAN €€
(☑0433 8 62 27; www.sauris811.it; Località La Maina 10; meals €25-32; ⊙noon-2.30pm & 7.30-10.30pm) Part of Residence Sauris 811 (ste €150-210; 🅿@🛜🌊), this is a surprisingly urban space, with dramatic black-slate floors, long rustic-modern fir tables and contemporary Italian chairs, and an equally dramatic view out of floor-to-ceiling windows. The food has a casual sophistication, too: plump homemade ravioli is stuffed with forest mushrooms or wild greens, while house frico comes in both soft and crispy varieties.

🛍 Shopping

Tessitura di Sauris ARTS & CRAFTS
(☑0433 8 62 08; www.tessiturasauris.com; Sauris di Sotto; ⊙10am-noon & 2-6pm Mon-Fri) Hand-loomed rugs, tapestries, scarves and shawls in wool, hemp and linen bearing traditional geometric patterns.

ℹ️ Information

Tourist Office (📞 0433 8 60 76; www.sauris.
org; Sauris di Sotto 91a; ⏱ 9am-1pm & 2-6pm
Mon-Sat, 9am-1pm Sun mid-Jun–mid-Sep) Located in Sauris di Sotto not far from the ski lift.

ℹ️ Getting There & Away

Buses run from Tolmezzo or Gemona with a
change at Ampezzo. By car it's one to 1½ hours
from Udine via the A23 and SS52 to Ampezzo,
then the dramatic SP73.

Sappada

POP 1320 / ELEV 1217M

Voted one of the most beautiful villages in
Italy and winner of a sustainability award
in 2019, Sappada (Plodn in dialect) is a
picture-postcard Alpine village set on a sunny slope surrounded by dramatic Dolomitic
peaks. The village sits on the border of the
Veneto, Carnia and Carinthia (Austria) and
was settled by families from East Tyrol. As
such, it remains a linguistic island and the
inhabitants proudly maintain their unique
culture and traditions.

Wander Sappada Vecchia's flower-
fringed lanes along a 2km cobbled path
that rises up just above the main road and
passes through **Borgata Mülbach** and
Borgata Puiche, passing 17th- and 18th-
century houses. Neighbours vie to out-do
each other with their flower displays and
decorative wood-stacking. In the older
Borgata Cima, you'll find a charming
house-museum (€1.50; ⏱ 4-7pm daily Aug,
5-7pm Tue, Thu & Sat Jun, Jul & Sep), which illustrates what life was like in the village in times
past. There's also a small **museum** (📞 0435
46 91 31; Borgata Mülbach, Località Cascatelle;
⏱ 10am-noon & 4-7pm Tue-Fri mid-Jun–mid-Sep)
FREE dedicated to WWI when numerous
Sappadini, made suspect by their Germanic
sounding dialect, were forcibly transferred
to Arezzo.

Sappada is a year-round destination offering idyllic hiking and biking in summer
and good winter sports facilities. For skiing
and snowboarding there are 17km of slopes
between 1250m and 2000m, most of which
are blue and red runs. For information see
Sappada Ski (www.sappadaski.it). Sappada is
also the location of **Nevelandia** (📞 0435 46
91 22; www.nevelandia.it; Borgata Bach 92; all-day
admission €39; ⏱ 9.30am-4.30pm), one of the
largest winter leisure parks in Italy.

🎊 Festivals & Events

⭐ **Plodar Vosenocht**   CARNIVAL
(⏱ Feb-Mar) A fascinating event involving
masked characters sporting hand-carved
wooden masks and heavy bear-like fur outfits. Locals dress in traditional garb and
there's even a masked ski race. It's a serious
and vibrant folkloric festival.

🛏 Sleeping

⭐ **B&B Graz Trojar Haus**   B&B €
(📞 0435 46 97 04; www.antichecasesappada.com;
Borgata Cima 73; d €80-100; 🅿 🛜) One of just
two historic blockbau homes where you can
bed down for the night. Warm wooden bedrooms are furnished with traditional carved
beds dressed with Alpine-style linens. Breakfast is a spoiling affair of homemade goodies
and local produce and your hosts can give
you tips on activities in the local area.

Hotel Haus Michaela   HOTEL €€
(📞 0435 46 93 77; www.hotelmichaela.com; Borgata Fontana 40; d €145-215; 🅿 🛜 🏊) Sappada's most well-equipped hotel enjoys all the
character of a traditional chalet, plus top-
notch facilities including a swimming pool,
a Swedish sauna and hot tub, and a solarium
with views over the Piave valley. Parking is
free and bikes are available to hire. It also
runs a shuttle to Trieste Airport.

🍴 Eating

⭐ **Ristorante Laite**   FRIULIAN €€€
(📞 0435 46 90 70; www.ristorantelaite.com; Borgata Hoffe 10; menu €80-120; ⏱ noon-3pm & 7-10pm
Fri-Tue, noon-3pm Thu Jul-Sep & Nov-May) Sappada's Michelin-starred Laite ihas just 18
seats set in two romantic 18th-century *Stube*
(traditional Alpine restaurant). Each morning ingredients are foraged in the woods
presenting wild asparagus, nettles and rare
mountain chicory with roe deer, woodcock
and cheese from the local dairy. Highlights
are the chamois tartare and the trout with
mountain herbs.

⭐ **Ristorante Mondschein**   FRIULIAN €€€
(📞 0435 46 95 85; www.ristorantemondschein.
it; Borgata Bach 96; meals €45-60; ⏱ 9am-mid-
night) Presided over by the meticulous
Paolo Kratter, who wears his embroidered
leather lederhosen with tremendous style,
Mondschein is a stunning restaurant. The
fabulous wooden interior is both cosy and
elegant and the menu balances tradition

and innovation perfectly. The mushroom risotto with a thin layer of bilberry sauce is ingenious. Ask your server to recommend one of their excellent regional varietals.

ℹ Information

Tourist Infopoint (☑ 0435 46 91 31; www.sappadadolomiti.com; Borgata Bach 9; ☺ 9am-12.30pm & 4-7pm summer, 9am-1pm & 2-6pm winter) The tourist office's website details all the popular hikes in the area. For information on Alpine guides and activities contact the Italian Alpine Club (caisappada.org).

ℹ Getting There & Away

The fastest way to reach Sappada is by car on the A23 from Udine. Exit at Amaro onto the SS52, then turn onto the SR355.

SAF (☑ 0432 60 81 11; www.saf.ud.it) buses link Sappada with Tolmezzo (€5.90, 1¼ hours), Udine and Trieste. The nearest train station is in Calalzo di Cadore, in the Veneto.

The Giulie Alps

Named after Julius Caesar, the Giulie Alps' dramatic limestone monoliths bear more than a passing resemblance to their more famous Dolomite cousins. These frigid peaks are shared with Slovenia, with the Triglavski Narodni Park just across the border. A cross-border ski lift links the still pristine ski slopes which retain a feeling of wildness. As the area stands at the meeting point of three different cultures, hikers should get ready to swap their congenial *salve* (Italian) for a *grüss gott* (German) or *dober dan* (Slovenian).

Tarvisio

☑ 0428 / POP 4270

Tarvisio (Tarvis in Friulian and German) is 7km short of the Austrian border and 11km from Slovenia. Down to earth and prettily wedged into the Val Canale between the Giulie and eastern Carnic Alps, it's a good base for both winter and summer activities. Most of the action takes place on the slopes, including in the neighbouring resort of Sella Nevea (www.sellanevea.net), which has red runs and respected freeride and backcountry skiing. In both resorts, thanks to a unique micro-climate, the season lasts to the end of April.

🛏 Sleeping

Casa Oberrichter BOUTIQUE HOTEL **€**
(☑ 3482 71 31 57; www.casa-oberrichter.com; Via Superiore 4, Malborghetto; d €100) Located in a village 12km to the west, Casa Oberrichter is something of a destination in itself, a special place with interiors that take the Friulian-folk aesthetic to a new level, beautiful earthy dining rooms and a calendar of events and exhibitions. Rooms are decorated simply, in traditional style with painted and carved furniture and beds tucked beneath wooden beams.

★ Hotel Edelhof HOTEL **€€**
(☑ 0428 4 00 81; www.hoteledelhof.com; Via Diaz 13; s €75-92, d €150; P ☎) This is a beautiful traditional hotel with overhanging eaves, wooden balconies and a cosy wooden interior warmed by fires in winter. Rooms have a minimalist style enlivened by painted wooden beds and chests. There's a basement spa and the restaurant is famous for its traditional cuisine, particularly the game dishes. Situated right by the ski lifts, it has a seven-night minimum in high season.

🍴 Eating

Ristorante Italia RISTORANTE **€**
(☑ 0428 26 37; www.ristoranteitaliatarvisio.it; Via Roma 131; meals €25; ☺ noon-2pm & 7-9pm Thu-Mon) A historic restaurant that fires up the *'fogolar friulano'*, a slow-burning stove, and serves up venison, mushroom or radicchio risotto and other hearty mountain dishes.

Osteria Hladik OSTERIA **€€**
(☑ 0428 64 41 20; Via Romana 33; meals €25-30; ☺ 11am-2pm & 5.30-9.30pm Wed-Sat) Hladik accommodates just 25 tables and a small bar beneath its low vaulted ceiling where locals come for home soup, venison goulash and warming plates of risotto. Be sure to finish with a shot of celery schnapps.

ℹ Information

Tourist Office (☑ 0428 21 35; Via Roma 14; ☺ 9am-1pm & 2-7pm Mon-Sat, 9am-1pm summer, reduced hours winter) Has trekking maps and details on Alpine conditions.

ℹ Getting There & Away

Trains connect Tarvisio with Udine (€9.65, 1¼ hours, six daily). The quickest route by car is via the A23/E55 autostrada from Udine.

Torre degli Asinelli (p467)
STARMARO/SHUTTERSTOCK ©

Emilia-Romagna & San Marino

E milia-Romagna boasts some of Italy's most hospitable people, some of its most productive land, some of its fastest vehicles and most soul-satisfying food. Since antiquity, the verdant Po lowlands have sown enough agricultural riches to feed a nation and finance an unending production line of lavish products: luxury cars, regal *palazzi* (mansions), Romanesque churches, prosperous towns and a gigantic operatic legacy (Verdi and Pavarotti, no less).

And then there's Emilia-Romagna's treasure trove of oft-neglected destinations: vibrant Bologna with its photogenic porticoes, Ravenna with its dazzling mosaics, posh Parma and Rimini, the Roman frontier town turned beach resort. Wherever you go, you'll be welcomed with the trademark warmth of Emilia-Romagna's people.

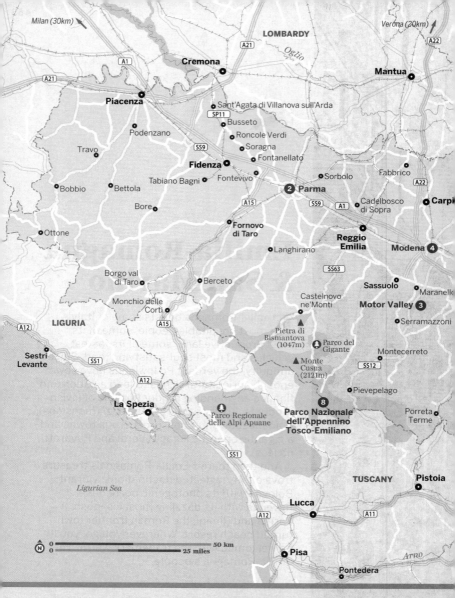

Milan (30km) ↗

LOMBARDY

Verona (20km) ↗

A21

Oglio

A22

Cremona

Mantua

A1

A21

Piacenza

Sant'Agata di Villanova sull'Arda

SP11

Busseto

Podenzano

Roncole Verdi

SS9

Soragna

Travo

Fontanellato

Fabbrico

Fidenza

Fontevivo

Sorbolo

A22

Bobbio

Bettola

Tabiano Bagni

2 Parma

Carpi

Bore

A15

SS9

A1

Cadelbosco di Sopra

Fornovo di Taro

Reggio Emilia

Modena **4**

Ottone

Langhirano

SS63

Borgo val di Taro

Berceto

Sassuolo

Maranello

Castelnovo ne'Monti

Motor Valley 3

LIGURIA

Monchio delle Corti

A15

Serramazzoni

▲ Pietra di Bismantova (1047m)

⌂ Parco del Gigante

Montecerreto

Sestri Levante

SS1

▲ Monte Cusna (2121m)

SS12

A12

A12

⌂ Pievepelago

La Spezia

⌂ Parco Regionale delle Alpi Apuane

8 Parco Nazionale dell'Appennino Tosco-Emiliano

Porreta Terme

SS1

TUSCANY

Pistoia

Ligurian Sea

Lucca

A12

A11

0   50 km

N   0   25 miles

Pisa

Arno

Pontedera

Emilia-Romagna & San Marino Highlights

1 **Ravenna** (p494) Marvelling at the intricate beauty of Italy's most gorgeous mosaics.

2 **Parma** (p483) Soothing your senses with opera or an early-evening *aperitivo* among

spectacular religious sights and iconic gastronomy.

3 **Motor Valley** (p488) Revving your engines among the world's iconic supercars.

4 **Modena** (p477) Savouring a very slow and very delicious

lunch at one of the city's delightfully down-to-earth eateries.

5 **Bologna** (p466) Strolling under the graceful porticoes, climbing tilted towers and indulging in the fabled

Padua (10km)

VENETO

Adige

A13

Valle Berluzzi

Po

Mirandola

Bondeno

Copparo

Ferrara

Pomposa

Cento

revalcore

Reno

A13

SS64

Ostellato

Comacchio

Porto Garibaldi

Consandolo

Argenta

Parco del Delta del Po

Valle di Comacchio

San Biagio

SS9

A1

Bologna Guglielmo Marconi Airport

Bologna

Conselice

Marina di Ravenna

Sasso Marconi

SS9

A14

Fluno

A14 dir

Russi

Ravenna

Adriatic Sea

Dozza

Imola

Vergato

Parco Regionale della Venna del Gesso Romagnola

Faenza

A14

Cervia

A1

Brisighella

Forlì

SS16

SS9

Igea Marina

Cesena

Viserba

Savignano sul Rubicone

Rimini

Rivazurra

Prato

Parco Nazionale delle Foreste Casentinesi

SS3bis

Federico Fellini Airport

Riccione

Cattolica

Bagno di Romagna

SAN MARINO

LE MARCHE

Florence

A1

gastronomy of this vibrant university city.

6 Brisighella (p499) Gazing at this pristinely preserved medieval village from castle-topped mountains.

7 Ferrara (p489) Cycling around the muscular medieval walls of this Renaissance beauty.

8 Parco Nazionale dell'Appennino Tosco-Emiliano (p482) Leaving the

flat lands behind and heading out for a day of hiking on Pietra di Bismantova.

9 Rimini (p500) Discovering Roman treasures and beachside pleasures in this coastal charmer.

EMILIA-ROMAGNA

Bologna

☑ 051 / POP 388,400

Fusing haughty elegance with down-to-earth grit in one beautifully colonnaded medieval grid, Bologna is a city of two intriguing halves. One side is a hard-working, high-tech city located in the super-rich Po valley where suave opera-goers waltz out of regal theatres and into some of the nation's finest restaurants. The other is a bolshie, politically edgy city that hosts the world's oldest university and is famous for its graffiti-embellished piazzas filled with mildly inebriated students swapping Gothic fashion tips.

No small wonder Bologna has earned so many historical monikers. *La Grassa* (the fat one) celebrates a rich food legacy (*ragù* or bolognese sauce was first concocted here). *La Dotta* (the learned one) doffs a cap to the city university founded in 1088. *La Rossa* (the red one) alludes to the ubiquity of the terracotta medieval buildings adorned with miles of porticoes, as well as the city's long-standing penchant for left-wing politics.

◎ Sights

★ San Colombano – Collezione Tagliavini   MUSEUM
(www.genusbononiae.it; Via Parigi 5; adult/reduced €7/5; ⊙ 11am-7pm Tue-Sun) An absolutely stunningly restored church with original frescoes and a medieval crypt rediscovered in 2005, the San Colombano hosts a wonderful collection of over 80 musical instruments amassed by the late octogenarian organist Luigi Tagliavini. Many of the assembled harpsichords, pianos and oboes date from the 1500s and, even more surprisingly, are still in full working order. Listen out for regular free concerts and charge up your phone – this is one of Bologna's most photogenic museums.

Museo della Storia di Bologna   MUSEUM
(www.genusbononiae.it; Via Castiglione 8; adult/reduced €10/8; ⊙ 10am-7pm Tue-Sun) Walk in a historical neophyte and walk out an A-grade honours student in Bologna's golden past. This magnificent interactive museum, opened in 2012 and skillfully encased in the regal Palazzo Pepoli, is – in a word – an 'education'. Using a 3D film, a mock-up of an old Roman canal and super-modern presentations of ancient relics, the innovative displays start in a futuristic open-plan lobby and progress through 35 chronologically themed rooms that make Bologna's 2500-year history at once engaging and epic.

There are many hidden nuggets (who knew Charles V was crowned Holy Roman Emperor in the city?). The only glaring omission is that there isn't too much talk of Mussolini, who was born 'down the road' in Forli.

★ Basilica di Santo Stefano   BASILICA
(www.abbaziassstefano.wixsite.com/abbaziassstefano; Via Santo Stefano 24; ⊙ 9.15am-7.15pm Apr-Sep, to 6pm Oct-Mar) Bologna's most unique religious site is this atmospheric labyrinth of interlocking ecclesiastical structures, whose architecture spans centuries of Bolognese history and incorporates Romanesque, Lombard and even ancient Roman elements. Originally there were seven churches – hence the basilica's nickname Sette Chiese – but only four remain intact today: Chiesa del Crocefisso, Chiesa della Trinità, Chiesa del Santo Sepolcro and Santi Vitale e Agricola.

Entry is via the 11th-century **Chiesa del Crocefisso**, which houses the bones of San Petronio and leads through to the **Chiesa del Santo Sepolcro**. This austere octagonal structure probably started life as a baptistery. Next door, the **Cortile di Pilato** is named after the central basin in which Pontius Pilate is said to have washed his hands after condemning Christ to death. In fact, it's an 8th-century Lombard artefact. Beyond the courtyard, the **Chiesa della Trinità** connects to a modest cloister and a small **museum**. The fourth church, the **Santi Vitale e Agricola**, is the city's oldest. Incorporating recycled Roman masonry and carvings, the bulk of the building dates from the 11th century. The considerably older tombs of two saints in the side aisles once served as altars.

★ Basilica di San Petronio   BASILICA
(☑ 051 23 14 15; www.basilicadisanpetronio.org; Piazza Maggiore; photo pass €2; ⊙ 7.45am-1.30pm & 2.30-6.30pm Mon-Sat, 7.45am-1.30pm & 2.30-7pm Sun) Bologna's hulking Gothic basilica is Europe's sixth-largest church, measuring 132m by 66m by 47m. Work began on it in 1390, but it was never finished, and still today its main facade remains incomplete. Inside, look for the huge sundial that stretches 67.7m down the eastern aisle. Designed in 1656 by Gian Cassini and Domenico Gugliel-

mi, this was instrumental in discovering the anomalies of the Julian calendar and led to the creation of the leap year.

Torre degli Asinelli   TOWER

(www.duetorribologna.com; Piazza di Porta Ravegnana; adult/reduced €5/3; ☺9.30am-7.30pm Mar–5 Nov, to 5.45pm 6 Nov–Feb) Bologna's two leaning towers are the city's main symbol. The taller of the two, the 97.2m-high Torre degli Asinelli (the tallest leaning medieval tower in the world), is open to the public, though it's not advisable for the weak-kneed (there are 498 newly re-stabilised steps) or for superstitious students (local lore says if you climb it you'll never graduate). Built by the Asinelli family between 1109 and 1119, it today leans 2.2m off vertical.

Its shorter twin, the 47m-high Torre Garisenda is sensibly out of bounds given its drunken 3.2m tilt. Tickets must be purchased in advance in 45-minute increments from the official website or at Bologna Welcome (p476), or on site by QR code.

Quadrilatero   AREA

To the east of Piazza Maggiore, the grid of streets around Via Clavature (Street of Locksmiths) sits on what was once Roman Bologna. Known as the Quadrilatero, this compact district is a great place for a wander with its market stalls, happening cafes and lavishly stocked gourmet delis.

Palazzo Fava   MUSEUM

(www.genusbononiae.it; Via Manzoni 2; ☺10am-7pm Tue-Sun) This exhibition space encased in a Renaissance mansion is frequently the site of blockbuster temporary art shows, which range in price from €6 to €14 (adult) and €5 to €10 (reduced). Beyond the exhibitions themselves, the palace's biggest draw is the group of heavily frescoed rooms on the 1st floor, in particular the Sala di Giasone, painted in bright naturalistic style by the precocious young Carraccis (brothers Annibale and Agostino and their cousin Ludovico) in the 1580s, to say nothing of the stunning coffered ceiling.

Pinacoteca Nazionale   MUSEUM

(www.pinacotecabologna.beniculturali.it; Via delle Belle Arti 56; adult/reduced €6/2; ☺8.30am-7.30pm Tue-Sun Sep-Jun, 8.30am-2pm Tue & Wed, 1.45-7.30pm Thu-Sun Jul & Aug) The city's main art gallery has a powerful collection of works by Bolognese artists from the 14th century onwards, including a number of important canvases by the late-16th-century Carraccis. Among the founding fathers of Italian baroque art, the Carraccis were deeply influenced by the Counter-Reformation sweeping through Italy in the latter half of the 16th century. Much of their work is religious, and their imagery is often highly charged and emotional.

Palazzo Poggi   PALACE

(www.sma.unibo.it/it/il-sistema-museale/museo-di-palazzo-poggi; Via Zamboni 33; adult/reduced €5/3; ☺10am-4pm Tue-Fri, 10am-6pm Sat & Sun) Three university museums are housed inside this 14th-century palace. At Museo di Palazzo Poggi, you can peruse terracotta uteri in the Obstetrics exhibition; remarkable anatomical models with wax muscular systems on top of actual human bones; and impressive exhibitions dedicated to 16th and 17th century ships models, stunning old maps, military architectural planning and physics (don't miss Ramsden's 18th-century electrostatic generator, visible in Antonio Muzzi's 1862 painting with Luigi Galvani to its left).

At the guided-tour-only Observatory Museum (adult/reduced €5/3), you can climb the 272 steps of Bologna's first tower built for scientific study (as opposed to defence), which was erected in 1726. Along the way, take in various rooms housing an astounding collection of 13th- to 18th-century astrological and navigational instruments, celestial and territorial globes, and a mesmerising Chinese constellation map on rice paper from 1634. The view is one of Bologna's best. Reserve ahead for three daily tours Tuesday through Sunday (10.30am, noon and 3.30pm; maximum 15 persons). The free European Student Museum (MeuS) covers student life from medieval times to the 1960s.

Teatro Anatomico   HISTORIC BUILDING

(www.archiginnasio.it/teatro.htm; Piazza Galvani 1; €3; ☺10am-6pm Mon-Fri, to 7pm Sat, to 2pm Sun) Housed in Palazzo dell'Archiginnasio (☺10am-6pm Mon-Fri, to 7pm Sat, to 2pm Sun), the fascinating 17th-century Teatro Anatomico is where public body dissections were held under the sinister gaze of an Inquisition priest, ready to intervene if proceedings became too spiritually compromising. Cedar-wood tiered seats surround a central marble-topped table while a sculptured Apollo looks down from the ceiling. The canopy above the lecturer's chair is supported by two skinless figures carved into the wood.

Bologna

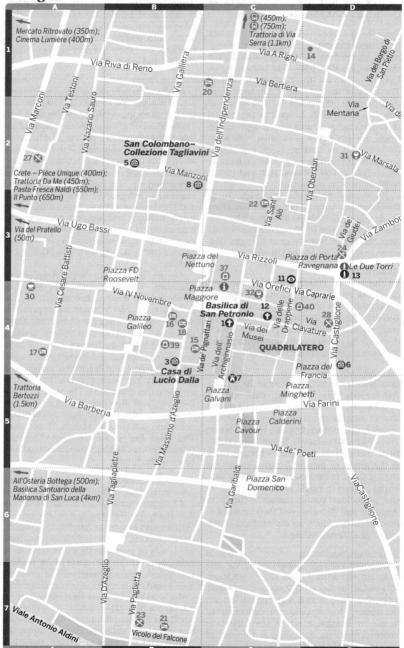

Bologna

EMILIA-ROMAGNA & SAN MARINO BOLOGNA

WORTH A TRIP

LA ROCCHETTA MATTEI

You'll find one of Emilia-Romagna's most fascinating and curious sights at **La Rocchetta Mattei** (www.rocchetta-mattei.it; SP62 Riola-Savignano, Riola di Vergato; adult/reduced €10/5; ⊘ 9.30am-1pm & 3-5.30pm Sat & Sun summer, 10am-3pm Sat & Sun winter), a captivating hilltop castle 50km southwest of Bologna. La Rocchetta Mattei was the home of eccentric Italian homeopath Count Cesare Mattei, who invented a quack medical procedure called 'electro-homoeopathy' that, despite being considered total insanity by the medical and scientific communities then and now, had its share of believers and 'cured' cancer patients in the late 19th century when it was one of the most practiced alternative medicines.

Mattei's pseudoscience, however, brought him great wealth, resulting in the outlandish marriage of medieval Gothic and Moorish architecture that pervades throughout this labyrinthine castle in the Apennines. Jarringly mismatched rooms, winding staircases, striking courtyards (such as *Il Cortile dei Leoni*, or Lion's Courtyard, a recreation of the courtyard of the Alhambra of Granada in Spain) and a thoroughly mesmerising black-and-white-striped chapel (a reproduction of the interior of Cordoba's Mezquita) are wildly out of place and well worth exploration. Moorish arches and turrets, onion-shaped domes and minarets feature prominently. After Mattei's death in 1896 (his tomb sits above the chapel), the castle bounced between various states of private ownership and abandonment (including being ransacked/occupied by both Nazi and American troops in WWII) before a 10-year restoration project saw it finally open to the public in 2015. To reach the castle (weekends only!), take a train from Bologna Centrale to Riola (€4.75) and walk the remaining 1.1km.

★**Casa di Lucio Dalla**   MUSEUM
(☑051 27 35 30; www.fondazioneluciodalla.it; Via D'Azeglio 15; adult/reduced €15/7.50; ⊘tours Fri, closed Jul-Aug) The 15th-century Palazzo Casa Fontana poi Gamberini – the fascinating, pricier-than-the-Colosseum home of eccentric Italian singer-songwriter Lucio Dalla (1943–2012) – opened publicly in 2019 and has become a thrilling addition to Bologna's cultural arsenal. Dalla, one of Italy's most world-renowned contemporary songwriters, lived here between 1993 until his death and amassed an extraordinary collection of art. Highlights include numerous 18th-century Neapolitan nativity scenes and many provocative works (see the life-sized bronzed flasher in the music room!).

★**Museo Internazionale e Biblioteca della Musica di Bologna**   MUSEUM
(www.museibologna.it/musica; Strada Maggiore 34; adult/reduced €5/3; ⊘10am-6pm Tue-Sun) This mouthful of a museum inside Palazzo Sanguinetti – the former home of Napoleon's Italian minister – chronicles six centuries of European musical history and is one of the pillars of Bologna's designation as a Unesco Creative City of Music. It houses one of the most astonishing collections of musical artefacts in the world, including extinct instruments (cornets, chromatic harps, lutes, trumpet marine etc) and documents (manuals, sheets, notes, scores etc) curated from the lifelong collection of Giambattista Martina, considered a human Wikipedia of musical history.

Santuario di Santa Maria della Vita CHURCH
(Via Clavature 8-10; Compianto adult/reduced €4/2, with Oratorio & museum €8/5; ⊘10am-7pm Tue-Sun) In the heart of the Quadrilatero, this 17th-century shrine is one of Bologna's most beautiful and important, not only for its 13th-century foundation by the Congregation of Flagellati (named for their custom of flagellating themselves for penitence), but also as the home of *Compianto del Cristo Morto* (Lamentation over the Dead Christ), a masterpiece of Italian Early Renaissance sculpture by Niccolò dell'Arca.

FICO Eataly World   MARKET
(Fabbrica Italiana Contadina; www.eatalyworld.it; Via Paolo Canali 8; ⊘10am-11pm Sun-Fri, to midnight Sat) FICO, the world's largest agri-food park, opened in 2017 to equal parts cheering and sneering in a formerly dilapidated wholesale farmers' market 7km northeast of Piazza Maggiore. Love it or hate it, the 100,000-sq-metre culinary theme park, is a gastronomic juggernaut. It features 45 restaurants, including ventures from Michelin-starred chefs like Enrico Bartolini; and

Trattoria da Amerigo (p474), a detour-worthy restaurant in Emilia-Romagna's truffle territory. It also includes endless speciality shops and kiosks slinging Italy's greatest culinary accomplishments and drool-worthy wine and beer sections.

Basilica Santuario della
Madonna di San Luca BASILICA
(www.santuariobeataverginesanluca.org; Via di San Luca 36; ⊘ 7am-12.30pm & 2.30-6pm Mon-Sat, 9am-6pm Sun) About 3.5km southwest of the city centre, this hilltop basilica occupies a powerful and appropriately celestial position overlooking the teeming red-hued city below. The basilica houses a black representation of the Virgin Mary, supposedly painted by St Luke and transported from the Middle East to Bologna in the 12th century. The 18th-century sanctuary is connected to the city walls by the world's longest portico, held aloft by 666 arches, beginning at Piazza di Porta Saragozza.

🍴 Courses

CIBO - Culinary Institute
of Bologna COOKING
(📞 370 3698230; www.cookingclassesinbologna. com; Via Agamennone Zappoli 5) Bologna's most heralded cooking school isn't cheap, but top-notch classes will have you opening your own trattoria in no time. Choose from handmade pasta (€165), tack on a market visit (€245) or go all in for a multiday culinary vacation (three days from €945).

☞ Tours

⭐ Italian Days
Food Experience FOOD & DRINK
(📞 338 4216659; www.italiandays.it; tour €150) Maybe Emilia-Romagna's best time for gluttons and gastronauts, Italian Days' take on the region's most popular day trip – the *parmigiano reggiano*, balsamic vinegar and prosciutto combo tour – is the brain child of charismatic owner Alessando Martini's decade-long palette-pleasing perfection.

✨ Festivals & Events

Tour-Tlen FOOD & DRINK
(www.tour-tlen.it; Piazza Maggiore1, Palazzo del Re Enzo; €5-20; ⊘ Oct 4) 'Tour-Tlen' means 'tortellino' (Bologna's most famous pasta) in Bolognese dialect, and this culinary extravaganza features 24 local chefs reinterpreting the traditional *tortellino in brodo* (pork-stuffed pasta in broth) recipe. Palazzo del Re Enzo, one of the city's iconic 13th-century palaces, becomes a foodie free-for-all of the most gluttonous proportions.

🛏 Sleeping

Accommodation in Bologna is geared to the business market, with a glut of midrange to top-end hotels in the convention zone to the north of the city. If possible, avoid the busy spring and autumn trade-fair seasons when hotels get heavily booked, advance reservations are essential, and standard prices can literally double or triple. There is a city tax levied on top of room rates that runs between €1.50 and €5 per person per night depending on the rack rate.

Casa Isolani B&B €
(📞 338 2881153; www.casaisolani.com; Via D'Azeglio 1; s/d from €90/100; ❄ 🛜) Occupying two meticulously renovated historic residences (one superbly located mere steps from Piazza Maggiore; the other at Via Santo Stefano 16), Casa Isolani offers a bevy of well-equipped, good-value city-centre rooms, many with original details like terracotta ceilings and period furnishings. It's a DIY choice (no reception or personal services), but there are some epic Bologna views on offer.

We Bologna HOSTEL €
(📞 051 039 79 00; www.we-gastameco.com; Via de' Carracci 69/14; dm €15-25, tw €35-60; 🅿 ❄ @ 🛜) On the suburb side of the ring road 1km north of the train station, this massive hostel is a world unto itself, evoking an upscale American university dormitory aesthetic. The 92 rooms are made up of excellent four-bed dorms with private bathrooms and colourful twin private rooms with huge desks, minibars, closets and hot-water kettles.

You can rent a bike, watch a movie in the mini-cinema or whip up some *tagliatelle* in the modern kitchen. From October to July, half the rooms are turned over to university students, so there's always a great vibe. To get here, catch bus 30 from Via Rizzoli just near Le Due Torri, which drops you within a few hundred metres.

Dopa Hostel HOSTEL €
(📞 051 095 24 61; www.dopahostel.com; Via Irnerio 41; dm €20-28, d €60-80, tr without bathroom €60-90; ❄ @ 🛜) Barely a kilometre from the train station, this stylish hostel, the baby of detail-oriented owner Paris, features all manner of recycled design touches (Mason-style jars as light covers, beer crates reincarnated as wall shelving), classy tiled bathrooms and

EMILIA-ROMAGNA & SAN MARINO BOLOGNA

GELATO MUSEUM

Opened in 2012, the family-friendly **Gelato Museum Carpigiani** (📞051 650 53 06; www.gelatomuseum.com; Via Emilia 45, Anzola; adult/reduced €7/5, classes €20-50; ⏰9am-6pm Tue-Sat; 🚗) – run by Carpigiani, Italy's most famous gelato-machine manufacturer – traces the history of frozen desserts from ancient times to the present. Discover 19th-century ice-cream carts, try out vintage gelato-making equipment and sample a flavour or two on the Taste Gelato History tour, or don an apron and create your own gelato under the expert guidance of teachers from the adjacent Gelato University.

a communal kitchen that's above and beyond with an induction stovetop.

⭐ **Bologna nel Cuore**   B&B €€
(📞329 2193354; www.bolognanelcuore.it; Via Cesare Battisti 29; s €90-120, d €125-150, apt €140-145; 🅿🌬🤖) This centrally located, immaculate and well-loved B&B features a pair of bright, high-ceilinged rooms with pretty tiled bathrooms and endless mod cons, plus two comfortable, spacious apartments with kitchen and laundry facilities. Owner and art historian Maria generously shares her knowledge of Bologna and serves breakfasts featuring jams made with fruit picked near her childhood home in the Dolomites.

⭐ **Hotel Metropolitan**   BOUTIQUE HOTEL €€
(📞051 22 93 93; www.hotelmetropolitan.com; Via dell'Orso 6; d €140-180, ste €220-300; 🅿🌬@🤖) One of Bologna's few design hotels, the 45-room Met mixes functionality with handsome modern furnishings. It injects peace and tranquillity into its frenetic city-centre location with unexpected touches such as superior rooms upstairs surrounding a small courtyard with olive trees and newer slate-toned deluxe 4th-floor rooms with terraces. The rooftop courtyard is superb sundowner territory.

Porta San Mamolo   BOUTIQUE HOTEL €€
(📞051 58 30 56; www.hotel-portasanmamolo. it; Vicolo del Falcone 6; s/d/tr from €70/90/120, ste €150-250; 🌬🤖) Probably the city's most romantic choice, Porta San Mamolo's 48 rooms are spread about five adjoining buildings centred on an ivy-draped courtyard and

patio dominated by a persimmon tree. Standard rooms are steeped in classic elegance but lack wow – you're better off springing for a superior with an intimate terrace. Hardwood desks and wardrobes and gold-leaf light fixtures feature prominently.

Arthotel Orologio   DESIGN HOTEL €€
(📞051 745 74 11; www.bolognarthotels.it; Via IV Novembre 10c; s €109-255, d €129-282, ste €185-430; 🅿🌬@🤖) Affiliated with the upmarket Bologna Art Hotels mini-chain, this refined pile with a prime location just off Piazza Maggiore seduces guests with its slick service, smart rooms furnished in elegant gold, blue and burgundy, swirling grey-and-white marble bathrooms, antique clocks and complimentary chocs. It also sponsors rotating art shows on the hotel walls and in the sweet *piazzetta* out front. Free bicycles for guests.

Two sister hotels within a two-block radius of the Orologio offer similarly enticing amenities: the **Arthotel Commercianti** (📞051 745 75 11; Via de' Pignattari 11; s €100-180, d €150-260, ste €220-340; 🅿🌬@🤖) and the more modern **Arthotel Novecento**.

⭐ **Prendiparte B&B**   B&B €€€
(📞335 5616858; www.prendiparte.it; Piazzetta Prendiparte 5; d €500; 🤖) You will never – repeat, *never* – stay anywhere else like this. Forget the B&B tag: you don't just get a room here, you get an entire 900-year-old tower (Bologna's second tallest). The living area (bedroom, kitchen and lounge with newly renovated bathroom) is spread over three floors and there are nine more levels to explore, with outstanding views from the terrace up top.

The price includes breakfast, a welcome drink on the panoramic terrace and a personal tour of the tower with the convivial owner, Matteo Giovanardi. For another couple of hundred euros, you can have a private dinner catered by a professional chef or a private jazz concert. Find a millionaire to shack up with and pretend you're an errant medieval prince(ss) for the night!

🍴 Eating

Bologna is the kind of city where you can be discussing Chomsky with a leftie newspaper-seller one minute, and eating like an erstwhile Italian king in a fine restaurant the next. Two meals into your Bologna stay and you'll start to understand why the city's known as *La Grassa*.

Mercato Ritrovato   MARKET
(www.facebook.com/mercatoritrovato; Via Azzo Gardino 65, Cortile della Cineteca; ⊗ 9am-2pm Sat) 🍃 This lively, eco-focused Saturday market is a wonderful spot to escape fellow tourists and wander among booths of craft beer, wine, artisanal cheeses, sweets and ready-made meals. Locals plant themselves on picnic tables in the Cinema Lumière (p475) courtyard, chowing down on fried sardines, vegan pastas, *tigella* sandwiches and other farm-to-table goodies while shopping for organic produce and other sundries.

⭐ **Cremeria Santo Stefano**   GELATO €
(www.facebook.com/CremeriaSantoStefano; Via Santo Stefano 70; small/medium/large €2.50/3/3.50, closed Jan; ⊗ 11am-11pm) Offering a welcoming rustic-chic ambience, this locally recommended, family-run gelateria shakes things up among the usual Italian artisanal suspects and brings imported ingredients into the mix, like Turkish pistachios (for the absolutely excellent salted pistachio flavour) and Venezuelan chocolate.

La Sorbetteria Castiglione   GELATO €
(www.lasorbetteria.it; Via Castiglione 44d; small/medium/large €2.80/3.40/4; ⊗ 11.30am-midnight summer, 12.30-3pm & 7.30pm-11pm rest of year) A beloved Bologna institution since 1994, this temple to gelati is a bit peripheral to the centre but well worth the walk for decadently creamy flavours like pistachio, *gianduia* (chocolate mixed with hazelnuts) or salted caramel.

Pasta Fresca Naldi   EMILIAN €
(www.facebook.com/pastafrescanaldi; Via del Pratello 69; dishes €6-8; ⊗ noon-2.30pm & 7-11pm Tue-Sun) Owner Valeria keeps an army of nonnas in line at this simple pasta lab tucked among myriad bars on Bologna's booziest street. Pasta is sold raw or cooked and is handmade before your eyes. The rich *tortellini al pasticcio* (pork-stuffed pasta with fresh cream and *ragù*) is immensely satisfying, while *tagliatelle* with prosciutto and lemon is a tart and refreshing change of pace.

Bottega Portici   ITALIAN €
(www.bottegaportici.it; Piazza di Porta Ravegnana 2; meals €5-9; ⊗ 7.30am-10pm) This trendy pit stop under the shadow of the towers is great for high-quality Bologna specialities (such as tortellini in *brodo* or with sage and butter, and *tagliatelle al ragù*) served up lightning fast or to go.

It doubles as a gourmet provisions shop (pick up the famous Bolognese broth to go), and the impressive, high-tech Faema E71 espresso machine (which costs significantly more than most Fiats!) means it's a great choice for a stunning *caffè* as well.

Sfoglia Rina   EMILIAN €
(www.sfogliarina.it; Via Castiglione 5b; mains €9.50-11; ⊗ shop 8am-8pm Mon-Sat, 9am-8pm Sun, restaurant 11.30am-7pm; 🕎) Hurry up and wait at this famous Casalecchio di Reno transplant – it's impossible to walk by without salivating over its fresh pasta. Started in 1963 in the Bolognese suburbs, the modern and hip city location attracts oodles of in-the-know pasta lovers for both the traditional (*tagliatelle*, tortellini, *tortelloni*) and weekly-changing creative takes.

Communal seating (write your name, table number and order on the paper provided) under the pasta-basket-draped ceiling and a counter by the fresh pasta shop are the fastest to be seated. No reservations.

⭐ **Trattoria Da Me**   TRATTORIA €€
(☑ 051 55 54 86; www.facebook.com/trattoriadame; Via San Felice 50; meals €29-38; ⊗ noon-2.30pm & 7.30-10.30pm) Bologna's most exciting reinvention is this formerly uneventful trattoria transformed by chef Elisa Rusconi, who triumphed on Italian television show *4 Ristoranti* and upgraded her grandfather's restaurant – at it since 1937 – into a daring, must-stop dining destination in the city's culinary landscape.

⭐ **Trattoria Bertozzi**   EMILIAN €€
(☑ 051 614 14 25; Via Andrea Costa 84; meals €26-40; ⊗ noon-3pm & 7-10.30pm Mon, Fri & Sat, 7-10.30pm Tue-Thu) Often touted as Bologna's best restaurant by in-the-know culinarians – especially locals – this unassuming neighbourhood trattoria is both a rousing good-time and a deeply serious dive into Bologna's famed specialities. It's run by a jovial pair who excel as much with hospitality and wine-swilling as they do with *tagliatelle al ragù*, meatballs with peas, and *gramigna* pasta with saffron, *guanciale* (cured pork cheeks) and zucchini.

Come to escape tourists, but not sport fans (on local game days, it becomes party HQ for superfans). It's located 2km west of Piazza Maggiore in Quartiere Saragozza. Reserve.

⭐ **Trattoria di Via Serra**   TRATTORIA €€
(☑ 051 631 23 30; www.trattoriadiviaserra.it; Via Luigi Serra 9b; meals €25-32; ⊗ 7pm-midnight

WORTH A TRIP

TRATTORIA DA AMERIGO

Emilia-Romagna's best dining experience awaits in truffle territory. In the small village of Savigno, a 30km detour west of Bologna, the fantastic **Trattoria da Amerigo** (🗷 051 670 83 26; www.amerigo1934.it; Via Marconi 14-16, Savigno; meals €45-55, tasting menus €38-50; ⊗ 7.30-10.30pm Tue-Fri, noon-2.30pm & 7.30-10.30pm Sat & Sun) armed with a Michelin star (but lacking any pretension) is the domain of legendary pastamaker Nonna Giuliana Vespucci (you wish she was *your* grandmother!), executive chef Alberto Bettini and his talented young apprentice, Giacomo Orlandi.

Together, their traditional takes and seasonal creations are the Italian dishes of your culinary dreams. Think *tortelli* stuffed with *parmigiano reggiano* and wood-fired prosciutto, gnocchi with regional truffles, Parmesan basket-cradled poached egg with regional mushrooms and shaved truffles — we could go on and on... You could drop a pay cheque on the in-house provisions at the attached gourmet shop. Book a bed, too (singles/doubles from €50/80). You'll want breakfast!

Tue-Wed, noon-4pm & 7pm-midnight Thu-Sat; 🗟)
🍽 Book at least three weeks in advance at this seemingly unassuming trattoria in Bolognina, just a step outside the city centre. Flavio and Tommaso came down from their established destination restaurant in the mountains in Zocca seven years ago wielding recipes (carefully outlined on the short menu) that forge a bridge between classic Emilian and hilltop twists.

⭐ **All'Osteria Bottega** OSTERIA €€
(🗷 051 58 51 11; Via Santa Caterina 51; meals €36-41; ⊗ 12.30-2.30pm & 8-10.30pm Tue-Sat) At Bologna's temple of culinary contentment, owners Daniele and Valeria lavish attention on every table between trips to the kitchen for astonishing plates of *culatello di Zibello* ham, tortellini in capon broth, Petroniana-style veal cutlets (breaded and fried, then topped with *prosciutto di Parma* and *parmigiano reggiano,* and pan-sauteed in broth), off-menu speciality pigeon and other Slow Food delights.

Oltre GASTRONOMY €€
(🗷 051 006 60 49; www.oltrebologna.it; Via Majani 1; meals €36-43; ⊗ 12.30-2.30pm & 7.30-10.30pm Mon & Thu-Sun, 7.30-10.30pm Wed; 🗟) Hip Oltre (Beyond) bucks tradition with its trendy Instagrammable dining space, an absolute detour from Bologna down to nearly every detail. Chalk up the Michael Jordan and skateboard-accented decor to youthful foolishness; it's the adventurous kitchen of Chef Daniele Bendanti that has the city's gastronauts in a frenzy.

Al Sangiovese TRATTORIA €€
(🗷 051 58 30 57; www.alsangiovese.com; Vicolo del Falcone 2; meals €24-40; ⊗ 12.15-2.30pm &

7-10.30pm Mon-Sat; 🗟) A convivial husband-and-wife team as generous with their portions as they are with their hospitality runs this somewhat off-the-beaten-path trattoria in the centre. On a cold day, the savoury *passatelli in brodo* (*passatelli* pasta in broth) is immensely satisfying, but heaping platefuls of *tagliatelle al ragù* and *strozzapreti* pasta with porcini mushrooms, peas and prosciutto are nearly impossible to overlook.

🍷 Drinking & Nightlife

Hit the graffiti-strewn, slightly seedy streets of the university district (Via Petroni) after sunset and the electrifying energy is enough to make any jaded 30- or 40-something feel young again. For a more upmarket, dressier scene head to the Quadrilatero. Try the more down-to-earth Via del Pratello for the city's coolest concentration of bars.

⭐ **Le Serre dei Giardini Margherita** BAR
(🗷 370 3336439; www.vetro.kilowatt.bo.it; Via Castiglione 134; ⊗ 8am-1am Mon-Fri, 9am-1am Sat & Sun Mar-Dec, to 8pm Mon-Wed, to midnight Thu-Sat, 9am-8pm Sun Jan-Feb; 🗟) 🍽 Bologna's best time: parking yourself, an Aperol *spritz* (cocktail made with Prosecco; €4) in hand, among the cool kids and digital nomads at these once-abandoned city greenhouses. They have been transformed into an immensely cool and highly recommended co-working space, vegetarian/vegan restaurant (Vetro) and community gardens in the heart of Giardini Margherita, the city's largest green space.

⭐ **Ranzani 13** CRAFT BEER
(🗷 051 849 37 43; www.ranzani13.it; Via Camillo Ranzani 5/12; ⊗ noon-2.30pm & 7pm-1am Mon-Thu, to 2am Fri, 7pm-2am Sat, 7pm-1am Sun; 🗟) Ditch

the city centre and venture just outside Bologna's ring road to a distinctly unremarkable apartment block where one of the city's best craft-beer bars and gastropubs awaits. Twelve rotating taps (beers €3 to €6; good Belgian and Danish choices) complement a delectable selection of gourmet pizzas like Happy Pork (slow-cooked pork shoulder, burrata, basil and Parmesan) and more.

Il Punto CRAFT BEER
(www.puntobologna.com; Via San Rocco 1g; ⊘5.30pm-1.30am; ⊚) Bologna's best and most Italian-focused craft-beer bar offers eight taps of *birra artigianale* (including one hand-pump; draught beers €3.50 to €6) and over 150 mostly local and Belgian choices by the bottle, which you can take at the small bar or at one of the informal hardwood tables inside or out.

Aroma COFFEE
(www.ilpiaceredelcaffe.it; Via Porta Nova 12b; ⊘8am-6pm Mon-Sat) You'd walk right past this seemingly typical Italian *caffè* and never think twice, the wince-inducing logo certainly not helping matters. But inside, Alessandro Galtieri's passion and fierce dedication to single-origin and micro-lot speciality coffee (five espressos on offer per day; €1.20 to €2.80) is the city's best (to say nothing of his third place at the 2019 World Brewers Cup).

Antica Drogheria Calzolari WINE BAR
(www.anticadrogheriacalzolari.it; Via Giuseppe Petroni 9; ⊘8am-2pm & 4-8.30pm Mon-Sat) This standing-room-only wine bar is one of Bologna's most social, attracting an eccentric early-evening crowd – bohemian art professors, seasoned drunks, wayward wanderers – who spill out onto the sidewalk along lively Via Petroni.

Caffè Rubik BAR
(www.cafferubik.com; Via Marsala 31d; ⊘7am-1am Mon-Sat, 8am-1pm Sun; ⊚) This bohemian pop-art coffee and amaro bar packs a wallop of soul into a tiny space. Cassette tapes and old school lunchboxes line the walls, and the exquisite espresso – among Bologna's best – is unexpectedly served in Japanese porcelain. For something stiffer, the amaro selection is the city's best.

Osteria del Sole BAR
(www.osteriadelsole.it; Vicolo Ranocchi 1d; ⊘10.30am-10.30pm Mon-Sat) The sign outside this ancient Quadrilatero dive bar tells you all you need to know – 'vino'. Bring in your own food, and elbow past the alley-filling cacophony of smashed students, mildly inebriated grandpas and the occasional Anglo tourist for a sloppily poured glass of chianti, Sangiovese or Lambrusco. It's a spot-on formula that's been working since 1465.

☆ Entertainment

Bologna, courtesy of its large student population, knows how to rock – but it also knows how to clap politely at the opera. The most comprehensive listing guides are bilingual Bologna Welcome (www.bolognawelcome.it; check under 'Live') and Bologna Agenda Cultura (http://agenda.comune.bologna.it/cultura). During the summer, Cineteca di Bologna (☑051 219 48 26; www.cinetecadibologna.it; Piazza Re Enzo 1; ⊘10am-7.30pm) hosts films in Piazza Maggiore on the biggest open-air cinema screen in Europe.

Covo Club LIVE MUSIC
(www.covoclub.it; Viale Zagabria 1) The city's best alternative-rock club, located about 5km northeast of the centre. It has drawn the likes of Franz Ferdinand, Mars Volta, the Decemberists, Modest Mouse and the XX in recent years.

Oratorio di Santa Cecilia LIVE MUSIC
(www.sangiacomofestival.it; Via Zamboni 15) The annual San Giacomo Festival brings regular free chamber-music recitals to this lovely space. Check the website or the board outside for upcoming events.

Cinema Lumière CINEMA
(☑051 219 53 11; www.cinetecadibologna.it; Via Azzo Gardino 65; tickets €7) One of Italy's top indie cinemas, run by the world-renowned Cineteca di Bologna. Films are shown in their original language. Tickets are reduced to €5 on Wednesdays.

Cantina Bentivoglio JAZZ
(☑051 26 54 16; www.cantinabentivoglio.it; Via Mascarella 4b; cover €4.50; ⊘8pm-2am) Bologna's top jazz joint, the Bentivoglio is a jack of all trades: part wine bar (over 600 labels), part restaurant (eat elsewhere) and part jazz club (live music six nights a week most of the year). This much-loved institution oozes cosy charm, with its labyrinth of chambers sporting ancient brick floors, arched ceilings and shelves full of wine bottles.

Bravo Caffè LIVE MUSIC
(www.bravocaffe.it; Via Mascarella 1; ⊘8pm-late) Hosting the university district's most dependable and varied mix of live music,

Bravo begins nightly operations as a resto-bar with homemade Bolognese specialities and a 300-label wine cellar. It then moves into club mode, with an eclectic mix of rock, blues, funk, jazz and more. Throughout Emilia-Romagna, it's renowned as a live-music reference.

Teatro Comunale THEATRE
(✆051 52 90 19; www.tcbo.it; Largo Respighi 1; ⊙box office 2-6pm Tue-Fri, 11am-3pm Sat) This venerable theatre, where Wagner's works were heard for the first time in Italy, is still Bologna's leading opera and classical-music venue.

🛍 Shopping

If you came for the food, head for the Quadrilatero, a haven of family-run delis and speciality local food shops; head to FICO Eataly World (p470) for Italian-wide specialities. You'll find myriad Italian boutiques and upscale shopping along main avenues like Via Rizzolo, Via Ugo Bassi and Via dell'Indipendenza. Don't miss the **Mercato Antiquario Città di Bologna** (Bologna Antique Market; Piazza Santo Stefano; ⊙8.30am-6pm, closed Jul & Aug).

New Dandy CLOTHING
(www.newdandy.it; Via Marescalchi 4; ⊙10am-2pm & 3-8pm Mon-Sat) For those looking for a true made-to-measure Italian suit, an exquisite experience awaits at this fiercely artisanal tailor, where Leonardo and Gianluca will take you (and your suit) on a journey of old-school craftsmanship that forges a creative bridge between classic Napolese tailoring and English sensibility.

Paolo Atti FOOD
(www.paoloatti.com; Via delle Drapperie 6; ⊙7.30am-7.15pm Mon-Thu, to 7.30pm Fri & Sat) This shop in Bologna's famed Quadrilatero neighbourhood specialises in beautifully packaged boxes of traditional Bolognese tortellini stuffed with prosciutto, *mortadella* (pork cold cut), fresh Parmesan and nutmeg. Decorative boxes run €10 or €18 empty, and then can be filled with as much as 1kg or 3kg of pasta (€37.90 per kg).

Crete – Pièce Unique DESIGN
(www.cretepieceunique.it; Via San Felice 48a; ⊙9.30am-1.30pm & 3.30-7.30pm Tue-Sat) An interesting shop for unique, nearly 100% Italian-made (there's one Spaniard represented) jewellery, funky ceramics and interior design pieces, many of which are created in the design studio out the back.

ℹ Information

Bologna Welcome (Tourist Office; ✆051 658 31 11; www.bolognawelcome.it; Piazza Maggiore 1e; ⊙9am-7pm Mon-Sat, 10am-5pm Sun) Bologna's official tourist-information hub offers daily, two-hour morning and afternoon walking tours (€15), among other excursions, and can help with bookings. It puts out a handy daily news and events brochure in English and sells the **Bologna Welcome Card** (www.bolognawelcome.com/en/richiedicard; Easy/Plus card €25/40) and 24-hour bus passes (€5). Also

---

THE PATH OF GODS

Few would argue that Emilia-Romagna and Tuscany offer two of Italy's most idyllic and bucolic countryside landscapes – why not make a week of walking it? The ancient 130km Via degli Dei (www.viadeglidei.it) connecting Bologna and Florence through the Tuscan-Emilian Apennines mountains was once traipsed upon by Etruscans and Romans, but it had remained largely lost until its discovery by mountaineers Cesare Agostini and Franco Santi in 1979.

In 2018 the two regions joined forces, stepping up both the infrastructure and their marketing of the trekking route, leading to 10,000 hikers legging the path that same year. The route can be covered on foot (five to eight days) or bike (two to three days), taking in a variety of landscapes, including centuries-old chestnut groves and the dramatic rock formations making up Riserva Naturale Contrafforte Pliocenico in Emilia-Romagna to olive tree-draped hillsides of Tuscany; in parts, the Roman-laid Flaminia Militare road (dating back to 187 BC) leads to Medicean villas and of course there's an abundance of traditional *osterie* and trattorias along the route.

The path remains open year-round, leaving from Piazza Maggiore in Bologna and finishing in Piazza della Signoria in Florence. There is a network of campgrounds, *agriturismi*, hotels and B&Bs along the way to rest your weary head (and feet!). Weatherwise, April, May, June, September and October are your best bets.

has an office at the **airport** (☎ 051 647 22 01; Via Triumvirato 84, Guglielmo Marconi Airport; ◷ 9am-7.30pm Mon-Sat, to 5pm Sun) as well as an affiliate at **FICO Eataly World** (Via Paolo Canali 8; ◷ 10am-10pm).

Ospedale Maggiore (☎ 051 647 81 11; Largo Nigrisoli 2) West of the city centre.

❶ Getting There & Away

AIR

Bologna's **Guglielmo Marconi airport** (☎ 051 647 96 15; www.bologna-airport.it; Via Triumvirato 84) is 8km northwest of the city. It's served by more than 40 airlines, including Ryanair, easyJet and British Airways.

BUS

Intercity buses leave from the **Autostazione di Bologna** (Bus Station; ☎ 051 24 54 00; www.autostazionebo.it; ◷ 24hr) off Piazza XX Settembre, just southeast of the train station. However, for nearly all destinations, the train is a better option.

CAR & MOTORCYCLE

Bologna is linked to Milan, Florence and Rome by the A1 Autostrada del Sole. The A13 heads directly to Ferrara, Padua and Venice, and the A14 to Rimini and Ravenna. Bologna is also on the SS9 (Via Emilia), which connects Milan to the Adriatic coast. The SS64 goes to Ferrara.

Major car-hire companies are represented at Guglielmo Marconi airport and outside the train station. City offices include **Budget** (☎ 051 634 16 32; www.budgetautonoleggio.it; Via Nicolo dall'Arca 2d; ◷ 8am-8pm Mon-Fri, to 6pm Sat, 8.30am-12.30pm Sun) and **Hertz** (☎ 344 1908587; www.hertz.it; Via Boldrini 4; ◷ 8am-7pm Mon-Sat). Recommended **B-Rent** (☎ 334 8593840; www.b-rent.it; Via de' Carracci; ◷ 8am-7.30pm Mon-Sat, to 1pm Sun) is the only agency operating from within the train station itself.

TRAIN

Bologna is a major transport junction for northern Italy, with most trains arriving at **Bologna Centrale station** (☎ 89 20 21; www.trenitalia.com; Piazza Medaglie d'Oro 2; ◷ 24hr, ticket windows 6am-9pm). The high-speed train to Florence (from €17) takes only 35 minutes. Other lightning-quick *Frecciarossa* links include Venice (from €17, 1¼ hours), Milan (from €23, 1¼ hours), Rome (from €27, 2¼ hours) and Naples (from €36, 3½ hours). Slower, less expensive trains also serve these destinations. Check Italo (www.italotreno.it), Trenitalia's upstart competition, for alternative departures and prices.

Do as locals do and ask taxis to drop you directly at the underground high-speed platforms ('Stazione Alta Velocità') at the station (though occasionally *Freccia* trains are moved elsewhere).

Frequent trains connect Bologna with cities throughout Emilia-Romagna, including Modena, Parma, Ferrara, Ravenna and Rimini.

❶ Getting Around

BICYCLE

BikeinBo (☎ 347 0017996; www.bikeinbo.it; Via dell'Indipendenza 69a; bike rental per day/week €15/58; ◷ 9am-8pm) Delivers a rental bike to your door anywhere in Bologna. Rates include helmet, lock, maps and front basket; an optional child seat costs €2 extra.

MoBike (https://mobike.com/it) Bologna's bike-share scheme offers 2200 bikes at 200 stations around the city. Download the app to get moving – fares start at €0.30 per 30 minutes with a €20 deposit.

PUBLIC TRANSPORT

Bologna has an efficient bus system, run by **TPER** (☎ 051 29 02 90; www.tper.it), with information booths at Bologna Centrale train station and the nearby Autostazione di Bologna. Navetta (shuttle) A or bus 27 from Piazza XX Settembre are the most direct of several buses that connect the train station with the city centre. A single costs €1.50 (€2 on board; transfers are free within a 75-minute window of your ticket validation); a 24-hour ticket (*giornaliero*) is €6 and a 10-trip City Pass is €14.

Tickets can be purchased at tobacco stands (*tabaccherias*), newstands (*edicolas*) or on board; as well as via the bilingual **Roger** app (iOS/Android; www.rogerapp.it).

Fines are issued regularly for those without valid tickets.

Modena

☎ 059 / POP 186,000

If Italy were a meal, Modena would be the main course. Here, on the flat plains of the slow-flowing Po, lies one of the nation's great gastronomic centres, the creative force behind *real* balsamic vinegar, giant tortellini stuffed with tantalising fillings, and sparkling Lambrusco wine. It boasts backstreets crammed with some of the best restaurants no one's ever heard of, and one, Osteria Francescana, that everybody's heard of – it was awarded top spot on the coveted 'World's 50 Best Restaurants' list in 2016, and again in 2018, the first Italian restaurant to nab the honour.

For those with bleached taste buds, the city has another equally lauded legacy: cars. The famous Ferrari museum (p488) is situated in the nearby village of Maranello. Modena is also notable for its haunting

Modena

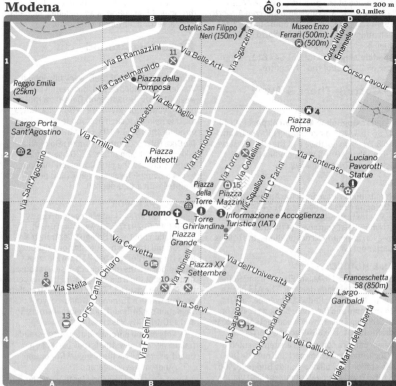

Romanesque cathedral and as the birth-place of the late Italian opera singer Pavarotti, whose former home is a worthwhile museum just outside town.

◉ Sights

Several of Modena's museums and galleries, including Galleria Estense and Musei Civico, are conveniently housed together in the Palazzo dei Musei on the western fringes of the historic centre. A Unesco World Heritage Site combo ticket (€6) – buy at **Modenatur** (🖥weekdays 059 22 00 22, weekends 059 203 26 88; www.modenatur.it; Via Scudari 8; ⏱2.30-6.30pm Mon, 9am-1.30pm & 2.30-6.30pm Tue-Fri) or at each venue – includes admission to Torre Ghirlandina, Musei del Duomo and Palazzo Comunale.

★ Duomo   CATHEDRAL

(Cattedrale Metropolitana di Santa Maria Assunta e San Geminiano; www.duomodimodena.it; Corso Duomo; ⏱7am-12.30pm & 3.30-7.30pm Mon, 7am-7pm Tue-Sat, 7.30am-7pm Sun) Modena's celebrated duomo combines the austerity of the Dark Ages with throwback traditions from the Romans in a style known as Romanesque. The church stands out among Emilia-Romagna's many other ecclesiastical relics for its remarkable architectural purity. It is, by popular consensus, the finest Romanesque church in Italy, and in 1997 was listed as a Unesco World Heritage Site.

Museo Enzo Ferrari   MUSEUM

(www.museomodena.ferrari.com; Via Paolo Ferrari 85; adult/reduced €16/14, incl Maranello museum €26/22; ⏱9.30am-7pm Apr-Oct, to 6pm Nov-Mar) While Maranello's Museo Ferrari (p488) focuses on the supersonic cars, this museum near Modena's train station, inaugurated in 2012, celebrates Signor Enzo Ferrari himself. The memorabilia is cleverly juxtaposed in two separate buildings. The traditional house where Enzo was born in 1898 includes the Museum of Engines, while a

Modena

slick curvaceous modern building painted in bright 'Modena yellow' acts as a gigantic car showroom, with plenty of Ferraris to gawp at, though specific vehicles and exhibition themes change yearly.

A shuttle bus (day pass €12) connects to Modena's train station and the Maranello museum six times daily between 9.40am and 5pm (last bus back at 6pm).

Casa Museo Luciano Pavarotti   MUSEUM
(www.casamuseolucianopavarotti.it; Stradello Nava 6; adult/reduced €10/8; ⊙10am-6pm) Legendary tenor Luciano Pavarotti's final home is prettily perched in the Modenese countryside 8.5km southeast of the city. The building was turned into a museum in 2015; 40-minute self-guided audio tours in nine languages take visitors through the modest home in which Pavarotti lived from 2004 until his death in 2007. Highlights of the tour include access to intimate private areas like his bedroom and bathroom, his buttery ellow kitchen and to personal letters from Frank Sinatra, Bono and Princess Di.

Musei del Duomo   MUSEUM
(www.duomodimodena.it; Via Lanfranco 6; adult/child €4/3; ⊙ 9.30am-2.30pm & 3.30-6.30pm Tue-Sun Apr-Sep, 9.30am-12.30pm & 3-6pm Tue-Sun Oct-Mar) Tucked down an alley along the left side of the cathedral, the duomo's side-by-side museums operate like two exhibitions within the same space. **Musei del Duomo** focuses on religious artefacts belonging to San Geminianus, the patron saint of Modena, including his portable altar dating to 1106. **Museo Lapidario** displays more captivating stonework by famed 12th-century

sculptor Wiligelmo, as well as eight monstrous metopes by an unidentified sculptor who probably worked in Wiligelmo's workshop, which graced the duomo's rooftop until 1948.

Galleria Estense   GALLERY
(www.gallerie-estensi.beniculturali.it; Palazzo dei Musei, Largo Porta Sant'Agostino 337; adult/reduced €6/3; ⊙ 8.30am-7.30pm Tue-Sat, 10am-6pm Sun) Reopened in 2015 after a three-year closure (due to earthquake damage), this delightful gallery features the Este family's collection of northern Italian paintings from late medieval times to the 18th century. There are also some fine Flemish works and a canvas or two by Velázquez, Correggio and El Greco.

Palazzo Ducale   PALACE
(Piazza Roma; adult/reduced €8/6; ⊙ tours Sat & Sun by reservation) Construction began in 1634 on this massive palace, a baroque masterpiece that absolutely dominates the northeast end of Modena's historic centre. Today, it houses the Accademia Militare di Modena, Italy's most prestigious military academy, but the former seat of the princely House of Este is open for one-hour guided tours on weekends – check the schedule and book via the tourist office (p482) at least a week prior.

⌕ Tours

Emilia Delizia   FOOD & DRINK
(☑ 3511726074; www.emiliadelizia.com) It's undeniably pricey, but this UK-based foodie tour company and its wonderful, Modena-based guide, Paolo, will take you on a wonderful and comprehensive gastronomic adventure

fuelled by artisanal balsamic vinegar, *parmigiano reggiano* and Parma ham with generous tastings, intimate interactions with producers and invaluable insight.

🛏 Sleeping

Ostello San Filippo Neri   HOSTEL €
(☏ 059 23 45 98; www.ostellomodena.it; Via Santa Orsola 48-52; dm/s/d/tr €22/40/59/60; P @ 🛜) Modena's businesslike HI hostel has 76 beds in single-sex dorms and family units. Pluses include the convenient location between the train station and downtown Modena, a guest kitchen and cafe/bar, disabled access, large lockers, spacious and uncrowded rooms (maximum three beds per dorm) and a bike-storage area. Each room also has a private bathroom, though not inside the room.

★ Hotel Cervetta 5   HOTEL €€
(☏ 059 23 84 47; www.hotelcervetta5.com; Via Cervetta 5; s €80-104, d €120-150; ❄🛜) Cervetta is about as hip as Modena gets without pandering to the convention crowd. Adjacent to the intimate Piazza Grande, it has quasi-boutique facilities, including rooms that complement the wonderfully soothing, candlelit lobby with rustic-chic additions like African iron light covers, unfinished concrete bathrooms and roped Edison lighting.

★ Casa Maria Luigia   B&B €€€
(www.casamarialuigia.com; Stradello Bonaghino 56, San Damaso; d €450-750; ☻closed Sun-Mon; P ❄🛜🏊) Aiming to capitalise on the worldwide foodie frenzy created by Osteria Francescana, top chef Massimo Bottura and his American wife, Lara Gilmore, transformed this Emilian countryside villa just outside Modena into a food- and art-focused B&B in 2019.

The 12 rooms and common areas are deluged with fascinating and provocative art (Damien Hirst, Tracey Ermin, Ai Weiwei), Bottura's personal vinyl collection and discerning furniture and antiques. The fantastic grounds include sculptures, a pool and tennis court, an artificial pond, a vegetable and tulip garden, 1920s street lamps and massive oak trees. Fancy a guaranteed reservation at Osteria Francescana? Make a non-refundable, paid-in-advance booking and you're in!

🍴 Eating

Modena would easily make a top-10 list of best Italian culinary towns. Its beauty lies not just in the food, but in the way it is presented in simple, unpretentious eateries shoehorned up blind alleys or hidden inside faceless office blocks, often without signage.

★ Mercato Albinelli   MARKET
(www.mercatoalbinelli.it; Via Luigi Albinelli 13; ☻6.30am-2.30pm year-round, plus 4.30-7pm Sat Oct-May) Modena's covered municipal market cradles a cornucopia of local delights. Foodies should head straight here for Bible-sized hunks of *parmigiano reggiano*, bottles of Vecchia Modena Lambrusco or aged balsamic vinegar, just-stuffed tortellini and tortelloni, piles and piles of fresh produce, and a million other things you will be dying to try. You can assemble a picnic of Last Supper proportions here.

★ Trattoria Ermes   TRATTORIA €
(☏ 059 23 80 65; Via Ganaceto 89; meals €20; ☻noon-2.30pm Mon-Sat) In business since 1963, this fabulous, affordable little lunch spot is tucked into a single wood-panelled room at the northern edge of downtown Modena. Gregarious patron Ermes Rinaldi runs the place with his wife Bruna: she cooks, he juggles plates and orders while excessively bantering with the customers, though these days he often sits out for health reasons.

Trattoria Aldina   TRATTORIA €
(☏ 059 23 61 06; Via Albinelli 40; meals €16-25; ☻noon-2.30pm Mon-Thu, noon-2.30pm & 8-10.30pm Fri & Sat) Cloistered upstairs in a utilitarian apartment block, Aldina feels like a precious secret guarded loyally by local shoppers from the adjacent produce market. The menu features the kind of no-nonsense homemade grub that only an Italian *nonna* raised on hand-shaped pasta could possibly concoct. Despite a written menu, you'll be offered what's in the pot and revel in the people-watching potential.

If the lasagna is in the pot, don't miss it. Cash only; no reservations.

La Piazzetta del Gusto   EMILIAN €€
(☏ 059 54 62 55; www.lapiazzettadelgusto.com; Via Roma 24, Nonantola; meals €28-33; ☻12.30-2.30pm & 7-10.30pm Tue-Fri, 7-10.30pm Sat, noon-2.30pm Sun; 🛜) If you know anything about *passatelli,* Emila-Romagna's stringy pasta made from *parmigiano reggiano,*

breadcrumbs and eggs, you know it's not often found outside Italy, and you know it's amazing. So a restaurant specialising in it is worth travelling for.

About 12km from Modena, owner Max offers some 15 types of *passatelli asciutti* (dry, as opposed to in broth) as well as immensely satisfying pasta. A visit to this small-town charmer in Nonantola pairs perfectly with a visit to the famous Romanesque abbey down the street. Want off-menu perfection? Split servings of *passatelli* with fresh basil, *datterino* tomatoes, almonds and olive oil and *orecchie elefante* (elephant ear!) pasta with peas and *gambuccio* (the sweeter ends of prosciutto). *Prego!*

Ristorante da Danilo   ITALIAN **€€**
(☑ 059 21 66 91; www.ristorantedadanilomodena. it; Via Coltellini 31; meals €25-30; ⊘noon-3pm & 7pm-midnight Mon-Sat) Speedy waiters glide around juggling bread baskets and wine bottles in this deliciously traditional choice where first dates mingle with animated families and local characters. The impressive antipasti spread and perfect *gnocchi fritti* (fried dough; eat it with local prosciutto) are divine, but don't overdo it – the Vecchia Modena-style tortelloni (ricotta and spinach with bacon cream sauce) is nothing short of transcendent.

★ **Osteria Francescana**   GASTRONOMY **€€€**
(☑ 059 22 39 12; www.osteriafrancescana.it; Via Stella 22; tasting menus €250-270, with wine €390-450; ⊘12.30pm or 1pm & 8pm or 8.30pm Tue-Sat) Reserve months in advance (or pray for a waiting-list miracle) at this fabled 12-table restaurant, where reimagined Italian fare is art and tasting menus top out at €270. Owner Massimo Bottura is onto his third Michelin star (earned in 2011), and the restaurant claimed the number-one spot on the influential 'World's 50 Best Restaurants' list in 2016 and 2018.

Six tables per meal are now set aside for pre-paid reservation holders at their new Casa Maria Luigia B&B, so dropping €450 for a room is actually the most surefire route for a table here. For creative international cuisine with a more moderate price tag, try Bottura's equally diminutive bistro Franceschetta 58 (☑ 059 309 10 08; www. franceschetta58.it; Via Vignolese 58; meals €35-40, tasting menus €50-70, 3-course lunch €25; ⊘12.30-3pm & 7.30pm-midnight Mon-Sat; ☎), 1km southeast of the centre.

🍷 Drinking & Nightlife

★ **Menomoka**   COFFEE
(www.facebook.com/menomoka; Corso Canal Chiaro 136a; ⊘7am-10pm Sun-Thu, to midnight Fri & Sat; ☎) Step up your coffee game at this trendy, barista-driven cafe that produces Modena's best espresso, pulled from 100% Arabica specialty blends from around the world. Coffee connoisseurs will also find siphon and V60 methods served here, along with wine and craft beer.

FM23   CRAFT BEER
(www.facebook.com/fm23beerstro; Via Antonio Scarpa 23; ⊘5pm-midnight Sun-Thu, to 1am Fri & Sat; ☎) The big personality behind the now-closed rock-and-roll craft-beer bar Maltomania is one of the partners behind Modena's newest and best destinations for *birra artigianale*. Part brewpub, part rustic-chic contemporary restaurant (a *beer-stró!*), the 10 taps (two hand pumps) focus on Belgian and Italian sour and funk but always offer well-rounded selections, including a house-brewed ESB, a session IPA and/ or porter.

⭐ Entertainment

**Teatro Comunale
Luciano Pavarotti**   THEATRE
(☑ 059 203 30 10; www.teatrocomunalemodena. it; Corso Canal Grande 85) It will come as no surprise that the birthplace of Pavarotti has a decent opera house. The Comunale opened in 1841 and has 900 seats and 112 boxes. Following the death of the city's exalted native son in September 2007, it was renamed in his honour. Outside the theatre is a life-sized bronze statute of Pavarotti (at the corner of Via Carlo Goldoni and Corso Canal Grande).

🛍 Shopping

La Consorteria 1966   FOOD & DRINKS
(www.facebook.com/laconsorteria1966; Piazza Mazzini 9; ⊘11am-6pm Mon-Sat) Modena's best shop for balsamic vinegar represents 20 or so DOP producers belonging to the strictest and biggest of the three consortiums affiliated with Modena's most famous product. Carry-on-friendly 100ml bottles – designed by famed automobile designer Giorgetto Giugiaro – cost between €50 and €150. Prepare to taste a few before committing.

EMILIA-ROMAGNA & SAN MARINO MODENA

❶ Information

Tourist Office (☑ 059 203 26 60; www. visitmodena.it; Piazza Grande 14; ⊙ 9am-6pm Mon-Sat, to 6pm Sun) Provides city maps and a wealth of info about the surrounding area as well as books the Discover Ferrari and Pavarotti Land tour, Unesco Combo ticket and tours of Palazzo Ducale and Teatro Comunale Luciano Pavarotti. Also organises walking tours (€8; 11pm and 3.30pm, subject to availability).

❶ Getting There & Away

By car, take the A1 Autostrada del Sole if coming from Rome or Milan, or the A22 from Mantua and Verona.

The **train station** (☑ 06 6847 5475; www. ferroviedellostato.it; Piazza Dante Alighieri) is north of the historic centre, fronting Piazza Dante Alighieri. Destinations include Bologna (from €3.85, 30 minutes, half-hourly), Parma (from €5.40, 30 minutes, half-hourly) and Milan (regional from €15.50, 2¼ hours, hourly; express from €29, 1¾ hours, every two hours).

Parco Nazionale dell'Appennino Tosco-Emiliano

In the late 1980s Italy had half a dozen national parks. Today it has 25. One of the newer additions is Parco Nazionale dell'Appennino Tosco-Emiliano (☑0585 94 72 00; www.parcoappennino.it), a 260-sq-km parcel of land that straddles the border between Tuscany and Emilia-Romagna. Running along the spine of the Apennine mountains, the park is notable for its hiking potential, extensive beech forests and small population of wolves.

In 2015 the park achieved Unesco's Man and Biosphere Reserve status.

🏃 Activities

The park offers a wealth of hiking and climbing options, including at least seven or so organised Club Alpino Italiano paths, highlighted by the 5km trek Pietra di Bismantova (1047m). The imposing limestone outcrop is also considered Emilia-Romagna's most diverse rock climb. Other activities available in the park include cycling, cross-country skiing and fishing.

Hiking

Day-hikers should take on the 5km trek to Pietra di Bismantova (Castelnovo ne' Monti), reachable from the car park in front of For-

esteria San Benedetto or from tiny Eremo di Bismantova monastery, which dates from 1400. From here various paths fan out to the rock's summit (25 minutes). You can also circumnavigate the rock on the lovely 5km Anello della Pietra or even tackle it on a difficult *via ferrata* (trail with permanent cables and ladders), with the proper equipment.

Of the park's many majestic peaks, the highest is 2121m Monte Cusna, easily scalable from the village of Civago, near the Tuscan border, on a path (*sentiero* No 605) that passes the region's best mountain hut, the Rifugio Cesare Battisti (☑ 348 5954241, 0522 89 74 97; www.rifugio-battisti.it; Lama Lite di Ligonchio; dm incl half-board €48). The *rifugio* sits alongside one of Italy's great longdistance walking trails: the three-week, 375km-long Grande Escursione Appennenica (GEA), which bisects the park in five stages from Passo della Forbici (near the Rifugio Cesare Battisti) up to its termination point just outside the park's northwest corner in Montelungo. Sections of the GEA can be done as day walks. *Trekking in the Apennines: The Grande Escursione Appenninica Through Tuscany and Emilia-Romagna* by Gillian Price provides an excellent detailed guide of the whole route.

🛏 Sleeping

⭐ Foresteria San Benedetto   LODGE €
(☑ 0522 61 17 52; www.foresteriasanbenedetto.it; Viale Bismantova 43a, Castelnovo ne' Monti; s/d/ tr/q €45/80/105/140, half board/full board per person extra €15/25) Picturesquely set at the foot of the dramatic Pietra di Bismantova, this simple but cosy lodge offers rooms housing up to six people, along with hearty meals for hikers.

❶ Information

Tourist Office (☑ 0522 81 23 13; www. appenninoreggiano.it; Via Franceschini 1a, Castelnovo ne' Monti; ⊙ 9.30am-12.30pm Mon & Wed, 9am-12.30pm & 2-4.30pm Fri & Sat) The large village of Castelnovo ne' Monti has an ultra-helpful tourist office that stocks stacks of free information and sells cheap maps of the region for hikers, cyclists and equestrians.

❶ Getting There & Away

One of the best gateways to the park is the village of Castelnovo ne' Monti, about 40km south of Reggio Emilia along the winding SS63 on a delightfully scenic ACT bus route. To reach Castelnovo ne' Monti via public transport, take bus 3B44 from Reggio Emilia (€4.50, 1½ hours, seven to 15 daily), operated by **SETA** (⌨ 840 000216; www.setaweb.it; Piazzale Europa).

Parma

⌨ 0521 / POP 187,000

If reincarnation ever becomes an option, pray you come back as a Parmesan. Where else do you get to cycle to work through streets virtually devoid of cars, lunch on fresh-from-the-attic prosciutto and aged *parmigiano reggiano,* quaff crisp, refreshing Lambrusco wine in regal art-nouveau cafes, and spend sultry summer evenings listening to classical music in architecturally dramatic opera houses?

Starting from its position as one of Italy's most prosperous cities, Parma has every right to feel smug. More metropolitan than Modena, yet less clamorous than Bologna, this is the city that gave the world a composer called Verdi and enough ham and cheese to start a deli chain. Stopping here isn't an option, it's a duty.

◎ Sights

★ **Duomo**   CATHEDRAL
(Cattedrale di Santa Maria Assunta; www.piazza-duomoparma.com; Piazza del Duomo; ⊙ 7.30am-7.15pm) Another daring Romanesque beauty? Well, yes and no. Consecrated in 1106, Parma has a classic Lombard-Romanesque facade, but inside, the gilded pulpit and ornate lamp-holders scream baroque. Take note: there are some genuine treasures here. Up in the dome, Antonio da Correggio's *Assunzione della Vergine* (Assumption of the Virgin) is a kaleidoscopic swirl of cherubs and whirling angels, while in the southern transept, Benedetto Antelami's *Deposizione* (Descent from the Cross; 1178) relief is considered a masterpiece of its type.

★ **Battistero**   CHRISTIAN SITE
(www.piazzaduomoparma.com; Piazza del Duomo; adult/reduced incl Museo Diocesano €8/6; ⊙ 10am-6pm Apr-Oct, to 5pm Nov-Mar) Overshadowing even the cathedral, the octagonal pink-marble baptistery on the south side of the piazza is one of the most important such structures in Italy. Its architecture is a hybrid of Romanesque and Gothic, and its construction started in 1196 on the cusp of the two great architectural eras. The interior is particularly stunning, with its interplay of pencil-thin marble columns and richly coloured 13th-century frescoes in the Byzan-

CASTELLO DI TORRECHIARA

Castello di Torrechiara (www.castellidelducato.it; Borgo del Castello 1, Torrechiara; adult/reduced €5/2; ⊙ 8.10am-1.50pm Mon-Sat, 10am-7pm Sun Sep-Jun, 8.10am-1.50pm Mon-Sat, 10am-4pm Sun Jul-Aug) Magnifico Pier Maria Rossi's impressive Torrechiara Castle is one of the most important examples of Italian castle architecture and is considered one of Emilia-Romagna's most storybook fortresses. Built between 1448 and 1460, its outer structure, featuring five massive square towers, is extraordinarily preserved while its interiors, though empty, harbour a series of grotesque, colourful and remarkably intact 15th- and 16th-century frescoes.

tine style, interspersed at irregular intervals with statues and bas-reliefs.

Architect and sculptor Benedetto Antelami oversaw the project and it contains his best work, including a celebrated set of figures representing the months, seasons and signs of the zodiac. The baptistery wasn't completed until 1307 thanks to several interruptions, most notably when the supply of pink Verona marble ran out.

★ **Galleria Nazionale**   GALLERY
(www.pilotta.beniculturali.it; Piazza della Pilotta 5; adult/reduced incl Teatro Farnese & Museo Archeologico Nazionale €10/5; ⊙ 8.30am-7pm Tue-Sat, 1-7pm Sun) The Galleria Nazionale displays Parma's main art collection in dark and ambiently affective environs. Alongside works by local artists Correggio and Parmigianino, you'll find paintings by Fra Angelico, Canaletto and sometimes El Greco. Don't miss Leonardo da Vinci's 16th-century *La Scapigliata,* a striking High Renaissance–style oil painting on wood. You also access the stage of Teatro Farnese (p485) from here, a copy of Andrea Palladio's Teatro Olimpico in Vicenza. Constructed entirely out of wood, it was almost completely rebuilt after being bombed in WWII.

Parco della Cittadella   PARK
(Viale delle Rimembranze 5a; ⊙ 7am-9pm Apr-Oct, to 8pm Sep-Mar) FREE Parma's favourite city park is set inside a cinematic 16th-century pentagonal fortress surrounded by an intact 10m-high wall. Restored and made into a

Parma

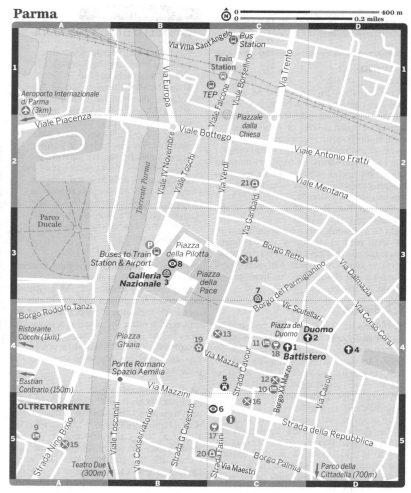

EMILIA-ROMAGNA & SAN MARINO PARMA

park in 2009, it's a great spot for picnics, adventures with kiddos (there is a playground and a giant trampoline) or a workout: a 1.6km jogging trail flanks the ramparts.

Pinacoteca Stuard   MUSEUM
(www.comune.parma.it/cultura; Borgo del Parmigianino 2; ⊙10am-5pm Mon & Wed-Fri, 10.30am-6.30pm Sat & Sun) **FREE** Giuseppe Stuard was a 19th-century Parmese art collector who amassed 600 years worth of epoch-defining art linking the Tuscan masters of the 1300s to 1950s modern art. In 2002 the collection was moved into a wing of this 10th-century Benedictine convent dedicated to St Paul,

where it has been artfully laid out over 22 rooms on the site of an old Roman home.

Chiesa & Monastero di
San Giovanni Evangelista   CHURCH
(www.monasterosangiovanni.com; Piazzale San Giovanni; ⊙church 8-11.45am & 3-7.45pm Mon-Sat, monastery 9-11.30am & 3-5.30pm Mon-Wed, Fri & Sat Oct-May, 3-5.30pm Mon-Wed, Fri & Sat Jun-Sep) Directly behind the duomo, this abbey church is noteworthy for its 16th-century mannerist facade and Correggio's magnificent frescoed dome, which was highly influential for its time and inspired many later works. The adjoining monastery is known

Parma

EMILIA-ROMAGNA & SAN MARINO PARMA

as much for the oils and unguents that its monks produce as for its Renaissance cloisters. Upstairs, a library is adorned with huge old maps that hang from the walls of a musty reading room.

Teatro Farnese   THEATRE
(www.pilotta.beniculturali.it; Piazzale della Pilotta 15; adult/reduced incl Galleria Nazionale & Museo Archeologico Nazionale €10/5; ⊙8.30am-7pm Tue-Sat, 1-7pm Sun) Rebuilt to original plans after WWII bombing, this stunning theatre is almost entirely made out of wood. The great Monteverdi, frustrated by the theatre's acoustic problems before its inaugural event in 1628, was forced to put his orchestra in a pit below the stage – long before 19th-century composer Wagner established this modern practice. The stage is accessed via Galleria Nazionale (p483).

Piazza Garibaldi   PIAZZA
On the site of the ancient Roman forum, Piazza Garibaldi is Parma's cobbled hub bisected by the city's main east–west artery, Via Mazzini, and its continuation, Strada della Repubblica. On the square's north side, the facade of the 17th-century **Palazzo del Governatore** (www.palazzodelgovernatore.it), these days municipal offices, sports a giant sundial, added in 1829.

☞ Tours

Tastybus   FOOD & DRINK
(☑0521 22 97 85; www.maestrotravelexperience. com; Piazza Garibaldi; adult/child from €65/44) Leaving from Piazza Garibaldi Monday to

Friday at 9.30am, this minibus tour (maximum 18 people) is the most convenient (read: *not* the most intimate) way to hit both production farms of *parmigiano reggiano* and *prosicutto di Parma* in one half-day tour. A full day tour extends the experience to lunch and a balsamic vinegar producer.

🛏 Sleeping

★**B&B Pio**   B&B €
(☑347 7769065; www.piorooms.it; Borgo XX Marzo 14; s/d from €70/80; 🔊) Location, comfort and hospitality all come together at this B&B run by a gregarious owner with a passion for local food and wine. Four lower-floor doubles and a kitchenette-equipped upper-floor suite share attractive features such as beamed ceilings, antique textiles and ultra-modern fixtures.

Al Ducale   B&B €
(☑0521 28 11 71; www.bbalducale.it; Via della Costituente 11; s/d/tr/q from €55/75/95/115, apt €55-115; ❄🔊) Opera-loving, English-speaking Giovanni is a consummate host at this sensible Oltretorrente choice, which offers well-equipped rooms, studios and one-, two- and three-bedroom apartments. All are within pleasant walking distance of the historical centre, yet are far enough removed from the hubbub to make you feel like a local.

Fruits and breads are delivered to your door each morning, along with any city tips you could ever want or need. It's especially popular with composers, actors and singers, whose autographed messages dot the B&B.

DON'T MISS

THE WORLD'S LARGEST MAZE

The 2015 opening of the world's largest maze, **Labirinto della Masone** (☏ 0521 82 70 81; www.labirintodifrancomariaricci.it; Strada Masone 121, Fontanellato; adult/reduced €18/12; ⏱ 10.30am-7pm Wed-Mon Apr-Oct, 9.30am-6pm Wed-Mon Nov-Mar; 🅿), fulfilled a lifetime dream of art publisher Franco Maria Ricci, who once published what many considered to be the most beautiful art magazine in the world, *FMR*. Ricci's 7-hectare bamboo labyrinth in the countryside in Fontanellato 17km west of Parma is perhaps Emilia-Romagna's quirkiest unmissable attraction. Kids and adults alike love getting lost en route to an interior courtyard – set aside an hour – which includes two luxury suites (€950 per night).

But in addition to the maze, Ricci's extraordinary personal art collection, amassed over 50 years, includes Napoleonic busts, mannerist works, paintings spanning the 17th to 19th centuries, original illustrations of Luigi Serafini's *Codex Seraphinianus,* a wooden model of Milan's duomo, countless *FMR* magazine covers and a thoroughly fascinating room devoted to morbid 17th-century still-life vanitas. Unfortunately, you'll need personal transport to reach the park.

Palazzo dalla Rosa Prati   BOUTIQUE HOTEL €€€
(☏ 0521 38 64 29; www.palazzodallarosaprati.it; Strada al Duomo 7; d €100-300, ste & apt €200-400; ❋ 🛜) Kick back like Marie Antoinette in regal digs right next to Parma cathedral. Choose from among nine posh and palatial renovated historic suites, 10 modern apartments and two smaller, less expensive doubles. Corner suite 5 is especially alluring, with views into the baptistery's upper window directly across the street (a trade-off for the gaudy pink bedspread).

Parking costs €14. Downstairs, sip wine or coffee at the modish **T-Cafe** (⏱ 8am-8pm Mon-Wed & Sun, to 3pm Thu, to 9pm Fri & Sat; 🛜).

🍴 Eating

Most of Parma's specialities need no introduction to anyone familiar with the food of planet Earth. Both *prosciutto di Parma* (Parma ham) and *parmigiano reggiano* make excellent antipasto plates, accompanied by a good Sangiovese red, and are readily available throughout city centre restaurants. And then there's the horse meat...

Ciacco Lab   GELATO €
(www.ciaccolab.it; Via Garibaldi 11; extra small/small/medium/large €2.50/3/3.40/4; ⏱ noon-11pm Sun-Fri, to midnight Sat Apr-Oct, shorter hours Nov-Mar) 🍃 This experimental farm-to-table gelataria wants nothing to do with additives, preservatives, hydrogenated vegetable oils, added fats or starches, and works directly with Emilian producers to concoct ace flavours. The pistachio is the best we've had in Emilia-Romagna, and surprising choices like green-tea matcha or *nero ardente* (with

Trinidadian cacao, *añejo* rum and habanero peppers) have some serious bite!

Oven   PIZZA €
(☏ 0521 06 18 46; www.oven-restaurant.com; Strada Nino Bixio 52a; pizza €5.50-9; ⏱ 7-11.30pm Mon & Sat, noon-2.30pm & 7-11.30pm Tue-Fri; 🛜) Parma's best pizzeria is this hip hotspot in Oltretorrente started by young upstarts from Campania. It's all about authentic pizza *napoletana* and trendy cocktails like pink pepper negronis. Stars here include *Crudaiola* (aged prosciutto, artisanal *fior di latte, stracciatella* from Puglia, grape tomatoes, olive oil and basil), but the dough/crust is so good, you might be content to simply go with that.

Pepèn   SANDWICHES €
(Borgo Sant'Ambrogio 2; sandwiches €2.50-6; ⏱ 9am-2.45pm & 4-7.15pm Tue-Sat) Prepare to battle the throngs of locals that crowd into this buzzing little sandwich shop, where *panini* get piled high with *prosciutto di Parma,* cheeses and countless other tasty ingredients. After seven decades, it's a dearly beloved Parma institution, though getting served can be an exercise in elbow-throwing frustration for non-Italian speakers.

⭐ **Ristorante Cocchi**   EMILIAN €€
(☏ 0521 98 19 90; www.ristorantecocchi.it; Viale Antonio Gramsci 16a; meals €27-45; ⏱ 12.15-2.15pm & 7.30-10.15pm Sun-Fri; 🛜) You'll need to venture across the river to Oltretorrente for a traditional Parmigiano experience untainted by the city's influx of culinary tourism. Classy yet unpretentious, father and son duo Corrado and Daniele Cocchi woo you with tradition at this top restaurant.

★ **Borgo 20**   ITALIAN €€

(☑ 0521 23 45 65; www.borgo20.it; Borgo XX Marzo 14/16; meals €21-37; ☺ 12.15-2.10pm & 7.30-10pm Tue-Sat; ☜) A father-son team has taken over from a formerly starred Michelin chef at this wonderful contemporary bistro in the city centre, but the concept – and, more importantly, the food – hasn't skipped a beat. Inventive culinary treats made from Parma's classic local ingredients along with special, tri-flour pizza leavened for 70 hours (€9 to €16; available in taster portions!) are dazzling.

La Greppia   GASTRONOMY €€

(☑ 0521 23 36 86; www.ristorantelagreppia.axele roweb.it; Via Garibaldi 39a; meals €26-38; ☺ 12.30-2.30pm & 7.30-10.30pm Tue-Sun; ☜) La Greppia is hallowed ground for the kind of Emilia-Romagna gourmands who know their *ragù* from their bolognese. Sticking tradition and modernity in the same blender, the Pugliese chef has come up with wheel-shaped lasagna with 24-month aged *parmiggiano reggiano* fondue and arugula pesto, and wonderfully soft, red, beer-braised beef with apricots. Service is impeccable.

🍷 Drinking & Nightlife

★ **Bastian Contrario**   CRAFT BEER

(☑ 347 8113440; www.bastiancontrarioparma.it; Strada Inzani 34a; ☺ 6pm-1am Sun-Thu, to 2am Fri & Sat; ☜) Owner Marco has done up this cosy neighbourhood bar, fashioning a draught distribution system made from recycled farming irrigation piping, with tap handles hand-carved by his father – a retired doctor who surely must harbour an admiration for the monolithic statues of Easter Island!

★ **Tabarro**   BAR

(www.tabarro.net; Strada Farini 5b; ☺ 5.30pm-12.45am Sun-Mon & Wed-Thu, to 1.45am Fri, noon-3pm & 5.30pm-1.45am Sat; ☜) In the heart of Parma's animated Strada Farini drinking scene is this classy but friendly wine bar run by a personable ex-rugby player. In warm weather, aficionados crowd the street out front, sipping fine vintages by the glass (€4 to €8) at barrels draped with tablecloths. For some fine people-watching, grab one of the pavement tables tucked across the street on Borgo della Salina.

☆ Entertainment

There are few better places in Italy to see live opera, concerts and theatre. Check out

Italian-only *Teatri* (www.teatridiparma. it) for comprehensive theatre and concert listings.

Teatro Due   THEATRE

(☑ 0521 23 02 42; www.teatrodue.org; Borgo della Salnitrara 12a; ☺ box office 10am-1pm & 5-7.30pm Mon-Fri, 10.30am-1pm & 5-7.30pm Sat) Presents the city's top drama.

Teatro Regio   THEATRE

(☑ 0521 20 39 99; www.teatroregioparma.it/en/homepage; Via Garibaldi 16a; ☺ box office 11am-1pm & 5-7pm Tue-Sat, plus 90min before performances) Offers a particularly rich program of music and opera, even by exacting Italian standards.

🛍 Shopping

La Prosciutteria   FOOD

(www.silvanoromaniparma.com; Strada Farini 9c; ☺ 8.30am-1.30pm & 3.30-7.45pm Mon-Fri, 8.30am-7.45pm Sat, 9am-1pm Sun) An arsenal of strung-up Parma ham hangs above the counter at Silvano Romani's temple of swine, one of Parma's absolute best for cured meats: prosciutto, *culatello*, salami and *strolghino*, among others. Also offers *parmigiano reggiano*, local wine and pasta dishes.

Salumeria Garibaldi   FOOD

(www.salumeriagaribaldi.com; Via Garibaldi 42; ☺ 8am-8pm Mon-Sat) Tempting new visitors just steps from the train station is this bountiful delicatessen dating to 1829, with dangling sausages, shelves of Lambrusco wines, slabs of Parma ham and wheel upon wheel of *parmigiano reggiano*.

ℹ Information

Tourist Office (☑ 0521 21 88 89; www.turismo. comune.parma.it; Piazza Garibaldi 1; ☺ 9am-7pm) Parma's helpful tourist information sits handily on Piazza Garibaldi.

ℹ Getting There & Away

AIR

Parma's **Aeroporto Internazionale di Parma** (Giuseppe Verdi Airport; ☑ 0521 95 15 11; www. parma-airport.it; Via Licinio Ferretti 40) is a mere 3km from the city centre. Ryanair (www. ryanair.com) offers service to Cagliari; and FlyOne (www.flyone.md) to Chişinău (Moldova). **Bus 6 Aeroporto** (Viale Toschi), best caught heading north along Viale Toschi near Palazzo della Pilotta, links to both the train station and airport (€1.20).

FERRARI FANTASIES & LAMBORGHINI LEGENDS

Fiats might be functional, but to appreciate the true beauty of Italian artisanship, you must visit the small triangle of land between Modena and Bologna – sometimes called 'Motor Valley' – where the world's finest luxury cars, namely Ferrari, Lamborghini and Pagani, are made. Here, serious aficionados can bliss out for a day or two touring the region's six motor-vehicle museums, two devoted to Ferraris – including the Museo Enzo Ferrari (p478) in Modena – and two to Lamborghinis, among others.

Museo Ferrari (www.museomaranello.ferrari.com; Via Ferrari 43, Maranello; adult/reduced €17/15; ⊘9.30am-7pm Apr-Oct, to 6pm Nov-Mar)

Mudetec (Museum of Technologies; www.lamborghini.com; Via Modena 12, Sant'Agata Bolognese; adult/reduced €15/12, with factory tour €75/72; ⊘9.30am-7.30pm Apr-Oct, to 6pm Nov-Mar)

Museo Ferruccio Lamborghini (☑051 86 33 66; www.museolamborghini.com; Via Galliera 319, Argelato; adult/reduced €15/10; ⊘10am-1pm & 2-6pm Mon-Fri, Sat & Sun by appointment only)

Museu Horacio Pagani (p489)

Museo Ducati (www.ducati.com; Via Antonio Cavalieri Ducati 3; museum adult/reduced €15/10, with factory tour €30/20; ⊘9am-6pm Thu-Tue Apr-Oct, closed Sun Sep-Mar)

BUS
From the **bus station** (Via Villa Sant'Angelo), attached to the north side of Parma's train station, **TEP** (☑0521 21 41; www.tep.pr.it; Piazzale dalla Chiesa 11; ⊘8.10am-12.50pm & 2.15-4.30pm Mon-Fri) operates buses throughout the region; and Flixbus (www.flixbus.com) goes to Rome, Milan, Naples and Perugia, among others.

TRAIN
There are trains once or twice hourly from Parma's modern **Stazione Ferroviaria di Parma** (www.trenitalia.com; Piazzale dalla Chiesa 11; ⊘4.30am-1.30am) to Milan (regional/express from €11.10/15, 1¼ to 1¾ hours), Bologna (from €7.50, one to 1¼ hours), Modena (from €5.50, 30 minutes) and Piacenza (from €5.50, 40 minutes, half-hourly).

The taxi queue is unsigned from inside the station and difficult to find on arrival. It's on the -2 level along Viale Falcone on the west side of the station. A taxi to the airport from the station runs around €10.

Busseto & Verdi Country

During the 'golden age of opera' in the second half of the 19th century, only Wagner came close to emulating Giuseppe Verdi, Italy's operatic genius who was born in the tiny village of Roncole Verdi in 1813. You can discover his extraordinary legacy starting in the town of Busseto (35km northwest of Parma), a pleasant place imbued with history and endowed with some good cafes and restaurants. There are enough sights for a decent musical day out.

◉ Sights

★**Teatro Verdi**   THEATRE
(Piazza Verdi; adult/reduced €4/3; ⊘9.30am-12.30pm & 3-6pm Tue-Sun Apr-Oct, to 5pm Nov-Mar) This stately theatre on Busseto's aptly named Piazza Verdi was built in 1868, although Verdi himself initially pooh-poohed the idea. It opened with a performance of his masterpiece *Rigoletto*. Guided tours in English (and sometimes German or French) take place every 30 minutes.

Villa Verdi   MUSEUM
(www.villaverdi.org; Via Verdi 22, Sant'Agata di Villanova sull'Arda; adult/reduced €9/5; ⊘9.30-11.45am & 2.30-6.15pm Tue-Sun Apr-Oct, shorter hours Nov-Mar) Verdi's 56-room villa, where he composed many of his major works, is 5km northwest of Busseto. Verdi lived and worked here from 1851 onwards and literally willed it to remain just as he left it, leaving behind a fascinating array of furniture, personal artefacts and art, just as it was the day he passed. Guided visits through the five rooms open to the public (descendants of Verdi's second cousin still occupy the rest) start every 30 minutes.

Museo Nazionale Giuseppe Verdi   MUSEUM
(www.museogiuseppeverdi.it; Via Provesi 35; adult/reduced €9/7; ⊘10am-6.30pm Tue-Sun Apr-Oct, shorter hours Nov-Mar) Take a trip through the

rooms of this fine country mansion turned museum, which cleverly maps out the story of Verdi's life through paintings, music and audio guides (€1; available in English, German and French). As you explore, you'll undoubtedly recognise numerous stanzas from classic operas such as *Il Trovatore* and *Aida*, still fresh after two centuries.

Casa Natale di Giuseppe Verdi MUSEUM
(www.casanataleverdi.it; Strada Processione 1, Roncole Verdi; adult/reduced €5/4; ⊘9.30am-1pm & 2.30-6pm Tue-Sun Apr-Oct, shorter hours Nov-Mar) The humble, sparsely furnished cottage where Giuseppe Verdi was born in 1813 is now a small museum. Grab a tablet at the entrance to take advantage of multimedia exhibits highlighting the composer's life and music. It's in the hamlet of Roncole Verdi, 5km southeast of Busseto.

✖ Eating

⭐ **Antica Corte Pallavicina** GASTRONOMY €€€
(☑0524 93 65 39; www.anticacortepallavicina relais.com; Strada Palazzo due Torri 3, Polesine Parmense; 7-course tasting menu €90-98, with wines €120-170; ⊘noon-2.30pm & 7.30-10pm Tue-Sun; 🖘) Picking favourites at this 14th-century castle is excruciating: there's the castle itself, especially when enveloped in cinematic Po river fog; the ageing cave, where 5000 of the world's very best *salumi* (cured meats) hang alongside namecards of their owners (Prince Charles, Monaco's Prince Albert II); the 11 rooms with enchanting free-standing bathtubs; or Massimo Spigaroli's one-star Michelin foodgasm.

ℹ Information

A combined ticket covering three of the main Verdi-related sights costs €11 (€9.50 with the free Tourist Card). For more information, contact Busseto's **tourist office** (☑0524 9 24 87; www.bussetolive.com; Piazza Verdi 10; ⊘9.30am-1pm & 3-6.30pm Tue-Sun Apr-Oct, shorter hours Nov-Mar).

ℹ Getting There & Away

The train from Parma to Busseto (€3.85, 30 to 45 minutes) requires a change in Fidenza. The **train station** (www.trenitalia.it; Piazzale Stazione) is 700m south of Piazza Guiseppe Verdi.

Alternatively, **TEP** (☑0521 21 44 44; www. tep.pr.it) offers a handful of direct but slow bus departures between Parma and Busseto (€4.50, 1½ hours) daily on route 2120.

Ferrara

☑0532 / POP 135,000

A heavyweight Renaissance art city peppered with colossal palaces and still ringed by its intact medieval walls, Ferrara jumps out at you like an absconded Casanova (he once stayed here) on the route between Bologna and Venice. But, like any city situated in close proximity to La Serenissima ('The Most Serene' Venetian Republic), it is serially overlooked, despite its Unesco World Heritage status. As a result, Venice avoiders will find Ferrara's bike-friendly streets and frozen-in-time *palazzi* relatively unexplored and deliciously tranquil.

Historically, Ferrara was the domain of the powerful Este clan, rivals to Florence's Medici in power and prestige, who endowed

EMILIA-ROMAGNA & SAN MARINO FERRARA

DON'T MISS

MUSEU HORACIO PAGANI
··

If peeking at the assembly lines at Ferrari and Lamborghini is like glimpsing inside a well-oiled machine, a day behind the scenes at **Museu Horacio Pagani** (☑0592 2 00 22; www.pagani.com; Via dell'Industria 26, San Cesario sul Panaro; adult/reduced €18/15, with factory tour €50/25; ⊘9.30am-5pm Mon-Fri, to 12.30pm Sat) is like peering into an artisan's workshop. Argentine-Italian Horacio Pagani produces a measly 40 or so unique, made-to-order hypercars per year (base price: €1.3 to €2.5 million!), which are assembled by hand, including hundreds of pieces cast from composite materials baked in giant autoclaves, at this astonishing factory 13km east of Modena.

Factory tours, booked through Modenatur (p478), include the new Museu Horacio Pagani, a small but fascinating glimpse into Pagani's life and cars, including some of his earliest designs, forged from balsa wood when he was 10-years-old!). But coming here without visiting the showroom factory (no robotic machinery or assembly lines; so quiet and hand-crafted you can nearly hear a pin drop) would be a major injustice for any fan of life's finer things.

Ferrara

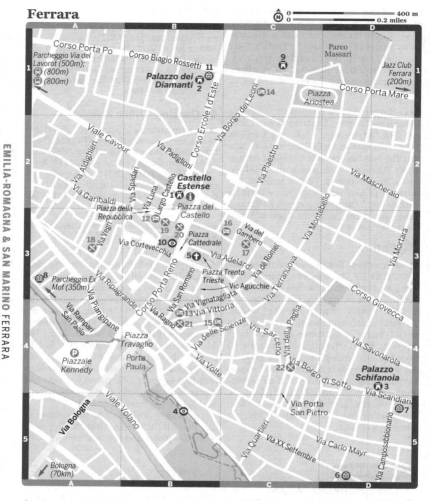

the city with its signature building – a huge castle complete with moat positioned slapbang in the city centre. Ferrara suffered damage from bombing raids during WWII, but its historical core remains intact. Of particular interest is the former Jewish ghetto, the region's largest and oldest, which prevailed from 1627 until 1859.

◉ Sights

Renaissance palaces reborn as museums are Ferrara's tour de force. Also check out the fascinating and wonderfully preserved medieval old town and its one-time Jewish ghetto. Note that most museums are closed on Monday.

Many of Ferrara's top sights sustained damage in a 2012 earthquake and were still closed at the time of research, although some were due to reopen in 2021; check the websites for Palazzo Schifanoia, Museo Lapidario, the Duomo and all museums at Palazzo Massari (Corso Porta Mare 9).

★ **Castello Estense** CASTLE
(www.castelloestense.it; Viale Cavour; adult/reduced €8/6; ⏰ 9.30am-5.30pm Tue-Sun Oct-Feb, 9.30am-5.30pm Mar-Sep) Complete with moat and drawbridge, Ferrara's towering castle

Ferrara

EMILIA-ROMAGNA & SAN MARINO FERRARA

was commissioned by Nicolò II d'Este in 1385. Initially it was intended to protect him and his family from the town's irate citizenry, who were up in arms over tax increases, but in the late 15th century it became the family's permanent residence. Although sections are now used as government offices, a few rooms, including the royal suites, are open for viewing.

Highlights are the **Sala dei Giganti** (Giants' Room), **Salone dei Giochi** (Games Salon), **Cappella di Renée de France**, the claustrophobic **dungeon** and the superb panoramic Ferrara views from the **Torre dei Leoni** (122 steps up!). It was here in 1425 that Duke Nicolò III d'Este had his young second wife, Parisina Malatesta, and his son, Ugo, beheaded after discovering they were lovers, providing the inspiration for Robert Browning's *My Last Duchess*.

Linked to the castle by an elevated passageway, the 13th-century crenellated **Palazzo Municipale** (Palazzo Ducale; Piazza del Municipio 1; ☉9am-1pm Mon, Wed & Fri, to 1pm & 3-5pm Tue & Thu) **FREE** was the Este family home until they moved next door to the castle. Nowadays, it's largely occupied by administrative offices, but you can wander around its twin courtyards (though one, Giardino delle Duchesse, was closed for renovation at the time of writing).

City Walls
WALLS

Only Lucca in Tuscany can claim a more complete set of walls than Ferrara, though with a total circumference of 9km, Ferrara's are longer and among the most impressive in Italy. Adorned with a well-marked set of paths, unbroken on the northern and eastern sections, the walls make a pleasant walking or cycling loop.

★ Palazzo dei Diamanti
PALACE

(www.palazzodiamanti.it; Corso Ercole I d'Este 21) Named after the spiky diamond-shaped ashlar stones on its facade, the late-15th-century 'diamond palace' was built for Sigismondo d'Este. It houses Ferrara's Pinacoteca Nazionale, where you can contemplate the genius of the 16th- to 17th-century 'Ferrara school'. High-profile special exhibits are held in the adjacent **Spazio Espositivo** (adult/reduced €13/11; ☉9am-7pm).

★ Palazzo Schifanoia
PALACE

(www.artecultura.fe.it/159/museo-schifanoia; Via Scandiana 23; adult/reduced €3/2; ☉9.30am-6pm Tue-Sun) Dating to 1385, the Este's 14th-century pleasure palace suffered significant earthquake damage in May 2012 and underwent major restorations and upgrades. Its highlight – the **Salone dei Mesi** (Room of the Months) harbours one of Ferrara's most famous frescoes, executed by Francesco del Cossa in 1470, which depicts the months, seasons and signs of the zodiac and constitutes an exceptionally fine and cohesive example of secular Renaissance art.

Covered by the same ticket is the nearby **Museo Lapidario** (www.artecultura.fe.it/159/museo-schifanoia; Via Camposabbionario; ☉9.30am-6pm Tue-Sun), with its small collection of Roman and Etruscan stele, tombs and inscriptions.

Pinacoteca Nazionale
GALLERY

(www.gallerie-estensi.beniculturali.it/pinacoteca-nazionale; 1st fl, Palazzo dei Diamanti, Corso Ercole I d'Este 21; adult/reduced €6/3; ☉10.30am-5.30pm Tue-Sun) Ferrara's art gallery is the perfect spot to contemplate the genius of the 16th- to 17th-century 'Ferrara school', spearheaded by artists with odd nicknames such as Guercino (the squinter) and Il Maestro degli Occhi Spalancati (master of the wide-open eyes). Free audio guides enhance the experience.

Duomo
CATHEDRAL

(Cattedrale di San Giorgio; Piazza Cattedrale; ⊘7.30am-noon & 3.30-6.30pm Mon-Sat, 7.30am-12.30pm & 3.30-7pm Sun) The outstanding feature of the pink-and-white 12th-century cathedral is its three-tiered marble facade combining Romanesque and Gothic styles on the lower and upper tiers respectively. Much of the upper level is a graphic representation of *The Last Judgment,* and heaven and hell (notice the four figures clambering out of their coffins). The cathedral's interiors were closed for renovation at the time of research; after reopening, work on the facade will continue for five years.

★ Museo Nazionale dell'Ebraismo Italiano e della Shoah
MUSEUM

(MEIS; www.meisweb.it; Via Piangipane 81; adult/reduced €10/8; ⊘10am-6pm) 🕭 Born by an Italian Parliamentary decree to create a National Holocaust Museum, the National Museum of Italian Judaism and the Shoah partially opened in 2017 in the renovated buildings of Ferrara's 1900s prison. The museum chronicles 2200 years of Italian-Jewish history (Italy was once the cradle of Jewish culture in Europe and it remains the oldest active Jewish community in the Western world) via restrained, audio-visually stunning exhibitions told from the perspective of Jewish-Roman historian Josephus Flavius.

At the time of writing, two of the museum's four buildings were completed (and represent Italy's first historic buildings to receive Green Building Council certification) and were housing long-running temporary exhibitions, parts of which will eventually be incorporated into the permanent collection. Don't miss the Holy Arc dating to 1472, an extraordinarily detailed 1st-century statue of Titus once buried under Pompeii, vibrant Renaissance paintings by Andrea Mantegna and the 24-minute introductory film *Through the Eyes of Italian Jews,* which puts the whole experience here into perspective. It's expected to be completed in 2021; the buildings will be connected via five massive, inscripted brise-soleil solar panels of diffused light bearing inscriptions from the five books of the Torah – a remarkable modern architectural twist to the otherwise historic setting.

★ Museo Archeologico Nazionale
MUSEUM

(www.archeoferrara.beniculturali.it; Via XX Settembre 122; adult/reduced €6/2; ⊘9.30am-5pm Tue-Sun) Housed within what is arguably Ferrara's most beautifully preserved palace – the 1505 Palazzo Costabili – the city's national archaeological museum is mainly devoted to what some consider to be the most important collection of Greek and Etruscan ceramics in the world. Recovered from some 4000 ancient tombs at the Etruscan city of Spina buried in the Po Delta, there are in fact so many extraordinary 6th- to 3rd-century BC Attic volute-kraters (decorative mixing bowls) here that the museum has even set aside a few *you can touch.*

But highlights here run far deeper than spun clay. The museum has a remarkable collection of colourful Phoenician and Rhodian molten glass, and amber and golden jewellery dating to the 5th and 6th centuries BC. Not to mention two 12- to 15m-long Roman pirogues (dugout canoes) and the astonishing 16th-century frescoed ceiling – complete with a rose window in gilded wood – in the Treasure Hall. And there are wonderful gardens, too.

☆ Festivals & Events

Il Palio
SPORTS

(www.paliodiferrara.it; ⊘May) On the last Sunday of May each year, the eight *contrade* (districts) of Ferrara compete in a horse race that momentarily turns Piazza Ariostea into medieval bedlam. Claimed to be the oldest race of its kind in Italy, Ferrara's Palio was first held in 1259, and was officially enshrined as an annual competition in 1279.

🛏 Sleeping

★ Le Stanze di Torcicoda
B&B €

(📱380 9068718; www.lestanze.it; Vicolo Mozzo Torcicoda 9; s €60-75, d €85-100; ❉🛇) Tucked down a crooked lane in Ferrara's old Jewish quarter, this cosy, long-established B&B offers four rooms of varying sizes in a late 14th-century *cassero* (medieval house). Owner Pietro Zanni keeps things environmentally friendly with outstanding made-from-scratch, organic-leaning breakfasts, green cleaning products and cyclist-friendly features, including an enclosed bike garage.

Locanda Borgonuovo B&B €

(☑ 0532 21 11 00; www.borgonuovo.com; Via Cairoli 29; s €50-60, d €80-100; P ❄ @ 🛜) Around the corner from the duomo, this small, classically styled gem is Italy's oldest B&B. Four refined rooms and two apartments, each decorated with antiques, come with polished wood floors, minibars, safes, flat-screen TVs and wi-fi. Breakfast in the elegant upstairs sitting room, or retire to the central patio. Parking costs €10 to €15. Guests have free access to bikes.

Albergo degli Artisti GUESTHOUSE €

(☑ 0532 76 10 38; www.albergoartisti.it; Via Vittoria 66; s/d €40/60, without bathroom €28/50; 🛜) Ferrara's most economical option, run by a doting ex-Yugoslavian, offers 20 immaculate rooms at an unbeatable price on a back alley within a five-minute walk of the duomo and Castello Estense. Attractive common spaces include a sunny upstairs terrace and a teeny but cheerful guest kitchen. Book ahead for the three rooms with bathroom. No breakfast.

★**Alchimia B&B** B&B €€

(☑ 0532 186 46 56; www.alchimiaferrara.it; Via Borgo dei Leoni 122; s €90, d €130, apt €110; P ❄ 🛜) Occupying a lovingly remodelled 15th-century home with a spacious, green backyard, this classy six-room B&B seamlessly blends wood-beamed high ceilings with modern comforts such as memory-foam beds, electric tea kettles, state-of-the-art bathrooms, fantastic air-con, rock-solid wi-fi and self-serve wine fridges. Two new apartments are even more modern, with wood-framed flat-screen TVs and subway-tiled walls.

Albergo Annunziata HOTEL €€

(☑ 0532 20 11 11; www.annunziata.it; Piazza della Repubblica 5; d €80-130, ste €150-180; P ❄ @ 🛜) At this top-notch, centrally located four-star hotel, romantics can be forgiven for glimpsing Casanova apparitions (the man himself once stayed here). Six of the sharp modernist rooms with mosaic bathrooms come with direct views of Castello Estense. Guests enjoy convenient bike rental (per day €8), along with an often-fawned-over breakfast, while kids love the complimentary table football.

✖ Eating

Like all Emilian cities, Ferrara has its gastronomic nuances. Don't leave town without trying *cappellacci di zucca,* a hat-shaped pasta pouch filled with pumpkin and herbs, and brushed with sage and butter.

Salama da sugo is a stewed pork sausage, while *pasticcio di maccheroni* is an oven-baked macaroni pie topped with Parmesan. Even Ferrarese bread is distinctive, shaped into a crunchy twisted knot.

★**Trattoria le Nuvole** SEAFOOD €€

(☑ 347 2591995; www.trattorialenuvole.it; Via Fondobanchetto 5; meals €34-37, tasting menus €45-50; ⊙ 7.30-10pm Tue-Fri, 12.30-2.30pm & 7.30-10pm Sat, 12.30-2.30pm Sun; 🛜) This quaint, crafty-chic charmer lit by candlelight and tucked away in Ferrara's medieval quarter is the city's seafood superstar. The hip and beautiful swarm in (reserve two weeks in advance for weekends) for innovative modern dishes with occasional foreign flourishes such as guacamole and yuzo mayo.

★**Trattoria da Noemi** TRATTORIA €€

(☑ 0532 76 90 70; www.trattoriadanoemi.it; Via Ragno 31a; meals €28-42; ⊙ noon-2.30pm & 7.30-10.30pm Wed-Mon; 🛜) Ferrara's classic dishes are delivered *con molto amore* (with much love) at this back-alley eatery named after the hardworking, independent-spirited mother of proprietor Maria Cristina Borgazzi. Arrive early (yes, it's busy) to get some of the city's best *cappellacci di zucca* (pumpkin-stuffed pasta), grilled meats, macaroni pie and a wonderfully messy and extraordinary *zuppa inglese* (liqueur-soaked sponge and custard dessert) to finish.

Osteria degli Angeli OSTERIA €€

(☑ 0532 76 43 76; www.osteriadegliangeliferrara .it; Via delle Volte 4; meals €29-39; ⊙ noon-2.30pm & 7-10.30pm Wed-Mon; 🛜) A perfect modern choice on a Monday evening when many restaurants are closed, this traditional-with-a-twist *osteria* (casual tavern) and its very open kitchen (you can practically hover over the culinary magic) does *Ferrarese* staples, but also offers special non-conformist options like the black *cime di rapa* (turnip greens) ravioli with sausage and *pecorino* cream, and the aglianico-braised beef.

Ca' d' Frara ITALIAN €€

(☑ 0532 20 50 57; www.ristorantecadfrara.it; Via del Gambero 6; meals €26-38; ⊙ 12.15-2pm & 7.15-10pm Thu-Mon, 7.15-10pm Tue-Wed; 🛜) Looking for a reasonably priced place to sample Ferrara's full gamut of culinary specialities? Step into this classy back-alley trattoria and order the 'Tradizione Ferrarese' menu (€28), a seemingly endless parade of courses that includes antipasti, *cappellacci di zucca, pasticcio di maccheroni,* and *salama da sugo* with mashed potatoes and dessert, all served in a smart modern dining room.

Osteria Savonarola
OSTERIA €€

(☑ 0532 20 02 14; Piazza Savonarola 18; meals €24-30; ⊙ 12.30-3.30pm & 7pm-midnight Tue-Sun) Friendly, efficient service and outdoor seating on an arcaded pavement with prime Castello Estense views make this an enjoyable warm-weather spot that's wildly popular with Ferraresi for lunch or dinner. The menu is classically Ferrarese, and prices are easy on the wallet.

Osteria Quattro Angeli
ITALIAN €€

(☑ 0532 21 18 69; www.osteriadegliangeliferrara.it; Piazza del Castello 10; meals €25-36; ⊙ 8am-1am Tue-Sun) Relax beneath fat, sausage-shaped salamis opposite the castle and demolish enormous portions of Ferrarese classics – there's a divine *cappellacci di zucca al ragù* (pumpkin-stuffed pasta with meat sauce) supplemented by cuts of local cured meat. Come 6pm, the tented section out front becomes a busy *aperitivi* bar, upping the noise levels and heightening the atmosphere.

☆ Entertainment

★ Jazz Club Ferrara
JAZZ

(☑ 331 4323840; www.jazzclubferrara.com; 167 Rampari di Belfiore; ⊙ 7.30pm-2am Mon, Fri & Sat) There are few places in the solar system more cinematic than this extraordinary and intimate house of swing and syncopation occupying a restored Renaissance defence tower dating to 1493. Considered one of Europe's top jazz clubs, it draws ace talent from around the world – especially the USA and Brazil – and seeing a show here is a privilege indeed.

ⓘ Information

Tourist Office (IAT; ☑ 0532 20 93 70; www.ferrararaterraeacqua.it; Viale Cavour, Castello Estense; ⊙ 9am-6pm Mon-Sat, 9.30am-5.30pm Sun) In Castello Estense's courtyard.

ⓘ Getting There & Away

Ferrara Bus & Fly (☑ 333 2005157; www.ferrarabusandfly.it) offers direct transfers eight times daily between Bologna's Guglielmo Marconi airport and Ferrara (€15, one hour, 4.45am to 10.30pm). From Ferrara, buses leave from the train station and Viale Cavour.

Buses (Piazzale della Stazione) to Bologna airport and Comacchio leave from just in front of the train station.

From **Stazione di Ferrara** (www.trenitalia.it; Piazzale della Stazione 28), 1.5km west of the centre, trains run frequently to Bologna (from €4.75, 30 to 50 minutes, half-hourly) and Ravenna (from €6.50, one to 1½ hours, hourly) as well as other destinations throughout Emilia-Romagna.

ⓘ Getting Around

BICYCLE

Get in the saddle and join the hundreds of other pedallers in one of Italy's most cycle-friendly cities. Many places rent bikes, such as **Pirani e Bagni** (☑ 339 2814002; Piazza della Stazione 2; bike rental per 1hr/3hr/day €2/5/7; ⊙ 4.45am-8pm Mon-Fri, 6.30am-2pm Sat) beside the train station, and **Ferrara Store** (www.ferrara-store.it; Piazza della Repubblica 23/25; per hr/day €3/12; ⊙ 8am-7pm Mon-Wed & Fri & Sat, to 3pm Thu, 9am-5pm Sun) near Castello Estense. The latter is an in-town representative for **BiciDeltaPo** (www.bicideltapo.it) and bicycles must be reserved in advanced. The tourist office can provide info on the region's well-developed network of bike routes; look for the spiral-bound *Bike Book*, which details itineraries throughout Ferrara and the Po Delta.

BUS

TPER (☑ 0532 59 94 11; www.tper.it) operates frequent local buses along Viale Cavour between the train station and the centre (€1.30, five minutes) – take No 1, 6 or 9. For Castello Estense, get off at Cavour Giardini. A day pass runs €3.50.

Punto Bus (☑ 0532 59 94 90; www.tper.it; Piazzale della Stazione 24; ⊙ 7am-7pm Mon-Sat, 8am-2pm Sun), inside the train station, provides bus information and tickets; you can also purchase tickets with the bilingual **Roger** app (iOS/Android; www.rogerapp.it).

Ravenna

☑ 0544 / POP 160,000

For mosaic lovers, Ravenna is an earthly paradise. Spread out over several churches and baptisteries around town is one of the world's most dazzling collections of early Christian mosaic artwork, enshrined since 1996 on Unesco's World Heritage list. Wandering through the unassuming town centre today, you'd never imagine that for a three-century span beginning in AD 402, Ravenna served as capital of the Western Roman Empire, chief city of the Ostrogoth Kingdom of Italy and nexus of a powerful Byzantine exarchate. During this prolonged golden age, while the rest of the Italian peninsula flailed in the wake of Barbarian invasions, Ravenna became a fertile art studio for skilled craftsmen, who covered the city's terracotta brick churches in heart-rendingly beautiful mosaics.

◉ Sights

Ravenna revolves around its eight Unesco World Heritage Sites (seven scattered about town, one 5km to the southeast). A *biglietto cumulativo* (combo ticket, €9.50), good for seven days, grants access to five of the sites: Basilica di San Vitale, Mausoleo di Galla Placidia. Basilica di Sant'Apollinare Nuovo, Museo Arcivescovile and Battistero Neoniano. Three others – Basilica di Sant'Apollinare in Classe , Mausoleo di Teodorico and Battistero degli Ariani – require individual tickets. Tickets are purchased at the L'Opera di Religione della Diocesi di Ravenna Ticket Office (☎0544 54 16 88; www.ravennamosaici.it; Via Argentario 22; ⊙9am-6.45pm) near San Vitale.

The city's brilliant 4th- to 6th-century gold, emerald and sapphire masterpieces will leave you struggling for adjectives. A suitably impressed Dante once described them as a 'symphony of colour' and spent the last few years of his life admiring them. Romantic toff Lord Byron added further weight to Ravenna's literary credentials when he spent a couple of years here before decamping to Greece.

★Mausoleo di
Galla Placidia   HISTORIC BUILDING
(www.ravennamosaici.it; Via San Vitale; 5-site combo ticket €9.50 plus summer-only surcharge €2; ⊙9am-7pm Mar-Oct, 10am-5pm Nov-Feb) In the same complex as Basilica di San Vitale, the small but equally incandescent Mausoleo di Galla Placidia was constructed for Galla Placidia, the half-sister of Emperor Honorius, who initiated construction of many of Ravenna's grandest buildings. The mosaics here are the oldest in Ravenna, probably dating from around AD 430.

★Basilica di
Sant'Apollinare Nuovo   BASILICA
(www.ravennamosaici.it; Via di Roma 52; 5-site combo ticket €9.50; ⊙9am-7pm Mar-Oct, 10am-5pm Nov-Feb) An old legend states that Pope Gregory the Great once ordered the Apollinare's mosaics to be blackened as they were distracting worshippers from prayer. A millennium and a half later, the dazzling Christian handiwork is still having the same

effect. It's almost impossible to take your eyes off the 26 white-robed martyrs heading towards Christ with his apostles on the right (south) wall. On the opposite side, an equally expressive procession of virgins bears similar offerings for the Madonna.

The basilica dates originally from the 560s, and its architectural fusion of Christian east and west can be seen in its marble porticoes and distinctive conical bell tower.

★Basilica di San Vitale   BASILICA
(www.ravennamosaici.it; Via San Vitale; 5-site combo ticket €9.50; ⊙9am-7pm Mar-Oct, 10am-5pm Nov-Feb) Sometimes, after weeks of strolling around dark Italian churches, you can lose your sense of wonder. Not here! The lucid mosaics that adorn the altar of this ancient church consecrated in 547 by Archbishop Massimiano invoke a sharp intake of breath in most visitors. Gaze in wonder at the rich greens, brilliant golds and deep blues bathed in shafts of soft yellow sunlight.

The mosaics on the side and end walls inside the church represent scenes from the Old Testament: to the left, Abraham prepares to sacrifice Isaac in the presence of three angels, while the one on the right portrays the death of Abel and the offering of Melchizedek. Inside the chancel, two magnificent mosaics depict the Byzantine emperor Justinian with San Massimiano and a particularly solemn and expressive Empress Theodora, who was his consort.

★Basilica di
Sant'Apollinare in Classe   CHURCH
(Via Romea Sud 224; adult/reduced €5/2.50; ⊙8.30am-7.30pm Mon-Sat, 1-7.30pm Sun) This signature early Christian basilica, lighter than Ravenna's other churches, is situated 5km southeast of town in the former Roman port of Classe. Its magnificent central apse mosaic, featuring Ravenna's patron Sant'Apollinare flanked by sheep and juxtaposed against a stunningly green landscape, is surmounted by a brilliant star-spangled triumphal arch displaying symbols of the four evangelists.

Other mosaics in the apse depict Byzantine Emperor Constantine IV (652–685) and biblical figures such as Abel and Abraham. The basilica – architecturally the city's most 'perfect' – was built in the early 6th century on the burial site of Ravenna's patron saint, who converted the city to Christianity in the 2nd century.

Ravenna

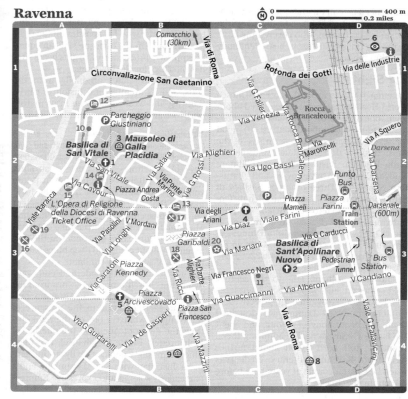

To get here, take a local train to Classe (€1.50, five minutes), one stop in the direction of Rimini, or catch bus 4 opposite the train station. There's free admission on the first Sunday of the month.

Battistero Neoniano
CHRISTIAN SITE

(www.ravennamosaici.it; Piazza del Duomo 1; 5-site combo ticket €9.50; ⊙9am-7pm Mar-Oct, 10am-5pm Nov-Feb) Roman ruins aside, this is Ravenna's oldest intact building, constructed over the site of a former Roman bathing complex in the late 4th century. Built in an octagonal shape, as was the custom with all Christian baptisteries of this period, it was originally attached to a church (since destroyed). The mosaics, which thematically depict Christ being baptised by St John the Baptist in the River Jordan, were added at the end of the 5th century.

Museo Arcivescovile
MUSEUM

(www.ravennamosaici.it; Piazza Arcivescovado 1; 5-site combo ticket €9.50; ⊙9am-7pm Mar-Oct, 10am-5pm Nov-May) A museum with a difference, this religious gem is on the 2nd floor of the Archiepiscopal Palace. It hides two not-to-be-missed exhibits: an exquisite ivory throne carved for Emperor Maximilian by Byzantine craftsmen in the 6th century (the surviving detail on the 27 engraved panels is astounding) and a stunning collection of mosaics in the 5th-century chapel of San Andrea, which has been cleverly incorporated into the museum's plush modern interior.

Battistero degli Ariani
CHRISTIAN SITE

(Via degli Ariani; adult/reduced €1/0.50; ⊙8.30am-7.15pm) The €1 entry here (unique among Ravenna's Unesco sites) is no reflection of the quality of the artistry inside. The baptistery's breathtaking dome mosaic, depicting the baptism of Christ encircled by the 12 apostles, was completed over a period of years beginning in the 5th century.

Ravenna

◉ Top Sights
1 Basilica di San Vitale...............................A2
2 Basilica di Sant'Apollinare Nuovo.........C3
3 Mausoleo di Galla Placidia....................B2

◉ Sights
4 Battistero degli Ariani.............................C3
5 Battistero Neoniano B3
6 Mausoleo di Teodorico........................... D1
7 Museo Arcivescovile...............................B4
8 Museo d'Arte della Città di
  Ravenna...D4
9 Museo TAMO..B4

⊕ Activities, Courses & Tours
10 Gruppo Mosaicisti...................................A2
11 Mosaic Art School...................................C3

⊟ Sleeping
12 Ai Giardini di San Vitale..........................A1
13 Albergo Cappello B2
14 Le Case di San Vitale..............................A2
15 M Club Deluxe A2

⊗ Eating
16 La Cucina del Condominio....................A3
17 La Piadina del Melarancio....................B3
18 Osteria dei Battibecchi.........................B3
19 Osteria L'Acciuga..................................A3

⊕ Entertainment
20 Teatro Alighieri.......................................C3

Museo TAMO   MUSEUM
(www.tamoravenna.it; Via Nicolò Rondinelli 2; adult/
reduced €4/3; ⊙ 10am-6.30pm Mon-Fri, 26 Dec–6
Jan & Mar–2 Jun, to 2pm 3 Jun–6 Oct, to 5pm 7 Oct–
24 Dec) This newer museum doubles-down
on Ravenna's extraordinary history of mosaic work by chronicling 12 centuries of
history, using technology and multimedia
presentations with a particular emphasis on
contemporary work.

**Museo d'Arte della
Città di Ravenna**   GALLERY
(www.mar.ra.it; Via di Roma 13; adult/reduced €6/5;
⊙ 9am-6pm Tue-Sat, 2-6pm Sun) Arranged in a
converted 15th-century monastery abutting
a public garden, Ravenna's permanent art
collection is backed up by regular temporary
expos. The ground floor features some rather fetching modern mosaics, first brought
together in the 1950s, including one *(Le Coq
Bleu)* based on a design by Marc Chagall.

Mausoleo di Teodorico   TOMB
(Via delle Industrie 14; adult/reduced €4/2;
⊙ 8.30am-5.30pm Oct-Mar, to 7pm Apr-Sep) Historically and architecturally distinct from
Ravenna's other Unesco sites (there are no
mosaics here), this two-storey mausoleum
was built in 520 for Gothic king Teodorico,
who ruled Italy as a Byzantine viceroy. It is
notable for its Gothic design features and
throwback Roman construction techniques:
the huge blocks of stone were not cemented
by any mortar. At the heart of the mausoleum is a Roman porphyry basin recycled as a
sarcophagus. It's 2km from the city centre;
take bus 5.

🎓 Courses

Gruppo Mosaicisti   ARTS & CRAFTS
(☑ 0544 3 47 99; www.gruppomosaicisti.it; Via
Fiandrini 8; courses from €550) Tucked around
the side of San Vitale, this school offers a
variety of mosaic-making courses for beginners, experienced artists and those involved
in professional restoration work.

Mosaic Art School   ARTS & CRAFTS
(☑ 0544 6 70 61; www.mosaicschool.com; Via
Francesco Negri 14) Offers five-day intensive
mosaic-making courses for all skill levels
(€690).

🎊 Festivals & Events

Ravenna Festival   MUSIC
(www.ravennafestival.org; ⊙ Jun & Jul) Renowned
Italian conductor Riccardo Muti has close
ties with Ravenna and is intimately involved
with this classical-music festival each year.
Concerts are staged at venues all over town,
including the **Teatro Alighieri** (☑ 0544 24 92
11; www.teatroalighieri.org; Via Mariani 2; ⊙ box office 10am-1pm Mon-Wed & Fri, to 1pm & 4-6pm Thu).

🛏 Sleeping

★ **M Club Deluxe**   B&B €
(☑ 333 9556466; www.m-club.it; Piazza Baracca
26; s €70-90, d €80-130; P ❋ 🛜) Two minutes
from San Vitale's gorgeous mosaics, industrious young owner Michael Scapini Man-
tovani has converted this old family home
into a luxurious B&B. Historical touches
(ancient beamed ceilings, a stuffed crocodile
brought from Ethiopia by a great uncle, Michael's father's decades-old collection of *National Geographics*) coexist with countless

modern conveniences, including super-comfy beds and wi-fi routers in every room.

Ai Giardini di San Vitale
B&B €

(☑ 0544 3 35 53; www.g-sanvitale.it; Via Don Giovanni Minzoni 63; s €59-89, d €89-98, tr €114-135; ✳ ⬥) It's not necessarily about the rooms (simple but spacious) at this family-run, six-room B&B, but rather the jungly back gardens, which sit right next door to Basilica di San Vitale, though you'd never know it – the tourist soundtrack is drowned out by chirping birds in this wonderfully peaceful urban retreat.

★ Albergo Cappello
BOUTIQUE HOTEL €€

(☑ 0544 21 98 13; www.albergocappello.it; Via IV Novembre 41; d €139-189; P ✳ @ ⬥) Colour-themed rooms come in three categories at this finely coiffed seven-room boutique hotel smack in the town centre. Murano glass chandeliers, original 15th-century frescoes and coffered ceilings are set against modern fixtures and flat-screen TVs; some rooms boast Venetian silk wallpaper and wood-panelled bathrooms. The ample breakfast features pastries from Ravenna's finest *pasticceria*. There's also an excellent restaurant and wine bar attached.

Le Case di San Vitale
BOUTIQUE HOTEL €€

(☑ 0544 21 83 04; www.lecasedisanvitale.it; Via San Vitale 36; d €144-165, ste €232; ✳ ⬥) A relative newcomer in a renovated historic building that offers six well-appointed rooms and suites across the street from Basilica di San Vitale. It's both ultra-modern (internal glass elevator, RFID entry) and dripping in period detail (vaulted stone ceilings supported by rustic timber, fantastic hardwood flooring) with bonuses such as an internal patio and complimentary wet bar. Hands-off staff.

✖ Eating

La Piadina del Melarancio
FAST FOOD €

(www.lapiadina.biz; Via IV Novembre 31; piadine €4.50-5.50; ⊙ 11.30am-10pm; ⬥) This simple city-centre spot is a great place to try Romagna's classic snack food: a hot, fresh *piadina* (stuffed flatbread). Fillings range from *squacquerone* cheese with caramelised figs to roasted pork and smoked *scamorza* cheese. Place your order at the front counter and wait until your number is called.

★ La Cucina del Condominio
TRATTORIA €€

(☑ 327 6803847; www.cucinadelcondominio.it; Via Guglielmo Oberdan 36; meals €21-38; ⊙ 10am-7.30pm Mon-Fri, to 11pm Sat, to 4pm Sun) Raven-

na's best new restaurant is brought to you by the same chef-owner as the excellent Osteria L'Acciuga next door. Evoking a haute version of Sunday lunch at grandma's house, the warm and always-packed space perfectly complements fantastic dishes like the house speciality broth-boiled meatballs and fresh pasta preparations like *passatelli* with ham, arugula and fresh tomatoes or the sublime *cappelletti ragù*.

Reservations essential. Save room for the chocolate salami with zabaglione cream!

Osteria L'Acciuga
SEAFOOD €€

(☑ 0544 21 27 13; www.osterialacciuga.it; Viale Baracca 74; meals €35-45; ⊙ 12.30-2.30pm & 7.30-10.30pm Tue-Sat; ⬥) For an inventive change of culinary pace, head to this classy seafooder far enough away from Ravenna's Unesco sites to feel authentic, but close enough to walk. Impressive interiors were forged from a decommissioned submarine, and the changing menu is dependent upon the daily catch.

Osteria dei Battibecchi
OSTERIA €€

(☑ 0544 21 95 36; www.osteriadeibattibecchi.it; Via della Tesoreria Vecchia 16; meals €22-30; ⊙ noon-3pm & 7pm-midnight) Simple Romagna food done right is the hallmark of this Slow Food–recommended local favourite. Offerings range from the basket of warm *piadina* bread that comes unbidden to your table through to scrumptious plates of pasta, grilled vegetables, meat and fish, and homemade desserts like *zuppa inglese*.

🍷 Drinking & Nightlife

★ Darsenale
MICROBREWERY

(www.facebook.com/darsenaleristopub; Viale Giovanna Bosi Maramotti; ⊙ 6.30pm-1.30am Sun & Tue-Thu, to 2am Fri & Sat; ⬥) This 1200-sq-metre brewpub and beer garden is the most ambitious craft-beer undertaking in Emilia-Romagna yet. Local brewery Birra Bizantina flipped this long-abandoned former fertiliser warehouse along the docks into a hophead playground in 2019, opening with 18 beers on draught and a great pub menu of *pala*-style (rectangular) pizza, burgers etc. It now anchors the city's revitalising Darsena district.

ℹ Information

Tourist Office (☑ 0544 48 28 38; www.turismo.ravenna.it; Piazza San Francesco 7; ⊙ 8.30am-7pm Mon-Sat, 9.30am-5.30pm Sun) Helpful office with maps and printed material; can also help with booking accommodation and

PO DELTA

Italy's greatest river dissolves into the Adriatic Sea in the Po Delta (Foci del Po), an area of dense pine forests and extensive wetlands often doused in an eerie fog, especially in winter. The wetlands, protected in the Unesco-recognised Parco del Delta del Po, are one of Europe's largest and are notable for their birdlife – 300 species have been registered here.

The delta's main centre, Comacchio, a picturesque fishing village of canals and brick bridges, harbours a good tourist office offering reams of information about hiking, cycling, birdwatching, horse riding and boat excursions, and a fascinating new museum, **Museo Delta Antico** (www.museodeltaantico.com; Via Agatopisto 2; adult/reduced €6/3; ☺9.30am-1pm & 3-6.30pm Tue-Sun Mar-Aug, shorter hours Sep-Feb).

Boat excursions (Stazione Foce; adult/reduced €12/9) leave from Stazione Foce, 4km from Comacchio. Contact **Po Delta Tourism** (☑0533 813 02; www.podeltatourism.it).

From Ferrara, TPER (p494) bus 331 (€5, one hour) departs about 10 times daily to Comacchio, leaving from the bus station across from Ferrara's train station; from Ravenna, TPER bus 333 (€4.50, one hour) departs about five times daily.

organises mosaic-themed guided tours (€5 to €9.50). An additional **outlet** (☑0544 4 51 39; www.turismo.ravenna.it; Via delle Industrie 14; ☺9.30am-12.30pm & 3.30-6.30pm May-Sep, 9.30am-3.30pm Oct-Apr) is at Mausoleo di Teodorico.

ℹ Getting There & Away

Frequent trains connect **Stazione di Ravenna** (www.trenitalia.com; Piazza Farini) with Bologna (€7.50, one to 1½ hours), Ferrara (€6.50, 1¼ hours), Rimini (from €4.75, one hour) and the south coast. From the **bus station** (www.startromagna.it; Piazzale Aldo Moro) bus 333 departs for Comacchio five or so times daily (€4.50, one hour).

Ravenna is on a branch (A14 dir) of the main east-coast A14 autostrada. The SS16 (Via Adriatica) heads south to Rimini and on down the coast.

Brisighella

☑0546 / POP 7660

Romagna's storybook medieval village is cinematically set on the slopes of the Tosco-Romagna Apennines, cradled by pastoral green hills peppered with vineyards and olive plantations. Founded in the 12th century, Brisighella is defined by its trio of iconic hilltop structures: La Rocca (The Rock), La Torre (The Tower) and Il Monticino, the three of which overlook the sunset-hued rooftops of one of Italy's most picturesque villages. In town is one of the country's unique sights: a wonderfully photogenic 700-year-old walkway that evolved from the town's first defensive wall into a commercial thoroughfare used mostly by cart-pulling donkeys – hence its name, the Via degli Asini (Donkey's Street).

Today, Brisighella is best known for its award-winning olive oils which, of course, go down mighty fine alongside the local cuisine, which you can enjoy in a village that is still lightly touristed by international travellers.

◉ Sights

★**Via degli Asini**   HISTORIC SITE
(Via del Borgo) Hidden behind a colourful patchwork of warped homes, this low-slung, wood-beamed, delightfully uneven medieval walkway dates to 1290. It's unique in Italy because it began life as a defensive wall that was later incorporated into the town's commercial space (as an elevated pathway for donkeys carrying gypsum from nearby quarries). Today, former donkey stables now hide private homes (and one dental office) that sit atmospherically along 100m of picturesque, non-uniform arches, flanked by at least one surviving guard tower.

★**Rocca di Brisighella**   FORTRESS
(Via Rontana 64; €3; ☺10am-12.30pm & 3-7pm Sat & Sun May-Sep, shorter hours Oct-Apr) Standing sentinel high above town on a gypsum hilltop, this medieval fortress, along with the Torre dell'Orologio and Santuario del Monticino on neighbouring hilltops, forms the postcard-perfect view of Brisighella. Construction dates to 1310 – with two later renovations, including the expansion of the western bastion by the Venetians between 1503 and 1506. The fortress features two watchtowers of varying heights. The views

from here, both of town and across to the Torre dell'Orologio, are the reason you have come to Brisighella.

✖ Eating

★ Framboise
ITALIAN €€

(☎329 0740862; www.facebook.com/Framboise cucinina; Via Porta Fiorentina 15; meals €26-30; ⊙noon-2.30pm & 7-10pm Tue-Sun) A true family affair, where owner Pier Luigi, along with his wife and daughter, will shower you with seasonally changing local delicacies. It's a great spot to try *spoja lorda* (dirty pasta), and the pulled black pork *panino* (sandwich), cooked sous vide for half a day, is a true delight. It's worth coming in spring for the in-season Moretto artichoke menu (mid-April to mid-May), too.

ℹ Information

Tourist Office (IAT; ☎0546 8 11 66; www.brisighella.org; Piazzetta Porta Gabolo 5; ⊙9.30am-12.30pm & 3.30-5.30pm Mon-Sat, 3.30-6.30pm Sun Apr-Oct, shorter hours Nov-Mar)

ℹ Getting There & Away

Brisighella sits 12km southwest of Faenza off the SS9. To reach the village by train requires a switch in Faenza (reachable on lines from Bologna, Ancona, Florence and Ravenna), from where there are trains mostly hourly (€2.20). **Cooperativa Trasporti di Riolo Terme** (www.cooptrasportiriolo.it) also runs bus No 2/525 five to six times daily (except Sunday) from Faenza's Stazione della Corriere (€2.10, 30 minutes).

Rimini

☎0541 / POP 146,000

Roman relics, jam-packed beaches, hedonistic nightclubs and the memory of film director and native son Federico Fellini make sometimes awkward bedfellows in seaside Rimini. Although there's been a settlement here for over 2000 years, Rimini's coast was just sand dunes until 1843, when the first bathing establishments took root next to the ebbing Adriatic. The beach huts gradually morphed into a megaresort that was sequestered by a huge nightclub scene in the 1990s. Despite some interesting history, Fellini-esque movie memorabilia and a decent food culture, 95% of Rimini's visitors come for its long, boisterous, sometimes tacky beachfront.

◉ Sights

★ Museo della Città
MUSEUM

(www.museicomunalirimini.it; Via Tonini 1; adult/reduced incl Domus del Chirurgo €7/5; ⊙10am-7pm Tue-Sun Jun & Sep, 10am-7pm Tue-Sun, plus 9-11pm Wed Jul-Aug, shorter hours Oct-May) This rambling museum is best known for its Roman section. Spread over several rooms, with excellent bilingual (Italian/English) signage, are finds from two nearby Roman villas, including splendid mosaics, a rare and exquisite representation of fish rendered in coloured glass, and the world's largest collection of Roman surgical instruments. Other highlights include the colourful and imaginative doodlings of Federico Fellini.

Museum tickets also include admission to the adjacent **Domus del Chirurgo** (www.domusrimini.com; ⊙10am-7pm Tue-Sun Jun & Sep, 10am-7pm Tue-Sun, plus 9-11pm Wed Jul-Aug, shorter hours Oct-May), which holds the remains of three excavated Roman homes with several fine floor mosaics still partially intact.

★ Ponte di Tiberio
LANDMARK

The majestic five-arched Tiberius' Bridge dates from AD 21. In Roman times it marked the start of the Via Emilia – the important arterial road between the Adriatic Coast (at Rimini) and the Po river valley (at Piacenza) – which linked up here with the Via Flaminia from Rome. These days, the bridge still connects Rimini's city centre to the old fishing quarter of Borgo San Giuliano and rests on its original foundations consisting of an ingenious construction of wooden stilts.

★ Tempio Malatestiano
CHURCH

(Via IV Novembre 35; ⊙8.30am-noon & 3.30-6.30pm Mon-Fri, to 7pm Sat, 9am-12.30pm & 3.30-6.30pm Sun) Built originally in 13th-century Gothic style and dedicated to St Francis, Rimini's cathedral was radically transformed in the mid-1400s into a Renaissance Taj Mahal for the tomb of Isotta degli Atti, beloved mistress of roguish ruler Sigismondo Malatesta. Sigismondo hired Florentine architect Leon Battista Alberti to redesign the church in 1450, and the resulting edifice, while incomplete, is replete with Alberti's grandiose Roman-inspired touches, along with elements that glorify Sigismondo and Isotta, including numerous medallions bearing the two lovers' initials.

Arco di Augusto
LANDMARK

(Corso d'Augusto) This Roman triumphal arch, the oldest of its kind in northern Italy, was commissioned by Emperor Augustus in 27 BC and stands an impressive 17m high on modern-day Corso d'Augusto. It was once the end point of the ancient Via Flaminia that linked Rimini with Rome. Buildings that had grown up around the arch were demolished in 1935 to accentuate its stature.

Borgo San Giuliano
AREA

Just over the Ponte di Tiberio, Rimini's old fishing quarter has been freshened up and is now a colourful patchwork of cobbled lanes, trendy trattorias, wine bars and trim terraced houses (read: prime real estate). Look out for the numerous murals.

Cinema Fulgor
THEATRE

(☎0541 70 95 45; www.cinemafulgorrimini.it; Corso d'Augusto 162; films adult/reduced €8/5) Legendary Italian film director Federico Fellini's restored hometown theatre, where he watched films as a child and developed his passion for cinema, was renovated according to original renderings of Oscar-winning set designer and Fellini protégé Dante Ferretti. The gorgeous results, a striking, art deco–esque marriage of red velvet and ornate, gold-leafed accents, reopened as a working cinema on Fellini's birthday in January 2018. Both Fellini and contemporary films are shown.

Tours are for groups only, but some city tours pop in on a regular basis. Part of the new **Museo Internazionale Federico Fellini** (www.museionline.info/musei/museo-fellini), a series of Fellini-related exhibits across the town, will be housed here; other works will be found at **Castel Sismondo** (Piazza Malatesta) and outdoors at CircAmarcord Piazza d'Arti. The museum, which is due to open in 2021, will include exhibitions on Fellini's work as told through poetry, photographs, drawings and film projects (including films never produced), as well as interactive and multimedia installations.

🛏 Sleeping

Ironically for a city with more than 1200 hotels, finding accommodation can be tricky. In July and August places can be booked solid and prices are sky-high, especially as many proprietors insist on full board. In winter a lot of places simply shut up shop. The per person per night tourist tax ranges from €0.70 (B&Bs and one-star hotels) to €4 (five-star accommodation).

Up Hotel
BOUTIQUE HOTEL €

(☎0541 37 88 60; www.uphotel.it; Viale Gubbio 7; s €50-150, d €65-200; [P][❄][@][🛜]) ✈ Apologetically dangling the high-tech carrot to millennials and digital nomads, this newer, design-forward 25-room boutique hotel is high-wired (USB ports built into the communal breakfast table, e-Bikes for guests) and prides itself on guest freedom – outside food and drink, for example, are welcome. The trendy decor marries vintage furniture with funky, oft-changing design elements, including vintage Italian bicycles and motorbikes.

Sunflower City Backpacker Hostel
HOSTEL €

(☎0541 2 51 80; www.sunflowerhostel.com; Viale Dardanelli 102; dm €12-30, s €21-42, d €32-70; [@][🛜]) Run by two ex-backpackers, the Sunflower welcomes travellers with its laundry and cooking facilities, retro Austin Powers–style wallpaper, in-house bar and organised pub crawls. It's in a leafy residential district halfway between the train station and the beach. Exuding an even livelier party vibe, Sunflower's beachside **branch** (☎0541 37 34 32; www.sunflowerhostel.com; Via Siracusa 25; dm €12-30, s €21-42, d €32-70; ⊙Mar–mid-Nov; [P][❄][@][🛜][🏊]), open only in the high seaso, has its own stage, with live music in summer.

★ Grand Hotel
HISTORIC HOTEL €€

(☎0541 5 60 00; www.grandhotelrimini.com; Parco Federico Fellini 1; s €120-150, d €130-180, ste €180-210; [P][❄][@][🛜][🏊]) One of Rimini's only five-star hotels and as much a monument as a place to stay. Despite a 1920 fire and serious damage incurred during WWII, it has remained true to its 1908 roots with rooms clad in authentic 18th-century Venetian antiques. Beloved by Fellini, the hotel has lured many other celebs with its pool, private beach and elegant gardens.

Il Brigitta B&B
B&B €€€

(☎339 4816486; ilbrigitta@alice.it; Via Sinestra del Porto 88/90; s/d €130/200; [🛜]) Enjoy all that Rimini has to offer without committing to the overwrought beach-resort experience at this adorable new three-room B&B overlooking the picturesque Porto Canale. Artist and interior designer Brigitta speaks little English, but her nautical driftwood art and penchant for Provence ensure a cosy, shabby-chic stay. It's all drenched in lavender – a perfectly romantic hideaway.

Rimini

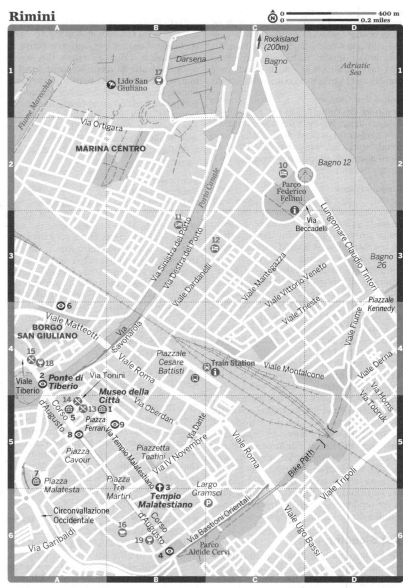

EMILIA-ROMAGNA & SAN MARINO RIMINI

🍴 Eating

Rimini's cuisine is anchored by the *piadina* and *pesce azzurro* (oily fish), especially sardines and anchovies. The favourite tipple is Sangiovese wine.

Nud e Crud SANDWICHES €
(www.nudecrud.it; Viale Tiberio 27/29; piadina €5-13; ⊙ 11am-4pm & 6pm-midnight Sun-Thu, to 1am Fri & Sat; 🛜🌱) Avoid the tourist onslaught along the waterfront and head to quaint Borgo San Giuliano where locals – includ-

Rimini

ing the mayor – go year-round for gourmet *piadine*. Plop down on the colourful patio and dig into stuffed treats: anchovy, chicory, lettuce and spring onion; *moro romagnola* sausage, radicchio and onion; and grilled vegetables with melted *squacquerone* cheese, among others.

★ **Il Pescatore del Canevone**   SEAFOOD €€
(📞 366 3541510; www.ilpescatodelcanevone.it; Via Luigi Tonini 34; meals €25-36; ⊙ 12.30-2.30pm & 7.30-11pm Sun & Tue-Fri, 7.30-11pm Sat; 🖥) This contemporary, family-run seafooder sits steps from Museo della Città and Domus del Chirurgo but you'd never know it – its fuss-free demeanour is decidedly anti-hubbub. The daily-changing, chalkboard menu is short on choice but long on freshness. Surefire options: perfectly fried *sardoncini* (European anchovies) with sweet red Tropea onions, seafood risotto or stewed octopus with candied lemons, seasonal vegetables and cherry tomatoes.

★ **Abocar Due Cucine**   FUSION €€€
(📞 0541 2 22 79; www.abocarduecucine.it; Via Farini 13; meals €44-52, tasting menus €49-65; ⊙ 7.30-11pm Tue-Thu, 12.30-2.30pm & 8-10.30pm Fri & Sat, 12.30-3pm Sun; 🖥) Opened in 2014

by the daughter of fabled local restaurateur Tonino Il Lurido (owner of one of Fellini's former haunts), this Argentine-Italian affair snagged a Michelin star in 2018. It crafts three monthly changing, carefully curated tasting menus, revolving around fish, meat or a combination of the two. And it isn't afraid to inject the best of Latin America (Chipotle! Avocados! *Dulce de leche!)* into a firmly Italian pedigree.

🍷 Drinking & Nightlife

Some come to Rimini in search of Roman relics. Others seek out its lavish modern nightclubs. Rimini first garnered a reputation for mega-hip nightclubbing in the 1990s when an electric after-dark scene took off in the hills of **Misano Monte** and **Riccone** several kilometres to the south of the city centre. Far from being a tacky re-run of Torremolinos or Magaluf, Rimini's new clubs quickly established themselves as modish, fashionable affairs with an appeal that extended beyond simply the 18- to 30-year-old demographic. That's not to say they were boring.

Darsena Sunset Bar   COCKTAIL BAR
(📞 340 6825842; www.darsenasunsetbar.it; Viale Ortigara 78/80; ⊙ 8am-1am; 🖥) It's a good idea to reserve a prime spot in advance at this trendy cocktail bar hidden away in Rimini's marina (Darsena). You have entered the domain of the beautiful people, here to ogle the sunset, groove to loungy, DJ-spun vinyl and sip on exquisitely mixed libations (Instagramming it all along the way).

Enoteca del Teatro   WINE BAR
(Via Ortaggi 12; wines by the glass €3-12; ⊙ 9.30am-12.45pm & 4.30-9.30pm Mon & Wed-Sat, to 12.45pm Tue) 🍷 In quaint Borgo San Giuliano, this is Rimini's best spot for a sophisticated glass of *vino* without the hubbub that comes along with major European beach resorts. The tiny, standing-room-only candlelit bottleshop features 20 or so choices by the glass, often from small and/or organic producers. Let genial owner Ricky guide you to a glass outside your wheelhouse.

Cocoricò   CLUB
(www.cocorico.it; Viale Chieti 44, Riccione; ⊙ 11pm-6am Mon-Fri, 10pm-8am Sat & Sun, Sat only Oct-Dec & Feb-Apr) Dancing under Cocoricò's glass pyramid, 2000 clammy strangers (straight, bi, gay, whatever) quickly become friends to the sounds of techno, house and underground at Rimini's top club. World-famous DJs pop in

EMILIA-ROMAGNA & SAN MARINO RIMINI

on Fridays and Saturdays, while drag queens enliven the scene on 'Tunga party' nights. In summer Cocoricò hosts poolside dance parties at the nearby Aquafàn water park.

Nécessaire   BAR
(www.facebook.com/bottegagourmet; Via XX Settembre 1870; ⊙7am-midnight; 🔊) For an adult *aperitivo*, this trendy newcomer is a solid bet. This spot boasts excellently mixed cocktails and sophisticated tapas led by a creation after our own hearts: the *scarpetta* (tomato sauce with shallots and black olives; €5.50). It's a genius take on the Italian act to '*fare la scarpetta*' (sopping up your leftover sauce with bread), served as simply the sauce itself. Fantastic!

Bar Lento   CAFE
(www.facebook.com/barlentorimini; Via Aurelio Bertola 52; ⊙8am-9pm Tue-Sat, 9am-1pm & 4-9pm Sun; 🔊) This artsy cafe is the domain of Rimini's alterna-hipsters, wandering bohemians and the anti-beach brigade. It's a great spot for settling in with a coffee and a book (or laptop). It's all about creativity and attitude.

FOB   CRAFT BEER
(www.birreria-fob.it; Via Castracane 17; ⊙5.30pm-2am Mon-Thu, to 3am Fri & Sat, 4.30pm-2am Sun; 🔊) FOB, named after the Foam on Beer draught head control system installed above its 34 taps (pints €5 to €6.50), is one of Emilia-Romagna's most visually impressive craft-beer drinking dens. It has a long hardwood bar, denim-covered bar seats, and its larger, orange-slathered room comes with chapel-like windows stained not with glass but with colourful beer cans from around the world.

Byblos   CLUB
(www.byblosclub.com; Via Pozzo Castello 24, Misano Adriatico; ⊙9pm-5am Fri-Sun Jun-Aug, swimming pool 4-11pm Sun Jun-Aug) Feeling more like a hedonistic Beverly Hills house party than a club, Rimini's poshest after-dark venue occupies a converted villa complex with a swimming pool, a restaurant and highly acclaimed DJs. It's populated with ridiculously beautiful people and pop stars.

❶ Information

Rimini has three helpful tourist information points, one inside the **train station** (📞0541 5 33 99; www.riminiturismo.it; Piazzale Cesare Battisti 1; ⊙8.15am-7.15pm Jun–mid-Sep, to 6pm Mon-Sat mid-Sep–May), another at the **waterfront** (📞0541 5 33 99; www.riminiturismo. it; Piazzale Fellini 3; ⊙8.30am-7.30pm Mon-Sat Jun-Aug, to 1pm Mon-Fri Sep-May) near Parco Federico Fellini and a third at **aRimini Caput Viarum** (www.riminiromana.it; Corso d'Augusto 235; ⊙10am-1pm & 4.30-7.30pm Tue & Thu-Sat, plus 8-10pm Fri, 9.30am-12.30pm Sun Jun-Sep, shorter hours Oct-May).

Ospedale Infermi (📞0541 70 52 52; www.ausl. rn.it; Viale Settembrini 2) Located 2.5km southeast of the centre.

❶ Getting There & Away

Rimini's **Federico Fellini International Airport** (📞0541 37 98 00; www.riminiairport.com; Via Flaminia 409), 8km south of the city centre, offers direct flights to Scandinavia with Finnair, to Russia with Rossiya and Ural Airlines, and to various other European cities, including with seasonal charter flights.

Benedettini (📞0549 90 38 54; www.bened ettinispa.com) and **Bonelli Bus** (📞0541 66 20 69; www.bonellibus.it) operate 12 buses daily from a bus stop outside Rimini's train station to San Marino (6.55am to 8.40pm, €5, 50 minutes) in summer (service drops slightly in winter). From the same stop, **Shuttle Rimini Bologna** (📞0541 60 01 00; www.shuttleriminibologna. it) runs shuttles direct to Bologna's airport eight times per day (3.30am to 10.15pm, from €20, 1¾ hours). Bonelli buses to Rome also leave from here daily at 3.10pm (€29, 5½ hours) in summer; 6.50am and 2.50pm Friday and Sunday, respectively, in winter.

By car, you have a choice of the A14 (south into Le Marche or northwest towards Bologna and Milan) or the toll-free but very busy SS16.

Hourly trains run from **Stazione di Rimini** (www.trenitalia.com; Piazzale Cesare Battisti 1; ⊙5am-midnight) down the coast to the ferry ports of Ancona (from €8, one to 1¼ hours) and Bari (Intercity/Frecciabianca €27/40, 4¾ to six hours). Up the line, they serve Ravenna (from €4.75, one hour, hourly) and Bologna (from €10, one to 1½ hours, half-hourly).

SAN MARINO

📞 0549 / POP 31,800

Of Earth's 196 independent countries, San Marino is the fifth smallest and – arguably – the most curious. How it exists at all is something of an enigma. A sole survivor of Italy's once powerful city-state network, this landlocked micronation clung on long after the more powerful kingdoms of Genoa and Venice folded. And still it endures, secure in its status as the world's oldest surviving sovereign state and its oldest republic (since AD 301). San Marino also enjoys one of the planet's highest GDP per capita, but some say it retains a curious absence of heart and soul.

Measuring 61 sq km, the country is larger than many outsiders imagine, being made up of nine municipalities each hosting its own settlement. The largest 'town' is Dogana (on the bus route from Italy), a place 99.9% of the two million annual visitors skip en transit to its Unesco-listed capital, Città di San Marino.

◉ Sights

Città di San Marino's highlights are its spectacular views, its Unesco-listed streets, and a stash of rather bizarre museums dedicated to vampires, torture, wax dummies and strange facts (pick up a list in the tourist office). Ever popular in summertime is the hourly changing of the guard (⊙hourly 8.30am-12.30pm & 2.30-6.30pm Mon-Fri, 10.30am-5.30pm Sat & Sun summer) in Piazza della Libertà.

Torre Guaita CASTLE
(Prima Torre; www.museidistato.sm; Salita alla Rocca; adult/reduced €4.50/3.50; ⊙8am-8pm 20 Jun–10 Sep, 9am-5pm 11 Sep–19 Jun) The oldest and largest of San Marino's castles, Torre Guaita dates from the 11th century. It was still being used as a prison as recently as 1975.

Torre Cesta CASTLE
(Seconda Torre; www.museidistato.sm; Salita alla Cesta; adult/reduced €4.50/3.50; ⊙8am-8pm 20 Jun–10 Sep, 9am-5pm 11 Sep–19 Jun) Dominating the skyline and offering superb views towards Rimini and the coast, the Cesta castle dates from the 13th century and sits atop 750m Monte Titano. Today you can walk its ramparts and peep into its four-room **museum** devoted to medieval armaments.

Museo di Stato MUSEUM
(www.museidistato.sm/mds; Piazza Titano 1; adult/reduced €4.50/3.50; ⊙8am-8pm Jun 20-Sep 10, 9am-5pm Sep 11-Jun 19) San Marino's best museum by far is the well laid out if disjointed state museum, which displays art, history, furniture and cultural objects.

Don't miss the Domagnano Treasure, an Ostrogothic trove of jewels dating back to the 5th and 6th centuries.

🍴 Sleeping & Eating

Balsimelli 12 B&B €
(☑0549 99 01 02; www.balsimelli12.com; Contrada dei Magazzeni 12; s €60-65, d €90-125; 🕾) Well-known Italian actor Fabrizio Raggi – along with his three adorable Jack Russells, Rocco, Viola and Asso – has renovated his grandfather's historic, late-1800s house into a discerning two-room B&B beautifully tucked away in the centre of everything. Book the attic room – you'll trade a lower ceiling for a stupendous terrace, on which Riggi can arrange an *aperitivo* with local wine or in-room massages.

Ristorante Righi SAMMARINESE €€€
(☑0549 99 11 96; www.ristoranterighi.com; Piazza della Libertà 10; meals €35-52, tasting menus €40-90; ⊙12.30-2pm & 7.30-10.30pm Tue-Sat, 12.30-2.30pm Sun; 🕾) This Michelin one-star affair, awash in beige and brick, is San Marino's most coveted table. Don't miss Chef Luigi's Sartini's sublime signature lasagne, spread thin and topped with knife-cut *ragù* and *pecorino* fondue. There are also plenty of themed tasting menus, including seafood and vegetarian options.

ℹ️ Information

Tourist Office (Ufficio del Turismo; ☑0549 88 23 90; www.visitsanmarino.com; Contrada Omagnano 20; ⊙8.15am-6pm Mon-Fri, 9am-1pm & 2-6pm Sat & Sun) You can get your passport stamped with a San Marino visa for €5 here (cash only). In 2021, the office is expected to move to Piazza Garibaldi 1, inside the new Museo Filatelico e Numismatico, which will re-open in the historic centre after closing in Borgo Maggiore in the 1980s.

ℹ️ Getting There & Away

Bonelli Bus (☑0541 66 20 69; www.bonellibus.it) and **Benedettini** (☑0549 90 38 54; www.benedettinispa.com) operate 12 buses daily to/from Rimini in summer (one-way €5, 50 minutes, 6.45am to 8.40pm), arriving at Piazzale Calcigni in Città di San Marino. Service drops off slightly in winter.

The SS72 leads up from Rimini. Leave your car at one of Città di San Marino's numerous car parks and walk up to the *centro storico*. Alternatively, park at **Parcheggio 11** (Piazzale Campo della Fiera; per day €8) and take the **funivia** (cable car; Piazzale Campo della Fiera 10; return €4.50; ⊙7.45am-1am Jul-Sep, shorter hours Oct-Jun). In the opposite direction, the **funivia** (Via Eugipo; return €4.50; ⊙7.45am-1am Jul-Sep, shorter hours Oct-Jun) leaves from next to the tourist office.

Piazza della Signoria (p510)
SERGEY ANDREEVICH/SHUTTERSTOCK ©

Florence & Tuscany

Life is sweet around Florence, a fashionable city known for its truly extraordinary treasure trove of world-class art and architecture, and its seasonally driven cuisine. Away from its urban heart the pace slows as magnificent landscapes and the gentle beat of the seasons cast their seductive spell.

This part of Italy has been working on its remarkable heritage since Etruscan times. Explore a World Heritage Site in the morning, visit a vineyard in the afternoon and bunk down in a palatial villa or cinematically rural *agriturismo* (farm stay) with indigenous black pigs and chickens nearby. Renaissance paintings and Gothic cathedrals? Check. Spectacular trekking and sensational Slow Food? You bet. Hills laden with vines and ancient olive groves? More than you can possibly imagine.

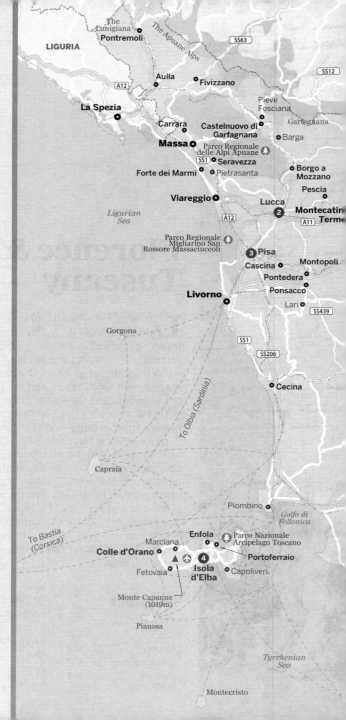

Tuscany Highlights

❶ Uffizi (p512) Swooning over Florence's treasures: the world's finest collection of Renaissance paintings at the Uffizi and the dome of Brunelleschi's Duomo.

❷ Lucca City Walls (p605) Pedalling and picnicking atop stone walls encircling Lucca.

❸ Leaning Tower (p598) Getting lost in medieval Pisa and scaling its iconic tower at sunset.

❹ Elba (p595) Setting sail for the Mediterranean isle and sleeping on an olive estate scented with orange blossoms and olive groves.

❺ Chianti (p562) Vineyard-hopping through Chianti and lunching at a family estate.

❻ Siena (p551) Gorging on Gothic architecture and almond biscuits.

❼ Abbazia di Sant'Antimo (p578) Being spellbound by Gregorian chants in the compelling abbey near Montalcino.

❽ Città del Tufo (p586) Exploring Etruscan heritage in southern Tuscany.

❾ Arezzo (p610) Marvelling at frescoes in Cappella Bacci and the beautiful Tuscan square.

FLORENCE

📞 055 / POP 382,250

Return time and again and you still won't see it all. Stand on a bridge over the Arno river several times in a day and the light, mood and view change every time. Surprisingly small as it is, Florence (Firenze) looms large on Europe's 'must-see' list. Host to the tourist masses that flock here to feast on world-class art, Tuscany's largest city buzzes with romance and history. Towers and palaces evoke a thousand tales of its medieval past; designer boutiques and artisan workshops pearl its streets; and the local drinking and dining scene is second to none. Cradle of the Renaissance and home of Machiavelli, Michelangelo and the Medici, Florence is magnetic, romantic and brilliantly absorbing.

◉ Sights

Florence's wealth of museums and galleries house many of the world's most exquisite examples of Renaissance art, and its architecture is unrivalled. Yet don't feel pressured to see everything: combine your personal pick of sights with ample meandering through the city's warren of narrow streets broken by cafe and *enoteca* (wine bar) stops.

Churches enforce a strict dress code for visitors: no shorts, sleeveless shirts or plunging necklines. Photography with no flash is allowed in museums, but leave the selfie stick at home – they are officially forbidden.

◉ Piazza della Signoria & Around

Piazza della Signoria   PIAZZA
(Map p524) The hub of local life since the 13th century, Florentines flock here to meet friends and chat over early-evening *aperitivi* (predinner drinks) at historic cafes. Presiding over everything is Palazzo Vecchio (p522), Florence's city hall, and the 14th-century **Loggia dei Lanzi**, an open-air gallery showcasing Renaissance sculptures, including Giambologna's *Rape of the Sabine Women* (c 1583), Benvenuto Cellini's bronze *Perseus* (1554) and Agnolo Gaddi's *Seven Virtues* (1384–89).

In centuries past, townsfolk congregated on the piazza whenever the city entered one of its innumerable political crises. The people would be called for a *parlamento* (people's plebiscite) to rubber-stamp decisions that frequently meant ruin for some ruling families and victory for others. Scenes of great pomp and circumstance alternated with those of terrible suffering: it was here that vehemently pious preacher-leader Savonarola set fire to the city's art – books,

---

ℹ️ MUSEUM TICKETS

In July, August and other busy periods such as Easter, unbelievably long queues are a fact of life at Florence's key museums – if you haven't prebooked your ticket, you could well end up standing in line for four hours or so.

For a fee of €3 per ticket (€4 for the Uffizi and Galleria dell'Accademia), tickets to nine *musei statali* (state museums) can be reserved, including the Uffizi, Galleria dell'Accademia (where *David* lives), Palazzo Pitti, Museo del Bargello and the Medicean chapels (Cappelle Medicee). In reality, the only museums where prebooking is vital are the Uffizi and the Accademia – to organise your ticket, book online through Firenze Musei (p523), with ticketing desks at Door 2 of the **Uffizi** (Piazzale degli Uffizi; ⊗8.15am-6.05pm Tue-Sun), **Palazzo Pitti** (📞055 29 48 83; Piazza dei Pitti; ⊗8.15am-6.05pm Tue-Sun) and inside the Via del Cimatori entrance of Chiesa e Museo di Orsanmichele (p527).

At the Uffizi, signs point prebooked ticket holders to Door 3 opposite the main gallery where tickets can be collected; once you've got the ticket you go to Door 1 of the museum (for prebooked tickets only) and queue again to enter the gallery. It's annoying, but you'll still save hours of queuing time overall. Many hotels in Florence also prebook museum tickets for guests.

Admission to all state museums, including the Uffizi and Galleria dell'Accademia, is free on the first Sunday of each month between October and March, for six days in the first week of March during Italy's National Museum Week, and on 18 February, the day Anna Maria Louisa de' Medici (1667–1743) died. The last of the Medici family, it was she who bequeathed the city its vast cultural heritage.

Visitors aged under 18 and over 65 get into Florence's state museums for free, while EU citizens aged 18 to 25 pay just €2. Have your ID with you at all times. Note that museum ticket offices usually shut 30 minutes before closing time.

Florence

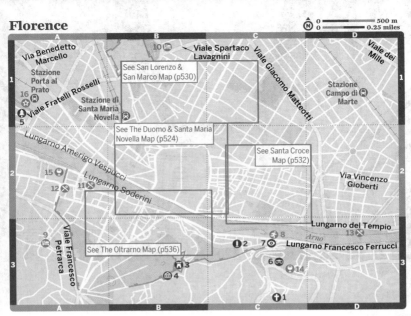

Florence

paintings, musical instruments, mirrors, fine clothes and so on – during his famous 'Bonfire of the Vanities' in 1497, and where he was hung in chains and burnt as a heretic, along with two other supporters, a year later.

The same spot where both fires burned is marked by a bronze plaque embedded in the ground. Nearby, Ammannati's **Fontana di Nettuno**, with pin-headed bronze satyrs and divinities frolicking at its edges, dazzles again thanks to a €1.5-million restoration in 2017–19 funded by Florentine fashion house Salvatore Ferragamo. It was originally unveiled in 1565 to celebrate the wedding of Francesco I de' Medici and the Grand Duchess Giovanna d'Austria.

Equally impressive are the equestrian statue of Cosimo I by Giambologna in the centre of the piazza, the copy of Michelangelo's *David* guarding the western entrance to the Palazzo Vecchio since 1910 (the original stood here until 1873), and two copies of important Donatello works: *Marzocco*, the heraldic Florentine lion – for the original, visit the Museo del Bargello (p523) – and *Giuditta e Oloferne* (Judith and Holofernes; c 1455; original inside Palazzo Vecchio).

Continued on p522

TOP SIGHT
GALLERIA DEGLI UFFIZI

Home to the world's greatest collection of Italian Renaissance art, Florence's premier gallery occupies the vast U-shaped Palazzo degli Uffizi. The world-famous collection, displayed in chronological order, spans the gamut of art history from ancient Greek sculpture to 18th-century Venetian paintings. But its core is the Renaissance collection – a morning can be spent enjoying its unmatched collection of Botticellis alone.

The Nuovo Uffizi

As part of a gargantuan €65-million refurbishment, the Uffizi has been under constant renovation since 1995, with exhibition space doubling and artworks reorganised to fill – at the last count – some 100 rooms across two floors. The contemporary loggia, designed by Japanese architect Arata Isozaki in 1998 for the gallery's exit, appears something of a pipe dream these days: future project work will focus more on areas earmarked for temporary exhibitions and conferences. When planning a visit, check on the museum website which rooms are closed that day.

Tuscan 13th-Century Art

Arriving in the Primo Corridoio (First Corridor) on the 2nd floor, the first room to the left of the staircase (Room 2) is designed like a medieval chapel to reflect its fabulous contents: three large altarpieces from Florentine churches by Tuscan masters Duccio di Buoninsegna, Cimabue and Giotto. They show the transition from Gothic to nascent Renaissance style.

DON'T MISS

➡ Sala del Botticelli (2nd Floor, Rooms 10 to 14)

➡ Leonardo da Vinci (2nd Floor, Room 35)

➡ Michelangelo (2nd Floor, Room 41)

PRACTICALITIES

➡ Uffizi Gallery

➡ Map p524

➡ ☏ 055 29 48 83

➡ www.uffizi.it

➡ Piazzale degli Uffizi 6

➡ adult/reduced Mar-Oct €20/2, Nov-Feb €12/2

➡ ◷ 8.15am-6.50pm Tue-Sun

Sienese 14th-Century Art
The highlight in Room 3 is Simone Martini's shimmering *Annunciazione* (1333), painted with Lippo Memmi and setting the Madonna in a sea of gold. Also of note is *Madonna con il bambino in trono e angeli* (Madonna with Child and Saints; 1340) by Pietro Lorenzetti, which demonstrates a realism similar to Giotto's; unfortunately, both Pietro and his artistic brother Ambrogio died of the plague in Siena in 1348.

Renaissance Pioneers
Perspective was a hallmark of the early-15th-century Florentine school (Room 8) that launched the Renaissance. One panel from Paolo Uccello's striking *Battle of San Romano* (1436–40), which celebrates Florence's victory over Siena in 1432, shows the artist's efforts to create perspective with amusing effect as he directs the lances, horses and soldiers to a central disappearing point. In the same room, don't miss the exquisite *Madonna con bambino e due angeli* (Madonna and Child with Two Angels; 1460–65) by Fra' Filippo Lippi, a Carmelite monk who had an unfortunate soft spot for earthly pleasures and scandalously married a nun from Prato. This work clearly influenced his pupil, Sandro Botticelli.

Duke & Duchess of Urbino
In the same room (Room 8), revel in the realism of Piero della Francesca's 1465 warts-and-all portraits of the Duke and Duchess of Urbino. The crooked-nosed duke lost his right eye in a jousting accident, hence the focus on his left side only, while the duchess is deathly stone-white to convey the fact that the portrait was painted posthumously.

Botticelli
Learn about the seven cardinal and theological values of 15th-century Florence with the huge painting *The Seven Virtues* by brothers Antonio and Piero del Pollaiolo in Room 9, commissioned for the merchant's tribunal in Piazza della Signoria. The only canvas in the series not to be painted by the Pollaiolos is *Fortitude* (1470), the first documented work by Botticelli.

The spectacular Sala del Botticelli, numbered 10 to 14 but really two light and graceful rooms, is always packed. Of the many Botticelli works displayed in the Uffizi, his iconic *La nascita di Venere* (The Birth of Venus; c 1485), *Primavera* (Spring; c 1482) and *Madonna del Magnificat* (Madonna of the Magnificat; 1483) are the best-known by the Renaissance master known for his ethereal figures. Take time to study the lesser known *Annunciazione*

PALAZZO DEGLI UFFIZI
Cosimo I de' Medici commissioned Vasari to build the huge U-shaped Palazzo degli Uffizi in 1560 as a government office building (*uffizi* means 'offices'). Following Vasari's death in 1564, architects Alfonso Parigi and Bernado Buontalenti took over, with Buontalenti modifying the upper floor to house the artworks keenly collected by Cosimo I's son, Francesco I. In 1580 the building was complete. When the last Medici died in 1743, the family's enormous private art collection was bequeathed to Florence on the strict proviso that it never leave the city.

To exit quick after admiring the 2nd-floor Renaissance stars, take the 'quick exit' route signposted next to the cafe.

THE CLOSED DOOR
Spot the closed door next to Room 25 leading to the Medici's Corridoio Vasariano (p523), a 1km-long covered passageway connecting Palazzo Vecchio (p522) with the Uffizi and Palazzo Pitti (p534). It was designed by Vasari in 1565 to allow the Medicis to wander between palaces in privacy and comfort. It is due to reopen in 2022.

(Annunciation), a 6m-wide fresco painted by Botticelli in 1481 for the San Martino hospital in Florence.

Northern Influences

In the next room (Room 15) don't miss the single work by Botticelli: *Flagellazione di Cristo* (Flagellation of Christ; 1505–10), part of a cycle of paintings illustrating the life of Christ; it was one of Botticelli's last works before his death from illness and old age in 1510.

Room 15 otherwise explores the clear influence northern European artists had on Florentine artists during the Renaissance with works by Flemish painter Hugo van der Goes (1430–82). His monumental *Portinari Altarpiece* (1476–78), a triptych 2.5m tall and 3m wide representing the Adoration of the Shepherds, arrived in Florence in 1483 and was displayed in the church inside Florence's Santa Maria Novella hospital. Van der Goes painted it for Tommasso Portinari, director of the Medici bank in Bruges – admire his portrait and that of his wife and their three children on the side panels.

The Tribune

The Medici clan stashed away their most precious art in this octagonal-shaped treasure trove (Room 18), created by Francesco I between 1581 and 1586. Designed to amaze, it features a small collection of classical statues and paintings on its upholstered silk walls and 6000 crimson-varnished mother-of-pearl shells encrusting the domed ceiling.

Michelangelo & Räphael

Room 34, with sage-green painted walls, displays sculptures from classical antiquity – of great influence on the young Michelangelo – and from the Medici-owned sculpture garden in San Marco where Michelangelo studied classical sculpture as an apprentice from the age of 13.

Michelangelo's dazzling *Doni Tondo,* a depiction of the Holy Family, hangs in Room 41. The composition is unusual and the colours as vibrant as when they were first applied in 1504–06. It was painted for wealthy Florentine merchant Agnolo Doni (who hung it above his bed) and bought by the Medici for Palazzo Pitti in 1594.

The other High Renaissance masterpiece in this room is Raphael's *Madonna col Bambino e San Giovanni* (Madonna with Child and St John; 1505–06), otherwise known as Madonna of the Goldfinch after the red-feathered goldfinch cradled in the chubby hands of a baby John the Baptist. Raphael painted it during his four-year sojourn in Florence and it has been in the Uffizi since 1704.

Medici Portraits

Rooms 64 and 65 showcase Agnolo Bronzino (1503–72), who worked as official portrait artist at the court of Cosimo I from 1539 until 1555 (when he was replaced by Vasari). His 1545 portraits of the Grand Duchess Eleonora of Toleto and her son Giovanni together, and the 18-month-old Giovanni alone holding a goldfinch – symbolising his calling into the church – are considered masterpieces of 16th-century European portraiture. Giovanni was elected a cardinal in 1560 but died of malaria two years later.

Leonardo Da Vinci

Three early Florentine works by Leonardo da Vinci are shown off to perfection in Room 35. His *Annunciazione* (Annunciation; 1472) was deliberately painted to be admired not face on (from where Mary's arm appears too long, her face too light and the angle of buildings not quite right), but rather from the lower right-hand

side of the painting. *Adoration of the Magi* (1481–82), originally commissioned for the altar of the monastery of San Donato a Scopeto near Florence and never finished, is typical of Florentine figurative painting in the 15th century. *Battesimo di Cristo* (Baptism of Christ; 1475) depicts John the Baptist baptising a very naturalistic Christ on the banks of the Jordan.

Caravaggio

Rooms 96 and 97 are filled with paintings by Caravaggio, deemed vulgar at the time for his direct interpretation of reality. The *Head of Medusa* (1598–99), commissioned for a ceremonial shield, is supposedly a self-portrait of the young artist, who later died at the age of 39. The biblical drama of an angel steadying the hand of Abraham as he holds a knife to his son Isaac's throat in Caravaggio's *Sacrifice of Isaac* (1601–02) is glorious in its intensity.

CEILING ART

Take time to study the make-believe grotesque monsters and unexpected burlesques (spot the arrow-shooting satyr outside Room 15) waltzing across the eastern corridor's fabulous frescoed ceiling. Admire more compelling art in Rooms 19 to 23, whose ornate vaulted ceilings were frescoed in the 16th and 17th centuries depicting military objects and allegories, as well as illustrations of historical battles and traditional festivals that took place on Florence's many beautiful and distinctive piazzas.

Head to the Uffizi's rooftop cafe for coffee, fresh air and fabulous views.

TICKETING TIME-SLOTS

The gallery is road-testing a new time-slot reservation system aimed at reducing queue time. Visitors wanting to buy a same-day ticket can simply print off a voucher with QR code and admission time from a 'digital kiosk' beneath the arches outside the gallery; they then return at the allotted time to purchase their ticket and enter the Uffizi.

The Uffizi
JOURNEY INTO THE RENAISSANCE

Navigating the Uffizi's chronologically-ordered art collection is straightforward enough: knowing which of the 1500-odd masterpieces to view before gallery fatigue strikes is not. Swap your bag (travel light) for floor plan and audioguide on the ground floor, then meet 16th-century Tuscany head-on with a walk up the *palazzo's* magnificent bust-lined staircase (skip the lift – the Uffizi is as much about masterly architecture as art).

Allow four hours for this journey into the High Renaissance. At the top of the staircase, on the 2nd floor, show your ticket, turn left and pause to admire the full length of the first corridor sweeping south towards the Arno river. Then duck left into room 2 to witness first steps in Tuscan art – shimmering altarpieces by ❶ **Giotto** et al. Journey through medieval art to room 8 and ❷ **Piero della Francesca's** impossibly famous portrait. After Renaissance heavyweight ❸ **Botticelli** (don't miss his solitary work hidden in Room 15), duck out into the corridor to break beneath playful ❹ **ceiling art**. Stroll past the Tribuna (potential detour) and enjoy the daylight streaming in through the vast windows and panorama of the ❺ **riverside second corridor**. Lap up soul-stirring views of the Arno, crossed by Ponte Vecchio and its echo of four bridges drifting towards the Apuane Alps on the horizon. Then saunter into the third corridor, pausing between rooms 25 and 34 to ponder the entrance to the enigmatic Vasari Corridor. Give a nod to the teenage Michelangelo in the ❻ **San Marco sculpture garden**, enjoy a brilliant encounter with ❼ **Leonardo da Vinci**, and end on a High Renaissance high with ❽ **Michelangelo and Raphael**.

Giotto's Madonna
Room 2
Draw breath at the shy blush and curvaceous breast of Giotto's humanised Madonna and Child (*Maestà di Ognissanti;* 1306–1310) – so feminine compared with those of Duccio and Cimabue painted just 25 years before.

Portraits of the Duke & Duchess of Urbino
Room 8
Revel in realism's voyage with these uncompromising, warts-and-all portraits (1472–75) by Piero della Francesca. No larger than A3 size, they originally slotted into a portable, hinged frame that folded like a book.

Start of Vasari Corridor (linking the Palazzo Vecchio with the Uffizi and Palazzo Pitti)

Entrance to 2nd Floor Gallery

Palazzo Vecchio

Piazza della Signoria

Grotesque Ceiling Frescoes
First Corridor
Take time to study the make-believe monsters and most unexpected of burlesques (spot the arrow-shooting satyr outside room 15) waltzing across this eastern corridor's fabulous frescoed ceiling (1581).

ALIZADA STUDIOS/SHUTTERSTOCK ©

The Genius of Botticelli
Room 10–14

Botticelli's tondo twinset, *Madonna of the Pomegranate* (c 1487) and *Madonna of the Magnificat* (c 1483) hang in heavy gilt frames. Both are round, a sure sign during the Renaissance that they were commissioned for a private home rather than church.

EMI CRISTEA/SHUTTERSTOCK©

View of the Arno

Indulge in intoxicating city views from this short glassed-in corridor – an architectural masterpiece. Near the top of the hill, spot one of 73 outer towers built to defend Florence and its 15 city gates below.

Second Corridor

First Corridor

Tribuna

Arno River

Original entrance to Vasari Corridor

❶ ❷ ❸ ❹ ❺ ❻ ❼ ❽

San Marco sculpture garden
Room 34

A 13-year-old Michelangelo studied classical sculpture as an apprentice at Lorenzo de Medici's sculpture school in San Marco. Admire relief-sculpted sarcophagi that had such a massive influence on this artist.

Leonardo da Vinci
Room 41

Futuristic climate-controlling, anti-glare, anti-terrorist glass cases protect three early masterpieces by Leonardo da Vinci, including *Adoration of the Magi*, still unfinished when da Vinci left Florence for Milan in 1482 and a Uffizi treasure since 1670.

Third Corridor

Stairs by cafe to 1st Floor Gallery and Ground Floor 'Quick Exit'

Tribuna

No room in the Uffizi is so tiny or so exquisite. It was created in 1851 as a 'treasure chest' for Grand Duke Francesco and in the days of the Grand Tour, the Medici Venus here was a tour highlight.

Doni Tondo
Room 41

The creator of *David*, Michelangelo, was essentially a sculptor and no painting expresses this better than *Doni Tondo* (1506–08). Mary's muscular arms against a backdrop of curvaceous nudes are practically 3D in their shapeliness.

MATTER OF FACT

The Uffizi collection spans the 13th to 18th centuries, but its 15th- and 16th-century Renaissance works are second to none.

VALUE LUNCHBOX

Try the Uffizi rooftop cafe or – better value – gourmet *panini* at 'Ino (www. ino-firenze.com; Via dei Georgofili 3-7r).

 TOP SIGHT
DUOMO

Properly titled Cattedrale di Santa Maria del Fiore (Cathedral of St Mary of the Flower), but known as the Duomo (cathedral), this is Florence's iconic landmark. Designed by Sienese architect Arnolfo di Cambio, construction began in 1296 and took almost 150 years. The result – with Brunelleschi's distinctive red-tiled cupola, graceful *campanile* (bell tower) and pink, white and green marble facade – is breathtaking.

Facade

The neo-Gothic facade was designed in the 19th century by architect Emilio de Fabris to replace the uncompleted original. The oldest and most clearly Gothic part of the structure is its south flank, pierced by the **Porta dei Canonici** (Canons' Door), a mid-14th-century High Gothic creation (you enter here to climb to the dome).

Interior

After taking in the incredibly richly adorned facade as best as one can, the spartan nature of the *duomo's* vast interior – 155m long and 90m wide – comes as something of a visual relief. Most of its artistic treasures have been removed and those that remain are unexpectedly secular, reflecting the fact that the *duomo* was built with public funds as a *chiesa di stato* (state church).

Down the left aisle two immense frescoes of equestrian statues portray two *condottieri* (mercenaries) – on the left Niccolò da Tolentino by Andrea del Castagno (1456), and on the right Sir John Hawkwood (who fought in the service of Florence in the 14th century) by Paolo Uccello (1436). In the same aisle, *La Commedia illumina Firenze* (1465) by Domenico

DON'T MISS

→ Climbing inside Brunelleschi's cupola

→ City view from atop the *campanile*

→ Sala del Paradiso, Museo dell'Opera del Duomo

→ Michelangelo's *La Pietà*

PRACTICALITIES

→ Cattedrale di Santa Maria del Fiore

→ Map p524

→ 📞 055 230 28 85

→ www.museumflorence.com

→ Piazza del Duomo

→ ⏰10am-5pm Mon-Wed & Fri, to 4.30pm Thu & Sat, 1.30-4.45pm Sun

di Michelino depicts poet Dante Alighieri surrounded by the three afterlife worlds he describes in the *Divine Comedy:* purgatory is behind him, his right hand points towards hell, and Florence is paradise.

Mass Sacristy

Between the left (north) arm of the transept and the apse is the Sagrestia delle Messe (Mass Sacristy), accessible only by guided tour. All four walls are panelled in a marvel of inlaid wood carved by Benedetto and Giuliano da Maiano between 1436 and 1468. The fine bronze doors were executed by Luca della Robbia – his only known work in the material. Above the doorway is his glazed terracotta *Resurrezione* (Resurrection).

Crypt of Santa Reparata

Excavated remains of the very first church that stood on this site, the 5th-century Chiesa di Santa Reparata, can be admired in the Duomo's Cripta Santa Reparata (adult/reduced incl cupola, baptistry, campanile & museum €18/3; ☺10am-5pm Mon-Wed & Fri, to 4.30pm Thu & Sat) – access it from the staircase, not far from the main entrance, in the south aisle. Down below, secreted among the ancient stones, are the cathedral gift shop, remains of Roman dwellings, marble floor mosaics (for early Christians the peacock was a symbol of eternal life) and the tomb of 15th-century architect Filippo Brunelleschi.

Cupola

When Michelangelo went to work on St Peter's in Rome, he reportedly said, 'I go to build a greater dome, but not a fairer one', referring to the huge but graceful terracotta-brick dome (Brunelleschi's Dome; adult/reduced incl baptistry, campanile, crypt & museum €18/3; ☺8.30am-7pm Mon-Fri, to 5pm Sat, 1-4pm Sun) atop Florence's *duomo*. It was constructed between 1420 and 1436 to a design by Filippo Brunelleschi and is a highlight of any visit to Florence. Its sheer scale alone is breathtaking: 45m wide and 90m high (116m with the crowning lantern).

One of the finest masterpieces of the Renaissance, the cupola crowning the Duomo is a feat of engineering and one that cannot be fully appreciated without climbing its 463 interior stone steps. Taking his inspiration from Rome's Pantheon, Brunelleschi arrived at an innovative engineering solution of a distinctive octagonal shape of inner and outer concentric domes resting on the drum of the cathedral rather than the roof itself, allowing artisans to build from the ground up without needing a wooden support frame. Over four million bricks were used in the construction, all of them laid in consecutive rings in horizontal courses using a vertical herringbone pattern.

TICKETS

Entry to the cathedral itself is free. The combined ticket (adult/reduced €18/3) covers the cupola, crypt, bell tower, baptistry and museum, and is valid for 72 hours (one visit per sight); purchase at www.museumflorence.com or at the Duomo ticket office (Piazza San Giovanni 7; ☺8.15am-6.45pm), opposite the baptistry entrance at Piazza di San Giovanni 7.

Dress code is strict: no shorts, miniskirts or sleeveless tops.

A MATHEMATICAL WHIZZ

Architect, mathematician, engineer and sculptor, Filippo Brunelleschi (1377–1446) spent an incredible 27 years working on the dome of Florence's *duomo*. Starting work in 1419, his mathematical brain and talent for devising innovative engineering solutions enabled him to do what many Florentines had thought impossible: deliver the largest dome to be built in Italy since antiquity.

The Climb

The climb up the spiral staircase is relatively steep, and should not be attempted if you are claustrophobic. Make sure to pause when you reach the balustrade at the base of the dome, which gives an aerial view of the octagonal coro (choir) of the cathedral below and the seven round stained-glass windows (by Donatello, Andrea del Castagno, Paolo Uccello and Lorenzo Ghiberti) that pierce the octagonal drum.

Look up and you'll see the flamboyant late-16th-century frescoes by Giorgio Vasari and Federico Zuccari, depicting the *Giudizio Universale* (Last Judgement) and covering a remarkable 4500 sq metres.

As you climb, snapshots of Florence can be spied through small windows. The final leg – a straight, somewhat hazardous flight up the curve of the inner dome – rewards with an unforgettable 360-degree panorama of one of Europe's most beautiful cities.

The Last Judgement

Don't forget to look upwards as you mount the stairs. Giorgio Vasari and Federico Zuccari's late-16th-century *Giudizio universale* (1572–79) fresco decorating the 4500-sq-metre surface of the cupola's inner dome is one of the world's largest paintings. Look for a spent Mother Nature with wrinkled breasts and the four seasons asleep at her feet. Less savoury are the poor souls in hell being sodomised with a pitch fork.

Bell Tower

Set next to the *duomo* is its slender campanile (adult/reduced incl baptistry, cupola, crypt & museum €18/3; ⊘8.15am-7pm), a striking work of Florentine Gothic architecture designed by Giotto, the artistic genius often described as the founding artist of the Renaissance. The steep 414-step climb up the square, 85m-tall tower offers the reward of a view that is nearly as impressive as that from the dome.

The first tier of bas-reliefs around the base of its elaborate Gothic facade are copies of those carved by Pisano depicting the creation of humanity and the *attività umane* (arts and industries). Those on the second tier depict the planets, the cardinal virtues, the arts and the seven sacraments. The sculpted prophets and sibyls in the upper-storey niches are copies of works by Donatello and others.

Baptistry

Across from the *duomo's* main entrance is the 11th-century Battistero di San Giovanni (Baptistry; adult/reduced incl campanile, cupola, crypt & museum €18/3; ⊘8.15-10.15am & 11.15am-7.30pm Mon-Fri, 8.15am-6.30pm Sat, 8.15am-1.30pm Sun), an octagonal, striped structure of white-and-green marble. Dante is among the famous people to have been dunked in its baptismal font – still used every third Sunday of the month to baptise babies born within the surrounding San Lorenzo parish.

The Romanesque structure is most celebrated, however, for its three sets of doors illustrating the story of humanity and the Redemption. The gilded bronze doors by Lorenzo Ghiberti's at the eastern entrance, the *Porta del Paradiso* (Gate of Paradise), are copies – the originals are in the Museo dell'Opera del Duomo (p521). Andrea Pisano executed the southern doors (1330), illustrating the life of St John the Baptist, and Lorenzo Ghiberti won a public competition in 1401 to design the northern doors, likewise replaced by copies today.

The baptistry's interior gleams with Byzantine-style mosaics. Covering the dome in five horizontal tiers, they include scenes from the lives of St John the Baptist, Christ and Joseph on one side, and a representation of the Last Judgement on the other. A choir of angels surveys proceedings from the innermost tier.

Buy tickets online or at the ticket office at Piazza di San Giovanni 7, opposite the baptistry entrance.

Campanile

Museo dell'Opera del Duomo

This awe-inspiring museum (Cathedral Museum; Piazza del Duomo 9; adult/reduced incl cathedral bell tower, cupola, baptistry & crypt €15/3; ⊙9am-7pm) tells the magnificent story of how the *duomo* was built through art and short films. Its spectacular main hall, Sala del Paradiso, is dominated by a life-size reconstruction of the original facade of the *duomo*, decorated with some 40 carved for the facade by 14th-century masters (including a rather spooky, glass-eyed Madonna by Arnolfo di Cambio, dating to 1300–1305). Building work began in 1296 but it was never finished and in 1587 the facade was eventually dismantled. This is also where you will find Ghiberti's original 15th-century masterpiece, *Porta del Paradiso* (Doors of Paradise; 1425–52) – gloriously golden, 16m-tall gilded bronze doors designed for the eastern entrance to the Baptistry – as well as those he sculpted for the northern entrance (1403–24). In 2019 the final set of doors (1330–36), designed for the southern door by Andrea Pisano, arrived in the museum after five painstakingly long years of restoration.

Michelangelo's achingly beautiful *La Pietà,* sculpted when he was almost 80 and intended for his own tomb, is displayed in the Tribuna di Michelangelo. Dissatisfied with the marble quality and his own work, Michelangelo broke up the unfinished sculpture, destroying the arm and left leg of the figure of Christ. Donatello's mid-15th-century, wooden sculpture of a gaunt, desperately desolate Mary Magdalene is the star of Room 8.

THE DUOMO CLOCK

Upon entering the *duomo*, look up to see its clock with fantastic, 4.6m-wide frescoed face resembling a flower. One of Europe's first monumental – and unconventional – clocks, it notably turns in an anticlockwise direction, counts in 24 hours starting at the bottom and begins the first hour of the day at sunset (rather than midnight). The clock was painted by eclectic Florentine painter Paolo Uccello (1397–1495) between 1440 and 1443. To this day, it is lovingly tended for by two caretakers who enter the tiny door on ground level below the clock, climb the steep narrow staircase hidden between the *duomo's* thick interior and exterior walls, and adjust the clock mechanism to take into account the changing hour of sunset.

Visit early in the morning to escape the crowds and avoid queuing in the hot sun.

CUPOLA RESERVATIONS

Reservations are obligatory for the *duomo's* cupola; book a time slot online or at a self-service Ticketpoint machine inside the Piazza di San Giovanni ticket office.

Continued from p511

The Loggia dei Lanzi at the piazza's southern end owes its name to the Lanzichenecchi (Swiss bodyguards) of Cosimo I, who were stationed here.

★ **Palazzo Vecchio**   MUSEUM
(Map p524; ☑ 055 276 85 58; www.musefirenze. it; Piazza della Signoria; adult/reduced museum €12.50/10, tower €12.50/10, museum & tower €17.50/15, museum & archaeological tour €16/ 13.50, combination ticket €19.50/17.50; ⊙ museum 9am-11pm Fri-Wed, to 2pm Thu Apr-Sep, 9am-7pm Fri-Wed, to 2pm Thu Oct-Mar, tower 9am-9pm Fri-Wed, to 2pm Thu Apr-Sep, 10am-5pm Fri-Wed, to 2pm Thu Oct-Mar) This fortress palace, with its crenellations and 94m-high tower, was designed by Arnolfo di Cambio between 1298 and 1314 for the *signoria* (city government). Today it is home to the mayor's office and the municipal council. From the top of the **Torre d'Arnolfo** (tower), you can revel in unforgettable views. Inside, Michelangelo's *Genio della Vittoria* (Spirit of Victory) sculpture graces the Salone dei Cinquecento, a magnificent painted hall created for the city's 15th-century ruling Consiglio dei Cinquecento (Council of 500).

During their short time in office the nine *priori* (consuls) – guild members picked at random – of the *signoria* lived in the palace. Every two months nine new names were pulled out of the hat, ensuring ample comings and goings.

In 1540 Cosimo I made the palace his ducal residence and centre of government,

---

ⓘ TIME SAVER

The **Firenze Card** (www.firenzecard. it; €85) is valid for 72 hours and covers admission to 70-plus museums, villas and gardens in Florence, as well as unlimited use of public transport and free wi-fi across the city. To add on unlimited public transport, pay an additional €7 for a Firenzecard+ add-on. The card's biggest advantage is reducing queueing time in high season – museums have a separate queue for card-holders. The downside of the Firenze Card is it only allows one admission per museum, plus you need to visit an awful lot of museums to justify the cost. Buy the card online (and collect upon arrival in Florence or download the Firenze Card App and store it digitally).

---

commissioning Giorgio Vasari to renovate and decorate the interior. What impresses is the 53m-long, 22m-wide **Salone dei Cinquecento** with swirling battle scenes, painted by Vasari and his apprentices. These glorify Florentine victories by Cosimo I over arch-rivals Pisa and Siena: unlike the Sienese, the Pisans are depicted bare of armour (play 'Spot the Leaning Tower'). To top off this unabashed celebration of his own power, Cosimo had himself portrayed as a god in the centre of the exquisite panelled ceiling – but not before commissioning Vasari to raise the original ceiling 7m in height. It took Vasari and his school, in consultation with Michelangelo, just two years (1563–65) to construct the ceiling and paint the 34 gold-leafed panels. The effect is mesmerising.

On the same floor, **Quartiere di Leo X** ensnares the private suite of apartments of Cardinal Giovanni de' Medici (1475–1521), the son of Lorenzo Il Magnifico, who became a cardinal at the tender age of 13 and became pope in 1513 – taking the name Leo X. The **Sala di Leo X** is a visual celebration of his life. In the stairwell off this room, admire the wall fresco of Palazzo Vecchio during 24 June celebrations in 1558.

Upstairs on the 2nd floor, the **Sala delle Carte Geografiche** (Map Room) houses Cosimo I's fascinating collection of 16th-century maps charting everywhere in the known world at the time, from the polar regions to the Caribbean. Continue through to the private apartments of Eleonora and her ladies-in-waiting, heavy-handed decor predictably blaring the glory of the Medici. The ceiling in the **Camera Verde** (Green Room) by Ridolfo del Ghirlandaio was inspired by designs from Nero's Domus Aurea in Rome. The **Sala dei Gigli**, named after its frieze of fleur-de-lis, representing the Florentine Republic, is home to Donatello's original *Judith and Holofernes*.

On rain-free days, don't miss the 418-step hike up the palace's striking Torre d'Arnolfo, also accessible from the palace's 2nd floor. No more than 35 people are allowed at any one time and on busy days you have just 30 minutes to lap up the city panorama.

Gucci Garden   MUSEUM
(Map p524; ☑ 055 7592 7010; www.gucci.com; Piazza della Signoria 10; adult/reduced €8/5; ⊙ 10am-8pm) Elegantly housed in 14th-century Palazzo della Mercanzia, Gucci Garden is an all-out whimsical ode to the Florentine fashion giant. The practically psychedelic, boudoir-styled boutique on the

WATCH THIS SPACE!

Florence's enigmatic covered passageway, the 1km-long **Corridoio Vasariano** (Vasari Corridor; Map p524; guided visit by reservation Mar-Oct €45, Nov-Feb €20), currently closed for restoration work, connects Palazzo Vecchio with the Uffizi (p512) and Palazzo Pitti (p534). Vasari designed it in 1565 to allow the Medici family to wander between their palaces in privacy and comfort. When the €10-million renovation is complete in 2022, visitors will follow in Medici footsteps past a line-up of antique statues, 16th-century frescoes once adorning the corridor's external walls, and memorials to Florence bombings in 1944 and 1993. Guided visits by **Firenze Musei** (Florence Museums; ☏ 055 265 43 21; www.firenzemusei.it) will be by reservation only.

In the 17th century the Medici strung the corridor with hundreds of artworks, including self-portraits of Andrea del Sarto, Rubens, Rembrandt and Canova.

The original promenade incorporated tiny windows (facing the river) and circular apertures with iron gratings (facing the street) to protect those who used the corridor from outside attacks. But when Hitler visited Florence in 1941, his chum and fellow dictator Benito Mussolini had big new windows punched into the corridor walls on Ponte Vecchio so that his guest could enjoy an expansive view down the Arno from the famous Florentine bridge.

On the Oltrarno, the corridor passes by Romanesque **Chiesa di Santa Felicità** (Map p536; Piazza di Santa Felicità; ⊗9.30am-noon & 3.30-5.30pm Mon-Sat), thereby providing the Medicis with a private balcony in the church where they could attend Mass without mingling with the minions.

ground floor is designed as much for experiential browsing as high-end shopping, while gallery rooms on the 1st and 2nd floors illustrate the Gucci story. Born in 1921, the brand's history is shown with clothing, accessories, video installations and a highly popular 'selfie' wall emblazoned with the famous double-G monogram, glossy red lips, stilettos and other 'walk the talk' emojis.

Museo Galileo   MUSEUM
(Map p524; ☏ 055 26 53 11; www.museogalileo.it; Piazza dei Giudici 1; adult/reduced €10/6; ⊗9.30am-6pm Wed-Mon, to 1pm Tue) On the Arno river next to the Uffizi in 12th-century Palazzo Castellani – look for the sundial telling the time on the pavement outside – is this state-of-the-art science museum, named after the great Pisa-born scientist Galileo Galilei, who was invited by the Medici court to Florence in 1610. Don't miss two of his fingers and a tooth displayed here.

★ **Museo del Bargello**   MUSEUM
(Map p524; ☏ 055 238 86 06; www.bargellomusei.beniculturali.it; Via del Proconsolo 4; adult/reduced €8/4; ⊗8.15am-2pm, closed 2nd & 4th Sun, 1st, 3rd & 5th Mon of month) It was behind the stark walls of Palazzo del Bargello, Florence's earliest public building, that the *podestà* (governing magistrate) meted out justice from the 13th century until 1502. Today the building safeguards Italy's most comprehensive collection of Tuscan Renaissance sculpture,

with some of Michelangelo's best early works and several by Donatello. Michelangelo was just 21 when a cardinal commissioned him to create the drunken grape-adorned *Bacchus* (1496–97). Unfortunately the cardinal didn't like the result and sold it.

Other Michelangelo works are in the ground-floor **Sala di Michelangelo e della Scultura del Cinque Cento** (first door on the right after entering the interior courtyard). Look out for the marble bust of *Brutus* (c 1539), the *David/Apollo* from 1530–32 and the large, uncompleted roundel of the *Madonna and Child with the Infant St John* (aka the Tondo Pitti; 1505). After Michelangelo left Florence for the final time in 1534, sculpture was dominated by Baccio Bandinelli (his 1551 *Adam and Eve,* created for the *duomo,* is also displayed here) and Benvenuto Cellini (look for his playful 1548–50 marble *Ganymede* in the same room).

Back in the interior courtyard, an open staircase leads up to the elegant, sculpture-laced **loggia** (1370) and, to the right, the **Salone di Donatello**. Here, in the majestic Sala del Consiglio where the city council met, works by Donatello and other early-15th-century sculptors can be admired. Originally on the facade of Chiesa di Orsanmichele and now within a tabernacle at the hall's far end, Donatello's wonderful *St George* (1416–17) brought a new sense of perspective and movement to Italian sculpture. Also look for

The Duomo & Santa Maria Novella

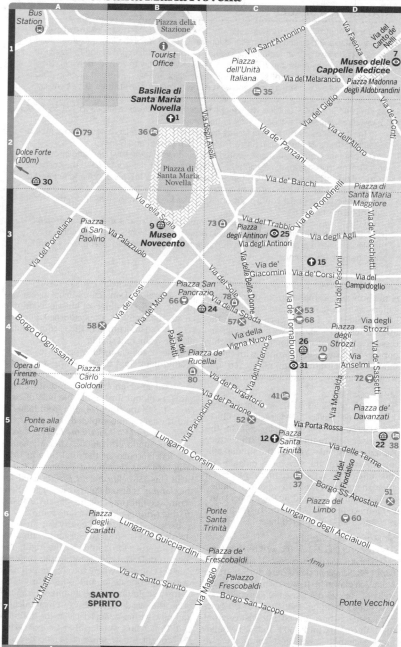

Bus Station

Piazza della Stazione

Tourist Office

Via Sant'Antonino

Piazza dell'Unità Italiana

Via del Melarancio

Museo delle Cappelle Medicee 7

Piazza Madonna degli Aldobrandini

35

Via Faenza

Via del Canto de' Nelli

Basilica di Santa Maria Novella 1

79

36

Via degli Avelli

Via de' Panzani

Via del Giglio

Via dell'Alloro

Via de' Conti

Dolce Forte (100m)

30

Piazza di Santa Maria Novella

Via de' Banchi

Piazza di Santa Maria Maggiore

Via della Scala

Via de' Rondinelli

Piazza di San Paolino

Via del Porcellana

Via Palazzuolo

9 **Museo Novecento**

73

Via del Trabbio

Piazza degli Antinori 25

Via degli Antinori

Via degli Agli

Via de' Vecchietti

15

Via de' Giacomini

Via de' Corsi

Via del Campidoglio

Via del Fossi

Via del Moro

Piazza San Pancrazio

66

Via del Sole

78

24

Via delle Belle Donne

Via della Spada

Via de' Tornabuoni

Via de' Pescioni

53

68

Piazza degli Strozzi

Via degli Strozzi

Via de' Sassetti

Borgo d'Ognissanti

58

Via del Palchetti

57

Via della Vigna Nuova

26

70

Via Anselmi

Opera di Firenze (1.2km)

Piazza Carlo Goldoni

Piazza de' Rucellai

80

Via dell'Inferno

31

Via del Purgatorio

41

72

Piazza de' Davanzati

Ponte alla Carraia

Via Parioncino

Via del Parione

52

Via Porta Rossa

Piazza Santa Trinità

12

Via Monalda

22 38

Via delle Terme

Lungarno Corsini

37

Borgo SS Apostoli

Via del Fiordaliso

Piazza del Limbo

51

Piazza degli Scarlatti

Lungarno Guicciardini

Ponte Santa Trinità

Piazza de' Frescobaldi

Lungarno degli Acciaiuoli

60

Arno

Via Maffia

Via di Santo Spirito

Via Maggio

SANTO SPIRITO

Palazzo Frescobaldi

Borgo San Jacopo

Ponte Vecchio

N 0   200 m
0   0.1 miles

Tourist
Office

81

Piazza San
Lorenzo

Piazza
Brunelleschi

Via de' Ginori
Via Cavour

11

Via de' Gori

Via dei Servi

Palazzo
Pucci

Via del Castellaccio

Via de' Biffi

14

Via de' Pucci

Via de' Martelli

34

Borgo San Lorenzo

75

Via de' Servi

Via Bufalini

Via Ricasoli

55

Via F. Zanetti

Via de' Cerretani

40

8

Piazza di
Santa
Maria
Nuova

Cupola del
Brunelleschi 4

Museo dell'Opera
del Duomo

Piazza del
Cavallari

13

17

5
Duomo

SANTA
CROCE

Via dell'Olio

Via Roma

Piazza di
San Giovanni
Infopoint
Bigallo

Via dei Pecori

2 Campanile

Piazza del Duomo

Via del
Campanile

Via dei Pecori

76

Piazza del
Adimari

Via della Canonica

Piazza delle
Pallottole

Via dell'Oriuolo

Via de' Brunelleschi

Via de' Tosinghi

45

Via delle Oche

Piazza de
SS Benedetto

Via de' Medici

62

Via de' Cavaiuoli

Piazza del
Giglio

59

74

Piazza
Santa
Elisabetta

69

Via Santa
Margherita

56

39 33

49

Via del Corso

Borgo degli Albizi

27

Piazza
della
Repubblica

71

Via Speziali

Piazza
de' Donati

44

Via del Presto

Via Pellicceria

50

67

Via del Pandolfini

Via Orsanmichele

46

16

54

Piazza dei
Cimatori

Via Dante Alighieri

Via de'
Lamberti

Via Calimala

Via dell'Arte
della Lana

Via dei Cimatori

Via del Proconsolo

Piazza de'
Cerchi

21

Via de' Giraldi

Via Ghibellina

Via della
Vigna Vecchia

Via Porta Rossa

77

Via della Condotta

Piazza
San
Firenze

Via delle Burella

Via del
Panico

47

Via di Capaccio

Via
Calimaruzza

Via dell'Anguillara

Via Vaccherreccia

63

Piazza di
Santa
Cecilia

28

Piazza della
Signoria

19

18

32

Via de'Gondi

10 Palazzo
Vecchio

Borgo dei Greci

20

Piazza
Saltarelli

Via del Corno

Via della
Mosca

Amici degli Uffizi
Welcome Desk

Piazza del
Grano

Via Vinegia

61

Piazza di
San Remigio

Piazza de'
Rustici

Via del Pesce

65

Piazza
de' Santo
Stefano

Via de'Girolami

48

Via Georgofili

6

Galleria
degli
Uffizi

Piazza
Castellani

42

Via de' Neri

64

Via delle Brache

Via de' Bracci

Vic dell'Oro

Via Por-Santa-Maria

Via Lambertesca

Piazza
del Pesce

29

3 Corridoio
Vasariano

Piazza dei
Giudici

23

Via Castello d'Altafronte

Via Osteria del Guanto

the bronze bas-reliefs created for the baptistry doors competition by Brunelleschi and Ghiberti.

Yet it is Donatello's two versions of *David,* a favourite subject for sculptors, that really fascinate: Donatello fashioned his slender, youthful dressed image in marble in 1408 and his fabled bronze between 1439 and 1443. The latter is extraordinary – the more so when you consider it was the first free-standing naked statue to be sculpted since classical times.

Criminals received their last rites before execution in the palace's 1st-floor **Cappella del Podestà**, also known as the Mary Magdalene Chapel, where Hell and Heaven are frescoed on the walls, as are stories from the lives of Mary of Egypt, Mary Magdalene and John the Baptist. These remnants of frescoes by Giotto were not discovered until 1840,

The Duomo & Santa Maria Novella

when the chapel was turned into a store-room and prison.

The 2nd floor moves into the 16th century with a superb collection of terracotta pieces by the prolific della Robbia family, including some of their best-known works, such as Andrea's *Ritratto idealizia di fanciullo* (Bust of a Boy; c 1475) and Giovanni's *Pietà* (1514). Instantly recognisable, Giovanni's works are more elaborate and flamboyant than either father Luca's or cousin Andrea's, using a richer palette of colours.

👁 Piazza della Repubblica & Around

Piazza della Repubblica   PIAZZA
(Map p524) The site of a Roman forum and heart of medieval Florence, this busy civic space was created in the 1880s as part of a controversial plan of 'civic improvements' involving the demolition of the old market, Jewish ghetto and slums, and the relocation of nearly 6000 residents. Vasari's lovely Loggia del Pesce (Fish Market) was saved and re-erected on Via Pietrapiana.

Chiesa e Museo di Orsanmichele   CHURCH
(Map p524; www.bargellomusei.beniculturali.it; Via dell'Arte della Lana; ⊘church 10am-4.50pm daily, closed Mon Aug, museum 10am-4.50pm Mon, 10am-12.30pm Sat) **FREE** This unusual and inspirational church, with a Gothic tabernacle by Andrea Orcagna, was created when the arcades of an old grain market (1290) were walled in and two storeys added during the 14th century. Its exterior is decorated with niches and tabernacles bearing statues representing the patron saints of Florence's many guilds, commissioned in the 15th and 16th centuries after the *signoria* (city government) ordered the guilds to finance the church's decoration.

Via de' Tornabuoni   LANDMARK
(Map p524) Renaissance palaces and Italian fashion houses border Via de' Tornabuoni, the city's most expensive shopping strip. Named after a Florentine noble family (which died out in the 17th century), it is referred to as the 'Salotto di Firenze' (Florence's Drawing Room). At its northern end is the 1461–69 **Palazzo Antinori** (Piazza degli Antinori 3), owned by the aristocratic Antinori family (known for wine production) since 1506. Opposite, huge stone steps lead up to 17th-century **Chiesa dei Santi Michele e Gaetano** (Piazza degli Antinori; ⊘ 7.30am-7.30pm Tue-Sat, 8am-8pm Sun, 2-7pm Mon).

Palazzo Strozzi   GALLERY
(Map p524; 🎫055 264 51 55; www.palazzostrozzi.org; Piazza degli Strozzi; exhibition adult/reduced €12/4; ⊘10am-8pm Fri-Wed, to 11pm Thu; 👪) This 15th-century Renaissance mansion was built for wealthy merchant Filippo Strozzi, one of the Medici's major political and commercial rivals. It hosts exciting art exhibitions spanning all periods and genres – its contemporary art events are particularly sensational. There's always a buzz about the place, with fashionable Florentines milling around the elegant interior courtyard and lingering over drinks at **Strozzi Caffè** (🎫055 28 82 36; ⊘8am-1am Thu-Sat, to 9.30pm Sun-Wed; 🛜); during major exhibitions, grab a coffee to take away from here to enjoy while waiting in line.

Basilica di Santa Trinità   CHURCH
(Map p524; Piazza Santa Trinità; ⊘ 7am-noon & 4-7pm) **FREE** Built in Gothic style and later given a mannerist facade, this 14th-century church shelters some of the city's finest frescoes. Right of the main altar, paintings (1483–85) by Ghirlandaio depict the life of St Francis of Assisi through portraits of illustrious Florentines of the time in **Cappella Sassetti**, (pop €0.50 in the slot to illuminate the frescoes). In **Cappella Bartholini Salimbeni**, the gated side chapel, Lorenzo Monaco's *Annunciation* (1422) sits above the altar and wall frescoes illustrate the life of the Virgin Mary.

★ Museo di Palazzo Davanzati   MUSEUM
(Map p524; 🎫055 064 94 60; www.bargellomusei.beniculturali.it; Via Porta Rossa 13; adult/reduced €6/3; ⊘8.15am-2pm Mon-Fri, 1.15-7pm Sat & Sun) Home to the wealthy Davanzati merchant family from 1578, this 14th-century *palazzo* (mansion) with a wonderful central loggia gives you a view into precisely how Florentine nobles lived in the 16th century. Spot the carved faces of the original owners on the pillars in the inner courtyard, and don't miss the 1st-floor **Sala Madornale** (Reception Room) with its painted wooden ceiling, exotic **Sala dei Pappagalli** (Parrot Room) and **Camera dei Pavoni** (Peacock Bedroom).

The 2nd and 3rd floors of the palace can only be visited by guided tours that run at 10am, 11am and noon on weekdays and at 3pm, 4pm and 5pm during weekends; reservations (by telephone or online) are obligatory. Note the windows in the beautiful **Camera delle Impannate** are not made from glass – a luxury only nobles could afford in Renaissance Florence – but from waxed cloth panels tacked to the wooden frame. The kitchen is placed on the top floor, to ensure living rooms remained cool and free of unsavoury cooking odours and possible fires.

◉ Santa Maria Novella

★ **Basilica di Santa Maria Novella** BASILICA
(Map p524; ☏ 055 21 92 57; www.smn.it; Piazza di Santa Maria Novella 18; adult/reduced €7.50/5; ⊙ 9am-7pm Mon-Thu, 11am-7pm Fri, 9am-6.30pm Sat, noon-6.30pm Sun Jul & Aug, shorter hours rest of year) The striking green-and-white marble facade of 13th- to 15th-century Basilica di Santa Maria Novella fronts an entire monastical complex, comprising romantic church cloisters and a frescoed chapel. The basilica itself is a treasure chest of artistic masterpieces, climaxing with frescoes by Domenico Ghirlandaio. The lower section of the basilica's striped marbled facade is transitional from Romanesque to Gothic; the upper section and the main doorway (1456–70) were designed by Leon Battista Alberti. Book in advance online to avoid queues.

As you enter, look straight ahead to see Masaccio's superb fresco *Trinità* (Holy Trinity; 1424–25), one of the first artworks to use the then newly discovered techniques of perspective and proportion. Hanging in the central nave is a luminous painted *Crucifix* by Giotto (c 1290).

The monumental main altar, **Altare Maggiore** (1858-61), sits within the **Cappella Maggiore**, which is decorated with frescoes by Domenico Ghirlandaio. Those on the right depict the life of John the Baptist; those on the left illustrate scenes from the life of the Virgin Mary. The frescoes were painted between 1485 and 1490, and are notable for their depiction of Florentine life during the Renaissance. Spot portraits of Ghirlandaio's contemporaries and members of the Tornabuoni family, who commissioned them.

The first chapel to the right of the altar, **Cappella di Filippo Strozzi**, features spirited late-15th-century frescoes by Filippino Lippi (son of Fra' Filippo Lippi) depicting the lives of St John the Evangelist and St Philip the Apostle.

To the far left of the altar, up a short flight of stairs in the western transept, is the **Cappella Strozzi di Mantova**, covered in 14th-century frescoes by Niccolò di Tommaso and Nardo di Cione depicting paradise, purgatory and hell. The altarpiece (1354–57) here was painted by the latter's brother Andrea, better known as Andrea Orcagna.

From the church, walk through a side door into the serene **Chiostro Verde** (Green Cloister; 1332–62), part of the vast monastical complex occupied by Dominican friars who arrived in Florence in 1219 and settled in Santa Maria Novella two years later. The tranquil cloister takes its name from the green earth base used for the frescoes on three of the cloister's four walls. On its north side is the spectacular **Cappellone degli Spagnoli** (Spanish Chapel), originally the friars' chapter house and named as such in 1566 when it was given to the Spanish colony in Florence. The chapel is covered in extraordinary frescoes (c 1365–67) by Andrea di Bonaiuto. The vault features depictions of the *Resurrection, Ascension* and *Pentecost,* and on the altar wall are scenes of the *Via Dolorosa, Crucifixion* and *Descent into Limbo.* On the right wall is a huge fresco of *The Militant and Triumphant Church* – look in the foreground for a portrait of Cimabue, Giotto, Boccaccio, Petrarch and Dante. Other frescoes in the chapels depict the *Triumph of Christian Doctrine,* 14 figures symbolising the arts and sciences, and the Life of St Peter.

By the side of the chapel, a passage leads into the **Chiostro dei Morti** (Cloister of the Dead), an atmospheric vaulted-cloister cemetery existent well before the arrival of the Dominicans to Santa Maria Novella. The tombstones embedded in the walls and floor date from the 13th and 14th centuries, a period when wealthy Florentine families assumed patronage of the tiny chapels here.

Head back to the Chiostro Verde and enter the passageway on the western (left) side of the cloister to access the 14th-century **Cappella degli Ubriachi** and vast **Refettorio** (Refectory; 1353–54) featuring a 1583 *Last Supper* by Alessandro Allori. These two rooms form a small museum displaying sacred treasures and ecclesiastical relics from the Santa Maria complex – including brilliantly restored frescoes of the Garden of Eden, originally in the Chiostro Verde, by Paolo Uccello (1397–1475).

Backtrack through the museum to end in the magnificently frescoed **Chiostro Grande** (Great Cloister; 1340–60), so named because of its majestic size; the crests of the wealthy Florentine families who helped pay for the cloister's sweep of 56 arches are carved on pillars in the loggia. On the cloister's northern side, admire the sweep of cross-vaults in the **Dormitorio Settentrionale** (Northern Dormitory). A staircase in the cloister's northwest corner leads to the

GREEN ESCAPES

Founded in 1545 to furnish medicine to the Medici, Florence's botanical garden **Giardino dei Semplici** (Orto Botanico; Map p530; Via Pier Antonio Micheli 3; adult/reduced €6/3; ⏰10am-7pm Thu-Tue summer, to 4pm Sat & Sun winter) – managed today by the university – is a wonderfully peaceful retreat in a stretch of the city with little green space. Its greenhouse is fragrant with citrus blossoms, and its 2.3 hectares are peppered with medicinal plants, Tuscan spices, 220 tree types and wildflowers from the Apennines. Don't miss the magnificent yew tree, planted in 1720, and an ornamental cork oak from 1805. Several themed footpaths wend their way through the gardens.

Across the river, behind high walls, lies the vast 'secret' garden of **Giardino Torrigiani** (Map p536; ☎055 22 45 27; www.giardinotorrigiani.it; Via de' Serragli 144; 1½hr guided tours by donation; ✉advance reservation via email) – Europe's largest privately owned green space within a historic centre. Designed at the height of the Romantic movement in the early 19th century, the idyllic oasis of green wrapped around the original 16th-century villa and subsequent early-19th-century house includes rare tree species, wide English-style lawns, herb and vegetables gardens, sculpted lions, a beautifully restored greenhouse, and remains of city walls built under Cosimo I in 1544.

exquisite **Cappella del Papa** (Papal Chapel; accessible only by guided tour), a chapel built to commemorate a visit by Medici pope Leo X to Florence in 1515. The wall fresco of Saint Veronica by Jacopo Carucci (better known as Pontormo) is one of the finest examples of 16th-century Florentine painting.

There are two entrances to the Santa Maria Novella complex: the main entrance to the basilica or through the tourist office (p550) opposite the train station on Piazza della Stazione (which brings you directly into the Chiostro dei Morti).

City-run **Mus.e** (☎055 276 85 58, 055 276 82 24; www.musefirenze.it; tours & activities €4; ⏰reservations 9.30am-1pm & 2.30-5pm Mon-Sat, 9.30am-12.30pm Sun) offers fantastic guided tours (€5, 1¼ hours) in English of both the basilica complex in general and Cappella del Papa; reserve in advance online or by phone.

⭐ **Museo Novecento** MUSEUM
(Museum of the 20th Century; Map p524; ☎055 28 61 32; www.museonovecento.it; Piazza di Santa Maria Novella 10; adult/reduced €9.50/4.50; ⏰11am-8pm Sat-Wed, to 2pm Thu, to 11pm Fri summer, 11am-7pm Fri-Wed, to 2pm Thu winter) Don't allow the Renaissance to distract you from Florence's fantastic modern art museum, at home in a 13th-century pilgrim shelter, hospital and school. A well-articulated itinerary guides visitors through modern Italian painting and sculpture from the early 20th century to the late 1980s. Installation art makes effective use of the outside space on the 1st-floor loggia. Fashion and theatre also get a nod, and the itinerary ends with a 20-minute cinematic montage of the best films set in Florence.

A highlight of Room 10 is Arturo Martini's exquisite sculpture *La Pisana* (1933), next to one of Marino Marini's signature bronze horses – both representative of the archaeological rediscovery of the ancient world expressed by artists in Italy in the 1920s and 1930s.

Captivating family-orientated guided tours and activities for children from age four upwards (€4) cap off the museum's first-class portfolio. Tours are run by Mus.e; reserve in advance by email or phone, or in situ directly at the museum or at the ticket desk inside Palazzo Vecchio (p522).

Museo Marino Marini GALLERY
(Map p524; ☎055 21 94 32; www.museomarinomarini.it; Piazza San Pancrazio 1; chapel adult/reduced €6/4; ⏰10am-7pm Sat-Mon, by online reservation only Tue-Fri) Deconsecrated in the 19th century, Chiesa di San Pancrazio is home to this small art museum displaying sculptures by Pistoia-born sculptor Marino Marini (1901–80) intertwined with various contemporary art exhibits (free admission). But the highlight is **Cappella Rucellai** with a tiny scale copy of Christ's Holy Sepulchre in Jerusalem – a Renaissance gem by Leon Battista Alberti. The chapel was built between 1458 and 1467 for the tomb of wealthy Florentine banker and wool merchant Giovanni Rucellai.

👁 San Lorenzo

⭐ **Museo delle Cappelle Medicee** MAUSOLEUM
(Medici Chapels; Map p524; ☎055 064 94 30; www.bargellomusei.beniculturali.it/musei/2/medicee; Piazza Madonna degli Aldobrandini 6; adult/

San Lorenzo & San Marco

San Lorenzo & San Marco

reduced €9/2; ⊙8.15am-2pm, closed 2nd & 4th Sun, 1st, 3rd & 5th Mon of month) Nowhere is Medici conceit expressed so explicitly as in the Medici Chapels. Adorned with granite, marble, semiprecious stones and some of Michelangelo's most beautiful sculptures, it is the burial place of 49 dynasty members. Francesco I lies in the dark, imposing **Cappella dei Principi** (Chapel of Princes) alongside Ferdinando I and II and Cosimo I, II and III. Lorenzo Il Magnifico is buried in the graceful **Sagrestia Nuova** (New Sacristy), which was Michelangelo's first architectural work.

It is also in the sacristy that you can swoon over three of Michelangelo's most haunting sculptures: *Dawn and Dusk* on the sarcophagus of Lorenzo, Duke of Urbino; *Night and Day* on the sarcophagus of Lorenzo's son Giuliano (note the unfinished face of 'Day' and the youth of the sleeping woman drenched in light aka 'Night'); and *Madonna and Child,* which adorns Lorenzo's tomb. Since 2019 clever lighting recreates the soft, indirect sunlight Michelangelo originally intended to illuminate his work.

★**Basilica di San Lorenzo**   BASILICA
(Map p524; ☎055 21 40 42; www.operamedicea laurenziana.org; Piazza San Lorenzo; €7, with Biblioteca Medicea Laurenziana €9.50; ⊙10am-5.30pm Mon-Sat) Considered one of Florence's most harmonious examples of Renaissance architecture, this unfinished basilica was the Medici parish church and mausoleum. It was designed by Brunelleschi in 1425 for Cosimo the Elder and built over a 4th-century church. In the solemn interior, look for Brunelleschi's austerely beautiful **Sagrestia Vecchia** (Old Sacristy) with its sculptural decoration by Donatello. Michelangelo was commissioned to design the facade in 1518, but his design in white Carrara marble was never executed, hence the building's rough, unfinished appearance.

Inside, columns of *pietra serena* (soft grey stone) crowned with Corinthian capitals separate the nave from the two aisles. The gilded funerary monument of Donatello – who was still sculpting the two bronze pulpits (1460–67) adorned with panels of the Crucifixion when he died – lies in the

Cappella Martelli (Martelli Chapel) featuring Fra' Filippo Lippi's exquisitely restored *Annunciation* (c 1440).

Donatello's actual grave lies in the basilica crypt, today part of the Museo del Tesoro di San Lorenzo (San Lorenzo Treasury Museum); the crypt entrance is in the courtyard beyond the ticket office. The museum displays chalices, altarpieces, dazzling altar cloths, processional crucifixes, episcopal brooches and other precious sacred treasures once displayed in the church. Across from the plain marble tombstone of Donatello is the tomb of Cosimo the Elder, buried inside the quadrangular pilaster in the crypt supporting the basilica presbytery – his funerary monument sits directly above, in front of the high altar in the basilica.

Biblioteca Medicea Laurenziana   LIBRARY
(Medici Library; Map p524; ☑ 055 293 79 11; www.bml.firenze.sbn.it; Piazza San Lorenzo 9; €3, incl Basilica di San Lorenzo €8.50; ⊗ 9.30am-1.30pm Mon-Fri) Beyond the Basilica di San Lorenzo ticket office lie peaceful cloisters framing a garden with orange trees. Stairs lead up the loggia to the Biblioteca Medicea Laurenziana, commissioned by Giulio de' Medici (Pope Clement VII) in 1524 to house the extensive Medici library (started by Cosimo the Elder and greatly added to by Lorenzo Il Magnifico). The extraordinary staircase in the vestibule, intended as a 'dark prelude' to the magnificent Sala di Lettura (Reading Room), was designed by Michelangelo.

◉ San Marco

★**Galleria dell'Accademia**   GALLERY
(Map p530; ☑ 055 098 71 00; www.galleriaaccademiafirenze.beniculturali.it; Via Ricasoli 58/60; adult/reduced €12/2; ⊗ 8.15am-6.50pm Tue-Sun) A queue marks the door to this gallery, built to house one of the Renaissance's most iconic masterpieces, Michelangelo's *David*. But the world's most famous statue is worth the wait. The subtle detail – the veins in his sinewy arms, the leg muscles, the change in expression as you move around the statue – *is* impressive. Carved from a single block of marble, Michelangelo's most famous work was his most challenging – he didn't choose the marble himself and it was veined.

And when the statue of the nude boy-warrior, depicted for the first time as a man in the prime of life rather than a young boy, assumed its pedestal in front of Palazzo Vecchio on Piazza della Signoria in 1504, Florentines immediately adopted it as a powerful emblem of Florentine power, liberty and civic pride.

Michelangelo was also the master behind the unfinished *San Matteo* (St Matthew; 1504–08) and four *Prigioni* ('Prisoners' or 'Slaves'; 1521–30), also displayed in the gallery. The prisoners seem to be writhing and struggling to free themselves from the marble; they were meant for the tomb of Pope Julius II, itself never completed. Adjacent rooms contain paintings by Andrea Orcagna, Taddeo Gaddi, Domenico Ghirlandaio, Filippino Lippi and Sandro Botticelli.

★**Museo di San Marco**   MUSEUM
(Map p530; ☑ 055 238 86 08; Piazza San Marco 3; adult/reduced €8/2; ⊗ 8.15am-1.50pm Mon-Fri, to 4.50pm Sat & Sun, closed 1st, 3rd & 5th Sun, 2nd & 4th Mon of month) At the heart of Florence's university area sits Chiesa di San Marco and an adjoining 15th-century Dominican monastery where both gifted painter Fra' Angelico (c 1395–1455) and the sharp-tongued Savonarola piously served God. Today the monastery, aka one of Florence's most spiritually uplifting museums, showcases the work of Fra' Angelico. After centuries of being known as 'Il Beato Angelico' (literally 'The Blessed Angelic One') or simply 'Il Beato' (The Blessed), the Renaissance's most blessed religious painter was made a saint by Pope John Paul II in 1984.

Enter via Michelozzo's Chiostro di Sant' Antonio (St Antoninus Cloister; 1440). Turn immediately right to enter the Sala dell'Ospizio dei Pellegrini (Pilgrims' Hospital Hall) where Fra' Angelico's attention to perspective and the realistic portrayal of nature come to life in a number of major paintings, including the *Deposition from the Cross* (1432).

Giovanni Antonio Sogliani's fresco *The Miraculous Supper of St Dominic* (1536) dominates the former monks' Refettorio (Refectory) in the cloister. Fra' Angelico's huge *Crucifixion and Saints* fresco (1441–42), featuring all the patron saints of the convent and city, plus the Medici family who commissioned the fresco, decorates the former Capitolo (Chapterhouse). But it is the 44 monastic cells on the 1st floor that are the most haunting: at the top of the stairs, Fra' Angelico's most famous work, *Annunciation* (c 1440), commands all eyes.

A stroll around each of the cells reveals snippets of many more religious reliefs by the Tuscan-born friar, who decorated the cells between 1440 and 1441 with deeply devotional frescoes to guide the meditation of his fellow friars. Most were completed by

Santa Croce

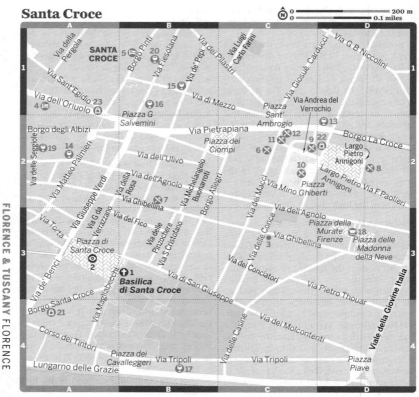

Fra' Angelico himself, with others by aides under his supervision, including Benozzo Gozzoli. Among several masterpieces is the magnificent *Adoration of the Magi* in the cell used by Cosimo the Elder as a meditation retreat (Nos 38 to 39); only 10 people can visit at a time. The frescoes in the cell of San Antonino Arcivescovo (neighbouring Fra' Angelico's *Annunciation*) are gruesome: they show Jesus pushing open the door of his sepulchre, squashing a nasty-looking devil in the process.

Contrasting with the pure beauty of these frescoes are the plain rooms (Cell VI) that Savonarola called home from 1489. Rising to the position of prior at the Dominican convent, it was from here that the fanatical monk railed against luxury, greed and corruption of the clergy. Kept as a kind of shrine to the turbulent priest, the three small rooms house a portrait, a few personal items, fragments of the black cape and white tunic Savonarola wore, his rosary beads and the linen banner

he carried in processions, and a grand marble monument erected by admirers in 1873.

★ **Museo degli Innocenti**   MUSEUM
(Map p530; ☑ 055 203 73 08; www.museodegl innocenti.it; Piazza della Santissima Annunziata 13; adult/reduced €7/5; ☉10am-7pm) Shortly after its founding in 1421, Brunelleschi designed the loggia for Florence's **Ospedale degli Innocenti**, a foundling hospital and Europe's first orphanage, built by the wealthy silk-weavers' guild to care for unwanted children. Inside, a highly emotive, state-of-the-art museum explores its history, climaxing with a sensational collection of frescoes and artworks that once decorated the hospital and a stunning rooftop-cafe terrace (fab city views). Brunelleschi's use of rounded arches and Roman capitals marks it as arguably the first building of the Renaissance.

Andrea della Robbia (1435–1525) added the facade's distinctive terracotta medallions of infants in swaddling clothes.

Santa Croce

In 1445 the first unwanted baby (female, as was commonly the case at the time) was found abandoned on the hospital's doorstep; by the end of the 15th century it was home to over 1000 children. In the 16th century, such was the demand that the hospital replaced the *pila* (a concave stone on which infants were left) with a revolving door in which newborns could be left in relative warmth. On display are the various sentimental objects that often appeared with a foundling – coins, rosary beads, a crucifix, ribbons, one half of a broken medal allowing parents to later identify their child. From 1667 the hospital also accepted young mothers as wet nurses, and by the mid-19th-century the orphanage was accepting 2000 unwanted children a year.

No museum visit is complete without a drink in the rooftop cafe, **Caffè del Verone** (Map p530; ☎ 392 4982559; www.facebook.com/CaffedelVeroneRooftopFlorence; ◷ 8.30am-7pm Mon, to 9pm Tue-Sat, 9am-7pm Sun; ☏), at home in the foundling hospital's *verone* (drying room) where linen was stretched and hung to dry in the 15th century.

Cenacolo di Sant'Apollonia CONVENT
(Map p530; ☎ 055 238 86 07; www.polomusealetoscana.beniculturali.it; Via XXVII Aprile 1; ◷ 8.15am-1.50pm daily, closed 1st, 3rd & 5th Sat & Sun of month) **FREE** Once part of a sprawling Benedictine monastery, this *cenacolo* (refectory) harbours arguably the city's most remarkable *Last Supper* scene. Painted by Andrea del Castagno in the 1440s, it is one of the first works of its kind to effectively apply Renaissance perspective. It possesses a haunting power with its vivid colours – espe-

cially the almost abstract squares of marble painted above the apostles' heads – as well as the dark, menacing figure of Judas.

◎ Santa Croce

Piazza di Santa Croce PIAZZA
(Map p532) This square was cleared in the Middle Ages to allow the faithful to gather when the church itself was full. In Savonarola's day, heretics were executed here. Such an open space inevitably found other uses, and from the 14th century it was often the colourful scene of jousts, festivals and *calcio storico* (historic football) matches. The city's 2nd-century amphitheatre took up the area facing the square's western end: Piazza dei Peruzzi, Via de' Bentaccordi and Via Torta mark the oval outline of its course.

★ **Basilica di Santa Croce** BASILICA
(Map p532; ☎ 055 246 61 05; www.santacroceopera.it; Piazza di Santa Croce 16; adult/reduced €8/6; ◷ 9.30am-5.30pm Mon-Sat, from 2pm Sun) The austere interior of this Franciscan basilica is a shock after the magnificent neo-Gothic facade enlivened by varying shades of coloured marble. Most visitors come to see the tombs of Michelangelo, Galileo and Ghiberti, but frescoes by Giotto in the chapels to the right of the altar are the real highlights. The basilica was designed by Arnolfo di Cambio between 1294 and 1385 and owes its name to a splinter of the Holy Cross donated by King Louis IX of France in 1258.

Fondazione Zeffirelli MUSEUM
(Map p524; ☎ 055 265 84 35; www.fondazionefrancozeffirelli.com; Piazza San Firenze 5; adult/reduced

€10/7; ⊙10am-6pm Tue-Sun) Opera buffs will adore this museum celebrating more than seven decades of work by the late, internationally renowned, Florence-born film director Franco Zeffirelli (1923–2019). Housed in the San Firenze Complex, a magnificent late-Baroque *palazzo* which previously served as the city's tribunal and courthouse (until it moved out of the historic centre to Novoli), the exhibition begins in 1953 and spans 20 'chapters' or rooms. Admire scene sketches, costumes, posters, flyers, set-design models, original drawings and behind-the-scenes photographs. The exquisite, ground-floor music room hosts occasional chamber-music concerts and film screenings.

◉ Oltrarno

Ponte Vecchio   BRIDGE

(Map p524) Dating from 1345, iconic Ponte Vecchio was the only Florentine bridge to survive destruction at the hands of retreating German forces in 1944. Above jewellery shops on the eastern side, Corridoio Vasariano (p523) is a 16th-century passageway between the Uffizi and Palazzo Pitti that runs around, rather than through, medieval Torre dei Mannelli at the bridge's southern end.

The first documentation of a stone bridge here, at the narrowest crossing point along the entire length of the Arno, dates from 972.

Floods in 1177 and 1333 destroyed the bridge, and in 1966 it came close to being destroyed again. Many of the jewellers with shops on the bridge were convinced the floodwaters would sweep away their livelihoods; fortunately the bridge held.

They're still here. Indeed, the bridge has twinkled with the glittering wares of jewellers, their trade often passed down from generation to generation, ever since the 16th century, when Ferdinando I de' Medici ordered them here to replace the often malodorous presence of the town butchers, who used to toss unwanted leftovers into the river.

★ Cappella Brancacci   CHAPEL

(Map p536; ☑ 055 238 21 95; www.museicivici fiorentini.comune.fi.it; Piazza del Carmine 14; adult/reduced Wed-Fri €8/6, Sat-Mon €10/7; ⊙10am-5pm Wed-Sat & Mon, 1-5pm Sun) Fire in the 18th century practically destroyed 13th-century Basilica di Santa Maria del Carmine (⊙6.15am-noon & 5-6.45pm Mon-Sat, 9.15am-1pm & 5-7pm Sun), but it spared its magnificent chapel frescoes – a treasure of paintings by Masolino da Panicale, Masaccio and Filippino Lippi commissioned by rich merchant

Felice Brancacci upon his return from Egypt in 1423. The chapel entrance is right of the main church entrance. Only 30 people can visit at a time, limited to 30 minutes in high season; pricier weekend tickets include admission to the Fondazione Salvatore Romano (Cenacolo di Santo Spirito; ☑ 055 28 70 43; Piazza Santo Spirito 29; adult/reduced €10/7; ⊙10am-4pm Sat-Mon).

★ Basilica di Santo Spirito   CHURCH

(Map p536; www.basilicasantospirito.it; Piazza Santo Spirito; ⊙8.30am-1pm & 3-6pm Mon, Tue & Thu-Sat, 11.30am-1.30pm & 3-6pm Sun) The facade of this Brunelleschi church, smart on Florence's most shabby-chic piazza, makes a striking backdrop to open-air concerts in summer. Inside, the basilica's length is lined with 38 semicircular chapels (covered with a plain wall in the 1960s), and a colonnade of grey *pietra forte* Corinthian columns injects monumental grandeur. Artworks to look for include Domenico di Zanobi's *Madonna of the Relief* (1485) in the Cappella Velutti, in which the Madonna wards off a little red devil with a club.

★ Palazzo Pitti   MUSEUM

(Map p536; ☑ 055 29 48 83; www.uffizi.it/en/pitti -palace; Piazza dei Pitti; adult/reduced Mar-Oct €16/8, Nov-Feb €10/5, combined ticket with Uffizi incl Giardino di Boboli Mar-Oct €38/21, Nov-Feb €18/11; ⊙8.15am-6.50pm Tue-Sun) Commissioned by banker Luca Pitti in 1458, this Renaissance palace was later bought by the Medici family. Over the centuries, it was a residence of the city's rulers until the Savoys donated it to the state in 1919. Nowadays it houses an impressive collection of silver and jewellery, a couple of art museums and a series of rooms recreating life in the palace during House of Savoy times. Stop by at sunset when its entire facade is coloured a vibrant pink.

★ Giardino di Boboli   GARDENS

(Map p536; ☑ 055 29 48 83; www.uffizi.it/en/ boboli-garden; Piazza dei Pitti; adult/reduced incl Giardino Bardini & Museo delle Porcellane Mar-Oct €10/2, Nov-Feb €6/2, combined ticket with Uffizi incl Palazzo Pitti Mar-Oct €38/21, Nov-Feb €18/11; ⊙8.15am-6.50pm summer, reduced hours winter, closed 1st & last Mon of month) Behind Palazzo Pitti, the fountain- and sculpture-adorned Boboli Gardens – slowly but surely being restored to their former pristine glory thanks to a €2 million investment by Florence's homegrown fashion house Gucci – were laid out in the mid-16th century to a design by architect Niccolò Pericoli. At the upper, southern limit, beyond the box-hedged rose

STREET ART

Take a break from Renaissance art with some urban street art. Exhibitions at the **Street Levels Gallery** (Map p524; ☑ 339 2203607; https://street-level-gallery.business.site; Via Palazzuolo 74r; ⊙3-7pm Tue-Sat) showcase the work of local artists, including the stencil art of Hogre, and Exit Enter whose work is easily recognisable by the red balloons holding up the matchstick figures he draws. A highlight is the enigmatic Blub, whose caricatures of historical figures wearing goggles and diving masks adorn many a city wall – his art is known as L'Arte Sa Nuotare (Art Knows how to Swim).

Should you notice something gone awry with street signs in Oltrarno – on a No Entry sign, a tiny black figure stealthily sneaking away with the white bar for example – you can be sure it is the work of French-born Clet Abraham, one of Florence's most popular street artists. In his Oltrarno **studio** (Map p511; ☑ 339 2203607, 347 3387760; Via dell'Olmo 8r; ⊙hours vary) you can buy stickers, postcards, T-shirts and tote bags featuring his hacked traffic signs and, if you're lucky, catch a glimpse of the rebellious artist at work.

Should you want your own little piece of Florence street art, head to Mio Concept (p549) for postcards, prints and the occasional, limited edition Clet street sign.

garden and **Museo delle Porcellane** (Porcelain Museum), beautiful views over the Florentine countryside unfold. Within the lower reaches of the gardens, don't miss the fantastical shell- and gem-encrusted **Grotta del Buontalenti**.

Villa e Giardino Bardini
GARDENS

(Map p536; ☑ 055 2006 6233; www.villabardini.it; Costa San Giorgio 2, Via de' Bardi 1r; adult/reduced villa €10/5, gardens €6/3, gardens with Giardino di Boboli ticket free; ⊙villa 10am-7pm Tue-Sun, gardens 8.15am-7.30pm summer, shorter hours winter, closed 1st & last Mon of month) This 17th-century villa and garden was named after the 19th-century antiquarian art collector Stefano Bardini (1836–1922), who bought it in 1913 and restored its ornamental medieval garden. It has all the features of a quintessential Tuscan garden, including artificial grottoes, orangery, marble statues and fountains. Inside the villa, the small **Museo Pietro Annigoni** displays works by Italian painter Pietro Annigoni (1910–88). End with city views from the romantic roof terrace.

Piazzale Michelangelo
VIEWPOINT

(Map p511; ☑13) Turn your back on the bevy of ticky-tacky souvenir stalls flogging *David* statues and boxer shorts and take in the spectacular city panorama from this vast square, pierced by one of Florence's two *David* copies. Sunset here is particularly dramatic. It's a 10-minute uphill walk along the serpentine road, paths and steps that scale the hillside from the Arno and Piazza Giuseppe Poggi; from Piazza San Niccolò walk uphill and bear left up the long flight of steps signposted Viale Michelangelo. Or take bus 13 from Stazione di Santa Maria Novella.

Torre San Niccolò
GATE

(Map p511; ☑ 055 276 85 58, 055 276 82 24; www.musefirenze.it; Piazza Giuseppe Poggi; guided visit every 30min €4; ⊙5-8pm late Jun-late Sep) Built in 1324, the best preserved of the city's medieval gates stands sentinel on the banks of the Arno. In summer, with a guide you can scale the steep stairs inside the tower to enjoy blockbuster river and city views. Visits organised by Mus.e (p529) are limited to 15 people at a time (no children under eight years) and advance reservations are essential; book online, by email or by phone. Tours are cancelled when it rains.

Behind the city gate a monumental staircase designed by Giuseppe Poggi winds its way up towards **Basilica di San Miniato al Monte** (Map p511; ☑ 055 234 27 31; www.sanminiatoalmonte.it; Via Monte alle Croci; ⊙9.30am-1pm & 3-7.30pm summer, to 7pm winter) **FREE**.

Forte di Belvedere
FORTRESS

(Map p511; Via di San Leonardo 1; ⊙hours vary) **FREE** Forte di Belvedere is a rambling fort designed by Bernardo Buontalenti for Grand Duke Ferdinando I at the end of the 16th century. From the massive bulwark, soldiers kept watch on four fronts – as much for internal security as to protect the Palazzo Pitti against foreign attack. Today the fort hosts summertime art exhibitions, which are well worth a peek if only to revel in the sweeping city panorama that can be had from the fort. Outside of exhibition times, the fort is closed.

🏃 Activities

Cooking, paddling along the Arno or indulging in a morning jog along its grassy riverbanks, up narrow stone-walled lanes to

The Oltrarno

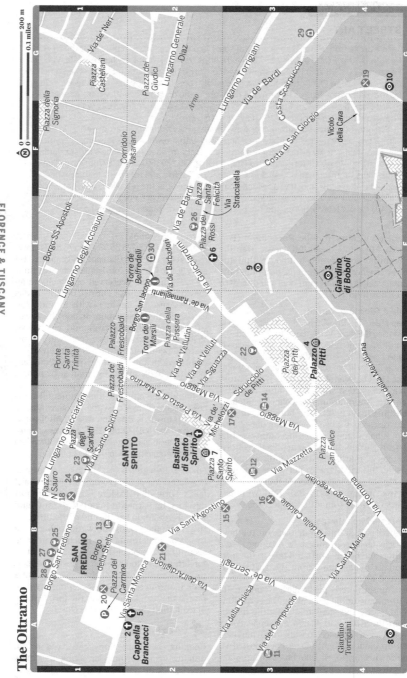

The Oltrarno

FLORENCE & TUSCANY FLORENCE

San Miniato al Monte or in city park **Parco delle Cascine** (Map p511; Viale degli Olmi) is as active as most Florentines get.

★**Urban Beach** BEACH
(Map p511; ☑ 055 234 11 12; www.easylivingfirenze. it; Piazza Giuseppe Poggi; ☺May-Sep) Be it relaxing beneath a parasol on a sun-lounger, playing beach volleyball or joining a sunset yoga class, Florence's sandy riverside beach is the place to be in summer. Run by the creative folks behind the neighbouring Easy Living (p547) kiosk, Urban Beach rocks with a buoyant crowd quaffing cocktails at the bar and snacking on salads and *panini* using organic products.

★**Firenze Rafting** RAFTING
(☑ 349 0921540; www.firenzerafting.it; €25; ☺Mar-Nov) View Ponte Vecchio, the Uffizi and other Florence landmarks from a different perspective – afloat a sturdy inflatable raft on the Arno. Trips, departing from the riverbanks across the Torre San Niccolò in the Oltrarno, last two hours and include an aperitif beneath the arches of Ponte Vecchio.

The same company can also organise SUP (stand-up paddleboard) and kayaking trips on the river.

Relax Firenze HEALTH & FITNESS
(Map p524; ☑ 055 28 46 83; www.relaxfirenze.com; Via degli Strozzi 2; ☺9am-8pm Mon-Fri, 10.30am-7pm Sat) This small-but-lovely spa overlooks Piazza della Repubblica. The soothing massages (€70/100 for 60/90 minutes), yoga and tai chi classes (€20) – not to mention the

invigorating Himalayan salt room (€25 for 40 minutes) and other wellness treatments – offered are, quite frankly, heaven on earth after a long day spent pounding the city's crowded cobbled streets. Advance reservations are essential.

☞ Tours

Curious Appetite TOURS
(☑ 391 4005956; www.curiousappetitetravel.com; 3hr group tour per person €85) Personalised bespoke and small-group culinary tours and tastings led by Italian-American Coral Sisk and her team of knowledgeable guides, most of whom are trained sommeliers too. Tours are themed: at the market, *aperitivi,* Italian food and wine pairings, 'dinner crawl', gelato etc. Cocktail lessons too with a Florentine mixologist.

500 Touring Club DRIVING
(☑ 346 8262324; www.500touringclub.com; Via Gherardo Silvani 149a) Hook up with Florence's 500 Touring Club for a guided tour in a vintage motor – with you behind the wheel! Every car has a name in this outfit's fleet of gorgeous vintage Fiat 500s from the 1960s. Motoring tours are guided (hop in your car and follow the leader) and themed – families love the picnic trip, couples the wine tasting.

Tuscany Bike Tours CYCLING
(Map p532; ☑ 339 1163495, 055 386 02 53; www. tuscany-biketours.com; Via Ghibellina 34r) Cycling tours in and around Florence, including a 2½-hour city bike tour with gelato break (adult/reduced €39/35) and a

full-day bike ride into the Chianti hills (adult/reduced €85/75). For the less energetic, consider a Chianti day trip by Audrey Hepburn–style scooter (adult/reduced/passenger €130/120/95, including lunch, castle visit and wine or olive-oil tasting) or Fiat 500 (driver/passenger €150/90, including lunch). Bike hire too.

Festivals & Events

Festa di Anna Maria Medici   CULTURAL
(⊙18 Feb) Florence's Feast of Anna Maria Medici marks the death in 1743 of the last Medici, Anna Maria Luisa de' Medici, with a costumed parade from Palazzo Vecchio to her tomb in the Cappelle Medicee.

Scoppio del Carro   FIREWORKS
(⊙Mar/Apr) A cart of fireworks is exploded in front of the cathedral on Piazza del Duomo at 11am on Easter Sunday.

Maggio Musicale Fiorentino   PERFORMING ARTS
(www.maggiofiorentino.com; ⊙Apr-Jun) Italy's oldest arts festival features world-class performances of theatre, classical music, jazz, opera and dance. Events are staged at the **Teatro del Maggio Musicale Fiorentino** (Map p511; ☑ 055 200 12 78; Piazzale Vittorio Gui 1; ⊙box office 10am-6pm Mon-Sat) and other key venues across the city.

Festa di San Giovanni   RELIGIOUS
(⊙24 Jun) Florence celebrates its patron saint, John, with a *calcio storico* (historic football) match on Piazza di Santa Croce and fireworks over Piazzale Michelangelo.

Sleeping

Florence is unexpectedly small, rendering almost anywhere in the city centre convenient. Advance reservations are essential between Easter and September, winter ushers in some great deals for visitors.

Duomo & Piazza della Signoria

Hotel Cestelli   HOTEL €
(Map p524; ☑ 055 21 42 13; www.hotelcestelli.com; Borgo SS Apostoli 25; d €100, s/d without bathroom €60/80; ⊙closed 2 weeks Jan & 10 days Aug; ⊛) Housed in a 12th-century *palazzo* a stiletto strut from fashionable Via de' Tornabuoni, this intimate eight-room hotel is a gem. Rooms reveal an understated style, tastefully combining polished antiques with spangly chandeliers, vintage art and silk screens. Owners Alessio and Asumi are a mine of local information and are happy to share their

knowledge. No breakfast. Ask about low-season discounts for longer stays.

★**Hotel Scoti**   PENSION €€
(Map p524; ☑ 055 29 21 28; www.hotelscoti.com; Via de' Tornabuoni 7; d/tr €140/165; ⊛) Wedged between designer boutiques on Florence's smartest shopping strip, this hidden *pensione* is a fab mix of old-fashioned charm and value for money. Its traditionally styled rooms are spread across the 2nd floor of a 16th-century *palazzo;* some have lovely rooftop views. Guests can borrow hairdryers, bottle openers etc and the frescoed lounge (1780) is stunning. Optional breakfast €5 extra.

★**Hotel Davanzati**   HOTEL €€
(Map p524; ☑ 055 28 66 66; www.hoteldavanzati. it; Via Porta Rossa 5; s/d from €140/229; ⊛@⊛) Twenty-six steps lead up to this family-run hotel. A labyrinth of enchanting rooms, frescoes and modern comforts, it oozes charm – as do Florentine brothers Tommaso and Riccardo, and father Fabrizio, who run the show. Rooms come with a mini iPad (meaning free wi-fi around town), direct messaging with the hotel, handy digital city guide and complimentary access to a nearby gym.

Hotel Pendini   HISTORIC HOTEL €€
(Map p524; ☑ 055 2 11 17; www.hotelpendini.it; Via degli Strozzi 2; d €120-205; ⊛@⊛) Very much part of city history, the Pendini opened in 1879 as an upmarket *pensione* – hence the giant 'Pensione Pendini' lettering dominating its privileged facade on Piazza della Repubblica. Its 44 comfortable rooms are up-to-the-minute, with polished parquet floors, antique furnishings, and beautiful floral fabrics and wallpapers. Historic B&W photographs adorn the corridors and classical music plays in the enchanting, vintage-styled lounge.

Hotel Perseo   HOTEL €€
(Map p524; ☑ 055 21 25 04; www.hotelperseo.it; Via de' Cerretani 1; s €160, d €181-195, tr €230-256, q €256-299; ⊛@⊛) Perseo is a perfect family choice with its 25 rooms, comfy lounge, Scandinavian-styled breakfast room and friendly hosts, New Zealander Louise and Italian husband Giacinto. Rooms come with kettle, tea and coffee, and fridge; those on the 5th floor (there's a lift as far as the 4th floor) smooch with the rooftops and gorgeous *duomo* views. Book online for the cheapest rates.

Santa Maria Novella

★**Student Hotel**   HOSTEL €
(Map p511; ☑ 055 062 18 55; www.thestudenthotel .com; Viale Spartaco Lavagnini 70; s/d from €92/

109; ❀ @ ❃ ⬱) Designed for anyone with a fun 'student-for-life' spirit, this hostel-hotel hybrid embodies 21st-century living – in a historic *palazzo* from 1864. Sharp interior design throws in a shiny grand piano for guests to tinkle on, co-working spaces, break-out zones and bags of communal space. Rooms, shared kitchens, and the 360-degree city views from the rooftop pool, gym and sky bar are positively hedonistic.

🛏 San Lorenzo & San Marco

★ Academy Hostel HOSTEL €
(Map p524; ☑ 055 239 86 65; www.academy hostel.eu; Via Ricasoli 9; dm €30-45, d €70-90; ❀ @ ❃) This classy hostel – definitely not a party hostel – sits on the 1st floor of Baron Ricasoli's 17th-century *palazzo*. The inviting lobby, with books to browse, was once a theatre and is a comfy spot to chill on the sofa over TV or a DVD. Dorms sport four, five or six beds, high moulded ceilings and brightly coloured lockers.

Hotel Monna Lisa HOTEL €€
(Map p532; ☑ 055 247 97 51; www.monnalisa.it; Borgo Pinti 27; d €140-200; P ❃; 🖫) At home in a Renaissance *palazzo* endowed with beautiful paintings and sculptures, Monna Lisa is one chic place. Its 45 rooms are old-world and four-star, but what really stuns are the communal spaces – the glorious loggia with painted ceiling; the period lounges; and the peaceful garden with gravel paths, jasmine and lime trees.

Hotel Morandi alla Crocetta BOUTIQUE HOTEL €€
(Map p530; ☑ 055 234 47 48; www.hotelmorandi. it; Via Laura 50; s/d €120/170; P ❀ ❃) This medieval convent-turned-hotel away from the madding crowd in San Marco is a stunner. Rooms are refined and traditional in look – think antique furnishings, wood beams and oil paintings – with a quiet, old-world ambience. Pick of the bunch is frescoed room No. 29, the former chapel.

🛏 Santa Croce

★ Hotel Dalí HOTEL €
(Map p532; ☑ 055 234 07 06; www.hoteldali.com; Via dell'Oriuolo 17; d €95, s/d without bathroom €40/70; P ❃) A warm welcome from hosts Marco and Samanta awaits at this lovely small hotel. A stone's throw from the *duomo*, it has 10 sunny rooms, some overlooking a leafy inner courtyard, decorated in a low-key modern way and equipped with kettles, coffee and tea. No breakfast, but – miraculous for central Florence – free parking in the rear courtyard. The icing on the cake is a trio of gorgeous self-catering apartments – one with a *duomo* view – sleeping three, four or six.

🛏 Oltrarno

Ostello Tasso HOSTEL €
(Map p511; ☑ 055 060 20 87; www.ostellotasso firenze.it; Via Villani 15; dm €38-40, s €55-58, d €130-150, without bathroom s €45-48, d €95-98; @ ❃) Hostel in style at this chic crash pad, a two-minute walk from Piazza Tasso. Coloured bed linen and floor rugs give three- to six-bed dorms a boutique charm, the courtyard garden is a dream and DJs spin tunes in the hip lounge bar (open to nonguests too). The hostel's monthly open-mic evening is a honeypot for local artists and performers.

★ Oltrarno Splendid B&B €€
(Map p536; ☑ 055 464 85 55; www.oltrarnosplen did.com; Via dei Serragli 7; d €160-240; @ ❃) Original frescoes and Toile de Jouy wall fabrics, decorative fireplaces and a wonderful collection of vintage curios create an enriching sense of home at this exquisite guesthouse – the latest on-trend creation by calligrapher Betty Soldi and partner Matteo. All 14 rooms enjoy romantic rooftop views of Florence, and the welcome from maître d' Alberto could not be warmer or more charming.

★ AdAstra B&B €€€
(Map p536; ☑ 055 075 06 02; www.adastra florence.com; Via del Campuccio 53; d €280-350; ☺ reception 8.30am-7.30pm; P ❀ @ ❃) There is no other address quite like it in Florence. Seductively at home in a 16th-century *palazzo* overlooking Europe's largest private walled garden, this uberchic guesthouse rocks. A creation of the talented British-Italian duo behind SoprArno Suites (Map p536; ☑ 055 046 87 18; www.soprarnosuites.com; Via Maggio 35; d €280-342; ❃), AdAstra sports 14 beautiful rooms adorned with Betty Soldi's calligraphy, Matteo's vintage collectibles, claw-foot bathtubs and the odd 19th-century fresco or wooden herringbone floor.

★ Hotel Palazzo Guadagni HOTEL €€€
(Map p536; ☑ 055 265 83 76; www.palaz zoguadagni.com; Piazza Santo Spirito 9; d/tr/q €250/270/310; ❀ ❃) This romantic midrange hotel overlooking Florence's liveliest summertime square is legendary – Zeffirelli shot scenes from *Tea with Mussolini* here. Housed in an artfully revamped Renaissance palace, it has 15 spacious rooms with

old-world high ceilings and the occasional fresco or fireplace (decorative today). In summer bartenders serve cocktails on the impossibly romantic loggia terrace with wicker chairs and predictably dreamy views.

✖ Eating

Quality ingredients and simple execution are the hallmarks of Florentine cuisine, climaxing with the *bistecca alla fiorentina,* a huge slab of prime T-bone steak rubbed with tangy Tuscan olive oil, seared on the chargrill, garnished with salt and pepper and served beautifully *al sangue* (bloody). Be it dining in a traditional trattoria or contemporary, designer-chic space, quality is guaranteed.

✖ Duomo & Piazza della Signoria

★ Osteria I Buongustai   OSTERIA €

(Map p524; ☑ 055 29 13 04; www.facebook.com/ ibuongustaifirenze; Via dei Cerchi 15r; meals €15-20; ⊙9.30am-3.30pm Mon-Sat) Run with breathtaking speed and grace by Laura and Lucia, 'The Gourmand' is unmissable. Lunchtimes heave with locals and savvy students who flock here to fill up on tasty Tuscan home cooking at a snip of other restaurant prices. The place is brilliantly no frills – watch women in hair caps at work in the kitchen, share a table and pay in cash. No credit cards.

ℹ STREET ETIQUETTE

In a bid to keep things clean and pretty in Renaissance Florence, the city mayor passed a law in 2018 banning al fresco eating at certain times on specific streets and squares in the historic centre – on Via de'Neri, Via della Ninna, Piazzale degli Uffizi and Piazza del Grano from noon to 3pm and 6pm to 10pm. The mayor also introduced stiff fines of up to €500 for those who dared disobey. In reality, however, street eating remains very much alive and well in town, with huge crowds happily gathering outside popular eateries at lunchtime to chow tripe-stuffed *panini* (sandwiches) and other Florentine street-food delights on the hop. To avoid the wrath of both the city mayor and city-proud Florentines, avoid littering and head for the riverbanks or a city park to dine al fresco.

Trattoria Le Mossacce   TRATTORIA €

(Map p524; ☑ 055 29 43 61; www.trattorialemossacce.it; Via del Proconsolo 55r; meals €20; ⊙noon-2.30pm & 7-9.30pm Mon-Fri) Strung with legs of ham and garlic garlands, this old-world trattoria lives up to its vintage promise of a warm *benvenuto* (welcome) and fabulous home cooking every Tuscan *nonna* would approve of. A family address, it has been the pride and joy of the Fantoni-Mannucci family for the last 50-odd years and their *bistecca alla fiorentina* (T-bone steak) is among the best in town.

Mangiafoco   TUSCAN €€

(Map p524; ☑055 265 81 70; www.mangiafoco.com; Borgo SS Apostoli 26r; meals €40; ⊙noon-midnight) Aromatic truffles get full-page billing at this small and cosy *osteria* (casual tavern) with buttercup-yellow walls, cushioned seating and an exceptional wine list. Whether you are a hardcore truffle fiend or a truffle virgin, there is something for you here: steak topped with freshly shaved truffles in season, truffle *tagliatelle* (ribbon pasta) or a simple plate of mixed cheeses with sweet truffle honey.

Obicà   ITALIAN €€

(Map p524; ☑055 277 35 26; www.obica.com; Via de' Tornabuoni 16; meals €30-50; ⊙noon-4pm & 6.30-11.30pm Mon-Fri, noon-11pm Sat & Sun) Given its exclusive location in Palazzo Tornabuoni, this designer address is naturally ubertrendy – even the table mats are upcycled from organic products. Taste 10 different types of mozzarella cheese in the cathedral-like interior or snuggle beneath heaters over pizza and salads on sofas in the enchanting star-topped courtyard. At *aperitivo* hour, nibble on *taglierini* (tasting boards loaded with cheeses, salami and deep-fried veg).

★ Irene   BISTRO €€€

(Map p524; ☑055 273 58 91; www.roccoforte hotels.com; Piazza della Repubblica 7; meals €60; ⊙7.30am-10.30pm) Named after the Italian grandmother of Sir Rocco Forte of the eponymous luxury hotel group, Irene (part of neighbouring Hotel Savoy) is a dazzling contemporary bistro with a pavement terrace (heated in winter) overlooking Piazza della Repubblica. Interior design is retro-chic 1950s and celebrity chef Fulvio Pierangelini cooks up playful, fabulous bistro cuisine.

✖ Santa Maria Novella

★ UqBar   CAFE €

(Todo Modo; Map p524; ☑055 239 91 10; www.todo modo.org; Via dei Fossi 15r; meals €15-25; ⊙10am-

WHAT TRIPE!

When Florentines fancy a fast munch-on-the-move, they flit by a *trippaio* – a cart on wheels or mobile stand – for a tripe *panino*. Think cow's stomach chopped up, boiled, sliced, seasoned and bunged between bread.

Those great bastions of good old-fashioned Florentine tradition still going strong include **Il Trippaio del Porcellino** (Map p524; ☑ 335 8070240; Piazza del Mercato Nuovo 1; tripe €4.50; ◷ 9am-6.30pm Mon-Sat) on the southwest corner of Mercato Nuovo; **L'Antico Trippaio** (Map p524; ☑ 339 7425692; Piazza dei Cimatori; dishes & panini €5; ◷ 9.30am-8pm); **Trippaio Sergio Pollini** (Map p532; Piazza Sant' Ambrogio; tripe €3.50; ◷ 9.30am-3.30pm Mon-Sat) in Santa Croce; and hole-in-the-wall **Da Vinattieri** (Map p524; www.facebook.com/davinattieri; panini €4.50; ◷ 11.30am-7pm) tucked down an alley next to Dante's Chiesa di Santa Margherita. Pay €4.50 to €5 for a *panino* with tripe doused in *salsa verde* (pea-green sauce of smashed parsley, garlic, capers and anchovies) or garnished with salt, pepper and ground chilli. Alternatively, opt for a meaty-sized bowl of *lampredotto* (cow's fourth stomach that is chopped and simmered for hours).

To watch tripe cooked up by some of the city's top chefs, hit February's **Funk e Frattaglie Festival** (www.facebook.com/funkfrattaglie), an alternative celebration of traditional offal and funk music.

8pm Tue-Sun, closed Sun May-Sep; ☎) Grab a vintage pew between book- and bottle-lined shelves inside the city's most dynamic independent bookshop, select a glass of well-chosen wine, and tuck into a tasty 'slow food' lunch that changes daily. Outside of lunch hours (12.30pm to 3.30pm), enjoy fresh coffee and homemade cakes in the company of a good book. *Aperitivo*, from 6pm, is the other hot date.

Trattoria Marione TRATTORIA €€
(Map p524; ☑ 055 21 47 56; Via della Spada 27; meals €30; ◷ noon-5pm & 7-11pm) For the quintessential 'Italian dining' experience, Marione is gold. It's busy, it's noisy, it's 99.9% local and the cuisine is right out of *nonna's* Tuscan kitchen. No one appears to speak English so go for Italian – the tasty and excellent-value traditional fare is worth it. If you don't get a complimentary *limoncello* (lemon liqueur) with the bill, you clearly failed the language test.

✕ San Lorenzo & San Marco

★ Mercato Centrale FOOD HALL €
(Map p530; ☑ 055 239 97 98; www.mercatocentrale.it; Piazza del Mercato Centrale 4; dishes €5-15; ◷ market 7am-3pm Mon-Fri, to 5pm Sat, food hall 8am-midnight; ☎) Wander the maze of stalls crammed with fresh produce at Florence's oldest and largest food market, on the ground floor of an iron-and-glass structure designed by architect Giuseppe Mengoni in 1874. Head to the 1st floor's buzzing, thoroughly contemporary food hall with dedicat-

ed cookery school and artisan stalls cooking steaks, burgers, tripe *panini*, vegetarian dishes, pizza, gelato, pastries and pasta.

★ Trattoria Mario TUSCAN €
(Map p530; ☑ 055 21 85 50; www.trattoria-mario.com; Via Rosina 2r; meals €25; ◷ noon-3.30pm Mon-Sat, closed 3 weeks Aug; ✱) Arrive by noon to ensure a spot at this noisy, busy, brilliant trattoria – a legend that retains its soul (and allure with locals) despite being in every guidebook. Charming Fabio, whose grandfather opened the place in 1953, is front of house while big brother Romeo and nephew Francesco cook with speed in the kitchen. No advance reservations; cash only.

Pugi BAKERY €
(Map p530; ☑ 055 28 09 81; www.focacceria-pugi.it; Piazza San Marco 9b; per kilogram €15-25; ◷ 7.45am-8pm Mon-Sat, closed 2 weeks mid-Aug) The inevitable line outside the door says it all. This bakery is a Florentine favourite for pizza slices and chunks of *schiacciata* (Tuscan flatbread) baked up plain, spiked with salt and rosemary, or topped or stuffed with whatever delicious edible goodies are in season.

★ La Ménagère INTERNATIONAL €€
(Map p530; ☑ 055 075 06 00; www.lamenagere.it; Via de' Ginori 8r; meals €15-70; ◷ 7am-2am; ☎) Be it breakfast, lunch, dinner, coffee or cocktails, this industrial-styled space lures Florence's hip social set. The concept store is a fashionable one-stop shop for chic china and tableware, designer kitchen gear and fresh flowers. For daytime dining, pick from retro sofas in the boutique, banquette seating or bar stools

in the bistro or a table between flower pots in the conservatory-style restaurant.

FAC
ITALIAN €€

(Fast and Casual; Map p524; ☑055 015 36 10; www.fastandcasual.com; Via de' Martelli 22; meals €30; ☺noon-10pm) Celebrated Florentine chef Simone Cipriani from Essenziale (p544) cooks up affordable, 'fast and casual' dining inside food emporium Eataly (p550). Head up to the 1st floor to savour Italian-inspired street food to share – pulled-beef taco with cabbage and coriander, polenta with squid-ink ragout, meatballs in tomato sauce – around shared picnic tables, or snag a table in the laid-back trattoria. A good-value *aperitivo* comprising a glass of wine or *spritz* (a type of cocktail made with prosecco) and tapas (€6) is served from 5pm, but a full-blown dinner can only be ordered from 7pm.

★ Regina Bistecca
STEAK €€€

(Map p524; ☑055 269 37 72; www.reginabistecca.com; Via Ricasoli 14r; menus €25-59, meals €40-50; ☺12.30-3pm & 7-10.30pm Tue-Sun; ☏) Plump for a high stool and beautifully mixed Negroni in the wood-panelled American bar, lined with bookshelves and vintage prints in homage to the space's former life as an antiquarian bookshop (since 1875). Or relax in the effortless elegance of the colonnaded, white-table-clothed restaurant where exquisitely cooked, charcoal-grilled steak reigns supreme. Sunday ushers in a hog roast, and the dessert trolley at this fashionable steak house is Italian heaven on earth.

✖ Santa Croce

★ Terrazza Menoni
STREET FOOD €

(Map p532; ☑055 248 07 78; www.terrazzamenoni.it; Piazza Ghiberti 11; meals €15-20; ☺noon-2.30pm Mon-Sat) Luca Menoni's meat stall inside the Sant'Ambrogio covered market has been a favourite with locals since 1921 (his father first ran the business) and now the Florentine artisan has struck gold with a sassy self-service, zero-kilometre *risto macelleria* (butcher's eatery) above his market stall. Everything is homemade and ingredients are sourced fresh from the morning market.

Brac
VEGETARIAN €

(Map p524; ☑055 094 48 77; www.libreriabrac.net; Via dei Vagellai 18r; meals €20; ☺noon-midnight, closed 2 weeks mid-Aug; ☏☑) This hipster cafe-bookshop – a hybrid dining-*aperitivo* address – cooks up inventive, home-style and strictly vegetarian and/or vegan cuisine. Its

---

BEST PANINI SPOTS

Count on paying €5 to €8 for a lavishly filled *panino*.

Mariano (Map p524; ☑055 21 40 67; Via del Parione 19r; panini €3.50-6; ☺8am-3pm & 5-7.30pm Mon-Fri, 8am-3pm Sat) Around since 1973, this brick-vaulted cellar near Via de' Tornabuoni buzzes with Florentines propped at the counter sipping coffee or wine or eating salads and *panini*.

Semel (Map p532; Piazza Ghiberti 44r; panini €3.50-5; ☺11.30am-2.30pm Mon-Sat) Florentines swear by this pocket-sized sandwich bar opposite Sant' Ambrogio food market. Pick from six gourmet combos, washed down with water or wine.

'Ino (Map p524; ☑055 21 45 14; www.inofirenze.com; Via dei Georgofili 3r-7r; panini €6-10; ☺noon-4.30pm) ✿ Artisan ingredients sourced locally and mixed creatively in a gourmet sandwich bar, handily placed near the Uffizi.

All'Antico Vinaio (Map p524; ☑349 3719947, 055 238 27 23; www.allanticovinaio.com; Via de' Neri 65r; tasting platters €10-30; ☺10am-4pm & 6-11pm Tue-Sat, noon-3.30pm Sun) The crowd spills out the door of this noisy Florentine thoroughbred in Santa Croce. Push your way to the tables at the back to taste cheese and salami in situ (advance reservations recommended). Or join the queue at the deli counter for a well-stuffed focaccia wrapped in waxed paper to take away – pour yourself a glass of wine while you wait.

I Due Fratellini (Map p524; ☑055 239 60 96; www.iduefratellini.com; Via dei Cimatori 38r; panini €4; ☺10am-7pm) This hole-in-the-wall near the *duomo* has been in business since 1875. Wash your pick of 30 different types of *panini* down with a beaker of wine and leave the empty glass on the wooden shelf outside.

S.Forno (Map p536; ☑055 239 85 80; www.facebook.com/sfornofirenze; Via Santa Monaco 3r; ☺7.30am-7.30pm Mon-Fri, from 8am Sat & Sun) Vintage bakery-cum–hipster favourite on the Oltrarno.

decor is recycled vintage with the occasional kid's drawing thrown in for that intimate homey touch; the vibe is artsy. Lunchtime ushers in a fantastic-value *piatto unico* (€15) comprising your choice of three dishes served on a single plate.

Le Vespe Café CAFE €
(Map p532; ☑055 388 00 62; www.levespecafe. com; Via Ghibellina 76r; meals €10-15; ☺9am-3pm Mon-Fri, from 10am Sat & Sun; ☑) A favourite with the vegetarian and vegan crowd, this retro-fashioned cafe is a hipster spot to hang out over freshly squeezed juices and cleansing green smoothies, ginger-spiced spinach bread and fabulous weekend brunches. The pocket-sized street terrace gets crammed and a constant queue marks the entrance.

★ Il Teatro del Sale TUSCAN €€
(Map p532; ☑055 200 14 92; www.teatrodelsale. com; Via dei Macci 111r; brunch/dinner €20/30; ☺noon-2.30pm & 7-11pm Tue-Fri, noon-3pm & 7-11pm Sat, noon-3pm Sun, closed Aug) Florentine chef Fabio Picchi is one of Florence's living treasures who steals the Sant'Ambrogio show with this eccentric, good-value, members-only club (everyone welcome, membership €7) inside an old theatre. He cooks up brunch and dinner, culminating at 9.30pm in a live performance of drama, music or comedy arranged by his wife, artistic director and comic actress Maria Cassi.

Dinners are hectic: grab a chair, serve yourself water, wine and antipasti, and wait for the chef to yell out what's about to be served before queuing at the glass hatch for your *primo* (first course) and *secondo* (second course). Note: this is the only Picchi restaurant to serve pasta! Dessert and coffee are laid out buffet-style prior to the performance.

Enoteca Pinchiorri TUSCAN €€€
(☑055 2 63 11; www.enotecapinchiorri.com; Via Ghibellina 87r; 7-/8-course menu €250/275; ☺7.30-10pm Tue-Sat, closed Aug) Niçoise chef Annie Féolde applies French techniques to her refined Tuscan cuisine and does it so well that this is the only restaurant in Tuscany to brandish three shiny Michelin stars. Imagine pigeon roasted in a cocoa-bean crust, with a salted-peanut emulsion and black-truffle sauce. The setting is a 16th-century *palazzo* hotel and the wine list is out of this world.

✕ Oltrarno

★ #Raw VEGAN €
(Map p536; ☑055 21 93 79; www.hashtagraw.it; Via Sant'Agostino 11r; meals €8-15; ☺10am-6pm Tue-

ⓘ FAVE GELATERIE

My Sugar (Map p530; ☑393 0696042; Via de' Ginori 49r; cones €2.50-4.50, tubs €2.50-5; ☺11-11pm summer, to 8.30pm winter, closed Jan & Feb) Sensational artisan gelateria near Piazza San Marco.

Grom (Map p524; ☑055 21 61 58; www. grom.it; Via del Campanile 2; cones & tubs €2.60-5.50; ☺10am-midnight Sun-Fri, to 1am Sat summer, 10.30am-10.30pm winter) Top-notch gelato, including outstanding chocolate, near the duomo.

Venchi (Map p524; ☑055 26 43 39; www.venchi.com; Via dei Calzaiuoli 65; 2-/3-/4-scoops €3.20/4/5; ☺10am-11pm Sun-Thu, to midnight Fri & Sat) Who can resist an entire wall flowing with melted chocolate?

Fri, 11am-8pm Sat & Sun; ☎☑) Should you desire a turmeric, ginger or aloe vera shot or a gently warmed, raw vegan burger served on a stylish slate-and-wood platter, innovative Raw hits the spot. Everything served here is freshly made and raw – to sensational effect. Herbs are grown in the biodynamic greenhouse of charismatic and hugely knowledgeable chef Caroline, a Swedish architect before moving to Florence.

★ Il Santo Bevitore TUSCAN €€
(Map p536; ☑055 21 12 64; www.ilsantobevitore. com; Via di Santo Spirito 64-66r; meals €40; ☺12.30-2.30pm & 7.30-11.30pm, closed Sun lunch & Aug) Reserve or arrive right on 7.30pm to snag the last table at this ever-popular address, an ode to stylish dining where gastronomes eat by candlelight in a vaulted, whitewashed, bottle-lined interior. The menu is a creative reinvention of seasonal classics: pumpkin gnocchi with hazelnuts, coffee and greenveined *blu di Capra* (goat's-milk cheese), *tagliatelle* with hare *ragù*, garlic cream and sweet Carmignano figs.

★ Gurdulù RISTORANTE €€
(Map p536; ☑055 28 22 23; www.gurdulu.com; Via delle Caldaie 12r; meals €40, tasting menu €55; ☺7.30-11pm Tue-Sat, 12.30-2.30pm & 7.30-11pm Sun; ☎) Gourmet Gurdulù seduces fashionable Florentines with razor-sharp interior design, magnificent craft cocktails and seasonal market cuisine from young local chef Gabriele Andreoni. A hybrid drink-dine, this address is as much about noshing gourmet *aperitivi* (predinner drinks) snacks over

expertly mixed cocktails (€12) or an expertly curated Tuscan wine flight (€25 for four wines) as it is about dining exceedingly well.

iO Osteria Personale
TUSCAN €€

(Map p511; ☑ 055 933 13 41; www.io-osteriapersonale.it; Borgo San Frediano 167r; 4-/5-/6-course tasting menus €40/49/57; ⊗ 7.30-10pm Mon-Sat) Persuade everyone at your table to order the tasting menu to avoid the torture of picking just one dish – everything on the menu at this fabulously contemporary and creative *osteria* (casual tavern) is to die for. Pontedera-born chef Nicolò Baretti uses only seasonal products, natural ingredients and traditional flavours – to sensational effect.

L'OV
VEGETARIAN €€

(Osteria Vegetariana; Map p536; ☑ 055 205 23 88; www.osteriavegetariana.it; Piazza del Carmine 4r; meals €30; ⊗ noon-2.45pm & 7-11pm; 🎵) The team behind gluten-free favourite Quinoa is the creative energy behind this appealing San Frediano address, a hit with vegetarians, vegans and coeliacs alike. The menu features no specific courses – rather a tantalising melody of seasonal dishes bursting with local produce: broccoli and bean burgers, violet artichokes with mint and pecorino, and so forth.

★ Essenziale
TUSCAN €€€

(Map p511; ☑ 055 247 69 56; www.essenziale.me; Piazza di Cestello 3r; 6-/8-course tasting menu €65/80; ⊗ 7-10pm Tue-Sat; 🐾) There's no finer showcase for modern Tuscan cuisine than this loft-style restaurant in a 19th-century warehouse. Preparing dishes at the kitchen bar in rolled-up shirt sleeves and navy

---

PIZZA FIX

Santarpia (Map p532; ☑ 055 24 58 29; www.santarpia.biz; Largo Pietro Annigoni 9c; pizza €8.50-15; ⊗ 7.30pm-midnight Tue-Sun; 🎵) Thin-crust Neapolitan pizza near Mercato di Sant'Ambrogio.

Gustapizza (Map p536; ☑ 055 28 50 68; www.facebook.com/GustapizzaFirenze; Via Maggio 46r; pizza €5-8; ⊗ 11.30am-3.30pm & 7-11.30pm Tue-Sun) Student favourite, Neapolitan-style, on the Oltrarno.

SimBIOsi (Map p530; ☑ 055 064 01 15; www.simbiosi.bio; Via de' Ginori 56r; pizza €6.50-11; ⊗ noon-11pm; 🎵) Hipster pizzeria cooking organic pizza, with craft beer and wine by small producers.

---

butcher's apron is dazzling young chef Simone Cipriani. Order one of his tasting menus to sample the full range of his inventive, thoroughly modern cuisine inspired by classic Tuscan dishes.

🍷 Drinking & Nightlife

Florence's drinking scene covers all bases. Be it historical cafes, contemporary cafes with barista-curated specialist coffee, traditional *enoteche* (wine bars, which invariably make great eating addresses too), trendy bars with lavish *aperitivo* buffets, secret speakeasies or edgy cocktail or craft-beer bars, drinking is fun and varied. Nightlife, less extravagant, revolves around a handful of dance clubs.

🍷 Duomo & Piazza della Signoria

Mayday Club
COCKTAIL BAR

(Map p524; ☑ 055 238 12 90; www.maydayclub.it; Via Dante Alighieri 16; cocktails €8-10; ⊗ 8pm-2am Tue-Sat) Strike up a conversation with passionate mixologist Marco Arduino at Mayday. Within seconds you'll be hooked on his mixers and astonishing infusions, all handmade using wholly Tuscan ingredients. Think artichoke- and thistle-infused vermouth, pancetta whisky and porcini liqueur. Marco's cocktail list is equally impressive – or tell him your favourite flavours and let yourself be surprised.

Amblé
BAR

(Map p524; ☑ 055 26 85 28; www.amble.it; Piazzetta dei Del Bene 7a; ⊗ 10am-midnight Tue-Sat, from noon Sun) 'Fresh food and old furniture' is the catchy strapline of this cafe-bar hidden in an alleyway near Ponte Vecchio. Vintage furniture – all for sale – creates a shabby-chic vibe and the tiny terrace feels delightfully far from the madding crowd on summer evenings. From the river, follow Vicolo dell'Oro to Hotel Continentale, then turn left along the alley running parallel to the river.

Tosca & Nino
CAFE

(Map p524; ☑ 055 493 34 68; www.toscanino.com; Piazza della Repubblica 1, La Rinascente; meals €25-35; ⊗ 9am-midnight Mon-Sat, from 10.30am Sun) 'Tasting Tuscany' is the driver behind the rooftop hybrid crowning central department store La Rinascente on people-busy Piazza della Repubblica. As much quality eatery as a fashionable place to drink: nip up here between boutiques to gloat with the birds over coffee, cocktails or wine on its rooftop terrace. Views of the *duomo* and Florentine hills beyond are predictably dreamy.

Shake Café
CAFE

(Map p524; ☑055 21 59 52; www.shakecafe.bio; Via del Corso 28-32; ⊙7.30am-8pm) Smoothie bowls with protein powder, kale and goji berries, cold-pressed juices and vitamin-packed elixir shots – to eat in or take away – satisfy wellness cravings at this laid-back cafe on people-busy Via del Corso. International newspapers, mellow music and a relaxed vibe make it a hipster place to hang. All-day wraps, salads and hearty, homemade soups (€6 to €8) too.

YAB
CLUB

(Map p524; ☑055 21 51 60; www.yab.it/en; Via de' Sassetti 5r; ⊙7pm-4am Mon & Wed-Sat Oct-May) Pick your night according to your age and tastes – disco, rock 'n' roll, groove or a 'UnYversal' bit of everything – at this very popular nightclub with electric dance floor, around since the 1970s, behind Palazzo Strozzi.

🍸 Santa Maria Novella

★Fabbricato Viaggiatori
BAR

(Map p530; ☑055 264 51 14; www.facebook. com/fabbricatoviaggiatori; Piazza del Stazione 50; ⊙8am-midnight) An experimental 'factory' of people, ideas, food, wine, cocktails and live music is the essence of this funky new hangout, at home in Palazzina Reale di Santa Maria Novella – the striking, white marble Rationalist building from the 1930s adjoining the central train station. Be it breakfast, daytime drinks or dining, DJ sets, wine tasting or late-night dancing, it's an upcoming hybrid to watch.

★Manifattura
COCKTAIL BAR

(Map p524; ☑055 239 63 67; www.facebook. com/Manifattura-6266; Piazza di San Pancrazio 1; ⊙6pm-1am Tue-Thu & Sun, to 2am Fri & Sat) 'Made in Italy' has never been such a pertinent buzzword in the city, hence this trendy cocktail bar – an unabashed celebration of Italian spirits and other drinks, both alcoholic and soft. Behind the bar, Fabiano Buffolini is one of Florence's finest mixologists, and tapas-style small plates of traditional Tuscan dishes make wonderful pairings and the music is undeniably retro (think 1950s Italian).

Tenax
CLUB

(☑393 9204279, 335 5235922; www.tenax.org; Via Pratese 46; admission varies; ⊙10pm-4am Thu-Sun Oct-Apr) The only club in Florence on the European club circuit, with great international guest DJs and wildly popular

A GARDEN ROMANCE

At home in the grounds of historic Villa Bardini, Michelin-starred **La Leggenda dei Frati** (Map p536; ☑055 068 05 45; www.laleggendadeifrati.it; Villa Bardini, Costa di San Giorgio 6a; menus €105 & €130, meals €90; ⊙12.30-2pm & 7.30-10pm Tue-Sun; 🛜) enjoys the most romantic terrace with a view in Florence. Veggies are plucked fresh from the vegetable patch, tucked between waterfalls and ornamental beds in Giardino Bardini, and contemporary art jazzes up the classically chic interior. Cuisine is Tuscan, gastronomic and well worth the vital advance reservation – it's summertime's hottest address.

'Nobody's Perfect' house parties on Saturday night; find the warehouse-style building out of town near Florence airport. Take bus 29 or 30 from Stazione di Santa Maria Novella.

🍸 San Lorenzo & San Marco

★PanicAle
COCKTAIL BAR

(Map p530; ☑335 5473530; www.facebook.com/ PanicAleFirenze; Via Panicale 7-9r; ⊙5.30pm-1am Mon-Wed & Sun, to 2am Thu-Sat) Still lovingly known as Lo Sverso (its original name) by many a Florentine socialite, this superstylish bar is a gem. In a part of town where hipster addresses are scarce, there's no finer spot for an expertly crafted cocktail mixed with homemade syrups (try the basil), craft beer on tap or home-brewed ginger ale. DJs spin tunes many a weekend.

★Buca 10
WINE BAR

(Map p532; ☑055 016 53 28; www.facebook.com/ enotecabuca10; Via Fiesolana 10r; ⊙3.30pm-midnight Tue-Thu, to 2am Fri & Sat; 🛜) 'Peace and Wine' is the alluring strapline of this contemporary *enoteca* (wine bar), run with an arty passion and creativity by Francesca and Daniele. Tasty *taglieri* (tasting boards) accompany the excellent wine list, there is a guitar and *cajón* (Peruvian percussion instrument) lying around for anyone to tinkle on, and the modern space hosts occasional photography exhibitions, film screenings and other local happenings.

Bitter Bar
COCKTAIL BAR

(Map p532; ☑340 5499258; www.bitterbarfirenze.it; Via di Mezzo 28r; ⊙9pm-2am Mon-Sat) The 1920s provide the sassy inspiration behind this speakeasy where ordering anything so mundane as a Sex on a Beach is simply not done. Mixologist Cristian Guitti experiments with plenty of unusual bitters, infusions and fresh ingredients to keep cocktail aficionados on their toes, while tasting notes on the tantalising menu – 'sweet smooth', 'fresh and delicate', 'for gin lovers' – pander to the less initiated.

Rex Café BAR

(Map p532; ☑055 248 03 31; www.rexfirenze.com; Via Fiesolana 25r; ⊗8pm-3am) A firm long-term favourite (since 1990), down-to-earth Rex maintains its appeal. Behind the bar Virginia and Lorenzo shake a mean cocktail, using homemade syrups and artisanal spirits like ginger- or carrot-flavoured vodka, pepper rum and laurel vermouth. The artsy, Gaudí-inspired interior is as much art gallery and nightlife stage as simple bar.

DJ sets at weekends and bags of fun events; check its Facebook page (www.facebook.com/rex.firenze) for the week's agenda.

Art. 17 Birreria CRAFT BEER

(Map p532; ☑055 234 66 94; www.articolo17birreria.it; Borgo La Croce 64r; ⊗5pm-2am; ☎) Craft-beer aficionados will simply adore this Santa Croce *birreria artigianale* (artisanal

HISTORIC CAFES

Caffè Gilli (Map p524; ☑055 21 38 96; www.gilli.it; Piazza della Repubblica 39r; ⊗7.30am-1am) The most famous of the historic cafes on the city's old Roman forum, serving delectable cakes, fruit tartlets and *millefoglie* (vanilla or custard slice) since 1733.

Procacci (Map p524; ☑055 21 16 56; www.procacci1885.it; Via de' Tornabuoni 64r; ⊗10am-9pm Mon-Sat, 11am-8pm Sun, closed 3 weeks Aug) The last remaining bastion of genteel old Florence on Via de' Tornabuoni, this tiny cafe was born in 1885. Order bite-sized *panini tartufati* (truffle pâté rolls) and prosecco (sparkling wine).

Caffè Rivoire (Map p524; ☑055 21 44 12; www.rivoire.it; Piazza della Signoria 4; ⊗7am-midnight Tue-Sun summer, to 9pm winter) Golden oldie from 1872 with an unbeatable people-watching terrace and exquisite chocolate (sadly only available in winter).

brewery) which provides night owls with an edgy fusion of Tuscan, Italian and international craft beer – there are some 50-odd bottled and on tap to choose from – and live music at weekends. 'Happy Hour' kicks in daily from 5pm to 9pm.

🍷 Santa Croce

⭐**Ditta Artigianale** CAFE

(Map p524; ☑055 274 15 41; www.dittaartigianale.it; Via de' Neri 32r; ⊗8am-10pm Mon-Thu, to midnight Fri, 9am-midnight Sat, to 11pm Sun; ☎) With industrial decor and laid-back vibe, this ingenious coffee roastery is a perfect place to hang at any time of day. The creation of three-times Italian barista champion Francesco Sanapo, it's famed for its first-class coffee and outstanding gin cocktails. If you're yearning for a flat white, cold-brew tonic or cappuccino made with almond milk, come here.

⭐**Locale** COCKTAIL BAR

(Map p532; ☑055 906 71 88; www.localefirenze.it; Via delle Seggiole 12; ⊗7.30pm-2am) At home in a 13th- to 15th-century *palazzo,* this tucked-away drinking and dining space is designed to stun. From the exquisite craft cocktails (€20 to €30) mixed at the bar, to the beautifully presented modern Tuscan fare and awe-inspiring interior design – a theatrical fusion of original architectural features, period furnishings and contemporary vegetal wall gardens – Locale is a true feast for the eyes (and appetite).

Le Murate CAFE

(Caffè Letterario Firenze; Map p532; ☑055 234 68 72; www.lemurate.it; Piazza delle Murate; ⊗10.30am-1am Mon-Fri, from 4pm Sat & Sun; ☎) This arty cafe-bar in Florence's former jail is where literati meet to talk, create and perform over coffee, drinks and light meals. The literary cafe hosts everything from readings and interviews with authors – Florentine, Italian and international – to film screenings, debates, live music and art exhibitions. Tables are built from recycled window frames and in summer everything spills outside into the brick courtyard.

Babylon Club CLUB

(Map p532; ☑347 3818294; www.facebook.com/BabylonClubOfficialPage; Via dei Pandolfini 26r; ⊗11pm-4am Mon, Tue & Thu-Sat) For late-night dancing, hit this swish nightclub with sleek black facade and three dance floors playing a mixed bag of sounds: latino, kizomba, reggae and lots of funky hip-hop and R&B. Check its Facebook page for the week's events.

SUMMER ROOFTOPS & RIVERSIDE SHACKS

Summer in the city all too often translates as hot, frenetic, overcrowded days when, quite frankly, the only place any savvy urbanite strives to be is by a pool or on a rooftop – away from the crowds.

Breezy (if you're lucky) hotspots up high to catch a brief respite from summertime's sizzling temperatures – over drinks and a dip during the day or after dusk – include **Three Sixty** at **Grand Hotel Minerva** (Map p524; ☑055 2 72 30; www.grandhotelminerva.com; Piazza di Santa Maria Novella 16) and American rooftop bar **Empireo** (Map p532; ☑055 262 35 00; www.hotelplazalucchesi.it; Lungarno della Zecca Vecchia 38; ⊙7.30am-midnight; ☎) at Plaza Hotel Lucchesi. Both seasonal bars open June to September, lure an insanely fashionable crowd, and come with cooling rooftop pool and weekly live jazz soirées.

Summer rooftop bar **La Terrazza Lounge Bar** (Map p524; ☑055 2726 5987, 342 1234710; www.lungarnocollection.com; Vicolo dell'Oro 6r; ⊙3.30-10.30pm Apr-Sep) at Hotel Continentale doesn't have a pool but the five-star view of Ponte Vecchio dished up with sophisticated cocktails at sunset is pretty damn good. By Santa Maria Novella train station, fashionistas while away sultry summer nights over drinks at the **B-Roof** bar atop **Grand Hotel Baglioni** (Map p524; ☑055 2 35 80; www.hotelbaglioni.it; Piazza dell'Unità Italiana 6). Across the river on Piazzale Michelangelo, Florentine sophisticates dress up to the nines to lounge, drink, dance until dawn – and swoon at the city by night beautifully laid out at their feet – at hilltop **Flò** (Map p511; ☑334 1080164, 334 1080164 055 65 07 91; www.flofirenze.com; Piazzale Michelangelo 84; ⊙7.30pm-4am late May-Sep).

On the banks of the Arno, riverside shacks mushroom after the rain during the sweltering summer months. Year-round snack shack **Easy Living** (Map p511; ☑055 234 11 12; www.easylivingfirenze.it; Piazza Giuseppe Poggi; snacks €3.50-4.50; ⊙9am-7pm Mon-Sat winter, longer hours summer) in San Niccolò morphs into an urban beach complete with sand, sun loungers, beach volleyball, sunset yoga classes, DJ sets and weekend beach parties. Watch for seasonal newcomers each year both here and directly across the water where, on the grassy riverbanks, you might also spot cherry-red food truck **La Toraia** (Map p511; www.latoraia.com; Lungarno del Tempio 3450; meals €5-10; ⊙noon-midnight mid-Apr–mid-Oct).

Blob Club   CLUB
(Map p524; ☑324 8043276; Via Vinegia 21r; ⊙10pm-4am) This small and edgy Santa Croce club lures an international crowd with its music theme nights – loads of 1960s, hip-hop, alternative rock; all sounds in fact.

🍷 Oltrarno

★**Santarosa Bistrot**   BAR
(Map p511; ☑055 230 90 57; www.facebook. com/santarosa.bistrot; Lungarno di Santarosa; ⊙8am-midnight; ☎) The living is easy at this hipster garden-bistro-bar, snug against a chunk of ancient city wall in the flowery Santarosa gardens. Comfy cushioned sofas built from recycled wooden crates sit al fresco beneath trees; food is superb (meals €30); and mixologists behind the bar complement an excellent wine list curated by Enoteca Pitti Gola e Cantina (p548) with serious craft cocktails. Spaghetti jazz soirées and other music events set the bar buzzing after dark. In warmer weather, grab a picnic

hamper for two and enjoy an intimate lunch amid greenery.

★**Le Volpi e l'Uva**   WINE BAR
(Map p536; ☑055 239 81 32; www.levolpieluva. com; Piazza dei Rossi 1; ⊙11am-9pm Mon-Sat) This humble wine bar remains as appealing as the day it opened in 1992. Its food and wine pairings are first class – taste and buy boutique wines by small Italian producers, matched perfectly with cheeses, cold meats and the finest crostini in town; the warm, melt-in-your-mouth *lardo di cinta senese* (wafer-thin slices of aromatic of pork fat) is absolutely extraordinary.

There are wine-tasting classes too – or simply work your way through the impressive 50-odd different wines available by the glass (€4.50 to €9).

★**Mad Souls & Spirits**   COCKTAIL BAR
(Map p536; ☑055 627 16 21; www.facebook. com/madsoulsandspirits; Borgo San Frediano 38r; ⊙6pm-2am; ☎) At this ubercool bar in San Frediano, cult alchemists Neri Fantechi and Julian Biondi woo a discerning crowd with

their expertly crafted cocktails, served in a tiny aqua-green and red-brick space that couldn't be more spartan. A potted cactus decorates each scrubbed wood table and the humorous cocktail menu is the height of irreverence. Check the 'Daily Madness' blackboard for specials.

★ **Gosh** COCKTAIL BAR
(Map p536; ☑ 055 046 90 48; www.facebook.com/goshfirenze; Via Santo Spirito 46r; ⊘ 7pm-midnight Tue-Thu, 6pm-2am Fri-Sun) Whimsical flamingo wallpaper, funky music, DJ sets and a subtle NYC vibe lures Florence's fashionable set to this buzzing cocktail bar across the river. Expect lots of fun variations of classic cocktails – blueberry mojitos, dozens of different Moscow mules and sensational basil-infused creations.

★ **Enoteca Pitti**
Gola e Cantina WINE BAR
(Map p536; ☑ 055 21 27 04; www.pittigolaecantina.com; Piazza dei Pitti 16; ⊘ 1pm-midnight Wed-Mon) Wine lovers won't do better than this serious wine bar opposite Palazzo Pitti, run with passion and humour by charismatic trio Edoardo, Manuele and Zeno – don't be surprised if they share a glass with you over wine talk. Floor-to-ceiling shelves of expertly curated, small-production Tuscan and Italian wines fill the tiny bar, and casual dining is around a handful of marble-topped tables. Look forward to excellent cured meats and pasta *fatta in casa* (housemade).

★ **Il Santino** WINE BAR
(Map p536; ☑ 055 230 28 20; http://ilsantobevitore.com; Via di Santo Spirito 60r; ⊘ 12.30-11pm) Kid sister to top-notch restaurant Il Santo Bevitore (p543) two doors down the same street, this intimate wine bar with exposed stone walls and marble bar is a stylish spot for pairing cured meats, cheeses and Tuscan staples with a carefully curated selection of wine – many by local producers – and artisanal beers.

Love Craft COCKTAIL BAR
(Map p536; ☑ 055 269 29 68; www.facebook.com/lovecraftfirenze; Borgo San Frediano 24r; ⊘ 6pm-2am) Florence's first dedicated whisky bar – named after illustrious American horror writer HP Lovecraft – has proved a hit from day one with a staunchly local crowd who flock here for a break from the norm. Two hundred-odd whiskies from around the globe jostle for the limelight with mixologist Manuel Petretto's Scotch whisky–based craft cocktails (from €7) and craft beers on tap.

Unsure what to order? Go for a well-curated, three- or four-tipple-strong tasting flight.

La Cité BAR
(Map p536; www.facebook.com/lacitelibreriacafe; Borgo San Frediano 20r; ⊘ 10am-2am Mon-Sat, from 2pm Sun; ☎) A hip cafe-bookshop with an eclectic choice of vintage seating, La Cité makes a wonderful, intimate venue for book readings, after-work drinks and fantastic live music – jazz, swing, world music. Check its Facebook page for the week's events.

🔒 Shopping

Tacky mass-produced souvenirs (boxer shorts emblazoned with *David's* packet) are everywhere, not least at city market **Mercato Nuovo** (Map p524; Piazza del Mercato Nuovo; ⊘ 8.30am-7pm Mon-Sat), awash with cheap imported handbags and other leather goods. But for serious shoppers keen to delve into a city synonymous with craftsmanship since medieval times, there are ample addresses.

★ **Benheart** FASHION & ACCESSORIES
(Map p524; www.benheart.it; Via dei Calzaivoli 78; ⊘ 10am-7.30pm) This flagship store of local superstar Ben, a Florentine-based fashion designer who set up the business with schoolmate Matteo after undergoing a heart transplant, is irresistible. The pair swore that if Ben survived, they'd go it alone – which they did, with huge success. For real-McCoy handcrafted leather designs – casual shoes, jackets and belts for men and women – there is no finer address.

★ **Officina Profumo-Farmaceutica di Santa Maria Novella** GIFTS
(Map p524; ☑ 055 21 62 76; www.smnovella.it; Via della Scala 16; ⊘ 9am-8pm) In business since 1612, this exquisite perfumery-pharmacy began life when Santa Maria Novella's Dominican friars began to concoct cures and sweet-smelling unguents using medicinal herbs cultivated in the monastery garden. The shop, with an interior from 1848, sells fragrances, skincare products, ancient herbal remedies and preparations for everything from relief of heavy legs to improving skin elasticity, memory and mental energy.

★ **Lorenzo Villoresi** PERFUME
(Map p536; ☑ 055 234 11 87; www.lorenzovilloresi.it; Via de' Bardi 14; ⊘ 10am-7pm Mon-Sat) Artisanal perfumes, bodycare products, scented candles and stones, essential oils and room fragrances crafted by Florentine perfumer Lorenzo Villoresi meld distinctively Tuscan elements such as laurel, olive, cypress and

iris with essential oils and essences from around the world. His bespoke fragrances are highly sought after and visiting his elegant boutique, at home in his family's 15th-century *palazzo*, is quite an experience.

★**Mio Concept**   HOMEWARES
(Map p524; ☑055 264 55 43; www.mio-concept. com; Via della Spada 34r; ◷10am-1.30pm & 2.30-7.30pm Mon-Sat) Design objects for the home – made in Italy and many upcycled – as well as jewellery, bags and belts crafted from old bicycle tyres and inner tubes by Turinese designers Cingomma, cram this stylish boutique created by German globetrotter Antje. Don't miss the prints of iconic designs by Italian street artists Blub and Exit Enter, and street-sign artworks by Florence's Clet (p535).

★**Luisa Via Roma**   FASHION & ACCESSORIES
(Map p524; ☑055 906 41 16; www.luisaviaroma. com; Via Roma 19-21r; ◷10.30am-7.30pm Mon-Sat, from 11am Sun) The flagship store of this historic store (think: small 1930s boutique selling straw hats) turned luxury online retailer is a must for the fashion-forward. Eye-catching window displays woo with giant screens, while seasonal themes transform the interior maze of rooms into an exotic Garden of Eden. Shop here for lesser-known designers as well as popular luxury-fashion labels.

Pre- or post-shop, hob-nob with the city's fashionista set over fair-trade coffee, organic cuisine and creative cold-press juices in Luisa's chic 1st-floor cafe-bar **Floret** (☑055 29 59 24; www.floret-bar.com; salads & bowls €12-16; ◷10.30am-7.30pm Mon-Sat, from 11am Sun; 🛜) 🥗.

★**Street Doing**   VINTAGE
(Map p524; ☑055 538 13 34; www.streetdoing vintage.it; Via dei Servi 88r; ◷10.30am-7.30pm Mon-Sat, from 2.30pm Sun) Vintage couture for men and women is what this extraordinary rabbit warren of a boutique – surely the city's largest collection of vintage – is about. Carefully curated garments and accessories are in excellent condition and feature all the top Italian designers: beaded 1950s Gucci clutch bags, floral 1960s Pucci dresses, Valentino shades from every decade. Fashionistas, *this* is heaven.

★**Aquaflor**   COSMETICS
(Map p532; ☑055 234 34 71; www.aquaflorexpe rience.com; Borgo Santa Croce 6; ◷10am-1pm & 2-7pm) This elegant Santa Croce perfumery in a vaulted 15th-century *palazzo* exudes romance and exoticism. Artisanal scents are crafted here with tremendous care and precision by master perfumer Sileno Cheloni, who

works with precious essences from all over the world, including Florentine iris. Organic soaps, cosmetics and body-care products make equally lovely gifts to take back home.

★**Uashmama**   HOMEWARES
(Map p536; ☑055 21 62 23; www.uashmama.com; Borgo San Jacopo 30r; ◷10.30am-7.30pm) Modern craftsmanship shines out of this loveable boutique, the pride and joy of the Marconi family, whose washable paper bags – tanned just like leather and, indeed, looking like leather too – are all the rage in contemporary Florence. Handbags, backpacks, sleek clutch bags and purses tempt fashionistas alongside a sleek array of paper tableware, cushions and lampshades.

Pineider   ARTS & CRAFTS
(Map p524; ☑055 28 46 56; www.pineider.com; Piazza de' Rucellai 4-7r; ◷10am-7pm) 'Writing the Future' is the inspired strapline of this iconic stationery company, in business in Florence since 1714. Stendhal, Byron, Shelley and Dickens are among the literary luminaries who have chosen to purchase its beautifully crafted, top-quality paper products, pens and leather goods. For a real treat, order your own bespoke writing paper.

Aprosio & Co   FASHION & ACCESSORIES
(Map p524; ☑055 21 01 27; www.aprosio.it; Via del Moro 75-77r; ◷10.30am-6.30pm Mon-Sat) Ornella Aprosio fashions teeny-tiny Murano glass and crystal beads into dazzling pieces

---

DESIGNER OUTLET MALLS

Mall (☑055 865 77 75; www.themall.it; Via Europa 8, Leccio Reggello; ◷9.30am-7.30pm Jun-Aug, 10am-7pm Sep-May) Find this luxury fashion designer outlet 35km from Florence; buses (adult/reduced single €7/3.50, return €13/7.50) depart every half hour from the SITA bus station across from the train station on Via Santa Caterina da Siena.

Barberino Designer Outlet (☑055 84 21 61; www.mcarthurglen.it; Via Meucci, Barberino di Mugello; ◷10am-9pm; 🛜) Previous season's collections by D&G, Prada, Roberto Cavalli, Missoni et al at discounted prices, 40km north of Florence. A shuttle bus (adult/reduced €13/8, 30 minutes) departs from in front of Florence' central train station on Piazza della Stazione two to four times daily. Check seasonal schedules and book tickets online.

of jewellery, hair accessories, animal-shaped brooches, handbags, even glass-flecked cashmere. It is all quite magical.

Sbigoli Terrecotte — CERAMICS

(Map p532; ☑ 055 247 97 13; www.sbigoliterrecotte. it; Via Sant'Egidio 4r; ☺ 9.30am-1pm & 2.30-7pm Mon-Sat) This family-run ceramics workshop and showroom, founded by the Sbigoli family in 1857, is littered with hundreds of handmade and painted tableware pieces. Traditions are kept alive by Antonella Chini Adami, who in her 80s is still painting and firing up her delicate creations in the on-site kiln alongside daughter Lorenza.

★C.BIO — FOOD & DRINKS

(Map p532; ☑ 055 247 92 71; www.cbeo.it; Via della Mattonaia 3a; ☺ 8.30am-8.30pm Mon-Sat) Be it bread baked in situ that morning, organic fruit, veg or wine made by a small Tuscan producer, homemade pasta or a white-truffle *panino* to take away, this artisanal grocery and deli is essential viewing for foodies. A fabulous showcase of Tuscany's rich bounty of seasonal produce, C.BIO – an acronym for *'cibo buono, italiano e onesto'* meaning 'good, honest, Italian food' – is the brainchild of celebrated chef Fabio Picchi of **Cibrèo** (Map p532; www.cibreo.com; Via dei Macci 122r; meals €30-35; ☺ 12.50-2.30pm & 6.50-11pm, closed Aug) fame. Shop here for your very own luxuriant, organic picnic to enjoy on the grocery's flowery terrace, riverside or in the nearby botanical gardens.

Eataly — FOOD & DRINKS

(Map p524; ☑ 055 015 36 01; www.eataly.net; Via de' Martelli 22r; ☺ 10am-10.30pm; 🐕) Eataly is a one-stop food shop for everything Tuscan. Peruse beautifully arranged aisles laden with oils, conserved vegetables, pasta, rice, biscuits and so on. There are fresh bakery and deli counters, fridges laden with seemingly every cheese under the Italian sun and a coffee bar with outdoor seating. Many products are local and/or organic; most are by small producers. Upstairs is a wine cellar with 600 labels, summer terrace and Florentine chef Simone Cipriani's fast and epicurean FAC (p542), serving Italian-inspired street food to go as well as tasty trattoria fare.

❶ Information

EMERGENCY

Police Station (Questura; ☑ 055 4 97 71, English-language service 055 497 72 68; http://questure.poliziadistato.it/it/Firenze; Via Zara 2; ☺ 24hr, English-language service 9.30am-1pm Mon-Fri)

MEDICAL SERVICES

24-Hour Pharmacy (☑ 055 21 67 61; Stazione di Santa Maria Novella; ☺ 24hr)

Dr Stephen Kerr: Medical Service (☑ 335 8361682, 055 28 80 55; www.dr-kerr.com; Piazza Mercato Nuovo 1; ☺ 3-5pm Mon-Fri, or by appointment 9am-3pm Mon-Fri)

Hospital (Ospedale di Santa Maria Nuova; ☑ 055 6 93 81; www.asf.toscana.it; Piazza di Santa Maria Nuova 1; ☺ 24hr)

TOURIST INFORMATION

Airport Tourist Office (☑ 055 31 58 74; www. firenzeturismo.it; Via del Termine 11, Florence Airport; ☺ 9am-7pm Mon-Sat, to 2pm Sun)

Infopoint Bigallo (Map p524; ☑ 055 28 84 96; www.firenzeturismo.it; Piazza San Giovanni 1; ☺ 9am-7pm Mon-Sat, to 2pm Sun)

Tourist Office (Map p524; ☑ 055 21 22 45; www.firenzeturismo.it; Piazza della Stazione 4; ☺ 9am-7pm Mon-Sat, to 2pm Sun)

❶ Getting There & Away

AIR

Also known as Aeroporto Amerigo Vespucci, **Florence Airport** (☑ 055 306 18 30, 055 3 06 15; www.aeroporto.firenze.it; Via del Termine 11) is 5km northwest of the city centre and is served by both domestic and European flights.

BUS

Services from the **bus station** (Autostazione Busitalia-Sita Nord; Map p524; ☑ 800 373760; www.fsbusitalia.it; Via Santa Caterina da Siena 17r; ☺ 5.45am-8.40pm Mon-Sat, 6.25am-8.30pm Sun), just west of Piazza della Stazione, are limited; the train is better. **Autolinee Chianti Valdarno** (www.acvbus.it) operates hourly buses to/from Greve in Chianti (line 365; €4.50 or €7 direct from the driver, one hour), and Siena is served with at least hourly buses by **Tiemma SpA** (www.tiemmespa.it; €7.80, 1¾ hours).

Flixbus (www.flixbus.com) buses to/from Florence and Siena (€4.99; 45 minutes) are cheaper and faster, but arrive/depart from the stop at Parcheggio Villa Costanza on Via della Costituzione, linked by tramline T1 to Stazione Santa Maria Novella in the town centre.

TRAIN

Florence's central train station is **Stazione di Santa Maria Novella** (www.firenzesantamaria novella.it; Piazza della Stazione). Leave luggage at well-organised **KiPoint Left Luggage** (Deposito Bagagliamano; ☑ 055 933 77 49; www.ki point.it; 1st 5hr €6, then per hour €1 up to 12hr, then per hour €0.50; ☺ 6am-11pm) on platform 16. Tickets for all trains are sold in the main ticketing hall, at staffed counters and touch-screen automatic ticket-vending machines.

FLORENCE & TUSCANY FLORENCE

Florence is on the Rome–Milan line. Services include the following:

Destination	Fare (€)	Time	Frequency
Bologna	29	35-40min	every 15-30min
Lucca	9.90	1½-1¾hr	twice hourly
Milan	56	1¾-2hr	at least hourly
Pisa	8.60	45min-1hr	every 15min
Pistoia	4.60	45min-1hr	every 10min
Rome	50	1¾-4¼hr	at least twice hourly
Venice	53	2hr	at least hourly

ⓘ Getting Around

TO/FROM THE AIRPORT
Tram

Tram line T2 links Florence Airport with Piazza della Unità and Stazione di Santa Maria Novella – a swift 22-minute journey – every few minutes between 5am and 12.30am Sunday to Thursday and until 2am on Friday and Saturday. A single ticket costs €1.50 from ticket-dispensing machines at tram stops or €2.50 on board from the driver.

Note passengers can only take one suitcase or bag weighing up to 10kg on board for free; each piece of luggage over 10kg (max 20kg) requires its own ticket.

Bus

ATAF (www.ataf.net) operates a **Volainbus** (☑ 800 373760; www.fsbusitalia.it; single/ return €6/10) shuttle (20 to 30 minutes) between Florence airport and Florence bus station every 30 minutes between 5am and 8.30pm, then hourly until 12.10am (from 5.30am to 12.30am from the airport). Bus drivers sell tickets.

CENTRAL TUSCANY

When people imagine classic Tuscan countryside, they usually conjure up images of silver-green olive groves, sloping fields of golden wheat gently rippling in the breeze, sun-kissed vineyards and artistically planted avenues of

ⓘ FLORENCE VIA PISA AIRPORT

The city's other handy airport is Pisa International Airport (Galileo Galilei Airport; ☑ 050 84 93 00; www.pisa-airport. com), 80km west of Florence, with flights to most major European cities.

Regular trains link Florence's Stazione di Santa Maria Novella with Pisa's central train station, Pisa Centrale (€8.60, 1½ hours, at least hourly from 4.30am to 10.25pm), with fully automated, super-speedy PisaMover trains (www.pisa-mover.com; single €5, five minutes, every five minutes from 6am to midnight) continuing to Pisa International Airport.

cypress tress. The real gems are the historic towns and cities, most of which are medieval and Renaissance time capsules magically transported to the modern day.

Siena

☑ 0577 / POP 53,900

Siena is a city where the architecture soars, as do the souls of many of its visitors. Effectively a giant, open-air museum celebrating the Gothic, Siena has spiritual and secular monuments that have retained both their medieval forms and their extraordinary art collections, providing the visitor with plenty to marvel at. The city's historic *contrade* (districts) are marvellous too, being as close-knit and colourful today as they were in the 17th century when their world-famous horse race, the Palio, was inaugurated. And within each *contrada* lie vibrant streets populated with artisanal boutiques, sweet-smelling *pasticcerie* (pastry shops) and tempting restaurants. It's a feast for the senses and an essential stop on every Tuscan itinerary.

◉ Sights

★ Piazza del Campo   PIAZZA

Popularly known as 'Il Campo', this sloping piazza has been Siena's social centre since being staked out by the ruling Consiglio dei Nove (Council of Nine) in the mid-12th century. Built on the site of a Roman marketplace, its paving is divided into nine sectors representing the members of the *consiglio,* and these days acts as a carpet on which young locals meet and relax. The cafes around its perimeter are the most

Siena

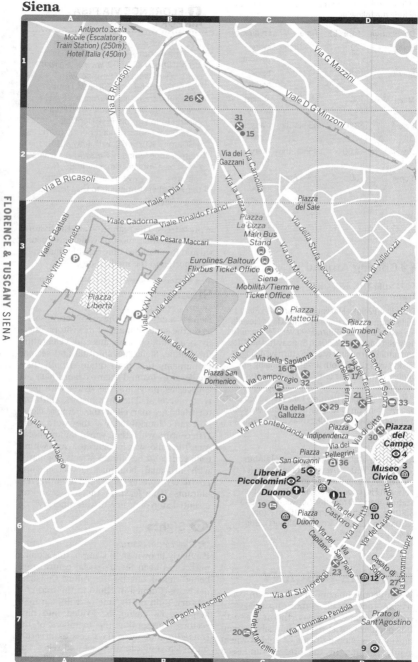

Siena

◎ Top Sights
1	Duomo	C6
2	Libreria Piccolomini	C5
3	Museo Civico	D5
4	Piazza del Campo	D5

◎ Sights
5	Battistero di San Giovanni	C5
6	Complesso Museale di Santa Maria della Scala	C6
	Cripta	(see 1)
7	Museo dell'Opera	D6
8	Oratorio di San Bernardino	E4
9	Orto Botanico dell'Università	D7
10	Palazzo Chigi Saracini	D6
	Palazzo Pubblico	(see 3)
11	Panorama del Facciatone	D6
12	Pinacoteca Nazionale	D7
13	Sinagoga di Siena	E5
14	Torre del Mangia	E5

◎ Activities, Courses & Tours
15	Fonte Giusta Cooking School	C2

◎ Sleeping
16	Albergo Bernini	C4
17	Antica Residenza Cicogna	D4
18	Hotel Alma Domus	C4
19	Ostello Casa delle Balie	C6
20	Pensione Palazzo Ravizza	C7

◎ Eating
21	Enoteca I Terzi	D5
22	La Prosciutteria	F5
23	La Vecchia Latteria	D6
24	Lievito M@dre	E5
25	Morbidi	D4
26	Osteria Il Vinaio	B1
27	Osteria La Taverna di San Giuseppe	D7
28	Ristorante All'Orto de' Pecci	E7
29	Ristorante Grotta di Santa Caterina da Bagoga	D5
30	Te Ke Voi?	D5
31	Trattoria Fonte Giusta	C2
32	Zest Ristorante & Wine Bar	C4

◎ Drinking & Nightlife
33	Bar Pasticcerie Nannini	D5
34	Bottega Roots	E5
35	UnTUBO	E5

◎ Shopping
36	Il Magnifico	D5

popular coffee and *aperitivo* (predinner drinks) spots in town.

Palazzo Pubblico
HISTORIC BUILDING

(Palazzo Comunale; Piazza del Campo) Built to demonstrate the enormous wealth, proud independence and secular nature of Siena, this 14th-century Gothic masterpiece is the visual focal point of the Campo (p551), itself the true heart of the city. Architecturally clever (notice how its concave facade mirrors the opposing convex curve) it has always housed the city's administration and been used as a cultural venue. Its distinctive bell tower, the Torre del Mangia (📞 0577 29 26 15; ticket@comune.siena.it; adult/family €10/25; 🕙 10am-6.15pm Mar–mid-Oct, to 3.15pm mid-Oct–Feb), provides magnificent views for those who brave the steep climb to the top.

★ Museo Civico
MUSEUM

(Civic Museum; 📞 0577 29 26 15; Palazzo Pubblico; adult/reduced €10/9, with Torre del Mangia €15, with Torre del Mangia & Complesso Museale di Santa Maria della Scala €20; 🕙 10am-6.15pm mid-Mar–Oct, to 5.15pm Nov–mid-Mar) Entered via the Palazzo Pubblico's Cortile del Podestà (Courtyard of the Chief Magistrate), this wonderful museum showcases rooms richly frescoed by artists of the Sienese school. Commissioned by the city's governing body rather than by the Church, some of the frescoes depict secular subjects – highly unusual at the time. The highlights are two huge frescoes: Ambrogio Lorenzetti's *Allegories of Good and Bad Government* (c 1338–40) and Simone Martini's celebrated *Maestà* (*Virgin Mary in Majesty*; 1315).

★ Duomo
CATHEDRAL

(Cattedrale di Santa Maria Assunta; 📞 0577 28 63 00; www.operaduomo.siena.it; Piazza Duomo; Mar-Oct €5, Nov-Feb free, when floor displayed €8; 🕙 10.30am-7pm Mon-Sat, 1.30-6pm Sun Mar-Oct, 10.30am-5.30pm Mon-Sat, 1.30-5.30pm Sun Nov-Feb) Consecrated on the former site of a Roman temple in 1179 and constructed over the 13th and 14th centuries, Siena's majestic *duomo* (cathedral) showcases the talents of many great medieval and Renaissance architects and artists: Giovanni Pisano designed the intricate white, green and red marble facade; Nicola Pisano carved the elaborate pulpit; Pinturicchio painted the frescoes in the extraordinary Libreria Piccolomini ; and Michelangelo, Donatello and Gian Lorenzo Bernini all produced sculptures.

★ Libreria Piccolomini
LIBRARY

(Piccolomini Library; 📞 0577 28 63 00; www.operaduomo.siena.it; Piazza Duomo; €2; 🕙 10.30am-6.30pm Mon-Sat & 1.30-5.30pm Sun Mar-Oct, 10.30am-5pm Mon-Sat & 1.30-5pm Sun Nov-Feb) Cardinal Francesco Todeschini Piccolomini, archbishop of Siena (later Pope Pius III), commissioned the building and decoration of this hall off the north aisle of the *duomo* in 1492 to house the books of his uncle, Enea Silvio Piccolomini (Pope Pius II). Come here not to see the books (only a series of huge choral tomes remains on display), but to enjoy the vividly coloured narrative frescoes (1503–08) by Pinturicchio (Bernardino di Betto), which depict events in the life of Pius II.

Battistero di San Giovanni
LANDMARK

(📞 0577 28 63 00; http://operaduomo.siena.it; Piazza San Giovanni; adult/child €6/1; 🕙 10.30am-6.30pm Mon-Sat & 1.30-5.30pm Sun Mar-Oct, 10.30am-5pm Mon-Sat & 1.30-5pm Sun Nov-Feb) The baptistry is lined with 15th-century frescoes and centres around a hexagonal marble font by Jacopo della Quercia, decorated with bronze panels depicting the life of St John the Baptist by artists including Lorenzo Ghiberti (*Baptism of Christ; St John in Prison*) and Donatello (*The Head of John the Bap-*

ⓘ SIENA MONEY-SAVING MUSEUM PASSES

OPA SI Pass Covers the Duomo, Libreria Piccolomini, Museo dell'Opera, Battistero di San Giovanni, Cripta and Oratorio di San Bernardino; €13 March to mid-August and last week of October, €8 November to February, valid for three days.

OPA SI + Pass Covers the list above plus Porta del Cielo tour; €20 March to December, valid for three days.

Acropoli Pass Covers the Duomo, Libreria Piccolomini, Museo dell'Opera, Battistero di San Giovanni, Cripta, Oratorio di San Bernardino and Complesso Museale di Santa Maria della Scala; €18 March to mid-August and last week of October, €20 from mid-August to late October, €13 November to February, valid for three days.

Acropoli + Pass Covers the list above, plus Porta del Cielo tour; €25 March to October, valid for three days.

tist Being Presented to Herod). Entry is included in the OPA SI and Acropoli passes.

Cripta
CHRISTIAN SITE

(☑0577 28 63 00; http://operaduomo.siena.it; Piazza San Giovanni; adult/child €6/1; ⊘10.30am-6.30pm Mon-Sat & 1.30-5.30pm Sun Mar-Oct, 10.30am-5pm Mon-Sat & 1.30-5pm Sun Nov-Feb) Remarkably, this vaulted space under the *duomo's* pulpit was totally filled with debris in the late 1300s and was only excavated and restored in 1999. Originally functioning as a cathedral entrance and confessional, it was decorated with 180 sq metres of richly coloured 13th-century *pintura a secco* ('dry' or mural paintings) covering walls, columns, pilasters, capitals and corbels. Fortunately, these managed to survive their ignominious treatment. Entry is included in the OPA SI and Acropoli passes.

Museo dell'Opera
MUSEUM

(☑0577 28 63 00; www.operaduomo.siena.it; Piazza Duomo; adult/child €6/1; ⊘10.30am-6.30pm Mon-Sat & 1.30-5.30pm Sun Mar–mid-Apr, from 10am mid-Apr–Oct, 10.30am-5pm Mon-Sat & 1.30-5pm Sun Nov-Feb) The highlight of this repository of artworks that formerly adorned the duomo is undoubtedly Duccio (di Buoninsegna)'s striking *Maestà* (1308–11), which was painted on both sides as a screen for the high altar. Duccio portrays the Virgin surrounded by angels, saints and prominent contemporary Sienese citizens; the rear panels (sadly incomplete) show scenes from the Passion of Christ. Entry to the Panorama del Facciatone is included in the entry ticket.

Panorama del Facciatone
TOWER

(☑0577 28 63 00; http://operaduomo.siena.it; Piazza Duomo; ⊘10.30am-6.30pm Mon-Sat & 1.30-5.30pm Sun Mar–mid-Apr, from 10am Mon-Sat mid-Apr–Oct, 10.30am-5pm Mon-Sat & 1.30-5pm Sun Nov-Feb) For an unforgettable view of Siena's unique cityscape, head up the 131-step, narrow corkscrew stairway to walk atop the unfinished facade of the Duomo Nuovo (New Cathedral). Entrance is included in the Museo dell'Opera ticket and in both the OPA SI and Acropoli passes. The entrance is via the museum's upstairs floors.

★Complesso Museale di Santa Maria della Scala
MUSEUM

(☑0577 28 63 00; www.santamariadellascala.com; Piazza Duomo 2; adult/reduced €9/7; ⊘10am-7pm Fri-Wed, to 10pm Thu mid-Mar–mid-Oct, to 5pm Mon, Wed & Fri, to 8pm Thu, to 7pm Sat & Sun mid-Oct–mid-Mar) Built as a hospice for pilgrims travelling the Via Francigena, this huge complex

opposite the *duomo* dates from the 13th century. Its highlight is the upstairs Pellegrinaio (Pilgrim's Hall), featuring vivid 15th-century frescoes by Lorenzo di Pietro (aka Vecchietta), Priamo della Quercia and Domenico di Bartolo. All laud the good works of the hospital and its patrons; the most evocative is di Bartolo's *Il governo degli infermi* (Caring for the Sick; 1440–41), which depicts many activities that occurred here.

★Pinacoteca Nazionale
GALLERY

(☑0577 28 11 61; http://pinacotecanazionale.siena.it; Via San Pietro 29; adult/reduced €8/2, free 1st Sun of month Oct-Mar; ⊘8.15am-7.15pm Tue-Sat) Siena's recently renovated art gallery, housed in 14th-century Palazzo Buonsignori since 1932, is home to an extraordinary collection of Gothic masterpieces from the Sienese school. These include works by Guido da Siena, Duccio (di Buoninsegna), Simone Martini, Niccolò di Segna, Lippo Memmi, Ambrogio and Pietro Lorenzetti, Bartolo di Fredi, Taddeo di Bartolo and Sano di Pietro.

Oratorio di San Bernardino
GALLERY

(☑0577 28 63 00; http://operaduomo.siena.it; Piazza San Francesco 10; adult/child €6/1; ⊘1.30am-6.30pm Mar-Oct) Nestled in the shadow of the huge Gothic church of San Francesco, this 15th-century oratory is dedicated to St Bernardino and decorated with Mannerist frescoes by Il Sodoma, Domenico (di Pace) Beccafumi and Girolamo del Pacchia. Upstairs, the small Museo Diocesano di Arte Sacra has some lovely paintings, including *Madonna del latte* (*Nursing Madonna;* c 1340) by Ambrogio Lorenzetti. Entry is included in the OPA SI and Acropoli passes.

BILDAGENTUR ZOONAR GMBH/SHUTTERSTOCK ©

SHAIITH/GETTY IMAGES ©

3

BALATE DORIN/SHUTTERSTOCK ©

1. Lucca (p603)

Lucca's monumental *mura* (wall) was built around the old city in the 16th and 17th centuries and remains in almost perfect condition.

2. Pisa (p598)

The world-famous Leaning Tower is just one of many noteworthy sights in this compelling city.

3. Isola d'Elba (p594)

Napoleon would think twice about fleeing Elba today, now an ever-glorious paradise of beach-laced coves, vineyards, azure waters and mind-bending views.

4. Val d'Orcia (p577)

This picturesque agricultural valley is a Unesco World Heritage site.

DON'T MISS

IL PALIO

Dating from the Middle Ages, this spectacular annual event includes a series of colourful pageants and a wild horse race in Piazza del Campo on 2 July and 16 August. Ten of Siena's 17 *contrade* (town districts) compete for the coveted *palio* (silk banner). Each contrada has its own traditions, symbol and colours, plus its own church and palio museum.

From about 5pm on race days, representatives from each *contrada* parade in historical costume, all bearing their individual banners. For scarcely one exhilarating minute, the 10 horses and their bareback riders tear three times around a temporarily constructed dirt racetrack with a speed and violence that makes spectators' hair stand on end.

The race is held at 7.45pm in July and 7pm in August. Join the crowds in the centre of the Campo at least four hours before the start if you want a place on the rails, but be aware that once there you won't be able to leave for toilet or drink breaks until the race has finished. Alternatively, the cafes in the Campo sell places on their terraces; these cost between €280 and €400 per ticket. The tourist office can supply information about how to book tickets; this should be done up to one year in advance.

Sinagoga di Siena SYNAGOGUE

(Museo Ebraico di Siena; ☑ 0577 27 13 45; www.jewishtuscany.it; Viccolo delle Scotte; adult/reduced €4/3; ◷ 10.45am-4.45pm Sun, Mon & Thu) Sheltering behind an anonymous facade, this Ashkenazi synagogue in Siena's former Ghetto once serviced a community of 500. Sadly, a mere 50 Jews now live in the city. Functioning since 1731, the synagogue's rococo-style interior with its distinctive green-and-white colour scheme resembles an ornate church and can be visited on an enjoyable guided tour in which the history of the building and of Jews in Siena is recounted. Tours depart every 30 minutes.

Palazzo Chigi Saracini MUSEUM

(☑ 333 9180012, 0577 2 20 91; http://eng.chigiana.it; Via di Città 89; guided tours adult/student €7/5, picture gallery €1; ◷ tours 11.30am Mon-Wed, 11.30am & 4pm Thu & Fri) Few buildings have pedigrees as splendid as this 13th-century palace. Home of the Piccolomini family (of which Pope Pius II was the most prominent member) during the Renaissance, it was acquired by the powerful Saracini family in the 18th century and inherited a century later by a scion of the wealthy Roman Chigi family. Today it houses the **Fondazione Accademia Musicale Chigiana** and its art-adorned interiors are a testament to the wealth, erudition and taste of the Saracini and Chigi families.

Orto Botanico dell'Università GARDENS

(Botanical Garden of the University; ☑ 0577 23 20 76; www.simus.unisi.it/musei/mb; Via Pier Andrea Mattioli 4; adult/reduced €5/2.50; ◷ 10am-7pm Jul-Sep, to 5pm Mar-Jun, to 4pm Oct-Feb) The tranquil terraces of this botanical garden (1856), which is spread over 2.5 hectares of the verdant Sant'Agostino Valley, provide gorgeous views across the valley and a welcome escape from the tourist crowds. Owned by the University of Siena, which operates it as a centre for research and education, it features three greenhouses filled with tropical and subtropical species, a citrus house and gardens planted with ornamental, medicinal and food plants. Native and endangered species are also represented.

☞ Tours

Associazione Centro Guide CULTURAL

(AGT; ☑ 0577 4 32 73; www.guidesiena.it/en) One of three official local guides' associations. Operates two-hour tours to the Complesso Museale di Santa Maria della Scala (p555) and the Museo Civico (p554) from 3pm every Monday, Friday and Saturday between mid-April and October (adult/child under 11 €25/free). This departs from outside the tourist office (p561) in the Santa Maria della Scala complex. Other tours are detailed on its website.

Centro Guide Turistiche Siena e Provincia CULTURAL

(☑ 0577 4 32 73; www.guidesiena.it) Accredited guides offer guaranteed daily departures of a two-hour 'Classic Siena' Walking Tour (adult/child seven to 12/child under seven €20/10/free) at 11am between April and October. This features key historical and cultural landmarks and includes entrance to the duomo (p554) or Santa Maria della Scala (p555). Tours in English and Italian depart from outside the tourist-information office in Santa Maria della Scala (p555).

🛏 Sleeping

Siena is blessed with a wide variety of accommodation types. Note that prices skyrocket and minimum-stay requirements are implemented during the Palio.

Ostello Casa delle Balie   HOSTEL €
(☑ 347 6137678; ostellosms@operalaboratori.com; Vicolo di San Girolamo 2; dm €18; ⊙ reception 11am-4.30pm & 7-9.15pm; ✱ @ 🛜) Siena's historic centre sorely lacks backpacker accommodation; the exception is this hostel just off Piazza Duomo. Though primarily catering to pilgrims walking the Via Francigena, it also welcomes others – book in advance. Rooms have bunk beds and small lockers (sheets and blankets provided); hot showers cost €0.50. Laundry facilities (charged), but no kitchen or lounge.

Albergo Bernini   PENSION €
(☑ 0577 28 90 47; www.albergobernini.com; Via della Sapienza 15; d €100, without bathroom €80; 🛜) The tiny terrace alone might prompt you to stay at this welcoming, family-run hotel – it sports grandstand views across to the *duomo* and is a captivating spot for a drink at sunset. The 10 bedrooms are traditional affairs and only a couple have air-con. Cash payment only.

Hotel Alma Domus   HOTEL €
(☑ 0577 4 41 77; www.hotelalmadomus.it; Via Camporegio 37; s €46-55, d €72-140; ✱ @ 🛜) Your chance to sleep in a convent: Alma Domus is owned by the church and is still home to several Dominican nuns. The economy rooms, although comfortable, are styled very simply and aren't as soundproofed as many would like. But the superior ones are lovely, with stylish decor and modern fittings; many have minibalconies with uninterrupted *duomo* views.

Antica Residenza Cicogna   B&B €€
(☑ 0577 28 56 13; www.anticaresidenzacicogna.it; Via delle Terme 76; s/d/ste €90/110/150; ✱ @ 🛜) You'll get a true feel for Siena's history in this 13th-century *palazzo* close to the Campo. Tiled floors, ornate lights and painted ceilings meet tones of yellow ochre and (suitably) burnt sienna. All of the rooms are charming, but we were particularly taken with the Stanza dei Paesaggi, which is named after the frescoed landscapes that decorate it.

Hotel Italia   HOTEL €€
(☑ 0577 4 42 48; www.hotelitalia-siena.it; Viale Cavour 67; s €70-122, d €140-175; Ⓟ ✱ @ 🛜) Close to both the train station and the busy shopping and eating strip of Via Camollia, this well-priced modern hotel offers a range of accommodation, including worn-but-comfortable standard rooms and swish, newly built executive rooms. Parking costs €10 per night, the breakfast buffet is generous and guests can use the swimming pool at a nearby hotel in the same group.

**★ Pensione
Palazzo Ravizza**   BOUTIQUE HOTEL €€€
(☑ 0577 28 04 62; www.palazzoravizza.it; Pian dei Mantellini 34; r €170-330; Ⓟ ✱ 🛜) Occupying a Renaissance-era *palazzo* located in a quiet but convenient corner of Siena, the Ravizza offers rooms perfectly melding traditional decor and modern amenities; the best face the large rear garden, which has a panoramic terrace. The breakfast buffet is generous, on-site parking is free if you book directly with the hotel and room rates are remarkably reasonable (especially in low season).

🍴 Eating

Among the many traditional local dishes served in Siena are *panzanella* (summer salad of soaked bread, basil, onion and tomatoes), *ribollita* (a rich vegetable, bean and bread soup), *pappardelle alla lepre* (ribbon pasta with hare), *panforte* (a rich cake of almonds, honey and candied fruit) and *ricciarelli* (sugar-dusted chewy almond biscuits). Keep an eye out for dishes featuring the region's signature *cinta senese* (indigenous Tuscan pig).

★ La Vecchia Latteria   GELATO €
(☑ 0577 05 76 38; www.facebook.com/GelateriaYo gurteriaLaVecchiaLatteria; Via San Pietro 10; gelato €2-4.50; ⊙ noon-11pm, to 8pm winter) Sauntering through Siena's historic centre is always more fun with a gelato in hand. Just ask one of the many locals who are regular customers at this *gelateria artigianale* (maker of handmade gelato) near the Pinacoteca Nazionale. Using quality produce, owners Fabio and Francesco concoct and serve fruity fresh

---

DON'T MISS

SWEET SIENA

Lorenzo Rossi is Siena's best baker, and his *panforte*, *ricciarelli* and *cavallucci* are a weekly purchase for most local households. Try them at **Il Magnifico** (☑ 0577 28 11 06; www.ilmagnifico.siena.it; Via dei Pellegrini 27; ⊙ 7.30am-7.30pm Mon-Sat), his bakery and shop behind the *duomo*, and you'll understand why.

ⓘ PICNIC PERFECT

Prosciutto is the focus at **La Prosciut-teria** (📞 0328 541 43 25; www.laprosci utteria.com; cnr Via Pantaneto & Vicolo Magalotti; panini €4-7, tasting boards from €10; 🕐 11.30am-3.30pm & 5.30pm-midnight Mon-Thu, 11.30am-12.30am Sat; 🛜). served in panini or on a *taglieri*; cheese is an optional extra. Order to take away – the Orto de' Pecci is close by – or claim one of the tables on the street and enjoy a glass of wine (€2.50) too. An *aperitivo* costs €5.

Near the Campo, popular bakery-cum-cafe **Lievito M@dre** (📞 0577 151 54 51; www.facebook.com/LievitoMadre Siena; Via di Pantaneto 59; meal deal €6.90, pizzas €6-12; 🕐 7.30am-11pm Sun-Thu, to midnight Fi & Sat; 🛜🖉) is a recommended address for filled panini and pizza slices to take away (or eat in).

or decadently creamy iced treats – choose from gelato or frozen yogurt.

Te Ke Voi?　　　　　　　FAST FOOD €

(📞 0577 4 01 39; Vicolo di San Pietro 4; burgers €10-14, pizza €7-10, focaccias €4.50-5.50; 🕐 noon-3.30pm & 6.30pm-midnight Mon-Thu, noon-1am Fri & Sat, noon-midnight Sun; 🖉) The name means 'Whaddya want?' and the answer is simple – cheap and tasty food prepared fast and served in pleasant surrounds. Beloved of local students, it serves focaccias, salads, risottos, pastas, pizzas and burgers (including veggie options). The *pasta cresciuta* (fried pasta) goes down a treat with a cold beer or glass of wine. Order at the counter.

Osteria Il Vinaio　　　　　　TUSCAN €

(📞 0577 4 96 15; Via Camollia 167; dishes €6.50-13; 🕐 10am-10pm Mon-Sat) Wine bars are thin on the ground here in Siena, so it's not surprising that Bobbe and Davide's neighbourhood *osteria* (casual tavern) is so popular. Join the multigenerational local regulars for a bowl of pasta or your choice from the generous antipasto display, washed down with a glass or two of eminently quaffable house wine.

Ristorante All'Orto de' Pecci　　TUSCAN €

(📞 0577 22 22 01; www.ortodepecci.it; Via di Porta Giustizia, Orto de' Pecci; pizza €6-9, meals €22; 🕐 noon-2.30pm & 7.30-10pm Tue-Sun) 🖉 Serving fruit and vegetables grown in the surrounding cooperative organic farm, this rustic eatery is an excellent spot for lunch – when soup and pasta are popular choices – or for a pizza on weeknights or all day on weekends. All profits go to supporting Cooperativa La Proposta, which works to support and rehabilitate people suffering social, intellectual or physical disadvantage.

Morbidi　　　　　　　　　　DELI €

(📞 0577 28 02 68; www.morbidi.com; Via Banchi di Sopra 75; lunch buffet €12; 🕐 8am-8pm Mon-Wed, to 9pm Thu & Fri, to 3pm Sat) Famed for top-quality produce, Morbidi's excellent-value basement lunch buffet (12.15pm to 2.30pm Monday to Saturday) includes freshly prepared antipasti, salads, risotto, pasta and dessert. Bottled water is supplied; wine and coffee cost extra. Buy your ticket upstairs before heading down. It also offers an *aperitivo* buffet from 6pm (€7 to €13 Monday to Thursday, €8 to €14 Friday and Saturday).

Enoteca I Terzi　　　　　　TUSCAN €€

(📞 0577 4 43 29; www.enotecaiterzi.it; Via dei Termini 7; meals €42; 🕐 12.30-3pm & 7.30-11pm Mon-Sat) Close to the Campo but off the well-beaten tourist trail, this *enoteca* (wine bar) is located in a vaulted medieval building but has a contemporary feel. It's popular with sophisticated locals, who linger over working lunches, *aperitivo* sessions and slow-paced dinners featuring Tuscan *salumi* (cured meats), delicate hand-made pasta, grilled meats and wonderful wines (many available by the glass).

Trattoria Fonte Giusta　　　　TUSCAN €€

(📞 0577 4 05 06; Via Camollia 102; meals €30; 🕐 7-11pm Mon-Fri, noon-2.30pm & 7-11pm Sat & Sun; 🖉) The huge slabs of Chianina beef displayed in a refrigerated cabinet in the window signals one of the specialities at this family-run trattoria on the historic Via Francigena pilgrimage route through town. Other draws include hand-made pasta, flavourful seasonal antipasti, house-made gelato and home-style cakes. The owners also run the highly regarded **Fonte Giusta Cooking School** (Fonte Giusta Scuola di Cucina; http://scuoladicucinafontegiusta.com; Via Camollia 78; per person €100; 🕐 4.30-7pm).

Zest Ristorante & Wine Bar　　TUSCAN €€

(📞 0577 4 71 39; http://zestsiena.com/en; Costa di Sant'Antonio 13; meals €38; 🕐 noon-2.30pm & 6.30-10pm; 🛜🖉) There are more vegetarian, seafood and gluten-free options on the menu of this contemporary eatery than is usual in Siena, and the cuisine is less traditional than the norm, featuring plenty of colour and fresh flavours. Sit inside or at one of the tables on the steep street.

Ristorante Grotta di Santa
Caterina da Bagoga   TUSCAN €€

(☑0577 28 22 08; www.bagoga.it; Via della Galluz-za 26; meals €35; ☺12.30-3pm & 7-10pm Tue-Sat, 12.30-3pm Sun) Pierino Fagnani ('Bagoga'), one of Siena's most famous Palio jockeys, swapped his saddle for an apron in 1973 and opened this much-loved restaurant. Now operated by his son Francesco, it serves traditional Tuscan palate-pleasers that are lauded by Slow Food Italia (this is one of only two Slow Food–accredited restaurants in the city). The set menus (€25 to €55) offer good value.

★Osteria La Taverna
di San Giuseppe   TUSCAN €€€

(☑0577 4 22 86; www.tavernasangiuseppe.it; Via Dupré 132; meals €49; ☺noon-2.30pm & 7-10pm Mon-Sat) Any restaurant specialising in beef, truffles and porcini mushrooms attracts our immediate attention, but not all deliver on their promise. Fortunately, this one does. A favoured venue for locals celebrating important occasions, it offers excellent food, an impressive wine list with plenty of local, regional and international choices, a convivial traditional atmosphere and efficient service.

🍹 Drinking & Nightlife

Via Camollia and Via di Pantaneto are Siena's major bar and coffee strips. Though atmospheric, be warned that the bars lining the Campo are expensive if you sit at a table.

Bar Pasticcerie Nannini   CAFE

(☑0577 23 60 09; www.pasticcerienannini.it/en; Via Banchi di Sopra 24; ☺7.30am-10pm Mon-Thu, to 11pm Fri & Sat, to 10pm Sun) Established in 1886, its good coffee and location near the Campo ensure that it remains a local favourite. It's a great place to sample Sienese treats like *cantuccini* (crunchy, almond-studded biscuits), *cavallucci* (chewy biscuits flavoured with aniseed and other spices), *ricciarelli* (chewy, sugar-dusted almond biscuits), and *panpepato* (*panforte* with pepper and hazelnuts).

Bottega Roots   BAR

(☑0577 89 24 82; www.facebook.com/bottegarootssiena; Via di Pantaneto 58; ☺10.30am-2am; 🛜) Located in Siena's student quarter, this bar stages live-music acts in a vaulted interior with a mezzanine area. Artisan beer is the tipple of choice. Check its Facebook page for the performance schedule.

UnTUBO   CLUB

(☑0577 27 13 12; www.untubo.it; Vicolo del Luparello 2; cover charge varies; ☺6.30pm-3am Tue-Sat) Live jazz acts regularly take the stage on Thursday and Friday nights at this intimate club near the Campo, popular with students and the boho set. Check the website for a full program – blues, pop and rock acts drop in for gigs too. Winter hours are often reduced.

ℹ Information

Tourist Office (☑0577 28 05 51; www.terresiena.it; Piazza Duomo 2, Santa Maria della Scala; ☺10am-6pm mid-Mar–Oct, to 4.30pm Nov–mid-Mar)

ℹ Getting There & Away

BUS

Siena Mobilità (☑800 922984; www.sienamobilita.it), part of the Tiemme network, links

FLORENCE & TUSCANY SIENA

SIENA MOBILITÀ BUSES

Routes operated by Siena Mobilità from Monday to Saturday include the following:

DESTINATION	FARE (€)	TIME	FREQUENCY	NOTES
Arezzo	7.60	90min	8 daily	
Colle di Val d'Elsa	3.90	30-40min	hourly	Onward connections for Volterra (€2.75, four daily)
Fiumicino Airport (Rome) via Grosseto	22	3¾hr	2 daily	
Florence (*Corse Rapide/*Express service via the *autostrada*)	8.40	75min	frequent	*Corse Ordinarie* services don't use the *autostrada;* add at least 20min
Montalcino	5.60	75min	6 daily	Departs train station
Montepulciano	7.60	90min	2 daily	Departs train station
Monteriggioni	2.60	25min	frequent	
Pienza	6.20	70min	2 daily	Departs train station
San Gimignano	6.20	60-90min	10 daily	Often changes in Poggibonsi (€4.35, 1hr, hourly)

Siena with the rest of Tuscany. It has a **ticket office** (www.tiemmespa.it; Piazza Antonio Gramsci; ☺6.30am-7.30pm Mon-Fri, from 7am Sat) underneath the **main bus station** (Piazza Antonio Gramsci) in Piazza Antonio Gramsci; there's also a daytime-only left-luggage office here (€5.50 per bag between 7am and 7pm).

TRAIN

Siena's rail links aren't that extensive; buses are usually a better option. There are direct *regionale* services to Florence (€9.30, 1½ to two hours, hourly) and Grosseto (€9.90, 1½ hours, nine daily). Rome requires a change of train at Chiusi-Chianciano Terme. For Pisa, change at Empoli.

A free *scala mobile* (escalator) connects the **train station** (Piazza Carlo Rosselli) with Viale Vittorio Emanuele II, near Porta Camollia in the historic centre.

ⓘ Getting Around

BUS

Within Siena, **Tiemme** (☑7am-7pm 199 16 81 82; www.tiemmespa.it) operates *pollicino* (city centre), *urbano* (urban) and *suburbano* (suburban) buses (€1.20 per 70 minutes). Buses 3 and 7 run between the train station and Piazza del Sale in the historic centre.

CAR & MOTORCYCLE

There's a ZTL (Zona a Traffico Limitato; Limited Traffic Zone) in Siena's historic centre, although visitors can often drop off luggage at their hotel; ask reception to report your licence number in advance, or risk a hefty fine.

There are large car parks operated by **Siena Parcheggi** (☑0577 22 87 11; www.sienaparcheggi.com) at the Stadio Comunale and around the Fortezza Medicea, both just north of Piazza San Domenico (the website is a useful resource). Hotly contested free street parking (look for white lines) is available in Viale Vittorio Veneto on the Fortezza Medicea's southern edge. The paid car parks at San Francesco and Santa Caterina (aka Fontebranda) each have a free *scala mobile* (escalator) going up into the centre.

Most car parks charge €2 per hour between 7am and 8pm.

Chianti

The vineyards in this picturesque part of Tuscany produce the grapes used in namesake Chianti and Chianti Classico: world-famous reds sold under the Gallo Nero (Black Cockerel/Rooster) trademark. It's a landscape where you'll encounter historic olive groves, honey-coloured stone farmhouses, dense forests, graceful Romanesque *pievi* (rural churches), handsome Renaissance villas and

imposing stone castles built in the Middle Ages by Florentine and Sienese warlords.

Though now part of the province of Siena, the southern section of Chianti (Chianti Senese) was once the stronghold of the Lega del Chianti, a military and administrative alliance within the city-state of Florence that comprised Castellina, Gaiole and Radda. Chianti's northern part sits in the province of Florence (Chianti Fiorentino) and is a popular day trip from that city. The major wine and administrative centres are Greve in Chianti, Castellina in Chianti and Radda in Chianti.

For regional information, including festivals and special events, see www.wechianti.com and www.chianti.com.

Greve in Chianti

☑0558 / POP 13,800

The main town in the Chianti Fiorentino, Greve is a hub of the local wine industry and has an amiable market-town air. It's not picturesque (most of the architecture is modern and unattractive), but it does boast an attractive, historic central square and a few notable businesses. The annual wine fair Expo del Chianti Classico (Chianti Classico Expo; www.expochianticlassico.com) is held in early September – if visiting at this time, book accommodation here and throughout the region well in advance.

⊙ Sights & Activities

Montefioralle   VILLAGE

Medieval Montefioralle crowns a rise just east of Greve, and can be accessed via a 2km walking path from the town centre (head up Via San Francesco, off Via Roma). Surrounded by olive groves and vineyards, the village was home to Amerigo Vespucci (1415–1512), an explorer who followed Columbus' route to America. Vespucci wrote so excitedly about the New World that he inspired cartographer Martin Waldseemüller (creator of the 1507 *Universalis Cosmographia*) to name the new continent in his honour.

Enoteca Falorni   WINE

(☑0558 54 64 04; www.enotecafalorni.it; Piazza delle Cantine 6; tastings by glass €0.60-30; ☺11am-5pm Mon, Thu & Fri, to 7pm Sat & Sun) A perfect place to let your palate limber up before visiting individual wineries, this *enoteca* stocks more than 1000 wines and offers 100 for tasting, including a huge array of Chianti Classico, IGTs and other Tuscan favourites. Leave your credit-card as a guarantee or buy a non-refundable prepaid wine card (€5 to €100) to test your tipples of choice.

Castello di Verrazzano   WINE
(☑0558 5 42 43; www.verrazzano.com; Via Citille 32a, Greti; tours €22-68; ⊘9.30am-6pm Mon-Sat, 10am-1pm & 3-6.30pm Sun) This hilltop castle 3km north of Greve was once home to Giovanni da Verrazzano (1485–1528), who explored the North American coast and is commemorated by the Verrazzano-Narrows Bridge in New York. Today it presides over a 225-hectare wine estate offering a wide range of tours.

🛏 Sleeping

Antico Pastificio Ulisse Mariotti APARTMENT €
(☑339 8485564; www.anticopastificio.com; Via dell'Arco 13; s/d €53/62, apt from €84; ❄🐾🛜🏊) In central Greve, two buildings of this former pasta factory have been converted into neat double rooms and basic self-catering apartments sleeping up to 10 guests. It offers swimming pool, table tennis, children's playground, shady grassed garden, BBQ area and a washing machine for guest use (€2 per load). Wi-fi (charged) is in common areas only. No breakfast; two-night minimum stay.

★ Borgo del Cabreo   AGRITURISMO €€€
(☑347 1174065, 0553 98 50 32; www.borgo delcabreo.it; Via Montefioralle Case Sparse 9; d €260-280, q villa €400; Ⓟ❄🛜🏊) Manager Michele works hard to ensure that guests enjoy their stay at this boutique *agriturismo* owned by the Tenuta di Nozzole winery, offering an efficient check-in, pouring a complimentary *aperitivo* on arrival and organising everything from restaurant bookings to bicycle hire. Rooms are classically elegant and extremely comfortable; facilities include a fabulous pool terrace overlooking the estate's olive groves.

🍴 Eating

There are plenty of eateries on or around Greve in Chianti's Piazza Giacomo Matteotti, but few are worthy of recommendation. At lunch, buy picnic provisions or enjoy a snack at **Antica Macelleria Falorni** (☑0558 5 30 29; www.falorni.it; Piazza Giacomo Matteotti 71; ⊘9am-1pm & 3-7pm Mon-Sat, from 10am Sun). For a sit-down meal, walk or drive up the hill to La Castellana. There's a weekly market on Saturday morning in Piazza Matteotti.

Bistro Falorni   DELI €
(☑0558 5 30 29; www.falorni.it; Piazza Giacomo Matteotti 71; taglieri €7-9, panini €4-5, lasagne €6; ⊘10am-7pm; 🛜) Italians do fast food differently, and what a wonderful difference it is. Greve's famous *macelleria* (butcher) and gourmet-provision shop operates this cafeteria attached to the *macelleria,* and it's popular with both locals and tourists. Choose from the range of *taglieri* (tasting boards), *panini* and meat or vegetable lasagnes on offer, and enjoy a glass of wine (€4) too.

La Castellana   TUSCAN €€
(☑0558 5 31 34; www.ristorantelacastellana.it; Via di Montefioralle 2, Montefioralle; meals €40; ⊘12.30-2pm & 7.30-9.30pm Tue-Sun summer, hr vary winter) Located in a hamlet 2km above Greve, this well-regarded trattoria has six indoor tables and a hillside terrace overlooking cypresses, olive trees and vines. The home-style Tuscan cooking is wonderful – highlights include handmade ravioli stuffed with mushrooms and truffles, and succulent slices of rosemary-studded beef – and the wine list features many Chianti highlights.

CYCLING CHIANTI

Exploring Chianti by bicycle is a true highlight. The Greve in Chianti tourist office (p566) can supply information about local cycling routes, and the town is home to the well-regarded **Discovery Chianti** (☑328 6124658; www.discoverychianti.com; Via I Maggio 32, Greve in Chianti; ⊘Mar-Oct), which runs guided cycling tours. It's also possible to rent bicycles from **Ramuzzi** (☑055 85 30 37; www.ramuzzi.com; Via Italo Stecchi 23; mountain or hybrid bike per day/week €20/130, e-bike/scooter per day €35/€65; ⊘9am-1pm & 3-7pm Mon-Fri, 9am-1pm Sat) in Greve's town centre. A number of companies offer guided cycling tours (including by Discovery Chianti) leaving from Florence:

Florence by Bike (☑0554 8 89 92; www.florencebybike.it; Chianti guided bike tour adult/reduced €83/75; ⊘daily Mar-Oct)

I Bike Italy (☑342 9352395; www.ibikeitaly.com; 2-day Chianti guided bike tour road bike/e-bike €450/550; ⊘Mon, Wed & Fri mid-Mar–Oct)

We Bike Tuscany (☑USA 1-800-850-6832; www.webiketuscany.com; prices on application)

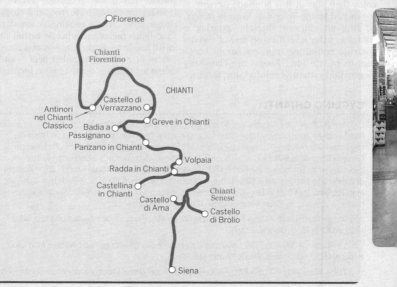

Florence

Chianti
Fiorentino

CHIANTI

Castello di
Verrazzano

Antinori
nel Chianti
Classico

Greve in Chianti

Badia a
Passignano

Panzano in Chianti

Volpaia

Radda in Chianti

Castellina
in Chianti

Chianti
Senese

Castello
di Ama

Castello
di Brolio

Siena

4 DAYS Wine Tour of Chianti

Tuscany has more than its fair share of highlights, but few can match the glorious indulgence of a leisurely drive through Chianti. On offer is an intoxicating blend of scenery, fine dines and ruby-red wine.

From **Florence** (p510), take the *superstrada* (expressway) towards Siena, exit at Bargino and follow the signs to **Antinori nel Chianti Classico** (p567), a state-of-the-art wine estate featuring an architecturally innovative ageing cellar. Take a tour, prime your palate with a wine tasting and enjoy lunch in the estate's Rinuccio 1180 restaurant.

Head southeast along the SS2, SP3 and SS222 (Via Chiantigiana) towards Greve in Chianti. Stop at historic **Castello di Verrazzano** (p563) for a tasting en route.

On the next day, make your way to **Greve in Chianti** (p562) to test your new-found knowledge over a self-directed tasting at Enoteca Falorni. For lunch, eat a Tuscan-style burger at Dario DOC in **Panzano in Chianti** (p569). Your destination in the afternoon should be **Badia a Passignano** (p566), an 11th-century, still-functioning Vallombrosan abbey surrounded by an Antinori wine estate. Enjoy a tasting in the *enoteca* (wine bar) and consider staying for an early pizza dinner at L'Antica Scuderia opposite the abbey, where you'll be able to watch the sun set over the vineyards.

On day three, pop into the pretty hilltop hamlet of **Volpaia** near **Radda in Chianti** (p568) and take a tour of the **Castello di Volpaia cellars** (☑0577 73 80 66; www.volpaia.it; Località Volpaia; ⊙enoteca 9am-1pm & 2.30-5pm Mon-Fri Apr-Nov) before relaxing over lunch at the innovative Ristorante Taverna Squarcialupi in **Castellina in Chianti** (p568).

Hit **Siena** (p551) on the last day. En route tour **Castello di Brolio** (p570), ancestral home of the aristocratic Ricasoli family. Their wine estate is the oldest in Italy, so be sure to sample some Baron Ricasoli Chianti Classico at the estate's *cantina* (cellar) or over lunch in its *osteria* (casual tavern). Afterwards, enjoy award-winning wines and contemporary art at **Castello di Ama** (p569).

Top: Antinori nel Chianti Classico (p567; architect Marco Casaminti)
Bottom: Enoteca Falorni (p562)

ⓘ Information

The **tourist office** (☑ 0558 54 62 99, 0558 5 36 06; www.helloflorence.net; Piazza Matteotti 11; ☺10.30am-1.30pm late Mar–mid-Oct, to 6.30pm Easter-Aug) is located in Greve's main square.

ⓘ Getting There & Away

Buses travel between Greve in Chianti and Florence (€4.50, one hour, hourly) and between Greve and Panzano in Chianti (€1.50, 15 minutes, frequent). The bus stop is on Piazza Trento, 100m from Piazza Giacomo Matteotti. Purchase tickets from the tourist office or from Caffè Annando (open Thursday to Tuesday) in Galleria delle Cantine next to the Coop Supermarket on the main road.

Badia a Passignano

Chianti doesn't get much more atmospheric than Badia a Passignano, a Benedictine Vallombrosan abbey set amid vineyards run by the legendary Antinori dynasty. Head here to visit the historic church and abbey buildings, admire the views over the vineyards, and taste wines in the Antinori *enoteca* or in one of a number of good eateries located here.

ⓞ Sights & Activities

Chiesa di San Michele Arcangelo   CHURCH
(Abbey of Passignano; Via di Passignano; ☺10am-noon & 3-5pm Mon-Wed, Fri & Sat, 3-5pm Sun) An 11th-century church on this site was destroyed in the 13th century and replaced by this structure, which was subsequently heavily altered over the centuries. Dedicated to St Michael the Archangel (look for the 12th-century statue of him slaying a dragon next to the high altar), it is home to frescoes and paintings of varying quality – the best are by Domenico Cresti (known as 'Il Passignano') on the side walls of the transept.

Abbazia di San Michele
Arcangelo a Passignano   MONASTERY
(☑ English 0558 07 23 41, Italian 0558 07 11 71; Via di Passignano; by donation; ☺tours by reservation) The four Vallombrosan monks who call this medieval abbey home open their quarters to visitors on regular guided tours. The highlight is the refectory, which was remodelled in the 15th century and is presided over by Domenico Ghirlandaio's utterly marvellous, recently restored 1476 fresco *The Last Supper*. The tours also visit the monastery's garden cloister and historic kitchen. It's best to book in advance, as tour times can vary.

La Bottega di Badia a Passignano   WINE
(☑ 055 807 12 78; www.osteriadipassignano.com; Via di Passignano 33; ☺10am-7.30pm Mon-Sat) Taste or purchase Antinori wine in this *enoteca* beside the prestigious Osteria di Passignano restaurant. A tasting of three wines by the glass will cost between €25 and €60, and there is a variety of guided tours of the cellars and vineyards on offer – check the website for details. Wines by the glass cost between €6 and €25.

🛏 Sleeping & Eating

Torre di Badia   B&B €€
(☑ 0550 16 41 60; www.torredibadia.com; Via Passignano 22; r €110-180; ❋🛜) Offering five comfortable rooms, this B&B in a recently restored medieval tower on the Badia di Passignano estate is a good choice for those wanting to explore the local area. In winter, the open fire and honesty bar in the lounge make for a welcoming retreat; in summer the garden terrace overlooking the Antinori vineyard beckons.

Fattoria di Rignana   AGRITURISMO €€
(☑ 0558 5 20 65; www.rignana.it; Via di Rignana 15, Rignana; d from €100; ☺Apr-Nov; 🅿@🛜❋) The historic *fattoria* (farmhouse) of this wine estate has its very own chapel and bell tower, which reveal themselves after you brave a long, rutted access road. You'll also find glorious views, a large swimming pool and a nearby eatery. Sleep in rustic en suite rooms in the *fattoria*. Find it 4km from Badia a Passignano.

★ **L'Antica Scuderia**   TUSCAN €€
(☑055 807 16 23, 335 8252669; www.ristorolanti cascuderia.com; Via di Passignano 17; meals €45, pizza €10-18; ☺12.30-2.30pm & 7.30-10.30pm Wed-Mon; ❋🛜🍴) The large terrace at this restaurant overlooks one of the Antinori vineyards and is perfect for summer dining. In winter, the elegant dining room comes into its own. Lunch features antipasti, pastas and traditional grilled meats, while dinner sees plenty of pizza-oven action. Kids love the playground set; adults love the fact that it keeps the kids occupied. Huge wine list.

Osteria di Passignano   ITALIAN €€€
(☑055 807 12 78; www.osteriadipassignano.com; Via di Passignano 33; meals €85, tasting menus €90, wine pairing €140; ☺12.15-2.15pm & 7.30-10pm Mon-Sat; 🅿🛜🍴) This elegant Michelin-starred eatery in the centre of Badia a Passignano has long been one of Tuscany's best-loved dining destinations. Intricate, Tuscan-inspired dishes fly the local-produce

flag and the wine list is mightily impressive, with Antinori offerings aplenty. Vegetarians are well catered for, with a dedicated tasting menu available.

❶ Getting There & Away

There is no public transport connection to Badia a Passignano. The easiest road access is via Strada di Badia off the SP94.

San Casciano in Val di Pesa

📞 0588 / POP 17,200

Almost totally destroyed by Allied bombs in 1944, San Casciano in Val di Pesa, to the south of Florence, was fully rebuilt and is now a busy hub for the local wine and olive-oil industries. There are no sights of note within the town itself, but the surrounding countryside is home to a number of impressive *agriturismi* (farmstay accommodation) and villas.

🏃 Activities

⭐ **Antinori nel Chianti Classico**   WINE

(📞0552 35 97 00; www.antinorichianticlassico.it; Via Cassia per Siena 133, Località Bargino; tours & tastings from €35; ⏱10am-5pm Mon-Fri, to 5.30pm Sat & Sun winter, to 6.30pm Sat & Sun summer) Marco Casaminti's sculptural building set into the hillside is a landmark sight from the *autostrada* just south of Florence, and is one of the world's most impressive examples of contemporary winery design. Daily guided tours (in English and Italian) include a short film presentation, a visit to the winemaking and fermentation areas and a guided tasting; in the 'Bottaia' tour, the latter is often held in a glass tasting room cantilevered over the barriques in the cathedral-like ageing cellar. Bookings essential.

The Antinori family has been in the winemaking business since 1180. You can taste or purchase their wines in the stylish *enoteca* or enjoy a glass or two over lunch in the Rinuccio 1180 restaurant. Alternatively, book for the 'Bottaia Cru' tour (€160), which includes tastings of seven of the vineyard's wines as well as lunch.

Bargino is 7km south of San Casciano in Val di Pesa and 20km northwest of Greve.

🛏 Sleeping

The best accommodation options are outside the centre of San Casciano.

⭐ **Villa I Barronci**   HOTEL €€

(📞0558 2 05 98; www.ibarronci.com; Via Sorripa 10; s/d/ste from €165/185/330; P❄@🛜🏊) Exemplary service, superb amenities and high comfort levels ensure this country hotel on the northwestern edge of San Casciano is one to remember. You can relax in the bar, rejuvenate in the spa, laze by the pool, dine in the excellent restaurant (meals €36) or take day trips to Pisa, Lucca, Florence, Volterra, San Gimignano and Siena. Amazing low-season rates.

Il Paluffo   AGRITURISMO €€

(📞0571 66 42 59; www.paluffo.com; Via Citerna 144, Località Fiano; B&B r from €125, apt from €170; P❄@🛜🏊) 🅿 Hidden in the hills 14km southwest of San Casciano, this clever conversion of a centuries-old olive farm has seen the former fermentation room transformed into a comfortable guest lounge, farm buildings into self-catering apartments, and upstairs rooms of the frescoed farm villa into elegant B&B rooms with modern bathrooms. Views from the terraces stretch as far as San Gimignano's towers.

Staff can arrange wine tasting and truffle hunting, while cookery courses cover everything from pasta making to Tuscan dinner parties. Add a luscious bio-filtered swimming pool, an honesty bar stacked with Tuscan wines and a delicious breakfast featuring organic local produce (included in B&B room cost, charge levied for apartment guests). There's a two-night minimum stay.

🍴 Eating

⭐ **L'Osteria di Casa Chianti**   TUSCAN €€

(📞0571 66 96 88; www.osteriadicasachianti.it; Località Case Nuove 77, Fiano; meals €38; ⏱7-10pm Tue-Sat, 12.30-2.30pm & 7-10pm Sun; 🪑) The type of restaurant that fuels fantasies of moving permanently to Tuscany, Massimiliano Canton's ultrafriendly *osteria* bakes its own bread, makes pasta by hand, grills *bistecca* on a wood fire, specialises in truffle and porcini dishes, and has an exceptional wine list. Families appreciate the keenly priced kids' menu (€5 to €12) too. Book ahead. You'll find it on the SP79 between Fiano and Certaldo, 14km southwest of San Casciano in Val di Pesa.

Rinuccio 1180   TUSCAN €€

(📞0552 35 97 20; www.antinorichianticlassico.it; Via Cassia per Siena 133, Bargino; meals €42; ⏱noon-4pm) Built on the rooftop of the sleek Antinori winery, this restaurant seats diners on an expansive outdoor terrace with a 180-degree Dolby-esque surround of hills, birdsong and pea-green vines. In cooler weather, the dining action moves into a glass dining space. Cuisine is Tuscan, modern, seasonal and sassy (Chianti burger, anyone?). Book ahead.

Bargino is 6.7km south of San Casciano in Val do Pesa and 20km northwest of Greve.

ℹ Getting There & Away

San Casciano is on the SP92, just off the Florence–Siena *autostrada*. **Busitalia/Autolinee Chianti Valdarno** (ACV; www.acvbus.it) operates services between the town and Florence (€3.50, 35 minutes, frequent).

Castellina in Chianti

☑ 0577 / POP 2850

Established by the Etruscans and fortified by the Florentines in the 15th century as a defensive outpost against the Sienese, sturdy Castellina in Chianti is now a major centre of the wine industry, as the huge silos brimming with Chianti Classico on the town's approaches attest. The town's location on the SR222 makes it a convenient overnight or meal stop for those travelling between Florence and Siena.

🛏 Sleeping & Eating

Il Colombaio B&B €

(☑ 0577 74 04 44; www.albergoilcolombaio.it; Via Chiantigiana 29; s/d/tr €90/100/130; P 🛜 🐝) A tasteful conversion has turned this 14th-century farmhouse on the edge of Castellina into a welcoming *albergo* (hotel) with 15 rooms and a rich heritage feel: tapestry-covered chairs frame lace curtains and oil paintings; wood-beamed ceilings and iron bedheads add plenty of character. Breakfast is served in the vaulted wine cellar or in the garden, where there is also a pool.

Palazzo Squarcialupi HOTEL €€

(☑ 0577 74 11 86; www.squarcialupirelaxinchianti .com; Via Ferruccio 22; r €138-175; ⊘ closed Nov-early Apr; P @ 🛜 🐝) You've gotta love a hotel that offers four-star facilities for three-star prices. And that's what this well-run hotel in a 15th-century *palazzo* in Castellina's historic centre does. Rooms are comfortable and well sized; those in the superior category have views. Facilities include an excellent restaurant, bar, large swimming pool, panoramic terrace and spa (free for guests).

Ristorante Taverna Squarcialupi TUSCAN €€

(☑ 0577 74 14 05; www.tavernasquarcialupi.it; Via Ferruccio 26; meals €40; ⊘ noon-3pm Thu-Tue, 7-10pm Thu-Mon) Interesting and highly successful flavour combinations characterise

the menu at this huge *taverna* (tavern) in the centre of Castellina. The handmade pasta dishes are delicious – grab a seat on the panoramic rear terrace and enjoy one with a glass or two of wine from the nearby La Castellina wine estate.

ℹ Getting There & Away

Tiemme (www.tiemmespa.it) buses link Castellina in Chianti with Radda in Chianti (€2.60, 10 minutes, three to five daily Monday to Saturday) and with Siena (€3.50, 40 minutes, seven daily Monday to Saturday). The most convenient bus stops are on the main road near Via delle Mura; buy tickets from **Tabacchi Piattellini** in Via Ferruccio (open Monday to Saturday).

Radda in Chianti

☑ 0577 / POP 1580

The age-old streets in pretty Radda in Chianti fan out from its central square, where the heraldic shields of the 16th-century Palazzo del Podestà add a touch of drama to the scene. A historic wine town, it's the home of the Consorzio di Chianti Classico and is an appealing albeit low-key base for visits to some classic Tuscan vineyards, including those surrounding the historic hilltop hamlet of Volpaia, approximately 7km north of town.

◉ Sights

Casa Chianti Classico MUSEUM

(☑ 0577 73 81 87; www.casachianticlassico.it; Monastery of Santa Maria al Prato, Circonvallazione Santa Maria 18; self-guided tour with glass of wine €7; ⊘ tours & tastings 11am-5pm Thu-Sat, to 3pm Sun Mar-Oct) FREE Occupying an 18th-century convent complex attached to a 10th-century church, this facility is operated by the Consorzio di Chianti Classico and pays homage to the region's favourite product. Self-guided tours of the **Wine Museum** on the 1st floor introduce the terroir and history of the denomination and include an enjoyable multimedia quiz in which participants test their newly acquired oenological knowledge by analysing a glass of local wine (included in tour price).

The complex also has a tasting room off the main cloister (glass of wine €5 to €8), and a bistro incorporating a downstairs *enoteca* with a lovely terrace overlooking vineyards – perfect for a leisurely lunch or late-afternoon glass of wine. To find it, head downhill from Radda's main piazza.

🛏 Sleeping & Eating

Palazzo Leopoldo HOTEL €€
(📞 0577 73 56 05; www.palazzoleopoldo.it; Via
Roma 33; s from €120, d from €135, ste from €240;
🅿 ❄ 🛜 ⛱) Like the idea of staying in a luxury hotel in an elegant 15th-century building
but fear your budget won't stretch that far?
This meticulously presented hotel may well
be the answer. Well-equipped rooms and
suites are located in the main building and
an annexe; many have valley views. It has an
indoor pool, outdoor hot tubs and a restaurant (meals €36).

Bistro Casa Chianti Classico TUSCAN €
(📞 0577 73 81 87; www.chianticlassico.com; Monastery of Santa Maria al Prato, Circonvallazione Santa
Maria 18; meals €23; ⊙ noon-5pm Tue-Sun mid-
Mar–Oct) Offering a seasonally driven menu
and boasting (of course) a wonderful wine
list, this bistro in the Chianti complex seats
diners in the former kitchen and cloisters
of an 18th-century convent, as well as in a
downstairs *enoteca* with a terrace overlooking an adjoining vineyard. Try the signature
pici del convento (pasta with confit tomato,
almonds, olives and herbs).

ℹ Information

Tourist Office (📞 0577 73 84 94; www.face
book.com/proradda; Piazza del Castello 2;
⊙ 10am-1pm Mon-Sat; 🛜)

ℹ Getting There & Away

Radda is linked with Siena by the SP102 and
with Castellina in Chianti by the SR429. **Tiemme**
(www.tiemmespa.it) buses link the town with
Castellina (€2.60, 10 minutes, three to five daily
Monday to Saturday) and with Siena (€4.50, one
hour, four daily Monday to Saturday). Buses stop
on Via XX Settembre (SR429) near La Botte di
Bacco restaurant; buy tickets at Porciatti Alimentari on Piazza IV Novembre.

Gaiole in Chianti

📞 0577 / POP 2760

Surrounded by majestic medieval castles
and atmospheric *pievi* (rural churches), this
small town has few attractions but is sometimes visited en route to Castello di Brolio
(p570) or Castello di Ama.

👁 Sights

★ **Castello di Ama** WINERY
(📞 0577 74 60 69; www.castellodiama.com; Località
Ama; guided tours adult/child under 16yr €25/free;
⊙ enoteca 10am-7pm, tours by appointment) At
Castello di Ama, centuries-old winemaking
traditions meet cutting-edge contemporary
art in a 12th-century *borgo* (agricultural estate). As well as vineyards and a winery producing internationally acclaimed wines such
as 'L'Apparita' merlot, the estate also features
a boutique hotel, a restaurant and a sculpture
park showcasing 14 impressive site-specific
pieces by artists including Louise Bourgeois,

FLORENCE & TUSCANY CHIANTI

TUSCANY'S CELEBRITY BUTCHER

The small town of Panzano in Chianti, 10km south of Greve in Chianti, is known throughout Italy as the location of **L'Antica Macelleria Cecchini** (📞 0558 5 20 20; www.
dariocecchini.com; Via XX Luglio 11; ⊙ 9am-4pm), a butcher's shop owned and run by the
ever-extroverted Dario Cecchini. This Tuscan celebrity has carved out a niche for himself
as a poetry-spouting guardian of the *bistecca* (steak) and other Tuscan meaty treats,
and he operates three eateries clustered around the *macelleria*: **Officina della Bistecca** (📞 0558 5 20 20; www.dariocecchini.com; Via XX Luglio 11; set menu adult/child under 10
€50/25; ⊙ sittings 1-1.30pm & 8-8.30pm), with a set menu built around the famous *bistecca*; **Solociccia** (📞 0558 5 27 27; www.dariocecchini.com; Via XX Luglio; set meat menu adult/
child under 10 €30/15; ⊙ sittings 1-1.30pm, 8pm & 9pm), where guests sample meat dishes
other than steak; and **Dario DOC** (📞 0558 5 21 76; www.dariocecchini.com; Via XX Luglio 11;
burgers €10 or €15 Mon-Fri, €15 Sat, meat sushi €20; ⊙ noon-3pm Mon-Sat), his casual lunch-
time-only eatery. Book ahead for the Officina and Solociccia.

Pre- or post-lunch, motor to neighbouring **Pieve di San Leolino** (Strada San Leolino,
Località San Leolino; ⊙ 10am-7pm, reduced hours winter, mass 10am Sun), a beautiful Romanesque *pieve* (rural church with baptistry) on a hilltop just outside Panzano in Chianti. Artworks inside include a 1421 polyptych behind the high altar by Mariotto di Nardo (1421),
two glazed terracotta tabernacles by Giovanni della Robbia, and a luminous 13th-century
triptych by the master of Panzano.

Chen Zhen, Anish Kapoor, Kendell Geers and Daniel Buren. This can be visited on a guided tour; advance bookings essential.

A paid wine tasting (€60, including guide tour) includes the Chianti Classico Riserva DOCG, Haiku IGT (a blend of Sangiovese, cabernet franc and merlot) and a third wine.

The estate is 11km south of Radda in Chianti, near Lecchi in Chianti.

Castello di Brolio   CASTLE

(📞 0577 73 02 80; www.ricasoli.it; Località Madonna a Brolio; garden, chapel & crypt €5, museum €3; ⊙10am-5.30pm mid-Mar–Oct) The ancestral estate of the aristocratic Ricasoli family dates from the 11th century and is the oldest winery in Italy. Currently home to the 32nd baron, it opens its formal garden, panoramic terrace and small but fascinating museum to day trippers, who often adjourn to the excellent on-site *osteria* for lunch after enjoying a morning tour and tasting.

Occupying three rooms in the castle's tower, Brolio's museum is dedicated to documenting the life of the extravagantly mustachioed Baron Bettino Ricasoli (1809–80), the second prime minster of the Republic of Italy, a man of many identities (scientist, farmer, winemaker, statesman and businessman) and a leading figure in the Risorgimento. One of his great claims to fame is inventing the formula for Chianti Classico that is enshrined in current DOC regulations. Entry is by guided tour only, and these must be booked in advance.

The *castello*'s chapel dates from the early 14th century; beneath it is a crypt where

---

A VINTAGE BIKE RIDE

Each year on the first Sunday in October cyclists gather in Gaiole in Chianti to compete in Eroica (www.eroicagaiole.com). The original event in a now-global phenomenon, Chianti's famous cycling race was launched in 1997 to raise funds and awareness for the protection and preservation of gravel roads in Tuscany. Cyclists follow five routes of varying difficulty (45km to 209km) throughout Chianti and the Crete Senese. Participants ride 'vintage' bikes – no modern racing, mountain or e-bikes are allowed.

May ushers in a similar Eroica (www.eroicamontalcino.it) in nearby Montalcino: cyclists follow five routes (27km to 171km) starting in Montalcino.

---

generations of Ricasolis are interred. The estate produces wine and olive oil, and the huge terrace commands a spectacular view of the vineyards and olive groves.

The Classic Tour (€30, two hours) takes in the wine-making facilities and features a tasting; it runs at least three times weekly. The Vineyard Tour (€45, two hours, 3pm Thursday) sees you exploring three of the estate's different terrains and sampling vintages beside the vines. It is essential to book online in advance.

A *bosco inglese* (English garden) surrounds the estate; in it (near the car park) you'll find the estate's **Osteria del Castello** (📞0577 73 02 90; Località Madonna a Brolio; meals €40; ⊙noon-2.30pm 2nd half of Mar–Oct and Sun-Wed Nov-Dec, 7-10pm Apr-Oct and Fri-Sat 2nd half of Mar, closed Jan–mid-Mar). Just outside the estate's entrance gates, on the SP484, is a modern **cantina** (📞0577 73 02 20; https://ricasoli.com/en; Madonna a Brolio; ⊙10am-7pm mid-Mar-late Oct, to 6pm late Oct–Dec, 10am-5pm Mon-Fri early Jan–mid-Mar), or cellar, where you can taste the estate's well-regarded Chianti Classico.

❶ Getting There & Away

Gaiole is on the SP408 between Siena and Montevarchi. **Tiemme** (www.tiemmespa.it) bus 127 travels between Gaiole and Via Lombardi behind Siena's railway station (€3.50, 40 minutes, seven daily Monday to Saturday). The bus stop in Gaiole is on the main road, opposite the elementary school.

San Gimignano

📞0577 / POP 7770

As you crest the nearby hills, the 14 towers of the walled town of San Gimignano rise up like a medieval Manhattan. Originally an Etruscan village, the settlement was named after the bishop of Modena, San Gimignano, who is said to have saved the city from Attila the Hun. It became a *comune* (local government) in 1199, prospering in part because of its location on the Via Francigena. Building a tower taller than their neighbours' (there were originally 72 of them) became a popular way for prominent families to flaunt their power and wealth. In 1348 plague wiped out much of the population and weakened the local economy, leading to the town's submission to Florence in 1353. Today, not even the plague would deter the swarms of summer day trippers, who are lured by a palpable sense of history, an intact medieval streetscapes and the enchanting rural setting.

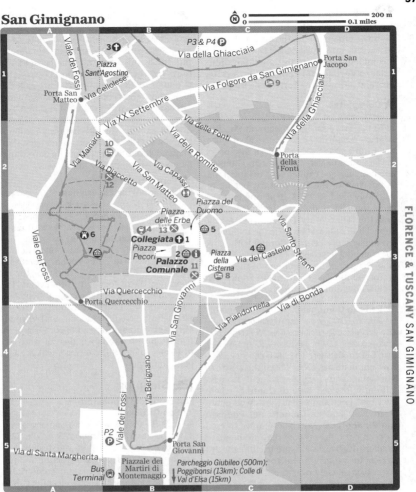

FLORENCE & TUSCANY SAN GIMIGNANO

⊙ Sights

San Gimignano's triangular **Piazza della Cisterna** is named after the 13th-century cistern at its centre. In Piazza del Duomo, the cathedral looks across to the late-13th-century **Palazzo Vecchio del Podestà** (Piazza del Duomo) and its tower, the **Torre della Rognosa**.

★ Collegiata   CHURCH

(Duomo; Basilica di Santa Maria Assunta; ☑ 0577 28 63 00; www.duomosangimignano.it; Piazza del Duomo; adult/reduced €4/2; ⊘ 10am-7.30pm Mon-Fri, to 5.30pm Sat, 12.30-7.30pm Sun Apr-Oct, shorter hours Nov-Mar) Parts of San Gimignano's Romanesque cathedral were built in the second half of the 11th century, but its remarkably vivid frescoes, depicting episodes from the Old and New Testaments, date from the 14th century. Look out, too, for the Cappella di Santa Fina, near the main altar – a Renaissance chapel adorned with naive and touching frescoes by Domenico Ghirlandaio, depicting the life of one of the town's patron saints. These featured in Franco Zeffirelli's 1999 film *Tea with Mussolini*.

★ Palazzo Comunale   MUSEUM

(☑ 0577 28 63 00; www.sangimignanomusei.it; Piazza del Duomo 2; combined Civic Museums ticket adult/reduced €9/7; ⊘ 10am-7.30pm Apr-Sep, 11am-5.30pm Oct-Mar) The 13th-century Palazzo Comunale has always been the centre of San Gimignano's local government; its magnificently frescoed **Sala di Dante** is where the great poet addressed the town's council in 1299 and its **Camera del Podestà** and **Pinacoteca** (Art Gallery) once housed government offices – now they are home to wonderful artworks. Be sure to climb the 218 steps of the *palazzo's* 54m **Torre Grossa** for a spectacular view over the town and surrounding countryside.

Chiesa di Sant'Agostino   CHURCH

(Piazza Sant'Agostino; ⊘ 10am-noon & 3-7pm Apr-Oct, to 6pm Nov & Dec, 4-6pm Mon, 10am-noon & 3-6pm Tue-Sun Jan-Mar) **FREE** This late-13th-century church is best known for Benozzo Gozzoli's charming fresco cycle (1464–65) illustrating the life of St Augustine. You'll find it in the choir behind the altar. Gozzoli also painted the fresco featuring San Sebastian on the north wall, which shows the saint protecting the citizens of San Gimignano during the 1464 plague. What makes the image highly unusual is that he's helped by a bare-breasted Virgin Mary; this symbolises her maternal love for humanity.

★ Galleria Continua   GALLERY

(☑ 0577 94 31 34; www.galleriacontinua.com; Via del Castello 11; ⊘ 10am-1pm & 2-7pm) **FREE** It may seem strange to highlight contemporary art in this medieval time capsule of a town, but there's good reason to do so. This is one of the best commercial art galleries in Europe, showing the work of big-name artists such as Ai Weiwei, Daniel Buren, Antony Gormley and Mona Hatoum. Spread over four venues (an old cinema, a medieval tower, a vaulted cellar and an apartment on Piazza della Cisterna), it's one of San Gimignano's most compelling attractions.

★ Vernaccia di San Gimignano Wine Experience   MUSEUM

(☑ 0577 94 12 67; www.sangimignanomuseovernaccia.com; Via della Rocca 1; ⊘ 11.30am-7.30pm Apr-Oct, to 6.30pm Nov & Mar, closed Dec-Feb) **FREE** San Gimignano's famous wine, Vernaccia, is celebrated at this museum and *enoteca* next to the **rocca (fortress)** (⊘ 24hr) **FREE**. Interactive exhibits on the 1st floor trace the history of the product and the surrounding land, and the ground-floor *enoteca* offers both tastings (tasting card €10 to €25, leftover credit refunded) and **Vernaccia master classes** (class €15-60; ⊘ Mar-Nov). It's also possible to buy a glass of wine (€4 to €7) to enjoy on the terrace, which has a panoramic view.

🛏 Sleeping

Foresteria del Monastero di San Girolamo   HOSTEL €

(☑ 0577 94 05 73; www.monasterosangirolamo.it; Via Folgore da San Gimignano 26; s/tw/tr €32/60/90; 🅿) This is a first-rate backpacker choice. Run by friendly Benedictine Vallumbrosan nuns, it has basic but comfortable and impeccably clean rooms sleeping two to four people in single beds; all have attached bathrooms. Parking costs €4 per night, breakfast costs €3 and there are two rooms set up for guests in wheelchairs (a rarity in town). Sadly, no wi-fi.

Hotel L'Antico Pozzo   BOUTIQUE HOTEL €€

(☑ 0577 94 20 14; www.anticopozzo.com; Via San Matteo 87; s €95, d €120-190; ⊘ closed mid-Jan–mid-Feb; ✳@ 🛜) The sense of heritage here is palpable: stone arches and winding stairs lead to a handsome breakfast salon, and some rooms have frescoes and period furniture. The sun-drenched rear courtyard is a great retreat from the madding crowds. Room types are named after Italian poets – those in the Boccaccio category are cramped but the Dante suites are elegant and extremely desirable.

Al Pozzo dei Desideri　　GUESTHOUSE €€
(✆370 3102538, 0577 90 71 99; www.alpozzodei
desideri.it; Piazza della Cisterna 32; d €110, tr €120,
q €160; ❄️🎧) Three rooms with a view (two
over the countryside and one over the main
piazza) are on offer in this 13th-century building; though well worn, they are comfortable
and relatively well priced. There's no breakfast, but this is town-centre Tuscany: there
are plenty of cafes close by.

★**Locanda dell' Artista**　　AGRITURISMO €€€
(✆0577 94 60 26; www.locandadellartista.com;
Lucignano 43, Canonica; r €325, ste €450; ⊗mid-
Mar–mid-Oct; 🅿️❄️🎧🏊) American Baker
Bloodworth left a career in Hollywood to
open this boutique retreat with his Italian
partner Cristian Rovetta, the culinary force
behind the property's Michelin-starred restaurant, Al 43 (menus €85 to €95). The seven rooms and suites are as elegant as they
are comfortable, and facilities include a
pool terrace with wonderful views over olive
groves towards nearby San Gimignano. No
children under 14.

🍴 Eating & Drinking

Many San Gimignano restaurants focus on
the tourist trade and serve mediocre food
at inflated prices. Higher-standard eateries
gravitate toward fresh local produce, including the town's famous *zafferano* (saffron).
Purchase meat, vegetables, fish and takeaway food at the **Thursday morning market**
(⊗8am-1.30pm) on and around Piazzas Cisterna, Duomo and delle Erbe. A small produce market also operates on the latter on
Saturday morning.

★**Gelateria Dondoli**　　GELATO €
(✆0577 94 22 44; www.gelateriadipiazza.com; Piazza della Cisterna 4; gelato €2.50-5; ⊗9am-11pm
summer, to 7.30pm winter, closed mid-Dec–mid-Feb)
Think of it less as ice cream, more as art. Former gelato world champion Sergio Dondoli
is known for creations including Crema di
Santa Fina (saffron cream) gelato and Vernaccia sorbet. His creations are so delicious
that some devotees even sign up for a two-hour gelato-making workshop (www.dondoli
gelatoclass.com, price on application).

★**Ristorante La Mandragola**　　TUSCAN €€
(✆348 3023766; www.locandalamandragola.it;
Via Diaccetto 26; meals €38; ⊗12.15-2.30pm &
7-9.30pm; 🎧) Nestled beneath the crumbling
walls of the rocca, La Mandragola (The Man-

drake) is deservedly popular – book ahead,
especially if you're keen to dine in the gorgeous courtyard. It's not exactly tourist-free,
but the welcome is genuine and the food is
delicious, especially the handmade pasta
dishes, which feature unusual sauces and
stuffings.

D!Vineria　　WINE BAR
(✆0577 94 30 41; www.divineria.it; Via della Rocca
2c; ⊗10am-10pm mid-Mar–Oct) Massimo Delli, the owner of this tiny wine bar on the
street leading up to the rocca, will enthusiastically suggest local wines to try (consider
ordering Montenidoli's Fiore or Rubicini's
Etherea – both excellent Vernaccias). A glass
costs between €3.50 and €25, and Massimo
also stocks a good range of local salami and
cheese (*taglieri* €20).

🛈 Information

Tourist Office (✆0577 94 00 08; www.
sangimignano.com; Piazza del Duomo 1;
⊗10am-1pm & 3-7pm Mar-Oct, 10am-1pm &
2-6pm Nov-Feb)

🛈 Getting There & Away

BUS
San Gimignano's **bus station** (Piazzale dei
Martiri di Montemaggio) is next to the *carabinieri*
(police station) at Porta San Giovanni. The tourist office sells bus tickets.

Florence (€6.80, 1¼ to two hours, 14 daily)
Change at Poggibonsi.

Monteriggioni (€4.50, 55 minutes, eight daily
Monday to Saturday)

Poggibonsi (€2.60, 30 minutes, frequent)

Siena (€6.20, one to 1½ hours, 10 daily Monday
to Saturday)

Head to Colle di Val d'Elsa (€3.50, 35 minutes)
to take a connecting bus to Volterra (€3.50, 50
minutes). These run four times daily from Monday to Saturday.

TRAIN
The closest train station to San Gimignano is
Poggibonsi.

Volterra

✆0588 / POP 10,300

Volterra's well-preserved medieval ramparts give the windswept town a proud,
forbidding air that author Stephenie Meyer
deemed ideal for the discriminating tastes of
the planet's principal vampire coven in her
wildly popular *Twilight* series. Fortunately,
the reality is considerably more welcoming,

as a wander through the winding cobbled streets dotted with Roman, Etruscan and medieval structures attests. Known for its artisanal heritage – alabaster carving in particular – the town is a particularly satisfying stop for those seeking to stock up on Tuscan art and handicrafts.

◉ Sights

The **Volterra Card** (adult/reduced/family €16/13/24, valid 72 hours) gives admission to Volterra's key sights. Buy it at any museum.

★**Museo Etrusco Guarnacci**   MUSEUM
(✆0588 8 63 47; www.volterratur.it/en/come/arts-culture/the-museum/guarnacci-etruscan-museum; Via Don Minzoni 15; adult/reduced €8/6; ☉9am-7pm mid-Mar–Oct 10am-4.30pm Nov–mid-Mar) The vast collection of artefacts exhibited here makes this one of Italy's most impressive Etruscan collections. Found locally, they include some 600 funerary urns carved mainly from alabaster and tufa – perhaps the pick is the *Urna degli sposi* (Urn of the Spouses), a strikingly realistic terracotta rendering of an elderly couple. The finds are displayed according to subject and era; the best examples (those dating from later periods) are on the 2nd and 3rd floors.

★**Museo Diocesano d'Arte Sacra Volterra**   MUSEUM
(Sacred Art Museum; ✆0588 8 77 33; Piazza XX Settembre; adult/reduced €5/3; ☉11am-6pm Tue-Sun Easter-Oct, to 5pm Fri-Sun Oct-Easter) Offering an innovative and particularly satisfying museum experience, this collection of sacred art is housed in the still-functioning Chiesa di San Agostino, ensuring that works are presented in a proper context. Drawn from the churches of the diocese of Volterra, they include three magnificent *Madonnas Enthroned with Child:* 15th-century versions by Neri di Bicci and Taddeo di Bartoli, and a 16th-century example from Rosso Fiorentino. Don't miss the particularly beautiful 14th-century carved wooden *Madonna of the Annunciation.*

Cattedrale di Santa Maria Assunta   CATHEDRAL
(Duomo di Volterra; Piazza San Giovanni) A handsome coffered ceiling is the standout feature of Volterra's *duomo,* which was built in the 12th and 13th centuries and remodelled in the 16th. The **Chapel of Our Lady of Sorrows**, to the left as you enter from Piazza San Giovanni, has two sculptures by Andrea della Robbia and a small fresco of the *Procession of the Magi* by Benozzo Gozzoli. In front of the duomo is a 13th-century **baptistry** featuring a Sansovino font (1502).

Pinacoteca Comunale   GALLERY
(✆0588 8 75 80; www.volterratur.it/en/come/arts-culture/the-museum/art-gallery; Via dei Sarti 1; adult/reduced incl Ecomuseo dell'Alabastro €8/6; ☉9am-7pm mid-Mar–Oct, 10am-4.30pm Nov–Mar) Local, Sienese and Florentine art holds sway in this modest collection in the Palazzo Minucci Solaini. Taddeo di Bartolo's *Madonna Enthroned with Child* (1411) is exquisite, while Rosso Fiorentino's *Deposition from the Cross* (1521) appears strikingly modern. .

Ecomuseo dell'Alabastro   MUSEUM
(✆0588 8 75 80; www.volterratur.it/en/come/arts-culture/the-museum/ecomuseum-of-alabaster; Via dei Sarti 1; adult/reduced incl Pinacoteca Comunale €8/6; ☉9am-7pm mid-Mar–Oct, 10am-4.30pm Nov–mid-Mar) As befits a town that's hewn the precious material from nearby quarries since Etruscan times, Volterra is the proud possessor of an alabaster museum. It's an intriguing exploration of everything related to the rock, from production and working to commercialisation. Contemporary creations feature strongly; there are also choice examples from Etruscan times onwards, as well as a recreated artisan's workshop.

🛏 Sleeping

Ostello Chiosco delle Monache   HOSTEL €
(✆0588 8 66 13; www.ostellovolterra.it; Via del Teatro 4, Località San Girolamo; dm €20-22, B&B s/d €65/75; ☉late Mar-Oct; [P][☏]) This excellent hostel occupies a 13th-century monastery complete with a frescoed refectory where breakfast is served. Airy rooms overlook the cloisters and have good beds and bathrooms; dorms sleep five. Breakfast (for those in dorms) costs €7. It's 1km from the centre of Volterra. Local bus 1 from Piazza Martiri della Libertà stops right outside the entrance (€1.50).

★**La Primavera**   B&B €
(✆0588 8 72 95; www.affittacamere-laprimavera.com; Via Porta Diana 15; s/d/tr €50/75/100; ☉mid-Apr–mid-Nov; [P][☏]) This home-style B&B in a former alabaster workshop is a cosy affair, with a knick-knack-adorned lounge, a pretty garden, polished parquet floors and meticulously presented bedrooms featuring soothing pastel colour schemes. It's in an excellent location just outside the city walls, a 10-minute walk from Piazza dei Priori. The free on-site parking is a definite plus. No credit cards.

Volterra

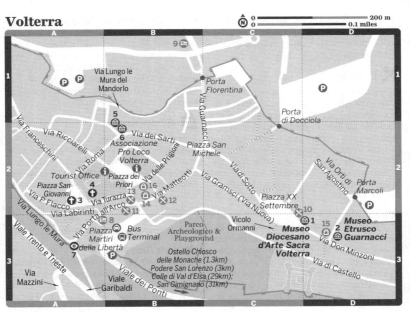

Volterra

Hotel Volterra In   HOTEL **€**
(☑0588 8 68 20; www.hotelvolterrain.it; Via Porta all'Arco 37-41; s €75, d €90-110, ste €160-170; ✿ ❊) There are no top-end or boutique hotels in the centre of Volterra, so the recent opening of this small three-star establishment close to the **Porta all'Arco** (Via Porta all'Arco) is to be applauded. Though it doesn't deserve its self-claimed boutique label, the rooms are pleasant and have bathrooms so clean they gleam. Guests rave about the breakfast.

Podere San Lorenzo   AGRITURISMO **€**
(☑0588 3 90 80; www.agriturismo-volterra.it; Via Allori 80; B&B d €100, 2-/3-/4-bed apt without break-

fast €105-165; ❊❊) In this tranquil model of slow tourism you dip straight into a rural idyll. A spring-fed swimming pool is located next to an enviable veggie garden; apartments sleep between two and four (some have private terraces) and rooms are quiet. Dinners (per person €30 including wine) are served in a former 12th-century chapel.

Walking, biking and hands-on olive-oil production opportunities are available, as are cooking classes. The farm is located some 3km outside Volterra, accessed via a narrow, almost hidden road that is signed off the SS68 (right-hand-side) as you drive up to the town from the direction of Siena,

Florence and San Gimignano. Staff are happy to drop off or pick up guests from a bus stop a short distance away, making trips to and from town easy.

✖ Eating

Decent dining options are somewhat limited in Volterra. Those we've recommended tend to serve local specialities including white Marzuolo truffles, mushrooms (porcini and ovuli), *zuppa volterrana* (thick vegetable and bread soup), *pappardelle* with hare or wild boar sauce, *trippa alla volterrana* (tripe cooked with tomato, sausage and herbs) and *ossi di morto* (bones of the dead) almond biscuits.

★ L'Incontro   CAFE €
(☑ 0588 8 05 00; Via Matteotti 18; panini €2-4, biscuits €1.50-2.50; ⊙ 6am-midnight, to 2am summer, closed Wed winter; 🛜) L'Incontro's rear *salone* is a top spot to grab a quick antipasto plate or *panino* for lunch, and its front bar area is always crowded with locals enjoying a coffee or *aperitivo*. The house-baked biscuits are noteworthy – try the chewy and nutty *brutti mai buoni* (ugly but good) or its alabaster-coloured cousin, *ossi di morto*.

VolaTerrA   CAFE €
(☑ 0588 8 87 65; www.volaterra.it; Via G Turazza 5-7; bruschette €6-12.50, salads €9, cakes €4-6; ⊙ 11am-10pm, to midnight Fri & Sat Jul-Sep; ❉🛜) Owner Jonni is a fifth-generation member of the Guarguaglini family, owners of the Frantoio dei Colli Toscani olive estate. His casual bistro and wine bar is a great spot to enjoy a light meal, coffee or *aperitivo* as standards are high. You can also purchase picnic provisions here, or sign up for a guided olive-oil tasting (€8, bookings essential).

Life Bistro   VEGAN €
(☑ 0588 8 53 71; www.lifebistro.com; Via Porta all'Arco 15; dishes €8-18, pizzas €8-15; ⊙ noon-10pm Apr-Oct; 🖼) 🌿 Catering to vegans, vegetarians and anyone keen on organic plant-based cooking, this casual bistro stocks its bain-marie with an array of dishes that's changed daily and charged by weight. It also serves veggie pizzas, artisan beer and local wine. The glass floor of the dining area protects a Roman-era archaeological site.

La Carabaccia   TUSCAN €€
(☑ 0588 8 62 39; www.lacarabacciavolterra.it; Piazza XX Settembre 4-5; meals €26; ⊙ 12.30-2.30pm Tue-Sun, 7.30-9.30pm Tue-Sat, reduced hours winter; 🛜🖼) Mother and daughters

Sara, Ilaria and Patrizia have put their heart and soul into this charming trattoria with a country-style interior and attractive front terrace. Named after a humble Tuscan vegetable soup (one of the specialities of the house), it's the city's best lunch option. The small seasonal menu changes daily and always features fish on Fridays.

🛍 Shopping

Volterra's centuries-old heritage as a town that mines and works alabaster ensures plenty of shops specialise in hand-carved alabaster items. The **Società Cooperativa Artieri Alabastro** (☑ 0588 8 61 35; www.artierialabastro.it; Piazza dei Priori 4-5; ⊙ 10.30am-6pm) showcases the impressive work of 23 local alabaster artisans. For information about local artisans, see www.arteinbottegavolterra.it.

★ Gloria Giannelli   ARTS & CRAFTS
(☑ 0588 8 40 30; www.gloriagiannellialabastri.it; Via Don Minzoni 13; ⊙ 10am-1pm & 3-7pm Mar-Oct) One of only four female alabaster carvers in Volterra, Gloria Giannelli creates elegant hand-carved pieces that are rich in fretwork detail – the vases, bowls and plates are particularly lovely. Worldwide shipping can be arranged.

Boutique del Tartufo   FOOD
(☑ 348 7121883; www.boutiquedeltartufo.it; Via Matteotti 5; ⊙ 10.30am-7.30pm Wed-Mon summer, 10.30am-12.30pm & 2.30-6.30pm winter) Stefania Socchi's husband Daniele is a professional truffle hunter, and sources the tasty fungi that are used to produce the products sold in this shop near Piazza dei Priori. Purchase whole truffles or opt for honey, polenta, pasta, oil or pastes made or infused with them. You can also order a *panino* made with truffle paste or truffle-infused cheese (€6).

Email to enquire about the possibility of going on a truffle hunt with Daniele and his dog – this is sometimes on offer.

There's another branch in Vicolo Ormani, off Piazza XX Settembre.

ℹ Information

Associazione Pro Loco Volterra (☑ 0588 8 61 50; www.provolterra.it; Piazza dei Priori 10; ⊙ 9am-12.30pm & 3-6pm Mon-Sat, 9am-12.30pm Sun) Helpful, volunteer-run service: tourist advice, bus tickets and luggage storage (two hours/extra hour/day €3/1/6).

Tourist Office (☑ 0588 8 60 99; www.volterratur.it; Piazza dei Priori 19; ⊙ 9.30am-1pm & 2-6pm)

❶ Getting There & Away

BUS

Volterra's **bus station** (Piazza Martiri della Libertà) is in Piazza Martiri della Libertà. Buy tickets at *tabacchi* or Associazione Pro Loco Volterra. Note bus services are greatly reduced on Sundays.

CTT (☑ 800 570530; www.pisa.cttnord.it) buses connect Volterra with Pisa (€6.90, two to 2½ hours, 11 daily Monday to Saturday, one Sunday) via Pontedera (€5.60, 1½ hours).

You'll need to go to Colle di Val d'Elsa (€3.50, 50 minutes, four Monday to Saturday) to catch a connecting **Tiemme** (www.tiemmespa.it)service (four Monday to Saturday, one Sunday) to San Gimignano (€3.50, 35 minutes), Siena (€3.90, 30 to 40 minutes) or Florence (€6.80, 65 minutes).

CAR & MOTORCYCLE

There is a ZTL (Limited Traffic Zone) in the historic centre. The most convenient car park is beneath Piazza Martiri della Libertà (€2/15 per hour/day).

Val d'Orcia

The picturesque agricultural valley of Val d'Orcia is a Unesco World Heritage site, as is the historic centre of the town of Pienza on its northeastern edge. The valley's distinctive landscape features flat chalk plains, out of which rise almost conical hills topped with fortified settlements and magnificent abbeys that were once important staging points on the Via Francigena.

For information about places, activities and events in the Val d'Orcia see www.parcodellavaldorcia.com.

Montalcino

☑ 0577 / POP 5920

Known globally as the home of one of the world's great wines, Brunello di Montalcino, the attractive hilltop town of Montalcino has a remarkable number of *enoteche* lining its medieval streets and is surrounded by picturesque vineyards. There's history to explore too: the town's efforts to hold out against Florence even after Siena had fallen earned it the title 'the Republic of Siena in Montalcino', and there are many well-preserved medieval buildings within the historic city walls.

◉ Sights & Activities

To save a couple of euros for your wine fund, purchase a combined ticket (adult/reduced €6/4.50) for entry to the **Fortezza's ramparts** (☑0577 84 92 11; Piazzale Fortezza; ramparts adult/reduced €4/2, courtyard free; ⊙9am-8pm Apr-Oct, 10am-6pm Nov-Mar) and the Museo Civico e Diocesano d'Arte Sacra. These are available from the tourist office (p578).

Museo Civico e
Diocesano d'Arte Sacra   MUSEUM
(☑0577 84 60 14; www.facebook.com/museociv icoed   iocesanoearcheologicamontalcino; Via Ricasoli 31; adult/reduced €4.50/3; ⊙10am-1pm & 2-5.40pm Tue-Sun Sep-Mar, 10am-1pm & 2-5.50pm Apr-Oct) Occupying the former convent of the neighbouring **Chiesa di Sant'Agostino**, this collection of religious art from the town and surrounding region includes a triptych by Duccio and a *Madonna and Child* by Simone Martini. Other artists represented include the Lorenzetti brothers, Giovanni di Paolo and Sano di Pietro.

Enoteca La Fortezza   WINE
(☑0577 84 92 11; www.enotecalafortezza.com; Piazzale Fortezza; ⊙9am-8pm, 10am-6pm in winter) The *enoteca* in Montalcino's medieval fortress offers a range of paid tastings, stocks a huge range of wine for sale and will ship overseas. Start with a tasting of three/five Brunellos (€14/20) and then consider graduating to two/three/five Riserva and Gran Selezioni vintages (€20/30/40).

🛏 Sleeping

Hotel Vecchia Oliviera   HOTEL €€
(☑0577 84 60 28; www.vecchiaoliviera.com; Via Landi 1; r €145-180; 🅿❋🛜🏊) Chandeliers, polished wooden floors and rugs lend this converted oil mill a refined, albeit slightly worn, air. Of the 11 rooms on offer, opt for one in the superior category as these have great views (number 9 is best). The pool is in an attractive garden setting and the terrace has wrap-around views. Breakfast is disappointing.

Albergo Il Giglio   HOTEL €€
(☑0577 84 81 67; www.gigliohotel.com; Via Soccorso Saloni 5; s €95, d €150; ❋🛜) There's a real old-world feel at this family-run place, something enhanced by the traditional Tuscan fireplace in the lounge and the brass bedsteads and arched ceilings in the 12 comfortable rooms. The views from upstairs windows are captivating – try to score room 1, which has its own panoramic terrace.

✕ Eating

Trattoria L'Angolo   TUSCAN €
(☑0577 84 80 17; Via Ricasoli 9; meals €22; ⊙noon-3pm Wed-Mon Sep-Jun, noon-3pm &

FLORENCE & TUSCANY VAL D'ORCIA

ABBAZIA DI SANT'ANTIMO

This serenely beautiful, Romanesque **abbey** (☑0577 28 63 00; www.antimo.it; Castelnuovo dell'Abate; ☺10am-7pm Apr-Oct, to 5pm Nov-Mar) **FREE** lies in an isolated valley just below the village of Castelnuovo dell'Abate, 11km from Montalcino.

Tradition tells us that Charlemagne founded the original monastery here in 781. The exterior of the abbey's church, built in pale travertine stone, is simple except for the stone carvings, which include various fantastical animals. Inside, study the capitals of the columns lining the nave, especially the one representing Daniel in the lion's den (second on the right as you enter). Below it is a particularly intense polychrome 13th-century *Madonna and Child* and there's a haunting 12th-century *Crucifixion* above the main altar. The church, crypt, upper loggia, chapel, pharmacy and garden can be visited with a rented videoguide (€6), and there is also a dedicated videoguide to the church (€3).

It's a two- to three-hour walk from Montalcino to the abbey. The route starts next to the police station near the main roundabout in town; many visitors choose to walk to the abbey and return by bus (€1.50, 10 minutes, four daily) – check the timetable with the tourist office in Montalcino.

7-11pm Wed-Mon Jul & Aug) We thought about keeping shtum about this place (everyone loves to keep a secret or two), but it seemed selfish not to share our love for its pasta dishes. Be it vegetarian (ravioli stuffed with ricotta and truffles) or carnivorous (*pappardelle* with wild-boar sauce), the handmade *primi* (first courses) here are uniformly excellent. *Secondi* aren't as impressive.

★ Re di Macchia   TUSCAN €€
(☑0577 84 61 16; redimacchia@alice.it; Via Soccorso Saloni 21; meals €35, set menus €35; ☺noon-2pm & 7-9pm Fri-Wed; 🖋) Husband-and-wife team Antonio and Roberta run this relaxed eatery in the centre of town with great aplomb. Roberta's cooking is much more sophisticated than the Tuscan average but retains the usual laudable focus on local, seasonal produce. Antonio's excellent and affordable wine list is one of the best in town. The four-course set menus (one vegetarian) offer excellent value.

Enoteca Osteria Osticcio   TUSCAN €€€
(☑0577 84 80 46; www.osticcio.it; Via Giacomo Matteotti 23; meal €75; ☺12.30-2.30pm & 7.30-10pm Tue-Sun mid-Feb–mid-Dec; 🏵) In a town overflowing with *enoteche,* this is definitely one of the best. Choose a bottle from a huge selection of Italian and European wines on offer (including loads of Brunello) and then relax over a selection of well-executed modern Tuscan dishes. You can order à la carte or opt for a six-course set menu with wine match (€130).

ℹ Information

Tourist Office (☑0577 84 93 31; www.prolocomontalcino.com; Costa del Municipio 1; ☺10am-1pm & 2-5.40pm, closed Mon winter) Just off the main square, this office can supply free copies of the *Consorzio del Vino Brunello di Montalcino* map of wineries and also books cellar-door visits and winery accommodation.

ℹ Getting There & Away

Tiemme (www.tiemmespa.it) buses run between Montalcino and Siena (€5.60, 75 minutes, six daily Monday to Saturday, two daily Sunday). The bus stop is near the Hotel Vecchia Oliviera (p577).

Pienza

☑0578 / POP 2080
Once a sleepy hamlet, pretty Pienza was transformed when, in 1459, Pope Pius II began turning his home village into an ideal Renaissance town. The result is magnificent – the church, papal palace, town hall and accompanying buildings in and around Piazza Pio II went up in just three years and haven't been remodelled since. In 1996 Unesco added the town's historic centre to its World Heritage list, citing the revolutionary vision of urban space. On weekends, Pienza draws big crowds; come midweek if you possibly can.

◉ Sights

A cumulative ticket (adult/student €5/3.50) covers access to both the Museo Diocesano and the baptistry.

Piazza Pio II
PIAZZA

Stand in this magnificent square and spin 360 degrees. You've just taken in an overview of Pienza's major monuments. Gems of the Renaissance constructed in a mere three years between 1459 and 1462, they're arranged according to the urban design of Bernardo Rossellino, who applied the principles of Renaissance town planning devised by his mentor, Leon Battista Alberti.

★ Duomo
CATHEDRAL

(Concattedrale di Santa Maria Assunta; Piazza Pio II; ☉ 7.30am-1pm & 2-7pm) Pienza's *duomo* was built on the site of the Romanesque Chiesa di Santa Maria, of which little remains. The Renaissance church with its handsome travertine facade was commissioned by Pius II, who was so proud of the building that he issued a papal bull in 1462 forbidding any changes to it. The interior is a strange mix of Gothic and Renaissance styles and contains a superb marble tabernacle by Rossellino housing a relic of St Andrew the Apostle, Pienza's patron saint.

★ Museo Diocesano
MUSEUM

(☑ 0578 74 99 05; www.palazzoborgia.it; Corso il Rossellino 30; adult/reduced €4.50/3; ☉ 10.30am-1.30pm & 2.30-6pm Wed-Mon mid-Mar–Oct, 10am-1pm & 2-5pm Sat & Sun Nov–mid-Mar) Set in the **Palazzo Borgia** (Palazzo Vescovile; Piazza Pio II), this museum displays an intriguing miscellany of artworks, illuminated manuscripts, tapestries and miniatures. Highlights include Pietro Lorenzetti's *Madonna col Bambino* (1310–20), Bartolo di Fredi's *Madonna della Misericordia* (c 1364) and the English-produced, Gothic-style *Cope di Pius II,* a richly embroidered early-14th-century cloak depicting the stories of the Virgin Mary, Margaret of Antioch and Catherine of Alexandria. Enter via Corso il Rossellino.

🛏 Sleeping

★ La Bellavita
B&B €€

(☑ 391 4392068; www.labellavitapienza.it; Via della Chiochina 1; r €90-140; ☉ closed Christmas; ❄ 🎧) Host Elisabetta goes out of her way to make guests feel at home in her cute four-room B&B. It can be hard to find – enter through the arch next to 81 Corso il Rossellino – but once you've arrived you'll be charmed by the clean and comfortable rooms, panoramic terrace and cute attic where a delicious buffet breakfast is served.

★ La Bandita Townhouse
BOUTIQUE HOTEL €€€

(☑ 0578 74 90 05; www.la-bandita.com/townhouse; Corso il Rossellino 111; r €350-€595;

RURAL RETREATS

Motor just a few kilometres away from towns to uncover these absolutely exquisite rural retreats – perfect bases for exploring the Val d'Orcia.

La Bandita (☑ 333 4046704; www.la-bandita.com; Podere La Bandita, Località La Foce; r €250-550, self-contained ste €550; ☉ Apr-early Nov; P ❄ @ 🎧 ☲) Sophisticated urban style melds with stupendous scenery at this rural retreat in one of the most stunning sections of the Val d'Orcia. Owned and operated by a former NYC music executive and his travel-writer wife (non–Lonely Planet, we hasten to add), it offers spacious rooms, amenities galore (we love the Ortigia toiletries), communal dinners (set menu €45 per person) and personalised service.

Foresteria Podere Brizio (☑ 0577 04 10 72; www.poderebrizio.it; Località Podere Brizio; r €230-255; ☉ closed Dec-Easter; P ❄ 🎧 ☲) A huge amount of thought has gone into the design and construction of this splendid hotel on a wine estate 8km southwest of Montalcino, near Tavernelle. Room rates are relatively restrained considering comfort and amenity levels in the spacious rooms and the wide array of facilities (huge swimming pool, restaurant, tennis court, spa).

Il Borgo (☑ 0577 87 77 00; www.castellobanfiilborgo.com; Castello Banfi, Poggio alle Mura, off SP117; r €450-1000, ste €700-1500; ☉ late Mar-late Nov; P ❄ 🎧 ☲) Most of the 14 rooms on offer at Banfi's flagship Tuscan wine state, wrapped around imposing medieval Castello di Poggio alla Mura, command wonderful views of vineyards and majestic Monte Amiata. Facilities include a heated pool, two formal restaurants and a pool bar serving drinks and light meals. Guests can use complimentary e-bikes to follow cycle routes through the vineyards.

DON'T MISS

IL LECCIO

Sometimes simple dishes are the hardest to perfect. And perfection is the only term to use when discussing Il Leccio (0577 84 41 75; www.illeccio.net; Via Costa Castellare 1/3, Sant'Angelo in Colle; meals €30; noon-3pm & 7-10pm Thu-Tue), a trattoria in Brunello heartland. Watching the chef make his way between his stove and kitchen garden to gather produce for each order puts a whole new spin on the word 'fresh', and both the results and the house Brunello are spectacular.

Sant'Angelo in Colle is 10km southwest of Montalcino along Via del Sole (or 10km west of the Abbazia di Sant'Antimo along an unsealed but signed road through vineyards).

mid-Mar–early Jan;) Aiming to provide their guests with a taste of Tuscan village life and Pienza with a world-class boutique hotel, the American owners of this boutique hotel purchased and renovated a Renaissance-era convent close to Piazza Pio – the result is both sensitive and supremely stylish. Facilities include a communal lounge with an honesty bar and a restaurant with a garden terrace.

Eating

Osteria Sette di Vino   TUSCAN €
(0578 74 90 92; Piazza di Spagna 1; snacks €3.50-7.50; noon-2.30pm & 7.30-10pm Thu-Tue) Known for its *zuppa di pane e fagioli* (bread and white-bean soup), bruschette, crostini and range of local *pecorino* (sheep's-milk cheese), this simple place has a clutch of tables inside and a scattering outside – book ahead.

Townhouse Caffè   ITALIAN €€
(0578 74 90 05; www.la-bandita.com/townhouse/the-restaurant; Via San Andrea 8; meals €40; noon-2.30pm Tue-Sun, 7.30-10pm daily mid-Mar–early Jan;) The menu at this chic eatery is pared back in more ways than one: there are around four choices per course, presentation is minimalist and the emphasis is on the quality of the produce rather than clever culinary tricks – bravo! In summer, guests dine in an atmospheric medieval courtyard; in winter, the action moves into a two-room space with open kitchen.

La Terrazza del Chiostro   ITALIAN €€€
(349 5676148, 0578 74 81 83; www.laterrazzadelchiostro.it; Via del Balzello; meals €55; 12.15-2.45pm & 7.15-10pm Thu-Tue, closed mid-Nov–mid-Mar, open Wed in high summer;) Dining on this gorgeous terrace with its panoramic view is the stuff of which lasting travel memories are made, and the food also has plenty of pizzazz – to fully appreciate it, opt for a set menu (from €45) and choose a wine match from the restaurant's impressive wine selection.

Drinking & Nightlife

★ **Idyllium**   BAR
(0578 74 81 76; www.facebook.com/idylliumbar; Via Gozzante 67; 11am-2am summer, reduced hours rest of year) Located underneath Palazzo Piccolomini and accessed via the staircase between the palace and the *duomo,* this hybrid cafe and cocktail bar in the former palace stables has a terrace with wonderful views over the Val d'Orcia and towards Monte Amiata. Owners Bledar Ndoci and Federico Fioravanti learned their mixology art in Milan and definitely make the best cocktails in town.

Bar Il Casello   BAR
(0578 74 91 05; Via del Casello 3; noon-8pm Wed, Thu & Sun, 6pm-midnight Fri, noon-midnight Sat) A local secret that we hereby expose, this bar next to the *belvedere* (scenic viewpoint) behind Piazza Pio II is a perfect place to enjoy an *aperitivo* – the sunset vistas are simply stupendous. It's also a popular spot for an afternoon coffee.

Information

Tourist Office (0578 74 99 05; info.turismo@comune.pienza.si.it; Corso il Rossellino 30; 10.30am-1.30pm & 2.30-6pm Wed-Mon mid-Mar–Oct, 10am-1pm & 2-5pm Sat & Sun Nov–mid-Mar)

Getting There & Away

Four **Tiemme** (www.tiemmespa.it) buses run Monday to Saturday between Siena and Pienza (€6, 70 minutes, two daily) and eight travel to/from Montepulciano (€2.60, 20 minutes). The bus stops are on Via della Madonnina, near the police station. Buy tickets at Pancaffè Il Chicco nearby.

Montepulciano

☑ 0578 / POP 14,000

Exploring the medieval town of Montepulciano, perched on a reclaimed narrow ridge of volcanic rock, will push your quadriceps to failure point. When this happens, self-medicate with a generous pour of the highly reputed Vino Nobile while also drinking in the spectacular views over the Val di Chiana and Val d'Orcia.

◉ Sights

Il Corso   STREET
Montepulciano's main street – called in stages Via di Gracciano, Via di Voltaia, Via dell'Opio and Via Poliziano – climbs up the eastern ridge of the town from Porta al Prato and loops to meet Via di Collazzi on the western ridge. To reach the centre of town (Piazza Grande), take a dog-leg turn into Via del Teatro.

Piazza Grande   PIAZZA
Elegant Piazza Grande is the town's highest point and main meeting place. If you think it looks familiar, it might be because it featured in *New Moon*, the second movie in the *Twilight* series based on Stephenie Meyer's vampire novels. They shot the main crowd scene here, despite the book being set in Volterra. More recently, it features in episodes of the television series *Medici: Masters of Florence*.

Palazzo Comunale   PALACE
(Piazza Grande; terrace & tower adult/reduced €5/2.50, terrace only €2.50; ⊙10am-6pm Apr-Christmas) Built in the 14th century in

Gothic style and remodelled in the 15th century by Michelozzo, the Palazzo Comunale still functions as Montepulciano's town hall. Head up the 67 narrow stairs to the tower to enjoy extraordinary views – you'll see as far as Pienza, Montalcino and even, on a clear day, Siena.

Duomo   CATHEDRAL
(Cattedrale di Santa Maria Assunta; www.montepulcianochiusipienza.it; Piazza Grande; ⊙8am-7pm) Montepulciano's 16th-century *duomo* is striking, largely because its unfinished facade gives the building a stern, heavily weathered look. Inside, don't miss Taddeo di Bartolo's ornate *Assumption* triptych (1401) behind the high altar and Sano di Pietro's *Madonna del pilastro* (Madonna of the Pillar; 15th century) on the eastern wall of the nave.

Museo Civico & Pinacoteca Crociani   MUSEUM
(☑ 0578 71 73 00; www.museocivicomontepulciano.it; Via Ricci 10; adult/reduced €6/4; ⊙10am-6.30pm Wed-Mon Apr-Oct, to 6pm Sat & Sun Nov-Mar) It was a curatorial dream come true: in 2011 a painting in the collection of this modest art gallery was attributed to Caravaggio. The work, *Portrait of a Man*, is thought to portray Cardinal Scipione Borghese, the artist's patron. It's now accompanied by a touch-screen interpretation that allows you to explore details of the painting, its restoration and diagnostic attribution. Other works here include two terracottas by Andrea Della Robbia, and Domenico Beccafumi's painting of the town's patron saint, Agnese.

FLORENCE & TUSCANY MONTEPULCIANO

WORTH A TRIP

A GARDEN ESCAPADE

Built in four stages between 1924 and 1939, the formal gardens of La Foce (☑ 0578 6 91 01; www.lafoce.com; Strada della Vittoria 61, off SP40; adult/child under 12 €10/free; ⊙ tour & entry 3pm, 4pm, 5pm & 6pm Wed, 11.30am, 3pm & 4.30pm Sat & Sun last weekend Apr-Oct) were commissioned by Anglo-American expat Iris Origo and her Italian husband Antonio. Designed by English architect Cecil Pinsent (1884–1963), who created many splendid gardens around Florence in the early decades of the 20th century, they surround a 16th-century former pilgrims' inn that was converted into a residence by the Origos after they purchased the La Foce estate in 1924. Visits are by 45-minute guided tour in English or Italian.

Post-tour, indulge in a lazy alfresco lunch at Dopolavoro La Foce (☑ 0578 75 40 25; www.dopolavorolafoce.it; meals €30, sandwiches €5-9; ⊙8am-11pm Tue-Sun late Mar-Oct; P🖥☑), a 1939 *dopolavoro* (recreational club) transformed into a contemporary space with Tuscan-chic rear garden. Equally on-trend, the menu features vegetarian pastas, burgers, flatbread sandwiches, craft beers and organic juices.

🏃 Activities

★ Enoliteca Consortile · WINE
(www.enolitecavinonobile.it; Fortezza di Montepulciano, Via San Donato 21; ⊙11am-7pm) Operated by Montepulciano's consortium of local wine producers, this recently opened showcase of Vino Nobile on the ground floor of the Medicean fortress has a modern tasting room offering over 70 wines for tasting and purchase. Buy a €10 or €15 card, use it to pour the tipples of your choice and direct your own tasting.

Cantina de' Ricci · WINE
(☎0578 75 71 66; www.cantinadericci.it; Via Ricci 11; ⊙10.30am-7pm mid-Mar–early Jan, Sat & Sun only early Jan–mid-Mar) **FREE** The most evocative of Montepulciano's wine cellars, this *cantina* lies at the foot of a steep winding staircase in the Renaissance-era **Palazzo Ricci** (☎0578 75 60 22; www.palazzoricci.com). Immense vaulted stone encasements surround two-storey-high barrels. Dimly lit and hushed, it's like a cathedral of wine. Entry is free, as will be your first two tastings.

Cantina Storica Talosa · WINE
(☎0578 75 79 29; www.talosa.it; Via Talosa 8; ⊙10.30am-7pm, reduced hours Jan & Feb) **FREE** The underground tunnels in this *cantina* were hewn out of tufa by the Etruscans and are now filled with huge oak barriques. Look out for the sea fossils in the tufa – they're five million years old. There's also an Etrus-

can tomb dating from the 6th century BC to visit. Tastings are free, but the expectation is that you'll purchase a bottle.

👉 Tours

★ Urban Bikery · CYCLING
(☎377 5453297; www.urbanbikery.it; Via Ricci 2; per 2hr/half-day/day €40/45/65; ⊙9.30am-7pm Mar-Oct, 11am-6pm Nov-Feb) What a clever idea! This recently established outfit rents out specially customised off-road e-bikes with attached GPS devices that have been programmed with cycling routes in the Montepulciano area. It also offers two guided tours: a four-hour, 22km e-bike experience that includes tastings at two wine estates (€110) and a four-hour, 22km experience passing through local landscapes immortalised in cinema (€99).

Strada del Vino Nobile di Montepulciano e dei Sapori della Valdichiana Senese · TOURS
(☎0578 71 74 84; www.stradavinonobile.it; Piazza Grande 7; ⊙9.30am-1.30pm & 2.30-6pm Mon-Fri, 10am-1pm & 2-5pm Sat, 10am-1pm Sun, closed Sat & Sun Jan-Mar) This organisation of local wine and food producers, hospitality businesses and municipalities organises a huge range of tours and courses, including cooking courses (€115 to €170), vineyard tours (€69 to €115) and vineyard walking tours that culminate in wine tasting (€49 to €69). Book in advance online or at its information office.

WORTH A TRIP

WINE TASTING AROUND MONTEPULCIANO

'Idyllic' best describes the **Palazzo Vecchio Winery** (☎0578 72 41 70; www.vinonobile.it; Via Terra Rossa 5; ⊙10am-5pm), atop a hill outside the town of Valiano, 15km northeast of Montepulciano. Its large 14th-century stone farmhouse is surrounded by fruit trees, the winery is in converted outbuildings, and 25 hectares of vineyards planted with Sangiovese, Canaiolo and Mammolo grapes cascade down the hillsides. A tour and tasting (€20 to €35 per person, €60 to €70 with lunch) are by reservation only.

Part of the legendary Avignonesi Winery company, **Le Capezzine** (☎0578 72 43 04; www.avignonesi.it; Via Colonica 1, Valiano; ⊙10am-6pm Mon-Fri Mar & Apr, 10am-7pm Mon-Sat, noon-6pm Sun May-Sep, 10am-6pm Mon-Sat Oct, 10am-5pm Mon-Fri Nov & Dec, closed Jan & Feb) is a 19-hectare organic estate known for its 'Round Vineyard', which was designed to establish to what extent the quality of wine is influenced by planting density. No bookings are needed to enjoy a guided tasting (from €15), glass of wine (from €5 per glass) and tasting board (€25) in the cantina. Other activities (requiring advance booking) include 90-minute vineyard tours, balloon rides with brunch, falconry lessons and so on. Four-course gourmet lunches with wine pairings are served in the estate's **restaurant** (☎0578 72 43 04; www.avignonesi.it/en/hospitality; 4-course menu incl wine match €95; ⊙12.30-3pm Mon-Sat late Mar-Nov; 🅿✳🍴) 🍷.

Festivals & Events

Montepulciano Calici di Stelle WINE
(Glasses of Stars; www.calicidistellemontepulciano.it; ⏲Aug) Organised by the Strada del Vino Nobile di Montepulciano e dei Sapori della Valdichiana Senese, this popular evening event features wine tastings, live music and performances of traditional flag throwing and drumming in Piazza Grande.

Bravio delle Botti CULTURAL
(www.braviodellebotti.com; ⏲Aug) Members of Montepulciano's eight *contrade* (districts) push 80kg wine barrels uphill in this race held on the last Sunday in August. There are also Renaissance-themed celebrations during the week before.

Sleeping

Camere Bellavista HOTEL €
(☎0578 75 73 48; www.camerebellavista.it; Via Ricci 25; r €70-120; P 📶) As this budget hotel is four storeys tall and sits on the edge of the old town, the views live up to its name. The styling is heritage rustic with exposed beams, hefty wooden furniture, brass bedsteads and smart new bathrooms. The owner isn't resident, so phone ahead to be met with the key. No breakfast; cash only.

Agriturismo Nobile AGRITURISMO €€
(☎340 7904752, 347 7252853; www.agriturismonobile.it; Strada per Chianciano, Località San Benedetto; d €100, apt €150-220; P 📶 🏊) In the 15th century they were sheds and hen houses; now they're five rustic-chic self-contained apartments. Some have big open fireplaces and many feature grandstand views of Montepulciano, which is only 1km away. There are also five cheaper, simpler rooms in the 15th-century farmhouse; rates for these include breakfast. In high season there's a three-night minimum stay. Very kid friendly.

Eating

Osteria Acquacheta TUSCAN €
(☎0578 71 70 86; www.acquacheta.eu; Via del Teatro 22; meals €24; ⏲12.30-3pm & 7.30-10.30pm Wed-Mon mid-Apr–Dec) Hugely popular with locals and tourists alike, this bustling *osteria* specialises in *bistecca alla fiorentina* (chargrilled T-bone steak), which comes to the shared tables in huge, lightly seared and exceptionally flavoursome slabs (don't even *think* of asking for it to be served otherwise). Phone to book ahead.

★ **La Dogana** ITALIAN €€
(☎339 5405196; www.ladoganaenoteca.it; Strada Lauretana Nord 75, Valiano; 4-course set lunch €35, meals €34; ⏲11am-3.30pm & 6-10pm Wed-Mon, closed Jan) Chef and cookbook writer Sunshine Manitto presides over the kitchen of this chic *enoteca* overlooking the Palazzo Vecchio Winery, 13km northeast of Montepulciano. Windows frame vistas of vines and cypress trees, but the best seats in the house are on the grassed rear terrace. The casual menu showcases seasonal produce (much of it grown in the kitchen garden).

★ **La Grotta** TUSCAN €€
(☎0578 75 74 79; www.lagrottamontepulciano.it; Via di San Biagio 15; meals €43; ⏲12.30-2pm & 7.30-10pm Thu-Tue, closed mid-Jan–late Mar) Located just below Montepulciano, overlooking the Renaissance splendour of the **Chiesa di San Biago**, the town's best restaurant serves traditional dishes with refined flavour and presentation. Service is exemplary, and the courtyard garden is a lovely place to enjoy a six-course tasting menu (€53) or your choice from the à la carte menu. Bookings advisable.

Drinking & Nightlife

★ **Caffè Poliziano** CAFE
(☎0578 75 86 15; www.caffepoliziano.it; Via di Voltaia 27; ⏲7am-9pm Mon-Fri, to 10.30pm Sat, to 9pm Sun; 📶) Established in 1868, Poliziano was lovingly restored to its original form 20 years ago and is the town's most atmospheric cafe. It serves excellent coffee but is most atmospheric for *aperitivo*, when the view of the sun setting over the Val di Chiana from the tables near the rear windows is simply magnificent.

La Vineria WINE BAR
(☎0578 85 01 53; www.facebook.com/lavineriadimontepulciano; Via di Gracciano nel Corso 101; ⏲10am-10pm) Specialising in local produce, this tiny place near the Porta al Prato is an excellent choice if you are keen to try a glass or two of Nobile or Rosso di Montepulciano, accompanied by a generously sized tasting board of *crostini* (toasts with toppings), pecorino cheese and cured meats (€15). It also offers filled *panini* at lunch.

E Lucevan Le Stelle WINE BAR
(☎0578 75 87 25; www.locandasanfrancesco.it; Piazza San Francesco 3; ⏲10am-midnight Easter-Oct, to 11pm Sat & Sun Nov-Easter, closed 2 weeks

WORTH A TRIP

A SLOW FOOD LUNCH

An easy 30-minute drive from Montelpuciano in Chiusi, Il Grillo è Buoncantore (☑ 0578 2 01 12; https://ilgrilloebuoncantore.wixsite.com/ristorante; Piazza XX Settembre 10; meals €30, pizzas €6-10; ☺ noon-2.30pm & 7-11pm, closed Mon winter; ✱ ☑) showcases the regional cuisine of passionate chef and sommelier Tiziana Tacchi. An acclaimed Slow Food destination, the restaurant's menu is grounded in local tradition but Tiziana's creations are executed with a contemporary sensibility and the results are truly delectable (the antipasti are a knockout). No pizzas at lunch.

Nov & 2 weeks Jan; ☎) The decked terrace of this ultrafriendly *osteria* is the top spot in Montepulciano to watch the sun go down. Inside, squishy sofas, modern art and jazz on the sound system give the place a chilled-out vibe. Snacks include *piandine* (filled flatbreads; €8), pastas (€9) and antipasto boards (€10 to €28).

ⓘ Information

Strada del Vino Nobile di Montepulciano Information Office (p582) Books accommodation in Montepulciano and arranges a wide range of courses and tours.

Tourist Office (☑ 0578 75 73 41; www.prolo comontepulciano.it; Piazza Don Minzoni 1; ☺ 9.30am-1pm & 3-7pm Apr-Sep. 9.30am-1pm & 3-6pm Mon-Sat Oct-Mar; ☎)

ⓘ Getting There & Away

BUS

The Montepulciano **bus station** (Piazzo Pietro Nenni) is next to Car Park No. 5, behind the Giardino di Poggiofanti. **Tiemme** (www.tiemmespa.it) runs four buses to/from Siena's train station daily from Monday to Saturday (€7.60, 1½ hours) stopping at Pienza (€2.60, 20 minutes) en route. There are also four extra services solely to/from Pienza.

TRAIN

Chiusi-Chianciano Terme railway station is in Chiusi Scalo, 22km southeast of Montepulciano. There are 12 daily *regionale* services to/from Siena (€8.60, 90 minutes) and Rome (€9.95, 1¾ hours). Regular buses (€3.50, 50 minutes) travel between the railway station and Montepulciano.

SOUTHERN TUSCANY

This is an intriguing part of Tuscany, home to wild scenery, dramatic coastlines, medieval hilltop villages and evocative reminders of Italy's Etruscan heritage.

Massa Marittima

☑ 0566 / POP 8290

Drawcards at this tranquil hill town in Tuscany's Colline Metallifere (metal-producing hills) include an eccentric yet endearing jumble of museums, an extremely handsome central piazza and largely intact medieval streets that are blessedly bereft of tour groups.

Briefly under Pisan domination, Massa Marittima became an independent *comune* (city-state) in 1225 but was swallowed up by Siena a century later. A plague in 1348 was followed by the decline of the region's lucrative mining industry, reducing the town to the brink of extinction, a situation made even worse by the prevalence of malaria in surrounding marshlands. Fortunately, the draining of marshes in the 18th century and the re-establishment of mining shortly afterwards brought it back to life.

The town is divided into three districts: the Città Vecchia (Old Town), Città Nuova (New Town) and Borgo (Borough). The medieval Arco Senese marks the boundary between the Città Vecchia and Città Nuova.

⊙ Sights

A cumulative ticket (adult/reduced €12/10) gives access to all of Massa Marittima's museums and monuments.

★ **Cattedrale di San Cerbone**   CATHEDRAL
(Piazza Garibaldi; ☺ 8am-noon & 3-7pm summer, to 6pm winter) Presiding over photogenic Piazza Garibaldi (aka Piazza Duomo), Massa Marittima's asymmetrically positioned 13th-century *duomo* (cathedral) is dedicated to St Cerbonius, the town's patron saint, always depicted surrounded by a flock of geese. Inside, don't miss the free-standing *Maestà* (Madonna and Child Enthroned in Majesty; 1316), attributed by some experts to Duccio di Buoninsegna.

The other treasures of the *duomo* include a carved marble urn known as the *Arca di San Cerbone* (St Cerbone's Ark; 1324) behind the high altar and an early-14th-century polychrome wooden crucifix carved by Giovanni Pisano on the altar itself. The facade's main doorway is topped by carved panels depicting scenes from the life of St Cerbonius.

Museo di Arte Sacra   MUSEUM
(Complesso Museale di San Pietro all'Orto; ☑ 0566 90 22 89; www.museidimaremma.it; Corso Diaz 36; adult/reduced €5/3; ☉ 10am-1pm & 4-7pm Tue-Sun Jul-Sep, 11am-1pm & 3-5pm Tue-Sun Apr-Jun & Oct, 3-5pm Fri & 10am-1pm & 3-5pm Sat & Sun Nov-Mar) A splendid *Maestà* (c 1335–37) by Ambrogio Lorenzetti, as well as sculptures by Giovanni Pisano that originally adorned the facade of the *duomo,* are the major attractions at this small museum housed in the former convent of San Pietro all'Orto in the Città Nuova. The collection of primitive grey-alabaster bas-reliefs also came from the *duomo,* but date from an earlier era.

Torre del Candeliere   TOWER
(Candlestick Tower; ☑ 0566 90 65 25; Piazza Matteotti; adult/reduced €3/2; ☉ 10am-1pm & 4-7pm Tue-Sun Jul-Sep, 11am-1pm & 3-5pm Tue-Sun Apr-Jun & Oct, 3-5pm Fri & 10am-1pm & 3-5pm Sat & Sun Nov-Mar) Climb to the top of this 13th-century, 30m tower on the border between the Città Vecchia and Città Nuova for views over the old town. It's the only part of the medieval city walls that can be walked on.

🛏 Sleeping

★ Casa della Pia   PENSION €
(☑ 333 9777614; www.casadellapia.eu; Via della Libertà 15; r €82; 🕸) The marital home of tragic Pia dei Tolomei, immortalised in Dante's *Divine Comedy,* this pension in a 13th-century *palazzo* (mansion) just off Piazza Garibaldi is run by the charming Costanza, who goes out of her way to make guests feel at home. One spacious and well equipped room is on offer, providing extremely comfortable accommodation. No breakfast.

Podere Riparbella   AGRITURISMO €€
(☑ 0566 91 55 57; www.riparbella.com; Località Sopra Pian di Mucini; s/d €68/116; ☉ closed early Jan—mid-Apr; ℗) 🌿 The Swiss owners of this 46-hectare estate, 5km outside of town, have built an ecologically sustainable farm operation where they cultivate grapes and olives and host guests in 11 small and simple guest rooms. Facilities include a communal lounge and a terrace. Meals featuring home-grown and local produce can be arranged (fully vegetarian on request). No credit cards and no wi-fi.

🍴 Eating & Drinking

Taverna del Vecchio Borgo   TUSCAN €€
(☑ 0566 90 21 67; taverna.vecchioborgo@libero.it; Via Norma Parenti 12; meals €32; ☉ 7.30-10pm Tue-Sun summer, 7.30-10pm Tue-Sat, 12.30-2.30pm Sun winter) Massa's best restaurant is as atmospheric as it is delicious. You'll sit in a dimly lit brick-vaulted wine cellar dating from the 16th century and dine on top-quality beef grilled on the wood-fired oven, fresh mushrooms in season or unusual dishes such as *testaroli* pasta with a pistachio sauce. The set four-course menu (€30) is a steal.

★ Il Bacchino   WINE BAR
(☑ 0566 94 02 29; www.facebook.com/pages/Il-Bacchino/140075709522677; Via Moncini 8; ☉ 10am-noon & 4-7pm Mon-Sat, 10am-noon Sun, closed Mon Nov-Feb) Owner Magdy Lamei may not be a local (he's from Cairo), but it would be hard to find anyone else as knowledgeable and passionate about local artisanal produce. Come to his classy *enoteca* (wine bar) to taste and buy local wines (€3.50 to €25 per glass), or to stock up on picnic provisions including jams, cheese and cured meats.

🛍 Shopping

Cantina Moris   WINE
(☑ 0566 91 91 35, 0566 91 80 10; www.morisfarms.com; Via Butigni 1; ☉ 8.30am-12.30pm & 4-7.30pm Thu-Tue) The best-known winery in the area, Morisfarms has a hugely atmospheric 15th-century *cantina* (wine cellar) in town where you can purchase wines, including its signature Avvoltore, a sophisticated Sangiovese, cabernet sauvignon and syrah blend. Call ahead to enjoy a tasting of seven wines (€20 per person, Monday to Saturday Easter to October) at its equally atmospheric *fattoria* (farm) in nearby Cura Nuova.

ℹ Information

Tourist Office (☑ 0566 90 65 54; www.turismomassamarittima.it; Via Todini 5; ☉ 10am-1pm & 3-5pm Wed-Mon Apr-Jun & Sep-Oct, 10am-1pm & 4-7pm daily Jul & Aug, 10am-1pm & 3-5pm Fri-Sun Nov-Mar; 🕸)

ℹ Getting There & Away

BUS
The bus station is in Piazza XXIV Maggio, near the Museo di Arte Sacra; the bus stop closest to Piazza Garibaldi is in Via Corridoni. **Tiemme** (www.tiemmespa.it) operates buses to Grosseto

(€5.60, one hour, four daily) and Siena (€7.60, two hours, one daily) from Monday to Saturday. To get to Volterra you'll need to change at Monterotondo Marittimo. **Massa Veternensis** (Piazza Garibaldi 18) sells bus and train tickets.

TRAIN

The nearest train station is in Follonica, 22km southwest of Massa Marittima; Tiemme buses (€3.50, 25 minutes, frequent Monday to Saturday, two services Sunday) travel between the station and the town.

Città del Tufo

☑ 0564

The picturesque towns of Pitigliano, Sovana and Sorano form a triangle enclosing a dramatic landscape where local buildings have been constructed from the volcanic porous rock tufa since Etruscan times. Known as the Città del Tufo (city of the tufa), the area incorporates Etruscan sites including tombs and *vie cave* (sunken roads with high walls carved out of the tufa), all protected as part of the Parco Archeologico 'Città del Tufo' (www.leviecave.it). For updates on activities in the archaeological park, check its Facebook page.

Pitigliano

☑ 0564 / POP 3760

Perched atop a volcanic rocky outcrop towering over the surrounding countryside, this spectacularly sited hilltop town is surrounded by gorges on three sides, constituting a natural bastion completed to the east by a fort. Within the town, twisting stairways disappear around corners, cobbled alleys bend tantalisingly out of sight beneath graceful arches, and reminders of the town's once-considerable Jewish community remain in the form of a 16th-century synagogue and a unique Jewish-flavoured local cuisine.

◉ Sights

Museo Civico Archeologico di Pitigliano   MUSEUM
(☎389 5933592; Piazza della Fortezza; adult/reduced €3/2; ◷10am-6pm Fri-Sun Jun, 10am-7pm Tue-Sun Jul-Sep, 9am-5pm Fri-Sun Oct, 10am-5pm Sat & Sun Nov, hours vary rest of year) Head up the stone stairs to this small but well-run museum, which has rich displays of finds from local Etruscan sites. Highlights include some huge intact *bucchero* (black earthenware pottery) urns dating from the 6th century BC and a collection of charming pinkish-cream clay oil containers in the form of small deer.

Museo Archeologico all'Aperto 'Alberto Manzi'   ARCHAEOLOGICAL SITE
(Alberto Manzi Open-Air Archaeology Museum; ☑0564 61 40 67, 389 5933592; SP127 Pantano, off SR74; adult/reduced €4/2; ◷10am-6pm Fri-Sun May & Jun, 10am-7pm Thu-Sun Jul, 10am-7pm

---

OFF THE BEATEN TRACK

VIE CAVE

There are at least 15 *vie cave* (sunken roads) hewn out of tufa in the valleys below Pitigliano. These enormous passages – up to 20m deep and 3m wide – are popularly believed to be sacred routes linking Etruscan necropolises and other religious sites. A more mundane explanation is that these strange ancient corridors were used to move livestock or as some kind of defence, allowing people to flit from village to village unseen. The Torciata di San Giuseppe is a procession through the Via Cava di San Giuseppe to mark the end of winter.

Two particularly good examples of *vie cave*, the Via Cava di Fratenuti FREE and the Via Cava di San Giuseppe FREE, are found 500m west of Pitigliano on the road to Sovana. Fratenuti has high vertical walls and Etruscan markings, and San Giuseppe passes the Fontana dell'Olmo, a fountain carved out of solid rock. From it stares the sculpted head of Bacchus, the god of wine and fertility.

There's a fine walk from Pitigliano to Sovana (8km) that incorporates parts of the *vie cave*. There's also an enjoyable 2km walk from the small stone bridge in the gorge below Sorano along the Via Cava San Rocco FREE to the Necropoli di San Rocco, another Etruscan burial site.

The open-air Museo Archeologico all'Aperto 'Alberto Manzi', south of Pitigliano on the road to Saturnia, contains sections of *vie cave* and several necropolises.

DON'T MISS

SPA TIME!

The sulphurous thermal baths at **Terme di Saturnia** (☑ 0564 60 08 14; www.termedisat urnia.it; pool park access Mon-Fri €26, Sat & Sun €31, after 2pm €21; ⊙ 9.30am-7pm summer, to 5pm winter, closed Jan) are some 2.5km downhill from the village of Saturnia, which is 25km west of Pitigliano. You can happily replicate the Romans and spend a whole day indulging in bathing and spa treatments at this luxury resort, or take the econo-bather option at the **Cascate del Gorello**, 1.8km south on the opposite side of the highway, where a cluster of gratis, open-air pools with temperatures at a constant 37.5°C can be found. These pools are hugely popular, but before you opt to bathe in them consider the fact that the pools are filled with water that has been expelled from the *terme* upriver, so they aren't particularly clean. And be sure not to leave any valuables in your car when bathing – thefts are a regular occurrence. Alternatively, overnight in the **Hotel Saturno Fonte Pura** (☑ 0564 60 13 13; www.hotelsaturnofontepura.com; Località la Croce; d with half-board 2/3 nights €400/594; P ✳ 🛜 🛍), a spa resort with its own thermal pool.

Tue-Sun Aug, 10am-6pm Fri-Sun Sep) This open-air museum south of Pitigliano on the road to Saturnia contains sections of *vie cave* and several Etruscan necropolises. The *vie cave* are fascinating to explore – popularly believed to be sacred routes linking the necropolises with other religious sites, they are impressive feats of construction that sit comfortably in the landscape and endow the site with a palpable sense of mystery and majesty.

A combination ticket to both this site and the Museo Civico Archeologico di Pitigliano (adult/reduced €6/3) is available for purchase at the ticket office.

La Piccola Gerusalemme   MUSEUM
(Little Jerusalem; ☑ 0564 61 42 30; www.lapiccola gerusalemme.it; Vicolo Manin 30; adult/reduced €5/4; ⊙ 10am-1pm & 2.30-6pm Sun-Fri summer, 10am-12.30 & 2-3.30pm Sun-Fri winter) Head down Via Zuccarelli and turn left at a sign indicating 'La Piccola Gerusalemme' to visit this fascinating time capsule of Pitigliano's historic but sadly near-extinct Jewish culture. It incorporates a tiny, richly adorned synagogue (established in 1598 and one of only five in Tuscany), ritual bath, kosher butcher, bakery, wine cellar and dyeing workshops.

✦ Festivals & Events

Torciata di San Giuseppe   CULTURAL
(⊙ 19 Mar) Every spring on the night of the equinox there is a torch-lit procession down the Via Cava di San Giuseppe, which culminates in a huge bonfire in Pitigliano's Piazza Garibaldi. The procession serves as a symbol of purification and renewal marking the end of winter.

🛏 Sleeping

La Casa degli Archi   APARTMENT €€
(☑ 349 4986298; www.lacasadegliarchi.com; r €129-149; 🛜) These apartment rentals, sleeping between two and six guests across three properties, make great bases for those visiting the region. Casa degli Archi is highly recommended and two of the three apartments in a second building, Case Nuove, are also good – the third, Casa Capitano, has a strangely sloping low roof and isn't as comfortable. Reception is in Via Roma 106.

Le Camere del Ceccottino   PENSION €€
(☑ 0564 61 42 73; www.ceccottino.com; Via Roma 159; r €100-130; ✳ 🛜) Owned and operated by the extremely helpful Chiara and Alessandro, who also run the nearby restaurant of the same name, this *pensione* boasts an excellent location near the *duomo* and five immaculately maintained and well-equipped rooms. Opt for a superior room if possible, as the standard versions are cramped. No breakfast.

🍴 Eating & Drinking

There are a few wine bars on and around Piazza della Repubblica and a popular cafe on Piazza Francesco Petruccioli near the main gate to the historic centre. The local DOC wine, Bianco di Pitigliano, is a crisp white with a good balance of floral and mineral notes. When here, try to sample Jewish specialities such as *sfratto pitiglianese* (a sweet made with honey and walnuts).

La Rocca TUSCAN €

(0564 61 42 67; Piazza della Repubblica 12; meals €30, pizzas €6-8.50; 9.30am-10pm, closed Mon in winter) Generous pourings of local wine are on offer at this cavernous restaurant and wine bar next to one of the panoramic viewpoints on Piazza della Repubblica. There are far more seafood options on the menu than is usual, which is a refreshing change in rural Tuscany. In summer, the terrace seating is popular.

Il Tufo Allegro TUSCAN €€

(0564 61 61 92; www.facebook.com/iltufoallegro; Vicolo della Costituzione 5; meals €42; 12.30-2.30pm & 7.30-9.30pm Wed-Sun) The aromas emanating from the kitchen door off Via Zuccarelli should be enough to draw you down the stairs and into the cosy dining rooms, which are carved out of tufa. Chef Domenico Pichini's menu ranges from traditional to modern and all of his creations rely heavily on local produce for inspiration. It's near La Piccola Gerusalemme (p587).

★Hostaria del Ceccottino TUSCAN €€€

(0564 61 42 73; www.ceccottino.com; Piazza San Gregorio VII 64; meals €53; 12.30-3pm & 7-10pm Fri-Wed mid-Mar–mid-Jan;) Specialising in *piatti tipici* (typical dishes), Ceccottino serves delicious versions of Tuscan classics such as *spezzatino di cinghiale* (wild-boar stew), but also offers less-common dishes inspired by local produce. There might be a *tagliatelle* made with *bottarga* (salted dried cod roe) from Orbetello, or a *tortelli* stuffed with fresh ricotta and *ortica* (nettles). Excellent local wine list too.

ⓘ Information

Tourist Office (0564 61 71 11; www. comune.pitigliano.gr.it; Piazza Garibaldi 12; 9am-12.30pm & 3.30-6.30pm Tue-Sat, 9am-12.30pm Sun, extended hours summer) In the piazza just inside the the main gate to the historic centre.

ⓘ Getting There & Away

Tiemme (www.tiemmespa.it) buses leave from Via Santa Chiara, just off Piazza Petruccioli. Some routes operate Monday to Saturday only; buy tickets at the newsagent next to La Rocca restaurant in Piazza della Repubblica. Services include the following:

Grosseto (€8.40, two hours, three daily)
Orbetello (€6.90, 90 minutes, one daily)
Siena (€12.20, three hours, one daily)
Sorano (€1.50, 15 minutes, three daily)
Sovana (€1.50, 20 minutes, one daily)

Sovana

 0564

The main attractions at this postcard-pretty village are a cobbled main street that dates from Roman times, two austerely beautiful Romanesque churches and a museum showcasing a collection of ancient gold coins.

◎ Sights & Activities

★Necropoli di Sovana ARCHAEOLOGICAL SITE

(0564 61 40 74; www.leviecave.it; €5; 10am-7pm summer, to 6pm Oct, to 5pm Sat & Sun Nov-Mar; Ⓟ) At Tuscany's most significant Etruscan tombs, part of the Parco Archeologico 'Città del Tufo', signs in Italian and English guide you around four elaborate burial sites. The headline exhibit is the Tomba Ildebranda, named after Pope Gregory VII, which preserves traces of its carved columns and stairs. The Tomba dei Demoni Alati (Tomb of the Winged Demons) features a recumbent headless terracotta figure.

The carving of a sea demon with huge wings that was the original centrepiece of that tomb is now protected in a roofed enclosure nearby. The Tomba del Tifone (Tomb of the Typhoon) is about 300m down a trail running alongside a rank of tomb facades cut from the rock face. Two arresting lengths of *vie cave* (one known as 'Cavone' and the other 'Poggio Prisca') are nearby.

On the opposite side of the site is the Tomba della Sirena and another *via cava*, San Sebastiano. The latter can be accessed at all times, not just within the Necropoli's official hours.

You'll find the Necropoli 1.5km east of town.

La Biagiola WINE

(366 676 64 00; www.labiagiola.it; Località Pianetti; by appointment) Those interested in wine and archaeology might want to combine the two by visiting this wine estate 7km north of Sovana. In 2004 the remains of an imperial Roman villa were discovered in the vineyard; the archaeologists leading an ongoing excavation welcome visitors to join them for hands-on experiences assisting on the dig in summer. See www.culturaterritorio.org for details.

🛌 Sleeping & Eating

Sovana Hotel & Resort   HOTEL €€
(📞 338 5802977, 0564 61 70 30; www.sovana
hotel.it; Via del Duomo 66; r €125-145; P🖥☀)
The huge garden surrounding this hotel
is nothing less than extraordinary, featuring a maze, Etruscan ruin, olive grove and
swimming pool grand enough for a Roman
emperor's villa. Rooms aren't quite as swish,
but they are perfectly comfortable and offer
good value. There's also a bar, restaurant
and communal lounge with open fire. Special two-night deals (weekdays/weekends
€298/328) include dinner.

★ **Vino al Vino**   TUSCAN €
(📞 0564 61 71 08; www.facebook.com/enoteca.vi
noalvino; Via del Duomo 10; cheese & salumi plates
€15, soup €8; ⊙ 10.30am-9pm Wed-Mon mid-Mar–
Dec, 10.30am-9pm Sat & Sun Jan–mid-Mar; 🌿)
Mellow jazz plays on the soundtrack, art
adorns every wall and the vibe is friendly
at this hybrid cafe and *enoteca* (wine bar)
on Sovana's main street. The speciality-roast
coffee is good; cakes (sourced in Pitigliano)
are even better.

At lunch or dinner, glasses of wine and
tasting plates of local produce reign supreme. Vegan and vegetarian soups and
bruschette are available.

ℹ Information

Tourist Office (📞 0564 61 40 74; Piazza del
Pretorio; ⊙ 10am-1pm & 3-7pm Fri-Wed mid-
Mar–Oct, 10am-1pm & 2-5pm Sat & Sun Nov
& Dec)

ℹ Getting There & Away

Between Monday and Saturday, **Tiemme** (www.
tiemmespa.it) buses travel to Pitigliano (€1.50,
30 minutes, five daily) and Sorano (€1.50, 15
minutes, two daily).

Sorano

📞 0564 / POP 3320
Sorano's setting is truly dramatic – sitting
astride a rocky outcrop, its weatherworn
stone houses are built along a ridge overlooking the Lente river and gorge. Below
the ridgeline are *cantine* (cellars) dug out of
tufa, as well as a series of terraced gardens,
many part-hidden from public view.

◉ Sights

Fortezza Orsini   FORT
(📞 0564 63 34 24; adult/reduced €5/3.50;
⊙ 10am-1pm & 3-7pm Tue-Sun summer, 10am-1pm
& 2-5pm Sat & Sun Nov & Dec) Work on this massive fortress started in the 11th century. Today it still stands sentinel over the town, its
sturdy walls linking two bastions surrounded by a dry moat. The highlight of any visit is
undoubtedly a guided tour of the evocative
subterranean passages (tour schedule
varies), which are noticeably chilly even in
the height of the Tuscan summer.

**Area Archeologica
di Vitozza**   ARCHAEOLOGICAL SITE
(⊙ 10am-dusk) FREE More than 200 caves
pepper a high rock ridge here, making it
one of the largest troglodyte dwellings in
Italy. The complex was first inhabited in
prehistoric times. To explore the site, you'll
need two hours and sturdy walking shoes.

FLORENCE & TUSCANY CITTÀ DEL TUFO

WORTH A TRIP

PARCO REGIONALE DELLA MAREMMA

Hundreds of acres of forests, mountains, marshy plains, 20km of pristine coastline,
countless activities and your chance to be a cowboy are all on offer in southern Tuscany's wild and wonderful regional park (📞 0564 39 32 38; www.parco-maremma.it; adult/
reduced from €6/4; ⊙ 8.30am-4pm Apr–mid-Jun, to 6pm mid-Jun–Oct, to 2pm Nov-Mar). It's
also a popular destination for beachgoers, who enjoy safe swimming at the 8km-long
sandy beach at Marina di Albarese.

Park access is limited to 12 signed walking trails ranging in length from 2.5km to
13km; the most popular are the easy 7km A2 ('Le Torri') and the demanding A1, a 7.8km
uphill hike to San Rabano Abbey and the Torre Uccellina. Mid-June to mid-September
you can only visit on a guided tour. There are also bicycle, horse-riding and canoe
trails. Pay your entry fee and pick up information at the main visitor centre (📞 0564
39 32 38; Via del Bersagliere 7-9, Alberese; ⊙ 8am-6pm mid-Jun–mid-Sep, to 4pm mid-Sep–mid-
Nov, to 2pm mid-Nov–mid-Jun) in Alberese.

It's 4km due east of Sorano; there's a signed walking path between Sorano and the site.

Sleeping & Eating

★ Sant'Egle   AGRITURISMO €€
(☎329 4250285; www.santegle.it; Case Sparse Sant'Egle 18; r €170-280, glamping €150; ☺closed mid-Jan–mid-Mar; P🅿🛜🕮) 🅿 If only all accommodation could be as sustainable and comfortable as this. Set on an organic multicrop farm, it offers individually designed bedrooms in a carefully renovated 17th-century customs house, one luxury glamping tent and a wonderfully tranquil garden environment in which to de-stress and relax. Four-night minimum stay in August.

Hosteria del Borgo   TUSCAN €€
(☎0564 63 84 31; www.hosteriadelborgo.it; Via del Borgo 46; meal €37; ☺noon-4pm & 6-10pm) The view from the terrace of this friendly *osteria* (casual tavern) is spectacular, making it a particularly popular choice in fine weather. The menu is traditionally Maremmese – your best bet is to order a pasta such as the hand-made *pappardelle* with wild-boar sauce, or opt for one of the rustic dishes made with locally grown beans and lentils. Good house wine too.

ℹ Information

Tourist Office (☎0564 63 30 99; Piazza Busatti; ☺10am-1pm & 3-7pm Thu-Tue Apr–Sep, 10am-1pm & 2-5pm Sat & Sun Oct-Dec)

ℹ Getting There & Away

From Monday to Saturday, **Tiemme** (www.tiemmespa.it) operates five daily services to Pitigliano (€1.50, 20 minutes); there are three services from Pitigliano. There are three services each way on Sundays.

CENTRAL COAST & ELBA

Despite possessing the types of landscapes that dreams are made of, much of this part of Tuscany feels far away from well-beaten tourist trails.

Livorno

🅿 0586 / POP 161,900

Tuscany's third-largest city is a quintessential port town with a colourful history and cosmopolitan heritage. A free port from the 17th century, Livorno (Leghorn in English) attracted traders from across the globe, who brought with them new customs and habits, exotic goods, slaves and foreign forms of worship. The result was a city famed throughout Europe for its multiculturalism. Today its seafood is the best on the Tyrrhenian coast, its shabby historic quarter threaded with Venetian-style canals is full of character, and its elegant belle-époque buildings offer evocative reminders of a prosperous past. An easy train trip from Florence, Pisa and Rome, it makes an understated but undeniably worthwhile stop on any Tuscan itinerary.

◎ Sights & Activities

The city's beach clubs open from May to September.

Piccola Venezia   AREA
(Little Venice) Piccola Venezia is a tangle of small canals built during the 17th century, using Venetian methods of reclaiming land from the sea. At its heart sits the remains of the Medici-era **Fortezza Nuova** (New Fort; Scali della Fortezza Nuova; ☺8am-8pm mid-Apr–mid-Sep, reduced hours rest of year) FREE. Canals link this with the slightly older, waterfront **Fortezza Vecchia** (Old Fort; Piazzale dei Marmi; ☺hours vary) FREE. The waterways can be explored by canalside footpaths but a boat tour is the best way to see its shabby-chic panoramas of faded, peeling apartments draped with brightly coloured washing, interspersed with waterside cafes and bars.

Terrazza Mascagni   STREET
(Viale Italia) No trip to Livorno is complete without a stroll along this seafront terrace with its dramatic black-and-white chessboard-style pavement. When it was built in the 1920s, it was called Terrazza Ciano after the leader of the Livorno fascist movement; it now bears the name of Livorno-born opera composer Pietro Mascagni (1863–1945).

Acquario di Livorno   AQUARIUM
(☎0586 26 91 11; www.acquariodilivorno.com; Piazzale Mascagni 1; adult €10-17, child €5-11; ☺10am-7pm Jul & Aug, to 6pm mid-Apr–Jun & early-mid Sep, 10am-6pm Sat & Sun mid-Sep–Mar) Livorno's seafront aquarium swims with black-tip reef and zebra sharks, seahorses, Madagascan spider tortoises, moon jellyfish and impressive green sea turtles. Among the 33 tanks on the ground floor, there is also a touching pool – a favourite with kids. Upstairs, the 1st floor showcases insects, amphibians and

FESTA DEL MADONNA

The story goes like this: in 1345, the Virgin Mary appeared to a shepherd, who led her to black mountain (monte nero), a haven of brigands. Needless to say, the brigands immediately saw the error of their ways and built a chapel on the mountain. Soon pilgrims arrived and the chapel was extended in stages; it reached its present form in 1774. Rooms and corridors surrounding the **Santuario della Madonna di Montenero** (☑ 0586 57 96 27; www.santuariomontenero.org; Piazza di Montenero 9; ⊙ 6.30am-12.30pm & 2.30-7pm summer, to 6pm winter) house a fascinating collection of 20,000 historic ex-votos thanking the Virgin for miracles.

The best time to visit is on 8 September, for the Festa del Madonna. To get here by public transport, take the LAM Rosso bus to Montenero (€1.50 or €2 on board, every 10 to 20 minutes) and get off at the last stop on Piazza delle Carrozze in Montenero Basso. From there, take the historic funicular (€2, every 10 to 20 minutes) up to the sanctuary.

reptiles, including a chameleon and glorious green iguana. End your visit on the panoramic terrace with sweeping sea views.

👉 Tours

Livorno in Battello   BOATING
(☑ 333 1573372; www.livornoinbattello.it; adult/child €12/5) One of a handful of local companies to offer daily one-hour guided tours of Livorno's Medicean waterways by boat, Livorno in Battello operates year-round (up to four departures daily in summer, limited departures December to February). The main departure jetty for boats is the pier opposite the **Monumento dei Quattro Mori** (Monument of the Four Moors; Piazza Giuseppe Micheli), but check online or at the tourist office when buying tickets.

🛏 Sleeping

Camping Miramare   CAMPGROUND €
(☑ 0586 58 04 02; www.campingmiramare.it; Via del Littorale 220; standard/seafront tent pitch €15/48, campsite adult/child/car €15/7/10; ⊙ reception 8am-10pm Jul & Aug, reduced hours rest of year; P 🛜 🏊) Be it a tent pitched beneath trees or the deluxe version with wooden terrace and sun lounges on the pebble beach, this pool-clad campground by the sea – open year-round thanks to its village of mobile homes, maxi caravans and bungalows – has it all. Rates outside of July and August are at least 50% lower. Find the campground 8km south of town in Antignano, near Montenero.

Hotel al Teatro   BOUTIQUE HOTEL €€
(☑ 0586 89 87 05; www.hotelalteatro.it; Via Mayer 42; s €78-85, d €99-115, tr 110-128; P 🛜) The eight rooms in this hotel near the **Goldoni**

Theatre (☑ 0586 20 42 90; www.goldoniteatro.it; Via Carlo Goldoni 83) are comfortable and clean, if a tad frumpy, but the real draw is the hidden garden out back. Here, guests can breakfast or lounge over coffee on wicker furniture beneath a breathtakingly beautiful, 300-year-old magnolia tree.

Grand Hotel Palazzo   HISTORIC HOTEL €€€
(☑ 0586 26 08 36; www.grandhotelpalazzo.com; Viale Italia 195; d from €225; P 🛜 @ 🏊) Livorno's grand dame of a belle-époque hotel, part of the MGallery by Sofitel, looks out to sea from its waterfront perch. The finest of its 123 spacious, elegant rooms enjoy big blue sea views – or simply head up to the rooftop infinity pool and restaurant-bar with panoramic balcony. There is no lovelier spot for a sunset *aperitivo* (predinner drink).

🍴 Eating

Livornese cuisine – particularly traditionally prepared seafood – is known throughout Italy for its excellence. Indeed, sampling the city's signature dish of *cacciucco* (pronounced kar-*choo*-ko), a mixed seafood stew, is reason enough to visit the city. Preferably made using the local Slow Food–accredited San Vincenzo tomatoes, it packs more than its fair share of flavour.

★ Scom Posto   TUSCAN €
(☑ 0586 88 75 96; www.dascomposto.it; Piazza dei Domenicani 17; sandwiches & platters €5-7, tartare €14; ⊙ 11am-3.30pm & 6pm-midnight Sun-Thu, to 2am Fri & Sat; 🛜) Everything about this water-edge bistro is sassy, fresh and on trend. Plump for a place around one huge long shared table outside or enjoy the romance of a candlelit, vaulted red-brick interior. Furnishings are crafted from chipboard and

Livorno

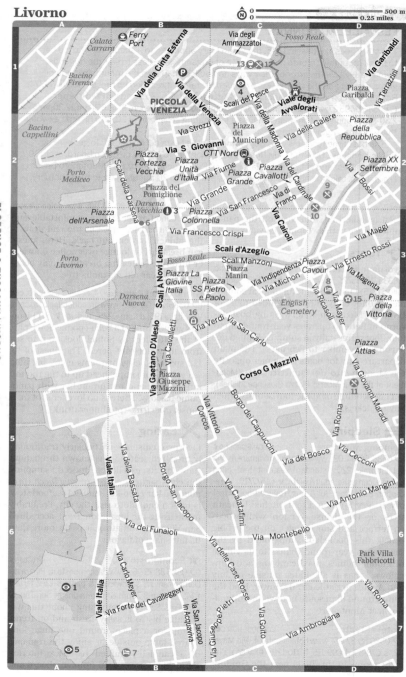

FLORENCE & TUSCANY LIVORNO

N 0 ──────── 500 m
0 ──────── 0.25 miles

Ferry Port

Calata Carrara

Bacino Firenze

Bacino Cappellini

Porto Mediceo

Porto Livorno

Via della Cinta Esterna

Via della Venezia

PICCOLA VENEZIA

Scali della Darsena

Piazza Fortezza Vecchia

Darsena Vecchia

Piazza dell'Arsenale

Darsena Nuova

Scali A Novi Lena

Scali A Novi Lena

Via Gaetano D'Alesio

Via Cavalletti

Via Cavalletti

Piazza Giuseppe Mazzini

Viale Italia

Viale Italia

Via della Bassata

Via Carlo Meyer

Via Forte dei Cavalleggeri

Via dei Funaioli

Borgo San Jacopo

Via degli Ammazzatoi

Fosso Reale

13   12

Via degli Ammazzatoi

Scali del Pesce

4

2

Viale degli Avvalorati

Via della Madonna   Via del Cardinale

Piazza del Municipio

Via delle Galere

Piazza Garibaldi

Via Garibaldi

Via Terrazzini

Piazza della Repubblica

Via Strozzi

Via S Giovanni

CTT Nord

Piazza Unità d'Italia

Piazza del Municipio

Piazza Cavallotti

Piazza XX Settembre

Via L Bossi

Plazza del Pomiglione

1

Via Fiume

Piazza Grande

Via Grande

9

Via di Franco

10

Via Francesco Crispi

3

Piazza Colonnella

Via San Francesco

Via Cairoli

Via Maggi

Via Ernesto Rossi

Scali d'Azeglio

Scali Manzoni

Piazza Manin

Piazza Cavour

Via Indipendenza

Via Magenta

Fosso Reale

Piazza La Giovine Italia

Piazza SS Pietro e Paolo

Via Michon

8

Via Ricasoli

Via Mayer

15

Piazza della Vittoria

English Cemetery

16

Via Verdi   Via San Carlo

Piazza Attias

11

Via Giovanni Marad

Corso G Mazzini

Via Vittorio Corcos

Borgo dei Cappuccini

Via Roma

Via Cecconi

Via del Bosco

Via Calatafimi

Via Antonio Mangini

Via dei Funaioli

Via Montebello

Park Villa Fabbricotti

1

Via delle Case Rosse

Via Giuseppe Pietri

Via San Jacopo In Acquaviva

Via Goito

Via Roma

5

7

Via Ambrogiana

Livorno

the dining choice is simple: Chianina beef tartare, cheese and salami platters, or gourmet *schiacciate* (sandwiches) already assembled or served loose on a wooden board.

★**Antica Torteria Al**
Mercato da Gagarin   SANDWICHES €
(☑0586 88 40 86; Via del Cardinale 24; sandwich €2.50-3.20; ⊙8am-2pm & 4.30-8.30pm Mon-Sat) There is no finer blast to old-world Livorno than this retro snack bar, little changed since its 1959 opening. Push through the plastic fly-net veiling the unmarked door and order the house speciality: a sensational 'five and five' sandwich (ask for a *cinque e cinque*) stuffed with scrumptious *torta di ceci* (chickpea pancake, fried in peanut oil and salted).

★**Alle Vettovaglie**   TUSCAN €
(☑347 7487020; www.allevettovaglie.com; Scali Saffi 27, Mercato Centrale; dishes €6.50-12; ⊙10am-3pm Tue-Thu, 10am-3pm & 7-11pm Fri & Sat) Owned by three sommeliers, this wine bar in the historic Mercato Centrale has a menu that changes according to what produce is fresh and plentiful on the day – it's just as likely to feature *triglie alla livornese* (mullet in tomato sauce) as it is pasta with an aromatic pesto. It also – unsurprisingly – offers an impressive selection of wine.

★**Cantina Nardi**   TUSCAN €€
(☑0586 80 80 06; www.cantinanardi.com; Via Leonardo Cambini 6-8; meals €20-30; ⊙8am-4pm & 5-9.30pm Mon-Thu, to 10.30pm Fri & Sat) They've been in business since 1965, so the friendly Nardis know how to keep their customers happy. As much an *enoteca* (wine bar) as it is Slow Food–hailed eatery, Cantina

Nardi has a 400-bottle wine list and an amazing 100 wines are offered by the glass. It is one of the city's best *aperitivo* spots, so come sit between bottle-filled shelves inside, or at a streetside table.

⬛ Drinking & Nightlife

Piazza Grande and Piazza Cavour are surrounded by cafes where locals meet for coffee or an *aperitivo* (predinner drink). Waterfront snack bars and cafes dot the seafront around the Terrazza Mascagni. In Piccola Venezia watch for new bar openings on and around Scali delle Ancore.

★**Le Botteghe & Makutu Tiki Bar**   BAR
(☑346 6217884; www.facebook.com/lebottegheli vorno; Piazza dei Domenicani 20; ⊙7.30pm-1.30am Sun-Thu, to 2am Fri & Sat) Live music, craft beer, creative bar cuisine and fabulous cocktails lure a local party set to this red-brick cellar bar, right by a canal in Piccola Venezia. Sultry summer nights are particularly fun when the drinking and dancing action spills onto the quayside in front.

ⓘ Information

Tourist Office (☑0586 89 42 36; Via Pieroni 18; ⊙9am-4pm summer, to 3pm winter) Hands out free maps and books boat tours.

ⓘ Getting There & Away

BOAT

Livorno is a major port. Regular ferries for Sardinia, Corsica and Sicily depart from the **ferry port** (Calata Carrara); ferries to Capraia use the smaller **Porto Mediceo** (Via del Molo Mediceo) near Piazza dell'Arsenale. Boats to Spain use Porto Nuovo, 3km north of the city.

DON'T MISS

SOUVENIR SHOPPING
....

Consider **Pesce Fresco** (Fresh Fish; 328 7210546; www.artpescefresco.com; Borgo dei Cappuccini 71; ☺hours vary) as a gift to take home. Livorno-born Stefano Pilato (b. 1965) is the creative talent behind the sculptures and collages crafted from recycled tools, scrap metal, old hooks and all sorts at his backstreet artist's studio. The funky fish, seahorses and other seafaring creatures – wonderfully fantastical with a subtle sci-fi vibe – come in all shapes and sizes, to either hang on the wall or string from the ceiling.

Corsica Ferries (www.corsica-ferries.co.uk) Up to seven ferries per week to Bastia, Corsica (from €60, four hours) and Golfo Aranci, Sardinia (from €90, 9½ hours).

Grimaldi Lines (www.grimaldi-lines.com) Daily sailings to/from Olbia, Sardinia (from €34, nine hours) and Palermo, Sicily (from €45, 18 hours).

Moby (www.moby.it) Year-round at least two services a day to Olbia, Sardinia (from €32, seven to 10 hours). Plus in the summer, several crossings a week to Bastia, Corsica (from €25, four hours).

Toremar (www.toremar.it) Several weekly crossings year-round to Capraia (€22, 2¾ hours).

TRAIN

From the central **train station** (Piazza Dante) walk westwards (straight ahead) along Viale Carducci, Via de Larderel and Via Grande to access Piazza Grande, Livorno's central square.

Services include the following:

Castiglioncello (€3.60, 20 minutes, at least hourly)

Florence (€9.90, 1¼ hours, hourly).

Pisa (€2.60, 15 minutes, frequent).

Rome (€22.85, 3¾ hours, at least seven daily).

San Vincenzo (€6.10, 40 minutes to one hour, at least hourly)

❶ Getting Around

LAM Blu buses operated by **CTT Nord** (0586 37 69 00; www.livorno.cttnord.it; Largo Duomo; ☺7am-7.30pm Mon-Sat) travel from the main train station into the city centre, stopping at Piazza Grande before continuing to Porto Mediceo and then along the seafront (valid 70 minutes €1.20, on board €2.50). If you're catching a ferry to Sardinia or Corsica, take bus 1 to Piazza Grande, then bus 5 from Via Cogorano, just off Piazza Grande.

Isola d'Elba

Napoleon would think twice about fleeing Elba today. Dramatically more congested than when the emperor was exiled here in 1814 (he managed to engineer an escape within a year), the island is an ever-glorious paradise of beach-laced coves, vineyards, azure waters, hairpin-bend motoring, a 1018m mountain (Monte Capanne) and mind-bending views. It's all supplemented by a fine seafaring cuisine, lovely island wines, and land and seascapes just made for hiking, biking and sea kayaking.

With the exception of high season (actually only August), when the island's beaches and roads are jam-packed, Elba is something of a Robinson Crusoe paradise. In springtime, early summer and autumn, when grapes and olives are harvested, there are plenty of tranquil nooks on this stunningly picturesque, 28km-long, 19km-wide island.

There is a wealth of information about the island at www.infoelba.com.

Portoferraio
0565 / POP 12,000

Portoferraio can be a hectic place, especially in August when holidaymakers pour off the ferries from Piombino on the mainland every 20 minutes or so. But wandering the streets and steps of the historic centre, indulging in the exceptional eating options and haggling for sardines with fishermen more than makes up for the squeeze.

Known to the Romans as Fabricia and later Ferraia (an acknowledgement of its important role as a port for iron exports), this small harbour was acquired by Cosimo I de' Medici in the mid-16th century, when its distinctive fortifications took shape.

◉ Sights

The Old Town's spiderweb of narrow streets and alleys staggers uphill from the old harbour to Portoferraio's defining twinset of forts, **Forte Falcone** (0565 94 40 24; www.visitaportoferraio.com; Via del Falcone; €5; ☺10am-8pm mid-June–mid-Sep, 10am-6pm mid-Apr–mid-June & mid-Sep–early Nov) and **Forte Stella** (0565 91 69 89; Via della Stella; adult/reduced €2/1.50; ☺10am-1pm & 3-6pm Easter-Sep), revealing deserted 16th-century ramparts to wander and seagulls freewheeling overhead.

From waterside square **Piazza Cavour** head uphill along Via Garibaldi to the foot of the monumental **Scalinata Medici**, a fabulous mirage of 140 wonky stone steps cascading up through every sunlit shade of amber to the dimly lit, 17th-century **Chiesa della Misericordia** (Via della Misericordia; ☺8am-5pm). Inside is Napoleon's death mask. Continue to the top of the staircase to reach the forts and **Villa dei Mulini**, where Napoleon lived when in Portoferraio.

Museo Nazionale della
Residenze Napoleoniche   MUSEUM
(Villa dei Mulini; ☑0565 91 58 46; Piazzale Napoleone; adult/reduced €5/2; ☺8.30am-7.30pm Mon-Sat, 8.30am-1.30pm Sun summer, 8.30am-1.30pm daily winter) Villa dei Mulini was home to Napoleon during his stint in exile on this small isle. With its Empire-style furnishings, splendid library, fig-tree-studded Italianate gardens and unbeatable sea view, the emperor didn't want for creature comforts – contrast this with the simplicity of the camp bed and travelling trunk he used when on campaigns. While that history lesson is nice, the dearth of actual Napoleonic artefacts here is a tad disappointing.

★**Museo Villa Napoleonica**
di San Martino   MUSEUM
(☑0565 91 58 46; San Martino; adult/reduced €5/2; ☺8.30am-1.30pm Tue, Thu, Sat & Sun, 2-5.30pm Wed & Fri summer, 9am-3pm Tue-Sun winter) Napoleon personally supervised the transformation of what had been a large farmhouse in the hills 5km southwest of Portoferraio into an elegant villa where he could escape the summer heat. Romanticism and hubris both came into play as he sought to give his new residence a Parisian sheen – the pretty **Room of the Love Knot** and grand **Egyptian Room** were particular triumphs. In the 1850s, a Russian nobleman purchased the villa and built a grandiose gallery at its base.

Bus 1 travels between the port at Portoferraio and San Martino at least eight times per day (€1, 15 minutes). The car park near the villa charges a whopping €3.50.

🛏 Sleeping

Accommodation options in central Portoferraio are lacklustre – you're better off sleeping elsewhere on the island; Schiop-parello, Magazzini and Otone are all handily close by.

B&B Porta del Mare   PENSION €
(☑328 8261441; www.bebportadelmarelba.com; Piazza Cavour 34; d €70-140, tr €90-170; 🛜) If you like being in the heart of things, the 4th-floor rooms in this elegant town house could work a treat. Three light, bright bedrooms have tall ceilings and filmy drapes; two have cracking harbour views. It's right in the middle of Portoferraio's main square (so expect some noise after dark). Owners Rossella and Bruno are gracious hosts.

Rosselba Le Palme   CAMPGROUND €
(☑0565 93 31 01; www.rosselbalepalme.it; Località Ottone; campsite adult/child €15/12, tent/car €20/5; ☺mid-Apr–Sep; P🛜🏊) Set around a botanical garden backed by Mediterranean forest, few campgrounds are as leafy or large. The beach is a 400m walk between trees while accommodation ranges from simple pitches to 'glamping' tents with bathtubs, or cute wooden chalets to villa apartments. Find the ground 9km east of Portoferraio near Ottone.

★**Agriturismo Due Palme**   AGRITURISMO €€
(☑338 7433736, 0565 93 30 17; www.agriturismo elba.it; Via Schiopparello 28, Schiopparello; r €120-140; P🛜) Utterly tranquil despite being just a few minutes from the Portoferraio–Magazzini road, this *agriturismo* (farmstay accommodation) is part of the only olive plantation on Elba to produce quality-stamped IGP olive oil. Its six simple but well-maintained self-catering cottages are dotted amid flowerbeds, citrus trees and 100-year-old olive groves. Tree-shaded deckchairs, a barbecue and a tennis court heighten the charm.

🍴 Eating

Il Castagnacciao   PIZZA €
(☑0565 91 58 45; www.ilcastagnacciaio.com; Via del Mercato Vecchio 5; pizza €6-10; ☺9.30am-2.30pm & 5pm-midnight daily summer, 10am-2.30 & 4.30-10.30pm Thu-Tue winter) They work the pizza chef so hard here that the dining room sometimes has a smoky tinge. To go local, start with a lip-smacking plate of *torta di ceci* (chickpea 'pizza'), then watch your rectangular, thin-crust supper go in and out of the wood-fired oven. But save space for dessert – *castagnaccio* baked over the same flames.

Osteria Libertaria

TUSCAN €€

(☑ 0565 91 49 78; www.facebook.com/osterialib
ertaria; Calata Giacomo Matteotti 12; meals €35;
⊙ noon-2.30pm & 7-10.30pm, reduced hours winter) Fish drives the menu of this traditional
osteria (casual tavern) – no wonder, as the
boats that land it are moored right outside.
Traditional dishes such as fried calamari
or *tonno in crosta di pistacchi* (pistachio-
encrusted tuna fillet) are superfresh and
very tasty. Dine at one of two tile-topped
tables on the traffic-noisy street or on the
back-alley terrace.

Bitta 20

SEAFOOD €€€

(☑ 0565 93 02 70; www.facebook.com/bitta20;
Calata Guiseppe Mazzini 20; meals €50; ⊙ noon-
3.30pm & 7-10.30pm Easter–mid-Oct) A Portoferraio favourite, this harbourside restaurant
has a long terrace overlooking a string of
bobbing yachts. White napery and efficient
service combine with fresh fish and seafood
to make it a good choice for lunch or dinner.
Book for the latter.

ℹ Information

**Parco Nazionale dell'Arcipelago Toscana
Office** (Info Park; ☑ 0565 90 82 31; www.
parcoarcipelago.info; Calata Italia 4; ⊙ 9am-
7pm Apr-Oct, to 10pm Tue & Thu Aug, 9am-
4pm Mon-Sat, to 3pm Sun Nov-Mar) Helpful
staff have abundant information on walking
and biking on the island. Find the office on the
seafront, near the ferry docks.

ℹ Getting There & Around

BOAT

Year-round, regular car and foot-passenger
ferries sail at least hourly between Stazione
Marittima (ferry port) in Piombino and Elba's
main town, Portoferraio – count on one hour
sailing time. Unless it's August or a summer
weekend, there's no need to book a ticket in advance; simply buy one from a booth at the port.
Fares (one way from €14/30 per person/car and
driver) vary according to the season.

Moby (www.mobylines.com)

Toremar (www.toremar.it)

Blu Navy (www.blunavytraghetti.com) Seasonal services only.

There are also seasonal ferry services operated
by **Aquavision** (www.aquavision.it) to/from San
Vincenzo on the mainland; €20/10 one way per
adult/child or €35/20 return.

BUS

Bus 118 travels between Portoferraio and Bagnaia (€2.60; 25 minutes) stopping at Schiopparello and Magazzini (€1.50) en route, but services
are scant.

More-frequent bus 117 (€2.60) connects
Portoferraio with Capoliveri (45 minutes), Porto
Azzurro (45 minutes), Rio Elba (65 minutes), Rio
Marina (1¼ hours) and Cavo (1½ hours) at least
eight times daily.

CAR & MOTORCYCLE

TWN Rent (☑ 329 2736412, 0565 91 46 66;
www.twn-rent.it; Viale Elba 32) Offers cars,
scooters, electric bicycles, mountain bikes
and city bikes from the office next to the port
in Portoferraio. Also has offices in Marina di
Campo, Lacona and Porto Azzurro.

Marciana Marina, Marciana & Poggio

☑ 0565 / POP 1975

Unlike many modern, cookie-cutter marinas, the attractive resort of Marciana Marina has character and history to complement
its pleasant pebble beaches. The port is
18km west along the coast from Portoferraio. From it, a twisting 9km mountain road
winds inland up to Marciana, the island's
oldest and highest village (375m).

Marciana's stone streets, arches and stone
houses with flower boxes and petite balconies are as pretty as a picture, and it's worth
exploring them before heading uphill from
the village to Elba's most important pilgrimage site: the Santuario della Madonna del
Monte.

Between the two Marcianas, along a twisting and precipitous road, is the mountain
village of Poggio. Set on the SP25, it's famous
for its spring water and has steep cobblestone alleys and stunning coastal views.

◎ Sights & Activities

Santuario della Madonna del Monte

CHAPEL

(⊙ 24hr) FREE To enjoy an invigorating
40-minute hike, head up through Marciana along Via della Madonna to reach
this much-altered hilltop chapel with its
13th-century fresco of the Madonna painted
on a slab of granite. A remarkable coastal
panorama unfolds as you make your way
here, past scented parasol pines, chestnut
trees, wild sage and thyme. Once you reach
the chapel (627m), emulate Napoleon and
drink from the old stone fountain across
from the church – a plaque commemorates
his visit in 1814.

★ **Cabinovia Monte Capanne**   CABLE CAR
(☑ 0565 90 10 20; www.cabinovia-isoladelba.it; Località Pozzatello; adult/reduced return €18/13; ⊙ 10am-1pm & 2.20-5.30pm Jul-Sep, to 5pm Apr-Jun & Oct) Elba's famous cable car transports passengers up to the island's highest point, Monte Capanne (1018m), in open, barred baskets – imagine riding in a canary-yellow parrot cage and you'll get the picture. After a 20-minute ride, passengers alight and can scramble around the rocky peak to enjoy an astonishing 360-degree panorama of Elba, the Tuscan Archipelago, Etruscan Coast, and Corsica 50km away. Keen hikers can buy a cheaper one-way ticket and take the 90-minute walk back down a rocky path.

 Eating

★ **La Svolta**   GELATO €
(☑ 0565 9 94 79; www.gelaterialasvolta.it; Via Cairoli 6, Marciana Marina; ⊙ 10.30am-late Tue-Sun Apr-Oct) The philosophy here is laudable:

FLORENCE & TUSCANY ISOLA D'ELBA

DON'T MISS

ELBA'S FINEST BEACHES

Given the wide range of bays on Elba's 147km-long coast it pays to know your *spiagge* (beaches). You'll find sandy strands on the south coast and in the Golfo della Biodola, on the western side of Capo d'Enfola; La Biodola has the nearest sandy beach to Portoferraio. The quietest, prettiest beaches are tucked in bijou rocky coves and often involve a steep clamber down. Parking is invariably roadside and scant.

Colle d'Orano & Fetovaia

The standout highlight of these two beach destinations on Elba's western coast is the dramatic 9km-long drive between the two along the SP25. Legend has it Napoleon frequented Colle d'Orano to sit and swoon over his native Corsica, which is visible across the water. Its rocky pebble beach, Spiaggia di Patresi (Via il Faro), is a beautiful and wild spot to watch the sun set. Heading south, a heavenly scented promontory covered in *maquis* (herbal scrubland) protects the brilliant golden sands of Spiaggia di Fetovaia, which is popular with families for its beach restaurant and canoe/pedalo/boat rentals on the sand. Not far away, nudists flop on granite rocks known as Le Piscine.

Enfola

Just 6km west of Portoferraio, it's not so much the grey pebbles as the outdoor action that lures crowds to this tiny fishing port. There are pedalos to rent, a beachside diving school, and a family-friendly 2.5km-long circular hiking trail around the green cape.

Morcone, Pareti & Innamorata

Find this trio of charming sandy-pebble coves framed by sweet-smelling pine trees some 5km south of Capoliveri in southeast Elba. Rent a kayak and paddle out to sea from Cala dell'Innamorata (SP31), the wildest of the three; or fine-dine and overnight on Pareti beach at Hotel Stella Maris (☑ 0565 96 84 25; www.albergostellamaris.it; Località Pareti; half-board per person d €70-100; P ✱ ☎), one of the few three-star hotels to be found on the sand.

Sansone & Sorgente

This twinset of cliff-ensnared, white-shingle and pebble beaches stands out for its crystal-clear, turquoise waters just made for snorkelling and kayaking. A footpath crosses the small rocky promontory dividing Spiaggia La Sorgente in the east from Spiaggia di Sansone (🏊) to the west. By car from Portoferraio, follow the SP24 for 5km towards Enfola. Parking is challenging.

Procchio & La Biodola

Just 10km west of Portoferraio, the beach town of Procchio and adjoining resort area of La Biodola draw the summer-time crowds thanks to one of Elba's longest stretches of golden sand.

use fresh local produce (organic where possible), ensure that the flavours are as natural as possible, and serve the almost-inevitably delectable result in cones or in biodegradable cups.

Chilli and black pepper, bread with butter and jam, and pumpkin with toasted almonds are among wacky flavours that simply have to be tried...more than once.

★**Ristorante Salegrosso** SEAFOOD €€
(☑ 0565 99 68 62; www.facebook.com/SaleGrosso Ristorante; Piazza della Vittoria 14, Marciana Marina; meals €40; ⊗ noon-3pm & 7.30-10pm Wed-Sun Mar-Dec) Those on the hunt for Elba's best fish dish need look no further – the fish stew here is a flavoursome pile of shellfish, tomato and saffron topped by a garlicky slice of *bruschetta*. Delicious! Dine on it or other fishy treats, including excellent homemade pasta, while watching locals take their *passeggiata* along the waterfront.

★**Osteria del Noce** SEAFOOD €€
(☑ 0565 90 12 84; www.osteriadelnoce.it; Via della Madonna 19, Marciana; meals €30; ⊗ noon-2pm & 7.30-9.30pm late Mar-Sep) This family-run bistro in hilltop Marciana is the type of place where the bread is homemade and flavoured with fennel, chestnut flour and other seasonal treats. The pasta (incredible walnut-pesto sauce!), seafood dishes and sweeping views from the terrace are all truly magnificent. To find it, follow the Madonna del Monte walking signs to the top of the village.

ℹ️ **Getting There & Away**

Bus 116 links Marciana Marina and Marciana with Portoferraio at least eight times per day (€2.60).

NORTHWESTERN TUSCANY

There's far more to this green corner of Tuscany than Italy's iconic Leaning Tower. Usually hurtled through en route to Florence and Siena's grand-slam queue-for-hours sights, this is the place to take your foot off the accelerator and go slowly – on foot or by bicycle or car. Allow for long lunches of regional specialities to set the pace for the day, before meandering around a medieval hilltop village or along an ancient pilgrimage route.

Pisa
☑ 050 / POP 90,500

Once a maritime power to rival Genoa and Venice, modern Pisa is best known for an architectural project gone terribly wrong. But the world-famous Leaning Tower is just one of many noteworthy sights in this compelling city. Education has fuelled the local economy since the 1400s, and students from across Italy compete for places in its elite university. This endows the centre of town with a vibrant cafe and bar scene, balancing an enviable portfolio of well-maintained Romanesque buildings, Gothic churches and Renaissance piazzas with a lively street life dominated by locals rather than tourists – a charm you will definitely not discover if you restrict your visit to Piazza dei Miracoli.

◉ **Sights**

Buy tickets for the Leaning Tower from one of two well-signposted ticket offices: the main **ticket office** (☑ 050 83 50 11; www.opa pisa.it; Piazza dei Miracoli; ⊗ 8am-7.30pm summer, to 5.30pm winter) behind the tower or the dramatically quieter ticket desk inside Museo delle Sinopie. To guarantee your visit to the tower and cut the long queue in high season, buy tickets in advance online (note tickets can only be bought 20 days before visiting).

Ticket offices in Pisa also sell combination tickets covering admission to the Battistero, Camposanto and Museo delle Sinopie: buy a ticket covering one/two/three sights costing €5/7/8 (reduced €3/4/5). Admission to the cathedral is free, but you need to show a ticket valid for another Piazza dei Miracoli sight or a fixed-time free pass issued at ticket offices.

◉ Piazza dei Miracoli

Pisans claim that this vast square, with pea-green lawns enclosed within 12th-century **city walls** (☑ 050 098 74 80; www.muradipisa. it; Piazza del Duomo; adult/reduced €3/2; ⊗ 9am-7pm Apr-Mat & Sep, 9am-7pm Mon-Thu, to 9pm Fri-Sun Jun-Aug, shorter hours rest of year; ♿) that can be scaled and strolled along, is one of the world's most beautiful urban spaces.

★**Leaning Tower** TOWER
(Torre Pendente; ☑ 050 83 50 11; www.opapisa. it; Piazza del Duomo; €18; ⊗ 8.30am-10pm mid-Jun–Aug, 9am-8pm Apr–mid-Jun & Sep, to 7pm Oct & Mar, to 6pm Nov-Feb) One of Italy's signature

sights, the Torre Pendente truly lives up to its name, leaning a startling 3.9 degrees off the vertical. The 58m-high tower, officially the Duomo's *campanile*, took almost 200 years to build, but was already listing when it was unveiled in 1372. Over time, the tilt, caused by a layer of weak subsoil, steadily worsened until it was finally halted by a major stabilisation project in the 1990s.

Building began in 1173 under the supervision of architect Bonanno Pisano, but his plans came a cropper almost immediately. Only three of the tower's seven tiers had been built when he was forced to abandon construction after it started leaning. Work resumed in 1272, with artisans and masons attempting to bolster the foundations but failing miserably. They kept going, though, compensating for the lean by gradually building straight up from the lower storeys. But once again work had to be suspended – this time due to war – and construction wasn't completed until the second half of the 14th century.

Over the next 600 years, the tower continued to tilt at an estimated 1mm per year. By 1993 it stood 4.47m out of plumb, more than 5 degrees from the vertical. To counter this, steel braces were slung around the 3rd storey and joined to steel cables attached to neighbouring buildings. This held the tower in place as engineers began gingerly removing soil from below the northern foundations. After some 70 tonnes of earth had been extracted from the northern side, the tower sank to its 18th-century level and, in the process, rectified the lean by 43.8cm. Experts believe that this will guarantee the tower's future for the next three centuries.

Access to the Leaning Tower is limited to 45 people at a time – children under eight are not allowed in/up. To avoid disappointment, book in advance online or go straight to a ticket office when you arrive in Pisa to book a slot for later in the day. Visits last 35 minutes and involve a steep climb up 251 occasionally slippery steps. All bags, handbags included, must be deposited at the free left-luggage desk next to the central ticket office – cameras are about the only thing you can take up.

★ **Duomo** CATHEDRAL
(Duomo di Santa Maria Assunta; ☑ 050 83 50 11; www.opapisa.it; Piazza del Duomo; ⊙10am-8pm Apr-Oct, to 6pm or 7pm Nov-Feb) FREE Pisa's magnificent *duomo* was begun in 1064 and consecrated in 1118. Its striking tiered exterior, with green-and-cream marble cladding, gives onto a columned interior capped by a gold wooden ceiling. The elliptical dome, the first of its kind in Europe at the time, was added in 1380.

Admission is free but you need a ticket from another Piazza dei Miracoli sight to enter or a fixed-timed free pass from the ticket office behind the Leaning Tower or inside Museo delle Sinopie.

★ **Battistero** CHRISTIAN SITE
(Battistero di San Giovanni; ☑ 050 83 50 11; www.opapisa.it; Piazza del Duomo; €5, combination ticket with Camposanto or Museo delle Sinopie €7, Camposanto & Museo delle Sinopie €8; ⊙8am-8pm Apr-Oct, 9am-6pm or 7pm Nov-Mar) Pisa's unusual round baptistry has one dome piled on top of another, each roofed half in lead, half in tiles, and topped by a gilt bronze John the Baptist (1395). Construction began in 1152, but it was remodelled and continued by Nicola and Giovanni Pisano more than a century later and finally completed in the 14th century. Inside, the hexagonal marble pulpit (1260) by Nicola Pisano is the highlight.

Camposanto CEMETERY
(☑ 050 83 50 11; www.opapisa.it; Piazza del Duomo; €5, combination ticket with Battistero or Museo delle Sinopie €7, Battistero & Museo €8; ⊙8am-8pm Apr-Jul, Sep & Oct, 8am-10pm Aug, 9am-7pm Nov, Dec & Mar, 9am-5pm Jan & Feb) Soil shipped from Calvary during the Crusades is said to lie within the white walls of this hauntingly beautiful resting place for many prominent Pisans, arranged around a garden in a cloistered quadrangle. During WWII, Allied artillery destroyed many of the cloisters' frescoes, but several have been salvaged and restored. Most notable are *Inferno* and *Triumph of Death* (both 1336–41), remarkable illustrations of Hell attributed to 14th-century painter Buonamico Buffalmacco; find them immediately to the right of the main entrance (second and fourth frescoes), in the southern cloister.

Museo delle Sinopie MUSEUM
(☑ 050 83 50 11; www.opapisa.it; Piazza del Duomo; €5, combination ticket with Battistero or Camposanto €7, Battistero & Camposanto €8; ⊙8am-8pm Apr-Nov, 9am-6pm or 7pm Nov-Feb) Home to some fascinating frescoes, this museum safeguards several *sinopie* (preliminary sketches), drawn by the artists in red earth pigment on the walls of the Camposanto

Pisa

in the 14th and 15th centuries before frescoes were painted over them. The museum is a compelling study in fresco painting, with short films and scale models filling in the gaps.

◉ Along the Arno

Palazzo Blu GALLERY
(☑ 050 220 46 50; www.palazzoblu.it; Lungarno Gambacorti 9; adult/reduced €3/2; ☉ 10am-7pm Mon-Fri, to 8pm Sat & Sun, shorter hours winter) Facing the river is this magnificently restored 14th-century building with a striking dusty-blue facade. Inside, its over-the-top 19th-century interior decoration is the perfect backdrop for the Foundation Pisa's art collection – predominantly Pisan works from the 14th to the 20th centuries on the 2nd floor. Admission includes an archaeological area in the basement and the noble residence of this aristocratic palace, furnished as it would have been in the 19th century, on the 1st floor.

Museo Nazionale di San Matteo MUSEUM
(☑ 050 54 18 65; Piazza San Matteo in Soarta 1; adult/reduced €5/2.50; ☉ 8.30am-7.30pm Tue-Sat, to 1.30pm Sun) This inspiring repository of medieval masterpieces sits in a 13th-century

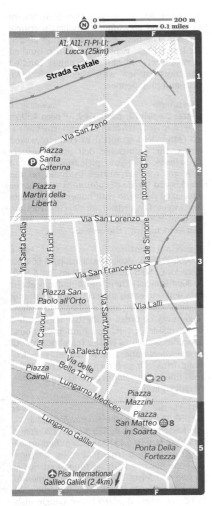

FLORENCE & TUSCANY PISA

tabernacles and statues. It was built between 1230 and 1233 to house a reliquary of a *spina* (thorn) from Christ's crown.

🛏 Sleeping

Hostel Pisa Tower ⠀⠀⠀⠀⠀⠀⠀⠀⠀⠀⠀⠀ HOSTEL €
(📞050 520 24 54; www.hostelpisatower.it; Via Piave 4; dm €25; @🛜) This super-friendly hostel occupies a suburban villa a couple of minutes' walk from Piazza dei Miracoli. It's bright and cheery, with colourful decor, female and mixed dorms, communal kitchen, and a summer-friendly terrace overlooking a small grassy garden. Dorms are named, meaning you can sleep with Galileo, Mona Lisa, Leonardo or Michelangelo.

Hotel Di Stefano ⠀⠀⠀⠀⠀⠀⠀⠀⠀⠀⠀⠀⠀ HOTEL €
(📞050 55 35 59; www.hoteldistefanopisa.com; Via Sant'Apollonia 35; d/q €140/160; P✳@🛜) This three-star hotel has been in business since 1969 for good reason. Partly tucked in a medieval town house, it fuses vintage charm with no-frills functionality and a warm, family-run ambience. Deluxe rooms have beamed ceilings, exposed brickwork and a balcony overlooking the small back garden. The rooftop terrace, with armchairs and

Benedictine convent on the Arno's northern waterfront boulevard. The museum's collection of paintings from the Tuscan school (c 12th to 14th centuries) is notable, with works by Lippo Memmi, Taddeo Gaddi, Gentile da Fabriano and Ghirlandaio. Don't miss Masaccio's *St Paul,* Fra' Angelico's *Madonna of Humility* and Simone Martini's *Polyptych of Saint Catherine.*

Chiesa di Santa Maria della Spina ⠀⠀ CHURCH
(Lungarno Gambacorti; ⊙10am-1pm Mon, 3-7pm Tue-Thu, 10am-1pm & 3-7pm Fri-Sun) Don't miss this waterside, triple-spired church, an exquisite Pisan-Gothic gem encrusted with

stunning sunset views, is accessible – fabulously so – to all.

★ **Hotel Pisa Tower**   HOTEL €€
(📞 050 520 00 19; www.hotelpisatower.com; Via Pisano 23; d/tr/q from €109/134/149; P ❋ 🛜) For peace, tranquillity and sundown drinks in a romantic walled garden after a busy day navigating the Pisa crowds, this outstanding three-star hotel hits the spot. Its 14 rooms are spacious, with high ceilings and country-style furnishings. Chandeliers, marble floors and framed antique prints adorn the lounge, and breakfasting al fresco on the elegant terrace is the perfect start to any Tuscan day.

Five cheaper rooms for four (€139) languish in the hotel annexe. Find the hotel a two-minute walk from Pisa San Rossore train station. The hotel rents out bicycles and runs daily shuttles to Pisa Centrale train station/Pisa International Airport (€5/6 per person).

✖ Eating

★ **Gelateria De' Coltelli**   GELATO €
(📞 345 4811903; www.decoltelli.it; Lungarno Pacinotti 23; small/medium/large €2.50/3/4.30; ⏱ 11.30am-10.30pm Sun-Thu, to 11.30pm Fri & Sat) Follow the crowd to this world-class gelateria, famed for its sensational artisanal, organic and 100% natural gelato. Flavours are as zesty and appealing as its bright-orange interior. The hard part is choosing: ginger, Sicilian orange, ricotta cheese with candied orange peel and chocolate chips, candied chestnuts, cashew with Maldon salt, kiwi, pear and pink pepper…

L'Ostellino   SANDWICHES €
(Piazza Cavallotti 1; panini €4-7; ⏱ noon-4.30pm Mon-Fri, to 7pm Sat & Sun) For a gourmet *panino* (sandwich) wrapped in crunchy waxed paper, this minuscule deli and *panineria* delivers. Take your pick from dozens of different combos written by hand on the blackboard (*lardo di colonnata* with figs or cave-aged *pecorino* with honey and walnuts are sweet favourites), await construction, then hit the green lawns of Piazza dei Miracoli to picnic with the crowds.

Pizzeria Il Montino   PIZZA €
(📞 050 59 86 95; Vicolo del Monte 1; pizza €6-8.50, foccacine €2.50-5, cecina €2; ⏱ 11am-3pm & 5.30-10.30pm Mon-Sat) There's nothing fancy about this down-to-earth pizzeria, an icon among Pisans, students and sophisticates alike. Take away or order at the bar then grab a table, inside or out, and munch on house specialities such as *cecina* (chickpea pizza), *castagnaccio* and *spuma* (sweet, nonalcoholic drink). Or go for a *focaccine* (small flat roll) filled with salami, pancetta or *porchetta* (suckling pig).

Osteria dei Cavalieri   TUSCAN €€
(📞 050 58 08 58; www.osteriacavalieri.pisa.it; Via San Frediano 16; meals €25-30; ⏱ 12.30-2pm & 7.45-10pm Mon-Fri, 7.45-10pm Sat) When an *osteria* cooks up a tripe platter for *antipasto*, bone marrow with saffron-spiced rice as *primo* and feisty T-bone steaks as *secondo*, you know you've struck Tuscan foodie gold. A trio of inspired *piatti unico* (single dishes) promise a quick lunch, or linger over themed multi-course menus (including, unusually, a vegetarian menu) packed with timeless Tuscan faves.

🍷 Drinking & Nightlife

Most drinking action takes place on and around Piazza delle Vettovaglie and student-packed Piazza Dante Alighieri. Sundashed Piazza Cairoli is another favourite for lingering al fresco over *un caffè* or gelato. Try to taste local wines produced in the Pisan hills under the DOCG Chianti delle Colline Pisane label.

LOCAL KNOWLEDGE

GREEN ESCAPE

For a Zen respite from the Piazza dei Miracoli crowd, explore **Orto e Museo Botanico** (Botanical Garden & Museum; 📞 050 221 13 10; www.ortomuseobot. sma.unipi.it; Via Roma 56; adult/reduced €4/2; ⏱ 8.30am-8pm Apr-Sep, 9am-5pm Mon-Sat, to 1am Sun Oct-Mar), a peaceful walled garden laced with centurion palm trees, flora typical to the Apuane Alps, a fragrant herb garden, vintage greenhouses and 35 orchid species. Showcasing the botanical collection of Pisa University, the garden dates to 1543 and was Europe's first university botanical garden, tended by the illustrious botanist Luca Ghini (1490–1556). The museum, inside Palazzo della Conchiglie, explores the garden's history, with exquisite botanical drawings, catalogues, maquettes etc.

Wood Coffee
COFFEE

(📞050 622 37 38; www.facebook.com/woodcof
feepisa; Via Santa Bibbiana 10; ⊙7.30am-6.30pm
Mon-Sat; 🔊) Chill in peace over a love heart–
topped cappuccino, French-press coffee,
Nutella-flavoured frappuccino or iced americano at this speciality coffee shop. Fittings
and furnishings are recycled from wooden
pallets and coffee bean sacks, and the kitch-
en cooks up a tasty selection of cookies, muffins, creatively stuffed bagels (€5 to €6) and
sassy lunchtime salads (€4 to €6.50).

La Stafetta
CRAFT BEER

(www.lastaffetta.com; Lungarno Pacinotti 24;
⊙6pm-1am Mon-Thu, 7pm-2am Fri & Sat, 4-11pm
Sun) Squat on a bench outside or grab a pew
inside this funky riverside tap room, the
creation of three ale-loving Pisan students:
Matteo, Davide and Francesco. Inside, order
one of the small microbrewery's own brews:
taste English hops in Wilson (a dark-red bitter with hints of coffee, chocolate and liquorice) or go for a light and golden May Ale.

Keith
CAFE

(📞050 50 31 35; www.facebook.com/keithcafe;
Via Zandonai 4; ⊙7am-11pm summer, to 9pm winter; 🔊) This trendy cafe stares face to face
with *Tuttomondo* (1989), a mural on the facade of a Pisan church – and the last mural
American pop artist Keith Haring painted
just months before his death. Sip a coffee or
cocktail on the terrace and lament the fading, weather-beaten colours of Haring's 30
signature prancing, dancing men.

Bazeel
BAR

(📞349 0880688; www.bazeel.it; Lungarno Pacinotti 1; ⊙7am-1am Sun-Thu, to 2am Fri & Sat) A
dedicated all-rounder, Bazeel is a hotspot
from dawn to dark. Laze over breakfast, linger over a pizza or hang out with the A-list
crowd over a generous *aperitivo* spread,
live music and DJs. Its chapel-like interior is
nothing short of fabulous, as is its pavement
terrace out the front. Check its Facebook
feed for what's on.

❶ Information

Tourist Office (📞050 55 01 00; www.turismo.
pisa.it/en; Piazza del Duomo 7; ⊙9.30am-
5.30pm Mar-Oct, 9am-5pm Nov-Feb; 🔊)

❶ Getting There & Around

TO/FROM THE AIRPORT

Fully automated, super-speedy PisaMover
(http://pisa-mover.com) trains link Pisa International Airport (p551) with Pisa Centrale train

---

WORTH A TRIP

SAN MINIATO

There is one delicious reason to visit
this enchantingly sleepy, medieval
hilltop town almost equidistant (50km)
between Pisa and Florence: to eat, hunt
and dream about the *Tuber magnatum
pico* (white truffle).

It's also home to **Peperino** (📞0571
41 95 23; Via IV Novembre 1; menu incl
bottle champagne & wine €250; ⊙by
appointment only), the world's smallest
restaurant. Decor is in-your-face romantic, furnishings are period and the waiter
only comes when diners ring the bell.
Reserve months in advance.

---

station (€5, five minutes, every five minutes
from 6am to midnight).

The LAM Rossa (red) bus line (€1.20, 10 minutes, every 10 to 20 minutes) run by **CPT** (📞050
520 51 00; www.cpt.pisa.it; Via Cesare Battisti
53; ⊙ticket office 7.20am-7.40pm) passes
through the city centre and by the train station
en route to/from the airport. Buy tickets from
the blue ticket machine next to the bus stops to
the right of the train station exit.

A taxi between the airport and city centre
should cost no more than €10. To book, call **Radio Taxi Pisa** (📞050 54 16 00; www.cotapi.it).

BUS

From its **bus station** (Piazza Sant'Antonio 1)
hub, Pisan bus company **CPT** (www.cpt.pisa.it)
runs buses to/from Volterra (€6.40, two hours,
up to 10 daily) with change of bus in Pontedera.

TRAIN

There is a handy **left-luggage counter** (Deposito Bagagli; 📞050 2 61 52; www.deposito
bagaglipisa.it; bag per day €5; ⊙7am-9pm)
at **Pisa Centrale** (Piazza della Stazione) train
station – not to be confused with north-of-town
Pisa San Rossore (Via Giunta) station. Regional
train services to/from Pisa Centrale include the
following:

Florence (€8.60, 1¼ hours, frequent)
Livorno (€2.60, 15 minutes, frequent)
Lucca (€3.60, 30 minutes, every 30 minutes)
Viareggio (€3.60, 15 minutes, every 20
minutes)

Lucca

📞0583 / POP 89,200

Lovely Lucca endears itself to everyone who
visits. Hidden behind imposing Renaissance
walls, its cobbled streets, handsome piazzas

Lucca

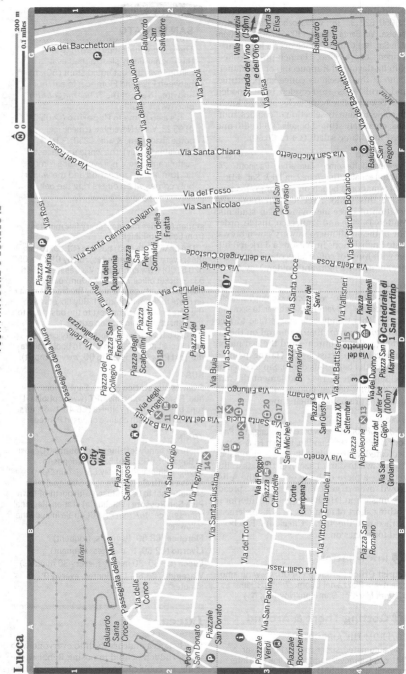

Baluardo Santa Croce

Porta San Donato

Via delle Conce

Passegiata della Mura

Piazzale Verdi

Piazzale San Donato

Piazzale Boccherini

Via San Paolino

Via Galli Tassi

Via del Toro

Via Santa Giustina

Via San Giorgio

Via Tegrimi

Piazza Sant'Agostino

Piazza San Romano

Via Vittorio Emanuele II

Via di Poggio

Piazza Cittadella

Corte Campana

Piazza San Michele

Via San Girolamo

Via Veneto

Piazza San Giusto

Piazza XX Settembre

Piazza Napoleone

Via del Giglio

Piazza del Surfer Joe (100m)

Via Cenami

Via del Battistero

Via del Molinetto

Via Fillungo

Via Santa Lucia

Via Buia

Via del Moro

Via degli Angeli

Via Battisti

Piazza del Collegio

Piazza degli Scalpellini

Piazza San Frediano

Via della Cavallerizza

Via della Quarquonia

Via del Fiumeno

Piazza Santa Maria

Passegiata della Mura

Via Santa Gemma Galgani

Via della Quarquonia

Piazza San Francesco

Via dei Bacchettoni

Baluardo San Salvatore

Via Paoli

Via Santa Chiara

Via del Fosso

Via del Fosso

Via Rosi

Piazza San Pietro Somaldi

Via della Fratta

Via Mordini

Piazza del Carmine

Piazza Anfiteatro

Piazza Sant'Andrea

Via Canuleia

Via dell'Angelo Custode

Via Guinigi

Via Santa Croce

Piazza dei Servi

Piazza Bernardini

Via dei Servi

Via Santa Croce

Piazza San Martino

Piazza del Duomo

Via Vallisneri

Piazza Antelminelli

Cattedrale di San Martino

Via del Giardino Botanico

Via della Rosa

Porta San Gervasio

Via San Nicolao

Via San Micheletto

Strada del Vino e dell'Olio

Villa Lucrezia (150m)

Porta Elisa

Via Elisa

Baluardo della Libertà

Baluardo del Bacchettoni

Baluardo San Regolo

Moat

Moat

1 Cattedrale di San Martino
2 City Wall
3
4
5
6
7
8
9 Piazza Cittadella
10
11
12
14
15
16
17
18
19
20

and shady promenades make it a perfect destination to explore by foot – as a day trip from Florence or in its own right. At the day's end, historic cafes and restaurants tempt visitors to relax over a glass or two of Lucchesi wine and a slow progression of rustic dishes prepared with fresh produce from nearby Garfagnana.

If you have a car, the hills to the east of Lucca demand exploration. Home to historic villas and belle époque Montecatini Terme, where Puccini lazed in warm spa waters, they are easy and attractive day-trip destinations from Lucca.

◎ Sights

Stone-paved Via Fillungo, with its fashion boutiques and car-free mantra, threads its way through the medieval heart of the old city. East is one of Tuscany's loveliest piazzas: oval cafe-ringed Piazza Anfiteatro, named for the amphitheatre that was here in Roman times. Spot remnants of the amphitheatre's brick arches and masonry on the exterior walls of the medieval houses ringing the piazza.

★**City Wall**   WALLS
Lucca's monumental *mura* (wall) was built around the old city in the 16th and 17th centuries and remains in almost perfect condition. It superseded two previous walls, the first built from travertine stone blocks in the 2nd century BC. Twelve metres high and 4.2km long, today's ramparts are crowned with a tree-lined footpath looking down on the historic centre and – by the Baluardo San Regolo (San Regolo Bastion) – the city's vintage Orto Botanico (Botanical Garden; ☑ 0583 58 30 86; www.lemuradilucca.it/orto

-botanico; Casermetta San Regolo; adult/reduced €4/3; ☺ 10am-7pm Jul-Sep, to 6pm May & Jun, to 5pm Mar, Apr & Oct) with its magnificent centurion cedar trees.

★**Cattedrale di San Martino**   CATHEDRAL
(☑ 0583 49 05 30; www.museocattedralelucca.it; Piazza San Martino; €3, incl campanile, Museo della Cattedrale & Chiesa e Battistero dei SS Giovanni & Reparata adult/reduced €9/6; ☺ 9.30am-6.30pm Mon-Fri, to 6.45pm Sat, noon-6.30pm Sun) Lucca's predominantly Romanesque cathedral dates from the 11th century. Its stunning facade was constructed in the prevailing Lucca-Pisan style and designed to accommodate the pre-existing *campanile*. The reliefs over the left doorway of the portico are believed to be by Nicola Pisano, while inside, treasures include the Volto Santo (literally, Holy Countenance) crucifix sculpture and a wonderful 15th-century tomb in the sacristy. The cathedral interior was rebuilt in the 14th and 15th centuries with a Gothic flourish.

★**Museo della Cattedrale**   MUSEUM
(Cathedral Museum; ☑ 0583 49 05 30; www.museocattedralelucca.it; Piazza San Martino; adult/reduced €4/3, with cathedral sacristy & Chiesa e Battistero dei SS Giovanni e Reparata €9/6; ☺ 10am-6pm) The cathedral museum safeguards elaborate gold and silver decorations made for the cathedral's *Volto Santo,* including a 17th-century crown and a 19th-century sceptre.

Chiesa e Battistero dei SS Giovanni e Reparata   CHURCH
(☑ 0583 49 05 30; www.museocattedralelucca.it; Piazza San Giovanni; adult/reduced €4/3, with cathedral sacristy & Museo della Cattedrale €9/5;

Lucca

⊙10am-6pm) The 12th-century interior of this deconsecrated church is a hauntingly atmospheric setting for summertime opera and concert recitals (www.puccinielasua lucca.com), staged daily at 7pm; buy tickets (adult/reduced €25/20) in advance inside the church or at a cheaper rate before 6pm from the tourist office – €20 instead of €25.

In the north transept, the Gothic baptistry crowns an **archaeological area** comprising five building levels going back to the Roman period. Don't miss the hike up the red-brick **bell tower**.

★**Torre Guinigi** TOWER
(Via Sant'Andrea 45; adult/reduced €4/3; ⊙9.30am-7.30pm Jun-Sep, to 6.30pm Apr & May, to 5.30pm Oct & Mar, to 4.30pm Nov & Dec) The bird's-eye view from the top of this medieval, 45m red-brick tower adjoining 14th-century **Palazzo Guinigi** is predictably magnificent. But what impresses even more are the seven oak trees planted in a U-shaped flower bed at the top of the tower. Legend has it that upon the death of powerful Lucchese ruler Paolo Guinigi (1372–1432) all the leaves fell off the trees. Count 230 steps to the top.

★**Palazzo Pfanner** PALACE
(☑0583 95 21 55; www.palazzopfanner.it; Via degli Asili 33; palace or garden adult/reduced €4.50/4, both €6.50/5.50; ⊙10am-6pm Apr-Nov) Fire the romantic in you with a stroll around this beautiful 17th-century palace where parts of *Portrait of a Lady* (1996), starring Nicole Kidman and John Malkovich, were shot. Its baroque-styled garden – the only one of substance within the city walls – enchants with ornamental pond, lemon house and 18th-century statues of Greek gods posing between potted lemon trees. Summertime chamber-music concerts hosted here are absolutely wonderful.

⛱ Sleeping

From charm-rich B&Bs to small boutique hotels on quiet cobbled lanes, Lucca delivers. The tourist office has accommodation lists and, if you visit in person, can make reservations for you (free of charge). For accommodation amid vines, consider a winery along the idyllic **Strada del Vino e dell'Olio** (☑0583 49 51 69; www.stradavinoeoliolucca.it; Porta Elisa; ⊙9.30am-7pm).

★**Villa Lucrezia** B&B €
(☑0583 95 42 86; www.luccainvilla.it; Viale Cadorna 30; d/q €98/150; 🅿🛜) A particularly

handy address for those arriving by car, this 10-room B&B is a two-minute walk from the city walls, inside a graceful 19th-century villa with a jasmine-scented garden. Rooms are spacious and light-filled, with big windows, contemporary design furnishings and sharp en suite bathrooms. Complimentary tea, coffee and cakes are at hand throughout the day in the basement breakfast room.

Piccolo Hotel Puccini HOTEL €
(☑0583 5 54 21; www.hotelpuccini.com; Via di Poggio 9; s/d €75/100; ✳🛜) In a brilliant central location, this welcoming three-star hotel hides behind a discreet brick exterior. Its small guest rooms are attractive with wooden floors, vintage ceiling fans and colourful, contemporary design touches. Breakfast, optional at €3.50, is served at candlelit tables behind the small reception area. Rates are at least 30% lower in winter.

2italia APARTMENT €€
(☑392 9960271; www.2italia.com; apt for 2 adults & up to 4 children per night/week €240/1250; 🛜) Not a hotel but a handful of family-friendly self-catering apartments in the historic centre. Available on a nightly basis (minimum two nights), the project is the brainchild of well-travelled parents-of-three, Kristin (English) and Kaare (Norwegian). Spacious apartments sleep five to 10 people, have a fully equipped kitchen and washing machine, and come with sheets and towels.

★**Alla Corte degli Angeli** BOUTIQUE HOTEL €€€
(☑0583 46 92 04; www.allacortedegliangeli.com; Via degli Angeli 23; d from €180; ✳@🛜) This four-star boutique hotel sits in a couple of terraced 15th-century town houses on a peaceful lane. Its 24 sunny suites and doubles – named after flowers – feature frescoed ceilings, patches of exposed brick, romantic landscape murals and some lovely pieces of period furniture. Up-to-the-minute bathrooms have hot tubs and power-jet showers. The hotel restaurant and cocktail bar is an address in its own right.

The stylish lounge begs relaxation beneath yet another vintage beamed ceiling. It also hosts fantastic wine-tasting workshops with the hotel sommelier (30-minute/one hour class €25/50), and fun two-hour cooking classes kicking off with a bike ride with the chef through town to shop for the ingredients (€50).

✕ Eating

Surfer Joe AMERICAN €
(☑ 0583 4 82 80; www.surferjoe.it; Corso Garibaldi
68; ⊙ noon-3pm & 7-11pm Tue-Fri, 10am-midnight
Sat, 10am-11pm Sun) Find Lucca's beautiful,
young, music-loving things lingering over
burgers, pancakes, smoothies and all-day
breakfasts at this fun, all-day hangout – a
much-welcomed offshoot of the Livorno
original. The look is retro 1950s American
diner – think turquoise banquette seating
and vinyl sleeves on the wall – and surf music is the sound. Check its Facebook page for
the month's party line-up.

Pizza Da Felice PIZZA €
(☑ 0583 49 49 86; www.pizzeriadafelice.it; Via Buia
12; focaccia & pizza slices €1-5; ⊙ 11am-8.30pm
Mon, 10am-8.30pm Tue-Sat) This buzzing spot
behind Piazza San Michele is where the locals come for wood-fired pizza, *cecina* and
castagnaccio. Eat in or take away, *castagnaccio* comes wrapped in crisp white paper,
and my, it's good married with a chilled bottle of Moretti beer.

Trattoria da Leo TRATTORIA €
(☑ 0583 49 22 36; Via Tegrimi 1; meals €25;
⊙ 12.30-2pm & 7.30-10.30pm Mon-Sat) Veteran Leo is famed for its friendly ambience
and cheap food – ranging from plain-Jane
acceptable to grandma delicious. Enticing
sides include baked fennel with parmesan,
oven-baked baby onions and *peperonata*
(stewed peppers). Arrive early to snag one
of a handful of tables squashed beneath
parasols on the street outside. Otherwise
it's noisy dining inside amid 1970s decor. No
credit cards.

★ La Parte degli Angeli TUSCAN €€
(☑ 346 8079791, 0583 46 92 04; www.facebook.
com/lapartedegliangeli; Via degli Angeli 23; meals
€30-40; ⊙ 7pm-midnight Tue-Sun) For a stylish
cocktail with a herb-infused gin perhaps,
followed by dinner amid romantic frescoes,
look no further than 'The Angels' Share', an
intimate restaurant named after the portion
of whisky lost to evaporation during the
ageing process. Mixologist, chef and owner
Leonardo is a huge whisky fan, works with
his own homemade syrups and cooks creative Tuscan in the kitchen.

★ Ristorante Giglio TUSCAN €€
(☑ 0583 49 40 58; www.ristorantegiglio.com; Piazza del Giglio 2; meals €40-50, 4-/5-course tasting
menus €45/55; ⊙ 12.15-2.45pm & 7.30-10.30pm

FLORENCE & TUSCANY LUCCA

A WALLTOP PICNIC

When in Lucca, picnicking atop its city walls – on grass or at a wooden picnic table – is
as lovely (and typical) a Lucchesi lunch as any.

Buy fresh-from-the-oven pizza and focaccia with a choice of fillings and toppings
from fabulous bakery **Forno Amedeo Giusti** (☑ 0583 49 62 85; www.facebook.com/
PanificioGiusti; Via Santa Lucia 20; pizzas & filled focaccias per kg €10-15; ⊙ 7am-7.30pm Mon-
Sat, to 1.30pm Sun), then nip across the street for a bottle of Lucchesi wine and Garfag-
nese *biscotti al farro* (spelt biscuits) at **La Bodega di Prospero** (☑ 0583 49 48 75; Via
Santa Lucia 13; ⊙ 9am-7pm); look for the old-fashioned shop window stuffed with sacks of
beans, lentils and other local pulses.

Complete the perfect picnic with a slice of *buccellato*, a traditional sweet bread loaf
with sultanas and aniseed seeds, baked in Lucca since 1881. Devour the rest at home,
either with butter, dipped in egg and pan-fried, or dunked in sweet Vin Santo. Buy it at
pastry shop **Taddeucci** (☑ 0583 49 49 33; www.buccellatotaddeucci.com; Piazza San Michele
34; buccellato loaf per 300/600g €4.50/9; ⊙ 8.30am-7.45pm, closed Thu winter).

Swill down the picnic with your pick of Italian craft beers from microbrewery **De
Cervesia** (☑ 0583 49 30 81; www.decervesia.it; Via Fillungo 92; ⊙ noon-midnight Wed-Fri,
noon-1am Sat, 5pm-midnight Sun), which has a small shop on Lucca's main shopping
street and a tap room for serious tasting (open 5pm to 10pm Tuesday to Sunday) a few
blocks away at Via Michele Rosi 20. Should a shot of something stronger be required to
aid digestion, nip into historic **Antica Farmacia Massagli** (☑ 0583 49 60 67; Piazza San
Michele 36; ⊙ 9am-8pm Mon-Sat) for a bottle of China elixir, a heady liqueur of aromatic
spices and herbs first concocted in 1855 as a preventive measure against the plague.
Lucchese typically drink the natural alcoholic drink (no colouring or preservatives) at the
end of a meal.

Thu-Mon, 7.30-10.30pm Wed) Splendidly at home in frescoed 18th-century Palazzo Arnolfini, Giglio is stunning. Sip a complimentary prosecco, watch the fire crackle in the marble fireplace and savour traditional Tuscan fare with a modern twist: think fresh artichoke salad served in an edible parmesan-cheese wafer 'bowl', or risotto simmered in Chianti. End with Lucchese *buccellato* (sweet bread) filled with ice cream and berries.

In summer dining spills out onto Giglio's pretty terrace overlooking the town's historic theatre.

🍷 Drinking & Nightlife

⭐ **Bistrot Undici Undici** CAFE
(📷 0583 189 27 01; www.facebook.com/undiciundi ci11.11; Piazza Antelminelli 2; ⊙10am-8pm Tue-Thu, to 1am Fri-Sun) With a giant canvas cream parasol providing shade and a tinkling stone fountain the atmospheric soundtrack, cafe terraces don't get much better than this. And then there is the view from this bucolic cafe on Piazza San Miniato of the almighty facade of Lucca's lovely cathedral. Kick back over an Aperol spritz at sundown and enjoy occasional live music after dark.

Bollicine d'Autore BAR
(📷347 7655596; https://bollicinedautore.com; Via Calderia 12; ⊙10am-midnight Fri-Wed) Food pairings with fine wine and bubbles is the speciality of this glamorous *enoteca* (wine bar), *champagneria* (champagne cellar) and bistro in central Lucca. Pick from Italy's top sparkling wines – an Uberti or Bellavista Franciacorta Brut from Lombardy perhaps, a Ferrari Trento from Trentino-Alto Adige or a timeless prosecco DOC – or go French with a Pommery or Laurent Perrier champagne.

ℹ️ Information

Tourist Office (📷 0583 58 31 50; www.turismo.lucca.it; Piazzale Verdi; ⊙9.30am-6.30pm)

ℹ️ Getting There & Around

BICYCLE

Pedalling the 4.2km circumference of Lucca's romantic city walls is always fun. There are plenty of outlets, ranging from touristy to those aimed squarely at serious cyclists, to rent wheels.

Biciclette Poli (📷 0583 49 37 87; www.bicic lettepoli.com; Piazza Santa Maria 42; per hr/ day €4/16; ⊙9am-7pm summer)

Cicli Bizzarri (📷 0583 49 66 82; www.cicli bizzarri.net; Piazza Santa Maria 32; per hr/day €4/16; ⊙8.30am-12.30pm & 2-7.30pm)
Tourist Center Lucca (📷 0583 49 44 01; www. touristcenterlucca.com; Piazzale Ricasoli 203; bike per 3hr/day €8/12; ⊙9am-7pm)

BUS

From the bus stops around Piazzale Verdi, **CTT Lucca** (www.lucca.cttnord.it) runs services throughout the region, including the following:
Bagni di Lucca (€3.60, 50 minutes, eight daily)
Castelnuovo di Garfagnana (€4.40, 1½ hours, eight daily)
Pisa airport (€4, 45 minutes to one hour, 30 daily)

TRAIN

The train station is south of the city walls: take the path across the moat and through the (dank and grungy) tunnel under Baluardo San Colombano. Regional train services include the following:
Florence (€7.80, 1¼ to 1¾ hours, hourly)
Pietrasanta (€4.60, 50 minutes, hourly)
Pisa (€3.60, 30 minutes, half-hourly)
Pistoia (€5.70, 45 minutes to one hour, half-hourly)
Viareggio (€3.60, 25 minutes, hourly)

Pietrasanta

📷 0584 / POP 23,700

Often overlooked by Tuscan travellers, this refined art town – an easy day trip from Pisa or Florence – sports a bijou historic heart (originally walled) peppered with tiny art galleries, workshops and fashion boutiques – perfect for a day's amble broken only by lunch.

Founded in 1255 by Guiscardo da Pietrasanta, the *podestà* (governing magistrate) of Lucca, the town was seen as a prize by Genoa, Lucca, Pisa and Florence, all of which jostled for possession of its marble quarries and bronze foundries. Florence won out and Leo X (Giovanni de' Medici) took control in 1513, putting the town's quarries at the disposal of Michelangelo, who came here in 1518 to source marble for the facade of Florence's San Lorenzo. Artists continue to work here, including internationally lauded Colombian-born sculptor Fernando Botero (b 1932), whose work can be seen here.

⊙ Sights

From Pietrasanta train station on Piazza della Stazione head straight across Piazza Carducci, through the Old City gate and onto Piazza del Duomo, the main square, which doubles as an outdoor gallery for sculptures and other seasonal, generally very large works of art.

Duomo di San Martino   CATHEDRAL

(📞0584 79 01 77; www.duomodipietrasanta.org; Piazza del Duomo; ⊙hours vary) Grandiose white-marble steps flank Pietrasanta's attractive cathedral, built in the 14th century on the site of an earlier church dating from 1250. Its distinctive 36m-tall, freestanding, red-brick bell tower is actually unfinished; the red brick was intended to have a marble cladding when designed by Donato Benti in the 15th century. The cathedral interior dates from the 17th century, with fine frescoes by Florentine painter Luigi Ademello (1764–1849) in the dome and nave.

Watch for organ concerts in the cathedral and summertime art exhibitions that occasionally open up the bell tower and the unusual helix-shaped staircase hidden inside – a treat not to be missed – to visitors.

Via della Rocca   VIEWPOINT

(Piazza del Duomo) Next to Chiesa di Sant'Agostino, a steep path known as Via della Rocca leads up to the remnants of Pietrasanta's ancient fortifications. The crenellated city walls date from the early 1300s and what remains of Palazzo Guinigi was built as a residence for the *signore* of Lucca, Paolo Guinigi, in 1408. Views of the city and the deep-blue Mediterranean beyond are worth the short climb.

Museo dei Bozzetti   MUSEUM

(Maquettes Museum; 📞0584 79 55 00; www.museodeibozzetti.it; Via Sant'Agostino 1; ⊙2-7pm Mon & Sat, 9am-1pm & 2-7pm Tue-Fri, 4-7pm Sun) **FREE** Inside the convent adjoining Chiesa di Sant'Agostino, this small museum explores the evolution of modern sculpture through 700-odd *bozzetti* (maquettes or models) and plaster moulds of famous sculptures cast or carved in Pietrasanta by some 350 artists from all over the world since the early 20th century.

Don't leave without enquiring about the latest additions to the museum's informal Parco della Scultura (Sculpture Park), an open-air trail leading to 70 public works of art in and around town. Check the museum's website for a complete list of artworks.

🛏 Sleeping & Eating

The historic heart spoils for choice with its many arty addresses spilling onto flower-pot-adorned summer terraces. Pedestrian Via Stagio Stagi, parallel to main street Via Mazzini, has several appealing restaurants.

★Hotel Palagi   HOTEL €€

(📞0584 7 02 49; www.hotelpalagi.it; Piazza Carducci 23; s/d/tr €90/140/150; ℗ ❄ @) The tender love and care lavished on this outstanding three-star hotel by owner Eliza and her friendly staff seeps out of every last perfectly plumped cushion, potted plant and modern artwork. Thirteen rooms in soft muted hues are spacious with white marble bathrooms, and the shared romantic rooftop terrace is pure gold. Breakfast includes heaps of freshly cut fruit and homemade cakes.

FLORENCE & TUSCANY PIETRASANTA

DON'T MISS

CARNIVAL IN VIAREGGIO

This hugely popular sun-and-sand resort of Viareggio – an easy trip by train from Pisa, Pietrasanta, Lucca or Florence – is known as much for its flamboyant Carnevale (📞0584 58 07 55; http://viareggio.ilcarnevale.com; ⊙Feb & Mar), second only to Venice for party spirit, as for its dishevelled line-up of once-grand art-nouveau facades along its seafront, which recall the town's 1920s and '30s heyday.

This annual four weeks of glory happens during February and early March when the city goes carnival-wild – a festival of floats, many featuring giant satirical effigies of political and other topical figures. It also includes fireworks and rampant dusk-to-dawn spirit. Tickets for the 3pm Sunday processions (adult/reduced €20/17) can be bought on the same day from ticket kiosks on the procession circuit or in advance via the online box office. The tourist office (📞0584 96 22 33; Viale Carducci 10; ⊙9am-1pm Mon, Fri & Sat, 9am-1pm & 3-6pm Tue & Thu), across from the clock on the cafe-lined water front, also has info.

★ **Filippo** TUSCAN €€
(☑0584 7 00 10; https://filippopietrasanta.it;
Via Barsanti 45; meals €40-50; ⊙12.30-2.30pm
& 7.30pm-1am, bar 6pm-midnight) This foodie address never disappoints. From the
homemade bread and focaccia brought
warm to your table, to the industrial-
meets-lime-green-velour interior and contemporary part-glass kitchen, this hybrid
lounge-bistro-cocktail bar is sensual and
chic. Cuisine mixes tripe-type classics with
modern dishes (the deep-fried artichoke
with creamed potato and bacon is glorious)
and, just like the menu, the wall art by the
bar changes each season.

🍷 Drinking & Nightlife

★ **L'Enoteca Marcucci** WINE BAR
(☑0584 79 19 62; www.enotecamarcucci.it; Via
Garibaldi 40; ⊙10am-1pm & 5pm-1am Tue-Sun)
Taste fine Tuscan wine on bar stools at high
wooden tables or beneath big parasols on
the street outside. Whichever you pick, the
distinctly funky, arty spirit of Pietrasanta's
best-loved *enoteca* enthrals.

❶ Getting There & Away

Regional train services include the following:
Florence (with change of train in Pisa; €10.80,
1¾ hours, at least hourly)
Lucca (with change of train in Pisa or Viareg-
gio; €4.60, one hour, every 30 minutes)
Pisa (€4.60, 30 minutes, every 30 minutes)
Viareggio (€2.60, 10 minutes, every 10
minutes)

EASTERN TUSCANY

The eastern edge of Tuscany is beloved by
both Italian and international film directors, who have immortalised its landscape,
hilltop towns and oft-quirky characters in
several critically acclaimed and visually
splendid films.

Arezzo

☑0575 / POP 99,400
Arezzo may not be a Tuscan centrefold,
but those parts of its historic centre that
survived merciless WWII bombings are as
compelling as any destination in the region
– the city's central square is as beautiful as it
appears in Roberto Benigni's classic film *La
vita è bella* (Life is Beautiful; 1997).

Once an important Etruscan trading post,
Arezzo was later absorbed into the Roman
Empire. A free republic as early as the 10th
century, it supported the Ghibelline cause
in the violent battles between pope and
emperor and was eventually subjugated by
Florence in 1384.

Today the city is known for its churches, museums and fabulously sloping Piazza
Grande, across which a huge antiques fair
spills each month. Come dusk, Arentini (locals of Arezzo) spill along the length of shop-
clad Corso Italia for the ritual late-afternoon
passeggiata (stroll).

◎ Sights

A combined ticket (adult/reduced €12/8)
covers admission to Cappella Bacci, Museo Archeologico Nazionale, Museo di Casa
Vasari and Museo Nazionale d'Arte Medievale e Moderna. It's valid for two days and can
be purchased at each museum.

★ **Chiesa di Santa
Maria della Pieve** CHURCH
(Corso Italia 7; ⊙8am-12.30pm & 3-6.30pm) FREE
This 12th-century church – Arezzo's oldest –
has an exotic Romanesque arcaded facade
adorned with carved columns, each individually decorated. Above the central doorway
are 13th-century carved reliefs called *Cyclo
dei Mesi* representing each month of the
year. The plain interior's highlight – being
restored at the RICERCA Restoration Studio (p612) at the time of research – is Pietro
Lorenzetti's polyptych *Madonna and Saints*
(1320–24). Below the altar is a 14th-century
silver bust reliquary of the city's patron
saint, San Donato.

Other treasures include a 13th-century
crucifix by Margarito di Arezzo (left of the
altar by the door to the sacristy) and a fresco
on a column (across from the sacristy door)
of Sts Francesco and Domenico by Andrea di
Nerio (1331–69).

Piazza Grande PIAZZA
This lopsided and steeply sloping piazza
is overlooked at its upper end by the porticoes of the **Palazzo delle Logge Vasariane**, completed in 1573. Construction of the
churchlike **Palazzo della Fraternità dei
Laici** (☑0575 2 46 94; www.fraternitadeilaici.
it; adult/child €5/free; ⊙10.30am-6pm) in the
northwest corner commenced in 1375 in
the Gothic style and was completed after
the onset of the Renaissance. The piazza is
the hub of the city's famous antiques fair

Arezzo

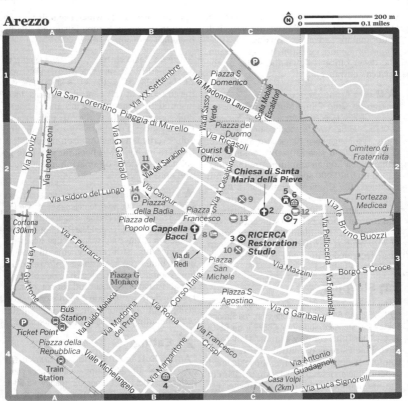

N 0 ▬▬▬▬▬▬ 200 m
   0 ▬▬▬▬▬▬ 0.1 miles

FLORENCE & TUSCANY AREZZO

Arezzo

(Arezzo Antique Fair; www.fieraantiquaria.org; ⊘9am-7pm), which is held on the first Sunday and preceding Saturday of each month.

★ **Cappella Bacci**   CHURCH
(☑0575 35 27 27; www.pierodellafrancesca. it; Piazza San Francesco; adult/reduced €8/5;

⊘9am-6pm Mon-Fri, to 5.30pm Sat, 1-5.30pm Sun, extended hours summer) This chapel, in the apse of 14th-century **Basilica di San Francesco**, safeguards one of Italian art's greatest works: Piero della Francesca's fresco cycle of the *Legend of the True Cross*. Painted between 1452 and 1466, it relates the story of the cross on which Christ was crucified. Only 30 people are allowed in every half hour, making advance booking (by telephone or email) essential in high season. The ticket office is down the stairs by the basilica's entrance.

★ Museo Archeologico
Nazionale 'Gaio Cilnio Mecenate'   MUSEUM

(Gaius Cilnius Maecenas Archeological Museum; ☑ 0575 2 08 82; www.facebook.com/archeologico arezzo; Via Margaritone 10; adult/reduced €6/3; ⊘ 8.30am-7.30pm Mon-Sat) Overlooking the remains of a Roman amphitheatre that once seated up to 10,000 spectators, this museum – named after Gaius Maecenas (68–8 BC), a patron of the arts and trusted advisor to Roman Emperor Augustus – exhibits Etruscan and Roman artefacts in a 14th-century convent building. The highlight is the *Cratere di Euphronios,* a 6th-century-BC Etruscan vase decorated with vivid scenes showing Hercules in battle.

🛏 Sleeping

Casa Volpi   HOTEL €

(☑ 0575 35 43 64; www.casavolpi.com; Via Simone Martini 29; standard/superior r €85/95, ste €140; [P] 🛜) This 18th-century manor, 4km from the cobbled streets of central Arezzo, has 15 comfortable but worn rooms; those deemed superior have views towards Arezzo. Family run, its main draw is the good on-site restaurant (meals €34), which expands its seating into the pretty garden in summer. Sadly, breakfast is disappointing.

Graziella Patio Hotel   BOUTIQUE HOTEL €€

(☑ 0575 40 19 62; www.hotelpatio.it; Via Cavour 23; d €160-180, ste €210-285; [✳] [@] 🛜) Each of the 10 rooms at this central hotel has decor inspired by Bruce Chatwin's travel space. Pink-kissed Arkady is the 'Australia room', Fillide exudes a distinctly Moroccan air and Cobra Verde is a green Amazon-inspired loft. Every room has a Macbook for guests to go online; wi-fi access on smartphones is pretty well non-existent.

★ Villa Fontelunga   BOUTIQUE HOTEL €€€

(☑ 0575 66 04 10; www.fontelunga.com; Via Cunicchio 5, Foiano della Chiana; d €240-410, villa per week €2730-4830; ⊘ mid-Mar–Oct; [P] [✳] 🛜 🐕) Gorgeous is the only word to use when describing this 19th-century villa in Foiano della Chiana, 35km southwest of Arezzo. Its nine rooms are the perfect balance of traditional Tuscan elegance and jet-set pizzazz. Leisure facilities include a tennis court, gorgeous pool and mountain-bike use. Dinner (€39 including wine) is offered twice weekly.

🍴 Eating

L'Antica Bottega di Primo   SANDWICHES €

(☑ 0575 04 01 24; https://it-it.facebook.com/ Bottegadiprimo; Via Cavour 92; panini €2.50-4; ⊘ 7.30am-9pm Mon-Thu, to 11pm Fri-Sun; 🛜) A delectable array of local cheese and cured meats awaits at this popular *alimentari* (grocery store), which fills fresh *panini* (sandwiches) and foccacias to order and also sells delicious freshly baked biscuits and pastries. Eat in or take away.

★ Antica Osteria Agania   TUSCAN €

(☑ 0575 29 53 81; www.agania.com; Via Mazzini 10; meals €20; ⊘ noon-3pm & 6-10.30pm Tue-Sun) Operated by the Ludovichi family since 1905, Agania serves the type of diehard traditional fare that remains the cornerstone of Tuscan dining. Specialities include sensational antipasti (with lots of vegetarian options), rustic soups, homemade pasta and *secondi* ranging from *lumache* (snails) to *grifi* (lambs' cheeks) with polenta, *baccalà* (cod) with chickpeas, and sausages with beans.

★ Aliciati   ITALIAN €€

(☑ 0575 2 72 41; www.aliciati.com; Via Bicchieraia 16-18; meals €38; ⊘ 12.30-2.30pm & 7.30-10pm Tue-Sun) At his eponymous restaurant, chef

---

DON'T MISS

BEHIND THE SCENES

Art lovers will adore visiting the RICER-CA Restoration Studio (☑ 0575 2 86 70, 333 2851179; www.ricercarestauro. wordpress.com; Via Mazzini 1; by donation; ⊘ by appointment). The base of Art Angels Arezzo (www.artangelsarezzo.org), a group of professional art historians and conservators dedicated to restoring important Arentini works of art, it welcomes visitors interested in learning about restoration techniques and seeing the painstaking process underway. Past projects have included Vasari's La Pala Albergotti from the Badia, and when we recently visited, Pietro Lorenzetti's exquisite Madonna and Saints altarpiece from the Chiesa di Santa Maria della Pieve (p610) was being returned to its original glory.

Giovanni Aliciati reimagines classic Italian dishes using top-quality ingredients and incorporating French and Spanish techniques and flavours. The refined results are as good to taste as they are to look at. The interior of the restaurant, which is near Piazza Grande (p610), is equally impressive, with contemporary glass light fittings throwing golden light on stone walls.

🍷 Drinking & Nightlife

Caffè Vasari CAFE

(📞0575 04 36 97; Piazza Grande 15; ⊙7.30am-9pm summer, 8.30am-6pm winter) Bathed in Tuscan sunrays from dawn to dusk, this cafe is the perfect spot for lapping up the ancient elegance and beauty of Piazza Grande over a coffee or *aperitivo* (predinner drink). Find it enviably squirrelled beneath the cinematic porticoes of Palazzo delle Logge Vasariane (p610).

No Sugar Please CAFE

(www.sugar.it; rear 60 Corso Italia; ⊙4-8pm Mon, 10am-8pm Tue-Sat) Accessed via the arched corridor between the two Corso Italia storefronts of ultra-fashionable clothing retailer Sugar, which is housed in Renaissance–era Palazzo Lambardi, this espresso bar serves excellent coffee, cakes and *panini*. Sit inside or in the courtyard, from which you can also access a room paved with Roman mosaics now protected by a glass floor.

ℹ Information

Tourist Office (Centro Accoglienza Turistica; 📞0575 40 19 45; www.arezzointuscany.it; Piazza della Libertà; ⊙10am-4pm)

ℹ Getting There & Away

BUS

Buses operated by **Tiemme** (www.tiemmespa. it) travel to/from Siena (€7.60, 1½ hours, eight daily Monday to Saturday, four Sunday), Sansepolcro (€5.60, one hour, hourly Monday to Saturday, two Sunday), Anghiari (€4.50, 45 minutes, hourly Monday to Saturday, two Sunday) and Cortona (€4.50, 65 minutes, 10 daily Monday to Saturday). Buy tickets from the **ticket point** (Via Piero della Francesca 1; ⊙6.10am-8pm Mon-Sat year-round, 6.30am-noon Sun summer, 8am-12.30pm Sun winter) to the left as you exit the train station; buses leave from the bus bay opposite.

TRAIN

Arezzo is on the Florence–Rome train line, and there are frequent services to Florence (*region-*

MARKET TALK

A treasure trove of locally grown and produced foodstuffs, **Mercato Logge del Grano** (📞0575 2 06 46; www.face book.com/loggedelgrano; Piazzetta a delle Loggia del Grano; ⊙9am-2.30pm & 4.30-8pm Mon-Sat) is a superb organic market selling fresh meat, fruit and vegetables, olive oil, dried pasta and legumes, bread, wine and dairy products including milk and cheese. It's a sensational resource for self-caterers. Free tastings are offered every Saturday and also at special openings on the first Sunday of each month.

ale €8.60, 45 minutes to 1½ hours) and Rome (Intercity €27.50, 2¼ hours; *regionale* €15.15, 2¾ hours) from the train station in Piazza della Repubblica on the southwest edge of the city centre. There are also twice-hourly regional trains to Camucia-Cortona (€3.60, 20 minutes).

Sansepolcro

📞0575 / POP 15,900

This hidden gem is a town that truly deserves that description. Dating from the year 1000, Sansepolcro (called 'Borgo' by locals) reached its current size in the 15th century and was walled in the 16th century. Its historic centre is littered with *palazzi* (mansions) and churches squirrelling away Renaissance works of art or bejewelled with exquisite terracotta Andrea della Robbia medallions. Spend a day wandering from dimly lit church to church, following in the footsteps of Sansepolcro's greatest son, Renaissance artist Piero della Francesca.

◉ Sights

★ **Museo Civico** MUSEUM

(📞0575 73 22 18; www.museocivicosansepolcro. it; Via Niccolò Aggiunti 65; adult/reduced €10/8.50, with Casa di Piero della Francesca €11/9.50; ⊙10am-1.30pm & 2.30-6.40pm mid-Jun–mid-Sep, reduced hours est of year) The town's flagship museum is home to a small but top-notch collection of artworks, including two Piero della Francesca masterpieces – *Resurrection* (1458–74) and the *Madonna della Misericordia* (Madonna of Mercy; 1445–56) polyptych – as well as two fresco fragments portraying *San Ludovico* (Saint Ludovic;

1460) and *San Giuliano* (Saint Julian; 1460). Also of note are works from the studio of Andrea della Robbia, including a beautiful tondo (circular sculpture) known as the *Virgin and Child with Manetti Coat of Arms* (1503).

🛏 Sleeping & Eating

★ Dolce Rosa

PENSION €

(📞 366 3973527; www.dolcerosa.it; Via Niccolò Aggiunti 74; s/d €45/60; ❄) It's rare to find budget accommodation that is well located, super-clean and extremely comfortable, but that's what's on offer at this excellent pension near the Museo Civico (p613). Host Rodolfo looks after his guests well, providing kettles and mini-fridges stocked with complimentary water and soft drinks. No breakfast, but at these prices, who's quibbling?

★ Pasticceria Chieli

CAFE €

(📞 0575 74 20 26; www.pasticceriachieli.it; Viale Vittorio Veneto 35; ⊗ 6am-8pm Tue-Fri, to 8.30pm Sat, 6.30am-1.30pm Sun; ❄) Just outside the historic town walls, Sansepolcro's best cafe bustles at all times of the day. It's a go-to destination whether you're after a morning coffee and pastry, a lunchtime *panino*, a cake in the afternoon or an *aperitivo* (predinner drink). Staff are friendly and there's plenty of seating too.

★ Ristorante Al Coccio

TUSCAN €€

(📞 0575 74 14 68; www.alcoccio.com; Via Niccolò Aggiunti 83; meals €40; ⊗ 12.30-2.30pm & 7.30-9.30pm Wed-Mon; ❄) 🍴 Sisters Sara and Loide Battistelli head the kitchen and dining room of this elegant restaurant, which serves organic produce and plenty of gluten-free choices. The locally sourced beef is a highlight – order a *tagliata* of dry-aged Chianina or a carpaccio topped with shaved black truffle and *parmigiano reggiano*. Great desserts too.

★ Ristorante Da Ventura

TUSCAN €€

(📞 0575 74 25 60; www.albergodaventura.it; Via Niccolò Aggiunti 30; meals €30; ⊗ 12.30-2.15pm & 7.30-9.45pm Tue-Sat, 12.30-2.15pm Sun; 🍴) This old-world eatery is a culinary joy. Trolleys laden with feisty joints of pork, beef stewed in *chianti classico* and roasted veal shank are pushed from table to table, the bow-tied waiters intent on piling plates high. Vegetarians are well catered for with a feast of a mixed house antipasti followed by black truffle omelette or buttered *tagliatelle*.

ℹ Information

Tourist Office (📞 0575 74 05 36; www.valtiberinaintoscana.it; Via Giacomo Matteotti 8; ⊗ 10am-1pm & 2.30-6.30pm mid-Mar–Oct, shorter hours winter; 🛜)

ℹ Getting There & Away

Tiemme (www.tiemmespa.it) operates buses to/from Arezzo (€5.60, one hour, hourly Monday to Saturday, two Sunday), stopping in Anghiari (€1.50, 15 minutes) en route. **Sulga** (www.sulga.it) operates a daily service to Rome and Leonardo da Vinci Airport (€19.50, 3½ to 4¼ hours); check schedules and buy tickets for this service online. All buses use the **bus interchange** on Via Guglielmo Marconi, near Porta Fiorentina; purchase tickets at Bar Autostazione here.

Cortona

📞 0575 / POP 22,100

Rooms with a view are the rule rather than the exception in this spectacularly sited hilltop town. At the beginning of the 15th century Fra' Angelico lived and worked here, and fellow artists Luca Signorelli and Pietro da Cortona were both born within the walls – all three are represented in the Museo Diocesano's small but sensational collection. Large chunks of *Under the Tuscan Sun*, the 2003 film of the book by Frances Mayes, were shot here and the town has been a popular tourist destination ever since.

◉ Sights

★ Museo Diocesano di Arte Sacra

MUSEUM

(📞 0575 6 28 30; Piazza del Duomo 1; adult/reduced €5/3; ⊗ 10am-6.30pm Apr-Oct, 11am-4pm Tue-Fri, 10am-5pm Sat & Sun Nov-Mar) Highlights of this small museum in the decommissioned 16th-century Chiesa del Gesù include a number of works by Pietro Lorenzetti, a *Madonna and Child* (c 1336) by Niccolò di Segna and two beautiful works by Fra' Angelico: *Annunciation* (1436) and *Madonna with Child and Saints* (c 1438). Upstairs, the Sala Signorelli is home to two paintings by the Cortona-born artist, including *Lamentation Over the Dead Christ* (1502).

Museo dell'Accademia Etrusca e della Città di Cortona

MUSEUM

(MAEC; 📞 0575 63 04 15; www.cortonamaec.org; Piazza Signorelli 9; adult/reduced €10/7; ⊗ 10am-7pm Apr-Oct, to 5pm Tue-Sun Nov-Mar) Spread over five floors and 40 rooms in the

13th-century **Palazzo Casali**, the collection here includes substantial local Etruscan and Roman finds, Renaissance globes, 18th-century decorative arts and an eclectic array of paintings. The Etruscan collection is the highlight – don't miss the extraordinary hanging bronze lamp on the 2nd floor. Paintings to look out for include Luca Signorelli's sinister *Madonna with Child and Saint Protectors of Cortona* (1512) and Gino Severini's exquisite *Maternità* (1916).

🛏 Sleeping & Eating

Villa Marsili　　　　　　　HOTEL €€
(☑0575 60 52 52; www.villamarsili.net; Viale Cesare Battisti 13; s €75-85, d €110-220; ☉Apr-Nov; P❋🛜) Service is the hallmark at this attractive villa wedged against the city walls and a short walk downhill from Cortona centre. Guests rave about the helpful staff, lavish breakfast buffet and early-evening *aperitivo* served in the garden. Pricier suites have hot tubs and wonderful views across the Val di Chiana to Lago Trasimeno. Advance, non-refundable rates are considerably reduced.

Monastero di Cortona
Hotel & Spa　　　　　LUXURY HOTEL €€€
(☑0575 178 58 39; www.monasterodicortona.com; Via del Salvatore; r €195-300, ste €350; P❋🛜🏊) The monks who once called this monastery home wouldn't recognise their quarters these days, as a makeover has transformed the heritage building into an alluring luxury hotel. Rooms are elegant and well equipped, and facilities include an atmospheric spa with indoor pool, garden with plunge pool, and bar with 17th-century frescoes.

✖ Eating

Taverna Pane e Vino　　　　TUSCAN €
(☑0575 63 10 10; www.pane-vino.it; Piazza Signorelli 27; bruschette €4, cheese & meat boards €7-13; ☉noon-11pm Tue-Sun) Simple seasonal dishes are the trademark of this vaulted cellar, a hotspot with local bon vivants who come to indulge in their pick of Tuscan and Italian wines in the company of *bruschette* and generous platters of local cheese and cured meats.

La Bucaccia　　　　　　　TUSCAN €€
(☑0575 60 60 39; www.labucaccia.it; Via Ghibellina 17; meals €38; ☉12.30-2.30pm & 7-10.30pm Tue-Sun) Occupying the medieval stable of a Renaissance *palazzo*, Cortona's best-regarded restaurant has close-set tables where diners enjoy refined versions of Cortonese specialities – beef, game and handmade pasta feature on the menu. Owner Romano Magi ripens his own cheeses and starting or ending your meal with a cheese course is recommended. There's an excellent wine list too. Reservations essential.

ℹ Information

Tourist Office (☑0575 63 72 23; www.comune dicortona.it/turismo-e-cultura/info-cortona; Piazza Signorelli 9; ☉10am-7pm Apr-Oct, 9am-1pm Mon-Thu, 10am-5pm Fri-Sun Nov-Mar)

ℹ Getting There & Away

Tiemme (www.tiemmespa.it) buses connect the town with Arezzo (€4.50, 65 minutes, 10 daily Monday to Saturday) via Castiglion Fiorentino (€2.60, 35 minutes). There are bus stops in Piazzale Garibalidi and Piazzale del Mercato.

FLORENCE & TUSCANY CORTONA

AT A GLANCE

POPULATION
2.38 million

CAPITAL
Perugia

BEST PORCHETTA
Antica Salumeria
Granieri Amato
(p626)

BEST LIVE MUSIC
Umbria Jazz (p624)

**BEST ORGANIC
FARM**
Locanda della Valle
Nuova (p666)

WHEN TO GO
Feb & Mar Celebrate
all things truffle-
related at Norcia's
Nero Norcia food
festival.

May Hit Le Marche's
beaches, as wild-
flowers bloom on the
Piano Grande.

Jun & Jul Get lost in
music at the Spoleto
Festival and Peru-
gia's Umbria Jazz.

Perugia (p620)
ARTMEDIAFACTORY/SHUTTERSTOCK ©

Umbria &
Le Marche

S waths of billowing green slopes cloaked
by olive groves and sun-ripened wheat
fields, castle-topped medieval towns and
snow-capped Apennine peaks. No, not Tuscany
but Umbria, its quieter and less-trodden
neighbour, and Le Marche, one of Italy's great
unsung regions.

This lush and often sparsely populated
part of central Italy is made for slow travel,
for snaking along winding back roads to
enchanting hill towns such as Perugia, Assisi,
Gubbio and Urbino, and for revelling in fine
food and wine. The cultural menu is equally
rich, and Renaissance masterpieces grace
many of the regions' churches and museums.
Music lovers are also well served, with summer
opera in Macerata, Pesaro and Spoleto, and
jazz in Perugia.

Umbria & Le Marche Highlights

1 Basilica di San Francesco (p635) Gazing heavenwards at the extraordinary frescoes that adorn Assisi's signature basilica.

2 Parco del Conero (p661) Revelling in the magical seascapes of this glorious stretch of Adriatic coastline.

3 Palazzo Ducale – Galleria Nazionale delle Marche (p664) Taking in world-famous Renaissance art in Urbino, home town of the artist Raphael.

4 Duomo (p651) Marvelling at the architectural and artistic glories of Orvieto's breathtaking cathedral.

5 Funivia Colle Eletto (p633) Savouring vast views as you soar above medieval Gubbio on this birdcage-like cable car.

6 Galleria Nazionale dell'Umbria (p621) Browsing Umbria's finest art collection in Perugia's showpiece Gothic palace.

7 Ascoli Piceno (p669) Snacking on fried olives in Ascoli Piceno's elegant historic centre.

8 Lago Trasimeno (p629) Slipping into the relaxed groove of lake life at Italy's fourth-largest lake.

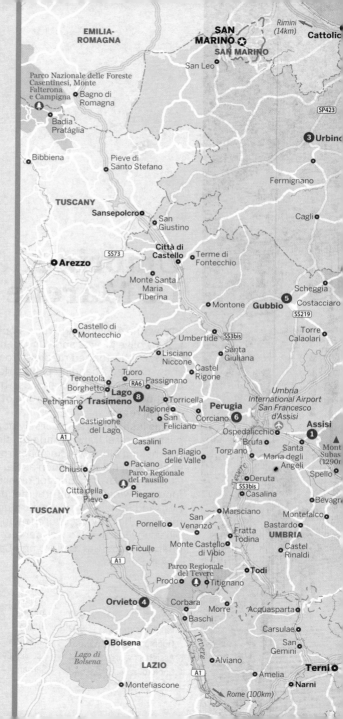

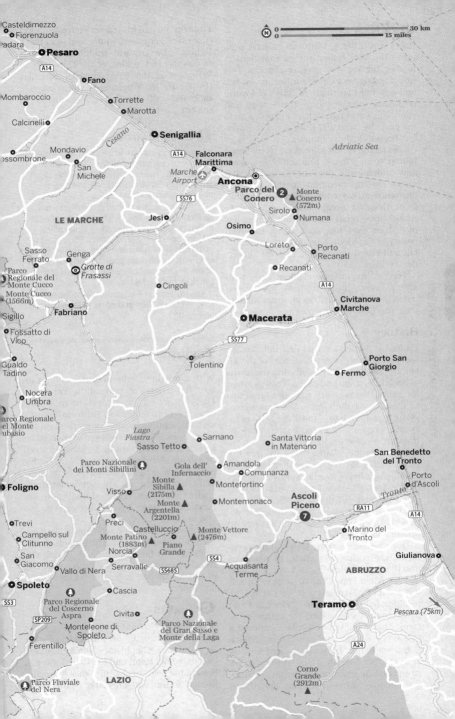

UMBRIA

Italy's green heart, Umbria is a land unto itself, the only Italian region that borders neither the sea nor another country. This isolation has kept outside influences at bay and ensured that many of Italy's old-world traditions survive today. Travel here and you'll still see grandmothers in aprons making pasta by hand and front doors that haven't been locked in centuries.

The region is best known for its medieval hilltop towns, many beautifully preserved and dramatically set. The Etruscans, Romans, feuding medieval families and Renaissance artists have all left an imprint, from Orvieto's great Gothic cathedral to Assisi's fresco-clad basilica. But nature has played its part too, contrasting the wild beauty of the Monti Sibillini with the gentle fall and rise of green hills and wildflower-flecked meadows.

Foodies are in their element here, with *tartufi neri* (black truffles), fine cured meats and full-bodied local wines finding their way onto regional menus.

History

Umbria is named after its first inhabitants, the Umbri tribe, who settled east of the Tiber around 1000 BC, establishing the towns of Spoleto, Gubbio and Assisi. They jockeyed for regional supremacy with the Etruscans to the west of the river – the founders of Perugia and Orvieto – until the 3rd century BC, when the Romans came marching through, conquering them both.

Following the collapse of the Western Roman Empire, the region spent much of the Middle Ages being fought over by advocates of the Holy Roman Empire (Ghibellines) and supporters of the pope (Guelphs). Intriguingly, it was during this turbulent period that peace-loving St Francis came to prominence in Assisi.

Over the course of the 15th and 16th centuries, the region was gradually absorbed into the Papal States. Events came to a head in 1540 when Pope Paul III imposed a salt tax and Perugia rose up in rebellion. The resulting Salt War saw the city crushed and papal control established for centuries to come. Under the popes, Umbria endured a period of economic and cultural immobility.

But while history has been hard on Umbria, art has flourished and Perugia has a strong artistic tradition. In the 15th century it was home to fresco painters Bernardino

Pinturicchio and his master Pietro Vannucci (known as Perugino), who would later teach Raphael. Its cultural tradition continues to this day in the form of the University of Perugia and the Università per Stranieri (University for Foreigners), which attracts thousands of international students to the city.

ⓘ Getting Around

While having your own wheels certainly makes it easier to reach those off-the-radar hill towns and Umbria's rural corners, it is possible to get around on public transport with a little pre-planning (and patience).

Train services are limited in the region, but **Busitalia** (☑ 075 963 76 37; www.fsbusitalia.it; Piazza Partigiani, Perugia; ⓣ ticket office 6.15am-8pm Mon-Sat, 7.30am-7.30pm Sun) fills in the blanks with bus and ferry services. Buses link Perugia with many towns in the area; check at the city's tourist office (p627) or bus station (p628) for exact details.

A useful resource for mountain biking and road-cycling is **Bike in Umbria** (www.bikein umbria.it).

Perugia

POP 165,700

With a pristine medieval centre and an international student population, Perugia is Umbria's largest and most cosmopolitan city. Its *centro storico* (historic centre), seemingly little changed in more than 400 years, rises in a helter-skelter of cobbled alleys, arched stairways and piazzas framed by solemn churches and magnificent Gothic *palazzi* (mansions). Reminders of its lively and often bloody past are everywhere, from ancient arches and medieval basilicas to Renaissance frescoes by the likes of Perugino and Raphael.

But while history reverberates all around, Perugia knows how to party. University students pep up the nightlife and fill cafe terraces, while music-lovers swarm to the city in July for Umbria Jazz, one of Europe's top jazz festivals.

◎ Sights

★ **Piazza IV Novembre**　　　　PIAZZA
In Perugia all roads seem to lead to Piazza IV Novembre. This historic square, flanked by Palazzo dei Priori and the Cattedrale, has been at the heart of civic life since it was the Roman forum and later the political and

geographic centre of the medieval city. Nowadays, people from all walks of life gather here to sit on the cathedral steps, soak up the sun and watch the street entertainers work their magic.

Cattedrale di San Lorenzo   CATHEDRAL
(☑ 075 572 38 32; Piazza IV Novembre; ⊙ 7.30am-12.30pm & 3.30-6.45pm Mon-Sat, 8am-12.45pm & 4-7pm Sun) Lording it over Piazza IV Novembre is Perugia's stark medieval cathedral. A church has stood here since the 900s, but the version you see today was begun in 1345 from designs created by Fra Bevignate. Building continued until 1587, although the main facade was never completed. Inside you'll find dramatic late-Gothic architecture, an altarpiece by Signorelli and sculptures by Duccio. The steps in front of the facade are where seemingly all of Perugia congregates; they overlook the pink-and-white Fontana Maggiore.

Fontana Maggiore   FOUNTAIN
(Piazza IV Novembre) The centrepiece of Piazza IV Novembre, the delicate pink-and-white marble Fontana Maggiore was designed by Fra Bevignate and built by father-and-son team Nicola and Giovanni Pisano between 1275 and 1278. Some 50 bas-reliefs and 24 statues grace the two-tier polygonal basin, representing scenes from the Old Testament, the founding of Rome, the seven 'liberal arts', the signs of the zodiac, a griffin and a lion.

★ Palazzo dei Priori   HISTORIC BUILDING
(Corso Vannucci 19) Flanking Corso Vannucci, this Gothic palace, constructed between the 13th and 14th centuries, is architecturally striking with its tripartite windows, ornamental portal and fortress-like crenellations. It was formerly the headquarters of the local magistracy, but now houses the city's main art gallery, the Galleria Nazionale dell'Umbria, and a series of historic rooms and suites: the Nobile Collegio del Cambio, the Nobile Collegio della Mercanzia and the Sala dei Notari.

★ Galleria Nazionale dell'Umbria   GALLERY
(☑ 075 572 10 09; www.gallerianazionaleumbria.it; Palazzo dei Priori, Corso Vannucci 19; adult/reduced €8/4; ⊙ 8.30am-7.30pm Tue-Sun year-round, plus from noon Mon mid-Mar–Oct) Umbria's foremost art gallery is housed in Palazzo dei Priori on Perugia's main strip. Its collection, chronologically displayed over 40 rooms,

is one of central Italy's finest, numbering more than 3000 works, ranging from Byzantine-inspired 13th-century paintings to Gothic works by Gentile da Fabriano and Renaissance masterpieces by home-town heroes Pinturicchio and Perugino.

Important works include Gentile da Fabriano's *Madonna con il Bambino e angeli* (early 15th century), the *Pala di Santa Maria dei Fossi* altarpiece (1496–98) by Pinturicchio, and Benedetto Bonfigli's fresco cycle for the *Cappella dei Priori* (c 1454–80).

★ Nobile Collegio del Cambio   HISTORIC BUILDING
(Exchange Hall; ☑ 075 572 85 99; www.collegiodelcambio.it; Palazzo dei Priori, Corso Vannucci 25; €4.50, incl Nobile Collegio della Mercanzia €5.50; ⊙ 9am-12.30pm & 2.30-5.30pm Mon-Sat, 9am-1pm Sun) Seat of Perugia's Moneychanger's Guild between 1452 and 1457, the extravagantly adorned Nobile Collegio del Cambio has three rooms: the Sala dei Legisti (Jurists' Hall), with 17th-century wooden stalls carved by Giampiero Zuccari; the Sala dell'Udienza (Audience Chamber), with inlaid wooden furniture and outstanding Renaissance frescoes by Perugino; and the Cappella di San Giovanni Battista (Chapel of San Giovanni Battista), painted by a student of Perugino's, Giannicola di Paolo.

Nobile Collegio della Mercanzia   HISTORIC BUILDING
(Merchant's Hall; ☑ 075 573 03 66; www.collegiomercanzia.it; Palazzo dei Priori, Corso Vannucci 15; €1.50, incl Nobile Collegio del Cambio €5.50; ⊙ 9am-1pm & 2.30-5.30pm Tue-Sat & 9am-1pm Sun summer, shorter hours winter) The Nobile Collegio della Mercanzia, HQ of Perugia's medieval merchants guild, features a 14th-century audience chamber with exquisite wood panelling.

Sala dei Notari   HISTORIC BUILDING
(Notaries' Hall; Palazzo dei Priori, Piazza IV Novembre; ⊙ 9am-1pm & 3-7pm Tue-Sun) **FREE** The Sala dei Notari was built from 1293 to 1297 and is where the nobility met. The arches supporting the vaults are Romanesque, covered with vibrant frescoes depicting biblical scenes and Aesop's fables. To reach the hall, walk up the steps from Piazza IV Novembre.

Pozzo Etrusco   HISTORIC SITE
(Etruscan Well; ☑ 075 573 36 69; www.pozzoetrusco.it; Piazza Danti 18; adult/reduced €3/2, incl Casa Museo di Palazzo Sorbello €6; ⊙ 10am-1.30pm & 2.30-6pm summer, Tue-Sun spring & autumn,

Perugia

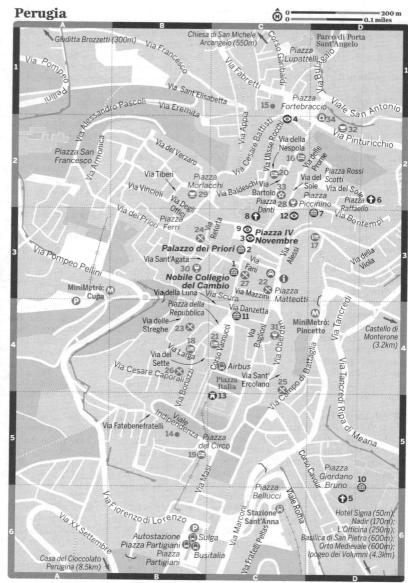

11am-1.30pm & 2.30-5pm Tue-Sun winter) Just north of Piazza IV Novembre, you can venture down an Etruscan well. Dating from the 3rd century BC, the 37m-deep cylindrical shaft was the main water source for the Etruscan city, and, more recently, provided water during WWII bombing raids.

Casa Museo di Palazzo Sorbello MUSEUM
(☏ 075 573 27 75; www.casamuseosorbello.org; Piazza Piccinino 9; adult/reduced €4/3, incl Pozzo Etrusco €6; ☉ guided tours 10.30am-2pm, shorter hours winter) This exquisite 17th-century mansion, once owned by the aristocratic Sorbello family, has been restored to its fres-

Perugia

coed, gilt-clad, chandelier-lit, 18th-century prime. Guided tours (in Italian and English) let you admire the family's almost ludicrously opulent collection of art, porcelain, embroidery and manuscripts.

Cappella di San Severo CHAPEL
(☑ 075 947 17 66; Piazza Raffaello; adult/reduced €4/2; ⊙ 11am-1.30pm & 2.30-5pm Tue-Sun Jan-Mar & Nov-Dec, 10am-6pm Apr & Aug, 10am-1.30pm & 2.30-6pm Tue-Sun May-Jul & Sep-Oct) From the outside, this rather bland church northeast of Piazza IV Novembre looks nothing special. But step inside and you'll find a tiny chapel decorated with a fresco by Raphael. *Trinità e santi* (Trinity with Saints), which was painted during the artist's residence in Perugia between 1505 and 1508 and later completed by his mentor Perugino, is the only painting by Raphael in Perugia.

Arco Etrusco GATE
(Etruscan Arch; Piazza Fortebraccio) The most impressive of Perugia's ancient city gates, this landmark arch is one of Umbria's most important Etruscan monuments. It was originally built in the 3rd century BC but was later modified by the emperor Augustus

– hence the inscription 'Augusta Perusia' and its alternative name, Arco di Augusto.

★**Chiesa di San Michele Arcangelo** CHURCH
(Tempio di San Michele Arcangelo; ☑ 075 572 26 24; Via del Tempio; ⊙ 9am-4pm) Also known as the Chiesa or Tempio di Sant'Angelo, this 5th-century Romanesque church is one of the oldest in Italy (and the most appealing in Perugia). It was first built over an earlier Roman temple – hence the circular form and recycled columns in the interior – but it has since been modified and the main portal dates from a 14th-century Gothic makeover.

Palazzo Baldeschi al Corso MUSEUM
(☑ 075 573 47 60; www.fondazionecariperugiaarte. it; Corso Vannucci 66; €4; ⊙ 3-7pm Fri-Sun, plus 10am-1pm Sat & Sun) Originally dating from the 14th century, Palazzo Baldeschi features a series of palatial rooms decorated with stunning Murano chandeliers and frescoes from the 1850s, including Mariano Piervittori's vivid Sala della Muse. The museum displays the private collection of art historian Alessandro Marabottini (mainly paintings and sculptures spanning the 16th to 20th centuries) and the Fondazione Cassa di

Risparmio di Perugia's renowned collection of Renaissance ceramics.

Rocca Paolina   FORTRESS
(Piazza Italia; ☉6.15am-2am) **FREE** Commissioned by Pope Paolo III in the 1540s, this fortress wiped out entire sections of a formerly wealthy neighbourhood. Its insides have long since been hollowed out to make way for *scale mobili* (escalators) up to the historic centre, but it's still a fascinating sight with its mighty walls, moody lighting and dark nooks and crannies, and is sometimes used to host temporary exhibitions. Up above is a small park, the **Giardini Carducci** (Corso Vannucci; ☉24hr).

**Museo Archeologico
Nazionale dell'Umbria**   MUSEUM
(MUNA; ☎075 572 71 41; www.polomusealeumbria. beniculturali.it; Piazza Giordano Bruno 10; adult/reduced €5/2.50; ☉10am-7.30pm Mon, from 8.30am Tue-Sun) Housed in the former convent of the **Basilica di San Domenico** (☉7am-noon & 4-7pm), Umbria's regional archaeology museum harbours an encyclopaedic collection of Etruscan and prehistoric artefacts – carved funerary urns, coins and Bronze Age statuary – dating as far back as the 16th century BC. One of its star pieces is the *Cippo Perugino* (Perugian Memorial Stone), which has the longest Etruscan-language engraving ever found, offering a rare window into this obscure culture.

**Cattedrale e Abbazia
di San Pietro**   BASILICA
(www.fondazioneagraria.it; Borgo XX Giugno 74; adult/reduced €3/2; ☉9am-7pm Mon-Sat, 3-7pm Sun summer, to 6pm winter) South of the town centre, past the Porta di San Pietro, is this atmospheric 10th-century basilica complex. The basilica, overlooked by a landmark bell tower, is stunning inside, with opulent displays of gilt and marble and some wonderful works of art, including a *Pietà* (a painting of the dead Christ supported by the Madonna) by Perugino.

Ipogeo dei Volumni   HISTORIC SITE
(www.archeopg.arti.beniculturali.it; Via Assisana 53, Località Ponte San Giovanni; adult/reduced €3/2; ☉9am-6.30pm Mon-Sat, to 1.30pm Sun) About 5km southeast of the city, the Ipogeo dei Volumni is part of the Palazzone necropolis, a vast 2nd-century-BC Etruscan burial site. The tomb, which according to the custom of the time was built to resemble a house, holds the funerary urns of the Volumni, a local noble family. The surrounding grounds are a massive expanse of partially unearthed burial chambers, with several buildings housing locally found artefacts.

To get there, take bus F022 from Viale Roma; by car, take the Bonanzano exit off the southbound E45.

🍴 Courses

Università per Stranieri   LANGUAGE
(☎075 574 65 59; www.unistrapg.it; Piazza Fortebraccio 4) This is Italy's foremost academic institution for foreigners, offering courses in language, literature, history, art, music, opera and architecture. Monthly language courses will set you back €600 (elementary and intermediate levels) or €680 (advanced level). See the website for details.

👉 Tours

Studio Moretti Caselli   ART
(☎340 7765594; www.studiomoretticaselli.it; Via Fatebenefratelli 2; tour contribution per person €5; ☉10am-12.30pm Tue & Wed or by appt) Explore the colourful world of stained glass on a tour of this family-run studio. It was originally founded in 1860 by master glasspainter Francesco Moretti, whose work peppers historic churches and buildings in Perugia, throughout Italy and across the world.

🎊 Festivals & Events

Check the tourist office's website (http:// turismo.comune.perugia.it) or www.bella umbria.net for details on Perugia's gazillions of festivals, concerts, summertime outdoor film screenings and *sagre* (traditional festivals).

★ **Umbria Jazz**   MUSIC
(www.umbriajazz.com; ☉Jul) Ever since making its debut in 1973, Perugia's swinging 10-day

---

ℹ MUSEUM CARD
....
Planning on ticking off several sights? Invest in a **Perugia Città Museo Card** (www.perugiacittamuseo.it; adult/reduced €14/10), which provides admission to five museums of your choice as well as reduced entry to other museums and exhibitions, and discounts at several restaurants. Valid for 48 hours, it's available at the main tourist office and participating sights – see the website for details.

July festival, Umbria Jazz, has put the city firmly on the world jazz map, with such headline acts as BB King, Van Morrison, James Brown, Sting, Chet Baker, Diana Krall and, more recently, Thom Yorke, Nick Mason and Paolo Conte.

Eurochocolate FOOD & DRINK
(www.eurochocolate.com; ⊘ mid-Oct) Perugia celebrates the cocoa bean over 10 days. More than a million chocoholics flock to the city for choc-crazy exhibitions, cookery classes, giant chocolate sculptures and – the real reason everyone is here – to hoover up the free samples.

🛏 Sleeping

B&B San Fiorenzo B&B €
(☑ 393 3869987; www.sanfiorenzo.com; Via Alessi 45; d €70-90, q €100-120, apt per week €450-560; ☜) Buried in Perugia's medieval centre is this charming B&B, where Luigi and Monica make you welcome in one of three suites, each with its independent entrance. Mod cons and marble bathrooms have been skilfully incorporated into spacious quarters with brick vaulting, lime-washed walls and antique furnishings; the Maior suite even has a shower built into an 11th-century well.

Hotel Rosalba HOTEL €
(☑ 075 572 82 85; www.hotelrosalbaperugia.com; Piazza del Circo 7; s €47-65, d €55-75, q €90-100; ✳☜) An inviting budget option, the two-star Rosalba occupies a hard-to-miss pink town house just off the escalator up from Piazza Partigiana. Facilities are modest but its clean, simply attired rooms offer top value for money. The best come with balconies and views, though one, downstairs, is a tad dark. Breakfast is €4.50 extra.

Little Italy HOSTEL €
(☑ 075 966 19 97; www.littleitalyhostel.it; Via della Nespola 1; dm €16-25, d €39-99, q €59-125; @☜) History and cutting-edge design cavort at this slick and intimate hostel. Pair the central location with modern dorms (bunk beds, heated flooring, individual lockers, lights and plugs), rooms housed in a re-vamped 12th-century church (complete with original vaults and frescoes), a kitchen, and 24-hour lounge area, and you're looking at one fine place to stay.

Alla Maison di Alessia B&B €
(☑ 345 0784208; www.allamaisondialessia.it; Via Bartolo 55-61; s €35-50, d €60-100; ☜) Alessia and Enrico have waved magic wands

PERUGIA'S HOUSE OF CHOCOLATE

To visit the Wonka-esque world of Perugian chocolate, sign up for a 1¼-hour guided tour (in Italian or English; times vary) of the **Casa del Cioccolato Perugina** (☑ 800 800 907; www.perugina.it; Van San Sisto 207, Località San Sisto; adult/reduced €9/7; ⊘ 9am-1pm & 2-5.30pm Mon-Fri, 10am-4pm Sat; 🖶) **FREE**. After visiting the museum, you'll wend your way through an enclosed sky bridge, watching as the white-outfitted Oompa Loompas, er, factory workers, go about their chocolate-creating business.

The Casa is located at Nestlé's large, nondescript factory in the outskirts of town – drive through the factory entrance, or take the bus to San Sisto (€1.50, 25 minutes).

over this historic house near the Università per Stranieri. There are just four spacious, great-value rooms – three doubles and one single – but each has been lovingly dressed in bright, cheery colours and features artistic renditions of musicians and actors. Breakfast is a sweet affair playing up Italian produce.

Hotel Signa HOTEL €
(☑ 075 572 23 93; www.hotelsigna.it; Via del Grillo 9; s €34-64, d €49-109, tr €59-119, q €69-159; ✳☜) Slip down an alley off Corso Cavour to reach Signa, one of Perugia's best budget picks. The petite rooms are simple, bright and well kept, and many have balconies with cracking views of the city and countryside. Rooms at the cheaper end of the scale forgo minibars and air-con. The friendly owner, Mario, hands out maps and tips freely. Breakfast costs an extra €7.

Hotel Fortuna HISTORIC HOTEL €€
(☑ 075 573 50 40; www.hotelfortunaperugia.com; Via Luigi Bonazzi 19; s €69-88, d €77-147, tr €134-181, q €173-218; ✳@☜) Behind a weathered stone facade draped in ivy, this historic three-star hotel hides 14th-century walls and secrets like its former past as a love motel. Past the welcoming front desk, you'll find original frescoes on the 3rd floor, Murano chandeliers in the breakfast room and classic decor that instils a sense of place in its 52 guest rooms.

★ **Castello di Monterone** HOTEL €€€

(☑ 075 572 42 14; www.castellomonterone.com; Strada Montevile 3; r €110-250; P ✳ ☏ ☰) This fairy-tale castle comes with all the turreted, ivy-clad, vaulted trappings you would imagine. Its 18 individually designed rooms have been finished to great effect, with low timber-beamed ceilings, exposed stone, custom wood furniture, handmade wrought-iron beds, antiques and the odd Etruscan and medieval artefact. Superior rooms come with views over the rolling countryside to Perugia's centre, 3km away.

★ **Locanda della Posta** BOUTIQUE HOTEL €€€

(☑ 075 572 89 25; www.locandadellapostahotel. it; Corso Vannucci 97; d €130-280, ste €200-500; ✳ @ ☏) Perugia's oldest hotel dates from 1786, but a complete makeover has turned it into one of the city's sleekest digs. Stunning 18th-century frescoes juxtapose with glistening marble flooring, contemporary art and a minimalist grey-and-white colour scheme. None of the 17 rooms are the same, but modish elements like hardwood flooring and textured shower walls feature in several.

✕ Eating

★ **Antica Salumeria**
Granieri Amato SANDWICHES €

(Piazza Matteotti; sandwiches €3-4.50, with glass of wine €5; ☉ 11am-8pm Mon-Sat, hours vary Sun) Sitting inconspicuously in a no-fanfare grey kiosk on Piazza Matteotti is this Perugian street-food institution. Its speciality is succulent *porchetta* (herbed roast pork) piled high and served – crispy skin and all – in a crusty bread roll for €4.50. Get in line and *buon appetito*!

Sandri CAFE €

(www.sandridal1860.it; Corso Vannucci 32; pastries from €1.50; ☉ 7.30am-9pm) Perugia's most celebrated cafe, this city institution has been serving coffee and cake since 1860. Its delicately frescoed, chandelier-lit interior provides the perfect backdrop for exquisite-looking pastries, chocolates and cakes, enticingly presented in floor-to-ceiling cabinets. Specialities include delicate pink macarons (€7.50 for 10) and decadent chocolate postcards (€8.50).

★ **L'Officina** UMBRIAN €€

(☑ 075 572 16 99; www.l-officina.net; Borgo XX Giugno 56; meals €30-35, 6-course tasting menus €25-40; ☉ 12.30-3.30pm & 6.30-midnight Mon-Sat; ☏) Gourmet food at everyday prices

make L'Officina one of Perugia's hottest dining tickets. Passionate owner Yannis shares his 30 years of Italian food and wine experience at this, his meandering restaurant set inside a former factory. The vibe is casual and the food modern and exciting with seasonally driven menus (including a vegetarian tasting menu) and inventive, artfully presented dishes.

★ **La Taverna** RISTORANTE €€

(☑ 075 572 41 28; www.ristorantelataverna.com; Via delle Streghe 8; meals €35-40; ☉ 12.30-2.30pm & 7.30-10.30pm; ☏) La Taverna consistently wins the praise of local foodies. Brick vaults and candlelit tables create an intimate backdrop for Chef Claudio Brugolossi's seasonal dishes, from homemade ravioli with black truffles to a bevy of diverse *secondi* (expertly grilled steaks, lamb stew with flat bread, chicken curry), all paired with superb wines.

★ **Osteria a Priori** UMBRIAN €€

(☑ 075 572 70 98; www.osteriaapriori.it; Via dei Priori 39; meals €30-35; ☉ 12.30-2.30pm & 7.30-10pm Mon-Sat; ☏) ✒ Located above an *enoteca* (wine bar/shop), this fashionable *osteria* (tavern) specialises in local wines and fresh regional cuisine prepared with seasonal ingredients. Umbrian cheeses and cured meats feature alongside black truffles, Chianina beef and autumnal mushrooms. Reservations recommended.

Osteria i Birbi OSTERIA €€

(☑ 075 988 90 41; www.osteriaibirbi.com; Via Campo di Battaglia 10-14; meals €35; ☉ 7.30-10.30pm Thu-Tue, plus 12.30-2.30pm Fri-Sun) A romantic setting in a quiet corner of the medieval centre goes hand in hand with creative Italian cuisine at this cosy *osteria*. Run by husband-and-wife team Luca and Amanda, it serves an imaginative menu that sets classic regional hits such as pasta with Norcia black truffles alongside dishes centred on *baccalà* (cod) and Iberian ham.

Ristorante Altromondo UMBRIAN €€

(☑ 075 572 61 57; https://ristorante-perugia-altro mondo.business.site; Via Caporali 11; meals €30-35; ☉ noon-3pm & 7-10pm Mon-Sat) Visiting university professors join locals and out-of-towners at this handsome brick-vaulted restaurant. Meals get off to a cracking start with a complimentary taster of *fagioli* (beans) before *antipasti* of cured meats, crisp fried zucchini flowers and cheesy focaccia set you up for the well-executed grilled meats.

🍷 Drinking & Nightlife

⭐ Pinturicchio Cafe & Kitchen   CAFE
(🖉 340 4610715; www.pinturicchiocafe.com; Via Pinturicchio 26; ⏰8am-midnight Mon, to 1.30am Tue-Fri, 3pm-1.30am Sat, 11am-3pm Sun) This cool hang-out draws a steady stream of students and trendy urbanites throughout the day, for coffee and bagels at breakfast, light lunches, craft beers on tap and wines by the glass. Mismatched furniture and lived-in sofas create a relaxed living-room vibe, while regular events ensure there's always something going on.

⭐ Kundera   BAR
(🖉 075 372 54 35; www.facebook.com/Kundera-CaffeBistrot; Via Oberdan 23; ⏰6.30pm-11pm Tue-Thu & Sun, to midnight Fri, to 1am Sat; 🛜) Follow the lead of students and clued-up locals by searching out this artsy little backstreet bar for an early evening *aperitivo*. Until 9.30pm you can pair a drink (including a fine €4.50 spritz) with your choice of tasty appetiser platters (up to €5) – you can even ask for vegetarian and gluten-free options. Snag a table on the terrace when it's warm.

Elfo Pub   CRAFT BEER
(www.facebook.com/elfopubperugia; Via Sant'Agata 20; pints from €5; ⏰6pm-2am; 🛜) Hophead central in Perugia, this snug pub turned to craft beer a decade ago and has never looked back. Artisanal beer geeks can choose between 10 taps or a 200-strong bottle menu, guided by knowledgeable staff who will enthusiastically take you through the lists of international guest brews. Birra Perugia and Assisi's Birra dell'Eremo often feature.

Bottega del Vino   WINE BAR
(🖉 075 571 61 81; www.labottegadelvino.net; Via del Sole 1; wine by the glass from €3.50; ⏰noon-3pm & 7pm-midnight, closed Sun & Mon lunch; 🛜) A classic stone building, live jazz (on Wednesday evenings) and hundreds of wine bottles lining its woody, art-clad interior create a cosy, convivial air at this central bar. You can taste dozens of Umbrian wines, which you can purchase with the help of sommelier-like experts.

Caffè Morlacchi   CAFE
(🖉 075 850 11 30; www.facebook.com/caffemorlacchi; Piazza Morlacchi 6/8; ⏰7am-10pm Mon, to midnight Tue-Sat, from 3pm Sun; 🛜) Students, professors and all comers flock to this chandeliered, blissfully relaxed hang-out for coffee by day and cocktails to the backbeat of DJ tunes by night.

☆ Entertainment

Some of the venues and clubs in the outskirts of town run a shuttle bus to/from the Università per Stranieri, starting around 11pm. Students hand out flyers on Corso Vannucci, so check with them or ask at the steps. Most places get going around midnight, so it's worth remembering that the *scale mobili* (escalators) stop running at 2am.

Marla   LIVE MUSIC
(🖉 347 1878420; www.facebook.com/marla.perugia; Via Bartolo 9; ⏰8pm-1.30am Tue-Sat; 🛜) A favourite among a 30s and 40s alternative crowd, this bohemian haunt hosts acts from across the musical spectrum (jazz, rock, soul, reggae, electronic) as well as art installations and mismatched vintage furniture. DJs spin house, techno and/or disco on Saturdays. The music generally gets going around 10.30pm to 11pm.

🛍 Shopping

Giuditta Brozzetti   ARTS & CRAFTS
(🖉 075 4 02 36; www.brozzetti.com; Via Tiberio Berardi 5; ⏰by appt 8.30am-12.30pm & 3-6pm Mon-Fri) Inside a 13th-century Franciscan church, fourth-generation weaver Marta Cucchia is one of the few artisans still working with 19th-century Jacquard looms. Her extraordinary and fascinating workshop resurrects previously lost medieval and Renaissance textile styles and patterns – some seen in Leonardo da Vinci's *The Last Supper* – weaving them into everything from bookmarks and cushions to table runners and custom-made tablecloths.

Marta also leads guided group tours of the workshop, available in English on request.

Augusta Perusia
Cioccolato e Gelateria   CHOCOLATE
(🖉 075 573 45 77; www.cioccolatoaugustaperusia.it; Via Pinturicchio 2; per 100g €6; ⏰10.30am-8pm; ♿) Founded in 2000 by Giacomo Mangano, an expert chocolatier who learned his craft at Perugina (p625), Augusta Perusia is a renowned chocolate maker. This, the company's original shop, is a magical showroom for all sorts of chocolatey delights, from slabs of rich dark choc spiked with zesty candied orange to melt-in-your-mouth pralines and creamy spreads.

ℹ Information

Ospedale S. Maria della Misericordia (🖉 075 57 81; www.ospedale.perugia.it; Piazza Menghini 1, Località Sant'Andrea delle Fratte; ⏰24hr)

Perugia's main hospital, 7km southwest of the city centre.

Tourist Office (☑ 075 573 64 58; http://turismo.comune.perugia.it; Piazza Matteotti 18; ☉ 9am-6pm) Housed in the 14th-century Loggia dei Lanari, Perugia's main tourist office has stacks of info on the city, including maps (€0.50) and guides (€2.50), and can provide up-to-date bus and train timetables.

❶ Getting There & Away

AIR

Umbria International Airport San Francesco d'Assisi (☑ 075 59 21 41; www.airport.umbria.it; Via dell'Aeroporto, Sant'Egidio), 12km east of the city, is served by Ryanair flights to/from London, Brussels, Catania and Malta; and Albawings and Blu-Express flights to/from Tirana.

BUS

Busitalia (☑ 075 963 76 37; www.fsbusitalia.it) operates most intercity buses from Perugia. Services depart from the **Autostazione Piazza Partigiani** (Piazza Partigiani; ☉ ticket office 6.15am-8pm Mon-Sat, 7.30am-7.30pm Sun) to the south of the historic centre – take the *scale mobili* (escalators) through the Rocca Paolina to/from Piazza Italia.

Rome buses are operated by **Sulga** (☑ 800 099661; www.sulga.eu; Piazza Partigiani). These run from the Autostazione to Rome's Tiburtina bus station (€17, 2½ hours, five daily Monday to Saturday, four on Sundays) and Terminal 3 at Rome's Fiumicino airport (€22, 3¼ hours, four daily Monday to Saturday, two on Sundays).

Buses to Florence are run by **Flixbus** (www.flixbus.it) and depart from the train station and Piazzale Umbria Jazz.

Services go to the following destinations (with additional services possible in summer):

Destination	Fare (€)	Duration	Frequency (daily)
Assisi	4.20	45min	6
Castiglione del Lago	6.10	1¼hr	7
Deruta	3.60	30min	up to 8
Florence	9-16	1¾-2½hr	5-11
Gubbio	5.50	1¼hr	up to 10
Todi	6.30	1½hr	7
Torgiano	2.50	30min	4

CAR & MOTORCYCLE

To reach Perugia from Rome, leave the A1 at the Orte exit and follow signs for Terni. Once there, take the SS3bis/E45 for Perugia. From the north, exit the A1 at Valdichiana and take

dual-carriageway RA6 *(raccordo autostradale)*. To the east of Perugia, the SS75 connects the city with Assisi.

Rental companies have offices at the airport and train station.

TRAIN

In the southwest of town, Perugia's main **train station** (Perugia Fontivegge; ☑ 075 963 78 91; Piazza Vittorio Veneto) has trains to destinations across Umbria and Tuscany, and down to Rome. Note, however, that most services to Orvieto and Rome involve a change, as do some trains to Arezzo and Florence.

Destination	Fare (€)	Duration	Frequency
Arezzo	7.55-13	1hr	10 daily
Assisi	2.70	25min	hourly
Florence	14.65-21.25	2-2½hr	17 daily
Fossato di Vico-Gubbio	7.55-11	1hr	7 daily
Orvieto	8.05-14.25	1½-2hr	hourly
Rome	12.10-27.75	2¼-3½hr	at least hourly
Spello	3.50	40min	hourly

❶ Getting Around

If you're not carrying too much luggage, the simplest way of getting from Perugia's intercity bus station to the town centre is by hopping aboard the *scale mobili* (escalator) linking Piazza Partigiani with **Piazza Italia** (www.fsbusitalia.it; ☉ 6.15am-1.45pm). Alternatively, you can catch bus TS to the centre (€1.50). There are also *scale mobili* from the car park at **Piazzale della Cupa** (www.fsbusitalia.it; ☉ 6.45am-1.45am) up to Via dei Priori.

TO/FROM THE AIRPORT

The easiest way from the airport to Perugia city centre is on the **Airbus** (☑ 075 500 96 41; www.acap.perugia.it; Piazza Italia; one way/return €8/14), which runs up to Piazza Italia via the train station. Departure times vary depending on flight schedules, but you'll find an updated timetable on the website (in the news section). Buy tickets on board.

A taxi from the airport to the city centre costs €30. Drive time is approximately 25 minutes.

BUS

It's a steep 1.5km climb from the train station, so a bus is highly recommended (and essential for those with luggage). The TS bus takes you to Piazza Italia. Tickets for the 15-minute ride cost €1.50 from the train-station kiosk or €2 on board. Validate your ticket on board to avoid a fine. A 10-ticket pass costs €12.90.

UMBRIAN CUISINE

Umbrian cuisine has long lived under the international food radar but the region produces some of Italy's finest produce, and its cured meats and truffles are celebrated across the country.

For a taste, look out for these specialities on your travels:

Cinghiale Richly gamey but tender, wild boar is often served over pasta or stewed in sauce.

Farro Emmer wheat still graces tables today. Classic *zuppa di farro* is rich, nutty and distinctly Umbrian, perfect for a warm lunch on a cold, misty day in the hills.

Lenticchie These small, thin lentils from Castelluccio are at their best in a thick rustic soup drizzled with virgin olive oil.

Strangozzi Also known as *stringozzi*, this flat spaghetti-like pasta is often served with tomato sauce, black truffles or porcini mushrooms.

Tartufi neri Umbrian black truffles give menus an earthy edge, especially in the autumn harvest months.

CAR & MOTORCYCLE
Perugia is notoriously difficult to navigate and much of the historic centre is off-limits to unauthorised traffic. Your best bet is to leave your car in one of the big, signposted car parks (€1.10 to €1.90 per hour; open 24 hours) – Piazza Partigiani and the Mercato Coperto are the most convenient.

MINIMETRÒ
The **Minimetrò** (www.minimetrospa.it; ⊙7am-9.20pm Mon-Sat, 9am-9pm Sun) is a system of single-car people-movers that runs from the train stationup to Pincetto just off Piazza Matteotti in the historic centre. Tickets cost €1.50. From the train station, facing the tracks, head right up a long platform.

TAXI
Call **Radio Taxi Perugia** (☏075 500 48 88; www.perugiataxi.it; ⊙24hrs) to arrange a pickup. A ride from the city centre to the main train station will cost about €10 to €15. Tack on €1 for each suitcase.

Lago Trasimeno

A splash of inky blue on the hilly landscape, Lago Trasimeno is where Umbria spills over into Tuscany. Italy's fourth-largest lake is a prime spot if you want to tiptoe off the well-trodden trail and slip into the languid rhythm of lake life. All around the 128-sq-km lake, olive groves, woods of oak and cypress trees, vines and sunflower fields frame castle-topped medieval towns, such as Castiglione del Lago and Passignano, draped along its shores like a daisy chain.

But while the scenery is bucolic and the atmosphere slow, at least outside peak summer months, the area has a turbulent past and it was here that Hannibal destroyed a Roman army in 217 BC.

Castiglione del Lago on the lake's western flank is the area's main centre.

⊙ Sights

Isola Polvese   ISLAND
This island, accessible by ferry from San Feliciano, is a delight – not so much for its sights, of which there aren't many, but for its glorious unspoiled countryside and soothing silence. From the ferry docking area, where the Centro di Educazione Ambientale di Isola Polvese (www.polvese.it) has its base and runs environmental workshops and group tours, several paths lead across the island, providing easy-going walking and fine views.

Isola Maggiore   ISLAND
The only one of Lago Trasimeno's islands with a permanent, albeit tiny, population, Isola Maggiore was reputedly a favourite with St Francis, who spent time here in 1211. Once you've wandered around its small fishing village, you can visit the hilltop Chiesa di San Michele Arcangelo, which contains a crucifixion painted by Bartolomeo Caporali dating from around 1460.

Palazzo della Corgna   PALACE
(☏075 95 10 99; www.palazzodellacorgna.it; Piazza Gramsci, Castiglione del Lago; adult/reduced incl Rocca del Leone €9/3; ⊙9.30am-7pm, shorter hours winter) Crowning Castiglione del Lago's

hilltop centre, this 16th-century ducal palace boasts a series of impressive frescoes by Giovanni Antonio Pandolfi Mealli and Salvio Savini. The admission ticket also covers entry into the adjacent **Rocca del Leone**, the forbidding fortress that dominates Castiglione's skyline. Dating from the 13th century, this pentagonal-shaped structure is a stellar example of medieval military architecture.

🏃 Activities

Lago Trasimeno is well set up for outdoor escapades. Horse riding is available at centres around the area, including the agriturismo **Le Case Rosse di Montebuono** (☑ 075 528 85 56; www.lecaserosse.com; Via Case Sparse di Monte Buono 15, Magione; 1hr with instructor €25, 2hr ride €50), or you can take to waymarked trails on foot or by bike – pick up a bike at **Cicli Valentini** (☑ 075 95 16 63; www.ciclivalentini.it; Via Firenze 68b, Castiglione del Lago; per half-day/day/week €9/12/59; ⊙ 9am-1pm & 3.30-8pm Mon-Sat) in Castiglione del Lago. The lake also offers swimming, sailing and kayaking.

🛏 Sleeping

★ **Fattoria Il Poggio**   HOSTEL €
(☑ 075 965 95 50; www.fattoriaisolapolvese.com; Isola Polvese; dm/d/q/apt €25/70/100/120, meals per adult/child €18/15; ⊙ Mar-Oct; @ 🛜) 🍴 A little corner of Eden, this eco-minded hostel sits in glorious isolation on the unspoiled Isola Polvese. It's housed in a converted farmstead set amid olive groves and lush greenery and offers basic, spick-and-span rooms, sloping gardens and gorgeous lake views. Super-hospitable owners Michele and Paola also serve up wholesome meals prepared with organic produce and home-grown herbs.

La Casa sul Lago   HOSTEL €
(☑ 075 840 00 42; www.lacasasullago.com; Via del Popolo 8, Torricella di Magione; dm €15-18, s €30-50, d €40-80, meals €15; 🅿 @ 🛜 ⛱) Housed in a big ivy-clad building about 50m from the lakeshore, this top hostel scores across the board. It has beds in dorms and attractive hotel-quality rooms (some with four-poster beds and parquet floors), and guests have access to every amenity known to hostel-kind: bicycles, games, home-cooked meals, a garden with hammocks and even an outdoor swimming pool.

Il Torrione   B&B €
(☑ 075 95 32 36; www.iltorrionetrasimeno.com; Via delle Mura 4, Castiglione del Lago; s €60, d €80-100, q €120, apt €80-120; ❄ 🛜) Romance abounds at this artistically minded retreat in Castiglione del Lago's historic centre. Housed in a 16th-century tower, its six rooms and two mini-apartments are cosy and rustically furnished with terracotta floors and colourful artworks. Best of all is the panoramic flower-filled garden on top of Castiglione's medieval walls, which commands grandstand views over the placid lake below.

Albergo La Torre   HOTEL €
(☑ 075 95 16 66; www.latorretrasimeno.com; Via Vittorio Emanuele 50, Castiglione del Lago; s €40-80, d €45-105, tr €70-135, q €80-150; ❄ 🛜) Handily situated on the main drag through Castiglione's historic centre, La Torre extends a warm family welcome. The spotless, old-style rooms, decorated in florals and pastel hues, are spacious and come with comfortable beds. Breakfast costs €7.50 extra.

STRADA DEL VINO COLLI DEL TRASIMENO

Vines and olives thrive in the microclimate of Lago Trasimeno, which yields some top-quality DOC (*Denominazione di origine controllata*) red and white wines, as well as gold-green DOP (*Denominazione d'origine protetta*) olive oils. You can pick up a bottle anywhere, but you'll get more out of a tasting at one of the *cantine* (cellars) that open their doors to visitors.

The Wine Route of the Trasimeno Hills, the **Strada del Vino Colli del Trasimeno** (☑ 333 9854593; www.stradadelvinotrasimeno.it; Passignano; ⊙ 10am-12.30pm & 3-6pm Thu-Sun), takes in wineries offering tastings (you almost always need to call ahead), restaurants and *agriturismi* (farm stays), where you can sleep off the overindulgence.

For details of participating wineries and tasting tours (from €60 per person) see the website or pop into the Strada's info centre at Piazza Trento e Trieste 6 in Passignano.

🍴 Eating

Restaurants line Lago Trasimeno, with the highest concentration on Via Vittorio Emanuele in Castiglione del Lago's hilltop centre. Specialities of the Trasimeno area include *fagiolina* (little white beans), carp in *porchetta* (cooked in a wood oven with garlic, fennel and herbs) and *tegamaccio*, a kind of soupy stew of local fish cooked in olive oil, white wine and herbs.

⭐ **DivinPeccato**   RISTORANTE **€€**
(📞 075 528 02 34; www.ristorantedivinpeccato. com; Strada Pievaiola 246, Capanne; meals €35; ⏰ 7.30-10pm Tue-Sun, plus 12.30-2pm Sun; 🐾) Chef Nicola works culinary magic at this wonderful roadside restaurant, a favourite for wedding receptions and special occasions some 27km southeast of Castiglione del Lago. The menu fizzes with seasonal oomph, featuring fresh springtime combos such as *gnocchi con fave e asparagi* (with broad beans and asparagus) and fantastic seafood creations.

Ristorante Monna Lisa   UMBRIAN **€€**
(📞 075 95 10 71; www.facebook.com/ristorante monnalisa; Via del Forte 2, Castiglione del Lago; meals €30-40; ⏰ 12.30-2.30pm & 7.30-10.30pm Thu-Tue; 🐾) You can imagine Mona Lisa giving a wry smile of approval to the food served at this intimate, art-strewn restaurant in the heart of town. You, too, will be smiling about specialities like *tegamaccio*, a rustic soup of lake fish, and *baci di Giuda*, handmade pockets of pasta stuffed with mint-infused burrata and served on a cream of *pecorino* and saffron.

🍷 Drinking & Nightlife

Cafes and wine bars line Via Vittorio Emanuele (considered Lago Trasimeno's main drag) in Castiglione del Lago. Be sure to try *vino* from the town's best winery, **Poggio Bertaio** (red fans will love their Stucchio and Cimbolo Sangioveses), and sample Lake, a Belgian-style blonde ale brewed with *fagiolina* (little white beans).

⭐ **L'Angolo del Buon Gustaio**   WINE BAR
(📞 329 3168456; www.angolodelbuongustaio.com; Via Vittorio Emanuele 40, Castiglione del Lago; wines by the glass from €4; ⏰ 8am-8.30pm Wed-Mon, longer hours summer; 🐾) This is the most consistently packed spot on Castiglione del Lago's main drag, and for good reason. Ricardo, armed with a wealth of wine knowledge, assembles epic *taglieri* (cheese and charcuterie platters; €8 to €12) and expertly pairs them with local wines like Poggio Beltraio. Definitely reserve ahead.

ℹ️ Information

Tourist Office (📞 075 965 82 92; www.lago trasimeno.net; Piazza Gramsci 1, Castiglione del Lago; ⏰ 8.30am-1pm & 3.30-7pm Mon-Fri, 9.30am-7pm Sat & Sun) Housed in Palazzo della Corgna – on the ground floor from Monday morning to Friday lunchtime, and on the 1st floor from Friday afternoon to Sunday – it can advise on accommodation and activities in the area as well as provide maps.

ℹ️ Getting There & Around

BUS

Busitalia (📞 075 963 76 37; www.fsbusitalia.it) Bus E017 links Perugia with Passignano (€4.20, one hour, four daily), while the E018 runs to Castiglione del Lago (€6.10, 1¼ hours, seven daily). Services are increased during school term time.

CAR & MOTORCYCLE

Two major highways skirt Lago Trasimeno: the SR71, which runs to Castiglione del Lago from Arezzo in the north and Chiusi in the southwest; and the RA6 *(raccordo autostradale)* Bettolle–Perugia, which follows the north end of the lake en route from the A1 autostrada to Perugia.

FERRY

Busitalia (www.fsbusitalia.it) ferries serve Isola Maggiore and Isola Polvese from late March to late September. The frequencies quoted here are for high season, from 7 July to 1 September.

For Isola Polvese, take the **ferry** (📞 075 963 77 02; www.fsbusitalia.it) from San Feliciano (€6 return, 10 minutes, 10 daily).

For Isola Maggiore, there are boats from Tuoro (€6.70 return, 10 minutes, 18 daily), Castiglione del Lago (€8.80 return, 30 minutes, eight daily) and Passignano (€8 return, 25 minutes, 13 daily).

Ferries stop running around 7pm.

TRAIN

Direct trains run roughly hourly from Perugia to Passignano (€3.50, 30 minutes). Services from Perugia to Castiglione del Lago (€5, 65 minutes to 1½ hours, hourly) require a change at Terontola-Cortona.

Gubbio

POP 31,700

Angular, sober and imposing, Gubbio appears like something out of medieval fresco. Tightly packed grey buildings cluster

UMBRIA & LE MARCHE GUBBIO

Gubbio

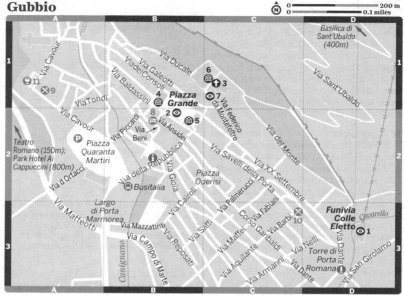

together on the steep slopes of Monte Ingino in a picturesque jumble of tiled roofs, Gothic towers and 14th-century turrets. There are unforgettable views from Piazza Grande, the town's starkly beautiful central square, and from the open-air *funivia* (cable car) that glides high above the higgledy-piggledy rooftops.

⊙ Sights

★ Piazza Grande   PIAZZA

This panoramic piazza, the result of an ambitious 14th-century urban development plan, is medieval Gubbio's showpiece square. Commanding huge valley views, it's book-ended by two of the town's signature buildings: **Palazzo dei Consoli** on its western flank and, on the eastern side, **Palazzo del Podestà**.

Museo Civico   MUSEUM

(☑ 075 927 42 98; www.palazzodeiconsoli.it; Palazzo dei Consoli, Piazza Grande; adult/reduced €10/5; ⊙10am-1pm & 3-6pm Mon-Fri, 10am-6pm Sat & Sun, shorter hours winter) Housed in Palazzo dei Consoli, this museum is home to the celebrated Iguvine Tables (also known as the Eugubian Tables or Tablets), seven bronze tablets inscribed with ancient text. Discovered in 1444 and dated to between 300 BC and 100 BC, these are considered the finest

existing samples of the ancient Umbrian language. Further archaeological finds are also on show alongside a rich coin collection.

Upstairs is a picture and ceramics gallery featuring works from the medieval Gubbian school.

Via Federico da Montefeltro   STREET

Snaking up to the top of town, Via Federico da Montefeltro is a steep, narrow lane that leads to three of Gubbio's main historic buildings: the 12th-century **Museo Diocesano** (☑ 075 922 09 04; www.museogubbio.it; Via Federico da Montefeltro 3; adult/reduced €6/3; ⊙10am-6pm Tue-Sun summer, 10.30am-5pm Thu-Sun winter), the 13th-century cathedral and the Renaissance Palazzo Ducale.

Palazzo Ducale   MUSEUM

(☑ 075 927 58 72; www.polomusealeumbria.beni culturali.it; Via Federico da Montefeltro 2; adult/reduced €5/2.50; ⊙1-7pm Mon, 8.30am-7.30pm Tue-Sun) The 15th-century Palazzo Ducale was built by the Duke of Montefeltro's family as a scaled-down version of their palatial residence in Urbino. Its walls hide an impressive Renaissance courtyard, built over an earlier medieval piazza, and excavated vestiges of pre-existing medieval buildings. Inside, works by 13th- to 18th-century Umbrian artists hang in the airy halls.

Gubbio

Cattedrale di Gubbio　　　　CATHEDRAL
(Via Federico da Montefeltro; donations welcome;
⊙10am-5pm summer, to 4pm winter) Gubbio's
fading pink 13th-century cathedral boasts
an atmospheric interior, capped by unadorned ribbed arches and lit by sunlight
entering through a 12th-century stained-
glass window. Also of note are several baroque frescoes by Antonio Gherardi.

★Funivia Colle Eletto　　　　CABLE CAR
(☎075 927 38 81; www.funiviagubbio.it; Via San Girolamo; adult/reduced one way €4/3, return €6/4;
⊙9am-8pm daily Jul-Aug, shorter hours rest of
year) Although the Basilica di Sant'Ubaldo is
a perfectly lovely church, the real adventure
is getting there on the *funivia*. The word
funivia suggests an enclosed cable car,
but this is more like a glorified ski lift that
whisks you up the steep hillside in a hanging
metal basket.

Basilica di Sant'Ubaldo　　　　BASILICA
(Via Monte Ingino 5; ⊙basilica 8am-6pm, museum 10am-12.30pm & 2.30-5.30pm Mon-Fri, 10am-
12.30pm & 3-6pm Sat & Sun) FREE Perched high
on Monte Ingino, and accessible by the *funivia* or a steep 30-minute walk from Palazzo
Ducale, this landmark basilica has housed
the body of Sant'Ubaldo, the town's patron
saint, since the late 12th century – it's in a
glass coffin above the altar. The basilica also
contains the three massive statues *(ceri)* that
are carried through town during the annual
Corsa dei Ceri.

🎉 Festivals & Events

★Corsa dei Ceri　　　　CULTURAL
(www.ceri.it) Gubbio's headline festival culminates in the 'Corsa dei Ceri', a centuries-old
race held each 15 May to celebrate the town's
patron saint, Sant'Ubaldo. It involves three
teams, each carrying a *cero* (a massive
wooden pillar weighing 300kg to 400kg)
bearing the statue of a saint (Sant'Ubaldo, St
George and St Antony), racing through the
city's medieval streets.

Palio della Balestra　　　　CULTURAL
On the last Sunday in May, Gubbio gets
out its medieval crossbows for its annual
archery competition with historic rival Sansepolcro. The festival, which features much
costumed pageantry and flag waving, is kept
alive throughout the year in the form of
scary-looking crossbow paraphernalia in the
tourist shops.

🛏 Sleeping

Hotel Gattapone　　　　HOTEL €€
(☎075 927 24 89; www.hotelgattapone.net; Via
Beni 11; s €54-95, d €60-140; ❋🤶) A smiling
welcome, comfortable, country-style rooms
and an excellent location – handy for both
the car park on Piazza Quaranta Martiri and
the historic centre – combine to winning effect at this friendly three-star. It's particularly good value in low season.

Park Hotel Ai Cappuccini　　　　HOTEL €€€
(☎075 92 34; www.parkhotelaicappuccini.it; Via
Tifernate; s €130-190, d €160-280, meals €40-50;
P ❋ 🤶 ☷) Silence hangs like a monk's habit over this luxurious four-star, exquisitely
housed in a 17th-century monastery. Its
rooms, soberly styled with parquet and subdued colours, are divided between the original monastery and a larger modern wing.
Facilities are excellent, including a fine restaurant serving Mediterranean cuisine, an
indoor pool and spa, and beautiful gardens.

> ### ⓘ GUBBIO TURISTCARD
> The tourist office (p634) sells the
> good-value **Turisticard**, which comes
> in two versions. A €5 version provides
> an audio guide (in Italian or English), a
> 50% reduction on museum entry and
> discounts on the funivia and in partic-
> ipating shops and restaurants. For €3,
> you get the same as above minus the
> audio guide.

✕ Eating & Drinking

Don't miss *crescia,* Gubbio's version of Umbria's classic *torta al testo* (a thick and savoury stuffed flatbread), and *friccò,* a hearty stew-like concoction of chicken, rabbit and lamb flavoured with garlic, rosemary and white wine. *Brustengo,* a fried bread served with local prosciutto, is another local speciality.

La Cresceria   UMBRIAN €

(✆ 075 375 15 09; www.lacresceria.net; Via Cavour 23; meals €15; ⊙ noon-3pm & 7-11pm Wed-Mon; 🛜) Gubbio's *crescia* (flat bread) is the star turn at this casual, and often busy, *centro storico* restaurant. Stuffed with all manner of locally sourced goodies (prosciutto, *porchetta,* pancetta, *scamorza* cheese), they go perfectly with cool craft beer, here blissfully served in proper glass pint mugs.

Picchio Verde   UMBRIAN €

(✆ 075 375 51 80; www.ristorantepicchioverde.com; Via Savelli della Porta 65; meals €15-30; ⊙ 12.30-2.30pm & 7.30-9.30pm Wed-Mon) Huddled away in the upper part of the old town, this inviting trattoria attracts a faithful local following for its cosy vaulted interior, authentic food and modest prices. Homemade pasta (try the *strozzapreti* with mushrooms) seg-

ues smoothly into mains of perfectly chargrilled meats.

★ Don Navarro   CRAFT BEER

(✆ 075 927 14 88; www.facebook.com/aldon sepuede; Piazza Bosone 2; ⊙ 11am-1am Tue-Fri, to 2am Sat, to midnight Sun; 🛜) With its industrial grey decor and youthful energy, this bar provides a burst of modernity on medieval Piazza Bosone. It's named after a legendary rum kingpin, although it's the craft beer that stars here and there's a surprisingly eclectic mix of international and Italian brews. A generous evening aperitif adds to the appeal.

ⓘ Information

Tourist Office (✆ 075 922 06 93; www. comune.gubbio.pg.it; Via della Repubblica 15; ⊙ 9am-1pm & 2-6pm) Sells the Turisticard (p633) and rents out multilingual audio guides (€3).

ⓘ Getting There & Around

To reach Gubbio by car, take the SR298 from Perugia or the SS76 from Ancona, and follow the signs. In town, there's a 24-hour car park on Piazza Quaranta Martiri at the foot of the historic centre.

Busitalia (✆ 075 963 70 01; www.fsbusitalia. it) services run to Perugia (€5.50, 1¼ hours, up to 10 daily Monday to Saturday) from Piazza Quaranta Martiri. Services drop off considerably on Sundays. Buy your tickets at the newsstand on the square.

Gubbio is gloriously walkable, but if you aren't into climbing the steep streets, there are a few public elevators to whisk you up to important locations like Piazza Grande – from **Via Baldassini** (⊙ 9am-6.30pm) – and Palazzo Ducale, from **Via XX Settembre** (⊙ 9am-6.20pm).

OFF THE BEATEN TRACK

RURAL HIDEAWAY

Everything else seems a world away as you settle into **La Cuccagna** (✆ 348 7792330; www.lacuccagna.com; Frazione Santa Cristina 22; s €80-150, d €100-150; 🅿🛜🏊), a charming farm stay high in the hills between Gubbio and Perugia. Surrounded by wooded slopes and olive groves, Sarah and Salvatore's country house is pin-drop peaceful and big on rustic charm with its timber beams and stone walls. Outside, you can bask in soothing views from the garden and infinity pool.

Breakfasts feature lovely organic produce and your super-helpful hosts do everything in their power to ensure you have an enjoyable stay, offering everything from pizza nights to pasta classes and seasonal olive-picking holidays.

Note there's a minimum three-night stay.

Assisi

POP 28,400

With the plains spreading picturesquely below and Monte Subasio rearing steep and wooded above, the mere sight of Assisi in the rosy glow of dusk is enough to send pilgrims' souls spiralling to heaven. It's at this hour, when the day trippers have left and the town is shrouded in saintly silence, that the true spirit of St Francis of Assisi, born here in 1181, can be felt most keenly. However, you don't have to be religious to be struck by Assisi's beauty and enjoy its pristine *centro storico* (historic centre) and Unesco-listed Basilica di San Francesco, home to one of Italy's most celebrated artistic masterpieces.

PARCO REGIONALE DEL MONTE CUCCO

In Umbria's wild northeastern fringes, the **Parco Regionale del Monte Cucco** (📞 075 917 10 46; www.discovermontecucco.it; Costacciaro; ⊗ info point 9am-12.30pm & 3-5pm) `FREE` is a gorgeous swath of wildflower-speckled meadows, gentle slopes brushed with beech, yew and silver fir trees, waterfalls, deep ravines and karst cave systems, all topped by the oft-snowcapped Monte Cucco (1566m). Some 120km of waymarked trails snake through the 105-sq-km park, which offers everything from hiking and mountain biking to hang-gliding and cross-country skiing.

Deep in the heart of the park, the **Grotta Monte Cucco** (📞 351 2827335; www.grotta montecucco.umbria.it; Località Pian di Monte; tours adult/reduced from €14/12; ⊗ info point 9am-1pm daily Jul & Aug, shorter hours spring & autumn) is one of Europe's most spectacular limestone caves, with 30km of galleries reaching depths of 900m. Those up for a challenge can delve into its underground forest of stalactites and stalagmites on a guided two- to three-hour 'discovery' tour. For more expert cavers, there's a longer four- to five-hour 'crossing' tour (adult/reduced €20/18; pre-booking necessary). Times and dates vary – check the website or stop by the Grotta's info point in the village of Costacciaro (Via Valentini 31).

◉ Sights

★ **Basilica di San Francesco** BASILICA
(www.sanfrancescoassisi.org; Piazza Superiore di San Francesco; ⊗ basilica superiore 8.30am-6.50pm, basilica inferiore 6am-6.50pm summer, shorter hours winter) `FREE` Visible for miles around, the Basilica di San Francesco is the crowning glory of Assisi's Unesco-listed historic centre. The 13th-century complex is comprised of two churches: the Gothic **Basilica Superiore** (Upper Church), with its celebrated cycle of Giotto frescoes, and beneath, the older **Basilica Inferiore** (Lower Church) where you'll find works by Cimabue, Pietro Lorenzetti and Simone Martini. Also here, in the **Cripta di San Francesco**, is St Francis' much-venerated tomb.

The Basilica Superiore, which was built immediately after the lower church and consecrated in 1253, is home to one of Italy's most famous works of art – a cycle of 28 frescoes depicting the life of St Francis. Vibrant and colourful, these are generally attributed to a young Giotto, though some art historians contest this, claiming that stylistic discrepancies suggest they were created by several different artists. To view them in the correct sequence, start on the right wall near the altar and work your way around in a clockwise order.

From outside the upper church, stairs lead down to the Romanesque Basilica Inferiore and yet more glorious works of art. Almost every inch of the vaulted, dimly lit church, constructed between 1228 and 1230, is adorned with frescoes by Giotto and fellow Sienese and Florentine masters Cimabue, Lorenzetti and Martini. Among the works to look out for are four vault frescoes (aka *vele* or 'sails') above the main altar. Attributed to Giotto and collaborators, including the mysterious Maestro delle Velle, these depict *The Glory of St Francis* and the *Allegories of the Franciscan Virtues* (poverty, chastity and obedience).

The basilica has its own **information office** (📞 075 819 00 84; ⊗ 9am-5.30pm Mon-Sat winter, to 6pm summer), on the piazza in front of the lower church, where you can pick up an audio guide in 10 languages (€6). Groups of 10 or more can schedule guided tours (in various languages), led by a resident Franciscan friar – check the website or call ahead for booking details.

Foro Romano ROMAN SITE
(Roman Forum; 📞 848 004000; www.coopculture. it; Via Portica 2; adult/reduced €5/3, incl Rocca Maggiore €9/6; ⊗ 10am-7pm summer, to 5pm winter) In among the churches and medieval streets you can still find a few traces of Assisi's Roman past. Extending beneath Piazza del Commune are the remains of the town's ancient forum, discovered during archaeological digs in the 19th century. Above ground, the piazza is dominated by the columned facade of the 1st-century-BC **Tempio di Minerva** (Temple of Minerva; Piazza del Comune 14; ⊗ 7am-7.30pm Mon-Sat, from 8am Sun) `FREE`, now hiding a rather uninspiring 16th-century church.

The Saint of Assisi

That someone could found a successful movement based on peace, love, compassion, charity and humility in any age is remarkable; that Francis Bernardone was able to do it in war-torn 13th-century Umbria was nothing short of a miracle. But then again, in his early years Francis was very much a man of the times – and anything but saintly.

Not-So-Humble Beginnings

Born in Assisi in 1181, the son of a wealthy cloth merchant and a French noblewoman, Francis was a worldly chap: he studied Latin, spoke passable French, had a burning fascination with troubadours and spent his youth carousing. In 1202 Francis joined a military expedition to Perugia and was taken prisoner for nearly a year until his father paid a ransom. Following a spate of ill health, he enlisted in the army of the Count of Brienne and was Puglia-bound in 1205 when a holy vision sparked his spiritual awakening.

Life & Death

Much to the shock, horror and ridicule of his rich, pleasure-seeking friends, Francis decided to renounce all his possessions in order to live a humble, 'primitive' life in imitation of Christ, preaching and helping the poor. He travelled widely around Italy and beyond, allegedly performing miracles such as curing the sick and communicating with animals, spending hermit-like months praying in a cave, and founding monasteries. Before long, his wise words and good deeds had attracted a faithful crowd of followers.

1. Basilica di San Francesco (p635), Assisi **2.** Basilica di San Giovanni in Laterano (p125), Rome **3.** Greccio, Lazio

St Francis asked his followers to bury him in Assisi on a hill known as Colle d'Inferno (Hell Hill), where people were executed at the gallows until the 13th century, to be in keeping with Jesus, who had died on the cross among criminals and outcasts.

Saintly Spots

Today various places claim links with St Francis, including Greccio in Lazio where he supposedly created the first (live) nativity scene in 1223; Bevagna in Umbria where he is said to have preached to the birds; and La Verna in Tuscany where he received the stigmata shortly before his death at the age of 44. He was canonised just two years later, after which the business of 'selling' St Francis began in earnest. Modern Assisi, with its glorious churches and thriving souvenir industry, seems an almost wilfully ironic comment on Francis' ascetic and spiritual values.

TOP ST FRANCIS SITES

Assisi (p634) His home town and the site of his birth and death, his hermitage, his chapel, the first Franciscan monastery and the giant basilica containing his tomb.

Gubbio (p631) Where the saint supposedly brokered a deal between the townsfolk and a man-eating wolf – Francis tamed the wolf with the promise that it would be fed daily.

Rome Francis was given permission by Pope Innocent III to found the Franciscan order at the Basilica di San Giovanni in Laterano (p125).

Assisi

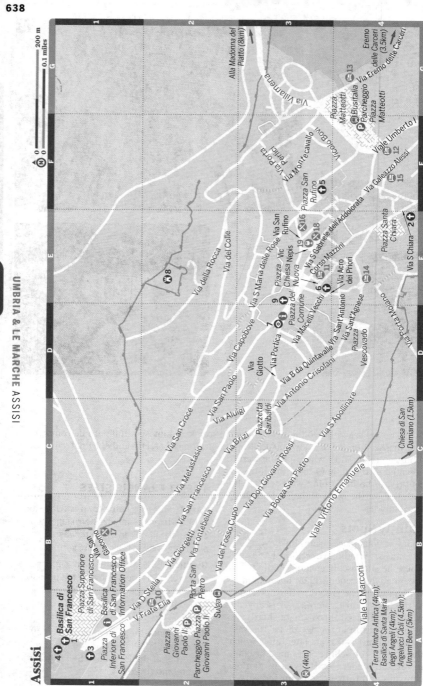

Map labels:

Basilica di San Francesco
1 San Francesco
4
3
Piazza Superiore di San Francesco
Basilica di San Francesco
Information Office
Piazza Inferiore di San Francesco
San Francesco Information Office

Via D Stella
V. Frate Elia 10
Piazza Giovanni Paolo II
Parcheggio Piazza Giovanni Paolo II
Porta San Pietro
Sulga

Via Giotto
17
Via San Giacomo
Via Capobove

Alla Madonna del Piatto (8km)

Eremo delle Carceri (3.5km)
Via Eremo delle Carceri
13
Busitalia
Piazza Matteotti
Parcheggio
Piazza Matteotti
Viale Umberto I
12
Via Galeazzo Alessi
15

Via Villamena
Vicolo Bovi
Via Montecavallo
Via Porta Perlici
Piazza San Rufino
5
16
18
19
Via San Rufino
Via San Gabriele dell'Addolorata
Via S Gabriele dell'Addolorata
Piazza Santa Chiara
Via S Chiara
2

Via della Rocca
Via del Colle
Via S Maria delle Rose
8
Piazza Vic Chiesa Nepis Nuova
6
9
7
Piazza del Comune
Via Macelli Vecchi
11
Corso Mazzini
Via Arco dei Priori
14
Via Sant'Antonio
Via Sant'Agnese
Piazza Vescovado
Via Portica
Via B da Quintavalle
Via Antonio Crisofani
Via S Apollinare
Via Porta Moiano

Via San Paolo
Via San Croce
Via Metastasio
Via San Francesco
Via Giorgetti
Via Fontebella
Via Aluigi
Via Brizi
Piazzetta Garibaldi
Via Don Giovanni Rossi
Via Borgo San Pietro
Viale Vittorio Emanuele
Via del Fosso Cupo

Viale G Marconi

Terra Umbra Antica (4km); Basilica di Santa Maria degli Angeli (4km); Angelucci Cicli (4.5km); Umami Beer (5km)

Chiesa di San Damiano (1.5km)

(4km)

0   200 m
0   0.1 miles

Cattedrale di San Rufino
CHURCH

(Piazza San Rufino; ⊘7.30am-7pm) This 13th-century Romanesque church, remodelled by Galeazzo Alessi in the 16th century, contains the font where St Francis and St Clare were baptised. The square facade, punctuated by three doors and three rose windows, is adorned with grotesque figures and fantastic animals.

Rocca Maggiore
FORT

(⊘848 004000; www.coopculture.it; Via della Rocca; adult/reduced €6/4, incl Foro Romano €9/6; ⊘10am-8pm, shorter hours winter) Looming over Assisi is the 14th-century Rocca Maggiore, an oft-expanded, pillaged and rebuilt fortress that commands inspiring 360-degree views of Perugia to the north and the surrounding valleys below. Walk up winding staircases and claustrophobic passageways to reach the archer slots that served the Assisians as they fought off various medieval invaders.

Eremo delle Carceri
CHRISTIAN SITE

(⊘075 81 23 01; www.eremodellecarceri.it; Via Eremo delle Carceri; ⊘6.30am-7pm Mon-Sat, from 7.30pm Sun summer, to 6pm winter) FREE

Assisi

⊙ **Top Sights**

⊙ **Sights**

⊚ **Sleeping**

⊗ **Eating**

⊙ **Drinking & Nightlife**

Perched on the forested slopes of Monte Subasio, this monastery is set around the caves where St Francis and his followers prayed and contemplated spiritual matters. The *carceri* (isolated places, or 'prisons') are as peaceful today as in St Francis' time, even though they're now surrounded by religious buildings. It's a claustrophobic walk down to Francesco's **Grotta** (cave), where he prayed and slept on a stone bed in his later years.

Chiesa Nuova
CHURCH

(Piazza Chiesa Nuova; ⊘8am-12.30pm & 2.30-6pm) Just southeast of Piazza del Comune, this baroque domed church is a peaceful place for contemplation. It was built by King Philip III of Spain in 1615 over the remains of a house reputed to be the home of St Francis' family. A bronze statue of the saint's parents stands outside.

Basilica di Santa Chiara
BASILICA

(www.assisisantachiara.it; Piazza Santa Chiara; ⊘6.30am-noon & 2-7pm summer, to 6pm winter) Built in a 13th-century Romanesque style, with muscular flying buttresses and a striking pink-and-white striped facade, this church is dedicated to St Clare, a spiritual contemporary of St Francis and founder of the *Sorelle Povere di Santa Chiara* (Order of the Poor Ladies), now known as the Poor Clares. She is buried in the church's crypt, alongside the original **Crocifisso di San Damiano**, a Byzantine cross before which St Francis was praying when he is said to have received his mission from God in 1205.

Chiesa di San Damiano
CHURCH

(⊘075 81 22 73; www.santuariosandamiano.org; Via San Damiano 7; ⊘10am-noon & 2-6pm summer, to 4.30pm winter) Set amid lush olive groves 1.5km southeast of Assisi's historic centre, this atmospheric sanctuary is where St Francis is said to have heard the voice of God in 1205 and later wrote his *Cantico delle Creature* (Canticle of the Creatures). Signs point the way through the various fresco-slathered rooms, a small Canticle museum and gorgeous cloister. You can also see a copy of the Crocifisso di San Damiano here; the original is in the Basilica di Santa Chiara.

Basilica di Santa Maria degli Angeli
BASILICA

(www.porziuncola.org; Piazza Porziuncola 1, Santa Maria degli Angeli; ⊘6.15am-12.40pm & 2.30-7.30pm Mon-Sat, 6.45am-12.50pm & 2.30-7.30pm Sun) The enormous domed church you see as you approach Assisi along the Tiber valley is the 16th-century Basilica di Santa Maria degli Angeli, some 4km beneath Assisi proper. Built between 1565 and 1685, its vast interior houses the Porziuncola chapel, a humble stone church where St Francis first took refuge after he'd renounced his worldly goods, which is generally regarded as the place where the Franciscan movement started. Nearby, the Cappella del Transito stands on the site where St Francis died.

🏃 Activities

To experience Assisi's spirituality, do as St Francis did and take to the surrounding wooded hills. Popular walks include the 4km-trek to the Eremo delle Carceri (p639) and the downhill stroll to the Chiesa di San Damiano (p639). The tourist office (p642) can provide information on routes, including paths in the nearby Monte Subasio and St Francis' Way, a long, multi-leg trail that traverses Umbria.

Bicycle rentals are available at Angelucci Cicli (☎075 804 25 50, 393 1304680; www.angeluccicicli.it; Via Risorgimento 54a; bike hire per hour/day €5/20, e-bike €13/39; ☺8.30am-12.30pm & 3.30-7.30pm Mon-Sat) in Assisi's suburb of Santa Maria degli Angeli.

🎉 Festivals & Events

Festa di Calendimaggio   CULTURAL
(www.calendimaggiodiassisi.com) This four-day festival sees Assisi take a joyous leap into spring with flamboyant costumed parades, flag waving, jousting and other medieval fun. It starts the first Wednesday after 1 May.

🛏 Sleeping

There's plenty of accommodation in Assisi, but you'll still need to book well in advance for peak periods such as Easter, August, September and the Festa di San Francesco (3 and 4 October). The tourist office (p642) can provide a list of private rooms, religious institutions, flats and *agriturismi* (farm-stay accommodation) in and around Assisi.

Hotel Alexander   HOTEL €
(☎075 81 61 90; www.hotelalexanderassisi.it; Piazza Chiesa Nuova 6; s €55-75, d €75-110, ste €120-140; ❈🐾) On a small cobbled piazza by the Chiesa Nuova, this attractive hideaway offers nine spacious rooms and a communal terrace with wonderful rooftop views. The modern decor – pale wooden floors and earthy brown tones – contrasts well with the wood-beamed ceilings and carefully preserved antiquity all around.

Alla Madonna del Piatto   AGRITURISMO €
(☎328 7025297; www.incampagna.com; Via Petrata 37, Pieve San Nicolò; d €90, apt for 2/4/6 people per week €650/700/750; ☺Mar-Nov; 🅿) 🌿 Waking up to views of lush green meadows and olive groves will put a spring in your step at this ecofriendly *agriturismo* (farm stay), less than 15 minutes' drive from Assisi. Its six rooms and spacious self-catering apartment have all been tastefully designed and feature wrought-iron beds, antique furnishings and intricate handmade fabrics. Note there's a minimum two-night stay.

St Anthony's Guesthouse   B&B €
(☎075 81 25 42; atoneassisi@tiscali.it; Via Galeazzo Alessi 10; s/d/tr €50/70/90; ☺Mar–mid-Nov; 🅿📶) A serene convent run by Franciscan sisters, this guesthouse makes for a lovely base. It's a modest affair but rooms are clean and some even come with balconies and breathtaking views. Breakfast is served in an 800-year-old dining room, while outside there's a small garden and a statue of St Francis feeding the birds.

There's a two-night minimum stay and an 11pm curfew.

⭐ **Gallery Hotel Sorella Luna**   HOTEL €€
(☎075 81 61 94; www.hotelsorellaluna.it; Via Frate Elia 3; r €53-150; ❈📶) This artistic hideaway, ideally located about 200m from the Basilica di San Francesco and five minutes' walk from the Parcheggio Piazza Giovanni Paolo II, is a real find. Its 15 rooms are bright and tastefully low-key with clean white walls, unobtrusive modern furniture and smooth brick-tiled floors. Breakfast is a further plus and well worth getting up for.

Hotel Ideale   HOTEL €€
(☎075 81 35 70; www.hotelideale.it; Piazza Matteotti 1; s €40-60, d €75-145; 🅿❈📶) Ideal indeed, this welcoming family-run hotel is conveniently located near the bus stops on Piazza Matteotti. Many of its bright, simply decorated rooms open onto balconies with uplifting views over the rooftops to the valley beyond. Breakfast is done properly, with fresh pastries, fruit, cold cuts and frothy cappuccino, and is served in the garden when the weather's fine.

⭐ **Nun Assisi**   BOUTIQUE HOTEL €€€
(☎075 815 51 50; www.nunassisi.com; Via Eremo delle Carceri 1a; s €285-335, d €350-400, ste €325-450; 🅿❈📶🏊) An air of Zen-like calm hangs over this super-stylish boutique hotel. Housed in a converted stone convent, it

exudes understated class with a decor that elegantly pairs original trappings with a clean, modern aesthetic. Stone arches and wood beams feature alongside discreet mod cons and minimalist furniture in the cool, pared-down rooms.

Residenza D'Epoca
San Crispino HISTORIC HOTEL €€€
(⌨ 075 804 32 57; www.assisibenessere.it; Via Sant'Agnese 11; s €99-149, d €139-309; ❄ 🛜) This is the real deal: a charming 14th-century mansion complete with a garden and soul-stirring views over Assisi. Each of its seven spacious suites is different, but all have oodles of character, with original vaulted ceilings, stone-flagged floors, fireplaces and four-poster beds. Its location is a further plus, in the centre near the Basilica di Santa Chiara.

🍴 Eating

Terra Umbra Antica SANDWICHES €
(⌨ 075 804 36 96; Via Patrono d'Italia 10, Santa Maria degli Angeli; panini €2-3; ⏰ 8am-1pm & 4-7.30pm Mon-Sat, to 7pm Sun) A fat, well-stuffed *panino*, perhaps with tangy *pecorino* cheese or sweet *prosciutto crudo* (Parma ham), makes for a handy, on-the-hoof lunch. This small food shop near the basilica in Santa Maria degli Angeli prepares them on the spot, as well as serving cheese and cured-meats platters and selling Umbrian wines, olive oils, conserves and pastas.

★Osteria La
Piazzetta dell'Erba OSTERIA €€
(⌨ 075 81 53 52; www.osterialapiazzetta.it; Via San Gabriele dell'Addolorata 15a; meals €30-35; ⏰ 12.30-2.30pm & 7.30-10pm Tue-Sun; 🛜) Tables at this local favourite are always highly coveted: in winter in the cosy stone-vaulted interior, in summer outside on a small, flower-strewn square. The big draw is the kitchen's inventive cuisine and a seasonally driven menu that's flecked with Asian and European influences (hummus, sauerkraut and wasabi regularly pop up in dishes).

★Osteria Eat Out GASTRONOMY €€
(⌨ 075 81 31 63; www.eatoutosteriagourmet.it; Via Eremo delle Carceri 1a; meals €50, tasting menu €110; ⏰ 7.30-10.30pm daily, plus 12.30-2.30pm Sat & Sun; 🛜) With its dreamy al fresco terrace and casually chic interiors, you might expect the glass-fronted restaurant of the five-star Nun Assisi hotel to be all style over substance. Not so. Polished service and an exciting wine list are well matched by chef Emanuele Mazzella's refined and creative take on seasonal Italian cuisine.

Hostaria Terra Chiama OSTERIA €€
(⌨ 075 819 90 51; www.hostariaterrachiama.it; Via San Rufino 16; meals €25-35; ⏰ 11am-11pm; 🛜) Annarita is your hospitable host at this casual, brick-arched *osteria*, where enquires for a glass of local red are met with a barrage of tasting options. Its menu, designed to showcase regional ingredients, tempts with simple but honed preparations like pasta with Norcia black truffles and pork shank with roast potatoes.

La Locanda del Podestà UMBRIAN €€
(⌨ 075 81 65 53; www.locandadelpodesta.it; Via San Giacomo 6; meals €25-30; ⏰ noon-2.45pm & 7-9.30pm Thu-Tue) A short hop from the Basilica di San Francesco, this inviting restaurant is big on old-world charm, with low arches and stone walls. The menu is similarly traditional, featuring Umbrian staples such as black truffles, *strangozzi* pasta (like a square spaghetti) and *ragù di cinghiale* (wild boar meat sauce), all expertly matched with regional wines.

🍸 Drinking & Nightlife

Umami Beer CRAFT BEER
(⌨ 392 2043500; www.umamibeer.it; Via Los Angeles 145, Santa Maria degli Angeli; ⏰ 7pm-11.45pm Sun-Thu, to 1am Fri & Sat; 🛜) A far cry from the medieval-styled wine bars up the road in Assisi, this modern roadside outfit is all about the uncomplicated pleasures of beer and burgers. Owner and expert beer sommelier Roberto oversees a choice selection of Italian and international craft brews, while the kitchen cooks up mountainous burgers forged from top Chianina beef and veggie substitutes (€9 to €15).

Bibenda Assisi WINE BAR
(⌨ 075 815 51 76; www.bibendaassisi.it; Vicolo Nepis 9; wines by the glass from €3.50; ⏰ 11.30am-11pm Wed-Mon; 🛜) Aficionados and wine enthusiasts love this inviting, rustic-chic bar. Owner Nila, a highly knowledgeable Ukrainian transplant, will talk you through the wine list she has assembled from small, boutique producers and tiny appellations – all served in proper Riedel glassware and paired with tasting platters of local *salumi e formaggi* (cured meats and cheese). At busy times, call ahead to reserve a table.

UMBRIA & LE MARCHE ASSISI

ℹ Information

Tourist Office (✆075 813 86 80; www.visit
-assisi.it; Piazza del Comune 10; ⊙9am-7pm)
Stop by here for maps, leaflets and accommodation lists.

ℹ Getting There & Around

BUS

Busitalia (www.fsbusitalia.it) runs buses from
Assisi to Perugia (€4.20, 70 minutes, six daily
Monday to Saturday) from Piazza Matteotti.

  Sulga (✆075 500 96 41; www.sulga.eu) buses
serve Rome's Stazione Tiburtina (€18.50, 3¼
hours, 1.45pm and 4.30pm daily) from Porta
San Pietro.

CAR & MOTORCYCLE

To reach Assisi from Perugia take the SS75, exit
at Ospedalicchio and follow the signs.

  Daytime parking is all but banned in Assisi's
historic centre, but there are convenient car
parks (www.sabait.it) just outside the old town
at **Piazza Giovanni Paolo II** (per hour €1.25;
⊙24hrs) – the closest to the basilica – and
Piazza Matteotti (per hour €1.30; ⊙24hrs).

TAXI

For a taxi, call **Radio Taxi Assisi** (✆075 81 31
00; www.radiotaxiassisi.it).

TRAIN

Assisi is on the Foligno–Terontola train line with
regular services to Perugia (€2.70, 25 minutes,
hourly). There are also direct trains to Florence
(€15.80 to €23.50, two to three hours, seven
daily) and Rome (€10.95 to €21.90, two to three
hours, six daily).

  Assisi's **train station** (www.trenitalia.it) is
4km west of town in Santa Maria degli Angeli;
local bus C (€1.30 or €2 on board, 13 minutes)
runs between the train station and Piazza Matteotti every 30 minutes or so. Buy tickets from the
station *tabaccaio* (tobacconist) or in town.

Spello

POP 8560

Sprawling down a steep hillside, pretty
Spello is the archetypal postcard-pretty
medieval town. Action is centred on the
historic centre, an attractive ensemble of
immaculate honey-tinted stone houses and
churches, encircled by ancient Roman walls
and chess-piece towers.

  Come summer, the green-fingered locals
try to outdo each other with their billowing
hanging baskets and flowerpots, turning
the skinny streets into a riot of colour and
scents.

◉ Sights

**Chiesa di Santa
Maria Maggiore**   CHURCH
(Piazza Matteotti; Cappella Baglioni €3; ⊙9.30am-
12.30pm & 3.30-5pm Tue-Sun) The impressive
12th-century Chiesa di Santa Maria Maggiore houses Spello's main draw – a wonderful cycle of frescoes by the Perugia-born
artist Pinturicchio. These beautiful works
adorn the **Cappella Baglioni**, depicting episodes from the the life of Christ. When in the
chapel, look down as well as up to admire its
16th-century Deruta majolica floor.

Belvedere Cappuccini   VIEWPOINT
(Via Cappuccini) Head to this viewing balcony
at the top of town for a living postcard view
across the bucolic countryside below – on a
clear day you can make out Assisi (it's off to
the right, just under the horizon).

Villa dei Mosaici di Spello   MUSEUM
(✆0742 30 19 09; www.villadeimosaicidispello.it;
Via Paolina Schicchi Fagotti 7; adult/reduced €6/2;
⊙10.30am-1pm & 3-6.30pm Tue-Sun summer,
shorter hours winter) Just outside the historic
centre, this cracking little museum showcases a series of floor mosaics unearthed at a
Roman villa in 2005. Raised walkways allow
you to look at the polychrome mosaics, all
in situ and some depicting wild animals and
mythical creatures, while screen displays illustrate what the villa would originally have
looked like.

Chiesa di Sant'Andrea   CHURCH
(Piazza Matteotti; ⊙hours vary but typically 9am-
12.30pm & 3-7pm) On the main drag through
the village, this much-modified Gothic
church features some fine 16th-century
artworks. Its prize feature is Pinturicchio's
Madonna con Bambino e santi (Madonna
with Child and Saints; 1507–8) in the right
transept.

🎉 Festivals & Events

Infiorata del Corpus Domini   RELIGIOUS
(www.infiorataspello.it; ⊙Jun) The people of
Spello celebrate Corpus Domini (the ninth
Sunday after Easter) by decorating streets
in the historic centre with fresh flowers in
colourful designs. Come on the Saturday
evening before the Sunday procession to
see the floral fantasies being laid out (from
about 9pm). The Corpus procession begins
at 11am on Sunday.

🛏 Sleeping

La Residenza dei Cappuccini   APARTMENT **€**
(📞 331 4358591; www.residenzadeicappuccini.
it; Via Cappuccini 5; s €50-85, d €60-90; 🛜) At
the top of the village, this gem of an *affittacamere* (room rental) plays up the historic
charm with its stepped entrance of exposed
stone and beams. Its three rooms all come
with kitchenettes and a DIY breakfast basket. Additional apartments are found in two
other annexes around town.

★**Agriturismo il Bastione**   AGRITURISMO **€€**
(📞 340 5973402; www.agriturismoilbastione.it; Via
Fontemonte 3; d €90-120, incl half-board €140-170;
🅿 ✳ 🛜 ➿) Some 3km from Spello, this medieval farmstead is a delight. Surrounded
by silent olive groves on the slopes of Monte
Subasio, it commands stirring views over
patchwork plains and hills. Its rooms have a
cosily rustic flavour, with wrought-iron beds,
wood beams and 1000-year-old stone walls.
Dinner, served in the barrel-vaulted restaurant, is a feast of home-grown produce.

🍴 Eating & Drinking

Osteria del Buchetto   OSTERIA **€€**
(📞 0742 30 30 52; www.osteriadelbuchetto.it; Via
Cappuccini 19; meals €25-30; ⊙ 7.30-10.30pm
Mon, Tue & Thu-Sat, 12.30-2.30pm Sun) This modest *osteria* is at its best on warm summer
evenings when you can sit outside and bask
in romantic views over the valley towards
Assisi. Its food is genuine and proudly local, and lingering is positively encouraged.
Perhaps start with baked *pecorino* cheese
and ham before progressing onto *tagliatelle* with black truffles or an expertly grilled
steak.

Enoteca Properzio   WINE BAR
(📞 0742 30 15 21; www.enotecaproperzio.com;
Palazzo dei Canonici, Piazza Matteotti 8; ⊙ 10am-
10pm; 🛜) One of Umbria's top *enoteche*
(wine bars), here you can mingle among
master sommeliers while trying local wines
and snacking on platters of cheese (€13),
cured meats (€13) and *bruschette* (€10).

ℹ Information

Infopoint (Tourist Office; 📞 0742 30 19 09;
www.villadeimosaicidispello.it; c/o Villa dei
Mosaici di Spello, Via Paolina Schicchi Fagotti
7; ⊙ 10.30am-1pm & 3-6.30pm Tue-Sun summer, shorter hours winter) The ticket office at
the Villa dei Mosaici di Spello also serves as the
town's tourist office.

ℹ Getting There & Away

Spello is on the SS75 between Perugia and
Foligno.

There are services from the **train station** (Via
Pasciana) at least hourly to Perugia (€3.50,
40 minutes) and Assisi (€1.85, 10 minutes). If
the station is unstaffed, buy your tickets at the
self-service ticket machine. It's about a 1km walk
into town from the station.

Spoleto

POP 38,000

Presided over by a formidable medieval fortress and backed by the broad-shouldered
Apennines, their summits iced with snow
in winter, hillside Spoleto is visually stunning. Ancient arches and a virtually intact
amphitheatre tell of its past as a strategic
Roman colony, while a series of Romanesque churches testifies to a golden age in
the early Middle Ages. In 570 the Lombards
made it capital of their duchy and over the
next three centuries it flourished, becoming
for a brief period one of the most important
towns in Italy.

Today, Spoleto is best known for its mammoth summer festival (p645), a 17-day bonanza of opera, dance, music and art.

👁 Sights

★**Duomo**   CATHEDRAL
(Cattedrale di Santa Maria Assunta; www.duomo
spoleto.it; Piazza del Duomo; ⊙ 10.30am-6pm Mon-
Sat, from 12.30pm Sun summer, 10.30am-5pm Mon-
Sat, from 12.30pm Sun winter) A flight of steps
sweeps down to Spoleto's pale-stone cathedral, photogenically set on a graceful hillside
piazza. Originally constructed to a Romanesque design in the 12th century, it later
underwent various modifications, including
the addition of a Renaissance portico in the
late 15th century. The interior, revamped in

ℹ SPOLETO CARD

Valid for seven days, the Spoleto
Card (www.spoletocard.it; adult/reduced
€9.50/8) offers significant savings, giving access to six of the town's museums
for less than a tenner. You can pick it up
at participating museums, at the Spoleto Card Info Point (www.spoletocard.
it; Piazza della Libertà; ⊙ 10am-1.30pm Tue-
Thu, 10am-1pm & 3-6pm Fri-Sun summer,
shorter hours winter) or online.

Spoleto

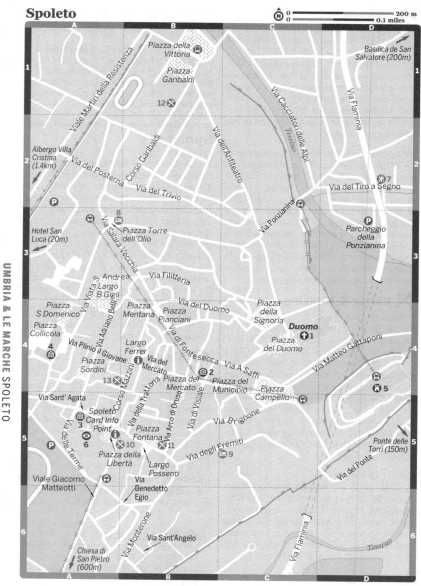

UMBRIA & LE MARCHE SPOLETO

a 17th-century baroque makeover, features a Cosmati marble floor and frescoes by Pinturicchio and, in the domed apse, by Filippo Lippi and pupils. This rainbow-coloured design depicts stories from the life of the Virgin Mary.

Lippi died before completing the frescoes and Lorenzo de Medici travelled to Spoleto from Florence and ordered Lippi's son, Filippino, to build a mausoleum for the artist. This now stands in the right transept.

Spoleto

Rocca Albornoziana   FORTRESS
(☑ 0743 22 49 52; Piazza Campello; adult/reduced €7.50/3.75; ⊙ 9.30am-7pm Tue-Sun, to 1.30pm Mon summer, to 6pm Tue-Sun winter) Dominating the skyline above Spoleto, this formidable fortress was built on the summit of Colle Sant'Elia as part of a 14th-century campaign to reassert papal authority over central Italy. Nowadays, it houses the **Museo Nazionale del Ducato**, a small museum tracing the history of the Spoleto duchy through a series of Roman, Byzantine, Carolingian and Lombard artefacts, ranging from 5th-century sarcophagi to Byzantine jewellery.

★ Ponte delle Torri   BRIDGE
(Via Giro del Ponte) Many people gasp the first time they glimpse the medieval Ponte delle Torri, a 10-arch bridge that spectacularly spans a steeply wooded gorge – a scene beautifully captured by Turner in his 1840 oil painting *The Ponte Delle Torri*. The bridge, which tops off at 80m and runs for 230m, was erected in the 14th century on the foundations of a Roman aqueduct. However, it was damaged in the August 2016 earthquake and at the time of research was closed.

Casa Romana   HISTORIC BUILDING
(Roman House; ☑ 0743 4 02 55; Via di Visiale 6; adult/reduced €3/2; ⊙ 10am-1.30pm & 2-5.30pm Wed-Mon) With its intact floor mosaics and vaulted ceilings, this small house gives visitors a peek into what a typical Roman villa would have looked like in the 1st century AD.

Palazzo Collicola Arte Visive   MUSEUM
(☑ 0743 4 64 34; www.palazzocollicola.it; Piazza Collicola; adult/reduced €6.50/4; ⊙ 10.30am-1pm & 3.30-7pm Wed-Mon summer, 10.30am-1pm & 3-5.30pm Wed-Mon winter) The 18th-century Palazzo Collicola houses Spoleto's premier collection of modern art. The collection, named after its late former director and noted art critic, Giovanni Carandente, is displayed in 15 halls and contains works by major Italian and international artists such as Leonardo Leoncillo, Alexander Calder and Alberto Burri. Upstairs on the 1st floor is the *Piano nobile* (Noble Apartment), decorated with ornate 18th-century furniture, some of it from the *palazzo* itself, and paintings from the 16th to 19th centuries.

Museo Archeologico   MUSEUM
(☑ 0743 22 32 77; www.polomusealeumbria.beniculturali.it; Via Sant'Agata 18; adult/reduced €4/2; ⊙ 8.30am-7.30pm) Spoleto's archaeological museum, housed in a 15th-century monastery on the western edge of Piazza della Libertà, holds a well-curated collection of Roman and Etruscan bits and bobs, illustrating the town's ancient origins as far back as the Bronze Age. Tickets also include access to the adjacent 1st-century-BC **Teatro Romano**.

Basilica di San Salvatore   CHURCH
(☑ 0743 21 86 20; Piazza Mario Salmi 1; ⊙ 8am-7pm summer, to 6pm spring & autumn, to 5pm winter) Spoleto's Romanesque basilica, listed as a Unesco World Heritage Site as part of the 'Longobards in Italy, Places of the Power (568-774 AD)' group, dates from the 4th or 5th century. Unfortunately, it was off limits at the time of research after suffering damage in the August 2016 earthquake. You can, however, look inside through the main doorway, which is opened during the day.

★★ Festivals & Events

Spoleto Festival   PERFORMING ARTS
(Festival dei Due Mondi; ☑ 0743 77 64 44; www.festivaldispoleto.it; Via Filitteria 1; ⊙ late Jun–mid-Jul, box office 10am-1pm & 3-6pm mid-Apr–mid-Jun, 10am-7pm mid-Jun–Jul) Conceived by the Italian-American composer Gian Carlo Menotti in 1958, the Festival dei Due Mondi (Festival of Two Worlds, aka the Spoleto Festival) has given the town a worldwide reputation. Events at the 17-day festival range from opera and theatre performances to ballet and art exhibitions. For details and tickets, visit the website.

UMBRIA & LE MARCHE SPOLETO

SPOLETO'S PANORAMIC PATH

The 6km **Giro dei Condotti** walk is an irresistible draw for photographers, keen walkers and anyone who appreciates jaw-dropping panoramas. From Via del Tiro a Segno, the path leads along sun-dappled woodland trails, offering classic postcard views of the Ponte delle Torri and hilltop Rocca Albornoziana. Be sure to wear flat, comfortable shoes.

🛏 Sleeping

⭐ **L'Aura**   B&B €

(☑ 347 2210013; Piazza Torre dell'Olio 5; s €50-60, d €70-80; 🛜) This B&B is a real home away from home, albeit one perched on top of a 200-year-old *palazzo*. It's a tidy, cosy place, with bright, wood-beamed rooms, original 16th-century brickwork and a terrace overlooking rooftops to the hills beyond. Your host, Claudia, makes you very welcome and gives excellent tips on Spoleto.

Albergo Villa Cristina   HOTEL €

(☑ 0743 4 80 36; www.albergovillacristina.com; Via Fabiano Benedetti Valentini 55; s €50-80, d €60-110; [P] 🛜) Owner Anna Maria is the star at this lovely family-run hotel. She cheerfully welcomes you to her lovingly restored 18th-century home set in tranquil countryside just outside town. Its traditional, tile-floored rooms sport a restrained rustic look, while outside a garden terrace presents dreamy views over verdant, cypress-plumed hillsides. Homemade cakes and honey are served with bread, ricotta and coffee at breakfast.

The hotel is in the tiny *frazione* (fraction) of Collerisana, about a 1.6km walk west of Piazza della Libertà.

Hotel San Luca   BOUTIQUE HOTEL €€

(☑ 0743 22 33 99; www.hotelsanluca.com; Via Interna delle Mura 21; 🛜 s €70-130, d €90-240, ste €190-300; [P] [✳] [@] 🛜) Once a tannery and now a peaceful boutique hotel, the San Luca offers friendly service, refined interiors and a leisurely, relaxed atmosphere. Bold colours and antique furnishings feature in the individually decorated rooms set around an immaculate internal courtyard. The homemade cakes are the stars of the breakfast buffet.

⭐ **Palazzo Leti**   BOUTIQUE HOTEL €€€

(☑ 0743 22 49 30; www.palazzoleti.com; Via degli Eremiti 10; s €100-200, d €120-280; [✳] 🛜) This exquisitely converted 13th-century palace exudes charm down to the last detail, from the delicate breakfast china to the historical oak and wrought-iron furnishings. Outside, romance takes the form of magical views from a small, but perfectly landscaped, panoramic garden. And such is the sense of peace, you can easily forget you're only a three-minute walk from the centre of town.

🍴 Eating

Signature Spoleto staples include *strangozzi alla spoletina,* a thin, fettuccine-like pasta served with tomato, garlic and chilli pepper, and *attorta,* a sweet pastry filled with apples and chocolate.

⭐ **Novecento**   UMBRIAN €€

(☑ 338 1622612; www.9centocasualrestaurant. com; Corso Garibaldi 58; meals €25-30; ⏱ 11am-11.45pm) An oasis of modern design, this self-styled 'casual' restaurant marries kooky decor, including a canoe on the wall and colourful hanging lamps, with inventive and astonishingly good-value Umbrian cuisine. Kick off with a *pecorino* flan doused in lentil cream and crispy bacon before diving into a decadent plate of black *Venere* rice coated in cheese sauce and crowned by shavings of black truffles.

Sabatini   ITALIAN €€

(☑ 0743 4 72 30; www.ristorantesabatinispoleto. it; Corso Mazzini 54; meals €30-40, tasting menus €25-30; ⏱ noon-2.30pm & 7-10.45pm Tue-Sun; 🛜) Forget studying the menu – just go for one of the tasting menus and loosen a belt notch in readiness for dish after delectable dish. This is home cooking at its best with a pinch of seasonality – as simple as 24-month dry-cured prosciutto sliced by hand, ravioli with ricotta, taleggio and saffron, and wild boar stewed with mushrooms, thyme and juniper berries.

Il Tempio del Gusto   ITALIAN €€

(☑ 0743 4 71 12; www.iltempiodelgusto.com; Via Arco di Druso 11; meals €30-40; ⏱ 12.30-3pm & 7-11pm Fri-Wed; 🛜) Intimate, inventive and unmissable, Tempio del Gusto is fine dining without the Michelin-starred price tag. Chef Eros Patrizi takes an experimental approach, creating dishes that, while undeniably Umbrian, are also creative and originally composed. Typical of his approach is a decadent risotto with scallops and seasonal black truffles.

Bar Canasta ITALIAN €€
(☑ 0743 402 05; Piazza della Libertà 14; meals €20-30; ⊙ kitchen 12.30-3pm & 7.30-10.30pm Thu-Tue; ☎) With prime Piazza della Libertà patio seating and an airy dining room overlooking the Teatro Romano, this simple cafe restaurant serves a well-rounded surf-and-turf menu offering classic Italian and Umbrian staples. Its signature dish is its highly rated *spaghetti alla carbonara,* served here with an optional (and decidedly untraditional) shaving of truffle.

ℹ Information

Tourist Office (☑ 0743 21 86 20; www.comune.spoleto.pg.it/turismoecultura; Largo Ferrer 6; ⊙ 9am-1pm & 3-7pm Mon-Sat, 10am-1pm & 3-5.30pm Sun summer, 9am-1pm & 2.30-6.15pm Mon-Sat, 9.30am-1pm & 3-5pm Sun winter) Just off central Corso Mazzini. Helpful English-speaking staff can provide maps and local information.

ℹ Getting There & Away

BUS

Busitalia services depart to Norcia (€6.10, 55 minutes, five daily Monday to Saturday, three Sunday) from Spoleto's train station, stopping a few minutes later at the **bus station** (Piazza della Vittoria).

CAR & MOTORCYCLE

Spoleto is on the SS3 (Via Flaminia) and is an easy connection via the SS209 to the Valnerina.

Vehicle traffic in the hillside *centro storico* is heavily restricted, but there are several car parks (parcheggi) in the lower part of town. These generally charge about €1.20 per hour.

TRAIN

From the **station** (www.trenitalia.it; Piazzale Giovanni Polvani) trains connect with Rome (€8.85 to €16.50, 65 minutes to 1¾ hours, 17 daily), Perugia (€5.45 to €13.70, one to 1¼ hours, 16 daily) and Assisi (€4.25, 40 minutes, 17 daily). Note, however, that some services require a change.

From the station, about 1km from the centre, take any city bus that reads 'Centro' to Piazza della Libertà (€1.30).

ℹ Getting Around

Spoleto's hillside centre is compact and best explored on foot. To access it, there are free elevators, escalators and travelators:

Route 1 A series of travelators and elevators runs from **Parcheggio Spoletosfera** (Viale Giacomo Matteotti 6; per hour/day €1-1.20/10; ⊙ 7am-1am) to Piazza della Libertà (7am to 8.30pm weekdays, from 9am Sundays).

Route 2 Escalators go from near **Parcheggio della Ponzianina** (Via Ponzianina 3; per hour/day €1/5; ⊙ 24hr) to Rocca (7.30am to 8pm weekdays, from 8.30am Sundays) from where an elevator ascends to the Rocca Albornoziana (p645) (8.30am to 7.30pm daily).

Route 3 A string of travelators and elevators links **Parcheggio della Posterna** (Via della Posterna 2; per hour/day €1-1.20/10; ⊙ 24hr) with Piazza Campello (7am to 9pm Sundays to Thursdays, to 1am Fridays and Saturdays).

All three routes have various stations along the way – many decorated with art exhibits or archaeological ruins.

Norcia & the Valnerina

Surrounded by silent green hills in Umbria's far eastern reaches, remote Norcia is the main town in the Valnerina. With its uplifting scenery and small mountain towns, this gloriously unspoilt river valley is ideal for leisurely exploring. Norcia itself is renowned as the birthplace of San Benedetto (St Benedict) and as a foodie hotspot – its *tartufo nero* (black truffle), *prosciutto di Norcia* (dry-cured ham) and *salame di cinghiale* (spicy wild-boar sausage) are known and appreciated throughout Italy.

Unfortunately, the town is still struggling to bounce back from the devastating effects of the 2016 earthquakes that all but destroyed its best-known church, the Basilica di San Benedetto, and severely damaged many other buildings. However, as reconstruction continues, the town remains open for business.

◉ Sights

Piazza San Benedetto PIAZZA
Centred on a statue of St Benedict, Norcia's most famous son, this small piazza is flanked by the town's most impressive medieval buildings, many of which are still closed after the 2016 earthquake. Most obviously, the **Basilica di San Benedetto** is in ruins save for its facade. Next to it, the 14th-century **Palazzo Comunale** is intact, but at the time of research its portico and belfry were hidden behind scaffolding. Opposite is the **Castellina**, a 16th-century papal fortress that houses a small museum (closed).

✪ Festivals & Events

Nero Norcia
FOOD & DRINK

(www.nero-norcia.it; ⊙Feb/Mar) Visitors, gourmets and bon viveurs descend on Norcia for three weekends in late February and early March to pay homage to the town's *tartufo nero* (black truffle). The prize tuber is the star of this annual food fest, which sees stalls take over the historic centre, offering everything from truffles and cured meats to Sicilian candies, Tuscan cheeses and much more besides.

🛏 Sleeping & Eating

★ Palazzo Seneca
HISTORIC HOTEL €€€

(🖉 0743 81 74 34; www.palazzoseneca.com; Via Cesare Battisti 12; s €128-176, d €150-300, ste €400-800; 🅿 ✳ 🛜) Live like the local nobility at this refined family-run hotel, one of the few still operating in Norcia's historic centre. Its spacious rooms are a picture of rustic-chic styling, seamlessly melding four-poster beds and marble bathrooms with stone walls and oak wood floors. The public areas exude class, with leather armchairs set around a fireplace and artfully arranged coffee-table books.

Locanda del Teatro
UMBRIAN €€

(🖉 0743 81 78 57; www.locandadelteatro.it; Piazza Vittorio Veneto 10; meals €25-30; ⊙noon-3pm & 7-10pm Wed-Mon) A trattoria that's busy on a wet winter's night is usually doing something right. And that's the case at this relaxed spot in the heart of Norcia's historic centre. Here the welcome is warm and traditional Umbrian food generous and full of big country flavours.

★ Vespasia
RISTORANTE €€€

(🖉 0743 81 74 34; http://vespasianorcia.com; Via Cesare Battisti 12; tasting menus €80-154; ⊙noon-

3pm & 7-10pm) Few places elevate Umbria's earthy cuisine to such heights as Michelin-starred Vespasia. Elegantly housed in a 16th-century *palazzo* and furnished with bright modern art, chef Valentino Palmisano's fine-dining restaurant serves three tasting menus (plus a €48 weekday lunch menu), showcasing his contemporary approach in dishes such as *lenticchie* (lentil) soup with aged Parmesan foam, and truffle mousse paired with olive oil gelato.

🛍 Shopping

Ansuini do Mastro Peppe
FOOD & DRINKS

(🖉 0743 81 66 43; www.norcineriaansuini.it; Via Anicia 105; ⊙7.30am-7.30pm Fri-Wed) You can't miss the extravagant display of wild boars outside the entrance to this classic gourmet deli, one of the best places in town to stock up on local *salume,* cheeses and other gourmet goodies, including craft beer from Amatrice.

ⓘ Information

Norcia Tourist Office (🖉 328 1797616; Via Novelli 1; ⊙9.30am-12.30pm & 3-6pm) Temporarily housed in a car park just outside the town walls, it has a few basic information leaflets that it sells for €2 each.

ⓘ Getting There & Away

To reach Norcia and the Valnerina by car from Spoleto, take the northbound SS3 to connect with the SP209 and SS685. The closest train station is in Spoleto (p647).

Buses run to and from Spoleto (€6.10, 55 minutes, five daily Monday to Saturday, three Sunday) and Perugia (€7.50, two hours, one daily Monday to Friday). Buses depart from **Porta Ascolana** (Porta Masari), also stopping at Porta Romana before leaving town.

OFF THE BEATEN TRACK

PIANO GRANDE

What sounds like a finely tuned instrument is in fact a lyrical mountain plain. Tucked in the far-eastern corner of Umbria, the 1270m-high Piano Grande is a karstic plateau framed by the bare-backed peaks of the Sibilline mountains. It's a dramatic sight at any time of the year but is especially beautiful between May and June when the snows have melted and wildflowers carpet the grassy plain. Poppies, cornflowers, wild tulips, daisies, crocuses and narcissi produce an extraordinary display of reds, golds, violets and whites to add to the greens and browns of the surrounding slopes.

The Piano is best accessed from Norcia via the winding mountain SP477 – it's about 26km in total (follow signs to Castelluccio).

Torgiano

POP 6660

Vineyards and olive groves sweep up to the tiny medieval town of Torgiano, on a hilltop perch overlooking the confluence of the Chiascio and Tiber rivers. The town, centred on a walled red-brick core, has an irresistible draw for gastronomes: it's renowned for its thick, green extra-virgin olive oil and spicy, peppery red wines such as Rubesco Rosso DOC, produced with 70% Sangiovese grapes.

◉ Sights & Activities

Museo del Vino   MUSEUM

(Wine Museum; ☑ 075 988 02 00; www.lungarotti. it/fondazione/muvit; Corso Vittorio Emanuele 31; adult/reduced incl Museo dell'Olivo e dell'Olio €7/5; ☺ 10am-1pm & 3-5pm Tue-Sun Oct-Mar, to 6pm Tue-Sun Apr-Jun, 10am-6pm daily Jul-Sep) Housed in an aristocratic 17th-century mansion, this is one of Italy's premier wine museums. Greek, Etruscan and Roman ceramics, jugs and vessels, glassware and various wine-making implements are displayed in its 20 rooms, racing you from the Bronze Age to the present day and covering topics such as wine as medicine and its role in mythology.

Museo dell'Olivo e dell'Olio   MUSEUM

(☑ 075 988 02 00; www.lungarotti.it/fondazione/ moo; Via Garibaldi 10; adult/reduced incl Museo del Vino €7/5; ☺ 10am-1pm & 3-5pm Tue-Sun Oct-Mar, to 6pm Tue-Sun Apr-Jun, 10am-6pm daily Jul-Sep) Showcasing mills, presses and crafts, this, the sister museum of the Museo del Vino, is an ode to olive oil and its symbolic, medicinal and dietary uses.

Cantine Giorgio Lungarotti   WINE

(☑ 075 988 66 49; www.lungarotti.it; Viale Giorgio Lungarotti 2; tastings from €12; ☺ 9am-1pm & 3-7pm Mon-Fri, 9.30am-1pm & 3.30-6pm Sat) A historic name in these parts, the Lungarotti have done more than anyone to put Torgiano (and Umbria) on Italy's wine map. The family, whose company was founded by Giorgio Lungarotti in the early 1960s, have two estates: one in Montefalco and one here, near the entrance to town. A range of tours and tastings is available – see the website for details.

🛏 Sleeping & Eating

Al Grappolo d'Oro   HOTEL €

(☑ 075 982 22 53; www.algrappolodoro.net; Via Principe Umberto 24; s €60-70, d €90-100; P ☀ 🛜 🖳) The view across lush, green vineyards from the tree-rimmed pool is soothingly beautiful at this friendly three-star hotel in the centre of town. Rooms are sunny and classically furnished with parquet and polished wood furniture, while the common areas are a riot of bric-a-brac and cheerful wine-country kitsch. Free parking is a further plus.

Ristorante Siro   ITALIAN €€

(☑ 075 98 20 10; www.hotelsirotorgiano.it; Via Giordano Bruno 16; meals €25-30; ☺ noon-2.30pm & 7-10pm; 🛜) This convivial, picture-plastered restaurant is big on old-school charm and classic Umbrian cuisine. Its signature starter for two – a piled-high platter of cured meats, cheeses, fried nibbles, veggies and bruschette – would feed a small family. Next, loosen a belt notch for mains such as wild-boar stew and butter-soft steaks.

ℹ Getting There & Away

Torgiano sits around 2.3km east of the SS3bis, about 16km south of Perugia.

Busitalia (☑ 075 963 76 37; www.fsbusitalia. it) buses connect Torgiano to Perugia (€2.50, 40 minutes, at least four daily).

Todi

POP 16,600

A collage of soft-stone houses, *palazzi* and belfries pasted to a hillside, Todi looks freshly minted for a fairy tale. Wandering its steep backstreets is like playing a game of medieval snakes and ladders. The pace of life inches along, keeping time with the wildflowers and vines that bloom and ripen in the valley below.

Like rings around a tree, Todi is encircled by three sets of concentric walls, each from a different historical era: the innermost is Etruscan in origin, the middle ones date from the town's Roman period, and the 'new' medieval walls survive from Todi's heyday as a prosperous centre in the Middle Ages.

◉ Sights

⭐ **Piazza del Popolo**   PIAZZA

(Piazza del Popolo) Just try to walk through Piazza del Popolo without trying to photograph it from every angle. The rectangular piazza is one of Umbria's finest medieval squares and is flanked by a series of notable buildings: the Cattedrale di Santa Maria Annunziata at the northern end; the 13th-century Palazzo del Capitano and Palazzo del Popolo, together home to the **Museo**

Pinacoteca Comunale (www.coopculture.
it; adult/reduced €5/2.50; ⊙10am-1pm Mon &
Wed-Fri, to 6pm Sat & Sun summer, 10am-1pm
Fri, 10am-1pm & 2-5pm Sat & Sun winter), in the
southeastern corner; and, on the southern
flank, the 14th-century Palazzo dei Priori.

La Cattedrale di Santa
Maria Annunziata   CATHEDRAL
(☑075 894 30 41; Piazza del Popolo; crypt €2;
⊙8am-1pm & 3-6pm) Todi's 12th-century Duomo sits at the head of Piazza del Popolo
on the site of an earlier Roman temple. Its
solemn square facade sports a magnificent
central rose window, actually added in the
16th century, and an intricately decorated
main portal. Inside, look out for *The Last
Judgment,* a fresco by Ferraù Fenzoni (aka Il
Faenzone) inspired by Michelangelo's more
celebrated Sistine Chapel version.

Chiesa di San Fortunato   CHURCH
(Via San Fortunato; ⊙10.30am-1pm & 2-4.30pm
Tue-Fri, 10am-1pm & 2-5pm Sat & Sun) With its
never-finished facade and vaulted, light-
filled Gothic interior, the 15th-century
Chiesa di San Fortunato boasts fragments
of frescoes by Masolino da Panicale and the
tomb of Beato Jacopone, Todi's beloved patron saint.

While here, it's worth climbing the
church's bell tower, the **Campanile di San
Fortunato** (adult/reduced €2/1.50; ⊙10.30am-
1pm & 2-4.30pm Tue-Fri, 10am-1pm & 2-5pm Sat &
Sun), to enjoy memorable views of the surrounding hills and castles.

Tempio di Santa Maria
della Consolazione   CHURCH
(☑075 895 62 27; Via della Consolazione;
⊙9.30am-12.30pm & 3-6.30pm Wed-Mon, shorter
hours winter) Todi's architectural pride and
joy is this stunning landmark church, attributed to Donato Bramante. Completed in
1607 outside the town's medieval walls, the
distinctive structure is considered a masterpiece of late Renaissance architecture with
its geometrically perfect Greek-cross plan
and soaring 50m-high dome.

🎊 Festivals & Events
Todi Festival   CULTURAL
(www.todifestival.it) Held for 10 days spanning late August and early September, this
festival brings together a mix of classical
and jazz concerts, theatre, dance, art exhibitions, food and wine tastings, and author
presentations.

🛏 Sleeping
San Lorenzo Tre   B&B €
(☑075 894 45 55; www.sanlorenzo3.it; Via San
Lorenzo 3; d €95-110, ste €130-150; @🕾) Five
generations of the same family have lived
at this 17th-century abode. Awaiting guests
on the 3rd floor are rooms full of character,
with polished brick floors, delicately painted beams and carefully chosen antiques.
There's no TV, but there are books to browse,
in keeping with the blissfully laid-back vibe,
and a roof terrace with magical views.
No lift.

★ Il Ghiottone Umbro   B&B €€
(☑339 1321509, 075 894 84 44; www.ilghiottone
umbro.com; Frazione San Giorgio 45, Vocabolo Molino; r €110-130; P 🌂 🕾) What a delight! Danish duo Thomas and Lisbeth bring together
old-stone farmhouse charm with Scandi cool
at their gorgeous boutique B&B. The rooms
combine historic features like beams, terracotta tiles and fireplaces with canopy beds,
free-standing baths and Nordic furnishings.
Breakfast is a sumptuous spread of muesli,
fresh fruits, juices and homemade pastries.

🍴 Eating
Vineria San Fortunato   UMBRIAN €
(☑075 372 11 80; Piazza Umberto I 5; meals €25-
30; ⊙noon-2am Tue-Sun) Wine lovers are in
their element at this slick wine bar, where
Umbrian and Tuscan wines are perfectly
matched with delicious tasting platters of
salumi e formaggi (cured meats and cheeses) and daily specials such as tender lamb
and olive stew or *scafata* (a stew of broad
beans, peas and artichokes).

Bar Pianegiani   GELATO €
(☑075 894 23 76; www.barpianegiani.it; Corso Cavour 40; cones & tubs €2-3; ⊙7am-midnight summer, to 8pm winter; 🕾) For around 50 years,
this central, and much frequented, cafe has
been serving some of Umbria's best gelato. The choice is fairly limited but flavours
are right on the money – try the *amarena*
(black cherry), *nocciola* (hazelnut) or the
house speciality: cream with pine nuts.
It also serves small pastries and savoury
panini, along with coffees and drinks.

★ Pane & Vino   RISTORANTE €€
(☑075 894 54 48; www.panevinotodi.com; Via Augusto Ciuffelli 33; meals €30-35; ⊙12.30-2.30pm
& 7.30-10.30pm Thu-Tue) It simply doesn't get
any more Umbrian than this: a lovely, warm
interior with tables set on a rough wooden

NARNI

Said to mark Italy's exact geographical centre, Narni often slips under the radar. Yet the town boasts an inviting hilltop centre with all the trimmings: medieval churches, quaint piazzas and noble *palazzi*. Further relics await at Narni Sotterranea (Narni Underground; ☑ 0744 72 22 92; www.narnisotterranea.it; Piazza San Bernardo 12; adult/reduced €6/3; ☉ by guided tour), an extraordinary underworld hiding a 13th-century church, Roman cistern, ancient aqueducts and, most chillingly, an Inquisition courtroom and cell.

In ancient times Narni, or Narnia as it was then known, was an important Roman settlement. Little survives from that period but its name lives on courtesy of CS Lewis, who chose it for his fictional kingdom after seeing it in an ancient atlas.

Narni lies 21km south of Todi, just east of the A1 autostrada (from the south take the Magliano Sabina exit; from the north the Orte exit). It's well served by Busitalia (www.fsbusitalia.it) buses, mostly from Terni (€2.50, 30 minutes, up to 10 daily).

---

floor and wall dressers packed with wine bottles. The earthy regional food plays its part too, with dishes like smoked pork with porcini mushrooms and black truffles leaving you happy and full fit to burst.

ⓘ Information

Tourist Office (☑ 075 895 62 27; iat.todi@ coopculture.it; Piazza del Popolo 29/30; ☉10am-1pm & 2-5pm Mon-Fri, to 6pm Sat & Sun, longer hours summer) Helpful office on Todi's main square.

ⓘ Getting There & Away

By car, Todi is easily reached on the SS3bis-E45, which runs between Perugia and Terni. Alternatively, take the A1 autostrada and exit at the Orvieto turn-off.

In town, park at the **Parcheggio Porta Orvietana** (Viale Montesanto; per hour €1.20; ☉24hr), from where there's an elevator up to the historic centre. If that isn't working, however, there are free shuttle buses every 15 minutes.

Busitalia (☑ 075 963 76 37; www.fsbusitalia. it) operates buses to/from Perugia (€6.30, 1½ hours, up to seven daily). These depart from Piazza Consolazione near the Tempio di Santa Maria della Consolazione.

Orvieto

POP 20,300

Set atop a gigantic plug of rock above fields streaked with vines, olive groves and cypress trees, Orvieto is one of Umbria's star attractions. Its austere medieval centre is a classic of its kind, with weaving lanes, brown stone houses and cobbled piazzas, and its location between Rome and Florence ensures a constant stream of visitors. But what sets the town apart from its medieval neighbours is its breathtaking cathedral. This extraordinary vision, one of Italy's greatest Gothic churches, is stunning inside and out, with a sensational facade and frescoes that are said by some to rival Michelangelo's in the Sistine Chapel.

◉ Sights

★ **Duomo**   CATHEDRAL
(☑ 0763 34 24 77; www.opsm.it; Piazza Duomo 26; €4, incl Museo dell'Opera del Duomo di Orvieto €5; ☉ 9.30am-7pm Mon-Sat, 1-5.30pm Sun summer, shorter hours winter) Nothing can prepare you for the visual feast that is Orvieto's soul-stirring Gothic cathedral. Dating from 1290, it sports a black-and-white banded exterior fronted by what is perhaps the most astonishing facade to grace any Italian church: a mesmerising display of rainbow frescoes, jewel-like mosaics, bas-reliefs and delicate braids of flowers and vines. Head inside and the show continues, most spectacularly in the form of Luca Signorelli's mesmerising *Giudizio Universale* (Last Judgment) fresco in the Cappella di San Brizio.

The building took 30 years to plan and three centuries to complete. It was started by Fra Bevignate and later additions were made by Sienese master Lorenzo Maitani, Andrea Pisano (of Florence Cathedral fame) and his son Nino, Andrea Orcagna and Michele Sanmicheli.

Of the art on show inside, it's Luca Signorelli's *Giudizio Universale* that's the star turn. The artist began work on this vast fresco in 1499 and over the course of the next four years covered every inch of the Cappella di San Brizio with a swirling, and at times grotesque, depiction of the *Last Judgment*. Michelangelo is said to have taken

UMBRIA & LE MARCHE ORVIETO

Orvieto

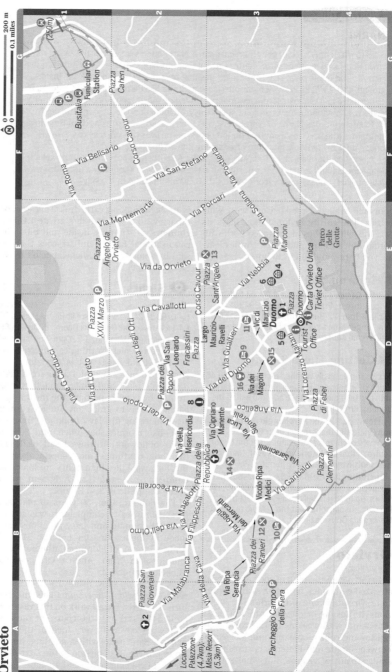

inspiration from it. Indeed, to some, Michelangelo's masterpiece runs a close second to Signorelli's creation.

On the other side of the transept, the **Cappella del Corporale** houses a 13th-century altar cloth stained with blood that is believed to have miraculously poured from the communion bread of a priest who doubted the transubstantiation.

Museo dell'Opera del Duomo di Orvieto
MUSEUM
(☑0763 34 24 77; www.opsm.it; Piazza Duomo 26; €4, incl Duomo €5; ⊙9.30am-7pm daily summer, to 5pm Tue-Sun winter) Housed in a complex of papal palaces, the Palazzi Papali, this museum showcases a fine collection of religious relics from the Duomo and paintings by artists such as Arnolfo di Cambio and the three Pisanos (Andrea, Nino and Giovanni). A separate exhibition in Palazzo Soliano is dedicated to sculptor and medallist Emilio Greco (1913–95).

The ticket also covers admission to the ex-**Chiesa di Sant'Agostino** (Piazza San Giovenale) where the museum's sculptural collection is on show.

Museo Archeologico Nazionale
MUSEUM
(☑0763 34 10 39; Palazzo Papale, Piazza Duomo; adult/reduced €4/2; ⊙8.30am-7.30pm) Housed in the medieval Palazzo Papale behind the Duomo, Orvieto's archaeological museum holds plenty of interesting artefacts, some over 2500 years old. Etruscan ceramics, necropolis relics, bronzes and frescoed chamber tombs feature among the items on display.

Orvieto Underground
HISTORIC SITE
(☑0763 340680; www.orvietounderground.it; Piazza Duomo 23; adult/reduced €7/5; ⊙visits 11am, 12.15pm, 4pm & 5.15pm) The coolest place in Orvieto (literally), this series of 440 caves

(out of 1200 in the system) has been used for millennia by locals for various purposes – WWII bomb shelters, refrigerators, wine cellars, wells and, during many a pesky Roman or barbarian siege, as dovecotes to trap the usual one-course dinner: pigeon (still seen on local menus as *palombo*).

Museo Claudio Faina e Civico
MUSEUM
(☑0763 34 15 11; www.museofaina.it; Piazza Duomo 29; adult/reduced €4.50/3; ⊙9.30am-6pm summer, 10am-5pm winter, closed Mon Nov-Feb) Stage your own archaeological dig at this fantastic museum opposite the Duomo. It houses one of Italy's foremost collections of Etruscan finds, comprising plenty of stone sarcophagi, terracotta pieces and some amazing bronzeware. Also of note are a series of decorative Greek amphorae.

Torre del Moro
TOWER
(Moor's Tower; ☑0763 34 45 67; Corso Cavour 87; adult/reduced €2.80/2; ⊙10am-8pm summer, shorter hours winter) This 47m-high tower has loomed over Orvieto's *centro* since the 13th century, though the clock was only added in 1866. Climb all 250 steps for sweeping 360-degree views of the city.

Chiesa di Sant'Andrea
CHURCH
(☑328 1911316; www.parrocchiadisantandrea-it.it; Piazza della Repubblica; ⊙8.30am-12.30pm & 3.30-7.30pm) This 12th-century church, with its curious decagonal bell tower, presides over Piazza della Repubblica, once Orvieto's Roman forum and now a cafe-lined square in the medieval centre. Call ahead for an archaeologist-led tour of ancient Etruscan and Roman buildings and an early Christian church in the basement (€5).

Chiesa di San Giovenale
CHURCH
(Piazza San Giovenale; ⊙9am-12.30pm & 3.30-6.30pm) This tufa-brick church at the

❶ CARTA UNICA ORVIETO

The Carta Orvieto Unica (adult/reduced €20/17) is a discount card that covers entry to the town's nine main attractions, including the Duomo, Museo Claudio Faina e Civico, Orvieto Underground, Torre del Moro and Museo dell'Opera del Duomo di Orvieto. It also includes one return trip on the funicular (and another on a city bus). Buy it at participating sites or at the Carta Orvieto Unica ticket office (☑ 0763 34 06 88; Piazza Duomo 23; ⊙ 10.30am-12.15pm & 3.30-5.15pm Mon-Fri, 10.30am-12.30pm & 3.30-5.30pm Sat & Sun) next to the tourist office.

western end of town is one of Orvieto's oldest, dating from 1004. A solemn example of Romanesque-Gothic architecture, it boasts some wonderful 12th to 15th-century frescoes and a notable marble altar from 1170.

In front of the church, you can enjoy expansive views of the countryside from the town walls.

★☆ Festivals & Events

Umbria Jazz Winter   MUSIC
(www.umbriajazz.com; ⊙ late Dec-early Jan) Jazz and gospel music take to the *palazzi* and streets of Orvieto's historic centre to shake off the winter blues. Events culminate in a big party on New Year's Eve.

🛏 Sleeping

★ B&B Ripa Medici   B&B €
(☑ 328 7469620, 0763 34 13 43; www.ripamedici.com; Vicolo Ripa Medici 14; s €50, d €75-90; ◗✸�) Hugging the walls on the edge of Orvieto's old town, this gracious B&B takes the concept of a 'room with a view' to another level, gazing out across undulating countryside. But the dreamy views are just one of its attractions. The immaculate guest room and two apartments ooze charm and are lovingly furnished with antique pieces, timber beams and English farmhouse decor.

B&B La Magnolia   B&B €
(☑ 349 4620733, 0763 34 28 08; www.bblamagnolia.it; Via del Duomo 29; s €45-60, d €60-85, apt €55-140; ✸�) A short hop from the Duomo, this lovely B&B makes a handy base for the historic centre. It's a relaxed set-up with four light-filled rooms and three apartments, all

decorated in simple, cosy style and some boasting original 18th-century frescoes. The English-speaking owner Serena extends a friendly welcome and is a mine of local information.

★ Misia Resort   BOUTIQUE HOTEL €€
(☑ 0763 34 23 36; www.misiaresort.it; Località Rocca Ripesena 51; s/d/ste €80/130/160; ◗✸�) You won't regret going the extra mile to this boutique hotel in Rocca Ripesena, a panoramic hilltop hamlet 6km west of Orvieto. Its light, spacious rooms and suites, in the main hotel building and spread across the stone village, feature soft, earthy tones and stylish vintage touches – a chesterfield sofa here, a distressed wood beam there.

Hotel Duomo   HOTEL €€
(☑ 0763 34 18 87; www.orvietohotelduomo.com; Vicolo di Maurizio 7; s €70-90, d €100-130, ste €120-150; ◗✸@�) Bunk down in the shadow of the Duomo at this friendly three-star where the church bells will most likely be your wake-up call. Orvieto-born artist Livio Orazio Valentini has left bold, abstract paintings in some of the 18 guest rooms, which are tastefully decorated in polished woods and subdued cream colours.

🍴 Eating

Umbrichelli, a thick, spaghetti-like pasta, served *all'arrabbiata* (with spicy tomato sauce), stews of wild boar and – like most of Umbria – truffled *everything* are just a few of the delicacies that pair nicely with the town's renowned DOC wines.

Trattoria La Palomba   UMBRIAN €
(☑ 0763 34 33 95; Via Cipriano Manente 16; meals €30-35; ⊙ 12.30-2.15pm & 7.30-10pm Thu-Tue; �) If you want to know what a genuine Italian trattoria experience is all about, head to this family-run local favourite. Wood panelling and old-school house wine labels abound, and the food – heavy on homemade pastas, hearty game sauces and aromatic local truffles – hits the spot perfectly. Bookings highly recommended.

Trattoria La Pergola   TRATTORIA €€
(☑ 0763 34 30 65; www.lapergolaorvieto.com; Via dei Magoni 9B; meals €25-30; ⊙ 12.15-3pm & 7.15-10pm Thu-Tue) This charming backstreet trattoria disproves any theories that you can't eat well near major tourist sites. A family-run outfit, it cooks up hearty regional food near the Duomo, serving the likes of gnocchi

with bacon, spinach and truffle sauce, and casseroled wild boar, in a cosy front room or a walled courtyard at the back.

Al Pozzo Etrusco   UMBRIAN €€

(☑0763 34 10 50; www.alpozzoetruscodagiovanni. it; Piazza dei Ranieri 1a; meals €30-35; ⊙12.30-2.30pm & 7.30-9.30pm Wed-Mon; 🐾) Named after an ancient Etruscan well that graces its basement, this is a firm local favourite. Your host, Giovanni, will guide you through his seasonal menu of updated Umbrian delights, best enjoyed al fresco on the charming candlelit terrace. Pastas are seasoned with herbed meats and flavoursome vegetables, paving the way for original mains such as beef cheeks stewed in red beer.

★ I Sette Consoli   ITALIAN €€€

(☑0763 34 39 11; www.isetteconsoli.it; Piazza Sant'Angelo 1a; meals €40-45, tasting menu €45; ⊙12.30-3pm & 7.30-10pm, closed Wed & dinner Sun) This refined restaurant walks the culinary high wire in Orvieto, serving inventive, artfully presented dishes, from joyful starters such as *panzanella* (a bread-based salad typical of central Italy) with vegetables and anchovies to pasta so light it almost floats off the fork. In good weather, try to get a table in the back garden. Dress for dinner and reserve ahead.

🍷 Drinking & Nightlife

Bottega Vera   WINE BAR

(☑349 4300167; www.casaveraorvieto.it/it/bottega.html; Via del Duomo 36; ⊙8.30am-8.30pm Mon-Fri & Sun, to 10pm Sat; 🐾) This stylish gourmet deli and wine shop has been pouring the good stuff since 1938, when it was started by grandmother of current host Cesare, who will expertly guide you through his daily selections of wine by the glass (from €3). Of Cesare's 120 wines or so, half are from Orvieto.

❶ Information

Tourist Office (☑0763 34 17 72; Piazza Duomo 24; ⊙8.15am-1.50pm & 4-7pm Mon-Fri, 10am-6pm Sat & Sun) Helpful office opposite the Duomo. Can supply city maps and up-to-date information on the principal sights.

❶ Getting There & Away

BUS

Busitalia (☑075 963 76 37; www.fsbusitalia.it) services depart from the **bus station** (Piazza Cahen), often also stopping at the train station (p656). Destinations include Todi (€6.30, two hours, one daily Monday to Saturday during school term time) and Terni (€6.90, 2¼ hours, one daily Monday to Saturday).

ORVIETO'S WINE COUNTRY

Now renowned for its white DOC wines, Orvieto has been a wine-producing area for more than 2000 years. It was the Etruscans who first introduced viticulture to the region, recognising in its climate and volcanic soil the ideal conditions for growing vines. They carved caves into the soft tufa rock that underlies much of the surrounding countryside and left the grapes to slowly ferment. Today, wine is still stored in cool underground cellars cut into the tufa.

From the Middle Ages, Orvieto became famous in Italy and beyond for its super-sweet gold-coloured wines. Nowadays these have largely given way to drier blends, such as Orvieto DOC and Orvieto Classico.

To really immerse yourself in Orvieto's wine heritage, spend a night or two at the Locanda Palazzone (☑0763 39 36 14; www.locandapalazzone.com; Rocca Ripesena 67; ste from €200, apt €300-385; P🐾🏊), a highly respected local winery offering tastings and wine-making tours. These range from a simple three-wine tasting (€15) to tours of the winery (€25 to €45 including appetisers or a light lunch) and four-course wine-tasting dinners (€70).

Another winery worth searching out is Decugnano dei Barbi (☑0763 30 82 55; www.decugnanodeibarbi.com; Località Fossatello 50) 🚗, 18km east of Orvieto. You can tour its cellars – wines are stored in Etruscan tombs – and taste its minerally whites and Orvieto Classico reds (tastings €30 to €50 per person). For something more hands-on, sign up for one of its four-hour cookery classes (€95 to €150 per person).

CAR & MOTORCYCLE

Orvieto is on the Rome–Florence A1 autostrada, while the SS71 heads north to Lago Trasimeno. Your best bet for parking is the **Parcheggio Campo della Fiera** (per hour/day €1.50/12), which has a free lift up to the historic centre. There's also metered parking on Piazza Cahen.

TRAIN

Orvieto's **train station** (www.trenitalia.com; Via Antonio Gramsci) is 4km west of the *centro storico* (historic centre) in Orvieto Scalo. Direct trains run to/from Rome (€8.25 to €17.50, one to 1½ hours, hourly) and Florence (€14.90 to €16.70, two to 2½ hours, eight daily). Services to Perugia (€8.05 to €14.25, 1½ to two hours, hourly) involve a change at Orte or Terontola-Cortona.

ⓘ Getting Around

A century-old **funicular** (€1.30; ⊘ every 10min 7.15am-8.30pm Mon-Sat, every 15min 8am-8.30pm Sun) creaks up the wooded hill from Orvieto's train station (west of the centre) to Piazza Cahen. The fare includes a bus ride from Piazza Cahen to Piazza Duomo. Outside of funicular hours, bus 1 runs up to the old town from the train station (€1.30).

Local bus A (€1.30) connects Piazza Cahen with Piazza Duomo.

LE MARCHE

From white-pebble beaches and cliff-backed Adriatic bays to medieval hill towns and snow-capped peaks, Le Marche is one of Italy's least-known treasures.

Sandwiched between the Apennines and the Adriatic coast, this hilly region boasts a string of exquisite provincial towns. Chief among them is Urbino, whose beautifully preserved *centro storico* (historic centre) recalls its heyday as a Renaissance cultural centre and birthplace of the artist Raphael. Ascoli Piceno is another highlight, a refined, animated town famous for its fantastic food. Music fans should make a beeline for Macerata, whose hilltop centre rings to the sound of opera each summer.

In the region's western reaches, and bleeding over into neighbouring Umbria, the wild Parco Nazionale dei Monti Sibillini boasts dramatic mountain scenery and thrilling outdoor pursuits. The area suffered terribly in the 2016 earthquakes, but it has continued to rebuild.

ⓘ Getting There & Away

Drivers have two options for travelling along Le Marche's coastline: the A14 autostrada toll route or the parallel SS16. Inland, roads are either secondary or tertiary and much slower.

Regular trains ply the coast on the Bologna–Lecce main line, with spurs branching inland to Macerata and Ascoli Piceno.

Marche Airport (p659) in Ancona is the main aerial gateway, served by Lufthansa, EasyJet and Ryanair.

Ancona

POP 100,900

Ancona is often written off as just another gritty port. In fact, there's more to this historic city than ferries and transport connections, and to bypass it would be to miss much. It was founded by Greek settlers from Syracuse around 387 BC and its old town, crowned by a dramatically sited cathedral, harbours many reminders of its long history: archaeological artefacts, Roman arches, Romanesque churches, and Renaissance *palazzi* that glow softly in the evening light. Linger long enough in the hilltop parks, lively boulevards and cafe-rimmed piazzas and you'll start to see another, more likeable side to Le Marche's seafront capital.

◉ Sights

★**Pinacoteca Comunale di Ancona**   MUSEUM
(☑071 222 50 47; www.facebook.com/Pinacoteca Ancona; Palazzo Bosdari, Vicolo Foschi 4; adult/reduced €6/3; ⊘5-8pm Tue-Thu, from 10am Fri, 10am-1pm & 5-8pm Sat & Sun summer, 4-7pm Tue-Fri, from 10am Sat & Sun winter) Ancona's fascinating civic art gallery houses Le Marche's most important art collection. Spread over two 16th- to 17th-century *palazzi*, the museum traces the development of art in the region, skilfully juxtaposing modern and medieval works with daring disregard for either tradition or expectation. Unmissable masterpieces include the *Pala Gozzi* (1520), the first painting signed and dated by Titian, and Carlo Crivelli's absolutely flooring *Madonna col Bambino* (Madonna and Child; c 1480).

★**Museo Archeologico Nazionale delle Marche**   MUSEUM
(☑071 20 26 02; www.facebook.com/Museo ArcheologicoAncona; Via Ferretti 6; adult/reduced €5/2; ⊘8.30am-7.30pm Tue-Sun) Housed in

Ancona

the beautiful 16th-century **Palazzo Ferretti**, whose ceilings are covered with original frescoes and bas-reliefs, this museum presents a fascinating romp through time, from the Palaeolithic to the Middle Ages. Among its treasures are Neolithic flint daggers, richly embellished Attic vases, Etruscan votive bronzes, Celtic gold (the torques and crowns are stunning) and a pristine copy of the famous bronzes of Pergola (50–30 BC).

Cattedrale di San Ciriaco   CATHEDRAL
(Piazzale del Duomo; ☉8am-noon & 3-7pm summer, to 6pm winter) A stiff but scenic climb up from the old town, Ancona's domed cathedral dominates the city skyline. Guarded by two marble lions, it commands sweeping views from its perch atop the Colle Guasco (Guasco Hill), formerly the site of an ancient pagan temple. The church's origins date from the 6th century, but it took on much of its current form between the 12th and 13th centuries and today features an architectural

EXPLORING ANCONA'S ARCHES

At the northern end of the port stands one of Ancona's most high-profile ancient landmarks: the **Arco di Traiano** (Trajan's Arch; Banchina Nazario Sauro), a Roman triumphal arch built by Apollodorus of Damascus between AD 110 and 116 to honour the Emperor Trajan. Beyond it, and accessible by a walkway along a defensive wall, is Luigi Vanvitelli's grand **Arco Clementino** (Clementine's Arch; Molo Nord), inspired by Apollodorus' arch and dedicated to Pope Clement XII.

From the arch, backtrack and follow the seafront road south for approximately 1.7km to the **Mole Vanvitelliana** (☑ 071 281 19 35; www.museoomero. it; Banchina Da Chio 28; ⊗ museum 5-8pm Tue-Thu & Sat, 10am-1pm & 5-8pm Fri & Sun, shorter hours winter) **FREE**, a vast pentagonal building designed by Luigi Vanvitelli in 1732. Just before it, the baroque **Porta Pia** (Largo Caduti sul Mare 27) was built as a monumental town entrance in the late 18th century at the behest of Pope Pius VI.

potpourri of Byzantine, Romanesque and Gothic features.

Wandering downhill from the cathedral along Piazza Anfiteatro, you'll see the remains of the city's Roman **amphitheatre**, believed to have been built during the reign of Emperor Augustus.

Piazza del Plebiscito
PIAZZA

Crowned by the baroque **Chiesa di San Domenico** (⊗ 8.30am-noon & 5-6pm), this sloping cafe-lined square has been Ancona's favourite meeting spot since medieval times. At its head, set in a grand staircase, sits a gigantic statue of Pope Clement XII, the 18th-century pontiff who was honoured by the city for giving it free port status – hence the square's alternative name, Piazza del Papa.

The nearby fountain is a more recent addition, dating from the 19th century.

Chiesa di Santa Maria della Piazza
CHURCH

(Piazza Santa Maria; ⊗ hours vary but typically 10.30am-12.30pm & 4.30-7.30pm) Contrasting sharply with the industrial scenery of the nearby port, the Chiesa di Santa Maria della Piazza is one of Ancona's showpiece churches. Its distinct Romanesque form, which comprises a fine marble facade and elaborate arched portal, dates from the 13th century when it was built over an earlier paleo-Christian basilica. Remains of this early basilica can still be seen beneath the main church – particularly striking are the mosaic floors and traces of 4th- to 6th-century frescoes.

🛏 Sleeping

Casa Scotty
B&B €

(☑ 391 7044102; www.bnbcasascotty.it; Piazza Antonio da Sangallo 9; r per person €35-45; P ❄ 🐾) Affable hosts Ferruccio and Fabio (along with Ice, their Scottish terrier) greet you with a warm smile at this hilltop B&B. Situated about 10 minutes' walk from the centre, it's a homey apartment set-up with two pristine bedrooms (no TVs but good wi-fi), a shared bathroom and a lounge/kitchen whose large windows offer dizzying views of the port and waterfront.

La Mansarda di Lorenzo
APARTMENT €

(☑ 071 918 88 03, 335 6196326; www.facebook. com/LaMansardaDiLorenzo; Via Cuneo 1, Falconara Marittima; apt €50-80; P ❄ 🐾) Handily placed near the airport in Falconara Marittima, this penthouse apartment is a delight – spacious, immaculate, homey and run by the amiable Lorenzo. Sleeping up to four people, it's kitted out with lounge and dining areas, a huge terrace and a proper kitchen with breakfast goodies. Give Lorenzo a call and he'll even pick you up from the airport.

★ SeePort Hotel
BOUTIQUE HOTEL €€

(☑ 071 971 51 00; www.seeporthotel.com; Rupi di Via XXIX Settembre 12; d €84-159, ste €189-259; P ❄ 🐾) This sleek, sea-facing four-star sets the standard in Ancona. Housed in a converted 1950s brick building overlooking the port, it sports a crisp minimalist look, all cool whites, plate-glass windows and slate-greys, and its light, parquet-floored rooms are among the most stylish in town.

Grand Hotel Passetto
HOTEL €€

(☑ 071 3 13 07; www.hotelpassetto.it; Via Thaon de Revel 1, Passetto; s €86-141, d €108-215, ste €192-259; P ❄ @ 🐾 ☀) Enjoying a lovely location near Ancona's white-shingle beach, this genteel hotel is a classic seaside pile. There's something slightly old-fashioned about the place, but staff extend a warm welcome and its sunny, light-filled rooms are attractive with hardwood floors and crisp white linen.

Extras include sea views, a heated pool and garage parking (€15 per night).

✗ Eating

The two main strips, Corso Garibaldi and Corso Mazzini, are lined with restaurants, cafes and sliced-pizza takeaways, some of which can be fiercely packed at lunchtime (aim to arrive early). The city's culinary claim to fame is *stoccafisso all'anconetana* (stockfish – similar to salted cod but somewhat milder – with potatoes, tomatoes, *verdicchio* wine and a boatload of olive oil).

Alice's Restaurant   SEAFOOD €
(🖉 071 3 31 37; Circolo Tennis, Viale della Vittoria 44; €20-25; ⊗12.15-2.30pm & 7.30-10.30pm, closed Sun & Mon evenings) Hidden away in a tennis club near the Passetto, this workaday fish restaurant is as authentic as it gets. Every lunch, crowds of hungry locals – everyone from construction workers to besuited business folk and families – descend for simple seafood staples prepared well and served quickly. Don't expect silver service, though: it's all cheerfully rough and ready.

★ Osteria del Pozzo   SEAFOOD €€
(🖉 071 207 39 96; www.osteriadelpozzo.net; Via Bonda 2; meals €25-35; ⊗noon-2.30pm & 7.30-10pm Mon-Sat; 🥢) Unless you've booked ahead, you'll be lucky to grab one of the cheek-by-jowl tables at this long-standing favourite. The big draw is its coveted seafood, washed down with inexpensive house wine and served in brisk, efficient style. Everything is good, but standouts include a *millefoglie* (mille-feuille) starter of *baccalà* (salt-dried cod) and puréed potato, and the oven-baked sea bass.

La DegOsteria   RISTORANTE €€
(🖉 071 20 30 31; www.ladegosteria.it; Via Ciriaco Pizzecolli 3; meals €40-45; ⊗12.30-3pm & 7.30-10.30pm, closed Mon & Sat lunch; 🥢) This fashionable restaurant, set virtually on top of the Chiesa di Santa Maria della Piazza, cuts a contemporary dash in the heart of the historic centre. With its clapboard red-and-white flooring and modish modern decor, its interior sets a stylish setting for creative, forward-looking cuisine.

🍷 Drinking & Nightlife

Piazza del Plebiscito – known to locals as Piazza del Papa – is one of the most popular spots for an al fresco drink, with several cafes and bars ringing the pretty square.

Bar Torino   BAR
(www.facebook.com/bartorinoancona1860; Corso Garibaldi 49; cocktails €6-7; ⊗6.30pm-midnight, to 9pm in winter) Slinging cocktails since 1860, this righteously retro bar is one of Ancona's liveliest *aperitivo* haunts. The Americano and Negroni *Marchigiano* (with the vermouth traded for *verdicchio* wine) are fantastic, as are the abundant accompanying snacks. But the headline act is the Torino Special, a spiky blend of red vermouth, Campari, vanilla liqueur and bitter orange.

The name comes from the bar's claim to be the first in Italy outside of Turin to serve Vermouth.

❶ Information

Tourist Office (🖉 071 207 64 31; www.turismo.marche.it; Banchina Nazario Sauro 50; ⊗9am-6pm daily summer, to 2pm Mon-Fri & 2.30-6pm Tue & Thu winter) Down at the ferry port, this is the tourist office for Ancona and Le Marche province. Stop by for leaflets, maps, itineraries and more.

❶ Getting There & Away

AIR
Marche Airport (🖉 071 2 82 71; www.aeroportomarche.it; Piazzale Sandro Sordoni, Falconara Marittima) Lufthansa, EasyJet and Ryanair (with regular flights to London Stansted) are among the airlines that fly into Marche Airport, some 19km west of Ancona.

BUS
Most buses leave from Piazza Cavour inland from the port – it's a five-minute walk east of the seafront along Corso Giuseppe Garibaldi. An exception are summer services to Portonovo, which depart from the train station.

Destination	Fare (€)	Duration	Frequency
Macerata	4.10	1½hr	13 daily
Marche Airport	5.50	30min	based on flight times
Numana	2.60	40min	up to 15 daily
Portonovo	1.25	35min	up to 16 daily summer

CAR & MOTORCYCLE
Ancona is on the A14 autostrada, linking Bologna with Bari. The SS16 coastal road runs parallel to the autostrada and provides a toll-free alternative if you're not looking to get anywhere fast. The SS76 connects Ancona with Perugia and Rome.

Parking is a challenge in Ancona with space at a premium and street parking expensive in the centre (€1.20 to €2.70 per hour). A good option is the multi-storey **Parcheggio Degli Archi** (☑ 071 20 37 48; www.anconaparcheggi. it; Via Terenzio Mamiani; per hour/day €0.50/2; ◷5.30am-9pm Mon-Sat) near the train station, which has economical all-day parking from Monday to Saturday.

You'll find all the major car hire companies at the airport, including **Europcar** (☑071 916 22 40; www.europcar.it; ◷8.30am-7pm Mon-Fri, to 4pm Sat, to 12.30pm Sun), **Avis** (☑071 5 22 22; www.avisautonoleggio.it; ◷8.30am-8.30pm & 10.30-11.30pm Mon-Fri, 8.30am-10.30pm Sat, 9-11am & 2-6pm Sun) and **Hertz** (☑071 207 37 98; www.hertz.it; ◷8.30am-10pm Mon, to 6.30pm Tue-Sat, 8.30am-12.30pm Sun); **Maggiore** (☑071 4 26 24; www.maggiore.it; Piazza Carlo e Nello Rosselli; ◷8.30am-1pm Mon-Sat, plus 3-7pm Mon-Fri) is at the train station.

FERRY

Direct ferries operate from Ancona to Greece, Croatia and Albania.

TRAIN

Ancona is on the Bologna–Lecce main line. Direct trains serve the following destinations from the **train station** (Piazza Carlo e Nello Rosselli):

Destination	Fare (€)	Duration	Frequency
Bari	39.50-58	3¾-4¾hr	hourly
Bologna	16.50-33.50	1¾-2¾hr	twice hourly
Milan	39.90-66	3¼-5hr	15 daily
Pesaro	5.20-13	25-45min	twice hourly
Rome	17.75-32.50	4hr	seven daily

❶ Getting Around

TO/FROM THE AIRPORT

From Castelferreti station, opposite the terminal at Marche Airport, trains run frequently to Ancona (€2.15, 15 to 25 minutes, 13 daily).

FERRIES ACROSS THE ADRIATIC

The port of Ancona is a jumping-off point for three countries: Greece, Croatia and Albania. Check ferry websites for a comprehensive list of schedules and prices.

Greece

Anek Lines (☑071 207 23 46; www.anekitalia.com; Via XXIX Settembre 2/o; ◷8.30am-7pm Mon-Fri, 9am-1pm Sat) and **Superfast Ferries** (☑071 20 20 34; www.superfast.com; Webtours, Via XXIX Settembre 4/E; ◷9am-7pm Mon-Fri, 10am-1pm Sat) Sail to Igoumenitsa (8¼ hours) and Patras (22½ hours) six to seven times weekly, and to Corfu twice weekly in July and August. Fares range from €63 to €85 for a deck ticket, and €273 to €385 for a luxe cabin (based on double occupancy).

Minoan Lines (☑071 20 17 08; www.minoan.it; Frittelli Maritime, Lungomare Vanvitelli 18; ◷9am-1pm & 3-7pm Mon-Fri, 9am-1pm Sat) Serves Igoumenitsa and Patras from four to six times weekly (check the website for sailing times). Fares range from €69 to €91 on deck, and €269 to €369 for a luxe cabin (based on double occupancy).

Croatia

Jadrolinija (☑071 228 41 00; www.jadrolinija.hr; Agenzia Marittima Amatori, Via della Loggia 20; ◷9am-1pm & 3-7pm Mon-Fri) Runs year-round services to Split (deck €34 to €48, luxe cabin €119 to €150) two to four times weekly. In June and September it also runs four to five weekly ferries to Zadar (deck €40 to €55, luxe cabin €125 to €157, 8½ hours). In August a single weekly ferry stops at Stari Grad (deck €37 to €55, luxe cabin €139 to €157, 10 hours).

Snav (☑081 428 55 55; www.snav.it) From mid-April to October, sails to Split (11 hours) four to six times weekly. Fares are €40 for deck passage, and €102 to €142 for a seaview cabin (based on double occupancy).

Albania

Adria Ferries (☑071 5021 1621; www.adriaferries.com; Frittelli Maritime, Lungomare Vanvitelli 18; ◷9am-1pm & 3-7pm Mon-Fri, to 1pm Sat) Sails to Durrës (20 hours) on Tuesdays, Thursdays and Saturdays. Fares range from €75 to €95 for desk passage, and €175 to €215 for a luxe suite (based on double occupancy).

Alternatively, **Conero Bus** (☑ 071 283 74 11; www.conerobus.it) runs the Aerobus Raffaelo to/from Piazza Cavour and Piazza Kennedy in the centre. Services are set to coincide with flight arrivals and departures – check Conero's website for the latest times; the trip costs €5.50 one way and takes around 30 minutes.

A taxi to central Ancona will cost around €35 and takes approximately 30 minutes.

BUS

Conero Bus (☑ 071 283 74 11; www.conerobus. it) runs Ancona's bus services. Numbers 1/3 and 1/4 connect the main train station with Piazza Cavour, while number 12 runs from the station to the **ferry port** (Via Luigi Einaudi). A single ticket costs €1.25.

Parco del Conero

Only minutes from Ancona but a world unto itself, the Parco del Conero is stunning, with limestone cliffs plunging into the cobalt blue Adriatic and arching white-pebble bays backed by fragrant woods of pine, oak, beech, broom and oleander trees. Walking trails thread through the 60-sq-km regional park, which is remarkably still off the radar for many travellers and retains a peaceful, unspoilt air found nowhere else on the coast of Le Marche. Its highest peak is the 572m-high **Monte Conero**, which takes a spectacular nosedive into the sea and provides fertile soil for the vineyards that taper down its slopes, giving rise to the excellent, full-bodied Rosso Conero red wine.

The park encompasses the resorts of **Portonovo**, **Sirolo** and **Numana**, all of which make fine bases for exploring. Boat trips from Numana or Sirolo are the best way to cove- or beach-hop.

🛏 Sleeping

Camping Internazionale   CAMPGROUND €
(☑ 071 933 08 84; www.campinginternazionale. com; Via San Michele 10, Sirolo; camping 2 people, car & tent €26-54, for sea view add €5-12, bungalows €60-220; ☉ mid-May–mid-Sep; @ 🛜 🛝) Shaded in trees just a few minutes' (steep) walk above Sirolo's beaches, this coastal campground boasts a prime location, stunning sea views and excellent facilities: a swimming pool, pizzeria, bar, grocery store and children's club with plenty of activities to keep the little ones amused.

★**Acanto Country House**   GUESTHOUSE €€
(☑071 933 11 95; www.acantocountryhouse.com; Via Ancarano 18, Sirolo; s €70, d €90-140, ste €100-150; P ✻ 🛜 🛝) Set back from Sirolo's beaches and surrounded by cornfields, meadows and olive groves, this converted farmhouse is a gorgeous country hideaway. Named after flowers like peony and rose, its rooms have been designed with the utmost attention to detail, with gleaming wood floors, exposed stone and embroidered bedspreads. Outside, you can relax in the gardens and enjoy bucolic views from the panoramic saltwater pool.

🍴 Eating

Osteria Sara   SEAFOOD €€
(☑ 071 933 07 16; Corso Italia 9, Sirolo; ☉12.30-2.30pm & 7.30-9.45pm Thu-Tue) An old-school *osteria* serving excellent seafood on Sirolo's main square. Its small dining room, all white walls and ageing framed pictures, fills quickly as diners pour in to sample marinated anchovies and tuna carpaccio starters followed by seafood risotto and mains such as grilled catch of the day.

★**Ristorante da Giacchetti**   SEAFOOD €€
(☑ 071 80 13 84; www.ristorantedagiacchetti.it; Località Portonovo 171; meals €35-50; ☉12.30-3pm & 7.45-10.30pm Mar-Oct) Beachfront eating hits the heights at this, the best of Portonovo's wildly popular seaside restaurants. To keep it local, try the *moscioli di Portonovo* (mussels), a renowned speciality in these parts, and *stoccafisso all'anconetana,* Ancona's trademark stockfish stew, perhaps paired with a crisp regional *verdicchio* (white wine).

La Torre   SEAFOOD €€
(☑ 071 933 07 47; www.latorrenumana.it; Via la Torre 1, Numana; fixed-price lunch menu €28, meals €40; ☉12.30-2.30pm & 7.30-10.30pm) Floor-to-ceiling glass walls maximise the wrap-around sea views from this sleek fish restaurant located on a panoramic point in Numana. Oysters, prawns, tuna and *baccalà* (cod) appear in artfully crafted *antipasti,* while pastas and mains make tasty use of sea urchins, clams, cuttlefish and the like. Its weekday lunch menu offers a taste at a snip of the regular price.

ℹ Information

Parco del Conero Visitor Centre (☑ 071 933 11 61; www.parcodelconero.org; Via Peschiera 30a, Sirolo; ☉ visitor centre 9am-noon Sat &

UMBRIA & LE MARCHE PARCO DEL CONERO

PARCO DEL CONERO'S BEACHES

With its spectacular coastal scenery and magical blue waters, the Parco del Conero boasts some of the Adriatic's best beaches.

The most celebrated is the Spiaggia delle Due Sorelle, a remote white-pebble beach named after two rock stacks (the *Due Sorelle* or two sisters) that rise out of the turquoise sea. It's an idyllic spot but it can get very busy in summer, despite the fact it's only accessible by sea. Ferries run to the beach from mid-June to September, sailing from the port at Numana up to four times daily and less frequently from the Spiaggia San Michele at Sirolo. Bank on a return fare of around €20. Alternatively, you can rent a kayak and paddle your own way there.

Easier to access are Sirolo's two beaches: Spiaggia Urbani and Spiaggia San Michele. Both can be reached on foot, or by a summer shuttle bus from Sirolo, and both are quite beautiful: gentle arcs of sand and shingle backed by white cliffs cloaked in ever-green trees and aromatic Mediterranean *macchia* (shrubland).

Sun spring, longer hours summer, offices 9am-1pm Mon-Fri & 3-6pm Tue & Thu) The park's visitor centre can provide information on the park and sells maps. If the main visitor centre is closed, ask at the admin offices in the building behind.

ℹ️ Getting There & Away

Conero Bus (☑ 071 283 74 11; www.conerobus. it) runs summer buses to Portonovo (€1.25, 35 minutes, up to 16 daily) from Ancona's train station, and to Numana (€2.60, 40 minutes, up to 15 daily) from Piazza Cavour in Ancona. That said, the area is much easier to explore with your own wheels.

Pesaro

POP 95,000

Summer seaside fun goes hand in hand with high culture in Pesaro, Le Marche's second-largest city. It's not an immediately attractive place, but look beyond the concrete high-rise hotels and crowds of bronzed holidaymakers jostling for beach space in August and you'll find a lot to like. Its setting is perfect, with beaches of fine golden sand fringing the Adriatic and a backdrop of undulating hills, and it has a handsome historic centre of Liberty-style villas and Renaissance *palazzi*. The composer Rossini was born here, and every year opera fans pour into town for the renowned Rossini Opera Festival.

◉ Sights

Musei Civici   MUSEUM
(www.pesaromusei.it; Piazza Toschi Mosca 29; adult/reduced incl Casa Rossini €10/8; ⊙10am-1pm & 4.30-7.30pm Tue-Sun, shorter hours winter) Once the residence of a powerful noble fam-
ily, the 16th-century Palazzo Mosca provides the aristocratic setting for Pesaro's premier museum. Of the paintings on display, the main draw is Giovanni Bellini's *Incoronazione della Vergine* (Coronation of the Virgin), a striking altarpiece painted in around 1475. The museum also showcases Pesaro's stunning 700-year-old pottery tradition, with one of Italy's best collections of majolica ceramics.

Casa Rossini   MUSEUM
(www.pesaromusei.it; Via Rossini 34; adult/reduced incl Musei Civici €10/8; ⊙10am-1pm & 4.30-7.30pm Tue-Sun, shorter hours winter) In 1792 composer Gioachino Rossini was born in this four-storey town house on what is now the main drag through Pesaro's historic centre. The small museum is dedicated to the maestro, with prints, personal items, portraits, even a small piano, illustrating his life and famous operas, such as the 1816 bestseller, *Il barbiere di Siviglia* (The Barber of Seville).

✷ Festivals & Events

Rossini Opera Festival   MUSIC
(☑ 0721 380 02 94; www.rossinioperafestival.it; ⊙Aug) This two-week festival is a love letter to Pesaro's favourite son. Productions of Rossini's operas and concerts are staged at the Teatro Rossini and Vitrifrigo Arena. Tickets go for anything from €20 to €160, with substantial discounts for students and on last-minute purchases.

🛏️ Sleeping & Eating

Pesaro is a seaside resort town and the city offers a huge range of accommodation covering all budgets and styles. And while many places are uninspiring 1960s concrete blocks, there are some real charmers tucked away among them. You'll need to book ahead for the summer when many places impose minimum stays. Many hotels shut up shop from October to Easter. For help with accommodation, contact the **Associazione Pesarese di Albergatori** (⌨0721 6 79 59; www.apahotel.it; Piazzale della Libertà 10; ⊙9am-1pm Mon-Fri & 3-7pm Tue).

Hotel Clipper   HOTEL €€
(⌨0721 3 09 15; www.hotelclipper.it; Viale Guglielmo Marconi 53; s €40-170, d €44-203; [P][❄][🛜]) On first sight, the Clipper appears to be just another old seaside hotel with a cavernous lobby and tired 1970s-style decor. But stay here and you'll discover its rooms are bright and modern, staff are welcoming, breakfast is a feast and its location, near the beach and within walking distance of the historic centre, is ideal.

L'Angolo di Mario   SEAFOOD, PIZZA €€
(⌨0721 6 58 50; www.angolodimario.it; Via Nazario Sauro; pizza €2.50-11, meals €25-35; ⊙noon-2.45pm & 7-11pm Mar-Nov; 🛜) A popular seafront set-up, L'Angolo di Mario couples views with contemporary decor, swift service and reliably good food. Bag a table on the terrace to gaze across the Adriatic as you dig into octopus salad, perhaps followed by a heaped-high plate of *tagliolini ai frutti di mare* (noodles with mixed seafood). Booking recommended at weekends.

Antica Osteria La Guercia   TRATTORIA €€
(⌨0721 3 34 63; www.osterialaguercia.it; Via Baviera 33; meals €25; ⊙12.30-2.30pm & 7.30-11pm Mon-Sat) In a 15th-century backstreet building off Piazza del Popolo, this old-school trattoria is straight out of central casting with its timber beams, exposed brick and rough wooden tables. It's all just right for a meal of no-nonsense regional fare – chickpea soup with clams and pasta squares, roast pork and potatoes, and cheese with fig marmalade.

☆ Entertainment

Teatro Rossini   THEATRE
(⌨0721 38 76 20; www.teatridipesaro.it; Piazza Lazzarini 1; ⊙box office 5-7.30pm Wed-Sat, on performance days 10am-1pm & 5-9pm Mon-Sat, 10am-1pm Sun) With its grand ceiling and ornate box seats, Pesaro's historic theatre sets a lavish stage for theatrical performances, concerts and opera, especially during the Rossini Opera Festival.

ℹ Information

Tourist Office (⌨0721 6 93 41; www.turismo.marche.it; Piazzale della Libertà 11; ⊙9am-1pm Mon, Wed & Fri, 9am-1pm & 2.30-5.30pm Tue & Thu, longer hours summer) Friendly office with maps and excellent information (in English) on bike paths, accommodation, sights and events.

WORTH A TRIP

A PILGRIMAGE TO LORETO

Straddling a hilltop south of Ancona, Loreto is dominated by the domed **Basilica della Santa Casa** (www.santuarioloreto.it; Piazza della Madonna; ⊙615am-7.30pm summer, to 7pm winter). This majestic sanctuary is one of Italy's most celebrated pilgrimage sites. The basilica, built between 1469 and 1587, is a stunning hybrid of Gothic and Renaissance styles, with a white two-tier facade, soaring dome and 75m-high bell tower by Luigi Vanvitelli. Inside, the chief focus is the **Santa Casa di Loreto**, a tiny brick house that is said to be where the Virgin Mary grew up and the Archangel Gabriel told her of her impending maternity.

Each year, thousands of pilgrims flock to the Casa, now enclosed in an ornate marble screen by Bramante. According to legend, a host of angels brought the house from Nazareth in 1294 after the Crusaders were expelled from Palestine.

As well as the Madonna's mythical home, Loreto can also offer Michelin-starred dining at the **Ristorante Andreina** (⌨071 97 01 24; www.ristoranteandreina.it; Via Buffolareccia 14; tasting menus €75-100, meals €60-70; ⊙noon-3pm & 8-10.30pm, closed lunch Tue & Wed), a renowned restaurant known for its superlative grilled meats.

Loreto sits 3km or so west of the A14 autostrada (exit Loreto–Porto Recanati). It's easily reached by train from Ancona (€3.20, 20 minutes, at least hourly).

❶ Getting There & Away

BUS

Pesaro's **bus station** (☑ 800 664332, 0722 37 67 38; www.adriabus.eu) is next to the train station on Piazzale Giovanni Falcone e Paolo Borsellino, about 1.5km southwest of the seafront.

Adriabus (☑ 0722 37 67 38, 800 664332; www.adriabus.eu; Piazzale Giovanni Falcone e Paolo Borsellino; ☺ ticket office 7.30am-1pm Mon-Sat) operates a weekday 5.40am bus to Rome (€35, five hours), and half-hourly buses to Urbino, alternating between normal (€3.40, 1¼ hours) and express services (€3.70, 40 minutes).

TRAIN

Pesaro's **train station** (www.trenitalia.com; Viale del Risorgimento) is on the Bologna–Lecce train line and you can reach Rome (€21.75 to €40.50, 3½ to 8¾ hours, 10 daily) directly once a day; other trains require a change in Falconara Marittima or Ancona. There are at least hourly services to Ancona (€5.20 to €18, 35 to 50 minutes), Rimini (€3.85 to €12, 20 to 35 minutes) and Bologna (€11.10 to €22.50, 1¼ to 2¼ hours).

The train station is on the western edge of town, about 1.5km from the beach.

Urbino

POP 14,600

Birthplace of the artist Raphael, Unesco-listed Urbino is both a vibrant university town and a model Renaissance city. Its immaculate *centro storico* appears to have changed little since the 15th century when it enjoyed a golden age under the powerful Duca Federico da Montefeltro, one of the giants of the Italian Renaissance.

◉ Sights

★ Palazzo Ducale – Galleria Nazionale delle Marche   MUSEUM

(☑ 0722 32 26 25; www.gallerianazionalemarche. it; Piazza Duca Federico; adult/reduced €8/5; ☺ 8.30am-7.15pm Tue-Sun, to 2pm Mon) Urbino's great architectural masterpiece, the 15th-century Palazzo Ducale provides the monumental setting for the Galleria Nazionale delle Marche and its stunning collection of Renaissance art. The palace's cavernous halls are lined with paintings by the likes of Titian, Signorelli, Guido Reni and Piero della Francesca, whose intriguing *Flagellazione di Cristo* (Flagellation of Christ) hangs in what was once the Duke of Urbino's library. Other highlights include Raphael's enigmatic *La Muta* (Portrait of a

Young Woman) and Luciano Laurana's *Città Ideale* (Ideal City).

The main part of the collection is displayed on the *piano nobile* (literally 'noble floor'), accessible via a grand staircase from the inner courtyard, the **Cortile d'Onore**. Works are hung in a seemingly endless series of rooms culminating in the immense **Salone del Trono**, a vast 35m-long and 17m-high space that served as the banqueting hall for Federico da Montefeltro, the powerful duke who had the palace built in the 1450s.

The duke, under whom Urbino became an important Renaissance centre, enlisted the foremost artists and architects of the age to create his showpiece residence. For the best views of the complex, head to Corso Garibaldi and look up at the **Facciata dei Torricini**, the building's signature facade with its trio of arched loggias and two circular towers.

Duomo   CATHEDRAL

(Via Puccinotti; ☺ currently closed) Rebuilt in the early 19th century in neoclassical style, the interior of Urbino's *duomo* commands much greater interest than its austere facade. Particularly memorable is Federico Barocci's *Ultima cena* (Last Supper).

At the time of research, the cathedral was closed for restoration work, but the adjacent **Museo Diocesano Albani** (☑ 0722 322 59; www.museodiocesanourbino.it; Piazza Pascoli 1; €3.50; ☺ 9.30am-1.30pm & 2-6pm Sat & Sun) was open at weekends.

Casa Natale di Raffaello   MUSEUM

(☑ 0722 32 01 05; www.casaraffaello.com; Via Raffaello 57; €3.50; ☺ 9am-1pm & 3-7pm Mon-Sat, 10am-1pm & 3-6pm Sun Mar-Oct, 9am-2pm Mon-Sat, 10am-1pm Sun Nov-Feb) This 15th-century house is where Renaissance artist Raphael was born in 1483 and spent his first 16 years. The museum, which displays copies of many of his celebrated masterpieces, takes a touching look at Raphael's family life. A highlight is the *Madonna con Bambino* (Madonna with Child) on the 1st floor, reckoned to be one of the artist's earliest frescoes.

Oratorio di San Giovanni   CHURCH

(☑ 0722 91 02 59; Via Barocci 31; adult/reduced €2.50/1.50; ☺ 10am-1pm & 3-6pm Mon-Sat, 10am-1pm Sun) This 14th-century red-brick church features a series of brightly coloured frescoes by Lorenzo and Giacomo Salimbeni. Behind the main altar is a gripping depiction of the *Crocefissione* (Crucifixion) while

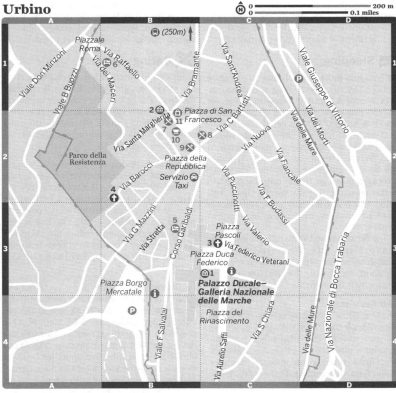

Urbino

◎ Top Sights

◎ Sights

🛏 Sleeping

✖ Eating

🍷 Drinking & Nightlife

🛍 Shopping

the right wall is given over to the life of St John the Baptist.

🎭 Festivals & Events

Urbino boasts a year-round calendar of festivals and cultural events. As well as the headline Festa del Duca, key dates include **Urbino Musica Antica Festival Internazionale** in late July and the **Urbino Plays Jazz Festival** in early August. The first Sunday in September is time for the **Festa dell'Aquilone**, a bright, multi-coloured kite festival.

Festa del Duca CULTURAL
(www.urbinofestadelduca.it; ⊙ 2nd or 3rd Sun Aug) For three or four days in August, Urbino

time-travels back to the Middle Ages, with medieval fun hitting the streets in the form of costumed pageants, markets and the re-enactment of a horseback tournament.

🛏 Sleeping

★**Locanda della Valle Nuova** AGRITURISMO €
(☑0722 33 03 03, 329 8975940; www.vallenuova. it; La Cappella 14, Sagrata di Fermignano; d €56, apt €80-150, dinners per person €30; ☺late Apr-early Nov; P@🛜🌊) 🍴 What a delight this organic farm is, with bright, immaculate rooms and lovely, soothing views across wooded hills to the mountains beyond. Whether you want to rustle up an Italian feast with a cookery class, go truffle hunting or learn basket-weaving, friendly owner Giulia will oblige. She is also a terrific cook and dinners (book in advance) are feasts of homegrown goodies.

The farm is 16km south of Urbino (follow signs to Fermignano, then Sagrata), but the English-speaking owners will assist you with transport and visiting the local towns. Minimum stay is three nights.

B&B Albornoz B&B €
(☑347 2987897; www.bbalbornoz.com; Via dei Maceri 23; s/d €50/80; 🛜) Wedged in a quiet old-town corner, this B&B offers boutique style for a pinch of the price. A spiral staircase links three contemporary designed studio flats, with murals, funky lighting and bold artworks, from the monochromatic 'You and Me' to the floral, lilac-kissed romance of 'Osaka'. All come with kitchenettes and espresso machines.

★**Tenuta Santi Giacomo e Filippo** AGRITURISMO €€
(☑0722 58 03 05; www.tenutasantigiacomoe filippo.it; Via San Giacomo in Foglia 7, Pantiere; s €79-149, d €99-189, ste €109-209, meals €30-40; P❄🛜🌊) 🍴 You can't help but unwind the minute you check into this gorgeous country retreat. Surrounded by vineyards, aromatic gardens and verdant hills, it sits in glorious isolation some 13km north of Urbino, offering stylish, individually decorated rooms spread across six tastefully converted stone buildings.

Albergo Italia HOTEL €€
(☑0722 27 01; www.albergo-italia-urbino.it; Corso Garibaldi 32; s €50-75, d €80-130; ❄🛜) Set under the porticoes on Corso Garibaldi, the three-star Italia is well located for pretty much everything – it's a hop from the historic centre action and it's near the staircase/lift up from the Borgo Mercatale car park. Rooms are spacious and comfortable, if rather functional, and staff are helpful.

🍴 Eating

Urbino's ubiquitous local speciality is *crescia sfogliata*. Similar to Emilia-Romagna's *piadina* (flat bread), the *urbinate* version is enhanced with eggs, salt and pepper, then stuffed with all sorts of goodness – the most common combo is *prosciutto* (ham) and local *pecorino* cheese.

Sorbetto del Duca GELATO
(www.sorbettodelduca.com/; Via Raffaello 1; tubs & cones €2.50-4.50; ☺11.30am-10pm) Set on prime Piazza della Repubblica real estate, this ever-popular gelateria is perfectly placed for a cooling break. The house speciality is pomegranate gelato, but there are plenty of other flavours to choose from, including a lick-your-lips *caramello al sale* (salted caramel).

La Trattoria del Leone TRATTORIA €€
(☑0722 32 98 94; www.latrattoriadelleone.it; Via Cesare Battisti 5; meals €25-30; ☺6.30-10.30pm Mon-Sat, plus 12.30-2.30pm Sat & Sun) 🍴 This cosy basement trattoria raids Le Marche's larder for the best regional produce. Platters of cheese and cold cuts whet appetites for dishes such as ravioli with local Casciotta cheese and roast pork seasoned with spices. Save an inch for the excellent chocolate cake.

★**Antica Osteria da la Stella** OSTERIA €€€
(☑0722 32 02 28; www.anticaosteriadalastel la.com; Via Santa Margherita 1; meals €45-50; ☺12.30-2.15pm & 7.30-10.30pm, closed Sun dinner & Mon lunch; 🛜) Duck down a quiet side street to this elegant, wood-beamed restaurant, occupying what was once a 15th-century inn patronised by the likes of Piero della Francesca. Legendary in these parts, it serves a menu of updated regional dishes prepared with seasonal, locally sourced ingredients and dreamy, homemade pastas. Skipping dessert is unwise.

🍸 Drinking & Nightlife

Caffè Raffaello CAFE
(Via Raffaello 41; ☺6am-8pm Mon-Sat) For much of the day this unassuming cafe quietly goes about its business, but come 7pm it springs to life as crowds of students and middle-aged urbanites stop by for their nightly *aperitivo*. Armed with glasses of excellent

marchigiana wine, they spill out onto the street, only to disperse an hour or so later as the cafe shuts for the day.

🛍 Shopping

⭐ **Raffaello Degusteria**   FOOD & DRINKS
(☑ 0722 32 95 46; www.raffaellodegusteria.it; Via Bramante 8; ⊙ 9am-1pm & 4-8pm Mon-Sat) The best spot in town for local products, with an encyclopeadic selection of *casciotta d'Urbina* cheeses, *salumi, biscotti* (biscuits), wines, craft beers, honeys, grappas, olive oils, truffles and even local saffron. At least 90% of their inventory counts as *marchigiana* (from Le Marche).

ℹ Information

Tourist Infopoint (☑ 0722 26 31; www.urbino servizi.it; Piazza Borgo Mercatale; ⊙ 7am-8pm Mon-Fri, from 8am Sat) Pick up free maps and other tourist info at this small tourist information office at the entrance of the lift up to the historic centre.

Tourist Office (☑ 0722 26 31; www.facebook.com/Urbino.iat.turismo; Via Puccinotti 35; ⊙ 9am-1pm Mon-Fri & 3-5.45pm Tue & Fri, longer hours summer) Urbino's main tourist information office is in the old town, across from Palazzo Ducale.

ℹ Getting There & Around

BUS
Adriabus (☑ 800 664332, 0722 376738; www.adriabus.eu) runs a fast bus service (No 46)

from the **Terminal Bus** (Viale Antonio Gramsci) to Pesaro (€3.70, 40 minutes, hourly Monday to Saturday, eight on Sundays), from where you can pick up onward trains. These buses leave from Stall A.

To reach the Terminal Bus, take the elevator from outside Porta San Lucia. You'll actually need to take two elevators: one down to level 6 and then another from inside the Porta Santa Lucia Centro Commerciale down to level 0.

Buy tickets for buses at the Terminal.

CAR & MOTORCYCLE
Urbino is 37km or so southwest of Pesaro along the SP423.

Most vehicles are banned from Urbino's walled centre. There are car parks outside the city gates, including the main one at Borgo Mercatale. Parking here costs €1.50 per hour or €10 per day.

Macerata

POP 41,800

Set amid low-lying green hills, Macerata is a charming provincial town with a wonderfully preserved hilltop centre and an animated student population – its university is one of Europe's oldest, dating from 1290. Its old town, threaded through by skinny cobblestone streets lined by honey-coloured brick *palazzi*, springs to life in summer for the town's celebrated month-long opera festival (p668).

(p668)

WORTH A TRIP

GROTTE DI FRASASSI

Deep in the hill country near the remote village of Genga, the Grotte di Frasassi (☑ 800 166250; www.frasassi.com; adult/reduced €18/12; ⊙ 10am-6pm summer, to 5pm winter; 🅿) is one of Europe's largest cave systems. This karst wonderland, gouged out by the river Sentino and discovered by a team of climbers in September 1971, can be explored on a 75-minute guided tour. This takes in features such as the Ancona Abyss, a cavernous 200m-high, 180m-long chamber, and the so-called Gran Canyon full of parallel stalactites resembling pipe organs and waxy stalagmites that rise up like melted candles.

Tours in English depart at 11.40am, 1.40pm and 3.40pm daily from mid-May to June, with an additional 5.15pm departure in July and August, but it's worth calling ahead to check times. Outside of these months, tours are in Italian (with the exception of pre-reserved groups of 10 or more people). English-language audio guides are available, though these require earphones (either bring your own or buy them at the site for €3).

Wear comfortable shoes and bring an extra layer of clothing, as the 14°C temperature can feel nippy in summer.

To reach the caves from Ancona, take the SS76 off the A14 and look for the Genga-Sassoferrato exit. The car park, 1.5km east of the cave entrance at San Vittore Terme, is where you buy your tickets and catch the free shuttle bus to the caves. The closest train station, Genga-San Vittore Terme, is also next to the car park and ticket office.

⊙ Sights

★ Musei Civici di
Palazzo Buonaccorsi   MUSEUM
(📞0733 25 63 61; www.maceratamusei.it; Via Don Minzoni 24; adult/reduced €10/8, incl Arena Sferisterio; ⊙10.30am-1pm & 2.30-5.30pm Tue-Sun) Deep in the historic centre, the 17th-century Palazzo Buonaccorsi houses three of Macerata's best museums. The **Museo delle Carozza** boasts an extensive collection of horse-drawn carriages, while, upstairs, the picture gallery is dedicated to **Arte Antica** with works from the 13th to the 19th centuries. Best of all is the 2nd-floor **Galleria di Arte Moderna**, which showcases works by regional artists such as Macerata-born Ivo Pannaggi, a driving force behind Italian futurism in the 1920s and '30s.

Torre Civica   TOWER
(Piazza della Libertà) Conceived as early as 1492 but not completed until 1653, Macerata's 64m-tall civic tower looms over Piazza della Libertà. It's most obvious feature is its striking astronomical clock, in fact an exact replica of the original 16th-century clock that kept time here for some three centuries until 1882. It features an immense blue dial with concentric circles that indicate the hour, the phases of the moon and the movement of celestial bodies.

Arena Sferisterio   THEATRE
(📞0733 27 17 09; www.maceratamusei.it; Piazza Mazzini 10; adult/reduced €10/8, incl Palazzo Buonaccorsi, Palazzo Ricci & City Tour; ⊙10.30am-1pm & 2.30-5.30pm Tue-Sun) A stunning outdoor theatre, the neoclassical Arena Sferisterio is a grand colonnaded affair that was built between 1820 and 1829 to resemble an ancient Roman arena. It's a vast structure, measuring 90m by 36m and boasting superlative acoustics, most notably enjoyed during Macerata's summer opera festival.

★★ Festivals & Events

Macerata Opera Festival   MUSIC
(📞0733 23 07 35; www.sferisterio.it) From mid-July to mid-August, Macerata's Arena Sferisterio provides the stage for the Macerata Opera Festival, one of Italy's foremost musical events, attracting the cream of the operatic world.

🛏 Sleeping

Le Case   AGRITURISMO €€
(📞0733 23 18 97; www.ristorantelecase.it; Via Mozzavinci 16/17; s/d/ste Mon-Fri €75/100/200, Sat & Sun €90/120/230; 🅿❄🛜🏊) 🍃 Once you make it to this lovely rural retreat you won't want to go anywhere in a hurry. Nestled in verdant countryside 9km west of Macerata, it offers spacious rooms decorated with original trappings like timber beams, flagstone floors and period furniture, and a long list of facilities including a spa, indoor pool and two restaurants.

Hotel Arcadia   HOTEL €€
(📞0733 23 00 63; www.arcadiahotelmacerata.it; Via Matteo Ricci 134; s €50-80, d €70-130, tr €90-150; 🅿❄🛜) On a quiet lane in the *centro storico* (historic centre), the Arcadia offers slick three-star comfort at wallet-friendly prices. Rooms sport a contemporary look, with warm hues, parquet floors and flat-screen TVs. Light sleepers should be aware that the walls are quite thin. Parking, a useful extra in this part of town, is available for €8.

Albergo Arena   HOTEL €€
(📞0733 23 09 31; www.albergoarena.com; Vicolo Sferisterio 16; s €50-85, d €62-130; 🅿❄🛜) Bang in the heart of Macerata's old town, this shuttered stone house makes a convenient base for exploring the historic centre. Its carpeted rooms are spacious and spotlessly clean, if a little anonymous, and staff are hospitable. Parking is available for €8 per night.

🍴 Eating

Macerata specialities include *vincisgrassi alla maceratese,* a regional version of lasagna that differs from the usual in that the *ragù* contains a mix of pork, beef and lamb, and *ciauscolo,* a soft, spreadable *salume* that's wonderful slathered on bread.

Frecandò   TRATTORIA €
(📞0733 171 01 89; www.frecando.it; Vicolo Viscardi 10; meals €25; ⊙7.30-11pm Thu-Tue, plus 1-3pm Sun) Trying to find an open restaurant on Sunday night in Macerata is not a simple operation. Which is where Frecandò comes in. This casual trattoria is an oasis in a desert, providing flavoursome, value-for-money food – cured meat and cheese starters, grilled steaks, pizzas – and a laid-back atmosphere, abetted by ambient jazz music.

Da Secondo   ITALIAN €€
(📞0733 26 09 12; www.ristorantedasecondo.it; Via Pescheria Vecchia 26/28; meals €30-35; ⊙12.30-3pm & 7.30-10pm Tue-Sun) One of Macerata's

best-known restaurants, Da Secondo is a welcoming spot for regional *maceratese* specialities like *vincisgrassi* and *frittura mista* (fried veggies, beef-stuffed olives and other goodies). Alternatively, you can go for something completely different, perhaps a chicken curry or veal with tuna sauce.

Osteria dei Fiori   OSTERIA €€
(☑ 0733 26 01 42; www.osteriadeifiori.it; Via Lauro Rossi 61; meals €25-30; ☺ noon-3pm & 7-11pm Mon-Sat; ☑) Laid-back and casual, this popular backstreet *osteria* has a low-key vibe and al fresco seating in summer. Sit down to inventive dishes prepared with regional ingredients and given a slight modern twist: starters of ham paired with candied figs, for example, and mains of roast rabbit with wild fennel. Vegetarians are also well catered for here.

🍷 Drinking & Nightlife

Beer Bang   CRAFT BEER
(☑ 0733 23 27 17; www.facebook.com/beerbang macerata; Via Francesco Crispi 41; beers €2-8.50; ☺ 6pm-2am; 🎵) If the flavour of your beer counts more than any fancy decor, this dark, atmospheric pub is the place for you. There are eight Italian and international beers on tap – the friendly bar staff will happily introduce them all – or you can go for a bottle from the fridge of mainly Belgian and German brews.

ℹ️ Information

Tourist Office (☑ 0733 23 48 07; www.turismo.provinciamc.it; Corso della Repubblica 32; ☺ 9am-1pm Mon, 9am-1pm & 3-6pm Tue-Sat) Pick up info on Macerata and its surrounds here.

ℹ️ Getting There & Around

BUS

Marche Roma (☑ 800 037737; https://marcheroma.contram.it) runs services to/from Rome (€20, four hours, two daily Monday to Saturday, one Sunday).

Contram (☑ 800 037737; www.contram.it; Piazza Piazzarello) operates services to regional destinations and the Monti Sibillini National Park.

Buy tickets and check timetables at the **bus station** (Terminal Extraurbano; ☑ 0733 23 08 75; Piazza Piazzarello; ☺ ticket office 7.30am-2.30pm Mon-Sat & 4-7pm Tue & Thu).

CAR & MOTORCYCLE

The SS77 connects Macerata with the A14 autostrada to the east and roads for Rome to the west.

There's paid parking (€1.20 per hour) from 8am to 8pm along the city walls. Alternatively, use the **Parcheggio Centro Storico** near the Giardino Diaz. You'll pay €3 per day Monday to Saturday, but it's free on Sundays.

TRAIN

From Macerata's **train station** (☑ 0733 24 03 54; www.trenitalia.com; Piazza XXV Aprile 8/10) there are direct services to Ancona (€6.65, 1¼ hours, eight daily) and trains via Fabriano to Rome (€18.50 to €33, four to five hours, eight daily). To reach Ascoli Piceno (€9, 1¾ to 2¾ hours, 10 daily), change trains at Civitanova Marche-Montegranaro.

Buses run every 20 minutes or so from the train station to Piazza della Libertà in the historic centre. A single ticket costs €1.25.

Ascoli Piceno

POP 48.800

With a continuous history dating from the Sabine tribe in the 9th century BC, Ascoli Piceno is one of Le Marche's most refined and attractive towns. Its historic centre, mercifully flat after so many steeply stacked hillside towns, is a charming pocket of medieval streets punctuated by grand churches and photogenic piazzas. There's a sense of grandeur here too, especially on its central squares: Piazza Arringo and Piazza del Popolo. Foodies are in for a treat: Ascoli is the birthplace of Italy's much-loved *olive all'ascolana* (meat-stuffed fried olives) and wherever you go in town you're never far from a tempting takeaway or trendy bar.

◉ Sights

⭐**Piazza del Popolo**   PIAZZA
This harmonious piazza has been Ascoli's *salotto* (drawing room) since Roman times. The elegant rectangular space is flanked by the Chiesa di San Francesco (p670) and, on the west, the 13th-century **Palazzo dei Capitani del Popolo**. The 'Captain's Palace' served as the seat of the city's Pontifical Governors for centuries and today houses municipal offices and temporary art exhibitions. The statue of Pope Paul III above the main entrance was erected in recognition of his efforts to bring peace to the town.

Chiesa di San Francesco CHURCH

(Via del Trivio 49; ⊙ 7am-12.30pm & 3.30-8pm) This monumental church, its southern flank edging onto Piazza del Popolo, is named after St Francis, who is said to have visited Ascoli in 1215. It was consecrated in 1371, but construction, which started in 1258, took some 300 years and it wasn't until 1549 that the church was completed.

In the austere interior, look out for a 15th-century cross in the left nave that miraculously survived a 1535 fire at the **Palazzo dei Capitani**, and has reputedly spilled blood twice.

Annexed to the church is the **Loggia dei Mercanti**, built in the 16th century by the powerful guild of wool merchants to hide their rough-and-tumble shops.

★ **Pinacoteca** GALLERY

(☑ 0736 29 82 13; www.ascolimusei.it; Piazza Arringo 7; adult/reduced €8/5; ⊙ 10am-7pm Tue-Sun summer, 10am-1pm & 3-6pm Tue-Fri, 11am-6pm Sat & Sun winter) Set around a tree-shaded courtyard, the second-largest art gallery in Le Marche sits inside the 17th-century **Palazzo Comunale**. The palace's aristocratic halls are lined with outstanding works of art and sculpture by major Italian artists such as Titian, Carlo Crivelli and Guido Reni, as well as a collection of religious artefacts. Highlights include Titian's *San Francesco riceve le stigmate* (Saint Francis Receiving the Stigmata) and a stunning embroidered 13th-century papal cape worn by Ascoli-born Pope Nicholas IV.

Cattedrale di Sant'Emidio CATHEDRAL

(Duomo; Piazza Arringo; ⊙ 8am-noon & 4-8pm) Topped by a pair of mismatched towers, Ascoli's cathedral was built in the 16th century and dedicated to St Emidio, the city's patron saint. Its most prized possession is the three-section *Polittico di Sant'Emidio* (Polyptych of Saint Emidio; 1473) by the Venetian painter Carlo Crivelli in the **Cappella del Sacramento**. An extraordinary work of 15th-century pictorial art, the work is still in its original frame and has never once left its current spot.

Museo Archeologico MUSEUM

(☑ 0736 25 35 62; www.facebook.com/Museo ArcheologicoAscoli; Piazza Arringo 28; adult/reduced €4/2; ⊙ 8.30am-7.30pm Tue-Sun) Ascoli's archaeological museum holds a small collection of artefacts from the Piceni and other European peoples dating back to the first cen-

turies AD, as well as a fantastic mosaic floor featuring a stunning centrepiece: a dual-sided depiction of an old/young Roman god Janus (an optical illusion depending on your viewpoint).

Galleria d'Arte Contemporanea Osvaldo Licini GALLERY

(☑ 0736 29 82 13; www.ascolimusei.it; Corso Mazzini 90; adult/reduced €4/2; ⊙ 3-6pm Thu-Fri, 10am-1pm & 3-6pm Sat & Sun, by reservation only Tue & Wed) Housed in an ex-convent, this gallery has a small collection of Italian contemporary art, including a number of graphic works. There are works by several artists on show, but the spotlight is very much on paintings by Osvaldo Licini, one of Italy's best-known abstract artists.

Museo dell'Arte Ceramica MUSEUM

(☑ 0736 29 82 13; www.ascolimusei.it; Piazza San Tommaso; adult/reduced €4/2; ⊙ 10am-1pm & 3-6pm Sat & Sun, 11am-3.30pm by reservation only Tue-Fri summer, shorter hours winter) The Museo dell'Arte Ceramica traces the development of ceramic production in Ascoli and displays works from Italy's famous pottery towns, including Deruta, Faenza and Genoa. Don't miss Francesco and Carlo Grue's 18th-century framed pictorials, a sort of Old World comic strip.

🎺 Festivals & Events

Quintana CULTURAL

(☑ 0736 29 82 23; www.quintanadiascoli.it; ⊙ late Jul/early Aug) This is one of Italy's most famous medieval festivals, and for good reason. Expect thousands of locals dressed in typical medieval garb: knights in armour, flag-throwers and ladies in flamboyant velvet robes. Processions and flag-waving contests take place throughout July and August, but the big draw is the Quintana joust, when the town's six *sestieri* (districts) face off.

🛏 Sleeping

★ **Villa Fortezza** B&B €

(☑ 328 4131656; www.villafortezza.it; Via Fortezza Pia 5; s €50-80, d €60-100, q €120, 3-bedroom house €250; 🅿 ❄ 🛜) On its hilltop perch above Ascoli's historic centre, and reached by a seemingly never-ending flight of steps, this villa is a delight. Salvatore, your kindly host, welcomes you to his art-strewn home, where the individually designed, parquet-floored rooms swing from classic to contemporary.

Hotel Palazzo
dei Mercanti   HISTORIC HOTEL €€
(☑0736 25 60 44; www.palazzodeimercanti.it; Corso Trento e Trieste 35; d €75-150, ste €120-200; 🅿❄🛜) Housed in a 16th-century *palazzo*, once part of the Sant'Egido convent, this fab four-star offers a soothing stay in the heart of the action. Its decor combines columns and original stone vaults with contemporary design touches, resulting in refined modern rooms furnished with hand-crafted furniture, Nespresso machines and bathrobes (handy for the spa's whirlpool, sauna and hammam).

Palazzo Guiderocchi   BOUTIQUE HOTEL €€
(☑0736 25 47 53; www.hotelguiderocchi.com; Via Cesare Battisti 3; s €69-129, d €89-149, ste €119-190; 🅿❄@🛜) This welcoming hotel boasts history, atmosphere and comfort, all in the handsome confines of a noble 16th-century *palazzo*. Rising around an inner courtyard, it offers attractive spacious rooms and romance in the form of vaulted roofs, low wood-beamed ceilings, frescoes and original doors.

🍴 Eating

⭐**Vittoria Ristorante**   RISTORANTE €
(☑0736 25 95 35; www.vittoriaristorante.it; Via dei Bonaccorsi 7; meals €20-25, weekday fixed-price menu €15; ☺noon-2.30pm & 7.30-10.30pm, closed Wed & Sun) This welcoming spot is a great example of what Italy does so well: a casual, friendly restaurant, in this case decorated with white arches and bright lights, cooking up fabulous local food at honest prices. The menu includes Ascoli's renowned fried olives and a brilliant *amatriciana* (pancetta and tomato sauce), here served with *mezze maniche* (thick pasta rings).

Degusteria 25 Doc & Dop   ITALIAN €
(☑0736 31 33 24; Via Panichi 3; meals €15; ☺11.45am-3pm & 7.30pm-midnight Tue-Sun) Strings of garlic and chilli dangle from the ceiling of this pocket-sized deli-*enoteca*, where locals squeeze in or spill out onto the terrace for fine wines and tasting platters of regional *salumi*, cheese and, of course, *olive all'ascolana*.

Siamo Fritti   FAST FOOD €
(☑0736 25 99 09; www.siamofritti.ap.it; Piazza Simonetti 87; fried snacks €3.50-4.50; ☺11am-2.30pm & 5pm-midnight, closed Wed lunch) This ever-popular spot is a classic Ascoli *friggi-*

FRIED FOOD FESTIVAL

Ascoli celebrates the joys of fried food during the **Fritto Misto all'Italiana** (www.frittomistoallitaliana.it; Piazza Arringo; ☺late Apr), an annual bonanza of eating and drinking. Along with Ascoli's legendary *olive all'ascolana*, stalls dish out all manner of international snacks, from Sicilian *arancini* (fried rice balls) to *panzerotti* (fried pizza pies) from Puglia, and even fish and chips from the UK. Oiling the fun is widely available craft beer.

toria, a takeaway cafe specialising in crisp fried snacks. Ascoli's trademark *olive all'as-colana* headline the menu and they make a fine accompaniment to a glass of local wine, perhaps a fizzy red Fiori di Seta.

Piccolo Teatro   ITALIAN €€
(☑0736 26 15 74; www.alpiccoloteatro.it; Via Carlo Goldoni 2; meals €30-35; ☺11.30am-11.30pm Tue-Sun) Ensconced in a typical stone building, this cosy, barrel-vaulted restaurant blends historic charm with a dash of style and a strong sense of place. Dishes are seasonally driven and feature fine regional ingredients such as pungent black truffles and *pecorino* cheese from the nearby Sibillini mountains. Bookings recommended, particularly at weekends.

🍷 Drinking & Nightlife

⭐**La Birrita**   CRAFT BEER
(☑0736 52 04 73; www.facebook.com/labirretta.ap; Largo Carlo Crivelli 1; ☺6.30pm-2am; 🛜) If you're aching for a *birra* that's not Peroni or Moretti, leg it to Le Marche's best craft-beer bar and choose between the industrial-hip interior (hanging Edison lighting, cool indie tunes) or a table on distinctly low-key Piazza Carlo Crivelli.

ℹ Information

Tourist Office (☑0736 28 83 34; www.visit ascoli.it; Piazza Arringo 7; ☺9am-6pm Mon-Sat, 10am-7pm Sun) Ascoli's helpful tourist office is stocked with maps and leaflets on the city's sights and hikes in the nearby Monti Sibillini. It also rents out bikes for €5/10/15 per two/four/eight hours.

UMBRIA & LE MARCHE ASCOLI PICENO

ℹ Getting There & Around

BUS

Services leave from **Piazzale della Stazione** (Piazzale della Stazione), in front of the train station in the new part of town, east of the Castellano river. **Start** (☑ 800 443040; www.startspa.it; Piazzale della Stazione) runs buses to/from Rome's Tiburtina bus station (€17.50, three hours, seven daily) and Fiumicino Airport (€20.50, 3¾ hours, three daily).

CAR & MOTORCYCLE

Ascoli is on the RA11, which connects the city with the coastal A14 autostrada and the SS4 (Via Salaria).

To park in the city, your best bet is the 24-hour **Parcheggio Torricella**, which costs €10 per day and has lifts up to the historic centre.

TRAIN

Trains to Ancona (€9.90, two hours, 16 daily) occasionally involve a change in Porto d'Ascoli or San Benedetto Del Tronto. Services to Macerata (€9, 2¼ hours, 10 daily) require one or two changes. The **train station** (www.trenitalia.com; Piazza della Stazione) is a 1.2km walk east of the centre.

A free shuttle bus connects Ancona's train station to Piazza Arringo in the city centre every 20 minutes between 7.40am and 2pm and then from 3pm to 8pm.

Monti Sibillini National Park

Straddling the Le Marche–Umbria border in rugged splendour, the wild and wonderfully unspoiled Parco Nazionale dei Monti Sibillini never looks less than extraordinary, whether visited in winter, when its peaks – 10 of which tower above 2000m - are covered in snow, or in summer, when its highland meadows are carpeted with poppies and cornflowers.

The area was hit hard by the 2016 earthquakes; while you can still see evidence of their destructive force, life has since returned to normal in most places and the majority of roads and trails are now open.

Main gateways include Norcia (p647) to the southwest and Amandola in the northeast. Just to the north of the park, Sarnano is the largest and prettiest town in the area. From there, the SS78 leads to Sasso Tetto, the main ski area in the Monti Sibillini.

◉ Sights & Activities

The park is a magnet for hikers and outdoor enthusiasts, with an expansive network of walking trails and mountain-biking circuits, and a series of summer *rifugi* (mountain huts) offering hearty meals and warm beds. Most trails are now open after the 2016 earthquakes but a number of *rifugi* remain closed – check the park website (www.sibillini.net) for updates. Information is also available from the **park information office** (☑ 0736 85 64 62; www.sibillini.net; Via Roma, Montemonaco; ⊘ 9.30am-12.30pm & 3.30-6.30pm July & Aug, Sat & Sun only Sep & Oct).

Gola dell'Infernaccio GORGE
(Montefortino) There's fine walking to be had in the spectacular mountain country near the village of Montefortino. A stunning, and relatively accessible route, leads through the Gola dell'Infernaccio (Gorge of Hell), a thrilling canyon wedged between walls of vertiginous rock face. Silence hangs over the rugged peaks and ancient woodland, broken only by birdsong and the sound of the fast-flowing River Tenna.

The Gola is signposted off the SP83 north of Montefortino – follow the road, which becomes unsurfaced as it approaches a small parking area at the trailhead.

🛏 Sleeping

Villa delle Rose BOUTIQUE HOTEL €
(☑ 0736 84 74 68; www.sibillinihotels.it; Piazza Umberto I, Amandola; s €50-60, d €80-100; ⊠ ⓟ 🛜) In the small town of Amandola on the northeastern fringes of the park, this is a lovely five-bedroom hotel. A warm welcome and classically furnished rooms await at the elegant 1920s villa, which is set in its own garden at the top of the historic centre (follow signs to Hotel Paradiso).

ℹ Getting There & Around

Realistically, you'll need your own wheels to explore the park. You can take buses to towns such as Amandola on the eastern edge of the park, but few services venture further into the mountains. For details, check with the bus companies – **Contram** (www.contram.it) in Macerata or **Start** (☑ 800 443040; www.startspa.it; Piazzale della Stazione) in Ascoli Piceno.

By car, the main approach roads to the park are: from Macerata and the northeast, the SS77 and SS78; from the south and east, the SS4; and from Terni and the southwest, the SS209.

The nearest train stations are in Ascoli Piceno to the south and Tolentino to the north.

Sarnano

POP 3220

Spilling photogenically down a steep hillside, Sarnano looks every inch the model Italian hill town, particularly when its red-brick facades glow warmly in the late-afternoon sun. It's best known for its spas, but with its charming medieval centre and good road links it makes an ideal base for exploring Monti Sibillini National Park. There's excellent hiking in the vicinity and skiing at the nearby resort of Sassotetto-Santa Maria Maddalena.

◉ Sights

Centro Storico OLD TOWN

Sarnano's medieval centre sprawls up the hillside in a tangle of steep cobbled lanes and attractive red-brick houses. Climb to the top and you'll come to Piazza Alta, a lovely pint-sized square framed by historic buildings: **Palazzo del Popolo**, home of a 19th-century theatre; **Palazzo dei Priori**; and, most impressively, the **Chiesa di Santa Maria Piazza Alta**, a robust brick church with a splendid Gothic portal. All around are stirring views out to the brooding Monti Sibillini.

🛏 Sleeping & Eating

★ **Agriturismo Serpanera** AGRITURISMO €€

(☑ 334 1220242; www.serpanera.com; Contrada Schito 447; apt €79-169, per week €500-1200; P❋🐾🛜🐕) 🐾 Quite the rural idyll, this 17th-century farmhouse resides in 10 hectares of orchards, vines and woodlands just outside Sarnano. Besides its spotless apartments, it invites lingering with its bucolic mountain views, panoramic pool, spa and barbecue area. For more active stays, you can explore nature trails or saddle up and take to the hills on horseback.

La Marchigiana RISTORANTE €

(☑ 0733 65 72 11; www.la-marchigiana.it; Via Campanotico 199; meals €20-25; ☺ noon-2.30pm & 7.15-10pm Wed-Mon) About 1km north of Sarnano on the SP78, this hotel-restaurant is ideal for a break from the road. Join the locals who regularly stop by to greet convivial manager, Max, and fill up on fantastically generous helpings of country food. Perhaps start with a selection of local cheese before moving onto a bowl of wild boar slow-cooked in rich red wine.

❶ Information

Tourist Office (☑ 0733 65 73 43; www.sarnanoturismo.it; Borgo Garibaldi 88c; ☺ 9am-1pm Mon-Fri, plus 3-5.45pm Tue & Thu) The Sarnano tourist office can provide information about activities and accommodation in Monti Sibillini National Park.

❶ Getting There & Away

Sarnano is on the SP78, about 20km south of the Caldarola exit off the SS71.

Buses depart from a stop on the SP78 on the north side of Piazza della Libertà. **SASP** (☑ 0733 66 31 37; www.autolineesasp.it) buses run to/from Macerata (€3.40, one hour, hourly). For Ascoli Pisceno, Contram (p669) runs buses to Comunanza (€2.60, 35 minutes, four daily), where you can catch a connecting **Start** (☑ 800 443040; www.startspa.it) bus on to Ascoli (€2.60, 45 minutes, eight daily).

POPULATION
1.59 million

CAPITAL
L'Aquila

BEST HIKE
Corno Grande (p678)

**BEST HILLTOP
TOWN**
Opi (p685)

BEST FOCCACIA
La Cucineria (p687)

WHEN TO GO
Jan & Feb Grab
some skis and head
for one of the
Abruzzo-Molise ski
areas.

Jul Sulmona holds
its medieval festival,
while Pescara hosts
a major jazz festival.

May, Jun & Sep
Spring wildflowers,
summer sun or
autumn leaves –
perfect conditions
for hiking.

Chapel at Rocca Calascio (p679)

Abruzzo & Molise

Bisected by the spinal Apennine mountains, Abruzzo and Molise make up Italy's forgotten quarter, blessed more with natural attractions than cultural colossi. A major national-park-building effort in the 1990s created an almost unbroken swath of protected land that stretches from the harsh, isolated Monti della Laga in the north to the round-topped Majella mountains further south.

Dotted in their midst are some of Italy's most unspoiled mountain villages. Sometimes, a visit here feels like a trip back to the 1950s – a world of wheezing trains, ruined farmhouses and poppy-filled pastures.

Sulmona is the best base for mountain excursions, Pescara on the Adriatic coast satisfies those with traditional beach urges, while diminutive Molise hides vestiges of the Roman past.

Abruzzo & Molise Highlights

1 Parco Nazionale d'Abruzzo, Lazio e Molise (p685) Keeping an eye out for rare Marsican bears while hiking in this fabulous wilderness.

2 Saepinum (p690) Pacing the foundations of one of Italy's most complete provincial Roman towns.

3 Sulmona (p679) Joining the *passeggiata* to scope out which Abruzzese trattoria you'll eat in next.

4 Museo Archeologico Nazionale d'Abruzzo (p688) Coming face to face with masterpieces of pre-Roman Italy in Chieti.

5 Santo Stefano di Sessanio (p678) Enjoying a comfortable room in a primitive house in Gran Sasso's mountain village.

6 Parco Nazionale della Majella (p682) Taking a walk through history on the Sentiero della Libertà.

7 Isernia La Pineta (p690) Digging up the 700,000-year-old roots of European humankind at this intriguing archaeological site.

8 Gole di Sagittario (p685) Driving the winding switchbacks of this ravishingly beautiful gorge, between Sulmona and Scanno.

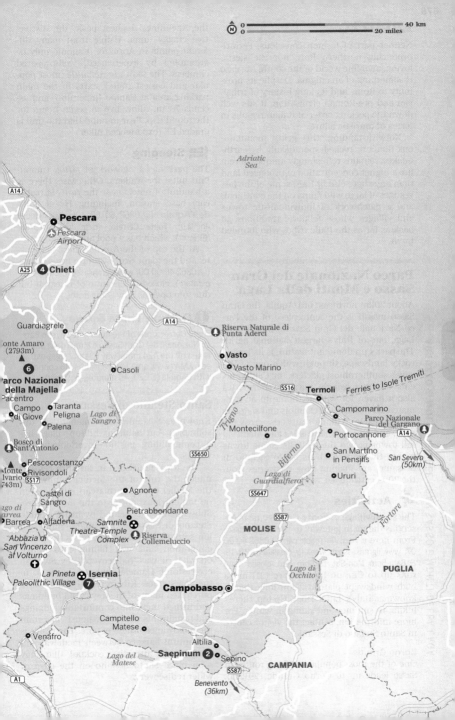

Adriatic
Sea

0 ——————————— 40 km
0 ——————————— 20 miles

A14

Pescara
✈ Pescara
Airport

A25 **4** **Chieti**

Guardiagrele

A14

⚐ Riserva Naturale di
Punta Aderci

onte Amaro
(2793m) **6**

●Casoli

Vasto
●Vasto Marino

**Parco Nazionale
della Majella**
Pacentro

Campo ●Taranta
di Giove ●Peligna
●Palena

SS16 ●**Termoli** Ferries to Isole Tremiti

Campomarino

Parco Nazionale
del Gargano

●Portocannone **A14**

●Montecilfone

●San Martino
in Pensilis

Lago di
Sangro

Trigno

Biferno

San Severo
(50km)

Bosco di
⚐Sant'Antonio

▲
Monte
lvario
'43m) **SS17**

●Pescocostanzo
●Rivisondoli

Lago di
arrea
●Barrea ●Alfadena

●Agnone

Pietrabbondante

Castel di
Sangro

SS650

Lago di
Guardialfiera

SS647

●Ururi

MOLISE

SS87

Fortore

PUGLIA

Samnite
Theatre-Temple
Complex

⚐Riserva
Collemeluccio

Abbazia di
San Vincenzo
al Volturno

Lago di
Occhito

La Pineta ☢**Isernia**
Paleolithic Village **7**

Campobasso ◉

●Venafro

Campitello
Matese

A1

Lago del
Matese

●Altilia
Saepinum **2**
●Sepino

SS87

CAMPANIA

Benevento
(36km)

ABRUZZO

Neither part of fashion conscious, Ferrari-producing northern Italy, nor the siesta-loving, anarchic world of the south, Abruzzo is something of an enigma. Despite its proximity to Rome and its long history of tribalism and pre-Roman civilisation, it sits well down the pecking order of Italian regions in terms of touristic allure.

Notwithstanding, this gritty mountainous domain, rocked sporadically by earthquakes, remains refreshingly unique. Herein lies a higher concentration of protected land than anywhere else in Italy, some of the last vestiges of large wild fauna on the continent, and a patchwork of individualistic towns and villages whose folkloric traditions go back as far as the Italic tribes who founded them.

Parco Nazionale del Gran Sasso e Monti della Laga

About 20km northeast of L'Aquila, the Gran Sasso massif is the centrepiece of the Parco Nazionale del Gran Sasso e Monti della Laga, one of Italy's largest national parks. The park's predominant feature is its jagged rocky landscape, through which one of Europe's southernmost glaciers, the Calderone, cuts its (increasingly narrow) course. It's also a haven for wildlife, home to an estimated 40 wolves, 350 chamois and six pairs of royal eagles. Hiking trails criss-cross the park, and atmospheric castles and medieval hill towns crown the foothills. Some towns within the park, such as Santo Stefano di Sessanio, are making slow recoveries from the 2009 earthquake.

🏃 Activities

The small village of Fonte Cereto near Assergi is the main gateway to the Gran Sasso. From here a funivia (cable car; ☎ 0862 40 00 07; www.ilgransasso.it; weekday/weekend €10/15; ⏱ 8am-5pm Mon-Sat, to 6pm Sun, closed May) runs up to Campo Imperatore (2117m), a high windswept plateau 27km long that is known as Italy's 'Little Tibet'. Up top, there's hiking in summer and skiing in winter. For more information, contact the visitor centre in Santo Stefano di Sessanio.

Corno Grande   HIKING
One of the most popular trekking routes in Sasso leads up to Corno Grande (2912m),

the Apennines' highest peak, the distinctive craggy dome visible from many different points in Abruzzo. It should only be attempted by experienced, well-prepared climbers. The 9km *via normale* (most popular and easiest route) starts in the main parking area at Campo Imperatore and ascends 782m. Allow five to seven hours for the round trip. Bear in mind that the trail is graded EE (experienced hiker).

🛏 Sleeping

The park has a network of *rifugi* (mountain huts) for walkers. Otherwise, there is a handful of hotels near the *funivia* (cable car) base station, including Hotel Nido dell'Aquila (☎ 0862 60 68 40; www.nidodellaquila.it; Fonte Cerreto; d/tr from €70/85; ⓟ 🛜 ❄), which has a pool and restaurant.

At the top of the *funivia* there is a hostel and the giant Hotel Campo Imperatore (☎ 0862 40 00 00; www.ilgransasso.it; Campo Imperatore), closed at the time of research but due to reopen as a five-star hotel.

ℹ Getting There & Away

Fonte Cerreto, one of the main gateways to Parco Nazionale del Gran Sasso e Monti della Laga, is just off the A24 motorway (clearly signposted). AMA (www.ama.laquila.it) bus M6 connects with L'Aquila (€1.20, 40 minutes, six daily).

Santo Stefano di Sessanio

Known as Sextantio in Roman times, this somnolent but haunting hilltop village has a commanding position overlooking two valleys.

The town flourished in the 16th century under the rule of the Medici family, and the Medici coat of arms can still be seen on the entrance portal to the main piazza. Subsequently left behind by history, Santo Stefano di Sessanio, like many rural Italian settlements, lost most of its people to emigration and was falling into oblivion when it was 'rediscovered' by Swedish eco-restorer Daniele Kihlgren in 1999. In the years since, Kihlgren and others have purchased many of the town's old buildings and turned them into comfortable lodgings and restaurants that meticulously maintain the mossy ancientness of yore. The result is a beautiful balance between medieval and modern, an attractive cocktail that may soon place Santo Stefano on the cusp of wider rediscovery.

⊙ Sights & Activities

Located within the borders of Gran Sasso e Monti della Laga national park, Santo Stefano di Sessanio sits on the cusp of some good walking country. The most popular local hike is to the mountaintop fortress of Rocca Calascio (one hour), visible on a ridge to the southeast. Built between the 10th and 13th centuries, the castle has been used in several films including *The Name of the Rose*.

Centro Visite Museo
Terre della Baronia MUSEUM
(✆ 0862 89 91 17, 347 3159855; www.centrovisite santostefanodisessanio.it; Via del Municipio; ☺ 10am-7pm summer, to 3pm Sat & Sun winter) The main visitor centre for the Gran Sasso national park also houses the Museo Terre della Baronia, a museum that showcases the environment, history and culture of the region, with information displayed on large panels with diagrams and photos (some in English). There are also some local costumes on show.

⊨ Sleeping & Eating

★ **Sextantio** DESIGN HOTEL €€
(✆ 0862 89 91 12; www.sextantio.it; Via Principe Umberto; d/ste from €162/320; ☎) ✦ This enchanting *albergo diffuso*, with 28 distinctive rooms and suites scattered throughout the village, was what helped rescue Santo Stefano from oblivion. Designed to reignite Italy's lesser-known settlements without scrimping on luxury, they marry traditional handmade bedspreads and rustic furniture with under-floor heating, mood lighting and divinely deep bathtubs. Everything was restored using local materials.

★ **Locanda Sotto gli Archi** ABRUZZESE €€
(✆ 0862 89 91 16; http://santostefano.sextantio. it; Via degli Archi; meals €32-38; ☺ 7.30-11pm Wed-Mon, plus 12.30-3pm Sat & Sun) Sextantio hotel's restaurant makes imaginative use of an arched, 16th-century dining room. Furniture and crockery are designed to re-create the austere quality of bygone times (picture a *Game of Thrones* banquet), and the excellent food uses time-honoured ingredients and techniques native to the region.

❶ Getting There & Away

Taking the SS17, Santo Stefano di Sessanio is 27km from L'Aquila. You'll need to fork left just outside the village of Barisciano to cover the last 10km.

There are four **TUA** (✆ 800 762622; www.tua bruzzo.it) buses a day running between L'Aquila bus station and Santo Stefano di Sessanio (€3, 50 minutes), but none on Sundays.

Sulmona
☑ 0864 / POP 24,500

An underappreciated city of fantastic restaurants, narrow medieval streets and half-discovered mountain magic, Sulmona sits strategically on a plateau surrounded by three national parks, making it the ideal base for outdoor excursions in Abruzzo. It's easy to reach from Pescara or Rome, and simple to navigate once you arrive (trails fan out from the city limits). The city can trace its history back to the Roman town of Sulmo, where the poet Ovid (of *Metamorphoses* fame) was born in 43 BC. It is also known within Italy for its *confetti* – the almond sweets, not the coloured paper scattered at weddings.

⊙ Sights

Most sights are on or near the main street, Corso Ovidio, which runs southeast from the Villa Comunale park to Piazza Garibaldi, Sulmona's main square. A five-minute stroll away is Piazza XX Settembre, with its statue of Ovid – a popular meeting point.

Piazza Garibaldi PIAZZA
The large town square is home to Sulmona's extensive Wednesday and Saturday morning market: you'll find fresh fish, veg, fruit and flowers, as well as the ubiquitous *porchetta* van, selling pork in a roll. Along Corso Ovidio is a striking series of arches, all that remains of a 13th-century aqueduct. In the centre of the piazza, the Renaissance Fontana del Vecchio (Fountain of the Old One) is said by some to depict Solimo, the founder of Sulmona.

To the northeast, the 14th-century Chiesa di San Filippo Neri displays its impressive Gothic portal against a backdrop of often snow-covered mountains. To the southwest, beyond the aqueduct, lies the Rotonda, once the monumental entrance and apse of the Chiesa di San Francesco della Scarpa, but cut off from the functional church when it was salvaged from the 1706 earthquake. It's used for exhibitions and other events.

ABRUZZO & MOLISE SULMONA

Cattedrale di San Panfilo CATHEDRAL

(Piazza del Duomo; ⊙ 7.30am-noon & 3-7pm)
Slightly out of the centre, the Gothic-meets-baroque cathedral is like many things in Sulmona: understated and underrated. The fantastically restored interior guards some precious old artefacts, including a 14th-century wooden crucifix. The highlight, however, is a subterranean room (opened in 2009) containing the relics of hermit-turned-pope Pietro da Morrone (1215–96), including his slippers and a piece of his heart. The original church built here replaced a temple of Apollo and Vesta.

Museo Civico MUSEUM

(☑ 0864 21 02 16; Palazzo dell'Annunziata, Corso Ovidio; adult/reduced €4/2; ⊙ 9am-1pm & 3.30-6.30pm Tue-Sun) Inside the **Palazzo dell'Annunziata** is the four-in-one Museo Civico, with sections dedicated to archaeology, religious art, Abruzzese-Molisiano culture and the remains of the Roman *domus* (villa) over which the *palazzo* stands. The brilliant Abruzzese-Molisiano folk costumes are particularly worth seeing. Signs are in Italian.

Museo dell'Arte Confettiera MUSEUM

(☑ 0864 21 00 47; www.pelino.it; Via Stazione Introdacqua 55; ⊙ 8am-12.30pm & 3-7pm Mon-Sat) **FREE** This museum is housed in the **Fabbrica Confetti Pelino** (established 1783), Sulmona's most famous manufacturer of *confetti* (the confectionery product). With its antique sweet-making equipment, the reconstructed laboratory looks more like an old-time science lab than a sweet-making plant.

🛏 Sleeping

Excellent, charismatic *locandas* (inns) and *alberghi diffusi* (diffused accommodation; generally with one central reception) are easily found in Sulmona's medieval heart.

★ Legacy Casa Residencia B&B €

(☑ 377 9766036; www.legacycasaresidencia.it; Vico dell'Ospedale 54; d/apt €75/135; P ❋ 🛜) A beautifully curated and professionally run B&B right in the centre of Sulmona with a choice of double rooms or miniapartments. All the accommodation skilfully combines convenience and comfort with the distinct sense that you're in the heart of traditional Italy. The apartments can be let on self-catering and (discounted) weekly bases and cooking, painting and hiking packages are available.

Albergo Stella HOTEL €

(☑ 0864 5 26 53; www.albergostella.info; Via Panfilo Mazara 18; s/d/ste €80/90/130; P ❋ @ 🛜) Compact family-run hotel in Sulmona's historic centre that has kept up with the trends, with subtle style accents in its large minimalist rooms. The real *stelle* (stars) here though are the staff who work out of a smart little reception area and cafe on the ground floor; they are tirelessly generous with their help, welcomes and local tips.

🍴 Eating

Diminutive Sulmona displays a wealth of good honest trattorias plying genuine Abruzzese food. Look out for the typical *spaghetti alla chitarra,* a long egg pasta made with a unique guitar-like cutter.

★ Ristorante Gino ABRUZZESE €

(☑ 0864 5 22 89; www.lalocandadigino.it; Piazza Plebiscito 12; meals €23-26; ⊙ 12.30-2.45pm) Occupying handsome arched chambers that have been used as an inn or wine shop for centuries, the restaurant of **La Locanda di Gino** (☑ 0864 5 22 89; www.lalocandadigino.it; Via Serafini 1; s/d/tr/q €80/90/130/160; 🛜) calls on *molta experienza*. Proudly advertising the provenance of its produce (red garlic of Sulmona, lentils from Santo Stefano di Sessanio, saffron from an Abruzzese collective), the menu is a paean to the best of Abruzzo.

WORTH A TRIP

POPE'S HERMITAGE

The cliff-clinging hermitage **Eremo di Sant'Onofrio al Morrone** (Contrada Morrone; ⊙ hours vary), with its 15th-century ceiling, 13th-century frescoes, narrow oratory and arched porticoes, cowers under a massive rock face in the Morrone mountains. It was here in a grotto beneath the present church that Pietro da Morrone was apparently told he was to become pope in 1294. It's a steep 20-minute walk from a car park just outside Badia to reach the hermitage. The views of Sulmona and the Valle Peligna below are superb.

Opening hours vary; check ahead with the tourist office in Sulmona.

★ **Il Vecchio Muro**   ABRUZZESE **€€**
(☎0864 5 05 95; Via M D'Eramo 20; meals €28;
☺12.45-2.30pm & 7.45-10.30pm, closed Wed Oct-
Apr) One of Sulmona's best restaurants, the
'old wall' is notable for spot-on Abruzzese
fare such as wholewheat pasta with lentils
and *guanciale* (cured pork jowl). The rest
of the menu – especially the bits involving
sausage and mushroom – is wonderfully
executed, and even the pizza is well above
average.

The *cacio e pepe* (pasta with cheese and
pepper) is served in a *crosta di parmigiano*
(dish-shaped cheese crust).

You can eat outside in a secluded garden,
weather permitting.

La Cantina di Biffi   ABRUZZESE **€€**
(☎0864 3 20 25; Via Barbato 1; meals €30-33;
☺12.30-2.30pm & 8-11pm Tue-Sun) Dedicated
to the food and wine of Abruzzo, this stone-
walled *cantina* is a handsome place to eat,
with its open kitchen and blackboard of
seasonal specialities. An antipasto of cheese
and cured meats with a wine accompaniment sets you up nicely for the main deal.
Think asparagus on poached egg with *grana* cheese or thick lardons of *guanciale*.

Buonvento   ABRUZZESE **€€**
(☎0864 95 00 10; Piazza Plebiscito 21; meals €24-
28; ☺noon-midnight Mon & Wed-Sat, noon-3pm
Sun) Books help furnish the rooms at Buonvento (great stacks of them piled up on the
floor) along with avant-garde art and a global array of souvenirs from miniature Bud-
dhas to vintage phones. The food is more of
an Abruzzo affair – simple and economical
dishes that rarely break €10.

Peruse the blackboard for *chitarra*
(Abruzzo-style spaghetti) and *ragù*, pesto
and courgette lasagne, and lamb cooked
multiple ways. The restaurant is split into
several small rooms to give a feeling of
intimacy.

🍷 Drinking & Nightlife

Multiple old-fashioned cafe-bars are prominent on the Corso Ovidio and Piazzas Garibaldi and Annunziata, while nearby a few
less traditional 'pubs' are less easily spotted.

ℹ️ Information

Tourist Office (☎0864 21 02 16; www.comune.
sulmona.aq.it; Corso Ovidio 208, Palazzo
Annunziata; ☺9am-1pm & 3.30-7.30pm) *Molto*
helpful staff. The office also sells local bus
tickets.

ℹ️ Getting There & Away

BUS
Buses leave from a confusing array of points,
including Villa Comunale, the hospital and beneath Ponte Capograssi. The tourist office will
point you in the right direction.

TUA (☎800 762622; www.tuabruzzo.it) buses
go to and from L'Aquila (€6.30, 1½ hours, up to
eight daily) and Pescara €6.30, one hour, four
daily). There are also regular buses to Scanno,
Campo di Giove and Pacentro.

TRAIN
Trains link Sulmona with L'Aquila (€5.90, one
hour, frequent), Pescara (€5.90, 1¼ hours,
frequent) and Rome (€11.30, 2½ hours, 10 daily).
The train station is 2km northwest of the historic centre; the half-hourly bus A runs between
the two.

L'Aquila
📍0862 / POP 69.600

From tragedy springs hope. In the years
years since 2009, when a powerful earthquake killed 308 of its citizens and toppled
copious historic buildings, L'Aquila has rebuilt and is back in business. It welcomes
visitors who come not just to admire the
durability of the town's churches and fountains, but also to study the meticulous renovation work that has returned many of the
sights to their former glory – in some cases
even surpassing them.

👁️ Sights

A slew of L'Aquila's sights have reopened including the Basilica di Santa Maria di Collemaggio, the magnificently restored Basilica
di San Bernardino (p682) and the city's impressive **Fontana delle 99 Cannelle** (Fountain of 99 Spouts; Piazza San Vito).

At the time of research the Duomo and
the San Giorgio castle remained closed, although the castle's erstwhile museum had
been temporarily reopened at a different
site.

**Basilica di Santa Maria
di Collemaggio**   BASILICA
(www.santamariadicollemaggio.it; Piazzale di Collemaggio; ☺9.30am-12.30pm & 3-6pm) With its
distinctive chequerboard facade and strong
links to Italy's much admired hermit-pope
Celestino V (whose remains are interred
inside), the 12th-century Collemaggio is the
church for which Aquilinos reserve most
affection. Structurally damaged in the 2009

ABRUZZO & MOLISE L'AQUILA

earthquake, its lengthy renovation project (initiated in 2012) took five years to complete. The details of how it was done are chronicled inside and provide an interesting coda to the church's roller-coaster history.

Basilica di San Bernardino BASILICA
(www.basilicasanbernardino.it; Via San Bernardino; ☺7am-12.30pm & 3-7.30pm) A marvel of post-earthquake restoration, the 15th-century San Bernardino gleams like a salvaged *Titanic* brought to the surface to sail once more. Position yourself under the huge central dome to fully admire the richly embroidered ceiling, the grand gold-leafed organ above the main door, and the relics of San Bernardino of Siena encased in an elaborate mausoleum.

🛏 Sleeping & Eating

Hotel L'Aquila HOTEL €
(☑ 0862 58 12 37; www.hotel-laquila.com; Via Simonetto 5A; r €75-100; 🖘) Fresh from a recent renovation, the rooms at this quietly elegant hotel are doused in pretty yellows and greens, and are spacious by Italian standards. There's free parking at a nearby municipal car park.

Arrosticini Divini ABRUZZESE €
(☑ 0862 41 38 52; www.arrosticinidivini.it; Via Castello 13; meals €15-20; ☺noon-3pm & 7-11.30pm) A casual restaurant that specialises in Abruzzo's classic street food, *arrosticini*. These charcoal-grilled lamb skewers are seasoned with olive oil and rosemary, and served wrapped in foil in ceramic jugs or mugs. *Arrosticini*'s best *amici* (friends) are *bruschette* and a glass of Montepulciano d'Abruzzo wine, both of which are listed on the restaurant's refreshingly short menu.

❶ Getting There & Away

BUS
The **bus terminal** (Via Caldora) is on the edge of town close to the Basilica di Santa Maria di Collemaggio (p681). An 800m-long underground tunnel (with escalators) links it with the centrally located Piazza Duomo.

Bus links to L'Aquila are good: Flixbus (www.flixbus.com) runs several services a day between L'Aquila and Rome/Rome Fiumicino (from €14/20, 1½ to 2½ hours), while **TUA** (☑ 800 762622; www.tuabruzzo.it) runs frequent services to Pescara (from €8.80, 1½ hours, 10 daily) and Sulmona (€6.30, 1½ hours, up to eight daily).

TRAIN
Frequent Trenitalia (www.trenitalia.com) trains connect L'Aquila with Rome (from €12.95, three to 3½ hours, via Terni), Perugia (from €11.80, 3¾ to 4½ hours, via Terni) and Sulmona (€5.90, one to 1¼ hours).

Parco Nazionale della Majella

History, geology and ecology collide in 750-sq-km Parco Nazionale della Majella, Abruzzo's most diverse park, where wolves roam in giant beech woods, ancient hermitages speckle ominous mountains, and 500km of criss-crossing paths and a handful of ski areas cater to the hyperactive. Monte Amaro, the Apennines' second-highest peak, surveys all around it from a lofty 2793m vantage point.

From Sulmona the two easiest access points are Pacentro, a mountain foothills town 10km to the east, and the lovely town of Pescocostanzo, 33km south of Sulmona along the SS17.

❶ Getting There & Away

TUA (☑ 800 762622; www.tuabruzzo.it) buses run from Sulmona to Roccaraso (€3.60, 50 minutes, three daily), near Pescocostanzo. There are also regular buses to Campo di Giove (€2.40, 45 minutes, four daily) and Pacentro (€2.40, 35 minutes, nine daily).

Pescocostanzo
☑ 0864 / POP 1110
Set amid verdant highland plains, Pescocostanzo is practically alpine. It's a surprisingly grand hilltop town, whose historical core has changed little in more than 500 years. Much of the cobbled centre dates from the 16th and 17th centuries when it was an important town on the 'Via degli Abruzzi', the main road linking Naples and Florence.

◉ Sights

The triangular **Piazza del Municipio** is flanked by a number of impressive *palazzi*, including **Palazzo Comunale**, with its distinctive clock tower, and **Palazzo Fanzago** (Piazza Municipio; ☺11am-1pm & 5-8pm Sat & Sun) FREE, designed by the Lombardy-born architect Cosimo Fanzago in the early 17th century. Don't be deceived by the fancy win-

THE WARTIME PATH TO FREEDOM

During WWII, with the Allies advancing swiftly through southern Italy, the inmates at one of the country's most notorious POW camps – Fonte d'Amore (Campo 78), 5km north of Sulmona – began to sniff freedom.

Their excitement wasn't unfounded. When the Italian government surrendered in September 1943, the camp's Italian guards deserted their posts and promptly disappeared. Their boots were quickly filled by German soldiers invading Italy from the north but, in the confusion of the changeover, many POWs escaped.

Using the Apennines as a natural refuge, the prisoners fanned out into the surrounding mountains. With the help of local partisans, most fled east across the Majella range from German-occupied Sulmona to Casoli on the Sangro River, which had been held by the Allies since September 1943. The rugged and dangerous escape route – nicknamed the Sentiero della Libertà (Freedom Trail; www.ilsentierodellaliberta.it) – was used multiple times by escaped Allied POWs during the exceptionally cold winter of 1943–44, when the Allied advance was temporarily halted by German troops dug in along the Gustav Line (a fortified defensive line built by the Germans across central Italy in 1943 to stem the Allied advance).

Having to negotiate well-guarded checkpoints and rugged, mountainous terrain, not all the escapees made it. On a windswept mountain pass known as Guado di Coccia, halfway between Campo di Giove and the small mountain village of Palena, a stone monument memorialises Ettore De Conti, an Italian partisan captured and executed by the Germans in September 1943. It acts as an enduring symbol of the underground resistance.

Today, the Sentiero della Libertà has been turned into a historic long-distance hiking trail that cuts across the peaks and plateaus of the Parco Nazionale della Majella. Well-signposted with red and white markers, the 60km-long path starts at the eastern suburbs of Sulmona and is usually tackled over three to four days with stops in Campo di Giove and Taranta Peligna. Since 2001, a commemorative communal march along the trail has been held in late April attracting up to 700 people. See the Sentiero della Libertà website for entry details.

The foreboding fences and watchtowers of the now disused Campo 78 still rise above the village of Fonte d'Amore.

dows: they're fake, serving a purely decorative function.

🛏 Sleeping & Eating

⭐ **Albergo La Rua**   HOTEL €
(☑ 0864 64 00 83; www.larua.it; Via Rua Mozza 1/3; d/tr €80/115; ᐧ) Hikers should head straight for this charming little hotel in Pescocostanzo's historic centre. The look is country cosy, with low, wood-beamed ceilings, parquet floors, and stone walls and fireplaces. Super-friendly owner Giuseppe is a mine of local knowledge on the town's distinctive domestic architecture, fine jewellery and dialect, while his brother Luigi is an experienced guide who can organise treks.

⭐ **Ristorante da Paolino**   ABRUZZESE €€
(☑ 0864 64 00 80; www.ristorantedapaolino.com; Strada Vulpes 34; meal €35; ⏱ 1-3pm & 8pm-midnight Tue-Sun) Be sure to book ahead at this bustling and popular little inn-restaurant in the heart of Pescocostanzo. Pasta dishes make expert use of earthy ingredients in season, such as truffles, mushrooms and chestnuts. Follow up with *secondi* of rabbit with oranges, or polenta spread on a bread board and topped with mince and black truffles. The coda? A creamy pudding.

ℹ Information

Tourist Office (Pro Loco Pescocostanzo; ☑ 0864 64 10 54; www.visit-pescocostanzo.it; Via delle Carceri 6; ⏱ 9am-1pm & 3-6pm Mon-Fri Sep-Jun, 9am-1pm & 4-7pm daily Jul & Aug) Off the central Piazza del Municipio. Also see the Parco Nazionale della Majella's comprehensive website (www.parcomajella.it).

ℹ Getting There & Away

TUA (☑ 800 762622; www.tuabruzzo.it) buses run from Sulmona to Roccaraso (€3.60, 50 minutes, three daily) from where you can catch another bus to Pescocostanzo (€1.20, 15 minutes, four daily).

Pacentro

📞 0864 / POP 1140

Set on a knoll above the Sulmona plateau in the foothills of the Parco Nazionale della Majella, Pacentro is a gorgeous hill town, its three slim Renaissance towers evoking those of Tuscany's San Gimignano. It has never expanded far beyond its medieval boundaries and remains free of the unsightly modern sprawl that encircles some of its bigger neighbours. Largely off the standard tourist circuit and – unlike Pescocostanzo and Scanno – not affiliated with a ski resort, its pleasantly tangled streets remain quiet and authentic. It's a good place to mingle with the locals, taste home cooking in low-key trattorias, or use as a base for some nearby national-park walks.

Of interest to modern visitors are the mostly 14th-century **Caldora Castle** (Largo del Castello; admission €2; ⊙ 10am-1pm & 3-6pm) with its three famous towers, the mannerist-meets-baroque **Chiesa Santa Maria della Misericordia**, and a slew of grand nobles' houses that beautify the lanes between Piazza del Popolo and Piazza Umberto I.

🏃 Activities

Zipline Majella ADVENTURE SPORTS
(📞 366 7279724; www.ziplinemajella.com; Piazza del Popolo 13; single ride €40-45; ⊙ 10am-6.30pm daily Jul & Aug, Sat & Sun only Sep-Jun) In 2019 central Italy's first zip line was installed in the foothills of the Majella mountains. Measuring just shy of 1km, it catapults human bullets above the medieval towers, piazzas and roofs of Pacentro at 80km/h.

Book online. It also offers zip line–hiking combo packages.

🛏 Sleeping & Eating

B&B In Centro a Pacentro B&B €
(📞 349 7841697; www.incentroapacentro.it; Via San Marco 5; s/d from €40/75; 🐕) A wonderful family heirloom of a house, full of precious furniture, photos and mementos of the owner's parents and grandparents (some of whom emigrated to the USA). A breakfast terrace offers stunning views across Pacentro to the mountains beyond. Excellent hands-on service and full village immersion is assured.

Ristorante-Pizzeria Majella ABRUZZESE €€
(📞 0864 77 33 91; Via Santa Maria Maggiore 146; meals €25-35; ⊙ 11.30am-3pm & 7-11pm Tue-Sun, 6-11pm Mon) You could easily walk right past this restaurant; it doesn't brag about its existence. Instead, its reputation is carried by word of mouth – which in small-town Pacentro travels fast. The pizzas are excellent, but the menu apogee is the *arrosticini*, an old Abruzzo classic comprising lamb skewers wrapped in foil and served in a sloping ceramic pot.

ℹ Information

Centro Informazioni Parco Nazionale Majella (Majella National Park Information Centre; 📞 0864 4 13 04; www.parcomajella.it; Piazza del Popolo 7, Palazzo Tonno; ⊙ 10am-1pm & 4-8pm May-Sep, weekend only Oct-Apr) Information on the town and the wider national park.

PACENTRO'S BAREFOOT RUNNING RACE

Pacentro's most bizarre festival involves a running race with one very painful difference: participants must complete it barefoot.

Undertaken on rugged paths immediately surrounding the village, the **Corsa degli Zingari** has been going on in some form or other for over 550 years. Its origins are the subject of conjecture. Some claim it evolved from an old hunting rite practised by Italic tribes; others suggest it was part of a medieval military initiation. The word *zingaro* in the local dialect means 'one who walks barefoot', which in medieval Italy meant a poor person.

Run on the first Sunday in September, the race starts atop a steep escarpment on the hillside opposite Pacentro. Runners (the bulk of whom are young men) hurtle down a steep path covered in brambles and sharp stones, before athletically fording the Vella River and climbing a steep slope on the opposite bank into the village. The finish line is the diminutive baroque Chiesa della Madonna di Loreto where participants – their feet, by now, a bloody mess – collapse in front of the altar. Afterwards the winners are carried through town on the shoulders of an enthusiastic crowd, foot pain momentarily forgotten.

❶ Getting There & Away

Pacentro lies 10km east of Sulmona along the SS487. Regular **TUA** (📞 800 762622; www.tua bruzzo.it) buses run between the two towns (€2.40, 35 minutes, nine daily).

Scanno

📞 0864 / POP 1820

A tangle of steep alleyways and sturdy, grey-stone houses, Scanno is a dramatic and atmospheric *borgo* (medieval town), known for its finely worked filigree gold jewellery. For centuries a centre of wool production, it is one of the few places in Italy where you can still see women wearing traditional dress.

Be sure to take the exhilarating drive or bus ride up to Scanno from Sulmona through the rocky Gole di Sagittario, a World Wildlife Fund reserve and gorge, and past tranquil Lago di Scanno, where there's a scattering of bars and cafes, and where you can hire boats in summer.

🛏 Sleeping & Eating

⭐ Il Palazzo   B&B €

(📞 0864 74 78 60; www.ilpalazzobb.it; Via Ciorla 25; s/d €55/95; 🅿🛜) Who wouldn't want to stay at a B&B called 'The Palace'? This elegant and gently welcoming place occupies the 2nd floor of Casa Parente, an 18th-century *palazzo* in Scanno's historic centre. The six amply sized rooms are decorated with sturdy antique furnishings, and breakfast is served under a frescoed ceiling. The building was commandeered for a military hospital by the Germans in WWII.

Pizzeria Trattoria
Vecchio Mulino   TRATTORIA €

(📞 0864 74 72 19; Via Silla 50; pizzas/meals from €8/28; ⊘ noon-3pm & 7pm-midnight, closed Wed winter) This old-school eatery is a good bet for a classic wood-fired pizza, lentil soups, pastas (perhaps ravioli with mushroom and ricotta) and roasted *salsicce* (sausage). In summer the pretty street-side terrace provides a good perch from which to people-watch (read: tourist-watch). The excellent bread and pasta are homemade and the cheeses are all local.

❶ Information

Tourist Office (📞 0864 7 43 17; Piazza Santa Maria della Valle 12; ⊘ 9am-1pm Mon-Fri &

5-8pm Tue & Thu year-round, & 9am-1pm & 3-6pm Sat & Sun Jul-Sep) In the village centre.

❶ Getting There & Away

TUA (📞 800 762622; www.tuabruzzo.it) buses run to and from Sulmona (€3.20, one hour, seven daily). Service is pared back to two buses on Sundays.

Parco Nazionale d'Abruzzo, Lazio e Molise

Italy's second-oldest national park is also one of its most ecologically rich. Established by royal decree in 1923, it began as a modest 5-sq-km reserve that, little by little, morphed into the 440-sq-km protected area it is today. The evolution wasn't easy. The park was temporarily abolished in 1933 by the Mussolini government. It returned to the fold in 1950 only to face further encroachment from housing construction, road building and ski developers.

The park has managed to remain at the forefront of Italy's conservation movement, reintroducing and protecting wild animals such as the Abruzzo chamois, Apennine wolf, lynx, deer and – most notably – Marsican bear (the park has Italy's largest surviving enclave of these threatened animals).

Today the park extends over three regions, with over half of it covered in thick beech forest. Thanks to its long history, it receives more visitors than other parks – around two million annually.

⊙ Sights

Right in the middle of the park, the red-roofed town of Pescasseroli has the open, airy feel of a large village. Narrow streets and medieval churches suggest a rich history, but the lure of the wilderness is never far away. The Centro di Visita di Pescasseroli (📞 0863 911 32 21; www.parcoabruzzo.it; Viale Colli dell'Oro, Pescasseroli; adult/reduced €6/4; ⊘ 10am-5.30pm) harbours some rescued bears and wolves, but for a better rundown of the park's flora and fauna, head 17km southeast to Civitella Alfedena, whose wolf museum doubles as an info centre.

Situated on a hilltop 6km from Pescasseroli is Opi, a *borgo più bella d'Italia* (one of Italy's most beautiful towns). It's one of the highest settlements in the park (1250m), makes an attractive base and is home to the little Centro Visita del Camoscio (www.parcoabruzzo.it; Via Affacciata, Opi; ⊙9am-1pm & 3.30-7.30pm summer, 10am-1pm & 3.30-6.30pm winter) **FREE**, a wildlife sanctuary that studies the Apennine chamois.

On the park's eastern edge and about 17km from Opi is the calm-inducing Lago di Barrea, with the venerable and handsome town of Barrea positioned on a rocky spur above the lake.

At the opposite end of the lake, much smaller Civitella Alfedena is a seductive hamlet reached via a bridge across the water. Here you can learn about the Appenine wolf and other fauna (and flora) at the **Museo del Lupo Appenninico** (Appenine Wolf Museum; ☑0864 89 01 41; Via Santa Lucia; adult/reduced €3/2; ⊙10am-1.30pm & 3-6.30pm Apr-Sep, to 5.30pm Oct-Mar).

🏃 Activities

Hiking opportunities abound, whether you want to go it alone or with an organised group. There are numerous outfits, including **Ecotur** (☑0863 91 27 60; www.ecotur.org; Via Piave 9, Pescasseroli; ⊙9am-1pm & 4-7.30pm), offering guided excursions. Between May and October, there are horse treks with **Centro Ippico Vallecupa** (☑0863 91 04 44; www.agriturismomomaneggiovallecupa.it; Via della Difesa Monte Tranquillo, Pescasseroli).

Rocca Ridge   HIKING

An adventurous day hike that takes you through an atmospheric beech forest and up to a long ridge from where it's possible to view large tracts of the national park – and possibly sight a distant bear. The hike starts and finishes in the village of Pescasseroli, passes two *rifugi* (mountain huts) and a mountain chapel, and takes in several peaks (the highest rising to 1924m).

🛏 Sleeping & Eating

★**La Fattoria di Morgana**   AGRITURISMO €

(☑334 1564908; Via Fonte Dei Cementi Snc, Opi; s/d/tr €60/80/120) It's hard to imagine a lovelier place in which to base yourself than this *agriturismo* (farm stay) below the stunning village of Opi. Surrounded by forest-clad mountains, you'll not only have gregarious farmers Simon and Claudia for company, but also their menagerie of ducks, goats, pigs, horses and adorable Abruzzo sheepdogs, usually including litters of puppies.

It's worth the extra €20 for Claudia's excellent cooking.

★**Albergo Antico Borga La Torre**   HOTEL €

(☑0864 89 01 21; www.albergolatorre.com; Via Castello 3, Civitella Alfedena; s/d €50/70; [P] [🛜]) Housed in an atmospheric *palazzo* incorporating Civitella Alfedena's oldest (medieval) tower, this attractive and spotless hotel is deservedly popular with hikers. Rooms are simple and small with tiny bathrooms, but the building itself is loaded with atmosphere, plus there's a garden for alfresco relaxation. Also in-house is the Ristorante La Torre, serving fresh Abruzzese food, after which the owner might treat you to his homemade (and eye-wateringly strong) *digestivo*.

Il Duca degli Abruzzi   ITALIAN €€

(☑0863 91 10 75; Piazza Duca degli Abruzzi 5, Pescasseroli; meals €25-30; ⊙7.30-10.30pm Fri & Sat, 1-3.30pm Sun) This handsome hotel-restaurant located on a quiet square in Pescasseroli's *centro storico* (historic centre) is a little more gourmet than your average salt-of-the-earth village trattoria, but doesn't shirk on the rustic charm either. Everything is homemade and utterly delicious: try the truffle pasta or potato gnocchi, and follow up with baked cod or grilled pork, washed down with Montepulciano d'Abruzzo.

ℹ Getting There & Away

Pescasseroli, Civitella Alfedena and other villages in the national park are linked by **TUA** (☑800 762622; www.tuabruzzo.it) buses.

Buses head from Pescasseroli to Avezzano (€5, 1½ hours, six daily) from where you can change for L'Aquila, Pescara and Rome (either bus or train).

Buses also head into the park from Castel di Sangro calling at Civitella Alfedena, Opi and Pescasseroli (€3.90, 1¼ hours, six daily). In Castel di Sangro, change for buses to Sulmona and Naples.

Pescara

☑085 / POP 120,400

Abruzzo's largest city is a heavily developed seaside resort, with one of the biggest marinas on the Adriatic. The city was heavily bombed during WWII, reducing much of the centre to rubble. It's a lively place with an animated seafront, especially in summer, but unless you're coming for the 16km of sandy beaches, there's no great reason to hang around. A couple of mildly diverting museums and some fresh-from-the-Adriatic seafood restaurants could fill a lazy half-day.

⊙ Sights

**Museo Casa Natale
Gabriele D'Annunzio** MUSEUM
(☏ 085 6 03 91; Corso Manthonè 116; admission
€4; ⊗ 8.30am-7.30pm) The birthplace of controversial proto-fascist poet Gabriele D'Annunzio is small but excellently curated,
with nine rooms displaying furniture, documents, photos and his death mask resting in
a polished glass case. A short film (in Italian)
is given as an introduction.

Museo delle Genti d'Abruzzo MUSEUM
(☏ 085 451 00 26; www.gentidabruzzo.com; Via
delle Caserme 24; adult/reduced €6/3; ⊗ 9am-1pm
Mon-Fri, 9am-1pm & 4.30-7.30pm Sat, 4.30-7.30pm
Sun) An extensive (if slightly dated) display
of Abruzzo culture that squeezes rather a lot
into 13 interconnecting rooms, covering the
Bronze Age to the Risorgimento and beyond.
The labelling is mainly in Italian with some
sporadic English and the presentation is, at
times, a little cluttered. But there's a lot of
history backed up by exhibits of a more folkloric bent (including numerous costumes).
Most illuminating is the little-told story of
Abruzzo's Italic shepherd warriors who gave
the peninsula its name.

🛌 Sleeping

★ G Hotel BOUTIQUE HOTEL €€
(☏ 085 2 76 89; www.ghotelpescara.it; Via Stazione
Ferroviaria 100; s/d €105/130; P ❄ 🛜 🐾) The G
is the Alfa Romeo of Pescara's hotels: smart,
well-designed and quietly luxurious, but at
the same time, not ridiculously expensive.
Located a mere 100m dash from the train
station, it instantly impresses with a large
modern-minimalist lobby-lounge where
generous *aperitivo* snacks are rolled out
every afternoon. Tech-savvy rooms have
huge mirrors, rain showers, crisp duvets and
atmospheric lighting.
Even the toilets are shapely.

Hotel Victoria BOUTIQUE HOTEL €€
(☏ 085 37 41 32; www.victoriapescara.com; Via
Piave 142; s/d €80/110; P ❄ @ 🛜) A top-notch
hotel in a handsome building in the city centre, the Victoria is a memorable place with
Impressionist paintings etched onto bedroom doors, curvaceous balconies and an
excellent downstairs cafe. Best of all is the
service, which goes above and beyond the
call of duty. Bonuses include a fitness centre
and a spa.

Hotel Alba HOTEL €€
(☏ 085 38 91 45; www.hotelalbapescara.com; Via
Michelangelo Forti 14; s/d/tr €75/85/100; P ❄ @)
A glitzy three-star place with decorative columns and gilt furniture in the brightly frescoed lobby, the Alba provides comfort and
a central location. Rooms vary but the best
sport polished wood, firm beds and plenty of
sunlight. Rates are lowest at weekends, and
garage parking costs €10.

🍴 Eating

La Bottega del 40 ABRUZZESE €
(☏ 085 66 28 5; www.ristorantelabottegadel40.it;
Via delle Caserme 54; meals €18-25; ⊗ 8-11.45pm
Thu-Tue) A small abode encased under a
stone archway in Pescara's diminutive old
town where the *primi* prices rarely break
double figures. This is a good place for a
light economical dinner served *veloce* (fast)
with a basket of bread and a glass of the
house plonk. There aren't many tables, but
the turnover is fast.
The gnocchi with sausages and saffron is
simple but sublime. Cash only.

★ La Cucineria ABRUZZESE €€
(☏ 335 5459990; Via Clemente de Cesaris 26;
meals €28-35; ⊗ 12.30-2.30pm & 7.30-10.30pm
Mon-Sat, 7.30-10.30pm Sun) Sitting pretty in a
city full of seafood, Cucineria relies more on
the fat of the *terra* (land) with *chitarrina*
(Abruzzo's spaghetti) tossed with mountain herbs and sun-dried tomatoes, cheesy
Roman favourite *cacio e pepe*, and a whole
section of the menu dedicated to different
focaccie made with locally milled flour that's
been left to rise for 72 hours.

ℹ Information

Info Point (☏ 331 6706473; www.abruzzo
turismo.it; Piazza della Rinascita; ⊗ 9am-1pm
& 4-7pm Jun-Sep, 9am-1pm & 3-6pm Oct-May)
A glass box in the main pedestrianised square,
run by Abruzzo Turismo.

ℹ Getting There & Away

AIR
Abruzzo International Airport (☏ 895
8989512; www.abruzzoairport.com; Via Tiburtina Km 229) Pescara's airport is 3km out of
town and easily reached by bus 38 (€1.10, 20
minutes, every 15 minutes) from in front of the
train station. Ryanair flies to London Stansted,
and Alitalia flies to Milan.

BUS

TUA (☑ 800 762622; www.tuabruzzo.it) buses leave from Piazzale della Repubblica in front of the train station for L'Aquila (€8.80, 1½ hours, 10 daily), Sulmona (€6.80, one hour, 11 daily), Naples (€26, four hours, five daily), Rome (€7 to €15, three hours, 11 daily) and towns throughout Abruzzo and Molise. There's a small ticket office and cafe on the edge of the car park.

Flixbus (www.flixbus.com) runs buses to Rome's Tiburtina station (€11, three hours, four daily) and Isernia (€10, 2½ hours, one daily).

TRAIN

Pescara's huge main train station (called Pescara Centrale) looks more like an airport terminal. Direct trains run to Ancona (from €11 to €22, 1¼ to 2¼ hours, frequent), Bari (from €33.50, 2¾ to 4¾ hours, frequent), Rome (from €14.50, 3½ to 5½ hours, seven daily) and Sulmona (€5.90, 1¼ hours, 20 daily).

Chieti

☑ 0871 / POP 51,300

Overlooking the Aterno valley, Chieti is a sprawling hilltop town with roots dating back to pre-Roman times when, as capital of the Marrucini tribe, it was known as Teate Marrucinorum. Later, in the 4th century BC, it was conquered by the Romans and incorporated into the Roman Republic.

The *comune* of Chieti splits into two parts: Chieti Scalo is the new commercial district, while hilltop Chieti Alta is of more interest to travellers thanks to two fine archaeology museums and handsome streets lined with dignified buildings and dotted with Roman remains.

◎ Sights

★ **Museo Archeologico Nazionale d'Abruzzo – Villa Frigerj**   MUSEUM
(☑ 0871 40 43 92; www.archeoabruzzo.benicultur ali.it; Via Costanzi 2, Villa Comunale; adult/reduced €4/2; ⊙ 8.30am-7.30pm Tue-Sat, 8.30am-2pm Sun) Housed in a neoclassical villa in the Villa Comunale park, Abruzzo's best archaeological museum displays a comprehensive collection of local finds, illuminating Chieti's three millennia of existence. While the primary focus is on the vanished worlds of the Marrucini, Aequi, Marsi, Sabini and other tribes that inhabited central Italy prior to Roman expansion, there are also plenty of Roman artefacts. Of particular note are impressive coin hoards and classical sculpture – including a colossal seated Hercules from the 1st century BC.

The museum's undoubted pride of place goes to the 6th-century-BC 'Warrior of Capestrano', considered the most important pre-Roman find in central Italy. Mystery surrounds the identity of the warrior, but there are some who reckon it to be Numa Pompilio, the second king of Rome, and successor to Romulus.

Museo Archeologico Nazionale d'Abruzzo – La Civitella   MUSEUM
(☑ 0871 6 31 37; www.archeoabruzzo.benicultur ali.it; Via Pianell; adult/reduced €4/2; ⊙ 8.30am-7.30pm Tue-Sat, 2-8pm Sun) 'La Civitella' is more modern than its museum twin across the road. It curls around a Roman amphitheatre built at the city's highest point in the 1st century AD, and was restored in 2000. Exhibits charting the history of Chieti and the area since Palaeolithic times include relics of the pre-Roman Marrucini, and statuary and items from early Imperial Rome.

🍴 Sleeping & Eating

Chieti is oddly undersupplied with restaurants, although street food such as focaccia stuffed with *porchetta* (roast pork) is cheap and excellent.

Grande Albergo Abruzzo   HOTEL €
(☑ 0871 4 19 40; www.albergoabruzzo.it; Via Herio 20; s/d/tr from €45/53/71; 🅿 🛜) Well located on the lip of Chieti Alta, this economical *albergo* (hotel) offers panoramic views of coast and mountains. The Grande's decor is either unfashionably dated or agreeably 'olde' depending on your taste for flowery sofas and rotary dial phones, but there are other perks – such as the outdoor terrace, left-luggage facility, on-site restaurant and bar, and free parking.

❶ Getting There & Away

Frequent **TUA** (☑ 800 762622; www.tuabruzzo. it) buses head down to Pescara (€2.40, 30 minutes) from Largo Cavallerizza on the cusp of Chieti's *centro storico*.

If you're catching a bus from Pescara, get off in Chieti Alta and not industrial Chieti Scalo, which is 7km short of the hilltop town.

Vasto & Around

On Abruzzo's southern coast, the hilltop town of Vasto has an atmospheric medieval quarter and superb sea views. Much of the *centro storico* dates from the 15th century, a period in which the city was known as 'the Athens of the Abruzzi'; it's also distinguished as the birthplace of the poet Gabriele Rossetti.

Two kilometres downhill is the blowsy resort of **Vasto Marina**, a strip of hotels, restaurants and campgrounds fronting a long sandy beach. About 10km north of town a wilder flavour prevails at the beautiful **Spiaggia di Punta Penna** set inside the **Riserva Naturale di Punta Aderci** (www.puntaderci.it).

In summer the action is on the beach at Vasto Marina. In the old town, interest revolves around the small historic centre, guarded on the seaward side by the romantic **Loggia Amblingh**, a walkway with long-distance views.

Sights

Palazzo d'Avalos MUSEUM
(☎0873 36 77 73; www.museipalazzodavalos.it; Piazza Pudente; palazzo & museums adult/reduced €5/3.50; ⏲10am-1pm & 6pm-midnight Jul & Aug, shorter hours rest of year) The Renaissance Palazzo d'Avalos houses a quartet of museums: the **Museo Archeologico**, with its eclectic collection of ancient bronzes, glasswork and paintings; the **Pinacoteca Comunale**, featuring paintings by the Palizzi brothers and other 19th-century artists; the **Galleria d'Arte Contemporanea**, with 80 works by contemporary Italian and Spanish artists; and the **Museo del Costume**, with donated Abruzzese folk outfits dating back to the early 19th century.

On the seaward side of the *palazzo* there's also a delightful **Neapolitan Garden** replete with arches, stand-alone columns, a profusion of blooms and hilltop views of the coastline.

Sleeping & Eating

★**Residenza Amblingh** HOTEL €€
(☎0873 36 27 02; www.amblingh.it; Via Portone Panzotto 13, Loggia Amblingh; ste €149-169; ❄📶) Don't even think about leaving Vasto off your itinerary when you can stay at this debonair accommodation offering four beautifully decorated suites (two with epic Vasto sea views) that make luxurious use of a handsome 18th-century *palazzo* (mansion). The state-of-the-art rooms integrate bare stone walls, sloping ceilings, skylights, giant bath tubs and funky staircases with lights under each step. It's beautifully (and subtly) done.

Once checked in you can savour customised bathrobes, an honesty bar, a minilibrary, *à la carte* pillows, and a lovely breakfast room with views that stretch as far south as the Tremiti Islands.

Breakfasts are made using local Molise coast ingredients. The whole place has been renovated using original building materials.

Trattoria da Peppe GRILL €€
(☎0873 36 21 69; Via Laccetti 16; meals €28-40; ⏲8-11.30pm Tue-Sat, noon-3.30pm Sun) Vasto's grill king runs a small eight-table operation in the old town. The emphasis is on charcoal-grilled meat – namely lamb, beef and sausages – backed up by various appetiser plates and pasta cut and cooked right under your nose. It's as much fun to watch as it is to eat here, with flavours that linger on the palate.

Getting There & Away

The train station (Vasto-San Salvo) is about 2km south of Vasto Marina and 4km from the old town. Trains run frequently to Pescara (€4.80, one hour) and Termoli (from €2.60, 15 minutes). From the station take bus 1 or 4 for Vasto Marina and the town centre (€1.50, half-hourly).

MOLISE

Of Italy's 20 regions, Molise probably ranks 20th in terms of name recognition. In fact, until 1970, it was part of Abruzzo, the adjacent region it closely resembles. Mountains and hills, rather than people, crowd the interior, while flatter plains guard a short 35km stretch of Adriatic coast. Although Campobasso is the largest city, its brightest attractions are Termoli, a higgledy-piggledy coastal town characterised by its *trabucchi* (fishing platforms), and Isernia and Saepinum, for glimpses of the Palaeolithic and Roman past. Molise has suffered steady depopulation since the late 19th century, adding to its sense of isolation.

Isernia

☎0865 / POP 21,800

With roots stretching back to the pre-Roman Samnites and beyond (to our proto-human ancestors), the city known to the Romans as *Aesernia* is historically rich. This may not be immediately apparent, as earthquakes and a massive WWII bombing raid have spared little of its original *centro storico*. But spend

---

WORTH A TRIP

SAEPINUM

One of Molise's hidden treasures, the Roman ruins of Saepinum (⊙9am-7pm) are among the best preserved and least visited in the country. Unlike Pompeii and Ostia Antica, which were both major ports, Saepinum was a small provincial town of no great importance. It was originally established by the Samnites but the Romans conquered it in 293 BC, paving the way for an economic boom in the 1st and 2nd centuries AD. Some 700 years later, it was sacked by Arab invaders.

The walled town retains three of its four original gates and its two main roads, the *cardo maximus* and the *decamanus*. Highlights include the forum, basilica and theatre – where you'll find the Museo della Città e del Territorio (adult/reduced €3/2; ⊙9.30am-6.30pm Tue-Sun).

It's not easy to reach Saepinum by public transport, but the bus from Campobasso to Sepino (€1.20, six daily on weekdays) generally stops near the site at Altilia, although it's best to ask the driver.

---

some time and you'll discover an undemonstrative old town harbouring sights such as the Fontana Fraterna, a 19th-century fountain built of ancient Roman stones, and the 14th-century Cattedrale di San Pietro Apostolo and various Roman and medieval arches and statuary. Among all that, you'll also stumble across some wonderful trattorias doing real Molise food for mainly local clientele.

The main historical draw is La Pineta, a 700,000-year-old archaeological site that is one of Europe's oldest proto-human links. It has an intriguing museum.

⊙ Sights

★ Museo Paleolitico di Isernia   MUSEUM
(☑0865 29 06 87; Contrada Ramiera Vecchia; adult/reduced €4/2; ⊙8am-7pm Tue-Sun) Built around the adjacent 730,000-year-old archaeological site of La Pineta, this intriguing museum stands next to a pavilion that protects the site of the original find. The modern open-plan building focuses mainly on the story of human development from prehistoric times, using large picture boards, mock-up dwellings and detailed captions (mostly in Italian). The site itself with its piles of elephant bones, remains of ancient lions, fossils, and stone tools left by our ancestor, *Homo erectus*, is reproduced on the museum floor.

Uncovered by road workers in 1978, La Pineta is basically a huge abattoir in which butchered kills were hidden from predators in the mud. Excavations are ongoing, and in 2014 archaeologists found the tooth of a young child dated to around 586,000 years ago.

The museum is poorly signposted but only a 1.5km walk from Isernia train station. It's rarely busy, apart from the odd school party. There are no refreshments on site.

Museo Civico Isernia   MUSEUM
(Piazza Celestino V; ⊙9.30am-1.30pm & 3-7pm Mon & Wed-Sat, 9.30am-1.30pm & 4-8pm Sun) FREE World War II doesn't get a lot of coverage in Italy, which makes this small museum chronicling the events of 10 September 1943, when Isernia was heavily bombed by the Allies, all the more interesting. Old photos, discarded possessions of American, British and German soldiers, and stories of local heroism add to the poignancy.

🛏 Sleeping & Eating

Residenze Portacastello Graffolus   B&B €
(☑0865 23 45 79; www.residenzeportacastello. it; Vico Storto Castello 42; s/d/apt €55/65/75; P🛜) A renovated, early-17th-century stone building in Isernia's historic heart is the setting for this welcoming and well-run B&B. Spread over three floors, the seven rooms and two apartments (with kitchenettes) feature parquet floors, exposed stone walls, mood lighting, good-quality beds and (in some) fireplaces.

★ O'Pizzaiuolo   OSTERIA €€
(☑0865 41 27 76; www.ristoranteopizzaiuolo.it; Corso Marcelli 253; meals €18-30; ⊙12.30-3.30pm & 7.30-11.30pm) If the bread's good, usually all else will follow and so it goes in this old town cantina-restaurant whose single arched entrance leads into a labyrinth of brick-lined alcoves creatively decorated with bottles of wine. The menu's an extravaganza of underrated Molise food, simple but effective rec-

ipes like *cacio e pepe* with added pancetta, stewed meats, and creamy herb-laden risottos. Even the chips are fabulous.

❶ Getting There & Away

BUS

From the bus station next to the train station on Piazza della Repubblica, **ATM** (📞 0874 6 47 44; www.atm-molise.it) runs buses to Campobasso (€3.50, one hour, eight daily), Termoli (€4.90, 1½ hours, three daily), and Castel San Vincenzo (€1.50, 35 minutes, three daily), a 1km walk from Abbazia di San Vincenzo al Volturno. Get tickets from Bar Ragno d'Oro on Piazza della Repubblica.

From Isernia, **SATI** (📞 0874 6 01 59; www.satiautobus.com) buses serve Pietrabbondante (€1.65, 35 minutes, two daily) and Agnone (€2.05, one hour, five daily).

TRAIN

Trains connect Isernia with Sulmona (from €8.50 to €14.40, three to four hours, one to two changes, two daily), Campobasso (€3.60, one hour, 14 daily), Naples (€7.55, two hours, four direct services daily) and Rome (€12.50, 2¼ hours, seven direct services daily).

Termoli

📞 0875 / POP 33,700

Despite its touristy trattorias and brassy bars, Molise's top beach resort retains a winning, low-key charm. At the eastern end of the seafront, the pretty *borgo antico* (old town) juts out to sea like a massive pier, dividing the sandy beach from Termoli's small harbour. From the seawall you'll see several typical Molisan *trabucchi* (special fishing platforms).

Guarding the entrance to the old town is Termoli's iconic 13th-century Castello Svevo (Swabian Castle; 📞 0875 71 23 54; Largo Castello; ☺ by request); beyond, through a tangle of narrow streets, pastel-coloured houses and souvenir shops, lies its beautiful 12th-century cathedral (📞 0875 70 80 25; Piazza Duomo; ☺ 7.30-11.50am & 4.30-8pm).

🍴 Sleeping & Eating

★ **Residenza Sveva**　　　　　HOTEL €
(📞 0875 70 68 03; www.residenzasveva.com; Piazza Duomo 11; s/d/tr/q from €60/90/120/140; ❄ �) This historic *albergo diffuso* (dispersed hotel) has its reception on Piazza Duomo,

near the cathedral, but the 21 rooms are squeezed into several *palazzi* in the *borgo* (old town). The style is summery with plenty of gleaming blue tiles and traditional embroidery. There's also an excellent, elegant seafood restaurant, Svevia (📞 0875 55 02 84; www.svevia.it; Via Vecchio 24; meals €35-50; ☺ 12.30-2.30pm & 8-10.30pm Tue-Sun), on site.

Ristorante Da Nicolino　　　SEAFOOD €€
(📞 0875 70 68 04; www.ristorantenicolino.it; Via Roma 13; meals from €35; ☺ 12.30-3pm & 7.30-11pm Fri-Wed) Well regarded by locals, this discreet restaurant near the entrance to the old town serves some of the best seafood in a town not short on seafood. It's made a name for its *brodetto alla termolese,* a large terracotta bowl literally brimming with assorted fish and crustaceans 'swimming' in a sweet, spicy soup. The stuffed squid comes a close second.

❶ Information

Tourist Office (📞 0875 70 39 13; www.termoli.net; 1st fl, Piazza Bega 42; ☺ 8am-2pm & 3-6pm Mon & Wed, 8am-2pm Tue, Thu & Fri) Helpful but hard to find, Termoli's tourist office is tucked away in a dodgy-looking car park behind a small shopping gallery, 100m east of the train station.

❶ Getting There & Away

BOAT

Termoli is the only port with year-round ferries to the Isole Tremiti. **Tirrenia Navigazione** (📞 049 6111 4020; www.tirrenia.it) runs a year-round ferry and **Navigazione Libera del Golfo** (📞 0875 70 48 59; www.navlib.it; ☺ Apr-Sep) operates a quicker hydrofoil in summer. Buy tickets online or at the port (east of the old town).

BUS

Termoli's bus station is beside Via Martiri della Resistenza. **SATI** (📞 0874 6 01 59; www.satiautobus.com) has services to/from Campobasso (€3.20, 1¼ hours, 10 daily), Isernia (€4.90, 1½ hours, three daily) and Pescara (from €5.40, 1¾ hours, three daily. Flixbus (www.flixbus.com) runs two direct daily buses to Rome (from €14, 5¼ hours).

TRAIN

Direct trains serve Bologna (from €46, four to five hours, 10 daily), Lecce (from €42, 3½ to 4½ hours, 10 daily) and stations along the Adriatic coast.

POPULATION
5.71 million

POPULATION DENSITY: NAPLES
8,306 per sq km

BEST PIZZA
Concettina Ai Tre
Santi (p714)

BEST VIEW
Seggiovia del Monte
Solaro (p740)

BEST SPA
Negombo (p744)

WHEN TO GO

May Best month to
visit. Warm days,
with many special
events.

Jun & Sep Summer
heat without the
August crowds and
traffic.

Aug Hottest month;
many shops and
restaurants close for
a few weeks.

Positano p749
GONZH/SHUTTERSTOCK ©

Naples & Campania

Campania is a rich *ragù* of Arabesque street life, decadent palaces, pastel-hued villages and aria-inspiring vistas.

Few corners of Europe can match the cultural conundrums here. Should you spend the morning waltzing through chandeliered Bourbon bedrooms or the frescoed villa of a Roman emperor's wife? And which of Caravaggio's canvases shouldn't you miss: the multiscene masterpiece inside Naples' Pio Monte della Misericordia, or the artist's swansong inside the city's belle époque Palazzo Zevallos?

Campania's mountains and coastline offer their own plethora of options, from horse-riding the slopes of Mt Vesuvius to sailing the Amalfi Coast and soaking in thermal waters on Ischia.

Naples & Campania Highlights

1 Pompeii (p728) Channelling the ancients on the ill-fated streets of this erstwhile Roman city.

2 Grotta Azzurra (p740) Being bewitched by Capri's ethereal blue cave.

3 Sentieri degli Dei (p753) Walking with the gods on the Amalfi Coast.

4 Cappella Sansevero (p701) Re-evaluating artistic ingenuity in Naples.

5 Procida (p747) Lunching by lapping waves on the pastel-hued smallest island of the Bay of Naples.

6 Negombo (p744) Indulging in a little thermal therapy on Ischia.

7 Villa Rufolo (p758) Attending a concert at this dreamy Ravello villa and its cascading gardens.

8 Reggia di Caserta (p720) Pretending you're royalty at this monumental Unesco-listed palace complex.

9 Paestum (p762) Admiring ancient Hellenic ingenuity in the colossal ruins of Magna Graecia.

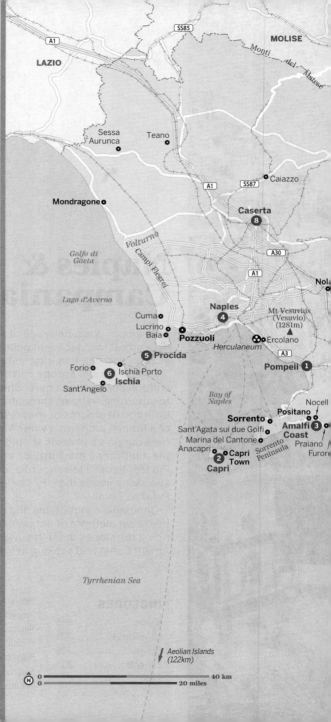

NAPLES

♩ 081 / POP 966,145

Naples is raw, high-octane energy, a place of soul-stirring art and panoramas, spontaneous conversations and unexpected, inimitable elegance. Welcome to Italy's most unlikely masterpiece.

History

After founding nearby Cuma in the 8th century BC, the ancient Greeks settled the city in around 680 BC, calling it Parthenope. Under the Romans, the area became an ancient Miami of sorts: a sun-soaked spa region that drew the likes of Virgil. Dampening the bonhomie was Mt Vesuvius' eruption in AD 79.

Naples fell into Norman hands in 1139 before the French Angevins took control a century later, boosting the city's cred with the mighty Castel Nuovo (p709). By the 16th century, Naples was under Spanish rule and riding high on Spain's colonial riches. By 1600,

it was Europe's largest city and a burgeoning baroque beauty adorned by artists like Luca Giordano, Jusepe de Ribera and Caravaggio.

Despite a devastating plague in 1656, Naples soared under the Bourbons (1734–1860), with epic constructions such as the Teatro San Carlo (p717) and the Reggia di Caserta (p720) sealing the city's showcase reputation.

An ill-fated attempt at republican rule in 1799 was followed by a short stint under the French and a final period of Bourbon governance before nationalist rebel Giuseppe Garibaldi inspired the city to snip off the puppet strings and join a united Italy in 1860.

The Nazis took Naples in 1943, but they were quickly forced out by a series of popular uprisings between 26 and 30 September, famously known as the *Quattro giornate di Napoli* (Four Days of Naples). Led by locals, especially by young *scugnizzi* (Neapolitan for 'street urchins') and ex-soldiers, the street battles paved the way for the Allies to enter the city on 1 October.

Naples

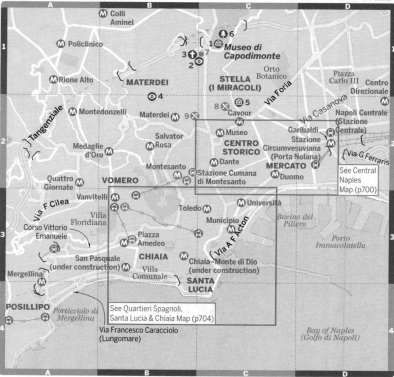

After setting up a provisional government in Naples, the Allies were confronted with an anarchic mass of troops, German prisoners of war and bands of Italian fascists all competing with the city's starving population for food. Overwhelmed, Allied authorities turned to the underworld for assistance. As long as the Allies agreed to turn a blind eye to their black-market activities, the Mafia was willing to help. And so the Camorra (Neapolitan Mafia) was given a boost.

On 23 November 1980, a devastating earthquake struck the mountainous area of Irpinia, 100km east of Naples. The quake, which left more than 2700 people dead and thousands more homeless, caused extensive damage in Naples. It is believed that US$6.4 billion of the funds that poured into the region to assist the victims and rebuilding ended up in the pockets of the Camorra.

In 2011, Neapolitan voters elected the city's current mayor, Luigi de Magistris, a youthful former public prosecutor and vocal critic of both the Mafia and government corruption. Determined to improve the city's liveability, de Magistris has pushed through a number of initiatives, including the transformation of the Lungomare from a traffic-clogged thoroughfare into a pedestrian and bike-friendly waterfront strip.

While De Magistris is not without his critics, his progressive, anticorruption agenda has hit the right note with many Neapolitans. In 2016, the Gen-X independent was re-elected city mayor, beating rival Gianni Lettieri of the centre-right Forza Italia party.

Naples

◉ Sights

◉ Centro Storico

★**Complesso Monumentale di Santa Chiara** BASILICA
(Map p700; ☑081 551 66 73; www.monasterodisantachiara.it; Via Santa Chiara 49c; basilica free, Complesso Monumentale adult/reduced €6/4.50; ⊙basilica 7.30am-1pm & 4.30-8pm, Complesso Monumentale 9.30am-5.30pm Mon-Sat, 10am-2.30pm Sun; ▥Dante) Vast, Gothic and cleverly deceptive, the mighty Basilica di Santa Chiara stands at the heart of this tranquil monastery complex. The church was severely damaged in WWII: what you see today is a 20th-century recreation of Gagliardo Primario's 14th-century original. Adjoining it are the basilica's cloisters, adorned with brightly coloured 17th-century majolica tiles and frescoes.

While the Angevin porticoes date back to the 14th century, the cloisters took on their current look in the 18th century thanks to the landscaping work of Domenico Antonio Vaccaro. The walkways that divide the central garden of lavender and citrus trees are lined with 72 ceramic-tiled octagonal columns connected by benches. Painted by Donato and Giuseppe Massa, the tiles depict various rural scenes, from hunting sessions to vignettes of peasant life. The four internal walls are covered with soft, whimsical 17th-century frescoes of Franciscan tales.

Adjacent to the cloisters, a small and elegant museum of mostly ecclesiastical props also features the excavated ruins of a 1st-century spa complex, including a remarkably well-preserved *laconicum* (sauna).

Commissioned by Robert of Anjou for his wife Sancia di Maiorca, the monastic complex was built to house 200 monks and the tombs of the Angevin royal family. Dissed as a 'stable' by Robert's ungrateful son Charles of Anjou, the basilica received a luscious baroque makeover by Domenico Antonio Vaccaro, Gaetano Buonocore and Giovanni Del Gaizo in the 18th century. It took a direct hit during an Allied air raid on 4 August 1943 and its reconstruction was completed in 1953. Features that did survive the fire resulting from the bombing include part of a 14th-century fresco to the left of the main door and a chapel containing the tombs of the Bourbon kings from Ferdinand I to Francesco II.

Continued on p701

NAPLES & CAMPANIA NAPLES

TOP SIGHT
MUSEO ARCHAEOLOGICO NAZIONALE

The stuff history dreams are made of, Naples' Museo Archeologico Nazionale houses an extraordinary collection of ancient art and artefacts. Its assets include many of the finest frescoes, mosaics and epigraphs from the ancient settlements below Mt Vesuvius, not to mention the largest single sculpture from antiquity unearthed to date, the epic *Toro Farnese* (Farnese Bull).

Toro Farnese & Hercules

The undisputed star of the ground-floor Farnese collection of colossal Greek and Roman sculptures is the *Toro Farnese* (Farnese Bull). Mentioned in the *Natural History* of Pliny the Elder, the early-3rd-century masterpiece – most likely a Roman copy of a Greek original – is the largest single sculpture recovered from antiquity. Unearthed in Rome in 1545, the piece was restored by Michelangelo before being escorted to Naples by warship in 1788. Sculpted from a single block of marble, the masterpiece depicts the humiliating demise of Dirce, Queen of Thebes, tied to a raging bull and violently dragged to her death. Directly opposite the work is mighty *Ercole* (Hercules), also discovered at Rome's Baths of Caracalla, albeit without his legs. Michelangelo commissioned Guglielmo della Porta to sculpt replacement pins. The original legs were later uncovered and reinstated by the Bourbons. An inscription on the rock below Hercules' club attributes the work to Athenian sculptor Glykon.

DON'T MISS

➡ Toro Farnese & Hercules statues

➡ Alexander the Great mosaic from the Casa del Fauno

➡ Gabinetto Segreto (Secret Chamber)

➡ Frescoes of *Perseus and Andromeda*, *Theseus the Liberator*, *Bacchus and Vesuvius* and the *Riot between Pompeians and Nucerians*.

➡ Villa dei Papiri sculptures

PRACTICALITIES

➡ Map p700

➡ 📞 848 800288

➡ www.museoarcheologico napoli.it

➡ Piazza Museo Nazionale 19

➡ adult/reduced €18/2

➡ 🕙 9am-7.30pm Wed-Mon

➡ Ⓜ Museo, Piazza Cavour

Mezzanine Mosaics & Ancient Erotica

The museum's mezzanine level is awash with precious mosaic panels, most of which hail from ancient Pompeii. Room LIX is home to the playful *Scena di commedia: Musici ambulanti*, depicting four roaming musicians, as well as the allegorical *Memento mori*, in which a skull represents death, a butterfly the soul, and the wheel fate. The mosaics in rooms LX and LXI are even more impressive. Once adorning the largest home in Pompeii, the Casa del Fauno, they include an action-packed mural of Alexander the Great in battle against Persian king Darius III. Considered one of the most important works of art from antiquity, it's a precise copy of a famous Hellenistic painting from the second half of the 4th century BC. The mosaics found in the Casa del Fauno were created by lauded craftsmen from Alexandria, Egypt, active in Italy between the end of the 2nd century BC and the beginning of the 1st century BC. The mezzanine is also home to the Gabinetto Segreto (Secret Chamber), a small, once-scandalous collection of erotically themed artworks and objects. Its most famous piece is a marble sculpture of the mythical half-goat, half-man Pan copulating with a nanny goat. The collection's bounty of erect members is testament to the common use of phallic symbols in Roman homes, considered symbols of good fortune, success and fertility.

First-Floor Frescoes & Sculptures

The 1st floor is a tour-de-force of ancient frescoes, pottery, glassware and sculpture. From the Sala del Meridione, the collection commences with frescoes retrieved from Vesuvian villas. Room LXXII is home to the largest known depiction of Perseus and Andromeda, in which the hero rescues his young bride after slaying a sea monster. More beast slaying occurs in Room LXXIII, home to a notable depiction of *Theseus the Liberator*. In Room LXXV, *Bacchus and Vesuvius* is believed to represent Vesuvius as it looked before the eruption of 79 AD, with one summit instead of two. A notorious clash between rival spectators at Pompeii's amphitheatre in 59 AD is captured in Room LXXVIII's *Riot between Pompeians and Nucerians*. At the end of the building is a collection of impressive sculptures found at the Villa dei Papiri. Room CXVI houses the five bronzes known collectively as the *Daughters of Danaus*. Dating from the Augustan period (27 BC–14 AD), the figures represent mythical siblings condemned to pouring water for eternity after murdering their cousins (and bridegrooms) to appease their father, who sought revenge on his own sibling, Aegyptus.

BASEMENT TREASURES

The museum's basement claims one of the world's most important collections of ancient Greek, Italic and Latin epigraphs (stone inscriptions), representing both public and private life in ancient times. Adjoining it is a collection of Egyptian treasures, which, in Italy, is outshone only by Turin's Museo Egizio.

Before tackling the collection, consider investing in the *National Archaeological Museum of Naples* (€12), published by Electa; if you want to concentrate on the highlights, audio guides (€5) are available in English.

MUSEUM ARCHITECTURE

The museum occupies the Palazzo degli Studi, built in the late 16th century as a cavalry barracks. It was extended and modified over the centuries by architects including Giulio Cesare Fontana, the son of the late-Renaissance architect Domenico Fontana. The building's pièce de résistance is its 1st-floor Salone della Meridiana (Hall of the Sundial), featuring a vault fresco by Pietro Bardellino honouring King Ferdinand IV and Maria Carolina of Austria.

Central Naples

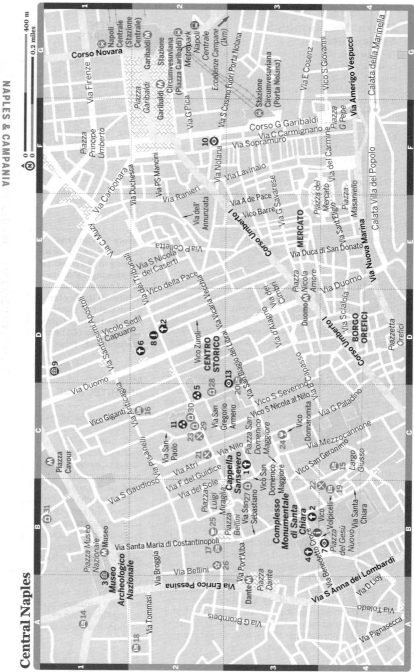

400 m
0.2 miles

Corso Novara

Napoli Centrale (Stazione Centrale) Ⓜ
Stazione Circumvesuviana Ⓜ
Piazza Garibaldi Ⓜ
Garibaldi Ⓜ
Stazione Circumvesuviana (Piazza Garibaldi) Ⓜ

Via Firenze

Piazza Principe Umberto

Metropark Napoli Centrale

Eccellenze Campane (1km)

Via S Cosmo Fuori Porta Nolana

Stazione Circumvesuviana (Porta Nolana) Ⓜ

Corso G Garibaldi
Via C Carmignano
Via Sopramuro

Piazza G Pepe

Via Amerigo Vespucci

Via E Cosenz
Vico S Giovanni

Calata della Marinella

Via G Pica

Via Duchesca

Via Carbonara

Via PS Mancini

Via Ranieri

Via Nolana

10

Via Lavinaio

Via A de Pace
Vico Barre

Via G Savarese

MERCATO

Piazza del Mercato
Piazza Masaniello

Via del Carmine
Via del Mercato di San Sant'Eligio

Calata Villa del Popolo

Via dell'Annunziata

Corso Umberto I

Via Duca di San Donato

Via Nuova Marina

Calata della Marinella

Via C Minzi

Via Santissimi Apostoli

Vicolo Sedil Capuano

Via P Colletta

Via S Nicola dei Caserti

Via dei Tribunali

Vico della Pace

6
8
12

CENTRO STORICO

Via Duomo

9

Vico Zuroli

Via Vicaria Vecchia

Via dei Cimbri

Via S Bago del Libraio

Duomo Ⓜ

Piazza Nicola Amore

BORGO OREFICI

Piazzetta Orefici

Via Duomo

Corso Umberto I

Via Scialoja

Piazza Cavour Ⓜ

Vico Giganti

Via Anticaglia

16

30
5
28

13
20

Via San Gregorio Armeno

Vico S Severino
Vico S Nicola al Nilo

Corso Capasso

Via G Paladino

Via Donnaromita

11
23
29

Via San Paolo

Via S Gaudioso

Via San Nilo

Piazza San Domenico Maggiore

Via Mezzocannone

Vico San Geronimo

Largo Giusso

15

Via Atri

Via F del Guidice

21

Cappella Sansevero

1

Vico San Domenico Maggiore

24

19

Via del Sole

Piazza Luigi Miraglia

San 27

Via San Sebastiano

22

Piazza Bellini

25

17

Complesso Monumentale di Santa Chiara

26

Via Santa Maria di Costantinopoli

Via Broggia

Via Bellini

Via PortʼAlba

Vico Volpicelli

2

7

Piazza del Gesù Nuovo

Via Santa Chiara

4

Via S Anna dei Lombardi

Museo Archeologico Nazionale

3

Piazza Museo Nazionale

Museo Ⓜ

14

18

Via Tommasi

Via Enrico Pessina

Dante Ⓜ

Piazza Dante

Via G Brombeis

Via S Benedetto Croce

Via D Lioy

Via Toledo

Via Pignasecca

31

Central Naples

Continued from p697

The church forecourt makes a cameo in Pier Paolo Pasolini's film *Il Decameron* (The Decameron), itself based on Giovanni Boccaccio's 14th-century novel.

★**Cappella Sansevero**   CHAPEL
(Map p700; ☑081 551 84 70; www.museo sansevero.it; Via Francesco de Sanctis 19; adult/ reduced €7/5; ⊙9am-7pm Wed-Mon; Ⓜ Dante) It's in this Masonic-inspired baroque chapel that you'll find Giuseppe Sanmartino's incredible sculpture, *Cristo velato* (Veiled Christ), its marble veil so realistic that it's tempting to try to lift it and view Christ underneath. It's one of several artistic wonders that include Francesco Queirolo's sculpture *Disinganno* (Disillusion), Antonio Corradini's *Pudicizia* (Modesty) and riotously colourful frescoes by Francesco Maria Russo that have remained untouched since their creation in 1749.

Originally built around the end of the 16th century to house the tombs of the di Sangro family, the chapel was given its current baroque fit-out by Prince Raimondo di Sangro, who, between 1749 and 1766, commissioned the finest artists to adorn the interior. In Queirolo's *Disinganno*, the man trying to untangle himself from a net represents Raimondo's father, Antonio, Duke of Torremaggiore. After the premature death of his wife, Antonio abandoned the young Rai-

mondo, choosing instead a life of travel and hedonistic pleasures. Repentant in his later years, he returned to Naples and joined the priesthood, his attempt to free himself from sin represented in Queirolo's masterpiece.

Even more poignant is Antonio Corradini's *Pudicizia*, whose veiled female figure pays tribute to Raimondo's mother, Cecilia Gaetani d'Aquila d'Aragona. Raimondo was only 11 months old when she died, and the statue's lost gaze and broken plaque represent a life cruelly cut short.

The chapel's original polychrome marble flooring was badly damaged in a major collapse involving the chapel and the neighbouring Palazzo dei di Sangro in 1889. Designed by Francesco Celebrano, the flooring survives in fragmentary form in the passageway leading off from the chapel's right side. The passageway leads to a staircase, at the bottom of which you'll find two meticulously preserved human arterial systems – one of a man, the other of a woman. Debate still circles the models: are the arterial systems real or reproductions? And if they are real, just how was such an incredible state of preservation achieved? More than two centuries on, the mystery surrounding the alchemist prince and his abilities lives on.

Queues here can be notoriously long so consider purchasing your ticket online in advance for fast-track entry into the chapel; it's worth the extra €2 booking fee, especially during peak holiday periods.

NAPLES & CAMPANIA NAPLES

Chiesa del Gesù Nuovo
CHURCH

(Map p700; ☑ 081 557 81 51; Piazza del Gesù Nuovo; ⊘ 7.15am-12.45pm & 4-8pm Mon-Sat, 8am-2pm & 4-9pm Sun; Ⓜ Dante) The extraordinary Chiesa del Gesù Nuovo is an architectural Kinder Surprise. Its shell is the 15th-century, Giuseppe Valeriani–designed facade of Palazzo Sanseverino, converted to create the 16th-century church. Inside, *piperno*-stone sobriety gives way to a gob-smacking blast of baroque that could make the Vatican blush: a vainglorious showcase for the work of top-tier artists such as Francesco Solimena, Luca Giordano and Cosimo Fanzago.

The church is the final resting place of much-loved local saint Giuseppe Moscati (1880–1927), a doctor who served the city's poor. Adjacent to the right transept, the Sale di San Giuseppe Moscati (Rooms of St Joseph Moscati) include a recreation of the great man's study, complete with the armchair in which he died. Scan the walls for *ex-voti,* gifts offered by the faithful for miracles purportedly received. The church itself received a miracle of sorts on 4 August 1943, when a bomb dropped on the site failed to explode. Its shell is aptly displayed beside the *ex-voti.*

The church flanks the northern side of beautiful Piazza del Gesù Nuovo, a favourite late-night hang-out for students and lefties. At its centre soars Giuseppe Genuino's lavish Guglia dell'Immacolata (Piazza del Gesù Nuovo), an obelisk built between 1747 and 1750. On 8 December, the Feast of the Immacolata, a firefighter scrambles up to the top to place a wreath on the statue of the Virgin Mary.

Via San Gregorio Armeno
STREET

(Map p700; Ⓜ Dante) Dismissed by serious collectors, this narrow street nonetheless remains famous across Italy for its *pastori* (nativity-scene figurines). Connecting Spaccanapoli with Via dei Tribunali, the *decumanus maior* (main road) of ancient Neapolis, its clutter of shops and workshops peddle everything from doting donkeys to kitsch celebrity caricatures. At No 8 you'll find the workshop of Ferrigno (☑ 081 552 31 48; www.arteferrigno.com), whose terracotta figurines are the most famous and esteemed on the strip.

Complesso Monumentale di San Lorenzo Maggiore
ARCHAEOLOGICAL SITE

(Map p700; ☑ 081 211 08 60; www.lanapolisotterrata.it; Via dei Tribunali 316; church free, museum & excavations guided tour adult/reduced €10/7.50; ⊘ church 8am-7pm, excavations & museum 9.30am-5.30pm; Ⓜ Dante) The basilica at this richly layered religious complex is deemed one of Naples' finest medieval buildings. Aside from Ferdinando Sanfelice's facade, the Cappella al Rosario and the Cappellone di Sant'Antonio, its baroque makeover was stripped away last century to reveal its austere, Gothic elegance. Beneath the basilica is a sprawl of extraordinary Graeco-Roman ruins, accessible on a one-hour guided tour.

Napoli Sotterranea
ARCHAEOLOGICAL SITE

(Underground Naples; Map p700; ☑ 081 29 69 44; www.napolisotterranea.org; Piazza San Gaetano 68; adult/reduced €10/8; ⊘ English tours 10am, noon, 2pm, 4pm & 6pm; Ⓜ Dante) This evocative guided tour leads you 40m below street level to explore Naples' ancient labyrinth of aqueducts, passages and cisterns.

The passages were originally hewn by the Greeks to extract tufa stone used in construction and to channel water from Mt Vesuvius. Extended by the Romans, the network of conduits and cisterns was more recently used as an air-raid shelter in WWII. Part of the tour takes place by candlelight via extremely narrow passages – not suitable for expanded girths!

★ Pio Monte della Misericordia
CHURCH, MUSEUM

(Map p700; ☑ 081 44 69 44; www.piomontedellamisericordia.it; Via dei Tribunali 253; adult/reduced €7/5; ⊘ 9am-6pm Mon-Sat, to 2.30pm Sun; Ⓜ Piazza Cavour) The 1st-floor gallery of this octagonal, 17th-century church delivers a satisfying, digestible collection of Renaissance and baroque art, including works by Francesco de Mura, Jusepe de Ribera, Andrea Vaccaro and Paul van Somer. It's also home to contemporary artworks by Italian and foreign artists, each inspired by Caravaggio's masterpiece *Le sette opere di Misericordia* (The Seven Acts of Mercy). Considered by many to be the most important painting in Naples, you'll find it above the main altar in the ground-floor chapel.

Magnificently demonstrating the artist's chiaroscuro style, which had a revolutionary impact in Naples, *Le sette opere di Misericordia* was considered unique in its ability to illustrate the various acts in one seamlessly choreographed scene. Pio Monte della Misericordia's archives are home to the *Declaratoria del 14 Ottobre 1607,* an original church document acknowledging payment of 400 ducats to Caravaggio for the painting. A photocopy of the document is on display in the 1st-floor gallery, where you can also view the painting from the gallery's Sala del Coretto (Coretto Room).

On the opposite side of the street stands the Guglia di San Gennaro (Piazza Riario Sforza). Dating back to 1636, with stonework by Cosimo Fanzago and a bronze statue by Tommaso Montani, the obelisk is a soaring *grazie* (thank you) to the city's patron saint for protecting Naples from the 1631 eruption of Mt Vesuvius.

★ **Duomo** CATHEDRAL
(Map p700; ☑ 081 44 90 97; Via Duomo 149; cathedral/baptistry free/€2; ☉ cathedral 8.30am-1.30pm & 2.30-7.30pm Mon-Sat, 8.30am-1.30pm & 4.30-7.30pm Sun, baptistry 8.30am-12.30pm & 3.30-6.30pm Mon-Sat, 8.30am-1pm Sun, Cappella di San Gennaro 8.30am-1pm & 3-6.30pm Mon-Sat, 8.30am-1pm & 4.30-7pm Sun; ☐ 147, 182, 184 to Via Foria, Ⓜ Piazza Cavour) Whether you go for Giovanni Lanfranco's fresco in the Cappella di San Gennaro (Chapel of St Janarius), the 4th-century mosaics in the baptistry, or the thrice-annual miracle of San Gennaro, do not miss Naples' cathedral. Kick-started by Charles I of Anjou in 1272 and consecrated in 1315, it was largely destroyed in a 1456 earthquake. It has had copious nips and tucks over the subsequent centuries.

Among these is the gleaming neo-Gothic facade, only completed in 1905. Step inside and you'll immediately notice the central nave's gilded coffered ceiling, studded with late-mannerist art. The high sections of the nave and the transept are the work of baroque overachiever Luca Giordano.

Off the right side of the nave, the Cappella di San Gennaro (also known as the Chapel of the Treasury) was designed by Theatine priest and architect Francesco Grimaldi, and completed in 1646. The most sought-after artists of the period worked on the chapel, creating one of Naples' greatest baroque legacies. Highlights here include Jusepe de Ribera's gripping canvas *St Gennaro Escaping the Furnace Unscathed* and Giovanni Lanfranco's dizzying dome fresco. Hidden away in a strongbox behind the altar is a 14th-century silver bust in which sit the skull of San Gennaro and the two phials that hold his miraculously liquefying blood.

The next chapel eastwards contains an urn with the saint's bones and a cupboard full of femurs, tibias and fibulas. Below the high altar is the Cappella Carafa, a Renaissance chapel built to house yet more of the saint's remains.

Off the left aisle lies the 4th-century Basilica di Santa Restituta, the subject of an almost complete makeover after the earthquake of 1688. From it you can access the Battistero di San Giovanni in Fonte. It is Western Europe's oldest baptistry and is encrusted with fragments of glittering 4th-century mosaics.

The Duomo's subterranean archaeological zone, which includes fascinating remains of Greek and Roman buildings and roads, remains closed indefinitely.

MADRE GALLERY
(Museo d'Arte Contemporanea Donnaregina; Map p700; ☑ 081 1973 7254; www.madrenapoli.it; Via Settembrini 79; adult/reduced €8/4; ☉ 10am-7.30pm Mon & Wed-Sat, to 8pm Sun; Ⓜ Piazza Cavour) When *Madonna and Child* overload hits, reboot at Naples' museum of modern and contemporary art. In the lobby, French conceptual artist Daniel Buren sets the mood with his playful, mirror-panelled installation *Work in Situ*, with other specially commissioned installations from heavyweights like Anish Kapoor, Rebecca Horn and Sol LeWitt on level one. Level two houses the bulk of MADRE's permanent collection of painting, sculpture, photography and installations from other prolific 20th- and 21st-century artists, designers and architects.

Mercato di Porta Nolana MARKET
(Porta Nolana; ☉ 8am-2pm; ☐ R2 to Corso Umberto I, Ⓜ Garibaldi) Naples at its most vociferous and intense, the Mercato di Porta Nolana is a heady, gritty street market where bellowing fishmongers and greengrocers collide with fragrant delis and bakeries, contraband cigarette vendors and Bangladeshi takeaways and grocery stores. Dive in for anything from luscious tomatoes and mozzarella to golden-fried street snacks, cheap luggage and bootleg CDs.

⊙ Vomero

★ **Certosa e Museo di San Martino** MONASTERY, MUSEUM
(Map p704; ☑ 081 229 45 03; www.polomusealecampania.beniculturali.it/index.php/certosa-e-museo; Largo San Martino 5; adult/reduced €6/3; ☉ 8.30am-7.30pm Tue & Thu-Sat, to 6.30pm Sun; Ⓜ Vanvitelli, ☐ Montesanto to Morghen) The high point (quite literally) of the Neapolitan baroque, this charterhouse-turned-museum was built as a Carthusian monastery between 1325 and 1368. Centred on one of the most beautiful cloisters in Italy, it has been decorated, adorned and altered over the

Quartieri Spagnoli, Santa Lucia & Chiaia

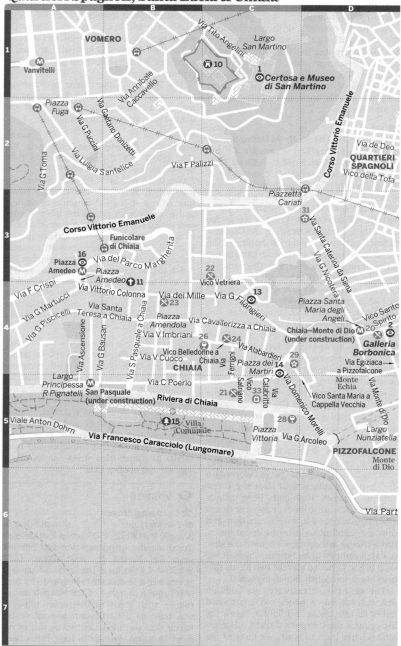

VOMERO

Vanvitelli

Via Tito Angelini

Largo
San Martino

10

1
Certosa e Museo
di San Martino

Via Annibale
Caccavello

Piazza
Fuga

Via G Puccini

Via Gaetano Donizetti

Via de Deo

QUARTIERI
SPAGNOLI
Vico della Tofa

Via Luigia Sanfelice

Via G Toma

Via F Palizzi

Corso Vittorio Emanuele

Piazzetta
Cariati

31

Corso Vittorio Emanuele

Funicolare
di Chiaia

Via Santa Caterina da Siena

Via G Nicotera

16

Piazza
Amedeo

Via del Parco Margherita

Piazza
Amedeo

11

22

Vico Vetriera

13

Piazza Santa
Maria degli
Angeli

Vico Santo
Spirito

Via F Crispi

Via Vittorio Colonna

Via dei Mille

Via G Filangieri

23

Via G Martucci

Via Santa
Teresa a Chiaia

Piazza
Amendola

Via Cavallerizza a Chiaia

Chiaia–Monte di Dio
(under construction)

20

2

Via G Piscicelli

Via Ascensione

Via G Bausan

Via S Pasquale a Chiaia

Via V Imbriani

26

24

Via Alabardieri

Galleria
Borbonica

29

Via Egiziaca
a Pizzofalcone

Vico V Cuoco

Vico Belledonne a
Chiaia

CHIAIA

Via Ferrigni

Piazza dei
Martiri

14

Monte
Echia

Largo
Principessa
R Pignatelli

San Pasquale
(under construction)

Via C Poerio

Riviera di Chiaia

21

Vico Satriano

33

Via Calabritto

Via Domenico Morelli

Vico Santa Maria a
Cappella Vecchia

Via Monte di Dio

Viale Anton Dohrn

15

Villa
Comunale

Piazza
Vittoria

28

Via G Arcoleo

Largo
Nunziatella

PIZZOFALCONE

Monte
di Dio

Via Francesco Caracciolo (Lungomare)

Via Part

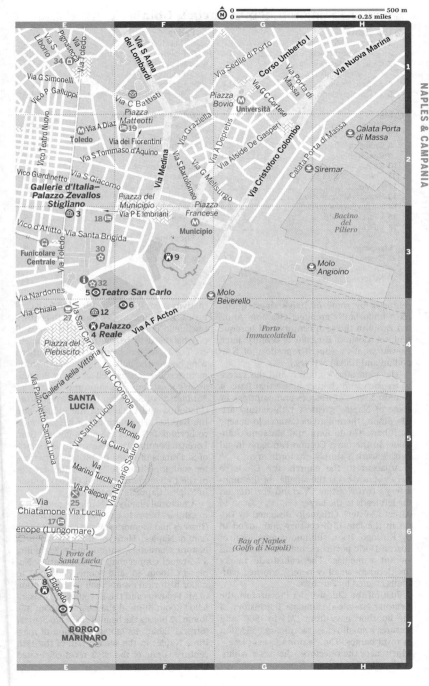

Quartieri Spagnoli, Santa Lucia & Chiaia

centuries by some of Italy's finest talent, most importantly architect Giovanni Antonio Dosio in the 16th century and baroque sculptor Cosimo Fanzago a century later. Nowadays, it's a superb repository of Neapolitan and Italian artistry.

The monastery's church and the sacristy, treasury and chapter house that flank it contain a feast of frescoes and paintings by some of Naples' greatest 17th-century artists, among them Battista Caracciolo, Jusepe de Ribera, Guido Reni and Massimo Stanzione. In the nave, Cosimo Fanzago's inlaid marble work is simply extraordinary.

Adjacent to the church, the Chiostro dei Procuratori is the smaller of the monastery's two cloisters. A grand corridor on the left leads to the larger Chiostro Grande (Great Cloister). Originally designed by Dosio in the late 16th century and added to by Fanzago, it's a sublime composition of Tuscan-Doric porticoes, marble statues and vibrant camellias. The balustrade marks the Certosa's small cemetery, adorned with skulls created by Fanzago.

Just off the Chiostro dei Procuratori, the Sezione Navale documents the history of the Bourbon navy from 1734 to 1860, and features a small yet extraordinary collection of royal barges. The Sezione Presepiale – which faces the refectory – houses a whimsical collection of rare Neapolitan presepi

(nativity scenes) from the 18th and 19th centuries, including the colossal 19th-century Cuciniello creation, which covers one wall of what used to be the monastery's kitchen. The Quarto del Priore in the southern wing houses the bulk of the monks' historic picture collection, as well as one of the museum's most famous sculptures, the tender *Madonna col Bambino e San Giovannino* (Madonna and Child with the Infant John the Baptist). The piece is the work of Pietro Bernini, father of the more famous Gian Lorenzo Bernini. Also noteworthy is a statue of St Francis of Assisi by 18th-century master sculptor Giuseppe Sanmartino, creator of the *Cristo velato* (Veiled Christ) housed in Naples' Cappella Sansevero.

A pictorial history of Naples is told in Immagini e Memorie della Città e del Regno (Images and Memories of the City and Kingdom of Naples). Here you'll find portraits of historic characters; antique maps, including a 35-panel copper map of 18th-century Naples in Room 45; and rooms dedicated to major historical events such as the eruption of Mt Vesuvius and the Revolt of the Masaniello (Room 36) and the plague (Room 37). Room 32 boasts the beautiful *Tavola Strozzi* (Strozzi Table); its fabled depiction of maritime Naples in the second half of the 15th century is one of the city's most celebrated historical records.

It's worth noting that some sections of the museum are only open at various times of the day; see the website for specific times.

Below the Certosa is the imposing **Sotterranei Gotici** (Gothic basement). The austere vaulted space holds around 150 marble sculptures and epigraphs.

Castel Sant'Elmo CASTLE
(Map p704; ☑ 081 558 77 08; www.polomusealecampania.beniculturali.it/index.php/il-castello; Via Tito Angelini 22; adult/reduced Wed-Mon €5/2.50, Tue €2.50/1.25; ⊙ castle 8.30am-7.30pm daily, museum 9.30am-5pm Wed-Mon, reduced hours winter; MVanvitelli, 🚠Montesanto to Morghen) Star-shaped Castel Sant'Elmo was originally a church dedicated to St Erasmus. Some 400 years later, in 1349, Robert of Anjou turned it into a castle before Spanish viceroy Don Pedro de Toledo had it further fortified in 1538. Used as a military prison until the 1970s, it's now famed for its jaw-dropping panorama, which takes in much of the city, its bay, islands and beyond. It's also known for its **Museo del Novecento**, dedicated to 20th-century Neapolitan art.

◉ Via Toledo & Quartieri Spagnoli

★**Gallerie d'Italia – Palazzo Zevallos Stigliano** GALLERY
(Map p704; ☑ 081 42 50 11; www.palazzozevallos.com; Via Toledo 185; adult/reduced €5/3; ⊙10am-7pm Tue-Fri, to 8pm Sat & Sun; MMunicipio) Built for a Spanish merchant in the 17th century and reconfigured in belle-époque style by architect Luigi Platania in the early 20th century, Palazzo Zevallos Stigliano houses a compact yet stunning collection of Neapolitan and Italian art spanning the 17th to early 20th centuries. Star attraction is Caravaggio's mesmerising swansong, *The Martyrdom of St Ursula* (1610). Completed weeks before the artist's lonely death, the painting depicts a vengeful king of the Huns piercing the heart of his unwilling virgin-bride-to-be, Ursula.

La Pignasecca MARKET
(Via Pignasecca; ⊙8am-1pm; MToledo) Naples' oldest street market is a multisensory escapade into a world of wriggling seafood, fragrant delis and clued-up *casalinghe* (homemakers) on the hunt for perfect produce. Fresh produce aside, the market's street-side stalls flog everything from discounted perfume and linen to Neapolitan hip-hop CDs and oh-so-snug nonna slippers.

◉ Santa Lucia & Chiaia

★**Palazzo Reale** PALACE
(Royal Palace; Map p704; ☑081 40 05 47; www.coopculture.it; Piazza del Plebiscito 1; adult/reduced €6/3; ⊙9am-8pm Thu-Tue; 🚌R2 to Via San Carlo, MMunicipio) Envisaged as a 16th-century monument to Spanish glory (Naples was under Spanish rule at the time), the magnificent Palazzo Reale is home to the **Museo del Palazzo Reale**, a rich and eclectic collection of baroque and neoclassical furnishings, porcelain, tapestries, sculpture and paintings, spread across the palace's royal apartments.

Among the many highlights is the **Teatrino di Corte**, a lavish private theatre created by Ferdinando Fuga in 1768 to celebrate the marriage of Ferdinand IV and Marie Caroline of Austria. Incredibly, Angelo Viva's statues of Apollo and the Muses set along the walls are made of papier mâché.

Sala (Room) VIII is home to a pair of vivid, allegorical 18th-century French tapestries representing earth and water respectively. Further along, Sala XII will leave you sniggering at the 16th-century canvas *Gli esattori delle imposte* (The Tax Collectors). Painted by Dutch artist Marinus Claeszoon Van Reymerswaele, it confirms that attitudes to tax collectors have changed little in 500 years. Sala XIII used to be Joachim Murat's study in the 19th century, but was used as a snack bar by Allied troops in WWII. Meanwhile, what looks like a waterwheel in Sala XXIII is actually a nifty rotating reading desk made for Queen Maria Carolina of Austria by Giovanni Uldrich in the 18th century.

The Cappella Reale (Royal Chapel) houses an 18th-century *presepe napoletano* (Neapolitan nativity scene). Fastidiously detailed, its cast of *pastori* (nativity-scene figurines) were crafted by a series of celebrated Neapolitan artists, including Giuseppe Sanmartino, creator of the *Cristo velato* (Veiled Christ) sculpture in the Cappella Sansevero.

The palace is also home to the **Biblioteca Nazionale di Napoli** (National Library; ☑081 781 91 11; www.bnnonline.it; ⊙8.30am-7pm Mon-Fri, to 1.30pm Sat, papyri exhibition by appointment only, Sezione Lucchesi Palli 8.30am-6.45pm Mon-Thu, to 3.30pm Fri) **FREE**, its own priceless treasures including at least 2000 papyri discovered at Herculaneum. You will need to email the library a month ahead to organise a viewing of its ancient papyri, retrieved from Herculaneum. Thankfully, you won't

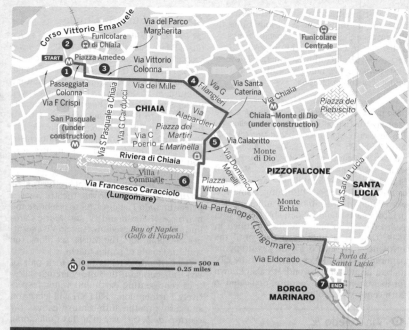

🏃 City Walk
An Architectural Saunter

START PIAZZA AMEDEO
END CASTEL DELL'OVO
LENGTH 2.2KM; 1.5 HOURS

Begin the walk outside Piazza Amedeo metro station on ❶ **Piazza Amedeo.** Just off its northern end stands former hotel ❷ **Villa Maria** (Map p704; Via del Parco Margherita 1; ⓜ Piazza Amedeo), one of Naples' finest examples of art nouveau architecture. From the southeast side of Piazza Amedeo, slip into Via Vittorio Colonna (which becomes Via dei Mille). To your left you'll pass the unapologetically baroque ❸ **Chiesa di Santa Teresa a Chiaia** (Map p704; ☎ 081 41 42 63; Via Vittorio Colonna 22; ⏱ 7.30-11am Mon-Sat, 8.30am-noon & 5-7.30pm Sun), designed by Cosimo Fanzago and home to paintings by Luca Giordano. Via dei Mille eventually kinks southeast, becoming Via Filangieri. It's here that you'll find art nouveau ❹ **Palazzo Mannajuolo** (Map p704; Via Filangieri 36; ⏱ 8am-9pm; 🚌 E6 to Piazza dei Martiri). Wander inside to admire its

spiral staircase, famously featured in *Napoli velata* (Naples in Veils), a film by prolific Turkish-Italian director Ferzan Özpetek. Continue along Via Filangieri, then turn right into Via Santa Caterina. The street leads to dashing ❺ **Piazza dei Martiri**, its 19th-century centrepiece dedicated to Neapolitan martyrs. The monument's four lions represent the anti-Bourbon uprisings of 1799, 1820, 1848 and 1860. At No 30 is Palazzo Calabritto, designed by architect Luigi Vanvitelli, most famous for his monumental Reggia di Caserta. Head south on exclusive Via Calabritto, cross busy Piazza Vittoria – which flanks former Bourbon garden ❻ **Villa Comunale** (Map p704; Piazza Vittoria; ⏱ 7am-midnight) – and turn left into Via Partenope (Lungomare), a pedestrianised seafront promenade popular with everyone from love-struck teens to boisterous families. The strip leads to Via Eldorado and the ancient islet of Borgo Marinaro, home to the ❼ **Castel dell'Ovo** and its silver screen–worthy rooftop views.

need to book ahead to view the library's exquisite **Biblioteca Lucchesi Palli** (Lucchesi Palli Library; closed Saturday). Crafted by some of Naples' most celebrated 19th-century artisans, it's home to numerous fascinating artistic artefacts, including letters by composer Giuseppe Verdi. Bring photo ID to enter the Biblioteca Nazionale. Theatre and opera fans can buy the combination ticket (€11) for entry to both the Palazzo Reale and adjoining MeMus theatre museum.

★ **Galleria Borbonica**   HISTORIC SITE
(Map p704; ☑ 081 764 58 08, 366 2484151; www.galleriaborbonica.com; Vico del Grottone 4; 1hr standard tour adult/reduced €10/5; ⊙ standard tour 10am, noon, 3pm & 5pm Fri-Sun; ☐ R2 to Via San Carlo, ⓜ Chiaia-Monte di Dio) Traverse five centuries along Naples' Bourbon Tunnel. Conceived by Ferdinand II in 1853 to link the Palazzo Reale to the barracks and the sea, the never-completed escape route is part of the 17th-century Carmignano Aqueduct system, itself incorporating 16th-century cisterns. The standard tour does not require prebooking, though the Adventure Tour (85 minutes; adult/reduced €15/10) and adults-only Speleo Light Tour (90 minutes; €15) do.

MeMus   MUSEUM
(Museum & Historical Archive of the Teatro San Carlo; Map p704; http://memus.squarespace.com; Palazzo Reale, Piazza del Plebiscito; adult/reduced €6/5; ⊙ 9am-7pm Mon, Tue & Thu-Sat, to 3pm Sun; ☐ R2 to Via San Carlo, ⓜ Municipio) Located inside the Palazzo Reale (p707) – purchase tickets at the palace ticket booth – MeMus hosts long-running temporary exhibitions linked to the rich history of Europe's oldest working opera house, the Teatro San Carlo (p717). Exhibitions showcase everything from original stage-design sketches, costumes, posters and letters, to the personal artefacts of legends of the theatre and opera world.

Castel Nuovo   CASTLE
(Map p704; ☑ 081 795 77 22; Piazza Municipio; adult/reduced €6/3; ⊙ 8.30am-6pm Mon-Sat, 10am-1pm Sun; ⓜ Municipio) Locals know this 13th-century castle as the Maschio Angioino (Angevin Keep), and its Cappella Palatina is home to fragments of frescoes by Giotto; they're on the splays of the Gothic windows. You'll also find Roman ruins under the glass-floored Sala dell'Armeria (Armoury Hall). The castle's upper floors (closed on Sunday) house a collection of mostly 17th- to early-20th-century Neapolitan paintings. The top floor houses the more interesting works, including landscape paintings by Luigi Crisconio and a watercolour by architect Carlo Vanvitelli.

The history of the castle stretches back to Charles I of Anjou, who upon taking over Naples and the Swabians' Sicilian kingdom found himself in control not only of his new southern Italian acquisitions but also of possessions in Tuscany, northern Italy and Provence (France). It made sense to base the new dynasty in Naples, rather than Palermo in Sicily, and Charles launched an ambitious construction program to expand the port and city walls. His plans included converting a Franciscan convent into the castle that still stands in Piazza Municipio.

Christened the Castrum Novum (New Castle) to distinguish it from the older Castel dell'Ovo and **Castel Capuano**, it was completed in 1282, becoming a popular hang-out for the leading intellectuals and artists of the day – Giotto repaid his royal hosts by painting much of the interior. Of the original structure, however, only the Cappella Palatina remains; the rest is the result of Aragonese renovations two centuries later, as well as a meticulous restoration effort prior to WWII.

The two-storey Renaissance triumphal arch at the entrance – the **Torre della Guardia** – commemorates the victorious entry of Alfonso I of Aragon into Naples in 1443, while the stark stone **Sala dei Baroni** (Hall of the Barons) is named after the barons slaughtered here in 1486 for plotting against King Ferdinand I of Aragon. Its striking ribbed vault fuses ancient Roman and Spanish late-Gothic influences.

Castel dell'Ovo   CASTLE
(Map p704; ☑ 081 795 45 92; Borgo Marinaro; ⊙ 9am-7.30pm Mon-Sat, to 2pm Sun Apr-Oct, reduced hours Nov-Mar; ☐ E6, 128 to Via Santa Lucia) **FREE** Built by the Normans in the 12th century, Naples' oldest castle owes its name (Castle of the Egg) to Virgil. The Roman scribe reputedly buried an egg on the site where the castle now stands, warning that when the egg breaks, the castle (and Naples) will fall. Thankfully, both are still standing, and walking up to the castle's ramparts will reward you with a breathtaking panorama.

Used by the Swabians, Angevins and Alfonso of Aragon, who modified it to suit his military needs, the castle sits on the rocky, restaurant-lined 'island' of **Borgo Marinaro**. According to legend, the heartbroken siren Partenope washed ashore here after failing to seduce Ulysses with her song. It's also

 TOP SIGHT
SUBTERRANEAN NAPLES

Lurking beneath Naples' loud and greasy streets is one of the world's most thrilling urban wonderlands, a silent, mostly undiscovered sprawl of Greek-era grottoes, paleo-Christian burial chambers, catacombs and ancient ruins. Search out these places for a glimpse of the city's fascinating *sottosuolo* (underground).

History

Speleologists (cave specialists) estimate that about 60% of Neapolitans live and work above this *sottosuolo* network. Since the end of WWII, some 700 cavities have been discovered, from original Greek-era grottoes to palaeo-Christian burial chambers and royal Bourbon escape routes. According to the experts, this is simply a prelude, with another 2 million sq metres of troglodytic treats to unfurl.

Naples' dedicated caving geeks are quick to tell you that their underworld is one of the largest and oldest on earth. Sure, Paris might claim a catacomb or two, but its subterranean offerings don't come close to this giant's 2500-year history.

And what a history it is. Naples' most famous saint, San Gennaro, was interred in the Catacombe di San Gennaro in the 5th century. A century later, in 536, Belisario and his troops caught Naples by surprise by storming the city through the ancient tunnels. According to legend, Alfonso of Aragon used the same trick in 1442, undermining the city walls by using an underground passageway leading into a tailor's shop and straight into town. Even the city's dreaded Camorra has got in on the act. In 1992 the notorious Stolder clan was busted for running a subterranean drug lab, with escape routes heading straight to the clan boss's pad.

DON'T MISS

➡ Early-Christian frescoes at the Catacombe di San Gennaro

PRACTICALITIES

➡ Map p696

➡ ☎ 081 744 37 14

➡ www.catacombe dinapoli.it

➡ Via Capodimonte 13

➡ adult/reduced €9/6

➡ ⏱ 1hr tours hourly 10am-5pm Mon-Sat, to 2pm Sun

➡ 🚌 R4, 178 to Via Capodimonte

Catacombe di San Gennaro

Naples' oldest and holiest catacombs harbour three types of ancient tombs, including the open-room *cubiculum* preferred by the city's wealthiest denizens. One of these features an especially beautiful funerary fresco of a mother, father and child: it's made up of three layers of fresco, one commissioned for each death. From the 5th to the 9th centuries, the remains of San Gennaro – Naples' most famous patron saint – were buried in the catacombs' *basilica minore* (minor basilica). The painting on the side of San Gennaro's tomb – depicting the saint with Mt Vesuvius and Mt Somma in the background – is the first known image of San Gennaro as Naples' protector. Lovingly restored, the catacombs now also host occasional special events, including theatrical and live-music performances; see the website for updates.

Galleria Borbonica

During WWII, Naples' subterranean cisterns and former quarries were turned into civilian shelters. The lakes of rubbish that had filled many of them were compacted and covered, old passageways were enlarged, toilets were built and new staircases were erected. As bombs showered the city above, tens of thousands took refuge in the dark, damp spaces below. One of these spaces was the Galleria Borbonica (p709). Used as an air-raid shelter and makeshift hospital, the restored labyrinth rekindles the past with evocative wartime artefacts, from toys and stretchers to moving graffiti.

Complesso Monumentale di San Lorenzo Maggiore

Architecture and history buffs shouldn't miss this richly layered religious complex (pictured; p702), whose subterranean ruins include ancient bakeries, wineries, laundries and barrel-vaulted rooms that once formed part of ancient Neapolis' two-storey *macellum* (market). The onsite Museo dell'Opera di San Lorenzo Maggiore includes a model of the area as it appeared in ancient times, while the 13th-century basilica itself upcycles ancient columns in its nave. Catherine of Austria, who died in 1323, is buried here in a beautiful mosaic tomb. Legend has it that this was where Boccaccio first fell for Mary of Anjou, the inspiration for his character Fiammetta, while the poet Petrarch called the adjoining convent home in 1345.

NEED TO KNOW

For more on Naples' underground wonders check out www.napoli unplugged.com/ locations-category/ subterranean-naples.

For a gourmet break from your underground adventuring, head to the famed Da Ettore (p715), near the Tunnel Borbonico.

TOURS

Tours of the Catacombe di San Gennaro are run by the Cooperativa Sociale Onlus 'La Paranza' (p712), whose ticket office is to the left of the Chiesa di Madre di Buon Consiglio (Map p696; ☑ 081 741 00 06; Via Capodimonte 13), a snack-sized replica of St Peter's in Rome completed in 1960. Tickets can also be purchased in advance online. The cooperative also runs a fascinating Sunday-morning walking tour called *Il Miglio Sacro* (The Holy Mile; adult/reduced €15/13), which explores the neighbouring Sanità district. The Holy Mile tour must be prebooked and is offered in Italian unless requested in English, French or Spanish in advance; see the website for details.

where the Greeks first settled the city in the 7th century BC, calling the island Megaris. Its commanding position wasn't wasted on the Roman general Lucullus either, who had his villa here long before the castle hit the skyline. Views aside, the castle is also the setting for temporary art exhibitions, special events, and no shortage of posing brides and grooms.

◎ Capodimonte & La Sanità

★ Museo di Capodimonte   MUSEUM
(Map p696; ☑ 081 749 91 11; www.museocapodimonte.beniculturali.it; Via Miano 2; adult/reduced €12/8; ⊘ 8.30am-7.30pm Thu-Tue; ☐ R4, 178 to Via Capodimonte, ☐ Shuttle Capodimonte) Originally designed as a hunting lodge for Charles VII of Bourbon, the monumental Palazzo di Capodimonte was begun in 1738 and took more than a century to complete. It's now home to the Museo di Capodimonte, southern Italy's largest and richest art gallery. Its vast collection – much of which Charles inherited from his mother, Elisabetta Farnese – was moved here in 1759 and ranges from exquisite 12th-century altarpieces to works by Botticelli, Caravaggio, Titian and Warhol.

The gallery is spread over three floors and 160 rooms; for most people, a full morning or afternoon is enough for an abridged best-of tour. The 1st floor includes works by greats such as Michelangelo, Raphael and Titian, with highlights including Masaccio's *Crocifissione* (Crucifixion), Botticelli's *Madonna col Bambino e due angeli* (Madonna with Child and Angels), Bellini's *Trasfigurazione* (Transfiguration) and Parmigianino's *Antea*, all of which are subject to room changes within the museum.

The floor is also home to the royal apartments, a study in regal excess. The Salottino di Porcellana (Room 52) is an outrageous example of 18th-century chinoiserie, its walls and ceiling dense with whimsically themed porcelain 'stucco'. Originally created between 1757 and 1759 for the Palazzo Reale in Portici, it was transferred to Capodimonte in 1867.

Upstairs, the 2nd-floor galleries display work by Neapolitan artists from the 13th to the 19th centuries, including de Ribera, Giordano, Solimena and Stanzione. It's also home to some spectacular 16th-century Belgian tapestries. The piece that many come to see, however, is Caravaggio's *Flagellazione* (Flagellation of Christ; 1607–10), which hangs in reverential solitude in Room 78. Rooms 88 to 95 are dedicated to paintings of the Neapolitan baroque period.

Accessed from the 2nd floor, a small mezzanine level hosts a rotating selection of modern works from artists including Andy Warhol, Mimmo Jodice and John Armleder.

Once you've finished in the museum, the Real Bosco di Capodimonte (www.boscodicapodimonte.it; ⊘ 7am-7.30pm Apr-Sep, to 6pm Feb, Mar & Oct, to 5pm Nov-Jan;) FREE – the palace's 134-hectare estate – provides a much-needed breath of fresh air.

The museum offers a convenient, hourly shuttle-bus service, Shuttle Capodimonte, that runs between central Naples and the museum. Buses depart from Piazza Trieste e Trento (opposite Teatro San Carlo) and stop at Piazza Dante and the Museo Archeologico Nazionale en route. Tickets (which include museum entry) can be purchased directly on the bus.

★ Cimitero delle Fontanelle   CEMETERY
(Map p696; ☑ 081 1925 6964; www.cimiterofontanelle.com; Via Fontanelle 80; ⊘ 10am-5pm; ☐ C51 to Via Fontanelle, ☐ Materdei) FREE Holding about eight million human bones, the ghoulish Fontanelle Cemetery was first used during the 1656 plague, before becoming Naples' main burial site during the 1837 cholera epidemic. At the end of the 19th century it became a hot spot for the *anime pezzentelle* (poor souls) cult, in which locals adopted skulls and prayed for their souls. Lack of information at the site makes joining a tour much more rewarding; reputable outfits include Cooperativa Sociale Onlus 'La Paranza' (Map p696; ☑ 081 744 37 14; www.catacombedinapoli.it; Via Capodimonte 13; ⊘ information point 10am-5pm Mon-Sat, to 2pm Sun; ☐ R4, 178 to Via Capodimonte).

★☆ Festivals & Events

Maggio dei Monumenti   CULTURAL
(www.comune.napoli.it; ⊘ May) A month-long cultural feast, with a bounty of concerts, performances, exhibitions, guided tours and other events across Naples. The festival program is usually released on the Comune di Napoli (Naples City Council) website.

★ Napoli Teatro Festival Italia   THEATRE
(www.napoliteatrofestival.it; ⊘ Jun/Jul) One month of local and international theatre, dance and performance art, staged in conventional and unconventional venues.

Wine & The City   WINE
(www.wineandthecity.it; ⊘ May) A 10-day celebration of regional vino, with free wine tastings and cultural events in palaces,

museums, boutiques and eateries across the city.

Festa di San Gennaro RELIGIOUS
(Duomo; ⊙ Sat before 1st Sun in May, 19 Sep, 16 Dec) The faithful flock to the Duomo to witness the miraculous liquefaction of San Gennaro's blood three times a year.

🛏 Sleeping

Where to slumber? The *centro storico* (historic centre) is studded with important churches and sights, artisan studios and student-packed bars. Seafront Santa Lucia delivers grand hotels, while sceney Chiaia is best for fashionable shops and *aperitivo* bars. The lively, laundry-strung Quartieri Spagnoli is within walking distance of all three neighbourhoods.

★The Church B&B €
(Map p700; ☑081 1952 9272; www.thechurch.it; Via San Biagio dei Librai 39; d €50-100, tr €70-130; ❄🛜; 🚊R2 to Corso Umberto I) On the 4th floor of an anecdote-rich 16th-century *palazzo*, this intimate, cultured B&B is decorated with contemporary Neapolitan photography and cleverly upcycled objects, from coffee percolators turned plant pots to an African tek tree turned bookshelf. The four minimalist rooms are equally whimsical; the top-floor room is the most coveted and comes with a striking in-room shower and private terrace.

★Magma Home B&B €
(Map p700; ☑320 4360272, 338 3188914; http://magmahome.it; Via San Giuseppe dei Nudi 18; d €70-150; ❄🛜; 🚇Museo) 🏷 Contemporary artworks, cultural soirées and impeccable hospitality plug you straight into Naples' cultural scene at Magma. Its eight rooms – each designed by a local artist – intrigue with their mix of Italian design classics, upcycled materials and specially commissioned artworks. There's a large, contemporary communal kitchen and living area, plus two inviting rooftop terraces with views of the city and Mt Vesuvius.

★Schiara B&B €
(Map p700; ☑081 033 09 77, 338 9264453; www.maisonsdecharme.it; Vico Volpicelli 20; s €30-85, d €50-100, tr €65-110, q €80-125; ❄🛜; 🚇Dante) Freshly minted B&B Schiara offers five contemporary rooms, each with en-suite bathroom and playful artisan details inspired by southern Italian themes. The 'Miti' room comes with its own in-room soaking tub, while the upstairs 'Riti' room has a kitchenette and private rooftop terrace. All guests

have access to a gorgeous outdoor terrace and communal rooftop garden with sunbeds and bewitching views.

★Dimora dei Giganti B&B €
(Map p700; ☑081 033 09 77, 338 9264453; www.maisonsdecharme.it/dimoradeigiganti; Vico Giganti 55; s €40-60, d €55-80, tr €70-95, q €85-105; 🅿❄🛜; 🚇Piazza Cavour, Museo) Run by a warm and personable team, this urbane B&B offers four colour-coordinated bedrooms with specially commissioned sculptural lamps, ethnic-inspired furnishings and designer bathrooms. It has a modern kitchen, a cosy lounge and a charming majolica-tiled terrace. Best of all, its quiet side-street location is only steps away from the buzzing heart of the *centro storico*.

B&B Arte e Musei B&B €
(Map p700; ☑081 1950 4479, 333 6962469; www.facebook.com/bnbarteemusei; Via Salvator Rosa 345; s €40-70, d €60-120, tr €80-150; ❄🛜; 🚇Museo, Piazza Cavour) Close to the Museo Archeologico Nazionale, this artful B&B is adorned with Neapolitan-themed paintings and ceramics by gracious owner and artist Federica. Both the double and triple room include a small balcony and spotless en-suite bathroom, while the smaller single room (with double bed) has its private bathroom in the hallway.

★Atelier Inès B&B €€
(Map p696; ☑349 4433422; www.atelierinesgallery.com; Via dei Cristallini 138; d €135-170; ❄🛜; 🚊C51, C52 to Via dei Vergini, 🚇Piazza Cavour) A stylish, eclectic oasis in the earthy Sanità district, this three-suite B&B is a homage to the late Neapolitan sculptor and designer Annibale Oste, whose **workshop** (www.annibaleoste.com/esperienza-oste; ⊙ usually 9am-6pm Mon-Fri) shares a leafy courtyard. Everything from the lamps and spiral towel racks to the one-of-a-kind sculptural bedheads are Oste's whimsical designs, complemented by heavenly mattresses, a choice of pillows, and Vietri-ceramic bathrooms with satisfyingly hot water.

Neapolitan Trips HOSTEL €€
(Map p704; ☑B&B 081 551 8977, hostel 081 1836 6402, hotel 081 1984 5933; www.neapolitantrips.com; Via dei Fiorentini 10; hostel dm €15-35, B&B d €45-90, hotel d €80-160; ❄🛜; 🚇Toledo) Neapolitan Trips is a unique beast, with a clean, next-gen hostel on one floor, and both B&B and hotel rooms on another. The hostel is the standout, boasting a hip communal lounge-bar complete with electric guitars,

amps and a piano for impromptu evening jams, a modern guest kitchen with complimentary pasta to cook, and mixed-gender dorms with USB ports by each bed.

★ Hotel Piazza Bellini   BOUTIQUE HOTEL €€
(Map p700; ☑ 081 45 17 32; www.hotelpiazza bellini.com; Via Santa Maria di Costantinopoli 101; d €90-190; ❄@⛅; Ⓜ Dante) Only steps from the bars and nightlife of Piazza Bellini, this sharp, hip hotel occupies a 16th-century *palazzo,* its pure-white spaces spiked with original majolica tiles, vaulted ceilings and *piperno*-stone paving. Rooms are modern and functional, with designer fittings, fluffy duvets and chic bathrooms with excellent showers. Four rooms on the 5th and 6th floors feature panoramic terraces.

Check the hotel website for decent discounts.

Decumani Hotel de Charme   BOUTIQUE HOTEL €€
(Map p700; ☑ 081 551 81 88; www.decumani.it; Via San Giovanni Maggiore Pignatelli 15; d from €116; ❄@⛅; Ⓜ Università) This classic boutique hotel occupies the former *palazzo* of Cardinal Sisto Riario Sforza, the last bishop of the Bourbon kingdom. Its simple, stylish 42 rooms feature high ceilings, parquet floors, 19th-century furniture and modern bathrooms with spacious showers. Deluxe rooms crank up the *dolce vita* with personal hot tubs. The pièce de résistance, however, is the property's breathtaking baroque salon.

★ La Ciliegina Lifestyle Hotel   BOUTIQUE HOTEL €€€
(Map p704; ☑ 081 1971 8800; www.cilieginahotel .it; Via PE Imbriani 30; d from €200; ❄@⛅; Ⓜ Municipio) An easy walk from the hydrofoil terminal, this chic, contemporary slumber spot is a hit with fashion-conscious urbanites. Spacious white rooms are splashed with blue and red accents, each with top-of-the-range Hästens beds, flat-screen TVs and marble-clad bathrooms with a water-jet jacuzzi shower (one junior suite has a jacuzzi tub).

Breakfast in bed or on the rooftop terrace, which comes with sunbeds, hot tub and a view of Vesuvius. Complimentary iPad use is a nice touch, and it's always a good idea to check the hotel website for decent discounts.

Grand Hotel Vesuvio   HOTEL €€€
(Map p704; ☑ 081 764 00 44; www.vesuvio.it; Via Partenope 45; d from €260; ❄@⛅; ☐128, E6 to Via Santa Lucia) Known for hosting legends – past guests include Rita Hayworth and Humphrey Bogart – this five-star veteran seduces with its dripping Murano chandeliers, period antiques and strangely appealing, faded glory. Rooms are a suitable mix of luxury linen sheets, sumptuous mattresses and Echia spa products, though it's the sea-view rooms that really justify the price of slumbering here.

Count your lucky stars at the rooftop bar and restaurant, which is better for sunset drinks than a forgettable dinner.

✖ Eating

Naples is one of Italy's gastronomic darlings, and the bonus of a bayside setting makes for some seriously memorable meals. While white linen, candlelight and €50 bills are readily available, some of the best bites await in the city's spit-and-sawdust trattorias, where two courses and house wine can cost under €20.

★ Concettina Ai Tre Santi   PIZZA €
(Map p696; ☑ 081 29 00 37; www.pizzeriao liva.it; Via Arena della Sanità 7; pizzas from €5; ⏱ noon-midnight Mon-Sat, to 5pm Sun; ⛅; Ⓜ Piazza Cavour, Museo) Head in by noon (or 7.30pm at dinner) to avoid a long wait at this hot-spot pizzeria, made famous thanks to its young, driven *pizzaiolo* Ciro Oliva. The menu is an index of fastidiously sourced artisanal ingredients, used to top Ciro's flawless, wood-fired bases. Traditional Neapolitan pizza aside, you'll also find a string of creative seasonal options.

These might include the slider-like *Annarella*, its pizza-dough buns filled with artichoke prepared three ways (boiled, creamed and fried), *provola* (provolone cheese), *culatello* (cured ham) and lemon peel. The pizzeria includes a casual takeaway outlet next door, though the pizzas at the latter are not quite as spectacular.

Pasticceria Mennella   PASTRIES €
(Map p704; ☑ 081 42 60 26; www.pasticceria mennella.it; Via Carducci 50-52; pastries from €1.50; ⏱ 6.30am-9.30pm Mon-Fri, to 10.30pm Sat, 7am-9.30pm Sun; Ⓜ Piazza Amedeo) If you eat only one sweet treat in Naples (good luck with that!), make it Mennella's spectacular *frolla al limone,* a shortbread pastry filled with heavenly lemon cream. Just leave room for the *mignon* (bite-size) version of its *sciù* (choux pastry) with *crema di nocciola* (hazelnut cream). Before you go feeling guilty, remember that everything is free of preservatives and artificial additives.

Mennella also makes its own almond milk, a sweet, refreshing must for lovers of marzipan flavour. If you're more in the mood for a cold treat, you'll find a branch of Mennella's exceptional gelateria across the street at number 45.

★**Pizzeria Starita**   PIZZA €

(Map p696; ☑ 081 557 36 82; www.pizzeriestarita. it; Via Materdei 28; pizzas from €4; ⏲ noon-3.30pm & 7pm-midnight Tue-Sun; M Materdei) The giant fork and ladle hanging on the wall at this historic pizzeria were used by Sophia Loren in *L'oro di Napoli*, and the kitchen made the *pizze fritte* sold by the actress in the film. While the 60-plus pizza varieties include a tasty *fiorilli e zucchine* (zucchini, zucchini flowers and *provola*), our allegiance remains to its classic *marinara*.

Serafino   SICILIAN €

(Map p700; ☑ 081 557 14 33; Via dei Tribunali 44; arancini, cannoli €2.50; ⏲ 10.30am-10.30pm Mon-Thu, to midnight Fri-Sun) A veritable porthole to Sicily, this takeaway stand peddles authentic island street food. Savoury bites include various types of *arancini* (deep-fried rice balls), among them *al ragù* (with meat sauce) and *alla Norma* (with fried aubergine and ricotta). The real reason to head here, however, is for the crisp, flawless cannoli, filled fresh with silky Sicilian ricotta and sprinkled with pistachio crumbs. Bliss.

Pizzeria Gino Sorbillo   PIZZA €

(Map p700; ☑ 081 44 66 43; www.sorbillo.it; Via dei Tribunali 32; pizzas from €4; ⏲ noon-3.30pm & 7-11.30pm Mon-Sat; ☎; M Dante) Day in, day out, this cult-status pizzeria is besieged by hungry hordes. While debate may rage over whether Gino Sorbillo's pizzas are the best in town, there's no doubt that his giant, wood-fired discs – made using organic flour and tomatoes – will have you licking fingertips and whiskers. Head in superearly or prepare to wait.

★**Da Ettore**   NEAPOLITAN €€

(Map p704; ☑ 081 764 35 78; Via Gennaro Serra 39; meals €25; ⏲ 1-3pm & 8-10pm Tue-Sat, 1-3pm Sun; ☎; ☒ R2 to Via San Carlo, M Chiaia-Monte di Dio) This homey, eight-table trattoria has an epic reputation. Scan the walls for famous fans like comedy great Totò, and a framed passage from crime writer Massimo Siviero, who mentions Ettore in one of his tales. The draw is solid regional cooking, which includes one of the best *spaghetti alle vongole*

(spaghetti with clams) in town. Book two days ahead for Sunday lunch.

★**Salumeria**   NEAPOLITAN €€

(Map p700; ☑ 081 1936 4649; www.salumeria upnea.it; Via San Giovanni Maggiore Pignatelli 34/35; sandwiches from €5.50, charcuterie platters from €8.50, meals around €30; ⏲ 12.30-5pm & 7.15pm-midnight Thu-Tue; ☎; M Dante) Small producers, local ingredients and contemporary takes on provincial Campanian recipes drive bistro-inspired Salumeria. Nibble on quality charcuterie and cheeses or fill up on artisanal *panini*, hamburgers or Salumeria's sublime *ragù napoletano* (pasta served in a rich tomato-and-meat sauce slow-cooked over two days). Even the ketchup here is made in-house, using DOP Piennolo tomatoes from Vesuvius.

Pescheria Mattiucci   SEAFOOD €€

(Map p704; ☑ 081 251 2215; www.pescheriamat tiucci.com; Vico Belledonne a Chiaia 27; crudo €25, cooked dishes €12-15; ⏲ 12.30-3pm & 7-10.30pm Tue-Sat; ☒ E6 to Piazza dei Martiri, M Piazza Amedeo) Run by brothers Francesco, Gennaro and Luigi, this local Chiaia fishmonger transforms daily into a wonderfully intimate, sociable seafood eatery. Perch yourself on a bar stool, order a vino, and watch the team prepare your superfresh, tapas-style *crudo* (raw seafood) to order. You'll also find a number of simple, beautifully cooked surf dishes.

If they're on the menu, order the scampi with fresh pineapple and mustard as well as the salted *alici* (anchovies), the latter served with toasted bread and butter. For the best experience, go early in the week, when the crowds are thin and the ambience *much* more relaxed.

★**L'Ebbrezza di Noè**   ITALIAN €€

(Map p704; ☑ 081 40 01 04; www.lebbrezzadi noe.com; Vico Vetriera 9; meals €35-40, cheese & charcuterie platters €10; ⏲ 6-11pm Tue-Thu, to midnight Fri & Sat, 1-3pm Sun; ☎; M Piazza Amedeo) A wine shop by day, 'Noah's Drunkenness' transforms into an intimate culinary hot spot by night. Slip inside for *vino* and conversation with sommelier Luca at the bar, or settle into one of the bottle-lined dining rooms for seductive, market-driven dishes such as house special *paccheri fritti* (fried pasta stuffed with aubergine and served with fresh basil and a rich tomato sauce).

Dialetti   ITALIAN €€

(Map p704; ☑ 081 248 1158; www.facebook.com/ DialettiNapoli; Vico Satriano 10; meals around

€32; ☉noon-3.30pm & 6pm-midnight Mon-Sat; ☎; ☒128, 140, 151 to Riviera di Chiaia) On-point Dialetti takes its cues from cities like New York, London and Sydney. You'll find a snug, vintage-pimped lounge corner at the front, a communal dining table with views of the glassed-in kitchen, and a softly lit dining room beyond it. Service is attentive and the daily changing menu champions gorgeous ingredients, cooked beautifully and with subtle contemporary tweaks.

Ristorantino dell'Avvocato   NEAPOLITAN €€

(Map p704; ☎081 032 00 47; www.ilristoran tinodellavvocato.it; Via Santa Lucia 115-117; meals €40-45; ☉noon-3pm & 7.30-11pm Tue-Sat, noon-3pm Sun; ☎; ☒128, E6 to Via Santa Lucia) This elegant yet welcoming restaurant is a favourite of Neapolitan gastronomes. Apple of their eye is affable lawyer turned head chef Raffaele Cardillo, whose passion for Campania's culinary heritage merges with a knack for subtle, refreshing twists – think coffee papardelle served with mullet *ragù*.

The degustation menus (€50 to €60) are good value. Book ahead.

🍷 Drinking & Nightlife

Although Neapolitans aren't big drinkers, Naples offers an increasingly varied selection of venues in which to imbibe. You'll find well-worn wine bars and a new wave of options focused on craft beer, cocktails and even speciality coffee. The main hubs are the *centro storico* and Chiaia. The former is generally cheaper and more alternative, the latter more fashionable and scene-y.

★L'Antiquario   COCKTAIL BAR

(Map p704; ☎081 764 53 90; www.facebook. com/AntiquarioNapoli; Via Gaetani 2; ☉7.30pm-2.30am; ☒151, 154 to Piazza Vittoria) If you take your cocktails seriously, slip into this sultry, speakeasy-inspired den. Wrapped in art nouveau wallpaper, it's the domain of Neapolitan barkeep Alex Frezza, a finalist at the 2014 Bombay Sapphire World's Most Imaginative Bartender Awards. Straddling classic and contemporary, the drinks are impeccable, made with passion and meticulous attention to detail. Live jazz-centric tunes add to the magic on Wednesdays.

★Barril   BAR

(Map p704; ☎393 9814362; www.barril.it; Via G Fiorelli 11; ☉7pm-2am Tue-Thu & Sun, to 3am Fri & Sat; ☎; Ⓜ Piazza Amedeo) From street level, stairs lead down to this softly lit, buzzing garden bar, where grown-up, fashionable types mingle among birdcage seats and vintage Cinzano posters. Fresh cocktails include giant, creamy piña coladas, and you'll also find over 40 gins with numerous tonic waters for a customised G&T. Bites include cheese and charcuterie platters, plus a decent selection of complimentary *aperitivo*-time snacks.

★Caffè Gambrinus   CAFE

(Map p704; ☎081 41 75 82; www.grancaffegam brinus.com; Via Chiaia 1-2; ☉7am-1am Sun-Fri, to 2am Sat; ☒R2 to Via San Carlo, Ⓜ Municipio) Gambrinus is Naples' oldest and most venerable cafe, serving superlative Neapolitan coffee under flouncy chandeliers. Oscar Wilde knocked back a few here and Mussolini had some rooms shut to keep out left-wing intellectuals. Sit-down prices are steep, but the *aperitivo* nibbles are decent and sipping a *spritz* or a luscious *cioccolata calda* (hot chocolate) in its belle-époque rooms is something worth savouring.

Shanti Art Musik Bar   BAR

(Map p700; ☎081 551 49 79; www.facebook.com/ ShantiSPACCANapoli; Via Giovanni Paladino 56; ☉10.30am-2.30am Mon-Wed, 11am-3am Thu-Sat; ☎; Ⓜ Dante) Under Tibetan prayer flags, shabby Shanti draws a cosmopolitan crowd of arty and indie types, both local and foreign. While the place serves lunchtime grub, head here in the evenings, when party people congregate at upcycled, candlelit tables to chat, flirt and party well into the night. Drinks are well priced.

Spazio Nea   CAFE

(Map p700; ☎081 45 13 58; www.spazionea.it; Via Costantinopoli 53; ☉9am-2am, to 3am Fri & Sat; ☎; Ⓜ Dante) Aptly skirting bohemian Piazza Bellini, this whitewashed gallery features its own cafe-bar speckled with books, flowers, cultured crowds and al fresco seating at the bottom of a baroque staircase. Eye up exhibitions of contemporary Italian and foreign art, then kick back with a *caffè* or a *spritz*. Check Nea's Facebook page for upcoming readings, live-music gigs or DJ sets.

☆ Entertainment

Although Naples is no London or Milan on the entertainment front, it does offer world-class opera, ballet, classical music and jazz, thought-provoking theatre and in-the-know DJs. To see what's on, scan Italian-language *Corriere del Mezzogiorno* (https://corriere delmezzogiorno.corriere.it/napoli) or *La Repubblica* (http://napoli.repubblica.it), or ask at the tourist office.

⭐ **Teatro San Carlo**   OPERA, BALLET
(Map p704; ☑box office 081 797 23 31; www.teatro
sancarlo.it; Via San Carlo 98f; ⊙box office 10am-9pm
Mon-Sat, to 6pm Sun; ☑R2 to Via San Carlo, ⓂMu-
nicipio) San Carlo's opera season runs from
November or December to June, with occasional summer performances. Sample prices:
a place in the 6th tier (from €35), the stalls
(€75 to €130) or the side box (from €40). Ballet season runs from late October to April or
early May; tickets range from €30 to €110. Although the original 1737 theatre burnt down
in 1816, Antonio Niccolini's 19th-century reconstruction is pure Old World opulence. If
you can't make it to a performance, consider
taking one of the 45-minute guided tours of
the venue; tickets (adult/reduced €9/7) can
be purchased at the theatre up to 15 minutes
before each tour begins.

⭐ **Stadio San Paolo**   FOOTBALL
(Piazzale Vincenzo Tecchio; Ⓜ Napoli Campi Flegrei)
Naples' football team, Napoli, is the fourth
most supported in Italy after Juventus, AC
Milan and Inter Milan, and watching it play
in the country's third-largest stadium is a
rush. The season runs from late August to
late May; seats cost from around €20 to
€100. Tickets are available from selected
tobacconists, the agency inside **Feltrinelli** (Map p704; ☑ 081 032 23 62; www.azzurroser
vice.net; La Feltrinelli bookstore, Piazza dei Martiri
23; ⊙11am-2pm & 3-8pm Mon-Sat; ☑E6 to Piazza
dei Martiri), or **Box Office** (Map p704; ☑081 551
91 88; www.boxofficenapoli.it; Galleria Umberto I 17;
⊙9.30am-8pm Mon-Fri, 10am-1.30pm & 4.30-8pm
Sat; ☑R2 to Piazza Trieste e Trento, ⓂMunicipio);
bring photo ID. On match days, tickets are
also available at the stadium itself.

**Centro di Musica Antica
Pietà de' Turchini**   CLASSICAL MUSIC
(Map p704; ☑ 081 40 23 95; www.turchini.it;
Via Santa Caterina da Siena 38; adult/reduced
€10/7; ☑ Centrale to Corso Vittorio Emanuele)
Classical-music buffs are in for a treat at this
beautiful deconsecrated church, an evocative setting for concerts of mostly 17th- to
19th-century Neapolitan works. Upcoming
concerts are listed on the venue's website.
Note that some concerts are held at other
venues, including the Palazzo Zevallos Stigliano (p707).

Bourbon Street   JAZZ
(Map p700; ☑338 8253756; www.bourbon
streetjazzclub.com; Via Bellini 52; ⊙8.30pm-2am
Tue-Thu & Sun, to 3am Fri & Sat; closed Jul-early
Sep; ⓂDante) Bourbon Street is one of the

top spots for live jazz and blues, drawing
a mixed crowd of seasoned jazz nerds and
rookies. Acts are mostly local, with Wednesday, Thursday and Sunday nights featuring
'JamJazz' sessions, when musicians hit the
stage for impromptu collaborations. Check
the venue's Facebook page (Bourbon Street
Napoli Jazz Club) to see who's up next.

🛍 **Shopping**

⭐ **Omega**   FASHION & ACCESSORIES
(Map p700; ☑081 29 90 41; www.omegasrl.com; Via
Stella 12; ⊙8.30am-6pm Mon-Fri; ⓂPiazza Cavour,
Museo) Despite hiding away on the 3rd floor
of a nondescript building, Paris, New York
and Tokyo know all about this family-run
glove factory, whose clients include Dior and
Hermes. Omega's men's and women's leather
gloves are meticulously handcrafted using a
traditional 25-step process, and best of all,
they retail for a fraction of the price charged
by the luxury fashion houses.

Expect to pay between €30 and €110 for
a pair of gloves, depending on the style. The
workshop is now run by the fourth and fifth
generations of the family: affable Mauro
Squillace and his son Alberto. Mauro offers
free 45-minute tours of the workshop and
glove-making process if he's not busy, and
no reservations are necessary to drop by the
place, whether to shop or simply take a peek.

⭐ **Bottega 21**   FASHION & ACCESSORIES
(Map p700; ☑081 033 55 42; www.bottegaventu
no.it; Vico San Domenico Maggiore 21; ⊙9.30am-
8pm Mon-Sat) Top-notch Tuscan leather and
traditional, handcrafted methods translate
into coveted, contemporary leather goods at
Bottega 21. Block colours and clean, simple
designs underline the range, which includes
stylish totes, handbags, backpacks and duf-
fel bags, as well as wallets and coin purses,
unisex belts, gloves, sandals, tobacco pouch-
es and, occasionally, notebook covers.

There's a second branch further down the
street at No 11.

⭐ **E Marinella**   FASHION & ACCESSORIES
(Map p704; ☑081 764 32 65; www.emarinella.
com; Via Riviera di Chiaia 287; ⊙6.30am-8pm
Mon-Sat, 9am-1pm Sun; ☑C25 to Piazza Vittoria,
E6 to Piazza dei Martiri) One-time favourite of
Luchino Visconti and Aristotle Onassis, this
pocket-sized, vintage boutique is *the* place
for prêt-à-porter and made-to-measure silk
ties in striking patterns and hues. Match
them with an irresistible selection of luxury

accessories, including shoes, heritage colognes and scarves for female style queens.

⭐ **La Scarabattola**   ARTS & CRAFTS
(Map p700; ☑081 29 17 35; www.lascarabattola.it; Via dei Tribunali 50; ☉10.30am-2pm & 3.30-7.30pm Mon-Fri, 10am-8pm Sat; Ⓜ Dante) La Scarabattola's handmade sculptures of *magi* (wise men), devils and Neapolitan folk figures constitute Jerusalem's official Christmas crèche, and the artisanal studio's fans also include fashion designer Stefano Gabbana and Spanish royalty. Figurines aside, sleek ceramic creations (like Pulcinella-inspired place-card holders) inject Neapolitan folklore with refreshing contemporary style.

Limonè   FOOD & DRINKS
(Map p700; ☑081 29 94 29; www.limoncellodinapoli.it; Piazza San Gaetano 72; ☉11am-8.30pm; Ⓜ Dante) For a take-home taste of Napoli, stock up on a few bottles of Limonè's homemade *limoncello* (lemon liqueur), made with organic lemons from the Campi Flegrei. For something a little sweeter, opt for the *crema di limone*, a gorgeous lemon liqueur made with milk. Other take-home treats include lemon pasta and risotto, lemon-infused chocolate, jars of rum-soaked *babà*, even lemon-infused grappa.

Ask nicely for a sample of the liqueurs. If the shop isn't too busy, you might even get shown the foundations of an ancient Greek temple hidden out the back.

ⓘ Information

MEDICAL SERVICES
Loreto Mare Hospital (Ospedale San Maria di Loreto Nuovo; ☑081 254 21 11; www.aslnapolicentro.it/818; Via Vespucci 26; ☐154 to Via Vespucci) Central-city hospital with an emergency department.

Pharmacy (Napoli Centrale; ☉7am-9.30pm Mon-Sat (to 9pm in winter), 8am-9pm Sun; Ⓜ Garibaldi, ☐Napoli Centrale) Pharmacy inside the main train station.

POST
Main Post Office (Map p704; ☑081 428 98 14; www.poste.it; Piazza Matteotti 2; ☉8.20am-7pm Mon-Fri, to 12.30pm Sat; Ⓜ Toledo) Naples' curvaceous main post office is famous for its fascist-era architecture.

TOURIST INFORMATION
Tourist Information Office (Map p700; ☑081 551 27 01; www.inaples.it; Piazza del Gesù Nuovo 7; ☉9am-5pm Mon-Sat, to 1pm Sun; Ⓜ Dante) In the *centro storico*.

Tourist Information Office (Map p704; ☑081 40 23 94; www.inaples.it; Via San Carlo 9; ☉9am-5pm Mon-Sat, to 1pm Sun; ☐R2 to Via San Carlo, Ⓜ Municipio) At Galleria Umberto I, directly opposite Teatro San Carlo.

ⓘ Getting There & Away

AIR
Naples International Airport (Capodichino; ☑081 789 62 59; www.aeroportodinapoli.it; Viale F Ruffo di Calabria), 7km northeast of the city centre, is southern Italy's main airport. It's served by a number of major airlines and low-cost carriers, including easyJet, which operates flights to Naples from London, Paris, Amsterdam, Vienna, Berlin and several other European cities.

BOAT
Fast ferries and hydrofoils for Capri, Ischia, Procida and Sorrento depart from **Molo Beverello** (Map p704; Ⓜ Municipio) in front of Castel Nuovo; hydrofoils for Capri, Ischia and Procida also sail from Mergellina.

High-speed ferry and hydrofoil operators include the following:

Alilauro (☑081 497 22 38; www.alilauro.it; Molo Beverello) Runs up to six daily services to/from Naples and Sorrento (€13). Also runs up to 10 daily services to/from Naples and Ischia (€20).

Caremar (☑081 1896 6690; www.caremar.it; Molo Beverello) Operates up to four daily services between Naples and Capri (€18). Also runs up to six daily services to/from Naples and Ischia (€18) and up to eight daily services to/from Procida (€14.50).

Navigazione Libera del Golfo (NLG; ☑081 552 07 63; www.navlib.it; Marina Grande) Runs up to nine daily services to/from Naples and Capri (from €19). Also runs one daily services to/from Naples and Sorrento (€13).

SNAV (☑081 428 55 55; www.snav.it; Molo Beverollo, Naples) Runs up to nine daily services between Naples and Capri (from €22.50). Also runs up to eight daily services to Ischia (from €20) and up to four daily services to Procida (from €17.50).

Slow ferries for Sicily, the Aeolian Islands and Sardinia sail from **Molo Angioino** (Map p704; Ⓜ Municipio), which is right beside Molo Beverello, and neighbouring **Calata Porta di Massa** (Map p704; Ⓜ Municipio). Car ferries to Ischia and Procida also depart from Calata Porta di Massa.

Slow-ferry operators include the following:
Caremar (☑081 1896 6690; www.caremar.it; Molo Beverello) Runs ferries to/from Naples and Capri (from €12.50) three times daily. Runs up to eight times daily to/from Naples and

Ischia (€12.50) and up to seven times daily to/from Naples and Prodica (€10.50).

Medmar (☑ 081 333 44 11; www.medmar group.it; Calata Porta di Massa, Naples) Runs ferries to/from Naples and Ischia (from €12.50) three times daily.

Siremar (Map p704; ☑ 800 627414; www.siremar.it; Calata Porto di Massa, Naples) Operates overnight ferries to the Isole Eolie (Aeolian Islands) and Milazzo in Sicily (from €57.50) twice weekly.

SNAV (www.snav.it; Calata Porta di Massa) Runs to/from Naples and the Isole Eolie (Aeolian Islands) several times weekly (from €58) from June to early September.

Tirrenia (☑ 199 303040; www.tirrenia.it; Calata Porta di Massa) Runs ferries from Naples to Cagliari in Sardinia (from €47) twice weekly. Also runs once daily from Naples to Palermo in Sicily (from €56.50).

BUS

Most national and international buses leave from **Metropark Napoli Centrale** (Map p700; ☑ 800 650006; Corso Arnaldo Lucci; Ⓜ Garibaldi), on the southern side of Napoli Centrale train station. The bus station is home to **Biglietteria Vecchione** (☑ 331 88969217; Corso Arnaldo Lucci, Terminal Bus Metropark; ⊙ 6.30am-9.15pm Mon-Fri, to 7pm Sat, 7am-7pm Sun; Ⓜ Garibaldi), a ticket agency selling national and international bus tickets.

Metropark Napoli Centrale serves numerous bus companies offering regional and inter-regional services, among them FlixBus (https://global.flixbus.com), **CLP** (☑ 081 531 17 07; www.clpbus.it; Metropark Napoli Centrale, Corso Arnaldo Lucci), **Marino** (☑ 080 311 23 35; www.marinobus.it; Metropark Napoli Centrale, Corso Arnaldo Lucci), **Miccolis** (☑ 080 531 53 34; www.miccolis-spa.it; Metropark Napoli Centrale, Corso Arnaldo Lucci) and **SAIS** (☑ 091 617 11 41; www.saistrasporti.it; Metropark Napoli Centrale, Corso Arnaldo Lucci). It also serves **Fiumicino Express** (☑ 391 3998081; www.fiumicino express.com), which runs to and from Rome's Fiumicino and Ciampino airports via Caserta.

The bus stop for **SITA Sud** (☑ 342 6256442; www.sitasudtrasporti.it) services to the Amalfi Coast is just around the corner on Via Galileo Ferraris (in front of the hulking Istituto Nazionale della Previdenza Sociale office building).

CAR & MOTORCYCLE

Naples is on the north–south Autostrada del Sole, the A1 (north to Rome and Milan) and the A3 (south to Salerno and Reggio di Calabria).

Among other locations, the following car-rental agencies have branches at Naples International Airport:

Avis (☑ 081 28 40 41; www.avisautonoleggio.it; Piazza Garibaldi 92, Starhotels Terminus; ⊙ 8am-7.30pm Mon-Fri, 8.30am-4.30pm Sat, 9am-1pm Sun)

Europcar (☑ 081 780 56 43; www.europcar.it; Naples International Airport (Capodichino); ⊙ 7.30am-11.30pm)

Hertz (☑ 081 20 28 60; www.hertz.it; Corso Arnaldo Lucci 171; ⊙ 8.30am-1pm & 2.30-7pm Mon-Fri, 8.30am-1pm Sat)

Maggiore (☑ 081 28 78 58; www.maggiore.it; Napoli Centrale; ⊙ 8.30am-7.30pm Mon-Fri, to 6pm Sat, to 12.30pm Sun)

For scooter rental, contact **Vespa Sprint** (☑ 081 764 34 52; http://vespasprint.it/noleggio-vespa-scooter-napoli; Via Santa Lucia 36, Naples; scooter hire per day from €60; ⊙ 8am-8pm Mon-Sat, 10am-6pm Sun), in the city's Santa Lucia district.

TRAIN

Naples is southern Italy's rail hub and on the main Milan–Palermo line, with good connections to other Italian cities and towns.

The city's main train station is **Napoli Centrale** (Stazione Centrale; ☑ 081 554 31 88; Piazza Garibaldi), just east of the *centro storico*. From here, the national rail company **Trenitalia** (☑ 892021; www.trenitalia.com) runs regular direct services to Rome (2nd class €13 to €48, 70 minutes to three hours, around 66 daily). High-speed private rail company **Italo** (☑ 892020; www.italotreno.it) also runs daily direct services to Rome (2nd class €15 to €40, 70 minutes, around 20 daily). Most Italo services stop at Roma Termini and Roma Tiburtina stations.

ⓘ Getting Around

BUS

ANM (☑ 800 639525; www.anm.it) operates city buses in Naples. There's no central bus station, but most buses pass through Piazza Garibaldi. Buses generally run from around 5.30am to about 11pm, depending on the route and day. Some routes do not run on Sunday. A small number of routes run through the night, marked with an 'N' before their route number.

Useful city routes include the following:

140 Santa Lucia to Posillipo (via Mergellina)

154 Port area to Chiaia (along Via Volta, Via Vespucci, Via Marina, Via Depretis, Via Acton, Via Morelli and Piazza Vittoria)

C51 Piazza Cavour to La Sanità (along Via Foria, Via Vergini, Via Sanità and Via Fontanelle)

E6 Piazza Trieste e Trento to Chiaia (along Via Monte di Dio, Via Santa Lucia, Via Morelli, Piazza dei Martiri and Via Filangieri)

R2 Napoli Centrale to Piazza Trento e Trieste (along Corso Umberto I and Piazza Municipio)

R4 Via Toledo to Capodimonte (via Piazza Dante and Via Santa Maria di Costantinopoli)

FUNICULAR

Three services connect central Naples to Vomero, while a fourth connects Mergellina to Posillipo. All operate from 7am to 10pm daily. ANM transport tickets are valid on funicular services.

Funicolare Centrale (www.anm.it; ⊘7am-10pm) Travels from Piazzetta Augusteo to Piazza Fuga.

Funicolare di Chiaia (www.anm.it; ⊘7am-10pm) Travels from Via del Parco Margherita to Via Domenico Cimarosa.

Funicolare di Montesanto (www.anm.it; ⊘7am-10pm) Travels from Piazza Montesanto to Via Raffaele Morghen.

Funicolare di Mergellina (www.anm.it; ⊘7am-10pm) Connects the waterfront at Via Mergellina with Via Manzoni.

METRO

Metro Line 1 (Linea 1; www.anm.it) runs from Garibaldi (Stazione Centrale) to Vomero and the northern suburbs via the city centre. Useful stops include Duomo and Università (southern edge of the *centro storico*), Municipio (hydrofoil and ferry terminals), Toledo (Via Toledo and Quartieri Spagnoli), Dante (western edge of the *centro storico*) and Museo (National Archaeological Museum).

Metro Line 2 (Linea 2; www.trenitalia.com) runs from Gianturco to Garibaldi (Stazione Centrale) and on to Pozzuoli. Useful stops include Piazza Cavour (La Sanità and northern edge of *centro storico*), Piazza Amedeo (Chiaia) and Mergellina (Mergellina ferry terminal). Change between Lines 1 and 2 at Garibaldi or Piazza Cavour (known as Museo on Line 1).

Metro Line 6 (Linea 6; www.anm.it) is expected to open in 2021. When completed, it will run from Municipio to Mostra, with useful stops

---

WORTH A TRIP

REGGIA DI CASERTA

Italy's swansong to the baroque, the colossal **Reggia di Caserta** (Palazzo Reale; ☑0823 44 80 84; www.reggiadicaserta.beniculturali.it; Viale Douhet 22, Caserta; adult/reduced €12/6; ⊘palace 8.30am-7.30pm Wed-Mon, park to 7pm Wed-Mon Apr-Sep, reduced hours Oct-Mar, Giardino Inglese to 6pm Wed-Mon Apr-Sep, reduced hours Oct-Mar; ▣Caserta) began life in 1752 after Charles VII ordered a palace to rival Versailles. Not one to disappoint, Neapolitan architect Luigi Vanvitelli delivered a palace bigger than its French rival. With its 1200 rooms, 1790 windows, 34 staircases and 250m-long facade, it was reputedly the largest building in 18th-century Europe.

Vanvitelli's immense staircase leads up to the Royal Apartments, lavishly decorated with frescoes, art, tapestries, period furniture and crystal.

The back rooms off the Sala di Astrea (Room of Astraea) house an extraordinary collection of historic wooden models of the Reggia, along with architectural drawings and early sketches of the building by Luigi Vanvitelli and his son, Carlo. The apartments are also home to the Mostra Terrea Motus, an underrated collection of international modern art commissioned after the region's devastating earthquake in 1980. Among the contributors are US heavyweights Cy Twombly, Robert Mapplethorpe and Keith Haring, as well as local luminaries like Mimmo Paladino and Jannis Kounellis.

The complex has appeared in numerous films, including *Mission: Impossible III, Star Wars: Episode 1 – The Phantom Menace,* and *Star Wars: Episode II – Attack of the Clones,* moonlighting as Queen Amidala's palace in the latter two.

To clear your head afterwards, explore the elegant landscaped park, which stretches for some 3km to a waterfall and a fountain of Diana. Within the park is the famous Giardino Inglese (English Garden), a romantic oasis of intricate pathways, exotic flora, pools and cascades. Bicycle hire (from €4) is available at the back of the palace building, as are pony-and-trap rides (€50 for 40 minutes, up to five people).

If you're feeling peckish, consider skipping the touristy palace cafeteria for local cafe **Martucci** (☑0823 32 08 03; www.facebook.com/martucci.caffe; Via Roma 9, Caserta; pastries from €1.50, sandwiches from €3.50, salads €7.50; ⊘5am-10.30pm; ☎), located 250m east of the complex.

Regular trains connect Naples to Caserta (€3.40, 30 to 50 minutes); always plan ahead and check times online before hitting the station. Caserta train station is located directly opposite the palace grounds. If you're driving from Naples, exit the A1 (E45) at Caserta Sud and follow signs for Caserta and the Reggia.

including Chiaia–Monte di Dio (just west of Piazza del Plebiscito), San Pasquale (Chiaia and the Lungomare) and Mergellina.

TAXI

Official taxis are white and metered. Always ensure the meter is running.

The minimum starting fare is €3.50 (€6.50 on Sunday), with a baffling range of additional charges, all of which are listed at www.taxi napoli.it/tariffe. These extras include the following:

➡ €1.50 for a radio taxi call
➡ €4 for an airport run
➡ €5 for trips starting at the airport and €0.50 per piece of luggage in the boot (trunk). Guide dogs, wheelchairs and strollers are carried free of charge.

There are taxi stands at most of the city's main piazzas. Book a taxi by calling any of the following companies:

Consortaxi (☑ 081 22 22; www.consortaxi. com)

Radio Taxi Partenope (☑ 081 01 01; www. radiotaxilapartenope.it)

Taxi Napoli (☑ 081 88 88; www.taxinapoli.it)

SOUTH OF NAPLES

Herculaneum (Ercolano)

Ercolano is an uninspiring Neapolitan suburb that's home to one of Italy's best-preserved ancient sites: Herculaneum. A superbly conserved fishing town, the site is smaller and less daunting than Pompeii, allowing you to visit without the nagging feeling that you're bound to miss something.

◎ Sights

★ **Ruins of Herculaneum**   ARCHAEOLOGICAL SITE
(☑ 081 777 70 08; http://ercolano.beniculturali.it; Corso Resina 187, Ercolano; adult/reduced €13/2; ⊙ 8.30am-7.30pm, last entry 6pm Apr-Oct, 8.30am-5pm, last entry 3.30pm Nov-Mar; P; R Circumvesuviana to Ercolano–Scavi) Herculaneum harbours a wealth of archaeological finds, from ancient advertisements and stylish mosaics to carbonised furniture and terror-struck skeletons. Indeed, this superbly conserved Roman fishing town of 4000 inhabitants is easier to navigate than Pompeii, and can be explored with a map and highly recommended audio guide (€8).

To reach the ruins from Ercolano–Scavi train station, walk downhill to the very

end of Via IV Novembre and through the archway across the street. The path leads down to the ticket office, which lies on your left. Ticket purchased, follow the walkway around to the actual entrance to the ruins, where you can also hire audio guides.

Herculaneum's fate runs parallel to that of Pompeii. Destroyed by an earthquake in AD 62, the AD 79 eruption of Mt Vesuvius saw it submerged in a 16m-thick sea of mud that essentially fossilised the city. This meant that even delicate items, such as furniture and clothing, were discovered remarkably well preserved. Tragically, the inhabitants didn't fare so well; thousands of people tried to escape by boat but were suffocated by the volcano's poisonous gases. Indeed, what appears to be a moat around the town is in fact the ancient shoreline. It was here in 1980 that archaeologists discovered some 300 skeletons, the remains of a crowd that had fled to the beach only to be overcome by the terrible heat of clouds surging down from Vesuvius.

The town itself was rediscovered in 1709 and amateur excavations were carried out intermittently until 1874, with many finds carted off to Naples to decorate the houses of the well-to-do or ending up in museums. Serious archaeological work began again in 1927 and continues to this day; with much of the ancient site buried beneath modern Ercolano, it's slow going.

Note that at any given time some houses will invariably be shut for restoration.

Casa d'Argo   ARCHAEOLOGICAL SITE
(Argus House) This noble house would originally have opened onto Cardo II (as yet unearthed). Its porticoed garden opens onto a *triclinium* (dining room) and other residential rooms.

Casa dello Scheletro   ARCHAEOLOGICAL SITE
(House of the Skeleton) The modest Casa dello Scheletro features five styles of mosaic flooring, including a design of white arrows at the entrance to guide the most disoriented of guests. In the internal courtyard, don't miss the skylight, complete with the remnants of an ancient security grill. Of the house's mythically themed wall mosaics, only the faded ones are originals; the others now reside in Naples' Museo Archeologico Nazionale (p698).

Terme Maschili   ARCHAEOLOGICAL SITE
(Men's Baths) The Terme Maschili were the men's section of the **Terme del Foro** (Forum Baths). Note the ancient latrine to the left of

the entrance before you step into the *apodyterium* (changing room), complete with bench for waiting patrons and a nifty wall shelf for sandal and toga storage. While those after a bracing soak would pop into the *frigidarium* (cold bath) to the left, the less stoic headed straight into the *tepadarium* (tepid bath) to the right. The sunken mosaic floor here is testament to the seismic activity preceding Mt Vesuvius' catastrophic eruption. Beyond this room lies the *caldarium* (hot bath), as well as an exercise area.

Decumano Massimo ARCHAEOLOGICAL SITE

Herculaneum's ancient high street is lined with shops, and fragments of advertisements; look for the wall fresco advertising wines by colour code and price per weight. Note the one to the right of the Casa del Salone Nero. Further east along the street, a crucifix found in an upstairs room of the Casa del Bicentenario (Bicentenary House) provides possible evidence of a Christian presence in pre-Vesuvius Herculaneum.

Casa del Bel Cortile ARCHAEOLOGICAL SITE

(House of the Beautiful Courtyard) The Casa del Bel Cortile is home to three of the 300 skeletons discovered on the ancient shore by archaeologists in 1980. Almost two millennia after the volcanic eruption, it's still poignant to see the forms of what are understood to be a mother, father and young child huddled together in the last, terrifying moments of their lives.

Casa di Nettuno e Anfitrite ARCHAEOLOGICAL SITE

(House of Neptune & Amphitrite) This aristocratic pad takes its name from the extraordinary mosaic in the *triclinium* (dining room), which also features a mosaic-encrusted *nymphaeum* (fountain and bath as a shrine to the water nymph). The warm colours in which the sea god and his nymph bride are depicted hint at how lavish the original interior must have been.

Casa del Tramezzo di Legno ARCHAEOLOGICAL SITE

(House of the Wooden Partition) Unusually, this house features two atria, which likely belonged to two separate dwellings that were merged in the 1st century AD. The most famous relic here is a wonderfully well-preserved wooden screen, separating the atrium from the *tablinum,* where the owner talked business with his clients. The second room off the left side of the atrium features the remains of an ancient bed.

Casa dell'Atrio a Mosaico ARCHAEOLOGICAL SITE

(House of the Mosaic Atrium; ⊘ closed for restoration) An ancient mansion, the House of the Mosaic Atrium harbours extensive floor tilework, although time and nature have left the floor buckled and uneven. Particularly noteworthy is the black-and-white chessboard mosaic in the atrium.

Casa del Gran Portale ARCHAEOLOGICAL SITE

(House of the Large Portal) Named after the brick Corinthian columns that flank its main entrance, the House of the Large Portal is home to some well-preserved wall paintings.

Casa dei Cervi ARCHAEOLOGICAL SITE

(House of the Stags) The Casa dei Cervi is an imposing example of a Roman noble family's house that, before the volcanic mud slide, boasted a seafront address. Constructed around a central courtyard, the two-storey villa contains murals and some beautiful still-life paintings. Waiting for you in the courtyard is a diminutive pair of marble deer assailed by dogs, and an engaging statue of a drunken, peeing Hercules.

Terme Suburbane ARCHAEOLOGICAL SITE

(Suburban Baths) Marking Herculaneum's southernmost tip is the 1st-century-AD Terme Suburbane, one of the best-preserved Roman bath complexes in existence, with deep pools, stucco friezes and bas-reliefs looking down upon marble seats and floors. This is also one of the best places to observe the soaring volcanic deposits that smothered the ancient coastline.

MAV MUSEUM

(Museo Archeologico Virtuale; ☑ 081 777 68 43; www.museomav.com; Via IV Novembre 44; adult/reduced €10/8; ⊘ 9am-5.30pm daily Mar-May, 10am-6.30pm daily Jun-Sep, to 4pm Tue-Sun Oct-Feb; ⛪; Ⓡ Circumvesuviana to Ercolano–Scavi) Using computer-generated recreations, this 'virtual archaeological museum' brings ruins such as Pompeii's forum and Capri's Villa Jovis back to virtual life. Some of the displays are in Italian only. The short documentary gives an overview of the history of Mt Vesuvius and its infamous eruption in AD 79... in rather lacklustre 3D. The museum is on the main street linking Ercolano–Scavi train station to the ruins of Herculaneum.

🍴 Eating

Viva Lo Re NEAPOLITAN €€

(☑ 081 739 02 07; www.vivalore.it; Corso Resina 261, Ercolano; meals €32; ⊘ noon-3.30pm & 7.30-

11.30pm Tue-Sat, noon-3.30pm Sun; 🐾) Whether you're after an inspired meal or a simple glass of vino, this refined yet relaxed *osteria* (casual tavern) is a solid choice. The wine list is extensive and impressive, while the menu offers competent, produce-driven regional cooking with subtle modern twists. For an appetite-piquing overview, start with the multitaste *antipasto Viva Lo Re*.

The *osteria* lies 500m southeast of the Herculaneum ruins on Corso Resina; dubbed the *Miglio d'Oro* (Golden Mile) for its once glorious stretch of 18th-century villas.

ℹ️ Information

Tourist Office (☑️081 788 13 75; Via IV Novembre 44; ⊙9am-2pm Mon-Fri & 2.30-5pm Tue & Thu; 🚉Circumvesuviana to Ercolano– Scavi) Ercolano's tourist office is in the same building as MAV, between the Circumvesuviana Ercolano–Scavi train station and the Herculaneum *scavi* (ruins).

ℹ️ Getting There & Away

If travelling by **Circumvesuviana** (☑️800 211388; www.eavsrl.it) train (€2.20 from Naples or €2.90 from Sorrento), get off at Ercolano–Scavi station and walk 500m downhill to the ruins – follow the signs for the *scavi* down the main street, Via IV Novembre.

If driving from Naples, the A3 runs southeast along the Bay of Naples. To reach the ruins of Herculaneum, exit at Ercolano Portico and follow the signs to car parks near the site. From Sorrento, head north along the SS145, which spills onto the A3.

From mid-March to early November, tourist train *Campania Express* runs four times daily between Naples (Porta Nolana and Piazza Garibaldi Circumvesuviana stations) and Sorrento, stopping at Ercolano–Scavi and Pompei Scavi–Villa dei Misteri en route. One-day return tickets from Naples to Ercolano (€7) or from Sorrento to Ercolano (€11) can be purchased at the stations or online at **EAV** (☑️800 211388; www.eavsrl.it).

Mt Vesuvius

Rising formidably beside the Bay of Naples, Mt Vesuvius forms part of the Campanian volcanic arch, a string of active, dormant and extinct volcanoes that include the Campi Flegrei's Solfatara and Monte Nuovo, and Ischia's Monte Epomeo. Infamous for its explosive Plinian eruptions and surrounding urban sprawl, it's also one of the world's most carefully monitored volcanoes. Anoth-

er full-scale eruption would be catastrophic. More than half a million people live in the so-called 'red zone', the area most vulnerable to pyroclastic flows and crushing pyroclastic deposits in a major eruption. Yet, despite government incentives to relocate, few residents are willing to leave.

👁️ Sights

Mt Vesuvius   VOLCANO

(☑️081 239 56 53; www.parconazionaledelvesuvio. it; crater adult/reduced €10/8; ⊙crater 9am-6pm Jul & Aug, to 5pm Apr-Jun & Sep, to 4pm Mar & Oct, to 3pm Nov-Feb, ticket office closes 1hr before crater) Since exploding into history in AD 79, Vesuvius has blown its top more than 30 times. What redeems this slumbering menace is the spectacular panorama from its crater, which takes in Naples, its world-famous bay, and part of the Apennine Mountains. Vesuvius is the focal point of the Parco Nazionale del Vesuvio (Vesuvius National Park; ☑️081 239 56 53; www.parconazionaledelvesuvio. it), with nine nature walks around the volcano – download a simple map from the park's website. Horse Riding Tour Naples (☑️345 8560306; www.horseridingnaples.com; guided tour €60) also runs daily horse-riding tours.

The mountain is widely believed to have been higher than it currently stands, claiming a single summit rising to about 3000m rather than the 1281m of today. Its violent outburst in AD 79 not only drowned Pompeii in pumice and pushed the coastline back several kilometres but also destroyed much of the mountain top, creating a huge caldera and two new peaks. The most destructive explosion after that of AD 79 was in 1631, while the most recent was in 1944.

ℹ️ Getting There & Away

Vesuvius can be reached by bus from Pompeii and Ercolano.

The cheapest option is to catch the public **EAV** (☑️800 211388; www.eavsrl.it) bus service, which departs from Piazza Anfiteatro in Pompeii and stops outside Pompei Scavi–Villa dei Misteri train station en route. Buses depart every 50 minutes from 8am to 3.30pm and take around 50 minutes to reach the summit car park. Once here, purchase your entry ticket to the summit area (adult/reduced €10/8) and follow the 860m gravel path up to the crater (roughly a 25-minute climb). In Pompeii, ignore any touts telling you that the public bus only runs in summer; they are merely trying to push private tours. Bus tickets cost €3.10 one-way and can be purchased on board.

1. Complesso Monumentale di San Lorenzo Maggiore (p702),
Naples 2. Tempio di Cerere (p762), Paestum 3. Pompeii (p726)
4. Mosaic, Herculaneum (p721)

©IMAS/SHUTTERSTOCK©

Historical Riches

Few Italian regions can match Campania's historical legacy. Colonised by the ancient Greeks and loved by the Romans, it's a sun-drenched repository of A-list antiquities, from World Heritage wonders to lesser-known archaeological gems.

Paestum

Great Greek temples never go out of vogue and those at Paestum (p762) are among the greatest outside Greece itself. With the oldest structures stretching back to the 6th century BC, this place makes Rome's Colosseum feel positively modern.

Herculaneum

A bite-sized Pompeii, Herculaneum (p721) is even better preserved than its nearby rival. This is the place to delve into the details, from once-upon-a-time shop advertisements and furniture, to vivid mosaics and even an ancient security grille.

Pompeii

Short of stepping into the Tardis, Pompeii (p726) is your best bet for a little time travel. Locked in ash for centuries, its excavated streetscapes offer a tangible encounter with the ancients and their daily lives. It has everything from luxury homes to a racy brothel.

Subterranean Naples

Eerie aqueducts, mysterious burial crypts and ancient streetscapes: beneath Naples' hyperactive streets lies a wonderland of Graeco-Roman ruins. For a taste, head below the Complesso Monumentale di San Lorenzo Maggiore (p702) or follow the leader on a tour of the evocative Catacombe di San Gennaro (p711).

In Ercolano, private company **Vesuvio Express** (☑ 081 739 36 66; www.vesuvioexpress. it; Piazzale Stazione Circumvesuviana, Ercolano; return incl admission to summit €20; ☺ every 40min, 9.30am-5pm Jul & Aug, to 4pm Apr-Jun & Sep, to 2.10pm Oct-Mar) runs buses to the summit car park from Piazzale Stazione Circumvesuviana, outside Ercolano–Scavi train station. A word of warning: this company has received very mixed reviews, with numerous claims of unreliability from travellers.

When the weather is bad the summit path is shut and bus departures are suspended.

If travelling by car, exit the A3 at Ercolano Portico and follow signs for the Parco Nazionale del Vesuvio. From the summit car park (€5), a shuttle bus (return €3) reaches the ticket office and entry point further up the volcano.

Pompeii

Modern-day Pompeii (Pompei in Italian) may feel like a nondescript satellite of Naples, but it's here that you'll find Europe's most compelling archaeological site: the ruins of Pompeii. Sprawling and haunting, the site is a stark reminder of the destructive forces that lie deep inside Vesuvius.

◉ Sights

Terme Suburbane   ARCHAEOLOGICAL SITE
Just outside ancient Pompeii's city walls, this 1st-century-BC bathhouse is famous for several erotic frescoes that scandalised the Vatican when they were revealed in 2001. The panels decorate what was once the *apodyterium* (changing room). The room leading to the colourfully frescoed *frigidarium* (cold bath) features fragments of stuccowork, as well as one of the few original roofs to survive at Pompeii. Beyond the *tepadar-*

ium (tepid bath) and *caldarium* (hot bath) rooms are the remains of a heated outdoor swimming pool. The bathhouse was closed at the time of research.

Tempio di Apollo   ARCHAEOLOGICAL SITE
(Temple of Apollo) The oldest and most important of Pompeii's religious buildings, the Tempio di Apollo largely dates from the 2nd century BC, including the striking columned portico. Fragments remain of an earlier version dating from the 6th century BC. The statues of Apollo and Diana (depicted as archers) on either side of the portico are copies; the originals are housed in Naples' Museo Archeologico Nazionale (p698).

Basilica   ARCHAEOLOGICAL SITE
The basilica was the 2nd-century-BC seat of Pompeii's law courts and exchange. The semicircular apses would later influence the design of early Christian churches.

Foro   ARCHAEOLOGICAL SITE
A huge rectangle flanked by limestone columns, the *foro* was ancient Pompeii's main piazza, as well as the site of gladiatorial games before the Anfiteatro (p729) was constructed. The buildings surrounding the forum are testament to its role as the city's hub of civic, commercial, political and religious activity. At its northern end are the remains of the Tempio di Giove (Capitolium), the heart of religious life in Pompeii.

Granai del Foro   ARCHAEOLOGICAL SITE
(Forum Granary) The Granai del Foro is now used to store hundreds of amphorae and a number of body casts that were made in the late 19th century by pouring plaster into the hollows left by disintegrated bodies. Among these casts is a pregnant slave; the belt

---

OFF THE BEATEN TRACK

OPLONTIS

Buried beneath the unappealing streets of Torre Annunziata, Oplontis (☑ 081 857 53 47; www.pompeiisites.org; Via dei Sepolcri, Torre Annunziata; adult/reduced incl Boscoreale €7/2; ☺ 8.30am-7.30pm, last entry 6pm Apr-Oct, 8.30am-5pm, last entry 3.30pm Nov-Mar; ℝ Circumvesuviana to Torre Annunziata) was once a blue-ribbon seafront suburb under the administrative control of Pompeii. First discovered in the 18th century, only two of its houses have been unearthed; only one, Villa Poppaea, is open to the public. This villa is a magnificent example of an *otium* villa (a residential building used for rest and recreation), thought to have belonged to Sabina Poppaea, Nero's second wife. Particularly outstanding are the richly coloured 1st-century wall paintings in the *triclinium* (dining room) and *calidarium* (hot bath) in the west wing. Marking the villa's eastern border is a garden with a swimming pool (17m by 61m). The villa is a straightforward 300m walk from Torre Annunziata Circumvesuviana train station.

Old Pompeii

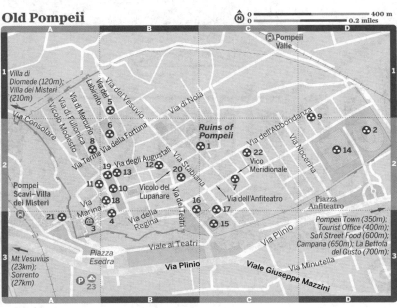

NAPLES & CAMPANIA POMPEII

Old Pompeii

around her waist would have displayed the name of her owner.

Macellum ARCHAEOLOGICAL SITE
Dating from the 2nd century BC, the *macellum* was the city's main produce market. Note the 12 bases at the centre of the market, which were once stands for the timber poles that supported the market's conical roof. Surviving frescoes reveal some of the goods for sale, including prawns.

Casa dei Vettii ARCHAEOLOGICAL SITE
The Casa dei Vettii is home to a famous depiction of Priapus with his gigantic phallus

balanced on a pair of scales...much to the anxiety of many a male observer. The image symbolised the impressive wealth of its sibling owners, Aulus Vettius Restitutus and Aulus Vettius Conviva, who made their fortune trading in wine and agricultural produce.

Via dell'Abbondanza ARCHAEOLOGICAL SITE
(Street of Abundance) The Via dell'Abbondanza was one of ancient Pompeii's main streets. The elevated stepping stones allowed people to cross the street without stepping into the waste that washed down the thoroughfare.

TOP SIGHT
RUINS OF POMPEII

The ruins of Pompeii are a veritable time machine, hurling visitors back to the time of emperors and Latin chatter. Here, time remains paused at 79 AD, the city's frescoed homes, businesses and baths still waiting for their occupants to return. Few archaeological sites offer such an intimate connection to the past, and few are as deeply haunting and evocative.

A Site Reborn

An injection of both national and EU funding over the past decade has fuelled Pompeii's ongoing rehabilitation, turning the once-forlorn site into a hub of archaeological activity and restoration work. Ongoing digs in Cardio V, located to the north of the main archaeological park, have unearthed numerous news-worthy treasures in recent years, including one of Pompeii's most elaborate domestic shrines. While these most recent discoveries may not yet be accessible to the public, Campania's top archaeological drawcard is not short of highlights, including the following.

Villa dei Misteri

This restored, 90-room villa is one of the most complete structures left standing in Pompeii. The Dionysiac frieze, the most important fresco still on-site, spans the walls of the large dining room. One of the largest paintings from the ancient world, it vividly depicts the initiation of a bride-to-be into the cult of Dionysus, the Greek god of wine. A farm for much of its life, the villa's vino-making area is still visible at its northern end.

DON'T MISS

➡ Dionysiac frieze inside Villa dei Misteri

➡ Stucco decoration in the Terme Stabiane

➡ Canine floor mosaic at Casa del Poeta Tragico

➡ Anfiteatro

PRACTICALITIES

➡ ☎ 081 857 53 47

➡ www.pompeiisites.org

➡ entrances at Porta Marina & Piazza Anfiteatro

➡ adult/reduced €16/2

➡ ⊙ 9am-7.30pm Mon-Fri, from 8.30am Sat & Sun, last entry 6pm Apr-Oct, 9am-5.30pm Mon-Fri, from 8.30am Sat & Sun, last entry 3.30pm Nov-Mar

➡ 🚆 Circumvesuviana to Pompei Scavi–Villa dei Misteri

Casa del Poeta Tragico

The 1st-century-AD Casa del Poeta Tragico (House of the Tragic Poet) features the world's first-known 'beware of the dog' – *cave canem* – warnings. Visible through a protective glass panel, the floor mosaic is one of the best preserved at the ruins. The house itself is featured in Edward Bulwer-Lytton's 1834 novel *The Last Days of Pompeii*.

Terme Stabiane

At this typical 2nd-century-BC bathing complex, bathers would enter from the vestibule, stop off in the vaulted *apodyterium* (changing room), and then pass through to the *tepidarium* (tepid bath) and *caldarium* (hot bath). Particularly impressive is the stuccoed vault in the men's changing room, complete with whimsical images of *putti* (winged babies) and nymphs.

Casa del Menandro

Better preserved than the larger Casa del Fauno, luxurious Casa del Menandro has an outstanding, elegant peristyle (a colonnade-framed courtyard; pictured) beyond its beautifully frescoed atrium. On the peristyle's far right side a doorway leads to a private bathhouse, lavished with exquisite frescoes and mosaics. The central room off the far end of the peristyle features a striking fresco of the ancient Greek dramatist Menander, after whom the rediscovered villa was named.

Lupanare

Ancient Pompeii's only dedicated brothel, Lupanare is a tiny two-storey building with five rooms on each floor. Its collection of raunchy frescoes was a menu of sorts for clients. The walls in the rooms are carved with graffiti – including declarations of love and hope written by the brothel workers – in various languages.

Anfiteatro

Gladiatorial battles thrilled up to 20,000 spectators at the grassy anfiteatro (Amphitheatre). Built in 70 BC, it's the oldest known Roman amphitheatre in existence. In 59 AD, the venue witnessed violent clashes between spectators from Pompeii and Nucera, documented in a fresco now found in Naples' Museo Archeologico Nazionale.

TOURS

You'll almost certainly be approached by a guide outside the *scavi* (excavations) ticket office: note that authorised guides wear identification tags. If considering a guided tour of the ruins, reputable tour operators include **Yellowsudmarine Food Art & Tours** (📱 329 1010328; www. yellowsudmarine.com; 2hr Pompeii guided tour €150, plus entrance fee) and **Walks of Italy** (www. walksofitaly.com; 3hr Pompeii guided tour per person €59), both of which also offer excursions to other areas of Campania.

Buy your ticket online to avoid long queues, especially in high season, and allow at least three or four hours (longer if you want to go into detail).

THEATRE AT THE RUINS

In the summer, Naples' Teatro Stabile presents an acclaimed season of classical theatre at Pompeii's ancient Teatro Grande. See the theatre company's website (www.teatrostabile napoli.it/pompeii-thea trum-mundi) for more details.

Tragedy in Pompeii

24 AUGUST AD 79

8am Buildings including the ❶ **Terme Suburbane** and the ❷ **Foro** are still undergoing repair after an earthquake in AD 63 caused significant damage to the city. Despite violent earth tremors overnight, residents have little idea of the catastrophe that lies ahead.

Midday Peckish locals pour into the ❸ **Thermopolium di Vetutius Placidus**. The lustful slip into the ❹ **Lupanare**, and gladiators practise for the evening's planned games at the ❺ **Anfiteatro**. A massive boom heralds the eruption. Shocked onlookers witness a dark cloud of volcanic matter shoot some 14km above the crater.

3pm–5pm Lapilli (burning pumice stone) rains down on Pompeii. Terrified locals begin to flee; others take shelter. Within two hours, the plume is 25km high and the sky has darkened. Roofs collapse under the weight of the debris, burying those inside.

25 AUGUST AD 79

Midnight Mudflows bury the town of Herculaneum. Lapilli and ash continue to rain down on Pompeii, bursting through buildings and suffocating those taking refuge within.

4am–8am Ash and gas avalanches hit Herculaneum. Subsequent surges smother Pompeii, killing all remaining residents, including those in the ❻ **Orto dei Fuggiaschi**. The volcanic 'blanket' will safeguard frescoed treasures like the ❼ **Casa del Menandro** and ❽ **Villa dei Misteri** for almost two millennia.

TOP TIPS

➡ Visit in the afternoon.
➡ Allow three hours.
➡ Wear comfortable shoes and a hat.
➡ Bring drinking water.
➡ Don't use flash photography.

CRYSTALITE / GETTY IMAGES ©

Villa dei Misteri
Home to the world-famous *Dionysiac Frieze* fresco. Other highlights at this villa include *trompe l'oeil* wall decorations in the *cubiculum* (bedroom) and Egyptian-themed artwork in the *tablinum* (reception).

Villa di Diomede

Casa del Poeta Tragico

Porta Ercolano

Casa d Faune

Basilica

Tempio di Apollo

Porta Marina

❶

❷

Terme del Foro

Macellum

Teatro Grande

Quadriportico dei Teatri

Porta di Stabia

Teatro Piccolo

❹

❽

Foro
An ancient Times Square of sorts, the forum sits at the intersection of Pompeii's main streets and was closed to traffic in the 1st century AD. The plinths on the southern edge featured statues of the imperial family.

PHIODEY / GETTY IMAGES ©

Lupanare

The prostitutes at this brothel were often slaves of Greek or Asian origin. Mattresses once covered the stone beds and the names engraved in the walls are possibly those of the workers and their clients.

Thermopolium di Vetutius Placidus

The counter at this ancient snack bar once held urns filled with hot food. The *lararium* (household shrine) on the back wall depicts Dionysus (the god of wine) and Mercury (the god of profit and commerce).

Casa dei Vettii

Porta del Vesuvio

EYEWITNESS ACCOUNT

Pliny the Younger (AD 61–c 112) gives a gripping, first-hand account of the catastrophe in his letters to Tacitus (AD 56–117).

Porta di Nola

Casa della Venere in Conchiglia

Porta di Sarno

③

⑦

Grande Palestra

⑥

⑤

Tempio di Iside

Orto dei Fuggiaschi

The Garden of the Fugitives showcases the plaster moulds of 13 locals seeking refuge during Vesuvius' eruption – the largest number of victims found in any one area. The huddled bodies make for a moving scene.

Casa del Menandro

This dwelling most likely belonged to the family of Poppaea Sabina, Nero's second wife. A room to the left of the atrium features Trojan War paintings and a polychrome mosaic of pygmies rowing down the Nile.

Anfiteatro

Magistrates, local senators and the games' sponsors and organisers enjoyed front-row seating at this veteran amphitheatre, home to gladiatorial battles and the odd riot. The parapet circling the stadium featured paintings of combat, victory celebrations and hunting scenes.

Teatro Grande   ARCHAEOLOGICAL SITE

The 2nd-century-BC Teatro Grande was a huge 5000-seat theatre carved into the lava mass on which Pompeii was originally built. The site hosts the annual **Pompeii Theatrum Mundi** (www.teatrostabilenapoli.it/pompeii-theatrum-mundi; ⊙ Jun-Jul), a summer season of classical theatre.

Quadriportico dei Teatri   ARCHAEOLOGICAL SITE

Behind the Teatro Grande's stage, the porticoed Quadriportico dei Teatri was initially used as a place for the audience to stroll between acts and later as a barracks for gladiators.

Teatro Piccolo   ARCHAEOLOGICAL SITE

(Odeon) The Teatro Piccolo was once an indoor theatre renowned for its acoustics.

Casa della Venere
in Conchiglia   ARCHAEOLOGICAL SITE

(House of the Venus Marina, House of Venus in a Shell) Casa della Venere in Conchiglia harbours a lovely peristyle looking onto a small, manicured garden. It's here in the garden that you'll find the large, striking Venus fresco, after which the house is named. Venus – whose hairstyle in this depiction reflects the style popular during Emperor Nero's reign – was the patron goddess of the city.

Palestra Grande   ARCHAEOLOGICAL SITE

Lithe ancients kept fit at the Palestra Grande, an athletics field with an impressive portico dating from the Augustan period. Used both as a training ground for gladiators and as a meeting centre for youth associations, its huge, portico-flanked courtyard includes the remains of a swimming pool. The site is now used to host temporary exhibitions.

Antiquarium   MUSEUM

Pompeii's small museum hosts rotating exhibitions showcasing the site's archaeological finds and exploring various aspects of ancient Roman culture. The space also includes an impressive multimedia presentation that digitally reconstructs a number of ancient Pompeii's buildings, making it a helpful stop before roaming the ruins themselves.

🛏 Sleeping & Eating

Although the town of Pompeii has a number of mainly nondescript hotels, you're better off basing yourself in Sorrento or Naples and exploring the ruins as an easy day trip.

★President   CAMPANIAN €€€

(✆081 850 72 45; www.ristorantepresident.it; Piazza Schettini 12; meals €80, tasting menus €80-

120; ⊙noon-3.30pm & 7pm-late Tue-Sun; ☒FS to Pompei, Circumvesuviana to Pompei Scavi–Villa dei Misteri) At the helm of this Michelin-starred standout is charming owner-chef Paolo Gramaglia, whose passion for local produce, history and culinary whimsy translates into bread made to ancient Roman recipes, yellowtail carpaccio with bitter orange and citrus zest, lemon emulsion and buffalo mozzarella, or impeccably glazed duck breast lifted by vinegar cherries, orange sauce and nasturtium. The menu's creative and visual brilliance is matched by sommelier Laila Buondonno's swoon-inducing wine list, which features around 600 drops from esteemed and lesser-known Italian winemakers; best of all, the staff are happy to serve any bottle to the value of €100 by the glass.

Note: if you plan on catching a *treno regionale* (regional train) back to Naples from nearby Pompei station (a more convenient option than the Pompei Scavi–Villa dei Misteri station on the Circumvesuviana train line), check train times first as the last service from Pompei can depart as early as 9.53pm.

ℹ Getting There & Away

To reach the *scavi* (ruins) by **Circumvesuviana** (✆800 211388; www.eavsrl.it) train (€2.80 from Naples, 36 minutes; €2.40 from Sorrento, 30 minutes), alight at Pompei Scavi–Villa dei Misteri station, located beside the main entrance at Porta Marina. Regional trains (www.trenitalia.com) stop at Pompei station in the centre of the modern town.

From mid-March to mid-October, tourist train *Campania Express* runs four times daily between Naples (Porta Nolana and Piazza Garibaldi Circumvesuviana stations) and Sorrento, stopping at Ercolano–Scavi, Torre Annunziata (Oplontis), Pompei Scavi–Villa dei Misteri, Castellammare and Vico Equense en route. One-day return tickets from Naples to Pompeii (€11, 29 minutes) or from Sorrento to Pompeii (€7, 24 minutes) can be purchased at the stations or online at **EAV** (✆800 211388; www.eavsrl.it).

If driving from Naples, head southeast on the A3, using the Pompei exit and following the signs to Pompei Scavi. Car parks are clearly marked and vigorously touted. Close to the ruins, **Camping Spartacus** (✆081 862 40 78; www.campingspartacus.it; Via Plinio 127; adult/child per night €7.50/4, car/camper/caravan €5/10/12; 📶 ☒) offers good-value, all-day parking (€5). This is a much cheaper option than the main car park located directly north of the Circumvesuviana train station.

From Sorrento, head north along the SS145, which connects to the A3 and Pompeii.

Sorrento

081 / POP 16,400

A small resort with a big reputation, Sorrento is a town of lemons, high-pedigree hotels and plunging cliffs that cut through the heart of the historical core.

The town's longstanding popularity stems from its location at the western gateway to the Amalfi. It's also on the train line to Pompeii and has regular fast-ferry connections to Naples and Capri.

Tourism has a long history here. It was a compulsory stop on the 19th-century 'Grand Tour' and interest in the town was first sparked by the poet Byron, who inspired a long line of holidaying literary geniuses – including Goethe, Dickens and Tolstoy – to sample the Sorrentine air. The romance persists. Wander through Piazza Tasso on any given Sunday and you'll be exposed to one of Italy's finer *passeggiate* (strolls), snaking past palatial hotels, magnificent marquetry shops and simple Campanian restaurants serving *gnocchi alla sorrentina* finished off with a shot of ice-cold *limoncello*.

Sights

Museo Correale di Terranova MUSEUM
(081 878 18 46; www.museocorreale.it; Via Correale 50; adult/reduced €8/5; 9.30am-6.30pm Mon-Sat, to 1.30pm Sat) East of the city centre, this wide-ranging museum is well worth a visit whether you're a clock collector, an archaeological egghead or into delicate ceramics. In addition to the rich assortment of 16th- to 19th-century Neapolitan arts and crafts (including extraordinary examples of marquetry), you'll discover Japanese, Chinese and European ceramics, clocks, fans and, on the ground floor, ancient and medieval artefacts. Among these is a fragment of an ancient Egyptian carving uncovered in the vicinity of Sorrento's **Sedile Dominova** (Via San Cesareo).

**Chiesa & Chiostro
di San Francesco** CHURCH
(081 878 12 69; Via San Francesco; 7am-7pm) Located next to the Villa Comunale Park, this church is best known for the peaceful 14th-century cloister abutting it, which is accessible via a small door from the church. The courtyard features an Arabic portico and interlaced arches supported by octagonal pillars. Replete with bougainvillea and birdsong, they're built on the ruins of a 7th-century monastery. Upstairs in the

Sorrento International Photo School, the **Gallery Celentano** (344 0838503; www.raffaelecelentano.com; adult/reduced €3.50/free; 10am-9pm Mar-Dec) exhibits black-and-white photographs of Italian life and landscapes by contemporary local photographer Raffaele Celentano. The cloisters host classical-music concerts in the summer.

**Museo Bottega
della Tarsia Lignea** MUSEUM
(081 877 19 42; Via San Nicola 28; adult/reduced €8/5; 10am-6.30pm Apr-Oct, to 5pm Nov-Mar) Since the 18th century, Sorrento has been famous for its *intarsio* (marquetry) furniture, made with elaborately designed inlaid wood. Some wonderful historical examples can be found in this museum, many of them etched in the once fashionable picaresque style. The museum, housed in an 18th-century palace complete with beautiful frescoes, also has an interesting collection of paintings, prints and photographs depicting the town and the surrounding area in the 19th century.

Duomo CATHEDRAL
(081 878 22 48; Corso Italia; 8am-12.30pm & 4.30-9pm) Sorrento's cathedral features a striking exterior fresco, a triple-tiered bell tower, four classical columns and an elegant majolica clock. Inside, take note of the marble bishop's throne (1573), as well as both the wooden choir stalls and stations of the cross, decorated in the local *intarsio* (marquetry) style. Although the cathedral's original structure dates from the 15th century, the building has been altered several times, most recently in the early 20th century when the current facade was added.

Activities

Nautica Sic Sic BOATING
(081 807 22 83; www.nauticasicsic.com; Via Marina Piccola 43, Marina Piccola; Apr-Oct) Seek out the best beaches by rented boat, with or without a skipper. This outfit rents a variety of motor boats, starting at around €50 per hour or from €150 per day plus fuel. It also organises boat excursions and wedding shoots.

Bagni Regina Giovanna SWIMMING
Sorrento lacks a decent beach, so consider heading to Bagni Regina Giovanna, a rocky beach with clear, clean water about 2km west of town, amid the ruins of the Roman Villa Pollio Felix. It's possible to walk here (follow Via Capo), but wear good shoes as it's a bit of a scramble. Alternatively, you can

Sorrento

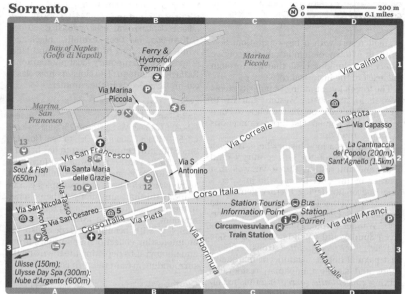

Sorrento

◎ Sights

1 Chiesa & Chiostro di San
    Francesco A2
2 Duomo A3
  Gallery Celentano .... (see 1)
3 Museo Bottega della Tarsia Lignea A3
4 Museo Correale di Terranova D1
5 Sedile Dominova B3

◎ Activities, Courses & Tours

6 Nautica Sic Sic B1

◎ Sleeping

7 Casa Astarita A3
8 Palazzo Marziale A2

◎ Eating

9 Acqu' e Sale B2

◎ Drinking & Nightlife

10 Bollicine A2
11 Cafè Latino A3
12 D'Anton B2
13 La Pergola A2

take the SITA Sud bus headed for Massa Lubrense to save your strength.

Ulysse Day Spa SPA

(☑ 081 807 35 81; www.spaulysse.it; Via del Mare 22; ⊙ baths 11am-10pm Mon, Wed & Fri, 3-10pm Tue & Thu, 11am-8pm Sat, 10am-7pm Sun, massage centre 9am-8pm Mon-Sat, 10am-7pm Sun) Ischia might be the spa capital of Campania, but Sorrento gets its oar in with the Ulysse where you can unwind in the spa (€25) or rev up in the gym (€10). There's also a long massage and beauty menu (extra cost). Spa facilities include an indoor pool and a jacuzzi, plus a cave-like Turkish bath and a chill-out lounge. The centre shares digs with deluxe hostel Ulisse.

★ Festivals & Events

Settimana Santa RELIGIOUS

(Holy Week) Famed throughout Italy; the first procession takes place at midnight on the Thursday preceding Good Friday, with robed and hooded penitents in white; the second occurs on Good Friday, when participants wear black robes and hoods to commemorate the death of Christ.

Sant'Antonino RELIGIOUS

(⊙ 14 Feb) The city's patron saint, Sant'Antonino, is remembered annually with processions and huge markets. The saint is credited with having saved Sorrento during WWII when Salerno and Naples were heavily bombed.

🛌 Sleeping

Accommodation is thick on the ground in Sorrento, although if you're arriving in high summer (July and August), you'll need to book ahead. Most of the big city-centre hotels are geared towards package tourism and prices are correspondingly high. There are, however, some excellent choices, particularly on Via Capo, the coastal road west of the centre.

Ulisse HOSTEL €

(☎081 877 47 53; www.ulissedeluxe.com; Via del Mare 22; dm from €35, d from €139; P❄🅿🛜💦) Although it calls itself a hostel, the Ulisse is about as far from a backpackers' pad as a hiking boot from a stiletto. Most rooms are plush, spacious affairs with swish if bland fabrics, gleaming floors and large en-suite bathrooms. There are two single-sex dorms, and quads for sharers. Breakfast is included in some rates but costs €10 with others. At the adjacent wellness centre Ulysse Day Spa guests get to use the facilities for a daily rate of €10.

Nube d'Argento CAMPGROUND €

(☎081 878 13 44; www.nubedargento.com; Via Capo 21; camping per 2 people, car & tent €26-42, 2-person bungalows €70-95, 4-person bungalows €100-130; ☺late Mar-early Jan; 🛜💦) Remarkably central for a campground, this sloping affair set in a ravine above the Maria Grande has pitches and wooden chalet-style bungalows spread out beneath a canopy of olive trees – a source of much-needed summer shade – and the facilities are excellent. Kids in particular will enjoy the open-air swimming pool, table-tennis table, slides and swings.

Hotel Cristina HOTEL €€

(☎081 878 35 62; www.hotelcristinasorrento.it; Via Privata Rubinacci 6, Sant'Agnello; d/tr/q from €150/220/240; ☺Mar-Oct; P❄🛜💦) Located high above Sant'Agnello, this hotel has superb views, particularly from the swimming pool. The spacious rooms have sea-view balconies and combine inlaid wooden furniture with contemporary flourishes such as Philippe Starck chairs. There's an in-house restaurant and a free shuttle bus to/from Sorrento's Circumvesuviana train station.

Casa Astarita B&B €€

(☎081 877 49 06; www.casastarita.com; Corso Italia 67; d €90-140, tr €115-165; ❄🛜) Housed in an 18th-century *palazzo* (mansion) on Sorrento's main strip, this charming B&B has a colourful, eclectic look with original vaulted ceilings, brightly painted doors and tiled floors. Its eight rooms are simple but well equipped, with breakfast served on a large rustic table in the B&B's central parlour.

★ Palazzo Marziale BOUTIQUE HOTEL €€€

(☎081 807 44 06; www.palazzomarziale.com; Largo San Francesco 2; d/ste from €220/455; ❄🛜) From cascading vines, Chinese porcelain urns and Persian rugs in the lobby lounge, to antique furniture, *objets* and artworks in the hallways, and inlaid wood in the lift, this sophisticated, 11-room hideaway is big on details. The family's elegant tastes extend to the rooms, resplendent with high ceilings, chaise longues and classy mattresses and linens.

La Tonnarella HOTEL €€€

(☎081 878 11 53; www.latonnarella.com; Via Capo 31; d €160-300, ste €333-410; ☺Apr-Oct & Christmas; P❄🅿🛜) A splendid choice atop a cliff to the west of town, La Tonnarella is a dazzling canvas of majolica tiles, antiques and chandeliers. Rooms, most with their own balcony or small terrace, continue the sumptuous classical theme with traditional furniture and discreet mod cons. The hotel also has its own lift-accessible private beach and a highly regarded terrace restaurant.

🍴 Eating

The centre of town heaves with bars, cafes, trattorias, restaurants and even the odd kebab takeaway shop. Many places, particularly those with waistcoated waiters stationed outside (or eateries displaying sun-bleached photos of the dishes), are tourist traps serving bland food at inflated prices. Don't leave without a dose of *gnocchi alla sorrentina* (gnocchi with tomato sauce and mozzarella).

La Cantinaccia del Popolo NEAPOLITAN €

(☎366 1015497; Vico Terzo Rota 3; meals €21; ☺11am-3pm & 7-11pm Tue-Sun) Festooned with garlic and with cured hams hanging from the ceiling, this down-to-earth favourite proves that top-notch produce and simplicity are the keys to culinary success. A case in point is the *spaghetti al pomodoro*, a basic dish of pasta and tomato that bursts with flavour, vibrancy and balance. For extra authenticity, it's served directly to you in the pan.

La Cantinaccia's also plies its own cured meats and some interesting Campanian cheeses straight out of the glass deli counter.

Acqu' e Sale   NEAPOLITAN €€

(☑ 081 1900 5967; www.acquesale.it; Piazza Marinai D'Italia 2; pizzas from €7, meals €35-40; ⊙ 7am-11.30pm; 🕿) This so-called 'water and salt' restaurant with a dazzling blue-and-white interior is right next to the ferry terminal. Seafood here is worth getting excited about and it also offers fine Neapolitan-style pizzas with a creative choice of bases, including a very local lemon-flavoured option (*al limone*).

With its generous opening times and proximity to the port, Acqu' e Sale is a good place to catch a last-minute breakfast before heading across the water.

Soul & Fish   SEAFOOD €€

(☑ 081 878 21 70; www.soulandfish.com; Via Marina Grande 202; meals €38-46; ⊙ noon-2.30pm & 7-10.30pm, closed Nov-Easter; 🕿) Soul & Fish has a hipper vibe than Marina Grande's no-nonsense seafood restaurants. Your bread comes in a bag, your dessert might come in a Kilner jar and your freshly grilled fish with a waiter ready to slice it up before your eyes. The decor is more chic beach shack than sea-shanty dive bar, with wooden decks, director chairs and puffy cushions.

🍷 Drinking & Nightlife

⭐ D'Anton   LOUNGE

(☑ 333 1543706; Piazza Sant'Antonio 3/4; ⊙ 10am-11pm mid-Mar–early Jan, to 1.30am summer; 🕿) Welcome to a new and very Italian concept: a cocktail bar doubling up as an interior-design store. That elegant sofa you're sipping a negroni on is for sale. So is that glistening chandelier and that enchanting mirror. Add them to your drinks bill if you're feeling flush, or just admire the candelabras and lampshades over savoury *antipasti* and wicked chocolate-and-almond cake.

Bollicine   WINE BAR

(☑ 081 878 46 16; Via Accademia 9; ⊙ 6pm-late Mar-Nov; 🕿) The wine list at this unpretentious bar with a dark, woody interior includes all the big Italian names and a selection of interesting local labels. If you can't decide what to go for, the amiable bar staff will advise you. There's also a small menu of *panini* (sandwiches), bruschettas and one or two pasta dishes.

Cafè Latino   BAR

(☑ 081 877 37 18; www.cafelatinosorrento.it; Vico Fuoro 4a; ⊙ 10am-1am Easter-Oct; 🕿) Think locked-eyes-over-cocktails time. This is the

place to impress your date with cocktails (€8) on the candlelit terrace, surrounded by orange, lemon and banana trees. Sip a spicy Hulk (vodka, grapefruit, sugar cane and jalapeño) or a glass of chilled white wine. If you can't drag yourselves away, you can also eat here (pizzas from €7, meals around €40).

La Pergola   BAR

(☑ 081 878 10 24; www.bellevue.it; Hotel Bellevue Syrene, Piazza della Vittoria 5; ⊙ 10.30am-11pm) When love is in the air, put on your best Italian shoes and head for a predinner libation at the Hotel Bellevue Syrene's swoon-inducing terrace bar–restaurant. With its commanding clifftop view across the Bay of Naples towards Mt Vesuvius, it never fails to glam up an otherwise ordinary evening.

ℹ Information

Main Tourist Office (☑ 081 807 40 33; www.sorrentotourism.com; Via Luigi de Maio 35; ⊙ 9am-7pm Mon-Sat, to 1pm Sun Jun-Oct, 9am-4pm Mon-Fri, to 1pm Sat Nov-May; 🕿) In the Circolo dei Forestieri (Foreigners' Club); lists ferry and train times. Ask for the useful publication *Surrentum*, published monthly from March to October.

Post Office (www.poste.it; Corso Italia 210; ⊙ 8.20am-7pm Mon-Fri, to 12.30pm Sat) Just north of the train station.

ℹ Getting There & Away

BOAT

Sorrento is the main jumping-off point for Capri and also has ferry connections to Naples and Amalfi coastal resorts during the summer months from its **ferry and hydrofoil terminal** (Via Luigi de Maio).

Caremar (☑ 081 807 30 77; www.caremar.it) Runs fast ferries to Capri (€14.40, 25 minutes, four daily).

Alilauro (☑ 081 807 18 12; www.alilauro.it) Runs year-round hydrofoils to Naples (€13, 20 minutes, up to six daily) and Capri (€20.50, 20 minutes, up to 13 daily), as well as seasonal services to Ischia (€23, one hour, two to three daily), Positano (€20, 30 minutes, two daily) and Amalfi (€21, 50 minutes, two daily).

BUS

SITA Sud (www.sitasudtrasporti.it) buses serve Naples, the Amalfi Coast and Sant'Agata, leaving from the **bus station** (Piazza Giovanna Battista de Curtis) across from the entrance to the Circumvesuviana train station. Buy tickets at the station or from shops bearing the blue SITA sign.

TRAIN

Sorrento is the last stop on the **Circumvesuviana** (☑ 800 211388; www.eavsrl.it) line from Naples. Trains run every 30 minutes for Naples (€3.90, 70 minutes), via Pompeii (€2.40, 30 minutes) and Ercolano (€2.90, 50 minutes).

THE ISLANDS

Capri

☑ 081 / POP 14,120

Capri is beautiful – seriously beautiful. There's barely a grubby building or untended garden to blemish the splendour. Steep cliffs rise majestically from an impossibly blue sea; elegant villas drip with wisteria and bougainvillea; even the trees seem to be carefully manicured.

Long a preserve of celebrities and the super-rich, this small, precipitous island off the west end of the Sorrento Peninsula has a tangible deluxe feel. Your credit card can get a lot of exercise in its expensive restaurants and museum-quality jewellery shops – a cappuccino alone can cost €7. But, regardless of this, Capri is worth visiting, whatever your budget. Glide silently up craggy Monte Solaro on a chairlift. Relive erstwhile poetic glories in Villa Lysis. Find a quiet space in the sinuous lanes of Anacapri. In the process, you'll enjoy some sublime moments.

⊙ Sights

⊙ Capri Town & Around

With its whitewashed stone buildings and tiny, car-free streets, Capri Town exudes a cinematic air. A diminutive model of upmarket Mediterranean chic, it's a well-tended playground of luxury hotels, expensive bars, smart restaurants and high-end boutiques. In summer the centre swells with crowds of camera-wielding day trippers and yacht-owning playboys (and girls), but don't be put off from exploring the atmospheric and ancient side streets, where the crowds quickly thin. The walk east out of town to Villa Jovis is especially wonderful.

★ **Villa Jovis**   RUINS

(Jupiter's Villa; Via A Maiuri; adult/reduced €6/4; ⊙10am-7pm Jun-Sep, to 6pm Apr, May & Oct, to 4pm Mar, Nov & Dec, closed Jan & Feb) Villa Jovis was the largest and most sumptuous of 12

Roman villas commissioned by Roman Emperor Tiberius (AD14–37) on Capri, and his main island residence. This vast complex, now reduced to ruins, famously pandered to the emperor's supposedly debauched tastes, and included imperial quarters and extensive bathing areas set in dense gardens and woodland. It's located a 45-minute walk east of Capri Town along Via Tiberio.

The villa's spectacular location posed major headaches for Tiberius' architects. The main problem was how to collect and store enough water to supply the villa's baths and 3000-sq-metre gardens. The solution they eventually hit upon was to build a complex canal system to transport rainwater to four giant storage tanks, whose remains you can still see today.

Beside the ticket office, which closes 45 minutes before site closing time, is the 330m-high Salto di Tiberio (Tiberius' Leap), a sheer cliff from where, as the story goes, Tiberius had out-of-favour subjects hurled into the sea. True or not, the stunning views are real enough; if you suffer from vertigo, tread carefully.

★ **Villa Lysis**   HISTORIC BUILDING

(www.villalysiscapri.com; Via Lo Capo 12; €2; ⊙10am-7pm Thu-Tue Jun-Aug, to 6pm Apr, May, Sep & Oct, to 4pm Nov & Dec) This beautifully melancholic art-nouveau villa is set on a clifftop on Capri's northeast tip and was the one-time retreat of French poet Jacques d'Adelswärd-Fersen, who came to Capri in 1904 to escape a gay sex scandal in Paris. Unlike other stately homes, the interior has been left almost entirely empty; this is a place to let your imagination flesh out the details. It's a 40-minute walk from Piazza Umberto I and rarely crowded.

One notable curiosity is the 'Chinese room' in the basement, which includes a semicircular opium den with a swastika emblazoned on the floor. Fersen became addicted to opium following a visit to Ceylon in the early 1900s; the swastika is the Sanskrit symbol for well-being. Equally transfixing is the sun-dappled garden, a triumph of classical grandiosity half given over to nature.

The €2 entry fee includes an explanatory pamphlet available in Italian and English. Afterwards, it is possible to take a steep, winding path, the Sentiero delle Calanche, to Villa Jovis (20 minutes away).

Fersen's scandal-plagued life ended in 1923 with a lethal cocaine-champagne cocktail.

Capri

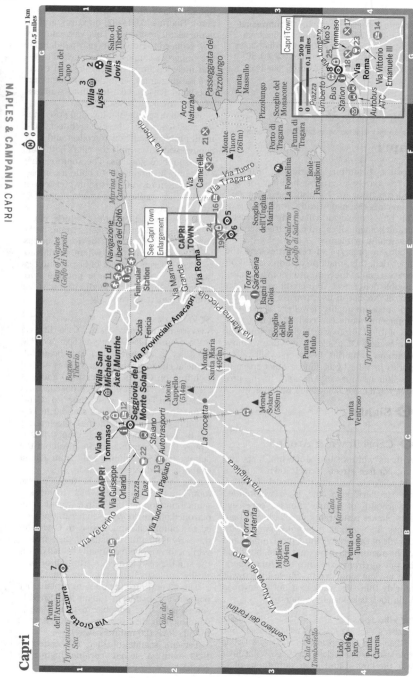

Capri

Giardini di Augusto　　　　　　GARDENS
(Gardens of Augustus; €1; ⊙9am-7.30pm summer, reduced hours rest of year) As their name suggests, these gardens near the Certosa di San Giacomo were founded by Emperor Augustus. Rising in a series of flowered terraces, they lead to a lookout point offering breathtaking views over to the Isole Faraglioni, a group of three limestone stacks rising out of the sea.

From the gardens, pretty, hairpin Via Krupp winds down to Marina Piccola and past a bust of Vladimir Lenin overlooking the road from a nearby platform. The Russian revolutionary visited Capri in 1908, during which time he was famously snapped engaged in a game of chess with fellow revolutionary Alexander Bogdanov. Looking on in the photograph is Russian writer Maxim Gorky, who called the island home between 1906 and 1909.

Certosa di San Giacomo　　　MONASTERY
(⊠081 837 62 18; Viale Certosa 40; adult/reduced €6/2; ⊙10am-6pm Tue-Sun Apr-Sep, to 3pm Oct-Mar) Founded in 1363, this substantial monastery is generally considered to be the finest remaining example of Caprese architecture and today houses a school, a library, a temporary exhibition space and a museum with some evocative 17th-century paintings. Be sure to look at the cloisters, which have a real sense of faded glory (the smaller is 14th-century, the larger 16th-century).

To get here take Via Vittorio Emanuele III, east of Piazza Umberto I, which meanders down to the monastery.

The monastery's history is a harrowing one: it became the stronghold of the island's powerful Carthusian fraternity and was viciously attacked during Saracen pirate raids in the 16th century. A century later, monks retreated here to avoid the plague and were rewarded by an irate public (whom they should have been tending), who tossed corpses over the walls. There are some soothing 17th-century frescoes in the church, which will hopefully serve as an antidote as you contemplate the monastery's dark past.

Piazza Umberto I　　　　　　　PIAZZA
Located beneath the 17th-century clock tower and framed by see-and-be-seen cafes, this showy, open-air salon is central to your Capri experience, especially in the evening when the main activity in these parts is dressing up and hanging out. Be prepared for the cost of the front-row seats – the moment you sit down for a drink, you're going to pay handsomely for the grandstand views (around €7 for a cappuccino and €18 for a couple of glasses of white wine).

⦿ Anacapri & Around

Traditionally Capri Town's more subdued neighbour, Anacapri is no stranger to tourism. The focus is largely limited to Villa San Michele di Axel Munthe and the souvenir shops on the main streets. Delve further, though, and you'll discover that Anacapri is still, at heart, the laid-back, rural village that it's always been.

★ **Seggiovia del Monte Solaro**   CABLE CAR

(☑ 081 837 14 38; www.capriseggiovia.it; Via Capsocurò; single/return €8/11; ⊕ 9.30am-5pm May-Oct, 9am-4pm Mar & Apr, to 3.30pm Nov-Feb) Sitting in an old-fashioned chairlift above the white houses, terraced gardens and hazy hillsides of Anacapri as you rise to the top of Capri's highest mountain, the silence broken only by a distant dog barking or your own sighs of contentment, has to be one of the island's most sublime experiences. The ride takes an all-too-short 13 minutes, but when you get there, the views, framed by dismembered classical statues, are outstanding.

★ **Villa San Michele di Axel Munthe**   MUSEUM, GARDENS

(☑ 081 837 14 01; www.villasanmichele.eu; Via Axel Munthe 34; €8; ⊕ 9am-6pm May-Sep, reduced hours rest of year) The former home of Swedish doctor, psychiatrist and animal-rights advocate Axel Munthe, San Michele di Axel Munthe should be included on every visitor's itinerary. Built on the site of the ruins of a Roman villa, the gardens make a beautiful setting for a tranquil stroll, with pathways flanked by immaculate flowerbeds. There are also superb views from here, plus some fine photo props in the form of Roman sculptures.

🏃 Activities

Banana Sport   BOATING

(☑ 348 5949665; Marina Grande; 2hr/day rental 5-person boat €80/220; ⊕ May–mid-Oct) Located on the eastern edge of the waterfront, Banana Sport hires out five-person motorised dinghies, allowing you to explore secluded coves and grottoes. You can also visit the popular swimming spot **Bagno di Tiberio** (€10), a small inlet west of Marina Grande; it's said that Tiberius once swam here.

★ **Capri Whales**   BOATING

(☑ 081 837 58 33; www.capriwhales.it; Marina Grande 17; 2hr private boat tours from per boat €150, day trip to Positano from €650, boat hire 2hr/full day €100/250, children under 6yr free; ⊕ year-round; 🚗) A congenial business based on the main quay offering guided boat tours

---

DON'T MISS

GROTTA AZZURRA

Capri's most famous attraction is the Grotta Azzurra (Blue Grotto; €14; ⊕ 9am-5pm), an unusual sea cave illuminated by an otherworldly blue light. The easiest way to visit is to take a boat tour (☑ 081 837 56 46; www.motoscafisticapri.com; Private Pier 0; Grotta Azzurra/island trip €15/€18) from Marina Grande; tickets include the return boat trip, but the rowing boat into the cave and admission are paid separately. Beautiful though it is, the Grotta is extremely popular in the summer. The crowds, coupled with long waiting times and tip-hungry guides, can make the experience underwhelming for some.

The grotto had long been known to local fisherfolk when it was rediscovered by two Germans – writer August Kopisch and painter Ernst Fries – in 1826. Subsequent research revealed that Emperor Tiberius had built a quay in the cave around AD 30, complete with a *nymphaeum* (shrine to the water nymph). Remarkably, you can still see the carved Roman landing stage towards the rear of the cave.

Measuring 54m by 30m and rising to a height of 15m, the grotto is said to have sunk by up to 20m in prehistoric times, blocking every opening except the 1.3m-high entrance. And this is the key to the magical blue light. Sunlight enters through a small underwater aperture and is refracted through the water; this, combined with the reflection of the light off the white sandy seafloor, produces the vivid blue effect to which the cave owes its name.

The Grotta can also be accessed from land. Take a bus from Marina Grande to Anacapri and then another bus to the road's end at Grotta Azzurra. From here, a staircase leads down to a small dock where rowing boats await to take passengers into the adjacent cave.

Bear in mind that the time actually spent in the Grotta during a tour amounts to 10 minutes maximum. The singing row-boat 'captains' are included in the price, so don't feel any obligation if they push for a tip.

The grotto is closed if the sea is too choppy and swimming in it is forbidden, although you can swim outside the entrance.

of the island as well as longer full-day trips to Positano. Alternatively, you can hire your own boat for three hours or a full day. Trips are family-friendly, with a child life vest and water toys provided.

🛏 Sleeping

You can't fully discover Capri in one day; stay the night and you'll see the island in a different light. Accommodation is strictly seasonal, which means bed space is tight and, in general, costly – although there are a few relative bargains to be had, mainly in Anacapri. At the top end of the market, you'll find some of Italy's most opulent hotels. Book well ahead in the summer.

⭐ Casa Mariantonia BOUTIQUE HOTEL €€
(☑ 081 837 29 23; www.casamariantonia.com; Via Orlandi 80, Anacapri; d €120-300; ⊙ late Mar-Oct; P ❄ 🛜 🏊) A family-run boutique hotel with a history (*limoncello di Capri* was supposedly invented here), boasting nine fabulous rooms, a giant swimming pool, a prestigious restaurant and a heavyweight list of former guests – philosopher Jean-Paul Sartre among them. If the tranquillity, lemon groves and personal *pensione* feel doesn't sooth your existential angst, nothing will.

Hotel Villa Eva HOTEL €€
(☑ 081 837 15 49; www.villaeva.com; Via La Fabbrica 8, Anacapri; d €120-200, tr €150-220, apt per person €60-90; ⊙ Apr-Oct; ❄ @ 🛜 🏊) Villa Eva is all about the garden, which is lush and immense. This is about as bucolic as it gets in Capri. The 10-room villa is fairly self-contained, with a swimming pool, a snack bar, and sunny rooms and apartments. Whitewashed domes, terracotta floors, stained-glass windows and vintage fireplaces add character, while the location ensures peace and quiet.

⭐ Capri Palace HOTEL €€€
(☑ 081 978 01 11; www.capripalace.com; Via Capodimonte 2b, Anacapri; d/ste from €410/1070; ⊙ mid-Apr–mid-Oct; ❄ 🛜 🏊) This really lives up to the 'palace' in its name – a regal mix of chicness, opulence and unashamed luxury that takes the concept of *la dolce vita* to dizzying heights. Lily-white communal areas set the scene for the lavish guestrooms – some even have their own terraced garden and private plunge pool with Warhol-esque motifs decorating the tiles.

⭐ La Minerva BOUTIQUE HOTEL €€€
(☑ 081 837 70 67; www.laminervacapri.com; Via Occhio Marino 8, Capri Town; d €190-650; ⊙ late Mar-early Nov; ❄ 🛜 🏊) This gleaming establishment is a model of Capri style and considered by many to be one of the best hotels in Italy. The 19 rooms, which cascade down the hillside, feature ravishing blue and white ceramic tiles, silk drapes and cool 100% linen sheets, while terraces come with sun loungers, jacuzzis and obligatory sea views.

And then there's the gorgeous pool, surrounded by a veritable arboretum of trees, as well as the genteel lobby bar with its unique cocktails, and the general pinch-yourself atmosphere of pure bliss.

Room prices start at €190 and head north, but there's one single room (€100 to €140) and a cheaper double (from €140) available without views.

Grand Hotel Quisisana HOTEL €€€
(☑ 081 837 07 88; www.quisisana.com; Via Camerelle 2, Capri Town; r from €360; ⊙ Apr–mid-Oct; ❄ 🛜 🏊) The Quisisana is Capri's most prestigious address, just a few espadrille-clad steps from Piazza Umberto I. A slumber palace since the 19th century, it's a bastion of unashamed opulence, with two swimming pools, a fitness centre and spa, restaurants, bars and subtropical gardens. Rooms are suitably palatial, with off-white colour schemes and mostly classic, conservative furniture.

🍴 Eating

Traditional Campanian food served in traditional trattorias is what you'll mainly find on Capri. Prices are high but drop noticeably the further you get from Capri Town. The island's culinary gift to the world is *insalata caprese,* a salad of fresh tomatoes, basil and silky mozzarella drizzled with olive oil.

Many restaurants, like hotels, close over winter and reopen at Easter.

Gelateria Buonacore FAST FOOD €
(☑ 081 837 78 26; Via Vittorio Emanuele III 35, Capri Town; snacks €2-10, gelato from €2.50; ⊙ 8am-midnight Jul-Sep, reduced hours rest of year, closed Tue Oct-Jun; 🚸) Ideal for quick takeaways, this popular, down-to-earth snack bar does a roaring trade in savoury and sweet treats. Hit the spot with *panini* (sandwiches), stuffed peppers, waffles and the legendary ice cream. Hard to beat, though, are the delicate but filling *sfogliatelle*

(cinnamon-infused ricotta in a puff-pastry shell; €2.50) and the feather-light speciality *caprilu al limone* (lemon and almond cakes).

★ La Palette
ITALIAN €€
(📞 081 837 72 83; www.lapalette.it; Via Matermània 36; meals from €35; ⏰ 11am-midnight Apr-early Nov) Local Caprese ingredients are combined into the most flavour-filled, creative dishes possible here. Expect the delights of zucchini flowers stuffed with ricotta, fresh and tangy octopus salad, and an aubergine *parmigiana* that seems to taste so much better than everyone else's. An easy 10-minute walk from Capri Town, it has swooningly romantic bay views.

★ È Divino
ITALIAN €€
(📞 081 837 83 64; www.edivinocapri.com/divino; Via Sella Orta 10a, Capri Town; meals €33-48; ⏰ 8pm-1am daily Jun-Aug, 12.30-2.30pm & 7.30pm-midnight Tue-Sun rest of year; 📶) Proudly eccentric (what other restaurant has a bed in its dining room?), this diligent purveyor of Slow Food is a precious secret to those who know it. Whether dining among lemon trees in the garden or among antiques, chandeliers and contemporary art (and that bed!) inside, expect a thoughtful, regularly changing menu dictated by what's fresh from the garden and market.

Le Grottelle
ITALIAN €€
(📞 081 837 57 19; Via Arco Naturale 13; meals €30-40; ⏰ noon-2.30pm & 7-11pm Fri-Wed summer, noon-3pm Fri-Wed Apr, May & Oct, closed Nov-Mar; 📶) This is a great place to impress someone – not so much for the food, which is decent enough, but for the dramatic setting: its two dining areas are set in a cave and on a hillside terrace with sea views. Dishes are rustic, from homemade *fusilli* pasta with shrimps and courgettes to rabbit with onions, garlic and rosemary.

★ Il Geranio
SEAFOOD €€€
(📞 081 837 06 16; www.geraniocapri.com; Via Matteotti 8, Capri Town; meals €45-50; ⏰ noon-3pm & 7-11pm mid-Apr–mid-Oct) Time to pop the question or quell those predeparture blues? The terrace at this sophisticated spot offers heart-stealing views over the pine trees to Isole Faraglioni. Seafood is the speciality, particularly the salt-baked fish. Other fine choices include octopus salad and linguine with saffron and mussels. Book at least three days ahead for a terrace table in high season.

🍷 Drinking & Nightlife

Taverna Anema e Core
CLUB
(📞 329 4742508; www.anemaecore.com; Via Sella Orta 39e, Capri Town; ⏰ 11pm-late Jun-Aug, closed Wed Apr, May, Sep & Oct, closed rest of year) Behind a humble exterior is one of the island's most famous nightspots, run by the charismatic Guido Lembo. This smooth and sophisticated bar-club attracts an appealing mix of superchic and casually dressed punters, here for the relaxed atmosphere and regular live music, including unwaveringly authentic Neapolitan guitar strumming and singing.

Caffè Michelangelo
CAFE
(📞 333 7784331; Via Orlandi 138, Anacapri; ⏰ 8am-2am Jul & Aug, to 1am Sep-Jun, closed Thu Nov & Dec; 📶) On a street flanked by tasteful shops and near two lovely piazzas, this is the best place in Anacapri to park your gluteus maximus for a bit of tourist-watching. Rate the passing parade over a *spritz con Cynar*, a less-sweet take on the classic Aperol *spritz*, made using a herbacious Italian bitter liqueur. It also does wine by the glass.

🛍 Shopping

★ La Parisienne
FASHION & ACCESSORIES
(📞 081 837 02 83; www.laparisiennecapri.it; Piazza Umberto I 7, Capri Town; ⏰ 9am-10pm) First opened in 1906 (yes, that is not a misprint!) and best known for introducing Capri pants in the 1960s – famously worn by Audrey Hepburn, who bought them here – La Parisienne can run you up a made-to-measure pair within a day. It also sells off-the-hook Capri pants (from €250).

Jackie O was a customer, and Clark Gable apparently favoured the fashions here, particularly the Bermuda shorts, which (believe it or not) were considered quite raffish in their day.

Limoncello Capri Canale Massimo
DRINKS
(📞 081 837 29 27; www.limoncello.com; Via Capodimonte 27, Anacapri; ⏰ 9am-7.30pm, closed mid-Jan–mid-Feb) Don't be put off by the gaudy yellow display: this historic shop stocks some of the island's best *limoncello*. In fact, it was here that the drink was first concocted (or at least that is the claim). Apparently, the grandmother of current owner Massimo made the tot as an after-dinner treat for the guests in her small guesthouse.

Carthusia I Profumi di Capri   COSMETICS
(🖉 081 837 53 93; www.carthusia.it; Via Matteotti
2d, Capri Town; ⊙ 9am-8pm Apr-Sep, to 5pm rest
of year) Allegedly, Capri's famous floral perfume was established in 1380 by the prior
of the Certosa di San Giacomo. Caught un-
awares by a royal visit, he displayed the island's most beautiful flowers for the queen.
Changing the water in the vase, he discovered a floral scent. This became the base of
the classic perfume now sold at this smart
laboratory outlet.

ℹ Information

Post Office (www.poste.it; Via Roma 50, Capri
Town; ⊙ 8.20am-7pm Mon-Fri, to 12.30pm Sat;
🖥) Located just west of the bus terminal.

Tourist Office (🖉 081 837 06 34; www.capri
tourism.com; Banchina del Porto; ⊙ 8.30am-
4.15pm, closed Sat & Sun Jan-Mar & Nov) Can
provide a map of the island, plus accommodation listings, ferry timetables and other useful
information.

ℹ Getting There & Away

The two major ferry routes to Capri are from
Naples and Sorrento, although there are also
seasonal connections with Ischia and the Amalfi
Coast (Amalfi, Positano and Salerno).

Caremar (🖉 081 837 07 00; www.caremar.it;
Marina Grande) Operates hydrofoils and ferries
to/from Naples (€12.50 to €18, 40 minutes to
1¼ hours, up to seven daily) and hydrofoils to/
from Sorrento (€14.40, 25 minutes, four daily).

Navigazione Libera del Golfo (NLG; 🖉 081
552 07 63; www.navlib.it; Marina Grande)
Operates hydrofoils to/from Naples (from €19,
45 minutes, up to nine daily).

SNAV (🖉 081 428 55 55; www.snav.it; Marina
Grande) Operates hydrofoils to/from Naples
(from €22.50, 45 minutes, up to nine daily).

ℹ Getting Around

BUS
Autobus ATC (🖉 081 837 04 20; Bus Station,
Via Roma, Capri Town; tickets €2, day pass
€6) Runs buses between Marina Grande, Capri
Town, Marina Piccola and Anacapri.

Staiano Autotrasporti (🖉 081 837 24 22;
www.staianotourcapri.com; Bus Station, Viale
de Tommaso, Anacapri; tickets €2) Runs
regular buses to the Grotta Azzurra and Punta
Carena *faro* (lighthouse) from Anacapri.

FUNICULAR
Funicular (Via Colombo 18; tickets €2;
⊙ 6.30am-9.30pm) The first challenge facing
visitors is how to get from Marina Grande to
Capri Town. The most enjoyable option is the
funicular, if only for the evocative en-route
views over the lemon groves and surrounding
countryside. The ticket booth in Marina Grande
is not at the funicular station itself; it's behind
the tourist office (turn right onto Via Marina
Grande from the ferry port). Note that the
funicular usually closes from January through
March for maintenance; a substitute bus
service is in place during this period.

SCOOTER
Capri Scooter (🖉 338 3606918, 081 362 00
83; www.capriscooter.com; Via Marina Grande
280, Marina Grande; per 2/24hr €30/65)
If you're looking to hire a scooter at Marina
Grande, stop here. There's another outlet in
Anacapri (🖉 081 837 38 88; www.capriscooter.
com; Piazza Barile 20, Anacapri; per 2/24 hr
€30/65).

TAXI
Taxi (🖉 in Anacapri 081 837 11 75, in Capri
Town 081 837 66 57) From Marina Grande, a
taxi costs from €17 to Capri Town and from €23
to Anacapri; from Capri Town to Anacapri costs
around €18. These rates include one bag per
vehicle. Each additional bag (with dimensions
exceeding 40cm by 20cm by 50cm) costs an
extra €2.

Ischia
🖉 081 / POP 64,110

The volcanic outcrop of Ischia is the most
developed and largest of the islands in the
Bay of Naples. An early colony of Magna
Graecia, first settled in the 8th century BC,
Ischia today is famed for its thermal spas,
manicured gardens, striking Aragonese castle and unshowy, straightforward Italian
airs – a feature also reflected in its food.
Ischia is a refreshing antidote to glitzy Capri.

Most visitors head straight for the north-
coast towns of Ischia Porto, Ischia Ponte,
Forio and Lacco Ameno. Of these, Ischia
Porto boasts the best bars, while Forio and
Lacco Ameno have the prettiest spas and
gardens. On the calmer south coast, the
car-free perfection of Sant'Angelo offers
a languid blend of a cosy harbour and
lazy beaches. In between the coasts lies a
less-trodden landscape of chestnut forests,
vineyards and volcanic rock, loomed over by
Monte Epomeo, Ischia's highest peak.

⦿ Sights

★ **Castello Aragonese**   CASTLE
(Aragon Castle; 🖉 342 9618566, 081 99 28 34; www.
castelloaragoneseischia.com; Rocca del Castello, Ischia Ponte; adult/reduced €10/6; ⊙ 9am-sunset)

ISCHIA'S BEST BEACHES

Spiaggia dei Maronti Long, sandy and very popular; the sand here is warmed by natural steam geysers. Reach the beach by bus from Barano, by water taxi from Sant'Angelo (€3 one way) or on foot along the path leading east from Sant'Angelo.

Baia di San Montano Due west of Lacco Ameno, this gorgeous bay is the place for warm, shallow, crystal-clear waters. You'll also find the Negombo spa park here. Take the bus to Lacco Ameno and walk the last 500m.

Baia di Sorgeto (Via Sorgeto) Not a beach as such, but an intimate cove complete with bubbling thermal spring. Perfect for a winter dip. Catch a water taxi from Sant'Angelo (€5 one way) or get here on foot from the town of Panza.

Spiaggia dei Pescatori (Fishermen's Beach; 📷) Wedged between Ischia Porto and Ischia Ponte is the island's most down-to-earth and popular seaside strip; it's perfect for families. It's accessible by the island's main bus line.

Punta Caruso Located on Ischia's northwestern tip, this secluded rocky spot is perfect for a swim in clear, deep water. To get here, follow the walking path that leads off Via Guardiola down to the beach. Not suitable for children or when seas are rough.

There are castles and then there's Ischia's Castello Aragonese, a veritable fort-city set on its own craggy islet, looking like a cross between Harry Potter's Hogwarts and Mont Saint Michel. While Syracusan tyrant Gerone I built the first fortress here in 474 BC, the bulk of the current structure dates from the 1400s, when King Alfonso of Aragon gave the older Angevin fortress a thorough makeover, building the fortified bastions, current causeway and access ramp cut into the rock.

⭐ **La Mortella**   GARDENS
(Place of the Myrtles; ☎ 081 98 62 20; www.la mortella.it; Via F Calese 39; adult/reduced €12/10; ⏱ 9am-7pm Tue, Thu, Sat & Sun Apr–early Nov) A symphony of plants, La Mortella (the myrtles) is the former home and gardens of the late British composer William Walton (1902–83) and his Argentine wife, Susana. Designed by Russell Page and inspired by the Moorish gardens of Spain's Alhambra, it is recognised as one of Italy's finest botanical gardens. Stroll among terraces, pools, palms, fountains and more than 1000 rare and exotic plants from all over the world.

The lower section of the garden is humid and tropical, while the upper level features Mediterranean plants and beautiful views over Forio and the coast.

The Waltons first came here in 1949 to establish a new home where they subsequently entertained such venerable house guests as Sir Laurence Olivier, Maria Callas and Charlie Chaplin. Walton's life is commem-

orated in a small on-site museum, while his ashes are buried beneath a monument in the garden's upper reaches. The gardens host chamber-music recitals and concerts and there's also a rather elegant cafe where you can enjoy a cup of tea amid the greenery.

Monte Epomeo   MOUNTAIN
To anyone of average fitness, an ascent of Ischia's slumbering volcanic peak is practically obligatory. The views from the rocky summit are superb. And, if that's not enough, a rustic restaurant sheltered beneath a precipitous crag lures hikers with what is possibly the best tomato bruschetta in the viewable vicinity (which, on a clear day, is a long way).

The quickest way to climb Epomeo is from the village of Fontana located on the island's southern flank. The route (signposted from a bend in the road where the bus stops) weaves up a paved road, diverts onto a track and finishes on a steep-ish path. Total distance: 2.5km.

🏊 Activities

⭐ **Negombo**   SPA
(☎ 081 98 61 52; www.negombo.it; Baia di San Montano; all day adult/reduced €35/23, from 3.30pm €23/19; ⏱ 8.30am-7pm mid-Apr–early Oct) This is arguably the best thermal spa on an island full of them, courtesy of its multifaceted attractions. Sure, there are the Zen-like thermal pools, a hammam and private beach, but Negombo is also part of the Grandi Giardini Italiani network, home to more than 500 exotic plant species. Furthermore,

it ranks as an 'art park' with avant-garde sculptures incorporated into the greenery.

Attractive pools (13 of them) are arranged amid floral foliage, plus there's a Japanese labyrinth pool for weary feet, a decent *tavola calda* (snack bar), and a full range of massage and beauty treatments. A private beach on the Baia di San Montano lies out front, meaning Negombo tends to draw a younger crowd than many other Ischian spa spots.

Those arriving by car or scooter can park all day on-site (car/scooter €5/€3).

Ischia Diving   DIVING
(📞 081 99 18 52; www.ischiadiving.net; Via Iasolino 106, Ischia Porto; single dive €40) This well-established diving outfit offers some attractively priced dive packages, such as five dives including equipment for €180.

🛏 Sleeping

Camping Mirage   CAMPGROUND €
(📞 347 3781562; www.campingmirage.it; Via Maronti 37, Spiaggia dei Maronti, Barano d'Ischia; camping 2 people, car & tent €38-46; ⊙ Apr-Oct; 🅿) Located on Spiaggia dei Maronti, one of Ischia's best beaches, and within walking distance of Sant'Angelo, this shady campground offers 50 places, as well as showers, laundry facilities, a bar and a restaurant dishing up local speciality *tubettoni, cozze e pecorino* (pasta with mussels and sheep cheese).

Hotel Noris   HOTEL €
(📞 081 99 13 87; www.norishotel.it; Via Sogliuzzo 2, Ischia Ponte; d €50-150; ⊙ Easter–mid-Oct; 🕸🛜) This place has a great price and a great position within easy strolling distance of the Ponte sights. Comfortable, decent-sized rooms are decked out in blue and white, and breakfast is a generous Continental buffet. If you can, take a front room with a balcony for views towards Procida and partial glimpses of the magnificent Castello Aragonese.

Semiramis Hotel de Charme   HOTEL €€
(📞 081 90 75 11; www.hotelsemiramisischia.it; Via Giovanni Mazzella 236, Forio; d €143-215; ⊙ mid-Apr–mid-Oct; 🅿🕸🛜🛋) A few minutes' walk from the Poseidon spa complex, this bright hotel has a tropical-oasis feel with its outdoor thermal pools surrounded by lofty palms. Rooms are large and beautifully tiled in the traditional yellow-and-turquoise pattern, and the garden is equally glorious, with fig trees, vineyards and sea views.

★ Albergo Il Monastero   HOTEL €€
(📞 081 99 24 35; www.albergoilmonastero.it; Castello Aragonese, Rocca del Castello, Ischia Ponte; s €65-90, d €105-145; ⊙ mid-April–mid-Oct; 🕸🛜) Monastery stays offer some of Italy's best bargains but you know you're onto something really special when the digs are inside Ischia's huge castle. The former monks' cells here still have a certain appealing sobriety about them, with their dark-wood furniture, white walls and vintage terracotta tiles. Elsewhere, the hotel exudes a pleasing sense of space and style.

Relax and enjoy the vaulted ceilings, plush sofas, antiques and contemporary art by the late owner and artist Gabriele Mattera. There are no TVs but the views more than make up for this.

🍴 Eating

★ La Casereccia   CAMPANIAN €€
(📞 081 98 77 56; www.lacasereccia.com; Via Baiola 269; meals €28-40; ⊙ 1-3pm & 7.30pm-1am, closed Mon-Wed Feb) Safe in the hands of Mamma Tina, Casereccia delivers plenty of full-flavoured *casereccia* (homemade food). The very Ischian menu pushes seafood, doughy pizzas, island-produced wine and that much vaunted local speciality – *coniglio* (rabbit). Try it either roasted or packaged in delicate ravioli. It's a little out of town on the flanks of Monte Epomeo, but worth the detour.

★ Il Focolare   ITALIAN €€
(📞 081 90 29 44; www.trattoriailfocolare.it; Via Creajo al Crocefisso 3, Barano d'Ischia; meals €30-35; ⊙ 12.30-2.45pm Thu-Sun & 7.30-11.30pm daily Jun-Oct, closed Wed Nov-May, closed Feb) A good choice for those seeking a little turf instead of surf, this is one of the island's best-loved restaurants. Family run, homely and rustic, it has a solidly traditional meat-based menu with steaks, lamb cutlets and specialities including *coniglio all'Ischitana* (typical local rabbit dish with tomatoes, garlic and herbs). On the sweet front, the desserts are homemade and exquisite.

Owner Riccardo D'Ambra (who runs the restaurant together with his wife, Loretta, and their children) is a leading local advocate of the Slow Food movement. If you want seafood, coffee or soft drinks, you'll have to go elsewhere; they're not on the menu here.

★ Ristorante Pietratorcia   ITALIAN €€
(📞 081 90 72 32; www.ristorantepietratorcia.it; Via Provinciale Panza 401; menus €35, wine

LOCAL KNOWLEDGE

ISCHIA ON A FORK

If you wanted to stick the best parts of Ischian cuisine on a fork, you'd need to make it a big one. The island's insularity and rich volcanic soil have thrown up a rich melange of recipes over the years, many of them subtly different from dishes found elsewhere in Campania.

A popular Ischian starter is *caponata*. Unlike Sicilian *caponata* (made with aubergines), the Ischian dish resembles tomato bruschetta with added tuna and olives. It was originally a poor person's food, made for farmers out in the fields from the leftovers of the previous day's stale bread.

For the main course, there's an enticing choice between land and sea. Classic seafood dishes adhere to a cooking method known as *acqua pazza* (crazy water): white fish poached in a herb-heavy broth with locally grown *pomodorini* (cherry tomatoes), garlic and parsley. Typical local fish include *pesce bandiera* (sailfish), the flat castagna, lampuga and *palamide* (a small tuna). Smaller seafood, such as squid, prawns and anchovies, are best enjoyed fried in a *frittura di parzana* (meaning 'from the trawler') and served simply with lemon.

Plump local *pomodorini* reappear in the most classic of all Ischian dishes, *coniglio all'ischitana*, a rabbit stew cooked on the hob in a large terracotta pot with a sauce of olive oil, unpeeled garlic, tomato, chilli, basil, thyme and white wine. Traditionally, rabbits were caught wild, but by the late 20th century cage-bred rabbits had become standard fare on Ischia. In recent years, in a nod to the Slow Food movement, farmers have started to return to rearing rabbits *di fossa* (semiwild in burrows).

Despite its high population density and limited agricultural terrain, Ischia still supports an estimated 800 hectares of vineyards, most of them terraced on the lower slopes of Monte Epomeo. Wine production in Ischia goes back to the ancient Greeks and the island harbours some of Italy's oldest DOCs. With fish or pasta, try a Forastera or a Biancolella (both whites). With the rich *coniglio all'ischitana* go for a ruby red Piedirosso.

If you've room for dessert, opt for chocolate and almond cake (an import from nearby Capri), helped down with an obligatory ice-cold limoncello.

degustations from €20; 11am-2pm & 5.30pm-midnight Tue-Sun Easter-Oct;) Enjoying a bucolic setting among tumbling vines, wild fig trees and rosemary bushes, this A-list winery is a showcase for Ischian cooking. Tour the old stone cellars, sip a local drop and eye up a competent, seasonal turf-and-surf menu that is led by rabbit, served with pasta or slow-cooked island style with wine and potatoes. Book ahead in high season.

The CD and CS buses stop within metres of the winery's entrance; ask the driver to advise you when to alight.

Montecorvo   ITALIAN €€
(081 99 80 29; www.montecorvo.it; Via Montecorvo 33; meals €30; 7.30pm-midnight daily yr round, 12.30-3pm Sun mid-Sep–mid-Jun, closed Wed Nov-Mar;) Part of the dining room at hillside Montecorvo is tunnelled into a cave, while the verdant terrace offers spectacular sunset views. Owner Giovanni prides himself on the special dishes he makes daily.

There's an emphasis on grilled meat and fish, and an especially popular dish of local rabbit, cooked in a woodfired oven.

ℹ Information

Tourist Office (081 507 42 31; www.info ischiaprocida.it; Via Iasolino 7, Ischia Porto; 9am-2pm & 3-8pm Mon-Sat Apr-Sep, 9am-2pm Mon-Fri Oct-Mar) A slim selection of maps and brochures, next to the ferry port.

ℹ Getting There & Away

Hydrofoils and ferries are the most likely way of getting to the islands. Note that services departing to/from Positano and Amalfi operate solely from around May to September or October. At other times of the year, you will have to catch services from Naples or Sorrento. In Naples, hydrofoils leave from Molo Beverello, with slower ferries leaving from the adjacent Calata Porta Massa. Generally, there is no need to book: just turn up around 35 minutes before departure in case there's a queue.

Ischia's main ferry terminal is in Ischia Porto. However, there are also other smaller terminals in Casamicciola and Forio.

Caremar (☑ 081 98 48 18; www.caremar.it; Via Iasolino) Operates up to six daily hydrofoils from Naples to Ischia Porto (€17.90, 45 minutes) and Procida (€8.70, 20 minutes), as well as ferries.

Alilauro (☑ 081 497 22 42; www.alilauro.it) Operates hydrofoils from Naples to Ischia Porto (€20.10, 50 minutes, up to 12 daily) and up to six hydrofoils daily between Forio and Naples (€21.50). There are also two daily ferries to Sorrento (€22.90, one hour) from Ischia Porto.

SNAV (☑ 081 428 55 55; www.snav.it) Operates hydrofoils from Naples to the Ischian town of Casamicciola (€20.20 to €21.20, one hour, five daily).

ℹ Getting Around

Ischia's main circular highway can get clogged with traffic in the height of summer. This, combined with the penchant the local youth have for overtaking on blind corners and the environmental impact of just too many cars, means that you may want to consider riding the excellent network of buses (cheap!) or hopping in a taxi (not cheap!) to get around. The distance between attractions and the lack of pavements on the busy roads makes walking unappealing.

The island's main **bus station** (cnr Via Iasolino & Via della Foce) is a one-minute walk west of the **ferry and hydrofoil terminal** (Via Iasolino), at Ischia Porto, with buses servicing all other parts of the island.

Procida

☑ 081 / POP 10,465

The Bay of Naples' smallest island is also its best-kept secret. Off the mass-tourist radar, Procida is like the Portofino prototype and is refreshingly real. August aside – when beach-bound mainlanders flock to its shores – its narrow, sun-bleached streets are the domain of the locals: kids clutch fishing rods, parents push prams and old seafolk swap yarns. Here, the hotels are smaller, fewer waiters speak broken German and the island's welcome hasn't been changed by a tidal wave of visitors.

If you have the time, Procida is an ideal place to explore on foot. The most compelling areas (and where you will also find most of the hotels, bars and restaurants) are Marina Grande, Marina Corricella and Marina di Chiaiolella. Beaches are not plentiful here, apart from the Lido di Procida,

where, aside from August, you shouldn't have any trouble finding some towel space.

◉ Sights

Abbazia di San
Michele Arcangelo   CHURCH, MUSEUM
(☑ 334 8514252, 334 8514028; www.abbaziasanmicheleprocida.it; Via Terra Murata 89, Terra Murata; ⏰10am-12.45pm Mon-Sat, from 10.30am Sun) **FREE** Soak up the dizzying bay views at the belvedere before exploring the adjoining Abbazia di San Michele Arcangelo. Built in the 11th century and remodelled between the 17th and 19th centuries, this one-time Benedictine abbey houses a small museum with some arresting pictures created in gratitude by shipwrecked sailors, plus a church with a spectacular coffered ceiling and an ancient Greek alabaster basin converted into a font.

The church apse features four paintings by Neapolitan artist Nicola Russo. Dating back to 1690, these works include a depiction of St Michael the Archangel protecting Procida from Saracen attack on 8 May 1535. The painting is especially fascinating for its depiction of Marina Grande in the 16th century. Free guided tours can be arranged between April and October.

Isola di Vivara   ISLAND
(☑ 347 7858256; www.comune.procida.na.it; adult/reduced €10/5; ⏰guided tours 10am & 3pm Fri-Sun) Linked to Procida by pedestrian bridge, pocket-sized Vivara is what remains of a volcanic crater dating back some 55,000 years. The island is home to unique flora and abundant birdlife, while archaeological digs have uncovered traces of a Bronze-Age Mycenaean settlement as well as pottery fragments dating back to early Greek colonisation. Book online 15 days in advance.

⚑ Activities

Blue Dream Yacht
Charter Boating   BOATING
(☑ 081 896 05 79, 339 5720874; www.bluedreamcharter.com; Via Emanuele 14, Marina Grande; 6/8-person yacht per week from €1600/2800) If you have 'champagne on the deck' aspirations, you can always charter your very own yacht or catamaran from here.

Sprint   CYCLING
(☑ 339 8659600; www.sprintprocida.com; Via Roma 28, Marina Grande; standard/electric bike per day €10/20; ♿) One of several bike-hire

places on the port at Marina Grande. Bikes are an excellent way of exploring this small, relatively flat island.

Tours

Cesare Boat Trips
BOATING

(☑333 4603877; 2½hr tour per person €25; ⊙Mar-Oct) On the harbour at Marina Corricella, ask for friendly Cesare in your best Italian. Check at one of the beach bars or by La Gorgonia restaurant – he won't be far away. Cesare runs some great boat trips.

Festivals & Events

Procession of the Misteri
RELIGIOUS

Good Friday sees a solemn procession when a wooden statue of Christ and the Madonna Addolorata, along with life-size plaster and papier-mâché tableaux illustrating events leading to Christ's crucifixion, are carted across the island. Men dress in blue tunics with white hoods, while many of the young girls dress as the Madonna.

The procession starts in the Piazza dei Martiri, just behind Marina della Corricella.

Sleeping

Bed & Breakfast La Terrazza
B&B €

(☑081 896 00 62; Via Faro 26, Marina Grande; s €50-70, d €75-90; ⊙Easter-Oct; 🖨) Attractive budget option tucked into one of the timeless lanes that characterise central Procida, the Terrazza is run by an equally timeless couple who rent three compact rooms with low ceilings and carefully chosen seafaring decor. The highlight is the broad terracotta-tiled roof terrace where generous breakfasts are served.

★ Hotel La Vigna
BOUTIQUE HOTEL €€

(☑081 896 04 69; www.albergolavigna.it; Via Principessa Margherita 46, Terra Murata; d €110-180, ste €160-230; ⊙Easter-Oct; P❈🛜🏊) Enjoying a discreet cliffside location, this crenelated 18th-century villa is a gorgeous retreat, complete with rambling garden, vines and swimming pool. Five of the spacious, simply furnished rooms offer direct access to the garden. The hotel also has its own vineyard, produces its own wine (served in a chic wine bar) and offers wine therapy treatments at its small spa.

Casa Sul Mare
HOTEL €€

(☑081 896 87 99; www.lacasasulmare.it; Salita Castello 13, Marina Corricella; d €126-162; ⊙early Mar-Oct; ❈🛜) A crisp, white-washed place

with the kind of evocative views that helped make *The Talented Mr. Ripley* such a memorable film (parts were filmed in Procida). Overlooking the pastel-hued fishing village of Marina Corricella, near the ruined Castello d'Avalos, its rooms are simple yet elegant, with fetching tiled floors, wrought-iron bedsteads and the odd piece of antique furniture.

The hotel treats its guests well: during summer there's a boat service to the nearby Spiaggia della Chiaia (Chiaia Beach), and the morning cappuccino, courtesy of Franco, may be the best you'll find outside Turin.

Eating

Prime waterfront dining here needn't equal an overpriced disappointment, with portside trattorias serving fresh, classic food. Several inland trattorias use home-grown produce and game in their cooking. Try the zesty *insalata al limone,* a lemon salad infused with chilli oil. Marina Grande is the place to mix with the fisherfolk at one of the earthy local bars.

★ Da Mariano
ITALIAN €

(☑081 896 73 50; Marina di Chiaiolella; meals €20-25; ⊙noon-3pm & 7pm-midnight Easter-Nov; 🖨) Hugely popular with locals, thanks to simple yet perfectly executed dishes like stuffed calamari and *spaghetti alle vongole* (spaghetti with clams). The fish, including swordfish, is jumping fresh, and you eat looking out at the bay. Round off a meal with the signature *la Procidana,* a *caprese*-style cake made with white chocolate and the juice and rind of local lemons.

Da Giorgio
TRATTORIA €

(☑081 896 79 10; Via Roma 36, Marina Grande; meals €24; ⊙noon-3pm & 7-11.30pm Mar-Oct, closed Tue Nov-Feb) A retro, no-frills neighbourhood trattoria close to the port. The menu holds few surprises, but the ingredients are fresh; try the *spaghetti con frutti di mare* (seafood spaghetti) with some spongy *casareccio* (home-style) bread.

Information

Pro Loco (☑081 010 07 24; www.prolocodi procida.it; Via Roma, Stazione Marittima, Marina Grande; ⊙10am-1pm daily, 3-5pm Sat & Sun Apr-Oct) Located at the Ferry & Hydrofoil Ticket Office, this modest office has sparse printed information but should be able to advise on activities, accommodation and the like.

❶ Getting There & Away

The **Ferry & Hydrofoil Terminal** (Via Roma, Stazione Marittima, Marina Grande) is in Marina Grande.

Caremar (☑ 081 896 72 80; www.caremar.it; Via Roma, Stazione Marittima, Marina Grande) Operates hydrofoils to/from Naples (€14.50, 40 minutes, up to eight daily) and Ischia (from €13, 20 minutes, up to six daily). It also runs slower ferries to/from both destinations.

SNAV (☑ 081 428 55 55; www.snav.it; Via Roma, Stazione Marittima, Marina Grande) Operates up to four hydrofoils daily to/from Naples (from €17.50, 25 minutes).

THE AMALFI COAST

The Amalfi Coast is one of Italy's most memorable destinations. Here, mountains that plunge into the sea in a nail-biting vertical scene of precipitous crags, cliff-clinging abodes and verdant woodland.

Its string of fabled towns read like a Hollywood cast list. There's jet-set favourite Positano, a pastel-coloured cascade of chic boutiques, spritz-sipping pin-ups and sun-kissed sunbathers. Further east, ancient Amalfi lures with its Arabic-Norman cathedral, while mountaintop Ravello stirs hearts with its cultured villas and Wagnerian connection. To the west lies Amalfi Coast gateway Sorrento, a handsome clifftop resort that has miraculously survived the onslaught of package tourism.

The region also boasts well-marked hiking trails providing the chance to escape the star-struck coastal crowds.

❶ Getting There & Away

BOAT

Year-round hydrofoils run between Naples and Sorrento (€13, 20 minutes, up to six daily), as well as between Sorrento and Capri (€20.50, 20 minutes, up to 13 daily). From around April/May to October, ferry services connect Sorrento to Positano (€20, 30 minutes, two daily) and Amalfi (€21, 50 minutes, two daily), from where ferries continue to Salerno.

BUS

The Circumvesuviana train runs from Naples' Piazza Garibaldi to Sorrento, from where there is a regular and efficient **SITA Sud** (www.sitasudtrasporti.it) bus service to Positano, Amalfi and Salerno.

TRAIN

The **Circumvesuviana** (☑ 800 211388; www.eavsrl.it) runs every 30 minutes between Naples' Garibaldi station (beside Napoli Centrale station) and Sorrento (€3.90, 70 minutes). Trains stop in Ercolano (Herculaneum) and Pompeii en route. **Trenitalia** (☑ 892021; www.trenitalia.com) runs frequent services between Napoli Centrale station and Salerno (€4.70, 40 minutes).

Positano

☑ 089 / POP 3915

Dramatic, deluxe and more than a little dashing, Positano is the Amalfi Coast's front-cover splash, with vertiginous houses tumbling down to the sea in a cascade of sun-bleached peach, pink and terracotta. No less photo-worthy are its steep streets and steps, flanked by wisteria-draped hotels, smart restaurants and fashionable retailers.

Look beyond the facades and the fashion, however, and you will find reassuring signs of everyday reality: crumbling stucco, streaked paintwork and even, on occasion, a faint whiff of drains. There's still a southern-Italian-holiday feel about the place, with sunbathers eating pizza on the beach, kids pestering parents for gelato and chic *signore* from Milan browsing the boutiques. The fashionista history runs deep – *moda Positano* was born here in the '60s and the town was the first in Italy to import bikinis from France.

◉ Sights & Activities

Positano's most memorable sight is its pyramidal townscape, with pastel-coloured houses stacked up on the hillsides.

Getting around town is largely a matter of walking. If your knees can take the slopes, dozens of narrow alleys and stairways make strolling around relatively straightforward and joyously traffic-free. The easy option is to take the local bus to the top of the town and wind your way down on foot.

Chiesa di Santa Maria Assunta CHURCH
(☑ 089 87 54 80; Piazza Flavio Gioia; ⊙ 9am-noon & 4-7pm Mon-Sat) Omnipresent in most Positano photos is the colourful majolica-tiled dome of its main church (and the town's only real sight). If you are visiting at a weekend you will probably have the added perk of seeing a wedding; it's one of the most

Positano

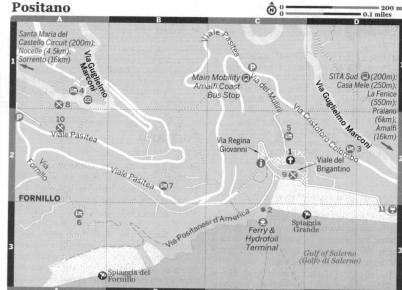

popular churches in southern Italy for exchanging vows.

The church is known for a 13th-century Byzantine *Black Madonna and Child* above the main altar. The icon was supposedly stolen from Constantinople by pirates and smuggled west.

Santa Maria del Castello Circuit   HIKING
For those travelling on foot, there's no real way out of Positano that doesn't involve climbing steep stone staircases – lots of 'em! The advantage of this particular circuitous route is that it enjoys a bit of shade in its early stages as you plod heavenward amid a thick and gnarly holm-oak forest.

The walk starts on the main coast road (SS163) close to the Montepertuso turn-off

by a ruined building and climbs steeply through trees before breaking into dryer Mediterranean scrub higher up. The coastal views open out as the path (#333a) traverses the hills above Positano, with the hulk of Monte Sant'Angelo standing sentinel in the background. Turn left 2km up the ascent and then right at the top to join a wider trail towards the hike's high point; the tiny village of **Santa Maria del Castello** (670m) is accessible by diverting along a narrow, paved road. At this ancient crossing point around 5km into the hike, you'll find a small bar and a church. Take the narrow road back down to the main path; turn left (trail #333), proceed around the headland and then head right on a path that leads steeply down via a series of well-constructed staircases to Positano, visible in all its glory directly below. The walk ends beside the Bar Internazionale (p754) in Upper Positano. The total distance is 9km.

L'Uomo e il Mare · BOATING

(☑089 81 16 13; www.escursioniluomoeilmare.it; ☺9am-8pm Easter-Oct) Offers a range of tours, including Capri and Amalfi day trips (from €65 to €80), out of a kiosk near the ferry terminal. It also organises private sunset tours to Li Galli, complete with champagne (from €200 for up to 12 people). Private tours should be organised at least a day in advance.

🛏 Sleeping

Positano is a glorious place to stay, but be aware that prices are, overall, high. Like everywhere on the Amalfi Coast, it gets very busy in summer, so book ahead, particularly on weekends and in July and August. Ask at the tourist office about rooms or apartments in private houses.

Villa Nettuno · HOTEL €

(☑089 87 54 01; www.villanettunopositano.it; Viale Pasitea 208; d €80-150; ☺Apr-Oct; ❋🅯) Hidden behind a barrage of perfumed foliage, lofty Villa Nettuno is not short on charm. Go for one of the original rooms in the 300-year-old part of the building, decked out in robust rustic decor and graced with a communal terrace. Bathrooms are a little old fashioned, but this place is all about the view.

Pensione Maria Luisa · PENSION €€

(☑089 87 50 23; www.pensionemarialuisa.com; Via Fornillo 42; d €129-179; ☺Mar-Oct; ❋@🅯) Carlo the ceramicist is the main man at Maria Luisa; he's an extremely congenial (and multilingual) host who'll make your stay in glitzy Positano feel pleasantly homely. Simple rooms have extravagant views over town (get one with a balcony) and handy fridges, and there's a small rooftop terrace. It's in the Fornillo neighbourhood, a short walk via steps from the beach. Breakfast is €8 extra.

Hostel Brikette · HOSTEL €€

(☑089 87 58 57; www.hostel-positano.com; Via Guglielmo Marconi 358; dm €40-73, d €160-220; ☺mid-Mar–mid-Oct; ❋🅯) Though more expensive than most hostels, cheerful Brikette is relatively cheap by Positano standards as long as you opt for a dorm. The top-of-the-town building has wonderful views and a range of sleeping options, from doubles

to three different types of dorm. Premium dorms have private bathrooms and terraces; all have handy bunk-side USB sockets and reading lights.

La Fenice · B&B €€

(☑089 87 55 13; www.lafenicepositano.com; Via Guglielmo Marconi 8; d €180; ☺Easter-Oct; ❋🅯🏊) With hand-painted Vietri tiles, high ceilings and the odd piece of antique furniture, the rooms at this friendly family-run place are simple but smart; most have their own balcony or terrace with dreamy views. As with everywhere in Positano, you'll need to be good at stomping up and down steps to stay here – it's 1km east of the town centre.

Albergo California · HOTEL €€

(☑089 87 53 82; www.hotelcaliforniapositano.it; Via Cristoforo Colombo 141; d €160-250; ☺Mar-mid-Oct; P❋🅯) If you were to choose the best place to take a quintessential Positano photo, it might be from the balcony of this hotel. But the view isn't all you get. The rooms in the older part of this grand 18th-century palace are magnificent, with original ceiling friezes and decorative doors. New rooms are simply decorated but tasteful, spacious and minimalist.

★Hotel Palazzo Murat · HOTEL €€€

(☑089 87 51 77; www.palazzomurat.it; Via dei Mulini 23; d from €310; ☺late Mar-early Nov; ❋@🅯🏊) Positano personified. Hidden behind an ancient wall away from the tourists who surge along the pedestrian thoroughfares daily, this magnificent hotel occupies the 18th-century *palazzo* (mansion) that the one-time king of Naples used as his summer residence. Rooms are regal quarters (one even has a crown over the bed) with sumptuous antiques, original oil paintings and gleaming marble.

🍴 Eating

Positano excels in deluxe restaurants with fine food and romantic settings, but you can also get by on a budget if you know where to look. Generally, the nearer you get to the seafront, the more expensive everything becomes. Many places close over winter, making a brief reappearance for Christmas and New Year.

★C'era Una Volta · TRATTORIA, PIZZA €

(☑089 81 19 30; Via Marconi 127; meals €20-30; ☺noon-3pm Wed-Mon, 6-11pm daily) Calling like a siren to any cash-poor budget traveller who thought Positano was for celebs only, this heroically authentic trattoria at the top of town specialises in honest, down-to-earth Italian grub. No need to look further than the *gnocchi alla sorrentina* (gnocchi in a tomato and basil sauce) and Caprese salad. Pizzas start at €4.50; beer €2. In Positano, no less!

It also runs a free shuttle to/from anywhere in Positano in the summer.

La Cambusa SEAFOOD €€
(☑089 87 54 32; www.lacambusapositano.com; Piazza Vespucci 4; meals €40; ☺noon-11pm, closed Nov-mid-Dec; 🛜) Sporting summery pastel hues and a seafront terrace, La Cambusa is on the front line, which, given the number of cash-rich tourists in these parts, could equal high prices for less-than-average food. Happily, that is not the case. Ingredients are top-notch and shine brightly in dishes such as homemade crab-filled ravioli and seafood risotto.

★ Casa Mele ITALIAN €€€
(☑089 81 13 64; www.casamele.com; Via Guglielmo Marconi 76; tasting menus €75-100; ☺7pm-midnight Tue-Sun Apr-Nov; 🛜) Something of a rarity in this land of traditional trattorias, Casa Mele is one of those cool contemporary restaurants with a lengthy tasting menu and food presented as art – and theatre. The slick open kitchen is a window into a high-powered food laboratory from which emerge whimsical pastas, delicate fish in subtle sauces, and outstanding desserts. Service is equally sublime.

★ Donna Rosa ITALIAN €€€
(☑089 81 18 06; www.drpositano.com; Via Montepertuso 97-99, Montepertuso; meals €45-65; ☺11am-2pm & 5.30-10pm Wed-Mon Apr-Oct, closed lunch Aug) Once a humble trattoria, Donna Rosa is now considered an Amalfi Coast classic despite its out-of-the-way location in the village of Montepertuso. The reason? Jolly good food served by three generations of the original Rosa's family and a nod of admiration from that well-known food-campaigning Italophile, Jamie Oliver. Reservations are highly recommended for dinner and obligatory for lunch.

Next2 ITALIAN €€€
(☑089 812 35 16; www.next2.it; Viale Pasitea 242; meals €65, 6-course menu €80; ☺6.30-11pm Apr-Oct; 🛜) Local produce and polished takes on tradition underscore sophisticated Next2. Standouts include the signature *conchigli-* *oni ripieni di ragù alla bolognese e stracciatella*, shell-shaped pasta served with pork-mince *ragù* and *stracciatella* cheese. The kitchen boasts a top-range charcoal oven, put to fine use in dishes like tender octopus and mackerel with chickpea purée and cherry tomatoes. In summer, reserve a table on the terrace.

🍷 Drinking & Nightlife

Music on the Rocks CLUB
(☑089 87 58 74; www.musicontherocks.it; Via Grotte dell'Incanto 51; cover charge €10-30; ☺10pm-4am Apr-Oct; 🛜) This is one of the town's few genuine nightspots and one of the best clubs on the coast. The venue is dramatically carved into the tower at the eastern end of Spiaggia Grande. Join a lively crowd and some of the region's top DJs spinning anything from mainstream house to retro disco.

ℹ️ Information

Post Office (www.poste.it; Via Guglielmo Marconi 318; ☺8.20am-1.45pm Mon-Fri, to 12.45pm Sat) On the main highway passing through town.

Tourist Office (☑089 87 50 67; www.azienda turismopositano.it; Via Regina Giovanna 13; ☺8.30am-5pm Mon-Sat, to 3pm Sun) Provides lots of information, from sightseeing and tours to transport information. Also supplies a free hiking map.

ℹ️ Getting There & Away

BOAT

Positano has excellent ferry connections to the coastal towns and islands between April and October from its ferry and hydrofoil terminal.

TraVelMar (☑089 87 29 50; www.travelmar. it) Sails to numerous coastal destinations between April and October, including Amalfi (€8, 25 minutes, six daily) and Salerno (€12, 70 minutes, six daily). To reach Minori (€11), Maiori (€11) and Cetara (€12), transfer in Amalfi.

Lucibello Positano (☑089 87 50 32; www. lucibello.it) Operates three daily services to Capri (€22, 30 minutes) from mid-April to mid-October.

BUS

About 16km west of Amalfi and 18km from Sorrento, Positano is on the main SS163 coastal road. There are two Sita Sud main bus stops: coming from Sorrento and the west, the first stop you come to is opposite Bar Internazionale; arriving from Amalfi and the east, the stop is at the top of Via Cristoforo Colombo. To get into

WALK OF THE GODS

The Sentiero degli Dei (Path of the Gods) is the best-known walk on the Amalfi Coast for two reasons: first, it's spectacular from start to finish; and second, unlike most Amalfi treks, it doesn't involve inordinate amounts of stair-climbing. The walk starts in the village of Bomerano (a subdivision of Agerola), easily accessible from Amalfi town by SITA bus.

Beginning in the main square, where several cafes supply portable snacks, follow the red-and-white signs along Via Pennino. The start of the walk proper is marked by a **monument** inscribed with quotes by Italo Calvino and DH Lawrence. Views of terraced fields quickly open out as the path contours around a cliff-face and passes beneath the overhanging **Grotta del Biscotto** (Biscuit Cave). From here, the trail continues its traverse of the mountainside with some minor undulations. Periodically it dips into thickets of trees and sometimes you'll be required to negotiate rockier sections, but, in the main, the going is relatively easy.

The first main landmark after the Grotta is a path junction at **Colle Serra**. Here you get a choice between a low route or a high route. The low route is more exposed and threads its way through vineyards and rockier sections, with magnificent views of Praiano below. Roughly 800m along its course, it is possible to make a short diversion south to the **San Domenico Monastery**. The more popular high route (#327a) sticks to the rocky heights with broad, sweeping vistas. Both paths converge at a point called **Cisternulo**, 1.5km further on. Just below Colle Serra, a path from the Sentiero degli Dei's alternative start in Praiano joins the main trail. Bear in mind that starting in Praiano involves a thigh-challenging climb up 1000 steps before you reach the trail proper.

After Cisternulo, the path kinks around some half-obscured *grotte* (caves) and descends into the Valle Grarelle before climbing back up to the finish point in the tiny village of **Nocelle**. A small kiosk selling cold drinks and coffee, served on a charming terrace, greets you as you enter the village. Alternatively, head a little further through the village to Piazza Santa Croce, where a stall dispenses freshly squeezed orange and lemon juice.

From here you have three options: 1) take stairs (around 1500 of them!) down through the village to be deposited on the coast road 2km out of Positano; 2) catch a bus from the end of Nocelle's one interconnecting road to Positano – small minibuses run by Mobility Amalfi Coast (p754) depart 10 times a day; 3) a much nicer if longer option – especially if you're weary of steps at this point – is to continue along the path that leads west out of Nocelle towards Montepertuso. Don't miss the huge hole in the centre of the cliff at Montepertuso where it looks as though an irate giant has punched through the slab of limestone. In Montepertuso cut down past the church via a series of staircases to hit the northern fringes of Positano.

The CAI (Club Alpino Italiano; Italian Alpine Club) has a website dedicated to the Monti Lattari area (www.caimontilattari.it). Alternatively, the best printed map is from the cart&guide series (map #3) and available in most local bookshops/newsagents (€5). If you prefer a guided hike, reliable local guides include American **Frank Carpegna** (www.positanofrankcarpegna.com), a longtime resident here, and **Zia Lucy** (www.zialucy.it).

The Sentiero degli Dei is not advised for acute vertigo sufferers – if in doubt, take the less exposed upper path (#327a). The trail itself (Bomerano to Nocelle) measures just under 6km one-way, but you'll add on another 3km to 4km if you continue by foot to Positano at the end. Bring a rucksack and plenty of water, and wear proper walking shoes. You may want to pack swimming gear too and end the walk with a refreshing plunge into the sea.

Inclement weather and/or landslides can sometimes lead to trail closures. Check ahead. Tourist offices in Praiano (p755) and **Bomerano** (☏081 879 10 64; Piazza Paolo Capasso, Bomerano; ☺8am-1pm & 3-8pm Easter-Sep, 8am-1pm & 2-7pm rest of year; ☎) can provide more guidance.

town from the former, follow Viale Pasitea; from the latter (a far shorter route), take Via Cristoforo Colombo. When departing, buy bus tickets at **Bar Internazionale** (Via Guglielmo Marconi 306; ⊘7am-1am) or from the **tabaccheria** (☑089 81 21 33; Via Cristoforo Colombo 5; ⊘9.30am-9pm) at the bottom of Via Cristoforo Colombo.

SITA Sud (www.sitasudtrasporti.it) runs up to 28 daily buses to Sorrento (€2, one hour). It also runs up to 25 daily services to Amalfi (€2, 50 minutes), from where buses continue east to Salerno.

Nocelle
☑089 / POP 140

A tiny, still relatively isolated mountain village, located 2km southeast of Montepertuso, Nocelle (450m) commands some of the most spectacular views on the entire coast. A world apart from touristy Positano, it's a sleepy, silent place where not much ever happens and where the small population of residents are happy to keep it that way. The Sentiero degli Dei officially ends here.

Very handy as you stumble off the Sentiero degli Dei with wobbly legs, **Villa della Quercia** (☑089 812 34 97; http://villa laquercia.com; Via Nocelle 5; d €75-85; ⊘Apr-mid-Oct; ☜) is a delightful B&B in a former hilltop monastery in Nocelle. It comes armed with a tranquil garden and spectacular, goat's-eye views of the coast. All six simple rooms have a terrace or balcony for languid lounging and the hosts welcome you with small-village friendliness. To reach the property, catch a local bus (€1.30) from Amalfi to Nocelle. The B&B is about a 10-minute walk from the bus stop.

Modest **Trattoria Santa Croce** (☑089 81 12 60; www.ristorantesantacrocepositano.com; Via Nocelle 19; meals €22; ⊘noon-3.30pm & 7-9.30pm Apr-Oct) has spectacular views over the coast and is located just past the finishing post on the Sentiero degli Dei. The menu is short and traditional, with a mix of good (if not memorable) surf-and-turf dishes such as rustic lentil soup, tagliatelle alla genovese (pasta with a rich, onion-based Neapolitan sauce) and freshly caught fish with local herbs.

❶ Getting There & Away
Small minibuses run by **Mobility Amalfi Coast** (☑089 81 30 77) depart for Positano (€1.30, 30 minutes) via Montepertuso 10 times a day. Catch the bus from the end of Nocelle's one inter-

connecting road. Note that tickets purchased onboard (as opposed to those purchased from *tabaccheria* shops) cost €1.80.

A return from Positano costs an extortionate €35 to €40: avoid.

It's a 3km walk to Positano – downhill all the way.

Praiano
☑089 / POP 2020

An ancient fishing village, a low-key summer resort and, increasingly, a popular centre for the arts, Praiano is a delight. With no centre as such, its whitewashed houses pepper the verdant ridge of Monte Sant'Angelo as it slopes towards Capo Sottile. Formerly an important silk-production centre, it was a favourite of the Amalfi *doges* (dukes), who made it their summer residence.

Praiano is glued to a steep bluff 120m above sea level and exploring it inevitably involves lots of steps. There are also several trails that start from town, including a dreamy walk – particularly romantic at sunset – that leaves from beside the San Gennaro church, descending due west to the Spiaggia della Gavitelli, via 300 steps, and carrying on to the medieval defensive Torre di Grado. The town also acts as an alternative starting point for the Sentiero degli Dei (Path of the Gods; p753).

The spread-out settlement stretches east and down to the sea at Marina di Praia, a sheltered cove with restaurants, a beach and a couple of diving operators.

🛏 Sleeping & Eating
Fish and seafood dominate the menus in this old fishing town. Its most famous traditional dish is *totani e patate alla praianese*, a soulful combination of soft calamari rings, sliced potato, *datterini* tomatoes, garlic, croutons, *peperoncino* (chilli) and parsley.

Hotel Onda Verde   HOTEL €€€
(☑089 87 41 43; www.hotelondaverde.com; Via Terramare 3, Praiano; d from €250; ⊘Apr-Oct; ℗❋☜☒) The 'Green Wave' enjoys a commanding cliffside position overlooking secluded Marina di Praia. The interior is tunnelled into the stone cliff face, which makes it wonderfully cool in the height of summer. Elegant rooms have lashings of white linen, satin bedheads, Florentine-inspired furniture and majolica-tiled floors.

Some spoil guests with terraces and deck-chairs for panoramic contemplation.

The **restaurant** (☑089 87 41 43; www.on daverde.it; Via Terramare 3; meals €38; ☉12.30-9.30pm Apr-Nov) comes highly recommended.

Da Armandino   SEAFOOD €€
(☑089 87 40 87; Via Praia 1, Marina di Praia; meals €35; ☉1-4pm & 7pm-midnight Apr-Nov) Seafood-lovers should head for this widely acclaimed, no-frills restaurant located in a former boatyard on the beach at Marina di Praia. Da Armandino is great for fish fresh off the boat. There's no menu; just opt for the dish of the day – it's all excellent.

The holiday atmosphere and appealing setting – at the foot of sheer cliffs towering up to the main road – round things off nicely.

🍸 Drinking & Nightlife

★**Africana Famous Club**   CLUB
(☑089 81 11 71; www.africanafamousclub.com; Via Terramare 2; €10-35; ☉10pm-late May-Sep, bar opens 8pm; 🕾) All Amalfi nightlife converges in the unlikely setting of Marina di Praia. But this is no run-of-the-mill nightclub: Africana's been going since the '60s, when Jackie Kennedy was a regular guest. It has an extraordinary cave setting (complete with natural blowholes), a mix of DJs and live music, plus a glass dance floor with fish swimming beneath your feet.

ℹ Information

Tourist Office (☑089 87 45 57; www.praiano. org; Via G Capriglione 116b; ☉9am-1pm & 4.30-8.30pm Mon-Sat) Can provide maps and information for the area's hiking trails.

ℹ Getting There & Away

SITA Sud (www.sitasudtrasporti.it) runs up to 27 daily buses to Sorrento (€2.40, 1¼ hours). It also runs up to 25 daily services to Amalfi (€1.30, 25 minutes) from where buses continue east to Salerno. Reduced services on Sunday.

Amalfi

☑089 / POP 5100

It is hard to grasp that pretty little Amalfi, with its sun-filled piazzas and small beach, was once a maritime superpower with a population of more than 70,000. For one thing, it's not a big place – you can easily walk from one end to the other in about 20 minutes. For another, there are very few his-torical buildings of note. The explanation is chilling: most of the old city, and its inhabitants, simply slid into the sea during an earthquake in 1343.

Despite this, the town exudes history and culture, most notably in its over-sized Byzantine-influenced cathedral and diminutive Paper Museum. And while the permanent population is now a fairly modest 5000 or so, the numbers swell significantly during summer.

Just around the headland, neighbouring **Atrani** is a dense tangle of whitewashed alleys and arches centred on an agreeably lived-in piazza and small scimitar of beach; don't miss it.

◉ Sights & Activities

★**Cattedrale di Sant'Andrea**   CATHEDRAL
(☑089 87 35 58; Piazza del Duomo; adult/reduced €3/1 between 10am-5pm; ☉7.30am-8.30pm, closed Nov-Mar) A melange of architectural styles, Amalfi's cathedral is a bricks-and-mortar reflection of the town's past as an 11th-century maritime superpower. It makes a striking impression at the top of a sweeping 62-step staircase. Between 10am and 5pm, the cathedral is only accessible through the adjacent **Chiostro del Paradiso** (☑089 87 13 24; adult/reduced €3/1; ☉9am-7.45pm Jul & Aug, shorter hours Sep-early Jan & Mar-Jun, closed early Jan & Feb), part of a four-section museum, incorporating the cloisters, the 9th-century Basilica del Crocefisso, the crypt of St Andrew and the cathedral itself. Outside these times, you can enter the cathedral for free.

The cathedral dates in part from the early 13th century. Its striped facade has been rebuilt twice, most recently at the end of the 19th century. It was constructed next to an older cathedral, the Basilica del Crocefisso, to which it long remained interconnected. The still-standing basilica now serves as a museum.

The cathedral was originally built to house the relics of St Andrew the Apostle, which arrived here from Constantinople in 1208. Architecturally the building is a hybrid. The Sicilian Arabic-Norman style predominates outside, particularly in the two-tone masonry, mosaics and 13th-century bell tower. The huge bronze doors, the first of their type in Italy, were commissioned by a local noble and made in Syria before being shipped to Amalfi. The interior is primarily baroque with some fine statues at the altar, along with some interesting 12th- and 13th-century mosaics.

Museo della Carta
MUSEUM

(Paper Museum; ☑089 830 45 61; www.museo dellacarta.it; Via delle Cartiere 23; adult/reduced €4/2.50; ⊙10am-6.30pm daily Mar-Oct, to 4pm Tue-Sun Nov-late Jan) Amalfi's Paper Museum is housed in a rugged, cave-like 13th-century paper mill (the oldest in Europe). It lovingly preserves the original paper presses, which are still in full working order, as you'll see during the 30-minute guided tour (in English). The tour explains the original cotton-based paper production and the subsequent wood-pulp manufacturing. Afterwards you might be inspired to pick up some of the stationery sold in the gift shop, including calligraphy sets and paper pressed with flowers.

Grotta dello Smeraldo
CAVE

(admission €5; ⊙9am-4pm) Four kilometres west of Amalfi, this grotto is named after the eerie emerald colour that emanates from the water. Stalactites hang down from the 24m-high ceiling, while stalagmites grow up to 10m tall. Buses regularly pass the car park above the cave entrance (from where you take a lift or stairs down to the rowing boats). Alternatively, **Coop Sant'Andrea** (☑089 87 31 90; www.coopsantandrea.com; Lungomare dei Cavalieri 1) runs boats from Amalfi (€10 return, plus cave admission). Allow 1½ hours for the return trip.

Amalfi Marine
BOATING

(☑338 3076125; www.amalfiboatrental.com; Spiaggia del Porto, Lungomare dei Cavalieri 7) Amalfi Marine hires out boats (without a skipper from €220 per day per boat excluding petrol; maximum six passengers). Private day-long tours with a skipper start from €600.

🛏 Sleeping

Despite its reputation as a day-trip destination, Amalfi has plenty of places to stay. It's not especially cheap, though, and most hotels are in the midrange to top-end price bracket. Always try to book ahead, as the summer months are very busy and many places close over winter. If you're coming by car, consider a hotel with a car park, as finding on-street parking can be especially painful.

Albergo Sant'Andrea
HOTEL €

(☑089 87 11 45; www.albergosantandrea.it; Salita Costanza d'Avalos 1; s/d €70/100; ⊙Mar-Dec;

✳🤶) Enjoy the atmosphere of busy Piazza del Duomo from the comfort of your own room. This modest two-star place has basic rooms with brightly coloured tiles and coordinating fabrics. Double glazing has helped cut down the piazza hubbub, which can reach fever pitch in high season – this is one place to ask for a room with a (cathedral) view.

★ DieciSedici
B&B €€

(☑089 87 22 52; www.diecisedici.it; Piazza Municipio 10-16; d from €145; ⊙Mar-Oct; ✳) DieciSedici (1016) dresses up an old medieval palace in the kind of style that only the Italians can muster. The half-dozen rooms dazzle with chandeliers, mezzanine floors, glass balconies and gorgeous linens. Two rooms (the Junior Suite and Family Classic) come complete with kitchenettes. All have satellite TV, air-con and Bose sound systems.

Breakfast is laid on in a cafe in the nearby Piazza del Duomo.

Residenza del Duca
HOTEL €€

(☑089 873 63 65; www.residencedelduca.it; Via Duca Mastalo II 3; d from €135; ⊙mid-Mar–Oct; ✳🤶) This family-run hotel has just six rooms, all of them light, sunny and prettily furnished with antiques, majolica tiles and the odd chintzy cherub. The jacuzzi showers are excellent. Call ahead if you are carrying heavy bags, as it's a seriously puff-you-out staircase climb to reach here and a luggage service is included in the price.

Hotel Lidomare
HOTEL €€

(☑089 87 13 32; www.lidomare.it; Largo Duchi Piccolomini 9; s/d €65/145; ✳🤶) This gracious, old-fashioned, family-run hotel has no shortage of character. The large, luminous rooms have an air of gentility, with their appealingly haphazard decor, vintage tiles and fine antiques. Some have spa baths, others have sea views and a balcony; some have both. Rather unusually, breakfast is laid out on top of a grand piano.

Hotel Centrale
HOTEL €€

(☑089 87 26 08; www.amalfihotelcentrale.it; Largo Duchi Piccolomini 1; d/tr/q €159/180/220; ✳🤶) Central it is, with small, functional rooms berthed in a building accessed via a tiny little piazza in the *centro storico*. The joy is not the rooms themselves (which are visually boring), but the window seat they offer over the buzzing Piazza del Duomo below. Be sure to ask for a front-facing room with a balcony.

Hotel Luna Convento HOTEL €€€

(☑ 089 87 10 02; www.lunahotel.it; Via Pantaleone Comite 33; d from €340; ☺ mid-Mar–Dec; P❄@☎☂) This former convent was founded by St Francis in 1222 and has been a hotel for some 170 years. Rooms in the original building are in the former monks' cells, but there's nothing poky about the bright tiles, balconies and seamless sea views. The newer wing is equally beguiling, with religious frescoes over the beds. The cloistered courtyard is magnificent.

✗ Eating

La Pansa CAFE €

(☑ 089 87 10 65; www.pasticceriapansa.it; Piazza del Duomo 40; cornetti from €1, pastries from €1.80; ☺ 7.30am-midnight Wed-Mon, closed early Jan-early Feb) A marbled and mirrored fifth-generation cafe on Piazza del Duomo where black-bow-tied waiters serve minimalist Italian breakfasts: freshly made *cornetti* (croissants), full-bodied espresso and deliciously frothy cappuccino. Standout pastries include the crisp, flaky *coda di aragosta con crema di limone*, a lobster-tail-shaped concoction filled with a rich yet light lemon-custard cream.

Le Arcate ITALIAN €€

(☑ 089 87 13 67; www.learcateatrani.it; Largo Orlando Buonocore, Atrani; pizzas from €6, meals €30; ☺ 12-3.30pm & 7-11pm daily Jul & Aug, closed Mon Sep-Jun; ☎) If you've had it with the tourist tumult of Amalfi, try temporarily relocating to its quieter cousin Atrani to eat al fresco at one of its traditional restaurants. Arcate is right on the seafront with huge parasols shading its sprawl of tables, and a dining room in a stone-walled natural cave.

★ Ristorante La Caravella ITALIAN €€€

(☑ 089 87 10 29; www.ristorantelacaravella.it; Via Matteo Camera 12; meals €50-135; ☺ noon-2.30pm & 7-11pm Wed-Mon; ❄) A restaurant of artists, art and artistry, Caravella once hosted Andy Warhol. No surprise that it doubles up as a de-facto gallery with frescoes, creative canvases and a ceramics collection. And then there's the food on the seven-course tasting menu, prepared by some of the finest culinary Caravaggios in Italy.

Despite its fame, Michelin-starred Caravella, in business since 1959, remains an unpretentious and discreet place that's true to its seafood roots.

Not to be missed are the anchovy croquettes, fish with fennel and sun-dried tomatoes and – the *Mona Lisa* on the menu – a fine lemon *soufflé*. The wine list is, arguably, the best on the Amalfi Coast. Reservations essential.

ⓘ Information

Post Office (www.poste.it; Corso delle Repubbliche Marinare 31; ☺ 8.20am-7pm Mon-Fri, to 12.30pm Sat) Next door to the tourist office.

Tourist Office (☑ 089 87 11 07; www.amalfitouristoffice.it; Corso delle Repubbliche Marinare 27; ☺ 8.30am-1pm & 2-6pm Mon-Sat Apr-Oct, 8.30am-1pm Mon-Sat Nov-Mar; ☎) Just off the main seafront road in a small courtyard.

ⓘ Getting There & Away

BOAT

The ferry terminal is a simple affair with several ticket offices located a short hop from the bus station on the seafront.

TraVelMar (☑ 089 87 29 50; www.travelmar.it) Runs a reliable April to October water taxi to/from Positano (€8, 25 minutes, daily), Minori (€3, 10 minutes, seven daily), Cetara (€5, 40 minutes, six daily) and Salerno (€8, 35 minutes, up to 12 daily).

Alilauro (☑ 081 497 22 38; www.alilauro.it) Runs ferries to Sorrento (€21, one hour, two daily) via Positano, and to Capri (€24, 1¼ hours, one daily) from around April to October.

BUS

Amalfi's **bus station** (Lungomare dei Cavalieri) in Piazza Flavio Gioia is little more than a car park, but it is the main transport nexus on the coast.

SITA Sud (☑ 342 6256442; www.sitasudtrasporti.it; Piazza Flavio Gioia) runs up to 27 buses daily to Ravello (€1.30, 25 minutes). Eastbound, it runs up to 20 buses daily to Salerno (€2.40, 1¼ hours) via Maiori (20 minutes). Westbound, it runs up to 25 buses daily to Positano (€2, 40 minutes) via Praiano (€1.30, 25 minutes). Many continue to Sorrento (€2.90, 1¾ hours).

You can buy tickets from the *tabacchi* (tobacconist) on the corner of Piazza Flavio Gioia and Via Duca Mansone I (the side street that leads to Piazza del Duomo).

Ravello

☑ 089 / POP 2490

It cured Richard Wagner's writer's block, provided inspiration for DH Lawrence as he nurtured the plot of *Lady Chatterley's*

Lover, and impressed American writer Gore Vidal so much that he stayed for 30 years and became an honorary local. Ravello has a metamorphic effect on people.

Founded in the 5th century as a sanctuary from barbarian invaders fresh from sacking Rome, this lofty Amalfi town was built, in contrast to other Amalfi settlements, up on a hill rather than down on the coast. It's second only to Positano in its style and glamour.

Ravello's refinement is exemplified in the town's polished main piazza, where debonair diners relax under the canopies of alfresco cafes. It's also reflected in its lush villas (many now turned into palatial hotels), manicured gardens and one of Italy's finest musical festivals (thank Wagner's wife for that).

◉ Sights

Even if you have absolutely no sense of direction and a penchant for going round in circles, it's difficult to get lost in this town; everything is clearly signposted from the main Piazza Duomo. Explore the narrow backstreets, however, and you will discover glimpses of a quieter, traditional lifestyle: dry-stone walls fronting simple homes surrounded by overgrown gardens, neatly planted vegetable plots and basking cats.

★ **Villa Rufolo**   GARDENS
(☑ 089 85 76 21; www.villarufolo.it; Piazza Duomo; adult/reduced €7/5; ☉ 9am-9pm summer, reduced hours winter, tower museum 10am-7pm summer, reduced hours winter) To the south of Ravello's cathedral, a 14th-century tower marks the entrance to this villa, famed for its beautiful cascading gardens. Created by a Scotsman, Sir Francis Neville Reid, in 1853, they are truly magnificent, commanding divine panoramic views packed with exotic colours, artistically crumbling towers and luxurious blooms. Note that the gardens are at their best from May till October; they don't merit the entrance fee outside those times.

The villa was built in the 13th century for the wealthy Rufolo dynasty and was home to several popes as well as King Robert of Anjou. Wagner was so inspired by the gardens when he visited in 1880 that he modelled the garden of Klingsor (the setting for the second act of the opera *Parsifal*) on them.

The 13th-century Torre Maggiore (Main Tower) now houses the **Torre-Museo**, an interactive museum that sheds light on the villa's history and characters. Among the

latter is Reid, the Scottish botanist who purchased and extensively restored the property in the 19th century. The museum also showcases art, archaeological finds and ceramics linked to the villa. Stairs inside the tower lead up to an outdoor viewing platform, affording knockout views of the villa and the Amalfi Coast.

Today Villa Rufolo's gardens stage world-class concerts during the town's annual arts festival.

★ **Villa Cimbrone**   GARDENS
(☑ 089 85 74 59; www.hotelvillacimbrone.com/gardens; Via Santa Chiara 26; adult/reduced €7/4; ☉ 9am-sunset) If you could bottle up a take-away image of the Amalfi, it might be the view from the **Belvedere of Infinity**, classical busts in the foreground, craggy coast splashed with pastel-shaded villages in the background. It's yours to admire at this re-fashioned 11th-century villa (now an upmarket hotel) with sublime gardens. Open to the public, the gardens were mainly created by a British peer, Ernest Beckett, who reconfigured them with rose-beds, temples and a Moorish pavilion in the early 1900s.

The villa (also owned by Beckett) was something of a bohemian retreat in its early days; it was frequented by Greta Garbo and her lover Leopold Stokowski as a secret hideaway. Other illustrious former guests include Virginia Woolf, Winston Churchill, DH Lawrence and Salvador Dalí. The house and gardens sit atop a crag that's a 10-minute walk south of Piazza Duomo.

✖ Festivals & Events

★ **Ravello Festival**   PERFORMING ARTS
(☑ 089 85 84 22; www.ravellofestival.com; ☉ Jul-Aug) The Ravello Festival – established in 1953 – turns much of the town centre into a stage. Events range from orchestral concerts and chamber music to ballet performances, film screenings and exhibitions. The festival's most celebrated (and impressive) venue is the overhanging terrace in the Villa Rufolo gardens.

⛱ Sleeping

Ravello is an upmarket town and the accommodation reflects this, both in style and in price. There are some superb top-end hotels, several lovely midrange places and a fine *agriturismo* (farm stay) nearby. Book well ahead for summer – especially if you're planning to visit during the music festival.

Agriturismo Monte Brusara AGRITURISMO €
(☑089 85 74 67; www.montebrusara.com; Via Monte Brusara 32; d €94-100; ◎yr-round; 🛜) 🍴 A working farm, this mountainside *agriturismo* (farm stay) is located a tough half-hour walk of about 1.5km from Ravello's centre (call ahead to arrange to be picked up). It's especially suited to families or those who simply want to escape the crowds and drink in the bucolic views.

Villa Casale APARTMENT €€
(☑340 9479909; www.ravelloresidence.it; Via Orso Papice 4; apt €99-206, ste €179-280; ❄🛜🏊) Practically next to the Villa Rufolo and enjoying the same glamorous view, Villa Casale consists of a handful of elegant suites and apartments arranged around a large pool. Top billing goes to the suites, graced with antiques and occupying the original 14th-century building. All the suites and apartments come with a self-contained kitchen and the property has tranquil gardens.

★ **Belmond Hotel Caruso** HOTEL €€€
(☑089 85 88 01; www.grandluxuryhotels.com; Piazza San Giovanni del Toro 2; d from €935; ◎mid-Apr-Oct; 🅿❄🛜🏊) There can be no better place to swim than the Caruso's sensational infinity pool. Seemingly set on the edge of a precipice, its blue waters merge with the sea and sky to magical effect. Inside, the sublimely restored 11th-century *palazzo* (mansion) is no less impressive, with 15th-century vaulted ceilings, high-class ceramics and Moorish arches doubling as window frames.

✗ **Eating**

Babel CAFE €
(☑089 858 62 15; Via Trinità 13; meals €20; ◎11.30am-5pm & 6.30-10.30pm daily May-Sep, closed Wed late Mar, Apr & Oct, closed Nov-late Mar; 🛜) A cool little deli-cafe with a compact menu of what you could call 'Italian tapas', affordable bites including Italian *gazpacho* (cold soup), bruschetta, dry polenta and creative salads with combos such as lemon and orange with goat's cheese and chestnut honey. It offers an excellent range of local wines, smooth jazz on the sound system, and Vietri-school ceramics for sale.

Da Salvatore ITALIAN €€
(☑089 85 72 27; Via della Repubblica 2; meals €38-45, pizzas from €5; ◎12.30-3pm & 7.30-10pm Tue-Sun Easter-Nov) Located just before the bus stop, Da Salvatore doesn't merely rest on the laurels of its spectacular terrace views.

This is one of the coast's best restaurants, serving arresting dishes that showcase local produce with creativity, flair and whimsy; your premeal *benvenuto* (welcome) may include an *aperitivo* of Negroni encased in a white-chocolate ball.

ℹ️ **Information**

Tourist Office (☑089 85 70 96; www.ravello time.it; Piazza Fontana Moresca 10; ◎9am-7pm summer, to 5pm rest of year) Shares digs with the police station. Provides brochures and maps, and can also assist with accommodation.

ℹ️ **Getting There & Away**

From the bus stop on the eastern side of Amalfi's Piazza Flavio Gioia, **SITA Sud** (☑342 6256442; www.sitasudtrasporti.it) runs up to 27 buses daily to Ravello (€1.30, 25 minutes).

SALERNO & THE CILENTO

Salerno
☑089 / POP 133,970
Salerno may initially seem like a bland big city, but the place has a charming, if gritty, individuality, especially around its ostensibly tatty *centro storico*, where medieval churches and neighbourhood trattorias echo with the addictive bustle of southern Italy. The city has invested in various urban-regeneration programs centred on this historic neighbourhood, which features a tree-lined seafront promenade widely considered to be one of the cheeriest and most attractive in Italy.

◎ **Sights**

Although Salerno is a sprawling town, you can easily visit it in one day and on foot, as the main sights (castle aside) are concentrated in and around the historic centre. Don't miss having a walk along the seafront promenade.

★ **Duomo** CATHEDRAL
(☑089 23 13 87; www.cattedraledisalerno.it; Piazza Alfano; ◎8.30am-8pm Mon-Sat, 8.30am-1pm & 4-8pm Sun) One of Campania's strangely under-the-radar sights, Salerno's impressive cathedral is considered by aficionados to be the most beautiful medieval church in Italy. Built by the Normans in the 11th century and later aesthetically remodelled in the

18th century, it sustained severe damage in a 1980 earthquake. It is dedicated to San Matteo (St Matthew), whose remains were reputedly brought to the city in 954 and now lie beneath the main altar in the vaulted crypt.

Take special note of the magnificent main entrance, the 12th-century **Porta dei Leoni**, named after the marble lions at the foot of the stairway. It leads through to a beautiful, harmonious courtyard, surrounded by graceful arches and overlooked by a 12th-century bell tower. Carry on through the huge bronze doors (similarly guarded by lions), which were cast in Constantinople in the 11th century. When you come to the three-aisled interior, you will see that it is largely baroque, with only a few traces of the original church. These include parts of the transept and choir floor and the two raised pulpits in front of the choir stalls. Throughout the church you can see highly detailed 13th-century mosaic work redolent of the extraordinary early-Christian mosaics in Ravenna.

In the right-hand apse, don't miss the **Cappella delle Crociate** (Chapel of the Crusades), containing powerful frescoes and more wonderful mosaics. It was so named because crusaders' weapons were blessed here. Under the altar stands the tomb of 11th-century pope Gregory VII.

Museo Archeologico Provinciale   MUSEUM
(☑ 089 23 11 35; www.museoarcheologicosalerno.it; Via San Benedetto 28; adult/reduced €4/2; ⊙ 9am-7.30pm Tue-Sun) The province's restored and revitalised main archaeological museum is an excellent showcase for the excavated history of the surrounding area, dating back to cave dwellers and the colonising Greeks. The pièce de résistance is the 1st-century BC *Testa bronzea di Apollo* (bronze head of Apollo). Showcased in its own small room upstairs, the head is thought to have been part of a larger statue; it was found by a fisherman in the Gulf of Salerno in 1930.

Castello di Arechi   CASTLE
(☑ 089 296 40 15; www.ilcastellodiarechi.it; Via Benedetto Croce; adult/reduced €4/2; ⊙ 9am-5pm Tue-Sat, to 3.30pm Sun) Hop on bus 19 from Piazza XXIV Maggio to visit Salerno's most famous landmark, the forbidding Castello di Arechi, dramatically positioned 263m above the city. Originally a Byzantine fort, it was built by the Lombard duke of Benevento, Arechi II, in the 8th century and subse-quently modified by the Normans and Aragonese, most recently in the 16th century.

🛏 Sleeping

The little accommodation that Salerno offers is fairly uninspiring, although, conveniently, there are several reasonable hotels in the town centre. Prices tend to be considerably lower than on the Amalfi Coast.

Ostello Ave Gratia Plena   HOSTEL €
(☑ 089 23 47 76; www.ostellodisalerno.it; Via dei Canali; dm/s/d €16/45/65; @ 🛜) Housed in a 16th-century convent, Salerno's excellent HI hostel is right in the heart of the *centro storico* action. Inside, there's a charming central courtyard and a range of bright rooms, from dorms to great-bargain doubles with private bathroom. The 2am curfew is for dorms only.

Hotel Montestella   HOTEL €€
(☑ 089 22 51 22; www.hotelmontestella.it; Corso Vittorio Emanuele II 156; d €90-125, tr €95-160; ❄ @ 🛜) Within walking distance of just about anywhere worth going to, the modern, if slightly bland, Montestella is on Salerno's main pedestrian thoroughfare, halfway between the *centro storico* and train station. Although some rooms are quite small, all are light and contemporary, with firm beds and patterned feature walls.

🍴 Eating

Cicirinella   ITALIAN €€
(☑ 089 22 65 61; Via Genovesi 28; meals €25; ⊙ 8pm-midnight daily, 1-3pm Sat & Sun; 🛜) This place, tucked behind the cathedral, has that winning combination of an earthy and inviting atmosphere and unfailingly good, delicately composed dishes. Exposed stone, shelves of wine and an open-plan kitchen set the scene for traditional Campanian cuisine like pasta with seafood and chickpeas, or a mussel soup that tastes satisfyingly of the sea.

Sant'Andrea   ITALIAN €€
(☑ 328 727274; www.ristorantesantandrea.it; Piazza Sedile del Campo 58; pizzas €4-6, meals €25-30; ⊙ 12.30-3pm & 8pm-midnight Tue-Sun; 🛜) There's an earthy southern Italian flavour at this classic old-town trattoria with its terrace surrounded by historic houses decorated with last night's pajamas hung out to dry. Choices are more innovative than you would expect, and include such seafood dishes as

Salerno

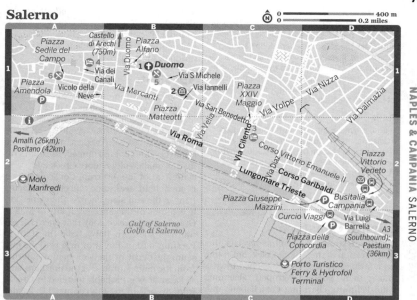

squid with porcini mushrooms and cuttlefish with creamed vegetables.

ℹ️ Information

Post Office (Piazza Vittorio Veneto 7; ⏱ 8.20am-1.30pm Mon-Fri, to 12.30pm Sat) Beside the train station.

Tourist Office (☑ 089 23 14 32; Lungomare Trieste 7; ⏱ 9am-7pm Mon-Sat) Located right on the promenade. Has limited information.

ℹ️ Getting There & Away

BOAT

TraVelMar (☑ 089 87 29 50; www.travelmar. it) Sails seasonally to Amalfi (€8, 35 minutes, 12 daily) and Positano (€12, 70 minutes, eight daily), as well as to Cetara (€5, 15 minutes, six daily), Maiori (€7, 30 minutes, six daily) and Minori (€7, 40 minutes, six daily).

Alicost (☑ Mon-Fri 089 87 14 83, Sat & Sun 089 948 36 71; www.alicost.it) Runs one daily seasonal ferry service to Capri (€25.40, 2¼ hours) via Minori (€7), Amalfi (€8) and Positano (€12).

Navigazione Libera del Golfo (NLG; www. navlib.it) Runs one daily hydrofoil service to Capri (€26) from Easter to mid-October.

TraVelMar services depart from the **Porto Turistico**, 200m down the pier from Piazza della Concordia. You can buy tickets from the booths by the embarkation point. Alicost and Navigazi-

Salerno

◎ Top Sights
1 Duomo...B1

◎ Sights
2 Museo Archeologico Provinciale........B1

🛏 Sleeping
3 Hotel Montestella.............................C2
4 Ostello Ave Gratia Plena A1

🍴 Eating
5 Cicirinella B1
6 Sant'Andrea......................................A1

one Libera del Golfo services depart from **Molo Manfredi**, 1.8km further west.

BUS

SITA Sud (www.sitasudtrasporti.it) buses for Amalfi depart at least hourly from the bus station on Piazza Vittorio Veneto, beside the train station, stopping en route at Vietri sul Mare, Cetara, Maiori and Minori. For Pompeii, take **Busitalia Campania** (☑ 089 984 72 86; www.fsbusitaliacampania.it) bus 4 from nearby Corso Garibaldi (at the corner of Via Luigi Barrella). For the south coast and Paestum, take bus 34 from Piazza della Concordia near the Porto Turistico ferry terminal. Bus 34 runs roughly every one to two hours from Monday to Saturday, with no service on Sunday.

CAR & MOTORCYCLE

Salerno is on the A3 between Naples and Reggio di Calabria; the A3 is toll-free from Salerno south. Take the Salerno exit and follow signs to the *centro*. If you want to hire a car, there's a **Europcar** (☑ 089 258 07 75; www.europcar. com; Via Clemente Mauro 18; ☺ 8.30am-1pm & 2.30-6.30pm Mon-Fri, 8.30am-1pm Sat) agency not far from the train station.

TRAIN

Salerno is a major stop on southbound routes to Calabria, and the Ionian and Adriatic coasts. From the **train station** (Piazza Vittorio Veneto) there are regular services to Naples (from €4.70, 35 to 45 minutes), Rome (Intercity from €30.50, three hours) and Agropoli (€3.40, 40 minutes).

Cilento Coast

The Cilento stretch of coastline may lack the sophistication of the Amalfi Coast, but it too has a string of craggy, sun-bleached towns, among them popular Agropoli, gleaming white Palinuro, charming Castellabate and the evocative ruined temples of Paestum. The Cilento can even afford to have a slight air of superiority when it comes to its beaches: a combination of secluded coves and long stretches of golden sand with fewer overpriced ice creams and sunbeds. Yet Campania's southern bookend is about more than its waterside appeal. It's here that you'll find the ancient Greek temples of Paestum and a large coastal tract of the Parco Nazionale del Cilento, Vallo di Diano e Alburni, also a Unesco World Heritage site.

Paestum

Paestum is home to one of Europe's most glorious archaeological zones. Deemed a World Heritage site by Unesco, it includes three of the world's best-preserved ancient Greek temples, as well as an engrossing museum crammed with millennia-old frescoes, ceramics and daily artefacts. Among these is the iconic *Tomba del tuffatore* (Tomb of the Diver) funerary fresco.

Paestum – or Poseidonia as the city was originally called, in honour of Poseidon, the Greek god of the sea – was founded in the 6th century BC by Greek settlers and fell under Roman control in 273 BC. Decline set in following the demise of the Roman Empire. Savage raids by the Saracens and periodic outbreaks of malaria forced the steadily dwindling population to abandon the city altogether.

Today, Paestum offers visitors a vivid, to-scale glimpse of the grandeur and sophistication of the area's past life.

⊙ Sights

★ **Paestum's Temples**   ARCHAEOLOGICAL SITE
(Area Archeologica di Paestum; ☑ 0828 81 10 23; www.museopaestum.beniculturali.it; adult/reduced incl museum €12/2, ruins only €8/2; ☺ 8.30am-7.30pm daily, last entry 6.50pm, museum closed Mon) Very different to Pompeii, Paestum's ruins are smaller, older, more Greek and – crucially – a lot less overrun. Consequently, it is possible to steal some reflective moments here as the sun slants across the giant Doric columns of this once great city of Magna Graecia (the Greek colony that once covered much of southern Italy). Take the train to Paestum station. Buy your tickets in the museum, just east of the site, before entering from the main entrance at the northern end.

Paestum was probably founded by Greeks from Sybaris in the 6th century BC. It later became a Roman city, but was abandoned in the Middle Ages. The ruins were rediscovered in the 1760s, but not fully unearthed and excavated until the 1950s.

The first structure is the 6th-century-BC **Tempio di Cerere** (Temple of Ceres); originally dedicated to Athena, it served as a Christian church in medieval times.

As you head south, you can pick out the basic outline of the large rectangular forum, the heart of the ancient city. Among the partially standing buildings are the vast domestic housing area and, further south, the amphitheatre. Both provide evocative glimpses of daily life here in Roman times. In the former houses you'll see mosaic floors, and a marble *impluvium* (cistern) that stood in the atrium and collected rainwater.

The **Tempio di Nettuno** (Temple of Neptune), dating from about 450 BC, is the largest and best preserved of the three temples at Paestum; only parts of its inside walls and roof are missing. The two rows of double-storied columns originally divided the outer colonnade from the *cella*, or inner chamber, where a statue of the temple deity would have been displayed. Despite its commonly used name, many scholars believe that the temple was actually dedicated to the Greek goddess Hera, sister and wife of Greek god Zeus.

Almost next door, the so-called **basilica** (a temple to the goddess Hera) is Paestum's oldest surviving monument. Dating from the middle of the 6th century BC, it's a magnificent sight, with nine columns across and 18 along the sides. Ask someone to take your photo next to one of the columns: it's a good way to appreciate the scale.

Save time for the **museum** (☑0828 81 10 23; adult/reduced incl temples €9.50/4.75; ☺8.30am-7.30pm, last entry 6.50pm, closes 1.40pm 1st & 3rd Mon of month), which covers two floors and houses a collection of interesting bas-relief friezes, plus numerous frescoes dating back to the 5th century BC.

The archaeological site and adjoining museum are particularly evocative in spring when they are surrounded by scarlet poppies.

🛏 Sleeping & Eating

There are various restaurants in close proximity to the ruins at Paestum, most serving mediocre food at inflated prices. A much better alternative is Nonna Sceppa, located around 4km northwest of the ruins. Alternatively, head south to Agropoli for more options or book ahead to dine at one of the Cilento's rustic *agriturismi* (farm stays).

⭐ **Casale Giancesare**

Villa Agricola B&B €

(☑0828 199 96 14; www.casalegiancesare.com/en; Via Giancesare 8, Capaccio Paestum; s €50-120, d €60-150, 4-person apt from €80-185; P❄@ ☎⛲) A 19th-century former farmhouse, this elegantly decorated, stone-clad B&B is run by the delightful Voza family, who will happily ply you with their homemade wine, *limoncello* and marmalades; they even make their own olive oil. The B&B is located 2.5km from Paestum and is surrounded by vineyards and olive and mulberry trees; views are marvellous, particularly from the swimming pool.

There are seven farmhouse-chic rooms and three apartments on offer.

Nonna Sceppa ITALIAN €€

(☑0828 85 10 64; Via Laura 53; meals €35; ☺12.30-3pm & 7.30-11pm Fri-Wed; ☎⛲) Seek out the superbly prepared, robust dishes at Nonna Sceppa, a family-friendly restaurant that's gaining a reputation throughout the region for excellence. Dishes are firmly seasonal and, during summer, concentrate on fresh seafood, like the refreshingly simple grilled fish with lemon. Other popular choices include risotto with zucchini and artichokes, and spaghetti with lobster.

ⓘ Information

Tourist Office (☑0828 81 10 16; www.info paestum.it; Via Magna Grecia 887; ☺9am-1pm & 2-4pm) Across the street from the archaeological site, this helpful tourist office offers a map of the archaeological site, as well as information on the greater Cilento region.

ⓘ Getting There & Away

Trains run around 16 times daily from Salerno to Paestum (€2.90, 30 minutes). The temples are a pleasant 10-minute stroll from the station.

Busitalia Campania (www.fsbusitalia campania.it) bus 34 goes to Paestum from Piazza della Concordia in Salerno (€2.70, one hour). Bus 34 runs roughly every one to two hours from Monday to Saturday, with no service on Sunday.

Parco Nazionale del Cilento e Vallo di Diano

Proving the perfect antidote to the holiday mayhem further north, the Parco Nazionale del Cilento, Vallo di Diano e Alburni combines dense woods and flowering meadows, with dramatic mountains, rivers and waterfalls. It is the second-largest national park in Italy, covering 1810 sq km, including 80 towns and villages. To get the best out of the park, you will probably need a car, although the coastal strip from Castellabate down to Palinuro has reasonable pubic transport. The Cilento is known for its orchids, vast underground cave complexes and handsome hilltop villages. Sitting on the cusp of the park proper are the ruins of Paestum and the Certosa di San Lorenzo, both crucial to it gaining Unesco World Heritage status in 1998.

Compared to the Amalfi, the Cilento is not so well set up for tourism and the network of walking trails is less well marked. If in doubt, join a guided excursion.

⊙ Sights

⭐ **Grotte di Castelcivita** CAVE

(☑0828 77 23 97; www.grottedicastelcivita.com; Piazzale N Zonzi, Castelcivita; adult/reduced €10/8; ☺standard tours 10.30am, noon, 1.30pm & 3pm, 4.30pm & 6pm Apr-Sep, 10.30am, noon, 1.30pm & 3pm Mar & Oct; P⛲) The grottoes are fascinating, otherworldly caves that date from prehistoric times: excavations have revealed that they were inhabited 42,000 years ago, making them the oldest known settlement in Europe. Don't forget a jacket, and leave the high heels at home, as paths are wet and slippery. Hard hats (provided) and a certain level of fitness and mobility are required. Located 40km southeast of Salerno on the northwest cusp of the national park, the complex is refreshingly noncommercial.

Although it extends over 4800m, only around half of the complex is open to the public. The one-hour tour winds through a route surrounded by extraordinary stalagmites and stalactites, and a mesmerising play of colours, caused by algae, calcium and iron, which tint the naturally sculpted rock shapes.

The tour culminates in a cavernous lunar landscape – think California's Death Valley in miniature – called the Caverna di Bertarelli. The caves are still inhabited – by bats – and visitors are instructed not to take flash photos for fear of disturbing them.

Certosa di San Lorenzo   MONASTERY
(✆ 0975 7 77 45; www.polomusealecampania.be niculturali.it; Viale Certosa, Padula; adult/reduced €6/3; ⊙ 9am-7pm Wed-Mon) A giant among monasteries, even by Italian standards, the Certosa di San Lorenzo dates from 1306 and covers 250,000 sq metres. Numerologists can get a kick out of ticking off the supposed 320 rooms and halls, 2500m of corridors, galleries and hallways, 300 columns, 500 doors, 550 windows, 13 courtyards, 100 fireplaces, 52 stairways and 41 fountains – in other words, it is *huge*. The monastery is just outside the hillside town of Padula.

As it is unlikely that you will have time to see everything, be sure to visit the highlights, including the vast central courtyard (a venue for summer classical-music concerts), the magnificent wood-panelled library, frescoed chapels, and the kitchen with its grandiose fireplace and famous tale: apparently this is where the legendary 1000-egg omelette was made in 1534 for Charles V's passing army. Unfortunately, the historic frying pan is not on view – just how big was it, one wonders.

Within the monastery you can also peruse the modest collection of ancient artefacts at the **Museo Archeologico Provinciale della Lucania Occidentale** (✆ 0975 7 71 17; Certosa di San Lorenzo, Viale Certosa, Padula; ⊙ 9am-7pm Wed-Mon; ⊕) FREE.

Grotte di Pertosa-Auletta   CAVE
(✆ 0975 39 70 37; www.grottedipertosa-auletta. it; Pertosa; guided visits adult/reduced 100min €20/15, 60min €13/10; ⊙ tour times vary, see website; P ⊕) (Re)discovered in 1932, the Grotte di Pertosa-Auletta date back 35 million years. Used by the Greeks and Romans as places of worship, the caves burrow for some 2500m, with long underground passages and lofty grottoes filled with stalagmites and stalactites. The first part of the tour is a boat (or raft) ride on the river; you disembark just before the waterfall (phew!) and continue on foot for around 800m, surrounded by marvellous rock formations and luminous crystal accretions.

🏃 Activities

The park has 15 listed **nature trails** that vary from 1km to 8km in length. But this isn't the Amalfi. Don't expect abundant signage, well-trodden paths and a surfeit of trail-side cafes selling cappuccinos or lemonade.

The countryside in the park can be dramatic and in spring you'll experience real flower power: delicate narcissi, wild orchids and tulips hold their own among blowsier summer drifts of brilliant yellow ox-eye daisies and scarlet poppies.

Thickets of silver firs, wild chestnuts and beech trees add to the sumptuous landscape, as do the dramatic cliffs, pine-clad mountains and fauna, including wild boars, badgers and wolves and, for bird-watchers, the increasingly rare golden eagle.

Even during the busier summer season, the sheer size of the park means that hikers are unlikely to meet others on the trail to swap tales and muesli bars – so getting lost could become a lonely, not to mention dangerous, experience if you haven't done some essential planning before striding out. In theory, the tourist offices should be able to supply you with a guide to the trails. In reality, they frequently seem to have run out of copies. Failing this, you can buy the *Parco Nazionale del Cilento, Vallo di Diano e Alburni: Carta Turistica e dei Sentieri* (Tourist and Footpath Map; €7) or the excellent *Monte Stella: Walks & Rambles in Ancient Cilento,* published by the Comunita' Montana Alento Monte Stella (€3). Most of the *agriturismi* (farm stays) in the park can also organise guided treks.

A popular self-guided hike, where you are rewarded with spectacular views, is a climb of Monte Alburno (1742m). There's a choice of two trails, both of which are clearly marked from the centre of the small town of Sicignano degli Alburni and finish at the mountain's peak. Allow approximately four hours for either route. The less experienced may prefer to opt for a guide.

Another good access area for hikers is the Trentova-Tresino (Via Fontana dei Monaci; P) nature reserve just south of Agropoli, which has four well-marked coastal walks and a visitor centre.

There are some excellent *agriturismi* (farm-stay accommodation) here that offer additional activities, including guided hikes, painting courses and horse-riding.

🛏 Sleeping & Eating

★ **Agriturismo i Moresani**   AGRITURISMO €
(☑ 0974 90 20 86; www.agriturismoimoresani. com; Località Moresani; d €90-110; ☺ Mar-Oct; ❄ 🛜 ☂) 🖉 For tranquillity and fabulous food, head to this family-run *agriturismo* 1.5km west of Casal Velino. The setting is bucolic: rolling hills interspersed with grapevines, grazing pastures and olive trees. The sprawling farm produces its own *caprino* goat's cheese, wine, olive oil and preserves, and home-grown organic products are the protagonists in its notable restaurant. The rooms themselves are simple and classic in style.

Trattoria degli Ulivi   ITALIAN €
(☑ 334 2595091; www.tavolacaldadegliulivi.it; Viale Certosa, Padula; set menus €10-16; ☺ 11am-4pm Wed-Mon; 🛜) After your marathon walk through the endless corridors of the Certoza di San Lorenzo, head to this uncomplicated restaurant, a short 50m stumble from the main entrance. The decor is canteen-like, but the daily specials are affordable, flavour-filled and generously proportioned. It serves snacks as well as four-course blow-out lunches.

ℹ Information

Alpine Rescue (☑ 118) For emergencies.

Parks.it (www.parks.it/parco.nazionale. cilento/Eindex.php) Useful online information about the national park.

Sicignano degli Alburni Pro Loco (☑ 0828 97 37 55; www.scoprisicignano.it; Piazza Plebiscito 13, Sicignano degli Alburni; ☺ 9am-1.30pm & 2.30-5pm Mon-Sat) Tourist information office with very basic info on the national park.

Tourist Office (p763) In Paestum; this office has info on the Parco Nazionale del Cilento.

ℹ Getting There & Away

SITA Sud (www.sitasudtrasporti.it) Runs three daily services between Salerno and Pertosa (Monday to Saturday), two of which continue to Polla. It also runs one daily bus between Salerno and Castelcivita (weekdays only).

Busitalia Campania (☑ 089 984 72 86; www. fsbusitaliacampania.it) Runs daily buses between Salerno, Agropoli, Castellabate and Acciaroli.

Infante Viaggi (☑ 089 82 57 65; www.agenzia infanteviaggi.it) A twice-weekly bus runs to/ from Rome stopping in Salerno, Sicignano degli Alburni, Padula and Palinuro.

NAPLES & CAMPANIA PARCO NAZIONALE DEL CILENTO E VALLO DI DIANO

AT A GLANCE

POPULATION
6.4 million

CAPITAL
Bari

BEST TRABUCCO
Al Trabucco da Mimì
(p780)

BEST ECO-HOTEL
Palazzo Papaleo
(p796)

**BEST
THRILL-SEEKING**
Il Volo dell'Angelo
(p807)

WHEN TO GO
Apr–Jun Spring wild-
flowers are blooming:
perfect for hiking in
Parco Nazionale del
Pollino.

Jul & Aug Summer
beach weather and
festivals in towns
such as Lecce and
Matera.

Sep & Oct Thinner
crowds, mild weather
and mushrooms
sprouting in Parco
Nazionale della Sila.

Alberobello (p782)

Puglia, Basilicata & Calabria

The Italian boot's heel (Puglia), instep (Basilicata) and toe (Calabria) are where the 'Mezzogiorno' (southern Italy) shows all its throbbing intensity. Long stereotyped as the poorer, more passionate cousins of Italy's sophisticated northerners, these regions are finally being appreciated for their true richness. You *will* see washing on weather-worn balconies, scooters speeding down medieval alleys and ancient towns crumbling under Mediterranean suns. But look past the pasta-advert stereotypes and you'll find things altogether more complex and wonderful: gritty, unsentimental cities with pedigrees stretching back thousands of years, dramatically broken coastlines that have harboured fisherfolk and pirates for millennia, and above all, proud and generous people who are eager to share these delights with you.

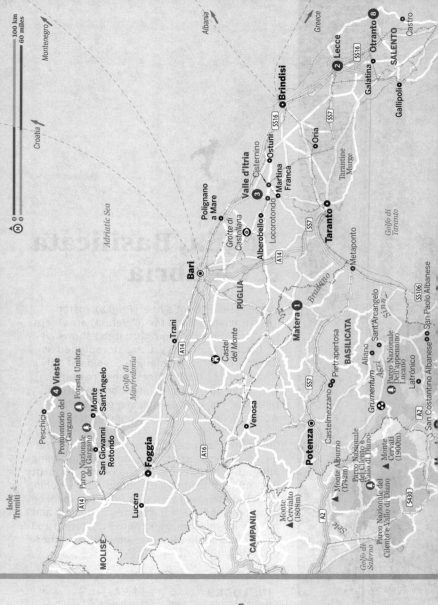

Puglia, Basilicata & Calabria Highlights

1 Matera (p800)
Marvelling at the contrast between miserable caves and soaring cathedrals in this ancient city.

2 Lecce (p782)
Learning to love the ornate excesses of the city's baroque architecture.

3 Valle d'Itria (p782) Eating the best of Mediterranean cuisine in the valley's gorgeous hill towns.

4 Vieste (p776)
Searching for early morning photo ops around the cream-coloured lanes of this divine coastal town.

5 Maratea (p795)
Driving with the top down and the sea in your nostrils around an impossibly

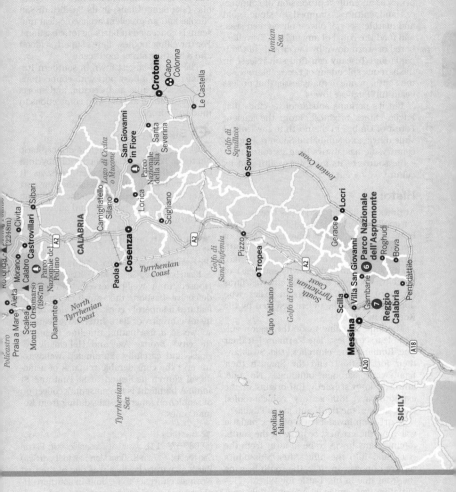

beautiful string of coastal towns.

6 Parco Nazionale dell'Aspromonte (p818) Rambling in the wild, lonely uplands of this mysterious Calabrian wilderness.

7 Museo Nazionale di Reggio Calabria (p819) Getting up close and personal with the godlike Riace Bronzes.

8 Otranto Cathedral (p795) Viewing macabre skulls and magnificent mosaics in this unique Norman basilica.

PUGLIA

Puglia can surely now take its place in the first rank of Italy's famous regions. Clearly, everything the Italophile craves is there in abundance: ancient towns heavy with the tangible past; extravagant churches dreamt up by Europe's finest architects; the footprints of an endless procession of conquerors and cultures, stamped in stone, gold and marble; seas of olives; olive-green seas; and food the equal of any in Italy. Travellers bored or worn down by the crowds of Campania and Tuscany can find still release in the baroque splendour of Lecce, 'Florence of the South', or one of many lesser (but no less beautiful) Pugliese towns.

But it's perhaps outside of its cities that Puglia shines brightest. From the ancient Forest of Umbra in the north to the fruitful Valle d'Itria and sun-baked Salento, Puglia's countryside has always been its foundation – the source of its food, its wealth and its culture.

History

At times Puglia feels and looks Greek – and for good reason. This tangible legacy dates from when the Greeks founded a string of settlements along the Ionian coast in the 8th century BC. A form of Greek dialect (Griko) is still spoken in some towns southeast of Lecce. Historically, the major city was Taras (Taranto), settled by Spartan exiles who dominated until they were defeated by the Romans in 272 BC.

The long coastline made the region vulnerable to conquest. The Normans left their fine Romanesque churches, the Swabians their fortifications and the Spanish their flamboyant baroque buildings. No one, however, knows exactly the origins of the extraordinary 16th-century conical-roofed stone houses, the *trulli,* unique to Puglia.

Apart from invaders and pirates, malaria was long the greatest scourge of the south, forcing many towns to build away from the coast and into the hills. After Mussolini's seizure of power in 1922, the south became the front line in his 'Battle for Wheat'. This initiative was aimed at making Italy self-sufficient when it came to food, following the sanctions imposed on the country after its conquest of Ethiopia. Puglia is now covered in wheat fields, olive groves and fruit arbours.

Bari

☑ 0805 / POP 324,200

Most travellers skip Bari on their way to Puglia's big-hitter, Lecce (the towns have a long-standing rivalry, especially over soccer), but Bari doesn't lack history or culture. The old town contains the bones of St Nicholas (aka Santa Claus) in its Basilica di San Nicola, and an excellent archaeological museum is concealed in Bari's historic bastions. For travelling foodies, there's superb seafood and a bustling street food scene.

The second-largest town in southern Italy, Bari is also a busy port with connections to Greece, Albania and Croatia, and sports an international airport with connections to much of Europe.

◎ Sights

Most sights are in or near the atmospheric old town, Bari Vecchia, a medieval labyrinth of tight alleyways and graceful piazzas. It fills a small peninsula between the new port to the west and the old port to the southeast, cramming in 40 churches and more than 120 shrines.

★ Museo Archeologico
di Santa Scolastica   MUSEUM
(Piazzale Cristoforo Colombo; adult/reduced €5/3; ⊙10am-5pm Wed-Sat & Mon, 10am-2pm Sun) Housed in a well-preserved 16th-century defensive bastion, this excellent museum features a superbly curated overview of the historic origins of Bari. Interactive features showcase a fascinating timeline including the city's Bronze Age and Hellenistic periods, and carefully illuminated walkways traverse the considerable remains of a medieval church dedicated to St Paul and St John. A highlight is the museum's collection of sepulchral funerary slabs dating from Roman times.

★ Basilica di San Nicola   BASILICA
(☑080 573 71 11; www.basilicasannicola.it; Piazza San Nicola; ⊙7am-8.30pm Mon-Sat, to 10pm Sun) Bari's signature basilica was one of the first Norman churches to be built in southern Italy, and is a splendid (if square and solid) example of Pugliese-Romanesque architecture. Dating to the 12th century, it was originally constructed to house the relics of St Nicholas (better known as Father Christmas), which were stolen from Turkey in 1087 by local fishing folk. Today, it is an impor-

Bari

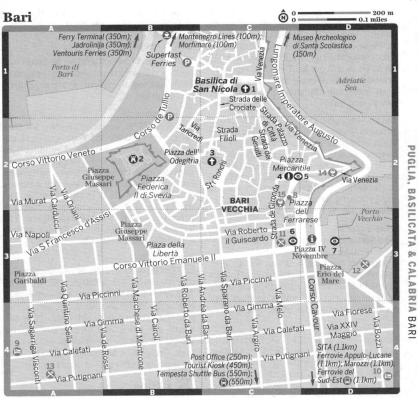

Bari

tant place of pilgrimage for both Catholics and Orthodox Christians.

Cathedral CATHEDRAL
(☏080 521 06 05; www.arcidiocesibaribitonto.it; Piazza dell'Odegitria; ⊙8am-7pm Mon-Sat, 8-10am & 11am-7pm Sun) Built over the original Byzantine church, the 12th- to 13th-century Romanesque cathedral, dedicated to San Sabino, is technically Bari's most important church, although its fame pales alongside San Nicola. Inside, the plain walls are

punctuated with deep arcades and the eastern window is a tangle of plant and animal motifs. The highlight lies in the subterranean **Museo del Succorpo della Cattedrale** (Padult/reduced €3/2; ⊙9.30am-4pm Mon, Wed, Sat & Sun, to 12.30pm Tue, Thu & Fri), where excavations have revealed remnants left over from an ancient Christian basilica and various Roman ruins.

Teatro Margherita
ARTS CENTRE

(Piazza IV Novembre; ⊙vary by exhibition) Originally constructed from 1912 to 1914, this historic theatre was restored and reopened in 2018 and is now used for travelling art and photographic exhibitions. To see inside the beautifully restored interior, ask at the nearby tourist information office if any exhibitions are currently scheduled.

Spazio Murat
CULTURAL CENTRE

(www.facebook.com/spaziomurat; Piazza del Ferrarese; ⊙11am-8pm Tue-Sun) Check out this repurposed heritage building for an ever-changing series of interesting and innovative cultural and art displays, part of the nexus of galleries and exhibition spaces taking shape near the edge of Bari's harbour.

Castello Svevo
CASTLE

(Swabian Castle; ☑ 080 521 37 04; Piazza Federico II di Svevia; adult/reduced €9/3.50; ⊙8.30am-7.30pm Wed-Mon) Roger the Norman originally built this castle in the 12th century over the ruins of a Byzantine structure. Later, Frederick II of Swabia built over the existing castle, incorporating it into his design and leaving intact the two towers of the Norman structure that still stand. The bastions, with corner towers overhanging the moat, were added in the 16th century during Aragonese rule. Excavation is ongoing and the largely sparse interior is used for occasional art and sculpture exhibitions.

Piazza Mercantile
PIAZZA

This beautiful piazza is fronted by the Sedile, the headquarters of Bari's Council of Nobles. In the square's northeast corner is the **Colonna della Giustizia** (Column of Justice), where debtors were once tied and whipped.

⚜ Festivals & Events

Festa di San Nicola
RELIGIOUS

(⊙7-9 May) The Festival of St Nicholas is Bari's biggest annual shindig, celebrating the 11th-century arrival of St Nicholas' relics from Turkey. On the first evening a procession leaves Castello Svevo for the Basilica di San Nicola. The next day there's a deafening

fly-past and a fleet of boats carries the statue of St Nicholas along the coast.

🛏 Sleeping

Most of Bari's hotels tend to be bland and overpriced, aimed at business clientele. B&Bs and rental apartments are generally a better option.

Bozzi 1910
APARTMENT €

(☑ 328 8167829; www.bozzi1910.com; Via Bozzi 39; s/d from €60/85; 🛜) Four stylish studio apartments are in a heritage building near Bari's waterfront. Well-equipped kitchenettes include coffee machines, bathrooms are modern and include laundry facilities, and interesting art enlivens the walls. The friendly owners can also arrange transfers from Bari airport or to the train station. The location is quiet, but it's just a short stroll to good bars and restaurants.

B&B Casa Pimpolini
B&B €

(☑ 333 9580740, 0805 21 99 38; www.casapimpolini. com; Via Calefati 249; s €50-65, d €75-90; ❄🛜) This lovely B&B in Bari's new town is within easy walking distance to shops, restaurants and Bari Vecchia (the old town). The two rooms are warm and welcoming, and the superb homemade breakfast is an absolute treat. Great value and great hospitality from the friendly, well-travelled owner, Dyria.

🍴 Eating

Seafood Market
SEAFOOD €

(Molo San Nicola 6; ⊙11am-2pm Mon-Sat) Just maybe Puglia's freshest raw seafood – including squid, oysters and briny sea urchins – is served outside at simple tables by Bari's wise-cracking fisherfolk. Around €5 will buy a plateful, and local custom is to devour it with a frosty bottle of Peroni beer. An essential Bari experience.

Mastro Ciccio
SANDWICHES €

(☑0805 21 00 01; www.facebook.com/mastrociccio bari; Corso Emanuele 15; from €5; ⊙9am-midnight) 🖋 Top-notch salads and panini sandwiches crammed with local products including octopus, ham, buffalo mozzarella cheese and pistachios make Mastro Ciccio a great place for lunch or a less formal, good-value dinner. Order at the counter and combine your snack with a beer or glass of wine.

Terranima
PUGLIAN €€

(☑0805 21 97 25, 334 6608618; www.terranima. com; Via Putignani 213; meals €30-35; ⊙noon-3pm daily, 7-11pm Mon-Sat) Peep through the lace curtains into the cool interior of this rustic trattoria, where worn flagstone floors and period furnishings make you feel like you're dining in someone's front room. The menu features fabulous regional offerings such as veal, lemon and caper meatballs, and *sporcamuss,* a sweet flaky pastry.

🍷 Drinking & Nightlife

La Bitta   CRAFT BEER
(☑391 7703075; www.facebook.com/labittanew; Via Manfredi Re 36; ☺11am-3am) Our favourite of the bars and cafes along narrow Via Manfredi Re on the edge of Bari's old town. Six beer taps feature a rotating selection and the fridge is packed with top drops from top Italian breweries including CR/AK and Extraomnes. La Bitta's music is usually great and the friendly bar staff can rustle up cheese and charcuterie platters.

Reverso Unconventional Bistrot   WINE BAR
(☑347 9123522; www.facebook.com/reversobistrot; Strada Vallisa 79; ☺7pm-late Tue-Sun; 🛜) Tucked away in a laneway in Bari Vecchia, the cosy Reverso combines an excellent Puglian wine list, interesting bar snacks and platters, and a welcoming and inclusive vibe. Drop by to see if any live music is scheduled, often from Thursday to Saturday from around 9pm.

ℹ️ Information

From Piazza Aldo Moro, in front of the main train station, streets heading north will take you to Corso Vittorio Emanuele II, which separates the old and new parts of the city.

Hospital (☑800 34 93 49; Piazza Cesare 11)
Post Office (☑0805 25 01 50; Piazza Umberto I 33a; ☺8.30am-7pm Mon-Fri, to 12.30pm Sat)
Tourist information office (www.viaggiarein puglia.it; Piazza del Ferrarese 29; ☺9am-7.30pm) English is spoken at this very helpful office. City maps are provided and it's a good source of information on bus and train travel to Matera and Alberobello.
Tourist Kiosk (☑0805 82 14 11; Piazza Aldo Moro 32; ☺9am-1pm & 3-7pm Mon-Sat) Convenient to Bari's central train station and packed with information on the city and Puglia generally.

ℹ️ Getting There & Away

AIR
Bari's **Karol Wojtyła Airport** (☑0805 80 02 00; www.aeroportidipuglia.it; Viale Ferrari), 10km northwest of the city centre, is served by a host of international and budget airlines, including easyJet, Alitalia and Ryanair.

Pugliairbus (www.aeroportidipuglia.it) connects Bari airport with Foggia and Brindisi airports. It also has services to Matera, Vieste and Taranto.

BOAT
Ferries run from Bari to Albania, Croatia, Greece and Montenegro. All boat companies have offices at the **ferry terminal**, accessible on bus 20 from the main train station. Fares vary considerably among companies and it's easier to book with a travel agent such as **Morfimare** (☑0805 7 98 15; www.morfimare.it; Corso de Tullio 36-40).

The main companies and their routes:
Jadrolinija (☑0805 27 54 39; www.jadrolinija.hr; Nuova Stazione Marittima di Bari) For Dubrovnik, Croatia (from €55, 10 hours, up to six times per week) and Bar, Montenegro (from €59, 10 hours, two per week).
Montenegro Lines (☑382 30 31 11 64; www.montenegrolines.net; Corso de Tullio 36) For Bar (Montenegro, from €59, 10 hours, two per week) and Dubrovnik (Croatia, from €59, 10 hours, up to six times per week).
Superfast (☑0805 28 28 28; www.superfast.com; Corso de Tullio 6) For Corfu (from €75, nine hours), Igoumenitsa (from €64, 10 hours) and Patras (from €64) in Greece.
Ventouris Ferries (☑080 876 14 51; www.ventouris.gr; Nuova Stazione Marittima di Bari) For Corfu, Cephalonia and Igoumenitsa (Greece; from €74, 10 hours) and daily ferries to Durrës (Albania; from €75, nine hours).

BUS
Intercity buses leave from two main locations. From Via Capruzzi, south of the main train station, **SITA** (☑0805 79 01 11; www.sitabus.it) covers local destinations. **Ferrovie Appulo-Lucane** (☑0805 72 52 29; http://ferrovie appulolucane.it) buses serving Matera (€4.90, 1¾ hours, six daily) also depart from here, plus **Marozzi** (☑0805 79 02 11; www.marozzivt.it) buses for Rome (from €34.50, 4½ to 5½ hours, six daily – note that the overnight bus departs from Piazza Moro in front of the railway station) and other long-distance destinations.

Buses operated by **Ferrovie del Sud-Est** (FSE; ☑080 546 21 11; www.fseonline.it) leave from Largo Ciaia, south of Piazza Aldo Moro and service the following places:
Alberobello (€5, 1½ hours, hourly); continues to Locorotondo (€5.70, 1¾ hours) and Martina Franca (€5.70, two hours)
Grotte di Castellana (€2.80, one hour, frequent)
Taranto (from €8.60, three hours with change, four per day)

WORTH A TRIP

GROTTE DI CASTELLANA

These spectacular limestone caves, 40km southeast of Bari, are Italy's longest natural subterranean network. The interlinked galleries contain an incredible range of underground landscapes, with extraordinary stalactite and stalagmite formations. The highlight is the Grotta Bianca (White Grotto), an eerie alabaster cavern hung with stiletto-thin stalactites. 'Speleonights' take small torch-wielding groups into the caves after dark, among the bats, beetles, and crustacea that live there.

There are two tours in English: a 1km, 50-minute tour that doesn't include the Grotta Bianca (€12, on the half hour); and a 3km, two-hour tour (€16, on the hour) that does include it. Temperatures inside the cave average 18°C, so take a light jacket.

In the same complex, you'll also find a speleology **museum** (☑ 080 499 82 30; www.grottedicastellana.it; ⊙ 9.30am-1pm & 3.30-6.30pm mid-Mar–Oct, 10am-1pm Nov–mid-Mar) **FREE** and an **observatory** (☑ 080 499 82 13; www.osservatorio.grottedicastellana.it; adult/6-14yr €5/3; ⊙ tours by appointment Jul & Aug).

Grotte di Castellana can be reached by rail from Bari on the FSE Bari–Taranto train line (€3.20, 1¼ hours, roughly hourly).

TRAIN

A web of train lines spreads out from Bari. Note that there are fewer services on the weekend.

From the **Bari Centrale Station** (☑ 0805 24 43 86), Trenitalia trains go to Puglia and beyond: Destinations include Brindisi (from €8.60, one hour, frequent and Rome (from €40, four hours, four per day).

Ferrovie Appulo-Lucane (☑ 0805 72 52 29; http://ferrovieappulolucane.it) serves Matera (€5, 1¾ hours, 12 daily) and Potenza (€11.60, 3¾ hours, four daily).

Ferrovie del Sud-Est (FSE; ☑ 0805 46 21 11; www.fseonline.it) trains leave from the southern side of the station where they have their own separate ticket office: Destinations include:

Alberobello (€5, 1¾ hours, hourly)

Martina Franca (€5.70, 3¼ hours, five per day)

Taranto (from €6.40, 2½ hours, nine daily)

❶ Getting Around

Central Bari is compact – a 15-minute walk will take you from Piazza Aldo Moro to the old town. For the ferry terminal, take bus 20 (tickets €1.50) from Piazza Moro.

Street parking is migraine-inducing. There's a large parking area (€1) south of the main port entrance; otherwise, there's a large multistorey car park between the main train station and the FSE station. Another car park is on Via Zuppetta, opposite Hotel Adria.

TO/FROM THE AIRPORT

To and from the airport, the most direct option is to catch the **train** (www.ferrovienordbarese.it; Piazza Aldo Moro; €5) to Bari Centrale's Ferrovie Nord terminal (€5, 20 minutes, 6am to midnight). Another option is to take the **Tempesta shuttle bus** (www.autoservizitempesta.it), also from Bari Centrale (€4, 30 minutes, hourly),

with pickups at Piazza Garibaldi and the corner of Via Andrea da Bari and Via Calefati. A taxi trip from the airport to town costs around €25.

Around Bari

The *Terra di Bari*, or 'land of Bari', surrounding the capital is rich in olive groves and orchards, and has an impressive architectural history, with some magnificent cathedrals, an extensive network of castles along its coastline, charming seaside towns like Trani and the mysterious inland Castel del Monte.

Trani

☑ 0883 / POP 56,100

Known as the 'Pearl of Puglia', beautiful Trani has a sophisticated feel, particularly in summer when well-heeled visitors pack the array of marina-side bars. The marina is the place to promenade and watch the white yachts and fishing boats in the harbour, while the historic centre, with its medieval churches, glossy limestone streets, historic Jewish quarter and faded yet charming *palazzi* is an enchanting area to explore. But it's the cathedral, pale against the deep-blue sea, that is the town's most arresting sight.

❍ Sights

Cathedral   CATHEDRAL
(www.cattedraletrani.it; Piazza del Duomo; campanile €5; ⊙ 8.30am-12.30pm & 3.30-7pm Mon-Sat, 9am-12.30pm & 4-8.30pm Sun Apr-Oct, shorter hours Nov-Mar) This dramatic seafront cathedral is dedicated to St Nicholas the Pilgrim, a Greek Christian who wandered through Puglia crying '*Kyrie eleison*' ('Lord, have

mercy'). First thought to be a simpleton, he was posthumously revered after several miracles attributed to him occurred. Below the church is the crypt, a forest of ancient columns that predates the current structure, and where the bones of St Nicholas are kept beneath the altar. You can also visit the campanile (bell tower).

Castello
CASTLE

(☏080 528 52 49; www.castelloditrani.beniculturali.it; Piazza Manfredi 16; adult/reduced €5/2.50; ☺8am-7pm) Two hundred metres north of the cathedral is one of Trani's major landmarks, the vast, almost modernist Swabian castle built by Frederick II in 1233. Charles V later strengthened the fortifications and it was used as a prison from 1844 to 1974. While the moat is now dry, the ingenious engineers originally devised a system allowing the level of seawater in it to be precisely controlled.

Scolanova Synagogue
SYNAGOGUE

(☏0883 48 17 99; Via Scolanova 23; ☺hours vary) This synagogue, one of four once established in Trani's ancient Jewish quarter, has been reborn after over 600 years. Persecutions, forced conversions and confiscations periodically beset the Jews of Trani, culminating in their forced expulsion in 1510. This 13th-century synagogue was converted to a Christian church in an earlier wave of hate, around 1380. Abandoned by the mid-20th century, it has been deconsecrated and re-turned to life as the Jewish house of worship it originally was.

Ognissanti Church
CHURCH

(Via Ognissanti; ☺hours vary) Traditionally (but controversially) thought to be built by the Knights Templar in the 12th century, this church became a place of blessing for those setting out on Crusade. Legend has it that it was in this austere and dignified building that the knights of the First Crusade swore allegiance to their leader, Bohemond I of Antioch, before setting off to 'liberate' the Holy Lands. Whatever the truth, it's a treasured example of Pugliese-Romanesque architecture of the period.

🛌 Sleeping

B&B Centro Storico Trani
B&B €

(☏0883 50 61 76; www.bbtrani.it; Via Leopardi 28; s/d €40/60; ☏) This simple, old-fashioned B&B inhabits the 14th-century Palazzo Morola in the old Jewish quarter, and is run by a lovely elderly couple. It's basic, but the rooms are large and 'Mama' makes a mean *crostata* (jam tart). There's a terrace, laundry and wi-fi in communal areas.

Palazzo Filisio
HOTEL €€

(☏0883 50 09 31; www.palazzofilisio.it; Piazza Addazi 2; d/ste €145/190; P❀☏) A lovely building facing the cathedral and the Adriatic, the 18th-century Palazzo Filisio houses this charmingly understated grand hotel.

WORTH A TRIP

FREDERICK II'S TOY CASTLE

You'll see Castel del Monte (☏0883 56 99 97; www.casteldelmonte.beniculturali.it; adult/reduced €10/3.50; ☺10.30am-7.30pm Apr-Sep, 9am-6.30pm Oct-Mar), an inhumanly exact geometric shape on a hilltop, from miles away. Mysterious and perfectly octagonal, it's one of southern Italy's most talked-about landmarks and a Unesco World Heritage Site. No one knows why Frederick II built it – there's no nearby town or strategic crossroads. It was not built to defend anything, as it has no moat or drawbridge, no arrow slits, and no trapdoors for pouring boiling oil on invaders.

Some theories claim that, according to mid-13th-century beliefs in geometric symbolism, the octagon represented the union of the circle and square, of God-perfection (the infinite) and human-perfection (the finite). The castle was therefore nothing less than a celebration of the relationship between humanity and God.

The castle has eight octagonal towers. Its interconnecting rooms have decorative marble columns and fireplaces, and the doorways and windows are framed in corallite stone. Many of the towers have washing rooms with what are thought to be Europe's first flushing loos – Frederick II, like the Arab world he admired, set great store by cleanliness. Audio guides (€3) are a worthwhile investment to maximise your visit.

To get to the castle without a car, take the Ferrovia Bari-Nord train from Bari to Andria, then bus number 6 from Andria station to the castle (35 minutes, five daily, April to October only). The castle is about 35km from Trani; there's no parking, but a nearby site charges €5 for a car, and €1 for a shuttle up the short, steepish 500m to the castle.

WORTH A TRIP

POLIGNANO A MARE

Located around 34km south of Bari on the S16 coastal road, Polignano a Mare is spectacularly built on the edge of a craggy ravine pockmarked with caves. The town is thought to be one of the most important ancient settlements in Puglia and was later inhabited by successive invaders ranging from the Huns to the Normans. On Sunday the *logge* (balconies) are crowded with day trippers from Bari who come here to view the crashing waves, visit the caves and crowd out the *cornetterias* (shops specialising in Italian croissants) in the atmospheric centro storico. **Polignano Made in Love** (☑080 321 77 58; www.polignanomadeinlove.com; Via Anemone 39; tours per person €25-100) offers a wide range of culinary experiences, including cookery classes, as well as biking tours, SUP (stand-up paddleboarding) and boat trips exploring the spectacular coastline. The town is also home to **MINT Cucina Fresca** (www.mintcucinafresca.com; Via San Benedetto 32; meals €25-35; ⏰12.30-2.30pm & 7-10pm Tue-Sat, 12.30-4pm Sun; ☑) ✿, a notable eatery known for its vegetarian focus.

Regular trains (€2.50, 35 minutes) link Bari Centrale to Polignano a Mare.

Stylish rooms have been renovated with colours referencing the cobalt Adriatic and the location is superb. The in-house Regia restaurant (meals €60) maintains the up-market vibe with dishes such as risotto with prawns, asparagus and black truffle.

✕ Eating

Paninart　SEAFOOD €
(Via Statuti Marittimi 78; meals €7-12; ⏰noon-3pm & 6-11.30pm; 🔊) This compact and happening spot soundtracked by classic soul music combines good-value gourmet salads and *panini* sandwiches with a thoughtful selection of local wines and Puglian craft beers. There's brilliant harbourfront seating outside and excellent service from the young waitstaff. Try the U Purp sandwich, crammed with tender lemon-marinated octopus.

★ Corteinfiore　SEAFOOD €€
(☑0883 50 84 02; www.corteinfiore.it; Via Ognissanti 18; meals €40-45; ⏰1-2.15pm Tue-Sun, 8-10.15pm Tue-Sat) The decking, stiff tablecloths and marquee setting of this famed Trani seafood restaurant set hopes racing, and the food, wine and service deliver in full. Expect lots of seafood, and expect it to be excellent: try the *frutti di mari antipasti*, or the Gallipoli prawns with candied lemon. Also rents delightful rooms (double €120) decked out in pale colours.

ℹ Information

Tourist Office (☑0883 58 88 30; https:// viaggiareinpuglia.it; 1st fl, Palazzo Palmieri, Piazza Trieste 10; ⏰10.30am-12.30pm & 5.30-7.30pm Mon-Sat) Located 200m south of the cathedral. Offers free guided walking tours most days in the peak season at 8pm.

ℹ Getting There & Away

STP (☑0883 49 18 00; www.stpspa.it) has frequent bus services to Bari (€4.20, 45 minutes). Services depart from **Bar Stazione** (Piazza XX Settembre 23), which has timetables and tickets.

Trani is on the main train line between Bari (€3.20, 30 to 45 minutes, frequent) and Foggia (€6.50, 40 to 50 minutes, frequent).

Promontorio del Gargano

The coast surrounding this expansive promontory seems permanently bathed in a pink-hued, pearly light, providing a painterly contrast to the sea, which softens from intense to powder blue as the evening draws in. It's one of Italy's most beautiful corners, encompassing white limestone cliffs, fairy-tale grottoes, sparkling sea, ancient forests, rare orchids and tangled, fragrant maquis (dense scrub vegetation).

Once connected to what is now Dalmatia (in Croatia), the 'spur' of the Italian boot has more in common with the land mass across the sea than with the rest of Italy. Creeping urbanisation was halted in 1991 by the creation of the **Parco Nazionale del Gargano** (www.parcogargano.gov.it) FREE. Aside from its magnificent national park, the Gargano is home to pilgrimage sites and the lovely seaside towns of Vieste and Peschici.

Vieste

☑0884 / POP 13,950

Like a young belle who's beautiful without even realising it, the town of Vieste clings modestly to a spectacular promontory on the Gargano Promontory. It resembles nothing so much as a cross between Naples and Dubrovnik, with a bit of Puglian magic mixed in. The narrow alleys of the old town, draped with lines of drying clothes and patrolled by slinking cats and the odd friendly dog, are atmospheric day or night, high or low season. Wedged up against the old town is the equally unpretentious new town, ghostly in winter, but packed with holidaying humanity in summer, especially during the *passeggiata* (evening stroll).

Vieste is strategically placed atop the steep Pizzomunno cliffs between two sweeping sandy beaches. The gritty harbour offers water sports, while the surrounding Parco Nazionale del Gargano is perfect for cycling and hiking.

◉ Sights

Cathedral
CATHEDRAL

(Via Duomo; ⊙7.30am-noon & 4-11pm) Built by the Normans on the ruins of a Vesta temple, this 11th-century 'co-cathedral' (so called because its bishopric is shared with another) is in Pugliese-Romanesque style with a fanciful tower that resembles a cardinal's hat. Of note are its beautiful paintings, swirling interior columns and Latin-inscribed altar.

Chianca Amara
HISTORIC SITE

(Bitter Stone; Via Cimaglia) Vieste's most gruesome sight is this worn and polished stone where thousands were beheaded when Turks sacked Vieste in the 16th century.

🏃 Activities

Superb sandy beaches surround the town: in the south are Spiaggia del Castello, Cala San Felice and Cala Sanguinaria; due north, head for the area known as La Salata. Diving is popular around the promontory's rocky coastline, which is filled with marine grottoes. From May to September fast boats zoom to the Isole Tremiti.

For hiking ideas, pick up a *Guida al Trekking sul Gargano* brochure from the tourist office. A section of walk 4 is doable from Vieste. It starts 2.5km south of town off the Lungomare Enrico Mattei, where a track cuts up through olive groves into increasingly wild terrain.

👉 Tours

Motobarca Desirèe
BOATING

(☑360 262386; www.grottemarinegargano.com; Lungomare Vespucci; adult/child €23/10; ⊙Apr-Oct) These boat tours of the various caves, arches and *trabucchi* (Pugliese fishing structures) that characterise the Gargano coast are spectacular, though the boats can get crowded. There are two departures a day (9am and 2.30pm); buy tickets port-side. Other boat operators offer similar trips.

Explora Gargano
CYCLING

(☑340 7136864, 0884 70 22 37; www.exploragargano.it/contatti.html; Vieste-Peschici km 5.5; tours from €50) To get off the beach for a day or two, take one of the many tours on offer at Explora Gargano. As well as hiking and mountain biking (half day from €70) in the Foresta Umbra, it offers quad tours and 4WD safaris.

🛏 Sleeping

Albergo Labotte
B&B €

(☑0884 70 75 13; Lungomare Mattei 14; d from €60; P 🐾) With a location opposite Vieste's main beach, Albergo Labotte is well placed for a convenient stay. All rooms have been refurbished to a modern and very comfortable standard and there is also off-street, secure parking. The owners don't speak much English, but they are unfailingly friendly and helpful. Bathrooms are particularly spacious.

B&B Rocca sul Mare
B&B €

(☑0884 70 27 19; www.roccasulmare.it; Via Mafrolla 32; r from €80; 🐾) In a former convent in the old quarter, this is a popular, charming and reasonably priced place with comfortable high-ceilinged rooms. There's also a rooftop terrace with panoramic views, a suite with a steam bath and simple, tasty meals (€25 for four courses). Bike hire is available, and your hosts can arrange fishing trips and cook your catch that evening.

Relais Parallelo 41
B&B €€

(☑0884 35 50 09; www.bbparallelo41.it; Via Forno de Angelis 3; r €120; ⊙Mar-Oct; 🕸🐾) This small B&B in an updated *palazzo* in the midst of the old town has five renovated rooms decorated with hand-painted ceilings, luxurious beds and super modern bathrooms. Breakfasts consist of a buffet, and the reception area acts as a mini information centre for local activities. Note that there are minimum stays in July and August.

🍴 Eating & Drinking

Osteria degli Archi
ITALIAN €€

(☑0884 70 51 99; www.osteriadegliarchivieste.it; Via Ripe 2; meals €35-40; ⊙noon-2.30pm & 7-11pm) A classy cut above other Vieste restaurants, Osteria degli Archi offers innovative spins on established flavours and recipes. Stand-out dishes include tartare of red tuna and gossamer-light ravioli stuffed with smoked cheese, mint and fennel. Wine bottles lining the stone walls hint at the restaurant's excellent wine list with many Puglian and Salento labels available. Bookings recommended on summer weekends.

Carpenter
WINE BAR
(☑ 320 6989512; Via Seggio 9; ⊗ 11am-late Apr-Oct; 🛜) Vieste's go-to for *aperitivi* is this popular spot where locals line their refreshing drinks up on a rustic sea wall. Look forward to ocean views on the edge of the old town and a selection of Italian craft beers and wine. During the day it's a more laid-back espresso bar. The location used to be a carpenter's workshop.

ℹ️ Information

POST OFFICE
Post Office (☑ 0884 70 28 49; Via Vittorio Veneto 7; ⊗ 8.30am-7pm Mon-Sat)

TOURIST INFORMATION
Tourist Office (☑ 0884 70 88 06; Piazza Garibaldi; ⊗ 8am-8pm Mon-Sat) You can weigh yourself down with useful brochures here.

ℹ️ Getting There & Away

BOAT
Vieste's port is to the north of town, about a five-minute walk from the tourist office. In summer, several companies, including **Linee Marittime Adriatico** (☑ 0884 96 20 23; Corso Garibaldi 32), head to the Isole Tremiti. Tickets can be bought port-side and at agencies in town.

THE RICH FLAVOURS OF CUCINA POVERA

In Italy's less wealthy 'foot', traditional recipes evolved through economic necessity rather than experimental excess. Local people used whatever ingredients were available to them, plucked directly from the surrounding soil and seas, and kneaded and blended using recipes passed down through generations. The result is called *cucina povera* (literally 'food of the poor'), which, thanks to a recent global obsession with farm-to-table purity, has become increasingly popular.

If there is a mantra for *cucina povera*, it is 'keep it simple'. Pasta is the south's staple starch. Made with just durum wheat and water (and no eggs, unlike some richer northern pastas) it is most commonly sculpted into *orecchiette* ('little ears') and used as the starchy platform on which to serve whatever else might be growing readily and inexpensively. For the same reasons, vegetables feature prominently: eggplants, mushrooms, tomatoes, artichokes, olives and many other staple plants grow prodigiously in these climes and are put to good use in the dishes.

Meat, though present in *cucina povera*, is used more sparingly than in the north. Lamb and horsemeat predominate and are usually heavily seasoned. Unadulterated fish is more common, especially in Puglia, which has a longer coastline than any other mainland Italian region. Popular fish dishes incorporate mussels, clams, octopus (in Salento), swordfish (in northern Calabria), cod and prawns.

A signature Pugliese *primi* (first course) is *orecchiette con cima di rape*, a gloriously simple blend of rapini (a bitter green leafy veg with small broccoli-like shoots) mixed with anchovies, olive oil, chilli peppers, garlic and *pecorino*. Another popular *orecchiette* accompaniment is *ragù di carne di cavallo* (horsemeat), sometimes known as *ragù alla barese*. Bari is known for its starch-heavy *riso, patate e cozze*, a surprisingly delicious marriage of rice, potatoes and mussels that is baked in the oven. Another wildly popular vegetable is wild chicory, which, when combined with a fava bean purée, is reborn as *fave e cicorie*.

Standard cheeses of the south include *burrata*, which has a mozzarella-like shell and a gooey centre, and *pecorino di filiano*, a sheep's-milk cheese from Basilicata. There are tons of bread recipes, but the horn-shaped crusty bread from Matera is king.

Recommended traditional restaurants include Terranima (p772) in Bari and Alle due Corti (p792) in Lecce. Awaiting Table (p789) in Lecce and Charming Tours (p782) in Alberobello offer cookery classes, and tours with Velo Service in Bari (☑ 389 6207353; www.veloservice.org; Strada Vallisa 81; tours from €15; ⊗ 10am-7pm) and Lecce (p790) explore the region's hearty street food.

BUS

From Piazzale Manzoni, where intercity buses terminate, a 10-minute walk east along Viale XXIV Maggio, which becomes Corso Fazzini, brings you into the old town and the Marina Piccola's attractive promenade. In summer buses terminate at Via Verdi, a 300m walk from the old town down Via Papa Giovanni XXIII.

SITA (0881 35 20 11; www.sitabus.it) buses run between Vieste and Foggia via Manfredonia. There are also services to Monte Sant'Angelo (€5) via Macchia Bivio Monte.

From May to September, **Pugliairbus** (080 580 03 58; www.aeroportidipuglia.it) runs a service (€20, three hours, four daily) to the Gargano, including Vieste and Peschici, from Bari airport.

Monte Sant'Angelo

0884 / POP 12,550 / ELEV 796M

One of Europe's most important pilgrimage sites, this isolated mountain-top town has an extraordinary atmosphere. Pilgrims have been coming here for centuries – and so have the hustlers, pushing everything from religious kitsch to parking spaces.

The object of devotion is the Santuario di San Michele. Here, in AD 490, St Michael the Archangel is said to have appeared in a grotto to the Bishop of Siponto.

During the Middle Ages, the sanctuary marked the end of the Route of the Angel, which began in Mont St-Michel (in Normandy) and passed through Rome. In 999 the Holy Roman Emperor Otto III made a pilgrimage to the sanctuary to pray that prophecies about the end of the world in the year 1000 would not be fulfilled. His prayers were answered, the world staggered on and the sanctuary's fame grew.

The sanctuary has been a Unesco World Heritage Site since 2011.

Sights

Santuario di San Michele   CAVE
(0884 56 11 50; www.santuariosanmichele.it; Via Reale Basilica; 7.30am-7.30pm Jul-Sep, shorter hours rest of year) FREE Over the centuries this sanctuary has expanded to incorporate a large complex of religious buildings that overlay its original shrine. The double-arched entrance vestibule at street level stands next to a distinctive octagonal bell tower built by Carlo I of Naples in 1282. As you descend the staircase inside, look for the 17th-century pilgrims' graffiti. The grotto/shrine where St Michael is said to have left

a footprint in stone is located at the bottom of the staircase.

Because of St Michael's footprint, it became customary for pilgrims to carve outlines of their feet and hands into the stone. Etched Byzantine bronze and silver doors, cast in Constantinople in 1076, open into the grotto itself. Inside, a 16th-century statue of the Archangel Michael covers the site of St Michael's footprint. Audio guides cost €3, and it's €5 to get into the museum (or €7 for both together).

Tomba di Rotari   TOMB
(0884 56 11 50; Largo Tomba di Rotari; €1; 9am-noon & 3-7pm Apr-Oct, to 4.30pm Nov-Mar) A short flight of stairs opposite the Santuario di San Michele leads to a 12th-century baptistry with a deep sunken basin for total immersion. You enter the baptistry through the facade of the Chiesa di San Pietro with its intricate rose window squirming with serpents – all that remains of the church, destroyed in a 19th-century earthquake. The Romanesque portal of the adjacent 11th-century Chiesa di Santa Maria Maggiore has some fine bas-reliefs.

Castle   CASTLE
(0884 56 54 44; Largo Roberto Giuscardo 2; €2; 9am-1pm & 2.30-7pm) At the highest point of Monte Sant'Angelo is this rugged fastness, first built by Orso I, who later became Doge of Venice, in the 9th century. One 10th-century tower, Torre dei Giganti, survives, but most of what you can see are Norman, Swabian and Aragonese additions. The views alone are worth the admission.

Sleeping & Eating

Hotel Michael   HOTEL €
(0884 56 55 19; Via Reale Basilica 86; s/d €50/65;) A small hotel with shuttered windows, located on the main street across from the Santuario di San Michele, this traditional place has spacious rooms, some with extremely pink bedspreads, and walls spruced up with devotional art. Ask for a room with a view, or just enjoy it as you breakfast on the rooftop terrace.

Casa li Jalantuúmene   TRATTORIA €€
(0884 56 54 84; www.li-jalantuumene.it; Piazza de Galganis 5; meals €45; noon-3pm & 7.30-10.30pm Wed-Mon;) This renowned restaurant owned by well-known chef Gegè Mangano serves excellent fare amid an intimate setting. The seasonal menu always

features good vegetarian options, there's a select wine list and, in summer, tables spill onto the piazza. There are also four suites on-site (from €100), decorated in traditional Pugliese style. Chef Gegè has also opened an informal wine bar (☑ 087 97 63 21; Via Gambadoro 27; ☉ 7.30pm-late) nearby.

❶ Getting There & Away

SITA (☑ 0881 35 20 11; www.sitasudtrasporti. it) buses run to and from Foggia (€7, 1½ hours, four daily) and Vieste via Macchia Bivio Monte.

Peschici

☑ 0884 / POP 4500

Perched above a turquoise sea and tempting beach, Peschici, like Vieste, is a cliff-clinging Amalfi lookalike. Its tight-knit old walled town of Arabesque whitewashed houses acts as a hub to a wider resort area. The small town gets crammed in summer, so book in advance. Boats zip across to the Isole Tremiti in high season, and there are a couple of excellent places to eat.

◉ Sights

Castello di Peschici   CASTLE
(adult/reduced €4/2; ☉ 9.30am-1.30pm & 4-9pm Jun-Sep) Peschici's medieval hilltop castle stands sentinel over the town's port, and inside there is a fascinating Museum of Torture with life-sized replicas of some of history's most devious and chilling methods to extract information through extreme coercion.

🛏 Sleeping & Eating

Peschici's ample accommodation stocks can come under stress when it seems half of Puglia heads to Gargano in August.

Locanda al Castello   B&B €€
(☑ 0884 96 40 38; www.peschicialcastello.it; Via Castello 29; s/d €70/120; P ✳ 🤶) Staying here is like entering a large, welcoming family home. It's by the cliffs with fantastic views and it's air-conditioned, should you visit in the height of summer. Enjoy hearty home cooking in the restaurant (meals €25) while the owners' kids run around playing football – indoors!

★ Al Trabucco da Mimì   SEAFOOD €€
(☑ 0884 96 25 56; www.altrabucco.it; Localita Punta San Nicola; meals €40-45; ☉ 12.30-2pm & 7-11pm Easter-Oct) Mimì sadly passed away in 2016, but his extended family keep this delightful place ticking. Sitting on wooden trestles beneath the *trabucco* (a traditional Pugliese wooden fishing platform) you'll eat the freshest seafood, prepared with expertise but no fuss, as you watch the sun sink behind Peschici. Local Gargano craft beers complete a relaxed experience. Bookings are recommended for weekends.

There are three simple rooms for rent, at €50 per person. There's also occasional live music (usually jazz) and *aperitivo* in summer.

Porta di Basso   ITALIAN €€€
(☑ 0884 35 51 67; www.portadibasso.it; Via Colombo 38; menus €45-60; ☉ noon-2.30pm & 7-11pm, closed Jan & Feb) 🥢 Superb views of the ocean drop away from the floor-to-ceiling windows beside intimate alcove tables at this adventurous and stylish clifftop restaurant. Choose from one of three degustation menus, and prepare to be delighted by dishes such as smoked bluefish with Jerusalem artichokes, foie gras and honey vinegar.

❶ Information

Tourist Office (☑ 0884 96 49 66; Via Magenta 3; ☉ 10am-1pm & 4.30-7pm Mon-Sat)

❶ Getting There & Away

The bus terminal is beside the sports ground, uphill from the main street, Corso Garibaldi.

From April to September, ferry companies, including Linee Marittime Adriatico (p778), serve the Isole Tremiti (adult/child €30/18, 1½ hours). Day trips to the islands are also possible daily during July and August, and around key holiday weekends.

Foresta Umbra

The 'Forest of Shadows' is the Gargano's enchanted interior – thickets of tall, epic trees interspersed with picnic spots bathed in dappled light. It's the last remnant of Puglia's ancient forests: Aleppo pines, oaks, yews and beech trees cloak the hilly terrain. More than 65 different types of orchid have been discovered here, and the wildlife includes roe deer, wild boar, foxes, badgers and the increasingly rare wild cat. Walkers and mountain bikers will find plenty of well-marked trails within the forest's 5790 sq km.

There is a small *centro visitatori* in the middle of Foresta Umbra that houses a museum and nature centre (SP52bis, Foresta Umbra; €1.50; ☉ 9.30am-6.30pm mid-Apr–mid-Oct, 4-10pm Easter) with fossils, photographs, and stuffed animals and birds. Half-day guided hikes are available by reservation (€10 per person) and you can hire bikes (per hour/day €5/25) and buy walking maps (€2.50). The centre is on SP52bis close to the junction with SP528.

Located en route from Vieste to Foresta Umbra, **Gargano Bike** (☑ 329 315 76 47; www.gargano.bike; Mandrione; rental/tours from €20/30) can arrange mountain-bike rental, provide advice on recommended local trails and also organise half-day mountain-bike tours.

In the middle of the Foresta Umbra, 5km north of the visitor centre on the way to Vico di Gargano, cosy **Rifugio Sfilzi** (☑ 338 3345544; www.rifugiosfilzi.com; SP528; adult €45, incl half-/full board €85/100, child 4-12 incl full board €50) offers eight rooms with three- and four-bed configurations, making them ideal for groups or families. It also has a small shop selling locally made products such as jams and oils, and a cafe-restaurant with homemade cake and coffee. Three-course menus (€525) are also available.

ℹ Getting There & Away

You'll need your own transport to get in and out of the forest.

Isole Tremiti

POP 490

This beautiful archipelago of three islands, 36km offshore, is a picturesque composition of ragged cliffs, sandy coves and thick pine woods, surrounded by the glittering dark-blue sea.

Unfortunately, the islands are no secret, and in July and August some 100,000 holidaymakers head over. If you want to savour the islands in tranquillity, visit during the shoulder season. In the low season most tourist facilities close down and the few permanent residents resume their quiet and isolated lives.

The islands' main facilities are on San Domino, the largest and lushest island, formerly used to grow crops. It's ringed by alternating sandy beaches and limestone cliffs; inland grows thick maquis flecked with rosemary and foxglove. The centre harbours a nondescript small town with several hotels.

Small San Nicola island is the traditional administrative centre; a castle-like cluster of medieval buildings rises up from its rocks. The third island, Capraia, is uninhabited.

◉ Sights

San Domino   ISLAND

Head to San Domino for walks, grottoes and coves. It has a pristine, marvellous coastline and the islands' only sandy beach, **Cala delle Arene**. Alongside the beach is the small cove **Grotta dell'Arene**, with calm clear waters for swimming. You can also take a boat trip (around €20 from the port) around the island to explore the grottoes: the largest, Grotta del Bue Marino, is 70m long. A tour of all three islands costs around €25.

Diving in the translucent sea is another option with **Tremiti Diving Center** (☑ 337 648917; www.tremitidivingcenter.com; Via Federico II, Villaggio San Domino; 1-tank day-/night-dive from €40/50). There's an undemanding, but enchanting, walking track around the island, starting at the far end of the village.

San Nicola   ISLAND

Medieval buildings thrust out of San Nicola's rocky shores, the same pale-sand colour as the barren cliffs. In 1010, Benedictine monks founded the **Abbazia e Chiesa di Santa Maria** here; for the next 700 years the islands were ruled by a series of abbots who accumulated great wealth.

Capraia   ISLAND

The third of the Isole Tremiti, Capraia (named after the wild caper plant) is uninhabited. Birdlife is plentiful, with impressive flocks of seagulls. There's no organised transport, but trips can be negotiated with local fishing folk.

🛏 Sleeping & Eating

La Casa di Gino   B&B €€

(☑ 0882 46 34 10; www.hotel-gabbiano.com; Via dei Forni, San Nicola; d €140-165; ✳) A tranquil accommodation choice on San Nicola, away from the frenzy of San Domino, this B&B run by the Hotel Gabbiano has stylish white-on-white rooms. Great views and quiet space to amble or relax are two of its most delightful aspects.

Hotel Gabbiano   HOTEL €€

(☑ 0882 46 34 10; www.hotel-gabbiano.com; Via Garibaldi 5, Villaggio San Domino; d from €120; ✳ 🛜) An established icon on San Nicola and run for decades by the same Neapolitan family, this smart hotel has pastel-coloured rooms with balconies overlooking the town and the sea. It also has a seafood restaurant, spa and gym.

Archititiello
SEAFOOD €€

(☑ 0882 46 30 54; Via Salita delle Mura 5, San Domino; meals €30-35; ⊙noon-3pm & 7.30-11pm Apr-Oct) A class act with a sea-view terrace, this place specialises in – what else? – fresh fish.

❶ Getting There & Away

Boats for the Isole Tremiti depart from several points on the Italian mainland: Manfredonia, Vieste and Peschici in summer, and Termoli in nearby Molise year-round. Most boats arrive at San Domino. Small boats regularly make the brief crossing to San Nicola (€6 return) in high season; from October to March a single boat makes the trip after meeting the boat from the mainland.

Valle d'Itria

Between the Ionian and Adriatic coasts rises the great limestone plateau of the Murgia (473m). It has a strange karst geology: the landscape is riddled with holes and ravines through which small streams and rivers gurgle, creating what is, in effect, a giant sponge. At the heart of the Murgia lies the idyllic Valle d'Itria.

The rolling green valley is criss-crossed by drystone walls, vineyards, almond and olive groves, and winding country lanes. This is the part of Puglia most visited by foreign tourists and is the best served by hotels and luxury *masserias* (working farms) or manor farms.

Alberobello

☑ 080 / POP 10,750

Unesco World Heritage Site Alberobello resembles an urban sprawl – for gnomes. The *zona dei trulli* on the westernmost of the town's two hills is a dense mass of 1500 beehive-shaped houses, white-tipped as if dusted by snow. These drystone buildings are made from local limestone; none are older than the 14th century.

The town is named after the primitive oak forest Arboris Belli (beautiful trees) that once covered this area. It's an amazing place, but also something of a tourist trap – from May to October busloads of tourists pile into *trullo* homes, drink in *trullo* bars and shop in *trullo* shops. Try to visit in the morning to avoid the arrival of tourist buses and the inevitable throng of visitors.

If you park in Lago Martellotta, follow the steps up to Piazza del Popolo, where the Bel-

vedere Trulli lookout offers fabulous views over the whole higgledy-piggledy picture.

◉ Sights

Rione Monti
AREA

Within the old town quarter of Rione Monti more than 1000 *trulli* cascade down the hillside, many of which are now souvenir shops. The area is surprisingly quiet and atmospheric in the late evening, once the day trippers have left and the gaudy stalls have been stashed away.

Rione Aia Piccola
AREA

On the eastern side of Via Indipendenza is Rione Aia Piccola. This neighbourhood is much less commercialised than Rione Monti, with 400 *trulli,* many still used as family dwellings. You can climb up for a rooftop view at many shops, although most do have a strategically located basket for donations.

Trullo Sovrano
MUSEUM

(☑ 080 432 60 30; www.trullosovrano.eu; Piazza Sacramento 10; adult/reduced €1.50/1; ⊙10am-1.30pm & 3.30-7pm Apr-Oct, to 6pm Nov-Mar) Trullo Sovrano dates in parts to the early 17th century, and is Alberobello's only two-floor *trullo.* Built by a wealthy priest's family, it's now a small 'living' museum recreating *trullo* life, with sweet, rounded rooms that include a recreated bakery, bedroom and kitchen. The souvenir shop here has a wealth of literature on the town and surrounding area, plus Alberobello recipe books.

☞ Tours

Charming Tours
FOOD & DRINK

(☑ 080 432 38 29; www.charmingtours.it; Piazza Sacramento 8; tours per person from €120) Offering food-based tours and cookery classes in Alberobello and the surrounding region. Shopping at food markets, cheese-making and visits to local farms can all be arranged, and cultural and historical tours to destinations including Matera, Lecce and Otranto are available. Ask about special tours negotiating Valle d'Itria's sleepy rural byways on a retro Vespa or in a vintage Fiat 500.

🛏 Sleeping

Casa Albergo Sant'Antonio
HOTEL €

(☑ 080 432 29 13; www.santantonioalbergo.com; Via Isonzo 8a; s/d/tr/q €53/80/95/110; 🖧) Excellent value right in the heart of the Rione Monti neighbourhood, this simple hotel is in an old monastery located next to a unique *trulli*-style church with a conical roof. The tiled rooms are relatively monastic and spartan, but will do the trick for the unfussy.

Trullidea RENTAL HOUSE €€
(☎080 432 38 60; www.trullidea.it; Via Monte Sabotino 24; trulli from €140; 📶) Based on the *albergo diffuso* concept, Trullidea has numerous renovated, quaint, cosy and atmospheric *trulli* in Alberobello's historic centre available on a self-catering, B&B, or half- or full-board basis. Half-board is €30 person, and a buffet breakfast is included in the price.

Eating

Trattoria Amatulli TRATTORIA €
(☎080 432 29 79; Via Garibaldi 13; meals €20-25; ⌚12.30-3pm & 7.30-11.30pm Tue-Sun) The cheerily cluttered interior of this excellent trattoria is papered with photos of smiley diners, obviously put in the best mood by dishes like *orecchiette scure con cacioricotta pomodoro e rucola* ('little ears' pasta with cheese, tomato and arugula). Wash it down with the surprisingly drinkable house wine, only €5 a litre. It won't add much to an invariably reasonable bill.

Trattoria Terra Madre VEGETARIAN €€
(☎080 432 38 29; www.trattoriaterramadre.it; Piazza Sacramento 17; meals €26-57; ⌚12.15-2.45pm & 7.15-9.45pm Tue-Sat, 12.15-2.45pm Sun; ✓) Vegetables take pride of place in Italian kitchens, especially at this enthusiastic vegetarian-ish (some meat is served) restaurant. The farm-to-table ethos rules – most of what you eat comes from the organic garden outside. Start with the huge vegetable antipasti and save room for *primi* like *capunti* 'Terra Madre' (pasta with eggplant, zucchini and peppers) and the perfect house-baked desserts.

Information

The main **tourist information office** (☎080 432 28 22; www.prolocoalberobello.it; Monte Nero 1; ⌚9am-7pm) is in the *zona dei trulli*. There is another smaller **tourist office** (☎080 432 51 71; cnr Via Independenza & Largo Martellotta; ⌚10am-1pm & 3-6pm) that opens only during peak times.

Getting There & Away

Alberobello is easily accessible from Bari (€5, 1½ hours, hourly) on the FSE Bari–Taranto train line. From the station, walk straight ahead along Via Mazzini, which becomes Via Garibaldi, to reach Piazza del Popolo (a journey of around 500m).

Locorotondo

☎080 / POP 14,160

Locorotondo is endowed with a whisper-quiet pedestrianised *centro storico*, where everything is shimmering white aside from the blood-red geraniums that tumble from the window boxes. Situated on a hilltop on the Murge Plateau, it's a *borgo più bella d'Italia* (see http://borghipiubellid italia.it) – that is, it's rated as one of the most beautiful towns in Italy. There are few 'sights' as such – rather, the town itself is a sight. The streets are paved with smooth ivory-coloured stones, with the church of **Santa Maria della Graecia** as their sun-baked centrepiece.

From **Villa Comunale**, a public garden, you can enjoy panoramic views of the surrounding valley. You enter the compact historic quarter directly across from here.

Not only is this deepest *trulli* country, it's also the liquid heart of the Pugliese wine region. Sample some of the local *verdeca* at Controra (p784).

Sleeping

Locorotondo and the surrounding country are blessed when it comes to quality accommodation. If you're going to stay on a *masseria* or in a *trullo* whilst in Puglia, this is the place to do it.

Truddhi AGRITURISMO €
(☎080 443 13 26; www.truddhi.com; Contrada Trito 161; d per 5 nights from €440; P ❄) This charming cluster of 11 self-catering *trulli* in the hamlet of Trito near Locorotondo is surrounded by olive groves and vineyards. It's a tranquil place and you can take cooking courses (per day €80) with Mino, a lecturer in gastronomy. The *trulli* sleep between two and six people, depending on size.

★**Sotto le Cummerse** APARTMENT €€
(☎080 4313298; www.sottolecummerse.it; Via Vittorio Veneto 138; apt incl breakfast from €125; ❄📶) At this *albergo diffuso* (dispersed hotel) you'll stay in one of 13 tastefully furnished apartments scattered throughout Locorotondo's *centro storico*. The apartments are traditional buildings that have been beautifully restored and furnished, and you can book activities such as horse riding, cooking classes and historical tours. A delightful base for exploring the Valle d'Itria.

✖ Eating & Drinking

Quanto Basta
PIZZA €

(☑ 080 431 28 55; www.facebook.com/qbpizzeria; Via Morelli 12; pizza €6-13; ⊙ 12.30-3pm & 7.30-11.30pm; 🐾) Craft beer and pizza make an excellent combination at this quietly stylish old town restaurant with wooden tables, soft lighting and stone floors. It's hard to stop at *quanto basta* (just enough) when the pizza, carpaccio, salads and antipasti are so good, to say nothing of the lovely Itrian wines. Try the superb Golosa pizza with local Itrian almonds and sausage.

La Taverna del Duca
TRATTORIA €€

(☑ 080 431 30 07; www.tavernadelducascatigna. it; Via Papatodero 3; meals €38; ⊙ noon-3pm & 7.30pm-midnight Tue-Sat, noon-3pm Sun & Mon) In a narrow side street off Piazza Vittorio Emanuele, this well-regarded trattoria serves robust Itrian fare such as pork cheek in a *primitivo* reduction and donkey stew. If they sound daunting, there's always Puglia's favourite pasta (*orecchiette* 'little ears' pasta), thick vegetable soup and other familiar foods.

Controra
WINE BAR

(☑ 339 6874169; www.facebook.com/controralo corotondo; Via Nardelli 67; ⊙ noon-late) Treat this laid-back little place either as a sandwich shop or wine bar, sampling *prosit* (sparkling rose), *verdeca* and other niche wines of the Valle d'Itria, all partnered with amazing sandwiches, platters of regional produce, and Locorotondo's uniformly stunning views of olive groves and *trulli*. Welcome to the best seats in town.

ℹ Information

Tourist Office (☑ 080 431 30 99; www.prolo colocorotondo.it; Piazza Emanuele 27; ⊙ 9am-1pm & 5-7pm) Offers free internet access. Only open Saturday and Sunday outside of the peak season.

ℹ Getting There & Away

Locorotondo is easily accessible via frequent trains from Bari (€5.70, 1½ to two hours) on the FSE Bari–Taranto train line.

Cisternino

☑ 080 / POP 11,600

An appealing, whitewashed hilltop town, slow-paced Cisternino has a charming *centro storico* beyond its bland modern outskirts; with its kasbah-like knot of streets, it has been designated as one of the country's *borghi più belli* (most beautiful towns). Beside its 13th-century **Chiesa Matrice** and **Torre Civica** there's a pretty communal garden with rural views. If you take Via Basilioni next to the tower you can amble along an elegant route right to the central piazza, Vittorio Emanuele.

✖ Eating

Micro
VEGETARIAN €

(☑ 340 5315463; www.facebook.com/micropuglia; Via Santa Lucia 53; meals €20-25; ⊙ 10am-3pm & 6-11pm Wed-Mon; 🍴) 🌿 This charismatic little juice bar/lunch spot is the necessary counterbalance to the meaty excesses Cisternino is famous for. Market-fresh vegetables and herbs arrive each morning and are turned into soups, salads, torte, vegetarian sushi and more. There are some choices for carnivores, but for once it's they who are the afterthought. Organic wines and Italian craft beers complete the picture.

Rosticceria L'Antico Borgo
BARBECUE €€

(☑ 080 444 64 00; www.rosticceria-lanticoborgo. it; Via Tarantini 9; meals €30-35; ⊙ 6.30-11pm daily summer, Mon-Sat winter) A classic *fornello pronto* (half butcher's shop, half trattoria), this is the place for a cheerful, no-frills meat fest. The menu is brief, listing a few simple pastas and various meat options (priced per kilo), including Cisternino's celebrated *bombette* (skewered pork wrapped around a piece of cheese). Choose your roast meat and eat it with red wine, chips and salad.

ℹ Getting There & Away

Cisternino is accessible by regular FSE trains from Bari (€5, 45 minutes). STP Brindisi runs hourly buses between Cisternino and Ostuni.

Martina Franca

☑ 080 / POP 49,030

The old quarter of this town is a picturesque scene of winding alleys, blinding white houses and blood-red geraniums. There are graceful baroque and rococo buildings here too, plus airy piazzas and curlicue ironwork balconies that almost touch above the narrow streets. This town is the highest in the Murgia, and was founded in the 10th century by refugees fleeing the Arab invasion of Taranto. It only started to flourish in the 14th century when Philip of Anjou granted tax exemptions (*franchigie,* hence Franca); the town became so wealthy that a castle and defensive walls complete with 24 solid bastions were built.

◉ Sights

The best way to appreciate Martina Franca's beauty is to wander around the narrow lanes and alleyways of the *centro storico*.

Passing under the baroque **Arco di Sant'Antonio** at the western end of pedestrianised Piazza XX Settembre, you emerge into Piazza Roma, dominated by the imposing, 17th-century rococo **Palazzo Ducale** (☑ 080 480 57 02; Piazza Roma 28; ☉ 9am-8pm Mon-Fri, from 10am Sat & Sun mid-Jun–Sep, shorter hours rest of year) **FREE**, whose upper rooms have semirestored frescoed walls and host temporary art exhibitions.

From Piazza Roma, follow the fine Corso Vittorio Emanuele, with baroque townhouses, to reach Piazza Plebiscito, the centre's baroque heart. The piazza is overlooked by the 18th-century **Basilica di San Martino**, its centrepiece a statue of city patron, St Martin, swinging a sword and sharing his cloak with a beggar.

✴ Festivals & Events

Festival della Valle d'Itria   MUSIC
(☑ 080 480 51 00; www.festivaldellavalleditria.it; event tickets from €15; ☉ Jul & Aug) This summer music festival takes over Martina Franca's venues from mid-July to early August. Musical theatre, especially opera, tops the bill, but concertos and other recitals also abound. For information, contact the Centro Artistico Musicale Paolo Grassi in the Palazzo Ducale.

🛏 Sleeping & Eating

B&B San Martino   B&B €
(☑ 080 48 56 01; www.bandbsanmartino.com; Via Abate Fighera 32; s/d €33/85; ❋ ⊛) A stylish B&B in a historic palace with rooms overlooking gracious Piazza XX Settembre. The rooms have exposed stone walls, shiny parquet floors, wrought-iron beds and small kitchenettes (only one has a working cooker) and there's a compact pool to take a dip in when it's hot.

Cibando   BISTRO €
(☑ 080 798 42 22; https://cibando.business.site; Piazza Roma 18; platters from €10; ☉ 11am-3pm & 6pm-late) A friendly delicatessen and cafe showcasing Slow Food ingredients from around the Valle d'Itria, Cibando is a good place to try the area's renowned smoked burrata cheese and *capocollo* (pork neck salami). Local wines and interesting craft brews on tap reinforce the proclamation on the door, *Non abbiamo birre normali!* (We don't have normal beers!)

★**Nausikaa**   ITALIAN €€
(☑ 080 485 82 75; www.ristorantenausikaa.it; Vico Arco Fumarola 2; meals €35; ☉ noon-3pm Tue-Sun, 7.30-11.30pm Tue-Sat) Tucked away down a dogleg alley off Martina Franca's main pedestrian drag is this lovely little modern Italian place, run by brothers Francesco and Martino. Tradition is not sacrificed to forward-thinking, and vice versa – a 'caprese' salad, for instance, is stuffed inside a silky pasta bundle, anointed with 'basil pearls'. The Puglia-focused wine list is a joy.

ℹ Information

Tourist Office (☑ 080 480 57 02; www.agenziapugliapromozione.it; Piazza XX Settembre 3; ☉ 10.30am-1.30pm & 4.30-7pm Jul & Aug, shorter hours rest of year)

ℹ Getting There & Away

The FSE train station is downhill from the historic centre. From the train station, go right along Viale della Stazione, continue along Via Alessandro Fighera to Corso Italia, then continue to the left along Corso Italia to Piazza XX Settembre.

FSE (☑ 080 546 21 11; www.fseonline.it) trains run to/from Bari (€5.70, 2¼ hours, hourly) and Taranto (€2.50, 50 minutes, four per day).

FSE buses run to Alberobello (€1.10, 20 minutes, frequent).

Ostuni

☑ 0831 / POP 31,150

Chic Ostuni shines like a pearly white tiara, extending across three hills with the magnificent gem of a cathedral as its sparkling centrepiece. It's the end of the *trulli* region and the beginning of the hot, dry Salento. With some excellent restaurants, stylish bars and swish yet intimate places to stay, it's packed in summer.

Ostuni is surrounded by olive groves, so this is the place to buy some of the region's DOC 'Collina di Brindisi' olive oil – either delicate, medium or strong – direct from producers.

◉ Sights & Activities

The surrounding countryside is perfect for cycling. **Ciclovagando** (☑ 330 985255; www.ciclovagando.com; Via Savoia 19, Mesagne; bike rental per day from €20), based in Mesagne, 30km south of Ostuni, rents basic and high-end bikes at reasonable rates, and will deliver them free within a 10km radius of its office in Mesagne (any further and there is a charge). It also guides half- and full-day tours (€35/70), including bike rental and helmets, with a choice of three or four itineraries, departing daily from Lecce, Matera, Trani and Castellana Grotte.

Museo di Civiltà Preclassiche della Murgia
MUSEUM

(☑ 0831 33 63 83; www.ostunimuseo.it; Via Cattedrale 15; adult/reduced €5/3; ⊙10am-7pm) Located in the Convento delle Monacelle, the museum's most famous exhibit is Delia, a 25,000-year-old expectant mother. Pregnant at the time of her death, her well-preserved skeleton was found in a local cave. Many of the finds here come from the Palaeolithic burial ground, now the Parco Archeologico e Naturale di Arignano (☑ 083 133 63 83; www.ostunimuseo.it; ⊙10am-1pm Sun, or by appointment).

Cathedral
CATHEDRAL

(Piazza Beato Giovanni Paolo II; by donation; ⊙9am-noon & 3.30-7pm) Dedicated to the Assumption of the Virgin Mary, Ostuni's dramatic 15th-century cathedral has an unusual Gothic-Romanesque-Byzantine facade with a frilly rose window and an inverted gable. The 18th-century sacred art covering the ceiling and altars is well worth stepping inside to see.

✵ Festivals & Events

La Cavalcata
RELIGIOUS

Ostuni's annual feast day is held on 26 August, when processions of horsemen dressed in glittering red-and-white uniforms (resembling Indian grooms on their way to be wed) follow the statue of Sant'Oronzo around town.

🛏 Sleeping

Le Sole Blu
B&B €

(☑ 0831 30 38 56; https://bed-and-breakfast-sole blu-ostuni.business.site; Corso Vittorio Emanuele II 16; d & apt €70) Located in the 18th-century (rather than medieval) part of town, Le Sole Blu only has one room available: it's large, fully renovated and has a separate entrance. The two self-catering apartments nearby are also excellent value. It's just a short stroll to good cafes and Ostuni's shimmering marble main square.

La Terra
HOTEL €€

(☑ 0831 33 66 51; www.laterrahotel.it; Via Petrarolo 16; d from €130; P ❋ ❂) This 13th-century former *palazzo* offers atmospheric and stylish accommodation with original niches, dark-wood beams and furniture, and contrasting light stonework and whitewash. There's a colonnaded terrace, wi-fi throughout, a more-than-decent restaurant and a truly cavernous bar – tunnelled out of a cave.

★ Il Frantoio
AGRITURISMO €€€

(☑ 0831 33 02 76; www.masseriailfrantoio.it; SS16 km 874, Ostuni; d €220; P ❋ @ ❂ ⛱) Stay at this charming, whitewashed farmhouse and estate where the owners still live and work producing high quality olive oil. Even if you're not staying here, book in for one of the marathon eight-course lunches – the food is local, organic and superb. Il Frantoio's new swimming pool is a welcome addition for warmer Puglian days.

Il Frantoio lies 5km outside Ostuni along the SS16 in the direction of Fasano. You'll see the sign on your left-hand side when you reach the km 874 marker.

✗ Eating

Osteria Ricanatti
ITALIAN €€

(☑ 0831 1561831; Corso Cavour 37; meals €35-45; ⊙noon-3pm & 7-11pm Wed-Mon) Puglian classics are given a thoroughly modern makeover at the stylish and elegant Osteria Ricanatti. Seafood is often the star, including superb tuna and octopus, while the savvy chef also has a winning way with local vegetables like eggplant and zucchini. The optional five-course menu (€35) is good value. Delve into the wine list with a few top Salento varietals.

Porta Nova
ITALIAN €€€

(☑ 0831 33 89 83; www.ristoranteportanova.com; Via Petrarolo 38; meals €50-55; ⊙12.30-3.30pm & 7.30-11pm) Scenically installed in the Aragonese fortifications, this terraced restaurant is a special occasion charmer. Seafood is wonderful here, with a whole section of the menu devoted to *crudo mare* (raw fish). Ease into what will be a splendid hour or so of indulgence with sea-bass carpaccio, then ramp it up with rosemary-scented Gallipoli prawns on beech-smoked potato.

ⓘ Information

Tourist Office (☑ 0831 30 12 68, 0831 33 96 27; Corso Mazzini 6; ⊙8am-2pm & 3-8pm)

ℹ Getting There & Away

STP Brindisi (www.stpbrindisi.it) buses run to Brindisi (€3.10, 50 minutes, six daily) and to Martina Franca (€2.10, 45 minutes, three daily), leaving from Piazza Italia in the newer part of Ostuni.

Trains run frequently to Brindisi (€2.90, 25 minutes) and Bari (€5.70, 50 minutes). A half-hourly local bus covers the 2.5km between the station and town.

Salento

The Penisola Salentina, better known simply as Salento, is hot, dry and remote, retaining a flavour of its Greek past. It stretches across Italy's heel from Brindisi to Taranto and down to Santa Maria di Leuca. Here the lush greenery of Valle d'Itria gives way to flat, ochre-coloured fields hazy with wildflowers in spring, and endless olive groves.

Lecce

📞 0832 / POP 95,000

Bequeathed with a generous stash of baroque buildings by its 17th-century architects, Lecce has a completeness and homogeneity that other southern Italian metropolises lack. Indeed, so distinctive is Lecce's architecture that it has acquired its own moniker, *barocco leccese* (Lecce baroque), an expressive and hugely decorative incarnation of the genre replete with gargoyles, asparagus columns and cavorting gremlins. Swooning 18th-century traveller Thomas Ashe thought it 'the most beautiful city in Italy', but the less-impressed Marchese Grimaldi said the facade of Basilica di Santa Croce made him think a lunatic was having a nightmare.

◉ Sights

Lecce has more than 40 churches and at least as many *palazzi*, all built or renovated between the 17th and 18th centuries, giving the city an extraordinary cohesion. Two of the main proponents of *barocco leccese* (the craziest, most lavish decoration imaginable) were brothers Antonio and Giuseppe Zimbalo, who both had a hand in the fantastical Basilica di Santa Croce.

Admission fees are charged for a selection of the city's most popular churches. Full tickets (€9) cover admission to the Cathedral, Basilica di Santa Croce, Chiesa di San Matteo, Chiesa di Santa Chiara and the Museo Diocesano d'Arte Sacra, while a secondary ticket (€3) allows admission to only two of these.

★ **Basilica di Santa Croce**　　　　BASILICA
(📞 0832 24 19 57; Via Umberto I; full ticket incl admission to 4 other churches €9, incl admission to 1 other church €3; ⊙ 9am-9pm) It seems that hallucinating stonemasons have been at work on the basilica. Sheep, dodos, cherubs and beasties writhe across the facade, a swirling magnificent allegorical feast. Throughout the 16th and 17th centuries, a team of artists under Giuseppe Zimbalo laboured to work the building up to this pitch. The interior is more conventionally baroque, and deserves a look. Spare a thought for the expelled Jewish families whose land the basilica was built on.

Piazza del Duomo　　　　　　　　PIAZZA
Piazza del Duomo is a baroque feast, the city's focal point and a sudden open space amid the surrounding enclosed lanes. During times of invasion the inhabitants of Lecce would barricade themselves in the square, which has conveniently narrow entrances. Lecce's 12th-century cathedral, Palazzo Vescoville (Episcopal Palace) and museum of sacred art (📞 0832 24 47 64; http://museo.diocesilecce.org; full ticket incl admission to 4 other churches €9, incl admission to 1 other church €3; ⊙ 9am-9pm) face one another in silent dignity across the square.

Cathedral　　　　　　　　　　CATHEDRAL
(📞 0832 30 85 57; Piazza del Duomo; full ticket incl admission to 4 other churches €9, incl admission to 1 other church €3; ⊙ 9am-9pm) Giuseppe Zimbalo's 1659 reconstruction of Lecce's original 12th-century cathedral is recognised as being among his finest work. Zimbalo, Lecce's famous 17th-century architect, was also responsible for the thrusting, tiered bell tower, 72m high. The cathedral is unusual in that it has two facades, one on the western end and the other, more ornate, facing the piazza. It's framed by the 17th-century Palazzo Vescovile (Episcopal Palace) and the 18th-century Seminario, designed by Giuseppe Cino.

★ **Museo Faggiano**　　　　　　　MUSEUM
(📞 0832 30 05 28; www.museofaggiano.it; Via Grandi 56/58; €5; ⊙ 9.30am-8pm) Descend through Lecce's rich historical strata in this fascinating home-turned-museum, where sewerage excavations led to the chance discovery of an archaeological treasure trove. The deepest finds take you all the way back

Lecce

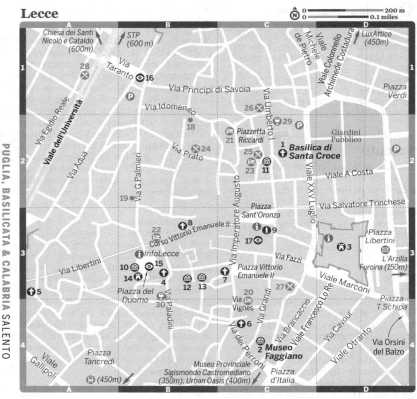

to the Messapii culture of the 5th century BC; you then ascend through Roman crypts, medieval walls, Jewish insigna and Knights Templar symbols in the rooftop tower.

Museo Ebraico   MUSEUM

(Jewish Museum Lecce; ☑ 0832 24 70 16; www. palazzotaurino.com; Via Umberto 9; adult/reduced €5/4; ⏲ 10am-1pm & 3-7pm Mon-Sat, 10.30am-1.30pm Sun) This fascinating museum outlines the Jewish history of Lecce and the greater Salento region. Entry is by 30-minute guided tour only, running every 45 minutes from 10am to 1pm and 3pm to 6.15pm. Excellent maps (€1.50) covering other nearby Jewish heritage sites are a good option for self-drive travellers. On Thursday evenings at 6.30pm the museum hosts *Sarah's Stories* (€12), a poignant spoken-word and audiovisual performance by Italian actor, Giustina de Iaco. Booking ahead is recommended.

MUST   GALLERY

(Museo Storico Citta di Lecce; ☑ 0832 24 10 67; www.mustlecce.it; Via degli Ammirati 11; adult/reduced €4.50/2.50; ⏲ noon-7pm Tue-Sun) The beautifully restored 15th-century Monastery of Santa Chiara houses this civic museum and gallery, and has a great view of the Roman theatre from the back window. Exhibits focus on the history of Lecce, from the Messapians of 2500 years ago to the present day, while the work of modern Leccese artists hangs in the ground-floor gallery.

Castello di Carlo V   CASTLE

(☑ 0832 24 65 17; www.castellocarlov.it; Via XXV Luglio; adult/reduced €10/8; ⏲ 9am-8.30pm Mon-Fri, from 9.30am Sat & Sun, closes later in summer) While the Normans built the original castle in the 12th century, it became associated with the Spanish Holy Roman Emperor Charles V, who enlarged it extensively in the 16th century. Bound within enormous

Lecce

trapezoidal walls cornered with stout bastions, it is Puglia's largest castle, and has been used as a prison, court, military barracks and now the headquarters of Lecce's cultural authorities. You can wander around inside, catch a recital, and visit the on-site **papier-mâché museum**.

Museo Provinciale
Sigismondo Castromediano   MUSEUM
(🖋 0832 68 35 03; www.facebook.com/MuCastro mediano; Viale Gallipoli 30; ⊙ 8.30am-7.30pm Mon-Sat, 9am-1pm Sun) 𝗙𝗥𝗘𝗘 This museum stylishly covers 10,000 years of history, from Palaeolithic and Neolithic bits and bobs to a handsome display of Greek and Roman jewels, weaponry and ornaments. The stars of the show are the Messapians, whose jaunty Mycenaean-inspired jugs and bowls date back 2500 years. There's also an interesting collection of 15th- to 18th-century paintings.

Roman Amphitheatre   AMPHITHEATRE
(Piazza Sant'Oronzo) Below the ground level of the piazza is this restored 2nd-century-AD amphitheatre, discovered in 1901 by construction workers. It was excavated in the 1930s to reveal a perfect horseshoe that actually extends under the rest of the square to originally seat 15,000. A little colonised by weeds, it's nonetheless an impressive centrepiece to Lecce's main communal square. Walking tours available at the nearby tourist office (p792) include the history of the amphitheatre.

Museo Teatro Romano   MUSEUM
(🖋 0832 27 91 96; Via degli Ammirati 5; adult/reduced €3/2; ⊙ 9.30am-1pm Mon-Sat) Exhibiting artefacts revealed during the excavation of the adjacent Roman theatre, this museum also has displays recreating classical Roman life, including a reconstruction of Roman Lupiae (Lecce). The museum is housed in a handsome 17th-century *palazzo*.

Colonna di Sant'Oronzo   MONUMENT
(Piazza Sant'Oronzo) Two Roman columns once marked the end of the Appian Way in Brindisi. When one of them crumbled in 1582 some of the pieces were rescued and subsequently donated to Lecce (the base and capital remain in Brindisi). The old column was rebuilt in 1666 with a statue of Lecce's patron saint placed on top. Sant'Oronzo is venerated for supposedly saving the city of Brindisi from a 1656 plague.

Porta Napoli   GATE
The main city gate, Porta Napoli, was erected in 1548 in anticipation of a state visit from Charles V. It's a typically bombastic effort by Gian dell'Acaja (builder of Lecce's fortified walls), who modelled it on a Roman triumphal arch and gave it a pointy pediment carved with toy weapons and an enormous Spanish coat of arms.

🥢 Courses

Awaiting Table   COOKING
(🖋 334 7676970; www.awaitingtable.com; Via Idomeneo 41; day/week €265/1995) Silvestro

PUGLIA, BASILICATA & CALABRIA SALENTO

LECCE'S NOTABLE CHURCHES

Lecce's unique baroque style is perhaps best seen in its churches; the city harbours dozens of them.

Chiesa dei Santi Nicolò e Cataldo (Via Cimitero; ⊙9am-noon & 5-7pm Jun-Aug, shorter hours rest of year) Located in the monumental cemetery outside the city walls, this outstanding church was built by the Normans in 1180. It got caught up in the city's baroque frenzy and was revamped in 1716 by the prolific Giuseppe Cino, who retained the Romanesque rose window and portal. The 16th-century fresco cycles inside tell stories from the saints' lives.

Chiesa di Santa Chiara (Piazzetta Vittorio Emanuele II; full ticket incl admission to 4 other churches €9, incl admission to 1 other church €3; ⊙9am-9pm) A 15th-century church given a baroque makeover between 1687 and 1691. Inside, every niche and surface swirls with twisting columns and ornate statuary. The ceiling is 18th-century Leccese *cartapestra* (papier mâché) masquerading as wood.

Chiesa di Sant'Irene (Corso Vittorio Emanuele II; ⊙7.30-11am & 4-6pm) Dedicated to Lecce's former patron saint and modelled on Rome's Basilica di Sant'Andrea della Valle, this church was completed in 1639. Inside you'll find a magnificent pair of mirror-image baroque altarpieces, facing each other across the transept.

Chiesa di San Matteo (Via dei Perroni 29; full ticket incl admission to 4 other churches €9, incl admission to 1 other church €3; ⊙9am-9pm) Known by the locals as Santa Maria della Luce, this graceful little church bears the fingerprints of Giuseppe Zimbalo, as much of baroque Lecce does. The famed architect completed the building, with its elaborate facade and more restrained interior, when the original architect died before completion.

Chiesa del Rosario (Via Libertini 5; ⊙8.30-11.30am & 5-6pm) Also known as the Chiesa di San Giovanni Battista (Church of John the Baptist), this elaborately fronted church was prodigious Leccese architect Giuseppe Zimbalo's last commission. He died before it was completed, and a quick-fix wooden roof was put up, instead of the dome he had intended.

Silvestori's splendid culinary and wine school provides day- or week-long courses with market shopping, tours, tastings, noteworthy lecturers and lots of hands-on cooking. Week-long courses are held in Silvestro's home, but you'll need to arrange your own accommodation. Book well in advance as courses fill up rapidly.

Tours

Velo Service TOURS
(☎389 6207353; www.veloservice.org; Via Palmieri 32; tours from €15; ⊙10am-7pm) Offers various guided tours of Lecce including street food, papier mâché and shopping. Alternative ways to negotiate the city include by bicycle, in a rickshaw, by foot or on a Segway. Velo Service can also arrange six-hour tours exploring Puglia's olive oil scene. Booking ahead is recommended for all tours. Bicycle rental is also available along with ideas for day excursions.

Sleeping

Urban Oasis HOSTEL €
(☎0832 30 00 50; www.urbanoasishostel.com; Via Cataldi 3; dm/d from €17/45; �) Lecce's only hostel is a winner with options in a restored heritage townhouse including dorms for a maximum of six guests, and stylish double and triple rooms. Bathrooms are uniformly modern and there's a hip vibe enlivened by colourful decor. At the rear of the building is a wonderful garden perfect for end-of-day drinks.

B&B Idomeneo 63 B&B €
(☎333 9499838; www.bebidomeneo63.it; Via Idomeneo 63; d/ste €80/120; ☎) You'll be looked after like a VIP at this wonderfully curated B&B in the midst of Lecce's baroque quarter, complete with six colour-coded rooms and a funky entrance lounge. Decked out boutique-hotel style, it manages to seamlessly incorporate older features like stone ceiling arches. The two 'apartments', with kitchenettes, are great value.

Azzurretta B&B
B&B €

(☑ 0832 24 22 11; www.bblecce.it; Via Vignes 2; d/tr €80/90; [P][🏠]) Tullio runs this arty B&B located in a historic *palazzo*. Of the four rooms, ask for the large double with a balcony, wooden floors and vaulted ceiling. Massage is available in your room or on the roof terrace – also a splendid place to take a sundowner. You get a cafe voucher for breakfast.

There is also a tiny studio flat, which is a little dark but a good option if you're self-catering on a budget.

Palazzo Rollo
B&B €

(☑ 0832 30 71 52; www.palazzorollo.it; Corso Vittorio Emanuele II 14; s/d/ste from €75/90/100; [P][✱][@]) This tastefully restored 17th-century *palazzo* – the Rollo family seat for more than 200 years – makes a delightful base from which to explore Lecce. The grand B&B suites (with kitchenettes) have high curved ceilings and chandeliers while, downstairs, contemporary-chic studios open onto an ivy-hung courtyard. There are also self-catering apartments (from €120) and a rooftop garden with wonderful views.

Centro Storico B&B
B&B €

(☑ 328 8351294, 0832 24 27 27; www.centrostoricolecce.it; Via Vignes 2; s/d/ste €70/90/110; [P][✱][🏠]) This friendly and well-run B&B located in the 16th-century Palazzo Astore features big rooms, double-glazed windows and a classy heritage makeover with sparkling new bathrooms and stylish furniture. Perfect for end of day relaxation, the huge rooftop terrace has sunloungers, views of Lecce's rooftops and a popular Jacuzzi. Vouchers are provided for breakfast at a nearby cafe.

LuxAttico
B&B €€

(☑ 328 1233450; https://luxattico.it; Via Lubello Formoso 2; s/d €90/120; [P][🏠]) Hosted by the friendly Luisa, LuxAttico has stylish rooms in a quiet residential area a short walk from Lecce's historic centre. Breakfast includes Lecce's finest baked goods, and there's a sunny terrace with views across the rooftops to Lecce's cathedral.There's a handy car park in the building (per day €5), and Luisa can recommend the best of Lecce's restaurants.

Patria Palace Hotel
HOTEL €€

(☑ 0832 24 51 11; http://patriapalace.com; Piazzetta Riccardi 13; d from €127; [P][✱][@][🏠]) This sumptuous hotel is traditionally Italian with large mirrors, dark-wood furniture and wistful murals. The location is wonderful, the bar gloriously art deco with a magnificent carved ceiling, and the shady roof terrace has views over the Basilica di Santa Croce. The attached restaurant, Atenze (☑ 0832 24 51 11; https://patriapalace.com/it/ristorante-atenze; meals €50; ⏰ 12.30-3pm & 7-11pm), is one of Lecce's finest.

★ Masseria Trapana
AGRITURISMO €€€

(☑ 0832 18 32 101; www.trapana.com; Strada Vicinale Masseria Trapana 9; ste from €600; [P][✱][🏠]) Surrounded by citrus groves, this modern reinvention of a 16th-century farmhouse is 12km north of Lecce. Ten suites combine with shared areas enlivened by Oriental textiles, and the Moroccan-style firepit is ideal for *aperitivi*. A subterranean vault houses a romantic plunge pool, the property makes its own mandarin liqueur, and excellent Puglian cuisine and superb breakfasts both feature.

🍴 Eating

La Succursale
PIZZA €

(☑ 391 4977749; www.facebook.com/lasuccursale.lecce; Viale dell'Università 15; pizza €7-10; ⏰ 6pm-midnight Tue-Sun) Lecce is an important university town and this boisterous pizzeria combining gourmet pizzas with decent wine and craft beer is hugely popular with local students. Grab a table outside in warmer weather and feast on wood-fired goodness harnessing ingredients like spicy sausage, almonds and blue cheese. Other snacking highlights include *polpette* meatballs.

Baldo Gelato
GELATO €

(☑ 328 0710290; www.facebook.com/Baldogelato; Via Idomeneo 78; medium cone or cup €3; ⏰ 11am-10pm Mon-Thu, to midnight Fri-Sun) The couple behind Baldo Gelato make the best gelato in Lecce, hands down. The dark chocolate may be the most intensely chocolatey thing you've ever put in your mouth.

★ La Cucina di Mamma Elvira
PUGLIAN €€

(☑ 331 5795127; www.mammaelvira.com; Via Maremonti 33; meals €30-35; ⏰ 12.30pm-midnight) An offshoot of the stylish Enoteca Mamma Elvira, 'The Kitchen' makes use of a bigger space than that available to its older sibling to deliver more ambitious and substantial food. There's a focus on Pugliese wine, simply augmented by a seasonal menu that offers seafood antipasti, lovely vegetarian options, robust Pugliese pastas and more. Booking ahead is recommended.

L'Arzilla Furcina   ITALIAN €€

(☑391 3320419; www.larzillafurcina.it; Via Bacile 25; meals €30-35; ☉7.30-11.30pm Tue-Sun, 12.30-2.30pm Tue, Thu & Sun) Tucked away down a shopping street in Lecce's New Town, L'Arzilla Furcina features a compact and stylish space showcasing seasonal and local ingredients and Salento wines. Traditional Puglian recipes are given a modern spin and could feature local seafood such as *cozze* (mussels). Thoroughly unpretentious and friendly service also makes L'Arzilla Furcina worth the short detour from Lecce's historic centre.

Alle due Corti   PUGLIAN €€

(☑0832 24 22 23; www.alleduecorti.com; Via Prato 42; meals €30-35; ☉12.30-2pm & 7.30-11pm Mon-Sat, closed Jan) Rosalba de Carlo, a noted repository of Salento gustatory wisdom, is the presiding authority in this authentic-as-it gets Pugliese kitchen. 'The Two Courts' keeps it strictly seasonal and local, dishing up classics such as *ciceri e tria* (crisply fried pasta with chickpeas) and *turcineddhi* (offal of kid) in a relaxed, traditional restaurant environment.

🍸 Drinking & Nightlife

★**Quanta Basta**   COCKTAIL BAR

(☑347 0083176; www.facebook.com/quantobasta lecce; Via Paladini 17; ☉8pm-2am Thu-Tue) Just maybe Lecce's best Negroni cocktail is a fine reason to adjourn to Quanta Basta's outdoor tables for your nightly *aperitivi* session. Further rationale is provided by friendly service from the hip, bearded bartenders and a superb location framed by twilight shadows, historic architecture and Lecce's beautiful golden light.

★**Enoteca Mamma Elvira**   WINE BAR

(☑0832 169 20 11; www.mammaelvira.com; Via Umberto I 19; ☉8am-3am; 🛜) All you need to know about Salento wine will be imparted by the hip staff at this cool joint near the Santa Croce church. Taster glasses are dispatched liberally if you order snacks. You'll need to order a few if you're going to properly research the 250+ Pugliese wines it stocks. Italian craft beers also feature.

ℹ Information

MEDICAL SERVICES

Hospital (Ospedale Vito Fazzi; ☑0832 66 11 11; Piazza Filippo) About 2km south of the centre on the Gallipoli road.

POST

Post Office (Piazza Libertini 5; ☉8.30am-7pm Mon-Fri, to 12.30pm Sat)

TOURIST INFORMATION

InfoLecce (☑0832 52 18 77; www.infolecce. it; Piazza del Duomo 2; ☉9.30am-1.30pm & 3.30-7.30pm Mon-Fri, 10am-1.30pm & 3.30-7pm Sat & Sun) Independent and helpful tourist information office. Has guided tours and bike rental (per hour/day €3/15).

Puglia Blog (www.thepuglia.com) An informative site run by Fabio Ingrosso with articles on culture, history, food, wine, accommodation and travel in Puglia.

Tourist Office (☑0832 24 20 99; Piazza Sant'Oronzo; ☉10am-1pm & 4-6pm) One of two main government-run offices. The other is in **Castello di Carlo V** (☑0832 24 65 17; ☉9am-8.30pm Mon-Fri, 9.30am-8.30pm Sat & Sun, closes later in summer).

ℹ Getting There & Away

BUS

The city bus terminal is located to the north of Porta Napoli. Brindisi is best reached by train.

Pugliairbus (www.aeroportidipuglia.it/home pagebrindisi) Connects with Brindisi airport (€7.50, 40 minutes, nine daily).

STP (☑0832 35 91 42; www.stplecce.it) Runs buses to Gallipoli (€4.40, 1¼ hours, frequent) and Otranto (€4.40, one hour, frequent) from the **STP bus station** (☑800 43 03 46; Viale Porta D'Europa).

TRAIN

The main train station, 1km southwest of Lecce's historic centre, runs frequent services.

Bari from €10.80, 1½ to two hours

Bologna from €53.50, 7½ to 9½ hours

Brindisi from €2.90, 30 minutes

Naples from €49.30, 5½ hours (transfer in Caserta)

Rome from €56, 5½ to nine hours

FSE trains head to Otranto, Gallipoli and Martina Franca; the ticket office is located on platform 1.

Brindisi

☑0831 / POP 87,800

Like all ports, Brindisi has its seamy side, but it's also surprisingly slow paced and balmy, particularly along the palm-lined Corso Garibaldi and the promenade stretching along the interesting *lungomare* (seafront).

The town was the end of the ancient Roman road Via Appia, down whose length

Brindisi

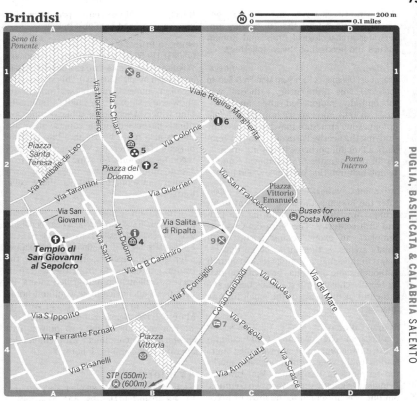

trudged weary legionnaires and pilgrims, crusaders and traders, all heading to Greece and the Near East.

◉ Sights

★ Tempio di San Giovanni al Sepolcro   CHURCH

(☑ 0831 52 30 72; Piazzetta San Giovanni al Sepolcro; ⊙ 8am-2pm & 2.30-8.30pm) FREE This 12th-century church, a brown bulk of Norman stone conforming to the circular plan the Templars so loved, is a wonderfully evocative structure, austere and bare. You'll see vestigial medieval frescoes on the walls, and glimpses of the crypt below. The church was a popular stop for Crusaders travelling to and from the Holy Land. Don't miss the expansive gardens at the rear of the building.

Museo Archeologico Provinciale Ribezzo   MUSEUM

(☑ 0831 56 55 01; Piazza del Duomo 6; adult/reduced €5/3; ⊙ 9.30am-1.30pm Wed-Sat, 9.30am-

1.30pm & 3.30-6.30pm Tue) This superb museum has several floors of well-documented exhibits (in English), including some 3000 bronze sculptures and fragments in

Hellenistic Greek style. There are also terracotta figurines from the 7th century, underwater archaeological finds, and Roman statues and heads (not always together).

Cathedral
CATHEDRAL

(Piazza del Duomo; ⊗8am-9pm Mon-Fri & Sun, to noon Sat) This 12th-century cathedral was substantially remodelled after an earthquake in 1743. You can see how the original Romanesque structure may have looked by studying the nearby Porta dei Cavalieri Templari, a fanciful portico with pointy arches – it's all that remains of a medieval Knights Templar church that once also stood here.

Porta dei Cavalieri Templari
RUINS

After the Romans, the next big event to hit Brindisi was the Crusades during the 12th and 13th centuries. The Porta dei Cavalieri Templari, an exotic-looking portico with pointy arches, is thought to be all that remains of the Knights Templar's main church (although some doubt has been cast on that by recent scholarship). It stands beside the cathedral in the heart of the small historic quarter.

Roman Column
MONUMENT

(Via Colonne) The gleaming white column above a sweeping set of sun-whitened stairs leading to the waterfront promenade marks the terminus of the Roman Via Appia at Brindisi. Originally there were two columns, but one was presented to the town of Lecce back in 1666 as thanks to Sant'Oronzo for having relieved Brindisi of the plague.

Palazzo Granafei-Nervegna
MUSEUM

(Via Duomo 20; ⊗8am-8.30pm) FREE This 16th-century Renaissance-style palace is named for the two different families who owned it. The building is of interest because it houses the huge ornate capital that used to sit atop one of the Roman columns that marked the end of the Appian Way (the rest of the column is in Lecce). Also on site are Brindisi's tourist office, a pleasant cafe, a bookshop, exhibition spaces and the archaeological remains of a Roman *domus* (house).

🛏 Sleeping & Eating

Hotel Orientale
HOTEL €

(⊘0831 56 84 51; www.hotelorientale.it; Corso Garibaldi 40; r €99; P❄🠶) This sleek, modern hotel overlooks the long palm-lined *corso*. Rooms are pleasant, the location is good and

it has a small fitness centre, private car park and (rare) cooked breakfast option.

Numero Primo
ITALIAN €€

(⊘0831 179 55 37; www.vinotecanumeroprimo.it; Viale Regina Margherita 46; meals €25-30; ⊗11am-3pm & 6pm-midnight Tue-Sun) This stylish glass pavilion along Brindisi's seafront is the showcase restaurant for Puglia's Tenute Rubino winery. Local seafood like octopus and tuna is harnessed for the concise menu and there's also more hearty fare like gourmet burgers. The attentive waitstaff have good recommendations on wine matches from Tenute Rubino's diverse range. See www.tenuterubino.com for details about cellar tours.

Trattoria Pantagruele
TRATTORIA €€

(⊘0831 56 06 05; www.facebook.com/brindisitrattoria; Via Salita di Ripalta 1; meals €33; ⊗12.30-2.30pm Mon-Sat, 7.30-10.30pm Mon-Fri) Named after the Rabelaisian giant Pantagruel, this trattoria three blocks from the waterfront serves excellent fish and grilled meats. Expect fresh anchovies in season, and homemade pasta in all seasons. Begin with the Mare e Terra (Sea & Land) *antipasti,* and we can recommend the raw prawns with *salmoriglio* (a condiment with lemon juice, olive oil, garlic and fresh herbs).

ℹ Information

Post Office (⊘0831 22 55 95; Piazza Vittoria 10; ⊗8.30am-7pm Mon-Fri, to 12.30pm Sat)
Tourist Office (⊘0831 52 30 72; www.visitbrindisi.it; Via Duomo 20, Palazzo Granafei-Nervegna; ⊗10am-6pm Mon, 8am-8pm Tue-Sun; 🛜)

ℹ Getting There & Away

AIR

From Brindisi's small **airport** (BDS; ⊘0831 411 74 06; www.aeroportidipuglia.it; Contrada Baroncino) there are domestic flights to Rome, Bologna, Naples, Turin and Milan. Airlines include Alitalia, Ryanair and easyJet. There are also direct flights from London Stansted with Ryanair.

BOAT

Ferries, all of which take vehicles, leave Brindisi for Greece and Albania.

Ferry companies have offices at Costa Morena (the newer port), which is 4km from the train station. A free bus connects the two.
Grimaldi Lines (⊘0831 54 81 16; www.grimaldi-lines.com; Costa Morena Terminal) Frequent

year-round ferries to Igoumenitsa (from €41, nine hours), Corfu (from €41, seven hours) and Patras (from €55, 17 hours) in Greece.

Red Star Ferries (☑ 0831 57 52 89; www. directferries.co.uk/red_star_ferries.htm; Costa Morena Terminal) To Vlorë in Albania, once a day (€42, five hours).

BUS

Pugliairbus (www.aeroportidipuglia.it) Services to Bari airport (€10, 1¾ hours) and Lecce (€7.50, 40 minutes) from Brindisi's airport.

Ferrovie del Sud-Est Buses serving local towns leave from Via Bastioni Carlo V, in front of the train station.

Marozzi (☑ 0831 52 16 84; www.marozzivt.it) Runs to Rome's Stazione Tiburtina (from €28, 6½ to 8½ hours, four daily) from Viale Arno.

STP Brindisi (p787) Buses go regularly to Ostuni (€3.20, 50 minutes, frequent), Lecce (€6.30, 35 minutes, nine daily) and other towns throughout the Salento. Most leave from Via Bastioni Carlo V, in front of the train station.

TRAIN

Brindisi's train station has regular services to the following destinations:

Bari from €8.60, 1¼ hours

Lecce from €2.90, 30 minutes

Milan from €43.80, 8½ to 11 hours

Rome from €28, eight to 12 hours

Taranto from €5, one hour

ℹ Getting Around

Major and local car-rental firms are represented at the airport. To reach the airport by bus, take the STP-run **Cotrap** (☑ 800 232042; www. stpbrindisi.it; ticket €1) bus from Via Bastoni Carlo V.

A free minibus connects the train station and old ferry terminal with Costa Morena. It departs two hours before boat departures. You'll need a valid ferry ticket.

Otranto

☑ 0836 / POP 5750

Bloodied and bruised by an infamous Turkish massacre in 1480, Otranto is best appreciated in its amazing cathedral, where the bones of 813 martyrs are displayed in a glass case behind the altar. The city has back-heeled quite a few invaders over the centuries and been brutally kicked by others – most notably the Turks. Sleuth around its compact old quarter and you can peel the past off in layers – Greek, Roman, Turkish and Napoleonic.

WORTH A TRIP

GALATINA

With a charming historic centre, Galatina, 18km south of Lecce, is at the core of the Salentine Peninsula's Greek past. It is almost the only place where the ritual *tarantismi* (Spider Music) is still practised. The tarantella folk dance evolved from this ritual, and each year on the feast day of St Peter and St Paul (29 June), it is performed at the (now deconsecrated) church. Galantina's essential sight is the astounding 14th-century **Basilica di Santa Caterina d'Alessandria** (Piazzetta Orsini; ⊙ 4-6.30pm daily, 8.30am-12.30pm Mon-Sat Apr-Sep, shorter hours rest of year), its interior a kaleidoscope of frescoes. **Ferrovie del Sud** (www.fseonline.it) runs frequent trains between Lecce and Galatina (€2.10, 30 minutes).

◉ Sights

★ **Cathedral**   CATHEDRAL

(☑ 0836 80 27 20; Piazza Basilica; ⊙ 7am-noon & 3-8pm, shorter hours in winter) Mosaics, skulls, crypts and biblical-meets-tropical imagery: Otranto's cathedral is like no other in Italy. It was built by the Normans in the 11th century, incorporating Romanesque, Byzantine and early Christian styles with their own, and has been given a few facelifts since. Covering the entire floor is its pièce de résistance, a vast 12th-century mosaic of a stupendous tree of life balanced on the back of two elephants.

Castello Aragonese Otranto   CASTLE

(☑ 0836 210 0 94; www.castelloaragoneseotranto. com; Piazza Castello; adult/reduced €6/4; ⊙ 10am-8pm) Built in the late 15th century, when Otranto was more populous and important than today, and not long after the Ottoman raid that resulted in the execution of hundreds for refusing Islam, the castle is a blunt and grim structure, well preserved internally and offering views from the outer walls. It is also famous from Horace Walpole's *The Castle of Otranto* (1764), recognised as the first Gothic novel. Ask about guided tours (adult/reduced €3/2) of the castle's underground area.

L'Approdo
PUBLIC ART

Dubbed *L'Approdo* (The Landing) and located in Otranto's new port area, this striking installation by the Greek artist Costas Varostos was erected in 2012. Sheathed in shards of green glass, it is based on the rusting infrastructure of the *Kateri i Rades,* a boat that foundered near Otranto in 1997 with the loss of 87 Albanian asylum seekers. More than 20 years after the tragedy, *L'Approdo* remains a poignant memorial to those seeking refuge across the Mediterranean in southern Europe.

Chiesa di San Pietro
CHURCH

(Via San Pietro; ☺10am-noon & 4-8pm Jun-Sep, by request rest of year) The origins of this cross-shaped Byzantine church are uncertain, but some think they may be as remote as the 5th century. The present structure seems to be a product of the 10th century, to which the oldest of the celebrated frescoes decorating its three apses dates.

🏃 Activities

There are some great beaches north of Otranto, especially Baia dei Turchi, with its translucent blue water. South of Otranto a spectacular rocky coastline makes for an impressive drive down to Castro. To see what goes on underwater, speak to Scuba Diving Otranto (☎0836 80 27 40; www.scubadiving.it; Via del Porto 1; 1-/2-tank dive incl equipment €48/75; ☺7am-10pm).

🛏 Sleeping

Palazzo de Mori
B&B €€

(☎0836 80 10 88; www.palazzodemori.it; Bastione dei Pelasgi; d €160; ☺Apr-Oct; ❄@) In Otranto's historic centre, this charming B&B serves fabulous breakfasts on the sun terrace overlooking the port. The rooms are decorated in soothing white on white.

★ Palazzo Papaleo
HOTEL €€€

(☎0836 80 21 08; www.hotelpalazzopapaleo.com; Via Rondachi 1; r from €230; P❄@🤖) Located next to the cathedral, this sumptuous hotel, the first to earn the EU Eco-label in Puglia, has magnificent rooms with original frescoes, exquisitely carved antique furniture and walls washed in soft greys, ochres and yellows. Soak in the panoramic views while enjoying the rooftop spa, or steam yourself pure in the hammam. The staff are exceptionally friendly.

🍴 Eating

SoFish
SEAFOOD €

(☎331 9867387; Corso Garibaldi 39; meals €10-15; ☺noon-11pm) A modern update on a traditional *friggitoria,* SoFish features excellent fried seafood, good salads – the one with huge slabs of seared tuna almost overflows the plate – and a concise drinks list with Salento wines by the glass and a rather good selection of Italian craft beers. The fried calamari and octopus are both also very good.

★ L'Altro Baffo
SEAFOOD €€

(☎0836 80 16 36; www.laltrobaffo.com; Via Cenobio Basiliano 23; meals €40-45; ☺12-2.30pm & 7.30pm-midnight Tue-Sun) This elegant modern restaurant near the castle stands out in Otranto's competitive dining scene. It stays in touch with basic Pugliese and Italian principles, but ratchets things up several notches: the 'carbonara' made with sea-urchin roe is a daring instant classic. The menu is mainly seafood, but there are a few vegetarian dishes that are anything but afterthoughts.

ℹ Information

Tourist Office (☎0836 80 14 36; Castello Aragonese Otranto; ☺9am-1pm & 3-6pm) Located in the entrance to the castle.

ℹ Getting There & Away

Otranto can be reached from Lecce by FSE train (€3.50, 1½ hours). It is on a small branch line, which necessitates changing in Maglie and sometimes Zollino too. Services are reduced on Sundays. By bus, STP links directly from Lecce (€4.40, one hour, frequent).

Castro

☎0836 / POP 2450

One of Salento's most striking coastal settlements, the walled commune of Castro has a pedigree that predates the Romans, who gave it the name *Castrum Minervae,* or 'Minerva's Castle'. The castle and walls that remain today date to the 16th-century rule of the Aragonese, who built atop foundations laid by the Angevins and Byzantines before them. The charming old town, which also has a 12th-century cathedral, the remains of a Byzantine church and a clifftop piazza with delightful sea views, sits above a marina (which really comes alive in summer) and terraced olive groves leading to a limestone coast riddled with spectacular caves.

⊙ Sights

Grotta Zinzulusa   CAVE
(☑0836 94 38 12; Via Zinzulusa; adult/reduced €6/3; ⊙9.30am-7pm Jul & Aug, shorter hours rest of year; ℗) An aperture on the Ionian coast below Castro leads into the magnificent stalactite-festooned Cave of Zinzulusa, one of the most significant coastal limestone karst formations in Italy. The portion accessible to the public stretches hundreds of metres back from the cliff face, terminating in a chamber grand enough to justify the sobriquet 'Il Duomo'. Divided into three distinct geomorphological sections, Zinzulusa is home to endemic crustacea and other 'living fossils' known nowhere else on the planet.

Castello Aragonese   CASTLE
(☑0836 94 70 05; Via Sant Antonio 1; adult/reduced €2.50/2; ⊙10am-1pm & 3-7.30pm) Primarily the work of the Aragonese who ruled southern Italy in the 16th century, this sturdy redoubt retains elements built by the Angevins in previous centuries, on earlier Byzantine foundations. Partly ruinous by the 18th century, it's been thoroughly restored, and now houses the small Antonio Lazzari Civic Museum, exhibiting Messapian, Greek and Roman archaeology uncovered in Castro and the surrounding area. Its prize piece is a torso of the goddess Minerva (Athena), buried at the ancient city gates.

❶ Getting There & Away

STP Lecce runs a daily bus between Castro and Lecce (€4, 90 minutes).

Gallipoli

☑0833 / POP 20,700

Like Taranto, Gallipoli is a two-part town: the modern hub is based on the mainland, while the older *centro storico* inhabits a small island that juts out into the Ionian Sea. With a raft of serene baroque architecture usurped only by Lecce, it is, arguably, the prettiest of Salento's smaller settlements.

⊙ Sights

Gallipoli has some fine beaches, including the Baia Verde, just south of town. Nature enthusiasts will want to take a day trip to Parco Regionale Porto Selvaggio, about 20km north – a protected area of wild coastline with walking trails among the trees and diving off the rocky shore.

Cattedrale di Sant'Agata   CATHEDRAL
(www.cattedralegallipoli.it; Via Duomo 1; ⊙hours vary) On the island, Gallipoli's 17th-century cathedral is a baroque beauty that could compete with anything in Lecce. Not surprisingly, Giuseppe Zimbalo, who helped beautify Lecce's Santa Croce basilica, worked on the facade. Inside, it's lined with paintings by local artists.

Frantoio Ipogeo   HISTORIC SITE
(☑0833 26 42 42; Via Antonietta de Pace 87; €1.50; ⊙10am-1pm & 3-6pm) This is only one of some 35 olive presses buried in the tufa rock below the town. It was here, between the 16th and early 19th centuries, that local workers pressed Gallipoli's olive oil, which was then stored in one of the 2000 cisterns carved beneath the old town.

🛌 Sleeping

Insula   B&B €
(☑329 8070056, 0833 20 14 13; www.bbinsula gallipoli.it; Via Antonietta de Pace 56; d €80; ⊙Apr-Oct; ❄@) A magnificent 16th-century building houses this memorable B&B. The five rooms are all different but share the same princely atmosphere with exquisite antiques, vaulted high ceilings and cool pastel paintwork. Directly adjacent to the cathedral, it couldn't be any more central.

Hotel Palazzo del Corso   HOTEL €€€
(☑0833 26 40 40; www.hotelpalazzodelcorso. it; Corso Roma 145; r/ste €220/370; ℗❄🛋) It's worth forking out a bit extra for this beautiful town hotel, if you fancy a bit of luxury. The rooms are furnished distinctively enough to avoid looking too corporate, there's a gym and a fantastic terrace complete with a small swimming pool. There's also a fine terrace restaurant, La DolceVita, serving lots of seafood (meals €40 to €45).

🍴 Eating

Gallipoli is famous for its red prawns and its soothing *spumone* layered gelato.

Baguetteria de Pace   SANDWICHES €
(www.facebook.com/baguetteriadepace; Via Sant'Angelo 8; baguettes €6-8; ⊙11am-3pm & 7-11pm) The Italian art of making exceptional sandwiches is practised assiduously here. Choose the dense Italian bread (or a baguette if you're feeling fluffy) and have the friendly staff stuff it with top-notch smallgoods, cheeses, vegetables and whatever else takes your fancy. Especially good

is the black pork salami with local burrata cheese. Salento wines and craft beer are also available.

La Puritate
SEAFOOD €€€

(📋 0833 26 42 05; Via Sant'Elia 18; meals €50; ⏰ 12.30-3pm & 7.30-10.30pm, closed Wed winter) Book ahead to ensure your table at *the* place for fish in this seafood-loving town. Follow the practically obligatory seafood *antipasti* with delicious *primi* (first courses). Anything fishy is good (especially the prawns, swordfish and tuna) and the picture windows allow splendid views of the waters whence it came.

🛈 Information

Tourist Office (📋 0833 26 25 29; Via Antonietta de Pace 86; ⏰ 8am-9pm summer, 8am-1pm & 4-9pm Mon-Sat winter) Near the cathedral in the old town.

🛈 Getting There & Away

FSE (www.fseonline.it) buses and trains head direct to Lecce (€4.40, 1¾ hours, frequent).

Taranto

📋 099 / POP 199,560

Not generally considered to be on the tourist circuit, Taranto is rimmed by modern industry, including a massive steelworks, and is home to Italy's second biggest naval base after La Spezia. Thanks to an illustrious Greek and Roman history, it has been bequeathed with one of the finest Magna Graecia museums in Italy. For this reason alone, it's worth a stopover.

👁 Sights

★ Museo Nazionale Archeologico di Taranto
MUSEUM

(📋 099 453 21 12; www.museotaranto.org; Via Cavour 10; adult/reduced €5/2.50; ⏰ 9am-7.30pm) Sitting unassumingly in a side street in Taranto's new town is one of Italy's most important archaeological museums, chiefly dedicated to the archaeology of ancient Taras (Taranto). It houses, among other artefacts, the largest collection of Greek terracotta figures in the world. Also on display are fine collections of 1st-century-BC glassware, classic black-and-red Attic vases and stunning gold and jewellery from Magna Graecia, such as a 4th-century-BC bronze and terracotta crown.

Cathedral
CATHEDRAL

(Piazza Duomo; ⏰ 4.30-7.30pm daily, 7.30am-noon Sat & Sun) The 11th-century cathedral is one of Puglia's oldest Romanesque buildings and an extravagant treat. It's dedicated to San Cataldo, an Irish monk who lived and was buried here in the 7th century. Within, the **Capella di San Cataldo** is a baroque riot of frescoes and polychrome marble inlay.

Castello Aragonese
CASTLE

(📋 099 775 34 38; www.castelloaragonesetaranto. com; Piazza Castello; ⏰ 9.30am-1.30am summer, shorter hours rest of year) **FREE** Guarding the swing bridge that joins the old and new parts of town, this impressive 15th-century structure, built on Norman and Byzantine predecessors, was once a prison and is currently occupied by the Italian navy, which has restored it. Multilingual and free guided tours, mandatory to get inside, are led by naval officers throughout the day. Opposite are the two remaining columns of the ancient **Temple of Poseidon**.

★ Festivals & Events

Le Feste di Pasqua
RELIGIOUS

Taranto is famous for its Holy Week celebrations – the biggest in the region – when bearers in Ku Klux Klan–style robes carry icons around the town. There are three processions: the Perdoni, celebrating pilgrims; the Addolorata (lasting 12 hours but covering only 4km); and the Misteri (even slower at 14 hours to cover 2km).

🛏 Sleeping

Hotel Akropolis
HOTEL €€

(📋 099 470 41 10; www.hotelakropolis.it; Vico Seminario 3; s/d/ste €90/120/160; ❄ @ 🛜) If Taranto's richly historic yet crumbling old town is ever to be reborn, it will be due to businesses such as this hotel – a converted medieval *palazzo* with a heavy Greek theme. It offers 13 stylish cream-and-white rooms, beautiful majolica-tiled floors, a panoramic rooftop terrace and an atmospheric bar and restaurant, decked out in stone, wood and glass.

🍴 Eating & Drinking

Trattoria al Gatto Rosso
TRATTORIA €€

(📋 340 5337800, 099 452 98 75; www.ristorante gattorosso.com; Via Cavour 2; meals €35-40; ⏰ 12.30-3pm & 7.30-11pm Tue-Sun) Unsurprisingly, seafood is the thing at the Red Cat. Relaxed and unpretentious, its heavy tablecloths, deep wine glasses and solid cutlery

Taranto

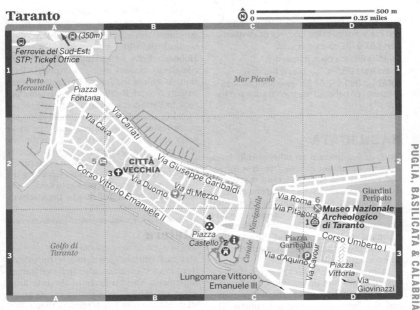

set the scene for full enjoyment of dishes such as spaghetti with local clams and slow-cooked swordfish with eggplant *caponata* (sweet-and-sour vegetable salad). Rooms at Gatto Rosso's adjacent Baylon Guesthouse are stylish and colourful and include an excellent breakfast.

Cibo per la Mente BAR
(Caffe Letterario; ☑ 099 400 75 20; www.facebook. com/pg/CiboPerLaMenteTaranto; Palazzo Gennarini, Via Duomo; ⊙ 9am-11pm Mon-Thu, to 1am Fri & Sat; 🛜) Inspiring the reinvigoration of Taranto's *centro storico* is this cool and compact cafe. Local cats mooch around on bench seats outside, while the interior adorned with books and quirky prints of David Bowie is good for a coffee or cocktail. Light snacks are available, and the space is used occasionally for live music and literary events.

ℹ Information

Tourist office (☑ 334 2844098; Castello Aragonese; ⊙ 9am-8pm summer, shorter hours rest of year)

ℹ Getting There & Away

BUS
Buses heading north and west depart from Porto Mercantile. **FSE** (☑ 080 546 21 11; www.

fseonline.it) buses go to Bari (€8.60, 3¼ hours, four per day); **STP** (☑ 080 975 26 19) buses go to Lecce, with a change at Monteparano (€6.80, two hours, four daily).

 Marozzi (☑ 080 5799 0211; www.marozzivt. it) has express services serving Rome's Stazione Tiburtina (from €32, six to eight hours, four daily); **Autolinee Miccolis** (☑ 099 470 44 51; www.busmiccolis.it) serves Naples (from €16, four hours, three daily).

 The bus **ticket office** (⊙ 6am-1pm & 2-7pm) is at Porto Mercantile.

PUGLIA, BASILICATA & CALABRIA SALENTO

TRAIN

From **Taranto Centrale** (Piazza Moro), Trenitalia and FSE trains go to the following destinations:

Bari €8.60, 1¼ hours, frequent

Brindisi €5, one hour, frequent

Rome from €52.50, six hours, five daily

AMAT (☑ 099 452 67 32; www.amat.taranto. it) buses run between the train station and the new city.

BASILICATA

Much of Basilicata is an otherworldly landscape of mountain ranges, trackless forests and villages that seem to sprout organically from the granite. Not easily penetrated, it is strategically located, and has been dominated by the Lucanians, Greeks, Romans, Germans, Lombards, Byzantines, Saracens, Normans and others. Being the plaything of such powers has not been conducive to a quiet or happy fate.

In the north the landscape is a fertile zone of gentle hills and deep valleys; the interior is dominated by the Lucanian Apennines and the Parco Nazionale del Pollino. The Tyrrhenian coast is a fissured wonderland of rocky coves and precariously sited villages. Here, Maratea is one of Italy's most charming seaside resorts.

But it is inland Matera, where primitive *sassi* (caves) lurk under grand cathedrals, that is Basilicata's most precious gem. The third-oldest continuously inhabited city in the world, it's intriguing, breathtaking and tragic in equal measures.

History

Basilicata spans Italy's 'instep', and is landlocked apart from slivers of Tyrrhenian and Ionian coastline. It was known to the Greeks and Romans as Lucania, after the Lucani tribe who lived here as far back as the 5th century BC. The name survives in the 'Lucanian Dolomites', 'Lucanian cooking' and elsewhere. The Greeks also prospered in ancient Basilicata, possibly settling along the coastline at Metapontum and Erakleia as far back as the 8th century BC. Roman power came next, and the Punic Wars between that expanding power and Carthage. Hannibal, the ferocious Carthaginian general, rampaged through the region, making the city of Grumentum his base.

In the 10th century, the Byzantine Emperor Basil II (976–1025) bestowed his title, 'Basileus', on the region, overthrew the Saracens in southern Italy and reintroduced Christianity. The pattern of war and overthrow continued throughout the Middle Ages right up until the 19th century, as the Normans, Hohenstaufens, Angevins and Bourbons ceaselessly tussled over this strategic location. As talk of the Italian unification began to gain ground, Bourbon-sponsored loyalists took to Basilicata's mountains to oppose political change. Ultimately, they became the much-feared bandits of local lore who make scary appearances in writings from the late 19th and early 20th centuries. In the 1930s, Basilicata was used as a kind of open prison for political dissidents – most famously the painter, writer and doctor Carlo Levi – sent into exile to remote villages by the fascists.

Matera

☑ 0835 / POP 60,350 / ELEV 405M

Matera, Basilicata's jewel, may be the world's third-longest continuously inhabited human settlement. Natural caves in the tufa limestone, exposed as the Gravina cut its gorge, attracted the first inhabitants perhaps 7000 years ago. More elaborate structures were built atop them. Today, looking across the gorge to Matera's huddled *sassi* (cave dwellings) it seems you've been transported back to the ancient Holy Land.

Old Matera is split into two sections – the Sasso Barisano and the Sasso Caveoso – separated by a ridge upon which sits Matera's gracious *duomo* (cathedral). The *sassi*, many little more than one-room caves, once contained such appalling poverty and unthinkable living conditions that in the 1950s Matera was denounced as the 'Shame of Italy', and the *sassi*-dwellers were moved on. Only in later decades has the value of this extraordinarily built environment been recognised, and in 2019 the city was recognised as a European Capital of Culture.

◉ Sights

The two *sassi* districts – the more restored, northwest-facing Sasso Barisano and the more impoverished, northeast-facing Sasso Caveoso – are both extraordinary, riddled with serpentine alleyways and staircases, and dotted with frescoed *chiese rupestri* (cave churches) created between the 8th and 13th centuries. Modern Matera still contains some 3000 habitable caves.

The *sassi* are accessible from several points. There's an entrance off Piazza San

Francisco, or take Via delle Beccherie to Piazza del Duomo and follow the tourist itinerary signs to enter either Barisano or Caveoso. Sasso Caveoso is also accessible from Via Ridola.

For a great photograph, head out of town for about 3km on the Taranto–Laterza road and follow signs for the *chiese rupestri*. This takes you up on the Murgia Plateau to the belvedere (Contrada Murgia Timone), from where you have fantastic views of the plunging ravine and Matera.

◎ Sasso Barisano

★Chiesa San Pietro Barisano   CHURCH
(⊡342 0319991; www.oltrelartematera.it; Piazza San Pietro Barisano; adult/reduced €3.50/2.50, incl Chiesa di Santa Lucia alle Malve & Chiesa di Santa Maria di Idris €7/5; ⊙9am-8pm Apr-Oct, 10am-5pm Nov-Mar) Dating in its earliest parts to the 12th century, St Peter's, the largest of Matera's rupestrian churches, overlays an ancient honeycomb of niches where corpses were placed for draining. At the entrance level can be found 15th- and 16th-century frescoes of the Annunciation and a variety of saints. The empty frame of the altarpiece graphically illustrates the town's troubled recent history: the church was plundered when Matera was partially abandoned in the 1960s and '70s.

Chiesa di Madonna delle Virtù
& Chiesa di San Nicola del Greci   CHURCH
(⊡377 4448885; www.caveheritage.it; Via Madonna delle Virtù; ⊙10am-8pm Jun-Sep, shorter hours rest of year) FREE This monastic complex, one of the most important monuments in Matera, comprises dozens of chambers carved into the tufa limestone over two floors. Chiesa di Madonna delle Virtù was built in the 10th or 11th century and restored in the 17th century. Above it, the simple Chiesa di San Nicola del Greci is rich in frescoes. The complex was used in 1213 by Benedictine monks of Palestinian origin. The churches are sometimes used for art installations (admission charges apply).

◎ Sasso Caveoso

★Casa Noha   MUSEUM
(⊡0835 33 54 52; www.fondoambiente.it/casa-noha-eng; Recinto Cavone 9; adult/reduced €6/2; ⊙9am-7pm Apr-Oct, shorter hours rest of year) Highly recommended as a precursor to visiting the *sassi* themselves, this wonderful 25-minute multimedia exhibit, spread across three rooms of a 16th-century family home donated to the Fondo Ambiente Italiano, relates the astonishing and often painful social history of the town and its *sassi*. Your appreciation of Matera's unique history and renaissance, and the tribulations of the *sassi* dwellers, will be transformed.

Museo della Scultura
Contemporanea   MUSEUM
(MUSMA; ⊡366 9357768; www.musma.it; Via San Giacomo; adult/reduced €5/3.50; ⊙10am-8pm Apr-Sep, to 6pm Oct-Mar) The setting of this fabulous museum of contemporary sculpture – deeply recessed caves and the frescoed

---

EXPLORING THE GRAVINA GORGE

In the picturesque landscape of the Murgia Plateau, the Matera Gravina cuts a rough gouge in the earth, a 200m-deep canyon pockmarked with abandoned caves and villages and roughly 150 mysterious *chiese rupestri* (cave churches). The area is protected as the Parco della Murgia Materana, an 80-sq-km wild park formed in 1990 and, since 2007, included in Matera's Unesco World Heritage Site. You can hike from the *sassi* into the gorge; steps lead down from the parking place near the Monasterio di Santa Lucia (Via Madonna delle Virtù; ⊙7.30am-1pm & 5-8.30pm). At the bottom of the gorge you have to ford a river and then climb up to the belvedere on the other side; this takes roughly two hours.

Cave churches accessible from the belvedere include San Falcione, Sant'Agnese and Madonna delle Tre Porte. The belvedere is connected by road to the Jazzo Gattini (p806) visitor centre, housed in an old sheepfold. Guided hikes can be organised here, as can walks to the nearby Neolithic village of Murgia Timone. For longer forays into the park, including a long day trek to the town of Montescaglioso, consider a guided hike with Ferula Viaggi (⊡0835 33 65 72; www.ferulaviaggi.it; Via Cappelluti 34; ⊙9am-1.30pm & 3.30-7pm Mon-Sat). Beware: paths and river crossings in the park can be treacherous during and after bad weather.

Matera

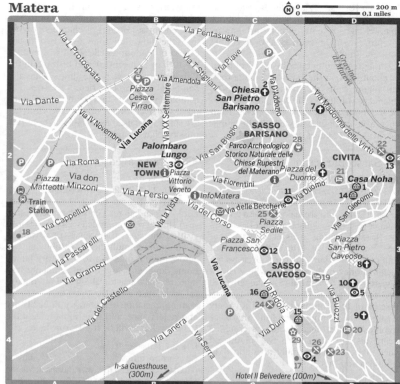

rooms of the 16th-century Palazzo Pomarici – is as extraordinary as the exhibits. Italian sculpture from the late 19th century to the present day is the principal focus, but you can also see beautiful examples of graphic art, jewellery and ceramics.

Chiesa di San Pietro Caveoso   CHURCH

(☑0835 31 15 10; Piazza San Pietro Caveoso 1; ⓧMass 7pm Mon-Sat, 11am & 7pm Sun) **FREE** The only church in the *sassi* not dug into the tufa rock, Chiesa di San Pietro Caveoso was originally built in 1300 and has a 17th-century Romanesque-baroque facade and frescoed timber ceiling.

Chiesa di Santa Maria di Idris   CHURCH

(☑344 2763197; www.oltrelartematera.it; Piazza San Pietro Caveoso; adult/reduced €3.50/2.50, incl Chiesa San Pietro Barisano & Chiesa di Santa Lucia alle Malve €7/5; ⓧ9am-8pm Apr-Oct, 10am-5pm Nov-Mar) Dug into the Idris rock, this church has an unprepossessing facade, but the narrow corridor communicating with

the recessed church of San Giovanni in Monterrone is richly decorated with 12th- to 17th-century frescoes.

Chiesa di Santa Lucia alle Malve   CHURCH

(☑342 0919624; www.oltrelartematera.it; Rione Malve; adult/reduced €3.50/2.50, incl Chiesa San Pietro Barisano & Chiesa di Santa Maria di Idris €7/5; ⓧ9am-8pm Apr-Oct, 10am-5pm Nov-Mar) Dating to the 8th century, when it was built as the Benedictine Order's first foothold in Matera, this cliff-face church has a number of 13th-century frescoes, including an unusual breastfeeding Madonna. The church originally comprised three aisles, with two later adapted as dwellings.

Casa-Grotta di Vico Solitario   HISTORIC SITE

(€3; ⓧ9.30am-late) For a glimpse of life in old Matera, visit this historic *sasso* off Via Bruno Buozzi. There's a bed in the middle, a loom, a room for manure and a section for a pig and a donkey. You also have access to a couple of neighbouring caves: in one

Matera

there's, a black-and-white film depicting gritty pre-restoration Matera.

⦿ New Town

The nucleus of the new town is **Piazza Vittorio Veneto**, an excellent, bustling meeting point for a *passeggiata* (sociable evening stroll). It's surrounded by elegant churches and richly adorned *palazzi* with their backs deliberately turned on the *sassi:* an attempt by the bourgeois to block out the shameful poverty the *sassi* once represented.

★**Palombaro Lungo**   HISTORIC SITE
(☎339 3638332; Piazza Vittorio Veneto; guided tour €3; ⊙10am-1pm & 3-6pm) This giant cistern, arguably as magnificent as a subterranean cathedral, is one of Matera's great sights. Lying under the city's main square with arches carved out of the existing rock, it is mind-boggling in its scale and ingenuity, and was still supplying water to Materans within living memory. Book ahead for a 25-minute tour with the multilingual guides, who explain its conception and history (English-language tours generally leave at 10.30am, 12.30pm, 3.30pm and 5.30pm).

Museo Nazionale d'Arte Medievale e Moderna della Basilicata   MUSEUM
(☎0835 25 62 11; www.musei.basilicata.beniculturali.it; Piazzetta Pascoli 1, Palazzo Lanfranchi; adult/reduced €3/1.50; ⊙9am-8pm Thu-Tue, from 11am Wed) The Palazzo Lanfranchi, built as a seminary incorporating an earlier church in the 17th century, now houses this intriguing museum of sacred and contemporary art. The stars of the show here are Carlo Levi's paintings, including the panoramic mural *Lucania '61* depicting peasant life in biblical technicolour. There are also some centuries-old sacred art from the *sassi*.

Cathedral   CATHEDRAL
(☎0835 33 29 08; www.matera-irsina.chiesacattolica.it; Piazza del Duomo; ⊙9am-7pm) Set high up on a spur between the two natural bowls of the *sassi*, the wan, graceful exterior of the 13th-century Pugliese-Romanesque cathedral makes the neobaroque excess within all the more of a surprise. Following 13 years of renovation, it's possible once again to admire the ornate capitals, sumptuous chapels, 17th-century frescoes, 13th-century Byzantine Madonna and two 12th-century frescoed crypts, uncovered in the works. Note the pediments mounted on the cathedral's altars, which come from Greek temples at Metaponto.

Museo Nazionale Ridola   MUSEUM
(☎0835 31 00 58; www.musei.basilicata.beniculturali.it; Via Ridola 24; adult/reduced €2.50/1.25; ⊙9am-8pm Tue-Sun, 2-8pm Mon) This impressive collection includes local Neolithic finds and some remarkable Greek pottery, such as

PUGLIA, BASILICATA & CALABRIA MATERA

PUGLIA, BASILICATA & CALABRIA MATERA

CRIPTA DEL PECCATO ORIGINALE

A fascinating Benedictine site dating to the Lombard period, the Cripta del Peccato Originale (☑320 3345323; www.criptadelpeccatooriginale.it; Contrada Pietrapenta; adult/reduced €10/8; ⊙10am-1.30pm & 4-7.30pm Tue-Sun Apr-Sep, shorter hours rest of year) houses well-preserved 8th-century frescoes – depicting vivid scenes from both Old and New Testaments – that have earned it a reputation as the 'Sistine Chapel' of Matera's cave churches. It's 7km south of Matera: all visits must be booked through the website, then joined at the ticket office (at Azienda Agricola Dragone on Contrada Pietrapenta) 30 minutes prior to the scheduled starting time.

the *Cratere Mascheroni*, a huge urn more than 1m high.

🏃 Activities

Eldorado Ranch   HORSE RIDING
(☑328 7610502; www.eledoradoranch.it; Strada Statale 7; 1hr ride €30; ⊙9am-7pm) A few kilometres south of Matera, this well-run horseback-riding outfit takes tours (one to two hours) through the Gravina gorge, or south, to the Cripta del Peccato Originale. It's a delightful day trip outside Matera, if you're here for a while.

🎓 Courses

Cook'n Fun at Mary's   COOKING
(☑320 6936553; www.cooknfunatmarys.com; Via Monsignor Macco 67a; per person €100) Fresh produce from the kitchen garden is the foundation of the traditional Lucanian recipes taught in Mary's relaxed domestic kitchen. Classes are in English, and culminate in a meal and glass of wine.

👉 Tours

Amy Weideman   TOURS
(☑339 2823618; www.materatours.net; half-day tour for 1-3 people €80, for 4 or more people €100) Amy Weideman offers an English-speaking expat's perspective on her adopted home of Matera, with tours ranging from 2½ hours to full-day excursions and trips further afield (to the delightful hilltop towns of Pie-

trapertosa and Castelmezzano, for example). Highly recommended.

Altieri Viaggi   TOURS
(☑346 6453440, 0835 31 43 59; www.altieriviaggi.it; Via Ridola 61; ⊙9am-9pm) Runs tours around the *sassi* and rupestrian churches of Matera and the Parco della Murgia, starting from €20 for a 50-minute tour (minimum four people). Altieri also offers plenty of other trips, including hiking and *sassi* tours by *ape calessino* (autorickshaw). Tours usually end with a tasting of typical local products.

🎉 Festivals & Events

Sagra della Madonna della Bruna   RELIGIOUS
(⊙2 Jul) This week-long celebration of Matera's patron saint has 14th-century roots. The culminating day, 2 July, begins at dawn with the colourful 'Procession of Shepherds', in which an image of the Virgin is carried through Matera's neighbourhoods. The finale is the *assalto al carro*, when the crowd descends on the ornately decorated main float and tears it to pieces.

🛏 Sleeping

Matera's unique appeal has seen accommodation options mushroom across the *sassi* and the new town. Take your pick: a smartly refurbished *sasso*, a room in a repurposed *palazzo*, or something more modern in the new town. Cheaper options can still be found.

h-sa Guesthouse   B&B €
(☑340 7062574; Via Pasquale Vena 87; d from €80; P🍴🛜) In a quiet residential neighbourhood around 1km walk from central Matera, the modern h-sa Guesthouse is an excellent option if you're travelling with a car. There's plenty of free off-street parking, and the friendly family owners provide an excellent breakfast. In warmer weather, stylish rooms open onto leafy gardens with outdoor seating and places to relax. Book through online booking websites.

La Dolce Vita B&B   B&B €
(☑328 7111121, 0835 31 03 24; www.ladolcevitamatera.it; Rione Malve 51; r €80; 🛜) 🌿 This delightful, ecofriendly B&B in Sasso Caveoso comprises two self-contained apartments with solar panels, rainwater recycling, a scenic terrace and cool, comfortable furnishings. Owners Vincenzo and Carla are passionate about Matera and are mines of information on the *sassi*.

Il Vicinato B&B €

(📞 380 1828935; www.ilvicinato.com; Piazzetta San Pietro Caveoso 7; s/d €60/90; ❀ 📶) Run by Luigi and Teresa, 'The Neighbourhood' is wonderfully located in Sasso Caveoso, in a building dating in parts to around 1600. Rooms are decorated in clean modern lines, with views across to the Murgia Plateau. As well as the standard rooms, there's a room with a balcony and a small apartment, each with an independent entrance.

⭐**Hotel Il Belvedere** HOTEL €€

(📞 0835 31 17 02; www.hotelbelvedere.matera. it; Via Casalnuovo 133; d from €135; ❀ 📶) This cave boutique looks unremarkable from its street-side perch on the edge of the Sasso Caveoso, but you'll feel your jaw start to drop as you enter its luxurious entrails and spy the spectacle of Old Matera sprawling below a jutting terrace. Cavernous rooms sport mosaics, mood lighting and curtained four-poster beds. Two-night minimums apply in August.

Palazzo Viceconte HOTEL €€

(📞 0835 33 06 99; www.palazzoviceconte.it; Via San Potito 7; d/ste from €158/220; ❀ 📶) You won't have trouble spotting the palatial features at this 17th-century *palazzo* near the cathedral with superb views of the *sassi* and gorge. The 14 rooms are elegantly furnished, the bathrooms all have baths and the rooftop terrace has panoramic views. Be king (or queen) for a day (or more) amid the courtyards, salons, frescoed ceilings and antiques.

Corte San Pietro BOUTIQUE HOTEL €€€

(📞 0835 31 08 13; www.cortesanpietro.it; Via Buozzi 97; d €230; ❀ 📶) Located in Sasso Caveoso, the family-owned Corte San Pietro is one of Matera's most comfortable boutique hotels. Each room is a different shape and size, designed to fit the idiosyncratic cave location, and the shadow and light interplay of the interior is sometimes used to showcase interesting art installations.

🍴 Eating

⭐**I Vizi degli Angeli** GELATO €

(📞 0835 31 06 37; www.ivizidegliangeli.it; Via Ridola 36; medium cone €23; ⊘ noon-11pm Thu-Tue) 'The Angels' Vices', an artisanal gelato 'laboratory' on the busy promenade of Via Domenico Ridola, is Matera's best. Alongside classics such as pistachio, you'll find experimental flavours such as grapefruit with pink pepper

and thyme and mallow, which taste even better than they read.

Da Zero PIZZA €

(📞 0835 165 23 69; www.cominciadazero.com; Via Madonna delle Virtu 12; pizza €10-12; ⊘ 12.30-3pm & 7.30pm-midnight Thu-Sun, 7.30pm-midnight Mon-Wed) Harnessing ingredients sourced from Slow Food producers around southern Italy, Da Zero is the best pizzeria in Matera. Interesting flavour combinations lift this cave eatery above the norm, and the wine and craft beer list focuses on interesting local drops from Basilicata and nearby Calabria. Good salads also feature at this quieter location away from the main tourist trail.

enoteca dai tosi ITALIAN €€

(📞 0835 31 40 29; www.enotecadaitosi.it; Via Buozzi 12; meals €30-35; ⊘ noon-3pm & 7pm-late Wed-Mon) Easily Matera's most spectacular wine bar and restaurant, enoteca dai tosi's subterranean space enlivened with shimmering green glass is a top place to partner wines from southern Italy with a concise selection of shared plates. Standout tapas-style dishes include fava bean and chicory croquettes and the stuffed calamari with zucchini. Tasting platters (€12 to €28) of cheese and charcuterie are good value.

La Gatta Buia ITALIAN €€

(📞 0835 25 65 10; www.lagattabuia.eu; Via delle Beccherie 90-92; meals €38; ⊘ 1-3pm & 7.30-11pm) With a sleekly decorated bar and dining areas and a menu that goes beyond Basilicatan classics, 'The Good Cat' is another feather in the cap of Matera's increasing sophistication. Wines from Lombardy, Piedmont and Abruzzo join the local drops to help you wash down veal cheeks braised in Aglianico wine, or Sicilianesque pasta with cod, raisins, pine nuts, tomatoes and olives.

L'Abbondanza Lucana ITALIAN €€

(📞 0835 33 45 74; Via Buozzi 11; meals €45; ⊘ noon-3pm Tue-Sun, 7-11pm Tue-Sat) The paradoxical bounty of Lucania's *cucina povera* is laid out before you in this stone cellar in Sasso Caveoso. For a fantastic introduction to a range of *prodotti tipici* from the region, start with the Lucanian tasting plate, laden with delights such as wild boar, baked ricotta and a soup of chestnuts with Sarconi's famous beans.

⭐**Vitoantonio Lombardo** ITALIAN €€€

(📞 0835 33 54 75; www.vlristorante.it; Via Madonna delle Virtu 13/14; meals €85-130; ⊘ 12.30-2pm

& 7.30-10pm Thu-Mon, 7.30-10pm Wed) Degustation menus from five to 12 courses provide a sumptuous experience of elevated Italian cuisine at Matera's most innovative restaurant. Menu options include lamb with fennel, lemon and liquorice, and a dessert of ravioli with salted ricotta cheese and a basil and tomato sorbet. Yes, it's pricey, but it will be the Materan meal you remember the most. Bookings essential.

Drinking & Nightlife

Options for drinking and socialising have mushroomed, along with Matera's renaissance. You'll find wine bars, pubs and *enotecas* along Via Domenico Ridola, Via Fiorentini, Via San Biagio and Via delle Beccherie, and also dotted throughout the *sassi*.

★ **Malto & Luppolo**　　　CRAFT BEER
(327 4405292; www.facebook.com/maltoelup polomatera; Piazza Firrao 25; ⊙6pm-midnight Tue-Sun) A short walk from Piazza Vittorio Veneto but off the tourist trail is this warm and welcoming bar specialising in Italian craft beer. Four rotating taps feature regular surprises and the bar fridge has interesting tipples like a nectarine-flavoured sour beer. The friendly owner's English is better than he thinks.

Vicolo Cieco　　　WINE BAR
(338 8550984; www.facebook.com/vicolocieco salsamenteria; Via Fiorentini 74; ⊙6pm-2am Tue-Thu, from noon Fri-Sun) Matera's renaissance and new-found relaxed vitality come to the fore at this wine bar in a typical cave-house off Sasso Barisano's main drag. The eccentric decor signals its friendly, upbeat spirit – retro jukeboxes, a wall-mounted Scalextric track, chairs cut in half and glued to the wall in the name of art, and a chandelier of repurposed cutlery.

☆ Entertainment

★ **Area 8**　　　LIVE MUSIC
(333 3369788; http://area8.it; Via Casalnuovo 15; ⊙7.30pm-3am Wed-Sun) This unusual cafe/bar and 'nano-theatre' is a production agency by day, but comes alive four nights a week to host film screenings, live music, product launches and other events beneath its beautiful creamy arches.

ℹ Information

POST

Post Office (0835 25 70 40; Via del Corso 15; ⊙8am-1.30pm Mon-Fri, to 12.30pm Sat; 🖥)
Post Office (0835 24 55 32; Via Passarelli 13B; ⊙8.30am-7pm Mon-Fri, to 12.30pm Sat; 🖥)

TOURIST INFORMATION

Basilicata Turistica (www.aptbasilicata.it) is the official tourist website with useful information on history, culture, attractions and sights. Sassiweb (www.sassiweb.it) is another informative website on Matera. Quite a few private operators also advertise themselves as tourist information offices. They're there to sell tours, generally, but can still give good (if not impartial) advice.

InfoMatera (0835 68 02 54; Piazza Veneto 39; ⊙9am-8pm) This private operator in Matera's new town offers advice on sights, accommodation, tours and more.

Jazzo Gattini (0835 33 22 62; www.ceamatera.it; Contrada Murgia Timone; ⊙9.30am-2.30pm & 4-6.30pm Apr-Oct, shorter hours rest of year) Home to the visitor centre of the Parco della Murgia Materana.

Parco Archeologico Storico Naturale delle Chiese Rupestri del Materano (0835 33 61 66; www.parcomurgia.it; Via Dolori 10; ⊙9.30am-6.30pm) For info on Parco della Murgia Materana.

Tourist Information Centre (Basilicata Open Space; www.basilicataturistica.it; Piazza Vittorio Veneto, Palazzo dell'Annunziata; ⊙9am-9pm) Centrally located. Includes galleries focusing on Matera's history.

ℹ Getting There & Away

BUS

The bus station is south of Piazza Matteotti, next to the subterranean **train station** (Piazza Matteotti).

Marino (www.marinobus.it) For Naples (€12, 4¾ hours, six daily).
Marozzi (06 225 21 47; www.marozzivt.it) For Rome (€30, six to seven hours, five daily), Siena (€39, 8¼ hours, one daily), Florence (€43, 9½ hours, one daily) and Pisa (€48, 11¾ hours, one daily).
Pugliairbus (080 579 02 11; www.aeroporti dipuglia.it) For Bari airport (€6, 1¼ hours, five daily).
SITA (0835 38 50 07; www.sitabus.it) For Taranto (from €8, 1¾ hours, three daily).

Ferrovie Appulo-Lucane (FAL; ☑ 800 050500; http://ferrovieappulolucane.it) For Bari (€5, 1¾ hours).

Appennino Lucano

The Appennino Lucano (Lucanian Apennines) bite Basilicata in half like a row of jagged teeth. Sharply rearing up south of Potenza, they protect the lush Tyrrhenian coast and leave the Ionian shores gasping in the semi-arid heat. Much of the area is protected by the Parco Nazionale Dell'Appennino Lucano, inaugurated in 2007 and the second-youngest of Italy's 25 national parks.

Aside from its gorgeous mountain terrain, the park's most iconic site is the abandoned Roman town of Grumentum, 75km south of Potenza and just outside the town of Grumento Nova. In the granite eyries of Pietrapertosa and Castelmezzano, it can also lay claim to two of Italy's most strikingly situated hill towns.

Castelmezzano & Pietrapertosa

The two mountaintop villages of Castelmezzano (elevation 985m) and Pietrapertosa (elevation 1088m), ringed by the Lucanian Dolomites, are spectacular. Basilicata's highest villages, they're often swathed in cloud, making you wonder why anyone would build here, in a territory best suited to goats.

Castelmezzano is surely one of Italy's most theatrical villages: the houses huddle along an impossibly narrow ledge that falls away in gorges to the Rio di Caperrino. Pietrapertosa is possibly even more amazing: the Saracen fortress at its pinnacle is difficult to spot as it is carved out of the mountain. Despite difficulties of access, the towns can be swarmed by Italian tourists on weekends and holidays. Foreign visitors are scarcer.

You can 'fly' between these two dramatic settlements courtesy of Il Volo dell'Angelo, two heart-in-mouth zip lines across the void. Another option is to walk 7km across the valley on the Sentiero Sette Pietre (Path of the Seven Stones).

🏃 Activities

★ Il Volo dell'Angelo   ADVENTURE SPORTS
(Angel's Flight; ☑ Castelmezzano 0971 98 60 20, Pietrapertosa 0971 98 31 10; www.volodellangelo.com; s €35-42, couples €63-75; ⊙ 9.30am-6.30pm May-Oct) The extraordinary situation of Pietrapertosa and Castelmezzano, two steepling Basilicatan hill towns, is the inspiration behind 'Angel's Flight', two zip lines running over 1400m between the peaks, dropping over 100m and reaching speeds of up to 120km/h. Tandem flights are possible, providing the couple's combined weight doesn't exceed 150kg. It's only open daily in August; check the website for details.

Dolomiti Discovery   ADVENTURE SPORTS
(☑ 320 8696246; www.dolomitidiscovery.it; Via Provinciale 4; ⊙ tours from €30) Operates self-drive quad bike excursions around the area with the option of riding in a 4WD with a driver. Also supplies climbing gear for tackling nearby Via Ferrata courses and provides advice on walking the 7km Sentiero Sette Pietre (Path of the Seven Stones) linking Castelmezzano and Pietrapertosa. Ask about organising a quad bike transfer from Pietrapertosa back to Castelmezzano.

PUGLIA, BASILICATA & CALABRIA APPENNINO LUCANO

WORTH A TRIP

GRUMENTUM

The Parco Archeologico di Grumentum (☑ 0975 6 50 74; Contrada Spineta, Grumento Nova; incl museum €2.50; ⊙ 9am-1hr before sunset Tue-Sun, from 2pm Mon; ℗) – sometimes known as Basilicata's 'Little Pompeii' – contains remains of a theatre, an amphitheatre, Roman baths, a forum, two temples and a *domus* (villa) with mosaic floors. Knowing something of its history ratchets up the interest: among its illustrious inhabitants was Hannibal, who made it his headquarters in the 3rd century BC. Its swansong came when the Saracen invasions of the 10th century forced its abandonment in favour of Grumento Nova, on a nearby hill.

Many of the artefacts found here are on display at the nearby and moderately interesting Museo Nazionale dell'Alta Val d'Agri (☑ 0975 6 50 74; www.musei.basilicata.beniculturali.it/; Contrada Spineta, Grumento Nova; incl archaeological site €2.50; ⊙ 9am-8pm Tue-Sun, 2-8pm Mon; ℗).

Surprises of the South

In the Mezzogiorno, the sun shines on a magical landscape: dramatic cliffs and sandy beaches fringed with turquoise seas; wild mountains and gentle forested slopes; rolling green fields and flat plains. Sprinkled throughout are elegant *palazzi* (mansions), ancient cave dwellings and gnome-like stone huts.

Valle d'Itria

In a landscape of rolling green hills, vineyards, orchards and picture-pretty fields, conical stone huts called *trulli* sprout from the ground en masse in the Disneyesque towns of Alberobello (p782) and Locorotondo (p783).

Matera

A European Capital of Culture in 2019, the ancient cave city of Matera (p800) has been inhabited since Paleolithic times. Explore the tangled alleyways, ponder frescoes in rock churches, and slumber in millennia-old *sassi* (former cave dwellings).

Promontorio del Gargano

Along with its charming seaside villages, sandy coves and crystalline blue waters, the Gargano (p776) is also home to the Parco Nazionale del Gargano. It's perfect for hikers, nature trippers and beach fiends alike.

Salento

Hot, dry plains covered in wildflowers and olive groves reach towards the gorgeous beaches of the Ionian and Adriatic Seas. This is the unspoilt 'heel' of Italy, with Lecce (p787) as its sophisticated capital.

Parco Nazionale dell'Aspromonte

In this wild park (p818), narrow roads lead to hilltop villages such as spectacularly sited Bova. Meanwhile, waterfalls, wide riverbeds, jagged cliffs and sandstone formations set the scene for some unforgettable hikes.

2

1. Alberobello (p782) 2. Matera (p800) 3. Beach, Vieste, Promontorio del Gargano (p776) 4. Beach, Salento (p787)

MARCIN KRZYZAK/SHUTTERSTOCK ©

4

PETRU STAN/SHUTTERSTOCK ©

🛏 Sleeping & Eating

La Casa di Penelope e Cirene   B&B **€**
(☑ 338 3132196; Via Garibaldi 32, Pietrapertosa; d €75) This delightful B&B, the 'House of Penelope and Cirene', offers just two handsomely furnished rooms in the heart of Pietrapertosa. There's a sitting room, kitchenette, and great views over the Lucanian Dolomites.

Al Becco della Civetta   RISTORANTE **€€**
(☑ 0971 98 62 49; www.beccodellacivetta.it; Vico I Maglietta 7, Castelmezzano; meals €35-40; ⊙ 1-3pm & 8-10pm) Don't miss this authentic Lucano restaurant in Castelmezzano, which serves excellent regional cuisine based on seasonal local ingredients. It also offers 22 traditionally furnished, simple whitewashed rooms (doubles €80), some with lots of dark wood, others with vivid murals, and many with fabulous views. Booking recommended.

ℹ Getting There & Away

SITA SUD (☑ 0971 50 68 11; www.sita sudtrasporti.it) bus 102 runs twice a day between Potenza and Castelmezzano (€5, 80 minutes) but you'll probably want your own wheels to explore properly.

Maratea

POP 5100

A sparkling, sun-drenched contrast to Basilicata's rugged interior, Maratea is a pure delight. In fact a disparate collection of placid coastal villages, rather than a single place, it's the centrepiece of Basilicata's Tyrrhenian coast. Embellished with lush vegetation, riven by rock-walled coves below well-tended hillside villages, Maratea's joys might be compared to those of the Amalfi. Perhaps the biggest, most welcome disparity is the number of tourists – far fewer here, and notably fewer non-Italians. You can climb the steep hill above Maratea to see the ruins of the prior settlement, take boat cruises and fishing trips, poke around venerable hilltop churches (44 of them), or just kick back with a coffee in a perfectly photogenic piazza, watching the sun play on the waters below.

◉ Sights & Activities

The deep green hillsides that encircle this tumbling conurbation offer excellent walking trails, providing a number of easy day trips to the surrounding hamlets of Acquafredda and Fiumicello, with its small sandy beach. The tourist office in Maratea Borgo's main square can provide an excellent map. Other activities including boating and kayaking.

Maratea Superiore   RUINS
FREE The ruins of the original settlement of Maratea, supposedly founded by the Greeks, are situated at a higher elevation than the current village on a rocky escarpment just below the Christ the Redeemer statue. Abandoned houses with trees growing in their midst, some thought to be over 1000 years old, have long been given over to nature.

Statue of Christ the Redeemer   STATUE
The symbol of Maratea, visible from multiple vantage points along the coast, this 22m-high statue of Christ faces inland towards the Basilica di San Biagio. Slightly smaller than Rio's Christ the Redeemer, it's made of concrete faced with Carrara marble and sits atop 644m-high Monte San Biagio. A dramatic winding asphalt road leads to the top, although it's more fun to walk the steep path (number 1) that starts off Via Cappuccini in Maratea Borgo.

Fly Maratea   ADVENTURE SPORTS
(☑ 333 7957286; www.flymaratea.it) This affiliation of local tour operators offers a range of different activities including coastal kayaking, mountain biking, trekking and paragliding. Check the website for contact details of specific guides specialising in each option. The local tourist office can also usually arrange introductions.

☞ Tours

Nautilus Escursioni   BOATING
(☑ 334 3545085; www.facebook.com/Maratea Escursioni; Porto di Maratea; ⊙ tours adult/child from €25/10) Friendly boat skipper and an excellent option to help you explore the spectacular surrounding coastline.

🛏 Sleeping

Locanda delle Donne Monache   HOTEL **€€**
(☑ 0973 87 61 39; www.locandamonache.com; Via Mazzei 4, Maratea Borgo; d/ste €180/300; ⊙ Apr-Oct; P 🅿 @ 🛜 🏊) Overlooking the *borgo* (medieval hamlet), this exclusive hotel is in a converted 18th-century convent with a suitably lofty setting. It's a hotchpotch of vaulted corridors, terraces and gardens fringed with bougainvillea and lemon trees. The rooms are elegantly decorated in pastel shades and there's a fitness centre, Jacuzzi and a stunning panoramic outdoor pool.

ℹ️ ORIENTATION

What is usually referred to as Maratea is actually a collection of small settlements split into several parts, some of them walkable if you're relatively fit and the weather co-operates. Maratea's main train station sits roughly in the middle.

The **Porto** is clustered around a small harbour and is about a 10-minute walk below the station (towards the sea). The 'village' of **Fiumicello** is in the same direction, but reached by turning right rather than left once you've passed under the railway bridge. The main historic centre, known as **Maratea Borgo**, is perched in the hills behind. A bus leaves every 30 minutes or so from the station, or you can walk up a series of steps and paths (approximately 5km; the town is always visible). It has plenty of cafes and places to eat. The **Marina di Maratea** is located 5km south along the coast and has its own separate train station. The village of **Acquafredda** is 8km in the other direction, kissing the border of Campania.

Hotel Villa Cheta Elite HOTEL €€€
(📞0973 87 81 34; www.villacheta.it; Via Canonica 48, Acquafredda; r from €230; ⊙Apr-Oct; 🅿✳🛜🌊) Set in an art-nouveau villa in Acquafredda, this hotel is like a piece of plush Portofino towed several hundred kilometres south. Enjoy a broad terrace with spectacular views of the Gulf of Policastro, a fabulous restaurant (1pm to 2pm and 8pm to 9.30pm), a pool and large rooms where antiques mix seamlessly with modern amenities. Bright Mediterranean foliage fills sun-dappled terraced gardens.

🍴 Eating

Il Sacello ITALIAN €€
(📞0973 87 61 39; www.facebook.com/ristoranteilsacellomaratea; Via Mazzei 4, Maratea Borgo; meals €40-45; ⊙12.30-2.30pm & 7.30-10pm; 🛜) The in-house *ristorante* of the Locanda delle Donne Monache hotel, Il Sacello serves wonderful Lucanian fare and seafood, overlooking the red rooftops of Maratea Borgo. Try the pasta with local sausage, the beef tartare or delicately wrought desserts such as the buffalo-ricotta souffle. Il Sacello sometimes closes on Monday or Tuesday night in June.

Lanterna Rossa SEAFOOD €€
(📞0973 87 63 52; www.facebook.com/lanternarossamarateaporto; Via Arenile, Maratea Porto; meals €35-40; ⊙11am-3pm & 7-11.30pm) This terrace restaurant, sitting above the Bar del Porto overlooking the marina, has been knocking out delightful Lucanian seafood for over 20 years. Sit either in the tastefully art-strewn interior or on the terrace to enjoy dishes such as *zuppa di pesce* (fish soup) and octopus with wild beans and fennel. Bookings are advised, especially in July and August.

ℹ️ Information

Maratea has two tourist offices: one in the **borgo** (📞0973 03 03 66; www.maratea.info; Piazza Vitolo 1, Maratea Borgo; ⊙10am-1pm & 5-10pm Mon-Fri, daily Jul & Aug) and one above the **marina** (📞0973 87 71 15, 371 1446350; www.maratea.info; Via Arenile 35, Maratea Porto; ⊙8am-1pm & 3-7pm Jun-Oct, shorter hours rest of year).

ℹ️ Getting There & Away

Maratea is easily accessed via the coastal train line. InterCity and regional trains on the Rome–Reggio line stop at Maratea train station. Some slower trains stop at Marina di Maratea.

Local buses (€1.20) connect the coastal towns and Maratea train station with Maratea Borgo, running more frequently in summer. Some hotels offer pickups from the station.

CALABRIA

If a Vespa-riding, siesta-loving, unapologetically chaotic Italy still exists, it's in Calabria. Rocked by recurrent earthquakes and lacking a Matera or Lecce to give it high-flying tourist status, this is a corner of Italy less globalised and homogenised. Its wild mountain interior and long history of poverty, Mafia activity and emigration have all contributed to its distinct culture, but there is so much more to Calabria than just its history - it's authentic, has great culinary experiences and utterly breathtaking landscapes. Calabria is unlikely to be the first place in Italy you'd visit. But if you're intent on seeing a candid and uncensored version of *la dolce vita* that hasn't been dressed up for tourist consumption, look no further, *ragazzi* (guys).

PARCO NAZIONALE DEL POLLINO

Italy's largest national park, the Parco Nazionale del Pollino (Pollino National Park; www.parcopollino.it), straddles Basilicata and Calabria and covers 1960 sq km. It acts like a rocky curtain separating the region from the rest of Italy and has the richest repository of flora and fauna in the south.

The park's most spectacular areas are Monte Pollino (2248m), Monti di Orsomarso (1987m) and the canyon of the Gole del Raganello. The mountains, often snowbound, are blanketed by forests of oak, alder, maple, beech, pine and fir. The park is most famous for its ancient *pino loricato* trees, which can only be found here and in the Balkans.

Your own vehicle is needed to explore within Pollino. To get there, however, there's a daily SLA Bus (☑ 0973 2 10 16; www.slasrl.it) between Naples and Rotonda, while SAM Autolinee (☑ 0973 66 38 35; www.samautolinee.com) buses operate around some of Pollino's Basilicatan villages.

Basilicata

In Basilicata the park's main centre is Rotonda (elevation 626m), home to the official park office, Ente Parco Nazionale del Pollino (☑ 0973 66 93 11; www.parcopollino.gov.it/en/live-the-park; Strada Provinciale 28, Rotonda; ⊙ 9am-1pm & 2-4pm Mon-Fri). It can recommend local guides, accommodation and nearby stores to buy good hiking maps.

Adjacent to the park office is the L'Ecomuseo del Pollino (www.parcopollino.gov.it/en/live-the-park/ecomuseum; Strada Provinciale 28, Rotonda; ⊙ 9am-1pm & 2-4pm Mon-Fri), offering a brilliant overview of the park's cultural, geological and natural heritage. Based in Rotonda, English-speaking guide Guiseppe Cosenza (☑ 347 2631462; www.viaggiarenelpollino.it; Rotonda) offers hiking, birdwatching and walking tours to see the park's ancient *pino loricato* trees. Water sports including canyoning and river tubing can be booked with Info Pollino (☑ 338 2333888; www.infopollino.com; Strada Provinciale 4, Viggianello) near Rotonda.

The unique, isolated Albanian villages of San Paolo Albanese and San Costantino Albanese fiercely maintain their mountain culture and the Greek liturgy is retained in the main churches. For local handicrafts, visit the town of Terranova di Pollino for wooden crafts, Latronico for alabaster, and Sant'Arcangelo for wrought iron. The chalet-style Picchio Nero (☑ 0973 9 31 70; www.hotelpicchionero.com; Via Mulino 1, Terranova di Pollino; s/d €65/78; ℗) in Terranova di Pollino is a popular hotel for hikers and includes a recommended restaurant.

Two highly recommended restaurants include Luna Rossa (☑ 0973 9 32 54; www.federicovalicenti.it; Via Marconi 18, Terranova di Pollino; meals €35-40; ⊙ noon-3pm & 7-10pm Thu-Tue) in Terranova di Pollino and Da Peppe (☑ 0973 66 12 51; Corso Garibaldi 13, Rotonda; meals €30-35; ⊙ noon-3pm & 7.30-11pm Tue-Sun) in Rotonda.

Calabria

Civita was founded by Albanian refugees in 1746. Other towns worth visiting are Castrovillari, with its well-preserved 15th-century Aragonese castle, and Morano Calabro. Naturalists should also check out the wildlife museum Centro Il Nibbio (☑ 0981 3 07 45; www.ilnibbio.it; Vico Il Annunziata 11, Morano Calabro; €4; ⊙ 9am-6pm Jul & Aug, shorter hours rest of year) in Morano.

White-water rafting down the spectacular Lao river is popular in the Calabrian Pollino. Centro Lao Action Raft (☑ 0985 9 10 33; www.laoraft.it; Via Lauro 10/12, Scalea) in Scalea can arrange rafting trips as well as canyoning, trekking and mountain biking. Ferula Viaggi (p801) in Matera runs mountain-bike excursions and treks into the Pollino.

The park has a number of *agriturismi*. Agriturismo Colloreto (☑ 347 3236914, 0981 3 12 55; www.colloreto.it; Contrada Colloreto, Morano Calabro; half board per person €60) near Morano Calabro, and Locanda di Alia (☑ 339 8346881, 0981 4 63 70; www.alia.it; Via letticelle 55, Castrovillari; s/d €100/110; ℗ ※ 🛜 🗶) in Castrovillari are noteworthy.

Calabria's gritty cities are of patchy interest. More alluring is its attractive Tyrrhenian coastline, broken by several particularly lovely towns (Tropea and Scilla stand out). The mountainous centre is dominated by three national parks, none of them particularly well explored. Its museums, collecting the vestiges of a rich classical past are probably its greatest treasure.

History

Traces of Neanderthal, Palaeolithic and Neolithic life have been found in Calabria, but the region only became internationally important with the arrival of the Greeks in the 8th century BC. They founded a colony at what is now Reggio Calabria. Remnants of this colonisation, which spread along the Ionian coast with Sibari and Crotone as the star settlements, are still visible. In 202 BC the cities of Magna Graecia came under the control of Rome, the rising power in Italy. The Romans did irreparable environmental damage, destroying the countryside's handsome forests. Navigable rivers became fearsome *fiumare* (torrents) dwindling to wide, dry, drought-stricken riverbeds in high summer.

Post-Rome, Calabria's fortified hilltop communities weathered successive invasions by the Normans, Swabians, Aragonese and Bourbons, and remained largely undeveloped. Although the late 18th-century Napoleonic incursion and the later arrival of Garibaldi and Italian unification inspired hope for change, Calabria remained a disappointed, feudal region and, like the rest of the south, was racked by malaria.

A byproduct of this tragic history was the growth of banditry and organised crime. Calabria's Mafia, known as the 'ndrangheta (from the Greek for heroism/virtue), inspires fear in the local community, but tourists are rarely the target of its aggression. For many, the only answer has been to get out and, for at least a century, Calabria has seen its young people emigrate in search of work.

Northern Tyrrhenian Coast

The good, the bad and the ugly all jostle cheek-by-jowl along Calabria's northern Tyrrhenian coast. The *Autostrada del Mediterraneo* (A2), one of Italy's great coastal drives, ties them all together. It twists and turns through mountains, past huge swathes of dark-green forest and flashes of cerulean-blue sea. But the Italian penchant for cheap summer resorts has taken its toll here and certain stretches, particularly in the south, are blighted by shoddy hotels and soulless stacks of flats.

A 30km stretch of wide, pebbly beach runs south from the border with Basilicata, from the popular and not-too-garish resort town of Praia a Mare to Diamante, a fashionable seaside town famed for its chillies and bright murals painted by local and foreign artists. Inland are the precariously perched, otherworldly villages of Aieta and Tortora, reached by a tortuously twisted but rewarding mountain drive. Further south, Paola is worth a stop to see its holy shrine.

◉ Sights

Santuario di San Francesco di Paola   CAVE
(🖉 0984 47 60 32; www.santuariopaola.it; Via San Francesco di Paola, Paola; ⊙ 6am-1pm & 2-8pm Apr-Sep, 6am-1pm & 2-6pm Oct-Mar) FREE Watched over by a crumbling castle, the Santuario di San Francesco di Paola is a curious, empty cave with tremendous significance to the devout. The saint lived and died in Paola in the 15th century and the sanctuary that he and his followers carved out of the bare rock has attracted pilgrims for centuries. The cloister is surrounded by naive wall paintings depicting the saint's truly incredible miracles. The original church contains an ornate reliquary of the saint.

Isola di Dino   ISLAND
Visible from the Praia a Mare seafront is an intriguing rocky chunk off the coast, the Isola di Dino. The tourist office has information on the island's sea caves; alternatively, expect to pay around €10 for a guided tour from the old boys who operate from the beach.

ⓘ Information

Just off the Praia a Mare seafront is the tourist office for the area, the **Consorzio Turistico del Tirreno** (Tyrrhenian Tourist Consortium; 🖉 0985 77 76 37; Via Amerigo Vespucci 4, Praia a Mare; ⊙ 9am-noon Mon-Fri).

ⓘ Getting There & Away

Paola is the main train hub for Cosenza, about 25km inland. From Praia a Mare, **Autolinee Preite** (🖉 0984 41 30 01; www.autoservizipreite.it) buses go to Cosenza via Diamante and to Aieta and Tortora, (6km and 12km from Praia respectively). **SITA** (🖉 0971 50 68 11; www.sitabus.it) buses run to Maratea and regular trains also pass through for Paola and Reggio Calabria.

Cosenza

📱 0984 / POP 67,600 / ELEV 238M

Stacked atop a steep hill, Cosenza's old town epitomises the authentic, unkempt charm of southern Italy. Time-warped and romantically dishevelled, its dark weathered alleys are full of drying clothes on rusty balconies, old curiosity shops and the freshly planted shoots of an arty renaissance. Welcome to a no-nonsense workaday town where tourists are incidental and local life, with all its petty dramas, takes centre stage

Cosenza's modern city centre is a typically chaotic Italian metro area that serves as a transport hub for Calabria and a gateway to the nearby mountains of Parco Nazionale della Sila.

👁 Sights

In the new town, pedestrianised Corso Mazzini provides a pleasant respite from the chaotic traffic and incessant car honking. The thoroughfare serves as an open-air museum with numerous sculptures lining the *corso*, including *Saint George and the Dragon* by Salvador Dalí.

In the old town, head up the winding, charmingly dilapidated Corso Telesio, which has a raw Neapolitan feel to it and is lined with ancient tenements and antiquated shopfronts, including shops housing a musical instrument maker, a Dickensian shoe mender and shops selling traditional crafts. Enlivened by an ever-changing gallery of street art, the side alleys are a study in urban decay. At the top is Cosenza's 12th-century cathedral (📱 0984 7 78 64; www.cattedraledi cosenza.it; Piazza del Duomo 1; ⊙ 8am-noon & 3-7.30pm).

Head further along the *corso* to Piazza XV Marzo, an appealing square fronted by the Palazzo del Governo and the handsome neoclassical Teatro Rendano (📱 0984 81 32 27; Piazza XV Marzo; tickets from €5).

From Piazza XV Marzo, follow Via Paradiso, then Via Antonio Siniscalchi for the route to the restored Norman castle (📱 0984 181 12 34; www.castellocosenza.it; Piazza Frederico II; adult/reduced €4/2; ⊙ 9.30am-6pm Tue-Sat, from 10am Sun).

Cosenza's culture is low-key, but you can piece bits of it together at the refurbished Galleria Nazionale (📱 0984 79 56 39; Via Gravina; ⊙ 10am-6pm Tue-Sun) FREE. Close by is the Museo dei Brettii e degli Enotri (📱 0984 2 33 03; www.museodeibrettiiedeglienotri.

it; Salita Agostino 3; adult/reduced €4/3; ⊙ 9am-1pm & 3.30-6.30pm Tue-Fri, 10am-1pm & 3.30-6.30pm Sat & Sun).

🛏 Sleeping

B&B Via dell'Astrologo   B&B €
(📱 338 9205394; www.viadellastrologo.com; Via Benincasa 16; s/d from €41/71; 🛜) A gem in the historic centre, this small B&B is tastefully decorated with polished wooden floors, white bedspreads and good-quality artwork. Host Marco is a mine of information on Cosenza and Calabria in general.

Royal Hotel   HOTEL €
(📱 0984 41 21 65; www.hotelroyalcosenza.it; Via delle Medaglie d'Oro 1; s/d/ste from €60/75/85; 🅿 ❄ 🛜) The best all-round hotel central Cosenza can provide, the four-star Royal is a short stroll from Corso Mazzini right in the heart of town. Rooms are fresh and businesslike, and there's a bar, restaurant and convenient parking on-site. Efficient and friendly front-desk service comes with good advice on where to eat in Cosenza.

🍴 Eating & Drinking

Gran Caffè Renzelli   CAFE €
(www.renzelli.com; Corso Telesio 46; cakes from €1.50; ⊙ 7am-9pm; 🛜) This venerable cafe behind the *duomo* has been run by the same family since 1803 when the founder arrived from Naples and began baking gooey cakes and desserts. Sink your teeth into *torroncino torrefacto* (a confection of sugar, spices and hazelnuts) or *torta telesio* (made from almonds, cherries, apricot jam and lupins).

Il Paesello   CALABRIAN €€
(📱 349 4385786; Via Rivocati 95; meals €30; ⊙ 7-11pm Mon-Sat, noon-3pm Sun) Beloved of the locals, this unpretentious trattoria is one of Cosenza's best. Simple, robust dishes such as *fagioli con cozze* (beans with mussels), tagliatelle with porcini mushrooms and anything plucked from the sea are executed with care and skill.

Bulldog Ale House   BAR
(📱 0984 181 14 43; www.facebook.com/bulldog cosenza; Corso Mazzini 39; ⊙ 6pm-2am; 🛜) More than 200 beers and a good selection of gin and whiskey combine at our favourite Cosenza bar. Grab a table outside on the city's main pedestrian thoroughfare and meet the friendly locals, including Cosenza's big student population. The beer taps feature a rotating selection of always interesting brews.

ℹ Getting There & Away

AIR

Lamezia Terme Airport (Sant'Eufemia Lamezia, SUF; ☑ 0968 41 43 85; www.sacal.it; Via Aeroporto 40, Lamezia Terme), 63km south of Cosenza, at the junction of the A2 and SS280 motorways, links the region with major Italian cities. The airport is served by Ryanair, easyJet and charters from northern Europe. A shuttle leaves the airport every 20 minutes for the airport train station, where **Autolinee Romano** (☑ 0962 2 17 09; www.autolineeromano. com) runs two buses a day to Cosenza (€7, 70 minutes).

BUS

Cosenza's main **bus station** (☑ 0984 41 31 24) is northeast of Piazza Bilotti. Services leave from here for Catanzaro and towns throughout La Sila. **Autolinee Preite** (☑ 0984 41 30 01; www.autoservizipreite.com) has buses heading daily along the north Tyrrhenian coast; **Autolinee Romano** serves Crotone as well as Rome and Milan.

TRAIN

Stazione Nuova (Via Vaglio Lise) is about 2km northeast of the centre. Regular trains go to Reggio Calabria (from €15, 2¾ hours) and Rome (from €54, four to six hours), both usually with a change at Paola, and Naples (from €119, three to four hours), as well as most destinations around the Calabrian coast.

Regular buses link the centre and the main train station, although they follow a roundabout route.

Parco Nazionale della Sila

'La Sila' is a big landscape, where wooded hills stretch to endless rolling vistas. Dotted with hamlets, it's cut through with looping roads that make driving a test of your digestion.

The park's 130 sq km are divided into three areas: the Sila Grande, with the highest mountains; the strongly Albanian Sila Greca (to the north); and the Sila Piccola (near Catanzaro), with vast forested hills.

The highest peaks, covered with tall Corsican pines, reach 2000m – high enough to generate enough winter snow to attract skiers. In summer the climate is coolly alpine; spring sees carpets of wildflowers; and there's mushroom hunting in autumn. Gigantic firs grow in the Bosco di Gallopane (Forest of Gallopane). There are several beautiful lakes, the largest of which is Lago di Cecita o Mucone near Camigliatello Si-

lano. There is plenty of wildlife here, including the light-grey Apennine wolf, a protected species.

◉ Sights

La Sila's main town, **San Giovanni in Fiore** (1049m), is named after the founder of its beautiful medieval abbey. Today, the abbey houses a home for the elderly and the **Museo Demologico** (☑0984 97 00 59; Abbazia Forense; adult/reduced €1.50/1; ⊙8.30am-6.30pm Mon-Sat year-round & 9.30am-12.30pm Sun mid-Jun–mid-Sep). San Giovanni's handsome old centre is famous for its Armenian-style hand-loomed carpets and tapestry. See how it's done at the studio and shop of master carpet maker **Domenico Caruso** (☑0984 99 27 24; http://carusotessiture.it; Via Gramsci 195, San Giovanni in Fiore; ⊙8.30am-8pm Mon-Sat).

A popular ski-resort town with 6km of slopes, **Camigliatello Silano** (1272m) looks much better under snow. A few lifts operate on Monte Curcio, about 3km to the south. Around 5.5km of slopes and a 1500m lift can be found near **Lorica** (1370m), on gloriously pretty **Lago Arvo** – the best place to camp in summer.

Scigliano (620m) is a small hilltop town located west of the Sila Piccola section of the park and 75km south of Cosenza.

⚞ Activities

Valli Cupe   TREKKING
(☑ 334 9174699, 333 8342866; www.riservanatura levallicupe.it) You can take fantastic trekking, 4WD or donkey trips with this cooperative in the area around Sersale in the southeast, where there are myriad waterfalls and the dramatic Canyon Valli Cupe. Specialising in botany, the guides also visit remote monasteries and churches. Check out their excellent English-language website for planning and contact information.

Cammina Sila   HIKING
(☑ 347 9131310; www.camminasila.com) Based in the town of San Giovanni in Fiore this outfit offers scheduled hiking and canoeing excursions in Parco Nazionale della Sila throughout June, July and August. Most tours are scheduled on Saturday or Sunday. Check the website for upcoming dates.

⚞ Festivals & Events

During August, **Sila in Festa** takes place, featuring traditional music. Autumn is mushroom season, when you'll be able to frequent mushroom festivals, including the Sagra del Fungo in Camigliatello Silano.

🛏 Sleeping & Eating

B&B Calabria
B&B €

(☏ 349 8781894; www.bedandbreakfastcalabria. it; Via Roma 7, Scigliano; s/d €40/60; ☺ Apr-Nov; P 🛜) This B&B in the mountains has five clean, comfortable and characterful rooms, all with separate entrances. Owner Raffaele is a great source of information on the region and can recommend places to eat, visit and go hiking. There's a wonderful terrace overlooking endless forested vistas. Mountain bikes are available and there's wi-fi in public areas. Cash only.

The B&B is west of the national park in the village of Scigliano, about an hour south of Cosenza by train.

Albergo San Lorenzo
HOTEL €

(☏ 0984 57 08 09; www.sanlorenzosialberga.it; Campo San Lorenzo; d/tr/q/ste €90/105/120/135; P ❄ 🛜) Above their famous restaurant, the owners of La Tavernetta have opened the area's most stylish sleep, with 21 large, well-equipped rooms done up in colourful, modernist style.

⭐ La Tavernetta
CALABRIAN €€€

(☏ 0984 57 90 26; www.sanlorenzosialberga. it; Campo San Lorenzo, near Camigliatello Silano; meals €50-55; ☺ 12.30-3pm & 7.30-11pm Tue-Sun) Among Calabria's best eats, La Tavernetta marries rough country charm with citified elegance in warmly colourful dining rooms. The food is first-rate and based on the best local ingredients, from wild anise seed and mushrooms to mountain-raised lamb and kid. Reserve ahead on Sundays and holidays.

🛍 Shopping

⭐ Alta Salumeria Campanaro
FOOD

(☏ 0984 57 80 15; https://altagastronomiacam panaro.it; Piazza Misasi 5, Camigliatello Silano; sandwiches €4; ☺ 9am-1.30pm & 3.30-8pm Thu-Tue) Even among Italian delicatessens, this long-established *salumeria* is something special. It's a temple to all things fungoid (get your Sila porcini here), as well as an emporium of fine meats, cheeses, pickles, sweetmeats and wines.

ℹ Information

Good-quality information in English is scarce. You can try the national park **visitors centre**

(☏ 0984 53 71 09; www.parcosila.it; Via Nazion-ale, Lorica; ☺ 10am-noon & 3-5pm Mon & Wed, 10am-noon Tue, Thu & Fri) at Lorica, 10km from Camigliatello Silano, or the **Pro Loco tourist office** (☏ 0984 57 81 59; www.prolococam igliatello.it; Via Roma, Camigliatello Silano; ☺ 9.30am-6.30pm Tue-Sun) in Camigliatello Silano. A useful internet resource is the official park website (www.parcosila.it). The people who run B&B Calabria in the park are extremely knowledgeable and helpful.

For a map, you can use *La Sila: Carta Turistico-Stradale ed Escurionistica del Parco Nazionale* (€7). *Sila for 4* is a miniguide in English that outlines a number of walking trails in the park. The map and booklet are available at tourist offices.

ℹ Getting There & Away

You can reach the park's two main hubs, Camigliatello Silano and San Giovanni in Fiore, via regular Ferrovie della Calabria buses from Cosenza or Crotone.

Ionian Coast

With its flat coastline and wide sandy beaches, the Ionian coast has some fascinating stops from Sibari to Santa Severina, with some of the best beaches around Soverato. However, it has borne the brunt of some ugly development and is mainly a long, uninterrupted string of resorts, thronged in the summer months and mothballed from October to May.

It's worth taking a trip inland to visit Santa Severina, a spectacular mountain-top town, 26km northwest of Crotone. The town is dominated by a Norman castle and is home to a beautiful Byzantine church. But the true glories of this long stretch of coast are its museums and archaeological sites, preserving what remains of the pre-Roman cities of Magna Graecia (Greater Greece).

Le Castella

☏ 0962 / POP 1103

This town is named for its impressive 16th-century Aragonese castle (☏ 0962 79 51 60; €3; ☺ 9am-midnight Jul & Aug, shorter hours rest of year, closed Mon Oct-Mar), a vast edifice linked to the mainland by a short causeway. The philosopher Pliny said that Hannibal constructed the first tower. Evidence shows it was begun in the 4th century BC, designed to protect Crotone in the wars against Pyrrhus. Le Castella is south of Capo Rizzu-to, a rare protected area along this coast, rich not only in nature but also in Greek history. For further information on the park, try www.riservamarinacaporizzuto.it.

🛏 Sleeping

With around 15 campgrounds near Isola di Capo Rizzuto to the north, this is the Ionian coast's prime camping area.

Da Annibale   HOTEL €

(📞 0962 79 50 04; Via Duomo 35; s/d €70/75; 🅿 ❄ @ 🛜) Right in the heart of Le Castella, Da Annibale is a seafood restaurant that doubles as a B&B with pleasant rooms.

La Fattoria   CAMPGROUND €

(📞 0962 79 11 65; Via del Faro, Isola di Capo Rizzuto; camping 2 people, car & tent €30, bungalow €65; ⊙ Jun-Sep) Around 1.5km from the coast, La

PUGLIA, BASILICATA & CALABRIA IONIAN COAST

FOOTPRINTS OF MAGNA GRAECIA

Long before the Romans colonised Greece, the Greeks were colonising southern Italy. Pushed out of their homelands by demographic, social and political pressures, the nebulous mini-empire they created between the 8th and 3rd centuries BC was often referred to as Magna Graecia by the Romans in the north. Many Greek-founded cities were located along the southern coast of present-day Puglia, Basilicata and Calabria. They included (south to north) Locri Epizephyrii, Kroton, Sybaris, Metapontum and Taras (now known, respectively, as Locri, Crotone, Sibari, Metaponto and Taranto).

Magna Graecia was more a loose collection of independent cities than a coherent state with fixed borders, and many of these cities regularly raged war against each other. The most notable conflict occurred in 510 BC when the athletic Krotons attacked and destroyed the hedonistic city of Sybaris (from which the word 'sybaritic' is derived).

Magna Graecia was the 'door' through which Greek culture entered Italy, influencing its language, architecture, religion and culture. Though the cities were mostly abandoned by the 5th century AD, the Greek legacy lives on in the Griko culture of Calabria and the Salento peninsula, where ethnic Greek communities still speak Griko, a dialect of Greek.

Remnants of Magna Graecia can be seen in numerous museums and architectural sites along Calabria's Ionian coast.

Locri

Museo Nazionale di Locri Epizephyrii (📞 0964 39 00 23; www.locriantica.it; Contrada Marasà, Locri; adult/reduced €6/3; ⊙ 9am-8pm Tue-Sun; 🅿 ♿) Situated 3km south of modern-day Locri, the Greek colony of Locri Epizephyrii was founded in 680 BC, later subsumed by Rome and finally abandoned following Saracen raids in the 10th century AD. The archaeological site is sprawling and full of interest, including harbour structures, the *centocamere* (hundred rooms) and the Casino Macri – a Roman bathhouse later repurposed as a farming villa. The attached museum is well curated, and includes artefacts found in the numerous nearby necropoli.

Sibari

Museo Archeologico Nazionale delle Sibaritide (📞 0981 7 93 91; Località Casa Bianca, Sibari; €3; ⊙ 9am-8pm Tue-Sun) Founded around 730 BC and destroyed by the Krotons in 510 BC, Sybaris was rebuilt twice: once as Thurii by the Greeks in 444 BC, and again in 194 BC by the Romans, who called it Copia. Prehistoric artefacts and evidence of all three cities are displayed at this important (if underpatronised) museum, 5km southeast of the modern beach resort of Sibari. The nearby archaeological park has been affected by flooding in the past: check ahead to ensure it's open.

Crotone

Museo Archeologico Nazionale di Crotone (📞 0962 2 30 82; Via Risorgimento 14, Crotone; €2; ⊙ 9am-8pm) Founded in 710 BC, the powerful city-state of Kroton was known for its sobriety and high-performing Olympic athletes. Crotone's museum is located in the modern town, while the main archaeological site is at Capo Colonna, 11km to the southeast. Votive offerings and other remnants of the famous Hera Lacinia Sanctuary at Cape Colonna are a highlight.

Fattoria has 100 grass campsites (generally shaded), plus games and hot showers.

Eating

Trattoria La Bussola SEAFOOD €€
(☑ 329 2769164; Via Annibale Barca; meals €25-30; ☺ 8-11.30pm) When your dad's a fisherman, it's easy to guarantee a good supply of the freshest seafood. There's nothing pretentious about this family-owned eatery, just a dedication to great seasonal dishes showcasing the best of local produce. Tables are limited, so try to book ahead. Don't leave without trying the hazelnut gelato and the homemade wild fennel and myrtle digestif.

Ristorante Da Annibale SEAFOOD €€
(☑ 0962 79 50 04; Via Duomo 35; meals €40; ☺ noon-3pm & 7.30-11pm) Da Annibale offers local seafood served in a wisteria-draped outdoor area. Swordfish, tuna carpaccio, stuffed pumpkin flowers and handmade pasta dishes are worth ordering. During the height of summer from July to August, an adjacent garden combines beer and pizza (€7 to €11) to good effect.

❶ Getting There & Away

Autolinee Romano buses connect Le Castella with Crotone (€3.20, 20 minutes, three per day).

Gerace

☑ 0964 / POP 2650

A spectacular medieval hill town, Gerace is worth a detour for the views alone – on one side the Ionian Sea, on the other, dark, interior mountains. Blessed with numerous handsome churches, some dating back to the Byzantine 9th century, it's dramatically sited on a rocky fastness rearing up from the inland plain. On the highest point is the photogenic ruin of a Norman castle that seems to sprout from the jagged stones.

Further inland is **Canolo**, a small village seemingly untouched by the 21st century.

◉ Sights

Cathedral CATHEDRAL
(Via Duomo 28; adult/reduced €3/2; ☺ 9.30am-12.30pm & 3-6.30pm) Gerace has Calabria's largest Romanesque cathedral. Dating from 1045, its three aisles are divided by columns salvaged from classical villas and temples in the area; later alterations have not robbed it of its majesty. The interior is wonderfully austere and admission includes entry to the attached Cathedral Treasury museum with a glittering array of tapestries and ecclesiastical riches.

Sleeping & Eating

L'Antico Borgo B&B €€
(☑ 327 2330095; https://lanticoborgogerace.it; Via IV Novembre 38; d €70; ☜) L'Antico Borgo's five rooms are tucked away in Gerace's medieval labyrinth adjacent to the restaurant and pizzeria of the same name. Decor is relatively simple, but rooms are kept spotless and are a good option to enjoy the hill town's shadowed streets and laneways after the day trippers have departed.

Ristorante A Squella CALABRIAN €
(☑ 0964 35 60 86; Via Ferruccio 21; meals €20-25; ☺ 12.30-2.30pm daily & 7.30-10.30pm Mon-Sat) For a taste of traditional Calabrian cooking, modest, welcoming Ristorante a Squella makes for a great lunchtime stop. It serves reliably good dishes, specialising in seafood and Calabrian pasta dishes. The views from just outside are spectacular and the service from the friendly family that owns the restaurant is warm and heartfelt. Try the delicious deep-fried doughnuts for dessert.

❶ Getting There & Away

Buses connect Gerace with Locri and also Canolo with Siderno, both of which link to the main coastal railway line. To explore these quiet hills properly, you'll need your own transport.

Parco Nazionale dell'Aspromonte

Most Italians think of the **Parco Nazionale dell'Aspromonte** (www.parcoaspromonte.gov. it) as a refuge used by Calabrian kidnappers in the 1970s and '80s. It's still rumoured to contain 'ndrangheta strongholds, but you're extremely unlikely to encounter any murky business. The park, Calabria's second-largest, is dramatic, rising sharply inland behind Reggio. Its highest peak, **Montalto** (1955m), is dominated by a huge bronze statue of Christ and offers sweeping views across to Sicily.

Subject to frequent mudslides and carved up by torrential rivers, Aspromonte's mountains are awesomely beautiful. Underwater rivers keep the peaks covered in coniferous forests and ablaze with flowers in spring. It's wonderful walking country and is crossed by several colour-coded trails. **Gambarie** is the main town and the easiest approach to the park. The roads are good and many activities are organised from here – you can ski and it's also the place to hire a 4WD – ask around in the town.

Extremes of weather and geography have resulted in some extraordinary villages, such as **Pentidàttilo** and **Roghudi**, clinging limpet-like to the craggy, rearing rocks and now all but deserted. It's worth the drive to explore these eagle-nest villages. Another mountain eyrie with a photogenic ruined castle is **Bova**, perched at 900m above sea level. The drive up the steep, dizzying road to Bova is not for the faint-hearted, but the views are stupendous.

🏃 Activities

Misafumera WALKING
(☑340 9024422, 347 0804515; www.facebook.com/www.misafumera.it; Via Nazionale 306d, Reggio Calabria Bocale 2; treks €690) Reggio-based Misafumera runs week-long trekking excursions (€690, April to November). Treks operate with a minimum of six participants.

Aspro Park ADVENTURE SPORTS
(☑342 8065010; https://aspropark.wordpress.com; Strada Redentore Gambarie; adult/child €15/10; ⊙10am-6pm Sun Jun–mid-Jul, 10am-6pm daily mid-Jul–Aug) Fifteen minutes' drive southwest of Gambarie is this outdoor adventure park with forested walking trails, mountain bike rental and tree-climbing and elevated ropes courses. A good option for travelling families.

🛏 Sleeping

Hotel Centrale HOTEL €
(☑0965 74 31 33; www.hotelcentrale.net; Piazza Mangeruca 22, Gambarie; s/d €50/100; 🅿️❄️🛜) Hotel Centrale in Gambarie is a large all-encompassing place with a decent restaurant, a comprehensive modern spa, renovated wood-finished rooms and the best cafe in town. Centrale also helps organise treks and other activities, and offers full and half pension for €20/30 more per person. The attached bookshop is a good place to pick up maps and local information.

**Azienda Agrituristica
Il Bergamotto** AGRITURISMO €
(☑347 6012338; www.naturaliterweb.it; Via Amendolea, Amendolea di Condofuri; per person €25) You can stay among the olives, donkeys and eponymous bergamot trees at this peaceful *agriturismo*. Ugo Sergi can arrange excursions, the rooms are simple and the food delicious.

ℹ Information

Maps are scarce. Try the **national park office** (☑0965 74 30 60; www.parcoaspromonte.gov.it; Via Aurora 1, Gambarie; ⊙10.30am-12.30pm Mon & Fri & 3-6pm Tue) in Gambarie or ask at the bookshop at the Hotel Centrale in Gambarie.

The cooperative **Naturaliter** (☑347 3046799; www.naturaliterweb.it; Condofuri), based in Condofuri, is an excellent source of information. **Co-operativa San Leo** (☑347 3046799; https://coopsanleobova.it/i-nostri-trekking; Bova), based in Bova, also provides guided tours and accommodation. In Reggio Calabria, you can book treks and tours with Misafumera.

ℹ Getting There & Away

To reach Gambarie, take ATAM city bus 319 from Reggio Calabria (€1, 1½ hours, up to six daily). Most of the roads inland from Reggio eventually hit the SS183 road that runs north to the town.

It's also possible to approach from the south, but the roads aren't as good.

Reggio Calabria
☑0965 / POP 182.550

Port, transport nexus and the main arrival and departure point for Sicily, Reggio seems more functional than fascinating. That is up until the point you set foot inside its fabulous national museum, custodian of some of the most precious artefacts of Magna Graecia known.

The city's architectural eclecticism is a result of its tectonic liveliness: in 1908 the last big quake triggered a tsunami that killed over 100,000. By Italian standards, little of historical merit remains, although the *lungomare*, with its views across the Messina Strait to smouldering Mt Etna is, arguably, one of the most atmospheric places in Italy for an evening *passeggiata*.

Fortunately, there's no need to doubt the food. Reggio hides some of Calabria's best salt-of-the-earth restaurants. You can work up an appetite for them by hiking in the nearby Parco Nazionale dell'Aspromonte, or exploring the coastline at nearby seaside escapes along the Tyrrhenian and Ionian coasts.

⊙ Sights

⭐**Museo Nazionale
di Reggio Calabria** MUSEUM
(☑0965 81 22 55; www.museoarcheologicoreggiocalabria.it; Piazza de Nava 26; adult/reduced €8/5; ⊙9am-8pm Tue-Sun; 🚹) Over several floors

Reggio Calabria

Reggio Calabria

in Southern Italy's finest museum you'll descend through millennia of local history, from Neolithic and Palaeolithic times through Hellenistic, Roman and beyond. The undoubted crown jewels are, probably, the world's finest examples of ancient Greek sculpture: the Bronzi di Riace, two extraordinary bronze statues discovered on the seabed near Riace in 1972 by a snorkelling chemist from Rome. You'll have to stand for three minutes in a decontamination cham-

ber to see the bronzes, but they're more than worth the wait. Larger than life, they depict the Greek obsession with the body; inscrutable, determined and fierce, their perfect form is more godlike than human. The finest of the two has ivory eyes and silver teeth parted in a faint *Mona Lisa* smile. No one knows who they are – whether human or god – and even their provenance is a mystery. They date from around 450 BC, and it's believed they're the work of two artists.

In the same room as the bronzes is the 5th-century-BC bronze *Philosopher's Head,* the oldest-known Greek portrait in existence. Also on display are impressive exhibits from Locri, including statues of Dioscuri falling from his horse.

Museo Nazionale
del Bergamotto   MUSEUM
(🖉 0340 7635968; www.facebook.com/museodel bergamotto; Via Filippini 50, Mercato Coperto; €3; ⊙ 9am-noon & 5-7pm Tue-Sat, 10.30-noon Sun) Housed in Reggio's former covered market, this museum showcases the interesting 300-year-old history of the region's bergamot growing industry. The zesty citrus fruit is grown almost exclusively in the Reggio and Aspromonte area. Sample the essential oils and bergamot-infused teas before trying *bergamotto* gelato at Reggio's beloved gelateria **Cèsare** (🖉 0965 88 99 77; www.gelato cesare.it; Piazza Indipendenza 2; gelato from €2.50; ⊙ 6am-1am).

Aragonese Castle   CASTLE
(Piazza Castello; ⊙ 9am-1pm & 2-7pm Tue-Sun)
FREE Only two towers, restored in 2000, remain of the Aragonese Castle damaged by earthquake and partially demolished in 1922. The site is used for events and performances today. It's worth a visit for the excellent views from the towers.

🛏 Sleeping

★ B&B Kalavria   B&B €
(🖉 347 5637038; ww.kalavriabb.com; Via Pellicano 21F; s/d €70/80; 🕏) Owner Domenico is a brilliant host at this modern and elegant B&B a few blocks from Reggio's waterfront *lungomare.* Bathrooms are particularly stylish, and in warmer months the rooftop terrace is a great place to relax. Breakfast features the best of local baked goods and Domenico can offer well-researched recommendations on where to eat and drink in his interesting hometown.

B&B Casa Blanca   B&B €
(🖉 340 9032992; www.bbcasablanca.it; Via Arcovito 24; s/d/tr €55/75/85; P❄🕏) A little gem in Reggio's heart, this 19th-century *palazzo* has three floors of spacious rooms gracefully furnished with white-on-white decor. There's a self-serve breakfast nook, a small breakfast table in each room and two apartments available. Breakfast is a celebration of fresh pastries.

🍴 Eating & Drinking

★ La Cantina del Macellaio   TRATTORIA €€
(🖉 0965 2 39 32; www.lacantinadelmacellaio.com; Via Arcovito 26/28; meals €35; ⊙ 12.30-3pm & 7.30-11.30pm Wed-Mon) One of the best restaurants in Reggio, serving *maccheroni al ragù di maiale* (handmade pasta with pork sauce) and *involtini di vitello* (veal rolls) in an open, tiled dining room with exposed stonework and green flasks on the walls. The mostly Calabrian wines are equally impressive, as is the service. Aficionados of excellent meat dishes should order the mixed grill.

La Vie del Gusto   CALABRIAN €€
(🖉 324 8844025; Via II Settembre 55; meals €30-35; ⊙ 7.30-11.30pm Tue-Sat, noon-4pm Sun) Local Calabrian flavours shine at this friendly and informal spot where the menu changes regularly on a seasonal basis. Meaty favourites like Calabrian sausage are a perennial favourite and La Vie del Gusto's sprawling *antipasti* plates are famous in Reggio. Great ambience and also great value.

Lievito   CRAFT BEER
(🖉 0965 81 30 88; www.pizzerialievito.it; Via dei Filippini 33; ⊙ 7pm-midnight) Street art and excellent pizza made from Slow Food ingredients combine with Lievito's own range of craft beers – the 9% Belgian-style Tripel is a smooth heavy hitter – and there's also a fridge full of other interesting Italian brews. Check out the artisan food products on sale before you leave; a good option for tasty gifts and souvenirs.

ℹ Information

MEDICAL SERVICES
Hospital (🖉 800 198629, emergency 118; www.ospedalerc.it; Via Melacrino; ⊙ 24hr) Reggio's main hospital has a 24-hour *pronto soccorso* (emergency department).

POST
Post Office (🖉 0965 31 51 11; Via Miraglia 14; ⊙ 8.30am-7pm Mon-Fri, to 12.30pm Sat)

TOURIST INFORMATION
Tourist Information Kiosk (🖉 0965 2 11 71; http://turismo.reggiocal.it; Via Roma 3; ⊙ 9am-noon & 4-7pm) There is also an information kiosk at the **airport** (🖉 0965 64 32 91; ⊙ 9am-5pm).

❶ Getting There & Away

AIR

Reggio's **airport** (REG; ☑ 0965 64 05 17; https://reggiocalabriaairport.it) is at Ravagnese, about 5km south. It has Alitalia flights to Rome, Turin and Milan.

BUS

Most buses terminate at the **Piazza Garibaldi bus station**, in front of the Stazione Centrale . Several different companies operate to towns in Calabria and beyond. Regional trains are more convenient than bus services to Scilla and Tropea.

ATAM (☑ 800 43 33 10; www.atam-rc.it) Runs to Gambarie (€1.50, 1½ hours, six daily) in the Aspromonte National Park.

Lirosi (☑ 0966 5 79 01; www.lirosiautoservizi. com) Buses to Rome (from €36, 9½ hours, two daily).

CAR & MOTORCYCLE

The A2 ends at Reggio, via a series of long tunnels. If you are continuing south, the SS106/ E90 hugs the coast around the 'toe', then heads north along the Ionian Sea.

TRAIN

Trains stop at **Stazione Centrale** (☑ 0965 32 41 91; Via Barlaam 1), the main train station at the town's southern edge. Of more use to ferry foot passengers and those visiting the Museo Nazionale is the **Stazione Lido** (Viale Zerbi), near the harbour. There are frequent trains to Milan, Rome and Naples. Regional services run along

---

❶ **ONWARD TO SICILY**

Reggio is the gateway to Sicily, via the island's main port, Messina.

Note that there are two main departure ports for Sicily: the **Stazione Marittima** in Reggio Calabria, and the ferry port in the town of Villa San Giovanni, 14km north of Reggio and easily accessible by train. Passenger ferries operated by **Blu Jet** (☑ 0340 1545091; www. blujetlines.it) depart from both Stazione Marittima (€3.50, 20 minutes, 16 daily Monday to Friday and six daily on weekends) and Villa San Giovanni (€2.50).

Car ferries from Villa San Giovanni (€29 with vehicle, 20 minutes, 28 per day) are run by **Caronte & Tourist** (☑ 800 62 74 14; www.carontetourist.it). This is also the port used by Trenitalia's train-ferry – carriages are pulled directly onto the ferry.

---

the coast to Scilla and Tropea, and also to Catanzaro and less frequently to Cosenza and Bari.

❶ Getting Around

Orange local buses run by **ATAM** (☑ 800 43 33 10; www.atam-rc.it) cover most of the city including regular buses between the port and Piazza Garibaldi outside Stazione Centrale. The Università–Aeroporto bus, bus 27, runs from Piazza Garibaldi to the airport and vice versa (15 minutes, hourly). Buy your ticket at ATAM offices, tobacconists or newsstands.

Southern Tyrrhenian Coast

North of Reggio Calabria, along the coast-hugging **Autostrada del Mediterraneo (A2)**, the scenery rocks and rolls to become increasingly beautiful and dramatic, if you can ignore the shoddy holiday camps and unattractive developments that sometimes scar the land. Like the northern part of the Tyrrhenian coast, it's mostly quiet in winter and packed in summer.

Scilla

☑ 0965 / POP 4900

In Scilla, cream-, ochre- and earth-coloured houses cling on for dear life to the jagged promontory, ascending in jumbled ranks to the hill's summit, which is crowned by a castle and, just below, the dazzling white confection of the **Chiesa Arcipretale Maria Immacolata**. Lively in summer and serene in winter, the town is split in two by the tiny port. The fishing district of Scilla Chianalea, to the north, harbours small hotels and restaurants off narrow lanes, lapped by the sea. It can only be visited on foot.

Scilla's high point is a rock at the northern end, said to be the lair of Scylla, the mythical six-headed sea monster who drowned sailors as they tried to navigate the Strait of Messina. Swimming and fishing off the town's glorious white sandy beach is somewhat safer today. Head for **Lido Paradiso** from where you can squint up at the castle while sunbathing on the sand.

◉ Sights

Castello Ruffo   CASTLE
(☑ 0965 70 42 07; Piazza San Rocco; admission €2; ☻ 8.30am-7.30pm) An imposing fortress surmounting the headland commanding Scilla, this castle has at times been a light-

house and a monastery. It houses a *luntre,* the original boat used for swordfishing, and on which the modern-day *passarelle* (a special swordfish-hunting boat equipped with a 30m-high metal tower) is based.

🛏 Sleeping

The old fishing village of Chianalea, on Scilla's eastern flank, holds some delightful sea-facing B&Bs.

B&B Sunshine · B&B €
(📞 339 7980266; www.sunshinescilla.com; Via Garibaldi 13; d €80-120; 🛜) Brilliant ocean views combine with friendly service from host Antonio at this sparkling hillside B&B around halfway between Chianalea and Scilla town. Sunshine's three colourful rooms have poetic names referencing Scilla's maritime climate. Our favourite is the romantic Rosa Dei Venti room. The Tramanto apartment includes a kitchen and accommodates up to five guests. Look forward to legendary breakfasts.

Hotel Principe di Scilla · HOTEL €€
(📞 0965 70 43 24; www.ubais.it; Via Grotte 2; ste from €150; ❋🛜) Get lulled to sleep by the sound of lapping waves in this grand old family residence on Scilla's seafront. Two suits of armour guard the front door while inside six individually themed suites are stuffed with countless antiques. In warm weather throw the windows open onto lovely views of the fishing village of Chianalea and, beyond, the sparkling Tyrrhenian.

🍴 Eating & Drinking

Osteria del Centro · ITALIAN €€
(📞 392 6440208; www.facebook.com/osteria delcentroscilla; Via Bastia 7; meals €30-35; ⏰12.30-3pm & 8-11.30pm Tue-Sun) Providing an elegant upper town alternative to the cafes and restaurants in Chianalea, this place comes recommended by locals for its excellent meat dishes.

Blue of You · SEAFOOD €€
(📞 0965 79 05 85; www.bleudetoi.it; Via Grotte 40; meals €35-40; ⏰noon-3pm & 8pm-midnight Wed-Mon) Soak up the atmosphere at this lovely little restaurant, where blue lampshades, a Blue Note soundtrack and glimpses of the blue Tyrrhenian set the mood. It has a terrace over the water and excellent seafood dishes made with local ingredients such as Scilla's renowned swordfish, perhaps with fresh pasta and eggplant. Ask for the homemade Amaro (herbal liqueur) to finish.

Casa Vella · WINE BAR
(📞 329 3649711; www.casavelascilla.it; Via Annunziata 18; 🛜) Good-value sandwiches and flatbreads combine with Calabrian craft beer and wine at this spot in Chianalea's pedestrian main drag. The friendly owners also run an adjacent B&B (doubles €60 to €120) and can advise on local walks and excursions. Don't miss the array of Calabrian artisan produce on sale inside.

ℹ Getting There & Away

Scilla is on the main coastal train line. Frequent trains run to Reggio Calabria (€2.40, 30 minutes). The train station is a couple of blocks from the beach.

Tropea
📞 0963 / POP 6400

Tropea, a puzzle of lanes and piazzas, is famed for its beauty, dramatic cliff's-edge site and spectacular sunsets. It sits on the Promontorio di Tropea, which stretches from Nicotera in the south to Pizzo in the north. The coast alternates between dramatic cliffs and icing sugar–soft sandy beaches, all edged by translucent sea. Unsurprisingly, hordes of Italian holidaymakers descend here in summer. If you hear English being spoken, it is probably from Americans visiting relatives: enormous numbers left to forge better lives in America in the early 20th century.

Despite the legend that Hercules founded the town, it seems this area has been settled as far back as Neolithic times. Tropea has been occupied by the Arabs, Normans, Swabians, Anjous and Aragonese, as well as being attacked by Turkish pirates. Perhaps they were all after the town's famous red onions, so sweet they can be turned into marmalade?

👁 Sights & Activities

Santa Maria dell'Isola · CHURCH
(📞 347 2541232; www.santuariosantamariadelliso latropea.it; garden & museum €2; ⏰9am-1pm & 3-7.30pm Apr-Jun, 9am-8.30pm Jul & Aug, shorter hours rest of year) Tropea's number-one photo op to opp is Santa Maria dell'Isola, a medieval monastic church given several facelifts over centuries of wear and tear (mainly attributable to earthquakes). Sitting on what was once its own rocky little island, it's now joined to the mainland by a causeway created by centuries of silt, and is reached via a flight of steps up the cliff face. Access to the

church is free, but the small museum and garden costs €2.

Cathedral
CATHEDRAL

(Largo Duomo 12; ⊙7am-noon & 4-8pm) The beautiful Norman cathedral has two undetonated WWII bombs near the door: it's believed they didn't explode due to the protection of the town's patron saint, Our Lady of Romania. A Byzantine icon (1330) of the Madonna hangs above the altar – she is also credited with protecting the town from the earthquakes that have pummelled the region.

CST Tropea
BOATING

(✑0963 6 11 78; www.csttropea.it; Largo San Michele 8-9) This Tropea-based company can arrange a wide variety of tours and activities around the area including boat trips and trekking on the island of Stromboli, mountain-bike rental, Vespa tours and horse riding. For travelling foodies options include cookery classes and excursions taking in the local wine and olive oil scene. Apartment rentals can be arranged through its website.

🛏 Sleeping

Keep an eye on seasonal fluctuations: a reasonable B&B room may become exorbitant, or simply unavailable, during the high summer season of August.

Donnaciccina
B&B €€

(✑0963 6 21 80; www.donnaciccina.com; Via Pelliccia 9; s/d/ste €75/150/200; ❈🐾) Look for the sign of a bounteous hostess bearing fruit and cake to find this delightful B&B, overlooking the main *corso*. The 17th-century *palazzo* retains a tangible sense of history with carefully selected antiques, canopy beds and terracotta tiled floors. There are nine restful rooms, a nearby suite (itself dat-

---

WORTH A TRIP

CAPO VATICANO

There are spectacular views from this rocky cape, around 7km south of Tropea, with its beaches, ravines and limestone sea cliffs. Birdwatchers' spirits should soar. There's a lighthouse, built in 1885, which is close to a short footpath from where you can see as far as the Aeolian Islands. Capo Vaticano beach is one of the balmiest along this coast.

---

ing to the 15th century) and a chatty parrot at reception.

Residenza il Barone
B&B €€

(✑0963 60 71 81; www.residenzailbarone.it; Largo Barone; ste from €130; ❈🐾) This graceful *palazzo* has six suites decorated in masculine neutrals and tobacco browns, with dramatic modern paintings by the owner's brother adding pizzazz to the walls. There's a computer in each suite and you can eat breakfast on the small roof terrace with views over the old city and out to sea.

🍴 Eating

Osteria del Pescatore
SEAFOOD €

(✑0963 60 30 18; Via del Monte 7; meals €22-25; ⊙noon-2.30pm & 8pm-midnight Wed-Mon) *Pesce spada* (swordfish) is a speciality on this part of the coast and it rates highly on the menu at this simple seafood place tucked away in the backstreets. Also arranges fishing trips in good weather.

Genus Loci
ITALIAN €€

(✑345 5896475; Largo Vaccari; €35-40; ⊙noon-2.30pm & 6.30-10.30pm) Dining options include a slender and modern dining room or an outside terrace with excellent views, both great locations to enjoy Genus Loci's light and innovative approach to the freshest of local seafood. Try the eggplant layered with shrimps and basil before a *secondi* course of baked grouper with anchovies. A concise wine list features mainly Calabrian varietals.

🛈 Information

Tourist Office (✑347 5318989, 0963 6 14 75; www.prolocotropea.eu; Piazza Ercole; ⊙9am-1pm & 4-8pm) In the old town centre.

🛈 Getting There & Away

Trains run to Pizzo-Lamezia (€2.40, 30 minutes, 12 daily), Scilla (€4.80, 1¼ hours, frequent) and Reggio (from €6.40, 1¾ hours, frequent). **Ferrovie della Calabria** (✑0961 89 62 39; www.ferroviedellacalabria.it) buses connect with other towns on the coast.

Pizzo

✑0963 / POP 9300

Stacked high up on a sea cliff, pretty little Pizzo is the place to go for *tartufo*, a death-by-chocolate ice-cream ball, and to see an extraordinary rock-carved grotto church. It's a popular and cheerful tourist stop. Piazza della Repubblica is the heart, set high above the sea with great views. Settle here at one of the many gelateria terraces for a gelato fix.

◎ Sights

Chiesetta di Piedigrotta   CHURCH
(☑ 0963 53 25 23; Via Riviera Prangi; adult/reduced €3/2.50; ☺ 9am-1pm & 3-7.30pm Jul & Aug, shorter hours rest of year) The Chiesetta di Piedigrotta is an underground cave full of carved stone statues. It was carved into the tufa rock by Neapolitan shipwreck survivors in the 17th century. Other sculptors added to it and it was eventually turned into a church. Later statues include the less-godly figures of Fidel Castro and John F Kennedy. It's a bizarre, one-of-a-kind mixture of mysticism, mystery and kitsch, especially transporting when glowing in the setting sun.

Castello Murat   CASTLE
(☑ 0963 53 25 23; www.castellomurat.it; Scesa Castello Murat; adult/reduced €3.50/2.50; ☺ 9am-11pm Jul & Aug, to 7pm Apr-Jun, Sep & Oct, shorter hours rest of year) This neat little 15th-century castle is named for Joachim Murat, brother-in-law of Napoleon Bonaparte and briefly King of Naples, captured in Pizzo and sentenced to death for treason in 1815. Inside the castle, you can see his cell and the details of his grisly end by firing squad, which is graphically illustrated with wax-works. Although Murat was the architect of enlightened reforms, the locals showed no great concern when he was executed.

Chiesa Matrice di San Giorgio   CHURCH
(Via San Giorgio 1; ☺ hours vary) In town, the 16th-century Chiesa Matrice di San Giorgio, with its splendid baroque facade and dressed-up Madonnas, houses the tomb of Joachim Murat.

🛏 Sleeping & Eating

Armonia B&B   B&B €
(☑ 0963 53 33 37; www.casaarmonia.com; Vico II Armonia 9; s/d €45/60; @) Run by the charismatic Franco in his 16th-century family home, this B&B has three relaxing rooms and spectacular sea views.

Piccolo Grand Hotel   BOUTIQUE HOTEL €€
(☑ 0963 53 32 93; www.piccolograndhotel.com; Via Chiaravalloti 32; s/d €110/130; ❄ 🛜) This pleasant four-star boutique hotel is hidden on an unlikely and rather dingy side street. But its exuberant blue-and-white design, upscale comforts and panoramic rooftop breakfasts make it one of Pizzo's top sleeps. There's also a small fitness area and e-bikes to rent.

Pepe Nero   SEAFOOD €€
(☑ 348 8124618; www.facebook.com/pg/pepe neropizzo; Via Marconi; meals €30-35) This family-owned restaurant just off Pizzo's main square has a stylish outdoor deck, the ideal spot to enjoy local seafood like *spada* (swordfish), prawn and lobster. We can also recommend the *calamaretti ripieni* (stuffed baby squid) and tuna tartare. Wine selections of local Calabrian varietals are also excellent. An essential stop for seafood fans.

❶ Getting There & Away

Pizzo is just off the major A2 autostrada. There are two train stations. Vibo Valentia-Pizzo is located 4km south of town on the main Rome–Reggio Calabria line. A bus service connects you to Pizzo. Pizzo-Lamezia is south of the town on the Tropea–Lamezia Terme line. Shuttle buses (€2) connect with trains or you can walk for 20 minutes along the coast road. Note the final walk up the hill is very narrow so consider taking a taxi (or a tuk-tuk during summer).

Teatro Greco (p853) Taormina
IORK KISLER/SHUTTERSTOCK ©

Sicily

Overloaded with art treasures and natural beauty, undersupplied with infrastructure, and continuously struggling against Mafia-driven corruption, Sicily's complexities sometimes seem unfathomable. To really appreciate this place, come with an open mind – and a healthy appetite. Despite the island's perplexing contradictions, one factor remains constant: the uncompromisingly high quality of the cuisine.

After 25 centuries of foreign domination, Sicilians are the heirs to an impressive cultural legacy, from the refined architecture of Magna Graecia to the Byzantine splendour and Arab craftwork of the island's Norman cathedrals and palaces. This cultural richness is matched by a startlingly diverse landscape that includes bucolic farmland, smouldering volcanoes and kilometres of island-studded aquamarine coastline.

INCLUDES

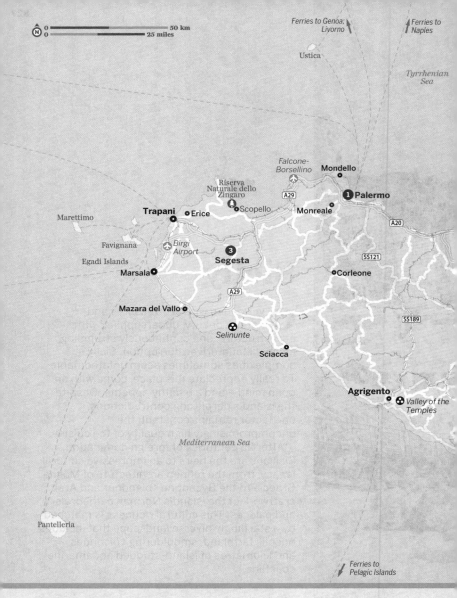

Sicily Highlights

1 Teatro Massimo (p837)
Joining the impeccably
dressed opera-goers at this
elegant theatre in Palermo.

2 Catania (p857) Bargaining
with fish vendors at dawn,

climbing sn active volcano in
the afternoon, and returning to
buzzing nightlife.

3 Segesta (p891) Marvelling
at the majesty of the 5th-
century ruins.

4 Taormina (p852)
Watching stars perform
against Mt Etna's breathtaking
backdrop at summer festivals.

5 Aeolian Islands (p844)
Observing Stromboli's

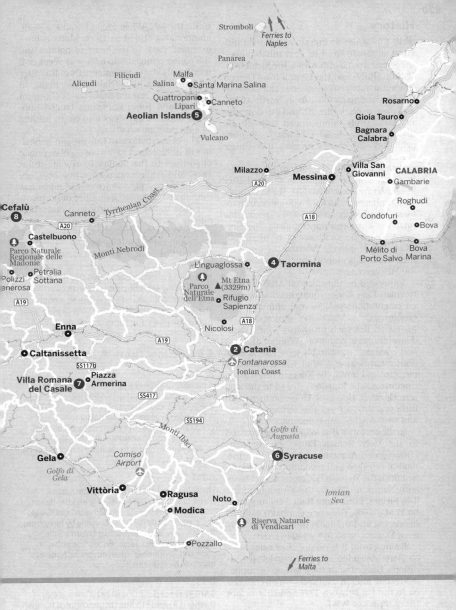

Stromboli

Ferries to
Naples

Panarea

Malfa
Filicudi   Salina
Alicudi   ● Santa Marina Salina
          Quattropani ●   ● Canneto
          Lipari ●
Aeolian Islands ❺

                                                    Rosarno ●
                                        Gioia Tauro ●
                                                    Bagnara
                                                    Calabra
                                    ● Villa San   **CALABRIA**
Vulcano   Giovanni
                    ● Milazzo ●   ● Gambarie
Cefalù   Messina ●
❽   Roghudi
    Canneto   *Tyrrhenian Coast*   Condofuri
    ● Castelbuono   A20   A18   ● Bova
    🅰 Parco Naturale   Mélito di   Bova
    Regionale delle   Porto Salvo   Marina
    Madonie
● Polizzi   Petralia   Linguaglossa ●   **Taormina** ❹
enerosa   Sottana ●
    A19   🅰 Parco
                               Naturale   ▲ Mt Etna
                               dell'Etna   (3329m)
    ● Enna   ● Rifugio
                                    Sapienza
    ● Caltanissetta   A19   ● Nicolosi
                  SS117b   A18
    Villa Romana ❼ ● Piazza   ❷ **Catania**
    del Casale   Armerina   ✈ Fontanarossa
                    SS417   *Ionian Coast*

                    SS194
    ● **Gela**   *Monti Iblei*   *Golfo di*
                Comiso   *Augusta*
                Airport ✈
                                    ❻ **Syracuse**
    Vittòria ●
                    ● **Ragusa**
                    ● **Modica**   Noto ●   *Ionian*
                                               Sea
                            🅰 Riserva Naturale
                               di Vendicari
                    ● Pozzallo
                                    Ferries to
                                    Malta

volcanic fireworks and hiking
on these stunningly scenic
islands.

❻ **Syracuse** (p865)
Wandering aimlessly in
Ortygia's atmospheric alleys

or stepping back in time at
an ancient Greek theatre
performance.

❼ **Villa Romana del Casale**
(p879) Admiring prancing wild
beasts and dancing bikini-

clad gymnasts on the mosaic
floors.

❽ **Cefalù** (p842) Being
dazzled by Byzantine mosaics
and splendid coastal sunsets.

History

Sicily's most deeply ingrained cultural influences originate from its first inhabitants – the Sicani from North Africa, the Siculi from Latium (Italy) and the Elymni from Greece. The subsequent colonisation of the island by the Carthaginians (also from North Africa) and the Greeks, in the 8th and 6th centuries BC respectively, compounded this cultural divide through decades of war when powerful opposing cities struggled to dominate the island.

Although part of the Roman Empire, Sicily didn't truly come into its own until after the Arab invasions of AD 831. Trade, farming and mining were all fostered under Arab influence and Sicily soon became an enviable prize for European opportunists. The Normans, desperate for a piece of the pie, invaded in 1061 and made Palermo the centre of their expanding empire and the finest city in the Mediterranean.

Impressed by the cultured Arab lifestyle, Norman king Roger squandered vast sums on ostentatious palaces and churches and encouraged a hedonistic atmosphere in his court. But such prosperity – and decadence (Roger's grandson, William II, even had a harem) – inevitably gave rise to envy and resentment and, after two centuries of pleasure and profit, the Norman line was extinguished. The kingdom passed to the austere German House of Hohenstaufen with little opposition from the seriously eroded and weakened Norman occupation.

In the centuries that followed, Sicily passed to the Holy Roman Emperors, Angevins (French) and Aragonese (Spanish) in a turmoil of rebellion and revolution that continued until the Spanish Bourbons united Sicily with Naples in 1734 as the Kingdom of the Two Sicilies. Little more than a century later, on 11 May 1860, Giuseppe Garibaldi planned his daring and dramatic unification of Italy from Marsala on Sicily's western coast.

Reeling from this catalogue of colonisers, Sicilians struggled in poverty-stricken conditions. Unified with Italy, but no better off, nearly one million men and women emigrated to the US between 1871 and 1914 before the outbreak of WWI.

Ironically, the Allies (seeking Mafia help in America for the re-invasion of Italy) helped in establishing the Mafia's stranglehold on Sicily. In the absence of suitable administrators, they invited the undesirable *mafioso* (Mafia boss) Don Calógero Vizzini

to do the job. When Sicily became a semi-autonomous region in 1948, Mafia control extended right to the heart of politics and the region plunged into a 50-year silent civil war. It only started to emerge from this after the anti-Mafia maxi-trials of the 1980s, in which Sicily's revered magistrates Giovanni Falcone and Paolo Borsellino hauled hundreds of Mafia members into court, leading to important prosecutions.

The assassinations of Falcone and Borsellino in 1992 helped galvanise Sicilian public opposition to the Mafia's inordinate influence, and while organised crime lives on, the thuggery and violence of the 1980s has diminished. A growing number of businesses refuse to pay the extortionate protection money known as the *pizzo*, and important arrests continue, further encouraging those who would speak out against the Mafia. On the political front, anti-Mafia crusader Leoluca Orlando, now serving his fifth term as mayor of Palermo, continues the fight.

Nowadays the hottest topics on everyone's mind are the island's continued economic struggles and conflict over Sicily's role as a major gateway for immigrants from northern Africa.

ℹ Getting There & Away

AIR

A number of airlines fly direct to Sicily's two main international airports, Palermo's Punta Raisi (PMO) and Catania's Fontanarossa (CTA). A few also serve the smaller airports of Trapani (TPS) and Comiso (CIY). Alitalia (www.alitalia.com) is the main Italian carrier, while Ryanair (www.ryanair.com) is the leading low-cost airline serving Sicily.

BOAT

Hydrofoils and car ferries cross the narrow Strait of Messina between Sicily and the Italian mainland ports of Villa San Giovanni and Reggio di Calabria. Sicily is also accessible by ferry from Naples, Genoa, Civitavecchia, Livorno, Salerno, Cagliari, Malta and Tunis. Prices rise between June and September, when advanced bookings may also be required.

BUS

SAIS Trasporti (☑ 091 617 11 41; www.sais trasporti.it) and **Flixbus** (https://global.flixbus.com; Via d'Amico, Catania) run long-haul services to Sicily from Rome and Naples.

TRAIN

For travellers originating in Rome and points south, Intercity trains cover the distance from mainland Italy to Sicily in the least possible time, without a change of train. If coming from Milan, Bologna or Florence, your fastest option is to take the ultra-high-speed Frecciarossa as far as Naples, then change to an Intercity train for the rest of the journey.

All trains enter Sicily at Messina, after being transported by ferry from Villa San Giovanni at the toe of Italy's boot. At Messina, trains branch west along the Tyrrhenian coast to Palermo, or south along the Ionian coast to Catania.

ⓘ Getting Around

BOAT

Efficient ferries and hydrofoils serve Sicily's outer islands. Main ports include Milazzo for the Aeolian Islands, Palermo for the island of Ustica, Trapani for the Egadi Islands and Porto Empedocle for the Pelagie Islands.

BUS

Buses are the best option for certain intercity routes, including Palermo–Trapani, Palermo–Syracuse and Catania–Agrigento. Also useful for some villages not served by train.

CAR & MOTORCYCLE

Having your own wheels is preferable for visiting smaller interior towns and remote archaeological sites (Segesta, Selinunte, Piazza Armerina etc). Car hire is readily available at airports and in many towns.

TRAIN

Trenitalia service is dependable and frequent along the Palermo–Messina and Messina–Syracuse coastal routes. Other well-served routes include Palermo to Agrigento, and Trapani to Marsala.

PALERMO & AROUND

Palermo

☑ 091 / POP 668,400

Having been the crossroads of civilisations for millennia, Palermo delivers a heady, heavily spiced mix of Byzantine mosaics, Arabesque domes and frescoed cupolas. This is a city at the edge of Europe and at the centre of the ancient world, a place where souk-like markets rub up against baroque churches, where date palms frame Gothic palaces and where the blue-eyed and fair have bronze-skinned cousins.

Centuries of dizzying highs and crushing lows have formed a complex metropolis. Here, crumbling staircases lead to gilded ballrooms, and guarded locals harbour hearts of gold. Just don't be fooled. Despite its noisy streets, Sicily's largest city is a shy beast, rewarding the inquisitive with citrus-filled cloisters, stucco-laced chapels and crooked side streets dotted with youthful artisan studios. Add to this Italy's biggest opera house and an ever-growing number of vibrant, new-school eateries and bars and you might find yourself falling suddenly, unexpectedly in love.

◉ Sights

Via Maqueda is the main street, running north from the train station, changing names to Via Ruggero Settimo as it passes the landmark Teatro Massimo, then finally widening into leafy Viale della Libertà north of Piazza Castelnuovo, the beginning of the city's modern district.

◉ Around the Quattro Canti

Forming the centre of the old city, the busy intersection of Corso Vittorio Emanuele and Via Maqueda is known as the **Quattro Canti** (Four Corners). This crossroads neatly divides the historic nucleus into four traditional quarters – Albergheria, Capo, Vucciria and La Kalsa.

★ **Chiesa e Monastero di Santa Caterina d'Alessandria** CONVENT
(☑ 091 271 38 37; Piazza Bellini; church, convent & rooftop adult/reduced €10/9, church only adult/reduced €3/2; ⊙ church 9am-7pm, convent & rooftop 10am-7pm) Built as a hospice in the early 14th century and transformed into a Dominican convent the following century, this monastic complex wows with its magnificent maiolica cloister, surrounded by unique balconied cells and punctuated by an 18th-century fountain by Sicilian sculptor Ignazio Marabitti. The convent's rooftop terraces offer spectacular views of the surrounding piazzas and city, while the church's baroque interior harbours works by prolific artists, among them Filippo Randazzo, Vito D'Anna and Antonello Gagini.

La Martorana CHURCH
(Chiesa di Santa Maria dell'Ammiraglio; ☑ 345 8288231; Piazza Bellini 3; adult/reduced €2/1; ⊙ 9.30am-1pm & 3.30-5.30pm Mon-Sat, 9-10.30am Sun) On the southern side of Piazza Bellini, this luminously beautiful 12th-century church was endowed by King Roger's Syrian emir, George of Antioch, and was originally planned as a mosque. Delicate Fatimid pillars support a domed cupola depicting Christ enthroned amid his archangels. The

SICILY PALERMO

Palermo

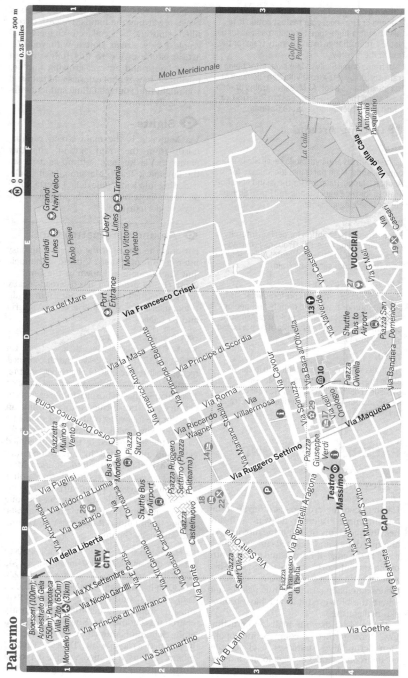

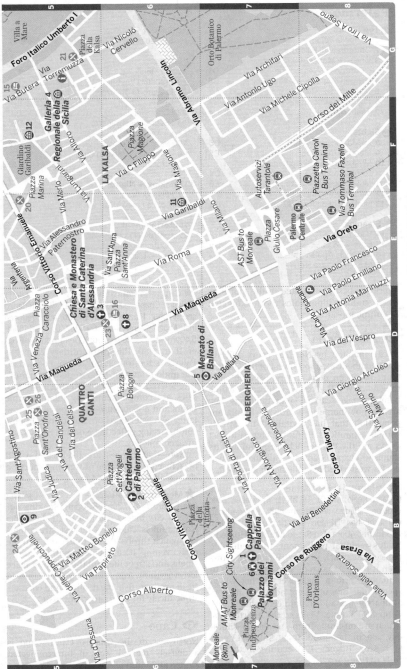

Palermo

interior is best appreciated in the morning, when sunlight illuminates the magnificent Byzantine mosaics.

◉ Albergheria

Once inhabited by Norman court officials, this neighbourhood southwest of the Quattro Canti has been poor and ramshackle since the end of WWII – you can still see wartime bomb damage scarring some buildings. The area is now home to a growing immigrant population that has revitalised the streets with its aspirations. By far the biggest tourist draws are the Palazzo dei Normanni and its exquisite chapel, Cappella Palatina, both at the far western edge of the neighbourhood,

★**Palazzo dei Normanni**　　　PALACE
(Palazzo Reale; ☎ 091 705 56 11; www.federicosec ondo.org; Piazza del Parlamento; adult/reduced incl exhibition Fri-Mon €12/10, Tue-Thu €10/8; ◷8.15am-5.40pm Mon-Sat, to 1pm Sun) Home to Sicily's regional parliament, this venerable palace dates back to the 9th century. However, it owes its current look (and name) to a major Norman makeover, during which spectacular mosaics were added to its royal apartments and magnificent chapel, the Cappella Palatina. Visits to the apartments, which are off-limits from Tuesday to Thursday, take in the mosaic-lined Sala dei Venti and King Roger's 12th-century bedroom, Sala di Ruggero II.

★**Cappella Palatina**　　　CHAPEL
(Palatine Chapel; ☎ 091 705 56 11; www.federico secondo.org; Piazza del Parlamento; adult/reduced incl Appartamenti Reali €9.50/7.50; ◷8.15am-5.40pm Mon-Sat, to 1pm Sun) Designed by Roger II in 1130, this extraordinary chapel is Palermo's top tourist attraction. Located on the middle level of Palazzo dei Normanni's three-tiered loggia, its glittering gold mosaics are complemented by inlaid marble floors and a wooden *muqarnas* ceiling, the latter a masterpiece of Arabic-style honeycomb carving reflecting Norman Sicily's cultural complexity.

Note that queues are likely, and you'll be refused entry if you're wearing shorts, a short skirt or a low-cut top.

★**Mercato di Ballarò**　　　MARKET
(Via Ballaro 1; ◷7.30am-8.30pm) Snaking for several city blocks southeast of Palazzo dei Normanni is Palermo's busiest street market, which throbs with activity well into the early evening. It's a fascinating mix of noises, smells and street life, and the cheapest place for everything from Chinese padded bras to fresh produce, fish, meat, olives and cheese – smile nicely for *un assaggio* (a taste).

◉ Capo

Northwest of the Quattro Canti, Capo is a densely packed web of interconnected streets and blind alleys.

★**Cattedrale di Palermo**   CATHEDRAL
(☏329 3977513; www.cattedrale.palermo.it; Corso Vittorio Emanuele; cathedral free, royal tombs €1.50, treasury & crypt €3, roof €5, all-inclusive ticket adult/reduced €8/4; ⏰7am-7pm Mon-Sat, 8am-1pm & 4-7pm Sun; royal tombs, treasury, crypt & roof 9am-1.30pm Mon-Sat, royal tombs & roof also 9am-12.30pm Sun) A feast of geometric patterns, ziggurat crenellations, maiolica cupolas and blind arches, Palermo's cathedral has suffered aesthetically from multiple reworkings over the centuries, but remains a prime example of Sicily's unique Arab-Norman architectural style. The interior, while impressive in scale, is essentially a marble shell whose most interesting features are the **royal Norman tombs** (to the left as you enter), the **treasury** (home to Constance of Aragon's gem-encrusted 13th-century crown) and the panoramic views from the **roof**.

Mercato del Capo   MARKET
(Via Sant'Agostino; ⏰7am-8pm Mon, Tue & Thu-Sat, to 1pm Wed & Sun) Running the length of Via Sant'Agostino, Capo's street market is a seething mass of colourful activity during the day, with vendors peddling fruit, vegetables, meat, fish, cheese and household goods of every description.

◉ **Vucciria**

Once the heart of poverty-stricken Palermo and a den of crime and filth, this neighbourhood northeast of the Quattro Canti illustrated the almost medieval chasm that existed between rich and poor in Sicily until the 1950s. Though it's still quite shabby, the winds of change are blowing.

Museo Archeologico Regionale Antonio Salinas   MUSEUM
(☏091 611 68 07; www.regione.sicilia.it/bbccaa/salinas; Piazza Olivella 24; admission €3; ⏰9am-6pm Tue-Sat, to 1.30pm Sun) Situated in a Renaissance monastery, this splendid, wheelchair-accessible museum houses some of Sicily's most valuable Greek and Roman artefacts, including the museum's crown jewel: a series of original decorative friezes from the temples at Selinunte. Other important finds in the museum's collection include Phoenician sarcophagi from the 5th century BC, Greek carvings from Himera, the Hellenistic *Ariete di bronzo di Siracusa* (Bronze Ram of Syracuse), Etruscan mirrors and the largest collection of ancient anchors in the world.

Oratorio di Santa Cita   CHAPEL
(www.ilgeniodipalermo.com; Via Valverde; €4, incl Oratorio di San Domenico €6; ⏰9am-6pm) This 17th-century chapel showcases the breathtaking stuccowork of Giacomo Serpotta, who famously introduced rococo to Sicilian churches. Note the elaborate *Battle of Lepanto* on the entrance wall. Depicting the Christian victory over the Turks, it's framed by stucco drapes held by a cast of cheeky cherubs modelled on Palermo's street urchins. Serpotta's virtuosity also dominates the side walls, where sculpted white stucco figures hold gilded swords, shields and a lute, and a golden snake (Serpotta's symbol) curls around a picture frame.

◉ **La Kalsa**

This quarter southeast of the Quattro Canti was long one of the city's most notorious neighbourhoods. A recent program of urban regeneration, however, has seen many of its long-derelict palazzos being restored and long-abandoned streets speckled with petite bohemian bars, trendy eateries, artisan studios and street art.

★**Galleria Regionale della Sicilia**   MUSEUM
(Palazzo Abatellis; ☏091 623 00 11; www.regione.sicilia.it/beniculturali/palazzoabatellis; Via Alloro 4; adult/reduced €8/4; ⏰9am-6.30pm Tue-Fri, to 1pm Sat & Sun) Housed in the stately 15th-century Palazzo Abatellis, this art museum – widely regarded as Palermo's best – showcases works by Sicilian artists dating from the Middle Ages to the 18th century. One of its greatest treasures is *Trionfo della morte* (Triumph of Death), a magnificent fresco (artist unknown) in which Death is represented as a demonic skeleton mounted on a wasted horse, brandishing a wicked-looking scythe while leaping over his hapless victims.

Museo dell'Inquisizione   MUSEUM
(Palazzo Chiaramonte-Steri; ☏091 2389 3788; Piazza Marina 61; adult/reduced €8/5; ⏰10am-6pm Tue-Sun) Housed in the lower floors and basements of 14th-century Palazzo Chiaromonte Steri, this fascinating museum explores the legacy of the Inquisition in Palermo. Thousands of 'heretics' were detained here between 1601 and 1782; the honeycomb of former cells has been painstakingly restored to reveal multiple layers of their graffiti and artwork (religious and otherwise). Visits are by one-hour guided tour only, conducted in English and Italian and departing roughly every 40 to 60 minutes from the ticket desk.

WORTH A TRIP

AROROUND PALERMO

A few kilometres outside Palermo's city limits, the beach town of Mondello and the dazzling cathedral of Monreale are both worthwhile day trips. Just off shore, Ustica makes a great overnight or weekend getaway.

Monreale

In the hills 8km southwest of Palermo, **Cattedrale di Monreale** (☑091 640 44 03; www.monrealeduomo.it; Piazza del Duomo; cathedral free, Roano chapel, terrace & cloister adult/reduced €10/7; ☺cathedral 8.30am-12.30pm & 2.30-5pm Mon-Sat, 8-9.30am & 2.30-5pm Sun, cloisters 9am-7pm Mon-Sat, to 1.30pm Sun) is considered the finest example of Norman architecture in Sicily, incorporating Norman, Arab, Byzantine and classical elements. Inspired by a vision of the Virgin, it was built by William II in an effort to outdo his grandfather, Roger II, who was responsible for the cathedral in Cefalù and the Cappella Palatina in Palermo. The interior, completed in 1184 and executed in shimmering mosaics, depicts 42 Old Testament stories. Outside the cathedral, the **cloister** is a tranquil courtyard with a tangible oriental feel. Surrounding the perimeter, elegant Romanesque arches are supported by an exquisite array of slender columns alternately decorated with mosaics. To reach Monreale, take AMAT bus 389 (€1.40, 35 minutes, every 1¼ hours) from Palermo's Piazza Indipendenza or AST's Monreale bus (€2.40, 40 minutes, every 60 to 90 minutes Monday to Saturday) from in front of Palermo Centrale train station.

Mondello

Tucked between dramatic headlands 12km north of Palermo, Mondello is home to a long, sandy beach that became fashionable in the 19th century, when people came to the seaside in their carriages, prompting the construction of the huge art nouveau pier that still graces the waterfront. Most of the beaches near the pier are private (two sunloungers and an umbrella cost from €15 to €22); however, there's a wide swath of public beach opposite the centre of town with all the requisite pedalos and jet skis for hire. Given its easygoing seaside feel, Mondello is an excellent base for families. To get here, take AMAT bus 806 (€1.40, 20 to 30 minutes) from Piazza Sturzo in Palermo.

Ustica

A 90-minute boat trip from downtown, the 8.7-sq-km island of Ustica was declared Italy's first marine reserve in 1986. The surrounding waters are a playground of fish and coral, ideal for snorkelling, diving and underwater photography. To enjoy Ustica's wild coastline and dazzling grottoes without the crowds, try visiting in June or September.

There are numerous dive centres, hotels and restaurants on the island, as well as some nice hiking. To get here from Palermo, take the once-daily ferry (from €97 including vehicle, three hours) operated by **Siremar** (☑090 57 37; https://carontetourist.it/it/siremar; ☺ticket office 9.30am-1pm & 3-6.15pm) or the faster, more frequent hydrofoils (€26, 1½ hours) operated by **Liberty Lines** (☑Ustica office 091 844 90 02, customer service 0923 87 38 13; www.libertylines.it; ☺ticket office 9.30am-1pm & 3-6.15pm). For more details on Ustica, see Lonely Planet's *Sicily* guide.

Museo delle Maioliche   MUSEUM
(Stanze al Genio; ☑340 0971561, 380 3673773; www.stanzealgenio.it; Via Garibaldi 11; adult/reduced €9/8; ☺guided tours in English 3pm Tue-Fri, 10am Sat, 11am Sun, in Italian 4pm Tue-Fri, 11am Sat & Sun) Lovers of hand-painted Italian maiolica should make a beeline for this unique museum, which contains a superlative private collection of almost 6000 tiles, most from Sicily and Naples, and spanning the 15th to 20th centuries. Amassed over three decades by founder Pio Mellina, the tiles fill the walls and floors of the lovingly restored 16th-century Palazzo Torre-Piraino, itself a work of art with vaulted and frescoed ceilings. The museum also houses a small collection of vintage Italian toys.

◉ New City

North of Piazza Giuseppe Verdi, Palermo's streets widen, the buildings lengthen, and the shops, restaurants and cafes become more elegant (and more expensive). Glorious neoclassical and Liberty examples from the last golden age in Sicilian architecture give the city an exuberant, belle-époque feel in stark contrast to the narrow, introspective vibe of the historic quarter.

⭐ **Teatro Massimo**   THEATRE
(✏️box office 091 605 35 80; www.teatromassimo.it; Piazza Giuseppe Verdi; guided tours adult/reduced €8/5; ⊙9.30am-6pm) Taking over 20 years to complete, Palermo's neoclassical opera house is the largest in Italy and the second-largest in Europe. The closing scene of *The Godfather: Part III*, with its visually arresting juxtaposition of high culture, crime, drama and death, was filmed here and the building's richly decorated interiors are nothing short of spectacular. Guided 30-minute tours are offered throughout the day in English, Italian, French, Spanish and German.

⭐ **Pinacoteca Villa Zito**   GALLERY
(✏️091 778 21 80; www.villazito.it; Via della Libertà 52; adult/reduced €5/3; ⊙9.30am-7.30pm Tue-Sun) Elegant 18th-century Villa Zito houses a sharply curated collection of mainly Sicilian-themed art spanning the 17th to 20th centuries. You'll find a number of fascinating historical depictions of Palermo, numerous paintings by Ettore De Maria Bergler (considered the foremost Italian painter of the Liberty era), as well as works by 20th-century heavyweights Ugo Attardi, Fausto Pirandello, Filippo De Pisis, Carlo Carrà and Renato Guttuso.

⭐ **Palazzina Cinese &**
Parco della Favorita   PALACE
(✏️091 707 14 03; Via Duca degli Abruzzi 1; ⊙9am-6pm Tue-Sat, plus 9am-1pm 1st Sun of month) Once a retreat for King Ferdinand IV and his wife Maria Carolina, this pagoda-inspired pavilion exemplifies the popularity of 'Oriental exotica' in 18th-century Europe. Chinese, Egyptian, Islamic and Pompeiian motifs decorate its many rooms, with particular highlights including a trompe l'oeil 'collapsed' ceiling by Giuseppe Velazquez and a nifty dining table connected to the kitchen below via a lift. To get here, catch bus 107 to Piazza Giovanni Paolo II and then bus 615 or 645 to Duca degli Abruzzi – Palazzina Cinese.

⭐ **Festivals & Events**

Festino di Santa Rosalia   RELIGIOUS
(U Fistinu; ⊙Jul) Palermo's biggest annual festival celebrates patron saint Santa Rosalia, beloved for having saved the city from a 17th-century plague. The most colourful festivities take place on the evening of 14

July, when the saint's relics are paraded aboard a grand chariot from the Palazzo dei Normanni through the Quattro Canti to the waterfront, where fireworks and general merriment ensue.

🛏️ **Sleeping**

A burgeoning crop of B&Bs in Palermo's historic centre offers an alternative to the city's established, oft-dated hotels. Be mindful that street noise can be a problem, and some accommodation occupies historic buildings where stairs rather than lifts provide the only access.

⭐ **Stanze al Genio Residenze**   B&B €
(✏️340 0971561; www.stanzealgeniobnb.it; Via Garibaldi 11; s €85-100, d €100-120; ❄️🛜) Speckled with Sicilian antiques, this B&B offers four gorgeous bedrooms, three with 19th-century ceiling frescoes. All four are spacious and thoughtfully appointed, with Murano lamps, old wooden wardrobes, the odd balcony railing turned bedhead, and top-quality, orthopaedic beds. That the property features beautiful maiolica tiles is no coincidence; the B&B is affiliated with the wonderful Museo delle Maioliche downstairs.

Palazzo Pantaleo   B&B €
(✏️091 32 54 71; www.palazzopantaleo.it; Via Ruggero Settimo 74h; s/d/ste €80/100/150; 🅿️🛜) Offering unbeatable comfort and a convenient location, Giuseppe Scaccianoce's elegant B&B occupies the top floor of an old *palazzo* (mansion) half a block from Piazza Politeama, hidden from the busy street in a quiet courtyard with free parking. Glowing with warm, earthy tones, five rooms and one spacious suite feature high ceilings, marble, tile or wooden floors, soundproof windows and modern bathrooms.

B&B Amélie   B&B €
(✏️328 8654824, 091 33 59 20; www.bb-amelie.it; Via Prinicipe di Belmonte 94; s €40-60, d €60-80, tr €90-100; ❄️@🛜) On a central, car-free street, affable, multilingual Angela has converted her grandmother's spacious 6th-floor flat into a cheery B&B. Rooms are simple, colourful and spotless. All have private bathroom (either as an ensuite or in the hallway) and two come with private terrace. Breakfast includes homemade cakes and jams, and Angela, a native Palermitan, is a font of local knowledge.

Massimo Plaza Hotel   HOTEL €€
(✏️091 32 56 57; www.massimoplazahotel.com; Via Maqueda 437; d €140-250; 🅿️❄️🛜) The intimate

Massimo Plaza sits in a prime location along vibrant, pedestrianised Via Maqueda. Tie-back curtains and wooden furniture give rooms a classic feel. Seven of the rooms offer a prime view of the iconic Teatro Massimo across the street. Breakfast can be delivered directly to your room at no extra charge.

Butera 28 APARTMENT €€
(📞 333 3165432; www.butera28.it; Via Butera 28; apt per day €85-265, per week €570-1780; 🅿 ❄ 🛜) Delightful multilingual owner Nicoletta rents 12 apartments in the 18th-century Palazzo Lanzi Tomasi, the last home of Giuseppe Tomasi di Lampedusa, author of *The Leopard.* Graced with family antiques, the units range from 30 to 180 sq metres, most sleeping a family of four or more. Five apartments face the sea and all feature laundry facilities, well-equipped kitchens and sound-proofed windows.

★ De Bellini Apartments APARTMENT €€€
(📞 331 8836589; http://debellinipalermo.it; Piazza Bellini 5; apt from €200; ❄ 🛜) In a 17th-century *palazzo* on one of Palermo's finest squares, these 10 architect-designed apartments are spectacular. Six have their own kitchen with high-tech appliances, and while all have different configurations and looks, all feature contemporary art, striking designer furniture, contemporary bathrooms and quality bedding. Bellini's balcony apartment is so close to the 12th-century La Martorana you can almost touch it from your private terrace.

Grand Hotel Villa Igiea HOTEL €€€
(📞 091 631 21 11; www.villa-igiea.com; Salita Belmonte 43; d from €289; 🅿 ❄ @ 🛜 🏊) What can you say about an art nouveau villa that was designed by Ernesto Basile for the Florio family (of tuna and Marsala-wine fame)? This is Palermo's top hotel, located around 3km north of the city centre and with its own private beach, swimming pool, tennis court, spa centre, gym and restaurants. The rooms are predictably elegant, with blissful beds and palatial bathrooms.

🍴 Eating

Palermo's restaurant scene ranges from heirloom trattorias serving faithful classics like *bucatini con le sarde* (pasta mixed with sardines, wild fennel, raisins, pine nuts and breadcrumbs) to next-gen hotspots. Hit the markets and street-food stalls for delicious bargain bites.

★ I Segreti del Chiostro SWEETS €
(📞 327 5882302; www.isegretidelchiostro.com; Monastero di Santa Caterina d'Alessandria, Piazza Bellini; sweets from €1; ⏰ 10am-7pm summer, to 6pm winter; 🍴 ♿) Countless blessings await at this extraordinary *pasticceria,* hidden away in a former convent. The culmination of endless hours of research, it uses once secret recipes to bake rare sweet treats from numerous Sicilian convents. Everything is made from scratch using premium ingredients, including the *fedde del Cancelliere,* a reckless concoction of apricot jam and *biancomangiare* (almond pudding) encased in marzipan clam shells.

★ Trattoria al Vecchio Club Rosanero SICILIAN €
(📞 349 4096880; Vicolo Caldomai 18; mains €3-12; ⏰ 1-3.30pm Mon-Sat & 8-11pm Thu-Sat; 🛜) A veritable shrine to the city's football team (*rosa nero* refers to the team's colours, pink and black), cavernous Vecchio Club scores goals with its generous, bargain-priced grub. Fish and seafood are the real fortes here; if it's on the menu, order the *caponata e pesce spada* (*caponata* with swordfish), a sweet-and-sour victory. Head in early to avoid a wait.

Archestrato di Gela PIZZA €
(📞 091 625 89 83; www.facebook.com/archestratodigelapalermo; Via Emanuele Notarbartolo 2f; pizzas €6.50-14; ⏰ 7.45pm-midnight Tue-Sun; 🛜🍴) If you're serious about wood-fired pie, book at least two days ahead at what many consider to be the best pizzeria in town. The puffy, Neapolitan-style crusts are charred to perfection and topped with speciality, artisan ingredients from across Italy. Standouts include the Priolo, a turf-meets-surf smash of Bronte pistachio pesto, aged *prosciutto crudo, burratina* cheese (made from mozzarella and cream) and Cetara tuna. Libations include cocktails.

★ Aja Mola SEAFOOD €€
(📞 091 611 91 59, 334 1508335; www.ajamolapalermo.it; Via Cassari 39; meals €35-40; ⏰ 12.30-3pm & 7.30-11pm Tue-Sun; 🛜) On-point Aja Mola is among Palermo's top seafood eateries. The interior's smart, subtle take on a nautical theme is reflected in the open kitchen, which eschews stock-standard cliches for modern, creative dishes. The result: appetite-piquing options like teriyaki-style tartare with caperberries, or surf-turf *tagliolini* pasta with succulent shrimps and pork jowl. Bar seating available; ideal for solo diners. Book ahead.

PALERMO'S STREET FOOD

Bangkok, Mexico City, Marrakesh and Palermo: worldly gluttons know that Sicily's capital is a street-food heavyweight. Palermitans are obsessed with eating (and eating well), and almost any time is a good time to feast. What they're devouring is *buffitieri* – little hot snacks prepared at stalls and designed for eating on the spot.

Kick off the morning with *pane e panelle,* Palermo's famous chickpea fritters – great for vegetarians and a welcome change from a sweet custard-filled croissant. You might also want to go for some *crocchè* (potato croquettes, sometimes flavoured with fresh mint) or *quaglie* (literally translated as quails, they're actually aubergines/eggplants cut lengthwise and fanned out to resemble a bird's feathers, then fried). Other options include *sfincione* (a spongy, oily pizza topped with onions and caciocavallo cheese) and *scaccie* (discs of bread dough spread with a filling and rolled up into a pancake). In the warmer months, locals find it difficult to refuse a freshly baked brioche jammed with gelato or *granita* (crushed ice mixed with fresh fruit, almonds, pistachios or coffee).

From 4pm onwards the snacks become decidedly more carnivorous, and you may just wish you hadn't read the following translations: how about some barbecued *stigghiola* (goat intestines filled with onions, cheese and parsley), for example? Or a couple of *pani ca meusa* (breadroll stuffed with sautéed beef spleen). You'll be asked if you want it *'schietta'* (single) or *'maritata'* (married). If you choose *schietta,* the roll will only have ricotta in it before being dipped into boiling lard; choose *maritata* and you'll get beef spleen as well.

You'll find stalls and kiosks selling street food all over town, especially in Palermo's street markets. Top choices include **Francu U Vastiddaru** (Corso Vittorio Emanuele 102; sandwiches €1.50-4; ⊙9am-1am), **Friggitoria Chiluzzo** (⛵329 0615929; Piazza della Kalsa; sandwiches €1-2.50; ⊙8am-5pm Mon-Sat, to 4pm Sun) and tiny **I Cuochini** (Via Ruggero Settimo 68; snacks from €0.70; ⊙8.30am-2.30pm Mon-Sat, plus 4.30-7.30pm Sat).

Ristorante Ferro
SICILIAN €€

(⛵347 1618373, 091 58 60 49; www.facebook.com/ristoranteferropalermo; Piazza Sant'Onofrio 42; meals €30-40; ⊙8-11pm Mon-Sat) All clean lines, timber panels and tinted mirrors, intimate, family-run Ferro wouldn't look out of place in London or Sydney. Whether you're savouring a soup of squid and mussels, earthy ravioli stuffed with porcini mushrooms, or a flawless steak, the food here is superb in its simplicity, favouring prime produce cooked beautifully and without fuss. Alas, wines by the glass are limited.

Le Angeliche
SICILIAN €€

(⛵091 615 70 95; www.leangeliche.it; Vicolo Abbadia 10; meals €25-35; ⊙9am-3pm Mon-Thu, to midnight Fri & Sat; 🎄) An oasis of potted plants and pastel hues, Le Angeliche is run by four women passionate about honouring and refreshing Sicily's rich, sometime obscure culinary traditions. Scan the menu and you might find a soup of cannellini beans, endive, chestnuts and pasta, or perhaps *cassatella di Montevago* – fried, ravioli-like pastries filled with sweetened sheep's milk ricotta, honey and lemon zest. Book ahead.

Bioesserì
HEALTH FOOD €€

(⛵091 765 71 42; www.bioesseri.it; Via Giuseppe La Farina 4; pizza €7.50-14, meals €30-35; ⊙7.30am-11pm Mon-Thu, to 11.30pm Fri, 8.30am-11.30pm Sat, to 11pm Sun; 🎄) Organic fare with flair awaits at this stylish Milanese import. Part cafe, part upmarket grocery store, its virtuous bites tap all bases, including vegan *cornetti* (croissants), smoothies and soy-milk *budini* (puddings), spelt-flour pizzas and well-executed, bistro-style dishes like *fregola* pasta in a fish-and-crustacean soup, or stuffed calamari paired with herbed potato purée.

Gagini
ITALIAN €€€

(⛵091 58 99 18; www.gaginirestaurant.com; Via Cassari 35; meals €45, 4-/5-/8-course degustation menu €70/85/110; ⊙12.30-3pm & 7.30-11.30pm; 🎄) Expect sharp professionals and serious gastronomes at Gagini's rustic, candlelit tables. In the kitchen are Massimiliano Mandozzi and Elnava De Rosa, whose passion for season, region and fresh thinking might offer a Sicilian twist on the kebab, a playful take on classic *pasta con le sarde* (pasta with sardines), or seafood unexpectedly paired with cracked wheat and hazelnuts. Book ahead.

🍷 Drinking & Nightlife

Popular drinking spots include bohemian Via Paternostro, Piazza della Rivoluzione, Discesa dei Giudici, as well as cheap, gritty Via Maccherronai. Further north, lively bars line Via Isidora la Lumia. You'll also find bars in the Champagneria district due east of Teatro Massimo, centred on Piazza Olivella, Via Spinuzza and Via Patania. Higher-end drinking spots are concentrated in the new city.

★ **Ferramenta** WINE BAR
(☑ 091 672 70 61; Piazza G Meli 8; ⊘ 6.30pm-1am Tue-Sun) Once a hardware store, this genuinely cool, piazza-side bar-eatery now fixes long days with well-mixed cocktails and clued-in vino. Rotating wines by the glass might include a natural white from western Sicily or an organic red from Etna, best paired with a *tagliere* (board) of top-notch charcuterie, seafood or vegetables (€10 to €18). More substantial dishes are also available, including pasta.

★ **Hic! La Folie du Vin** WINE BAR
(☑ 349 2693038; www.facebook.com/hiclafoliedu vin; Via G Mazzini 46; ⊘ 6.30-11.30pm, closed Sun mid-Jun–Jul & Sep, closed Mon Oct–mid-Jun, closed Aug) Hugely popular with 30- and 40-plus locals, Hic! is never short of a fun crowd, spilling out onto the footpath in a sea of banter and reasonably priced vino. The latter includes lots of Italian, French and German drops, each one approved by owner Giuseppe. Edibles include quality cheeses and cured meats, and the bar hosts live acoustic sets on Sunday evenings.

☆ **Entertainment**

★ **Teatro Massimo** OPERA
(☑ box office 091 605 35 80; www.teatromassimo. it; Piazza Giuseppe Verdi) Ernesto Basile's six-tiered art-nouveau masterpiece is Europe's second-largest opera house and one of Italy's most prestigious, right up there with La Scala in Milan, San Carlo in Naples and La Fenice in Venice. It stages opera, ballet and music concerts from September to June. Opera tickets range from around €20 to €140.

Teatro dei Pupi di Mimmo Cuticchio THEATRE
(☑ 091 32 34 00; www.facebook.com/TeatroDell OperaDeiPupi; Via Bara all'Olivella 95) This puppet theatre is a charming low-tech choice for children (and the child within), staging traditional, one-hour shows using exquisitely handcrafted Sicilian *pupi* (puppets). Check the theatre's Facebook page for upcoming performances.

🛍 **Shopping**

In the new city, Via della Libertà is lined with high-end fashion stores. More atmospheric is Palermo's historic centre, where crumbly streets harbour artisan workshops selling everything from ceramics to leather goods. Many belong to ALAB (www.alab palermo.it), an association of artisans helping to revitalise the area. For fresh edibles, hit Mercato di Ballarò or Mercato del Capo. Come Sunday morning, trawl the Mercatino Antiquariato Piazza Marina for antiques and decorative objects.

ℹ **Information**

Micro² Tourist Information Centre (☑ 091 732 02 48; www.visitpalermo.it; Via Torremuzza 15; ⊘ 10am-1pm & 2.30-5.30pm Mon-Sat, 10.30am-2pm Sun) Enthusiastic, privately run tourist-information office open seven days a week and able to book tours, transfers and accommodation.

Municipal Tourist Office (☑ 091 740 80 21; http://turismo.comune.palermo.it; Piazza Bellini; ⊘ 8.45am-6.15pm Mon-Fri, from 9.45am Sat) Main branch of Palermo's city-run information booths. Other locations include **Via Cavour** (⊘ 8.30am-1.30pm Mon-Fri), **Teatro Massimo** (Piazza Giuseppe Verdi; ⊘ 9.30am-1.30pm Mon-Fri), the Port of Palermo and Mondello, though these are only intermittently staffed, with unpredictable hours.

Ospedale Civico (☑ 091 666 55 17; www.arnas civico.it; Via Tricomi; ⊘ 24hr) Major hospital with 24-hour emergency department.

Police (Questura; ☑ 091 21 01 11; Piazza della Vittoria 8) Palermo's main station, located between Via Maqueda and Palazzo dei Normanni.

Tourist Information Office, Falcone-Borsellino Airport (☑ 091 59 16 98; www.gesap.it/en/ aeroporto/services/tourist-information-of fice; ⊘ 8.30am-7.30pm Mon-Fri, to 6pm Sat) Downstairs in the arrivals hall, run by Palermo Metropolitan City.

ℹ **Getting There & Away**

AIR

Palermo Falcone-Borsellino Airport (☑ 800 541880, 091 702 02 73; www.gesap.it) is at Punta Raisi, 31km northwest of Palermo on the E90 motorway. Alitalia and other major airlines such as Air France, Lufthansa and KLM fly from Palermo to destinations throughout Europe. Several cut-rate carriers also offer flights to/ from Palermo, including Ryanair, Volotea, Vueling and easyJet. Falcone-Borsellino is the hub airport for regular domestic flights to the islands of Pantelleria and Lampedusa.

BOAT

Ferry companies operate from Palermo's **port** (☑ 091 604 31 11; cnr Via Francesco Crispi & Via Emerico Amari), just east of the New City.

Grandi Navi Veloci (☎ 010 209 45 91, 091 6072 6162; www.gnv.it; Molo Piave, Porto Stazione Marittima) Runs ferries to Civitavecchia (from €43), Genoa (from €51), Naples (from €43) and Tunis (from €44).

Grimaldi Lines (☎ 081 49 65 55, 091 611 36 91; www.grimaldi-lines.com; Molo Piave, Porto Stazione Marittima) Operates twice-weekly ferries from Palermo to Salerno (from €25, 9½ to 11 hours) and Tunis (from €38, 10 to 13½ hours). Ferries run thrice weekly to Livorno (from €32, 18½ to 19½ hours).

Liberty Lines (☎ 091 32 42 55; www.liberty lines.it; Calata Marinai d'Italia) Operates one to five daily hydrofoil services (€26, 1½ hours) between Ustica and Palermo.

Siremar (☎ 090 57 37; https://carontetourist. it/it/siremar; ⊙ ticket office 9.30am-1pm & 3-6.15pm) Runs one daily car ferry (passenger including car from €95, three hours) between Ustica and Palermo.

Tirrenia (☎ 800 804020, 091 611 65 18; www. tirrenia.it; Calata Marinai d'Italia) Sails to Cagliari (from €45, 13 hours, once or twice weekly) and Naples (from €55, 10½ hours, daily).

BUS

Offices for all bus companies are located within a block or two of Palermo Centrale train station. The two main departure points are the Piazzetta Cairoli bus terminal, just south of the train station's eastern entrance, and the newer Via Tommaso Fazello bus terminal, beside the station's western entrance. Check locally with your bus company to make sure you're boarding at the appropriate stop.

AST (Azienda Siciliana Trasporti; ☎ 091 620 81 11; www.aziendasicilianatrasporti.it; Piazzetta Cairoli Bus Terminal) Services to southeastern destinations including Ragusa (€13.50, four hours, two to four daily) and Modica (€13.50, 4½ hours, two to four daily)

Autoservizi Tarantola (☎ 0924 310 20; www. facebook.com/groups/calecavincenzo; Via Paolo Balsamo) To Segesta (€7, 1¼ hours, three daily Mon-Sat Apr-Oct)

Cuffaro (☎ 091 616 15 10; www.facebook.com/ cuffaro.info; Via Paolo Balsamo 13) To Agrigento (€9, two hours, three to seven daliy)

Interbus (☎ 091 616 79 19; www.interbus.it; Piazzetta Cairoli Bus Terminal) To Syracuse (€13.50, 3½ hours, two to three daily)

SAIS Autolinee (☎ 800 211020, 091 616 60 28; www.saisautolinee.it; Piazzetta Cairoli Bus Terminal) To Messina (€14, 2¾ hours, four to seven daily) and Catania (€14, 2¾ hours, 10 to 14 daily)

Salemi (☎ 0923 98 11 20; www.autoservizi salemi.it; Piazzetta Cairoli Bus Station) To Trapani airport (€11, 1¾ hours, four to six daily) and Marsala (€9.50, 2¼ hours, four to six daily)

AST, Salemi, Segesta, SAIS and Interbus tickets are sold at the bus terminal building at Piazzetta Cairoli.

Cuffaro tickets can be purchased from the Cuffaro ticket office at Via Paolo Balsamo 13, just east of the train station, or on board.

CAR & MOTORCYCLE

Palermo is accessible on the A20–E90 toll road from Messina, and from Catania (A19–E932) via Enna. Trapani and Marsala are also easily accessible from Palermo by motorway (A29), while Agrigento and Palermo are linked by the SS121, a good state road through the interior of the island.

TRAIN

Regular services leave from **Palermo Centrale train station** (Piazza Giulio Cesare) to the following destinations:

Agrigento (€9, two hours, six to 13 daily)

Catania (€13.50, three hours, five to six Monday to Saturday, transfers required Sunday)

Cefalù (from €5.60, 45 minutes to one hour, eight to 17 daily)

Messina (€12.80; 2¾ to three hours, six to nine daily)

From Messina, Intercity trains continue to Reggio di Calabria, Naples and Rome.

Inside the station are ATMs, toilets and left-luggage facilities (first five hours €6 flat fee, next seven hours €1 per hour, all subsequent hours €0.50 per hour; office staffed 8am to 8pm).

ⓘ Getting Around

TO/FROM THE AIRPORT

Prestia e Comandè (☎ 091 58 63 51; www. prestiaecomande.it; Via Tommaso Fazello Bus Terminal; 1-way/return €6.50/11) runs efficient, half-hourly buses between Palermo and the airport. From the airport, buses run from 5am to 12.30am (1am May to October; 50 minutes). From Palermo, airport-bound buses run from 4am to 10.30pm, departing the Via Tommaso Fazello Bus Terminal beside Palermo Centrale train station and stopping at numerous points in central Palermo, including outside the Rinascente department store on Via Roma 289 and on Piazza Ruggero II. Purchase tickets on board or, for a small discount, online.

Trinacria Express (☎ 091 704 40 07; www. trenitalia.com) trains run between the airport (Punta Raisi station) and Palermo Centrale (€5.90, around one hour). Trains run every 15 to 60 minutes and tickets can be purchased online or at the station.

Societá Autolinee Licata (SAL; ☎ 0922 40 13 60; www.autolineesal.it) runs between the airport and Agrigento (€12.60, 2¾ hours, three daily Monday to Saturday).

SICILY PALERMO

There is a taxi rank outside the arrivals hall and the fare to/from Palermo is between €35 and €45, depending on your destination in the city.

All major car-hire companies are represented at the airport. You'll often save money by booking online before leaving home. Given the city's chaotic traffic and expensive parking, and the excellent public transport from Palermo's airport, it's generally best to postpone rental car pickup until you're ready to leave the city.

BICYCLE

Centrally located **Social Bike Palermo** (☑ 328 2843734; www.socialbikepalermo.com; Discesa dei Giudici 21; standard/electric bike half-day €8/15, guided bike tours €40-55; ☺ 9.30am-6.30pm) rents out folding, standard, electric and tandem bikes and runs bike tours of Palermo's *centro storico* (historic centre) and its Liberty (art nouveau) architecture.

CAR & MOTORCYCLE

Driving is frenetic in Palermo and best avoided. Many hotels have a *garage convenzionato*, a local garage that offers special rates to their guests (typically between €12 and €20 per day). Street parking spaces marked by blue lines require that you buy a ticket from a machine or a *tabaccheria* (tobacconist's shop); spaces marked by white lines are free.

PUBLIC TRANSPORT

Palermo's orange, white and blue city buses, operated by **AMAT** (☑ 091 35 01 11, 848 800817; http://amat.pa.it), are frequent but often overcrowded and slow. Tickets, valid for 90 minutes, cost €1.40 if pre-purchased from *tabaccherie* or from AMAT information kiosks, including one at Palermo Centrale train station. Tickets can also be purchased on board (€1.80). A day pass costs €3.50. Remember to validate your ticket at a machine when boarding. The free map handed out at Palermo tourist offices details the major bus lines; most stop at Palermo Centrale train station.

TAXI

Official taxis should have a *tassametro* (meter), which records the fare; check for this before embarking. The minimum starting fare is €3.81, with a range of additional charges, all listed at www.taxi.it/palermo. Hailing a passing taxi on the street is not customary; rather, wait at one of the taxi ranks at major travel hubs such as the train station, Piazza Ruggero Settimo, Teatro Massimo and Piazza Indipendenza, or order ahead by calling **Autoradio Taxi Palermo** (☑ 091 8481; www.autoradiotaxi.it) or using appTaxi (www.apptaxi.it).

TYRRHENIAN COAST

The coast between Palermo and Milazzo is studded with popular tourist resorts attracting a steady stream of holidaymakers, particularly between June and September. The best of these is Cefalù, a resort second only to the Ionian coast's Taormina in popularity. Just inland lie the two massive natural parks of the Madonie and Nebrodi mountains.

Cefalù

☑ 0921 / POP 14,300

Beautiful Cefalù offers a rare combination of tourist attractions: one of Sicliy's finest beaches side-by-side with one of its greatest Arab-Norman architectural masterpieces, all set against a dramatic mountain backdrop. Holidaymakers from all over Europe flock here to relax in resort hotels, stroll the narrow cobbled streets and sun themselves on the long sandy beach.

This popular holiday resort wedged between a dramatic mountain peak and a sweeping stretch of sand has the lot: a great beach, a truly lovely historic centre with a grandiose cathedral, and winding medieval streets lined with restaurants and boutiques. Avoid the height of summer when prices soar, beaches are jam packed and the charm of the place is tainted by bad-tempered drivers trying to find a car park.

Sights & Activities

★ **Duomo di Cefalù**   CATHEDRAL

(☑ 092 192 20 21; www.cattedraledicefalu.com; Piazza del Duomo; towers & apse or treasury & cloisters €5, combo ticket incl towers, apse, treasury & cloisters €8; ☺ 8.30am-6.30pm Apr-Oct, 8.30am-1pm & 3.30-5pm Nov-Mar) Cefalù's cathedral is one of the jewels in Sicily's Arab-Norman crown, only equalled in magnificence by the Cattedrale di Monreale and Palermo's Cappella Palatina. Filling the central apse, a towering figure of Cristo Pantocratore (Christ All Powerful) is the focal point of the elaborate Byzantine mosaics – Sicily's oldest and best preserved, predating those of Monreale by 20 or 30 years.

★ **Spiaggia di Cefalù**   BEACH

Cefalù's crescent-shaped beach is one of the most popular along the whole Sicilian coast. In summer it's packed, so arrive early to get a good spot. Though some sections require a ticket, the area closest to the old town is public and you can hire a beach umbrella and deckchair for around €15 per day.

★ La Rocca
HIKING

(adult/reduced €4/2; ⊙8am-7pm May-Sep, 9am-4pm Oct-Apr) Looming over Cefalù, this imposing rocky crag was once the site of an Arab citadel, superseded in 1061 by the Norman castle whose ruins still crown the summit. To reach the top, follow signs for Tempio di Diana, taking Vicolo Saraceni off Corso Ruggero or Via Giuseppe Fiore off Piazza Garibaldi. The 30- to 45-minute route climbs the **Salita Saraceni**, a winding staircase, through three tiers of city walls before emerging onto rock-strewn upland slopes with spectacular coastal views.

🛏 Sleeping & Eating

Bookings are essential in the summer.

★ B&B Agrodolce
B&B €

(☑338 7250863; www.agrodolcebb.it; Via Gioeni 44; d €80-110, tr €100-120; 🛜) Three flights of old stone steps lead to this lovely upper-floor B&B in Cefalù's historic centre. Architect Rita Riolo offers four bright and airy rooms with cool tiled floors and bathrooms, along with delicious lemon cake and other home-baked goodies served on a tiny breakfast terrace looking towards the Duomo.

La Plumeria
HOTEL €€

(☑0921 92 58 97; www.laplumeriahotel.it; Corso Ruggero 185; d €169-229; 🅿❄🛜) Midway between the Duomo and the waterfront, with free parking a few minutes away, this small hotel offers four-star service in a prime location. Rooms are mostly unexceptional but well appointed; the sweetest of the lot is room 301, a cosy top-floor eyrie with checkerboard tile floors and a small terrace looking up to the Duomo.

Bottega Tivitti
PIZZA €

(☑0921 92 26 42; www.bottegativitti.com; Lungomare Giardina 7; mains €6-15; ⊙11am-4pm & 7pm-midnight) This casual waterfront spot serves pizzas, salads and inventive 'Sicilian burgers' made with top-of-the-line local ingredients – like the Tivitti Burger, with sheep's-milk cheese, olive tapenade, sundried tomatoes and roasted eggplant. It's a great spot to watch the sunset while sampling Sicilian wines and microbrews and snacking on local cheese and meat platters.

Mandralisca 16 Bistrot
SICILIAN €€

(☑0921 99 22 45; www.facebook.com/mandralisca16; Via Mandralisca 16; meals €25-35; ⊙noon-3pm & 7-11pm Tue-Sun) Picturesque setting combines with scrumptious Sicilian cuisine at this relative newcomer with sidewalk seating in an alley gazing towards the Duomo's bell towers. Start with a perfect *caponata* (eggplant, olives, capers, onions and celery in a sweet-and-sour tomato sauce), then move on to chickpea, chard and sage soup or *involtini* (roulades) of fish with citrus, bay leaves and breadcrumbs.

Locanda del Marinaio
SEAFOOD €€

(☑0921 42 32 95; www.locandadelmarinaiocefalu. it; Via Porpora 5; meals €35-45; ⊙noon-2.30pm & 7-11pm Wed-Sun, 7-11pm Mon) Fresh seafood rules the chalkboard menu at this upscale eatery on the old town's main waterfront thoroughfare. Depending on the season, you'll find

---

WORTH A TRIP

THE MADONIE MOUNTAINS: CEFALÙ'S BACKYARD PLAYGROUND

Due south of Cefalù, the 400sq-km **Parco Naturale Regionale delle Madonie** incorporates some of Sicily's highest peaks, including the imposing Pizzo Carbonara (1979m). The park's wild, wooded slopes are home to wolves, wildcats, eagles and the near-extinct ancient Nebrodi fir trees that have survived since the last ice age. Ideal for hiking, cycling and horse trekking, the park is also home to several handsome mountain towns, including **Castelbuono**, **Petralia Soprana** and **Petralia Sottana**.

The region's distinctive rural cuisine includes roasted lamb and goat, cheeses, grilled mushrooms, and aromatic pasta with *sugo* (meat sauce). A great place to sample these specialties is **Nangalarruni** (☑0921 67 12 28; www.hostariananangalarruni.it; Via delle Confraternite 7; meals €29-45; ⊙12.30-3pm & 7-10pm Thu-Tue) in Castelbuono.

For information, contact the park headquarters in **Petralia Sottana** (Madonie Park Authority; ☑0921 68 40 11; www.parcodellemadonie.eu; Corso Paolo Agliata 16) or the branch office in **Cefalù** (☑0921 92 33 27; www.parcodellemadonie.eu; Corso Ruggero 116; ⊙8am-2pm Mon, to 6pm Tue-Sat).

Bus service to the park's main towns is limited; to fully appreciate the Madonie, you're better off hiring a car for a couple of days.

dishes such as red tuna carpaccio with toasted pine nuts, shrimp and zucchini on a bed of velvety ricotta, or grilled octopus served with thyme-scented potatoes, all accompanied by an excellent list of Sicilian wines.

❶ Information

Tourist Office (☏ 0921 42 10 50; www.turismocefalu.sicilia.it; Corso Ruggero 77; ⊙9am-7.30pm Mon-Fri, 8am-2pm Sat) English-speaking staff, lots of leaflets and good maps.

❶ Getting There & Away

Hourly trains go to Palermo (€5.60, 45 minutes to 1¼ hours), and virtually every other town on the coast.

AEOLIAN ISLANDS

The Aeolian Islands are a little piece of paradise. Stunning cobalt sea, splendid beaches, some of Italy's best hiking and an awe-inspiring volcanic landscape are just part of the appeal. The islands also have a fascinating human and mythological history that goes back several millennia: the Aeolians figured prominently in Homer's *Odyssey*, and evidence of the distant past can be seen everywhere, most notably in Lipari's excellent archaeological museum.

The seven islands of Lipari, Vulcano, Salina, Panarea, Stromboli, Alicudi and Filicudi are part of a huge 200km volcanic ridge that runs between the smoking stack of Mt Etna and the threatening mass of Vesuvius above Naples. Collectively, the islands exhibit a unique range of volcanic characteristics, which have earned them a place on Unesco's World Heritage List. The islands are mobbed with visitors in July and August, but out of season things remain delightfully tranquil.

❶ Getting There & Away

Liberty Lines (☏ 0923 87 38 13; www.liberty lines.it) operates the lion's share of hydrofoils to the islands, including summer-only services from Palermo that make stops on all seven islands. Check the Liberty Lines website for up-to-the-minute schedules.

Ferry service from Milazzo (cheaper but slower and less frequent than hydrofoil service) is provided by **Siremar** (☏ 090 57 37; www.caron tetourist.it/en/siremar) and **NGI Traghetti** (☏ 090 928 40 91; www.ngi-spa.it).

From Naples, Siremar runs twice-weekly car ferries to the islands, while **SNAV** (☏ 081 428 55 55; www.snav.it) operates summer-only hydrofoils.

❶ Getting Around

Liberty Lines (www.libertylines.it) runs frequent hydrofoils connecting all seven islands; ferries ply the same routes, costing less but taking twice as long.

Lipari, Vulcano and Salina are the only islands with significant road networks. Bringing your own car by ferry is expensive; you'll often save money by garaging it at Milazzo or Messina on the mainland (from €12 per day) and hiring a scooter on-site, or better yet, exploring the islands on foot or bike.

Lipari

☑090 / POP 12,800

Lipari is the largest, busiest and most accessible of the Aeolian Islands, yet still retains a charming, unhurried vibe. Visitors arriving from the mainland will likely experience it as a relaxing introduction to island life; on the other hand, if you've just come from the outer Aeolians, it may feel a bit like a big city!

The main focus is Lipari Town, the archipelago's principal transport hub and the nearest thing that islanders have to a capital city. A busy little port with a pretty, pastel-coloured seafront and plenty of accommodation, it makes the most convenient base for island-hopping. Away from the town, Lipari reveals a rugged and typically Mediterranean landscape of low-lying *macchia* (dense Mediterranean shrubbery), silent, windswept highlands, precipitous cliffs and dreamy blue waters.

⊙ Sights

Town Centre AREA
One of Lipari Town's great pleasures is simply wandering its streets, lapping up the laid-back island atmosphere. Lipari's liveliest street is **Corso Vittorio Emanuele**, a cheerful thoroughfare lined with bars, cafes and restaurants. The street really comes into its own in early evening, when it's closed to traffic and the locals come out for their *passeggiata* (evening stroll). Equally atmospheric is **Marina Corta**, down at the end of Via Garibaldi, a pretty little marina ringed by popular bars and restaurants.

★ Museo Archeologico Regionale Eoliano MUSEUM
(☏090 988 01 74; www.regione.sicilia.it/beniculturali/museolipari; Via Castello 2; adult/reduced €6/3; ⊙9am-7.30pm Mon-Sat, to 1.30pm Sun) A must-see for Mediterranean history buffs, Lipari's archaeological museum has one of Europe's

finest collections of ancient finds. Especially worthwhile are the Sezione Preistorica, devoted to locally discovered artefacts from the Neolithic and Bronze Ages to the Graeco-Roman era, and the Sezione Classica, the highlights of which include ancient shipwreck cargoes and the world's largest collection of miniature Greek theatrical masks. Pay admission fees at the ticket office, about 100m north of the Sezione Classica.

★ Quattrocchi   VIEWPOINT

Lipari's best coastal views are from a celebrated viewpoint known as Quattrocchi (Four Eyes), 3km west of town. Follow the road for Pianoconte and look on your left as you approach a big hairpin bend about 300m beyond the turnoff for Spiaggia Valle Muria. Stretching off to the south, great cliffs plunge into the sea, while in the distance plumes of sinister smoke rise from the dark heights of neighbouring Vulcano.

★ Spiaggia Valle Muria   BEACH

Lapped by clean waters and surrounded by sheer cliffs, this dark, pebbly beach on Lipari's southwestern shore is a dramatically beautiful swimming and sunbathing spot. From the signposted turnoff, 3km west of Lipari town towards Pianoconte, it's a steep 25-minute downhill walk; come prepared with water and sunscreen. In good weather, Lipari resident Barni (☑ 339 8221583, 349 1839555) sells refreshments from his rustic cave-like beach bar, and provides memorably scenic boat transfers to and from Lipari's Marina Corta (€5/10 one-way/return).

☞ Tours

Numerous agencies in town, including the dependable Da Massimo/Dolce Vita (☑ 090 601 98 41; www.damassimo.it; Via Maurolico 2), offer boat tours to the surrounding islands. Prices run around €20 for a tour of Lipari and Vulcano, €45 to visit Filicudi and Alicudi, €45 for a day trip to Panarea and Stromboli, or €80 for a late-afternoon trip to Stromboli with a guided trip up the mountain and a late-night return to Lipari.

🛏 Sleeping

Lipari is the Aeolians' best-equipped base for island-hopping, with plenty of places to stay, eat and drink. Note that prices soar in summer; avoid August if possible.

★ B&B Al Salvatore di Lipari   B&B €

(☑ 335 8343222; www.facebook.com/bbalsalvatore; Via San Salvatore, Contrada al Salvatore; d

€60-120; ⊙ Apr-Oct; 🛜) Once you reach this peaceful hillside oasis 2km south of town, you may never want to leave. Artist Paola and physicist Marcello have transformed their Aeolian villa into a green B&B that works at all levels, from dependable wi-fi to a panoramic terrace where delicious home-grown breakfasts are served, featuring produce from the adjacent garden, fresh-baked cakes and homemade marmalade.

★ Diana Brown   B&B €

(☑ 338 6407572, 090 981 25 84; www.dianabrown.it; Vico Himera 3; s €35-65, d €50-80, tr €65-105; ❄ 🛜) Now run by the daughter and son-in-law of longtime Lipari innkeeper Diana Brown, this delightful warren of rooms tucked down a narrow alley sports attractive features including in-room kettles, fridges, clothes-drying racks, satellite TV and a book exchange. Units downstairs are darker but have built-in kitchenettes. Its excellent buffet breakfast is served on the sunny terrace and solarium with deck chairs.

Enzo Il Negro   GUESTHOUSE €

(☑ 090 981 31 63; www.enzoilnegro.com; Via Garibaldi 29; s €45-50, d €75-90, tr €90-120; ❄ 🛜) Family-run for nearly 40 years, and perfectly placed in the pedestrian zone near picturesque Marina Corta, Enzo and Cettina's down-to-earth guesthouse offers spacious, tiled, pine-furnished rooms with fridges and air-con. Two panoramic terraces overlook the rooftops, the harbour and the castle walls.

🍴 Eating

Gilberto e Vera   SANDWICHES €

(☑ 090 981 27 56; www.gilbertoevera.it; Via Garibaldi 22; half/full sandwiches €3.50/5; ⊙ 7.30am-11pm mid-Mar–mid-Nov) Still run by the friendly couple who founded it four decades ago (ably assisted by daughter Alessia), this beloved shop sells two dozen varieties of *panini,* many named for now-grown locals who once stopped by here on their way to school. It's the perfect stop for morning hiking and beach-hopping provisions, or afternoon glasses of wine on the street-side terrace.

★ Sangre Rojo   SICILIAN €€

(☑ 338 2909524; www.facebook.com/ristorante sangrerojo; meals €34-39; ⊙ noon-2.30pm & 7pm-midnight Wed-Mon Easter–mid-Oct) Dazzling vistas of Salina, Filicudi and Alicudi floating in the Tyrrhenian are reason enough to visit

SICILY LIPARI

Lipari Town

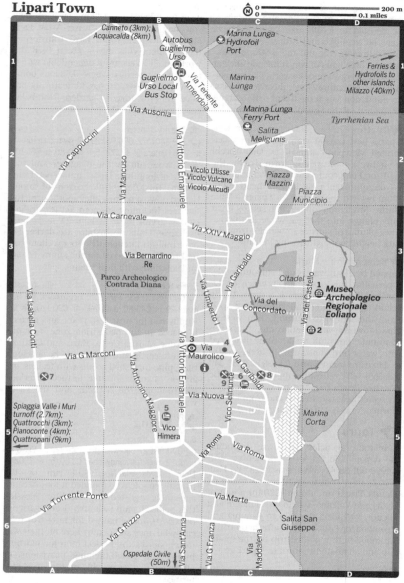

this hilltop restaurant near Lipari's northern tip. But the cuisine, based on fresh fish and classic Aeolian ingredients like wild fennel, capers, olives and mint, is the real clincher. Enjoy lunch on the gorgeous sun-drenched terrace or linger over dinner with a sunset view.

Kasbah   MEDITERRANEAN €€
(📱 090 921 37 42; www.kasbahlipari.it; Vico Selinunte 43; pizzas €10-12, meals €35, tasting menu €45; ⏱ 7-10.30pm Apr-Oct) Tucked down narrow Vico Selinunte, with a window where you can watch the chefs at work, this place serves everything from fancy pasta, fish and

Lipari Town

meat dishes to simple wood-fired pizzas (try the Kasbah, with smoked swordfish, rocket, lemon and black pepper). The stylish dining room with its grey linen tablecloths is complemented by a more casual outdoor terrace.

E Pulera   MODERN SICILIAN €€
(📞 090 981 11 58; www.pulera.it; Via Isabella Conti; meals €35-45; ⊙ 7.30-11.30pm late Apr–mid-Oct) With its serene garden setting, low lighting, tile-topped tables and exquisite food – from tuna carpaccio with blood oranges and capers for dinner to *cassata* (sponge cake, ricotta, marzipan, chocolate and candied fruit) served with sweet Malvasia wine for dessert – E Pulera makes an upscale but relaxed choice for a romantic dinner.

ℹ Information

Tourist Office (📞 090 988 00 95; Via Maurolico 17; ⊙ 9am-1pm Mon-Fri, plus 4-6pm Wed & Fri) Lipari's sporadically staffed office provides information covering all the Aeolian Islands.

ℹ Getting There & Around

BOAT
Lipari is the Aeolians' transport hub. The main port is Marina Lunga, where you'll find the **ticket office** (📞 090 981 24 48; ⊙ 5am-8.40pm) for hydrofoil operator Liberty Lines, and ferry operators NGI and Siremar. Hydrofoils run frequently to the mainland port of Milazzo (€16, one hour) and to the other Aeolian islands, including Vulcano (€6, 10 minutes), Salina (€9, 20 minutes) and Stromboli (€18, 1½ to 1¾ hours). Hydrofoil service to Messina (€26, 1½ to 3¼ hours) is less

frequent. In summer (late May through early September), **SNAV** (📞 081 428 55 55; www. snav.it) also runs daily hydrofoils from Naples to Lipari (from €62, 6½ hours).

BUS
Autobus Guglielmo Urso (📞 090 981 10 26; www.ursobus.com/Orario-ita.htm) runs buses from its stop opposite the Marina Lunga hydrofoil dock. One route serves the island's eastern shore, from Lipari Town to Canneto (five minutes) and Acquacalda (20 minutes); another runs from Lipari Town to the splendid Quattrocchi viewpoint and the western highland settlements of Pianoconte and Quattropani. Individual tickets range from €1.30 to €2.40; discounts are available for round-trip tickets or multiple rides (six/10/20 tickets for €10/14/28). Service is limited to nonexistent on Sundays.

CAR & MOTORCYCLE
Lipari's seafront road circles the entire island, a journey of about 30km. Various outfits at Marina Lunga, including **Da Marcello** (📞 090 981 12 34; www.noleggiodamarcello.com; Via Amendola), rent out bikes (about €10 per day), scooters (€15 to €40) and cars (€30 to €70).

Vulcano
POP 720

With its visibly smoking crater and vile sulphurous fumes, Vulcano makes an indelible first impression. The island's volcanic nature has long impressed visitors: the ancient Romans believed it to be the chimney of the fire god Vulcan's workshop. Vulcano's most obvious attractions – climbing the crater, strolling over to the mud baths and the black beaches at Porto di Ponente – are easily managed on a day trip from Lipari. Visitors who linger and explore beyond drab, dated and touristy Porto di Levante will discover a whole different island, swimming off Gelso's volcanic beaches, kayaking the wild coast or enjoying the rural tranquillity of the central plateau, filled with vegetable gardens, birdsong and a surprising amount of greenery.

Boats dock at Porto di Levante. To the right, as you face the island, are the mud baths and the small Vulcanello peninsula; to the left is the volcano. Straight ahead is Porto di Ponente, 700m west, where you will find the black sands of **Spiaggia Sabbie Nere**.

◎ Sights & Activities

For spectacular sea and island views without the physical exertion of climbing Fossa di Vulcano, follow the signposted road to **Capo**

SICILY VULCANO

Grillo, about 7km southeast of Vulcano port, near the mid-island settlement of Piano.

★**Fossa di Vulcano**　　　　　HIKING

Vulcano's star attraction is the straightforward trek up its 391m volcano (no guide required). Start early if possible and bring a hat, sunscreen and water. Follow the signs south along Strada Provinciale, then turn left onto the zigzag gravel track that leads to the summit. It's a 30- to 60-minute climb to the lowest point of the volcano's rim (290m), where you'll be rewarded with fine views of the steaming crater encrusted with red and yellow crystals.

Pozza dei Fanghi　　　　HOT SPRINGS

(Mud Baths; ☑ 338 8335514; www.geoterme.it; admission €3, shower/towel €1/2.60; ⊗ 7am-10pm Jul & Aug, 8am-7.45pm late Mar-Jun & Sep-early Nov) Backed by a *faraglione* (rock tower) and stinking of rotten eggs, Vulcano's harbourside pool of thick, coffee-coloured sulphurous gloop isn't exactly a five-star beauty farm. But the warm (29°C) mud is considered an excellent treatment for rheumatic pains and skin diseases, and rolling around in it can be fun if you don't mind smelling funny for a few days. Keep the mud away from your eyes (as the sulphur is acidic and can damage the cornea) and hair.

Sicily in Kayak　　　　　BOATING

(☑ 329 5381229; www.sicilyinkayak.com; excursions from €55) Kayaking enthusiast Eugenio Viviani heads this home-grown outfit offering everything from half-day explorations of Vulcano's sea caves to multiday paddling excursions visiting multiple islands in the Aeolian archipelago. Recent new initiatives include sailing tours and stand-up paddleboard excursions down Lipari's dramatic west coast. See the website or contact Eugenio directly for full details.

🛏 Sleeping & Eating

Vulcano isn't a great place for an overnight stay; the town is pretty soulless and the sulphurous fumes really do smell. Most people visit on day trips from nearby Lipari.

★**Malvasia**　　　　SANDWICHES €

(☑ 346 6039439; www.ristorantemalvasiavulcano.it; Via degli Eucaliptus; sandwiches from €12; ⊗ 11.30am-2.30pm & 7.30-11pm late Apr-early Oct) After years selling open-faced sandwiches from a cart near Vulcano's port, jovial owner Maurizio Pagano opened this popular restaurant and wine bar in 2015. Bask on the sunny front patio and enjoy his trademark *pane cunzatu eoliano* (tuna, olives, capers, tomatoes and buffalo-milk mozzarella on delectable toasted homemade bread drenched in extra-virgin olive oil), or go for salads and daily specials.

★**Trattoria da Pina**　　　　SEAFOOD €€

(☑ 368 668555; Gelso; meals €29-32; ⊗ 12.30-2.30pm & 8-9.45pm Apr–mid-Oct) With sea-blue tablecloths and an intimate outdoor porch overlooking the black-sand beach at Vulcano's southern tip, this down-to-earth trattoria serves up delicious pasta and fresh-caught fish in a wonderful end-of-the-line setting. Two local men do the fishing, and their families do the cooking. Save room for scrumptious desserts such as pistachio *semifreddo*, or homemade biscotti and sweet Malvasia wine.

ℹ Getting There & Around

BOAT

Vulcano is an intermediate stop between Milazzo (€15, 50 minutes) and Lipari (€5.80, 10 minutes). Both Liberty Lines and Siremar run multiple vessels in both directions throughout the day. The hydrofoil journey to or from Lipari takes only 10 minutes, making Vulcano an easy and popular day-trip destination.

CAR & MOTORCYCLE

Sprint da Luigi (☑ 347 7600275; www.nolosprintdaluigi.com; Porto di Levante; bike/electric bike/scooter/car rental per day from €7/20/25/50) Rent some wheels and get travel advice about the island from Luigi and

HYDROFOILS TO THE AEOLIAN ISLANDS

FROM	TO	COST (€)	DURATION	FREQUENCY
Messina	Lipari	31	1½-3½hr	5 daily in summer, 1 daily in winter
Milazzo	Lipari	21	1hr	12-17 daily
Milazzo	Vulcano	20	45min	12-16 daily
Milazzo	Stromboli	26	1¼-3hr	3-7 daily
Milazzo	Salina	23	1½hr	12 daily

Nidra, friendly multilingual owners of this well-signposted outfit just south of the port.

Salina

POP 4000

Ah, green Salina! In stark contrast to sulphur-stained Vulcano and lava-blackened Stromboli, Salina's twin extinct craters, Monte dei Porri and Monte Fossa delle Felci – nicknamed *didyme* (twins) by the ancient Greeks – are lushly wooded and invitingly verdant, a result of the numerous freshwater springs on the island. Wildflowers, thick yellow gorse bushes and serried ranks of grapevines carpet the hillsides in vibrant colours and cool greens, while its high coastal cliffs plunge dramatically towards beaches. The famous Aeolian capers grow plentifully here, as do the grapes used for making Malvasia wine.

◉ Sights & Activities

Salina's main villages are Santa Marina, on the east side of the island where most boats dock, and Malfa on the northwestern coast. Salina is famous for its dark-golden or light-amber sweet Malvasia wine. Wineries in Malfa and Lingua offer visits and tastings with advance notice.

Pollara   VILLAGE
Don't miss a trip to sleepy Pollara, sandwiched dramatically between the sea and the steep slopes of an extinct volcanic crater on Salina's western edge. The gorgeous beach here was used as a location in the 1994 film *Il Postino,* although the land access route to the beach has since been closed due to landslide danger.

★ Monte Fossa delle Felci   HIKING
For jaw-dropping views, climb to the Aeolians' highest point, Monte Fossa delle Felci (962m). The two-hour ascent starts from the Santuario della Madonna del Terzito, an imposing 19th-century church at Valdichiesa, in the valley separating the island's two volcanoes. Up top, gorgeous perspectives unfold on the symmetrically arrayed volcanic cones of Monte dei Porri, Filicudi and a distant Alicudi.

★ Signum Spa   SPA
(Salus Per Aquam; ☑ 090 984 42 22; www.hotel signum.it; Via Scalo 15, Malfa; €30, treatments extra; ◷ 10am-8pm Apr-Sep) Enjoy a revitalising hot spring soak or a cleansing sweat in a traditional adobe-walled steam house at Hotel Signum's fabulous spa. The complex includes several stylish Jacuzzis on a pretty flagstoned patio, and blissful spaces where you can immerse your body in salt crystals, get a massage or pamper yourself with natural essences of citrus, Malvasia and capers.

🛏 Sleeping & Eating

Salina remains relatively undisturbed by mass tourism, yet offers some of the Aeolians' finest hotels and restaurants.

★ Hotel Ravesi   HOTEL €€
(☑ 090 984 43 85; www.hotelravesi.it; Via Roma 66, Malfa; d €90-190, ste €160-290; ◷ mid-Apr–mid-Oct; ✱ ☀ 🤶 ⌨) Star attractions at this peach of a family-run hotel beside Malfa's town square include the delightful grassy lounge and bar area and the outdoor deck with infinity pool overlooking Panarea, Stromboli and the Mediterranean. Sea views are especially nice from corner room 12 upstairs and from the two brand-new honeymoon suites with antique furniture, decorative tiles and private terraces.

Capofaro   BOUTIQUE HOTEL €€€
(☑ 090 984 43 30; www.capofaro.it; Via Faro 3; d €260-680, ste €580-1200; ◷ May–mid-Oct; ✱ @ 🤶 ⌨) Immerse yourself in luxury at this five-star boutique resort surrounded by well-tended Malvasia vineyards, halfway between Santa Marina and Malfa. Sharp white decor prevails in the 20 rooms with terraces looking straight out to smoking Stromboli and six brand-new suites in the picturesque 19th-century lighthouse. Tennis courts, poolside massages, wine tasting and vineyard visits complete this perfect vision of island chic.

★ Da Alfredo   SANDWICHES, GELATERIA €
(Piazza Marina Garibaldi, Lingua; granite €3, sandwiches €10-14; ◷ 8am-11pm Jun-Sep, reduced hours Oct-May) Straddling a sunny waterfront terrace in Lingua, Alfredo's place is renowned Sicily-wide for its *granite:* ices made with coffee, fruit or locally grown pistachios, hazelnuts and almonds. For an affordable lunch, try its *pane cunzato,* open-faced sandwiches loaded with smoked tuna carpaccio, citrus, wild fennel, almond-caper pesto, ricotta, tomatoes, capers, olives and more; split one with a friend – they're huge!

★ A Cannata   SICILIAN €€
(☑ 090 984 31 61; www.acannata.it; Lingua; meals €35; ◷ 12.30-2.30pm & 7.30-10pm) Meals are built around locally sourced produce and seafood caught fresh daily by owner Santino

at this unassuming but excellent restaurant, run by the same family for four decades. Expect dishes such as squid-ink risotto, *maccheroni* (macaroni) with eggplant, pine nuts, mozzarella and ricotta, fresh grilled fish, sautéed wild fennel, almond *semifreddi* (a light frozen dessert) and local Malvasia wine.

★ **A Quadara**   TRATTORIA **€€**
(☑ 389 1519650; www.aquadaratrattoria.it; Via Roma 88, Malfa; meals €25-39; ☺ 6.30-11pm) Since opening in 2018, this restaurant has won a loyal following for its delicious, authentic Aeolian cuisine. The menu abounds in seasonal specials and enticing local recipes, from pasta with chickpeas and fennel, to rabbit stewed with veggies, pine nuts, almonds, lemon, cinnamon and capers. Scrumptious homemade *cannoli* and an excellent local wine selection are icing on the cake.

🍸 Drinking & Nightlife

★ **Maracaibo**   BAR
(☑ 331 6244981; Punta Scario, Malfa; ☺ 8am-11pm late May-Sep) This palm-thatched beach bar on the rocky shoreline of Punta Scario (just below Malfa town) makes a dreamy spot for a sunset drink. The friendly owners also rent out loungers, beach umbrellas and kayaks.

ℹ Getting There & Around

BOAT

Hydrofoils and ferries serve Santa Marina Salina and the small southern port of Rinella from Lipari and the other islands.You'll find ticket offices in both ports.

BUS

CITIS (☑ 090 984 41 50; www.trasportisalina. it) provides dependable local bus service year-round from Santa Marina to Lingua (€2, five to 10 minutes), Malfa (€2, 15 to 20 minutes) and Rinella (€2.80, 40 minutes). From Santa Marina to Pollara (€2.50, 25 minutes to 1½ hours), a change of bus in Malfa is always required. See schedules online.

CAR & MOTORCYCLE

Just above Santa Marina's port, **Antonio Bongiorno** (☑ 338 3791209; Via Risorgimento 222, Santa Marina Salina; ☺ 8am-8pm) hires scooters (from €20 per day) and cars (from €50 per day).

Stromboli

POP 500

For many the most captivating of the Aeolians, Stromboli conforms perfectly to one's childhood idea of a volcano, with its symmetrical, smoking silhouette rising dramatically from the sea. It's a hugely popular day-trip destination, but to best appreciate its primordial beauty, languid pace and the romance that lured Roberto Rossellini and Ingrid Bergman here in 1949, you'll need to give it at least a couple of days.

Volcanic activity has scarred and blackened much of the island, but the northeastern corner is inhabited, and it's here that you'll find the island's famous black beaches and the main settlement sprawled attractively along the volcano's lower slopes. Despite the picture-postcard appearance, life here is tough: food and drinking water have to be ferried in, there are no roads across the island, and until relatively recently there was no electricity in Ginostra, the diminutive second settlement on Stromboli's west coast.

⊙ Sights & Activities

★ **Stromboli Crater**   VOLCANO
For nature lovers, climbing Stromboli is one of Sicily's not-to-be-missed experiences. Since 2005 access has been strictly regulated: you can walk freely to 400m, but need a guide to continue any higher. Organised treks depart daily (between 3.30pm and 6pm, depending on the season), timed to reach the summit (924m) at sunset and to allow 45 minutes to an hour to observe the crater's fireworks.

The climb itself takes 2½ to three hours, while the descent back to Piazza San Vincenzo is shorter (1½ to two hours). All told, it's a demanding five- to six-hour trek up to the top and back; you'll need to have proper walking shoes, a backpack that allows free movement of both arms, clothing for cold and wet weather, a change of T-shirt, a handkerchief to protect against dust (wear glasses not contact lenses), a torch (flashlight), 1L to 2L of water and some food. If you haven't got any of these, **Totem Trekking** (☑ 090 986 57 52; www.totemtrekkingstromboli.com; Piazza San Vincenzo 4; ☺ 9.30am-1pm & 3.30-7pm Mar-Nov) hires out all the necessary equipment, including boots (€6), backpacks (€5), hiking poles (€4), torches (€3) and windbreakers (€5).

★**Sciara del Fuoco Viewpoint** VIEWPOINT
(Path of Fire) An alternative to scaling Stromboli's summit is the hour-long climb to this viewpoint (400m, no guide required), which directly overlooks the Sciara del Fuoco (the blackened laval scar running down Stromboli's northern flank) and offers fabulous if more distant views of the crater's explosions. Bring plenty of water, and a torch (flashlight) if walking at night. The trail (initially a switchbacking road) starts in Piscità, 2km west of Stromboli's port; halfway up, you can stop for pizza at L'Osservatorio.

Volcano Climbs

To climb to the top of Stromboli you'll need to go on an organised trek. Maximum group size is 20 people, and although there are usually multiple groups on the mountain, spaces can still fill up. To avoid disappointment, book early – if possible a week or more before you want to climb. The standard fee for group climbs is €28 per person.

Beside the church in the heart of town, **Magmatrek** (☑ 090 986 57 68; www.magmatrek.it; Via Vittorio Emanuele) is one of Stromboli's longest-established and most professional agencies, with experienced, multilingual (English-, German- and French-speaking) guides. Other agencies charging identical prices include **Stromboli Adventures** (☑ 090 98 60 95, 339 5327277; www.stromboliadventures.it; Via Vittorio Emanuele 17), **Stromboli Fire Trekking** (☑ 090 98 62 64; www.stromboli firetrekking.com; Via Vittorio Emanuele) and **Il Vulcano a Piedi** (☑ 090 98 61 44; www.ilvulcanoapiedi.it; Via Pizzillo).

Boat Tours

Numerous operators down by the port, including **Società Navigazione Pippo** (☑ 090 98 61 35, 348 0559296; www.facebook.com/pipponavigazionestromboli; Porto Scari) and **Antonio Caccetta** (☑ 339 5818200; Vico Salina 10), offer three-hour daytime circuits of the island (€25), 1½-hour sunset excursions to watch the Sciara del Fuoco from the sea (€20), and evening trips to Ginostra village on the other side of the island for dinner or *aperitivi* (€25).

Many private boat operators in Lipari offer day-trip packages including a guided excursion to the craters followed by return transport to Lipari the same evening.

Beaches

Stromboli's black sandy beaches are the best in the Aeolian archipelago. The most accessible swimming and sunbathing is at **Ficogrande**, about a 10-minute walk northwest of the hydrofoil dock. Further-flung beaches worth exploring are at **Piscità**, 2km to the west, and **Forgia Vecchia**, about 300m south of the port.

🛏 Sleeping

More than a dozen places offer accommodation, including B&Bs, guesthouses and fully fledged hotels.

★**Casa del Sole** GUESTHOUSE €
(☑ 090 98 63 00; www.casadelsolestromboli.it; Via Cincotta; dm €25-35, s €30-55, d €60-110) This cheerful Aeolian-style guesthouse is only 100m from a sweet black-sand beach in Piscità, the tranquil neighbourhood at the west end of town. Dorms, private doubles and a guest kitchen all surround a sunny patio, overhung with vines, fragrant with lemon blossoms, and decorated with the masks and stone carvings of sculptor-owner Tano Russo. It's a pleasant 25-minute walk or a €10 taxi ride from the port 2km away.

Pensione Aquilone GUESTHOUSE €
(☑ 090 98 60 80; www.aquiloneresidence.it; Via Vittorio Emanuele 29; s €30-50, d €50-70) Convenience and a peaceful location come together at this cheerful, long-established guesthouse tucked away above Stromboli's main drag, just west of the hilltop church square. Guests love the sunny, flowery central garden patio and shared terraces with views to the volcano and Strombolicchio. Three rooms come with cosy cooking nooks; otherwise, friendly owners Adriano and Francesco – both Stromboli natives –provide breakfast.

🍴 Eating

★**Lapillo Gelato** GELATO €
(Via Roma; gelato €3-5; ⊙ 10am-1pm & 3.30pm-midnight Jun-Aug, 10.30am-12.45pm & 3.30-8pm Sep-May) On the main street between the port and the church, this artisanal gelateria is a great place to fuel up with homemade gelato before making the big climb. The pistachio flavour is pure creamy bliss.

L'Osservatorio PIZZA €
(☑ 090 958 69 91; www.facebook.com/osservatorio stromboli; pizzas €8-11; ⊙ 10am-10pm Apr-Jun & Sep–mid-Nov, to 2am Jul & Aug) Sure, you could eat a pizza in town, but come on – you're on Stromboli! On clear evenings, nothing

compares to the full-on views of the volcano's eruptions from l'Osservatorio's panoramic outdoor terrace. From Piscità, 2km west of Stromboli's port, it's a 30-minute uphill trek or a bumpy ride on the free included shuttle (call ahead to be met at Piscità).

★ **Punta Lena** SICILIAN €€
(☑090 98 62 04; http://ristorantepuntalena.business.site; Via Marina 8; meals €36-45; ☉12.15-2.30pm & 7-10.30pm Thu-Tue, 7-10.30pm Wed May-Sep) For a romantic outing, head to this upscale waterfront restaurant with cheerful blue decor, lovely sea views and the soothing sound of waves lapping in the background. The food is among the island's finest, with signature dishes including fresh seafood, fish stewed with local olives and capers, and *spaghetti alla stromboliana* (with wild fennel, mint, anchovies, cherry tomatoes and breadcrumbs).

ℹ Information

Bring enough cash for your stay on Stromboli. Many businesses don't accept credit cards, and the village's lone ATM on Via Roma is sometimes out of service. Internet access here is limited and slow.

ℹ Getting There & Away

Liberty Lines (☑0923 87 38 13; www.libertylines.it) offers daily hydrofoil service to Salina (€16, one to 1¼ hours), Lipari (€19, one to two hours) and Milazzo (€21, 2¼ to three hours). **Siremar** (☑090 57 37; www.carontetourist.it/en/siremar) also runs car ferries from Stromboli to Naples (from €48, 10 hours), Milazzo and the other Aeolians, and **SNAV** (☑081 428 55 55; www.snav.it) runs a summer-only hydrofoil to Naples (from €62, 4½ hours, late May through early September). In bad weather service is often disrupted or cancelled altogether.

The **ticket office** (☑090 98 60 03; ☉6-8am, 9.30am-12.30pm & 3-5.30pm) is 150m north of Stromboli's **ferry dock**.

IONIAN COAST

The Ionian Coast is studded with enough Sicilian icons to fill a souvenir tea towel. It's here that you'll find the skinny Strait of Messina, mighty Mt Etna and the world's most spectacularly located ancient Greek theatre. Catania is the region's centre, a gritty, vibrant city packed with students, bars and nightlife. Its black-and-white baroque Piazza del Duomo is World Heritage–listed, while its hyperactive fish market is one of Sicily's most appetising sights. Halfway up a rocky mountainside, regal Taormina is sophisticated and exclusive, a favourite of holidaying VIPs and day-tripping tourists. Brooding menacingly on the city's doorstep, Mt Etna offers unforgettable hiking and is also a vino-making hotspot, dotted with celebrated wineries.

Taormina

☑0942 / POP 10,900 / ELEV 204M
Spectacularly perched on the side of a mountain, Taormina is one of Sicily's most popular summer destinations, a chic resort town popular with holidaying high-rollers and those wanting a taste of Sicilian *dolce vita*. Although unashamedly touristy and expensive, the town merits a couple of days for its stunning ancient theatre, people-watching and breathtaking vistas.

Founded in the 4th century BC, Taormina enjoyed great prosperity under the Greek ruler Gelon II and later under the Romans,

---

WORTH A TRIP

SICILY'S OFFSHORE ISLANDS

Sicily is an island lover's paradise, with more than a dozen offshore islands scattered in the seas surrounding the main island. Beyond the major Aeolian Islands of Lipari, Vulcano, Stromboli and Salina, you can detour to the smaller Aeolians: Panarea, Filicudi and Alicudi.

Alternatively, cast off from Trapani on Sicily's western coast to the slow-paced Egadi Islands or the remote, rugged volcanic island of Pantelleria.

South of Agrigento, the sand-sprinkled Pelagie Islands of Lampedusa, Linosa and Lampione offer some fantastic beaches.

Liberty Lines (☑0923 02 20 22; www.libertylines.it) and Siremar (☑090 57 37; www.carontetourist.it/siremar) provide hydrofoil and/or ferry services to all of these islands. For further information, see Lonely Planet's *Sicily* guide.

but fell into quiet obscurity after being conquered by the Normans in 1087. Its reincarnation as a tourist destination dates to the 18th century, when northern Europeans discovered it on the Grand Tour. Among its fans was DH Lawrence, who lived here between 1920 and 1923.

Taormina gets extremely busy in July and August and virtually shuts down between November and Easter. Ideally, head up in April, May, September or October.

◉ Sights & Activities

A short walk uphill from the bus station brings you to Corso Umberto I, a pedestrianised thoroughfare that traverses the length of the medieval town and connects its two historic town gates, Porta Messina and Porta Catania.

Lido Mazzarò is the nearest beach to Taormina, located directly beneath the town. It's well serviced with bars and restaurants, though it gets very crowded in the summer.

★ Teatro Greco   RUINS
(☑0942 2 32 20; Via Teatro Greco; adult/reduced €10/5; ⊙9am-1hr before sunset) Taormina's premier sight is this perfect horseshoe-shaped theatre, suspended between sea and sky, with Mt Etna looming on the southern horizon. Built in the 3rd century BC, it's the most dramatically situated Greek theatre in the world and the second largest in Sicily (after Syracuse). In summer, it's used to stage concerts and festival events. To avoid the high-season crowds, try to visit early in the morning.

Corso Umberto I   STREET
Taormina's chief delight is wandering this pedestrian-friendly, boutique-lined thoroughfare. Start at the tourist office in Palazzo Corvaja (Piazza Santa Caterina; ⊙varies), which dates back to the 10th century, before heading southwest for spectacular panoramic views from Piazza IX Aprile. Facing the square is the early-18th-century Chiesa di San Giuseppe (☑0942 2 31 23; ⊙8.30am-8pm). Continue west through the Torre dell'Orologio, the 12th-century clock tower, into Piazza del Duomo, home to an ornate baroque fountain (1635) that sports Taormina's symbol, a two-legged centaur with the bust of an angel.

Villa Comunale   PARK
(Parco Duchi di Cesarò; Via Bagnoli Croce; ⊙8am-midnight summer, to 6pm winter; ⊕) Created by Englishwoman Florence Trevelyan

in the late 19th century, these stunningly sited public gardens offer breathtaking views of the coast and Mt Etna. They're a wonderful place to escape the crowds, with tropical plants and delicate flowers punctuated by whimsical follies. You'll also find a children's play area.

Castelmola   VILLAGE
For eye-popping views of the coastline and Mt Etna, head for this cute hilltop village above Taormina, crowned by a ruined castle. If you're reasonably fit, head up on foot (one hour) for a good workout and sweeping panoramas. Alternatively, take the hourly Interbus service (one-way/return €1.90/3, 15 minutes). While you're up here, stop in for almond wine at Bar Turrisi (☑0942 2 81 81; www.barturrisi.com; Piazza Duomo; ⊙10am-late; ⊛), a multilevel bar with some rather cheeky decor.

Isola Bella   ISLAND
(www.parconaxostaormina.com; adult/reduced €4/2; ⊙9am-7pm May-Aug, to 6.30pm Apr & early–mid-Sep, reduced hours rest of year) Southwest of Lido Mazzarò is the minuscule Isola Bella, a beautiful nature reserve set in a stunning cove with fishing boats. Reached on foot via a narrow sandbar (take your shoes off!), the island was once home to Florence Trevelyan, creator of the Villa Comunale.

Gole Alcantara   SWIMMING
(☑0942 98 50 10; www.golealcantara.com; €1.50; ⊙8am-sunset; ⊕) This series of vertiginous lava gorges with swirling rapids, 20km west of Taormina, is a pretty spot for cooling off on a summer day. That said, some may be put off by the crowds and the heavy layers of tourist infrastructure. If driving, park in the main Gole Alcantara car park (tip optional), then walk 200m further up the main road to the public entrance, where you'll find a ticket booth and stairs leading down to the gorge.

🎭 Festivals & Events

Taormina Arte   PERFORMING ARTS
(☑391 7462146; www.taoarte.it; ⊙Jun-Sep) Taormina Arte oversees a plethora of cultural events in town, including the annual Taormina Film Fest (http://taofilmfest.it; ⊙Jun or Jul). The peak season for offerings is summer, when the Teatro Greco becomes a hub for world-class opera, dance, theatre and music concerts, with no shortage of internationally renowned acts. See the website for what's on.

Taormina

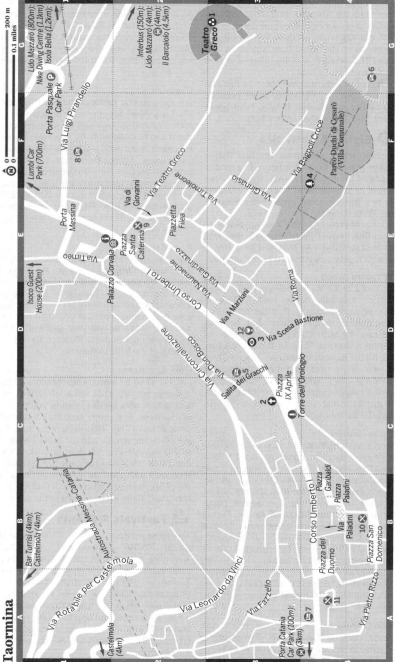

Bar Turrisi (4km);
Castelmola (4km)

Castelmola (4km)

Via Rotabile Per Castelmola

Via Rotabile Messina-Catania

Via Catania Car Park (100m);
Autostrada Messina-Catania (3km)

Via Leonardo da Vinci

Via Fazzello

Porta Catania
Car Park (3km)

Via Pietro Rizzo

Piazza San
Domenico

Piazza
Paladini

Via
Paladini

Piazza
Garibaldi

Corso Umberto I

Piazza del
Duomo

Via Don Bosco

Via Circonvallazione

Salita del Gracchi

Piazza
IX Aprile

Torre dell'Orologio

Via Scesa Bastione

Via A Marziani

Via Naumachie

Via Giardinazzo

Corso Umberto I

Via Roma

Piazzetta
Filea

Piazza
Santa
Caterina

Via di
Giovanni

Palazzo Corvajà

Via Timeo

Porta
Messina

Isoco Guest
House (200m)

Via Teatro Greco

Via Timoleone

Via Ginnasio

Via Bagnoli Croce

Parco Duchi di Cesarò
(Villa Comunale)

Teatro
Greco

Interbus (150m);
Lido Mazzarò (4km);
Il Barcaiolo (4.5km)

Lido Mazzarò (800m);
Nike Diving Centre (1.1km);
Isola Bella (1.2km)

Porta Pasquale
Car Park

Via Luigi Pirandello

Lumbi Car
Park (700m)

Lumbi Car Park

0   200 m
0   0.1 miles

Via Luigi Pirandello

🛏 Sleeping

Given its VIP reputation, it's not surprising that Taormina's accommodation scene tends towards the expensive. Still, there are a number of decent, centrally located midrange options. Book well in advance, especially if visiting during the summer, when demand (like the room rates) is at its highest.

Villa Nettuno   PENSION €

(☑ 0942 23 79 97; www.hotelvillanettuno.it; Via Pirandello 33; s €35-44, d €60-78; 🗶 🛜) A throwback to another era, this conveniently located salmon-pink *pensione* has been run by the Sciglio family for seven decades. Its low prices reflect a lack of recent updates, but the inviting lounge, pretty gardens (complete with olive trees and potted geraniums) and the sea views from the breakfast terrace offer a measure of charm you won't find elsewhere at this price. Breakfast costs €4.

Médousa Suites   BOUTIQUE HOTEL €€

(☑ 0942 38 87 38; www.medousa.it; Via Sesto Pompeo 1; junior ste €100-250, ste €150-600; 🗶 🛜) Set above a stylish garden bar-restaurant, these five high-end suites offer an on-point mix of oak panels, linen curtains, Milanese sofas and contemporary takes on Sicily's *cementine* (traditional cement floor tiles). The suites also include coffee machines, SMEG minibars, quality Parisian amenities and handy USB ports by the custom-made beds. Guests also have access to a small garden area dotted with citrus.

Isoco Guest House   GUESTHOUSE €€

(☑ 0942 23 36 79; www.isoco.it; Via Salita Branco 2; r €78-220; ☺ Mar-Nov; 🅿 🗶 @ 🛜) Each room at this welcoming, LGBT-friendly guesthouse is dedicated to an artist, from Botticelli to Keith Haring. While the older rooms are highly eclectic, the newer suites are chic and subdued, each with a modern kitchenette. Breakfast is served around a large table,

while a pair of terraces offer stunning sea views and a hot tub. Multinight or prepaid stays earn the best rates.

★ Casa Turchetti   B&B €€€

(☑ 0942 62 50 13; www.casaturchetti.com; Salita dei Gracchi 18/20; d €220-260, junior ste €360, ste €470; ☺ late Mar-Oct; 🗶 @ 🛜) Every detail is perfect at this painstakingly restored former music school turned luxurious B&B, on a back alley near Piazza IX Aprile. Vintage furniture and fixtures (including a giant four-poster bed in the suite), handcrafted woodwork and fine homespun sheets exude a quiet elegance. Topping it off is a breathtaking rooftop terrace and the warmth of Sicilian hosts Pino and Francesca.

★ Hotel Villa Belvedere   HOTEL €€€

(☑ 0942 2 37 91; www.villabelvedere.it; Via Bagnoli Croce 79; d €120-680, ste €390-890; ☺ Mar-late Nov; 🗶 @ 🛜 ☒) Built in 1902, the distinguished, supremely comfortable Villa Belvedere was one of Taormina's original grand hotels. Well positioned with fabulous views, luxuriant gardens and wonderful service, its highlights include plush, communal lounge areas and a swimming pool complete with century-old palm. Neutral hues and understated style typify the hotel's 55 rooms, with parking costing an extra €20 per day.

🍴 Eating & Drinking

Eating in Taormina is expensive, and service can be lacklustre. That said, there are some excellent restaurants, serving quality local produce and wines. Avoid touts and tourist menus and reserve up to a week ahead in the summer.

★ Minotauro   PASTRIES €

(☑ 0942 2 47 67; Via di Giovanni 15; pastries from €1, cannoli €2.50; ☺ 9am-8.30pm, to midnight mid-Jun-Aug, closed Dec–mid-Mar) Tiny Minotauro has an epic reputation for its calorific,

SICILY TAORMINA

Taormina

made-from-scratch treats. Scan the counters for old-school tempters such as artful marzipan, sticky *torrone* (nougat) and *paste di mandorla* (almond biscuits) with fillings like orange or pumpkin. Top billing goes to the silky ricotta *cannoli,* filled fresh to order and pimped with pistachio, cinnamon and candied orange.

⭐ **Il Barcaiolo**   SICILIAN €€
(☑0942 62 56 33; www.barcaiolo.altervista.org; Via Castellucci 43, Spiaggia Mazzarò; meals €33-45; ⊙1-2.30pm & 7-10.45pm Wed-Mon Jun-Aug, to 10pm Wed-Mon Apr, May, Sep-early Jan) Book five days ahead come summer, when every *buongustaio* (foodie) and hopeless romantic longs for a table at this fabulous trattoria. Set snugly in a boat-fringed cove at Mazzarò beach, it's celebrated for its sublimely fresh seafood, such as sweet *gamberi rossi marinati agli agrumi* (raw Mazzara shrimps served with citrus fruits) and *sarde a beccaficu* (stuffed sardines).

⭐ **Osteria Nero D'Avola**   SICILIAN €€
(☑0942 62 88 74; www.facebook.com/osterianerodavola; Piazza San Domenico 2b; meals €40-50; ⊙7-11pm daily mid-Jun–mid-Sep, noon-2.30pm & 7-11pm Tue-Sun rest of year; ☎) Owner Turi Siligato fishes, hunts and forages for his smart *osteria,* and if he's in, he'll probably share anecdotes about the day's bounty and play a few tunes on the piano. This is one of Taormina's top eateries, where seasonality, local producers and passion underpin outstanding dishes, such as grilled meatballs in lemon leaves, and fresh fish with Sicilian pesto.

Osteria RossoDiVino   SICILIAN €€€
(☑0942 62 86 53; www.osteria-rosso-divino.com; Vico De Spuches 8; meals €45-65; ⊙7pm-midnight Jul-early Sep, noon-3pm & 7-11pm Wed-Mon Mar-Jun & mid-Sep–Dec; ☎) With seating on an intimate, candlelit courtyard, this coveted nosh spot (book ahead!) is the passion project of siblings Jacqueline and Sara Ragusa. The day's offerings are dictated by the season, the local fishers' catch, and the siblings' own morning market trawl. Expect anything from heavenly anchovy tempura (the secret: mineral water in the batter) to *paccheri* pasta with gorgonzola crema and dehydrated pears.

⭐ **Morgana**   COCKTAIL BAR
(☑0942 62 00 56; www.morganataormina.it; Scesa Morgana 4; ⊙7.30pm-late daily Apr-Oct & mid-Dec–early Jan, 7.30pm-late Fri & Sat Nov–mid-Dec;

☎) This so-svelte cocktail-lounge sports a new look every year, with each concept inspired by Sicilian culture, artisans and landscape. It's the place to be seen, whether on the petite dance floor or among the prickly pears and orange trees in the dreamy, chichi courtyard. Fuelling the fun are gorgeous libations, made with local island ingredients, from wild fennel and orange to sage.

🛍 Shopping

Taormina is a window-shopper's paradise, particularly along pedestrianised Corso Umberto I, where you'll find a mix of high-end fashion, shoes and accessories, quality ceramic goods, lace and linen tableware and antique furniture, along with local culinary treats and wine. Side streets harbour some interesting boutiques and artisan studios.

❶ Information

Tourist Office (☑0942 2 32 43; Palazzo Corvaja, Piazza Santa Caterina; ⊙8.30am-2.15pm & 3.30-6.45pm Mon-Fri Jan-Dec, 9am-1pm & 4-6.30pm Sat summer) Handy for practical information, including transport timetables and town maps.

❶ Getting There & Away

BUS

Bus is the easiest way to reach Taormina. **Interbus** (☑0942 62 53 01; www.interbus.it; Via Luigi Pirandello) goes to Messina (€4.30, 55 minutes to 1¾ hours, one to five daily), Catania (€5.10, 1¼ to two hours, once or twice hourly) and Catania airport (€8.20, 1½ hours, once or twice hourly).

CAR & MOTORCYCLE

Taormina is on the A18 autostrada and the SS114. The historic centre is closed to nonresident traffic and Corso Umberto I is closed to all traffic. Some top-end hotels offer limited parking; otherwise, you'll have to leave your car in one of three car parks outside the historic centre: **Porta Catania**, **Porta Pasquale** or **Lumbi** (per 24hr €16 Jul & Aug, Sep-Jun €14). All three are within walking distance of Corso Umberto I, though Lumbi (the furthest) runs a free shuttle bus up to the centre.

TRAIN

Trains run frequently to Messina (from €4.30, 45 minutes to 1¼ hours) and Catania (€4.30, 35 minutes to one hour), but the awkward location of Taormina's station (a steep 4km below town) is a strong disincentive. If you arrive this way, catch a taxi (€15) or an Interbus coach (€1.90, 10 minutes) up to town.

Catania

📞 095 / POP 311,600

For all the noise, chaos and scruffiness that hit the visitor at first glance, Catania has a strong magnetic pull. This is Sicily at its most youthful, a city packed with cool and gritty bars, abundant energy and an earthy spirit in sharp contrast to Palermo's aristocratic airs.

Catania's historic core is a Unesco-listed wonder, where black-and-white *palazzi* tower over sweeping baroque piazzas. One minute you're scanning the skyline from a dizzying dome, the next perusing contemporary art in an 18th-century convent. Beneath it all are the ancient ruins of a town with over 2700 candles on its birthday cake. Indeed, food is another local forte. This is the home of Sicily's iconic *pasta alla Norma* and the extraordinary La Pescheria market.

Keeping an eye on it all is Catania's skyscraping frenemy, Mt Etna, a powerful presence that adds another layer of intensity and beauty to Sicily's second-biggest city.

🎯 Sights

Piazza del Duomo SQUARE

A Unesco World Heritage Site, Catania's central piazza is a set piece of contrasting lava and limestone, surrounded by buildings in the unique local baroque style and crowned by the grand Cattedrale di Sant'Agata. At its centre stands Fontana dell'Elefante (1736), a naive, smiling black-lava elephant dating from Roman times and surmounted by an improbable Egyptian obelisk. Another fountain at the piazza's southwest corner, Fontana dell'Amenano, marks the entrance to Catania's fish market.

⭐ La Pescheria MARKET

(Via Pardo; ⏰7am-2pm Mon-Sat) Catania's raucous fish market, which takes over the streets behind Piazza del Duomo every workday morning, is pure street theatre. Tables groan under the weight of decapitated swordfish, ruby-pink prawns and trays full of clams, mussels, sea urchins and all manner of mysterious sea life. Fishmongers gut silvery fish and high-heeled housewives step daintily over pools of blood-stained water. It's absolutely riveting. Surrounding the market are a number of good seafood restaurants.

⭐ Teatro Massimo Bellini THEATRE

(📞095 730 61 35, guided tours 344 2249701; www. teatromassimobellini.it; Via Perrotta 12; guided tour adult/child €6/4) Completed in 1890 and made for homegrown composer Vincenzo Bellini, Catania's opera house is suitably lavish, from the stucco-and-marble extravagance of the foyer (dubbed the *ridotto*) to the glory of the theatre itself, wrapped in four tiers of gilded boxes. Its painted ceiling, by Ernesto Bellandi, depicts scenes from four of Bellini's best-known operas. The Associazione Guide Turistiche Catania (www.guidecatania.it; info@ guidecatania.it) runs 45-minute guided tours; email to book a tour and call ahead to confirm times as the theatre isn't always open.

⭐ Monastero delle Benedettine CHURCH

(www.officineculturali.net/benedettine.htm; cnr Via Teatro Greco & Via Crociferi; adult/reduced €5/3; ⏰10am-5pm Tue, Fri & Sat, plus 11am-5pm 1st Sun of the month) The Monastero delle Benedettine covers two adjacent sites: a Benedictine convent and the Chiesa di San Benedetto. Top billing goes to the church, built between 1704 and 1713 and adorned with splendid stucco, marble and a late-18th-century altar made of Sicilian jasper. Standout artworks include Giovanni Tuccari's glorious ceiling frescoes and a graphic depiction of St Agatha being tortured in front of a curious sultan.

Parco Archeologico Greco Romano RUINS

(📞095 715 05 08; Via Vittorio Emanuele II 262; adult/reduced incl Casa Liberti €6/3; ⏰9am-7pm) West of Piazza del Duomo lie Catania's most impressive ancient ruins: the remains of a 2nd-century Roman Theatre and its small rehearsal theatre, the Odeon. The ruins are evocatively sited in a crumbling residential neighbourhood, with vine-covered buildings that appear to have sprouted organically from the half-submerged stage. Adjacent to the main theatre is the Casa Liberti (closed Sundays), an elegantly restored 19th-century apartment now home to two millennia worth of artefacts discovered during the excavation of the site.

Cattedrale di Sant'Agata CATHEDRAL

(📞095 32 00 44; Piazza del Duomo; ⏰7am-noon & 4-7pm Mon-Sat, 7.30am-12.30pm & 4.30-7.30pm Sun) Inside the vaulted interior of this cathedral, beyond its impressive marble facade sporting two orders of columns taken from the Roman amphitheatre, lie the relics of the city's patron saint. Its other famous resident

Catania

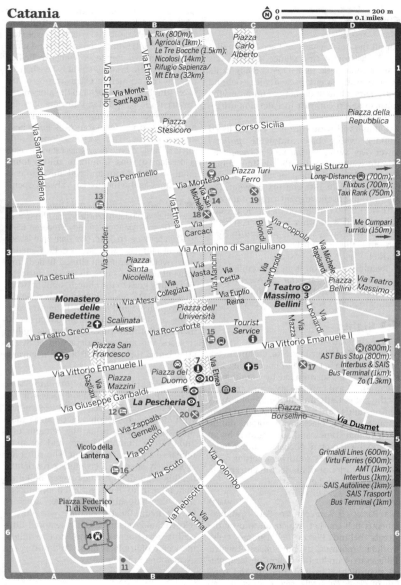

is the world-famous Catanian composer Vincenzo Bellini, his remains transferred here in 1876, 41 years after his death in France. Consider visiting the **Museo Diocesano** (☑ 095 28 16 35; www.museodiocesanocatania. com; Piazza del Duomo; adult/reduced €7/4, incl baths €10/6; ☺9am-2pm Mon, Wed & Fri, to 2pm

& 3-6pm Tue & Thu, to 1pm Sat) next door for access to the Roman baths directly underneath the church.

Castello Ursino CASTLE
(Piazza Federico II di Svevia) Catania's forbidding 13th-century castle once guarded the

Catania

SICILY CATANIA

city from atop a seafront cliff. However, the 1669 eruption of Mt Etna changed the landscape and the whole area to the south was reclaimed by the lava, leaving the castle completely landlocked. The castle now houses the **Museo Civico** (☏095 34 58 30; adult/reduced €6/3; ⊙9am-7pm), home to the valuable archaeological collection of the Biscaris, Catania's most important aristocratic family. Exhibits include colossal classical sculpture, Greek vases and some fine mosaics.

★☆ Festivals & Events

If you're visiting Catania in February or early March, don't miss Carnevale (www.carnevaleacireale.it) in nearby Acireale, one of Sicily's most colourful festivals.

Festa di Sant'Agata   RELIGIOUS
(www.festadisantagata.it; ⊙3-5 Feb) In Catania's biggest religious festival one million people follow the Fercolo (a silver reliquary bust of St Agatha) along the main street of the city. On the evening of 3 February, spectacular fireworks are set to music, with some folk heading into the square early in the afternoon to secure a good vantage point.

⌸ Sleeping

As Sicily's second-largest city, Catania offers a solid range of accommodation options, from chain and boutique hotels to unique B&Bs offering a taste of the city's creative and cultural spirit.

★**Palazzu Stidda**   APARTMENT €
(☏338 6505133, 095 34 88 26; www.palazzustiddacatania.com; Vicolo della Lanterna 2-5; d €80-100, q €140-160, main apt €150-300; 🌬🛜) Creative hosts Giovanni and Patricia Manidoro have poured their hearts into creating these four family-friendly apartments on a peaceful dead-end alley, with all the comforts of home plus a host of whimsical touches. All are decorated with the owners' artwork, handmade furniture, family heirlooms and upcycled vintage finds. The largest apartment, Ammiraglia, accommodates up to eight people, with three bedrooms, a kitchen and lounge.

★**B&B Crociferi**   B&B €
(☏095 715 22 66; www.bbcrociferi.it; Via Crociferi 81; d €75-85, tr €100-110, apt €98-110, ste €120-140; 🌬🛜) Perfectly positioned on pedestrianised Via Crociferi, this B&B in a beautifully decorated family home affords easy access to Catania's historic centre. Three palatial rooms (each with a private, refurbished bathroom across the hall) feature high ceilings, antique tiles, frescoes and artistic accoutrements from the owners' travels. The B&B also houses two apartments, the largest (called Lilla) has a spectacular, leafy panoramic terrace. Book ahead.

B&B Faro   B&B €
(☏349 4578856; www.bebfaro.it; Via San Michele 26; d/tr €80/100, apt €130-150; 🅿🌬🛜) Artist couple Anna and Antonio own this urbane B&B, set in a vibrant quarter dotted with galleries and bohemian bars. Anna's custommade furniture graces the rooms, which

feature double-glazed windows and modern bathroom fixtures. The fabulous apartments offer the convenience of kitchenettes, while the plush communal lounge makes for a wonderful spot to linger. Self check-in and nearby parking (€6) are available.

Ostello degli Elefanti HOSTEL €
(☑ 095 226 56 91; www.ostellodeglielefanti.it; Via Etnea 28; dm €19-26, d €55-70; ❄ 🛜) Housed in a 17th-century *palazzo* a stone's throw from the *duomo*, this clean, friendly hostel offers incredible location and value. Three dorms (one female-only) and one private room have lofty frescoed ceilings and panoramic balconies, with reading lights and curtains for every bed. The marble-floored former ballroom doubles as a lounge, while the rooftop terrace-bar offers incomparable Etna vistas.

★**Asmundo di Gisira** BOUTIQUE HOTEL €€
(☑ 095 097 88 94; www.asmundodigisira.com; Via Gisira 40; d from €125; ❄ 🛜) Not many B&Bs welcome you with a 3m-high pink flamingo at reception, but then this is no ordinary slumber pad. Its six 'Art Rooms' are designed by renowned Italian and international artists, each inspired by local mythological figures. The remaining five rooms find their muse in the 18th-century's Grand Tour era. All are airy, with lofty ceilings, stylish bathrooms and excellent amenities.

✕ Eating

Eating in Catania is a pleasure, whether by market stalls at La Pescheria or on trendy Via Santa Filomena. Classic street food bites include *arancini* (fried rice balls) and *cartocciate* (bread stuffed with ham, mozzarella, olives and tomato).

★**I Dolci di
Nonna Vincenza** SWEETS, GELATO €
(☑ 095 715 18 44; www.dolcinonnavincenza.it; Piazza San Placido 7; cannoli & arancini from €2.30; ⏲ 8.30am-8pm Mon-Sat, 9am-1.30pm Sun; 🚼) Nuns taught a young Nonna Vincenza the art of baking. Today, her fragrant sweets are the stuff of glutinous dreams. Under huge chandeliers, counters gleam with irresistible treats, among them cinnamon- and lemon-flavoured *geli* (jellies) and crisp *cannoli* filled with combos like ricotta and hazelnut. Take-home treats include cult-status *cassatella di Agira,* shortcrust biscuits filled with cocoa, cinnamon, almond and citrus zest.

La Deliziosa SICILIAN €
(☑ 095 668 18 06; www.deliziosacatania.it; Via Crociferi 77; meals €20-25; ⏲ 12.30-4pm & 5.30pm-midnight Tue-Sun; 🛜 🍴) Affable Aurora and Carminia run this adorable little eatery, with alfresco tables on atmospheric Via Crociferi. The weekly-changing menu celebrates regional produce and modern takes on Sicilian cooking, with staples including *facciazza,* a pizza-style concoction topped with uncooked ingredients like tomatoes, cheese and prosciutto. Those wanting to graze can drop in for an afternoon *aperitivo* of Sicilian nibbles, vino, beer and *spritz.*

Agricolab SICILIAN €
(☑ 095 1693 2878; www.agricolab.it; Via F Crispi 258; meals €20-27; ⏲ 12.30-3pm & 6-10.30pm Mon, Wed & Thu, to midnight Fri & Sat, winter times vary; 🛜 🍴 🚼) 🌱 Small Sicilian farms and producers are showcased at this hip, upbeat cafe-bistro, run by Singaporean Fawn and her Sicilian partner Giuseppe. Tuck into anything from sourdough bread with homemade spreads, to Agricolab's signature *pasta aglio e olio* (pasta with olive oil and garlic). Service is friendly, and the option of bar seating makes it perfect for solo diners. Book ahead on weekends.

La Cucina dei Colori VEGETARIAN €
(☑ 095 715 98 93; Via San Michele 9; mixed plates €10-14, meals €20; ⏲ 12.30-3pm & 7.30-11pm, closed Sun mid-Jun–Sep; 🍴 🚼) Take away or dine in at communal tables at this contemporary ode to seasonal, organic, meat-free nosh. Scan the counters for the daily-changing options, which might include wholewheat pasta with artichokes, sautéed seitan (wheat gluten) with vegetables, or an egg, vegetable and *caciocavallo* cheese flan. Vegan and gluten-free options are available and drinks include organic wines.

★**Mè Cumpari Turiddu** SICILIAN €€
(☑ 095 715 01 42; www.mecumparituriddu.it; Piazza Turi Ferro 36-38; meals €26-40; ⏲ 11.30am-12.30am; 🛜) Old chandeliers, recycled furniture and vintage mirrors exude a nostalgic air at this quirky bistro-restaurant-providore, where tradition and modernity meet to impressive effect. Small producers and Slow Food sensibilities underline sophisticated, classically inspired dishes like ricotta-and-marjoram ravioli in a pork sauce, soothing Ustica lentil stew or a playful 'deconstructed' *cannolo.* There's a fabulous selection of Sicilian cheeses, lighter bistro grub and cakes.

Pescheria Fratelli Vittorio SEAFOOD €€
(☑339 7733890; Via Dusmet 1; meals €25-40; ⏱11.30am-3.30pm & 7pm-midnight Tue-Sun, closed Sun dinner Nov–mid-May) Cats would kill for a table at Fratelli Vittorio, a cult-status eatery whose counter glistens with Catania's freshest fish and seafood. It's not surprising given that co-owner Giovanni is a fishmonger, handpicking the best ingredients from the nearby market. For an overview, order the *degustazione di antipasti del giorno,* or feel the love in the generous *zuppa di pesce* (seafood soup).

Le Tre Bocche SEAFOOD €€
(☑095 53 87 38; Via Ingegnere 11; meals €35-45; ⏱8.30-11.45pm, plus 1-3.30pm Sun) Reservations are essential at this Slow Food–recommended restaurant, which even has its own stand at La Pescheria market. The tasting of antipasti is a non-negotiable feast of fresh, vibrant coastal flavours. If you still have room, opt for a standout *primo* (first course), whether it be spaghetti soaked in sea urchins or squid ink, or perhaps a risotto of courgette and prawns.

🍷 Drinking & Entertainment

Catania has great nightlife. Dozens of cafes and bars dot town. Hubs include Piazza Bellini (a university-student favourite), Via Montesano, Via Santa Filomena, Via Penninello and Via Alessi. Catania's live-music and clubbing scenes are also notable, with regular live acts at many bars, plus dedicated venues serving up top-tier Italian and international names.

★Mercati Generali CLUB
(☑334 9197095, 095 57 14 58; www.mercatigenerali.org; Strada Statale 417, Contrada Lungetto; 9pm-4am Sat; 🛜) The 11km drive southwest of central Catania is worth it: this is one of Sicily's finest clubs, with top-tier Italian and international DJs and live-music acts, plus edgy exhibitions and other cultural events. Then there's the enchanting setting, in a converted 19th-century wine-pressing warehouse, complete with summertime courtyard. Attention to detail extends to the drinks and food, which include decent wood-fired pizzas.

★Bohéme Mixology Bar COCKTAIL BAR
(☑095 250 33 40; www.bohememixologybar.com; Via Montesano 27-29; ⏱7pm-3am; 🛜) There's no drinks list at this intimate cocktail den, decked out in mismatched furniture, gilded mirrors and the odd gramophone. Simply state your flavour and spirit preferences and let the barkeeps work their magic. While the cocktails aren't cheap (€8 to €12), they're better than most local offerings, with everything from the syrups to the grilled pineapple marmalade made from scratch.

★Rix COCKTAIL BAR
(www.facebook.com/ritzcatania; Via Pantano 54; ⏱7pm-1.30am Mon-Sat summer, Tue-Sun winter; 🛜) Svelte, convivial, urbane Rix takes its cocktails seriously. Each is made with passion and precision, from punchy Aviations to a very local Etna Kir (spumante Brut rosé, Etna cherry-liqueur, hazelnut crust). The bar harbours some lesser-known local craft spirits, and almost half of the wines are natural. Food options are seasonal and top notch, with some especially memorable desserts.

★Teatro Massimo Bellini THEATRE
(☑095 730 61 11; www.teatromassimobellini.it; Via Perrotta 12) Catania's premier theatre is named after the city's most famous son, composer Vincenzo Bellini. It's one of Italy's most glorious old theatres, staging annual seasons of world-class opera and classical music, as well as dance performances. Tickets, which are available online, start at around €20 and can rise to over €100 for a seat in the stalls.

ℹ Information

Airport Tourist Office (☑095 723 96 82; www.comune.catania.it/la-citta/turismo; ⏱8am-7pm, 8.30am-1.30pm Sun) In the arrivals hall.

Police (Questura; ☑095 736 71 11; Piazza Santa Nicolella 8) Just off Via Etnea.

Presidio Ospedaliero Garibaldi-Centro (☑095 759 11 11; www.ao-garibaldi.catania.it/presidio-osp-garibaldi; Piazza Santa Maria di Gesù 5) Major hospital with a 24-hour emergency department.

Tourist Office (☑095 742 55 73; www.comune.catania.it/la-citta/turismo; Via Vittorio Emanuele II 172; ⏱8am-7pm Mon-Sat, 8.30am-1.30pm Sun) City-run tourist office just off Piazza del Duomo.

ℹ Getting There & Away

AIR

Catania Fontanarossa (☑095 723 91 11; www.aeroporto.catania.it; 🛜) is located 7km southwest of the city centre. It's Sicily's busiest airport, with regular non-stop connections to major Italian cities and numerous destinations in Europe, as well as to Dubai.

SICILY CATANIA

BOAT

From Catania's **ferry terminal** (Via Dusmet) at the southeast edge of the historic centre, **Grimaldi Lines** (☑ 095 586 22 30; www. grimaldi-lines.com; Via Dusmet) operates overnight ferries to Salerno (passenger/with car from €23/57, 13 hours, one nightly Monday to Saturday).

From May through September, **Virtu Ferries** (☑ 095 703 12 11; www.virtuferries.com) runs daily catamarans from Pozzallo (south of Catania) to Malta (1¾ hours, same-day adult return €90 to €141, open return €118 to €166). Coach transfer between Catania and Pozzallo (€14 each way) adds two hours to the journey. Frequency is reduced from October to April.

BUS

All long-distance buses leave from a **terminal** (Via Archimede) 300m northwest of the train station, with ticket offices across the street on Via D'Amico.

Tickets for SAIS Autolinee, Salemi and Big Bus services can also be purchased at **Nafè** (☑ 095 219 45 50; https://coffeebarnafe.business. site; Piazza Papa Giovanni XXIII 6; ☺ 5.30am-8.30pm, closed Sun winter), a cafe-bar opposite Catania train station. Around the corner from Nafè, **TDS Service** (☑ 095 216 64 54; Via Sturzo 245; ☺ 9am-8pm Mon-Sat) is a good-value, cash-only left-luggage office (per hour/day €2/6). It also sells bus tickets for numerous long-distance bus companies, including SAIS Autolinee.

As a rule, buses are quicker than trains for most destinations.

Interbus (☑ 095 53 27 16; www.interbus.it; Via d'Amico 187) Runs to Syracuse (€6, 1½ hours, 10 to 20 daily), Taormina (€5, 1¼ to two hours, 15 to 20 daily), Ragusa (€8.50, two hours, eight to 14 daily) and Piazza Armerina (€9, 1¾ hours, two to six daily).

SAIS Autolinee (☑ 800 211020, 095 53 61 68; www.saisautolinee.it; Via d'Amico 181) Serves Palermo (€14, 2¾ hours, 10 to 14 daily).

SAIS Trasporti (☑ 090 601 21 36; www.sais trasporti.it; Via d'Amico 181) Runs to numerous destinations, including Agrigento (€13.50, three hours, 10 to 14 daily) and overnight to Rome (€44, one daily, 10½ hours).

Flixbus (https://global.flixbus.com; Via d'Amico) Operates direct long-distance buses from Catania to Italian mainland destinations, including Taranto (from €20, 7½ hours, one daily), Bari (from €23, eight to nine hours, twice daily) and Naples (from €26, 8½ to nine hours, twice daily).

CAR & MOTORCYCLE

Catania is easily reached from Messina on the A18 *autostrada* as well as from Palermo on the A19. From the *autostrada*, signs for the city centre direct you to Via Etnea.

TRAIN

Frequent trains depart from Catania Centrale station on Piazza Papa Giovanni XXIII. Destinations include Messina (€7.50, 1¼ to 2¼ hours), Syracuse (€7, one to 1½ hours) and Palermo (€13.50, three hours). Train services are significantly reduced on Sunday.

❶ Getting Around

TO/FROM THE AIRPORT

Shuttle-bus service **Alibus** (www.amt.ct.it; 🕿) runs to the airport from numerous stops in central Catania, including the train station (€4, 20 to 30 minutes, every 25 minutes). Tickets can be purchased on board using cash (carry the correct change) or credit card. A taxi will cost around €20 to €26. All major car hire companies have offices at the airport.

CAR & MOTORCYCLE

Driving in Catania is challenging due to limited parking and a complicated system of one-way streets. If you're bringing your own vehicle, consider a hotel or B&B with parking facilities; if you're hiring a car, you're best advised to pick up the car as you leave town and return it when you re-enter.

PUBLIC TRANSPORT

Several useful **AMT** (☑ 800 018696, 095 751 91 11; www.amt.ct.it) city bus routes terminate in front of Catania Centrale train station, including bus 2-5, which runs every 10 to 40 minutes from the station west to Via Etnea and southwest to Piazza Borsellino (just south of the Cattedrale di Sant'Agata). Also useful is bus D, which runs every 50 minutes from Piazza Borsellino to the local beaches south of the centre. Tickets, available from *tabacchi* (tobacconists), cost €1 and last 90 minutes. All-day tickets are also available (€2.50).

Catania's one-line metro currently has 11 stops, all on the periphery of the city centre. For tourists, it's mainly useful as a way of getting from Catania Centrale station to the Circumetnea train that circles Mt Etna. A 90-minute metro ticket costs €1. A two-hour combined metro-bus ticket costs €1.20.

TAXI

For a taxi, call **Radio Taxi Catania** (☑ 095 33 09 66; www.radiotaxicatania.org). You'll find taxi ranks at the train station and at the northwest corner of Piazza del Duomo.

Mt Etna

ELEV 3326M

Dominating the landscape of eastern Sicily, Mt Etna is a massive brooding presence. At 3326m it is Italy's highest mountain south of the Alps and the largest active volcano in Europe. It's in an almost constant state of activity and eruptions occur frequently, most spectacularly from the four summit craters, but more often, and more dangerously, from the fissures and old craters on the mountain's flanks. This activity, which is closely monitored by 120 seismic activity stations and satellites, means that it is occasionally closed to visitors. The park's varied landscape ranges from the severe, snowcapped mountaintop to lunar deserts of barren black lava, beech woods and lush vineyards where the area's highly rated DOC wine is produced.

◉ Sights & Activities

The southern approach to Mt Etna presents the easier ascent to the **craters**. The AST bus from Catania drops you off at **Rifugio Sapienza** (1923m) from where the **Funivia dell'Etna** (☑095 91 41 41; www.funiviaetna.com; return adult/child €30/23, incl bus & guide adult/child €65/48; ⊙9am-4pm) cable car runs up the mountain to 2500m. Once you're out of the cable car you can attempt the long walk (3½ to four hours return) up the winding track to the authorised crater area (2920m). Alternatively, you can opt for a 4x4 minibus to take you up to (and back down from) the crater area; the minibus option includes a 40-minute guided tour of the crater area. If you plan on walking up to the crater, make sure you leave yourself enough time to get up and down before the last cable car.

The gateway to Etna's quieter and more picturesque northern slopes is **Piano Provenzana** (1800m), a small ski station about 16km upslope from Linguaglossa. Further down the volcano, there's lovely summer walking in the pine, birch and larch trees of the **Pineta Ragabo**, a vast wood accessible from the Mareneve road between Linguaglossa and Milo. Note that you'll need your own car to get to Piano Provenzana and the Pineta Ragabo, as no public transport passes this way.

SICILY MT ETNA

DON'T MISS

SAVOURING ETNA: WINE & HONEY TASTING

Mt Etna's rich volcanic soils produce some of Italy's finest wines. This is the home of Etna DOC, one of 23 Sicilian wines to carry the Denominazione di Origine Controllata denomination. While there are numerous wineries offering wine degustations, many (including those listed below) require that you book at least a day ahead.

Among the area's standout wineries is **Planeta Feudo di Mezzo** (☑0925 195 54 60; https://planeta.it; Contrada Sciara Nuova, Passopisciaro), a highly acclaimed estate located 3.2km southwest of Passopisciaro. Wine degustations take place in a historic pressing room, with a tasting of five wines (€30 per person) including samples of typical local bites. A lunch of traditional recipes (€55 to €65) is also available.

For an especially intimate winery experience, make time for **Cantina Malopasso** (☑393 9728960; www.cantinamalopasso.it; Via Sguazzera 25, Zafferana Etnea). Just south of Zafferana Etnea on Etna's eastern flank, its young, talented winemakers are making waves with nuanced, small-batch wines, often blended with less-common local varietals. Degustations (€22, with a first course €27) are offered from mid-April to December.

Zafferana Etnea itself has a long tradition of apiculture, producing up to 35% of Italy's honey. For a taste, visit **Oro d'Etna** (☑095 708 14 11; www.orodetna.it; Via San Giacomo 135, Zafferana Etnea; ⊙8.30am-6.30pm), where you can try honey made from the blossoms of orange, chestnut and lemon trees.

The **Treno dei Vini dell'Etna** (Etna Wine Train; ☑392 6263404; www.stradadelvinodell etna.it/treno-vino-etna; train & tour adult €80, 11-17yr €40, 4-10yr €35) offers a handy way to explore Etna's wineries without a car. The train runs on selected dates from May to October, leaving Riposto train station at 9.15am and arriving in Randazzo at 10.24am. From here, a 'Wine Bus' service continues to a couple of wineries and towns on Etna's northern slopes. The tour includes wine tastings.

☞ Tours

Many operators offer guided tours up to the craters and elsewhere on the mountain. Tours typically involve some walking and 4WD transport. Recommended operators include Etna Guided Tours (☑ 340 5780924; www.facebook.com/EtnaGuidedTours), Gruppo Guide Alpine Etna Nord (☑ 348 0125167, 095 777 45 02; www.guidetnanord.com; Via Roma 81-83, Linguaglossa), Gruppo Guide Alpine Etna Sud (☑ 389 3496086, 095 791 47 55; www.etna guide.eu) and Etna Experience (☑ 349 3053021, 347 6620341; www.etnaexperience.com; Piazza Federico di Svevia 32). Etna Touring (☑ 095 791 80 00; www.etnatouring.com; Via Roma 1, Nicolosi) also offers guided mountain bike tours.

🛏 Sleeping & Eating

There's plenty of B&B accommodation around Mt Etna, particularly in the small, pretty town of Nicolosi.

Shalai   BOUTIQUE HOTEL €€
(☑ 095 64 31 28; www.shalai.it; Via Marconi 25, Linguaglossa; d €162-200, d with frescoed ceiling €247-285; ⊖ restaurant 7.30-10.30pm daily, plus 1-2.30pm Sat & Sun; P✳☎) After a day tackling Etna, retreat to this luxe spa hotel. Softly lit and in muted shades, the hotel's 13 rooms are minimalist and contemporary, with crisp white linen, flowing drapes, designer lighting and (in rooms 101 and 102) original frescoed ceilings. Then there's the stucco-adorned 19th-century lounge, the candlelit spa (for that post-trek massage), bar and fine-dining, Michelin-starred restaurant. Bliss.

★ Monaci delle
Terre Nere   BOUTIQUE HOTEL €€€
(☑ 095 708 36 38; www.monacidelleterrenere.it; Via Monaci, Zafferana Etnea; d from €360; P✳☎) 🖉 This is one of Sicily's top boutique hotels, set in a winery on Mt Etna's eastern flank, halfway between Catania and Taormina. The 27 rooms and suites – spread between a main villa and outbuildings – impeccably balance rustic architectural elements with contemporary artworks, designer furniture and antiques. Bathroom amenities are chemical-free, and the fabulous in-house restaurant serves plenty of homegrown and organic produce.

★ Cave Ox   SICILIAN €€
(☑ 0942 98 61 71; www.caveox.it; Via Nazionale Solicchiata 159, Solicchiata; meals €25-30, pizzas €5-10; ⊖noon-3.30pm & 7-11pm Wed-Mon) Modest Cave Ox is a fabulous spot to sample local produce, including *salumi* (charcuterie) made from local black pigs. Whether it's a bowl of carbonara tweaked with speck and asparagus, or spectacular pork and wild-fennel sausages, the dishes burst with flavour. Pizzas are available in the evenings and owner Sandro Dibella's impressive wine cellar includes his own collaboration with maverick local winemaker Frank Cornelissen.

ℹ Information

Nicolosi Tourist Office (☑ 095 91 44 88; Piazza Vittorio Emanuele 32, Nicolosi; ⊖9am-1pm daily, plus 4-6pm Wed & Thu) In central Nicolosi on Etna's southern side.

Parco dell'Etna (☑ 095 91 44 88; www. parcoetna.ct.it; Via del Convento 45, Nicolosi; ⊖9am-1.30pm Mon-Fri, also 4-6pm Wed & Thu) Offers specialist information about Mt Etna, including climbing and hiking information. About 1.3km north of the centre of Nicolosi.

Proloco Linguaglossa (☑ 095 64 30 94; Piazza Annunziata 5, Linguaglossa; ⊖9am-1pm & 4-7pm Mon-Sat, 9am-noon Sun) In central Linguaglossa on Etna's northern side.

ℹ Getting There & Away

BUS
AST (☑ 095 723 05 11; www.azienda sicilianatrasporti.it) runs daily buses from Catania to Rifugio Sapienza (one-way/return €3.40/6.50, two hours). Buses leave from the car park opposite Catania's train station at 8.15am, travelling via Nicolosi. The bus back to Catania departs Rifugio Sapienza at 4.30pm, arriving in Catania at 6.30pm.

CAR & MOTORCYCLE
Nicolosi is about 17km northwest of Catania on the SP10. From Nicolosi it's a further 18km up to Rifugio Sapienza. For Linguaglossa, take the A18 *autostrada* from Catania, exit at Fiumefreddo and follow the SS120 towards Randazzo.

TRAIN
Slow train **Ferrovia Circumetnea** (FCE; ☑ 095 54 11 11; www.circumetnea.it; Via Caronda 352a, Catania) follows a 114km route around the base of the volcano from Catania to Riposto, stopping at various small towns along the way. Most trains terminate at Randazzo (two hours, one-way/return €5.50/9) in the mountain's northern reaches.

SOUTHEASTERN SICILY

Sicily's southeast is the island at its most seductive. This is the cinematic *Sicilia* of TV series *Inspector Montalbano*, a swirl of luminous baroque hill towns, sweeping topaz beaches and olive-laden hillsides luring everyone from French artists to Milanese moguls in search of new beginnings.

The region's coastal protagonist is Syracuse (Siracusa), where Graeco-Roman ruins meet magnificent piazzas, boutique-studded side streets and crystalline waves. To the southwest lies the undulating Val di Noto, its string of late-baroque towns the most beautiful in Sicily. Noto, Modica, Ragusa and Scicli are the fairest of them all, each one a feast of architectural flourishes and gastronomic delights, from artisanal gelato and chocolate to Michelin-star-spangled chefs.

Then there is the region's countryside, a sun-bleached canvas of sleepy back roads lined with carob trees, rocky ravines pierced with prehistoric tombs, and rugged coastline dotted with crumbling *tonnare* (tuna fisheries), Mediterranean herbs and precious, migratory birdlife.

Syracuse

📞 0931 / POP 121,600

More than any other city, Syracuse (Siracusa) encapsulates Sicily's timeless beauty. Ancient Greek ruins rise out of lush citrus orchards, cafe tables spill onto dazzling baroque piazzas, and honey-hued medieval side streets lead down to the sparkling blue sea. It's difficult to imagine now, but in its heyday this was the largest city in the ancient world, bigger even than Athens and Corinth. Its 'once upon a time' begins in 734 BC, when Corinthian colonists landed on the island of Ortygia (Ortigia) and founded the settlement, setting up the mainland city four years later. Almost three millennia later, the ruins of that then-new city constitute the Parco Archeologico della Neapolis, one of Sicily's greatest archaeological sites. Across the water from the mainland, Ortygia remains Syracuse's most beautiful corner, a deeply atmospheric quarter with an ever-growing legion of fans enamoured with its beautiful streetscapes and attractive dining, drinking and shopping options.

👁 Sights

Syracuse's showpiece square, Piazza del Duomo, is a masterpiece of baroque town planning. A long, rectangular piazza flanked by flamboyant *palazzi,* it sits on what was once Syracuse's ancient acropolis (fortified citadel).

👁 Ortygia

⭐ Duomo   CATHEDRAL
(Map p866; Piazza del Duomo; adult/reduced €2/1; ⊙ 9am-6.30pm Mon-Sat Apr-Oct, to 5.30pm Nov-Mar) Built on the skeleton of a 5th-century BC Greek temple to Athena (note the Doric columns still visible inside and out), Syracuse's 7th-century cathedral became a church when the island was evangelised

---

DON'T MISS

LA GIUDECCA

Simply walking through Ortygia's tangled maze of nougat-coloured alleys is an atmospheric experience, especially down the narrow streets of Via della Maestranza, the heart of the old guild quarter, and the gentrifying Jewish ghetto of Via della Giudecca. At the Alla Giudecca hotel you can visit an ancient Jewish miqwe (Ritual Bath; Map p866; 📞 0931 2 14 67; Via Alagona 52; tours €5; ⊙ tours 10am-6pm May-Oct, reduced hours rest of year) some 20m below ground level. Blocked up in 1492 when the Jewish community was expelled from Ortygia, the baths were rediscovered during renovation work at the hotel.

A short walk away, Syracuse's much-loved puppet theatre, the Teatro dei Pupi (Map p866; 📞 0931 46 55 40; www.teatrodeipupisiracusa.it; Via della Giudecca 22; ⊙ 6 times weekly Mar-Jul, Sep & Oct, 6 to 18 times weekly Aug, fewer Nov-Feb), stages puppet shows re-enacting traditional tales involving magicians, love-struck princesses, knights and dragons. Just down the road, the small Museo dei Pupi (Map p866; 📞 328 5326600; www.museodeipupisiracusa.it; Palazzo Midiri-Cardona, Piazza San Giuseppe; adult/reduced €3/2; ⊙ 11am-1pm & 2-7pm Mon-Sat Mar-Nov) chronicles Sicily's rich history of puppet theatre.

Ortygia

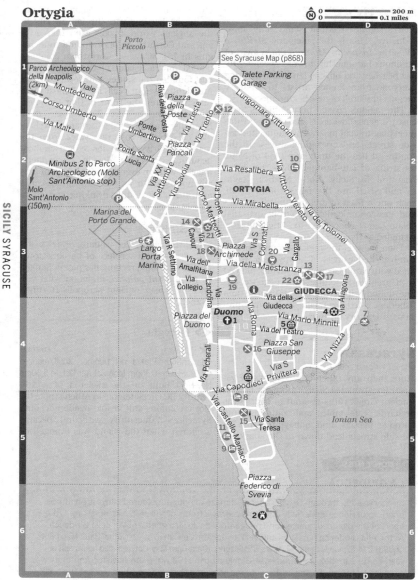

See Syracuse Map (p868)

by St Paul. Its most striking feature is the columned baroque facade (1728–53) added by Andrea Palma after the 1693 earthquake. A statue of the Virgin Mary crowns the rooftop, in the same spot where a golden statue of Athena once served as a beacon to homecoming Greek sailors.

Castello Maniace CASTLE
(Map p866; Piazza Federico di Svevia; adult/reduced €4/2; ⏱2.30-6.45pm Mon, 8.30am-1pm Tue-Fri & Sun, 8.30am-6.45pm Sat Apr-Sep, reduced hours rest of year) Guarding the island's southern tip, Ortygia's 13th-century castle is an evocative place to wander, gaze out over the

Ortygia

SICILY SYRACUSE

water and contemplate Syracuse's past glories. Built for Emperor Frederick II, it's an important example of Swabian (German) architecture, with a magnificent, vaulted central hall (Sala Ipostila). The grounds house a small antiquarium displaying archaeological objects from the site, including Norman-era ceramics and some curious-looking ceramic hand grenades from the 16th century.

**Galleria Regionale
di Palazzo Bellomo** GALLERY
(Map p866; ☑0931 6 95 11; www.regione.sicilia.it/beniculturali/palazzobellomo; Via Capodieci 16; adult/reduced €8/4; ⊙9am-7pm Tue-Sat, to 1.30pm Sun) Housed in a 13th-century Catalan-Gothic palace, this art museum's eclectic collection ranges from early Byzantine and Norman stonework to 19th-century Caltagirone ceramics. In between there's a good range of medieval sculpture, as well as medieval, Renaissance and baroque religious paintings. Among the latter is *Annunciation* (1474), executed by Sicily's greatest 15th-century artist, Antonella da Messina. The museum also claims a couple of storybook 18th-century Sicilian carriages.

⊙ Mainland Syracuse

★ **Parco Archeologico
della Neapolis** ARCHAEOLOGICAL SITE
(Map p868; ☑0931 6 62 06; Viale Paradiso 14; adult/reduced €10/5, incl Museo Archeologico €13.50/7; ⊙8.30am-1hr before sunset) For the classicist, Syracuse's real attraction is this archaeological park, home to the pearly **Teatro Greco**. Constructed in the 5th century BC and rebuilt in the 3rd century, the 16,000-capacity amphitheatre staged the last tragedies of Aeschylus (including *The Persians*), first performed here in his presence. From early May to early July it's brought to life with an annual season of classical theatre.

Beside the theatre is the mysterious **Latomia del Paradiso** (Garden of Paradise), a deep, precipitous limestone quarry out of which stone for the ancient city was extracted. Riddled with catacombs and filled with citrus and magnolia trees, it's also where the 7000 survivors of the war between Syracuse and Athens in 413 BC were imprisoned. The **Orecchio di Dionisio** (Ear of Dionysius), a 23m-high grotto extending 65m back into the cliffside, was named by Caravaggio after the tyrant Dionysius, who is said to have used the almost perfect acoustics of the quarry to eavesdrop on his prisoners.

Back outside this area you'll find the entrance to the 2nd-century **Anfiteatro Romano**, originally used for gladiatorial combats and horse races. The Spaniards, little interested in archaeology, largely destroyed the site in the 16th century, using it as a quarry to build Ortygia's city walls. West of the amphitheatre is the 3rd-century-BC **Ara di Gerone II** (Altar of Hieron II), a monolithic sacrificial altar to Hieron II, where up to 450 oxen could be killed at one time.

To reach the park, take Sd'A Trasporti minibus 2 (€1, 15 minutes) from Molo

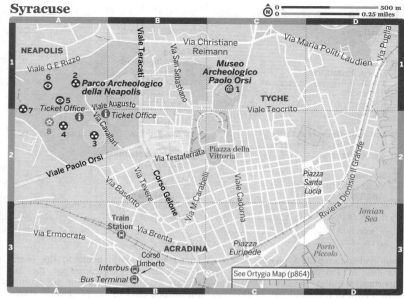

Syracuse

◎ Top Sights
1 Museo Archeologico Paolo Orsi..........	C1
2 Parco Archeologico della Neapolis...	A1

◎ Sights
3 Anfiteatro Romano...............................	A2
4 Ara di Gerone II	A2
5 Latomia del Paradiso	A1
6 Orecchio di Dionisio...........................	A1
7 Teatro Greco	A2

◎ Entertainment
8 Fondazione Inda Ticket Booth............	A2

Sant'Antonio, on the west side of the main bridge into Ortygia; purchase tickets on-board. Alternatively, walking from Ortygia will take about 30 minutes. If driving, there is limited free parking on Viale Augusto.

There are two ticket offices here: one office is located near the corner of Via Cavallari and Viale Augusto, opposite the main site, while the second outlet is located down the path leading to the actual ruins. Those wanting a break will find a cafe between the second ticket office and the Anfiteatro Romano.

★ **Museo Archeologico Paolo Orsi**   MUSEUM
(Map p868; ☑0931 48 95 11; www.regione.sicil ia.it/beniculturali/museopaoloorsi; Viale Teocrito 66; adult/reduced €8/4, incl Parco Archeologico €13.50/7; ☉9am-6pm Tue-Sat, to 1pm Sun) Located about 500m east of the archaeological park, Syracuse's archaeological museum claims one of Sicily's largest and most interesting collections of antiquities. Allow at least a couple of hours to investigate its various sprawling sections, which chart the area's prehistory, as well as the city's development from foundation to the late Roman period.

🏃 Activities

The **Forte Vigliena** (Map p866; Via Nizza) swimming platform, flanked by crenellated walls along Ortygia's eastern waterfront, is a favourite summertime hangout for swimming and sunbathing. Serious beach bunnies make the short trip south to **Lido Arenella** (Traversa Arenella), where sandy beaches await. In summer, **Compagnia del Selene** (Map p866; ☑347 1275680; www.com pagniadelselene.it; Foro Vittorio Emanuele II; 50min tour per adult/under 10yr €10/free) offers scenic sailing trips around Ortygia.

✦✦✦ Festivals & Events

★ Festival del Teatro Greco   THEATRE
(Festival of Greek Theatre; www.indafondazione.org;
☺ mid-May–early Jul) Syracuse claims the only
school of classical Greek drama outside Athens, and from early May to early July it hosts
live performances of Greek plays (in Italian)
at the Teatro Greco, attracting Italy's finest
performers. Tickets (from around €29 to
€55) are available online, from the **Fondazione Inda ticket office** (Map p866; ☎ office
0931 48 72 48, tickets 800 542644; www.indafon
dazione.org; Corso Matteotti 29; ☺ 10am-1pm Mon-
Sat) in Ortygia or at the **ticket booth** (Map
p868; ☎ 800 542644; ☺ 10am-5pm Mon, to 7pm
Tue-Sun) outside the theatre.

★ Ortigia Sound System   MUSIC
(www.ortigiasoundsystem.com; ☺ Jul) One of Sicily's top music festivals, OSS takes over Ortygia with five summery days of electronic
music spanning various styles. Events take
place across the island, with boat parties
and a stellar lineup of top-tier Italian and international artists. Past guests have included
Virgil Abloh (US), Danielle (UK) and Italy's
own 'Father of Disco' Giorgio Moroder.

🛏 Sleeping

The best place to slumber is on the atmospheric island of Ortygia, the historic heart
of Syracuse. Here you'll find everything
from boutique hotels to atmospheric B&Bs
and beautiful self-contained apartments in
historic *palazzi*.

B&B Aretusa Vacanze   B&B €
(Map p866; ☎ 0931 48 34 84; www.aretusava
canze.com; Vicolo Zuccalà 1; d €59-90, tr €70-120,

q €105-147; P ❄ 🛜) This great, family-run
budget option, elbowed into a tiny pedestrian street in a 17th-century building, has
large rooms and apartments with comfortable beds, kitchenettes and satellite TV. The
recently refurbished bathrooms feature
spacious showers and three of the 11 rooms
come with small balconies. Parking costs
€15 per day.

B&B dei Viaggiatori,
Viandanti e Sognatori   B&B €
(Map p866; ☎ 0931 2 47 81; www.bedandbreak
fastsicily.it; Via Roma 156; d €55-70, tr €70-80;
❄ 🛜) Enjoying a prime Ortygia location,
this relaxed, TV-free B&B exudes an easy,
boho vibe. It's a homely place, where books
and antiques mingle with the owners' children's toys. Rooms are simple yet imagina-
tively decorated, and the sunny roof terrace
– complete with sweeping sea views – is a
fine place for breakfast-time organic bread
and marmalade.

★ Hotel Gutkowski   HOTEL €€
(Map p866; ☎ 0931 46 58 61; www.guthotel.it;
Lungomare Vittorini 26; d €90-150, tr €150, q €160;
❄ 🛜) Book well in advance for one of the
sea-view rooms at this stylish, eclectic hotel
on the Ortygia waterfront, at the edge of the
Giudecca neighbourhood. Divided between
two buildings, its rooms are simple yet chic,
with pretty tiled floors, walls in teals, greys,
blues and browns, and a sharply curated
mix of vintage and industrial details.

Palazzo Blanco   APARTMENT €€€
(Map p866; ☎ 342 7672092; www.casedisicilia.com;
Via Castello Maniace; small apt per night €210-240,
large apt per night €230-260; ❄ 🛜) Two elegant

SICILY SYRACUSE

WORTH A TRIP

NECROPOLI DI PANTALICA

On a huge plateau above the Valle dell'Anapo, the **Necropoli di Pantalica** `FREE` is
Sicily's most important Iron and Bronze Age necropolis, with more than 5000 tombs of
various shapes and sizes honeycombed along the limestone cliffs. The site is incredibly
ancient, dating to between the 13th and 8th centuries BC, and its origins are largely mysterious, although it is thought to be the Siculi capital of Hybla, which gave the Greeks Me-
gara Hyblaea in 664 BC. Enshrined by Unesco as a World Heritage Site, Pantalica's ruins
are surrounded by the beautifully wild and unspoilt landscape of the **Valle dell'Anapo**,
a deep limestone gorge laced with walking trails.

   Maps posted at the archaeological site's entrance allow you to find your way, but the
site is remote, with no services; wear sensible hiking shoes and bring plenty of water.

   You'll need your own wheels to get here. From Syracuse, head northwest on the SS124
towards Palazzolo Acreide. After about 36km, turn right towards Ferla; the Necropoli di
Pantalica is 11km beyond the town.

apartments await in this *palazzo,* owned by a Milanese art collector. The larger apartment is utterly decadent, with luxurious sofas, king-size bed, dining table, precious artworks and stone, vaulted ceiling. There's a sea-view terrace and bathroom with original stonework and hydro-massage shower. The smaller apartment features floor-to-ceiling artwork and a romantic four-poster bed. Both have kitchenettes and can accommodate up to four.

Henry's House   HOTEL €€€

(Map p866; ☑ 0931 2 13 61; www.hotelhenrys house.com; Via del Castello Maniace 68; d €160-300, ste €260-400; ❈ 🕿) This waterfront 17th-century *palazzo* was restored by an antique collector. The period lounge is fabulously aristocratic, while the homely rooms blend antiques and modern art. If money isn't an issue, book one of the two upstairs suites (one with terrace, both with water views). The hotel offers free bike use and, for those who book directly through the hotel website, complimentary minibar.

🍴 Eating

Ortygia is the best place to eat. Its postcard-pretty streets heave with bustling trattorias, fashionable restaurants and cafes. While some are obvious tourist traps, many are not, and you'll have no trouble finding somewhere to suit your style. Expect plenty of seafood pasta and grilled catches of the day.

★Caseificio Borderi   SANDWICHES €

(Map p866; ☑ 329 9852500; www.caseificiobor deri.eu; Via Benedictis 6; sandwiches €6; ⊙ 7am-4pm Mon-Sat) No visit to Syracuse's market is complete without a stop at this colourful deli near Ortygia's far northern tip. Veteran sandwich-master Andrea Borderi stands out front with a table full of cheeses, olives, greens, herbs, tomatoes and other fixings and engages in nonstop banter with customers while creating free-form sandwiches big enough to keep you fed all day.

Fratelli Burgio   SICILIAN €

(Map p866; ☑ 0931 6 00 69; www.fratelliburgio. com; Piazza Cesare Battisti 4; panini €3.50-7.50, platters €12-20; ⊙ 7am-4pm Mon-Sat; 🖉) A hybrid deli, wine shop and eatery edging Ortygia's market, trendy Fratelli Burgio is all about artisanal grazing. Consider opting for a *tagliere,* a wooden platter of artful bites, from cheese, charcuterie and smoked fish,

to zesty *caponata* (sweet-and-sour vegetables). If you're euro-pinching, fill up on one of the gourmet *panini,* stuffed with a range of seasonal veggies, herbs, cured meats and cheeses.

★Moon   VEGAN €€

(Map p866; ☑ 0931 44 95 16; www.moonortigia. com; Via Roma 112; meals €22-30; ⊙ 6-11.30pm Wed-Mon, also open 12.30-3pm Wed-Mon Apr-Jun, Sep & Oct, closed mid-Jan–mid-Mar; 🕿 🖉) This moody, boho-chic restaurant and bar makes vegan food so good even a hardcore carnivore could convert. A cast of mostly organic and biodynamic ingredients beam in balanced, intriguing dishes that might see a tower of thinly sliced pears interlayered with a rich, soy-based cashew cream cheese, or chickpea and tofu conspiring in a smokey carbonara pasta as wicked as the Roman original.

★Sicilia in Tavola   SICILIAN €€

(Map p866; ☑ 392 4610889; www.siciliaintavola. eu; Via Cavour 28; meals €27-40; ⊙ 1-2.30pm & 7.30-10.30pm Tue-Sun) One of the longest established and most popular eateries on Via Cavour, this snug, wonderfully hospitable trattoria has built its reputation on delicious homemade pasta and seafood. To savour both at once, tuck into the *fettuccine allo scoglio* (pasta ribbons with mixed seafood) before sampling *secondi* (mains) like beautifully cooked octopus with chilli, garlic, potatoes and a sublime tomato *sugo.* Reservations recommended.

Retroscena   SICILIAN €€

(Map p866; ☑ 0931 185 42 78; www.facebook.com/ retroscenaristorante; Via della Maestranza 108; meals €40; ⊙ 7.30-11.30pm Mon-Sat summer, to 10.30pm winter; 🕿) After running a restaurant in Greece for 18 years, Syracuse local Fabio and his Greek partner Kiri are pleasing palates at their hotspot Ortygia restaurant. Vintage mirrors, midcentury lighting and velvet in shades of blue and dusty pink set a fashionable scene for creative, rotating options like trofie pasta with pesto, ricotta, sun-dried tomatoes and crispy zucchini ribbons, or mandarin-and-honey glazed prawns.

Il Pesce Azzurro   SEAFOOD €€

(Map p866; ☑ 366 2445056; Via Cavour 53; meals €30-35; ⊙ noon-3.30pm & 6.30-10.30pm) Seafood-loving locals swear by this easy-to-miss *osteria* (casual tavern), its white-and-blue interior somewhat reminiscent of a Greek-island taverna. The menu favours simplicity and top-notch produce, whether it's sweet, succulent Mazara shrimps drizzled in lime juice, plump *vongole* (clams) paired with spaghetti and garlic, or tender *polpo* (octopus) served *alla luciana* (in a rich tomato and onion sauce). Honest, flavour-packed goodness.

La Medusa   SICILIAN €€
(Da Kamel; Map p866; ☑0931 6 14 03; Via Santa Teresa 21-23; meals €26-45; ☉noon-3pm & 7-11pm Tue-Sun) This friendly, family-run spot made its name serving delicious couscous, but chef-owner Kamel also knows his way around a fish – the must-try *fritto misto* (mixed fish fry) is wonderfully light. If there's more than one of you, order the *pasta fibus*, an epic, plate-licking serve of *pennette* pasta with seafood, cherry tomatoes, radicchio and crunchy *pangrattato* (toasted breadcrumbs). Book ahead.

★ Don Camillo   SICILIAN €€€
(Map p866; ☑0931 6 71 33; www.ristorantedon camillo.it; Via della Maestranza 96; meals €45-75; ☉12.30-2.30pm & 8-10.30pm Mon-Sat; ☎☑) One of Ortygia's most elegant restaurants, Don Camillo specialises in sterling service and innovative Sicilian cuisine. Pique the appetite with a *crudo* of crustaceans paired with sweet-and-sour celery gelato, swoon over decadent braised-beef ravioli with butter, sage and *ragusano* cheese, or (discreetly) lick your whiskers over an outstanding *tagliata di tonno* (tuna steak) with red-pepper 'marmalade'. A must for Slow Food gourmands.

🍷 Drinking & Nightlife

A vibrant university and tourist town, Syracuse has a lively bar scene, with cafes, wine bars, pubs and cocktail hotspots spilling over the gorgeous streets of Ortygia.

★ Cortile Verga   COCKTAIL BAR
(Map p866; ☑333 1683212; www.facebook. com/cortilevergaortigia; Via della Maestranza 33; ☉11am-midnight summer, from 5.30pm winter, closed Jan–mid-Mar; ☎) Take an aristocratic courtyard, add an intimate interior kitted out in vintage coffee tables and a Chesterfield lounge, and you have Cortile Verga. This is one of Ortygia's top cocktail bars, crafting top-tier drinks like the Eleutheria, a blend of vermouth, mezcal, *amaro* (Italian herbal liqueur) and hibiscus tonic. While

they're not cheap (€8 to €10), they're a cut above the competition.

Biblios Cafè   CAFE
(Map p866; ☑0931 6 16 27; www.biblioscafe.it; Via del Consiglio Reginale 11; ☉5-11pm Wed-Sat) This beloved bookshop-cafe organises a whole range of cultural activities, including Italian language courses and regular literary events. It's also a great place to drop in for a restorative *caffè* (coffee), an *aperitivo* or simply to mingle.

🛍 Shopping

Browsing Ortygia's quirky boutiques is great fun. Good buys include papyrus paper, ceramics and handmade jewellery. You'll find a concentration of interesting boutiques and galleries on Via Cavour, Via Roma and Via della Giudecca.

❶ Information

Hospital (Ospedale Umberto I; ☑emergency department 0931 72 42 85, switchboard 0931 72 41 11; www.asp.sr.it/default.asp?id=424; cnr Via Testaferrata & Corso Gelone) Located just east of the Parco Archeologico.

Tourist Office (Map p866; ☑800 055500; www.provincia.siracusa.it; Via Roma 31; ☉7.30am-2pm Mon, Tue, Thu & Fri, to 4.30pm Wed) Offers a free city map and small selection of brochures.

❶ Getting There & Away

Syracuse's train and bus stations are a block apart from each other, halfway between Ortygia and the Parco Archeologico.

BUS
Buses are generally faster and more convenient than trains, with long-distance buses arriving and departing from the **bus terminal** (Map p868; Corso Umberto I), 180m southeast of the train station.

Interbus (Map p868; ☑091 611 95 35; www. interbus.it) runs buses to Catania (€6.20, 1½ hours, one to two hourly) and its airport, Noto (€3.60, 55 minutes, three to seven daily) and Palermo (€13.50, 3½ hours, two to three daily). Tickets can be purchased at the bus station ticket kiosk.

SAIS Autolinee (☑091 617 11 41; www.sais trasporti.it) runs an overnight service to Rome (€41, 12 hours, one nightly) and both daytime and overnight services to Bari (€40, 9½ to 11 hours, one to two daily). Purchase tickets from the train station *edicola* (newsagent).

Flixbus (https://global.flixbus.com) runs direct buses from Syracuse to numerous destinations on the Italian mainland, including Taranto (from €26, nine hours, one daily), Bari (from €26, 10½ hours, one nightly) and Naples (from €28, 10¼ hours, one nightly). Buy tickets on the Flixbus website.

CAR & MOTORCYCLE

The dual-carriageway SS114 heads north from Syracuse to Catania, while the SS115 runs south to Noto and Modica. While the approach roads to Syracuse are rarely very busy, traffic gets increasingly heavy as you enter town and can be pretty bad in the city centre.

If you're staying in Ortygia, the best place to park is the **Talete parking garage** (Parcheggio Talete; ☑ 0931 46 32 89) on Ortygia's northern tip, which charges a 24-hour maximum of €10 (payable by cash or credit card at the machine).

Note that most of Ortygia is a limited traffic zone, restricted to residents and those with special permission. On-street parking is hard to find during the week, less so on Sunday when it's often free.

TRAIN

From Syracuse's **train station** (Via Francesco Crispi), trains depart daily for Catania (€6.90, one to 1½ hours, 12 daily Monday to Saturday, six Sunday) and Messina (from €10.50, 2½ to 3¼ hours, 11 daily Monday to Saturday, five Sunday). Some go on to mainland Italy. Note that passengers travelling from Syracuse to Messina may need to change at Catania Centrale station.

There are also trains to Noto (€3.80, 30 to 45 minutes, seven daily Monday to Friday, six Saturday), Scicli (€6.90, 1½ to 1¾ hours, six daily Monday to Friday, five Saturday), Modica (€7.60, 1¾ to two hours, six daily Monday to Friday, five Saturday) and Ragusa (€8.30, 2¼ hours, five daily Monday to Friday, four Saturday).

❶ Getting Around

Siracusa d'Amare Trasporti (☑ 0931 175 62 32; 90min ticket €1) runs inexpensive electric minibuses around Syracuse and Ortygia. To reach Ortygia from the bus and train stations, catch **minibus 1**. To reach the Parco Archeologico della Neapolis, take **minibus 2** (Map p866) from Molo Sant'Antonio (just west of the bridge to Ortygia). Buses run every 20 minutes between 8am and 8pm from March to June and every 30 minutes between 9am and 9pm from July to December. Tickets can be purchased on board. Be warned that during the Ciclo di Rappresentazioni Classiche (p869) festival, minibus 2 can get extremely crowded, with lengthy delays.

Noto

☑ 0931 / POP 24,000 / ELEV 152M

Noto is an architectural supermodel, a baroque belle so gorgeous you might mistake it for a film set. Located less than 40km southwest of Syracuse, the town is home to one of Sicily's most beautiful historic centres. The pièce de résistance is Corso Vittorio Emanuele, an elegant walkway flanked by thrilling baroque *palazzi* and churches. Dashing at any time of the day, it's especially hypnotic in the early evening, when the red-gold buildings seem to glow with a soft inner light.

The Noto you see today dates to the early 18th century, when it was almost entirely rebuilt in the wake of the devastating 1693 earthquake. Creator of many of the finest buildings was Rosario Gagliardi, a local architect whose extroverted style also graces churches in Modica and Ragusa.

◉ Sights

About halfway along Corso Vittorio Emanuele is the graceful Piazza Municipio, flanked by Noto's cathedral and a series of elegant palaces, including Palazzo Landolina and Palazzo Ducezio (☑ 0931 83 64 62; www.comune.noto.sr.it/la-cultura/la-sala-degli -specchi; Sala degli Specchi €2, panoramic terrace €2; ☉ 10am-8pm).

Further west, Piazza XVI Maggio is overlooked by the beautiful Chiesa di San Domenico (☑ 327 0162589; www.oqdany.it; church free, guided tour of crypt €2; ☉ 10am-2pm & 4.30-9pm Jul & Aug, 10am-6pm Sep-Jun) and the adjacent Dominican monastery, both designed by Rosario Gagliardi. On the same square, Noto's elegant 19th-century Teatro Tina di Lorenzo (Teatro Vittorio Emanuele; ☑ 0931 83 50 73; www.fondazioneteatrodinoto.it; general visit €2, theatre tickets adult/reduced from €10/8; ☉ general visits 10am-6pm) is worth a look.

For sweeping views of Noto's baroque splendour, climb to the rooftop terrace at Chiesa di Santa Chiara (Corso Vittorio Emanuele; adult/reduced €2/1; ☉ 10.30am-1pm & 2.30-4pm) or the campanile (bell tower) of Chiesa di San Carlo al Corso (Corso Vittorio Emanuele; campanile €2; ☉ 10am-10pm Jul & Aug, to 8pm May, Jun & Sep, reduced hours rest of year).

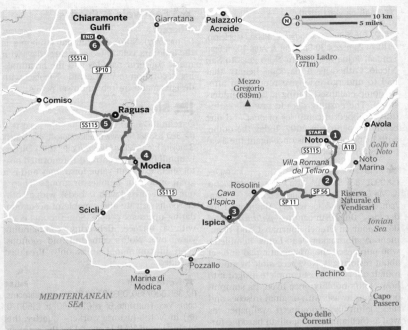

Driving Tour
Baroque Towns

START NOTO
END CHIARAMONTE GULFI
LENGTH 71KM; TWO DAYS

A land of remote rocky gorges, sweeping views and silent valleys, Sicily's southeastern corner is home to the 'baroque triangle', an area of Unesco-listed hilltop towns famous for their lavish baroque architecture. This tour takes in some of the finest, all within easy driving distance of each other.

Just over 35km south of Syracuse, **1 Noto** is home to what is arguably Sicily's most beautiful street – Corso Vittorio Emanuele, a pedestrianised boulevard lined with golden baroque *palazzi*. It's also home to a number of culinary hotspots, among them Ristorante Vicari and Manna. From Noto, head south along SP19, quickly pop into **2 Villa Romana del Tellaro** (☎0931 57 38 83; www.villaromanadeltellaro.com; ☺8.30am-7.30pm, last entry 6pm) **FREE** to admire its Roman mosaics. Continue on to Ispica, a hilltop town overlooking a huge canyon, **3 Cava d'Ispica** (☎0932 95 26 08; www.cavadispica.org; Crocevia Cava Ispica; adult/ reduced €4/2; ☺9am-6.30pm May-Oct, to 1.15pm Mon-Sat Nov & Dec), riddled with prehistoric tombs. Follow the SS115 for a further 18km to **4 Modica** (p875), a bustling town set in a deep rocky gorge. There's excellent accommodation and great restaurants, so it's a good place to stay overnight. The best of the baroque sights are up in Modica Alta, the high part of town, but make sure you have energy left for the *passeggiata* on Corso Umberto I and dinner at Accursio, Cappero or Ornato.

Next morning, a short, winding, up-and-down drive through rock-littered hilltops leads to **5 Ragusa** (p878). The town is divided in two – Ragusa Ibla is a claustrophobic warren of grey stone houses and elegant *palazzi* that opens up onto Piazza Duomo, a superb example of 18th-century town planning. Consider lunching at casual standout I Banchi, or save your appetite for **6 Chiaramonte Gulfi**, a tranquil hilltop town some 20km to the north along the SP10. Dubbed the Balcone della Sicilia (Sicily's Balcony) for its breathtaking panorama, it's famous for its coveted olive oil and blue-ribbon pork, the latter best savoured at Ristorante Majore.

★ Basilica Cattedrale di San Nicolò
CATHEDRAL

(☎327 0162589; www.oqdany.it; Piazza Municipio; ⏱10am-2pm & 4.30-9pm Jul & Aug, 10am-6pm Sep-Jun) Pride of place in Noto goes to San Nicolò Cathedral, a baroque beauty that had to undergo extensive renovation after its dome collapsed during a 1996 thunderstorm. The ensuing decade saw the cathedral scrubbed of centuries of dust and dirt before reopening in 2007. Today the dome, with its peachy glow, is once again the focal point of Noto's skyline.

★ Palazzo Castelluccio
PALACE

(☎0931 83 88 81; http://palazzocastelluccio. it; Via Cavour 10; adult/child €12/free; ⏱11am-7pm, closed Mon & Tue winter) Abandoned for decades, this 18th-century *palazzo* found its saviour in French journalist and documentary filmmaker Jean-Louis Remilleux, who purchased the aristocratic pad and set about restoring it. Now accessible by guided tour, it offers the most complete insight into how Noto's nobility once lived, its sumptuous rooms awash with original frescoes and tiles, faithfully reproduced wallpaper, as well as Sicilian and Neapolitan baroque furniture from the owner's collection.

Palazzo Nicolaci di Villadorata
PALACE

(☎338 7427022; www.comune.noto.sr.it/palazzo -nicolaci; Via Corrado Nicolaci; admission €4; ⏱10am-6pm mid-Mar–mid-Oct, 10am-1pm & 3-5pm rest of year) The fantastical facade of this 18th-century palace wows with its wrought-iron balconies, supported by a swirling pantomime of grotesque figures. Inside, the richly brocaded walls and frescoed ceilings offer an idea of the sumptuous lifestyle of Sicilian nobles, as brought to life in the Giuseppe Tomasi di Lampedusa novel *Il Gattopardo* (The Leopard).

Basilica del Santissimo Salvatore
CHURCH

(☎327 0162589; www.oqdany.it; Via Vincenzo Gioberti; ⏱10am-2pm & 4.30-9pm Jul & Aug, 10am-6pm Sep-Jun) Situated towards the grand Porta Reale is the Basilica del Santissimo Salvatore. Its recently restored interior is the most impressive in Noto, crowned by a glorious vault fresco by Antonio Mazza depicting the Holy Spirit's descent. Mazza is also responsible for the church's facade, completed in 1791 and showing influences of a more restrained neoclassical style. The adjoining Benedictine convent offers sweeping views from its bell tower.

★★ Festivals & Events

Infiorata
CARNIVAL

(⏱mid-May) Noto's big annual jamboree is the Infiorata, celebrated over three days with music concerts, parades and the breathtaking decoration of Via Corrado Nicolaci with designs made entirely of flower petals.

🛏 Sleeping

Ostello Il Castello
HOSTEL €

(☎320 8388869; www.ostellodinoto.it; Via Fratelli Bandiera 1; dm €20, s/d €35/70; P※🌐) Directly uphill from the centre, this renovated hostel offers excellent value for money and is a great option for families or groups. There's one dorm (mixed with 18 beds), with all other rooms private and capable of accommodating up to six people. Some rooms come with a terrace, delivering commanding views over Noto's cathedral and rooftops. Wi-fi in communal areas only. Breakfast included.

★ Nòtia Rooms
B&B €€

(☎366 5007350, 0931 83 88 91; www.notiarooms. com; Vico Frumento 6; d €130-150, tr €150-170; 🌐) In Noto's historic workers' quarter, this sophisticated B&B is owned by the gracious Giorgio and Carla, who gave up the stress of northern Italian life to open this three-room beauty. Crisp white interiors are accented with original artworks, Modernist Italian lamps and upcycled vintage finds. Rooms seduce with sublimely comfortable beds and polished modern bathrooms. Gorgeous breakfasts maintain the high standards.

★ Seven Rooms Villadorata
BOUTIQUE HOTEL €€€

(☎0931 83 55 75; https://7roomsvilladorata.it; Via Cavour 53; d from €275; P※🌐) This elegantly appointed boutique hotel occupies a wing of the 18th-century Palazzo Nicolaci, one of Noto's most celebrated aristocratic palaces. With their restrained colour palette, rooms are tactile and sophisticated, with artfully distressed furniture, beautiful artworks, alpaca throws, Nespresso machines and luxurious bathrooms stocked with high-quality amenities; the Deluxe Rooms are especially impressive. Quality extends to the breakfast, served at a communal table.

🍴 Eating & Drinking

Noto has a vibrant food scene, with a mix of innovative, sophisticated restaurants and old-school trattorias serving unfussy classics. The best spots are in the *centro storico* (historic centre), within walking distance of Corso Vittorio Emanuele. The corso and its piazzas constitute the town's social nerve centre, with evening crowds partaking in the evening *passeggiata* (stroll).

⭐**Caffè Sicilia**   GELATO **€**
(📞 0931 83 50 13; www.caffesicilia.it; Corso Vittorio Emanuele 125; pastries €2.50; ⏰ 8am-10pm Tue-Sun, closed Nov & early Jan-early Mar; 🚸) Dating from 1892 and especially renowned for its *granite,* this beloved place vies with its neighbour, Dolceria Corrado Costanzo, for the honours of Noto's best dessert shop. Frozen desserts are made with the freshest seasonal ingredients (wild strawberries in springtime, for example), while the delicious *torrone* (nougat) bursts with the flavours of local honey and almonds. It's also a good spot for an *aperitivo.*

⭐**Manna**   SICILIAN **€€**
(📞 0931 83 60 51; www.mannanoto.it; Via Rocco Pirri 15; meals €35-47; ⏰ noon-2.30pm & 7-10.30pm Wed-Mon Easter-Jul & Sep-Dec, 7-10.30pm daily Aug; 🎵) Divided into a hip front bar and sultry back dining rooms, Manna wows with its competent, contemporary creations. Premium produce dictates the menu, which might see *tagliatelle* pasta paired with duck ragù and Parmesan crisps, or mackerel fillet served with aromatic herbs, seaweed and a salted lemon *gelo* (Sicilian jelly). Staff are competent and friendly, and the wine list is focused on worthy drops.

⭐**Ristorante Vicari**   SICILIAN **€€€**
(📞 0931 83 93 22; www.ristorantevicari.it; Ronco Bernardo Leanti 9; meals €45-60; ⏰ 12.30-2pm Mon, Tue & Thu-Sat, plus 7-10pm daily Jul-Sep, 12.30-2pm Tue-Sat, plus 7-10pm Mon-Sat Oct-Jun) Low-slung lamps spotlight linen-clad tables at Vicari, and rightfully so. In the kitchen is young-gun chef Salvatore Vicari, who thrills with his whimsical takes on Sicilian produce: succulent squid stuffed with tomato and almonds and served on a pistachio cream, or ravioli stuffed with roast chicken and paired with a carrot, lemon and spinach cream. Reservations highly recommended.

⭐**Anche gli Angeli**   LOUNGE
(📞 0931 57 60 23; www.anchegliangeli.it; Via A da Brescia 2; ⏰ 8am-1am; 🎵) Sophisticated, LGBT-friendly and irrefutably cool, 'Even the Angels' is *the* place to schmooze in Noto. A cafe-bar, lounge, restaurant and concept store in one, it's as fabulous for a cappuccino and house-baked pastry as it is for browsing books, *aperitivo* sessions, a smashing modern-Sicilian dinner (meals €32 to €60) or a late-night tipple. Live music Wednesdays and Fridays, with DJ sets Fridays and Saturdays.

ℹ️ Information

Infopoint Noto (📞 339 4816218; www.notoin forma.it; Corso Vittorio Emanuele 135; ⏰ 10am-7pm Apr, May & Oct, to 8pm Jun & Sep, to 9pm Jul, to 10pm Aug, to 6pm rest of year) Offers maps, brochures, free computer access and a complimentary left-luggage service. Visitors can print boarding passes or other documents (€1), and the enthusiastic, multilingual staff also organise guided tours in Italian, English and French.

ℹ️ Getting There & Away

BUS

Noto's bus station is conveniently located just to the southeast of Porta Reale and the Giardini Pubblici. Buy tickets from **Bar Flora** (Hotel Flora, Via Pola 1), located at Hotel Flora, just west of the bus stop.

AST (📞 0931 46 27 11; www.aziendasiciliana trasporti.it) runs to Syracuse (€3.60, one hour, seven daily Monday to Saturday) and Catania (€7.50, 1½ hours, six daily Monday to Saturday, two Sunday). Buses to Catania stop at Catania airport en route.

Interbus (📞 091 611 95 35, 0935 2 24 60; www.interbus.it) also runs to Catania (€8.40, 1½ to 2½ hours, eight to nine daily Monday to Friday, six Saturday, three Sunday) and Syracuse (€3.60, one hour, four to five daily Monday to Friday, four Saturday, three Sunday).

TRAIN

Trains run daily except Sunday to Syracuse (€3.80, 30 to 40 minutes), Scicli (€4.30, one hour), Modica (€5.10, 1¼ hours) and Ragusa (€6.20, 1½ hours), but the station is inconveniently located 1km downhill from the historic centre.

Modica

📞 0932 / POP 54,500 / ELEV 296M

From early Greek and Roman roots, Modica rose to become one of Sicily's most powerful cities as the personal fiefdom of the Chiaramonte family in the 14th century. Modern-day Modica remains a superbly atmospheric town, with its medieval and baroque buildings climbing steeply up either side of a deep gorge. The multilayered town is divided into Modica Alta (Upper Modica) and Modica Bassa (Lower Modica). A devastating flood in 1902 resulted in the wide avenues of Corso Umberto and Via Giarrantana (the river was dammed and diverted), which remain the main axes of the town, lined by *palazzi* and tiled stone houses.

◉ Sights

Duomo di San Giorgio
CHURCH

(☑0932 94 12 79; Corso San Giorgio, Modica Alta; ⊙8am-12.30pm & 3.30-7pm) The high point of a trip to Modica – quite literally as it's up in Modica Alta – is the Duomo di San Giorgio, one of Sicily's most extraordinary baroque churches. Considered Rosario Gagliardi's great masterpiece, it stands in isolated splendour at the top of a majestic 250-step, 19th-century staircase, its sumptuous three-tiered facade towering above the medieval alleyways of the historic centre.

Duomo di San Pietro
CATHEDRAL

(Corso Umberto I 159, Modica Bassa; ⊙8.30am-12.30pm & 2-7pm Mon-Sat, to 8pm Sun) In Modica, the Duomo di San Pietro plays second fiddle only to the Cattedrale di San Giorgio. The original 14th-century church was damaged in the earthquake of 1693, leading to its reconstruction in 1697. Construction continued way into the 19th century; the rippling staircase, lined with life-sized statues of the Apostles, was only completed in 1876.

Chiesa di San Giovanni Evangelista
CHURCH

(Piazza San Giovanni, Modica Alta; ⊙hours vary) Attributed to Rosario Gagliardi and marking the top of Modica Alta is this grand baroque church. Prefaced by a sweeping staircase, the church underwent major restoration work in the 19th century, its current facade completed between 1893 and 1901. If the church is open, slip inside its elliptical interior for beautiful, neoclassical stuccowork. Nearby, at the end of Via Pizzo, a viewing balcony offers arresting views over the old town.

🛏 Sleeping

Sophisticated Modica offers a wide choice of accommodation in both the upper and lower towns; the latter is closer to the action, especially at night. Book ahead in summer and during busy periods such as April's Festa di San Giorgio.

★Masseria Quartarella
AGRITURISMO €

(☑360 654829; www.quartarella.com; Contrada Quartarella Passo Cane 1; s €40, d €75-80, tr €85-100, q €90-120; P🕸🛜🏊) Spacious rooms, welcoming hosts and ample breakfasts make this converted farmhouse in the countryside south of Modica an appealing choice for anyone travelling by car. Owners Francesco and Francesca are generous in sharing their love and encyclopaedic knowledge of local history, flora and fauna and can sug-

---

WORTH A TRIP

SCICLI

About 10km southwest of Modica, Scicli is the most authentic and relaxed of the Val di Noto's showpiece baroque towns. Its relatively compact, quickly gentrifying historic centre is awash with cultural sights, from beautiful churches and aristocratic *palazzi* (mansions) to eclectic museums and a time-warped apothecary. The town makes regular cameos on the hit TV series *Inspector Montalbano*, and visitors can visit two of the show's sets inside Palazzo Municipio.

Overlooking the town is a rocky peak topped by an abandoned church, the Chiesa di San Matteo. It's not too hard a walk up to the church to take in the sweeping views – simply follow the yellow sign up from Palazzo Beneventano and keep going for about 10 minutes.

For those who wish to linger overnight, Scicli Albergo Diffuso (☑392 8207857; www.sciclialbergodiffuso.it; Via Francesco Mormina Penna 15; r €77-177; 🕸🛜) offers fabulous digs in numerous locations across Scicli's historic core. Options range from simple rooms in restored *dammusi* (traditional stone abodes) to breathtaking suites in 19th-century palaces. Top of the heap are the frescoed rooms inside the 18th-century Palazzo Favacchio Patanè.

Trains run daily except Sunday to Modica (€1.70, 10 to 14 minutes), Ragusa (€3.10, 30 to 40 minutes), Noto (€4.30, 50 minutes to one hour) and Syracuse (€6.90, 1½ hours).

gest a multitude of driving itineraries in the surrounding area.

Palazzo Failla
HOTEL €€

(📞 0932 94 10 59; www.palazzofailla.it; Via Blandini 5, Modica Alta; s €55-65, d €69-125; 🅿@🛜) Smack in the heart of Modica Alta, this four-star, family-run hotel in a nostalgic 18th-century palace has retained much of its historical splendour, with original frescoed ceilings, hand-painted ceramic Caltagirone floor tiles, elegant drapes and heirloom antiques. Start the day with the generous breakfast buffet and end it at the hotel's well-regarded restaurant.

★ Casa Gelsomino
APARTMENT €€

(📞 335 8087841; www.casedisicilia.com; Via Raccomandata, Modica Bassa; per night €160-200, per week €1000-1260; 🅿🛜) It's easy to pretend you're a holidaying celebrity in this beautifully restored apartment, its balconies and private terrace serving up commanding views over Modica. Incorporating an airy lounge, fully equipped kitchen, stone-walled bathroom, laundry room, sitting room (with sofa bed) and separate bedroom, its combination of vaulted ceilings, antique floor tiles, original artworks and plush furnishings takes self-catering to sophisticated highs.

✖ Eating

Modica merits a stop on any Sicilian foodie trail, with both Slow Food trattorias and creative, high-end restaurants. The town is renowned for its grainy chocolate, a blend of bitter cocoa, sugar and spices worked at low temperature using an ancient method.

★ Caffè Adamo
GELATO €

(📞 0932 197 25 46; www.caffeadamo.it; Via Maresa Tedeschi 15-17, Modica Bassa; cup/cone from €2/2.50; ⊗ 6am-1am summer, to 11pm rest of year, closed Mon Sep-Mar; 🛜) There is great gelato and then there's gelato made by Antonio Adamo. The affable *modinese* makes all his confections from scratch; even the Agrigento pistachios are ground on-site. The result is ice cream packed with extraordinarily natural flavour and freshness. Gelato aside, Antonio's *cremolate* (water ices), Modica chocolate blocks and take-home jars of *babà* (rum-soaked sponge cake) are also outstanding.

★ Ornato
SEAFOOD €€

(📞 0932 94 24 23; http://ornato-ristorante-di-pesce.thefork.rest; Via Pozzo Barone 30, Modica Bassa; meals €35-50, tasting menu €60; ⊗ noon-2pm & 7-10.30pm Tue-Sun Sep-Jul, 7-10.30pm daily Aug; 🛜) The decorative tagines at stylish Ornato reflect Luca Ornato's love of global flavours, a fact also echoed in out-of-the-box dishes like *crudo* (raw seafood) with yuzu. The talented cook marries tradition and innovation with impressive skill, his menu as likely to offer flawless *spaghetti con frutti di mare* (spaghetti with seafood) as it is a sweet interpretation of the Caprese salad.

★ Cappero
SICILIAN €€

(📞 393 9078088; www.facebook.com/Cappero Bistrot; Corso Umberto I 156, Modica Bassa; meals €25-40; ⊗ noon-3pm & 7-10.30pm Fri-Wed, closed Aug; 🛜🍴) Small, quietly confident Cappero wows food lovers with beautiful cooking that's refined and comforting in equal parts. The house-made pasta is made using ancient grains, herbs are picked fresh from the restaurant's vertical herb garden, and the seasonal menu includes typically Modican dishes like broth with veal meatballs and noodles. If it's on the menu, sink your teeth into the succulent rabbit. Reservations recommended.

★ Accursio
SICILIAN €€€

(📞 0932 94 16 89; www.accursioristorante.it; Via Grimaldi 41, Modica Bassa; meals €80-90, tasting menus €90-150; ⊗ 12.30-2pm & 7.30-10pm Tue-Sat, 12.30-2pm Sun) While we love the modernist furniture and vintage Sicilian tiles, the food is the real thrill at this intimate, Michelin-starred maverick. Head chef Accursio Craparo specialises in boldly creative, nuanced dishes inspired by childhood memories and emblematic of new Sicilian thinking. For a well-rounded adventure, opt for a tasting menu.

🛍 Shopping

Antica Dolceria Bonajuto
CHOCOLATE

(📞 0932 94 12 25; www.bonajuto.it; Corso Umberto I 159, Modica Bassa; ⊗ 9am-8.30pm Sep-Jul, to midnight Aug) Sicily's oldest chocolate factory is the perfect place to taste Modica's famous chocolate. Flavoured with cinnamon, vanilla, orange peel and even hot peppers, it's a legacy of the town's Spanish overlords who imported cocoa from their South American colonies. Leave room for Bonajuto's *'mpanatigghi*, sweet local biscuits filled with chocolate, spices...and minced beef!

ℹ Information

Tourist Office (📞 0932 75 96 34, 346 6558227; www.comune.modica.rg.it; Corso Umberto I 141, Modica Bassa; ⏱ 8.30am-1.30pm & 3-7pm Mon-Fri, 9am-1pm & 3-7pm Sat) City-run tourist office in Modica Bassa.

ℹ Getting There & Away

BUS

Modica's bus station is at Piazzale Falcone-Borsellino at the top end of Corso Umberto I. **AST** (📞 0932 76 73 01; www.aziendasiciliana trasporti.it) runs to Noto (€3.90, 1½ to 1¾ hours, seven to 11 daily Monday to Saturday, one Sunday), Ragusa (€2.40, 25 to 30 minutes, 14 to 18 daily Monday to Saturday, two Sunday) and Catania (€9, 2¼ hours, seven to eight daily Monday to Saturday, four Sunday).

TRAIN

There are trains to Ragusa (€2.50, 20 to 30 minutes, nine daily Monday to Friday, seven Saturday), Scicli (€1.70, 10 minutes, six daily Monday to Friday, five Saturday) and Syracuse (€7.60, 1¾ hours, six daily Monday to Friday, five Saturday).

Ragusa

📞 0932 / POP 73,600 / ELEV 502M

Set amid the rocky peaks northwest of Modica, Ragusa is a town of two faces. Crowning the hilltop is Ragusa Superiore, a busy workaday town with sensible grid-pattern streets and all the trappings of a modern provincial capital, while etched into the hillside further down is Ragusa Ibla. This sloping area of tangled alleyways, grey stone houses and baroque *palazzi* on handsome squares is effectively Ragusa's historic centre and it's quite magnificent.

👁 Sights

⭐ **Ragusa Ibla**   AREA
Ragusa Ibla is a joy to wander, its labyrinthine lanes weaving through rock-grey *palazzi* to open onto beautiful, sun-drenched piazzas. It's easy to get lost but you can never go too far wrong, and sooner or later you'll end up at **Piazza Duomo**, Ragusa's sublime central square.

Facing the piazza, on Corso XXV Aprile, is **Palazzo Arezzo di Trifiletti** (📞 339 4000013, 349 6487463; www.palazzoarezzo.it; 20min tour €5, tour & aperitivo €15-40; ⏱ guided tours 10.30am-7pm daily Jun-Sep, by appt rest of the year), built between the 17th and early 19th centuries. Guided tours of the aristocratic palace in-clude its showpiece ballroom, graced with rare, late-18th-century Neapolitan majolica tiles and luminous 19th-century frescoes that have never needed touching up.

Opposite the palace, Via Novelli leads to the entrance of jewel-box **Teatro Donnafugata** (📞 334 2208186; www.teatrodonnafugata. it; Via Novelli 3; guided tour €10; ⏱ guided tours Apr-Oct, shows year-round), a 99-seat theatre that looks like a grand Italian opera house in miniature form. The theatre is a stop on the A Porte Aperte walking tour of Ragusa Ibla.

Via Novelli leads to Via Orfanotrofio, home to **Cinabro Carrettieri** (📞 340 8444804; www. cinabrocarrettieri.it; Via Orfanotrofio 22; 15/30min guided tour €3/5; ⏱ 10.30am-9pm), the colourful workshop of world-famous Sicilian cart craftsmen Biagio Castilletti and Damiano Rotella. The street continues south back to Corso XXV Aprile, where you're met by an eye-catching Gagliardi church, the elliptical **Chiesa di San Giuseppe** (Piazza Pola; ⏱ 9am-12.30pm & 3-7pm daily Jun-Sep, reduced hours rest of year), its cupola graced by Sebastiano Lo Monaco's fresco *Gloria di San Benedetto* (Glory of St Benedict, 1793).

Further downhill, the street to the right of the entrance of the **Giardino Ibleo** (📞 0932 65 23 74; Piazza Odierna) harbours the Catalan Gothic portal of what was once the large **Chiesa di San Giorgio Vecchio** (Via dei Normanni), now mostly ruined. The lunette features an interesting bas-relief of St George killing the dragon.

At the other end of Ragusa Ibla, the **Chiesa delle Santissime Anime del Purgatorio** (📞 0932 62 18 55; Piazza della Repubblica; ⏱ 10am-7pm daily Jun-Sep, reduced hours rest of year) is one of the few churches in town to have survived the great earthquake of 1693. Step inside to admire Francesco Manno's *Anime in Purgatorio* (Souls in Purgatory; 1800) at the main altar.

Duomo di San Giorgio   CATHEDRAL
(Piazza Duomo, Ragusa Ibla; ⏱ 10am-1pm & 3-6.30pm Apr-Oct & Dec, shorter hours rest of year) At the top end of the sloping Piazza Duomo is the town's pride and joy, the mid-18th-century cathedral with a magnificent neoclassical dome and stained-glass windows. One of Rosario Gagliardi's finest accomplishments, its extravagant convex facade rises like a three-tiered wedding cake, supported by gradually narrowing Corinthian columns and punctuated by jutting cornices.

VILLA ROMANA DEL CASALE

Near the town of Piazza Armerina in central Sicily is the stunning 3rd-century Roman Villa Romana del Casale (☑ 0935 68 00 36; www.villaromanadelcasale.it; adult/reduced €10/5, combined ticket incl Morgantina & Museo Archeologico di Aidone €14/7; ☺ 9am-11.30pm Apr-Oct, to 5pm Nov-May), a Unesco World Heritage Site and one of the few remaining sites of Roman Sicily. This sumptuous hunting lodge is thought to have belonged to Diocletian's co-emperor Marcus Aurelius Maximianus. Buried under mud in a 12th-century flood, it remained hidden for hundreds of years before its magnificent floor mosaics were discovered in the 1950s. Visit out of season or early in the day to avoid the crowds.

The mosaics cover almost the entire floor (3500 sq metres) of the villa and are considered unique for their narrative style, the range of subject matter and variety of colour – many are clearly influenced by African themes. Along the eastern end of the internal courtyard is the wonderful Corridor of the Great Hunt, vividly depicting chariots, rhinos, cheetahs, lions and the voluptuously beautiful Queen of Sheba. Across the corridor is a series of apartments, where floor illustrations reproduce scenes from Homer's Odyssey. But perhaps the most captivating of the mosaics is the so-called Room of the Ten Girls in Bikinis, with depictions of sporty girls in bikinis throwing a discus, using weights and throwing a ball; they would blend in well on a Malibu beach and are among Sicily's greatest classical treasures.

Travelling by car from Piazza Armerina, follow signs south of town to the SP15, then continue 5km to reach the villa. Getting here by public transport is more challenging. Buses operated by Interbus (☑ 095 53 27 16; www.interbus.it) run from Catania to Piazza Armerina (€9.20, 2 hours); from here catch a local bus (€1, 30 minutes, summer only) or a taxi (€20) for the remaining 5km.

Castello di Donnafugata   PALACE
(☑ 0932 67 65 00; www.comune.ragusa.gov.it; Contrada Donnafugata; adult/reduced €6/3; ☺ 9am-1pm & 2.30-7pm Tue-Sun summer, 9am-1pm & 2-4.45pm Tue-Sun winter) Located 18km southwest of Ragusa, this sumptuous neo-Gothic palace houses the Collezione Gabriele Arezzo di Trifiletti, an extraordinary fashion and costume collection. The easiest way to reach the *castello* is by car. From Monday to Saturday, trains run from Ragusa to Donnafugata (three to four daily, 20 to 25 minutes, €2.50), from where it's a 600m walk to the castle. Alternatively, Autotrasporti Tumino (☑ 0932 62 31 84; www.tuminobus.it; Via Zama) runs a very limited bus service from Ragusa (return €4.80); see the company website for times.

🏃 Activities

A Porte Aperte   WALKING
(☑ 366 3194177; www.facebook.com/aporte aperte; guided tour €10; 🕑) Cultural association 'Iblazon' runs 50-minute walking tours of three historic sites in Ragusa Ibla: the 'Circolo di Conversazione' (a club for Ragusan aristocrats), the private garden Palazzo Arezzo-Bertini and the Teatro Donnafugata, a jewel-box 19th-century theatre. Tours are

offered in Italian and English and must be booked at least a day ahead, either by email, SMS or calling.

🎊 Festivals & Events

⭐ **Scale del Gusto**   FOOD & DRINK
(www.scaledelgusto.it; ☺ Oct) For three days, Ragusa's squares, streets and Unesco-listed buildings not usually open to the public become evocative settings for this buzzing celebration of Sicilian food and artisan food producers. The program includes masterclasses by prolific chefs, talks, *aperitivo* sessions, pop-up restaurants, art exhibitions, live performances and light installations.

🛏 Sleeping

Tenuta Zannafondo   B&B €
(☑ 0932 183 89 19; www.tenutazannafondo.it; Contrada di Zannafondo; d €79-89; P ❄ 🕸) Set amid olive-sprinkled hillsides lined with stone walls, this converted 19th-century farmstead sits halfway between Ragusa and the coast (a 15-minute drive from each). Its charm lies in the tranquil cluster of independent stone-walled cottages, each with its own little patio; two rooms in the main house are less appealing. Dinner is available on request.

Delightful Desserts

From citrus-scented pastries filled with ricotta, to gelato served on brioche, to the marzipan fruits piled in every confectioner's window, Sicily celebrates the joys of sugar morning, noon and night.

Multicultural Roots

People from the Arabs to the Aztecs have influenced Sicily's culture of sweets: the former introduced sugar cane; the latter's fiery hot chocolate so impressed the Spaniards that they brought it to Sicily. The land also supplied inspiration, from abundant citrus, almond and pistachio groves to Mt Etna's snowy slopes, legendary source of the first *granita* (crushed ice made with coffee, fresh fruit or pistachios and almonds).

Sweet Sicilian Classics

The all-star list of Sicilian desserts starts with *cannoli*, crunchy pastry tubes filled with sweetened ricotta, garnished with chocolate, crumbled pistachios or a spike of candied citrus. Vying for the title of Sicily's most famous dessert is *cassata*, a coma-inducing concoction of sponge cake, cream, marzipan, chocolate and candied fruit. Feeling more adventurous? How about an *'mpanatigghiu*, a traditional Modican pastry stuffed with minced meat, almonds, chocolate and cinnamon?

A SUGAR-FILLED ISLAND SPIN

I Segreti del Chiostro (p838) Sweets using ancient recipes passed down by generations of Sicilian nuns.

Da Alfredo (p845) Dreamy *granita* made with almonds and wild strawberries.

Antica Dolceria Bonajuto (p877) Aztec-influenced chocolate with vanilla and hot peppers.

Caffè Sicilia (p875) Legendary *gelateria* satisfying Sicilian sweet tooths since 1892.

Maria Grammatico (p891) Marzipan fruit, almond pastries and toasted-nut *torrone* (nougat).

2

1. 'Mpanatigghi 2. Cassatine (miniature cassate) 3. Cannoli
4. Granita

4

L'Orto Sul Tetto
B&B €

(☑0932 24 77 85; www.lortosultetto.it; Via Tenente di Stefano 56, Ragusa Ibla; d €75-90; ❀⌖) This sweet little B&B behind the Duomo di San Giorgio offers an intimate experience, with simple, tastefully decorated rooms and a leafy roof terrace where a generous breakfast is served. Service is warm and obliging.

✗ Eating

★ I Banchi
ITALIAN €€

(☑0932 65 50 00; www.ibanchiragusa.it; Via Orfanotrofio 39, Ragusa Ibla; panini €6-6.50, meals €40-50, tasting menus €30-70; ⊙8.30am-11pm; ⌖▯) Michelin-star chef Ciccio Sultano is behind this contemporary, smart-casual eatery, which includes a dedicated bakery, specialist deli counter and the freedom to choose anything from *caffè* and just-baked pastries, to made-on-site gourmet *panini*, lazy wine-and-cheese sessions or more elaborate, creative dishes that put twists on Sicilian traditions, such as carob-glazed local pork with hummus and Modican chocolate salsa.

Agli Archi
SICILIAN €€

(☑0932 62 19 32; www.facebook.com/agliarchitrattoria; Piazza della Repubblica 15, Ragusa Ibla; meals €25-30; ⊙12.30-3pm & 7.30-10.30pm Fri-Wed, closed Jan & Feb; ⌖▯) With an outdoor terrace facing the pretty Chiesa delle Santissime Anime del Purgatorio, Agli Archi reveals a genuine passion for local ingredients and less-ubiquitous regional recipes. Rotating with the seasons, offerings might include *cavatelli* (elongated, shell-like pasta) with broccoli, anchovies and breadcrumbs, or succulent pork fillet cooked with oranges and served in a carob salsa.

★ Ristorante Duomo
SICILIAN €€€

(☑0932 65 12 65; www.cicciosultano.it; Via Capitano Bocchieri 31, Ragusa Ibla; tasting menus €135-150; ⊙12.30-2pm Mon, 12.30-2pm & 7.30-10.30pm Tue-Sat) Widely regarded as one of Sicily's finest restaurants, Duomo comprises a cluster of small rooms outfitted like private parlours behind its stained-glass door, ensuring a suitably romantic ambience for chef Ciccio Sultano's refined creations. The menu abounds in classic Sicilian ingredients such as pistachios, fennel, almonds and Nero d'Avola wine, combined in imaginative and unconventional ways. Reservations essential.

❶ Information

Tourist Office (☑0932 68 47 80; www.comune.ragusa.gov.it; Piazza San Giovanni, Ragusa Superiore; ⊙9am-7pm Mon-Fri year-round, 9am-2pm Sat & Sun Easter–mid-Oct & Dec) Ragusa's main tourist office, with friendly, helpful staff.

❶ Getting There & Around

BUS

Long-distance and municipal buses share a terminal on Via Zama in the upper town (Ragusa Superiore). Buy tickets at the ticket kiosk at the terminal or from the bar **Tre Passi Avanti** (☑0932 191 00 60; Via Zama 24; ⊙5am-9pm Mon-Sat), located 70m away.

AST (☑0932 76 73 01; www.aziendasiciliana trasporti.it; Via Zama) runs direct services to numerous destinations, including Modica (€2.70, 25 minutes, 15 to 17 daily Monday to Saturday, two Sunday) and Syracuse (€7.20, 3¼ hours, three daily Monday to Saturday).

Interbus (☑091 611 95 35; www.interbus. it; Via Zama) runs to Catania (€8.60, two hours, hourly Monday to Friday, every one to three hours Saturday, every one to two hours Sunday).

Flixbus (https://global.flixbus.com) operates direct services to the Calabrian port of Villa San Giovanni (from €14, 3¾ to five hours, three daily) on the Italian mainland.

Monday through Saturday, AST's city buses 11 and 33 (€1.20) run hourly between Via Zama bus terminal and Giardino Ibleo in Ragusa Ibla. On Sunday, bus 1 makes a similar circuit. Daily tickets are available (€2).

TRAIN

Trains run daily except Sunday to Modica (€2.50, 20 to 25 minutes), Scicli (€3.10, 30 to 35 minutes) and Syracuse (€8.30, two to 2½ hours).

CENTRAL SICILY & THE MEDITERRANEAN COAST

Central Sicily is a land of vast panoramas, undulating fields, severe mountain ridges and hilltop towns not yet sanitised for tourism. Moving towards the Mediterranean, the perspective changes, as ancient temples jostle for position with modern high-rise apartments outside Agrigento, Sicily's most lauded classical site and also one of its busier modern cities.

Agrigento

☑0922 / POP 59,600

Situated about 3km below the modern city of Agrigento, the Unesco-listed Valley of the Temples is one of the most mesmerising

Agrigento

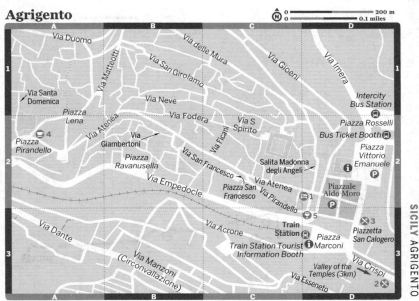

sites in the Mediterranean, with the best-preserved Doric temples outside Greece. On the travel radar since Goethe sang their praises in the 18th century, the temples now constitute Sicily's single biggest tourist site, with more than 600,000 visitors a year. As impressive as the temples are, what you see today are mere vestiges of the ancient city of Akragas, which was once the fourth-largest city in the known world.

Just uphill, Agrigento has an attractive medieval core, but beyond the elegant old town, the modern city is a chaos of elevated motorways converging on a ragged hilltop scarred by brutish tower blocks and riddled with choking traffic. Focus on the city's attractive old town and the proximity to the Valley of the Temples to maximise your enjoyment of a sojourn here.

Sights & Activities

For English-language tours of the ruins, contact **Associazione Guide Turistiche Agrigento** (☎ 345 8815992; www.agrigentoguide.org). After a day among the temples, roaming the lively, winding streets of medieval Agrigento makes a pleasant counterpoint. Start your exploration on Via Atenea, an attractive strip lined with smart shops, trattorias and bars. From here, narrow alleyways wind

Agrigento

Sleeping
1 PortAtenea D2

Eating
2 Aguglia Persa D3
3 Kalòs D3

Drinking & Nightlife
4 Caffè Concordia A2
5 Caffè San Pietro D3

upwards past tightly packed *palazzi* (mansions) interspersed with historic churches.

★ **Valley of the Temples** ARCHAEOLOGICAL SITE
(Valle dei Templi; ☎ 0922 183 99 96; www.parco valledeitempli.it; adult/reduced €12/7, incl Museo Archeologico €15.50/9, incl Museo Archeologico & Giardino della Kolymbetra €17/11; ⏱ 8.30am–8pm, to 11pm mid-Jul–mid-Sep) Sicily's most enthralling archaeological site encompasses the ruined ancient city of Akragas, highlighted by the stunningly well-preserved **Tempio della Concordia** (Temple of Concordia), one of several ridge-top temples that once served as beacons for homecoming sailors. The 13-sq-km park, 3km south of Agrigento, is split into eastern and western zones. Ticket offices with car parks are at the park's

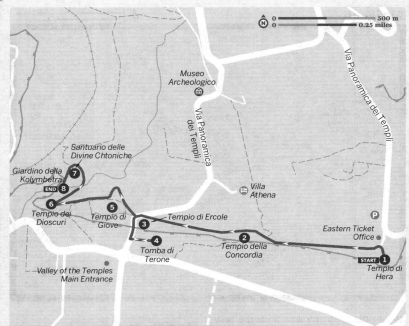

🚶 Archaeological Walking Tour
Valley of the Temples

START TEMPIO DI HERA
END GIARDINO DELLA KOLYMBETRA
LENGTH 3KM; THREE HOURS

Begin your exploration in the so-called Eastern Zone, home to Agrigento's best-preserved temples. From the Eastern Ticket Office, a short walk leads to the 5th-century-BC **❶ Tempio di Hera**, perched on the ridge top. Though partly destroyed by an earthquake, the colonnade remains largely intact, as does a long sacrificial altar. Traces of red are the result of fire damage likely dating to the Carthaginian invasion of 406 BC.

Next, descend past a gnarled 500-year-old olive tree and a series of Byzantine tombs to the **❷ Tempio della Concordia** (p883). This remarkable edifice, the model for Unesco's logo, has survived almost entirely intact since its construction in 430 BC, partly due to its conversion into a Christian basilica in the 6th century, and partly thanks to the shock-absorbing, earthquake-dampening quali-ties of the soft clay underlying its hard rock foundation.

Further downhill, the **❸ Tempio di Ercole** is Agrigento's oldest, dating from the end of the 6th century BC. Down from the main temples, the miniature **❹ Tomba di Terone** dates to 75 BC.

Cross the pedestrian bridge into the west-ern zone, stopping first at the **❺ Tempio di Giove**. This would have been the world's largest Doric temple had its construction not been interrupted by the Carthaginian sacking of Akragas. A later earthquake reduced it to the crumbled ruin you see today. Lying flat on his back amid the rubble is an 8m-tall *telamon* (a sculpted figure of a man with arms raised), originally intended to support the temple's weight. It's actually a copy; the original is in Agrigento's archaeological museum.

Take a brief look at the ruined 5th-century-BC **❻ Tempio dei Dioscuri** and the 6th-century-BC complex of altars and small buildings known as the **❼ Santuario delle Divine Chtoniche**, before ending your visit in the **❽ Giardino della Kolymbetra**, a lush garden in a natural cleft near the sanctuary, with more than 300 (labelled) species of plants and some welcome picnic tables.

southwestern corner (the main Porta V entrance) and at the northeastern corner near the Temple of Hera (Eastern Entrance).

★ **Museo Archeologico**　　　MUSEUM
(☑ 0922 40 15 65; Contrada San Nicola 12; adult/reduced €8/4, incl Valley of the Temples €13.50/7; ⊙ 9am-7.30pm Tue-Sat, to 1.30pm Sun & Mon) North of the temples, this wheelchair-accessible museum is one of Sicily's finest, with a huge collection of clearly labelled artefacts from the excavated site. Noteworthy are the dazzling displays of Greek painted ceramics and the awe-inspiring reconstructed *telamon,* a colossal statue recovered from the nearby Tempio di Giove.

🛏 Sleeping

★ **PortAtenea**　　　B&B €
(☑ 349 0937492; www.portatenea.com; Via Atenea, cnr Via Cesare Battisti; s/d/tr €50/70/90; ❄ 🖥) This five-room B&B wins plaudits for its panoramic roof terrace overlooking the Valley of the Temples, and its superconvenient location at the entrance to the old town, five minutes' walk from the train and bus stations. Best of all is the generous advice about Agrigento offered by hosts Sandra and Filippo (witness Filippo's amazing Google Earth tour of nearby beaches!).

★ **Fattoria Mosè**　　　AGRITURISMO €
(☑ 0922 60 61 15; www.fattoriamose.com; Via Pascal 4a; r per person €55, incl breakfast/half board €65/93, 2-/4-/6-person apt per week €550/850/1100; ❄) If Agrigento's urban jungle has got you down, head for this authentic organic *agriturismo* 6km east of the Valley of the Temples. Four suites, six self-catering apartments and a pool offer ample space to relax. Guests can opt for reasonably priced dinners (€28 including wine) built around the farm's organic produce, cook for themselves or even enjoy cooking courses on site.

★ **Villa Athena**　　　HISTORIC HOTEL €€€
(☑ 0922 59 62 88; www.hotelvillaathena.it; Via Passeggiata Archeologica 33; d €423-577, ste €505-1165; 🅿❄@🖥❄) With the Tempio della Concordia lit up in the near distance and palm trees lending an exotic *Arabian Nights* feel, this historic five-star hotel in an aristocratic 18th-century villa offers the ultimate luxury experience. The cavernous Villa Suite, floored in antique tiles with a free-standing spa bath and a vast terrace overlooking the temples, might well be Sicily's coolest hotel room.

🍴 Eating & Drinking

On a hot day, head for Caffè Concordia (Piazza Pirandello 36; almond milk €2; ⊙ 6am-9.30pm Tue-Sat) near Teatro Pirandello for a chilled glass of almond milk made from Agrigento's famous almonds, mixed with sugar, water and a hint of lemon rind.

★ **Aguglia Persa**　　　SEAFOOD €€
(☑ 0922 40 13 37; www.agugliapersa.it; Via Crispi 34; meals €30-40; ⊙ noon-3.30pm & 7-11pm Wed-Mon) Set in a mansion with a leafy courtyard just below the train station, this place is a welcome addition to Agrigento's fine-dining scene. Opened by the owners of Porto Empedocle's renowned Salmoriglio restaurant, it specialises in fresh-caught seafood in dishes such as citrus-scented risotto with shrimp and wild mint, or marinated salmon with sage cream and fresh fruit.

★ **Kalòs**　　　SICILIAN €€
(☑ 0922 2 63 89; www.ristorantekalos.it; Piazzetta San Calogero; meals €35-45; ⊙ 12.30-3pm & 7-11pm Tue-Sun) For fine dining, head to this restaurant just outside the historic centre. Tables on little balconies offer a delightful setting to enjoy homemade *pasta all'agrigentina* (with fresh tomatoes, basil and almonds), grilled lamb chops or *spada gratinata* (baked swordfish in breadcrumbs). Superb desserts, including homemade *cannoli* (pastry shells with a sweet filling) and almond *semifreddi* (a light frozen dessert), round out the menu.

Caffè San Pietro　　　WINE BAR
(☑ 0922 2 97 42; www.spaziotemenos.it/sanpietro; Via Pirandello 1; ⊙ 7.30am-late Oct-Apr, from 11am May-Sep, closed Mon) This hip cafe serves excellent coffee, Sicilian wines and evening *aperitivi,* but what really sets it apart is the adjacent 18th-century San Pietro church, accessed through a doorway just beyond the bar. Beautifully restored by the bar's owners over an eight-year period, the church sometimes serves as a lively venue for concerts, films and other cultural events.

ℹ Information

Ospedale San Giovanni di Dio (☑ 0922 44 21 11; Contrada Consolida; ⊙ 24hr) North of the centre.

Tourist Office (☑ 0922 59 32 27; www.living agrigento.it; Piazzale Aldo Moro 1; ⊙ 8am-7pm Mon-Fri, to 1pm Sat) In the provincial government building.

> ### WORTH A TRIP
>
> ## SCALA DEI TURCHI & TORRE SALSA
> ....
>
> With your own wheels, you'll find some dreamy beaches and beauty spots west of Agri-
> gento, all within an easy 30- to 45-minute drive of the city via the SS115.
>
> ### Scala dei Turchi
> One of the most beautiful sights in the Agrigento area, this blindingly white rock **out-
> crop**, shaped like a giant staircase, juts into the sea near Realmonte, 15km west of
> Agrigento. It's a popular spot with local sunseekers who come to sunbathe on the
> milky-smooth rock and dive into the indigo sea. To escape the crowds, walk another few
> hundred metres north along the white rocky shelf, and descend to the long sandy beach
> below.
>
> ### Riserva Naturale Torre Salsa
> This stunning 761-hectare natural **park** (www.wwftorresalsa.com), administered by the
> World Wildlife Fund, is signposted off the SS115. Exit at Siculiana Marina (a small coastal
> settlement with its own great sandy beach) or continue10km north to the second Mon-
> tallegro exit and follow the signs for WWF Riserva Naturale Torre Salsa. There's plenty
> of scope for walkers here, with well-marked trails and sweeping panoramic views of the
> surrounding mountains and coast. The long, deserted Torre Salsa beach (reached from
> the northern entrance) is especially beautiful, although the access road is rough.

❶ Getting There & Away

BUS
From most destinations, the bus is the easiest
way to get to Agrigento. The intercity bus station
and ticket booth are on Piazza Rosselli, just off
Piazza Vittorio Emanuele.

Buses to Palermo (€9, two hours) are operated by **Cuffaro** (☑ 091 616 15 10; www.facebook.
com/cuffaro.info) (eight Monday through Friday,
six on Saturday, three on Sunday) and **Camilleri**
(☑ 0922 47 18 86; www.camilleriargentoelat
tuca.it) (five Monday through Friday, four on
Saturday, one on Sunday), while **SAL** (Società
Autolinee Licata; ☑ 0922 40 13 60; www.auto
lineesal.it) serves Palermo's Falcone-Borsellino
Airport (€12.60, 2¾ hours, three to four Monday
through Saturday).

Lumia (☑ 0922 2 04 14; www.autolineelumia.
it) runs to Trapani and its Birgi airport (€11.90,
three to four hours, three daily Monday to Friday,
two on Saturday, one on Sunday).

SAIS Trasporti (☑ 0922 2 60 59; www.sais
trasporti.it) runs 10 to 14 buses daily to Catania
and its Fontanarossa airport (€13.40, three
hours).

CAR & MOTORCYCLE
Agrigento is easily accessible by road from all of
Sicily's main towns. The SS189 and SS121 connect with Palermo, while the SS115 runs along
the coast to Sciacca and Licata. For Catania,
take the SS640 via Caltanissetta.

Driving and parking in Agrigento can be a
nightmare. Via Atenea, the historic centre's main
street, is closed to traffic from 9am to 8pm, with

a short break during lunchtime when cars can
pass through the centre (for loading luggage).
There's metered parking at Piazza Vittorio Emanuele and on the streets around Piazzale Aldo
Moro, although you'll have to arrive early to find
a space.

TRAIN
Trains run regularly to/from Palermo (€9, two
hours, hourly). For Catania, the bus is a better
option as there are no direct trains. The train
station has left-luggage lockers (per 12 hours
€2.50).

❶ Getting Around

BUS
City bus 1, operated by **TUA** (Trasporti Urbani
Agrigento; ☑ 0922 41 20 24; www.trasportiurba
niagrigento.it), runs half-hourly from Agrigento's
bus and train stations to the archaeological
museum (15 minutes) and the Porta V entrance
to the temples (20 minutes). 'Bus 2/', as distinct
from 'bus 2' (which has a different route – watch
out for the hard-to-spot slash!) runs every hour
or so to the temples' eastern entrance near the
Tempio di Hera (10 to 15 minutes). Tickets cost
€1.20 if purchased in advance from a tobacconist, or €1.70 on board the bus.

CAR & MOTORCYCLE
From Agrigento's train station (Piazza Marconi),
take Via Francesco Crispi downhill. After 1.5km,
bear gently left onto Via Panoramica Valle dei
Templi to reach the valley's eastern entrance
and car park. To reach the main (Porta V) en-

trance and car park, bear right on Via Passeggiata Archeologica, then left on the SP4 and right on Viale Caduti di Marzabotto.

WESTERN SICILY

Situated directly across the water from North Africa and still retaining vestiges of the Arab, Phoenician and Greek cultures that once prevailed here, Sicily's windswept western coast is a feast for the senses – from Trapani's savoury fish couscous to the dazzling views from hilltop Erice and the wild coastal beauty of the Riserva Naturale dello Zingaro.

Marsala

POP 82,800

Many know about its sweet dessert wines, but few people realise what a charmer the town of Marsala is. Though its streets are paved in gleaming marble, lined with stately baroque buildings and peppered with graceful piazzas, Marsala has pleasures that are simple – a friendly *passeggiata* (evening stroll) most nights, plenty of *aperitivo* options and family-friendly restaurants aplenty.

◉ Sights & Activities

Piazza della Repubblica   PIAZZA

Marsala's most elegant piazza is dominated by the imposing Chiesa Madre. Just across the way, on the eastern side of the square, is the arcaded **Palazzo VII Aprile**, formerly known as the Palazzo Senatorio (Senatorial Palace) and now the town hall.

Cantine Florio   WINE

(⌨0923 78 13 05; www.duca.it/en/florio/ospitalita; Via Vincenzo Florio 1; standard tour adult/

reduced €13/5; ⊘9am-6pm Mon-Fri, to 1pm Sat, English-language tour 10am & 4pm Mon-Fri, 10am Sat) These venerable wine cellars, in a huge walled complex east of the centre and on the seafront since 1833, open their vintage doors to visitors to explain the Marsala-making process and the fascinating history of local viticulture. Afterwards, visitors can sample the goods in the sharp tasting room: tasting of four wines, accompanied by hors d'oeuvres, are included in the standard 1½-long tour.

★ Prokite Alby Rondina   KITESURFING

(⌨347 5373881; www.prokitealbyrondina.com; Via Passalacqua; 2/6hr lesson €150/370, 2hr lesson plus 1/2/5 days of equipment rental €200/330/440; ⊘Mar-Oct; ⊛) Handily located just 10 minutes from Trapani's Birgi airport and 14km north of Marsala, this highly professional kitesurfing resort combining school, **hotel** (⌨347 5373881; www.prokitealbyrondina.com; Via Passalacqua; s/d/tr from €60/85/115; ⊘Mar-Nov; ⓟ❄@⌶) and villa accommodation is a world-class spot to kite on a lagoon.

🛏 Sleeping & Eating

★ Il Profumo del Sale   B&B €

(⌨0923 189 04 72; www.ilprofumodelsale.it; Via Vaccari 8; s/d €40/65; ⌶) Perfectly positioned in Marsala's historic city centre, this lovely B&B offers three attractive rooms – including a palatial front unit with cathedral views from its small balcony – enhanced by welcoming touches like almond cookies, fine soaps and ample breakfasts featuring homemade bread and jams. Sophisticated owner Celsa is full of helpful tips about Marsala and the surrounding area.

★ Quimera   SANDWICHES €

(⌨349 0765524; www.facebook.com/quimerapub; Via Sarzana 34-36; sandwiches & salads from €5;

CELEBRATING COUSCOUS

Couscous (or cuscus), the beloved North African culinary treat cooked with gusto all over Western Sicily, is the delicious focus of **CousCousFest** (www.couscousfest.it; ⊘last week Sep), a six-day multicultural festival filling small-town San Vito Lo Capo with international chefs and foodies for one week in September. Food stands inviting festival goers to taste dozens of different couscous recipes from western Sicily, North Africa and the Mediterranean pop up on the beach and in town. Live cooking shows and music concerts fill the stage most evenings and the festival climaxes with – drum roll – the Couscous World Championships starring couscous chefs from 10 countries. Tickets (€15 to €25) are sold to be part of the tasting jury for the semifinals or finals. Otherwise, a 'tasting ticket' (€10) gives you access to dozens of stands on the beach and around town.

⊘ noon-3pm & 6.30pm-2am Mon-Sat, 6.30pm-2am Sun) Smack in the heart of Marsala's pedestrianised centre, this buzzy eating-drinking hybrid is the local hotspot for artisanal craft beers, gourmet sandwiches and meal-sized salads – all served with a big smile and bags of charm by the friendly young owners. Linger over a shared cutting board of cheeses or salami, or agonise over the choice of creatively filled *panini* and *piadine* (wraps).

🍷 Drinking & Nightlife

★ Ciacco Putia Gourmet   WINE BAR
(📞 347 6315684; www.ciaccoputia.it; Via Cammareri Scurti 3; ⊘ noon-3pm & 7-11pm Mon-Sat; 📶) Run by Tuscan-Sicilian couple Anna and Francesco, this irresistible *enoteca* is a gorgeous spot to quaff Marsala wines with locally sourced *salumi* (cold cuts), *panini* with *burrata* (cheese made from mozzarella and cream), anchovies and other snacks. The icing on the cake is the beautiful summertime terrace on a cobbled fountain-pierced square overlooking the showy baroque facade of 18th-century Chiesa del Purgatorio.

ℹ Information

Tourist Office (📞 0923 71 40 97, 0923 99 33 38; Via XI Maggio 100; ⊘ 8.30am-1.30pm & 3-8pm Mon-Fri, to 1.30pm Sat) Provides a limited range of maps and brochures, plus a list of wine cellars open by guided tour (but staff cannot make bookings for you).

ℹ Getting There & Away

Operators from Marsala's **bus station** (Piazza del Popolo) include Lumia (www.autolineelumia. it) to Agrigento (€10.10, 2¾ hours) and Salemi (www.autoservizisalemi.it) to Palermo (€11, 2¼ to 2½ hours). Train is the best way to get to Trapani (€3.80, 35 minutes). To reach Marsala's historic centre from the train station, walk 800m up Via Roma, which meets Via XI Maggio at Piazza Matteotti.

Selinunte

The ruins of Selinunte (Selinunte Archaeological Park; 📞 0924 4 62 77, 334 6040459; https://en.visitselinunte.com/archaeological-park; Via Selinunte, Castelvetrano; adult/reduced €6/3; ⊘ 9am-6pm Mar-Oct, to 5pm Nov-Feb) are the most impressively sited in Sicily. The huge city was built in 628 BC on a promontory overlooking the sea, and over the course of two-and-a-half centuries became one of the richest and most powerful in the world. It was de-

stroyed by the Carthaginians in 409 BC and finally fell to the Romans about 350 BC, at which time it went into rapid decline and disappeared from historical accounts.

The city's past is so remote that the names of the various temples have been forgotten and they are now identified by the letters A to G, M and O. The most impressive, Temple E, has been partially rebuilt, its columns pieced together from their fragments with part of its tympanum. Many of the carvings, particularly from Temple C, are now in the archaeological museum in Palermo. Their quality is on par with the Parthenon marbles and clearly demonstrates the high cultural levels reached by many Greek colonies in Sicily.

The ticket office and entrance to the ruins is located near the eastern temples. Try to visit in spring when the surroundings are ablaze with wildflowers. Escape the mediocre restaurants near the ruins by heading for Lido Zabbara (📞 0924 4 61 94; www.facebook.com/lidozabbara; Via Pigafetta, Marinella di Selinunte; buffet per person €12; ⊘ noon-3pm Mar-early Nov, plus 7.30-10.30pm Jun-Sep), a beachfront eatery in nearby Marinella di Selinunte that serves good grilled fish and a varied buffet. Alternatively, drive 15km east to Da Vittorio (📞 0925 7 83 81; www.ristorantevittorio. it; Via Friuli Venezia Giulia, Porto Palo; meals €30-45; ⊘ 12.30-2.30pm & 7-10pm) in Porto Palo, another wonderful spot to enjoy seafood, sunset and the sound of lapping waves.

ℹ Getting There & Away

Selinunte is midway between Agrigento and Trapani, about 10km south of the junction of the A29 and SS115 near Castelvetrano. Salemi (https://autoservizisalemi.it/tratte/selinunte) runs regular buses between Marinella di Selinunte and Castelvetrano train station (€1.50, 25 to 35 minutes), where you can make onward rail connections to Marsala (€4.30, 45 minutes) and Trapani (€6.20, 1¼ hours). For eastbound travellers, Lumia (www.autolineelumia.it) runs buses from Castelvetrano to Agrigento (€8.60, two hours, one to three daily).

Trapani

POP 67,900

Hugging the harbour where Peter of Aragon landed in 1282 to begin the Spanish occupation of Sicily, the sickle-shaped spit of land occupied by Trapani's old town once sat at the heart of a powerful trading network that

SCOPELLO & RISERVA NATURALE DELLO ZINGARO

Saved from development and road projects by local protests, the tranquil Riserva Naturale dello Zingaro (☑0924 3 51 08; www.riservazingaro.it; adult/child €5/3; ☉7am-7.30pm Apr-Sep, 8am-4pm Oct-Mar) is the star attraction on the Golfo di Castellammare, halfway between Palermo and Trapani. Founded in 1981, this was Sicily's first nature reserve. Zingaro's wild coastline is a haven for the rare Bonelli's eagle, along with 40 other species of bird. Mediterranean flora dusts the hillsides with wild carob and bright yellow euphorbia, and hidden coves, such as Capreria and Marinella Bays, provide tranquil swimming spots. The main entrance to the park is 2km north of the village of Scopello. Several walking trails are detailed on maps available for free at the entrance or downloadable from the park website. The main 7km trail along the coast passes by the visitor centre and five museums that document everything from local flora and fauna to traditional fishing methods.

Once home to tuna fishers, the tiny town of Scopello has morphed into a popular weekend getaway. The town's vintage *tonnara* (tuna factory), on the waterfront 1km below town, now houses the unusual Tonnara di Scopello (☑388 8299472; www.la tonnaradiscopello.it; Largo Tonnara Scopello; adult/child €5/free; ☉10am-7pm summer, shorter hours rest of year) museum, which documents traditional tuna fishing. In operation from the 13th century until its closure in 1984, the complex was greatly developed in the 15th and 16th centuries, and in 1874 the wealthy owners had the elegant, salmon-pink Palazzina Florio built right on the water. The setting alone – overlooking the fluorescent blue gulf, at the foot of dramatic rock formations capped by a medieval tower – makes it a worthwhile visit.

Pensione Tranchina (☑0924 54 10 99; www.pensionetranchina.com; Via Armando Diaz 7; B&B per person €35-50, half-board per person €60-75; ❋🛜) is the nicest of several accommodation options clustered around the cobblestoned courtyard at Scopello's village centre. Friendly owner Marisin offers comfortable rooms, a roaring fire on chilly evenings and superb home-cooked meals featuring local fish and home-grown fruit and olive oil.

stretched from Carthage to Venice. Traditionally the town thrived on coral and tuna fishing, with some salt and wine production. These days, Trapani's small port buzzes with ferry traffic zipping to and from the remote Egadi Islands and the mysterious volcanic rock island of Pantelleria, not far from Tunisia.

☉ Sights

Trapani's historic centre, with its small but compelling maze of gold-stone *palazzi* and 18th-century baroque gems such as the Cattedrale di San Lorenzo (☑0923 2 33 62; http://cattedraletrapani.it; Corso Vittorio Emanuele; ☉8am-4pm), is a mellow place to stroll, for both locals and travellers awaiting their next boat. From late afternoon onwards, car-free main street Via Garibaldi buzzes with what feels like the entire town out in force enjoying their lazy, absolute sacrosanct *passeggiata*. Join them.

Chiesa Anime Sante del Purgatorio   CHURCH
(☑329 7078896; Via San Francesco d'Assisi; by donation; ☉7.45am-noon & 4-7pm Mon-Sat, 10am-noon & 4-7pm Sun) Just off the *corso* in the heart of the city, this church houses the impressive 18th-century *misteri*, 20 life-sized wooden effigies depicting the story of Christ's Passion, which take centre stage during the city's dramatic Easter Week processions every year. Explanatory panels in English, Italian, French and German help visitors to understand the story behind each figure.

🛏 Sleeping & Eating

★ Room Mate Andrea   DESIGN HOTEL €€
(☑912 179287; https://room-matehotels.com/en/andrea; Viale Regina Margherita 31; d €79-135; 🅿❋@🛜🏊) Graceful Palazzo Platamone, with neoclassical caramel-coloured facade dating to the 1900s, is the grandiose setting for the Sicilian debut of Spanish urban

hotel group, Room Mate. Andrea is predictably stylish, with the city's only rooftop pool. Beautifully decorated, vintage-chic rooms mix original neoclassical fittings and fixtures with modern comforts. Breakfast costs €19.90 and is served until noon; the bar serves tip-top seasonal cocktails.

★ **La Bettolaccia** SICILIAN €€
(☑0923 2 59 32; www.labettolaccia.it; Via Enrico Fardella 25; meals €35-45; ⊙12.45-3pm & 7.45-11pm Mon-Fri, 7.45-11pm Sat) Unwaveringly authentic, this on-trend Slow Food favourite, squirrelled away down a sleepy side street, is the hotspot to feast on spicy couscous with fried fish or mixed seafood, *caponata* (eggplant and sun-dried tomatoes with capers in a sweet-and-sour sauce), the catch of the day, and other traditional Trapanese dishes in a sharp, minimalist white space. Reservations essential.

❶ Information

Tourist Office (☑0923 54 45 33; Piazzetta Saturno 3bis; ⊙9am-1pm Mon-Fri summer, 9am-2pm & 3-5pm Mon & Thu, 9am-2pm Tue, Wed & Fri winter) Just north of the port.

❶ Getting There & Around

AIR

Trapani's **Vincenzo Florio (Birgi) Airport** (☑0923 61 01 11; www.airgest.it) is served by budget flights from mainland Italy and the rest of Europe. **AST** (Azienda Siciliana Trasporti; ☑0923 2 10 21; www.astsicilia.it; Via Virgilio 20) runs hourly buses (€4.90, 20 minutes) to/from Trapani's port. A taxi between Birgi airport and Trapani costs a fixed €30. Marsala-based Salemi (https://autoservizisalemi.it) operates buses between the Birgi airport and Palermo (€11, 1¾ to two hours, five to six daily); buy tickets online or on the bus.

BOAT

Trapani's busy port is the main departure point for the Egadi Islands and the remote Mediterranean island of Pantelleria. Ferry and hydrofoil schedules are available from **Liberty Lines** (☑0923 87 38 13; https://eng.libertylines.it; Via Ammiraglio Staiti) and **Siremar** (☑090 57 37; https://carontetourist.it/en/siremar; Stazione Marittima, Porto Trapani). See Lonely Planet's Sicily guide for more information on the islands themselves.

BUS

AST (Azienda Siciliana Trasporti; ☑0923 2 10 21; www.astsicilia.it; Via Virgilio 20) buses to/from Vincenzo Florio (Birgi) airport

(€2.90, 55 minutes) use the bus stop in front of the hydrofoil docks. Buy tickets at **Egatour** (☑0923 2 17 54; www.egatourviaggi.it; Via Ammiraglio Staiti 13), located directly opposite. The same bus stop is used by Big Bus (www.bigbus.it) buses heading to/from Palermo train station (two hours), Marsala (50 minutes) and an overnight bus to/from Naples (13¾ hours, one daily) and Rome (14¼, one daily). Segesta Autolinee (www.segesta.it) buses connect Trapani with Palermo airport (€8, 65 minutes, at least hourly).

TRAIN

From Trapani's train station, 1km east of the centre on Piazza Umberto, 10 daily trains (five on Sunday) run to Marsala (€3.80, 25 to 40 minutes). For Palermo, the bus is a much faster option.

Erice

POP 27,900 / ELEV 751M

Medieval Erice watches over the port of Trapani from its giddy mountain perch atop the legendary peak of Eryx, spectacularly set 750m above sea level. It's a mesmerising, walled 12th-century village whose peculiar history, mountain charm and sensational sea-and-valley views are only enhanced by frequent unpredictable changes in weather that take you from brilliant sunshine to thick fog in the space of minutes.

Allow ample time for losing yourself in the atmospheric maze of stone-paved streets – all the more cinematic when the piercing sun plays peekaboo with swirling mist – and savouring a sweet old-world moment at Sicily's most famous pastry shop.

◉ Sights

The best views can be had from Giardino del Balio, which overlooks the turrets and wooded hillsides south to Trapani's salt-pans, the Egadi Islands and the sea. Looking north, there are equally staggering views of San Vito Lo Capo's rugged headlands.

Castello di Venere CASTLE
(Castle of Venus; ☑329 7823035; www.fondazioneericearte.org/castellodivenere.php; Via Castello di Venere; adult/reduced €4/2; ⊙10am-8pm Aug, to 7pm Jul & Sep, to 6pm Apr-Jun & Oct, 10am-1pm Sat & Sun Nov-Mar) This 12th- to 13th-century Norman castle was built over the Temple of Venus, long a site of worship for the ancient Elymians, Phoenicians, Greeks and Romans. Nowadays the castle's rooms are off-limits, but visitors can explore the grassy interior

courtyard, filled with ruined foundations and flanked by an impressive stone wall allegedly built by Daedalus. Stealing the show are the spectacular panoramic vistas extending to San Vito Lo Capo on one side and the Saline di Trapani on the other.

🛏 Sleeping & Eating

Hotels, many with their own restaurants, are scattered along Via Vittorio Emanuele, Erice's main street. After the day-trippers have gone, the town assumes a beguiling medieval air.

Erice has a tradition of *dolci ericini* (Erice sweets) made by local nuns. There are numerous pastry shops in town, the most famous being Maria Grammatico (☑0923 86 93 90; www.mariagrammatico.it; Via Vittorio Emanuele 14; pastries from €2; ⊙9am-midnight May-Sep, to 9pm Oct-Apr), revered for its *frutta martorana* (marzipan fruit) and almond pastries. If you like what you taste, you can even stick around and take cooking classes from Signora Grammatico herself.

Hotel Elimo   HOTEL €€
(☑0923 86 93 77; www.hotelelimo.it; Via Vittorio Emanuele 75; s €72-100, d €90-160, q €120; ❋ 🛜) Communal spaces at this atmospheric historic house are filled with tiled beams, marble fireplaces, intriguing art, knick-knacks and antiques. The bedrooms are more mainstream, although many (along with the hotel terrace and restaurant) have breathtaking vistas south and west towards the Saline di Trapani, the Egadi Islands and the shimmering sea.

❶ Getting There & Away

AST runs four to six buses daily between Erice and Trapani's bus terminal (€2.90, 40 minutes to one hour). Alternatively, catch the **funicular** (Cabinovia di Erice; ☑0923 56 93 06, 0923 86 97 20; www.funiviaerice.it; one way/return €5.50/9; ⊙1-8pm Mon, 8.30am-8pm Tue-Fri, 9am-9pm Sat, 9.30am-8.30pm Sun) opposite the car park at the foot of Erice village, across from Porta Trapani; the 10-minute descent drops you in Trapani near Ospedale Sant'Antonio

Abate, where you can catch local bus 21 or 23 into the centre of Trapani.

Segesta

Set on the edge of a deep canyon amid desolate mountains, the 5th-century BC ruins of Segesta (☑0924 95 23 56; Contrada Barbaro, SR22; adult/child €6/free; ⊙9am-7.30pm Apr-Sep, to 6.30pm Mar & Oct, to 5pm Nov-Feb) are among the world's most magical ancient sites.

Long before the arrival of the Greeks, Segesta was the principal city of the Elymians, an ancient civilisation claiming descent from the Trojans that settled in Sicily in the Bronze Age. The Elymians were in constant conflict with Greek Selinunte, whose destruction (in 409 BC) they pursued with bloodthirsty determination. More than 100 years later the Greek tyrant Agathocles slaughtered over 10,000 Elymians and repopulated Segesta with Greeks.

Little remains of ancient Segesta today, save its hilltop theatre and the never-completed Doric temple, yet the ruins' remarkable state of preservation and the majesty of their rural setting combine to make this one of Sicily's enduring highlights. Occasional music concerts and cultural events held beneath the stars in the theatre on hot summer nights are nothing short of magical.

❶ Getting There & Away

Tarantola (www.tarantolabus.com) operates a limited service to/from Trapani bus station and Segesta (single/return €4/6.60, 40 to 50 minutes). From April to October only, it also operates services to/from Palermo (single/return €7/11.20, 80 minutes, three daily Monday to Saturday). Check schedules carefully as times posted are not necessarily reliable; there are no buses on Sunday.

Visitors with their own vehicles must use the car park 1.5km from the hilltop ruins and continue to the temple on foot or by shuttle bus (€1.50, every 15 minutes). A second bus (€1.50) shuttles visitors between the temple and the theatre, another 1.25km uphill again.

POPULATION
1.61 million

CAPITAL
Cagliari

BEST SEAFOOD
Luigi Pomata (p901)

BEST WILDERNESS HIKE
Valle di Lanaittu (p930)

BEST COUNTRY COOKING
Su Gologone (p931)

WHEN TO GO

Feb Pre-Lenten shenanigans, from carnival madness to medieval jousting at Oristano's Sa Sartiglia.

Mar–May Spring wildflowers, Easter parades, and hiking without the heat and crowds.

Jun–Aug Sun-kissed beaches, open-air festivals and folksy fun at Nuoro's Sagra del Redentore.

Spiaggia della Pelosa (p917)
TRAVELWILD/SHUTTERSTOCK ©

Sardinia

As DH Lawrence so succinctly put it: 'Sardinia is different'. Indeed, where else but on this 365-village, four-million-sheep island could you travel from shimmering bays to near-alpine forests, granite peaks to snow-white beaches, rolling vineyards to one-time bandit towns – all in the space of a day? Sardinia baffles with its unique prehistory at 7000 nuraghic sites, dazzles with its kaleidoscopic blue waters, and whets appetites with island treats like spit-roasted suckling pig, sea urchins, crumbly *pecorino* (sheep's milk cheese), Vermentino whites and Cannonau reds.

Whether you're swooning over the mega-yachts in the Costa Smeralda's fjord-like bays or kicking back at a rustic *agriturismo* (farm stay accommodation), you can't help but appreciate this island's love of the good life.

Sardinia Highlights

1 Gola Su Gorropu (p931) Walking on the wild side in Sardinia's most spectacular gorge

2 Costa Verde (p906) Feeling the lure of the sea on the windswept beaches of Sardinia's southwest coast

3 Il Castello (p897) Wandering the medieval backstreets of Cagliari's rocky citadel

4 Costa Smeralda (p923) Rubbing bronzed shoulders with the rich and superfamous

5 Nuraghe Su Nuraxi (p907) Boning up on prehistory at Sardinia's sole World Heritage Site

6 Golfo di Orosei (p934) Dropping anchor in brilliant aquamarine waters

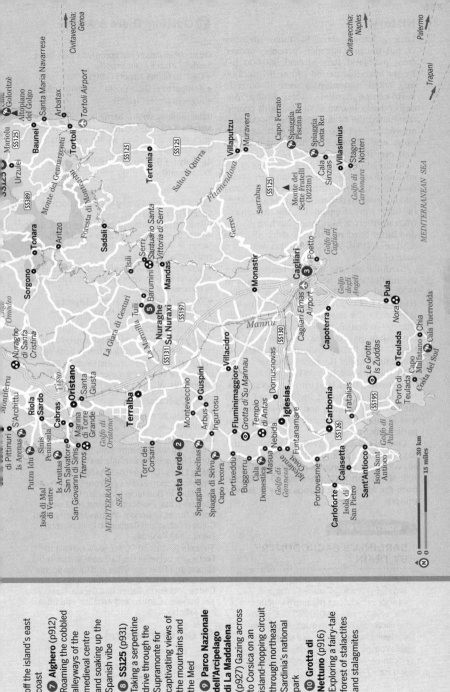

off the island's east
coast

7 Alghero (p912)
Roaming the cobbled
alleyways of the
medieval centre
and soaking up the
Spanish vibe

8 SS125 (p931)
Taking a serpentine
drive through the
Supramonte for
captivating views of
the mountains and
the Med

**9 Parco Nazionale
dell'Arcipelago
di La Maddalena**
(p927) Gazing across
to Corsica on an
island-hopping circuit
through northeast
Sardinia's national
park

**10 Grotta di
Nettuno** (p916)
Exploring a fairy-tale
forest of stalactites
and stalagmites

History

Little is known about Sardinia's prehistory, but the first islanders probably arrived from mainland Italy around 350,000 BC. By the neolithic period (8000 BC to 3000 BC), tribal communities were thriving in north-central Sardinia. Their Bronze Age descendants, known as the nuraghic people, dominated the island until the Phoenicians arrived around 850 BC. The Carthaginians came next, followed by the Romans, who took over in the 3rd century BC.

In the Middle Ages, the island was divided into four independent *giudicati* (kingdoms), but by the 13th century the Pisans and Genoese were battling for control. They in turn were toppled by the Aragonese from northern Spain, who also had to subdue bitter Sard resistance led by Eleonora d'Arborea (1340-1404), Sardinia's very own Joan of Arc.

Sardinia became Spanish territory after the unification of the Spanish kingdoms in 1479, and today there remains a tangible Hispanic feel to towns such as Alghero and Iglesias. In the ensuing centuries, Sardinia suffered as Spain's power crumbled; in 1720 the Italian Savoys took possession of the island. After Italian unity in 1861, Sardinia found itself under the boot of Rome.

In the aftermath of WWII, efforts were made to drag the island into the modern era. In 1946 a huge project was launched to rid the island of malaria and in 1948 Sardinia was granted its own autonomous regional parliament.

Coastal tourism arrived in the 1960s and has since become a mainstay of the Sardinian economy. Environmentalists breathed a sigh of relief in 2008 when NATO withdrew from the Maddalena islands after a 35-year sojourn.

WORTH A TRIP

SARDINIA'S BACKCOUNTRY BY TRAIN

If you're not in a rush, one of the best ways of exploring Sardinia's rugged interior is by taking the narrow-gauge Trenino Verde (☑070 265 76 12; www. treninoverde.com; ☉mid-Jun–Sep, some weekends May & Oct). There are five available routes: Mandas–Sadali, Mandas–Laconi, Arbatax–Gairo, Sindia–Bosa, and Palau–Tempio.

ⓘ Getting There & Away

AIR

Flights from Italian and European cities serve Sardinia's three main airports:
➔ Cagliari Elmas Airport (p903)
➔ Aeroporto di Olbia Costa Smeralda (p923)
➔ Alghero Airport (p915)

Italian airlines serving Sardinia:

Alitalia (☑892010, Sardinia flights 06 6585 9515, general info 06 6 56 40; www.alitalia.it) Italy's national carrier.

Air Italy (☑0789 5 26 82, 892928; www.airitaly.com)

BOAT

Sardinia is accessible by ferry from ports in Spain, France and Italy.
➔ The arrival points in Sardinia are Olbia, Golfo Aranci, Santa Teresa di Gallura and Porto Torres in the north; Arbatax on the east coast; and Cagliari in the south.
➔ Services are most frequent between mid-June and mid-September, when it is advisable to book well ahead.
➔ You can book tickets at travel agents throughout Italy or directly online.

Useful ferry websites:

AFerry (www.aferry.co.uk) Information on routes, ferry operators and online booking.

Traghetti Web (www.traghettiweb.it) Comprehensive site listing major routes and ferry companies. Also has online booking.

Ferry Operators

Three main ferry operators serve Sardinia from mainland Italy.

Grandi Navi Veloci (☑010 209 45 91; www.gnv.it; ☉booking centre 8am-9pm) From Porto Torres in northern Sardinia to Genoa.

Moby Lines (☑+49 (0)611-14020; www.mobylines.com) Ferries go from Santa Teresa di Gallura to Bonifacio (Corsica); Olbia to Civitavecchia, Piombino, Genoa and Livorno; Porto Torres to Genoa; Arbatax to Genoa and Civitavecchia; and Cagliari to Civitavecchia, Naples and Palermo.

Tirrenia (☑199 30 30 40; www.tirrenia.it) Ferries go between Cagliari and Civitavecchia, Naples and Palermo; Olbia and Civitavecchia and Genoa; Arbatax and Civitavecchia and Genoa; and Porto Torres and Genoa. Boats also sail between Cagliari and Arbatax, and Olbia and Arbatax.

ⓘ Getting Around

BUS

Azienda Regionale Sarda Trasporti (ARST; ☑800 865042; www.arst.sardegna.it) is

Sardinia's main bus company, running most local and long-distance buses.

CAR & MOTORCYCLE

Sardinia is best explored by road. There are rental agencies at all airports, along with downtown branches in Cagliari and other cities.

TRAIN

Trenitalia (☑892021; www.trenitalia.com) services link Cagliari with Oristano, Sassari, Porto Torres, Olbia and Golfo Aranci. Services are slow but generally reliable. Slow ARST trains serve Sassari, Alghero and Nuoro. Between mid-June and early September, ARST also operates a scenic tourist train service, the Trenino Verde.

CAGLIARI

☑070 / POP 154,100

The best way to arrive in Sardinia's historic capital is by sea; the city rises in a helter-skelter of golden-hued *palazzi*, domes and facades up to the rocky centrepiece, Il Castello. Although Tunisia is closer than Rome, Cagliari is the most Italian of Sardinia's cities. Vespas buzz down tree-fringed boulevards and locals hang out at busy cafes tucked under arcades in the seafront Marina district.

Like many Italian cities, Cagliari wears its history on its sleeve and everywhere you go you come across traces of its rich past: ancient Roman ruins, museums filled with prehistoric artefacts, centuries-old churches and elegant *palazzi*.

Edging east of town brings you to Poetto beach, the hub of summer life with its limpid blue waters and upbeat party scene.

⊙ Sights

★ **Il Castello** AREA
This hilltop citadel is Cagliari's most iconic image, its domes, towers and *palazzi*, once home to the city's aristocracy, rising above the sturdy ramparts built by the Pisans and Aragonese. Inside the battlements, the old medieval city reveals itself like Pandora's box. The university, cathedral, museums and Pisan palaces are wedged into a jigsaw of narrow high-walled alleys. Sleepy though it may seem, the area harbours a number of boutiques, bars and cafes popular with visitors, students and hipsters.

★ **Museo Archeologico Nazionale** MUSEUM
(☑070 6051 8245; http://museoarcheocagliari.beniculturali.it; Piazza Arsenale 1; adult/reduced €7/3, incl Pinacoteca Nazionale €9/4.50; ⊙9am-8pm Tue-Sun) Of the four museums at the Citta-della dei Musei, this is the undoubted star. Sardinia's premier archaeological museum showcases artefacts spanning thousands of years of history, from the early Neolithic, through the Bronze and Iron Ages to the Phoenician and Roman eras. Highlights include a series of colossal figures known as the Giganti di Monte Prama and a superb collection of *bronzetti* (bronze figurines), which, in the absence of any written records, are a vital source of information about Sardinia's mysterious nuraghic culture.

★ **Cattedrale di Santa Maria** CATHEDRAL
(☑070 864 93 88; www.duomodicagliari.it; Piazza Palazzo 4; ⊙8am-noon & 4-8pm Mon-Sat, to 1pm & 4.30-8.30pm Sun) Cagliari's graceful 13th-century cathedral stands proudly on Piazza Palazzo. Except for the square-based bell tower, little remains of the original Gothic structure: the clean Pisan Romanesque facade is a 20th-century imitation, added between 1933 and 1938. Inside, the once-Gothic church has all but disappeared beneath a rich icing of baroque decor, the result of a radical late-17th-century makeover. Bright frescoes adorn the ceilings, and the side chapels spill over with exuberant sculptural whirls.

★ **Bastione di Saint Remy** VIEWPOINT
This vast neoclassical structure, comprising a gallery space, monumental stairway and panoramic terrace, was built into the city's medieval walls between 1899 and 1902. The highlight is the elegant Umberto I terrace, which commands sweeping views over Cagliari's jumbled rooftops to the sea and distant mountains. To reach the terrace, you can try the stairway on Piazza Costituzione or take one of the elevators – eg from the Giardino Sotto Le Mure (Viale Regina Elena; ⊙7am-9pm winter, longer hours summer) or Piazza Yenne (p899) – although at the time of research they were closed and you needed to walk up via the streets.

★ **Santuario & Basilica di Nostra Signora di Bonaria** CHURCH
(☑070 30 17 47; www.bonaria.eu; Piazza Bonaria 2; ⊙6.30am-7.30pm) Crowning the Bonaria hill, around 1km southeast of Via Roma, this religious complex is a hugely popular pilgrimage site. Devotees come from all over the world to visit the understated 14th-century Gothic church sanctuary and pray to *Nostra Signora di Bonaria,* a statue of the Virgin Mary and Christ that supposedly saved a ship's crew during a storm. To the right of the sanctuary, and accessible through a

Cagliari

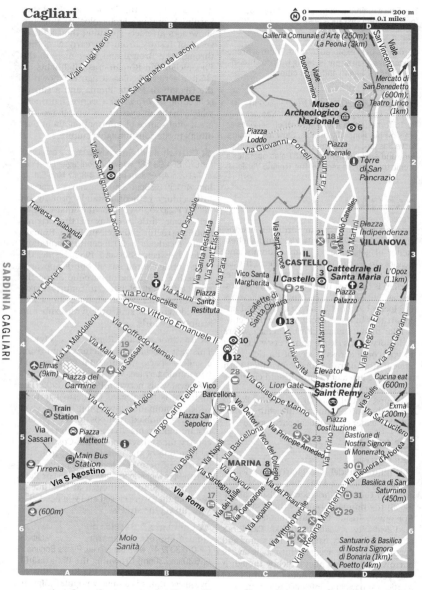

connecting door, the towering basilica still acts as a landmark to returning sailors.

Torre dell'Elefante   TOWER
(www.beniculturalicagliari.it; cnr Via Santa Croce & Via Università; adult/reduced €3/2; ⊙ closed at time of research) One of only two Pisan tow-

ers still standing, the Torre dell'Elefante was built in 1307 as a defence against the threatening Aragonese. Named after the sculpted elephant by the vicious-looking portcullis, the 42m-high tower became something of a horror show, thanks to the severed heads the city's Spanish rulers used to adorn it with.

Cagliari

The crenellated storey was added in 1852 and used as a prison for political detainees. Climb to the top for far-reaching views over the city's rooftops to the sea.

Galleria Comunale d'Arte GALLERY
(⌑070 677 75 98; www.museicivicicagliari.it; Giardini Pubblici; adult/reduced €6/2.50; ⊙10am-8pm Tue-Sun Jun-Aug, to 6pm Sep-May) Housed in a neoclassical villa in the Giardini Pubblici (Public Gardens) north of the Castello, this terrific gallery focuses on modern and contemporary art. Works by many of Sardinia's top artists are on show, alongside paintings and sculptures from the Collezione Ingrao, a formidable collection of 20th-century Italian art.

Chiesa di San Michele CHURCH
(Via Ospedale 2; ⊙8-11am & 7-9pm Mon-Sat, 10am-noon & 7-9pm Sun) Although consecrated in 1538, this Jesuit church is best known for its lavish 18th-century decor, considered the finest example of baroque styling in Sardinia. The spectacle starts outside with the ebullient triple-arched facade and continues through the vast colonnaded atrium into the magnificent octagonal interior. Here six heavily decorated chapels radiate out from the centre, capped by a grand, brightly frescoed dome. Also of note is the sacristy, with its vivid frescoes and intricate inlaid wood.

Pinacoteca Nazionale GALLERY
(⌑340 9824303; www.pinacoteca.cagliari.beniculturali.it; Piazza Arsenale; adult/reduced €4/2, incl

Museo Archeologico Nazionale €9/4.50; ⊙9am-8pm Tue-Sun) Cagliari's principal gallery showcases a prized collection of 15th- to 17th-century art. Many of the best works are *retablos* (grand altarpieces), painted by Catalan and Genoese artists. Of those by known Sardinian painters, the four 16th-century works by Pietro Cavaro, father of the so-called Stampace school and arguably Sardinia's most important artist, are outstanding. They include a moving *Deposizione* (Deposition) and portraits of St Peter, St Paul and St Augustine.

Orto Botanico GARDENS
(Botanic Gardens; ⌑070 675 35 12; www.ccb-sardegna.it; Viale Sant'Ignazio da Laconi 11; adult/reduced €4/2; ⊙9am-8pm Tue-Sun summer, to 6pm Apr, May, Sep & Oct, to 2pm winter) Established in 1858, the Orto Botanico is one of Italy's most famous botanical gardens. Today it extends over 5 hectares and nurtures 2000 species of flora. Leafy arches lead to trickling fountains and gardens bristling with palm trees, cacti and *ficus* trees with huge snaking roots.

Piazza Yenne PIAZZA
The focal point of the Marina district, and indeed of central Cagliari, is Piazza Yenne. The small square is adorned with a statue of King Carlo Felice to mark the beginning of the SS131 cross-island highway, the project for which the monarch is best remembered. On summer nights, the piazza heaves as a

WORTH A TRIP

SAND IN THE CITY

An easy bus ride from the centre, Cagliari's fabulous **Poetto Beach** extends for 7km beyond the green Promontorio di Sant'Elia, nicknamed the Sella del Diavola (Devil's Saddle). In summer much of the city's youth decamps here to sunbathe and party in the restaurants and bars that line the sand. Water sports are big and you can hire canoes at the beach clubs. To get to the beach, take bus PF or PQ from Piazza Matteotti.

young crowd flocks to its bars, *gelaterie* and pavement cafes.

Museo del Tesoro e Area Archeologica di Sant'Eulalia MUSEUM
(☎070 66 37 24; www.mutseu.org; Vico del Collegio 2; adult/reduced €5/2.50; ⏲9.30am-4pm Tue-Sun) In the heart of the Marina district, this museum contains a rich collection of religious art, as well as an archaeological area beneath the adjacent **Chiesa di Sant'Eulalia**. The main drawcard is a 13m section of excavated Roman road (constructed between the 1st and 2nd centuries AD), which archaeologists think would have connected with the nearby port.

Festivals & Events

★**Festa di Sant'Efisio** RELIGIOUS
(www.festadisantefisio.com; ⏲1-4 May) Visitors descend in droves for this saintly celebration in May. On the opening day the effigy of St Ephisius, Cagliari's patron saint, is taken from the Chiesa di Sant'Efisio and paraded through the streets on a bullock-drawn carriage before being carried to Nora, 40km away, and back again. Tickets for the stands (€15 to €35) are sold at Box Office Tickets (p902).

Sleeping

Il Cagliarese B&B €
(☎339 6544083; www.ilcagliarese.com; Via Vittorio Porcile 19; s €45-60, d €60-75; ❄@📶) Bang in the heart of the Marina district, this snug B&B is a real find. It has three immaculate rooms, each with homey touches such as embroidered fabrics and carved wooden furnishings. Breakfast is scrumptious, and Mauro, your welcoming host, bends over backwards to please.

Residenza Kastrum B&B €
(☎348 0012280; www.kastrum.eu; Via Nicolò Canelles 78; s €55-60, d €65-85, q €125-160; ❄📶) Escape the hurly-burly of the centre at this cosy B&B in the hilltop Castello district. Its simple white rooms are comfortable enough, with parquet floors and classic dark wood furniture, but what sets it apart are the memorable views from the small rooftop terrace. The quad rooms are ideal for families.

Marina di Castello B&B €
(☎335 8125881; www.bedandbreakfastcagliaricity.it; Via Roma 75a; d €75-120; ❄📶) Sabrina makes you feel instantly at ease at this B&B on Cagliari's main seafront boulevard. There's a clean, modern feel about the place with rooms tastefully done up in silver, bronze and gold, while patches of exposed brick and artistic flourishes add a boutique touch. Up top, the roof terrace overlooking the marina is a panoramic spot for a summer sundowner.

Maison Savoia GUESTHOUSE €
(☎070 67 81 81, 334 2088478; www.maisonsavoia.it; Piazza Savoia 2; s €60-70, d €80-90; ❄📶) This discreet guesthouse is brilliantly placed right in the heart of the action. It's surrounded by restaurants, bars and shops, yet its decently sized rooms are quiet. Decor is old school, with parquet floors, framed prints and heavy wood furniture. Note that breakfast is not always included in your room rate.

★**Hotel Nautilus** HOTEL €€
(☎070 37 00 91; www.hotelnautiluspoetto.com; Viale Poetto 158; d €150-210, tr €170-225; ❄📶) Nothing shouts holiday as much as the sight of sea and sand on your doorstep. This gleaming three-star hotel is one of the best on the Poetto beachfront, offering summery blue and white rooms, balconies and sea views. Rates plummet in the low season.

Stampace Apartments APARTMENT €€
(☎335 7850199; www.stampaceapartments.com; Via Sassari 68; apt from €90; @📶) Chic, newly renovated apartments in a centrally located townhouse make a perfect base for exploring the city. Each beautiful apartment is outfitted with the basics you'll need to cook for yourself, two have balconies and the Licia Roof Garden room also has a terrace with views.

★**Hotel Miramare** BOUTIQUE HOTEL €€€
(☎070 66 40 21; www.hotelmiramarecagliari.it; Via Roma 59; r €207-500; ❄📶) A fashion magazine spread waiting to happen, this boutique four-star exudes effortless chic with its

artistic interiors and classy rooms. Located on sea-facing Via Roma, it has individually styled rooms whose decor ranges from pared-down contemporary cool to full-on belle-époque glamour, with crimson walls, zebra-print chairs, pop art and art deco furniture. Elevator, too.

✕ Eating

It's not difficult to eat well in Cagliari. The city offers everything from classy fine-dining restaurants to humble neighbourhood trattorias, pizzerias, bars and takeaways. Marina is chock-full of places. Some are obviously touristy, but many are, in fact, popular with locals. Good eat streets include Via Sassari and Corso Vittorio Emanuele.

Pizzeria Nansen   PIZZA €
(🖉070 667 03 35; Corso Vittorio Emanuele II 269; pizzas €5-10; ⊙11.30am-2.30pm Tue-Fri, plus 6.30-11.30pm Tue-Sun) For a slice of *delizioso* pizza and a cool bottle of Ichnusa (Sardinian beer), head to this superfriendly pizzeria. The pizzas, served ready-cut on a tray, are finger-lickingly good with light fluffy bases and flavour-packed toppings. The setting – high stools, paper napkins and framed Roma football shirts (!) – is suitably relaxed.

★Martinelli's   ITALIAN €€
(🖉070 65 42 20; www.martinellis.it; Via Principe Amedeo 18; meals from €35; ⊙8.30-11.30pm Tue-Sat) Simplicity is the ethos underpinning this intimate, subtly lit bistro in the Marina district. Service is friendly without being overbearing, and the menu plays up seasonal, winningly fresh seafood along the lines of *tagliolini* (flat spaghetti) with octopus ink and sea bass cooked in Vernaccia wine.

★La Paillote   SEAFOOD €€
(🖉340 3948856; www.lapaillote.it; Viale Cala Mosca, Cala Fighera; meals €35-45; ⊙11am-11pm; 🛜) It doesn't get much cooler than this. Open-air dining on a rocky promontory between Cala Mosca and Cala Fighera with sea and fortress views, sunshine and delicious seafood. On-trend Cagliarians sip cocktails and savour beautifully presented and conceived dishes. Book ahead or plan on waiting for a table on one of the chic loungers.

★L'Imperfetto   SARDINIAN €€
(🖉070 461 99 09; www.facebook.com/imperfettoristorante; Via dei Genovesi 111; meals €30-40; ⊙8-11pm Tue-Sat, plus 12.45-2.45pm Sat, 12.45-3.15pm Sun) If you have only one swank meal out in Sardinia, make it at L'Imperfetto. Tucked into a quiet lane in the Castello, this

arched-stone dining room is both elegant and welcoming, with fantastic, fresh Sardinian fare. It's a chance to try the specialties of the island executed with flair and integrity. Reserve ahead.

★Luigi Pomata   SEAFOOD €€€
(🖉070 67 20 58; www.luigipomata.com; Viale Regina Margherita 14; meals restaurant €50-60, bistrot €25-30; ⊙1-3pm & 8-11pm Mon-Sat) There's always a buzz at chef Luigi Pomata's minimalist seafood restaurant, with pared-down decor and chefs skilfully preparing superfresh sushi. For a more casual eating experience, try the Pomata Bistrot, around the corner at Via Porcile 21, where you can dine on dishes such as stuffed squid with broccoli cream in a tranquil, relaxed setting.

Dal Corsaro   RISTORANTE €€€
(🖉070 66 43 18; www.stefanodeidda.it; Viale Regina Margherita 28; fixed-price menus €95-125; ⊙8-11pm Tue-Sun) One of only three Michelin-starred restaurants in Sardinia, Dal Corsaro has long been a bastion of high-end culinary creativity. Calling the shots is chef Stefano Deidda, whose artistic brand of cuisine marries technical brilliance with a passion for seasonal Sardinian ingredients. Typical of his style is his *maialino da latte, topinambur e aglio* (roast pork with Jerusalem artichoke and garlic). Bookings required.

🍷 Drinking & Nightlife

★Cucina.eat   WINE BAR
(🖉070 099 10 98; www.facebook.com/pg/Cucina.eat; Piazza Galileo Galilei 1; ⊙10.30am-4pm & 6-11.30pm Mon-Sat) A bookshop, a bar, a bistro? Cucina.eat is pretty much all these things with its central bar and ceiling-high shelves stocked with wines, olive oils, cookbooks and kitchen gadgets, all of which are available to buy. Cool and relaxed, it's a fine spot to spend an evening over a bottle of wine and a light meal (around €12 to €25).

★Caffè Libarium Nostrum   BAR
(🖉346 5220212; Via Santa Croce 33; ⊙7.30am-2am) Offering some of the best views in town, this modish Castello bar has panoramic seating on top of the city's medieval ramparts. If the weather's being difficult, make for the brick-lined interior and order yourself an Alligator, a formidable cocktail of Calvados and Drambuie created in honour of the hero of Massimo Carlotto's novels.

Inu   WINE BAR
(🖉070 667 04 14; www.facebook.com/InuSardinaWineBar; Via Sassari 50; ⊙6.30pm-2am Tue-Sun)

SARDINIA CAGLIARI

Get versed in Sardinian wine at this contemporary, high-ceilinged wine bar, which pairs throaty Cannonau reds and tangy Vermentino whites with platters of top-quality Sardinian cured meats and cheeses, prepared at the well-stocked counter.

Hop Corner   PUB
(☑070 67 31 58; www.hopcornerbirreria.com; Via Principe Amedeo 14; ☺7.30pm-1am Tue-Thu, to 2am Fri & Sat) This vaulted pub carved out of rock is an atmospheric spot for specialty craft beers and ales, which pair nicely with the excellent hamburgers and platters of Sardinian cured meats and cheeses. It hosts occasional live-music evenings with a retro vibe.

Tiffany   CAFE
(☑070 732 47 87; Via Baylle 133; ☺6am-9pm Mon-Sat) The outside tables at this handsome brick-vaulted cafe are *the* place to be for an early evening *aperitivo*. Come around 6.30pm and you'll find every seat taken as Cagliari's fashionable drinkers congregate to catch up on gossip, sip on *spritz* and look beautiful.

☆ Entertainment

Cagliari has a lively performance scene, comprising classical music, dance, opera and drama. The season generally runs from October to May, although some places also offer a summer line-up of events. For information on upcoming events ask at the tourist office, check online at Box Office Tickets (☑070 65 74 28; www.boxofficesardegna.it; Viale Regina Margherita 43; ☺10am-1pm & 5-8pm Mon-Fri winter, plus 10am-1pm Sat summer), or pick up a copy of the local newspaper *L'Unione Sarda*.

Teatro Lirico   THEATRE
(☑070 408 22 30; www.teatroliricodicagliari.it; Via Sant'Alenixedda) This is Cagliari's premier venue for classical music, opera and ballet. The line-up is fairly traditional, but quality is high and concerts are well attended. Tickets range from €10 to €35 for concerts, and from €15 to €75 for opera and ballet.

🛍 Shopping

Cagliari has a refreshingly small number of overtly touristy souvenir shops. Style-conscious shoppers will find plenty to browse on Via Giuseppe Manno and Via Giuseppe Garibaldi. Nearby Via Sulis has several fashion boutiques and jewellery stores. You'll also find various artisanal shops tucked away, particularly in the Ma-

rina district. Sunday is best for flea market and antique finds.

★ Mercato di San Benedetto   MARKET
(☑070 6775614; Via San Francesco Cocco Ortu 50; ☺7am-2pm Mon-Fri, to 3pm Sat) Cagliari's historic morning food market is exactly what a thriving market should be: busy, noisy and packed with fresh, fabulous produce such as fish, salami, heavy clusters of grapes, *pecorino* the size of wagon wheels, steaks and sushi, among other foodstuffs.

Enoteca Biondi 1959   WINE
(☑070 667 04 26; www.enotecabiondi.it; Viale Regina Margherita 83; ☺10am-1.30pm & 5-9pm Mon-Sat) One of Cagliari's best-stocked bottle shops, Enoteca Biondi sells wine and beer from all over the world, as well as a selection of Italian gourmet specialities: balsamic vinegar from Modena, Sicilian *torrone* (nougat), conserves, cheeses and truffles.

Intrecci   ARTS & CRAFTS
(☑070 332 87 08; www.facebook.com/artegianata; Viale Regina Margherita 63; ☺10am-1pm & 4.30-8.30pm Mon-Sat) This airy showroom is a cut above Cagliari's other souvenir shops. It showcases a range of products made by island artisans, including hand-crafted jewellery, paintings, ceramic work and objets d'art.

ℹ Information

Virtually all hotels and B&Bs now offer free wi-fi, as do many bars and cafes. The city is also dotted with free wi-fi zones, including Via Roma and Largo Carlo Felice, but annoyingly you can only log in if you have an Italian SIM card (the password is sent to your mobile phone).

Banks and ATMs are widely available, particularly around the port and train station, on Largo Carlo Felice and Corso Vittorio Emanuele.

InfoPoint (☑070 3791 9201; www.parcomolentargius.it; Edificio Sali Scelti, Via La Palma; ☺8am-6pm) Learn about the Parco Naturale Regionale Molentargius at its information point on the eastern fringes of town.

Ospedale Brotzu (☑070 53 92 10; www.aobrotzu.it; Piazzale Ricchi 1) Hospital with accident and emergency department. It's located northwest of the city centre; take bus 1 from Via Roma if you need to make a nonemergency visit.

Tourist Office (☑070 677 81 73; www.cagliariturismo.it; Via Roma 145, Palazzo Civico; ☺9am-8pm Apr-Oct, 10am-1pm & 2-6pm Mon-Sat, 10am-1pm Sun Nov-Mar) Helpful English-speaking staff can provide city information and maps. If you email them, they'll send you an audioguide of the town for your smartphone.

The office is just inside Palazzo Civico's main entrance, on the right.

ℹ Getting There & Away

AIR

Cagliari Elmas Airport (☎ 070 21 12 11; www.cagliariairport.it) is 9km northwest of the city centre, near Elmas. Flights connect with mainland Italian cities, including Rome, Milan, Bergamo, Bologna, Florence, Naples, Rome, Turin and Venice. There are also flights to/from European destinations, including Barcelona, London, Paris and Frankfurt. In summer, there are additional charter flights.

A number of major international airlines serve Cagliari, such as easyJet, Eurowings and Ryanair, as well as Italy's national carrier **Alitalia** (☎ 892010, Sardinia flights 06 6585 9515, general info 06 6 56 40; www.alitalia.it) and **Air Italy** (☎ 0789 5 26 82, 892928; www.airitaly.com).

Trains run from the airport to Cagliari station approximately every 20 to 30 minutes between 6.49am and 11pm. The journey takes six to 10 minutes; tickets cost €1.30. A taxi will set you back around €20.

BOAT

Cagliari's ferry port is located just off Via Roma. **Tirrenia** (☎ 070 66 60 65, 892123, agency 070 66 95 01; www.tirrenia.it; Via Sassari 3; ⊙ agency 9am-noon Mon-Sat, plus 4-7pm Mon-Wed, 5-8pm Thu, 4.30-7.30pm Fri, 5-7pm Sat) is the main ferry operator serving Cagliari, with year-round services to Civitavecchia (€56 to €66 per person with a *poltrona* seat), Naples (€56 to €98 per person) and Palermo (€58 to €70 per person). Book tickets at the port agency, online or at travel agencies.

BUS

From the **main bus station** (Piazza Matteotti), **ARST** (Azienda Regionale Sarda Trasporti; ☎ 800 865042; www.arst.sardegna.it; ⊙ ticket office 7am-7.55pm) buses serve Pula (€3.10, 50 minutes, hourly), Chia (€3.70, 1¼ hours, up to 10 daily) and Villasimius (€4.30, 1½ hours, at least six daily), as well as Oristano (€6.50, two hours, two daily), Nuoro (€12.50, 2¾ hours, two daily) and Iglesias (€4.30, 1½ hours, daily Monday to Friday). There's luggage storage (€8 per day).

Turmo Travel (☎ 0789 2 14 87; www.gruppoturmotravel.com) has services to Olbia (€16.50, 4½ hours, twice daily) and Santa Teresa di Gallura (€19.50, 5½ hours, daily).

CAR & MOTORCYCLE

The island's main dual-carriage, the SS131 'Carlo Felice', links the capital with Porto Torres via Oristano and Sassari; a branch road, the SS-131dcn, runs from Oristano to Olbia via Nuoro. The SS130 leads west to Iglesias.

TRAIN

The main train station is located on Piazza Matteotti. Direct trains serve Iglesias (€4.30, one hour, 11 daily), Sassari (€16.50, 2¾ to 3½ hours, five daily), Oristano (€6.50, 50 minutes to 1½ hours, 15 daily) and Olbia (€18, 3¼ hours, three daily).

ℹ Getting Around

BUS

CTM (Consorzio Trasporti e Mobilità; ☎ 800 078870; www.ctmcagliari.it; single/daily ticket €1.30/3.30) bus routes cover the city and surrounding area. You might use the buses to reach a handful of out-of-the-way sights, and they come in handy for Calamosca and Poetto beaches. Tickets are valid for 1½ hours. Try the smartphone app.

The most useful lines:

Bus 7 Circular route from Piazza Yenne up to Il Castello and back.

Bus 30 or 31 Along the seafront to near the sanctuary at Bonaria.

Bus PF or PQ From Piazza Matteotti to Poetto beach.

CAR & MOTORCYCLE

Driving in the centre of Cagliari is a pain, although given the geography of the town (one big hill), you might consider renting a scooter for a day or two.

Parking in the city centre from 9am to 1pm and 4pm to 8pm Monday to Saturday means paying. On-street metered parking (within the blue lines) costs €1 per hour. Alternatively, there's a 24-hour car park next to the train station, which costs €1 per hour or €10 for 24 hours. There's no maximum stay.

TAXI

Many hotels and guesthouses arrange airport pickups. There are taxi ranks at Piazza Matteotti, Piazza Repubblica and Piazza Yenne. Otherwise you can call the radio taxi firms **Radio Taxi 4 Mori** (☎ 070 40 01 01; www.cagliaritaxi.com) and **Rossoblù** (☎ 070 66 55; www.radiotaxirossoblu.com).

Around Cagliari

The Sarrabus, the triangular-shaped territory that covers Sardinia's southeastern corner, is one of the island's least populated and least developed areas. It might only be an hour or two by car from Cagliari, but it feels like another world, with its remote, thickly wooded mountains and snaking, silent roads. Its high point, Monte dei Sette Fratelli (1023m), is a miraculously unspoilt wilderness, home to some of the island's last remaining deer. The coastal scenery is every bit as impressive, featuring high cliff-bound coves and endless swaths of sand fronted by transparent azure waters.

Most people visit in summer, sticking to the well-known and correspondingly busy beach destinations of Villasimius and the Costa Rei, but venture inland and you'll discover there's some great hiking to be had in its mountainous hinterland.

Villasimius & Capo Carbonara

POP 3660

Once a quiet fishing village surrounded by pines and *macchia* (Mediterranean scrub), Villasimius is now one of Sardinia's most popular southern resorts. The town itself is about 1.5km inland, but it makes a handy base from which to explore the fabulous beaches and transparent waters that sparkle on the nearby coast. In summer it's a lively, busy place, but activity all but dies out in winter.

◎ Sights & Activities

★ **Capo Carbonara**   NATURE RESERVE
(www.ampcapocarbonara.it) If you embark on just one excursion from Villasimius, make it the 15-minute drive south to Capo Carbonara, a protected marine park. The promontory dips spectacularly into the crystal-clear waters of the Med. Besides perfect conditions for divers, the area has some gorgeously secluded bays with white quartz sand, backed by cliffs cloaked in *macchia* and wildflowers. Walking trails teeter off in all directions.

★ **Cala Giunco**   BEACH
The pick of Villasimius' *spiagge* (beaches), Cala Giunco is a vision of beach perfection: a long strip of silky white sand sandwiched between tropical azure waters and a silvery lagoon, the **Stagno Notteri**, where pink flamingos congregate in spring. To the north, *macchia*-clad hills rise on the blue horizon.

Fiore di Maggio   BOATING
(☑ 345 6032042; www.fioredimaggio.eu; per adult/child incl lunch €45/25) These daily boat tours are a superb way to see the hidden bays and islands of the Capo Carbonara marine reserve. Take your bathers if you fancy a dip.

🛏 Sleeping & Eating

Hotel Mariposas   HOTEL €€
(☑ 070 79 00 84; www.hotelmariposas.it; Via Mar Nero 1; s €80-190, d €120-250, ste €135-280;

P ❄ 🛜 🌊) Situated about halfway between the town centre and Spiaggia Simius, this lovely stone-clad hotel is set in glorious flower-strewn gardens. Its sunny spacious rooms all have their own terrace or balcony, and there's an attractive pool for whiling away those lazy afternoons.

Ristorante Le Anfore   MEDITERRANEAN €€
(☑ 070 79 20 32; www.hotelleanfore.com; Via Pallaresus 16; meals €35-45; ⊙ noon-2.30pm Tue-Sun & 7.30-10.30pm daily) The chef's love of fresh local produce shines through in Sardinian dishes such as *bottarga di muggine* (mullet roe) and *fregola con le vongole* (couscous-like pasta with clams) at this highly regarded hotel restaurant. Adding to the experience is the alfresco veranda overlooking the hotel gardens.

❶ Getting There & Away

ARST buses run to and from Cagliari (€4.30, 1½ hours, at least six daily) throughout the year.

Costa Rei

Stretching along Sardinia's southeastern seafront, the Costa Rei extends from Cala Sinzias, about 25km north of the resort Villasimius, to a rocky headland known as Capo Ferrato. Its lengthy beaches are stunning with soft, pearly-white sands and glorious azure waters.

Approaching from Villasimius, the first beach you hit is Cala Sinzias, a pretty sandy strip some 6km south of the main Costa Rei resort. The resort is typical of many in Sardinia, a functional holiday village of villas, shops, bars and eateries that's dead in winter but packed in the summer holiday months. In front of the resort, the **Spiaggia Costa Rei** is a lengthy strip of dazzling white sand lapped by astonishingly clear blue-green waters.

North of the resort, the fabulous **Spiaggia Piscina Rei** impresses with its blinding white sand and turquoise water. A couple more beaches fill the remaining length of coast up to Capo Ferrato, beyond which drivable dirt trails lead north.

You can pitch a tent under eucalyptus and mimosa trees at **Villaggio Camping Capo Ferrato** (☑ 070 99 10 12; www.campingcapoferrato.it; Località Costa Rei; 2 people, car & tent €22-45; ⊙ Apr-Oct; P 🛜), a well-organised campground by the southern entrance to Capo Rei. Facilities include a small food shop, tennis court, kids' playground and direct access to the adjacent beach. It also has small bungalows.

❶ Getting There & Away

Throughout the year, three weekday ARST buses connect the Costa Rei with Villasimius (€1.90, 45 minutes). In summer, there are at least a couple more services.

Costa del Sud & Chia

Extending from Porto di Teulada to Chia, the Costa del Sud is one of southern Sardinia's most beautiful coastal stretches. The main hub is Chia, a popular summer hangout centred on two glorious beaches. Elsewhere, you'll find several swimming spots on the Strada Panoramica della Costa del Sud, the stunning road that dips and twists its way along the rocky coastline.

◉ Sights & Activities

Chia   VILLAGE
More a collection of hotels, holiday homes and campgrounds than a traditional village, Chia is surrounded by rusty-red hills tufted with tough *macchia*. Its beaches are hugely popular, drawing an annual influx of sunseekers, windsurfers and water-sports enthusiasts. To see what all the fuss is about, head up to the Spanish watchtower and look to the west to **Spiaggia Sa Colonia**, the area's largest and busiest beach, and to the east to the smaller **Spiaggia Su Portu**.

**★ Strada Panoramica
della Costa del Sud**   SCENIC DRIVE
Running the 25km length of the Costa del Sud, this panoramic road – known more prosaically as the SP71 – snakes along the spectacular coastline between Chia and Porto di Teulada. It's a stunning drive whichever way you do it, with jaw-dropping views at every turn and a succession of bays capped by Spanish-era watchtowers.

Starting in Chia, you'll begin with a Spanish watchtower presiding over the small resort and its two fine beaches. From here the road climbs inland away from the water. For great coastal views, turn off along the narrow side road at **Porto Campana** and follow the dirt track to the lighthouse at **Capo Spartivento**. Along that stretch, watch out for signposts to Cala Cipolla (a gorgeous spot backed by pine and juniper trees), Spiaggia Su Giudeu and Porto Campana to detour out to the sea.

As the main road drops back to the coast, popular **Cala Teurredda** beach has vivid emerald-green waters, summer snack bars and a conveniently situated bus stop.

The road then twists past several coves as it rises to and descends from the high point of **Capo Malfatano**. As the road wriggles along the coast on the last stretch to Porto di Teulada, **Spiaggia Piscinni** is a great place for a dip with incredible azure waters.

🛏 Sleeping

Campeggio Torre Chia   CAMPGROUND €
(☑ 070 923 00 54; www.campeggiotorrechia.it; Via del Porto 21, Chia; 2 people, car & tent €26-34, 4-person cottage €70-135; ⊙ May-Oct) At the popular summer resort of Chia, this busy campground enjoys a prime location near the beach. It's fairly spartan with minimal facilities, tent pitches under pine trees and basic four-person cottages.

❶ Getting There & Away

Chia is located off the SS195, the main road that runs between Cagliari and Teulada. Regular ARST buses connect Cagliari with Chia (€4.30, 1¼ hours).

SOUTHWESTERN SARDINIA

Iglesias

🖉 0781 / POP 26,800
Surrounded by the skeletons of Sardinia's once-thriving mining industry, Iglesias is a historic town that bubbles in the summer and slumbers in the colder months. Its historic centre, an appealing ensemble of lived-in piazzas, sun-bleached buildings, churches and Aragonese-style wrought-iron balconies, creates an atmosphere that's as much Iberian as Sardinian – a vestige of its time as a Spanish colony. Visit at Easter to experience the city's extraordinary Settimana Santa (Holy Week) processions, featuring trains of sinister-looking, white-robed celebrants parading through the skinny lanes of the *centro storico* (historic centre).

◉ Sights

Cattedrale di Santa Chiara   CATHEDRAL
(Duomo; Piazza del Municipio; ⊙ 9am-12.30pm & 3-8pm) Dominating the eastern flank of Piazza del Municipio, the Cattedrale di Santa Chiara has a lovely Pisan-flavoured gold-hued facade and a checkerboard stone bell tower. The church was originally built in the late 13th century, but it was given a comprehensive makeover in the 16th century, which

WORTH A TRIP

ISOLE DI SANT'ANTIOCO & SAN PIETRO

The southwest's two islands, Isola di Sant'Antioco and Isola di San Pietro, display very different characters. The larger and more developed of the two, Isola di Sant'Antioco has a casual small-town vibe, but not the spectacular beauty that you'd ordinarily associate with small Mediterranean islands. It's got a rich history – it was founded by the Phoenicians in the 8th century BC, and its historic hilltop centre is littered with necropolises.

Barely half an hour across the water, Isola di San Pietro presents a pretty picture with its pastel houses and bobbing fishing boats. A mountainous trachyte island measuring about 15km long and 11km wide, it's named after St Peter, who, legend has it, was marooned here during a storm on the way to Karalis (now Cagliari). Its main town, Carloforte, is the very image of Mediterranean chic, with graceful *palazzi*, crowded cafes, palm trees along the waterfront and quaint cobbled streets. The island's restaurants dish up the world-famous local tuna.

Regular Delcomar (☑ 800 195344, Calasetta ticket office 342 1080330; www.delcomar.it; Calasetta; ⊙ 7.15am-5.50pm Mon-Sat, to 7pm Sun) ferries sail from Portovesme on the Sardinian 'mainland' to Carloforte (per person/midsize car €4.90/14, 30 minutes) and on to Calasetta (per person/midsize car €4.50/11, 13 daily) on Sant'Antioco. Alternatively, Sant'Antioco town is accessible by the SS126 road bridge.

accounts for its current Catalan Gothic look. Inside, the highlight is a gilded retable that once held the relics of St Antiochus.

Museo dell'Arte Mineraria　　　MUSEUM
(☑ 347 5176886; www.museoartemineraria.it; Via Roma 47; adult/reduced €5/4; ⊙ 6.30-8.30pm Sat & Sun Jun-Aug, by appointment rest of year) Just outside the historic centre, Iglesias' main museum is dedicated to the town's mining heritage. It displays up to 70 extraction machines, alongside tools and a series of thought-provoking B&W photos. But to get a real taste of the claustrophobic conditions in which the miners worked, duck down into the recreated tunnels. These were dug by mining students and were used to train senior workers until WWII when they were used as air-raid shelters.

🛏 Sleeping

★ **B&B Mare Monti Miniere**　　　B&B €
(☑ 0781 4 17 65, 348 3310585; www.maremonti miniere-bb.it; Via Trento 10; s €35-45, d €45-55, tr €65-80; ❋ 🐾) A warm welcome awaits at this cracking B&B. Situated in a quiet side street near the historic centre, it has two cheery and immaculately kept rooms in the main house and an independent studio with its own kitchen facilities. Thoughtful extras include beach towels and a regular supply of home-baked cakes and biscuits.

ℹ Getting There & Away

Twice-daily ARST buses run to Cagliari (€4.30, one to 1½ hours).

Costa Verde

Extending from Capo Pecora in the south to the small resort of Torre dei Corsari in the north, the Costa Verde (Green Coast) is one of Sardinia's great untamed coastlines, an unspoilt stretch of wild, exhilarating tawny sands and windswept dunes. Inland, woods and *macchia* (Mediterranean scrub) cover much of the mountainous hinterland.

The area's main drawcards are its two magnificent beaches – Spiaggia di Scivu and Spiaggia di Piscinas – and the former mining complex of Montevecchio. Elsewhere, keen hikers can summit Monte Arcuentu (785m), one of the last preserves of the *cervo sardo* (Sardinian deer), and lovers of quirky museums can learn about Sardinian knives at Arbus, a small mountain town sprawled along the slopes of Monte Linas.

◉ Sights

★ **Spiaggia di Piscinas**　　　BEACH
This magnificent beach is a picture of unspoilt beauty. A broad band of golden sand, it's sandwiched between a big-wave sea and a vast expanse of dunes flecked by hardy green *macchia*. These towering dunes, known as Sardinia's desert, rise to heights of up to 60m. Facilities are limited but in summer there's a hotel and two beach bars with showers, umbrellas and sunloungers.

The beach is signposted off the SS126 and is most accessible via Ingurtosu and a 9km dirt track.

Spiaggia di Scivu   BEACH

A 3km lick of fine sand backed by towering dunes and walls of sandstone, Spiaggia Scivu is the most southerly of the Costa Verde's beaches. To get there take the SS126 and head towards Arbus (if heading north) or Fluminimaggiore (if heading south) and follow the signs about 12km south of Arbus.

🛏 Sleeping & Eating

Agriturismo L'Oasi del Cervo   AGRITURISMO €

(🖉347 3011318; www.oasidelcervo.com; Località Is Gennas, off SP65, Montevecchio; d €60-70, half-board per person €55-60; 🅿🛜) With 12 modest rooms and a remote location amid *macchia*-cloaked hills, this working farm is a genuine country hideaway. It's very down to earth, but the rooms are comfortable enough, the views are uplifting, the owners are warm, and the homemade **food** (meals €25-30; ⊙reservation only) is delicious. You'll see a sign for the *agriturismo* off the SP65 between Montevecchio and Torre dei Corsari.

Hotel Le Dune Piscinas   HOTEL €€€

(🖉070 97 71 30; www.ledunepiscinas.com; Spiaggia di Piscinas; d from €200; ⊙mid-Apr–Aug; ❄@🛜) Location, location, location. This hotel is all about its prime spot on Spiaggia di Piscinas, one of the best beaches in Sardinia. It's a classic hotel, with understated decor and attentive service, but the reason to be here is to walk out onto that gorgeous stretch of tawny sand like it's your front yard.

❶ Getting There & Away

Travelling in this area is difficult without a car. You can get to Arbus by bus from Cagliari (€4.90, two hours, up to 11 daily weekdays) and Oristano (€4.30, 1¼ hours, up to seven daily weekdays), but beyond that you're pretty much on your own. Access to the area by road is via the inland SS126.

ORISTANO & THE WEST

Oristano

📞 0783 / POP 31,700

With its elegant shopping streets, ornate piazzas, popular cafes and some good restaurants, Oristano's refined and animated centre is a lovely place to hang out. Though there's not a huge amount to see beyond some churches and an interesting archaeological museum, the city makes a good base for the surrounding area.

👁 Sights

⭐**Piazza Eleonora d'Arborea**   PIAZZA

Oristano's elegant outdoor salon sits at the southern end of pedestrianised Corso Umberto I. An impressive, rectangular space, it comes to life on summer evenings when townsfolk congregate and children blast footballs against the glowing *palazzi*. The city's central square since the 19th century, it's flanked by grand buildings, including the neoclassical Municipio. In the centre stands an ornate 19th-century statue of Eleonora, raising a finger as if about to launch into a political speech.

**Cattedrale di Santa
Maria Assunta**   CATHEDRAL

(Duomo; Piazza Duomo; ⊙9am-7pm summer, to 6pm winter) Lording it over Oristano's skyline, the Duomo's onion-domed bell tower is one of the few remaining elements of the original 14th-century cathedral, itself a reworking of an earlier church damaged by fire in the late 12th century. The free-standing *campanile* (bell tower), topped by its conspicuous majolica-tiled dome, adds an exotic Byzantine feel to what is otherwise a typical 18th-century baroque complex.

SARDINIA ORISTANO

DON'T MISS

NURAGHE SU NURAXI

In the heart of the voluptuous green countryside near Barumini, the Nuraghe Su Nuraxi (🖉070 936 81 28; www.fondazionebarumini.it; SP44; adult/reduced €12/9; ⊙9am-8pm summer, to 5pm winter, last admission 1hr before closing) is Sardinia's sole World Heritage Site and the island's most visited *nuraghe*. The focal point is the 1500 BC tower, which originally stood on its own but was later incorporated into a fortified compound. Many of the settlement's buildings were erected in the Iron Age, and it's these that constitute the beehive of circular interlocking buildings that tumble down the hillside.

Hours vary by month – check the website. Visits are by guided tour only, in Italian or English. Queues are the norm in summer when it can get very hot on the exposed site.

Oristano

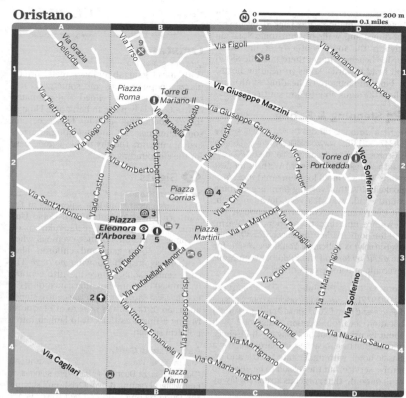

Oristano

◎ Top Sights

◎ Sights

◎ Sleeping

◎ Eating

Museo Archeologico
Antiquarium Arborense MUSEUM
(📞0783 79 12 62; www.antiquariumarborense.it; Piazza Corrias; adult/reduced €5/2.50; ◎9am-8pm Mon-Fri, to 2pm & 3-8pm Sat & Sun) Oristano's principal museum has one of the island's major archaeological collections, with prehistoric artefacts from the Sinis Peninsula and finds from Carthaginian and Roman Tharros. There's also a small collection of *retabli* (painted altarpieces), including the

16th-century *Retablo del Santo Cristo,* from the workshop of Pietro Cavaro. It depicts a group of apparently beatific saints, but look closer and you'll see they all sport the instruments of their torture slicing through their heads, necks and hearts.

★✦ Festivals & Events

★ Sa Sartiglia CARNIVAL
(◎Feb) Oristano's carnival is the most colourful on the island. It is attended by hun-

dreds of costumed participants and involves a medieval joust, horse racing and incredible, acrobatic riding.

🛏 Sleeping

★Eleonora B&B
B&B €

(☎0783 7 04 35, 347 4817976; www.eleonora-bed-and-breakfast.com; Piazza Eleonora d'Arborea 12; s €40-60, d €65-90, tr €80-110; 🌐🛜) This charming B&B scores on all counts: location – it's in a medieval *palazzo* on the central piazza; decor – rooms are decorated with a mix of antique furniture, exposed-brick walls and gorgeous old tiles; and hospitality – owners Andrea and Paola are helpful, hospitable hosts. It's excellent value for money.

★Hotel Regina d'Arborea
BOUTIQUE HOTEL €€

(☎0783 30 21 01; www.hotelreginadarborea.com; Piazza Eleonora 4; r €115-225) Palatial elegance and prime location are the twin attractions at this hotel on Oristano's main square. Four of the seven rooms are downright magnificent, with 7m-high ceilings, restored ceiling frescoes and original patterned floors. Book ahead for the Sofia room, crowned with a hexagonal cupola and wraparound windows that offer a bird's-eye view of Oristano's famous Eleonora d'Arborea statue.

✕ Eating

★Trattoria Gino
TRATTORIA €€

(☎0783 7 14 28; Via Tirso 13; meals €25-33; ⊙12.30-3pm & 8-11pm Mon-Sat) For excellent food and a bustling, authentic vibe, head to this old-school trattoria. Since the 1930s, locals and visitors alike have been squeezing into Gino's simple dining room to feast on tasty seafood and classic pastas. Don't miss the seafood antipasto, the butter-soft roast *seppie* (cuttlefish) and the scrumptious *seadas* (fried dough pockets with fresh *pecorino*, lemon and honey) for dessert.

La Brace
SARDINIAN €€

(☎0783 7 33 28; Via Figoli 41; lunch specials €15-20, meals €25-35; ⊙1-2.30pm & 8-11pm Tue-Sun) This restaurant's name refers to the glowing embers of a wood fire, and grilled meats and fish are indeed its speciality – but you'll also find a full range of Sardinian appetisers, homemade pastas and desserts.

❶ Information

Tourist Office (☎0783 368 32 10; www.gooristano.com; Piazza Eleonora d'Arborea 18; ⊙10am-2pm & 3-5pm Mon-Thu, to 7pm Fri-Sun) Ask for the useful booklet, *Oristano in Your Pocket*.

❶ Getting There & Away

From the main **bus station** (Via Cagliari), direct buses run to/from Santa Giusta (€1.30, 15 minutes, half-hourly), Cagliari (€6.50, two hours, two daily), Bosa (€4.90, two hours, five daily) and Sassari (€8, two hours, three daily).

The main train station is on Piazza Ungheria, east of the town centre. Up to 17 daily trains, some of which involve a change, run between Oristano and Cagliari (€6.70, 50 to 80 minutes). Direct trains serve Sassari (€11, two to 2¼ hours, two to three daily) and Olbia (€12.50, 2½ hours, three to four daily); there are additional services, but they require a change at Ozieri-Chilivani.

Tharros & the Sinis Peninsula

Spearing into the Golfo di Oristano, the Sinis Peninsula feels like a lush escape. Its limpid lagoons – the Stagno di Cabras, Stagno Sale Porcus and Stagno Is Benas – and snow-white beaches lend it an almost remote air, while the low-lying green countryside alternates agricultural fields with flower-filled meadows in spring. The area has been inhabited since the 5th century BC and *nuraghi* litter the landscape. The compelling Punic-Roman site of Tharros also stands testament to the area's historic importance. Water-sports enthusiasts will enjoy great surfing, windsurfing and fine diving.

Although summer is the obvious time to visit, early spring when wildflowers brighten the verdant landscape and flocks of migrating birds swarm to the lagoons is also wonderful. The queen of the show is the gorgeous pink flamingo.

◉ Sights

★Area Archeologica di Tharros
ARCHAEOLOGICAL SITE

(☎0783 37 00 19; www.tharros.sardegna.it; adult/reduced €5/4, incl tower €6/5, incl Museo Civico Cabras €8/6; ⊙9am-7pm Jun, Jul & Sep, to 8pm Aug, to 6pm Apr, May & Oct, to 5pm Nov-Mar) The choppy blue waters of the Golfo di Oristano provide a magnificent backdrop to the ruins of ancient Tharros. Founded by the Phoenicians in the 8th century BC, the city thrived as a Carthaginian naval base and was later taken over by the Romans. Much of what you see today dates to the 2nd and 3rd centuries AD, when the basalt streets were laid and the aqueduct, baths and other major monuments were built.

SARDINIA BOSA

EXPLORING THE SINIS PENINSULA

One of the peninsula's most famous beaches, Is Aruttas is a pristine arc of white sand fronted by translucent aquamarine waters. For years its quartz sand was carted off to be used in aquariums and on beaches on the Costa Smeralda, but it's now illegal to take the sand away. From San Salvatore on the main Oristano–Tharros road, follow signs 2km north along the SP7 then continue 5km west on the SP59 to reach the beach.

Backed by a motley set of holiday homes and beach bars, Putzu Idu's beach sits in the north of the peninsula. It's a picturesque strip of sand that's something of a water-sports hotspot with excellent surfing, windsurfing and kitesurfing. To the north, the Capo Mannu promontory is scalloped with a tantalising array of more secluded beaches and battered by some of the Mediterranean's biggest waves.

In business for more than 20 years, the Sinis Peninsula's top surf school, Is Benas Surf Club (☑ 0783 192 53 63; www.isbenas.com; Lungomare S'Arena Scoada, Putzu Idu) has it all – from lessons to equipment to accommodation to professional advice – for surfers, kitesurfers and stand-up paddleboarders. The main branch is just south of Putzu Idu at Arena Scoada beach, while the affiliated Capo Mannu Kite School is a few kilometres northwest at Sa Rocca Tunda.

★ Museo Civico   MUSEUM

(☑ 0783 29 06 36; www.museocabras.it; Via Tharros 121; adult/reduced €5/4, incl Tharros €8/6; ☺ 9am-1pm & 4-8pm Mon-Sat, to 1pm & 3-8pm Sun Apr-Oct, to 1pm & 3-7pm Tue-Sun Nov-Mar) Cabras' cultural highlight is the Museo Civico, and the real superstars here are the so-called Giants of Monte Prama, a series of towering nuraghic figures depicting archers, wrestlers and boxers. Also of interest are finds from Tharros and the prehistoric site of Cuccuru Is Arrius, along with obsidian and flint tools said to date back to the Neolithic cultures of Bonu Ighinu and Ozieri.

Chiesa di San Giovanni di Sinis   CHURCH

(SP6; ☺ 9am-5pm) Built from softly worn sandstone, Chiesa di San Giovanni di Sinis is one of the two oldest churches in Sardinia (Cagliari's Basilica di San Saturnino is older). It owes its current form to an 11th-century makeover, although elements of the 6th-century Byzantine original remain, including the characteristic red dome. Inside, the bare walls lend a sombre and richly spiritual atmosphere. Find it near the southern tip of the Sinis Peninsula, just beyond the car park at the foot of the Tharros access road.

🛏 Sleeping & Eating

Agriturismo Sinis   AGRITURISMO €€

(☑ 328 9312508, 0783 39 26 53; www.agriturismoilsinis.it; Località San Salvatore; half-board per person €55-65; ❋ 🐾) This working farm offers 12 guest rooms and serves wonderful earthy food. Rooms are frill-free but clean and airy, and views of the lush garden can be enjoyed from chairs on the patio.

★ Hotel Lucrezia   HOTEL €€

(☑ 0783 41 20 78; www.hotellucrezia.it; Via Roma 14a, Riola Sardo; r €164-184, ste €264-284; ❋ @) Housed in a 17th-century *cortile* (courtyard house), this elegant hideaway has rooms surrounding an inner garden complete with a wisteria-draped pergola and fig and citrus trees. The decor is rustic-chic, with high 18th-century antique beds, period furniture and eye-catching tiled bathrooms. Bikes are provided, and the welcoming staff regularly organise cooking classes. Note that there's a three-night minimum stay in August.

Sa Pischera 'e Mar 'e Pontis   SEAFOOD €€

(☑ 0783 39 17 74; www.consorziopontis.it; Strada Provinciale 6; menus €27-32; ☺ 1-2.30pm & 8-9.30pm) The Pontis fishing cooperative on the waterfront between Cabras and Tharros runs this atmospheric spot. The fresh seafood menu changes according to the daily catch, but pride of place goes to the local *muggine* (mullet) and prized *bottarga* (mullet roe). Booking recommended.

❶ Getting There & Away

Tharros is a 25-minute drive from Oristano. Take the SP6 to San Giovanni di Sinis, then continue south another 1km to the parking area.

Bosa

☑ 0785 / POP 7930

Bosa is one of Sardinia's most beautiful towns. Seen from a distance, its rainbow townscape resembles a vibrant Paul Klee canvas, with pastel houses stacked on a steep hillside, tapering up to a majestic, golden castle. In front, moored fishing boats bob on a glassy river elegantly lined with palm trees.

Bosa was established by the Phoenicians and thrived under the Romans. During the early Middle Ages it suffered repeat raids by Arab pirates, but in the early 12th century a branch of the noble Tuscan Malaspina family moved in and built their huge castle. In the 19th century, the Savoys established lucrative tanneries here, but these have since fallen by the wayside.

About 2.5km west of Bosa proper, at the mouth of the Fiume Temo, Bosa Marina is the town's seaside satellite. It's a busy summer resort set on a wide, 1km-long beach overlooked by a 16th-century Aragonese defensive tower.

◉ Sights

★**Castello Malaspina** CASTLE
(Castello di Serravalle; ☎0785 37 70 43; www.castellodibosa.com; Via Canonico Nino; adult/reduced €5.50/4.50; ☉10am-1hr before sunset Apr-Oct, 10am-1pm Sat & Sun Nov-Mar) Commanding huge views, this hilltop castle was built in the 12th and 13th centuries by the Tuscan Malaspina family. Little remains of the original structure except for its skeleton – imposing walls and a series of stone towers. Inside, a humble 14th-century chapel, the special **Chiesa di Nostra Signora di Regnos Altos**, is adorned with an extraordinary 14th-century fresco cycle depicting saints ranging from St George slaying the dragon to St Lawrence in the middle of his martyrdom on the grill.

★**Museo Casa Deriu** MUSEUM
(☎0785 37 70 43; Corso Vittorio Emanuele II 59; adult/reduced €4.50/3; ☉10.30am-1pm & 3-5pm Tue-Fri, to 6pm Sat & Sun) Housed in an elegant 19th-century townhouse, Bosa's main museum showcases local arts and crafts. Each floor has a different theme relating to the city and its past: the 1st floor hosts temporary exhibitions and displays of traditional hand embroidery; the 2nd floor displays the *palazzo*'s original 19th-century decor and furnishings; and the top floor is dedicated to Melkiorre Melis (1889–1982), one of Sardinia's most important modern artists.

⌖ Sleeping

★**Hotel Sa Pischedda** HOTEL €€
(☎0785 37 30 65; www.hotelsapischedda.com; Via Roma 8; d €95-170; ❄@🛜) The apricot facade of this restored 1890s hotel greets you just south of the Ponte Vecchio. Several rooms retain original frescoed ceilings, some are split-level, and a few (such as 305) have terraces overlooking the river. Additional perks include friendly staff, an excellent restaurant and thoughtful touches for families (witness the 4th-floor suite with its own elevator for easy stroller access).

✕ Eating & Drinking

★**Locanda di Corte** SARDINIAN €€
(☎340 2474823; www.facebook.com/Locanda DiCorte; Via del Pozzo 7; meals €30-35; ☉12.30-2.30pm & 7.30-10pm Tue-Sun) Wriggle through Bosa's backstreets to discover this sweet local trattoria on a secluded cobblestoned square. Owners Angelo and Angela work the small collection of tables adorned with

SARDINIA BOSA

WORTH A TRIP

THE SACRED WELL OF SANTA CRISTINA

Just off the SS131 north of Oristano, the **Nuraghe di Santa Cristina** (Sanctuary of Santa Cristina; www.archeotour.net; SS131; adult/reduced incl Museo Archeologico-Etnografico Paulilatino €5/2.50; ☉8.30am-sunset) is an important nuraghic complex. The nuraghic village's extraordinary Bronze Age *tempio a pozzo* (well temple) is one of the best preserved in Sardinia. The worship of water was a fundamental part of nuraghic religious practice, and there are reckoned to be about 40 sacred wells across the island – this is the most awe-inspiring example.

Dating back to the late Bronze Age (11th to 9th century BC), the *tempio a pozzo* is accessible through a finely cut basalt keyhole entrance and a flight of 24 superbly preserved steps. When you reach the bottom you can gaze up at the perfectly constructed tholos (conical tower), through which light enters the dark well shaft. Every 18 years, one month and two days, the full moon shines directly through the aperture into the well. Otherwise you can catch the yearly equinoxes on 21 March and 23 September, when the sun lights up the stairway down to the well.

red-and-white-checked cloths, while their son Nicola cooks up scrumptious Sardinian classics such as *fregola* pasta with mussels, clams and cherry tomatoes, or pork chops in Cannonau wine.

Cantina G Battista Columbu　　WINE BAR
(☑339 5731677; www.malvasiacolumbu.com; Via del Carmine 104; ⊙10.30am-1.30pm & 5.30-9pm) A wonderful venue for sampling Bosa's renowned Malvasia, this attractive cantina is operated by the Columbu family, which has been producing wine in the region for three generations. Sip glasses (€3 to €4) of smooth-as-silk, sherry-like Malvasia di Bosa and aromatic Alvariga, along with wines from other Sardinian vintners, accompanied by local *salumi* and *formaggi* (cold cuts and cheeses).

ⓘ Information

Pro Loco Bosa (☑ 349 9360900; www.face book.com/prolocobosa.info; ⊙10am-1pm & 3.30-7pm)

ⓘ Getting There & Away

There are weekday services from the bus stops on Piazza Zanetti to Alghero (€3.70, 55 minutes, two daily), Sassari (€5.50, 2¼ hours, three daily) and Oristano (€4.90, two hours, five daily). Buy tickets at **Edicola da Oscar** (Corso Vittorio Emanuele II 80; ⊙8am-1pm & 4-8pm Mon-Sat, to 1pm Sun).

ALGHERO & THE NORTHWEST

Alghero

☑079 / POP 44,000
One of Sardinia's most beautiful medieval cities, seafront Alghero is the main resort in the northwest. Although largely given over to tourism – its population can almost

quadruple in July and August – the town retains a proud and independent spirit. Its animated historic centre is a terrific place to hang out and, with so many excellent restaurants and bars, it makes an ideal base for exploring the beaches and beauty spots of the nearby Riviera del Corallo.

The main focus of attention is the picturesque *centro storico*, one of the best preserved in Sardinia. Enclosed by robust, honey-coloured sea walls, it's a tightly knit enclave of cobbled lanes, Gothic *palazzi* and cafe-lined piazzas. Below, yachts crowd the marina and long, sandy beaches curve away to the north. Presiding over everything is a palpable Spanish atmosphere, a hangover from the city's past as a Catalan colony.

◉ Sights

★**Sea Walls**　　WALLS
(Bastioni) Alghero's golden sea walls, built around the *centro storico* by the Aragonese in the 16th century, are a highlight of the town's historic cityscape. Running from Piazza Sulis in the south to Porta a Mare in the north, they're crowned by a pedestrianised path that commands superb views over to Capo Caccia on the blue horizon. Restaurants and bars line the walkway, providing the perfect perch to sit back and lap up the holiday atmosphere.

★**Campanile**　　TOWER
(Bell Tower; ☑ 079 973 30 41; Via Principe Umberto; adult/reduced €4/3; ⊙11am-1pm & 7-9pm Mon & Fri Jul & Aug, 11am-1pm Mon, Tue, Thu & Fri & 4-7pm Thu & Fri May, Jun, Sep & Oct, by request Dec & Jan, closed Feb-Apr) Rising above the historic centre, the Cattedrale di Santa Maria's 16th-century *campanile* is one of Alghero's signature landmarks. The tower, accessible through a Gothic doorway on Via Principe Umberto, is a fine example of Catalan Goth-

---

PREHISTORIC WONDERS

The strange *nuraghi* (prehistoric stone structures) that litter Sardinia's interior provide compelling windows into the world of the island's mysterious Bronze Age people. There are said to be up to 7000 *nuraghi* across the island, most built between 1800 and 500 BC. No one is absolutely certain what they were used for, although most experts think they were defensive watchtowers.

Even before they started building *nuraghi*, the Sardinians were busy digging tombs into the rock, known as *domus de janas* (fairy houses). More elaborate were the common graves fronted by stele called *tombe dei giganti* (giants' tombs).

Evidence of pagan religious practices is provided by *pozzi sacri* (well temples). Built from around 1000 BC, these were often constructed to capture light at the yearly equinoxes, hinting at a naturalistic religion as well as sophisticated building techniques.

Alghero

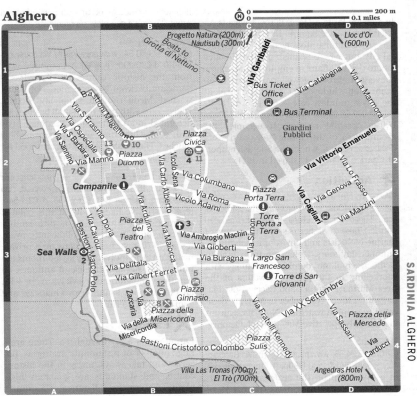

Alghero

⊚ Top Sights
1	Campanile	B2
2	Sea Walls	A3

⊚ Sights
3	Chiesa di San Francesco	B3
4	Palazzo d'Albis	B2
	Piazza Civica	(see 4)

🛏 Sleeping
5	B&B Benebenniu	B3

⊗ Eating
6	La Botteghina	B3
7	Mabrouk	A2
8	Prosciutteria Sant Miquel	B4
9	Trattoria Lo Romanì	B3

⊙ Drinking & Nightlife
10	Cafè Latino	B2
11	Caffè Costantino	B2
12	L'Altra Vineria	B3
13	SardOa	B2

ic architecture with its elegant octagonal structure and short pyramid-shaped spire. Climb to the top for amazing views.

★ **Chiesa di San Francesco** CHURCH
(☑ 079 97 92 58; www.diocesialghero-bosa.it; Via Carlo Alberto; €2, with bell tower €4; ☺ 9am-9pm) Alghero's finest church is a model of architectural harmony. Originally built to a Catalan Gothic design in the 14th century, it was later given a Renaissance facelift after it partially collapsed in 1593. Inside, interest is focused on the 18th-century polychrome marble altar and a strange 17th-century wooden sculpture of a haggard Christ tied to a column. Through the sacristy you can enter a beautiful 14th-century cloister, where the 22 columns connect a series of round arches.

Piazza Civica
PIAZZA

Just inside Porta a Mare, Piazza Civica is Alghero's showcase square. In a former life it was the administrative heart of the medieval city, but where Spanish aristocrats once met to debate affairs of empire, tourists now converge to browse jewellery displays in elegant shop windows, eat gelati and drink at the city's grandest cafe – Caffè Costantino (079 98 29 29; Piazza Civica 31; 7.30am-1.30am, closed Mon winter). It occupies the ground floor of the Gothic Palazzo d'Albis (Palazzo de Ferrera), where the Spanish emperor Charles V famously stayed in 1541.

🏃 Activities

Progetto Natura
TOURS

(392 1404069; www.progettonaturasardegna.com; Lungomare Barcellona; tours adult/reduced €40/25) Take to Alghero's seas with a crew of marine biologists and environmental guides. Summer day tours, which run from June to October, combine dolphin watching with snorkelling in the protected waters of the Area Marina Protetta Capo Caccia-Isola Piana; winter tours, November to May, are dedicated to dolphin watching. Note, its seafront kiosk is only operative May through October.

Nautisub
DIVING

(079 95 24 33; www.nautisub.com; Via Garibaldi 45; 9am-1pm & 2.30-6.30pm) Operating out of a dive shop on the seafront, this year-round outfit organises dives (from €45 or €60 with kit hire), snorkelling excursions (€35) and boat tours (€50 including lunch).

🛏 Sleeping

B&B Benebenniu
B&B €

(393 2836269; www.benebenniu.com; Via Carlo Alberto 70; r €60-105;) A home away from home, this laid-back B&B exudes warmth and familiarity. It's wonderfully located on a lively *centro storico* piazza and has three generously sized rooms with simple furnishings and plenty of natural light. Hosts Katya and Valeria are more than happy to share their local tips and recommendations. Minimum stays of three to six nights in summer.

Lloc d'Or
B&B €

(334 287130; www.llocdor.com; Via Amsicora 17; s/d from €55/80;) A cute budget B&B just a few minutes' walk from the seafront and harbour. Its two rooms and apartment are bright and simply furnished, and hosts Gemma and Giovanni go that extra mile to make you feel welcome – be it with beach towels, delicious breakfasts or tips on getting about town. There's a sea-view terrace, too.

Angedras Hotel
HOTEL €€

(079 973 50 34; www.angedras.it; Via Frank 2; s €75-110, d €90-200;) A 15-minute walk from the historic centre, the Angedras – Sardegna backwards – is a model of whitewashed Mediterranean simplicity. Rooms, which come with their own small balcony, are decorated in an understated Sardinian style with cool white tiles and aquamarine-blue touches. There's also an airy terrace, good for iced drinks on hot summer evenings.

★ Villa Las Tronas
HERITAGE HOTEL €€€

(079 98 18 18; www.hotelvillalastronas.it; Via Lungomare Valencia 1; s €269-350, d €317-540;) Live like royalty at this palatial seafront hotel. Housed in a 19th-century *palazzo* once used by holidaying royals, it's set in its own lush gardens on a private headland. The individually styled rooms are pure fin de siècle, with elegant antiques, oil paintings and glorious sea views. A spa with an indoor pool, sauna, hydro-massage and gym invites lingering.

🍴 Eating

Eating out is a joy in Alghero. There are a huge number of restaurants, trattorias, pizzerias and takeaways, many in the historic centre, and standards are generally high. Menus feature the full range of Sardinian staples, but seafood is the star. A local speciality is Catalan-style lobster, *aragosta alla catalana,* served with tomato and onion.

Prosciutteria Sant Miquel
SARDINIAN €

(348 4694434; www.facebook.com/ProsciutteriaSantMiquel; Via della Misericordia 20; meals €20; 11.30am-1am summer, shorter hours winter) A model wine bar complete with wooden ceiling, hanging hams and a menu of delicious Sardinian charcuterie and cheeses. Grab a table in the tiny, usually packed, interior and tuck into wafer-thin slices of ham and salami, wedges of aged *pecorino* and bowls of plump, glistening olives, all served on thick wooden boards.

★ Trattoria Lo Romanì
SARDINIAN €€

(079 973 84 79; Via Principe Umberto 29; meals €35; 12.30-2.30pm Tue-Sun & 7.30-10.30pm daily) Many Alghero restaurants serve *porcetto,* Sardinia's classic spit-roasted pork, but few places cook it to such buttery perfection. The crackling is spot on and the meat is sweet and packed with flavour. *Porcetto* apart, it's a delightful trattoria. Exposed sandstone walls and soft lighting create a warm, elegant atmosphere, service is attentive and the fresh island food is terrific.

⭐ **La Botteghina**   SARDINIAN €€
(☑ 079 973 83 75; www.labotteghina.biz; Via Principe Umberto 63; meals €35; ☺ 7-11.30pm Wed-Sun plus noon-3pm Sat & Sun) Cool, casual dining in a stylish *centro storico* setting – with blond-wood decor and low sandstone arches – is what La Botteghina is all about. In keeping with the upbeat, youthful vibe, the food is simple, seasonal and local, so expect steaks of *bue rosso* beef, cured meats and Sardinian cheeses, alongside inventive pizzas and Sardinian wines and craft beers.

Mabrouk   SEAFOOD €€
(☑079 97 00 00; http://mabroukalghero.com; Via Santa Barbara 4; meals €40; ☺6pm-midnight Tue-Sat, 1-3.30pm Sun) Reserve a table at this cosy, low-ceilinged stone restaurant and you never know what you're going to get. What you do know is that it'll be fish, it'll be fresh, and it'll be excellent. Dinner, which is served as a set menu, depends on the day's catch, but with several antipasti, three pasta dishes and three main courses included, you won't go hungry.

🍷 Drinking & Nightlife

⭐ **L'Altra Vineria**   CRAFT BEER
(☑ 079 601 49 54; Via Principe Umberto 66-68; ☺7pm-late) L'Altra Vineria is all about the pleasures of craft beer and island wine. The bar, run with warmth and infectious enthusiasm by Luca and Sonia, is a small, cosy place with barrels doubling as tables and a selection of terrific beers, including Sassari-brewed Speed.

⭐ **SardOa**   WINE BAR
(☑ 349 2212055; www.sardoadivino.it; Piazza Duomo 4; ☺6pm-late daily summer, noon-2.30pm & 6pm-late Sat & Sun winter) The Basque country lands in Alghero at this chilled wine bar. Under a vaulted stone ceiling, happy punters sit on wooden crates and sip Basque and Sardinian wines while munching on *pintxos* (Basque-style tapas) made with glistening anchovies and Iberic ham.

Cafè Latino   BAR
(☑079 97 65 41; www.cafelatino.it; Bastioni Magellano 10; ☺9am-2am daily summer, to 9.30pm Wed-Mon winter) Revel in harbour views over an evening *aperitivo* at this chic bar on the sea walls. Overlooking the marina, it has an ample menu of drinks and snacks.

❶ Information

Airport Tourist Office (☑ 079 93 50 11; ☺9am-11pm) In the arrivals hall.

InfoAlghero Office (☑ 079 97 90 54; www.algheroturismo.eu; Via Cagliari 2, Giardini Pubblici; ☺9am-1pm & 3.30-6.30pm Mon-Fri, to 1pm Sat & Sun) English-speaking staff can provide tourist information on the city and environs.

Ospedale Civile (☑ 079 995 51 11; www.aslsassari.it; Via Don Minzoni) The main hospital.

Police Station (☑ 079 972 00 00; Via Fratelli Kennedy; ☺8am-8pm Mon-Fri, to 2pm Sat & Sun)

❶ Getting There & Away

AIR

Alghero airport (Fertilia; ☑ 079 93 50 11; www.aeroportodialghero.it) is 10km northwest of town in Fertilia. It's served by **Alitalia** (☑ 892010; www.alitalia.com) and a number of low-cost carriers, including **Ryanair** (☑ 895 5895509; www.ryanair.com), which operates flights to mainland Italy and destinations across Europe, including Brussels, Eindhoven, Frankfurt, London and Munich.

BUS

Intercity buses serve the **bus terminal** (Via Catalogna) by the Giardini Pubblici. Note, however, that it's not much of a terminal, more a series of bus stops with a small **ticket office** (☑ 079 95 01 79; Via Catalogna; ☺ 6.25am-7.15pm Mon-Sat). Note there are no direct links with Olbia – you have to go via Sassari.

ARST (☑800 865042; www.arst.sardegna.it) Runs up to 11 daily buses to Sassari (€3.10, one hour), where you can pick up connections to destinations across the island. Also buses to/from Porto Torres (€3.70, one hour, five daily) and Bosa (€3.70, 1¼ hours, two daily with extra services in summer), as well as a single weekday service to Macomer (€5.50, two hours).

Digitur (☑ 0799 35 2 82; www.digitur.it) Runs buses from Alghero airport to Santa Teresa di Gallura.

Logudoro Tours (☑ 079 28 17 28; www.logudorotours.it) Runs two daily buses from the airport to Cagliari (€20, 3½ hours), via Oristano (€16, 2¼ hours) and Macomer (€12, 1¼ hours).

Redentours (☑ 0784 3 03 25; www.redentours.com) Operates two daily buses from Alghero airport to Nuoro (€18, 2¼ hours).

Sardabus (☑ 079 51 05 54; www.sardabus.it) Between June and mid-September operates five daily buses to Stintino from Alghero and Alghero airport (€6, 70 minutes).

CAR & MOTORCYCLE

There is no parking in the historic centre. The fast-running SS291 connects with Sassari,

WORTH A TRIP

TOP DROP

Sardinia's top wine producer, **Sella e Mosca** (☑ 079 99 77 00; www.sellaemosca.com; Località I Piani; guided tour free, tasting €15-50; ⊙ tour & tasting 10.30am-12.30pm & 3-5pm Mon-Fri, also Sat Jun-Sep, guided tour 5.30pm Mon-Sat summer, by request rest of year) **FREE**, has been based on this 650-hectare estate since 1899. To learn more about its history and production methods, join the free afternoon tour of the estate's historic cellars and lovingly tended museum. Afterwards, stock up at the beautiful **enoteca** (☑ 079 99 77 19; www.sellaemosca.it; Località I Piani; ⊙ 9am-8pm Mon-Sat summer, to 6pm winter). Private tastings can also be organised.

From Alghero, three weekday buses pass by the turnoff for Sella e Mosca (€1.90, 25 minutes).

40km to the northeast, where you can pick up the SS131, the island's main north–south artery. Snaking along the west coast, the scenic SP105 runs 46km southwards to Bosa.

TRAIN

The train station is 1.5km north of the old town on Via Don Minzoni. ARST (p915) operates up to 14 daily trains to/from Sassari (€3.10, 35 minutes).

❶ Getting Around

From the **bus stop** (Via Cagliari), bus line AF runs along the seafront and up to Fertilia. Tickets, available at newspaper stands and *tabacchi* (tobacconists), cost €1, although you can also buy them on board for €1.50.

Operating out of a hut on the seaward side of Via Garibaldi, **Cicloexpress** (☑ 079 98 69 50; www.cicloexpress.com; Via Garibaldi 49a; ⊙ 9am-1pm & 4-7.30pm Mon-Sat, 9.30am-noon Sun) hires out cars (from €60 per day), scooters (from €30) and bikes (from €5).

There's a taxi rank by the Giardini Pubblici at Via Vittorio Emanuele 1. Otherwise you can call for one by phoning **Alghero Radio Taxi** (☑ 079 989 20 28; www.taxialghero.it).

Riviera del Corallo

The Riviera del Corallo (Coral Riviera), named after the red coral for which the area is famous, encompasses Alghero's northwest coast and hinterland. The main focus of interest is Porto Conte, a scenic bay sprinkled with hotels and discreet villas, and Capo Caccia, a rocky headland famous for its cave complex, the Grotta di Nettuno. For sunseekers there are several great beaches, while history buffs can explore a couple of interesting archaeological sites.

◉ Sights

★ Grotta di Nettuno   CAVE

(☑ 079 94 65 40; adult/reduced €13/7; ⊙ 9am-7pm May-Sep, 10am-4pm Apr & Oct, 10am-2pm Nov-Mar) Capo Caccia's principal crowd-puller is the Grotta di Nettuno, a haunting fairyland of stalactites and stalagmites. The easiest way to get to the caves is to take a ferry from Alghero, but for those with a head for heights, there's a vertiginous 654-step staircase, the **Escala del Cabirol**, that descends 110m of sheer cliff from the car park at the end of the Capo Caccia road.

You can also reach the cave by tourist boat from Alghero or the signposted dock on the Capo Caccia road.

★ Le Prigionette

Nature Reserve   NATURE RESERVE

(☑ 079 94 21 11; Località Prigionette; on foot or by bike €3, per person in car €5; ⊙ 9am-6pm summer, to 4pm winter) This reserve, just west of Porto Conte at the base of Monte Timidone (361m), is a beautiful pocket of uncontaminated nature. Encompassing 12 sq km of woodland, aromatic *macchia* (Mediterranean scrub) and rocky coastline, it offers wonderful scenery and excellent walking with a network of well-marked tracks, suitable for hikers and cyclists. Wildlife flourishes – deer, albino donkeys, Giara horses and wild boar roam the woods, while griffon vultures and falcons fly the skies.

Nuraghe di Palmavera   ARCHAEOLOGICAL SITE

(☑ 329 4385947; www.coopsilt.it; Località Monte Palmavera; adult/reduced €6/4, incl Necropoli di Anghelu Ruju €8/6; ⊙ 9am-7pm Mon-Fri summer, 10am-2pm daily winter) A few kilometres west of Fertilia on the SS127bis road to Porto Conte, the Nuraghe di Palmavera is a 3500-year-old nuraghic village. At its centre stands a limestone tower and an elliptical building with a secondary sandstone tower. The ruins of smaller towers and fortified walls surround the central edifice; beyond are are the packed remnants of circular dwellings, of which there may originally have been about 50. Between April and September a single weekday bus runs to the site from Alghero (€1.30); otherwise you'll need a bike or car to get there.

Spiaggia Mugoni BEACH
The main focus of Porto Conte is Spiaggia Mugoni, a hugely popular beach that arcs around the bay's northeastern flank. With its fine white sand and protected waters, it makes an excellent venue for beginners to try their hand at water sports. The **Club della Vela** (☑ 338 1489583; www.clubdellavela alghero.it; Località Mugoni) offers windsurfing, canoeing, kayaking and sailing courses, and also rents out boats.

ℹ️ Getting There & Away
You can get to most places in this area by ARST bus from Alghero. That said, there might only be two or three weekday buses, and even fewer on Sundays and in winter. To explore the area in any depth, you'll really need your own transport.

Stintino & Isola dell'Asinara
POP 1630

Sardinia's remote northwestern tip has wild, unspoiled countryside and one of the island's most celebrated beaches, the stunning Spiaggia della Pelosa.

The only town of any note is Stintino, a former tuna-fishing village turned cute and breezy summer resort and the main gateway to the Isola dell'Asinara. This island, now a national park and wildlife haven, was for years home to one of Italy's most notorious prisons. North of Stintino, the road continues to **Capo Falcone**, a rugged headland peppered with hotels and holiday homes, and the fabled Pelosa beach.

Outside summer, the area is pretty deserted. Silence hangs over the empty landscape and the cold *maestrale* (northwesterly) wind blows through, blasting the tough *macchia* (Mediterranean scrubland) and bare rocks.

👁 Sights

⭐ Spiaggia della Pelosa BEACH
About 2.5km north of Stintino, the Spiaggia della Pelosa is a dreamy image of beach perfection: a salt-white strip of sand lapped by shallow, turquoise seas and fronted by strange, almost lunar, licks of rocky land. Completing the picture is an Aragonese watchtower and the craggy Isola Piana. The beach gets extremely busy in July and August, but is popular throughout the year,

especially with wind- and kitesurfers, who take to its waters when the *maestrale* wind whips through.

⭐ Parco Nazionale dell'Asinara NATIONAL PARK
(☑ 079 50 33 88; www.parcoasinara.org) Named after its resident *asini bianchi* (albino donkeys), the Isola dell'Asinara encompasses 51 sq km of *macchia,* rocky coastline and remote sandy beaches. The island, Sardinia's second largest, is now a national park, but for years was home to one of Italy's toughest maximum-security prisons. The only way to reach it is with a licensed boat operator from Stintino or Porto Torres. Once there, you can explore independently, although there's no public transport and access is restricted to certain areas.

🏃 Activities

Windsurfing Center Stintino WINDSURFING
(☑ 079 52 70 06; www.windsurfingcenter.it; Località l'Approdo, Le Saline) On the beach at Pelosa, this outfit rents out windsurfing rigs (from €18 per hour) and canoes (from €10 per hour), as well as offering windsurfing and sailing courses. If that all sounds far too energetic, it can also sort you out with an umbrella and sunloungers (€17 to €33 per day).

Asinara Scuba Diving DIVING
(☑ 079 52 71 75; www.asinarascubadiving.com; Viale la Pelosa, Località Porto dell'Ancora) Just before Pelosa beach, near the Club Hotel Ancora, this diving centre offers a range of dives around Capo Falcone and the protected waters of the Parco Nazionale dell'Asinara. Reckon on €45-plus for a dive and €20 for kit hire.

👉 Tours

Agenzia La Nassa TOURS
(☑ 079 52 00 60; www.agenzialanassa.it; Via Sassari 39; tours per person €20-70; ⏰ 8.30am-1pm & 4.30-8pm daily summer, Mon-Sat winter) This agency runs a number of tours around Parco Nazionale dell'Asinara. The cheapest option, available between June and September, covers your boat passage only, leaving you free to walk or cycle on designated paths on the island – you can download a map from the agency's website. More expensive packages include boat tours and visits with 4WD or bus transport.

🛏 Sleeping & Eating

Albergo Silvestrino HOTEL
(☑ 079 52 30 07; www.hotelsilvestrino.it; Via Sassari 14; s €55-75, d €70-130; ⏰ closed Dec ❄🐶) Stintino's oldest hotel is still

its best. Housed in a hard-to-miss red villa at the sea end of the main street, it offers summery rooms with cool aquamarine tiled floors, colourful paintings and unfussy furniture; some also have their own balcony. Downstairs, the excellent in-house restaurant specialises in local seafood.

Skipper ITALIAN €€
(☑ 079 52 34 60; Lungomare Cristoforo Colombo 57; panini €5, meals €30; ⊙ 11am-11pm daily summer, 10.30am-8pm Tue-Sun winter) This casual bar-restaurant, a long-standing favourite, is a jack of all trades. You can sit down on the waterfront terrace and order anything from coffee and cocktails to *zuppa di cozze* (mussel soup), hamburgers, salads and *panini*.

❶ Getting There & Away

Between June and mid-September, **Sardabus** (☑ 079 51 05 54; www.sardabus.it) operates five daily buses to Stintino from Alghero and Alghero airport (€6, 70 minutes).

There are at least four weekday ARST buses (two on Sundays) to Stintino from Porto Torres (€2.50, 45 minutes) and Sassari (€3.70, 70 minutes). Services increase between June and September.

From May to October daily power boats (return €20) and sailboats (return €75) sail for the Isola dell'Asinara from the Porto Turistico in Stintino. Departures are generally around 9am to 9.30am, returning 5pm to 6pm. Services are much reduced between November and April.

Sassari

☑ 079 / POP 127,500

Sassari, Sardinia's second-largest city, is a proud and cultured university town with a handsome historic centre and an unpretentious, workaday vibe. Like many Italian towns it hides its charms behind an outer shell of drab apartment blocks and confusing, traffic-choked roads. Once through to the inner sanctum it opens up, revealing a grand centre of wide boulevards, impressive piazzas and stately *palazzi*. In the evocative and slightly rundown *centro storico,* medieval alleyways hum with Dickensian activity as residents run about their daily business amid grimy facades and hidden churches.

◉ Sights

★ **Museo Nazionale Sanna** MUSEUM
(☑ 079 27 22 03; www.museosannasassari.beni culturali.it; Via Roma 64; adult/reduced €3/2, 1st Sun of month free; ⊙ 9am-8pm Tue-Sat & 1st Sun of month, to 1pm Sun) Sassari's premier museum, housed in a grand Palladian villa, has a comprehensive archaeological collection and an ethnographical section dedicated to Sardinian folk art. The highlight is the nuraghic bronzeware, including weapons, bracelets, votive boats and figurines depicting humans and animals. At the time of research it was closed indefinitely for renovations.

Duomo CATHEDRAL
(Cattedrale di San Nicola; Piazza Duomo; ⊙ 8.45am-noon Mon-Sat & 4.30-7pm Tue-Sat, 9-11.30am & 5-7pm Sun) Sassari's principal cathedral dazzles with its 18th-century baroque facade, a giddy free-for-all of statues, reliefs, friezes and busts. It's all a front, though, because inside the cathedral reverts to its true Gothic character. The facade masks a late-15th-century Catalan Gothic body, which was itself built over an earlier Romanesque church. Little remains of this, except for the 13th-century bell tower.

🛏 Sleeping

★ **Tanina B&B** B&B €
(☑ 346 1812404; www.taninabandb.com; Viale Trento 14; s/d/tr €30/50/70; ⊛) About 500m from Piazza Italia, this is a model B&B. Its three large guest rooms are lovingly maintained and decked out in old-school Italian style with original tiled floors, antique furniture and floral motifs. Each has its own external bathroom and there's a fully equipped communal kitchen for guest use.

Hotel Vittorio Emanuele HOTEL €€
(☑ 079 23 55 38; www.hotelvittorioemanuele.ss.it; Corso Vittorio Emanuele II 100-102; s €45-79, d €54-150; ⊛◎⊛) Occupying a renovated medieval *palazzo* (mansion), this friendly three-star provides corporate comfort at reasonable rates. Rooms are decent enough, if anonymous, and the location, on the main drag in the historic centre, is convenient for pretty much everywhere.

✕ Eating

Fainè alla Genovese Sassu SARDINIAN €
(☎079 23 64 02; www.facebook.com/fainesassu
viausai; Via Usai 17; meals €10-15; ⊗7-11.30pm Thu-
Tue) Modest, no-frills and much loved locally,
this bare, white-tiled eatery is the place to try
Sassari's famous *fainè*, thick pancakes made
with chickpea flour and cooked like pizzas.
There's nothing else on the menu, but with
various types to choose from – sausage, onions, mushrooms, anchovies – they're ideal
for a cheap, tasty fill-up.

L'Antica Hostaria RISTORANTE €€
(☎079 20 00 66; www.facebook.com/lanticahos
taria.eu; Via Cavour 55; meals €40; ⊗1-11.30pm
Mon-Sat) Hidden behind a chipped, low-key
exterior, L'Antica Hostaria is a consistently
top restaurant. In intimate, homey surroundings you're treated to inventive dishes
rooted in Italian culinary traditions. Desserts are also impressive, and there's an excellent list of island and Italian wines.

ℹ Information

Ospedale Civile SS Annunziata (☎079 206
10 00; www.aslsassari.it; Via De Nicola 14;
⊗24hr) Hospital south of the city centre.

Tourist Office (☎079 200 80 72; www.
turismosassari.it; Via Sebastiano Satta 13;
⊗9am-1.30pm & 3-6pm Tue-Fri, 9am-1.30pm
Sat) Helpful office with information on Sassari
and the surrounding area.

ℹ Getting There & Away

Sassari shares Alghero airport (p915), about
28km west of the city at Fertilia. Up to nine daily
buses run from the airport to Via Padre Zirano
(€3.10, 30 minutes).

Intercity buses depart from and arrive at **Via
Padre Zirano**, near the Chiesa di Santa Maria di
Betlem. There's a small **ticket office** (Via Padre
Zirano; ⊗6.30am-8pm Mon-Sat, 8am-2pm
& 5-8pm Sun) by the stops. Services run to/
from Alghero (€3.10, one hour, up to 10 daily),
Porto Torres (€1.90, 30 minutes, hourly) and
Castelsardo (€3.10, one hour, 11 weekdays, four
Sundays). Further afield, there are also buses to
Nuoro (€8, 1¾ hours, six daily) and Oristano (€8,
two hours, two daily).

The main train station is just beyond the
western end of the old town on Piazza Stazione.
Direct trains run to Cagliari (€16.50, three to
four hours, three daily), Oristano (€11, two to 2½
hours, four daily) and Olbia (€8, 1¾ hours, three
daily). There are also daily services to these
destinations via Ozieri-Chilivani.

OLBIA, THE COSTA SMERALDA & GALLURA

The Costa Smeralda evokes Sardinia's classic images: pearly-white beaches and weird,
wind-whipped licks of rock tapering into
emerald seas. The dazzling coastal strip
that the Aga Khan bought for a pittance is
today the playground of millionaires and
A-listers. Come summer, scandal-hungry paparazzi haunt the marinas, zooming in on
oligarchs cavorting with bikini-clad beauties
on yachts so big they eclipse the sun.

A few kilometres inland, a very different
vision of the good life emerges. Here, vine-
striped hills roll to deeply traditional villages and mysterious *nuraghi* (Bronze Age
fortified settlements), silent cork-oak woods
and granite mountains. Immune to time
and trends, the hinterland offers a refreshing contrast to the coast, best appreciated
during a multiday getaway at a country *agriturismo* (farm stay).

Further north the Gallura coast becomes
wilder, the preserve of the dolphins, divers
and windsurfers who splash around in the
startlingly blue waters of La Maddalena marine reserve.

Olbia

☎0789 / POP 59,000

Often ignored in the mad dash to the Costa
Smeralda, Olbia has more to offer than first
meets the eye. Look beyond its industrial
outskirts and you'll find a fetching city with
a *centro storico* (historic centre) crammed
with boutiques, wine bars and cafe-rimmed
piazzas. Olbia is a refreshingly authentic and
affordable alternative to the purpose-built
resorts stretching to the north and south.

◉ Sights

★**Museo Archeologico** MUSEUM
(☎0789 2 82 90; Isolotto di Peddone; ⊗10am-1pm
& 5-8pm Wed-Sun) **FREE** Architect Vanni Mac-
ciocco designed Olbia's strikingly contemporary museum near the port. The museum
spells out local history in artefacts, from Roman amulets and pottery to nuraghic finds.
The highlight is the relic of a Roman vessel
discovered in the old port. A multimedia display recreates the scene of the Vandals burning and sinking such ships in AD 450. Free
audioguides are available in English.

TRAVELWILD/SHUTTERSTOCK ©

1. Riviera del Corallo (p916)
One of the area's principal crowd-pullers is the Grotta di Nettuno, a haunting fairyland of stalactites and stalagmites.

2. Costa Smeralda (p923)
Billionaire jet-setters cruise into Costa Smeralda's marinas in mega-yachts like floating mansions, and models, royals, Russian oligarchs and balding media moguls come to frolic in its waters.

3. Alghero (p912)
The main focus of attention is the picturesque *centro storico* (historic centre), one of the best preserved in Sardinia.

4. Nuraghe Su Nuraxi (p907)
In the heart of the voluptuous green countryside near Barumini, the Nuraghe Su Nuraxi is Sardinia's sole World Heritage Site and the island's most visited *nuraghe* (Bronze Age edifice).

ARKADY ZAKHAROV/SHUTTERSTOCK ©

OFF THE BEATEN TRACK

EXPLORING GALLURA'S INTERIOR

Away from the preening millionaires on the beach, Gallura's granite interior is remote and resolutely rural. In fact, it was this fertile hinterland that attracted the waves of Corsican migrants who settled here to farm the cork forests and plant the extensive Vermentino vineyards. Cork has long been a mainstay of the local economy.

A few kilometres northwest of the deeply traditional village of Aggius you reach the Valle della Luna, a surreal and evocative landscape where huge granite boulders spill across rolling hills and farmland like giants' marbles. The lookout point on the SP74 commands fantastic views of the surrounding countryside, honeycombed with bizarrely sculpted rocks. The valley is a fantastic place for a bike ride, and the road through here down to the coast is tremendously scenic.

For a memorable overnight stay, head 20km east to the tiny village of Nuchis, where you'll find La Casa di Babbai (☑348 1721901, 079 63 12 89; Via Canonico Pes 6, Nuchis; r €50-115; 🖧), a thoughtfully restored grand 16th-century property owned by a former architect whose family has had the home for generations. Tasteful rooms are decked out in comfy combos of antiques, and the bathrooms are modern and large. The hosts are happy to share tips about the region.

Chiesa di San Simplicio   CHURCH
(Via San Simplicio; ⊗7.30am-1pm & 3.30-8pm) Considered to be Gallura's most important medieval monument, this Romanesque granite church was built in the late 11th and early 12th centuries on what was then the edge of town. It is a curious mix of Tuscan and Lombard styles with little overt decoration other than a couple of 13th-century frescoes depicting medieval bishops.

🛏 Sleeping

★ Porto Romano   B&B €
(☑349 1927996; www.bedandbreakfastportoroma no.it; Via A Nanni 2; d €65-90; ❋🖧) We love the chilled vibe and the heartfelt *benvenuto* at this welcoming B&B in an old family home near the train station. Light, spacious and well kept, the rooms have tiled floors and wood furnishings, and some come with balconies. Homey touches include the shared kitchen and barbecue area, and the friendly reception from owner Simonetta and her lovable dog, Lilly.

Hotel Panorama   HOTEL €€
(☑0789 2 66 56; www.hotelpanoramaolbia.it; Via Giuseppe Mazzini 7; s €95-140, d €110-200, ste €170-300; P❋🖧) The name says it all: the roof terrace and 5th-floor superior rooms enjoy peerless views over the rooftops of Olbia to the sea and Monte Limbara. Even the standard rooms are fresh and elegant, with gleaming wooden floors and marble bathrooms, and there's a whirlpool and a sauna for quiet moments. Plus it has parking lots for guests.

La Locanda del Conte Mameli   BOUTIQUE HOTEL €€
(☑0789 2 30 08; www.lalocandadelcontemameli. com; Via delle Terme 8; r €95-155; P❋🖧) Raising the style stakes is this boutique hotel, housed in an 18th-century *locanda* (inn) built for Count Mameli. A wrought-iron balustrade twists up to chic caramel-cream rooms with Orosei marble bathrooms. The vaulted breakfast room has a pair of unique treasures: an original Roman well and a 1960s-vintage Lambretta motorcycle.

🍴 Eating

★ Agriturismo Agrisole   SARDINIAN €€
(☑349 0848163; www.agriturismo-agrisole.com; Via Sole Ruiu 7, Località Casagliana; menu incl drinks €40; ⊗dinner by reservation Thu-Sun Apr-Sep) Tucked serenely away in the countryside around 10km north of Olbia, this Gallurese *stazzo* (farmhouse) dishes up a feast of home cooking. Monica, your charming host, brings dish after marvellous dish to the table – antipasti, *fregola* (granular pasta), *porceddu* (roast suckling pig) and ricotta sweets. From Olbia, take the SS125 towards Arzachena/Palau, turning left at the signs about 11km north of the city.

Dolceacqua   ITALIAN €€
(☑0789 196 90 84; http://ristorantedolceacqua. com; Via Giacomo Pala 4; meals €30-40; ⊗12.15-2.15pm & 7.30-10.30pm Tue-Sun, 7.30-10.30pm only mid-Jun–mid-Sep) This smart, intimate bistro has laid-back charm, warm service and an appetising Sardinian and Ligurian cuisine. Start with its decadent sampler of five sea-

food antipasti, then dig into Sardinian classics such as *culurgiones* (ravioli filled with cheese and potato) or creative alternatives like *millefoglie di orata alla ligure* (bream cooked in oil, garlic, olives and wine, served between thin pastry layers).

ℹ Information

Tourist Office (☑ 0789 5 22 06; www.olbia turismo.it; Via Dante 1; ⊙ 9am-8pm Mon-Fri, to 1pm & 4-8pm Sat & Sun Apr-Sep, reduced hours Oct-Mar) This helpful office should be your first port of call for info on Olbia.

ℹ Getting There & Away

AIR

Olbia's **Aeroporto di Olbia Costa Smeralda** (☑ 0789 56 34 44; www.geasar.it) is about 5km southeast of the centre and handles flights from major Italian and European airports. It's the home airport for Air Italy, which flies to two dozen cities. Low-cost operators include Air Berlin, easyJet and Volotea. Destinations served include most mainland Italian airports as well as London, Paris, Madrid, Barcelona, Berlin, Amsterdam and Zurich.

BOAT

Olbia's ferry terminal, Stazione Marittima, is on Isola Bianca, an island connected to the town centre by the 1km Banchina Isola Bianca causeway. All the major ferry companies have counters here, including **Moby Lines** (☑ +49 (0)611 14020; www.mobylines.com), **Grimaldi Lines** (☑ 0789 183 55 64; www.grimaldi-lines.com) and **Tirrenia** (☑ 02 7602 8132, 800 804020; www.tirrenia.it). There are frequent services, especially during the summer months, to Civitavecchia, Genoa, Livorno and Piombino.

You can book tickets at any travel agent in town, or directly at the port.

BUS

ARST (Azienda Regionale Sarda Trasporti; ☑ 800 865042, 0789 5 53 00; www.arst.sard egna.it) Buses run from Olbia to destinations across the island. Get tickets from **Bar della Caccia** (Corso Vittorio Veneto 28; ⊙ 5.30am-8pm Mon-Sat), just opposite the main **bus stops** on Corso Vittorio Veneto, or from the self-service **ARST ticket machine** (Corso Umberto 166e) behind Olbia's train station. Destinations include Arzachena (€2.50, 45 minutes, 12 daily) and Porto Cervo (€2.50, 1½ hours, five daily). Further afield you can get to Nuoro (€8, 2½ hours, eight daily), Santa Teresa di Gallura (€4.30, 1½ hours, seven daily) and Sassari (€8, 1½ hours, two daily) via Tempio Pausania (€3.70, 1¼ hours, seven daily). There are fewer connections on Sunday.

Sun Lines (☑ 0789 5 08 85, 348 2609881; www.sunlines.it) Operates buses between Olbia

and various destinations on the Costa Smeralda, including Porto Cervo, Baia Sardinia and Cannigione, as well as Palau, Porto Torres, Sassari and Alghero airport. Buses originate at Olbia's airport, passing through downtown Olbia (Piazza Crispi) and the port on their way north.

Turmo Travel (☑ 0789 2 14 87; www.gruppo turmotravel.com) Runs two buses from Olbia to Cagliari (€19, 4½ hours) – an early-morning weekday bus from Piazza Crispi, and a daily afternoon bus from Olbia's port that stops off at Olbia's airport en route. Get tickets at Stazione Marittima ferry terminal or on the bus.

TRAIN

The station is off Corso Umberto. There are direct trains to Cagliari (€18, 3¼ hours, three daily), Oristano (€12.50, 2½ hours, three daily), Sassari (€8, 1¾ hours, four daily) and Golfo Aranci (€2.50, 25 minutes, 10 daily).

Costa Smeralda & Around

Back in 1962, flamboyant millionaire Karim Aga Khan established a consortium to buy a strip of unspoiled coastline in northeastern Sardinia. Each investor paid roughly US$25,000 for a little piece of paradise, and the coast was christened Costa Smeralda (Emerald Coast) for its brilliant green-blue waters.

These days billionaire jet-setters cruise into Costa Smeralda's marinas in megayachts like floating mansions, and models, royals, Russian oligarchs and balding media moguls come to frolic in its waters.

Starting at the Golfo di Cugnana, 17km north of Olbia, the Costa stretches 55km northwards to the Golfo di Arzachena. The 'capital' is the yachtie haven of Porto Cervo, although Porto Rotondo, a second marina developed in 1963, attracts plenty of paparazzi with its Silvio Berlusconi connections and its attractive seafront promenade.

Inland from the Costa Smeralda, the mountain communities of San Pantaleo and Arzachena offer a low-key counterpoint to the coastline's glitz and glamour.

◉ Sights & Activities

Coddu Ecchju ARCHAEOLOGICAL SITE
(Località Capichera, off SP14; €3; ⊙ 9am-7pm) Taking the Arzachena–Luogosanto road south, you can follow signs to one of the most important *tombe dei giganti* in Sardinia. The most visible part of it is the oval-shaped central stele (standing stone). Both slabs of granite, one balanced on top of the other, show an engraved frame that

apparently symbolises a door to the hereafter, closed to the living. On either side of the stele stand further tall slabs of granite that form a kind of semicircular guard of honour around the tomb.

Tempio di Malchittu ARCHAEOLOGICAL SITE
(Località Malchittu, off SS125; €3; ⊙9am-6pm) Accessible via a 2km track from the Nuraghe di Albucciu ticket office, this temple dating back to 1500 BC is one of only a few of its kind in Sardinia. Experts aren't certain of its original purpose, but it appears it had a timber roof and was closed with a wooden door. Just as engaging as the ruins is the trail to get here, which affords lovely views over the surrounding countryside, strewn with granite boulders.

Cantine Surrau WINE
(✉0789 8 29 33; www.vignesurrau.it; Località Chilvagghja, SP59; ⊙10am-9pm May-Sep, reduced rest of year) Cantine Surrau takes a holistic approach to winemaking. Take a spin of the cellar and the gallery showcasing Sardinian art before tasting some of the region's crispest Vermentino white and beefiest Cannonau red wines. Service can be spotty, but the wine is delicious.

🛌 Sleeping

B&B La MeSenda B&B €
(✉0789 8 19 50; www.lamesenda.com; Località Malchittu; d €75-100; 🐾) Immersed in peaceful countryside along the Tempio di Malchittu trail, this converted stone-and-stucco farmhouse makes an idyllic spot for an overnight stay. Simple rooms with exposed beams face onto a courtyard with a 500-year-old olive tree, a hot tub and comfortable spaces for lounging. Owners Judith (from French Polynesia) and Mario (from Sardinia) serve a delicious homemade breakfast.

★ B&B Lu Pastruccialeddu B&B €€
(✉0789 8 17 77; www.pastruccialeddu.com; Località Lu Pastruccialeddu, Arzachena; s €50-100, d €80-120, ste €100-150; 🅿🐾🏊) This is the real McCoy, a smashing B&B housed in a typical stone farmstead, with pristine rooms, a beautiful pool and two resident donkeys. It's run by the ultra-hospitable Caterina Ruzittu, who prepares the sumptuous breakfasts – a vast spread of biscuits, yoghurt, freshly baked cakes, salami, cheese and cereals.

★ Ca' La Somara B&B €€
(✉0789 9 89 69; www.calasomara.it; off SP73; s €58-98, d €80-148; 🅿🐾🏊) Follow the donkey signs to Laura Lagattolla's welcoming

rural retreat, 1km north of San Pantaleo. A relaxed, ramshackle farm, it offers simple guest rooms and endless opportunities for downtime: swinging in a hammock, strolling the gardens, or lounging poolside surrounded by rocky crags. Marvellous breakfasts featuring home-grown produce are served in the rustic dining room.

B&B Smeralda B&B €€
(✉0789 9 98 11; www.bbsmeralda.com; Villaggio Faras, Lu Cumitoni; d €90-150; 🛁@🐾) Straddling a steep hillside 1km above Poltu Quatu's fjord-like harbour, this charming B&B offers three comfortable bedrooms with pretty tiled bathrooms. The real stars here are the outdoor whirlpool tub surrounded by sculpted rocks and the tantalising sea views from the veranda, where you can enjoy Luciana's freshly made breads and pastries at breakfast.

🍴 Eating

Aruanã Churrascaria BRAZILIAN €€
(✉0789 90 60 85; www.aruana.it; Via degli Oleandri; buffet €44; ⊙8pm-1am) With romantically lit tables set amid garden terraces that cascade down from a boulder-strewn hillside, this Brazilian steakhouse offers that rare combination of classy setting and top-notch food. Aruanã specialises in Brazilian-style grilled meats. Serve yourself at will from the all-you-can-eat buffet; drinks cost extra.

Ristorante Pizzeria La Rocca SARDINIAN €€
(✉0789 93 30 11; www.ristorante-larocca.com; Località Pulicinu, SP59; meals €20-45; ⊙noon-2.30pm & 7-11.30pm) With black-clad waiters and impeccably fresh seafood ('choose any shellfish living in the aquarium'), La Rocca offers dependable quality with a resolutely old-school vibe. It's the kind of place where you'll find Sardinian families lingering over a long lunch or celebratory dinner. Look for it southwest of town along the main road towards Cannigione.

Spinnaker ITALIAN €€€
(✉0789 9 12 26; www.ristorantespinnaker.com; Località Liscia di Vacca, SP59; meals €40-55; ⊙12.30-2.30pm & 7.30-11pm daily Jun-Sep, closed Wed Apr, May & Oct) This fashionable restaurant buzzes with a good-looking crowd, who come for the stylish ambience and fabulous seafood. Pair dishes such as calamari and fresh artichokes or rock lobster with a local Vermentino white. The restaurant is on the road (sadly, no sea view) between Porto Cervo and Baia Sardinia.

COSTA SMERALDA BEACH CRAWL

You'll need your own set of wheels to hop between the most sublime beaches on the Costa Smeralda, but it's worth the effort. They're super busy in July and August, so avoid peak summer season if you want these bays to yourself. The following (listed from north to south) are all between Porto Cervo and Porto Rotondo.

Spiaggia del Grande & Piccolo Pevero (off SP59) This twinset of stunning bays, 3km south of Porto Cervo, fulfil the Sardinian paradise dream with their floury sands and dazzlingly blue, shallow water. There's a small beach bar, too.

Spiaggia Romazzino (off Via Romazzino) Less busy than some, this curving sandy bay has remarkably clear water and is named after the rosemary bushes that grow in such abundance. Look beyond the main bay to smaller coves for more seclusion.

Spiaggia del Principe (off Via Romazzino) Also known as Portu Li Coggi, this magnificent crescent of white sand is bound by unspoiled *macchia* and startlingly clear blue waters. Apparently it's the Aga Khan's favourite. It's around 2.5km northeast of Capriccioli.

Spiaggia Capriccioli (SP160) Dotted with granite boulders and backed by fragrant *macchia*, this gorgeous half-moon bay has water that goes through the entire spectrum of blues and is shallow enough for tots. Several unique mini-beaches dot the promontory. Umbrellas and sunbeds are available to rent.

Spiaggia Liscia Ruia (off SP94) Though busy in peak season, this beach is a beauty – a long arc of pale, fine sand and crystal-clear water. It's close to the neo-Moorish fantasy that is Hotel Cala di Volpe.

❶ Getting There & Away

ARST and Sun Lines operate buses from Olbia to the Costa Smeralda, but to properly explore all the nooks and crannies of this beautiful coastline, you'll want your own wheels. The main coastal road changes names a time or two as you make your way along the coast: known as SP73 near Porto Redondo, it becomes SP94 closer to Porto Cervo, and SP59 as you continue west through Poltu Quatu to Baia Sardinia.

Santa Teresa di Gallura

☎0789 / POP 5230

Bright and breezy Santa Teresa di Gallura occupies a prime seafront position on Gallura's north coast. The resort gets extremely busy during high season, yet somehow manages to retain a distinct local character, making it a wonderful alternative to the more soulless resorts on the Costa Smeralda.

The town was established by Savoy rulers in 1808 to help combat smugglers, but the modern town grew up as a result of the tourism boom since the early 1960s. Santa Teresa's history is caught up with Corsica as much as it is with Sardinia. Over the centuries plenty of Corsicans have settled here, and the local dialect is similar to that of southern Corsica.

◎ Sights & Activities

★ **Spiaggia Rena Bianca** BEACH
The 'just like the Caribbean' comments come thick and fast when it comes to this bay – a glorious sweep of pale sand lapped by shallow, crystal-clear aquamarine water. From the eastern tip, a trail threads along the coastline past granite boulders and formations that fire the imagination with their incredible shapes.

★ **Capo Testa** WALKING
Four kilometres west of Santa Teresa, this extraordinary lighthouse-topped headland resembles a vast sculptural garden. Giant boulders lie strewn about the grassy slopes, their weird and wonderful forms the result of centuries of wind erosion. The Romans quarried granite here, as did the Pisans centuries later. A couple of beaches lie to either side of the narrow isthmus that leads out to the headland – **Rena di Levante** and **Rena di Ponente** – where you can rent surfing gear, beach umbrellas and sunloungers.

Consorzio delle Bocche BOATING
(☎0789 75 51 12; www.consorziobocche.com; Piazza Vittorio Emanuele; ⊙9am-1pm & 5-7.30pm May, Jun & Sep, to 12.30am Jul & Aug) This outfit runs various excursions, including trips to the Maddalena islands and down the Costa

Smeralda (summer only). These cost around €45/25 per adult/child and include lunch (excluding drinks).

🛏 Sleeping

★B&B Domus de Janas
B&B €€

(☑338 4990221; www.bbdomusdejanas.it; Via Carlo Felice 20a; s €70-100, d €80-160, q €130-170; ❉🐾) Daria and Simone are your affable hosts at this sumptuous six-room B&B smack in the centre of town (as photos on the wall attest, the rambling home has belonged to Daria's family since her great-great-grand-mother's days). The colourfully decorated rooms are spacious and regally comfortable, the rooftop terrace enjoys cracking sea views, and guests rave about the varied, abundant self-service breakfast.

Hotel Moderno
HOTEL €€

(☑0789 75 42 33, 393 9177814; www.moderno hotel.eu; Via Umberto 39; s €60-80, d €75-150, tr €110-180; ❉🐾) This is a homey, family-run pick near the piazza. Rooms are bright and airy with little overt decor but traditional blue-and-white Gallurese bedspreads and tiny balconies.

🍴 Eating

La Locanda dei Mori
SEAFOOD €€

(☑0789 75 51 68; www.locandadeimori.com; SP90, Km 5; menus €45; ⏰8-11pm Jun-Sep) In a country setting just off the main road 6km south of Santa Teresa, this lovely *agriturismo* spreads a sea of tables onto its open-air terrace each summer. Guests come from miles around for the Locanda's multicourse menu of fresh seafood. Wine, water, coffee and after-dinner drinks are all included in the price.

Il Grottino
MEDITERRANEAN €€

(☑0789 75 42 32; www.facebook.com/ilgrottino santateresa; Via del Mare 14; pizzas €5-14, meals €35-45; ⏰noon-3pm & 7-11.30pm summer, closed Jan–mid-Mar; 🐾) Il Grottino sets a rustic picture with bare, grey stone walls and warm, low lighting. In keeping with the look, the food is wholesome and hearty with no-nonsense pastas, fresh seafood, juicy grilled meats and wood-fired pizzas.

★Agriturismo Saltara
SARDINIAN €€€

(☑0789 75 55 97; www.agriturismosaltara.it; Località Saltara; meals €40-60; ⏰7-11pm; 🚗) Natalia and Gian Mario welcome you warmly at this *agriturismo*, 10km south of town off the SP90 (follow signs up a dirt track). Tables are scenically positioned under the trees for a home-cooked feast. Wood-fired

bread and garden-vegetable antipasti are a delicious lead to dishes such as *pulilgioni* (ricotta-filled ravioli with orange zest) and roast suckling pig or wild boar.

❶ Information

Tourist Office (☑0789 75 41 27; www. comunesantateresagallura.it; Piazza Vittorio Emanuele 24; ⏰9am-1pm & 4-6pm) Very helpful, with loads of information.

❶ Getting There & Away

Santa Teresa is the main embarkation point for Corsica. Two companies run car ferries on the 50-minute crossing to Bonifacio, although between November and March services are drastically reduced. In summer, **Moby Lines** (☑199 30 30 40, 0789 75 14 49; www.mobylines.com) has four daily departures in each direction, while **Blu Navy** (☑0789 75 55 70; www.blunavy traghetti.com) operates three to four daily crossings. Blu Navy tends to be cheaper, but in general a one-way adult fare averages about €29 and a small car around €35 to €50.

Intercity buses depart from the bus station on Piazza Bruno Modesto.

ARST (www.arst.sardegna.it) ARST buses run to/from Arzachena (€3.10, 1¼ hours, five daily), Olbia (€4.30, two hours, seven daily), Castelsardo (€4.90, 1½ hours, two daily) and Sassari (€6.50, 2½ hours, three daily).

Turmo Travel (☑0789 2 14 87; www.gruppo turmotravel.com) Operates a daily service to/from Cagliari (€19.50, six hours), as well as a summer service to Olbia airport (€4.30, 1½ hours, six daily June to September) via Arzachena and Palau.

Palau & Arcipelago di La Maddalena

Off Sardinia's northeastern tip, Palau is a lively summer resort crowded with surf shops, boutiques, bars and restaurants. It's also the main gateway to the wind-sculpted granite islands and jewel-coloured waters of Arcipelago di La Maddalena.

The only town of any size on the islands is La Maddalena, which makes a good base with its bustling core of guesthouses, restaurants and cafes. The adjacent Isola Caprera, reached by a causeway just east of La Maddalena, was the longtime home of 19th-century Italian revolutionary Giuseppe Garibaldi. To visit the archipelago's uninhabited smaller islands, check out the daily boat tours from Palau or La Maddalena, which stop in at some of Sardinia's most idyllic coves and beaches, or hire a Zodiac (no licence required).

◉ Sights & Activities

★ Parco Nazionale dell'Arcipelago
di La Maddalena   NATIONAL PARK

(www.lamaddalenapark.it) Established in 1996, Parco Nazionale dell'Arcipelago di La Maddalena consists of seven main islands and several smaller granite islets off Sardinia's northeastern coast. Over the centuries the prevailing *maestrale* (northwesterly wind) has helped mould the granite into the bizarre natural sculptures that festoon the archipelago. The spectacular seascapes of La Maddalena's outer islands are best explored by boat, although the two main islands have plenty of charm with their sun-baked ochre buildings, cobbled piazzas and infectious holiday atmosphere.

Roccia dell'Orso   VIEWPOINT

(trail adult/reduced €3/2, parking €3; ☺ 9am-sunset; 🅿) This weather-beaten granite sculpture sits on a high point 6km east of Palau. The Roccia dell'Orso (Bear Rock) looks considerably less bearlike up close, resembling more – dare we say it? – a dragon. Analogies aside, the granite formations are extraordinary, as are the far-reaching views of the coast from up here. From the parking lot, it's a climb of 10 to 15 minutes.

Fortezza di Monte Altura   FORT

(adult/reduced €5/2.50; ☺ guided tours 10.15am-12.15pm & 3.15-5.15pm daily, last tour 3.15pm Apr, May & Sep–mid-Oct) Standing sentinel on a rocky crag, this sturdy 19th-century bastion was built to help defend the north coast and Arcipelago di La Maddalena from invasion – something it was never called on to do. A guided 45-minute tour leads you to watchtowers and battlements with panoramic views out to sea. The fortress is signposted off the SS125, 3km west of town.

Nautilus Diving Centre   DIVING

(☑ 0789 70 90 58, 340 6339006; www.divesardegna.com; Via Roma 14; ☺ 9am-5.30pm) There's some excellent diving in the marine park. This PADI five-star dive centre runs dives to 40 sites, with single dives starting at around €75. Kids' Bubblemaker courses (€135) are available.

☞ Tours

Sardinia Island Tours/
Natour Sardinia   BOATING

(☑ Kevin 391 7327232, Rodolfo 339 4774472; www.sardiniaislandtours.com; Via Guerrazzi 4; full-day tour from €70) Sharing an office near the port, these two companies work in tandem to provide excellent multilingual tours of the Maddalena archipelago. In addition to visiting local beaches, guides Kevin and Rodolfo offer hikes to local fortresses dating back to WWII and Napoleon's ill-fated attempt to take over Isola Maddalena in 1793. Lunch, wine and water are included in the tour price.

Elena Tour Navigazioni   BOATING

(☑ 380   3032664;   www.elenatournavigazioni.com; Lungomare Via Amendola; ☺ office 10am-5.30pm) Elena Tour runs relaxed cruises to the fabulous hidden beaches and smaller, lesser-known islands of Arcipelago di La Maddalena, with plenty of time for chilling and swimming. Reckon on €35 to €40 per person for a full-day tour, including lunch. Itinerary details are given on the website.

🍽 Sleeping & Eating

L'Orso e Il Mare   B&B €

(☑ 331   2222000;   www.orsoeilmare.com;   Vicolo Diaz 1; d €60-110, tr €70-145; ❄ 🛜) Pietro gives his guests a genuinely warm welcome at this two-room B&B, just steps from Piazza Fresi. The spacious rooms sport cool blue-and-white colour schemes and homey amenities such as fridges, kettles and corkscrews in each room. Breakfast is a fine spread of cakes, biscuits and fresh fruit salad. Occasionally requires a three-night minimum.

Del Porticciolo   SARDINIAN €

(☑ 0789 70 70 51; Via Omero; pizzas €4-9, meals €25-35; ☺ 12.15-2pm & 7.15-10.30pm Sat-Thu) Locals swear by the authentic antipasti, pasta and fresh fish at this no-frills restaurant just south of the harbour. Stop by for a good-value lunch, or for pizza in the evening when chefs fire up the ovens.

ℹ Information

Tourist Office (☑ 0789 70 70 25; www.palauturismo.com; Palazzo Fresi, Piazza Fresi; ☺ 9am-1pm & 4-7pm) The multilingual staff can provide information about the surrounding area, including the Arcipelago di La Maddalena.

ℹ Getting There & Away

BOAT

Car ferries to Isola Maddalena are operated by **Delcomar** (☑ 0789 70 92 28; www.delcomar.it) and **Maddalena Lines** (☑ 0789 73 91 65; www.maddalenalines.it). Boats run every 15 to 40 minutes, then reduce to roughly hourly from midnight to 5.30am, with Delcomar offering the most frequent service. The 15-minute crossing costs between €3.70 and €4.20 per passenger and between €8 and €22 per car (one-way).

SARDINIA PALAU & ARCIPELAGO DI LA MADDALENA

BUS

ARST (www.arst.sardegna.it) Buses connect Palau port with Olbia (€3.10, 1¼ hours, eight daily), Santa Teresa di Gallura (€2.50, 45 minutes, five daily) and Arzachena (€1.90, 30 minutes, five daily).

Caramelli (☑ 079 67 06 13; www.caramelli tours.it) In summer runs frequent buses to other nearby destinations such as Isola dei Gabbiani and Capo d'Orso.

Turmo Travel (☑ 0789 2 14 87; www.gruppo turmotravel.com; ⊗ office 9am–1pm & 3.30–7.30pm) Offers year-round bus service from Palau to Olbia airport (€6, 50 minutes) and Santa Teresa di Gallura (€4, 35 minutes). Buses run six times daily from June through September, and once daily October to May.

EASTERN SARDINIA

Nowhere else in Sardinia is nature as overwhelming a force as it is in the wild, wild east, where the Supramonte's imperious limestone mountains roll down to the Golfo di Orosei's cliffs and startling aquamarine waters. Who knows where that winding country road might lead you? Perhaps to deep valleys concealing prehistoric caves and Bronze Age *nuraghi*, to the lonesome villages of the Barbagia steeped in bandit legends, or to forests where wild pigs snuffle amid centuries-old holm oaks. Neither time nor trend obsessed, this region is refreshingly authentic.

Outdoor action abounds: drop anchor along the coast in a string of pearly-white bays, multipitch climb upon cliffs thrusting up out of the sea, pedal mountain bikes along old mule trails, and hike atop peaks and through ravines only reachable on foot.

True, the Costa Smeralda attracts more celebrities, but the real rock stars and rolling stones are right here.

Nuoro

☑ 0784 / POP 36,900

Once an isolated hilltop village and a byword for banditry, Nuoro had its cultural renaissance in the 19th and early 20th centuries when it became a hotbed of artistic talent. Today museums in the historic centre pay homage to local legends including Nobel Prize–winning author Grazia Deledda, acclaimed poet Sebastiano Satta, novelist Salvatore Satta and sculptor Francesco Ciusa. Further enhancing Nuoro's modern-day cultural vitality are the local university, with its graduate program in environmental studies and sustainable development, and the city's recently renovated ethnographic museum.

Nuoro itself is a hodgepodge of modern buildings, but its spectacular backdrop is the granite peak of Monte Ortobene (955m), capped by a 7m-high bronze statue of the Redentore (Christ the Redeemer). The thickly wooded summit commands dress-circle views of the valley below and the limestone mountains enshrouding Oliena opposite.

◉ Sights

★ **Museo Etnografico Sardo**   MUSEUM
(Museo del Costume; ☑ 0784 25 70 35; www.isresardegna.it; Via Antonio Mereu 56; adult/reduced €5/3; ⊗ 10am–1pm & 3–8pm Tue–Sun mid-Mar–Sep, to 7pm Oct–mid-Mar) Beautifully renovated in 2016, this museum zooms in on Sardinian folklore, harbouring a peerless collection of filigree jewellery, carpets, tapestries, rich embroidery, musical instruments,

---

FESTIVALS OF NUORO'S INTERIOR

Nuoro province has some of Sardinia's most colourful and characteristic festivals. Topping the list is the Festa di Sant'Antonio Abate, held in mid-January in the town of Mamoiada, 20km south of Nuoro. Bonfires rage throughout town for two nights starting on 16 January, as half-human, half-animal *mamuthones* parade through the streets – clad in sheepskins and shaking heavy bells – accompanied by white-masked, red-jacketed *issohadores* who go about town lassoing young women.

The rest of the year, you can get a vicarious taste of Mamoiada's festivities at the small but engaging Museo delle Maschere Mediterranee (☑ 0784 56 90 18; www.museodellemaschere.it; Piazza Europa 15; adult/reduced €5/3; ⊗ 9am–1pm & 3-7pm Jun-Sep, closed Mon Oct-May). Film footage documents the making of masks and bells, along with the processions and bonfires that mark Mamoiada's big event. A second room displays masks and costumes from three of Nuoro province's most traditional carnivals (Mamoiada, Ovodda and Ottana) and from throughout the Mediterranean.

weapons and masks. The highlight is the traditional costume display – the styles, colours and patterns speaking volumes about the people and their villages. Look out for fiery red skirts from the fiercely independent mountain villages, the Armenian-influenced dresses of Orgosolo and Desulo finished with a blue-and-yellow silk border, and the burkalike headdresses of Ittiri and Osilo.

Museo Ciusa   MUSEUM
(Museo Tribu; ☑ 0784 25 21 10; www.comune.nuoro.it; Piazza Santa Maria della Neve; adult/reduced €3/2; ☉ 11am-8pm Tue-Sun Jun-Sep, 10am-1pm & 3-7pm Tue-Sun Oct-May) This museum houses the permanent collection of Nuoro's excellent art museum and has an entire wing devoted to the works of renowned Nuoro-born sculptor Francesco Ciusa (1883–1949). Displays include works by the island's top 20th-century artists, including painters Antonio Ballero, Giovanni Ciusa-Romagna and Mario Delitala, abstract artist Mauro Manca and sculptor Costantino Nivola.

Monte Ortobene   MOUNTAIN
About 7km east of Nuoro is the granite peak of Monte Ortobene (955m), covered in thick woods of ilex, pine, fir and poplar, and capped by a 7m-high bronze statue of the Redentore (Christ the Redeemer). A favourite picnic spot, the mountain is the focus of Nuoro's annual Sagra del Redentore festival. On 29 August, the brightly clothed faithful make a pilgrimage here from the cathedral, stopping for Mass at Chiesa di Nostra Signora del Monte, and again under the statue.

Festivals & Events

Sagra del Redentore   RELIGIOUS
The Sagra del Redentore (Feast of Christ the Redeemer), in the last week of August, is Nuoro's main event and one of Sardinia's most exuberant folkloric festivals, attracting costumed participants from across the island for parades, music making and dancing. On the evening of 28 August a torchlit procession, starting at the Chiesa della Solitudine (Viale della Solitudine), winds its way through the city.

Sleeping

Casa Solotti   B&B €
(☑ 328 6028975, 0784 3 39 54; www.casasolotti.it; Località Monte Ortobene; per person €26-35; ⓟ ❈ ☎) This B&B reclines in a rambling garden amid woods and walking trails near the

top of Monte Ortobene, 5km from central Nuoro. Decorated with stone and beams, the elegantly rustic rooms have tremendous views of the surrounding valley and the Golfo di Orosei in the distance. Staying here is a delight.

Nothing is too much trouble for your hosts, Mario and Frédérique, who can arrange everything from horse riding to packed lunches and guided hikes in the Supramonte.

Silvia e Paolo   B&B €
(☑ 0784 3 12 80; www.silviaepaolo.it; Corso Garibaldi 58; d with/without bathroom €65/55; ❈ ☎) Silvia and Paolo run this sweet B&B in the historic centre. Cheerful family decor makes you feel right at home in the bright, spacious rooms, while up top there's a roof terrace for observing the action on Corso Garibaldi by day and stargazing by night. Note that two of the three guest rooms share a bathroom.

Eating

Agriturismo Testone   SARDINIAN €€
(☑ 329 4115168, 328 3150592; www.agriturismotestone.com; Via Verdi 49, Testone; meals €30; ☑) You'll feel immediately part of *la famiglia* at this *agriturismo*, which rests in peaceful solitude in the countryside, 20km northwest of Nuoro. The welcome is heartfelt, mealtimes are cheerful and communal affairs, and the mostly home-grown food is terrific. The farm rears lamb and produces its own *formaggi, salumi,* honey, sweets, olive oil and wine.

Il Portico   SARDINIAN €€
(☑ 0784 21 76 41; www.ilporticonuoro.it; Via Monsignor Bua 13; meals €35-45; ☉ 12.30-2.30pm & 8-10.30pm Tue-Sat, 12.30-2.30pm Sun) You'll receive a warm welcome at this restaurant, where abstract paintings grace the walls and jazzy music plays. Behind the scenes, the talented Graziano and Vania rustle up a feast of local fare such as *spaghetti ai ricci* (spaghetti with sea urchins) and fresh gnocchi with lamb *ragù.* Save room for the delectable caramel-nougat semifreddo.

Information

Tourist Office (☑ 0784 23 87 94, 0784 44 18 23; www.provincia.nuoro.it; Piazza Italia 8; ☉ 7.30am-2pm Mon-Fri, plus 3-6.30pm Tue) Multilingual staff provide plenty of useful information on Nuoro and environs.

VALLE DI LANAITTU

Immerse yourself in the karst wilderness of the Supramonte by hiking, cycling or driving through this enchanting 7km valley, signposted off the Oliena–Dorgali road. Towering limestone mountains, cliffs and caves lord it over the narrow valley, scattered with natural and archaeological wonders. Rosemary and mastic, grapes and olives flourish in the valley, which attracts wildlife such as martens, birds of prey, wild boar and goats. Near the valley's southern end, it's possible to visit a pair of caves – **Grotta di Sa Ohe** (€5; ⊙ 9am-6pm Apr-Sep) and **Grotta Corbeddu** (☑ 0784 28 02 00; €5; ⊙ 9am-7pm Apr-Sep) – and the nuraghic site of **Sa Sedda 'e Sos Carros** (☑ 333 5808844; €5; ⊙ 9am-7pm Apr-Sep), with its unique circular Temple of the Sacred Well; buy tickets for all three sites at Rifugio Sa Ohe, a whitewashed hut down a nearby signposted dirt road.

ℹ️ Getting There & Away

BUS

ARST (☑ 0784 29 08 00; www.arst.sardegna. it) Runs buses from the bus station on Viale Sardegna to destinations throughout the province and beyond. These include Dorgali (€2.50, 45 minutes, six daily), Orosei (€3.70, 55 minutes, 10 daily), San Teodoro (€6, two hours, five daily), Olbia (€8, 2¾ to 3½ hours, three daily) and Tortolì (€5.50, two hours, five daily). There are also regular buses to Oliena (€1.90, 20 minutes) and Orgosolo (€2.50, 35 minutes). Two daily nonstop buses connect with Cagliari (€12.50, 2¾ hours).

Deplano (☑ 0784 29 50 30; www.deplanobus. it) Runs up to five daily buses to Olbia airport (€8, 1¾ hours) via San Teodoro (€6, 1¼ hours).

Redentours (☑ 0784 3 03 25; www.reden tours.com) Two daily buses (€18, 2¼ hours) to Alghero airport, for which bookings are required.

TRAIN

The train station is west of the town centre on Via Lamarmora. ARST operates trains from Nuoro to Macomer (€4.90, 70 minutes, six daily Monday to Saturday), where you can connect with mainline Trenitalia trains to Cagliari (from Macomer €11, 1½ to 2¼ hours, five daily).

Supramonte

Southeast of Nuoro rises the great limestone massif of the Supramonte, its sheer walls like an iron curtain just beyond Oliena. Despite its intimidating aspect, it's actually not as high as it seems – its peak, Monte Corrasi, only reaches 1463m – but it is impressively wild, the bare limestone plateau pitted with ravines and ragged defiles. The raw, uncompromising landscape is made all the more thrilling by its one-time notoriety as the heart of Sardinia's bandit country.

The Supramonte provides some magnificent hiking. But because much of the walking is over limestone, there are often few discernible tracks to follow, and in spring and autumn you should carefully check the weather conditions. You can engage a local guide in towns throughout the region, including Oliena, Dorgali and Baunei.

Oliena

☑ 0784 / POP 7110

Few images in Sardinia are as arresting as the magnificent peak of Monte Corrasi (1463m) when the dusky light makes its limestone summit glow. From Nuoro you can see Oliena's multicoloured rooftops cupped in the mountain's palm. The village itself is an unassuming place with a grey-stone centre, but it is a handy base for exploring the Supramonte.

Oliena was probably founded in Roman times, although its name is a reference to the Ilienses people, descendants of a group of Trojans who supposedly escaped Troy and settled in the area. The arrival of the Jesuits in the 17th century was better documented and set the scene for the village's modern fame. The eager fathers helped promote the local silk industry and encouraged farmers to cultivate the surrounding slopes. The lessons were learnt well, and now Oliena is famous for its beautiful silk embroidery and its blood-red Cannonau wine, Nepente di Oliena.

◎ Sights & Activities

★ **Su Gologone** SPRING
(☑ 328 5649983; www.sorgentisugologone.it; adult/reduced €2/1.50; ⊙ 9am-7pm) Tucked beneath sheer limestone cliffs, this gorgeous mountain spring is the final outflow point for Italy's largest underground river system.

Water percolating through the countless fissures and sinkholes in the Supramonte's high country eventually gathers here and flows out to join the Cedrino river. The spring is beautiful any time, but try to catch it around 1pm when the sun passes directly overhead, turning the water brilliant green. Afterwards, the adjacent tree-shaded park is perfect for a picnic or an afternoon swim in the reservoir.

Cooperativa Enis   ADVENTURE SPORTS
(☑0784 28 83 63; www.coopenis.it; Località Monte Maccione) This highly regarded adventure-sports company offers guided treks and 4WD excursions into the Supramonte and along the Golfo di Orosei. Destinations include Tiscali, Gola Su Gorropu, Cala Luna and the Supramonte di Orgosolo and Murales, with prices starting at €38 for a half-day trek or €44 for a full day. A packed lunch bumps up the cost by €5.

🛏 Sleeping & Eating

★**Agriturismo Guthiddai**   AGRITURISMO €
(☑0784 28 60 17; www.agriturismoguthiddai.com; Nuoro-Dorgali bivio Su Gologone; d €105-115, half-board per person €75-85; ❄🔊) On the road to Su Gologone, this bucolic, whitewashed farmstead sits at the foot of rugged mountains, surrounded by fig, olive and fruit trees. Olive oil, Cannonau wine and fruit and veg are all home produced. Rooms are tiled in pale greens and cobalt blues. From Oliena, head to Dorgali, taking the turnoff right towards Valle di Lanaittu.

★**Su Gologone**   HOTEL €€€
(☑0784 28 75 12; www.sugologone.it; Località Su Gologone; d from €290, incl half-board from €375; P❄🔊≋) Treat yourself to a spot of rural luxury at Su Gologone, nestled in glorious countryside 7km east of Oliena. Rooms are decorated with original artworks and handicrafts, and the facilities are top notch – it has a pool, a spa, a wine cellar and a **restaurant** (meals €35-50; ⊙12.30-3pm & 8-10pm), which is considered one of Sardinia's best.

❶ Getting There & Away

ARST runs frequent buses from Via Roma to Nuoro (€1.90, 20 minutes, up to 12 daily Monday to Saturday, six on Sunday).

Oliena is a 15-minute drive from Nuoro via the SP22, or a 30-minute drive from Dorgali via the SP46 (the latter reopened in 2020 after a seven-year bridge closure).

Dorgali & Around
☑0784 / POP 6500

Dorgali is a down-to-earth town with a grandiose backdrop, nestled at the foot of Monte Bardia and framed by vineyards and olive groves. Limestone peaks rear above the centre's pastel-coloured houses and steep, narrow streets, luring hikers and climbers to their summits.

For more outdoor escapades, the dramatic Golfo di Orosei and spectacularly rugged Supramonte are within easy striking distance.

◉ Sights

★**Gola Su Gorropu**   CANYON
(☑328 8976563, Chintula Company 389 4208595; www.gorropu.info; adult/reduced €5/3.50; ⊙10.30am-5.30pm) Sardinia's most spectacular gorge is flanked by limestone walls towering up to 500m in height. The endemic (and endangered) *Aquilegia nuragica* plant grows here, and at quieter times it's possible to spot mouflon and golden eagles. From the Rio Flumineddu riverbed you can explore about 1km into the boulder-strewn ravine without climbing gear; follow the markers. Near the narrowest point (just 4m wide) you reach the formidable **Hotel Supramonte**, a tough 8b multipitch climb up a vertical 400m rock face.

You can either hike into and out of the gorge, or book a ride in a jeep one way (€20, including canyon entrance fee) or both

WORTH A TRIP

ROAD TRIPPING THROUGH THE SUPRAMONTE

It's well worth driving the 60km stretch of the SS125 between Dorgali and Santa Maria Navarrese. Serpentine and at times hair-raising, the road threads through the mountaintops where the scenery is distractingly lovely: to the right the ragged limestone peaks of the Supramonte rear above wooded valleys and deep gorges; to the left mountains tumble down to the bright-blue sea. The first 20km to the Genna 'e Silana pass (1017m) are the most breathtaking. Aside from the odd hell-for-leather Fiat, traffic is sparse. Take care at dusk, when wild pigs, goats, sheep and cows rule the road and bring down rocks.

SARDINIA SUPRAMONTE

❶ GET A GUIDE

If you fancy striking out into the Supramonte, here's our pick of the best guides:

Cooperativa Gorropu (☑ Franco 347 4233650, Sandra 333 8507157; www.gorropu.com; Passo Silana SS125, Km 183) In business for over 20 years, local guides Sandra and Franco arrange all sorts of excursions, from trekking to canyoning and caving. They run a small info centre at Genna 'e Silana pass and also have a base in Urzulei.

Cooperative Ghivine (☑ 338 8341618; www.ghivine.com; Via Lamarmora 31) A one-stop action shop, arranging treks to places including Gola Su Gorropu and Tiscali. Trekking packages including accommodation are also available.

Corrado Conca (☑ 347 2903101; www.corradoconca.it; Via Barzini 15, Sassari) Based in Sassari, Sardinian hiking and climbing guru Corrado Conca is the ideal companion for excursions on the island. Book well in advance.

Sardegna Nascosta (☑ 0784 28 85 50, 349 4434665; www.sardegnanascosta.it; Via Masiloghi 35) Arranges trips and treks (€38 to €60 including lunch) with a cultural focus, from excursions to Monte Corrasi, Tiscali, Orgosolo, Gola Su Gorropu and the Valle di Lanaittu to canoeing in Lago del Cedrino.

ways (from €30) with Chintula Company – the Gola Su Gorropu website has details of packages.

To hike into the gorge, you'll need sturdy shoes and sufficient water. There are two main routes. The most dramatic begins from the car park opposite Hotel Silana at the **Genna 'e Silana** pass on the SS125 at Km 183. The 8km trail takes 1½ to two hours one way, so allow at least four hours for the return trek, longer if you plan to spend time exploring the gorge itself. While the descent is mostly easygoing, the climb back up is considerably tougher.

The hike weaves through holm oak woods, boulder-strewn slopes and cave-riddled cliffs. For a bird's-eye perspective of the gorge, you could take the 6km ridge trail from the car park to 888m **Punta Cucuttos**. It takes around 1½ hours one way.

The second and slightly easier hiking route (14km) to Gorropu is via the **Sa Barva bridge**, about 15km from Dorgali. To get to the bridge, take the SS125 and look for the sign on the right for the Gola Su Gorropu and Tiscali between Km 200 and Km 201. Follow this road for 10.5km until the asphalt finishes (about 20 minutes). Park here and cross the Sa Barva bridge, after which you'll see the trail for the Gola signposted off to the left. From here it's a scenic two-hour hike along the Rio Flumineddu to the mouth of the gorge (four hours return).

If you'd prefer to go with a guide, Sandra and Franco at the Cooperativa Gorropu arrange all sorts of excursions and activities, from trekking and canyoning to caving and

cookery courses; see the website for prices. Their base is in Urzulei, but they also run a small info centre at Genna 'e Silana pass.

★ Tiscali   ARCHAEOLOGICAL SITE

(☑ 338 8341618; www.museoarcheologicodorgali. it; adult/reduced €5/2; ☺ 9am-7pm daily May-Sep, to 5pm Oct-Apr, closed in rainy weather) Hidden in a mountaintop cave deep in the Valle di Lanaittu, the mysterious nuraghic village of Tiscali is one of Sardinia's must-see archaeological highlights. Dating from the 6th century BC and populated until Roman times, the village was discovered in the late 19th century. At the time it was relatively intact, but since then grave robbers have done a pretty good job of looting the place, stripping the conical stone-and-mud huts down to the skeletal remains that you see today.

Despite the fragmentary condition of the ruins themselves, Tiscali is an awe-inspiring sight, with jumbled stone foundations amid holm oak and turpentine trees huddled in the eerie twilight of the limestone overhang. The inhabitants of nearby Sa Sedda 'e Sos Carros (p930) used it as a hiding place from the Romans, and its inaccessibility ensured that the Sards were able to hold out here until well into the 2nd century BC.

Local guides lead hikes – tough and steeply uphill at times – to the site.

Grotta di Ispinigoli   CAVE

(adult/reduced €7.50/3.50; ☺ hourly tours 10am-6pm Jul & Aug, to 5pm Jun & Sep, 10am-noon & 3-5pm Apr, May & Oct) A short drive north of Dorgali, off the SS125, the fairy-tale-like Grotta di Ispinigoli is a veritable forest of glittering rock formations, including the world's second-tallest stalagmite (the highest is in Mexico and stands at 40m). Unlike most caves of this type, which you enter from the side, here you descend 60m inside a giant 'well', at whose centre stands the magnificent 38m-high stalagmite. Admire the tremendous rock formations, many of them sprouting from the walls like giant mushrooms and broccoli.

✕ Eating

★ **Ristorante Ispinigoli**   SARDINIAN €€
(📞0784 9 52 68; www.hotelispinigoli.com; off SS125; meals €30-36; ⏰12.30-2.30pm & 7.30-9.30pm) Linger for dinner and panoramic sunset views at the Ristorante Ispinigoli, just below the entrance to the Grotta di Ispinigoli. Located in Hotel Ispinigoli, the well-known restaurant rolls out local delights such as stone-bass-stuffed black ravioli with mullet roe, herb-infused roast kid and a waistline-expanding selection of *formaggi*. To get here, turn off the SS125 about 6km north of Dorgali and continue another 2km east.

ℹ Information

Tourist Office (📞0784 92 72 35; www.enjoy dorgali.it; Corso Umberto 37; ⏰10am-1pm & 4-8pm Mon-Fri) Can provide info on Dorgali and Cala Gonone, including contact details for local trekking outfits and accommodation lists.

ℹ Getting There & Away

ARST buses serve Nuoro (€2.50, 50 minutes, eight daily Monday to Saturday, four Sunday). Up to seven (four on Sundays) shuttle back and forth between Dorgali and Cala Gonone (€1.30, 20 minutes). You can pick up buses at several stops along Via Lamarmora. Buy tickets at the bar at the junction of Via Lamarmora and Corso Umberto.

By car or motorcycle, Dorgali is 15 minutes from Cala Gonone via the SP26, 35 minutes from Orosei via the SS125, and 45 minutes from Nuoro via the SP46 or SS129.

Note: the bridge on the SP46 between Dorgali and Oliena was closed for years but is due to reopen. Check ahead as you map your route.

Baunei & the Altopiano del Golgo

Clinging to a precipitous rocky ridge on the long, tortuous road between Arbatax and Dorgali, the old stone shepherd's village of Baunei is an agreeable mountain outpost and a welcome oasis in the middle of the rugged Supramonte. Whether or not you linger in town, be sure not to miss the region's uncontested highlight: the 10km detour up to the Altopiano del Golgo, a magical, otherworldly plateau where goats, pigs and donkeys graze in the *macchia* (Mediterranean scrub) and woodland. From here, one of Sardinia's best hiking trails descends to the coast at Cala Goloritzè, while a hardscrabble road snakes down to the rock spike

SARDINIA SUPRAMONTE

DON'T MISS

SELVAGGIO BLU

For serious hikers, the Selvaggio Blu is the stuff of myth: an epic seven-day, 45km trek along the Golfo di Orosei's wild and imperious coastline, traversing thickly wooded ravines and taking in bizarre limestone formations, caves and staggeringly sheer cliffs. Both the scenery and the walking are breathtaking (in every sense of the word!) on what is often hailed as Italy's toughest trek.

The trail follows the starkly eroded – and often invisible – trails of goatherds and charcoal burners, teetering around cliffs that plunge into the dazzlingly blue sea. Because of its challenging terrain, the trek requires a good level of fitness and some climbing experience for the short climbs and abseiling involved. The seven-day duration is based on the assumption that you will walk six to eight hours a day. You'll also need to come prepared with a bivi bag or an ultralight tent, climbing gear (including two 45m ropes), a roll mat, sturdy boots, a compass, a map and ample food.

A guide is recommended as the trail is not well signposted and there's no water en route (guides can arrange for it to be dropped off by boat).

Get Enrico Spanu's *Book of Selvaggio Blu*, and ask locally about current conditions. New laws in 2019 restrict where you can camp and some mainstay guides are not offering the trek as a result. This includes the author of *Arrampicare a Cala Gonone* (€18) and *Il Sentiero Selvaggio Blu* (€16), Corrado Conca, Sardinia's hiking and climbing guru, and a brilliant guide. Also consult www.selvaggioblu.it for the latest news.

at Cala Pedra Longa, a natural monument and also the southernmost starting point for Sardinia's star coastal trek, the Selvaggio Blu (p933).

Sights & Activities

Il Golgo
LANDMARK

FREE This remarkable feat of nature – a 270m abyss just 40m wide at its base – is tucked high up on the Altopiano del Golgo. Its funnel-like opening is now fenced off, but just peering into the dark opening is enough to bring on vertigo.

Cala Goloritzè Trail
HIKING

(€6; ⊙ trailhead 7.30am-4pm, beach to 6pm) Few experiences in Sardinia compare with this thrilling trek to Cala Goloritzè, one of the Mediterranean's most spectacular beaches. Suitable for families, the easygoing, well-signposted (if rocky and occasionally steep) hike along an old mule trail takes you through a gorgeous limestone canyon shaded by juniper and holm oaks, passing cliffs honeycombed with caves, dramatic rock arches, overhangs and pinnacles. From the trailhead at Bar Su Porteddu on the Altopiano del Golgo, it's 3.5km down to the beach (about 1¼ hours), longer hiking back up.

After an initial 15-minute climb, you'll get your first tantalising glimpses of the bay and a sea so blue it will make you gasp. Keep an eye out for a traditional sheepfold and the idiosyncratic spike of the Aguglia as you approach the bay. Steps lead down to the half-moon of bone-white pebbles; this is a perfect picnic spot. Bring along your bathers for a dip in the deliciously warm, astonishingly blue waters. Allow 1½ hours for the slightly more challenging, uphill return trip.

To reach the trailhead from downtown Baunei, drive up Via San Pietro, following signs for the Altopiano. After travelling 8.4km north on pavement, continue another 1.2km east on the signposted dirt road to the parking lot at Bar Su Porteddu.

Cooperativa Goloritzè
HIKING

(☑ 368 7028980; www.coopgoloritze.com; Località Golgo) This highly regarded cooperative organises excursions ranging from trekking to 4WD trips. Many treks involve a descent through canyons to the Golfo di Orosei's dreamy beaches. Staff at the refuge also arrange guides and logistical support for walkers attempting Sardinia's stunning Selvaggio Blu trek (p933).

Sleeping & Eating

Hotel Bia Maore
B&B €€

(☑ 0782 61 10 33; www.biamaore.it; Via San Pietro 19, Baunei; s €55-85, d €82-130, tr €107-150; P❄🌐) Perched like an eyrie above Baunei, this B&B has compelling views of the mountains and coast. The warm-hued rooms are decked out with handmade furnishings and Sardinian fabrics – the pick of them with a balcony overlooking the mountains and the Gulf of Ogliastra.

Locanda Il Rifugio
SARDINIAN €€

(☑ 368 7028980; www.coopgoloritze.com; Località Golgo; meals €25-35; ⊙ 12.30-3pm & 7.30-11pm Easter-Oct) Managed by Cooperativa Goloritzè, this converted farmstead puts on a generous spread of regional fare such as *ladeddos* (potato gnocchi) and spit-roasted kid and suckling pig, washed down with local Cannonau red. Afterwards, spare yourself the nail-biting drive back down to Baunei by camping (per person €7) or staying in one of the refuge's simple rooms (double including breakfast €60).

Getting There & Away

Baunei sits astride the SS125, about 20km north of Tortolì/Arbatax and 48km south of Dorgali. Several daily ARST buses run south to Tortolì (€1.90, 35 minutes), but for travel north to Dorgali or up to the Altopiano del Golgo, you're much better off with your own wheels.

Golfo di Orosei

For sheer stop-dead-in-your-tracks beauty, there are few places to match this gulf, forming the seaward section of the glorious **Parco Nazionale del Golfo di Orosei e del Gennargentu** (www.parcogennargentu.it). Here the high mountains of the Gennargentu abruptly meet the sea, forming a crescent of dramatic cliffs riven by false inlets, scattered with horseshoe-shaped bays and lapped by exquisitely aquamarine waters. Beach space is at a premium in summer, but there's room for everyone, especially in the rugged, elemental hinterland.

Cala Gonone

☑ 0784 / POP 1800

Climbers, divers, sea kayakers, beachcombers and hikers all find their thrill in Cala Gonone. Why? Just look around you: imperious limestone peaks frame grandstand views of the Golfo di Orosei, sheer cliffs dip into the brilliant-blue sea, trails wriggle through emerald-green ravines to pearly-white beaches. It is quite magnificent. Even getting here is an adventure, with each hairpin bend bringing you ever closer to a sea that spreads out before you like a giant liquid mirror.

Gathered along a pine-shaded promenade, this seaside resort still has the low-key, family-friendly vibe of the small fishing village it once was. August aside, the beaches tend to be uncrowded and the room rates affordable. Bear in mind that the resort slumbers in winter, closing from October until Easter.

👁 Sights & Activities

Boat tour and adventure sports operators are clustered down by the port, including **Prima Sardegna** (📞0784 9 33 67; www.primasardegna.com; Lungomare Palmasera 32; ☺9am-1pm & 4-8pm summer), **Cielomar** (📞0784 92 00 14; www.cielomar.it; Piazza del Porto 6), **Dolmen** (📞347 6698192; www.sardegnadascoprire.it; Piazza del Porto 3) and **Nuovo Consorzio Trasporti Marittimi** (📞0784 9 33 05; www.calagononecrociere.it; Piazza del Porto 1).

Cala Fuili   BEACH
About 3.5km south of town (follow Viale del Bue Marino) is this captivating rocky inlet backed by a deep green valley. From here you can hike over the clifftops to Cala Luna, about two hours (4km) away on foot. The trail cuts a scenic path through juniper and mastic trees and is easy to navigate, with triangle-circle symbols marking handy rocks. The coastal views are breathtaking as you approach Cala Luna.

Grotta del Bue Marino   CAVE
(adult/reduced Aug €11/5, Sep-Jul adult €8-10, reduced €4-5; ☺guided tours hourly 10am-noon & 3-5pm summer, 11am & 3pm winter, groups only Nov-Mar) It's a scenic 40-minute hike from Cala Fuili, or a speedy boat ride from Cala Gonone, to this enchanting grotto. It was the last island refuge of the rare monk seal ('bue marino' or 'sea ox' as it was known by local fishers). The watery gallery is impressive, with shimmering light playing on the strange shapes and Neolithic petroglyphs

DON'T MISS

THE BLUE CRESCENT

If you do nothing else in Sardinia, you should try to make an excursion along the 20km southern stretch of the Golfo di Orosei by boat. Either hire a Zodiac (about €100 and €35 for petrol) or buy tickets to excursion boats (€35 to €45 per person) in the port at Cala Gonone from one of the man portside operators. From the water, you'll see intimidating limestone cliffs plunge headlong into the sea, scalloped by exquisite beaches, coves and grottoes. With an ever-changing palette of sand, rocks, pebbles, seashells and crystal-clear water (no cliche, just truth!), the unfathomable forces of nature have conspired to create a sublime taste of paradise. The colours are at their best until about 3pm, when the sun starts to drop behind the higher cliffs.

From the port of Cala Gonone you head south to the Grotta del Bue Marino. The first beach after the cave is **Cala Luna**, a crescent-shaped strand closed off by high cliffs to the south. **Cala Sisine** is the next beach of any size, also a mix of sand and pebbles and backed by a deep, verdant valley. **Cala Biriola** quickly follows, and then several enchanting spots where you can bob below the soaring cliffs – look out for the patches of celestial-blue water.

Cala Mariolu is arguably one of the most sublime spots on the coast. Split in two by a cluster of bright limestone rocks, it has virtually no sand. Don't let the smooth white pebbles put you off, though. The water that laps these beaches ranges from a kind of transparent white at water's edge through every shade of light and sky blue and on to a deep purplish hue.

The last beachette of the gulf, **Cala Goloritzè** rivals the best. At the southern end, bizarre limestone formations soar away from the cliffside. Among them is jaw-dropping Monte Caroddi, also known as the **Aguglia**, a 148m-high needle of rock beloved of climbers. Many boat trips will take you here, or you can hike in from the **Altopiano del Golgo** on the beautiful, 3.5km Cala Goloritzè Trail. Note that the beach itself is rather small and can get crowded in summer; boats cannot land there as it's protected park.

within the cave. Guided visits take place up to seven times a day. In peak season you may need to book at the Cala Gonone portside kiosk for 'Comune di Dorgali'. Note: boat tickets do not include entry tickets to the cave, which must be paid in cash.

Nuraghe Mannu   ARCHAEOLOGICAL SITE
(adult/reduced €3/2; ☺9am-noon & 5-8pm Jul & Aug, 9am-noon & 4-7pm May, Jun & Sep, 10am-1pm & 3-6pm Apr & Oct) To get an eagle-eye view over the coast, follow the signs off the Cala Gonone–Dorgali road to this *nuraghe*. After 3km the rocky track peters out at a wild headland where you can see nearly the entire curve of the gulf. The location is idyllic, set above a lush gorge and with silver-grey blocks strewn beneath the olive trees. First inhabited around 1600 BC, the tower is a modest ruin, but you can still see niches in the central chamber.

🛏 Sleeping & Eating

★**Agriturismo Codula Fuili**   AGRITURISMO €
(☑340 2546208, 328 7340863; www.codulafuili.com; Località Pranos; r per person incl breakfast €35-60, half-board €65-90, camping 2 people, car & tent €16-20) You could be excused for fainting when you first see the spellbinding views from this end-of-the-road *agriturismo*. Perched high on the slopes above Nuraghe Mannu and Cala Fuili, it offers four rooms, campsites, a bungalow and a panoramic terrace. Dinners (€30) feature cheese from the family's free-ranging goats, plus homegrown olives, olive oil, meats and veggies.

Agriturismo Nuraghe Mannu   AGRITURISMO €
(☑0784 9 32 64, 328 8685824; www.agriturismonuraghemannu.com; Località Pranos; r per person incl breakfast €29-36, half-board €48-55, camping per person €10-12) 🏊 Immersed in greenery and with blissful sea views, this is an authentic, ecofriendly working farm with five simple rooms, a restaurant open to all, and home-produced bread, milk, ricotta and sweets at breakfast. For campers, there are also five tent pitches available.

Hotel Bue Marino   HOTEL €€
(☑0784 92 00 78; www.hotelbuemarino.it; Via Vespucci 8; s/d/tr from €75/86/91) Conveniently located just steps above the port, this blindingly white hotel has pleasant, cool blue rooms done up in traditional Sardinian fabrics. Adding to its appeal are friendly staff and magnificent sea views from many guest rooms, as well as from the upper-floor breakfast area, solarium and hot tub.

Hotel L'Oasi   B&B €€
(☑0784 9 31 11; www.loasihotel.it; Via Garcia Lorca 13; d €80-140; [P][❄][☎]) Perched on the cliffs above Cala Gonone and nestling in flowery gardens, this B&B offers enticing sea views from many of its breezy rooms. The friendly Carlesso family can advise on activities from climbing to diving. L'Oasi is a 700m uphill walk from the harbour.

Il Pescatore   SEAFOOD €€
(☑0784 9 31 74; www.ristoranteilpescatorecalagonone.com; Via Lungomare dell'Acqua Dolce 7; meals €35-50; ☺noon-2.30pm & 7-10.30pm; [👶]) Fresh seafood is what this authentic place is about. Sit on the terrace for sea breezes and fishy delights, such as pasta with *ricci* (sea urchins), and spaghetti with clams and *bottarga* (mullet roe). It also does a kids' menu (€15).

❶ Information

Namaste (☑0784 9 37 23; Viale Colombo 11; ☺8am-1pm & 4-8pm) Outdoor enthusiasts should check out this bookshop, which stocks an excellent selection of maps and guides for trekkers and climbers.

Tourist Office (☑0784 9 36 96; Viale del Bue Marino 1a; ☺9am-1pm & 3-7pm May-Sep, to 1pm Oct-Apr) A very helpful office in the small park off to the right as you enter town.

❶ Getting There & Away

Buses run to Cala Gonone from Dorgali (€1.30, 20 minutes, seven daily Monday to Saturday, four Sunday) and Nuoro (€3.10, 1¼ hours, six daily Monday to Saturday, three Sunday).

Understand
Italy

History

Italy has only been a nation since 1861, prior to which it was last unified as part of the Roman Empire. It has wielded powerful influence as Catholicism's headquarters, and Italy's dynamic city-states set the modern era in motion with the Renaissance. Italian unity was won in blood, fusing north and south in a dysfunctional yet enduring marriage. Even today, Italy feels like a powerfully distinct collection of regions, existing in a present that has roots in the past.

Etruscans, Greeks & Wolf-Raised Twins

Ancient Artefacts
....
Vatican Museums (Rome)
....
Capitoline Museums (Rome)
....
Museo Archeologico Nazionale (Naples)
....
Museo Archeologico Paolo Orsi (Syracuse)
....
Museo Nazionale Etrusco di Villa Giulia (Rome)

Of the many tribes that emerged from the millennia of the Stone Age in ancient Italy, it was the Etruscans who dominated the peninsula by the 7th century BC. Etruria was based on city-states mostly concentrated between the Arno and Tiber rivers. Among them were Caere (modern-day Cerveteri), Tarquinii (Tarquinia), Veii (Veio), Perusia (Perugia), Volaterrae (Volterra) and Arretium (Arezzo). The name of their homeland is preserved in the name Tuscany, where the bulk of their settlements were (and still are) located.

Most of what we know of the Etruscan people has been deduced from artefacts and paintings unearthed at their burial sites, especially at Tarquinia, near Rome. Argument persists over whether the Etruscans had migrated from Asia Minor. They spoke a language that today has barely been deciphered. An energetic people, the Etruscans were redoubtable warriors and seafarers, but lacked cohesion and discipline.

At home, the Etruscans farmed, and mined metals. Their gods were numerous, and they were forever trying to second-guess them and predict future events through such rituals as examining the livers of sacrificed animals. They were also quick to learn from others. Much of their artistic tradition (which comes to us in the form of tomb frescoes, statuary and pottery) was influenced by the Greeks.

Indeed, while the Etruscans dominated the centre of the peninsula, Greek traders settled in the south in the 8th century BC, setting up a series of independent city-states along the coast and in Sicily that together were known as Magna Graecia. They flourished until the 3rd century BC

TIMELINE	c 700,000 BC	2000 BC	474 BC
	Primitive tribes lived in caves and hunted elephants, rhinoceroses, hippopotamuses and other hefty wild beasts on the Italian peninsula.	The Bronze Age reaches Italy. Hunter-gatherers have settled as farmers. The use of copper and bronze to fashion tools and arms marks a new sophistication.	The power of the Etruscans in Italy is eclipsed after Greek forces from Syracuse and Cumae join to crush an Etruscan armada off the southern Italian coast in the Battle of Cumae.

and the ruins of magnificent Doric temples in Italy's south (at Paestum) and on Sicily (at Agrigento, Selinunte and Segesta) stand as testimony to the splendour of Greek civilisation in Italy.

Attempts by the Etruscans to conquer the Greek settlements failed and accelerated the Etruscan decline. The death knell, however, would come from an unexpected source – the grubby but growing Latin town of Rome.

The origins of the town are shrouded in myth, which says it was founded by Romulus (who descended from Aeneas, a refugee from Troy whose mother was the goddess Venus) on 21 April 753 BC on the site where he and his twin brother, Remus, had been suckled by a she-wolf as orphan infants. Romulus later killed Remus and the settlement was named Rome after him. At some point, legend merges with history. Seven kings are said to have followed Romulus and at least three were historical Etruscan rulers. In 509 BC, disgruntled Latin nobles turfed the last of the Etruscan kings, Tarquinius Superbus, out of Rome after his predecessor, Servius Tullius, had stacked the Senate with his allies and introduced citizenship reforms that undermined the power of the aristocracy. Sick of monarchy, the nobles set up the Roman Republic. Over the following centuries, this piffling Latin town would grow to become Italy's major power, sweeping aside the Etruscans, whose language and culture disappeared by the 2nd century AD.

Sandwiched between Emilia-Romagna and Le Marche, the Republic of San Marino was established in AD 301. The wealthy microstate is home to the world's oldest continuous constitution and is the only country on Earth with more cars than people.

The Roman Republic

Under the Republic, *imperium,* or regal power, was placed in the hands of two consuls who acted as political and military leaders and were elected for nonrenewable one-year terms by an assembly of the people. The Senate, whose members were appointed for life, advised the consuls.

Although from the beginning monuments were emblazoned with the initials SPQR (Senatus Populusque Romanus, or the Senate and People of Rome), the 'people' initially had precious little say in affairs. (The initials are still used and many Romans would argue that little has changed.) Known as plebeians (literally 'the many'), the disenfranchised majority slowly wrested concessions from the patrician class in the more than two centuries that followed the founding of the Republic. Some plebeians were even appointed as consuls, and by about 280 BC most of the distinctions between patricians and plebeians had disappeared. That said, the apparently democratic system was largely oligarchic, with a fairly narrow political class (whether patrician or plebeian) vying for positions of power in government and the Senate.

At first, the Romans were a rough-and-ready lot. Rome did not bother to mint coins until 269 BC, even though the neighbouring (and later conquered or allied) Etruscans and Greeks had long had their own currencies. The Etruscans and Greeks also brought writing to the attention

396 BC	264–241 BC	218–146 BC	133 BC
Romans conquer the key Etruscan town of Veio, north of Rome, after an 11-year siege. Celebrations are short-lived, as invading Celtic tribes sweep across Italy and sack Rome in 390 BC.	War rages between Rome and the empire of Carthage, stretching across North Africa and into Spain, Sicily and Sardinia. By the war's end Rome is the western Mediterranean's prime naval power.	Carthage sends Hannibal to invade Italy overland from the north in the Second Punic War. Rome invades Spain, Hannibal fails and Carthage is destroyed in a third war from 149–146 BC.	Rome gains control of Sardinia, Sicily, Corsica, mainland Greece, Spain, most of North Africa and part of Asia Minor.

of Romans, who found it useful for documents and technical affairs but hardly glowed in the literature department. Eventually, the Greek pantheon of gods formed the bedrock of Roman worship. Society was patriarchal and its prime building block was the household (*familia*). The head of the family (*pater familias*) had direct control over his wife, children and extended family. He was responsible for his children's education. Devotion to household gods (eg Panes, the spirits of the kitchen) was as strong as devotion to the pantheon of state gods, led at first by the Capitoline Triad of Jupiter (the sky god and chief protector of the state), Juno (the female equivalent of Jupiter and patron goddess of women) and Minerva (patron goddess of craftspeople). An earlier version of the triad included Mars (god of war) instead of Juno.

Slowly at first, then with gathering pace, Roman armies conquered the Italian peninsula. Defeated city-states were not taken over directly; they were instead obliged to become allies. They retained their government and lands but had to provide troops on demand to serve in the Roman army. This relatively light-handed touch was a key to success. Increasingly, the protection offered by Roman hegemony induced many cities to become allies voluntarily. Wars with Carthage and other rivals in the east led Rome to take control of Sardinia, Sicily, Corsica, mainland Greece, Spain, most of North Africa and part of Asia Minor by 133 BC.

As the empire grew, so did its ancient system of 'motorways'. With the roads came other bright concepts: postal services and wayside inns. Messages could be shot around the empire in a matter of days or weeks by sending dispatch riders. At ancient 'truck stops', the riders would change mounts, have a bite and continue on their way (more efficient than many modern European postal systems).

By the second half of the 2nd century BC, Rome was the most important city in the Mediterranean, with a population of 300,000. Most were lower-class freedmen or slaves living in often precarious conditions. Tenement housing blocks (mostly of brick and wood) were raised alongside vast monuments. Among the latter was the Circus Flaminius, the stage of some of the spectacular games held each year. These became increasingly important events for the people of Rome, who flocked to see gladiators and wild beasts in combat.

The Romans adopted the ancient Greek belief that left-handed people were unlucky or untrustworthy. The belief led both ancient Greeks and Romans to wear their wedding rings on the third finger of their left hand to ward off any misfortune brought on by the left-handed minority.

Hail, Caesar!

Born in 100 BC, Gaius Julius Caesar would prove to be one of Rome's most masterful generals and capable administrators, but his hunger for power was probably his undoing.

He was a supporter of the consul Pompey, who in 78 BC had become a leading figure in Rome after putting down rebellions in Spain and eliminating piracy. Caesar himself had been in Spain for several years

46 BC	30 BC	AD 79	100–138
Julius Caesar assumes dictatorial powers, alienating pro-republican senators. Among these are Cassius and Brutus, who orchestrate Caesar's assassination on 15 March 44 BC. Civil wars lead to the Republic's dissolution.	Octavian (Augustus) invades Egypt, Antony and Cleopatra commit suicide and Egypt becomes a province of Rome. Three years later, Octavian becomes the first emperor of the newly formed Roman Empire.	Mt Vesuvius showers molten rock and ash upon Pompeii and Herculaneum. Pliny the Younger later describes the eruption in letters, and the towns are only rediscovered in the 18th century.	The Roman Empire reaches its greatest extent, during the reign of Hadrian.

dealing with border revolts; on his return to Rome in 60 BC, he formed an alliance with Pompey and another important commander and former consul, Crassus. They backed Caesar's candidacy as consul.

To consolidate his position in the Roman power game, Caesar needed a major military command. This he received with a mandate to govern the province of Gallia Narbonensis, a southern swath of modern France stretching from Italy to the Pyrenees, in 59 BC. Caesar raised troops and in the following year entered Gaul proper (modern France) to head off an invasion of Helvetic tribes from Switzerland and subsequently to bring other tribes to heel. What started as a defensive effort soon became a full-blown campaign of conquest. In the next five years, he subdued Gaul and made forays into Britain and across the Rhine. In 51 BC he stamped out the last great revolt in Gaul, led by Vercingetorix. Caesar was generous to his defeated enemies and consequently won over the Gauls. Indeed, they became his staunchest supporters in coming years.

By now, Caesar also had a devoted veteran army behind him. Jealous of the growing power of his one-time protégé, Pompey severed his political alliance and joined like-minded factions in the Senate to outlaw Caesar in 49 BC. On 7 January, Caesar crossed the Rubicon river into Italy and civil war began. His three-year campaign in Italy, Spain and the eastern Mediterranean proved a crushing victory. Upon his return to Rome in 46 BC, he assumed dictatorial powers.

He launched a series of reforms, overhauled the Senate and embarked on a building program (of which the Curia and Basilica Giulia remain). By 44 BC it was clear Caesar had no plans to restore the Republic, and dissent grew in the Senate, even among former supporters like Marcus Junius Brutus, who thought he had gone too far. A small band of conspirators led by Brutus finally stabbed him to death in a Senate meeting on the Ides of March (15 March), two years after he had been proclaimed dictator for life.

In the years following Caesar's death, his lieutenant, Mark Antony (Marcus Antonius), and nominated heir, great-nephew Octavian, plunged into civil war against Caesar's assassins. Things calmed down as Octavian took control of the western half of the empire and Antony headed to the east, but when Antony fell head over heels for Cleopatra VII in 31 BC, Octavian went to war and finally claimed victory over Antony and Cleopatra at Actium, in Greece. The following year Octavian invaded Egypt, Antony and Cleopatra committed suicide and Egypt became a province of Rome.

At its height, the Roman Empire stretched from Portugal in the west to Syria in the east, and from Britain in the north to the North African deserts across the Mediterranean. It covered an area two-thirds the size of the US and had a population of around 120 million people.

Augustus & the Glories of Empire

Octavian was left as sole ruler of the Roman world and by 27 BC had been acclaimed Augustus (Your Eminence) and the Senate had conceded to him virtually unlimited power. In effect, he had become emperor.

HISTORY AUGUSTUS & THE GLORIES OF EMPIRE

476	568	754–56	902
Germanic tribal leader Odovacar proclaims himself king in Rome. The peninsula sinks into chaos and only the eastern half of the empire survives intact.	Lombards invade and occupy northern Italy, leaving just Ravenna, Rome and southern Italy in the empire's hands. Other tribes invade Balkan territories and cut the eastern empire off from Italy.	Frankish king Pepin the Short enters Italy at the request of Pope Stephen II, defeats the Lombards and declares the creation of the Papal States.	Muslims from North Africa complete the occupation of Sicily, encouraging learning of the Greek classics, mathematics and other sciences. Agriculture flourishes and Sicily is relatively peaceful for two centuries.

Under Augustus, the arts flourished – his contemporaries included the poets Virgil, Horace and Ovid, as well as the historian Livy. He encouraged the visual arts, restored existing buildings and constructed many new ones. During his reign the Pantheon was raised and he boasted that he had 'found Rome in brick and left it in marble'. The long period of comparatively enlightened rule that he initiated brought unprecedented prosperity and security to the Mediterranean.

By AD 100, the city of Rome was said to have had more than 1.5 million inhabitants and all the trappings of an imperial capital – its wealth and prosperity were obvious in the rich mosaics, marble temples, public baths, theatres, circuses and libraries. People of all races and conditions converged on the capital. Poverty was rife among an often disgruntled lower class. Augustus had created Rome's first police force under a city prefect *(praefectus urbi)* to curb mob violence, which had long gone largely unchecked.

Augustus carried out other far-reaching reforms. He streamlined the army, which was kept at a standing total of around 300,000 men. Military service ranged from 16 to 25 years, but Augustus kept conscription to a minimum, making it a largely volunteer force. He consolidated

IMPERIAL INSANITY

Bribes? *Bunga bunga* parties? Think they're unsavoury? Spare a thought for the ancient Romans, who suffered their fair share of eccentric leaders. We salute some of the Roman Empire's wackiest, weirdest and downright kinkiest rulers.

Tiberius (14–37) – A steady governing hand but prone to depression, Tiberius had a difficult relationship with the Senate and withdrew in his later years to Capri, where, they say, he devoted himself to drinking, orgies and throwing out-of-favour subjects into the sea.

Gaius (Caligula; 37–41) – 'Little Shoes' made grand-uncle Tiberius look tame. Sex (including with his sisters) and gratuitous, cruel violence were high on his agenda. He emptied the state's coffers and suggested making a horse consul, before being assassinated.

Claudius (41–54) – Apparently timid as a child, he proved ruthless with his enemies (among them 35 senators), whose executions he greatly enjoyed watching. According to English historian Edward Gibbon, he was the only one of the first 15 emperors not to take male lovers (unusual at the time).

Nero (54–68) – Augustus' last descendant, Nero had his pushy stage mum murdered, his first wife's veins slashed, his second wife kicked to death and his third wife's ex-husband killed. The people accused him of playing the fiddle while Rome burned to the ground in 64. He blamed the disaster on the Christians, executed the evangelists Peter and Paul and had others thrown to wild beasts in a grisly public spectacle.

962	1130	1202–03	1271
Otto I is crowned Holy Roman Emperor in Rome, the first in a long line of Germanic rulers. His meddling in Italian affairs leads to clashes between papacy and empire.	Norman invader Roger II is crowned King of Sicily, a century after the Normans landed in southern Italy, creating a united southern Italian kingdom.	Venice leads the Fourth Crusade to the Holy Land on a detour to Constantinople in revenge for attacks on Venetian interests there. The Crusaders topple the Byzantine emperor, installing a puppet ruler.	Venetian merchant Marco Polo embarks on a 24-year journey to Central Asia and China with his father and uncle. His written travel accounts help enlighten Europeans about Asia.

Rome's three-tier class society. The richest and most influential class remained the senators. Below them, the so-called equestrians filled posts in public administration and supplied officers to the army (control of which was essential to keeping Augustus' position unchallenged). The bulk of the populace filled the ranks of the lower class. The system was by no means rigid and upward mobility was possible.

A century after Augustus' death in AD 14 (at age 75), the Roman Empire reached its greatest extent. Under Hadrian (76–138), it stretched from the Iberian Peninsula, Gaul and Britain to a line that basically followed the Rhine and Danube rivers. All of the present-day Balkans and Greece, along with the areas known in those times as Dacia, Moesia and Thrace (considerable territories reaching to the Black Sea), were under Roman control. Most of modern-day Turkey, Syria, Lebanon, Palestine and Israel were occupied by Rome's legions and linked with Egypt. From there a deep strip of Roman territory stretched along the length of North Africa to the Atlantic coast of what is today northern Morocco. The Mediterranean was a Roman lake.

This situation lasted until the 3rd century. By the time Diocletian (245–305) became emperor, attacks on the empire from without and revolts within had become part and parcel of imperial existence. A new religious force, Christianity, was gaining popularity and persecution of Christians became common. This policy was reversed in 313 under Constantine I (c 272–337) in his Edict of Milan.

Inspired by a supposed vision of the cross, Constantine defeated his own rival, Maxentius, on Rome's Ponte Milvio (Milvian Bridge) in 312, becoming the Roman Empire's first Christian leader and commissioning Rome's first Christian basilica, San Giovanni in Laterano.

The empire was later divided in two, with the second capital in Constantinople (founded by Constantine in 330), on the Bosphorus in Byzantium. It was this, the eastern empire, which survived as Italy and Rome were overrun. This rump empire stretched from parts of present-day Serbia and Montenegro across to Asia Minor, a coastal strip of what is now Syria, Lebanon, Jordan and Israel down to Egypt and a sliver of North Africa as far west as modern Libya. Attempts by Justinian I (482–565) to recover Rome and the shattered western half of the empire ultimately came to nothing.

Papal Power & Family Feuds

Ironically, the minority religion that Emperor Diocletian had tried so hard to stamp out saved the glory of the city of Rome. Through the chaos of invasion and counter-invasion that saw Italy succumb to Germanic tribes, the Byzantine reconquest and the Lombard occupation in the north, the papacy established itself in Rome as a spiritual and secular force. It invented the Donation of Constantine, a document in which

Medieval Mystique

Assisi (Umbria)

Ravello (Campania)

San Gimignano (Tuscany)

Santo Stefano di Sessanio (Abruzzo)

Vieste (Puglia)

Tropea (Calabria)

1282	1309	1321	1348
Charles of Anjou creates enemies in Sicily with heavy taxes on landowners, who rise in the Sicilian Vespers revolt. They hand control of Sicily to Peter III, King of Aragon.	Pope Clement V shifts the papacy to Avignon, France, for almost 70 years. Clement had been elected pope four years earlier but refused to rule in a hostile Rome.	Dante Alighieri completes his epic poem La divina commedia (The Divine Comedy). The Florentine poet, considered Italy's greatest literary figure, dies the same year.	The Black Death (bubonic plague) wreaks havoc across Italy and much of the rest of Western Europe. Florence is said to have lost three-quarters of its populace.

Emperor Constantine I had supposedly granted the Church control of Rome and surrounding territory. What the popes needed was a guarantor with military clout. This they found in the Franks and a deal was done.

In return for formal recognition of the popes' control of Rome and surrounding Byzantine-held territories henceforth to be known as the Papal States, the popes granted the Carolingian Franks a leading (if ill-defined) role in Italy and their king, Charlemagne, the title of Holy Roman Emperor. He was crowned by Leo III on Christmas Day 800. The bond between the papacy and the Byzantine Empire was thus broken and political power in what had been the Western Roman Empire shifted north of the Alps, where it would remain for more than 1000 years.

The stage was set for a future of seemingly endless struggles. Similarly, Rome's aristocratic families engaged in battle for the papacy. For centuries, the imperial crown was fought over ruthlessly and Italy was frequently the prime battleground. Holy Roman emperors sought time and again to impose their control on increasingly independent-minded Italian cities, and even on Rome itself. In riposte, the popes continually sought to exploit their spiritual position to bring the emperors to heel and further their own secular ends.

The clash between Pope Gregory VII and Emperor Henry IV over who had the right to appoint bishops (who were powerful political players and hence important friends or dangerous foes) in the last quarter of the 11th century showed just how bitter these struggles could become. They became a focal point of Italian politics in the late Middle Ages, and across the cities and regions of the peninsula two camps emerged: Guelphs (Guelfi, who backed the pope) and Ghibellines (Ghibellini, in support of the emperor).

> Europe's first modern banks appeared in Genoa in the 12th century. The city claims the first recorded public bond (1150) and the earliest-known exchange contract (1156). Italy's Banca Monte dei Paschi di Siena is the world's oldest surviving bank, counting coins since 1472.

The Wonder of the World

The Holy Roman Empire had barely touched southern Italy until Henry, son of the Holy Roman Emperor Frederick I (Barbarossa), married Constance de Hauteville, heir to the Norman throne in Sicily in 1186. The Normans had arrived in southern Italy in the 10th century, initially as pilgrims en route from Jerusalem, later as mercenaries attracted by the money to be made fighting for rival principalities and against the Arab Muslims in Sicily. Of Henry and Constance's match was born one of the most colourful figures of medieval Europe, Frederick II (1194–1250), nicknamed *stupor mundi* (wonder of the world).

Crowned Holy Roman Emperor in 1220, Frederick was a German with a difference. Having grown up in southern Italy, he considered Sicily his natural base and left the German states largely to their own devices. A warrior and scholar, Frederick was an enlightened ruler with an absolutist vocation. A man who allowed freedom of worship to Muslims and

1506	1508–12	1534	1582
Work starts on St Peter's Basilica, to a design by Donato Bramante, on the site of an earlier basilica in Rome. Work would continue on Christendom's showpiece church until 1626.	Pope Julius II commissions Michelangelo to paint the ceiling frescoes in the Sistine Chapel. Michelangelo decides the content, and the central nine panels recount stories from Genesis.	The accession of Pope Paul III marks the beginning of the Counter-Reformation.	Pope Gregory XIII replaces the Julian calendar (introduced by Julius Caesar) with the modern-day Gregorian calendar. The new calendar adds the leap year to keep in line with the earth's rotation.

Jews, he was not to everyone's liking, as his ambition was to finally bring all of Italy under the imperial yoke.

A poet, linguist, mathematician and philosopher, Frederick founded a university in Naples and encouraged the spread of learning and translation of Arab treatises. Having reluctantly carried out a crusade (marked more by negotiation than the clash of arms) in the Holy Land in 1228 and 1229 on pain of excommunication, Frederick returned to Italy to find papal troops invading Neapolitan territory. Frederick soon had them on the run and turned his attention to gaining control of the complex web of city-states in central and northern Italy, where he found allies and many enemies, in particular the Lombard League. Years of inconclusive battles ensued, which even Frederick's death in 1250 did not end. Campaigning continued until 1268 under Frederick's successors, Manfredi (who fell in the bloody Battle of Benevento in 1266) and Corradino (captured and executed two years later by French noble Charles of Anjou, who had by then taken over Sicily and southern Italy).

America was named after Amerigo Vespucci, a Florentine navigator who, from 1497 to 1504, made several voyages of discovery in what would one day be known as South America.

Rise of the City-States

While the south of Italy tended to centralised rule, the north was heading the opposite way. Port cities such as Genoa, Pisa and especially Venice, along with internal centres such as Florence, Milan, Parma, Bologna, Padua, Verona and Modena, became increasingly hostile towards attempts by the Holy Roman Emperors to meddle in their affairs.

The cities' growing prosperity and independence also brought them into conflict with Rome. Indeed, at times Rome's control over some of its own Papal States was challenged. Caught between the papacy and the emperors, it was not surprising that these city-states were forever switching allegiances in an attempt to best serve their own interests.

Between the 12th and 14th centuries, they developed new forms of government. Venice adopted an oligarchic, 'parliamentary' system in an attempt at limited democracy. More commonly, the city-state created a *comune* (town council), a form of republican government dominated at first by aristocrats but then increasingly by the wealthy middle classes. The well-heeled families soon turned their attentions from business rivalry to political struggles, in which each aimed to gain control of the *signoria* (government).

In some cities, great dynasties, such as the Medici in Florence and the Visconti and Sforza in Milan, came to dominate their respective stages.

War between the city-states was constant and eventually a few, notably Florence, Milan and Venice, emerged as regional powers and absorbed their neighbours. Their power was based on a mix of trade, industry and conquest. Constellations of power and alliances were in constant flux, making changes in the city-states' fortunes the rule rather

1600	1714	1805	1814–15
Dominican monk and proud philosopher Giordano Bruno is burned alive at the stake in Rome for heresy after eight years of trial and torture at the hands of the Inquisition.	The end of the War of the Spanish Succession forces the withdrawal of Spanish forces from Lombardy. The Spanish Bourbon family establishes an independent Kingdom of the Two Sicilies.	Napoleon is proclaimed king of the newly constituted Kingdom of Italy, comprising most of the northern half of the country. A year later he takes the Kingdom of Naples.	After Napoleon's fall, the Congress of Vienna is held to reestablish the balance of power in Europe. The result for Italy is largely a return of the old occupying powers.

A WHIFF OF HELLFIRE

Politics in Italy's mercurial city-states could take a radical turn. When Florence's Medici clan rulers fell into disgrace (not for the last time) in 1494, the city's fathers decided to restore an earlier republican model of government.

Since 1481, the Dominican friar Girolamo Savonarola had been in Florence preaching repentance. His blood-curdling warnings of horrors to come if Florentines did not renounce their evil ways somehow captured everyone's imagination and the city submitted to a fiery theocracy. He called on the government to act on the basis of his divine inspiration. Drinking, whoring, partying, gambling, flashy fashion and other signs of wrongdoing were pushed well underground. Books, clothes, jewellery, fancy furnishings and art were burned on 'bonfires of the vanities'.

Pleasure-loving Florentines soon began to tire of this fundamentalism, as did Pope Alexander VI (possibly the least religious pope of all time) and the Dominicans' rivals, the Franciscan religious order. The local economy was stagnant and Savonarola seemed increasingly out to lunch. The city government, or *signoria*, finally had the fiery friar arrested. After weeks at the hands of the city rack-master, he was hanged and burned at the stake as a heretic, along with two supporters, on 22 May 1498.

than the exception. Easily the most stable, and long the most successful of them, was Venice.

In Florence, prosperity was based on the wool trade, finance and general commerce. Abroad, its coinage, the *firenze* (florin), was king.

In Milan, the noble Visconti family destroyed its rivals and extended Milanese control over Pavia and Cremona, and later Genoa. Giangaleazzo Visconti (1351–1402) turned Milan from a city-state into a strong European power. The policies of the Visconti (up to 1450), followed by those of the Sforza family, allowed Milan to spread its power to the Ticino area of Switzerland and east to the Lago di Garda.

The Milanese sphere of influence butted up against that of Venice. By 1450 the lagoon city had reached the height of its territorial greatness. In addition to its possessions in Greece, Dalmatia and beyond, Venice had expanded inland. The banner of the Lion of St Mark flew across northeast Italy, from Gorizia to Bergamo.

These dynamic, independent-minded cities proved fertile ground for the intellectual and artistic explosion that would take place across northern Italy in the 14th and 15th centuries – an explosion that would come to be known as the Renaissance and the birth of the modern world. Of them all, Florence was the cradle and launch pad for this fevered activity, in no small measure due to the generous patronage of the long-ruling Medici family.

1848	1860	1861	1889
European revolts spark rebellion in Italy, especially in Austrian-occupied Milan and Venice. Piedmont's King Carlo Alberto joins the fray against Austria, but within a year Austria recovers Lombardy and Veneto.	In the name of Italian unity, Giuseppe Garibaldi lands with 1000 men, the Red Shirts, in Sicily. He takes the island and lands in southern Italy.	By the end of the Franco-Austrian War (1859–61), Vittorio Emanuele II controls Lombardy, Sardinia, Sicily, southern Italy and parts of central Italy and is proclaimed king of a newly united Italy.	Raffaele Esposito invents pizza margherita in honour of Queen Margherita, who takes her first bite of the Neapolitan staple on a royal visit to the city.

A Nation Is Born

The French Revolution at the end of the 18th century and the rise of Napoleon awakened hopes in Italy of independent nationhood. Since the glory days of the Renaissance, Italy's divided ministates had gradually lost power and status on the European stage. By the late 18th century, the peninsula was little more than a tired, backward playground for the big powers and a Grand Tour hotspot for wealthy toffs of a romantic bent.

Napoleon marched into Italy on several occasions, finishing off the Venetian republic in 1797 (ending 1000 years of Venetian independence) and creating the so-called Kingdom of Italy in 1805. That kingdom was in no way independent, but the Napoleonic earthquake spurred many Italians to believe that a single Italian state could be created after the emperor's demise. But it was not to be so easy. The reactionary Congress of Vienna restored all the foreign rulers to their places in Italy.

Count Camillo Benso di Cavour (1810–61) of Turin, the prime minister of the Savoy monarchy, became the diplomatic brains behind the Italian unity movement. Through the pro-unity newspaper *Il Risorgimento* (founded in 1847) and the publication of a parliamentary *Statuto* (Statute), Cavour and his colleagues laid the groundwork for unity.

Cavour conspired with the French and won British support for the creation of an independent Italian state. His 1858 treaty with France's Napoleon III foresaw French aid in the event of a war with Austria and the creation of a northern Italian kingdom, in exchange for parts of Savoy and Nice.

The bloody Franco-Austrian War (also known as the Second Italian War of Independence; 1859–61), unleashed in northern Italy, led to the occupation of Lombardy and the retreat of the Austrians to their eastern possessions in the Veneto. In the meantime, a wild card in the form of professional revolutionary Giuseppe Garibaldi had created the real chance of full Italian unity. Garibaldi took Sicily and southern Italy in a military blitz in the name of Savoy king Vittorio Emanuele II in 1860. Southern Italy was thus conquered, rather than willingly forming a union with the north.

Spotting the chance, Cavour and the king moved to take parts of central Italy (including Umbria and Le Marche) and so were able to proclaim the creation of a single Italian state in 1861. In the following nine years, Tuscany, the Veneto and Rome were all incorporated into the fledgling kingdom. Unity was complete and parliament was established in Rome in 1871. However, Italy is a collection of discrete regions rather than a nation, and this is perhaps where many of its contemporary problems lie. As one of the architects of unification, Massimo d'Azeglio, said in his memoirs, 'We made a nation, now we have to make the Italians.'

1908	1915	1919	1922
On the morning of 28 December, Messina and Reggio di Calabria are struck by a 7.5-magnitude earthquake and a 13m-high tsunami. More than 80,000 lives are lost.	Italy enters WWI on the side of the Allies to win Italian territories still in Austrian hands after Austria's offer to cede some of the territories is deemed insufficient.	Former socialist journalist Benito Mussolini forms a right-wing militant group, the Fasci Italiani di Combattimento (Italian Combat Fasces), precursor to his Fascist Party.	Mussolini and his Fascists stage a march on Rome in October. Doubting the army's loyalty, a fearful King Vittorio Emanuele III entrusts Mussolini with the formation of a government.

The turbulent new state saw violent swings between socialists and the right. Giovanni Giolitti, one of Italy's longest-serving prime ministers (heading five governments between 1892 and 1921), managed to bridge the political extremes and institute male suffrage. Women, however, were denied the right to vote until after WWII.

From Trenches to Hanged Dictator

When war broke out in Europe in July 1914, Italy chose to remain neutral despite being a member of the Triple Alliance with Austria and Germany. Italy had territorial claims on Austrian-controlled Trento (Trentino), southern Tyrol, Trieste and even in Dalmatia (some of which it had tried and failed to take during the Austro-Prussian War of 1866). Under the terms of the Triple Alliance, Austria was due to hand over much of this territory in the event of occupying other land in the Balkans, but Austria refused to contemplate fulfilling this part of the bargain.

The Italian government was divided between noninterventionists and a war party. The latter, in view of Austria's intransigence, decided to deal with the Allies. In the London pact of April 1915, Italy was promised the territories it sought after victory. In May, Italy declared war on Austria and thus plunged into a 3½-year nightmare.

Italy and Austria engaged in a weary war of attrition, much of it fought in rugged mountainous terrain in the Dolomites. The Austro-Hungarian forces collapsed in November 1918, after which the Austrian Empire ceded South Tyrol, Trieste, Trentino and Istria to Italy in the postwar Paris Peace Conference. However, Italy failed to obtain additional territorial claims upon Dalmatia and Albania in the Treaty of Versailles, which left many Italians bitterly disappointed.

These were slim pickings after such a bloody and exhausting conflict. Italy lost 600,000 men and the war economy had produced a small concentration of powerful industrial barons while leaving the bulk of the civilian populace in penury. This cocktail was made all the more explosive as hundreds of thousands of demobbed servicemen returned home or shifted around the country in search of work. The atmosphere was perfect for a demagogue, who was not long in coming forth.

Benito Mussolini (1883–1945) was a young war enthusiast who had once been a socialist newspaper editor and one-time draft dodger. This time he volunteered for the front and returned only wounded in 1917. The experience of war and the frustration shared with many at the disappointing outcome in Versailles led him to form a right-wing militant political group that by 1921 had become the Fascist Party, with its black-shirted street brawlers and Roman salute. These were to become symbols of violent oppression and aggressive nationalism for the next 23 years. After his march on Rome in 1922 and victory in the 1924 elections,

1929	1935	1940	1943
Mussolini and Pope Pius XI sign the Lateran Pact, which declares Catholicism Italy's sole religion and the Vatican an independent state. Satisfied, the papacy acknowledges the Kingdom of Italy.	Italy seeks a new colonial conquest through the invasion of Abyssinia (Ethiopia) from Eritrea. The League of Nations condemns the invasion and imposes limited sanctions on Italy.	Italy enters WWII on Nazi Germany's side and invades Greece, which quickly proves to be a mistake. Greek forces counter-attack and enter southern Albania. Germany saves Italy in 1941.	Allies land in Sicily. King Vittorio Emanuele III sacks Mussolini. He is replaced by Marshall Badoglio, who surrenders after Allied landings in southern Italy. German forces free Mussolini.

Mussolini, who called himself Il Duce (the Leader), took full control of the country by 1926, banning other political parties, trade unions not affiliated to the party and the free press.

By the 1930s, all aspects of Italian society were regulated by the party. The economy, banking, a massive public works program, the conversion of coastal malarial swamps into arable land and an ambitious modernisation of the armed forces were all part of Mussolini's grand plan.

On the international front, Mussolini first showed a cautious hand, signing international cooperation pacts (including the 1928 Kellogg Pact solemnly renouncing war) and until 1935 moving close to France and the UK to contain the growing menace of Adolf Hitler's re-arming Germany.

That all changed when Mussolini decided to invade Abyssinia (Ethiopia) as the first big step to creating a 'new Roman empire'. This aggressive side of Mussolini's policy had already led to skirmishes with Greece over the island of Corfu and to military expeditions against nationalist forces in the Italian colony of Libya.

The League of Nations condemned the Abyssinian adventure (King Vittorio Emanuele III was declared Emperor of Abyssinia in 1936) and from then on Mussolini changed course, drawing closer to Nazi Germany. Italy backed the rebel General Franco in the three-year Spanish Civil War and in 1939 signed an alliance pact.

WWII broke out in September 1939 with Hitler's invasion of Poland. Italy remained aloof until June 1940, by which time Germany had overrun Norway, Denmark, the Low Countries and much of France. It seemed too easy and so Mussolini entered on Germany's side in 1940, a move Hitler must have regretted later. Germany found itself pulling Italy's chestnuts out of the fire in campaigns in the Balkans and North Africa and could not prevent Allied landings in Sicily in 1943.

By then, the Italians had had enough of Mussolini and his war and so the king had the dictator arrested. In September, Italy surrendered and the Germans, who had rescued Mussolini, occupied the northern two-thirds of the country and reinstalled the dictator.

The painfully slow Allied campaign up the peninsula and German repression led to the formation of the Resistance, which played a growing role in harassing German forces. Northern Italy was finally liberated in April 1945. Resistance fighters caught Mussolini as he fled north in the hope of reaching Switzerland. They shot him and his lover, Clara Petacci, before stringing up their corpses (along with others) in Milan's Piazzale Loreto. This was a far cry from Il Duce's hopes for a glorious burial alongside his ancient imperial idol, Augustus, in Rome.

Despite the Italians claiming it as their own, it was the Arabs who first introduced spaghetti to Italy, where 'strings of pasta' were documented by the Arab geographer Al-Idrissi in Palermo, Sicily, in 1150.

1944	1946	1957	1966
Mt Vesuvius explodes back into action on 18 March. The eruption is captured on film by USAAF (United States Army Air Forces) personnel stationed nearby.	Italians vote in a national referendum to abolish the monarchy and create a republic. King Umberto II leaves Italy and refuses to recognise the result.	Italy joins France, West Germany and the Benelux countries to sign the Treaty of Rome, creating the European Economic Community (EEC) as of 1 January 1958.	A devastating flood inundates Florence in early November, leaving around 100 people dead, 5000 families homeless and 14,000 movable artworks damaged. The flood is the city's worst since 1557.

GOING THE DISTANCE FOR THE RESISTANCE

In 1943 and 1944, the Assisi Underground hid hundreds of Jewish Italians in Umbrian convents and monasteries, while the Tuscan Resistance forged travel documents for them – but the refugees needed those documents fast, before they were deported to concentration camps by Fascist officials. Enter the fastest man in Italy: Gino Bartali, world-famous Tuscan cyclist, Tour de France winner and three-time champion of the Giro d'Italia. Three years after his death in 2003, documents revealed that during his 'training rides' throughout the war years, Bartali had carried Resistance intelligence and falsified documents to transport Jewish refugees to safe locations. Bartali was interrogated at the dreaded Villa Triste in Florence, where suspected anti-Fascists were routinely tortured – but he revealed nothing. Until his death, the long-distance hero downplayed, even to his children, his efforts to rescue Jewish refugees, saying, 'One does these things, and then that's that.'

The Grey & Red Years

In the aftermath of war, the left-wing Resistance was disarmed and Italy's political forces scrambled to regroup. The USA, through the economic largesse of the Marshall Plan, wielded considerable political influence and used this to keep the left in check.

Immediately after the war, three coalition governments succeeded one another. The third, which came to power in December 1945, was dominated by the newly formed right-wing Democrazia Cristiana (DC; Christian Democrats), led by Alcide De Gasperi. Italy became a republic in 1946 and De Gasperi's DC won the first elections under the new constitution in 1948, and remained prime minister until 1953.

Until the 1980s, the Partito Comunista Italiano (PCI; Communist Party), at first under Palmiro Togliatti and later the charismatic Enrico Berlinguer, played a crucial role in Italy's social and political development, despite being systematically kept out of government.

The popularity of the party led to a grey period in the country's history, the *anni di piombo* (years of lead) in the 1970s. Just as the Italian economy was booming, Europe-wide paranoia about the power of the communists in Italy fuelled a secretive reaction, that, it is said, was largely directed by the CIA and NATO. Even today, little is known about Operation Gladio, an underground paramilitary organisation supposedly behind various unexplained terror attacks in the country, apparently designed to create an atmosphere of fear in which, should the communists come close to power, a right-wing coup could be quickly carried out.

The 1970s were dominated by terrorism and considerable social unrest, especially in the universities. Neo-fascist terrorists struck with a

1970	1980	1980	1999
Parliament approves the country's first-ever divorce legislation. Unwilling to accept this 'defeat', the Christian Democrats call a referendum to annul the law in 1974. Italians vote against the referendum.	A bomb in Bologna kills 85 and injures hundreds more. The Red Brigades and a Fascist cell both claim responsibility. Analysis later points to possible para-state terrorism in Operation Gladio.	At 7.34pm on 25 November, a 6.8–Richter scale earthquake strikes Campania. The quake kills almost 3000 people and causes widespread damage, including in the city of Naples.	Italy becomes a primary base in NATO's air war on Yugoslavia. Air strikes are carried out from the Aviano airbase from 24 May until 8 June.

bomb blast in Milan in 1969. In 1978, the Brigate Rosse (Red Brigades, a group of young left-wing militants responsible for several bomb blasts and assassinations), claimed their most important victim – former DC prime minister Aldo Moro. His kidnap and murder some 54 days later (the subject of the 2003 film *Buongiorno, notte*) shook the country.

The 1970s was a time of positive change. In 1970, regional governments with limited powers were formed in 15 of the country's 20 regions (Sicily, Sardinia, Valle d'Aosta, Trentino-Alto Adige and Friuli Venezia Giulia already had strong autonomy statutes). The same year, divorce became legal. Abortion was legalised in 1978.

From Clean Hands to Berlusconi

A growth spurt in the aftermath of WWII saw Italy become one of the world's leading economies, but by the 1970s the economy had begun to falter, and by the mid-1990s a new and prolonged period of crisis had set in. High unemployment and inflation, combined with a huge national debt and mercurial currency (the erstwhile lira), led the government to introduce draconian measures to cut public spending, allowing Italy to join the single currency (euro) in 2001.

The 1990s saw the Italian political scene rocked by the Tangentopoli ('kickback city') scandal. Led by a pool of Milanese magistrates, including the tough Antonio di Pietro, investigations known as Mani Pulite (Clean Hands) implicated thousands of politicians, public officials and businesspeople in scandals ranging from bribery and receiving kickbacks to blatant theft.

The old centre-right political parties collapsed in the wake of these trials and from the ashes rose what many Italians hoped might be a breath of fresh political air. Media magnate Silvio Berlusconi's Forza Italia (Go Italy) party swept to power in 2001 and again in April 2008 (after a two-year interlude of centre-left government under Romano Prodi from 2006). A onetime cruise-ship crooner, Berlusconi's carefully choreographed blend of charisma and promises of tax cuts appealed to many Italian voters, and he has enjoyed a longevity that is incomprehensible to many outsiders.

Giuliano Procacci's *History of the Italian People* is one of the best general histories of the country in any language. It covers the period from the early Middle Ages until 1948.

However, Berlusconi's tenure saw Italy's economic situation deteriorate, while a series of laws were passed that protected his extensive business interests. In 2011, Berlusconi was finally forced to resign due to the deepening debt crisis. A government of technocrats, headed by economist Mario Monti, took over until the inconclusive elections of February 2013. After lengthy postelectoral negotiations, Enrico Letta, a member of the Partito Democratico (PD), was named prime minister, steering a precarious right-left coalition.

2001	2005	2006	2011
Silvio Berlusconi's right-wing Casa delle Libertà (Liberties House) coalition wins an absolute majority in national polls. The following five years are marked by economic stagnation.	Pope John Paul II dies at age 84, prompting a wave of sorrow and chants of *santo subito* (sainthood now). He is succeeded by Benedict XVI, the German Cardinal Ratzinger.	Juventus, AC Milan and three other top Serie A football teams receive hefty fines in a match-rigging scandal that also sees Juventus stripped of its 2005 and 2006 championship titles.	Berlusconi stands trial in Milan in April on charges of abuse of power and paying for sex with underaged Moroccan prostitute Karima El Mahroug (aka Ruby Heartstealer).

Coalitions & Populism

The downfall of Silvio Berlusconi ushered in a new era in Italian politics. In 2014, 39-year-old Matteo Renzi, former mayor of Florence, took over as leader of a right-left coalition, making him the third unelected prime minister since Berlusconi's fall (following Mario Monti and Enrico Letta). Renzi's cabinet became the youngest in Italian history and the first with an even gender balance, and under his leadership important reforms were introduced, such as the legalisation of same-sex civil unions.

From December 2016 to June 2018, former Foreign Affairs Minister, Paolo Gentiloni briefly held the tiller as prime minister. Considered a pro-European, progressive Christian leftist, Gentiloni passed health reforms and made changes to the electoral law. However, given the desperate refugee crisis borne by Italy's southern provinces, Gentiloni was forced to moderate his integrationist views on immigration.

Those twin forces – Europeanism and immigration – helped deliver Europe's first populist government in 2018 under Giuseppe Conte. Formed by an uneasy alliance of the Eurosceptic Five Star Movement and the anti-immigration Lega, the coalition collapsed in August 2019 when Lega leader Matteo Salvini sought to wrest control and break free of EU fiscal constraints. Subsequently, Conte's party, the Democratic Party, and M5S agreed to form a new government without Salvini and Conte was returned to office in September.

Despite having no prior political experience, during his second term Conte became increasingly popular. He introduced a guaranteed minimum income, passed constitutional reform to reduce the number of members in Italy's unwieldy parliament by one third, implemented stricter immigration policies, and nationalised the Italian highway company and Alitalia. When COVID-19 hit, Italy became the first European country to implement a national lockdown, and despite suffering one of Europe's highest death rates, Conte's strong response was widely approved. As was his success in securing the highest level of funding – €209 billion – from the European Recovery Fund to assist with the coronavirus recovery.

Subsequent debates about what course the economic recovery should take ultimately resulted in the collapse of Conte's government in January 2021, when Matteo Renzi – who sought more radical economic reforms – withdrew his support from the government. After various unsuccessful attempts to negotiate a new government, Italy's president, Sergio Mattarella, gave Mario Draghi, former president of the European Central Bank, the task of forming a new cabinet.

Italy lays claim to numerous revolutionary inventions. Istrian Santorio Santorio invented the first clinical thermometer in 1612. Como's Alessandro Volta introduced the electric battery in 1800, while Bologna's Guglielmo Marconi shook up global communications by introducing the world's first practical wireless telegraphy transmitters and receivers in the mid-1890s.

2014	2016	2020	2021
Matteo Renzi becomes the youngest prime minister in the republic's history and the third PM in succession to take control without an election. He resigns in 2016 after losing a referendum to change the constitution.	Central Italy is rocked by a series of powerful earthquakes. The deadliest measuring 6.2 on the Richter scale, hits the mountainous northeastern corner of Lazio on 24 August. Almost 300 people die.	In March the town of Bergamo in Lombardy becomes the European epicentre of the COVID-19 pandemic. The mortality rate in the town rises 400% compared with the previous year.	Italy's biggest mafia trial in decades commences. In dock are 355 members of Calabria's 'Ndrangheta crime syndicate. More than 900 witnesses will give evidence in a trial set to last over two years.

Italian Art & Architecture

The art and architecture of Italy has seduced visitors for hundreds of years. This rich legacy stretches back to before Roman times and continues today in the country's evolving contemporary scenes. While every epoch has its treasures and devotees, it's the Renaissance that is the most stunning, from Florence's elegant streetscapes and the otherworldly beauty of Venice's *palazzi* to the dizzying caches of works that line galleries and churches like the Uffizi in Florence and St Peter's Basilica in Rome.

Art

Italian art's long history underpins that of all Western art, from the classical, Renaissance and baroque to the explosive doctrine of the futurists and the conceptual play of Arte Povera in the 20th century. A roll call of Italian artists – Giotto, Botticelli, da Vinci, Michelangelo, Raphael, Caravaggio and Bernini – forged their vision into some of the greatest bodies of work of the millennia and are, centuries after their deaths, still household names the world over.

The Ancient & the Classical

Greek colonists settled many parts of Sicily and southern Italy as early as the 8th century BC, naming it Magna Graecia and building great cities such as Syracuse and Taranto. These cities were famous for their magnificent temples, many of which were decorated with sculptures modelled on, or inspired by, masterpieces by Praxiteles, Lysippus and Phidias. In art, as in so many other realms, the ancient Romans looked to the Greeks for inspiration.

Sculpture flourished in southern Italy into the Hellenistic period. It also gained popularity in central Italy, where the art of the Etruscans was greatly refined by the contribution of Greek artisans, who arrived to trade.

In Rome, sculpture, architecture and painting flourished first under the Republic and then the empire. But the art that was produced here during this period differed in key ways from the Greek art that influenced it. Essentially secular, it focused less on ideals of aesthetic harmony and more on accurate representation, taking sculptural portraiture to new heights of verisimilitude, as innumerable versions of Pompey, Titus and Augustus showing a similar visage attest.

8th–3rd Century BC Magna Graecia
Greek colonisers grace southern Italy with Stoic temples, sweeping amphitheatres and elegant sculptures that later influence their Roman successors.

6th Century BC– 4th Century AD Roman
Epic roads and aqueducts spread from Rome, alongside proud basilicas, colonnaded markets, sprawling thermal baths and frescoed villas.

4th–6th Century Byzantine
Newly Christian and based in Constantinople, the Roman Empire turns its attention to the construction of churches with exotic, Eastern mosaics and domes.

8th–12th Century Romanesque
Attention turns from height to the horizontal lines of a building. Churches are designed with a stand-alone bell tower and baptistry.

13th & 14th Century Gothic
Northern European Gothic gets an Italian makeover, from the Arabesque spice of Venice's Cá d'Oro to the Romanesque flavour of Siena's cathedral.

Late 14th–15th Century Early Renaissance
Filippo Brunelleschi's elegant dome graces the Duomo in Florence, heralding a return to classicism and a bold new era of humanist thinking and rational, elegant design.

Italy has more World Heritage–listed sites than any other country in the world; many of its 54 listings are repositories of great art.

The Roman ruling class understood art could be used as a political tool, one that could construct a unified identity and cement status and power. As well as portraiture, Roman narrative art often took the form of relief decoration recounting the story of great military victories – the Colonna di Traiano (Trajan's Column) and the Ara Pacis Augustae (Altar of Peace) in Rome exemplify this tradition. Both are magnificent, monumental examples of art as propaganda, exalting the emperor and Rome in a form that no Roman citizen could possibly ignore.

Wealthy Roman citizens also dabbled in the arts, building palatial villas and adorning them with statues looted from the Greek world or copied from Hellenic originals. Today, museums in Rome burst at the seams with such trophies, from the Capitoline Museums' 'Made in Italy' *Galata morente* (Dying Gaul, c 240–200 BC) to the Vatican Museums' original Greek *Laocoön and His Sons* (c 160–140 BC).

And while the Etruscans had used wall painting – most notably in their tombs at centres like Tarquinia and Cerveteri in modern-day Lazio, it was the Romans who refined the form, refocusing on landscape scenes to adorn the walls of the living. A visit to Rome's Museo Nazionale Romano: Palazzo Massimo alle Terme or to Naples' Museo Archeologico Nazionale offers sublime examples of the form.

The Glitter of the Byzantine Period

Emperor Constantine the Great, a convert to Christianity, made the ancient city of Byzantium his capital in 330 and renamed it Constantinople. The city became the great cultural and artistic centre of early Christianity and it remained so up to the time of the Renaissance, though its influence was not as fundamental as the art of ancient Rome.

The Byzantine period was notable for its sublime ecclesiastical architecture, its extraordinary mosaic work and – to a lesser extent – its ethereal painting. Drawing inspiration from the symbol-drenched decoration of the Roman catacombs and the early Christian churches, the Byzantine deemphasised the naturalistic aspects of the classical tradition and exalted the spirit over the body, glorifying God rather than humanity or the state. This was infused with the Near East's decorative traditions and love of luminous colour.

Italy's dedicated art police, the Comando Carabinieri Tutela Patrimonio Culturale (aka Carabinieri TPC), tackle the looting of priceless heritage. It's estimated that over 100,000 ancient tombs have been ransacked by *tombaroli* (tomb raiders) alone; contents are sold to private and public collectors around the world.

In Italy, the Byzantine virtuosity with mosaics was showcased in Ravenna, the capital of the Byzantine Empire's western regions in the 6th century. The Basilica di Sant'Apollinare (in nearby Classe) and the Basilica di San Vitale and Basilica di Sant'Apollinare Nuovo house some of the world's finest Byzantine art, their hand-cut glazed tiles (tesserae) balancing extraordinary naturalness with an epic sense of grandeur and mystery.

The Byzantine aesthetic is also evident in Venice, in the exoticism of the Basilica di San Marco, and in the technicolor interior of Rome's Chiesa di San Prassede. Byzantine, Norman and Arab influences in Sicily fused to create a distinct regional style showcased in the mosaic-encrusted splendour of Palermo's Cappella Palatina, as well as the cathedrals of Monreale and Cefalù.

The Not-so-Dark Ages

Italy, and Italian art, were born out of the so-called Dark Ages. The barbarian invasions of the 5th and 6th centuries began a process that turned a unified empire into a land of small independent city-states, and it was these states – or rather the merchants, princes, clergy, corporations and guilds who lived within them – that created a culture of artistic patronage that engendered the great innovations in art and architecture that would define the Renaissance.

Clarity of religious message continued to outweigh the notion of faithful representation in the art of the medieval period. To the modern eye, the simplicity and coded allegorical narrative of both the painting and sculpture of this period can look stiff, though a closer look usually reveals a sublimity and grace, as well as a shared human experience, that speaks across the centuries.

Gothic Refinement

The Gothic style in art, as in architecture, was much slower to take off in Italy than in the rest of Europe. But it steadily evolved, marking the transition from medieval restraint to the Renaissance, and seeing artists once again drawing inspiration from life itself rather than concentrating solely on religious themes. Occurring at the same time as the development of court society and the rise of civic culture in the city-states, its art was both sophisticated and elegant, highlighting attention to detail, a luminous palette and an increasingly refined technique. The first innovations were made in Pisa by sculptor Nicola Pisano (c 1220–84), who emulated the example of the French Gothic masters and studied classical sculpture in order to represent nature more convincingly, but the major strides forward occurred in Florence and Siena.

Giotto & the 'Rebirth' of Italian Art

Walk into an art gallery anywhere in Italy and it's not hard to discern which paintings hail from the Middle Ages. Medieval art was dominated by its overtly religious subject matter, a pious pastiche of two-dimensional human forms and zealous biblical scenes that paid little attention to the complexities of everyday life. The reason? Most of the art that was painted between Roman times and the Renaissance was commissioned by the all-powerful Catholic Church and designed to embellish the interiors of religious buildings. Iconic and spiritual in nature, its main purpose was to reinforce the prevailing Catholic doctrine. For over 500 years, few artists had the courage or audacity to break the mould. But as England and France took up arms in the Hundred Years' War and the Black Death raged indiscriminately across the continent, a skillful Italian draughtsman from Tuscany named Giotto di Bondone (1267–1337) began quietly pushing back against the accepted conventions.

Exhibiting the spirit and style of the Renaissance 200 years before Leonardo da Vinci grafted a smile onto the face of the Mona Lisa, Giotto was an artist way ahead of his time. Born near Florence, the Italian master is said to have spent his early life working as a shepherd boy before being discovered by the eminent Tuscan painter Cimabue who allegedly observed him etching naturalistic pictures of his sheep onto a rock. Taken under Cimabue's wing, Giotto quickly eclipsed the fame of his mentor. Despite working almost exclusively in the religious realm, he was one of the first painters to introduce the notion of perspective into European portrait painting, giving his figures three-dimensional features and drawing them accurately from real life. In another break with tradition, Giotto added grace and humanity

15th & 16th Century High Renaissance

Rome ousts Florence from its status as the centre of the Renaissance, its newly created wonders including Il Tempietto and St Peter's Basilica.

Late 16th–Early 18th Century Baroque

Renaissance restraint gives way to theatrical flourishes and sensual curves as the Catholic Church uses spectacle to upstage the Protestant movement.

Mid-18th–Late 19th Century Neoclassical

Archaeologists rediscover the glories of Pompeii and Herculaneum and architects pay tribute in creations like Vicenza's La Rotonda and Naples' Villa Pignatelli.

19th Century Industrial

A newly unified Italy fuses industrial technology, consumer culture and ecclesial traditions in Milan's cathedral-like Galleria Vittorio Emanuele II and Naples' Galleria Umberto I.

Late 19th–Early 20th Century Liberty

Italy's art nouveau ditches classical linearity for whimsical curves and organic motifs.

Early–Mid-20th Century Modernism

Italian modernism takes the form of futurism (technology-obsessed and antihistorical) and rationalism (seeking a middle ground between a machine-driven utopia and Fascism's fetish for classicism).

to the human form, endowing the faces of his subjects with a rich range of emotions from joy to despair.

Many Renaissance painters included self-portraits in their major works. Giotto didn't, possibly due to the fact that friends such as Giovanni Boccaccio described him as the ugliest man in Florence. With friends like those...

Giotto's most famous works are all in the medium of the fresco (where paint is applied on a wall while the plaster is still damp), and his supreme achievement is the cycle gracing the walls of Padua's Cappella degli Scrovegni (nominated a Unesco World Heritage Site in 2016). It's impossible to overestimate Giotto's achievement with these frescoes, which illustrate the stories of the lives of the Virgin and Christ. Abandoning popular conventions such as the three-quarter view of head and body, he presented his figures from behind, from the side or turning around, just as the story demanded. Giotto had no need for lashings of gold paint and elaborate ornamentation either, opting to convey the scene's dramatic tension through a naturalistic rendition of figures and a radical composition that created the illusion of depth.

Giotto remains one of the most ground-breaking and influential painters in the history of European art. His small but distinguished oeuvre both preempted and paved the way for the Renaissance.

The Sienese School

Giotto wasn't the only painter of his time to experiment with form, colour and composition and create a radical new style. The great Sienese master Duccio di Buoninsegna (c 1255–1319) successfully breathed new life into the old Byzantine forms using light and shade. His preferred medium was panel painting and his major work is probably his *Maestà* (Virgin Mary in Majesty; 1311) in Siena's Museo dell'Opera Metropolitana.

ART, ANGER & ARTEMESIA

Sex, fame and notoriety: the life of Artemesia Gentileschi (1593–1652) could spawn a top-rating soap opera. One of the early baroque's greatest artists, and one of the few females, Gentileschi was born in Rome to Tuscan painter Orazio Gentileschi. Orazio wasted little time introducing his young daughter to the city's working artists. Among her mentors was Michelangelo Merisi da Caravaggio, whose chiaroscuro technique would deeply influence her own style.

At the tender age of 17, Gentileschi produced her first masterpiece, *Susanna and the Elders* (1610), now in the Schönborn Collection in Pommersfelden, Germany. Her depiction of the sexually harassed Susanna proved eerily foreboding: two years later Artemesia would find herself at the centre of a seven-month trial, in which Florentine artist Agostino Tassi was charged with her rape.

Out of Gentileschi's fury came the gripping, technically brilliant *Judith Slaying Holofernes* (1612–13). While the original hangs in Naples' Museo di Capodimonte, you'll find a larger, later version in Florence's Uffizi. Vengeful Judith would make a further appearance in *Judith and her Maidservant* (c 1613–14), now in Florence's Palazzo Pitti. While living in Florence, Gentileschi completed a string of commissions for Cosimo II of the Medici dynasty, as well as becoming the first female member of the prestigious Accademia delle Arti del Disegno (Academy of the Arts of Drawing).

After separating from her husband, Tuscan painter Pietro Antonio di Vincenzo Stiattesi, Gentileschi headed south to Naples sometime between 1626 and 1630. Here her creations would include *The Annunciation* (1630), also in Naples' Museo di Capodimonte, and her *Self-Portrait as the Allegory of Painting* (1630), housed in London's Kensington Palace. The latter work received praise for its simultaneous depiction of art, artist and muse, an innovation at the time. Gentileschi's way with the brush was not lost on King Charles I of England, who honoured the Italian talent with a court residency from 1638 to 1641.

Despite her illustrious career, Gentileschi inhabited a man's world. Nothing would prove this more than the surviving epitaphs commemorating her death, focused not on her creative brilliance, but on the gossip depicting her as a cheating nymphomaniac.

It was in Siena, too, that two new trends took off: the introduction of court painters and the advent of purely secular art.

The first of many painters to be given ongoing commissions by one major patron or court, Simone Martini (c 1284–1344) was almost as famous as Giotto in his day. His best-known painting is the stylised *Maestà* (1315–16) in Siena's Museo Civico, in which he pioneered his famous iridescent palette (one colour transformed into another within the same plane).

Also working in Siena at this time were the Lorenzetti brothers, Pietro (c 1280–1348) and Ambrogio (c 1290–1348), who are considered the greatest exponents of what, for lack of a better term, can be referred to as secular painting. Ambrogio's magnificent *Allegories of Good and Bad Government* (1337–40) in the Museo Civico lauds the fruits of good government and the gruesome results of bad. In the frescoes, he applies the rules of perspective with an accuracy previously unseen, as well as significantly developing the Italian landscape tradition. In *Life in the Country,* one of the allegories, Ambrogio successfully depicts the time of day, the season, colour reflections and shadows – a naturalistic depiction of landscape that was unique at this time.

The Venetians

While Byzantine influence lingered longer in Venice than in many other parts of Italy, its grip on the city loosened by the early to mid-15th century. In *Polyptych of St James* (c 1450) by Michele Giambono (c 1400–62) in Venice's Gallerie dell'Accademia, the luscious locks and fair complexion of the archangel Michael channel the style of early Renaissance master Pisanello (c 1395–1455). The winds of change blow even stronger in fellow Accademia resident *Madonna with Child* (c 1455) by Jacopo Bellini (c 1396–1470). Featuring a bright-eyed baby Jesus and a patient, seemingly sleep-deprived Mary, it's an image any parent might relate to. Relatable emotions are equally strong in the biblical scenes of Andrea Mantegna (1431–1506); one can almost hear the sobbing in his *Lamentation over the Dead Christ* (c 1480) in Milan's Pinacoteca di Brera.

Tuscan painter Gentile da Fabriano (c 1370–1427) worked in Venice during the early stages of his transition to Renaissance realism, and his evolving style reputedly influenced Venetian Antonio Vivarini (c 1415–80), the latter's *Passion* polyptych radiating tremendous pathos. Antonio's brother, Bartolomeo Vivarini (c 1432–99), created a delightful altarpiece in Venice's I Frari, in which a baby Jesus wriggles out of the arms of his mother, squarely seated on her marble Renaissance throne.

In 1475, visiting Sicilian painter Antonello da Messina (c 1430–79) introduced the Venetians to oil paints, and their knack for layering and blending colours made for a luminosity that would ultimately define the city's art. Among early groundbreakers was Giovanni Bellini (c 1430–1516). The son of Jacopo Bellini, his Accademia *Annunciation* (1500) deployed glowing reds and ambers to focus attention on the solitary figure of the kneeling Madonna, the angel Gabriel arriving in a rush of geometrically rumpled drapery.

Bellini's prowess with the palette was not lost on his students, among them Giorgione (1477–1510) and Titian (c 1488–1576). Giorgione preferred to paint from inspiration without sketching out his subject first, as in his enigmatic *La Tempesta* (The Storm; 1500), also in the Accademia. The younger Titian set himself apart with brushstrokes that brought his subjects to life, from his early and measured *St Mark Enthroned* (1510)

The Renaissance

Of Italy's countless artistic highs, none surpass the Renaissance. The age of Botticelli, da Vinci and Michelangelo is defined by a rediscovery of classical learning and humanist philosophy, driven by the spirit of scientific investigation. It also marks a seismic shift of the artists' own role; once considered a mere craftsperson, the Renaissance artist is reborn as intellectual and philosopher.

Florence, Classicism & the Quattrocento

Giotto and the painters of the Sienese school introduced many innovations in art: the exploration of proportion, a new interest in realistic portraiture and the beginnings of a new tradition of landscape painting. At the start of the 15th century (Quattrocento), most of these were explored and refined in one city – Florence.

Sculptors Lorenzo Ghiberti (1378–1455) and Donatello (c 1382–1466) replaced the demure robe-clad statues of the Middle Ages with anatomically accurate figures evoking ancient Greece and Rome. Donatello's bronze *David* (c 1440–50) and *St George* (c 1416–17), both in Florence's Museo del Bargello, capture this spirit of antiquity.

Ghiberti's greatest legacy would be his bronze east doors (1424–52) for the baptistry in Florence's Piazza del Duomo. The original 10 relief panels heralded a giant leap from the late-Gothic art of the time, not only in their use of perspective, but also in the individuality bestowed upon the figures portrayed.

When the neighbouring Duomo's dome was completed in 1436, author, architect and philosopher Leon Battista Alberti called it the first great achievement of the 'new' architecture, one that equalled or even surpassed the great buildings of antiquity. Designed by Filippo Brunelleschi (1377–1446), the dome was as innovative in engineering terms as the Pantheon's dome had been 1300 years before.

A New Perspective

While Brunelleschi was heavily influenced by the classical masters, he was able to do something that they hadn't – discover the mathematical rules by which objects appear to diminish as they recede. In so doing, Brunelleschi gave artists a whole new visual perspective.

The result was a new style of masterpiece, including Masaccio's *Trinity* (c 1424–25) in Florence's Basilica di Santa Maria Novella and Leonardo da Vinci's fresco *The Last Supper* (1495–98) in the refectory of Milan's Chiesa di Santa Maria delle Grazie. Andrea Mantegna (1431–1506) was responsible for the painting that is the most virtuosic of all perspectival experiments that occurred during this period – his highly realistic *Dead Christ* (c 1480), now in Milan's Pinacoteca di Brera.

These innovations in perspective were not always slavishly followed, however. Sandro Botticelli (c 1444–1510) pursued a Neoplatonic concept of ideal beauty that, along with his penchant for luminous decoration, resulted in flat linear

---

1. Masaccio's *Trinity*, Basilica di Santa Maria Novella (p528), Florence

compositions and often improbable poses. *The Birth of Venus* (c 1485), now in Florence's Uffizi, is a deft and daring synthesis of poetry and politics, eroticism and spirituality, contemporary Florentine fashion and classical mythology.

High Renaissance Masters

By the early 16th century (Cinquecento), the epicentre of artistic innovation shifted from Florence to Rome and Venice. This reflected the political and social realities of the period, namely the transfer of power in Florence from the Medicis to the moral-crusading, book-burning friar Girolamo Savonarola (1452–98), and the desire of the popes in Rome to counter the influence of Martin Luther's Reformation through turning the city into a humbling showpiece. While the age delivered a bounty of talent, some of its luminaries shone exceedingly bright.

Donato Bramante

Donato Bramante (1444–1514) knew the power of illusion. In Milan's Chiesa di Santa Maria presso San Satiro, he feigned a choir using the trompe l'oeil technique. In Rome, his classical obsession would shine through in his perfectly proportioned Tempietto of the Chiesa di San Pietro in Montorio, arguably the pinnacle of High Renaissance architecture. The Urbino native would go on to design St Peter's Basilica, though his Greek-cross floor plan would never be realised.

Leonardo da Vinci

Leonardo da Vinci (1452–1519), the quintessential polymath Renaissance man, took what some critics have described as the decisive step in the history of Western art – abandoning the balance that had previously been maintained between colour and line in painting and choosing to modulate his contours using colour. This technique, called sfumato, is perfectly displayed in his *Mona Lisa* (now in the Louvre

1. Tempietto di Bramante (p123), Rome 2. Michelangelo's *Pietà*, St Peter's Basilica (p111)

in Paris). In Milan's Chiesa di Santa Maria delle Grazie, his *The Last Supper* bestowed dramatic individuality to each depicted figure.

Raphael Santi

Raphael Santi (1483–1520) would rise to the aforementioned challenge faced by the Quattrocento painters – achieving harmonious and accurate (in terms of perspective) arrangement of figures – in works such as *Triumph of Galatea* (c 1514) in Rome's Villa Farnesina and *La Scuola d'Atene* (The School of Athens) in the Vatican Museums' Stanza della Segnatur. Other inspiring works include his enigmatic *La Fornarina* in Rome's Galleria Nazionale d'Arte Antica: Palazzo Barberini, and *Portrait of Alessandro Farnese* in Naples' Palazzo Reale di Capodimonte.

Michelangelo Buonarroti

Michelangelo Buonarroti (1475–1564) saw himself first and foremost as a sculptor, creating incomparable works like the *Pietà* in St Peter's Basilica and *David* (1504) in Florence's Galleria dell'Accademia. As a painter, he would adorn the ceiling of Rome's Sistine Chapel, creating figures that were not just realistic, but emotive visual representations of the human experience. A true Renaissance Man, Michelangelo's talents extended to architecture – the dome atop St Peter's Basilica is another Michelangelo creation.

Andrea Palladio

Bramante's Tempietto would influence Andrea Palladio (1508–80) when he was designing his villas in and around the city of Vicenza and the wider Veneto region. Like Bramante, northern Italy's greatest Renaissance architect was enamoured of classicism. His Palladian villas, such as the Brenta Riviera's Villa Foscari, radiate an elegant mathematical logic, perfectly proportioned and effectively accentuated with pediments and loggias. Classical influences also inform his Chiesa di San Giorgio Maggiore in Venice.

in Venice's Chiesa di Santa Maria della Salute to his thick, textured swansong *Pietà* (1576) in the Accademia.

Titian raised the bar for a new generation of northern Italian masters, including Jacopo Robusti, aka Tintoretto (1518–94). Occasionally enhancing his palette with finely crushed glass, Tintoretto created action-packed biblical scenes that read like a modern graphic novel. His wall and ceiling paintings in Venice's Scuola Grande di San Rocco are nail-bitingly spectacular, laced with holy superheroes, swooping angels, and deep, ominous shadows. Paolo Caliari, aka Veronese (1528–88), was another 16th-century star, the remarkable radiance of his hues captured in *Feast in the House of Levi* (1573), another Accademia must-see.

Renaissance Highs

Rising in the wake of Giotto, the Renaissance, with its progressive ideas about humanism and individual expression, pushed the boundaries of painting and sculpture to a new level. Serving their apprenticeship in the late 1400s, Leonardo da Vinci, Michelangelo and Raphael emerged as the illustrious pathfinders of High Renaissance art. Commissioned by the wealthy guilds and merchants of Florence in an Italy divided into small duchies and kingdoms, these three prodigious geniuses personified the central tenets of Renaissance art, a period that saw a rebirth of interest in classical antiquity, are appreciation of ancient mythology and a noble quest to inject realism into art.

Using his vast scientific and anatomical knowledge, polymath Leonardo da Vinci (1452–1519) spearheaded numerous technical innovations, experimenting with light manipulation, linear perspective and the depiction of subtle emotions in the human face. He worked all these elements into his enigmatic magnum opus, *Mona Lisa*, which has gone on to become one of the most famous (and valuable) paintings of all time. Not to be outdone, Michelangelo (1475–1564) used his dynamic sculpting skills to create a wonderfully realistic study of strength and beauty in his statue of *David*, while Raphael (1483–1520) devoted his energy to fashioning a grandiose fresco, *The School of Athens*, in the Vatican. The painting is considered by many to be the greatest homage to classicism to come out of the Renaissance.

From Mannerism to Baroque

By 1520, artists such as Michelangelo and Raphael had pretty well achieved everything that former generations had tried to do and, alongside other artists, began distorting natural images in favour of heightened expression. This movement – which reached its heights in Titian's luminous *Assunta* (Assumption, 1516–18), in Venice's I Frari, and in Raphael's *La trasfigurazione* (The Transfiguration, 1517–20), in the Vatican Museums' Pinacoteca – was derided by later critics, who labelled it mannerism. Pejorative as the term once was, the stylish artificiality of Agnolo Bronzino's Florentine court portraits has an almost 21st-century seductiveness.

Milanese-born enfant terrible Michelangelo Merisi da Caravaggio (1573–1610) had no sentimental attachment to classical models and no respect for 'ideal beauty'. He shocked contemporaries in his relentless search for truth and his radical, often visceral, realism. But even his most ardent detractors could not fail to admire his skill with the technique of chiaroscuro (the bold contrast of light and dark) and his employment of tenebrism, where dramatic chiaroscuro becomes a dominant and highly effective stylistic device. One look at his *Conversion of St Paul* and the *Crucifixion of St Peter* (1600–01), both in Rome's Basilica di Santa Maria del Popolo, or his *Le sette opere di Misericordia* (The Seven Acts of Mercy) in Naples' Pio Monte della Misericordia, and the raw emotional intensity of his work becomes clear.

This creative intensity was reflected in the artist's life. Described by the writer Stendhal as a 'great painter [and] a wicked man', Caravaggio fled

---

Top Renaissance Sculptures

David, Michelangelo, Galleria dell'Accademia, Florence

David, Donatello, Museo del Bargello, Florence

Tomb of Pope Julius II, Michelangelo, Basilica di San Pietro in Vincoli, Rome

---

Michelangelo's *David* is no stranger to close calls. In 1527, the lower part of his arm was broken off in a riot. In 1843, a hydrochloric 'spruce-up' stripped away some of the original surface, while in 1991 a disturbed, hammer-wielding Italian painter smashed the statue's second left toe.

ITALIAN ARTISTS: THE EXCLUSIVE SCOOP

Painter, architect and writer Giorgio Vasari (1511–74) was one of those figures rightly described as a 'Renaissance Man'. Born in Arezzo, he trained as a painter in Florence, working with artists including Andrea del Sarto and Michelangelo (he idolised the latter). As a painter, he is best remembered for his floor-to-ceiling frescoes in the Salone dei Cinquecento in Florence's Palazzo Vecchio. As an architect, his most accomplished work was the elegant loggia of the Uffizi (he also designed the enclosed, elevated corridor that connected the Palazzo Vecchio with the Uffizi and Palazzo Pitti and was dubbed the 'Corridoio Vasariano' in his honour). But posterity remembers him predominantly for his work as an art historian. His *Lives of the Most Excellent Painters, Sculptors and Architects, from Cimabue to Our Time,* an encyclopedia of artistic biographies published in 1550 and dedicated to Cosimo I de' Medici, is still in print (as *The Lives of the Artists*). It's full of wonderful anecdotes and – dare we say it – gossip about his artistic contemporaries in 16th-century Florence. Memorable passages include his recollection of visiting Donatello's studio one day only to find the great sculptor staring at his extremely lifelike statue of the *Prophet Habakkuk* and imploring it to talk (we can only assume that Donatello had been working too hard). Vasari also writes about a young Giotto (the painter whom he credits with ushering in the Renaissance) painting a fly on the surface of a work by Cimabue that the older master then tried to brush away. The book makes wonderful predeparture reading for anyone planning to visit Florence and its museums.

to Naples in 1606 after killing a man in a street fight in Rome. Although his sojourn in Naples lasted only a year, it had an electrifying effect on the city's younger artists. Among these artists was Giuseppe (or Jusepe) de Ribera (1591–1652), an aggressive, bullying Spaniard whose *capo lavoro* (masterpiece), the *Pietà,* hangs in the Museo Nazionale di San Martino in Naples. Along with the Greek artist Belisiano Crenzio and Naples-born painter Giovanni Battista Caracciolo (known as Battistello), Ribera formed a cabal to stamp out any potential competition. Merciless in the extreme, they shied from nothing in order to get their way. Ribera reputedly won a commission for the Cappella del Tesoro in the Duomo by poisoning his rival Domenichino (1581–1641) and wounding the assistant of a second competitor, Guido Reni (1575–1642). Much to the relief of other nerve-racked artists, the cabal eventually broke up when Caracciolo died in 1642.

North of Rome, Annibale Caracci (1560–1609) was the major artist of the baroque Bolognese school. With his painter brother Agostino he worked in Bologna, Parma and Venice before moving to Rome to work for Cardinal Odoardo Farnese. In works such as his magnificent frescoes of mythological subjects in Rome's Palazzo Farnese, he employed innovative illusionistic elements that would prove inspirational to later baroque painters such as Cortona, Pozzo and Gaulli. However, Caracci never let the illusionism and energy of his works dominate the subject matter, as these later painters did. Inspired by Michelangelo and Raphael, he continued the Renaissance penchant for idealising and 'beautifying' nature.

Arguably the best known of all baroque artists was the sculptor Gian Lorenzo Bernini (1598–1680), who used works of religious art such as his *Ecstasy of St Theresa* in Rome's Chiesa di Santa Maria della Vittoria to arouse feelings of exaltation and mystic transport. In this and many other works he achieved an extraordinary intensity of facial expression and a totally radical handling of draperies. Instead of letting these fall in dignified folds in the approved classical manner, he made them writhe and whirl to intensify the effect of excitement and energy.

While creative boundary pushing was obviously at play, the baroque was also driven by the Counter-Reformation, with much of the work commissioned in an attempt to keep hearts and minds from the clutches of the Protestant church. Baroque artists were early adopters of the sex

The Italian equivalent of French Impressionism was the Macchiaioli movement based in Florence. Its major artists were Telemaco Signorini (1835–1901) and Giovanni Fattori (1825–1908). See their socially engaged and light-infused work in the Palazzo Pitti's Galleria d'Arte Moderna in Florence.

sells mantra, depicting Catholic spirituality, rather ironically, through worldly joy, exuberant decoration and uninhibited sensuality.

The New Italy

Discontent at years of foreign rule – first under Napoleon and then under the Austrians – may have been good for political and philosophical thinkers, but there was little innovation in art. The most notable product of this time was, ironically, the painting and engraving of views, most notably in Venice, to meet the demand of European travellers wanting Grand Tour souvenirs. The best-known painters of this school are Francesco Guardi (1712-93) and Giovanni Antonio Canaletto (1697-1768).

Despite all the talk of unity, the 19th-century Italian cities remained as they had been for centuries – highly individual centres of culture with sharply contrasting ways of life. Music was the supreme art of this period and the overwhelming theme in the visual arts was one of chaste refinement.

The major artistic movement of the day was neoclassicism and its greatest Italian exponent was the sculptor Antonio Canova (1757-1822). Canova renounced movement in favour of stillness, emotion in favour of restraint and illusion in favour of simplicity. His most famous work is a daring sculpture of Paolina Bonaparte Borghese as a reclining *Venere vincitrice* (Conquering Venus), in Rome's Museo e Galleria Borghese.

WHO'S WHO IN RENAISSANCE & BAROQUE ART

Giotto di Bondone (c 1266–1337) Said to have ushered in the Renaissance; two masterworks: the Cappella degli Scrovegni (1304–06) in Padua and the upper church (1306–11) in Assisi.

Donatello (c 1382–1466) Florentine born and bred; his *David* (c 1440–50) in the collection of the Museo del Bargello in Florence was the first free-standing nude sculpture produced since the classical era.

Fra' Angelico (1395–1455) Made a saint in 1982; his best-loved work is the *Annunciation* (c 1450) in the convent of the Museo di San Marco in Florence.

Sandro Botticelli (c 1444–1510) *Primavera* (c 1482) and *The Birth of Venus* (c 1485) are among the best-loved of all Italian paintings; both in the Uffizi.

Domenico Ghirlandaio (1449–94) A top Tuscan master; his frescoes include those in the Tornabuoni Chapel in Florence's Basilica di Santa Maria Novella.

Michelangelo Buonarroti (1475–1564) The big daddy of them all; everyone knows *David* (1504) in the Galleria dell'Accademia in Florence and the Sistine Chapel ceiling (1508–12) in Rome's Vatican Museums.

Raphael Santi (1483–1520) Originally from Urbino; painted luminous Madonnas and fell in love with a baker's daughter, immortalised in his painting *La Fornarina*, in Rome's Galleria Nazionale d'Arte Antica: Palazzo Barberini.

Titian (c 1490–1576) Real name Tiziano Vecelli; seek out his *Assumption* (1516–18) in the Chiesa di Santa Maria Gloriosa dei Frari (I Frari), Venice.

Tintoretto (1518–94) The last great painter of the Italian Renaissance, known as 'Il Furioso' for the energy he put into his work; look for his *Last Supper* in Venice's Chiesa di Santo Stefano.

Annibale Caracci (1560–1609) Bologna-born and best known for his baroque frescoes in Rome's Palazzo Farnese.

Michelangelo Merisi da Caravaggio (1573–1610) Baroque's bad boy; his most powerful work is the *St Matthew Cycle* in Rome's Chiesa di San Luigi dei Francesi.

Gian Lorenzo Bernini (1598–1680) The sculptor protégé of Cardinal Scipione Borghese; best known for his *Rape of Persephone* (1621–22) and *Apollo and Daphne* (1622–25) in Rome's Museo e Galleria Borghese.

Canova was the last Italian artist to win overwhelming international fame. Italian architecture, sculpture and painting had played a dominant role in the cultural life of Europe for some 400 years, but with Canova's death in 1822, this supremacy came to an end.

Modern Movements

Italy entered the 20th century still in the throes of constructing a cohesive national identity. Futurism, led by poet Filippo Tommaso Marinetti (1876–1944) and painter Umberto Boccioni (1882–1916), grew out of this sense of urgent nationalism and, as Italy's north rapidly industrialised, sought new ways to express the dynamism of the machine age. Futurists demanded a new art for a new world and denounced every attachment to the art of the past. Marinetti's *Manifesto del futurismo* (Futurist Manifesto, 1909) was reinforced by the publication of a 1910 futurist painting manifesto by Boccioni, Giacomo Balla (1871–1958), Luigi Russolo (1885–1947) and Gino Severini (1883–1966). The manifesto declared, 'Everything is in movement, everything rushes forward, everything is in constant swift change.' Boccioni's *Rissa in galleria* (Brawl in the Arcade, 1910), in the collection of Milan's Pinacoteca di Brera, clearly demonstrates the movement's fascination with frantic movement and with modern technology. After WWI, a number of the futurist painters, including Mario Sironi (1885–1961) and Carlo Carrà (1881–1966), became aligned with fascism, sharing a common philosophy of nationalism and violence. Milan's Museo del Novecento along with Trentino's Museo d'Arte Moderna e Contemporanea di Trento e Rovereto (MART) have the world's best collection of futurist works.

Paralleling futurism's bullying bluster, the metaphysical movement of Giorgio de Chirico (1888–1978) produced paintings notable for their stillness and sense of foreboding. He and Carlo Carrà depicted disconnected images from the world of dreams, often in settings of classical Italian architecture, as in *The Red Tower* (1913), now in Venice's Peggy Guggenheim Collection. Like futurism, the movement was short lived, but held powerful attraction for the French surrealist movement in the 1920s.

As Italy's north flourished in the 1950s, so did the local art scene. Artists such as Alberto Burri (1915–95) and the Argentine-Italian Lucio Fontana (1899–1968) experimented with abstraction. Fontana's punctured canvases were characterised by *spazialismo* (spatialism) and he also experimented with 'slash paintings', perforating his canvases with actual holes or slashes and dubbing them 'art for the space age'. Burri's assemblages were made of burlap, wood, iron and plastic and were avowedly antitraditional. *Grande sacco* (Large Sack) of 1952, housed in Rome's Galleria Nazionale d'Arte Moderna e Contemporanea, caused a major controversy when it was first exhibited.

Piero Manzoni (1933–63) created highly ironic work that questioned the nature of the art object itself, such as his canned *Artist's Shit* (1961), directly prefiguring conceptual art and earning him posthumous membership of the radical new movement of the 1960s, *Arte Povera* (Poor Art). Focused primarily in Turin and often using simple, everyday materials in installation or performance work, artists such as Mario Merz (1925–2003), Michelangelo Pistoletto (b 1933) and Giovanni Anselmo (b 1934), sought to make the art experience more 'real', and to attack institutional power.

The 1980s saw a return to painting and sculpture in a traditional (primarily figurative) sense. Dubbed 'Transavanguardia', this movement broke with the prevailing international focus on conceptual art and was thought by some critics to signal the death of avant-garde. The artists who were part of this movement include Sandro Chia (b 1946), Mimmo Paladino (b 1948), Enzo Cucchi (b 1949) and Francesco Clemente (b 1952).

While global interest in contemporary art and the art market has shown exponential growth in recent decades, Italian art-world insiders

ITALIAN ART & ARCHITECTURE ART

Modern Art Musts

Galleria Nazionale d'Arte Moderna e Contemporanea, Rome

Peggy Guggenheim Collection, Venice

Museo del Novecento, Milan

Castello di Rivoli, Turin

MADRE, Naples

MAMbo, Bologna

Museion, Bolzano

British art critic Andrew Graham-Dixon has written three authoritative books on Italian art: *Michelangelo & the Sistine Chapel* (2016); *Caravaggio: A Life Sacred & Profane* (2012); and *Renaissance* (2000), the companion book to the BBC TV series.

CAPITAL SCANDALS: CONTROVERSIAL ART IN ROME

The Last Judgment (1537–41), Michelangelo There were more than just arms and legs dangling from Michelangelo's Sistine Chapel fresco in Rome's Vatican Museums. The depiction of full-frontal nudity on the chapel's altar horrified Catholic Counter-Reformation critics. No doubt Michelangelo turned in his grave when the offending bits were covered up.

Madonna and Child with St Anne (1605–06), Caravaggio St Anne looks more 'beggar-woman' than 'beatified grandmother', but it's Mary who made the faithful blush on Caravaggio's canvas, her propped-up cleavage a little too 'flesh-and-bone' for the mother of God. The sexed-up scene was too much for the artist's client, who offered a 'Grazie, but no grazie'. The painting now hangs in Rome's Museo e Galleria Borghese.

St Matthew and the Angel (1602), Caravaggio In the original version, personal space (or the sheer lack of it) was the main problem for Caravaggio's client Cardinal del Monte. It features a sensual, handsome angel snuggling up to St Matthew – exactly what kind of inspiration the winged visitor was offering the saint was anybody's guess. And so Caravaggio went back to his easel, producing the prime-time version now gracing the Chiesa di San Luigi dei Francesi in Rome.

Conquering Venus (1805–08), Antonio Canova When asked whether she minded posing nude, Paolina Bonaparte Borghese provocatively replied 'Why should I?' Given her well-known infidelities, this marble depiction of Napoleon's wayward sister as the Roman goddess of love merely confirmed her salacious reputation. This fact was not lost on her husband, Italian prince Camillo Borghese, who forbade the sculpture from leaving their home. You'll find it at the Museo e Galleria Borghese.

bemoan the country's art scene, citing a dearth of institutional support, no real market to speak of and a backward-gazing population. That said, Italy does have a number of innovative, engaged contemporary-art champions, from museums such as Rome's MAXXI, Turin's Castello di Rivoli, Bologna's MAMbo and Museion in Bolzano. They are joined in Milan by a growing number of *fondazione* – private foundation collections, from the new Fondazione Giangiacomo Feltrinelli (opened in 2016) to the sprawling Fondazione Prada (opened in 2015) and the edgy Hangar Bicocca, along with the magnificent Palazzo Grassi in Venice, and the broadly roaming Museo Ettore Fico and small but astutely curated Fondazione Sandretto Re Rebaudengo, both in Turin. American art dealer Larry Gagosian set up a Roman gallery in 2007 and Milan's dealers continue to flourish. Naples and Turin also have a small but significant number of contemporary galleries.

Due to the influence of superstar Italian curators such as Francesco Bonami and Massimiliano Gioni, Italian contemporary artists are often celebrated as much, if not more, on the international stage as at home. Italian artists to watch both at home and abroad include Rudolf Stingel (b 1956), Paolo Canevari (b 1963), Maurizio Cattelan (b 1960), Vanessa Beecroft (b 1969), Rä di Martino (b 1975), and Paola Pivi (b 1971) – variously working in painting, sculpture, photography, installation, video and performance.

> Italy's major contemporary-art event is La Biennale di Venezia, held every odd-numbered year. It's the most important and most mythologised survey show on the international art circuit, welcoming over 300,000 visitors.

Architecture

Italian architecture has an enduring obsession with the 'classical', employing the principles of symmetry, order, elegance and refinement. The Greeks, who established the style, employed it in the southern cities they colonised; the Romans refined and embellished it; Italian Renaissance architects rediscovered and tweaked it; and the Fascist architects of the 1930s returned to it in their powerful modernist buildings. Even today, architects such as Richard Meier are designing buildings in Italy that clearly reference classical prototypes.

Classical

Only one word describes the buildings of ancient Italy: monumental. The Romans built an empire the size of which had never before been seen and went on to adorn it with buildings cut from the same pattern. From Verona's Roman Arena to Pozzuoli's Anfiteatro Flavio, giant stadiums rose above skylines. Spa centres like Rome's Terme di Caracalla were veritable cities of indulgence, exhibiting everything from giant marble-clad pools to gymnasiums and libraries. Aqueducts like those below Naples provided fresh water to thousands, while temples such as Pompeii's Tempio di Apollo provided the faithful with awe-inspiring centres of worship.

Having learned a few valuable lessons from the Greeks, the Romans refined architecture to such a degree that their building techniques, designs and mastery of harmonious proportion underpin much of the world's architecture and urban design to this day.

And though the Greeks invented the architectural orders (Doric, Ionic and Corinthian), it was the Romans who employed them in bravura performances. Consider Rome's Colosseum, with its ground tier of Doric, middle tier of Ionic and third tier of Corinthian columns. The Romans were dab hands at temple architecture too. Just witness Rome's exquisitely proportioned Pantheon, a temple whose huge but seemingly unsupported dome showcases the Roman invention of concrete, an ingredient as essential to the modern construction industry as Ferrari is to the F1 circuit.

Byzantine

After Constantine became Christianity's star convert, the empire's architects and builders turned their talents to the design and construction of churches. The emperor commissioned a number of such buildings in Rome, but he also expanded his sphere of influence east, to Constantinople in Byzantium. His successors in Constantinople, most notably Justinian and his wife, Theodora, went on to build churches in the style that became known as Byzantine. Brick buildings built on the Roman basilican plan but with domes, they had sober exteriors that formed a stark contrast to their magnificent, mosaic-encrusted interiors. Finding its way back to Italy in the mid-6th century, the style expressed itself on a grand scale in Venice's Basilica di San Marco, as well as more modestly in buildings like the Chiesa di San Pietro in Otranto, Puglia. The true stars of Italy's Byzantine scene, however, are the Basilica di San Vitale in Ravenna and the Basilica di Sant'Apollinare in nearby Classe, both built on a cruciform plan between 527 and 550.

Masterpiece Mosaics

Basilica di Sant'Apollinare in Classe, Ravenna

Basilica di San Vitale, Ravenna

Basilica di San Marco, Venice

Cattedrale di Monreale, Monreale

Romanesque

The next development in ecclesiastical architecture in Italy came from Europe. The European Romanesque style became momentarily popular in four regional forms – the Lombard, Pisan, Florentine and Sicilian Norman. All displayed an emphasis on width and the horizontal lines of a building rather than height, and featured churches where the bell tower *(campanile)* and baptistry *(battistero)* were separate to the church.

The use of alternating white and green marble defined the facades of the Florentine and Pisan styles, as seen in iconic buildings like Florence's Basilica di Santa Maria Novella and Duomo baptistry, as well as in Pisa's cathedral, baptistry (Italy's largest) and famous leaning tower.

The Lombard style featured elaborately carved facades and exterior decoration with bands and arches. Among its finest examples are the Lombard cathedral in Modena, Pavia's Basilica di San Michele and Brescia's unusually shaped Duomo Vecchio.

Down south, the Sicilian Norman style blended Norman, Saracen and Byzantine influences, from marble columns to Islamic-inspired pointed arches to glass tesserae detailing. One of the greatest examples of the form is the Cattedrale di Monreale, located just outside Palermo.

1. Piazza dei Miracoli and the Leaning Tower (p598) **2.** Florence's Duomo (p518) **3.** Colosseum (p86) **4.** Milan's Duomo (p262)

Architectural Wonders

Italy is Europe's architectural overachiever, bursting at its elegant seams with triumphant temples, brooding castles and dazzling basilicas. If you can't see it all in one mere lifetime, why not start with five of the best?

Duomo, Milan

A forest of petrified pinnacles and fantastical beasts, Italy's ethereal Gothic glory (p262) is pure Milan: a product of centuries of pillaging, trend spotting, one-upmanship and mercantile ambition. Head to the top for a peek at the Alps.

Duomo, Florence

Florence's most famous landmark (p518) is more than a monumental spiritual masterpiece. It's a living, breathing testament to the explosion of creativity, artistry, ambition and wealth that would define Renaissance Florence.

Piazza dei Miracoli, Pisa

Pisa (p598) promises a threesome you won't forget: the Duomo, the Battistero and the infamous Leaning Tower. Together they make up a perfect Romanesque trio, artfully arranged like objets d'art on a giant green coffee table.

Colosseum, Rome

Almost 2000 years on, Rome's mighty ancient stadium (p86) still has the X factor. Once the domain of gladiatorial battles and ravenous wild beasts, its 50,000-seat magnitude radiates all the vanity and ingenuity of a once-glorious, intercontinental empire.

Basilica di San Marco, Venice

It's a case of East–West fusion at this Byzantine beauty (p362), founded in AD 829 and rebuilt twice since. Awash with glittering mosaics and home to the remains of Venice's patron saint, its layering of eras reflects the city's own worldly pedigree.

Gothic

The Italians didn't wholeheartedly embrace the Gothic: its verticality, flying buttresses, grotesque gargoyles and over-the-top decoration were just too far from the classical ideal that seems to be integral to the Italian psyche. The local version was generally much more restrained, a style beautifully exemplified by Naples' simple, elegant Basilica di San Lorenzo Maggiore. There were, of course, exceptions. The Venetians used the style in grand *palazzi* (mansions) such as the Ca' d'Oro and on the facades of high-profile public buildings like the Palazzo Ducale.

Gothic appears in a number of hybrid cathedrals in Italy, several of which took hundreds of years to complete. Siena's cathedral mixes Gothic with Romanesque, Florence's cathedral fuses Gothic with elements of a nascent Renaissance. Milan's flamboyant Duomo took nearly 600 years to build and absorbed many different architectural influences, but it's often held up to be the finest (and largest) Gothic building in Italy.

Baroque

Unlike the gradual, organic spread of the styles that preceded it, Renaissance architecture's adoption was a highly conscious and academic affair, helped along by the invention of the printing press. The Florentine Filippo Brunelleschi and the Venetian Andrea Palladio spread a doctrine of harmonic geometry and proportion, drawing on classical Roman principles.

This insistence on restraint and purity was sure to lead to a backlash, and it's no surprise that the next major architectural movement in Italy was noteworthy for its exuberant – some would say decadent – form. The baroque took its name from the Portuguese word *barroco,* used by fishers to denote a misshapen pearl. Compared to the pure classical lines of Renaissance buildings, its output could indeed be described as 'misshapen' – Andrea Palma's facade of Syracuse's cathedral, Guarino Guarini's Palazzo Carignano in Turin and Gian Lorenzo Bernini's baldachin in St Peter's in Rome are dramatic, curvaceous and downright sexy structures that bear little similarity to the classical ideal.

The baroque's show-stopping qualities were not lost on the Catholic Church. Threatened by the burgeoning Reformation to the north of the Alps, the Church commissioned a battalion of grandiose churches, palaces and art to dazzle the masses and reaffirm its authority. Rome soon became a showcase of this baroque exuberance, its impressive new statements including Giacomo della Porta's Chiesa del Gesù. Commissioned to celebrate the newly founded Jesuit order, the church's hallucinatory swirl of frescoes and gilded interiors was produced by baroque greats such as Battista Gaulli (aka Il Baciccio), Andrea Pozzo and Pietro da Cortona.

Even more prolific was Gian Lorenzo Bernini, who expressed the popes' claim to power with his sweeping new design of St Peter's Square, its colonnaded arms 'embracing' the faithful with a majesty that still moves visitors today. Yet not everyone was singing Bernini's praise, especially the artist's bitter rival, Francesco Borromini (1599–1667). Reclusive and tortured, Borromini looked down on his ebullient contemporary's lack of architectural training and formal stone-carving technique. No love was lost: Bernini believed Borromini 'had been sent to destroy architecture'. Centuries on, the rivalry lives on in the works they left behind, from Borromini's Chiesa di San Carlo alle Quattro Fontane and Bernini's neighbouring Chiesa di Sant'Andrea al Quirinale to their back-to-back creations in Piazza Navona.

Glowing in the wealth of its Spanish rulers, 16th-century Naples also drew driven, talented architects and artists in search of commissions and fame. For many of Naples' baroque architects, however, the saying 'it's what's inside that counts' had a particularly strong resonance. Due in part to the city's notorious high density and lack of show-off piazzas, many invested less time on adorning hard-to-see facades and more on lavishing

For a Blast of Baroque

Lecce, Puglia

Noto, Sicily

Rome, Lazio

Naples, Campania

Catania, Sicily

TOP FIVE ARCHITECTS

Filippo Brunelleschi (1377–1446) Brunelleschi blazed the neoclassical trail, his dome for Florence's Duomo announcing the Renaissance's arrival.

Donato Bramante (1444–1514) After a stint as court architect in Milan, Bramante went on to design the tiny Tempietto and huge St Peter's Basilica in Rome.

Michelangelo (1475–1564) Architecture was but one of the many strings in this great man's bow; his masterworks are the dome of St Peter's Basilica and the Piazza del Campidoglio in Rome.

Andrea Palladio (1508–80) Western architecture's single-most influential figure, Palladio turned classical Roman principles into elegant northern Italian villas.

Gian Lorenzo Bernini (1598–1680) The king of the Italian baroque is best known for his work in Rome, including the magnificent baldachin, piazza and colonnades at St Peter's.

interiors. The exterior of churches like the Chiesa e Chiostro di San Gregorio Armeno gives little indication of the opulence inside, from cheeky cherubs and gilded ceilings to polychromatic marble walls and floors. The undisputed meister of this marble work form was Cosimo Fanzago, whose pièce de résistance is the church inside the Museo Nazionale di San Martino in Naples – a mesmerising kaleidoscope of inlaid colours and patterns.

Considering the Neapolitans' weakness for all things baroque, it's not surprising that the Italian baroque's grand finale would come in the form of the Palazzo Reale in Caserta, a 1200-room royal palace designed by Neapolitan architect Luigi Vanvitelli to upstage France's Versailles.

Arguably, Italy's most homogeneous baroque city is Lecce in Puglia, set off by half a dozen highly decorative churches.

The Industrial & the Rational

Upstaged by political and social upheaval, architecture took a back seat in 19th-century Italy. One of the few movements of note stemmed directly from the Industrial Revolution and saw the application of industrial innovations in glass and metal to building design. Two monumental examples of the form are Galleria Vittorio Emanuele II in Milan and its southern sibling Galleria Umberto I in Naples.

By century's end, the art-nouveau craze sweeping Europe inspired an Italian version, called *lo stile floreale* or 'Liberty' (after the British department store). It was notable for being more extravagant than most, evidenced in Giuseppe Sommaruga's Casa Castiglione (1903), a large block of flats at Corso Venezia 47 in Milan.

Italy's take on European modernism was rationalism, which strove to create an indigenous style that would fuse classical ideals with the charged industrial-age fantasies of the futurists. Its founding group was Gruppo 7, seven architects inspired by the Bauhaus; their most significant member, Giuseppe Terragni, designed the 1936 Casa del Fascio (now called Casa del Popolo) in Como. MIAR (Movimento Italiano per l'Architettura Razionale, the Italian Movement for Rational Architecture), a broader umbrella organisation, was led by Adalberto Libera, the influential architect best known for his Palazzo dei Congressi in EUR, a 20th-century suburb of Rome. EUR's most iconic building is the Palazzo della Civiltà del Lavoro (Palace of the Workers), designed by Giovanni Guerrini, Ernesto Bruno La Padula and Mario Romano, its arches and gleaming travertine skin graphically referencing the Colosseum and ancient Rome's glory. With most of these commissions at the behest of Mussolini's government, rationalism is often known simply as 'Fascist Architecture', although the architects' uncompromising modernism eventually fell out of favour as the regime turned to a theatrical pastiche of classical styles.

Into the Future

Italy's postwar boom may have driven an internationally acclaimed and cutting-edge design industry, but this was not reflected in its built environment. One of the few high points came in 1956, when architect Giò Ponti and engineer Pier Luigi Nervi designed Milan's slender Pirelli Tower. Ponti was the highly influential founding editor of the international architecture and design magazine *Domus*, which had begun publication in 1928; Nervi's innovations in reinforced concrete changed the face of modern architecture.

Architects such as Carlo Scarpa, Aldo Rossi and Paolo Portoghesi then took Italian architecture in different directions. Veneto-based Scarpa was well known for his organic forms, most particularly the Brion Tomb and Sanctuary at San Vito d'Altivole. Writer and architect Rossi was awarded the Pritzker Prize in 1990, and was known for both his writing (eg *The Architecture of the City* in 1966) and design work. Rome-based Paolo Portoghesi is an architect, academic and writer with a deep interest in classical architecture. His best-known Italian building is the Central Mosque (1974) in Rome, famed for its luminously beautiful interior.

Italy's most brilliant starchitect is, however, Renzo Piano, whose international projects include London's scene-stealing Shard skyscraper and the Centre Culturel Tjibaou in Nouméa, New Caledonia. At home, recent projects include Turin's rather uninteresting Intesa Sanpaolo tower (166m) and his far more bold Museo delle Scienze (MUSE) in Trento. Composed of a series of voids and volumes that seemingly float on water, its striking design echoes its dramatic mountain landscape. Further south in Rome, Piano's 2002 Auditorium Parco della Musica is considered one of his greatest achievements to date. He was also asked to help in earthquake reconstruction efforts and in developing anti-earthquake building codes. Piano's stature is so great, he was appointed as 'senator for life' in 2013.

Piano's heir apparent is Massimiliano Fuksas, whose projects are as whimsical as they are visually arresting. Take, for instance, his recent Nuovo Centro Congressi (New Congress Center) in Rome's EUR, dubbed the 'Nuvola' (Cloud) for its 'floating', glass-encased auditorium. Other Fuksas highlights include the futuristic Milan Trade Fair Building and the San Paolo Parish Church in Foligno.

High-profile foreign architects have also shaken things up. In Venice, David Chipperfield extended the Isola di San Michele's cemetery, while Tadao Ando oversaw the city's acclaimed Punta della Dogana and Palazzo Grassi renovation. In Rome, Richard Meier divided opinion with his 2006 Ara Pacis pavilion. The first major civic building in Rome's historic centre in more than half a century, the travertine, glass and steel structure was compared to a petrol station by popular art critic Vittorio Sgarbi. A little more love was given to Zaha Hadid's bold, sinuous MAXXI art gallery in northern Rome, which earned the Iraqi-British starchitect the prestigious RIBA (Royal Institute of British Architects) Sterling prize in 2010. One of Hadid's final works, the Messner Mountain Museum Kronplatz, opened in 2016, now also graces a stunning Dolomiti site.

Meanwhile, Milan's skyline has had a 21st-century makeover, with the ambitious redevelopment of its Porta Nuova district. Home to Italy's tallest building (the 231m César Pelli–designed UniCredit tower), the project also features Stefano Boeri's Bosco Verticale (Vertical Forest), a pair of eco-conscious apartment towers covered in the equivalent of a hectare of woodland. The city's ambitious CityLife project, a commercial, residential and parkland development, revolves around three experimental skyscrapers by Zaha Hadid, Arata Isozaki and Daniel Libeskind. Isozaki's 50-floor *Il Dritto* (the straight one) opened in 2015 as the HQ for the Allianz Group, Hadid's 44-floor *Lo Storto* (the twisted one) was completed in 2017, and Libeskind's *Il Curvo* (the curved one), inspired by the curvaceous lines of a Renaissance cupola, was inaugurated in 2019.

The Italian Way of Life

Time to employ a little creative thinking. Imagine you woke up tomorrow and discovered you were Italian. Aside from vastly superior pizza and a propensity to get operatically emotional every time your football team loses, how would life be different, and what could you discover about Italy in just one day as a local? It's more than you might think.

A Day in the Life of an Italian

Sveglia! You're woken not by an alarm but by the burble and clatter of the *caffettiera,* the ubiquitous stovetop espresso-maker. You're running late, so you bolt down your coffee scalding hot (an acquired Italian talent) and pause briefly to ensure your socks match before dashing out the door. Yet still you walk blocks out of your way to fuel your hard-to-kick cigarette habit (one you share with 23% of Italians). You purchase your low-tar smokes at the *tabaccheria* from Bucharest-born Nicolae who, as a Romanian, is part of Italy's largest migrant community. You chat briefly about his new baby – you may be late, but at least you're not rude.

There are 12 minority languages officially recognised in Italy, consisting of native languages Friulian, Ladin and Sardinian, and the languages of neighbouring countries, including French, Franco-Provençal, German, Catalan, Occitan, Slovene, Croatian, Albanian and Greek.

On your way to work you scan news sites on your phone: another 24-hour transport strike, more coalition-government infighting and an announcement of new EU regulations on cheese. Outrageous! The cheese regulations, that is; the rest is to be expected. At work, you're buried in paperwork until noon, when it's a relief to join friends for lunch and a glass of wine. Afterwards you toss back another scorching espresso at your favourite bar and find out how your barista's latest audition went – turns out you went to school with the sister of the director of the play, so you promise to put in a good word.

Back at work by 2pm, you multitask Italian-style, chatting with co-workers as you dash off work emails, text your schoolmate about the barista on your *telefonino* (mobile phone) and surreptitiously check *l'Internet* for employment listings – your work contract is due to expire soon. After a busy day like this, *aperitivi* are definitely in order, so at 6.30pm you head directly to the latest happy-hour hotspot. Your friends arrive, the decor is *molto design* and the vibe *molto fashion,* until suddenly it's time for your English class – everyone's learning it these days, if only for the slang.

By the time you finally get home, it's already 9.30pm and dinner will have to be reheated. *Peccato!* (Shame!) You eat, absent-mindedly watching the latest episode of *MasterChef Italia* while recounting your day and complaining about cheese regulations to whoever's home – no sense giving reheated pasta your undivided attention. While brushing your teeth, you dream of a vacation in Anguilla, though without a raise, it'll probably be Abruzzo again this year.

Finally you make your way to bed and check Instagram one last time; your colleague Marco seems to be acclimatising to life in Sydney. He's the third person you know who has moved to Australia in recent years. You wonder what it would be like to live in a nation so young and booming. They say hard work pays over there. Marco has already been promoted, without the need of favours or influential contacts. Once again you entertain the thought of following in his footsteps, but then ponder the distance and start to pine for your *famiglia e amici* (family and friends). As you drift off, you console yourself in the knowledge that while it mightn't be perfect, they don't call Italy the *bel paese* (beautiful country) for nothing.

Being Italian

The People

Who are the people you'd encounter every day as an Italian? Just over 23% of your fellow citizens are smokers and around 61% drive (or are driven) to work, compared to only 3.3% who cycle. The average Italian is 45.5 years old, up 0.8 years since 2015. The percentage of Italians aged over 65 is 21.6%, the highest ratio in the European Union. This explains the septuagenarians you'll notice on parade with dogs and grandchildren in parks, affably arguing about politics in cafes, and ruthlessly dominating bocce tournaments.

You might also notice a striking absence of children. Italy's birth rate is one of the lowest in the world; an average of 1.33 births per woman compared to 1.75 in the UK, 1.84 in Ireland and 1.85 in France.

North versus South

In his film *Ricomincio da tre* (I'm Starting from Three; 1980), acting great Massimo Troisi comically tackles the problems faced by Neapolitans forced to head north for work. Punchlines aside, the film reveals Italy's north–south divide; a divide that still lingers 40 years on. While the north is known for its fashion empires and moneyed metropolises, Italy's south (dubbed the 'Mezzogiorno') is often spotlit for its higher unemployment, poorer infrastructure and Mafia-related police raids. To many Italians, the terms *settentrionale* (northern Italian) and *meridionale* (southern Italian) remain weighed down by crude stereotypes: while the former is often considered modern, sophisticated and successful, the latter is still often seen as lazy, traditional and somewhat unrefined. From the Industrial Revolution to the 1960s, millions of southern Italians fled to the industrialised northern cities for factory jobs. Disparagingly nicknamed *terroni* (literally meaning 'of the soil'), these in-house 'immigrants' were often exposed to discriminatory attitudes from their northern cousins. Decades on, the overt discrimination may have dissipated but some prejudices remain. It's not uncommon to find northerners who resent their taxes being used to 'subsidise' the south – a sentiment that has been well exploited by the Lega Nord (Northern League) political party.

From Emigrants to Immigrants

From 1876 to 1976, Italy was a country of net emigration. With some 30 million Italian emigrants dispersed throughout Europe, the Americas and Australia, remittances from Italians abroad helped keep Italy's economy afloat during economic crises after independence and WWII.

The tables have since turned. Political and economic upheavals in the 1980s brought new arrivals from Central Europe, Latin America and North Africa, including Italy's former colonies in Tunisia, Somalia and Ethiopia. More recently, waves of Chinese and Filipino immigrants have given Italian streetscapes a Far Eastern twist. While immigrants account for just over 8% of Italy's population today, the number is growing. In 2001, the country's foreign population (a number that excludes

According to the OECD's 2018 Better Life Index, 92% of Italians surveyed knew of someone they could rely on in a time of need, more than the OECD average of 89%. On a scale from 0 to 10, general life satisfaction ranked 6.0, below the OECD average of 6.5.

Today, people of Italian origin account for more than 40% of the population in Argentina and Uruguay, more than 10% in Brazil, more than 5% in Switzerland, the US and Venezuela, and more than 4% in Australia and Canada.

foreign-born people who take Italian citizenship) was 1.3 million. By 2019, that number had almost quadrupled to over five million.

From a purely economic angle, these new arrivals are vital for the country's economic health. While most Italians today choose to live and work within Italy, the country's population is ageing and fewer young Italians are entering blue-collar agricultural and industrial fields. Without immigrant workers to fill the gaps, Italy would be sorely lacking in tomato sauce and shoes. From kitchen hands to hotel maids, it is often immigrants who take the low-paid service jobs that keep Italy's tourism economy afloat.

Despite this, not everyone is rolling out the welcome mat. In 2010, the shooting of an immigrant worker in the town of Rosarno, Calabria, sparked Italy's worst race riots in years. In 2013, a top-level football match between AC Milan and Roma was suspended after fans chanted racist abuse at Mario Balotelli, AC Milan's black, Italian-born striker. In 2017, Pescara midfielder Sulley Muntari walked off the field in response to racist chants during a Serie A game against Cagliari. The Ghanaian footballer was consequently penalised, receiving one yellow card for protesting about the abuse and another for leaving the field without following procedures. The Italian Football Federation subsequently withdrew the penalty (which equalled a one-match ban) in the face of widespread condemnation, including from the UK's Kick It Out antidiscrimination organisation.

According to official statistics there are around 1.4 million Muslims in Italy, a lot less than other European countries such as France and Spain. Furthermore, Islam is not officially recognised by the state.

Religion, Loosely Speaking

While almost 80% of Italians identify as Catholics, only around 15% of Italy's population regularly attends Sunday Mass. That said, the Church continues to exert considerable influence on public policy and political parties, especially those of the centre- and far-right.

But in the land of the double park, even God's rules are up for interpretation. Sure, *mamma* still serves fish on Good Friday, but while she might consult *la Madonna* for guidance, chances are she'll get a second opinion from the *maga* (fortune teller) on channel 32. It's estimated that around 13 million Italians use the services of psychics, astrologers and fortune tellers. While the uncertainties stirred up by Italy's still-stagnant economy help drive these numbers, Italians have long been a highly superstitious bunch. From not toasting with water to not opening umbrellas inside the home, the country offers a long list of tips to keep bad luck at bay.

Superstitious beliefs are especially strong in Italy's south. Here *corni* (horn-shaped charms) adorn everything from necklines to rearview mirrors to ward off the *malocchio* (evil eye) and devotion to local saints takes on an almost cultish edge. Every year in Naples, thousands cram into the *duomo* to witness the blood of San Gennaro miraculously liquefy in the phial that contains it. When the blood liquefies, the city breathes a sigh of relief – it symbolises another year safe from disaster. When it didn't in 1944, Mt Vesuvius erupted, and when it failed again in 1980, an earthquake struck the city that year. Coincidence?

At 83 years, Italy has one of the highest life expectancies in the world.

It's Not What You Know...

From your day as an Italian, this much you know already: conversation is far too important to be cut short by tardiness or a mouthful of toothpaste. All that chatter isn't entirely idle, either: in Europe's most ancient, entrenched bureaucracy, social networks are essential to get things done. Putting in a good word for your barista isn't just a nice gesture, but an essential career boost. According to Italy's Ministry of Labour, over 60% of Italian firms rely on personal introductions for recruitment. Indeed, *clientelismo* (nepotism) is as much a part of the Italian lexicon as *caffè* (coffee) and *tasse* (taxes); a fact that is satirised in Massimiliano Bruno's film *Viva l'Italia* (2012), about a crooked, well-connected senator who secures jobs for his three children, among them a talentless TV actress with a speech impediment.

In 2016, Raffaele Cantone – president of the Autorità Nazionale Anticorruzione (ANAC) – sparked a national debate after claiming that nepotism in Italian universities played a major role in the country's ongoing 'brain drain'. It's a sentiment echoed in a 2011 study conducted by the University of Chicago Medical Center. The study found an unusually high recurrence of the same surnames among academic staff at various Italian universities.

Over 160,000 Italians left the country in 2018 in search of better opportunities abroad, including a growing number of people from wealthy northern regions like Lombardy and the Veneto. Despite the fact that these northern regions enjoy a high per-capita GDP, a growing number of its people believe that better employment opportunities and quality of life can be found elsewhere. It's a cumulative problem. In the last decade some two million Italians – many of them young and highly skilled – have emigrated, with the vast majority remaining in Europe.

Hotel Mamma

If you're between the ages of 18 and 34, there's a 67% chance that's not a roommate in the kitchen making your morning coffee: it's mum or dad. The number of young Italian adults living at home is almost 20% higher than the European average, with only Slovakia claiming more young adults slumming it under their parents' roof.

This is not because Italy is a nation of pampered *bamboccioni* (big babies) – at least, not entirely. With a general unemployment rate of 10% and a youth unemployment rate hovering around 30% in mid-2019, it's no wonder that so many refuse to cut those apron strings. Yet high unemployment is only part of the picture. In general, Italians tend to graduate later than most Europeans. Once they do graduate, many end up in low-paying jobs or voluntary internships. It's a reality that has led to the adoption of the Spanish term *milleuristi* to describe the many young, qualified Italian adults living on a paltry *mille euro* (€1000) or less a month.

The World Economic Forum's 2018 Global Gender Gap Report ranked Italy 70th worldwide in terms of overall gender equality, down from 50th in 2016. It ranked 118th in female economic participation and opportunity, 61st in educational attainment and 38th in political empowerment.

While Italy's family-based social fabric provides a protective buffer for many during these challenging economic times, intergenerational solidarity has always been the basis of the Italian family. According to the time-honoured Italian social contract, you'd probably live with your parents until you start a career and a family of your own. Then after a suitable grace period for success and romance – a couple of years should do the trick – your parents might move in with you to look after your kids, and be looked after in turn.

As for those who don't live with family members, chances are they're still a quick stroll away, with over 50% living within a 30-minute walk of close relatives. All this considered, it's hardly surprising to hear that famous mobile-phone chorus at evening rush hour: '*Mamma, butta la pasta!*' (Mum, put the pasta in the water!).

Gender Equality

It might score straight As in fashion, food and design, but Italy's performance in the gender-equality stakes leaves much room for improvement. Despite the fact that many of Italy's current cabinet ministers are women – a conscious effort on the part of former prime minister Matteo

Renzi to redress the country's male-dominated parliament – sexism remains deeply entrenched in Italian society.

According to the European Commission's *2019 Report on Equality Between Women and Men in the EU*, only 53% of Italian women are in the workforce, compared to 80% in Sweden, 75% in Denmark and 68% in France. On average, Italian women earn significantly less than their male counterparts. And though successful Italian businesswomen do exist – among them Poste Italiane chairperson Bianca Maria Farina and Eni chairperson Emma Marcegaglia – almost 95% of public-company board members in Italy remain male, and of these, approximately 80% of them are older than 55.

Italian women fare no better on the domestic front. OECD figures reveal that Italian men spend 103 minutes per day cooking, cleaning or caring, less than a third as long as Italian women, who spend an average of 315 minutes per day on what the OECD labels unpaid work.

Italian Passions

Coordinated wardrobes, strong espresso and general admiration are not the only things that make Italian hearts sing. And while Italian passions are wide and varied, few define Italy like football and opera.

Better Living by Design

As an Italian, you actually did your coworkers a favour by being late to the office to give yourself a final once-over in the mirror. Unless you want your fellow employees to avert their gaze in dumbstruck horror, your socks had better match. The tram can wait as you *fare la bella figura* (cut a fine figure).

Italians have strong opinions about aesthetics and aren't afraid to share them. A common refrain is *Che brutta!* (How hideous!), which may strike visitors as tactless. But consider it from an Italian point of view – everyone is rooting for you to look good, so who are you to disappoint? The shop assistant who tells you with brutal honesty that yellow is *not* your colour is doing a public service, and will consider it a personal triumph to see you outfitted in orange instead.

If it's a gift, you must allow 10 minutes for the sales clerk to *fa un bel pacchetto,* wrapping your purchase with string and an artfully placed sticker. This is the epitome of *la bella figura* – the sales clerk wants you to look good by giving a good gift. When you do, everyone basks in the glow of *la bella figura:* you as the gracious gift-giver and the sales clerk as savvy gift consultant, not to mention the flushed and duly honoured recipient.

As a national obsession, *la bella figura* gives Italy its undeniable edge in design, cuisine, art and architecture. Though the country could get by on its striking good looks, Italy is ever mindful of delightful details. They are everywhere you look and many places you don't: the intricately carved cathedral spire only the bell-ringer could fully appreciate, the toy duck hidden inside your chocolate *uova di pasqua* (Easter egg), the absinthe-green silk lining inside a sober grey suit sleeve. Attention to such details earns you instant admiration in Italy – and an admission that, sometimes, non-Italians do have style.

Calcio (Football): Italy's Other Religion

Catholicism may be your official faith, but as an Italian your true religion is likely to be *calcio* (football). On any given weekend from September to May, chances are that you and your fellow *tifosi* (football fans) are at the *stadio,* glued to the TV or checking the score on your mobile

Italian Style Icons

Bialetti *coffee-maker*

Cinzano *vermouth*

Acqua di Parma *cologne*

Piaggio *Vespa*

Olivetti 'Valentine' *typewriter*

phone. Come Monday, you'll be dissecting the match by the office water cooler.

Football was introduced to Italy by the British at the tail-end of the 19th century. Not surprisingly, it didn't take long for the locals to stamp their characteristic panache on the 'beautiful game'. By the late 1930s, over a dozen teams were competing in an annual league known as Serie A, and the national side had taken home two out of three FIFA World Cups. Almost without realizing it, the Italians had elevated football into a tactical art where elegant attacking skill was backed up by a ruthless watertight defence.

In style-conscious Italy, it isn't just the football matches that are important, it's also the way they are played. Well-coiffured and self-aware Italian players prowl the field like Milanese models strutting the catwalk. In a nation that spawned Michelangelo, beauty is everything. There is no hoofing the ball in the air à la the English Premier League; Instead, it is manoeuvred skillfully across the playing surface waiting for that

FASHION FAMILY SAGAS

Tight as they may be, Italian families are not always examples of heart-warming domesticity. Indeed, some of Italy's most fashionable *famiglie* (families) prove that every clan has its problems, some small, some extra, extra large.

Consider the Versace bunch, fashion's favourite catwalking Calabrians. One of Italy's greatest exports, the familial dynasty was founded by Gianni, celebrity BFF and the man who single-handedly made bling chic. But not even the fashion gods could save the bearded genius, inexplicably shot dead outside his Miami mansion by serial killer Andrew Cunanan in 1997. With Gianni gone, creative control was passed to Donatella, Gianni's larger-than-life little sister. The subject of Anna Wintour's most unusual fashion memory – full-body spandex on horseback – the former coke-addled party queen flew herself to rehab on daughter Allegra's 18th birthday.

Then there are the Florentine fashion rivals, the Gucci clan. Established by Guccio Gucci in 1904, the family firm reads like a bad Brazilian soap – power struggles between Rodolfo and Aldo (Guccio's sons) in the 1950s; assault charges by Paolo (Aldo's son) against siblings Roberto and Giorgio, and cousin Maurizio Gucci, in 1982; and a major fallout between Paolo and father Aldo over the offshore siphoning of profits.

The last Gucci to run the company was Maurizio, who finally sold his share to Bahrain investment-bank Investcorp in 1993 for a healthy US$170 million. Two years later, Maurizio was dead, gunned down outside his Milan office on the order of ex-wife, Patrizia Reggiani. Not only had Reggiani failed to forgive her then ex-husband's infidelity, she was far from impressed with her US$500,000 annual allowance. After all, this was the woman who famously quipped that she'd rather weep in a Rolls Royce than be happy on a bicycle. Offered parole in 2011 from Milan's San Vittore prison on condition of finding employment, Reggiani stayed true to form, stating: 'I've never worked a day in my life; I'm certainly not going to start now'. Despite the now-infamous quip, fashion's 'black widow' did find herself a gig while on day release, working part-time in a Milanese jewellery store. Reggiani's most famous accessory while strutting Milan's upmarket streets was a live macaw, perched on her shoulder.

Having served only 18 years of her 26-year sentence, Reggiani was released early from custody in late 2016 for good behaviour. The widow's lucky streak continued in 2017 when an appeals court in Milan ruled that despite her conviction, Gucci's ex-wife remained entitled to an annual allowance of just over €1 million, a deal agreed to by Maurizio in 1993. The court also ruled that Reggiani was owed over €18 million in back payments accrued during her time behind bars. No doubt the windfall will fuel Reggiani's infamous spending, which reputedly includes €10,000 a month on orchids.

all-important moment of divine inspiration that lights up many Italian games. Ironically, the genius is countered by another distinctly Italian football trait: guile. Serie A games are renowned for their fake playacting and theatrical attempts to curry favour with the referee, and it isn't always pretty.

The guile went a stretch too far in 2006 when Juventus and four other Italian clubs were implicated in a match-fixing scandal known as *Calciopoli* that shook Italian football to its foundations.

Scandals aside, football in Italy remains a great cultural leveller. You'll see plenty of flag-waving in the streets and squares of tourist cities on big game days when the result can – for better or worse – affect the public mood. Bank on far better service in Naples if local heroes Napoli have just won 4-0, but don't expect too much sleep in Rome on nights when Lazio are playing local rivals, AS Roma.

In July 2006, an estimated 715 million people watched as Italy won the World Cup against France. In bars and businesses across the nation, life practically stopped for 120 minutes and only ecstatically restarted when native Roman Fabio Grosso slotted in the winning penalty. For unbiased observers watching from the sidelines, this highly charged moment seemed to epitomise the passion, emotion, energy and excitement of Italian football, a game of style and skill that, for all its associated baggage, is as closely reflective of the Italian personality as Puccini or pizza.

Opera: Let the Fat Lady Sing

At the stadium, your beloved *squadra* (team) hits the field to the roar of Verdi. OK, so you might not be first in line to see *Rigoletto* at La Fenice, but Italy's opera legacy remains a source of pride. After all, not only did you invent the art form, you gave the world some of its greatest composers and compositions. Gioachino Rossini (1792–1868) transformed Pierre Beaumarchais' *Le Barbier de Séville* (The Barber of Seville) into one of the greatest comedic operas, Giuseppe Verdi (1813–1901) produced the epic *Aida,* while Giacomo Puccini (1858–1924) delivered staples such as *Tosca, Madama Butterfly* and *Turandot.*

Lyrical, intense and dramatic – it's only natural that opera bears the 'Made in Italy' label. Track pants might be traded in for tuxedos, but Italy's opera crowds can be just as ruthless as their pitch-side counterparts. A centuries-old tradition, the dreaded *fischi* (mocking whistles) still possess a mysterious power to blast singers right off stage. In December 2006, a substitute in street clothes had to step in for Sicilian-French star tenor Roberto Alagna when his off-night aria met with vocal disapproval at Milan's legendary La Scala. Best not to get them started about musicals and 'rock opera', eh?

The word diva was invented for legendary sopranos such as Parma's Renata Tebaldi and Italy's adopted Greek icon Maria Callas, whose rivalry peaked when *Time* quoted Callas saying that comparing her voice to Tebaldi's was like comparing 'champagne and Coca-Cola'. Both were fixtures at La Scala, along with the wildly popular Italian tenor to whom others are still compared, Enrico Caruso. Tenor Luciano Pavarotti (1935–2007) remains beloved for attracting broader public attention to opera, while bestselling blind tenor Andrea Bocelli became a controversial crossover sensation with what critics claim are overproduced arias sung with a strained upper register. Newer generations of stars include soprano Fiorenza Cedolins, who performed a requiem for the late Pope John Paul II, recorded *Tosca* arias with Andrea Bocelli and scored encores in Puccini's iconic *La Bohème* at the Arena di Verona Festival. Younger still is celebrated tenor Francesco

Italy's culture of corruption and *calcio* (football) is captured in *The Dark Heart of Italy,* in which English expat author Tobias Jones wryly observes, 'Footballers or referees are forgiven nothing; politicians are forgiven everything.'

Genoa airport has an exception to the standard 100ml restriction on liquids allowed in cabin luggage – but only for Genovese pesto. Tourists may carry up to 500g of pesto. The catch – you must first donate 50 cents to a children's charity.

MUSIC FOR THE MASSES

Most of the music you'll hear booming out of Italian cafes to inspire sidewalk singalongs is Italian *musica leggera* (popular music), a term covering homegrown rock, jazz, folk, hip-hop and pop ballads. The scene's annual highlight is the Sanremo Music Festival (held at San Remo's Teatro Ariston and televised on RAI1), a Eurovision-style song comp responsible for launching the careers of chart-topping contemporary acts like Eros Ramazzotti, Giorgia, Laura Pausini and, more recently, singer-songwriter Marco Mengoni. In 2013, Mengoni won Sanremo for his ballad 'L'essenziale', using the same song later that year to represent Italy at Eurovision. Two years later, operatic pop trio Il Volo took their winning hit 'Grande amore' to Eurovision, the soaring anthem winning Italy third place. The trend was continued in 2019, when Sanremo champion Mahmood took the song 'Soldi' to Europe's campy song comp. The Sardinian-speaking Italian who has an Egyptian father and professes to sing 'Moroccan pop' was runner-up to Holland's Duncan Laurence.

In the early 1960s, Sanremo helped launch the career of living music legend, Mina Mazzini. Famed for her powerful, three-octave voice and a musical versatility spanning pop, soul, blues, R&B and swing, the songstress dominated the charts throughout the 1960s and 1970s, her emancipated image and frank tunes about love and sex ruffling a few bourgeois feathers.

Towering over all is the legendary songwriter and producer Giorgio Moroder. Hailing from South Tyrol, Moroder made his name in Germany in the early 1970s where he built a career writing and producing pioneering electronic and disco acts. He is often called the 'Father of Disco' for his part in producing and cowriting the 1977 Donna Summer hit 'I Feel Love'. Moroder later gravitated into film music where he won three Academy Awards, most notably for the song 'Take my Breath Away' from the movie *Top Gun*. He has also amassed numerous Grammys and Golden Globes and worked with a who's who of rock and pop artists from Bowie and Blondie to Janet Jackson and Daft Punk.

Meli, a regular fixture at many of the world's great opera houses. Much sadder, however, was the fate of promising tenor Salvatore Licitra. Famed for stepping in for Pavarotti on his final show at New York's Metropolitan Opera, the 43-year-old died tragically after a motorcycle accident in 2011.

Italy on Page & Screen

From ancient Virgil to the recently deceased Umberto Eco, Italy's literary canon is awash with world-renowned scribes. The Renaissance alone coughed up Boccaccio, Petrarch and Dante Alighieri, a language-shaping trio who, communally, are often referred to as the *tre corone* (three crowns) of Italian literature. The nation's film stock is equally robust. Sift through movie credits packed with visionary directors like Fellini and Rossellini, iconic stars such Marcello Mastroianni and that trademark Italian pathos.

Literature

Latin Classics

Roman epic poet Virgil (aka Vergilius) from Mantua spent 11 years and 12 books tracking the outbound adventures and inner turmoil of Trojan hero Aeneas, from the fall of Troy to the founding of Rome. Virgil died in 19 BC with just 60 lines to go in his *Aeneid,* a kind of sequel to Greek epic poet Homer's *Iliad* and *Odyssey.* As Virgil himself observed: 'Time flies'.

Fellow Roman Ovid (Ovidius) from Abruzzo was also skilled at telling a ripping tale. His *Metamorphoses* chronicled civilisation from murky mythological beginnings to Julius Caesar, and his how-to seduction manual *Ars amatoria* (The Art of Love) inspired countless Casanovas. Despite his popularity, Ovid was banished to the ancient Black Sea settlement of Tomis by Augustus in 8 AD. The emperor's motive remains a mystery to this day, with theories ranging from Ovid's association with people opposed to his rule, to the poet's knowledge of a supposedly incestuous relationship between Augustus and his daughter or granddaughter.

Timeless Poets

Some literature scholars claim that Shakespeare stole his best lines and plot points from earlier Italian playwrights and poets. Debatable though this may be, the Bard certainly had stiff competition from 13th-century Dante Alighieri as the world's finest romancer. Dante broke with tradition in *La divina commedia* (The Divine Comedy; c 1307–21) by using the familiar Italian, not the formal Latin, to describe travelling through the circles of hell in search of his beloved Beatrice. Petrarch (aka Francesco Petrarca), a contemporary and pen pal of Boccaccio, added wow to Italian woo with his eponymous sonnets, applying a strict structure of rhythm and rhyme to romance the idealised Laura.

If sonnets aren't to your taste, try 1975 Nobel laureate Eugenio Montale, who wrings poetry out of the creeping damp of everyday life, or Ungaretti, whose WWI poems hit home with a few searing syllables.

Cautionary Fables

The most universally beloved Italian fabulist is Italo Calvino, whose titular character in *Il barone rampante* (The Baron in the Trees; 1957) takes to the treetops in a seemingly capricious act of rebellion that makes others rethink their own earthbound conventions. In Dino Buzzati's *Il deserto dei Tartari* (The Tartar Steppe; 1940), an ambitious officer posted to a mythical Italian border is besieged by boredom, thwarted expectations

For Dante with a pop-culture twist, check out Sandow Birk and Marcus Sanders' satirical, slangy translation of *The Divine Comedy,* which sets *Inferno* in hellish Los Angeles traffic, *Purgatorio* in foggy San Francisco and *Paradiso* in New York.

and disappearing youth while waiting for enemy hordes to materialise – a parable drawn from Buzzati's own dead-end newspaper job.

Over the centuries, Niccolo Machiavelli's *Il principe* (The Prince; 1532) has been referenced as a handy manual for Mussolini types, but also as a cautionary tale against unchecked 'Machiavellian' authority.

Crime Pays

Crime fiction and *gialli* (mysteries) dominate Italy's best-seller list, and one of its finest writers is Gianrico Carofiglio, the former head of Bari's anti-Mafia squad. Carofiglio's novels include the award-winning *Testimone inconsapevole* (Involuntary Witness; 2002), which introduces the shady underworld of Bari's hinterland. The scribe's latest novel is *L'estate fredda* (The Cold Summer; 2016), a hard-hitting tale set against the especially gruesome Mafia violence that marked 1992.

Art also imitates life for judge and novelist Giancarlo de Cataldo, whose best-selling novel *Romanzo criminale* (Criminal Romance; 2002) spawned both a TV series and film. Another crime writer with page-to-screen success is Andrea Camilleri, his savvy Sicilian inspector Montalbano starring in capers like *Il gioco degli specchi* (Game of Mirrors; 2011).

Umberto Eco gave the genre an intellectual edge with his medieval detective tale *Il nome della rosa* (The Name of the Rose; 1980) and *Il pendolo di Foucault* (Foucault's Pendulum; 1988). In Eco's *Il cimitero di Praga* (The Prague Cemetery; 2010), historical events merge with the tale of a master killer and forger.

Historical Epics

Set during the Black Death in Florence, Boccaccio's *Decameron* (c 1350–53) has a visceral gallows humour that foreshadows Chaucer and Shakespeare. Italy's 19th-century struggle for unification parallels the story of star-crossed lovers in Alessandro Manzoni's *I promessi sposi* (The Betrothed; 1827, definitive version released 1842), and causes an identity crisis among Sicilian nobility in Giuseppe Tomasi di Lampedusa's *Il gattopardo* (The Leopard; published posthumously in 1958).

Wartime survival strategies are chronicled in Elsa Morante's *La storia* (History; 1974) and in Primo Levi's autobiographical account of Auschwitz in *Se questo è un uomo* (If This Is a Man; 1947). WWII is the uninvited guest in *Il giardino dei Finzi-Contini* (The Garden of the Finzi-Continis; 1962), Giorgio Bassani's tale of a crush on a girl whose aristocratic Jewish family attempts to disregard the rising tide of anti-Semitism. In Margaret Mazzantini's *Venuto al mondo* (Twice Born; 2008), it's the Bosnian War that forms the backdrop to a powerful tale of motherhood and loss.

Social Realism

Italy has always been its own sharpest critic and several 20th-century Italian authors captured their own troubling circumstances with unflinching accuracy. Grazia Deledda's *Cosima* (1937) is her fictionalised memoir of coming of age and into her own as a writer in rural Sardinia. Deledda became one of the first women to win the Nobel Prize for Literature (1926) and set the tone for such bittersweet recollections of rural life as Carlo Levi's *Cristo si è fermato a Eboli* (Christ Stopped at Eboli; 1945).

Jealousy, divorce and parental failings are grappled with by pseudonymous author Elena Ferrante in her brutally honest *I giorni dell'abbandono* (The Days of Abandonment; 2002). In 2014, Ferrante published *Storia della bambina perduta* (The Story of the Lost Child), the final installment in her so-called Neapolitan series, four novels exploring the life-long friendship of two women born into a world of poverty, chaos and violence in Naples.

Confronting themes also underline Alessandro Pipero's *Persecuzione* (Persecution; 2010), which sees an esteemed oncologist accused of child

Italy's most coveted literary prize, the Premio Strega, is awarded annually to a work of Italian prose fiction. Its youngest recipient to date is physicist and writer Paolo Giordano, who, at 26, won for his debut novel *La solitudine dei numeri primi* (The Solitude of Prime Numbers; 2008).

Italy's north–south divide is the focus of Luca Miniero's comedy smash *Benvenuti al Sud* (Welcome to the South; 2010). An adaptation of French film *Bienvenue chez les Ch'tis* (Welcome to the Sticks; 2008), it tells of a northern postmaster sent to a small Campanian town, bulletproof vest in tow.

molestation. Its sequel, *Inseparabili* (2012), won the 2012 Premio Strega literature prize.

Cinema

Neorealist Grit

Out of the smouldering ruins of WWII emerged unflinching tales of woe, including Roberto Rossellini's *Roma, città aperta* (Rome: Open City; 1945), a story of love, betrayal and resistance in Nazi-occupied Rome. In Vittorio De Sica's Academy-awarded *Ladri di biciclette* (The Bicycle Thieves; 1948), a doomed father attempts to provide for his son without resorting to crime in war-ravaged Rome, while Pier Paolo Pasolini's *Mamma Roma* (1962) revolves around an ageing prostitute trying to make an honest living for herself and her deadbeat son. More recently, Gianfranco Rosi's Oscar-nominated documentary *Fuocoammare* (Fire at Sea; 2016) has drawn comparisons to the neorealist movement in its confronting, moving exploration of the European refugee crisis as played out on the island of Lampedusa.

Crime & Punishment

Italy's acclaimed contemporary dramas combine the truthfulness of classic neorealism, the taut suspense of Italian thrillers and the psychological revelations of Fellini. Among the best is Matteo Garrone's brutal Camorra exposé *Gomorra* (2008). Based on Roberto Saviano's award-winning novel, the film won the Grand Prix at the 2008 Cannes Film Festival before inspiring a successful spin-off TV series.

Paolo Sorrentino's *Il divo* (2008) explores the life of former prime minister Giulio Andreotti, from his migraines to his alleged Mafia ties. The entanglement of organised crime and Rome's political class is at the heart of Stefano Sollima's neo-noir *Suburra* (2015), while Mafiosi also appear in the deeply poignant *Cesare deve morire* (Caesar Must Die; 2012). Directed by octogenarian brothers Paolo and Vittorio Tavianian, this award-winning documentary tells the story of maximum-security prisoners preparing to stage Shakespeare's *Julius Caesar*. Italy's political and social ills drive Gabriele Mainetti's acclaimed film *Lo chiamavano Jeeg Robot* (They Call Me Jeeg; 2015), which gives Hollywood's superhero genre a gritty local twist.

Romance all'Italiana

It's only natural that a nation of hopeless romantics should provide some of the world's most tender celluloid moments. In Michael Radford's *Il postino* (The Postman; 1994), exiled poet Pablo Neruda brings poetry and passion to a drowsy Italian isle and a misfit postman, played with heartbreaking subtlety by the late Massimo Troisi. Another classic is Giuseppe Tornatore's Oscar-winning *Nuovo cinema paradiso* (Cinema Paradiso; 1988), a bittersweet tale about a director who returns to Sicily and rediscovers his true loves: the girl next door and the movies. In Silvio Sordini's *Pane e tulipani* (Bread and Tulips; 2000), a housewife left behind at a tour-bus pit stop runs away to Venice, where she befriends an anarchist florist, an eccentric masseuse and a suicidal Icelandic waiter – and gets pursued by an amateur detective. Equally contemporary is Ferzan Özpetek's *Mine vaganti* (Loose Cannons; 2010), a situation comedy about two gay brothers and their conservative Pugliese family.

Spaghetti Westerns

Emerging in the mid-1960s, Italian-style Westerns had no shortage of high-noon showdowns featuring flinty characters and Ennio Morricone's terminally catchy whistled tunes (*doodle-oodle-ooh, wah wah wah...*). Top of the directorial heap was Sergio Leone, whose Western debut *Per un pugno di dollari* (A Fistful of Dollars; 1964) kick-started a young Clint Eastwood's

Italian acting greats Sophia Loren and the late Marcello Mastroianni appeared together in 13 films, including Vittorio De Sica's classics *Ieri, oggi, domani* (Yesterday, Today, Tomorrow; 1963) and *Matrimonio all'italiana* (Marriage Italian Style; 1964). Their last on-screen union was in Robert Altman's catwalk comedy *Prêt-à-Porter* (1994).

Rome's Cinecittà is Europe's largest film studio complex and the historic hub of the Italian film industry. Aside from homegrown productions, the complex has served as a shooting location for numerous Hollywood films, including *Ben-Hur* (1959) and *Cleopatra* (1963), as well as the small-screen hit *The New Pope* (2019).

LOCATION! LOCATION!

Italy's cities, hills and coastlines set the scene for countless celluloid classics. Top billing goes to Rome, where Gregory Peck gives Audrey Hepburn a fright at the Bocca della Verità in William Wyler's *Roman Holiday* (1953) and Anita Ekberg cools off in the Trevi Fountain in Federico Fellini's *La dolce vita* (The Sweet Life; 1960). Fellini's love affair with the Eternal City culminated in his silver-screen tribute, *Roma* (1972), while Woody Allen paid tribute to the city in the romantic comedy *To Rome with Love* (2012).

Florence's Piazza della Signoria recalls James Ivory's *Room with a View* (1985). Siena's Piazza del Palio and Piazza della Paglietta both featured in the 22nd James Bond instalment, *Quantum of Solace* (2008). Venice enjoys a cameo in *The Talented Mr Ripley* (1999), while fans of *Il postino* (The Postman; 1994) will recognise Procida's pastel-hued Corricella. The cavernous landscape of Basilicata's Matera moonlights as Palestine in Mel Gibson's *Passion of the Christ* (2004). Naples' elegant *palazzi,* fin-de-siècle cafes and tailors are flaunted in Gianluca Migliarotti's fashion-documentary film *E poi c'è Napoli* (And Then There is Naples; 2014). The city also stars in Turkish-Italian director Ferzan Özpetek's thriller, *Napoli velata* (2018).

movie career and morphed into a now-legendary trilogy that helped reshape world cinema (ironically the movies were filmed in Spain). Leone followed up with his 'Once Upon a Time' trilogy starting in 1968 when he relaunched the career of Henry Fonda in *C'era una volta il West* (Once Upon a Time in the West; 1968), a story about a revenge-seeking widow.

Tragicomedies

Italy's best comedians pinpoint the exact spot where pathos intersects with the funny bone. A group of ageing pranksters turn on one another in Mario Monicelli's *Amici miei* (My Friends; 1975), a satire reflecting Italy's own postwar midlife crisis. Midlife crisis also underscores Paolo Sorrentino's Oscar-winning *La grande bellezza* (The Great Beauty; 2013), a Fellini-style tale that revolves around Jep Gambardella, an ageing, hedonistic bachelor haunted by lost love and memories of the past.

Contemporary woes feed Massimiliano Bruno's biting *Viva l'Italia* (2012), its cast of corrupt politicians and nepotists cutting close to the nation's bone. Italy is slapped equally hard by Matteo Garrone's *Reality* (2012). Winner of the Grand Prix at the 2012 Cannes Film Festival, the darkly comic film centres on a Neapolitan fishmonger desperately seeking fame through reality TV. The foibles of modern Italian life are also pulled into sharp focus in Paolo Genovese's *Perfetti sconosciuti* (Perfect Strangers; 2016), an award-winning comedy-drama in which three couples and a bachelor disclose each other's private text messages and phone calls in an attempt to prove they have nothing to hide.

Darkest of all, however, remains actor-director Roberto Benigni's Oscar-winning *La vita è bella* (Life is Beautiful; 1997), in which a father tries to protect his son from the brutalities of a Jewish concentration camp by pretending it's all a game.

Shock & Horror

Sunny Italy's darkest dramas deliver more style, suspense and falling bodies than Prada platform heels on a slippery Milan runway. In Michelangelo Antonioni's *Blow-Up* (1966) a swinging-'60s fashion photographer spies dark deeds unfolding in a photo of an elusive Vanessa Redgrave. Gruesome deeds unfold at a ballet school in Dario Argento's *Suspiria* (1977), while in Mario Monicelli's *Un borghese piccolo piccolo* (An Average Little Man; 1977), an ordinary man goes to extraordinary lengths for revenge. The latter stars Roman acting great Alberto Soldi in a standout example of a comedian nailing a serious role.

It may be an international staple these days, but the term paparazzi stems from Federico Fellini's La dolce vita (1960), which features a newspaper photographer named Paparazzo. It's said that Fellini's inspiration for the character's name was a word in dialect used to describe the buzzing sound of a mosquito.

Survival Guide

Directory A–Z

Accessible Travel

Italy is not an easy country for travellers with disabilities. Cobblestone streets and pavements blocked by parked cars and scooters make getting around difficult for wheelchair users. And while many buildings have lifts, they are not always wide enough for wheelchairs. Not a lot has been done to make life easier for hearing- or vision-impaired travellers either. However, awareness of accessibility issues and a culture of inclusion are steadily growing.

If you have an obvious disability and/or appropriate ID, many museums and galleries offer free admission for yourself and a companion.

Arriving in Italy

→ Airline companies will arrange assistance at airports if you notify them of your needs in advance. For help at Rome's Fiumicino or Ciampino airports contact ADR Assistance (www.adrassistance.it).

→ To reach Rome from Fiumicino Airport, the wheelchair-accessible

Leonardo Express (www.trenitalia.com; one-way €14) train runs to Stazione Termini. Private wheelchair-accessible transfers are also available 24/7 from both Fiumicino and Ciampino airports – book online at www.transfers-rome-civitavecchia.com/wheelchair-rome-taxi-transfers.

Getting Around

→ If travelling by train, you can arrange assistance through SalaBlu online (https://salabluonline.rfi.it) or by calling 800 90 60 60 (from a landline) or 02 32 32 32 (from a landline or mobile).

→ Visit the information page of Rete Ferroviaria Italiana (www.rfi.it/rfi-en/for-persons-with-disability) for full details of services offered and barrier-free stations.

→ Many urban buses are wheelchair-accessible; however some of the stops may not be – ask before you board.

→ Some taxis are equipped to carry passengers in wheelchairs; ask for a taxi for a *sedia a rotelle* (wheelchair).

→ If you are driving, EU disabled parking permits

are recognised in Italy, giving you the same parking rights that local drivers with disabilities have.

Travel Agencies

Rome & Italy (☑06 4425 8441; www.romeanditaly.com/tourism-for-disabled; Via Giuseppe Veronese 50; ⊘9am-8pm) This mainstream travel agency has a well-developed accessible-tourism arm that offers customised tours, accessible accommodation, and equipment and vehicle hire. Its Wheely Trekky service, which uses a specially designed sedan/rickshaw with sherpas, allows wheelchair users to access many otherwise inaccessible archaeological sites.

Fausta Trasporti (☑06 540 33 62; http://accessibletransportationrome.com) Has a fleet of wheelchair-accessible vehicles that can carry up to seven people, including three wheelchair users. It's based in Rome, but operates day trips to Lazio, Tuscany, Umbria and Campania.

Accessible Italy (www.accessibleitaly.com) A San Marino–based nonprofit company that runs guided tours and provides services for people with disabilities, including equipment rental and adapted-vehicle hire, and can arrange personal assistants.

Sage Traveling (www.sagetraveling.com) A US-based accessible-travel agency that offers tailor-made tours to assist mobility-impaired travellers in Europe. Check out its website for detailed access guides to Florence, Naples, Rome and Venice.

BOOK YOUR STAY ONLINE

For more accommodation reviews by Lonely Planet authors, check out http://lonelyplanet.com/hotels/. You'll find independent reviews, as well as recommendations on the best places to stay. Best of all, you can book online.

Resources

Village for All (www.villageforall.net/en) Performs on-site audits of tourist facilities in Italy and San Marino. Most of the 67 facilities are accommodation providers, ranging from camping grounds to high-class hotels.

Tourism without Barriers (www.turismosenzabarriere.it) Has a searchable database of accessible accommodation and tourist attractions in Tuscany, with a scattering of options in other regions.

Fondazione Cesare Serono (www.fondazioneserono.org/disabilita/spiagge-accessibili/spiagge-accessibili) A list (in Italian) of accessible beaches.

Lonely Planet (http://shop.lonelyplanet.com/accessible-travel) Download Lonely Planet's free Accessible Travel guide.

Accommodation

For information on accommodation and the best places to stay in Italy, please see the Accommodation chapter (p32).

Customs Regulations

Entering Italy from a non-EU country you can bring in the following duty-free.

Spirits & liqueurs	1L
Wine	4L (or 2L of fortified wine)
Cigarettes	200
Other goods	up to a value of €300/430 (travelling by land/sea)

On leaving the EU, non-EU citizens can reclaim value-added tax (IVA) on any purchases over €154.94. For more information, see www.italia.it/en/useful-info/rights-for-tourists/customs.html.

Discount Cards

Italy's state museums and sites are free to EU citizens under the age of 18. Discounts also apply to people aged 18 to 25.

Some cities or regions offer their own discount passes, such as the **Roma Pass** (www.romapass.it), which provides free public transport and free or reduced admission to many of Rome's museums.

In many places around Italy, you can also save money by purchasing a *biglietto cumulativo*, a ticket that covers admission to a number of associated sights.

Emergency & Important Numbers

From outside Italy, dial your international access code, Italy's country code (39) then the number (including the first '0').

Country code	☑39
International access code	☑00
Ambulance	☑118
Police	☑112, ☑113
Fire	☑115

Electricity

Type F
230V/50Hz

Type L
220V/50Hz

DISCOUNT CARDS

CARD	WEBSITE	COST	ELIGIBILITY
European Youth Card (Lazio Youth Card)	www.eyca.org	€14	14-30yr
International Student Identity Card (ISIC)	www.isic.org	€15	full-time student
International Teacher Identity Card (ITIC)		€15	full-time teacher
International Youth Travel Card (IYTC)		€15	under 31yr

EATING PRICE RANGES

The following price ranges refer to a meal of two courses (antipasto/*primo* and *secondo*), a glass of house wine, and *coperto* (cover charge) for one person.

€ less than €25

€€ €25–45

€€€ more than €45

These figures represent a halfway point between expensive cities such as Milan and Venice and the considerably cheaper towns across the south. Indeed, a restaurant rated as midrange in rural Sicily might be considered dirt cheap in Milan. Note that most eating establishments add a *coperto* of around €2 to €3. Some also include a *servizio* (service charge) of 10% to 15%.

Food & Drink

For detailed information on eating and drinking in Italy, see Eat & Drink Like a Local (p46).

Health

Before You Go
HEALTH INSURANCE

Italy has a public health system (*Servizio Sanitario Nazionale, SSN*) that is legally bound to provide emergency care to everyone.

EU nationals are entitled to reduced-cost, sometimes free, medical care with a **European Health Insurance Card** (EHIC), available from your home health authority. Non-EU citizens should take out medical insurance.

If you need insurance, make sure to get a policy that covers you for the worst possible scenario, such as an accident requiring emergency repatriation.

Find out in advance if your insurance plan will make payments directly to providers or reimburse you later for overseas health expenditures.

Also, check if there is a reciprocal arrangement between your country and Italy. If there is, you may be covered for essential medical treatment and some subsidised medications. Australia,

for instance, has such an agreement; carry your Medicare card.

VACCINATIONS

No jabs are required to travel to Italy, though the World Health Organization (WHO) recommends that all travellers should be covered for diphtheria, tetanus, the measles, mumps, rubella, polio and hepatitis B.

In Italy
AVAILABILITY & COST OF HEALTH CARE

Health care is readily available throughout Italy, but standards can vary significantly.

Pharmacists can advise on medical matters and sell over-the-counter medications for minor illnesses. They can also point you in the right direction if you need more specialised help.

In large city-centre pharmacies (*farmacie*), you'll probably find someone who speaks a little English.

Pharmacies, marked by a green cross, generally keep shop hours, typically opening from 8.30am to 7.30pm Monday to Friday and on Saturday mornings. Outside these hours, they open on a rotational basis. When closed, a pharmacy is legally required to post a list of places open in the vicinity.

In the larger cities, English-speaking doctors are often available for house calls or appointments through private clinics.

For emergency treatment, head to the *pronto soccorso* (casualty department) of an *ospedale* (public hospital), where you can also get emergency dental treatment.

If you need an ambulance anywhere in Italy, call 118.

TAP WATER

Tap water in Italy is safe to drink. The only exception is where a tap is marked '*Acqua non potabile*' (Water not suitable for drinking).

Insurance

A travel-insurance policy to cover theft, loss and medical problems is a very good idea. It may also cover you for cancellation or delays to your travel arrangements.

Paying for tickets with a credit card can often provide limited travel accident insurance and you may be able to reclaim payments if the operators don't deliver. Ask your credit-card company what it will cover.

Worldwide travel insurance is available at www.lonelyplanet.com/travel-insurance. You can buy, extend and claim online anytime – even if you're already on the road.

Internet Access

➡ Free wi-fi is widely available in hotels, hostels, B&Bs and *agriturismi* (farm stays), though signal quality varies. Some places also provide laptops/computers.

➡ Many bars and cafes offer free wi-fi.

➡ Numerous Italian cities and towns offer public wi-fi hotspots, including Rome, Milan, Bologna, Florence and Venice. To use them, you'll need to register online using a credit card or an Italian mobile number.

➡ A free smartphone app, wifi.italia.it, allows you to connect to participating networks through a single login. It gets mixed reports.

Language Courses

Italian language courses are run by private schools and universities throughout Italy. Rome and Florence are teeming with schools, while most other cities and major towns have at least one. For a list, see Saena Iulia (www.saenaiulia.it); click on 'Schools in Italy'.

Università per Stranieri di Perugia (Map p622;☑075 574 65 59; www.unistrapg.it; Piazza Fortebraccio 4) Italy's foremost academic institution for foreigners, Perugia's University for Foreigners offers courses in language, literature, history, art, music, opera and architecture.

Università per Stranieri di Siena (www.unistrasi.it) As well as degree courses for international students, this Siena institution runs language and cultural courses in one of Italy's most beautiful medieval cities.

Italian Foreign Ministry (www.esteri.it) Its website lists 83 worldwide branches of the *Istituto Italiano di Cultura* (IIC), a government-sponsored organisation that promotes Italian culture and language. It's an excellent resource for studying Italian before you leave or finding out more about learning opportunities in Italy. Locations include Australia (Melbourne and Sydney), the UK (London and Edinburgh), Ireland (Dublin), Canada (Toronto and Montreal) and the USA (Los Angeles, San

Francisco, Chicago, New York and Washington, DC). Click on 'Foreign Policy', then 'Culture Diplomacy' and 'The Network of Italian Cultural Institutes'.

Legal Matters

The most likely reason for a brush with the law is to report a theft. If you have something stolen and you want to claim it on insurance, you must make a statement to the police, as insurance companies won't pay without official proof of a crime.

Drugs & Alcohol

➡ If you're caught with what the police deem to be a dealable quantity of hard or soft drugs, you risk prison sentences of between two and 22 years.

➡ Possession for personal use is punishable by administrative sanctions, although first-time offenders might get away with a warning.

➡ The legal limit for blood-alcohol when driving is 0.05%; it's zero for drivers under 21 and those who have had a licence for less than three years. Random breath tests do occur.

Police

The Italian police is divided into three main bodies: the *polizia*, who wear navy-blue jackets; the *carabinieri*, in a black uniform with a red stripe; and the grey-clad *guardia di finanza* (fiscal police), responsible for fighting tax evasion and drug smuggling. If you run into

trouble, you're most likely to end up dealing with the *polizia* or *carabinieri*.

Your Rights

➡ You should be given verbal and written notice of the charges laid against you within 24 hours by arresting officers.

➡ You have no right to a phone call upon arrest, though the police will inform your family with your consent. You may also ask the police to inform your embassy or consulate.

➡ The prosecutor must apply to a judge for you to be held in pre-trial custody (depending on the seriousness of the offence) within 48 hours of arrest.

➡ Once you've been arrested a lawyer is appointed by the state to assist you. Alternatively, you can appoint a lawyer for yourself at any time after your arrest.

➡ You have the right not to respond to questions without the presence of a lawyer.

LGBTQ+ Travellers

Homosexuality is legal (over the age of 16) and even widely accepted, but Italy is fairly conservative in its attitudes and discretion is still wise. Overt displays of affection by LGBTQ+ couples can attract a negative response, especially in smaller towns.

There are gay venues in Rome, Milan and Bologna, and a handful in places such as Florence and

ITALIAN POLICE ORGANISATIONS

POLIZIA DI STATO (STATE POLICE)	GENERAL CRIME AND MAINTENANCE OF PUBLIC ORDER AND SECURITY
Carabinieri (military police)	General crime and public order (often overlapping with the *polizia di stato*)
Vigili Urbani (local traffic police)	Parking tickets, towed cars, municipal administration
Guardia di Finanza	Financial crime, tax evasion, drug smuggling
Corpo Forestale	Environmental protection

Naples. Some coastal towns and resorts (such as the Tuscan town of Torre del Lago, Taormina in Sicily and Gallipoli in Puglia) are popular gay holiday spots in summer.

Arcigay (☎051 095 72 41; www.arcigay.it; Via Don Minzoni 18, Cassero LGBT Center; ⌚9.30am-5pm Mon-Fri) Bologna-based national organisation for the LGBTQ+ community.

Circolo Mario Mieli di Cultura Omosessuale (☎06 541 39 85, Rainbow Help Line 800 110611; www.mariomieli.org; Via Efeso 2a; ⌚11am-6pm Mon-Fri; Ⓜ Basilica San Paolo) Rome-based cultural centre that organises debates, cultural events and social functions.

Coordinamento Lesbiche Italiano (www.clrbp.it; Via San Francesco di Sales 1b; 🚌 Lungotevere della Farnesina) The national organisation for lesbians holds regular conferences, literary evenings and cultural events at its Rome headquarters.

Gay.it (www.gay.it) Website featuring LGBTQ+ news, features and gossip.

Pride (www.prideonline.it) Culture, politics, travel and health with an LGBTQ+ focus.

Maps

The city maps provided by Lonely Planet, combined with the free local maps available at tourist offices, will be sufficient for most needs.

For more specialised maps, try bookseller Feltrinelli (www.lafeltrinelli.it).

Touring Club Italiano (www.touringclubstore.com) Italy's largest map publisher offers a comprehensive 1:200,000, 592-page road atlas of Italy (€54.90), as well as 1:400,000 maps of northern, central and southern Italy (€8.50). It also produces 15 regional maps at 1:200,000 (€8.50), as well as a series of walking guides with maps (€14 to €16). Discounts are available for online purchases.

Tabacco (www.tabaccoeditrice.com) Publishes 1:25,000 scale walking maps (€9.20), covering the northeast Alps and Dolomites.

Kompass (www.kompass-italia.it) Publishes 1:25,000 and 1:50,000 scale hiking maps of various parts of Italy, plus a nice series of 1:70,000 cycling maps.

Stanfords (www.stanfords.co.uk) Excellent UK-based shop that stocks many useful maps, including cycling maps.

Money

ATMs

- ATMs (known as *bancomat*) are widely available in Italy, and most will accept cards tied into the Visa, MasterCard, Cirrus and Maestro systems.
- Beware of transaction fees. Every time you withdraw cash, you'll be hit by charges – typically your home bank will charge a foreign-exchange fee and a transaction fee. These might be a flat rate or a percentage of around 1% to 3%. Fees can sometimes be reduced by withdrawing cash from banks affiliated with your home banking institution; check with your bank.
- If an ATM rejects your card, try another one before assuming the problem is with your card.

Credit Cards

- Major cards such as Visa, MasterCard, Eurocard, Cirrus and Eurocheques are widely accepted. Amex is also recognised, although it's less common than Visa or MasterCard.
- Virtually all midrange and top-end hotels accept credit cards, as do most restaurants and large shops. Some cheaper *pensioni* (pensions), trattorias and pizzerias only accept cash. Don't rely on credit cards at smaller museums or galleries.
- Note that using your credit card in ATMs can be costly. On every transaction there's a fee, which can reach US$10 with some credit-card issuers, as well as interest per withdrawal. Check with your issuer before leaving home.
- If your card is lost, stolen or swallowed by an ATM, phone to have an immediate stop put on its use.
- Always inform your bank of your travel plans to avoid your card being blocked for payments made in unusual locations.

Currency

Italy's currency is the euro. The seven euro notes come in denominations of €500, €200, €100, €50, €20, €10 and €5. The eight euro coins are in denominations of €2 and €1, then 50, 20, 10, five, and two cents, and finally one cent.

Changing Money

- You can change money at a *cambio* (exchange office) or post office. Some banks might change money, though many now only do this for account holders. Post offices and banks offer the best rates; exchange offices keep longer hours, but watch for high commissions and inferior rates.
- Take your passport or photo ID when exchanging money.

Exchange Rates

Australia	A$1	€0.62
Canada	C$1	€0.69
Japan	¥100	€0.83
New Zealand	NZ$1	€0.57
Switzerland	Sfr1	€0.91
UK	UK£1	€1.16
US	US$1	€0.90

For current exchange rates, see www.xe.com.

Tipping

Italians are not big tippers. The following is a rough guide.

Taxis Optional, but most round up to the nearest euro.

Hotels Tip porters about €5 at high-end hotels.

Restaurants Service (*servizio*) is generally included – otherwise, a euro or two is fine in pizzerias and trattorias, and 5% to 10% in smart restaurants.

Bars Not necessary, although many leave small change if drinking coffee at the bar, usually €0.10 or €0.20.

Opening Hours

Opening hours vary throughout the year. We've provided high-season hours, which are generally in use over summer. Summer refers to the period between April and September (or October); winter is October (or November) to March.

Banks 8.30am–1.30pm and 2.45pm–4.30pm Monday to Friday

Bars & cafes 7.30am–8pm, sometimes to 1am or 2am

Clubs 10pm–4am or 5am

Restaurants noon–3pm and 7.30pm–11pm (later in summer)

Shops 9am–1pm and 3.30pm–7.30pm (or 4pm to 8pm) Monday to Saturday. In main cities some shops stay open at lunchtime and on Sunday mornings. Some shops close Monday mornings.

Post

➜ Italy's postal system, **Poste Italiane** (☏ 803 160; www.poste.it), is reasonably reliable.

➜ To locate a post office and check postage rates see www.poste.it (in Italian).

➜ Opening hours vary but for large post offices they are typically 8.20am to 7pm Monday to Friday, to 12.35pm Saturdays. All post offices close two hours earlier than normal on the last business day of the month.

➜ Stamps (*francobolli*) are available at post offices and authorised tobacconists (look for the official sign: a white 'T' on a black background).

Rates

Letters up to 20g cost €1.10 to destinations in Italy, €1.15 to Zone 1 (Europe and the Mediterranean basin), €2.40 to Zone 2 (other countries in Africa, Asia and the Americas) and €3.10 to Zone 3 (Australia and New Zealand). For more important items, use registered mail (*raccomandata*), which costs €5.40 to Italian addresses, €7.10 to Zone 1, €8.40 to Zone 2 and €9.05 to Zone 3.

Public Holidays

Most Italians take their annual holiday in August. Many businesses and shops close for at least part of the month, particularly around *Ferragosto* (Feast of the Assumption) on 15 August. *Settimana Santa* (Easter Holy Week) is another busy holiday period.

National public holidays include the following:

Capodanno (New Year's Day) 1 January

Epifania (Epiphany) 6 January

Pasquetta (Easter Monday) March/April

Giorno della Liberazione (Liberation Day) 25 April

Festa del Lavoro (Labour Day) 1 May

Festa della Repubblica (Republic Day) 2 June

Ferragosto (Feast of the Assumption) 15 August

Festa di Ognisanti (All Saints' Day) 1 November

Festa dell'Immacolata Concezione (Feast of the Immaculate Conception) 8 December

Natale (Christmas Day) 25 December

Festa di Santo Stefano (Boxing Day) 26 December

Safe Travel

Italy is generally a safe country to travel in. Note, however, petty theft can be a problem – pickpockets and thieves are active in touristy areas and on crowded public transport. In case of theft or loss, always report the incident to the police within 24 hours and ask for a statement.

Telephone

Mobile Phones

➜ Italian mobile phones operate on the GSM 900/1800 network, which is compatible with the rest of Europe and Australia but not always with the North American GSM or CDMA systems – check with your service provider.

GOVERNMENT TRAVEL ADVICE

The following government websites offer up-to-date travel advisories.

Australian Department of Foreign Affairs & Trade (www.smartraveller.gov.au)

British Foreign & Commonwealth Office (www.gov.uk/foreign-travel-advice)

Global Affairs Canada (www.travel.gc.ca/travelling/advisories)

New Zealand Ministry of Foreign Affairs & Trade (www.safetravel.govt.nz)

US Department of State (https://travel.state.gov)

➡ The cheapest way of using your mobile is to buy a prepaid (*prepagato*) Italian SIM card. TIM (*Telecom Italia Mobile*; www.tim.it), Wind (www.wind.it), Vodafone (www.vodafone.it) and Tre (www.tre.it) all offer SIM cards and have retail outlets across the country. You can then top up as you go, either online or at one of your provider's shops.

➡ Note that by Italian law all SIM cards must be registered in Italy, so make sure you have your passport or ID card when you buy one.

Domestic Calls

➡ Italian area codes begin with 0 and consist of up to four digits. They are an integral part of all phone numbers and must be dialled even when calling locally.

➡ Mobile-phone numbers begin with a three-digit prefix starting with a 3.

➡ Toll-free numbers are known as *numeri verdi* and usually start with 800.

➡ Some six-digit national rate numbers are also in use (such as those for Alitalia and Trenitalia).

International Calls

➡ To call Italy from abroad, dial your country's international access code, then Italy's country code (39) followed by the area code of the location you want (including the first zero) and the rest of the number.

➡ To call abroad from Italy dial 00, then the country code, followed by the full number.

➡ Avoid making international calls from hotels, as rates are high.

➡ The cheapest way to call is to use an app such as Skype or Viber, connecting through the wi-fi at your hotel/B&B etc.

Time

➡ All of Italy occupies the Central European Time Zone, which is one hour ahead of GMT. When it is noon in London, it is 1pm in Italy.

➡ Daylight-saving time (when clocks move forward one hour) starts on the last Sunday in March and ends on the last Sunday in October.

➡ Italy operates on a 24-hour clock, so 3pm is written as 15:00.

Toilets

Besides in museums, galleries, department stores and train stations, there are few public toilets in Italy. If you're caught short, the best thing to do is to nip into a cafe or bar. The polite thing to do is to order something at the bar.

You may need to pay to use some public toilets (usually €0.50 to €1.50).

Tourist Information

Italy's national tourist board, **ENIT – Agenzia Nazionale del Turismo**, has offices across the world. Its website, www.italia.it, provides both practical information and inspirational travel ideas.

Tourist Offices

➡ Most cities and towns in Italy have a tourist office that can provide maps, lists of local accommodation and information on sights in the area.

➡ In larger towns and major tourist areas, English is generally spoken, along with other languages, depending on the region (for example, German in Alto Adige, French in Valle d'Aosta).

➡ Most tourist offices will respond to written or telephone requests for information.

➡ Office hours vary: in major tourist destinations, offices generally open daily, especially in the summer high season. In smaller centres, they generally observe regular office hours and open Monday through to Friday, perhaps also on Saturday mornings.

➡ Affiliated information booths (at train stations and airports, for example) may keep slightly different hours.

➡ Tourist offices in Italy go under a variety of names, depending on who they're administered by (the local municipality, province, or region), but most perform similar functions. On the ground, look for signs to the Ufficio Turistico.

Regional Tourist Authorities

Regional offices are generally more concerned with marketing and promotion than offering a public information service. However, they have useful websites.

TOURIST OFFICES

OFFICE NAME	DESCRIPTION	MAIN FOCUS
Informazione e Accoglienza Turistica (IAT) or Azienda Autonoma di Soggiorno e Turismo (AAST)	Municipal tourist office in larger towns and cities	Town-specific information only (bus routes, museum opening times etc)
Pro Loco	Local tourist office in smaller towns and villages	Similar to IAT and AAST

PRACTICALITIES

Newspapers Key national dailies include centre-left *la Repubblica* (www.repubblica.it) and its conservative rival *Corriere della Sera* (www.corriere.it). For the Vatican's take on affairs, *L'Osservatore Romano* (www.osservatoreromano.va) is the Holy See's official newspaper.

Television The main terrestrial channels are Rai 1, 2 and 3 run by Rai (www.rai.it), Italy's state-owned national broadcaster, and Canale 5, Italia 1 and Rete 4 run by Mediaset (www.mediaset.it), the commercial TV company founded and still partly owned by Silvio Berlusconi.

Radio As well as the principal Rai channels (Radiouno, Radiodue, Radiotre), there are hundreds of commercial radio stations operating across the country. Popular Rome-based stations include Radio Capital (www.capital.it) and Radio Città Futura (www.radio cittafutura.it). Vatican Radio (www.radiovaticana.va) broadcasts in Italian, English and other languages.

Weights & Measures Italy uses the metric system.

Smoking Banned in enclosed public spaces, which includes restaurants, bars, shops and public transport.

Abruzzo (www.abruzzoturismo.it)

Basilicata (www.basilicata turistica.it)

Calabria (www.turiscalabria.it)

Campania (www.incampania.com)

Emilia-Romagna (www.emilia romagnaturismo.it)

Friuli Venezia Giulia (www. turismo.fvg.it)

Lazio (www.visitlazio.com)

Le Marche (www.turismo. marche.it)

Liguria (www.lamialiguria.it)

Lombardy (www.in-lombardia.it)

Molise (www.visitmolise.eu)

Piedmont (www.piemonte italia.eu)

Puglia (www.viaggiareinpuglia.it)

Sardinia (www.sardegna turismo.it)

Sicily (www.visitsicily.info)

Trentino-Alto Adige (www.visit trentino.it)

Tuscany (www.visittuscany.com)

Umbria (www.umbriatourism.it)

Valle d'Aosta (www.lovevda.it)

Veneto (www.veneto.eu)

Visas

➡ Italy is one of the 26 European countries making up the Schengen area. There are no customs controls when travelling between Schengen countries, so the visa rules that apply to Italy apply to all Schengen countries.

➡ EU citizens do not need a visa to enter Italy.

➡ Nationals of some other countries, including Australia, Canada, Israel, Japan, New Zealand, Switzerland and the USA, do not need a visa for stays of up to 90 days.

➡ Nationals of other countries will need a Schengen tourist visa – to check requirements see www.schengenvisainfo. com/tourist-schengen-visa.

➡ All non-EU and non-Schengen nationals entering Italy for more than 90 days or for any reason other than tourism (such as study or work) may need a specific visa. Check http:// vistoperitalia.esteri.it for details.

➡ Ensure your passport is valid for at least six months beyond your departure date from Italy.

Electronic Authorisation

In July 2018, the European Parliament approved plans for an electronic vetting system for travellers to the Schengen area.

Under the terms of the European Travel Information & Authorisation System (ETIAS), all non-EU travellers will have to fill in an online form and pay a €7 fee before they can travel to a Schengen country.

The system is set to come into force in 2022.

For further details, see www.etiaseurope.eu.

Permesso di Soggiorno

➡ A *permesso di soggiorno* (permit to stay, also referred to as a residence permit) is required by all non-EU nationals who stay in Italy longer than three months. In theory, you should apply for one within eight days of arriving in Italy.

➡ EU citizens do not require a *permesso di soggiorno*, but are required to register with the local registry office (Ufficio Anagrafe) if they stay for more than three months.

➡ Check exact requirements on www.poliziadistato.it – click on the English tab and then follow the links.

➡ Further information is also available at www. portaleimmigrazione.it.

Volunteering

Concordia International Volunteer Projects (www.concordiavolunteers.org.uk) Lists opportunities for short-term community-based projects covering the environment, archaeology and the arts.

European Youth Portal (www.europa.eu/youth) Has various links suggesting volunteering options across Europe. Navigate to the Volunteering page.

Legambiente (http://international.legambiente.it) Italy's best known conservation group offers environmentally focused volunteering opportunities.

World Wide Opportunities on Organic Farms (www.wwoof.it) For a membership fee of €35 this organisation provides a list of farms looking for volunteer workers.

Women Travellers

Italy is not a dangerous country for women to travel in. That said, solo women travellers may occasionally be subjected to unwanted attention and harassment.

Intense staring is common in Italy, though note that this is not necessarily limited to women travellers.

If ignoring unwanted male attention doesn't work, tell your interlocutor that you're waiting for your *marito* (husband) or *fidanzato* (boyfriend). If necessary, walk away.

If you feel yourself being groped on a crowded bus or metro, a loud '*che schifo!*' (how disgusting!) will draw attention to the incident. Otherwise take all the usual precautions you would in any other part of the world.

You can report incidents to the police, who are required to press charges.

Due to the presence in certain areas of African women who have been trafficked into prostitution, there have been reports of some black travellers being mistaken for sex workers.

Work

EU citizens and nationals of Norway, Iceland, Switzerland and Liechtenstein are legally entitled to work in Italy. To stay in the country for more than three months you are simply required to register at your local registry office (*ufficio anagrafe*).

Non-EU citizens will need a work visa to enter Italy, and a *permesso di soggiorno per lavoro* (permit to stay for work) to stay in the country.

For the visa, you'll first need to secure a job offer. Your prospective employer will then apply for work authorisation for you. If the application is successful, your local Italian embassy or consulate will be informed and you will be issued with a work visa. Note, however, that Italy operates a visa quota system for most occupations,

so a visa will only be offered if the relevant quota has not been met by the time your application is processed.

Once in Italy, you'll need to apply for a *permesso di soggiorno* (permit to stay). You'll have to do this within eight days of arriving in the country. See www.poliziadistato.it for details on the application process.

Italy has reciprocal, working-holiday visa agreements with Canada, Australia, New Zealand and South Korea. With this type of visa, you can stay in Italy for one year and work for six months. To be eligible you must be aged between 18 and 30. Contact your local Italian embassy for more information.

Popular jobs in Italy include English teaching, either at a language school or as a freelancer. While some language schools take on teachers without professional qualifications, the more reputable (and better-paying) establishments will require you to have a TEFL (Teaching of English as a Foreign Language) certificate.

Useful job-seeker websites for English-language teachers include ESL Employment (www.eslemployment.com) and TEFL (www.tefl.org.uk/tefl-jobs-centre).

Au pairing is another popular work option; check www.aupairworld.com for more information on work opportunities and tips.

Transport

GETTING THERE & AWAY

A plethora of airlines link Italy with the rest of the world. In Europe, competition between low-cost carriers has led to a significant reduction in the cost of flying from other European countries. Alternatively, there are excellent rail and bus connections, especially to destinations in northern Italy, while car and passenger ferries serve Italian ports from across the Mediterranean.

Flights, cars and tours can be booked online at lonely planet.com/bookings.

Entering the Country

Entering Italy from most other parts of the EU is generally uncomplicated, with no border checkpoints and no customs thanks to the Schengen Agreement. Document and customs checks apply if arriving from (or departing to) a non-Schengen country.

Passport

➡ EU and Swiss citizens can travel to Italy with a national identity card. All other nationalities must have a valid passport and may be required to fill out a landing card (at airports).

➡ By law you are supposed to carry your passport or an ID card with you at all times in Italy.

➡ You'll need to present an ID card/passport when you check in at a hotel/B&B etc.

➡ In theory there are no passport checks at land crossings from neighbouring countries, but random controls do occasionally take place.

Air

Airports & Airlines

Italy's main intercontinental airports are Rome's **Fiumicino Airport** (Leonardo da Vinci International Airport; ☑06 6 59 51; www.adr.it/fiumicino), officially known as Leonardo da Vinci, and Milan's **Aeroporto Malpensa** (MXP; ☑02 23 23 23; www.milanomalpensa-airport.com; ®Malpensa Express). Both are served by nonstop flights from around the world. Venice's **Marco Polo Airport** (☑flight information 041 260 92 60; www.venice airport.it; Via Galileo Gallilei 30/1, Tessera) is also served by a handful of intercontinental flights.

Dozens of international airlines compete with the country's national carrier, **Alitalia** (☑89 20 10; www.alitalia.com), rated a three-star airline by UK aviation research company Skytrax. If you're flying from Africa or Oceania, you'll generally need to change planes at least once en route to Italy.

Cross-European flights serve plenty of other Italian cities. Europe's leading national carriers include Alitalia, Air France, British Airways, Lufthansa and KLM.

Low-cost carriers, led by Ryanair and easyJet, fly from a growing number of European cities to more than two dozen Italian destinations, typically landing in smaller airports such as Rome's **Ciampino Airport** (☑06 6 59 51; www.adr.it/ciampino).

Departure Tax

Departure tax is included in the price of a ticket.

Land

There are plenty of options for entering Italy by train, bus or private vehicle.

Border Crossings

Aside from the coastal roads linking Italy with France and Slovenia, border crossings into Italy mostly involve tunnels through the Alps (open year-round) or mountain passes (seasonally closed and requiring snow chains). The list below outlines the major points of entry.

Austria From Innsbruck to Bolzano via A22/E45 (Brenner Pass); Villach to Tarvisio via A23/E55.

CLIMATE CHANGE & TRAVEL

Every form of transport that relies on carbon-based fuel generates CO_2, the main cause of human-induced climate change. Modern travel is dependent on aeroplanes, which might use less fuel per kilometre per person than most cars but travel much greater distances. The altitude at which aircraft emit gases (including CO_2) and particles also contributes to their climate change impact. Many websites offer 'carbon calculators' that allow people to estimate the carbon emissions generated by their journey and, for those who wish to do so, to offset the impact of the greenhouse gases emitted with contributions to portfolios of climate-friendly initiatives throughout the world. Lonely Planet offsets the carbon footprint of all staff and author travel.

France From Nice to Ventimiglia via A10/E80; Modane to Turin via A32/E70 (Fréjus Tunnel); Chamonix to Courmayeur via A5/E25 (Mont Blanc Tunnel).

Slovenia From Sežana to Trieste via SR58/E70.

Switzerland From Martigny to Aosta via SS27/E27 (Grand St Bernard Tunnel); Lugano to Como via A9/E35.

Bus

Buses are the cheapest overland option to Italy but services are less frequent, less comfortable and significantly slower than the train.

Eurolines (☑0861 199 19 00; www.eurolines.eu) A consortium of coach companies with offices throughout Europe. Italy-bound buses run to Milan, Rome, Bologna, Venice and other Italian cities.

FlixBus (☑02 9475 9208; www.flixbus.it) German-owned company offering both international and inter-regional routes. Direct international routes to Italy include: Milan from Paris, Lyon, Nice, Zurich, Geneva, Basel and Munich; Venice from Ljubljana, Vienna, Budapest, Zurich, Lyon and Paris. The InterFlix bus pass (€99) allows travel on five FlixBus European routes in a three-month period.

Car & Motorcycle

FROM CONTINENTAL EUROPE

➡ Every vehicle travelling across an international border should display the nationality plate of its country of registration.

➡ Always carry the vehicle's registration certificate and evidence of third-party insurance. If driving an EU-registered vehicle, your home country insurance is sufficient. Ask your insurer for a European Accident Statement (EAS) form, which can simplify matters in the event of an accident. The form can also be downloaded from http://cartraveldocs.com/european-accident-statement.

➡ A European breakdown assistance policy is a good investment and can be obtained through Italy's national automobile association, the **Automobile Club d'Italia** (ACI; ☑80 31 16, from a foreign mobile 800 116800; www.aci.it).

➡ Italy's scenic roads are tailor-made for motorcycle touring, and motorcyclists swarm into the country every summer. With a motorcycle you can often enter restricted-traffic areas in cities. Crash helmets and a motorcycle licence are compulsory.

FROM THE UK

You can take your car to Italy, via France, by ferry or the Eurotunnel Shuttle rail service (www.eurotunnel.com). The latter runs up to four times per hour between Folkestone and Calais (35 minutes) at peak times.

For breakdown assistance, both the **AA** (www.theaa.com) and the **RAC** (www.rac.co.uk) offer comprehensive packages covering Italy.

Train

Regular trains on two western lines connect Italy with France (one along the coast and the other from Turin into the French Alps). Trains from Milan head north into Switzerland and on towards the Benelux countries. Further east, two main lines head for the main cities in Central and Eastern Europe. Those crossing the Brenner Pass go to Innsbruck, Stuttgart and Munich. Those crossing at Tarvisio proceed to Vienna, Salzburg and Prague. The main international train line to Slovenia crosses near Trieste.

Depending on distances covered, rail can be highly competitive with air travel. Those travelling from neighbouring countries to northern Italy will find it's frequently more comfortable, less expensive and only marginally more time-consuming than flying.

Those travelling longer distances (say, from London, Spain, northern Germany or Eastern Europe) will generally find flying cheaper and quicker. Bear in mind, however, that the train is a much greener way to go – a trip by rail can contribute up to 10 times fewer carbon dioxide emissions per person than the same trip by air.

Useful resources include **Oui-sncf** (https://en.oui.sncf/en), an online booking service run by France's national rail operator, and **Deutsche Bahn** (www.deutschebahn.com/en), the website of Germany's national rail company.

FROM CONTINENTAL EUROPE

➤ The comprehensive European Rail Timetable (UK£19.99, digital version UK£13.99), updated regularly, is available for purchase at www.europeanrailtimetable.eu, as well as at a handful of bookshops in the UK and continental Europe (see the website for details).

➤ Reservations on international trains to/from Italy are always advisable, and sometimes compulsory.

➤ Some international services include transport for private cars.

➤ Consider taking long journeys overnight, as the supplemental fare for a sleeper will often cost less than an Italian hotel.

FROM THE UK

➤ Trains to Italy from the UK involve a change in France.

➤ The high-velocity Eurostar (www.eurostar.com) connects London with Paris, Lyon, Avignon and Marseille. Direct trains to Italy then run from Paris, Lyon and

Marseille. Alternatively, you can get a train ticket that includes crossing the Channel by ferry.

➤ For fare information and ticket bookings, check out **Loco 2** (www.loco2.com), a clear and easy-to-use booking site.

Sea

Multiple ferry companies connect Italy with ports across the Mediterranean. Some routes only operate in summer, when ticket prices also rise. Fares for vehicles depend on the size of the vehicle.

The helpful website www.directferries.co.uk allows you to search routes and compare prices between international ferry companies. Another useful resource for Italy–Greece ferries is www.ferries.gr.

International ferry companies that serve Italy:

Adria Ferries (☏071 5021 1621; www.adriaferries.com) Runs ferries from Trieste, Ancona and Bari to Durrës (Albania).

Anek Lines (☏071 207 23 46; www.anekitalia.com) Runs ferries from Venice, Ancona and Bari to Greece.

GNV (Grandi Navi Veloci; ☏010 209 45 91; www.gnv.it) Services from Genoa, Civitavecchia and

Naples to Sicily and Sardinia. International routes include Palermo (Sicily) to Tunis, Genoa to Barcelona, Tunis and Tangier, Civitavecchia to Tunis, and Bari to Durrës.

Grimaldi Lines (☏081 49 64 44; www.grimaldi-lines.com) International routes include Venice, Ancona and Brindisi to Corfu, Igoumenitsa and Patras (Greece); Civitavecchia to Barcelona (Spain) and Tunis (Tunisia); Savona to Barcelona and Tangier (Morocco); Salerno and Palermo to Tunis; Catania and Salerno to Malta.

Jadrolinija (☏071 228 41 00; www.jadrolinija.hr) Runs ferries from Ancona to Zadar, Split and Stari Grad (Croatia). It also sails from Bari to Dubrovnik (Croatia) and Bar (Montenegro).

Minoan Lines (☏071 20 17 08; www.minoan.it) Runs ferries from Venice and Ancona to Corfu, Igoumenitsa and Patras (Greece).

Moby Lines (☏800 804020; www.moby.it) International routes include Genoa, Livorno, Piombino and Santa Teresa di Gallura (Sardinia) to Corsica.

Montenegro Lines (☏Bar +382 3030 3469; www.montenegrolines.net) Operates ferries from Bari to Bar (Montenegro) and Dubrovnik (Croatia).

SNAV (☏081 428 55 55; www.snav.it) Runs ferries from Ancona to Croatia (Split).

TRANSPORT SEA

DIRECT TRAINS TO ITALY FROM CONTINENTAL EUROPE

FROM	TO	FREQUENCY	DURATION (HR)	COST (€)
Geneva	Milan	4 daily	4	49-85
Geneva	Venice	1 daily	7	119
Munich	Rome	1 nightly	13	119
Munich	Florence	1 nightly	10	70
Munich	Venice	1 daily/1 nightly	6½	60-80
Paris	Milan	3 daily/1 nightly	7½/10¼	69-125
Paris	Turin	3 daily	5½-6	69-84
Paris	Venice	1 nightly	14½	127
Vienna	Milan	1 nightly	14	50
Vienna	Rome	1 nightly	14	99
Zurich	Milan	6 daily	3¾	29-61

Superfast (☎Athens +30 210 891 97 00; www.superfast.com) Sails from Ancona, Bari and Venice to Corfu, Igoumenitsa and Patras (Greece).

Venezia Lines (☎041 847 09 03; www.venezialines.com; ⊗9am-5pm daily May-Sep, Mon-Fri Oct-Apr; ⊗San Basilio)

Ventouris (☎080 876 14 51; www.ventouris.gr; Nuova Stazione Marittima di Bari)

Virtu Ferries (☎Catania 095 703 12 11; www.virtuferries.com)

GETTING AROUND

Air

Italy offers an extensive network of internal flights. Airport taxes are included in the price of your ticket.

Italy's flag carrier, **Alitalia** (☎89 20 10; www.alitalia.com), flies domestically, serving cities across the Italian mainland and on Sicily and Sardinia. Several low-cost airlines also operate in the country.

Air Italy (☎89 29 28; www.airitaly.com) Olbia-based airline operating domestic and international flights.

Blue Panorama (☎895 8988985; www.blue-panorama.

INTERNATIONAL FERRY ROUTES FROM ITALY

DESTINATION COUNTRY	DESTINATION PORT(S)	ITALIAN PORT(S)	COMPANY
Albania	Durrës	Bari	Ventouris, GNV
	Durrës	Bari, Ancona, Trieste	Adria Ferries
Croatia	Dubrovnik	Bari	Jadrolinija, Montenegro Lines
	Split	Ancona	SNAV
	Split, Zadar, Stari Grad	Ancona	Jadrolinija
	Umag, Poreč, Rovinj, Pula	Venice	Venezia Lines
France (Corsica)	Bastia	Livorno, Genoa, Piombino	Moby Lines
	Bonifacio	Santa Teresa di Gallura	Moby Lines
Greece	Corfu, Igoumenitsa, Patras	Bari	Superfast, Anek Lines
	Corfu, Igoumenitsa, Zakynthos, Cephalonia	Bari	Ventouris
	Igoumenitsa, Patras	Brindisi	Grimaldi Lines
	Igoumenitsa, Patras	Ancona	Superfast, Anek Lines, Grimaldi Lines, Minoan Lines
	Igoumenitsa, Patras	Venice	Superfast, Anek Lines, Grimaldi Lines, Minoan Lines
Malta	Valletta	Pozzallo	Virtu Ferries
Montenegro	Bar	Bari	Montenegro Lines, Jadrolinija
Morocco	Tangier	Genoa	GNV
	Tangier	Savona	Grimaldi Lines
Slovenia	Piran	Venice	Venezia Lines
Spain	Barcelona	Genoa	GNV
	Barcelona	Civitavecchia, Savona, Porto Torres	Grimaldi Lines
Tunisia	Tunis	Genoa, Civitaveccchia, Palermo	GNV
	Tunis	Civitavecchia, Palermo, Salerno	Grimaldi Lines

com) Operates flights from Rome and Milan to Lampedusa and from Milan and Bologna to Reggio Calabria.

easyJet (☑199 201840; www.easyjet.com) Operates domestic flights to cities across the country, including Milan, Naples, Bari, Palermo and Olbia.

Ryanair (☑02 8998 0500; www.ryanair.com) Operates domestic routes to mainland airports, as well as to/from Sardinia and Sicily.

Volotea (☑06 9450 2850; www.volotea.com) Operates international and domestic flights to Italian destinations.

Useful websites for comparing fares include: www.skyscanner.com; www.kayak.com; www.azfly.it.

Bicycle

Cycling is very popular in northern Italy, less so in the south. The following tips will help ensure a pedal-happy trip.

➡ If bringing your own bike, you'll need to disassemble and pack it for the journey. You may need to pay an airline surcharge.

➡ Make sure to bring tools, spare parts, a helmet, lights and a secure bike lock.

➡ Bikes are prohibited on Italian *autostrade* (motorways).

➡ Bikes can be wheeled onto regional trains displaying the bicycle logo. Simply purchase a separate bicycle ticket (*supplemento bici*), valid for 24 hours (€3.50). Certain international trains also allow transport of assembled bicycles for €12, paid on board. Bikes dismantled and stored in a bag can be taken for free, even on night trains. For more information, see the dedicated page on Trenitalia's website: www.trenitalia.com/en/services/travelling_with_yourbike.html.

➡ Bikes are sometimes free to transport on ferries. On some routes, you might have to pay a small supplement.

➡ In the UK, Cycling UK (www.cyclinguk.org) can help you plan your tour or organise a guided tour. Membership costs £46.50 for adults, £29.50 for seniors and £22 for students.

➡ Bikes are available for hire in most Italian towns. City bikes start at €10/50 per day/week; mountain bikes a bit more. A growing number of Italian hotels also offer free bikes for guests.

Boat

Craft *Navi* (large ferries) sail to Sicily and Sardinia, while *traghetti* (smaller ferries) and *aliscafi* (hydrofoils) serve the smaller islands. Most ferries carry vehicles; hydrofoils do not.

Routes Main embarkation points for Sicily and Sardinia are Genoa, Livorno, Civitavecchia and Naples. Ferries for Sicily also leave from Villa San Giovanni and Reggio di Calabria. Main arrival points in Sardinia are Cagliari, Arbatax, Olbia and Porto Torres; in Sicily, Palermo, Catania, Trapani and Messina.

Timetables and tickets Comprehensive website Direct Ferries (www.directferries.co.uk) allows you to search routes, compare prices and book tickets for Italian ferry routes.

Cabins and Seating Travellers can book a two- to four-person cabin or a *poltrona*, an airline-style armchair. Deck class (which allows you to sit/sleep in lounge areas or on deck) is available only on some ferries.

Bus

Buses are particularly useful in mountainous territories and remote inland areas where there's little rail infrastructure.

Routes Bus companies provide everything from meandering local routes to fast, reliable intercity connections.

Timetables These are available on bus-company websites and at tourist offices. Local coastal services are often seasonal with more buses in summer holiday periods. Conversely, in small towns and villages, there'll often be more buses in school term time.

Tickets Tickets are generally competitively priced with the train. In larger cities most intercity bus companies have ticket offices (usually at or near the main bus station) or sell tickets through agencies. In villages and even some good-sized towns, tickets are sold in bars or on the bus.

Advance booking Generally not required, but advisable for overnight or long-haul trips in high season.

Car & Motorcycle

Italy has an extensive network of roads. Most are in good condition but a lack of maintenance in some areas means that you should be prepared for potholes and bumpy surfaces, particularly on smaller, secondary roads.

➡ Autostrada (Italy's toll-charging motorways). On road signs they're marked by a white 'A' and number on a green background. The main north–south artery is the A1, aka the Autostrada del Sole (the 'Motorway of the Sun'), which runs from Milan to Naples via Bologna, Florence and Rome. The main road south from Naples to Reggio di Calabria is the A3. To drive on an autostrada pick up a ticket at the entry barrier and pay (by cash or credit card) as you exit.

➡ *Strade statali* (state highways) – Represented on maps by 'S' or 'SS'. Vary

LIMITED TRAFFIC ZONES

Many Italian cities, including Rome and Florence, have designated their historic centres as Limited Traffic Zones (ZTL). These areas are off-limits to unauthorised vehicles and entry points are covered by street cameras. If you're caught entering one without the necessary permission you risk a fine. Contact your hotel or accommodation supplier if you think you'll need to access a ZTL.

from four-lane highways to two-lane roads. The latter can be extremely slow, especially in mountainous regions.

➡ *Strade regionali* (regional highways) – Like SS roads but administered by regional authorities rather than the state. Coded 'SR' or 'R'.

➡ *Strade provinciali* (provincial highways) – Smaller and slower roads. Coded 'SP' or 'P'.

For information about distances, driving times and fuel costs, see https://en.mappy.com. Additional information, including traffic conditions and toll costs, is available at www.auto strade.it.

Automobile Associations

Italy's national automobile association, the **Automobile Club d'Italia** (ACI; ☎80 31 16, from a foreign mobile 800 116800; www.aci.it) is a driver's best resource in Italy. It offers 24-hour roadside assistance, available on a pay-per-incident system, and its website has comprehensive information on driving in Italy (www.aci.it/laci/driving-in-italy/driving-in-italy-information-for-visiting-motorists.html).

Driving Licences

All EU driving licences are valid in Italy. Travellers from other countries should obtain an International Driving Permit (IDP) through their national automobile association.

A licence is required to ride a scooter – a car licence will do for bikes up to 125cc; for anything over 125cc you'll need a motorcycle licence.

Fuel

➡ Staffed filling stations (*benzinai*, *stazioni di servizio*) are widespread. Smaller stations tend to close between about 1pm and 3.30pm and sometimes also on Sunday afternoons.

➡ Many stations have self-service (*fai da te*) pumps that you can use 24 hours a day. To use one insert a bank note into the payment machine and press the number of the pump you want.

➡ Unleaded petrol is marked as *benzina senza piombo*; diesel as *gasolio*.

➡ Prices vary from one station to another. At the time of writing, unleaded petrol was averaging €1.46 per litre; diesel €1.29 per litre.

Hire

CAR

➡ Prebooking costs less than hiring a car once you arrive in Italy.

➡ Online booking agency Rentalcars.com compares the rates of numerous rental companies.

➡ Renters must generally be 21 or over, with a credit card and home-country driving licence or IDP.

➡ Consider hiring a small car. Doing so will reduce your fuel expenses and make it

easier to negotiate narrow city lanes and tight parking spaces.

➡ Check with your credit-card company to see if it offers a Collision Damage Waiver, which covers you for additional damage if you use the card to pay for your car.

➡ The following companies have pick-up locations throughout Italy.

Auto Europe (www.autoeurope.it)

Avis (www.avisautonoleggio.it)

Budget (www.budgetinter national.com)

Europcar (www.europcar.it)

Hertz (www.hertz.it)

Italy by Car (www.italybycar.it)

Maggiore (www.maggiore.it)

Sixt (www.sixt.it)

MOTORCYCLE

Agencies throughout Italy rent motorbikes, ranging from small Vespas to large touring bikes. Prices start at around €35/150 per day/week for a 50cc scooter; upwards of €80/400 per day/week for a 650cc motorcycle.

Road Rules

➡ Drive on the right; overtake on the left.

➡ It's obligatory to wear seat belts (front and rear), to drive with your headlights on outside built-up areas, and to carry a warning triangle and fluorescent waistcoat in case of breakdown.

➡ Wearing a helmet is compulsory on all two-wheeled vehicles.

➡ Motorbikes can enter most restricted traffic areas in Italian cities, and traffic police generally turn a blind eye to motorcycles or scooters parked on footpaths.

➡ The blood alcohol limit is 0.05%; it's zero for drivers under 21 and for those who have had their licence for less than three years.

Unless otherwise indicated, speed limits are as follows.

➡ 130km/h on autostradas

➡ 110km/h on main roads outside built-up areas

➡ 90km/h on secondary roads outside built-up areas

➡ 50km/h in built-up areas

Local Transport

Major cities all have good transport systems, including bus, tram and metro networks. In Venice, the main public transport option are the *vaporetti* (small passenger ferries) which ply the city's waterways.

Bus & Metro

➡ Extensive *metropolitane* (metros) exist in Rome, Milan, Naples and Turin, with smaller metros in Genoa and Catania. The *Minimetrò* in Perugia connects the train station with the city centre.

➡ Cities and towns of any size will have an *urbano* (urban) and *extraurbano* (suburban) bus network. Services are generally limited on Sundays and public holidays.

➡ Purchase bus, tram and metro tickets before boarding, then validate them once on board or at metro entry barriers. If you're caught with an unvalidated ticket you risk a fine (between €50 and €110).

➡ Buy tickets at *tabaccai* (tobacconist's shops), newsstands and ticket booths, or from dispensing machines at bus and metro stations. Tickets usually cost around €1 to €2. Many cities offer good-value 24-hour or daily travel cards.

Taxi

➡ You'll find taxi ranks outside most train and bus stations. Alternatively, phone for a radio taxi. Radio taxi meters start running from the moment you call for them rather than when you're picked up.

➡ Charges vary from one region to another. As a rough guide, most short city journeys will cost between €10 and €15. Generally, no more than four people are allowed in a single taxi.

➡ Uber is not widespread in Italy – only Uber Black is available and that only in Rome and Milan. An alternative app is MyTaxi.

Train

➡ Trains in Italy are convenient and relatively cheap compared with other European countries. The better train categories are fast and comfortable.

➡ Most trains are run by **Trenitalia** (☑892021; www.trenitalia.com), Italy's national train operator.

➡ Privately owned **Italo** (☑892020; www.italotreno.it) runs high-velocity trains to/from Turin, Milan, Verona, Venice, Bologna, Florence, Rome, Naples and Salerno.

➡ Tickets for regional trains must be validated in the green machines (usually found at the head of platforms) before boarding. Failure to do so could result in a fine.

➡ You do not need to validate tickets printed at home or tickets for Frecciarossa, Frecciargento, Frecciabianca, Italo, InterCity and EuroCity trains as these are valid for a specific train and include a seat reservation.

Italy operates several types of trains.

Regionale The slowest and cheapest trains. They generally stop at all or most stations.

InterCity (IC) Faster services operating between major cities. Their international counterparts are called EuroCity (EC).

Alta Velocità (AV) High-velocity Frecciarossa, Frecciargento, Frecciabianca and Italo trains, with speeds of up to 300km/h and connections to major cities.

Classes & Costs

➡ Ticket prices vary according to the type of train, class of service, time of travel and how far in advance you book.

➡ Most Italian trains have 1st- and 2nd-class seating; a 1st-class ticket typically costs from a third to half more than 2nd-class.

➡ On Frecciarossa trains, 1st class is known as Business Class and 2nd class as Standard.

Reservations

➡ Seat reservations are obligatory on InterCity, Frecciabianca, Frecciargento and Frecciarossa trains.

POPULAR HIGH-VELOCITY TRAIN ROUTES

FROM	TO	DURATION (HR)	PRICE FROM (€)
Turin	Naples	5¾- 6	58
Milan	Rome	3-3½	95
Venice	Florence	2¼	57
Rome	Naples	1¼-1¾	39
Florence	Bologna	35min	29

EURAIL & INTERRAIL PASSES

Generally speaking, you'll need to cover a lot of ground to make a rail pass worthwhile. Before buying, consider where you intend to travel and compare the price of a rail pass to the cost of individual tickets – get prices on the Trenitalia website (www. trenitalia.com).

InterRail (www.interrail.eu) passes, available online and at most major stations and student-travel outlets, are for people who have been a resident in Europe for more than six months. A **Global Pass** encompassing 31 countries comes in 10 versions, ranging from three days' travel within a one-month period to three month's unlimited travel. There are four price categories: youth (12 to 27), adult (28 to 59), senior (60+) and child (4 to 11), with different prices for 1st and 2nd class. The InterRail one-country **Italy Pass** can be used for three to eight days in one month. A **Premium Italy Pass** also exists which includes free seat reservations. The standard Italy Pass doesn't cover reservations which are required on all Italian trains except for slow *regionale* trains. See the website for details and prices.

Eurail (www.eurail.com) passes, available for non-European residents, are good for travel in 31 European countries. They can be purchased online or from travel agencies outside Europe. The Eurail **Global Pass** offers a number of options, from three days of travel within a one-month period to three months of unlimited travel. The **Italy Pass** allows three to eight days of travel in Italy within a one-month period. Like the InterRail pass, Eurail passes do not cover seat reservations, which are necessary on most Italian trains.

Note also that neither InterRail or Eurail passes are valid on Italo trains.

➡ Reservations can be made on the **Trenitalia** (☑892021; www.trenitalia.com) and **Italo** (☑892020; www.italotreno.it) websites, at railway station counters, and self-service ticketing machines, as well as through travel agents.

➡ Both Trenitalia and Italo offer advance purchase discounts. Basically, the earlier you book, the greater the saving. Discounted tickets are limited, and refunds and changes are highly restricted. For all ticket options and prices, see the Trenitalia and Italo websites.

Train Passes

Trenitalia offers various discount passes, including the Carta Verde (€40, for 12- to 26-year-olds) and Carta d'Argento (€30, for over-60s), but these are mainly useful for residents or long-term visitors, as they only pay for themselves with regular use over an extended period.

More interesting for short-term visitors are Eurail and InterRail passes.

Language

Standard Italian is taught and spoken throughout Italy. Regional dialects are an important part of identity in many parts of the country, but you'll have no trouble being understood anywhere if you stick to standard Italian, which we've also used in this chapter.

The sounds used in spoken Italian can all be found in English. If you read our coloured pronunciation guides as if they were English, you'll be understood. The stressed syllables are indicated with italics. Note that ai is pronounced as in 'aisle', ay as in 'say', ow as in 'how', dz as the 'ds' in 'lids', and that r is a strong and rolled sound. Keep in mind that Italian consonants can have a stronger, emphatic pronunciation – if the consonant is written as a double letter, it should be pronounced a little stronger, eg *sonno son*·no (sleep) versus *sono so*·no (I am).

BASICS

Hello.	*Buongiorno.*	bwon·*jor*·no
Goodbye.	*Arrivederci.*	a·ree·ve·*der*·chee
Yes./No.	*Sì./No.*	see/no
Excuse me.	*Mi scusi.* (pol)	mee *skoo*·zee
	Scusami. (inf)	*skoo*·za·mee
Sorry.	*Mi dispiace.*	mee dees·*pya*·che
Please.	*Per favore.*	per fa·*vo*·re
Thank you.	*Grazie.*	*gra*·tsye
You're welcome.	*Prego.*	*pre*·go

WANT MORE?

For in-depth language information and handy phrases, check out Lonely Planet's *Italian Phrasebook*. You'll find it at **shop.lonelyplanet.com**, or you can buy Lonely Planet's iPhone phrasebooks at the Apple App Store.

How are you?		
Come sta/stai? (pol/inf)		*ko*·me sta/stai
Fine. And you?		
Bene. E lei/tu? (pol/inf)		*be*·ne e lay/too
What's your name?		
Come si chiama? (pol)		*ko*·me see *kya*·ma
Come ti chiami? (inf)		*ko*·me tee *kya*·mee
My name is ...		
Mi chiamo ...		mee *kya*·mo ...
Do you speak English?		
Parla/Parli		*par*·la/*par*·lee
inglese? (pol/inf)		een·*gle*·ze
I don't understand.		
Non capisco.		non ka·*pee*·sko

ACCOMMODATION

campsite	*campeggio*	kam·*pe*·jo
guesthouse	*pensione*	pen·*syo*·ne
hotel	*albergo*	al·*ber*·go
youth hostel	*ostello della gioventù*	os·*te*·lo de·la jo·ven·*too*
Do you have a ... room?	*Avete una camera ...?*	a·*ve*·te oo·na *ka*·me·ra ...
double	*doppia con letto matrimoniale*	*do*·pya kon *le*·to ma·tree·mo·*nya*·le
single	*singola*	*seen*·go·la
How much is it per ...?	*Quanto costa per ...?*	*kwan*·to *kos*·ta per ...
night	*una notte*	oo·na *no*·te
person	*persona*	per·*so*·na
air-con	*aria condizionata*	*a*·rya kon·dee·tsyo·*na*·ta
bathroom	*bagno*	*ba*·nyo
window	*finestra*	fee·*nes*·tra

LANGUAGE DIRECTIONS

KEY PATTERNS

To get by in Italian, mix and match these simple patterns with words of your choice:

When's (the next flight)?
A che ora è
(il prossimo volo)?
a ke o·ra e
(eel pro·see·mo vo·lo)

Where's (the station)?
Dov'è (la stazione)?
do·ve (la sta·tsyo·ne)

I'm looking for (a hotel).
Sto cercando
(un albergo).
sto cher·kan·do
(oon al·ber·go)

Do you have (a map)?
Ha (una pianta)?
a (oo·na pyan·ta)

Is there (a toilet)?
C'è (un gabinetto)?
che (oon ga·bee·ne·to)

I'd like (a coffee).
Vorrei (un caffè).
vo·ray (oon ka·fe)

I'd like to (hire a car).
Vorrei (noleggiare
una macchina).
vo·ray (no·le·ja·re
oo·na ma·kee·na)

Can I (enter)?
Posso (entrare)?
po·so (en·tra·re)

Could you please (help me)?
Può (aiutarmi),
per favore?
pwo (a·yoo·tar·mee)
per fa·vo·re

Do I have to (book a seat)?
Devo (prenotare
un posto)?
de·vo (pre·no·ta·re
oon po·sto)

DIRECTIONS

Where's ...?
Dov'è ...?
do·ve ...

What's the address?
Qual'è l'indirizzo?
kwa·le leen·dee·ree·tso

Could you please write it down?
Può scriverlo,
per favore?
pwo skree·ver·lo
per fa·vo·re

Can you show me (on the map)?
Può mostrarmi
(sulla pianta)?
pwo mos·trar·mee
(soo·la pyan·ta)

EATING & DRINKING

What would you recommend?
Cosa mi consiglia?
ko·za mee kon·see·lya

What's the local speciality?
Qual'è la specialità
di questa regione?
kwa·le la spe·cha·lee·ta
dee kwe·sta re·jo·ne

Cheers!
Salute!
sa·loo·te

That was delicious!
Era squisito!
e·ra skwee·zee·to

Please bring the bill.
Mi porta il conto,
per favore?
mee por·ta eel kon·to
per fa·vo·re

I'd like to reserve a table for ...
Vorrei prenotare un tavolo per ...
vo·ray pre·no·ta·re oon ta·vo·lo per ...

(eight) o'clock
le (otto)
le (o·to)

(two) people
(due) persone
(doo·e) per·so·ne

I don't eat ...
Non mangio ...
non man·jo ...

eggs uova wo·va
fish pesce pe·she
nuts noci no·chee

Key Words

bar	locale	lo·ka·le
bottle	bottiglia	bo·tee·lya
breakfast	prima colazione	pree·ma ko·la·tsyo·ne
cafe	bar	bar
dinner	cena	che·na
drink list	lista delle bevande	lee·sta de·le be·van·de
fork	forchetta	for·ke·ta
glass	bicchiere	bee·kye·re
knife	coltello	kol·te·lo
lunch	pranzo	pran·dzo
market	mercato	mer·ka·to
menu	menù	me·noo
plate	piatto	pya·to
restaurant	ristorante	ree·sto·ran·te
spoon	cucchiaio	koo·kya·yo
vegetarian	vegetariano	ve·je·ta·rya·no

Meat & Fish

beef	manzo	man·dzo
chicken	pollo	po·lo
herring	aringa	a·reen·ga
lamb	agnello	a·nye·lo
lobster	aragosta	a·ra·gos·ta
mussels	cozze	ko·tse
oysters	ostriche	o·stree·ke
pork	maiale	ma·ya·le
prawn	gambero	gam·be·ro
salmon	salmone	sal·mo·ne
scallops	capasante	ka·pa·san·te

shrimp	gambero	gam·be·ro
squid	calamari	ka·la·ma·ree
trout	trota	tro·ta
tuna	tonno	to·no
turkey	tacchino	ta·kee·no
veal	vitello	vee·te·lo

Fruit & Vegetables

apple	mela	me·la
beans	fagioli	fa·jo·lee
cabbage	cavolo	ka·vo·lo
capsicum	peperone	pe·pe·ro·ne
carrot	carota	ka·ro·ta
cauliflower	cavolfiore	ka·vol·fyo·re
cucumber	cetriolo	che·tree·o·lo
grapes	uva	oo·va
lemon	limone	lee·mo·ne
lentils	lenticchie	len·tee·kye
mushroom	funghi	foon·gee
nuts	noci	no·chee
onions	cipolle	chee·po·le
orange	arancia	a·ran·cha
peach	pesca	pe·ska
peas	piselli	pee·ze·lee
pineapple	ananas	a·na·nas
plum	prugna	proo·nya
potatoes	patate	pa·ta·te
spinach	spinaci	spee·na·chee
tomatoes	pomodori	po·mo·do·ree

Other

bread	pane	pa·ne
butter	burro	boo·ro
cheese	formaggio	for·ma·jo
eggs	uova	wo·va
honey	miele	mye·le
jam	marmellata	mar·me·la·ta
noodles	pasta	pas·ta
oil	olio	o·lyo
pepper	pepe	pe·pe
rice	riso	ree·zo
salt	sale	sa·le
soup	minestra	mee·nes·tra
soy sauce	salsa di soia	sal·sa dee so·ya
sugar	zucchero	tsoo·ke·ro
vinegar	aceto	a·che·to

Drinks

beer	birra	bee·ra
coffee	caffè	ka·fe
juice	succo	soo·ko
milk	latte	la·te
red wine	vino rosso	vee·no ro·so
tea	tè	te
water	acqua	a·kwa
white wine	vino bianco	vee·no byan·ko

EMERGENCIES

Help!
Aiuto! a·yoo·to

Leave me alone!
Lasciami in pace! la·sha·mee een pa·che

I'm lost.
Mi sono perso/a. (m/f) mee so·no per·so/a

Call the police!
Chiami la polizia! kya·mee la po·lee·tsee·a

Call a doctor!
Chiami un medico! kya·mee oon me·dee·ko

Where are the toilets?
Dove sono i do·ve so·no ee
gabinetti? ga·bee·ne·tee

I'm sick.
Mi sento male. mee sen·to ma·le

SHOPPING & SERVICES

I'd like to buy ...
Vorrei comprare ... vo·ray kom·pra·re ...

I'm just looking.
Sto solo guardando. sto so·lo gwar·dan·do

Can I look at it?
Posso dare un'occhiata? po·so da·re oo·no·kya·ta

How much is this?
Quanto costa questo? kwan·to kos·ta kwe·sto

It's too expensive.
È troppo caro. e tro·po ka·ro

There's a mistake in the bill.
C'è un errore nel conto. che oo·ne·ro·re nel kon·to

SIGNS

Closed	Chiuso
Entrance	Entrata/Ingresso
Exit	Uscita
Men	Uomini
Open	Aperto
Prohibited	Proibito/Vietato
Toilets	Gabinetti/Servizi
Women	Donne

NUMBERS

1	uno	oo·no
2	due	doo·e
3	tre	tre
4	quattro	kwa·tro
5	cinque	cheen·kwe
6	sei	say
7	sette	se·te
8	otto	o·to
9	nove	no·ve
10	dieci	dye·chee
20	venti	ven·tee
30	trenta	tren·ta
40	quaranta	kwa·ran·ta
50	cinquanta	cheen·kwan·ta
60	sessanta	se·san·ta
70	settanta	se·tan·ta
80	ottanta	o·tan·ta
90	novanta	no·van·ta
100	cento	chen·to
1000	mille	mee·lel

ATM	Bancomat	ban·ko·mat
post office	ufficio postale	oo·fee·cho pos·ta·le
tourist office	ufficio del turismo	oo·fee·cho del too·reez·mo

TIME & DATES

What time is it?
Che ora è?   ke o·ra e

It's (two) o'clock.
Sono le (due).   so·no le (doo·e)

Half past (one).
(L'una) e mezza.   (loo·na) e me·dza

in the morning	di mattina	dee ma·tee·na
in the afternoon	di pomeriggio	dee po·me·ree·jo
in the evening	di sera	dee se·ra
yesterday	ieri	ye·ree
today	oggi	o·jee
tomorrow	domani	do·ma·nee

Monday	lunedì	loo·ne·dee
Tuesday	martedì	mar·te·dee
Wednesday	mercoledì	mer·ko·le·dee
Thursday	giovedì	jo·ve·dee
Friday	venerdì	ve·ner·dee
Saturday	sabato	sa·ba·to
Sunday	domenica	do·me·nee·ka

TRANSPORT

boat	nave	na·ve
bus	autobus	ow·to·boos
ferry	traghetto	tra·ge·to
metro	metropolitana	me·tro·po·lee·ta·na
plane	aereo	a·e·re·o
train	treno	tre·no

bus stop	fermata dell'autobus	fer·ma·ta del ow·to·boos
ticket office	biglietteria	bee·lye·te·ree·a
timetable	orario	o·ra·ryo
train station	stazione ferroviaria	sta·tsyo·ne fe·ro·vyar·ya

... ticket	un biglietto ...	oon bee·lye·to
one way	di sola andata	dee so·la an·da·ta
return	di andata e ritorno	dee an·da·ta e ree·tor·no

Does it stop at ...?
Si ferma a ...?   see fer·ma a ...

Please tell me when we get to ...
Mi dica per favore quando arriviamo a ...   mee dee·ka per fa·vo·re kwan·do a·ree·vya·mo a ...

I want to get off here.
Voglio scendere qui.   vo·lyo shen·de·re kwee

I'd like to hire a ...	Vorrei noleggiare una ...	vo·ray no·le·ja·re oo·na ...
bicycle	bicicletta	bee·chee·kle·ta
car	macchina	ma·kee·na
motorbike	moto	mo·to

bicycle pump	pompa della bicicletta	pom·pa de·la bee·chee·kle·ta
child seat	seggiolino	se·jo·lee·no
helmet	casco	kas·ko
mechanic	meccanico	me·ka·nee·ko
petrol	benzina	ben·dzee·na
service station	stazione di servizio	sta·tsyo·ne dee ser·vee·tsyo

Is this the road to ...?
Questa strada porta a ...?   kwe·sta stra·da por·ta a ...

Can I park here?
Posso parcheggiare qui?   po·so par·ke·ja·re kwee

GLOSSARY

abbazia – abbey
agriturismo – farm-stays
(pizza) al taglio – (pizza) by the slice
albergo – hotel
alimentari – grocery shop
anfiteatro – amphitheatre
aperitivo – pre-dinner drink and snack
APT – Azienda di Promozione Turistica; local town or city tourist office
autostrada – motorway; highway

battistero – baptistry
biblioteca – library
biglietto – ticket
borgo – archaic name for a small town, village or town sector

camera – room
campo – field; also a square in Venice
cappella – chapel
carabinieri – police with military and civil duties
Carnevale – carnival period between Epiphany and Lent
casa – house
castello – castle
cattedrale – cathedral
centro storico – historic centre
certosa – monastery belonging to or founded by Carthusian monks
chiesa – church
chiostro – cloister; covered walkway, usually enclosed by columns, around a quadrangle
cima – summit
città – town; city
città alta – upper town
città bassa – lower town
colonna – column
comune – equivalent to a municipality or county; a town or city council; historically, a self-governing town or city
contrada – district
corso – boulevard

duomo – cathedral

enoteca – wine bar
espresso – short black coffee

ferrovia – railway
festa – feast day; holiday
fontana – fountain
foro – forum
funivia – cable car

gelateria – ice-cream shop
giardino – garden
golfo – gulf
grotta – cave

isola – island

lago – lake
largo – small square
lido – beach
locanda – inn; small hotel
lungomare – seafront road/promenade

mar, mare – sea
masseria – working farm
mausoleo – mausoleum; stately and magnificent tomb
mercato – market
monte – mountain

necropoli – ancient name for cemetery or burial site
nord – north
nuraghe – megalithic stone fortress in Sardinia

osteria – casual tavern or eatery

palazzo – mansion; palace; large building of any type
palio – contest
parco – park
passeggiata – evening stroll
pasticceria – cake/pastry shop
pensione – guesthouse
piazza – square
piazzale – large open square
pietà – literally 'pity' or 'compassion'; sculpture, drawing or painting of the dead Christ supported by the Madonna
pinacoteca – art gallery
ponte – bridge

porta – gate; door
porto – port

reale – royal
rifugio – mountain hut; accommodation in the Alps
ristorante – restaurant
rocca – fortress

sala – room; hall
salumeria – delicatessen
santuario – sanctuary; 1. the part of a church above the altar; 2. an especially holy place in a temple (antiquity)
sassi – literally 'stones'; stone houses built in two ravines in Matera, Basilicata
scalinata – staircase
scavi – excavations
sestiere – city district in Venice
spiaggia – beach
stazione – station
stazione marittima – ferry terminal
strada – street; road
sud – south
superstrada – expressway; highway with divided lanes

tartufo – truffle
tavola calda – literally 'hot table'; pre-prepared meals, often self-service
teatro – theatre
tempietto – small temple
tempio – temple
terme – thermal baths
tesoro – treasury
torre – tower
trattoria – simple restaurant
Trenitalia – Italian State Railways; also known as Ferrovie dello Stato (FS)
trullo – conical house in Perugia

vaporetto – small passenger ferry in Venice
via – street; road
viale – avenue
vico – alley; alleyway
villa – town house; country house; also the park surrounding the house

Behind the Scenes

SEND US YOUR FEEDBACK

We love to hear from travellers – your comments keep us on our toes and help make our books better. Our well-travelled team reads every word on what you loved or loathed about this book. Although we cannot reply individually to your submissions, we always guarantee that your feedback goes straight to the appropriate authors, in time for the next edition. Each person who sends us information is thanked in the next edition – the most useful submissions are rewarded with a selection of digital PDF chapters.

Visit **lonelyplanet.com/contact** to submit your updates and suggestions or to ask for help. Our award-winning website also features inspirational travel stories, news and discussions.

Note: We may edit, reproduce and incorporate your comments in Lonely Planet products such as guidebooks, websites and digital products, so let us know if you don't want your comments reproduced or your name acknowledged. For a copy of our privacy policy visit lonelyplanet.com/privacy.

Brett Atkinson

Exploring southern Italy and Sicily with my LP hat on was a great experience thanks to Anna Rita in Bari, Luisa in Lecce and Domenico in Reggio Calabria. Thanks also to Amy in Matera for helping me negotiate the town's storied laneways, and to Tony in Vieste for securing me a slow boat to the Isole Tremiti. Special thanks to Anna Tyler for the commission, and to Carol on our gelato- and *aperitivi*-fuelled reconnaissance trip 12 months earlier.

Alexis Averbuck

Ahhh, Sardinia. My thanks go to this ever-fascinating and gorgeous island, and its warm and welcoming people. It has been a lifelong dream to get to know Sardinia and reality exceeded all fantasies. Huge thanks to my road-warrior sister and Zodiac-skipper, Rachel Averbuck, for dropping everything and joining me in our zippy Fiat cabriolet when I told her how grand it is! Many thanks to Anna Tyler who helmed the project with superb attention to detail, guidance and grace.

Cristian Bonetto

Grazie infinite to all those who shared their love and intimate knowledge of the Mezzogiorno. In Sicily, special thanks to Ornella Tuzzolino, Giorgio Ferravioli and Carla Bellavista, Pierfrancesco Palazzotto, Lorenzo Chiaramonte, Rosario Fillari, Giorgio Puglisi, Gennaro Mattiucci, Ernesto Magri, Giovanni Gurrieri, Joe Brizzi, Giuseppe Savà, Luigi Nifosì, Antonio Adamo, Cesare Setmani, Norma Gritti and Cristina Delli Fiori. In Campania, *grazie di cuore* to my *Re e Regina di Napoli*, Federica Rispoli and Ivan Palmieri, as well as to Igor Milanese.

Gregor Clark

Grazie mille to the many dozens of people who shared their love and knowledge of Sicily, Trentino and South Tyrol with me, especially Fausto Ceschi, Fabiana Mariotti, Micol Beittel, Stefano Musaico, Mark, Giovanna, Angela, Francesco, Marcello, Paola, Carmelina, Marian, Diego and Patrizia. Back in Vermont, big hugs to Gaen, Meigan and Chloe, who always make coming home the best part of the trip.

Peter Dragicevich

I still pinch myself that my work continues to allow me to spend time in such a magical city as Venice, and for that I have editor extraordinaire Anna Tyler to thank. Many thanks to Lonely Planet Local Jo-Ann Titmarsh for your good company and excellent advice on this assignment, and for the wealth of new listings that you had already uncovered. My eternal gratitude goes to my dear friend Bain Duigan, who accompanied me in spirit at least.

Duncan Garwood

A big *grazie* to all the locals and tourist office staff who helped and offered advice: Sara Cappelli, Roberta Magi, Elisa Fabri, Barbara Ravaglia, Cinzia at Narni, Silvia in Perugia, Nicola Santarelli, Luana Fringuelli, Carolina Grisanti, Vania Di Cicco, Ilaria Lucentini and Giulia in Tarquinia. Thanks also to Anna Tyler at Lonely Planet for all her support. Finally, a huge hug to Lidia and the boys, Ben and Nick.

Paula Hardy

Mille grazie to all the creative and passionate people who shared their insights with me. In Venice: Luisella Romeo, Gioele and Heiby Romanelli, Emanuele dal Carlo, Valeria Duflot, Sebastian Fagarazzi, Fabio Carrera, Jo-Ann Titmarsh, Alice Braveri and Anat at the Comunità Ebraica di Venezia. In Friuli: Tatjana Familio, Laura Fiorino, Maja de'Simoni, Roberto Mezzina, Cristiana Fiandra, Susanna Guerrato, Chiara Pigni, Fabio Tarlao, Francesca Boscarol, Alessia Drigo, Elisa Nervi, Anna Cleva, Monica Bertarelli, Raffaella Grasselli, Sonia Macor, and Fabio Stulin for his incredible patience on the road. And thank you Rob for sharing my love of the *bel paese*.

Virginia Maxwell

As always, many locals assisted me in my research for this project. Many thanks to Ilaria Crescioli, Elisa Grisolaghi, Serena Nocciolini, Sean Lawson, Valentina de Pamphilis, Rodolfo Ademollo, Sonia Corsi, Elena Giovenco, Eleonora Sandrelli, Valentina Pierguidi, Maria Guarriello and the staff at Strada Vino Nobile Montepulciano e Sapori Valdichiana Senese, Maja Malbasa, Lucrezia Lorini, Vanessa Brezzi, Roberta Benini, Gerardo Giorgi, Caterina Mori and Silvia Fiorentini. Thanks to Anna Tyler for giving me this and many past Italy gigs, and thanks and much love to my favourite travelling companion, Peter Handsaker, who loves Italy as much as I do.

Stephanie Ong

A big heartfelt thanks to Anna Tyler for trusting me with this update, Duncan Garwood for his sage writerly advice and the LP team for their great work. I'd also like to thank all the Milan locals, especially DJ Uabos for his nightlife tips and Jackie DeGiorgio for her foodie insight. Last but not least, I'd like to thank my partner in crime and life, Alessandro Sorci, for always being close to me and keeping me sane with regular post-work gelato.

Kevin Raub

Thanks to Anna Tyler and all my fellow partners in crime at LP. On the road, Alice Brignani, who puts out cultural fires, uncovers hidden gems, even leaps buildings in a single bound (all well beyond her Bologna borders!) and still wants to share an Italian IPA with me after it's all said and done.

Claudia Valentini, Francesca Soffici, Franca Rastelli, Sara Laghi, Fabrizio Raggi, Errica Dall'Ara, Maria Grazia Martini and Giovanni Pellegrini, too!

Brendan Sainsbury

Many thanks to all the skilled bus drivers, helpful tourist information staff, generous hotel owners, expert cappuccino makers, dogs that didn't growl at me, and numerous passers-by who helped me, unwittingly or otherwise, during my research trip. Special thanks to my wife Liz and my son Kieran for keeping the home fires burning while I was away.

Regis St Louis

I'm grateful to countless Italians and expats who provided tips and insight into Liguria, Valle d'Aosta and Piemonte while on the road. Special thanks to Catherina Unger, Eugenio Bordoni and Arbaspàa staff in Cinque Terre, Erika Carpaneto and Gloria Faccio in Turin, and Alberto and Fulvio Peluffo in Noli. Hugs to Cassandra and our daughters Magdalena and Genevieve, who joined for the great Ligurian adventure.

Nicola Williams

Heartfelt thanks to those who shared their love and insider knowledge with me: family tour guide & art historian extraordinaire Molly McIlwrath; Ambra Nepi and Avila Fernandez (Duomo); Doreen and Carmello (Hotel Scoti); Betti Soldi; Coral Sisk (@curiousappetite); Nardia Plumridge (@lostin florence); Katja Meier, Ilaria and Stella (Mus.e); Mary Gray; Anne Davis; Georgette Jupe (@girlin florence); and Paolo Bresci (Pistoia tourist office). Finally, kudos to my very own expert, trilingual, family-travel research team: Niko, Mischa and Kaya.

ACKNOWLEDGEMENTS

Climate map data adapted from Peel MC, Finlayson BL & McMahon TA (2007) 'Updated World Map of the Köppen-Geiger Climate Classification', *Hydrology and Earth System Sciences*, 11, 1633–44.

Illustrations pp92-3, pp382-3, pp516-17, pp730-1 by Javier Zarracina.

Cover photograph: Scooter, Tuscany, Bim/Getty Images ©

THIS BOOK

This 15th edition of Lonely Planet's *Italy* guidebook was researched and written by Brett Atkinson, Alexis Averbuck, Cristian Bonetto, Gregor Clark, Peter Dragicevich, Duncan Garwood, Paula Hardy, Virginia Maxwell, Stephanie Ong, Kevin Raub, Brendan Sainsbury, Regis St Louis and Nicola Williams. The previous edition was researched and written by the same authors.

This guidebook was produced by the following:

Destination Editor Anna Tyler
Senior Product Editors Elizabeth Jones, Fergus O'Shea
Regional Senior Cartographer Anthony Phelan
Product Editors Will Allen, Kate James
Book Designers Virginia Moreno, Mazzy Prinsep
Assisting Editors James Appleton, Michelle Coxall, Peter Cruttenden, Kate Daly, Andrea Dobbin, Emma Gibbs, Victoria Harris, Jennifer Hattam, Jodie Martire, Alison Morris, Anne Mulvaney, Susan Paterson, Gabrielle Stefanos, Maja Vatrić, Simon Williamson

Assisting Cartographers David Connolly, Julie Dodkins
Cover Researcher Ania Bartoszek

Thanks to Alexandra Bruzzese, Gemma Graham, Martin Heng, Alice Osterwalder, Joe Revill, Sophia Seymour, Jo-Ann Titmarsh, Robin Vermoesen, Brana Vladisavljevic

Index

INDEX Q-T

Map Legend

Sights

- Beach
- Bird Sanctuary
- Buddhist
- Castle/Palace
- Christian
- Confucian
- Hindu
- Islamic
- Jain
- Jewish
- Monument
- Museum/Gallery/Historic Building
- Ruin
- Shinto
- Sikh
- Taoist
- Winery/Vineyard
- Zoo/Wildlife Sanctuary
- Other Sight

Activities, Courses & Tours

- Bodysurfing
- Diving
- Canoeing/Kayaking
- Course/Tour
- Sento Hot Baths/Onsen
- Skiing
- Snorkelling
- Surfing
- Swimming/Pool
- Walking
- Windsurfing
- Other Activity

Sleeping

- Sleeping
- Camping
- Hut/Shelter

Eating

- Eating

Drinking & Nightlife

- Drinking & Nightlife
- Cafe

Entertainment

- Entertainment

Shopping

- Shopping

Information

- Bank
- Embassy/Consulate
- Hospital/Medical
- Internet
- Police
- Post Office
- Telephone
- Toilet
- Tourist Information
- Other Information

Geographic

- Beach
- Gate
- Hut/Shelter
- Lighthouse
- Lookout
- Mountain/Volcano
- Oasis
- Park
- Pass
- Picnic Area
- Waterfall

Population

- Capital (National)
- Capital (State/Province)
- City/Large Town
- Town/Village

Transport

- Airport
- Border crossing
- Bus
- Cable car/Funicular
- Cycling
- Ferry
- Metro station
- Monorail
- Parking
- Petrol station
- S-Bahn/Subway station
- Taxi
- T-bane/Tunnelbana station
- Train station/Railway
- Tram
- U-Bahn/Underground station
- Other Transport

Routes

- Tollway
- Freeway
- Primary
- Secondary
- Tertiary
- Lane
- Unsealed road
- Road under construction
- Plaza/Mall
- Steps
- Tunnel
- Pedestrian overpass
- Walking Tour
- Walking Tour detour
- Path/Walking Trail

Boundaries

- International
- State/Province
- Disputed
- Regional/Suburb
- Marine Park
- Cliff
- Wall

Hydrography

- River, Creek
- Intermittent River
- Canal
- Water
- Dry/Salt/Intermittent Lake
- Reef

Areas

- Airport/Runway
- Beach/Desert
- Cemetery (Christian)
- Cemetery (Other)
- Glacier
- Mudflat
- Park/Forest
- Sight (Building)
- Sportsground
- Swamp/Mangrove

Note: Not all symbols displayed above appear on the maps in this book

Brendan Sainsbury

Milan & the Lakes; Abruzzo & Molise; Naples & Campania Born and raised in the UK in a town that never merits a mention in any guidebook (Andover, Hampshire), Brendan spent the holidays of his youth caravanning in the English Lake District and didn't leave Blighty until he was 19. Making up for lost time, he's since squeezed 70 countries into a sometimes precarious existence as a writer and professional vagabond. In the last 11 years, he has written over 40 books for Lonely Planet. When not scribbling research notes, Brendan likes partaking in ridiculous 'endurance' races, strumming old Clash songs on the guitar, and experiencing the pain and occasional pleasures of following Southampton Football Club. Brendan also wrote the Understand section.

Regis St Louis

Turin, Piedmont & the Cinque Terre Regis grew up in a small town in the American Midwest – the kind of place that fuels big dreams of travel – and developed an early fascination with foreign dialects and world cultures. He spent his formative years learning Russian and a handful of Romance languages, which has served him well on journeys across much of the globe. Regis has contributed to more than 50 Lonely Planet titles, covering destinations across six continents. His travels have taken him from the mountains of Kamchatka to remote island villages in Melanesia, and to many grand urban landscapes. When not on the road, he lives in New Orleans. Follow him on Instagram @regisstlouis.

Nicola Williams

Florence & Tuscany; Sicily Border-hopping is way of life for British writer, runner, foodie, art aficionado and mum-of-three Nicola Williams who has lived in a French village on the southern side of Lake Geneva for more than a decade. Nicola has authored more than 50 guidebooks on Paris, Provence, Rome, Tuscany, France, Italy and Switzerland for Lonely Planet and covers France as a destination expert for the *Telegraph*. She also writes for the *Independent*, *Guardian*, lonelyplanet. com, *Lonely Planet Magazine*, *French Magazine*, *Cool Camping France* and others. Catch her on the road on Twitter and Instagram @tripalong. Nicola also wrote the Plan section.

Peter Dragicevich

Venice & the Veneto After a successful career in niche newspaper and magazine publishing, both in his native New Zealand and in Australia, Peter finally gave into Kiwi wanderlust, giving up staff jobs to chase his diverse roots around much of Europe. Over the last decade he's written dozens of guidebooks for Lonely Planet on an oddly disparate collection of countries, all of which he's come to love. He once again calls Auckland, New Zealand, his home – although his current nomadic existence means he's often elsewhere.

Duncan Garwood

Rome & Lazio; Umbria & Le Marche From facing fast bowlers in Barbados to sidestepping hungry pigs in Goa, Duncan's travels have thrown up many unique experiences. These days he largely dedicates himself to the Mediterranean and Italy, his adopted homeland where he's been living since 1997. He's worked on around 50 Lonely Planet titles, including guidebooks to Italy, Rome, Sardinia, Sicily, Spain and Portugal, and has contributed to books on world food and epic drives. He's also written on Italy for newspapers, websites and magazines. Duncan also wrote the Survival Guide section.

Paula Hardy

Venice & the Veneto; Fruili Venezia Giulia Paula Hardy is an independent travel writer and editorial consultant, whose work for Lonely Planet and other flagship publications has taken her from nomadic camps in the Danakil Depression to Seychellois beach huts and the jewel-like bar at the Gritti Palace on the Grand Canal. Over two decades, she has authored more than 30 Lonely Planet guidebooks and spent five years as commissioning editor of Lonely Planet's bestselling Italian list. These days you'll find her hunting down new hotels, hip bars and up-and-coming artisans primarily in Milan, Venice and Marrakesh. Get in touch at www.paulahardy.com.

Virginia Maxwell

Rome & Lazio; Florence & Tuscany Although based in Australia, Virginia spends at least half of her year updating Lonely Planet destination coverage across the globe. The Mediterranean is her major area of interest – she has covered Spain, Italy, Turkey, Syria, Lebanon, Israel, Egypt, Morocco and Tunisia – but she also covers Finland, Bali, Armenia, the Netherlands, the US and Australia for LP products. Follow her @maxwellvirginia on Instagram and Twitter.

Stephanie Ong

Milan & the Lakes Stephanie Ong is a writer/editor who's lived in Melbourne, Barcelona, London and now finds herself based in Milan, Italy. She's written travel pieces for various publications, including coffee-table books and guidebooks for Lonely Planet and Le Cool Publishing. When she's not immersed in the world of writing and travel, she's eating well and complaining about tax – like every good Italian.

Kevin Raub

Emilia-Romagna & San Marino Atlanta native Kevin Raub started his career as a music journalist in New York, working for *Men's Journal* and *Rolling Stone* magazines. He ditched the rock 'n' roll lifestyle for travel writing and has written for over 95 Lonely Planet guides, focused mainly on Brazil, Chile, Colombia, the USA, India, the Caribbean and Portugal. Raub also contributes to a variety of travel magazines in both the USA and the UK. Along the way, the self-confessed hophead is in constant search of wildly high IBUs in local beers. Follow him on Twitter and Instagram @ RaubOnTheRoad.

OUR STORY

A beat-up old car, a few dollars in the pocket and a sense of adventure. In 1972 that's all Tony and Maureen Wheeler needed for the trip of a lifetime – across Europe and Asia overland to Australia. It took several months, and at the end – broke but inspired – they sat at their kitchen table writing and stapling together their first travel guide, *Across Asia on the Cheap*. Within a week they'd sold 1500 copies. Lonely Planet was born.

Today, Lonely Planet has offices in Tennessee, Dublin and Beijing, with a network of over 2000 contributors in every corner of the globe. We share Tony's belief that 'a great guidebook should do three things: inform, educate and amuse'.

OUR WRITERS

Brett Atkinson

Puglia, Basilicata & Calabria; Sicily Brett is based in Auckland, New Zealand, but is frequently on the road for Lonely Planet. He's a full-time travel and food writer specialising in adventure travel, unusual destinations, and surprising angles on well-known destinations. He is featured regularly on the Lonely Planet website, and in newspapers, magazines and websites across New Zealand and Australia. Since becoming a Lonely Planet author in 2005, Brett has covered areas as diverse as Vietnam, Sri Lanka, the Czech Republic, New Zealand, Morocco, California and the South Pacific.

Alexis Averbuck

Rome & Lazio; Sardinia Alexis Averbuck has travelled and lived all over the world, from Sri Lanka to Ecuador, Zanzibar and Antarctica. In recent years she's lived on the Greek island of Hydra, in the wilds of NYC, and on the California coast. For Lonely Planet she explores the cobbled lanes of Rome and the azure seas of Sardinia, samples oysters in Brittany and careens through hill-top villages in Provence. A travel writer for over two decades, Alexis has written books on her journeys through Asia, Europe and the Americas. She's also a painter – visit www.alexisaverbuck. com – and promotes travel and adventure on video and television.

Cristian Bonetto

Naples & Campania; Sicily Cristian has contributed to over 30 Lonely Planet guides to date, including *New York City, Italy, Venice & the Veneto, Naples & the Amalfi Coast, Denmark, Copenhagen, Sweden* and *Singapore*. Lonely Planet work aside, his musings on travel, food, culture and design appear in numerous publications around the world, including the *Telegraph* (UK) and *Corriere del Mezzogiorno* (Italy). When not on the road, you'll find the reformed playwright and TV scriptwriter slurping espresso in his beloved hometown, Melbourne. Instagram: @rexcat7

Gregor Clark

Trentino & South Tyrol; Sicily Gregor is a US-based writer whose love of foreign languages and curiosity about what's around the next bend have taken him to dozens of countries on five continents. Chronic wanderlust has also led him to visit all 50 states and most Canadian provinces on countless road trips through his native North America. Since 2000, Gregor has regularly contributed to Lonely Planet guides, with a focus on Europe and the Americas. Gregor earned his degree in Romance Languages at Stanford University and has remained an avid linguist throughout career in publishing, teaching, translation and tour leadership.

OVER MORE
PAGE WRITERS

Published by Lonely Planet Global Limited
CRN 554153
15th edition – September 2021
ISBN 978 1 78868 414 9
© Lonely Planet 2021   Photographs © as indicated 2021
10 9 8 7 6 5 4 3 2 1
Printed in Singapore